D0855535

The Municipal Year Book 1985

The authoritative source book of urban data and developments

The Municipal Year Book

1985

Washington DC

For over sixty years ICMA has been the professional association of appointed administrators serving cities, counties, regional councils, and other local governments. Its primary goals include strengthening the quality of local government through professional management and developing and disseminating new concepts and approaches to management through a wide range of information services, training programs, and publications.

As an educational and professional association, ICMA is interested in the dissemination and application of knowledge for better local government management. To further these ends, the association supports a comprehensive research, data collection, and information dissemination program to facilitate reference and research by local government officials, university professors and students, researchers, and others concerned with local affairs.

Comprehensive Research, Data Collection, and Information Dissemination Program

The Municipal Year Book

Urban Data Service
 Monthly statistical reports
 Survey data resources

Management Information Service
 Monthly management reports
 Inquiry service
 Special reports

Research Projects and Publications

Volume 52, 1985

ISBN: 0–87326–960–8
ISSN: 0077–2186

Library of Congress Catalog Card Number: 34–27121

Printed in the United States of America

The views expressed in this Year Book are those of individual authors and are not necessarily those of the International City Management Association.

Suggested citation for use of material in this Year Book: Jane S. Author [and John N. Other], "Title of Article," in *The Municipal Year Book 1985* (Washington, D.C.: International City Management Association, 1985), pp. 00–000.

Acknowledgments

The Municipal Year Book, which provides local government officials with information on questions and issues associated with local government management, represents an important part of the ICMA's extensive research program. Each year, local officials are surveyed on a variety of topics, and the data derived from their responses to questionnaires constitute the primary information source for the Year Book. Articles are prepared by authors from local, state, and federal government agencies, universities, public interest groups, and ICMA staff. These articles analyze the data collected and examine trends and developments affecting local governments.

We would like to express our appreciation to the thousands of city and county managers, clerks, finance officers, personnel directors, police chiefs, fire chiefs, and other officials who patiently and conscientiously responded to ICMA questionnaires. It is only because of their often time-consuming efforts that we are able to provide the information in this volume.

The Municipal Year Book is published by the International City Management Association. The Year Book was developed and prepared by Mary A. Schellinger, Editor of the Year Book, with the help of the staff of ICMA's Municipal Data Service; Gregg Jackson, Sherman Landau, Ross H. Hoff, Donna Andrews, Elena Mina, and Lisa Babic. The Municipal Data Service is part of the ICMA's Office of Information Services, Donald J. Borut, Director, and Cheryl Farr, Director of Data and Information.

Christine Ulrich did the final edit for the Year Book and Emily Evershed prepared the Index. Dawn M. Leland supervised production and Rebecca Geanaros and Karen Peacock did the art for this edition. Hugh Guidi provided considerable assistance in the preparation of data for the Year Book. Special thanks go to Amy Cohen Paul and Ann Anajjar for their help in producing this book.

Washington, D.C.
January, 1985

William H. Hansell
Executive Director
International City
Management Association

Table of
Contents

Introduction

A Local Government Profiles

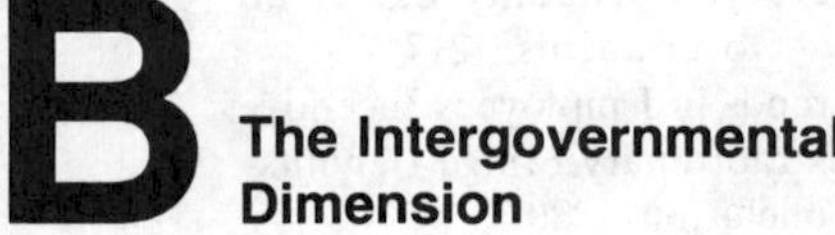

B The Intergovernmental Dimension

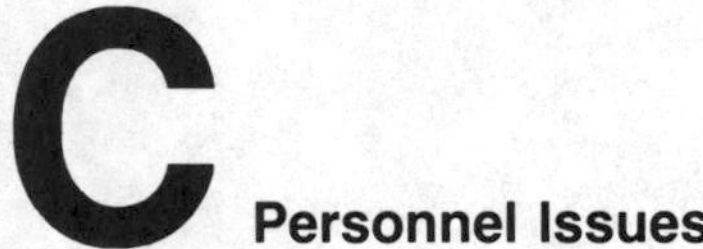

D Management Trends and Issues

Directories

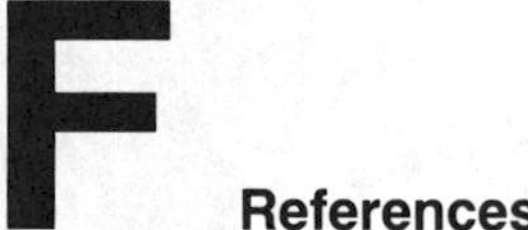

References

*Table listing individual local governments.

Inside the Year Book

The past year has been an introspective one. From our mid-decade vantage point we've taken a look at what we've accomplished in five years. For all of us, the most staggering change has been in the way we do business. The technological revolution that was predicted late in the 1970s is now in place (although it's fairly likely that we won't recognize its embryonic features when we look back on it five years from now). How much a part of our everyday lives the likes of electronic mail, office automation, and alternative telephone systems have become. The microcomputer could well become the logo of the 1980s.

But while all of us were spending time programming our phones and learning DOS, local governments were also forced to wrestle with changes that challenged the foundations of the local structure. What services are local governments responsible for providing? How much of what has in the recent past been thought of as local government's responsibility should be picked up by the private sector? Or by citizens themselves? And where is the money going to come from to pay for it?

One thing is certain in the wake of all this upheaval. And that is that while local governments are reassessing their roles vis-à-vis citizens' needs and service delivery, they are still concentrating many of their resources on "the basics."

The 1985 *Municipal Year Book* addresses this local government concern with providing an appropriate level of basic services within the constraints of limited resources. The articles in this edition of the Year Book focus on finances, on government employees and the incentives their employers are offering them, on the policies of state governments that affect local entities, on annexations and boundary changes, and on managers as the professionals who are trying to ride the waves of change.

The 1985 *Municipal Year Book* presents data from surveys conducted by the staff of the International City Management Association (ICMA), along with information from the best additional sources of local government data. These data are presented in individual and aggregate tables along with thoughtful analyses and timely information about local government operations for public officials, researchers, academicians, and others interested in local governments.

OVERVIEW

The *Municipal Year Book* is organized into six chapters: Local Government Profiles; The Intergovernmental Dimension; Personnel Issues; Management Issues and Trends; Directories; and References.

Local Government Profiles. For nearly ten years the Profiles of Individual Cities (PICs) have presented demographic information, data on the organizational structure of local governments, and considerable financial information about the cities as government entities and as clusters of citizens. Two years ago, the Profiles of Individual Counties, originally a part of the *County Year Book*, reappeared in the *Municipal Year Book,* presenting information on counties similar to that published for cities in the Profiles of Individual Cities.

Data for the PICs have been drawn from ICMA surveys, U.S. Bureau of the Census information, and the work of other major local government data collectors. Nowhere else is there such a rich accumulation of local government data in a single source.

The 1985 Profiles of Individual Cities include for each municipality 10,000 and over in population, the county in which it is located, its form of government, its metropolitan status, and its population. These characteristics can be used to classify governments.

The PICs also include the U.S. Bureau of the Census population estimates for 1982. A broad range of financial data are presented for cities. These data include: total general revenue for fiscal year 1983; total utility revenue; and per capita amounts for intergovernmental revenue, property taxes, other taxes, and charges and miscellaneous general revenue. The expenditure data shown include: total general expenditures for fiscal 1983; total utility expenditures; and per capita expenditures for police, fire, streets, and sewers and sanitation. To round out the financial picture for the communities listed in the PICs the long term debt per capita is shown.

Two features of public personnel are shown for October 1983: total full time equivalent employment and the average monthly salary for a full time municipal employee.

The Profiles of Individual Counties show most of the same data sets as the Profiles of Individual Cities. However, utility revenues and expenditures are not shown for counties. For counties, per capita expenditures are shown for law enforcement, streets, hospitals, welfare, and finance and administration.

In his article preceding the PICs tables, Ross H. Hoff describes the data sets shown in the PICs in detail. Hoff includes state and national summary data and analyzes the trends illustrated by the summary data in "Profiles of Individual Cities and Counties" (A/1).

The Intergovernmental Dimension. Analyzing the reports from the Year Book correspondents, Jay Muzychenko uncovered a trend toward improving relationships between states and local governments. Taking advantage of the economic recovery, many states created or increased aid programs to local governments. A number of states passed legislation that enhanced cities' and counties' ability to raise their own revenues. In his article, "State Actions Affecting Local Governments: Increased Flexibility in Conducting Business" (B/1), Muzychenko discusses these and other trends. Reports from each of the state correspondents follow the article.

Joel C. Miller brings Year Book readers up to date on corporate changes in his article, "Municipal Annexation and Boundary Changes: 1980–83" (B/2). Miller reports that annexation activity is down from the 1970 level. Miller also looks at detachments, incorporations, and disappearing places in his article.

Personnel Issues. One of the most basic personnel issues is compensation. This section provides salary data and benefits information for a variety of local officials.

In "Salaries of Municipal Officials for 1984" (C/1), Ross H. Hoff looks at the salaries of 26 municipal officials at the department head level and how the officials in those positions fared when measured against inflation. Salaries are those reported for 1 January 1984.

Amy Cohen Paul weighs the salaries of 12 county officials at the department head level against the same inflation measure in "Salaries of County Officials for 1984" (C/2). The data for county officials are as of 1 July 1984.

"Police, Fire, and Refuse Collection and Disposal Departments: Personnel, Compensation, and Expenditures" (C/3) presents the following in tabular form: total personnel, the number that are uniformed, the number of hours worked per week, entrance and maximum salaries, information on longevity pay, and a breakdown of departmental expenditures. Introductory comments and aggregate tables are taken from a Baseline Data Report written by Gerard J. Hoetmer (see note at the beginning of C/3 for the citation).

Management Issues and Trends. The real nuts and bolts of local government are the provision of basic services in response to citizen needs and the allocation of resources to get the job done efficiently.

Professional management of our local governments is a development of this century. Since the appointment of the first city manager in 1908, the profession has evolved and the men and women who make up the profession have changed remarkably. In "Local Government Administrators: Profiles of the Professionals in a Maturing Profession" (D/1), Mary A. Schellinger looks at some of the characteristics of professional administrators and the way they've changed over time.

In "The Irish City and County Management System" (D/2), Joseph F. Zimmerman describes the council-manager plan as it operates in Ireland as well as the roles of the managers and councils under this system. While the council-manager plan is universally used throughout Ireland, there is strong central control which severely limits local discretionary authority.

Lori M. Henderson, in "Intergovernmental Service Arrangements and the Transfer of Functions" (D/3), reports that "in an effort to do more with less, local officials have increasingly sought more economical alternatives to delivering services using only their employees." In her article, Henderson discusses the intergovernmental alternatives to direct service delivery.

President Reagan's efforts to reduce the size of the federal government have altered the traditional lines of human services delivery. Local governments are being forced to add human services programs to their lists of core programs to support their "social infrastructure" and preserve the "human stock" of their communities. In their article, "Human Services in Local Government: Patterns of Service at Metropolitan Levels" (D/4), Robert Agranoff and Alex N. Pattakos analyze the results of the first national survey of local human services programs since the Reagan cuts.

Amy Cohen Paul reports the results of a survey on a topic of continual importance to local governments. In her article, "Motivating Local Government Employees with Incentives" (D/5), Paul traces the use of six incentive programs and their increased prevalence in recent years.

Directories. The directories section (E/1/1 through E/1/10) encourages Year Book users to turn to sources beyond the Year Book—state municipal leagues, state agencies for community affairs, state management associations, and colleagues in other municipalities, counties, and regional councils—to exchange information and set up informal networks. The Year Book directories provide the names of nearly 70,000 contacts in United States local governments and a means of getting in touch with them—a phone number and in some cases an address. A new directory in this edition of the Year Book lists chief appointed administrators in countries outside the United States.

Professional Organizations. A special directory in the Year Book is "Professional, Special Assistance, and Educational Organizations Serving Local and State Governments" (E/2). The organizations included in this directory provide educational and research services to members or others on a cost-of-service basis and in this way strengthen professionalism in government administration.

References. The "Sources of Information" (F/1), the last section of the 1985 *Municipal Year Book*, provides annotated bibliographic listings of the latest books and periodicals in 2 basic reference categories and 15 functional area categories: basic references; basic statistical resources; emergency management; environment and energy; fire protection; housing; human resources and services; information technologies; intergovernmental relations; law enforcement and criminal justice; local government organization and management; personnel and labor relations; planning and development; public finance; public works and utilities; recreation and leisure; and transportation and roads. One of these sections—information technologies—is a new section this year. This addition to the Year Book bibliographies reflects the extent to which technology has been integrated into our lives.

PROFESSIONAL MUNICIPAL MANAGEMENT

Professional municipal management in the United States and Canada has its roots in the council-manager plan, as does the International City Management Association. The first appointment to a position similar to a city manager was 77 years ago, in 1908, in Staunton, Virginia, where a "general manager" was employed to oversee the administrative functions of the municipality. The first adoption of the council-manager plan in the United States is usually considered to have been in Sumter, South Carolina, in 1912, and in Canada during the next year at Westmount, Québec. Dayton, Ohio, in 1914, was the first community of substantial size to adopt the council-manager plan, and in 1930 Durham County, North Carolina, became the first county to institute professional management.

The council-manager plan grew steadily from 1914, slowed only as a result of the difficulties of war and depression. By 1918 there were 98 council-manager municipalities. In 1930 the total had increased to 418, and by 1945 it had reached 622. By the end of 1969, 2,252 municipalities in the United States and Canada were using the council-manager plan. Since that time the number of places using the plan has increased by 506 so that by 21 November 1984 ICMA had verified the existence of the plan in 2,626 cities and counties in the United States and 131 in Canada.

During the sixties the profile of local government had begun to show significant changes. Not only were there new problems, but variations in organization and structure became evident. Many cities, towns, and counties began providing for an appointed official responsible for overall administrative affairs without adopting the council-manager plan as it was originally conceived. Similarly, the development of councils of governments and regional councils brought new and innovative structures to local government. It became obvious to ICMA that, in many cases, professional management positions were being developed which did not significantly vary from the role of the traditional city and county manager positions provided for in the council-manager plan.

Therefore, in July 1969, the International City Managers' Association changed its name to the International City Management Association and provided for full professional recognition of these positions. To distinguish these municipalities from those recognized as council-manager municipalities, they were designated "general management municipalities." Criteria were established for recognition, and the incumbents in these positions were made eligible for Corporate (voting) Membership in ICMA.

Between June 1969 and 21 November 1984 ICMA recognized 1,097 governments in the United States and Canada under the general management criteria. Included in this total are 794 municipalities, 157 counties, and 146 councils of governments.

Recognized Municipalities. All management executives are selected by municipalities on the basis of relevant education and experience. While professional management is defined by a common set of functions, the association has not sought to control entrance into the profession by completion of a specified education program. The primary emphasis of entrance has been on demonstrated competence in a position with significant management responsibility and authority.

The procedure for this definition of professional positions is the establishment of a set of criteria describing the characteristics of overall professional management. The present criteria include a statement for recognition of a position in the council-manager form of government and of a position of general management which applies to a wide variety of governmental forms and to councils of governments.[1]

Table 1 indicates, by ICMA regions, the number of municipalities recognized. ICMA regions are determined by the Executive Board in accordance with the relative number of corporate members in the various geographic areas. The ICMA regions are: *Northeast:* Connecticut, Delaware, the District of Columbia, Maine, Maryland, Massachusetts, New Hampshire, New Jersey, New York, Pennsylvania, Rhode Island, and Vermont; *Southeast:* Alabama, Florida, Georgia, Kentucky, Mississippi, North Carolina, South Carolina, Tennessee, Virginia, and West Virginia; *Midwest:* Illinois, Indiana, Iowa, Michigan, Minnesota, Missouri, Ohio, and Wisconsin; *Mountain-Plains:* Arizona, Arkansas, Colorado, Idaho, Kansas, Louisiana, Montana, Nebraska, New Mexico, North Dakota, Oklahoma, South Dakota, Texas, Utah, and Wyoming; *West Coast:* Alaska, California, Hawaii, Nevada, Oregon, and Washington. The Canadian information is reported as for an independent region. (Although all members in countries outside of North America are currently represented in the association through a region which includes Canada, data for these countries are excluded from the table.) Further information on these recognized places, including legal basis, title of position, form of government, and year of recognition, is presented in the annual ICMA publication, *Who's Who in Professional Local Government Management.*

Organizational Goals. Beginning in the fall of 1983, the association undertook an extensive self-analysis and strategic planning process which resulted in a revision of ICMA's organizational goals. Adopted by the executive board in January 1985, these goals, the framework for ICMA services, are as follows:

1. To provide professional development programs and publications for local government professionals that improve their skills, increase their knowledge of local government, and strengthen their commitment to the values and ideals of professional management.
2. To support professional management in all forms of local government and specifically to encourage local governments in the United

Table 1 RECOGNIZED MUNICIPALITIES BY ICMA REGION[1]

	Council-Manager (CM)			General-Management (GM)				
ICMA region	Cities, towns, etc.	Counties	Total CM	Cities, towns, etc.	Counties	COGs	Total GM	Total CM & GM
Northeast	546	5	551	273	12	13	298	849
Southeast	537	59	596	70	86	38	194	790
Midwest	484	1	485	234	20	26	280	765
Mountain-Plains	526	6	532	124	7	41	172	704
West Coast	450	13	463	71	30	26	127	590
U.S. total	2,543	84	2,626	772	155	144	1,071	3,697
Canada total	125	6	131	22	2	2	26	157
Grand total	2,668	90	2,758	794	157	146	1,097	3,855

[1] Data in this table are as of 21 November 1984.

States and in other countries to adopt and retain the council-manager or the general management plan.

3. To improve the recruiting process for professional local government administrators, in order to ensure the future of the profession and increase professional management opportunities for women and minorities.
4. To serve as a national and international clearinghouse for the collection, analysis, and dissemination of local government-related information and to conduct research and offer contractual technical consulting services in areas that address local government needs.
5. To promote professional local government management by working in cooperation with and serving as a resource for public interest groups directly involved in the formulation of public policy.
6. To offer services and programs that respond to personal and family needs of members.

ORGANIZATION OF DATA

Most of the tabular data for the 1985 *Municipal Year Book* were obtained from public officials through questionnaires developed and administered by the International City Management Association. ICMA's Municipal Data Service maintains a computer-based municipal information file of all data collected through ICMA surveys.

Every city of 2,500 and over in population, all council-manager places under 2,500 population, and all counties were surveyed by questionnaire for this Year Book. However, not every city[2] and county were surveyed for each municipal function and activity included in the various sections. Each questionnaire is reviewed by municipal authorities and pretested before drafting in final form. All governments surveyed for each study receive a separate mail questionnaire; if they do not respond to the first mailing, a second request is sent. Third requests are distributed as necessary.

All survey questionnaires are edited by the ICMA staff to eliminate respondent errors and to assure that questionnaire responses are keypunched as accurately as possible for computer tabulation. Each Year Book author determines the analysis and the tables required from the computer as the basis for his or her article.

Summary data preceding individual city and county data are not necessarily based on the same number of places that appear in the individual city and county tables. The summary articles indicate trends and should be read when using the tables.

Government Definitions. There are over 82,000 governments in the United States today. Fifty-one of these are non-local governments; the remainder are all local governments—counties, municipalities, townships, school districts, and special districts. Table 2 indicates both the absolute counts and the trends with respect to numbers and types of governments in the United States.[3]

A municipality, by Census definition, is a "political subdivision within which a municipal corporation has been established to provide general local government for a specific population concentration in a defined area." This definition includes all active governmental units officially designated as cities, boroughs (except in Alaska), villages, or towns (except in Minnesota, New York, New England, and Wisconsin).[4] The definition generally includes all places incorporated under the procedures established by the several states.

Counties are the primary political administrative divisions of the states. In Louisiana these units are called parishes. Alaska has 11 county-type governments called boroughs. There are certain unorganized areas of some states that have a county designation from the Census Bureau for strictly administrative purposes which are not included in the Year Book data base. These comprise 12 areas in Alaska; 2 areas in South Dakota; 5 areas in Rhode Island; 8 areas in Connecticut; and 1 area in Montana.[5]

Year Book Data Base. This edition of the Year Book uses the Census Bureau's 1980 census counts for grouping local governments in the United States into population groups for tabular presentation.

It is possible to show information for 6,627 cities and other urban places 2,500 and over in population and 381 council-manager and general management places under 2,500 population. While the selection of cities 2,500 and over in population largely corresponds to the criteria established by the Bureau of the Census, there are some variations. Selection of council-manager and general management places under 2,500 population is based on recognition by the International City Management Association. The Year Book data base shows 3,043 counties.

City Classification. The Year Book data are presented by population group, geographic region, geographic division, metro status, and form of government.

Table 3 details the distribution of all municipalities of 2,500 and over in population (and all municipalities under 2,500 recognized by ICMA as providing for the council-manager plan or providing for a position of overall general management) by population, geographic region, metro status, and form of government.

Population. The population categories are self-explanatory.

Geographic Classification. Nine geographic divisions and four regions are used by the Bureau of the Census (see Figure 1). The nine divisions are: *New England:* Connecticut, Maine, Massachusetts, New Hampshire, Rhode Island, and Vermont; *Mid-Atlantic:* New Jersey, New York, and Pennsylvania; *East North Central:*

Table 2 NUMBER OF GOVERNMENTS IN THE UNITED STATES

Type of government	1982	1977	1972
Total	82,341	79,913	78,269
U.S. government	1	1	1
State governments	50	50	50
Local governments	82,290	79,862	78,218
County	3,041	3,042	3,044
Municipal	19,076	18,862	18,517
Township	16,734	16,822	16,991
School district	14,851	15,174	15,781
Special district	28,588	25,962	23,885

Illinois, Indiana, Michigan, Ohio, and Wisconsin; *West North Central:* Iowa, Kansas, Minnesota, Missouri, Nebraska, North Dakota, and South Dakota; *South Atlantic:* Delaware, the District of Columbia, Florida, Georgia, Maryland, North Carolina, South Carolina, Virginia, and West Virginia; *East South Central:* Alabama, Kentucky, Mississippi, and Tennessee; *West South Central:* Arkansas, Louisiana, Oklahoma, and Texas; *Mountain:* Arizona, Colorado, Idaho, Montana, New Mexico, Nevada, Utah, and Wyoming; and *Pacific Coast:* Alaska, California, Hawaii, Oregon, and Washington.

For the Year Book the regions are further consolidated as follows: *Northeast:* Connecticut, Maine, Massachusetts, New Hampshire, New Jersey, New York, Pennsylvania, Rhode Island, and Vermont; *North Central:* Illinois, Indiana, Iowa, Kansas, Michigan, Minnesota, Missouri, Nebraska, North Dakota, Ohio, South Dakota, and Wisconsin; *South:* Alabama, Arkansas, Delaware, the District of Columbia, Florida, Georgia, Kentucky, Louisiana, Maryland, Mississippi, North Carolina, Oklahoma, South Carolina, Tennessee, Texas, Virginia, and West Virginia; and *West:* Alaska, Arizona, California, Colorado, Hawaii, Idaho, Montana, Nevada, New Mexico, Oregon, Utah, Washington, and Wyoming.

Metro Status. Metro status refers to the status of a municipality within the context of the U.S. Office of Management and Budget definition of a metropolitan statistical area. The criteria for defining metropolitan statistical areas were revised in 1983 to allow greater latitude in identifying urban areas and surrounding communities that share an economic and social identity. The new criteria allow for three levels of classification: metropolitan statistical areas, primary metropolitan statistical areas, and consolidated metropolitan statistical areas.

Table 3 CUMULATIVE DISTRIBUTION OF U.S. MUNICIPALITIES

Classification	All cities	Cities 2,500 & over	Cities 5,000 & over	Cities 10,000 & over	Cities 25,000 & over	Cities 50,000 & over	Cities 100,000 & over	Cities 250,000 & over	Cities 500,000 & over	Cities over 1,000,000
Total, all cities	7,008	6,627	4,349	2,605	1,064	449	170	57	23	6
Population group										
Over 1,000,000	6	6	6	6	6	6	6	6	6	6
500,000-1,000,000	17	17	17	17	17	17	17	17	17	
250,000- 499,999	34	34	34	34	34	34	34	34		
100,000- 249,999	113	113	113	113	113	113	113			
50,000- 99,999	279	279	279	279	279	279				
25,000- 49,999	615	615	615	615	615					
10,000- 24,999	1,541	1,541	1,541	1,541						
5,000- 9,999	1,744	1,744	1,744							
2,500- 4,999	2,278	2,278								
Under 2,500[1]	381									
Geographic region										
Northeast	1,954	1,836	1,288	753	263	100	23	6	3	2
North Central	2,028	1,941	1,240	751	291	112	39	14	6	2
South	2,054	1,941	1,169	655	252	115	61	23	8	1
West	972	909	652	446	258	122	47	14	6	1
Metro status										
Central	508	508	508	508	475	300	151	57	23	6
Suburban	3,740	3,637	2,537	1,513	477	149	19			
Independent	2,760	2,482	1,304	584	122					
Form of government										
Mayor-council	3,794	3,698	2,084	1,108	406	180	76	35	18	6
Council-manager	2,537	2,302	1,852	1,251	586	248	87	20	5	
Commission	177	176	136	101	47	16	7	2		
Town meeting	419	370	219	100	6	1				
Rep. town meeting	81	81	58	45	19	4				

[1] Limited to municipalities recognized by the International City Management Association as providing for the council-manager plan or providing for a position of overall general management.

Metropolitan Statistical Areas (MSAs). These areas have either a city of at least 50,000 population or a Bureau of the Census urbanized area of at least 50,000 *and* a total metropolitan statistical area population of at least 100,000. Each MSA has at least one central city and one central county and may include outlying counties with strong economic and social ties to the central components of the area. Outlying counties must also meet requirements relating to commuting level and "urban character" to be included in an MSA.

MSAs are not closely associated with other metropolitan statistical areas and are surrounded by nonmetropolitan counties.

Primary Metropolitan Statistical Areas (PMSAs). Metropolitan statistical areas of over 1,000,000 population can be designated as primary metropolitan statistical areas if there is local support for separate recognition and the area has at least 100,000 population, at least 60% of its population is urban, and less than 50% of its resident workers commute to jobs outside the county.

If any area within a metropolitan statistical area is recognized as a primary metropolitan statistical area, the remaining area of that statistical area is designated as a separate primary metropolitan statistical area.

Consolidated Metropolitan Statistical Areas (CMSAs). A metropolitan statistical area in which primary statistical areas have been identified is designated as a consolidated metropolitan statistical area. If no primary metropolitan statistical areas are identified within an MSA, the term metropolitan statistical area applies.

In New England, the city and town are administratively more important than the county, and a wide range of data is compiled locally for such entities. Here, towns and cities are the units used in defining metropolitan statistical areas. Because cities and towns are generally smaller in area than counties, the total MSA population requirement is lower in the six New England states (75,000) than in the other states (100,000).

The Office of Management and Budget currently identifies 335 metropolitan areas. Of this number 257 are MSAs and 78 are PMSAs. There are 23 CSMAs.

Form of Government. Form of government relates primarily to the organization of the legislative and executive branches of municipalities and townships. In the mayor-council form, an elected mayor generally acts as the chief executive officer with the amount of administrative authority dependent on state law and variations in local organization. These variations include the scope of the powers of the elected council and the delegation of some authority to appointed professional administrators, to special boards, and to commissions.

Many cities with a mayor-council form of government have appointed city administrators. These officials are appointed by the elected representatives (council) and are responsible to them for the execution of their duties. However, their administrative authority is limited—they often do not directly appoint department heads or other key city personnel, and their responsibility for budget preparation and administration, while significant, is subordinate to that of the elected officials.

Under the council-manager form, a manager is appointed by and responsible to an elected council to serve as chief administrative officer to oversee personnel, development of the budget, proposing policy alternatives, and general implementation of policies and programs adopted by the council.

The commission form of government operates with an elected commission performing both legislative and executive functions, generally with departmental administration divided among the commissioners.

The town meeting form of government is a system in which all qualified voters of a municipality meet annually (or more often if necessary) to set policy and choose selectmen to carry out the basic policies they have established.

Under the representative town meeting form

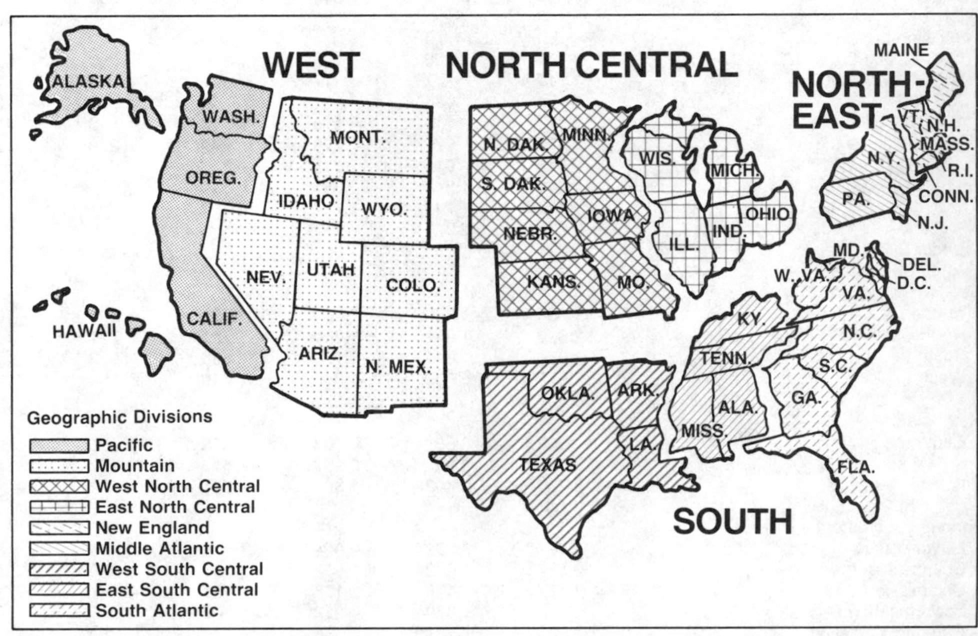

Figure 1 *U.S. Bureau of the Census geographic regions and divisions*

of government, the voters select a large number of citizens to represent them at the meeting(s). All citizens can participate in the meeting(s) but only the representatives actually have a direct vote.

County Classification. Counties are the primary political administrative divisions of the states. In Louisiana, these units are called parishes. The county-type governments in Alaska are called boroughs. Table 4 details the distribution of counties throughout the nation, utilizing the same categories as Table 3. The population categories are self-explanatory and the geographic regions have been described above in the discussion of Table 3.

Metropolitan status, for counties, refers to the status of a county within the context of the U.S. Office of Management and Budget definition of a metropolitan statistical area (MSA). "Metro" means a county is located within an MSA; "nonmetro" indicates that it is located outside the boundaries of an MSA.

Form of government relates to the structural organizations of the legislative and executive branches of counties; counties are classified as being with or without an administrator.

There are three basic forms of county government: commission, council-administrator, and council-elected executive. The commission form of county government is characterized by a governing board which shares the administrative and, to an extent, legislative responsibilities with several independently elected functional officials. Counties with this form of government are designated as being without an administrator.

Counties with the council-administrator form, in which an administrator is appointed by, and responsible to, the elected council to carry out directives, are designated under form of government as "with administrator." The council-elected executive form features two branches of government: the executive and the legislative. The independently elected executive is considered the formal head of the county. This form of government is also included in the designation "with administrator."

The use of varying types of local government is an institutional response to the needs, requirements, and articulated demands of citizens at the local level. Within each type of local government, structures are developed to provide adequate services. These structural adaptations are a partial result of the geographic location, population, metropolitan status, and form of government of the jurisdiction involved.

Table 4 CUMULATIVE DISTRIBUTION OF U.S. COUNTIES

Classification	All counties	Counties 2,500 & over	Counties 5,000 & over	Counties 10,000 & over	Counties 25,000 & over	Counties 50,000 & over	Counties 100,000 & over	Counties 250,000 & over	Counties 500,000 & over	Counties over 1,000,000
Total, all counties	3,043	2,942	2,766	2,317	1,358	747	374	156	68	20
Population group										
Over 1,000,000	20	20	20	20	20	20	20	20	20	20
500,000-1,000,000	48	48	48	48	48	48	48	48	48	
250,000- 499,999	88	88	88	88	88	88	88	88		
100,000- 249,999	218	218	218	218	218	218	218			
50,000- 99,999	373	373	373	373	373	373				
25,000- 49,999	611	611	611	611	611					
10,000- 24,999	959	959	959	959						
5,000- 9,999	449	449	449							
2,500- 4,999	176	176								
Under 2,500	101									
Geographic region										
Northeast	196	196	195	189	178	132	84	42	18	5
North Central	1,053	1,018	934	754	410	204	107	37	15	4
South	1,375	1,347	1,107	1,107	609	297	119	45	18	4
West	419	381	267	267	161	114	64	32	17	7
Metro status										
Metro	683	683	682	678	631	508	354	156	68	20
Nonmetro	2,360	2,259	2,084	1,639	727	239	20			
Form of government										
Without administrator	2,399	2,302	2,129	1,712	899	408	163	49	16	4
With administrator	644	640	637	605	459	339	211	107	52	16

USES OF STATISTICAL DATA

The Municipal Year Book uses both primary and secondary data. Primary data are collected and published by the same organization, while secondary data are published by an organization that did not collect the data. After the data have been collected and scrutinized, relationships or problems concerning the data may be put into proper perspective.

Misinterpretation of data or statistical tables will lead to erroneous conclusions. The user of the data and the statistics presented in this Year Book must analyze each tabular presentation completely. A careful study should be made of each table heading and any explanation prefacing or footnoting each table. Full recognition must be given to the limitations of the data and statistics presented.

Two types of statistical presentations may be discerned in the Year Book: descriptive and inductive. Descriptive statistics present numerical data in tabular and/or graphic form and make no generalizations or projections of data. Extreme care must be taken that the reasoning behind any generalization does not go beyond the data supplied. While many of the articles in this Year Book use inductive statistical interpretation, the tables are strictly descriptive in nature. Once the data have been collected and tabulated, they are described by measures of central tendency (the most common are means and medians), percentages, index numbers, and other common statistics.

Measures of Central Tendency. Many of the tables presented summarize the data collected into population and geographic groups. The two most often used summarizing statistics are the arithmetic mean and the median.

The arithmetic mean (also called the simple average) characterizes a set of data with one representative statistic. There are several advantages to using an arithmetic mean to describe a data set. First, for any set of numerical data a mean always exists and may be calculated. Second, there is only one mean for each set of numerical data, and its calculation accounts for every item in the data set. Finally, most people understand what is implied when discussing an "average."

The mean is calculated by summing all the items in a set of data and dividing by the number of items summed. For example, given the salaries of $6,200, $5,300, $6,800, $8,600, and $10,300, the mean is calculated to be $7,440 ($37,200 ÷ 5).

There are two distinct disadvantages in using a mean. First, a mean is not always the most meaningful descriptor, especially when considering small sets of numerical data. Second, a mean is affected by very large or small numbers. For example, if the above data set contained a sixth value of $40,500 the mean would be $12,950 ($77,700 ÷ 6). For this example, the median would be a better descriptor.

The median is the central value of a set of data that have been arranged in order of increasing size. For an odd number of items, the median is the middle item, while for an even number of items the median is the mean of the two middle items (i.e., one-half of the items fall above and one-half fall below the median). For example, given the above data set of six items arranged in magnitude as follows: $5,300, $6,200, $6,800, $8,600, $10,300, and $40,500, the median is calculated to be $7,700 ($6,800 + $8,600 ÷ 2).

The median is extremely difficult to calculate with large numbers of items in a data set. However, unlike the arithmetic mean, the median is not affected by very large or small values. Moreover, the median is difficult to use statistically since no algebraic basis exists for its calculation.

The mean and median represent only a characteristic or middle value of a data set. For inductive interpretation the mean, relatively more stable and reliable from data sample to data sample, is the better statistic.

Additional Measures of Location. The weighted mean takes account of the "relative importance" of additional data so that the computation of an average would not otherwise be meaningless. If a survey asks for a rating, on a scale of 1 to 5 to a particular question, we know that the scale is insufficient for computing the "average" rating since, for every question, it would be 3.0. However, if we know how many responses were given for each rating we could "weight" the average. For example, if the following numbers of responses were noted for each rating on the scale,

Number responding	*Rating*
300	1
600	2
400	3
200	4
100	5

we could multiply each rating by the number of respondents and divide by the total number of respondents. For this example, we would obtain a weighted mean of 2.5, which is much more representative of the "average" rating.

There is no limitation, other than reasonableness, about what to use as a weighting factor. Other commonly used weights are population, employment, and income.

The weighted mean must be used with particular care since it is affected by extreme values of the weighting factor. For example, if 1,000 people gave a rating of 1 and 1,000 people gave a rating of 5 to a question, the weighted mean would be 3.0. This value distorts the true distribution of responses to the question. In this case a complete explanation of the data distribution would be needed in order to use the statistic.

Quartiles divide a data set into four equal parts. When the data are ordered by increasing size, the first quartile is the value below which one-fourth of the items fall, the second quartile is the median (see above), and the third quartile is the value below which three-fourths of the items fall. The first and third quartiles are used in conjunction with the median to describe the distribution of a data set.

The final measure of location used in this Year Book is the largest and smallest items of a data set, which is self-explanatory.

Quartiles and the largest and smallest values

of a data set are presented in various tables throughout this book and are used to describe the distribution of the data. They are not measures of dispersion. A measure of dispersion indicates the variability of the data and evaluates the accuracy of an estimate or generalization. Two measures of dispersion that may be computed from the statistics found in this Year Book are the range and the interquartile range.

The range is, by definition, the difference between the largest and the smallest items of a data set. While easy to compute, the range only indicates the variation between the extreme values and not the dispersion of a data set. The interquartile range is the difference between the first and third quartiles. This measure describes the middle 50% of the data and is a more valuable statistic because it is unaffected by very large and very small values.

Explanations of the more indicative measures of dispersion, the standard deviation and the coefficient of variation, may be found in any introductory statistics text.

Additional Statistical Measures. Two additional statistics that can be found in the Year Book are percentages (not to be confused with percentiles—which divide a distribution into 100 equal parts) and index numbers.

In the Year Book, percentages are used in several ways. In some instances, percentages are used to show the distribution of the items in a data set or to characterize the relationship between one item in a data set and the remainder of the data set. In other instances, percentages show the rate of change of a particular data set from one time period to another. This change rate is computed by taking the value of the current year and dividing by the value of an earlier year. The result, if greater than 1.00 is reduced by 1.00 and then multiplied by 100 to show the percent of increase. If the result is less than 1.00 it is subtracted from 1.00 and multiplied by 100 to represent a decrease. Decreases are generally presented in parentheses in this publication.

Percentages are primitive index numbers. Index numbers compare the relative change between two or more items which may further be weighted by some other relevant data (e.g., population or income). Most indices used in this book are of the primitive type. Given a base year (base year = 100), the index number shows each additional year's data as a percentage of the base year. Therefore, if the table showed an employment index of 129 for the year 1963, with 1960 the base year, this would indicate an increase in employment of 29% since the year 1960.

Index numbers are becoming increasingly important for decision makers in government. While the responsibility of the statistician or researcher is to construct pertinent and viable indices, the decision maker must be aware of the strengths and weaknesses of index numbers.

Many indices attempt to measure the significance of an administration or a local government service, usually defined as productivity measurements. There must be a differentiation between the efficiency or productivity of a service and the effectiveness of a service. For example, for fire protection service, showing the amount of burnable property in a city and the fire losses per $1,000 of burnable property would allow some measurement of the effectiveness of the fire protection. However, showing the output (service performed) based on the inputs for the service (e.g., employment, expenditures, or equipment) suggests an indication of the efficiency of the fire protection service.

What data the index is based on are of prime importance. Measurement of fire protection on a per capita basis would be inadequate since fire risk is correlated more with the amount of burnable property in a city than with the population of a city.

Comparisons of indices for an individual city computed over time are valid as long as the data and computations remain standard. However, difficulties arise in attempting to make comparisons between cities. Unless there is data reporting compatibility between cities or some computational adjustments, there can be no valid comparisons between cities of any computed indices.

Limitations of the Statistics. The statistics presented in this Year Book are only as good as the data used in their computations. Besides the previously mentioned limitations of the statistics, limitations exist on the data collected and tabulated.

For most of the tables presented, the data originate from responses to questionnaires returned by individual cities and counties. Each local government has its own record keeping system, and therefore the data lack uniformity. In addition, biases in the data result from inconsistent interpretations of individual questions by persons responding to the questionnaires.

The statistics compiled from the questionnaire data are subject to additional bias. This additional bias tends to skew the data distribution and results because not all cities and counties return their questionnaires, many questionnaires are returned incomplete, and many answers have internal inconsistencies associated with them and must be eliminated.

Using the Statistics. Even with the limitations on the data and the statistics, there is still justification for their publication. First, the tables that summarize population and geographic groups are valuable for indicating trends in costs, performance, and accomplishments. Second, comparison of the figures for individual cities and counties with the descriptive statistics for governments of similar size is a starting point for further analysis. Third, with due care this information for individual cities and counties enables officials to compare their community with others in a similar situation.

---

[1] The criteria for council-manager and general management recognitions are laid out in International City Management Association, *Who's Who in Professional Local Government Management* (Washington, D.C.: International City Management Association, 1985).

[2] The terms *city* and *cities,* as used in this volume, refer to cities, villages, towns, townships, and boroughs.

[3] U.S., Department of Commerce, Bureau of the Census, *1982 Census of Governments,* vol. 1 no. 1: *Governmental Units in 1982,* GC82(1) (Washington, D.C.: Government Printing Office, 1982), Table A.

[4] Ibid., p. viii.

[5] Ibid., p. 346.

A Local Government Profiles

1 Profiles of Individual Cities and Counties

A 1

Profiles of Individual Cities and Counties*

Ross H. Hoff
International City Management Association

The year immediately following an election, especially one decided by a landslide, is predictably a time for the victorious administration to assert that a mandate has been given to its campaign platform. Constrained by his own political philosophy and the challenges of his opponent in the 1984 election, President Reagan faces his second term with the firm resolve to make inroads on the burgeoning federal deficit while steadfastly refusing to raise taxes. Still elusive is tax reform that will alleviate "loopholes" and strengthen the federal government's ability to collect revenue on an equitable basis from taxpayers.

With deficit reduction a goal and increased revenue dubious at best, the inexorable algebraic conclusion is that federal spending must be cut dramatically. And of the spending for the broad budget categories of domestic social programs and defense, cuts in the latter are as dogmatically shunned by the current administration in Washington as are tax increases.

At the time of this writing, the President has sent a budget to Congress proposing far-reaching reductions in or elimination of a variety of domestic spending programs, many of which would directly and devastatingly affect local governments. While Congress is likely to make some changes in the President's budget, it is equally likely to cut back or eliminate general revenue sharing, community development block grants, water and sewer grants, mass transit subsidies, and urban development action grants. The Profiles of Individual Cities and Counties (PICs) presented in *The Municipal Year Book 1985* provide comparative data on revenues and expenditures of local government operations in fiscal year 1983, a year in which those governments were already finding it necessary to tighten their belts and adjust service levels. As local governments face further decline in intergovernmental revenue, revenue from other sources will have to make up the difference, the alternative being decreases in expenditures for services provided by local governments.

THE 1985 PICS

The 1985 PICS include 2,570 municipalities that have a population of 10,000 or greater according to the 1982 Census Bureau population estimates and 1,358 counties that have a population of 25,000 or greater.

Information is presented for 18 data sets in the Profiles of Individual Cities and for 17 data sets in the Profiles of Individual Counties. These data sets are described below and in the introductory notes preceding Tables 1/9 and 1/10. The source notes for each data set appear at the end of the tables.

Listing of Governments. In the PICs tables, the governments are listed alphabetically in state groupings. For a municipality that is not legally constituted as a city, there is a designation following the name of the place indicating whether it is a borough, village, town, township, city-county consolidation, or independent city (see the key preceding Table 1/9 for an explanation of the designation codes used in the Profiles of Individual Cities).

The name of the county in which the munic-

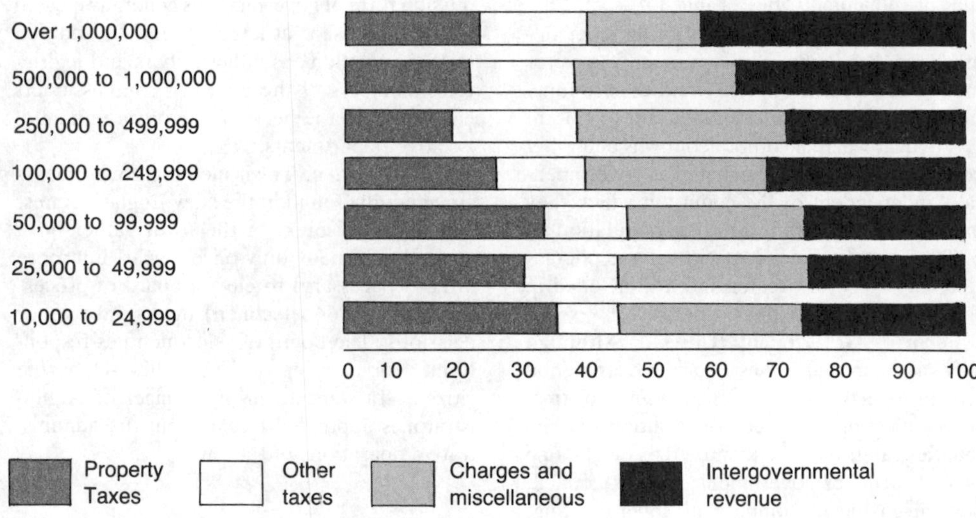

Figure 1/1 *Proportionate distribution of selected revenue items—cities by population group*

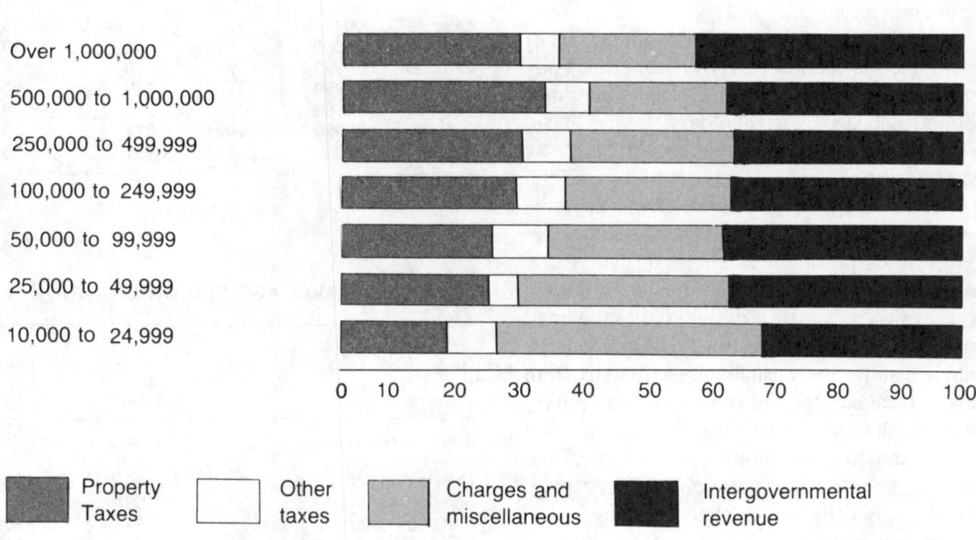

Figure 1/2 *Proportionate distribution of selected revenue items—counties by population group*

*The term cities used in this article refers to boroughs, cities, villages, and selected towns and townships. Some townships (primarily in New Jersey and Pennsylvania) that have been included in earlier Profiles of Individual Cities (PICs) are not included in this table. Only those townships that have historically been included in ICMA's survey universe are included here.

ipality is located is given in parentheses following the municipal designation. The county equivalent is shown for cities in Louisiana and Alaska where parishes and boroughs, respectively, perform county-type functions. For those places located in more than one county, the county in which the greatest portion of the municipality lies is the one given.

In the Profiles of Individual Counties, the name of each county is followed by the name of the county seat in parentheses.

Consolidations and Independent Cities. The merger of one or more municipalities with a county to form a city-county consolidation or metropolitan government performing the functions of both cities and counties has occurred in 19 instances where the population of the resulting consolidation is 10,000 or greater. Data for these consolidations are shown in the Profiles of Individual Cities (Table 1/9).[1]

In the United States a total of 44 cities operate independently from any county government and perform both city and county functions. Most of the independent cities (41) are in Virginia, where incorporated towns and other communities may be designated as governmentally independent of the county in which they are located after they reach a population of 5,000. Thirty independent cities have populations of 10,000 or greater and are included in the Profiles of Individual Cities.[2]

Form of Government (Cities). Although there are many variations in local governmental structure in this country, with minor distinctions reflecting local need or tradition, municipalities can usually be identified as having one of five forms of government: mayor–council, council–manager, commission, town meeting, and representative town meeting. Determination of the form of government for each of the cities in the PICs was made on the basis of a survey administered to all cities in the summer of 1981 as well as from information in the master file of the association. That file is updated as necessary when communities advise the association of changes in their legal forms of government.

Mayor–Council. The mayor–council form of government is characterized by a legislative body (generally called a city council, but sometimes termed a board of freeholders, board of selectmen, or commission) elected at large, by ward or district, or by some combination of the two, and a separately elected chief executive (usually called the mayor, but sometimes referred to as president or chairman where the individual is selected by the council from among its ranks). The mayor is designated as the head of the city government, but the extent of the mayor's authority is usually prescribed by state law or local charter and can range from purely ceremonial functions to full-scale responsibility for the day-to-day operations of the city. The mayor generally has veto power over ordinances passed by the council. In some cities, the mayor may assume largely a policy role, and responsibility for day-to-day operations may be delegated to an administrator appointed by and responsible to the mayor.

Council–Manager. The council–manager form of government also has an elected legislative body. The size of the council is generally smaller than that of a mayor–council municipality, and council elections are usually nonpartisan. Typically, the mayor is recognized as the political head of the municipality but is a member of council and does not have the power to veto council actions. The mayor and council as a collegial body are responsible for setting policy, approving the budget, and determining the tax rate. They hire a city manager or city administrator to carry out their policies. The manager or administrator serves at the pleasure of the council and has responsibility for preparing the budget, directing day-to-day operations, hiring and firing city personnel, and serving as the council's chief advisor.

Commission. The legislative body in the commission form of government is generally elected in a nonpartisan, at-large system. In addition to their functions as policymakers and legislators, members of the board of commissioners each serve as the head of one or more administrative departments.

Town Meeting. Town meeting governments are generally found in the New England states. All qualified voters of the town gather on a given day (usually only once a year, but more often if necessary) to elect a board of officers (generally called selectmen) and to make policy decisions. The board of selectmen has responsibility for carrying out the policy set by the citizens. In some towns a manager or administrator is appointed to carry out the administrative operations of the town.

Representative Town Meeting. The representative town meeting form of government is structured in much the same way as the town meeting form, with the exception that a large number of citizens are chosen by the general electorate to represent them in voting. All citizens can attend the meetings and participate in the debates, but only those chosen as representatives have a direct vote.

Recognition Status. The symbol to the left of the form of government in the Profiles of Individual Cities (Table 1/9) indicates that the municipality has been recognized by ICMA as having a position of professional management. An asterisk (*) indicates that the municipality is recognized as having the council–manager form of government; a section mark (§) indicates that the municipality provides for a position of overall general management.

Form of Government (Counties). There are three basic forms of county government: commission, council–administrator, and council–elected executive.

Commission. The commission form of government in counties is characterized by a central governing board whose members are generally elected by district; this board is often called the board of commissioners or supervisors. One of the members is selected by the board to be its presiding officer. Members of the governing board traditionally act as department heads over specific functions. The governing board shares the administrative and, to an extent, legislative functions with independently elected officials such as the clerk, the treasurer, the sheriff, the

Text continues on page 6

Table 1/1 AVERAGE PER CAPITA CITY REVENUES BY POPULATION GROUP

Population group	All Cities	Property taxes ($)	Other taxes ($)	Charges and miscellaneous sources ($)	Inter-governmental sources ($)
Total, all cities	2,570	165.03	98.14	168.98	234.07
Over 1,000,000	6	296.96	230.18	247.34	597.03
500,000–1,000,000	18	193.75	145.90	234.27	379.88
250,000– 499,999	33	116.30	121.59	207.77	203.56
100,000– 249,999	119	151.59	83.12	176.39	205.06
50,000– 99,999	286	154.07	66.32	134.67	136.76
25,000– 49,999	617	130.99	54.63	136.33	120.22
10,000– 24,999	1,491	125.67	39.35	109.16	106.45

Table 1/2 AVERAGE PER CAPITA COUNTY REVENUES BY POPULATION GROUP

Population group	All counties	Property taxes ($)	Other taxes ($)	Charges and miscellaneous sources ($)	Inter-governmental sources ($)
Total, all counties	1,358	88.62	22.08	77.24	126.99
Over 1,000,000	19	105.95	23.76	78.30	169.07
500,000–1,000,000	53	115.21	29.74	80.28	146.45
250,000– 499,999	89	80.23	19.12	69.21	103.21
100,000– 249,999	230	76.88	17.68	70.24	102.74
50,000– 99,999	369	69.28	22.91	81.53	114.67
25,000– 49,999	594	65.65	16.31	87.66	104.11
10,000– 24,999	4	46.57	15.83	107.19	77.70

Table 1/3 AVERAGE PER CAPITA CITY REVENUES BY STATE

State	All cities	Property taxes ($)	Other taxes ($)	Charges and miscellaneous sources ($)	Inter-governmental sources ($)
Total, all cities	2,570	165.03	98.14	168.98	234.07
Alabama	40	24.31	126.27	241.36	57.54
Alaska	3	245.28	44.54	794.68	1,373.13
Arizona	17	45.74	128.10	172.39	227.06
Arkansas	29	23.88	52.89	178.99	124.66
California	256	83.20	137.37	178.25	125.05
Colorado	25	67.62	225.05	250.37	130.99
Connecticut	84	527.79	6.89	91.77	248.10
Delaware	3	119.08	30.66	227.73	166.77
District of Columbia	1	578.45	825.55	323.59	1,322.48
Florida	95	110.52	95.32	217.91	101.17
Georgia	39	103.89	104.22	224.30	132.57
Hawaii	1	257.07	64.00	102.45	114.70
Idaho	11	101.13	10.20	138.24	96.45
Illinois	176	96.97	134.32	101.15	133.97
Indiana	61	150.39	4.98	130.73	179.89
Iowa	29	151.44	9.84	215.50	128.79
Kansas	34	95.75	45.73	231.10	82.51
Kentucky	30	62.12	32.41	111.79	111.29
Louisiana	34	62.72	156.75	190.15	169.23
Maine	18	399.83	4.55	100.70	236.25
Maryland	17	264.81	55.16	204.88	752.88
Massachusetts	151	499.44	7.40	125.43	399.83
Michigan	90	155.47	16.23	189.69	241.83
Minnesota	65	114.90	28.77	295.23	215.29
Mississippi	27	78.31	16.87	149.56	159.74
Missouri	51	50.10	172.17	148.45	135.55
Montana	9	128.78	17.73	169.94	78.50
Nebraska	12	103.28	83.59	161.79	119.62
Nevada	6	38.92	76.06	115.41	217.19
New Hampshire	21	390.15	10.04	113.22	144.52
New Jersey	183	163.36	7.79	60.52	205.51
New Mexico	13	52.54	95.23	356.97	274.42
New York	86	426.49	256.28	291.24	885.89
North Carolina	42	153.92	16.12	136.29	162.66
North Dakota	9	72.41	14.87	273.39	123.49
Ohio	149	37.11	8.61	100.73	88.03
Oklahoma	33	25.19	209.63	185.36	63.71
Oregon	29	157.51	50.21	188.01	126.53
Pennsylvania	163	98.18	37.32	99.48	140.79
Rhode Island	27	462.65	4.36	57.02	282.69
South Carolina	26	103.62	49.07	89.59	91.24
South Dakota	9	97.59	96.05	171.61	112.49
Tennessee	37	115.10	38.49	136.10	331.98
Texas	151	109.66	94.56	164.51	60.28
Utah	22	58.01	91.82	138.14	54.51
Vermont	8	134.08	2.47	30.69	100.53
Virginia	33	299.73	190.46	150.71	392.63
Washington	36	83.79	170.60	193.41	161.65
West Virginia	15	49.52	150.39	314.88	145.64
Wisconsin	56	256.42	7.86	138.02	267.24
Wyoming	8	21.46	22.65	239.82	469.97

Table 1/4 AVERAGE PER CAPITA COUNTY REVENUES BY STATE

State	All counties	Property taxes ($)	Other taxes ($)	Charges and miscellaneous sources ($)	Inter-governmental sources ($)
Total, all counties	1,358	88.62	22.08	77.24	126.99
Alabama	41	20.18	22.24	6.85	33.01
Alaska	1	190.48	30.49	168.96	1,282.65
Arizona	11	80.26	4.36	102.32	111.48
Arkansas	28	26.45	11.14	82.40	33.58
California	43	122.57	18.50	87.54	315.19
Colorado	12	90.52	17.35	68.70	93.39
Delaware	3	46.29	2.40	76.58	38.54
Florida	39	122.73	17.92	145.37	95.83
Georgia	49	105.32	69.44	47.89	51.40
Hawaii	3	342.29	69.94	92.23	185.10
Idaho	9	49.12	3.60	87.21	32.07
Illinois	51	43.79	13.04	35.75	37.58
Indiana	56	56.46	0.79	127.02	71.91
Iowa	24	108.33	2.62	47.99	56.44
Kansas	20	71.59	16.80	154.85	35.85
Kentucky	37	19.29	3.28	13.72	37.16
Louisiana	36	65.96	56.22	179.97	71.32
Maine	15	15.53	0.03	3.89	4.93
Maryland	20	310.68	51.58	173.21	322.44
Massachusetts	11	13.58	0.18	9.44	4.01
Michigan	51	59.76	1.39	85.11	123.50
Minnesota	36	114.58	1.69	71.01	192.83
Mississippi	30	57.24	3.49	181.83	53.73
Missouri	31	42.50	51.92	35.26	30.79
Montana	6	152.97	9.74	89.47	38.44
Nebraska	11	62.88	10.55	73.29	49.77
Nevada	2	91.53	98.21	419.76	165.54
New Hampshire	10	32.16	0.00	12.16	28.20
New Jersey	21	133.90	1.55	42.05	118.14
New Mexico	15	52.32	17.28	41.03	29.97
New York	54	123.21	108.08	93.34	188.75
North Carolina	65	147.46	44.84	112.11	384.77
North Dakota	5	54.01	1.85	17.15	54.46
Ohio	77	39.65	13.47	64.97	94.71
Oklahoma	35	42.59	0.37	26.33	35.57
Oregon	20	54.79	10.43	44.63	102.19
Pennsylvania	58	57.06	0.82	30.59	79.58
South Carolina	34	54.35	2.17	120.49	48.91
South Dakota	3	44.78	9.38	19.34	24.30
Tennessee	45	91.62	57.31	108.35	106.94
Texas	80	75.53	5.18	51.13	18.61
Utah	8	66.47	20.89	49.53	49.39
Vermont	9	2.34	0.00	0.14	0.43
Virginia	39	346.85	105.46	111.60	324.26
Washington	24	64.91	19.63	52.97	90.05
West Virginia	29	41.37	0.99	68.60	29.85
Wisconsin	45	82.13	0.65	114.83	160.42
Wyoming	6	257.72	80.12	320.04	111.53

Table 1/5 AVERAGE PER CAPITA CITY EXPENDITURES BY POPULATION GROUP

Population group	All cities	Police ($)	Fire ($)	Streets ($)	Sewers and sanitation ($)
Total, all cities	2,570	76.51	44.15	30.18	46.86
Over 1,000,000	6	126.31	55.98	30.51	58.05
500,000–1,000,000	18	99.07	51.77	24.22	59.53
250,000– 499,999	33	83.38	54.34	28.06	51.24
100,000– 249,999	119	72.55	51.04	31.98	49.06
50,000– 99,999	286	64.84	43.79	30.06	40.94
25,000– 49,999	617	58.26	37.93	30.53	41.03
10,000– 24,999	1,491	53.07	27.09	32.57	38.22

Table 1/6 AVERAGE PER CAPITA COUNTY EXPENDITURES BY POPULATION GROUP

Population group	All counties	Law enforcement ($)	Hospitals ($)	Streets ($)	Welfare ($)	Administration and finance
Total, all counties	1,358	28.81	34.76	16.79	52.95	31.03
Over 1,000,000	19	42.23	51.44	8.64	76.23	40.57
500,000–1,000,000	53	34.76	38.35	11.02	70.18	34.11
250,000– 499,999	89	25.76	23.84	15.01	53.77	28.47
100,000– 249,999	230	23.19	19.34	18.78	39.63	28.24
50,000– 99,999	369	20.55	33.66	24.29	31.91	24.53
25,000– 49,999	594	17.25	39.59	31.89	26.17	24.17
10,000– 24,999	4	14.12	64.38	50.07	62.10	14.51

assessor, the coroner, and the recorder. There is no single administrator to oversee the county's operations. In some commission form counties, the structure has been adapted to include an official (generally full-time), such as the county judge, who is independently elected, at large, to be the presiding officer of the governing board.

Council–Administrator. The council–administrator form of government for counties is similar to the council–manager form for cities. Three distinct variations are identifiable, however. In its strongest variation, the council–administrator form provides for an elected county board or council and an appointed administrator. The county board adopts ordinances and resolutions, adopts the budget, and sets policy. The administrator, appointed by the board, develops the budget, implements it after its adoption, hires and fires department heads, and recommends policy and legislation to the board.

In some counties, where a "weaker" version of the council–administrator plan is in place, the administrator usually has less direct responsibility for overall county operations and less authority in hiring and firing, and may consult with the board on policy issues.

A third variation of the plan is a compromise between the council–administrator plan and the commission form. Here, an assistant to the presiding officer of the governing board or a specific functional officer may serve in the capacity of administrator. For example, in Michigan the auditor/controller, appointed by the governing board to audit the county's finances, may serve as administrator; in other states the county clerk, who is by statute clerk to the governing board, may have some administrative responsibility.

Council–Elected Executive. This form is characterized by two branches of government—legislative and executive. The county council or board assumes responsibility for county policies, adopts the budget, and audits the financial performance of the county. The executive, elected at large, is considered the chief elected official of the county, and often has veto power which can be overridden by the council. The executive prepares the budget; carries out the administration of the county operations; appoints department heads, usually with the consent of the council; suggests policy to the governing board; carries out appropriations, ordinances, and resolutions passed by the board; and generally acts as the spokesperson for the county. Where the executive is considered the chief political spokesperson, he or she often delegates the administrative responsibility for the day-to-day county operations to a chief administrator.

Metropolitan Status. The U.S. Office of Management and Budget (OMB) program of statistical classification of the country based on population density and degree of economic and social integration was revamped as of 30 June 1983. Based on the demographic data collected in the 1980 decennial census and the adoption of new classification standards, the criteria for Standard Metropolitan Statistical Areas that had been in effect since 1971 were redefined; the

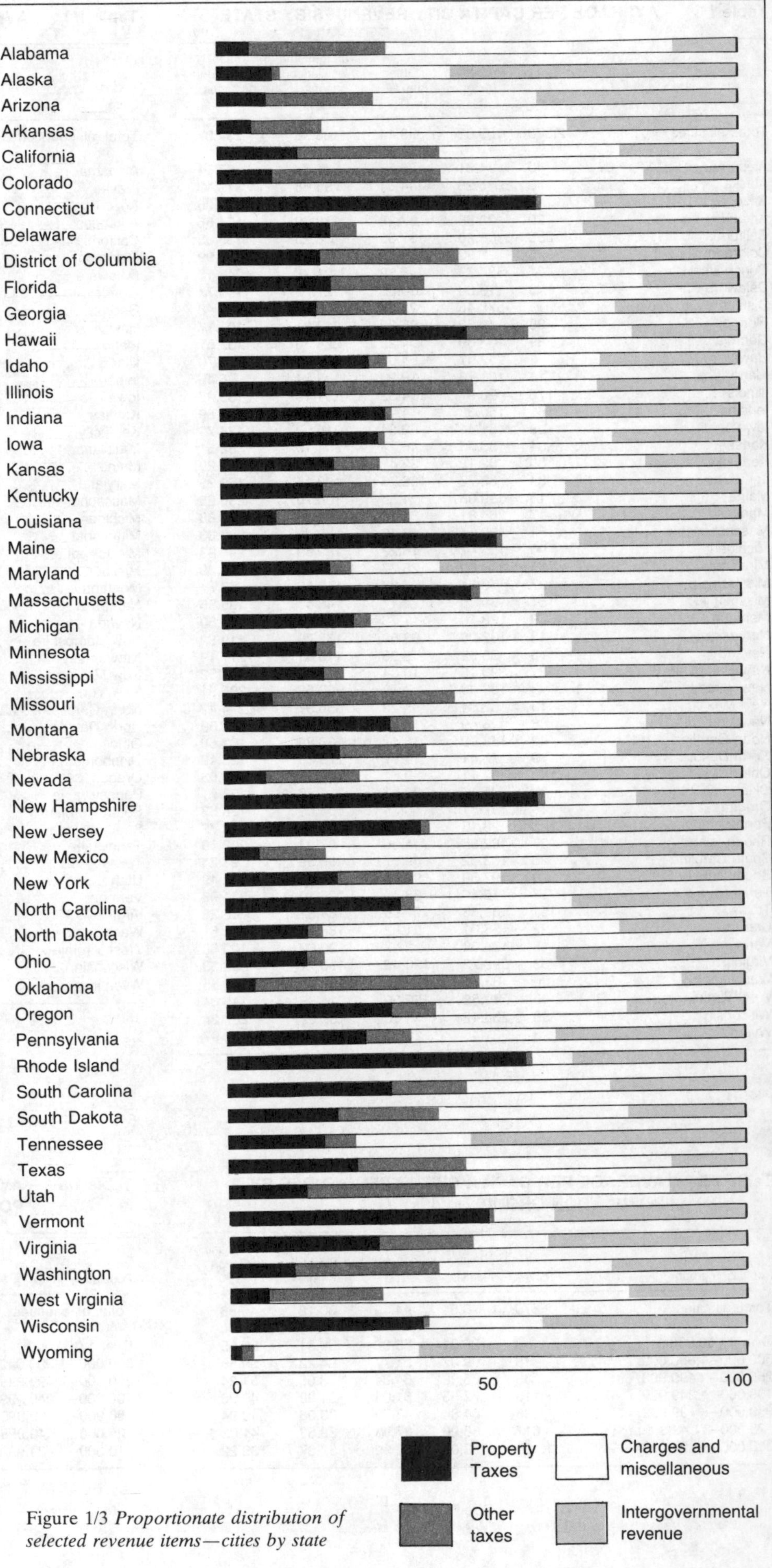

Figure 1/3 *Proportionate distribution of selected revenue items—cities by state*

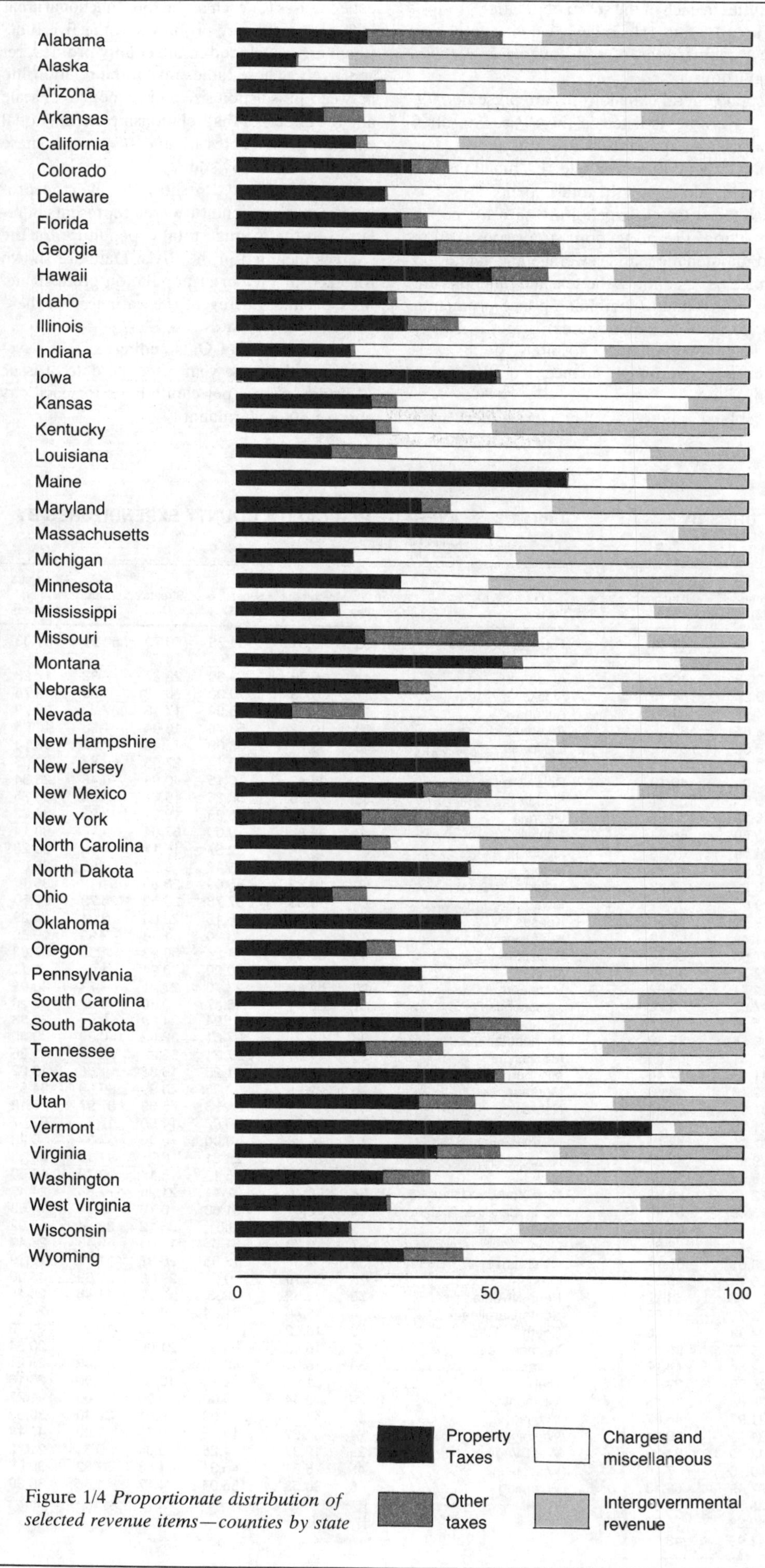

Figure 1/4 *Proportionate distribution of selected revenue items—counties by state*

designation for areas meeting the classification criteria has been changed as well. The new term for these areas is Metropolitan Statistical Areas (MSAs). To be classified as an MSA an area must include a city with a population of at least 50,000 or an urbanized area of at least 50,000 with a total metropolitan population of at least 100,000. The OMB further groups metropolitan areas of over 1,000,000 population into consolidated metropolitan statistical areas (CMSAs) and primary metropolitan statistical areas (PMSAs). Metro status as listed in the PICs describes the relationship of a municipality or county to an MSA.

Central cities are the core cities of an MSA and must have a population of at least 25,000 and meet two commuting requirements: at least 40% of the employed residents of the city must work within the city and there must be at least 75 jobs for each 100 residents who are employed. Cities between 15,000 and 25,000 population may also be considered central cities if they are at least one-third the size of the MSA's largest city and meet the two commuting requirements. *Suburban* cities are the other cities, towns, and incorporated places in an MSA. *Independent* cities are incorporated places not located in an MSA.

Counties that are located in an MSA are classified in a way similar to that for cities. *Central* counties are those counties in which central cities are located. *Suburban* counties are the other counties located within an MSA. Counties that are not located in an MSA are considered *independent*.

Population. The population figures listed in the PICs are 1982 estimates prepared by the U.S. Bureau of the Census. These are data which correspond most closely to the fiscal year 1983 revenue and expenditure statistics that follow.

General Revenues and Expenditures. City and county government revenue and expenditure data presented in the PICs are derived from information collected for fiscal year 1983 by the Governments Division of the U.S. Bureau of the Census as part of their annual studies of state and local financial transactions.

For both city and county governments total general revenue is presented and defined as all governmental revenue except that from utility systems, liquor stores, and locally maintained employee retirement funds. Total revenue from municipally operated utilities follows as a separate item in the city PICs and includes revenue from water supply systems, electric power, gas supply, and local transit systems as appropriate. Utility revenue is not reported for counties since relatively few county governments provide those services.

Intergovernmental revenue figures are presented on a per capita basis and include sums received from state governments, directly from the federal government and from other local governments (mainly county transfers to city govermnments). General revenue sharing funds distributed by the federal government are reported in this category. Per capita figures are further displayed for the governments' revenue from their own sources: property taxes, other locally imposed taxes (including general and selective sales taxes, income taxes, license and miscellaneous other taxes), and charges and miscellaneous other revenues.

Tables 1/1 and 1/2 display per capita revenues for each of the four revenue sources included in the city and county profiles, respectively, distributed among seven population groups. These tables can be used in comparing the per capita revenues for any individual government with the average figure for governments of its size class or with the country as a whole. Tables 1/3 and 1/4 provide these same data distributed by state.

Figures 1/1 and 1/2 use bar graphs to display the average proportion each revenue source represents of the average total revenue from the four sources included in the PICs. These figures present the information for cities and counties in each of the seven population groups. Figures 1/3 and 1/4 similarly use bar graphs to show comparisons of state averages of these proportions.

Total general expenditures are presented for the governments listed in the PICs. For cities total utility expenditures are also shown. Per capita expenditures for selected functions are displayed along with the total expenditures. For cities the selected expenditures are for police protection, fire protection, street construction and maintenance, and sewerage and sanitation services. For counties the selected functions are law enforcement (combining police protection and corrections expenditures), street construction and maintenance, hospitals, public welfare, and government finance and administration.

Table 1/5 and 1/6 display average per capita expenditures for each of the four functional areas included in the city profiles and the five functional areas included in the county profiles, respectively. These tables reveal the relationship between jurisdiction size and economics of scale and the effects of that relationship on functional expenditures. Tables 1/7 and 1/8 provide these data distributed by state.

Figures 1/5 and 1/6 show the average proportion each expenditure area represents in relation to the average total expenditure for the sources included in the PICs. Data are shown for each of the seven population groups. Figures 1/7 and 1/8 reveal the variances in these proportions by states.

Long Term Debt Outstanding. Debt payable more than one year after the date of issue is displayed on a per capita basis for each city and county government.

Table 1/7 AVERAGE PER CAPITA CITY EXPENDITURES BY STATE

State	All cities	Police ($)	Fire ($)	Streets ($)	Sewers and sanitation ($)
Total, all cities	2,570	76.51	44.15	30.18	46.86
Alabama	40	51.92	42.39	19.32	40.21
Alaska	3	166.49	105.26	173.28	104.15
Arizona	17	78.97	40.74	24.53	44.66
Arkansas	29	39.64	30.08	25.65	39.85
California	256	84.47	43.37	26.06	32.12
Colorado	25	77.45	39.52	40.81	39.81
Connecticut	84	62.46	40.03	40.08	40.19
Delaware	3	115.21	67.12	19.54	123.97
District of Columbia	1	240.95	77.01	40.39	132.28
Florida	95	80.60	43.71	25.80	56.74
Georgia	39	66.94	41.51	24.54	61.58
Hawaii	1	71.25	34.26	18.69	42.16
Idaho	11	48.92	39.50	18.22	57.12
Illinois	176	91.85	40.46	29.05	32.31
Indiana	61	56.00	42.49	29.10	48.56
Iowa	29	56.64	41.24	41.40	53.16
Kansas	34	50.51	33.03	27.63	28.58
Kentucky	30	58.01	46.19	22.35	38.43
Louisiana	34	60.27	37.08	24.71	49.92
Maine	18	45.76	45.86	47.62	42.22
Maryland	17	99.76	50.84	37.59	73.55
Massachusetts	151	66.28	60.35	39.38	35.39
Michigan	90	97.91	47.46	36.61	69.55
Minnesota	65	55.15	32.60	41.43	54.44
Mississippi	27	46.62	38.63	30.18	42.60
Missouri	51	83.09	37.58	31.04	30.95
Montana	9	44.46	35.68	31.23	48.09
Nebraska	12	51.47	37.80	37.65	42.10
Nevada	6	95.63	57.93	28.95	37.03
New Hampshire	21	53.14	46.96	55.68	38.26
New Jersey	183	74.23	36.63	22.39	39.81
New Mexico	13	70.26	38.68	25.48	51.48
New York	86	109.38	60.28	33.84	60.62
North Carolina	42	66.46	41.98	33.77	58.67
North Dakota	9	47.02	25.25	35.61	30.11
Ohio	149	68.80	43.98	25.13	48.93
Oklahoma	33	49.08	41.35	21.72	33.17
Oregon	29	79.93	57.64	32.32	43.98
Pennsylvania	163	75.54	28.87	27.38	44.26
Rhode Island	27	58.09	51.23	35.77	39.44
South Carolina	26	59.07	38.04	22.54	49.17
South Dakota	9	43.78	30.51	36.85	29.72
Tennessee	37	60.25	46.36	26.68	70.46
Texas	151	56.73	38.46	21.97	46.87
Utah	22	57.42	35.40	31.79	30.91
Vermont	8	47.71	30.02	43.80	21.20
Virginia	33	64.03	44.63	40.10	57.16
Washington	36	78.49	59.25	37.49	69.13
West Virginia	15	58.80	53.68	38.53	68.98
Wisconsin	56	89.73	53.29	52.39	75.76
Wyoming	8	73.82	42.23	43.49	43.04

Table 1/8 AVERAGE PER CAPITA COUNTY EXPENDITURES BY STATE

State	All counties	Law enforcement ($)	Hospitals ($)	Streets ($)	Welfare ($)	Administration and finance
Total, all counties	1,358	28.81	34.76	16.79	52.95	31.03
Alabama	41	16.26	4.39	26.27	2.82	17.23
Alaska	1	0.03	0.00	6.88	0.95	114.75
Arizona	11	34.70	46.52	17.18	37.23	39.70
Arkansas	28	10.32	53.75	16.84	1.88	16.05
California	43	53.71	53.09	15.43	167.86	58.53
Colorado	12	23.75	0.14	27.53	67.87	30.03
Delaware	3	23.43	0.15	0.88	0.48	25.34
Florida	39	47.25	38.26	19.61	9.56	35.25
Georgia	49	31.00	18.35	19.21	2.93	34.22
Hawaii	3	98.89	0.00	57.64	24.18	80.14
Idaho	9	18.64	52.57	15.11	4.95	30.28
Illinois	51	17.62	21.12	9.58	7.05	26.67
Indiana	56	13.23	86.09	23.35	51.22	36.16
Iowa	24	16.33	37.78	29.52	26.79	36.50
Kansas	20	15.89	15.15	22.63	3.31	24.29
Kentucky	37	17.05	3.90	11.14	2.99	9.69
Louisiana	36	38.31	114.24	30.93	1.36	27.83
Maine	15	8.21	0.00	0.94	1.01	5.11
Maryland	20	54.22	23.70	27.21	1.73	30.92
Massachusetts	11	6.14	6.47	0.36	0.08	3.20
Michigan	51	25.69	31.94	24.89	20.91	32.56
Minnesota	36	32.21	37.61	32.62	160.29	39.35
Mississippi	30	11.67	127.71	32.29	2.64	19.26
Missouri	31	18.00	21.25	15.83	1.68	19.02
Montana	6	22.28	2.25	25.99	30.68	34.55
Nebraska	11	17.49	25.98	25.39	37.97	36.12
Nevada	2	93.92	190.83	14.60	17.75	91.67
New Hampshire	10	9.88	0.00	0.00	53.33	8.28
New Jersey	21	21.23	26.81	8.95	97.16	25.43
New Mexico	15	18.25	35.13	15.17	2.79	16.50
New York	54	60.40	32.41	24.25	177.84	24.43
North Carolina	65	16.41	31.60	0.10	41.04	14.83
North Dakota	5	12.72	0.81	25.12	22.64	15.02
Ohio	77	16.78	31.65	18.04	68.46	26.49
Oklahoma	35	7.56	13.95	26.32	1.11	16.39
Oregon	20	35.19	0.00	29.98	7.69	45.00
Pennsylvania	58	13.52	3.85	2.67	41.46	25.15
South Carolina	34	18.46	81.14	9.82	3.91	20.66
South Dakota	3	16.62	1.43	20.36	10.27	23.79
Tennessee	45	16.68	86.88	21.06	6.70	20.34
Texas	80	16.01	40.15	12.32	2.68	28.21
Utah	8	21.91	2.96	10.37	3.09	26.16
Vermont	9	0.44	0.00	0.00	0.00	1.27
Virginia	39	47.64	0.00	9.01	32.40	39.83
Washington	24	34.62	14.56	30.78	1.02	40.14
West Virginia	29	12.37	4.25	0.04	0.31	21.72
Wisconsin	45	26.81	46.31	31.48	58.32	30.08
Wyoming	6	30.53	186.04	24.77	4.35	36.30

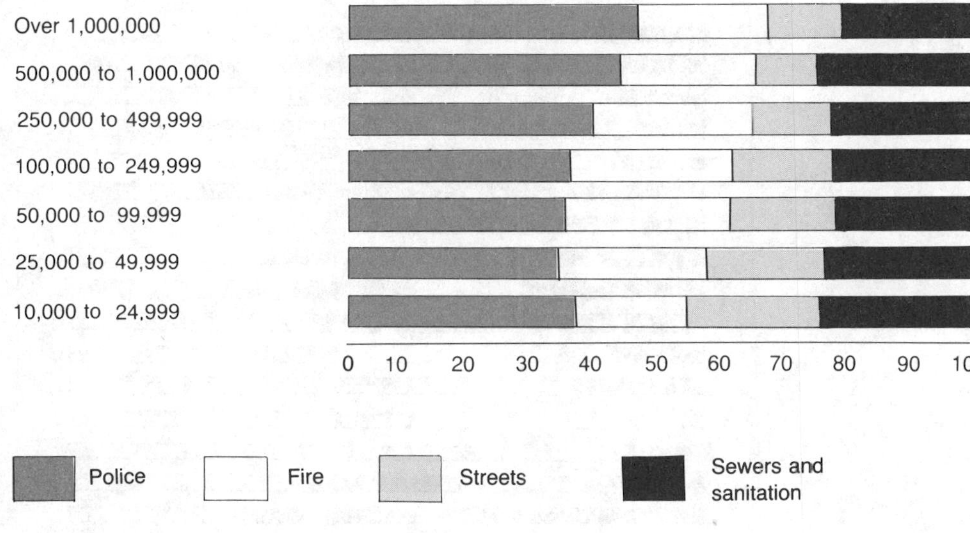

Figure 1/5 *Proportionate distribution of selected expenditure items—cities by population group*

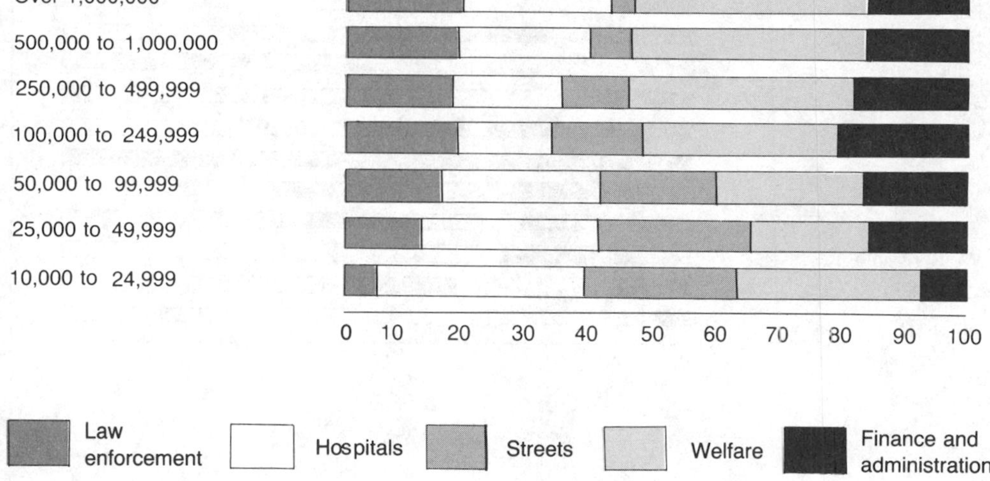

Figure 1/6 *Proportionate distribution of selected expenditure items—counties by population group*

Government Employment. The last data set in the PICs contains information on the total number of full-time equivalent employees working for city and county governments in October 1983 and their average full-time monthly salary. The full-time equivalent measure is used to convert any part-time employment to a full-time basis, using the average full-time salary as a criterion.

USE OF THE PICS

The format of the 1985 PICs is consistent with that of the PICs in earlier editions of *The Municipal Year Book* and *The County Year Book,* thereby facilitating use of the series as a unit. Cities and counties are listed in alphabetical order by states.

The total number of data sets presented in the Profiles of Individual Cities since their inception in 1976 is 204. Appendix A shows the data sets that have appeared in the Profiles of Individual Cites and the years in which they appeared. Many of these data sets have been included in more than one year's PICs to reflect updated information as it became available.

Appendix B provides information on the data sets that have appeared in the Profiles of Individual Counties. In addition to the Profiles of Individual Counties that appeared in *The Municipal Year Book 1983* and *The Municipal Year Book 1984*, two earlier versions of the county PICs appeared in *The County Year Book* in 1977 and 1978. (*The County Year Book* ceased publication after 1978.)

[1]The 19 consolidations 10,000 and over in population are listed below, followed by the year in which they were organized (city-county consolidations are designated in the individual table that follows this article by a "c" after the consolidation name): Anaconda–Deer Lodge County, Mont. (1976); Anchorage–Anchorage Area Borough, Alaska (1975); Baton Rouge–East Baton Rouge Parish, La. (1947); Boston–Suffolk County, Mass. (1821); Butte–Silver Bow County, Mont. (1976); Carson City–Ormsby County, Nev. (1969); Columbus–Muscogee County, Ga. (1970); Denver–Denver County, Colo. (1904); Honolulu–Honolulu County, Hawaii (1907); Houma–Terrebonne Parish, La. (1984); Indianapolis–Marion County, Ind. (1969); Jacksonville–Duval County, Fla. (1967); Juneau–Greater Juneau Borough, Alaska (1969); Lexington–Fayette County, Ky. (1972); Nashville–Davidson County, Tenn. (1962); New Orleans–Orleans Parish, La. (1805); New York–New York County, N.Y. (1847); Philadelphia–Philadelphia County, Pa. (1854); San Francisco–San Francisco County, Calif. (1856).

[2]The 30 independent cities that are 10,000 and over in population and that are included in the PICs table (where they are indicated by an "i" after the city name) are listed below (only those cities which became independent after 1 January 1960 are followed by an effective date): Washington, D.C.; Baltimore, Md.; St. Louis, Mo.; and in Virginia: Alexandria, Bristol, Charlottesville, Chesapeake (1962), Colonial Heights, Danville, Fairfax (1961), Fredericksburg, Hampton, Harrisonburg, Hopewell, Lynchburg, Manassas (1975), Martinsville, Newport News, Norfolk, Petersburg, Portsmouth, Radford, Richmond, Roanoke, Salem (1968), Staunton, Suffolk (1972), Virginia Beach (1962), Waynesboro, and Winchester.

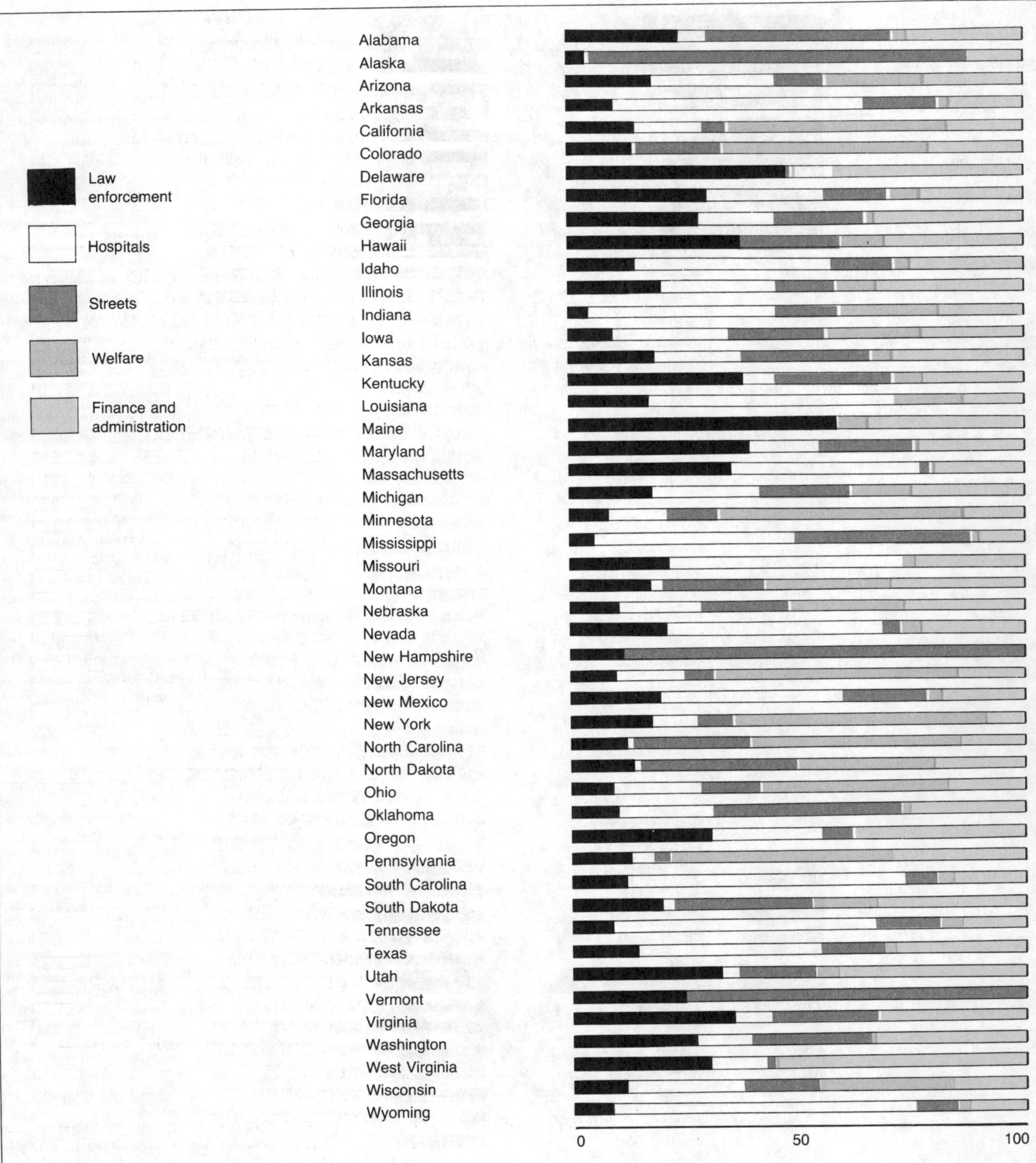

Figure 1/7 *Proportionate distribution of selected expenditure items—counties by state*

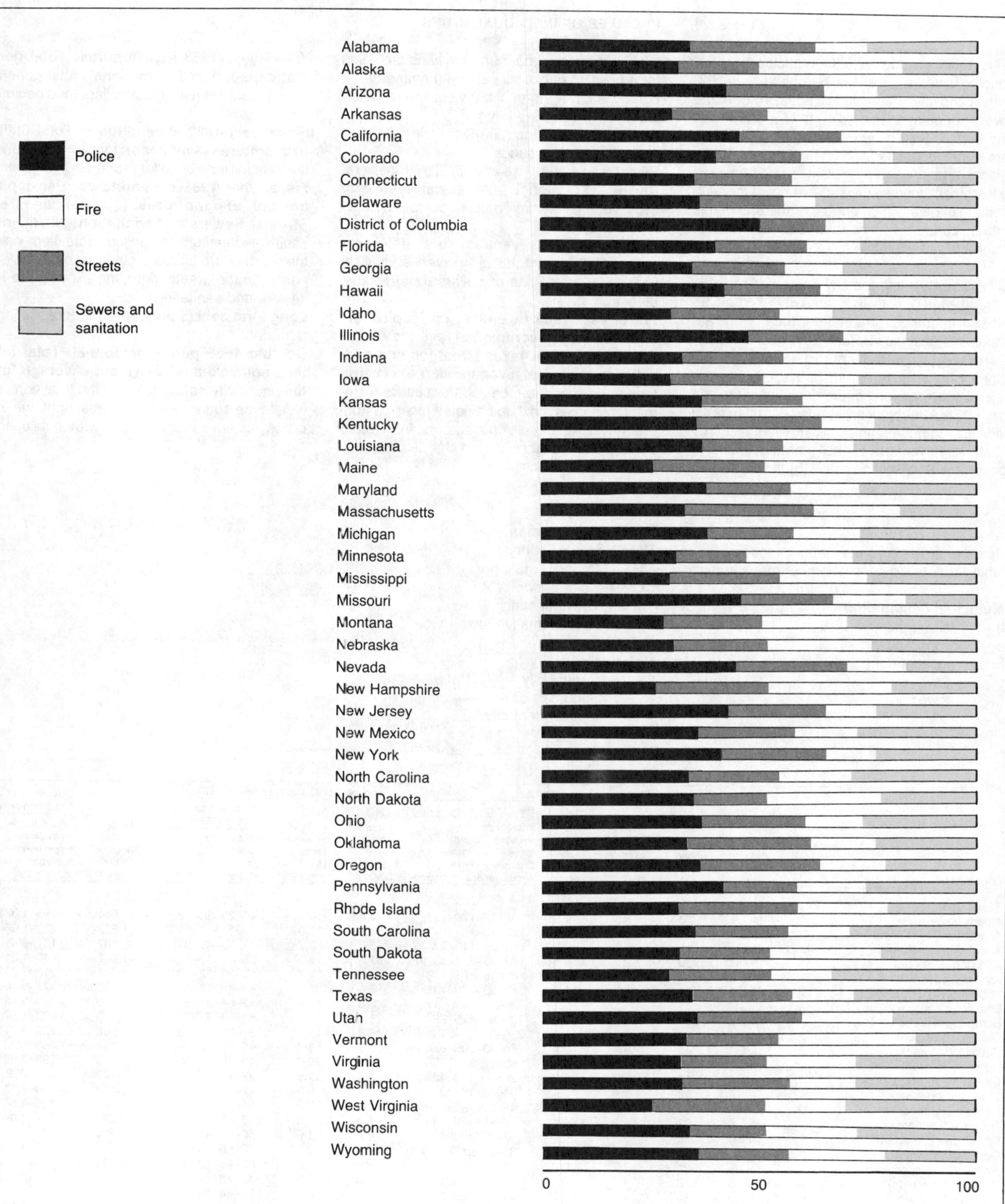

Figure 1/8 *Proportionate distribution of selected expenditure items—cities by state*

Table 1/9 PROFILES OF INDIVIDUAL CITIES

This table includes 2,570 municipalities (including cities as well as boroughs, selected towns and townships, and villages) 10,000 and over in population according to U.S. Bureau of the Census population estimates for 1982. Data are from the master file of the International City Management Association (ICMA), and from U.S. government sources (see source notes for each column of data, which appear at the end of this table). Leaders (...) indicate data are not reported or not available.

City (county): left, the city name, followed, in parentheses ( ), by the name of the county in which it is located. Small letter symbols indicate municipal designation (see key).
Form of government–metro status: left, the city's form of government (the symbol to the left of the form of government indicates the city's ICMA recognition status: an asterisk [*] indicates that the municipality is recognized by ICMA as having the council–manager form of government, a section mark [§] indicates that ICMA recognizes the municipality as providing for a position of overall general management); right, the city's status vis-à-vis a metropolitan statistical area. (See key.)
Est. 1982 population (000): the estimated 1982 population in thousands.
Fiscal year 1983 revenues: Total general revenue ($ millions): total general revenue for fiscal year 1983 in millions of dollars (one decimal place).
Fiscal year 1983 revenues: Total utility revenue ($ millions): total utility revenue for fiscal year 1983 in millions of dollars (one decimal place).
Fiscal year 1983 revenues: Per capita revenue ($): Intergovernmental revenue–Property taxes–Other taxes–Charges and miscellaneous general revenue: left, the per capita amount of revenue received from intergovernmental sources; next, the amount received from property taxes; next, the amount from other taxes; right, the amount from charges and miscellaneous revenue.
Fiscal year 1983 expenditures: Total general expenditures ($ millions): total general expenditures in millions of dollars (one decimal place).
Fiscal year 1983 expenditures: Total utility expenditures ($ millions): total utility expenditures in millions of dollars (one decimal place).
Fiscal year 1983 expenditures: Per capita current expenditures ($): Police–Fire–Streets–Sewers and sanitation: left, the per capita expenditure for police protection; next, the expenditure for fire protection; next, the expenditure for streets; right, the expenditure for sewers and sanitation.
Long term debt ($ per capita): Per capita long term debt.
October 1983 public personnel: Total full-time equivalent employment–Average full-time monthly salary ($): left, the total number of full-time equivalent employees; right, the average full-time monthly salary of public employees.

Key
See the article and the notes preceding this table for detailed descriptions of these items.

Municipal designation
b borough
c consolidation
i independent city
t town
tp township
v village

Form of government
MC Mayor–council
CM Council–manager
CO Commission
TM Town meeting
RT Representative town meeting

Metro status
C Central city
S Suburban city
I Independent city

			Fiscal year 1983 revenues			Fiscal year 1983 expenditures				October 1983 public personnel
City (county)	Form of government–Metro status	Est. 1982 population (000)	Total general revenue ($ millions)	Total utility revenue ($ millions)	Per capita revenues ($) Intergovernmental revenue–Property taxes–Other taxes–Charges and miscellaneous general revenue	Total general expenditures ($ millions)	Total utility expenditures ($ millions)	Per capita current expenditures ($) Police–Fire–Streets–Sewers and sanitation	Long term debt ($ per capita)	Total full time equivalent employment–Average full time monthly salary ($)
ALABAMA										
Albertville (Marshall)	MC-S	13	5.3	14.9	67–22–176–157	4.0	14.8	46–25–36–72	611	195–1,071
Alexander City (Tallapoosa)	MC-I	14	8.2	10.2	254–15–154–147	8.9	12.0	50–31–11–49	1,322	226–1,068
Andalusia (Covington)	MC-I	11	2.7	6.0	44–27–110–77	3.0	5.7	34–23–43–39	187	131–982
Anniston (Calhoun)	*CM-C	30	62.1	2.1	123–39–226–1,664	57.6	3.1	55–44–43–33	1,202	1,349–1,213
Athens (Limestone)	MC-S	15	5.8	21.7	41–18–161–178	5.2	24.2	45–23–32–69	941	213–1,239
Auburn (Lee)	*CM-I	29	10.0	1.2	47–33–142–125	8.4	1.2	48–45–18–47	282	325–1,166
Bessemer (Jefferson)	CO-S	31	...	...	...–...–...–...	8.8	17.2	59–54–31–32	0	368–1,494
Birmingham (Jefferson)	MC-C	283	171.7	0.0	109–60–175–262	76.7	0.0	69–57–5–24	0	3,420–1,576
Cullman (Cullman)	MC-I	13	7.5	11.6	230–32–67–243	6.9	11.1	51–36–43–75	686	227–1,311
Decatur (Morgan)	MC-I	42	48.1	62.9	64–49–205–830	46.7	58.7	45–39–29–68	1,109	1,208–1,221
Dothan (Houston)	†MC-I	51	19.9	33.0	63–12–162–150	26.8	30.7	49–40–17–58	1,361	696–1,288
Enterprise (Coffee)	MC-I	19	4.7	0.7	27–30–143–43	3.9	1.6	32–16–16–43	142	325–922
Eufaula (Barbour)	MC-I	12	5.8	0.4	104–19–159–210	5.1	0.5	41–32–15–19	532	99–1,111
Fairfield (Jefferson)	MC-S	13	6.3	0.0	49–50–142–246	5.0	0.0	51–35–23–18	98	105–1,659
Florence (Lauderdale)	†MC-C	37	13.9	44.4	57–40–126–148	11.2	47.6	53–41–0–57	923	1,222–1,061
Fort Payne (De Kalb)	MC-I	12	5.3	0.9	37–8–157–242	4.7	1.0	56–41–45–70	930	144–1,005
Gadsden (Etowah)	CO-C	47	20.5	2.7	85–24–256–72	19.5	2.5	62–66–20–69	265	717–1,284
Homewood (Jefferson)	MC-S	21	7.7	0.0	41–88–195–42	7.8	0.0	62–65–19–32	1,141	206–1,559
Hoover t (Jefferson)	MC-S	22	4.3	0.0	23–27–130–17	4.0	0.0	42–43–14–45	0	...–...
Hueytown (Jefferson)	MC-S	15	1.7	0.0	24–13–65–11	1.7	0.0	25–24–14–11	49	...–...
Huntsville (Madison)	MC-C	145	143.3	135.1	77–41–166–702	111.7	131.0	40–36–35–36	783	3,107–1,514
Jasper (Walker)	*CM-S	12	5.7	3.6	42–42–286–101	4.8	4.5	87–30–61–29	1,957	164–1,192
Mobile (Mobile)	CO-C	205	104.5	7.3	55–17–198–241	90.8	10.7	52–40–13–56	952	2,135–1,373
Montgomery (Montgomery)	MC-C	182	60.8	10.9	67–30–163–74	55.7	13.3	48–35–17–35	371	2,246–1,257
Mountain Brook (Jefferson)	*CM-S	20	6.9	0.0	28–101–168–54	6.0	0.0	66–74–33–42	36	210–1,455
Northport (Tuscaloosa)	MC-S	15	3.6	0.9	109–23–53–55	3.1	0.6	41–39–3–23	121	125–1,222
Opelika (Lee)	CO-I	24	13.8	13.1	83–29–196–275	15.6	12.8	60–45–33–29	651	362–1,126
Ozark (Dale)	MC-I	14	4.9	0.7	90–20–144–104	4.0	0.6	33–20–15–38	1,031	120–964
Phenix City (Russell)	*CM-S	27	46.9	7.2	52–27–128–1,534	34.8	6.8	32–27–26–37	1,010	1,040–994
Prattville (Autauga)	†MC-S	19	4.4	0.0	40–11–130–53	4.3	0.0	43–35–25–43	144	...–...
Prichard (Mobile)	MC-S	40	7.4	2.1	49–4–92–42	7.8	1.6	42–43–11–27	222	308–1,097

Table 1/9 continued **PROFILES OF INDIVIDUAL CITIES**

City (county)	Form of govern-ment–Metro status	Est. 1982 popu-lation (000)	Fiscal year 1983 revenues: Total general revenue ($ millions)	Total utility revenue ($ millions)	Per capita revenues ($): Intergovernmental revenue–Property taxes–Other taxes–Charges and miscellaneous general revenue	Fiscal year 1983 expenditures: Total general expenditures ($ millions)	Total utility expenditures ($ millions)	Per capita current expenditures ($): Police–Fire–Streets–Sewers and sanitation	Long term debt ($ per capita)	October 1983 public personnel: Total full time equivalent employment–Average full time monthly salary ($)
ALABAMA continued										
Scottsboro (Jackson)	MC-I	15	18.7	15.3	25–42–156–1,021	8.7	14.9	36–28–51–34	1,151	205–1,152
Selma (Dallas)	MC-I	28	14.1	1.2	75–55–212–169	12.1	0.8	48–36–5–34	127	427–1,026
Sheffield (Colbert)	CO-S	11	9.1	23.3	448–35–162–150	9.9	23.6	47–33–40–42	908	204–1,546
Sylacauga (Talladega)	MC-I	13	20.6	13.9	72–24–167–1,338	18.2	12.5	56–31–29–62	1,134	657–1,046
Talladega (Talladega)	CO-I	20	4.6	1.3	32–17–141–43	4.4	0.5	36–17–21–8	642	193–1,017
Troy (Pike)	CO-I	13	3.7	6.6	45–12–130–95	4.6	6.7	53–26–22–34	325	...–...
Tuscaloosa (Tuscaloosa)	CO-C	74	28.0	4.3	124–27–142–87	22.7	5.0	62–51–25–49	519	786–1,439
Tuskegee (Macon)	MC-I	13	...	...	...–...–...–...	4.4	5.9	10–7–35–27	0	276–1,102
Vestavia Hills (Jefferson)	MC-S	16	5.3	0.0	31–116–158–29	4.7	0.0	44–64–12–36	374	112–1,561
ALASKA										
Anchorage c (Anchorage)	†MC-C	195	540.7	35.4	1,565–305–51–857	656.2	64.4	177–103–189–105	3,187	7,607–3,186
Fairbanks (Fairbanks North Star)	*CM-I	27	57.3	13.4	1,097–13–35–988	48.2	17.0	153–129–97–107	1,901	227–3,154
Juneau c (Juneau)	*CM-I	22	...	...	...–...–...–...	69.9	3.7	86–93–126–90	0	986–2,963
ARIZONA										
Casa Grande (Pinal)	*CM-I	16	7.2	0.0	202–36–138–89	6.7	0.0	93–37–78–49	46	150–1,774
Chandler (Maricopa)	*CM-S	37	20.8	3.6	136–34–122–277	23.3	2.0	70–35–21–74	770	324–1,749
Douglas (Cochise)	CM-I	13	5.1	0.6	185–16–105–75	5.0	0.8	68–42–32–40	51	168–1,332
Flagstaff (Coconino)	*CM-I	35	22.9	3.6	258–85–129–185	19.3	9.3	66–50–39–51	793	437–1,751
Glendale (Maricopa)	*CM-S	106	40.5	7.0	154–29–69–128	32.8	11.8	50–25–23–24	680	905–1,994
Lake Havasu City (Mohave)	*CM-I	17	9.7	1.2	197–283–19–90	6.8	3.0	63–92–85–65	863	174–1,881
Mesa (Maricopa)	*CM-S	172	83.4	41.6	169–8–116–192	78.9	43.2	91–44–29–50	547	1,450–1,989
Nogales (Santa Cruz)	MC-I	16	4.9	0.9	169–8–79–48	4.8	1.1	50–21–61–45	191	183–1,109
Paradise Valley t (Maricopa)	*CM-S	13	3.2	0.0	126–8–76–48	1.7	0.0	61–0–21–1	19	47–2,002
Peoria (Maricopa)	*CM-S	14	8.5	1.0	176–28–173–241	6.6	1.2	73–20–31–96	689	...–...
Phoenix (Maricopa)	*CM-C	824	523.2	54.5	280–60–116–179	510.2	99.8	95–43–18–48	868	8,551–1,978
Prescott (Yavapai)	*CM-I	21	11.1	2.6	162–43–122–196	9.7	4.4	72–58–62–51	365	295–1,540
Scottsdale (Maricopa)	*CM-S	94	48.8	5.7	153–44–188–132	46.5	6.0	78–28–53–51	250	858–1,916
Sierra Vista (Cochise)	*CM-I	28	8.6	0.0	133–29–70–75	8.3	0.0	34–15–40–41	63	172–1,604
Tempe (Maricopa)	*CM-S	113	54.1	9.2	162–47–119–154	31.9	13.1	21–29–3–48	640	942–1,987
Tucson (Pima)	*CM-C	352	226.6	37.6	231–29–181–203	225.9	57.1	73–46–25–31	944	3,861–1,930
Yuma (Yuma)	*CM-I	45	19.0	3.2	169–54–127–74	17.2	2.5	67–45–27–50	291	450–1,819
ARKANSAS										
Arkadelphia (Clark)	*CM-I	10	2.0	0.4	52–6–91–50	1.8	0.4	35–9–25–41	45	73–1,139
Benton (Saline)	†MC-S	18	3.3	7.4	83–14–36–50	2.9	7.3	27–28–23–25	131	163–1,245
Blytheville (Mississippi)	MC-I	24	9.6	1.7	62–17–27–296	4.9	1.3	32–19–17–36	80	192–937
Camden (Ouachita)	*CM-I	16	4.8	0.7	111–17–35–140	3.5	2.3	30–33–21–30	192	150–994
Conway (Faulkner)	MC-I	20	4.7	0.0	69–24–71–65	3.3	0.0	34–23–19–27	24	133–1,287
El Dorado (Union)	MC-I	25	8.8	1.4	166–20–20–141	5.8	1.4	41–26–33–54	141	254–1,232
Fayetteville (Washington)	*CM-C	36	...	...	...–...–...–...	10.5	2.9	27–21–37–46	0	327–1,309
Forrest City (St. Francis)	MC-I	14	2.8	0.7	61–15–28–100	2.5	0.7	40–14–24–41	175	139–1,039
Fort Smith (Sebastian)	*CM-C	71	19.7	3.6	82–25–28–141	16.9	3.6	37–29–14–37	238	537–1,344
Hope (Hempstead)	*CM-I	10	2.3	7.4	59–11–11–144	2.9	7.4	38–20–36–50	340	102–1,076
Hot Springs (Garland)	MC-I	36	14.5	2.6	78–16–127–181	14.2	2.4	40–37–49–72	398	399–1,105
Jacksonville (Pulaski)	MC-S	29	13.8	2.0	61–17–49–349	13.1	2.0	29–26–14–29	432	436–1,249
Jonesboro (Craighead)	MC-I	31	17.0	17.0	193–19–32–303	9.0	30.4	27–29–29–41	2,291	330–1,344
Little Rock (Pulaski)	*CM-C	168	94.4	13.9	220–38–97–207	90.9	15.7	48–38–26–43	440	1,684–1,364
Magnolia (Columbia)	MC-I	12	7.1	0.7	54–11–33–490	6.9	0.7	27–15–34–16	108	266–890
Malvern (Hot Spring)	†MC-I	10	1.3	0.3	59–12–30–30	1.1	0.3	27–21–18–8	73	54–1,132
North Little Rock (Pulaski)	MC-C	64	23.4	27.7	138–34–47–145	21.9	26.4	59–48–32–50	376	702–1,473
Paragould (Greene)	MC-I	15	5.9	5.6	99–11–9–262	3.5	5.0	27–18–16–32	106	169–1,021
Pine Bluff (Jefferson)	MC-C	56	16.7	0.1	101–25–53–118	14.8	0.4	42–27–24–31	41	436–1,273
Rogers (Benton)	MC-S	19	7.1	1.2	49–28–55–239	5.6	2.0	39–33–26–28	54	142–1,281
Russellville (Pope)	MC-I	16	3.4	0.0	56–15–34–108	3.3	0.0	31–18–21–50	96	125–1,095
Searcy (White)	MC-I	14	2.2	0.0	55–18–30–59	2.1	0.0	23–19–18–27	0	91–1,011
Sherwood (Pulaski)	MC-S	11	3.0	0.0	76–15–23–150	2.4	0.0	35–0–20–15	212	67–1,218
Springdale (Washington)	MC-C	24	7.5	1.8	135–31–29–115	5.4	1.7	40–32–25–29	120	193–1,261
Stuttgart (Arkansas)	MC-I	11	9.4	0.6	154–25–45–634	8.7	0.5	34–17–38–54	192	363–1,085
Texarkana (Miller)	*CM-C	22	18.3	3.9	364–33–83–365	14.4	2.9	63–46–38–63	679	325–1,282
Van Buren (Crawford)	MC-S	12	2.4	0.7	59–24–38–73	2.0	0.6	21–20–21–22	222	79–1,177
West Helena (Phillips)	MC-I	11	1.9	0.4	96–8–18–47	1.4	0.3	28–19–14–24	13	81–1,087
West Memphis (Crittenden)	MC-S	28	10.5	15.2	113–20–32–213	8.1	15.7	40–32–18–38	1,020	264–1,173
CALIFORNIA										
Alameda (Alameda)	*CM-S	68	17.3	22.7	59–67–82–58	17.5	20.1	81–70–36–0	0	390–2,374
Albany (Alameda)	*CM-S	15	4.4	0.0	57–75–126–32	3.7	0.0	76–46–14–5	20	...–...
Alhambra (Los Angeles)	*CM-S	67	21.4	2.0	57–71–76–114	35.5	1.8	54–36–25–30	314	383–2,073
Anaheim (Orange)	*CM-C	226	120.7	137.4	72–90–143–227	148.8	174.9	101–48–37–30	2,017	2,065–2,238
Antioch (Contra Costa)	*CM-S	45	...	...	...–...–...–...	10.1	2.4	77–0–24–8	0	155–2,288
Arcadia (Los Angeles)	*CM-S	46	19.7	2.3	57–50–162–158	16.6	2.9	84–64–24–7	9	306–2,426
Arcata (Humboldt)	*CM-I	14	4.7	0.6	131–28–71–114	4.7	0.8	68–0–22–30	130	...–...
Arroyo Grande (San Luis Obispo)	*CM-I	12	3.0	0.8	65–49–92–37	2.3	0.8	44–9–30–12	46	...–...
Artesia (Los Angeles)	*CM-S	15	2.7	0.0	64–9–74–39	2.7	0.0	40–0–11–36	0	...–...
Atascadero (San Luis Obispo)	†MC-I	18	3.5	0.0	70–32–70–24	3.3	0.0	46–21–16–1	0	73–1,876
Atwater (Merced)	*CM-I	18	4.8	0.4	73–50–40–102	4.3	0.3	51–11–16–48	32	...–...
Azusa (Los Angeles)	*CM-S	31	13.0	10.5	67–43–74–230	12.7	11.6	51–31–40–16	0	225–1,824
Bakersfield (Kern)	*CM-C	116	44.0	5.7	72–70–166–73	54.3	2.5	106–63–39–71	196	877–2,168
Baldwin Park (Los Angeles)	*CM-S	54	9.9	0.0	74–30–41–40	10.1	0.0	57–0–32–0	61	173–2,014
Banning (Riverside)	*CM-S	15	4.7	6.1	74–71–62–107	4.6	6.4	79–33–18–38	211	194–1,619
Barstow (San Bernardino)	*CM-S	19	15.6	0.1	64–65–123–553	15.6	0.8	69–0–32–44	418	315–1,709

Table 1/9 continued **PROFILES OF INDIVIDUAL CITIES**

City (county)	Form of govern-ment–Metro status	Est. 1982 popu-lation (000)	Fiscal year 1983 revenues: Total general revenue ($ millions)	Total utility revenue ($ millions)	Per capita revenues ($): Intergovernmental revenue–Property taxes–Other taxes–Charges and miscellaneous general revenue	Fiscal year 1983 expenditures: Total general expenditures ($ millions)	Total utility expenditures ($ millions)	Per capita current expenditures ($): Police–Fire–Streets–Sewers and sanitation	Long term debt ($ per capita)	October 1983 public personnel: Total full time equivalent employment–Average full time monthly salary ($)
CALIFORNIA continued										
Bell (Los Angeles)	*CM-S	27	7.4	0.0	78–45–129–25	6.9	0.0	94–0–22–10	26	...–...
Bell Gardens (Los Angeles)	*CM-S	36	6.2	0.0	76–27–35–34	5.2	0.0	55–0–12–1	0	86–1,971
Bellflower (Los Angeles)	*CM-S	55	8.2	0.5	61–1–60–26	7.1	0.5	38–0–20–0	2	104–1,668
Belmont (San Mateo)	*CM-S	24	7.0	0.0	41–99–63–85	5.6	0.0	58–0–40–30	60	88–2,274
Benicia (Solano)	*CM-S	18	7.4	2.1	50–158–95–111	7.1	1.6	64–53–27–34	869	138–2,138
Berkeley (Alameda)	*CM-S	103	70.9	0.0	179–96–132–278	68.9	0.0	78–52–26–49	55	1,498–1,424
Beverly Hills (Los Angeles)	*CM-S	32	53.8	4.0	65–226–689–716	42.6	3.7	287–182–109–71	812	710–2,405
Brawley (Imperial)	*CM-I	17	4.9	0.8	105–41–66–84	6.0	0.5	56–27–41–24	14	...–...
Brea (Orange)	*CM-S	31	20.7	1.9	67–247–161–193	20.9	2.8	103–60–18–27	1,034	...–...
Buena Park (Orange)	*CM-S	64	20.9	2.5	63–47–139–76	24.3	2.7	91–52–26–15	33	388–2,339
Burbank (Los Angeles)	*CM-S	85	61.9	58.1	136–181–191–217	57.8	62.5	124–86–35–43	446	1,154–2,407
Burlingame (San Mateo)	*CM-S	26	13.5	1.5	56–77–239–143	14.4	1.4	80–89–38–69	21	248–1,759
Calexico (Imperial)	*CM-I	16	5.5	0.6	118–31–80–119	5.1	0.6	55–30–41–30	4	222–1,423
Camarillo (Ventura)	*CM-S	40	10.0	2.2	63–21–71–93	9.2	1.9	45–0–47–31	51	88–2,037
Campbell (Santa Clara)	*CM-S	33	9.8	0.0	51–45–133–71	10.6	0.0	83–58–19–8	164	185–2,733
Carlsbad (San Diego)	*CM-S	38	19.9	1.7	99–110–164–156	15.3	2.2	72–53–28–34	57	323–2,004
Carpinteria (Santa Barbara)	*CM-S	11	2.5	0.0	87–37–76–27	2.7	0.0	79–0–43–3	0	...–...
Carson (Los Angeles)	*CM-S	83	34.7	0.0	103–77–133–104	34.7	0.0	50–0–26–1	820	297–2,005
Ceres (Stanislaus)	*CM-S	15	4.3	0.5	75–35–82–101	4.2	0.2	73–7–21–31	68	78–1,685
Cerritos (Los Angeles)	*CM-S	54	29.0	2.6	65–155–152–164	26.3	2.5	54–0–13–14	635	180–1,962
Chico (Butte)	*CM-C	28	14.4	0.0	114–73–171–158	14.9	0.0	88–62–48–27	709	220–1,935
Chino (San Bernardino)	*CM-S	43	12.3	1.8	57–56–59–114	14.1	1.4	84–36–25–37	164	187–1,976
Chula Vista (San Diego)	*CM-S	87	26.8	0.0	55–74–90–89	29.5	0.0	49–25–30–23	711	474–2,026
Claremont (Los Angeles)	*CM-S	32	9.5	0.0	65–53–59–118	9.6	0.0	61–0–14–28	38	150–1,768
Clovis (Fresno)	*CM-S	36	9.6	1.0	66–43–85–76	10.2	1.0	59–32–28–58	76	234–1,802
Colton (San Bernardino)	*CM-S	22	11.3	10.8	82–73–138–217	11.6	10.2	99–72–31–54	367	226–1,899
Commerce (Los Angeles)	*CM-S	12	19.4	1.3	171–296–1020–194	13.4	1.7	193–386–90–0	760	...–...
Compton (Los Angeles)	*CM-S	85	34.2	2.1	117–150–77–60	32.4	3.0	36–34–45–17	227	603–2,093
Concord (Contra Costa)	*CM-S	104	40.7	0.0	49–79–123–141	40.7	0.0	86–0–20–31	298	507–2,415
Corona (Riverside)	*CM-S	40	16.2	3.7	76–91–92–145	17.4	3.4	85–57–12–23	708	337–1,607
Coronado (San Diego)	*CM-S	20	10.2	0.1	74–125–116–201	8.4	0.8	68–55–27–58	122	...–...
Costa Mesa (Orange)	*CM-S	85	33.5	0.0	47–72–182–94	34.1	0.0	85–41–38–4	192	562–2,329
Covina (Los Angeles)	*CM-S	39	13.4	1.3	61–81–130–75	13.2	1.3	74–46–30–20	403	238–2,423
Cudahy (Los Angeles)	*CM-S	19	3.5	0.0	101–13–46–26	2.3	0.0	43–0–7–1	0	...–...
Culver City (Los Angeles)	*CM-S	38	36.1	0.7	132–261–421–134	35.9	2.5	180–107–89–80	1,116	542–2,485
Cupertino (Santa Clara)	*CM-S	37	11.8	0.7	52–12–163–88	8.0	0.8	66–0–18–0	165	88–2,335
Cypress (Orange)	*CM-S	41	12.0	0.0	51–58–68–115	10.1	0.0	68–0–38–3	15	158–2,179
Daly City (San Mateo)	*CM-S	80	17.3	3.1	44–53–67–53	18.0	3.1	44–31–14–11	52	397–2,294
Davis (Yolo)	*CM-S	37	16.4	0.6	108–83–73–175	15.4	1.2	54–34–42–81	189	254–2,106
Delano (Kern)	*CM-S	18	6.6	0.7	139–35–78–122	6.5	0.6	77–24–37–57	97	135–1,679
Downey (Los Angeles)	*CM-S	83	22.3	2.7	70–35–108–56	27.5	2.2	75–46–24–4	0	416–2,248
Duarte (Los Angeles)	*CM-S	19	13.7	0.0	81–106–57–481	12.4	0.0	39–0–27–18	308	...–...
El Cajon (San Diego)	*CM-S	78	23.2	0.5	62–36–112–89	19.4	1.7	49–32–23–25	23	482–1,813
El Centro (Imperial)	*CM-I	26	...	...	...–...–...–...	27.4	1.0	73–53–27–72	0	563–1,618
El Cerrito (Contra Costa)	*CM-S	23	6.9	0.0	55–90–83–76	5.5	0.0	72–41–12–18	12	...–...
El Monte (Los Angeles)	*CM-S	85	20.5	0.3	73–53–86–29	20.7	0.4	64–35–22–3	29	374–2,099
El Segundo (Los Angeles)	*CM-S	14	12.8	3.4	86–79–447–311	16.7	3.0	309–251–81–64	0	...–...
Escondido (San Diego)	*CM-S	70	23.0	6.4	50–42–125–111	19.2	7.2	60–37–23–46	181	449–2,004
Eureka (Humboldt)	*CM-I	24	25.7	1.2	634–95–173–162	25.5	1.6	75–72–155–36	282	...–...
Fairfield (Solano)	*CM-C	62	40.1	3.4	68–75–100–407	36.0	4.2	72–21–29–4	1,784	355–2,069
Folsom (Sacramento)	*CM-S	13	4.1	0.5	62–50–110–91	3.6	0.6	55–34–16–27	428	...–...
Fontana (San Bernardino)	*CM-S	43	11.0	0.0	67–68–72–48	10.4	0.0	74–0–21–16	47	...–...
Foster City (San Mateo)	*CM-S	24	9.5	1.2	56–125–52–170	11.9	1.2	64–50–23–56	2,916	143–2,142
Fountain Valley (Orange)	*CM-S	55	13.5	2.4	52–79–64–51	14.9	2.2	64–36–30–14	5	230–2,327
Fremont (Alameda)	*CM-S	138	38.4	0.0	50–54–81–95	43.4	0.0	63–38–26–0	315	628–2,307
Fresno (Fresno)	*CM-C	245	107.1	7.1	104–81–119–134	101.6	19.2	84–57–35–60	107	2,243–2,083
Fullerton (Orange)	*CM-S	105	35.3	6.3	58–75–93–112	33.9	6.0	80–44–30–21	128	678–1,988
Garden Grove (Orange)	*CM-C	126	33.0	4.0	80–61–76–45	30.8	4.7	67–43–32–2	103	502–2,398
Gardena (Los Angeles)	*CM-S	46	21.1	0.8	201–35–184–38	16.6	3.8	108–63–21–3	0	390–2,358
Gilroy (Santa Clara)	*CM-S	23	10.0	0.7	89–33–174–132	10.0	0.7	69–33–47–55	362	...–...
Glendale (Los Angeles)	*CM-S	142	101.4	59.8	163–85–137–329	77.3	60.5	81–71–39–35	615	1,406–2,473
Glendora (Los Angeles)	*CM-S	39	10.9	2.8	62–69–75–73	10.0	2.4	72–0–48–17	115	188–2,136
Hanford (Kings)	*CM-I	22	7.6	1.2	63–42–111–125	7.6	1.1	70–35–22–62	52	160–1,762
Hawaiian Gardens (Los Angeles)	*CM-S	11	5.5	0.0	97–124–53–207	4.5	0.0	55–0–13–0	229	...–...
Hawthorne (Los Angeles)	*CM-S	58	22.1	1.2	81–48–115–139	23.5	1.3	112–62–15–70	745	328–2,605
Hayward (Alameda)	*CM-S	96	36.1	4.8	61–70–127–118	37.0	4.7	90–63–38–24	368	629–2,321
Hemet (Riverside)	*CM-S	25	8.9	0.7	78–48–106–121	9.4	0.7	64–53–26–38	12	180–2,255
Hermosa Beach (Los Angeles)	*CM-S	18	...	0.0	...–...–...–...	...	0.0	...–...–...–...	0	...–...
Hillsborough t (San Mateo)	*CM-S	10	3.9	1.1	55–226–32–61	4.0	1.3	121–113–24–54	0	...–...
Hollister (San Benito)	*CM-I	13	...	...	...–...–...–...	3.2	0.5	49–21–16–37	0	98–1,591
Huntington Beach (Orange)	*CM-S	176	58.3	5.9	61–81–127–62	54.8	6.0	82–45–27–17	39	968–2,421
Huntington Park (Los Angeles)	*CM-S	48	35.3	1.5	106–59–77–486	27.7	1.2	77–0–33–10	0	192–2,009
Imperial Beach (San Diego)	*CM-S	23	4.6	0.0	46–35–26–90	4.2	0.0	40–18–11–52	9	...–...
Indio (Riverside)	*CM-S	23	7.8	1.1	80–55–137–58	6.9	1.2	94–56–38–4	25	164–1,811
Inglewood (Los Angeles)	*CM-S	97	44.8	4.9	81–54–177–149	48.9	6.0	129–57–51–62	371	744–2,566
Irvine (Orange)	*CM-S	71	27.3	0.0	60–60–181–80	27.3	0.0	83–0–48–14	319	422–2,305
La Canada Flintridge (Los Angeles)	*CM-S	20	4.0	0.0	50–17–71–60	2.3	0.0	44–0–34–2	0	...–...
La Habra (Orange)	*CM-S	47	15.8	2.2	81–57–75–126	15.7	2.3	69–38–24–16	22	240–2,036
La Mesa (San Diego)	*CM-S	51	14.3	0.1	61–41–100–76	13.7	0.4	51–38–34–25	36	256–1,990
La Mirada (Los Angeles)	*CM-S	41	12.0	0.0	69–43–78–106	9.8	0.0	51–0–22–0	196	78–2,016

Table 1/9 continued **PROFILES OF INDIVIDUAL CITIES**

City (county)	Form of govern-ment–Metro status	Est. 1982 popu-lation (000)	Fiscal year 1983 revenues: Total general revenue ($ mil-lions)	Total utility reve-nue ($ mil-lions)	Per capita revenues ($): Intergovernmental revenue–Property taxes–Other taxes–Charges and miscella-neous general revenue	Fiscal year 1983 expenditures: Total general expendi-tures ($ mil-lions)	Total utility expendi-tures ($ mil-lions)	Per capita current expenditures ($): Police–Fire–Streets–Sewers and sanitation	Long term debt ($ per capita)	October 1983 public personnel: Total full time equivalent employment–Average full time monthly salary ($)
CALIFORNIA continued										
La Palma (Orange)	*CM-S	16	3.2	1.0	32–49–40–83	2.7	0.5	67–2–21–4	58	...–...
La Puente (Los Angeles)	*CM-S	31	5.7	0.0	78–0–51–54	4.9	0.0	56–0–18–4	0	30–1,671
La Verne (Los Angeles)	*CM-S	25	6.4	2.5	58–67–57–75	6.8	2.3	70–37–57–22	122	...–...
Lafayette (Contra Costa)	*CM-S	23	2.7	0.0	38–2–58–22	2.9	0.0	31–0–36–0	60	...–...
Laguna Beach (Orange)	*CM-S	18	13.4	0.1	104–149–163–323	12.2	0.5	123–73–37–61	31	...–...
Lakewood (Los Angeles)	*CM-S	74	16.7	2.0	65–25–77–57	14.6	2.3	51–0–21–22	35	186–1,960
Lancaster (Los Angeles)	*CM-S	51	12.3	0.0	88–3–108–42	10.5	0.0	49–0–24–3	0	61–1,422
Larkspur (Marin)	*CM-S	11	3.5	0.0	39–110–95–72	4.1	0.0	73–66–38–17	431	71–2,051
Lawndale (Los Angeles)	*CM-S	24	4.3	0.0	69–0–63–46	4.5	0.0	52–0–11–3	0	...–...
Lemon Grove (San Diego)	*CM-S	21	3.8	0.0	45–23–73–34	4.3	0.1	43–37–30–1	0	41–1,971
Livermore (Alameda)	*CM-S	50	19.9	0.7	125–42–67–167	21.5	0.6	64–37–24–44	285	239–2,314
Lodi (San Joaquin)	*CM-S	37	14.5	16.2	69–65–95–163	16.7	12.8	67–46–23–73	110	300–2,016
Loma Linda (San Bernardino)	*CM-S	11	3.2	0.7	60–57–75–98	3.3	0.8	35–43–39–56	111	47–1,807
Lomita (Los Angeles)	*CM-S	19	3.8	0.0	120–9–51–18	3.2	0.0	41–0–17–2	0	...–...
Lompoc (Santa Barbara)	*CM-C	28	14.1	8.6	165–33–80–223	11.2	7.1	54–28–19–95	76	247–1,711
Long Beach (Los Angeles)	*CM-C	371	368.8	173.4	236–93–166–499	376.1	184.8	145–93–33–48	526	4,729–2,158
Los Alamitos (Orange)	*CM-S	12	3.6	0.0	84–40–133–54	3.4	0.0	104–0–24–0	0	...–...
Los Altos (Santa Clara)	*CM-S	26	7.4	0.0	30–59–69–124	8.1	0.0	47–56–26–32	103	141–2,318
Los Angeles (Los Angeles)	†MC-C	3,022	1,808.4	1,233.7	121–109–175–193	1,673.2	1,127.6	107–46–21–25	862	40,342–2,488
Los Banos (Merced)	*CM-I	11	4.6	0.3	152–41–89–139	4.7	0.4	89–7–42–61	37	...–...
Los Gatos (Santa Clara)	*CM-S	27	8.6	0.0	53–54–148–64	6.9	0.0	74–0–28–6	76	...–...
Lynwood (Los Angeles)	*CM-S	51	13.2	1.4	117–36–47–59	11.9	1.1	65–39–23–13	57	127–2,062
Madera (Madera)	*CM-I	24	6.9	1.1	96–40–80–74	6.3	0.7	61–34–27–23	52	...–...
Manhattan Beach (Los Angeles)	*CM-S	32	13.7	1.6	60–74–129–160	12.2	2.2	114–49–37–54	4	243–2,333
Manteca (San Joaquin)	*CM-S	27	7.1	0.5	58–34–69–100	6.6	0.6	42–25–16–37	16	...–...
Marina (Monterey)	*CM-S	23	2.6	0.0	57–20–21–14	2.3	0.0	48–0–15–0	4	...–...
Martinez (Contra Costa)	*CM-S	24	6.6	2.0	48–70–76–83	6.5	1.6	89–0–28–1	401	133–1,937
Maywood (Los Angeles)	†MC-S	23	3.2	0.0	68–23–33–15	3.2	0.0	50–0–40–0	0	...–...
Menlo Park (San Mateo)	*CM-S	26	10.7	1.0	73–66–132–138	10.0	1.0	89–0–42–22	89	167–2,361
Merced (Merced)	*CM-I	40	18.0	1.3	116–68–104–164	17.7	2.1	70–46–26–61	443	356–1,798
Mill Valley (Marin)	*CM-S	13	7.2	0.0	67–151–118–223	7.5	0.0	92–65–29–54	84	105–2,276
Millbrae (San Mateo)	*CM-S	20	5.8	1.0	42–47–113–86	5.5	0.8	50–37–27–25	66	...–...
Milpitas (Santa Clara)	*CM-S	40	18.7	2.3	49–157–110–152	14.6	1.8	73–49–21–38	225	215–2,465
Modesto (Stanislaus)	*CM-C	114	38.9	2.9	84–35–128–94	38.4	4.4	73–43–30–39	100	855–2,065
Monrovia (Los Angeles)	*CM-S	31	13.8	1.8	93–110–94–148	14.9	1.8	95–50–25–27	501	212–2,054
Montclair (San Bernardino)	*CM-S	24	8.2	0.0	68–54–160–60	9.8	0.0	107–77–23–37	20	171–2,064
Montebello (Los Angeles)	*CM-S	55	23.1	1.5	122–126–101–74	22.2	4.7	85–53–9–0	435	378–2,098
Monterey (Monterey)	*CM-C	28	19.1	0.0	64–66–325–221	15.7	0.0	82–59–27–11	670	277–2,018
Monterey Park (Los Angeles)	*CM-S	57	15.2	1.9	46–84–65–73	16.0	1.9	61–33–22–24	298	297–2,201
Moraga t (Contra Costa)	*CM-S	15	1.7	0.0	37–25–33–21	1.8	0.0	40–0–14–0	0	33–2,266
Morgan Hill (Santa Clara)	*CM-S	18	8.2	1.0	39–67–76–263	7.1	0.7	65–37–19–29	275	...–...
Mountain View (Santa Clara)	*CM-S	60	33.5	4.2	61–98–181–219	33.0	3.6	76–53–38–84	522	434–2,487
Napa (Napa)	*CM-C	53	16.5	4.2	76–69–77–91	17.1	6.0	68–47–27–0	418	286–2,123
National City (San Diego)	*CM-S	54	15.9	0.2	76–43–118–60	11.4	0.5	55–28–22–16	39	255–1,948
Newark (Alameda)	*CM-S	33	...	0.0	...–...–...–...	9.3	0.0	66–39–26–0	0	159–2,222
Newport Beach (Orange)	*CM-S	65	40.4	5.6	76–141–170–238	41.6	2.6	151–73–50–40	0	696–2,303
Norco (Riverside)	*CM-S	21	4.0	1.1	52–32–39–65	4.0	1.0	31–26–13–22	163	61–1,690
Norwalk (Los Angeles)	*CM-S	86	21.0	1.0	99–8–78–58	16.7	3.5	39–0–19–20	0	244–1,824
Novato (Marin)	*CM-S	45	7.2	0.0	37–29–58–37	6.9	0.0	49–0–18–0	0	134–2,157
Oakland (Alameda)	*CM-C	345	307.0	0.0	150–135–179–427	295.5	0.0	101–62–23–8	884	3,493–2,375
Oceanside (San Diego)	*CM-S	84	44.1	7.8	47–69–93–316	51.1	7.8	80–50–40–90	429	561–2,007
Ontario (San Bernardino)	*CM-C	97	31.6	5.8	65–56–82–123	36.1	5.1	52–34–19–36	182	673–1,879
Orange (Orange)	*CM-S	95	28.4	5.5	55–57–124–63	31.6	5.2	82–60–37–18	31	609–2,257
Oxnard (Ventura)	*CM-C	116	43.1	6.1	59–64–78–54	29.4	4.9	11–5–26–93	0	893–1,965
Pacific Grove (Monterey)	*CM-S	16	5.6	0.0	79–52–144–80	4.7	0.0	76–41–39–9	161	117–1,861
Pacifica (San Mateo)	*CM-S	37	9.2	0.0	49–58–33–111	8.6	0.0	56–29–23–42	49	154–2,132
Palm Desert (Riverside)	*CM-S	13	14.1	0.0	68–227–351–440	20.9	0.0	55–28–124–0	1,445	50–2,036
Palm Springs (Riverside)	*CM-S	34	34.7	0.0	172–208–293–354	31.5	0.0	122–56–64–45	239	465–2,094
Palmdale (Los Angeles)	*CM-S	14	13.1	0.0	106–119–133–556	11.3	0.0	65–0–31–0	685	...–...
Palo Alto (Santa Clara)	*CM-S	55	38.4	47.7	78–66–216–339	45.4	35.3	105–105–39–109	366	852–2,404
Palos Verdes Estates (Los Angeles)	*CM-S	14	...	0.0	...–...–...–...	...	0.0	...–...–...–...	0	...–...
Paradise t (Butte)	†MC-S	23	4.5	0.0	69–52–46–26	4.6	0.0	47–57–16–0	30	88–2,019
Paramount (Los Angeles)	*CM-S	39	14.1	1.3	110–56–98–99	12.7	2.7	71–0–10–0	602	119–1,829
Pasadena (Los Angeles)	*CM-S	121	78.5	62.6	161–68–232–188	68.2	56.6	104–60–45–41	798	1,523–2,306
Petaluma (Sonoma)	*CM-S	35	14.2	2.0	124–61–102–116	14.5	2.9	65–41–27–29	132	208–1,965
Pico Rivera (Los Angeles)	*CM-S	55	12.1	1.7	87–22–63–49	11.4	0.9	45–0–19–2	0	168–1,549
Piedmont (Alameda)	†MC-S	10	4.3	0.0	48–144–154–73	4.4	0.0	99–77–43–25	0	...–...
Pinole (Contra Costa)	*CM-S	14	5.1	0.0	38–114–74–126	4.5	0.0	72–38–20–36	269	...–...
Pittsburg (Contra Costa)	*CM-S	36	27.1	1.3	129–71–45–500	24.7	1.2	79–0–22–6	35	163–2,355
Placentia (Orange)	*CM-S	37	7.8	0.0	46–46–95–27	8.3	0.0	66–34–19–1	84	147–2,012
Pleasant Hill (Contra Costa)	*CM-S	27	10.0	0.0	54–33–145–141	8.8	0.0	83–0–30–1	78	99–2,267
Pleasanton (Alameda)	*CM-S	36	15.3	1.7	42–75–112–199	65.0	1.5	69–44–31–68	2,022	197–2,332
Pomona (Los Angeles)	*CM-S	100	75.4	4.4	84–81–133–452	75.8	4.5	99–70–38–24	391	724–2,532
Port Hueneme (Ventura)	*CM-S	18	8.1	0.3	108–116–46–171	8.3	0.6	61–0–27–81	499	92–1,779
Porterville (Tulare)	*CM-C	22	9.1	0.8	112–29–132–143	8.4	0.9	66–31–20–62	61	165–1,617
Rancho Cucamonga (San Bernardino)	*CM-S	59	10.8	0.0	53–26–63–40	6.9	0.0	49–0–13–2	0	82–1,772
Rancho Palos Verdes (Los Angeles)	*CM-S	37	5.8	0.0	69–9–49–31	6.7	0.0	37–0–30–0	0	31–1,654
Redding (Shasta)	*CM-C	44	19.7	15.8	95–55–159–142	19.3	13.3	89–60–36–65	766	458–2,174
Redlands (San Bernardino)	*CM-S	47	16.5	2.7	66–80–81–126	16.9	3.7	72–37–26–49	370	326–1,906
Redondo Beach (Los Angeles)	*CM-S	59	34.8	0.0	71–89–163–269	31.6	0.1	96–44–41–17	150	452–2,237

Table 1/9 continued **PROFILES OF INDIVIDUAL CITIES**

City (county)	Form of govern-ment–Metro status	Est. 1982 popu-lation (000)	Fiscal year 1983 revenues: Total general revenue ($ mil-lions)	Total utility reve-nue ($ mil-lions)	Per capita revenues ($): Intergovernmental revenue–Property taxes–Other taxes–Charges and miscella-neous general revenue	Fiscal year 1983 expenditures: Total general expendi-tures ($ mil-lions)	Total utility expendi-tures ($ mil-lions)	Per capita current expenditures ($): Police–Fire–Streets–Sewers and sanitation	Long term debt ($ per capita)	October 1983 public personnel: Total full time equivalent employment–Average full time monthly salary ($)
CALIFORNIA continued										
Redwood City (San Mateo)	*CM-S	55	27.0	3.5	73–141–115–161	25.6	4.1	91–61–34–39	596	456–2,147
Reedley (Fresno)	†MC-S	12	4.0	0.4	138–28–77–105	3.8	0.3	64–5–41–38	29	70–1,745
Rialto (San Bernardino)	*CM-S	42	10.1	1.7	50–54–61–76	11.0	1.1	60–44–21–17	155	224–1,708
Richmond (Contra Costa)	*CM-S	76	61.4	0.0	114–188–100–406	50.3	0.0	85–50–25–28	954	675–2,207
Ridgecrest (Kern)	†MC-S	22	...	...	...–...–...–...	3.9	0.3	37–0–17–12	0	87–1,760
Riverside (Riverside)	*CM-C	174	85.3	101.5	123–47–129–191	76.9	121.3	82–47–42–54	1,215	1,685–2,088
Rohnert Park (Sonoma)	*CM-S	26	7.8	0.8	47–35–93–125	6.6	0.7	40–17–30–56	135	98–2,125
Rosemead (Los Angeles)	*CM-S	44	9.8	0.0	70–40–56–56	8.1	0.0	46–0–30–2	46	47–1,699
Roseville (Placer)	*CM-S	26	14.8	8.8	71–46–174–270	18.8	6.2	80–53–28–71	1,346	311–1,962
Sacramento (Sacramento)	*CM-C	289	156.1	8.2	66–54–85–166	152.6	12.9	104–68–21–64	0	2,858–2,211
Salinas (Monterey)	*CM-C	84	31.8	C.0	100–54–145–77	26.0	0.0	81–45–23–6	161	552–2,122
San Anselmo (Marin)	*CM-S	12	3.0	0.0	41–108–64–40	3.1	0.0	73–70–27–0	0	81–1,975
San Bernardino (San Bernardino)	†MC-C	124	69.5	4.5	92–90–168–209	70.3	6.0	77–55–35–61	883	1,354–1,718
San Bruno (San Mateo)	*CM-S	35	14.0	1.5	53–40–140–167	12.2	1.3	63–34–17–62	4	189–2,310
San Buenaventura (Ventura)	*CM-C	81	38.3	5.5	100–58–166–151	32.2	3.8	69–38–21–57	222	516–1,898
San Carlos (San Mateo)	*CM-S	25	8.3	0.0	40–69–120–104	7.5	0.0	80–60–39–39	71	91–2,243
San Clemente (Orange)	*CM-S	29	13.3	1.9	47–82–77–258	11.5	2.2	81–46–24–84	66	...–...
San Diego (San Diego)	*CM-C	916	404.4	57.2	115–62–113–152	341.9	78.1	65–31–15–46	149	7,276–2,019
San Dimas (Los Angeles)	*CM-S	26	6.1	0.0	49–53–60–73	5.9	0.0	38–0–37–3	303	...–...
San Fernando (Los Angeles)	*CM-S	18	6.9	0.6	65–115–115–82	6.0	0.6	94–58–38–15	151	...–...
San Francisco (San Francisco)	†MC-C	692	1,513.6	155.7	846–329–366–647	1,141.2	299.4	140–79–5–53	1,447	23,456–2,294
San Gabriel (Los Angeles)	*CM-S	31	7.1	0.0	51–49–91–38	6.7	0.0	78–48–24–3	0	154–2,308
San Jose (Santa Clara)	*CM-C	659	368.1	3.0	130–72–146–210	262.4	3.4	68–40–15–32	277	4,097–2,659
San Juan Capistrano (Orange)	*CM-S	20	6.6	0.0	65–70–93–97	7.9	0.0	37–0–68–68	25	68–2,021
San Leandro (Alameda)	*CM-S	65	31.4	0.0	64–51–213–158	32.6	0.0	75–54–29–58	66	492–2,504
San Luis Obispo (San Luis Obispo)	*CM-I	34	16.1	2.8	133–49–187–100	14.3	4.0	85–64–24–24	88	292–1,941
San Marcos (San Diego)	*CM-S	19	4.0	0.0	45–30–104–34	3.7	0.0	35–0–41–29	103	...–...
San Marino (Los Angeles)	*CM-S	13	...	0.0	...–...–...–...	...	0.0	...–...–...–...	0	...–...
San Mateo (San Mateo)	*CM-S	78	34.5	0.0	79–87–149–128	31.0	0.0	79–53–20–47	108	575–1,900
San Pablo (Contra Costa)	*CM-S	21	14.9	0.0	110–108–82–415	15.3	0.0	72–0–42–0	628	98–2,055
San Rafael (Marin)	*CM-S	44	19.4	0.0	51–95–173–118	20.8	0.0	71–73–39–1	391	356–2,059
Sanger (Fresno)	*CM-S	13	3.7	0.4	47–48–59–127	3.7	0.3	69–46–14–88	83	88–1,719
Santa Ana (Orange)	*CM-C	217	81.9	8.2	103–65–119–90	87.5	9.5	97–50–22–17	417	1,328–2,316
Santa Barbara (Santa Barbara)	*CM-C	75	49.5	5.8	104–80–208–271	43.0	7.5	102–58–29–35	429	779–2,061
Santa Clara (Santa Clara)	*CM-S	88	63.7	75.1	140–103–189–291	62.9	75.4	88–74–22–99	890	888–2,784
Santa Cruz (Santa Cruz)	*CM-C	42	24.2	4.2	90–66–124–291	25.4	4.3	73–40–24–78	326	550–1,894
Santa Fe Springs (Los Angeles)	*CM-S	15	25.3	1.6	206–517–671–338	26.7	2.2	182–264–109–10	3,067	242–2,651
Santa Maria (Santa Barbara)	*CM-C	42	22.0	1.9	80–56–156–229	17.2	5.4	76–30–33–43	5	328–1,959
Santa Monica (Los Angeles)	*CM-S	89	78.2	12.3	251–83–225–318	58.7	24.0	90–46–31–51	207	1,350–2,073
Santa Paula (Ventura)	*CM-S	21	5.4	0.0	94–45–47–65	6.0	0.0	49–5–26–31	8	89–1,798
Santa Rosa (Sonoma)	*CM-C	87	43.9	7.1	95–67–142–202	42.5	9.1	67–39–35–33	1,107	667–2,181
Santee (San Diego)	*cm-s	44	8.6	0.0	59–52–71–13	5.8	0.0	48–0–21–2	0	37–1,645
Saratoga (Santa Clara)	*CM-S	29	...	0.0	...–...–...–...	4.1	0.0	31–0–22–0	0	49–2,059
Seal Beach (Orange)	*CM-S	26	9.4	1.1	38–94–110–124	8.4	0.7	65–55–17–20	178	124–2,216
Seaside (Monterey)	*CM-C	38	6.0	0.1	48–22–60–27	6.1	0.1	29–18–21–0	45	144–2,026
Selma (Fresno)	†MC-S	12	2.7	0.0	75–28–83–49	2.8	0.0	74–19–28–0	0	...–...
Sierra Madre (Los Angeles)	*CM-S	11	2.8	0.6	25–98–34–100	2.9	0.6	53–12–22–35	183	...–...
Simi Valley (Ventura)	*CM-C	81	25.6	3.8	78–26–57–153	21.8	5.9	55–0–28–50	138	298–1,969
South El Monte (Los Angeles)	*CM-S	18	4.7	0.0	81–10–139–33	4.0	0.0	59–0–19–2	3	...–...
South Gate (Los Angeles)	*CM-S	72	19.5	1.6	85–52–72–61	16.7	1.9	76–0–27–11	0	311–2,127
South Lake Tahoe (El Dorado)	*CM-I	21	11.5	0.5	82–108–265–93	12.3	1.3	122–88–68–0	13	230–2,211
South Pasadena (Los Angeles)	*CM-S	23	6.5	1.1	55–111–65–52	6.3	1.2	60–49–27–2	68	...–...
South San Francisco (San Mateo)	*CM-S	50	27.2	0.0	137–82–168–155	36.0	0.0	102–77–48–60	571	378–2,337
Stanton (Orange)	*CM-S	25	5.6	0.0	51–28–93–52	4.7	0.0	75–47–20–0	0	...–...
Stockton (San Joaquin)	*CM-C	162	80.2	2.9	114–54–155–174	79.2	3.5	99–70–28–69	248	1,329–2,332
Suisun City (Solano)	*CM-S	13	2.9	0.2	121–16–53–39	2.9	0.2	39–8–18–4	51	...–...
Sunnyvale (Santa Clara)	*CM-S	107	61.8	5.1	122–82–163–213	53.9	4.5	70–56–39–87	0	649–2,725
Temple City (Los Angeles)	*CM-S	30	5.0	0.0	50–15–51–54	3.6	0.0	35–0–30–2	95	32–1,956
Thousand Oaks (Ventura)	*CM-S	91	29.8	3.2	87–33–91–118	25.7	4.4	46–0–23–37	138	339–1,897
Torrance (Los Angeles)	*CM-S	130	65.8	6.0	120–53–242–90	61.7	11.7	135–67–36–21	244	1,247–2,468
Tracy (San Joaquin)	*CM-S	20	8.3	1.4	83–52–73–199	9.1	1.0	65–32–22–124	422	144–1,841
Tulare (Tulare)	*CM-C	24	10.0	0.9	71–44–136–169	9.6	1.0	68–36–40–66	133	191–1,724
Turlock (Stanislaus)	*CM-S	29	8.1	0.8	64–31–91–96	5.7	2.5	52–28–3–22	103	177–1,721
Tustin (Orange)	*CM-S	38	11.1	3.6	58–77–112–43	12.1	2.6	92–35–32–6	257	168–2,233
Ukiah (Mendocino)	*CM-I	12	7.3	6.7	274–28–139–152	8.3	5.5	96–66–43–40	25	124–2,294
Union City (Alameda)	*CM-S	42	9.4	0.1	60–54–70–37	9.4	0.7	76–34–24–0	90	172–2,709
Upland (San Bernardino)	*CM-S	50	14.9	2.8	47–57–85–109	14.9	3.5	66–39–33–59	90	289–1,926
Vacaville (Solano)	*CM-S	47	14.8	2.5	83–53–61–118	13.1	2.5	57–43–33–28	243	220–2,278
Vallejo (Solano)	*CM-C	86	28.9	6.2	95–52–121–69	25.7	7.6	77–56–43–0	138	430–2,521
Victorville (San Bernardino)	*CM-S	17	7.5	0.0	95–39–183–135	6.9	0.0	60–30–37–86	184	...–...
Visalia (Tulare)	*CM-C	53	23.8	0.1	79–35–134–201	18.6	0.3	57–21–20–62	0	383–1,600
Vista (San Diego)	*CM-S	40	27.3	0.0	516–46–71–57	16.8	0.0	35–62–40–8	35	147–1,853
Walnut Creek (Contra Costa)	*CM-S	56	20.0	0.0	43–57–145–110	16.0	0.0	76–0–27–2	210	258–2,137
Watsonville (Santa Cruz)	*CM-S	25	14.1	1.6	154–89–88–242	14.9	2.5	67–38–28–54	775	...–...
West Covina (Los Angeles)	*CM-S	87	31.1	1.6	65–61–117–116	28.0	1.4	72–42–32–2	339	411–2,321
Westminster (Orange)	*CM-S	73	14.5	2.7	49–26–96–28	15.2	2.3	73–48–25–3	21	294–2,845
Whittier (Los Angeles)	*CM-S	69	21.9	1.5	77–35–113–93	20.5	1.8	73–1–29–23	35	362–2,120
Woodland (Yolo)	*CM-S	31	13.1	1.0	114–75–78–150	12.6	0.9	65–45–30–81	261	213–1,858
Yorba Linda (Orange)	*CM-S	31	6.5	0.0	39–0–61–109	6.1	0.0	46–1–22–0	320	...–...

Table 1/9 continued **PROFILES OF INDIVIDUAL CITIES**

City (county)	Form of govern-ment–Metro status	Est. 1982 popu-lation (000)	Fiscal year 1983 revenues: Total general revenue ($ mil-lions)	Fiscal year 1983 revenues: Total utility reve-nue ($ mil-lions)	Fiscal year 1983 revenues: Per capita revenues ($) Intergovernmental revenue–Property taxes–Other taxes–Charges and miscella-neous general revenue	Fiscal year 1983 expenditures: Total general expendi-tures ($ mil-lions)	Fiscal year 1983 expenditures: Total utility expendi-tures ($ mil-lions)	Fiscal year 1983 expenditures: Per capita current expenditures ($) Police–Fire–Streets–Sewers and sanitation	Long term debt ($ per capita)	October 1983 public personnel: Total full time equivalent employment–Average full time monthly salary ($)
CALIFORNIA continued										
Yuba City (Sutter)	*CM-C	20	8.0	1.4	62–69–115–159	7.6	1.0	80–47–39–57	248	164–1,924
COLORADO										
Arvada (Jefferson)	*CM-S	88	25.7	4.8	43–25–160–62	22.2	9.7	55–0–17–21	583	441–1,937
Aurora (Arapahoe)	*CM-S	184	104.5	11.0	45–51–296–176	89.1	29.1	63–46–46–29	1,016	1,936–1,645
Boulder (Boulder)	*CM-C	78	39.8	4.1	62–52–239–156	32.8	3.9	57–33–64–25	320	771–2,031
Brighton (Adams)	*CM-S	13	4.2	0.6	63–27–129–93	3.9	2.0	50–8–27–12	876	...–...
Broomfield (Boulder)	*CM-S	22	7.2	2.0	29–71–114–109	7.0	2.5	65–0–31–27	488	122–1,720
Canon City (Fremont)	*CM-I	13	4.3	1.0	71–13–121–117	3.5	1.3	51–40–34–3	325	126–1,567
Colorado Springs (El Paso)	*CM-C	232	139.3	207.1	102–44–140–315	119.4	213.8	61–35–39–28	1,433	3,964–1,854
Commerce City (Adams)	*CM-S	17	9.9	0.0	87–44–289–176	7.8	0.0	92–0–66–25	604	125–1,839
Denver c (Denver)	MC-C	506	644.7	63.2	283–149–342–501	509.5	82.3	124–66–46–66	1,094	11,636–1,997
Durango (La Plata)	*CM-I	12	1.8	0.6	0–0–0–149	7.5	0.7	87–38–54–60	347	...–...
Englewood (Arapahoe)	*CM-S	31	...	...	...–...–...–...	18.0	3.6	29–29–57–44	0	451–1,965
Fort Collins (Larimer)	*CM-C	69	38.1	30.5	103–45–177–231	42.4	30.6	57–39–31–30	650	807–1,970
Golden (Jefferson)	*CM-S	13	4.0	1.4	32–43–138–85	4.3	1.1	66–7–31–52	23	102–1,652
Grand Junction (Mesa)	*CM-I	31	28.0	2.3	308–59–296–238	19.4	3.6	86–67–79–49	359	407–1,661
Greeley (Weld)	*CM-C	54	21.9	4.0	88–44–191–88	20.7	8.2	65–33–32–28	606	495–1,723
Lakewood (Jefferson)	*CM-S	118	32.8	0.2	59–16–173–28	29.7	0.3	70–0–39–12	126	655–2,038
Littleton (Arapahoe)	*CM-S	32	18.6	0.0	164–43–240–136	16.9	0.0	61–90–56–56	161	301–2,074
Longmont (Boulder)	*CM-S	46	...	...	...–...–...–...	17.5	15.2	41–25–17–52	0	488–1,492
Loveland (Larimer)	*CM-S	32	10.6	15.5	35–33–103–155	13.6	14.9	42–19–17–53	1,025	323–1,759
Northglenn (Adams)	*CM-S	30	13.9	5.0	33–11–206–210	16.5	5.8	60–0–39–44	1,738	211–1,758
Pueblo (Pueblo)	*CM-C	101	42.1	10.4	105–50–151–111	38.1	12.2	63–48–34–23	377	899–1,668
Sterling (Logan)	*CM-I	12	5.1	0.4	84–62–140–148	3.6	0.6	60–17–47–40	313	125–1,303
Thornton (Adams)	*CM-S	44	20.4	5.3	33–53–183–191	22.0	9.7	57–37–28–60	874	402–1,859
Westminster (Adams)	*CM-S	55	31.5	3.1	117–15–256–184	29.8	12.0	53–24–28–33	333	462–1,861
Wheat Ridge (Jefferson)	†MC-S	31	9.0	0.0	32–16–208–37	8.3	0.0	57–0–49–1	0	157–1,852
CONNECTICUT										
Ansonia	MC-I	19	...	0.0	...–...–...–...	13.0	0.0	37–7–53–55	0	356–1,307
Avon t	*CM-S	12	12.5	0.0	116–804–11–101	11.6	0.0	100–12–60–9	645	331–2,064
Berlin t	TM-S	15	15.3	0.2	200–664–6–127	15.6	0.3	50–12–83–42	478	413–1,590
Bethel t	TM-S	17	13.3	0.3	197–547–6–55	13.4	0.3	43–4–38–30	418	416–1,572
Bloomfield t	*CM-S	19	...	0.0	...–...–...–...	22.1	0.1	94–0–62–28	0	624–1,618
Branford t	RT-S	24	...	0.0	...–...–...–...	19.0	0.0	43–21–17–30	0	503–1,575
Bridgeport	MC-C	144	163.9	0.0	427–565–5–143	177.7	0.0	85–98–17–37	408	4,181–1,791
Bristol	MC-C	58	51.2	1.7	268–562–3–55	48.8	1.8	49–43–34–21	178	1,392–1,684
Brookfield t	MC-S	13	12.0	0.0	176–632–12–76	11.7	0.0	48–5–33–4	199	348–1,693
Cheshire t	*CM-S	22	20.8	0.0	228–600–9–99	21.1	0.0	42–4–41–14	604	569–1,822
Clinton t	TM-S	11	9.7	0.0	272–514–6–60	10.7	0.0	56–19–67–17	170	275–1,500
Cromwell t	TM-S	10	9.1	0.0	214–515–8–132	8.7	0.0	41–0–33–32	1,035	259–1,493
Danbury	MC-C	62	56.0	2.4	202–613–4–79	56.3	2.4	58–49–38–38	450	1,541–1,874
Darien t	RT-S	19	...	0.0	...–...–...–...	22.0	0.0	80–9–36–63	0	518–2,210
Derby	MC-S	12	9.0	0.0	216–469–3–49	8.9	0.0	61–15–48–45	348	215–1,569
East Hartford t	MC-S	52	46.6	0.0	256–591–5–46	45.6	0.0	59–65–31–25	105	1,326–1,901
East Haven t	MC-S	25	23.8	0.0	326–490–7–125	22.2	0.0	49–41–34–46	795	488–1,734
East Lyme t	TM-S	14	13.0	0.5	232–614–13–54	12.4	0.4	21–21–77–14	358	438–1,541
Enfield t	*CM-S	43	34.9	0.0	264–482–4–69	33.6	0.0	48–0–44–32	289	1,071–1,821
Fairfield t	RT-S	55	55.8	0.0	130–786–6–99	54.7	0.0	78–68–62–23	452	1,399–1,859
Farmington t	*CM-S	17	17.3	0.0	149–755–12–122	16.5	0.0	70–15–38–36	458	409–2,004
Glastonbury t	*CM-S	25	...	0.0	...–...–...–...	23.9	0.0	60–10–61–25	0	937–1,568
Greenwich t	RT-S	60	78.9	0.0	177–933–16–186	85.1	0.0	89–35–40–53	41	2,035–2,082
Groton	MC-I	10	4.2	34.8	142–125–3–153	4.8	31.5	107–51–64–82	734	202–2,009
Groton t	*CM-S	40	34.1	0.0	365–358–2–119	34.8	0.0	30–2–51–36	592	975–1,745
Guilford t	TM-S	18	17.8	0.0	205–705–13–75	16.7	0.0	61–15–33–15	579	511–1,553
Hamden t	MC-S	51	49.0	0.0	222–681–4–50	47.0	0.0	57–64–40–46	476	1,228–1,829
Hartford	*CM-C	136	247.7	0.0	890–680–13–234	249.4	0.0	102–94–37–15	736	5,564–1,879
Killingly t	*CM-I	15	11.9	0.0	382–314–7–106	11.2	0.0	1–0–40–49	385	433–1,508
Ledyard t	MC-S	14	11.5	0.0	323–458–7–28	11.8	0.0	17–6–45–7	32	391–1,540
Madison t	TM-S	15	12.8	0.0	161–636–9–67	12.2	0.0	47–20–34–5	117	386–1,651
Manchester t	*CM-S	49	41.9	2.8	196–529–4–118	46.0	6.3	58–53–32–39	514	1,373–1,778
Mansfield t	*CM-I	20	9.5	0.0	174–255–3–35	9.1	0.0	8–21–33–1	80	221–1,608
Meriden	*CM-C	58	58.3	1.9	279–466–8–261	58.6	1.7	45–39–23–20	0	1,760–1,607
Middletown	MC-I	39	38.0	1.6	297–567–3–110	37.7	1.7	67–37–52–39	605	1,020–1,753
Milford	MC-S	50	50.6	0.0	231–708–11–67	49.0	0.0	70–73–33–53	552	1,249–1,872
Monroe t	*CM-S	15	14.4	0.0	233–668–15–72	15.0	0.0	62–24–42–14	463	396–1,564
Montville t	MC-S	17	10.1	0.0	222–330–10–39	11.1	0.0	12–9–35–11	92	372–457
Naugatuck t	MC-S	27	...	0.0	...–...–...–...	21.9	0.0	33–32–48–56	0	697–1,447
New Britain	MC-C	73	66.2	2.2	311–489–9–94	68.6	3.6	73–65–41–78	439	1,538–1,944
New Canaan t	TM-S	18	23.5	0.0	113–1066–19–103	21.9	0.0	86–19–53–34	475	571–2,850
New Fairfield t	TM-S	12	...	0.0	...–...–...–...	8.4	0.0	20–9–26–5	0	307–1,810
New Haven	MC-C	125	150.4	0.0	396–617–6–180	157.5	0.0	89–99–40–83	732	4,092–1,379
New London	*CM-C	29	29.5	1.8	392–433–4–176	29.5	1.9	66–58–25–77	323	857–1,485
New Milford t	MC-S	20	16.0	0.0	192–530–3–63	16.3	0.0	39–4–45–11	306	530–1,875
Newington t	*CM-S	29	...	0.0	...–...–...–...	23.3	0.0	2–6–35–55	0	601–2,053
Newtown t	MC-S	20	17.5	0.0	188–633–8–56	16.4	0.0	38–6–61–2	168	508–1,439
North Branford t	*CM-S	12	11.4	0.0	310–537–14–111	11.7	0.0	39–10–31–7	481	269–1,684
North Haven t	TM-S	22	25.3	0.0	220–786–9–136	23.4	0.0	63–46–64–34	336	723–1,606
Norwalk	MC-C	79	90.1	0.0	204–833–11–94	88.1	0.0	59–51–34–64	825	2,088–1,768

Table 1/9 continued PROFILES OF INDIVIDUAL CITIES

City (county)	Form of govern-ment–Metro status	Est. 1982 popu-lation (000)	Fiscal year 1983 revenues: Total general revenue ($ mil-lions)	Fiscal year 1983 revenues: Total utility reve-nue ($ mil-lions)	Fiscal year 1983 revenues: Per capita revenues ($) Intergovernmental revenue–Property taxes–Other taxes–Charges and miscella-neous general revenue	Fiscal year 1983 expenditures: Total general expendi-tures ($ mil-lions)	Fiscal year 1983 expenditures: Total utility expendi-tures ($ mil-lions)	Fiscal year 1983 expenditures: Per capita current expenditures ($) Police–Fire–Streets–Sewers and sanitation	Long term debt ($ per capita)	October 1983 public personnel: Total full time equivalent employment–Average full time monthly salary ($)
CONNECTICUT continued										
Norwich	*CM-C	39	30.3	27.3	358–324–5–98	32.3	24.4	49–60–61–42	328	914–1,565
Orange t.	TM-S	13	12.4	0.0	114–771–8–52	13.3	0.0	80–3–45–10	162	264–1,728
Plainfield t	TM-I	13	8.6	0.0	350–257–5–36	8.3	0.0	22–0–25–44	482	349–1,378
Plainville t.	*CM-S	17	...	0.0	...–...–...–...	14.4	0.0	55–11–30–46	0	405–1,623
Plymouth t	MC-S	11	10.8	0.0	393–473–3–116	12.7	0.0	37–11–53–34	1,019	288–2,454
Ridgefield t.	TM-I	21	...	0.0	...–...–...–...	21.4	0.0	42–24–46–11	0	698–1,582
Rocky Hill t.	*CM-S	15	14.0	0.0	198–619–7–100	13.3	0.0	65–14–40–47	870	333–1,803
Seymour t	TM-I	14	...	0.0	...–...–...–...	10.7	0.0	48–3–47–39	0	310–1,320
Shelton.	MC-S	32	23.2	0.0	194–450–11–63	20.5	0.0	31–19–18–22	403	656–1,471
Simsbury t	TM-S	21	22.1	0.0	165–713–9–141	22.6	0.0	48–0–46–18	463	625–1,935
South Windsor t.	*CM-S	18	18.9	0.0	240–719–6–101	18.5	0.0	45–20–54–44	279	562–1,724
Southbury t	TM-S	14	9.3	0.0	70–523–23–31	8.9	0.0	25–7–40–19	20	...–...
Southington t	*CM-S	37	...	...	...–...–...–...	36.7	0.7	37–18–27–19	0	940–1,507
Stamford	MC-C	104	148.4	0.0	193–1057–19–163	145.9	0.0	82–95–44–74	970	3,361–1,785
Stonington t	TM-S	16	14.3	0.0	221–535–4–109	16.4	0.0	59–1–53–57	575	380–1,636
Stratford t.	*CM-S	51	40.0	0.0	130–619–4–32	42.6	0.0	58–65–48–59	0	1,174–1,859
Torrington.	MC-I	31	25.6	0.0	278–496–5–37	23.7	0.0	48–50–58–59	128	704–1,566
Trumbull t.	MC-S	33	33.2	0.0	142–734–11–112	32.1	0.0	58–20–65–24	511	854–1,924
Vernon t.	†MC-S	29	...	0.0	...–...–...–...	24.3	0.1	61–13–43–71	0	758–1,480
Wallingford t.	MC-S	37	33.6	25.5	258–529–10–104	34.6	24.1	53–43–40–22	566	921–1,613
Waterbury	MC-C	103	101.3	4.1	406–485–10–84	106.6	5.8	76–80–18–41	496	2,999–1,676
Waterford t.	RT-S	18	...	...	...–...–...–...	32.7	0.4	79–52–78–30	0	525–1,762
Watertown t	*CM-S	20	17.7	0.4	257–531–2–117	17.2	0.5	44–11–42–27	411	522–1,550
West Hartford t.	*CM-S	61	64.5	0.0	134–818–7–104	69.9	0.0	102–71–52–68	336	1,572–2,190
West Haven	MC-C	53	41.2	0.0	219–511–2–39	37.4	0.0	62–0–35–38	118	1,132–1,614
Westport t	RT-S	26	43.1	0.0	196–1306–19–153	39.8	0.0	98–92–53–45	756	917–2,503
Wethersfield t.	*CM-S	26	20.6	0.0	158–584–8–52	22.6	0.0	72–9–59–52	187	628–1,815
Willimantic	*CM-I	15	...	0.0	...–...–...–...	...	0.0	...–...–...–...	...	...–...
Wilton t.	TM-S	15	19.3	0.0	124–1000–16–106	18.9	0.0	74–42–50–18	346	436–2,163
Winchester t.	*CM-S	11	9.7	0.2	294–546–4–47	8.3	0.8	50–10–71–31	310	216–1,258
Windham t	TM-I	21	...	0.0	...–...–...–...	14.3	0.0	1–0–14–21	0	511–1,416
Windsor t	*CM-S	26	25.5	0.0	195–696–7–94	24.2	0.0	56–11–49–42	716	810–1,662
Windsor Locks t.	TM-S	12	16.7	0.0	616–685–7–72	17.0	0.0	61–17–66–33	229	297–1,742
Wolcott t.	MC-S	13	12.1	0.0	309–518–6–111	11.5	0.0	48–7–39–34	674	393–1,396
DELEWARE										
Dover (Kent).	*CM-I	23	7.0	38.5	85–90–17–111	6.7	35.8	83–6–15–68	1,225	316–1,399
Newark (New Castle).	*CM-S	25	5.6	15.4	41–62–2–117	7.4	12.8	61–1–16–88	284	214–1,462
Wilmington (New Castle)	†MC-C	70	64.2	11.8	239–149–224–306	78.7	7.4	145–111–22–156	1,409	1,294–1,784
DISTRICT OF COLUMBIA										
Washington (Washington)	†MC-C	633	2,371.2	31.1	1,322–578–1519–324	2,337.1	63.7	241–77–40–132	2,993	38,251–2,280
FLORIDA										
Altamonte Springs (Seminole)	CM-S	24	8.6	4.6	98–79–125–58	6.0	4.5	58–42–12–0	924	301–1,400
Bartow (Polk).	*CM-S	16	4.9	12.3	101–22–51–142	6.5	10.6	57–21–21–59	20	239–1,416
Belle Glade (Palm Beach)	*CM-S	17	5.6	2.3	112–45–66–108	5.2	2.4	81–20–28–40	544	202–1,285
Boca Raton (Palm Beach)	*CM-C	54	33.5	9.6	98–203–139–185	32.2	23.0	82–73–41–43	1,407	768–1,660
Boynton Beach (Palm Beach)	*CM-S	38	11.7	4.6	56–106–66–81	11.9	9.2	67–47–12–24	512	442–1,793
Bradenton (Manatee)	MC-C	34	13.6	4.8	106–69–90–133	10.5	5.6	46–48–30–33	418	396–1,294
Cape Coral (Lee)	*CM-C	39	20.2	6.0	46–132–35–308	8.7	17.5	47–25–17–0	1,180	399–1,386
Casselberry (Seminole)	MC-S	17	...	...	...–...–...–...	2.6	5.6	54–25–7–0	0	149–1,336
Clearwater (Pinellas)	*CM-S	90	56.2	12.9	113–104–122–283	50.1	14.1	78–44–54–100	448	1,326–1,595
Cocoa (Brevard).	*CM-C	17	8.5	6.3	77–49–61–301	6.4	7.7	71–51–34–67	671	250–1,269
Cocoa Beach (Brevard)	*CM-S	12	5.9	0.0	41–123–120–211	5.4	0.0	58–40–41–74	511	171–1,184
Cooper City (Broward)	†MC-S	12	2.6	0.0	39–60–97–21	2.6	0.0	60–12–22–0	54	120–1,313
Coral Gables (Dade)	*CM-S	43	31.1	0.1	44–223–196–255	28.2	0.1	138–83–31–114	583	771–2,045
Coral Springs (Broward).	*CM-S	45	11.5	2.9	41–76–79–61	9.8	4.7	60–5–22–0	438	362–1,700
Dania (Broward).	*CM-S	12	7.3	0.7	94–135–123–239	6.5	0.8	100–64–41–43	109	...–...
Davie t (Broward).	CM-S	32	5.5	1.5	35–43–70–21	5.8	2.3	57–31–20–0	51	189–1,809
Daytona Beach (Volusia)	*CM-C	56	34.2	6.7	151–87–106–273	27.8	14.8	116–44–25–92	524	862–1,414
De Land (Volusia)	*CM-S	16	6.1	1.1	68–71–97–150	5.1	1.0	73–39–26–51	270	220–1,306
Deerfield Beach (Broward).	*CM-S	41	15.4	5.9	61–123–46–143	14.1	7.2	61–47–11–24	512	436–1,833
Delray Beach (Palm Beach).	*CM-S	40	20.4	6.3	85–161–85–184	17.3	9.1	87–39–19–53	622	362–1,488
Dunedin (Pinellas)	*CM-S	31	15.1	2.7	68–83–200–134	11.4	2.9	62–31–27–41	2,354	329–1,387
Fort Lauderdale (Broward).	*CM-C	154	103.2	14.8	113–147–148–263	88.4	24.9	131–61–22–75	743	2,134–1,360
Fort Myers (Lee)	MC-C	38	23.7	4.4	118–82–107–311	19.6	4.4	70–49–34–37	710	632–1,340
Fort Pierce (St. Lucie)	*CM-I	36	17.3	36.3	83–53–50–294	14.8	38.5	63–0–64–63	939	554–1,553
Fort Walton Beach (Okaloosa).	*CM-C	22	9.3	0.9	89–62–76–201	7.4	1.0	50–33–26–67	253	285–1,276
Gainesville (Alachua)	*CM-C	84	41.9	98.8	94–65–57–285	34.8	109.7	80–46–42–42	3,265	1,415–1,616
Gulfport (Pinellas)	*CM-S	11	3.7	1.5	72–36–76–140	3.6	1.5	59–6–12–30	67	...–...
Haines City (Polk)	*CM-S	12	3.7	0.4	132–39–59–83	3.1	0.3	45–23–18–46	373	126–1,201
Hallandale (Broward)	*CM-S	37	18.5	2.2	64–111–110–214	14.8	2.4	90–57–11–86	62	425–1,822
Hialeah (Dade).	MC-S	155	61.0	4.0	69–123–86–117	49.2	7.3	70–47–8–64	384	1,094–1,426
Hollywood (Broward)	*CM-C	122	57.6	5.2	86–105–111–170	49.1	8.8	107–62–28–66	315	1,375–1,926
Homestead (Dade).	*CM-S	22	...	...	...–...–...–...	12.3	17.8	4–1–15–3	0	638–1,456
Jacksonville (Duval).	MC-C	556	390.8	407.6	169–158–60–315	332.3	401.7	74–43–20–54	1,247	7,888–1,694
Jacksonville Beach (Duval)	*CM-S	17	5.1	19.6	64–74–26–139	5.7	22.8	77–53–33–1	918	263–1,345
Key West (Monroe)	*CM-I	25	12.5	34.5	87–126–24–260	11.8	38.2	60–53–20–79	2,968	292–1,583
Kissimmee (Osceola).	*CM-S	19	7.6	30.1	90–70–52–193	7.9	40.2	76–40–41–15	3,662	385–1,451
Lake Worth (Palm Beach)	*CM-S	28	14.0	23.4	81–68–53–298	15.8	21.2	81–41–18–144	1,266	494–1,506

Table 1/9 continued **PROFILES OF INDIVIDUAL CITIES**

City (county)	Form of govern-ment–Metro status	Est. 1982 popu-lation (000)	Fiscal year 1983 revenues: Total general revenue ($ mil-lions)	Total utility reve-nue ($ mil-lions)	Per capita revenues ($): Intergovernmental revenue–Property taxes–Other taxes–Charges and miscella-neous general revenue	Fiscal year 1983 expenditures: Total general expendi-tures ($ mil-lions)	Total utility expendi-tures ($ mil-lions)	Per capita current expenditures ($): Police–Fire–Streets–Sewers and sanitation	Long term debt ($ per capita)	October 1983 public personnel: Total full time equivalent employment–Average full time monthly salary ($)
FLORIDA continued										
Lakeland (Polk)	*CM-C	52	25.8	93.8	93–45–54–306	24.4	123.5	76–48–62–54	4,839	1,195–1,922
Largo (Pinellas)	*CM-S	60	22.6	0.0	85–17–83–192	17.6	0.0	51–27–11–55	0	524–1,596
Lauderdale Lakes (Broward)	MC-S	27	4.5	0.0	48–38–45–37	4.3	0.0	47–29–13–0	0	...–...
Lauderhill (Broward)	MC-S	39	9.2	3.4	47–38–82–70	9.2	5.8	54–42–18–0	836	226–1,427
Leesburg (Lake)	*CM-I	14	6.9	20.5	75–69–11–346	7.8	19.8	74–51–28–102	1,362	277–1,351
Lighthouse Point (Broward)	MC-S	11	2.8	0.0	44–126–51–25	2.7	0.0	86–38–4–15	0	...–...
Longwood (Seminole)	CM-S	11	1.8	0.4	42–39–53–21	1.6	0.4	49–21–24–0	0	80–1,503
Margate (Broward)	*CM-S	39	10.0	7.2	57–53–82–67	8.1	6.1	76–21–17–0	476	336–1,752
Melbourne (Brevard)	*CM-C	50	18.8	7.2	67–69–85–156	15.4	9.5	58–44–28–0	622	610–1,213
Miami (Dade)	*CM-C	383	202.3	0.0	114–191–127–97	217.2	0.0	103–65–29–47	539	3,864–2,305
Miami Beach (Dade)	*CM-S	94	78.3	5.1	85–297–201–253	72.2	4.2	110–41–11–77	564	1,558–1,872
Miami Springs (Dade)	*CM-S	12	6.3	0.5	56–124–113–228	5.7	0.5	107–0–12–76	1,434	137–1,579
Miramar (Broward)	MC-S	35	7.2	2.3	55–41–79–32	6.3	2.5	50–22–10–0	119	229–1,721
Naples (Collier)	*CM-I	19	11.8	5.3	58–120–144–293	9.9	7.0	90–38–27–52	2,261	400–1,306
New Port Richey (Pasco)	*CM-S	12	4.0	1.6	62–76–87–101	3.0	1.8	64–34–32–0	152	131–1,213
New Smyrna Beach (Volusia)	*CM-S	14	11.5	12.8	58–149–90–512	7.1	18.0	88–65–38–110	2,259	229–1,131
North Lauderdale (Broward)	*CM-S	20	3.7	1.6	47–33–66–38	3.8	1.6	57–16–16–0	259	159–1,492
North Miami (Dade)	*CM-S	43	15.0	6.6	47–107–111–84	13.0	7.9	65–0–12–30	612	418–1,816
North Miami Beach (Dade)	*CM-S	36	17.7	6.0	54–105–109–219	14.9	6.2	88–0–5–81	353	405–1,906
North Palm Beach v (Palm Beach)	*CM-S	12	4.5	0.0	47–133–85–117	4.8	0.0	65–8–27–39	159	...–...
Oakland Park (Broward)	*CM-S	24	10.9	3.0	59–110–146–143	10.8	3.8	111–51–22–68	355	283–1,873
Ocala (Marion)	*CM-C	41	10.5	44.0	70–49–17–121	14.6	39.7	72–40–21–42	545	735–1,337
Opa-Locka (Dade)	*CM-S	15	4.8	1.7	73–123–52–63	4.3	1.5	96–0–16–25	166	182–1,363
Orlando (Orange)	MC-C	134	166.0	155.9	183–104–124–827	142.9	189.9	124–75–33–104	4,072	3,131–1,429
Ormond Beach (Volusia)	*CM-S	24	9.3	1.7	45–66–81–203	6.9	4.2	55–18–35–60	607	287–1,316
Palatka (Putnam)	*CM-I	11	4.5	1.1	148–68–65–144	3.3	2.9	62–41–28–28	328	...–...
Palm Bay (Brevard)	*CM-S	26	5.6	0.7	46–28–116–24	5.5	0.7	51–26–21–0	63	...–...
Palm Beach Gardens (Palm Beach)	*CM-S	17	3.6	0.0	44–91–51–19	4.5	0.0	48–9–0–0	4	120–1,409
Panama City (Bay)	*CM-C	35	17.9	1.4	182–50–144–142	15.9	7.0	45–45–39–67	243	449–1,230
Pembroke Pines (Broward)	*CM-S	42	10.6	4.5	60–48–84–62	9.6	5.4	62–30–8–0	179	418–1,592
Pensacola (Escambia)	*CM-C	59	33.5	24.8	139–31–106–293	40.1	22.0	79–76–26–42	388	817–1,571
Pinellas Park (Pinellas)	*CM-S	36	13.4	2.4	71–45–82–178	10.8	3.5	44–28–46–84	521	308–1,486
Plant City (Hillsborough)	*CM-S	18	6.4	1.7	107–66–82–107	5.4	1.3	60–28–41–36	249	220–1,209
Plantation (Broward)	MC-S	51	19.4	3.9	48–63–117–149	15.7	8.4	61–7–5–0	757	371–1,522
Pompano Beach (Broward)	*CM-S	58	35.0	5.6	64–164–125–249	31.9	3.7	128–56–33–99	273	722–1,983
Port Orange (Volusia)	*CM-S	23	6.2	3.8	90–38–59–85	4.5	5.7	40–33–42–23	173	256–1,290
Port St. Lucie (St. Lucie)	CM-I	23	3.6	0.0	38–50–47–23	3.4	0.0	36–0–24–25	0	...–...
Riviera Beach (Palm Beach)	*CM-S	28	13.6	5.0	71–151–75–181	16.2	5.9	98–49–30–41	613	326–1,692
Rockledge (Brevard)	*CM-S	13	3.5	0.0	45–70–78–82	3.3	0.0	46–26–27–82	75	130–1,144
St. Augustine (St. Johns)	*CM-S	12	6.5	1.0	84–89–91–257	5.4	1.3	74–51–54–97	1,173	198–1,306
St. Petersburg (Pinellas)	*CM-C	241	130.3	17.9	126–102–80–233	102.6	34.4	81–38–37–78	817	2,904–1,663
Sanford (Seminole)	*CM-S	26	9.4	1.1	61–47–89–169	8.4	1.9	59–40–39–41	110	272–1,437
Sarasota (Sarasota)	*CM-C	51	33.2	4.5	94–126–129–306	26.6	15.2	102–86–30–97	738	859–1,564
South Miami (Dade)	*CM-S	11	3.5	0.0	49–97–99–81	3.7	0.0	97–0–17–69	94	...–...
Sunrise (Broward)	MC-S	45	19.9	10.1	52–78–121–195	19.5	11.1	67–45–14–37	1,509	443–1,849
Tallahassee (Leon)	*CM-C	103	60.3	100.2	166–34–54–333	66.2	88.9	58–31–46–79	1,730	1,923–1,431
Tamarac (Broward)	*CM-S	31	10.5	4.0	45–103–67–126	7.8	4.8	74–30–11–22	438	291–1,748
Tampa (Hillsborough)	MC-C	276	179.3	17.9	143–102–139–266	179.4	25.4	89–51–24–91	726	4,179–1,509
Tarpon Springs (Pinellas)	*CM-S	14	6.6	2.5	80–75–99–215	5.3	2.3	54–29–31–51	882	...–...
Temple Terrace (Hillsborough)	*CM-S	12	5.3	1.3	67–88–97–209	3.4	3.0	74–31–31–28	580	154–1,380
Titusville (Brevard)	*CM-C	35	9.4	3.2	64–47–80–79	8.5	2.4	45–32–22–27	214	323–1,253
Venice (Sarasota)	*CM-S	13	9.2	2.4	78–107–129–380	6.9	6.4	93–56–52–82	282	...–...
Vero Beach (Indian River)	*CM-I	17	9.7	33.3	50–68–65–372	9.9	35.4	82–0–30–54	2,320	463–1,476
West Palm Beach (Palm Beach)	*CM-C	66	39.9	5.7	75–129–119–279	37.7	7.4	85–48–33–101	445	1,100–1,627
Wilton Manors (Broward)	†MC-S	13	3.9	0.7	43–88–77–100	3.0	0.9	90–6–3–34	307	72–1,905
Winter Haven (Polk)	*CM-C	22	11.4	1.1	85–93–105–243	9.7	2.0	64–37–31–103	794	330–1,264
Winter Park (Orange)	*CM-S	22	11.6	4.1	87–98–170–165	10.2	2.6	89–48–29–75	128	360–1,397
Winter Springs (Seminole)	*CM-S	13	1.8	0.0	36–25–54–19	1.6	0.0	30–24–10–0	44	...–...
GEORGIA										
Albany (Dougherty)	*CM-C	85	30.4	61.2	138–58–46–116	28.9	56.5	54–41–12–57	120	1,157–1,368
Americus (Sumter)	MC-I	17	5.6	3.1	130–86–61–63	6.8	3.0	52–29–24–32	117	181–1,100
Athens (Clarke)	MC-C	43	13.6	2.5	150–3–84–80	15.7	7.2	60–0–25–59	578	547–1,308
Atlanta (Fulton)	†MC-C	428	459.3	37.2	193–198–147–535	367.4	36.8	93–46–30–86	2,295	7,387–1,461
Augusta (Richmond)	MC-C	46	29.6	6.3	219–93–82–243	23.0	5.3	64–45–20–38	377	1,025–1,088
Bainbridge (Decatur)	*CM-I	11	4.0	2.6	140–78–42–112	3.8	2.5	55–29–52–53	246	189–1,089
Brunswick (Glynn)	*CM-I	18	9.6	2.3	197–66–95–178	9.2	1.8	89–39–20–87	317	363–1,097
Carrollton (Carroll)	*CM-I	15	5.4	1.1	104–51–100–112	4.3	0.9	67–33–24–49	262	179–1,193
College Park (Fulton)	*CM-S	25	7.5	10.2	16–70–115–95	7.4	10.3	67–46–12–85	257	263–1,541
Columbus c (Muscogee)	*CM-C	174	62.0	1.0	83–87–150–35	59.5	2.1	43–30–21–16	180	2,245–1,053
Cordele (Crisp)	*CM-I	11	4.7	2.0	222–77–55–65	3.6	2.5	54–29–53–54	420	168–902
Covington (Newton)	*CM-S	12	4.2	10.7	160–0–60–134	6.2	10.1	76–47–41–83	447	172–1,296
Dalton (Whitfield)	MC-I	20	21.4	61.1	208–209–87–557	12.1	58.0	66–54–121–117	268	456–1,122
Decatur (De Kalb)	*CM-S	18	6.5	0.0	50–121–99–86	6.1	0.0	60–49–15–32	97	177–1,515
Douglas (Coffee)	*CM-I	11	3.5	9.0	140–38–41–96	5.1	7.8	62–40–43–46	210	188–1,140
Dublin (Laurens)	*CM-I	16	4.8	6.6	107–35–66–82	4.5	6.2	49–37–12–46	216	184–1,253
East Point (Fulton)	*CM-S	38	10.8	15.7	28–94–51–108	11.6	12.2	47–45–8–37	312	420–1,467
Fitzgerald (Ben Hill)	†MC-I	10	1.8	1.8	80–15–25–48	1.9	1.0	35–25–20–34	11	147–933
Forest Park (Clayton)	*CM-S	18	5.6	1.2	22–106–77–101	5.6	1.5	48–45–27–102	140	198–1,125
Gainesville (Hall)	*CM-I	15	11.9	3.9	202–162–171–248	10.5	5.6	95–68–47–141	834	385–1,307

Table 1/9 continued PROFILES OF INDIVIDUAL CITIES

City (county)	Form of govern-ment–Metro status	Est. 1982 popu-lation (000)	Fiscal year 1983 revenues: Total general revenue ($ mil-lions)	Total utility reve-nue ($ mil-lions)	Per capita revenues ($): Intergovernmental revenue–Property taxes–Other taxes–Charges and miscella-neous general revenue	Fiscal year 1983 expenditures: Total general expendi-tures ($ mil-lions)	Total utility expendi-tures ($ mil-lions)	Per capita current expenditures ($): Police–Fire–Streets–Sewers and sanitation	Long term debt ($ per capita)	October 1983 public personnel: Total full time equivalent employment–Average full time monthly salary ($)
GEORGIA continued										
Griffin (Spalding)	*CM-I	22	6.7	8.4	21–59–62–168	6.6	8.8	63–48–24–77	158	332–1,179
Hinesville (Liberty)	MC-I	13	3.0	0.4	67–60–58–45	2.7	0.4	46–19–21–54	438	137–1,150
La Grange (Troup)	*CM-I	25	9.7	23.1	152–65–54–117	12.0	18.0	66–52–16–49	174	348–1,190
Macon (Bibb)	†MC-C	119	43.9	...	91–75–160–44	45.3	0.7	64–59–17–28	205	1,370–1,358
Marietta (Cobb)	*CM-S	34	14.2	32.0	42–99–102–178	35.1	32.3	70–60–21–167	402	542–1,346
Milledgeville (Baldwin)	MC-I	13	4.6	1.0	103–49–80–114	4.2	1.0	57–35–15–57	195	161–1,114
Moultrie (Colquitt)	*CM-I	16	6.2	10.4	226–51–40–85	6.0	11.9	52–38–25–45	67	236–1,213
Newnan (Coweta)	*CM-I	12	2.5	0.0	104–13–69–29	2.9	0.0	59–38–14–37	2	167–1,356
Rome (Floyd)	*CM-I	30	16.1	2.5	171–104–117–139	13.9	9.7	68–105–42–63	279	588–1,241
Roswell (Fulton)	†MC-S	26	7.1	0.6	10–96–77–88	6.3	0.5	49–12–18–56	138	193–1,137
Savannah (Chatham)	*CM-C	146	71.7	7.6	178–54–63–197	71.6	7.4	79–36–17–63	276	1,706–1,243
Smyrna (Cobb)	MC-S	20	7.2	1.4	15–125–93–121	5.7	1.2	61–46–22–65	18	220–1,186
Statesboro (Bulloch)	MC-I	15	3.0	4.6	35–53–61–51	3.3	4.6	42–12–25–47	325	176–948
Thomasville (Thomas)	*CM-I	19	8.2	18.0	125–59–49–204	7.9	15.8	51–46–17–69	132	376–1,210
Tifton (Tift)	*CM-I	14	4.9	4.5	156–10–65–114	7.2	4.9	63–25–31–60	446	189–1,063
Valdosta (Lowndes)	*CM-I	39	12.6	2.4	93–41–60–133	10.6	2.3	23–41–29–55	230	425–1,159
Vidalia (Toombs)	*CM-I	11	2.5	0.4	55–80–53–49	2.1	0.4	37–11–20–36	205	93–867
Warner Robins (Houston)	MC-S	42	9.3	16.3	15–70–45–90	9.2	16.0	41–30–17–45	229	413–1,091
Waycross (Ware)	*CM-I	20	7.1	0.9	163–30–65–104	7.4	2.2	59–29–28–66	410	260–1,041
HAWAII										
Honolulu c (Honolulu)	MC-C	782	420.8	58.1	115–257–64–102	367.5	102.4	71–34–19–42	310	8,336–1,771
IDAHO										
Blackfoot (Bingham)	MC-I	10	2.4	0.4	51–86–7–96	2.5	0.4	48–28–19–40	25	110–1,202
Boise City (Ada)	MC-C	105	39.6	0.5	71–109–13–186	42.9	2.2	54–51–3–72	128	716–1,699
Caldwell (Canyon)	MC-I	18	6.1	0.6	119–93–4–131	4.9	0.4	38–27–27–49	34	132–1,216
Coeur d'Alene (Kootenai)	†MC-I	22	6.5	1.1	53–105–14–127	6.6	1.4	43–29–20–48	510	170–1,556
Idaho Falls (Bonneville)	MC-I	41	15.2	14.1	112–105–9–146	14.4	15.4	59–48–24–51	1,139	447–1,777
Lewiston (Nez Perce)	*CM-I	28	9.6	0.7	110–135–6–93	9.6	0.8	48–55–33–61	118	228–1,542
Moscow (Latah)	†MC-I	17	4.6	0.6	56–54–16–139	5.6	1.0	49–9–25–42	91	...–...
Nampa (Canyon)	MC-I	26	7.7	0.7	67–78–11–138	8.0	0.5	40–29–29–67	98	166–1,501
Pocatello (Bannock)	*CM-I	46	14.2	2.1	85–113–10–98	12.8	1.7	43–33–17–45	49	379–1,764
Rexburg (Madison)	MC-I	12	1.6	0.3	48–34–4–46	1.6	0.2	34–13–22–25	148	48–1,330
Twin Falls (Twin Falls)	*CM-I	27	14.2	1.6	291–101–5–129	13.4	1.5	56–40–29–57	41	192–1,568
ILLINOIS										
Addison v (Du Page)	†MC-S	30	12.8	0.7	61–56–98–205	12.4	0.7	63–0–32–39	199	180–1,944
Alsip v (Cook)	MC-S	17	0.7	2.2	0–0–0–42	5.1	1.8	70–53–26–5	280	...–...
Alton (Madison)	MC-S	34	13.6	0.0	77–64–110–155	13.8	0.0	55–49–30–51	187	303–1,565
Arlington Heights v (Cook)	*CM-S	66	23.8	6.3	49–134–96–79	18.8	17.0	56–42–28–0	1,043	494–1,750
Aurora (Kane)	MC-S	82	...	...	...–...–...–...	25.7	4.5	65–42–33–10	0	633–2,149
Bartlett v (Cook)	MC-S	14	3.8	0.4	38–68–30–128	3.0	0.7	54–0–22–26	409	62–1,826
Batavia (Kane)	MC-S	13	...	...	...–...–...–...	5.0	5.8	69–24–19–63	0	81–2,030
Belleville (St. Clair)	MC-S	41	11.8	0.0	48–44–107–86	10.3	0.0	42–35–16–41	36	265–1,643
Bellwood v (Cook)	MC-S	20	7.0	1.3	55–145–96–55	5.3	1.7	68–36–38–21	253	...–...
Belvidere (Boone)	MC-S	15	4.5	0.5	64–77–62–88	3.8	0.6	46–34–35–41	121	...–...
Bensenville v (Du Page)	†MC-S	16	6.7	0.9	53–53–168–138	5.3	1.2	71–51–40–72	214	122–1,769
Berwyn (Cook)	MC-S	46	10.7	2.3	41–66–85–41	9.0	1.9	51–40–32–35	101	262–1,524
Bloomingdale v (Du Page)	MC-S	13	5.4	0.8	37–80–145–148	4.5	0.8	68–0–25–48	901	87–1,781
Bloomington (Mc Lean)	*CM-C	45	21.8	2.2	81–100–144–155	17.6	1.9	50–41–32–32	347	398–1,764
Blue Island (Cook)	MC-S	22	...	0.0	...–...–...–...	...	0.0	...–...–...–...	0	...–...
Bolingbrook v (Will)	*CM-S	39	19.7	0.6	52–78–74–303	14.3	1.0	52–36–27–18	302	187–2,065
Bourbonnais v (Kankakee)	MC-S	14	...	0.0	...–...–...–...	...	0.0	...–...–...–...	0	...–...
Bradley v (Kankakee)	MC-S	11	0.2	0.4	0–0–0–14	2.6	0.6	50–8–52–21	55	...–...
Bridge View v (Cook)	MC-S	14	6.2	1.1	62–148–117–112	4.9	0.8	71–66–26–28	446	...–...
Brookfield v (Cook)	*CM-S	19	4.8	1.5	45–60–75–68	4.4	1.3	50–22–22–26	95	98–1,943
Buffalo Grove v (Cook)	*CM-S	24	7.4	1.4	37–89–69–120	6.4	5.6	62–34–36–48	828	130–2,069
Burbank (Cook)	MC-S	28	4.5	0.0	39–54–52–14	4.4	0.0	52–32–31–0	143	115–1,550
Cahokia v (St. Clair)	MC-S	19	4.9	0.3	83–52–69–58	3.6	0.3	66–0–28–21	105	86–1,885
Calumet City (Cook)	MC-S	40	11.4	2.5	46–54–135–52	7.9	2.3	52–27–19–22	392	253–1,813
Canton (Fulton)	MC-I	14	0.9	0.7	0–0–0–64	3.7	0.5	44–30–25–33	206	...–...
Carbondale (Jackson)	*CM-I	26	16.7	1.4	249–35–144–204	17.1	2.4	63–35–28–47	1,408	324–1,589
Carol Stream v (Du Page)	*CM-S	18	5.2	0.9	31–39–141–83	3.8	0.7	64–0–34–29	161	99–1,867
Carpentersville v (Kane)	*CM-S	23	4.8	0.6	55–39–71–43	3.8	1.0	61–0–25–44	77	90–1,931
Centralia (Marion)	*CM-I	15	6.6	1.4	182–82–88–87	5.3	1.2	51–35–36–47	283	153–1,577
Champaign (Champaign)	*CM-C	59	49.1	0.0	68–84–130–551	44.8	0.0	59–37–27–12	133	1,125–1,581
Charleston (Coles)	CO-I	19	4.9	1.6	58–57–45–94	4.1	1.7	38–24–31–19	377	128–1,217
Chicago (Cook)	MC-C	2,997	2,062.5	158.2	248–126–213–101	2,086.7	104.4	142–49–25–42	282	43,848–2,039
Chicago Heights (Cook)	MC-S	36	14.4	1.4	93–95–135–75	12.7	5.1	66–46–14–34	206	374–1,494
Chicago Ridge v (Cook)	MC-S	14	0.6	0.9	0–0–0–43	3.0	1.1	65–8–26–23	128	...–...
Cicero t (Cook)	MC-S	61	14.8	4.8	54–98–59–31	12.6	4.3	50–32–41–7	38	405–1,674
Collinsville (Madison)	CO-S	20	5.5	0.7	48–64–89–81	4.8	0.9	53–34–44–43	249	125–2,036
Country Club Hills (Cook)	MC-S	15	...	...	...–...–...–...	1.8	1.0	53–0–29–10	0	52–1,620
Crestwood v (Cook)	MC-S	11	2.0	0.4	56–39–51–30	1.8	0.6	35–6–22–14	161	...–...
Crystal Lake (Mc Henry)	*CM-S	19	7.1	0.6	84–76–121–99	6.6	0.8	66–26–12–48	187	136–1,790
Danville (Vermilion)	CO-I	38	15.1	0.1	152–61–82–101	16.3	0.6	73–56–27–26	154	282–1,578
Darien (Du Page)	†MC-S	16	2.1	0.9	32–27–65–12	2.3	0.6	47–3–22–0	187	52–1,926
De Kalb (De Kalb)	*CM-I	33	9.2	1.2	82–37–96–64	7.3	1.1	49–40–37–11	116	175–2,112
Decatur (Macon)	*CM-C	93	27.9	6.1	69–54–97–80	24.5	6.9	45–35–19–7	310	561–1,799
Deerfield v (Lake)	*CM-S	17	7.0	0.9	51–137–98–119	5.7	0.8	84–0–28–80	209	92–2,267

Table 1/9 continued **PROFILES OF INDIVIDUAL CITIES**

City (county)	Form of govern-ment–Metro status	Est. 1982 popu-lation (000)	Fiscal year 1983 revenues: Total general revenue ($ mil-lions)	Total utility reve-nue ($ mil-lions)	Per capita revenues ($): Intergovernmental revenue–Property taxes–Other taxes–Charges and miscella-neous general revenue	Fiscal year 1983 expenditures: Total general expendi-tures ($ mil-lions)	Total utility expendi-tures ($ mil-lions)	Per capita current expenditures ($): Police–Fire–Streets–Sewers and sanitation	Long term debt ($ per capita)	October 1983 public personnel: Total full time equivalent employment–Average full time monthly salary ($)
ILLINOIS continued										
Des Plaines (Cook)	MC-S	56	19.3	3.9	51–91–116–87	16.5	3.5	69–54–51–29	523	390–2,111
Dixon (Lee)	MC-I	15	0.7	0.7	0–0–0–46	4.3	0.5	46–26–41–43	62	...–...
Dolton v (Cook)	MC-S	24	4.8	1.3	42–80–59–16	4.7	1.3	60–22–28–18	97	122–1,996
Downers Grove v (Du Page)	*CM-S	43	17.8	1.8	43–96–105–172	15.8	1.4	49–29–48–4	79	277–1,968
East Moline (Rock Island)	MC-S	22	8.7	1.2	92–102–115–94	10.2	1.6	64–47–36–101	427	180–2,129
East Peoria (Tazewell)	CO-S	22	10.1	0.6	107–108–57–178	12.2	0.6	51–30–24–40	900	111–2,101
East St. Louis (St. Clair)	MC-S	53	21.8	0.0	176–59–74–66	17.0	0.0	47–43–16–16	0	398–1,334
Edwardsville (Madison)	MC-S	12	8.7	0.7	448–97–70–79	9.5	0.5	51–30–21–32	328	94–1,805
Effingham (Effingham)	CO-I	11	0.6	0.8	0–0–0–56	3.7	0.8	63–37–57–53	101	...–...
Elgin (Kane)	*CM-S	64	23.0	4.1	79–109–67–102	21.1	11.3	76–52–27–15	509	449–2,191
Elk Grove Village v (Cook)	*CM-S	30	12.5	1.9	73–95–167–86	12.6	2.1	89–98–57–17	78	304–2,142
Elmhurst (Du Page)	*CM-S	44	15.8	1.4	48–105–92–111	13.3	1.5	56–31–48–39	178	281–2,145
Elmwood Park v (Cook)	*CM-S	24	5.1	1.4	41–114–40–22	4.9	1.2	50–32–38–22	3	132–1,908
Evanston (Cook)	*CM-S	73	41.4	4.3	73–235–130–128	39.9	3.4	81–47–26–28	714	855–2,012
Evergreen Park v (Cook)	†MC-S	22	6.5	1.2	44–113–109–31	5.2	1.1	69–20–29–20	451	152–1,710
Fairview Heights (St. Clair)	MC-S	12	3.9	0.0	45–6–254–19	4.1	0.0	80–0–72–0	0	92–1,798
Forest Park v (Cook)	CO-S	15	5.3	1.1	62–134–105–45	5.7	0.8	74–43–62–20	120	...–...
Franklin Park v (Cook)	MC-S	18	9.0	2.7	91–219–133–69	7.9	3.5	107–101–49–43	233	...–...
Freeport (Stephenson)	MC-I	26	6.6	0.7	48–46–70–87	5.6	0.6	36–36–26–39	98	185–1,519
Galesburg (Knox)	*CM-I	34	12.0	1.4	71–91–85–105	11.3	1.3	48–35–37–15	81	247–1,849
Glen Ellyn v (Du Page)	†MC-S	24	10.1	1.1	39–94–123–167	10.7	2.1	57–2–31–135	241	197–1,717
Glendale Heights v (Du Page)	†MC-S	25	5.7	1.4	48–41–57–82	5.4	0.8	52–0–24–28	296	123–1,718
Glenview v (Cook)	*CM-S	33	10.1	3.7	42–87–127–49	10.6	3.3	59–38–40–15	349	202–2,000
Glenwood v (Cook)	MC-S	10	...	0.0	...–...–...–...	...	0.0	...–...–...–...	0	...–...
Granite City (Madison)	MC-S	36	10.9	0.0	69–69–90–75	9.7	0.0	52–38–24–56	190	248–1,714
Hanover Park v (Cook)	*CM-S	31	6.5	1.6	45–57–43–68	4.7	1.2	45–1–19–21	336	...–...
Harvey (Cook)	CO-S	36	11.6	3.4	94–105–92–34	10.4	3.6	80–44–24–20	68	255–1,876
Hazel Crest v (Cook)	*CM-S	14	0.4	1.3	0–0–0–26	2.4	1.1	54–21–30–6	215	...–...
Herrin (Williamson)	MC-I	11	2.4	0.8	43–52–57–76	2.1	1.0	33–19–23–32	86	71–1,428
Hickory Hills (Cook)	MC-S	14	...	...	...–...–...–...	2.3	0.5	53–0–34–16	0	58–1,788
Highland Park (Lake)	*CM-S	31	15.6	2.1	51–182–177–97	11.3	2.2	81–53–57–0	514	276–2,470
Hinsdale v (Du Page)	*CM-S	17	6.8	1.5	42–177–96–95	6.3	0.8	52–27–59–44	255	105–2,004
Hoffman Estates v (Cook)	†MC-S	39	8.0	2.7	39–90–46–32	6.6	2.2	46–33–26–15	111	207–1,629
Homewood v (Cook)	*CM-S	19	1.7	1.4	0–0–0–86	9.2	4.6	71–27–56–34	670	...–...
Jacksonville (Morgan)	MC-I	20	6.5	1.1	80–61–89–96	5.6	2.0	46–32–61–44	229	154–1,528
Joliet (Will)	*CM-S	77	53.5	4.9	77–150–103–366	36.0	5.3	67–51–49–39	394	627–2,262
Justice v (Cook)	MC-S	10	1.5	0.1	35–38–29–44	1.7	0.2	59–10–29–10	46	...–...
Kankakee (Kankakee)	MC-C	29	10.9	0.0	98–67–132–76	8.6	0.0	58–56–44–20	267	229–1,746
Kewanee (Henry)	MC-S	14	6.0	0.4	112–97–67–172	5.7	0.4	48–50–20–45	131	103–1,373
La Grange v (Cook)	*CM-S	16	8.3	1.6	216–126–96–93	4.5	1.5	75–52–41–8	206	...–...
La Grange Park v (Cook)	*CM-S	13	2.5	0.7	37–71–58–21	1.8	0.8	68–5–17–3	16	...–...
La Salle (La Salle)	MC-I	10	2.2	0.5	55–52–79–36	1.9	0.3	45–15–29–26	139	55–1,562
Lake Forest (Lake)	*CM-S	16	11.0	1.2	39–284–158–226	9.8	1.3	88–48–52–39	379	202–1,939
Lansing v (Cook)	MC-S	28	7.4	1.2	42–111–51–56	7.6	1.6	63–19–18–21	380	137–2,040
Libertyville v (Lake)	*CM-S	17	...	...	...–...–...–...	6.0	1.2	73–46–33–35	0	106–1,998
Lincoln (Logan)	MC-I	16	4.3	0.0	56–64–67–86	4.4	0.0	46–30–41–73	102	...–...
Lincolnwood v (Cook)	MC-S	12	4.0	0.8	42–121–125–46	3.4	0.9	86–5–54–19	2	...–...
Lisle v (Du Page)	†MC-S	15	4.6	0.5	44–43–88–135	3.8	0.3	66–0–32–14	83	69–1,859
Lombard v (Du Page)	*CM-S	38	13.6	1.3	47–88–126–98	12.3	1.1	57–37–31–48	465	222–1,895
Loves Park (Winnebago)	MC-S	14	2.4	0.9	32–3–98–35	2.0	0.8	42–11–23–3	116	57–1,597
Mc Henry (Mc Henry)	MC-S	12	3.2	0.2	47–57–89–78	3.1	0.3	78–1–41–20	95	73–1,731
Macomb (Mc Donough)	MC-I	21	6.4	1.0	91–44–68–106	5.8	1.3	44–31–28–45	171	130–1,653
Marion (Williamson)	CO-I	14	14.7	0.6	79–11–132–811	14.2	0.6	28–22–56–52	112	460–1,306
Markham (Cook)	MC-S	16	2.7	0.8	46–47–54–27	3.3	0.9	52–9–31–24	33	88–1,793
Matteson v (Cook)	MC-S	11	4.2	0.5	48–81–207–53	3.4	0.3	100–42–34–21	14	...–...
Mattoon (Coles)	CO-I	19	7.9	0.9	77–74–126–132	6.0	1.3	51–45–41–49	63	128–1,668
Maywood v (Cook)	*CM-S	28	8.8	1.5	71–125–75–47	9.6	1.7	66–41–19–23	206	244–1,407
Melrose Park v (Cook)	MC-S	21	1.1	3.3	0–0–0–54	9.3	3.8	101–96–45–32	245	...–...
Midlothian v (Cook)	MC-S	14	2.5	0.8	40–22–73–44	2.4	1.1	50–28–18–29	78	...–...
Moline (Rock Island)	†MC-C	46	41.4	1.8	84–119–104–587	46.1	2.7	56–44–36–52	245	940–1,748
Monmouth (Warren)	MC-I	10	...	...	...–...–...–...	8.8	0.9	40–35–35–41	0	317–1,108
Morton v (Tazewell)	MC-S	14	3.2	3.0	43–39–87–59	2.7	2.7	45–6–17–42	75	70–1,779
Morton Grove v (Cook)	MC-S	24	...	...	...–...–...–...	7.0	1.8	69–48–27–21	0	177–2,172
Mount Prospect v (Cook)	*CM-S	53	14.4	2.2	50–112–85–27	12.8	1.6	45–43–27–26	138	279–2,150
Mount Vernon (Jefferson)	*CM-I	18	7.8	1.6	123–61–128–130	7.8	1.9	56–45–37–77	397	180–1,843
Mundelein v (Lake)	†MC-S	17	4.2	0.6	55–65–78–50	4.1	0.5	62–26–33–33	127	86–1,953
Naperville (Du Page)	*CM-S	46	25.5	30.0	75–129–148–204	18.1	31.0	54–32–66–37	1,055	378–2,090
Niles v (Cook)	*CM-S	30	10.9	2.0	55–69–209–32	9.9	2.4	76–53–25–19	129	209–2,210
Normal t (Mc Lean)	*CM-C	36	9.9	1.5	58–45–83–92	11.2	1.5	39–30–26–17	261	207–1,778
Norridge v (Cook)	MC-S	16	3.5	0.9	38–28–130–20	2.5	0.7	53–0–20–24	256	59–1,885
North Chicago (Lake)	MC-S	41	6.0	1.6	58–17–53–18	5.2	1.9	39–16–22–4	98	150–1,777
Northbrook v (Cook)	*CM-S	31	11.7	1.6	55–122–134–63	10.6	1.4	95–63–27–16	435	244–2,312
Northlake (Cook)	*CM-S	12	...	0.0	...–...–...–...	...	0.0	...–...–...–...	0	...–...
O'Fallon (St. Clair)	MC-S	13	2.7	1.4	33–52–37–84	2.3	1.2	41–1–32–37	177	56–1,819
Oak Forest (Cook)	†MC-S	27	4.0	1.3	36–36–42–36	4.1	2.1	48–23–13–26	113	...–...
Oak Lawn v (Cook)	*CM-S	59	17.1	5.6	45–99–97–57	16.2	6.4	57–52–19–28	0	401–1,982
Oak Park v (Cook)	*CM-S	55	25.5	3.0	104–133–123–107	23.2	2.6	111–67–33–27	385	536–1,972
Orland Park v (Cook)	*CM-S	24	8.6	1.8	40–93–165–55	6.3	1.5	66–0–38–17	424	...–...
Ottawa (La Salle)	MC-I	18	1.0	0.5	0–0–0–56	4.0	0.4	33–32–22–20	75	...–...
Palatine v (Cook)	*CM-S	33	10.6	4.5	68–70–70–111	11.1	7.7	61–49–23–13	1,156	203–2,117

Table 1/9 continued **PROFILES OF INDIVIDUAL CITIES**

City (county)	Form of govern-ment–Metro status	Est. 1982 popu-lation (000)	Fiscal year 1983 revenues: Total general revenue ($ mil-lions)	Total utility reve-nue ($ mil-lions)	Per capita revenues ($): Intergovernmental revenue–Property taxes–Other taxes–Charges and miscella-neous general revenue	Fiscal year 1983 expenditures: Total general expendi-tures ($ mil-lions)	Total utility expendi-tures ($ mil-lions)	Per capita current expenditures ($): Police–Fire–Streets–Sewers and sanitation	Long term debt ($ per capita)	October 1983 public personnel: Total full time equivalent employment–Average full time monthly salary ($)
ILLINOIS continued										
Palos Heights (Cook)	MC-S	11	3.0	1.0	44–21–136–68	2.0	1.0	76–0–38–0	139	...–...
Palos Hills (Cook)	MC-S	17	2.8	0.9	46–38–34–53	2.5	1.0	55–0–17–22	55	...–...
Park Forest v (Cook)	*CM-S	26	6.8	1.5	56–75–66–63	5.8	1.4	38–24–14–13	149	154–2,059
Park Ridge (Cook)	*CM-S	38	16.2	2.3	44–153–123–109	10.9	2.3	53–46–32–23	375	236–2,129
Pekin (Tazewell)	CO-S	34	22.3	0.4	67–142–68–388	17.5	0.4	57–55–25–56	6	201–1,933
Peoria (Peoria)	*CM-C	122	66.0	0.0	184–140–101–115	75.7	0.0	73–55–14–40	524	912–2,079
Peru (La Salle)	MC-I	11	3.8	4.6	73–54–143–94	3.4	5.6	64–16–28–45	511	85–1,689
Pontiac (Livingston)	MC-I	11	4.7	0.0	192–76–63–89	4.3	0.0	42–19–33–61	33	80–1,640
Prospect Heights (Cook)	†MC-S	13	1.2	0.0	33–1–46–16	1.2	0.0	35–0–16–0	36	...–...
Quincy (Adams)	MC-I	42	19.4	2.0	138–61–79–180	16.8	2.5	48–44–26–52	290	401–1,581
Rantoul v (Champaign)	MC-C	21	1.8	4.5	0–0–0–86	2.8	4.6	28–3–19–29	121	...–...
River Forest v (Cook)	CM-S	12	4.5	0.9	42–156–122–56	3.7	0.7	87–55–39–33	80	87–2,458
River Grove v (Cook)	MC-S	10	2.6	0.8	77–80–72–32	1.9	0.8	69–13–19–20	40	...–...
Riverdale v (Cook)	MC-S	13	2.3	1.1	60–67–33–13	3.4	0.8	48–15–43–14	0	...–...
Rock Falls v (Whiteside)	MC-I	11	1.0	4.7	0–0–0–94	4.2	4.5	75–0–32–34	475	...–...
Rock Island (Rock Island)	*CM-C	47	26.9	2.7	101–143–50–285	24.6	2.7	69–42–57–39	545	473–1,876
Rockford (Winnebago)	MC-C	138	52.4	4.9	119–115–92–53	48.0	7.6	68–51–31–23	109	994–1,762
Rolling Meadows (Cook)	*CM-S	21	8.4	1.2	45–80–217–64	7.4	1.4	76–59–35–31	13	179–2,035
Romeoville v (Will)	†MC-S	15	5.2	0.4	52–107–106–73	4.9	0.5	83–22–26–53	385	101–1,887
Roselle v (Du Page)	MC-S	18	1.2	0.7	0–0–0–68	3.9	0.6	57–7–21–27	70	...–...
Round Lake Beach v (Lake)	MC-S	13	2.5	0.5	43–29–68–48	2.3	0.4	49–0–16–27	125	70–1,446
St. Charles (Kane)	MC-S	18	...	...	...–...–...–...	7.6	13.4	110–0–78–67	0	152–2,205
Sauk Village v (Cook)	MC-S	11	1.6	0.4	47–55–22–20	2.0	0.4	43–11–19–3	76	...–...
Schaumburg v (Cook)	*CM-S	56	19.5	4.5	55–4–185–104	15.6	4.2	67–61–23–0	65	414–2,231
Schiller Park v (Cook)	MC-S	12	4.6	1.0	57–147–158–35	4.1	0.9	107–53–36–18	108	...–...
Skokie v (Cook)	*CM-S	60	22.9	3.3	56–173–112–42	19.8	3.4	68–58–30–26	91	536–2,102
South Holland v (Cook)	MC-S	24	...	...	...–...–...–...	4.4	1.4	47–17–24–22	0	167–1,632
Springfield (Sangamon)	CO-C	99	41.0	71.9	95–94–101–123	36.4	77.3	64–51–64–10	1,658	1,414–1,932
Sterling (Whiteside)	*CM-I	16	...	0.0	...–...–...–...	14.8	0.0	51–41–21–35	0	460–1,056
Streamwood v (Cook)	*CM-S	24	4.1	1.6	43–57–52–19	3.9	1.5	54–25–24–0	169	111–2,000
Streator (La Salle)	MC-I	14	0.2	0.0	0–0–0–17	2.8	0.0	44–23–27–25	15	...–...
Summit v (Cook)	MC-S	10	2.5	0.6	52–95–80–19	2.8	0.6	74–5–41–20	56	...–...
Taylorville (Christian)	MC-I	11	4.3	0.9	184–77–84–46	3.7	1.8	36–20–41–17	209	...–...
Tinley Park v (Cook)	†MC-S	27	6.0	1.9	43–55–74–47	5.3	1.8	50–9–35–0	315	94–2,072
Urbana (Champaign)	†MC-C	36	13.9	0.0	79–64–114–132	13.9	0.0	42–34–53–10	146	206–1,889
Villa Park v (Du Page)	*CM-S	23	...	...	...–...–...–...	8.1	1.0	68–32–70–27	0	153–2,080
Washington (Tazewell)	†MC-S	10	0.6	0.3	0–0–0–62	2.4	0.3	56–11–32–37	219	...–...
Waukegan (Lake)	MC-S	69	28.7	3.6	73–60–140–142	27.4	4.8	64–39–40–14	247	468–1,884
West Chicago (Du Page)	*CM-S	13	0.9	0.5	0–0–0–68	3.4	0.5	81–0–50–35	62	...–...
Westchester v (Cook)	*CM-S	17	5.2	1.4	16–121–79–83	3.8	1.2	56–38–26–34	213	...–...
Western Springs v (Cook)	*CM-S	13	3.6	0.9	38–106–70–65	3.3	1.0	54–9–16–18	97	...–...
Westmont v (Du Page)	*CM-S	18	5.2	1.0	39–56–126–70	5.0	0.9	78–15–32–13	74	104–2,069
Wheaton (Du Page)	*CM-S	44	10.4	1.6	37–69–74–56	10.1	1.1	48–19–26–18	199	233–1,956
Wheeling v (Cook)	*CM-S	25	19.2	1.4	87–80–84–523	10.6	1.2	63–44–21–0	738	...–...
Wilmette v (Cook)	*CM-S	28	10.2	2.5	39–148–127–55	8.6	2.5	64–48–15–55	185	217–2,163
Winnetka v (Cook)	*CM-S	13	6.0	6.9	39–295–59–78	5.9	5.9	123–92–54–119	157	163–2,362
Wood Dale (Du Page)	*CM-S	11	3.0	0.3	39–65–74–89	2.7	0.4	85–0–30–44	160	67–1,890
Wood River (Madison)	*CM-S	12	4.0	0.6	65–66–94–102	3.7	0.4	56–24–36–49	38	78–1,735
Woodridge v (Du Page)	†MC-S	23	6.8	1.0	38–67–70–122	5.3	0.7	59–0–14–0	343	104–1,974
Woodstock (Mc Henry)	*CM-S	12	4.3	0.8	60–131–83–86	3.6	1.2	67–5–28–31	403	87–1,745
Worth v (Cook)	MC-S	12	2.0	0.8	50–53–50–15	1.7	0.8	71–11–22–2	270	...–...
Zion (Lake)	†CO-S	18	...	...	...–...–...–...	5.5	0.9	82–42–48–24	0	120–1,893
INDIANA										
Anderson (Madison)	MC-C	62	25.6	28.3	140–149–2–120	23.9	28.0	60–66–33–71	445	842–1,361
Bedford (Lawrence)	MC-I	14	4.0	1.1	136–119–0–35	4.5	0.7	66–67–33–56	171	195–1,246
Beech Grove (Marion)	MC-S	13	3.6	0.0	102–109–2–69	5.1	0.0	56–45–26–25	91	100–1,313
Bloomington (Monroe)	MC-C	53	18.0	3.4	105–90–2–143	17.4	3.8	36–35–33–53	322	513–1,302
Carmel (Hamilton)	MC-S	19	9.5	2.6	315–95–2–102	10.0	2.5	47–60–18–40	399	142–1,420
Clarksville t (Clark)	CO-S	15	5.1	0.0	109–94–0–139	6.7	0.0	43–47–23–54	131	129–1,164
Columbus (Bartholomew)	MC-I	31	15.3	2.1	150–177–0–166	19.8	1.5	63–66–48–81	433	406–1,173
Connersville (Fayette)	MC-I	17	5.1	0.7	111–126–0–68	6.0	0.8	55–59–30–49	203	182–1,246
Crawfordsville (Montgomery)	MC-I	13	5.0	11.5	78–136–1–170	4.7	12.6	61–48–35–80	217	200–1,331
Crown Point (Lake)	MC-S	16	4.5	1.3	63–100–1–109	5.1	1.7	48–12–19–44	248	92–1,520
East Chicago (Lake)	MC-C	38	28.5	2.7	327–321–1–92	35.5	2.6	123–92–33–66	1,016	898–1,176
Lake Station (Lake)	MC-S	15	2.6	0.4	57–83–0–33	2.7	0.3	44–9–29–40	7	130–1,097
Elkhart (Elkhart)	MC-C	41	17.0	4.3	155–137–2–120	17.8	3.9	80–70–42–52	172	657–1,292
Elwood (Madison)	MC-S	10	2.3	0.5	64–84–0–73	2.2	0.3	39–41–24–43	213	...–...
Evansville (Vanderburgh)	MC-C	130	53.9	19.3	164–120–0–129	53.3	18.6	48–42–35–42	369	1,244–1,311
Fort Wayne (Allen)	MC-C	168	85.3	18.3	232–128–0–148	93.9	17.2	64–50–23–57	387	1,394–1,564
Frankfort (Clinton)	MC-I	15	5.6	9.1	117–102–0–142	6.0	9.3	48–57–23–164	481	198–1,382
Franklin (Johnson)	MC-S	12	6.4	0.0	183–155–1–217	6.5	0.0	8–62–23–45	280	116–1,138
Gary (Lake)	MC-C	148	62.9	0.0	205–141–1–79	72.0	0.0	49–51–27–38	217	1,773–1,280
Goshen (Elkhart)	MC-S	20	5.3	0.6	103–80–1–85	6.0	1.0	43–45–28–68	166	154–1,368
Greenfield (Hancock)	MC-S	11	5.1	4.0	97–96–0–255	2.8	5.5	47–14–19–53	361	113–1,129
Greenwood (Johnson)	MC-S	21	3.6	0.0	66–45–0–64	4.0	0.0	36–6–25–51	75	90–1,123
Griffith t (Lake)	MC-S	16	4.6	0.7	54–83–1–141	3.9	0.6	52–4–29–45	135	65–1,416
Hammond (Lake)	MC-C	92	27.6	3.4	82–132–3–84	28.9	3.8	72–62–33–41	402	983–1,301
Highland t (Lake)	MC-S	25	4.5	0.9	55–71–0–54	5.2	0.9	44–11–22–63	60	102–1,528
Hobart (Lake)	MC-S	23	5.0	0.0	58–95–0–66	4.1	0.0	41–28–23–31	27	136–1,215

Table 1/9 continued **PROFILES OF INDIVIDUAL CITIES**

City (county)	Form of govern-ment–Metro status	Est. 1982 popu-lation (000)	Fiscal year 1983 revenues: Total general revenue ($ mil-lions)	Total utility reve-nue ($ mil-lions)	Per capita revenues ($): Intergovernmental revenue–Property taxes–Other taxes–Charges and miscella-neous general revenue	Fiscal year 1983 expenditures: Total general expendi-tures ($ mil-lions)	Total utility expendi-tures ($ mil-lions)	Per capita current expenditures ($): Police–Fire–Streets–Sewers and sanitation	Long term debt ($ per capita)	October 1983 public personnel: Total full time equivalent employment–Average full time monthly salary ($)
INDIANA continued										
Huntington (Huntington)	MC-I	16	4.9	1.2	124–105–0–85	5.3	1.1	50–60–28–68	445	...–...
Indianapolis c (Marion)	MC-C	708	480.2	6.1	247–217–17–198	467.3	21.5	62–29–29–53	531	11,025–1,448
Jeffersonville (Clark)	MC-S	21	6.3	0.0	90–145–0–65	6.4	0.0	61–60–43–40	82	223–1,316
Kokomo (Howard)	MC-C	46	20.2	0.0	113–176–0–150	19.6	0.0	70–69–25–97	269	524–1,349
La Porte (La Porte)	MC-I	22	5.5	1.0	74–111–0–65	5.6	1.1	44–51–21–44	145	219–1,217
Lafayette (Tippecanoe)	MC-C	44	13.7	2.0	91–113–1–107	13.6	1.8	54–59–41–59	199	507–1,288
Lawrence (Marion)	MC-S	25	3.9	0.5	60–52–1–41	4.9	0.6	35–12–22–0	205	97–1,232
Lebanon (Boone)	MC-S	12	2.3	6.3	42–65–0–80	2.9	5.2	36–32–15–44	447	121–1,494
Logansport (Cass)	MC-I	18	6.7	14.9	116–87–1–177	9.4	20.5	52–66–17–63	1,103	258–1,365
Madison (Jefferson)	MC-I	12	3.4	0.6	75–111–0–100	4.3	0.7	56–9–18–41	349	104–1,097
Marion (Grant)	MC-I	35	22.4	1.4	433–145–0–66	24.2	1.6	55–63–34–37	420	311–1,198
Martinsville (Morgan)	MC-S	12	2.5	0.4	92–60–0–61	2.5	0.6	36–26–35–67	113	105–1,247
Merrillville (Lake)	MC-S	28	2.7	0.0	43–45–1–9	2.7	0.0	38–0–30–0	0	72–1,325
Michigan City (La Porte)	MC-I	37	16.1	2.3	88–190–1–160	16.6	2.2	67–71–18–37	168	446–1,176
Mishawaka (St. Joseph)	MC-S	41	11.2	18.5	98–139–1–36	12.0	13.1	44–38–23–30	133	420–1,301
Muncie (Delaware)	MC-C	76	25.0	0.0	116–142–0–73	28.6	0.0	51–42–31–25	98	596–1,387
Munster t (Lake)	†MC-S	21	4.8	1.8	75–110–1–45	3.0	1.9	3–0–60–0	192	78–1,521
New Albany (Floyd)	MC-S	38	9.9	0.0	75–93–0–93	10.8	0.0	46–58–17–59	174	323–1,156
New Castle (Henry)	MC-I	19	10.4	1.0	342–125–0–77	11.3	1.0	48–36–47–73	122	238–998
Noblesville (Hamilton)	MC-S	12	3.8	0.0	118–111–0–78	3.8	0.0	36–36–23–33	159	96–1,121
Peru (Miami)	MC-I	13	8.1	7.8	225–100–2–284	3.6	9.3	54–62–19–56	481	217–1,294
Portage (Porter)	MC-S	28	12.2	0.0	256–76–1–97	12.0	0.0	44–34–22–35	552	174–1,383
Richmond (Wayne)	MC-I	41	32.7	24.8	563–146–1–92	30.7	20.6	56–56–35–17	262	657–1,406
Schererville t (Lake)	†MC-S	14	5.1	1.1	51–87–1–28	5.2	0.7	2–0–26–57	247	...–...
Seymour (Jackson)	MC-I	15	4.9	0.0	86–102–0–131	4.8	0.1	36–31–60–37	141	139–999
Shelbyville (Shelby)	MC-S	15	12.3	0.0	81–105–1–639	12.2	0.0	48–42–18–28	548	358–1,241
South Bend (St. Joseph)	MC-C	108	47.6	4.7	180–165–1–97	49.0	4.9	70–60–24–41	214	1,407–1,483
Speedway (Marion)	MC-S	13	3.2	0.7	80–86–3–82	3.7	0.6	63–60–39–56	148	104–1,404
Terre Haute (Vigo)	MC-C	60	22.0	0.0	140–148–1–75	19.0	0.0	48–37–33–28	459	580–1,024
Valparaiso (Porter)	MC-S	23	9.6	1.5	202–114–0–107	9.7	1.4	48–31–23–67	341	197–1,613
Vincennes (Knox)	MC-I	21	5.4	0.9	97–89–2–64	7.1	0.9	33–44–15–45	113	175–1,148
Wabash (Wabash)	MC-I	12	3.3	0.0	94–86–0–85	3.5	0.0	53–56–17–59	180	93–1,315
Warsaw (Kosciusko)	MC-I	11	7.0	0.0	332–201–0–113	7.2	0.0	67–45–69–66	197	118–1,181
Washington (Daviess)	MC-I	12	1.9	5.1	66–53–0–42	1.7	5.1	26–26–28–28	4	110–953
West Lafayette (Tippecanoe)	MC-C	22	4.5	0.0	88–76–0–44	4.5	0.0	43–31–20–45	54	134–1,332
IOWA										
Ames (Story)	*CM-I	46	...	...	...–...–...–...	29.7	12.3	37–31–26–36	0	1,017–1,490
Ankeny (Polk)	*CM-S	16	3.8	0.7	77–104–7–53	5.8	1.0	23–6–39–27	870	90–1,698
Bettendorf (Scott)	MC-S	28	10.5	...	104–149–6–121	10.0	0.2	52–4–35–46	516	161–1,867
Boone (Boone)	MC-I	13	5.2	0.5	110–145–5–151	3.5	0.5	46–38–51–24	449	...–...
Burlington (Des Moines)	MC-I	29	21.8	2.4	178–161–5–404	22.5	2.6	51–51–48–46	969	263–1,561
Cedar Falls (Black Hawk)	MC-C	36	18.9	20.6	86–134–3–300	19.3	15.4	39–28–41–28	1,282	653–1,563
Cedar Rapids (Linn)	MC-C	109	75.9	5.6	189–226–9–273	64.3	12.6	70–46–49–97	368	1,231–1,684
Clinton (Clinton)	MC-I	32	21.8	0.2	130–163–4–376	15.9	0.7	44–42–30–38	138	220–1,638
Council Bluffs (Pottawattamie)	*CM-S	57	25.2	2.7	112–154–9–169	21.4	2.4	64–44–24–49	350	549–1,598
Davenport (Scott)	†MC-C	104	49.3	0.4	104–201–13–161	40.0	2.3	44–44–33–44	0	827–1,707
Des Moines (Polk)	*CM-C	192	119.2	11.2	168–192–22–240	142.3	14.4	71–52–66–48	440	2,111–1,832
Dubuque (Dubuque)	*CM-C	61	31.6	2.7	174–150–11–181	30.6	4.2	50–54–34–77	292	528–1,794
Fort Dodge (Webster)	CO-I	29	13.3	1.8	163–165–4–130	14.3	3.8	54–35–33–53	361	251–1,510
Fort Madison (Lee)	*CM-I	13	10.7	1.0	142–173–3–496	8.8	2.5	69–56–40–64	505	144–1,437
Indianola (Warren)	*CM-S	11	5.5	3.6	129–67–4–312	2.4	3.6	37–8–5–32	373	71–1,645
Iowa City (Johnson)	*CM-C	52	27.4	2.4	198–155–7–170	21.5	4.8	43–25–22–45	406	542–1,620
Keokuk (Lee)	MC-I	14	11.0	2.0	141–189–6–477	9.5	1.0	66–44–78–139	934	195–1,360
Marion (Linn)	*CM-S	20	5.3	0.6	69–116–3–79	5.3	0.6	49–24–36–39	170	100–1,759
Marshalltown (Marshall)	MC-I	27	11.9	1.6	106–169–4–158	16.0	1.4	51–33–45–38	1,100	219–1,674
Mason City (Cerro Gordo)	MC-I	30	11.9	1.1	127–133–4–132	10.8	1.1	50–37–30–37	47	280–1,409
Muscatine (Muscatine)	*CM-I	24	28.1	21.0	94–159–10–896	27.8	44.0	44–40–39–152	1,481	487–1,812
Newton (Jasper)	MC-I	15	13.7	0.9	136–209–6–553	12.3	1.0	69–63–57–67	237	329–1,481
Oskaloosa (Mahaska)	†MC-I	11	3.6	1.1	101–112–3–108	3.4	1.2	49–25–46–41	263	...–...
Ottumwa (Wapello)	CO-I	27	11.2	2.3	144–152–6–113	12.2	2.0	46–42–62–40	391	279–1,522
Sioux City (Woodbury)	*CM-C	82	53.9	3.2	194–190–23–249	48.5	5.9	70–52–39–50	1,410	783–1,744
Spencer (Clay)	MC-I	12	14.4	5.7	102–169–3–969	11.8	5.9	54–12–39–70	923	356–1,275
Urbandale (Polk)	*CM-S	19	5.5	1.0	60–158–18–51	5.9	1.1	55–5–39–31	308	93–1,706
Waterloo (Black Hawk)	MC-C	76	38.4	2.7	132–199–8–163	38.6	2.3	68–55–34–42	690	662–1,766
West Des Moines (Polk)	*CM-S	22	9.6	1.1	71–157–13–196	8.4	0.5	47–4–14–14	341	107–1,757
KANSAS										
Arkansas City (Cowley)	*CM-I	14	11.1	0.9	121–82–58–551	9.7	0.9	49–28–36–52	357	337–1,297
Atchison (Atchison)	*CM-I	12	3.6	0.8	52–113–50–91	3.4	0.9	47–39–32–41	268	113–1,235
Chanute (Neosho)	*CM-I	11	10.6	9.1	509–65–54–320	7.9	8.4	43–26–34–28	591	159–1,433
Coffeyville (Montgomery)	*CM-I	16	16.4	10.9	74–114–11–857	17.7	10.3	55–45–38–20	1,533	588–1,379
Dodge City (Ford)	*CM-I	19	8.4	0.8	37–88–41–285	10.0	2.9	41–25–25–65	924	160–1,343
El Dorado (Butler)	*CM-S	12	7.5	0.9	302–120–30–183	8.8	0.9	34–34–35–52	468	113–1,335
Emporia (Lyon)	*CM-I	27	...	...	...–...–...–...	10.6	1.7	39–33–25–47	0	237–1,371
Garden City (Finney)	*CM-I	20	30.8	8.8	62–100–15–1,357	31.5	9.2	52–5–14–43	519	203–1,381
Great Bend (Barton)	†MC-I	18	7.9	0.0	63–189–34–163	9.4	0.0	51–37–36–34	480	155–1,496
Hays (Ellis)	*CM-I	18	5.5	1.4	33–106–21–157	4.9	1.1	32–20–16–38	578	121–1,284
Hutchinson (Reno)	*CM-I	40	14.9	1.3	65–129–29–144	15.3	1.4	39–44–21–33	509	339–1,676
Independence (Montgomery)	*CM-I	11	4.3	0.8	37–103–58–191	2.9	0.6	36–27–31–39	376	125–1,247
Junction City (Geary)	*CM-I	20	5.6	1.2	86–79–21–88	7.0	1.0	65–33–28–33	570	215–1,186

Table 1/9 continued **PROFILES OF INDIVIDUAL CITIES**

City (county)	Form of govern-ment–Metro status	Est. 1982 popu-lation (000)	Fiscal year 1983 revenues: Total general revenue ($ mil-lions)	Total utility reve-nue ($ mil-lions)	Per capita revenues ($): Intergovernmental revenue–Property taxes–Other taxes–Charges and miscella-neous general revenue	Fiscal year 1983 expenditures: Total general expendi-tures ($ mil-lions)	Total utility expendi-tures ($ mil-lions)	Per capita current expenditures ($): Police–Fire–Streets–Sewers and sanitation	Long term debt ($ per capita)	October 1983 public personnel: Total full time equivalent employment–Average full time monthly salary ($)
KANSAS continued										
Kansas City (Wyandotte)	CO-C	162	103.9	0.0	197–141–34–271	108.2	0.0	54–51–47–55	0	1,530–1,562
Lawrence (Douglas)	*CM-C	54	38.7	5.1	86–101–59–466	35.1	3.8	44–26–31–41	713	840–1,632
Leavenworth (Leavenworth)	*CM-I	34	9.9	1.7	41–77–41–136	9.8	1.9	36–29–24–38	350	231–1,542
Leawood (Johnson)	†MC-S	14	5.8	0.0	190–118–46–66	5.6	0.0	57–43–36–31	239	102–1,642
Lenexa (Johnson)	MC-S	21	15.6	1.2	126–118–102–411	15.9	1.2	87–39–25–13	761	162–1,856
Liberal (Seward)	*CM-I	16	8.8	0.8	286–78–29–153	10.8	0.9	50–14–33–42	350	130–1,366
Mc Pherson (Mc Pherson)	MC-I	12	10.3	16.4	34–124–17–683	9.2	14.7	38–27–52–46	2,202	144–1,765
Manhattan (Riley)	*CM-I	33	13.9	1.2	115–122–55–125	10.1	1.3	50–22–27–21	492	208–1,435
Merriam (Johnson)	†MC-S	11	5.8	0.0	79–64–134–260	4.6	0.0	51–22–35–0	3,834	62–1,686
Newton (Harvey)	*CM-I	17	7.2	0.8	56–144–25–206	6.4	0.7	35–36–20–41	596	140–1,490
Olathe (Johnson)	*CM-S	42	17.4	2.9	61–104–61–187	17.1	12.4	40–22–18–30	1,028	337–1,733
Ottawa (Franklin)	*CM-I	11	4.8	6.1	79–107–51–202	4.5	6.1	40–37–44–15	1,284	127–1,494
Overland Park (Johnson)	*CM-S	84	24.3	0.0	70–38–102–79	23.3	0.0	55–0–52–0	165	330–1,864
Parsons (Labette)	*CM-I	13	...	...	...–...–...–...	4.3	0.8	5–26–0–41	0	144–1,207
Pittsburg (Crawford)	*CM-I	19	7.8	1.2	108–106–66–135	6.7	1.2	35–30–15–22	261	162–1,366
Prairie Village (Johnson)	†MC-S	24	5.7	0.0	73–53–56–51	5.1	0.0	47–0–34–19	91	90–1,605
Salina (Saline)	*CM-I	42	16.4	2.4	39–129–28–190	12.4	2.5	33–30–23–29	363	341–1,399
Shawnee (Johnson)	*CM-S	31	5.1	0.0	46–44–44–32	6.0	0.0	53–10–20–0	194	94–1,692
Topeka (Shawnee)	CO-C	120	62.7	8.3	114–157–73–177	60.2	7.8	75–62–38–29	557	1,394–1,578
Wichita (Sedgwick)	*CM-C	289	193.1	14.9	116–140–51–362	184.9	18.9	51–33–8–13	781	2,857–1,756
Winfield (Cowley)	*CM-I	12	10.8	10.2	53–75–37–717	11.2	8.7	43–36–24–53	498	384–1,422
KENTUCKY										
Ashland (Boyd)	*CM-C	26	12.8	2.2	166–103–84–131	18.0	1.6	52–48–36–49	6,912	381–1,153
Bowling Green (Warren)	*CM-I	44	18.9	25.0	84–44–160–144	16.5	25.8	50–50–24–40	760	468–1,460
Covington (Kenton)	*CM-S	48	20.5	0.0	181–42–145–56	20.3	0.0	63–65–16–33	240	365–1,334
Danville (Boyle)	*CM-I	13	3.7	1.2	40–31–90–128	3.0	1.1	42–29–14–29	225	118–1,095
Elizabethtown (Hardin)	MC-I	16	12.1	7.0	467–42–109–125	17.2	6.9	37–34–29–33	388	189–1,220
Erlanger (Kenton)	MC-S	15	1.8	0.0	26–46–41–12	1.9	0.0	38–6–10–16	13	35–1,327
Florence (Boone)	MC-S	16	3.1	0.9	28–51–39–69	4.4	1.1	41–14–20–21	1,507	53–1,469
Fort Thomas (Campbell)	†MC-S	16	3.0	0.0	24–74–53–41	2.6	0.0	42–29–20–20	19	84–1,417
Frankfort (Franklin)	*CM-I	26	9.7	19.4	110–45–120–100	9.4	18.7	47–42–21–62	268	345–1,489
Georgetown (Scott)	MC-S	11	2.1	0.6	36–18–64–68	1.9	0.7	32–4–5–65	382	48–978
Glasgow (Barren)	MC-I	13	5.0	10.6	106–51–115–123	5.6	8.4	36–39–29–44	1,149	177–1,236
Henderson (Henderson)	*CM-S	25	11.4	31.1	93–59–35–268	9.0	39.0	34–34–26–52	5,750	400–1,271
Hopkinsville (Christian)	MC-C	28	8.8	16.8	117–36–69–91	7.2	17.7	36–42–28–26	1,067	300–1,261
Jeffersontown (Jefferson)	MC-S	16	2.1	0.0	18–68–47–4	2.4	0.0	52–0–7–31	378	75–1,091
Lexington c (Fayette)	MC-C	208	96.8	1.2	78–55–215–119	111.0	3.3	64–59–21–36	800	2,543–1,553
Louisville (Jefferson)	MC-C	294	126.4	3.2	136–90–186–19	107.8	3.2	82–53–27–37	0	4,463–1,500
Madisonville (Hopkins)	MC-I	17	6.6	12.1	124–33–134–95	5.2	8.8	44–71–25–68	795	271–1,225
Mayfield (Graves)	MC-I	10	4.8	5.7	166–63–94–143	4.4	6.1	43–59–25–38	180	148–1,287
Middlesborough (Bell)	MC-I	12	...	0.0	...–...–...–...	0.4	0.0	0–0–0–0	0	...–...
Murray (Calloway)	MC-I	14	16.6	12.0	240–48–39–851	18.2	11.8	36–34–13–66	1,117	138–1,149
Newport (Campbell)	*CM-S	21	5.4	1.3	48–49–130–27	4.4	1.6	45–39–20–20	81	214–1,162
Nicholasville (Jessamine)	CO-S	11	5.5	3.4	350–35–56–50	9.1	3.1	43–0–24–11	940	70–1,192
Owensboro (Daviess)	*CM-C	55	41.3	51.3	64–61–80–547	54.4	54.9	48–42–22–62	3,571	1,946–1,432
Paducah (Mc Cracken)	*CM-I	29	19.0	24.5	191–94–203–163	16.1	35.1	48–62–37–43	1,817	497–1,595
Radcliff (Hardin)	MC-I	16	2.2	0.0	36–24–34–41	2.0	0.0	33–3–16–15	200	55–1,216
Richmond (Madison)	*CM-I	22	7.9	5.3	149–28–85–100	6.2	9.2	29–31–13–33	1,229	226–1,148
St. Matthews (Jefferson)	MC-S	14	1.8	0.0	17–77–22–7	1.8	0.0	39–7–16–15	0	...–...
Shively (Jefferson)	MC-S	16	1.9	0.0	26–51–42–2	2.1	0.0	38–37–3–26	125	71–1,243
Somerset (Pulaski)	†MC-I	11	3.4	5.5	62–45–47–163	4.3	5.2	59–42–11–89	128	113–1,186
Winchester (Clark)	†MC-S	16	5.0	1.2	67–32–87–139	6.2	1.0	49–63–18–60	1,284	183–1,160
LOUISIANA										
Abbeville t (Vermilion)	MC-I	13	3.7	5.5	67–13–114–85	4.0	4.6	39–33–40–57	330	193–997
Alexandria (Rapides)	MC-C	52	30.2	43.5	252–29–164–141	29.0	47.2	49–45–18–74	0	918–946
Baker (East Baton Rouge)	MC-C	14	2.5	2.3	26–8–138–12	2.5	2.1	44–21–13–13	75	141–1,247
Bastrop (Morehouse)	MC-I	16	...	0.0	...–...–...–...	...	0.0	...–...–...–...	0	...–...
Baton Rouge (East Baton Rouge)	MC-C	362	248.8	2.2	166–68–204–250	221.4	4.4	70–32–39–37	296	5,105–1,529
Bogalusa (Washington)	MC-I	17	1.2	0.6	0–0–0–70	6.0	0.3	53–45–44–29	356	...–...
Bossier City (Bossier)	MC-S	55	43.0	1.8	169–48–117–454	38.0	2.4	48–40–16–41	739	581–1,198
Crowley (Acadia)	MC-I	16	7.0	0.0	56–33–138–196	6.2	0.0	34–31–25–41	250	170–1,021
De Ridder (Beauregard)	*CM-I	11	0.6	0.4	0–0–0–54	3.6	0.5	20–11–45–30	551	...–...
Eunice (St. Landry)	MC-I	13	...	...	...–...–...–...	2.5	3.5	15–27–7–23	0	170–1,039
Gretna (Jefferson)	MC-S	21	9.4	1.1	223–97–67–62	6.8	1.1	102–17–37–83	141	199–1,117
Hammond (Tangipahoa)	MC-I	17	0.6	0.4	0–0–0–33	6.3	1.6	46–38–33–36	302	...–...
Harahan (Jefferson)	MC-S	11	2.2	0.0	84–30–28–54	1.8	0.0	44–6–23–36	106	73–1,004
Houma (Terrebonne)	MC-I	100	13.5	26.9	73–5–10–47	12.6	26.0	22–13–10–20	304	452–1,164
Jennings (Jefferson Davis)	MC-I	12	1.1	1.1	0–0–0–87	3.8	1.0	56–31–20–34	65	...–...
Kenner (Jefferson)	MC-S	71	20.0	0.0	125–36–25–95	17.8	0.0	49–25–14–49	183	409–1,073
Lafayette (Lafayette)	MC-C	86	78.1	98.3	182–39–209–483	81.9	136.2	45–34–31–74	4,292	1,274–1,437
Lake Charles (Calcasieu)	MC-C	76	32.4	0.1	140–59–142–84	26.1	1.7	33–32–25–41	151	787–1,312
Minden (Webster)	CO-S	15	...	...	...–...–...–...	3.2	7.1	26–17–21–43	0	172–1,258
Monroe (Ouachita)	MC-C	57	34.8	3.4	107–84–158–262	24.8	5.5	54–58–11–39	973	1,012–1,058
Morgan City (St. Mary)	MC-I	16	10.2	14.0	432–36–32–125	9.1	15.5	95–57–31–64	1,313	261–1,575
Natchitoches (Natchitoches)	MC-I	17	4.0	9.4	54–12–97–77	3.6	8.8	39–32–24–32	746	229–1,101
New Iberia (Iberia)	MC-I	35	14.6	0.0	125–38–179–71	13.5	0.0	44–40–39–50	350	346–1,335
New Orleans (Orleans)	MC-I	565	518.0	33.3	298–108–259–252	462.8	40.2	86–49–19–69	719	11,013–1,477
Opelousas (St. Landry)	MC-I	20	...	...	...–...–...–...	5.5	7.6	50–19–17–33	0	281–1,157

Table 1/9 continued **PROFILES OF INDIVIDUAL CITIES**

City (county)	Form of govern-ment–Metro status	Est. 1982 popu-lation (000)	Fiscal year 1983 revenues: Total general revenue ($ mil-lions)	Total utility reve-nue ($ mil-lions)	Per capita revenues ($): Intergovernmental revenue–Property taxes–Other taxes–Charges and miscella-neous general revenue	Fiscal year 1983 expenditures: Total general expendi-tures ($ mil-lions)	Total utility expendi-tures ($ mil-lions)	Per capita current expenditures ($): Police–Fire–Streets–Sewers and sanitation	Long term debt ($ per capita)	October 1983 public personnel: Total full time equivalent employment–Average full time monthly salary ($)
LOUISIANA continued										
Pineville (Rapides)	MC-S	13	1.0	0.7	0–0–0–75	4.1	1.2	39–24–18–60	410	...–...
Ruston (Lincoln)	MC-I	21	1.5	11.6	0–0–0–69	5.0	10.9	25–34–11–55	754	272–1,217
Shreveport (Caddo)	†MC-C	211	108.5	11.3	151–75–148–141	108.3	18.4	51–48–27–46	690	2,758–1,247
Slidell (St. Tammany)	MC-S	30	12.1	1.1	168–77–113–45	8.2	6.9	57–0–46–24	351	238–1,305
Sulphur (Calcasieu)	CO-S	21	2.1	0.5	0–0–0–100	8.1	0.5	38–30–28–52	503	...–...
Tallulah (Madison)	MC-I	11	0.2	0.0	0–0–0–21	2.0	0.0	26–11–14–32	175	...–...
Thibodaux (Lafourche)	MC-I	17	7.0	2.8	63–33–113–213	7.2	5.4	53–8–39–63	1,411	160–979
West Monroe (Ouachita)	MC-S	15	...	...	...–...–...–...	9.7	0.4	47–36–20–37	0	205–1,061
Westwego (Jefferson)	MC-S	12	3.1	0.4	108–22–32–91	2.8	0.4	28–11–13–33	329	73–1,256
MAINE										
Auburn (Androscoggin)	*CM-C	23	18.6	0.0	336–406–3–65	18.6	0.0	41–59–89–34	358	677–1,443
Augusta (Kennebec)	*CM-I	22	14.8	0.0	231–401–2–51	15.5	0.0	42–40–47–15	231	613–1,226
Bangor (Penobscot)	*CM-C	31	31.4	0.3	251–503–5–241	30.4	0.4	57–75–65–27	356	1,003–1,503
Bath (Sagadahoc)	*CM-I	10	9.8	0.0	350–480–2–112	10.2	0.0	46–44–24–61	613	338–1,386
Biddeford (York)	MC-I	20	...	0.0	...–...–...–...	12.9	0.0	50–44–36–21	0	429–1,283
Brunswick t (Cumberland)	*CM-I	17	11.5	0.0	240–376–4–43	11.5	0.0	41–30–32–16	142	484–1,330
Gorham t (Cumberland)	*CM-S	10	5.7	0.0	228–296–3–35	6.1	0.0	26–10–31–17	353	245–1,097
Lewiston (Androscoggin)	*CM-C	40	25.9	0.6	228–333–4–82	28.3	0.7	40–51–44–34	292	982–1,366
Orono t (Penobscot)	*CM-S	10	4.6	0.0	209–214–1–35	4.0	0.0	20–22–22–30	386	162–1,413
Portland (Cumberland)	*CM-C	61	70.1	0.0	344–591–12–196	71.5	0.0	63–61–50–116	1,074	2,146–1,404
Presque Isle (Aroostook)	*CM-I	11	5.1	0.0	118–277–3–54	5.4	0.0	38–41–58–7	0	101–1,368
Saco (York)	*CM-S	13	8.6	0.0	223–352–5–65	9.6	0.0	33–34–42–48	109	234–1,331
Sanford t (York)	RT-I	18	12.5	0.0	286–356–2–43	12.4	0.0	44–39–52–13	117	482–1,341
Scarborough t (Cumberland)	*CM-S	12	7.6	0.0	180–423–4–52	8.0	0.0	42–14–66–15	268	302–1,287
South Portland (Cumberland)	*CM-S	23	19.8	0.1	201–559–6–109	19.0	0.6	48–53–46–54	384	600–1,486
Waterville (Kennebec)	†MC-I	18	11.3	0.0	231–378–3–30	10.8	0.0	41–30–27–24	366	434–1,399
Westbrook (Cumberland)	†MC-S	15	14.5	0.0	223–539–2–202	15.4	0.0	52–42–49–25	604	410–1,861
Windham t (Cumberland)	*CM-S	12	...	0.0	...–...–...–...	7.9	0.0	18–13–30–12	0	323–1,262
MARYLAND										
Aberdeen t (Harford)	*CM-S	12	2.9	0.4	89–81–7–77	3.2	0.3	67–3–33–73	142	89–1,440
Annapolis (Anne Arundel)	MC-S	32	19.9	1.5	129–243–49–202	17.8	1.4	85–58–28–79	390	413–1,660
Baltimore i	MC-C	774	1,392.2	34.3	1,045–328–178–248	1,261.7	32.3	124–66–39–83	595	32,648–1,661
Bowie (Prince George's)	*CM-S	34	7.3	0.6	79–55–4–74	6.2	0.6	0–0–25–39	436	117–1,511
Cambridge (Dorchester)	MC-I	11	3.9	0.8	104–128–12–94	3.4	0.7	63–3–28–67	491	108–1,304
College Park (Prince George's)	*CM-S	23	4.3	0.0	81–40–13–54	3.7	0.0	0–0–31–15	20	67–1,424
Cumberland (Allegany)	CM-C	25	10.2	1.4	147–155–5–96	11.1	1.4	59–55–39–80	271	284–1,452
Frederick (Frederick)	MC-I	31	15.6	0.9	190–162–15–141	13.3	2.5	68–30–49–48	468	327–1,364
Gaithersburg (Montgomery)	*CM-S	28	5.5	0.0	65–71–20–36	7.4	0.0	7–0–27–8	102	97–1,769
Greenbelt (Prince George's)	*CM-S	17	4.3	0.0	77–93–17–71	4.3	0.0	57–0–30–14	377	95–1,721
Hagerstown (Washington)	MC-C	33	17.3	13.5	268–119–12–119	16.6	13.7	88–31–23–75	49	429–1,471
Hyattsville (Prince George's)	MC-S	12	3.0	0.0	89–98–4–55	3.2	0.0	52–1–54–24	2	82–1,526
Laurel t (Prince George's)	MC-S	12	3.9	0.0	89–172–27–27	3.9	0.0	92–11–42–22	166	92–1,606
New Carrollton (Prince George's)	MC-S	12	1.3	0.0	58–26–19–5	1.5	0.0	6–0–27–33	34	...–...
Rockville (Montgomery)	*CM-S	44	23.0	2.1	93–171–22–237	24.1	1.4	23–0–48–92	544	352–1,627
Salisbury (Wicomico)	†MC-I	16	9.2	1.0	185–228–18–126	8.4	0.9	85–54–64–68	410	235–1,490
Takoma Park (Montgomery)	†MC-S	15	5.4	0.0	114–129–7–104	5.4	0.0	65–0–25–27	1,152	103–1,638
MASSACHUSETTS										
Abington t (Plymouth)	TM-S	14	7.6	0.5	191–308–3–54	10.0	0.6	51–47–32–15	426	312–1,588
Acton t (Middlesex)	†TM-S	17	16.2	0.0	134–741–6–51	15.9	0.0	44–56–48–0	127	298–1,992
Adams t (Berkshire)	RT-S	10	...	0.0	...–...–...–...	5.5	0.0	56–0–49–63	0	...–...
Agawam t (Hampden)	*CM-S	27	20.9	1.1	303–410–4–67	20.3	0.9	45–44–38–32	398	588–1,514
Amesbury t (Essex)	RT-S	14	20.2	0.9	368–448–5–600	19.1	0.8	51–43–45–27	432	601–1,459
Amherst t (Hampshire)	*RT-I	33	19.7	1.1	275–234–6–82	15.6	1.1	27–23–11–22	210	401–1,413
Andover t (Essex)	*TM-S	27	29.5	1.3	241–756–2–103	33.2	0.9	62–65–58–33	745	821–1,958
Arlington t (Middlesex)	*CM-S	47	44.2	1.2	295–587–4–57	42.4	0.6	67–64–48–32	326	1,209–1,713
Athol t (Worcester)	RT-I	11	3.3	0.4	176–90–3–38	3.7	0.2	46–38–40–23	26	106–1,485
Attleboro (Bristol)	MC-S	34	28.0	1.1	323–403–6–89	28.9	0.9	49–46–26–29	418	892–1,540
Auburn t (Worcester)	RT-S	15	12.2	0.0	271–458–10–94	12.3	0.0	45–8–32–25	192	374–1,677
Barnstable t (Barnstable)	RT-I	33	34.3	0.0	202–687–27–133	30.3	0.0	66–0–36–19	301	854–1,659
Bedford t (Middlesex)	†TM-S	13	17.0	0.6	333–885–8–107	16.8	1.2	71–49–87–29	428	345–2,229
Bellingham t (Norfolk)	TM-S	14	10.6	0.3	369–346–5–29	11.2	0.3	51–19–41–6	105	402–1,423
Belmont t (Middlesex)	RT-S	26	25.1	7.1	150–741–1–82	25.7	6.5	87–76–42–43	96	710–2,040
Beverly (Essex)	MC-S	38	32.1	1.1	231–543–4–73	31.7	1.2	58–76–45–29	300	824–1,792
Billerica t (Middlesex)	†RT-S	37	40.0	0.4	309–713–8–39	32.9	1.4	56–56–29–12	504	932–1,785
Boston c (Suffolk)	MC-C	561	1,007.8	29.8	862–608–25–302	847.9	25.3	116–90–30–60	949	19,359–1,846
Bourne t (Barnstable)	TM-I	14	13.1	0.0	354–484–12–65	13.7	0.0	56–57–45–13	133	456–2,370
Braintree t (Norfolk)	RT-S	36	33.8	26.9	229–599–2–107	33.9	29.9	67–56–37–62	571	974–1,935
Bridgewater t (Plymouth)	TM-S	17	...	...	...–...–...–...	10.1	0.3	44–39–33–11	0	290–1,759
Brockton (Plymouth)	MC-C	97	88.1	3.6	467–405–3–38	97.1	3.4	70–77–32–39	380	2,423–1,772
Brookline t (Norfolk)	†TM-S	54	61.8	2.8	184–805–3–149	62.0	1.3	85–100–58–41	172	1,493–1,938
Burlington t (Middlesex)	RT-S	23	35.9	0.8	266–1201–8–79	27.8	0.7	85–77–43–46	668	712–2,003
Cambridge (Middlesex)	*CM-S	94	146.6	4.8	469–713–26–355	161.9	3.5	96–87–39–51	431	3,118–2,095
Canton t (Norfolk)	TM-S	18	16.9	0.6	229–625–12–73	17.2	0.3	78–65–46–24	181	455–2,297
Chelmsford t (Middlesex)	TM-S	31	27.3	0.0	293–549–7–31	26.7	0.0	53–61–34–19	61	941–1,580
Chelsea t (Suffolk)	MC-S	26	26.7	0.9	735–241–9–63	29.6	0.4	85–105–47–26	31	742–1,832
Chicopee (Hampden)	MC-C	56	34.2	20.6	405–154–3–53	43.6	22.5	51–60–28–29	553	1,454–1,818
Clinton t (Worcester)	TM-I	12	11.1	0.2	511–340–2–35	10.1	0.3	40–35–45–0	382	302–1,509
Concord t (Middlesex)	*TM-S	16	19.2	9.3	129–959–6–73	19.0	9.3	61–54–38–32	328	471–1,972

Table 1/9 continued **PROFILES OF INDIVIDUAL CITIES**

City (county)	Form of govern-ment–Metro status	Est. 1982 popu-lation (000)	Fiscal year 1983 revenues: Total general revenue ($ mil-lions)	Total utility reve-nue ($ mil-lions)	Per capita revenues ($): Intergovernmental revenue–Property taxes–Other taxes–Charges and miscella-neous general revenue	Fiscal year 1983 expenditures: Total general expendi-tures ($ mil-lions)	Total utility expendi-tures ($ mil-lions)	Per capita current expenditures ($): Police–Fire–Streets–Sewers and sanitation	Long term debt ($ per capita)	October 1983 public personnel: Total full time equivalent employment–Average full time monthly salary ($)
MASSACHUSETTS continued										
Danvers t (Essex)	*RT-S	24	...	...	...–...–...–...	40.7	18.9	55–62–56–44	0	1,254–1,528
Dartmouth t (Bristol)	†RT-S	25	16.7	0.7	240–369–6–65	15.5	1.2	46–0–29–12	367	561–1,631
Dedham t (Norfolk)	RT-S	25	21.5	0.0	208–616–9–38	20.3	0.0	69–57–44–29	95	601–1,454
Dennis t (Barnstable)	†TM-I	13	9.9	0.0	68–541–34–122	9.8	0.0	70–44–70–14	114	142–1,487
Dracut t (Middlesex)	TM-S	22	19.9	0.1	308–540–7–42	14.9	0.0	43–33–40–20	259	484–1,910
Duxbury t (Plymouth)	TM-S	12	14.8	0.7	268–812–2–120	13.9	0.5	75–64–38–15	763	426–1,941
East Longmeadow t (Hampden)	TM-S	13	11.6	0.4	265–581–4–76	12.0	0.4	54–18–70–30	95	355–1,592
Easthampton t (Hampshire)	RT-S	16	10.2	0.3	323–290–3–34	10.0	0.2	39–33–30–26	261	299–1,570
Easton t (Bristol)	*TM-S	17	13.0	0.6	254–460–6–35	12.6	0.9	52–40–30–9	285	401–1,915
Everett (Middlesex)	MC-S	37	37.3	1.2	272–708–1–31	36.0	0.4	63–72–46–16	419	890–1,883
Fairhaven t (Bristol)	RT-S	16	12.4	0.4	307–421–4–61	12.2	0.4	47–28–58–39	320	376–1,491
Fall River (Bristol)	MC-C	93	93.6	2.6	693–234–4–73	82.3	2.8	62–68–28–41	339	2,427–1,506
Falmouth t (Barnstable)	RT-I	24	25.5	1.3	277–697–10–66	24.3	1.1	59–62–41–79	209	720–1,767
Fitchburg (Worcester)	MC-C	40	35.0	0.6	457–314–3–105	34.6	0.9	46–55–36–59	95	934–1,331
Foxborough t (Norfolk)	TM-S	14	13.2	0.6	271–560–7–80	12.3	0.6	47–33–51–7	190	395–1,782
Framingham t (Middlesex)	†RT-S	65	60.8	1.3	228–629–7–66	57.7	1.2	46–69–51–46	100	1,630–1,864
Franklin t (Norfolk)	†TM-S	18	16.2	0.3	306–479–5–89	15.0	0.4	46–21–39–50	352	488–1,626
Gardner (Worcester)	MC-I	18	18.2	0.5	475–498–2–40	14.4	0.6	46–57–31–27	263	378–1,546
Gloucester (Essex)	MC-I	28	26.1	1.0	212–645–8–72	30.6	2.0	79–79–49–24	584	854–1,687
Grafton t (Worcester)	TM-S	12	8.7	0.0	309–382–4–58	8.0	0.0	40–13–45–35	208	235–1,465
Greenfield t (Franklin)	RT-I	18	17.9	0.4	476–429–5–72	16.9	0.3	42–35–65–32	121	491–1,532
Hanover t (Plymouth)	†MC-S	11	10.7	0.7	309–568–6–49	11.0	0.6	48–31–42–18	163	349–1,862
Harvard t (Worcester)	TM-I	12	5.7	0.0	188–243–1–33	4.7	0.0	15–4–39–3	71	127–1,853
Haverhill (Essex)	MC-C	47	58.3	1.6	410–373–7–447	77.6	3.9	66–61–29–52	924	1,960–1,594
Hingham t (Plymouth)	TM-S	20	22.2	8.8	221–814–5–55	20.3	9.1	71–92–57–34	62	652–1,890
Holbrook t (Norfolk)	TM-S	11	8.1	0.4	365–346–1–22	9.9	0.3	51–59–52–9	43	248–1,740
Holden t (Worcester)	*CM-S	13	6.6	5.6	193–251–2–45	9.8	6.6	32–12–48–26	194	266–1,711
Holliston t (Middlesex)	TM-S	13	7.9	0.4	288–279–4–52	10.9	0.3	52–13–46–23	131	350–1,693
Holyoke (Hampden)	MC-C	43	48.0	35.6	686–287–3–127	50.9	35.7	72–74–50–54	606	1,248–1,691
Hudson t (Middlesex)	†TM-I	17	11.5	10.9	377–248–10–47	14.6	10.5	47–46–52–18	354	487–1,684
Ipswich t (Essex)	*TM-I	11	9.6	5.6	251–493–7–90	10.0	5.7	48–35–36–36	106	325–1,577
Lawrence (Essex)	CO-C	64	64.8	2.8	584–365–5–55	63.2	1.7	60–79–29–42	226	1,773–1,260
Leominster (Worcester)	MC-C	35	31.8	1.2	481–389–2–45	31.1	1.2	47–53–32–37	242	717–1,845
Lexington t (Middlesex)	†RT-S	29	35.1	1.1	190–929–5–82	35.1	0.2	62–55–83–37	96	899–2,076
Longmeadow t (Hampden)	TM-S	16	20.2	0.5	214–932–3–98	15.6	0.3	55–26–47–42	203	516–1,604
Lowell (Middlesex)	*CM-C	93	76.5	2.1	455–304–5–62	73.6	2.4	62–74–31–35	453	2,114–1,850
Ludlow t (Hampden)	RT-S	18	15.0	0.0	405–354–5–63	15.8	0.0	44–33–46–28	241	415–1,866
Lynn (Essex)	MC-S	79	104.4	1.7	788–448–6–75	94.4	2.3	69–88–30–26	167	2,157–2,014
Lynnfield t (Essex)	TM-S	11	10.4	0.0	201–693–8–37	10.8	0.0	69–26–59–15	42	278–1,966
Malden (Middlesex)	MC-S	53	42.0	1.2	448–240–6–95	55.1	0.5	65–69–29–33	509	1,117–1,936
Mansfield t (Bristol)	*TM-I	14	20.4	11.1	878–515–6–69	22.8	11.9	42–48–29–22	416	371–1,889
Marblehead t (Essex)	TM-S	20	22.2	7.0	142–766–7–203	23.3	6.1	70–60–24–40	108	651–1,882
Marlborough (Middlesex)	MC-I	31	29.8	0.6	340–508–7–113	26.4	1.8	46–48–65–27	492	710–1,615
Marshfield t (Plymouth)	TM-S	21	21.3	1.1	289–628–8–70	19.8	0.7	80–49–52–22	455	574–1,882
Medfield t (Norfolk)	*TM-S	10	9.7	0.2	261–596–6–79	9.2	0.9	58–8–55–19	322	273–1,739
Medford (Middlesex)	*CM-S	58	48.3	1.9	332–467–4–31	48.5	0.8	49–55–34–36	76	1,407–1,830
Melrose (Middlesex)	MC-S	29	25.2	0.8	300–513–2–42	25.0	0.3	55–55–39–31	197	705–2,172
Methuen (Essex)	*CM-S	37	29.7	1.7	295–433–6–65	27.5	4.0	43–55–44–43	233	813–1,887
Middleborough t (Plymouth)	*TM-I	17	14.5	10.4	317–485–2–61	12.1	9.9	62–34–38–18	65	495–1,550
Milford t (Worcester)	RT-I	24	19.7	0.0	345–398–6–86	18.3	0.0	35–40–41–23	487	526–1,633
Millbury t (Worcester)	TM-S	12	9.3	0.0	383–356–4–53	9.5	0.1	53–6–35–25	341	275–1,458
Milton t (Norfolk)	†RT-S	26	26.9	0.8	143–846–1–53	21.6	0.5	74–61–49–24	49	561–1,993
Natick t (Middlesex)	RT-S	30	33.2	1.0	259–793–13–53	27.3	0.6	62–76–41–35	77	840–1,674
Needham t (Norfolk)	†RT-S	28	41.7	1.1	153–834–1–528	42.2	0.6	65–83–42–30	72	1,071–2,136
New Bedford (Bristol)	MC-C	99	83.8	4.0	552–270–4–25	33.2	1.2	6–6–3–3	0	2,889–1,423
Newburyport (Essex)	MC-I	16	16.2	0.9	381–542–4–71	18.3	1.0	60–50–45–41	390	434–1,636
Newton (Middlesex)	MC-S	83	99.1	2.9	197–917–10–73	99.7	1.6	94–75–87–47	137	2,351–2,030
North Adams (Berkshire)	MC-I	17	14.3	0.3	522–256–3–42	12.6	0.3	57–46–50–27	269	450–1,437
North Andover t (Essex)	TM-S	21	10.7	0.7	208–263–3–43	16.0	0.6	55–55–43–28	185	465–1,797
North Attleborough t (Bristol)	TM-S	21	16.5	8.6	308–394–4–60	15.0	10.0	48–43–29–19	345	550–1,544
North Reading t (Middlesex)	†TM-S	11	10.7	0.4	273–632–7–43	11.0	0.4	57–57–57–13	144	355–1,768
Northampton (Hampshire)	MC-S	29	28.0	0.6	500–365–4–97	24.6	0.4	48–49–41–20	266	663–1,538
Northborough t (Worcester)	*TM-S	10	6.6	0.3	243–338–4–47	9.2	0.2	54–12–37–23	289	210–1,808
Northbridge t (Worcester)	TM-S	12	8.7	0.2	352–280–3–82	9.2	0.2	36–18–45–18	191	280–1,522
Norton t (Bristol)	TM-S	13	10.9	0.3	381–433–3–39	11.2	0.8	36–39–23–6	303	364–2,064
Norwood t (Norfolk)	*CM-S	29	33.3	16.6	237–804–2–99	28.0	16.0	71–56–42–47	159	788–1,779
Oxford t (Worcester)	*TM-S	12	9.2	0.0	445–290–2–43	9.0	0.0	37–10–26–7	45	309–1,421
Palmer t (Hampden)	TM-S	12	6.7	0.0	347–157–5–70	7.7	0.0	36–0–40–40	233	214–1,527
Peabody (Essex)	MC-S	46	53.2	23.8	287–506–2–356	53.1	24.7	59–54–50–47	960	1,223–1,029
Pembroke t (Plymouth)	TM-S	14	9.9	0.4	212–464–1–36	9.4	0.2	53–42–42–0	127	233–1,796
Pittsfield (Berkshire)	MC-C	51	44.6	1.4	364–435–3–78	44.1	1.0	47–64–50–42	280	1,892–1,240
Plymouth t (Plymouth)	†RT-I	37	29.2	1.0	188–547–7–46	31.9	1.0	74–77–31–19	93	754–1,522
Quincy (Norfolk)	MC-S	84	129.5	3.4	410–568–2–562	132.8	1.9	100–98–26–30	306	2,861–1,845
Randolph t (Norfolk)	RT-S	28	30.8	0.5	315–704–3–62	26.0	0.5	56–44–38–33	298	660–2,046
Reading t (Middlesex)	RT-S	23	24.0	36.1	329–627–1–98	23.7	35.6	57–60–72–34	403	669–1,785
Revere (Suffolk)	MC-S	42	...	0.0	...–...–...–...	36.3	0.1	60–64–24–16	0	833–1,781
Rockland t (Plymouth)	TM-S	16	14.5	0.8	446–394–3–75	14.6	0.7	55–50–30–49	442	402–1,694
Salem (Essex)	MC-S	38	44.9	1.3	345–556–8–267	47.7	1.7	50–66–39–50	565	1,176–1,620
Saugus t (Essex)	*RT-S	25	25.8	0.4	257–559–5–210	25.5	0.3	56–45–28–26	358	565–1,836

Table 1/9 continued **PROFILES OF INDIVIDUAL CITIES**

City (county)	Form of govern-ment–Metro status	Est. 1982 popu-lation (000)	Fiscal year 1983 revenues: Total general revenue ($ mil-lions)	Total utility reve-nue ($ mil-lions)	Per capita revenues ($): Intergovernmental revenue–Property taxes–Other taxes–Charges and miscella-neous general revenue	Fiscal year 1983 expenditures: Total general expendi-tures ($ mil-lions)	Total utility expendi-tures ($ mil-lions)	Per capita current expenditures ($): Police–Fire–Streets–Sewers and sanitation	Long term debt ($ per capita)	October 1983 public personnel: Total full time equivalent employment–Average full time monthly salary ($)
MASSACHUSETTS continued										
Scituate t (Plymouth)	*TM-S	17	18.0	0.5	76–903–6–51	17.3	0.4	54–81–107–52	173	515–1,727
Seekonk t (Bristol)	TM-S	12	13.4	0.0	188–834–5–56	9.4	0.0	72–31–34–10	53	332–1,589
Sharon t (Norfolk)	†TM-S	14	12.9	0.6	251–625–0–56	13.0	0.6	56–36–66–0	249	392–1,917
Shrewsbury t (Worcester)	*RT-S	22	16.4	9.6	192–452–4–81	17.1	12.0	42–35–40–25	289	514–1,772
Somerset t (Bristol)	TM-S	19	18.4	0.4	179–780–3–34	17.5	0.5	41–38–42–34	633	548–1,769
Somerville (Middlesex)	MC-S	77	66.6	1.0	457–390–4–16	62.9	0.7	53–55–39–35	244	1,632–1,827
South Hadley t (Hampshire)	RT-S	16	7.8	6.3	267–157–2–56	10.5	6.0	36–0–30–29	336	374–1,533
Southbridge t (Worcester)	*CM-I	17	12.3	0.0	430–272–3–32	12.8	0.0	37–39–40–26	173	360–1,707
Spencer t (Worcester)	TM-S	11	7.0	0.2	338–265–3–34	7.3	0.4	37–8–72–18	119	199–1,498
Springfield (Hampden)	MC-C	152	143.9	6.6	491–332–4–123	162.4	5.2	80–67–23–46	245	5,260–1,816
Stoneham t (Middlesex)	*TM-S	22	24.0	0.7	236–794–5–63	20.2	0.3	64–59–52–35	253	526–1,867
Stoughton t (Norfolk)	*TM-S	27	22.4	0.9	227–540–4–60	20.8	0.6	49–44–25–34	201	675–1,651
Sudbury t (Middlesex)	†TM-S	14	16.1	0.0	218–892–7–47	16.0	0.0	58–62–76–1	61	336–2,128
Swampscott t (Essex)	RT-S	14	...	0.0	...–...–...–...	13.8	0.1	83–86–42–36	0	336–1,641
Swansea t (Bristol)	TM-S	16	10.0	0.0	249–361–3–32	10.8	0.0	69–6–30–17	183	341–1,669
Taunton (Bristol)	MC-I	46	35.8	33.2	423–291–3–69	32.1	31.0	50–59–29–48	937	1,266–1,546
Tewksbury t (Middlesex)	TM-S	24	29.4	0.8	620–493–5–83	39.1	0.5	62–64–51–7	549	719–1,550
Wakefield t (Middlesex)	TM-S	25	28.0	12.6	266–813–3–44	25.6	12.2	54–56–74–32	24	740–1,779
Walpole t (Norfolk)	*RT-S	19	18.7	0.5	256–615–6–100	17.5	0.8	62–25–47–26	258	488–1,702
Waltham (Middlesex)	MC-S	58	49.6	2.7	209–579–2–61	55.9	2.1	59–69–37–55	199	1,362–1,934
Wareham t (Plymouth)	*TM-I	19	...	0.0	...–...–...–...	15.4	0.0	54–13–57–20	0	447–1,582
Watertown t (Middlesex)	*CM-S	34	33.9	0.9	313–611–5–78	33.2	0.2	64–83–42–43	218	769–1,863
Wayland t (Middlesex)	†TM-S	12	17.7	0.4	433–931–5–81	19.3	0.3	52–50–53–70	133	508–1,587
Webster t (Worcester)	TM-S	14	12.6	0.3	466–350–3–54	11.0	0.2	41–7–34–34	556	280–1,491
Wellesley t (Norfolk)	RT-S	27	30.8	13.3	175–848–8–114	33.3	14.0	70–60–66–65	73	862–1,946
West Springfield t (Hampden)	RT-S	27	20.7	0.7	215–489–4–57	22.8	0.6	71–56–46–30	203	696–1,741
Westborough t (Worcester)	TM-S	13	15.8	0.4	265–826–16–81	13.2	0.5	33–26–110–13	210	367–1,991
Westfield (Hampden)	MC-S	37	30.5	23.3	347–442–3–37	27.6	27.3	49–47–24–19	232	988–1,529
Westford t (Middlesex)	TM-S	14	15.3	0.4	265–776–7–47	11.7	0.9	56–10–55–0	154	380–1,732
Weston t (Middlesex)	TM-S	11	14.8	0.4	216–1025–0–99	15.7	0.2	91–77–75–26	565	440–2,575
Westport t (Bristol)	TM-S	14	9.7	0.0	246–406–5–43	9.3	0.0	45–31–36–2	252	312–1,536
Westwood t (Norfolk)	TM-S	13	10.4	0.0	278–449–0–61	16.9	0.0	80–64–47–32	402	373–1,715
Weymouth t (Norfolk)	RT-S	55	44.7	1.8	325–447–5–41	45.3	2.0	58–52–39–38	358	1,357–1,775
Whitman t (Plymouth)	TM-S	14	9.4	0.4	272–384–2–26	8.7	0.4	47–35–54–12	25	281–1,740
Wilbraham t (Hampden)	TM-S	12	8.4	0.2	139–498–3–66	9.8	0.2	53–47–32–30	203	258–1,657
Wilmington t (Middlesex)	*TM-S	17	20.0	1.0	366–698–5–81	18.9	0.8	60–48–69–26	423	498–1,851
Winchester t (Middlesex)	*RT-S	20	31.5	0.6	234–1275–7–47	22.2	0.6	67–65–53–39	247	684–1,794
Winthrop (Suffolk)	TM-S	19	13.3	0.7	325–336–2–42	13.8	0.6	46–44–41–33	94	424–1,710
Woburn (Middlesex)	MC-S	37	28.9	0.6	254–492–6–36	30.7	0.8	55–51–64–21	181	1,019–1,695
Worcester (Worcester)	*CM-C	161	212.2	5.4	633–381–3–299	215.6	3.6	73–69–33–29	332	6,012–1,394
Yarmouth t (Barnstable)	†TM-I	19	11.9	1.3	110–420–16–80	13.6	1.5	66–39–39–16	365	198–1,684
MICHIGAN										
Adrian (Lenawee)	*CM-I	21	8.0	1.1	122–128–1–133	6.9	1.6	63–42–17–60	239	168–1,798
Albion (Calhoun)	*CM-S	11	9.9	0.3	125–68–55–668	9.7	0.3	116–5–2–43	271	...–...
Allen Park (Wayne)	MC-S	32	11.4	2.4	90–194–5–62	9.3	2.2	65–35–38–17	86	179–2,091
Alpena (Alpena)	*CM-I	12	6.1	0.6	142–237–3–128	5.6	0.8	68–83–62–60	20	135–1,696
Ann Arbor (Washtenaw)	*CM-C	105	63.3	6.8	124–196–6–277	52.4	12.5	64–40–24–86	453	864–2,311
Battle Creek (Calhoun)	*CM-C	56	28.4	3.0	161–103–82–166	30.4	4.5	72–53–24–92	634	614–1,964
Bay City (Bay)	*CM-C	41	21.2	15.0	194–188–3–134	19.4	14.6	74–67–36–84	721	435–1,922
Benton Harbor (Berrien)	*CM-C	14	...	0.0	...–...–...–...	...	0.0	...–...–...–...	0	...–...
Berkley (Oakland)	*CM-S	18	5.6	1.6	77–158–12–60	5.3	1.5	62–33–33–35	145	...–...
Beverly Hills v (Oakland)	*CM-S	11	2.9	0.9	66–138–4–49	3.2	1.0	120–0–27–36	5	...–...
Big Rapids (Mecosta)	*CM-I	14	4.8	0.6	119–37–44–141	5.8	1.3	29–20–20–57	444	...–...
Birmingham (Oakland)	*CM-S	21	17.9	1.1	81–328–8–436	14.6	0.9	98–89–45–98	290	201–2,071
Burton (Genesee)	MC-S	29	7.1	0.5	77–83–8–77	6.8	0.6	36–6–15–63	258	87–1,997
Cadillac (Wexford)	*CM-I	10	5.4	0.5	234–146–2–139	5.5	1.2	56–42–47–90	207	...–...
Clawson (Oakland)	*CM-S	15	3.6	1.0	84–121–11–36	3.3	1.3	46–5–34–27	16	78–1,742
Dearborn (Wayne)	MC-S	87	63.5	3.3	149–339–7–238	62.9	3.4	109–64–33–110	33	1,051–2,014
Dearborn Heights (Wayne)	MC-S	65	16.6	4.6	96–130–5–25	18.4	5.0	81–46–2–24	7	330–2,168
Delta tp (Lansing)	*CM-S	23	6.1	0.6	43–82–2–132	5.6	1.0	22–29–7–38	78	76–1,988
Detroit (Wayne)	MC-C	1,139	1,351.5	130.7	607–159–239–182	1,282.8	206.0	162–52–75–123	655	18,107–2,026
East Detroit (Macomb)	*CM-S	37	9.3	2.9	74–141–3–34	8.9	2.4	74–34–15–27	0	194–1,828
East Grand Rapids (Kent)	*CM-S	11	3.8	0.5	66–194–1–77	3.7	0.5	68–48–15–40	82	81–1,829
East Lansing (Ingham)	*CM-C	49	14.7	1.4	93–96–3–109	14.9	1.3	38–29–26–68	188	345–1,928
Ecorse (Wayne)	MC-S	14	...	0.0	...–...–...–...	0.4	0.0	13–13–0–0	0	...–...
Escanaba (Delta)	*CM-I	14	6.1	7.0	137–119–0–170	6.6	7.0	106–9–30–83	205	147–1,698
Farmington (Oakland)	*CM-S	11	3.5	1.0	83–162–3–83	2.9	1.1	78–0–19–16	248	...–...
Farmington Hills (Oakland)	*CM-S	61	19.2	...	77–136–6–96	18.6	1.5	69–14–32–15	150	244–1,991
Ferndale (Oakland)	*CM-S	26	11.0	1.1	128–193–11–96	12.7	1.1	97–70–28–110	121	194–1,940
Flint (Genesee)	MC-C	154	179.5	10.5	192–120–110–743	186.7	10.4	89–96–34–75	610	3,791–2,020
Fraser (Macomb)	*CM-S	14	6.2	0.7	131–195–5–102	6.1	0.4	122–0–18–77	115	98–2,380
Garden City (Wayne)	†MC-S	34	9.2	2.5	94–135–3–40	11.1	2.2	65–30–21–86	23	239–1,744
Grand Haven (Ottawa)	*CM-S	12	10.7	9.9	147–145–3–612	5.6	32.3	74–37–28–79	7,566	205–1,751
Grand Rapids (Kent)	*CM-C	183	94.4	11.4	160–84–92–181	82.3	10.0	76–54–22–38	278	1,759–1,821
Grandville (Kent)	*CM-S	13	5.0	0.4	93–107–3–196	4.5	0.4	39–8–24–68	332	63–1,746
Grosse Pointe Farms (Wayne)	*CM-S	10	...	0.0	...–...–...–...	...	0.0	...–...–...–...	0	...–...
Grosse Pointe Park (Wayne)	*CM-S	14	5.0	1.3	72–250–5–37	4.9	1.1	93–54–30–46	19	...–...
Grosse Pointe Woods (Wayne)	*CM-S	18	7.3	1.7	70–242–3–84	6.5	1.8	115–10–34–24	94	96–2,269
Hamtramck (Wayne)	MC-S	20	12.3	1.8	287–143–56–127	8.5	3.8	68–46–15–18	0	...–...

Table 1/9 continued **PROFILES OF INDIVIDUAL CITIES**

City (county)	Form of govern-ment–Metro status	Est. 1982 popu-lation (000)	Fiscal year 1983 revenues: Total general revenue ($ mil-lions)	Total utility reve-nue ($ mil-lions)	Per capita revenues ($): Intergovernmental revenue–Property taxes–Other taxes–Charges and miscella-neous general revenue	Fiscal year 1983 expenditures: Total general expendi-tures ($ mil-lions)	Total utility expendi-tures ($ mil-lions)	Per capita current expenditures ($): Police–Fire–Streets–Sewers and sanitation	Long term debt ($ per capita)	October 1983 public personnel: Total full time equivalent employment–Average full time monthly salary ($)
MICHIGAN continued										
Harper Woods (Wayne)	*CM-S	15	6.9	1.5	108–286–4–47	6.0	1.2	111–63–25–32	44	132–1,962
Hazel Park (Oakland)	*CM-S	21	8.2	0.7	121–174–4–98	7.9	0.5	95–43–26–63	105	128–2,219
Highland Park (Wayne)	MC-S	26	13.8	0.1	167–166–159–43	10.0	0.1	81–65–5–34	43	306–1,695
Holland (Ottawa)	*CM-S	27	14.8	17.9	120–148–4–277	14.8	19.1	80–37–27–83	1,245	349–1,921
Inkster (Wayne)	*CM-S	34	8.3	2.9	94–125–2–24	7.8	2.5	63–28–21–5	130	180–1,870
Jackson (Jackson)	*CM-C	39	21.5	2.7	239–106–101–112	17.2	2.6	105–90–41–40	134	445–1,768
Kalamazoo (Kalamazoo)	*CM-C	79	44.1	5.1	171–163–3–221	67.3	9.6	92–69–37–78	1,061	961–1,843
Kentwood (Kent)	MC-S	32	6.5	0.6	55–72–6–70	5.3	0.6	32–12–16–19	100	101–1,974
Lansing (Ingham)	MC-C	128	76.7	110.4	139–100–108–250	86.2	104.7	86–51–26–56	767	2,284–1,995
Lincoln Park (Wayne)	MC-S	44	...	...	...–...–...–...	19.7	1.4	156–92–44–40	0	228–2,081
Livonia (Wayne)	MC-S	101	42.6	4.7	102–177–3–138	39.8	4.3	73–43–17–41	211	647–2,007
Madison Heights (Oakland)	*CM-S	35	13.1	1.2	98–164–6–109	13.0	2.0	77–44–18–86	49	233–2,327
Marquette (Marquette)	*CM-I	22	11.9	16.0	196–131–2–200	11.2	19.3	41–29–73–63	3,551	319–1,769
Melvindale (Wayne)	MC-S	12	6.5	0.7	173–233–4–133	5.1	0.8	76–41–39–23	58	94–1,663
Menominee (Menominee)	MC-I	10	3.1	1.3	120–124–11–62	2.5	1.1	40–33–35–17	152	...–...
Meridian tp (Ingham)	*CM-S	29	4.9	2.3	60–74–1–31	4.3	2.4	26–28–0–17	85	112–2,002
Midland (Midland)	*CM-I	37	17.2	0.1	127–234–4–96	18.4	8.6	60–63–45–65	996	351–2,047
Monroe (Monroe)	†MC-S	23	16.1	2.2	161–281–5–268	14.8	2.2	90–68–43–114	262	264–1,997
Mount Clemens (Macomb)	*CM-S	19	9.2	1.5	119–181–2–183	7.3	1.7	72–46–14–98	253	165–2,040
Mount Pleasant (Isabella)	*CM-I	23	8.8	0.7	153–76–1–154	7.2	0.7	30–14–14–31	346	...–...
Muskegon (Muskegon)	*CM-C	40	13.5	1.8	112–133–3–90	14.7	1.5	82–55–45–55	546	292–1,824
Muskegon Heights (Muskegon)	*CM-C	14	4.1	1.1	110–97–4–77	5.3	0.7	72–34–26–72	117	111–1,541
Niles (Berrien)	MC-S	13	8.6	5.3	172–221–1–290	4.4	5.6	71–53–36–73	15	153–1,821
Norton Shores (Muskegon)	†MC-C	22	5.4	0.9	80–83–2–85	5.0	1.2	45–19–31–27	48	82–1,817
Novi (Oakland)	*CM-S	23	9.3	2.2	69–166–12–155	10.7	3.0	77–12–19–0	573	118–2,092
Oak Park (Oakland)	*CM-S	31	...	...	...–...–...–...	15.3	1.3	124–7–41–81	0	224–2,270
Owosso (Shiawassee)	*CM-S	16	7.0	1.0	103–117–1–223	6.8	0.8	45–58–33–62	238	115–1,752
Pontiac (Oakland)	*CM-S	73	120.3	5.3	301–322–3–1,019	114.5	7.7	128–60–25–49	2,127	2,188–1,925
Port Huron (St. Clair)	*CM-S	34	23.7	1.9	164–149–75–319	21.3	1.8	85–69–25–103	386	319–1,891
Portage (Kalamazoo)	*CM-C	39	12.2	0.6	94–136–4–82	12.9	0.9	57–32–25–31	379	230–1,982
River Rouge (Wayne)	MC-S	12	10.6	1.7	189–476–4–200	9.6	1.5	126–62–30–0	61	...–...
Riverview (Wayne)	*CM-S	14	8.5	0.9	88–203–5–308	6.1	1.0	65–21–10–13	310	...–...
Romulus (Wayne)	MC-S	24	8.1	2.8	116–151–3–66	6.0	2.8	48–11–33–0	85	162–1,468
Roseville (Macomb)	*CM-S	53	19.6	1.4	135–140–4–92	19.2	1.8	90–35–27–70	77	283–2,107
Royal Oak (Oakland)	*CM-S	68	35.1	2.9	169–160–13–172	21.4	2.6	46–33–28–88	87	374–2,064
Saginaw (Saginaw)	*CM-C	75	42.6	6.7	178–94–96–197	39.4	10.2	86–85–24–45	634	699–1,931
St. Clair Shores (Macomb)	*CM-S	73	...	...	...–...–...–...	24.5	4.4	67–38–14–56	0	345–2,099
Sault Ste. Marie (Chippewa)	*CM-I	14	5.3	0.9	188–143–1–38	3.8	0.9	45–35–30–0	104	...–...
Southfield (Oakland)	*CM-S	73	42.6	8.1	106–336–7–132	36.7	7.4	107–71–26–13	380	659–2,287
Southgate (Wayne)	MC-S	31	11.5	2.3	107–200–6–61	8.9	2.5	62–32–20–25	214	166–1,884
Sterling Heights (Macomb)	*CM-S	108	34.4	4.7	68–158–3–88	34.3	4.4	80–38–13–55	27	623–2,107
Taylor (Wayne)	MC-S	74	30.9	2.8	118–197–3–100	23.5	2.7	63–34–20–30	128	398–1,453
Traverse City (Grand Traverse)	*CM-I	15	8.7	10.8	196–165–4–200	7.5	9.9	75–53–53–77	167	224–2,040
Trenton (Wayne)	MC-S	22	13.4	2.1	123–336–2–157	10.4	2.7	102–70–34–26	0	199–2,181
Troy (Oakland)	*CM-S	67	28.6	3.5	73–222–8–123	29.9	4.5	98–12–2–60	69	359–2,305
Walker (Kent)	MC-S	15	3.2	0.0	67–75–4–61	3.3	0.0	42–10–34–0	211	55–1,982
Warren (Macomb)	MC-S	156	58.9	6.4	108–171–4–94	55.2	5.5	77–53–16–50	123	983–2,352
Wayne (Wayne)	*CM-S	21	7.6	2.1	112–206–3–48	9.0	2.7	98–47–24–60	217	...–...
Westland (Wayne)	MC-S	82	23.7	4.7	102–155–3–31	21.0	5.0	59–35–7–20	97	388–1,806
Woodhaven (Wayne)	MC-S	11	4.2	1.2	109–234–5–37	3.7	1.1	91–13–11–0	172	...–...
Wyandotte (Wayne)	MC-S	33	64.4	10.5	91–203–2–1,683	52.9	13.2	69–42–19–78	883	1,345–1,661
Wyoming (Kent)	*CM-S	60	18.8	3.2	84–97–3–126	19.1	3.9	64–21–21–45	310	368–1,945
Ypsilanti (Washtenaw)	*CM-S	24	8.3	0.0	139–178–3–27	8.4	0.1	96–52–20–15	48	126–2,118
MINNESOTA										
Albert Lea (Freeborn)	*CM-I	19	9.2	0.4	138–76–48–217	9.3	0.6	67–48–35–53	809	165–1,779
Anoka (Anoka)	*CM-S	16	5.9	9.3	108–83–5–179	7.4	8.6	55–15–112–58	393	110–2,016
Apple Valley (Dakota)	MC-S	24	9.9	2.0	77–63–7–256	8.5	4.3	38–4–26–36	779	90–1,910
Austin (Mower)	MC-I	22	11.5	23.0	195–78–4–234	11.5	22.5	66–53–60–76	319	170–1,861
Bemidji (Beltrami)	*CM-I	11	4.9	2.2	149–60–7–231	4.4	2.1	76–24–41–53	445	...–...
Blaine (Anoka)	*CM-S	31	10.5	1.8	75–39–7–221	10.3	1.7	38–6–15–52	706	99–1,938
Bloomington (Hennepin)	*CM-S	83	35.5	3.8	92–101–40–192	31.8	3.4	47–20–36–47	564	453–2,022
Brainerd (Crow Wing)	MC-I	11	5.2	6.6	248–54–6–152	4.3	5.7	46–20–35–21	320	...–...
Brooklyn Center (Hennepin)	*CM-S	32	14.0	3.0	98–73–8–262	10.1	2.9	43–5–38–32	243	147–1,943
Brooklyn Park (Hennepin)	*CM-S	47	20.7	1.3	72–65–13–295	18.6	1.3	40–6–32–25	608	169–2,080
Burnsville (Dakota)	*CM-S	38	17.5	1.3	87–102–8–262	12.1	2.7	57–26–22–28	3,743	161–2,225
Cloquet (Carlton)	MC-I	11	5.2	1.1	256–74–4–141	5.0	1.5	48–42–66–52	325	80–1,878
Columbia Heights (Anoka)	*CM-S	20	7.4	1.7	118–64–8–189	6.8	1.7	47–22–27–46	590	101–1,929
Coon Rapids (Anoka)	*CM-S	39	21.5	3.2	94–59–22–380	17.4	4.9	42–21–21–24	476	203–2,117
Cottage Grove (Washington)	CM-S	20	5.6	0.5	88–65–5–121	5.3	0.8	42–20–24–29	499	76–2,137
Crystal (Hennepin)	*CM-S	25	6.7	0.7	109–45–8–107	5.9	0.6	36–4–16–30	64	98–2,107
Duluth (St. Louis)	†MC-C	90	67.0	29.7	255–115–61–310	63.7	39.3	53–48–59–61	653	1,300–1,901
Eagan (Dakota)	†MC-S	24	21.8	0.8	64–85–13–748	10.4	1.9	48–5–18–35	1,462	87–1,952
Eden Prairie (Hennepin)	*CM-S	19	14.9	2.1	91–192–22–480	23.1	3.0	41–7–46–50	3,722	141–1,987
Edina (Hennepin)	*CM-S	46	13.6	6.7	74–87–7–129	13.6	6.5	41–26–28–49	278	240–2,111
Fairmont (Martin)	MC-I	12	6.1	9.1	163–61–3–292	5.5	7.6	46–8–54–26	994	123–1,837
Faribault (Rice)	†MC-I	17	8.7	0.4	267–87–5–168	8.0	0.6	60–37–46–25	664	...–...
Fergus Falls (Otter Tail)	†MC-I	12	7.9	2.0	189–89–3–359	6.2	1.7	53–10–45–62	506	105–1,676
Fridley (Anoka)	*CM-S	30	12.4	2.4	78–92–12–234	10.1	2.3	53–12–29–37	307	140–2,010
Golden Valley (Hennepin)	*CM-S	23	10.0	1.0	133–116–16–174	9.3	0.4	60–13–33–48	360	110–2,264

Table 1/9 continued **PROFILES OF INDIVIDUAL CITIES**

City (county)	Form of government–Metro status	Est. 1982 population (000)	Fiscal year 1983 revenues: Total general revenue ($ millions)	Total utility revenue ($ millions)	Per capita revenues ($): Intergovernmental revenue–Property taxes–Other taxes–Charges and miscellaneous general revenue	Fiscal year 1983 expenditures: Total general expenditures ($ millions)	Total utility expenditures ($ millions)	Per capita current expenditures ($): Police–Fire–Streets–Sewers and sanitation	Long term debt ($ per capita)	October 1983 public personnel: Total full time equivalent employment–Average full time monthly salary ($)
MINNESOTA continued										
Hastings (Dakota)	†MC-S	13	5.4	0.3	161–87–7–158	4.6	0.3	40–22–32–42	583	65–2,032
Hibbing (St. Louis)	MC-S	21	14.1	10.4	321–59–4–285	12.6	13.6	46–44–67–42	1,018	253–1,983
Hopkins (Hennepin)	*CM-S	15	6.1	0.5	143–129–12–130	5.5	0.4	54–7–48–60	160	94–1,914
Inver Grove Heights (Dakota)	*CM-S	18	8.1	0.4	89–74–7–286	6.9	0.6	37–8–13–23	1,157	58–2,002
Lakeville (Dakota)	†MC-S	15	5.7	1.5	102–67–6–196	5.1	1.8	47–6–23–41	969	70–1,260
Mankato (Blue Earth)	*CM-I	29	17.5	1.6	201–175–7–228	14.2	1.8	48–37–50–41	800	237–1,626
Maple Grove (Hennepin)	†MC-S	24	12.8	0.5	82–79–8–354	10.8	2.0	21–4–29–28	1,516	94–1,931
Maplewood (Ramsey)	*CM-S	28	13.5	0.2	90–99–13–278	10.5	0.1	55–23–31–61	813	128–1,844
Marshall (Lyon)	†MC-I	11	11.5	5.9	165–72–6–778	12.4	5.4	48–11–62–33	1,461	226–1,549
Minneapolis (Hennepin)	†MC-C	369	356.1	20.7	376–215–49–324	318.0	17.1	87–57–65–83	1,281	4,603–2,238
Minnetonka (Hennepin)	*CM-S	41	22.3	1.6	104–95–12–340	16.0	2.6	48–7–31–38	1,911	169–2,149
Moorhead (Clay)	MC-C	30	24.0	9.4	395–77–4–334	23.7	7.8	40–25–34–60	978	246–1,913
Mounds View (Ramsey)	†MC-S	13	4.8	0.2	97–40–6–224	3.4	0.7	32–6–9–58	420	...–...
New Brighton (Ramsey)	*CM-S	23	...	...	...–...–...–...	4.5	2.8	32–4–12–39	0	87–1,797
New Hope (Hennepin)	*CM-S	23	6.2	0.6	83–65–5–114	5.6	0.7	43–6–20–32	374	68–1,855
New Ulm (Brown)	*CM-I	14	...	...	...–...–...–...	7.2	15.7	50–6–45–56	0	160–1,390
North St. Paul (Ramsey)	*CM-S	12	3.0	3.0	85–51–5–110	2.5	2.6	40–5–22–43	456	51–2,131
Northfield (Rice)	†MC-I	13	8.9	1.5	121–79–10–465	9.3	1.4	44–7–31–23	544	...–...
Oakdale (Washington)	†MC-S	13	3.4	0.2	60–44–5–150	3.5	0.5	37–11–18–40	504	31–2,113
Owatonna (Steele)	MC-I	18	15.0	17.7	156–95–4–557	12.7	22.4	34–14–53–15	685	173–1,824
Plymouth (Hennepin)	*CM-S	37	22.3	0.8	60–86–8–454	14.3	2.0	39–5–31–72	1,343	124–2,163
Ramsey (Anoka)	MC-S	11	1.9	0.0	63–39–4–73	1.9	0.0	21–3–11–1	338	...–...
Red Wing (Goodhue)	†MC-I	14	11.2	0.7	153–338–8–305	12.2	1.0	65–69–82–75	836	168–1,631
Richfield (Hennepin)	*CM-S	37	12.6	6.8	126–74–11–127	12.9	6.0	40–24–17–25	845	235–2,070
Robbinsdale (Hennepin)	*CM-S	14	5.6	1.5	157–95–18–121	4.7	1.4	58–10–26–53	311	90–1,920
Rochester (Olmsted)	†MC-C	59	61.3	26.4	498–111–26–403	56.3	26.8	55–46–50–28	379	666–2,011
Roseville (Ramsey)	*CM-S	36	9.9	2.1	60–75–14–130	8.8	2.2	39–9–20–37	387	117–2,037
St. Cloud (Stearns)	†MC-C	43	28.8	1.3	258–108–30–281	28.1	1.3	49–40–48–33	830	332–1,883
St. Louis Park (Hennepin)	*CM-S	43	20.1	1.1	115–126–14–212	13.1	1.2	42–17–27–61	428	237–1,992
St. Paul (Ramsey)	†MC-C	270	248.4	15.4	391–134–74–319	264.7	16.6	64–63–45–79	2,127	2,916–2,223
Shoreview (Ramsey)	†MC-S	19	7.1	0.4	74–41–10–258	4.6	1.3	18–6–20–29	725	39–1,978
South St. Paul (Dakota)	MC-S	21	10.1	0.6	166–117–33–165	7.8	0.4	44–33–33–74	533	101–2,178
Stillwater (Washington)	†MC-S	13	5.0	0.4	107–74–6–210	6.0	1.3	41–20–31–65	981	62–1,895
Virginia (St. Louis)	MC-S	11	24.0	7.0	440–139–3–1,651	23.8	6.9	75–70–54–59	1,682	670–1,603
West St. Paul (Dakota)	*CM-S	18	7.0	0.0	105–85–27–169	5.5	0.0	45–33–27–44	425	87–2,033
White Bear Lake (Ramsey)	*CM-S	23	8.6	0.7	81–46–15–229	8.3	0.8	47–10–17–72	590	...–...
Willmar (Kandiyohi)	MC-I	16	30.1	7.2	214–72–5–1,562	32.3	10.7	47–12–41–43	1,947	639–1,236
Winona (Winona)	*CM-I	25	10.6	0.5	173–112–12–129	9.0	0.6	57–67–38–21	115	190–1,804
Woodbury (Washington)	†MC-S	12	7.9	0.3	69–91–11–481	5.9	1.1	47–10–33–41	1,531	45–2,045
Worthington (Nobles)	MC-I	10	12.2	5.2	189–61–5–949	11.8	4.8	47–9–53–78	1,065	304–1,499
MISSISSIPPI										
Biloxi (Harrison)	MC-C	50	13.4	2.6	114–92–22–38	12.3	2.8	36–29–31–12	392	438–1,077
Brookhaven (Lincoln)	MC-I	11	4.0	0.7	188–75–17–78	4.7	0.5	37–29–36–53	323	157–972
Canton (Madison)	MC-I	11	2.6	7.4	131–26–4–85	3.0	6.9	31–26–68–46	30	117–1,035
Clarksdale (Coahoma)	MC-I	22	6.6	9.8	143–60–8–91	7.3	9.7	30–41–16–40	813	241–1,117
Cleveland (Bolivar)	MC-I	14	10.0	0.4	371–76–14–232	9.8	0.6	43–8–24–39	196	107–1,027
Clinton t (Hinds)	MC-S	15	2.1	0.5	52–49–14–24	2.1	0.8	33–27–15–29	29	82–1,136
Columbus (Lowndes)	MC-I	29	7.8	17.3	125–63–6–75	6.6	16.9	35–36–20–52	216	338–1,103
Corinth (Alcorn)	MC-I	13	17.6	3.1	142–54–13–1,167	24.6	2.8	37–43–35–39	1,229	578–1,104
Greenville (Washington)	MC-I	41	11.7	1.6	110–72–18–85	10.6	0.9	47–31–23–50	145	453–931
Greenwood (Leflore)	MC-I	21	...	...	...–...–...–...	17.8	11.1	48–45–32–52	0	903–901
Grenada (Grenada)	*CM-I	13	3.5	0.4	114–31–15–114	2.9	0.7	40–24–37–17	187	101–1,080
Gulfport (Harrison)	CO-C	41	37.8	1.8	115–80–26–706	38.3	2.8	43–48–59–31	1,135	1,317–1,261
Hattiesburg (Forrest)	CO-I	42	15.0	2.1	190–85–22–59	12.9	1.9	50–35–42–46	208	599–942
Jackson (Hinds)	CO-C	204	107.2	7.0	221–120–17–167	99.9	8.5	51–44–32–45	593	2,699–1,243
Laurel (Jones)	CO-I	23	10.5	1.3	255–70–37–101	9.6	1.4	79–56–49–45	191	365–1,055
Mc Comb (Pike)	MC-I	12	4.8	0.5	269–51–24–46	5.1	0.7	48–34–48–37	112	644–976
Meridian (Lauderdale)	*CM-I	46	20.2	2.0	210–83–23–121	16.1	2.5	47–37–21–49	501	608–1,093
Moss Point (Jackson)	MC-C	19	4.0	2.4	52–58–14–84	3.1	2.2	39–29–15–37	270	119–1,233
Natchez (Adams)	MC-I	23	7.8	0.9	193–63–20–64	7.6	1.0	60–35–16–56	382	249–1,222
Ocean Springs (Jackson)	MC-S	15	3.8	0.4	81–58–17–93	2.9	0.5	39–30–31–33	154	110–1,154
Pascagoula (Jackson)	*CM-C	30	10.3	4.9	155–80–24–81	8.3	4.6	53–41–22–37	473	324–1,335
Pearl (Rankin)	MC-S	20	5.6	1.0	132–56–12–83	4.6	1.3	30–32–14–51	354	167–1,065
Picayune (Pearl River)	*CM-I	11	3.3	2.4	148–31–18–106	3.1	2.2	61–51–34–49	161	128–1,151
Starkville (Oktibbeha)	*CM-I	17	4.6	11.2	91–45–5–133	5.8	10.3	39–31–24–43	216	185–1,033
Tupelo (Lee)	MC-I	25	...	...	...–...–...–...	9.1	27.0	47–45–34–36	0	308–1,289
Vicksburg (Warren)	CO-I	26	8.2	7.0	140–76–15–87	8.1	6.3	55–53–21–70	221	351–1,088
Yazoo City (Yazoo)	MC-I	12	3.3	6.4	126–69–3–81	3.3	5.6	56–43–7–69	251	183–1,042
MISSOURI										
Arnold (Jefferson)	†MC-S	19	3.8	0.0	35–15–105–39	4.0	0.0	59–0–26–27	50	96–1,549
Ballwin (St. Louis)	*CM-S	13	3.7	0.0	145–15–68–54	2.5	0.0	70–0–38–1	159	67–1,637
Bellefontaine Neighbors (St. Louis)	MC-S	12	1.9	0.0	78–7–54–18	1.7	0.0	45–0–32–0	82	49–1,638
Belton (Cass)	*CM-S	13	3.7	1.3	25–36–142–80	2.8	4.3	42–12–32–18	365	75–1,526
Berkeley (St. Louis)	*CM-S	16	5.0	0.0	110–45–127–30	4.7	0.0	66–37–31–8	20	126–1,603
Blue Springs (Jackson)	*CM-S	28	7.2	1.7	50–48–112–49	8.2	1.6	37–0–66–18	290	120–1,727
Bridgeton (St. Louis)	MC-S	18	6.6	0.0	203–14–93–58	6.4	0.0	121–0–62–16	172	138–2,031
Cape Girardeau (Cape Girardeau)	*CM-I	34	10.7	0.0	43–27–166–72	9.6	0.0	48–36–27–37	6	284–1,304
Carthage (Jasper)	†MC-S	11	9.0	8.1	30–43–100–627	8.4	8.8	54–59–29–25	89	316–1,156
Clayton (St. Louis)	*CM-S	14	7.4	0.0	182–44–189–111	6.8	0.0	112–54–52–22	273	178–1,868

M U N I C I P A L P I C S

Table 1/9 continued PROFILES OF INDIVIDUAL CITIES

City (county)	Form of government–Metro status	Est. 1982 population (000)	Fiscal year 1983 revenues: Total general revenue ($ millions)	Total utility revenue ($ millions)	Per capita revenues ($): Intergovernmental revenue–Property taxes–Other taxes–Charges and miscellaneous general revenue	Fiscal year 1983 expenditures: Total general expenditures ($ millions)	Total utility expenditures ($ millions)	Per capita current expenditures ($): Police–Fire–Streets–Sewers and sanitation	Long term debt ($ per capita)	October 1983 public personnel: Total full time equivalent employment–Average full time monthly salary ($)
MISSOURI continued										
Columbia (Boone)	*CM-C	63	34.8	32.2	193–20–151–186	34.3	34.1	51–42–27–52	547	839–1,690
Crestwood (St. Louis)	†MC-S	13	3.7	0.0	149–20–91–34	3.4	0.0	61–55–28–1	0	...–...
Creve Coeur (St. Louis)	†MC-S	12	6.2	0.0	263–10–133–127	5.0	0.0	120–0–43–19	0	73–1,815
Excelsior Springs (Clay)	*CM-S	10	9.6	0.5	97–41–106–675	8.9	0.6	50–22–38–31	223	321–1,062
Ferguson (St. Louis)	*CM-S	24	5.6	0.0	96–26–67–46	5.6	0.0	78–27–31–22	44	133–1,663
Florissant (St. Louis)	MC-S	55	8.9	1.3	95–9–31–28	9.9	0.9	35–0–22–1	50	199–1,687
Fulton (Callaway)	MC-I	11	3.1	9.2	46–18–125–100	3.3	8.5	49–29–44–52	358	156–1,169
Gladstone (Clay)	*CM-S	25	5.8	0.8	21–31–107–70	6.0	0.8	37–22–24–19	281	105–1,673
Grandview (Jackson)	*CM-S	25	6.7	0.0	22–52–111–88	7.4	0.0	53–35–14–22	365	136–1,694
Hannibal (Marion)	MC-I	19	7.9	6.0	105–50–110–148	6.8	6.6	43–39–20–37	108	215–1,416
Hazelwood (St. Louis)	*CM-S	16	5.6	0.0	187–36–91–42	5.7	0.0	90–65–17–0	37	131–1,774
Independence (Jackson)	*CM-S	112	38.2	29.8	64–31–147–101	37.7	30.7	50–42–23–39	488	992–1,742
Jefferson City (Cole)	†MC-I	35	13.8	0.1	56–56–178–108	11.6	0.5	54–39–28–19	129	315–1,371
Jennings (St. Louis)	MC-S	17	4.6	0.0	135–23–61–51	5.0	0.0	94–41–40–18	0	...–...
Joplin (Jasper)	*CM-C	39	14.7	0.0	77–48–168–80	13.2	0.0	37–32–25–30	66	348–1,335
Kansas City (Jackson)	*CM-C	445	360.4	26.8	163–66–378–203	338.5	28.6	119–51–39–44	512	7,219–1,720
Kennett (Dunklin)	CM-I	10	2.8	3.6	37–28–88–119	1.9	3.8	41–13–28–3	234	96–1,273
Kirksville (Adair)	*CM-I	17	5.4	1.5	72–32–127–81	5.0	3.2	30–21–26–49	404	135–1,165
Kirkwood (St. Louis)	CO-S	28	8.1	7.0	99–41–83–66	7.7	6.1	60–37–28–26	192	260–1,628
Lee's Summit (Jackson)	†MC-S	31	10.0	3.2	22–77–115–114	9.2	4.1	50–54–34–31	791	216–1,649
Liberty (Clay)	†MC-S	17	6.9	1.1	76–69–118–139	6.7	1.4	56–42–30–31	424	122–1,786
Maplewood (St. Louis)	CM-S	10	3.4	2.6	135–60–99–30	2.9	2.2	63–38–45–11	212	80–1,579
Marshall (Saline)	MC-I	13	5.3	10.1	61–37–141–170	5.1	8.2	43–30–33–70	665	176–1,450
Mexico (Audrain)	*CM-I	12	...	0.0	...–...–...–...	...	0.0	...–...–...–...	0	...–...
Moberly (Randolph)	*CM-I	13	4.8	0.9	73–35–176–78	4.4	0.7	54–28–40–33	12	146–1,312
Overland (St. Louis)	MC-S	19	4.5	0.0	131–8–74–23	4.3	0.0	76–0–63–21	0	109–1,544
Poplar Bluff (Butler)	*CM-I	17	5.2	5.8	47–37–147–74	4.2	5.5	60–38–45–0	189	258–1,414
Raytown (Jackson)	MC-S	31	8.0	0.0	27–33–119–75	6.9	0.0	50–0–29–35	108	135–1,554
Richmond Heights (St. Louis)	CO-S	11	3.8	0.0	132–61–103–39	3.7	0.0	63–41–45–32	26	...–...
Rolla (Phelps)	†MC-I	14	4.9	6.6	81–34–128–112	4.1	6.7	38–23–30–57	0	163–1,253
St. Ann (St. Louis)	MC-S	15	4.9	0.0	195–6–58–62	4.1	0.0	52–0–55–19	148	89–1,533
St. Charles (St. Charles)	MC-S	46	12.2	1.5	31–37–138–60	11.6	1.2	43–29–37–28	95	303–1,588
St. Joseph (Buchanan)	MC-C	76	27.7	0.0	85–60–121–101	22.4	0.0	36–38–31–31	174	685–1,211
St. Louis i.	MC-C	437	414.6	16.3	258–79–417–195	405.9	16.7	141–49–25–22	402	9,938–1,662
St. Peters (St. Charles)	†MC-S	18	4.8	0.7	26–52–119–73	5.0	2.0	57–0–45–23	670	121–1,487
Sedalia (Pettis)	MC-I	20	19.6	1.0	70–50–152–693	17.7	2.4	46–36–33–41	132	371–1,149
Sikeston (Scott)	*CM-I	18	7.0	50.8	45–35–95–226	3.9	63.3	52–15–17–25	1,403	267–1,660
Springfield (Greene)	*CM-C	134	64.5	124.4	101–27–151–201	71.8	116.4	43–33–23–53	1,251	2,114–1,893
University City (St. Louis)	*CM-S	43	12.8	0.0	104–57–83–56	11.1	0.0	60–30–34–25	49	330–1,715
Warrensburg (Johnson)	*CM-I	13	...	0.0	...–...–...–...	2.3	0.0	27–15–10–26	0	69–1,250
Webster Groves (St. Louis)	*CM-S	23	6.1	0.8	83–43–76–59	5.6	0.8	55–43–24–31	11	162–1,779
MONTANA										
Anaconda c (Deer Lodge)	CM-I	12	...	0.0	...–...–...–...	7.2	0.0	54–31–7–4	0	100–1,572
Billings (Yellowstone)	*CM-C	69	43.5	6.6	69–160–30–372	37.6	9.6	45–40–25–73	870	645–1,640
Bozeman (Gallatin)	*CM-I	23	9.1	1.5	159–90–15–140	5.5	1.3	29–24–17–30	638	158–1,614
Butte c (Silverbow)	MC-I	36	21.6	0.1	132–328–25–120	24.0	0.3	55–39–50–49	35	709–1,444
Great Falls (Cascade)	*CM-C	57	...	...	...–...–...–...	19.3	5.2	37–33–29–51	0	415–1,478
Havre (Hill)	MC-I	11	4.5	0.5	32–92–7–263	3.3	0.5	32–22–38–51	569	83–1,482
Helena (Lewis And Clark)	*CM-I	24	10.5	1.8	78–102–30–221	8.5	1.1	38–27–25–48	1,078	243–1,519
Kalispell (Flathead)	MC-I	11	4.7	0.5	111–161–27–143	4.5	0.4	63–42–85–46	71	121–1,601
Missoula (Missoula)	MC-I	33	14.8	0.0	154–164–14–115	13.0	0.0	56–46–32–19	383	228–1,645
NEBRASKA										
Beatrice (Gage)	†MC-I	13	4.1	4.9	108–87–17–107	6.1	5.2	47–36–24–12	221	88–1,491
Bellevue (Sarpy)	†MC-S	22	...	...	...–...–...–...	6.5	0.7	47–9–42–43	0	169–1,554
Columbus (Platte)	†MC-I	18	4.6	0.4	74–72–17–86	4.8	0.8	38–14–37–26	214	127–1,291
Fremont (Dodge)	†MC-I	24	8.9	14.1	70–103–4–193	6.3	15.1	31–25–32–45	1,326	273–1,410
Grand Island (Hall)	†MC-I	35	6.8	19.2	0–0–0–196	13.9	16.8	31–30–32–26	2,897	359–1,595
Hastings (Adams)	MC-I	24	10.0	17.4	129–99–7–187	7.4	16.5	34–17–41–18	3,134	307–1,387
Kearney (Buffalo)	*CM-I	22	6.2	0.8	65–61–14–138	6.8	1.7	35–3–47–34	502	163–1,528
Lincoln (Lancaster)	MC-C	177	108.5	80.6	118–109–82–304	95.7	110.9	45–33–26–32	2,270	3,023–1,655
Norfolk (Madison)	†MC-I	20	10.7	0.9	161–98–14–261	9.1	0.8	44–25–43–31	550	154–1,430
North Platte (Lincoln)	†MC-I	23	8.4	9.3	115–79–74–95	7.5	9.3	57–39–33–25	208	304–1,488
Omaha (Douglas)	MC-C	329	159.0	0.0	134–124–130–96	147.9	0.0	62–50–44–55	485	2,848–2,060
Scottsbluff (Scotts Bluff)	*CM-I	14	10.4	0.5	452–143–6–132	11.9	1.6	61–41–45–42	615	135–1,510
NEVADA										
Carson City c (Ormsby)	†MC-I	35	...	...	...–...–...–...	25.2	1.8	63–44–30–25	0	663–1,807
Henderson (Clark)	*CM-S	33	18.9	3.5	318–12–52–199	20.3	3.4	44–41–30–25	495	239–2,254
Las Vegas (Clark)	*CM-C	180	80.5	0.0	239–50–79–81	72.3	0.0	100–60–26–24	31	1,317–1,850
North Las Vegas (Clark)	*CM-S	45	21.0	4.4	249–26–45–143	21.1	2.0	97–56–33–50	223	423–2,008
Reno (Washoe)	*CM-C	107	54.6	0.0	201–37–110–163	53.0	0.0	123–71–28–46	247	984–2,107
Sparks (Washoe)	*CM-S	45	23.8	0.0	232–63–91–140	28.0	0.0	73–43–36–71	500	362–1,920
NEW HAMPSHIRE										
Berlin (Coos)	*CM-I	13	10.6	...	327–401–6–101	10.9	0.2	50–48–71–40	539	352–1,367
Claremont (Sullivan)	*CM-I	15	4.1	1.0	61–171–10–34	4.0	1.0	47–42–58–21	440	125–1,366
Concord (Merrimack)	*CM-I	31	25.3	1.6	332–278–12–203	29.1	3.1	57–62–41–67	799	471–1,551
Derry t (Rockingham)	*TM-S	20	4.3	0.3	40–123–7–46	6.7	0.3	35–0–32–17	77	138–1,625
Dover (Strafford)	*CM-C	23	22.5	1.5	197–512–9–265	25.1	0.9	76–58–79–47	462	532–1,502

Table 1/9 continued **PROFILES OF INDIVIDUAL CITIES**

City (county)	Form of govern-ment–Metro status	Est. 1982 popu-lation (000)	Fiscal year 1983 revenues: Total general revenue ($ mil-lions)	Total utility reve-nue ($ mil-lions)	Per capita revenues ($): Intergovernmental revenue–Property taxes–Other taxes–Charges and miscella-neous general revenue	Fiscal year 1983 expenditures: Total general expendi-tures ($ mil-lions)	Total utility expendi-tures ($ mil-lions)	Per capita current expenditures ($): Police–Fire–Streets–Sewers and sanitation	Long term debt ($ per capita)	October 1983 public personnel: Total full time equivalent employment–Average full time monthly salary ($)
NEW HAMPSHIRE continued										
Durham t (Strafford)	RT-S	11	2.8	0.1	56–115–3–67	2.5	0.3	30–17–32–25	377	42–1,636
Exeter t (Rockingham)	*CM-I	11	4.1	0.5	65–221–8–69	3.8	0.5	62–40–60–40	73	97–1,450
Goffstown t (Hillsborough)	TM-S	12	2.9	0.0	49–167–6–23	3.0	0.0	37–23–48–9	0	85–1,502
Hampton t (Rockingham)	*CM-S	11	6.0	0.0	60–349–9–135	5.4	0.0	87–91–125–7	111	122–1,575
Hudson t (Hillsborough)	CM-I	15	5.1	0.0	41–243–15–45	5.8	0.0	46–63–43–10	277	87–1,443
Keene (Cheshire)	*CM-I	22	8.1	0.6	82–213–9–70	10.0	0.5	54–44–51–21	96	197–1,493
Laconia (Belknap)	*CM-I	16	14.9	0.6	154–643–7–154	12.3	0.5	65–55–73–93	244	403–1,188
Lebanon (Grafton)	*CM-I	11	...	...	...–...–...–...	4.7	0.5	26–47–78–62	0	112–1,512
Londonderry t (Rockingham)	RT-S	14	3.7	...	43–173–7–36	3.7	0.3	41–26–35–12	87	74–1,477
Manchester (Hillsborough)	MC-C	92	89.4	4.0	225–560–10–175	91.7	5.8	50–51–65–55	339	2,476–1,657
Merrimack t (Hillsborough)	*TM-S	16	7.3	0.0	87–199–11–160	6.6	0.0	56–33–45–83	528	139–1,534
Nashua (Hillsborough)	MC-C	70	51.9	0.0	103–562–10–63	49.9	0.0	61–60–57–25	398	1,613–1,621
Portsmouth (Rockingham)	*CM-C	27	25.2	1.1	181–521–30–197	25.3	1.2	71–49–35–36	337	874–1,532
Rochester (Strafford)	MC-C	22	14.3	0.2	161–442–8–29	14.3	0.2	28–19–35–12	684	471–1,195
Salem t (Rockingham)	*CM-S	24	8.8	0.7	52–241–7–64	12.0	0.7	55–50–64–15	384	222–1,711
Somersworth (Strafford)	MC-S	11	8.9	0.3	251–485–8–101	8.5	0.3	48–35–38–69	393	266–1,284
NEW JERSEY										
Asbury Park (Monmouth)	*CM-C	17	...	0.0	...–...–...–...	9.6	0.0	91–80–42–47	0	248–1,692
Atlantic City (Atlantic)	CO-C	38	...	0.0	...–...–...–...	80.3	0.0	268–223–71–30	0	2,450–1,597
Bayonne (Hudson)	MC-S	64	50.6	1.9	289–419–6–74	53.7	1.6	71–71–15–33	87	1,705–1,598
Belleville t (Essex)	CO-S	35	...	...	...–...–...–...	10.6	1.2	68–57–17–35	0	317–1,883
Bellmawr b (Camden)	MC-S	14	2.3	0.3	80–69–3–18	2.4	0.9	42–4–30–9	33	64–1,416
Bergenfield b (Bergen)	MC-S	26	6.7	...	71–178–4–10	6.8	0.2	68–11–37–35	21	173–1,639
Berkeley Heights tp (Union)	†MC-S	12	...	0.0	...–...–...–...	10.1	0.0	68–6–39–24	0	79–1,762
Bernards tp (Somerset)	†MC-S	13	4.5	0.0	113–183–10–47	5.8	0.0	61–8–66–3	454	97–1,643
Bloomfield tp (Essex)	†MC-S	47	15.5	1.8	112–197–4–15	15.8	1.5	68–56–15–41	119	482–1,526
Bridgeton (Cumberland)	MC-C	19	6.9	1.3	226–61–4–76	7.2	1.6	73–19–31–59	58	206–1,395
Bridgewater tp (Somerset)	†MC-S	29	9.5	0.0	194–29–11–94	13.2	0.0	64–8–56–45	605	193–1,738
Burlington (Burlington)	MC-S	10	15.7	0.2	1,277–76–5–144	16.0	0.6	120–14–89–43	95	368–1,897
Camden (Camden)	MC-S	84	41.4	2.2	244–171–6–73	45.4	2.7	111–87–22–71	155	1,110–1,453
Carteret b (Middlesex)	MC-S	20	7.1	0.0	135–202–5–7	5.8	0.0	66–31–17–36	64	...–...
Cedar Grove tp (Essex)	*CM-S	12	4.2	0.5	107–116–6–108	3.9	0.8	63–13–30–38	155	...–...
Cherry Hill tp (Camden)	*CM-S	69	19.1	0.0	100–85–8–83	18.5	0.0	55–0–7–49	275	390–1,628
Cinnaminson tp (Burlington)	MC-S	16	3.3	0.0	118–52–6–28	2.6	0.0	44–9–38–0	22	...–...
Clark tp (Union)	MC-S	16	4.3	0.0	114–96–3–47	3.9	0.0	65–12–34–28	217	119–1,575
Cliffside Park b (Bergen)	MC-S	21	5.5	0.0	56–195–5–4	5.6	0.0	55–27–25–38	10	...–...
Clifton (Passaic)	*CM-C	75	45.5	0.0	192–359–4–56	52.2	0.0	61–58–13–67	262	1,335–1,991
Collingswood b (Camden)	CO-S	16	3.1	0.5	67–78–3–48	3.5	0.6	44–16–18–49	98	98–1,594
Cranford tp (Union)	MC-S	24	9.2	0.0	138–172–5–65	9.3	0.0	65–41–26–32	61	189–1,733
Delran tp (Burlington)	†MC-S	15	2.1	0.0	72–51–4–15	2.0	0.0	40–1–25–16	8	56–1,471
Denville tp (Morris)	†MC-S	14	4.3	0.6	112–108–8–70	4.3	0.6	64–9–37–18	81	98–1,708
Deptford tp (Gloucester)	*CM-S	24	...	0.0	...–...–...–...	4.4	0.0	51–0–18–10	0	135–1,283
Dover t (Morris)	†MC-S	15	...	...	...–...–...–...	4.3	0.8	52–9–51–21	0	112–1,532
Dumont b (Bergen)	MC-S	18	4.2	0.0	77–140–2–11	4.6	0.0	63–8–26–47	180	80–1,842
East Brunswick tp (Middlesex)	MC-S	38	13.1	1.7	103–183–8–51	12.5	1.7	83–3–9–23	367	294–1,612
East Orange (Essex)	MC-S	77	77.9	3.8	547–411–9–48	78.5	4.4	69–49–22–36	323	3,498–1,457
East Windsor tp (Mercer)	*CM-S	22	5.8	0.0	78–140–8–45	5.7	0.0	64–3–15–10	315	113–1,990
Eatontown b (Monmouth)	MC-S	13	...	0.0	...–...–...–...	3.5	0.0	81–5–26–2	0	69–1,818
Edison tp (Middlesex)	†MC-S	72	76.2	2.5	315–609–11–125	73.8	3.2	80–51–33–65	552	1,789–2,283
Elizabeth (Union)	MC-S	107	97.4	5.9	504–358–5–45	101.8	4.4	64–57–11–58	488	4,158–1,785
Elmwood Park b (Bergen)	†MC-S	18	...	0.0	...–...–...–...	...	0.0	...–...–...–...	0	...–...
Englewood (Bergen)	†MC-S	24	...	0.0	...–...–...–...	32.3	0.0	117–56–41–43	0	747–2,076
Evesham tp (Burlington)	*CM-S	23	...	0.0	...–...–...–...	4.9	0.0	41–0–18–9	0	86–1,883
Ewing tp (Mercer)	MC-S	35	9.2	0.0	151–50–5–59	8.4	0.0	45–10–22–75	90	206–1,248
Fair Lawn b (Bergen)	*CM-S	32	9.0	2.0	120–144–4–16	7.9	1.8	51–5–15–59	66	219–1,795
Fairview b (Bergen)	MC-S	10	3.0	0.0	97–170–6–19	3.4	0.0	72–9–31–36	161	...–...
Fort Lee b (Bergen)	MC-S	33	10.9	0.0	54–240–9–31	11.5	0.0	79–11–18–72	178	228–1,888
Franklin tp (Somerset)	*CM-S	32	8.3	1.2	102–123–9–23	9.1	1.0	58–4–28–0	288	194–1,810
Freehold b (Monmouth)	MC-S	10	3.8	0.7	93–160–9–114	3.1	0.7	73–2–46–59	233	...–...
Freehold tp (Monmouth)	*CM-S	19	5.9	0.8	178–27–11–88	4.7	1.3	53–3–26–7	337	126–1,754
Galloway tp (Atlantic)	*CM-S	14	3.0	0.0	87–53–11–66	3.0	0.0	53–6–31–40	19	81–1,424
Garfield (Bergen)	*CM-S	27	...	...	...–...–...–...	14.4	0.8	49–7–16–47	0	103–1,717
Glassboro b (Gloucester)	MC-S	15	4.1	0.5	131–85–3–63	3.8	0.8	57–5–49–48	184	109–1,351
Glen Rock b (Bergen)	MC-S	11	4.0	0.0	85–224–9–32	4.2	0.0	64–6–49–54	92	83–1,978
Gloucester tp (Camden)	*CM-S	47	7.7	0.0	77–73–2–11	8.5	0.0	53–0–9–19	69	157–1,872
Gloucester City (Camden)	MC-S	13	3.3	0.6	169–63–5–16	3.3	0.5	51–26–41–7	10	103–1,419
Hackensack (Bergen)	*CM-S	36	37.3	0.0	281–676–13–66	36.5	0.0	81–72–13–54	402	381–1,714
Haddon tp (Camden)	CO-S	16	2.9	0.2	74–70–3–37	2.8	0.3	45–1–23–42	113	73–1,447
Haddonfield b (Camden)	†CO-S	12	3.4	0.5	81–94–5–98	3.8	0.6	57–14–18–58	66	...–...
Hamilton tp (Mercer)	MC-S	83	29.3	0.0	182–76–5–90	23.2	0.0	50–0–15–50	248	675–1,697
Hammonton t (Atlantic)	MC-S	12	2.7	0.5	93–64–4–58	2.6	0.3	50–5–37–28	150	...–...
Harrison t (Hudson)	MC-S	12	...	...	...–...–...–...	13.4	0.7	146–139–50–57	0	342–1,962
Hasbrouck Heights b (Bergen)	MC-S	12	3.4	0.0	94–159–3–28	3.2	0.0	68–10–17–48	22	...–...
Hawthorne b (Passaic)	CO-S	18	3.6	0.9	85–71–4–37	3.4	0.8	40–6–16–45	8	...–...
Hazlet tp (Monmouth)	†MC-S	23	4.0	0.0	67–87–5–18	3.4	0.0	45–11–20–0	72	...–...
Highland Park b (Middlesex)	MC-S	13	3.4	1.0	75–165–4–13	3.2	1.2	79–14–13–20	56	94–1,654
Hillsdale b (Bergen)	MC-S	10	3.9	0.0	122–211–3–45	3.7	0.0	73–15–35–56	340	66–1,738
Hillside tp (Union)	MC-S	21	...	0.0	...–...–...–...	8.1	0.0	106–78–23–49	0	195–1,733
Hoboken (Hudson)	MC-S	42	...	...	...–...–...–...	39.9	2.7	67–82–12–45	0	457–1,833

Table 1/9 continued **PROFILES OF INDIVIDUAL CITIES**

City (county)	Form of government–Metro status	Est. 1982 population (000)	Fiscal year 1983 revenues: Total general revenue ($ millions)	Fiscal year 1983 revenues: Total utility revenue ($ millions)	Fiscal year 1983 revenues: Per capita revenues ($) Intergovernmental revenue–Property taxes–Other taxes–Charges and miscellaneous general revenue	Fiscal year 1983 expenditures: Total general expenditures ($ millions)	Fiscal year 1983 expenditures: Total utility expenditures ($ millions)	Fiscal year 1983 expenditures: Per capita current expenditures ($) Police–Fire–Streets–Sewers and sanitation	Long term debt ($ per capita)	October 1983 public personnel: Total full time equivalent employment–Average full time monthly salary ($)
NEW JERSEY continued										
Hopatcong b (Sussex)	MC-I	16	3.3	0.0	51–120–4–36	3.3	0.0	44–1–40–0	53	...–...
Hopewell tp (Mercer)	†MC-S	11	2.8	0.0	138–81–7–28	2.4	0.0	49–3–43–2	0	65–1,458
Irvington t (Essex)	MC-S	62	16.2	0.0	91–144–4–19	17.6	0.0	57–52–23–21	130	537–1,643
Jackson tp (Ocean)	†CO-I	26	5.5	0.0	83–97–6–24	4.8	0.0	65–0–34–0	68	150–1,581
Jefferson tp (Morris)	†MC-S	16	5.1	0.4	125–137–7–42	3.8	1.7	53–9–49–2	70	80–1,663
Jersey City (Hudson)	†MC-C	223	268.0	12.4	628–337–6–231	315.9	15.5	116–92–13–40	527	8,057–1,683
Keansburg b (Monmouth)	*CM-S	11	2.8	0.1	87–115–8–49	2.9	0.0	78–8–26–9	129	64–1,445
Kearny t (Hudson)	MC-S	36	20.4	1.4	508–26–14–26	18.0	1.0	104–102–7–48	497	434–2,104
Lakewood tp (Ocean)	*CM-I	39	10.0	0.0	97–136–5–21	9.2	0.0	64–7–25–14	182	256–1,484
Lawrence tp (Mercer)	*CM-S	20	8.3	0.0	156–152–12–89	7.9	0.0	78–8–36–69	72	148–1,791
Linden (Union)	MC-S	37	24.3	0.0	545–18–4–80	24.6	0.0	105–111–63–35	361	622–1,916
Lindenwold b (Camden)	MC-S	18	...	0.0	...–...–...–...	...	0.0	...–...–...–...	0	...–...
Little Falls tp (Passaic)	MC-S	12	2.3	0.0	106–57–5–18	2.4	0.0	46–8–35–14	80	57–1,538
Livingston tp (Essex)	*CM-S	28	7.2	1.1	118–61–7–74	5.9	1.4	56–6–26–19	74	192–1,495
Lodi b (Bergen)	MC-S	24	7.1	0.8	86–171–8–31	7.0	1.3	38–5–14–38	170	146–1,480
Long Branch (Monmouth)	MC-C	30	...	0.0	...–...–...–...	10.5	0.0	86–24–34–17	0	274–1,369
Lyndhurst tp (Bergen)	CO-S	20	6.1	0.9	87–181–8–28	5.1	0.9	63–3–20–51	0	...–...
Madison b (Morris)	†MC-S	15	5.2	6.5	87–205–9–38	6.3	6.6	74–21–50–40	366	164–1,816
Mahwah tp (Bergen)	†MC-S	12	...	...	...–...–...–...	5.7	1.2	105–10–40–47	0	92–2,013
Manville b (Somerset)	MC-S	11	3.0	0.5	117–114–4–29	2.4	0.4	47–3–32–28	217	70–1,680
Maple Shade tp (Burlington)	*CM-S	20	3.0	0.8	66–33–4–42	4.2	0.8	47–7–18–39	282	85–1,568
Maplewood tp (Essex)	MC-S	23	7.8	0.0	91–213–3–40	7.6	0.0	63–56–14–21	130	229–1,632
Medford tp (Burlington)	*CM-S	18	4.3	0.4	92–68–6–67	3.6	0.2	45–3–14–29	100	94–1,771
Metuchen b (Middlesex)	†MC-S	14	...	0.0	...–...–...–...	4.5	0.0	82–12–33–52	0	86–1,702
Middlesex b (Middlesex)	MC-S	13	4.0	0.0	115–150–5–32	3.9	0.0	57–11–29–39	364	...–...
Middletown tp (Monmouth)	†MC-S	64	17.0	0.0	79–158–8–21	13.6	0.0	34–8–40–0	368	386–1,560
Millburn tp (Essex)	†MC-S	19	10.5	0.0	219–227–6–91	10.7	0.0	101–81–43–32	154	217–1,921
Millville (Cumberland)	CO-C	25	21.5	0.8	480–253–3–125	22.3	0.7	77–6–23–44	283	825–1,420
Montclair t (Essex)	CO-S	38	40.6	1.8	280–672–13–100	40.5	2.8	75–52–19–45	270	1,217–1,868
Montville tp (Morris)	†MC-S	14	3.7	0.0	122–74–13–45	3.5	0.0	61–20–40–24	159	76–1,831
Moorestown tp (Burlington)	*CM-S	16	5.3	0.9	124–111–8–98	6.0	1.1	73–0–40–46	352	152–1,941
Morristown t (Morris)	MC-S	17	14.2	0.0	184–230–14–431	11.1	0.1	98–49–50–44	1,717	165–1,916
Mount Holly tp (Burlington)	*CM-S	11	2.3	0.0	114–75–5–17	2.4	0.0	69–9–23–10	40	...–...
Mount Laurel tp (Burlington)	*CM-S	20	4.1	0.0	79–69–8–54	3.9	0.0	46–9–17–13	113	...–...
Mount Olive tp (Morris)	†MC-S	19	4.6	0.3	78–117–7–35	3.8	0.5	47–4–23–41	117	104–1,702
Neptune tp (Monmouth)	CO-S	29	...	0.0	...–...–...–...	7.7	0.0	56–0–17–35	0	227–1,435
New Brunswick (Middlesex)	CO-C	41	32.4	2.4	377–340–8–67	43.7	2.8	85–73–14–54	68	1,111–1,584
New Hanover tp (Burlington)	CO-S	16	0.6	0.0	27–1–1–9	0.5	0.0	7–0–2–1	0	14–1,281
New Milford b (Bergen)	MC-S	17	3.6	0.0	95–107–2–10	4.0	0.0	72–10–23–37	9	...–...
New Providence b (Union)	MC-S	12	4.4	0.0	109–204–4–36	3.9	0.0	60–3–43–62	102	...–...
Newark (Essex)	†MC-C	321	265.3	16.3	556–108–43–121	255.9	25.8	130–88–2–71	409	4,882–1,693
North Arlington b (Bergen)	MC-S	16	4.1	0.8	76–129–10–33	4.3	0.5	74–3–19–23	201	88–1,781
North Bergen tp (Hudson)	CO-S	47	16.1	0.0	111–171–8–51	22.1	0.0	50–60–10–38	820	447–1,552
North Brunswick tp (Middlesex)	TM-S	23	8.2	1.3	149–100–14–94	9.0	1.7	84–4–25–40	143	197–1,678
North Plainfield b (Somerset)	MC-S	19	4.8	0.0	77–116–4–56	5.8	0.0	67–38–31–26	202	110–1,746
Nutley t (Essex)	CO-S	29	...	...	...–...–...–...	9.6	0.9	61–23–20–64	0	233–1,779
Oakland b (Bergen)	*CM-S	13	4.2	0.7	85–208–5–18	3.2	0.7	73–4–27–14	239	...–...
Ocean tp (Monmouth)	*CM-S	24	6.8	0.0	78–171–9–29	5.6	0.0	67–0–35–23	255	169–1,690
Ocean City (Cape May)	MC-I	15	11.0	0.0	171–431–35–125	11.7	0.1	112–97–52–50	908	265–1,875
Old Bridge tp (Middlesex)	*CM-S	52	11.2	0.0	90–105–9–14	9.3	0.0	64–2–12–7	0	310–1,837
Orange (Essex)	MC-S	31	28.6	1.1	515–348–6–62	27.3	1.1	91–71–24–35	222	...–...
Palisades Park b (Bergen)	MC-S	14	3.4	0.0	72–141–5–30	4.3	0.0	63–9–34–48	24	...–...
Paramus b (Bergen)	MC-S	26	11.3	0.0	164–135–17–113	12.8	0.0	130–14–24–58	386	277–1,720
Parsippany-Troy Hill t (Morris)	MC-S	50	19.7	2.1	101–131–9–153	24.4	2.3	67–2–23–78	539	372–1,627
Passaic (Passaic)	*CM-C	53	18.1	0.0	150–167–6–16	14.7	0.1	59–49–11–0	51	490–1,842
Paterson (Passaic)	MC-C	139	125.8	...	503–306–3–93	134.2	0.2	83–57–19–56	515	3,891–1,721
Pemberton tp (Burlington)	†MC-S	31	4.8	0.6	72–67–6–11	4.5	0.4	38–2–21–0	348	119–1,699
Pennsauken tp (Camden)	CM-S	34	12.1	0.0	174–116–8–58	12.4	0.0	100–14–22–36	377	270–1,644
Pequannock tp (Morris)	*CM-S	14	4.3	0.2	109–146–11–47	3.7	0.3	48–3–21–23	44	...–...
Perth Amboy (Middlesex)	†MC-C	39	12.7	2.4	136–137–5–47	12.6	2.3	68–32–17–39	284	457–1,752
Phillipsburg t (Warren)	*CM-S	17	...	0.0	...–...–...–...	3.6	0.0	46–5–39–20	0	101–1,480
Piscataway tp (Middlesex)	†MC-S	43	12.2	0.0	114–90–8–72	11.9	0.0	63–1–25–38	234	260–1,951
Plainfield (Union)	†MC-S	46	43.7	0.0	505–387–4–58	48.1	0.0	43–59–14–29	267	1,403–1,858
Pleasantville (Atlantic)	MC-S	13	...	0.0	...–...–...–...	...	0.0	...–...–...–...	0	...–...
Point Pleasant b (Ocean)	MC-I	18	3.9	0.4	69–71–7–72	4.2	0.4	55–3–18–51	321	86–1,574
Pompton Lakes b (Passaic)	MC-S	11	3.0	0.0	92–132–3–49	2.4	0.0	62–5–30–20	98	...–...
Princeton b (Mercer)	MC-S	12	5.0	0.0	96–159–11–148	4.8	0.0	72–6–30–97	39	...–...
Princeton tp (Mercer)	*CM-S	14	5.4	0.0	117–162–6–99	4.9	0.0	64–7–28–74	86	102–1,670
Rahway (Union)	†MC-S	27	9.9	1.7	120–226–2–22	9.6	1.7	81–60–35–44	76	274–1,768
Ramsey b (Bergen)	MC-S	13	6.2	0.5	127–281–10–58	5.4	0.4	71–2–22–95	648	96–1,728
Randolph tp (Morris)	*CM-S	18	...	0.0	...–...–...–...	5.5	0.0	59–6–32–15	0	110–2,036
Red Bank b (Monmouth)	MC-S	12	4.7	0.9	177–115–11–91	5.1	0.9	101–7–32–72	161	140–1,418
Ridgefield b (Bergen)	MC-S	10	8.1	0.0	754–2–6–36	8.8	0.0	114–12–66–76	111	100–1,726
Ridgefield Park v (Bergen)	CO-S	13	3.6	0.0	89–150–5–41	3.7	0.0	71–12–27–39	34	64–1,810
Ridgewood v (Bergen)	*CM-S	25	9.9	2.5	86–232–7–70	8.8	1.8	51–40–29–37	168	329–1,738
Ringwood b (Passaic)	†MC-S	13	3.4	0.6	83–161–4–16	3.1	0.7	59–6–43–18	98	83–1,546
River Edge b (Bergen)	MC-S	11	3.9	0.0	97–195–8–60	3.2	0.0	65–9–34–50	134	...–...
Rockaway tp (Morris)	†MC-S	20	...	...	...–...–...–...	6.3	0.4	62–9–46–4	0	132–1,698
Roselle b (Union)	MC-S	21	...	0.0	...–...–...–...	5.6	0.0	54–39–24–63	0	105–1,765

Table 1/9 continued **PROFILES OF INDIVIDUAL CITIES**

City (county)	Form of govern-ment–Metro status	Est. 1982 popu-lation (000)	Fiscal year 1983 revenues: Total general revenue ($ mil-lions)	Total utility reve-nue ($ mil-lions)	Per capita revenues ($): Intergovernmental revenue–Property taxes–Other taxes–Charges and miscella-neous general revenue	Fiscal year 1983 expenditures: Total general expendi-tures ($ mil-lions)	Total utility expendi-tures ($ mil-lions)	Per capita current expenditures ($): Police–Fire–Streets–Sewers and sanitation	Long term debt ($ per capita)	October 1983 public personnel: Total full time equivalent employment–Average full time monthly salary ($)
NEW JERSEY continued										
Roselle Park b (Union)	MC-S	13	3.1	0.0	74–127–3–29	3.2	0.0	61–8–25–36	149	75–1,547
Rutherford b (Bergen)	†MC-S	19	5.9	0.0	77–200–5–32	6.7	0.0	71–9–26–37	30	205–1,347
Saddle Brook tp (Bergen)	MC-S	14	4.0	1.0	125–149–7–8	4.0	1.0	68–5–36–43	92	84–1,541
Sayreville b (Middlesex)	MC-C	30	14.6	2.0	376–31–5–73	13.9	2.2	86–4–41–57	747	284–1,614
Scotch Plains tp (Union)	*CM-S	21	5.4	0.0	94–112–7–41	4.4	0.0	60–12–31–17	56	164–1,582
Secaucus t (Hudson)	MC-S	14	9.5	0.0	143–436–16–62	9.2	0.0	132–13–45–125	591	...–...
Somers Point (Atlantic)	MC-S	10	2.6	0.0	84–150–8–10	2.5	0.0	60–7–21–17	96	52–1,517
Somerville b (Somerset)	MC-S	12	...	0.0	...–...–...–...	5.3	0.0	95–10–28–76	0	98–1,612
South Brunswick tp (Middlesex)	†MC-S	17	9.2	1.7	235–46–39–213	8.4	4.1	86–6–18–122	1,123	170–1,789
South Orange Village tp (Essex)	CO-S	16	7.7	1.1	114–324–4–52	8.0	1.3	110–64–45–23	462	199–1,708
South Plainfield b (Middlesex)	MC-S	20	7.5	0.0	124–123–6–112	8.5	0.0	76–15–43–70	721	134–1,832
South River b (Middlesex)	MC-S	14	3.4	3.3	58–141–6–34	4.0	3.5	61–2–17–44	367	124–1,555
Sparta tp (Sussex)	*CM-I	13	3.5	0.0	77–151–6–29	4.0	0.0	68–7–45–6	13	72–1,955
Springfield tp (Union)	MC-S	14	...	0.0	...–...–...–...	...	0.0	...–...–...–...	0	...–...
Summit (Union)	MC-S	21	22.1	0.0	238–670–8–134	23.3	0.0	63–49–21–74	550	608–2,136
Teaneck tp (Bergen)	*CM-S	39	15.4	0.0	86–272–7–30	14.7	0.0	66–58–19–26	32	374–1,759
Tenafly b (Bergen)	MC-S	13	...	0.0	...–...–...–...	5.9	0.0	85–12–55–80	0	121–1,858
Totowa b (Passaic)	MC-S	11	3.1	0.6	133–89–6–42	3.1	0.5	52–4–24–44	318	72–1,624
Trenton (Mercer)	†MC-C	91	52.7	6.9	259–208–7–103	59.2	9.8	108–67–11–40	160	1,609–1,815
Union tp (Union)	MC-S	50	18.3	0.0	133–158–5–67	19.5	0.0	90–81–15–49	155	453–1,832
Union City (Hudson)	CO-S	57	21.0	0.0	135–217–4–13	20.3	0.0	62–54–11–32	0	578–1,480
Ventnor City (Atlantic)	MC-S	12	...	0.0	...–...–...–...	6.0	0.0	50–48–12–17	0	225–1,517
Verona b (Essex)	†MC-S	14	...	0.0	...–...–...–...	...	0.0	...–...–...–...	0	...–...
Vineland (Cumberland)	†MC-C	54	45.3	25.0	478–293–7–66	46.4	23.3	52–11–29–3	481	1,695–1,749
Waldwick b (Bergen)	MC-S	11	3.8	0.4	191–142–9–17	3.4	0.3	58–6–19–80	230	53–1,930
Wall tp (Monmouth)	†MC-S	19	6.1	0.5	146–81–9–81	5.3	0.7	84–0–22–45	292	131–1,659
Wallington b (Bergen)	MC-S	11	...	0.0	...–...–...–...	...	0.0	...–...–...–...	0	...–...
Wanaque b (Passaic)	MC-S	10	1.8	0.3	69–82–6–14	1.8	0.3	53–4–18–20	157	...–...
Washington tp (Morris)	†MC-S	12	3.4	0.0	78–156–11–37	3.3	0.0	52–4–43–1	260	61–1,847
Wayne tp (Passaic)	MC-S	47	20.7	2.3	112–179–8–142	21.8	1.9	64–3–24–75	691	435–1,675
Weehawken tp (Hudson)	CO-S	13	...	0.0	...–...–...–...	5.7	0.0	86–101–11–14	0	141–1,543
West Caldwell b (Essex)	MC-S	11	...	...	...–...–...–...	4.4	0.6	67–4–28–43	0	...–...
West Milford tp (Passaic)	*CM-S	23	6.5	0.0	98–144–5–30	6.2	0.1	54–9–45–31	206	152–1,680
West New York t (Hudson)	CO-S	41	32.4	0.0	433–342–4–11	32.6	0.0	91–63–12–28	233	435–1,577
West Orange t (Essex)	MC-S	40	...	0.0	...–...–...–...	13.1	0.0	66–60–34–22	0	357–1,959
West Paterson b (Passaic)	MC-S	11	2.4	0.3	77–103–7–21	2.5	0.2	44–5–14–28	335	57–1,440
Westfield t (Union)	MC-S	30	8.7	0.0	92–115–7–73	8.8	0.0	54–37–31–17	60	224–1,653
Westwood b (Bergen)	MC-S	11	3.2	0.0	112–165–5–19	2.8	0.0	75–11–42–20	140	...–...
Willingboro tp (Burlington)	*CM-S	40	7.6	0.0	79–79–2–31	7.6	0.0	66–3–24–22	76	169–1,769
Woodbridge tp (Middlesex)	MC-S	91	25.9	0.0	226–38–5–18	26.0	0.0	50–0–22–34	0	818–1,204
Woodbury (Gloucester)	MC-S	10	...	...	...–...–...–...	3.3	0.6	78–17–28–73	0	88–1,557
Wyckoff tp (Bergen)	MC-S	16	4.2	0.0	74–131–4–57	4.3	0.0	34–3–29–66	300	103–1,347
NEW MEXICO										
Alamogordo (Otero)	*CM-I	25	...	...	...–...–...–...	6.9	1.8	51–8–20–33	0	253–1,328
Albuquerque (Bernalillo)	†MC-C	342	265.4	29.8	315–92–103–265	224.4	52.1	74–43–15–49	1,242	4,677–1,771
Artesia (Eddy)	MC-I	11	6.1	0.6	350–8–104–94	5.2	0.9	60–30–24–21	21	116–1,427
Carlsbad (Eddy)	*CM-I	27	11.6	2.3	245–8–106–77	10.3	2.6	60–29–68–46	289	289–1,554
Clovis (Curry)	*CM-I	33	...	0.0	...–...–...–...	9.8	0.0	45–40–28–23	0	275–1,412
Farmington (San Juan)	*CM-I	36	106.4	38.0	315–7–140–2,523	103.8	43.4	105–62–1–173	4,533	651–1,784
Gallup t (Mc Kinley)	*CM-I	20	11.6	11.3	290–21–136–121	9.0	12.5	68–47–38–57	393	392–1,335
Grants (Mora)	*CM-I	11	4.9	0.7	248–25–69–107	4.3	0.8	74–24–27–32	246	123–1,210
Hobbs (Lea)	*CM-I	32	18.9	1.5	363–17–121–98	14.1	5.9	95–53–30–17	220	359–1,588
Las Cruces (Dona Ana)	*CM-C	46	55.2	11.8	217–28–87–856	49.4	11.2	61–26–64–72	751	1,404–1,149
Las Vegas (San Miguel)	*CM-I	16	4.5	4.5	150–7–61–72	4.1	3.9	60–13–30–42	93	165–1,120
Roswell (Chaves)	*CM-I	42	20.5	3.9	189–12–94–189	18.0	4.3	55–36–52–29	348	470–1,443
Santa Fe (Santa Fe)	*CM-I	51	33.5	0.0	389–19–106–144	34.8	0.0	62–27–23–47	346	646–1,333
NEW YORK										
Albany (Albany)	MC-C	100	62.8	4.6	292–246–19–90	62.4	5.0	94–74–30–74	0	1,961–1,352
Amsterdam (Montgomery)	MC-S	21	...	...	...–...–...–...	7.6	2.2	57–41–36–44	0	212–1,337
Auburn (Cayuga)	*CM-I	32	...	...	...–...–...–...	14.9	1.1	54–68–21–58	0	369–1,885
Babylon v (Suffolk)	MC-S	12	...	0.0	...–...–...–...	2.8	0.0	1–10–36–28	0	...–...
Batavia (Genesee)	*CM-I	16	7.1	0.7	148–56–141–92	6.5	0.7	64–75–41–58	46	155–1,666
Beacon (Dutchess)	CO-S	13	...	...	...–...–...–...	5.6	2.0	63–24–40–98	0	107–1,746
Binghamton (Broome)	MC-C	55	39.6	2.0	411–230–14–67	33.8	2.2	59–72–18–76	422	855–1,302
Buffalo (Erie)	MC-C	348	477.8	15.7	903–277–33–160	503.2	10.6	82–67–29–95	618	10,724–1,862
Canandaigua (Ontario)	*CM-S	11	7.2	1.2	343–118–138–72	5.0	0.8	54–32–33–51	802	107–1,629
Cohoes (Albany)	MC-S	18	9.3	0.7	273–133–11–99	8.6	0.6	41–56–39–37	327	188–1,575
Corning (Steuben)	MC-I	13	...	...	...–...–...–...	6.6	0.5	52–59–42–31	0	...–...
Cortland (Cortland)	MC-I	20	6.9	0.4	165–99–14–71	6.9	0.5	45–46–35–42	23	190–1,485
Depew v (Erie)	MC-S	19	...	...	...–...–...–...	5.7	0.3	48–5–28–64	0	114–1,361
Dobbs Ferry v (Westchester)	†MC-S	10	...	0.0	...–...–...–...	3.4	0.0	76–11–29–36	0	...–...
Dunkirk (Chautauqua)	MC-I	15	8.0	0.8	193–201–24–113	7.6	0.8	48–48–62–87	246	197–1,426
East Rockaway v (Nassau)	MC-S	11	...	0.0	...–...–...–...	1.1	0.0	0–1–2–39	0	...–...
Elmira (Chemung)	*CM-C	34	...	...	...–...–...–...	16.3	2.0	64–67–29–15	0	411–1,578
Endicott v (Broome)	MC-S	14	...	...	...–...–...–...	13.2	2.0	17–99–94–75	0	237–1,509
Floral Park v (Nassau)	MC-S	17	6.4	0.0	40–277–10–55	6.0	0.0	89–13–41–31	106	...–...
Fredonia v (Chautauqua)	CM-I	11	4.1	0.4	204–82–13–70	3.3	0.3	33–11–43–47	415	...–...
Freeport v (Nassau)	MC-S	39	...	...	...–...–...–...	17.2	10.6	80–9–29–45	0	412–1,624
Fulton (Oswego)	MC-S	13	8.1	0.6	239–111–198–68	8.8	0.8	66–65–68–38	659	229–1,456

Table 1/9 continued **PROFILES OF INDIVIDUAL CITIES**

City (county)	Form of govern-ment–Metro status	Est. 1982 popu-lation (000)	Fiscal year 1983 revenues: Total general revenue ($ mil-lions)	Total utility reve-nue ($ mil-lions)	Per capita revenues ($): Intergovernmental revenue–Property taxes–Other taxes–Charges and miscella-neous general revenue	Fiscal year 1983 expenditures: Total general expendi-tures ($ mil-lions)	Total utility expendi-tures ($ mil-lions)	Per capita current expenditures ($): Police–Fire–Streets–Sewers and sanitation	Long term debt ($ per capita)	October 1983 public personnel: Total full time equivalent employment–Average full time monthly salary ($)
NEW YORK continued										
Garden City v (Nassau)	†MC-S	23	...	...	...–...–...–...	13.6	0.9	82–54–36–73	0	284–1,870
Geneva (Ontario)	*CM-S	15	6.7	1.0	152–109–77–120	6.3	0.8	55–35–52–43	434	145–1,533
Glen Cove (Nassau)	MC-S	24	18.1	1.3	367–193–76–110	18.8	1.5	83–11–31–90	601	251–1,549
Glens Falls (Warren)	MC-C	16	8.8	0.6	204–176–93–72	9.7	0.5	51–58–46–28	234	...–...
Gloversville (Fulton)	MC-I	17	9.4	1.1	394–62–11–73	8.8	1.5	49–51–37–121	109	212–1,560
Hamburg v (Erie)	MC-S	10	...	0.0	...–...–...–...	2.7	0.0	5–9–44–66	0	...–...
Harrison (Westchester)	MC-S	23	...	0.0	...–...–...–...	...	0.0	...–...–...–...	0	...–...
Hempstead v (Nassau)	MC-S	40	16.9	1.6	60–303–8–48	16.8	1.4	90–18–18–39	226	391–1,610
Hornell (Steuben)	MC-I	10	...	...	...–...–...–...	4.5	0.7	47–46–37–34	0	...–...
Ithaca (Tompkins)	MC-I	28	14.0	1.3	148–135–123–89	13.1	1.1	56–47–47–39	177	371–1,508
Jamestown (Chautauqua)	MC-I	36	34.8	16.6	275–155–10–535	36.0	13.6	52–56–26–41	309	1,183–1,466
Johnson City v (Broome)	MC-S	17	...	...	...–...–...–...	5.6	0.6	8–6–59–52	0	152–1,596
Kenmore v (Erie)	MC-S	18	...	...	...–...–...–...	4.3	0.6	5–1–42–59	0	...–...
Kingston (Ulster)	MC-I	24	17.9	1.3	208–183–98–251	18.9	1.2	91–95–30–70	223	470–1,455
Lackawanna (Erie)	MC-S	22	23.3	0.0	534–406–23–97	23.9	0.0	92–88–45–76	194	299–1,623
Lancaster v (Erie)	MC-S	13	...	...	...–...–...–...	2.9	0.9	40–5–31–14	0	...–...
Lindenhurst v (Suffolk)	MC-S	27	...	0.0	...–...–...–...	3.4	0.0	0–13–33–15	0	80–1,327
Lockport (Niagara)	MC-S	25	11.9	1.7	235–138–20–93	12.0	1.5	51–61–52–56	303	341–1,304
Long Beach (Nassau)	*CM-S	34	...	...	...–...–...–...	16.6	2.0	5–4–1–86	0	399–1,709
Lynbrook v (Nassau)	MC-S	20	...	0.0	...–...–...–...	6.4	0.0	92–12–31–32	0	149–1,703
Mamaroneck v (Westchester)	*CM-S	17	7.6	0.0	40–342–15–46	7.3	0.0	93–11–28–37	10	190–1,624
Massapequa Park v (Nassau)	MC-S	19	...	0.0	...–...–...–...	2.0	0.0	3–0–23–6	0	...–...
Massena v (St. Lawrence)	MC-I	12	...	...	...–...–...–...	3.7	0.4	42–18–39–35	0	...–...
Middletown (Orange)	MC-C	22	8.6	1.1	155–186–15–41	8.4	0.9	55–42–37–30	70	223–1,552
Mineola v (Nassau)	MC-S	20	...	...	...–...–...–...	4.8	0.7	0–7–45–44	0	...–...
Mount Vernon (Westchester)	MC-S	66	33.3	1.5	155–212–79–58	34.6	1.3	74–56–7–40	168	806–1,748
New Rochelle (Westchester)	*CM-S	71	44.5	0.0	188–267–99–75	43.1	0.0	102–83–30–46	217	793–1,793
New York City	MC-C	7,086	19,288.3	1,364.2	1,133–540–681–368	16,411.6	2,547.3	128–64–35–64	1,292	336,671–2,110
Newark v (Wayne)	MC-S	10	2.6	0.6	55–152–12–44	2.6	0.4	41–11–26–33	86	68–1,363
Newburgh (Orange)	*CM-C	24	9.9	1.2	185–147–36–53	10.2	1.3	96–85–34–43	232	299–1,510
Niagara Falls (Niagara)	*CM-S	68	53.2	5.0	420–182–24–151	67.1	3.1	62–58–28–113	634	1,027–1,808
North Tonawanda (Niagara)	MC-S	35	15.9	1.3	223–96–19–109	15.2	1.7	43–44–37–64	273	328–1,692
Ogdensburg (St. Lawrence)	*CM-I	12	5.6	0.4	199–93–84–87	5.3	0.4	61–84–38–40	75	152–1,342
Olean (Cattaraugus)	MC-I	18	...	...	...–...–...–...	8.5	0.9	44–47–41–47	0	...–...
Oneida (Madison)	MC-S	11	28.1	1.5	1,377–91–122–1,086	29.2	3.8	49–48–62–29	878	598–1,212
Oneonta (Otsego)	MC-I	15	7.0	0.6	247–117–28–78	6.0	0.9	40–33–28–30	291	...–...
Ossining v (Westchester)	*CM-S	21	...	...	...–...–...–...	8.1	1.5	69–12–29–31	0	147–1,927
Oswego (Oswego)	MC-S	19	17.4	0.8	202–411–198–90	16.4	1.8	70–80–53–94	495	366–1,552
Patchogue v (Suffolk)	MC-S	11	...	0.0	...–...–...–...	2.4	0.0	1–11–30–35	0	...–...
Peekskill (Westchester)	*CM-S	19	9.6	1.1	214–246–10–49	9.7	1.1	71–38–29–29	362	458–1,551
Plattsburgh (Clinton)	MC-I	20	10.1	10.1	164–76–96–156	8.9	13.3	50–53–25–100	822	...–...
Port Chester v (Westchester)	*CM-S	23	...	0.0	...–...–...–...	11.0	0.0	82–24–22–40	0	173–1,984
Potsdam v (St. Lawrence)	MC-I	11	...	...	...–...–...–...	4.6	3.6	7–4–3–35	0	71–1,580
Poughkeepsie (Dutchess)	*CM-C	30	22.3	2.1	343–189–109–110	18.3	2.6	60–73–33–81	373	360–1,648
Rochester (Monroe)	*CM-C	244	341.5	15.8	758–426–51–164	350.6	11.1	93–74–44–39	845	7,491–2,097
Rockville Centre v (Nassau)	MC-S	25	10.9	9.1	51–285–9–85	12.8	7.9	83–17–34–51	250	256–2,122
Rome (Oneida)	MC-C	44	33.9	1.6	159–130–73–418	32.0	1.8	39–47–43–19	305	1,000–1,396
Rye (Westchester)	*CM-S	15	8.2	0.0	86–300–33–117	8.5	0.0	82–35–34–70	45	...–...
Saratoga Springs (Saratoga)	MC-S	24	9.7	1.3	191–78–91–47	10.0	0.9	54–48–62–11	64	265–1,519
Scarsdale v (Westchester)	*CM-S	17	...	0.0	...–...–...–...	5.5	0.1	3–79–19–79	0	252–1,940
Schenectady (Schenectady)	MC-C	68	34.3	3.2	195–194–44–72	35.1	2.2	84–68–10–62	0	833–1,675
Spring Valley v (Rockland)	MC-S	21	...	0.0	...–...–...–...	5.5	0.0	53–6–6–30	0	100–1,879
Suffern v (Rockland)	MC-S	11	...	...	...–...–...–...	6.8	0.4	65–8–41–31	0	...–...
Syracuse (Onondaga)	MC-C	166	190.9	4.8	705–257–16–171	211.5	5.1	85–73–32–33	524	5,396–1,592
Tarrytown v (Westchester)	†MC-S	11	...	...	...–...–...–...	4.2	0.7	6–12–45–33	0	107–1,760
Tonawanda (Erie)	MC-S	18	8.5	0.8	205–139–12–102	8.3	0.7	49–42–58–67	96	185–1,639
Troy (Rensselaer)	*CM-C	56	23.4	2.6	169–134–59–57	25.8	2.7	82–93–24–21	308	630–1,434
Utica (Oneida)	MC-C	74	39.1	4.1	241–146–62–82	39.7	4.8	57–60–23–28	400	1,043–1,369
Valley Stream v (Nassau)	MC-S	35	...	0.0	...–...–...–...	9.4	0.0	2–13–35–45	0	191–1,584
Watertown (Jefferson)	*CM-I	27	...	...	...–...–...–...	28.0	3.1	64–94–31–54	0	403–1,497
Watervliet (Albany)	*CM-S	11	4.5	0.8	221–80–11–86	4.3	0.8	52–57–34–39	397	123–1,296
Westbury v (Nassau)	MC-S	14	...	0.0	...–...–...–...	2.1	0.0	1–0–5–45	0	...–...
White Plains (Westchester)	MC-S	46	103.1	2.7	188–397–315–1,342	56.2	1.7	218–147–62–77	966	805–1,955
Yonkers (Westchester)	*CM-S	192	203.3	8.2	326–438–217–77	170.1	0.2	4–4–13–22	0	4,147–2,335
NORTH CAROLINA										
Albemarle (Stanly)	*CM-I	15	5.1	11.7	97–86–3–158	4.8	12.3	52–42–33–102	502	244–1,148
Asheboro (Randolph)	*CM-S	15	6.1	1.9	152–189–11–47	4.4	2.8	52–49–39–27	660	210–1,041
Asheville (Buncombe)	*CM-C	53	28.0	16.3	221–157–17–132	27.0	14.1	77–62–32–34	242	881–1,248
Boone t (Watauga)	*CM-I	11	2.6	1.0	122–93–4–26	1.8	1.5	48–6–27–25	497	80–1,135
Burlington (Alamance)	*CM-C	37	17.9	5.8	190–138–11–140	15.4	5.4	58–43–18–64	245	504–1,274
Cary t (Wake)	*CM-S	24	10.9	1.2	107–180–11–157	8.5	8.1	23–22–14–62	783	206–1,396
Chapel Hill t (Orange)	*CM-S	32	14.3	0.6	211–171–6–54	10.1	3.6	54–36–22–27	242	371–1,520
Charlotte (Mecklenburg)	*CM-C	324	182.8	16.9	154–202–45–163	163.4	26.2	62–47–38–56	707	3,832–1,640
Concord (Cabarrus)	*CM-C	18	9.0	16.3	173–103–5–227	11.6	13.3	61–48–27–284	188	355–1,350
Durham (Durham)	*CM-C	101	44.9	6.8	139–142–9–153	44.1	8.4	98–21–36–65	398	1,236–1,502
Eden t (Rockingham)	*CM-I	16	4.6	1.9	131–130–3–26	4.1	1.9	54–21–39–29	510	180–1,196
Elizabeth City (Pasquotank)	*CM-I	14	3.7	11.4	141–71–7–42	4.2	11.0	53–47–21–34	277	232–1,072
Fayetteville (Cumberland)	*CM-C	62	26.0	73.3	186–103–10–123	23.4	70.7	70–50–28–63	344	1,078–1,295
Gastonia (Gaston)	*CM-C	48	12.2	30.6	129–83–6–35	15.0	26.0	50–33–26–26	97	756–1,213

Table 1/9 continued **PROFILES OF INDIVIDUAL CITIES**

City (county)	Form of govern-ment–Metro status	Est. 1982 popu-lation (000)	Fiscal year 1983 revenues: Total general revenue ($ mil-lions)	Total utility reve-nue ($ mil-lions)	Per capita revenues ($): Intergovernmental revenue–Property taxes–Other taxes–Charges and miscella-neous general revenue	Fiscal year 1983 expenditures: Total general expendi-tures ($ mil-lions)	Total utility expendi-tures ($ mil-lions)	Per capita current expenditures ($): Police–Fire–Streets–Sewers and sanitation	Long term debt ($ per capita)	October 1983 public personnel: Total full time equivalent employment–Average full time monthly salary ($)
NORTH CAROLINA continued										
Goldsboro (Wayne)	*CM-I	35	10.7	1.2	112–101–4–88	9.1	2.0	46–36–26–42	79	359–1,140
Greensboro (Guilford)	*CM-C	157	74.6	17.1	159–172–14–129	69.4	16.5	77–43–33–69	166	2,116–1,611
Greenville (Pitt)	*CM-I	37	15.5	45.8	190–105–7–120	13.6	47.9	42–38–23–47	562	686–1,321
Havelock t (Craven)	CM-I	19	2.2	0.4	53–27–2–35	1.8	0.3	20–5–12–20	59	...–...
Henderson (Vance)	*CM-I	16	5.7	1.4	125–106–5–121	5.7	1.5	50–36–38–66	231	201–1,059
Hickory (Catawba)	*CM-C	24	11.9	2.7	192–199–11–93	9.0	4.6	64–57–38–29	269	438–1,067
High Point (Guilford)	*CM-C	63	41.3	38.5	259–165–6–221	42.0	35.7	61–50–26–65	623	1,055–1,279
Jacksonville (Onslow)	*CM-C	24	7.9	1.0	112–126–8–84	6.7	0.8	66–44–22–47	138	303–1,107
Kinston (Lenoir)	*CM-I	25	7.5	19.9	107–89–10–94	9.6	15.7	63–50–16–47	205	451–1,262
Laurinburg (Scotland)	*CM-I	12	2.7	5.9	145–56–3–23	2.9	5.2	43–11–22–24	253	117–1,211
Lenoir (Caldwell)	*CM-I	14	5.5	3.6	159–210–5–31	5.2	3.0	58–68–27–15	505	261–1,086
Lexington (Davidson)	*CM-S	16	5.6	28.8	107–82–1–164	6.7	27.0	81–62–38–54	497	381–1,243
Lumberton (Robeson)	*CM-I	18	6.3	12.2	109–83–8–146	6.7	10.4	59–45–25–72	54	281–1,177
Monroe (Union)	*CM-S	15	7.7	20.8	187–118–4–195	7.3	19.8	99–0–44–82	461	240–1,166
Morganton (Burke)	*CM-I	15	6.3	12.1	114–114–6–185	7.0	10.9	85–30–46–77	337	265–1,269
New Bern (Craven)	*CM-I	15	4.7	15.5	105–70–8–124	5.8	13.0	50–33–36–69	58	273–1,078
Raleigh (Wake)	*CM-C	154	82.1	18.1	184–191–15–142	66.7	29.2	62–41–29–57	601	1,958–1,454
Reidsville (Rockingham)	*CM-I	12	5.9	2.9	185–153–2–134	5.4	2.8	77–42–42–91	352	...–...
Roanoke Rapids (Halifax)	*CM-I	15	4.3	0.0	149–114–9–18	4.3	0.0	50–40–41–31	0	...–...
Rocky Mount (Nash)	*CM-I	43	13.4	45.6	134–86–4–88	21.3	39.9	61–41–46–57	324	699–1,297
Salisbury (Rowan)	*CM-C	23	10.9	2.0	151–185–5–144	7.4	2.1	59–43–46–78	186	365–1,172
Sanford (Lee)	*CM-I	15	5.2	3.9	144–148–2–45	4.8	3.7	70–42–52–35	240	198–1,178
Shelby (Cleveland)	*CM-I	15	5.3	24.0	195–43–4–102	7.3	21.4	76–54–36–59	70	269–1,157
Statesville (Iredell)	*CM-I	19	6.9	17.8	151–165–4–50	8.1	14.9	71–62–43–32	383	362–1,173
Thomasville (Davidson)	*CM-S	14	5.2	1.2	153–187–2–21	4.9	1.1	55–55–34–33	178	197–1,111
Wilmington (New Hanover)	*CM-C	45	21.0	5.0	188–158–12–113	16.9	6.3	65–60–30–26	140	639–1,315
Wilson (Wilson)	*CM-I	35	16.1	43.3	125–105–6–231	13.1	44.1	48–45–32–69	208	555–1,245
Winston-Salem (Forsyth)	*CM-C	141	86.8	23.1	198–185–17–217	69.6	31.0	96–38–51–86	466	1,878–1,552
NORTH DAKOTA										
Bismarck (Burleigh)	CO-C	46	24.1	2.4	130–97–6–292	21.5	2.8	44–23–35–25	818	399–1,719
Dickinson (Stark)	CO-I	19	6.6	1.4	78–57–5–210	4.7	2.4	46–8–23–17	1,448	114–1,522
Fargo (Cass)	CO-C	63	36.8	2.5	99–65–25–398	37.6	2.2	54–35–37–20	1,452	480–1,873
Grand Forks (Grand Forks)	MC-C	44	26.0	2.9	245–68–19–257	27.7	2.8	45–36–26–42	1,059	382–1,659
Jamestown (Stutsman)	MC-I	16	5.4	0.7	91–74–6–162	3.2	0.6	38–11–24–28	499	94–1,412
Mandan (Morton)	CO-S	16	5.5	0.9	68–62–7–208	4.0	0.7	36–7–33–28	989	82–1,532
Minot (Ward)	*CM-I	33	13.8	2.1	87–78–14–235	15.4	2.3	49–31–52–45	796	300–1,676
West Fargo (Cass)	CO-S	11	3.0	0.5	50–48–4–166	2.1	0.3	36–7–25–37	1,021	40–1,674
Williston (Williams)	CO-I	17	7.1	0.9	135–78–25–189	12.3	1.6	57–16–61–36	1,581	144–1,726
OHIO										
Akron (Summit)	MC-C	232	89.9	16.7	170–47–20–150	97.9	21.1	77–0–4–60	0	2,605–1,738
Alliance (Stark)	MC-S	24	...	...	...–...–...–...	3.6	1.5	1–1–27–18	0	244–1,260
Amherst (Lorain)	MC-S	11	2.4	3.9	39–26–56–101	2.3	3.9	46–10–29–22	653	52–1,665
Ashland (Ashland)	MC-I	20	...	...	...–...–...–...	6.4	0.8	37–35–32–47	0	216–1,299
Ashtabula (Ashtabula)	MC-I	23	...	0.0	...–...–...–...	5.5	0.0	39–32–34–37	0	183–1,526
Athens (Athens)	MC-I	20	...	...	...–...–...–...	2.5	1.2	1–5–2–32	0	147–1,359
Avon Lake (Lorain)	MC-S	13	5.3	1.5	67–98–123–110	5.1	1.5	54–50–54–74	710	118–1,888
Barberton (Summit)	MC-S	29	...	0.0	...–...–...–...	8.3	0.1	52–51–0–45	0	230–1,776
Bay Village (Cuyahoga)	MC-S	18	...	0.0	...–...–...–...	...	0.0	...–...–...–...	0	...–...
Beavercreek v (Greene)	MC-S	33	...	0.0	...–...–...–...	0.2	0.0	1–0–0–0	0	...–...
Bedford (Cuyahoga)	*CM-S	15	...	...	...–...–...–...	5.7	0.6	70–39–46–46	0	147–1,813
Bedford Heights (Cuyahoga)	MC-S	13	...	0.0	...–...–...–...	7.9	0.0	104–70–48–90	0	154–2,026
Bellefontaine (Logan)	MC-I	12	3.6	0.5	50–16–97–133	3.8	0.8	54–38–43–52	34	100–1,441
Berea (Cuyahoga)	MC-S	19	...	0.0	...–...–...–...	0.3	0.0	1–1–0–0	0	...–...
Bexley (Franklin)	MC-S	13	...	...	...–...–...–...	3.2	0.4	52–24–17–51	0	79–1,652
Bowling Green (Wood)	MC-S	25	...	...	...–...–...–...	5.0	12.5	42–28–0–52	0	254–1,570
Brecksville (Cuyahoga)	MC-S	10	...	0.0	...–...–...–...	0.1	0.0	0–0–0–0	0	...–...
Broadview Heights (Cuyahoga)	MC-S	11	2.6	0.0	46–50–104–36	3.1	0.0	57–11–39–10	75	...–...
Brook Park (Cuyahoga)	MC-S	26	11.8	0.0	53–77–300–34	10.0	0.0	70–60–54–61	11	252–1,720
Brooklyn (Cuyahoga)	MC-S	12	6.0	0.0	50–73–305–69	4.5	0.0	89–76–41–42	16	119–1,759
Brunswick (Medina)	*CM-S	29	4.2	0.0	34–32–47–35	4.9	0.0	33–5–23–10	140	78–1,620
Bucyrus (Crawford)	MC-I	13	...	0.0	...–...–...–...	0.2	0.0	0–4–4–0	0	...–...
Cambridge (Guernsey)	MC-I	13	...	...	...–...–...–...	4.7	0.7	52–32–30–28	0	140–1,367
Campbell (Mahoning)	MC-S	11	2.5	0.5	86–18–99–21	2.5	0.4	37–25–16–32	26	81–1,329
Canton (Stark)	MC-C	91	...	...	...–...–...–...	26.5	4.9	2–61–8–21	0	1,080–1,660
Centerville (Montgomery)	*CM-S	19	3.7	0.0	31–34–101–25	3.9	0.0	34–0–24–16	103	67–1,689
Chillicothe (Ross)	MC-I	24	...	0.0	...–...–...–...	0.6	0.0	1–0–2–0	0	...–...
Cincinnati (Hamilton)	*CM-C	380	308.4	31.7	205–83–286–238	307.5	31.0	113–87–30–111	452	5,966–1,930
Circleville (Pickaway)	MC-S	12	3.9	0.6	67–24–110–128	3.3	0.4	42–33–25–47	9	249–1,214
Cleveland (Cuyahoga)	MC-C	559	370.3	91.4	196–78–279–109	335.2	91.3	148–75–29–36	651	8,777–1,834
Cleveland Heights (Cuyahoga)	*CM-S	56	25.2	3.8	100–75–189–88	26.6	1.7	67–44–27–82	46	489–1,753
Columbus (Franklin)	MC-C	571	290.8	55.2	128–22–174–186	305.9	100.6	93–52–21–61	954	6,198–1,745
Conneaut (Ashtabula)	MC-I	14	...	...	...–...–...–...	5.3	0.6	47–29–5–28	0	141–1,259
Coshocton (Coshocton)	MC-I	13	...	0.0	...–...–...–...	...	0.0	...–...–...–...	0	...–...
Cuyahoga Falls (Summit)	MC-S	43	...	...	...–...–...–...	10.2	14.6	57–48–0–26	0	446–1,901
Dayton (Montgomery)	*CM-C	188	123.5	16.8	161–65–249–181	144.4	10.7	80–61–35–48	403	2,877–1,809
Defiance (Defiance)	†MC-I	16	5.6	1.5	93–35–99–114	5.9	1.2	49–33–35–56	335	152–1,466
Delaware (Delaware)	*CM-S	19	5.8	1.2	44–23–109–122	5.8	1.1	51–44–27–49	174	160–1,705
Dover (Tuscarawas)	MC-I	12	...	...	...–...–...–...	1.8	3.8	1–1–28–41	0	122–1,613

Table 1/9 continued **PROFILES OF INDIVIDUAL CITIES**

City (county)	Form of govern-ment–Metro status	Est. 1982 popu-lation (000)	Fiscal year 1983 revenues: Total general revenue ($ millions)	Total utility revenue ($ millions)	Per capita revenues ($): Intergovernmental revenue–Property taxes–Other taxes–Charges and miscellaneous general revenue	Fiscal year 1983 expenditures: Total general expenditures ($ millions)	Total utility expenditures ($ millions)	Per capita current expenditures ($): Police–Fire–Streets–Sewers and sanitation	Long term debt ($ per capita)	October 1983 public personnel: Total full time equivalent employment–Average full time monthly salary ($)
OHIO continued										
East Cleveland (Cuyahoga)	*CM-S	37	11.0	1.2	60–42–101–97	11.1	1.4	60–39–21–77	24	302–1,729
East Liverpool (Columbiana)	MC-I	17	...	...	...–...–...–...	3.9	1.0	7–7–31–40	0	131–1,317
Eastlake (Lake)	MC-S	22	6.7	0.0	68–46–114–75	6.3	0.0	52–44–34–66	125	139–1,879
Elyria (Lorain)	MC-C	57	20.0	3.4	71–34–99–144	20.6	3.7	46–51–37–54	303	461–1,813
Englewood (Montgomery)	*CM-S	11	3.0	0.4	52–38–92–85	3.2	0.3	53–0–63–46	227	...–...
Euclid (Cuyahoga)	MC-S	58	29.7	0.0	87–121–191–112	27.5	0.0	74–57–30–89	220	657–1,661
Fairborn (Greene)	*CM-S	29	9.1	1.2	73–41–69–130	8.5	0.6	55–52–19–38	217	213–1,784
Fairfield (Butler)	*CM-S	32	...	...	...–...–...–...	6.7	1.3	35–7–33–36	0	178–1,735
Fairview Park (Cuyahoga)	MC-S	19	5.9	0.0	60–88–88–81	6.9	0.0	60–54–25–132	28	...–...
Findlay (Hancock)	MC-I	36	11.2	2.5	47–24–141–97	11.8	2.4	57–43–29–20	132	303–1,649
Forest Park (Hamilton)	*CM-S	19	2.8	0.0	47–36–56–12	2.9	0.0	38–8–35–0	62	50–1,881
Fostoria (Seneca)	MC-S	16	...	...	...–...–...–...	0.5	0.8	0–0–0–0	0	...–...
Franklin (Warren)	*CM-S	11	...	...	...–...–...–...	2.8	0.3	43–14–20–92	0	53–1,583
Fremont (Sandusky)	MC-I	18	...	0.0	...–...–...–...	0.3	0.0	1–0–4–0	0	...–...
Gahanna (Franklin)	MC-S	19	...	0.0	...–...–...–...	0.1	0.0	0–0–2–0	0	...–...
Galion (Crawford)	MC-I	12	...	...	...–...–...–...	4.0	6.0	66–46–35–44	0	119–1,648
Garfield Heights (Cuyahoga)	MC-S	34	9.5	0.0	50–65–62–100	8.6	0.0	47–36–23–21	724	217–1,735
Girard (Trumbull)	MC-S	13	...	...	...–...–...–...	3.0	0.6	38–30–15–31	0	116–1,609
Greenville (Darke)	MC-I	13	4.7	1.1	66–56–129–118	5.0	1.0	45–42–23–65	313	...–...
Grove City (Franklin)	MC-S	17	3.2	0.2	63–22–59–41	3.1	0.2	55–0–17–12	111	...–...
Hamilton (Butler)	*CM-C	64	26.6	44.2	112–29–137–138	23.2	47.1	68–56–12–73	728	703–1,887
Ironton (Lawrence)	MC-S	14	5.0	0.6	102–23–109–128	3.1	0.6	42–31–19–42	64	...–...
Kent (Portage)	*CM-S	28	8.9	1.5	82–25–112–104	8.1	1.6	55–35–32–35	272	129–2,034
Kettering (Montgomery)	*CM-S	60	19.6	0.0	55–55–169–46	17.7	0.0	58–27–29–0	6	381–2,015
Lakewood (Cuyahoga)	MC-S	61	64.2	2.0	99–87–114–753	59.6	2.3	42–28–19–53	0	1,796–1,612
Lancaster (Fairfield)	MC-S	35	10.7	11.7	77–23–99–104	10.9	11.2	48–51–29–35	46	374–1,508
Lima (Allen)	MC-C	47	12.7	3.0	98–18–6–149	18.2	3.9	53–46–23–63	981	425–1,599
Lorain (Lorain)	MC-C	75	16.8	3.5	69–45–7–104	23.0	3.0	29–28–8–38	156	620–1,730
Lyndhurst (Cuyahoga)	MC-S	17	4.7	0.0	47–75–101–49	4.7	0.0	67–44–23–26	33	122–1,753
Mansfield (Richland)	MC-C	53	19.5	2.8	101–28–110–129	18.9	1.9	49–47–29–33	173	478–1,599
Maple Heights (Cuyahoga)	MC-S	29	9.1	2.0	64–98–122–31	8.7	1.7	59–46–26–36	205	247–1,991
Marietta (Washington)	MC-C	17	...	...	...–...–...–...	3.8	0.2	41–39–7–26	0	210–1,177
Marion (Marion)	MC-I	37	34.5	0.0	72–31–100–736	34.6	0.1	50–54–30–70	90	909–1,288
Massillon (Stark)	MC-S	31	...	0.0	...–...–...–...	10.4	0.0	43–36–23–68	0	224–1,572
Maumee (Lucas)	MC-S	16	8.8	0.8	90–52–187–222	9.7	0.6	83–12–73–75	1,401	122–1,917
Mayfield Heights (Cuyahoga)	MC-S	21	5.0	0.0	50–73–88–31	5.5	0.0	69–42–29–31	47	...–...
Medina (Medina)	MC-S	16	...	...	...–...–...–...	3.5	1.2	53–6–22–31	0	113–1,585
Mentor (Lake)	*CM-S	43	15.7	0.0	57–45–138–127	17.9	0.0	59–40–39–6	228	284–1,829
Miamisburg (Montgomery)	*CM-S	16	7.0	0.6	76–25–233–107	6.5	0.9	82–52–44–45	376	150–1,819
Middleburg Heights (Cuyahoga)	MC-S	16	5.7	0.0	42–79–161–81	5.3	0.0	79–37–18–47	239	88–1,942
Middletown (Butler)	*CM-C	44	...	...	...–...–...–...	29.0	4.6	21–4–30–72	0	541–1,826
Montgomery (Hamilton)	MC-S	11	2.0	0.0	21–41–109–21	1.6	0.0	52–1–15–11	153	...–...
Mount Vernon (Knox)	MC-I	15	5.6	0.8	51–33–116–183	5.1	0.6	45–34–24–36	91	...–...
New Philadelphia (Tuscarawas)	MC-I	17	...	0.0	...–...–...–...	0.3	0.0	1–1–6–0	0	...–...
Newark (Licking)	MC-C	42	12.1	2.5	62–23–114–89	11.6	2.1	42–47–40–25	126	342–1,498
Niles (Trumbull)	MC-S	23	...	...	...–...–...–...	4.5	11.7	38–33–23–26	0	216–1,534
North Canton (Stark)	MC-S	15	...	...	...–...–...–...	3.9	1.4	42–3–28–54	0	102–1,476
North College Hill (Hamilton)	MC-S	11	1.6	0.0	34–24–62–21	1.4	0.0	45–7–23–9	0	...–...
North Olmsted (Cuyahoga)	MC-S	36	...	...	...–...–...–...	8.6	4.0	3–3–30–62	0	308–1,816
North Ridgeville (Lorain)	MC-S	22	...	...	...–...–...–...	4.4	0.9	37–27–22–29	0	97–1,436
North Royalton (Cuyahoga)	MC-S	18	4.3	0.0	37–60–84–54	4.1	0.0	44–23–15–25	264	...–...
Norton (Summit)	MC-S	12	...	0.0	...–...–...–...	1.7	0.0	50–15–12–0	0	42–1,817
Norwalk (Huron)	MC-I	14	4.8	0.6	67–44–72–152	4.9	0.5	50–30–30–54	131	119–1,419
Norwood (Hamilton)	MC-S	26	11.1	0.9	76–35–260–58	10.7	1.1	64–76–19–57	72	225–1,654
Oregon (Lucas)	MC-S	19	7.1	0.6	51–64–179–88	6.5	1.9	90–34–36–57	146	163–2,125
Oxford (Butler)	*CM-S	17	...	...	...–...–...–...	2.7	0.4	42–3–14–32	0	82–1,789
Painesville (Lake)	*CM-S	17	8.2	8.6	72–18–143–254	6.6	8.4	60–41–21–82	650	254–1,789
Parma (Cuyahoga)	MC-S	91	20.9	0.0	41–35–132–23	20.3	0.0	36–35–24–18	287	545–1,754
Parma Heights (Cuyahoga)	MC-S	23	6.0	0.0	53–74–94–42	5.7	0.0	54–34–25–18	228	129–1,758
Perrysburg (Wood)	MC-S	11	4.2	0.7	48–70–175–101	3.6	0.8	63–21–33–66	66	96–1,767
Piqua (Miami)	*CM-S	20	...	...	...–...–...–...	9.5	12.2	18–37–34–48	0	213–1,740
Portsmouth (Scioto)	*CM-I	25	...	...	...–...–...–...	6.8	1.5	12–12–27–38	0	245–1,550
Ravenna (Portage)	MC-S	12	6.0	0.9	75–17–167–239	3.9	5.3	58–49–35–55	615	113–1,722
Reading (Hamilton)	MC-S	12	4.8	0.5	79–34–166–107	4.7	0.7	74–50–20–54	301	81–1,821
Reynoldsburg (Franklin)	MC-S	22	3.2	0.7	37–11–50–52	3.0	0.8	54–0–11–24	97	69–1,761
Richmond Heights (Cuyahoga)	MC-S	10	2.6	0.0	40–79–120–19	2.5	0.0	70–36–29–14	62	...–...
Rocky River (Cuyahoga)	MC-S	21	15.9	0.0	380–75–173–144	9.7	0.0	65–51–50–71	49	184–1,727
Salem (Columbiana)	MC-I	13	...	0.0	...–...–...–...	0.2	0.0	0–0–6–0	0	...–...
Sandusky (Erie)	*CM-I	31	10.4	1.8	53–30–137–113	10.0	1.8	51–54–20–39	107	249–1,670
Seven Hills (Cuyahoga)	MC-S	13	3.4	0.0	32–33–109–77	2.4	0.0	31–7–14–32	61	...–...
Shaker Heights (Cuyahoga)	MC-S	32	18.9	0.0	68–135–291–102	16.8	0.0	104–83–41–51	111	361–1,841
Sharonville (Hamilton)	MC-S	10	6.4	0.0	62–78–378–101	5.0	0.0	112–25–42–16	136	76–2,060
Sheffield Lake (Lorain)	MC-S	10	1.9	0.3	39–46–31–67	1.7	0.3	32–28–17–40	65	44–1,544
Sidney (Shelby)	*CM-I	18	...	...	...–...–...–...	5.3	0.6	60–45–37–58	0	154–1,725
Solon (Cuyahoga)	MC-S	15	14.4	0.0	74–130–340–416	12.7	0.0	88–67–111–138	640	194–2,024
South Euclid (Cuyahoga)	MC-S	25	...	0.0	...–...–...–...	7.2	0.0	52–39–19–34	0	139–1,549
Springdale (Hamilton)	†MC-S	10	5.9	0.0	60–79–319–107	4.2	0.0	94–21–37–10	727	71–2,017
Springfield (Clark)	*CM-C	71	16.0	3.1	112–13–12–87	26.6	2.5	59–57–23–27	238	652–1,717
Steubenville (Jefferson)	MC-C	26	10.7	1.3	107–49–131–133	9.5	1.7	51–51–32–44	552	248–1,364

Table 1/9 continued **PROFILES OF INDIVIDUAL CITIES**

City (county)	Form of government–Metro status	Est. 1982 population (000)	Fiscal year 1983 revenues: Total general revenue ($ millions)	Total utility revenue ($ millions)	Per capita revenues ($): Intergovernmental revenue–Property taxes–Other taxes–Charges and miscellaneous general revenue	Fiscal year 1983 expenditures: Total general expenditures ($ millions)	Total utility expenditures ($ millions)	Per capita current expenditures ($): Police–Fire–Streets–Sewers and sanitation	Long term debt ($ per capita)	October 1983 public personnel: Total full time equivalent employment–Average full time monthly salary ($)
OHIO continued										
Stow (Summit)	MC-S	26	...	0.0	...–...–...–...	4.4	0.0	41–25–30–0	0	135–1,990
Strongsville (Cuyahoga)	MC-S	30	10.1	0.0	35–96–105–102	10.6	0.0	51–39–50–76	174	155–1,934
Struthers (Mahoning)	MC-S	13	2.5	0.0	59–19–77–34	2.4	0.0	42–22–14–29	29	53–1,446
Sylvania (Lucas)	MC-S	16	...	...	...–...–...–...	5.3	0.8	59–1–33–82	0	78–1,749
Tallmadge (Summit)	MC-S	15	...	...	...–...–...–...	4.2	0.4	53–17–1–37	0	91–1,786
Tiffin (Seneca)	MC-I	19	...	0.0	...–...–...–...	0.2	0.0	0–0–0–0	0	...–...
Toledo (Lucas)	*CM-C	351	161.2	15.4	122–28–183–127	160.2	13.1	70–50–37–69	257	2,903–1,977
Troy (Miami)	†MC-S	19	9.8	1.3	58–34–121–294	8.7	0.8	50–45–42–64	68	198–1,635
University Heights (Cuyahoga)	MC-S	15	4.8	0.0	47–71–155–41	4.4	0.0	77–62–24–24	87	...–...
Upper Arlington (Franklin)	*CM-S	35	...	...	...–...–...–...	10.7	0.7	39–55–27–23	0	221–1,846
Urbana (Champaign)	†MC-S	11	...	0.0	...–...–...–...	0.1	0.0	7–7–0–0	0	...–...
Van Wert (Van Wert)	MC-S	11	...	0.0	...–...–...–...	0.2	0.0	0–0–0–4	0	...–...
Vandalia (Montgomery)	*CM-S	13	4.3	0.7	50–55–120–108	4.3	0.7	68–12–21–39	145	91–1,647
Vermilion (Erie)	MC-S	11	2.8	0.5	33–74–40–106	2.6	0.4	68–7–34–75	137	...–...
Wadsworth (Medina)	MC-S	15	5.6	8.9	43–22–93–211	5.3	8.5	53–6–42–58	113	131–1,406
Warren (Trumbull)	MC-C	56	11.6	3.4	100–22–10–76	17.1	3.3	47–41–29–47	135	518–1,891
Warrensville Heights (Cuyahoga)	MC-S	16	...	0.0	...–...–...–...	0.1	0.0	8–0–0–0	0	...–...
Washington (Fayette)	*CM-I	13	9.0	0.0	506–34–42–121	13.0	0.0	42–33–22–43	11	...–...
West Carrollton (Montgomery)	*CM-S	13	4.3	0.4	59–26–169–65	4.0	0.3	57–16–25–27	22	87–1,715
Westerville (Franklin)	*CM-S	24	...	...	...–...–...–...	6.5	11.6	40–25–15–48	0	174–1,800
Westlake (Cuyahoga)	MC-S	20	12.6	0.0	55–121–109–341	13.3	0.0	60–45–44–48	1,654	141–1,824
Whitehall (Franklin)	MC-S	22	...	0.0	...–...–...–...	2.1	0.0	1–37–1–12	0	123–1,715
Wickliffe (Lake)	MC-S	16	6.3	0.0	73–113–140–59	5.3	0.0	66–52–26–83	520	104–1,843
Willoughby (Lake)	MC-S	20	11.6	0.0	84–70–203–234	12.4	0.0	97–57–73–116	258	206–1,869
Willowick (Lake)	MC-S	17	5.0	0.0	66–92–56–72	3.9	0.0	53–25–11–52	172	87–1,604
Wilmington (Clinton)	MC-I	11	...	0.0	...–...–...–...	...	0.0	...–...–...–...	0	...–...
Wooster (Wayne)	MC-I	20	10.4	1.3	105–43–172–208	9.2	0.9	73–49–33–48	63	203–1,687
Worthington (Franklin)	*CM-S	16	...	0.0	...–...–...–...	0.1	0.0	0–0–0–0	0	...–...
Xenia (Greene)	*CM-S	25	...	...	...–...–...–...	13.3	3.5	56–40–19–54	0	187–1,637
Youngstown (Mahoning)	MC-C	111	50.3	6.9	170–31–189–61	44.3	6.8	75–56–31–30	357	1,086–1,522
Zanesville (Muskingum)	MC-I	29	10.1	1.4	81–17–157–96	9.9	1.7	62–34–27–54	170	306–1,395
OKLAHOMA										
Ada (Pontotoc)	*CM-I	17	6.9	1.3	38–4–266–109	4.7	1.0	51–38–38–40	62	190–1,295
Altus (Jackson)	MC-I	23	6.6	9.2	31–10–155–89	9.1	7.1	45–22–12–23	240	228–1,248
Ardmore (Carter)	*CM-I	25	8.6	1.5	37–9–221–80	8.8	1.3	28–25–21–44	644	285–1,161
Bartlesville (Washington)	*CM-S	37	18.8	2.2	104–44–238–118	17.8	4.7	42–46–25–57	275	389–1,533
Bethany (Oklahoma)	*CM-S	22	9.1	0.8	24–27–98–261	9.2	1.0	33–28–14–48	217	297–1,487
Broken Arrow (Tulsa)	*CM-S	42	...	...	...–...–...–...	5.6	2.3	21–25–10–18	0	285–1,430
Chickasha (Grady)	*CM-I	17	6.2	0.9	49–13–164–138	5.5	1.2	46–42–15–27	454	210–999
Claremore (Rogers)	MC-S	13	11.0	7.7	51–0–176–605	10.4	6.4	37–27–84–37	137	363–1,234
Del City (Oklahoma)	*CM-S	29	5.1	1.2	16–9–94–60	5.4	1.0	30–25–12–45	151	196–1,506
Duncan (Stephens)	*CM-I	24	9.1	8.1	43–4–167–161	7.2	10.1	44–26–17–31	307	235–1,454
Durant (Bryan)	*CM-I	12	4.9	0.7	61–2–221–113	3.9	1.1	44–37–32–35	707	...–...
Edmond (Oklahoma)	*CM-S	40	13.8	16.1	16–25–146–160	12.5	15.7	47–36–24–38	279	473–1,430
El Reno (Canadian)	*CM-S	17	7.1	0.9	65–7–151–192	6.1	1.1	31–24–13–33	203	318–1,124
Enid (Garfield)	*CM-C	54	20.3	2.6	35–0–232–105	19.8	9.4	41–39–36–51	0	563–1,512
Guthrie (Logan)	*CM-I	11	4.0	0.6	61–3–179–134	2.9	1.1	44–32–16–34	193	128–1,199
Lawton (Comanche)	*CM-C	86	26.9	4.6	65–10–141–97	26.7	2.3	53–41–21–43	154	744–1,649
Mc Alester (Pittsburg)	*CM-I	18	6.8	0.9	71–15–218–83	5.7	0.9	37–43–20–23	295	204–1,195
Miami (Ottawa)	CO-I	14	3.4	6.4	31–3–138–70	4.4	5.9	51–43–49–38	27	184–1,343
Midwest City (Oklahoma)	*CM-S	53	34.9	2.0	32–18–147–464	31.9	1.7	53–44–11–38	280	1,082–1,595
Moore (Cleveland)	*CM-S	39	7.9	1.6	19–22–97–67	6.2	4.1	37–28–12–36	329	401–1,326
Muskogee (Muskogee)	*CM-I	41	40.4	2.5	42–15–221–718	38.5	6.0	49–45–33–59	552	469–1,376
Norman (Cleveland)	*CM-S	73	61.8	3.5	34–27–207–577	53.2	6.8	42–33–14–34	440	1,408–1,673
Oklahoma City (Oklahoma)	*CM-C	428	232.7	19.8	89–51–230–174	182.5	31.5	55–45–20–27	803	4,512–1,625
Okmulgee (Okmulgee)	*CM-I	17	5.1	1.7	63–3–156–85	5.0	1.7	40–33–29–43	201	169–1,192
Ponca City (Kay)	*CM-I	28	10.7	14.5	68–15–141–160	10.7	10.6	56–51–28–57	58	423–1,425
Sand Springs (Tulsa)	*CM-S	14	5.2	0.0	33–4–235–96	5.2	0.0	46–42–17–25	0	186–1,194
Sapulpa (Creek)	*CM-S	17	4.7	1.1	55–1–136–86	4.7	0.6	35–41–29–38	88	165–1,260
Shawnee (Pottawatomie)	*CM-S	28	10.8	1.7	56–3–220–114	8.1	2.7	61–41–24–40	197	266–1,346
Stillwater (Payne)	*CM-I	39	23.7	15.1	69–16–169–345	14.1	16.3	32–27–19–46	385	398–1,426
The Village (Oklahoma)	*CM-S	12	2.6	0.0	13–0–143–63	2.6	0.0	48–34–11–48	0	...–...
Tulsa (Tulsa)	CO-C	375	202.4	23.3	84–25–289–141	174.0	42.9	59–52–24–25	466	4,149–1,182
Woodward (Woodward)	*CM-I	16	6.7	0.6	40–2–304–65	4.3	0.7	36–28–26–36	0	160–1,486
Yukon (Canadian)	*CM-S	20	4.6	0.9	26–19–140–46	3.5	1.1	26–23–15–19	141	137–1,361
OREGON										
Albany (Linn)	*CM-I	28	11.8	...	134–129–30–122	11.2	0.3	49–55–30–43	236	213–1,751
Ashland (Jackson)	†MC-S	15	10.9	5.1	126–42–118–437	10.2	6.3	66–48–26–37	220	285–1,644
Beaverton (Washington)	MC-S	33	23.7	2.7	108–338–70–196	23.3	1.9	60–74–33–49	1,264	256–2,083
Bend (Deschutes)	*CM-I	17	7.6	1.1	117–105–56–163	7.2	1.8	80–81–19–45	938	...–...
Coos Bay (Coos)	*CM-I	15	4.6	1.7	92–90–32–85	4.2	1.6	74–28–23–40	338	99–1,634
Corvallis (Benton)	*CM-I	41	18.7	1.8	90–93–43–227	16.9	2.5	49–39–34–43	569	315–1,924
Eugene (Lane)	*CM-C	104	65.5	97.4	129–187–23–294	67.0	81.7	78–67–26–43	2,304	1,464–2,140
Forest Grove (Washington)	*CM-S	12	6.6	3.5	299–97–13–156	3.6	3.5	56–34–9–6	661	101–1,913
Grants Pass (Josephine)	*CM-I	15	7.0	1.4	145–79–60–175	6.7	6.6	81–51–32–48	1,018	122–1,823
Gresham (Multnomah)	*CM-S	35	12.2	1.5	65–105–42–138	10.6	1.6	63–42–18–45	323	180–1,991
Hillsboro (Washington)	*CM-S	29	9.7	1.9	102–78–49–103	6.9	2.4	50–39–22–44	494	157–1,781
Klamath Falls (Klamath)	*CM-I	17	8.8	1.3	270–98–36–105	9.3	1.3	63–55–21–23	521	258–1,569
La Grande (Union)	*CM-I	12	3.8	0.6	72–103–35–107	3.6	0.5	54–37–20–29	176	96–1,432

Table 1/9 continued — PROFILES OF INDIVIDUAL CITIES

City (county)	Form of govern-ment–Metro status	Est. 1982 popu-lation (000)	Fiscal year 1983 revenues: Total general revenue ($ mil-lions)	Total utility reve-nue ($ mil-lions)	Per capita revenues ($): Intergovernmental revenue–Property taxes–Other taxes–Charges and miscella-neous general revenue	Fiscal year 1983 expenditures: Total general expendi-tures ($ mil-lions)	Total utility expendi-tures ($ mil-lions)	Per capita current expenditures ($): Police–Fire–Streets–Sewers and sanitation	Long term debt ($ per capita)	October 1983 public personnel: Total full time equivalent employment–Average full time monthly salary ($)
OREGON continued										
Lake Oswego (Clackamas)	*CM-S	23	10.1	2.1	88–178–53–121	12.4	1.9	61–74–9–49	601	212–1,807
Lebanon (Linn)	*CM-I	11	3.8	0.0	100–110–26–121	3.7	0.0	56–40–34–38	176	...–...
Mc Minnville (Yamhill)	†MC-I	15	5.1	8.2	78–99–48–122	4.2	8.1	46–24–16–22	350	158–1,772
Medford (Jackson)	*CM-C	40	15.7	2.0	92–118–53–125	15.6	1.8	74–69–34–35	252	336–2,693
Milwaukie (Clackamas)	*CM-S	18	5.7	0.7	73–122–32–90	5.8	0.4	71–67–25–52	181	117–1,850
Newberg (Yamhill)	†MC-I	11	11.5	0.3	79–147–34–787	9.0	0.9	73–22–19–42	760	248–1,454
Oregon City (Clackamas)	*CM-S	15	...	...	...–...–...–...	5.3	0.8	79–78–47–5	0	138–1,882
Pendleton (Umatilla)	*CM-I	15	5.6	0.8	130–98–41–115	5.6	0.6	56–55–26–26	131	130–1,589
Portland (Multnomah)	CO-C	367	230.4	28.1	152–199–72–205	215.6	52.2	108–68–42–53	1,234	4,073–2,233
Roseburg (Douglas)	*CM-I	16	6.5	1.9	98–154–42–108	5.4	1.8	69–62–57–28	654	150–1,656
Salem (Marion)	*CM-C	90	52.2	3.9	152–189–38–199	56.9	4.9	76–56–30–53	748	971–2,454
Springfield (Lane)	*CM-C	41	14.6	19.5	100–108–15–131	14.1	22.1	62–44–32–19	1,001	414–1,971
The Dalles (Wasco)	*CM-I	11	4.1	1.0	79–118–54–123	3.4	1.9	54–35–33–43	397	96–1,774
Tigard (Washington)	*CM-S	18	5.5	0.0	84–38–47–140	6.3	0.0	55–0–13–48	161	77–1,814
West Linn (Clackamas)	*CM-S	12	3.2	0.6	73–114–28–43	2.7	0.5	54–19–30–10	151	48–1,929
Woodburn (Marion)	*CM-S	11	3.8	0.5	100–117–29–96	4.1	0.5	76–39–23–36	458	119–1,494
PENNSYLVANIA										
Abington tp (Montgomery)	†CO-S	59	14.6	0.0	49–98–32–69	16.9	0.0	48–9–25–61	240	299–1,644
Aliquippa b (Beaver)	MC-S	17	2.8	0.0	35–90–29–16	3.0	0.0	33–16–47–15	138	83–1,594
Allentown (Lehigh)	†MC-C	104	38.9	3.6	99–105–68–100	34.5	3.7	47–33–30–48	104	901–1,754
Altoona (Blair)	MC-C	56	13.8	0.0	82–80–40–45	12.9	0.0	40–34–29–19	0	513–1,173
Aston tp (Delaware)	†MC-S	15	1.8	0.0	30–57–16–21	1.7	0.0	49–5–19–12	14	40–1,935
Baldwin b (Allegheny)	CM-S	24	4.2	0.0	24–71–37–39	4.1	0.0	31–5–23–39	4	63–1,614
Beaver Falls (Beaver)	MC-S	12	2.2	0.0	29–48–41–62	2.3	0.0	44–25–38–37	7	65–1,453
Bellevue b (Allegheny)	MC-S	10	2.0	0.0	26–83–65–27	2.1	0.0	55–10–45–12	0	...–...
Bensalem tp (Bucks)	*CM-S	54	6.6	0.0	19–66–20–15	7.2	0.0	64–8–17–0	98	142–1,952
Berwick b (Columbia)	CM-I	12	1.5	0.0	30–31–33–40	1.4	0.0	31–3–22–21	17	...–...
Bethel Park (Allegheny)	*CM-S	35	6.8	0.0	26–45–75–49	6.4	0.0	34–3–29–36	25	130–1,678
Bethlehem (Northampton)	†MC-C	70	22.0	3.3	74–105–50–85	23.9	2.4	53–35–32–19	205	654–1,705
Bethlehem tp (Northampton)	MC-S	12	2.1	0.0	34–30–47–62	2.4	0.0	28–5–30–18	96	30–1,910
Bloomsburg t (Columbia)	MC-I	12	1.7	0.0	43–37–37–26	1.5	0.0	27–4–29–0	113	34–1,464
Bradford (Mc Kean)	*CM-I	11	3.7	0.7	65–71–56–148	4.2	0.5	43–39–46–89	21	133–1,281
Brentwood b (Allegheny)	MC-S	11	2.1	0.0	25–95–42–24	2.1	0.0	43–6–27–36	20	...–...
Bristol b (Bucks)	†MC-S	11	1.7	0.0	29–76–10–45	1.7	0.0	41–12–33–25	11	55–1,641
Bristol tp (Bucks)	*CM-S	59	8.4	0.0	39–66–6–30	8.7	0.0	40–8–14–19	4	147–1,694
Butler (Butler)	MC-I	17	3.3	0.0	47–71–54–22	3.4	0.0	45–42–34–0	6	92–1,838
Canonsburg b (Washington)	*CM-S	10	2.5	0.0	50–54–40–101	3.7	0.0	43–7–21–192	20	39–1,533
Carbondale (Lackawanna)	†MC-S	11	1.2	0.0	27–44–32–4	1.2	0.0	23–13–17–18	20	49–1,350
Carlisle b (Cumberland)	*CM-S	19	4.3	1.0	56–51–42–81	4.2	1.0	34–14–30–49	55	107–1,434
Carnegie b (Allegheny)	MC-S	10	1.8	0.0	30–75–41–31	1.7	0.0	46–13–39–10	27	...–...
Castle Shannon b (Allegheny)	MC-S	10	1.5	0.0	22–75–38–19	1.5	0.0	42–4–40–20	11	...–...
Chambersburg b (Franklin)	*CM-I	16	6.5	12.6	111–62–43–178	5.9	12.2	60–24–27–106	150	172–1,657
Cheltenham tp (Montgomery)	†MC-S	35	8.7	0.0	22–122–23–78	8.9	0.0	68–11–23–45	169	201–1,843
Chester (Delaware)	MC-S	45	16.3	0.0	62–106–124–70	17.7	0.0	68–38–36–19	128	368–1,524
Clairton (Allegheny)	MC-S	12	5.1	0.0	237–125–38–15	5.0	0.0	46–29–40–19	50	...–...
Coatesville (Chester)	†MC-S	11	3.1	0.0	31–138–51–62	2.7	0.0	64–21–24–54	14	63–1,524
Columbia b (Lancaster)	*CM-S	11	1.1	0.0	23–33–32–10	1.1	0.0	38–5–19–6	6	30–1,428
Connellsville (Fayette)	MC-I	10	1.7	0.0	53–52–41–25	1.7	0.0	37–26–25–0	44	53–1,318
Cumru tp (Berks)	†CO-S	12	2.3	0.0	40–33–67–53	2.2	0.0	37–3–28–28	4	33–1,683
Darby b (Delaware)	†MC-S	11	1.8	0.0	21–68–12–59	1.7	0.0	50–7–18–33	28	36–1,486
Darby tp (Delaware)	CO-S	12	1.7	0.0	26–45–13–55	1.9	0.0	37–1–14–22	31	...–...
Derry tp (Dauphin)	*CM-S	18	3.2	0.0	23–25–97–38	3.3	0.0	37–4–28–9	38	68–1,680
Dormont b (Allegheny)	†MC-S	11	2.5	0.0	43–96–35–52	2.3	0.0	40–12–31–21	19	...–...
Doylestown tp (Bucks)	†MC-S	12	0.9	0.0	17–42–14–5	0.9	0.0	29–5–11–0	5	...–...
Dunmore b (Lackawanna)	MC-S	17	1.9	0.0	30–52–28–7	2.2	0.0	32–32–16–12	28	85–1,396
Duquesne (Allegheny)	MC-S	10	2.9	0.7	106–100–32–51	3.4	0.4	60–40–43–40	82	...–...
East Norriton tp (Montgomery)	†MC-S	13	2.6	0.0	27–12–83–79	3.0	0.0	41–13–21–47	44	...–...
East Pennsboro tp (Cumberland)	CO-S	14	3.4	0.0	42–21–44–139	4.5	0.0	36–3–38–79	437	60–1,594
Easton (Northampton)	MC-C	26	7.7	2.1	63–78–46–110	8.6	2.8	47–33–27–43	477	270–1,501
Emmaus b (Lehigh)	MC-S	11	2.4	0.3	13–75–55–71	2.3	0.4	42–13–38–28	235	62–1,577
Ephrata b (Lancaster)	†MC-S	11	2.4	4.6	16–16–41–141	3.0	4.0	45–2–24–58	0	69–1,450
Erie (Erie)	MC-C	118	46.7	6.0	136–128–37–93	37.8	5.3	56–48–37–68	181	1,049–1,644
Exeter tp (Berks)	MC-S	15	2.5	0.0	27–12–49–79	2.2	0.0	20–5–27–23	0	33–1,665
Fairview tp (York)	*CM-S	12	1.5	0.0	24–11–49–39	1.5	0.0	28–5–29–25	0	27–1,777
Falls tp (Bucks)	*CM-S	36	4.4	0.0	21–67–18–14	4.1	0.0	37–9–21–14	0	87–1,747
Greensburg (Westmoreland)	MC-S	17	4.2	0.0	33–99–46–64	3.6	0.0	46–9–29–3	53	53–1,566
Hampden tp (Cumberland)	†MC-S	18	4.1	0.0	38–12–61–115	4.2	0.0	22–6–20–35	37	70–1,573
Hampton tp (Allegheny)	†MC-S	15	3.9	0.0	23–53–54–134	4.0	0.0	46–9–41–29	14	...–...
Hanover b (York)	*CM-S	15	3.6	1.4	36–45–49–116	3.6	1.4	35–25–23–60	294	116–1,163
Harrisburg (Dauphin)	MC-C	53	32.6	2.3	188–114–57–261	36.0	1.1	85–42–37–202	803	716–1,604
Harrison tp (Allegheny)	CO-S	13	2.2	0.0	27–80–41–25	2.1	0.0	43–5–35–19	148	33–1,811
Hatfield tp (Montgomery)	†CO-S	14	1.9	0.0	35–47–23–27	2.0	0.0	49–6–18–4	31	40–1,619
Haverford tp (Delaware)	†CO-S	52	10.1	0.0	21–88–15–71	10.0	0.0	61–5–27–38	79	197–1,578
Hazleton (Luzerne)	MC-C	27	5.8	0.0	92–46–37–42	5.8	0.0	24–23–31–7	38	136–1,257
Hempfield tp (Westmoreland)	CO-S	44	3.6	0.0	19–10–41–12	3.5	0.0	0–3–27–1	19	47–1,591
Hermitage (Mercer)	*CM-S	17	3.5	0.0	41–28–82–52	3.4	0.0	44–6–42–29	16	73–1,677
Hopewell tp (Beaver)	†CO-S	14	2.2	0.0	23–33–48–48	2.3	0.0	25–4–46–29	20	45–1,505
Horsham tp (Montgomery)	*CM-S	17	2.3	0.0	23–71–27–16	2.2	0.0	49–9–20–0	31	56–1,773
Indiana b (Indiana)	†MC-I	16	2.5	0.0	34–44–26–52	2.5	0.0	41–3–15–20	13	...–...

Table 1/9 continued **PROFILES OF INDIVIDUAL CITIES**

City (county)	Form of govern-ment–Metro status	Est. 1982 popu-lation (000)	Fiscal year 1983 revenues: Total general revenue ($ mil-lions)	Total utility reve-nue ($ mil-lions)	Per capita revenues ($): Intergovernmental revenue–Property taxes–Other taxes–Charges and miscella-neous general revenue	Fiscal year 1983 expenditures: Total general expendi-tures ($ mil-lions)	Total utility expendi-tures ($ mil-lions)	Per capita current expenditures ($): Police–Fire–Streets–Sewers and sanitation	Long term debt ($ per capita)	October 1983 public personnel: Total full time equivalent employment–Average full time monthly salary ($)
PENNSYLVANIA continued										
Jeannette (Westmoreland)	MC-S	13	3.5	0.0	69–79–36–87	3.3	0.0	37–11–31–55	83	63–1,550
Johnstown (Cambria)	MC-C	34	13.5	0.0	154–102–41–100	12.0	0.0	42–38–42–39	63	322–1,578
Kingston b (Luzerne)	†MC-S	16	3.9	0.0	117–46–69–19	4.4	0.0	33–21–14–13	12	73–1,337
Lancaster (Lancaster)	MC-C	56	16.3	4.5	74–95–42–83	17.6	3.6	54–43–25–43	37	573–1,512
Lancaster tp (Lancaster)	MC-S	11	0.9	0.0	16–7–49–7	0.8	0.0	20–2–14–0	0	...–...
Lansdale b (Montgomery)	*CM-S	17	3.7	8.0	38–48–12–121	5.7	6.9	53–5–31–78	402	101–1,844
Lansdowne b (Delaware)	†MC-S	12	2.5	0.0	49–85–12–71	2.4	0.0	50–4–20–40	15	47–1,515
Latrobe b (Westmoreland)	†MC-S	10	2.5	0.0	45–79–37–75	2.4	0.0	42–8–31–31	73	48–1,585
Lebanon (Lebanon)	CO-I	26	9.0	2.0	116–63–36–129	8.0	1.5	42–24–39–28	85	157–1,306
Logan tp (Blair)	†MC-S	12	2.1	0.0	27–36–52–51	1.9	0.0	32–7–40–26	8	38–1,630
Lower Allen tp (Cumberland)	†MC-S	15	3.0	0.0	19–21–54–113	3.7	0.0	30–12–24–91	0	58–1,637
Lower Burrell (Westmoreland)	MC-S	13	2.2	0.0	28–52–40–46	2.1	0.0	27–3–41–17	12	36–1,481
Lower Makefield tp (Bucks)	*CM-S	19	4.4	0.0	25–82–19–108	4.9	0.0	35–8–17–29	455	53–1,567
Lower Merion tp (Montgomery)	†MC-S	59	22.1	0.0	43–176–39–114	23.4	0.0	93–14–47–80	305	399–1,820
Lower Moreland tp (Montgomery)	†MC-S	13	2.9	0.0	23–147–22–42	2.6	0.0	63–8–28–21	29	48–1,755
Lower Paxton tp (Dauphin)	†MC-S	36	3.9	0.0	24–14–53–18	3.7	0.0	28–5–18–4	27	91–1,644
Lower Providence tp (Montgomery)	*CM-S	19	2.0	0.0	22–16–57–8	1.9	0.0	33–4–17–0	4	...–...
Lower Southampton tp (Bucks)	†CO-S	19	2.8	0.0	22–66–25–33	2.9	0.0	42–11–17–15	122	52–1,650
Mc Candless t (Allegheny)	*CM-S	26	4.1	0.0	20–54–67–14	4.1	0.0	34–4–68–0	11	...–...
Mc Keesport (Allegheny)	MC-S	30	8.2	0.0	52–89–76–59	8.3	0.0	49–36–33–30	198	190–1,593
Manheim tp (Lancaster)	†CO-S	26	4.1	0.0	18–42–22–73	3.6	0.0	40–2–15–35	0	78–1,532
Marple tp (Delaware)	†MC-S	23	5.2	0.0	24–69–36–98	5.4	0.0	56–4–30–27	69	101–1,686
Meadville (Crawford)	*CM-I	15	4.0	0.8	41–86–48–86	5.3	0.7	37–27–34–35	148	150–1,395
Middletown tp (Bucks)	*CM-S	35	6.6	0.8	24–60–38–65	5.4	0.9	45–6–21–24	264	110–1,803
Middletown tp (Delaware)	*CM-S	13	1.3	0.0	29–23–35–13	1.1	0.0	2–11–14–0	12	...–...
Middletown b (Dauphin)	*CM-S	10	2.5	2.0	71–18–43–111	2.8	1.2	36–7–16–63	42	72–1,492
Millcreek tp (Erie)	MC-S	44	7.5	0.0	27–47–41–54	7.3	0.0	40–1–45–30	8	149–1,826
Monessen (Westmoreland)	†MC-S	11	3.4	0.0	150–75–30–42	3.3	0.0	37–12–30–13	55	62–1,229
Monroeville (Allegheny)	*CM-S	31	8.5	0.0	25–57–136–57	7.9	0.0	51–4–49–34	327	134–1,896
Moon tp (Allegheny)	†CO-S	21	3.3	0.0	24–63–61–11	2.8	0.0	36–3–25–4	45	51–1,858
Mt. Lebanon (Allegheny)	*CM-S	34	10.8	0.0	22–148–76–71	10.8	0.0	53–16–37–23	162	153–1,975
Munhall b (Allegheny)	MC-S	14	2.8	0.5	36–113–35–12	2.9	0.6	45–5–36–26	18	61–1,591
Murrysville (Westmoreland)	†MC-S	16	2.5	0.0	26–53–61–13	2.7	0.0	37–2–29–8	14	45–1,746
Nanticoke (Luzerne)	MC-S	13	1.4	0.0	23–32–31–19	1.3	0.0	20–17–19–17	19	68–1,163
Nether Providence tp (Delaware)	CO-S	13	1.7	0.0	16–65–13–40	1.5	0.0	35–4–21–1	61	25–1,930
New Castle (Lawrence)	†MC-I	33	8.6	0.0	62–113–43–45	8.8	0.0	48–41–36–32	97	173–1,540
New Kensington (Westmoreland)	MC-S	18	4.4	0.0	31–78–42–98	5.6	0.0	42–9–30–45	139	73–1,490
Newtown tp (Delaware)	†MC-S	12	1.9	0.0	19–59–25–56	1.8	0.0	37–7–25–4	0	30–1,856
Norristown b (Montgomery)	†MC-S	35	...	0.0	...–...–...–...	8.4	0.0	70–13–29–35	0	195–1,592
North Huntingdon tp (Westmoreland)	CM-S	31	3.2	0.0	22–33–38–8	2.8	0.0	22–3–21–0	5	47–1,120
North Versailles tp (Allegheny)	MC-S	13	1.9	0.0	29–71–41–7	1.9	0.0	26–7–36–21	13	...–...
Northampton tp (Bucks)	†MC-S	29	2.9	0.0	17–48–13–22	3.2	0.0	31–6–14–0	35	63–1,800
Oil City (Venango)	*CM-I	14	5.1	0.7	130–82–42–112	5.0	0.6	37–31–28–47	6	115–1,412
Penn Hills (Allegheny)	†MC-S	57	12.2	0.0	45–47–81–42	12.3	0.0	56–4–31–48	124	219–1,927
Peters tp (Washington)	†MC-S	14	2.3	0.0	24–51–69–24	2.2	0.0	36–12–20–8	83	41–1,580
Philadelphia C	MC-C	1,665	1,846.7	564.9	343–141–431–194	1,821.5	578.1	139–47–26–72	1,366	32,421–1,816
Phoenixville b (Chester)	*CM-S	14	3.5	1.1	25–67–51–103	3.8	1.3	61–6–29–57	379	93–1,590
Pittsburgh (Allegheny)	MC-C	415	274.2	19.9	152–199–221–88	270.5	19.2	98–65–24–34	536	6,128–1,878
Plum b (Allegheny)	CM-S	26	3.2	0.0	20–22–42–40	3.2	0.0	29–4–25–34	17	67–1,739
Plymouth tp (Montgomery)	†MC-S	17	3.8	0.0	29–92–35–69	3.9	0.0	56–7–25–63	75	65–1,774
Pottstown b (Montgomery)	*CM-S	23	5.8	1.1	69–57–40–84	6.1	0.8	58–19–22–57	43	120–1,557
Pottsville (Schuylkill)	CO-I	18	3.0	0.0	69–44–47–9	3.1	0.0	38–8–28–0	46	...–...
Radnor tp (Delaware)	†MC-S	28	7.0	0.0	23–120–32–76	7.3	0.0	57–3–31–29	200	141–1,743
Reading (Berks)	CO-C	79	31.0	4.1	144–111–54–84	31.1	3.2	57–32–26–9	187	769–1,571
Ridley tp (Delaware)	†CO-S	33	6.6	0.0	32–73–17–77	6.2	0.0	47–5–23–44	11	119–1,776
Ross tp (Allegheny)	†MC-S	35	4.9	0.0	21–48–58–11	4.9	0.0	34–6–34–4	24	105–1,485
Salisbury tp (Lehigh)	*CM-S	12	2.0	0.2	21–35–47–56	2.3	0.1	23–6–42–41	66	40–1,595
Scott tp (Allegheny)	†CO-S	20	3.1	0.0	22–60–58–16	3.0	0.0	42–5–31–9	49	...–...
Scranton (Lackawanna)	MC-C	86	33.5	0.0	147–63–113–66	30.4	0.0	44–49–10–42	25	681–1,471
Shaler tp (Allegheny)	†MC-S	33	4.6	1.5	28–40–41–29	4.6	1.4	29–3–26–1	0	98–1,652
Shamokin (Northumberland)	MC-I	10	1.3	0.0	25–31–42–27	1.1	0.0	31–6–23–0	39	...–...
Sharon (Mercer)	MC-C	18	5.3	0.0	49–158–50–44	4.7	0.0	44–34–39–36	385	143–1,450
South Park tp (Allegheny)	†MC-S	14	2.6	0.0	26–58–43–54	2.5	0.0	42–4–23–49	33	...–...
South Whitehall tp (Lehigh)	*CM-S	16	4.7	0.5	76–63–94–58	3.4	0.2	28–2–33–18	161	73–1,604
Spring tp (Berks)	MC-S	17	2.6	0.0	29–17–53–50	2.4	0.0	21–5–27–29	84	35–1,694
Spring Garden tp (York)	MC-S	11	2.6	0.0	21–49–76–96	2.3	0.0	39–25–24–68	43	37–1,750
Springettsbury tp (York)	*CM-S	20	4.0	0.0	22–15–74–90	4.0	0.0	31–19–15–43	0	80–1,720
Springfield tp (Delaware)	CO-S	25	6.7	0.0	21–111–25–113	5.9	0.0	53–4–17–38	210	122–1,223
Springfield tp (Montgomery)	*CM-S	20	3.5	0.0	24–94–15–44	3.7	0.0	43–9–27–46	2	78–1,255
State College b (Centre)	†MC-C	35	7.0	0.0	30–25–40–103	7.3	0.1	39–2–11–38	129	158–1,587
Sunbury (Northumberland)	MC-I	12	1.4	0.0	26–23–37–29	1.6	0.0	32–5–28–4	0	...–...
Susquehanna tp (Dauphin)	†MC-S	18	2.1	0.0	21–36–53–8	2.4	0.0	34–11–31–3	0	50–1,564
Swissvale b (Allegheny)	MC-S	11	2.2	0.0	56–94–35–9	2.2	0.0	55–15–27–15	33	57–1,492
Towamencin tp (Montgomery)	*CM-S	12	2.3	0.0	16–35–29–110	1.8	0.0	36–4–12–5	5	...–...
Tredyffrin tp (Chester)	†MC-S	24	5.3	0.0	22–91–25–86	5.5	0.0	63–5–36–38	66	84–1,851
Uniontown (Fayette)	MC-I	14	3.5	0.0	47–88–34–82	3.8	0.0	49–23–16–56	89	...–...
Upper Allen tp (Cumberland)	†MC-S	11	2.0	0.0	24–9–51–99	2.1	0.0	21–2–13–34	760	31–1,179
Upper Darby tp (Delaware)	†MC-S	83	18.7	0.0	45–94–16–70	14.9	0.0	54–10–19–35	0	489–1,311
Upper Dublin tp (Montgomery)	*CM-S	22	6.4	0.0	35–157–20–73	6.3	0.0	47–7–34–47	206	110–1,561
Upper Merion tp (Montgomery)	*CM-S	26	...	0.0	...–...–...–...	7.1	0.0	59–10–47–59	0	148–1,772

Table 1/9 continued **PROFILES OF INDIVIDUAL CITIES**

City (county)	Form of govern-ment–Metro status	Est. 1982 popu-lation (000)	Fiscal year 1983 revenues: Total general revenue ($ mil-lions)	Total utility reve-nue ($ mil-lions)	Per capita revenues ($): Intergovernmental revenue–Property taxes–Other taxes–Charges and miscella-neous general revenue	Fiscal year 1983 expenditures: Total general expendi-tures ($ mil-lions)	Total utility expendi-tures ($ mil-lions)	Per capita current expenditures ($): Police–Fire–Streets–Sewers and sanitation	Long term debt ($ per capita)	October 1983 public personnel: Total full time equivalent employment–Average full time monthly salary ($)
PENNSYLVANIA continued										
Upper Moreland tp (Montgomery)	†MC-S	26	4.1	0.0	27–85–26–22	4.2	0.0	43–16–27–14	32	94–1,742
Upper St. Clair tp (Allegheny)	*CM-S	19	5.1	0.0	24–81–108–53	5.2	0.0	63–6–49–19	134	96–1,988
Upper Southampton tp (Bucks)	†MC-S	16	2.2	0.0	26–75–12–26	1.9	0.0	51–2–16–11	12	58–1,522
Warminster tp (Bucks)	†MC-S	36	4.0	0.0	22–55–14–17	4.0	0.0	39–8–18–0	17	92–1,678
Warren b (Warren)	*CM-I	12	3.8	0.0	48–83–127–58	4.1	0.0	52–57–43–34	279	91–1,780
Warrington tp (Bucks)	†MC-S	11	1.1	0.0	19–57–13–15	1.1	0.0	30–8–14–0	20	...–...
Washington (Washington)	MC-S	18	3.4	0.0	49–65–45–23	3.3	0.0	36–32–30–9	62	103–1,353
West Chester b (Chester)	*CM-S	18	4.1	0.0	25–55–58–90	4.4	0.0	59–6–41–49	312	100–1,648
West Goshen tp (Chester)	*CM-S	17	...	0.0	...–...–...–...	2.5	0.0	33–4–12–30	0	41–1,723
West Mifflin b (Allegheny)	MC-S	26	5.6	0.0	33–107–59–15	5.6	0.0	42–4–46–56	19	135–1,660
West Norriton tp (Montgomery)	CO-S	14	1.7	0.0	21–16–57–28	1.7	0.0	37–4–18–1	4	...–...
Whitehall b (Allegheny)	MC-S	15	3.0	0.0	23–77–84–18	2.8	0.0	41–3–30–38	55	...–...
Whitehall tp (Lehigh)	MC-S	22	3.8	0.0	28–65–60–21	3.9	0.0	46–4–51–10	33	97–1,383
Whitemarsh tp (Montgomery)	*CM-S	15	3.8	0.0	35–98–35–81	3.6	0.0	58–9–22–49	35	60–1,787
Whitpain tp (Montgomery)	†CO-S	13	2.2	0.0	61–69–20–23	2.1	0.0	44–7–23–0	12	...–...
Wilkes-Barre (Luzerne)	†MC-C	51	20.4	0.0	158–71–124–50	18.2	0.0	50–51–35–18	17	466–1,378
Wilkinsburg b (Allegheny)	*CM-S	23	5.1	0.0	38–118–35–26	4.2	0.0	41–20–25–26	28	131–1,769
Williamsport (Lycoming)	MC-C	33	10.3	0.4	143–79–53–40	8.6	1.1	48–51–45–0	260	219–1,464
Yeadon b (Delaware)	†MC-S	12	1.8	0.0	21–78–5–43	1.9	0.0	35–3–19–14	57	34–1,672
York (York)	MC-C	45	19.0	0.0	107–91–51–177	21.5	0.0	58–52–36–123	344	373–1,485
York tp (York)	†MC-S	17	2.9	0.0	28–14–51–80	2.5	0.0	33–6–17–32	10	32–1,805
RHODE ISLAND										
Barrington t	*CM-S	16	18.0	0.0	240–805–3–73	18.2	0.0	43–56–63–33	1,807	420–1,755
Bristol t	TM-S	20	12.9	0.0	237–383–7–18	13.7	0.0	45–14–47–28	69	389–1,704
Burrillville t	MC-S	14	10.2	0.0	336–365–2–32	10.5	0.0	32–0–32–22	527	286–1,656
Central Falls	MC-S	17	12.8	0.0	407–313–4–23	12.4	0.0	55–54–28–14	253	359–1,803
Coventry t	*CM-S	28	20.3	0.0	282–425–4–17	20.1	0.0	54–3–28–9	264	572–1,826
Cranston	MC-S	72	77.1	0.1	427–529–8–113	74.9	1.5	57–62–35–17	469	2,018–1,938
Cumberland t	MC-S	27	19.2	0.4	277–426–2–12	19.9	0.5	36–10–36–17	231	614–1,781
East Greenwich t	*CM-S	10	12.0	0.0	332–775–7–68	11.7	0.0	72–0–60–48	136	336–1,732
East Providence	*CM-S	51	38.5	2.3	191–528–4–28	40.4	0.9	66–72–40–68	309	1,193–1,589
Johnston t	MC-S	25	18.5	0.0	238–465–6–28	18.3	0.0	51–48–23–40	195	552–1,700
Lincoln t	MC-S	17	14.8	0.7	240–613–3–17	13.3	0.9	51–9–52–10	149	362–2,200
Middletown t	*CM-I	17	13.1	0.0	325–361–5–69	13.4	0.0	44–31–26–30	244	416–1,787
Narragansett t	*CM-S	12	13.4	0.4	244–709–9–132	11.8	0.3	72–43–46–41	712	292–1,787
Newport	*CM-I	30	...	...	...–...–...–...	27.1	1.8	112–105–29–44	0	902–1,710
North Kingstown t	*CM-S	23	21.2	0.7	350–530–5–49	22.0	0.5	67–78–30–3	296	700–1,738
North Providence t	MC-S	30	19.7	0.0	172–439–3–46	18.3	0.0	40–27–28–48	108	539–1,794
Pawtucket	MC-C	72	...	...	...–...–...–...	48.0	3.5	11–11–30–30	0	1,618–1,950
Portsmouth t	MC-S	15	12.7	0.0	292–546–3–18	12.4	0.0	51–45–38–9	369	355–1,937
Providence	MC-C	156	179.4	8.9	447–598–6–101	166.4	7.2	80–90–47–78	548	3,937–1,940
Smithfield t	MC-S	17	14.5	0.1	224–496–6–126	13.8	0.1	65–44–49–48	736	359–2,114
South Kingstown t	*CM-S	21	17.0	0.3	203–505–4–99	16.5	0.2	60–4–33–44	508	458–1,771
Tiverton t	TM-S	14	...	0.0	...–...–...–...	1.2	0.0	36–1–0–7	0	298–1,861
Warren t	TM-S	11	9.8	0.0	399–503–3–8	8.9	0.0	42–13–39–58	435	216–1,758
Warwick	MC-C	87	86.8	1.9	270–671–5–55	84.3	1.5	73–73–28–23	668	2,326–1,833
West Warwick t	TM-S	27	21.4	0.0	317–414–3–45	21.1	0.0	46–51–24–38	630	565–1,770
Westerly t	*CM-S	19	14.2	1.2	179–479–6–96	14.1	1.8	53–0–49–40	317	437–1,683
Woonsocket	MC-S	45	42.0	1.2	428–428–4–69	42.7	1.4	54–64–28–41	230	1,108–1,787
SOUTH CAROLINA										
Aiken (Aiken)	*CM-S	16	7.3	1.6	83–147–50–188	6.2	1.5	60–26–44–76	185	213–1,319
Anderson (Anderson)	*CM-C	28	7.8	0.0	77–99–42–63	8.0	0.0	45–34–28–71	85	314–1,010
Cayce (Lexington)	*CM-S	12	2.7	0.7	66–59–42–58	2.6	0.8	48–20–10–33	282	...–...
Charleston (Charleston)	MC-C	71	33.7	8.8	125–164–75–112	45.5	17.2	88–54–30–71	1,117	1,291–1,276
Columbia (Richland)	*CM-C	101	35.4	11.2	76–101–49–123	45.1	18.4	65–53–22–71	593	1,466–1,321
Conway (Horry)	MC-I	11	3.7	0.5	138–81–39–82	3.9	1.8	59–18–24–41	308	106–1,132
Easley (Pickens)	MC-S	15	3.1	8.1	73–57–21–59	2.4	7.8	35–21–0–21	71	144–1,090
Florence (Florence)	*CM-C	30	9.1	2.2	65–121–52–63	9.3	2.3	57–44–24–49	280	327–1,294
Gaffney (Cherokee)	†MC-I	13	2.5	0.0	68–81–25–13	2.1	0.0	34–22–18–36	4	175–983
Georgetown (Georgetown)	†MC-I	10	3.7	4.9	95–140–41–85	4.0	4.0	81–45–39–47	307	164–1,158
Goose Creek (Berkeley)	†MC-S	21	2.2	0.5	42–19–18–26	1.8	0.6	26–7–0–9	50	83–1,088
Greenville (Greenville)	*CM-C	57	25.5	12.6	93–162–82–106	21.3	25.0	77–55–26–24	827	875–1,432
Greenwood (Greenwood)	*CM-I	22	5.8	21.1	105–103–28–25	6.6	23.5	54–41–25–25	301	303–1,267
Greer (Greenville)	†MC-S	11	3.8	13.1	82–71–26–174	4.0	14.8	61–23–14–51	278	189–1,157
Hanahan (Berkeley)	†MC-S	14	3.4	0.0	98–69–20–62	3.1	0.0	33–24–5–30	95	72–1,145
Laurens (Laurens)	MC-I	11	2.7	10.4	86–70–21–74	3.2	9.4	43–19–21–24	10	136–1,118
Mount Pleasant t (Charleston)	MC-S	17	7.3	1.0	202–87–35–114	3.3	4.7	30–27–4–76	233	135–1,051
Myrtle Beach (Horry)	*CM-I	20	13.8	2.2	191–177–118–203	15.5	3.1	92–39–43–93	871	274–1,291
North Augusta (Aiken)	*CM-S	14	4.2	0.8	57–78–34–127	3.2	2.0	54–0–3–49	312	...–...
North Charleston (Charleston)	MC-C	68	9.7	0.0	44–51–36–12	9.3	0.0	38–21–10–12	15	379–1,098
Orangeburg (Orangeburg)	*CM-I	15	4.9	36.2	86–50–31–154	6.5	33.9	60–44–26–82	437	295–1,285
Rock Hill (York)	*CM-C	36	10.2	17.5	88–89–15–90	12.1	15.2	42–31–15–67	184	506–1,188
Spartanburg (Spartanburg)	*CM-C	44	17.6	5.3	121–142–68–74	15.7	6.0	72–48–31–37	452	590–1,343
Sumter (Sumter)	*CM-I	26	9.0	2.2	110–88–57–96	9.5	2.2	63–49–55–54	293	384–1,011
Union (Union)	MC-I	10	2.2	10.8	39–39–23–110	1.9	10.3	45–15–22–48	72	120–1,199
West Columbia (Lexington)	MC-S	11	3.4	1.1	115–51–63–77	2.9	0.8	56–31–14–43	107	96–1,146

Table 1/9 continued **PROFILES OF INDIVIDUAL CITIES**

City (county)	Form of govern-ment–Metro status	Est. 1982 popu-lation (000)	Fiscal year 1983 revenues: Total general revenue ($ mil-lions)	Total utility reve-nue ($ mil-lions)	Per capita revenues ($): Intergovernmental revenue–Property taxes–Other taxes–Charges and miscella-neous general revenue	Fiscal year 1983 expenditures: Total general expendi-tures ($ mil-lions)	Total utility expendi-tures ($ mil-lions)	Per capita current expenditures ($): Police–Fire–Streets–Sewers and sanitation	Long term debt ($ per capita)	October 1983 public personnel: Total full time equivalent employment–Average full time monthly salary ($)
SOUTH DAKOTA										
Aberdeen (Brown)	CO-I	26	9.0	1.2	81–103–76–80	8.1	5.1	29–33–38–27	242	235–1,349
Brookings (Brookings)	CO-I	15	14.0	6.5	64–68–65–719	13.6	6.0	52–9–49–54	426	375–1,492
Huron (Beadle)	CO-I	13	4.8	0.6	46–133–76–113	4.2	1.0	49–24–49–43	249	119–1,240
Mitchell (Davison)	MC-I	14	6.5	0.4	66–126–76–201	4.8	0.7	43–22–35–30	248	137–1,193
Pierre (Hughes)	CO-I	12	2.7	4.7	16–68–87–49	3.6	3.8	44–10–29–23	109	116–1,368
Rapid City (Pennington)	MC-I	48	20.1	2.1	71–71–133–142	16.3	3.2	49–43–38–30	133	473–1,249
Sioux Falls (Minnehaha)	CO-C	83	44.0	5.0	198–124–97–108	38.7	7.9	41–40–31–22	264	752–1,758
Watertown (Codington)	MC-I	16	8.2	9.9	51–69–86–295	6.8	9.5	42–8–39–35	86	197–1,569
Yankton (Yankton)	*CM-I	12	5.8	0.9	124–43–90–220	5.8	0.7	57–8–47–43	193	109–1,287
TENNESSEE										
Athens (Mc Minn)	*CM-I	12	8.2	20.3	397–113–27–144	8.6	19.6	46–31–48–65	727	420–1,266
Bartlett t (Shelby)	MC-S	21	4.4	1.3	70–94–20–24	4.7	2.4	41–28–35–21	430	135–1,340
Bristol (Sullivan)	*CM-C	24	17.9	28.4	392–157–52–148	17.0	28.0	38–33–43–48	1,833	631–1,299
Chattanooga (Hamilton)	CO-C	168	153.2	208.7	537–184–32–158	174.0	210.0	57–52–40–59	349	5,453–1,641
Clarksville (Montgomery)	MC-C	60	14.1	36.9	95–40–22–79	12.0	37.7	32–25–30–19	499	478–1,236
Cleveland (Bradley)	CO-I	27	19.5	29.5	373–82–100–180	16.5	34.7	43–44–26–58	501	715–1,389
Columbia (Maury)	*CM-I	27	7.9	18.1	124–49–24–100	6.4	19.0	40–35–32–53	308	362–1,309
Cookeville (Putnam)	*CM-I	21	25.7	20.0	133–48–35–983	23.2	19.6	50–30–19–12	1,669	843–1,185
Dyersburg (Dyer)	MC-I	16	7.1	21.0	139–76–83–148	10.6	20.5	48–55–34–33	518	504–1,209
East Ridge t (Hamilton)	CO-S	21	3.2	0.0	89–36–22–9	3.4	0.0	33–0–18–50	98	101–1,279
Elizabethton (Carter)	*CM-S	13	20.1	19.0	422–131–27–1,019	18.8	16.8	48–35–54–53	470	735–1,218
Franklin t (Williamson)	MC-S	14	4.2	3.5	101–90–33–68	3.8	3.3	53–30–6–73	159	159–1,267
Gallatin (Sumner)	MC-S	18	5.7	18.7	125–75–30–93	4.5	22.5	51–40–24–30	781	231–1,227
Germantown (Shelby)	†MC-S	24	8.7	0.9	81–161–21–95	7.4	2.3	29–26–52–41	490	165–1,377
Greeneville t (Greene)	MC-I	14	14.5	31.4	515–227–39–269	12.2	29.1	44–39–43–77	964	643–1,279
Hendersonville (Sumner)	*CM-S	27	4.7	0.0	81–35–15–38	4.8	0.0	40–17–16–24	151	117–1,352
Humboldt (Gibson)	MC-I	10	6.7	10.2	378–114–24–149	6.0	10.0	44–37–25–27	258	342–1,199
Jackson (Madison)	CO-I	49	31.4	64.7	309–126–45–156	29.0	64.6	59–53–33–88	914	2,711–955
Johnson City (Washington)	*CM-C	44	28.2	52.2	303–125–73–140	29.6	52.4	72–39–36–48	593	1,783–1,181
Kingsport (Sullivan)	*CM-C	32	32.5	2.8	491–187–86–253	85.6	14.3	67–53–30–781	899	1,130–1,306
Knoxville (Knox)	MC-C	175	165.5	227.0	523–206–49–166	140.5	243.4	75–73–10–124	1,031	5,404–1,406
Lawrenceburg (Lawrence)	MC-I	10	3.2	18.4	149–59–11–97	3.1	18.0	78–28–56–61	541	165–1,058
Lebanon (Wilson)	MC-S	12	4.0	14.5	140–46–37–119	3.5	14.6	49–42–51–60	544	196–1,024
Mc Minnville (Warren)	MC-I	10	3.2	9.0	74–91–21–116	2.6	9.5	52–27–22–44	638	156–1,088
Maryville (Blount)	*CM-S	17	15.5	14.6	564–131–27–166	13.7	16.1	44–43–79–47	1,071	459–1,508
Memphis (Shelby)	MC-C	646	619.6	661.5	558–170–62–169	544.9	655.8	65–54–19–65	835	22,463–1,828
Millington (Shelby)	MC-S	18	3.1	0.3	87–27–15–48	3.0	0.2	35–17–14–17	13	92–1,223
Morristown (Hamblen)	*CM-I	21	22.9	19.3	597–178–54–269	21.9	17.6	67–54–61–47	639	824–1,227
Murfreesboro (Rutherford)	*CM-S	35	17.8	26.7	231–132–34–119	14.1	29.4	40–45–19–64	479	684–1,460
Nashville c (Davidson)	MC-C	455	482.3	355.9	265–281–244–269	463.0	369.0	68–39–26–46	0	15,522–1,680
Oak Ridge (Anderson)	*CM-S	28	23.0	15.4	420–212–53–142	22.7	15.8	56–50–42–57	294	877–1,525
Paris (Henry)	*CM-I	11	3.7	16.2	140–32–42–129	3.5	16.2	53–50–58–52	579	168–1,377
Red Bank (Hamilton)	*CM-S	13	2.0	0.0	79–27–14–29	1.9	0.0	42–16–26–28	11	65–1,228
Shelbyville t (Bedford)	*CM-I	14	5.7	9.5	102–107–51–164	4.5	9.1	43–38–56–55	70	202–1,150
Springfield (Robertson)	CO-S	11	2.9	10.3	101–39–75–56	3.3	10.2	49–33–33–49	1,121	139–1,352
Tullahoma (Coffee)	†MC-I	17	22.8	11.5	430–87–31–834	12.5	9.8	44–30–47–38	683	524–1,360
Union City (Obion)	*CM-I	10	...	...	...–...–...–...	6.1	12.7	52–53–31–94	0	333–1,292
TEXAS										
Abilene (Taylor)	*CM-C	104	38.6	6.3	51–93–113–113	32.6	8.4	47–35–20–39	325	1,115–1,519
Alice (Jim Wells)	*CM-I	22	1.3	2.2	0–0–0–59	7.6	1.8	46–27–29–41	50	...–...
Alvin (Brazoria)	*CM-S	18	5.4	0.8	9–117–72–102	4.5	0.8	41–5–37–51	547	127–1,638
Amarillo (Potter)	*CM-C	155	104.0	9.3	65–130–89–384	93.2	10.2	51–28–34–45	295	2,722–1,492
Andrews (Andrews)	*CM-I	12	0.9	0.8	0–0–0–73	2.2	0.5	28–3–14–32	31	...–...
Angleton (Brazoria)	*CM-S	15	8.1	0.6	307–72–64–103	4.0	0.6	44–4–29–40	576	103–1,294
Arlington (Tarrant)	*CM-S	183	72.8	13.6	32–112–92–162	69.9	21.8	41–30–30–33	1,209	1,302–1,571
Athens (Henderson)	*CM-I	11	2.6	0.5	13–49–92–93	2.0	0.4	28–20–9–40	244	...–...
Austin (Travis)	*CM-C	368	258.7	361.5	85–123–94–400	253.7	396.3	8–40–18–44	2,246	8,482–1,824
Balch Springs (Dallas)	MC-S	15	...	0.0	...–...–...–...	2.7	0.0	37–20–15–13	0	78–1,304
Bay City (Matagorda)	MC-I	17	...	0.0	...–...–...–...	...	0.0	...–...–...–...	0	...–...
Baytown (Harris)	*CM-S	61	30.0	4.0	83–147–82–177	30.9	4.5	62–37–24–42	485	546–1,819
Beaumont (Jefferson)	*CM-C	123	63.3	5.6	125–141–96–150	65.1	8.0	70–54–49–59	706	1,342–1,772
Bedford (Tarrant)	*CM-S	25	...	...	...–...–...–...	2.7	1.1	25–8–9–10	0	120–1,306
Beeville (Bee)	*CM-I	15	1.2	0.4	0–0–0–79	3.0	0.3	29–6–22–32	89	...–...
Bellaire (Harris)	*CM-S	15	8.0	0.8	12–230–120–167	6.7	1.0	86–41–36–78	185	181–1,751
Belton (Bell)	*CM-S	11	1.2	0.8	0–0–0–108	2.8	0.8	32–22–19–33	86	...–...
Benbrook (Tarrant)	*CM-S	15	0.9	0.0	0–0–0–57	3.1	0.0	47–5–21–16	358	...–...
Big Spring (Howard)	*CM-I	27	8.5	2.1	17–72–92–134	8.5	3.1	50–39–26–20	231	264–1,411
Borger (Hutchinson)	*CM-I	17	5.1	1.5	56–60–94–81	5.4	1.6	38–33–30–40	276	...–...
Brenham (Washington)	†MC-I	12	3.4	11.3	16–34–117–109	5.3	11.0	40–20–15–60	144	138–1,389
Brownfield (Terry)	*CM-I	11	0.7	4.8	0–0–0–60	2.6	4.0	44–12–34–60	135	...–...
Brownsville (Cameron)	*CM-C	91	32.2	41.7	100–57–66–129	32.3	46.2	34–19–12–55	718	1,137–1,227
Brownwood (Brown)	*CM-I	20	1.9	1.7	0–0–0–98	5.2	1.4	30–21–21–38	225	...–...
Bryan (Brazos)	*CM-C	53	15.5	41.9	19–66–78–129	19.1	42.3	35–30–24–37	1,257	688–1,608
Burkburnett (Wichita)	*CM-S	11	0.6	0.7	0–0–0–53	1.6	0.6	36–9–24–36	66	...–...
Burleson (Johnson)	*CM-S	13	3.0	0.6	10–69–57–92	2.6	1.1	41–2–15–44	284	87–1,365
Canyon (Randall)	*CM-S	11	0.7	0.7	0–0–0–63	1.3	0.1	29–16–17–21	38	...–...
Carrollton (Dallas)	*CM-S	49	20.8	2.9	10–176–99–142	23.1	5.4	53–48–45–60	560	477–1,645
Cleburne (Johnson)	*CM-S	20	5.7	1.3	51–75–74–85	6.8	0.7	40–47–28–39	408	208–1,419
College Station (Brazos)	*CM-C	43	13.1	21.2	27–53–78–150	15.1	19.7	42–38–12–15	1,086	440–1,483

Table 1/9 continued **PROFILES OF INDIVIDUAL CITIES**

City (county)	Form of govern-ment–Metro status	Est. 1982 popu-lation (000)	Fiscal year 1983 revenues: Total general revenue ($ mil-lions)	Total utility reve-nue ($ mil-lions)	Per capita revenues ($): Intergovernmental revenue–Property taxes–Other taxes–Charges and miscella-neous general revenue	Fiscal year 1983 expenditures: Total general expendi-tures ($ mil-lions)	Total utility expendi-tures ($ mil-lions)	Per capita current expenditures ($): Police–Fire–Streets–Sewers and sanitation	Long term debt ($ per capita)	October 1983 public personnel: Total full time equivalent employment–Average full time monthly salary ($)
TEXAS continued										
Conroe (Montgomery)	MC-S	20	6.3	0.9	16–73–148–76	7.4	0.9	54–33–38–66	266	230–1,496
Copperas Cove t (Coryell)	*CM-S	21	2.0	1.4	0–0–0–95	3.8	1.3	33–26–13–39	259	...–...
Corpus Christi (Nueces)	*CM-C	246	105.4	40.9	96–96–96–140	106.7	50.4	46–30–28–40	469	2,861–940
Corsicana (Navarro)	*CM-I	23	6.5	1.6	26–78–77–103	5.4	3.2	35–30–16–53	398	239–1,192
Dallas (Dallas)	*CM-C	944	512.1	99.3	65–170–144–163	477.4	124.8	87–48–19–52	668	14,116–1,882
De Soto (Dallas)	CM-S	17	4.3	1.1	9–131–49–67	4.0	1.6	40–46–14–13	681	117–1,716
Deer Park (Harris)	*CM-S	24	11.8	0.7	10–285–56–142	15.2	2.3	61–10–24–72	999	197–1,918
Del Rio (Val Verde)	*CM-I	32	5.5	3.3	21–37–58–57	4.2	3.7	27–16–14–17	13	253–1,243
Denison (Grayson)	*CM-C	24	7.6	1.4	36–81–67–133	10.9	1.9	33–25–32–63	541	269–1,262
Denton (Denton)	*CM-S	50	27.1	34.2	21–99–68–357	29.9	34.5	45–51–26–48	920	991–1,573
Dumas (Moore)	†MC-I	13	1.0	2.2	0–0–0–78	2.3	1.8	48–15–28–24	380	...–...
Duncanville (Dallas)	*CM-S	29	...	...	...–...–...–...	4.2	1.4	36–0–4–17	0	197–1,803
Eagle Pass (Maverick)	*CM-I	23	2.5	1.0	0–0–0–108	4.7	2.1	24–17–15–25	76	...–...
Edinburg (Hidalgo)	*CM-C	28	16.6	1.5	108–60–60–364	17.2	1.0	24–3–22–41	106	625–995
El Campo (Wharton)	*CM-I	11	2.0	0.5	0–0–0–186	3.5	0.5	51–16–38–60	271	...–...
El Paso (El Paso)	MC-C	445	188.5	23.3	104–85–63–172	145.1	28.5	51–32–16–27	119	4,316–1,445
Ennis (Ellis)	*CM-S	13	4.5	0.9	82–112–65–98	4.5	0.8	51–24–32–59	233	140–1,401
Euless (Tarrant)	*CM-S	27	6.7	1.7	10–81–64–95	5.8	1.4	44–27–12–35	326	185–1,717
Farmers Branch (Dallas)	*CM-S	26	17.3	2.2	21–240–262–150	16.7	3.2	72–61–66–93	445	354–1,879
Forest Hill (Tarrant)	*CM-S	12	0.2	1.1	0–0–0–16	1.6	1.1	46–17–20–0	249	...–...
Fort Worth (Tarrant)	*CM-C	401	193.7	27.1	98–132–95–158	190.0	46.3	64–46–26–54	699	4,743–1,641
Freeport (Brazoria)	*CM-S	13	5.4	0.9	16–110–92–195	5.1	0.6	61–17–27–65	681	146–1,467
Friendswood (Galveston)	*CM-S	12	4.2	0.5	27–157–47–115	3.4	0.5	61–10–34–65	667	...–...
Gainesville (Cooke)	*CM-I	14	4.8	0.7	40–94–89–110	3.4	0.6	56–29–32–31	342	162–1,246
Galveston (Galveston)	*CM-C	63	59.1	5.7	96–132–114–602	52.2	7.0	69–43–44–55	1,169	1,070–1,760
Garland (Dallas)	*CM-S	149	41.4	94.8	23–93–53–109	49.9	86.0	38–26–25–47	982	1,342–1,922
Grand Prairie (Dallas)	*CM-S	77	30.0	4.4	52–105–76–156	23.0	6.4	43–30–25–44	434	553–1,757
Grapevine (Tarrant)	*CM-S	15	8.0	1.2	26–137–186–194	6.1	1.0	77–49–27–32	1,065	197–1,632
Greenville (Hunt)	*CM-I	24	6.8	16.5	14–75–62–137	10.2	15.2	33–54–32–11	1,561	301–1,606
Groves (Jefferson)	*CM-S	17	6.2	0.7	69–110–67–113	4.4	1.0	26–13–15–56	158	100–1,774
Haltom City (Tarrant)	*CM-S	30	5.5	2.4	13–50–73–44	5.0	2.1	31–22–14–17	337	173–1,630
Harlingen (Cameron)	*CM-C	47	19.9	2.4	101–72–92–159	16.8	2.4	32–29–17–61	232	499–1,268
Henderson (Rusk)	CM-I	11	1.3	0.5	0–0–0–112	2.9	0.4	38–19–29–62	424	...–...
Hereford (Deaf Smith)	*CM-I	15	0.9	0.7	0–0–0–59	3.0	0.5	43–5–27–37	110	...–...
Houston (Harris)	MC-C	1,726	1,002.8	134.3	75–167–143–196	1,065.9	151.6	87–65–14–63	1,055	17,614–1,867
Huntsville (Walker)	*CM-I	29	3.2	2.7	0–0–0–110	6.2	2.3	31–6–2–48	634	...–...
Hurst (Tarrant)	*CM-S	33	12.0	2.0	12–93–135–125	8.9	2.1	47–29–20–14	477	245–1,918
Irving (Dallas)	*CM-S	114	49.9	6.0	13–129–100–194	45.5	9.2	40–38–18–56	618	1,047–1,818
Jacksonville (Cherokee)	*CM-I	13	0.9	1.3	0–0–0–70	2.9	1.4	27–20–18–41	443	...–...
Kerrville (Kerr)	*CM-I	16	1.2	1.6	0–0–0–75	3.8	1.8	41–33–16–38	332	...–...
Kilgore (Gregg)	*CM-S	12	8.6	0.7	22–93–233–377	6.9	2.4	50–85–12–56	442	344–1,191
Killeen (Bell)	*CM-C	51	13.2	2.5	48–67–60–86	11.6	2.6	53–30–14–21	115	404–1,443
Kingsville (Kleberg)	*CM-I	30	8.2	1.5	47–77–62–89	6.9	1.8	37–22–23–48	147	317–1,249
La Marque (Galveston)	*CM-S	16	4.1	1.2	10–77–45–129	3.3	1.0	37–15–26–58	80	107–1,646
La Porte (Harris)	*CM-S	20	11.8	1.1	196–191–74–143	9.7	1.0	62–25–75–61	411	218–2,059
Lake Jackson (Brazoria)	*CM-S	20	6.4	0.8	20–62–85–153	6.2	0.8	46–5–29–46	459	159–1,602
Lamesa (Dawson)	*CM-I	12	0.5	1.1	0–0–0–40	2.3	1.5	39–20–44–20	77	...–...
Lancaster (Dallas)	*CM-S	16	...	0.0	...–...–...–...	...	0.0	...–...–...–...	0	...–...
Laredo (Webb)	MC-C	100	32.9	5.7	51–38–95–145	35.8	6.4	38–35–37–26	265	959–1,177
League City (Galveston)	MC-S	20	...	...	...–...–...–...	13.2	1.0	35–5–29–30	0	147–1,317
Levelland (Hockley)	*CM-I	15	1.2	0.8	0–0–0–80	2.4	0.6	40–12–19–30	152	...–...
Lewisville (Denton)	*CM-S	25	8.3	2.0	18–135–89–87	6.7	2.0	46–35–17–17	946	241–1,604
Longview (Gregg)	*CM-C	69	22.8	5.0	45–92–113–80	21.5	5.7	40–33–21–29	593	699–1,480
Lubbock (Lubbock)	*CM-C	177	62.5	48.0	58–91–90–114	56.6	59.7	43–43–17–30	522	1,769–1,750
Lufkin (Angelina)	*CM-I	30	12.7	1.9	32–74–124–192	10.2	2.4	36–44–43–62	289	306–1,377
Mc Allen (Hidalgo)	*CM-C	72	30.9	4.3	45–35–138–211	28.3	4.9	53–25–32–54	451	733–1,174
Mc Kinney (Collin)	*CM-S	17	7.7	1.2	78–116–77–171	7.5	2.6	44–40–31–50	546	169–1,527
Marshall (Harrison)	*CM-C	26	7.3	2.0	52–76–75–82	7.2	1.7	38–30–0–39	317	268–1,257
Mercedes (Hidalgo)	*CM-S	12	2.8	0.5	48–36–26–115	3.0	0.6	32–1–12–23	27	93–874
Mesquite (Dallas)	*CM-S	71	24.2	3.1	37–89–83–131	23.1	6.4	50–39–17–42	439	582–1,774
Midland (Midland)	*CM-C	84	39.8	6.2	13–98–153–209	35.6	8.6	69–42–41–42	666	896–1,846
Mineral Wells (Palo Pinto)	*CM-I	15	1.7	1.2	0–0–0–112	5.3	1.6	36–8–34–42	209	...–...
Mission (Hidalgo)	*CM-S	25	5.8	1.2	50–54–46–76	4.6	0.6	28–7–12–38	83	212–1,012
Missouri City (Fort Bend)	†MC-S	30	5.6	0.0	3–100–63–19	5.0	0.0	45–30–21–0	202	110–1,038
Mount Pleasant (Titus)	*CM-I	12	1.2	1.2	0–0–0–100	3.1	1.5	31–17–16–68	395	...–...
Nacogdoches (Nacogdoches)	*CM-I	28	12.4	1.9	180–88–86–89	10.2	4.3	41–42–38–43	455	246–1,254
Nederland (Jefferson)	*CM-S	17	5.3	0.8	47–116–67–79	3.7	0.7	25–15–21–47	549	104–1,832
New Braunfels (Comal)	*CM-S	24	6.7	28.3	16–53–77–135	6.3	30.2	44–40–16–66	373	352–1,483
North Richland Hills (Tarrant)	*CM-S	33	9.0	4.2	9–98–70–96	7.7	4.9	37–31–24–22	465	205–1,724
Odessa (Ector)	*CM-C	102	37.5	7.9	29–85–130–122	30.8	7.4	40–32–30–25	120	840–1,796
Orange (Orange)	*CM-C	24	8.0	0.9	42–98–73–118	9.1	1.2	50–41–31–50	219	277–1,496
Palestine (Anderson)	*CM-I	17	3.2	1.0	0–0–0–188	8.1	1.0	48–36–25–50	600	...–...
Pampa (Gray)	*CM-I	23	5.6	1.3	10–61–97–79	6.0	0.9	41–38–33–31	161	213–1,341
Paris (Lamar)	*CM-I	25	2.5	2.1	0–0–0–100	8.5	1.7	35–29–51–44	122	...–...
Pasadena (Harris)	MC-S	122	43.5	6.0	59–131–72–95	39.6	6.2	69–6–28–52	420	958–1,823
Pearland (Brazoria)	CM-S	14	5.5	0.7	9–149–113–120	5.4	1.0	61–6–46–83	974	96–1,742
Pecos (Reeves)	*CM-I	13	1.1	1.0	0–0–0–80	2.7	0.9	42–6–12–22	284	...–...
Pharr (Hidalgo)	CO-C	23	5.7	1.2	64–47–79–58	6.4	0.7	33–13–15–29	252	192–969
Plainview (Hale)	*CM-I	22	2.0	1.2	0–0–0–88	5.7	1.3	55–27–18–49	138	...–...

Table 1/9 continued PROFILES OF INDIVIDUAL CITIES

City (county)	Form of govern-ment–Metro status	Est. 1982 popu-lation (000)	Fiscal year 1983 revenues: Total general revenue ($ mil-lions)	Total utility reve-nue ($ mil-lions)	Per capita revenues ($): Intergovernmental revenue–Property taxes–Other taxes–Charges and miscella-neous general revenue	Fiscal year 1983 expenditures: Total general expendi-tures ($ mil-lions)	Total utility expendi-tures ($ mil-lions)	Per capita current expenditures ($): Police–Fire–Streets–Sewers and sanitation	Long term debt ($ per capita)	October 1983 public personnel: Total full time equivalent employment–Average full time monthly salary ($)
TEXAS continued										
Plano (Collin)	*CM-S	84	33.7	5.0	20–141–82–157	38.1	6.4	52–35–15–65	1,156	724–1,835
Port Arthur (Jefferson)	*CM-C	65	40.6	3.3	112–275–68–167	35.4	7.0	52–43–29–84	458	801–1,745
Port Lavaca (Calhoun)	*CM-I	12	4.0	0.7	31–71–88–148	4.1	0.8	33–22–31–54	330	91–1,319
Port Neches (Jefferson)	*CM-S	15	5.1	0.6	9–193–46–104	4.7	0.7	50–31–36–55	696	88–2,040
Portland (San Patricio)	*CM-S	13	0.8	0.6	0–0–0–65	2.4	0.7	49–3–17–34	348	...–...
Richardson (Dallas)	*CM-S	76	25.3	4.3	9–105–108–111	27.2	6.5	65–45–14–57	450	702–1,752
Robstown (Nueces)	MC-S	13	2.3	7.5	21–59–33–69	2.8	7.3	47–14–22–72	262	155–1,369
Rosenberg (Fort Bend)	MC-S	19	4.6	0.8	14–54–84–85	4.5	0.4	47–16–25–41	266	178–1,415
Round Rock (Williamson)	*CM-S	16	1.2	1.0	0–0–0–78	3.3	0.8	28–15–21–39	1,175	...–...
San Angelo (Tom Green)	*CM-C	79	25.2	4.2	56–113–79–69	26.8	4.6	40–31–24–17	222	792–1,422
San Antonio (Bexar)	*CM-C	819	291.3	681.8	81–60–63–152	354.1	729.4	51–28–20–42	1,863	11,316–1,675
San Benito (Cameron)	*CM-C	19	1.0	0.6	0–0–0–54	3.8	0.6	33–14–11–33	76	...–...
San Marcos (Hays)	*CM-S	24	4.2	0.9	0–0–0–177	7.3	0.5	36–19–15–32	107	...–...
Seguin (Guadalupe)	MC-S	18	8.7	9.1	16–37–58–362	10.1	6.8	43–24–17–43	216	362–956
Sherman (Grayson)	*CM-C	31	12.0	3.0	38–123–105–125	10.4	2.5	49–45–24–59	328	376–1,429
Snyder (Scurry)	*CM-I	14	3.2	0.7	18–47–89–82	2.5	0.9	48–22–25–50	9	...–...
South Houston t (Harris)	MC-S	14	4.3	0.4	38–78–98–88	4.4	0.5	60–3–40–28	10	110–1,470
Stephenville (Erath)	*CM-I	12	5.4	0.6	0–0–0–442	3.8	0.6	43–20–26–41	148	...–...
Sulphur Springs (Hopkins)	*CM-I	13	1.6	1.5	0–0–0–120	4.1	1.0	47–29–25–87	516	...–...
Sweetwater (Nolan)	*CM-I	13	4.1	1.4	24–107–74–115	3.6	1.2	41–32–33–52	39	301–1,111
Taylor (Williamson)	*CM-S	11	2.2	0.5	0–0–0–201	2.9	0.4	30–26–27–41	140	...–...
Temple (Bell)	*CM-C	42	14.4	3.4	33–88–94–128	14.5	2.8	44–28–14–44	467	449–1,384
Terrell (Kaufman)	*CM-S	13	...	...	...–...–...–...	3.5	1.2	44–15–26–50	0	111–1,481
Texarkana (Bowie)	*CM-C	32	...	...	...–...–...–...	7.2	3.4	54–34–5–67	0	466–1,209
Texas City (Galveston)	CO-C	43	23.9	2.0	34–164–115–248	21.2	3.8	39–32–38–47	453	400–1,560
The Colony (Denton)	*CM-S	19	1.6	0.0	13–40–17–14	1.4	0.0	25–8–5–0	40	56–1,662
Tyler (Smith)	*CM-C	73	26.2	4.1	52–78–114–115	22.2	4.9	47–33–32–44	402	836–1,374
Universal City (Bexar)	*CM-S	11	1.1	0.5	0–0–0–100	2.6	0.5	53–21–27–58	221	...–...
University Park (Dallas)	*CM-S	22	8.9	1.3	3–121–92–181	9.5	2.4	56–43–24–63	607	234–1,661
Uvalde (Uvalde)	*CM-I	15	1.0	2.0	0–0–0–71	2.7	1.7	34–7–22–49	37	...–...
Vernon (Wilbarger)	*CM-I	13	0.9	2.9	0–0–0–71	2.5	2.5	26–21–25–38	134	...–...
Victoria (Victoria)	*CM-C	55	21.0	2.6	25–115–116–126	18.4	3.3	69–28–37–55	587	567–1,423
Vidor (Orange)	MC-S	13	0.3	0.0	0–0–0–26	1.4	0.0	41–0–24–19	0	...–...
Waco (Mc Lennan)	*CM-C	102	42.0	6.0	96–90–98–127	38.5	6.0	51–41–30–53	153	1,209–1,430
Watauga (Tarrant)	MC-S	13	0.2	0.0	0–0–0–19	1.6	0.0	36–2–16–0	217	...–...
Waxahachie (Ellis)	*CM-S	15	6.3	0.7	16–68–96–242	4.9	0.5	48–29–21–52	307	150–1,251
Weatherford (Parker)	*CM-S	13	6.5	8.9	172–77–73–172	6.5	7.9	57–19–50–50	201	174–1,416
Weslaco (Hidalgo)	*CM-S	21	5.2	1.0	34–59–64–91	4.2	0.7	40–16–10–42	102	195–1,087
West University Place (Harris)	*CM-S	12	6.8	0.6	221–122–55–179	6.6	1.0	56–48–24–66	140	123–1,473
White Settlement (Tarrant)	*CM-S	15	2.8	0.6	8–41–74–61	1.9	0.8	23–4–8–20	230	74–1,163
Wichita Falls (Wichita)	*CM-C	100	35.2	6.1	43–111–85–114	32.5	6.3	47–33–51–43	285	1,045–1,416
UTAH										
American Fork (Utah)	MC-S	14	2.7	0.4	29–35–52–76	2.8	0.6	33–4–20–46	194	55–1,637
Bountiful (Davis)	*CM-S	34	7.6	5.9	19–41–67–99	8.6	5.0	37–14–20–14	36	174–1,868
Brigham City (Box Elder)	MC-I	16	3.6	3.7	47–33–43–101	4.2	2.2	58–8–37–26	362	115–1,654
Cedar City (Iron)	†MC-I	12	3.2	0.7	47–62–78–87	3.2	0.6	39–11–35–16	408	72–1,428
Clearfield (Davis)	*CM-S	20	4.3	0.5	32–41–30–112	3.9	0.5	31–4–14–20	18	61–1,700
Layton (Davis)	MC-S	29	4.4	1.0	23–41–47–41	3.9	0.9	35–9–23–18	35	40–1,141
Logan (Cache)	MC-I	28	7.4	10.2	33–24–66–137	8.6	9.0	41–36–41–42	193	214–1,818
Midvale (Salt Lake)	MC-S	11	3.0	0.3	60–39–98–76	2.0	0.2	68–12–32–12	86	...–...
Murray (Salt Lake)	CO-S	27	10.8	13.7	55–47–139–163	10.5	16.9	65–32–29–23	482	274–1,738
Ogden (Weber)	*CM-C	66	27.1	3.1	57–79–126–148	28.5	3.3	60–53–33–36	39	560–1,757
Orem (Utah)	*CM-C	56	13.4	1.7	43–40–70–85	12.7	1.1	37–19–8–26	146	289–1,638
Pleasant Grove (Utah)	MC-S	12	2.1	0.3	27–49–30–69	2.2	0.3	28–2–17–42	82	37–1,488
Provo (Utah)	MC-C	77	...	...	...–...–...–...	18.2	14.3	31–25–12–34	0	463–1,740
Roy (Weber)	†MC-S	21	4.1	0.4	30–28–52–88	2.9	1.4	31–12–14–0	23	76–1,648
St. George (Washington)	†MC-I	15	7.7	5.0	34–56–78–362	6.5	4.3	50–4–26–25	618	114–1,376
Salt Lake City (Salt Lake)	CO-C	164	120.5	13.0	130–123–186–298	131.6	24.5	110–85–62–46	784	2,266–1,790
Sandy City (Salt Lake)	†MC-S	57	11.7	2.8	34–39–57–75	10.3	4.1	36–19–20–10	103	224–1,649
South Ogden (Weber)	MC-S	12	1.7	0.2	18–40–39–52	1.9	0.2	48–7–10–37	0	43–1,759
South Salt Lake (Salt Lake)	MC-S	11	5.8	0.4	76–46–263–129	4.6	0.4	76–52–48–37	0	91–1,551
Springville (Utah)	MC-S	13	2.6	3.1	60–30–24–88	4.3	1.8	40–7–26–38	58	105–1,493
Tooele (Tooele)	†MC-S	15	3.1	0.9	27–70–56–57	3.1	0.7	49–5–35–28	293	80–1,426
West Jordan (Salt Lake)	*CM-S	33	7.2	1.2	23–38–57–104	6.3	1.3	40–12–35–32	280	124–1,468
VERMONT										
Bennington t (Bennington)	†TM-I	16	4.5	0.6	78–143–2–57	3.8	0.4	40–5–59–18	153	97–1,256
Brattleboro t (Windham)	*CM-I	12	10.1	0.5	501–264–5–78	10.1	0.6	53–38–61–39	59	144–1,422
Burlington (Chittenden)	MC-C	38	...	...	...–...–...–...	18.0	20.7	48–47–34–27	0	531–1,843
Colchester t (Chittenden)	*CM-S	13	1.8	0.0	24–95–4–12	1.8	0.0	30–15–25–5	17	42–1,551
Essex t (Chittenden)	*TM-S	15	6.0	0.2	259–125–2–15	6.0	0.2	39–4–25–5	130	48–1,460
Rutland (Rutland)	MC-I	18	6.1	0.7	67–224–2–47	6.4	0.5	56–46–52–31	18	187–1,426
South Burlington (Chittenden)	*CM-S	11	3.6	0.5	27–233–7–60	3.3	0.5	66–24–47–30	220	77–1,520
Springfield t (Windsor)	*TM-I	10	3.5	0.7	48–261–3–34	3.5	1.1	54–35–69–0	145	94–1,358
VIRGINIA										
Alexandria i	*CM-S	104	160.8	0.0	340–748–259–194	170.8	0.0	98–67–77–88	1,199	3,290–1,905
Blacksburg t (Montgomery)	*CM-I	31	5.9	1.4	58–35–41–60	5.9	2.1	39–5–21–45	105	169–1,346
Bristol i	*CM-C	19	19.0	18.2	426–222–184–180	18.1	18.0	59–48–44–91	493	774–1,264
Charlottesville i	*CM-C	40	...	...	...–...–...–...	38.2	20.5	57–36–47–61	0	1,403–1,351

Table 1/9 continued PROFILES OF INDIVIDUAL CITIES

City (county)	Form of govern-ment–Metro status	Est. 1982 popu-lation (000)	Fiscal year 1983 revenues: Total general revenue ($ mil-lions)	Fiscal year 1983 revenues: Total utility reve-nue ($ mil-lions)	Fiscal year 1983 revenues: Per capita revenues ($): Intergovernmental revenue–Property taxes–Other taxes–Charges and miscella-neous general revenue	Fiscal year 1983 expenditures: Total general expendi-tures ($ mil-lions)	Fiscal year 1983 expenditures: Total utility expendi-tures ($ mil-lions)	Fiscal year 1983 expenditures: Per capita current expenditures ($): Police–Fire–Streets–Sewers and sanitation	Long term debt ($ per capita)	October 1983 public personnel: Total full time equivalent employment–Average full time monthly salary ($)
VIRGINIA continued										
Chesapeake i	*CM-S	120	115.7	6.9	431–263–148–125	114.5	7.3	52–41–56–35	594	4,123–1,483
Christiansburg t (Montgomery)	*CM-I	11	2.6	0.5	91–47–37–64	2.2	0.7	42–4–42–52	140	...–...
Colonial Heights i	*CM-C	17	13.9	1.4	311–312–115–75	13.5	1.0	39–4–30–44	648	516–1,314
Danville i	*CM-C	45	35.8	51.6	403–143–108–144	41.2	47.5	55–46–28–92	487	1,762–1,377
Fairfax i	*CM-S	20	25.8	2.9	169–594–326–173	25.1	3.2	136–79–95–127	892	245–1,835
Fredericksburg i	*CM-I	16	15.8	0.7	423–321–177–99	15.7	0.8	68–30–60–62	919	585–1,236
Front Royal t (Warren)	*CM-I	11	2.8	4.3	84–57–27–85	3.1	3.7	46–5–32–48	484	111–1,246
Hampton i	*CM-C	125	117.7	0.0	430–272–162–78	104.0	0.0	57–36–13–24	465	3,618–1,533
Harrisonburg i	*CM-I	25	15.0	15.1	169–122–165–137	21.8	15.6	29–16–35–76	988	593–1,417
Herndon t (Fairfax)	*CM-S	13	5.0	0.8	80–99–78–134	4.5	0.5	77–0–21–58	342	120–1,690
Hopewell i	*CM-C	24	29.2	0.0	391–340–123–365	29.3	0.0	53–41–51–375	125	816–1,366
Lynchburg i	*CM-C	67	70.8	4.0	411–259–233–149	76.1	4.8	56–53–35–33	935	2,210–1,389
Manassas i	CM-S	17	20.8	8.1	305–530–178–205	18.7	8.1	52–5–41–113	1,376	553–1,559
Martinsville i	*CM-I	18	15.6	9.5	388–198–158–119	16.7	9.6	71–32–40–75	41	712–1,338
Newport News i	*CM-C	151	150.8	18.7	445–289–140–124	143.1	16.1	44–44–23–46	696	5,181–1,407
Norfolk i	*CM-C	267	310.9	19.6	467–283–229–186	291.0	14.1	71–52–38–41	688	9,418–1,467
Petersburg i	*CM-C	40	41.7	2.4	451–307–180–100	41.0	2.9	71–56–41–62	362	1,581–1,326
Portsmouth i	*CM-C	106	124.9	6.9	485–242–185–269	120.5	11.5	69–55–34–50	908	4,172–1,318
Pulaski t (Pulaski)	*CM-I	10	3.4	0.4	132–53–62–95	2.9	0.4	57–23–38–45	37	130–1,051
Radford i	*CM-I	13	8.3	8.0	304–150–90–93	8.1	7.1	42–23–35–40	568	342–1,343
Richmond i	*CM-C	218	301.8	98.4	479–420–288–196	342.3	119.8	95–81–55–72	1,456	9,593–1,631
Roanoke i	*CM-C	100	124.0	3.1	495–301–215–226	117.2	5.3	48–46–44–64	744	3,502–1,537
Salem i	*CM-S	24	18.5	12.9	135–339–164–135	18.8	11.9	58–41–35–129	1,299	762–1,364
Staunton i	*CM-I	22	16.7	1.1	295–227–149–85	17.7	1.2	67–15–46–45	370	549–1,380
Suffolk i	*CM-S	48	39.5	0.9	425–214–144–49	33.8	1.8	33–23–16–26	270	1,397–1,193
Vienna t (Fairfax)	*CM-S	16	5.3	2.1	76–116–116–18	5.6	1.7	60–1–32–45	159	139–1,852
Virginia Beach i	*CM-C	283	274.2	15.5	370–273–204–123	256.2	19.8	59–29–37–45	890	8,704–1,526
Waynesboro i	*CM-I	15	14.5	0.6	325–323–172–138	13.6	0.2	56–23–50–47	193	528–1,387
Winchester i	*CM-I	20	18.9	1.4	277–317–194–143	19.6	1.8	67–25–28–45	715	642–1,295
WASHINGTON										
Aberdeen (Grays Harbor)	MC-I	18	11.1	0.9	186–85–160–171	9.9	1.4	83–70–51–86	1,704	192–2,204
Auburn (King)	MC-S	29	14.2	1.3	51–87–81–269	14.6	1.9	79–58–22–91	318	233–1,950
Bellevue (King)	*CM-S	74	40.5	5.8	90–114–170–172	37.9	6.7	59–48–53–66	658	690–2,327
Bellingham (Whatcom)	MC-C	45	22.6	4.1	104–55–190–150	24.3	5.2	71–61–78–51	603	527–1,934
Bremerton (Kitsap)	CO-C	34	...	...	...–...–...–...	14.1	4.3	60–49–32–35	0	318–2,241
Centralia (Lewis)	CO-I	12	6.7	6.0	286–48–75–143	4.6	5.3	57–44–33–49	58	...–...
Edmonds (Snohomish)	†MC-S	27	9.1	1.8	62–65–73–137	6.9	1.2	55–21–20–31	311	179–1,951
Ellensburg (Kittitas)	*CM-I	12	5.0	9.0	100–49–118–161	5.4	8.5	49–41–32–53	410	132–1,893
Everett (Snohomish)	MC-C	57	43.2	7.4	253–114–213–183	29.3	32.8	83–97–48–25	978	683–2,458
Kelso (Cowlitz)	*CM-I	11	5.8	0.6	131–46–122–223	4.8	0.7	70–47–65–70	273	95–1,807
Kennewick (Benton)	*CM-C	38	15.2	1.9	78–65–96–159	15.8	3.0	58–22–48–28	764	230–2,049
Kent (King)	†MC-S	24	24.5	2.1	360–159–169–351	25.2	2.9	115–92–88–162	738	325–2,176
Kirkland (King)	*CM-S	19	12.0	0.9	106–88–119–308	10.1	1.1	70–32–47–80	573	...–...
Lacey (Thurston)	*CM-S	14	4.4	1.2	60–64–70–110	4.1	1.3	68–26–33–24	653	81–2,066
Longview (Cowlitz)	*CM-I	31	15.5	1.9	168–60–120–152	14.0	2.9	83–42–40–83	363	302–2,113
Lynnwood (Snohomish)	MC-S	23	9.8	1.2	63–86–135–138	8.4	1.4	72–41–39–35	493	168–2,246
Mercer Island (King)	*CM-S	21	6.9	1.3	43–113–68–104	8.3	1.2	60–42–14–54	276	146–2,228
Moses Lake (Grant)	*CM-I	10	4.9	1.0	139–55–121–150	5.0	1.1	77–37–27–69	307	98–1,898
Mount Vernon (Skagit)	MC-I	14	4.9	0.0	39–67–101–149	4.9	0.0	77–38–31–51	108	131–1,551
Mountlake Terrace (Snohomish)	*CM-S	16	6.2	0.9	97–56–87–152	6.1	1.0	54–16–28–69	353	105–2,170
Oak Harbor (Island)	MC-I	12	2.8	0.5	52–40–39–104	2.6	0.4	57–12–25–37	163	65–2,023
Olympia (Thurston)	†CO-C	28	18.6	1.1	286–85–142–152	20.8	1.1	82–50–58–100	470	290–2,047
Pasco (Franklin)	*CM-C	19	10.6	1.5	94–72–148–232	7.8	2.3	75–41–35–19	741	140–2,071
Port Angeles (Clallam)	*CM-I	17	...	...	...–...–...–...	8.1	12.7	77–35–44–60	0	194–2,115
Pullman (Whitman)	†MC-I	23	5.2	0.7	79–31–63–53	5.1	1.4	36–15–24–21	111	130–1,686
Puyallup (Pierce)	*CM-S	19	20.6	1.4	750–58–131–160	15.1	8.9	90–52–53–64	894	141–2,244
Redmond (King)	MC-S	25	11.6	0.9	79–107–122–150	14.7	1.1	68–45–37–36	609	197–2,196
Renton (King)	MC-S	33	23.6	2.0	130–150–170–258	29.5	3.0	90–82–58–91	754	352–2,426
Richland (Benton)	*CM-C	35	14.9	16.2	97–55–101–172	15.8	20.5	60–38–25–69	1,038	370–2,326
Seattle (King)	MC-C	490	418.6	173.3	244–100–249–262	360.5	207.8	98–68–21–79	1,325	8,529–2,372
Spokane (Spokane)	*CM-C	172	76.8	8.7	104–57–143–143	73.8	17.8	63–62–40–62	239	1,729–2,060
Tacoma (Pierce)	*CM-C	161	100.9	138.6	141–87–212–185	117.7	104.7	80–84–58–78	1,827	2,725–2,461
Vancouver (Clark)	*CM-S	43	29.5	5.5	105–131–160–288	28.4	8.5	72–58–45–143	901	425–1,843
Walla Walla (Walla Walla)	*CM-I	26	11.6	1.1	158–49–99–145	9.8	1.8	53–43–24–64	268	240–1,650
Wenatchee (Chelan)	CO-I	17	7.6	0.9	78–69–150–142	6.8	2.5	77–54–39–70	503	168–1,862
Yakima (Yakima)	*CM-C	50	22.3	2.0	106–77–127–135	24.2	3.1	74–54–34–61	304	480–1,913
WEST VIRGINIA										
Beckley (Raleigh)	MC-I	20	8.0	0.0	78–31–208–73	7.3	0.0	82–70–65–31	96	199–1,544
Bluefield (Mercer)	*CM-I	16	8.3	0.0	58–28–113–321	8.1	0.0	52–50–38–79	429	178–1,084
Charleston (Kanawha)	MC-C	62	53.7	0.0	323–67–254–224	57.7	0.0	72–63–56–78	531	903–1,505
Clarksburg (Harrison)	*CM-I	22	7.8	1.4	49–25–121–159	7.8	1.5	54–44–53–105	311	234–1,158
Fairmont (Marion)	*CM-I	23	36.7	2.1	267–68–131–1,105	34.7	2.0	53–52–34–51	824	1,015–1,446
Huntington (Cabell)	*CM-C	62	33.9	0.0	168–31–143–204	34.3	0.1	63–67–17–65	567	732–1,344
Martinsburg (Berkeley)	*CM-I	13	5.0	0.9	39–22–85–235	4.8	0.9	52–50–26–67	114	133–1,346
Morgantown (Monongalia)	*CM-I	28	11.6	2.7	70–54–109–173	11.0	3.5	50–38–44–53	644	265–1,377
Moundsville (Marshall)	*CM-S	12	2.4	0.0	36–37–80–39	2.3	0.0	43–36–23–19	22	89–1,373
Parkersburg (Wood)	MC-C	39	52.8	3.0	253–20–114–950	68.3	13.2	57–56–16–143	1,409	1,225–1,493
St. Albans (Kanawha)	MC-S	12	4.8	0.8	101–34–127–135	5.0	1.5	41–40–37–80	241	160–1,194

Table 1/9 continued **PROFILES OF INDIVIDUAL CITIES**

City (county)	Form of government–Metro status	Est. 1982 population (000)	Fiscal year 1983 revenues: Total general revenue ($ millions)	Total utility revenue ($ millions)	Per capita revenues ($): Intergovernmental revenue–Property taxes–Other taxes–Charges and miscellaneous general revenue	Fiscal year 1983 expenditures: Total general expenditures ($ millions)	Total utility expenditures ($ millions)	Per capita current expenditures ($): Police–Fire–Streets–Sewers and sanitation	Long term debt ($ per capita)	October 1983 public personnel: Total full time equivalent employment–Average full time monthly salary ($)
WEST VIRGINIA continued										
South Charleston (Kanawha)	†MC-S	15	6.7	0.0	34–135–151–114	7.5	0.0	52–52–35–56	1,527	184–1,360
Vienna (Wood)	MC-S	12	2.3	0.3	60–20–52–64	2.5	0.5	40–7–22–34	20	73–1,088
Weirton (Hancock)	*CM-C	24	17.9	1.5	78–62–183–411	20.3	1.6	63–27–60–62	290	257–1,351
Wheeling (Ohio)	*CM-C	43	15.9	1.9	36–80–139–119	17.0	2.1	55–68–46–41	489	521–1,496
WISCONSIN										
Allouez t (Brown)	MC-S	15	4.2	0.5	118–59–2–96	3.8	0.6	12–24–38–54	186	29–1,266
Appleton (Outagamie)	MC-C	61	46.6	4.0	261–349–6–153	30.1	4.2	64–46–61–110	681	633–1,714
Ashwaubenon v (Brown)	MC-S	15	...	...	...–...–...–...	5.3	0.4	26–13–39–81	0	73–1,505
Beaver Dam (Dodge)	MC-I	14	5.5	0.4	206–90–4–88	6.0	0.5	74–30–48–44	740	130–1,354
Beloit (Rock)	*CM-C	34	...	...	...–...–...–...	42.7	0.7	94–73–46–69	0	347–1,658
Brookfield (Waukesha)	MC-S	34	12.4	0.5	116–155–13–85	13.7	0.9	64–42–46–71	520	239–1,563
Brown Deer v (Milwaukee)	*CM-S	13	5.4	0.4	130–128–3–158	4.6	0.5	74–32–32–52	664	74–2,117
Chippewa Falls (Chippewa)	MC-S	13	12.1	0.5	291–526–5–142	7.0	0.6	78–52–75–52	1,331	140–1,599
Cudahy (Milwaukee)	MC-S	19	13.4	0.9	203–364–10–114	7.4	0.8	77–30–65–101	258	151–2,038
De Pere (Brown)	†MC-S	15	14.0	0.3	398–269–5–233	14.5	0.6	66–53–44–102	1,117	151–1,869
Eau Claire (Eau Claire)	*CM-C	53	43.3	2.7	289–341–12–175	26.7	5.0	68–45–60–41	516	587–1,798
Fond du Lac (Fond du Lac)	*CM-I	36	27.6	0.9	232–366–6–164	30.4	1.8	68–68–31–93	926	406–1,789
Franklin (Milwaukee)	MC-S	18	6.0	0.1	111–94–6–125	7.0	0.3	68–29–32–42	561	91–1,917
Germantown v (Washington)	CM-S	11	3.7	0.2	136–102–8–79	4.3	0.6	77–10–43–68	259	60–1,856
Glendale (Milwaukee)	†MC-S	14	11.5	0.7	176–501–25–120	8.1	0.8	119–54–43–82	458	123–1,496
Green Bay (Brown)	MC-C	90	83.7	4.4	341–371–6–213	63.5	7.2	80–85–92–129	840	1,064–1,804
Greendale v (Milwaukee)	*CM-S	17	5.3	0.5	108–138–2–71	4.7	0.5	70–32–32–52	212	99–1,899
Greenfield (Milwaukee)	MC-S	32	13.8	0.0	158–109–4–165	15.6	0.0	72–44–38–73	900	142–1,817
Janesville (Rock)	*CM-C	51	31.3	0.8	204–308–4–94	20.9	2.1	59–51–46–42	404	457–1,839
Kaukauna (Outagamie)	MC-S	12	8.2	15.5	226–388–2–90	5.1	15.8	57–45–43–69	1,033	135–1,470
Kenosha (Kenosha)	MC-C	76	44.9	3.8	358–135–4–91	49.7	6.6	88–52–43–48	600	737–1,954
La Crosse (La Crosse)	MC-C	48	39.9	2.3	243–434–12–140	29.7	3.5	67–68–61–58	742	618–1,628
Madison (Dane)	MC-C	173	156.3	12.0	287–460–13–146	93.3	21.6	94–60–36–62	0	2,246–2,174
Manitowoc (Manitowoc)	MC-I	33	24.8	14.6	296–294–9–157	17.0	16.1	69–50–77–56	396	419–1,716
Marinette (Marinette)	MC-I	12	9.4	0.7	235–455–7–85	5.9	0.8	57–45–40–64	851	119–1,521
Marshfield (Wood)	MC-I	19	14.3	10.9	245–363–5–148	13.4	11.4	67–39–69–60	744	248–1,705
Menasha (Winnebago)	MC-S	15	17.5	6.9	611–428–3–147	17.2	7.8	96–79–48–103	823	230–1,834
Menomonee Falls v (Waukesha)	†MC-S	27	11.5	0.6	147–162–4–106	11.7	0.7	95–11–76–42	323	201–1,773
Menomonie (Dunn)	*CM-I	13	6.1	0.4	265–85–5–116	7.6	0.6	71–49–50–38	642	...–...
Mequon (Ozaukee)	†MC-S	16	5.4	0.0	98–133–5–97	6.5	0.0	84–11–77–42	377	93–2,122
Middleton (Dane)	MC-S	13	4.0	0.3	123–96–6–94	5.3	0.3	56–3–27–53	499	63–1,191
Milwaukee (Milwaukee)	MC-C	632	419.4	22.2	334–153–9–169	392.6	27.9	122–56–46–95	436	8,778–2,055
Monroe (Green)	MC-I	10	3.9	0.4	145–111–5–126	4.7	0.4	70–8–74–98	582	...–...
Muskego (Waukesha)	MC-S	16	4.0	0.0	117–79–4–59	4.5	0.0	58–8–29–34	543	72–1,781
Neenah (Winnebago)	MC-S	23	20.6	0.9	285–528–4–98	14.5	0.9	80–66–67–87	779	239–1,862
New Berlin (Waukesha)	MC-S	30	11.6	0.8	93–89–5–193	11.6	2.6	70–8–44–38	837	155–1,861
Oak Creek (Milwaukee)	MC-S	17	17.9	1.0	259–456–11–302	15.9	0.9	98–73–107–93	1,392	187–2,018
Oshkosh (Winnebago)	*CM-C	50	33.8	1.8	284–270–7–111	24.3	4.7	68–58–57–55	601	554–1,724
Racine (Racine)	MC-C	84	53.6	4.9	343–156–4–131	48.7	6.4	113–74–61–69	411	983–2,172
St. Francis (Milwaukee)	†MC-S	10	4.1	0.0	213–134–3–62	3.5	0.0	77–57–68–37	156	...–...
Sheboygan (Sheboygan)	MC-C	48	39.9	1.9	306–372–5–143	31.0	3.2	79–60–43–94	795	601–1,795
Shorewood v (Milwaukee)	*CM-S	15	4.9	0.3	121–135–3–78	5.5	0.5	57–45–39–62	61	...–...
South Milwaukee (Milwaukee)	MC-S	21	13.7	0.7	165–378–4–104	7.9	0.7	73–43–52–78	314	142–2,096
Stevens Point (Portage)	MC-I	22	20.3	0.7	284–551–12–79	13.1	1.4	64–52–78–39	767	212–1,628
Sun Prairie (Dane)	MC-S	14	3.6	4.0	108–73–4–77	3.8	4.2	58–3–33–43	433	71–1,618
Superior (Douglas)	MC-C	29	23.4	0.0	372–300–33–89	17.8	0.0	92–77–103–77	470	328–1,795
Two Rivers (Manitowoc)	*CM-I	13	8.8	3.9	264–272–3–118	5.5	4.3	70–49–44–73	159	152–1,627
Watertown (Jefferson)	MC-I	18	7.0	0.5	211–91–4–79	6.1	1.2	55–33–68–55	307	...–...
Waukesha (Waukesha)	MC-S	51	37.2	2.8	179–439–6–101	22.8	3.4	68–33–51–77	633	458–1,837
Wausau (Marathon)	MC-C	32	29.6	1.6	278–462–5–177	15.6	1.6	58–50–96–54	41	344–1,618
Wauwatosa (Milwaukee)	†MC-S	51	43.6	2.1	159–579–15–106	25.3	1.9	87–76–39–67	522	556–1,222
West Allis (Milwaukee)	MC-S	65	36.9	2.2	256–183–9–124	34.0	2.5	98–77–57–75	307	691–1,999
West Bend (Washington)	†MC-S	21	9.2	0.6	167–148–8–107	10.5	0.8	67–34–65–79	756	196–1,801
Whitefish Bay v (Milwaukee)	*CM-S	15	4.9	0.3	106–157–2–65	4.8	0.3	75–45–33–65	13	...–...
Whitewater (Walworth)	*CM-I	12	3.7	0.3	174–43–5–97	3.4	0.3	69–2–34–67	597	69–1,639
Wisconsin Rapids (Wood)	MC-I	19	21.7	8.6	429–649–6–88	16.1	10.2	88–53–67–53	1,307	290–1,823
WYOMING										
Casper (Natrona)	*CM-C	53	37.6	3.0	487–25–17–175	31.4	6.4	80–53–53–45	5	555–1,456
Cheyenne (Laramie)	MC-I	49	42.5	3.7	375–26–34–427	28.6	4.8	51–47–28–51	289	647–1,527
Gillette (Campbell)	*CM-I	18	14.0	10.1	515–17–19–207	16.2	11.2	94–0–52–45	1,416	175–2,045
Green River (Sweetwater)	†MC-I	14	14.5	0.0	478–17–17–522	15.4	0.0	90–8–32–55	37	113–1,977
Laramie (Albany)	*CM-I	25	10.6	1.2	306–21–17–75	10.7	2.0	62–66–49–34	212	194–1,971
Rawlins (Carbon)	*CM-I	12	7.3	0.8	470–27–18–93	5.5	1.7	89–20–63–44	375	146–1,596
Rock Springs (Sweetwater)	MC-I	22	16.3	0.0	557–3–28–163	20.4	0.0	85–44–39–23	67	210–1,731
Sheridan (Sheridan)	MC-I	16	15.6	0.7	790–27–19–145	15.9	0.7	80–45–40–42	172	163–1,680

Sources: Form of government and metro status: Master computer file of the International City Management Association; Population: U.S. Department of Commerce, Bureau of the Census, magnetic computer tape; Government finances: U.S. Department of Commerce, Bureau of the Census, *City Government Finances in 1982–83* GF83–4 (Washington, D.C.: Government Printing Office, 1984); Government employment: U.S. Department of Commerce, Bureau of the Census, *City Employment in 1983* GE83–2 (Washington, D.C.: Government Printing Office, 1984).

Table 1/10 PROFILES OF INDIVIDUAL COUNTIES

This table includes 1,358 counties, boroughs (in Alaska), and parishes (in Louisiana) 25,000 and over in population according to U.S. Bureau of the Census population estimates for 1982. Data on county-type governments—city-county consolidations and independent cities—are included in the Profiles of Individual Cities table immediately preceding this table. Data are from the master file of the International City Management Association (ICMA) and from U.S. government sources (see source notes for each column of data, which appear at the end of this table). Leaders (...) indicate data are not reported or not available.

County (county seat): left, the name of the county, followed, in parentheses ( ), by the name of the county seat.

Form of government–Metro status: left, the county's form of government (see key); right, the county's status vis-à-vis a metropolitan statistical area.

Est. 1982 population (000): the estimated 1982 population.

Fiscal year 1983 revenues: Total general revenue ($ millions): total general revenue for fiscal year 1983 in millions of dollars (one decimal place).

Fiscal year 1983 revenues: Per capita revenues ($): Intergovernmental revenue–Property taxes–Other taxes–Charges and miscellaneous general revenue: left, the per capita amount of revenue from intergovernmental sources; next, the amount from property taxes; next, the amount from other taxes; right, the amount from charges and miscellaneous sources.

Fiscal year 1983 expenditures: Total general expenditures ($ millions): total general expenditures in millions of dollars (one decimal place).

Fiscal year 1983 expenditures: Per capita current expenditures ($): Law enforcement–Streets–Hospitals–Welfare–Finance and administration: left, the per capita expenditure for law enforcement; next, the amount for streets; next, the amount for hospitals; next, the amount for welfare; right, the amount for finance and administration.

Long term debt ($ per capita): Per capita long term debt.

October 1983 public personnel: Total full-time equivalent employment–Average full-time monthly salary ($): left, the total number of full-time equivalent employees; right, the average full-time monthly salary of public employees.

Key

See article and notes preceding this table for detailed descriptions of these items.

Form of government

CO Council–commission
CA Council–administrator
CE Council–elected executive

Metro status

C Central county of an MSA
S Noncentral county included in an MSA
I Independent of an MSA

County (county seat)	Form of government–Metro status	Est. 1982 population (000)	Fiscal year 1983 revenues: Total general revenue ($ millions)	Fiscal year 1983 revenues: Per capita revenues ($): Intergovernmental revenue–Property taxes–Other taxes–Charges and miscellaneous general revenue	Fiscal year 1983 expenditures: Total general expenditures ($ millions)	Fiscal year 1983 expenditures: Per capita current expenditures ($): Law enforcement–Streets–Hospitals–Welfare–Finance and administration	Long term debt ($ per capita)	October 1983 public personnel: Total full time equivalent employment–Average full time monthly salary ($)
ALABAMA								
Autauga (Prattville)	CO-S	32	3.6	49–20–37–3	3.2	10–31–0–2–11	13	113–1,129
Baldwin (Bay Minette)	CA-S	83	7.3	46–18–15–8	6.6	16–21–0–2–17	0	243–1,048
Blount (Oneonta)	CO-I	37	5.0	50–35–43–8	4.2	12–28–0–4–12	0	...–...
Calhoun (Anniston)	CO-C	124	7.5	29–18–3–9	3.1	4–0–0–0–13	0	216–1,186
Chambers (Lafayette)	CO-I	40	4.3	30–25–44–8	4.8	15–37–0–1–11	20	208–973
Chilton (Clanton)	CO-I	31	3.8	53–27–33–11	4.8	15–68–0–0–14	66	...–...
Clarke (Grove Hill)	CO-I	29	2.7	65–19–3–9	2.7	11–41–0–0–9	24	...–...
Coffee (Elba)	CO-I	40	3.4	42–23–6–12	2.6	8–29–0–0–13	1	...–...
Colbert (Tuscumbia)	CO-S	54	5.9	50–26–26–6	4.9	14–22–0–0–11	37	178–1,090
Covington (Andalusia)	CO-I	37	4.3	53–22–40–3	4.7	9–60–0–0–2	24	134–1,075
Cullman (Cullman)	CO-I	63	13.3	59–15–99–38	12.2	16–52–0–2–15	230	188–1,175
Dale (Ozark)	CO-I	49	4.0	36–12–27–7	4.0	7–19–0–2–10	3	135–913
Dallas (Selma)	CO-I	56	5.5	68–24–5–2	5.4	15–28–0–1–9	13	227–978
De Kalb (Fort Payne)	CO-I	55	5.8	60–19–17–9	4.5	9–39–0–2–15	16	...–...
Elmore (Wetumpka)	CO-S	44	3.4	43–16–13–6	3.4	14–35–0–1–14	16	...–...
Escambia (Brewton)	CO-I	37	5.0	88–26–12–10	3.8	9–41–0–3–26	6	...–...
Etowah (Gadsden)	CO-C	103	10.6	48–30–17–8	11.0	13–27–0–0–16	105	284–1,084
Franklin (Russellville)	CO-I	29	4.0	73–25–35–6	3.8	11–45–0–0–10	12	...–...
Houston (Dothan)	CO-I	78	9.6	43–60–9–13	8.5	24–33–0–2–15	95	302–1,124
Jackson (Scottsboro)	CO-I	52	5.7	46–21–42–2	5.4	11–21–0–1–18	20	...–...
Jefferson (Birmingham)	CO-C	673	160.2	67–37–71–54	149.8	23–27–23–10–26	0	3,440–1,442
Lauderdale (Florence)	CO-C	82	7.4	39–19–27–5	7.5	12–26–0–1–13	8	205–1,099
Lawrence (Moulton)	CO-I	31	4.2	63–20–50–3	4.1	18–36–0–3–19	0	...–...
Lee (Opelika)	CO-I	79	6.1	37–22–17–1	5.4	11–17–0–0–7	5	187–1,137
Limestone (Athens)	CO-S	46	5.9	58–20–38–12	5.2	16–41–0–1–16	86	141–1,225
Macon (Tuskeegee)	CO-I	27	2.6	58–15–26–1	2.5	14–48–0–0–7	0	...–...
Madison (Huntsville)	CO-C	202	16.4	27–24–20–10	16.5	10–23–0–0–12	41	607–1,189
Marengo (Linden)	CO-I	25	3.2	79–29–9–12	3.3	12–67–0–1–13	29	...–...
Marion (Hamilton)	CO-I	30	3.8	50–14–47–14	4.5	10–74–0–0–13	68	96–1,044
Marshall (Guntersville)	CO-S	67	5.2	43–15–10–9	5.5	14–34–0–1–18	14	183–1,152
Mobile (Mobile)	CA-C	375	43.4	41–47–16–11	41.1	21–15–0–1–21	73	1,131–1,244
Montgomery (Montgomery)	CA-C	202	22.1	29–16–53–12	20.8	21–12–0–2–16	2	579–1,113
Morgan (Decatur)	CO-I	91	...	...–...–...–...	5.7	13–1–0–1–14	0	278–1,196
Pike (Troy)	CO-I	28	3.9	63–33–34–6	3.2	10–48–0–0–10	0	119–993
Russell (Phenix City)	CO-S	47	3.3	37–16–6–10	3.3	11–21–0–0–8	66	181–887
St. Clair (Ashville)	CO-S	42	4.1	47–31–14–6	4.2	18–39–0–3–19	10	131–1,150
Shelby (Columbiana)	CO-S	70	11.0	41–60–49–6	10.4	29–22–0–3–28	48	222–1,332
Talladega (Talladega)	CO-I	75	...	...–...–...–...	6.8	9–30–0–3–13	0	242–1,027
Tallapoosa (Dadeville)	CO-I	40	3.4	54–20–9–3	3.5	11–38–0–1–11	48	...–...
Tuscaloosa (Tuscaloosa)	CO-C	138	24.3	47–24–89–15	24.3	20–29–0–1–17	31	451–1,285
Walker (Jasper)	CO-S	69	11.3	66–29–58–11	11.3	13–35–0–0–16	70	211–1,159

Table 1/10 continued **PROFILES OF INDIVIDUAL COUNTIES**

County (county seat)	Form of government–Metro status	Est. 1982 population (000)	Fiscal year 1983 revenues: Total general revenue ($ millions)	Fiscal year 1983 revenues: Per capita revenues ($): Intergovernmental revenue–Property taxes–Other taxes–Charges and miscellaneous general revenue	Fiscal year 1983 expenditures: Total general expenditures ($ millions)	Fiscal year 1983 expenditures: Per capita current expenditures ($): Law enforcement–Streets–Hospitals–Welfare–Finance and administration	Long term debt ($ per capita)	October 1983 public personnel: Total full time equivalent employment–Average full time monthly salary ($)
ALASKA								
Fairbanks North Star (Fairbanks)	CE-I	60	100.8	1,283–190–30–169	128.0	0–7–0–1–115	1,358	1,665–2,939
ARIZONA								
Apache (St. Johns)	CA-I	52	25.9	72–7–0–416	26.2	14–18–0–8–29	4	163–1,385
Cochise (Bisbee)	CA-I	90	...	...–...–...–...	25.8	38–20–34–0–57	0	593–1,377
Coconino (Flagstaff)	CA-I	77	16.7	139–6–5–65	18.1	33–33–0–46–46	0	457–1,500
Gila (Globe)	CO-I	40	26.2	161–157–2–336	25.8	35–40–129–12–47	47	444–1,130
Maricopa (Phoenix)	CA-C	1,609	414.6	116–66–5–72	443.9	30–13–50–37–35	253	7,060–1,668
Mohave (Kingman)	CA-I	62	25.8	130–98–5–181	27.6	58–34–142–59–71	5	772–1,334
Navajo (Holbrook)	CO-I	69	13.6	116–23–2–57	13.3	28–36–0–14–38	21	327–1,338
Pima (Tucson)	CA-C	568	257.5	114–145–4–191	252.8	46–15–49–42–45	406	4,493–1,701
Pinal (Florence)	CA-I	96	29.7	109–123–2–75	32.7	40–26–63–43–47	0	1,087–1,196
Yavapai (Prescott)	CA-I	76	15.5	94–89–14–8	15.2	30–33–0–47–48	0	352–1,187
Yuma (Yuma)	CA-I	82	16.5	113–59–6–24	17.1	42–24–0–66–42	120	326–1,382
ARKANSAS								
Ashley (Hamburg)	CE-I	27	2.5	55–27–1–10	2.7	13–35–0–0–17	0	...–...
Baxter (Mountain Home)	CE-I	28	13.0	53–37–0–371	13.3	15–36–333–28–17	28	133–905
Benton (Bentonville)	CE-S	80	5.2	27–31–0–7	4.4	7–15–0–0–21	0	176–963
Boone (Harrison)	CE-I	27	17.2	50–33–0–562	13.9	7–25–433–1–14	106	495–1,054
Columbia (Magnolia)	CE-I	27	3.5	81–28–0–18	3.2	13–66–0–0–18	0	100–987
Craighead (Jonesboro)	CE-I	63	4.9	27–33–0–17	3.8	6–13–0–1–20	32	136–1,325
Crawford (Van Buren)	CE-S	38	3.4	59–19–0–11	2.9	9–23–0–0–15	0	...–...
Crittenden (Marion)	CE-S	50	...	...–...–...–...	1.2	7–3–0–1–1	0	203–928
Faulkner (Conway)	CE-I	47	2.5	25–24–0–5	2.5	7–23–0–1–13	0	100–776
Garland (Hot Springs)	CE-I	71	13.0	36–37–1–108	5.7	15–17–0–2–22	44	188–921
Greene (Paragould)	CE-I	31	1.9	36–18–0–7	1.9	8–18–0–2–14	0	71–830
Hot Spring (Malvern)	CE-I	27	7.3	44–36–0–194	6.8	10–24–177–1–15	96	87–1,035
Independence (Batesville)	CE-I	32	3.3	47–33–10–16	2.8	15–22–0–0–20	0	118–903
Jefferson (Pine Bluff)	CE-C	90	28.9	34–46–1–238	16.8	10–19–0–0–19	11	222–1,067
Lonoke (Lonoke)	CE-I	35	3.4	36–23–0–38	2.5	7–27–0–0–12	0	89–802
Miller (Texarkana)	CE-C	38	2.8	41–20–0–11	2.8	13–24–0–2–14	0	...–...
Mississippi (Blytheville)	CE-I	59	17.5	57–20–0–218	16.6	15–15–182–7–14	185	702–1,019
Ouachita (Camden)	CE-I	31	9.7	48–31–0–228	10.1	10–47–218–0–20	2	387–1,017
Phillips (Helena)	CE-I	34	5.4	58–38–48–13	3.1	12–32–0–1–15	0	...–...
Poinsett (Harrisburg)	CE-I	26	2.1	49–23–0–8	2.0	12–22–0–2–14	0	...–...
Pope (Russellville)	CE-I	40	6.7	48–64–0–55	5.4	15–35–0–1–14	49	174–1,042
Pulaski (Little Rock)	CE-C	345	42.5	20–25–35–43	31.7	11–6–0–3–17	0	776–1,203
St. Francis (Forrest City)	CE-I	31	2.8	48–29–0–14	2.7	9–26–0–4–16	59	77–924
Saline (Benton)	CE-S	54	12.6	29–24–19–160	11.7	6–15–153–0–12	21	429–1,431
Sebastian (Fort Smith)	CE-C	95	10.6	47–24–0–39	9.3	11–10–0–0–16	2	228–1,121
Union (El Dorado)	CE-I	49	17.5	51–29–54–226	15.4	13–13–181–3–17	29	521–1,058
Washington (Fayetteville)	CE-C	102	33.6	35–26–17–251	24.2	6–1–201–0–15	0	873–1,004
White (Searcy)	CE-I	51	10.1	33–21–0–141	9.8	9–23–133–1–9	0	98–919
CALIFORNIA								
Alameda (Oakland)	CA-C	1,138	555.0	312–99–10–66	546.9	51–9–65–177–66	25	9,413–1,824
Butte (Oroville)	CA-C	152	75.8	358–73–28–40	74.9	46–40–0–152–56	0	1,574–1,496
Contra Costa (Martinez)	CA-S	678	373.2	303–142–19–87	367.2	58–21–84–149–56	65	6,875–1,885
El Dorado (Placerville)	CA-I	94	47.3	269–156–33–46	46.9	88–45–0–123–86	121	912–1,805
Fresno (Fresno)	CA-C	535	364.3	444–106–21–109	367.6	59–19–122–231–56	32	6,738–1,789
Humboldt (Eureka)	CA-I	110	60.0	394–92–20–40	62.4	70–43–27–200–81	21	1,189–1,565
Imperial (El Centro)	CA-I	98	50.3	346–77–17–74	52.4	91–27–0–149–64	0	1,069–1,596
Kern (Bakersfield)	CA-C	434	293.9	311–219–51–96	315.0	101–35–99–158–77	0	6,256–1,964
Kings (Hanford)	CA-I	78	43.7	371–117–27–46	45.9	64–33–0–190–64	0	944–1,591
Lake (Lakeport)	CO-I	41	30.8	454–176–46–81	33.0	105–55–0–221–128	0	602–1,419
Los Angeles (Los Angeles)	CA-C	7,678	4,461.5	349–145–9–78	4,159.8	54–10–81–191–56	68	71,264–2,126
Madera (Madera)	CA-I	69	38.1	342–122–35–55	37.3	72–47–0–175–58	0	693–1,470
Marin (San Rafael)	CA-S	223	108.5	222–144–16–104	103.2	48–34–2–69–60	31	1,983–1,731
Mendocino (Ukiah)	CA-I	69	51.5	479–134–40–90	53.7	65–69–42–219–76	0	1,130–1,752
Merced (Merced)	CA-I	142	112.9	432–120–21–220	121.4	51–34–135–270–70	0	2,799–1,500
Monterey (Salinas)	CA-C	304	139.1	217–98–21–120	144.7	59–23–67–123–64	34	2,608–2,008
Napa (Napa)	CA-C	101	45.3	258–98–34–58	44.2	55–24–0–102–68	35	938–1,812
Nevada (Nevada City)	CO-I	60	29.2	267–121–45–57	28.4	66–58–0–125–80	69	624–1,624
Orange (Santa Ana)	CA-C	2,014	746.3	180–101–12–78	702.2	32–9–0–98–45	12	11,385–2,060
Placer (Auburn)	CA-S	126	73.3	310–144–47–81	74.0	72–45–0–153–98	77	1,413–1,846
Riverside (Riverside)	CA-C	715	410.7	348–118–23–86	399.7	66–18–52–168–58	34	7,358–1,752
Sacramento (Sacramento)	CA-C	829	593.2	410–105–50–151	580.0	71–16–1–267–72	141	6,779–1,935
San Benito (Hollister)	CO-I	27	11.6	284–73–19–56	11.9	42–28–5–125–49	60	318–1,638
San Bernardino (San Bernardino)	CA-C	965	550.6	360–104–20–87	521.6	57–11–46–204–57	31	8,564–1,996
San Diego (San Diego)	CA-C	1,962	770.7	252–80–11–50	715.4	36–10–3–138–49	4	10,515–1,827
San Joaquin (Stockton)	CA-C	372	247.1	407–108–18–133	255.2	60–28–84–303–71	0	4,183–1,827
San Luis Obispo (San Luis Obispo)	CA-I	167	89.2	216–155–26–138	87.7	54–33–56–96–74	122	1,804–1,629
San Mateo (Redwood City)	CA-S	590	267.2	226–117–19–91	244.6	63–13–59–80–55	3	4,471–2,161
Santa Barbara (Santa Barbara)	CA-C	308	158.7	240–142–24–109	153.9	60–19–0–95–68	16	3,173–1,888
Santa Clara (San Jose)	CA-C	1,329	779.4	317–115–48–106	669.6	44–7–72–136–56	15	10,959–2,040
Santa Cruz (Santa Cruz)	CA-C	196	94.7	249–99–29–107	97.1	59–29–0–123–77	59	1,727–1,799
Shasta (Redding)	CA-C	122	80.3	408–93–24–135	84.2	70–39–96–236–59	0	1,513–1,732
Siskiyou (Yreka)	CA-I	41	27.0	429–114–20–90	28.3	54–92–0–165–106	17	523–1,660
Solano (Fairfield)	CA-C	254	96.8	227–101–7–46	97.7	37–14–0–149–53	20	1,715–1,868
Sonoma (Santa Rosa)	CA-C	313	182.0	243–143–30–165	174.8	60–43–77–130–58	142	3,376–1,924

Table 1/10 continued **PROFILES OF INDIVIDUAL COUNTIES**

County (county seat)	Form of govern-ment–Metro status	Est. 1982 popu-lation (000)	Fiscal year 1983 revenues: Total general revenue ($ mil-lions)	Fiscal year 1983 revenues: Per capita revenues ($): Intergovernmental rev-enue–Property taxes–Other taxes–Charges and miscellaneous general revenue	Fiscal year 1983 expenditures: Total general expendi-tures ($ mil-lions)	Fiscal year 1983 expenditures: Per capita current expenditures ($): Law enforcement–Streets–Hospitals–Welfare–Finance and administration	Long term debt ($ per capita)	October 1983 public personnel: Total full time equivalent employment–Average full time monthly salary ($)
CALIFORNIA continued								
Stanislaus (Modesto)	CA-C	280	173.3	391–87–19–121	170.7	63–28–84–210–54	0	2,957–1,631
Sutter (Yuba City)	CA-C	55	40.0	394–140–28–163	39.6	87–47–82–165–90	0	832–1,743
Tehama (Red Bluff)	CO-I	41	26.0	379–124–24–106	26.9	72–63–46–171–80	1	530–1,560
Tulare (Visalia)	CA-C	258	164.6	448–98–28–63	162.6	60–36–0–263–62	1	2,523–1,672
Tuolumne (Sonora)	CA-I	36	25.5	288–143–51–223	22.7	70–56–22–151–87	0	616–1,363
Ventura (Ventura)	CA-C	558	308.0	273–156–13–110	290.1	60–12–45–100–63	54	5,453–1,994
Yolo (Woodland)	CA-S	117	69.8	322–121–43–112	75.2	53–28–53–165–104	22	1,419–1,694
Yuba (Marysville)	CA-S	51	38.3	392–99–25–237	35.5	64–29–0–281–57	2,722	539–1,529
COLORADO								
Adams (Brighton)	CA-S	262	93.8	120–89–3–148	83.9	20–20–0–89–36	40	1,165–1,538
Arapahoe (Littleton)	CO-S	332	46.7	40–80–4–16	48.0	28–15–0–35–28	47	802–1,880
Boulder (Boulder)	CO-C	200	43.5	76–115–4–22	43.6	24–23–0–57–24	22	945–1,052
Douglas (Castle Rock)	CO-S	29	7.9	53–157–24–39	8.0	39–67–0–19–50	41	194–1,333
El Paso (Colorado Springs)	CO-C	331	59.7	71–75–1–34	59.7	17–22–0–59–21	0	1,242–1,269
Fremont (Canon City)	CO-I	30	10.1	194–74–26–43	8.3	14–37–0–130–45	121	176–1,333
Jefferson (Golden)	CA-S	393	105.7	58–90–33–88	105.4	21–38–0–41–32	12	1,659–1,695
La Plata (Durango)	CO-I	29	12.9	137–71–110–120	11.4	33–52–0–85–46	19	159–1,433
Larimer (Fort Collins)	CA-C	158	45.7	110–93–31–55	48.3	25–39–0–65–28	50	602–1,734
Mesa (Grand Junction)	CA-I	94	48.2	207–76–102–129	52.6	32–55–3–83–34	462	562–1,520
Pueblo (Pueblo)	CO-C	126	56.6	196–106–1–147	55.6	25–20–0–188–34	277	771–1,241
Weld (Greeley)	CO-C	127	38.7	143–113–9–41	37.1	32–22–0–98–36	0	1,906–1,505
DELAWARE								
Kent (Dover)	CO-I	99	...	...–...–...–...	15.1	1–0–1–2–12	0	195–1,061
New Castle (Wilmington)	CE-C	401	86.0	49–61–3–101	93.5	34–1–0–0–30	265	1,312–1,875
Sussex (Georgetown)	CA-I	99	12.3	37–32–3–52	9.2	2–0–0–1–21	120	168–982
FLORIDA								
Alachua (Gainesville)	CA-C	162	37.6	52–115–2–63	36.6	47–17–0–9–36	504	960–1,058
Bay (Panama City)	CA-C	104	28.3	55–72–4–139	16.4	34–31–7–2–19	117	425–1,053
Brevard (Titusville)	CA-C	303	75.4	53–101–12–83	82.6	27–40–1–6–37	533	2,194–1,265
Broward (Fort Lauderdale)	CA-C	1,073	309.1	60–124–12–92	332.6	44–10–0–1–35	276	5,600–1,703
Charlotte (Port Charlotte)	CA-I	68	26.1	54–175–32–126	22.7	46–82–0–9–51	55	639–1,192
Citrus (Inverness)	CA-I	64	36.0	71–125–7–359	35.1	38–35–187–1–39	245	728–1,194
Clay (Green Cove Springs)	CO-S	74	14.4	30–104–13–48	14.3	34–29–0–3–23	80	376–1,189
Collier (Naples)	CA-I	101	41.3	55–169–38–147	40.1	81–42–0–5–66	406	1,204–1,234
Columbia (Lake City)	CA-I	38	7.0	67–78–10–32	5.9	30–26–1–0–28	0	...–...
Dade (Miami)	CA-C	1,717	1,325.3	250–168–50–305	1,121.8	70–10–111–13–44	766	26,591–1,786
Escambia (Pensacola)	CA-C	249	101.3	113–108–5–181	76.4	51–12–41–8–37	244	1,514–1,441
Gadsden (Quincy)	CO-I	43	8.2	68–51–2–71	8.2	21–28–61–3–25	312	...–...
Hernando (Brooksville)	CO-I	56	...	...–...–...–...	10.5	35–27–0–0–23	0	762–1,000
Highlands (Sebring)	CA-I	53	13.4	64–123–7–58	11.1	40–68–0–5–38	115	371–1,312
Hillsborough (Tampa)	CA-C	688	323.2	69–119–21–261	354.5	53–23–132–14–41	597	7,738–1,581
Indian River (Vero Beach)	CA-I	68	16.2	50–104–15–68	15.4	50–43–0–7–43	0	...–...
Jackson (Marianna)	CO-I	40	5.2	43–60–2–26	5.0	21–17–0–5–23	126	158–1,092
Lake (Tavares)	CO-I	114	19.8	58–66–7–44	20.1	23–47–0–8–25	16	548–1,044
Lee (Fort Myers)	CA-C	231	105.6	82–154–16–204	81.0	33–34–0–12–53	780	1,736–1,303
Leon (Tallahassee)	CA-C	159	24.5	47–75–5–28	25.0	34–14–0–1–27	151	570–1,272
Manatee (Bradenton)	CA-C	162	71.6	72–160–6–204	61.8	46–54–10–5–42	732	1,306–1,440
Marion (Ocala)	CO-C	139	22.6	57–76–5–24	22.6	43–17–7–3–29	3	587–1,281
Martin (Stuart)	CA-I	73	21.0	50–155–15–68	19.7	53–28–0–7–37	27	...–...
Monroe (Key West)	CA-I	67	24.2	87–153–21–99	24.9	65–39–0–12–59	181	574–1,075
Nassau (Fernandina Beach)	CO-S	36	7.0	63–101–3–30	6.2	35–42–0–1–27	119	224–1,280
Okaloosa (Crestview)	CA-C	119	20.7	54–51–3–66	16.9	18–22–0–0–27	52	543–1,179
Orange (Orlando)	CA-C	503	160.7	76–143–17–84	180.4	55–15–0–14–29	542	4,209–1,386
Osceola (Kissimmee)	CO-S	60	14.7	58–98–35–55	12.9	48–27–0–7–40	38	407–1,258
Palm Beach (West Palm Beach)	CA-C	647	196.6	75–153–7–69	214.9	45–16–0–25–26	301	3,868–1,530
Pasco (New Port Richey)	CA-S	217	62.4	46–87–10–145	52.0	32–18–63–3–25	469	1,230–1,299
Pinellas (Clearwater)	CA-C	760	219.5	61–112–10–106	226.6	34–7–0–17–31	335	3,517–1,498
Polk (Bartow)	CA-C	342	79.6	58–89–6–80	66.8	35–20–36–8–26	24	2,448–1,318
Putnam (Palatka)	CO-I	54	18.2	60–105–7–167	17.4	42–46–0–4–30	30	344–1,198
St. Johns (St. Augustine)	CA-S	57	14.9	52–123–8–76	14.0	53–44–3–6–38	132	368–1,142
St. Lucie (Fort Pierce)	CA-I	102	24.8	51–122–6–64	21.7	54–20–0–7–31	25	779–1,346
Santa Rosa (Milton)	CO-S	60	29.0	129–80–6–269	25.2	32–53–208–1–26	73	711–1,614
Sarasota (Sarasota)	CA-C	220	54.2	47–118–36–45	51.9	43–22–0–5–42	0	1,371–1,310
Seminole (Sanford)	CA-S	200	60.8	45–92–7–159	50.9	31–17–78–2–27	25	1,102–1,525
Volusia (De Land)	CA-C	282	62.4	57–110–11–44	58.9	44–23–0–2–21	21	1,612–1,328
GEORGIA								
Baldwin (Milledgeville)	CO-I	37	7.2	61–44–63–28	6.1	22–22–2–3–23	0	165–1,124
Bartow (Cartersville)	CO-I	42	14.5	51–112–4–177	15.4	17–48–3–1–25	147	252–1,024
Bibb (Macon)	CA-C	153	29.1	48–89–18–35	29.3	27–14–14–6–39	166	532–1,307
Bulloch (Statesboro)	CO-I	36	6.0	88–51–6–21	6.2	17–22–0–2–15	30	...–...
Carroll (Carrollton)	CO-I	59	8.9	33–36–65–16	6.6	21–36–0–1–15	3	155–992
Catoosa (Ringgold)	CO-S	38	5.8	27–41–54–30	4.2	0–32–4–1–20	0	...–...
Chatham (Savannah)	CA-C	210	50.5	47–87–92–13	40.2	29–19–17–3–30	30	926–1,253
Cherokee (Canton)	CO-S	57	6.3	28–59–10–15	5.2	12–11–0–0–16	0	171–965
Clarke (Athens)	CA-C	76	21.6	57–103–96–30	17.6	39–5–6–1–42	38	446–1,352
Clayton (Jonesboro)	CA-S	156	36.8	34–148–11–43	35.7	52–17–2–1–48	15	995–857
Cobb (Marietta)	CO-S	321	90.7	41–145–19–77	78.8	35–11–6–1–44	429	2,200–1,502

Table 1/10 continued **PROFILES OF INDIVIDUAL COUNTIES**

County (county seat)	Form of govern-ment–Metro status	Est. 1982 popu-lation (000)	Fiscal year 1983 revenues: Total general revenue ($ mil-lions)	Fiscal year 1983 revenues: Per capita revenues ($): Intergovernmental rev-enue–Property taxes–Other taxes–Charges and miscellaneous general revenue	Fiscal year 1983 expenditures: Total general expendi-tures ($ mil-lions)	Fiscal year 1983 expenditures: Per capita current expenditures ($): Law enforcement–Streets–Hospitals–Welfare–Finance and administration	Long term debt ($ per capita)	October 1983 public personnel: Total full time equivalent employment–Average full time monthly salary ($)
GEORGIA continued								
Coffee (Douglas)	CO-I	28	4.2	38–39–59–18	3.8	15–37–3–1–22	6	...–...
Colquitt (Moultrie)	CA-I	36	4.6	46–69–1–12	4.5	20–19–0–1–20	65	109–975
Columbia (Appling)	CO-S	44	7.5	24–52–55–39	6.0	20–19–0–0–21	335	203–1,126
Coweta (Newnan)	CA-I	41	10.7	40–63–89–68	9.9	42–40–3–3–18	24	158–1,248
De Kalb (Decatur)	CA-C	492	225.0	69–156–114–117	176.3	51–17–45–2–45	270	3,864–1,497
Decatur (Bainbridge)	CO-I	26	4.4	62–15–67–23	4.0	34–17–3–2–25	25	98–1,027
Dougherty (Albany)	CA-C	103	22.0	51–51–83–29	16.7	20–15–4–1–23	44	327–1,498
Douglas (Douglasville)	CO-S	59	13.8	62–78–57–37	16.2	24–26–7–3–21	315	388–1,200
Fayette (Fayetteville)	CO-S	34	7.3	25–84–55–52	6.6	23–19–0–0–19	276	190–1,253
Floyd (Rome)	CA-I	79	22.3	63–83–107–28	22.7	33–25–5–0–28	123	319–1,189
Forsyth (Cumming)	CA-S	30	4.6	37–43–54–20	4.7	23–28–0–2–32	45	114–1,154
Fulton (Atlanta)	CA-C	601	227.8	50–173–122–34	217.8	25–7–63–9–47	111	3,614–1,482
Glynn (Brunswick)	CA-I	56	20.2	67–115–129–49	19.6	77–34–0–1–52	79	611–1,271
Gordon (Calhoun)	CA-I	31	4.8	50–24–68–16	4.7	17–46–0–1–21	64	124–1,038
Gwinnett (Lawrenceville)	CA-S	192	61.4	64–167–21–67	52.1	42–36–1–8–32	1,087	1,361–1,453
Habersham (Clarkesville)	CO-I	26	3.2	36–74–2–11	2.9	12–23–3–4–27	7	93–1,057
Hall (Gainesville)	CA-I	78	19.5	67–79–83–21	17.5	41–23–4–3–40	13	392–1,300
Henry (Mc Donough)	CA-S	38	10.2	33–123–63–49	8.8	41–32–0–1–32	0	248–1,315
Houston (Warner Robins)	CO-S	80	11.2	39–74–6–22	10.2	21–8–0–1–23	48	237–1,195
Jackson (Jefferson)	CO-S	26	4.1	43–50–45–19	3.9	27–37–6–1–25	0	...–...
Laurens (Dublin)	CO-I	38	9.1	108–42–73–19	7.0	13–49–0–1–21	0	152–1,110
Liberty (Hinesville)	CO-I	41	6.0	42–36–43–27	4.5	16–12–0–1–17	3	135–1,088
Lowndes (Valdosta)	CA-I	69	14.2	63–27–79–37	11.0	20–24–0–1–19	33	228–943
Newton (Covington)	CO-S	37	6.6	33–63–53–27	7.4	19–29–8–2–28	35	125–921
Paulding (Dallas)	CO-S	27	4.9	32–95–38–15	4.2	23–43–8–2–24	6	111–968
Polk (Cedartown)	CO-I	33	6.4	38–89–52–15	4.6	16–40–0–1–25	0	...–...
Richmond (Augusta)	CA-C	183	43.8	42–39–100–58	35.1	32–12–23–0–31	101	1,102–1,107
Rockdale (Conyers)	CO-S	39	8.5	26–138–15–36	9.0	37–30–0–0–31	165	202–1,173
Spalding (Griffin)	CA-I	50	6.9	21–71–9–36	7.1	27–11–0–1–24	34	184–1,111
Sumter (Americus)	CO-I	30	5.8	82–26–62–22	5.1	26–22–2–2–20	0	...–...
Thomas (Thomasville)	CA-I	39	6.5	73–78–3–14	6.5	24–22–1–1–24	0	...–...
Tift (Tifton)	CO-I	34	9.1	58–46–73–94	7.6	18–23–0–1–32	25	148–1,135
Troup (La Grange)	CA-I	51	10.0	66–45–69–17	7.7	20–19–1–1–20	0	185–1,086
Upson (Thomaston)	CA-I	27	3.9	39–46–54–8	3.3	24–21–1–1–16	5	...–...
Walker (La Fayette)	CO-S	57	8.1	41–31–41–30	7.7	13–18–8–1–18	133	144–1,044
Walton (Monroe)	CO-S	31	5.0	38–53–48–24	4.6	20–27–8–1–30	0	139–1,054
Ware (Waycross)	CO-I	37	9.3	88–67–76–19	6.7	15–16–0–1–26	161	155–937
Whitfield (Dalton)	CA-I	66	13.2	63–28–95–15	11.8	20–45–5–1–25	18	265–1,049
HAWAII								
Hawaii (Hilo)	CE-I	99	63.0	160–367–63–49	63.8	105–52–0–0–80	561	1,463–1,670
Kauai (Lihue)	CE-I	41	30.6	262–341–71–67	26.7	92–60–0–11–71	461	785–1,609
Maui (Wailuku)	CE-I	76	55.4	176–312–78–162	58.3	95–63–0–62–85	251	1,100–1,673
IDAHO								
Ada (Boise)	CO-C	181	17.3	15–52–4–25	17.6	27–0–0–8–35	22	553–1,348
Bannock (Pocatello)	CO-I	68	22.2	31–51–4–242	29.4	17–23–231–4–33	159	750–1,266
Bingham (Blackfoot)	CO-I	37	...	...–...–...–...	...	...–...–...–...–...	0	267–1,414
Bonneville (Idaho Falls)	CO-I	67	7.7	41–53–2–18	7.7	15–30–0–6–26	7	209–1,392
Canyon (Caldwell)	CO-I	86	10.0	44–48–3–21	10.2	18–14–0–5–34	0	292–1,257
Kootenai (Coeur d'Alene)	CO-I	62	9.3	58–59–8–26	9.1	22–21–0–2–39	0	232–1,176
Latah (Moscow)	CO-I	30	3.7	38–46–2–39	5.3	15–20–0–3–25	64	78–1,131
Nez Perce (Lewiston)	CO-I	33	9.8	43–84–3–168	9.3	18–46–0–7–30	0	104–1,370
Twin Falls (Twin Falls)	CO-I	55	26.4	44–40–3–398	23.9	9–20–311–2–23	0	573–1,318
ILLINOIS								
Adams (Quincy)	CO-I	72	9.1	44–41–6–36	7.2	17–23–0–1–22	0	218–1,339
Boone (Belvidere)	CO-S	29	5.3	57–44–13–69	4.2	29–16–0–35–22	7	165–1,121
Bureau (Princeton)	CO-I	38	7.5	47–53–8–87	7.9	15–50–0–44–33	0	263–1,123
Champaign (Urbana)	CO-C	172	20.2	33–38–9–38	21.9	17–6–0–21–26	28	524–1,206
Christian (Taylorville)	CO-I	35	5.2	52–30–28–39	5.6	20–46–0–3–24	0	...–...
Clinton (Carlyle)	CO-S	33	...	...–...–...–...	2.9	7–23–0–0–4	0	88–1,340
Coles (Charleston)	CO-I	52	6.2	36–52–4–25	5.5	18–2–0–1–24	0	141–1,206
Cook (Chicago)	CE-C	5,256	794.2	39–51–20–40	779.6	19–5–43–3–30	42	21,989–1,545
De Kalb (Sycamore)	CA-I	75	12.8	70–54–4–44	11.3	21–11–0–36–21	4	303–1,451
Du Page (Wheaton)	CA-C	682	114.0	50–68–6–44	115.0	12–7–0–9–20	144	2,016–1,571
Effingham (Effingham)	CO-I	31	3.9	45–27–7–48	3.2	12–29–0–0–26	8	...–...
Franklin (Benton)	CO-I	43	3.8	39–19–9–21	4.1	11–19–0–0–15	0	...–...
Fulton (Lewistown)	CO-I	43	6.8	62–54–11–33	9.3	19–39–0–15–25	0	147–1,311
Grundy (Morris)	CO-I	30	6.9	53–79–5–90	6.5	27–31–0–52–27	23	219–1,199
Henry (Cambridge)	CO-S	55	...	...–...–...–...	4.4	8–23–0–34–0	0	316–1,031
Iroquois (Watseka)	CO-I	33	6.4	87–68–7–34	5.9	19–16–0–3–27	0	131–1,239
Jackson (Murphysboro)	CO-I	62	7.9	39–41–7–38	8.4	15–21–0–33–15	0	170–1,263
Jefferson (Mount Vernon)	CO-I	38	3.6	51–6–13–26	4.3	15–32–0–0–22	0	...–...
Kane (Geneva)	CO-S	281	26.9	22–41–5–27	25.0	18–14–0–0–23	18	704–1,399
Kankakee (Kankakee)	CA-C	102	8.7	30–30–6–19	9.0	19–27–0–0–21	0	264–1,153
Kendall (Yorkville)	CO-I	37	4.3	43–46–9–17	4.5	16–18–0–8–28	0	116–1,831
Knox (Galesburg)	CO-I	60	9.1	51–46–4–52	8.4	17–19–0–36–25	11	299–1,073
La Salle (Ottawa)	CO-I	110	13.6	48–41–6–30	15.1	11–30–0–20–30	0	315–1,128
Lake (Waukegan)	CO-S	452	45.3	22–40–5–33	58.1	15–8–0–13–25	124	1,735–1,480
Lee (Dixon)	CO-I	35	6.3	42–46–9–80	6.1	18–19–0–29–32	0	163–1,102

Table 1/10 continued **PROFILES OF INDIVIDUAL COUNTIES**

County (county seat)	Form of govern- ment– Metro status	Est. 1982 popu- lation (000)	Fiscal year 1983 revenues: Total general revenue ($ mil- lions)	Fiscal year 1983 revenues: Per capita revenues ($) Intergovernmental rev- enue–Property taxes– Other taxes–Charges and miscellaneous general revenue	Fiscal year 1983 expenditures: Total general expendi- tures ($ mil- lions)	Fiscal year 1983 expenditures: Per capita current expenditures ($) Law enforcement– Streets–Hospitals– Welfare–Finance and administration	Long term debt ($ per capita)	October 1983 public personnel: Total full time equivalent employment– Average full time monthly salary ($)
ILLINOIS continued								
Livingston (Pontiac)	CO-I	41	6.9	76–35–8–51	7.3	18–33–0–33–40	0	...–...
Logan (Lincoln)	CO-I	31	6.4	44–68–7–88	6.3	26–74–0–0–31	0	...–...
Mc Donough (Macomb)	CO-I	38	5.6	52–44–3–47	5.9	15–42–0–30–25	3	...–...
Mc Henry (Woodstock)	CO-S	150	14.2	32–35–12–16	12.4	20–9–0–7–20	0	372–1,367
Mc Lean (Bloomington)	CA-C	121	15.6	50–48–4–28	16.4	19–21–0–15–23	0	457–1,287
Macon (Decatur)	CO-C	130	14.7	48–38–3–25	13.3	18–8–0–1–23	0	350–1,220
Macoupin (Carlinville)	CO-I	49	5.7	47–33–17–19	4.9	14–45–0–1–25	0	97–1,282
Madison (Edwardsville)	CA-S	245	35.9	70–35–7–35	33.7	17–7–0–8–28	31	665–1,345
Marion (Salem)	CO-I	44	3.5	34–16–3–25	3.1	10–13–0–0–20	0	81–1,225
Montgomery (Hillsboro)	CO-I	32	5.6	75–31–21–45	5.0	14–60–0–0–21	2	...–...
Morgan (Jacksonville)	CO-I	37	5.8	56–77–6–20	4.6	20–38–0–1–27	0	157–1,103
Ogle (Oregon)	CO-I	45	7.0	41–61–7–45	6.1	26–30–0–6–26	0	...–...
Peoria (Peoria)	CA-C	199	...	...–...–...–...	27.0	21–15–0–17–28	0	720–1,297
Randolph (Chester)	CO-I	36	5.8	45–44–17–58	5.8	13–36–0–42–24	101	...–...
Rock Island (Rock Island)	CO-C	167	18.4	32–30–2–46	18.9	13–8–1–14–23	4	589–1,176
St. Clair (Belleville)	CA-S	267	...	...–...–...–...	20.6	6–10–0–0–23	0	753–1,211
Saline (Harrisburg)	CO-I	29	3.6	67–25–16–17	2.2	14–22–0–0–24	0	103–1,154
Sangamon (Springfield)	CO-C	176	16.4	34–30–6–24	15.2	18–6–0–0–20	1	566–1,105
Stephenson (Freeport)	CA-I	50	7.5	64–46–7–34	6.5	23–10–0–30–23	1	223–1,119
Tazewell (Pekin)	CO-S	131	11.2	33–27–3–21	10.3	11–12–0–0–16	0	253–1,267
Vermilion (Danville)	CO-I	93	...	...–...–...–...	13.1	7–16–0–18–33	0	446–992
Whiteside (Morrison)	CO-I	65	8.1	51–47–7–21	3.5	11–9–0–7–10	0	243–1,220
Will (Joliet)	CO-S	327	29.7	24–26–6–36	38.4	19–7–0–10–27	15	1,067–1,332
Williamson (Marion)	CO-I	57	7.0	40–38–15–30	5.8	15–32–0–13–21	0	143–1,255
Winnebago (Rockford)	CA-C	250	26.1	34–22–8–41	33.0	28–11–0–18–27	10	919–1,283
Woodford (Eureka)	CO-S	33	3.4	38–32–7–25	3.7	26–25–0–10–23	1	...–...
INDIANA								
Adams (Decatur)	CO-S	29	10.4	77–77–0–199	16.7	20–30–152–32–41	132	295–987
Allen (Fort Wayne)	CO-C	291	42.8	74–56–0–16	49.6	17–15–0–50–38	25	1,481–1,204
Bartholomew (Columbus)	CO-I	65	49.0	84–63–61–549	45.4	12–18–433–53–41	202	1,252–1,415
Boone (Lebanon)	CO-S	38	12.8	60–50–1–227	11.8	10–35–177–20–29	11	351–1,173
Cass (Logansport)	CO-I	40	17.2	71–25–47–283	17.4	9–47–229–35–25	245	525–1,123
Clark (Jeffersonville)	CO-S	89	37.2	72–42–0–302	32.2	11–15–222–51–22	17	1,033–1,205
Clinton (Frankfort)	CO-I	32	12.4	81–59–49–198	15.9	13–48–171–39–33	144	337–1,032
Daviess (Washington)	CO-I	29	14.5	78–43–25–359	11.8	8–40–224–34–32	143	457–1,041
De Kalb (Auburn)	CO-S	33	6.4	70–41–52–29	7.5	12–30–0–29–42	0	133–1,056
Dearborn (Lawrenceburg)	CO-S	35	19.7	66–40–1–456	18.5	12–42–342–31–30	149	526–1,142
Delaware (Muncie)	CO-C	126	20.9	72–61–0–33	21.3	12–13–0–61–36	1	568–1,089
Dubois (Jasper)	CO-I	34	3.9	52–43–1–19	6.1	5–75–0–19–28	0	145–894
Elkhart (Goshen)	CO-C	137	28.1	71–45–59–29	31.1	15–20–0–60–40	0	691–1,257
Fayette (Connersville)	CO-I	28	4.0	71–49–0–21	4.3	12–27–0–38–45	1	136–887
Floyd (New Albany)	CO-S	62	37.7	61–48–0–494	37.7	7–22–375–52–39	144	943–1,221
Gibson (Princeton)	CO-S	34	7.1	82–101–1–23	7.6	8–34–0–31–37	0	...–...
Grant (Marion)	CO-I	78	11.0	73–49–1–17	13.3	12–35–0–54–36	1	298–857
Greene (Bloomfield)	CO-I	31	10.0	70–52–1–203	8.5	7–43–90–37–31	80	305–1,045
Hamilton (Noblesville)	CO-S	85	22.8	45–49–1–175	23.4	11–16–148–15–33	23	629–1,407
Hancock (Greenfield)	CO-S	44	20.2	51–45–62–304	19.3	13–30–231–17–51	53	506–1,228
Harrison (Corydon)	CO-I	29	8.9	74–59–0–179	9.9	8–40–163–27–28	35	305–1,032
Hendricks (Danville)	CO-S	72	20.3	43–33–34–174	21.0	14–16–153–16–27	185	548–1,281
Henry (New Castle)	CO-I	52	26.0	76–53–0–374	23.6	9–33–286–43–28	201	724–1,118
Howard (Kokomo)	CO-C	85	29.3	69–57–1–217	33.7	19–26–191–89–37	70	844–1,459
Huntington (Huntington)	CO-I	34	12.7	69–45–43–214	13.8	22–41–184–37–43	172	310–1,042
Jackson (Brownstown)	CO-I	37	13.9	77–55–1–239	14.7	10–39–222–35–28	45	500–973
Jasper (Rensselaer)	CO-I	27	11.6	82–54–46–250	11.5	13–19–197–24–41	197	295–1,089
Jefferson (Madison)	CO-I	29	4.2	74–52–1–16	4.4	11–39–0–14–33	0	...–...
Johnson (Franklin)	CO-S	80	43.8	42–35–57–416	28.5	13–13–186–19–28	47	809–1,107
Knox (Vincennes)	CO-I	43	37.8	80–52–2–754	38.1	36–34–652–46–32	533	1,133–1,401
Kosciusko (Warsaw)	CO-I	60	6.9	56–39–0–19	9.1	8–39–0–22–28	49	159–973
La Porte (La Porte)	CO-I	109	18.8	73–76–1–23	19.6	17–20–0–49–44	29	558–1,028
Lagrange (Lagrange)	CO-I	26	7.9	66–55–1–182	8.5	11–44–152–17–35	4	245–1,159
Lake (Crown Point)	CO-C	514	112.0	104–87–2–25	125.2	17–8–0–116–32	12	2,870–1,023
Lawrence (Bedford)	CO-I	41	17.5	60–34–48–280	16.4	8–35–208–26–28	301	457–1,148
Madison (Anderson)	CO-C	135	18.3	69–47–1–18	19.7	9–23–0–49–37	13	552–1,091
Marshall (Plymouth)	CO-S	40	11.9	68–49–51–131	14.3	16–42–102–31–39	44	359–1,140
Miami (Peru)	CO-I	38	17.6	173–78–1–213	13.4	11–43–188–33–32	173	460–1,021
Monroe (Bloomington)	CO-C	101	16.5	43–29–0–91	13.7	9–19–0–29–22	0	314–962
Montgomery (Crawfordsville)	CO-I	35	8.5	46–41–1–152	9.2	10–43–115–25–26	6	121–876
Morgan (Martinsville)	CO-S	53	20.1	57–30–57–238	17.5	8–23–175–32–26	88	465–1,136
Noble (Albion)	CO-I	35	6.2	68–42–46–19	6.0	14–30–0–24–44	11	...–...
Porter (Valparaiso)	CO-S	123	56.2	46–59–0–351	55.5	13–21–302–18–53	35	1,621–1,257
Posey (Mount Vernon)	CO-S	27	4.9	82–66–1–36	6.0	14–60–0–35–47	153	...–...
Putnam (Greencastle)	CO-I	30	10.2	67–53–1–224	14.4	10–54–204–21–51	164	341–949
Randolph (Winchester)	CO-I	29	8.8	86–38–42–138	10.0	11–60–112–41–34	0	...–...
St. Joseph (South Bend)	CO-C	240	39.1	72–57–0–33	40.1	14–16–12–55–30	23	1,062–1,205
Shelby (Shelbyville)	CO-S	40	5.4	61–42–1–31	5.5	18–24–0–32–33	0	176–895
Tippecanoe (Lafayette)	CO-C	124	15.9	47–58–1–22	16.4	10–22–0–30–31	11	411–1,068
Vanderburgh (Evansville)	CO-C	167	25.1	61–62–1–26	28.1	9–14–0–66–64	0	742–1,206
Vigo (Terre Haute)	CO-C	112	18.9	71–68–1–29	19.1	9–13–0–60–53	43	787–897
Wabash (Wabash)	CO-I	35	14.0	70–42–49–232	14.7	14–38–214–37–34	222	439–1,096

Table 1/10 continued PROFILES OF INDIVIDUAL COUNTIES

County (county seat)	Form of government–Metro status	Est. 1982 population (000)	Fiscal year 1983 revenues: Total general revenue ($ millions)	Fiscal year 1983 revenues: Per capita revenues ($) Intergovernmental revenue–Property taxes–Other taxes–Charges and miscellaneous general revenue	Fiscal year 1983 expenditures: Total general expenditures ($ millions)	Fiscal year 1983 expenditures: Per capita current expenditures ($) Law enforcement–Streets–Hospitals–Welfare–Finance and administration	Long term debt ($ per capita)	October 1983 public personnel: Total full time equivalent employment–Average full time monthly salary ($)
INDIANA continued								
Warrick (Boonville)	CO-S	44	6.9	68–26–0–62	8.2	10–32–0–30–29	448	195–976
Wayne (Richmond)	CO-I	75	15.4	91–51–46–17	15.5	24–28–0–59–39	0	337–1,091
Wells (Bluffton)	CO-S	25	8.6	77–43–28–193	9.9	9–61–151–34–37	95	231–1,078
Whitley (Columbia City)	CO-I	26	11.0	71–78–0–274	11.4	8–42–242–26–28	77	334–1,041
IOWA								
Black Hawk (Waterloo)	CO-C	138	23.1	52–92–2–21	23.3	12–13–9–38–40	10	706–1,215
Boone (Boone)	CO-I	26	13.5	71–128–2–318	13.2	13–59–276–38–33	14	377–1,398
Cerro Gordo (Mason City)	CO-I	48	8.9	60–101–2–21	8.2	16–57–11–13–36	0	...–...
Clinton (Clinton)	CO-I	57	10.9	60–97–2–32	10.1	16–37–17–29–30	15	245–1,309
Dallas (Adel)	CO-I	29	11.6	76–152–3–163	12.0	17–65–111–52–34	37	299–1,124
Des Moines (Burlington)	CO-I	46	8.0	44–100–2–30	8.6	17–34–10–24–27	0	201–1,240
Dubuque (Dubuque)	CO-C	93	17.6	64–99–2–25	17.9	13–28–8–12–25	15	394–1,222
Fayette (West Union)	CO-I	25	5.7	97–91–5–35	5.6	13–72–7–23–37	0	161–1,284
Jasper (Newton)	CO-I	36	10.0	101–125–2–46	9.4	17–67–10–71–32	8	240–1,131
Johnson (Iowa City)	CO-C	84	15.4	54–100–2–28	14.3	14–28–6–31–33	13	288–1,561
Lee (Fort Madison)	CO-I	43	8.3	52–124–1–17	8.3	10–34–14–32–38	41	216–1,124
Linn (Cedar Rapids)	CO-C	169	35.9	63–115–3–31	35.4	20–21–12–28–37	60	672–1,439
Marion (Knoxville)	CO-I	30	6.3	92–89–3–26	6.0	7–61–7–16–24	4	137–1,190
Marshall (Marshalltown)	CO-I	42	10.7	77–134–2–42	9.1	11–40–11–43–42	52	323–1,088
Muscatine (Muscatine)	CO-I	42	16.4	43–117–2–230	15.0	13–35–203–27–27	81	357–1,452
Polk (Des Moines)	CO-C	307	81.2	49–140–4–71	80.8	21–9–97–24–49	195	1,743–1,649
Pottawattamie (Council Bluffs)	CO-S	87	14.8	68–78–2–21	15.7	16–47–17–14–33	18	325–1,355
Scott (Davenport)	CA-C	162	24.3	23–97–2–27	24.9	17–11–10–12–34	28	538–1,411
Sioux (Orange City)	CO-I	31	7.1	81–110–2–37	6.1	12–63–10–5–24	0	...–...
Story (Nevada)	CO-I	73	14.1	44–75–2–73	14.8	16–28–47–29–26	5	326–1,267
Wapello (Ottumwa)	CO-I	40	7.6	59–102–2–28	7.9	8–41–20–47–45	2	...–...
Warren (Indianola)	CO-S	35	4.7	54–56–2–22	6.2	15–54–13–14–29	0	133–1,377
Webster (Fort Dodge)	CO-I	45	10.7	67–132–3–36	10.3	20–59–13–44–42	90	232–1,218
Woodbury (Sioux City)	CO-C	101	18.6	63–97–2–22	19.2	18–28–21–33–40	0	412–1,361
KANSAS								
Barton (Great Bend)	CO-I	33	6.6	24–74–7–96	6.3	12–35–0–0–22	4	118–978
Butler (El Dorado)	CO-S	47	6.7	24–80–4–32	5.3	14–35–0–0–16	27	137–1,146
Cowley (Winfield)	CO-I	38	7.4	19–70–3–101	7.2	10–24–0–0–22	0	103–1,135
Crawford (Girard)	CO-I	38	7.7	24–89–2–86	7.8	12–40–0–0–21	121	255–837
Douglas (Lawrence)	CO-C	70	11.4	24–101–4–35	10.3	16–10–0–15–25	158	233–1,291
Ellis (Hays)	CO-I	28	6.2	30–145–5–43	5.7	13–71–0–0–22	27	114–1,253
Geary (Junction City)	CO-I	31	12.7	22–46–51–296	13.1	18–20–183–0–20	142	276–1,129
Harvey (Newton)	CA-I	31	4.8	28–92–4–30	4.4	13–35–5–0–25	120	112–1,236
Johnson (Olathe)	CO-S	282	82.3	93–57–45–98	70.5	15–12–0–5–30	220	1,219–1,527
Labette (Oswego)	CO-I	26	17.1	27–93–47–497	15.8	12–41–253–0–18	156	447–1,148
Leavenworth (Leavenworth)	CO-I	56	10.9	30–78–3–83	11.0	15–38–0–20–29	10	251–1,104
Lyon (Emporia)	CO-I	37	130.9	22–89–3–3440	19.2	13–46–341–0–24	248	601–1,166
Mc Pherson (Mc Pherson)	CO-I	27	6.0	31–143–13–33	5.9	13–82–0–0–26	0	117–1,165
Montgomery (Independence)	CO-I	44	5.6	24–80–2–22	5.6	9–33–0–0–29	7	157–976
Reno (Hutchinson)	CO-I	65	13.0	26–79–36–58	15.0	15–27–0–5–15	86	235–1,260
Riley (Manhattan)	CO-I	63	3.1	0–0–0–48	8.2	7–13–5–4–14	9	226–1,336
Saline (Salina)	CO-I	49	13.7	22–86–4–163	13.1	16–31–0–3–18	6	143–1,480
Sedgwick (Wichita)	CA-C	382	66.2	28–70–8–67	65.0	16–25–0–4–20	84	1,196–1,485
Shawnee (Topeka)	CO-C	158	34.6	20–92–4–103	32.5	31–11–0–0–31	69	594–1,420
Wyandotte (Kansas City)	CO-C	174	21.9	26–48–26–25	22.1	15–6–2–0–29	9	586–1,266
KENTUCKY								
Barren (Glasgow)	CO-I	34	2.5	41–25–5–2	2.2	5–20–0–0–10	11	...–...
Bell (Pineville)	CO-I	34	3.7	72–24–4–7	1.9	16–9–0–0–7	0	...–...
Boone (Burlington)	CO-S	48	7.9	59–44–49–14	12.7	18–12–0–0–6	4,283	130–1,239
Boyd (Catlettsburg)	CO-C	55	4.4	33–41–4–1	1.7	0–0–0–0–4	0	61–1,175
Boyle (Danville)	CO-I	25	2.2	37–24–20–7	1.5	9–5–0–2–7	54	57–984
Bullitt (Shepherdsville)	CO-S	44	2.8	32–24–4–3	2.1	11–12–0–1–7	0	71–1,231
Calloway (Murray)	CO-I	30	2.1	35–28–6–2	1.1	3–15–0–0–4	0	395–916
Campbell (Newport)	CO-S	83	9.3	44–38–17–14	5.7	14–8–0–2–8	670	132–1,170
Carter (Grayson)	CO-I	25	2.0	56–17–2–4	2.2	5–22–0–0–5	444	52–1,065
Christian (Hopkinsville)	CO-C	68	12.8	149–21–3–16	4.6	10–11–0–1–7	308	91–1,046
Clark (Winchester)	CO-S	29	2.3	38–31–6–6	2.9	9–14–0–2–10	2,321	...–...
Daviess (Owensboro)	CO-C	87	8.1	40–36–9–8	6.5	6–22–0–3–5	4	125–1,346
Floyd (Prestonsburg)	CO-I	50	3.2	45–17–1–1	5.1	3–16–0–1–7	655	93–1,209
Franklin (Frankfort)	CO-I	43	4.0	38–45–5–5	2.4	5–7–0–0–6	0	...–...
Graves (Mayfield)	CO-I	33	2.5	45–25–4–3	1.8	3–14–0–0–5	0	57–1,153
Greenup (Greenup)	CO-S	39	2.2	27–25–3–2	1.7	3–15–0–0–4	0	...–...
Hardin (Elizabethtown)	CO-I	87	5.4	28–19–6–9	3.7	3–7–0–0–5	104	100–977
Harlan (Harlan)	CO-I	43	5.4	89–19–2–15	4.2	7–22–0–2–9	47	...–...
Henderson (Henderson)	CO-S	41	4.1	61–29–6–3	3.0	1–26–0–2–6	173	94–1,045
Hopkins (Madisonville)	CO-I	47	4.9	62–31–5–7	6.9	9–19–0–1–4	1,232	79–1,204
Jefferson (Louisville)	CO-C	682	164.2	55–50–53–84	145.6	43–3–3–8–20	0	2,703–1,248
Jessamine (Nicholasville)	CO-S	27	2.0	36–27–10–2	1.6	5–14–0–2–7	2	...–...
Kenton (Covington)	CO-S	137	29.1	30–28–22–132	28.6	11–12–14–2–2	449	421–1,209
Knox (Barbourville)	CO-I	30	6.8	106–17–2–97	5.5	2–12–97–0–6	74	186–1,015
Laurel (London)	CO-I	40	2.7	40–20–4–3	2.5	1–15–0–0–5	47	...–...
Letcher (Whitesburg)	CO-I	31	2.6	68–12–4–1	2.3	1–25–0–5–8	9	183–962

Table 1/10 continued PROFILES OF INDIVIDUAL COUNTIES

County (county seat)	Form of government–Metro status	Est. 1982 population (000)	Fiscal year 1983 revenues: Total general revenue ($ millions)	Fiscal year 1983 revenues: Per capita revenues ($): Intergovernmental revenue–Property taxes–Other taxes–Charges and miscellaneous general revenue	Fiscal year 1983 expenditures: Total general expenditures ($ millions)	Fiscal year 1983 expenditures: Per capita current expenditures ($): Law enforcement–Streets–Hospitals–Welfare–Finance and administration	Long term debt ($ per capita)	October 1983 public personnel: Total full time equivalent employment–Average full time monthly salary ($)
KENTUCKY continued								
Mc Cracken (Paducah)	CO-I	61	4.8	39–27–9–3	3.1	7–18–0–1–5	662	131–852
Madison (Richmond)	CO-I	55	3.7	44–18–4–2	2.0	0–8–0–1–4	2	...–...
Marshall (Benton)	CO-I	26	5.8	57–43–32–90	7.3	5–39–95–0–10	213	66–870
Muhlenberg (Greenville)	CO-I	32	4.2	96–25–3–7	4.6	4–32–3–0–8	806	86–953
Nelson (Bardstown)	CO-I	28	2.7	45–35–5–10	2.9	9–20–0–1–6	0	...–...
Oldham (La Grange)	CO-S	29	2.4	35–32–6–12	2.0	15–14–0–1–8	0	45–866
Perry (Hazard)	CO-I	34	3.1	66–18–4–3	2.6	7–14–0–1–7	0	47–1,178
Pike (Pikeville)	CO-I	82	9.2	75–25–4–8	1.9	0–0–0–0–0	541	188–1,062
Pulaski (Somerset)	CO-I	46	4.0	49–26–10–3	2.7	3–22–0–3–5	36	119–999
Warren (Bowling Green)	CO-I	80	5.4	34–22–5–6	7.5	9–18–0–1–7	352	112–907
Whitley (Williamsburg)	CO-I	34	3.0	66–17–4–1	1.7	15–24–0–0–4	0	...–...
LOUISIANA								
Acadia (Crowley)	CA-I	59	19.2	84–38–2–204	18.3	31–40–164–0–23	73	455–856
Ascension (Donaldsonville)	CA-S	53	24.4	73–78–62–249	21.6	47–23–126–1–26	107	177–1,042
Avoyelles (Marksville)	CO-I	42	6.9	58–19–0–85	7.0	20–30–63–0–17	72	120–865
Beauregard (De Ridder)	CO-I	31	13.2	60–59–1–304	14.1	37–35–172–0–25	208	149–1,148
Bossier (Benton)	CA-C	87	12.0	91–28–1–19	10.1	19–24–0–12–17	23	334–1,185
Caddo (Shreveport)	CA-C	259	34.9	42–64–1–28	43.1	31–10–6–0–18	139	974–1,223
Calcasieu (Lake Charles)	CA-C	174	78.1	71–96–5–276	74.8	38–42–88–0–20	229	1,380–1,305
De Soto (Mansfield)	CO-I	26	2.5	0–0–0–95	6.4	28–33–0–2–46	0	...–...
Evangeline (Ville Platte)	CO-I	34	6.1	103–36–2–37	5.6	20–41–0–7–27	11	128–932
Iberia (New Iberia)	CO-I	68	29.8	125–43–4–263	26.0	30–18–154–3–28	213	295–1,217
Iberville (Plaquemine)	CA-I	33	17.5	122–136–129–141	15.2	80–71–0–3–29	320	275–1,149
Jefferson (Gretna)	CE-S	470	379.0	96–133–175–401	363.8	62–45–234–0–42	715	7,759–1,287
Jefferson Davis (Jennings)	CO-I	33	1.0	0–0–0–32	5.3	32–37–0–0–27	37	...–...
Lafayette (Lafayette)	CO-C	164	37.2	83–44–38–61	32.8	36–13–0–3–21	167	736–1,062
Lafourche (Thibodaux)	CO-I	87	51.4	122–92–9–367	45.1	50–25–266–1–32	268	1,377–1,070
Lincoln (Ruston)	CO-I	41	...	...–...–...–...	...	...–...–...–...–...	0	...–...
Livingston (Livingston)	CO-S	65	15.1	76–31–3–125	16.7	35–25–90–1–35	55	221–1,068
Morehouse (Bastrop)	CO-I	35	17.5	78–55–1–364	16.8	18–39–338–1–18	155	444–1,106
Natchitoches (Natchitoches)	CO-I	40	20.5	117–60–21–312	18.9	35–38–270–3–43	257	505–1,087
Ouachita (Monroe)	CA-C	141	25.8	69–55–20–39	21.6	27–20–0–0–18	81	751–1,048
Plaquemines (Pointe a la Hache)	CA-I	27	...	...–...–...–...	42.5	93–290–55–0–190	0	115–823
Rapides (Alexandria)	CO-C	137	31.6	82–38–68–43	34.5	25–13–0–2–24	68	471–1,389
Sabine (Many)	CA-I	26	...	...–...–...–...	3.7	26–48–0–1–24	0	141–1,115
St. Bernard (Chalmette)	CA-S	66	...	...–...–...–...	25.9	63–33–0–5–24	0	538–994
St. Charles (Hahnville)	CA-I	40	36.1	166–214–98–432	29.9	111–48–119–3–66	746	205–1,001
St. John the Baptist (Laplace)	CA-I	36	13.0	101–114–10–135	10.3	66–38–0–4–36	339	233–1,148
St. Landry (Opelousas)	CA-I	88	...	...–...–...–...	32.7	20–20–244–2–23	0	625–1,095
St. Martin (St. Martinville)	CA-I	43	...	...–...–...–...	9.9	29–26–37–2–29	0	200–1,273
St. Mary (Franklin)	CO-I	67	61.1	95–86–327–410	58.0	39–27–340–1–21	377	1,028–1,225
St. Tammany (Covington)	CO-S	123	45.6	43–44–3–281	47.4	28–22–193–1–17	91	938–1,115
Tangipahoa (Amite)	CA-I	85	...	...–...–...–...	26.0	35–16–148–1–20	0	180–1,206
Terrebonne (Houma)	CA-I	100	93.3	165–159–235–371	93.6	42–38–203–0–41	940	951–1,228
Vermilion (Abbeville)	CO-I	51	34.8	158–93–107–322	27.5	35–74–248–1–41	276	373–1,045
Vernon (Leesville)	CO-I	59	5.7	48–31–2–15	4.4	18–20–0–0–11	15	200–908
Washington (Franklinton)	CO-I	45	...	...–...–...–...	10.5	3–19–136–0–5	0	190–938
Webster (Minden)	CO-S	45	...	...–...–...–...	...	...–...–...–...–...	0	...–...
MAINE								
Androscoggin (Auburn)	CO-C	100	1.6	2–11–0–4	1.7	6–0–0–1–4	0	57–1,084
Aroostook (Houlton)	CO-I	90	2.5	9–13–0–4	2.4	9–2–0–1–6	0	76–1,031
Cumberland (Portland)	CO-C	218	5.3	6–15–0–3	4.5	8–0–0–1–4	10	163–1,198
Franklin (Farmington)	CO-I	28	1.2	6–30–0–6	2.2	15–5–0–2–5	44	55–1,053
Hancock (Ellsworth)	CO-I	43	1.5	7–21–0–7	1.2	9–0–0–2–10	8	43–1,218
Kennebec (Augusta)	CO-I	111	1.7	3–10–0–2	1.7	6–0–0–1–4	0	73–1,011
Knox (Rockland)	CO-I	34	1.1	3–23–0–7	1.1	11–0–0–1–6	12	46–1,287
Lincoln (Wiscasset)	CO-I	26	1.2	5–36–0–6	1.2	17–0–0–0–11	6	38–1,110
Oxford (South Paris)	CO-I	49	1.4	5–20–0–4	1.6	8–2–0–1–6	0	43–1,116
Penobscot (Bangor)	CO-C	138	2.8	6–12–0–2	2.1	5–0–0–1–4	0	76–1,255
Sagadahoc (Bath)	CO-I	29	0.8	3–19–0–4	0.7	10–0–0–0–7	0	26–1,315
Somerset (Skowhegan)	CO-I	45	1.2	4–16–0–5	1.5	9–6–0–1–6	0	44–1,077
Waldo (Belfast)	CO-S	29	0.8	5–20–0–4	0.8	13–1–0–1–6	0	33–1,020
Washington (Machias)	CO-I	34	1.3	9–25–0–5	1.2	9–8–0–2–7	0	26–1,067
York (Alfred)	CO-S	145	2.9	2–13–0–4	2.6	8–0–0–1–5	5	86–1,043
MARYLAND								
Allegany (Cumberland)	CO-C	79	54.4	329–136–112–109	56.5	7–27–0–0–12	160	2,118–1,455
Anne Arundel (Annapolis)	CE-S	382	375.6	330–238–230–187	349.0	51–37–0–0–40	898	9,477–2,028
Baltimore (Towson)	CE-S	659	650.3	263–299–255–169	683.5	73–30–0–5–27	615	17,494–2,090
Calvert (Prince Frederick)	CA-I	36	42.9	333–595–69–184	42.7	55–18–0–0–34	310	1,054–1,724
Carroll (Westminster)	CA-S	101	77.3	314–206–165–82	78.2	15–53–0–2–29	297	2,220–1,551
Cecil (Elkton)	CO-S	63	49.2	387–184–129–80	52.0	21–14–0–0–20	165	1,502–1,719
Charles (La Plata)	CA-S	78	75.0	431–251–166–118	80.6	61–0–0–0–18	457	2,261–1,678
Dorchester (Cambridge)	CO-I	30	23.6	422–192–113–51	22.2	18–72–0–0–22	283	691–1,581
Frederick (Frederick)	CA-I	120	100.1	354–223–169–89	106.4	14–36–0–4–28	201	3,284–1,672
Garrett (Oakland)	CA-I	27	27.1	546–290–117–57	26.8	17–171–0–0–22	224	981–1,303
Harford (Bel Air)	CE-S	149	129.1	381–223–163–102	126.4	34–56–0–0–26	468	3,791–1,650
Howard (Ellicott City)	CE-S	127	150.8	353–408–281–147	144.1	78–31–0–0–64	1,290	4,058–1,787
Montgomery (Rockville)	CE-S	594	784.8	287–527–355–151	812.0	68–19–0–0–33	840	18,536–2,423

Table 1/10 continued **PROFILES OF INDIVIDUAL COUNTIES**

County (county seat)	Form of govern-ment–Metro status	Est. 1982 popu-lation (000)	Fiscal year 1983 revenues: Total general revenue ($ mil-lions)	Fiscal year 1983 revenues: Per capita revenues ($): Intergovernmental rev-enue–Property taxes–Other taxes–Charges and miscellaneous general revenue	Fiscal year 1983 expenditures: Total general expendi-tures ($ mil-lions)	Fiscal year 1983 expenditures: Per capita current expenditures ($): Law enforcement–Streets–Hospitals–Welfare–Finance and administration	Long term debt ($ per capita)	October 1983 public personnel: Total full time equivalent employment–Average full time monthly salary ($)
MARYLAND continued								
Prince George's (Upper Marlboro)	CE-S	669	779.7	362–287–201–315	730.6	67–12–122–2–33	304	19,634–1,969
Queen Annes (Centreville)	CA-I	27	22.7	401–228–124–102	23.9	18–71–0–0–25	124	797–1,512
St. Marys (Leonardtown)	CA-I	61	46.1	366–178–129–79	47.1	24–0–0–5–21	744	1,367–1,544
Talbot (Easton)	CA-I	26	15.3	179–204–126–75	15.0	18–0–0–0–22	93	494–1,943
Washington (Hagerstown)	CA-C	112	73.1	289–165–130–69	79.5	12–25–0–0–20	66	2,480–1,698
Wicomico (Salisbury)	CA-I	65	46.4	313–175–129–94	47.9	13–30–0–0–19	337	1,498–1,613
Worcester (Snow Hill)	CA-I	31	24.9	216–385–104–88	23.5	29–52–1–0–32	35	918–1,598
MASSACHUSETTS								
Barnstable (Barnstable)	CO-I	154	10.0	5–26–0–34	9.1	14–0–18–1–7	4	338–1,483
Berkshire (Pittsfield)	CO-C	142	3.3	2–17–0–4	3.1	8–1–0–0–3	6	113–1,577
Bristol (Taunton)	CO-C	479	8.3	2–12–0–3	10.9	4–0–0–0–3	17	243–1,533
Essex (Salem)	CO-C	639	15.1	6–14–0–4	13.4	4–0–0–0–4	9	423–1,417
Franklin (Greenfield)	CO-I	65	2.2	7–21–0–6	1.9	11–0–0–3–5	0	66–1,510
Hampden (Springfield)	CO-C	442	10.9	2–18–0–5	10.2	10–0–0–0–2	24	338–1,423
Hampshire (Northampton)	CO-S	139	5.9	16–17–0–9	6.1	10–0–14–1–4	18	200–1,441
Middlesex (East Cambridge)	CO-C	1,365	36.5	3–13–0–10	32.7	6–0–8–0–3	15	1,164–1,488
Norfolk (Dedham)	CO-S	604	18.2	8–9–0–13	19.5	4–1–14–0–3	10	615–1,402
Plymouth (Plymouth)	CO-C	413	10.2	2–11–0–11	9.6	5–0–8–0–3	2	370–1,406
Worcester (Worcester)	CO-C	649	17.8	2–14–0–12	16.2	7–1–8–0–3	4	618–1,421
Allegan (Allegan)	CO-I	83	19.1	137–65–1–29	17.7	24–37–1–33–23	86	445–1,429
MICHIGAN								
Alpena (Alpena)	CO-I	32	27.5	213–66–0–582	29.2	16–57–493–17–37	951	147–1,428
Barry (Hastings)	CO-S	46	10.3	134–49–2–39	11.4	21–50–1–66–26	302	195–1,561
Bay (Bay City)	CE-C	118	35.3	90–96–3–110	27.4	14–45–3–49–14	0	726–1,565
Berrien (St. Joseph)	CA-C	165	48.9	121–62–1–112	47.3	25–25–58–18–27	374	1,214–1,413
Branch (Coldwater)	CO-I	39	29.8	248–67–4–443	27.9	24–51–304–68–36	149	760–1,433
Calhoun (Marshall)	CA-C	140	33.7	145–48–1–47	30.9	13–27–3–39–40	327	584–1,566
Cass (Cassopolis)	CO-I	48	10.0	130–65–1–11	10.2	24–16–2–47–29	59	...–...
Chippewa (Sault Ste. Marie)	CO-I	29	20.7	399–55–1–257	17.4	19–73–298–15–31	128	154–1,302
Clinton (St. Johns)	CO-S	55	12.1	113–53–2–52	12.4	21–43–1–12–31	303	196–1,527
Delta (Escanaba)	CO-I	39	8.3	124–47–1–40	8.4	14–54–0–13–27	87	...–...
Dickinson (Iron Mountain)	CO-I	25	17.7	345–82–1–271	17.4	13–50–394–10–25	88	417–1,221
Eaton (Charlotte)	CO-C	88	15.8	85–53–1–41	15.0	26–29–1–27–25	126	275–1,612
Genesee (Flint)	CA-C	440	83.6	72–56–2–60	91.1	21–22–24–24–35	494	1,662–2,058
Grand Traverse (Traverse City)	CO-I	56	22.0	208–104–5–76	19.7	63–43–3–63–43	299	416–1,400
Gratiot (Ithaca)	CA-I	39	8.7	82–56–1–82	7.3	17–66–1–14–27	117	163–1,508
Hillsdale (Hillsdale)	CO-I	41	...	...–...–...–...	0.4	4–0–0–5–0	0	...–...
Houghton (Houghton)	CO-I	38	13.1	148–45–0–153	13.2	9–82–0–117–24	140	...–...
Huron (Bad Axe)	CO-I	36	15.5	240–74–2–111	13.9	26–64–0–49–25	230	352–1,279
Ingham (Lansing)	CA-C	272	98.9	86–63–2–213	93.7	20–24–154–36–35	187	2,736–1,530
Ionia (Ionia)	CO-S	52	10.0	113–37–1–42	9.8	14–50–0–13–29	180	...–...
Iosco (Tawas City)	CO-I	29	...	...–...–...–...	0.2	1–0–0–0–0	0	...–...
Isabella (Mount Pleasant)	CA-I	53	16.0	161–51–3–85	13.2	12–42–2–49–24	12	...–...
Jackson (Jackson)	CA-C	148	38.9	126–48–2–86	34.4	14–37–1–45–28	293	745–1,447
Kalamazoo (Kalamazoo)	CO-C	214	53.8	116–58–3–74	54.4	34–16–2–17–30	193	841–1,669
Kent (Grand Rapids)	CO-C	452	116.6	118–43–1–96	106.0	24–21–38–20–23	136	2,028–1,683
Lapeer (Lapeer)	CO-S	70	35.9	122–52–1–340	35.4	19–50–236–74–28	315	1,028–1,504
Lenawee (Adrian)	CO-I	89	20.1	113–62–1–50	17.3	23–5–0–37–28	321	574–1,359
Livingston (Howell)	CO-S	100	23.6	102–63–2–68	20.9	19–41–1–15–32	161	389–1,428
Macomb (Mount Clemens)	CA-S	688	146.0	122–53–1–36	122.8	20–14–12–6–25	141	2,069–1,685
Marquette (Marquette)	CA-I	73	22.6	154–72–1–83	20.9	19–34–27–19–35	181	409–1,746
Mason (Ludington)	CO-I	26	9.4	129–95–2–128	8.4	24–74–2–88–42	39	...–...
Mecosta (Big Rapids)	CO-I	37	17.2	70–52–2–343	17.2	17–59–273–14–24	232	...–...
Menominee (Menominee)	CO-I	26	12.4	113–61–3–303	10.4	16–0–246–17–28	347	139–1,437
Midland (Midland)	CA-I	74	...	...–...–...–...	19.5	32–42–0–0–53	0	280–1,715
Monroe (Monroe)	CA-S	132	54.2	169–89–2–151	49.7	38–40–0–21–37	484	681–1,515
Montcalm (Stanton)	CO-I	49	12.5	114–48–2–93	10.0	21–40–0–11–31	96	...–...
Muskegon (Muskegon)	CA-C	156	42.0	112–49–2–106	43.3	22–32–4–35–37	502	982–1,535
Newaygo (White Cloud)	CO-I	36	13.2	240–55–7–66	13.4	20–79–0–73–38	340	169–1,503
Oakland (Pontiac)	CE-S	1,000	256.5	143–66–2–46	245.9	27–19–5–7–43	535	3,415–1,985
Ottawa (Grand Haven)	CO-S	160	40.7	121–47–1–87	41.8	13–42–0–14–20	360	523–1,704
Saginaw (Saginaw)	CO-C	223	72.8	137–68–0–121	66.2	24–31–72–20–29	202	1,399–1,654
St. Clair (Port Huron)	CA-S	138	60.0	204–75–0–156	55.3	24–37–0–19–39	468	739–1,699
St. Joseph (Centreville)	CO-I	57	12.6	117–50–2–52	14.0	15–19–1–39–28	225	172–1,492
Sanilac (Sandusky)	CO-I	40	11.5	172–73–2–39	12.0	27–61–1–49–35	147	...–...
Shiawassee (Corunna)	CO-S	70	16.5	132–57–2–46	16.2	18–50–1–72–30	193	431–1,326
Tuscola (Caro)	CO-I	56	14.5	169–44–2–45	14.8	23–54–2–54–21	123	183–1,407
Van Buren (Paw Paw)	CO-S	66	19.8	196–57–1–44	18.6	12–56–0–25–27	102	279–1,294
Washtenaw (Ann Arbor)	CA-C	261	69.1	152–67–1–45	83.2	37–20–2–14–43	309	1,331–1,670
Wayne (Detroit)	CO-C	2,241	616.9	115–69–1–90	643.7	33–14–37–15–35	156	5,235–2,179
Wexford (Cadillac)	CO-I	26	8.1	189–71–2–54	8.4	28–68–2–19–33	320	...–...
MINNESOTA								
Anoka (Anoka)	CA-S	204	61.7	173–86–3–40	60.7	28–34–0–102–39	32	944–1,765
Becker (Detroit Lakes)	CO-I	30	11.0	240–70–5–55	9.9	30–57–0–181–34	16	...–...
Beltrami (Bemidji)	CO-I	33	18.1	341–79–4–129	16.6	24–42–0–334–39	39	321–1,350
Benton (Foley)	CO-S	26	7.5	183–84–1–22	6.6	17–43–0–120–31	0	...–...
Blue Earth (Mankato)	CO-I	53	18.2	168–119–3–55	18.9	28–43–0–128–35	42	297–1,580
Brown (New Ulm)	CO-I	29	8.0	150–82–2–46	7.0	19–48–0–87–31	42	128–1,505

Table 1/10 continued **PROFILES OF INDIVIDUAL COUNTIES**

County (county seat)	Form of government–Metro status	Est. 1982 population (000)	Fiscal year 1983 revenues: Total general revenue ($ millions)	Fiscal year 1983 revenues: Per capita revenues ($): Intergovernmental revenue–Property taxes–Other taxes–Charges and miscellaneous general revenue	Fiscal year 1983 expenditures: Total general expenditures ($ millions)	Fiscal year 1983 expenditures: Per capita current expenditures ($): Law enforcement–Streets–Hospitals–Welfare–Finance and administration	Long term debt ($ per capita)	October 1983 public personnel: Total full time equivalent employment–Average full time monthly salary ($)
MINNESOTA continued								
Carlton (Carlton)	CO-I	30	...	...–...–...–...	13.5	28–52–0–216–71	0	211–1,713
Carver (Chaska)	CO-S	38	...	...–...–...–...	12.7	38–32–0–78–39	0	239–1,693
Chisago (Center City)	CO-S	27	10.7	170–124–2–103	9.8	41–45–0–178–34	57	288–1,215
Clay (Moorhead)	CA-C	49	12.6	143–68–2–43	11.6	23–58–0–98–26	7	...–...
Crow Wing (Brainerd)	CO-I	42	17.8	282–87–1–52	17.4	35–60–0–210–50	30	...–...
Dakota (Hastings)	CA-S	205	48.8	111–79–0–48	49.2	13–31–0–68–29	0	648–1,840
Douglas (Alexandria)	CO-I	28	20.9	219–85–6–427	21.0	20–86–366–107–27	270	512–1,304
Freeborn (Albert Lea)	CO-I	36	11.5	175–104–4–38	10.9	24–57–0–131–42	59	186–1,623
Goodhue (Red Wing)	CO-I	39	12.0	150–113–2–37	11.8	24–99–0–90–37	13	193–1,576
Hennepin (Minneapolis)	CA-C	958	452.3	215–157–2–97	438.8	35–13–98–166–47	56	6,797–2,024
Itasca (Grand Rapids)	CO-I	43	36.5	346–189–1–303	36.6	40–124–202–277–50	13	611–1,376
Kandiyohi (Willmar)	CO-I	38	...	...–...–...–...	12.5	22–91–0–128–31	0	195–1,456
Lyon (Marshall)	CO-I	26	14.8	448–89–0–41	14.4	11–107–0–385–19	17	...–...
Mc Leod (Glencoe)	CO-I	30	8.6	132–101–0–52	9.1	20–58–0–83–32	104	...–...
Morrison (Little Falls)	CA-I	30	11.7	275–84–4–34	11.0	19–79–0–161–41	0	...–...
Mower (Austin)	CO-I	40	13.2	189–114–1–29	11.8	27–45–0–132–35	9	...–...
Nicollet (St. Peter)	CO-I	28	7.5	135–93–2–41	6.9	14–25–0–85–35	120	115–1,429
Olmsted (Rochester)	CA-C	94	32.1	168–94–2–77	32.8	28–27–42–112–43	15	642–1,684
Otter Tail (Fergus Falls)	CO-I	52	15.9	203–73–4–24	14.7	21–43–0–97–29	6	260–1,436
Polk (Crookston)	CA-S	34	13.8	240–114–2–45	13.0	22–57–0–150–28	93	...–...
Ramsey (St. Paul)	CA-C	467	189.6	216–131–1–59	188.6	56–16–11–225–37	82	2,784–2,028
Rice (Faribault)	CA-I	47	...	...–...–...–...	18.3	19–41–122–115–29	0	359–1,581
St. Louis (Duluth)	CO-C	219	114.0	289–130–2–99	112.3	29–63–0–298–43	0	2,643–1,601
Scott (Shakopee)	CA-S	46	18.5	180–156–4–65	16.1	38–36–0–131–71	43	275–1,655
Sherburne (Elk River)	CO-S	32	9.2	143–111–1–36	8.7	31–33–0–127–34	0	152–1,551
Stearns (St. Cloud)	CO-C	110	24.0	124–56–3–34	21.2	17–26–0–87–23	0	351–1,538
Steele (Owatonna)	CA-I	30	11.3	157–119–0–97	11.1	24–55–0–148–41	53	204–1,492
Washington (Stillwater)	CA-S	119	35.2	143–96–2–55	32.1	29–14–0–101–39	30	546–1,834
Winona (Winona)	CO-I	46	12.5	155–83–3–29	11.2	20–40–0–92–24	16	205–1,442
Wright (Buffalo)	CA-S	61	20.7	211–99–2–29	18.0	31–29–0–136–25	0	264–1,571
MISSISSIPPI								
Adams (Natchez)	CO-I	40	22.8	69–98–7–400	20.3	16–53–342–1–31	207	625–782
Alcorn (Corinth)	CO-I	33	4.8	39–75–0–34	3.4	10–48–0–4–14	48	69–1,452
Bolivar (Cleveland)	CA-I	45	18.0	131–79–0–189	14.7	11–47–153–3–18	145	517–737
Coahoma (Clarksdale)	CO-I	36	19.6	69–70–2–401	20.8	11–51–388–2–22	82	197–1,036
Copiah (Hazlehurst)	CO-I	26	7.7	87–63–0–145	7.4	15–40–106–1–19	167	263–796
De Soto (Hernando)	CO-S	56	8.6	38–64–2–51	8.0	9–34–0–0–20	133	162–991
Forrest (Hattiesburg)	CO-I	68	43.9	54–64–0–528	41.6	11–29–507–1–20	21	236–1,037
Harrison (Gulfport)	CO-C	166	32.0	44–72–32–45	28.7	15–19–3–3–22	197	523–893
Hinds (Jackson)	CO-C	253	36.7	0–0–0–145	54.3	12–25–111–4–15	63	1,502–718
Jackson (Pascagoula)	CO-C	123	82.0	65–98–1–501	76.4	23–41–326–2–26	275	1,396–1,420
Jones (Laurel)	CO-I	65	36.2	52–68–0–442	28.5	7–26–293–2–22	219	974–1,021
Lafayette (Oxford)	CO-I	32	3.6	59–44–0–11	2.5	9–29–0–1–13	66	76–898
Lauderdale (Meridian)	CA-I	77	8.0	38–56–0–9	7.4	13–26–0–1–21	61	196–827
Lee (Tupelo)	CO-I	58	8.7	40–62–0–47	7.7	7–33–0–3–15	0	193–878
Leflore (Greenwood)	CO-I	42	7.7	87–68–0–27	7.1	10–34–0–2–25	201	129–962
Lincoln (Brookhaven)	CO-I	31	5.2	89–52–0–26	4.9	7–35–0–1–18	54	104–775
Lowndes (Columbus)	CO-I	60	27.9	45–62–1–357	26.2	8–29–265–1–20	101	776–890
Madison (Canton)	CO-I	44	8.4	52–55–0–87	7.8	10–40–52–20–14	48	250–961
Marion (Columbia)	CO-I	27	12.2	176–52–0–224	10.1	9–22–212–3–20	36	364–706
Marshall (Holly Springs)	CO-I	30	6.5	64–42–0–109	6.1	11–38–94–4–21	40	177–838
Monroe (Aberdeen)	CO-I	37	8.5	65–55–0–108	4.6	10–54–1–2–14	75	94–872
Oktibbeha (Starkville)	CO-I	37	10.3	45–44–0–187	9.2	7–22–165–0–15	55	327–1,009
Panola (Batesville)	CO-I	29	9.3	109–66–0–149	7.7	10–66–117–4–18	256	271–961
Pearl River (Poplarville)	CO-I	36	4.3	44–54–0–23	3.5	10–26–4–2–17	10	...–...
Pike (Magnolia)	CO-I	37	6.3	81–56–1–36	5.6	6–39–0–1–23	191	139–877
Rankin (Rankin)	CO-C	76	17.2	71–63–0–93	13.8	7–12–83–2–20	133	367–1,111
Sunflower (Indianola)	CO-I	36	12.3	68–46–0–226	11.5	12–40–173–1–18	26	337–1,118
Warren (Vicksburg)	CO-I	52	8.8	53–80–0–37	6.5	21–43–0–1–18	56	213–813
Washington (Greenville)	CO-I	73	35.1	58–65–0–356	24.5	8–27–208–3–12	162	814–1,058
Yazoo (Yazoo City)	CO-I	27	5.9	113–83–0–21	5.8	11–52–0–3–30	109	...–...
MISSOURI								
Audrain (Mexico)	CO-I	26	14.2	23–49–0–468	14.0	10–29–446–1–19	197	627–1,348
Boone (Columbia)	CO-C	104	9.7	14–33–27–20	8.8	12–14–0–15–15	79	1,317–1,482
Buchanan (St. Joseph)	CO-C	87	6.9	17–31–28–4	6.9	8–10–0–1–24	0	189–978
Butler (Poplar Bluff)	CO-I	38	2.1	14–8–23–10	2.1	7–25–0–0–12	0	...–...
Callaway (Fulton)	CO-I	32	3.5	23–74–0–10	2.5	12–17–0–1–24	0	92–1,053
Cape Girardeau (Jackson)	CO-I	60	3.6	9–10–31–9	2.8	8–10–0–1–16	0	135–1,110
Cass (Harrisonville)	CO-S	53	5.8	19–34–15–42	4.4	8–16–34–0–14	0	110–1,196
Clay (Liberty)	CO-C	137	15.7	17–42–33–22	14.3	18–11–0–1–15	100	320–1,219
Cole (Jefferson City)	CO-I	59	4.0	22–34–1–12	4.5	15–13–0–1–18	0	148–1,091
Dunklin (Kennett)	CO-I	36	7.1	18–18–0–160	7.6	8–5–163–0–14	7	361–1,119
Franklin (Union)	CO-S	73	3.9	16–32–1–5	3.5	11–18–0–0–12	0	183–1,065
Greene (Springfield)	CO-C	188	10.1	14–33–1–6	10.1	8–16–0–2–13	0	332–989
Howell (West Plains)	CO-I	29	1.3	20–21–0–5	1.4	6–12–0–2–17	0	...–...
Jackson (Kansas City)	CE-C	630	103.2	48–49–37–29	99.3	21–4–10–2–21	238	1,258–1,270
Jasper (Carthage)	CO-C	89	5.0	10–24–15–8	5.0	11–13–0–1–18	0	166–982

Table 1/10 continued **PROFILES OF INDIVIDUAL COUNTIES**

County (county seat)	Form of government–Metro status	Est. 1982 population (000)	Fiscal year 1983 revenues: Total general revenue ($ millions)	Fiscal year 1983 revenues: Per capita revenues ($) Intergovernmental revenue–Property taxes–Other taxes–Charges and miscellaneous general revenue	Fiscal year 1983 expenditures: Total general expenditures ($ millions)	Fiscal year 1983 expenditures: Per capita current expenditures ($) Law enforcement–Streets–Hospitals–Welfare–Finance and administration	Long term debt ($ per capita)	October 1983 public personnel: Total full time equivalent employment–Average full time monthly salary ($)
MISSOURI continued								
Jefferson (Hillsboro)	CO-S	151	8.4	14–15–19–8	10.9	12–12–0–1–14	46	321–1,076
Johnson (Warrensburg)	CO-I	39	10.1	18–42–17–184	8.9	9–20–174–0–13	0	78–978
Lafayette (Lexington)	CO-I	30	2.2	14–31–0–27	2.4	13–20–0–1–25	0	...–...
Lawrence (Mount Vernon)	CO-I	29	1.7	20–15–16–7	1.6	9–14–0–4–17	2	50–982
Marion (Palmyra)	CO-I	29	2.1	9–30–24–8	2.0	0–25–0–7–17	0	...–...
Newton (Neosho)	CO-S	41	2.3	21–13–12–8	1.9	7–11–0–0–12	0	...–...
Pettis (Sedalia)	CO-I	36	2.7	20–20–26–10	2.9	9–17–0–0–17	0	106–1,044
Phelps (Rolla)	CO-I	35	22.1	44–25–18–549	21.8	9–18–491–1–17	439	775–1,209
Platte (Platte City)	CO-C	48	5.2	20–57–21–10	4.5	17–22–0–6–23	35	121–1,107
Pulaski (Waynesville)	CO-I	44	4.4	8–12–0–79	4.2	3–7–74–0–7	1	158–929
Randolph (Huntsville)	CO-I	26	2.3	14–38–24–13	1.6	10–12–0–1–17	0	...–...
St. Charles (St. Charles)	CO-S	154	12.3	17–27–24–12	14.5	12–22–0–2–18	69	356–1,255
St. Francois (Farmington)	CO-I	42	2.3	10–24–18–2	2.5	11–15–0–0–14	0	...–...
St. Louis (Clayton)	CE-S	976	265.5	46–64–127–35	255.5	29–25–19–1–23	92	4,175–1,668
Scott (Benton)	CO-I	40	2.6	16–15–22–14	2.6	9–9–0–2–18	0	92–914
Stoddard (Bloomfield)	CO-I	29	1.4	27–14–0–9	1.3	6–10–0–0–15	0	...–...
MONTANA								
Cascade (Great Falls)	CO-C	80	22.8	48–157–13–67	24.1	19–25–0–52–28	0	555–1,299
Flathead (Kalispell)	CO-I	52	18.7	65–209–19–65	18.3	26–45–0–36–35	3	380–1,425
Gallatin (Bozeman)	CO-I	45	13.6	36–180–14–69	13.5	25–25–0–26–28	46	209–1,396
Lewis and Clark (Helena)	CO-I	44	16.4	55–202–16–97	15.9	26–22–21–18–35	198	309–1,262
Missoula (Missoula)	CO-I	75	8.3	0–0–0–110	35.3	34–28–0–25–55	280	393–1,684
Yellowstone (Billings)	CO-C	113	39.6	39–196–6–109	31.6	12–18–0–24–28	12	461–1,452
NEBRASKA								
Adams (Hastings)	CO-I	31	4.8	51–59–11–30	4.2	15–32–2–19–34	0	112–1,035
Buffalo (Kearney)	CO-I	37	5.6	51–71–13–17	5.7	14–49–1–15–29	0	166–1,110
Dodge (Fremont)	CO-I	36	21.4	47–58–13–477	20.7	14–37–409–13–28	78	462–1,175
Douglas (Omaha)	CO-C	402	77.7	38–62–11–83	80.7	17–20–25–40–46	12	1,383–1,720
Hall (Grand Island)	CO-I	49	8.5	62–77–9–24	9.5	17–26–1–27–25	0	193–1,039
Lancaster (Lincoln)	CO-C	199	42.5	69–68–10–66	39.6	20–18–1–73–34	2	916–1,316
Lincoln (North Platte)	CO-I	35	5.3	53–70–13–16	5.4	20–32–2–18–28	0	195–1,187
Madison (Madison)	CO-I	32	4.0	47–56–14–10	4.4	11–49–2–15–26	0	94–1,042
Platte (Columbus)	CO-I	29	4.4	53–70–12–17	4.5	13–64–2–12–20	1	115–1,174
Sarpy (Papillion)	CO-S	91	11.9	43–48–7–32	11.7	20–19–0–11–26	0	278–1,518
Scotts Bluff (Gering)	CO-I	39	6.5	73–59–10–26	6.6	13–35–1–37–29	0	170–1,031
NEVADA								
Clark (Las Vegas)	CA-C	511	403.8	166–102–109–414	446.0	109–9–114–15–94	1,162	6,403–1,951
Washoe (Reno)	CA-C	208	153.4	163–66–72–435	155.6	57–29–380–24–87	218	3,532–1,845
NEW HAMPSHIRE								
Belknap (Laconia)	CO-I	44	4.7	28–63–0–15	4.8	20–0–0–53–17	15	170–1,136
Carroll (Ossipee)	CO-I	29	4.0	40–66–0–31	4.0	22–0–0–80–16	35	161–1,003
Cheshire (Keene)	CO-I	64	...	...–...–...–...	6.3	5–0–0–49–9	0	172–1,138
Coos (Berlin)	CO-I	35	...	...–...–...–...	5.7	9–0–0–134–7	0	201–1,086
Grafton (Woodsville)	CO-I	67	...	...–...–...–...	5.5	10–0–0–47–7	0	191–1,130
Hillsborough (Nashua)	CO-C	286	17.9	20–32–0–10	17.6	10–0–0–40–6	16	522–1,224
Merrimack (Concord)	CA-S	101	12.6	60–43–0–23	10.9	11–0–0–76–9	82	369–1,083
Rockingham (Exeter)	CO-C	198	16.8	31–37–0–17	14.5	9–0–0–42–9	26	440–1,153
Strafford (Dover)	CO-C	89	7.8	45–37–0–6	7.5	7–0–0–45–7	41	258–1,080
Sullivan (Newport)	CO-I	37	5.0	64–45–0–26	5.4	9–0–0–99–10	21	49–1,076
NEW JERSEY								
Atlantic (Atlantic City)	CE-C	195	81.9	143–187–15–76	84.3	22–13–14–135–48	71	1,983–1,393
Bergen (Hackensack)	CA-S	841	210.0	55–122–2–71	210.0	17–5–62–24–20	124	6,059–1,480
Burlington (Mount Holly)	CO-S	370	90.8	95–114–1–34	101.0	15–10–22–61–14	137	2,680–1,343
Camden (Camden)	CA-S	478	196.3	182–192–1–35	186.4	18–9–12–182–24	0	4,662–1,238
Cape May (Cape May Court House)	CO-I	85	34.8	93–248–6–61	34.2	28–20–7–41–31	164	1,129–1,342
Cumberland (Bridgeton)	CA-C	133	53.6	233–138–0–30	53.7	27–12–16–207–19	107	1,102–1,220
Essex (Newark)	CO-C	839	400.8	267–175–1–34	376.8	42–6–18–210–35	71	8,979–1,346
Gloucester (Woodbury)	CA-S	204	49.2	70–118–1–53	54.1	19–10–8–69–22	68	1,490–1,320
Hudson (Jersey City)	CE-C	559	201.5	190–133–1–36	203.8	20–3–62–138–24	44	4,134–1,174
Hunterdon (Flemington)	CA-I	89	20.1	35–159–2–31	23.8	17–27–10–25–27	63	446–1,479
Mercer (Trenton)	CE-C	308	112.6	145–175–1–44	111.6	25–11–12–122–23	100	2,928–1,516
Middlesex (New Brunswick)	CA-C	602	183.1	101–156–1–46	200.8	19–6–35–61–24	129	4,707–1,693
Monmouth (Freehold)	CA-C	510	152.6	121–132–1–44	158.1	17–9–11–90–18	88	3,441–1,463
Morris (Morristown)	CA-S	411	110.3	91–132–2–44	110.0	15–12–14–43–26	106	2,801–1,626
Ocean (Toms River)	CA-I	358	96.1	86–141–2–40	108.3	17–17–5–53–26	112	2,387–1,463
Passaic (Paterson)	CA-C	452	130.3	131–124–2–32	137.8	19–4–30–116–27	107	3,086–1,452
Salem (Salem)	CO-S	65	17.3	64–143–0–59	23.9	28–18–16–49–33	7	676–1,305
Somerset (Somerville)	CA-S	205	59.9	78–169–2–44	63.2	20–11–6–40–26	226	1,588–1,537
Sussex (Newton)	CA-I	118	22.7	49–122–1–20	23.9	12–31–11–22–19	36	834–1,338
Union (Elizabeth)	CA-S	503	141.4	103–133–1–43	147.4	16–6–38–66–33	61	2,948–1,559
Warren (Belvidere)	CO-S	85	22.1	73–124–2–63	23.6	17–29–1–87–19	4	650–1,270
NEW MEXICO								
Bernalillo (Albuquerque)	CA-C	435	41.3	15–72–1–8	33.8	21–4–20–1–10	74	715–1,334
Chaves (Roswell)	CA-I	54	17.0	40–27–29–216	13.7	17–21–150–2–17	54	443–1,346
Cibola (Grants)	CO-I	28	2.4	42–38–0–6	2.3	12–15–0–0–22	30	67–1,133
Curry (Clovis)	CO-I	44	2.1	18–27–0–3	2.4	11–18–0–0–16	0	...–...

Table 1/10 continued **PROFILES OF INDIVIDUAL COUNTIES**

County (county seat)	Form of govern-ment–Metro status	Est. 1982 popu-lation (000)	Fiscal year 1983 revenues: Total general revenue ($ mil-lions)	Fiscal year 1983 revenues: Per capita revenues ($): Intergovernmental rev-enue–Property taxes–Other taxes–Charges and miscellaneous general revenue	Fiscal year 1983 expenditures: Total general expendi-tures ($ mil-lions)	Fiscal year 1983 expenditures: Per capita current expenditures ($): Law enforcement–Streets–Hospitals–Welfare–Finance and administration	Long term debt ($ per capita)	October 1983 public personnel: Total full time equivalent employment–Average full time monthly salary ($)
NEW MEXICO continued								
Dona Ana (Las Cruces)	CA-C	100	27.8	33–31–17–199	25.5	15–10–191–0–11	49	212–1,240
Eddy (Carlsbad)	CA-I	50	7.8	49–36–49–21	8.1	24–58–0–0–20	0	148–1,474
Grant (Silver City)	CA-I	29	8.2	42–55–1–187	7.9	25–20–176–2–25	0	92–1,271
Lea (Lovington)	CA-I	60	11.2	38–27–89–32	14.6	21–57–0–0–17	0	151–1,528
Mc Kinley (Gallup)	CA-I	61	7.2	33–71–3–10	4.3	14–11–0–3–18	40	99–1,307
Otero (Alamogordo)	CA-I	48	4.1	41–33–0–11	3.5	10–18–0–0–19	127	154–1,092
Rio Arriba (Tierra Amarilla)	CA-I	30	5.9	71–16–90–18	5.0	15–24–0–14–58	0	194–953
San Juan (Aztec)	CA-I	92	15.1	36–69–41–17	12.4	15–18–1–4–18	102	229–1,423
Sandoval (Bernalillo)	CO-S	35	4.2	60–40–3–15	3.6	14–15–0–0–28	0	100–1,011
Santa Fe (Santa Fe)	CA-I	78	7.9	25–44–26–7	8.0	19–10–0–25–20	92	216–1,107
Valencia (Los Lunas)	CA-I	31	3.3	61–31–1–12	3.1	17–23–0–0–29	0	127–964
NEW YORK								
Albany (Albany)	CE-C	284	222.4	504–44–188–47	198.9	28–24–0–244–24	0	2,923–1,114
Allegany (Belmont)	CO-I	52	22.3	218–87–100–28	22.3	19–72–0–193–20	0	362–1,172
Broome (Binghamton)	CE-C	213	109.6	161–60–160–134	122.6	20–24–0–178–20	0	2,228–1,389
Cattaraugus (Little Valley)	CO-I	86	45.1	210–74–131–111	48.0	22–81–0–221–25	40	927–1,190
Cayuga (Auburn)	CO-I	80	42.1	213–105–102–108	43.1	16–63–0–158–19	6	713–1,792
Chautauqua (Mayville)	CE-I	146	67.9	187–55–135–89	72.7	25–50–0–211–24	59	1,144–1,369
Chemung (Elmira)	CE-C	95	56.0	226–105–126–130	56.8	26–30–0–238–19	146	889–1,289
Chenango (Norwich)	CO-I	50	18.3	148–91–64–65	19.0	13–49–0–109–22	0	...–...
Clinton (Plattsburgh)	CO-I	81	31.1	189–46–112–39	32.2	14–40–0–156–16	16	627–1,053
Columbia (Hudson)	CO-I	60	26.9	166–117–85–82	26.6	23–61–0–150–19	46	636–1,239
Cortland (Cortland)	CO-I	48	23.8	189–108–136–59	23.9	27–79–0–162–23	1	433–1,189
Delaware (Delhi)	CO-I	46	20.8	227–150–2–68	21.3	10–99–0–200–18	0	...–...
Dutchess (Poughkeepsie)	CE-C	246	102.7	165–111–58–84	106.5	26–25–0–120–19	68	2,152–1,592
Erie (Buffalo)	CE-C	996	717.5	317–127–151–126	724.4	30–12–68–263–22	319	9,926–1,654
Essex (Elizabethtown)	CO-I	36	22.3	277–70–146–120	22.0	18–83–0–273–39	0	...–...
Franklin (Malone)	CO-I	44	23.1	267–48–109–101	24.4	23–34–0–258–25	26	579–1,106
Fulton (Johnstown)	CO-I	55	24.8	153–104–92–101	25.3	19–30–0–210–17	3	549–1,119
Genesee (Batavia)	CA-I	59	34.3	218–75–119–167	35.7	28–58–0–182–15	83	824–1,285
Greene (Catskill)	CO-I	41	...	...–...–...–...	29.2	22–82–204–209–24	0	970–1,025
Herkimer (Herkimer)	CO-S	67	25.4	184–139–4–55	25.4	11–55–0–118–15	46	567–1,164
Jefferson (Watertown)	CO-I	87	49.5	219–92–134–124	46.5	19–52–0–182–19	103	740–1,315
Lewis (Lowville)	CO-I	25	19.4	194–132–48–409	17.8	22–58–257–245–21	79	534–1,095
Livingston (Geneseo)	CO-S	57	24.7	139–73–69–149	27.6	30–33–0–215–19	43	573–1,096
Madison (Wampsville)	CO-S	65	23.7	137–106–50–72	24.5	18–66–0–134–18	24	628–1,069
Monroe (Rochester)	CA-C	707	473.2	259–107–167–136	495.7	42–15–32–189–27	335	5,324–1,668
Montgomery (Fonda)	CO-S	53	30.2	200–111–106–155	28.6	18–44–0–208–12	46	682–1,153
Nassau (Mineola)	CE-C	1,316	1,029.1	221–231–190–140	1,072.8	189–15–82–122–36	601	17,405–1,959
Niagara (Lockport)	CO-S	222	121.6	212–103–144–87	125.2	30–13–18–198–20	91	1,773–1,456
Oneida (Utica)	CE-C	252	105.4	211–108–15–84	107.1	16–22–0–183–12	0	2,029–1,298
Onondaga (Syracuse)	CE-C	459	311.5	229–170–157–122	322.1	41–24–0–211–22	395	5,439–1,495
Ontario (Canandaigua)	CO-S	89	47.7	165–68–147–153	47.4	32–32–0–125–25	99	812–1,418
Orange (Goshen)	CE-C	265	98.5	171–118–3–79	106.7	19–17–0–164–20	0	2,488–1,325
Orleans (Albion)	CO-S	39	17.7	189–68–91–109	18.2	36–45–0–211–22	51	405–1,177
Oswego (Oswego)	CO-S	114	...	...–...–...–...	51.8	23–76–0–165–21	0	826–1,345
Otsego (Cooperstown)	CO-I	59	22.0	141–65–70–97	24.0	10–66–0–194–16	0	532–1,080
Putnam (Carmel)	CO-S	79	24.4	99–107–69–35	26.2	37–39–0–76–36	41	492–1,631
Rensselaer (Troy)	CE-C	151	75.7	232–62–61–146	88.8	21–24–0–190–20	0	1,913–1,407
Rockland (New City)	CO-C	260	150.9	244–167–5–165	171.2	24–12–71–180–23	219	3,213–1,512
St. Lawrence (Canton)	CO-I	113	46.7	213–45–112–44	46.7	21–43–0–190–16	0	773–1,191
Saratoga (Ballston Spa)	CA-S	155	59.4	126–107–69–84	58.1	17–21–0–145–15	0	954–1,253
Schenectady (Schenectady)	CA-C	149	62.4	164–137–1–117	64.3	14–20–0–223–15	69	1,277–953
Schoharie (Schoharie)	CO-I	29	10.7	169–172–2–20	10.6	20–80–0–117–18	6	243–1,169
Seneca (Waterloo)	CO-I	33	...	...–...–...–...	13.3	21–39–0–85–20	0	...–...
Steuben (Bath)	CO-I	98	42.1	168–102–105–55	39.4	20–72–0–178–28	3	846–1,205
Suffolk (Hauppauge)	CE-C	1,285	719.6	189–164–145–62	748.4	128–5–0–131–28	622	11,602–1,746
Sullivan (Monticello)	CO-I	64	...	...–...–...–...	47.4	51–113–0–186–43	0	1,059–1,279
Tioga (Owego)	CO-S	50	16.2	132–91–74–30	16.7	25–25–0–140–16	0	...–...
Tompkins (Ithaca)	CO-I	88	33.3	172–20–114–73	34.9	18–46–0–126–18	221	762–1,358
Ulster (Kingston)	CO-I	159	75.4	206–67–140–63	79.3	17–48–0–175–23	74	1,748–1,296
Warren (Lake George)	CO-C	55	29.4	193–53–196–96	28.9	31–55–0–168–23	60	589–1,183
Washington (Fort Edward)	CO-S	55	30.9	202–74–84–203	30.7	19–55–0–168–19	0	698–1,322
Wayne (Lyons)	CO-S	86	36.1	156–101–73–90	34.4	24–42–0–133–19	23	630–1,252
Westchester (White Plains)	CE-S	861	561.7	253–207–71–121	578.3	34–4–107–211–26	227	8,799–1,801
Wyoming (Warsaw)	CO-I	40	26.9	146–122–95–304	25.3	20–114–230–86–21	2	694–1,170
NORTH CAROLINA								
Alamance (Graham)	CA-C	101	66.9	369–151–45–99	59.3	17–0–0–32–17	80	2,374–1,353
Anson (Wadesboro)	CA-I	26	30.0	737–124–24–271	25.2	19–0–183–46–17	92	897–1,140
Beaufort (Washington)	CA-I	42	23.8	298–127–41–105	27.0	13–0–0–40–16	42	1,201–1,267
Bladen (Elizabethtown)	CA-I	31	26.6	520–128–23–198	25.1	15–0–145–48–25	3	1,103–1,241
Brunswick (Bolivia)	CA-S	39	34.7	444–266–41–138	31.3	19–0–69–33–33	594	1,135–1,284
Buncombe (Asheville)	CO-C	164	109.2	372–169–53–74	99.2	19–0–4–30–14	26	3,852–1,301
Burke (Morganton)	CA-I	74	38.9	305–124–2–94	38.5	11–0–0–34–11	5	1,568–1,403
Cabarrus (Concord)	CA-C	89	80.3	349–111–39–403	81.4	29–0–346–29–12	124	2,865–1,288
Caldwell (Lenoir)	CA-I	68	40.2	390–106–30–64	38.5	15–0–0–29–10	107	1,696–1,344
Carteret (Beaufort)	CA-I	44	25.1	330–132–53–60	24.8	17–0–0–30–16	163	1,024–1,233

Table 1/10 continued PROFILES OF INDIVIDUAL COUNTIES

County (county seat)	Form of govern-ment–Metro status	Est. 1982 popu-lation (000)	Fiscal year 1983 revenues: Total general revenue ($ mil-lions)	Fiscal year 1983 revenues: Per capita revenues ($) Intergovernmental rev-enue–Property taxes–Other taxes–Charges and miscellaneous general revenue	Fiscal year 1983 expenditures: Total general expendi-tures ($ mil-lions)	Fiscal year 1983 expenditures: Per capita current expenditures ($) Law enforcement–Streets–Hospitals–Welfare–Finance and administration	Long term debt ($ per capita)	October 1983 public personnel: Total full time equivalent employment–Average full time monthly salary ($)
NORTH CAROLINA continued								
Catawba (Newton)	CA-C	108	74.2	367–121–56–144	80.3	17–0–128–36–18	125	3,150–1,354
Chatham (Pittsboro)	CA-I	34	18.3	309–139–26–59	20.1	21–0–0–30–16	86	705–1,284
Cleveland (Shelby)	CA-I	84	49.6	353–123–35–81	55.1	15–1–0–41–11	207	2,254–1,322
Columbus (Whiteville)	CO-I	51	34.7	459–130–31–57	36.8	18–0–0–44–12	112	1,625–1,265
Craven (New Bern)	CA-I	74	45.8	409–104–45–63	46.1	14–0–0–47–13	108	2,729–1,230
Cumberland (Fayetteville)	CA-C	250	153.3	384–132–38–59	144.2	21–0–0–42–10	108	7,985–1,309
Davidson (Lexington)	CA-S	115	64.7	373–112–30–48	63.0	16–0–0–29–9	62	2,676–1,334
Duplin (Kenansville)	CA-I	41	26.6	439–114–28–67	27.2	15–0–0–40–15	15	1,400–1,244
Durham (Durham)	CA-C	156	103.8	347–216–50–53	100.4	13–0–11–52–11	154	3,900–1,332
Edgecombe (Tarboro)	CA-I	57	32.5	375–110–25–61	30.7	13–0–0–60–15	101	1,343–1,253
Forsyth (Winston-Salem)	CA-C	250	158.3	344–175–55–60	150.6	17–0–0–46–18	208	5,204–1,535
Franklin (Louisburg)	CA-I	31	18.7	287–125–21–176	21.2	14–0–137–37–13	57	857–1,272
Gaston (Gastonia)	CA-C	166	97.8	368–123–37–61	98.8	20–0–0–34–12	157	3,982–1,334
Granville (Oxford)	CO-I	35	22.6	316–122–26–178	23.2	13–0–104–34–14	11	932–1,268
Guilford (Greensboro)	CA-C	321	219.1	370–184–59–70	205.5	19–0–0–48–24	213	7,937–1,334
Halifax (Halifax)	CA-I	56	38.1	435–124–35–92	45.5	16–0–0–85–15	173	1,787–1,242
Harnett (Lillington)	CA-I	61	33.7	374–109–27–43	30.5	15–0–0–41–11	0	1,386–1,274
Haywood (Waynesville)	CA-I	47	42.6	399–131–39–335	41.6	14–0–268–33–13	251	1,691–1,252
Henderson (Hendersonville)	CA-I	62	49.2	345–120–46–285	49.2	18–0–192–31–15	158	1,706–1,255
Iredell (Statesville)	CA-I	84	51.5	383–101–38–88	49.3	14–0–0–31–14	18	1,996–1,323
Jackson (Sylva)	CA-I	27	18.5	452–115–36–96	20.1	16–0–0–73–27	184	644–1,356
Johnston (Smithfield)	CA-I	72	57.0	460–114–32–182	53.2	11–0–129–35–11	117	2,289–1,249
Lee (Sanford)	CO-I	38	31.0	492–162–49–120	29.8	21–0–0–49–17	234	1,097–1,420
Lenoir (Kinston)	CA-I	60	59.9	479–121–41–357	59.4	11–0–283–43–9	666	2,495–1,263
Lincoln (Lincolnton)	CA-I	43	29.5	448–141–26–67	23.5	17–0–0–32–8	189	949–1,333
Mc Dowell (Marion)	CA-I	36	22.7	404–111–32–84	21.6	16–0–0–44–11	50	900–1,275
Martin (Williamston)	CA-I	26	27.6	516–194–33–310	27.9	14–0–0–68–24	119	811–1,298
Mecklenburg (Charlotte)	CA-C	419	325.1	389–236–73–77	306.7	21–0–13–49–18	291	10,972–1,492
Moore (Carthage)	CA-I	52	35.2	429–132–43–77	33.0	13–0–0–35–20	75	1,360–1,363
Nash (Nashville)	CA-I	68	52.6	523–110–56–80	48.2	11–0–0–50–17	35	2,102–1,306
New Hanover (Wilmington)	CA-C	107	83.1	421–184–90–79	86.8	27–0–0–52–22	296	2,749–1,347
Onslow (Jacksonville)	CA-C	117	51.2	273–71–38–57	47.2	13–0–0–27–12	165	2,106–1,303
Orange (Hillsborough)	CA-S	78	39.2	246–172–48–35	39.9	14–1–0–32–19	95	1,573–1,330
Pasquotank (Elizabeth City)	CA-I	29	31.8	457–100–52–497	30.1	7–0–422–37–16	148	818–1,310
Person (Roxboro)	CA-I	30	29.0	482–208–35–250	26.5	16–0–1–53–18	182	935–1,191
Pitt (Greenville)	CA-I	93	61.1	426–130–43–58	56.7	11–0–0–46–15	122	2,499–1,305
Randolph (Asheboro)	CA-C	94	50.9	352–99–27–65	46.3	12–0–0–20–12	144	2,033–1,307
Richmond (Rockingham)	CA-I	45	29.0	441–103–38–64	27.4	20–0–0–36–13	338	1,233–1,252
Robeson (Lumberton)	CA-I	104	80.3	570–102–30–73	80.4	12–3–0–47–9	204	3,252–1,268
Rockingham (Wentworth)	CA-I	84	57.2	392–158–36–92	53.7	19–1–0–40–16	5	2,178–1,389
Rowan (Salisbury)	CA-C	101	49.6	323–84–34–51	50.9	13–0–0–34–10	13	2,138–1,339
Rutherford (Rutherfordton)	CA-I	56	33.6	384–134–33–54	33.0	16–0–0–34–14	44	1,369–1,321
Sampson (Clinton)	CA-I	50	34.8	481–138–26–53	33.7	17–0–0–57–15	116	1,442–1,246
Scotland (Laurinburg)	CA-I	33	22.8	420–154–35–82	23.3	18–0–0–56–16	314	874–1,361
Stanly (Albemarle)	CA-I	49	30.0	373–149–32–62	28.8	13–0–0–31–15	147	1,163–1,357
Stokes (Danbury)	CA-S	34	25.0	369–166–17–179	25.9	22–0–128–35–14	167	1,017–1,241
Surry (Dobson)	CA-I	60	46.9	391–125–42–228	46.2	15–0–141–31–15	98	1,428–1,359
Union (Monroe)	CA-S	74	48.6	399–140–34–89	50.6	18–0–0–46–18	432	1,832–1,306
Vance (Henderson)	CO-I	37	32.9	501–114–39–227	24.8	15–0–0–56–16	62	1,093–1,284
Wake (Raleigh)	CA-C	315	268.5	330–193–66–264	202.1	12–0–5–37–12	277	6,788–1,446
Watauga (Boone)	CA-I	33	15.5	260–117–52–37	15.4	15–0–0–35–17	167	646–1,266
Wayne (Goldsboro)	CA-I	98	76.9	385–95–36–272	78.1	9–0–203–40–9	35	3,185–1,373
Wilkes (Wilkesboro)	CA-I	59	36.5	407–103–33–72	35.0	11–0–0–39–12	170	1,438–1,396
Wilson (Wilson)	CA-I	64	46.7	461–152–35–84	43.1	17–0–0–62–15	3	1,888–1,263
Yadkin (Yadkinville)	CA-S	29	19.3	346–102–26–190	18.7	16–0–114–33–13	30	619–1,343
NORTH DAKOTA								
Burleigh (Bismarck)	CO-C	57	7.3	64–51–1–14	7.4	18–27–0–43–15	0	187–1,412
Cass (Fargo)	CO-C	91	9.9	43–52–4–11	10.5	15–16–0–19–14	0	225–1,416
Grand Forks (Grand Forks)	CO-C	67	7.3	46–49–1–13	5.6	8–27–4–12–13	0	163–1,265
Morton (Mandan)	CO-S	26	6.3	93–98–1–53	5.5	18–67–0–21–25	7	140–1,526
Ward (Minot)	CO-I	60	7.4	57–47–2–18	5.8	8–17–0–21–14	32	181–1,372
OHIO								
Allen (Lima)	CA-C	110	25.2	128–26–23–52	23.2	19–33–0–73–24	39	881–1,139
Ashland (Ashland)	CO-I	47	11.8	109–38–19–87	8.5	19–32–0–30–25	2	...–...
Ashtabula (Jefferson)	CA-I	103	28.0	108–51–15–98	26.3	16–23–0–80–22	30	847–1,162
Athens (Athens)	CO-I	58	12.3	126–39–11–36	12.2	8–21–0–51–20	21	357–1,198
Auglaize (Wapakoneta)	CO-S	43	8.7	84–34–17–67	8.1	19–41–0–44–22	9	...–...
Belmont (St. Clairsville)	CA-S	82	20.8	110–40–4–101	13.8	13–27–0–45–21	45	449–1,212
Brown (Georgetown)	CO-I	33	...	...–...–...–...	13.1	0–34–215–37–0	0	410–1,247
Butler (Hamilton)	CA-C	263	47.5	106–31–3–40	52.5	12–22–0–54–17	106	1,165–1,454
Carroll (Carrollton)	CO-S	26	4.8	99–43–4–39	4.9	19–60–0–33–24	35	...–...
Champaign (Urbana)	CO-S	34	10.2	141–35–4–123	8.9	18–38–0–101–29	0	...–...
Clark (Springfield)	CA-C	149	39.5	154–38–16–58	38.9	20–18–0–94–22	193	999–1,175
Clermont (Batavia)	CA-S	134	36.4	109–50–17–96	44.1	16–14–0–43–20	275	675–1,412
Clinton (Wilmington)	CO-I	35	16.7	93–50–19–321	16.3	19–20–242–45–29	53	551–1,349
Columbiana (Lisbon)	CO-I	114	15.3	71–30–3–31	15.2	12–23–0–24–18	15	458–1,202
Coshocton (Coshocton)	CO-I	36	9.6	115–68–16–65	8.7	32–38–0–73–25	1	307–1,154
Crawford (Bucyrus)	CO-I	50	8.2	96–26–14–31	8.7	13–25–0–50–27	0	...–...

Table 1/10 continued **PROFILES OF INDIVIDUAL COUNTIES**

County (county seat)	Form of govern- ment– Metro status	Est. 1982 popu- lation (000)	Fiscal year 1983 revenues: Total general revenue ($ mil- lions)	Fiscal year 1983 revenues: Per capita revenues ($) Intergovernmental rev- enue–Property taxes– Other taxes–Charges and miscellaneous general revenue	Fiscal year 1983 expenditures: Total general expendi- tures ($ mil- lions)	Fiscal year 1983 expenditures: Per capita current expenditures ($) Law enforcement– Streets–Hospitals– Welfare–Finance and administration	Long term debt ($ per capita)	October 1983 public personnel: Total full time equivalent employment– Average full time monthly salary ($)
OHIO continued								
Cuyahoga (Cleveland)	CA-C	1,473	548.0	181–75–26–90	548.1	19–10–94–119–45	176	14,121–1,510
Darke (Greenville)	CO-I	54	10.8	102–36–13–49	11.6	17–25–0–34–20	52	294–1,088
Defiance (Defiance)	CO-I	39	8.1	117–31–3–57	7.6	10–32–0–45–21	6	...–...
Delaware (Delaware)	CO-S	56	10.9	91–27–13–65	10.8	15–31–0–33–23	0	321–1,215
Erie (Sandusky)	CA-I	79	26.6	139–46–25–130	26.3	23–29–0–63–33	105	573–1,284
Fairfield (Lancaster)	CO-S	96	29.2	72–29–15–189	28.5	12–25–160–25–22	33	429–1,146
Fayette (Washington Court House)	CO-I	27	...	...–...–...–...	12.4	6–50–210–51–26	0	424–1,157
Franklin (Columbus)	CA-C	884	235.2	119–53–7–87	217.9	16–6–0–89–21	0	4,654–1,073
Fulton (Wauseon)	CO-S	38	9.6	103–41–18–90	8.5	13–48–4–50–30	35	246–1,126
Gallia (Gallipolis)	CO-I	30	7.2	140–53–13–35	6.0	13–52–0–39–29	0	185–1,160
Geauga (Chardon)	CA-S	75	18.1	104–50–7–80	18.4	17–32–0–42–21	36	469–1,316
Greene (Xenia)	CA-S	131	31.7	98–39–15–89	35.6	13–24–2–54–31	163	764–1,307
Guernsey (Cambridge)	CO-I	42	10.8	93–58–27–80	9.4	12–40–0–49–32	64	260–1,140
Hamilton (Cincinnati)	CA-C	872	271.5	134–78–30–69	243.9	31–11–53–60–30	98	4,543–1,550
Hancock (Findlay)	CO-I	65	12.9	91–46–4–57	13.3	16–29–0–45–28	71	301–1,195
Hardin (Kenton)	CO-I	32	6.2	62–43–4–83	6.5	10–43–0–74–23	59	259–1,093
Henry (Napoleon)	CO-I	28	7.3	126–40–17–79	7.1	17–37–0–40–29	0	...–...
Highland (Hillsboro)	CO-I	34	...	...–...–...–...	0.2	1–0–0–0–3	0	...–...
Holmes (Millersburg)	CO-I	30	9.3	114–47–17–130	9.1	18–53–92–33–31	21	277–1,153
Huron (Norwalk)	CA-I	55	10.9	100–38–17–44	10.8	12–41–0–47–23	7	301–1,244
Jackson (Jackson)	CO-I	30	6.7	136–31–13–42	5.9	12–52–0–53–26	0	...–...
Jefferson (Steubenville)	CO-C	90	16.7	109–36–15–26	16.8	9–23–0–41–19	47	541–1,203
Knox (Mount Vernon)	CO-I	47	10.2	107–42–17–50	10.1	12–27–0–52–24	106	277–1,234
Lake (Painesville)	CA-S	215	92.8	63–54–25–289	87.9	13–13–173–25–30	100	2,011–1,077
Lawrence (Ironton)	CO-S	63	21.3	119–30–0–187	20.9	11–26–154–55–28	8	667–1,235
Licking (Newark)	CO-C	124	27.8	132–29–23–40	22.9	14–22–0–44–23	5	495–1,330
Logan (Bellefontaine)	CO-I	39	11.2	130–43–17–96	12.1	19–38–0–71–28	0	...–...
Lorain (Elyria)	CA-C	274	52.5	89–42–1–60	48.7	13–14–0–50–17	9	1,275–1,277
Lucas (Toledo)	CA-C	469	118.4	120–57–29–46	104.8	18–10–0–87–23	17	2,675–1,329
Madison (London)	CO-S	34	...	...–...–...–...	7.0	14–47–0–38–5	0	218–1,176
Mahoning (Youngstown)	CA-C	284	73.0	152–38–18–49	56.7	6–17–0–104–4	0	1,378–1,308
Marion (Marion)	CA-I	67	19.1	124–57–2–98	16.6	15–23–0–93–28	19	531–1,106
Medina (Medina)	CO-S	115	25.0	75–43–17–82	24.0	12–19–0–25–25	63	576–1,252
Mercer (Celina)	CO-I	39	8.4	129–34–17–39	7.1	15–38–0–43–21	11	...–...
Miami (Troy)	CO-S	90	18.5	99–45–16–45	16.0	17–22–0–22–28	23	476–1,264
Montgomery (Dayton)	CA-C	568	...	...–...–...–...	174.6	19–7–0–66–34	0	3,691–1,021
Morrow (Mount Gilead)	CO-I	27	9.3	132–48–8–157	9.0	14–54–123–50–28	17	269–1,151
Muskingum (Zanesville)	CO-I	85	24.7	138–47–27–79	19.9	14–34–0–68–20	0	610–1,146
Ottawa (Port Clinton)	CO-S	40	12.8	135–71–21–94	27.5	24–49–0–89–34	450	368–1,151
Perry (New Lexington)	CO-I	31	5.4	109–23–13–28	6.7	11–58–0–73–30	0	...–...
Pickaway (Circleville)	CO-S	43	6.8	90–56–2–11	6.0	20–27–0–20–22	44	205–1,082
Portage (Ravenna)	CA-S	138	58.7	91–54–1–280	59.1	15–28–217–53–30	63	1,876–1,264
Preble (Eaton)	CO-S	38	8.8	111–38–11–73	9.3	11–42–0–39–22	38	194–1,232
Putnam (Ottawa)	CO-S	33	8.2	111–46–14–76	6.6	18–35–0–52–20	7	...–...
Richland (Mansfield)	CO-C	130	24.8	102–36–8–44	25.0	13–22–0–51–18	8	700–1,206
Ross (Chillicothe)	CO-I	66	15.6	129–47–17–44	18.5	22–40–0–37–28	184	410–1,124
Sandusky (Fremont)	CA-I	62	15.7	98–35–18–101	14.5	14–36–0–81–25	64	450–1,190
Scioto (Portsmouth)	CO-I	84	20.9	170–25–14–39	20.3	10–26–0–67–17	82	393–1,191
Seneca (Tiffin)	CO-I	61	10.6	99–30–2–42	9.8	8–21–0–44–19	1	255–1,119
Shelby (Sidney)	CO-I	44	10.0	115–44–18–52	10.7	15–36–0–70–24	0	334–1,101
Stark (Canton)	CA-C	379	78.8	92–37–7–72	76.7	18–14–12–33–18	13	1,808–1,012
Summit (Akron)	CA-C	518	154.2	117–69–30–81	142.4	15–12–18–79–25	0	4,259–1,047
Trumbull (Warren)	CO-C	241	54.2	101–38–3–84	53.9	11–16–33–61–22	30	1,256–1,483
Tuscarawas (New Philadelphia)	CO-I	85	17.7	100–37–1–69	14.1	10–25–0–47–22	26	398–1,204
Union (Marysville)	CO-I	30	19.0	152–65–3–405	18.0	34–56–274–92–29	0	584–1,243
Van Wert (Van Wert)	CO-S	30	7.1	114–52–15–56	7.1	18–39–0–52–32	17	...–...
Warren (Lebanon)	CO-S	101	20.9	82–30–22–74	18.6	13–17–0–35–26	43	458–1,111
Washington (Marietta)	CO-C	65	13.2	103–40–3–58	12.3	14–32–0–46–18	18	320–1,211
Wayne (Wooster)	CO-I	99	19.1	92–30–23–48	19.9	21–26–0–41–27	3	570–1,138
Williams (Bryan)	CO-I	36	8.8	89–39–18–97	6.4	14–47–0–32–24	0	...–...
Wood (Bowling Green)	CA-S	109	27.4	104–32–19–96	26.6	14–27–0–45–21	95	741–1,266
OKLAHOMA								
Bryan (Durant)	CO-I	31	8.4	50–33–0–187	9.8	7–40–176–0–14	61	330–1,212
Caddo (Anadarko)	CO-I	33	6.6	140–38–0–18	5.5	10–87–0–0–24	38	125–1,202
Canadian (El Reno)	CO-C	64	7.2	58–43–0–12	7.1	7–59–0–0–17	0	160–1,330
Carter (Ardmore)	CO-I	46	6.3	88–33–0–16	6.2	11–76–0–0–17	0	159–1,005
Cherokee (Tahlequah)	CO-I	31	2.0	38–18–0–9	2.1	5–24–0–0–9	14	...–...
Cleveland (Norman)	CO-C	146	20.3	18–33–2–86	19.7	4–16–0–0–8	20	265–1,247
Comanche (Lawton)	CO-C	121	8.6	38–23–0–9	6.9	7–15–6–0–9	40	973–1,329
Creek (Sapulpa)	CO-S	64	5.6	44–31–1–12	6.2	5–49–0–1–14	11	153–1,120
Custer (Arapaho)	CO-I	31	6.8	101–55–1–62	4.3	10–51–0–1–15	119	...–...
Garfield (Enid)	CO-C	67	8.2	52–53–0–16	8.3	7–54–0–1–20	34	223–1,203
Garvin (Pauls Valley)	CO-I	30	3.6	78–34–0–8	3.8	6–73–0–1–14	0	118–1,155
Grady (Chickasha)	CO-I	43	18.8	96–30–0–306	18.1	8–79–277–1–15	24	509–1,367
Jackson (Altus)	CO-I	30	...	...–...–...–...	16.4	7–60–379–0–42	0	496–1,281
Kay (Newkirk)	CO-I	52	4.7	38–46–0–6	4.8	9–32–0–1–18	57	...–...
Le Flore (Poteau)	CO-S	42	...	...–...–...–...	3.6	5–2–66–1–0	0	129–990
Lincoln (Chandler)	CO-I	28	3.1	63–31–0–17	3.0	5–27–0–0–18	0	105–932

Table 1/10 continued **PROFILES OF INDIVIDUAL COUNTIES**

County (county seat)	Form of government–Metro status	Est. 1982 population (000)	Fiscal year 1983 revenues: Total general revenue ($ millions)	Fiscal year 1983 revenues: Per capita revenues ($): Intergovernmental revenue–Property taxes–Other taxes–Charges and miscellaneous general revenue	Fiscal year 1983 expenditures: Total general expenditures ($ millions)	Fiscal year 1983 expenditures: Per capita current expenditures ($): Law enforcement–Streets–Hospitals–Welfare–Finance and administration	Long term debt ($ per capita)	October 1983 public personnel: Total full time equivalent employment–Average full time monthly salary ($)
OKLAHOMA continued								
Logan (Guthrie)	CO-I	29	8.7	66–42–0–194	8.9	10–50–179–1–22	93	103–1,059
Mc Curtain (Idabel)	CO-I	36	2.8	31–40–0–8	2.7	6–40–0–1–11	33	278–805
Mayes (Pryor)	CO-S	34	2.5	36–29–0–9	2.7	6–28–0–1–15	0	91–1,184
Muskogee (Muskogee)	CO-I	68	6.3	32–50–0–10	4.5	7–9–0–0–14	0	203–997
Oklahoma (Oklahoma City)	CO-C	602	54.7	20–51–0–19	47.7	6–12–0–2–16	22	1,220–1,310
Okmulgee (Okmulgee)	CO-I	40	2.9	39–24–1–9	2.9	4–30–0–1–12	2	104–951
Osage (Pawhuska)	CO-C	41	6.1	103–29–0–16	6.4	13–100–0–0–22	20	157–1,123
Ottawa (Miami)	CO-I	33	2.0	30–25–0–5	2.0	5–20–0–0–9	0	86–1,050
Payne (Stillwater)	CO-I	66	4.0	27–21–0–12	4.4	5–24–0–0–13	27	146–1,113
Pittsburg (Mc Alester)	CO-I	41	4.1	62–29–0–8	4.7	3–67–0–0–23	0	...–...
Pontotoc (Ada)	CO-I	34	3.6	58–38–0–11	3.7	7–18–0–0–14	20	...–...
Pottawatomie (Shawnee)	CO-S	59	4.6	44–26–0–9	5.3	7–30–0–1–16	0	280–1,185
Rogers (Claremore)	CO-S	51	5.7	31–69–1–11	5.6	7–32–0–0–20	55	148–1,186
Seminole (Wewoka)	CO-I	29	3.2	59–41–0–13	3.0	8–51–0–0–16	4	135–982
Sequoyah (Sallisaw)	CO-S	31	1.8	35–17–0–5	1.5	4–17–0–1–8	0	...–...
Stephens (Duncan)	CO-I	47	...	...–...–...–...	5.0	6–65–0–1–13	0	116–881
Tulsa (Tulsa)	CO-C	499	53.7	25–66–1–16	43.4	12–7–0–3–22	10	1,680–1,352
Wagoner (Wagoner)	CO-S	46	2.6	28–23–1–6	2.9	5–22–0–0–14	0	92–1,088
Washington (Bartlesville)	CO-I	52	3.4	21–37–1–7	3.5	6–24–0–0–15	25	110–1,209
OREGON								
Benton (Corvallis)	CO-I	68	12.2	87–55–4–33	14.2	21–27–0–2–32	188	298–1,520
Clackamas (Oregon City)	CO-C	249	50.2	83–48–6–65	57.8	33–28–0–13–41	294	1,013–1,725
Clatsop (Astoria)	CA-I	33	14.8	365–48–1–36	9.8	30–33–0–1–60	51	155–1,610
Columbia (St. Helens)	CO-I	37	6.3	101–33–2–35	7.7	19–23–0–2–40	0	...–...
Coos (Coquille)	CO-I	62	12.3	110–24–1–62	12.8	33–36–0–0–45	1	275–1,472
Deschutes (Bend)	CO-I	64	13.7	91–64–19–40	14.8	26–41–0–1–37	40	288–1,593
Douglas (Roseburg)	CO-I	93	30.9	233–16–3–82	38.6	35–60–0–16–77	0	848–1,562
Jackson (Medford)	CA-C	135	20.9	104–14–4–32	26.9	27–26–0–6–47	1	475–1,701
Josephine (Grants Pass)	CO-I	60	12.3	141–5–6–53	16.7	45–25–0–9–59	0	346–1,659
Klamath (Klamath Falls)	CO-I	59	16.3	142–40–9–83	16.6	34–68–0–33–32	23	434–1,151
Lane (Eugene)	CA-C	273	59.4	127–37–4–50	77.3	32–32–0–13–60	148	1,745–1,469
Lincoln (Newport)	CO-I	37	10.8	132–99–14–51	12.0	34–62–0–7–80	0	321–1,271
Linn (Albany)	CO-I	91	15.8	118–28–3–26	15.8	28–43–0–1–28	0	352–1,518
Malheur (Vale)	CO-I	28	5.0	115–39–2–26	4.8	19–33–0–0–32	0	128–1,203
Marion (Salem)	CO-C	209	27.7	70–39–4–19	33.0	29–19–0–0–33	0	744–1,532
Multnomah (Portland)	CE-C	566	127.7	89–80–25–32	142.5	50–14–0–10–52	10	2,246–1,817
Polk (Dallas)	CO-C	46	7.0	86–50–5–12	8.4	26–22–0–0–47	1	178–1,464
Umatilla (Pendleton)	CO-I	60	8.2	72–46–0–17	9.7	18–19–0–1–37	0	...–...
Washington (Hillsboro)	CA-C	259	67.1	64–108–14–73	69.9	36–51–0–3–25	172	1,073–1,836
Yamhill (Mc Minnville)	CO-I	57	8.5	65–44–6–35	8.3	24–21–0–0–31	0	231–1,424
PENNSYLVAINA								
Adams (Gettysburg)	CO-S	70	7.0	40–34–3–22	6.6	15–1–0–34–20	26	271–996
Allegheny (Pittsburgh)	CA-C	1,433	438.1	124–119–2–61	430.5	15–7–24–32–31	359	7,838–1,485
Armstrong (Kittanning)	CO-I	78	9.0	71–22–2–20	9.8	6–2–0–65–20	0	285–1,160
Beaver (Beaver)	CO-S	203	41.9	113–57–0–37	41.9	10–3–17–79–26	69	494–1,116
Bedford (Bedford)	CO-I	48	3.2	21–23–3–20	3.2	6–2–0–5–22	1	...–...
Berks (Reading)	CO-C	315	49.6	95–31–0–32	54.8	15–1–0–55–22	3	1,472–896
Blair (Hollidaysburg)	CO-C	136	18.0	71–40–0–21	20.1	15–3–0–41–24	59	527–1,104
Bradford (Towanda)	CO-I	64	9.0	65–44–0–31	7.3	9–2–0–52–24	3	324–1,027
Bucks (Doylestown)	CO-S	496	78.9	66–69–0–23	81.3	17–1–0–23–25	63	1,813–1,306
Butler (Butler)	CA-I	150	23.7	82–41–3–33	25.5	6–1–0–40–18	46	518–1,207
Cambria (Ebensburg)	CO-C	179	34.3	102–50–0–39	32.6	11–2–0–80–22	66	1,085–1,049
Carbon (Jim Thorpe)	CO-S	54	11.5	133–39–1–40	11.0	6–2–0–101–33	2	283–860
Centre (Bellefonte)	CO-C	114	14.9	75–28–0–27	14.3	6–1–0–51–22	5	444–1,188
Chester (West Chester)	CO-S	326	60.5	80–66–0–40	66.3	18–1–0–38–36	49	1,459–1,320
Clarion (Clarion)	CO-I	43	...	...–...–...–...	...	...–...–...–...–...	0	...–...
Clearfield (Clearfield)	CO-I	83	6.2	19–42–3–11	6.3	14–1–0–8–17	29	172–992
Clinton (Lock Haven)	CO-I	39	3.1	25–41–2–11	3.0	13–2–0–12–31	0	...–...
Columbia (Bloomsburg)	CO-I	62	4.2	26–26–3–12	4.1	8–1–0–9–19	0	178–1,017
Crawford (Meadville)	CO-I	90	10.5	62–34–3–18	11.1	15–2–0–32–22	1	408–1,054
Cumberland (Carlisle)	CO-S	182	21.8	81–21–3–15	25.9	9–1–0–58–20	99	802–1,126
Dauphin (Harrisburg)	CO-C	234	40.0	92–50–0–29	50.3	17–0–0–95–26	103	1,329–1,137
Delaware (Media)	CA-S	551	118.8	107–71–0–37	121.2	22–2–0–46–34	82	2,782–1,235
Elk (Ridgway)	CO-I	38	2.0	19–19–2–12	2.3	5–3–0–9–19	30	81–1,075
Erie (Erie)	CE-C	281	53.8	118–56–0–18	53.4	18–2–0–71–24	22	732–1,434
Fayette (Uniontown)	CA-I	158	10.5	35–22–2–8	9.9	8–3–0–5–18	2	284–1,145
Franklin (Chambersburg)	CO-I	115	14.1	73–32–0–17	11.7	10–1–0–34–13	0	367–1,069
Greene (Waynesburg)	CO-I	41	6.2	76–56–3–16	5.9	11–3–0–65–26	39	...–...
Huntingdon (Huntingdon)	CO-I	43	5.2	26–39–2–54	5.0	12–3–0–63–22	34	189–1,012
Indiana (Indiana)	CO-I	93	7.7	34–32–2–14	6.4	7–0–0–21–15	6	229–1,038
Jefferson (Brookville)	CO-I	48	7.7	90–28–3–39	8.7	6–0–0–90–28	187	...–...
Lackawanna (Scranton)	CO-C	226	25.0	55–41–0–15	24.9	10–7–0–32–17	26	767–1,064
Lancaster (Lancaster)	CA-C	372	41.0	61–29–0–20	44.2	16–2–0–38–22	43	1,241–1,151
Lawrence (New Castle)	CO-I	106	12.0	61–36–0–16	11.7	10–6–0–21–20	26	344–1,008
Lebanon (Lebanon)	CO-I	111	15.6	83–35–0–22	15.2	13–2–1–68–23	44	739–1,134
Lehigh (Allentown)	CE-C	275	52.2	86–62–0–42	56.5	23–1–0–78–28	111	1,642–1,300
Luzerne (Wilkes-Barre)	CO-C	340	38.0	42–50–0–21	31.0	7–4–0–26–20	25	1,191–1,096
Lycoming (Williamsport)	CA-C	117	19.3	74–58–0–32	18.7	16–2–0–42–28	86	456–1,184

Table 1/10 continued PROFILES OF INDIVIDUAL COUNTIES

County (county seat)	Form of govern-ment–Metro status	Est. 1982 popu-lation (000)	Fiscal year 1983 revenues: Total general revenue ($ mil-lions)	Fiscal year 1983 revenues: Per capita revenues ($) Intergovernmental rev-enue–Property taxes–Other taxes–Charges and miscellaneous general revenue	Fiscal year 1983 expenditures: Total general expendi-tures ($ mil-lions)	Fiscal year 1983 expenditures: Per capita current expenditures ($) Law enforcement–Streets–Hospitals–Welfare–Finance and administration	Long term debt ($ per capita)	October 1983 public personnel: Total full time equivalent employment–Average full time monthly salary ($)
PENNSYLVANIA continued								
Mc Kean (Smethport)	CO-I	49	6.1	60–32–3–28	6.1	13–2–2–55–21	1	251–1,088
Mercer (Mercer)	CO-C	127	18.4	73–49–3–20	17.5	13–1–0–40–24	18	443–843
Mifflin (Lewistown)	CO-I	46	3.1	19–30–3–16	2.7	7–3–0–6–16	72	82–1,067
Monroe (Stroudsburg)	CA-S	73	9.8	42–70–1–22	10.2	19–0–0–40–39	26	257–1,026
Montgomery (Norristown)	CO-S	651	96.1	62–59–0–27	96.6	13–1–1–25–27	20	2,218–1,290
Northampton (Easton)	CE-C	228	47.9	114–66–0–31	41.6	17–1–0–69–32	62	1,106–1,468
Northumberland (Sunbury)	CO-I	100	16.3	106–31–3–24	15.1	10–2–0–61–22	0	664–860
Perry (New Bloomfield)	CO-S	37	2.5	24–30–3–10	2.6	5–1–0–11–20	0	...–...
Schuylkill (Pottsville)	CO-I	159	23.3	75–41–2–30	21.3	7–3–0–46–20	9	1,032–743
Snyder (Middleburg)	CO-I	34	1.9	16–27–0–11	1.6	6–0–0–4–19	43	91–1,241
Somerset (Somerset)	CO-S	82	8.5	24–39–3–38	8.2	10–2–0–34–25	45	354–1,016
Susquehanna (Montrose)	CO-S	38	0.8	0–0–0–22	2.6	7–1–0–12–29	0	...–...
Tioga (Wellsboro)	CO-I	41	5.0	47–43–2–31	5.1	28–3–0–25–29	0	165–1,068
Union (Lewisburg)	CO-I	33	2.6	24–41–3–10	2.5	7–1–0–9–21	35	...–...
Venango (Franklin)	CO-I	65	10.1	82–33–3–38	9.8	4–1–0–50–25	0	323–1,137
Warren (Warren)	CO-I	48	9.8	119–52–3–31	10.0	15–3–0–101–23	21	...–...
Washington (Washington)	CO-S	217	31.3	81–38–0–25	26.2	5–3–0–29–22	73	714–1,165
Wayne (Honesdale)	CO-I	36	3.9	54–42–0–12	4.4	10–4–0–17–35	0	155–1,093
Westmoreland (Greensburg)	CA-S	391	65.0	87–55–0–24	65.0	8–2–0–43–24	92	1,304–1,221
Wyoming (Tunkhannock)	CO-I	27	1.8	20–33–2–11	1.8	8–1–0–7–27	0	...–...
York (York)	CO-C	317	37.5	60–37–0–21	34.4	14–1–0–27–18	21	1,138–1,110
SOUTH CAROLINA								
Aiken (Aiken)	CA-S	108	15.2	40–49–1–51	14.8	19–9–0–16–21	145	399–1,088
Anderson (Anderson)	CO-C	137	14.6	36–46–0–24	13.1	16–12–0–0–17	235	319–1,177
Beaufort (Beaufort)	CA-I	75	20.2	48–81–7–134	21.5	26–11–92–1–31	197	626–1,261
Berkeley (Moncks Corner)	CO-S	103	21.7	81–38–1–91	26.2	13–14–0–1–24	184	323–1,147
Charleston (Charleston)	CA-C	288	56.3	40–77–3–75	55.2	24–8–44–1–21	151	1,540–1,168
Cherokee (Gaffney)	CA-I	41	7.6	37–27–1–121	7.7	14–11–106–0–17	0	422–1,059
Chester (Chester)	CA-I	31	14.5	56–55–3–361	13.0	19–13–237–2–18	47	163–1,095
Chesterfield (Chesterfield)	CA-I	38	5.3	41–29–2–67	3.6	13–8–2–2–17	46	114–913
Clarendon (Manning)	CA-I	28	8.5	37–39–0–230	6.7	20–6–148–0–22	56	265–910
Colleton (Walterboro)	CO-I	32	3.7	53–18–1–45	3.9	19–7–0–7–24	5	163–1,018
Darlington (Darlington)	CA-I	64	5.8	40–36–1–14	5.6	17–6–0–1–12	0	121–1,030
Dillon (Dillon)	CA-I	32	3.3	48–23–3–29	2.8	17–1–0–1–19	0	...–...
Dorchester (St. George)	CA-S	64	10.0	95–40–2–18	10.1	16–9–0–2–21	60	231–942
Florence (Florence)	CA-C	112	12.0	44–43–1–20	12.0	14–12–0–1–22	27	329–1,189
Georgetown (Georgetown)	CA-I	44	7.3	58–64–4–41	7.3	19–13–0–2–44	9	...–...
Greenville (Greenville)	CA-C	294	42.4	59–61–4–21	43.7	22–7–0–5–22	203	1,131–1,201
Greenwood (Greenwood)	CA-I	59	37.6	44–45–1–545	35.9	15–9–482–1–14	249	222–1,101
Horry (Conway)	CA-I	109	16.1	41–73–7–26	13.6	16–8–0–0–29	64	520–1,134
Kershaw (Camden)	CA-I	40	18.0	49–46–1–355	14.5	21–11–224–1–27	76	552–1,140
Lancaster (Lancaster)	CA-I	55	6.7	40–46–0–35	6.7	19–8–1–21–24	69	226–1,164
Laurens (Laurens)	CO-I	53	4.1	38–28–2–11	3.8	15–9–5–1–13	10	134–1,097
Lexington (Lexington)	CA-S	147	56.3	51–92–2–239	49.1	19–9–186–0–17	150	1,506–1,438
Marion (Marion)	CA-I	34	3.9	61–35–1–16	3.7	11–19–0–0–19	2	129–956
Marlboro (Bennettsville)	CO-I	32	...	...–...–...–...	0.8	3–1–0–1–0	0	105–876
Newberry (Newberry)	CA-I	31	10.5	51–55–0–227	9.5	21–7–194–0–23	111	327–855
Oconee (Walhalla)	CO-I	50	7.6	56–68–2–25	7.2	20–35–3–2–21	71	202–890
Orangeburg (Orangeburg)	CA-I	84	21.8	39–32–1–189	22.1	13–13–155–1–14	273	1,052–1,020
Pickens (Pickens)	CA-S	83	6.9	34–40–0–10	7.6	13–14–0–0–12	3	197–1,101
Richland (Columbia)	CA-C	276	114.3	56–76–3–279	104.7	24–6–234–15–27	93	3,017–1,382
Spartanburg (Spartanburg)	CA-C	204	85.5	50–51–2–316	85.0	21–14–243–1–20	125	2,530–1,216
Sumter (Sumter)	CA-I	91	11.1	56–41–1–25	10.4	18–10–0–3–20	323	365–1,164
Union (Union)	CO-I	31	8.4	50–38–0–184	8.5	17–12–175–4–18	224	109–1,059
Williamsburg (Kingstree)	CO-I	38	10.9	82–38–0–164	10.8	14–16–149–1–15	6	344–1,105
York (York)	CA-C	110	13.4	35–30–3–53	8.1	16–4–0–6–15	44	235–1,287
SOUTH DAKOTA								
Brown (Aberdeen)	CO-I	37	5.6	33–76–9–31	5.2	10–51–0–8–25	0	107–1,050
Minnehaha (Sioux Falls)	CO-C	113	9.6	22–37–10–17	10.1	15–16–2–12–20	6	242–1,436
Pennington (Rapid City)	CO-I	73	6.6	24–41–9–17	9.5	22–12–1–10–30	0	236–1,100
TENNESSEE								
Anderson (Clinton)	CA-S	68	27.3	187–176–7–32	24.5	11–17–0–1–11	162	1,005–1,182
Bedford (Shelbyville)	CO-I	28	19.3	219–119–64–285	18.9	9–51–251–1–7	359	864–1,016
Blount (Maryville)	CO-S	79	37.5	169–121–109–74	44.7	12–25–0–2–18	550	1,019–1,166
Bradley (Cleveland)	CO-I	69	50.2	153–159–81–339	46.1	13–17–228–30–11	350	1,424–1,258
Campbell (Jacksboro)	CO-I	35	...	...–...–...–...	13.9	0–0–0–0–0	0	901–1,006
Carroll (Huntingdon)	CO-I	28	...	...–...–...–...	4.2	11–37–15–2–11	0	220–1,074
Carter (Elizabethton)	CO-S	51	18.2	173–104–48–31	18.4	12–19–0–0–14	188	792–1,010
Cocke (Newport)	CO-I	29	17.5	238–99–74–191	16.3	10–36–151–2–11	275	708–1,138
Coffee (Manchester)	CO-I	40	13.6	116–63–108–53	13.8	12–18–0–0–8	217	442–1,137
Cumberland (Crossville)	CO-I	29	15.1	245–112–106–53	14.0	12–28–0–0–13	354	678–1,131
Dickson (Charlotte)	CO-S	30	14.5	224–93–94–66	13.8	14–23–0–18–17	180	558–1,053
Dyer (Dyersburg)	CO-I	34	25.3	154–92–99–387	14.0	18–27–0–1–15	76	461–1,238
Fayette (Somerville)	CO-I	25	...	...–...–...–...	8.6	12–71–0–0–16	0	633–959
Franklin (Winchester)	CO-I	32	25.8	227–84–50–433	19.2	12–25–218–0–10	587	978–1,157
Gibson (Trenton)	CO-I	49	9.7	42–78–63–14	9.6	10–34–0–3–10	138	337–1,033
Greene (Greeneville)	CO-I	55	20.7	165–101–66–45	19.2	10–37–0–0–13	220	824–1,016
Hamblen (Morristown)	CO-I	51	...	...–...–...–...	7.3	15–17–0–5–18	0	513–1,145

Table 1/10 continued PROFILES OF INDIVIDUAL COUNTIES

County (county seat)	Form of govern-ment–Metro status	Est. 1982 popu-lation (000)	Fiscal year 1983 revenues: Total general revenue ($ mil-lions)	Fiscal year 1983 revenues: Per capita revenues ($) Intergovernmental rev-enue–Property taxes–Other taxes–Charges and miscellaneous general revenue	Fiscal year 1983 expenditures: Total general expendi-tures ($ mil-lions)	Fiscal year 1983 expenditures: Per capita current expenditures ($) Law enforcement–Streets–Hospitals–Welfare–Finance and administration	Long term debt ($ per capita)	October 1983 public personnel: Total full time equivalent employment–Average full time monthly salary ($)
TENNESSEE continued								
Hamilton (Chattanooga)	CA-C	287	223.0	100–157–105–414	243.8	16–13–299–34–21	530	5,897–1,127
Hawkins (Rogersville)	CO-C	44	25.3	226–157–48–137	24.0	13–39–77–1–23	348	887–1,124
Henry (Paris)	CO-I	29	20.7	172–127–67–344	23.9	16–159–241–44–21	63	829–989
Jefferson (Dandridge)	CO-I	32	13.7	229–93–57–42	13.4	13–29–0–1–9	218	866–1,103
Knox (Knoxville)	CO-C	328	144.8	115–151–116–59	142.7	18–12–0–13–25	183	3,408–1,267
Lawrence (Lawrenceburg)	CO-I	34	14.2	234–92–56–37	14.5	10–33–0–0–12	214	745–1,182
Lincoln (Fayetteville)	CO-I	26	19.1	222–83–68–362	16.4	10–37–220–0–10	314	565–976
Loudon (Loudon)	CO-I	30	19.4	183–131–64–266	19.9	20–25–128–0–20	318	590–1,302
Mc Minn (Athens)	CA-I	42	23.5	174–164–80–136	21.3	12–35–102–1–9	431	711–1,111
Madison (Jackson)	CO-I	75	...	...–...–...–...	45.4	12–25–298–4–25	0	775–1,615
Maury (Columbia)	CO-I	51	34.3	199–130–75–262	30.4	12–23–136–0–12	349	1,632–1,145
Monroe (Madisonville)	CO-I	29	12.1	230–73–77–33	11.4	10–32–0–1–13	118	582–953
Montgomery (Clarksville)	CO-C	89	53.3	179–120–96–201	57.0	15–23–162–10–19	404	2,059–1,238
Obion (Union City)	CO-I	33	...	...–...–...–...	12.0	2–52–0–0–14	0	954–1,035
Putnam (Cookeville)	CA-I	49	...	...–...–...–...	4.5	11–20–0–1–0	0	861–1,198
Roane (Kingston)	CO-I	49	19.5	195–86–61–57	17.5	10–16–0–0–13	279	716–1,150
Robertson (Springfield)	CO-S	37	24.6	230–143–70–214	23.5	18–37–172–2–12	422	692–1,099
Rutherford (Murfreesboro)	CO-S	90	40.1	169–133–84–61	37.3	12–21–0–1–15	354	1,385–1,484
Sevier (Sevierville)	CO-I	44	20.5	199–110–127–34	17.9	18–17–0–3–10	325	886–1,076
Shelby (Memphis)	CE-C	784	403.1	90–164–92–172	289.2	28–6–94–0–37	0	6,115–1,334
Sullivan (Blountville)	CO-C	146	72.0	134–217–89–54	71.4	17–30–0–3–12	308	2,318–1,253
Sumner (Gallatin)	CO-S	88	53.9	187–134–59–230	57.2	10–25–176–0–9	348	1,811–1,271
Tipton (Covington)	CO-S	34	...	...–...–...–...	8.9	6–48–0–0–22	0	607–1,132
Warren (Mc Minnville)	CO-I	33	17.4	220–62–63–183	16.3	15–23–125–2–8	212	791–974
Washington (Jonesboro)	CO-C	91	32.9	118–103–108–34	32.0	8–29–0–1–10	213	936–1,314
Weakley (Dresden)	CO-I	33	13.4	184–97–52–76	13.1	8–39–0–45–13	245	804–997
Williamson (Franklin)	CO-S	62	45.9	158–194–67–325	40.3	13–35–203–0–11	593	1,172–1,118
Wilson (Lebanon)	CO-S	57	22.4	152–152–51–37	23.8	9–29–0–1–15	493	746–1,298
TEXAS								
Anderson (Palestine)	CO-I	43	14.9	12–65–11–262	13.3	17–22–213–1–20	3	481–1,235
Angelina (Lufkin)	CO-I	68	7.8	5–30–8–72	7.7	7–11–0–0–20	52	185–1,242
Atascosa (Jourdanton)	CO-I	26	3.5	18–86–12–19	3.5	23–30–0–1–24	34	...–...
Bee (Beeville)	CO-I	27	2.7	11–43–12–36	2.4	17–18–0–1–30	11	94–1,205
Bell (Belton)	CO-C	159	11.4	9–39–2–22	8.9	12–12–0–2–21	11	444–1,203
Bexar (San Antonio)	CO-C	1,046	130.0	19–61–3–41	127.5	14–3–58–2–21	29	4,997–1,250
Bowie (Boston)	CO-C	77	5.8	13–37–7–19	5.9	10–21–0–1–20	84	180–1,102
Brazoria (Angleton)	CO-S	180	27.7	15–108–4–26	25.0	17–50–0–2–23	43	691–1,330
Brazos (Bryan)	CO-C	108	10.3	6–41–5–43	8.3	10–9–0–1–24	96	259–1,418
Brown (Brownwood)	CO-I	35	3.3	9–36–10–42	2.6	10–17–0–0–21	36	...–...
Cameron (Brownsville)	CO-C	226	15.6	15–18–5–31	15.9	10–7–0–3–23	21	669–1,162
Cass (Linden)	CO-I	30	3.9	14–39–10–64	3.3	14–23–0–0–19	0	...–...
Cherokee (Rusk)	CO-I	39	3.9	11–54–9–25	3.1	11–30–0–4–17	0	...–...
Collin (Mc Kinney)	CO-S	165	12.3	5–43–3–23	11.8	13–16–1–0–18	45	345–1,623
Comal (New Braunfels)	CO-S	40	3.8	11–4–10–73	5.2	19–14–0–1–35	14	143–1,049
Cooke (Gainesville)	CO-I	29	1.1	0–0–0–37	4.4	19–43–0–2–37	0	...–...
Coryell (Gatesville)	CO-S	58	2.1	8–12–4–12	2.0	5–8–0–1–12	3	...–...
Dallas (Dallas)	CO-C	1,638	278.7	26–91–4–49	284.1	19–4–63–3–39	170	6,766–1,705
Denton (Denton)	CO-S	166	9.6	8–33–5–12	9.4	10–12–0–1–19	15	303–1,391
Ector (Odessa)	CO-C	135	55.0	15–100–8–285	51.9	19–20–247–8–25	110	1,482–1,575
El Paso (El Paso)	CO-C	505	61.8	21–49–3–49	53.4	11–3–33–2–9	50	2,034–1,155
Ellis (Waxahachie)	CO-S	63	4.3	7–27–8–27	4.0	11–21–0–1–15	6	142–1,122
Fort Bend (Richmond)	CO-C	160	30.3	7–112–5–66	26.3	22–23–0–1–25	23	556–1,334
Galveston (Galveston)	CO-C	208	60.2	24–86–2–178	66.4	27–17–112–4–41	253	1,523–1,826
Gray (Pampa)	CO-I	28	4.8	10–86–15–60	3.8	19–40–0–2–30	0	105–1,396
Grayson (Sherman)	CO-C	92	11.7	24–60–7–35	11.6	8–11–0–0–22	113	313–1,192
Gregg (Longview)	CO-C	110	17.9	6–93–3–62	15.8	15–24–0–2–33	319	396–1,345
Guadalupe (Seguin)	CO-S	49	4.5	8–45–7–30	5.1	9–21–14–2–24	1	154–1,009
Hale (Plainview)	CO-I	38	...	...–...–...–...	...	...–...–...–...–...	0	...–...
Hardin (Kountze)	CO-S	43	4.8	9–63–6–35	4.9	11–18–18–1–29	0	...–...
Harris (Houston)	CO-C	2,674	633.0	30–142–8–57	617.6	17–11–55–4–37	234	11,519–1,744
Harrison (Marshall)	CO-C	56	7.1	8–67–8–45	5.9	14–26–0–3–23	12	168–1,217
Hays (San Marcos)	CO-S	44	...	...–...–...–...	2.7	7–16–1–0–18	0	163–914
Henderson (Athens)	CO-I	46	9.2	9–63–8–119	9.6	13–35–100–1–16	37	126–1,139
Hidalgo (Edinburg)	CO-C	310	20.5	14–38–1–12	17.7	14–5–0–3–18	28	859–1,014
Hill (Hillsboro)	CO-I	26	2.3	7–35–8–38	2.2	16–34–0–2–20	4	...–...
Hopkins (Sulphur Springs)	CO-I	26	3.2	8–75–9–27	3.3	11–38–0–0–22	61	...–...
Howard (Big Spring)	CO-I	36	6.4	10–87–12–70	5.3	14–31–0–1–30	0	...–...
Hunt (Greenville)	CO-I	59	4.4	9–39–7–18	3.8	13–27–0–1–12	61	148–1,235
Hutchinson (Stinnett)	CO-I	29	10.5	13–133–11–203	10.0	24–22–158–3–42	22	311–1,261
Jasper (Jasper)	CO-I	32	3.0	15–47–13–21	2.6	13–20–0–2–24	2	...–...
Jefferson (Beaumont)	CO-C	260	30.3	8–76–4–26	25.9	16–14–0–4–32	0	831–1,709
Jim Wells (Alice)	CO-I	39	5.5	18–81–14–29	4.9	15–36–0–7–34	0	191–1,134
Johnson (Cleburne)	CO-S	74	4.3	7–34–4–13	4.4	11–17–0–2–14	13	142–1,079
Kaufman (Kaufman)	CO-S	42	3.9	19–43–9–22	3.3	14–7–0–1–24	9	122–1,220
Kerr (Kerrville)	CO-I	31	4.0	11–70–14–34	3.2	16–15–0–0–27	29	117–1,056
Kleberg (Kingsville)	CO-I	34	15.8	25–123–12–298	14.2	17–25–220–14–44	282	405–1,116
Lamar (Paris)	CO-I	43	3.7	13–40–9–26	3.5	21–25–0–2–19	1	...–...
Liberty (Liberty)	CO-S	52	5.8	12–74–7–20	5.8	19–37–0–6–23	36	200–1,111

Table 1/10 continued **PROFILES OF INDIVIDUAL COUNTIES**

County (county seat)	Form of govern-ment–Metro status	Est. 1982 popu-lation (000)	Fiscal year 1983 revenues: Total general revenue ($ mil-lions)	Fiscal year 1983 revenues: Per capita revenues ($) Intergovernmental rev-enue–Property taxes–Other taxes–Charges and miscellaneous general revenue	Fiscal year 1983 expenditures: Total general expendi-tures ($ mil-lions)	Fiscal year 1983 expenditures: Per capita current expenditures ($) Law enforcement–Streets–Hospitals–Welfare–Finance and administration	Long term debt ($ per capita)	October 1983 public personnel: Total full time equivalent employment–Average full time monthly salary ($)
TEXAS continued								
Lubbock (Lubbock)	CO-C	215	43.6	6–50–4–143	36.0	12–5–117–1–17	36	456–1,264
Mc Lennan (Waco)	CO-C	175	16.3	20–44–4–25	15.6	17–14–2–4–19	34	480–1,433
Matagorda (Bay City)	CO-I	37	...	...–...–...–...	7.2	27–44–0–5–31	0	169–1,472
Maverick (Eagle Pass)	CO-I	34	1.2	0–0–0–35	2.3	8–13–0–0–13	2	...–...
Midland (Midland)	CO-C	100	9.9	6–64–7–22	9.1	20–14–0–1–26	7	307–1,552
Montgomery (Conroe)	CO-C	161	26.2	14–95–5–49	22.0	24–29–0–2–22	24	646–1,405
Nacogdoches (Nacogdoches)	CO-I	48	4.0	12–38–10–22	3.4	13–19–0–0–21	15	125–1,124
Navarro (Corsicana)	CO-I	37	4.4	11–51–8–48	3.1	13–30–0–0–21	4	134–1,321
Nueces (Corpus Christi)	CO-C	285	86.9	38–95–4–168	80.3	24–17–164–5–30	63	2,580–1,360
Orange (Orange)	CO-C	88	9.1	12–63–2–26	9.6	20–26–0–2–26	48	403–1,173
Parker (Weatherford)	CO-S	48	4.8	7–64–9–20	4.3	10–35–0–0–26	7	141–1,155
Potter (Amarillo)	CO-C	102	12.0	9–81–7–21	11.1	32–6–0–3–41	0	338–1,496
Randall (Canyon)	CO-C	79	4.7	5–32–8–15	4.3	13–10–0–1–21	20	151–1,462
Rusk (Henderson)	CO-I	43	5.8	10–97–7–22	4.8	14–30–0–2–23	0	155–1,209
San Patricio (Sinton)	CO-S	62	10.0	25–90–7–38	9.6	29–33–0–8–31	96	279–1,196
Smith (Tyler)	CO-C	137	10.7	7–44–6–22	9.6	12–16–0–1–21	25	389–1,299
Starr (Rio Grande City)	CO-I	30	4.5	24–98–13–15	3.9	19–36–0–1–34	2	261–835
Tarrant (Fort Worth)	CO-C	930	116.7	23–58–4–41	128.0	13–8–42–3–26	92	2,937–1,535
Taylor (Abilene)	CO-C	118	8.7	10–40–7–16	7.5	12–6–0–2–24	101	260–1,324
Tom Green (San Angelo)	CO-C	91	7.6	6–42–7–29	7.7	12–13–0–1–19	20	263–1,378
Travis (Austin)	CO-C	453	47.4	20–55–1–28	41.4	20–13–0–2–32	0	1,294–1,667
Upshur (Gilmer)	CO-I	32	2.8	9–54–9–17	2.4	14–25–0–0–24	35	...–...
Val Verde (Del Rio)	CO-I	38	0.8	0–0–0–20	3.0	14–12–0–1–26	0	...–...
Van Zandt (Canton)	CO-I	33	3.3	10–51–11–28	3.0	10–12–0–0–26	11	118–1,133
Victoria (Victoria)	CO-C	74	27.1	14–71–9–270	26.5	21–12–214–2–30	191	844–1,303
Walker (Huntsville)	CO-I	47	4.2	18–47–6–19	4.6	19–17–0–1–26	33	...–...
Webb (Laredo)	CO-C	108	11.4	22–66–6–11	11.0	33–9–0–2–38	1	455–1,213
Wharton (Wharton)	CO-I	41	8.0	11–133–12–38	7.3	22–37–0–2–32	5	183–1,261
Wichita (Wichita Falls)	CO-C	127	12.5	9–40–5–45	11.3	11–6–1–6–26	43	293–1,308
Williamson (Georgetown)	CO-S	87	6.5	8–37–6–24	6.9	11–24–0–1–20	0	194–1,167
Wise (Decatur)	CO-S	28	4.3	23–82–10–38	4.0	15–49–0–1–32	26	136–1,129
UTAH								
Box Elder (Brigham City)	CO-I	35	5.9	53–30–10–74	5.9	24–33–0–51–26	12	102–1,407
Cache (Logan)	CO-I	62	5.1	25–39–2–15	4.9	18–14–0–1–15	6	121–1,447
Davis (Farmington)	CO-S	159	18.8	34–47–13–24	14.8	15–3–0–1–15	11	385–1,611
Salt Lake (Salt Lake City)	CO-C	660	168.3	63–91–37–64	169.4	31–13–0–1–31	36	3,106–1,799
Tooele (Tooele)	CO-S	28	7.9	68–38–12–169	8.1	19–22–145–9–38	0	231–1,225
Utah (Provo)	CO-C	232	18.6	10–27–3–40	18.1	8–5–0–0–18	3	362–1,621
Washington (St. George)	CO-I	29	4.3	56–46–6–39	4.5	14–19–0–0–30	84	79–1,226
Weber (Ogden)	CO-C	151	23.6	72–68–3–14	26.6	11–7–0–8–28	0	562–1,577
VERMONT								
Addison (Middlebury)	CO-I	30	0.1	1–2–0–0	0.1	1–0–0–0–1	0	...–...
Bennington (Bennington)	CO-I	34	0.1	0–2–0–0	0.1	0–0–0–0–2	0	...–...
Caledonia (St. Johnsbury)	CO-I	26	...	...–...–...–...	0.1	0–0–0–0–1	0	...–...
Chittenden (Burlington)	CO-C	118	0.3	0–2–0–0	0.2	0–0–0–0–1	4	...–...
Franklin (St. Albans)	CO-S	35	0.1	0–2–0–0	0.1	1–0–0–0–1	0	...–...
Rutland (Rutland)	CO-I	58	0.2	0–2–0–0	0.1	0–0–0–0–1	0	...–...
Washington (Montpelier)	CO-I	53	0.1	0–2–0–0	0.2	1–0–0–0–1	0	...–...
Windham (Brattleboro)	CO-I	37	0.2	0–4–0–0	0.1	2–0–0–0–2	0	10–905
Windsor (Woodstock)	CO-I	52	0.1	0–2–0–0	0.1	1–0–0–0–1	0	...–...
VIRGINIA								
Accomack (Accomac)	CA-I	31	20.0	360–130–58–96	23.8	16–0–0–103–30	223	754–1,203
Albemarle (Charlottesville)	CA-S	57	39.8	245–271–131–44	38.2	18–4–0–25–37	273	1,263–1,207
Amherst (Amherst)	CA-S	29	14.7	302–121–43–41	13.7	19–0–0–17–23	304	573–1,311
Arlington (Arlington)	CA-S	153	203.4	356–598–242–135	194.0	126–79–0–77–69	774	4,189–2,094
Augusta (Staunton)	CA-I	54	32.0	324–143–66–63	32.3	29–1–0–21–37	65	1,206–1,197
Bedford (Bedford)	CA-I	36	21.4	366–144–26–55	20.8	23–0–0–30–18	207	976–1,186
Buchanan (Grundy)	CA-I	38	33.6	406–166–236–72	30.0	26–0–0–31–30	506	1,256–1,120
Campbell (Rustburg)	CA-S	46	26.3	346–147–36–45	24.3	23–0–0–27–26	154	913–1,424
Carroll (Hillsville)	CA-I	28	13.7	346–96–22–27	13.5	19–0–0–24–20	174	603–1,148
Chesterfield (Chesterfield)	CA-S	152	148.5	342–344–93–196	156.4	56–2–0–41–39	879	4,849–1,472
Fairfax (Fairfax)	CA-S	638	855.8	308–666–158–210	829.2	57–1–0–33–50	984	22,848–1,895
Fauquier (Warrenton)	CA-I	37	25.1	270–291–73–37	23.5	22–0–0–19–37	538	824–1,339
Franklin (Rocky Mount)	CA-I	36	18.0	318–96–56–28	18.3	27–0–0–21–23	187	812–1,301
Frederick (Winchester)	CA-I	35	25.0	327–228–74–89	23.6	30–0–0–20–58	355	885–1,302
Halifax (Halifax)	CA-I	30	17.9	430–96–50–23	18.0	25–0–0–38–21	124	897–1,314
Hanover (Hanover)	CA-S	51	35.3	296–248–77–71	35.2	41–0–0–15–34	591	1,300–1,285
Henrico (Richmond)	CA-S	186	181.9	337–327–159–156	169.1	93–38–0–27–64	561	5,211–1,569
Henry (Collinsville)	CA-I	56	36.4	344–152–96–54	31.7	32–0–0–23–25	117	1,510–1,205
Lee (Jonesville)	CA-I	26	16.4	467–102–29–24	16.1	29–0–0–42–28	53	733–1,215
Loudoun (Leesburg)	CA-S	59	59.5	339–501–106–59	53.3	44–0–0–44–54	396	1,966–1,490
Mecklenburg (Boydton)	CA-I	29	15.6	366–95–50–25	15.1	29–0–0–28–16	209	759–1,156
Montgomery (Christiansburg)	CA-I	64	32.0	239–183–43–30	27.3	18–0–0–29–17	176	1,067–1,334
Pittsylvania (Chatham)	CA-S	66	33.1	349–82–23–44	31.2	25–0–0–16–13	14	1,325–1,334
Prince George (Prince George)	CA-S	26	15.6	385–124–39–52	15.3	32–0–0–14–28	209	594–1,321
Prince William (Manassas)	CA-S	157	166.5	387–487–76–112	153.2	74–2–0–20–43	460	5,245–1,624
Pulaski (Pulaski)	CA-I	35	20.2	367–119–47–39	19.2	25–0–0–34–28	85	786–1,280
Roanoke (Salem)	CA-S	74	...	...–...–...–...	37.7	17–1–0–26–24	0	2,260–1,456

Table 1/10 continued **PROFILES OF INDIVIDUAL COUNTIES**

County (county seat)	Form of government–Metro status	Est. 1982 population (000)	Fiscal year 1983 revenues: Total general revenue ($ millions)	Fiscal year 1983 revenues: Per capita revenues ($) Intergovernmental revenue–Property taxes–Other taxes–Charges and miscellaneous general revenue	Fiscal year 1983 expenditures: Total general expenditures ($ millions)	Fiscal year 1983 expenditures: Per capita current expenditures ($) Law enforcement–Streets–Hospitals–Welfare–Finance and administration	Long term debt ($ per capita)	October 1983 public personnel: Total full time equivalent employment–Average full time monthly salary ($)
VIRGINIA continued								
Rockingham (Harrisonburg)	CA-I	53	30.4	297–150–61–68	28.8	23–0–0–17–30	135	1,006–1,441
Russell (Lebanon)	CA-I	32	...	...–...–...–...	23.9	15–0–0–32–27	0	819–1,266
Scott (Gate City)	CA-S	25	13.7	379–86–42–32	12.8	26–0–0–24–19	142	629–1,077
Shenandoah (Woodstock)	CA-I	28	14.9	286–171–51–31	14.1	22–0–0–24–19	115	644–1,150
Smyth (Marion)	CA-I	33	17.6	374–90–37–30	16.2	27–0–0–36–19	73	681–1,277
Spotsylvania (Spotsylvania)	CA-I	36	26.5	363–219–76–77	26.0	19–0–0–23–35	849	991–1,392
Stafford (Stafford)	CA-I	44	34.9	364–330–51–50	31.0	32–7–0–20–57	897	1,220–1,351
Tazewell (Tazewell)	CA-I	52	30.7	348–140–73–35	29.1	22–0–0–40–23	280	1,171–1,266
Washington (Abingdon)	CA-S	47	24.0	337–108–36–30	22.9	23–0–0–28–23	313	1,010–1,358
Wise (Wise)	CA-I	44	34.1	408–92–203–65	31.0	26–67–0–25–21	151	1,072–1,526
Wythe (Wytheville)	CA-I	26	14.0	371–101–48–25	13.3	33–0–0–29–22	112	646–1,086
York (Yorktown)	CA-S	37	38.8	505–271–62–216	34.1	31–0–0–38–40	592	1,171–1,567
WASHINGTON								
Benton (Prosser)	CO-C	117	18.7	55–41–29–35	22.6	24–18–0–0–37	48	284–1,753
Chelan (Wenatchee)	CO-I	46	14.5	192–65–19–37	16.9	48–55–0–0–54	0	341–1,544
Clallam (Port Angeles)	CA-I	52	14.5	83–66–14–119	13.0	51–64–0–1–59	44	366–1,499
Clark (Vancouver)	CO-S	200	36.7	86–64–21–13	38.9	36–37–0–4–34	36	955–1,560
Cowlitz (Kelso)	CO-I	79	28.1	129–126–19–79	24.1	42–83–0–0–52	30	481–1,796
Franklin (Pasco)	CO-C	37	8.3	98–81–17–30	7.8	64–44–0–0–60	33	207–1,451
Grant (Ephrata)	CO-I	50	11.6	103–79–12–41	11.9	36–79–0–1–41	0	304–1,450
Grays Harbor (Montesano)	CO-I	66	24.3	155–65–77–73	18.8	47–87–0–1–46	13	422–1,550
Island (Coupeville)	CO-I	46	8.2	67–65–18–29	7.3	26–41–0–0–38	4	219–1,530
King (Seattle)	CE-C	1,312	331.1	82–75–21–74	325.3	37–11–46–0–38	255	4,858–2,183
Kitsap (Port Orchard)	CO-C	156	28.1	78–54–16–33	26.8	20–29–0–0–40	55	545–1,814
Lewis (Chehalis)	CO-I	57	19.6	176–73–31–61	18.5	50–88–0–1–50	43	371–1,767
Mason (Shelton)	CO-I	33	9.2	112–89–38–41	9.2	59–62–0–0–53	12	194–1,567
Okanogan (Okanogan)	CO-I	32	10.2	193–59–12–54	10.1	34–103–0–0–58	0	201–1,399
Pierce (Tacoma)	CO-C	510	99.9	93–53–15–36	95.1	24–17–0–3–37	14	1,634–1,879
Skagit (Mount Vernon)	CO-I	67	18.2	114–85–16–58	16.7	28–66–0–0–42	25	371–1,507
Snohomish (Everett)	CO-C	356	67.7	66–53–19–51	69.7	32–34–0–2–36	49	1,159–1,790
Spokane (Spokane)	CA-C	349	69.2	78–49–18–53	68.9	36–38–0–1–41	130	1,187–1,705
Stevens (Colville)	CO-I	30	7.2	109–72–19–37	7.4	29–91–0–0–52	13	165–1,495
Thurston (Olympia)	CA-C	133	27.5	88–69–15–34	26.7	30–33–0–1–37	3	553–1,736
Walla Walla (Walla Walla)	CO-I	49	11.5	116–78–13–30	12.2	96–62–0–0–41	0	249–1,310
Whatcom (Bellingham)	CO-C	110	28.1	113–76–15–51	29.1	31–46–0–0–59	48	655–1,650
Whitman (Colfax)	CO-I	40	8.4	104–67–8–32	9.1	25–80–0–0–39	0	220–1,346
Yakima (Yakima)	CO-C	176	32.7	101–45–13–28	36.0	33–29–0–0–38	0	729–1,525
WEST VIRGINIA								
Berkeley (Martinsburg)	CO-I	49	3.3	16–35–1–15	2.8	10–0–0–0–24	0	...–...
Boone (Madison)	CO-I	31	8.7	88–54–0–141	7.5	17–0–108–2–31	9	212–1,244
Brooke (Wellsburg)	CO-C	31	5.3	18–51–1–102	5.2	14–0–0–0–20	0	66–1,145
Cabell (Huntington)	CO-C	106	13.6	50–31–1–46	14.0	18–0–0–0–17	4	373–999
Fayette (Fayetteville)	CO-I	57	7.5	21–46–1–62	6.5	10–0–0–0–23	0	105–1,066
Greenbrier (Lewisburg)	CO-I	37	4.7	23–32–1–70	3.8	13–0–0–0–26	0	...–...
Hancock (New Cumberland)	CO-C	40	5.5	10–54–2–71	3.4	13–0–0–1–19	0	93–1,047
Harrison (Clarksburg)	CO-I	78	5.7	22–42–1–8	5.2	10–0–0–0–20	0	209–1,007
Jackson (Ripley)	CO-I	26	4.9	22–49–1–113	5.2	11–0–0–1–29	0	91–1,122
Jefferson (Charles Town)	CO-I	31	2.0	13–28–4–18	2.0	5–0–0–0–37	0	...–...
Kanawha (Charleston)	CO-C	230	37.3	29–70–0–63	43.4	10–0–0–0–16	414	721–1,199
Logan (Logan)	CO-I	51	4.5	37–36–0–16	3.6	14–0–0–1–26	30	...–...
Mc Dowell (Welch)	CO-I	49	3.9	36–32–0–12	4.2	19–0–0–0–31	0	159–964
Marion (Fairmont)	CO-I	65	7.8	30–40–1–49	7.0	11–0–0–0–25	0	145–1,158
Marshall (Moundsville)	CO-S	41	18.2	35–50–1–357	15.6	16–0–0–1–35	0	119–1,267
Mason (Point Pleasant)	CO-I	27	16.4	20–56–0–532	16.0	11–0–0–0–27	0	57–1,037
Mercer (Princeton)	CO-I	75	5.1	12–25–0–30	5.2	9–0–0–1–16	1	138–1,009
Mineral (Keyser)	CO-S	28	2.3	35–26–2–22	1.9	8–0–0–1–22	0	...–...
Mingo (Williamson)	CO-I	38	3.1	41–31–1–10	2.9	19–0–0–0–26	0	94–1,082
Monongalia (Morgantown)	CO-I	77	9.8	44–28–0–54	8.3	9–1–0–0–18	221	127–1,119
Nicholas (Summersville)	CO-I	28	3.8	46–44–1–43	3.5	19–0–0–0–28	0	93–938
Ohio (Wheeling)	CO-C	61	7.8	14–32–2–79	8.2	12–0–0–1–22	521	141–989
Preston (Kingwood)	CO-I	31	6.8	29–30–1–160	6.4	19–0–115–0–26	0	103–1,064
Putnam (Winfield)	CO-S	39	10.7	25–58–1–189	11.0	13–0–0–0–35	0	...–...
Raleigh (Beckley)	CO-I	87	9.2	28–30–1–48	8.6	15–0–0–1–15	0	145–1,186
Randolph (Elkins)	CO-I	29	2.5	25–44–1–17	2.7	8–0–0–0–21	23	58–960
Wayne (Wayne)	CO-C	46	4.6	17–29–1–51	4.4	10–0–0–0–17	2	78–1,071
Wood (Parkersburg)	CA-C	93	9.0	29–29–1–37	10.2	11–0–0–0–19	10	144–1,098
Wyoming (Pineville)	CO-I	36	3.7	54–39–0–10	3.5	16–0–0–0–23	0	105–982
WISCONSIN								
Barron (Barron)	CO-I	39	9.4	142–59–1–38	10.0	16–33–0–52–22	36	218–1,270
Brown (Green Bay)	CE-C	180	46.3	132–57–1–68	44.0	30–25–0–35–18	77	986–1,659
Calumet (Chilton)	CO-S	32	9.8	132–94–1–82	9.0	25–55–0–31–22	18	269–1,057
Chippewa (Chippewa Falls)	CO-S	53	16.5	123–35–1–149	15.9	16–36–0–49–19	56	454–1,432
Clark (Owen)	CO-I	33	13.6	164–56–0–189	17.5	28–37–0–76–21	283	474–1,148
Columbia (Portage)	CO-I	43	14.7	148–53–0–136	14.4	29–63–0–81–20	3	366–1,423
Dane (Madison)	CE-C	332	80.7	122–66–1–54	81.5	28–21–0–49–27	45	1,475–1,955
Dodge (Juneau)	CO-I	76	25.5	120–81–1–135	24.5	25–55–0–35–24	58	777–1,325
Door (Sturgeon Bay)	CO-I	26	8.3	160–116–2–45	8.8	36–69–0–34–32	0	...–...
Douglas (Superior)	CO-C	45	16.3	162–70–2–131	16.5	32–39–0–50–33	31	456–1,318

Table 1/10 continued PROFILES OF INDIVIDUAL COUNTIES

County (county seat)	Form of govern-ment–Metro status	Est. 1982 popu-lation (000)	Fiscal year 1983 revenues: Total general revenue ($ mil-lions)	Fiscal year 1983 revenues: Per capita revenues ($) Intergovernmental rev-enue–Property taxes–Other taxes–Charges and miscellaneous general revenue	Fiscal year 1983 expenditures: Total general expendi-tures ($ mil-lions)	Fiscal year 1983 expenditures: Per capita current expenditures ($) Law enforcement–Streets–Hospitals–Welfare–Finance and administration	Long term debt ($ per capita)	October 1983 public personnel: Total full time equivalent employment–Average full time monthly salary ($)
WISCONSIN continued								
Dunn (Menomonie)	CA-I	35	16.3	156–74–0–234	17.6	23–113–163–30–23	136	483–1,064
Eau Claire (Eau Claire)	CO-C	82	22.7	133–62–0–83	23.5	22–32–0–55–26	94	465–1,449
Fond du Lac (Fond du Lac)	CE-I	90	26.2	133–56–0–104	26.1	21–45–0–41–26	86	622–1,427
Grant (Lancaster)	CO-I	52	13.5	125–53–0–83	13.9	19–44–0–51–17	26	445–1,150
Green (Monroe)	CO-I	30	11.6	141–105–1–139	11.3	32–59–0–41–23	49	332–1,223
Jefferson (Jefferson)	CA-I	67	24.9	161–90–1–121	24.4	31–44–0–28–18	6	687–1,258
Kenosha (Kenosha)	CO-C	122	39.3	144–74–0–105	39.1	44–31–0–70–39	80	720–1,781
La Crosse (La Crosse)	CO-C	93	27.9	135–45–1–119	26.1	14–23–0–57–16	75	734–1,297
Lincoln (Merrill)	CO-I	27	11.2	146–108–0–163	10.6	29–81–0–49–28	125	321–1,176
Manitowoc (Manitowoc)	CO-I	84	...	...–...–...–...	27.4	26–41–0–36–17	0	687–1,360
Marathon (Wausau)	CA-C	113	58.0	200–88–0–228	38.6	21–30–117–41–21	92	1,256–1,293
Marinette (Marinette)	CO-I	40	22.2	164–80–1–311	27.3	30–56–196–49–29	179	607–841
Milwaukee (Milwaukee)	CE-C	962	526.7	259–134–1–154	505.9	23–12–162–103–53	264	10,520–1,667
Monroe (Sparta)	CO-I	36	14.3	169–78–0–151	13.6	25–61–0–56–22	28	386–1,159
Oconto (Oconto)	CA-I	29	8.4	155–79–1–53	7.5	28–79–0–39–24	31	...–...
Oneida (Rhinelander)	CO-I	32	8.8	151–88–1–41	8.9	28–40–0–32–34	132	182–1,334
Outagamie (Appleton)	CE-C	132	37.8	141–52–1–92	39.2	20–31–0–38–21	145	843–1,520
Ozaukee (Port Washington)	CO-S	67	17.4	106–70–1–82	16.7	29–39–0–23–19	13	430–1,493
Pierce (Ellsworth)	CO-I	32	9.2	142–96–0–52	8.8	28–81–0–27–31	0	213–1,544
Polk (Balsam Lake)	CO-I	34	10.4	135–77–1–97	9.5	26–65–0–45–25	27	220–1,512
Portage (Stevens Point)	CA-I	57	16.1	127–81–1–74	18.2	31–62–0–18–28	34	487–1,394
Racine (Racine)	CE-C	173	50.8	139–76–0–77	52.0	37–21–0–63–28	10	1,043–1,740
Rock (Janesville)	CA-C	139	40.3	141–60–1–88	42.3	35–22–0–65–27	67	1,017–1,501
St. Croix (Hudson)	CO-S	45	16.1	140–90–1–130	17.8	29–60–0–32–26	112	215–1,499
Sauk (Baraboo)	CO-I	45	17.0	130–91–1–160	17.8	42–55–0–49–27	40	480–1,197
Shawano (Shawano)	CO-I	36	9.5	116–63–1–83	9.0	29–51–0–43–22	25	233–1,234
Sheboygan (Sheboygan)	CO-C	102	36.2	141–79–1–134	36.6	34–45–37–38–22	79	782–1,021
Trempealeau (Whitehall)	CO-I	26	11.1	186–72–0–162	12.1	22–90–0–75–25	80	271–1,373
Vernon (Viroqua)	CO-I	26	8.6	159–61–0–105	8.2	16–70–0–50–19	82	276–854
Walworth (Elkhorn)	CO-I	72	43.4	131–115–1–358	40.4	51–39–182–43–33	93	1,031–1,620
Washington (West Bend)	CO-C	86	23.0	101–70–1–95	19.8	30–29–0–37–19	58	548–1,473
Waukesha (Waukesha)	CO-S	283	67.6	113–68–1–57	71.2	23–17–0–36–18	33	1,386–1,569
Waupaca (Waupaca)	CO-I	43	11.3	122–51–1–86	10.7	22–82–0–33–20	0	299–1,281
Winnebago (Oshkosh)	CE-C	133	39.2	138–52–1–104	43.8	27–25–0–51–22	63	1,322–1,040
Wood (Wisconsin Rapids)	CO-I	75	22.0	128–53–0–113	22.0	24–34–36–55–22	67	648–1,374
WYOMING								
Albany (Laramie)	CO-I	30	5.4	71–94–0–14	5.4	27–17–0–1–27	37	123–1,319
Fremont (Lander)	CO-I	38	16.9	84–318–1–41	18.0	32–47–0–0–39	217	208–1,519
Laramie (Cheyenne)	CO-I	71	38.0	94–147–68–230	30.9	34–17–188–2–27	2	653–1,346
Natrona (Casper)	CO-C	77	78.0	145–239–138–489	67.0	26–22–330–3–42	70	1,392–1,315
Sheridan (Sheridan)	CO-I	26	16.5	94–138–66–329	18.3	19–28–277–5–34	70	347–1,598
Sweetwater (Green River)	CO-I	46	67.3	142–583–127–599	51.2	40–26–165–16–45	43	350–1,237

Sources: Form of government and metro status: Master computer file of the International City Management Association; Population: U.S. Department of Commerce, Bureau of the Census; Government finances: U.S. Department of Commerce, Bureau of the Census, *City Government Finances in 1982–83* GF83–4 (Washington, D.C.: Government Printing Office, 1984); Government employment: U.S. Department of Commerce, Bureau of the Census, *City Employment in 1983* GE83–2 (Washington, D.C.: Government Printing Office, 1984).

Appendix A

PROFILES OF INDIVIDUAL CITIES (PICS) DATA SETS BY YEAR

Included in this appendix is a listing of all of the data sets included in the Profiles of Individual Cities (PICs) since they appeared for the first time in the 1976 *Municipal Year Book*. (There were no PICs in the 1979 *Municipal Year Book*.)

The listing is broken into six sections: demography, economics, employment and payroll (municipal), finance, government structure, and other areas. Each category is further broken down into subtopics. These subtopics are followed by the year(s) in which the data set(s) appeared (76 for 1976, 77 for 1977, and so forth).

DEMOGRAPHY

Age: Percent population under 18—76, 83; percent population 25 and over—77; percent population 65 and over—76, 83.

Education: Median years—77; percent of population 18 and over that has not completed high school—84; percent of population 18 and over that has completed high school only—84; percent of population 18 and over that has completed some college work—84; percent of population 18 and over with a college degree—84.

Housing: Number of year-round units—77, 82, 83; percent of structures that are one-unit—77; percent of units built before 1940—83; percent of units built since 1969—83; percent of units that are occupied—77; percent of units that are owner-occupied—77, 83; percent change in number of units 1970–1980—82.

Income and Employment: Per capita income—76, 78, 80, 81, 83; percent change 1969–1975—80; percent change 1969–1977—81; percent of population 16 and over that is employed—83; percent of population under poverty level—77.

Land Area: Land area—76.

Metro Status: Metro status—76, 80, 81, 82, 83, 84, 85.

Nonworker–Worker Ratio: Nonworker–worker ratio—77.

Population Density: Population density—77.

Population Totals: 1960—81; 1970—76, 81;

1973—76, 77; 1975—78, 80, 81; 1980—82, 83, 84; 1982—85; percent change 1960–1970—76, 81; percent change 1970–1973—76; percent change 1970–1975—78, 80, 81; percent change 1970–1980—82, 84.

Race and Ethnic Background: Percent black—82; percent Hispanic—82; percent nonwhite—76, 83; percent white—82.

Sex: Percent female—83.

Work Force Classification: Percent employed in business—83; percent employed in industry—83; percent employed in public administration—83; percent employed in public utilities—83; percent employed in services—83; percent employed in trade—83.

ECONOMICS

Manufacturing: Number of employees—77, 81; percent change in number of employees 1972–1977—81; number of establishments—77, 81; percent change in number of establishments 1972–1977—81.

Retail: Number of employees—81; percent change in number of employees 1972–1977—81; number of establishments—77, 81; percent change in number of establishments 1972–1977—81; amount of sales—77, 81; percent change in retail sales 1972–1977—81.

Service: Number of employees—81; percent change in number of employees 1972–1977—81; number of establishments—77, 81; percent change in number of establishments 1972–1977—81.

EMPLOYMENT AND PAYROLL (MUNICIPAL)

Municipal Employees: Number of employees—76, 78, 80, 84, 85; number for administration—80; percent for administration—84; percent for education—84; percent for streets—84; percent for parks and recreation—84.

Payroll: October total—80; average October earnings—80; average full-time monthly salary—85.

FINANCE

Bond Rating: Bond rating—76, 77, 78, 80, 81, 82, 83.

Debt: Per capita debt that is long term—85; percent of debt that is full faith and credit—80; percent of debt that is nonguaranteed—78; percent of debt that is short term—84; total debt—78, 80, 84.

Expenditure: General expenditure—84, 85; per capita for fire—85; per capita for police—85; per capita for sewers and sanitation—85; per capita for streets—85; percent for administration—84; percent for education—84; percent for parks and recreation—84; percent for streets—84; percent of expenditure other than capital outlay—78, 80, 84; total expenditure—83; total expenditure less capital outlay—76.

Revenue: City personal income tax—77; estimated assessed property valuation—77, 81; general revenue—78, 80, 84, 85; per capita from charges and miscellaneous sources—85; per capita from intergovernmental sources—85; per capita from other taxes—85; per capita from property taxes—85; percent from charges and miscellaneous sources—84; percent from intergovernmental sources—83, 84; percent from other taxes—84; percent from property tax—80, 84; property tax rate—77, 81; revenue from own sources—76; sales tax receipts—77; total revenue—83; utility revenue—85.

GOVERNMENT STRUCTURE

Ballot Type: Ballot type—76, 78.

Council: Councilmember compensation—82; number of members—76, 78, 82; number of members elected at large—78, 82; number of members elected by ward or district—78, 82; terms of office for councilmembers—78, 82; overlapping terms—78.

Provisions for Direct Democracy: Initiative, referendum, and recall—82.

Election Type: Election type—76, 78, 82.

Form of Government: Form of government—76, 77, 78, 80, 81, 82, 83, 84, 85; year form adopted—78.

Mayor: Membership on council—77, 82; method of election—76, 78, 82; salary—82; term—78, 82; voting power—78.

Manager/CAO Employed: Manager/CAO employed—78.

OTHER AREAS

Municipally Operated Utilities: Municipally operated utilities—76.

Fire Rating: Fire rating—76.

Appendix B

PROFILES OF INDIVIDUAL COUNTIES (PICs) DATA SETS BY YEAR

Included in this appendix is a listing of all the data sets included in the Profiles of Individual Counties (PICs) since they appeared for the first time in 1977.

The listing is broken into four sections: demography, employment and payroll (county), finance, and government structure. Each category is further broken down into subtopics. These subtopics are followed by the year(s) in which the data set(s) appeared (77 for 1977, 78 for 1978, and so forth). PICs data sets for 1977 and 1978 can be found in the *County Year Book* for the respective years and data sets for 1983, 1984, and 1985 can be found in the *Municipal Year Book* for those respective years.

DEMOGRAPHY

Age: Percent of the population under 18—77, 83; percent of the population 65 and over—77, 83.

Education: Percent of the population 18 and over that has not completed high school—84; percent of the population 18 and over that has completed high school only—84; percent of the population 18 and over that has completed some college work—84; percent of the population 18 and over with a college degree—84.

Housing: Number of units—83; percent of units built before 1940—83; percent of units built since 1969—83; percent of units that are owner occupied—83.

Income and Employment: Per capita income—77, 78, 83; percent of the population 16 and over that is employed—83.

Land Area: Land area—83.

Metro Status: Metro status—77, 78, 83, 84, 85.

Net Migration: Percent net migration—77.

Population Density: Population density—77.

Population Living in Urbanized Areas: Percentage of population living in urbanized areas—83.

Population Totals: 1970—77; 1975—77, 78; 1980—83, 84; 1982—85; percent change 1960–1970—77; percent change 1970–1975—77, 78; percent change 1970–1980—84.

Race and Ethnic Background: Percent of population that is nonwhite—77, 83.

Sex: Percent of population that is female—83.

Work Force Classification: Percent of population employed in business—83; percent employed in industry—83; percent employed in public administration—83; percent employed in public utilities—83; percent employed in services—83; percent employed in trade—83.

EMPLOYMENT AND PAYROLL (COUNTY)

County Employees: Number of county employees—77, 78, 84, 85; percent educational employees—78, 84; percent administrative employees—84; percent highway employees—84; percent hospital employees—84; percent welfare employees—84.

Payroll: Average earnings for nonteaching employees—78; average earnings for teaching employees—78; average full-time monthly salary—85.

FINANCE

Bond Rating: Bond rating—77, 78.

Debt: Per capita debt that is long term—85.

Expenditure: Expenditure for highways—78; expenditure for hospitals—78; expenditure for public welfare—78; general expenditure—78, 84, 85; per capita for finance and administration—85; per capita for hospitals—85; per capita for law enforcement—85; per capita for streets—85; per capita for welfare—85; percent for administration—84; percent for education—84; percent for highways—84; percent for hospitals—84; percent for welfare—84; percent other than capital outlay—84; total expenditure—83; total expenditure less capital outlay—77.

Revenue: Assessed value of real property—77; charges and miscellaneous revenue—78; general revenue—78, 84, 85; intergovernmental revenue—77; per capita from charges and miscellaneous sources—85; per capita from intergovernmental sources—85; per capita from other taxes—85; per capita from property taxes—85; percent from charges and miscellaneous sources—84; percent from intergovernmental sources—77, 78, 83, 84; percent from other taxes—84; percent from property tax—84; percent of real property that is personal property—77; property tax rate—77; total revenue—83; tax revenue—78.

GOVERNMENT STRUCTURE

Form of Government: Form of government—77, 84, 85.

Local Governments within County: Number of municipalities in county—84; number of townships in county—84; number of school districts in county—84; number of special districts in county—84.

B The Intergovernmental Dimension

1 State Actions Affecting Local Governments: Increased Flexibility in Conducting Business

2 Municipal Annexation and Boundary Changes: 1980–83

B 1

State Actions Affecting Local Governments: Increased Flexibility in Conducting Business

Jay Muzychenko
Dealer Bank Association

The past several years have been difficult ones for both state and local governments. Two back-to-back recessions followed by cutbacks in federal grants-in-aids programs have pressured all levels of government and often brought them into conflict. However, it seems that with the current economic recovery, local governments have fared well in their relationships with the states. By and large, laws have been passed that have given cities and counties more tools with which to conduct their business.

Fundamental to any unit of government's ability to function is its financial situation. With the economic recovery under way, many states took the opportunity to create or increase aid programs to local governments. Grants to support road and highway maintenance and construction programs were increased in several states. Additional financial help is going to the construction of wastewater treatment facilities.

More fundamental, though, is the enhanced ability of local governments to raise their own revenue. In states all across the country, cities and counties have been granted greater flexibility in their revenue raising capacity. In some states this has meant that as the pressure to exploit all revenue sources has eased, the legislature has restored traditional revenue sources to local governments. Other states have set new frameworks in place to give more flexibility to cities and counties to raise revenue. Examples of these new frameworks include laws governing new taxing authority that can be exercised at local option, flexibility in issuing of bonds, and broader use for certain funds.

States were also sensitive to local governments' need to use alternative ways to provide services. Greater authority to use intergovernmental agreements for service delivery was granted. In at least one state, efforts to limit contracting with the private sector were turned back, so that flexibility could be maintained.

Another area crucial to local governments is personnel management. Cities and counties this year were granted a broader range of authority in handling their employee benefit programs, especially pension funds. Furthermore, while some states passed legislation broadening the union rights of employees, they also responded to local government needs by not forcing binding arbitration and other such actions.

Finally, in the area of land use, where states often have their own goals and seek to limit the power of local governments to implement local plans, at least two states addressed this inherent conflict. Both gave authority to local governments that will act as a counterweight to state authority.

Despite the progress that has been made in striking a more equitable balance in state and local relationships, potential problems still exist. One problem concerns the issue of mandates. On a vast array of issues, states were supportive of local governments, but there seems to be an increasing tendency for states to mandate standards, despite the fact that they have backed away from mandating actual programs. Another potential problem concerns finances. If another recession comes in 1986 or 1987, as some predict, the recent financial generosity of states may again be curtailed. However, if the actions of the state legislatures during the 1983-84 session can be interpreted as the beginnings of a trend, the range of tools local governments can choose from to carry out their missions is growing. This increased flexibility may, in fact, be local governments' salvation if deficit reduction at the federal level or a poor economic situation put additional pressures on state and local governments. In any case, the progress that cities and counties made this past year will be the foundation for next year's agenda.

STATE AID PROGRAMS

By and large, state aid to local governments increased in 1983-84. In Maine, the percentage of state revenue going to local governments increased from 4% to 4.75% on 1 August 1984 and will go up to 5.1% after 1 July 1985. Payments made to local governments in lieu of taxes increased in Connecticut, and in Massachusetts the latest budget increased formula aid to local governments by $157 million to offset the effects of Proposition 2½. In Vermont, there was no further erosion of state aid to local governments or of state programs (requiring local governments to pick up the slack); there was an increase in spending for education and roads.

In at least one state there was a recognition of the importance of these revenues to local service provision and the obligation that the state has incurred to deliver these revenues promptly. Michigan will begin paying interest if it does not make revenue sharing or tax reimbursement payments on time.

Illinois was the one state that cut back the dollars in its grant programs.

In addition to increases in general aid programs, there were many aid programs set up or funded for specific projects, for example, wastewater treatment. In Tennessee, money was allocated for wastewater treatment plants. In Rhode Island, the Sewer and Water Supply Failure Fund was established for the same purpose.

In Arizona, funding to assist the chronically mentally ill was passed; the legislation removed the requirement for local match funds for residential treatment planning.

Another area where specific aid programs were enhanced is roads and highways. In Connecticut, this type of aid increased by 25%. In Maine, the Highway Allocation Act increased the highway block grant by 18.18%. In both Massachusetts and Vermont, the state support for roads was increased.

Schools also benefited from targeted state aid programs in some of the states where schools are a responsibility of the local government. In Connecticut, the courts mandated that the state fund the education equalization grant at 100% of full funding, an opinion which is now on appeal. The legislature approved funding at the 95% level. In Massachusetts, aid was increased for schools.

State aid from specific sources also rose in 1983-84. In Idaho, city and county revenue sharing was established, funded out of a one cent increase in the sales tax. This program represents the largest increase in state assistance to local governments in the state's history. One half of 1% of the state of South Carolina's income tax will be returned to municipalities based on population.

The Kentucky Municipal League got a bill passed changing the state's vehicle ad valorem tax collection procedures. This will result in increased revenues to cities. In Alabama, municipalities will receive a portion of the new increase in state gas inspection fees, license taxes, and registration fees on truck and truck-tractors. In Oregon, revenue from vehicle operating licenses going to the local level will increase.

In many cases, aid to local governments derived from specific sources was earmarked for specific uses. In Idaho, $4.8 million of the state sales tax will provide the Water Pollution Control Act with matching dollars for sewage treatment. In Wyoming, the state set aside one-third of the state's community development block grant (CDBG) allocation for local government economic development programs that create or retain permanent jobs. Pennsylvania voters passed a $190 million bond authorization to finance the economic revitalization efforts of local governments. Eight million dollars of a Massachusetts energy bond issue is earmarked for local governments.

Revenue from the state of New Jersey's new surcharge on drunk driving fines will go to local governments to enhance enforcement of the drunk driving laws. In Oklahoma, municipalities are entitled to half of the costs levied for the prosecution of driving while intoxicated (DWI) cases. The money goes to the local government where the person was arrested to encourage municipalities to prosecute DWI cases at the state level (rather than the local level) so convictions will go on the driver's record.

LOCAL REVENUE GENERATION

Sales Taxes. During 1983-84, there was an increase in the number of states allowing local governments to use the sales tax as a revenue raising tool. In Tennessee, municipalities can raise their local option sales tax by one-half cent if they get voter approval. Also in Tennessee, muncipalities can increase their local base of a countywide sales tax, even if the county they are in does not do so. In North Carolina, the state now allows an extra one-half cent to be added to the sales tax at local option. Resort cities in Idaho that are under 10,000 in population are allowed a city sales tax; these are the only cities in the state that are allowed such a tax.

States also approved a variety of local option sales taxes to be used for specific purposes. Wyoming now allows a countywide option of 1%, but for specific capital projects. In South Carolina, a 2% accommodation tax was passed; 25% goes for tourist promotion and 75% goes to offset the costs related to the tourist industry. Permanent authority was granted to cities in Missouri to levy a transportation sales tax.

This proliferation of local sales taxes has led at least two states to establish committees to study the resulting patchwork quilt of sales tax bases. In Colorado, a study committee was set up to examine the effects on local government if the state establishes a uniform sales and use tax. In Arizona, a Municipality Sales Tax Study Commission will review city sales tax ordinances and the differences between the system in each city and the state's system.

User Fees. Legislation passed during 1983–84 allowed greater flexibility in the use of service charges. In Massachusetts, for example, water boards can now use surplus revenue to maintain, repair, and reconstruct their water systems. Counties in West Virginia can charge fees for fire service. In Arizona, local governments can charge for the costs they incur as a result of negligent use, storage, or transportation of hazardous materials. Following the lead of the state legislatures, the Colorado Supreme Court upheld the validity of minimum service expansion fees.

Property Taxes. A major problem that local governments face is the erosion of their property tax base due to state-mandated exemptions from the property tax. This erosion was stemmed in some states this year. In Mississippi, the state now reimburses counties, municipalities, and school districts for tax losses resulting from the state's increased homesteading exemptions. Vermont did not repeal any property tax exemptions, but neither did it grant any new ones.

In Tennessee, on the other hand, the courts held that property held for lease is now exempt from property tax; it will be treated like inventory held for sale. This new exemption will cut local governments' revenue bases. In South Dakota, the state legislature passed legislation to allow a property tax exemption for civic centers. (In fact, this action supported Rapid City's sale and leaseback of its municipal convention center.)

Another aspect of the property tax as a revenue tool is the regulation of assessments. Some states addressed this issue in 1983–84. In New Jersey, municipalities in the "Pinelands Preservation Area" will get state dollars to stabilize property taxes. Since the preserve was created development has been curtailed, which means assessments of vacant lands have dropped and localities have raised taxes on existing development in order to continue to finance services. The state payments will counter the loss of property tax revenues due to the restrictions on development. In Vermont, towns can appeal assessments of state Environmental Conservation lands. In Hawaii and Connecticut there was clarification of property tax assessment.

A popular tool in the repertoire of local government revenue generating techniques is tax increment financing. South Carolina passed tax increment financing and in South Dakota it was upheld by the courts. In Kansas, tax increment bonds are now allowed with voter approval. On the other hand, the Connecticut governor vetoed legislation authorizing tax increment financing in his state.

In Kentucky, cities and counties were granted expanded authority for issuing bonds. They can issue bonds for industrial buildings and pollution control facilities. Also there is increased flexibility in the use of bonds for municipal electrical plant construction or acquisition.

Several states revised laws and set up mechanisms to make bonds more marketable. In Oregon, industrial development bonds (IDBs) were expanded to include umbrella bonds. They can be issued for as little as $100,000, and the legislation broadens their use. Illinois established a municipal bond bank. In Minnesota, regulations on issuing bonds were broadened and a state allocation mechanism for IDB issuance authority was established. The cap on bond interest rates was removed in Vermont for financing parking lots. The rate was previously limited to 6%; now market rates apply. In Tennessee, bonds can be issued for sewage treatment plants, to be covered by state shared taxes.

Restraints were placed on bonding powers in one state. In West Virginia, the State Supreme Court of Appeals would not allow municipalities to develop schemes to force early redemption of callable bonds. In order for a jurisdiction to do so, it must exercise this option at the time of the sale or forfeit it. (Some would argue, however, that removing the ability to recall the bonds early improves their marketability.)

Tax Limitations. Changes to tax limitations made during 1983–84 will have varied impacts on local governments. In Massachusetts, amendments to Proposition 2½ were passed that allow greater flexibility in applying the law. There were two actions in California that loosened the strictures of Proposition 13. In one, a state supreme court's interpretation of Proposition 13 said that a special tax is for a special purpose and, therefore, needs a two-thirds vote of the people. Furthermore, the court said local governments could raise property taxes to retire debt obligations already approved by the voters. But, at the same time, Jarvis 4 was put on the ballot to further restrict the taxing authority of local governments.

In Missouri, several state supreme court decisions strictly interpreted the tax lid which requires a vote of the public on all tax license or user fee increases.

In Oregon, which relies heavily on the property tax, a relief package which was to be financed by a sales tax was proposed. Such a plan would require an amendment to the state constitution. The proposal provided that the plan be referred to the voters only if requested by a majority of the 588 local governments in the state. However, the courts overturned the process that was used stating that only the legislature could place a constitutional amendment before the voters—the legislature did not reconvene to take the necessary action. The state, therefore, faced a 1.5% property tax limitation initiative.

Pension Funds. In 1983–84 local governments in several states were given greater flexibility in handling their pension system finances. In Kentucky, local governments formerly required to finance pension funds out of the property tax can now use funds from any revenue source for this purpose. The state of Pennsylvania established a state recovery fund to eradicate the $3 billion unfunded liability of government pension programs. On the other hand, municipalities in Mississippi are allowed to reallocate taxes earmarked for funding retirement systems.

Other Actions. There were other actions in the revenue area that will have an effect on how local governments raise money. In North Carolina, an attempt to repeal an intangibles tax was defeated. A Minimum Investment Fund was authorized in Rhode Island. Indiana counties can have a county income tax, at their option. The Montana state supreme court allowed reinstatement of a franchise tax on banks and savings and loans. In California, taxing authority that the state had usurped to meet its revenue needs was restored to local governments. The taxing authority of general law cities was broadened to equal that of charter cities.

In Wyoming, a county court ruled that a city does not own the mineral rights under city streets and, therefore, cannot collect mineral royalties. A Pennsylvania court decision striking down a city tax threatened to wreak havoc on home rule. But, after considerable lobbying by home rule municipalities, the state legislature clarified the home rule laws, restoring the power to set tax rates.

OPERATIONAL FLEXIBILITY

Several states passed laws that should give local governments greater flexibility in how they conduct their business.

Government Structure. Changes in the laws regulating the structure of local government were passed in at least three states. South Dakota now allows more flexibility in how local governments can be structured. In Idaho local governments can create council districts for city elections. However, in Vermont, municipal charter changes must now have an affirmative vote of the legislature. These changes used to be automatic unless the legislature voted "no," but recent U.S. Supreme Court cases called the legislative veto into question. The state of Montana started its decennial process of reassessing local government structure.

Open Meetings. Open meeting laws have often posed problems for local governments in the past. In at least two states greater flexibility in closing meetings was given to local governments during the past year: a Mississippi court upheld closed meetings for the purpose of discussing litigation. And in Oregon the state refused to expand the sections of the open meetings law dealing with personnel evaluation. Local jurisdictions can, therefore, still close meetings unless the discussion concerns agency goals or similar topics.

Purchasing. With one exception the laws governing the procurement of goods and services were also made more flexible. In Tennessee, purchasing laws were liberalized and more flexibility was granted to Oregon local governments for procuring contracts. Laws requiring prevailing wage rates to be paid in state and local contracts were repealed in Arizona. A Washington court upheld a county's rejection of a bid because the bidder failed to comply with an affirmative action requirement. In Massachusetts, efforts to prevent municipalities from contracting for services from outside providers were defeated. A move to require binding arbitration in construction contract disputes between contractors and local governments was also defeated. Only in Mississippi were restrictions placed on local governments in this area—and these restrictions were fiscal rather than procedural. The state prohibited municipal governments from spending or contracting more than one-quarter of their budget between April and July.

STATE MANDATES

Local governments are constantly concerned about efforts by state governments to require, or "mandate," that cities and counties implement certain programs, often without adequate funding on the part of the state. In 1983–84 local governments fared relatively well in this intergovernmental tug-of-war. Although the Illinois legislature did not implement a policy against unfunded mandates, they did not make any additional requirements of local governments either. In Oregon, local governments were able to defeat most mandate proposals. The Vermont legislature also refrained from mandating additional programs. In Connecticut, the workfare quota was decreased for municipal governments. Also in Connecticut, new mandates or changes in existing ones now have to go to the Appropriations Committee for cost estimates and reimbursement.

Fiscal notes must be attached to bills in the Alabama legislature that affect local revenues prior to their third reading. Last, but not least, in New Hampshire a constitutional convention succeeded in having put onto the ballot a prohibition of mandates that require additional local expenditures.

LIABILITY ISSUES

In recent years erosion of the principle of sovereign immunity has proven costly to local governments. In Rhode Island, tort liability limits were raised from $50,000 to $100,000 for cities and towns; however, several states acted to reduce local government exposure. In Illinois, state immunity now extends to cities. In Massachusetts, efforts to increase the financial limits of liability, and thus the exposure of municipalities, were defeated. In Idaho, the Tort Claims Act created a $500,000 combined single limit.

A tort immunity bill that was passed in Arizona limits state and local government liability. "Deep pocket" issues were also addressed in Arizona in a bill regulating tort feasor contributions. The new law sets a local government's liability at a level that is proportional to its responsibility in an action.

In Oklahoma, broad new exemptions from legal liability were granted; liability is limited to $1 million; and immunity is granted from punitive damages. In Mississippi, sovereign immunity was extended to all political subdivisions until 1 October 1985. At that time the law will be liberalized in certain cases, but a two-year statute of limitations and a $500,000 maximum liability will be imposed.

California local governments were unable to change soverign immunity laws that they consider detrimental to their interests.

There were also liability laws passed regarding specific situations. In Kentucky, local governments are now protected in the area of planning and zoning if they substantially conform to established legal processes. Georgia communities are now exempt from liability over suits from 911 responses except in cases of willful misconduct, gross negligence, or bad faith. In Tennessee, the definition of "governmental employee" was expanded to include volunteer and auxiliary public safety employees. In addition, Tennessee local governments can determine through intergovernmental agreements the status of personnel "loaned" for tort liability purposes.

In Iowa, property owners, rather than the local governments, are liable for accidents caused by faulty sidewalks or snow and ice. Immunity is now granted to cities and counties in Kentucky against liability in cleaning up hazardous waste spills; such activities are considered "good Samaritan" acts. However, the Michigan Supreme Court ruled that a city was liable for negligence in a high-speed police pursuit even though there was no contact between police and the injured party's vehicle.

Antitrust liability has become an issue in recent years. Action was taken in at least two states to clarify the status of local governments vis-à-vis state law. In Georgia, the immunity enjoyed by state officials from antitrust liability was extended to local governments in cases where they are exercising authority granted by state law. The Maine legislature passed a law clearly authorizing municipalities to regulate cable television, to protect them from antitrust suits.

PERSONNEL MANAGEMENT

An issue of ongoing concern to local governments is collective bargaining. In Vermont, efforts to extend collective bargaining to part-time employees were defeated. On the November 1984 ballot in Arizona there was a consitutional amendment that prohibits both public employee strikes and binding arbitration. Ohio now allows collective bargaining by public employees with provisions for binding arbitration in the case of public safety employees. Other Ohio public employees are allowed to strike. In Florida, local governments and unions can jointly waive special master proceedings in binding arbitration and can therefore go to the legislative bodies more quickly. Even though no legislation exists in West Virginia allowing collective bargaining, a court decision stated that a city can enter into an agreement or contract with employees under its existing powers to enter into contracts.

Compensation. Some states also took actions that affect the compensation policies of local governments. In Minnesota, comparable worth was addressed. Local governments must evaluate jobs and establish equitable compensation "relationships between classes," and identify those "female dominated" classes where pay inequality exists. Massachusetts state courts upheld a city's position that police and fire personnel may not accumulate fringe benefits while receiving injury pay. The Mississippi Civil Service Commission also supported local authority by upholding a city's classification of an employee.

Fringe Benefits. Fringe benefits were addressed, specifically in the area of pensions and retirement. In Alabama, any municipality under 5,000 in population can exercise the same options formerly held by larger communities to create or abolish a civil service system and choose to have its officers and employees under the state retirement system. Vermont employees can now buy into that state's retirement system.

In some states local governments lost some flexibility. The Kentucky pension system was revised so that many local systems must be closed to new members; they will not go into the County Employees' Retirement System. All current members can transfer to this system. The state gave cities authority to levy a special property tax to help effect the transfer. Kansas converted its retirement system to a deferred compensation plan so that employee contributions are not taxed. In Maine, local option to join the state retirement system was removed.

Several states addressed occupational health. Massachusetts legislation states that employees have a right to know if hazards exists in the work place. In Iowa, the right of fire departments to be fully informed about hazardous materials stored in plants and warehouses in their communities was established in law. In Illinois, legislation is pending to have the Illinois Occupational Safety and Health Act apply to state and local government employers only.

Other Personnel Issues. Several additional actions in the personnel area should prove interesting. Massachusetts now allows a hearing officer to hear civil service appeals if both sides agree. Also in Massachusetts, legislation was defeated that would have allowed city employees to be elected as city officials. The legislature in Montana removed veterans' and handicapped preference in employee hiring, to allow more flexibility in hiring. In West Virginia, the State Supreme Court of Appeals upheld a Human Rights Commission finding that two volunteer fire departments discriminated against women. The department was ruled to be "a place of public accommodations" and was covered as such.

In Minnesota, local residency requirements were prohibited; however, municipal needs were taken into account by allowing for job-related exceptions, for instance, to meet response time requirements in public safety departments. Similarly, Indiana removed the option of towns under 10,000 to set residency requirements for police officers, and instead set uniform statewide residency requirements.

LAND USE

Local governments' control over land use affects their ability to chart their own destinies. Conflicts between the goals and needs of the state, the counties, and the cities make this a thorny issue in many states.

States typically regulate annexation. In 1983–84, many states passed legislation that provides local governments additional annexation opportunities. Florida cities gained the right to leap-frog county-owned parks to annex land. Also in Florida, state growth management legislation was defeated that would have diminished home rule powers. As it stands, local governments retain control over independent development districts once a comprehensive plan is developed under state procedures. Indiana broadened its definition of the areas that can be annexed, giving towns greater flexibility. Mississippi courts upheld liberal annexation power for cities. The Colorado Supreme Court now allows a municipal utility to begin service in annexed areas already served by a utility certified by the state Public Utilities Commission. This should give localities more control over growth.

In Kentucky, greater annexation controls were enacted: cities cannot annex part of another city and taxes cannot be levied on annexed property until services are actually provided. In addition, a process was established for reducing a city's boundaries.

State laws regarding land use and zoning passed during 1983–84 generally favored local governments. In Kansas, the laws were clarified for cities wishing to exercise zoning control for territory within three miles of city limits when a county is not controlling zoning. In Tennessee, the definition of "subdivision" was broadened to allow local review if new road or utility construction is required.

In West Virginia, the state liquor board now *must* turn down a license request if a municipality protests because granting the license would violate the permitted or conditional use clauses in the local zoning law. The liquor board retains the option to turn down a request if the municipality protests on the basis of a conflict with the local government's plan for rehabilitation and revitalization of an area. In Massachusetts, local governments defeated an effort to impose a three-year freeze on dimensional changes in zoning laws.

In some cases greater restrictions on land use were imposed. Oregon increased restrictions on local governments in land use master planning and Colorado prohibited municipalities from passing regulations that effectively exclude manufactured housing.

COMMUNITY AND ECONOMIC DEVELOPMENT

By and large local governments' ability to implement community and economic development policies increased. In West Virginia, while the attorney general prohibited local governments from establishing revolving funds for local private business and industrial enterprises out of their general funds, municipalities may funnel public monies through a nonprofit, nonstock, development corporation. Kentucky allows cities to acquire and dispose of blighted or deteriorated vacant property.

The Illinois Department of Commerce and Community Affairs, in a pilot project with the U.S. Small Business Administration, gives long-term, low-interest loans to small companies so they can acquire fixed assets or working capital. Local governments will be contributing funding.

In South Carolina, a new law grants local governments powers to package redevelopment activities for urban improvements. Massachusetts local governments defeated efforts to allow drivers to appeal parking districts to the courts. Also in Massachusetts, an attorney general's opinion stated that only a governing board can regulate rights-of-way for private utilities. The same historic preservation authority that was granted to municipalities in Illinois was extended to counties.

Colorado, however, asserted state control. A new law in that state requires that by 1 July 1987 all building codes in the state must contain provisions with "approved design" language for fireplaces.

SERVICE DELIVERY ALTERNATIVES

Local governments are looking increasingly towards alternative ways to deliver services, relying less on municipal employees. State legislation largely fostered this process.

Intergovernmental Agreements. In several states, local ability to use intergovernmental agreements to provide a wide range of services was expanded. Kentucky allows agreements that enable counties to maintain city streets. New Jersey allows intergovernmental agreements to establish joint insurance funds for personal injury, liability, property damage liability, or workers' compensation.

The Minnesota legislature expanded and clarified joint powers agreements for police services. In Tennessee, the attorney general ruled that that office does not have to approve joint powers agreements.

Several actions were taken specifically in wastewater management. Illinois cities and counties can now create sewage treatment agencies through intergovernmental agreement. Kentucky also now allows certain classifications of cities and counties to create joint sewer agencies and to issue revenue bonds. In Vermont, municipalities can now contract, lease, or lease-purchase sewage disposal plants and can do so with other public or private entities.

Special Districts. Another tool that local governments are using to meet their needs is the special district. Again, greater flexibility was given to localities.

Missouri improved its special assessment statutes, and, in Colorado, greater flexibility to create municipal general improvement districts was granted. A court decision in Kansas was handed down that said a landowner has up to two years to challenge special assessment districts, instead of the state's standard 30-day limit. The legislature responded by changing the limit on assessment challenges to 90 days.

Maryland municipalities or counties can now create a "commercial district management authority" with a special fee or tax for promotion, marketing, security, maintenance, or amenities. Arizona communities can also set up improvement districts for planning and promotional purposes.

There were several other actions affecting other types of single purpose governments. While Minnesota broadened the authority of water management districts, it retains local approval. Arizona hospital districts can now provide ambulance services, by levying property taxes and letting service contracts. In Colorado, a committee was established to study the consolidation of special districts (i.e., limited purpose local governments) and to review the authority of general purpose governments to utilize special tax districts as an alternative to forming new special districts.

Fire Volunteers. Several state legislatures acknowledged that using volunteers is another way to stretch the local pocketbook. Volunteer fire services are a tradition in the United States and changes in state laws are making them even more effective. West Virginia allows creation of both county fire associations that can include volunteer fire departments, and county fire boards. The legislation allows counties to contract with paid municipal fire departments for services. In Tennessee, mutual aid agreements for fire services are now allowed between municipalities and volunteer fire departments. Municipalities or counties in New Jersey can appropriate money for volunteer ambulance or rescue squad associations.

INFORMATION PREPARED BY YEAR BOOK CORRESPONDENTS

Alabama

1. The legislature passed a measure that allows municipalities of 7,000 or more population to vote to allow the sale of alcoholic beverages even though they are located in counties which prohibit the sale of alcoholic beverages.
2. The legislature established the Birmingham Horse Racing Commission. Approved by city and county voters, the commission will oversee horse racing and pari-mutuel betting at the new Birmingham track.
3. A fiscal note must be attached to bills in the legislature that affect local revenues.
4. The legislature increased gasoline inspection fees, license taxes, and registration fees on trucks and truck-tractors. Municipalities will receive additional revenues as a result of these increases.
5. The legislature gave municipalities with populations of less than 5,000 the authority to abolish or create a civil service system and to choose to have its officers and employees come under the state retirement system. Previously, these privileges were extended only to larger municipalities.
6. The Alabama Court of Criminal Appeals ruled that municipal judges can direct search warrants to municipal law enforcement officers and are not required to utilize the services of the county sheriff's department.

Arizona

1. The legislature passed a tort immunity bill, which limits state and local government liability.
2. The legislature passed a bill requiring two or more persons or groups liable for the same negligent act, which results in injury to an individual or property, to pay a share of the judgment based on their relative responsibility for the negligent act. This act is expected to alleviate the "deep pocket" problem big companies and governments often face when they are only partially involved in a negligent act.
3. A bill was passed that allows local governments to charge the costs for extraordinary emergency services to persons negligent in use, storage, or transportation of hazardous materials.

Arkansas

1. A special session of the legislature was called to address the needs of education. As a result, the sales tax was increased by one cent to provide additional resources for public schools and educational reforms.

California

1. Broader taxing authority was given to general law cities; these cities now have the same authority as charter cities.
2. Taxes that the state had usurped to meet its revenue needs were restored or "given back" to local governments.
3. A state supreme court interpretation of Proposition 13 defines a special tax as one that is levied for a special purpose and that, therefore, needs a two-thirds vote of the people.
4. The supreme court said local governments could raise property taxes to retire debt obligations already approved by a vote of the people.

Colorado

1. A new law prohibits municipalities from enacting local regulations that have the effect of excluding manufactured homes from the municipality if such housing meets or exceeds, on the basis of performance engineering, the municipality's building and other code standards and regulations. The act allows municipalities to apply to manufactured homes certain features of their local building regulations that are applicable as well to existing or new housing.
2. The legislature has given the state Air Quality Control Commission authority to regulate emission standards, testing procedures and criteria, and certification of new wood stoves. The act also requires every county or municipality with a building code to adopt a code provision containing design specifications for fireplaces by 1 July 1987.
3. A new law provides for the formation of municipal general improvement districts. The law allows waiving of notice, publication, and hearing requirements for organizing a district under certain circumstances; allows bonds issued by the district to be sold at a private sale if it is in the best interest of the district; and deletes the 25% assessed valuation limitation on a district's bond issues.
4. The legislature created an office of consumer counsel to represent the public interest, particularly the interests of residential, agricultural, and small business consumers, in proceedings before the Colorado Public Utilities Commission.
5. The legislature established two legislative interim committees: a business issues committee to study the simplification of state and local sales and use taxes, to evaluate the differences between state and local government sales and use tax bases, and to examine the impact of the implementation of a uniform sales and use tax structure on the fiscal condition of local governments; and a special districts committee to study the consolidation of special districts and review the authority of general purpose governments to utilize special taxing districts as an alternative to forming new special districts.
6. Favorable decisions were rendered in two state supreme court cases: one involved the validity of a municipal service expansion fee, and the other involved the right of a municipal utility to serve an annexed area that is already being served by a utility certificated by the state Public Utilities Commission.
7. In another case, the Colorado Supreme Court held that the right to use the public ways for a cable television system is a proper subject for a franchise and that the Colorado Constitution prohibits a home rule municipality from granting by ordinance a permit to a cable television company.

Connecticut

1. The legislature passed a measure providing municipalities with state funding of the education equalization grant (guaranteed tax base) at $421.4 million—95% of full funding. In a related matter, a Connecticut superior court recently ruled in *Horton* v. *Meskill* that the state must immediately implement 100% funding. This decision is currently on appeal to the Connecticut Supreme Court.
2. State grants to municipalities for Payment in Lieu of Taxes (PILOT) increased by a total of $3 million. Two PILOT grants are designed to reimburse municipalities for money lost on tax-exempt property owned by private colleges and hospitals ($1.5 million grant increase) and the state ($1.5 million grant increase).
3. Two laws clarifying the valuation of property were passed. One states that market rent, rather than contract rent, should be used in determining fair market value for income-producing commercial property. The other requires owners to give assessors the income and expense data necessary for valuing property using the capitalization of income approach.
4. In recognition of local infrastructure needs the legislature increased the town road aid grant for every municipality by 25%. This brings the total funding to $25 million statewide.
5. The maximum participation state-mandated workfare program for municipalities was lowered from 85% to 67% of employable general assistance (welfare) recipients.
6. Each bill or floor amendment creating or expanding a state mandate to local governments must be referred to the legislature's Appropriations Committee for determination of the new local cost and the reimbursement level, if any, that is recommended to the General Assembly.

Delaware

1. The legislature increased the municipal street aid fund, which transfers revenues from the state gasoline tax to municipalities for the repair of local roads. The municipal street aid fund had remained at a fixed amount for several years despite increasing gasoline tax revenues.

Florida

1. State growth management legislation was defeated. If passed it would have reduced home rule powers. As it stands, once a comprehensive plan is developed under state procedures, local governments have control over independent development districts.
2. Cities can leap-frog county-owned parks to annex land.
3. Local governments and unions can jointly waive special master proceedings in binding

arbitration and can, therefore, go to the legislative bodies more quickly.

Georgia

1. Elected members of city and county governing bodies are subject to a new law providing for suspension-with-pay of public officials upon indictment in state court for any felony related to the work performance or activities of such official.
2. City and county governments have been prohibited from enacting or enforcing any rent control ordinance that would regulate the rent charged for privately owned, single family or multiple unit residential property.
3. The state auditor will henceforth review all city and county government audits to assure their compliance with state law. A note of any deficiencies will be sent to local officials as well as all state legislators whose districts include those cities or counties. Should the deficiencies go uncorrected, the auditor is required to post notice in local newspapers.
4. State and local governments and their employees have been exempted from liability for damages arising from "911" emergency telephone systems, except in cases of willful misconduct, gross negligence, or bad faith.
5. When exercising powers specifically granted by state law, local governing authorities have been granted immunity from antitrust liability to the same degree as enjoyed by state officials.

Hawaii

1. A new law states public employees hired after 1 July 1984 shall participate in a noncontributory public pension plan while employees employed before that date may still choose between contributory and noncontributory plans.
2. The legislature established a temporary study committee on comparable worth in state and local government.
3. The legislature repealed the mandatory retirement age of 70 years old for public sector employees.
4. The legislature authorized the use of tax increment financing by the counties for redevelopment purposes. However, this measure was later vetoed by the governor with no attempt by the legislature to override his action.
5. A recent decision in the state court mandated the use of the income method of valuation for commercial property by the counties' real property assessors. The question remains whether or not the income approach is to be a *legal* alternative method of assessment.

Idaho

1. The legislature created a city–county revenue sharing program, which will be funded out of a portion of the 1 cent increase in the state sales tax. The creation of this program represents the largest increase in state assistance to cities in the state's history.
2. Funding for the Water Pollution Control Account was greatly enhanced by the dedication of $4.8 million annually from state sales tax revenue. The account provides matching monies for sewage treatment projects.
3. Resort cities with populations of less than 10,000 were granted the authority to impose, with voter approval, a city sales tax. No other Idaho cities have local option taxation authority.
4. The policy limits specified under the Idaho Tort Claims Act were combined into a $500,000 single limit.
5. Cities were given the authority to assign numbers to council seats and/or create districts for city council elections. If a city should adopt either of these procedures, it may also provide for a run-off election if no candidate receives a majority.

Illinois

1. The Department of Commerce and Community Affairs established a pilot program in combination with the Small Business Administration to provide long-term, low interest loans to small companies for acquiring fixed assets or working capital. A portion of the funds for such loans will come from local governments.
2. The legislature reorganized the Chicago Area's Regional Transportation Authority to provide proximate balance on the authority's governing board to Chicago and suburban representatives. The act also gave the authority's board veto authority over the budgets of three transit agencies, including the Chicago Transit Authority.
3. The General Assembly overrode a gubernatorial amendatory veto and extended the state's immunity from federal antitrust laws to municipalities. The legislature clarified the power of local governments to award franchises for services such as cable television and taxi cabs regardless of the effect a franchise has on competition in the industry. The governor's veto attempted to limit the bill's application to home rule municipalities.
4. The legislature authorized the Illinois Housing Development Authority to consolidate the revenue bonding powers of individual municipalities to establish a statewide housing development pool. Municipalities must individually agree to join the pool. By midwinter (1983–84), 32 cities and counties had joined the pool, permitting the issuance of $130 million in bonds.
5. An act was passed that created an infrastructure bond bank for Illinois local governments. At their option, municipalities under 325,000 may request that their bonding needs for sewer, water, or street projects be met through a pooled bond issue by the Illinois Development Finance Authority. A special committee was given the power to screen out projects from the pool.

Indiana

1. The legislature broadened the definition of areas that can be annexed, giving towns greater flexibility.
2. The legislature removed the local option for towns under 10,000 to set residency requirements for police officers and fire fighters and set uniform residency requirements for town police officers.
3. Legislation was approved that gives counties an income tax, at their option.

Iowa

1. The legislature passed an act requiring local law enforcement officers to act immediately rather than wait for a specified period of time on missing children reports.
2. A new law states that Iowa libraries are not open to inspection by police without judicial permission.
3. Iowans elected to city, county, state, or federal office have the right to a leave of absence without pay for up to six years.
4. Fire departments have a right to be fully informed about hazardous chemicals stored in plants and warehouses.
5. Local property owners and not city governments will be liable for torts (e.g., accidents caused by faulty sidewalks or accidents caused by snow and ice on sidewalks).
6. Automobile inspections will no longer be required when individuals sell vehicles.
7. Restaurants and certain taverns will be allowed to serve liquor for four additional hours on Sundays. New hours will be 10 A.M. until midnight.

Kansas

1. A supreme court decision held that a landowner has up to two years to challenge the validity of special assessments.
2. A new state law establishes 90 days as the maximum period in which a federal civil rights suit dealing with special assessments may be brought against local units.
3. A law was enacted that revises the Kansas public employees' retirement system so that the employee retirement contribution is not considered as part of salary for federal income tax purposes.
4. The state tax increment financing statute for downtown redevelopment was revised permitting the issuance of full faith and credit tax increment bonds.
5. A new law clarifies cities' authority to adopt and enforce zoning regulations affecting territory within three miles of the city if a county is not exercising zoning control over the same area.
6. Legislation was enacted that broadens the authority of the state utility regulatory agency to regulate utility rates.

Kentucky

1. An amendment to existing legislation states that license fees and taxes imposed under the law shall not apply to group health insurance policies.
2. A law was passed that requires the county clerk to collect all ad valorem taxes on motor vehicles including ad valorem taxes levied by cities and urban county governments.
3. The legislature passed a law which requires

many city pension systems to be closed to new members in favor of entry into the County Employees' Retirement System.

4. A new annexation law states that an accurate map of area annexed to or severed from a city must be filed in the county clerk's office and the secretary of state's office within 60 days of the action and that taxes cannot be levied on property until services are provided; in addition, the law eliminates the possibility of a city annexing all or part of another city.
5. The Blighted and Deteriorated Properties Act allows cities to acquire and dispose of vacant properties that have been determined to be blighted or deteriorated.
6. A new law allows the compensation of mayors and city council members to be adjusted in accordance with the annual change in the Consumer Price Index.

Louisiana

1. A new law requires clean up of contaminated water and provides for shutting down hazardous waste sites in cases of water contamination.
2. The legislature authorized municipal public utilities to extend services to combinations of parishes, municipalities, or political subdivisions outside their territorial boundaries in accordance with service agreements with such parties.
3. A new law imposes a penalty for refusal to supply information to a municipality conducting an audit.
4. The laws relating to the establishment and designation of municipalities were consolidated.
5. Municipalities were authorized to acquire and resell vacant and underdeveloped real property at prices that will stimulate new housing construction for low and moderate income families.
6. Funding was provided for moving utility installations to accommodate state or interstate highway improvements in cases where the funds are not available out of the utility company's earnings for the fiscal year affected or if the cost exceeds the utility's annual income by 10%.

Maine

1. The percentage of state revenues being shared with municipalities was increased from 4% to 4.75% effective 1 August 1984 and to 5.1% effective 1 July 1985.
2. The Highway Allocation Act was amended to increase highway block grant allocations to all municipalities by 18.18%. This amendment took effect 1 January 1985.
3. The Maine State Retirement System abolished the authority of participating local districts to determine membership in the system by requiring all employees, including temporary and part-time employees, to become members.
4. A new law states that when a municipality is the prevailing party in a land use case, it shall recover its attorney's fees and other court costs.
5. A law was passed clearly establishing the authority of municipalities to regulate basic cable television services. Its purpose is to protect municipalities from antitrust liability.
6. In *Jackson* v. *Inhabitants of the Town of Searsport, et al.*, the court ruled that the town's failure to follow the statutory procedures for processing the plaintiff's general assistance applications does not infringe on constitutionally protected property interests of the plantiff. Furthermore, even if a legitimate property interest were involved, the state procedure available and invoked by plaintiff was sufficient to satisfy the due process requirement of the Fourteenth Amendment; thus, the plaintiff was not entitled to attorney's fees under the Civil Rights Attorney's Fees Award Act.

Maryland

1. The legislature authorized municipalities or counties to create commercial district management authorities. The local governments are authorized to charge a special fee or tax, which is not payable to the general fund but must be used to promote the district and aid marketing and to provide security, maintenance, or other amenities within the special district.
2. A new law allows municipalities to increase the maximum penalty for violation of municipal ordinances from $500 to $1,000 and from 90 days to six months imprisonment.

Massachusetts

1. The state attorney general issued an opinion stating that only a governing board (such as the board of selectmen) can pass measures regulating the rights-of-way of private utilities.
2. The Division of Local Mandates, which was created at the time Proposition 2½ was enacted, began issuing rulings. The purpose of the division is to determine whether a state mandate carries an additional financial burden for local governments. Proposition 2½ stipulated that local governments must be reimbursed for additional costs of activities imposed by the state.
3. The new state policy on the disposition of Chapter 90 funds for construction and maintenance of roads that service two or more communities permits cities and towns using these funds greater latitude in allocating costs to specific projects. Heretofore, the funds could be expended only for the actual physical work performed.
4. The State Ethics Commission issued a statement clarifying the definition of a "special employee" in cities and towns. The commission also issued guidelines for the classification of special employees.
5. The legislature enacted into law a $1.5 million measure to improve management capacity in the cities and towns.
6. The Massachusetts Appeals Court has ruled that police officers and firefighters who are on leave because of duty-related injuries are not entitled to accrue vacation and sick pay. In the case in point, the collective bargaining agreement between the town and the police did not specifically address the issue.

Michigan

1. The state court upheld the lobbying statute adopted as Public Act 472 of 1978; it went into effect on 1 January 1984. The act regulates lobbyists, lobbyist agents, and lobbying activities and requires registration of and reports from lobbyists and lobbyist agents.
2. For the first time in the state's history, Michigan voters recalled two state senators. The recalls were a reaction to the legislators' support of a 38% increase in the state income tax to help erase a $900 million budget deficit.
3. Three new acts require the state to pay interest if state revenue sharing or single business tax inventory reimbursement payments are delayed.
4. The first of four scheduled income tax reductions occurred on 1 January 1984 when the state income tax rate of 6.35% rolled back to 6.1%, resulting in an estimated $165 million cut in state income taxes for 1984. In June the legislature agreed to move up the second scheduled tax rollback to September 1984 from January 1985. At that time the state income tax will drop to 5.35%, reducing state income tax revenues by $570 million.
5. In *Stafford's Restaurant, Inc.* v. *City of Oak Park*, the Michigan Court of Appeals ruled that the state had not preempted the right of a municipality to limit the number of licenses for the sale of intoxicating liquor for consumption on the premises to fewer than the maximum permitted by the statute.
6. In *Fiser* v. *City of Ann Arbor*, the Michigan Supreme Court ruled that the city was liable for negligence in a high speed police pursuit even though there was no contact between the police vehicle and the injured party's vehicle.

Minnesota

1. A new law requires all governmental units to adopt a job evaluation system that ensures equitable compensation between male dominated and female dominated job classes by 1 August 1987.
2. A law was passed which prohibits residency requirements for municipal employment. Cities, however, are allowed to impose reasonable area and response time requirements if a demonstrated, job-related necessity exists.
3. The third Monday in January has been established as an official holiday honoring Martin Luther King. Cities and counties must allow employees to take unpaid leave and cannot conduct public business unless deemed necessary.
4. The legislature established an allocation mechanism for industrial development bond issuance authority.

5. The supreme court issued a ruling that prohibits municipal utilities from imposing payment obligations for services on someone who has not actually incurred the debt unless a contract or lien exists (*Cascade Motor Hotel, Inc.* v. *City of Duluth*).
6. The supreme court ruled to allow the public employer to offset the amount of unemployment compensation benefits to a discharged employee against the amount of back pay the employee receives because of veteran status.

Mississippi

1. In *Mississippi Public Service Commission* v. *Coast Waterworks, Inc.*, the state supreme court affirmed that the Public Service Commission is vested with broad discretion in determining whether to hear applications for rate increases. Even though the consolidation of water and sewer applications for rate increases would have facilitated a better understanding of the highly integrated water and sewer operations of a metropolitan area, the court could not say the commission abused its discretion when it refused to consolidate the applications.
2. In *Mayor and Aldermen of the City of Vicksburg and the City of Vicksburg Planning Commission* v. *Vicksburg Printing and Publishing Co.*, the Vicksburg Planning Commission was ruled to be a "public body" within the meaning of the state's Open Meetings Law, even though it only has advisory powers. Ordinarily its meetings with two expert city planners to consider extension of the corporate boundaries of the city are covered by that law; however, a meeting that is in substance a strategy session with respect to proposed litigation is a legitimate exception to the law and the press and public can be excluded from such a meeting.
3. In the *Matter of Extension of Counties of the City of Clinton*, the court ruled that the city has the power to annex adjoining territory in spite of landowners' objections that they already have most of the services that annexation would provide, if the city has need for expansion, the area to be annexed is reasonably within the path of expansion, and the city has the financial ability to make the improvements and furnish the municipal services called for by annexation.
4. Municipalities are required to furnish their tax collectors with serially numbered tax receipts. Tax collectors can obtain these receipts on their signatures from the city clerk and reconcile them annually. Tax collectors are required to stamp notice of delinquent taxes on the current tax receipt.
5. A new law increased the maximum amount of a fine that may be imposed by a municipal ordinance to $1,000.
6. A new bill provides for the disciplining (including removal) for cause of municipal employees under civil service and lays out the procedures to be followed in such actions and in appeals by municipalities from orders of the civil service commission.
7. The legislature extended sovereign immunity for all political subdivisions of the state until 1 October 1985; allowed certain suits (with a two-year statute of limitations and a $500,000 maximum single-act liability) against them after that date; and required certain steps by them to provide funds for paying judgments.
8. A new law prohibits any municipality from expending for or contracting for an obligation against its official budget more than one-fourth of any item of its budget between the first day of April and the first Monday of the following July.
9. The homestead exemption law was revised to allow a $7,500 exemption and to reimburse counties, municipalities, and school districts for the tax losses they would suffer from the increased exemption.
10. The legislature eliminated the necessity for dual voter registration for county and municipal elections and provided for "one-stop" registration for voting in both elections.
11. The legislature passed a bill that allows municipalities to reallocate proceeds from tax levies that were authorized for funding retirement systems.
12. Every arrest ticket or summons issued by a municipal police officer must be on a uniform arrest ticket.

Missouri

1. Bills were passed that eroded municipal home rule authority in the following areas: utility tax rates, personnel ordinances, firearms regulations, and control of real estate signs.
2. The state Department of Revenue may revoke the driver's license of any individual charged in municipal court with driving while intoxicated.
3. The legislature passed a measure giving permanent authority to cities to levy a transportation sales tax.
4. Several Missouri Supreme Court decisions stringently interpreted the state tax lid which requires a vote of the public on all tax, license, or user fee increases.

Montana

1. The state supreme court allowed reinstatement of franchise tax on banks and savings and loans institutions.
2. The state started its decennial process of reassessing local government structure.
3. The Montana legislature removed veterans' and handicapped preference in employee hiring and now allows more flexibility.

Nebraska

1. A new uniform recall law, covering all elected offices in all classes of cities, counties, school districts and water boards, has been enacted. In order to recall an officer there must be a petition containing voter signatures to equal 35% of the votes cast for that office at the last general election. Recalled officials will be replaced according to the basic law of that local government.
2. The initiative and referendum statute covering local governments has been amended. The district court may be petitioned regarding any question(s) arising under the initiative and referendum statute. Petitions may include, but are not limited to, a determination of whether a measure is properly the subject for a referendum or appropriate for enactment through the initiative process.
3. State courts may require convicted offenders sentenced to probation to pay all or a portion of the reasonable costs of pre-trial incarceration in county jails or other local facilities. All sums paid shall be deposited in the general fund of the county.
4. A recent interpretation of the state's Public Meetings Law as it relates to civil actions rejects "good faith" or "good intention" pleas as irrelevant to the question of compliance with the "closed session" application of that statute. The supreme court ruled further that the prohibition against formal actions in closed sessions forbids "crystallization of secret decisions . . . just short of ceremonial acceptance" in a *pro forma* public vote.
5. The state's highest court ruled that the matter of a nuclear freeze is an improper one for an initiative because no law would be enacted regardless of the initiative result.
6. The court reduced the assessed value of a motel by 44% and ruled that the long-standing practice of using different methods for valuing agricultural land and improved real property is unconstitutional.

Nevada

The legislature did not meet during the reporting period.

New Hampshire

1. Under the New Hampshire Constitution, a *non partisan* constitutional convention is called every ten years to consider proposals to amend the constitution. To be placed on the ballot in November, proposals must receive at least 240 affirmative votes from the 400 delegates. The 1984 Constitutional Convention considered 175 proposals and passed 10 on to the voters. Several proposals affect local governments. These include a proposal to prohibit the state from mandating new or expanded local programs and responsibilities that require the expenditure of additional local revenues without also providing full state funding; a prohibition of footnotes and sections in state budget bills that amend permanent statutes and are unrelated to the budget itself; a requirement that all voting places be accessible to elderly and handicapped voters; a requirement for full funding, on an actuarial basis, of the state and local employees' retirement system; and a prohibition of the diversion of retirement system assets to uses other than employee retirement.

New Jersey

1. A law was passed authorizing two or more local units (i.e., counties or municipalities)

to join together to establish a joint fund for insuring against personal injury, liability, property damage liability, and/or workers' compensation.
2. An existing law was amended that permits any county or municipality to appropriate such additional sums as it may deem necessary for the purchase of first aid vehicles, equipment, supplies, and materials for use by volunteer ambulance or rescue squad associations. The law stipulates that the title for any such purchases shall remain with the county or municipality, provided that the funds are controlled and disbursed by the county or municipality.
3. A law, called the "Pinelands Municipal Property Tax Stabilization Act," was passed providing state aid to municipalities located in, or partially in, the Pinelands Preservation Area, to stabilize property tax rates of those municipalities. The state assistance is designed to counter the effects of development restrictions of the "Pinelands Protection Act," a shift of the tax burden from vacant lands to developed properties as owners of vacant lands have received assessment reductions through the tax appeals process.
4. The legislature approved a measure that requires anyone convicted of drunk driving to pay a $100 surcharge in addition to any fine imposed. The monies collected will be used to increase the enforcement of the drunk driving law through such measures as the financing of additional patrols at peak violation periods and the purchasing of portable breath testing units.
5. The legislature passed an act which permits the leasing of county or municipal real property to private individuals and nonprofit corporations or associations for gardening or recreation. This leased real property may not be used for profit-making enterprises. Prior to this act, the law did not permit leasing to any religious association or corporation, or leasing to any private person other than by public letting to the highest bidder.

New Mexico
1. Major funding legislation was passed in the areas of wastewater treatment, community development, water supply, and highways.
2. A new bill was passed that provides assistance to small cities. It raises the assistance floor to $15,000 and increases the funding from 5% of the compensating tax to 8%.
3. The legislature authorized $70,000 to study the need for a fire academy, its location, and related issues.
4. Application, approval, and administration of community assistance and community development block grants was centralized and a Community Development Council was created to approve grants for all types of infrastructure needs.

North Carolina
1. The state assumed responsibility for the small cities community development program. Provisions for strong local government involvement in regulation of the program are included.
2. The state legislature enacted an additional one-half cent local option sales tax.

North Dakota
The legislature did not meet during the 1983–84 reporting period.

Ohio
1. A collective bargaining bill was passed which covers state and local public employees. The bill includes binding arbitration for safety employees and the right to strike for non-safety employees.

Oklahoma
1. A new law gives half of the costs levied by state district courts for driving while intoxicated convictions to the municipality in which the convicted person was arrested. Such funds are to be used to defer costs of prosecution. This action is designed to encourage municipalities to file driving while intoxicated charges in state court rather than municipal court so that the charges become part of an individual's driving record.
2. Cities and other governmental bodies have been given broad exemptions from legal liability. New state law limits a jurisdiction's liability to $1 million for all claims from a single action and provides immunity from punitive damages. The law lists 27 instances in which a jurisdiction cannot be sued, including instances of claims based on legislative acts, discretionary acts, and failure to inspect for safety or negligence in making an inspection.

Oregon
1. The state's industrial development bond program was expanded to create a program of "umbrella" revenue bonds. The program enables issues in amounts as little as $100,000. Also, property for research and development was added to the list of authorized uses.
2. Fees for vehicle operator licenses were increased. They will now generate about $2 million per year. Cities receive 12% of the increase.
3. The legislature passed the "Uniform Revenue Bond Act" establishing statewide procedures on revenue bonds issued by municipalities.
4. The secretary of state was empowered to subpoena witnesses and accounts in auditing municipalities.
5. The Oregon Attorney General ruled that Rajneeshpuram is a religious commune and, therefore, ineligible for municipal status, nullifying its charter of incorporation.

Pennsylvania
1. In April voters authorized $190 million in bonds for economic revitalization programs. A total of $68 million in bond revenue will fund grants and loans over a three-year period for the Business Infrastructure Development program and the Recreational Improvement Rehabilitation Act.
2. To counter a court ruling that removed the flexibility home rule municipalities have to establish local tax rates, a new law was passed clarifying the state's home rule law.
3. The general assembly created an innovative program to award community development block grant funds to small cities on a modified entitlement basis.
4. A comprehensive municipal pension reform bill was passed that modifies the formulas for distribution of foreign fire and casualty insurance company taxes, standardizes actuarial reporting for local governments, and mandates funding levels for municipal pension systems.

Rhode Island
1. A Rhode Island Vehicle Value Commission was established for the purpose of determining values for excise taxes.
2. A Sewer and Water Supply Failure Fund was established to provide state grants to individual cities and towns.
3. Minimum requirements for firefighters' protective clothing, equipment, training, and respiratory protection were established.
4. A municipal investment fund was authorized.
5. The legislature now requires businesses engaged in revaluing property for cities and towns to be certified by the state Department of Community Affairs.
6. Governmental tort liability limits were raised from $50,000 to $100,000 for Rhode Island cities and towns.

South Carolina
1. The legislature enacted a statewide 2% accommodation tax law. Revenues will be returned to the point of collection. One-quarter of the monies is to be devoted to the promotion of tourism; the remaining 75% is to be spent by city and county governments on tourist-related services (such as police, fire, and beach facilities).
2. One-half of one percent of the state income tax will be returned to municipal governments. Allocation will be based on population. This measure will provide $5.5 million for municipalities.
3. A new law was passed that uses the tax increment concept to aid cities in the redevelopment of blighted urban areas.
4. The new Urban Development Law allows a city council to sit as a redevelopment commission. The law gives commissions the power to package redevelopment activities for urban improvement (housing, commercial, recreational, industrial).
5. The legislature established a South Carolina Advisory Commission on Intergovernmental Relations, and provided for its budget requirements. The new commission will employ full-time staff and adopt a full complement of programs.

South Dakota

1. The legislature passed a measure that permits aldermanic form governments to increase the term of mayor from two years to four years. The same law allows the term for commissioners (including mayor) in commission form governments to be reduced from five years.
2. Governor Janklow announced in his 1984 budget message that state sales tax collections, which include collection of optional city sales taxes, would remain on a bimonthly basis. Monthly collections were authorized in the previous legislative session.
3. The South Dakota Supreme Court upheld the tax increment financing law enacted in 1978. Under the law, cities creating tax increment districts may dedicate taxes resulting from development to financing such developments.
4. The city of Springfield became the first South Dakota city to approve home rule since the adoption of the new home rule constitutional provision in 1972. The charter confers upon the city the power to obtain and operate the University of South Dakota/Springfield, which was closed by the 1984 legislature.
5. The city of Rapid City completed the sale and leaseback of their municipal convention center, made possible by a property tax exemption for civic centers passed by the 1984 legislature. This transaction was coupled with a $42 million industrial revenue bond issue, which will enable the city to finance $190 million in city improvements, and was accomplished in time to avoid the federal legislation limiting tax advantages from real estate depreciation in the sale-leaseback of public facilities.

Tennessee

1. The Comprehensive Education Reform Act of 1984 establishes career ladders for teachers, principals, and supervisors, and holds local governments harmless for the additional salaries, pay supplements, and other costs involved.
2. The state sales tax was increased from 4.5% to 5.5% and was extended to apply to club memberships and most amusements. Food will be taxed at progressively lower rates beginning 1 June 1985. The state sales tax on food items will be removed altogether by 1 June 1987.
3. Cities and counties were authorized to levy an additional one-half cent on the local sales tax rate in order to maintain the maximum local levy at half of the state rate. The local sales tax on food will apply even after the state tax on food is phased out.
4. The legislature appropriated $13 million for state grants to local governments for construction of wastewater treatment facilities.
5. In Tennessee, items held as inventory for sale by merchants have been exempt from personal property taxation. A lower court decision in 1984 held that property held for lease is also exempt from taxation as personal property. The Tennessee Supreme Court refused certiorari in appeal.
6. The legislature acted to include members of volunteer and auxiliary public safety organizations within the statutory definition of "governmental employee" for tort liability purposes. This law provides that local governments, by intergovernmental agreement, can determine the status of "loaned" personnel for tort liability purposes.
7. The legislature broadened the definition of "subdivision" so that more developments will be subject to local regulation.
8. The state law regulating municipal purchasing was liberalized by exempting intergovernmental and emergency transactions and purchases of under $1,000 from advertisement and competitive bidding requirements.

Texas

1. Cities gained an estimated $48 million in fiscal 1984 and $55 million in 1985 as a result of the omnibus tax bill passed by the legislature, which repealed a variety of exemptions from sales taxation.
2. The legislature completely rewrote the laws governing the taxation of banks by cities and counties. Under the new law cities will be able to tax banks' tangible personal property, but bank stock will be exempted from ad valorem taxation. Banks will be subject to a state franchise tax, which will be remitted back to local taxing jurisdictions.

Vermont

1. Governor Snelling pointed out the necessity to institute "state general aid to Vermont's cities and towns whose general government burdens are out of proportion to the already stretched capacity of the property tax." Supporting this commitment, the legislature refused to burden further the property tax base by mandating additional programs that local governments would have to fund.
2. Towns can now appeal assessments of state-owned Environmental Conservation lands.

Washington

1. The legislature enacted the Court Improvement Act, which is the most extensive reorganization and consolidation of municipal and county district courts in the state since 1961.
2. The legislature comprehensively revised the state law relating to recall of public officers, including city elected officials. One aspect of the law dealt with the requirements to be fulfilled by those making the charges.
3. The legislature enacted the Domestic Violence Prevention Act, which creates significant new duties for municipal courts. The law allows victims to seek relief through a petition for an order for protection.
4. In *King County* v. *City of Algona*, the Washington Supreme Court reversed an earlier decision and held that one municipal subdivision may not impose a tax on another municipal subdivision without express statutory authorization from the state.
5. In *City of Seattle* v. *State* the court ruled that the Seattle campaign financing ordinance, which provides funds to match private donations to a candidate's campaign for public office, does not constitute an unconstitutional gift of public funds but rather serves a valid public interest.
6. In *Southwest Washington Chapter, National Electrical Contractors Assoc.* v. *Pierce County*, the court ruled that a county can reject a bid on a public works project because the bidder fails to comply with an affirmative action requirement in the bid.

West Virginia

1. County commissions cannot directly appropriate money from general funded or revolving loan funds for local private businesses and industrial enterprises. They may, however, become members of and appropriate public monies from their general fund to a nonstock, nonprofit area development corporation as authorized by statute.
2. The state's Human Rights Commission determined that two volunteer fire departments had discriminated against women by excluding them from membership. The Shepherdstown volunteer fire department appealed the decision and the court ruled that "a volunteer fire department, organized and operated pursuant to the laws of the State . . . which receives funding from public sources, is a place of public accommodations as defined by W. Va. Code . . . , and is thereby subject to the provisions of the West Virginia Human Rights Act . . . ."
3. The state supreme court of appeals ruled that municipalities have no authority to develop schemes requiring early redemption of callable bonds. They must allow the option to call bonds early or not to do so.
4. Despite the fact that the West Virginia legislature has never passed a collective bargaining enabling statute, the state supreme court of appeals ruled that the city of Huntington's collective bargaining agreement with city sanitation workers was enforceable. The decision was grounded on the fact that the state code gives cities the authority to make contracts.
5. In an action that will affect most counties and municipalities, the legislature passed a bill to study and develop plans for improving transportation in the state.
6. The legislature passed a bill authorizing the creation of county fire associations (including volunteer fire departments but excluding full-time, paid fire departments), county fire boards, and county service fees. The act also gives counties authority to contract with full-time paid fire departments (cities) to provide fire protection services to county residents.
7. The legislature passed a bill authorizing municipalities by charter or ordinance to grant a recorder, municipal court clerk, or deputy clerk the authority to issue warrants for arrest, to administer oaths, and to accept and approve securities and bonds in the absence of mayor, police court, or municipal judges.
8. The legislature passed a bill that removes

the distinction between farm, industrial, and manufacturing land inside or outside urban areas with regard to making improvements to the land for continuance of a preexisting use. The act also addresses abandonment of a preexisting use under zoning rules and regulations.

9. The legislature passed a bill requiring persons seeking a private club license (liquor by the drink) within a municipality to file an intent notice with that municipality. The municipality may file written comment with the state alcohol beverage commissioner (ABCC), who can deny the license if the proposed private club is not a permitted or conditional use under the municipal zoning ordinance or is not compatible with a plan for revitalization or rehabilitation.

Wyoming

1. The state legislature passed three bills revising several sections of Title XV, Wyoming's Municipal Code, to update, remove archaic language, and clarify the authority of cities and towns and the roles and relationships of mayors and councils.
2. The Wyoming Supreme Court upheld the authority of a mayor to remove a police chief without cause.
3. The state legislature approved legislation allowing the levy of an additional 1% countywide local option sales tax for specific capital projects.
4. A county court ruled that a Wyoming city does not own the mineral rights under its city streets and, therefore, cannot collect mineral royalties from extraction of such minerals.
5. The state of Wyoming decided to set aside one-third of the state's community development block grant allocation for grants to local governments to promote economic development that creates or retains permanent jobs in Wyoming.

THE YEAR BOOK STATE CORRESPONDENTS

Alabama Philip B. Coulter
University of Alabama
Alaska Doug Griffin
Alaska Local Affairs Agency
Arizona Catherine F. Connolly
League of Arizona Cities and Towns
Arkansas Don A. Zimmerman
Arkansas Municipal League
California Don Benninghoven
League of California Cities
Colorado Tami A. Tanoue
Colorado Municipal League
Connecticut Kathryn Feidelson
Connecticut Conference of Municipalities
Delaware Jerome R. Lewis
University of Delaware
Florida Annie Mary Hartsfield
Florida State University
Georgia Edwin L. Jackson
University of Georgia
Hawaii Lowell L. Kalapa
Tax Foundation of Hawaii
Idaho James B. Weatherby
Association of Idaho Cities
Illinois James M. Banovetz
Northern Illinois University
Indiana John Myrland
Indianapolis Chamber of Commerce
Iowa Russell M. Ross
University of Iowa
Kansas E. A. Mosher
League of Kansas Municipalities
Kentucky Edwin L. Griffin
Kentucky Municipal League
Louisiana Susan Gordon
Louisiana Municipal Association
Maine Kathryn J. Rand
Maine Municipal Association
Maryland Leon F. Shore
City of College Park
Massachusetts Robert J. M. O'Hare
U.S. Office of Personnel Management
Michigan Kevin Rulkowski
Michigan Municipal League
Minnesota Donald Slater
League of Minnesota Municipalities
Mississippi Thomas H. Handy
Mississippi State University
Missouri Gary S. Markenson
Missouri Municipal League
Montana Alec N. Hansen
Montana League of Cities and Towns
Nebraska A. B. Winter
University of Nebraska
Nevada G. P. Etcheverry
Nevada League of Cities
New Hampshire John B. Andrews
New Hampshire Municipal Association
New Jersey William H. Struwe
New Jersey Department of Community Affairs
New Mexico William F. Fulginiti
New Mexico Municipal League
New York Cheryl Parsons Reul
New York Department of State
North Carolina Fred P. Baggett
North Carolina League of Municipalities
North Dakota Jerald Hjelmstad
North Dakota League of Cities
Ohio John P. Coleman
Ohio Municipal League
Oklahoma David R. Morgan
University of Oklahoma
Oregon Stephen C. Bauer
League of Oregon Cities
Pennsylvania Jay D. Himes
Pennsylvania League of Cities
Rhode Island Joseph E. Coduri
Rhode Island Department of Community Affairs
South Carolina J. McDonald Wray
Municipal Association of South Carolina
South Dakota Loren M. Carlson
University of South Dakota
Tennessee Ed Young
Tennessee Municipal League
Texas Dick Brown
Texas Municipal League
Utah Herschel G. Hester III
Utah League of Cities and Towns
Vermont Steven E. Joffrey
Vermont League of Cities and Towns
Virginia Julian F. Hirst
City of Norfolk
Washington Patrick W. Mason
Municipal Research and Services Center of Washington
West Virginia David A. Bingham
West Virginia University
Wisconsin LeRoy A. Lokken
League of Wisconsin Municipalities
Wyoming Rick O. Curneal
Wyoming Association of Municipalities

B 2

Municipal Annexation and Boundary Changes: 1980–83*

Joel C. Miller
U.S. Bureau of the Census

Municipal annexation increased slightly during 1983, with approximately 200,000 persons added to incorporated places of 5,000 or more population. The 562 square miles of land area added was not greatly changed from 1981 and 1982 levels, but was once again less than the nearly 900 square miles added in 1980. Detachments, while few in number, affected more area and population (nearly 70 square miles and 4,000 people) than in any year since 1980. In total, over three quarters of a million people living in 2,500 square miles (an area larger than Delaware) have been added to the nation's municipalities between January 1980 and December 1983.

Annexations. Annexation activity appears to be somewhat diminished from the 1970s, but comparisons are not exact since the principle data source—the Census Bureau's annual Boundary and Annexation Survey—currently includes only places of 5,000 or more population as of 1980. Prior to 1980, the Boundary and Annexation Survey covered all places. The Bureau plans to expand the survey to include all incorporated places of 2,500 or more in 1986 and all incorporated places in 1988. All of the figures from the Boundary and Annexation Survey and most figures cited in this article are estimates provided by local governments.

Number of Changes. A state-by-state listing of places reporting annexations of more than 1,000 persons with the number of actions and the estimated area added is shown in Table 2/1. The number of boundary changes varies greatly by state, depending in part on state annexation laws. In four years, 12,000 persons were added to Virginia municipalities by only 13 annexation actions. Similar populations were annexed through 239 actions in Kentucky and 319 actions in Washington. In both California and Il-

Table 2/1 MAJOR ANNEXATIONS BY PLACES OF 5,000 OR MORE POPULATION, 1980–83[1]

Place	No. of actions	Estimated annexation: Population (000)	Estimated annexation: Square miles	1980 Census population (000)[2]
United States	18,802	786.4	2,546.4	226,549.4
Alabama	536	44.3	141.1	3,894.0
Alabaster	1	4.0	14.0	7.1
Birmingham	55	1.1	1.9	284.4
Hoover	16	1.9	5.5	19.8
Hueytown	53	1.0	0.2	13.5
Montgomery	1	29.1	78.0	177.9
Alaska[3]	13	0.4	3.4	401.9
Arizona	228	23.9	161.8	2,718.4
Glendale	8	2.2	6.4	97.2
Mesa	20	4.6	15.5	152.5
Scottsdale	5	1.1	57.2	88.6
Tucson	8	9.7	9.0	330.5
Yuma	12	1.0	2.1	42.5
Arkansas	275	19.8	38.7	2,286.4
Fayetteville	5	1.3	2.4	36.6
Little Rock	18	8.9	4.2	158.9
Russellville	17	1.5	2.9	14.0
Sherwood	15	1.9	1.3	10.4
California	2,368	146.7	255.4	23,667.9
Arcata	7	1.1	0.6	12.8
Bakersfield	11	3.7	2.7	105.6
Brawley	5	1.5	1.1	15.0
Campbell	28	4.5	0.9	26.9
Compton	7	1.5	0.1	81.2
Covina	18	5.2	0.7	32.7
Cupertino	46	2.5	0.8	34.3
Cypress	1	1.4	0.2	40.4
El Monte	3	1.3	0.2	79.5
Escondido	67	1.5	4.3	64.4
Fontana	12	4.2	8.9	36.8
Fresno	216	26.0	25.0	217.5
Garden Grove	4	1.5	0.1	123.3
Glendora	17	1.1	0.5	38.5
Hemet	19	1.6	4.4	22.5
Lafayette	5	3.0	1.6	20.8
Los Altos	4	1.1	0.3	25.8
Manhattan Beach	2	1.1	0.1	31.5
Modesto	44	4.7	2.3	107.0
Napa	47	1.7	0.8	50.9
Oxnard	18	1.3	0.8	108.2
Porterville	15	1.3	0.5	19.7
Rancho Palos Verdes	1	8.1	1.1	36.6
Redding	36	2.6	15.5	42.0
Redondo Beach	1	1.6	0.2	57.1
Ridgecrest	1	4.0	7.5	15.9
San Bernardino	13	1.2	2.0	118.8
San Buenaventura	70	4.3	1.5	73.8
San Jose	196	6.7	10.3	629.4
Stockton	18	1.4	1.5	149.8
Sunnyvale	23	2.2	0.4	106.6
Thousand Oaks	22	8.3	1.7	77.1
Tustin	11	4.1	1.1	32.3
Visalia	25	2.2	1.1	49.7
West Covina	9	1.4	0.3	27.4
Colorado	604	26.6	91.4	2,889.7
Colorado Springs	49	20.8	26.3	215.1
Craig	6	1.0	0.9	8.1
Connecticut[3]	0	0	0	3,107.6
Delaware[3]	19	0	0.3	594.3
Florida	1,562	60.1	143.3	9,747.2
Davie	38	6.1	6.6	20.9
Delray Beach	70	6.5	0.9	34.3
Lakeland	39	4.9	6.7	47.4
Pembroke Pines	2	1.7	17.1	35.8
Pompano Beach	5	10.8	6.1	52.6
Tallahassee	12	25.0	24.0	81.5
Georgia	1,021	15.1	45.8	5,463.0
Albany	3	9.8	14.5	74.4
Hawaii[3]	0	0	0	964.7
Idaho	146	2.7	9.1	944.1
Coeur d'Alene	18	2.4	2.7	19.9

*Author's note: Richard L. Forstall of the Population Division of the Bureau of the Census provided valuable advice and consultation on this article. Clarissa S. Curtis, Mary Ann Hall, and Barbara Esworthy provided clerical support. Most of the information in this article was obtained from the Geography Division's Boundary and Annexation Survey.

Table 2/1 MAJOR ANNEXATIONS BY PLACES OF 5,000 OR MORE POPULATION, 1980–83[1] continued

Place	No. of actions	Estimated annexation: Population (000)	Estimated annexation: Square miles	1980 Census population (000)[2]
Illinois	2,420	16.6	69.1	11,427.4
Des Plaines	7	1.8	0.6	53.7
Indiana	339	10.3	22.5	5,490.2
Fort Wayne	22	2.0	4.2	172.4
Greenwood	8	1.3	0.9	19.3
Iowa[3]	147	0.5	10.7	2,913.8
Kansas	620	6.7	48.9	2,364.2
Wichita	77	2.3	10.3	279.8
Winfield	34	1.6	2.8	10.7
Kentucky	239	12.3	32.6	3,660.3
Jeffersontown	13	4.1	2.1	15.8
Owensboro	56	1.1	0.7	54.5
St. Matthews	4	1.0	0.3	13.5
Louisiana	427	32.1	40.4	4,206.1
Baton Rouge	10	21.2	11.3	220.4
Bossier City	7	1.3	0.5	50.8
Hammond	9	1.2	1.9	15.2
Lafayette	76	2.9	4.9	80.6
Shreveport	72	1.8	4.2	205.8
Maine[3]	0	0	0	1,125.0
Maryland	56	1.7	6.2	4,216.9
Gaithersburg	7	1.5	0.6	26.4
Massachusetts[3]	0	0	0	5,737.1
Michigan	145	21.9	37.7	9,262.0
Battle Creek	2	20.6	25.6	35.7
Minnesota[3]	215	1.4	12.4	4,076.0
Mississippi	20	5.0	9.5	2,520.7
Clarksdale	2	1.3	1.7	21.1
Gulfport	1	1.5	2.4	39.7
Indianola	1	1.4	0.2	8.1
Missouri	296	15.6	187.1	4,916.8
Florissant	5	2.5	2.5	55.1
Hazelwood	2	3.0	0.7	13.1
St. Charles	14	6.3	5.9	37.4
St. Peters	17	1.0	2.2	15.7
Montana	159	1.9	6.6	786.7
Billings	44	1.1	3.1	66.8
Nebraska	219	32.7	16.5	1,569.8
Bellevue	34	9.4	2.2	21.8
Grand Island	1	4.6	6.2	33.2
Omaha	46	13.5	4.1	313.9
Papillion	5	1.7	0.3	6.4
Nevada[3]	146	0.6	16.9	800.5
New Hampshire[3]	0	0	0	920.6
New Jersey[3]	4	0.1	0.1	7,365.0
New Mexico	175	3.8	39.1	1,303.3
Hobbs	8	1.1	0.8	29.2
Silver City	3	1.1	2.5	9.9
New York[3]	20	0	0.4	17,558.2
North Carolina	919	80.4	101.3	5,881.4
Asheville	11	5.6	3.1	54.0
Charlotte	6	8.7	6.2	315.5
Gastonia	17	1.7	3.1	47.3
Goldsboro	23	3.7	3.2	31.9
Greenville	24	1.4	1.9	35.7
Henderson	13	2.2	1.9	13.5
Hickory	35	2.8	4.0	20.8
High Point	14	3.2	9.1	63.5
Jacksonville	12	4.7	3.3	18.2
Kernersville	14	1.3	1.3	5.9

Balance of table on page 82.

linois about 2,400 annexations were reported, and in Florida, Georgia, and Texas, over 1,000.

In contrast, there was a single annexation (in Vermont) reported for all of New England. The Middle Atlantic states of New York, Pennsylvania, and New Jersey reported 27 actions, involving very little population. These annexations constitute less than 0.2% of the nation's 18,802 annexations, despite the fact that about 16% of the nation's population is concentrated within the boundaries of these states. Annexations are rare in the northeastern states because generally a relatively strong town or township would have to give up territory for a city to expand its boundaries.

State Annexation Totals. The state where the most people (146,700) have been added to municipalities by annexation between 1980 and 1983 is California, which ranked fifth in the 1970s. North Carolina (80,400), Texas (76,700), and Florida (60,100) follow. Annexation has been widespread among California and North Carolina municipalities since 1980. Thirty-five places of 5,000 or more in California and 18 in North Carolina reported annexations of 1,000 or more people. Florida's annexations were larger in population than those in the 1970s but only seven places reported annexing 1,000 or more persons. Tallahassee, which ranks third in the nation in population annexed since January 1980, accounted for nearly half of the Florida total. Alabama's strong fifth place showing in the state-by-state ranking is primarily due to a 1 January 1980 annexation by Montgomery of nearly 30,000 persons. This annexation is counted in the 1980 census because the January 1 boundaries were used for census purposes.

Nebraska, not prominent in 1970s annexation data, ranks sixth in the 1980s. There have been sizable annexations by several Nebraska cities, the largest being to Omaha (13,500) and Bellevue (9,400). Bellevue reported the second most populous annexation in the United States during 1983 (Table 2/2). In 1984 Omaha added another 7,000 persons; this recent annexation is not reflected in the tables of this report.

Tennessee remains relatively high in the ranking of annexing states (eleventh), due to numerous annexations by smaller places. However, Memphis, one of the top annexing cities in the nation during the 1970s, has reported no boundary changes since 1977.

In Michigan, one annexation accounted for about 95% of the reported annexed population in that state. Battle Creek's absorption of Battle Creek Township brought in 20,600 persons. On the other hand, Ohio reported annexations totalling 7,000 population with no place annexing as many as 1,000 people. Similarly, only one Illinois community contributed more than 1,000 persons to that state's total of 16,600 annexed population. Des Plaines annexed a total of 1,800 people.

Effects of City Size. Much of the 1980s annexation activity takes place in medium-sized cities. Populous annexations (totalling 500 or more persons) occurred most frequently in cities of 250,000 to 499,999 population (no table shown). Nearly one quarter of all cities this size added territory with at least 500 persons between 1980 and 1983. This compared with a 14% rate for the largest cities (those over 500,000), 20% for cities 100,000 to 249,999, 17% for cities 50,000 to 99,999, 9% for cities 25,000 to 49,999, 6% for cities 10,000 to 24,999, and less than 3% for places of 5,000 to 9,999 population. Houston is the only city with a population over half a million that reported annexating more than 10,000 people.

During the period 1980–83, several places annexed areas containing more than 25% of their total 1980 populations. For example, Davie, Florida, whose 1980 population was 20,877, annexed 6,100 people. Des Moines, Washington, added 2,500 people to a 1980 count of 7,378. Harrisonburg, Virginia, whose 1980 population was 19,671, annexed 5,500.

A few places that are too small to be included in the Census Bureau's Boundary and Annexation Survey reported annexations that are even more dramatic—Lyndon, Kentucky, nearly tripled in size by adding 2,714 persons; Middletown, Kentucky, increased tenfold through annexation from a population of 414 to 4,262. Parlier, California, another small community, recently doubled its population through annexation.

Land Area of Changes. Twenty places with populations over 5,000 that annexed more than 1,000 people added more than ten square miles to their land area. The greatest gains were reported by Montgomery, Alabama (78.0 square miles), followed by Scottsdale, Arizona (57.2 square miles), St. George, Utah (32.3), Colorado Springs, Colorado (26.3), Battle Creek, Michigan (25.6), Fresno, California (25.0), Tallahassee, Florida (24.0), and Austin, Texas (22.2). In 1980, part of Scottsdale was so sparsely populated that the Census Bureau designated it as rural. The newly annexed areas are very rural, averaging fewer than 20 persons per square mile. Some annexations were very densely settled—especially in California. Thousand Oaks added 8,300 persons in 1.7 square miles; Compton added 1,500 in only 78.5 acres (about a tenth of a square mile).

Detachments. Detachments in the 1980–83 period removed 147 square miles and approximately 11,600 persons from municipal jurisdiction. The largest detachments were from Jenks, Oklahoma (2,600), and Denver, Colorado (2,500). The Jenks detachments were offset by annexations.

Flint, Michigan, and Wewoka, Oklahoma, experienced a net change of zero despite a flury of activity when they each annexed an area and later detached the area they annexed.

Lanett, Alabama, detached nearly one quarter (1,900) of its residents. The only other reported detachments of more than 200 persons were from Oxnard, California (600), Darien, Illinois (300), and Vernal, Utah (300). Parsons, Kansas, Greenville, Texas, and Riverton and Sandy, Utah, each detached about 200 persons. Some of these detachments were also offset by annexations.

Incorporations. The Census Bureau has received reports of 149 places that incorporated between 1 January 1980 and 31 December 1983.

Table 2/1 MAJOR ANNEXATIONS BY PLACES OF 5,000 OR MORE POPULATION, 1980–83[1] continued

Place	No. of actions	Estimated annexation: Population (000)	Estimated annexation: Square miles	1980 Census population (000)[2]
North Carolina (cont'd)				
Kinston	23	1.4	1.3	25.2
Mint Hill	23	2.2	4.2	7.9
Monroe	20	1.9	4.0	12.6
Morganton	21	1.2	2.2	13.8
Raleigh	41	8.2	6.4	150.3
Rocky Mount	17	2.6	3.1	41.5
Tarboro	6	1.9	5.1	8.7
Winston-Salem	13	12.5	8.7	131.9
North Dakota[3]	97	1.3	15.1	652.7
Ohio[3]	467	7.0	39.7	10,797.6
Oklahoma	445	15.4	91.3	3,025.5
Jenks	10	1.8	4.3	5.9
Oregon	573	16.1	45.6	2,633.2
Albany	20	1.3	2.4	26.5
Klamath Falls	6	1.5	0.8	16.7
Portland	72	4.9	5.7	368.1
Salem	43	1.2	3.0	89.2
Tigard	50	2.5	1.8	14.8
Pennsylvania[3]	3	0.1	0.1	11,864.7
Rhode Island[3]	0	0	0	947.2
South Carolina	702	18.8	30.6	3,122.7
Charleston	60	1.9	10.0	69.9
Hartsville	5	1.3	0.3	7.6
Mount Pleasant	24	2.7	3.6	14.5
Summerville	65	3.0	0.4	6.5
Sumter	33	1.0	0.9	24.9
South Dakota	83	2.5	10.5	690.8
Sioux Falls	20	2.2	3.3	81.3
Tennessee	303	20.3	47.4	4,591.1
Bartlett	2	1.5	0.6	17.1
Clinton	6	2.2	6.6	5.2
Germantown	27	2.6	1.1	21.5
Johnson City	27	4.1	2.7	39.8
Morristown	31	1.3	0.6	19.6

An additional 23 communities incorporated in 1984.

Large new places continue to appear—there are already 20 new places this decade with populations exceeding 10,000. In comparison 23 such places incorporated during all of the 1970s. The latest large additions during 1983 and 1984 include Bullhead City, Arizona; East Palo Alto and West Hollywood, California; Fitchburg, Wisconsin, and Rochester Hills and Auburn Hills, Michigan (all three town or township governments incorporating as cities); and the textile mill community of Kannapolis, North Carolina (Table 2/3). For decades Kannapolis was the largest unincorporated place in North Carolina and one of the largest nonsuburban unincorporated places in the United States. West Hollywood, which incorporated in late 1984, includes the Sunset Strip area between Los Angeles and Beverly Hills.

Some of the new communities have colorful names—among them Pippa Passes, Kentucky; Birdsong, Arkansas; and Bar Nunn, Wyoming.

Texas reported the most incorporations (27) in this decade followed by California with 15, Kentucky with 14, and Alabama, North Carolina, and Oklahoma, with 10 each. California leads, as it did in the 1970s, in the size of populations incorporated. The total population of the California new incorporations is 245,000, about triple that of second-place Utah (74,300). The smallest new place in California (La Quinta with 4,027 people) was larger than the largest incorporation in most states. Most new places are quite small. For example, the smallest new incorporations are Seven Fields and Valley Hi, Pennsylvania, with 1980 populations of only 6 and 8, respectively.

In the 1980s, three states—Maryland, Montana, and Nevada—reported new incorporations for the first time in at least a decade. Several communities appearing in post-1980 Census records incorporated long before 1980 but were not reported to the Bureau until after the 1980 Census. Concord, Kentucky, was reputedly incorporated in 1830.

A referendum was held in California on the possible formation of a new county in the South Lake Tahoe area. The proposal was defeated. As population increased in some of the very

Table 2/1 MAJOR ANNEXATIONS BY PLACES OF 5,000 OR MORE POPULATION, 1980–83[1] continued

Place	No. of actions	Estimated annexation Population (000)	Square miles	1980 Census population (000)[2]
Texas	1,322	76.7	525.2	14,227.8
Abilene	7	1.3	16.1	98.3
Austin	57	3.9	22.2	345.9
Bryan	5	2.4	6.3	44.3
Corpus Christi	35	3.1	12.8	232.1
Edinburg	5	1.7	3.4	24.1
Friendswood	7	3.5	4.0	10.7
Houston	13	22.4	8.8	1,595.1
Huntsville	12	1.2	7.2	23.9
La Porte	4	2.7	1.4	14.1
Laredo	2	1.3	2.6	91.4
Longview	1	4.2	9.7	62.8
Midland	5	3.1	11.9	70.5
San Antonio	24	4.7	5.8	785.9
Utah	263	6.5	74.1	1,461.0
St. George	4	2.5	32.3	11.4
Vermont[3]	1	0	0.1	511.5
Virginia	13	12.0	35.1	5,346.8
Fairfax	5	1.1	0.2	19.4
Fredericksburg	1	2.8	4.4	15.3
Harrisonburg	1	5.5	11.4	19.7
Leesburg	2	1.5	8.1	8.4
Washington	319	13.2	33.9	4,132.4
Des Moines	2	2.5	0.6	7.4
Kennewick	32	3.2	2.0	34.4
Marysville	8	1.1	1.8	5.1
West Virginia[3]	61	2.5	4.8	1,950.2
Wisconsin[3]	528	3.4	20.8	4,705.6
Wyoming	284	7.7	23.8	469.6
Casper	27	1.3	0.2	51.0
Cheyenne	67	2.7	0.9	47.3
Cody	5	1.5	2.4	6.6
Gillette	43	1.6	2.7	12.1

Source: Unpublished data from the Census Bureau's Boundary and Annexation Survey.

[1]This table includes places of 5,000 or more population annexing populations of 1,000 or more (local estimates), net of detachments. State totals include all annexations to places of 5,000 or more.

[2]The populations in this column do not include the populations of the annexed areas.

[3]There were no cases of communities of 5,000 or more population annexing populations of 1,000 or more in this state.

Table 2/2 LARGEST ANNEXATIONS OF 1983

Annexation	Population (local estimate)
Battle Creek, Mich.	20,600
Bellevue, Neb.	9,400
Rancho Palos Verdes, Calif.	8,100
Fresno, Calif.	6,400
Pompano Beach, Fla.	6,000
Asheville, N.C.	5,000
Grand Island, Neb.	4,600
Portland, Ore.	4,500
Mesa, Ariz.	4,300
Tallahassee, Fla.	4,200
Longview, Tex.	4,200
Jeffersontown, Ky.	4,000
Winston-Salem, N.C.	4,000
Friendswood, Tex.	3,500
Bakersfield, Calif.	3,300
High Point, N.C.	3,200
Baton Rouge, La.	3,000

Source: Unpublished data from the Census Bureau's Boundary and Annexation Survey.

Table 2/3 LARGEST INCORPORATIONS OF 1983–84

Incorporation	Population (1980 Census)
Rochester Hills, Mich.	40,597
Kannapolis, N.C.	30,303
West Hollywood, Calif.	35,703[1]
East Palo Alto, Calif.	18,106
Hermitage, Pa.	16,365
Auburn Hills, Mich.	15,388
Fitchburg, Wis.	11,965
Bullhead City, Ariz.	10,719
Moorpark, Calif.	7,798
Wesley Hills, N.Y.	4,402
Meadows, Tex.	4,321
Sunland Park, N.M.	4,313
Mammoth Lakes, Calif.	4,089
New Hempstead, N.Y.	4,020

Source: Populations shown are 1980 Census counts derived from official census records.

[1]The population shown for West Hollywood is that of the census designated (unincorporated) place. The official determination of population is not yet complete.

large counties in the West, the pressure for governmental services resulted in the creation of new counties. La Paz, Arizona, was formed from a part of Yuma County with 12,557 population. Similarly, Cibola, New Mexico, was carved out of a large county.

Disappearing Places. A number of municipalities have been "lost" since 1980. Some, like Yost, Utah, and Carter, South Dakota, have disincorporated (Table 2/4). Others like Carrville, Alabama; McHenry Shores, Illinois; Eastside, Oregon; and Griffing Park, Texas, have merged with larger adjacent communities (Table 2/5). Others seem to fade in and out of existence, governmentally active at times, dormant at others.

Most disincorporating places are quite small. Wittenberg, Missouri, had nearly 300 people early in the twentieth century but dwindled to only 4 persons in 1980 before its disincorporation. Willimantic, Connecticut, with a 1980 population of 14,652, and Putnam, Connecticut (6,855 population), were unusually large communities to disincorporate. They merged with their parent towns of Windham and Putnam, respectively. Liberty City, Texas, and Phelps, Kentucky, both over 1,000 population, also disincorporated.

All of the boroughs and towns in Essex County, New Jersey, have become townships. Governmental powers of the township, village, borough, town, and city governments in New Jersey are identical. The motivating factor in the Essex County shifts appears to be the general revenue sharing formula, which in some counties favors township governments.

Penn Run Number One, Kentucky, enjoyed city status for only one year—it incorporated in April 1979 and disincorporated the following April.

Still other places reincarnate, although sometimes in different forms. Reston, Virginia, one of the largest and best known of the "new towns" in America, surrounds the once tiny incorporated town of Wiehle, a railroad stop with a bourbon distillery. The Wiehle government disbanded in the 1940s, but never officially disincorporated. A group of Reston citizens briefly investigated reactivating Wiehle so that Reston could join with Wiehle and become a municipal

Table 2/4 DISINCORPORATIONS SINCE 1 JANUARY 1980

Place	Population (1980 Census)
Willimantic, Conn.	14,652
Putnam, Conn.	6,855
Valley View, Ill.	2,112
Phelps, Ky.	1,126
Liberty City, Tex.	1,121
Elizabethtown, N.Y.	659
Akiachak, Alaska	438
Yost, Utah	67
Painter's Hill, Fla.	40
Ardmore, S.D.	16
Carter, S.D.	7
Loyalton, S.D.	6
Wittenberg, Mo.	4

government. On its own, Reston could not incorporate as a municipality because Fairfax County, the county in which Reston is located, has an urban county charter which prohibits any new incorporations within its boundaries. Cripple Creek, Colorado (1980 population 655) is thriving again without a name change, though it is still far short of its 1900 peak population of 10,147. Lists of the larger post-1980 disincorporations and mergers are in Table 2/4 and 2/5, respectively.

Census Counts for Annexed Areas. To indicate the population growth in annexed areas, the population counts at the beginning and end of the decade for 14 cities that made major annexations during the 1970s are shown in Table 2/6. The 1970 and 1980 population counts are shown within both 1970 and 1980 boundaries and for the annexed areas. The local estimates of the annexed population at the time of boundary changes are also provided.

Of the 14 cities, 12 realized net increases in population between 1970 and 1980, but only Raleigh, North Carolina, and Houston, Texas, showed increases within their 1970 boundaries. When the percentage changes between 1970 and 1980 for the population within these cities' 1970 boundaries are compared with those for their 1980 boundaries, the expanded areas showed population changes eight percentage points higher on the average. The population change figures in Table 2/6 should be used with caution. If these cities had had no annexations during the decade, it does not necessarily follow that their 1980 populations would have been the same as shown under "1980 population in 1970 boundaries." Development is often tied to the availability of utility hook-up, school location and quality, and other political, social, demographic, and economic considerations. Some of the growth experienced in the annexed fringe may have occurred instead within existing corporate limits if an annexation had not taken place. Nevertheless, the figures provide some clues to the significant contribution of annexation to city growth.

In four cases—Memphis, Raleigh, Houston, and San Antonio—the population within the annexed areas doubled or even tripled during the decade. Some population increase occurred in all the annexed territory of each of the 14 cities except that of Gary, Indiana. For the 14 cities combined, the population of the annexed areas increased 97% between 1970 and 1980.

Most of the 1980 population counts for the annexed areas exceeded the local estimates at the time of annexation. Apparently, many cities annex territory planned for or under development. Consequently, the number of persons living in annexed areas at the end of the decade generally exceeds that reported by the localities on the Boundary and Annexation Survey or determined by the Census Bureau at the time of the last census.

Table 2/5 MERGERS SINCE 1 JANUARY 1980

Place	Population (1980 Census)	Merged with
East Layton, Utah	3,531	Layton
Brownville, Ala.	2,386	Birmingham
Griffing Park, Tex.	1,802	Port Arthur
Eastside, Ore.	1,601	Coos Bay
Illmo, Mo.	1,368	Scott City
McHenry Shores, Ill.	1,041	McHenry
Carrville, Ala.	820	Tallahassee
Ridgeview Heights, Ky.	729	Independence
Norristown, Ark.	625	Russellville
Pleasant Valley, Ky.	342	Pikeville
Schuermann Heights, Mich.	234	Woodson Terrace
Hacienda Village, Fla.	126	Davie
Highley Heights, Mo.	100	Desloge

Table 2/6 POPULATION CHANGES FOR 1970 BOUNDARIES, 1980 BOUNDARIES, AND ANNEXED AREAS OF 14 SELECTED CITIES

	1970 boundaries			1980 boundaries			Annexed area			
Municipality	1970 population	1980 population	% change	1970 population	1980 population	% change	1970 population	1980 population	% change	Local estimate of annexed population
Savannah, Ga.	118,349	108,890	(8.0)	144,737	141,654	(2.1)	26,388	32,764	24.2	35,300
Gary, Ind.	175,415	141,969	(19.1)	188,398	151,968	(19.3)	12,983	9,999	(23.0)	13,000
Muncie, Ind.	69,082	60,553	(12.3)	84,500	77,216	(8.6)	15,418	16,663	8.1	16,700
Baton Rouge, La.	165,921	163,700	(1.3)	205,509	220,394	7.2	39,588	56,694	43.2	49,700
Jackson, Miss.	153,968	152,485	(1.0)	180,816	202,895	12.2	26,848	50,410	87.8	34,200
Charlotte, N.C.	241,420	220,147	(8.8)	291,875	315,474	8.1	50,455	95,327	88.9	84,700
Raleigh, N.C.	122,830	128,031	4.2	127,576	150,255	17.8	4,746	22,224	368.2	6,800
Portland, Or.	379,967	358,837	(5.6)	388,810	368,139	(5.3)	8,843	9,302	5.2	8,000
Chattanooga, Tenn.	119,923	112,889	(5.9)	167,838	169,565	1.0	47,915	56,669	18.3	53,800
Memphis, Tenn.	623,988	577,215	(7.5)	657,400	646,174	(1.7)	33,412	68,959	106.4	50,700
Houston, Tex.	1,233,535	1,344,243	9.0	1,311,029	1,595,138	21.7	77,494	250,895	223.8	208,400
San Antonio, Tex.	654,153	653,739	(0.1)	708,582	795,940	10.9	54,429	132,201	142.3	76,100
Lynchburg, Va.	54,083	51,335	(5.1)	64,583	66,743	3.3	10,500	15,408	46.7	13,800
Roanoke, Va.	92,115	85,053	(7.7)	105,618	100,220	(5.1)	13,503	15,167	12.3	13,400

Note: Numbers in parentheses indicate percentage decreases.

C Personnel Issues

1

Salaries of Municipal Officials for 1984*

Ross H. Hoff
International City Management Association

Trends in the 1984 salaries paid to municipal officials compare favorably with the state of the economy as a whole, according to a survey conducted by the International City Management Association in the winter of 1983–84 (Table 1/1). Though salary increases are less again this year than in the previous year, the increases still are running ahead of inflation, on average. The Consumer Price Index for All Urban Consumers (CPI-U)[1] rose 3.8% over the 12 months ending 31 December 1983 as compared with a 3.9% increase for the year ending 31 December 1982 and an 8.9% increase for the year ending 31 December 1981. Meanwhile, the average salaries for the 24 positions shown in Table 1/2 increased 5.7% for the period 1 January 1983 to 1 January 1984[2]. Although this is less than the average increases in the previous years (6.6% for the period ending 1 January 1983 and 9.2% for the period ending 1 January 1982[3]), it is still above the 3.8% increase in the CPI-U over the same period. Nevertheless, the average salaries for 19 of the 24 positions examined in this report increased by a smaller percentage in 1983 than in 1982.

The average annual rate of increase during the period 1979 to 1984 calculated for the salaries of the 24 positions in Table 1/2 was 8.2% (not shown in table). On an individual basis within the same time frame, salaries of assistant city managers/assistant chief administrative officers (CAOs) increased 9.3%, the largest average salary increase of the officials surveyed. This was followed closely by salaries of chief personnel officers, which increased 8.9%, and salaries of directors of data processing and directors of budget and research, which both increased 8.8% during the period. Although salaries of school superintendents increased the least of all municipal officials during the period (6.6%), that figure is still well above the increase in the CPI-U. However, school superintendents averaged the highest average annual salary for 1984 ($46,563). These positions continue to represent the extremes in average annual increases and actual salaries as they have for the past several years.

Table 1/3 presents salaries for four municipal government positions in selected central cities and suburban areas located in standard metropolitan statistical areas (SMSAs)[4]. In all cases but one (police chiefs in the Oakland SMSA) municipal administrators, police chiefs, fire chiefs, and public works directors in central cities earned higher salaries than did their counterparts in the suburbs. The greatest disparities between average central city and suburban salaries appear in the Cincinnati SMSA for city administrators (154%) and public works directors (168%); in the Houston SMSA for public works directors (147%), fire chiefs (141%), and police chiefs (136%); and in the Kansas City SMSA for city administrators (142%). The smallest differentials appear in the Newark SMSA for police chiefs (5%), city administrators (23%), and public works directors (23%); in the Boulder and Washington, D.C. SMSAs for fire chiefs (13% and 18%, respectively); and in the Oakland SMSA for public works directors (19%) and police chiefs, the only case among the considered SMSAs in which the salary of the suburban officials is higher on average (26%) than that of the central city (Oakland) official.

The extent to which parity between salaries of police chiefs and those of fire chiefs has been established in central cities can also be seen in Table 1/3. The cities of Atlanta, Fort Worth, Hartford, Houston, St. Paul, Newark, Philadelphia, Pittsburgh, St. Louis, Oakland, and Washington, D.C. have equalized the salaries paid to their police chiefs and fire chiefs. None of the suburban components of the SMSAs listed in Table 1/3 exhibit salary parity in the literal sense. Many of the figures, however, are close enough to justify the assumption that parity does exist in some of the jurisdictions included in the average for suburbs in each SMSA and that the average figure has been skewed by an occasional exception to the principle of parity.

Table 1/4 shows the 1984 mean, median, first quartile, and third quartile salaries for 26 municipal officials (the 24 positions of Table 1/2 with the addition of mayor and chief administrative officer) displayed by population group and distributed by geographic region, city type,[4] and form of government. City manager salaries in the 2,071 reporting municipalities average $40,609, an increase of 4.8% over 1983. Man-

Table 1/1 SURVEY RESPONSE

Classification	No. of cities surveyed (A)	Number responding	
		No.	% of (A)
Total, all cities[1]	6,983	5,106	73.1
Population group			
Over 1,000,000	6	4	66.7
500,000–1,000,000	17	15	88.2
250,000– 499,999	34	33	97.1
100,000– 249,999	113	105	92.9
50,000– 99,999	278	237	85.3
25,000– 49,999	613	506	82.5
10,000– 24,999	1,536	1,160	75.5
5,000– 9,999	1,739	1,272	73.1
2,500– 4,999	2,271	1,504	66.2
Under 2,500[2]	376	270	71.8
Geographic region[3]			
Northeast	1,949	1,203	61.7
North Central	2,022	1,580	78.1
South	2,048	1,510	73.7
West	964	813	84.3
Geographic division[4]			
New England	796	489	61.4
Mid-Atlantic	1,153	714	61.9
East North Central	1,321	1,008	76.3
West North Central	701	572	81.6
South Atlantic	839	682	81.3
East South Central	468	306	65.4
West South Central	741	522	70.4
Mountain	355	283	79.7
Pacific Coast	609	530	87.0
Metro status[5]			
Central	432	385	89.1
Suburban	3,695	2,674	72.4
Independent	2,856	2,047	71.7
Form of government[6]			
Mayor-council	3,780	2,558	67.7
Council-manager	2,526	2,161	85.6
Commission	177	115	65.0
Town meeting	419	227	54.2
Rep. town meeting	81	45	55.6

[1] The term *cities* is used in this and the other tables to refer to cities, villages, towns, townships, and boroughs.
[2] Only cities recognized by ICMA as having the council-manager form of government or providing for a position of overall professional management are included in this group.
[3] *Geographic regions: Northeast*—the New England and Mid-Atlantic Divisions; *North Central*—the East and West North Central Divisions; *South*—the South Atlantic and the East and West South Central Divisions; *West*—the Mountain and Pacific Coast Divisions. See footnote 4 for states included in the regions.
[4] *Geographic divisions: New England*—the states of Connecticut, Maine, Massachusetts, New Hampshire, Rhode Island, and Vermont; *Mid-Atlantic*—the states of New Jersey, New York, and Pennsylvania; *East North Central*—the states of Illinois, Indiana, Michigan, Ohio, and Wisconsin; *West North Central*—the states of Iowa, Kansas, Minnesota, Missouri, Nebraska, North Dakota, and South Dakota; *South Atlantic*—the states of Delaware, Florida, Georgia, Maryland, North Carolina, South Carolina, Virginia, and West Virginia, plus the District of Columbia; *East South Central*—the states of Alabama, Kentucky, Mississippi, and Tennessee; *West South Central*—the states of Arkansas, Louisiana, Oklahoma, and Texas; *Mountain*—the states of Arizona, Colorado, Idaho, Montana, Nevada, New Mexico, Utah, and Wyoming; *Pacific Coast*—the states of Alaska, California, Hawaii, Oregon, and Washington.
[5] *Metro status: Central*—the city(ies) actually appearing in the standard metropolitan statistical area (SMSA) title; *Suburban*—the city(ies) located within an SMSA; *Independent*—the city(ies) not located within an SMSA.
[6] *Forms of government: Mayor-council*—an elected council serves as the legislative body with a separately elected head of government; *Council-manager*—the mayor and council make policy and an appointed administrator is responsible for the administration of the city; *Commission*—a board of elected commissioners serves as the legislative body and each commissioner is responsible for administration of one or more departments; *Town meeting*—qualified voters meet to make basic policy and choose a board of selectmen to carry out the policy; *Representative town meeting*—representatives selected by citizens vote at meetings, which may be attended by all town citizens.

*Data for this article were collected from the survey *Salaries of Municipal Officials* (SAL/84) by the International City Management Association, Washington, D.C., 1984.

Table 1/2 AVERAGE SALARIES OF MUNICIPAL OFFICIALS[1]

Title	No. of cities included[2]	1979 ($)	1980 ($)	% increase from 1979	1981 ($)	% increase from 1980	1982 ($)	% increase from 1981	1983 ($)	% increase from 1982	1984 ($)	% increase from 1983
Manager	1,452	28,943	31,427	9	34,387	9	37,383	9	39,885	7	42,153	6
Clerk	2,069	15,158	16,589	9	18,214	10	19,966	10	21,245	6	22,493	6
Finance director	935	23,148	25,419	10	28,092	11	30,816	10	32,931	7	34,930	6
Controller	170	22,460	24,489	9	26,719	9	29,018	9	30,740	6	32,443	6
Auditor	164	19,377	21,461	11	23,258	8	25,507	10	27,152	6	28,861	6
Treasurer	584	16,320	17,780	9	19,425	9	21,257	9	22,555	6	23,684	5
Engineer	676	24,405	26,587	9	29,173	10	31,825	9	33,953	7	35,732	5
Director of public works	1,688	21,512	23,499	9	25,825	10	28,200	9	29,962	6	31,524	5
Superintendent of streets	1,642	16,590	18,153	9	19,965	10	21,821	9	23,236	6	24,516	6
Fire chief	1,425	21,263	23,377	10	25,740	10	28,161	9	30,008	7	31,774	6
Police chief	2,929	20,032	21,950	10	24,096	10	26,370	9	28,159	7	29,795	6
Planning director	733	23,650	26,030	10	28,816	11	31,470	9	33,535	7	35,314	5
Chief personnel officer	499	21,398	23,644	10	26,309	11	28,839	10	30,884	7	32,767	6
Attorney	492	27,379	29,963	9	32,877	10	35,835	9	38,278	7	40,381	5
Health officer	226	22,705	24,416	8	26,439	8	28,753	9	30,419	6	31,803	5
Director of parks and recreation	812	20,175	22,124	10	24,409	10	26,669	9	28,468	7	30,142	6
Superintendent of parks	572	16,933	18,652	10	20,664	11	22,677	10	24,181	7	25,459	5
Director of recreation	503	17,845	19,662	10	21,717	10	23,581	9	25,179	7	26,721	6
Librarian	846	16,713	18,156	9	20,029	10	22,006	10	23,676	8	25,071	6
Superintendent of schools	182	33,777	35,722	6	38,238	7	41,221	8	44,057	7	46,563	6
Director of data processing	301	22,495	24,817	10	27,402	10	30,261	10	32,484	7	34,332	6
Director of budget and research	80	26,248	29,169	11	32,315	11	35,619	10	38,049	7	40,061	5
Asst. city mgr./asst. cao.	399	22,765	25,102	10	27,838	11	30,816	11	33,177	8	35,560	7
Chief building inspector	1,372	17,519	19,189	10	21,155	10	23,065	9	24,539	6	25,805	5

[1] This table is based on those cities that reported salary data for each of the six years 1979 to 1984. All data are as of 1 January.

[2] Number of cities included are those cities of the original base of cities that reported data for the position indicated for each of the six years.

Table 1/3 AVERAGE SALARIES FOR CENTRAL CITY AND SUBURBAN OFFICIALS: 1 JANUARY 1984

Central city	No. of cities reporting in SMSA	City manager/chief administrative officer: Central city	Suburban[1]	% diff.	Police chief: Central city	Suburban[1]	% diff.	Fire chief: Central city	Suburban[1]	% diff.	Public works director: Central city	Suburban[1]	% diff.
Atlanta, Ga.	31	49,356	32,356	53	40,360	23,442	72	40,360	26,416	53	55,726	24,273	130
Chicago, Ill.	156	73,000	44,462	64	80,000	35,505	125	76,000	36,358	109	72,000	34,308	110
Cincinnati, Oh.	48	77,219	30,391	154	55,513	25,205	120	51,881	24,845	109	57,005	21,223	168
Cleveland, Oh.	47	. . .	41,114	. . .	53,563	32,312	66	52,498	32,313	62	43,528	32,264	35
Dallas, Texas[2]	55	95,240	45,548	109	75,577	33,342	127	77,980	36,751	112	75,413	33,086	128
Fort Worth, Texas[2]		86,278		89	57,264		72	57,264		56	57,264		73
Dayton, Oh.	25	53,383	37,607	42	44,530	29,265	52	43,575	31,070	40	43,795	28,669	53
Denver, Colo.[2]	23	. . .	53,716	. . .	. . .	43,149	. . .	62,124	43,002	44	62,943	41,066	53
Boulder, Colo.[2]		70,522		31	56,701		31	48,501		13	. . .		. . .
Hartford, Conn.	28	59,832	43,797	37	52,182	32,547	60	52,182	35,965	45	52,182	32,907	59
Houston, Texas	34	. . .	42,594	. . .	74,984	31,783	136	74,984	31,102	141	83,319	33,786	147
Kansas City, Mo.[2]	29	102,000	42,173	142	63,144	31,600	100	45,120	31,827	42	61,200	32,210	90
Kansas City, Ks.[2]		. . .		. . .	42,894		36	43,095		35	39,756		23
Los Angeles, Calif.[2]	67	96,779	56,770	70	106,968	52,937	102	95,944	52,110	84	. . .	46,678	. . .
Long Beach, Calif.[2]		82,000		44	73,334		39	70,779		36	78,449		68
Milwaukee, Wis.	29	. . .	38,153	. . .	67,517	33,544	101	63,580	34,210	86	61,146	33,645	82
Minneapolis, Mn.[2]	76	64,298	42,186	52	56,212	37,798	49	54,054	36,707	47	64,298	36,163	78
St. Paul, Mn.[2]		58,980		40	61,930		64	61,930		69	61,930		71
Newark, N.J.	44	50,000	40,772	23	38,192	36,482	5	38,192	38,216	. . .	44,669	36,400	23
Philadelphia, Pa.	101	62,500	34,222	83	55,000	31,627	74	55,000	24,932	121	55,000	29,022	90
Phoenix, Ariz.	16	84,011	48,246	74	74,568	38,706	93	63,627	39,910	59	66,706	40,738	64
Pittsburgh, Pa.	85	51,740	27,131	91	49,350	25,612	93	49,350	24,343	103	. . .	23,194	. . .
St. Louis, Mo.	64	. . .	35,384	. . .	52,500	28,180	86	52,500	30,240	74	. . .	29,512	. . .
San Francisco, Calif.[2]	52	88,166	54,141	63	81,536	47,256	73	81,536	48,776	67	86,000	49,913	72
Oakland, Calif.[2]		78,528		45	35,100		−26	60,864		25	59,520		19
Washington, D.C.	32	69,600	40,242	73	63,700	32,585	95	63,700	53,780	18	63,700	32,637	95

Leaders (. . .) indicate data not applicable or not reported.

[1] Average salary within the SMSA of the central city; does not include central city salary.

[2] The cities paired by brackets (}) are the central cities of one SMSA. Central city data are shown for each city, suburban data for the entire SMSA.

ager salaries in the nine population groups listed below increased for 1984 over 1983 as follows:

Population	*Increase*
500,000–1,000,000	0.5%
250,000– 499,999	8.4%
100,000– 249,999	4.9%
50,000– 99,999	5.0%
25,000– 49,999	5.7%
10,000– 24,999	5.1%
5,000– 9,999	4.6%
2,500– 4,999	6.7%
Under 2,500	3.3%

Managers of municipalities with populations under 10,000 earn an average of $9,438 less than the mean salary for all city managers. They earned $8,966 less in 1983 and $8,306 less in 1982. This indicates an increasing gap between the salaries of managers in municipalities this size (47% of the total number of managers reporting in 1984) and the average salaries for all city managers.

Managers of municipalities 250,000 and over, who account for less than 1% of all managers reporting, earn an average of $38,986 more than the mean salary for all managers, a 5.2% increase in the differential from 1983. Managers of municipalities with populations from 50,000 to 249,999 (10% of the total number of managers reporting) earn $20,545 more than the mean for all city managers, a 5.4% increase over 1983. Managers in cities with populations from 10,000 to 49,999 earn an average of $4,804 more than the mean, an increase of 9.7% from the previous year.

With the general economy currently on an upswing it may be that rates of salary increase for public officials will have gone as low as they are going to go. In the pattern of delayed reaction that has been the rule for these positions, it may be that salary increases next year will be greater than they are for 1984.[5]

[1]The Consumer Price Index (CPI) measures the price change of a constant market basket of goods and services over time. As a price index and not a cost of living index the CPI has limitations in wage and salary analyses, but it remains useful, nevertheless, because of its importance as an indicator of inflation.

The Consumer Price Index used in this report is the Consumer Price Index of All Urban Consumers (CPI-U), which covers approximately 80% of the total noninstitutional civilian population. The CPI-U is a refinement of the pre-1977 Consumer Price Index for Urban Wage Earners and Clerical Workers (CPI-W), which measured only about 40% of the population and was made up primarily of wage earners and clerical workers. The CPI-U includes groups that historically have been excluded from the CPI-W (professional, managerial, and technical workers, the self-employed, short-term workers, the unemployed, and retirees and others not in the labor force). The inclusion of white collar workers in the CPI-U makes its use in the analysis of salaries of municipal officials much more valid than was the case with the CPI-W.

[2]Salary data for this report are as of 1 January 1984. Salary data for previous years are as of 1 January of the year specified. Since municipalities have different fiscal years, the data collected are assumed to be sufficient for the total year of their collection. Therefore, for 1 January 1984 the data are assumed to hold for the total year 1984.

[3]The data presented in and extrapolated from Table 1/2 are based solely on those cities that reported salary data for each year from 1979 to 1984. Because of this, calculations of average salaries and percentage changes for previous years may not correspond precisely with the data for the same position and year in previous Salaries of Municipal Officials Reports.

[4]References to SMSAs in this report are based on the U.S. Office of Management and Budget 1980 definition of a standard metropolitan statistical area. Under this definition, each SMSA must include one city with a population of 50,000 or more, or a city of at least 25,000 inhabitants which, with the addition of contiguous places having a population density of at least 1,000 persons per square mile, constitutes for general economic and social purposes a single community with a combined population of at least 50,000, provided that the county (or counties) in which the city and contiguous places are located has a total population of at least 100,000.

[5]For a consideration of compensation of local government managers and selected department heads on an individual basis, including information on the important element of fringe benefits, see *Compensation 84: An Annual Report on Local Government Salaries and Fringe Benefits,* another publication of ICMA's Municipal Data Service.

Table 1/4 SALARIES OF MUNICIPAL OFFICIALS: 1 JANUARY 1984

Salary data for the 26 selected municipal officials in this table are based on information reported by municipal officials as of 1 January 1984. Data are reported by position title only and, while representing similar job responsibilities, do not purport to represent identical duties and responsibilities.

For the position of city manager, data are shown for only those municipalities recognized by the International City Management Association as having the council-manager form of government; for the position of the chief administrative officer (CAO) data are shown for all other reporting municipalities.

Except for the position of mayor, which does include part-time salaries, this table excludes: (1) salaries of part-time officials, (2) salaries for vacant positions, (3) salaries of acting officials, (4) those paid in whole or in part by fees, and (5) all salaries below $8,000. All salaries for position of mayor below $100 are also excluded. Salaries are presented for 10 population groups and are further classified by geographic region, city type, and form of government. Cities under 2,500 population include only cities recognized by the International City Management Association as providing for positions of overall professional management.

Classifications having less than three cities reporting were excluded because meaningful statistics cannot be computed. Quartiles are not shown when only three cities reported.

Title of official	No. of cities reporting	Mean ($)	First quartile ($)	Median ($)	Third quartile ($)
		Distribution of 1984 salaries			
All Cities					
Mayor					
Total	4092	7,226	1,286	3,000	6,500
Geographic region					
Northeast	945	7,624	1,065	2,250	6,000
North Central	1393	7,323	1,443	3,000	7,000
South	1165	7,434	1,222	3,150	7,200
West	589	5,945	1,800	2,800	5,143
City type					
Central	338	22,467	4,800	16,016	37,563
All cities continued					
Suburban	2084	6,305	1,500	2,880	5,800
Independent	1670	5,290	1,200	2,400	5,400
Form of government					
Mayor-council	2209	9,672	1,800	3,600	12,000
Council-manager	1559	3,473	1,200	2,100	4,000
Commission	102	11,084	2,400	4,900	14,000
Town meeting	185	7,439	656	1,440	11,888
Rep. town meeting	37	7,591	1,400	1,800	3,750

Table 1/4 continued **SALARIES OF MUNICIPAL OFFICIALS: 1 JANUARY 1984**

Title of official	No. of cities reporting	Distribution of 1984 salaries: Mean ($)	First quartile ($)	Median ($)	Third quartile ($)
All cities continued					
City manager					
Total	2071	40,609	30,519	39,000	49,229
Geographic region					
Northeast	373	32,727	24,110	31,668	40,327
North Central	479	40,514	32,019	39,468	47,076
South	713	38,375	28,850	36,210	45,723
West	506	49,657	39,474	49,499	58,104
City type					
Central	214	56,492	46,645	55,000	64,478
Suburban	1045	43,285	33,943	42,000	51,498
Independent	812	32,979	26,000	32,330	39,500
Form of government					
Mayor-council	4	31,334	19,200	30,817	33,200
Council-manager	1994	41,136	31,161	39,536	49,537
Town meeting	64	22,974	16,200	20,055	29,349
Rep. town meeting	8	38,999	28,000	39,700	44,000
Chief administrative officer					
Total	1185	31,573	24,247	30,030	37,990
Geographic region					
Northeast	345	30,926	22,822	30,100	37,760
North Central	366	32,371	25,440	31,186	38,970
South	304	28,964	21,000	27,497	34,020
West	170	35,831	27,973	33,371	40,693
City type					
Central	62	49,482	39,326	47,857	56,298
Suburban	718	31,945	25,446	31,187	38,356
Independent	405	28,171	22,410	27,375	33,128
Form of government					
Mayor-council	1012	31,891	25,000	30,459	38,093
Council-manager	67	31,163	26,175	29,000	35,000
Commission	29	33,120	25,700	31,292	40,000
Town meeting	54	26,407	18,960	23,329	34,003
Rep. town meeting	23	28,910	19,836	26,658	37,654
City clerk					
Total	3511	21,409	15,900	20,010	25,428
Geographic region					
Northeast	792	20,651	15,204	19,551	24,617
North Central	1015	21,010	16,000	20,000	24,913
South	1161	20,043	15,000	18,526	23,387
West	543	26,185	19,720	25,024	31,526
City type					
Central	321	29,248	21,725	27,200	34,996
Suburban	1753	21,928	16,538	20,791	26,493
Independent	1437	19,026	14,616	18,000	22,357
Form of government					
Mayor-council	1784	20,172	15,000	19,000	24,180
Council-manager	1482	23,230	17,524	21,986	27,855
Commission	76	23,445	17,016	21,059	29,000
Town meeting	135	16,711	13,119	16,000	19,298
Rep. town meeting	34	21,048	15,763	21,305	24,287
Finance director					
Total	1680	32,822	25,000	32,000	39,816
Geographic region					
Northeast	253	29,943	22,914	29,500	35,167
North Central	435	32,529	25,788	32,500	38,754
South	533	30,294	22,033	28,800	36,536
West	459	37,623	29,997	36,982	44,862
City type					
Central	297	41,201	34,360	40,129	47,421
Suburban	924	32,829	25,500	32,151	39,811
Independent	459	27,387	21,294	27,000	32,465
Form of government					
Mayor-council	489	29,863	22,076	29,717	35,827
Council-manager	1120	34,318	26,190	34,029	41,580
Commission	26	31,461	23,445	32,076	37,068
Town meeting	32	25,380	19,500	24,957	29,603
Rep. town meeting	13	36,338	21,740	35,736	45,910
Controller					
Total	363	30,368	21,500	29,136	37,101
Geographic region					
Northeast	110	29,383	21,225	28,584	36,998
North Central	119	30,127	23,859	28,891	35,128
South	84	29,893	20,717	28,418	36,608
West	50	33,906	20,939	33,822	45,716
City type					
Central	113	36,664	28,263	35,465	43,755
Suburban	161	29,665	20,908	29,136	37,043
Independent	89	23,646	17,760	23,014	28,000
Form of government					
Mayor-council	178	30,674	21,500	29,176	36,973
Council-manager	149	31,015	23,592	29,765	37,988

Title of official	No. of cities reporting	Distribution of 1984 salaries: Mean ($)	First quartile ($)	Median ($)	Third quartile ($)
All cities continued					
Commission	13	29,189	21,625	29,584	31,073
Town meeting	18	21,368	14,396	19,440	28,274
Rep. town meeting	5	35,650	30,227	35,677	37,030
Auditor					
Total	335	26,668	19,058	24,440	32,862
Geographic region					
Northeast	122	23,260	17,662	23,053	26,927
North Central	103	24,795	17,631	23,472	30,817
South	82	30,950	22,687	28,365	38,142
West	28	35,862	24,132	36,286	43,788
City type					
Central	118	33,681	24,109	30,878	38,754
Suburban	134	24,385	17,050	24,203	31,083
Independent	83	20,381	16,509	20,268	23,496
Form of government					
Mayor-council	145	25,695	18,000	23,592	31,997
Council-manager	120	30,003	22,565	27,980	35,835
Commission	17	28,242	20,060	28,193	34,096
Town meeting	39	19,505	14,485	19,220	23,433
Rep. town meeting	14	26,194	22,288	26,870	29,477
Treasurer					
Total	1104	22,215	15,511	20,196	27,362
Geographic region					
Northeast	377	21,052	15,096	20,065	26,201
North Central	316	21,962	16,300	20,184	26,959
South	248	21,413	14,332	18,817	25,974
West	163	26,620	17,940	24,200	33,399
City type					
Central	155	32,970	25,961	31,732	38,801
Suburban	563	22,150	16,300	20,900	27,146
Independent	386	17,991	13,475	17,000	20,928
Form of government					
Mayor-council	516	21,130	15,000	19,021	25,730
Council-manager	475	23,839	17,123	22,249	29,301
Commission	27	24,558	17,298	22,110	32,176
Town meeting	64	17,651	12,480	16,927	21,850
Rep. town meeting	22	23,006	15,506	22,994	27,998
City engineer					
Total	1280	34,452	29,114	33,967	39,500
Geographic region					
Northeast	266	32,059	27,359	31,923	37,558
North Central	390	34,116	29,786	34,304	38,383
South	347	32,670	26,684	32,620	37,598
West	277	39,456	32,416	38,556	44,872
City type					
Central	287	38,458	32,765	37,805	42,880
Suburban	563	35,411	30,328	34,866	40,472
Independent	430	30,524	25,228	30,339	35,060
Form of government					
Mayor-council	490	32,573	27,401	32,270	37,903
Council-manager	697	36,075	30,056	35,364	41,616
Commission	41	34,318	30,708	34,031	38,424
Town meeting	33	29,378	25,240	30,000	33,227
Rep. town meeting	19	32,492	30,394	32,809	35,002
Director of public works					
Total	3112	30,004	22,000	28,000	36,129
Geographic region					
Northeast	595	28,740	22,287	28,052	33,485
North Central	936	30,187	23,150	28,764	35,945
South	995	26,427	18,939	24,132	31,475
West	586	37,066	26,628	35,490	45,942
City type					
Central	311	42,532	34,252	41,558	49,095
Suburban	1643	31,065	23,264	29,539	37,411
Independent	1158	25,134	19,366	23,862	29,465
Form of government					
Mayor-council	1399	27,398	20,801	26,112	32,541
Council-manager	1536	32,571	23,500	30,797	40,308
Commission	54	30,766	22,953	30,006	37,000
Town meeting	89	25,064	18,436	23,760	30,472
Rep. town meeting	34	32,976	23,513	32,757	40,943
Superintendent of streets					
Total	2918	23,484	18,212	22,297	27,400
Geographic region					
Northeast	625	23,289	19,104	22,750	26,835
North Central	991	23,663	18,889	22,894	27,462
South	900	20,678	15,891	19,374	23,839
West	402	29,633	23,124	28,620	34,806
City type					
Central	306	30,852	24,750	29,670	34,933
Suburban	1382	24,783	19,685	24,381	28,860

Table 1/4 continued **SALARIES OF MUNICIPAL OFFICIALS: 1 JANUARY 1984**

Title of official	No. of cities reporting	Distribution of 1984 salaries: Mean ($)	First quartile ($)	Median ($)	Third quartile ($)
All cities continued					
Independent	1230	20,193	16,588	19,500	23,005
Form of government					
Mayor-council	1451	21,913	17,369	21,000	25,500
Council-manager	1258	25,323	19,438	24,147	29,921
Commission	78	24,814	19,526	23,775	29,187
Town meeting	105	21,677	17,891	21,000	24,440
Rep. town meeting	26	25,502	19,174	25,086	29,981
Fire chief					
Total	2197	30,380	22,448	28,886	36,553
Geographic region					
Northeast	330	31,360	24,562	30,135	37,154
North Central	651	30,189	24,189	29,732	35,967
South	798	26,102	18,930	24,226	30,783
West	418	38,071	29,316	37,050	46,506
City type					
Central	362	39,262	31,699	37,373	44,400
Suburban	1000	32,400	24,750	31,500	39,276
Independent	835	24,110	19,000	23,438	28,238
Form of government					
Mayor-council	900	27,656	20,224	25,795	33,400
Council-manager	1137	32,615	24,607	30,992	39,795
Commission	65	28,912	21,327	26,960	33,744
Town meeting	65	29,037	23,175	28,658	33,439
Rep. town meeting	30	33,477	24,800	34,950	39,544
Police chief					
Total	4648	28,516	20,928	26,521	34,452
Geographic region					
Northeast	1018	28,956	22,510	28,000	34,575
North Central	1472	27,778	21,200	26,467	33,500
South	1442	24,969	18,197	22,447	29,737
West	716	36,550	26,880	34,266	44,580
City type					
Central	375	44,413	33,452	40,147	46,922
Suburban	2375	39,680	23,500	29,500	36,473
Independent	1898	23,260	18,482	22,035	26,790
Form of government					
Mayor-council	2348	25,860	19,454	24,000	31,054
Council-manager	2003	31,662	23,167	29,856	38,546
Commission	107	28,164	20,950	26,685	34,127
Town meeting	148	27,295	22,162	27,024	33,062
Rep. town meeting	42	32,155	22,855	32,023	41,328
Planning director					
Total	1356	32,731	25,143	31,636	39,060
Geographic region					
Northeast	232	28,777	23,112	27,771	33,860
North Central	324	31,376	25,610	30,472	37,180
South	358	30,666	22,900	29,555	36,721
West	442	37,472	29,929	37,386	43,860
City type					
Central	312	38,086	30,208	36,398	44,000
Suburban	690	33,565	26,039	33,026	40,186
Independent	354	26,385	21,206	26,009	30,950
Form of government					
Mayor-council	417	29,745	23,000	28,620	34,968
Council-manager	865	34,558	27,047	34,000	40,946
Commission	35	29,706	24,000	28,660	33,606
Town meeting	20	24,485	18,200	23,258	29,499
Rep. town meeting	19	29,359	22,868	28,067	30,670
Chief personnel officer					
Total	925	30,432	22,139	29,004	37,496
Geographic region					
Northeast	119	28,165	21,894	26,290	32,627
North Central	201	30,511	23,836	30,659	35,952
South	365	27,259	19,570	25,356	33,112
West	240	36,317	29,286	36,612	42,075
City type					
Central	309	35,428	28,002	34,200	40,915
Suburban	409	30,475	23,080	29,239	37,496
Independent	207	22,891	18,092	21,726	27,128
Form of government					
Mayor-council	290	28,034	19,984	26,345	33,830
Council-manager	597	31,746	23,641	31,164	38,663
Commission	23	27,956	20,635	27,144	31,473
Town meeting	5	25,645	19,285	24,489	26,003
Rep. town meeting	10	29,683	20,531	24,173	35,504
Attorney					
Total	906	35,429	22,295	35,000	47,000
Geographic region					
Northeast	165	28,870	20,110	27,500	36,256
North Central	283	30,453	18,032	29,500	40,271
South	214	38,294	23,994	39,948	50,535

Title of official	No. of cities reporting	Distribution of 1984 salaries: Mean ($)	First quartile ($)	Median ($)	Third quartile ($)
All cities continued					
West	244	43,123	32,000	44,924	55,980
City type					
Central	281	44,799	35,447	44,772	54,238
Suburban	372	35,271	22,084	34,179	47,469
Independent	253	25,254	15,000	23,358	33,993
Form of government					
Mayor-council	403	28,434	16,950	25,920	37,292
Council-manager	468	41,897	31,669	42,189	52,196
Commission	24	30,782	19,200	30,637	37,704
Town meeting	7	24,456	13,875	25,938	29,707
Rep. town meeting	4	30,498	18,285	31,354	32,001
Health officer					
Total	421	30,380	20,828	27,153	35,259
Geographic region					
Northeast	216	27,097	20,013	25,996	33,074
North Central	120	31,640	22,932	28,196	35,604
South	70	35,434	19,308	28,638	50,582
West	15	43,986	23,003	30,492	62,780
City type					
Central	117	41,740	28,225	35,604	55,290
Suburban	220	27,767	21,464	26,812	33,200
Independent	84	21,401	16,993	20,000	24,096
Form of government					
Mayor-council	185	30,547	21,206	27,229	35,790
Council-manager	172	31,869	21,492	29,580	36,120
Commission	17	29,718	19,128	23,360	31,665
Town meeting	28	22,229	17,485	21,426	26,120
Rep. town meeting	19	27,881	20,453	25,462	30,346
Director of parks and recreation					
Total	1507	27,998	19,790	26,282	34,503
Geographic region					
Northeast	251	24,588	18,575	24,750	29,272
North Central	420	26,827	19,843	25,223	32,427
South	518	25,997	17,749	23,802	31,361
West	318	35,497	27,264	35,358	43,290
City type					
Central	265	37,168	29,894	36,414	43,884
Suburban	744	28,416	21,000	26,811	34,869
Independent	498	22,495	17,115	21,300	27,084
Form of government					
Mayor-council	598	24,197	17,292	22,314	29,920
Council-manager	825	31,134	23,059	29,616	38,235
Commission	33	27,968	20,250	25,854	31,651
Town meeting	37	20,340	15,304	21,330	24,842
Rep. town meeting	14	25,898	16,875	25,204	30,565
Superintendent of parks					
Total	1062	24,461	18,894	23,140	29,126
Geographic region					
Northeast	163	24,335	20,156	23,376	27,307
North Central	334	22,836	17,641	21,705	27,029
South	311	22,436	17,648	21,000	25,840
West	254	29,160	22,858	28,835	34,791
City type					
Central	235	30,095	23,732	29,017	34,932
Suburban	458	25,184	19,772	24,261	29,909
Independent	369	19,977	16,336	19,687	22,841
Form of government					
Mayor-council	401	22,878	17,469	22,000	26,030
Council-manager	598	25,723	20,000	24,382	30,383
Commission	34	21,750	16,913	21,493	23,714
Town meeting	18	21,617	17,658	21,018	23,452
Rep. town meeting	11	26,634	22,069	27,034	29,670
Director of recreation					
Total	971	24,841	17,928	23,296	30,430
Geographic region					
Northeast	222	22,402	16,447	21,384	27,152
North Central	246	23,087	17,273	21,808	27,762
South	282	23,066	17,035	21,461	27,655
West	221	31,507	24,089	31,500	37,587
City type					
Central	209	29,596	23,595	29,300	34,533
Suburban	476	25,854	18,866	24,962	31,692
Independent	286	19,679	15,500	18,386	22,979
Form of government					
Mayor-council	340	22,490	16,464	21,354	26,896
Council-manager	552	26,744	19,212	25,684	33,120
Commission	31	22,612	17,819	21,880	25,195
Town meeting	33	19,217	14,760	17,175	24,643
Rep. town meeting	15	25,068	18,757	24,847	28,408
Librarian					
Total	1387	23,401	15,483	21,050	29,035

Table 1/4 continued SALARIES OF MUNICIPAL OFFICIALS: 1 JANUARY 1984

Title of official	No. of cities reporting	Mean ($)	First quartile ($)	Median ($)	Third quartile ($)
		Distribution of 1984 salaries			
All cities continued					
Geographic region					
Northeast	365	22,565	16,630	21,325	27,448
North Central	405	21,329	14,866	19,496	26,259
South	325	22,079	12,985	20,022	27,163
West	292	28,789	17,712	26,532	39,270
City type					
Central	181	35,293	27,122	33,940	40,780
Suburban	679	24,482	16,833	22,675	30,019
Independent	527	17,924	12,604	16,900	21,525
Form of government					
Mayor-council	539	20,583	13,419	18,168	25,001
Council-manager	697	26,062	17,493	24,180	33,485
Commission	41	21,567	17,585	20,030	24,385
Town meeting	78	19,711	15,061	19,002	23,863
Rep. town meeting	32	24,245	17,919	25,007	27,990
Superintendent of schools					
Total	327	45,663	38,706	45,000	52,000
Geographic region					
Northeast	252	44,757	38,500	45,000	50,500
North Central	23	51,573	44,582	49,704	57,216
South	46	45,840	35,310	41,865	57,136
West	6	59,659	38,441	64,838	70,250
City type					
Central	46	53,791	45,000	52,177	60,000
Suburban	181	46,608	40,000	47,000	52,915
Independent	100	40,213	34,996	39,824	44,742
Form of government					
Mayor-council	98	47,536	40,000	47,276	54,000
Council-manager	124	46,037	38,500	45,000	51,000
Commission	7	49,607	40,261	50,865	53,900
Town meeting	81	41,661	35,625	42,135	47,261
Rep. town meeting	17	49,576	44,704	51,000	56,025
Director of data processing					
Total	609	31,537	23,693	31,304	37,892
Geographic region					
Northeast	104	29,350	24,503	28,639	33,878
North Central	139	30,649	23,005	31,000	36,751
South	235	30,084	21,426	29,711	37,375
West	131	36,822	30,255	35,797	42,996
City type					
Central	252	35,951	29,403	34,837	40,968
Suburban	216	31,973	25,440	32,725	38,142
Independent	141	22,981	16,842	22,148	27,116
Form of government					
Mayor-council	178	30,569	22,809	29,619	36,617
Council-manager	389	32,238	24,384	32,320	38,958
Commission	21	30,364	23,513	29,508	34,042
Town meeting	12	23,595	19,000	23,594	28,300
Rep. town meeting	9	33,702	28,534	33,878	36,838
Director of budget and research					
Total	178	36,336	28,110	34,274	44,351
Geographic region					
Northeast	35	31,143	24,660	32,175	34,901
North Central	35	36,415	26,979	34,287	45,075
South	73	37,369	28,622	35,745	43,597
West	35	39,294	30,408	37,462	46,998
City type					
Central	116	38,776	30,784	36,718	45,300
Suburban	47	34,774	25,578	33,580	43,865
Independent	15	22,357	14,750	22,605	24,700
Form of government					
Mayor-council	60	35,408	29,794	34,157	43,004
Council-manager	110	37,199	27,474	36,215	44,966
Commission	6	32,237	21,508	30,228	34,049
Rep. town meeting	2	28,967	...	28,967	...
Asst. city mgr./asst. CAO					
Total	984	32,080	22,308	29,630	40,500
Geographic region					
Northeast	195	23,706	18,826	23,000	27,117
North Central	244	30,371	23,682	28,859	35,395
South	319	31,792	21,701	30,016	40,224
West	226	41,558	31,434	41,872	49,924
City type					
Central	192	42,756	32,469	41,044	51,238
Suburban	568	31,422	22,524	29,418	39,728
Independent	224	24,599	18,200	23,520	29,516
Form of government					
Mayor-council	224	26,039	18,900	24,000	31,000
Council-manager	714	34,752	24,717	32,908	43,123
Commission	9	22,844	18,241	22,000	23,550

Title of official	No. of cities reporting	Mean ($)	First quartile ($)	Median ($)	Third quartile ($)
		Distribution of 1984 salaries			
All cities continued					
Town meeting	31	18,795	13,410	17,550	23,760
Rep. town meeting	6	22,209	14,625	24,051	25,447
Chief building inspector					
Total	2366	24,852	19,113	23,716	29,100
Geographic region					
Northeast	553	23,459	19,084	22,950	26,975
North Central	657	25,297	20,556	24,750	29,579
South	708	22,176	17,056	20,524	25,740
West	448	30,148	23,520	28,686	35,343
City type					
Central	327	31,303	24,296	30,014	36,154
Suburban	1291	25,633	20,479	25,008	30,038
Independent	748	20,685	16,870	19,989	23,616
Form of government					
Mayor-council	911	23,560	18,410	22,922	27,186
Council-manager	1276	26,069	20,020	24,730	31,020
Commission	59	23,713	18,559	21,677	27,993
Town meeting	88	21,358	17,811	20,851	24,000
Rep. town meeting	32	24,830	19,690	25,024	28,710
Over 1,000,000					
Mayor					
Total	4	72,030	60,000	73,433	76,865
City type					
Central	4	72,030	60,000	73,433	76,865
Form of government					
Mayor-council	4	72,030	60,000	73,433	76,865
Chief administrative officer					
Total	3	77,426	...	73,000	...
City type					
Central	3	77,426	...	73,000	...
Form of government					
Mayor-council	3	77,426	...	73,000	...
City clerk					
Total	3	53,967	...	48,069	...
City type					
Central	3	53,967	...	48,069	...
Form of government					
Mayor-council	3	53,967	...	48,069	...
Controller					
Total	4	57,455	46,119	56,850	63,700
City type					
Central	4	57,455	46,119	56,850	63,700
Form of government					
Mayor-council	4	57,455	46,119	56,850	63,700
Treasurer					
Total	3	57,648	...	55,000	...
City type					
Central	3	57,648	...	55,000	...
Form of government					
Mayor-council	3	57,648	...	55,000	...
City engineer					
Total	3	67,883	...	60,000	...
City type					
Central	3	67,883	...	60,000	...
Form of government					
Mayor-council	3	67,883	...	60,000	...
Director of public works					
Total	3	70,106	...	72,000	...
City type					
Central	3	70,106	...	72,000	...
Form of government					
Mayor-council	3	70,106	...	72,000	...
Superintendent of streets					
Total	4	59,141	51,360	53,630	55,000
City type					
Central	4	59,141	51,360	53,630	55,000
Form of government					
Mayor-council	4	59,141	51,360	53,630	55,000
Fire chief					
Total	4	75,482	55,000	75,492	76,000
City type					
Central	4	75,482	55,000	75,492	76,000
Form of government					
Mayor-council	4	75,482	55,000	75,492	76,000
Police chief					
Total	4	79,238	55,000	77,492	80,000
City type					

Table 1/4 continued **SALARIES OF MUNICIPAL OFFICIALS: 1 JANUARY 1984**

Title of official	No. of cities reporting	Distribution of 1984 salaries: Mean ($)	First quartile ($)	Median ($)	Third quartile ($)
Over 1,000,000 continued					
Central	4	79,238	55,000	77,492	80,000
Form of government					
Mayor-council	4	79,238	55,000	77,492	80,000
Planning director					
Total	3	58,117	...	60,000	...
City type					
Central	3	58,117	...	60,000	...
Form of government					
Mayor-council	3	58,117	...	60,000	...
Chief personnel officer					
Total	3	58,371	...	62,112	...
City type					
Central	3	58,371	...	62,112	...
Form of government					
Mayor-council	3	58,371	...	62,112	...
Attorney					
Total	3	76,925	...	85,000	...
City type					
Central	3	76,925	...	85,000	...
Form of government					
Mayor-council	3	76,925	...	85,000	...
Health officer					
Total	3	67,198	...	72,000	...
City type					
Central	3	67,198	...	72,000	...
Form of government					
Mayor-council	3	67,198	...	72,000	...
Librarian					
Total	4	64,673	49,896	65,426	67,852
City type					
Central	4	64,673	49,896	65,426	67,852
Form of government					
Mayor-council	4	64,673	49,896	65,426	67,852
Director of data processing					
Total	4	57,969	49,234	56,399	60,000
City type					
Central	4	57,969	49,234	56,399	60,000
Form of government					
Mayor-council	4	57,969	49,234	56,399	60,000
Chief building inspector					
Total	3	59,593	...	58,000	...
City type					
Central	3	59,593	...	58,000	...
Form of government					
Mayor-council	3	59,593	...	58,000	...
500,000–1,000,000					
Mayor					
Total	15	54,060	40,875	58,964	66,681
Geographic region					
North Central	4	61,086	57,881	59,482	60,000
South	7	47,337	3,680	57,185	63,976
West	4	58,799	37,500	54,204	66,408
City type					
Central	15	54,060	40,875	58,964	66,681
Form of government					
Mayor-council	11	65,887	57,707	60,000	69,601
Council-manager	4	21,535	2,600	20,770	37,500
City manager					
Total	4	87,216	83,448	85,088	86,165
City type					
Central	4	87,216	83,448	85,088	86,165
Form of government					
Council-manager	4	87,216	83,448	85,088	86,165
Chief administrative officer					
Total	7	63,033	50,765	60,372	69,957
Geographic region					
South	4	61,781	52,497	61,800	69,600
City type					
Central	7	63,033	50,765	60,372	69,957
Form of government					
Mayor-council	7	63,033	50,765	60,372	69,957
City clerk					
Total	13	49,084	39,905	52,000	54,777
Geographic region					
North Central	4	40,199	23,364	44,554	46,883
South	5	48,214	33,629	52,000	53,833
West	4	59,058	52,140	56,471	58,053
City type					

Title of official	No. of cities reporting	Distribution of 1984 salaries: Mean ($)	First quartile ($)	Median ($)	Third quartile ($)
500,000–1,000,000 continued					
Central	13	49,084	39,905	52,000	54,777
Form of government					
Mayor-council	9	46,829	33,629	46,883	53,247
Council-manager	4	54,159	52,000	53,292	54,444
Finance director					
Total	11	55,639	45,991	54,888	63,084
Geographic region					
South	7	57,529	46,563	55,484	63,796
City type					
Central	11	55,639	45,991	54,888	63,084
Form of government					
Mayor-council	8	53,698	45,364	48,742	54,888
Council-manager	3	60,815	...	62,878	...
Controller					
Total	13	47,895	37,013	45,000	51,142
Geographic region					
North Central	3	48,430	...	50,000	...
South	7	44,137	34,699	44,784	45,750
West	3	56,129	...	51,522	...
City type					
Central	13	47,895	37,013	45,000	51,142
Form of government					
Mayor-council	10	47,833	34,758	43,272	53,267
Council-manager	3	48,102	...	48,000	...
Auditor					
Total	14	47,742	37,128	47,194	55,975
Geographic region					
North Central	4	39,818	30,017	37,128	38,192
South	7	49,956	36,630	50,600	56,613
West	3	53,143	...	56,950	...
City type					
Central	14	47,742	37,128	47,194	55,975
Form of government					
Mayor-council	10	44,092	33,386	41,196	52,425
Council-manager	4	56,868	38,688	57,821	58,692
Treasurer					
Total	13	46,336	38,017	44,221	52,473
Geographic region					
North Central	3	45,929	...	42,224	...
South	6	43,133	31,800	39,150	46,910
West	4	51,446	44,221	48,678	50,292
City type					
Central	13	46,336	38,017	44,221	52,473
Form of government					
Mayor-council	10	47,046	35,640	46,258	54,867
Council-manager	3	43,968	...	44,221	...
City engineer					
Total	12	51,561	38,272	47,532	63,592
Geographic region					
North Central	4	44,156	35,730	38,651	39,029
South	4	51,002	37,805	45,395	47,040
West	4	59,525	48,024	58,967	64,314
City type					
Central	12	51,561	38,272	47,532	63,592
Form of government					
Mayor-council	8	47,293	37,805	41,390	48,024
Council-manager	4	60,097	47,040	58,967	64,314
Director of public works					
Total	14	58,425	45,807	56,694	65,203
Geographic region					
North Central	4	48,197	42,500	44,571	45,614
South	6	60,779	48,498	61,100	66,882
West	4	65,121	52,889	60,797	66,706
City type					
Central	14	58,425	45,807	56,694	65,203
Form of government					
Mayor-council	10	55,287	44,571	52,942	59,823
Council-manager	4	66,268	52,889	68,385	70,064
Superintendent of streets					
Total	12	44,356	32,703	44,340	46,202
Geographic region					
South	6	44,739	31,862	37,064	44,492
West	4	46,234	43,788	45,480	46,067
City type					
Central	12	44,356	32,703	44,340	46,202
Form of government					
Mayor-council	8	40,659	32,703	41,144	46,067
Council-manager	4	51,750	31,824	47,541	50,190
Fire chief					
Total	15	57,772	49,825	56,543	63,592

Table 1/4 continued **SALARIES OF MUNICIPAL OFFICIALS: 1 JANUARY 1984**

Title of official	No. of cities reporting	Distribution of 1984 salaries: Mean ($)	First quartile ($)	Median ($)	Third quartile ($)
500,000–1,000,000 continued					
Geographic region					
South	5	42,669	33,478	37,680	41,415
City type					
Central	9	41,125	32,776	37,000	41,415
Form of government					
Mayor-council	8	40,933	32,676	36,555	37,680
Librarian					
Total	11	54,401	47,877	51,857	55,708
Geographic region					
South	6	55,848	46,838	52,451	58,372
West	4	53,265	45,492	50,415	52,158
City type					
Central	11	54,401	47,877	51,857	55,708
Form of government					
Mayor-council	7	53,272	44,713	51,300	55,708
Council-manager	4	56,375	48,672	52,008	52,158
Superintendent of schools					
Total	3	74,964	...	78,630	...
Geographic region					
South	3	74,964	...	78,630	...
City type					
Central	3	74,964	...	78,630	...
Form of government					
Mayor-council	3	74,964	...	78,630	...
Director of data processing					
Total	12	52,760	43,620	52,009	56,950
Geographic region					
North Central	3	46,898	...	48,325	...
South	6	50,616	40,215	47,461	56,811
West	3	62,910	...	56,950	...
City type					
Central	12	52,760	43,620	52,009	56,950
Form of government					
Mayor-council	9	51,289	39,609	48,325	54,690
Council-manager	3	57,173	...	56,950	...
Director of budget and research					
Total	12	51,720	43,050	54,644	58,440
Geographic region					
South	7	50,642	36,162	54,400	59,277
West	3	55,521	...	54,888	...
City type					
Central	12	51,720	43,050	54,644	58,440
Form of government					
Mayor-council	8	49,964	37,975	54,644	56,533
Council-manager	4	55,232	47,465	55,157	61,788
Asst. city mgr./asst. CAO					
Total	9	62,523	47,168	60,265	69,157
Geographic region					
South	4	63,239	38,500	63,176	70,696
West	4	66,354	57,348	62,403	64,540
City type					
Central	9	62,523	47,168	60,265	69,157
Form of government					
Mayor-council	5	51,222	39,960	55,656	56,925
Council-manager	4	76,651	64,540	76,979	83,262
Chief building inspector					
Total	13	48,148	35,257	50,000	56,780
Geographic region					
North Central	3	39,849	...	39,029	...
South	6	46,854	32,882	47,250	53,580
West	4	56,312	48,024	54,265	55,640
City type					
Central	13	48,148	35,257	50,000	56,780
Form of government					
Mayor-council	9	45,581	32,323	44,500	57,866
Council-manager	4	53,922	50,000	54,265	55,640
Geographic region					
North Central	4	51,656	38,945	52,049	52,498
South	7	57,624	43,875	57,200	62,676
West	4	64,149	54,888	60,085	63,627
City type					
Central	15	57,772	49,825	56,543	63,592
Form of government					
Mayor-council	11	55,100	43,875	54,888	58,795
Council-manager	4	65,121	56,543	62,981	63,627
Police chief					
Total	15	60,162	52,041	58,440	64,654
Geographic region					
North Central	4	52,481	37,245	52,582	53,563
South	7	60,191	51,891	58,440	62,676

Title of official	No. of cities reporting	Distribution of 1984 salaries: Mean ($)	First quartile ($)	Median ($)	Third quartile ($)
500,000–1,000,000 continued					
West	4	67,792	54,888	67,372	74,568
City type					
Central	15	60,162	52,041	58,440	64,654
Form of government					
Mayor-council	11	57,252	51,450	54,888	59,755
Council-manager	4	68,164	60,176	68,451	74,568
Planning director					
Total	13	56,136	40,975	60,156	63,354
Geographic region					
North Central	3	46,507	...	36,750	...
South	6	56,242	42,950	54,927	62,735
West	4	63,198	54,888	61,237	62,317
City type					
Central	13	56,136	40,975	60,156	63,354
Form of government					
Mayor-council	9	51,947	37,313	48,084	61,497
Council-manager	4	65,561	60,156	62,044	62,317
Chief personnel officer					
Total	14	51,996	42,272	51,192	59,520
Geographic region					
North Central	4	43,281	38,325	42,272	44,339
South	6	51,841	43,071	51,192	55,362
West	4	60,942	54,888	60,562	60,907
City type					
Central	14	51,996	42,272	51,192	59,520
Form of government					
Mayor-council	11	49,818	40,188	50,257	52,647
Council-manager	3	59,982	...	60,216	...
Attorney					
Total	15	60,574	52,128	58,750	66,038
Geographic region					
North Central	4	53,613	46,359	52,250	55,000
South	7	59,495	51,003	58,750	61,310
West	4	69,424	54,888	73,155	73,260
City type					
Central	15	60,574	52,128	58,750	66,038
Form of government					
Mayor-council	11	56,799	48,715	55,000	59,961
Council-manager	4	70,956	60,513	73,155	73,260
Health officer					
Total	10	59,044	45,026	60,552	64,550
Geographic region					
North Central	3	50,963	...	45,364	...
South	6	58,649	50,844	60,552	62,812
City type					
Central	10	59,044	45,026	60,552	64,550
Form of government					
Mayor-council	8	58,667	44,688	60,350	65,400
Director of parks and recreation					
Total	12	54,084	44,000	49,745	58,823
Geographic region					
North Central	3	44,401	...	45,500	...
South	5	54,584	43,550	46,600	55,767
West	4	60,723	52,889	60,797	66,706
City type					
Central	12	54,084	44,000	49,745	58,823
Form of government					
Mayor-council	8	48,812	43,400	45,535	46,600
Council-manager	4	64,628	52,889	62,765	66,706
Superintendent of parks					
Total	9	38,839	32,037	37,000	38,963
Geographic region					
South	4	35,472	31,824	35,250	37,000
West	3	45,943	...	52,686	...
City type					
Central	9	38,839	32,037	37,000	38,963
Form of government					
Mayor-council	7	37,863	32,063	37,000	37,761
Director of recreation					
Total	9	41,125	32,776	37,000	41,415
250,000–499,999					
Mayor					
Total	32	34,011	12,000	40,608	51,871
Geographic region					
Northeast	3	54,833	...	55,000	...
North Central	8	39,446	29,581	40,608	43,743
South	15	29,610	8,750	25,000	50,000
West	6	27,354	8,704	19,500	35,920

Table 1/4 continued **SALARIES OF MUNICIPAL OFFICIALS: 1 JANUARY 1984**

Title of official	No. of cities reporting	Distribution of 1984 salaries: Mean ($)	First quartile ($)	Median ($)	Third quartile ($)
250,000–499,999 continued					
City type					
Central	32	34,011	12,000	40,608	51,871
Form of government					
Mayor-council	16	50,450	47,840	52,186	55,000
Council-manager	15	15,677	7,325	12,000	19,682
City manager					
Total	15	77,563	71,137	75,001	79,396
Geographic region					
North Central	4	77,859	59,150	75,143	77,219
South	7	78,851	70,268	75,001	91,424
West	4	75,011	67,000	75,522	78,528
City type					
Central	15	77,563	71,137	75,001	79,396
Chief administrative officer					
Total	10	52,315	47,175	50,870	55,278
Geographic region					
South	5	50,058	44,528	49,356	52,506
City type					
Central	10	52,315	47,175	50,870	55,278
Form of government					
Mayor-council	10	52,315	47,175	50,870	55,278
City clerk					
Total	27	39,549	32,002	39,998	43,960
Geographic region					
Northeast	3	41,047	...	41,212	...
North Central	5	40,469	36,594	41,424	42,261
South	13	38,794	28,907	39,998	44,893
West	6	39,670	34,830	38,653	41,317
City type					
Central	27	39,549	32,002	39,998	43,960
Form of government					
Mayor-council	13	39,093	30,408	41,212	44,086
Council-manager	14	39,973	33,083	38,653	41,294
Finance director					
Total	30	52,985	47,301	53,406	56,613
Geographic region					
Northeast	3	45,883	...	44,669	...
North Central	7	56,463	49,269	57,186	61,503
South	13	52,051	45,662	54,558	55,680
West	7	54,283	51,189	53,460	54,150
City type					
Central	30	52,985	47,301	53,406	56,613
Form of government					
Mayor-council	14	50,685	43,837	52,381	54,371
Council-manager	14	56,389	52,455	55,791	57,882
Controller					
Total	14	46,564	40,280	46,685	47,655
Geographic region					
Northeast	3	41,043	...	37,129	...
North Central	4	49,502	40,600	47,355	47,993
South	6	47,240	42,438	46,094	46,834
City type					
Central	14	46,564	40,280	46,685	47,655
Form of government					
Mayor-council	8	46,636	37,129	46,865	47,993
Council-manager	6	46,468	40,280	45,785	46,985
Auditor					
Total	20	42,104	34,953	39,385	46,020
Geographic region					
South	12	39,640	33,165	35,348	44,096
West	5	49,741	40,508	49,496	53,252
City type					
Central	20	42,104	34,953	39,385	46,020
Form of government					
Mayor-council	7	38,810	31,017	40,498	44,456
Council-manager	11	44,942	34,506	38,272	53,468
Treasurer					
Total	21	40,905	36,198	40,104	46,300
Geographic region					
Northeast	3	33,825	...	29,611	...
North Central	5	39,565	36,198	39,600	39,978
South	8	40,214	30,339	40,698	43,740
West	5	47,600	40,868	47,486	50,149
City type					
Central	21	40,905	36,198	40,104	46,300
Form of government					
Mayor-council	10	38,407	29,296	41,494	43,372
Council-manager	10	43,596	36,265	42,596	49,507
City engineer					
Total	26	46,521	41,506	45,762	51,420

Title of official	No. of cities reporting	Distribution of 1984 salaries: Mean ($)	First quartile ($)	Median ($)	Third quartile ($)
250,000–499,999 continued					
Geographic region					
Northeast	3	39,118	...	37,919	...
North Central	6	48,281	40,465	49,683	53,325
South	12	45,556	41,864	44,937	48,999
West	5	51,168	43,211	50,190	54,236
City type					
Central	26	46,521	41,506	45,762	51,420
Form of government					
Mayor-council	13	44,002	38,246	44,669	49,306
Council-manager	11	47,711	41,685	45,989	53,639
Director of public works					
Total	27	55,656	48,817	55,726	61,383
Geographic region					
North Central	7	56,288	49,330	57,005	61,383
South	13	53,910	44,317	54,588	59,322
West	6	60,531	50,513	60,384	62,096
City type					
Central	27	55,656	48,817	55,726	61,383
Form of government					
Mayor-council	11	51,760	41,629	53,000	61,824
Council-manager	14	58,528	50,908	57,135	60,604
Superintendent of streets					
Total	26	41,164	35,857	41,822	44,520
Geographic region					
Northeast	3	34,746	...	36,708	...
North Central	7	44,014	41,230	42,420	44,410
South	13	40,775	34,510	41,386	44,250
West	3	42,619	...	46,904	...
City type					
Central	26	41,164	35,857	41,822	44,520
Form of government					
Mayor-council	13	39,336	32,587	41,386	44,129
Council-manager	12	42,806	38,392	42,320	44,495
Fire chief					
Total	33	51,087	43,634	49,632	56,681
Geographic region					
Northeast	3	43,549	...	43,106	...
North Central	8	50,711	45,134	50,757	52,500
South	15	49,557	40,322	47,148	54,168
West	7	58,023	50,999	57,456	61,179
City type					
Central	33	51,087	43,634	49,632	56,681
Form of government					
Mayor-council	16	47,901	40,360	48,678	52,500
Council-manager	15	53,799	45,131	51,881	58,308
Police chief					
Total	32	52,370	44,990	52,323	55,513
Geographic region					
Northeast	3	43,549	...	43,106	...
North Central	8	54,588	49,920	54,007	56,212
South	15	51,833	43,995	50,400	53,942
West	6	55,169	44,049	54,167	58,091
City type					
Central	32	52,370	44,990	52,323	55,513
Form of government					
Mayor-council	15	47,274	42,420	48,465	50,752
Council-manager	15	57,206	51,187	54,588	61,722
Planning director					
Total	29	50,052	43,277	49,176	55,508
Geographic region					
Northeast	3	42,210	...	45,938	...
North Central	7	49,987	42,705	49,639	52,453
South	12	49,052	42,024	47,835	54,021
West	7	55,194	45,495	53,460	59,352
City type					
Central	29	50,052	43,277	49,176	55,508
Form of government					
Mayor-council	14	45,752	38,859	44,627	48,115
Council-manager	14	54,624	48,138	53,136	58,979
Chief personnel officer					
Total	31	48,771	41,671	48,506	53,517
Geographic region					
Northeast	3	38,196	...	32,845	...
North Central	7	50,348	39,874	47,736	55,316
South	14	47,898	39,734	46,733	52,333
West	7	53,472	48,267	53,460	56,660
City type					
Central	31	48,771	41,671	48,506	53,517
Form of government					
Mayor-council	15	44,103	35,143	43,139	48,717

Table 1/4 continued **SALARIES OF MUNICIPAL OFFICIALS: 1 JANUARY 1984**

Title of official	No. of cities reporting	Distribution of 1984 salaries: Mean ($)	First quartile ($)	Median ($)	Third quartile ($)
250,000–499,999 continued					
Council-manager	14	53,508	46,733	52,333	56,738
Attorney					
Total	33	57,989	49,513	60,060	64,255
Geographic region					
Northeast	3	47,226	...	47,658	...
North Central	8	60,078	52,650	62,725	64,298
South	15	58,895	48,524	60,132	64,594
West	7	58,273	48,752	59,000	61,683
City type					
Central	33	57,989	49,513	60,060	64,255
Form of government					
Mayor-council	16	53,184	44,669	51,327	60,132
Council-manager	15	63,814	58,727	62,888	67,326
Health officer					
Total	12	69,732	57,304	67,780	76,399
Geographic region					
North Central	7	63,855	57,135	62,020	66,200
City type					
Central	12	69,732	57,304	67,780	76,399
Form of government					
Mayor-council	5	64,368	52,142	57,304	58,631
Council-manager	7	73,563	63,970	75,623	77,829
Director of parks and recreation					
Total	29	48,760	43,628	48,906	54,282
Geographic region					
Northeast	3	41,094	...	37,225	...
North Central	6	50,360	43,901	48,703	51,963
South	14	47,766	39,524	47,429	52,488
West	6	53,315	47,882	52,777	55,428
City type					
Central	29	48,760	43,628	48,906	54,282
Form of government					
Mayor-council	14	44,531	38,000	43,784	49,677
Council-manager	13	53,099	47,047	53,400	56,032
Superintendent of parks					
Total	27	40,570	33,023	39,964	45,729
Geographic region					
North Central	8	44,194	33,180	39,502	56,642
South	11	37,069	30,793	38,272	41,679
West	6	43,916	38,031	46,599	46,967
City type					
Central	27	40,570	33,023	39,964	45,729
Form of government					
Mayor-council	12	40,898	29,611	40,356	45,534
Council-manager	14	40,226	34,632	39,118	44,404
Director of recreation					
Total	23	38,927	34,703	37,919	41,751
Geographic region					
North Central	6	43,071	36,841	40,120	45,950
South	9	33,875	28,899	34,823	36,273
West	6	45,181	37,423	43,992	46,205
City type					
Central	23	38,927	34,703	37,919	41,751
Form of government					
Mayor-council	9	35,049	25,862	35,784	37,786
Council-manager	13	41,578	35,677	38,780	42,333
Librarian					
Total	19	45,880	38,582	48,960	52,859
Geographic region					
North Central	4	52,238	40,000	54,537	59,073
South	9	39,061	31,595	39,127	45,177
West	6	51,870	48,733	51,960	53,376
City type					
Central	19	45,880	38,582	48,960	52,859
Form of government					
Mayor-council	10	42,462	31,596	40,154	52,045
Council-manager	9	49,678	47,340	51,420	52,448
Superintendent of schools					
Total	3	63,868	...	66,150	...
City type					
Central	3	63,868	...	66,150	...
Director of data processing					
Total	29	46,457	41,102	46,634	49,860
Geographic region					
North Central	6	45,582	37,710	47,245	49,916
South	14	46,302	39,191	45,494	47,921
West	7	50,364	47,344	48,600	50,565
City type					
Central	29	46,457	41,102	46,634	49,860

Title of official	No. of cities reporting	Distribution of 1984 salaries: Mean ($)	First quartile ($)	Median ($)	Third quartile ($)
250,000–499,999 continued					
Form of government					
Mayor-council	13	43,329	37,534	44,096	47,656
Council-manager	14	48,673	44,268	48,090	50,459
Director of budget and research					
Total	26	43,497	35,173	41,802	49,570
Geographic region					
Northeast	3	35,317	...	34,133	...
North Central	6	45,837	36,292	45,370	52,040
South	14	43,092	35,173	41,686	47,588
West	3	48,887	...	47,375	...
City type					
Central	26	43,497	35,173	41,802	49,570
Form of government					
Mayor-council	12	39,190	32,393	37,008	43,004
Council-manager	13	46,649	40,065	46,176	49,855
Asst. city mgr./asst. CAO					
Total	23	53,688	44,008	56,640	62,099
Geographic region					
North Central	6	58,195	51,810	60,366	61,632
South	11	50,614	37,861	54,021	58,802
West	4	61,200	56,640	62,201	62,604
City type					
Central	23	53,688	44,008	56,640	62,099
Form of government					
Mayor-council	9	44,375	35,958	42,024	53,167
Council-manager	14	59,675	55,209	60,598	63,322
Chief building inspector					
Total	28	41,271	35,472	39,917	46,800
Geographic region					
Northeast	3	33,082	...	32,393	...
North Central	7	45,936	35,847	45,259	53,462
South	12	37,765	29,442	38,220	41,386
West	6	46,936	39,048	46,258	50,189
City type					
Central	28	41,271	35,472	39,917	46,800
Form of government					
Mayor-council	13	38,411	29,669	37,919	44,291
Council-manager	13	43,644	37,131	42,624	51,197
100,000–249,999					
Mayor					
Total	96	25,592	8,800	24,750	42,500
Geographic region					
Northeast	15	38,876	29,875	43,200	47,750
North Central	21	33,825	21,260	38,485	43,132
South	34	23,404	8,600	13,750	41,250
West	26	14,141	3,600	8,210	23,186
City type					
Central	72	28,600	10,000	29,750	43,343
Suburban	24	16,571	3,600	8,750	16,356
Form of government					
Mayor-council	36	44,201	39,922	43,616	49,780
Council-manager	55	12,126	6,900	9,000	16,642
Commission	5	39,738	29,574	37,500	43,125
City manager					
Total	61	66,125	57,864	65,202	72,078
Geographic region					
Northeast	4	60,503	52,181	62,416	65,000
North Central	7	58,089	52,703	55,302	58,206
South	24	65,141	58,132	65,000	71,115
West	26	70,062	64,848	69,961	77,551
City type					
Central	41	64,232	56,639	64,498	70,260
Suburban	20	70,005	65,000	70,504	73,850
Form of government					
Council-manager	61	66,125	57,864	65,202	72,078
Chief administrative officer					
Total	14	52,197	42,500	51,768	59,584
Geographic region					
Northeast	4	42,471	33,000	40,645	41,000
North Central	3	52,307	...	48,000	...
South	5	57,649	44,834	59,000	63,890
City type					
Central	12	51,506	44,000	51,768	59,000
Form of government					
Mayor-council	12	50,236	41,000	47,669	59,000
City clerk					
Total	95	32,572	25,776	32,700	38,244

Table 1/4 continued **SALARIES OF MUNICIPAL OFFICIALS: 1 JANUARY 1984**

Title of official	No. of cities reporting	Distribution of 1984 salaries: Mean ($)	First quartile ($)	Median ($)	Third quartile ($)
100,000–249,999 continued					
Geographic region					
Northeast	15	30,554	23,364	32,700	35,088
North Central	22	32,311	24,967	30,875	39,292
South	34	30,281	23,993	29,014	34,904
West	24	37,318	34,200	36,953	40,000
City type					
Central	73	31,573	24,793	31,824	37,101
Suburban	22	35,886	29,296	35,883	39,550
Form of government					
Mayor-council	34	30,889	24,825	29,787	35,900
Council-manager	57	33,737	26,820	34,308	38,810
Commission	4	30,276	25,032	31,056	31,824
Finance director					
Total	82	47,274	41,477	47,341	53,538
Geographic region					
Northeast	10	42,600	34,550	41,463	52,091
North Central	14	42,221	36,126	44,610	46,999
South	31	46,450	39,941	47,182	52,094
West	27	52,570	46,389	54,228	56,284
City type					
Central	60	46,158	40,740	46,919	52,182
Suburban	22	50,318	44,264	52,901	54,971
Form of government					
Mayor-council	23	40,332	35,437	41,673	45,505
Council-manager	57	50,380	45,246	52,182	54,882
Controller					
Total	33	37,382	31,182	35,812	43,755
Geographic region					
Northeast	8	33,319	24,000	31,484	43,697
North Central	12	37,882	31,236	35,151	42,214
South	8	37,909	31,741	36,304	39,983
West	5	41,836	29,313	46,572	47,040
City type					
Central	28	36,810	31,164	35,753	43,697
Suburban	5	40,580	30,331	38,268	45,857
Form of government					
Mayor-council	19	36,425	27,957	34,608	44,109
Council-manager	12	38,649	34,300	37,438	40,147
Auditor					
Total	48	34,961	28,891	34,882	39,400
Geographic region					
Northeast	11	33,548	27,526	31,000	35,603
North Central	7	38,685	35,704	38,002	40,304
South	23	33,781	27,195	31,690	39,334
West	7	37,336	30,291	37,462	40,047
City type					
Central	38	34,301	28,474	33,898	37,793
Suburban	10	37,472	30,743	38,974	40,586
Form of government					
Mayor-council	15	34,419	27,866	34,000	38,010
Council-manager	29	35,365	29,405	35,001	39,378
Commission	4	34,067	26,616	33,197	38,002
Treasurer					
Total	51	35,686	32,096	36,080	39,941
Geographic region					
Northeast	11	31,558	25,801	32,496	35,495
North Central	15	35,299	32,675	34,200	36,523
South	14	37,258	31,875	38,966	40,642
West	11	38,339	35,681	37,200	40,653
City type					
Central	39	35,066	31,464	36,080	39,553
Suburban	12	37,701	34,020	37,190	41,028
Form of government					
Mayor-council	19	32,852	29,152	33,691	36,523
Council-manager	29	37,585	33,729	39,400	41,145
Commission	3	35,274	...	35,761	...
City engineer					
Total	80	43,218	38,502	41,561	47,528
Geographic region					
Northeast	13	39,908	33,447	40,039	44,831
North Central	21	40,285	34,468	40,123	44,054
South	28	42,278	39,100	41,198	45,390
West	18	50,493	44,825	51,291	54,905
City type					
Central	63	42,240	38,235	41,028	45,743
Suburban	17	46,844	39,588	47,528	53,218
Form of government					
Mayor-council	28	38,915	35,569	39,341	41,328
Council-manager	48	45,957	40,476	45,612	52,400
Commission	4	40,467	37,086	40,389	41,028
100,000–249,999 continued					
Director of public works					
Total	89	48,410	42,435	47,500	53,514
Geographic region					
Northeast	14	41,588	36,623	40,082	45,685
North Central	20	43,634	38,858	43,841	49,000
South	30	49,124	44,181	47,938	52,678
West	25	55,193	47,127	56,640	61,484
City type					
Central	68	46,660	42,016	46,665	50,419
Suburban	21	54,076	43,680	56,935	61,458
Form of government					
Mayor-council	31	42,415	36,842	41,252	46,410
Council-manager	53	52,282	46,821	50,960	59,428
Commission	5	44,533	40,575	45,516	45,579
Superintendent of streets					
Total	83	35,215	29,886	34,473	39,753
Geographic region					
Northeast	13	29,132	23,055	28,197	35,393
North Central	18	35,368	30,595	34,329	37,024
South	30	33,946	29,820	32,562	35,820
West	22	40,415	34,595	41,087	43,683
City type					
Central	64	33,699	28,475	33,024	37,918
Suburban	19	40,321	33,739	40,032	44,677
Form of government					
Mayor-council	25	31,508	24,749	32,715	34,401
Council-manager	53	37,131	31,758	35,874	42,995
Commission	5	33,441	28,787	30,380	34,343
Fire chief					
Total	98	45,388	38,812	44,678	52,189
Geographic region					
Northeast	15	43,621	37,360	45,923	50,052
North Central	23	41,140	35,840	41,751	43,945
South	34	42,976	38,582	42,492	45,780
West	26	53,318	49,722	54,102	58,250
City type					
Central	76	43,399	37,419	42,930	49,052
Suburban	22	52,259	42,812	54,267	57,630
Form of government					
Mayor-council	36	41,177	33,572	41,686	46,230
Council-manager	57	48,573	41,732	49,052	54,909
Commission	5	39,399	33,698	33,960	42,699
Police chief					
Total	101	48,152	42,315	47,050	54,227
Geographic region					
Northeast	14	43,707	36,632	45,010	50,301
North Central	22	42,225	37,816	43,067	45,938
South	36	46,872	42,253	46,908	51,792
West	29	56,384	53,354	56,935	59,999
City type					
Central	77	46,178	40,730	46,000	50,762
Suburban	24	54,487	45,650	55,767	58,932
Form of government					
Mayor-council	35	42,156	35,368	42,588	46,058
Council-manager	62	51,954	45,895	52,189	56,829
Commission	4	41,699	34,567	41,113	43,164
Planning director					
Total	92	43,413	37,419	43,319	48,192
Geographic region					
Northeast	14	37,004	27,677	38,350	42,726
North Central	21	39,999	32,959	41,737	44,497
South	32	43,689	37,575	42,733	47,606
West	25	49,518	43,730	50,049	54,238
City type					
Central	67	41,698	35,762	42,465	45,959
Suburban	25	48,010	42,335	47,606	54,082
Form of government					
Mayor-council	32	38,020	32,138	40,842	42,635
Council-manager	55	46,891	41,467	46,629	52,658
Commission	5	39,665	33,120	42,516	42,880
Chief personnel officer					
Total	96	40,302	34,415	39,876	46,440
Geographic region					
Northeast	15	36,127	27,455	33,759	41,884
North Central	19	37,851	34,158	37,772	41,179
South	36	39,290	34,457	39,182	41,954
West	26	45,904	39,982	48,853	50,430
City type					
Central	72	38,389	33,759	38,659	41,616
Suburban	24	46,041	39,537	48,853	50,556

Table 1/4 continued **SALARIES OF MUNICIPAL OFFICIALS: 1 JANUARY 1984**

Title of official	No. of cities reporting	Mean ($)	First quartile ($)	Median ($)	Third quartile ($)
		Distribution of 1984 salaries			
100,000–249,999 continued					
Form of government					
Mayor-council	35	35,612	31,673	35,000	41,010
Council-manager	57	43,668	38,033	44,824	50,000
Commission	4	33,383	23,696	34,518	39,312
Attorney					
Total	93	50,230	42,540	51,384	57,278
Geographic region					
Northeast	14	39,323	33,498	37,481	42,580
North Central	18	45,613	40,777	49,374	50,289
South	35	50,305	45,457	51,384	55,050
West	26	59,198	55,053	59,196	63,857
City type					
Central	70	48,188	39,231	50,173	55,099
Suburban	23	56,445	49,880	57,518	59,859
Form of government					
Mayor-council	30	41,876	34,750	42,580	50,263
Council-manager	58	54,819	49,591	55,099	60,542
Commission	5	47,123	38,516	49,440	49,442
Health officer					
Total	33	47,095	34,697	46,593	56,352
Geographic region					
Northeast	8	42,511	26,624	44,790	48,047
North Central	9	48,075	35,075	44,718	48,887
South	14	46,702	33,311	45,501	54,295
City type					
Central	24	48,463	34,364	47,749	62,480
Suburban	9	43,447	31,185	44,408	49,652
Form of government					
Mayor-council	14	46,549	35,031	47,320	50,370
Council-manager	17	44,415	33,077	44,408	50,627
Director of parks and recreation					
Total	87	42,009	36,401	41,754	45,989
Geographic region					
Northeast	10	37,312	30,000	35,223	42,653
North Central	20	37,643	35,000	38,135	41,700
South	35	41,222	36,479	41,621	44,846
West	22	49,366	44,532	50,538	53,284
City type					
Central	67	40,508	35,630	41,252	45,533
Suburban	20	47,039	40,666	45,547	51,688
Form of government					
Mayor-council	29	36,336	32,250	36,500	41,529
Council-manager	54	45,513	40,461	45,352	51,084
Commission	4	35,845	29,340	34,081	38,438
Superintendent of parks					
Total	73	32,948	26,179	34,404	37,563
Geographic region					
Northeast	12	30,639	23,376	30,872	35,968
North Central	12	32,966	27,082	32,517	34,766
South	27	30,370	24,820	29,474	34,667
West	22	37,362	34,595	37,122	40,080
City type					
Central	59	31,969	25,958	33,534	36,532
Suburban	14	37,073	32,639	37,561	40,746
Form of government					
Mayor-council	24	30,552	24,761	31,783	34,536
Council-manager	45	34,969	29,248	35,640	39,736
Commission	4	24,585	21,756	23,650	24,132
Director of recreation					
Total	65	32,730	26,994	32,815	37,911
Geographic region					
Northeast	13	29,867	24,361	30,593	33,330
North Central	10	28,712	21,517	29,994	31,800
South	23	31,769	25,313	30,004	35,025
West	19	37,966	33,818	38,268	40,410
City type					
Central	51	30,368	25,256	30,472	34,575
Suburban	14	41,334	36,091	40,920	44,733
Form of government					
Mayor-council	22	28,566	24,016	29,408	32,802
Council-manager	38	35,741	29,346	35,647	40,080
Commission	5	28,163	24,925	25,344	29,424
Librarian					
Total	59	40,972	34,497	40,836	47,481
Geographic region					
Northeast	8	37,103	32,519	36,668	40,551
North Central	9	39,640	34,910	37,419	41,762
South	24	39,336	34,174	38,502	43,356
West	18	45,541	41,173	48,074	50,570
City type					
Central	37	38,482	33,999	37,544	42,072

Title of official	No. of cities reporting	Mean ($)	First quartile ($)	Median ($)	Third quartile ($)
		Distribution of 1984 salaries			
100,000–249,999 continued					
Suburban	22	45,161	41,027	47,010	50,117
Form of government					
Mayor-council	16	36,717	32,800	36,326	42,229
Council-manager	41	43,108	36,865	42,718	49,919
Superintendent of schools					
Total	17	57,787	51,524	60,000	63,425
Geographic region					
Northeast	9	53,552	46,110	56,000	59,438
South	7	63,363	57,716	63,900	67,174
City type					
Central	13	56,261	49,795	56,871	61,500
Suburban	4	62,747	57,750	63,509	66,000
Form of government					
Mayor-council	6	50,755	38,640	54,750	56,875
Council-manager	10	62,699	58,436	62,950	66,110
Director of data processing					
Total	85	40,347	36,101	39,500	45,423
Geographic region					
Northeast	13	38,065	31,221	37,493	40,569
North Central	19	37,040	33,223	37,800	40,147
South	32	40,959	36,500	39,729	45,632
West	21	43,818	38,526	42,276	49,026
City type					
Central	65	39,159	35,538	38,521	42,499
Suburban	20	44,207	38,388	43,920	49,535
Form of government					
Mayor-council	28	35,768	31,150	37,388	38,521
Council-manager	52	43,193	38,235	42,336	48,651
Commission	5	36,385	32,802	34,394	38,176
Director of budget and research					
Total	50	39,292	33,347	40,196	44,904
Geographic region					
Northeast	10	39,125	31,804	37,977	42,939
North Central	8	40,156	30,482	44,346	45,300
South	24	38,449	33,000	37,268	43,650
West	8	41,166	37,200	42,245	44,076
City type					
Central	39	38,590	32,308	38,300	44,290
Suburban	11	41,781	34,338	43,611	45,059
Form of government					
Mayor-council	15	37,243	31,752	34,287	41,879
Council-manager	33	40,541	33,936	43,555	45,208
Asst. city mgr./asst. CAO					
Total	62	49,844	44,273	49,245	57,873
Geographic region					
Northeast	5	43,661	29,915	40,657	49,311
North Central	9	43,131	39,254	45,000	47,426
South	28	48,602	43,611	48,587	55,395
West	20	56,150	49,236	56,799	61,069
City type					
Central	46	48,279	40,708	48,411	55,491
Suburban	16	54,343	47,160	54,174	59,717
Form of government					
Mayor-council	10	36,805	29,312	38,575	39,849
Council-manager	52	52,352	45,996	51,449	58,851
Chief building inspector					
Total	88	35,795	30,836	35,935	41,606
Geographic region					
Northeast	15	33,283	26,790	32,496	36,698
North Central	18	32,515	26,531	32,416	37,034
South	33	34,374	30,002	35,429	38,073
West	22	42,323	37,923	41,883	45,298
City type					
Central	68	34,521	29,637	35,002	39,229
Suburban	20	40,127	35,429	40,634	44,876
Form of government					
Mayor-council	31	30,845	26,246	31,475	35,579
Council-manager	52	39,062	34,752	39,535	43,788
Commission	5	32,506	28,383	31,126	33,787
50,000–99,999					
Mayor					
Total	198	18,391	4,200	10,000	34,928
Geographic region					
Northeast	50	28,230	13,052	32,700	40,000
North Central	55	19,643	4,950	14,426	35,143
South	40	16,963	3,360	6,550	27,500
West	53	8,885	3,233	4,800	10,500
City type					
Central	91	21,256	4,800	16,032	36,069

Table 1/4 continued **SALARIES OF MUNICIPAL OFFICIALS: 1 JANUARY 1984**

Title of official	No. of cities reporting	Distribution of 1984 salaries: Mean ($)	First quartile ($)	Median ($)	Third quartile ($)
50,000–99,999 continued					
Suburban	107	15,954	3,743	8,000	30,090
Form of government					
Mayor-council	71	36,351	30,671	37,800	41,903
Council-manager	114	7,082	3,150	4,838	8,699
Commission	8	19,002	3,000	20,266	25,000
Rep. town meeting	4	24,375	700	24,400	47,300
City manager					
Total	147	58,946	50,815	59,000	65,799
Geographic region					
Northeast	11	49,316	44,600	49,882	51,219
North Central	32	54,529	48,000	55,340	58,999
South	39	56,608	47,630	56,679	64,665
West	65	64,154	58,334	63,470	69,260
City type					
Central	66	55,828	49,453	56,361	62,736
Suburban	81	61,487	54,825	62,000	67,453
Form of government					
Council-manager	146	59,045	50,919	59,020	65,818
Chief administrative officer					
Total	28	43,111	35,588	44,108	49,608
Geographic region					
Northeast	15	42,330	35,471	43,940	45,821
North Central	6	42,096	29,712	43,114	50,920
South	4	43,048	31,500	42,598	49,608
West	3	49,133	...	47,873	...
City type					
Central	13	43,885	35,680	45,422	51,255
Suburban	15	42,440	33,391	43,940	47,164
Form of government					
Mayor-council	24	42,109	34,021	42,195	49,608
City clerk					
Total	196	29,202	23,868	28,586	33,901
Geographic region					
Northeast	49	28,129	24,353	27,130	31,371
North Central	44	28,507	23,064	28,081	32,460
South	45	27,273	21,914	25,771	31,871
West	58	32,133	26,758	32,675	36,083
City type					
Central	92	26,762	22,000	25,361	31,224
Suburban	104	31,361	26,265	30,883	35,796
Form of government					
Mayor-council	61	27,920	23,274	27,000	32,319
Council-manager	126	29,879	24,240	29,151	34,560
Commission	4	27,238	20,802	23,687	24,310
Rep. town meeting	4	27,188	24,481	27,385	28,600
Finance director					
Total	185	41,705	35,650	41,340	46,594
Geographic region					
Northeast	33	37,068	31,853	34,798	40,611
North Central	46	40,112	36,317	40,237	44,539
South	46	39,539	34,950	38,466	44,613
West	60	47,138	43,201	46,846	51,480
City type					
Central	90	39,444	34,950	39,627	45,323
Suburban	95	43,847	37,104	44,166	49,293
Form of government					
Mayor-council	45	36,632	31,062	36,255	40,629
Council-manager	132	43,567	37,581	44,147	49,000
Commission	6	33,041	22,750	34,380	36,859
Controller					
Total	57	34,580	28,712	35,000	39,827
Geographic region					
Northeast	21	32,788	26,831	34,246	38,419
North Central	20	33,807	28,891	32,716	37,054
South	6	29,249	18,702	26,059	34,549
West	10	43,087	37,354	45,720	47,163
City type					
Central	30	31,026	25,520	29,903	37,182
Suburban	27	38,529	32,869	38,385	44,769
Form of government					
Mayor-council	27	32,517	25,985	33,826	37,106
Council-manager	26	37,054	29,282	37,377	43,941
Commission	3	30,435	...	30,305	...
Auditor					
Total	47	28,454	23,232	27,424	34,913
Geographic region					
Northeast	16	27,196	21,418	26,212	31,842
North Central	12	31,051	26,624	29,798	35,000
South	16	27,220	21,271	23,707	28,338
West	3	31,356	...	31,692	...
50,000–99,999 continued					
City type					
Central	26	25,594	21,229	23,405	27,849
Suburban	21	31,995	27,645	31,692	36,060
Form of government					
Mayor-council	18	29,557	23,298	29,871	35,321
Council-manager	24	27,680	22,764	24,648	30,610
Rep. town meeting	4	31,481	27,424	31,686	31,842
Treasurer					
Total	85	29,073	23,257	29,272	33,486
Geographic region					
Northeast	30	26,788	22,055	27,176	30,699
North Central	24	30,216	27,540	29,896	33,251
South	13	27,986	21,418	28,668	33,524
West	18	32,142	22,546	33,383	37,404
City type					
Central	38	27,160	21,710	28,064	31,290
Suburban	47	30,619	26,109	30,780	35,165
Form of government					
Mayor-council	29	28,406	22,750	29,272	32,932
Council-manager	47	29,926	23,590	30,480	33,815
Commission	5	23,386	12,875	22,110	26,183
Rep. town meeting	3	29,031	...	27,485	...
City engineer					
Total	161	38,424	33,764	37,886	42,948
Geographic region					
Northeast	38	33,957	29,750	33,559	37,993
North Central	49	37,922	35,042	37,656	41,517
South	37	36,934	34,164	37,398	39,693
West	37	45,169	42,578	46,128	48,475
City type					
Central	87	36,071	32,384	36,280	39,553
Suburban	74	41,191	35,571	41,618	45,182
Form of government					
Mayor-council	53	34,440	29,725	34,091	38,128
Council-manager	101	40,693	35,956	40,121	45,000
Commission	5	36,495	32,448	38,496	39,155
Director of public works					
Total	197	43,862	37,180	42,355	50,013
Geographic region					
Northeast	46	37,749	32,694	37,449	41,169
North Central	48	43,148	39,208	43,409	47,039
South	43	40,560	34,589	40,242	44,850
West	60	51,487	44,232	51,090	57,840
City type					
Central	91	40,992	34,680	40,242	44,813
Suburban	106	46,327	39,503	45,647	51,572
Form of government					
Mayor-council	59	37,547	32,817	37,180	40,845
Council-manager	128	47,067	40,630	45,806	53,940
Commission	5	33,160	24,201	33,000	34,856
Rep. town meeting	4	46,758	39,756	44,838	48,791
Superintendent of streets					
Total	185	31,362	26,578	30,801	35,444
Geographic region					
Northeast	50	28,336	24,727	28,478	31,179
North Central	48	31,766	28,861	31,994	34,881
South	41	28,396	24,331	26,901	31,038
West	46	36,873	32,116	36,900	40,570
City type					
Central	93	28,983	24,896	29,095	32,074
Suburban	92	33,766	29,795	33,853	37,128
Form of government					
Mayor-council	58	28,177	25,160	28,287	30,451
Council-manager	115	32,969	28,860	33,363	37,110
Commission	7	28,682	22,602	30,100	31,970
Rep. town meeting	4	34,375	28,067	34,033	36,472
Fire chief					
Total	203	40,849	35,003	40,102	46,430
Geographic region					
Northeast	47	37,807	32,709	37,100	41,577
North Central	55	39,306	36,214	39,818	43,039
South	51	37,151	33,014	35,820	41,175
West	50	49,179	45,370	50,284	53,559
City type					
Central	104	37,227	32,892	36,247	41,000
Suburban	99	44,654	38,625	43,706	49,520
Form of government					
Mayor-council	66	36,703	32,249	36,196	41,379
Council-manager	126	43,110	36,371	41,970	48,866
Commission	6	39,730	30,799	37,104	39,576

Table 1/4 continued **SALARIES OF MUNICIPAL OFFICIALS: 1 JANUARY 1984**

Title of official	No. of cities reporting	Mean ($)	First quartile ($)	Median ($)	Third quartile ($)
		Distribution of 1984 salaries			
50,000–99,999 continued					
Rep. town meeting	4	38,590	37,100	37,937	38,747
Police chief					
Total	222	43,246	36,787	42,356	48,646
Geographic region					
Northeast	54	39,165	33,906	38,611	42,984
North Central	58	40,763	37,168	41,064	44,031
South	50	39,702	34,804	40,720	44,819
West	60	52,274	48,500	53,358	56,701
City type					
Central	109	39,470	34,408	39,243	44,134
Suburban	113	46,890	39,429	46,127	53,265
Form of government					
Mayor-council	71	38,152	33,802	37,443	42,651
Council-manager	139	46,030	39,453	45,456	52,606
Commission	8	39,840	34,110	38,294	38,742
Rep. town meeting	3	43,211	...	41,886	...
Planning director					
Total	201	38,871	32,322	38,412	43,287
Geographic region					
Northeast	45	34,053	29,556	32,561	37,415
North Central	51	36,688	32,518	37,500	39,727
South	43	35,663	31,061	36,338	39,350
West	62	46,389	40,990	45,885	51,252
City type					
Central	94	35,787	30,848	35,794	39,090
Suburban	107	41,580	36,833	40,848	45,787
Form of government					
Mayor-council	61	33,473	28,813	32,088	38,375
Council-manager	130	41,783	36,338	40,518	45,922
Commission	5	31,442	25,149	29,544	35,499
Rep. town meeting	4	35,501	28,067	32,668	36,095
Chief personnel officer					
Total	191	34,991	28,684	35,126	40,116
Geographic region					
Northeast	36	31,518	26,290	30,828	35,126
North Central	49	33,388	29,788	33,436	37,488
South	49	32,632	27,072	31,776	37,844
West	57	40,592	37,371	40,440	45,096
City type					
Central	97	32,527	27,210	32,000	37,922
Suburban	94	37,534	32,119	37,530	41,984
Form of government					
Mayor-council	53	30,571	26,062	29,988	34,198
Council-manager	130	36,873	30,992	37,493	41,832
Commission	4	28,219	21,244	29,916	31,365
Rep. town meeting	3	39,436	...	35,881	...
Attorney					
Total	155	44,310	35,898	45,381	53,750
Geographic region					
Northeast	32	33,874	25,986	31,867	40,050
North Central	40	41,126	36,500	41,969	47,319
South	35	45,609	36,382	46,667	52,251
West	48	52,974	48,324	56,086	58,023
City type					
Central	81	42,272	35,147	43,500	49,724
Suburban	74	46,541	37,440	48,754	55,671
Form of government					
Mayor-council	45	36,068	27,325	35,590	41,473
Council-manager	106	48,430	41,437	49,360	56,095
Commission	4	27,854	21,533	26,802	31,273
Health officer					
Total	81	33,365	27,645	32,085	37,936
Geographic region					
Northeast	41	32,617	27,721	32,506	37,549
North Central	25	33,075	28,777	32,085	37,052
South	15	35,895	21,197	31,224	46,237
City type					
Central	43	33,121	24,215	31,798	37,535
Suburban	38	33,642	27,708	32,668	38,334
Form of government					
Mayor-council	35	32,013	27,196	30,415	37,535
Council-manager	34	34,904	28,281	33,625	38,751
Commission	7	28,450	19,726	31,266	32,717
Rep. town meeting	4	39,656	25,462	36,482	44,235
Director of parks and recreation					
Total	148	37,377	31,261	36,346	43,500
Geographic region					
Northeast	30	31,046	26,013	31,098	33,133
North Central	36	35,884	31,990	35,256	40,955
South	35	35.391	31,244	35,568	39,615

Title of official	No. of cities reporting	Mean ($)	First quartile ($)	Median ($)	Third quartile ($)
		Distribution of 1984 salaries			
50,000–99,999 continued					
West	47	44,039	39,444	44,588	48,084
City type					
Central	70	34,971	31,006	34,954	39,727
Suburban	78	39,536	32,182	39,888	45,774
Form of government					
Mayor-council	46	30,900	27,159	30,868	33,297
Council-manager	98	40,491	34,758	39,957	45,618
Superintendent of parks					
Total	138	30,015	25,047	29,724	34,850
Geographic region					
Northeast	29	26,247	22,186	24,541	29,630
North Central	31	29,426	26,198	29,703	32,382
South	35	26,682	22,220	26,771	29,875
West	43	35,695	32,042	35,652	39,114
City type					
Central	75	27,674	23,399	27,637	31,215
Suburban	63	32,802	29,058	33,192	36,185
Form of government					
Mayor-council	38	26,984	22,337	25,984	31,220
Council-manager	96	31,302	27,466	31,380	35,580
Director of recreation					
Total	115	31,154	25,521	31,616	35,753
Geographic region					
Northeast	22	25,537	21,440	26,649	28,331
North Central	24	29,162	25,766	30,304	33,529
South	33	29,226	24,751	29,187	32,296
West	36	37,683	34,175	36,178	41,280
City type					
Central	61	28,208	22,783	28,561	32,622
Suburban	54	34,482	28,557	34,742	37,382
Form of government					
Mayor-council	30	26,492	23,247	27,078	31,022
Council-manager	78	33,059	27,539	32,958	36,497
Commission	3	25,871	...	21,880	...
Rep. town meeting	3	31,557	...	33,952	...
Librarian					
Total	120	35,787	30,119	35,020	40,612
Geographic region					
Northeast	38	31,215	26,778	30,553	34,532
North Central	22	36,875	32,283	37,018	39,689
South	22	32,042	27,900	33,779	35,953
West	38	41,896	35,986	42,222	46,131
City type					
Central	50	32,284	27,469	31,899	35,898
Suburban	70	38,288	31,330	37,963	44,032
Form of government					
Mayor-council	33	31,756	27,227	31,000	36,666
Council-manager	76	37,984	32,000	37,018	43,160
Commission	6	29,336	22,113	29,308	32,182
Rep. town meeting	4	35,620	26,738	32,721	35,637
Superintendent of schools					
Total	26	54,431	48,889	52,988	58,188
Geographic region					
Northeast	24	54,355	48,500	52,988	57,900
City type					
Central	12	52,680	48,060	50,439	58,475
Suburban	14	55,933	50,210	54,853	57,300
Form of government					
Mayor-council	16	52,736	48,100	50,210	55,000
Council-manager	5	55,154	48,900	52,300	57,405
Rep. town meeting	3	58,589	...	56,700	...
Director of data processing					
Total	125	33,853	29,192	33,650	38,078
Geographic region					
Northeast	29	31,269	26,247	30,673	34,981
North Central	31	32,463	28,955	33,384	36,219
South	36	33,622	28,749	33,810	37,398
West	29	38,208	31,607	37,476	43,060
City type					
Central	73	31,647	28,371	31,920	35,465
Suburban	52	36,950	32,609	36,261	40,620
Form of government					
Mayor-council	42	29,472	25,395	29,992	32,850
Council-manager	77	36,280	32,060	35,472	39,932
Commission	3	28,738	...	28,368	...
Director of budget and research					
Total	41	34,627	27,911	32,400	37,533
Geographic region					
Northeast	10	29,802	24,555	31,401	33,476
North Central	6	38,304	29,650	34,142	41,250

Table 1/4 continued SALARIES OF MUNICIPAL OFFICIALS: 1 JANUARY 1984

Title of official	No. of cities reporting	Distribution of 1984 salaries: Mean ($)	First quartile ($)	Median ($)	Third quartile ($)
50,000–99,999 continued					
South	15	31,880	23,654	28,626	37,294
West	10	41,368	32,189	37,632	48,368
City type					
Central	27	30,434	26,062	30,701	33,382
Suburban	14	42,714	32,550	43,620	51,074
Form of government					
Mayor-council	8	32,087	29,794	32,839	33,695
Council-manager	31	35,797	27,420	32,999	42,243
Asst. city mgr./asst. CAO					
Total	132	41,792	33,529	41,488	49,356
Geographic region					
Northeast	19	29,978	22,785	31,716	34,748
North Central	32	36,665	29,292	36,857	42,494
South	36	41,973	35,304	40,538	46,260
West	45	50,282	45,030	50,897	54,376
City type					
Central	63	38,389	31,350	36,556	45,685
Suburban	69	44,899	36,123	44,720	52,451
Form of government					
Mayor-council	21	29,510	23,883	29,800	32,415
Council-manager	108	44,494	36,492	44,590	51,468
Chief building inspector					
Total	195	31,972	26,582	30,992	37,254
Geographic region					
Northeast	51	28,449	24,876	28,478	32,378
North Central	52	31,044	27,269	30,722	35,850
South	39	29,310	24,973	30,204	34,149
West	53	38,231	33,915	39,780	42,231
City type					
Central	99	29,158	24,578	28,791	33,234
Suburban	96	34,874	30,000	34,615	39,048
Form of government					
Mayor-council	65	27,722	24,114	27,215	32,053
Council-manager	119	34,264	28,679	34,176	39,402
Commission	6	30,657	25,551	31,448	33,498
Rep. town meeting	4	32,760	26,738	33,660	36,472
25,000–49,999					
Mayor					
Total	434	12,313	3,000	6,000	21,000
Geographic region					
Northeast	93	15,931	3,000	8,610	30,000
North Central	140	13,474	3,600	6,000	26,594
South	101	11,219	4,050	6,000	14,300
West	100	8,426	2,400	3,600	6,600
City type					
Central	95	12,842	3,450	7,000	20,194
Suburban	244	11,226	3,000	4,648	12,672
Independent	95	14,573	4,200	7,200	27,625
Form of government					
Mayor-council	159	24,045	10,654	26,236	34,513
Council-manager	249	4,236	2,400	3,900	6,000
Commission	19	19,821	5,700	25,000	30,625
Rep. town meeting	5	9,864	675	3,000	5,039
City manager					
Total	305	51,394	45,644	51,000	56,800
Geographic region					
Northeast	38	46,363	40,869	46,107	49,989
North Central	72	52,141	46,000	51,000	57,204
South	89	48,844	42,319	47,859	53,999
West	106	54,830	50,200	54,998	58,100
City type					
Central	63	50,372	43,967	49,998	55,383
Suburban	184	52,987	47,255	53,322	57,700
Independent	58	47,448	42,631	46,510	51,636
Form of government					
Council-manager	303	51,428	45,679	51,000	56,819
Chief administrative officer					
Total	73	40,890	37,059	42,033	47,099
Geographic region					
Northeast	38	39,418	33,015	40,656	45,950
North Central	24	43,827	40,000	44,450	47,460
South	6	35,737	28,593	37,364	37,980
West	5	44,167	33,645	46,908	48,852
City type					
Central	15	40,296	36,006	40,312	45,075
Suburban	48	41,766	37,440	42,353	47,898
Independent	10	37,576	29,855	41,714	43,527

Title of official	No. of cities reporting	Distribution of 1984 salaries: Mean ($)	First quartile ($)	Median ($)	Third quartile ($)
25,000–49,999 continued					
Form of government					
Mayor-council	62	40,988	37,076	42,248	47,142
Commission	6	40,681	33,503	38,810	41,204
Rep. town meeting	4	41,156	26,658	43,483	47,162
City clerk					
Total	377	26,238	21,441	25,665	30,865
Geographic region					
Northeast	94	26,666	22,306	24,750	30,260
North Central	106	23,493	18,799	23,019	27,616
South	95	26,150	21,057	24,133	30,869
West	82	29,398	25,206	28,742	32,355
City type					
Central	84	25,610	20,434	24,745	29,000
Suburban	210	27,514	22,972	27,416	31,942
Independent	83	23,647	19,369	22,957	26,604
Form of government					
Mayor-council	134	24,361	19,755	23,626	28,217
Council-manager	221	27,467	22,746	26,880	31,700
Commission	12	25,162	16,582	24,221	29,000
Rep. town meeting	8	24,703	19,559	24,027	29,144
Finance director					
Total	343	37,091	31,992	37,037	42,159
Geographic region					
Northeast	58	33,620	27,683	34,162	38,539
North Central	91	37,770	32,679	38,126	41,991
South	90	34,453	29,263	34,242	39,045
West	104	40,716	36,636	41,284	44,940
City type					
Central	77	35,536	31,386	35,734	39,103
Suburban	197	38,942	34,180	39,671	44,241
Independent	69	33,542	28,689	34,051	38,125
Form of government					
Mayor-council	77	32,651	27,148	32,500	36,345
Council-manager	252	38,568	34,216	39,000	43,541
Commission	8	30,998	22,567	30,756	32,760
Rep. town meeting	4	42,529	33,128	42,545	49,353
Controller					
Total	81	30,458	25,585	30,780	35,737
Geographic region					
Northeast	31	31,986	25,988	35,046	37,838
North Central	24	27,564	23,065	26,540	30,780
South	16	30,448	24,776	31,492	33,962
West	10	32,683	25,062	33,822	36,227
City type					
Central	23	28,173	23,756	27,839	34,188
Suburban	40	32,553	27,000	33,271	37,953
Independent	18	28,722	22,894	27,290	34,193
Form of government					
Mayor-council	43	28,721	22,281	28,000	35,071
Council-manager	32	32,125	27,456	32,322	36,634
Commission	3	32,267	...	30,800	...
Rep. town meeting	3	35,769	...	37,481	...
Auditor					
Total	54	25,876	22,957	25,334	29,656
Geographic region					
Northeast	24	26,415	23,088	24,893	28,809
North Central	13	26,976	19,310	25,762	33,176
South	12	22,669	17,846	23,647	25,891
West	5	28,123	20,738	31,632	32,207
City type					
Central	16	24,511	22,235	23,063	25,891
Suburban	22	27,506	23,721	28,068	32,016
Independent	16	24,999	20,000	24,585	26,777
Form of government					
Mayor-council	26	25,978	22,574	24,893	29,098
Council-manager	23	25,902	22,942	25,891	29,970
Treasurer					
Total	136	26,431	20,602	26,487	30,764
Geographic region					
Northeast	58	26,613	22,087	26,026	31,360
North Central	34	24,099	18,595	25,550	28,269
South	19	25,353	19,362	24,732	28,813
West	25	29,998	25,498	30,120	33,343
City type					
Central	32	26,366	21,710	26,871	31,620
Suburban	76	27,255	22,385	28,250	32,657
Independent	28	24,267	20,000	23,680	27,684
Form of government					
Mayor-council	54	25,560	20,158	25,012	30,163
Council-manager	72	26,906	22,789	27,247	30,409

Table 1/4 continued **SALARIES OF MUNICIPAL OFFICIALS: 1 JANUARY 1984**

Title of official	No. of cities reporting	Distribution of 1984 salaries: Mean ($)	First quartile ($)	Median ($)	Third quartile ($)
25,000–49,999 continued					
Commission	5	24,656	16,873	24,700	30,286
Rep. town meeting	4	30,103	15,155	33,039	37,530
City engineer					
Total	311	35,512	31,035	35,342	40,258
Geographic region					
Northeast	73	33,322	28,665	33,351	37,510
North Central	88	35,502	32,088	35,793	40,200
South	81	33,660	29,755	33,121	36,383
West	69	40,016	35,955	40,198	43,546
City type					
Central	82	34,019	29,518	34,555	38,690
Suburban	142	37,674	33,105	37,445	43,033
Independent	87	33,391	29,786	32,960	37,024
Form of government					
Mayor-council	98	32,775	28,000	32,887	37,046
Council-manager	191	37,044	32,721	36,378	42,035
Commission	13	33,855	29,633	34,031	37,620
Rep. town meeting	8	34,891	31,111	33,962	37,429
Director of public works					
Total	380	38,227	32,692	38,217	43,723
Geographic region					
Northeast	79	34,845	30,330	33,500	39,556
North Central	112	38,767	34,505	38,487	42,000
South	97	34,617	29,295	34,671	38,675
West	92	44,278	40,284	44,832	47,700
City type					
Central	82	36,440	30,176	35,820	41,680
Suburban	224	39,718	33,625	39,916	45,000
Independent	74	35,693	30,215	36,597	39,885
Form of government					
Mayor-council	115	34,662	30,180	34,516	39,200
Council-manager	246	40,088	34,607	40,025	45,977
Commission	11	32,361	25,287	35,640	37,750
Rep. town meeting	6	41,649	33,973	41,885	43,710
Superintendent of streets					
Total	349	28,062	24,154	27,650	31,152
Geographic region					
Northeast	76	27,611	24,043	27,891	30,300
North Central	108	28,151	25,104	28,174	31,000
South	91	24,504	22,326	24,381	26,582
West	74	32,772	28,626	31,984	35,424
City type					
Central	82	26,522	22,590	25,570	29,832
Suburban	183	29,919	26,064	29,547	33,459
Independent	84	25,521	22,797	25,185	28,908
Form of government					
Mayor-council	115	26,537	23,199	26,096	29,835
Council-manager	213	28,865	24,774	28,470	32,335
Commission	13	27,076	21,345	26,100	32,102
Rep. town meeting	6	30,302	26,536	29,981	31,798
Fire chief					
Total	390	35,462	30,188	35,076	40,394
Geographic region					
Northeast	65	35,767	30,268	35,484	40,453
North Central	128	34,089	30,400	34,112	38,159
South	108	31,946	27,314	31,166	35,652
West	89	41,481	36,819	40,500	46,696
City type					
Central	99	33,404	29,012	33,031	37,710
Suburban	189	38,703	33,988	39,000	43,232
Independent	102	31,454	27,092	31,096	35,000
Form of government					
Mayor-council	123	31,999	27,251	32,485	35,501
Council-manager	242	37,419	32,214	37,168	41,944
Commission	16	30,598	24,000	29,316	35,868
Rep. town meeting	8	38,404	33,911	38,850	40,057
Police chief					
Total	475	37,736	32,330	37,379	43,119
Geographic region					
Northeast	106	37,241	32,427	37,000	41,492
North Central	142	36,149	32,133	35,952	41,412
South	119	34,323	29,912	33,670	38,324
West	108	44,070	39,936	44,394	48,960
City type					
Central	105	35,679	30,579	35,821	40,417
Suburban	267	40,484	35,047	41,042	46,024
Independent	103	32,711	28,264	32,416	36,900
Form of government					
Mayor-council	155	34,290	29,655	34,486	39,000
Council-manager	292	39,778	34,200	39,547	45,000

Title of official	No. of cities reporting	Distribution of 1984 salaries: Mean ($)	First quartile ($)	Median ($)	Third quartile ($)
25,000–49,999 continued					
Commission	18	32,457	24,834	30,515	38,823
Rep. town meeting	8	41,626	35,801	43,250	46,248
Planning director					
Total	362	33,890	28,099	33,127	38,810
Geographic region					
Northeast	69	29,648	25,049	29,160	33,399
North Central	96	32,125	27,000	32,388	36,754
South	88	31,858	27,552	30,405	36,192
West	109	39,769	35,257	39,936	43,865
City type					
Central	87	32,524	27,309	31,452	36,710
Suburban	197	35,882	30,000	36,180	41,410
Independent	78	30,382	26,710	29,966	34,797
Form of government					
Mayor-council	100	29,535	25,050	29,455	33,183
Council-manager	238	36,217	30,669	36,287	41,328
Commission	16	28,285	24,000	28,316	30,000
Rep. town meeting	7	29,572	25,844	29,754	30,116
Chief personnel officer					
Total	272	29,568	24,000	29,434	34,200
Geographic region					
Northeast	36	25,320	22,062	24,021	27,872
North Central	65	29,109	25,119	29,516	33,683
South	94	27,316	22,680	26,604	31,528
West	77	34,690	30,840	34,418	38,955
City type					
Central	83	28,598	22,714	29,532	33,527
Suburban	128	31,168	25,012	31,341	36,144
Independent	61	27,529	23,200	27,216	31,111
Form of government					
Mayor-council	74	25,931	21,774	25,046	29,642
Council-manager	186	31,253	25,989	31,252	35,328
Commission	8	24,403	13,992	25,072	27,696
Rep. town meeting	4	28,798	20,562	24,173	24,500
Attorney					
Total	230	35,989	27,680	36,043	43,989
Geographic region					
Northeast	46	29,507	24,356	27,997	34,530
North Central	73	33,493	27,407	34,361	38,932
South	52	35,060	23,291	35,502	43,597
West	59	44,951	39,117	45,864	49,609
City type					
Central	66	35,859	28,725	36,392	42,244
Suburban	103	38,457	28,000	38,202	47,000
Independent	61	31,963	23,482	33,512	38,472
Form of government					
Mayor-council	84	29,879	22,500	29,043	36,036
Council-manager	137	40,448	34,063	40,986	47,142
Commission	7	24,239	17,650	21,000	25,878
Health officer					
Total	101	27,944	22,839	27,200	32,481
Geographic region					
Northeast	60	28,188	22,800	27,149	33,096
North Central	32	28,716	25,168	29,022	31,560
South	7	23,150	14,785	20,820	25,269
City type					
Central	21	28,147	22,719	27,500	31,218
Suburban	58	29,109	24,259	28,632	33,848
Independent	22	24,682	20,348	24,869	27,746
Form of government					
Mayor-council	47	27,313	21,919	26,264	31,104
Council-manager	43	29,412	24,641	29,400	33,463
Commission	4	18,368	10,330	18,246	20,292
Rep. town meeting	6	28,455	21,923	27,979	30,983
Director of parks and recreation					
Total	280	31,961	26,765	31,369	37,218
Geographic region					
Northeast	52	27,047	23,053	26,708	30,620
North Central	65	31,678	26,230	31,820	36,046
South	92	30,526	25,870	29,432	32,900
West	71	37,677	34,547	37,812	40,038
City type					
Central	62	31,028	25,723	30,629	37,018
Suburban	150	33,577	27,165	33,617	39,218
Independent	68	29,246	25,200	29,055	33,264
Form of government					
Mayor-council	82	28,076	23,523	28,602	31,326
Council-manager	181	34,053	28,559	34,512	38,973
Commission	12	28,799	23,803	28,553	31,800
Rep. town meeting	5	27,506	21,290	26,908	30,920

Table 1/4 continued **SALARIES OF MUNICIPAL OFFICIALS: 1 JANUARY 1984**

Title of official	No. of cities reporting	Distribution of 1984 salaries: Mean ($)	First quartile ($)	Median ($)	Third quartile ($)
25,000–49,999 continued					
Superintendent of parks					
Total	230	26,304	22,627	25,406	29,739
Geographic region					
Northeast	49	25,093	21,992	24,000	29,350
North Central	56	26,005	23,685	25,692	28,954
South	58	23,807	20,427	22,993	25,673
West	67	29,601	24,900	29,785	33,159
City type					
Central	53	25,603	22,137	25,174	28,898
Suburban	113	27,825	23,518	27,300	30,986
Independent	64	24,199	21,258	24,097	26,589
Form of government					
Mayor-council	73	25,074	22,406	24,682	27,193
Council-manager	143	27,113	22,956	26,333	30,348
Commission	8	21,278	16,700	19,050	21,804
Rep. town meeting	5	28,471	24,268	29,662	29,687
Director of recreation					
Total	226	26,765	21,017	26,348	31,383
Geographic region					
Northeast	53	25,013	18,616	24,847	30,246
North Central	56	25,149	19,900	24,052	28,525
South	50	22,689	18,180	22,660	26,075
West	67	32,543	27,817	32,808	37,629
City type					
Central	54	24,882	20,310	24,226	29,334
Suburban	119	29,156	22,115	29,745	35,097
Independent	53	23,314	19,211	23,234	27,767
Form of government					
Mayor-council	66	23,686	18,028	23,621	28,000
Council-manager	142	28,518	21,833	28,521	33,878
Commission	12	22,419	18,025	21,734	24,252
Rep. town meeting	4	27,436	21,394	26,113	27,378
Librarian					
Total	196	29,505	24,434	28,524	34,000
Geographic region					
Northeast	62	27,240	23,324	26,333	31,249
North Central	45	28,624	23,857	28,500	33,123
South	34	27,556	23,544	26,638	29,869
West	55	33,985	30,347	34,507	38,514
City type					
Central	42	28,796	24,417	27,556	33,753
Suburban	112	30,917	25,219	30,750	35,481
Independent	42	26,450	22,387	26,119	29,849
Form of government					
Mayor-council	52	26,561	23,516	25,960	29,245
Council-manager	124	31,263	26,172	31,324	35,381
Commission	10	22,728	16,558	23,109	24,843
Rep. town meeting	8	29,482	21,551	30,842	33,696
Superintendent of schools					
Total	48	47,530	42,846	46,849	52,000
Geographic region					
Northeast	38	47,859	42,923	46,849	51,234
North Central	4	53,300	43,000	55,600	56,000
South	5	45,923	38,376	46,000	47,400
City type					
Central	10	45,437	39,937	44,000	46,000
Suburban	29	49,771	44,775	48,500	54,207
Independent	9	42,634	38,125	43,500	48,759
Form of government					
Mayor-council	20	44,583	40,000	43,390	46,300
Council-manager	21	48,941	46,056	48,500	50,745
Rep. town meeting	4	52,984	43,500	55,450	56,600
Director of data processing					
Total	177	30,166	25,412	31,000	34,920
Geographic region					
Northeast	30	28,000	24,077	27,228	32,251
North Central	44	29,886	23,665	30,267	35,027
South	62	28,547	24,510	29,315	32,647
West	41	34,500	32,419	34,675	37,179
City type					
Central	61	29,473	25,453	30,347	32,975
Suburban	74	32,460	27,332	33,085	37,010
Independent	42	27,130	22,383	26,210	32,508
Form of government					
Mayor-council	38	27,855	23,556	28,566	31,780
Council-manager	126	31,159	25,984	31,937	35,664
Commission	8	25,999	20,000	26,074	29,508
Rep. town meeting	3	33,192	. . .	33,878	. . .
Director of budget and research					
Total	25	28,026	24,447	26,617	32,832

Title of official	No. of cities reporting	Distribution of 1984 salaries: Mean ($)	First quartile ($)	Median ($)	Third quartile ($)
25,000–49,999 continued					
Geographic region					
Northeast	5	23,952	14,627	25,837	26,422
North Central	4	28,828	23,430	25,816	28,104
South	10	29,467	24,670	29,937	33,046
West	6	28,486	24,708	26,843	30,204
City type					
Central	9	31,114	26,462	32,864	33,204
Suburban	12	27,639	24,420	26,638	31,470
Independent	4	22,242	17,938	23,018	23,430
Form of government					
Mayor-council	4	25,620	11,968	27,917	33,228
Council-manager	20	28,504	24,526	26,514	32,734
Asst. city mgr./asst. CAO					
Total	202	35,255	28,786	35,347	42,166
Geographic region					
Northeast	31	26,786	22,593	27,055	29,538
North Central	62	33,121	28,330	33,796	38,158
South	53	35,767	30,447	37,271	41,502
West	56	41,821	38,460	42,078	44,379
City type					
Central	41	35,111	29,275	35,395	40,800
Suburban	129	35,992	28,910	36,413	43,057
Independent	32	32,469	26,000	32,438	39,674
Form of government					
Mayor-council	27	28,705	23,744	27,303	33,219
Council-manager	171	36,476	30,778	36,858	42,935
Chief building inspector					
Total	415	27,551	22,854	26,974	32,112
Geographic region					
Northeast	98	26,661	22,584	26,066	29,427
North Central	119	27,289	23,255	26,728	31,989
South	108	24,716	20,257	23,810	28,176
West	90	32,267	28,295	32,825	35,640
City type					
Central	91	27,199	22,937	26,292	31,628
Suburban	233	29,287	25,212	28,772	33,447
Independent	91	23,454	20,218	22,988	26,268
Form of government					
Mayor-council	134	25,523	21,254	25,231	28,672
Council-manager	257	28,816	24,024	28,507	33,319
Commission	14	23,623	18,269	21,484	25,850
Rep. town meeting	8	27,955	25,463	27,792	28,710
10,000–24,999					
Mayor					
Total	946	7,680	1,800	3,600	8,353
Geographic region					
Northeast	246	6,970	1,500	2,500	6,351
North Central	326	9,217	2,550	5,000	12,600
South	250	7,995	1,800	3,958	7,440
West	124	4,411	1,800	2,400	4,800
City type					
Central	29	6,658	1,350	3,000	5,570
Suburban	591	7,272	1,800	3,500	7,200
Independent	326	8,510	1,800	4,518	12,000
Form of government					
Mayor-council	430	12,128	3,500	7,200	20,336
Council-manager	432	2,957	1,200	2,400	3,600
Commission	27	6,822	2,475	6,000	7,843
Town meeting	43	11,248	738	1,800	25,646
Rep. town meeting	14	7,472	1,100	1,750	4,250
City manager					
Total	567	42,196	36,809	41,526	46,919
Geographic region					
Northeast	115	39,096	34,314	37,757	42,625
North Central	133	42,823	38,314	42,500	46,000
South	198	40,361	35,589	40,000	45,199
West	121	47,456	40,863	47,810	51,552
City type					
Central	26	43,278	40,000	43,529	47,300
Suburban	348	43,615	37,800	43,114	48,504
Independent	193	39,493	36,000	39,130	43,000
Form of government					
Council-manager	549	42,289	36,827	41,749	46,989
Town meeting	13	38,016	33,027	37,757	40,645
Rep. town meeting	5	42,858	35,500	44,000	46,013
Chief administrative officer					
Total	244	36,358	30,900	36,963	42,000

Table 1/4 continued **SALARIES OF MUNICIPAL OFFICIALS: 1 JANUARY 1984**

Title of official	No. of cities reporting	Distribution of 1984 salaries Mean ($)	First quartile ($)	Median ($)	Third quartile ($)
10,000–24,999 continued					
Geographic region					
Northeast	101	34,055	28,909	34,000	38,288
North Central	83	38,068	33,113	40,000	43,346
South	38	36,524	30,980	37,541	39,998
West	22	40,197	34,686	40,000	45,357
City type					
Suburban	183	36,477	30,715	36,410	42,427
Independent	59	35,898	30,939	37,492	40,313
Form of government					
Mayor-council	201	37,004	32,000	37,332	42,324
Council-manager	7	36,291	29,130	38,948	40,061
Commission	9	30,519	26,125	28,210	31,029
Town meeting	20	33,841	28,890	35,464	38,500
Rep. town meeting	7	32,592	25,164	31,500	37,654
City clerk					
Total	790	22,382	18,017	21,605	26,511
Geographic region					
Northeast	238	21,499	17,447	20,422	25,000
North Central	226	22,339	18,000	21,472	26,974
South	241	21,782	18,008	21,132	25,012
West	85	26,669	22,745	26,270	30,114
City type					
Central	29	20,779	18,081	19,515	22,247
Suburban	488	22,668	18,163	22,448	26,750
Independent	273	22,040	17,872	21,000	25,971
Form of government					
Mayor-council	320	21,462	17,246	20,836	25,800
Council-manager	384	23,520	19,284	23,045	27,706
Commission	23	23,678	17,876	21,148	27,308
Town meeting	49	19,567	16,088	19,400	23,097
Rep. town meeting	14	19,913	16,679	19,705	22,497
Finance director					
Total	527	31,018	26,144	30,984	35,843
Geographic region					
Northeast	100	27,721	23,933	27,855	31,474
North Central	152	32,237	28,612	31,995	36,897
South	170	29,026	23,785	28,575	33,068
West	105	35,620	30,852	34,740	39,884
City type					
Central	27	31,189	26,480	31,990	34,020
Suburban	339	31,574	26,370	31,449	36,282
Independent	161	29,819	24,907	29,544	33,699
Form of government					
Mayor-council	142	29,497	25,190	29,686	33,371
Council-manager	357	31,806	26,691	31,465	36,175
Commission	4	27,608	23,406	27,636	30,792
Town meeting	19	28,229	22,524	27,922	32,440
Rep. town meeting	5	31,261	21,740	33,297	35,405
Controller					
Total	83	27,971	21,673	27,677	32,128
Geographic region					
Northeast	31	28,281	22,970	27,277	34,077
North Central	27	28,671	24,251	29,216	32,128
South	18	26,541	19,984	26,274	29,883
West	7	27,571	19,792	21,792	29,683
City type					
Suburban	51	29,273	22,323	28,319	35,352
Independent	31	25,789	20,350	26,000	28,441
Form of government					
Mayor-council	31	28,366	22,323	28,000	31,543
Council-manager	37	28,253	20,976	27,201	33,635
Commission	4	22,904	15,876	23,079	25,440
Town meeting	9	26,033	19,236	28,245	28,315
Auditor					
Total	82	21,578	17,220	21,209	24,567
Geographic region					
Northeast	41	21,630	17,450	21,700	24,584
North Central	31	22,353	17,694	21,060	24,237
South	8	16,396	13,000	15,291	17,602
City type					
Central	3	21,584	. . .	20,434	. . .
Suburban	45	21,939	16,078	21,400	26,881
Independent	34	21,100	17,629	21,209	23,220
Form of government					
Mayor-council	37	20,015	16,625	19,680	21,959
Council-manager	15	20,688	15,645	20,434	22,886
Commission	5	29,266	24,250	29,203	32,801
Town meeting	17	22,473	17,630	22,194	25,406
Rep. town meeting	8	23,771	21,427	23,209	26,847

Title of official	No. of cities reporting	Distribution of 1984 salaries Mean ($)	First quartile ($)	Median ($)	Third quartile ($)
10,000–24,999 continued					
Treasurer					
Total	271	21,465	16,800	21,340	25,979
Geographic region					
Northeast	119	21,233	16,342	21,340	25,473
North Central	70	20,944	16,650	20,592	25,792
South	58	21,788	15,979	21,436	26,728
West	24	23,353	18,270	22,389	28,543
City type					
Central	9	25,859	21,947	25,799	26,307
Suburban	170	22,053	17,137	21,914	26,650
Independent	92	19,948	15,500	19,000	23,900
Form of government					
Mayor-council	124	20,130	15,625	20,092	25,000
Council-manager	105	23,129	17,176	22,284	27,357
Commission	5	24,761	18,962	21,801	27,950
Town meeting	26	20,160	14,157	21,641	24,628
Rep. town meeting	11	22,212	15,508	22,350	26,470
City engineer					
Total	440	32,184	27,960	32,305	36,474
Geographic region					
Northeast	106	30,478	26,115	30,261	35,000
North Central	145	32,606	29,411	32,952	36,594
South	119	30,224	25,777	30,900	33,750
West	70	37,222	32,353	36,149	42,378
City type					
Central	14	29,756	22,465	31,606	33,952
Suburban	233	33,379	29,654	33,069	37,655
Independent	193	30,917	25,846	31,164	34,748
Form of government					
Mayor-council	156	31,440	26,540	31,796	36,660
Council-manager	239	33,009	28,745	32,922	36,674
Commission	14	29,548	24,000	32,145	33,756
Town meeting	22	31,075	28,455	31,845	33,769
Rep. town meeting	9	29,964	25,391	30,534	32,615
Director of public works					
Total	766	31,777	26,732	31,122	36,136
Geographic region					
Northeast	189	30,332	26,282	29,920	33,245
North Central	242	32,570	27,942	32,399	36,280
South	219	28,597	23,507	28,251	32,359
West	116	38,480	32,376	38,682	43,253
City type					
Central	26	30,972	25,326	30,005	35,845
Suburban	498	32,692	27,510	32,063	37,303
Independent	242	29,979	25,736	29,581	33,735
Form of government					
Mayor-council	290	30,192	25,500	29,868	34,840
Council-manager	416	32,969	27,709	32,126	37,128
Commission	12	29,313	23,406	28,176	32,640
Town meeting	34	30,729	25,784	31,483	34,178
Rep. town meeting	14	33,831	28,111	32,757	37,787
Superintendent of streets					
Total	719	24,692	20,464	24,369	28,019
Geographic region					
Northeast	152	24,995	22,050	24,697	26,978
North Central	252	25,890	22,536	25,612	29,100
South	228	21,375	17,771	20,600	24,173
West	87	29,386	24,609	29,028	32,574
City type					
Central	25	22,986	19,339	21,100	27,090
Suburban	417	26,033	22,493	25,500	29,486
Independent	277	22,828	19,172	22,437	25,518
Form of government					
Mayor-council	291	24,007	20,044	24,252	26,802
Council-manager	368	25,061	20,712	24,153	28,860
Commission	25	24,691	20,124	25,500	28,533
Town meeting	27	27,014	23,788	25,950	28,560
Rep. town meeting	8	24,779	22,935	24,812	25,238
Fire chief					
Total	725	28,800	23,858	28,002	32,693
Geographic region					
Northeast	128	29,474	24,866	28,001	32,295
North Central	244	28,928	24,964	28,974	33,000
South	248	25,494	21,711	24,989	28,665
West	105	35,488	30,219	34,700	39,897
City type					
Central	31	28,434	24,753	27,965	30,873
Suburban	382	30,897	25,647	30,730	34,960
Independent	312	26,268	22,533	25,674	29,049

Table 1/4 continued **SALARIES OF MUNICIPAL OFFICIALS: 1 JANUARY 1984**

Title of official	No. of cities reporting	Distribution of 1984 salaries: Mean ($)	First quartile ($)	Median ($)	Third quartile ($)
10,000–24,999 continued					
Form of government					
Mayor-council	283	26,802	22,268	26,243	31,093
Council-manager	376	29,926	25,002	28,685	33,737
Commission	17	25,471	21,225	23,452	29,515
Town meeting	38	32,138	27,782	32,279	35,514
Rep. town meeting	11	35,315	26,890	32,013	40,667
Police chief					
Total	1086	31,403	26,314	31,188	35,535
Geographic region					
Northeast	296	31,931	27,616	31,648	35,280
North Central	349	31,497	27,292	31,500	36,000
South	307	28,122	23,490	27,564	32,526
West	134	37,507	32,250	36,654	42,562
City type					
Central	34	31,327	28,283	31,360	33,973
Suburban	675	33,281	29,045	32,860	37,400
Independent	377	28,047	23,514	27,442	31,701
Form of government					
Mayor-council	455	29,707	24,552	30,000	34,700
Council-manager	533	32,703	27,741	32,370	36,699
Commission	29	28,516	24,048	29,652	31,506
Town meeting	52	33,354	28,881	33,159	37,548
Rep. town meeting	17	35,002	28,433	33,680	39,972
Planning director					
Total	411	28,289	22,684	27,792	33,071
Geographic region					
Northeast	83	25,276	21,650	24,406	28,000
North Central	102	27,374	21,949	27,990	31,064
South	113	25,088	20,671	24,000	29,549
West	113	34,529	29,250	33,696	39,741
City type					
Central	19	28,408	24,223	27,246	29,982
Suburban	241	29,885	23,116	29,500	35,988
Independent	151	25,727	21,483	25,610	29,599
Form of government					
Mayor-council	114	24,990	19,893	23,450	29,256
Council-manager	269	30,035	24,094	29,263	34,729
Commission	7	22,968	19,362	21,000	22,689
Town meeting	14	24,804	18,475	23,806	28,111
Rep. town meeting	7	27,203	22,376	25,080	27,853
Chief personnel officer					
Total	238	23,308	18,622	21,984	26,614
Geographic region					
Northeast	24	21,921	18,543	20,456	23,600
North Central	48	23,454	20,000	22,958	26,275
South	116	21,004	17,420	20,550	25,135
West	50	29,178	22,810	29,617	33,993
City type					
Central	9	26,617	17,642	30,472	33,577
Suburban	128	24,608	19,256	24,143	27,872
Independent	101	21,365	17,865	20,842	24,336
Form of government					
Mayor-council	69	20,604	15,850	19,947	23,591
Council-manager	158	24,646	19,937	23,841	27,911
Commission	4	19,565	17,666	19,939	20,389
Town meeting	4	22,461	19,146	22,095	24,489
Rep. town meeting	3	21,110	...	20,500	...
Attorney					
Total	215	28,424	19,228	27,967	35,568
Geographic region					
Northeast	51	25,116	17,624	22,084	31,265
North Central	76	24,964	17,500	23,449	30,000
South	41	27,464	18,250	30,000	35,750
West	47	38,447	32,231	37,356	45,410
City type					
Central	13	28,585	18,520	30,281	35,689
Suburban	110	29,315	20,000	27,979	37,242
Independent	92	27,337	18,600	26,500	34,020
Form of government					
Mayor-council	108	24,111	16,260	22,397	30,000
Council-manager	96	33,498	25,000	33,076	40,000
Town meeting	6	24,209	13,750	24,516	30,713
Rep. town meeting	3	30,429	...	32,001	...
Health officer					
Total	147	23,017	18,434	21,852	27,133
Geographic region					
Northeast	83	23,681	17,133	23,750	30,599
North Central	37	22,479	19,983	22,468	25,571
South	25	21,371	16,261	19,308	21,882

Title of official	No. of cities reporting	Distribution of 1984 salaries: Mean ($)	First quartile ($)	Median ($)	Third quartile ($)
10,000–24,999 continued					
City type					
Central	4	19,098	8,000	17,575	18,550
Suburban	98	24,509	19,831	24,973	29,443
Independent	45	20,118	16,374	19,500	21,996
Form of government					
Mayor-council	57	22,095	15,877	21,396	27,162
Council-manager	58	24,067	18,906	21,824	28,541
Town meeting	21	22,915	18,131	21,961	25,945
Rep. town meeting	9	22,266	17,687	21,730	25,166
Director of parks and recreation					
Total	494	26,032	21,146	25,233	30,186
Geographic region					
Northeast	101	23,274	19,032	23,500	26,119
North Central	145	26,339	21,373	25,227	30,702
South	165	23,948	19,589	23,320	27,338
West	83	32,993	26,739	32,482	37,851
City type					
Central	24	26,810	22,259	26,077	29,740
Suburban	289	27,146	22,315	26,115	31,753
Independent	181	24,149	19,739	23,144	28,133
Form of government					
Mayor-council	177	23,436	18,373	22,242	28,029
Council-manager	282	28,028	23,146	26,712	31,947
Commission	9	22,735	19,581	22,101	24,653
Town meeting	21	23,482	19,845	23,988	25,653
Rep. town meeting	5	21,949	14,417	24,131	25,300
Superintendent of parks					
Total	332	22,041	18,609	21,480	25,168
Geographic region					
Northeast	53	22,263	19,347	22,388	24,266
North Central	109	21,759	18,245	21,710	25,199
South	106	20,082	17,130	19,796	21,942
West	64	25,580	21,000	25,546	28,974
City type					
Central	10	21,606	17,551	20,929	23,553
Suburban	181	23,004	19,181	22,695	26,427
Independent	141	20,835	17,965	20,400	22,712
Form of government					
Mayor-council	121	21,511	17,789	21,653	24,509
Council-manager	187	22,352	18,680	21,228	25,318
Commission	9	20,969	16,489	21,377	22,375
Town meeting	11	22,957	19,558	22,388	24,444
Rep. town meeting	4	23,379	18,661	23,910	24,150
Director of recreation					
Total	286	22,872	17,910	21,851	26,890
Geographic region					
Northeast	78	21,810	16,624	20,608	26,164
North Central	75	21,813	17,262	21,550	26,010
South	79	21,577	17,837	20,548	23,660
West	54	27,774	23,162	27,341	32,040
City type					
Central	9	22,235	18,255	22,526	25,481
Suburban	180	23,890	18,555	23,221	28,032
Independent	97	21,044	16,308	20,422	23,980
Form of government					
Mayor-council	100	21,596	17,264	21,293	25,979
Council-manager	155	24,151	18,541	22,526	28,008
Commission	6	18,174	12,500	18,852	20,991
Town meeting	20	20,130	15,500	18,847	25,261
Rep. town meeting	5	25,361	20,496	27,034	27,944
Librarian					
Total	411	22,537	18,049	21,888	26,335
Geographic region					
Northeast	148	22,475	18,413	21,728	26,260
North Central	105	22,668	18,051	22,266	26,500
South	103	20,479	16,651	20,306	24,144
West	55	26,307	20,047	26,052	30,438
City type					
Central	18	22,869	19,790	21,873	25,357
Suburban	247	23,144	18,930	22,675	26,955
Independent	146	21,469	17,401	20,619	24,751
Form of government					
Mayor-council	129	21,171	17,034	20,500	25,034
Council-manager	215	23,517	19,010	22,793	27,440
Commission	15	18,878	17,323	18,144	21,100
Town meeting	37	23,185	19,347	23,505	26,607
Rep. town meeting	15	22,304	18,659	22,472	26,627
Superintendent of schools					
Total	107	46,392	40,975	46,629	50,557

Table 1/4 continued **SALARIES OF MUNICIPAL OFFICIALS: 1 JANUARY 1984**

Title of official	No. of cities reporting	Distribution of 1984 salaries: Mean ($)	First quartile ($)	Median ($)	Third quartile ($)
10,000–24,999 continued					
Geographic region					
Northeast	90	46,515	40,845	46,890	50,603
North Central	6	52,633	44,871	51,402	56,527
South	11	41,981	38,640	42,572	45,915
City type					
Central	4	42,992	40,789	42,589	42,605
Suburban	73	48,418	44,901	48,500	53,065
Independent	30	41,917	39,046	40,950	44,871
Form of government					
Mayor-council	23	44,994	39,177	46,729	51,022
Council-manager	42	44,460	40,000	44,443	49,198
Town meeting	32	48,783	44,039	47,587	50,510
Rep. town meeting	8	50,346	48,316	49,537	51,000
Director of data processing					
Total	132	23,953	18,643	23,218	28,412
Geographic region					
Northeast	25	24,968	18,918	26,475	28,563
North Central	28	23,457	19,140	22,809	26,760
South	65	22,521	17,616	21,432	26,349
West	14	29,783	23,411	27,402	35,045
City type					
Central	8	24,251	21,320	23,828	24,768
Suburban	60	25,516	20,000	23,940	30,742
Independent	64	22,451	17,186	21,631	26,760
Form of government					
Mayor-council	30	22,467	17,372	21,500	25,609
Council-manager	88	24,281	19,092	23,082	29,587
Commission	3	19,654	. . .	17,909	. . .
Town meeting	7	23,972	18,307	23,751	28,369
Rep. town meeting	4	31,065	26,654	30,853	33,176
Director of budget and research					
Total	12	27,163	23,604	24,770	28,621
Geographic region					
Northeast	3	24,999	. . .	24,675	. . .
North Central	4	25,566	16,000	27,142	30,679
South	3	24,845	. . .	24,864	. . .
City type					
Suburban	7	25,565	22,966	24,675	26,530
Independent	4	30,535	16,000	28,291	31,980
Form of government					
Mayor-council	5	25,388	17,901	24,675	29,178
Council-manager	6	28,864	22,770	24,733	26,743
Asst. city mgr./asst. CAO					
Total	298	27,819	22,206	26,738	32,701
Geographic region					
Northeast	75	23,920	19,489	23,502	26,207
North Central	80	26,773	22,128	27,135	30,679
South	93	28,160	22,674	27,312	33,255
West	50	34,707	27,406	35,242	40,646
City type					
Central	9	28,313	24,325	25,850	31,163
Suburban	211	28,578	22,640	27,518	33,496
Independent	78	25,708	20,209	24,681	29,330
Form of government					
Mayor-council	60	24,360	20,540	23,652	27,820
Council-manager	216	29,315	23,376	28,097	34,400
Commission	4	20,414	17,655	20,000	20,000
Town meeting	16	22,910	19,032	21,874	25,904
Chief building inspector					
Total	865	23,549	19,347	23,136	27,071
Geographic region					
Northeast	237	22,850	19,432	22,604	25,849
North Central	257	24,911	21,000	24,586	28,635
South	259	20,859	16,951	19,978	23,751
West	112	28,126	23,976	27,516	31,752
City type					
Central	25	22,667	19,426	22,493	24,935
Suburban	535	24,938	20,805	24,918	28,629
Independent	305	21,185	17,334	20,540	23,976
Form of government					
Mayor-council	326	22,811	18,500	22,999	26,445
Council-manager	456	24,255	19,974	23,343	27,768
Commission	20	20,270	16,061	20,620	22,628
Town meeting	48	23,185	20,500	23,163	26,400
Rep. town meeting	15	23,652	19,666	23,885	27,065
5,000–9,999					
Mayor					
Total	997	4,872	1,500	2,460	5,000

Title of official	No. of cities reporting	Distribution of 1984 salaries: Mean ($)	First quartile ($)	Median ($)	Third quartile ($)
5,000–9,999 continued					
Geographic region					
Northeast	256	4,169	1,200	1,800	3,500
North Central	340	4,967	1,800	3,000	5,500
South	275	6,125	1,500	3,000	6,195
West	126	3,308	1,800	2,325	3,900
City type					
Suburban	537	4,538	1,385	2,400	4,500
Independent	460	5,261	1,500	2,893	6,000
Form of government					
Mayor-council	565	6,134	2,100	3,600	7,000
Council-manager	350	2,120	975	1,755	2,500
Commission	19	5,114	2,400	3,150	5,325
Town meeting	59	9,198	1,000	1,929	18,488
Rep. town meeting	4	2,375	1,000	2,250	3,000
City manager					
Total	472	34,337	29,400	33,780	38,669
Geographic region					
Northeast	102	30,018	25,726	28,830	33,637
North Central	118	35,054	31,079	34,000	38,000
South	161	33,308	28,637	32,500	36,492
West	91	40,070	36,421	40,080	43,959
City type					
Suburban	240	35,847	30,000	35,693	40,812
Independent	232	32,775	28,500	32,387	36,938
Form of government					
Council-manager	465	34,468	29,618	33,967	38,762
Town meeting	5	24,608	22,099	24,000	24,369
Chief administrative officer					
Total	337	30,688	25,432	30,408	35,451
Geographic region					
Northeast	100	28,460	21,892	27,900	32,165
North Central	92	31,349	27,597	31,640	35,947
South	93	29,048	24,060	28,500	33,514
West	52	36,738	30,408	35,490	41,020
City type					
Suburban	225	31,377	25,904	31,432	37,347
Independent	112	29,305	24,510	28,600	32,640
Form of government					
Mayor-council	291	31,403	26,308	31,065	36,105
Council-manager	21	30,721	27,315	29,000	34,587
Commission	5	27,685	13,500	28,700	33,050
Town meeting	16	21,105	17,000	19,600	22,000
Rep. town meeting	4	20,565	19,282	20,148	20,276
City clerk					
Total	859	19,934	16,000	19,344	23,139
Geographic region					
Northeast	208	18,620	14,700	18,148	21,000
North Central	251	20,402	16,470	20,100	24,176
South	291	19,394	16,000	18,624	22,371
West	109	22,803	18,515	22,104	27,400
City type					
Suburban	467	20,205	16,322	19,570	23,609
Independent	392	19,611	15,650	18,848	22,902
Form of government					
Mayor-council	464	20,301	16,203	19,537	23,704
Council-manager	330	19,923	16,519	19,864	23,383
Commission	16	22,050	15,412	17,838	21,051
Town meeting	46	15,682	13,330	15,502	17,515
Rep. town meeting	3	18,178	. . .	17,270	. . .
Finance director					
Total	309	25,381	19,823	25,155	30,284
Geographic region					
Northeast	34	22,834	17,484	20,600	25,574
North Central	80	24,766	20,000	25,416	28,749
South	106	22,971	17,648	22,620	26,165
West	89	29,776	25,042	29,237	33,426
City type					
Suburban	184	25,965	19,437	25,900	31,284
Independent	125	24,520	20,000	23,908	27,598
Form of government					
Mayor-council	101	24,758	17,625	23,748	30,692
Council-manager	199	25,875	20,474	25,390	30,367
Town meeting	6	22,742	17,469	24,168	25,574
Controller					
Total	42	21,490	17,750	19,902	24,347
Geographic region					
Northeast	10	15,753	12,546	16,112	17,367
North Central	18	24,260	19,290	23,192	26,771
South	11	21,778	19,370	21,320	22,724
West	3	22,938	. . .	22,400	. . .

Table 1/4 continued **SALARIES OF MUNICIPAL OFFICIALS: 1 JANUARY 1984**

Title of official	No. of cities reporting	Distribution of 1984 salaries Mean ($)	First quartile ($)	Median ($)	Third quartile ($)
5,000–9,999 continued					
City type					
Suburban	23	21,207	18,150	19,804	22,295
Independent	19	21,832	16,982	22,137	25,836
Form of government					
Mayor-council	20	22,110	18,224	19,725	22,400
Council-manager	16	23,193	19,510	23,465	26,713
Town meeting	5	13,458	10,625	14,091	15,130
Auditor					
Total	56	17,999	14,295	17,565	21,201
Geographic region					
Northeast	24	16,989	14,295	16,336	19,600
North Central	28	18,847	13,800	18,250	23,220
City type					
Suburban	30	18,645	14,298	17,648	22,000
Independent	26	17,254	12,900	17,565	20,495
Form of government					
Mayor-council	23	17,214	11,880	16,500	19,120
Council-manager	13	20,277	17,074	19,600	21,207
Town meeting	18	16,762	13,982	15,271	19,887
Treasurer					
Total	250	18,850	15,000	18,127	22,359
Geographic region					
Northeast	98	17,489	13,325	16,525	20,105
North Central	74	20,186	16,025	19,272	23,578
South	51	18,558	14,674	18,634	22,277
West	27	20,676	16,084	18,792	23,604
City type					
Suburban	142	19,794	15,657	19,338	23,147
Independent	108	17,608	14,000	16,958	20,000
Form of government					
Mayor-council	121	18,970	15,000	18,000	21,975
Council-manager	96	19,523	15,780	19,000	22,466
Commission	6	18,679	14,646	17,293	19,471
Town meeting	26	15,905	12,540	15,588	19,597
City engineer					
Total	167	29,729	24,975	29,848	34,125
Geographic region					
Northeast	26	29,106	23,650	28,559	33,181
North Central	55	30,682	27,782	31,545	34,366
South	44	26,965	23,155	26,092	30,160
West	42	31,764	27,453	30,504	35,724
City type					
Suburban	73	31,705	28,094	31,545	35,298
Independent	94	28,195	23,565	28,525	32,402
Form of government					
Mayor-council	85	30,260	25,924	30,240	34,767
Council-manager	73	29,280	24,380	29,280	33,800
Town meeting	7	26,982	23,625	27,200	28,397
Director of public works					
Total	714	26,175	21,612	25,516	30,195
Geographic region					
Northeast	141	25,725	21,510	24,835	28,233
North Central	211	27,275	23,273	26,890	31,411
South	234	23,355	19,317	23,000	26,453
West	128	30,009	24,852	29,682	34,091
City type					
Suburban	409	26,958	22,274	26,195	31,500
Independent	305	25,124	20,895	24,607	28,412
Form of government					
Mayor-council	334	26,201	21,336	25,672	30,075
Council-manager	344	26,372	21,844	25,593	30,500
Commission	8	26,341	19,115	28,140	31,000
Town meeting	25	23,488	19,216	23,543	26,123
Rep. town meeting	3	22,540	. . .	21,060	. . .
Superintendent of streets					
Total	729	21,216	18,000	20,800	23,798
Geographic region					
Northeast	179	21,968	19,120	21,400	24,447
North Central	238	21,864	19,000	21,793	24,397
South	239	18,775	15,946	18,283	20,974
West	73	25,248	21,006	24,284	28,254
City type					
Suburban	362	22,125	18,610	21,684	25,200
Independent	367	20,319	17,583	19,752	22,500
Form of government					
Mayor-council	395	21,287	18,015	20,500	23,913
Council-manager	278	21,177	17,840	20,870	24,000
Commission	15	21,070	16,425	19,756	23,052
Town meeting	38	21,001	19,649	21,191	22,145
Rep. town meeting	3	18,842	. . .	18,366	. . .

Title of official	No. of cities reporting	Distribution of 1984 salaries Mean ($)	First quartile ($)	Median ($)	Third quartile ($)
5,000–9,999 continued					
Fire chief					
Total	491	23,266	18,647	22,500	26,651
Geographic region					
Northeast	58	23,100	19,950	21,923	25,451
North Central	151	23,862	19,500	24,037	26,949
South	208	20,721	17,098	19,724	23,448
West	74	29,337	24,780	29,526	33,180
City type					
Suburban	222	25,688	20,747	24,930	29,950
Independent	269	21,267	17,611	20,477	24,429
Form of government					
Mayor-council	233	22,616	17,689	21,144	25,875
Council-manager	220	24,066	19,598	23,716	26,832
Commission	13	21,787	16,913	21,200	24,859
Town meeting	21	23,444	20,105	22,000	27,013
Rep. town meeting	4	21,006	19,000	20,480	21,060
Police chief					
Total	1178	25,744	21,269	24,798	29,165
Geographic region					
Northeast	290	26,677	22,168	25,671	29,821
North Central	365	25,848	21,988	25,300	29,000
South	362	22,605	18,995	21,642	25,000
West	161	30,885	26,464	30,069	34,512
City type					
Suburban	647	27,611	22,730	27,081	31,805
Independent	531	23,469	20,017	22,842	26,591
Form of government					
Mayor-council	620	25,243	20,420	24,030	29,059
Council-manager	484	26,444	22,000	25,576	29,500
Commission	23	22,821	18,606	22,050	25,113
Town meeting	47	26,849	23,475	27,017	29,063
Rep. town meeting	4	22,387	19,500	22,282	23,463
Planning director					
Total	157	25,986	19,762	25,500	30,860
Geographic region					
Northeast	12	18,239	14,734	18,575	19,200
North Central	33	24,124	19,115	23,400	27,380
South	43	23,758	18,050	24,516	27,685
West	69	29,613	24,176	28,900	34,314
City type					
Suburban	89	27,329	21,738	27,780	32,795
Independent	68	24,229	19,040	24,237	28,224
Form of government					
Mayor-council	52	25,072	19,200	24,042	28,680
Council-manager	101	26,797	19,927	26,380	31,434
Town meeting	3	14,988	. . .	11,377	. . .
Chief personnel officer					
Total	54	19,794	15,482	18,245	22,278
Geographic region					
Northeast	3	17,028	. . .	17,576	. . .
North Central	8	21,502	11,897	21,806	23,850
South	31	19,015	14,594	17,500	21,095
West	12	21,358	17,659	20,910	23,233
City type					
Suburban	28	20,500	15,000	19,604	22,800
Independent	26	19,033	15,482	17,966	21,116
Form of government					
Mayor-council	20	18,657	13,660	16,695	21,112
Council-manager	34	20,462	16,776	19,354	22,278
Attorney					
Total	109	19,117	12,290	16,113	23,717
Geographic region					
Northeast	14	16,040	12,750	15,700	18,143
North Central	49	16,795	12,000	15,000	20,850
South	21	17,887	10,322	13,543	23,000
West	25	26,424	16,984	25,176	32,685
City type					
Suburban	42	19,519	14,975	17,389	23,433
Independent	67	18,865	11,098	15,246	23,049
Form of government					
Mayor-council	67	16,995	11,735	15,110	20,022
Council-manager	38	23,245	15,000	21,970	31,055
Commission	4	15,439	8,682	11,538	12,075
Health officer					
Total	22	19,735	15,575	19,374	23,395
Geographic region					
Northeast	18	19,508	13,443	19,374	23,356
North Central	3	19,915	. . .	19,000	. . .
City type					
Suburban	14	21,099	15,760	22,997	23,745

Table 1/4 continued — SALARIES OF MUNICIPAL OFFICIALS: 1 JANUARY 1984

Title of official	No. of cities reporting	Mean ($)	First quartile ($)	Median ($)	Third quartile ($)
		Distribution of 1984 salaries			
5,000–9,999 continued					
Independent	8	17,348	14,386	18,043	19,000
Form of government					
Mayor-council	10	24,133	22,997	23,570	23,908
Council-manager	6	16,666	12,193	17,892	19,253
Town meeting	5	14,771	11,429	12,500	17,361
Director of parks and recreation					
Total	301	20,732	16,369	19,500	23,794
Geographic region					
Northeast	39	18,908	14,200	18,512	20,899
North Central	103	21,296	18,000	20,790	24,289
South	112	18,877	15,600	17,526	21,162
West	47	25,430	20,392	25,648	30,395
City type					
Suburban	147	21,516	16,448	20,160	25,113
Independent	154	19,983	16,325	19,030	22,604
Form of government					
Mayor-council	156	19,609	15,996	18,529	22,815
Council-manager	128	22,706	18,283	21,822	25,929
Commission	3	18,120	...	16,500	...
Town meeting	13	15,873	12,212	14,412	17,956
Superintendent of parks					
Total	169	18,661	15,260	18,262	21,509
Geographic region					
Northeast	11	17,494	15,349	17,700	19,204
North Central	79	18,634	15,123	18,393	21,427
South	47	16,637	13,784	16,597	18,141
West	32	22,105	19,806	21,846	23,989
City type					
Suburban	61	19,696	17,134	19,050	22,859
Independent	108	18,077	15,000	18,002	21,120
Form of government					
Mayor-council	72	18,034	15,000	17,384	21,112
Council-manager	86	19,269	16,226	18,811	22,354
Commission	6	17,566	14,523	16,710	19,661
Town meeting	5	18,569	16,278	17,700	20,030
Director of recreation					
Total	160	18,528	15,297	17,953	21,133
Geographic region					
Northeast	39	17,034	14,787	16,614	18,918
North Central	51	18,686	15,619	17,955	21,427
South	47	17,747	14,060	16,800	19,672
West	23	22,310	19,508	20,760	24,042
City type					
Suburban	77	19,979	15,518	19,300	22,953
Independent	83	17,183	14,929	16,800	19,281
Form of government					
Mayor-council	65	18,008	15,166	17,955	20,572
Council-manager	82	19,590	16,259	18,889	22,718
Commission	3	16,803	...	15,960	...
Town meeting	9	13,472	10,569	13,100	14,787
Librarian					
Total	330	17,044	13,244	16,466	20,035
Geographic region					
Northeast	79	16,680	13,500	16,536	18,487
North Central	127	17,586	13,802	17,680	20,367
South	71	15,103	11,045	13,104	18,029
West	53	18,889	15,211	17,776	20,490
City type					
Suburban	151	17,810	13,773	17,464	21,011
Independent	179	16,399	12,727	15,965	19,321
Form of government					
Mayor-council	146	16,611	13,032	16,115	19,554
Council-manager	146	17,689	13,218	17,128	21,332
Commission	8	16,914	13,827	17,910	19,536
Town meeting	28	16,225	14,397	16,196	18,652
Superintendent of schools					
Total	72	39,906	35,500	39,777	44,023
Geographic region					
Northeast	53	39,964	35,678	40,000	44,115
North Central	6	46,958	41,347	45,709	47,517
South	12	33,994	30,000	35,660	37,485
City type					
Suburban	41	40,195	37,121	40,000	44,115
Independent	31	39,525	34,660	38,350	43,606
Form of government					
Mayor-council	17	43,776	33,733	44,023	51,500
Council-manager	28	38,985	35,464	38,563	42,000
Town meeting	26	38,354	35,603	39,692	43,977
Director of data processing					
Total	28	18,504	13,845	15,660	20,578

Title of official	No. of cities reporting	Mean ($)	First quartile ($)	Median ($)	Third quartile ($)
		Distribution of 1984 salaries			
5,000–9,999 continued					
Geographic region					
Northeast	3	15,123	...	14,525	...
North Central	4	14,299	13,655	13,910	14,040
South	15	16,991	13,089	15,000	19,182
West	6	26,782	17,064	24,604	26,659
City type					
Suburban	8	17,306	14,172	15,000	17,000
Independent	20	18,984	13,780	15,941	21,914
Form of government					
Mayor-council	7	15,089	12,758	13,780	16,332
Council-manager	20	19,899	14,172	16,581	22,995
Director of budget and research					
Total	6	17,961	8,000	16,285	22,285
Geographic region					
Northeast	3	18,398	...	11,000	...
City type					
Independent	4	15,893	8,000	16,285	21,570
Form of government					
Mayor-council	4	15,799	8,000	9,500	11,000
Asst. city mgr./asst. CAO					
Total	152	23,137	18,000	22,020	27,612
Geographic region					
Northeast	40	19,140	15,000	18,950	22,250
North Central	32	24,617	20,205	24,108	27,500
South	54	22,575	18,000	21,097	27,454
West	26	28,630	23,106	28,933	32,793
City type					
Suburban	90	23,255	18,262	22,325	28,103
Independent	62	22,965	16,826	21,832	27,304
Form of government					
Mayor-council	42	22,858	18,000	21,354	27,520
Council-manager	104	23,727	18,500	22,901	27,810
Town meeting	5	14,859	14,352	15,000	15,014
Chief building inspector					
Total	533	20,783	17,160	20,100	24,104
Geographic region					
Northeast	110	20,086	17,024	19,258	22,347
North Central	152	21,682	18,165	21,511	24,835
South	172	18,568	15,600	17,961	21,400
West	99	24,025	20,272	23,616	27,886
City type					
Suburban	295	21,950	18,026	21,583	25,499
Independent	238	19,336	16,209	18,810	21,731
Form of government					
Mayor-council	228	20,841	17,098	20,329	24,208
Council-manager	268	20,975	17,285	20,150	24,300
Commission	8	19,115	15,750	17,608	21,216
Town meeting	27	18,984	17,070	19,000	21,296
2,500–4,999					
Mayor					
Total	1196	3,033	1,000	1,800	3,500
Geographic region					
Northeast	242	2,822	735	1,310	3,000
North Central	437	2,644	1,000	1,800	3,000
South	390	3,694	1,200	2,100	3,960
West	127	2,742	1,200	1,800	3,600
City type					
Suburban	528	2,838	1,000	1,800	3,467
Independent	668	3,188	1,000	1,800	3,600
Form of government					
Mayor-council	860	3,266	1,200	2,100	3,600
Council-manager	244	1,776	600	1,200	1,980
Commission	23	3,301	1,200	1,800	3,479
Town meeting	59	4,915	604	1,440	6,500
Rep. town meeting	10	1,995	1,450	1,600	2,000
City manager					
Total	327	29,746	25,000	28,654	33,225
Geographic region					
Northeast	54	23,590	19,464	22,547	26,668
North Central	80	31,565	27,140	31,454	34,603
South	137	28,380	24,136	27,500	31,475
West	56	36,426	30,000	33,027	38,500
City type					
Suburban	133	31,668	26,530	31,200	36,075
Independent	194	28,428	23,366	27,500	31,500
Form of government					

Table 1/4 continued **SALARIES OF MUNICIPAL OFFICIALS: 1 JANUARY 1984**

Title of official	No. of cities reporting	Distribution of 1984 salaries: Mean ($)	First quartile ($)	Median ($)	Third quartile ($)
2,500–4,999 continued					
Council-manager	306	30,320	25,200	29,075	33,502
Town meeting	18	20,521	17,210	20,000	22,288
Chief administrative officer					
Total	415	25,995	21,008	26,000	30,000
Geographic region					
Northeast	75	22,537	17,950	22,000	27,206
North Central	129	27,527	24,068	27,500	30,538
South	138	23,979	19,520	23,234	28,000
West	73	30,654	26,114	29,368	33,876
City type					
Suburban	222	26,533	21,438	26,688	30,322
Independent	193	25,376	20,987	25,200	28,675
Form of government					
Mayor-council	351	25,969	21,104	26,000	30,000
Council-manager	37	29,226	24,024	27,864	34,000
Commission	5	27,257	18,663	23,276	31,589
Town meeting	15	20,831	16,763	20,000	24,368
Rep. town meeting	7	20,412	16,825	18,100	23,500
City clerk					
Total	1011	17,148	13,200	16,276	19,850
Geographic region					
Northeast	171	15,881	11,581	14,706	19,084
North Central	314	17,889	14,000	17,605	21,124
South	389	15,890	12,914	15,320	18,000
West	137	20,603	16,182	19,104	23,875
City type					
Suburban	421	17,633	13,689	16,952	20,546
Independent	590	16,802	13,012	15,884	19,398
Form of government					
Mayor-council	711	16,931	13,000	16,019	19,808
Council-manager	247	18,069	14,404	17,000	20,373
Commission	16	21,191	17,824	19,094	22,600
Town meeting	32	13,137	10,000	14,024	15,100
Rep. town meeting	5	15,191	11,225	15,220	15,232
Finance director					
Total	161	21,725	15,891	20,160	25,132
Geographic region					
Northeast	14	16,266	12,007	16,643	17,585
North Central	42	21,207	16,889	20,113	24,748
South	56	18,861	14,830	17,750	22,500
West	49	27,000	20,085	24,446	30,105
City type					
Suburban	80	21,943	16,500	21,319	25,498
Independent	81	21,508	15,374	19,138	24,619
Form of government					
Mayor-council	74	20,018	15,303	18,753	22,650
Council-manager	79	23,832	17,113	22,500	26,311
Town meeting	5	13,686	9,525	15,005	15,958
Controller					
Total	31	17,036	13,369	16,487	19,685
Geographic region					
Northeast	5	15,612	10,425	14,846	17,635
North Central	10	16,880	11,200	15,058	21,392
South	10	16,064	13,374	16,148	18,700
West	6	20,103	14,579	17,476	18,988
City type					
Suburban	14	16,746	12,662	16,622	19,277
Independent	17	17,275	12,929	15,252	19,602
Form of government					
Mayor-council	15	15,773	11,525	16,492	18,837
Council-manager	13	18,990	14,207	16,487	19,686
Town meeting	3	14,883	...	14,700	...
Auditor					
Total	13	14,988	9,665	15,000	19,058
Geographic region					
Northeast	5	14,304	9,665	12,172	17,286
North Central	6	15,944	11,609	16,302	18,342
City type					
Suburban	6	11,539	8,350	10,330	11,916
Independent	7	17,944	14,930	18,990	19,175
Form of government					
Mayor-council	8	14,340	8,500	14,859	19,080
Town meeting	3	14,511	...	12,172	...
Treasurer					
Total	241	16,393	12,762	15,884	19,010
Geographic region					
Northeast	52	14,993	10,500	13,927	17,345
North Central	76	17,255	14,000	17,684	19,249
South	71	14,929	12,419	13,728	17,448
West	42	19,042	14,770	19,000	22,071
2,500–4,999 continued					
City type					
Suburban	108	16,847	13,062	16,938	19,351
Independent	133	16,025	12,617	15,456	18,486
Form of government					
Mayor-council	139	15,542	12,048	15,215	18,068
Council-manager	89	18,099	13,850	18,110	20,139
Town meeting	8	12,558	9,500	10,756	15,305
Rep. town meeting	3	12,342	...	10,500	...
City engineer					
Total	70	27,785	21,929	26,694	31,373
Geographic region					
Northeast	5	24,189	20,471	22,500	25,095
North Central	21	25,483	20,747	27,210	29,845
South	20	24,363	20,424	24,203	26,687
West	24	33,402	26,500	31,440	39,180
City type					
Suburban	22	26,889	21,298	27,608	30,972
Independent	48	28,196	22,461	26,604	30,845
Form of government					
Mayor-council	44	26,164	20,424	26,510	30,000
Council-manager	23	31,215	24,071	28,800	33,972
Director of public works					
Total	784	22,220	18,200	21,530	25,139
Geographic region					
Northeast	109	21,458	18,375	20,712	23,854
North Central	250	23,363	19,903	22,690	26,556
South	304	19,685	16,480	18,923	22,339
West	121	26,914	21,612	24,900	29,048
City type					
Suburban	347	23,087	18,902	22,500	26,500
Independent	437	21,532	17,892	20,712	24,057
Form of government					
Mayor-council	511	22,020	18,000	21,465	25,438
Council-manager	235	22,990	18,876	22,000	25,000
Commission	10	22,690	17,464	21,465	24,038
Town meeting	21	18,837	16,030	17,950	21,011
Rep. town meeting	7	20,427	17,548	18,900	23,135
Superintendent of streets					
Total	719	18,482	15,500	17,853	21,000
Geographic region					
Northeast	134	18,508	16,362	18,452	20,292
North Central	282	19,199	16,204	18,710	21,840
South	224	16,124	13,567	15,656	17,846
West	79	22,561	19,036	21,708	25,863
City type					
Suburban	287	19,446	16,135	18,850	22,412
Independent	432	17,841	15,120	17,366	20,000
Form of government					
Mayor-council	512	18,173	15,212	17,645	20,776
Council-manager	160	19,427	15,965	18,474	21,609
Commission	12	19,745	16,151	19,276	20,008
Town meeting	30	18,315	16,362	17,993	19,500
Rep. town meeting	5	17,795	15,450	18,792	19,087
Fire chief					
Total	220	20,766	15,900	18,995	24,000
Geographic region					
Northeast	13	22,661	18,016	23,514	24,847
North Central	36	22,673	16,031	20,537	27,660
South	117	17,254	14,860	16,864	19,066
West	54	26,647	21,638	23,102	28,278
City type					
Suburban	81	23,045	17,217	21,126	26,770
Independent	139	19,438	15,259	17,492	21,701
Form of government					
Mayor-council	128	19,696	15,312	17,359	22,560
Council-manager	79	22,345	17,141	19,511	24,450
Commission	6	20,940	15,686	19,654	23,562
Town meeting	4	21,563	16,115	22,198	23,514
Rep. town meeting	3	23,410	...	24,000	...
Police chief					
Total	1338	21,487	17,498	20,406	24,438
Geographic region					
Northeast	231	21,770	17,900	20,904	24,349
North Central	462	21,889	18,171	21,080	24,875
South	469	18,896	15,863	18,200	20,892
West	176	26,969	22,200	25,500	29,316
City type					
Suburban	596	23,462	19,000	22,845	26,712
Independent	742	19,902	16,658	19,234	22,200
Form of government					

Table 1/4 continued **SALARIES OF MUNICIPAL OFFICIALS: 1 JANUARY 1984**

Title of official	No. of cities reporting	Distribution of 1984 salaries: Mean ($)	First quartile ($)	Median ($)	Third quartile ($)
2,500–4,999 continued					
Mayor-council	925	20,839	17,000	19,994	23,869
Council-manager	341	23,372	18,905	22,104	25,950
Commission	22	21,187	17,191	20,463	23,000
Town meeting	40	20,871	16,585	19,245	23,983
Rep. town meeting	10	20,327	16,738	21,005	22,055
Planning director					
Total	68	24,567	18,514	22,845	28,500
Geographic region					
Northeast	4	16,307	13,500	16,663	17,935
North Central	10	23,327	21,550	24,055	25,986
South	16	19,992	14,742	19,297	21,000
West	38	27,689	20,546	24,692	34,500
City type					
Suburban	28	26,159	20,000	24,189	28,500
Independent	40	23,452	17,935	21,206	25,200
Form of government					
Mayor-council	30	23,176	17,628	22,854	27,415
Council-manager	37	25,862	18,704	22,949	29,691
Chief personnel officer					
Total	22	17,840	13,437	17,009	20,922
Geographic region					
South	18	16,544	13,030	14,967	18,963
West	3	24,272	...	25,068	...
City type					
Suburban	7	16,822	13,268	15,840	17,700
Independent	15	18,314	13,192	19,200	21,628
Form of government					
Mayor-council	10	16,471	12,934	13,717	17,520
Council-manager	11	18,718	13,747	18,158	20,607
Attorney					
Total	48	18,092	12,000	14,801	18,060
Geographic region					
Northeast	4	16,154	11,449	14,582	17,163
North Central	14	14,772	10,926	13,950	17,795
South	7	18,222	10,350	12,000	17,730
West	23	20,411	12,900	16,628	24,398
City type					
Suburban	20	18,654	13,489	16,982	19,500
Independent	28	17,691	11,115	13,350	18,000
Form of government					
Mayor-council	37	15,891	11,622	14,400	17,956
Council-manager	11	25,496	13,012	18,000	26,477
Health officer					
Total	9	20,843	14,703	19,510	24,176
Geographic region					
Northeast	4	15,481	10,709	15,852	17,091
West	3	27,563	...	25,068	...
City type					
Suburban	3	17,895	...	14,975	...
Independent	6	22,317	15,852	20,505	23,284
Form of government					
Mayor-council	5	17,959	11,685	14,975	19,869
Council-manager	3	26,093	...	25,068	...
Director of parks and recreation					
Total	139	17,957	14,195	16,515	19,869
Geographic region					
Northeast	15	15,689	13,468	15,750	16,850
North Central	41	17,230	14,284	17,040	19,215
South	54	15,421	12,444	15,473	17,125
West	29	24,879	17,622	23,544	28,719
City type					
Suburban	57	18,011	14,233	17,118	21,553
Independent	82	17,919	14,168	16,373	19,070
Form of government					
Mayor-council	82	16,625	13,000	16,035	18,688
Council-manager	52	20,117	15,000	17,996	21,612
Town meeting	3	17,697	...	17,170	...
Superintendent of parks					
Total	77	16,898	14,000	16,360	19,167
Geographic region					
Northeast	6	19,381	14,856	20,177	22,379
North Central	35	16,269	14,620	16,000	17,865
South	20	15,262	11,100	15,392	18,171
West	16	19,389	14,160	18,736	21,000
City type					
Suburban	24	16,806	13,643	17,036	19,920
Independent	53	16,940	14,000	16,360	19,112
Form of government					
Mayor-council	49	16,294	13,715	15,984	18,831
Council-manager	23	17,737	14,474	16,744	19,192
2,500–4,999 continued					
Commission	4	20,200	14,760	20,778	22,555
Director of recreation					
Total	77	16,575	13,475	15,660	18,554
Geographic region					
Northeast	13	15,531	13,720	15,100	16,934
North Central	22	16,708	13,025	15,519	19,360
South	33	16,121	13,433	15,302	18,734
West	9	19,421	15,825	17,895	18,550
City type					
Suburban	28	16,628	13,300	16,422	19,406
Independent	49	16,544	13,475	15,500	18,031
Form of government					
Mayor-council	38	15,271	13,000	15,000	16,392
Council-manager	35	18,185	13,945	17,895	20,295
Librarian					
Total	215	13,825	10,740	12,738	15,635
Geographic region					
Northeast	29	12,781	10,005	12,300	14,755
North Central	84	13,936	11,099	13,150	16,500
South	50	12,036	9,578	11,261	13,629
West	52	15,947	11,762	14,257	17,304
City type					
Suburban	75	13,887	11,081	13,661	15,971
Independent	140	13,791	10,525	12,220	15,483
Form of government					
Mayor-council	135	13,227	10,331	12,400	15,512
Council-manager	67	15,355	11,100	14,140	16,950
Town meeting	10	12,215	9,500	11,625	14,750
Rep. town meeting	3	11,914	...	13,741	...
Superintendent of schools					
Total	41	37,079	31,640	35,500	42,000
Geographic region					
Northeast	32	34,512	30,000	35,000	38,000
North Central	3	51,935	...	49,704	...
South	5	36,725	31,279	35,000	37,625
City type					
Suburban	18	37,785	32,794	35,850	44,224
Independent	23	36,526	30,279	35,000	39,375
Form of government					
Mayor-council	10	42,768	34,500	40,150	47,728
Council-manager	9	40,525	30,421	37,600	38,500
Town meeting	20	33,774	26,765	35,000	38,000
Director of data processing					
Total	16	17,286	14,094	16,400	18,781
Geographic region					
North Central	3	15,641	...	15,621	...
South	4	13,852	10,400	13,906	14,094
West	8	19,405	15,404	16,884	21,200
City type					
Independent	14	17,671	14,175	16,400	18,098
Form of government					
Mayor-council	7	15,300	11,992	16,000	16,899
Council-manager	8	18,809	14,094	16,295	21,200
Director of budget and research					
Total	4	20,668	9,700	21,894	22,000
City type					
Independent	3	20,224	...	21,788	...
Asst. city mgr./asst. CAO					
Total	89	20,219	14,470	19,080	24,100
Geographic region					
Northeast	18	16,783	12,200	15,784	20,023
North Central	21	21,761	17,531	22,250	24,745
South	36	18,643	13,520	17,804	22,308
West	14	26,374	15,743	25,220	30,030
City type					
Suburban	47	20,273	13,726	20,124	24,970
Independent	42	20,157	14,563	18,082	23,442
Form of government					
Mayor-council	48	18,821	14,349	17,813	23,400
Council-manager	35	23,406	17,250	22,368	26,035
Town meeting	4	12,163	10,400	12,200	12,600
Chief building inspector					
Total	200	19,799	15,982	18,733	22,966
Geographic region					
Northeast	37	17,793	14,561	17,348	20,436
North Central	47	20,484	17,375	19,780	23,367
South	67	17,856	14,416	17,568	20,130
West	49	23,312	18,719	22,134	25,611
City type					
Suburban	105	20,393	17,000	19,780	24,120

Table 1/4 continued SALARIES OF MUNICIPAL OFFICIALS: 1 JANUARY 1984

Title of official	No. of cities reporting	Mean ($)	First quartile ($)	Median ($)	Third quartile ($)
		Distribution of 1984 salaries			
2,500–4,999 continued					
Independent	95	19,141	15,600	18,000	20,852
Form of government					
Mayor-council	100	19,666	16,227	18,689	22,766
Council-manager	85	20,382	15,938	19,704	24,013
Commission	3	21,352	...	19,554	...
Town meeting	9	16,699	15,882	17,256	17,340
Rep. town meeting	3	15,440	...	16,640	...
Under 2,500					
Mayor					
Total	174	1,083	500	750	1,200
Geographic region					
Northeast	39	740	375	500	683
North Central	61	891	435	720	1,200
South	52	1,406	600	1,040	1,500
West	22	1,462	600	1,050	1,200
City type					
Suburban	53	1,160	555	720	1,313
Independent	121	1,050	428	750	1,200
Form of government					
Mayor-council	57	1,061	600	960	1,200
Council-manager	96	1,158	500	775	1,200
Town meeting	21	801	385	500	719
City manager					
Total	174	25,262	17,870	22,553	28,617
Geographic region					
Northeast	49	16,918	13,032	16,500	20,425
North Central	33	25,220	21,275	24,786	28,056
South	57	22,936	18,000	22,000	26,011
West	35	40,769	27,898	39,504	52,449
City type					
Suburban	39	28,450	21,425	26,015	30,600
Independent	135	24,341	16,975	21,500	27,816
Form of government					
Council-manager	147	26,951	19,709	24,381	29,490
Town meeting	27	16,065	11,405	16,500	18,246
Chief administrative officer					
Total	54	23,936	19,000	23,508	26,541
Geographic region					
Northeast	9	25,204	17,875	24,251	28,671
North Central	25	21,990	17,888	23,000	25,034
South	11	21,292	16,675	20,000	23,624
West	9	31,308	23,713	30,314	35,668
City type					
Suburban	23	24,205	20,000	24,000	27,387
Independent	31	23,737	17,955	22,950	26,025
Form of government					
Mayor-council	51	24,148	19,000	23,518	26,986
City clerk					
Total	140	17,497	13,104	15,490	19,560
Geographic region					
Northeast	14	13,107	11,927	12,432	14,000
North Central	42	16,181	14,103	15,490	18,100
South	47	14,074	11,439	13,432	15,804
West	37	25,002	18,375	22,300	32,298
City type					
Suburban	41	16,833	13,788	16,139	18,264
Independent	99	17,773	12,960	15,457	19,592
Form of government					
Mayor-council	35	15,792	12,029	15,080	18,453
Council-manager	99	18,422	13,422	16,139	20,252
Town meeting	5	11,952	10,424	12,384	12,456
Finance director					
Total	30	26,710	16,051	21,879	35,232
Geographic region					
South	13	15,952	10,920	15,204	18,864
West	16	35,991	22,926	35,232	43,644
City type					
Suburban	7	21,898	17,178	20,832	23,702
Independent	23	28,175	14,778	22,926	40,420
Form of government					
Mayor-council	3	21,936	...	18,873	...
Council-manager	27	27,241	15,118	22,926	36,413
Controller					
Total	5	19,037	11,386	15,600	23,861
Geographic region					
West	4	21,046	12,544	21,108	26,615
City type					
Independent	4	19,896	11,000	19,580	26,615
Under 2,500 continued					
Form of government					
Council-manager	4	19,896	11,000	19,580	26,615
Treasurer					
Total	33	15,921	11,374	14,150	16,649
Geographic region					
Northeast	5	13,067	10,300	12,135	14,284
North Central	14	15,638	12,232	14,707	16,493
South	8	11,568	10,161	10,956	11,340
West	6	24,762	13,564	20,770	27,951
City type					
Suburban	8	16,058	13,440	14,607	15,683
Independent	25	15,877	11,235	12,688	16,649
Form of government					
Mayor-council	7	13,690	11,620	13,688	14,756
Council-manager	24	17,015	11,340	14,607	18,720
City engineer					
Total	10	30,830	19,317	29,035	38,765
Geographic region					
West	7	36,602	27,383	36,634	41,619
City type					
Independent	8	31,181	20,684	29,035	36,634
Form of government					
Council-manager	7	34,720	20,001	36,634	41,619
Director of public works					
Total	138	21,123	16,176	19,560	23,050
Geographic region					
Northeast	15	15,380	11,996	14,000	17,010
North Central	41	20,311	17,627	20,000	22,360
South	48	17,882	14,443	17,448	20,136
West	34	29,211	21,000	24,560	35,526
City type					
Suburban	38	20,498	16,825	19,264	22,022
Independent	100	21,361	15,750	19,823	23,672
Form of government					
Mayor-council	35	20,621	16,657	20,156	22,773
Council-manager	96	21,848	16,568	19,744	23,649
Town meeting	6	13,712	11,125	13,596	13,681
Superintendent of streets					
Total	92	18,065	14,300	16,753	19,785
Geographic region					
Northeast	17	17,105	14,400	16,348	17,865
North Central	35	19,073	16,462	18,512	20,000
South	27	13,861	12,199	13,832	14,880
West	13	25,335	18,515	21,970	30,662
City type					
Suburban	22	20,741	16,753	19,909	24,957
Independent	70	17,223	13,936	16,280	18,694
Form of government					
Mayor-council	30	18,341	15,190	17,632	19,909
Council-manager	55	18,372	13,948	16,440	19,300
Town meeting	7	14,466	11,700	14,300	15,690
Fire chief					
Total	18	24,907	14,370	20,687	34,227
Geographic region					
South	9	16,756	10,916	16,000	19,399
West	8	35,225	30,000	35,569	39,325
City type					
Suburban	5	28,600	19,500	26,978	31,972
Independent	13	23,486	11,964	16,000	33,613
Form of government					
Council-manager	18	24,907	14,370	20,687	34,227
Police chief					
Total	201	20,858	15,528	18,874	22,878
Geographic region					
Northeast	23	17,432	14,778	15,500	19,375
North Central	62	19,721	16,884	19,348	22,222
South	76	17,055	13,912	16,791	20,000
West	40	31,815	22,778	28,144	41,333
City type					
Suburban	56	21,723	17,043	20,997	24,578
Independent	145	20,524	15,050	18,360	22,481
Form of government					
Mayor-council	58	19,762	16,250	18,744	22,247
Council-manager	136	21,643	15,200	19,420	22,960
Town meeting	6	14,282	10,450	14,895	15,500
Planning director					
Total	20	28,767	21,884	25,416	35,596
Geographic region					
South	4	18,971	17,015	18,573	19,169
West	15	31,838	23,659	34,000	36,415
City type					

Table 1/4 continued **SALARIES OF MUNICIPAL OFFICIALS: 1 JANUARY 1984**

Title of official	No. of cities reporting	Mean ($)	First quartile ($)	Median ($)	Third quartile ($)
		Distribution of 1984 salaries			
Under 2,500 continued					
Suburban	3	25,025	...	22,464	...
Independent	17	29,427	21,912	26,832	35,711
Form of government					
Council-manager	17	28,955	21,791	24,000	36,015
Chief personnel officer					
Total	4	32,920	26,750	33,121	36,742
Geographic region					
West	4	32,920	26,750	33,121	36,742
City type					
Independent	4	32,920	26,750	33,121	36,742
Form of government					
Council-manager	4	32,920	26,750	33,121	36,742
Attorney					
Total	5	33,051	13,264	27,600	44,400
Geographic region					
West	5	33,051	13,264	27,600	44,400
City type					
Independent	5	33,051	13,264	27,600	44,400
Form of government					
Council-manager	3	44,200	...	50,000	...
Health officer					
Total	3	25,558	...	23,465	...
City type					
Independent	3	25,558	...	23,465	...
Director of parks and recreation					
Total	16	21,364	14,000	16,700	26,649
Geographic region					
South	5	15,884	11,656	16,697	16,702
West	9	26,571	14,306	26,649	35,306
City type					
Suburban	3	15,273	...	15,122	...
Independent	13	22,769	12,030	19,018	27,047
Form of government					
Mayor-council	3	16,813	...	14,000	...
Council-manager	13	22,414	14,281	16,703	25,087
Superintendent of parks					
Total	5	14,157	10,380	12,648	13,692
City type					
Independent	3	11,604	...	10,400	...
Form of government					
Mayor-council	3	12,354	...	12,648	...
Director of recreation					
Total	8	25,842	16,027	18,166	38,916
Geographic region					
West	5	31,695	16,826	38,916	40,545
City type					

Title of official	No. of cities reporting	Mean ($)	First quartile ($)	Median ($)	Third quartile ($)
		Distribution of 1984 salaries			
Under 2,500 continued					
Suburban	4	23,086	17,097	18,166	19,224
Independent	4	28,598	14,057	28,558	41,088
Form of government					
Council-manager	8	25,842	16,027	18,166	38,916
Librarian					
Total	22	16,981	9,815	12,771	19,357
Geographic region					
North Central	7	10,837	9,256	9,880	11,044
South	5	10,356	9,209	10,117	10,179
West	10	24,595	16,782	19,892	31,374
City type					
Independent	20	16,709	9,750	12,771	18,950
Form of government					
Mayor-council	7	11,348	9,256	10,600	12,422
Council-manager	15	19,610	10,025	17,844	21,774
Superintendent of schools					
Total	9	45,633	29,750	45,000	55,425
Geographic region					
Northeast	4	36,045	29,000	32,090	32,180
West	3	65,358	...	64,175	...
City type					
Independent	7	44,956	28,110	32,180	58,719
Form of government					
Council-manager	8	47,712	32,000	48,000	56,900
Asst. city mgr./asst. CAO					
Total	16	22,305	11,452	14,523	26,208
Geographic region					
Northeast	5	11,727	9,480	12,000	12,855
South	4	13,836	11,357	11,906	12,360
West	6	37,905	26,022	42,284	43,332
City type					
Suburban	6	26,888	12,249	23,006	35,028
Independent	10	19,555	11,186	12,968	20,839
Form of government					
Council-manager	10	28,689	13,915	26,022	42,284
Town meeting	5	11,727	9,480	12,000	12,855
Chief building inspector					
Total	26	23,642	17,211	20,768	30,251
Geographic region					
South	11	17,557	13,598	17,493	20,627
West	12	31,718	23,659	33,564	35,568
City type					
Suburban	7	22,674	17,394	20,800	24,087
Independent	19	23,999	14,190	20,736	33,885
Form of government					
Council-manager	22	25,108	17,447	21,171	33,564

2

Salaries of County Officials For 1984*

Amy Cohen Paul
International City Management Association

In the twelve-month period from July 1983 to July 1984 when inflation (as measured by the Consumer Price Index for All Urban Consumers, the CPI-U) slowed to only 4.1%, the salaries of most county officials increased by substantially more. The governing board chair/president/county judge showed the greatest increase on average (11.1%), followed by the chief financial officer (10.2%). County administrators' salaries increased the least during this period, averaging only 4.8%.

Of the 3,108 counties surveyed, over half (57.7%) responded to questionnaires mailed during the summer of 1984. Questionnaires were sent to all counties; those that did not respond to the first were sent a second request. Table 2/1 shows a breakdown of the counties surveyed by population, geographic region, geographic division, and metro status.

Table 2/2 exhibits average salaries of county officials by geographic region. As these data show, there is a great deal of disparity among salaries when regional averages are compared to the national average. County officials in the West consistently earn higher average salaries than their counterparts in the other regions. In three cases, the difference is greater than 25 percentage points. Governing board chairs earn 35% more on average in the West, while county managers and purchasing directors earn 27% more than their colleagues throughout the country.

While salaries in the West are consistently higher than the national average, those in the North Central region are consistently lower—in the case of the governing board chair, 35% lower. Health officers in the North Central region also earn considerably less than the average, as do chief finance officers and planning directors. Respectively, these officials earn 26%, 18%, and 17% less on average.

Table 2/3 provides another variation on salaries by examining the differential between average salaries for county officials in metropol-

*Data for this article were collected from the survey *Directory of County Officials* (KTYDIR) by the International City Management Association, Washington, D.C., 1984.

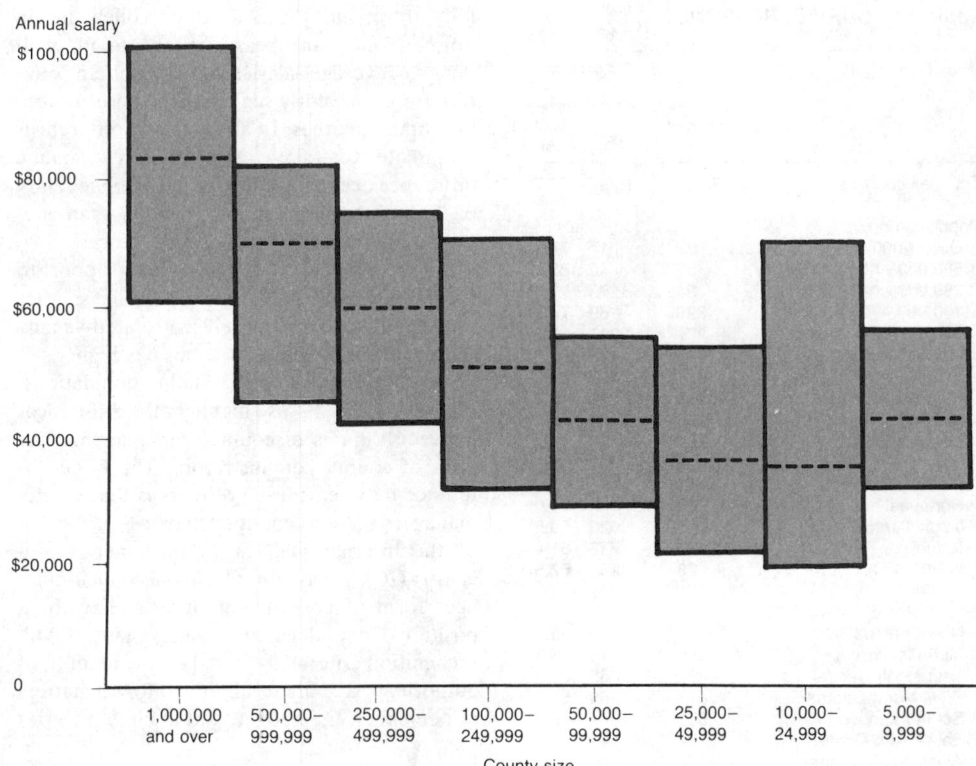

Figure 2/1 *Salaries of county managers as of 1 July 1984*

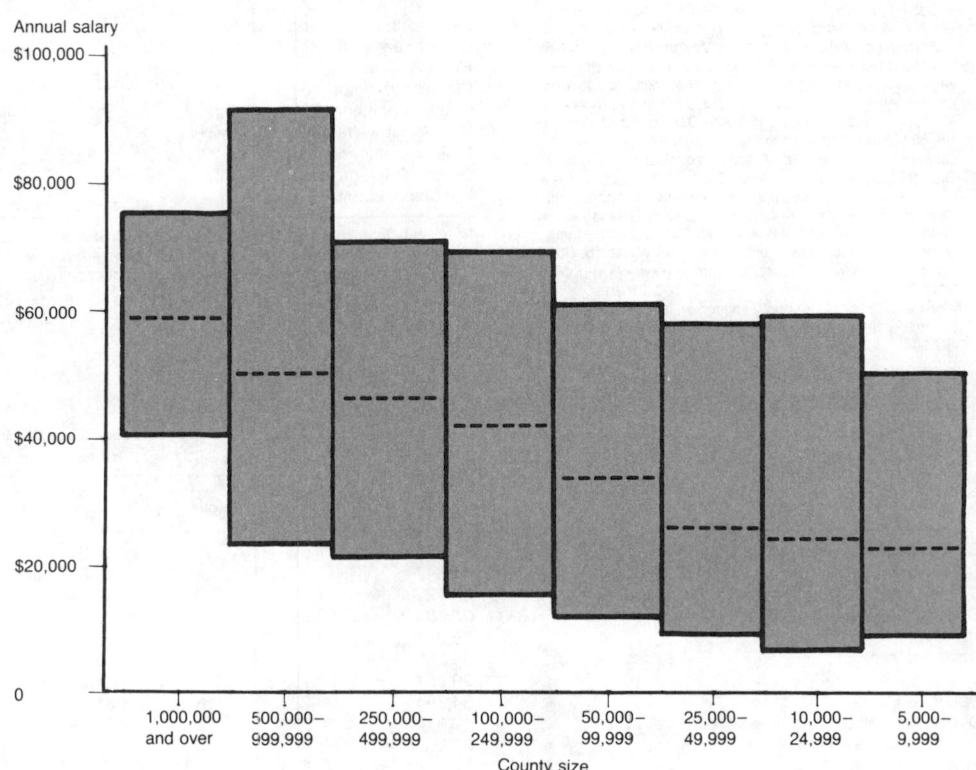

Figure 2/2 *Salaries of county administrators as of 1 July 1984*

Table 2/1 SURVEY RESPONSE

	No. of counties surveyed (A)	Counties responding No.	Counties responding % of (A)
Total, all counties	3,108	1,792	57.7
Population group			
Over 1,000,000	22	17	77.3
500,000–1,000,000	56	46	82.1
250,000– 499,999	94	73	77.7
100,000– 249,999	228	169	74.1
50,000– 99,999	375	237	63.2
25,000– 49,999	617	351	56.9
10,000– 24,999	974	497	51.0
5,000– 9,999	463	251	54.2
2,500– 4,999	178	95	53.4
Under 2,500	101	56	55.4
Geographic region[1]			
Northeast	200	142	71.0
North Central	1,055	628	59.5
South	1,425	733	51.4
West	428	289	67.5
Geographic division[2]			
New England	54	30	55.6
Mid-Atlantic	146	112	76.7
East North Central	437	268	61.3
West North Central	618	360	58.3
South Atlantic	591	371	62.8
East South Central	364	146	40.1
West South Central	470	216	46.0
Mountain	280	170	60.7
Pacific Coast	148	119	80.4
Metro Status[3]			
Metro	726	506	69.7
Nonmetro	2,382	1,286	54.0

[1] *Geographic regions: Northeast*—the New England and Mid-Atlantic Divisions; *North Central*—the East and West North Central Divisions; *South*—the South Atlantic and the East and West South Central Divisions; *West*—the Mountain and Pacific Coast Divisions. See footnote 2 for states included in the regions.

[2] *Geographic divisions: New England*—the states of Connecticut, Maine, Massachusetts, New Hampshire, Rhode Island, and Vermont; *Mid-Atlantic*—the states of New Jersey, New York, and Pennsylvania; *East North Central*—the states of Illinois, Indiana, Michigan, Ohio, and Wisconsin; *West North Central*—the states of Iowa, Kansas, Minnesota, Missouri, Nebraska, North Dakota, and South Dakota; *South Atlantic*—the states of Delaware, Florida, Georgia, Maryland, North Carolina, South Carolina, Virginia, and West Virginia, plus the District of Columbia; *East South Central*—the states of Alabama, Kentucky, Mississippi, and Tennessee; *West South Central*—the states of Arkansas, Louisiana, Oklahoma, and Texas; *Mountain*—the states of Arizona, Colorado, Idaho, Montana, Nevada, New Mexico, Utah, and Wyoming; *Pacific Coast*—the states of Alaska, California, Hawaii, Oregon, and Washington.

[3] *Metro status: Metro*—a county located within an SMSA; *Nonmetro*—a county located outside the boundaries of an SMSA.

itan areas and those of their colleagues in nonmetropolitan areas. As one might well imagine, average salaries in metropolitan counties are consistently higher than those in nonmetropolitan areas. In all cases, the differences are greater than 35%, with the most dramatic difference occurring between the average salary of the metropolitan and nonmetropolitan governing board chair—an 89% difference.

Figures 2/1 and 2/2 generally lend support to the findings in Table 2/3, indicating that salaries and population are loosely correlated—many counties with larger populations pay higher salaries than counties with smaller populations. Figures 2/1 and 2/2 also highlight the differences between salaries of county managers and salaries of county administrators. The basic difference between these positions is that county managers serve in counties that are recognized by the International City Management Association (ICMA) as either having a council-manager form of government or providing for a position of overall general management. ICMA recognition criteria are based on the amount of authority vested in the administrator on matters of personnel, the budget, and the like. Salaries for administrators in all other counties are listed under the category of "county administrator." The average county manager earns 42% more than the average administrator—$47,847 compared with $33,728 (not shown in figures).

The differences between county managers' and county administrators' salaries is also striking when compared by population group. In all cases, managers earn more on average than administrators. Managers in counties between 5,000 and 9,999 earn an average of 66% more than administrators in the same population group—$41,363 compared with $24,988. Although this highlights the greatest difference, managers in counties of over 1,000,000 population earn 42% more than administrators in the same population group. The difference is the least apparent in counties of 50,000 to 99,999 population, where managers earn only 16% more than administrators.

Individual differences by geographic region and metro status are provided in Table 2/4 where the mean, median, and first and third quartile data for each of twelve county officials are presented. Further comparison and analyses will most certainly uncover more variations.

Table 2/3 MEAN SALARIES FOR METROPOLITAN AND NONMETROPOLITAN COUNTIES

Position	Mean ($) Metro	Mean ($) Nonmetro	% diff.[1]
Governing board chair/president/county judge	22,981	12,183	89
County manager	54,595	37,820	44
County administrator	41,244	27,656	49
Clerk to the governing board	29,376	20,099	46
Chief finance officer	34,767	21,053	65
Health officer	48,038	27,315	76
Planning director	36,689	23,567	56
County engineer	40,256	29,677	36
Director of welfare/human services	39,873	27,058	47
Chief law enforcement officer	36,430	23,093	58
Purchasing director	31,360	21,777	44
Personnel director	35,030	24,804	41

[1] Percent difference is the difference between the metro mean and the nonmetro mean (e.g., for metro counties the county manager mean salary is 44% above the mean for nonmetro counties).

Table 2/2 MEAN SALARIES OF COUNTY OFFICIALS BY GEOGRAPHIC REGION

Position	All counties Mean ($)	Northeast Mean ($)	Northeast % diff.[1]	North Central Mean ($)	North Central % diff.[1]	South Mean ($)	South % diff.[1]	West Mean ($)	West % diff.[1]
Governing board chair/president/county judge	15,338	17,696	15	10,007	(35)	17,705	15	20,636	35
County manager[2]	47,847	47,591	(1)	47,860	. . .[3]	43,661	(9)	60,573	27
County administrator[2]	33,728	37,082	10	30,744	(9)	33,195	(2)	37,081	10
Clerk to the governing board	22,804	23,663	4	20,772	(9)	23,998	5	24,887	9
Chief finance officer	25,381	29,988	18	20,902	(18)	27,038	7	30,491	20
Health officer	36,268	42,962	19	26,728	(26)	42,289	17	44,983	24
Planning director	29,961	30,752	3	24,813	(17)	31,021	4	34,768	16
County engineer	34,194	39,233	15	31,363	(8)	32,950	(4)	41,237	21
Director of welfare/human services	32,370	36,583	13	29,796	(8)	30,636	(5)	39,776	23
Chief law enforcement officer	27,082	27,813	3	23,466	(13)	28,911	7	31,688	17
Purchasing director	27,139	27,166	. . .[3]	27,258	. . .[3]	24,547	(10)	34,577	27
Personnel director	31,099	28,616	(8)	30,502	(2)	29,385	(6)	37,029	19

[1] Percent difference is the difference between the regional mean and the mean for all counties (e.g., for the Northeast the county manager mean salary is 15% above the mean for all counties). Percentages in parentheses ( ) indicate that the regional mean is below the mean for all counties.

[2] In this table and throughout this article, a distinction is made between the county manager and the county administrator. County manager refers to the appointed chief administrative officer in only those counties recognized by the International City Management Association as either having the council-manager form of government or providing for a position of overall general management. County administrator refers to all other chief administrative officers.

[3] Leaders (. . .) indicate less than 0.5%.

Table 2/4 SALARIES OF COUNTY OFFICIALS: 1 JULY 1984

Salary data for the 12 selected county officials in this table are based on information reported by county officials as of 1 July 1984. Data are reported by position title only and, while representing similar job responsibilities, do not purport to represent identical duties and responsibilities.

For the position of county manager, data are shown for only those counties recognized by the International City Management Association as either having a council-manager form of government or providing for a position of overall general management. For the position of county administrator, data are shown for all other reporting counties.

Except for the position of governing board chairman/president/county judge which includes part-time salaries, this table excludes: (1) salaries of part-time officials, (2) salaries for vacant positions, (3) salaries of acting officials, (4) salaries of those paid in whole or in part by fees, and (5) all salaries below $8,000. Salaries are presented for 10 population groups and are further classified by geographic region, county type, and form of government.

Classifications having less than three counties reporting were excluded because meaningful statistics cannot be computed. Quartiles are now shown when only three counties reported.

		Distribution of 1984 salaries			
Title of official	No. of counties reporting	Mean ($)	First quartile ($)	Median ($)	Third quartile ($)
All counties					
Governing board chairman/ president/county judge					
Total	1266	15,338	5,946	11,605	21,841
Geographic region					
Northeast	120	17,696	8,500	15,000	22,800
North Central	461	10,007	4,800	7,530	12,500
South	496	17,705	5,200	15,915	27,504
West	189	20,636	8,063	18,885	26,753
County type					
Metro	370	22,981	9,531	20,000	30,932
Nonmetro	896	12,183	5,000	9,000	18,000
County manager					
Total	174	47,847	35,115	44,900	57,198
Geographic region					
Northeast	9	47,591	35,684	45,930	52,556
North Central	16	47,860	36,507	45,943	56,907
South	112	43,661	33,000	40,254	49,284
West	37	60,573	46,680	61,214	73,443
County type					
Metro	104	54,595	42,329	52,187	66,336
Nonmetro	70	37,820	31,130	35,629	41,691
County administrator					
Total	405	33,728	23,024	31,600	41,484
Geographic region					
Northeast	43	37,082	26,125	35,000	46,125
North Central	99	30,744	21,900	28,850	35,241
South	188	33,195	22,000	31,386	40,440
West	75	37,081	25,325	33,696	46,560
County type					
Metro	181	41,244	30,000	38,500	51,948
Nonmetro	224	27,656	19,200	26,874	33,770
Clerk to the governing board					
Total	1197	22,804	16,591	20,600	27,203
Geographic region					
Northeast	107	23,663	15,910	21,324	30,144
North Central	484	20,772	16,221	19,653	23,712
South	417	23,998	16,427	21,878	30,605
West	189	24,887	17,255	22,148	29,132
County type					
Metro	349	29,376	21,526	28,000	34,411
Nonmetro	848	20,099	15,600	18,621	23,005
Chief finance officer					
Total	1147	25,381	17,483	22,455	30,000
Geographic region					
Northeast	98	29,988	20,846	26,422	34,483
North Central	457	20,902	16,000	19,409	23,695
South	414	27,038	18,912	25,173	31,853
West	178	30,491	18,809	26,474	35,000
County type					
Metro	362	34,767	25,828	31,669	41,425
Nonmetro	785	21,053	16,113	19,500	24,438
Health officer					
Total	500	36,268	20,737	28,894	52,478
Geographic region					
Northeast	37	42,962	31,629	39,301	54,816
North Central	211	26,728	18,054	22,600	29,326
South	160	42,289	25,392	38,242	60,000
West	92	44,983	22,653	48,078	66,118
County type					
Metro	216	48,038	31,380	48,667	66,111
Nonmetro	284	27,315	18,060	22,790	31,308
Planning director					
Total	589	29,961	20,001	27,741	37,009
Geographic region					
Northeast	85	30,752	22,124	29,150	38,123
All counties continued					
North Central	182	24,813	17,711	21,875	30,080
South	181	31,021	22,539	29,172	37,305
West	141	34,768	23,010	33,252	44,256
County type					
Metro	287	36,689	28,154	35,281	44,178
Nonmetro	302	23,567	17,639	21,701	27,480
County engineer					
Total	658	34,194	26,500	33,600	39,748
Geographic region					
Northeast	53	39,233	28,330	38,000	44,184
North Central	310	31,363	24,810	32,347	37,000
South	177	32,950	25,089	32,700	39,839
West	118	41,237	31,854	39,567	51,774
County type					
Metro	281	40,256	31,465	37,750	46,283
Nonmetro	377	29,677	22,063	30,904	36,183
Director of welfare/human services					
Total	509	32,370	24,181	30,408	38,058
Geographic region					
Northeast	54	36,583	26,628	33,765	41,750
North Central	191	29,796	22,038	29,904	36,022
South	185	30,636	24,069	28,945	36,228
West	79	39,776	26,576	37,882	51,986
County type					
Metro	211	39,873	29,937	38,390	46,157
Nonmetro	298	27,058	22,011	26,805	32,516
Chief law enforcement officer					
Total	1267	27,082	19,800	24,400	31,371
Geographic region					
Northeast	108	27,813	20,400	25,119	32,000
North Central	495	23,466	18,356	21,871	26,007
South	485	28,911	21,602	28,405	32,934
West	179	31,688	20,125	27,500	37,275
County type					
Metro	379	36,430	27,500	33,833	42,501
Nonmetro	888	23,093	18,461	22,000	27,000
Purchasing director					
Total	479	27,139	18,297	25,872	32,978
Geographic region					
Northeast	66	27,166	19,950	24,571	31,975
North Central	76	27,258	18,000	27,176	34,000
South	251	24,547	16,970	23,171	30,491
West	86	34,577	25,686	31,552	42,832
County type					
Metro	268	31,360	23,171	30,120	37,802
Nonmetro	211	21,777	15,504	19,380	27,079
Personnel director					
Total	437	31,099	21,895	29,544	38,265
Geographic region					
Northeast	70	28,616	20,307	27,632	33,401
North Central	96	30,502	22,277	29,747	36,230
South	180	29,385	20,856	27,972	36,228
West	91	37,029	25,450	34,390	45,521
County type					
Metro	269	35,030	26,135	33,153	43,762
Nonmetro	168	24,804	18,300	23,579	30,143
Over 1,000,000					
Governing board chairman/ president/county judge					
Total	14	49,285	31,333	42,972	69,923
Geographic region					
Northeast	3	61,277	...	71,000	...

Table 2/4 continued **SALARIES OF COUNTY OFFICIALS: 1 JULY 1984**

Title of official	No. of counties reporting	Distribution of 1984 salaries			
		Mean ($)	First quartile ($)	Median ($)	Third quartile ($)
Over 1,000,000 continued					
South	4	46,309	6,000	50,658	64,740
West	6	46,933	29,255	38,634	57,230
County type					
Metro	14	49,285	31,333	42,972	69,923
County manager					
Total	8	84,056	72,800	83,919	93,554
Geographic region					
West	6	82,783	70,194	83,919	89,782
County type					
Metro	8	84,056	72,800	83,919	93,554
County administrator					
Total	8	59,089	41,436	58,887	71,520
Geographic region					
Northeast	3	55,107	...	48,000	...
North Central	3	65,845	...	71,520	...
County type					
Metro	8	59,089	41,436	58,887	71,520
Clerk to the governing board					
Total	14	46,316	39,223	48,737	51,030
Geographic region					
Northeast	3	49,079	...	50,000	...
South	3	47,869	...	51,708	...
West	6	46,937	36,642	46,433	49,585
County type					
Metro	14	46,316	39,223	48,737	51,030
Chief finance officer					
Total	13	61,781	56,528	64,463	68,383
Geographic region					
Northeast	3	57,543	...	64,463	...
South	4	62,589	54,999	62,303	63,490
West	5	68,735	64,294	68,182	68,383
County type					
Metro	13	61,781	56,528	64,463	68,383
Health officer					
Total	14	68,889	59,221	72,124	75,982
Geographic region					
Northeast	3	65,311	...	68,888	...
North Central	3	61,140	...	59,484	...
South	3	67,976	...	69,972	...
West	5	76,234	71,630	76,964	77,805
County type					
Metro	14	68,889	59,221	72,124	75,982
Planning director					
Total	15	56,872	47,578	58,566	63,221
Geographic region					
Northeast	3	58,080	...	63,131	...
North Central	3	45,899	...	45,916	...
South	3	59,163	...	63,490	...
West	6	60,609	57,142	58,818	59,945
County type					
Metro	15	56,872	47,578	58,566	63,221
County engineer					
Total	14	66,119	57,904	67,880	75,385
Geographic region					
North Central	3	51,085	...	47,400	...
South	3	67,803	...	72,749	...
West	6	70,774	61,872	71,592	77,229
County type					
Metro	14	66,119	57,904	67,880	75,385
Director of welfare/human services					
Total	14	63,546	53,704	63,688	73,301
Geographic region					
South	4	55,299	46,704	55,267	58,957
West	6	71,043	61,245	73,863	76,743
County type					
Metro	14	63,546	53,704	63,688	73,301
Chief law enforcement officer					
Total	14	66,130	59,078	67,389	69,535
Geographic region					
North Central	3	52,929	...	59,787	...
South	4	65,643	56,012	64,275	70,182
West	5	70,648	63,248	67,392	68,437
County type					
Metro	14	66,130	59,078	67,389	69,535
Purchasing director					
Total	17	45,579	36,853	48,173	50,885
Geographic region					
Northeast	4	39,280	19,900	41,765	51,179
North Central	3	40,221	...	36,744	...
South	4	49,953	37,802	47,822	50,004

Title of official	No. of counties reporting	Distribution of 1984 salaries			
		Mean ($)	First quartile ($)	Median ($)	Third quartile ($)
Over 1,000,000 continued					
West	6	49,540	41,939	48,646	49,145
County type					
Metro	17	45,579	36,853	48,173	50,885
Personnel director					
Total	14	54,676	50,155	56,704	59,064
Geographic region					
North Central	3	49,687	...	55,831	...
South	4	54,054	42,972	54,643	58,957
West	5	57,503	51,588	59,121	59,188
County type					
Metro	14	54,676	50,155	56,704	59,064
500,000-1,000,000					
Governing board chairman/president/county judge					
Total	30	43,067	29,619	37,220	51,500
Geographic region					
Northeast	7	35,231	14,462	34,024	37,500
North Central	8	47,110	34,600	46,491	50,000
South	9	46,386	33,025	50,000	56,140
West	6	41,838	23,375	33,287	40,479
County type					
Metro	30	43,067	29,619	37,220	51,500
County manager					
Total	15	70,375	62,935	71,250	77,925
Geographic region					
Northeast	3	59,525	...	60,070	...
South	6	70,730	65,493	69,459	72,766
West	4	80,242	77,664	80,156	81,605
County type					
Metro	15	70,375	62,935	71,250	77,925
County administrator					
Total	15	51,606	36,598	51,159	56,400
Geographic region					
Northeast	4	46,314	32,500	42,445	49,500
North Central	5	43,389	27,513	46,094	48,648
South	4	55,995	51,159	52,589	52,680
County type					
Metro	15	51,606	36,598	51,159	56,400
Clerk to the governing board					
Total	29	39,093	30,537	35,700	47,327
Geographic region					
Northeast	7	34,400	21,559	33,250	38,048
North Central	7	30,503	24,600	29,136	32,050
South	9	45,631	33,994	48,823	53,517
West	6	44,782	33,008	38,632	45,672
County type					
Metro	29	39,093	30,537	35,700	47,327
Chief finance officer					
Total	33	50,907	42,726	49,999	57,392
Geographic region					
Northeast	8	48,904	32,960	45,999	47,336
North Central	6	47,508	38,536	48,750	52,120
South	12	52,600	48,589	51,332	59,846
West	7	53,207	37,367	51,787	56,819
County type					
Metro	33	50,907	42,726	49,999	57,392
Health officer					
Total	25	64,176	56,508	69,681	74,665
Geographic region					
Northeast	4	61,037	40,376	64,328	72,155
North Central	5	55,514	36,645	59,999	60,754
South	9	63,605	55,125	69,681	73,621
West	7	72,891	63,722	72,542	77,394
County type					
Metro	25	64,176	56,508	69,681	74,665
Planning director					
Total	31	50,694	43,027	50,778	57,136
Geographic region					
Northeast	7	45,645	37,986	44,000	48,159
North Central	8	47,707	35,730	49,077	52,453
South	9	51,070	40,764	47,889	56,257
West	7	58,672	53,177	56,532	57,147
County type					
Metro	31	50,694	43,027	50,778	57,136
County engineer					
Total	28	52,606	42,494	53,519	61,210
Geographic region					
Northeast	8	51,967	39,000	53,906	59,776
North Central	6	47,063	31,969	47,202	52,348
South	8	50,964	41,000	50,972	55,868

Table 2/4 continued SALARIES OF COUNTY OFFICIALS: 1 JULY 1984

Title of official	No. of counties reporting	Distribution of 1984 salaries Mean ($)	First quartile ($)	Median ($)	Third quartile ($)
500,000-1,000,000 continued					
West	6	61,188	50,106	63,389	65,533
County type					
Metro	28	52,606	42,494	53,519	61,210
Director of welfare/human services					
Total	22	54,185	42,873	54,785	61,575
Geographic region					
Northeast	4	57,191	37,389	59,610	59,776
North Central	5	47,615	34,878	48,127	49,954
South	7	49,333	40,398	45,240	51,224
West	6	63,317	54,785	61,071	64,562
County type					
Metro	22	54,185	42,873	54,785	61,575
Chief law enforcement officer					
Total	29	50,184	38,737	52,188	60,896
Geographic region					
Northeast	7	40,112	26,932	34,985	43,858
North Central	6	47,778	32,300	45,691	53,708
South	10	56,622	49,225	55,892	63,642
West	6	53,613	41,006	58,084	60,460
County type					
Metro	29	50,184	38,737	52,188	60,896
Purchasing director					
Total	33	41,296	33,789	41,288	47,581
Geographic region					
Northeast	7	37,029	27,092	35,910	44,657
North Central	9	34,964	30,650	35,200	36,724
South	10	41,752	35,384	39,562	46,992
West	7	53,052	42,862	55,053	61,057
County type					
Metro	33	41,296	33,789	41,288	47,581
Personnel director					
Total	33	48,324	39,962	47,973	56,024
Geographic region					
Northeast	7	42,935	29,434	43,865	48,454
North Central	8	42,797	33,093	44,768	47,973
South	11	48,804	39,725	46,575	52,625
West	7	59,276	52,228	56,825	61,764
County type					
Metro	33	48,324	39,962	47,973	56,024
250,000-499,999					
Governing board chairman/ president/county judge					
Total	54	29,605	17,938	28,000	35,693
Geographic region					
Northeast	15	23,394	13,905	20,000	29,050
North Central	13	26,034	20,887	27,500	29,640
South	16	35,744	9,390	39,743	50,000
West	10	33,739	25,438	31,206	37,033
County type					
Metro	54	29,605	17,938	28,000	35,693
County manager					
Total	16	59,920	47,611	61,769	66,706
Geographic region					
North Central	3	59,536	...	60,320	...
South	8	58,114	45,000	57,800	67,008
West	5	63,042	48,432	66,336	66,614
County type					
Metro	16	59,920	47,611	61,769	66,706
County administrator					
Total	26	47,989	33,101	45,500	60,022
Geographic region					
Northeast	7	44,872	32,349	44,825	47,982
North Central	8	40,962	28,600	36,758	52,530
South	7	52,644	37,388	55,000	61,271
West	4	59,349	33,000	65,790	71,739
County type					
Metro	26	47,989	33,101	45,500	60,022
Clerk to the governing board					
Total	52	32,521	25,000	31,815	37,800
Geographic region					
Northeast	14	29,857	21,084	28,538	36,486
North Central	12	31,057	26,200	32,454	35,000
South	16	35,362	24,669	32,621	43,767
West	10	33,460	26,129	31,506	36,900
County type					
Metro	52	32,521	25,000	31,815	37,800
Chief finance officer					
Total	57	41,739	32,954	40,484	48,942
250,000-499,999 continued					
Geographic region					
Northeast	14	37,132	31,887	35,975	39,992
North Central	13	35,481	30,500	32,750	37,100
South	20	44,830	39,676	44,180	50,592
West	10	50,144	36,900	53,406	58,203
County type					
Metro	57	41,739	32,954	40,484	48,942
Health officer					
Total	39	58,381	45,103	64,976	70,462
Geographic region					
Northeast	6	55,634	43,163	56,250	61,988
North Central	12	41,477	20,578	42,088	51,063
South	12	67,926	64,314	69,064	72,080
West	9	70,023	61,562	71,900	73,748
County type					
Metro	39	58,381	45,103	64,976	70,462
Planning director					
Total	47	41,645	34,596	42,000	46,854
Geographic region					
Northeast	11	36,291	28,790	38,222	41,465
North Central	10	37,475	29,188	35,856	45,330
South	15	44,561	37,668	43,076	47,472
West	11	46,814	40,019	47,052	50,207
County type					
Metro	47	41,645	34,596	42,000	46,854
County engineer					
Total	49	44,338	35,500	43,368	52,475
Geographic region					
Northeast	11	40,192	28,726	39,527	49,672
North Central	12	40,313	35,500	37,000	45,032
South	15	41,819	33,959	42,511	44,624
West	11	56,311	48,792	58,872	60,066
County type					
Metro	49	44,338	35,500	43,368	52,475
Director of welfare/human services					
Total	37	43,035	34,465	43,512	48,641
Geographic region					
Northeast	9	42,404	32,943	43,035	44,055
North Central	8	39,622	33,592	37,929	44,944
South	11	37,461	28,300	42,276	43,128
West	9	53,512	47,067	52,153	55,599
County type					
Metro	37	43,035	34,465	43,512	48,641
Chief law enforcement officer					
Total	56	43,135	35,000	41,738	50,604
Geographic region					
Northeast	14	34,373	27,320	33,170	38,256
North Central	13	38,429	32,313	38,000	40,287
South	19	46,016	37,998	44,460	50,520
West	10	56,045	48,639	55,247	62,540
County type					
Metro	56	43,135	35,000	41,738	50,604
Purchasing director					
Total	51	33,947	26,546	32,368	41,409
Geographic region					
Northeast	13	32,734	23,850	31,908	38,870
North Central	11	31,228	21,672	29,700	37,310
South	19	33,318	26,373	32,368	37,860
West	8	41,153	38,448	42,142	43,520
County type					
Metro	51	33,947	26,546	32,368	41,409
Personnel director					
Total	50	39,006	30,000	37,961	45,292
Geographic region					
Northeast	9	36,681	29,029	35,820	40,715
North Central	11	35,830	23,404	36,780	42,347
South	19	37,563	28,487	36,228	42,139
West	11	46,575	37,520	45,552	51,878
County type					
Metro	50	39,006	30,000	37,961	45,292
100,000-249,999					
Governing board chairman/ president/county judge					
Total	131	20,561	9,640	20,100	27,732
Geographic region					
Northeast	29	17,814	9,406	16,950	24,252
North Central	33	15,972	7,678	15,180	24,858
South	46	20,572	9,200	17,775	28,129

Table 2/4 continued — SALARIES OF COUNTY OFFICIALS: 1 JULY 1984

Title of official	No. of counties reporting	Mean ($)	First quartile ($)	Median ($)	Third quartile ($)
		Distribution of 1984 salaries			
100,000-249,999 continued					
West	23	30,586	22,125	28,597	36,816
County type					
Metro	118	20,856	9,581	19,314	27,965
Nonmetro	13	17,884	9,250	21,000	24,059
County manager					
Total	42	50,384	42,511	48,852	57,032
Geographic region					
Northeast	5	42,880	33,175	45,147	45,734
North Central	7	45,977	39,709	44,635	49,088
South	21	50,575	42,455	48,984	54,034
West	9	57,535	49,478	60,902	63,086
County type					
Metro	37	50,663	42,728	48,984	56,337
Nonmetro	5	48,319	34,002	48,719	55,047
County administrator					
Total	58	41,980	30,671	37,877	51,672
Geographic region					
Northeast	11	34,710	23,325	32,476	40,213
North Central	18	36,189	28,336	35,900	40,000
South	19	46,121	31,183	37,586	62,262
West	10	52,533	43,070	50,626	57,026
County type					
Metro	54	42,646	31,020	38,334	53,340
Nonmetro	4	32,989	20,700	33,129	37,586
Clerk to the governing board					
Total	125	27,856	20,963	27,595	32,807
Geographic region					
Northeast	25	26,286	21,855	26,521	32,043
North Central	34	26,594	23,092	27,710	29,934
South	44	28,936	20,044	27,506	38,329
West	22	29,431	20,784	25,846	34,469
County type					
Metro	114	28,384	21,502	27,913	33,001
Nonmetro	11	22,388	14,743	20,988	23,950
Chief finance officer					
Total	125	32,616	25,894	30,000	38,506
Geographic region					
Northeast	27	26,770	21,468	24,178	28,553
North Central	35	29,638	25,965	28,000	31,882
South	42	35,827	27,434	35,867	43,303
West	21	38,676	32,675	35,438	41,840
County type					
Metro	113	33,262	26,368	31,312	38,719
Nonmetro	12	26,531	21,372	25,250	26,500
Health officer					
Total	75	46,506	34,466	45,073	60,111
Geographic region					
Northeast	8	36,965	28,787	34,777	38,000
North Central	27	39,888	27,094	38,981	46,781
South	26	50,710	36,367	57,726	60,290
West	14	56,913	46,297	58,273	65,225
County type					
Metro	69	46,690	35,351	45,073	60,112
Nonmetro	6	44,389	24,255	41,378	58,692
Planning director					
Total	103	35,122	29,335	34,933	40,281
Geographic region					
Northeast	22	32,453	26,876	33,838	36,075
North Central	27	31,685	25,736	32,403	35,437
South	35	35,275	28,954	33,000	40,508
West	19	42,816	36,108	43,452	47,291
County type					
Metro	93	36,071	30,359	35,513	40,604
Nonmetro	10	26,302	20,074	23,908	25,606
County engineer					
Total	100	38,169	33,000	37,008	44,088
Geographic region					
Northeast	16	34,194	27,685	34,631	40,480
North Central	28	36,484	33,000	35,946	42,383
South	37	37,801	32,234	36,900	42,584
West	19	44,718	35,509	44,324	52,507
County type					
Metro	92	38,464	33,000	37,201	44,088
Nonmetro	8	34,780	21,106	33,450	35,897
Director of welfare/human services					
Total	64	38,932	33,096	39,164	44,700
Geographic region					
Northeast	14	38,050	32,853	36,350	41,000
North Central	18	38,039	31,539	35,802	42,276
South	21	35,607	29,013	34,903	40,192
West	11	47,860	43,911	44,964	51,986

Title of official	No. of counties reporting	Mean ($)	First quartile ($)	Median ($)	Third quartile ($)
		Distribution of 1984 salaries			
100,000-249,999 continued					
County type					
Metro	58	38,938	31,834	39,371	44,793
Nonmetro	6	38,865	34,298	35,802	38,394
Chief law enforcement officer					
Total	134	35,459	29,158	34,109	41,665
Geographic region					
Northeast	28	28,504	21,786	26,075	34,000
North Central	37	33,275	28,250	31,704	36,591
South	48	37,740	32,022	35,668	43,087
West	21	43,371	35,799	41,579	48,112
County type					
Metro	121	35,973	30,329	35,000	41,734
Nonmetro	13	30,682	21,572	28,000	34,875
Purchasing director					
Total	103	28,491	23,044	27,324	33,139
Geographic region					
Northeast	23	24,819	20,225	23,406	26,992
North Central	18	27,590	20,099	27,176	33,485
South	42	28,061	23,306	27,671	32,144
West	20	34,428	27,324	32,189	38,088
County type					
Metro	94	28,808	23,413	27,831	33,171
Nonmetro	9	25,178	20,949	22,924	25,398
Personnel director					
Total	113	30,975	23,261	30,958	37,989
Geographic region					
Northeast	23	27,520	20,922	28,000	32,903
North Central	27	31,894	25,000	31,793	35,506
South	44	28,968	20,856	27,087	35,300
West	19	38,501	30,501	39,864	44,995
County type					
Metro	104	31,427	23,806	31,003	38,088
Nonmetro	9	25,758	17,411	21,964	29,556
50,000-99,999					
Governing board chairman/president/county judge					
Total	160	17,021	7,332	15,437	23,000
Geographic region					
Northeast	30	13,353	7,650	12,025	19,447
North Central	41	12,548	5,238	12,786	18,468
South	64	18,869	5,400	15,577	31,507
West	25	24,027	17,545	21,798	28,553
County type					
Metro	70	18,809	9,610	16,060	26,252
Nonmetro	90	15,631	5,450	14,553	21,896
County manager					
Total	31	41,245	34,998	41,153	46,712
Geographic region					
South	27	41,628	34,998	41,796	47,240
County type					
Metro	10	44,314	37,801	46,090	48,608
Nonmetro	21	39,783	34,721	37,032	45,885
County administrator					
Total	78	35,617	26,838	33,978	43,276
Geographic region					
Northeast	13	33,744	23,535	30,000	38,583
North Central	18	30,894	26,235	29,731	33,309
South	24	35,970	25,000	36,750	41,726
West	23	40,002	32,720	39,900	46,053
County type					
Metro	37	34,233	25,704	31,849	39,975
Nonmetro	41	36,865	30,036	36,000	44,331
Clerk to the governing board					
Total	151	24,311	18,625	23,650	28,583
Geographic region					
Northeast	25	21,179	16,740	20,030	24,188
North Central	45	24,044	20,535	24,000	26,454
South	55	25,300	17,856	24,839	30,680
West	26	25,693	19,646	23,464	29,372
County type					
Metro	64	26,225	21,000	25,072	31,380
Nonmetro	87	22,903	17,251	22,582	26,669
Chief finance officer					
Total	157	27,450	22,500	26,424	32,571
Geographic region					
Northeast	24	28,091	20,438	26,641	30,459
North Central	44	24,531	21,876	23,856	26,541
South	62	28,058	22,391	28,345	33,302
West	27	30,239	24,087	29,536	34,114

Table 2/4 continued — SALARIES OF COUNTY OFFICIALS: 1 JULY 1984

Title of official	No. of counties reporting	Mean ($)	First quartile ($)	Median ($)	Third quartile ($)
50,000-99,999 continued					
County type					
Metro	66	28,037	22,851	28,199	32,861
Nonmetro	91	27,023	22,500	26,202	31,571
Health officer					
Total	95	37,864	27,391	35,000	49,658
Geographic region					
Northeast	11	35,453	28,275	35,000	39,774
North Central	27	28,982	20,639	25,893	31,050
South	39	40,959	31,814	37,983	52,092
West	18	45,955	30,818	48,714	57,648
County type					
Metro	36	36,298	27,888	32,313	42,397
Nonmetro	59	38,819	26,210	35,464	52,030
Planning director					
Total	121	27,621	21,496	27,200	32,757
Geographic region					
Northeast	22	27,070	20,253	26,469	33,250
North Central	28	24,061	19,873	23,663	28,101
South	42	26,624	21,010	27,187	31,128
West	29	32,921	25,079	32,967	38,685
County type					
Metro	48	28,687	22,000	28,589	33,300
Nonmetro	73	26,920	21,041	26,400	31,558
County engineer					
Total	98	34,548	29,429	33,706	39,636
Geographic region					
Northeast	9	37,108	28,551	39,100	42,122
North Central	33	32,709	28,813	31,400	37,622
South	32	33,313	30,904	32,886	37,500
West	24	37,762	31,896	39,032	43,032
County type					
Metro	46	34,517	29,162	32,499	39,380
Nonmetro	52	34,574	30,600	34,631	39,612
Director of welfare/human services					
Total	84	31,784	25,841	32,774	37,057
Geographic region					
Northeast	10	30,033	24,416	29,595	31,775
North Central	25	31,547	25,792	30,867	36,527
South	36	32,250	27,792	35,134	37,424
West	13	32,297	23,668	34,428	39,867
County type					
Metro	32	32,724	23,566	34,114	38,480
Nonmetro	52	31,206	26,000	31,970	36,030
Chief law enforcement officer					
Total	165	30,116	25,838	30,480	34,066
Geographic region					
Northeast	27	25,979	20,429	26,500	30,550
North Central	48	28,125	24,800	28,006	31,500
South	63	31,867	28,582	31,507	34,743
West	27	33,707	28,403	32,900	38,555
County type					
Metro	71	30,654	25,950	30,500	34,413
Nonmetro	94	29,710	25,429	30,325	32,950
Purchasing director					
Total	92	23,809	17,950	23,088	28,600
Geographic region					
Northeast	17	20,101	16,243	18,364	23,152
North Central	11	26,015	17,838	24,626	30,847
South	48	22,735	17,047	21,547	26,426
West	16	29,456	24,772	30,030	31,827
County type					
Metro	37	24,723	19,306	23,800	28,966
Nonmetro	55	23,194	17,635	21,400	27,718
Personnel director					
Total	90	25,630	18,888	25,802	30,091
Geographic region					
Northeast	18	23,451	16,199	23,196	27,739
North Central	17	25,129	18,272	26,811	29,447
South	33	24,165	17,666	23,000	28,404
West	22	29,997	24,064	29,602	35,525
County type					
Metro	38	25,734	17,692	26,225	30,027
Nonmetro	52	25,554	19,675	25,004	30,115
25,000-49,999					
Governing board chairman/ president/county judge					
Total	243	13,970	5,138	11,870	21,315
Geographic region					
Northeast	25	13,010	4,775	14,400	19,000
25,000-49,999 continued					
North Central	91	9,759	5,500	8,731	14,819
South	106	16,717	4,350	15,477	29,542
West	21	19,488	10,897	21,500	25,445
County type					
Metro	56	15,034	5,426	12,929	22,037
Nonmetro	187	13,651	5,075	11,290	20,865
County manager					
Total	29	35,664	30,138	34,999	39,706
Geographic region					
South	25	35,635	30,138	35,033	39,706
County type					
Metro	10	38,179	28,596	39,425	41,813
Nonmetro	19	34,340	30,413	34,848	37,238
County administrator					
Total	82	28,644	21,000	28,185	33,733
Geographic region					
Northeast	4	23,144	16,174	22,000	26,500
North Central	25	25,209	18,768	27,352	30,635
South	43	29,856	20,749	28,350	35,740
West	10	34,218	25,938	32,068	38,794
County type					
Metro	27	30,072	16,600	30,000	36,870
Nonmetro	55	27,943	21,750	28,120	32,835
Clerk to the governing board					
Total	221	22,114	17,493	21,279	26,178
Geographic region					
Northeast	23	16,843	13,967	15,570	19,519
North Central	94	21,536	17,523	21,140	23,925
South	84	23,681	17,750	23,422	26,898
West	20	24,311	18,204	23,094	27,500
County type					
Metro	50	24,141	17,971	22,950	27,155
Nonmetro	171	21,521	17,162	21,060	25,060
Chief finance officer					
Total	217	23,799	19,500	23,160	27,507
Geographic region					
Northeast	15	22,422	18,000	23,002	24,413
North Central	93	21,219	18,141	21,000	24,134
South	90	25,453	20,531	26,152	31,417
West	19	29,684	23,538	28,896	32,655
County type					
Metro	54	26,224	20,500	26,044	31,170
Nonmetro	163	22,996	19,259	22,267	26,491
Health officer					
Total	102	28,337	19,711	25,084	32,029
Geographic region					
Northeast	4	28,528	17,500	29,393	33,285
North Central	51	21,796	15,643	22,272	25,359
South	34	37,546	25,629	32,029	52,630
West	13	29,854	15,471	26,147	34,067
County type					
Metro	27	31,577	21,915	25,296	49,102
Nonmetro	75	27,171	18,045	24,871	31,264
Planning director					
Total	119	24,051	17,792	22,575	27,679
Geographic region					
Northeast	15	22,037	17,156	22,497	25,104
North Central	48	20,986	16,478	19,577	24,699
South	38	25,776	18,506	24,368	30,500
West	18	30,264	23,216	30,048	33,376
County type					
Metro	36	25,832	18,050	25,000	28,704
Nonmetro	83	23,279	17,651	22,318	26,365
County engineer					
Total	126	31,827	26,493	31,730	37,800
Geographic region					
Northeast	7	28,007	23,425	27,862	30,428
North Central	66	32,649	28,200	33,550	38,000
South	36	28,638	21,500	27,870	33,666
West	17	36,961	33,583	36,600	39,357
County type					
Metro	37	31,414	26,804	29,738	36,919
Nonmetro	89	31,999	26,480	32,059	37,808
Director of welfare/human services					
Total	109	29,082	24,357	29,000	34,180
Geographic region					
Northeast	11	27,989	25,460	26,780	30,336
North Central	51	29,994	22,271	30,597	36,042
South	39	28,105	24,990	27,181	31,038
West	8	29,542	23,201	27,891	34,068

Distribution of 1984 salaries: Mean, First quartile, Median, Third quartile.

Table 2/4 continued **SALARIES OF COUNTY OFFICIALS: 1 JULY 1984**

Title of official	No. of counties reporting	Distribution of 1984 salaries: Mean ($)	First quartile ($)	Median ($)	Third quartile ($)
25,000-49,999 continued					
County type					
Metro	32	30,211	23,000	29,296	37,731
Nonmetro	77	28,613	24,357	29,000	33,902
Chief law enforcement officer					
Total	237	25,596	22,426	25,000	29,436
Geographic region					
Northeast	20	20,961	18,000	20,059	23,000
North Central	98	23,493	20,135	23,506	25,640
South	101	27,963	24,866	26,491	31,357
West	18	28,909	23,800	28,577	32,354
County type					
Metro	57	28,006	23,633	26,700	32,316
Nonmetro	180	24,832	22,000	24,319	27,655
Purchasing director					
Total	70	23,829	16,155	22,849	30,723
Geographic region					
North Central	7	26,437	17,105	30,846	31,812
South	51	22,635	14,769	20,710	28,955
West	10	29,005	18,548	27,819	31,120
County type					
Metro	23	25,270	16,123	21,848	32,284
Nonmetro	47	23,125	16,101	22,860	28,955
Personnel director					
Total	67	24,971	17,327	24,268	31,001
Geographic region					
Northeast	9	19,826	16,750	21,150	21,699
North Central	17	25,965	19,394	27,983	30,508
South	32	25,707	15,500	23,928	32,786
West	9	25,620	15,795	28,000	32,025
County type					
Metro	21	28,175	17,899	28,564	33,785
Nonmetro	46	23,509	17,274	22,754	28,906
10,000-24,999					
Governing board chairman/ president/county judge					
Total	352	11,904	5,810	9,570	16,224
Geographic region					
Northeast	8	8,388	1,620	8,150	14,000
North Central	148	8,400	6,240	7,700	10,860
South	154	14,817	4,800	14,345	24,293
West	42	14,239	7,600	13,122	19,502
County type					
Metro	24	11,991	4,000	6,622	24,116
Nonmetro	328	11,897	6,000	9,610	16,100
County manager					
Total	27	35,606	28,850	32,844	38,038
Geographic region					
South	20	32,470	27,500	30,872	35,912
West	6	46,961	33,948	46,060	50,875
County type					
Metro	7	36,557	29,225	33,000	37,359
Nonmetro	20	35,274	27,500	31,910	37,896
County administrator					
Total	91	27,285	18,997	25,050	32,825
Geographic region					
North Central	14	23,751	16,436	23,050	30,621
South	60	28,630	19,200	26,850	33,000
West	16	25,988	17,987	23,940	30,000
County type					
Metro	9	43,234	35,420	40,800	48,664
Nonmetro	82	25,534	18,489	23,940	31,090
Clerk to the governing board					
Total	330	20,718	16,750	19,668	24,000
Geographic region					
Northeast	7	15,936	12,887	15,100	15,650
North Central	161	20,018	17,604	19,604	21,440
South	123	21,564	14,952	19,780	28,075
West	39	21,799	17,482	21,708	24,000
County type					
Metro	21	24,943	19,302	24,282	30,505
Nonmetro	309	20,431	16,533	19,293	23,102
Chief finance officer					
Total	302	20,658	16,750	19,331	23,304
Geographic region					
Northeast	5	15,819	14,000	16,100	17,147
North Central	148	18,914	16,806	18,971	20,900
South	111	21,921	15,153	20,971	28,276
West	38	24,398	17,793	22,800	25,983

Title of official	No. of counties reporting	Distribution of 1984 salaries: Mean ($)	First quartile ($)	Median ($)	Third quartile ($)
10,000-24,999 continued					
County type					
Metro	20	26,668	19,800	26,478	31,417
Nonmetro	282	20,232	16,500	19,200	22,676
Health officer					
Total	96	22,175	19,000	21,326	23,594
Geographic region					
North Central	58	20,996	18,930	20,737	22,538
South	26	24,888	18,782	22,301	26,070
West	12	21,996	17,900	21,090	25,900
County type					
Metro	5	26,467	17,835	20,450	25,138
Nonmetro	91	21,939	19,015	21,405	23,224
Planning director					
Total	102	22,168	17,057	20,024	25,515
Geographic region					
Northeast	4	15,808	11,100	15,530	19,060
North Central	45	19,240	16,050	19,000	21,438
South	27	25,224	19,042	25,649	30,435
West	26	25,039	17,203	22,070	26,958
County type					
Metro	12	28,601	23,400	29,109	31,196
Nonmetro	90	21,310	16,720	19,278	24,500
County engineer					
Total	155	30,425	23,965	32,700	36,049
Geographic region					
North Central	98	32,320	28,320	33,746	36,354
South	38	23,970	13,531	22,600	31,795
West	19	33,562	26,469	33,100	39,688
County type					
Metro	13	30,912	22,800	32,718	35,672
Nonmetro	142	30,381	23,810	32,685	36,035
Director of welfare/human services					
Total	122	25,536	20,372	25,902	30,209
Geographic region					
Northeast	3	20,996	...	20,584	...
North Central	65	25,232	18,324	25,129	30,617
South	43	25,976	22,783	26,282	28,830
West	11	26,850	15,455	28,716	34,344
County type					
Metro	12	30,038	26,324	27,791	31,997
Nonmetro	110	25,045	19,923	24,938	29,918
Chief law enforcement officer					
Total	350	23,098	19,567	22,083	27,000
Geographic region					
Northeast	8	16,764	14,000	17,150	17,850
North Central	161	21,379	18,863	21,300	23,460
South	147	25,055	20,457	24,768	29,615
West	34	24,264	20,092	23,800	27,274
County type					
Metro	25	28,465	21,950	28,725	32,334
Nonmetro	325	22,685	19,396	21,861	25,888
Purchasing director					
Total	73	20,547	13,982	18,394	24,969
Geographic region					
North Central	11	18,180	14,726	17,785	19,243
South	53	19,419	13,513	18,360	23,358
West	9	30,083	19,490	30,000	33,410
County type					
Metro	11	25,875	19,616	25,214	27,912
Nonmetro	62	19,602	13,313	18,096	23,277
Personnel director					
Total	46	25,805	18,798	25,846	31,473
Geographic region					
North Central	11	23,161	18,105	19,372	27,761
South	26	25,762	18,797	25,634	31,939
West	9	29,164	21,013	30,000	32,736
County type					
Metro	7	30,913	25,986	32,208	34,843
Nonmetro	39	24,889	18,396	24,500	30,605
5,000-9,999					
Governing board chairman/ president/county judge					
Total	176	10,314	4,500	7,867	15,246
Geographic region					
Northeast	3	10,869	...	11,400	...
North Central	73	6,025	4,400	6,000	7,218
South	72	13,295	3,778	13,975	19,200
West	28	13,769	7,500	12,237	18,753

Table 2/4 continued **SALARIES OF COUNTY OFFICIALS: 1 JULY 1984**

Title of official	No. of counties reporting	Distribution of 1984 salaries: Mean ($)	First quartile ($)	Median ($)	Third quartile ($)
5,000-9,999 continued					
County type					
Metro	4	3,745	2,400	4,039	4,300
Nonmetro	172	10,467	4,545	8,050	15,720
County manager					
Total	6	41,363	31,459	37,131	46,750
Geographic region					
South	3	32,893	...	31,624	...
West	3	49,833	...	55,000	...
County type					
Nonmetro	5	42,483	31,376	38,500	50,875
County administrator					
Total	37	24,988	16,204	25,000	31,350
Geographic region					
North Central	6	17,494	11,477	17,054	19,540
South	26	27,564	17,430	26,000	34,000
West	5	20,582	13,275	21,012	25,241
County type					
Metro	5	40,002	31,052	40,000	43,750
Nonmetro	32	22,642	15,627	20,806	27,000
Clerk to the governing board					
Total	166	18,656	15,328	17,261	20,000
Geographic region					
Northeast	3	13,439	...	13,072	...
North Central	77	17,314	15,332	16,645	17,961
South	57	19,678	13,936	17,760	24,744
West	29	20,752	16,848	18,887	21,562
County type					
Metro	5	26,833	18,606	28,255	31,374
Nonmetro	161	18,402	15,280	17,032	19,844
Chief finance officer					
Total	145	18,851	15,510	16,966	20,971
Geographic region					
North Central	67	16,616	15,330	16,250	17,504
South	53	20,088	15,062	20,000	24,505
West	23	22,292	16,804	19,750	24,000
County type					
Metro	6	27,458	24,505	24,505	26,845
Nonmetro	139	18,479	15,332	16,900	20,289
Health officer					
Total	37	22,179	16,643	18,648	22,489
Geographic region					
North Central	19	18,410	16,226	17,500	19,530
South	11	30,474	19,484	22,000	28,155
West	6	19,948	12,524	19,002	24,030
County type					
Nonmetro	36	22,315	16,590	19,024	22,609
Planning director					
Total	38	22,912	16,204	20,146	25,416
Geographic region					
North Central	9	16,814	14,100	15,949	19,261
South	12	24,664	19,760	24,050	25,812
West	16	25,354	16,600	22,804	33,114
County type					
Metro	5	28,645	22,384	25,812	27,758
Nonmetro	33	22,043	15,561	19,760	24,733
County engineer					
Total	61	23,635	17,904	22,334	28,950
Geographic region					
North Central	41	22,968	17,551	21,000	28,750
South	6	22,383	14,819	21,299	25,028
West	14	26,124	17,996	25,256	28,919
County type					
Nonmetro	59	23,588	17,870	22,334	29,009
Director of welfare/human services					
Total	42	24,033	21,140	23,703	27,676
Geographic region					
North Central	11	22,406	17,448	19,776	26,571
South	20	23,937	21,972	23,490	26,300
West	10	26,597	25,380	28,064	29,766
County type					
Metro	4	26,584	22,723	25,530	27,579
Nonmetro	38	23,765	20,193	23,703	27,676
Chief law enforcement officer					
Total	173	20,769	17,337	19,200	22,687
Geographic region					
North Central	78	18,879	16,850	18,771	19,864
South	66	22,222	17,700	20,971	26,169
West	27	22,821	18,773	22,100	24,291
County type					
Metro	6	28,882	24,236	25,669	28,619
Nonmetro	167	20,478	17,231	19,032	22,025

Title of official	No. of counties reporting	Distribution of 1984 salaries: Mean ($)	First quartile ($)	Median ($)	Third quartile ($)
5,000-9,999 continued					
Purchasing director					
Total	28	19,353	13,852	18,025	22,830
Geographic region					
North Central	4	19,190	13,524	17,968	18,480
South	18	18,728	13,250	17,556	22,065
West	6	21,337	14,639	21,523	23,600
County type					
Nonmetro	26	19,030	13,688	17,556	22,415
Personnel director					
Total	16	21,025	10,466	19,458	27,300
Geographic region					
South	10	22,480	14,610	22,545	28,553
West	3	19,341	...	10,524	...
County type					
Nonmetro	14	19,860	10,268	18,790	26,150
2,500-4,999					
Governing board chairman/president/county judge					
Total	68	9,897	3,996	5,140	9,744
Geographic region					
North Central	37	5,031	3,900	4,545	5,790
South	15	17,595	11,500	18,600	22,848
West	16	13,934	3,600	5,950	9,200
County type					
Nonmetro	68	9,897	3,996	5,140	9,744
County administrator					
Total	5	21,825	14,109	16,700	26,863
County type					
Nonmetro	5	21,825	14,109	16,700	26,863
Clerk to the governing board					
Total	68	17,460	14,517	15,873	18,300
Geographic region					
North Central	35	16,330	14,475	15,332	16,178
South	15	17,730	12,775	17,833	19,338
West	18	19,433	14,521	16,518	18,408
County type					
Nonmetro	68	17,460	14,517	15,873	18,300
Chief finance officer					
Total	61	18,555	14,538	15,884	17,748
Geographic region					
North Central	32	15,772	14,500	15,037	15,880
South	13	19,091	11,585	17,833	20,593
West	16	23,687	16,200	16,818	18,966
County type					
Nonmetro	61	18,555	14,538	15,884	17,748
Health officer					
Total	13	21,526	12,500	15,284	17,810
Geographic region					
North Central	8	16,405	14,730	15,808	17,448
West	5	29,720	10,800	14,000	24,500
County type					
Nonmetro	13	21,526	12,500	15,284	17,810
Planning director					
Total	9	26,171	15,197	16,000	23,241
Geographic region					
North Central	3	17,846	...	15,037	...
West	6	30,333	15,747	17,689	21,953
County type					
Nonmetro	9	26,171	15,197	16,000	23,241
County engineer					
Total	21	19,454	14,950	16,950	22,267
Geographic region					
North Central	19	18,712	14,670	16,684	20,593
County type					
Nonmetro	21	19,454	14,950	16,950	22,267
Director of welfare/human services					
Total	9	24,686	16,602	22,488	31,241
Geographic region					
North Central	5	25,765	17,315	22,488	30,485
County type					
Nonmetro	9	24,686	16,602	22,488	31,241
Chief law enforcement officer					
Total	67	19,336	16,342	17,880	19,538
Geographic region					
North Central	34	17,390	15,730	17,298	18,356
South	15	19,657	14,156	19,500	21,851
West	18	22,745	16,659	18,490	19,908
County type					
Nonmetro	67	19,336	16,342	17,880	19,538

Table 2/4 continued — SALARIES OF COUNTY OFFICIALS: 1 JULY 1984

Title of official	No. of counties reporting	Mean ($)	First quartile ($)	Median ($)	Third quartile ($)
2,500-4,999 continued					
Purchasing director					
Total	10	24,892	15,288	17,775	26,824
Geographic region					
South	6	20,070	15,288	16,829	20,049
West	3	32,567	...	18,300	...
County type					
Nonmetro	10	24,892	15,288	17,775	26,824
Personnel director					
Total	6	37,973	14,700	24,550	32,068
Geographic region					
West	4	40,925	13,800	16,950	18,300
County type					
Nonmetro	6	37,973	14,700	24,550	32,068
Under 2,500					
Governing board chairman/ president/county judge					
Total	38	9,157	3,954	6,210	10,464
Geographic region					
North Central	16	3,734	2,000	3,954	4,800
South	10	17,790	8,410	17,813	21,353
West	12	9,195	5,750	8,334	9,888
County type					
Nonmetro	38	9,157	3,954	6,210	10,464
County administrator					
Total	5	17,439	11,834	16,000	16,711
Geographic region					
West	3	19,667	...	16,000	...
County type					
Nonmetro	5	17,439	11,834	16,000	16,711
Clerk to the governing board					
Total	41	16,137	14,000	15,450	17,194
Geographic region					
North Central	17	14,889	14,000	15,037	15,498
South	11	17,562	10,635	18,615	20,286
West	13	16,562	14,140	16,210	17,063
County type					
Nonmetro	41	16,137	14,000	15,450	17,194
Under 2,500 continued					
Chief finance officer					
Total	37	16,072	13,935	15,037	16,863
Geographic region					
North Central	18	14,560	13,050	15,037	15,482
South	7	19,179	13,250	18,615	20,303
West	12	16,528	14,114	16,232	17,250
County type					
Nonmetro	37	16,072	13,935	15,037	16,863
Health officer					
Total	4	20,870	8,493	12,984	15,000
Geographic region					
West	3	24,170	...	15,000	...
County type					
Nonmetro	4	20,870	8,493	12,984	15,000
Planning director					
Total	4	19,024	12,000	16,963	19,200
Geographic region					
West	3	20,456	...	19,200	...
County type					
Nonmetro	4	19,024	12,000	16,963	19,200
County engineer					
Total	6	24,974	15,709	25,320	27,000
Geographic region					
North Central	4	20,694	15,000	20,209	24,000
County type					
Nonmetro	6	24,974	15,709	25,320	27,000
Director of welfare/human services					
Total	6	20,676	14,244	20,784	23,526
Geographic region					
West	3	23,676	...	22,512	...
County type					
Nonmetro	6	20,676	14,244	20,784	23,526
Chief law enforcement officer					
Total	42	18,018	15,459	18,091	18,962
Geographic region					
North Central	17	16,544	15,025	16,980	18,356
South	12	19,209	15,125	18,962	21,145
West	13	18,846	16,157	18,181	19,421
County type					
Nonmetro	42	18,018	15,459	18,091	18,962

3

Police, Fire, and Refuse Collection and Disposal Departments: Personnel, Compensation, and Expenditures*

Gerard J. Hoetmer
International City Management Association

During 1983 the national economy grew in terms of real gross national product (GNP) by 6.2%. The early fears by many economists that the economic recovery would be a weak one proved to be off the mark, with the recovery actually being one of the strongest since World War II. During the first quarter of 1984 the GNP continued to grow at a very robust rate, with many economists foreseeing a "soft landing" in the final three quarters of the year, and the economy growing more moderately at a sustainable pace of growth. The consensus based on a survey of economists, published in the 21 March 1984 special issue of *Business Week*, is that the economy will grow at an average 4.4% from the fourth quarter in 1983 to the fourth quarter in 1984.

Prices have also continued to moderate. The inflation rate, as measured by the Consumer Price Index for all Urban Consumers (CPI-U), rose 3.8% from December 1982 to December 1983. During the period December 1981 to December 1982 the CPI-U rose 3.9%. As this article will show, employee salaries in the public sector as represented by police, fire, and refuse departments—although generally keeping pace with the inflation rate over the past year—have not risen as fast as the CPI-U over the past five years.

The data in this article were collected in January 1984. For this reason, the article represents the status of police, fire, and refuse departments in cities when the durability of the recovery was still questionable.

Methodology. The data in this article are based on responses to a mail survey conducted by ICMA in January 1984 as well as on responses to similar surveys in previous years. Surveys were sent to all municipalities in the United States with populations of 10,000 and over. (In this article, the terms cities and municipalities are used interchangeably to refer to cities, villages, towns, townships, and boroughs.) All data reported, except where specifically noted, are as of 1 January 1984.

This report again uses comparative data from previous years to show trends in the delivery of police, fire, and refuse collection and disposal services. From 1978 to 1981, survey universes included all cities 10,000 and over according to the 1975 U.S. Bureau of the Census population estimates, while the universes for earlier surveys were based on the 1970 population. The 1982, 1983, and 1984 surveys are based on the 1980 Census figures.

Personnel. Data on the size of the work force for each of the services, including both uniformed and nonuniformed personnel, are presented in Table 3/1. For all cities reporting, the average number of police department employees is 112, or 2.38 per 1,000 population. This is a decrease of 5.9% over last year's mean of 119. The number of fire department personnel decreased 5.4% to an average of 88 from previous year's average of 93. Refuse personnel decreased 8.7% from an average of 46 in 1983 to an average of 42 in 1984.

On a year-by-year basis the indicator of employees per 1,000 population gives a sharper distinction of the fluctuation in the average number of employees in each of these departments. Clearly, as can be seen in Figure 3/1, the size of these departments relative to population has been shrinking. The number of police employees per 1,000 population increased slightly (1.3%) in 1984 from 2.35 to 2.38 but decreased 8.8% since 1975 (from 2.61 to 2.38). The number of fire personnel per 1,000 population increased from 1983 to 1984 from 1.61 to 1.65 (2.5%), but is still significantly lower than the 1.75 employees per 1,000 population registered in 1975. Refuse collection departments also indicated a small increase in personnel on the basis of population from 0.70 to 0.71, or 1.4%, but again in comparison to 1975 is 50% lower on the per 1,000 population ratio.

The average number of civilian/non-uniformed personnel in police, fire, and refuse departments decreased over the past year. Nonuniformed police personnel averaged 26 per department (from 28 in 1983 and 29 in 1982); the civilian/nonuniformed fire personnel average decreased from 7 in 1983 to 6 in 1984 (no table shown). The average in 1982 was 9. Refuse departments also indicated a decrease in civilian personnel from an average of 28 in 1983 to an average of 25 in 1984.

As a percentage of total full-time paid personnel, refuse departments report the highest percentage of civilian/non-uniformed personnel (59.5%) while fire departments, where the use of civilians is still the exception rather than the rule, report the lowest percentage of civilian/uniformed personnel (6.8%) (no table shown).

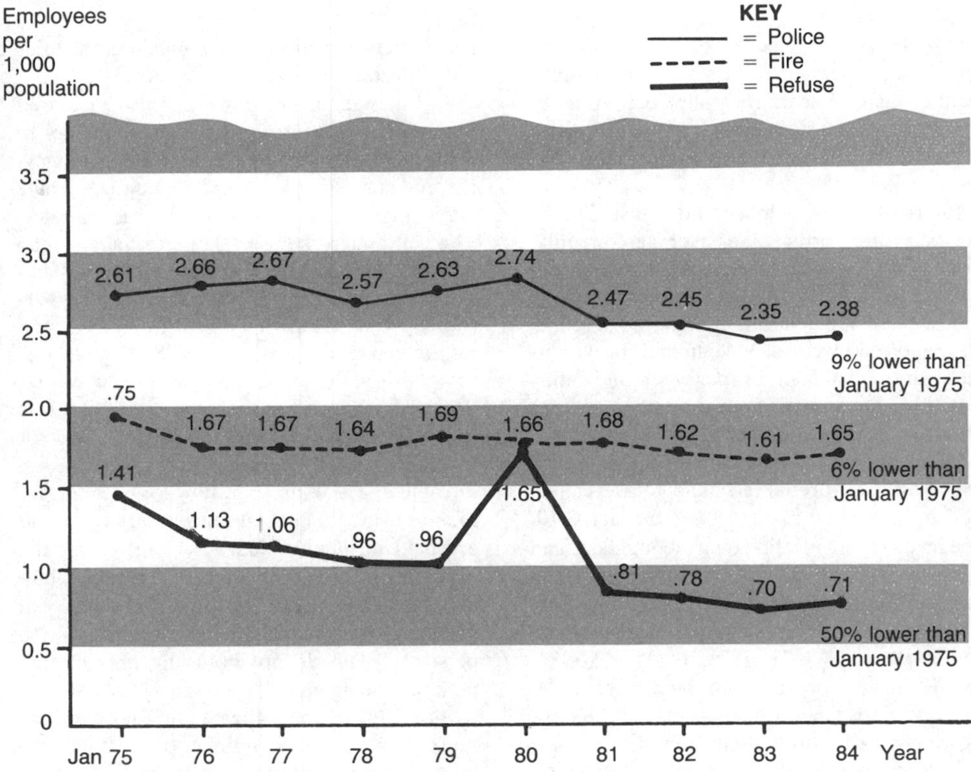

Figure 3/1 *Police, fire, and refuse department trends in employees per 1,000 population*

*Data for this article were collected from the survey *Police, Fire, and Refuse Collection and Disposal Personnel, Salaries, and Expenditures* (PFS–SAL/84) by the International City Management Association, Washington, D.C., 1984. A more detailed discussion of the data along with additional data tables aggregated by population group, geographic region and division, metro status, and/or form of government can be found in Gerard J. Hoetmer, *Police, Fire, and Refuse Collection,* Baseline Data Reports, vol. 16 no. 7 (Washington, D.C.: International City Management Association, July 1984).

Table 3/1 FULL-TIME PAID PERSONNEL[1]

Classification	Police department			Fire department			Refuse department		
	No. of cities reporting	Mean	Per 1,000 population	No. of cities reporting	Mean	Per 1,000 population	No. of cities reporting	Mean	Per 1,000 population
Total, all cities[2]	1,466	112	2.38	1,182	88	1.65	766	42	0.71
Population group									
Over 1,000,000	2	4,635	3.31	2	2,503	1.79	2	942	0.67
500,000–1,000,000	12	1,901	2.72	12	1,094	1.56	10	459	0.65
250,000– 499,999	23	980	2.82	23	615	1.77	19	212	0.60
100,000– 249,999	84	360	2.42	83	266	1.77	63	97	0.63
50,000– 99,999	177	147	2.16	164	112	1.65	94	49	0.70
25,000– 49,999	355	73	2.09	302	58	1.64	183	28	0.79
10,000– 24,999	813	34	2.12	596	24	1.46	395	15	0.92
Geographic division[3]									
New England	120	66	2.24	93	71	2.17	50	15	0.39
Mid-Atlantic	188	84	2.43	87	108	2.17	82	30	0.68
East North Central	320	90	2.21	262	68	1.47	141	30	0.52
West North Central	147	95	2.26	114	70	1.43	62	21	0.37
South Atlantic	188	143	2.96	173	100	1.97	162	55	1.05
East South Central	64	142	2.35	62	127	2.05	44	77	1.00
West South Central	155	127	2.35	140	98	1.69	129	51	0.86
Mountain	84	167	2.59	72	98	1.42	45	44	0.54
Pacific Coast	200	140	2.13	179	93	1.34	51	51	0.48
Form of Government[4]									
Mayor-Council	557	136	2.54	435	115	1.81	278	54	0.72
Council-Manager	828	99	2.25	689	73	1.51	452	36	0.70
Commission	38	122	2.30	26	125	1.87	24	32	0.65
Town Meeting	36	31	1.84	25	27	1.61	11	11	0.66
Representative Town Meeting	7	66	2.27	7	49	1.69	1	11	0.60

[1] Includes uniformed and nonuniformed personnel.
[2] The term *cities* is used in this and the following tables to refer to cities, villages, towns, townships, and boroughs.
[3] *Geographic divisions: New England*—the states of Connecticut, Maine, Massachusetts, New Hampshire, Rhode Island, and Vermont; *Mid-Atlantic*—the states of New Jersey, New York, and Pennsylvania; *East North Central*—the states of Illinois, Indiana, Michigan, Ohio, and Wisconsin; *West North Central*—the states of Iowa, Kansas, Minnesota, Missouri, Nebraska, North Dakota, and South Dakota; *South Atlantic*—the states of Delaware, Florida, Georgia, Maryland, North Carolina, South Carolina, Virginia, and West Virginia, plus the District of Columbia; *East South Central*—the states of Alabama, Kentucky, Mississippi, and Tennessee; *West South Central*—the states of Arkansas, Louisiana, Oklahoma, and Texas; *Mountain*—the states of Arizona, Colorado, Idaho, Montana, Nevada, New Mexico, Utah, and Wyoming; *Pacific Coast*—the states of Alaska, California, Hawaii, Oregon, and Washington.
[4] *Forms of government: Mayor-council*—an elected council serves as the legislative body with a separately elected head of government; *Council-manager*—the mayor and council make policy and an appointed administrator is responsible for the administration of the city; *Commission*—a board of elected commissioners serves as the legislative body and each commissioner is responsible for administration of one or more departments; *Town meeting*—qualified voters meet to make basic policy and choose a board of selectmen to carry out the policy; *Representative town meeting*—representatives selected by citizens vote at meetings, which may be attended by all town citizens.

Police departments reported that 23.2% of their total complement of full-time paid personnel were civilians. Except for police departments, where the use of civilians has increased, these ratios have remained relatively constant since the mid-1970s.

Hours of Work. Police and refuse departments in all reporting cities average 40 regular work hours per week (no table shown). Firefighters work an average of 52 hours (no table shown), with great variation in the work schedules reported by cities. Median and third quartile figures equal 56 hours per week, indicating that firefighters in the largest number of cities reporting average 56-hour work weeks.

Compensation. Salary data for full-time paid police officers, firefighters, and refuse collectors are presented in Tables 3/2 through 3/10. The mean (average), first quartile, median, and third quartile are shown for all salary figures in Tables 3/3 through 3/8.

Table 3/2 compares mean entrance and maximum salaries in 1973, 1978, 1983, and 1984. Salaries have more than doubled since 1973. All three departments have increased their entrance salaries by 107%. Maximum salaries have risen more sharply, 120% for police personnel, 117% for fire personnel, and 118% for refuse department personnel. The greater percentage spread between entrance and maximum salaries has reflected this difference.

Jurisdictions have, however, also increased the number of years it takes for employees to achieve maximum salaries (excluding longevity) and correspondingly decreased the average percentage gain for employees between grades. Thus, although the average percentage spread between entrance and maximum salaries has increased since 1973, specifically for police personnel by 40.5% (from 19.0% to 26.7%), and for fire and refuse personnel by 28.6% and 44%, respectively, the total salary cost over a twenty-year period at a hypothetical zero inflation rate has only increased 4.4% for police, 3.1% for fire, and 3.8% for refuse departments.

Tables 3/3, 3/4, and 3/5 show for each service the following: annual entrance salary (base salary paid during the first 12 months with the department, excluding uniform allowance, holiday pay, hazard pay, or any other additional compensation); maximum annual salary paid to personnel who do not hold any promotional rank (excluding uniform allowance, holiday pay, hazard pay, or any other additional compensation); and the mean number of years of service required to reach the maximum annual base salary.

Text continues on page 127

Table 3/2 COMPARISON OF MEAN ENTRANCE AND MAXIMUM SALARIES, 1973, 1978, 1983, AND 1984

Classification	Mean entrance salary ($)	Mean maximum salary ($)	% spread	No. of years to maximum	Average % increase/ year to maximum
Police					
1973	8,273	9,846	19.0	3	6.0
1978	11,472	14,026	22.3	4	5.2
1983	16,531	20,811	25.9	5	4.7
1984	17,120	21,691	26.7	5	4.8
Fire					
1973	7,954	9,480	19.2	3	6.0
1978	11,078	13,337	20.4	4	4.7
1983	15,858	19,695	24.2	4[1]	4.4
1984	16,473	20,534	24.7	5	4.5
Refuse					
1973	6,164	7,000	13.6	3	4.3
1978	8,600	9,997	16.2	4	3.8
1983	12,252	14,607	19.2	4	4.5
1984	12,776	15,282	19.6	5	3.6

[1] Cities 25,000 and over in population averaged 5 or more years to maximum.

Table 3/3 POLICE OFFICERS' ANNUAL BASE SALARIES, 1 JANUARY 1984

	Entrance salary					Maximum salary					No. of years to reach maximum	
Classification	No. of cities reporting	Mean	First quartile	Median	Third quartile	No. of cities reporting	Mean	First quartile	Median	Third quartile	No. of cities reporting	Mean
Total, all cities	1,453	$17,120	$14,644	$16,994	$19,399	1,439	$21,691	$18,410	$21,715	$24,979	1,167	5
Population group												
Over 1,000,000	2	20,838	...	20,838	...	2	26,313	...	26,313	...	2	7
500,000–1,000,000	12	18,973	15,852	18,273	20,916	12	24,849	21,696	24,024	26,125	11	6
250,000– 499,999	23	18,498	15,261	17,844	21,590	22	23,680	20,112	23,738	26,759	22	6
100,000– 249,999	85	18,345	15,392	18,150	20,571	85	23,678	20,236	23,064	26,267	74	6
50,000– 99,999	176	18,448	16,081	18,500	20,744	176	23,190	20,020	23,442	26,208	153	5
25,000– 49,999	351	17,719	15,188	17,772	19,847	349	22,456	19,098	22,917	25,437	292	5
10,000– 24,999	804	16,361	13,988	16,234	18,381	793	20,695	17,420	20,436	23,877	613	5

Table 3/4 FIREFIGHTERS' ANNUAL BASE SALARIES, 1 JANUARY 1984

	Entrance salary					Maximum salary					No. of years to reach maximum	
Classification	No. of cities reporting	Mean	First quartile	Median	Third quartile	No. of cities reporting	Mean	First quartile	Median	Third quartile	No of cities reporting	Mean
Total, all cities	1,145	$16,473	$13,776	$16,338	$18,752	1,130	$20,534	$17,402	$20,392	$23,709	919	5
Population group												
Over 1,000,000	2	20,838	...	20,838	...	2	26,313	...	26,313	...	2	7
500,000–1,000,000	12	18,553	15,676	17,405	20,784	12	24,076	21,696	23,112	25,192	12	6
250,000– 499,999	23	17,679	15,043	17,218	20,582	22	22,633	19,547	22,847	25,116	21	5
100,000– 249,999	82	17,603	15,059	17,583	19,828	82	22,548	19,309	22,013	25,284	73	6
50,000– 99,999	162	17,833	15,388	17,928	19,938	162	22,072	19,366	21,955	25,170	145	5
25,000– 49,999	295	16,979	14,622	17,062	19,206	293	21,289	18,461	21,356	24,056	238	5
10,000– 24,999	569	15,553	13,003	15,288	17,572	557	19,213	15,987	18,688	21,963	428	5

Table 3/5 REFUSE COLLECTORS' ANNUAL BASE SALARIES, 1 JANUARY 1984

	Entrance salary					Maximum salary					No. of years to reach maximum	
Classification	No. of cities reporting	Mean	First quartile	Median	Third quartile	No. of cities reporting	Mean	First quartile	Median	Third quartile	No. of cities reporting	Mean
Total, all cities	748	$12,776	$10,044	$12,461	$15,100	725	$15,282	$12,773	$15,046	$17,644	518	5
Population group												
Over 1,000,000	2	15,226	...	15,226	...	2	16,817	...	16,817	...	2	4
500,000–1,000,000	10	13,877	10,681	12,610	16,512	10	16,682	13,665	15,371	18,775	10	4
250,000– 499,999	18	13,356	10,931	13,694	15,107	18	16,846	13,556	16,287	18,531	18	4
100,000– 249,999	63	13,595	10,266	12,723	15,683	61	16,395	13,363	15,576	18,771	51	5
50,000– 99,999	91	13,678	11,631	13,494	15,320	91	16,165	13,656	16,066	18,292	72	5
25,000– 49,999	177	13,124	10,196	12,875	15,775	171	15,565	12,870	15,537	18,080	124	5
10,000– 24,999	387	12,204	9,563	11,736	14,519	372	14,633	12,085	14,325	16,786	241	5

Table 3/6 LONGEVITY PAY FOR POLICE OFFICERS, 1 JANUARY 1984

	Personnel can receive longevity pay					Maximum salary including longevity					No. of years service for maximum longevity	
		Yes		No								
Classification	No. of cities reporting (A)	No.	% of (A)	No.	% of (A)	No. of cities reporting	Mean	First quartile	Median	Third quartile	No. of cities reporting	Mean
Total, all cities	1,453	917	63.1	536	36.9	835	$23,109	$19,862	$22,778	$26,376	805	18
Population group												
Over 1,000,000	2	2	100.0	0	0.0	2	27,397	...	27,397	...	2	23
500,000–1,000,000	12	7	58.3	5	41.7	7	26,021	23,416	26,160	26,561	6	24
250,000– 499,999	23	20	87.0	3	13.0	19	25,187	21,051	26,489	28,031	19	20
100,000– 249,999	85	57	67.1	28	32.9	53	25,068	21,644	24,363	27,433	54	21
50,000– 99,999	177	114	64.4	63	35.6	107	24,136	20,704	23,930	26,484	106	19
25,000– 49,999	347	219	63.1	128	36.9	205	23,416	20,145	23,304	26,701	200	18
10,000– 24,999	807	498	61.7	309	38.3	442	22,328	18,851	21,923	25,831	418	17

Table 3/7 LONGEVITY PAY FOR FIREFIGHTERS, 1 JANUARY 1984

Classification	Personnel can receive longevity pay					Maximum salary including longevity					No. of years service for maximum longevity	
	No. of cities reporting (A)	Yes		No								
		No.	% of (A)	No.	% of (A)	No. of cities reporting	Mean	First quartile	Median	Third quartile	No. of cities reporting	Mean
Total, all cities	1,152	715	62.1	437	37.9	652	$21,872	$18,684	$21,472	$24,850	632	19
Population group												
Over 1,000,000	2	2	100.0	0	0.0	2	27,322	...	27,322	...	2	23
500,000–1,000,000	12	6	50.0	6	50.0	6	25,264	23,009	24,048	25,038	5	26
250,000– 499,999	23	20	87.0	3	13.0	19	24,367	20,348	25,027	26,535	19	21
100,000– 249,999	83	58	69.9	25	30.1	55	23,905	20,668	22,779	25,584	55	21
50,000– 99,999	163	111	68.1	52	31.9	104	23,062	20,051	22,325	26,001	102	18
25,000– 49,999	293	183	62.5	110	37.5	173	22,185	19,086	21,959	25,105	165	19
10,000– 24,999	576	335	58.2	241	41.8	293	20,615	17,624	19,980	23,274	284	18

Table 3/8 LONGEVITY PAY FOR REFUSE COLLECTORS, 1 JANUARY 1984

Classification	Personnel can receive longevity pay					Maximum salary including longevity					No. of years service for maximum longevity	
	No. of cities reporting (A)	Yes		No								
		No.	% of (A)	No.	% of (A)	No. of cities reporting	Mean	First quartile	Median	Third quartile	No. of cities reporting	Mean
Total, all cities	751	433	57.7	318	42.3	383	$16,735	$14,108	$16,539	$18,785	375	18
Population group												
Over 1,000,000	2	2	100.0	0	0.0	2	17,694	...	17,694	...	2	26
500,000–1,000,000	10	4	40.0	6	60.0	4	16,577	14,747	16,655	16,846	4	26
250,000– 499,999	18	14	77.8	4	22.2	13	17,346	14,408	16,539	18,204	14	20
100,000– 249,999	63	43	68.3	20	31.7	38	17,277	13,976	16,465	18,958	40	20
50,000– 99,999	93	62	66.7	31	33.3	58	17,609	15,308	17,878	19,228	57	20
25,000– 49,999	176	102	58.0	74	42.0	97	16,639	13,705	16,540	19,124	94	18
10,000– 24,999	389	206	53.0	183	47.0	171	16,319	13,904	16,013	18,042	164	17

Table 3/9 RATIO OF REFUSE COLLECTOR AND FIREFIGHTER SALARIES TO POLICE SALARIES, 1 JANUARY 1984

Classification	Refuse collector salary ratio				Firefighter salary ratio			
	Entrance		Maximum		Entrance		Maximum	
	Mean (%)	Median (%)	Mean (%)	Median (%)	Mean (%)	Median (%)	Mean (%)	Median (%)
Total, all cities	74.6	73.3	70.5	69.3	96.2	96.1	94.7	93.9
Population group								
Over 1,000,000	73.1	73.1	63.9	63.9	100.0	100.0	100.0	100.0
500,000–1,000,000	73.1	69.0	67.1	64.0	97.8	95.2	96.9	96.2
250,000– 499,999	72.2	76.7	71.1	68.6	95.6	96.5	95.6	96.2
100,000– 249,999	74.1	70.1	69.2	59.3	96.0	96.8	95.2	95.4
50,000– 99,999	74.1	72.9	69.7	68.5	96.7	96.9	95.2	93.7
25,000– 49,999	74.1	72.4	69.3	67.8	95.8	96.0	94.8	93.2
10,000– 24,999	74.6	72.3	70.7	70.1	95.1	94.2	92.8	91.4

Table 3/10 TRENDS IN POLICE OFFICERS', FIREFIGHTERS', AND REFUSE COLLECTORS' BASE AND MAXIMUM SALARIES (MEANS)[1]

Classification	No. of cities included[2]	1 Jan. 1979 ($)	1 Jan. 1980 ($)	% change from 1979	1 Jan. 1981 ($)	% change from 1980	1 Jan. 1982 ($)	% change from 1981	1 Jan. 1983 ($)	% change from 1982	1 Jan. 1984 ($)	% change from 1983	% change from 1979
Police													
Entrance salary	570	12,265	13,235	8	14,499	10	15,734	9	16,708	6	17,466	5	42.4
Maximum salary	562	15,155	16,477	9	18,101	10	19,802	9	21,062	6	22,146	5	46.1
Fire													
Entrance salary	462	11,769	12,746	8	13,967	10	15,147	8	16,069	6	16,764	4	42.4
Maximum salary	455	14,338	15,599	9	17,168	10	18,702	9	19,984	7	20,925	5	45.9
Refuse													
Entrance salary	303	8,896	9,703	9	10,617	9	11,523	9	12,196	6	12,761	5	43.4
Maximum salary	300	10,535	11,594	10	12,761	10	13,830	8	14,695	6	15,410	5	46.3

Except for average police entrance salaries, which increased only 3.6% (no table shown), mean entrance and maximum salaries since 1983 exceeded the increase in the CPI-U (3.8%) in all three services. Maximum salaries for police officers increased 4.2%. The mean entrance and maximum salaries for firefighters increased 3.9% and 4.3%, respectively. Refuse collectors' average entrance salaries increased 4.6%.

Tables 3/6, 3/7, and 3/8 show for each service the following: whether personnel can receive longevity pay (compensation over the regular maximum salary based on number of years of service); maximum salary including longevity that personnel holding no promotional rank can receive; and mean number of years of service required to reach the maximum annual salary with longevity. Only municipalities that reported an actual maximum salary including longevity were included.

Longevity pay has been adopted by the majority of cities responding to the survey. It is commonly used as an incentive to reduce employee turnover and to recognize employees who have reached the maximum salary and have limited promotional opportunities. Longevity pay may be a flat dollar amount, a percentage of base pay, a percentage of the maximum rate, or a normal step increase in the basic pay plan. The method of calculating longevity pay can have a significant effect on the extent of the burden on the personnel budget. On an average, longevity pay increases maximum salaries by 6.5% for police officers, 6.5% for firefighters, and 9.5% for refuse collectors.

The ratio of refuse collectors' and firefighters' salaries to police officers' salaries is shown in Table 3/9. Except for cities over 1,000,000, firefighters have consistently been paid less than police officers. Since ICMA began tracking these ratios in 1974 they have changed very little. For example, in 1974 refuse collector salary ratios for entrance and maximum for all cities averaged 73.0% and 70.4% respectively, of police salaries. Firefighter salary ratios for entrance and maximum for all cities averaged 98.5% and 94.9%, respectively.

Text continues on page 129

Table 3/11 TRENDS IN EXPENDITURES FOR POLICE, FIRE, AND REFUSE DEPARTMENTS (MEANS)[1]

Classification	No. of cities included [2]	1 Jan. 1979 ($000)	1 Jan. 1980 ($000)	% change from 1979	1 Jan. 1981 ($000)	% change from 1980	1 Jan. 1982 ($000)	% change from 1981	1 Jan. 1983 ($000)	% change from 1982	1 Jan. 1984 ($000)	% change from 1983	% change from 1979
Police													
Total salaries and wages	577	1,711	1,929	9	2,781	44	2,342	(16)	2,556	9	2,759	8	56
Capital outlay	439	100	127	27	127	0	121	(5)	161	33	186	16	86
Total expenditures	582	2,622	2,881	10	3,807	32	3,531	(7)	3,887	10	4,164	7	59
Fire													
Total salaries and wages	486	1,321	1,446	9	1,604	11	1,952	22	1,947	0	2,073	6	57
Capital outlay	328	115	87	(40)	94	8	112	19	126	13	107	(15)	(26)
Total expenditures	497	1,912	2,054	7	2,238	9	2,692	20	2,795	4	2,976	6	56
Refuse													
Total salaries and wages	316	589	580	(2)	632	9	668	6	702	5	707	1	20
Capital outlay	159	181	174	(4)	297	71	287	(3)	256	(11)	297	16	64
Total expenditures	324	1,165	1,213	4	1,607	32	1,510	(6)	1,644	9	1,672	2	44

Table 3/12 EXPENDITURES FOR SALARIES AND WAGES (CIVILIAN AND UNIFORMED)

Classification	Police			Fire			Refuse		
	No. reporting	Mean (000)	Per capita	No. reporting	Mean (000)	Per capita	No. reporting	Mean (000)	Per capita
Total, all cities	1,454	$ 2,684	$57.12	1,220	$ 2,099	$40.39	768	$ 686	$11.69
Population group									
Over 1,000,000	2	125,448	89.69	2	70,664	50.52	2	16,812	12.02
500,000–1,000,000	12	47,874	68.41	12	30,570	43.68	10	7,707	10.88
250,000– 499,999	23	24,610	70.80	23	16,483	47.40	18	4,504	12.61
100,000– 249,999	82	8,906	59.41	81	6,774	44.95	60	1,634	10.67
50,000– 99,999	171	3,538	52.00	160	2,693	39.63	95	772	11.19
25,000– 49,999	354	1,671	47.90	311	1,281	36.42	183	426	11.88
10,000– 24,999	810	721	45.47	631	468	28.98	400	214	13.27
Geographic region									
Northeast	306	1,832	57.50	195	1,932	50.04	132	458	11.03
North Central	462	2,270	55.44	397	1,617	35.97	205	518	9.16
South	405	2,774	53.01	377	2,195	39.92	335	786	13.89
West	281	4,163	63.37	251	2,846	41.31	96	1,007	10.70
Geographic division									
New England	118	1,414	49.31	98	1,448	46.86	50	257	6.88
Mid-Atlantic	188	2,095	61.86	97	2,421	52.18	82	580	13.18
East North Central	315	2,308	57.13	274	1,639	37.09	143	568	9.94
West North Central	147	2,189	51.96	123	1,566	33.58	62	402	7.29
South Atlantic	188	2,838	59.37	173	1,988	39.45	162	766	14.79
East South Central	64	2,741	45.25	62	2,517	40.64	44	1,000	14.20
West South Central	153	2,709	49.77	142	2,307	40.08	129	739	12.76
Mountain	84	4,067	63.06	74	2,493	36.75	44	903	11.07
Pacific Coast	197	4,204	63.50	177	2,994	43.17	52	1,096	10.45
Form of government									
Mayor-council	548	3,260	60.97	446	2,714	44.00	275	906	12.30
Council-manager	824	2,395	54.54	713	1,747	37.24	456	579	11.28
Commission	39	2,682	51.52	27	2,901	44.32	24	477	9.72
Town meeting	35	713	42.26	26	608	35.60	12	156	9.11
Representative town meeting	8	1,721	59.97	8	1,270	44.21	1	179	9.71

Table 3/13 TOTAL MUNICIPAL EXPENDITURES (CONTRIBUTIONS) FOR SOCIAL SECURITY AND STATE- AND CITY-ADMINISTERED EMPLOYEE RETIREMENT SYSTEMS (CIVILIAN AND UNIFORMED)

	Police department			Fire department			Refuse department		
Classification	No. of cities reporting	Mean (000)	Per capita	No. of cities reporting	Mean (000)	Per capita	No. of cities reporting	Mean (000)	Per capita
Total, all cities	1,365	$ 582	$12.25	1,112	$ 504	$ 9.41	725	$ 108	$1.80
Population group									
Over 1,000,000	2	47,772	34.16	2	20,978	15.00	2	3,182	2.28
500,000–1,000,000	12	12,353	17.65	12	9,548	13.64	10	1,124	1.59
250,000– 499,999	22	5,326	15.53	22	4,136	12.06	18	760	2.19
100,000– 249,999	77	1,849	12.52	76	1,498	10.09	57	252	1.64
50,000– 99,999	165	651	9.64	152	523	7.76	93	115	1.67
25,000– 49,999	334	297	8.47	286	259	7.31	172	62	1.71
10,000– 24,999	753	113	7.13	562	80	4.96	373	30	1.89

Table 3/14 TOTAL MUNICIPAL EXPENDITURES (CONTRIBUTIONS) FOR HEALTH, HOSPITAL, DISABILITY, AND LIFE INSURANCE PROGRAMS (CIVILIAN AND UNIFORMED)

	Police department			Fire department			Refuse department		
Classification	No. of cities reporting	Mean (000)	Per capita	No. of cities reporting	Mean (000)	Per capita	No. of cities reporting	Mean (000)	Per capita
Total, all cities	1,373	$ 190	$3.99	1,114	$ 143	$2.67	705	$ 69	$1.13
Population group									
Over 1,000,000	2	12,260	8.77	2	5,355	3.83	2	2,428	1.74
500,000–1,000,000	12	2,906	4.15	12	1,634	2.34	10	730	1.03
250,000– 499,999	22	1,650	4.81	22	1,090	3.18	18	397	1.14
100,000– 249,999	79	537	3.60	76	396	2.66	56	176	1.14
50,000– 99,999	166	262	3.86	154	195	2.88	90	73	1.06
25,000– 49,999	331	119	3.40	284	89	2.52	168	37	1.04
10,000– 24,999	761	52	3.30	564	35	2.17	361	18	1.13

Table 3/15 TOTAL PERSONNEL EXPENDITURES (CIVILIAN AND UNIFORMED)[1]

	Police department			Fire department			Refuse department		
Classification	No. of cities reporting	Mean (000)	Per capita	No. of cities reporting	Mean (000)	Per capita	No. of cities reporting	Mean (000)	Per capita
Total, all cities	1,454	$ 3,408	$ 72.53	1,220	$ 2,688	$51.72	768	$ 847	$14.44
Population group									
Over 1,000,000	2	185,479	132.63	2	96,997	69.36	2	22,422	16.03
500,000–1,000,000	12	63,132	90.21	12	41,752	59.66	10	9,561	13.50
250,000– 499,999	23	31,292	89.99	23	21,481	61.77	18	5,531	15.49
100,000– 249,999	82	11,160	74.44	81	8,552	56.74	60	2,032	13.27
50,000– 99,999	171	4,410	64.82	160	3,371	49.62	95	953	13.81
25,000– 49,999	354	2,061	59.07	311	1,600	45.30	183	518	14.46
10,000– 24,999	810	875	55.15	631	571	35.35	400	259	16.02
Geographic region									
Northeast	306	2,267	71.14	195	2,403	62.23	132	589	14.21
North Central	462	3,000	73.26	397	2,190	48.72	205	677	11.98
South	405	3,339	63.80	377	2,653	48.25	335	942	16.65
West	281	5,424	82.55	251	3,748	54.40	96	1,234	13.10
Geographic division									
New England	118	1,694	59.08	98	1,700	55.02	50	331	8.89
Mid-Atlantic	188	2,626	77.55	97	3,112	67.09	82	746	16.95
East North Central	315	3,134	77.57	274	2,260	51.13	143	760	13.29
West North Central	147	2,713	64.39	123	2,033	43.63	62	487	8.84
South Atlantic	188	3,469	72.56	173	2,448	48.57	162	930	17.96
East South Central	64	3,250	53.66	62	2,985	48.20	44	1,159	16.46
West South Central	153	3,216	59.07	142	2,759	47.94	129	884	15.25
Mountain	84	4,882	75.68	74	3,010	44.37	44	1,092	13.39
Pacific Coast	197	5,655	85.40	177	4,057	58.50	52	1,355	12.92
Form of government									
Mayor-council	548	4,213	78.81	446	3,541	57.40	275	1,131	15.35
Council-manager	824	2,993	68.17	713	2,200	46.90	456	709	13.81
Commission	39	3,506	67.36	27	3,792	57.94	24	587	11.95
Town meeting	35	826	48.89	26	679	39.78	12	187	10.88
Representative town meeting	8	1,920	66.79	8	1,396	48.56	1	189	10.50

[1]Includes total personnel expenditures, capital outlay, and all other department expenditures.

Trends in entrance and maximum salaries for police officers, firefighters, and refuse collectors are shown in Table 3/10. The average salaries presented are for 1 January 1979 through 1 January 1984. Mean figures for entrance and maximum salaries for each service are presented together with average percentage increases from year to year and for the entire period. Over a five-year period (December 1979–December 1984), the CPI-U rose faster than annual base salaries. During that period, the CPI-U increased 49.6%, while average entrance and maximum salaries for police officers increased 42.4% and 46.1%, respectively; for firefighters, 42.4% and 45.9%, respectively; and for refuse collectors, 43.4% and 46.3%, respectively (Table 3/10).

Expenditures. Data on expenditures for police, fire, and refuse departments appear in Tables 3/11 through 3/17.

Table 3/11 shows trends in expenditures for police, fire, and refuse departments from 1 January 1979 through 1 January 1984. The only expenditures to show a decrease were fire departments' capital outlay expenditures (a 15% reduction from 1983). In general, increases in expenditures exceeded the increase in the CPI-U over the five-year period.

Table 3/12 shows the amount expended on salaries and wages for all departmental personnel—permanent and temporary, full-time and part-time. (The survey requested the gross amount of salaries and wages, including longevity pay, hazard pay, holiday pay, etc., without deduction of withholding for income tax or employee contributions for social security or retirement coverage.)

Average expenditures, on a per capita basis, for salaries and wages for both civilian and uniformed personnel increased 6.0% for police departments, 9.2% for fire departments, and 4.0% for refuse departments since 1983. Refuse de-

Table 3/16 MUNICIPAL EXPENDITURES FOR CAPITAL OUTLAY[1]

Classification	Police department			Fire department			Refuse department		
	No. of cities reporting	Mean (000)	Per capita	No. of cities reporting	Mean (000)	Per capita	No. of cities reporting	Mean (000)	Per capita
Total, all cities	1,258	$ 131	$2.71	1,044	$ 97	$1.79	517	$ 179	$2.63
Population group									
Over 1,000,000	2	5,786	4.14	2	637	0.46	2	4,498	3.22
500,000–1,000,000	12	3,303	4.72	11	836	1.21	10	1,371	1.94
250,000– 499,999	19	584	1.70	21	496	1.43	14	931	2.65
100,000– 249,999	73	256	1.72	74	203	1.36	45	263	1.75
50,000– 99,999	155	184	2.71	140	158	2.31	71	184	2.60
25,000– 49,999	312	83	2.38	266	75	2.12	126	102	2.82
10,000– 24,999	685	43	2.70	530	43	2.68	249	77	4.76

[1]Including purchase and replacement equipment, purchase of land and existing structures, and construction.

Table 3/17 TOTAL EXPENDITURES[1]

Classification	Police department			Fire department			Refuse department		
	No. of cities reporting	Mean (000)	Per capita	No. of cities reporting	Mean (000)	Per capita	No. of cities reporting	Mean (000)	Per capita
Total, all cities	1,462	$ 4,003	$ 85.34	1,259	$ 2,928	$57.53	789	$ 1,547	$26.43
Population group									
Over 1,000,000	2	209,527	149.82	2	103,015	73.66	2	38,058	27.21
500,000–1,000,000	12	76,524	109.35	12	45,555	65.09	10	19,011	26.84
250,000– 499,999	23	35,894	103.22	23	23,814	68.48	19	9,776	27.68
100,000– 249,999	82	12,968	86.51	81	9,476	62.88	61	3,846	24.97
50,000– 99,999	173	5,156	75.94	161	3,803	56.05	99	1,834	26.45
25,000– 49,999	355	2,445	70.02	315	1,814	51.62	188	909	25.37
10,000– 24,999	815	1,062	66.89	665	654	40.72	410	443	27.52
Geographic region									
Northeast	309	2,496	78.06	223	2,325	64.50	139	859	20.86
North Central	463	3,411	83.40	401	2,404	53.85	210	1,305	23.25
South	407	4,095	78.42	383	2,941	54.07	342	1,663	29.10
West	283	6,482	99.18	252	4,277	62.29	98	2,634	28.31
Geographic division									
New England	119	1,971	68.32	101	1,876	60.89	51	631	16.44
Mid-Atlantic	190	2,825	83.25	122	2,697	66.77	88	990	23.17
East North Central	316	3,533	87.59	274	2,503	56.65	147	1,428	25.12
West North Central	147	3,150	74.78	127	2,190	47.99	63	1,019	18.70
South Atlantic	189	4,219	88.27	174	2,804	55.89	164	1,740	33.81
East South Central	64	3,928	64.85	62	3,352	54.13	45	1,953	25.98
West South Central	154	4,013	74.07	147	2,930	52.11	133	1,470	25.31
Mountain	85	5,809	90.95	75	3,545	52.85	45	2,457	30.72
Pacific Coast	198	6,771	102.60	177	4,587	66.15	53	2,785	26.75
Form of government									
Mayor-council	550	4,857	91.10	466	3,746	62.70	285	1,918	26.13
Council-manager	830	3,579	81.62	731	2,459	53.22	467	1,383	27.08
Commission	39	4,087	78.53	28	3,962	62.25	24	992	20.22
Town meeting	35	958	56.76	26	770	45.08	12	318	18.50
Representative town meeting	8	2,124	73.86	8	1,547	53.82	1	259	14.39

[1]Includes total personnel expenditures, capital outlay, and all other department expenditures.

partments spend a smaller percentage of their total departmental expenditures on salary and wages than police and fire departments. Refuse departments expended 44.4% of their total expenditures on salaries and wages while police departments expended 67% and fire department 71.7%.

Data showing municipal contributions (as opposed to employee contributions) for employee benefits are presented in Tables 3/13 and 3/14. Contributions to the following are shown for uniformed and civilian/nonuniformed personnel: federal social security and state- and city-administered employee retirement systems (Table 3/13); and health, hospital, disability, and life insurance programs (Table 3/14).

Per capita municipal contributions for employee retirement programs for police personnel decreased from 1983 by 2.5%. Per capita expenditures for retirement programs for fire and refuse personnel increased by 8.2% and 4.0%, respectively. Since 1979, or over a five-year period, expenditures for employee retirement programs for police, fire, and refuse personnel have increased by 40.2%, 37.0%, and 29.5%, respectively.

Per capita municipal expenditures for health, hospital, disability, and life insurance programs for police, fire, and refuse personnel increased 15.7%, 18.1%, and 28.4% respectively from 1983.

Total personnel expenditures (which include salaries and wages; contributions for employee benefits to federal social security and state- and city-administered employee retirement systems; and contributions to health, hospital, disability, and life insurance programs) are shown in Table 3/15. Average expenditures for police personnel have increased 4.9% per capita, from $69.12 in 1983 to $72.53 in 1984. Fire personnel expenditures per capita increased 9.3% from $47.32 in 1983 to $51.72 in 1984. Refuse personnel expenditures per capita increased 5.3% from $13.71 in 1983 to $14.44 in 1984.

Departmental expenditures for capital outlay, including purchase and replacement of equipment, purchase of land and existing structures, and construction, are presented in Table 3/16. Capital outlay expenditures on a per capita basis increased for both police and refuse departments by 4.2% and 8.2%, respectively. Fire departments indicated a decrease in capital outlay expenditures from 1983 by 4.3%.

Table 3/17 shows total expenditures, including total personnel, capital outlay, and all other department expenditures. Per capita expenditures for police departments increased in the past year by 4.9%; for fire departments by 9.4%; and for refuse departments by 6.1%.

Table 3/18 POLICE, FIRE, AND REFUSE COLLECTION AND DISPOSAL DEPARTMENTS: PERSONNEL, SALARIES, AND EXPENDITURES FOR CITIES OVER 10,000: 1984

This table includes 1,480 cities over 10,000 population (based on U.S. Bureau of the Census 1980 population). Data were collected in the spring of 1984. All personnel and salary figures are as of 1 January 1984; expenditure figures are for the fiscal year ended between 1 January 1983 and 1 January 1984. The numbers in parentheses following the names of cities are explained at the end of this headnote. Leaders (. . . or . .) indicate data not reported or not applicable.

Department: letter identifies department to which the line of data pertains: "P," police department; "F," fire department; "R," refuse collection and disposal department.

Total personnel, no. uniformed, duty hours per week: left, total actual (not authorized) number of full-time paid employees; middle, number of uniformed or sworn (not including civilian or nonuniformed) employees (for refuse, civilian or nonuniformed is meant to include drivers whose sole function is driving, foremen, equipment handlers, and others who do not perform trash and/or garbage collection work); regular work week (in hours) for each department.

Entrance, maximum salary ($): left, annual base salary of a full-time employee (patrol personnel, firefighter, refuse collector) during the first 12 months on the force; right, maximum annual base salary paid a full-time employee not holding any promotional rank.

Longevity pay, maximum ($), no. years to max.: left, indicates whether municipality has longevity pay—extra compensation over the regular maximum salary based on the number of years of service—("Y" yes); center, maximum salary with longevity; right, the number of years of service required for maximum salary with longevity.

Total expenditures (A) ($): sum of the other total figures (columns B, E, F). (This sum represents the total amount of department expenditures *reported* to the Year Book and may not, in all cases, be the complete expenditure figure for the department. Omissions can be found by examining the individual figures for each city.)

Total personnel expenditures (B), % of (A) ($): left, sum of columns C and D; right, total personnel expenditures as a percentage of the total reported expenditures (B ÷ A).

Salaries and wages (C) ($): amount of salaries and wages for all department personnel—regular, temporary, full-time, and part-time. (The gross amount is reported, including longevity pay, hazard pay, holiday pay, etc., without deduction of withholding for income tax or employee contributions for social security or retirement.)

City contributions to employee retirement, [to employee] insurance (D) ($): left, amount the municipality contributes to federal social security, to a state administered employee retirement system, and/or to a city administered employee retirement system for civilian and uniformed personnel; right, amount the municipality contributes to health, hospital, or disability, and to life insurance programs for civilian and uniformed personnel.

Capital outlay (E) ($): figure includes purchase and replacement of equipment, purchase of land and existing structures, and construction.

All other (F) ($): all other expenditures not reported in the above categories.

Numbers in parentheses after city names indicate:

1 - Fire department is primarily volunteer.
2 - Municipality contracts for fire services.
3 - Fire services are provided by a special district.
4 - Municipality contracts for police services.
5 - Municipality has a public safety department.
6 - Metropolitan government provides police/fire services.
7 - Municipality contracts for refuse collection service either totally or in addition to having its own refuse collection and disposal department. Expenditure figures may differ considerably if these municipalities are compared to municipalities of similar populations but dissimilar refuse collection and disposal arrangements.

City	Department	Total personnel, no. uniformed, duty hours per week	Entrance, maximum salary ($)	Longevity pay, maximum ($), no. years to max.	Reported expenditures (in thousands): Total expenditures (A) ($)	Total personnel expenditures (B), % of (A) ($)	Salaries and wages (C) ($)	City contrib. to employee retirement, insurance (D) ($)	Capital outlay (E) ($)	All other (F) ($)
OVER 1,000,000										
Chicago, Ill.	P	14,366-12,341-40	22,518-27,600	Y-32,634-30	528,700	504,639-95	443,860	60,515-264	1,980	22,081
	F	4,909-4,614-47	22,518-27,600	Y-32,634-30	201,697	187,989-93	162,509	25,396-84	1,219	12,489
	R	1,716-1,194-40	26,174-26,174	None	79,491	57,735-73	56,499	1,202-34	35	21,721
Detroit, Mich.	P	4,413-3,792-40	19,906-26,296	Y-27,159-21	250,922	230,396-92	137,320	72,907-20,169	5,460	15,066
	F	1,651-1,354-50	19,906-26,296	Y-27,009-21	89,166	82,795-93	49,234	26,101-7,460	700	5,671
	R	797-255-40	14,924-16,900	Y-17,350-26	41,865	21,785-52	14,584	3,546-3,655	8,978	11,102
Houston, Tex. (7)	P	4,856-2,444-40	21,770-26,330	Y-27,635-25	168,131	140,562-84	113,576	22,636-4,350	6,111	21,458
	F	3,355-3,132-47	21,770-26,330	Y-27,635-25	116,864	111,199-95	92,094	15,855-3,250	573	5,092
	R	1,087-613-35	15,527-16,733	Y-18,038-25	34,250	23,058-67	19,040	2,818-1,200	18	11,174

Table 3/18 continued **POLICE, FIRE, AND REFUSE COLLECTION AND DISPOSAL DEPARTMENTS: PERSONNEL, SALARIES, AND EXPENDITURES FOR CITIES OVER 10,000: 1984**

					Reported expenditures (in thousands)					
City	Department	Total personnel, no. uniformed, duty hours per week	Entrance, maximum salary ($)	Longevity pay, maximum ($), no. years to max.	Total expenditures (A) ($)	Total personnel expenditures (B), % of (A) ($)	Salaries and wages (C) ($)	City contrib. to employee retirement, insurance (D) ($)	Capital outlay (E) ($)	All other (F) ($)
500,000-1,000,000										
Baltimore, Md.	P	3,588-3,061-40	15,920-20,618	Y-22,575-25	115,157	91,506-79	72,928	12,246-6,332	24	23,627
	F	2,075-1,940-47	15,676-20,384	Y-22,322-25	66,730	58,978-88	46,786	7,960-4,232	...	7,752
	R	894-54-40	13,166-13,852	Y-14,747-25	32,767	15,835-48	13,027	1,303-1,505	2	16,930
Honolulu, Hawaii	P	1,967-1,611-40	18,312-22,248	Y-26,160-17	64,058	53,875-84	44,707	8,305-863	1,113	9,070
	F	995-967-56	17,964-21,864	Y-25,704-17	32,380	30,128-93	25,347	4,269-512	558	1,694
	R	513-244-40	15,936-17,700	None	17,280	12,023-70	9,512	2,237-274	1,901	3,356
Indianapolis, Ind. (7)	P	1,252-948-40	14,401-21,696	Y-23,696-..	45,378	36,622-81	26,182	9,684-756	577	8,179
	F	802-756-56	13,500-21,696	Y-23,696-..	31,454	27,934-89	17,919	9,553-462	387	3,133
	R	151-18-40	11,627-14,976	None	7,896	2,689-34	2,314	305-70	1,012	4,195
Jacksonville, Fla. (7)	P	1,603-973-40	18,234-24,348	Y-26,748-40	61,510	46,361-75	36,926	7,366-2,069	967	14,182
	F	759-745-56	16,128-21,972	Y-24,372-40	28,823	24,242-84	19,870	3,365-1,007	535	4,046
	R	195-30-40	10,056-14,064	Y-16,464-40	7,685	4,318-56	3,191	851-276	660	2,707
Memphis, Tenn. (7)	P	1,522-1,204-40	15,852-21,288	None	51,267	42,379-83	34,036	6,066-2,277	2,312	6,576
	F	1,481-1,416-56	15,108-20,583	None	44,929	41,587-93	33,366	6,080-2,141	1,094	2,248
	R	954-505-40	11,306-13,478	None	21,833	16,105-74	13,747	1,190-1,168	753	4,975
Milwaukee, Wis.	P	2,389-2,077-40	21,061-25,998	Y-26,498-14	91,756	85,720-93	63,781	15,729-6,210	1,211	4,825
	F	1,124-1,064-52	18,993-25,192	None	47,762	45,647-96	30,773	12,282-2,592	876	1,239
	R	508-390-40	18,106-19,849	None	34,721	13,589-39	10,098	2,221-1,270	982	20,150
New Orleans, La. (7)	P	1,874-1,417-40	16,846-23,700	Y-31,764-25	82,244	59,745-73	52,489	2,979-4,277	17,524	4,975
	F	1,010-939-48	16,846-23,700	Y-31,764-25	51,906	51,236-99	38,433	10,820-1,983	158	512
	R	445-445-40	8,946-12,562	Y-16,846-25	11,785	9,979-85	8,528	634-817	951	855
Phoenix, Ariz. (7)	P	2,371-1,680-40	20,916-28,824	None	85,663	67,205-78	56,804	6,226-4,175	6,950	11,508
	F	1,037-914-56	20,916-27,432	None	38,283	31,045-81	26,535	2,535-1,975	2,744	4,494
	R	261-164-40	17,088-20,340	None	23,728	6,224-26	5,020	725-479	4,018	13,486
San Antonio, Tex.	P	1,410-1,145-40	15,475-23,268	Y-24,708-25	51,760	37,682-73	30,899	4,881-1,902	493	13,585
	F	877-849-52	16,344-22,524	Y-23,724-25	35,010	32,829-94	28,079	3,477-1,273	536	1,645
	R	404-185-40	12,054-15,766	Y-18,251-15	15,873	8,157-51	6,275	791-1,091	1,625	6,091
San Diego, Calif.	P	1,812-1,340-40	19,417-26,125	None	70,158	57,197-82	45,126	9,250-2,821	5,717	7,244
	F	839-760-56	20,784-24,528	None	33,561	30,080-90	24,549	4,192-1,339	747	2,734
	R	265-233-40	20,488-24,232	None	16,538	6,695-40	5,359	982-354	1,804	8,039
San Francisco, Calif. (7)	P	1,898-1,243-40	24,726-28,626	None	146,947	128,202-87	72,285	54,267-1,650	1,451	17,294
	F	1,453-1,394-49	24,726-28,626	None	101,007	93,026-92	49,827	42,191-1,008	1,031	6,950
San Jose, Calif. (7)	P	1,123-915-40	26,520-31,450	None	52,393	51,092-98	38,320	11,235-1,537	1,301	...
	F	680-650-56	25,646-30,410	None	34,819	34,294-98	25,354	7,853-1,087	525	...
250,000-499,999										
Albuquerque, N.M.	P	883-585-40	12,896-21,778	Y-22,546-18	28,586	22,862-80	18,383	3,177-1,302	1,671	4,053
	F	491-471-56	15,093-20,326	Y-22,726-25	20,298	14,188-70	11,090	2,318-780	1,700	4,410
	R	201-98-40	14,144-17,763	Y-18,363-10	10,568	4,175-40	3,575	436-164	699	5,694
Baton Rouge, La.	P	753-650-40	13,572-16,968	Y-20,362-25	16,832	15,029-89	12,475	2,068-486	104	1,699
	F	581-571-56	13,572-16,968	Y-20,362-25	14,119	13,028-92	10,788	1,796-444	151	940
	R	331-155-48	13,503-16,748	Y-...-25	9,939	5,378-54	4,454	740-184	8	4,553
Birmingham, Ala.	P	784-642-40	16,754-19,864	Y-21,064-24	23,375	19,414-83	15,844	2,048-1,522	833	3,128
	F	625-603-52	16,754-19,864	Y-21,064-24	19,027	15,975-84	13,110	1,611-1,254	1,153	1,899
	R	122-84-40	10,306-11,128	Y-12,328-24	7,498	2,326-31	...	1,229-1,097	1,427	3,745
Buffalo, N.Y.	P	1,148-1,038-40	14,891-20,413	Y-21,013-25	40,619	39,037-96	26,592	10,921-1,524	244	1,338
	F	987-953-40	14,891-20,413	Y-21,013-25	34,406	32,366-94	22,070	9,000-1,296	528	1,512
	R	256-167-40	14,173-15,939	Y-16,539-25	7,452	6,072-81	4,701	1,056-315	1,347	33
Charlotte, N.C. (7)	P	797-633-40	15,952-20,359	Y-21,174-25	23,583	19,282-82	16,502	1,892-888	468	3,833
	F	644-605-52	15,192-19,390	Y-20,166-25	17,670	15,877-90	13,605	1,554-718	456	1,337
	R	329-309-40	10,797-13,780	Y-14,331-25	11,491	7,527-66	6,390	771-366	278	3,686
Cincinnati, Ohio	P	985-817-40	23,736-26,430	Y-26,905-20	41,499	37,642-91	29,058	6,613-1,971	62	3,795
	F	774-752-48	22,185-24,700	Y-25,175-20	33,161	30,806-93	22,136	6,794-1,876	55	2,300
	R	207-80-40	16,670-17,173	Y-17,523-20	9,757	5,912-61	4,391	712-809	120	3,725
Denver, Colo.	P	1,650-1,366-40	21,504-28,656	Y-29,856-24	63,991	58,298-91	48,208	6,790-3,300	1,211	4,482
	F	899-881-48	18,192-27,144	Y-28,644-24	37,893	35,957-95	29,612	4,519-1,826	703	1,233
	R	327-114-40	16,332-22,764	Y-23,800-7	18,565	11,959-64	9,979	1,345-635	537	6,069
Kansas City, Mo. (7)	P	1,652-1,151-40	17,844-28,380	None	54,364	48,297-89	40,658	5,263-2,376	688	5,379
	F	788-752-48	17,532-23,532	None	27,120	23,614-87	18,895	3,456-1,263	829	2,677
	R	95-13-40	11,076-14,784	None	7,238	1,951-27	1,588	227-136	66	5,221
Long Beach, Calif.	P	931-620-40	23,197-27,954	Y-30,823-10	70,454	59,520-84	47,975	9,391-2,154	157	10,777
	F	459-431-56	23,197-27,954	Y-30,823-10	42,729	35,535-83	28,307	6,168-1,060	93	7,101
	R	154-4-40	14,700-19,568	None	11,422	6,161-54	5,096	709-356	48	5,213
Minneapolis, Minn. (7)	P	775-690-40	22,681-29,989	Y-31,137-24	31,736	26,958-85	22,356	3,474-1,128	350	4,428
	F	474-455-55	20,913-28,710	Y-31,137-24	21,423	18,289-85	15,155	2,360-774	25	3,109
	R	80-48-40	15,514-24,096	Y-24,785-24	9,716	2,567-26	2,167	289-111	...	7,149
Nashville-Davidson, Tenn.	P	1,189-954-40	13,916-19,824	Y-20,674-20	30,236	24,768-82	24,768	...-...	...	5,468
	F	929-875-56	13,584-18,696	Y-19,546-20	22,735	19,690-87	19,690	...-...	878	2,167
	R	245-147-40	11,064-13,188	Y-14,038-20	6,912	3,456-50	3,456	...-...	...	3,456
Norfolk, Va.	P	694-624-40	13,332-17,628	Y-20,304-20	16,608	16,608-100	13,091	2,953-564	...	...
	F	433-422-56	13,332-17,628	Y-20,304-20	11,001	11,001-100	8,594	2,054-353	...	...
	R	222-222-40	9,960-13,332	Y-15,372-20	4,191	4,191-100	3,293	717-181	...	...
Oakland, Calif. (7)	P	912-631-40	25,476-...	Y-30,708-5	54,891	48,308-88	29,305	17,347-1,656	59	6,524
	F	494-473-52	23,352-...	Y-30,732-5	33,186	32,904-99	19,170	12,635-1,099	231	51
Omaha, Neb. (7)	P	731-571-38	21,462-25,409	Y-26,489-21	25,939	23,058-89	18,779	3,011-1,268	...	2,881
	F	565-545-56	20,472-24,420	Y-25,260-21	20,678	19,210-93	15,309	2,878-1,023	471	997
Pittsburgh, Pa.	P	1,365-1,276-40	18,870-24,534	Y-26,497-35	43,186	42,132-98	35,058	3,260-3,814	...	1,054
	F	1,094-1,006-42	14,351-23,251	Y-25,111-35	33,321	32,607-98	27,176	2,327-3,104	193	521
	R	355-70-40	17,914-22,392	None	14,067	12,670-90	9,189	2,377-1,104	...	1,397

Table 3/18 continued **POLICE, FIRE, AND REFUSE COLLECTION AND DISPOSAL DEPARTMENTS: PERSONNEL, SALARIES, AND EXPENDITURES FOR CITIES OVER 10,000: 1984**

					Reported expenditures (in thousands)					
City	Depart-ment	Total personnel, no. uniformed, duty hours per week	Entrance, maximum salary ($)	Longevity pay, maximum ($), no. years to max.	Total expendi-tures (A) ($)	Total personnel expendi-tures (B), % of (A) ($)	Salaries and wages (C) ($)	City contrib. to employee retirement, insurance (D) ($)	Capital outlay (E) ($)	All other (F) ($)
250,000-499,999 continued										
Portland, Ore. (7)	P	886-707-40	19,781-28,184	None	42,319	36,186-86	22,813	11,270-2,103	99	6,034
	F	664-618-56	18,200-28,184	None	31,808	30,319-95	20,510	8,150-1,659	135	1,354
Sacramento, Calif.	P	728-521-40	22,110-26,218	Y-26,518-25	30,654	24,478-80	20,072	3,131-1,275	99	6,077
	F	430-422-56	21,529-25,532	Y-25,832-25	20,666	17,266-84	14,198	2,227-841	31	3,369
	R	184-177-40	16,272-19,298	Y-19,598-25	7,276	4,403-61	3,711	414-278	...	2,873
St. Louis, Mo.	P	2,286-1,523-40	17,218-22,941	None	69,145	59,831-87	47,652	9,106-3,073	2,413	6,901
	F	728-714-52	17,218-22,941	None	28,029	27,633-99	18,836	8,176-621	...	396
	R	225-0-40	12,298-16,458	None	11,409	6,430-56	5,388	860-182	2,307	2,672
St. Paul, Minn.	P	614-505-40	21,847-27,088	Y-29,199-15	23,863	21,584-90	16,804	3,379-1,401	541	1,738
	F	470-448-56	21,847-27,088	Y-29,199-15	20,595	19,138-93	12,992	4,697-1,449	142	1,315
Tampa, Fla. (7)	P	888-721-43	16,862-22,874	Y-23,874-20	30,574	24,269-79	18,277	4,960-1,032	569	5,736
	F	567-545-52	15,502-18,090	Y-19,090-25	18,181	15,711-86	11,601	3,406-704	222	2,248
	R	173-99-40	11,461-15,454	Y-16,454-20	15,248	4,352-29	3,705	378-269	279	10,617
Tucson, Ariz.	P	765-565-40	19,632-25,128	Y-27,641-21	27,102	21,616-80	18,046	1,905-1,665	1,138	4,348
	F	398-371-56	17,784-22,752	Y-25,027-21	17,468	13,505-77	11,451	1,254-800	1,208	2,755
	R	293-167-40	13,884-16,116	Y-17,728-21	13,447	7,406-55	6,005	787-614	3,203	2,838
Virginia Beach, Va.	P	562-405-40	15,384-19,704	Y-21,768-11	15,934	13,749-86	11,240	1,748-761	233	1,952
	F	286-268-56	15,384-19,704	Y-21,768-11	9,009	7,042-78	5,739	902-401	1,079	888
	R	222-182-40	10,344-13,248	Y-14,640-11	9,020	4,841-54	3,895	618-328	2,486	1,693
Wichita, Kan. (7)	P	558-411-40	16,531-20,634	Y-...-..	20,072	16,795-84	12,293	3,459-1,043	162	3,115
	F	374-365-54	16,531-20,634	Y-...-..	13,210	12,413-94	9,078	2,699-636	140	657
	R	4-0-40	...-...	..-...-..	536	105-20	82	15-8	234	197
100,000-249,999										
Akron, Ohio (7)	P	459-423-40	20,654-24,128	Y-...-..	18,083	15,102-84	11,847	2,022-1,233	2	2,979
	F	398-373-40	20,654-24,128	Y-...-..	16,599	14,706-89	10,832	2,443-1,431	8	1,885
	R	66-30-40	12,459-15,122	Y-...-..	6,338	2,077-33	1,635	219-223	...	4,261
Allentown, Pa. (7)	P	184-160-40	20,024-21,568	Y-22,818-19	5,357	5,005-93	4,379	272-354	118	234
	F	152-142-42	19,181-21,585	Y-22,385-20	4,672	4,386-94	3,520	573-293	131	155
Amarillo, Tex.	P	240-240-40	15,792-21,828	Y-23,028-25	7,299	5,761-79	5,361	279-121	58	1,480
	F	208-208-56	15,168-20,304	Y-21,504-25	5,545	5,021-91	4,519	395-107	73	451
	R	97-95-40	15,012-18,984	Y-20,184-25	4,617	1,822-39	1,605	171-46	127	2,668
Anaheim, Calif. (7)	P	450-317-40	22,235-29,078	None	21,046	17,324-82	13,676	2,732-916	115	3,607
	F	202-195-56	18,972-27,352	None	11,144	9,689-87	7,485	1,630-574	278	1,177
Anchorage, Alaska (7)	P	373-279-40	36,264-47,070	Y-51,771-10	25,358	25,358-100	19,180	5,781-397	...	...
	F	288-258-56	28,246-40,360	Y-48,426-30	19,196	19,196-100	14,087	4,908-201	...	...
	R	70-10-40	31,158-31,158	Y-37,398-30	2,910	2,910-100	2,584	148-178	...	...
Arlington, Va. (7)	P	389-290-40	19,250-24,348	Y-24,764-13	16,212	13,605-84	9,967	3,094-544	78	2,529
	F	240-234-56	17,955-22,691	Y-23,107-13	9,957	9,127-92	6,573	2,178-376	35	795
	R	81-30-40	11,995-14,477	Y-14,893-13	5,473	2,302-42	1,820	355-127	39	3,132
Bakersfield, Calif. (7)	P	268-194-40	21,127-25,104	Y-27,363-20	12,304	9,721-79	7,312	2,002-407	37	2,546
	F	158-150-56	20,531-24,402	None	7,520	5,923-79	4,461	1,226-236	300	1,297
	R	39-0-40	17,419-20,654	None	3,979	1,202-30	978	156-68	...	2,777
Boise City, Idaho (7)	P	173-154-40	14,676-20,160	None	4,599	4,599-100	4,042	372-185	...	...
	F	157-150-54	15,516-20,820	None	4,811	4,811-100	3,742	896-173	...	...
Cedar Rapids, Iowa	P	201-157-40	15,641-19,822	Y-21,022-25	6,685	5,845-87	4,098	1,470-277	242	598
	F	153-145-56	15,229-19,335	Y-20,535-25	5,147	4,821-94	3,207	1,384-230	57	269
	R	55-28-40	13,516-15,200	Y-16,400-25	2,079	1,273-61	1,070	124-79	308	498
Chesapeake, Va. (5,7)	P	202-158-40	13,884-18,109	Y-20,976-16	6,390	5,179-81	4,270	704-205	345	866
	F	206-202-56	13,280-17,354	Y-19,920-16	4,865	4,273-88	3,511	588-174	60	532
	R	73-33-40	8,874-11,680	Y-13,280-16	2,619	1,381-53	1,160	166-55	275	963
Colorado Springs, Colo.	P	479-359-40	19,968-26,196	Y-27,456-25	17,307	14,783-85	12,400	1,578-805	408	2,116
	F	312-287-56	19,968-26,196	Y-27,456-25	11,034	9,999-91	7,934	1,540-525	383	652
Concord, Calif. (3,7)	P	182-125-40	26,484-31,404	None	8,949	8,119-91	5,936	1,397-786	72	758
Davenport, Iowa	P	178-151-40	19,783-21,647	Y-24,363-25	7,201	6,266-87	5,076	893-297	174	761
	F	138-136-54	18,241-19,881	Y-22,779-25	5,604	4,888-87	3,864	788-236	101	615
	R	47-23-40	14,557-15,808	Y-16,828-20	1,756	1,167-66	980	125-62	145	444
Dayton, Ohio	P	579-472-40	18,959-22,339	Y-22,489-15	20,688	18,941-92	14,667	2,994-1,280	350	1,397
	F	428-360-50	18,855-22,339	Y-22,739-20	16,564	15,737-95	11,723	3,224-790	226	601
	R	136-91-40	16,047-17,908	Y-18,058-20	6,250	3,963-63	3,180	443-340	219	2,068
Des Moines, Iowa	P	460-350-40	18,575-21,317	Y-22,587-26	15,330	12,861-84	9,559	2,195-1,107	49	2,420
	F	308-305-56	17,744-20,037	Y-21,239-26	10,786	9,819-91	6,752	2,319-748	96	871
	R	65-59-40	18,289-18,858	Y-19,989-25	2,799	1,634-58	1,309	155-170	4	1,161
Durham, N.C. (5)	P	386-327-42	17,351-17,351	Y-23,643-20	...	...-..	...	...-...	...	...
	F	75-67-56	13,935-13,935	Y-18,851-20	...	...-..	...	...-...	...	...
	R	105-90-40	11,463-11,463	Y-15,775-20	...	...-..	...	...-...	...	...
Elizabeth, N.J. (7)	P	361-290-..	18,694-22,509	Y-24,760-25	11,365	11,004-97	8,789	1,735-480	...	361
	F	259-250-..	18,694-22,509	Y-24,760-25	8,507	8,239-97	6,479	1,416-344	...	268
Erie, Pa. (7)	P	236-207-40	18,150-20,306	Y-21,666-32	6,799	6,228-92	5,050	565-613	43	528
	F	214-196-42	18,603-20,402	Y-21,762-32	6,090	5,779-95	4,745	501-533	64	247
	R	49-31-40	15,447-15,884	Y-16,724-28	1,773	1,007-57	748	114-145	43	723
Eugene, Ore. (7)	P	204-137-40	18,192-23,784	None	8,346	7,001-84	5,200	1,427-374	119	1,226
	F	162-144-56	18,528-24,696	None	7,046	6,221-88	4,612	1,300-309	72	753
Evansville, Ind. (7)	P	251-234-40	15,880-16,584	Y-19,650-30	5,147	5,050-98	4,557	127-366	97	...
	F	270-253-56	15,807-16,807	Y-19,755-30	5,375	5,179-96	4,572	213-394	196	...
Flint, Mich.	P	383-325-40	19,275-25,264	Y-26,685-20	18,741	16,753-89	11,165	4,177-1,411	64	1,924
	F	230-230-50	21,545-25,300	Y-27,249-20	12,462	11,147-89	6,698	3,488-961	48	1,267
	R	54-2-40	15,046-18,399	Y-19,423-20	2,641	1,713-65	1,157	394-162	...	928
Fort Lauderdale, Fla. (7)	P	634-421-40	17,415-24,724	Y-27,814-25	23,188	20,373-88	16,335	3,471-567	133	2,682
	F	277-272-48	17,193-21,722	Y-24,437-25	10,136	9,141-90	7,249	1,601-291	283	712

Table 3/18 continued POLICE, FIRE, AND REFUSE COLLECTION AND DISPOSAL DEPARTMENTS: PERSONNEL, SALARIES, AND EXPENDITURES FOR CITIES OVER 10,000: 1984

City	Department	Total personnel, no. uniformed, duty hours per week	Entrance, maximum salary ($)	Longevity pay, maximum ($), no. years to max.	Reported expenditures (in thousands): Total expenditures (A) ($)	Total personnel expenditures (B), % of (A) ($)	Salaries and wages (C) ($)	City contrib. to employee retirement, insurance (D) ($)	Capital outlay (E) ($)	All other (F) ($)
100,000-249,999 continued										
Fort Lauderdale, Fla. (cont'd)	R	24-9-40	11,675-15,318	Y-17,232-25	3,251	757-23	598	135-24	24	2,470
Fort Wayne, Ind. (7)	P	343-314-40	15,363-19,205	None	9,109	8,162-90	7,192	440-530	200	747
	F	252-244-56	18,160-18,210	None	7,496	6,226-83	5,523	266-437	356	914
Fresno, Calif.	P	501-345-40	25,212-29,028	None	20,655	17,191-83	12,064	4,303-824	21	3,443
	F	298-278-56	23,850-28,260	None	13,035	11,960-92	8,217	3,209-534	256	819
	R	151-10-40	16,818-20,256	None	7,914	3,263-41	2,570	422-271	...	4,651
Fullerton, Calif. (7)	P	200-142-43	22,044-28,363	None	8,622	7,675-89	5,784	1,518-373	175	772
	F	103-97-56	20,084-25,509	None	4,619	4,296-93	3,161	916-219	40	283
Garden Grove, Calif. (7)	P	188-143-40	22,668-27,540	None	8,456	7,723-91	5,756	1,543-424	33	700
	F	96-93-56	21,180-25,764	None	5,377	4,612-86	3,430	943-239	16	749
Garland, Tex.	P	220-167-40	19,271-26,291	Y-27,562-25	6,939	5,695-82	5,149	414-132	349	895
	F	173-168-56	20,675-22,392	Y-23,663-25	5,028	4,543-90	4,150	289-104	46	439
	R	80-0-40	12,220-19,594	None	3,112	1,487-48	1,262	177-48	700	925
Glendale, Calif.	P	257-183-40	23,730-30,180	None	11,688	9,878-85	6,929	1,925-1,024	192	1,618
	F	184-162-56	22,206-29,772	None	10,240	8,705-85	6,142	1,712-851	621	914
	R	72-32-40	16,524-21,024	None	4,087	1,925-47	1,483	257-185	543	1,619
Grand Rapids, Mich.	P	333-259-40	19,630-25,299	Y-25,889-25	13,983	11,603-83	8,841	2,075-687	102	2,278
	F	248-241-50	16,886-23,874	Y-24,534-25	9,878	9,001-91	6,819	1,640-542	10	867
	R	29-24-40	16,504-19,468	Y-20,128-25	2,085	708-34	565	93-50	1	1,376
Greensboro, N.C.	P	476-364-40	15,312-23,064	Y-24,794-20	12,534	10,546-84	9,416	755-375	645	1,343
	F	291-285-56	13,212-20,928	Y-22,498-20	6,885	6,292-91	5,740	315-237	73	520
	R	150-60-40	10,319-13,440	Y-14,448-20	4,987	2,552-51	2,183	263-106	152	2,283
Hampton, Va.	P	229-205-40	13,301-18,104	None	7,092	6,139-87	4,875	1,162-102	50	903
	F	185-173-60	13,301-18,104	None	6,020	4,903-81	3,935	900-68	138	979
	R	71-5-40	10,158-13,557	None	2,413	1,262-52	996	234-32	43	1,108
Hollywood, Fla.	P	451-299-40	20,187-26,304	Y-28,935-15	16,295	13,706-84	11,204	2,083-419	41	2,548
	F	213-201-48	17,859-22,793	Y-25,129-15	8,448	7,687-91	5,757	1,726-204	57	704
	R	62-37-40	13,658-17,006	Y-18,749-15	1,954	1,317-67	1,079	176-62	...	637
Huntsville, Ala.	P	323-240-40	15,704-19,074	Y-19,554-30	8,444	6,966-82	5,597	763-606	374	1,104
	F	282-260-56	14,934-18,158	Y-18,638-30	7,044	6,279-89	5,060	691-528	266	499
	R	171-96-40	11,170-12,938	Y-13,418-30	3,840	2,741-71	2,132	289-320	505	594
Independence, Mo. (7)	P	209-149-40	16,044-20,232	Y-22,482-25	5,795	5,193-90	4,169	695-329	43	559
	F	160-155-51	15,936-20,124	Y-22,224-25	4,829	4,615-96	3,618	707-290	21	193
Irving, Tex.	P	219-152-40	19,476-24,228	Y-24,420-4	5,329	5,097-96	4,550	399-148	21	211
	F	189-186-56	19,476-24,228	Y-24,420-4	5,542	5,059-91	4,458	474-127	340	143
	R	99-6-40	12,324-15,576	Y-15,768-4	2,674	1,935-72	1,717	151-67	690	49
Jackson, Miss. (7)	P	532-389-40	14,073-27,252	None	18,380	15,858-86	12,214	3,279-365	671	1,851
	F	424-417-56	13,652-27,252	None	15,604	14,733-94	11,464	2,942-327	102	769
	R	37-9-40	9,984-14,424	None	4,853	1,877-39	1,621	216-40	...	2,976
Jersey City, N.J.	P	965-907-40	19,011-25,481	Y-28,538-22	22,727	22,024-97	21,897	...-127	...	703
	F	726-719-42	19,429-26,041	Y-29,167-22	24,618	23,783-97	23,783	...-...	...	835
Knoxville, Tenn.	P	403-303-40	13,249-21,715	Y-24,128-25	13,469	10,978-82	8,873	1,433-672	450	2,041
	F	397-390-56	13,554-16,164	Y-18,564-25	12,634	10,555-84	8,431	1,416-708	78	2,001
	R	88-5-40	9,152-12,625	Y-14,185-25	2,425	1,325-55	1,080	181-64	271	829
Lakewood, Colo. (3)	P	287-188-40	21,715-30,617	None	9,833	8,649-88	7,568	686-395	104	1,080
Lansing, Mich.	P	317-243-40	17,102-24,545	Y-...-20	...	...-...	...	...-...	...	...
	F	243-239-56	...-...	Y-22,614-20	8,786	8,404-96	6,338	1,574-492	70	312
	R	18-18-40	18,019-18,855	Y-...-20	...	...-...	...	...-...	...	...
Las Vegas, Nev. (7)	P	1,095-722-40	18,630-25,476	Y-29,297-30	43,482	36,631-84	29,867	4,795-1,969	1,336	5,515
	F	330-294-56	18,168-24,886	Y-28,618-30	13,079	10,298-79	8,450	1,496-352	1,786	995
Lexington-Fayette, Ky.	P	439-354-40	12,555-20,488	Y-...-..	12,782	10,878-85	10,878	...-...	279	1,625
	F	391-375-56	12,555-20,488	Y-...-..	10,901	9,402-86	9,402	...-...	223	1,276
	R	178-105-40	10,671-16,006	Y-...-..	5,808	3,550-61	3,550	...-...	...	2,258
Lincoln, Neb.	P	231-158-40	17,077-20,758	None	6,820	6,706-98	6,373	98-235	114	...
	F	243-240-56	16,881-20,521	None	5,780	5,724-99	5,497	4-223	56	...
Little Rock, Ark.	P	393-308-40	14,310-19,545	Y-20,445-25	10,080	8,778-87	7,730	601-447	313	989
	F	318-316-56	13,600-18,291	Y-18,891-25	8,173	7,524-92	6,615	546-363	145	504
	R	151-82-40	8,970-12,866	Y-13,766-25	3,233	2,230-69	1,991	110-129	303	700
Livonia, Mich. (7)	P	155-140-40	22,963-26,124	Y-26,284-5	7,447	6,311-85	4,636	1,306-369	128	1,008
	F	93-90-56	22,963-26,124	Y-26,284-5	4,590	4,335-94	3,175	912-248	31	224
Lubbock, Tex.	P	272-230-40	15,974-21,819	Y-23,019-25	10,361	8,480-82	7,320	819-341	466	1,415
	F	277-265-56	15,974-21,819	Y-23,019-25	9,170	8,464-92	7,411	763-290	51	655
	R	82-4-40	11,648-16,348	Y-17,548-25	4,013	2,152-54	1,824	201-127	355	1,506
Macon, Ga.	P	304-258-40	12,917-18,221	None	8,729	6,988-80	5,997	696-295	549	1,192
	F	311-299-60	12,917-18,190	None	8,298	7,471-90	6,403	759-309	239	588
	R	204-62-40	8,798-12,376	None	3,311	2,067-62	1,718	246-103	200	1,044
Madison, Wis.	P	376-294-38	20,336-23,140	Y-25,685-19	17,302	14,926-86	10,969	3,190-767	42	2,334
	F	280-263-48	19,866-22,840	Y-25,350-19	14,771	12,501-85	8,847	3,023-631	824	1,446
	R	172-147-40	15,989-19,039	Y-21,133-19	11,088	7,000-63	3,988	709-2,303	829	3,259
Mesa, Ariz.	P	365-247-40	20,163-25,896	Y-28,485-20	13,298	11,426-86	9,534	1,062-830	1,026	846
	F	203-187-56	19,149-24,635	Y-27,100-20	7,075	6,140-87	5,351	302-487	514	421
	R	110-15-40	12,870-17,381	Y-19,120-20	6,428	2,458-38	1,977	261-220	829	3,141
Mobile, Ala.	P	468-349-40	12,804-17,148	None	10,899	9,182-84	6,403	1,533-1,246	...	1,717
	F	388-385-56	12,804-17,148	None	8,105	7,864-97	5,518	1,313-1,033	...	241
	R	148-148-40	9,552-12,804	None	2,466	2,184-89	1,418	372-394	...	282
Modesto, Calif. (7)	P	223-164-40	22,356-29,229	None	9,122	7,118-78	5,637	1,043-438	211	1,793
	F	141-135-56	19,790-25,875	None	5,231	4,596-88	3,643	717-236	232	403
	R	28-0-40	18,163-21,539	None	1,501	642-43	581	6-55	287	572
Montgomery, Ala.	P	448-372-40	12,037-15,514	None	10,240	8,223-80	8,223	...-...	485	1,532
	F	347-331-56	12,037-15,514	None	7,384	6,401-87	6,401	...-...	268	715

Table 3/18 continued POLICE, FIRE, AND REFUSE COLLECTION AND DISPOSAL DEPARTMENTS: PERSONNEL, SALARIES, AND EXPENDITURES FOR CITIES OVER 10,000: 1984

					Reported expenditures (in thousands)					
City	Department	Total personnel, no. uniformed, duty hours per week	Entrance, maximum salary ($)	Longevity pay, maximum ($), no. years to max.	Total expenditures (A) ($)	Total personnel expenditures (B), % of (A) ($)	Salaries and wages (C) ($)	City contrib. to employee retirement, insurance (D) ($)	Capital outlay (E) ($)	All other (F) ($)
100,000-249,999 continued										
Montgomery, Ala. (cont'd)	R	297-297-40	9,324-...	Y-9,805-..	5,439	3,549-65	3,549	...-...	503	1,387
New Haven, Conn.	P	394-358-40	17,478-21,237	Y-21,637-20	14,267	12,903-90	9,422	3,089-392	...	1,364
	F	455-439-42	17,421-21,396	Y-21,796-20	15,686	14,076-90	10,434	3,288-354	155	1,455
	R	29-17-40	14,203-14,203	Y-14,528-20	570	516-91	516	...-...	...	54
Newport News, Va.	P	242-195-40	13,150-18,750	None	7,120	6,226-87	4,842	1,111-273	63	831
	F	244-236-56	13,150-18,750	None	6,729	5,784-86	4,484	1,040-260	91	854
	R	113-87-40	8,944-10,608	None	3,181	2,193-69	1,775	315-103	15	973
Oxnard, Calif.	P	185-116-40	21,936-26,736	Y-27,538-15	8,949	6,920-77	5,153	1,579-188	79	1,950
	F	91-81-56	20,516-24,411	Y-25,143-15	4,505	3,559-79	2,736	730-93	26	920
	R	64-7-40	15,337-18,248	Y-18,795-15	4,319	1,261-29	1,099	108-54	15	3,043
Pasadena, Calif.	P	291-152-40	25,766-29,232	None	12,838	10,834-84	9,208	1,626-...	26	1,978
	F	136-131-56	17,949-31,242	None	7,178	5,933-83	4,930	1,003-...	27	1,218
	R	73-60-40	15,785-20,066	None	3,425	1,808-53	1,566	242-...	13	1,604
Peoria, Ill. (7)	P	...-...-..	20,649-30,647	Y-32,993-..	...	...-..	...	...-...	...	...
	F	203-195-56	19,209-25,268	Y-27,289-..	...	...-..	...	...-...	...	...
Portsmouth, Va.	P	205-174-40	13,642-18,592	Y-19,986-15	7,633	6,053-79	4,598	1,208-247	...	1,580
	F	203-198-56	13,642-18,592	Y-19,986-15	6,073	5,638-93	4,253	1,161-224	...	435
	R	54-47-52	10,302-14,250	Y-15,356-15	1,896	1,281-68	1,036	183-62	...	615
Providence, R.I. (7)	P	468-393-38	19,313-21,001	Y-...-5	12,590	12,151-97	12,086	...-65	439	...
	F	485-462-28	18,802-21,001	Y-...-5	12,899	12,508-97	12,343	...-165	391	...
	R	1-1-40	18,914-...	Y-...-5	21	21-100	21	...-...	...	...
Pueblo, Colo.	P	173-127-40	15,648-21,840	Y-22,500-20	6,940	5,863-84	4,761	709-393	184	893
	F	140-138-56	16,236-20,784	Y-21,444-20	4,742	4,302-91	3,331	742-229	22	418
Raleigh, N.C.	P	336-278-42	15,242-21,448	Y-21,984-5	10,975	8,959-82	7,666	974-319	453	1,563
	F	321-315-44	13,825-18,528	Y-18,991-5	7,438	7,047-95	6,021	764-262	41	350
	R	173-120-40	9,825-13,167	Y-13,496-5	4,897	3,340-68	2,810	357-173	232	1,325
Reno, Nev. (7)	P	412-291-40	18,179-25,783	Y-27,343-30	13,021	11,795-91	9,485	1,592-718	29	1,197
	F	186-184-56	21,279-22,152	Y-23,712-30	7,761	7,420-96	5,972	1,047-401	130	211
Richmond, Va. (7)	P	628-567-40	17,030-24,076	None	22,829	17,920-78	14,130	2,847-943	531	4,378
	F	542-538-56	17,030-24,076	None	18,506	14,146-76	11,098	2,322-726	721	3,639
	R	274-44-40	9,880-13,988	None	6,699	4,011-60	3,213	532-266	307	2,381
Riverside, Calif. (7)	P	234-146-40	21,414-30,864	None	15,529	12,379-80	9,265	2,571-543	347	2,803
	F	172-161-56	20,922-27,348	None	8,482	7,422-88	5,375	1,759-288	261	799
	R	84-82-40	13,872-18,132	None	4,377	1,950-45	1,623	194-133	435	1,992
Roanoke, Va.	P	258-184-40	13,657-17,005	Y-17,855-15	5,815	5,288-91	4,310	859-119	192	335
	F	244-242-56	13,657-17,005	Y-17,855-15	5,571	5,324-96	4,325	880-119	5	242
	R	100-66-40	9,706-12,085	Y-12,689-15	2,060	1,633-79	1,335	263-35	1	426
Rochester, N.Y.	P	740-597-40	21,138-25,436	Y-26,586-22	31,603	27,951-88	19,789	7,399-763	794	2,858
	F	594-572-40	21,138-25,436	Y-26,586-22	26,003	24,235-93	16,754	6,455-1,026	787	981
	R	122-0-40	16,414-19,825	Y-...-25	5,452	3,184-58	2,447	592-145	11	2,257
Rockford, Ill. (7)	P	273-247-40	14,550-16,575	Y-18,233-10	10,900	8,840-81	6,827	1,425-588	172	1,888
	F	259-252-52	13,570-21,873	Y-24,060-10	8,934	8,451-95	6,381	1,443-627	88	395
	R	2-0-40	12,491-14,614	Y-16,075-5	2,666	41-2	32	5-4	...	2,625
St. Petersburg, Fla.	P	612-402-40	16,746-22,530	None	20,927	17,776-85	13,856	3,194-726	84	3,067
	F	311-284-56	15,142-20,861	None	10,922	9,049-83	6,374	2,282-393	29	1,844
	R	207-27-40	11,086-15,413	None	14,307	4,641-32	3,857	520-264	4	9,662
Salt Lake City, Utah	P	463-329-40	16,560-24,276	Y-27,816-14	20,441	17,564-86	14,072	2,798-694	535	2,342
	F	334-310-56	16,560-24,276	Y-26,496-14	14,637	12,504-85	10,152	1,894-458	400	1,733
	R	35-13-40	15,649-17,388	Y-18,288-14	1,572	927-59	745	163-19	360	285
Santa Ana, Calif. (7)	P	503-349-40	26,806-32,479	None	21,201	17,977-85	14,280	2,845-852	40	3,184
	F	205-160-56	25,152-30,475	None	11,318	9,609-85	7,412	1,691-506	171	1,538
Savannah, Ga.	P	352-285-40	14,043-20,248	Y-20,968-40	10,608	7,419-70	6,253	743-423	118	3,071
	F	206-198-56	13,374-19,283	Y-20,003-40	5,540	4,209-76	3,623	343-243	32	1,299
	R	232-114-40	9,504-12,737	Y-13,457-40	5,943	3,276-55	2,637	360-279	24	2,643
Shreveport, La.	P	480-398-40	14,523-18,972	Y-26,560-26	14,931	13,612-91	9,830	3,284-498	...	1,319
	F	460-449-56	14,559-18,972	Y-20,712-26	14,272	12,482-87	8,955	3,034-493	...	1,790
	R	281-189-40	9,960-14,628	None	991	304-31	...	169-135	...	687
South Bend, Ind.	P	286-235-40	17,750-17,750	None	7,187	6,482-90	6,071	97-314	100	605
	F	247-243-56	15,750-15,750	None	6,285	5,447-87	5,115	6-326	433	405
	R	29-11-40	16,931-16,931	None	555	499-90	425	53-21	56	...
Spokane, Wash.	P	293-241-40	16,996-27,603	Y-29,775-20	13,270	11,126-84	8,398	2,353-375	91	2,053
	F	318-312-52	17,004-27,581	Y-29,751-20	12,200	11,340-93	9,981	845-514	86	774
	R	85-9-40	10,398-13,113	None	5,687	2,047-36	1,658	230-159	738	2,902
Springfield, Mo.	P	228-179-40	16,957-20,419	Y-21,619-20	7,242	6,234-86	4,774	1,305-155	235	773
	F	192-189-56	15,747-19,584	Y-20,784-20	5,803	5,131-88	3,853	1,186-92	142	530
	R	11-0-40	12,723-15,330	Y-16,530-20	806	309-38	271	32-6	178	319
Stockton, Calif. (7)	P	383-249-40	22,290-26,532	None	15,574	13,544-87	9,988	2,558-998	28	2,002
	F	226-215-56	21,312-25,368	None	11,323	10,161-90	7,492	1,970-699	46	1,116
	R	29-10-40	14,880-17,712	None	1,231	686-56	533	78-75	...	545
Syracuse, N.Y.	P	523-427-40	15,151-23,053	Y-24,053-30	19,289	17,474-91	12,568	4,489-417	459	1,356
	F	480-469-40	15,151-23,053	Y-24,053-30	18,682	16,995-91	12,021	4,595-379	566	1,121
	R	120-69-40	13,728-14,435	Y-15,059-25	4,592	2,317-50	1,820	415-82	400	1,875
Tacoma, Wash.	P	282-257-40	25,578-31,487	Y-34,006-20	13,934	10,227-73	9,235	565-427	27	3,680
	F	371-355-47	25,578-31,487	Y-34,006-20	15,424	13,676-89	12,416	732-528	306	1,442
	R	85-0-40	26,414-26,414	Y-27,471-20	7,244	3,724-51	2,813	470-441	73	3,447
Tempe, Ariz. (7)	P	252-187-40	18,990-25,634	None	7,909	6,795-86	5,789	668-338	182	932
	F	112-104-56	18,067-24,386	None	3,410	3,116-91	2,874	65-177	33	261
	R	46-19-40	15,541-20,997	None	3,990	1,067-27	871	118-78	574	2,349

Table 3/18 continued **POLICE, FIRE, AND REFUSE COLLECTION AND DISPOSAL DEPARTMENTS: PERSONNEL, SALARIES, AND EXPENDITURES FOR CITIES OVER 10,000: 1984**

City	Depart-ment	Total personnel, no. uniformed, duty hours per week	Entrance, maximum salary ($)	Longevity pay, maximum ($), no. years to max.	Reported expenditures (in thousands): Total expendi-tures (A) ($)	Total personnel expendi-tures (B), % of (A) ($)	Salaries and wages (C) ($)	City contrib. to employee retirement, insurance (D) ($)	Capital outlay (E) ($)	All other (F) ($)
100,000-249,999 continued										
Topeka, Kan.	P	299-213-40	15,480-20,580	Y-21,620-25	9,813	8,309-85	6,377	1,632-300	408	1,096
	F	239-228-56	15,972-20,484	Y-21,524-25	7,602	7,226-95	5,452	1,552-222	34	342
Torrance, Calif.	P	308-233-40	21,664-29,032	None	17,620	13,080-74	9,446	2,836-798	506	4,034
	F	165-152-56	21,036-27,502	Y-31,352-23	8,692	7,650-88	5,590	1,822-238	38	1,004
	R	32-3-40	15,234-18,518	Y-20,370-19	2,137	856-40	653	149-54	...	1,281
Waco, Tex.	P	230-175-40	16,740-20,220	Y-21,420-25	5,878	4,982-85	4,252	623-107	183	713
	F	169-168-63	16,380-19,860	Y-21,060-25	4,411	4,206-95	3,618	499-89	63	142
	R	77-77-40	8,700-10,980	Y-11,580-25	2,399	1,220-51	1,066	121-33	15	1,164
Winston-Salem, N.C.	P	436-349-40	16,412-20,197	Y-21,712-20	14,751	10,589-72	9,467	717-405	1,301	2,861
	F	193-184-56	14,976-18,408	Y-19,797-20	5,724	4,804-84	4,074	556-174	322	598
	R	227-125-40	10,442-12,792	Y-13,751-20	7,809	4,253-54	3,606	493-154	816	2,740
Worcester, Mass.	P	453-357-48	13,374-20,321	None	11,005	9,944-90	9,125	...-819	...	1,061
	F	476-453-42	15,187-18,540	Y-19,045-30	9,623	9,598-100	9,598	...-...	25	...
	R	70-47-40	11,667-13,337	None	2,321	2,147-93	1,038	502-607	174	...
Yonkers, N.Y.	P	538-450-36	20,962-27,561	Y-30,042-18	24,514	24,284-99	16,446	6,785-1,053	174	56
	F	438-430-38	23,217-29,116	Y-31,737-18	19,503	19,162-98	12,388	6,005-769	296	45
	R	97-56-40	22,178-22,178	Y-24,839-20	3,313	3,292-99	2,474	624-194	6	15
50,000-99,999										
Abilene, Tex.	P	197-153-40	15,480-19,392	Y-20,592-25	5,541	4,621-83	4,135	327-159	55	865
	F	170-160-56	13,824-17,928	Y-19,128-25	4,385	3,955-90	3,517	313-125	53	377
	R	55-8-40	11,232-13,932	None	3,004	1,551-52	1,300	171-80	47	1,406
Abington tp, Pa. (1)	P	104-89-40	17,472-24,430	Y-25,680-25	2,888	2,661-92	2,497	33-131	...	227
	R	26-11-40	16,994-18,054	Y-18,554-14	1,111	797-72	685	70-42	...	314
Albany, Ga.	P	209-185-40	12,126-12,272	None	5,234	4,194-80	3,406	520-268	228	812
	F	163-147-56	11,255-11,386	None	4,188	3,801-91	3,093	482-226	27	360
	R	104-63-40	8,486-8,590	None	2,861	1,578-55	1,254	192-132	134	1,149
Alhambra, Calif. (7)	P	122-86-40	21,432-26,040	None	5,948	4,766-80	3,327	833-606	50	1,132
	F	67-64-56	21,216-25,776	None	3,957	3,155-80	2,304	540-311	85	717
	R	...-...-..	...-...	..-...-..	1,547	...-..	...	...-...	...	1,547
Appleton, Wis.	P	121-95-39	19,020-22,080	Y-22,280-10	4,381	3,758-86	2,800	763-195	303	320
	F	98-97-40	19,776-21,696	Y-21,896-10	3,822	3,308-87	2,394	728-186	25	489
	R	29-9-40	17,888-18,782	Y-18,982-10	1,558	722-46	562	98-62	2	834
Arvada, Colo. (3,7)	P	154-111-40	19,728-27,120	Y-28,316-10	5,188	4,573-88	3,953	410-210	87	528
Asheville, N.C.	P	159-129-40	11,622-18,460	Y-19,198-20	4,151	3,224-78	2,531	693-...	122	805
	F	139-136-56	11,622-18,460	Y-19,198-20	3,355	2,914-87	2,641	273-...	36	405
	R	39-12-40	8,445-10,504	Y-10,924-20	1,121	654-58	599	55-...	21	446
Baldwin Park, Calif. (3,7)	P	57-37-40	22,282-27,092	None	3,856	3,644-95	2,956	533-155	8	204
Bayonne, N.J. (7)	P	185-157-40	15,844-22,523	Y-24,775-22	4,261	4,261-100	4,261	...-...	...	...
	F	184-184-42	14,835-20,176	Y-22,194-22	4,960	4,960-100	4,960	...-...	...	...
Baytown, Tex.	P	126-97-40	19,454-24,869	Y-26,069-25	3,576	3,245-91	2,890	335-20	330	1
	F	81-75-56	19,454-24,869	Y-26,069-25	2,243	2,236-100	1,986	237-13	7	...
	R	38-0-40	13,639-16,833	Y-18,033-25	959	790-82	701	83-6	168	1
Bellevue, Wash. (7)	P	152-108-40	20,544-28,452	Y-29,652-16	6,930	5,274-76	4,425	531-318	826	830
	F	126-113-50	21,900-30,324	None	6,066	4,294-71	3,799	230-265	869	903
Bellflower, Calif. (3,4,7)										
Bethlehem, Pa.	P	149-124-40	18,245-21,164	Y-22,289-20	4,838	4,457-92	3,747	237-473	161	220
	F	104-93-42	17,614-20,784	Y-21,784-20	3,229	3,162-98	2,620	195-347	13	54
	R	8-0-40	15,268-18,637	Y-19,637-20	330	192-58	152	17-23	...	138
Billings, Mont.	P	111-89-40	16,416-22,632	None	3,400	2,658-78	2,393	154-111	170	572
	F	114-95-44	14,862-18,660	Y-20,910-25	3,332	2,754-83	2,398	243-113	158	420
	R	40-7-40	14,172-19,008	Y-20,208-20	2,380	1,026-43	872	109-45	182	1,172
Bloomington, Ind.	P	76-57-40	16,100-16,100	Y-18,000-1	1,835	1,560-85	1,447	85-28	42	233
	F	78-77-40	17,238-17,238	Y-17,940-3	1,613	1,509-94	1,457	26-26	58	46
	R	14-9-40	12,334-12,334	None	346	211-61	187	21-3	1	134
Bloomington, Minn. (1)										
Boulder, Colo. (7)	P	150-108-40	20,792-29,255	None	5,813	4,751-82	4,017	444-290	28	1,034
	F	82-77-56	19,790-25,061	Y-26,261-4	3,206	2,664-83	2,218	311-135	70	472
Bristol, Conn.	P	97-89-38	18,013-20,029	None	4,018	3,686-92	2,440	947-299	65	267
	F	94-92-42	17,735-19,720	None	3,706	3,533-95	2,346	923-264	47	126
	R	28-18-40	13,312-14,123	None	894	607-68	458	71-78	137	150
Bristol tp, Pa. (7)	P	65-58-..	20,245-22,210	Y-...-20	899	774-86	...	444-330	125	...
Brownsville, Tex.	P	144-111-40	13,166-17,160	Y-18,360-25	4,482	3,017-67	2,545	343-129	962	503
	F	84-79-56	12,842-16,395	Y-17,595-25	2,406	1,863-77	1,570	221-72	419	124
	R	72-45-40	7,842-12,189	None	1,322	891-67	717	107-67	13	418
Buena Park, Calif. (7)	P	132-95-40	22,074-27,192	None	6,515	5,947-91	3,932	1,113-902	13	555
	F	72-65-56	20,454-25,164	Y-26,201-15	3,760	3,648-97	2,320	721-607	7	105
Burbank, Calif.	P	202-134-40	25,698-30,624	None	10,284	8,916-87	6,615	1,889-412	206	1,162
	F	126-122-56	25,344-30,204	None	7,252	6,493-90	4,800	1,386-307	99	660
	R	37-31-40	18,972-22,548	None	2,247	1,347-60	1,061	221-65	58	842
Cambridge, Mass.	P	283-256-40	18,579-23,325	Y-25,921-25	9,988	9,265-93	8,407	...-858	...	723
	F	285-281-42	18,632-23,393	Y-26,001-25	9,252	8,759-95	7,927	...-832	...	493
	R	39-24-40	15,743-17,345	Y-19,095-25	120	120-100	...	...-120	...	...
Carson, Calif. (3,4)										
Cerritos, Calif. (3,4,7)										
Champaign, Ill. (7)	P	108-82-40	20,822-22,385	Y-...-..	4,094	3,450-84	2,679	680-91	139	505
	F	78-75-56	18,735-21,645	Y-...-..	3,288	3,011-92	2,167	764-80	107	170
Charleston, S.C.	P	307-228-40	14,041-18,978	None	7,354	6,054-82	4,996	840-218	233	1,067
	F	196-187-60	12,129-15,629	None	3,920	3,696-94	3,150	414-132	35	189

Table 3/18 continued **POLICE, FIRE, AND REFUSE COLLECTION AND DISPOSAL DEPARTMENTS: PERSONNEL, SALARIES, AND EXPENDITURES FOR CITIES OVER 10,000: 1984**

					Reported expenditures (in thousands)					
City	De-part-ment	Total personnel, no. uniformed, duty hours per week	Entrance, maximum salary ($)	Longevity pay, maximum ($), no. years to max.	Total expendi-tures (A) ($)	Total personnel expendi-tures (B), % of (A) ($)	Salaries and wages (C) ($)	City contrib. to employee retirement, insurance (D) ($)	Capital outlay (E) ($)	All other (F) ($)
50,000-99,999 continued										
Charleston, S.C. (cont'd)	R	78-14-40	8,289-11,663	None	1,568	1,275-81	1,049	138-88	10	283
Charleston, W.Va.	P	204-170-40	15,956-17,437	Y-19,237-20	5,483	4,760-87	3,727	625-408	263	460
	F	147-144-56	15,956-17,437	Y-19,237-20	4,422	4,054-92	3,091	636-327	154	214
	R	81-3-40	11,740-12,655	None	1,895	1,454-77	1,097	175-182	2	439
Chula Vista, Calif. (7)	P	127-93-40	18,388-24,660	None	4,866	4,045-83	3,404	501-140	32	789
	F	65-63-56	18,146-24,326	None	2,460	2,218-90	1,872	281-65	13	229
Clarksville, Tenn.	P	120-118-40	12,026-12,943	Y-...-5	1,919	1,459-76	1,283	92-84	...	460
	F	95-95-60	12,026-12,943	Y-...-5	479	338-71	195	79-64	...	141
Clearwater, Fla.	P	264-185-40	16,867-21,519	Y-23,787-13	8,037	6,525-81	5,706	601-218	3	1,509
	F	175-167-56	16,124-20,591	Y-22,791-13	5,555	4,959-89	3,930	880-149	49	547
	R	104-58-40	12,691-14,649	Y-16,451-11	5,928	2,108-36	1,854	169-85	21	3,799
Cleveland Heights, Ohio	P	115-98-40	20,142-22,916	Y-23,716-20	3,619	3,137-87	2,380	405-352	...	482
	F	79-77-52	19,870-22,656	Y-23,456-20	4,752	2,391-50	1,823	311-257	2,200	161
	R	22-6-40	15,891-21,257	Y-22,057-20	1,223	831-68	639	83-109	...	392
Columbia, Mo.	P	121-102-40	14,149-17,000	None	4,190	3,091-74	2,579	390-122	332	767
	F	104-101-56	14,173-17,249	Y-17,896-20	3,969	2,814-71	2,517	188-109	718	437
	R	39-28-40	11,802-13,776	None	2,458	705-29	590	81-34	499	1,254
Columbia, S.C.	P	276-210-43	13,759-17,563	None	6,775	5,555-82	4,650	751-154	153	1,067
	F	260-236-56	12,482-15,927	None	5,629	5,009-89	4,165	703-141	207	413
	R	146-83-40	8,221-10,270	None	3,595	1,976-55	1,709	193-74	491	1,128
Compton, Calif. (7)	P	118-52-40	24,108-28,200	None	8,434	7,196-85	5,122	1,764-310	...	1,238
	F	73-71-56	22,080-25,836	None	3,814	3,428-90	2,448	822-158	...	386
Costa Mesa, Calif. (7)	P	175-135-40	23,268-28,296	Y-29,196-20	8,292	6,809-82	5,128	1,300-381	258	1,225
	F	105-101-56	21,108-25,668	Y-26,568-20	4,436	3,933-89	2,936	782-215	300	203
Council Bluffs, Iowa (7)	P	119-93-40	16,216-19,946	Y-20,886-22	3,607	2,877-80	2,316	384-177	65	665
	F	90-89-56	7,998-19,224	Y-19,704-25	2,687	2,557-95	1,908	507-142	...	130
	R	2-2-..	...-...	..-...-..	737	36-5	30	4-2	...	701
Cranston, R.I. (7)	P	161-134-38	17,503-19,682	Y-20,766-4	4,888	3,799-78	3,062	464-273	...	1,089
	F	179-174-42	17,933-20,162	Y-21,356-4	5,478	4,744-87	3,687	759-298	...	734
Daly City, Calif. (7)	P	124-99-40	23,166-28,184	None	4,710	4,197-89	3,368	629-200	80	433
	F	78-76-56	22,080-26,856	Y-27,528-5	3,253	2,977-92	2,391	455-131	41	235
Decatur, Ill. (7)	P	157-125-40	18,111-22,014	Y-22,039-5	5,131	4,310-84	3,405	737-168	97	724
	F	113-110-56	18,111-22,014	Y-22,039-5	4,396	4,020-91	2,716	1,142-162	148	228
Des Plaines, Ill. (7)	P	111-95-40	19,000-26,602	Y-29,060-20	4,568	3,912-86	2,984	623-305	135	521
	F	88-82-54	19,661-26,602	Y-29,150-20	3,955	3,556-90	2,504	817-235	39	360
	R	1-0-38	...-...	Y-...-..	962	20-2	16	2-2	...	942
Downey, Calif.	P	120-94-40	22,450-27,812	Y-30,148-..	...	...-..	...	...-...	...	...
	F	81-69-56	22,405-25,464	Y-27,603-..	...	...-..	...	...-...	...	...
Dubuque, Iowa (7)	P	86-76-40	19,520-20,862	Y-21,902-30	3,042	2,715-89	1,944	586-185	38	289
	F	93-89-56	19,520-20,862	Y-21,905-25	3,339	3,067-92	2,103	753-211	72	200
	R	25-15-40	16,744-17,285	Y-18,149-30	1,066	579-54	467	57-55	60	427
East Orange, N.J. (7)	P	231-231-..	16,300-22,801	Y-26,221-25	...	...-..	...	...-...	...	...
	F	176-176-..	16,300-22,801	Y-26,449-25	...	...-..	...	...-...	...	...
East Providence, R.I. (7)	P	114-97-38	16,475-19,435	Y-20,600-20	4,106	884-22	...	494-390	686	2,536
	F	110-104-42	16,585-19,905	Y-21,299-20	3,990	949-24	...	549-400	13	3,028
Eau Claire, Wis. (7)	P	99-75-39	17,320-21,054	Y-22,317-12	2,970	2,970-100	2,304	529-137	...	...
	F	88-86-56	17,668-20,523	Y-21,754-12	2,841	2,841-100	2,120	580-141	...	...
El Cajon, Calif. (7)	P	157-98-40	17,615-23,021	None	4,669	4,220-90	3,375	639-206	26	423
	F	92-80-56	16,363-22,478	None	2,972	2,719-91	2,157	440-122	55	198
El Monte, Calif. (7)	P	138-107-40	21,942-26,016	Y-27,576-20	6,123	5,445-89	4,011	1,094-340	184	494
	F	70-63-56	20,712-25,176	None	3,551	2,997-84	2,207	629-161	405	149
Elgin, Ill.	P	120-94-41	23,178-28,572	None	5,122	4,546-89	3,688	627-231	114	462
	F	85-76-56	23,094-27,660	None	3,751	3,485-93	2,566	745-174	41	225
	R	14-0-40	18,312-22,512	None	724	411-57	320	41-50	2	311
Enid, Okla.	P	104-83-40	15,600-19,860	Y-21,060-6	2,535	2,158-85	1,943	142-73	80	297
	F	85-82-56	14,820-18,960	Y-20,160-6	2,274	2,112-93	1,903	145-64	14	148
	R	79-51-40	12,120-15,600	Y-16,800-6	1,823	1,409-77	1,261	87-61	119	295
Escondido, Calif. (7)	P	104-70-40	19,938-24,828	None	3,283	3,257-99	2,514	566-177	26	...
	F	69-67-56	19,830-24,684	None	2,287	2,266-99	1,701	453-112	21	...
Euclid, Ohio	P	136-99-40	19,018-21,895	Y-23,428-20	5,043	4,358-86	3,365	636-357	122	563
	F	104-96-48	19,738-21,895	Y-23,428-20	3,946	3,626-92	2,789	600-237	35	285
	R	40-27-40	16,000-18,000	Y-19,260-20	1,634	1,376-84	1,038	143-195	68	190
Everett, Wash. (7)	P	102-70-40	22,272-29,292	Y-32,514-24	4,499	4,465-99	4,044	198-223	34	...
	F	143-140-42	21,300-30,432	Y-32,568-20	5,809	5,778-99	5,368	262-148	31	...
Fall River, Mass.	P	254-216-40	16,494-19,072	Y-19,272-5	7,961	7,431-93	5,653	1,383-395	128	402
	F	250-224-42	17,245-18,988	Y-19,388-6	8,398	8,050-96	6,281	1,307-462	50	298
	R	105-98-40	11,854-12,126	Y-12,476-5	3,410	2,170-64	1,486	531-153	50	1,190
Fargo, N.D.	P	100-83-40	17,712-24,948	Y-26,448-30	3,007	2,793-93	2,367	276-150	1	213
	F	86-80-56	17,712-24,948	Y-26,448-30	2,484	2,377-96	2,091	163-123	...	107
	R	39-19-40	13,392-18,864	Y-23,364-30	1,715	929-54	780	94-55	116	670
Farmington Hills, Mich. (1,7)	P	94-63-40	19,016-27,377	Y-30,662-22	4,128	3,393-82	2,717	411-265	155	580
	F	14-12-40	17,022-25,528	Y-27,060-15	1,021	660-65	580	45-35	152	209
Florissant, Mo. (3,7)	P	85-72-40	21,034-24,752	None	2,740	2,406-88	1,920	362-124	62	272
Fort Collins, Colo. (7)	P	108-82-40	18,408-25,792	None	4,200	3,114-74	2,757	231-126	207	879
	F	104-96-56	16,692-23,816	Y-...-..	4,101	3,244-79	2,900	221-123	272	585
Fountain Valley, Calif. (7)	P	78-59-40	22,372-27,168	None	3,634	2,972-82	2,311	487-174	105	557
	F	39-37-56	21,540-26,184	None	2,011	1,773-88	1,367	330-76	8	230

Table 3/18 continued **POLICE, FIRE, AND REFUSE COLLECTION AND DISPOSAL DEPARTMENTS: PERSONNEL, SALARIES, AND EXPENDITURES FOR CITIES OVER 10,000: 1984**

					Reported expenditures (in thousands)					
City	Depart-ment	Total personnel, no. uniformed, duty hours per week	Entrance, maximum salary ($)	Longevity pay, maximum ($), no. years to max.	Total expendi-tures (A) ($)	Total personnel expendi-tures (B), % of (A) ($)	Salaries and wages (C) ($)	City contrib. to employee retirement, insurance (D) ($)	Capital outlay (E) ($)	All other (F) ($)
50,000-99,999 continued										
Galveston, Tex.	P	180-137-40	18,622-20,723	Y-...-..	5,349	4,364-82	3,888	338-138	75	910
	F	122-115-56	18,622-20,723	Y-...-..	3,345	3,019-90	2,684	242-93	84	242
	R	76-76-40	11,895-13,640	Y-...-..	2,238	1,206-54	1,057	92-57	3	1,029
Glendale, Ariz.	P	205-160-40	19,500-25,000	None	5,068	4,575-90	4,575	...-...	65	428
	F	95-88-56	18,500-23,700	None	3,077	2,405-78	2,405	...-...	4	668
	R	52-0-40	13,700-17,600	None	189	145-77	145	...-...	22	22
Grand Prairie, Tex. (7)	P	135-94-40	19,176-23,868	Y-25,308-30	4,057	3,472-86	2,734	584-154	29	556
	F	83-81-72	18,030-22,428	Y-22,428-30	2,765	2,447-88	1,942	417-88	133	185
	R	5-3-40	15,228-19,908	Y-21,438-30	1,269	167-13	129	28-10	5	1,097
Great Falls, Mont.	P	88-63-40	12,000-19,728	Y-19,878-20	2,540	1,922-76	1,617	217-88	101	517
	F	73-71-42	14,646-19,992	Y-20,325-20	2,207	1,797-81	1,468	240-89	89	321
	R	21-8-40	18,595-18,595	Y-19,195-30	1,661	616-37	541	57-18	203	842
Green tp, Ohio	P	18-16-42	16,380-19,608	None	520	452-87	343	61-48	68	...
	F	11-10-45	17,550-21,013	None	206	171-83	142	19-10	35	...
Green Bay, Wis.	P	205-164-40	15,888-23,748	Y-24,108-15	7,746	7,153-92	5,150	1,526-477	107	486
	F	205-205-56	16,200-23,748	Y-24,108-15	8,284	7,831-95	5,518	1,836-477	109	344
	R	75-52-40	18,158-18,158	Y-18,518-15	2,215	1,246-56	907	164-175	195	774
Greenville, S.C.	P	171-136-40	14,789-18,886	Y-20,051-15	4,479	3,869-86	3,186	550-133	26	584
	F	134-130-40	14,789-18,886	Y-20,051-15	3,179	2,972-93	2,485	384-103	...	207
	R	66-4-40	9,485-12,189	Y-12,938-15	961	623-65	528	70-25	...	338
Greenwich t, Conn. (7)	P	172-147-35	18,398-23,205	None	6,733	6,035-90	4,921	835-279	248	450
	F	69-66-42	16,875-21,284	None	2,742	2,237-82	1,719	387-131	115	390
Hamden t, Conn. (7)	P	122-99-40	15,554-20,037	Y-20,738-25	3,643	3,186-87	2,567	415-204	130	327
	F	125-124-42	17,026-19,128	Y-19,797-25	3,984	3,452-87	2,796	446-210	40	492
Hamilton tp, N.J. (1,7)	P	146-122-40	18,371-26,543	Y-27,543-20	5,511	5,277-96	4,503	603-171	...	234
Hamilton, Ohio	P	101-96-40	19,249-23,615	Y-25,504-20	4,303	3,805-88	2,868	638-299	2	496
	F	101-100-53	18,798-22,490	Y-24,289-20	3,807	3,629-95	2,610	763-256	16	162
	R	16-6-30	13,260-17,680	Y-19,698-25	1,251	988-79	775	108-105	...	263
Hammond, Ind.	P	227-194-40	19,362-19,662	Y-20,082-8	6,122	5,064-83	4,481	183-400	156	902
	F	181-177-56	18,035-19,362	Y-19,902-13	4,489	3,905-87	3,544	127-234	39	545
	R	66-32-40	14,684-14,684	Y-15,224-13	1,596	1,249-78	979	126-144	...	347
High Point, N.C. (7)	P	178-156-40	13,195-18,664	Y-20,064-20	4,368	3,533-81	3,110	348-75	63	772
	F	169-166-56	12,595-17,844	Y-19,182-20	3,708	3,421-92	2,950	402-69	31	256
	R	84-33-40	7,907-11,833	Y-12,720-20	4,096	1,280-31	1,085	147-48	10	2,806
Inglewood, Calif. (7)	P	237-177-40	23,337-28,476	Y-30,228-14	13,480	11,250-83	8,249	2,165-836	6	2,224
	F	104-82-56	17,928-26,693	Y-28,335-15	6,133	5,011-82	3,680	923-408	136	986
	R	12-10-40	15,138-22,316	Y-24,407-20	4,944	388-8	297	55-36	30	4,526
Iowa City, Iowa	P	62-53-40	16,973-24,606	Y-24,806-20	2,001	1,729-86	1,354	313-62	...	272
	F	49-49-56	17,792-22,014	Y-22,214-20	1,819	1,537-84	1,113	362-62	...	282
	R	17-1-40	15,100-17,285	Y-17,485-20	1,007	364-36	316	31-17	...	643
Irvine, Calif. (2,7)	P	115-81-40	24,071-30,540	None	11,598	4,488-39	3,633	540-315	37	7,073
Janesville, Wis.	P	86-66-40	18,773-25,000	None	3,306	2,794-85	2,046	547-201	193	319
	F	85-83-56	19,101-24,321	None	3,821	3,111-81	2,203	690-218	555	155
	R	16-0-40	16,744-18,304	Y-18,512-..	485	305-63	233	42-30	1	179
Kalamazoo, Mich. (5,7)	P	347-314-46	20,744-30,902	Y-31,682-6	13,316	12,319-93	9,443	2,227-649	246	751
	R	1-1-..	...-...	..-...-..	293	36-12	31	5-...	16	241
Kenner, La. (7)	P	115-103-40	12,600-23,884	None	3,481	2,763-79	2,469	185-109	111	607
	F	67-65-48	14,856-16,841	None	1,867	1,600-86	1,369	168-63	59	208
Kenosha, Wis.	P	163-150-38	22,560-23,928	Y-24,228-25	6,647	5,890-89	4,377	1,044-469	251	506
	F	133-132-56	22,308-23,544	Y-23,844-25	4,670	4,531-97	3,299	860-372	25	114
	R	30-30-40	20,717-21,694	Y-21,994-25	1,156	874-76	680	119-75	20	262
Kettering, Ohio (1,7)	P	99-77-40	19,958-25,605	None	3,830	3,424-89	2,713	495-216	31	375
	F	45-40-40	19,802-25,480	None	1,849	1,513-82	1,145	265-103	25	311
La Mesa, Calif. (7)	P	50-38-40	...-...	None	2,474	2,153-87	1,630	393-130	33	288
	F	50-49-56	...-...	None	2,022	1,831-91	1,329	352-150	95	96
Lafayette, La.	P	210-164-40	16,162-17,826	None	4,917	3,637-74	3,154	315-168	279	1,001
	F	179-176-56	14,664-16,162	None	5,658	3,392-60	2,912	331-149	1,904	362
Lakewood, Calif. (3,4,7)										
Lakewood, Ohio	P	101-87-40	19,791-25,621	Y-26,221-25	4,107	3,345-81	2,428	624-293	7	755
	F	74-73-56	20,006-25,621	Y-25,909-25	3,215	2,930-91	2,015	665-250	161	124
	R	72-51-40	13,726-17,700	Y-17,875-20	2,152	1,583-74	1,294	115-174	181	388
Lancaster, Pa. (7)	P	140-113-40	14,245-21,110	Y-22,605-27	3,620	3,353-93	2,935	262-156	103	164
	F	115-112-42	14,500-20,710	Y-21,860-25	2,975	2,880-97	2,402	337-141	...	95
Largo, Fla.	P	125-79-40	16,349-21,299	None	3,745	3,206-86	2,963	186-57	233	306
	F	98-87-56	15,550-21,083	None	2,983	2,419-81	2,177	193-49	81	483
	R	35-0-44	10,754-14,061	None	1,879	787-42	724	41-22	217	875
Lawton, Okla.	P	169-135-40	14,945-18,637	Y-19,792-21	4,723	4,059-86	3,621	280-158	46	618
	F	123-122-56	15,392-19,178	Y-20,379-21	3,585	3,301-92	2,955	218-128	129	155
	R	83-0-40	11,305-14,082	Y-14,794-21	2,995	2,156-72	1,213	869-74	398	441
Longview, Tex.	P	173-143-40	20,022-20,022	Y-20,070-1	3,708	3,707-100	3,160	441-106	...	1
	F	133-127-56	19,288-19,288	Y-19,336-1	2,781	2,781-100	2,691	12-78	...	...
	R	77-53-40	10,338-10,338	Y-10,386-1	1,091	1,091-100	857	144-90	...	...
Lower Merion tp, Pa. (1)	P	151-124-40	18,500-24,491	Y-25,891-20	5,394	4,682-87	3,870	299-513	33	679
	F	4-3-..	...-...	..-...-..	900	126-14	99	10-17	8	766
	R	54-35-40	14,811-18,273	Y-19,473-20	2,278	1,309-57	1,044	109-156	56	913
Mc Allen, Tex.	P	177-112-40	14,778-14,778	Y-...-..	4,707	3,608-77	3,149	340-119	312	787
	F	105-96-56	13,745-13,745	Y-...-..	2,661	2,082-78	1,783	226-73	229	350
	R	68-28-40	7,530-7,530	Y-...-..	1,447	846-58	721	79-46	74	527

Table 3/18 continued **POLICE, FIRE, AND REFUSE COLLECTION AND DISPOSAL DEPARTMENTS: PERSONNEL, SALARIES, AND EXPENDITURES FOR CITIES OVER 10,000: 1984**

					Reported expenditures (in thousands)					
City	Department	Total personnel, no. uniformed, duty hours per week	Entrance, maximum salary ($)	Longevity pay, maximum ($), no. years to max.	Total expenditures (A) ($)	Total personnel expenditures (B), % of (A) ($)	Salaries and wages (C) ($)	City contrib. to employee retirement, insurance (D) ($)	Capital outlay (E) ($)	All other (F) ($)
50,000-99,999 continued										
Malden, Mass. (7)	P	108-100-40	19,195-20,457	None	3,168	2,888-91	2,604	...-284	51	229
	F	143-140-40	19,507-20,457	Y-21,057-20	3,998	3,750-94	3,427	...-323	...	248
Mansfield, Ohio	P	111-80-40	15,089-19,689	Y-20,449-20	3,074	2,920-95	2,295	375-250	75	79
	F	97-91-48	14,405-19,805	Y-20,545-20	3,211	3,018-94	2,264	532-222	141	52
	R	23-2-40	11,274-14,726	Y-15,391-20	788	499-63	388	54-57	...	289
Mesquite, Tex.	P	142-129-40	20,256-23,424	Y-24,624-25	5,027	3,234-64	2,755	406-73	45	1,748
	F	104-102-56	20,256-23,424	Y-24,624-25	3,495	3,158-90	2,725	368-65	132	205
	R	61-25-40	12,420-15,900	Y-17,100-25	2,111	1,301-62	1,048	217-36	236	574
Miami Beach, Fla.	P	392-294-40	20,186-27,726	Y-30,775-25	14,836	13,447-91	10,232	2,760-455	362	1,027
	F	161-152-50	20,675-20,726	Y-30,776-25	6,580	5,867-89	4,474	1,149-244	29	684
	R	107-81-40	15,301-15,301	Y-17,494-25	3,391	2,369-70	1,864	224-281	...	1,022
Monroe, La.	P	155-108-40	10,784-12,806	Y-14,606-9	2,751	2,358-86	1,557	621-180	125	268
	F	160-155-56	10,680-11,280	Y-14,907-3	2,466	2,334-95	1,670	431-233	14	118
	R	122-78-40	8,589-10,982	None	1,653	1,071-65	845	122-104	41	541
Montebello, Calif. (7)	P	93-67-40	19,818-24,684	None	4,561	3,903-86	2,874	722-307	10	648
	F	59-55-56	19,776-24,336	None	2,921	2,458-84	1,693	531-234	82	381
Monterey Park, Calif.	P	102-67-40	23,268-28,248	None	3,943	3,415-87	2,656	464-295	20	508
	F	43-42-56	22,788-27,684	None	2,527	1,988-79	1,578	280-130	368	171
Mount Prospect v, Ill. (7)	P	79-62-40	17,000-27,078	Y-27,778-6	3,093	2,722-88	2,194	419-109	108	263
	F	74-64-50	21,962-28,350	Y-29,050-6	3,307	2,920-88	2,385	433-102	225	162
Mountain View, Calif. (7)	P	98-73-40	24,690-30,015	None	4,758	3,876-81	3,105	512-259	118	764
	F	71-65-56	24,194-29,414	None	3,200	2,780-87	2,249	366-165	30	390
Muncie, Ind.	P	138-117-40	17,366-17,366	Y-18,582-10	3,965	3,785-95	2,564	924-300	13	167
	F	117-116-40	17,366-17,366	Y-18,582-10	3,625	3,242-89	2,196	822-224	232	151
	R	58-57-40	13,003-13,003	None	1,256	800-64	613	76-111	36	420
Nashua, N.H.	P	171-135-40	16,081-20,685	Y-20,985-7	5,223	4,672-89	3,908	551-213	...	551
	F	154-151-42	12,087-16,203	Y-16,303-10	3,857	3,641-94	2,944	511-186	...	216
	R	40-24-40	13,336-14,406	Y-15,872-..	5,410	2,103-39	2,005	41-57	1,378	1,929
New Britain, Conn. (7)	P	148-138-40	16,483-17,963	Y-21,487-20	4,306	4,055-94	3,647	16-392	...	251
	F	140-140-42	17,644-19,531	Y-19,881-20	3,969	3,796-96	3,466	...-330	...	173
	R	9-0-40	...-...	Y-16,307-20	1,961	159-8	143	15-1	...	1,802
New Rochelle, N.Y.	P	211-187-36	15,456-26,832	Y-27,182-15	9,083	8,489-93	5,638	2,443-408	194	400
	F	166-162-39	15,456-26,501	Y-26,951-15	8,222	7,602-92	5,244	2,034-324	78	542
	R	69-51-40	15,377-18,158	None	2,192	1,854-85	1,393	318-143	201	137
Newport Beach, Calif.	P	199-142-40	23,652-28,044	None	8,261	7,861-95	6,375	1,045-441	400	...
	F	110-107-56	21,594-25,608	None	4,551	4,315-95	3,425	662-228	236	...
	R	28-12-40	16,302-19,332	None	977	758-78	640	59-59	219	...
Newton, Mass. (7)	P	224-204-40	17,414-19,948	Y-20,448-20	...	...-..	...	...-...	...	...
	F	246-242-42	19,132-21,910	Y-22,410-20	...	...-..	...	...-...	...	...
Norman, Okla.	P	150-124-40	14,939-20,020	Y-20,320-5	4,899	3,405-70	2,875	359-171	1,227	267
	F	115-112-56	14,400-18,330	Y-18,630-5	2,910	2,468-85	2,176	151-141	373	69
	R	78-5-40	12,143-16,066	Y-16,366-5	1,822	1,263-69	1,070	105-88	249	310
North Charleston, S.C.	P	125-90-40	13,247-17,744	None	2,743	2,139-78	1,727	294-118	154	450
	F	82-80-72	11,949-16,004	None	1,472	1,230-84	995	168-67	49	193
	R	37-17-40	8,184-10,962	None	835	417-50	339	44-34	154	264
Norwalk, Calif. (3,4,7)										
Norwalk, Conn.	P	178-141-40	18,818-21,913	Y-22,043-8	6,671	5,788-87	4,042	1,214-532	273	610
	F	158-156-42	18,818-21,813	Y-21,953-8	5,895	5,489-93	3,671	1,343-475	72	334
	R	34-19-40	12,522-14,584	Y-14,759-8	1,548	874-56	629	145-100	269	405
Oak Lawn v, Ill. (7)	P	110-93-40	17,268-24,936	Y-26,376-20	4,242	3,656-86	3,051	340-265	60	526
	F	102-94-56	17,376-24,828	Y-26,268-20	3,772	3,174-84	2,813	120-241	35	563
Odessa, Tex.	P	223-205-40	18,144-21,996	Y-23,196-25	7,258	5,306-73	4,590	594-122	450	1,502
	F	156-153-56	17,220-20,976	Y-22,176-25	5,033	4,026-80	3,419	485-122	213	794
	R	61-1-40	14,908-17,148	Y-19,040-25	3,569	1,481-41	1,263	173-45	559	1,529
Ogden, Utah	P	133-105-40	15,643-23,288	None	4,258	3,651-86	2,956	477-218	273	334
	F	110-100-56	14,884-20,060	None	3,559	3,202-90	2,522	437-243	66	291
	R	16-14-40	12,198-16,441	None	1,318	361-27	267	57-37	165	792
Ontario, Calif.	P	139-106-40	19,896-24,288	None	7,306	5,533-76	3,819	1,294-420	412	1,361
	F	102-85-56	18,648-22,764	None	5,153	4,438-86	3,087	1,025-326	264	451
	R	33-0-40	13,152-18,276	None	2,334	971-42	702	159-110	43	1,320
Orange, Calif. (7)	P	161-116-40	21,132-25,056	None	7,589	6,571-87	5,441	789-341	25	993
	F	122-103-56	21,750-25,800	None	5,521	4,871-88	4,115	546-210	20	630
Orem, Utah	P	69-50-40	15,228-26,160	None	1,974	1,788-91	1,423	248-117	37	149
	F	32-31-56	14,928-25,692	None	1,050	979-93	732	186-61	54	17
	R	15-1-40	12,000-19,752	None	1,023	362-35	300	47-15	336	325
Owensboro, Ky.	P	123-100-40	13,615-16,657	Y-17,490-20	3,119	3,032-97	2,384	442-206	13	74
	F	99-99-48	13,615-16,657	Y-17,490-20	2,660	2,600-98	2,079	368-153	...	60
	R	77-7-40	10,967-13,661	Y-14,318-20	1,759	1,301-74	1,044	155-102	395	63
Parma, Ohio (7)	P	87-68-40	19,182-21,818	Y-23,018-25	2,394	2,394-100	2,394	...-...	...	...
	F	94-93-54	19,182-21,818	Y-23,018-25	2,262	2,262-100	2,262	...-...	...	...
Penn Hills, Pa. (1)	P	82-57-40	20,236-25,156	Y-25,781-5	3,500	2,882-82	2,636	92-154	97	521
	F	...-...-40	22,117-22,117	Y-22,742-5	35	30-86	23	5-2	...	5
Pensacola, Fla.	P	181-133-39	14,612-21,294	Y-23,426-30	5,177	4,508-87	3,733	676-99	63	606
	F	144-133-56	13,936-19,370	Y-21,320-30	5,095	4,403-86	3,481	841-81	34	658
	R	61-55-40	10,114-12,142	Y-13,364-30	3,716	1,380-37	1,129	216-35	1,671	665
Pico Rivera, Calif. (3,4,7)										
Pine Bluff, Ark. (7)	P	106-89-40	13,800-13,800	Y-18,600-..	2,516	2,024-80	1,839	97-88	211	281
	F	77-76-56	13,800-13,800	Y-18,600-..	1,571	1,468-93	1,353	57-58	24	79

Table 3/18 continued **POLICE, FIRE, AND REFUSE COLLECTION AND DISPOSAL DEPARTMENTS: PERSONNEL, SALARIES, AND EXPENDITURES FOR CITIES OVER 10,000: 1984**

City	Depart-ment	Total personnel, no. uniformed, duty hours per week	Entrance, maximum salary ($)	Longevity pay, maximum ($), no. years to max.	Reported expenditures (in thousands): Total expenditures (A) ($)	Total personnel expenditures (B), % of (A) ($)	Salaries and wages (C) ($)	City contrib. to employee retirement, insurance (D) ($)	Capital outlay (E) ($)	All other (F) ($)
50,000-99,999 continued										
Pittsfield, Mass. (7)	P	88-77-38	15,698-18,018	Y-18,518-20	3,586	3,322-93	2,522	621-179	120	144
	F	118-107-42	15,987-18,345	Y-18,845-30	4,501	4,256-95	3,231	788-237	100	145
Plano, Tex. (7)	P	176-123-40	20,112-24,216	Y-25,416-25	5,586	4,265-76	3,778	360-127	547	774
	F	125-112-56	18,240-21,528	Y-22,728-25	3,987	2,982-75	2,634	258-90	707	298
	R	36-36-40	12,528-14,868	Y-16,068-25	2,126	694-33	607	59-28	11	1,421
Pompano Beach, Fla. (7)	P	237-151-40	19,517-24,910	Y-27,463-17	8,115	7,089-87	5,883	993-213	10	1,016
	F	121-114-48	19,332-24,672	Y-27,201-17	4,794	4,251-89	3,545	597-109	86	457
Port Arthur, Tex.	P	135-124-40	20,460-24,216	Y-25,416-25	4,394	3,776-86	3,066	537-173	141	477
	F	106-99-56	19,614-22,584	Y-24,324-25	3,446	3,158-92	2,642	369-147	54	234
	R	87-86-40	14,269-14,982	Y-...-25	2,800	1,902-68	1,569	240-93	156	742
Portland, Me.	P	198-149-40	13,243-18,516	None	4,677	4,018-86	3,174	616-228	113	546
	F	228-207-42	13,137-17,102	None	4,468	3,927-88	3,354	349-224	113	428
	R	13-0-40	10,868-13,468	None	498	187-38	148	29-10	...	311
Provo, Utah	P	59-40-40	17,186-21,970	Y-22,857-10	2,926	2,570-88	2,161	337-72	83	273
	F	61-60-56	16,401-20,904	Y-21,748-10	2,430	2,201-91	1,828	300-73	108	121
	R	32-3-40	13,494-17,186	Y-17,880-10	2,326	749-32	622	88-39	287	1,290
Racine, Wis.	P	270-212-39	23,421-25,064	Y-26,318-15	10,475	9,647-92	7,299	1,749-599	286	542
	F	172-170-56	22,158-24,246	Y-25,458-15	6,866	6,509-95	4,780	1,324-405	149	208
	R	40-38-40	23,359-23,692	Y-24,876-15	1,926	1,021-53	797	154-70	149	756
Redondo Beach, Calif. (7)	P	142-92-40	22,308-27,132	Y-31,416-21	6,189	5,104-82	3,991	840-273	101	984
	F	70-65-56	22,416-27,240	Y-31,326-21	3,653	3,052-84	2,351	558-143	287	314
Redwood City, Calif. (7)	P	92-71-40	21,816-26,508	None	4,842	3,562-74	2,746	652-164	11	1,269
	F	73-67-56	19,296-25,992	None	3,096	2,757-89	2,117	516-124	24	315
Richardson, Tex.	P	166-106-40	20,448-24,384	Y-25,584-25	5,057	4,287-85	3,683	437-167	33	737
	F	119-115-56	21,060-23,172	Y-24,372-25	3,808	3,557-93	3,050	367-140	17	234
	R	45-5-40	14,040-17,280	Y-18,480-25	2,634	1,012-38	865	100-47	54	1,568
Rochester, Minn. (7)	P	113-96-40	20,776-25,776	None	4,062	3,764-93	2,919	611-234	63	235
	F	87-86-56	20,776-25,776	None	3,684	3,343-91	2,320	794-229	83	258
Roseville, Mich.	P	90-80-40	15,051-24,176	Y-26,593-25	4,160	3,688-89	2,859	534-295	76	396
	F	36-35-56	14,924-23,574	Y-25,931-25	1,880	1,719-91	1,346	248-125	8	153
	R	13-12-40	18,137-18,574	Y-20,431-25	876	387-44	264	83-40	...	489
Royal Oak, Mich. (7)	P	102-93-40	23,256-26,797	Y-28,140-25	4,322	4,092-95	3,018	743-331	5	225
	F	71-69-54	23,243-25,582	Y-28,140-25	2,852	2,740-96	2,000	513-227	3	109
	R	...-...-..	...-...	..-...-..	1,841	10-1	9	1-...	...	1,831
St. Joseph, Mo. (7)	P	132-124-40	12,171-14,830	None	2,994	2,459-82	2,315	20-124	152	383
	F	160-159-56	12,171-14,830	None	3,091	2,766-89	2,608	7-151	42	283
Salem, Ore. (7)	P	198-136-40	17,220-24,168	None	7,279	5,821-80	4,692	740-389	337	1,121
	F	142-135-56	16,464-23,316	None	5,378	4,461-83	3,642	546-273	349	568
Salinas, Calif. (7)	P	173-131-40	21,132-25,704	None	6,761	5,987-89	4,636	937-414	162	612
	F	97-94-56	20,843-25,319	None	3,648	3,015-83	2,410	497-108	385	248
San Angelo, Tex. (7)	P	160-127-40	17,304-17,304	Y-18,504-25	3,631	3,458-95	2,928	418-112	173	...
	F	136-124-56	17,304-17,304	Y-18,504-25	3,152	3,128-99	2,665	382-81	24	...
San Buenaventura, Calif. (7)	P	148-112-40	22,417-30,041	None	8,988	4,219-47	3,438	646-135	4,032	737
	F	73-70-56	22,909-28,542	None	2,927	2,554-87	2,063	414-77	56	317
San Leandro, Calif.	P	122-84-40	22,800-29,076	None	5,852	5,082-87	4,027	780-275	19	751
	F	93-91-56	21,444-28,752	None	4,273	3,955-93	3,120	624-211	30	288
	R	25-24-40	20,424-25,044	None	1,507	831-55	651	138-42	2	674
Sandy City, Utah (7)	P	59-46-40	13,674-23,150	None	1,975	1,482-75	1,210	193-79	46	447
	F	30-28-56	13,674-21,815	None	1,106	861-78	711	100-50	15	230
Santa Barbara, Calif. (7)	P	199-132-40	21,232-26,208	None	7,420	6,393-86	4,536	1,434-423	185	842
	F	111-101-56	19,292-26,026	None	4,763	4,266-90	2,791	1,260-215	39	458
Santa Clara, Calif. (7)	P	171-142-40	29,940-36,360	Y-38,196-15	9,575	8,006-84	6,548	1,154-304	320	1,249
	F	154-139-56	28,728-34,944	Y-36,672-15	8,917	7,014-79	5,629	1,056-329	1,036	867
	R	15-11-40	21,672-26,376	Y-27,660-15	1,013	364-36	287	49-28	187	462
Santa Monica, Calif.	P	267-163-40	23,952-29,568	Y-31,963-15	12,049	10,275-85	7,922	1,891-462	807	967
	F	114-102-56	21,465-26,501	None	5,731	5,256-92	3,921	1,112-223	162	313
	R	50-0-40	14,980-18,491	None	2,810	1,236-44	1,052	106-78	124	1,450
Santa Rosa, Calif. (7)	P	164-112-40	22,020-26,772	None	5,988	5,070-85	4,181	628-261	168	750
	F	98-94-56	20,172-24,192	None	3,841	3,041-79	2,509	388-144	418	382
Santee, Calif. (3,4,7)										
Schaumburg v, Ill. (7)	P	130-98-40	20,532-27,348	Y-28,848-25	4,469	4,007-90	3,400	285-322	101	361
	F	103-101-50	20,532-27,348	Y-28,848-25	3,945	3,415-87	2,987	220-208	280	250
Schenectady, N.Y.	P	171-150-40	16,060-23,459	Y-24,859-19	3,387	3,022-89	1,718	1,025-279	163	202
	F	177-172-40	16,060-23,459	Y-24,859-19	6,519	6,363-98	4,714	1,357-292	31	125
	R	66-44-40	13,874-13,874	Y-14,674-20	940	934-99	811	20-103	...	6
Scottsdale, Ariz. (2)	P	185-122-40	18,322-28,360	None	7,176	5,751-80	4,724	765-262	277	1,148
	R	45-0-40	13,377-21,100	None	3,360	1,054-31	872	119-63	11	2,295
Scranton, Pa.	P	157-153-40	19,456-20,196	Y-23,225-30	4,476	4,387-98	3,486	269-632	...	89
	F	202-201-42	18,999-19,649	Y-22,596-30	5,718	5,378-94	4,157	329-892	...	340
	R	91-32-40	14,914-14,914	Y-16,405-30	3,261	1,828-56	1,357	159-312	...	1,433
Simi Valley, Calif. (3,7)	P	112-77-40	18,624-23,100	None	4,632	3,610-78	2,710	685-215	129	893
Sioux City, Iowa (7)	P	141-101-40	19,499-22,655	Y-23,710-8	5,472	4,393-80	3,243	868-282	203	876
	F	122-117-56	18,754-22,225	Y-23,280-10	4,374	3,932-90	2,703	985-244	69	373
Sioux Falls, S.D.	P	136-117-40	17,260-23,352	None	4,242	3,591-85	3,073	416-102	194	457
	F	140-134-56	16,338-22,103	None	4,073	3,747-92	3,037	620-90	147	179
South Gate, Calif. (3)										
Southfield, Mich. (7)	P	176-141-40	21,260-29,030	Y-31,352-10	8,824	7,345-83	5,675	1,086-584	10	1,469
	F	115-101-56	21,318-29,030	Y-31,352-10	5,898	5,186-88	3,991	809-386	8	704
	R	..-...-..	...-...	..-...-..	972	...-..	...	...-...	...	972

Table 3/18 continued **POLICE, FIRE, AND REFUSE COLLECTION AND DISPOSAL DEPARTMENTS: PERSONNEL, SALARIES, AND EXPENDITURES FOR CITIES OVER 10,000: 1984**

					Reported expenditures (in thousands)					
City	Department	Total personnel, no. uniformed, duty hours per week	Entrance, maximum salary ($)	Longevity pay, maximum ($), no. years to max.	Total expenditures (A) ($)	Total personnel expenditures (B), % of (A) ($)	Salaries and wages (C) ($)	City contrib. to employee retirement, insurance (D) ($)	Capital outlay (E) ($)	All other (F) ($)
50,000-99,999 continued										
Springfield, Ohio	P	125-100-40	17,493-22,256	Y-23,591-25	4,663	3,945-85	3,150	560-235	157	561
	F	133-127-60	17,928-22,642	Y-...-..	4,382	4,138-94	3,139	729-270	71	173
	R	12-1-40	16,786-19,427	Y-20,398-20	678	278-41	210	39-29	149	251
Stratford t, Conn.	P	113-92-38	16,000-19,293	Y-19,893-20	3,653	3,085-84	2,614	246-225	78	490
	F	108-107-42	17,360-20,932	Y-21,732-20	3,961	3,060-77	2,623	233-204	24	877
	R	37-0-40	13,991-18,045	Y-18,815-25	1,917	856-45	681	104-71	...	1,061
Terre Haute, Ind. (7)	P	132-119-40	11,083-12,984	Y-13,744-..	...	...-..	...	...-...	...	...
	F	149-149-56	11,083-12,984	Y-13,744-..	...	...-..	...	...-...	...	...
Thousand Oaks, Calif. (3,4,7)										
Trenton, N.J.	P	427-358-40	18,500-24,000	Y-26,225-45	15,684	14,305-91	11,464	2,102-739	568	811
	F	277-267-42	18,500-24,000	Y-26,225-45	10,567	9,999-95	7,914	1,624-461	271	297
	R	62-49-40	13,187-15,485	Y-17,410-45	1,679	1,327-79	1,023	179-125	183	169
Troy, Mich. (1,7)	P	135-102-40	19,041-28,719	Y-30,919-19	6,650	5,498-83	4,277	787-434	94	1,058
	F	7-6-40	...-...	..-...-..	940	311-33	241	45-25	120	509
	R	...-...-..	...-...	..-...-..	1,402	...-..	...	...-...	...	1,402
Troy, N.Y.	P	144-124-40	14,914-20,245	Y-21,011-19	4,641	4,243-91	2,961	1,012-270	5	393
	F	175-170-48	13,743-19,549	Y-20,315-19	5,564	5,262-95	3,665	1,253-344	10	292
	R	33-0-40	9,336-13,482	Y-14,182-25	642	617-96	458	92-67	...	25
Tuscaloosa, Ala.	P	178-150-40	15,353-16,434	Y-17,875-9	4,250	3,555-84	3,057	311-187	52	643
	F	154-151-52	15,353-16,434	Y-17,875-9	4,070	3,834-94	3,313	345-176	2	234
	R	88-54-40	12,116-12,480	Y-12,979-20	1,923	1,276-66	1,120	78-78	106	541
Tyler, Tex.	P	140-108-40	16,830-19,380	Y-20,580-25	4,255	3,049-72	3,049	...-...	...	1,206
	F	118-111-64	16,152-18,816	Y-20,016-25	3,169	2,492-79	2,492	...-...	25	652
	R	106-65-40	9,859-13,000	Y-13,144-25	2,649	1,219-46	1,219	...-...	213	1,217
Union tp, N.J. (7)	P	151-130-40	19,399-25,112	Y-27,624-24	5,886	5,206-88	4,127	677-402	169	511
	F	133-130-42	19,399-25,112	Y-27,624-24	5,021	4,620-92	3,632	640-348	200	201
Union City, N.J. (7)	P	170-132-34	19,847-22,682	Y-24,950-15	4,188	4,188-100	4,188	...-...	...	...
	F	111-106-40	20,139-22,467	Y-24,659-15	2,939	2,939-100	2,939	...-...	...	...
Utica, N.Y. (7)	P	184-184-40	16,361-19,091	None	4,200	4,182-100	3,888	...-294	18	...
	F	220-220-40	14,725-18,729	None	4,934	4,719-96	4,356	...-363	215	...
Victoria, Tex.	P	113-71-40	16,464-18,696	None	3,380	2,591-77	2,164	328-99	38	751
	F	76-75-56	15,384-18,696	None	2,071	1,722-83	1,440	215-67	31	318
	R	56-56-40	10,440-13,728	None	1,609	941-58	775	119-47	47	621
Vineland, N.J. (7)	P	112-101-40	13,500-19,375	None	3,379	3,037-90	2,511	369-157	67	275
	F	19-18-56	13,300-22,000	None	698	606-87	509	71-26	11	81
Walnut Creek, Calif. (3)	P	91-71-40	23,604-28,668	None	4,261	3,548-83	2,575	784-189	183	530
Warren, Ohio	P	86-77-40	18,221-19,220	Y-...-..	3,239	3,037-94	2,381	417-239	...	202
	F	91-90-52	20,966-21,639	Y-...-..	3,144	2,987-95	2,236	506-245	...	157
	R	...-...-40	15,049-17,514	Y-18,564-25	1,172	692-59	554	77-61	...	480
Waterloo, Iowa	P	136-111-40	16,600-21,500	Y-23,060-30	6,007	4,980-83	3,802	852-326	281	746
	F	131-125-54	15,515-20,310	Y-21,870-30	4,168	3,402-82	3,070	10-322	112	654
	R	26-19-40	15,660-16,620	Y-18,036-26	1,138	586-51	470	67-49	158	394
Waukegan, Ill. (7)	P	138-106-40	17,950-24,480	None	4,999	4,328-87	3,334	713-281	121	550
	F	83-80-51	17,848-22,310	Y-24,830-21	3,386	3,190-94	2,216	718-256	103	93
Waukesha, Wis. (7)										
Wauwatosa, Wis. (7)	P	116-90-40	21,325-24,597	Y-24,909-25	4,517	4,128-91	3,178	754-196	81	308
	F	122-116-56	23,504-26,382	Y-26,696-25	4,996	4,748-95	3,543	985-220	41	207
	R	40-28-40	19,035-19,473	None	821	578-70	455	85-38	...	243
West Allis, Wis.	P	157-136-40	21,824-26,564	Y-26,864-25	6,702	6,302-94	4,452	1,469-381	137	263
	F	141-137-56	21,824-26,564	Y-26,864-25	5,661	5,445-96	3,976	1,127-342	47	169
	R	70-43-43	17,888-19,011	Y-19,311-25	3,296	1,779-54	1,398	258-123	416	1,101
West Covina, Calif. (7)	P	134-93-40	23,154-27,456	None	6,361	5,608-88	4,096	902-610	148	605
	F	73-70-56	22,878-27,132	None	3,663	3,310-90	2,485	535-290	46	307
West Hartford t, Conn.	P	165-135-40	17,979-20,982	Y-21,132-5	2,883	1,718-60	393	933-392	48	1,117
	F	104-102-42	17,979-20,982	Y-21,132-5	4,379	4,073-93	2,914	890-269	221	85
	R	43-29-40	16,068-17,097	Y-17,247-5	1,136	710-63	558	79-73	100	326
West Palm Beach, Fla.	P	208-168-40	18,720-22,188	Y-24,407-20	6,593	5,594-85	4,911	683-...	244	755
	F	147-141-48	15,966-19,884	Y-21,872-20	4,164	3,756-90	3,220	536-...	88	320
	R	80-23-40	13,626-14,664	Y-16,130-20	3,234	1,436-44	1,226	210-...	174	1,624
West Valley City, Utah (7)	P	89-70-40	14,419-25,272	None	3,410	2,508-74	1,977	345-186	450	452
	F	41-40-56	14,772-20,551	None	2,015	1,205-60	926	199-80	676	134
Westland, Mich. (7)	P	98-89-40	17,851-25,711	Y-26,211-14	4,809	4,210-88	3,066	838-306	18	581
	F	57-56-56	17,494-25,239	Y-25,739-14	2,708	2,603-96	1,863	541-199	4	101
Westminster, Calif.	P	114-80-40	25,818-30,120	Y-...-..	5,327	4,792-90	3,853	693-246	29	506
	F	64-62-56	24,270-28,296	None	3,450	3,104-90	2,491	464-149	24	322
Westminster, Colo. (7)	P	129-51-40	20,892-28,080	Y-30,900-20	4,328	3,567-82	3,108	309-150	297	464
	F	61-59-56	18,924-20,892	Y-22,980-20	1,852	1,603-87	1,393	132-78	55	194
Whittier, Calif. (3,7)	P	119-85-40	23,280-28,128	None	5,096	4,359-86	3,456	573-330	301	436
	R	24-8-40	13,494-18,288	None	1,476	759-51	575	53-131	25	692
Wichita Falls, Tex.	P	200-152-40	21,078-21,078	Y-21,335-16	5,685	4,573-80	4,063	409-101	325	787
	F	157-145-56	16,464-19,091	Y-19,738-4	3,883	3,412-88	3,008	324-80	118	353
	R	91-9-40	10,013-13,539	None	3,534	1,385-39	1,211	133-41	929	1,220
Wilkes-Barre, Pa.	P	110-95-40	18,950-20,200	Y-23,930-30	3,154	2,857-91	2,300	332-225	59	238
	F	111-104-42	19,150-20,200	Y-23,930-30	3,278	2,974-91	2,429	307-238	174	130
	R	21-13-40	15,174-15,174	None	689	369-54	305	34-30	...	320
Wilmington, Del.	P	285-226-40	15,489-25,695	None	10,027	8,955-89	7,598	864-493	30	1,042
	F	203-200-48	15,489-25,695	None	8,445	6,642-79	5,331	939-372	512	1,291
	R	64-44-40	14,750-15,910	None	2,271	1,322-58	1,112	97-113	...	949

Table 3/18 continued **POLICE, FIRE, AND REFUSE COLLECTION AND DISPOSAL DEPARTMENTS: PERSONNEL, SALARIES, AND EXPENDITURES FOR CITIES OVER 10,000: 1984**

					Reported expenditures (in thousands)					
City	Department	Total personnel, no. uniformed, duty hours per week	Entrance, maximum salary ($)	Longevity pay, maximum ($), no. years to max.	Total expenditures (A) ($)	Total personnel expenditures (B), % of (A) ($)	Salaries and wages (C) ($)	City contrib. to employee retirement, insurance (D) ($)	Capital outlay (E) ($)	All other (F) ($)
50,000-99,999 continued										
Wyoming, Mich.	P	97-71-40	21,424-26,395	Y-27,095-20	3,909	3,332-85	2,562	611-159	110	467
	F	27-26-42	17,472-21,840	Y-22,240-20	1,271	933-73	757	129-47	5	333
25,000-49,999										
Addison v, Ill. (3,7)	P	68-49-40	20,246-27,688	None	2,532	2,029-80	1,831	98-100	101	402
Albany, Ore. (7)	P	41-30-40	17,784-24,564	None	1,440	1,242-86	934	222-86	40	158
	F	52-46-56	16,212-23,820	None	1,923	1,506-78	1,133	267-106	28	389
Alton, Ill.	P	79-67-40	17,658-17,940	Y-20,004-20	2,229	1,971-88	1,669	241-61	68	190
	F	67-66-56	17,658-17,940	Y-20,004-20	1,952	1,810-93	1,505	254-51	57	85
	R	25-18-40	15,797-16,016	Y-17,867-20	657	450-68	368	58-24	46	161
Anderson, S.C.	P	70-70-42	12,492-15,380	..-..-..	1,637	1,354-83	1,110	184-60	78	205
	F	52-52-54	12,492-15,380	..-..-..	1,052	957-91	809	103-45	11	84
	R	61-38-40	9,256-11,367	..-..-..	1,080	826-76	679	98-49	75	179
Andover t, Mass. (7)	P	58-45-39	17,064-20,440	Y-21,090-5	1,940	1,690-87	1,480	158-52	72	178
	F	58-57-42	17,026-20,104	Y-20,754-5	1,932	1,703-88	1,488	158-57	140	89
	R	..-..-..	...-...	..-..-..	368	11-3	10	...-1	...	357
Annapolis, Md.	P	120-100-40	15,094-18,792	Y-19,929-15	4,906	4,148-85	2,314	1,655-179	127	631
	F	81-80-56	14,643-18,193	Y-19,294-15	3,773	3,048-81	1,621	1,314-113	33	692
	R	18-18-40	11,440-12,854	Y-13,832-20	676	378-56	294	59-25	3	295
Anniston, Ala. (7)	P	110-85-40	12,626-16,099	Y-16,339-20	2,125	1,702-80	1,491	159-52	105	318
	F	75-75-56	12,626-16,099	Y-16,339-20	1,578	1,422-90	1,258	123-41	22	134
Arcadia, Calif. (7)	P	84-69-40	24,720-29,316	Y-29,816-20	4,033	3,604-89	2,807	674-123	...	429
	F	65-55-56	23,730-28,140	Y-28,640-20	3,415	2,748-80	2,133	526-89	435	232
Auburn, N.Y.	P	60-51-40	18,120-20,900	Y-21,650-25	2,519	2,301-91	1,706	476-119	43	175
	F	86-85-40	18,320-21,061	Y-21,811-25	3,379	3,214-95	2,335	698-181	34	131
	R	15-1-40	14,966-16,777	Y-17,527-25	622	375-60	275	73-27	132	115
Auburn, Wash. (7)	P	62-62-40	24,144-30,451	Y-32,281-7	2,728	2,370-87	1,919	227-224	80	278
	F	45-43-50	21,204-27,300	Y-28,934-7	1,875	1,642-88	1,438	74-130	31	202
Azusa, Calif. (7)	P	70-49-40	21,876-25,488	None	3,204	2,300-72	1,724	480-96	44	860
Bangor, Me.	P	74-62-40	13,000-17,000	None	1,894	1,593-84	1,303	196-94	12	289
	F	108-103-48	13,000-17,000	None	2,664	2,297-86	1,860	288-149	7	360
	R	7-5-40	11,000-13,000	None	307	128-42	108	13-7	...	179
Barberton, Ohio (7)	P	39-39-40	19,749-21,884	Y-22,424-..	1,375	1,375-100	1,042	218-115	...	...
	F	39-39-52	19,749-21,884	Y-22,424-..	1,471	1,471-100	1,063	291-117	...	...
	R	2-2-40	15,660-16,660	Y-16,960-..	49	49-100	39	5-5	...	...
Bartlesville, Okla.	P	68-55-40	14,111-18,883	Y-19,500-5	1,643	1,376-84	1,147	161-68	80	187
	F	72-71-56	13,418-17,985	Y-18,585-5	1,783	1,596-90	1,417	96-83	59	128
	R	42-26-40	11,582-15,538	Y-15,849-5	1,433	756-53	649	64-43	122	555
Battle Creek, Mich. (7)	P	138-97-40	18,442-24,844	Y-...-..	5,494	4,603-84	3,468	654-481	11	880
	F	112-110-56	18,317-24,609	Y-...-..	4,551	4,313-95	3,293	714-306	80	158
Bay City, Mich.	P	77-71-40	16,286-24,826	Y-25,807-20	3,076	2,754-90	2,042	454-258	22	300
	F	72-71-56	17,275-27,769	Y-28,499-20	2,840	2,505-88	1,929	431-145	101	234
	R	14-14-40	17,142-19,502	Y-20,483-20	922	465-50	360	76-29	...	457
Beavercreek, Ohio (3,7)	P	36-28-40	16,598-23,674	None	1,073	921-86	748	111-62	35	117
Beaverton, Ore.	P	62-50-40	18,743-25,716	Y-27,000-10	2,450	2,096-86	1,554	400-142	41	313
	F	54-50-56	16,834-23,796	None	2,457	1,914-78	1,434	340-140	221	322
Bell, Calif. (2)										
Belleville, Ill.	P	69-59-40	17,572-23,092	None	2,379	2,146-90	1,446	587-113	61	172
	F	56-55-42	17,572-23,092	None	2,314	1,930-83	1,228	610-92	277	107
	R	16-16-40	16,638-...	None	487	332-68	263	46-23	...	155
Bellingham, Wash. (7)	P	107-69-40	20,760-26,310	Y-28,374-19	3,265	2,559-78	2,239	150-170	18	688
	F	96-93-52	20,058-25,068	Y-27,048-20	4,355	3,038-70	2,699	152-187	930	387
Beloit, Wis.	P	91-69-40	17,233-23,353	Y-24,146-18	3,190	2,796-88	2,109	494-193	96	298
	F	66-64-53	17,036-22,931	Y-23,855-15	2,890	2,420-84	1,769	478-173	12	458
	R	9-8-40	16,870-18,242	Y-18,658-10	440	167-38	127	23-17	...	273
Bergenfield b, N.J.	P	55-52-40	15,487-24,398	Y-26,350-27	1,536	1,536-100	1,536	...-...	...	...
	F	4-4-40	15,487-24,398	Y-26,350-27	114	114-100	114	...-...	...	...
	R	19-12-40	13,280-19,594	Y-21,162-27	467	438-94	438	...-...	29	...
Bessemer, Ala. (7)	P	73-60-40	16,260-20,238	Y-21,959-6	2,302	1,990-86	1,582	323-85	108	204
	F	73-69-52	16,260-20,238	Y-21,959-6	2,480	2,121-86	1,686	347-88	251	108
	R	52-13-40	10,941-10,941	Y-11,871-6	1,408	781-55	612	115-54	111	516
Bethel Park, Pa. (1)										
Bettendorf, Iowa	P	40-28-40	19,584-27,804	None	1,717	1,543-90	1,010	151-382	32	142
	F	4-4-40	18,550-20,591	None	144	123-85	78	6-39	1	20
	R	14-10-40	18,828-20,085	None	580	447-77	278	35-134	52	81
Beverly Hills, Calif.	P	169-117-40	26,970-30,877	None	9,433	7,197-76	5,437	1,456-304	523	1,713
	F	89-83-56	25,094-30,331	None	6,399	4,732-74	3,629	942-161	948	719
	R	24-0-40	19,805-23,880	None	2,178	896-41	729	106-61	161	1,121
Biloxi, Miss. (7)	P	111-77-40	11,918-13,139	None	2,705	2,111-78	1,577	403-131	60	534
	F	87-87-56	11,350-12,514	None	1,707	1,479-87	1,309	48-122	57	171
Blacksburg t, Va. (1,7)	P	37-25-40	13,196-17,372	None	1,222	978-80	821	117-40	35	209
	F	1-0-..	...-...	..-...-..	329	23-7	20	2-1	158	148
	R	...-...-..	...-...	..-...-..	129	101-78	83	12-6	...	28
Blaine, Minn. (7)	P	7-20-40	17,000-26,000	Y-29,000-16	1,261	1,067-85	921	101-45	43	151
Bloomington, Ill.	P	78-67-40	19,786-25,324	Y-28,002-20	2,738	2,420-88	2,054	286-80	8	310
	F	68-66-52	20,009-23,971	Y-27,088-25	2,499	2,306-92	1,747	489-70	9	184
	R	34-0-40	21,382-21,590	Y-24,398-25	994	625-63	553	37-35	1	368
Blue Springs, Mo. (3)	P	40-30-40	16,128-21,588	None	1,019	1,019-100	858	121-40	...	...

Table 3/18 continued POLICE, FIRE, AND REFUSE COLLECTION AND DISPOSAL DEPARTMENTS: PERSONNEL, SALARIES, AND EXPENDITURES FOR CITIES OVER 10,000: 1984

					Reported expenditures (in thousands)					
City	Depart-ment	Total personnel, no. uniformed, duty hours per week	Entrance, maximum salary ($)	Longevity pay, maximum ($), no. years to max.	Total expendi-tures (A) ($)	Total personnel expendi-tures (B), % of (A) ($)	Salaries and wages (C) ($)	City contrib. to employee retirement, insurance (D) ($)	Capital outlay (E) ($)	All other (F) ($)
25,000-49,999 continued										
Bolingbrook v, Ill. (7)	P	68-50-40	19,319-26,747	Y-27,962-20	2,584	2,196-85	1,914	166-116	72	316
	F	46-44-56	19,864-26,515	Y-27,730-20	2,082	1,855-89	1,493	262-100	30	197
Bossier City, La.	P	139-113-40	12,360-15,264	Y-27,864-23	2,991	2,797-94	2,051	738-8	194	...
	F	89-87-56	12,360-15,264	Y-27,864-23	2,530	2,475-98	1,616	855-4	55	...
	R	72-72-40	8,984-14,016	Y-16,997-23	1,023	865-85	771	41-53	158	...
Bountiful, Utah (1)	P	36-29-40	16,020-23,664	None	1,302	1,110-85	875	195-40	54	138
	F	11-11-40	15,048-22,260	None	517	408-79	309	58-41	27	82
	R	5-5-40	13,836-20,436	None	365	105-29	80	20-5	...	260
Bowie, Md. (2,4)	R	30-19-40	11,526-14,574	Y-16,412-15	992	583-59	461	53-69	23	386
Bowling Green, Ky. (7)	P	85-69-40	14,042-17,108	Y-17,158-20	2,572	2,475-96	1,872	432-171	84	13
	F	85-81-56	14,042-17,108	Y-17,158-20	2,637	2,491-94	1,844	478-169	14	132
Bowling Green, Ohio	P	41-31-40	16,786-21,819	Y-22,910-14	1,431	1,108-77	894	152-62	21	302
	F	24-23-52	16,786-21,819	Y-22,910-14	991	811-82	623	138-50	21	159
	R	3-0-40	14,498-18,845	Y-19,787-14	244	126-52	112	7-7	104	14
Boynton Beach, Fla.	P	93-77-40	17,181-20,925	Y-26,645-15	2,924	2,264-77	1,899	306-59	169	491
	F	65-62-48	16,370-19,906	Y-25,397-15	1,906	1,680-88	1,434	207-39	88	138
	R	32-13-40	12,210-14,830	Y-18,970-15	1,013	684-68	572	88-24	67	262
Bradenton, Fla.	P	66-52-40	15,803-16,277	Y-16,590-5	1,744	1,251-72	1,088	135-28	80	413
	F	72-64-56	13,832-16,389	Y-16,704-5	1,861	1,478-79	1,262	184-32	170	213
	R	57-0-40	9,739-11,247	Y-11,463-5	1,244	753-61	625	103-25	83	408
Brea, Calif. (7)	P	73-60-40	21,325-27,366	None	3,361	2,893-86	2,139	561-193	31	437
	F	43-40-56	20,480-26,280	None	2,107	1,828-87	1,337	373-118	52	227
Brighton t, N.Y. (3,7)	P	45-36-40	20,074-25,921	Y-26,921-20	1,957	1,750-89	1,278	407-65	...	207
Brook Park, Ohio	P	44-44-40	20,450-23,430	Y-24,430-5	1,909	1,510-79	1,177	202-131	184	215
	F	49-49-48	20,450-23,430	Y-24,430-5	1,794	1,520-85	1,088	293-139	174	100
	R	15-15-40	18,803-19,032	Y-20,032-5	612	461-75	355	50-56	...	151
Brookfield, Wis. (7)	P	65-51-39	23,049-24,943	Y-25,303-15	2,376	2,136-90	1,604	381-151	72	168
	F	42-42-56	19,338-20,671	Y-21,031-15	1,503	1,431-95	1,037	283-111	6	66
Brooklyn Park, Minn. (1)										
Brunswick, Ohio (1,7)	P	33-25-40	17,493-21,778	Y-22,778-22	1,096	921-84	716	125-80	49	126
	F	...-...-..	...-...	..-...-..	211	97-46	86	11-...	65	49
Bryan, Tex. (7)	P	73-56-40	17,790-22,104	Y-23,304-25	2,547	2,139-84	1,889	196-54	127	281
	F	81-80-56	16,044-19,920	Y-21,120-25	1,989	1,724-87	1,499	177-48	44	221
	R	56-28-40	10,119-10,899	None	1,470	829-56	723	75-31	235	406
Burlington, N.C.	P	103-84-40	13,296-17,004	Y-18,024-20	2,360	1,872-79	1,620	210-42	133	355
	F	81-75-56	12,720-16,260	Y-17,236-20	1,778	1,514-85	1,296	183-35	169	95
	R	43-24-40	9,354-11,916	Y-12,631-20	850	554-65	474	63-17	134	162
Burlington, Vt. (7)	P	94-73-40	15,586-18,960	Y-19,210-10	1,903	1,530-80	1,530	...-...	25	348
	F	85-83-56	14,461-20,513	Y-20,763-10	1,719	1,560-91	1,560	...-...	...	159
Burnsville, Minn. (5,7)	P	57-43-40	...-...	..-...-..	2,358	1,985-84	1,707	202-76	70	303
	F	23-23-56	...-...	..-...-..	1,146	898-78	775	92-31	81	167
Butte-Silver Bow, Mont. (7)	P	78-49-40	12,210-18,156	Y-18,246-2	1,842	1,588-86	1,316	178-94	1	253
	F	45-42-40	15,513-18,918	Y-19,008-1	1,392	1,205-87	980	166-59	2	185
Calumet City, Ill.	P	74-52-40	19,200-23,106	Y-25,417-10	1,795	1,795-100	1,795	...-...	...	...
	F	41-40-40	19,200-23,106	Y-25,417-10	1,058	1,058-100	1,058	...-...	...	...
	R	26-0-40	17,492-17,492	None	420	420-100	420	...-...	...	...
Camarillo, Calif. (3,4,7)										
Campbell, Calif. (7)	P	51-45-40	25,397-30,867	None	2,637	2,033-77	1,652	282-99	7	597
	F	38-36-56	23,774-28,891	None	1,758	1,546-88	1,254	220-72	11	201
Cape Coral, Fla.	P	80-60-40	14,456-22,402	None	1,744	1,628-93	1,356	174-98	116	...
	F	53-51-56	13,749-21,341	None	1,076	1,056-98	882	109-65	20	...
Carbondale, Ill.	P	68-48-40	16,514-19,094	Y-21,486-25	1,652	1,424-86	1,250	133-41	31	197
	F	32-32-56	16,514-18,841	Y-20,733-20	958	861-90	650	189-22	21	76
	R	4-4-40	11,612-15,075	Y-16,890-25	150	...-..	...	...-...	44	106
Carlsbad, Calif.	P	68-55-40	17,856-21,719	None	2,803	2,197-78	1,693	406-98	207	399
	F	52-50-56	19,352-23,530	None	2,004	1,810-90	1,341	386-83	46	148
Carlsbad, N.M.	P	51-42-40	17,950-...	None	1,305	1,074-82	1,074	...-...	30	201
	F	25-24-56	17,724-...	None	841	624-74	624	...-...	181	36
	R	23-2-40	18,387-...	None	806	410-51	410	...-...	177	219
Carrollton, Tex.	P	103-74-40	21,634-22,716	Y-26,316-25	3,151	2,469-78	2,200	122-147	285	397
	F	84-82-56	21,120-22,176	Y-23,976-25	2,640	2,353-89	2,125	125-103	57	230
	R	46-12-40	13,812-14,498	Y-15,698-25	1,959	868-44	732	39-97	376	715
Carson City, Nev. (7)	P	77-63-40	15,862-19,935	None	2,479	1,892-76	1,505	255-132	131	456
	F	49-46-56	16,620-20,244	None	1,377	1,203-87	950	161-92	63	111
Cedar Falls, Iowa	P	53-45-40	16,994-20,654	Y-21,998-35	1,575	1,327-84	1,113	102-112	78	170
	F	37-37-56	16,686-21,141	Y-22,485-35	1,139	1,044-92	818	129-97	...	95
	R	9-9-40	13,323-15,350	Y-16,238-28	637	196-31	152	19-25	53	388
Chandler, Ariz. (7)	P	100-64-40	19,224-24,684	None	3,111	2,586-83	2,238	259-89	105	420
	F	48-46-56	17,412-22,356	None	1,902	1,268-67	1,181	43-44	448	186
	R	9-0-40	12,264-15,756	None	1,927	110-6	95	10-5	436	1,381
Chapel Hill t, N.C.	P	73-63-42	14,749-20,754	None	1,842	1,606-87	1,407	131-68	91	145
	F	46-44-56	13,378-18,824	None	1,163	1,061-91	889	128-44	5	97
	R	39-20-40	9,507-13,378	None	966	723-75	596	88-39	81	162
Charlottesville, Va.	P	107-89-40	14,909-20,005	None	2,749	2,377-86	2,012	284-81	64	308
	F	67-65-56	14,196-19,048	None	1,681	1,537-91	1,290	195-52	16	128
	R	48-21-40	9,134-12,256	None	1,231	534-43	446	64-24	240	457
Chelmsford t, Mass. (7)	P	56-51-38	16,860-19,390	Y-21,717-20	1,889	1,651-87	1,468	107-76	50	188
	F	65-63-42	17,551-20,185	Y-22,607-20	2,115	1,948-92	1,724	137-87	12	155

Table 3/18 continued **POLICE, FIRE, AND REFUSE COLLECTION AND DISPOSAL DEPARTMENTS: PERSONNEL, SALARIES, AND EXPENDITURES FOR CITIES OVER 10,000: 1984**

City	Depart-ment	Total personnel, no. uniformed, duty hours per week	Entrance, maximum salary ($)	Longevity pay, maximum ($), no. years to max.	Reported expenditures (in thousands): Total expendi-tures (A) ($)	Total personnel expendi-tures (B), % of (A) ($)	Salaries and wages (C) ($)	City contrib. to employee retirement, insurance (D) ($)	Capital outlay (E) ($)	All other (F) ($)
25,000-49,999 continued										
Cheltenham tp, Pa. (1)	P	92-82-40	19,839-24,799	Y-26,999-40	2,954	2,637-89	2,237	154-246	20	297
	R	23-2-44	18,843-19,173	None	764	570-75	454	52-64	...	194
Chester, Pa. (7)	P	115-104-40	19,000-19,000	Y-24,200-15	3,861	3,351-87	2,749	60-542	120	390
	F	65-64-42	20,000-20,000	Y-22,800-21	2,338	2,103-90	1,637	211-255	35	200
	R	...-...-..	...-...	..-...-..	853	...-..	...	...-...	...	853
Cheyenne, Wyo.	P	109-84-40	15,170-24,381	None	4,163	2,960-71	2,339	427-194	222	981
	F	98-97-51	15,370-18,681	Y-19,881-14	3,681	2,655-72	2,005	393-257	293	733
	R	58-34-40	9,851-17,913	None	1,812	1,061-59	860	109-92	516	235
Chicago Heights, Ill. (7)	P	101-78-42	19,542-22,080	Y-22,800-12	3,108	2,811-90	2,246	375-190	109	188
	F	67-64-56	20,735-21,710	Y-22,490-12	2,379	2,222-93	1,553	536-133	29	128
Chico, Calif. (7)	P	65-42-40	18,980-22,526	Y-23,650-5	2,557	2,150-84	1,584	330-236	37	370
	F	41-39-56	16,715-19,802	None	1,682	1,447-86	1,072	236-139	26	209
Chino, Calif. (2)										
Claremont, Calif. (2)	P	48-35-40	20,652-24,492	None	2,308	1,983-86	1,676	256-51	17	308
	R	14-0-40	12,948-15,360	None	820	384-47	327	42-15	25	411
Clovis, Calif.	P	60-47-40	20,904-25,404	None	2,666	2,011-75	1,648	257-106	37	618
	F	39-38-56	18,060-21,948	None	1,437	1,299-90	1,045	188-66	11	127
	R	17-14-40	13,416-16,308	None	925	455-49	384	41-30	35	435
Coral Springs, Fla. (1,7)	P	126-83-40	18,724-25,180	Y-26,456-20	3,627	3,179-88	2,758	355-66	159	289
	F	...-...-..	...-...	..-...-..	353	101-29	95	6-...	34	218
Corona, Calif. (7)	P	81-49-40	18,456-24,744	..-...-..	3,250	2,827-87	1,911	528-388	21	402
	F	58-51-56	17,580-23,568	..-...-..	2,334	2,114-91	1,429	420-265	37	183
Covina, Calif.	P	63-53-40	21,684-25,728	None	2,808	2,445-87	2,040	243-162	5	358
	F	42-41-56	22,446-26,616	None	2,045	1,929-94	1,667	168-94	6	110
	R	13-12-40	16,488-19,572	None	890	371-42	288	55-28	32	487
Covington, Ky. (7)	P	114-96-40	13,498-16,713	Y-17,193-20	3,340	2,858-86	2,097	559-202	...	482
	F	117-113-48	13,073-19,732	Y-20,212-20	3,838	3,261-85	2,396	660-205	296	281
Crystal, Minn. (1,7)	P	31-30-40	17,364-26,688	Y-29,090-16	1,172	1,026-88	838	150-38	51	95
	F	...-...-..	...-...	..-...-..	163	127-78	82	45-...	17	19
Cumberland, Md. (7)	P	62-54-40	13,076-15,889	None	1,509	1,293-86	1,054	126-113	20	196
	F	64-63-48	13,004-15,807	None	1,406	1,315-94	1,045	159-111	26	65
Cupertino, Calif. (3,4,7)										
Cuyahoga Falls, Ohio	P	69-57-40	21,403-24,710	Y-25,091-14	2,487	2,200-88	1,706	307-187	66	221
	F	61-60-56	21,237-24,544	Y-25,048-19	2,588	2,115-82	1,576	371-168	36	437
	R	19-16-40	17,451-19,718	Y-19,947-20	1,033	536-52	424	59-53	22	475
Cypress, Calif. (2,7)	P	68-47-40	23,724-28,824	None	4,601	2,405-52	1,824	332-249	1,306	890
Danville, Va.	P	89-85-44	13,416-18,845	None	1,666	1,666-100	1,666	...-...	...	...
	F	91-91-56	13,416-18,845	None	1,608	1,608-100	1,608	...-...	...	...
	R	50-33-40	9,090-12,771	None	600	600-100	600	...-...	...	...
Davis, Calif. (7)	P	55-42-40	21,151-25,140	None	2,692	1,644-61	1,363	144-137	698	350
	F	31-30-56	20,023-23,793	None	1,294	1,056-82	877	94-85	58	180
De Kalb, Ill. (7)	P	52-43-..	19,531-25,940	Y-27,368-19	1,911	1,610-84	1,310	188-112	73	228
	F	43-42-..	16,392-23,343	Y-24,771-19	1,624	1,509-93	1,123	295-91	9	106
Decatur, Ala.	P	71-62-40	13,442-17,550	None	1,931	1,553-80	1,328	162-63	92	286
	F	82-82-56	11,648-15,158	None	1,770	1,600-90	1,351	166-83	10	160
	R	84-37-40	9,061-11,934	None	2,535	1,295-51	1,086	131-78	326	914
Deerfield Beach, Fla.	P	101-80-40	19,146-25,043	Y-27,047-20	3,400	3,127-92	2,659	354-114	20	253
	F	75-68-48	18,015-23,517	Y-25,399-20	2,499	2,442-98	2,078	288-76	...	57
	R	33-18-40	14,113-18,450	Y-19,925-20	1,296	718-55	595	79-44	20	558
Del City, Okla.	P	43-33-40	15,582-20,748	Y-22,188-18	868	868-100	695	124-49	...	...
	F	32-29-56	15,582-20,748	Y-22,188-18	738	738-100	634	56-48	...	...
	R	27-21-40	11,460-15,240	Y-16,680-18	455	455-100	359	64-32	...	...
Del Rio, Tex.	P	54-43-40	12,765-16,270	Y-18,070-25	929	929-100	830	96-3	...	...
	F	31-31-40	12,765-16,270	Y-18,070-25	652	652-100	582	68-2	...	...
	R	2-2-..	...-...	..-...-..	4	4-100	4	...-...	...	...
Delhi tp, Ohio (2)	P	20-18-..	20,855-24,268	Y-25,268-16	925	795-86	643	99-53	55	75
Denton, Tex.	P	82-73-40	18,005-20,841	Y-...-..	2,325	1,851-80	1,635	176-40	88	386
	F	97-92-56	16,336-18,957	Y-...-..	2,698	2,385-88	2,093	242-50	39	274
	R	30-1-40	11,057-13,041	Y-...-..	1,618	607-38	528	60-19	1	1,010
Dothan, Ala.	P	117-82-40	13,065-16,770	None	2,968	2,434-82	2,081	272-81	94	440
	F	103-101-56	13,065-16,770	None	2,187	2,110-96	1,796	237-77	4	73
	R	83-45-40	9,100-11,700	None	1,502	1,074-72	899	118-57	135	293
Downers Grove v, Ill. (7)	P	74-58-40	19,468-29,202	None	2,514	2,271-90	1,781	409-81	17	226
	F	33-24-44	16,761-25,141	None	1,444	1,128-78	990	98-40	130	186
Dunedin, Fla. (7)	P	61-47-40	16,027-21,866	Y-22,466-8	2,340	1,766-75	1,365	304-97	16	558
	F	37-36-56	14,790-20,650	Y-21,250-8	1,224	961-79	782	128-51	12	251
	R	33-21-40	10,208-14,309	Y-14,909-8	1,294	605-47	463	82-60	23	666
East Brunswick tp, N.J. (1,7)	P	91-79-..	22,620-26,436	Y-29,080-30	3,958	3,584-91	2,971	362-251	54	320
East Detroit, Mich.	P	53-47-40	20,247-23,997	Y-25,597-20	2,504	2,213-88	1,639	396-178	35	256
	F	25-24-56	18,890-22,640	Y-24,240-20	1,229	1,052-86	778	191-83	56	121
	R	16-16-40	17,108-17,576	Y-19,176-25	1,009	604-60	439	104-61	4	401
East Lansing, Mich.	P	66-50-40	17,368-24,066	Y-25,026-20	2,395	2,068-86	1,701	223-144	120	207
	F	51-50-50	18,097-23,378	Y-24,338-20	1,966	1,528-78	1,223	171-134	303	135
	R	12-0-40	16,390-19,406	Y-20,366-20	569	303-53	235	38-30	...	266
Easton, Pa.	P	59-48-40	16,453-18,672	Y-19,372-30	...	...-..	...	...-...	...	...
	F	42-42-56	17,410-18,672	Y-19,372-30	...	...-..	...	...-...	...	...
	R	11-0-40	14,144-14,144	Y-14,844-30	...	...-..	...	...-...	...	...
Edmond, Okla.	P	62-41-40	13,151-23,534	None	1,959	1,657-85	1,414	179-64	27	275
	F	63-56-56	12,536-21,765	None	1,668	1,337-80	1,193	84-60	246	85

Table 3/18 continued **POLICE, FIRE, AND REFUSE COLLECTION AND DISPOSAL DEPARTMENTS: PERSONNEL, SALARIES, AND EXPENDITURES FOR CITIES OVER 10,000: 1984**

City	Depart-ment	Total personnel, no. uniformed, duty hours per week	Entrance, maximum salary ($)	Longevity pay, maximum ($), no. years to max.	Reported expenditures (in thousands): Total expenditures (A) ($)	Total personnel expenditures (B), % of (A) ($)	Salaries and wages (C) ($)	City contrib. to employee retirement, insurance (D) ($)	Capital outlay (E) ($)	All other (F) ($)
25,000-49,999 continued										
Edmond, Okla. (cont'd)	R	52-34-40	11,152-16,228	None	1,202	867-72	737	84-46	130	205
Elk Grove Village v, Ill. (7)	P	83-74-40	20,553-29,918	None	3,230	2,591-80	2,212	239-140	216	423
	F	91-83-56	20,245-29,470	None	3,650	3,348-92	2,611	586-151	42	260
Elkhart, Ind.	P	101-96-40	16,947-18,547	Y-19,147-4	3,423	3,117-91	2,259	743-115	...	306
	F	103-102-56	16,809-18,516	Y-19,116-4	3,335	3,211-96	2,252	833-126	...	124
	R	13-13-40	16,723-...	Y-17,323-4	233	233-100	193	26-14	...	...
Elmhurst, Ill. (7)	P	70-57-40	18,909-24,955	Y-27,737-10	3,105	2,481-80	1,995	395-91	66	558
	F	39-38-56	18,201-24,465	Y-27,100-10	1,762	1,596-91	1,198	328-70	9	157
Elmira, N.Y.	P	88-85-40	15,090-18,195	Y-19,863-20	3,086	2,866-93	1,957	775-134	63	157
	F	100-99-40	15,281-20,594	Y-...-20	3,524	3,401-97	2,380	877-144	5	118
	R	16-11-40	12,313-13,832	Y-14,914-20	454	324-71	226	69-29	32	98
Emporia, Kan.	P	50-35-40	15,202-18,705	None	1,220	1,177-96	942	193-42	43	...
	F	43-43-56	14,560-18,705	None	1,060	1,039-98	836	170-33	21	...
	R	26-13-40	10,044-13,116	None	467	428-92	347	51-30	39	...
Enfield t, Conn. (3)	P	89-73-40	18,460-20,234	None	2,841	2,496-88	1,897	370-229	56	289
	R	13-0-40	17,160-17,160	None	555	265-48	213	24-28	...	290
Fairborn, Ohio	P	49-35-40	18,450-24,066	Y-24,547-20	1,817	1,434-79	1,140	190-104	20	363
	F	43-42-54	17,888-23,317	Y-23,783-20	1,587	1,375-87	1,046	234-95	29	183
	R	11-0-40	12,542-16,037	Y-16,412-25	766	264-34	214	30-20	...	502
Fairfield, Ohio (1,7)	P	44-37-40	17,014-21,986	Y-23,305-20	1,609	1,414-88	1,118	190-106	...	195
	F	..-...-..	.....-.....	..-...-..	288	161-56	152	9-...	...	127
Falls tp, Pa. (1,7)	P	45-39-40	17,388-22,952	Y-24,517-25	1,861	1,574-85	1,262	85-227	47	240
Farmington, N.M. (7)	P	119-93-40	13,813-23,753	Y-26,722-25	3,865	3,120-81	2,763	270-87	172	573
	F	74-71-56	13,182-22,284	Y-25,069-25	2,290	2,082-91	1,815	194-73	71	137
Ferndale, Mich. (7)	P	54-50-40	20,708-25,402	None	2,524	2,159-86	1,593	360-206	11	354
	F	38-38-54	19,322-24,336	None	1,946	1,733-89	1,333	254-146	27	186
Findlay, Ohio (7)	P	67-56-40	15,434-21,133	None	1,979	1,644-83	1,317	236-91	6	329
	F	58-57-56	15,434-21,133	None	1,769	1,554-88	1,191	279-84	31	184
Flagstaff, Ariz.	P	77-55-40	18,408-22,008	None	2,510	1,908-76	1,667	193-48	145	457
	F	63-62-56	17,592-21,048	None	1,804	1,545-86	1,421	84-40	92	167
	R	23-23-40	14,100-16,824	None	1,038	430-41	361	56-13	130	478
Florence, Ala.	P	83-62-40	12,559-15,912	None	2,041	1,567-77	1,249	183-135	106	368
	F	68-67-56	12,559-15,912	None	1,614	1,432-89	1,121	185-126	1	181
	R	43-20-40	10,944-11,440	None	1,077	701-65	538	83-80	38	338
Fond Du Lac, Wis.	P	71-63-39	17,321-21,457	Y-22,357-15	2,564	2,378-93	1,747	509-122	78	108
	F	71-70-56	19,477-20,994	Y-21,895-15	2,581	2,446-95	1,710	599-137	1	134
	R	13-13-40	16,966-17,383	None	624	313-50	248	43-22	...	311
Fontana, Calif.	P	79-54-40	20,406-27,000	None	3,402	2,833-83	1,862	388-583	17	552
Fort Dodge, Iowa	P	56-48-40	15,122-19,302	None	1,825	1,503-82	1,020	333-150	52	270
	F	37-37-56	14,394-21,278	None	910	841-92	747	...-94	11	58
	R	12-0-40	13,582-16,515	None	344	247-72	193	25-29	...	97
Fort Myers, Fla.	P	129-102-40	15,132-22,100	Y-29,000-16	5,746	2,691-47	2,314	268-109	2,334	721
	F	85-77-52	12,792-18,304	Y-18,654-16	2,845	1,884-66	1,532	282-70	667	294
	R	41-41-40	8,424-14,872	None	1,644	699-43	593	73-33	98	847
Fort Pierce, Fla. (3)	P	92-75-40	14,040-20,363	None	2,632	2,132-81	1,767	283-82	137	363
	R	24-0-40	11,710-16,973	None	1,365	343-25	283	40-20	136	886
Franklin tp, N.J. (1,7)	P	77-67-40	15,000-24,000	Y-26,000-25	2,728	2,449-90	1,981	299-169	56	223
	F	1-0-35	16,000-26,000	Y-26,000-21	34	25-74	22	3-...	...	9
Frederick, Md.	P	77-66-40	14,337-20,039	None	2,512	2,170-86	1,827	247-96	92	250
	F	21-21-56	15,054-20,039	None	773	703-91	597	59-47	70	...
	R	24-17-40	10,700-14,954	None	775	460-59	388	44-28	70	245
Fridley, Minn.	P	44-33-40	18,684-26,688	Y-29,090-15	1,374	1,108-81	918	129-61	74	192
	F	6-5-57	20,765-27,116	Y-27,980-15	311	241-77	212	20-9	4	66
Gadsden, Ala.	P	111-98-40	9,734-12,833	Y-13,860-25	3,355	2,727-81	2,060	435-232	141	487
	F	125-116-56	9,734-12,841	Y-13,868-25	3,498	3,115-89	2,363	498-254	56	327
	R	61-36-40	7,758-10,670	Y-11,524-25	1,829	1,039-57	793	122-124	325	465
Gaithersburg, Md.	P	8-7-40	16,299-21,829	None	217	184-85	153	22-9	12	21
Galesburg, Ill. (7)	P	65-49-49	17,191-20,896	Y-22,985-25	2,181	1,847-85	1,414	354-79	93	241
	F	50-50-56	17,191-19,901	Y-21,891-25	1,790	1,696-95	1,120	521-55	36	58
Gardena, Calif. (7)	P	101-82-40	22,920-27,840	Y-30,210-5	5,153	4,306-84	3,216	900-190	91	756
	F	51-49-56	23,532-28,620	Y-31,053-5	2,904	2,627-90	2,008	517-102	12	265
Garfield Heights, Ohio	P	47-47-40	18,404-22,642	Y-22,882-5	1,490	1,430-96	1,102	219-109	60	...
	F	40-40-56	18,370-22,580	Y-22,820-5	1,269	1,269-100	938	233-98	...	...
	R	51-31-40	16,245-17,077	Y-17,197-5	391	391-100	318	40-33	...	...
Gastonia, N.C. (7)	P	139-123-40	12,896-17,290	Y-17,940-20	3,011	2,460-82	2,219	144-97	184	367
	F	89-84-56	11,700-15,678	Y-16,328-20	1,769	1,689-95	1,547	79-63	21	59
	R	94-40-40	8,736-11,700	Y-12,350-20	1,820	1,289-71	1,037	189-63	278	253
Gates t, N.Y. (1,7)	P	28-24-..	19,528-25,123	Y-25,923-20	1,203	1,073-89	778	252-43	18	112
Glendora, Calif. (3,7)	P	62-43-40	23,894-29,043	None	3,474	2,975-86	2,585	267-123	5	494
Glenview v, Ill.	P	70-56-40	22,344-29,952	Y-30,652-..	2,699	2,244-83	2,244	...-...	26	429
	F	41-39-53	21,528-28,848	Y-29,548-..	1,600	1,318-82	1,318	...-...	34	248
Gloucester, Mass. (7)	P	74-67-40	19,000-19,770	Y-20,470-25	2,073	1,923-93	1,806	...-117	2	148
	F	86-85-42	18,744-19,769	Y-20,519-25	2,444	2,228-91	2,094	...-134	118	98
Gloucester tp, N.J. (3,7)	P	80-64-40	19,500-23,377	Y-29,069-20	3,073	2,620-85	2,050	405-165	100	353
Goldsboro, N.C.	P	87-68-40	11,702-16,121	Y-16,766-20	1,878	1,424-76	1,233	159-32	92	362
	F	67-66-56	11,122-15,357	Y-15,971-20	1,246	1,070-86	927	119-24	34	142
	R	46-22-40	8,711-11,985	Y-12,464-20	891	530-59	459	55-16	17	344
Grand Forks, N.D.	P	76-60-40	15,948-21,780	Y-21,835-20	2,249	2,019-90	1,730	195-94	29	201

Table 3/18 continued **POLICE, FIRE, AND REFUSE COLLECTION AND DISPOSAL DEPARTMENTS: PERSONNEL, SALARIES, AND EXPENDITURES FOR CITIES OVER 10,000: 1984**

City	Depart-ment	Total personnel, no. uniformed, duty hours per week	Entrance, maximum salary ($)	Longevity pay, maximum ($), no. years to max.	Reported expenditures (in thousands): Total expenditures (A) ($)	Total personnel expenditures (B), % of (A) ($)	Salaries and wages (C) ($)	City contrib. to employee retirement, insurance (D) ($)	Capital outlay (E) ($)	All other (F) ($)
25,000-49,999 continued										
Grand Forks, N.D. (cont'd)	F	65-64-56	15,948-21,780	Y-21,835-20	1,907	1,841-97	1,594	161-86	8	58
	R	38-0-40	13,248-17,988	Y-18,043-20	1,374	799-58	672	57-70	166	409
Grand Island, Neb. (7)	P	48-43-40	14,452-17,506	Y-19,257-10	1,419	1,138-80	945	116-77	40	241
	F	48-47-56	13,578-17,498	Y-19,248-10	1,503	1,312-87	943	301-68	65	126
	R	1-1-40	10,605-12,447	Y-13,662-10	35	20-57	17	1-2	...	15
Grand Junction, Colo.	P	99-67-40	19,398-25,428	None	2,625	1,994-76	1,749	153-92	99	532
	F	66-64-56	18,174-23,844	None	2,213	1,845-83	1,605	159-81	6	362
	R	17-4-40	15,867-19,812	None	748	414-55	372	22-20	10	324
Granite City, Ill. (7)	P	55-51-40	20,383-21,470	Y-23,188-15	2,103	1,777-84	1,358	302-117	63	263
	F	45-44-52	20,397-21,478	Y-23,196-15	1,607	1,510-94	1,116	298-96	...	97
Greenville, N.C.	P	91-75-40	13,520-18,637	Y-19,476-20	1,890	1,605-85	1,388	162-55	99	186
	F	79-77-56	12,262-18,637	Y-19,476-20	1,651	1,480-90	1,282	151-47	57	114
	R	61-39-40	9,579-12,563	Y-13,129-20	1,045	821-79	701	82-38	29	195
Gresham, Ore. (7)	P	61-32-40	16,650-23,496	None	2,228	1,803-81	1,320	302-181	44	381
	F	39-30-56	17,280-22,032	None	1,560	1,284-82	964	200-120	81	195
Groton t, Conn. (3)	P	53-46-40	17,456-21,088	Y-21,680-20	1,968	1,726-88	1,364	266-96	87	155
Gulfport, Miss. (7)	P	81-81-40	12,067-13,741	Y-15,421-20	1,934	1,323-68	1,136	116-71	79	532
	F	96-96-60	12,068-13,741	Y-15,421-30	2,045	1,705-83	1,529	81-95	15	325
Hagerstown, Md. (7)	P	106-86-40	12,925-18,450	None	2,792	2,427-87	1,984	337-106	52	313
	F	56-55-48	12,500-17,400	None	1,313	1,128-86	927	144-57	82	103
	R	...-...-..	...-...	...-...-..	255	...-...	...	...-...	...	255
Hallandale, Fla.	P	119-99-40	19,988-25,586	Y-...-..	3,936	3,281-83	2,638	441-202	107	548
	F	80-74-50	19,068-23,632	Y-28,360-20	2,399	2,183-91	1,768	291-124	24	192
	R	35-10-40	11,063-...	Y-...-..	1,164	800-69	608	109-83	53	311
Hattiesburg, Miss.	P	113-82-40	11,177-13,566	None	1,888	1,515-80	1,420	48-47	20	353
	F	93-92-..	11,177-13,566	None	1,512	1,355-90	1,307	...-48	1	156
	R	72-44-40	6,968-7,820	None	1,028	675-66	544	92-39	5	348
Hendersonville, Tenn. (7)	P	42-33-40	13,524-17,676	None	966	731-76	591	93-47	24	211
	F	21-20-48	12,264-16,008	None	486	392-81	331	41-20	8	86
Highland t, Ind. (1,7)	P	40-27-40	17,763-21,943	Y-...-20	1,219	1,201-99	981	79-141	18	...
	F	...-...-..	...-...	...-...-..	65	53-82	53	...-...	12	...
	R	2-0-40	...-...	Y-...-20	20	20-100	12	1-7	...	...
Highland Park, Ill. (7)	P	72-58-40	21,264-28,598	Y-29,742-20	3,024	2,583-85	2,054	417-112	22	419
	F	45-44-56	20,493-27,560	Y-28,662-20	2,129	1,933-91	1,462	383-88	40	156
Hilo, Hawaii	P	319-251-40	16,344-19,764	Y-23,136-18	10,405	7,195-69	7,195	...-...	409	2,801
	F	217-198-56	17,964-21,864	Y-25,704-18	6,937	5,047-73	5,047	...-...	1,087	803
Hobbs, N.M. (7)	P	98-65-40	19,560-25,560	None	2,886	2,549-88	2,162	318-69	127	210
	F	59-58-56	16,068-21,024	None	2,132	1,514-71	1,280	189-45	449	169
Hoffman Estates v, Ill. (7)	P	75-57-40	18,995-26,545	None	2,147	1,899-88	1,838	56-5	96	152
	F	54-53-56	18,173-26,250	None	1,673	1,353-81	1,304	44-5	175	145
Holland, Mich. (7)	P	59-50-40	20,665-24,544	Y-25,344-20	2,345	1,866-80	1,587	200-79	87	392
	F	26-26-56	20,051-23,593	Y-24,393-20	1,012	830-82	690	92-48	10	172
Hopkinsville, Ky.	P	49-44-40	11,226-13,786	None	967	656-68	560	57-39	29	282
	F	60-59-56	11,226-16,251	None	1,142	864-76	755	64-45	35	243
	R	76-48-40	7,280-10,319	None	1,323	891-67	745	95-51	117	315
Hot Springs, Ark. (7)	P	77-62-40	12,093-13,998	Y-14,598-20	1,553	1,237-80	1,111	61-65	38	278
	F	74-74-56	12,093-13,278	Y-13,878-20	1,406	1,254-89	1,137	47-70	19	133
	R	25-8-40	9,861-11,241	Y-11,841-20	1,052	343-33	278	49-16	82	627
Houma, La.	P	67-56-40	12,730-12,730	Y-12,927-..	2,468	1,856-75	1,564	172-120	101	511
	F	55-51-60	11,359-11,359	Y-11,556-..	1,554	1,310-84	1,116	106-88	8	236
	R	50-50-40	9,360-9,360	None	2,397	1,025-43	863	82-80	729	643
Huntington Park, Calif. (3)										
Hurst, Tex. (7)	P	72-47-40	20,856-22,800	Y-...-..	2,132	1,736-81	1,451	176-109	79	317
	F	40-38-56	20,856-22,800	Y-...-..	1,183	1,069-90	891	114-64	4	110
Hutchinson, Kan.	P	62-54-40	15,720-18,480	Y-19,930-25	2,250	1,852-82	1,375	368-109	91	307
	F	77-75-56	15,414-17,712	Y-19,752-34	2,454	2,197-90	1,614	473-110	35	222
	R	14-8-40	12,462-14,112	Y-15,612-25	611	302-49	255	27-20	52	257
Ithaca, N.Y.	P	72-65-40	14,960-18,427	Y-19,276-17	1,589	1,421-89	1,421	...-...	49	119
	F	57-55-40	16,539-22,703	None	1,486	1,273-86	1,273	...-...	18	195
	R	11-6-40	9,464-11,045	Y-11,245-21	254	166-65	166	...-...	37	51
Jackson, Mich. (7)	P	86-74-40	18,569-23,918	Y-25,757-18	4,091	3,553-87	2,373	1,001-179	43	495
	F	63-61-56	19,040-23,368	Y-25,207-18	3,518	3,223-92	2,161	930-132	34	261
Jackson tp, N.J. (1)	P	62-49-40	...-...	...-...-..	1,685	1,569-93	1,472	97-...	...	116
Jacksonville, Ark.	P	44-34-40	12,754-16,132	None	1,092	892-82	732	111-49	53	147
	F	45-45-56	13,113-18,523	None	986	877-89	797	31-49	15	94
	R	17-10-40	9,433-13,935	None	590	260-44	213	34-13	146	184
Jamestown, N.Y.	P	75-70-40	17,317-19,890	Y-20,430-20	2,560	2,314-90	1,650	567-97	65	181
	F	95-94-40	16,585-19,429	Y-19,949-20	3,069	2,898-94	2,069	701-128	13	158
	R	20-0-40	15,995-16,494	None	549	442-81	384	39-19	107	...
Johnstown, Pa. (7)	P	58-55-40	17,270-18,260	Y-19,860-10	1,978	1,725-87	1,278	146-301	84	169
	F	58-58-42	15,700-16,600	Y-18,200-10	1,717	1,577-92	1,148	140-289	...	140
Kennewick, Wash. (7)	P	58-46-40	19,800-25,500	Y-26,820-20	2,379	1,859-78	1,517	183-159	21	499
	F	34-33-50	20,172-25,428	Y-26,088-20	1,303	1,100-84	987	54-59	11	192
Kentwood, Mich. (7)	P	39-33-40	19,021-25,965	Y-26,965-25	1,215	1,056-87	876	119-61	1	158
	F	12-12-45	17,689-24,147	Y-25,147-25	435	380-87	323	41-16	1	54
Killeen, Tex.	P	129-97-40	14,343-19,236	Y-20,436-25	3,301	2,695-82	2,296	290-109	187	419
	F	69-62-56	13,452-17,604	Y-18,804-25	1,736	1,530-88	1,312	172-46	27	179
	R	41-0-40	9,102-11,328	Y-12,528-25	1,081	682-63	560	70-52	156	243

Table 3/18 continued **POLICE, FIRE, AND REFUSE COLLECTION AND DISPOSAL DEPARTMENTS: PERSONNEL, SALARIES, AND EXPENDITURES FOR CITIES OVER 10,000: 1984**

City	De- part- ment	Total personnel, no. uniformed, duty hours per week	Entrance, maximum salary ($)	Longevity pay, maximum ($), no. years to max.	Reported expenditures (in thousands): Total expendi- tures (A) ($)	Total personnel expendi- tures (B), % of (A) ($)	Salaries and wages (C) ($)	City contrib. to employee retirement, insurance (D) ($)	Capital outlay (E) ($)	All other (F) ($)
25,000-49,999 continued										
Kingsville, Tex.	P	60-44-40	14,658-17,904	Y-18,048-25	1,362	1,078-79	944	86-48	96	188
	F	33-32-56	11,817-16,461	Y-16,604-25	790	666-84	565	53-48	24	100
	R	34-15-40	9,288-11,016	No11,208	815	489-60	384	35-70	67	259
Kinston, N.C.	P	69-63-40	11,401-15,280	None	...	...-..	...	...-...	...	...
	F	81-74-56	10,858-14,552	None	...	...-..	...	...-...	...	...
	R	69-0-40	9,849-13,199	None	...	...-..	...	...-...	...	...
Kirkwood, Mo.	P	63-52-40	18,575-25,004	None	1,985	1,734-87	1,449	210-75	39	212
	F	39-39-63	17,199-24,079	None	1,213	1,015-84	872	93-50	29	169
	R	14-8-40	12,635-17,061	None	740	295-40	246	33-16	63	382
Kokomo, Ind.	P	127-100-40	17,095-17,275	Y-18,245-25	3,745	3,323-89	2,223	779-321	54	368
	F	123-122-56	17,050-17,230	Y-18,040-20	3,659	3,496-96	2,241	944-311	12	151
	R	29-27-40	14,394-14,394	None	770	692-90	555	64-73	...	78
La Crosse, Wis. (7)	P	104-85-38	...-...	..-...-..	...	...-..	...	...-...	...	...
	F	100-100-56	...-...	..-...-..	...	...-..	...	...-...	...	...
La Mirada, Calif. (3,4,7)										
La Puente, Calif. (2,4)										
Lakeland, Fla.	P	156-123-40	15,933-20,343	Y-20,823-20	4,256	3,505-82	3,203	221-81	74	677
	F	99-93-56	14,456-18,450	Y-18,930-20	2,619	2,290-87	2,086	144-60	55	274
	R	45-22-40	10,276-13,104	Y-13,584-20	2,012	701-35	633	43-25	19	1,292
Lakewood tp, N.J. (1)	P	82-82-40	17,577-27,015	Y-29,042-..	2,469	2,469-100	2,050	320-99	...	...
	F	3-3-40	17,577-27,015	Y-29,042-..	92	92-100	88	...-4	...	...
	R	18-18-40	10,510-17,383	Y-...-..	300	300-100	255	34-11	...	...
Lancaster, Calif. (3,4,7)										
Lauderdale Lakes, Fla. (4)										
Lauderhill, Fla. (7)	F	75-73-52	15,963-24,592	None	2,248	1,681-75	1,434	162-85	342	225
Lawrence, Ind. (7)	P	39-35-40	16,640-16,640	Y-19,115-2	796	717-90	673	4-40	79	...
	F	7-0-40	...-...	..-...-..	299	132-44	116	8-8	167	...
Leavenworth, Kan.	P	49-37-40	16,047-19,576	Y-19,936-15	1,474	1,177-80	937	119-121	4	293
	F	45-45-53	15,254-18,716	Y-19,076-15	1,069	1,002-94	813	103-86	...	67
	R	11-7-40	13,262-16,227	Y-16,587-15	475	268-56	217	23-28	...	207
Lee'S Summit, Mo.	P	63-49-40	15,674-24,069	None	1,809	1,335-74	1,150	118-67	128	346
	F	59-51-56	15,674-24,069	None	1,788	1,435-80	1,234	127-74	16	337
Lewiston, Idaho (7)	P	56-42-40	15,099-19,536	None	1,622	1,288-79	978	224-86	41	293
	F	48-46-56	14,998-18,694	Y-18,934-20	1,620	1,333-82	1,018	240-75	28	259
Lewiston, Me.	P	77-68-37	14,481-17,412	None	2,399	2,077-87	1,434	571-72	74	248
	F	102-101-42	13,392-15,752	None	2,558	2,295-90	1,598	599-98	28	235
	R	17-10-40	11,752-12,230	None	519	260-50	222	30-8	89	170
Lexington t, Mass. (7)	P	61-54-38	16,375-21,985	Y-22,435-20	1,786	1,604-90	1,530	60-14	37	145
	F	62-57-42	15,473-20,048	Y-20,448-20	1,666	1,543-93	1,437	92-14	...	123
Lima, Ohio (7)	P	92-78-40	16,908-20,138	Y-21,538-25	2,336	2,251-96	1,776	329-146	85	...
	F	83-82-56	16,908-20,138	Y-21,538-25	2,331	2,229-96	1,688	405-136	102	...
Linden, N.J.	P	134-124-37	17,655-26,326	Y-27,526-4	4,593	4,453-97	3,492	752-209	...	140
	F	135-131-42	17,958-24,060	Y-25,260-4	4,809	4,398-91	3,446	749-203	...	411
	R	27-0-40	17,118-19,115	Y-20,315-4	681	598-88	525	35-38	...	83
Littleton, Colo. (7)	P	62-53-40	21,240-28,512	None	2,214	1,925-87	1,678	122-125	22	267
	F	87-85-56	18,564-25,152	None	3,337	2,913-87	2,508	208-197	60	364
Livingston tp, N.J. (1,7)	P	47-41-40	14,753-24,482	Y-26,930-25	1,864	1,636-88	1,307	232-97	...	228
	F	...-...-..	...-...	..-...-..	227	132-58	88	13-31	...	95
Lodi, Calif. (7)	P	70-54-40	18,845-22,906	None	3,175	2,039-64	1,477	484-78	77	1,059
	F	49-48-56	17,436-21,193	None	2,423	1,588-66	1,139	394-55	80	755
Logan, Utah	P	46-41-40	16,187-23,338	None	1,039	952-92	818	77-57	53	34
	F	31-29-40	13,682-21,882	None	813	792-97	669	74-49	18	3
	R	30-4-40	12,200-18,766	None	606	579-96	469	74-36	20	7
Lombard v, Ill. (7)	P	62-50-40	17,223-25,440	None	2,494	2,066-83	1,689	299-78	33	395
	F	33-32-56	16,883-24,120	None	1,807	1,167-65	1,020	104-43	333	307
Longview, Wash.	P	57-48-40	22,920-28,176	Y-28,776-25	2,181	1,892-87	1,539	190-163	12	277
	F	41-40-51	23,274-27,036	Y-27,636-25	1,399	1,338-96	1,161	67-110	2	59
	R	21-0-40	21,132-26,544	Y-26,784-25	1,333	607-46	490	63-54	4	722
Los Altos, Calif. (7)	P	27-26-40	25,914-30,744	None	1,377	1,127-82	950	127-50	22	228
	F	39-39-56	25,092-29,712	None	1,933	1,540-80	1,273	192-75	81	312
Lufkin, Tex.	P	45-38-40	14,677-18,327	Y-20,730-25	1,361	1,082-80	950	105-27	82	197
	F	57-53-56	14,647-15,986	Y-18,389-25	1,430	1,290-90	1,156	99-35	25	115
	R	23-11-40	9,921-10,400	None	1,072	373-35	322	37-14	169	530
Lynwood, Calif. (4,7)	F	35-34-56	20,414-27,620	Y-28,370-15	2,017	1,705-85	1,085	582-38	17	295
Mc Candless t, Pa. (1,7)	P	31-27-40	19,200-24,000	Y-24,575-..	1,281	1,112-87	946	76-90	53	116
Mc Keesport, Pa. (7)	P	56-56-40	18,332-18,332	Y-...-..	1,249	1,249-100	1,249	...-...	...	...
	F	50-50-40	18,450-18,450	Y-...-..	1,005	1,005-100	1,005	...-...	...	...
Madison Heights, Mich.	P	62-55-40	21,315-25,240	Y-27,259-5	3,286	2,979-91	2,406	345-228	8	299
	F	37-37-54	21,360-26,136	Y-28,227-5	1,988	1,795-90	1,448	215-132	8	185
	R	9-0-40	18,470-20,342	Y-21,969-5	897	354-39	301	23-30	1	542
Manchester t, Conn. (7)	P	110-85-40	19,716-23,042	Y-23,442-20	3,802	3,094-81	2,297	640-157	134	574
	F	73-72-42	19,044-22,627	Y-23,027-20	2,662	2,125-80	1,715	274-136	26	511
	R	7-1-40	...-...	..-...-..	911	138-15	110	19-9	158	615
Manhattan, Kan. (4,7)	F	47-44-56	13,014-14,973	Y-15,273-..	1,105	1,048-95	732	233-83	10	47
Manhattan Beach, Calif. (7)	P	66-55-40	22,380-28,128	Y-...-10	3,674	2,770-75	2,032	650-88	...	904
	F	30-30-56	23,832-28,968	None	1,569	1,367-87	1,008	297-62	...	202
	R	...-...-..	...-...	..-...-..	1,455	461-32	391	44-26	...	994
Manheim tp, Pa. (1,7)	P	32-23-40	13,886-22,917	Y-23,942-25	1,104	913-83	827	46-40	38	153

Table 3/18 continued **POLICE, FIRE, AND REFUSE COLLECTION AND DISPOSAL DEPARTMENTS: PERSONNEL, SALARIES, AND EXPENDITURES FOR CITIES OVER 10,000: 1984**

					Reported expenditures (in thousands)					
City	Department	Total personnel, no. uniformed, duty hours per week	Entrance, maximum salary ($)	Longevity pay, maximum ($), no. years tc max.	Total expenditures (A) ($)	Total personnel expenditures (B), % of (A) ($)	Salaries and wages (C) ($)	City contrib. to employee retirement, insurance (D) ($)	Capital outlay (E) ($)	All other (F) ($)
25,000-49,999 continued										
Mankato, Minn. (7)	P	38-35-40	20,604-23,520	Y-25,872-30	2,395	1,729-72	1,616	56-57	24	642
	F	39-38-40	20,688-24,084	Y-26,492-30	1,706	1,633-96	1,531	44-58	5	68
Maple Heights, Ohio	P	49-47-40	20,696-22,817	Y-23,657-25	1,975	1,610-82	1,341	163-106	108	257
	F	44-43-54	20,696-22,817	Y-23,657-25	1,579	1,464-93	1,165	194-105	14	101
	R	19-12-40	15,845-18,969	Y-19,809-25	673	481-71	395	54-32	112	80
Maplewood, Minn. (2,7)	P	49-39-40	18,918-28,020	Y-30,540-16	2,065	1,565-76	1,342	163-60	168	332
Marietta, Ga.	P	116-96-40	12,856-19,956	None	2,965	2,335-79	1,894	441-...	153	477
	F	108-106-40	12,856-19,956	None	2,498	2,229-89	1,855	374-...	92	177
	R	42-22-40	8,698-14,178	None	1,211	515-43	449	66-...	247	449
Marion, Ind.	P	74-70-40	14,078-15,723	None	2,042	1,782-87	1,156	492-134	77	183
	F	81-80-56	14,078-15,723	None	2,205	2,067-94	1,329	585-153	...	138
	R	9-9-40	11,875-11,875	None	265	142-54	113	13-16	...	123
Marion, Ohio	P	36-35-40	19,219-23,774	Y-24,638-20	1,849	1,664-90	1,281	240-143	...	185
	F	38-38-48	19,194-23,762	Y-24,626-20	2,042	1,874-92	1,401	336-137	...	168
	R	31-15-40	14,997-18,429	Y-19,293-20	1,233	805-65	640	86-79	89	339
Marshalltown, Iowa (7)	P	49-40-40	17,285-20,093	Y-20,821-20	1,499	1,335-89	1,067	207-61	51	113
	F	34-34-53	18,408-20,632	Y-21,739-20	1,043	968-93	759	175-34	40	35
Massillon, Ohio	P	45-43-40	17,320-19,110	Y-20,282-30	1,727	1,661-96	1,262	236-163	66	...
	F	41-41-52	17,320-19,110	Y-20,282-30	1,298	1,259-97	923	217-119	39	...
	R	10-9-40	13,354-14,456	Y-15,558-30	329	299-91	227	32-40	30	...
Medford, Ore. (7)	P	80-63-40	19,644-24,408	None	3,202	2,761-86	2,077	509-175	77	364
	F	80-79-56	20,322-24,636	Y-24,901-20	2,814	2,606-93	1,971	476-159	29	179
Melbourne, Fla. (7)	P	...-...-..	...-...	..-...-..	1,467	491-33	...	394-97	...	976
	F	95-89-56	13,803-17,588	None	2,465	2,074-84	1,649	348-77	78	313
Melrose, Mass.	P	57-54-40	16,698-19,362	Y-20,112-10	1,628	1,501-92	1,450	...-51	4	123
	F	65-64-48	17,088-19,712	Y-20,462-10	1,706	1,637-96	1,566	...-71	...	69
	R	11-8-40	11,482-13,015	Y-13,480-10	405	149-37	138	...-11	...	256
Menlo Park, Calif. (3)	P	53-40-40	24,505-31,249	None	2,595	2,158-83	1,735	265-158	34	403
Menomonee Falls v, Wis. (7)	P	69-53-40	21,606-25,980	None	2,701	2,390-88	1,814	400-176	121	190
	F	4-4-40	19,774-21,959	None	483	213-44	166	33-14	...	270
Mentor, Ohio (7)	P	79-58-40	18,798-23,712	None	2,794	2,316-83	1,860	308-148	92	386
	F	45-38-56	18,798-23,712	None	2,022	1,830-91	1,445	293-92	16	176
Merced, Calif.	P	73-46-40	18,324-18,324	None	2,923	2,171-74	1,801	232-138	45	707
	F	52-49-56	18,156-18,156	None	1,898	1,631-86	1,276	167-188	35	232
	R	20-20-40	13,476-13,476	None	1,283	471-37	357	57-57	149	663
Meridian, Miss. (7)	P	131-95-40	12,646-18,325	Y-19,344-30	3,003	2,550-85	1,929	497-124	103	350
	F	103-98-56	12,334-16,203	Y-17,223-30	1,861	1,749-94	1,577	74-98	6	106
	R	78-46-40	8,528-11,190	Y-12,210-30	1,279	998-78	809	114-75	65	216
Michigan City, Ind.	P	93-84-40	14,912-14,912	Y-16,912-20	2,258	1,929-85	1,830	94-5	124	205
	F	81-80-56	14,725-14,985	Y-16,985-20	2,066	1,761-85	1,622	135-4	67	238
	R	25-0-40	12,875-12,875	None	694	487-70	427	59-1	92	115
Middletown, Ohio (7)	P	110-86-40	18,102-22,775	Y-23,459-20	3,468	3,370-97	2,687	509-174	34	64
	F	77-76-54	18,102-22,775	Y-23,459-20	2,988	2,680-90	2,010	506-164	101	207
	R	5-0-40	...-...	..-...-..	987	95-10	80	11-4	59	833
Middletown tp, Pa. (1,7)	P	56-45-40	20,934-25,143	Y-26,652-15	2,239	1,845-82	1,517	184-144	78	316
Midland, Mich.	P	47-44-40	20,795-26,215	Y-28,050-20	1,958	1,657-85	1,275	296-86	65	236
	F	45-44-56	21,770-24,895	Y-26,413-20	2,049	1,616-79	1,262	264-90	29	404
	R	21-0-40	19,254-19,906	None	1,032	394-38	300	62-32	14	624
Midwest City, Okla.	P	116-85-40	14,988-21,942	Y-23,142-20	2,659	2,596-98	2,154	299-143	...	63
	F	96-89-56	14,988-20,180	Y-22,664-20	2,272	2,188-96	1,938	135-115	...	84
	R	57-1-40	11,916-16,166	Y-17,366-20	1,310	1,054-80	850	130-74	...	256
Milford, Conn. (7)	P	116-107-40	18,696-21,205	Y-21,947-20	4,807	4,202-87	2,917	936-349	89	516
	F	118-111-42	18,696-21,491	Y-22,243-20	4,609	4,163-90	2,921	892-350	31	415
	R	27-21-40	13,853-15,642	Y-16,189-20	1,393	759-54	592	76-91	...	634
Minnetonka, Minn. (7)	P	52-43-40	23,307-28,296	None	1,913	1,546-81	1,330	159-57	78	289
	F	4-0-..	...-...	..-...-..	249	164-66	150	11-3	15	70
Minot, N.D. (7)	P	67-59-40	16,104-20,544	None	1,904	1,569-82	1,436	76-57	86	249
	F	46-43-56	16,104-20,544	None	1,213	1,109-91	998	72-39	38	66
	R	18-10-40	13,236-16,896	None	701	354-50	311	28-15	53	294
Miramar, Fla. (7)	P	74-62-40	18,028-24,175	None	2,194	2,194-100	1,865	277-52	...	...
	F	39-35-56	15,044-21,164	None	1,042	1,042-100	894	124-24	...	...
Mishawaka, Ind. (7)	P	80-70-48	15,037-16,325	None	1,662	1,488-90	1,386	100-2	104	70
	F	84-84-52	15,037-16,325	None	1,722	1,663-97	1,573	88-2	17	42
Missoula, Mont. (7)	P	67-53-40	16,226-18,690	Y-...-..	1,822	1,595-88	1,316	174-105	69	158
	F	50-49-41	15,468-18,492	Y-...-..	1,561	1,345-86	1,107	157-81	5	211
Moline, Ill. (7)	P	78-62-56	21,411-25,554	Y-26,717-14	3,198	2,867-90	2,163	577-127	64	267
	F	65-64-56	20,216-24,255	Y-25,322-14	2,794	2,685-96	1,805	760-120	14	95
	R	17-0-40	19,406-22,110	Y-23,212-14	814	509-63	420	58-31	...	305
Monroeville, Pa. (1)	P	49-43-40	23,039-24,923	Y-...-5	1,848	1,657-90	1,375	155-127	41	150
	R	25-9-50	17,807-17,807	..-...-.. 5	867	665-77	563	69-33	...	202
Monrovia, Calif. (7)	P	58-44-40	21,432-28,008	None	2,547	2,175-85	1,675	396-104	69	303
	F	33-29-56	21,912-27,972	None	1,312	1,207-92	909	244-54	13	92
Monterey, Calif. (7)	P	63-50-40	21,000-26,250	None	2,928	2,455-84	2,011	444-...	28	445
	F	50-47-48	19,500-24,400	None	2,179	1,905-87	1,522	383-...	71	203
Morgantown, W.Va.	P	50-47-40	...-16,747	Y-17,827-..	1,462	1,166-80	1,054	35-77	34	262
	F	45-44-52	...-16,747	Y-17,827-..	1,093	959-88	770	121-68	9	125
	R	28-28-40	11,616-12,498	Y-13,578-..	672	482-72	392	57-33	30	160
Murfreesboro, Tenn.	P	80-64-..	13,071-15,435	..-...-..	1,261	1,219-97	1,219	...-...	42	...

Table 3/18 continued **POLICE, FIRE, AND REFUSE COLLECTION AND DISPOSAL DEPARTMENTS: PERSONNEL, SALARIES, AND EXPENDITURES FOR CITIES OVER 10,000: 1984**

					Reported expenditures (in thousands)					
City	Department	Total personnel, no. uniformed, duty hours per week	Entrance, maximum salary ($)	Longevity pay, maximum ($), no. years to max.	Total expenditures (A) ($)	Total personnel expenditures (B), % of (A) ($)	Salaries and wages (C) ($)	City contrib. to employee retirement, insurance (D) ($)	Capital outlay (E) ($)	All other (F) ($)
25,000-49,999 continued										
Murfreesboro, Tenn. (cont'd)	F	96-93-..	13,071-15,435	..-...-..	1,541	1,525-99	1,525	...-...	16	...
	R	50-33-..	12,613-13,313	..-...-..	736	676-92	676	...-...	60	...
Muskegon, Mich. (7)	P	74-65-40	23,297-24,097	Y-...-25	3,022	2,319-77	1,762	315-242	...	703
	F	48-47-56	21,896-23,761	Y-...-25	1,907	1,689-89	1,278	231-180	...	218
	R	1-0-41	...-...	Y-...-25	790	23-3	20	3-...	...	767
Nacogdoches, Tex.	P	53-47-40	15,660-19,044	Y-20,244-25	1,278	954-75	823	107-24	60	264
	F	57-53-56	15,660-19,044	Y-20,244-25	1,715	1,203-70	1,038	136-29	300	212
	R	34-34-40	10,088-14,534	None	608	474-78	413	49-12	45	89
Nampa, Idaho (7)	P	42-32-40	15,135-18,411	None	899	887-99	714	114-59	12	...
	F	31-30-56	13,980-16,239	Y-18,852-20	738	736-100	549	139-48	2	...
National City, Calif. (7)	P	90-66-40	20,688-25,152	Y-25,182-25	3,355	2,535-76	2,008	440-87	49	771
	F	40-38-56	19,584-23,592	Y-23,622-25	1,744	1,308-75	1,033	224-51	156	280
Naugatuck t, Conn.	P	42-40-40	15,144-17,152	Y-17,302-20	1,066	880-83	748	38-94	34	152
	F	29-28-42	15,812-17,188	Y-17,388-20	986	636-65	534	40-62	13	337
	R	7-7-40	14,248-15,537	Y-15,687-20	318	182-57	137	33-12	...	136
Neptune tp, N.J. (1)	P	63-63-40	15,000-23,793	Y-25,293-25	1,912	1,912-100	1,912	...-...	...	...
	R	27-27-40	10,000-16,000	Y-16,280-25	430	430-100	430	...-...	...	...
New Berlin, Wis. (2,7)	P	65-52-39	21,467-25,298	Y-25,528-12	2,213	1,945-88	1,570	358-17	71	197
New Castle, Pa.	P	41-37-40	14,209-20,974	Y-22,414-30	1,187	1,084-91	913	42-129	21	82
	F	36-36-42	14,420-19,275	Y-20,463-30	1,112	1,004-90	778	120-106	...	108
	R	12-5-40	15,673-15,673	Y-16,072-20	323	240-74	205	10-25	32	51
New London, Conn.	P	83-76-40	18,176-20,116	Y-20,666-5	2,112	1,933-92	1,776	136-21	39	140
	F	72-71-42	18,248-19,681	Y-20,181-5	1,749	1,570-90	1,521	37-12	9	170
	R	16-2-40	13,520-14,560	Y-15,060-5	319	316-99	267	44-5	2	1
Newark, Calif.	P	54-42-40	23,112-27,312	None	2,552	1,783-70	1,528	161-94	117	652
	F	32-32-56	22,956-27,192	None	1,452	1,144-79	916	179-49	16	292
Newark, Ohio	P	57-50-40	12,084-17,388	Y-17,983-20	1,901	1,563-82	1,216	267-80	57	281
	F	68-64-42	12,105-16,182	Y-16,777-20	2,228	1,990-89	1,502	395-93	42	196
Newington t, Conn. (1,7)	P	51-47-40	16,978-21,658	Y-22,658-19	1,947	1,749-90	1,335	263-151	8	190
	F	...-...-...	...-...	..-...-..	181	25-14	25	...-...	...	156
Niles v, Ill. (7)	P	62-50-40	21,138-28,340	Y-29,430-15	2,685	2,370-88	1,976	265-129	18	297
	F	49-48-56	21,138-28,288	Y-29,376-15	1,976	1,786-90	1,413	267-106	24	166
North Las Vegas, Nev. (7)	P	128-98-40	20,752-25,944	Y-28,538-20	4,895	3,885-79	3,155	522-208	11	999
	F	60-59-56	18,169-24,887	Y-27,376-20	2,292	2,088-91	1,727	300-61	1	203
North Miami, Fla. (3)										
North Miami Beach, Fla.	P	109-93-40	20,291-25,614	Y-26,614-7	3,995	3,510-88	3,178	318-14	29	456
	R	37-37-40	13,004-...	Y-14,054-7	1,610	861-53	711	146-4	45	704
North Richland Hills, Tex. (7)	P	58-42-40	19,637-23,259	Y-24,219-20	1,419	1,195-84	1,112	41-42	85	139
	F	39-38-56	19,637-23,259	Y-24,219-20	1,128	953-84	888	35-30	44	131
North Tonawanda, N.Y.	P	53-50-40	18,030-21,444	Y-21,844-20	1,944	1,785-92	1,356	355-74	52	107
	F	58-57-40	18,021-21,435	Y-21,835-20	2,232	1,935-87	1,410	443-82	82	215
	R	23-15-40	13,781-16,140	Y-16,540-20	802	517-64	428	65-24	65	220
Northampton, Mass.	P	51-48-40	13,872-16,272	Y-18,192-25	1,116	1,109-99	1,063	...-46	...	7
	F	55-54-42	13,872-16,272	Y-18,192-25	1,436	1,261-88	1,214	...-47	100	75
Northampton tp, Pa. (1,7)	P	33-26-42	16,800-24,107	Y-26,885-15	1,510	1,338-89	885	323-130	27	145
Northglenn, Colo. (3)	P	61-48-40	18,857-26,535	Y-27,015-7	2,195	1,675-76	1,491	104-80	68	452
	R	7-0-40	16,596-22,314	Y-22,794-7	445	184-41	162	9-13	...	261
Norwood, Ohio (7)	P	53-52-36	19,443-22,660	None	1,854	1,633-88	1,217	253-163	68	153
	F	63-60-26	19,443-28,660	None	2,295	2,121-92	1,481	449-191	44	130
	R	19-7-40	12,771-16,556	None	642	465-72	344	57-64	...	177
Novato, Calif. (3)	P	61-46-40	20,796-25,284	..-...-..	2,245	1,887-84	1,559	328-...	53	305
Oak Forest, Ill. (7)	P	38-29-45	17,247-23,504	None	1,414	1,121-79	929	136-56	21	272
	F	15-14-56	17,247-24,454	None	660	538-82	452	70-16	25	97
Oak Ridge, Tenn. (7)	P	50-43-40	15,475-24,042	None	1,309	1,282-98	997	251-34	11	16
	F	40-40-56	15,475-24,042	None	1,259	1,232-98	968	236-28	4	23
Olathe, Kan.	P	77-71-40	17,709-27,789	None	2,578	2,094-81	1,657	333-104	145	339
	F	43-43-56	14,890-23,365	None	1,371	1,081-79	843	174-64	134	156
	R	21-21-40	15,743-20,282	None	887	517-58	436	47-34	150	220
Olympia, Wash.	P	63-48-40	21,696-26,856	None	2,761	1,965-71	1,722	115-128	31	765
	F	51-49-56	22,344-27,660	None	1,868	1,662-89	1,466	84-112	10	196
	R	16-2-40	18,168-22,068	Y-22,548-15	1,032	418-41	348	46-24	33	581
Oshkosh, Wis. (7)	P	94-89-40	19,007-23,085	Y-23,421-20	3,205	2,931-91	2,178	538-215	121	153
	F	99-98-56	15,331-21,840	Y-22,176-20	3,234	3,037-94	2,193	608-236	65	132
	R	21-20-40	17,513-18,075	Y-18,411-20	736	549-75	427	73-49	46	141
Pacifica, Calif. (7)	P	50-40-40	22,176-26,628	None	2,087	1,518-73	1,275	176-67	11	558
	F	25-24-56	19,956-24,984	None	1,122	839-75	710	98-31	50	233
Palm Springs, Calif. (7)	P	128-87-40	19,308-23,460	None	7,727	4,284-55	3,143	1,018-123	28	3,415
	F	65-63-56	19,380-23,592	None	3,395	2,404-71	1,826	484-94	32	959
Paramount, Calif. (2,4,7)										
Paramus b, N.J. (1)	P	109-90-40	18,143-28,351	Y-28,918-5	4,166	3,828-92	3,146	491-191	51	287
	F	...-...-...	...-...	..-...-..	79	77-97	67	6-4	...	2
	R	22-0-40	17,547-17,547	Y-17,898-5	583	546-94	468	46-32	23	14
Paris, Tex.	P	47-32-40	16,250-...	Y-16,298-25	1,016	848-83	720	87-41	47	121
	F	38-37-56	15,574-...	Y-15,622-25	835	738-88	660	53-25	...	97
	R	14-8-40	10,218-10,218	None	578	185-32	147	25-13	...	393
Parkersburg, W.Va.	P	80-62-40	15,194-17,347	Y-20,347-..	2,202	1,626-74	1,323	214-89	...	576
	F	75-73-48	14,437-17,984	Y-20,984-..	2,101	1,599-76	1,302	211-86	11	491
	R	17-17-40	12,334-14,518	None	619	309-50	253	38-18	15	295

Table 3/18 continued **POLICE, FIRE, AND REFUSE COLLECTION AND DISPOSAL DEPARTMENTS: PERSONNEL, SALARIES, AND EXPENDITURES FOR CITIES OVER 10,000: 1984**

City	De-part-ment	Total personnel, no. uniformed, duty hours per week	Entrance, maximum salary ($)	Longevity pay, maximum ($), no. years to max.	Reported expenditures (in thousands) Total expenditures (A) ($)	Total personnel expenditures (B), % of (A) ($)	Salaries and wages (C) ($)	City contrib. to employee retirement, insurance (D) ($)	Capital outlay (E) ($)	All other (F) ($)
25,000-49,999 continued										
Parsippany-Troy Hills tp, N.J. (1,7)	P	125-107-37	...-...	Y-...-15	3,840	3,311-86	3,311	...-...	...	529
Pekin, Ill. (7)	P	56-51-40	19,099-23,990	Y-25,670-15	2,051	1,701-83	1,511	33-157	77	273
	F	56-55-56	19,099-25,040	Y-27,044-20	1,893	1,722-91	1,502	22-198	20	151
Pennsauken tp, N.J. (7)	P	86-60-40	19,600-23,145	Y-24,533-..	4,021	3,442-86	2,635	335-472	...	579
	F	9-8-40	19,600-23,145	Y-24,533-..	727	328-45	248	33-47	160	239
Petaluma, Calif. (7)	P	66-47-40	21,084-25,008	None	2,197	1,925-88	1,562	260-103	106	166
	F	46-44-56	19,146-22,704	None	1,440	1,319-92	1,035	202-82	15	106
Petersburg, Va.	P	122-96-40	13,718-17,519	Y-20,282-10	2,187	2,187-100	1,819	248-120	...	...
	F	112-108-56	12,443-15,889	Y-18,392-10	2,218	2,218-100	1,828	249-141	...	...
	R	19-4-40	8,807-11,286	Y-13,057-10	371	371-100	304	40-27	...	...
Pinellas Park, Fla. (7)	P	56-43-40	16,536-22,797	None	1,827	1,263-69	1,137	92-34	98	466
	F	61-54-56	15,142-21,199	None	2,064	1,285-62	1,142	106-37	450	329
Piscataway tp, N.J. (1,7)	P	98-82-40	16,300-25,080	Y-28,968-25	3,358	3,196-95	2,631	326-239	53	109
	R	5-0-40	11,440-18,096	Y-19,905-25	200	115-58	94	12-9	...	85
Pittsburg, Calif. (3,7)	P	54-50-40	24,222-28,092	None	2,990	2,244-75	1,805	313-126	...	746
Placentia, Calif. (2,7)	P	60-44-40	23,063-27,714	None	2,305	1,915-83	1,478	332-105	48	342
Plantation, Fla. (1,7)	P	142-105-40	18,413-25,779	None	3,727	3,059-82	2,867	192-...	241	427
Pleasant Hill, Calif. (3,4)										
Pleasanton, Calif. (7)	P	57-41-40	21,012-25,608	None	2,524	2,187-87	1,570	392-225	21	316
	F	38-36-56	20,904-25,440	None	1,632	1,546-95	1,119	281-146	28	58
Plum b, Pa. (1)	P	25-20-40	16,400-23,600	Y-23,960-2	810	810-100	634	83-93	...	...
	R	11-11-40	19,011-20,009	None	223	223-100	209	14-...	...	...
Plymouth, Minn. (1,7)	P	38-30-40	21,900-30,120	None	1,522	1,118-73	967	103-48	7	397
	F	...-...-...	...-...	..-...-..	300	122-41	116	5-1	56	122
Pocatello, Idaho	P	87-67-40	16,500-21,384	Y-22,082-20	2,543	2,158-85	1,869	160-129	56	329
	F	70-67-56	18,500-20,653	Y-21,199-20	2,570	2,255-88	1,737	386-132	32	283
	R	21-1-40	16,900-17,940	Y-18,840-20	1,362	646-47	517	79-50	12	704
Ponca City, Okla.	P	61-49-40	14,442-17,131	Y-17,251-20	1,533	1,225-80	1,046	89-90	79	229
	F	69-68-50	13,756-16,340	Y-16,460-20	1,706	1,459-86	1,246	100-113	150	97
	R	43-23-40	12,780-12,780	Y-13,153-20	1,007	702-70	568	74-60	1	304
Port Huron, Mich.	P	73-56-40	18,745-21,179	Y-23,297-20	2,667	2,378-89	1,845	394-139	6	283
	F	57-55-56	19,545-22,083	Y-24,291-20	2,118	1,957-92	1,609	246-102	8	153
	R	9-0-40	18,720-18,720	Y-20,592-20	484	254-52	194	45-15	3	227
Portage, Ind.	P	46-36-40	14,800-19,336	Y-19,696-13	1,133	944-83	828	68-48	19	170
	F	39-38-60	14,800-19,634	Y-19,994-13	990	901-91	795	58-48	19	70
	R	12-8-40	13,146-13,146	None	284	197-69	171	15-11	...	87
Portage, Mich.	P	56-45-40	23,379-27,030	Y-27,571-5	2,283	1,602-70	1,602	...-...	11	670
	F	30-29-54	22,358-25,191	Y-25,391-5	1,173	836-71	836	...-...	24	313
Portsmouth, Ohio	P	44-39-40	14,892-17,976	None	1,230	1,112-90	821	156-135	...	118
	F	38-38-48	14,892-17,976	None	1,169	1,087-93	788	179-120	...	82
	R	16-15-40	13,041-15,267	Y-15,627-30	509	319-63	236	33-50	...	190
Poughkeepsie, N.Y.	P	82-73-40	19,226-21,795	Y-22,495-15	2,781	2,602-94	1,822	656-124	18	161
	F	67-62-40	18,850-20,630	Y-21,330-15	2,830	2,741-97	2,009	616-116	1	88
	R	16-7-40	11,241-12,956	Y-14,237-25	691	394-57	304	59-31	5	292
Poway, Calif. (4,7)	F	28-27-60	17,844-21,768	None	1,324	1,049-79	799	135-115	33	242
Quincy, Ill.	P	86-71-40	16,297-21,356	None	2,649	2,394-90	1,832	487-75	46	209
	F	80-73-56	16,017-21,356	None	2,532	2,408-95	1,690	648-70	22	102
	R	16-15-40	14,518-15,246	None	443	338-76	284	39-15	...	105
Rahway, N.J. (7)	P	77-72-37	17,942-25,177	Y-28,054-24	2,050	2,050-100	2,050	...-...	...	...
	F	62-62-42	18,177-23,968	Y-26,845-24	1,757	1,644-94	1,644	...-...	...	113
	R	...-...-...	...-...	..-...-..	506	...-..	...	...-...	...	506
Rancho Palos Verdes, Calif. (3,4,7)										
Raytown, Mo. (3)										
Redding, Calif.	P	68-38-40	19,481-30,000	None	3,953	3,323-84	2,522	552-249	172	458
	F	53-51-60	19,450-25,432	None	2,657	2,146-81	1,623	382-141	24	487
	R	40-38-40	19,377-22,362	None	1,660	1,285-77	985	199-101	...	375
Redlands, Calif.	P	77-57-40	20,460-24,876	None	2,985	2,872-96	2,075	741-56	113	...
	F	48-46-56	20,952-25,464	None	1,887	1,736-92	1,265	446-25	151	...
	R	33-19-40	14,171-17,017	None	1,063	911-86	657	223-31	152	...
Rialto, Calif. (7)	P	70-46-40	19,680-23,928	None	2,637	2,144-81	1,589	326-229	142	351
	F	48-45-56	18,744-22,788	None	1,898	1,582-83	1,123	263-196	103	213
Richfield, Minn. (5,7)	P	51-41-40	20,208-26,832	..-...-..	1,791	1,783-100	1,515	211-57	6	2
	F	25-24-56	22,185-27,330	Y-29,244-..	1,017	987-97	739	214-34	2	28
Richland, Wash.	P	55-44-40	23,304-26,400	None	2,506	2,233-89	1,655	489-89	78	195
	F	42-40-51	20,676-25,440	None	1,924	1,705-89	1,301	325-79	23	196
	R	20-19-40	19,164-22,128	None	1,735	687-40	537	72-78	341	707
Ridgewood v, N.J.	P	45-38-40	21,842-28,050	Y-30,855-21	1,436	1,367-95	1,105	206-56	...	69
	F	38-37-56	18,168-28,050	Y-30,855-21	1,276	1,205-94	1,027	133-45	...	71
	R	29-20-40	15,220-20,753	Y-22,828-21	583	526-90	473	22-31	...	57
Ridley tp, Pa. (1,7)	P	35-35-42	...-...	Y-...-..	1,766	1,336-76	1,090	73-173	42	388
	F	...-...-..	...-...	..-...-..	203	25-12	5	...-20	...	178
	R	27-27-..	...-...	None	632	490-78	459	31-...	...	142
Rock Hill, S.C.	P	79-64-40	12,626-17,742	None	1,980	1,642-83	1,345	228-69	1	337
	F	62-60-56	12,022-16,910	None	1,356	1,281-94	1,090	140-51	1	74
	R	55-23-40	9,422-12,626	None	1,230	771-63	647	81-43	16	443
Rock Island, Ill.	P	106-81-40	19,470-23,665	Y-26,065-20	4,398	3,486-79	2,601	788-97	121	791
	F	68-67-56	18,542-22,538	Y-24,938-20	3,005	2,502-83	1,712	725-65	43	460
	R	13-8-40	15,078-18,327	Y-20,727-20	687	400-58	347	40-13	...	287
Rockville, Md. (2)	P	35-25-..	17,438-22,254	Y-23,314-12	1,117	1,046-94	827	164-55	14	57

Table 3/18 continued **POLICE, FIRE, AND REFUSE COLLECTION AND DISPOSAL DEPARTMENTS: PERSONNEL, SALARIES, AND EXPENDITURES FOR CITIES OVER 10,000: 1984**

					Reported expenditures (in thousands)					
City	Department	Total personnel, no. uniformed, duty hours per week	Entrance, maximum salary ($)	Longevity pay, maximum ($), no. years to max.	Total expenditures (A) ($)	Total personnel expenditures (B), % of (A) ($)	Salaries and wages (C) ($)	City contrib. to employee retirement, insurance (D) ($)	Capital outlay (E) ($)	All other (F) ($)
25,000-49,999 continued										
Rockville, Md. (cont'd)	R	32-0-40	15,781-16,275	Y-17,903-12	1,380	930-67	719	159-52	...	450
Rockville Centre v, N.Y. (1)	P	57-52-40	21,670-30,185	Y-31,685-20	3,080	2,978-97	2,201	650-127	102	...
	F	...-...-..	...-...	..-...-..	44	...-..	...	...-...	44	...
	R	23-23-40	16,768-17,520	Y-18,705-16	698	693-99	499	143-51	5	...
Rocky Mount, N.C.	P	128-106-40	13,702-18,356	Y-19,266-25	3,281	2,755-84	2,267	390-98	196	330
	F	101-99-56	13,052-17,472	Y-18,356-25	2,147	2,009-94	1,649	283-77	14	124
	R	81-50-40	10,192-13,702	Y-14,378-25	2,005	1,279-64	1,039	179-61	135	591
Rome, Ga.	P	84-64-40	11,978-16,858	None	2,213	1,743-79	1,453	196-94	108	362
	F	155-151-56	11,978-16,858	None	3,814	3,136-82	2,751	211-174	312	366
	R	61-29-40	8,113-11,411	None	1,326	844-64	694	92-58	204	278
Rosemead, Calif. (3,4)										
Roseville, Minn. (1,7)	P	37-34-40	18,213-28,020	Y-30,541-16	1,438	1,245-87	1,058	128-59	36	157
Roswell, N.M.	P	108-88-42	15,824-19,702	Y-...-..	2,982	2,353-79	1,970	295-88	145	484
	F	87-86-56	15,069-18,764	Y-...-..	2,187	2,050-94	1,701	270-79	...	137
	R	52-31-40	10,710-13,335	Y-...-..	1,246	997-80	831	106-60	110	139
Saginaw tp, Mich. (1)	P	32-28-40	19,441-24,666	None	1,156	890-77	741	95-54	78	188
	F	3-2-40	...-...	None	501	184-37	170	8-6	145	172
St. Charles, Mo. (7)	P	86-78-40	16,275-19,361	Y-20,602-11	2,280	1,892-83	1,521	206-165	123	265
	F	65-63-56	15,300-18,268	None	1,908	1,589-83	1,282	181-126	210	109
St. Cloud, Minn. (1)	P	68-55-40	20,315-23,760	None	2,128	2,096-98	1,545	433-118	32	...
	F	52-51-56	20,170-23,436	None	1,819	1,813-100	1,289	424-100	6	...
	R	15-15-40	16,740-17,856	None	777	777-100	638	75-64	...	...
St. Louis Park, Minn. (5,7)	P	60-49-40	19,600-27,218	Y-29,668-13	2,444	2,087-85	1,687	305-95	62	295
	F	27-27-56	22,218-27,006	None	1,109	1,052-95	772	242-38	8	49
San Clemente, Calif. (7)	P	53-38-40	24,624-28,512	None	2,327	1,765-76	1,289	304-172	8	554
	F	24-22-..	28,788-33,324	None	1,410	1,071-76	838	169-64	47	292
San Gabriel, Calif. (7)	P	56-46-40	22,758-26,988	None	2,379	2,114-89	1,670	362-82	...	265
	F	35-34-56	21,996-26,088	None	1,464	1,387-95	1,087	248-52	...	77
San Luis Obispo, Calif. (7)	P	73-48-40	20,322-24,312	None	3,027	2,413-80	1,731	399-283	118	496
	F	49-45-56	20,664-24,720	None	2,077	1,676-81	1,354	242-80	64	337
San Rafael, Calif.	P	109-88-40	22,260-26,760	None	3,549	3,263-92	2,560	539-164	8	278
	F	95-93-56	21,024-25,308	None	4,064	3,689-91	2,846	659-184	184	191
Sandusky, Ohio (7)	P	41-35-40	18,876-19,824	Y-20,824-25	1,592	1,456-91	1,090	226-140	1	135
	F	52-52-52	18,876-19,824	Y-20,824-25	1,861	1,720-92	1,220	338-162	7	134
Santa Cruz, Calif.	P	76-54-40	21,480-25,668	None	3,066	2,641-86	2,110	442-89	117	308
	F	43-41-59	20,592-24,504	Y-25,117-10	1,614	1,440-89	1,155	243-42	15	159
	R	41-39-40	15,756-18,588	Y-19,053-10	1,895	967-51	797	127-43	50	878
Santa Fe, N.M.	P	120-87-40	10,564-14,886	None	3,326	2,496-75	2,020	383-93	6	824
	F	67-65-60	10,564-14,886	None	1,305	1,254-96	986	217-51	...	51
	R	47-6-40	8,714-12,231	None	1,159	603-52	512	66-25	278	278
Santa Maria, Calif.	P	76-60-40	20,953-25,580	None	3,196	2,515-79	1,907	505-103	3	678
	F	25-24-56	18,922-24,825	None	1,280	940-73	736	163-41	11	329
	R	21-3-40	14,563-18,682	None	1,826	526-29	411	84-31	537	763
Sarasota, Fla.	P	211-123-40	16,830-20,347	Y-22,202-25	5,998	4,885-81	4,143	620-122	209	904
	F	171-139-56	15,988-18,649	Y-20,341-25	5,189	4,235-82	3,440	696-99	445	509
	R	59-55-48	14,303-17,163	Y-18,879-25	2,610	1,186-45	1,016	132-38	148	1,276
Saratoga, Calif. (3,4)										
Seal Beach, Calif. (2,7)	P	53-42-40	22,359-27,192	None	2,481	2,067-83	1,581	360-126	...	414
Shaker Heights, Ohio	P	86-69-40	16,111-23,850	Y-24,850-18	3,444	3,051-89	2,305	463-283	57	336
	F	71-69-52	16,111-23,850	Y-24,850-18	2,816	2,594-92	1,850	502-242	24	198
	R	19-19-40	18,408-18,408	None	1,174	742-63	557	78-107	49	383
Shawnee, Kan. (1)	P	42-31-40	17,202-24,336	None	1,807	1,463-81	1,148	224-91	78	266
	F	7-7-40	17,202-24,336	None	382	185-48	152	33-...	57	140
Sheboygan, Wis.	P	112-94-39	18,623-21,099	Y-23,532-15	3,787	3,499-92	2,617	638-244	82	206
	F	89-84-56	19,084-21,699	Y-23,244-15	3,150	2,859-91	2,081	572-206	34	257
	R	29-0-40	17,576-18,179	Y-19,552-15	1,000	711-71	557	105-49	18	271
Shelton, Conn. (7)	P	37-33-40	16,156-17,443	None	1,116	937-84	745	104-88	52	127
	F	1-0-40	...-...	..-...-..	246	51-21	48	1-2	64	131
Sherman, Tex.	P	44-44-40	13,800-20,316	Y-21,036-..	1,867	1,507-81	1,266	170-71	72	288
	F	68-68-56	14,400-19,200	Y-19,920-..	1,737	1,572-91	1,320	172-80	53	112
	R	31-31-40	10,596-13,344	Y-14,064-..	1,069	609-57	501	70-38	119	341
Sierra Vista, Ariz.	P	34-23-40	17,508-27,168	None	961	897-93	757	99-41	25	39
	F	15-14-56	15,864-24,612	None	406	381-94	347	16-18	18	7
	R	8-1-40	12,384-19,224	None	466	152-33	124	18-10	...	314
South San Francisco, Calif. (7)	P	100-68-40	20,336-30,930	None	4,673	4,139-89	3,115	747-277	31	503
	F	82-79-56	20,064-23,791	None	4,132	3,569-86	2,562	730-277	19	544
Sparks, Nev. (7)	P	102-85-40	17,814-22,845	Y-22,974-5	4,243	3,571-84	3,025	381-165	159	513
	F	54-51-48	18,962-22,564	Y-20,686-5	2,159	2,033-94	1,670	233-130	35	91
Spartanburg, S.C.	P	128-123-40	13,166-16,515	None	2,828	2,344-83	1,800	435-109	141	343
	F	85-85-56	12,626-15,746	None	2,521	2,018-80	1,569	371-78	68	435
	R	67-32-40	8,715-10,878	None	1,448	960-66	729	172-59	146	342
Springfield, Ore.	P	68-54-40	18,492-24,456	None	2,304	2,179-95	1,679	357-143	50	75
	F	57-53-56	17,004-20,676	None	1,976	1,939-98	1,490	320-129	13	24
Springfield tp, Pa. (1)										
State College b, Pa. (1)	P	62-50-40	17,400-20,400	Y-21,400-16	1,737	1,404-81	1,244	90-70	58	275
	R	14-6-40	14,144-14,664	Y-15,064-16	606	303-50	254	33-16	16	287
Steubenville, Ohio	P	35-35-40	14,336-...	Y-15,086-...	1,162	1,089-94	761	149-179	...	73
	F	38-38-56	14,336-...	Y-15,086-..	1,278	1,203-94	792	210-201	13	62
	R	18-18-40	11,773-...	Y-12,523-..	555	359-65	265	38-56	90	106

Table 3/18 continued **POLICE, FIRE, AND REFUSE COLLECTION AND DISPOSAL DEPARTMENTS: PERSONNEL, SALARIES, AND EXPENDITURES FOR CITIES OVER 10,000: 1984**

City	Depart-ment	Total personnel, no. uniformed, duty hours per week	Entrance, maximum salary ($)	Longevity pay, maximum ($), no. years to max.	Reported expenditures (in thousands): Total expendi-tures (A) ($)	Total personnel expendi-tures (B), % of (A) ($)	Salaries and wages (C) ($)	City contrib. to employee retirement, insurance (D) ($)	Capital outlay (E) ($)	All other (F) ($)
25,000-49,999 continue										
Suffolk, Va. (7)	P	78-69-42	13,457-17,615	Y-19,228-14	1,958	1,615-82	1,290	215-110	79	264
	F	59-54-56	12,323-16,103	Y-17,615-14	1,363	1,168-86	931	155-82	13	182
	R	18-8-40	7,535-9,853	Y-10,786-14	1,158	266-23	208	35-23	89	803
Sunrise, Fla. (7)	P	119-92-40	17,500-17,500	None	3,774	3,085-82	2,467	402-216	296	393
	F	74-73-52	16,400-16,400	None	2,440	2,094-86	1,756	171-167	33	313
Tamarac, Fla. (7)	P	90-83-40	18,939-25,919	Y-26,438-20	2,418	2,406-100	2,029	242-135	12	...
	F	41-40-51	17,562-23,110	Y-23,572-20	987	986-100	819	105-62	1	...
Teaneck tp, N.J.	P	...-...-..	19,101-26,153	Y-29,291-24	2,758	2,629-95	2,629	...-...	...	129
	F	...-...-..	17,062-19,736	Y-22,104-24	2,282	2,227-98	2,227	...-...	...	55
Temple, Tex.	P	107-89-40	15,222-18,222	Y-19,422-25	2,616	2,058-79	1,823	159-76	97	461
	F	68-62-56	13,599-16,419	Y-17,619-25	1,726	1,329-77	1,261	28-40	38	359
	R	32-4-40	10,799-10,799	Y-11,999-25	1,285	442-34	398	34-10	417	426
Temple City, Calif. (3,4,7)										
Texarkana, Tex. (7)	P	92-68-40	14,296-16,128	Y-17,328-25	2,075	1,687-81	1,514	115-58	37	351
	F	72-71-56	13,602-15,360	Y-16,360-25	1,633	1,452-89	1,287	115-50	22	159
Thornton, Colo.	P	80-66-40	19,872-24,828	None	2,992	2,285-76	1,941	162-182	154	553
	F	55-53-56	18,624-24,900	Y-26,550-4	1,996	1,724-86	1,477	136-111	17	255
	R	11-11-40	18,870-23,568	None	516	314-61	265	27-22	1	201
Tinley Park v, Ill.	P	39-31-40	20,352-27,096	Y-28,056-19	1,788	1,511-85	1,239	178-94	102	175
	F	2-1-40	20,352-27,096	Y-28,056-19	388	241-62	219	18-4	56	91
Titusville, Fla.	P	71-52-40	13,042-18,408	None	1,759	1,389-79	1,166	145-78	79	291
	F	46-45-56	12,434-16,511	Y-16,802-11	1,203	979-81	818	104-57	20	204
	R	31-14-40	9,027-13,083	None	1,123	486-43	398	53-35	122	515
Torrington, Conn. (7)	P	62-60-40	15,756-16,952	Y-17,628-30	1,235	1,235-100	1,235	...-...	...	...
	F	59-59-42	16,266-17,627	Y-18,251-30	1,263	1,263-100	1,263	...-...	...	...
	R	2-2-40	13,728-16,411	Y-17,066-30	43	43-100	43	...-...	...	...
Trumbull t, Conn. (1)										
Turlock, Calif. (7)	P	56-42-40	16,945-22,596	None	1,798	1,546-86	1,170	299-77	...	252
	F	26-24-56	18,648-21,576	None	922	827-90	655	131-41	...	95
Tustin, Calif. (2,7)	P	72-52-40	23,892-28,336	None	2,958	2,574-87	2,190	233-151	12	372
Twin Falls, Idaho (7)	P	53-49-40	16,350-19,236	Y-19,836-25	1,435	1,274-89	1,031	159-84	24	137
	F	32-31-56	15,768-17,520	Y-18,120-25	986	949-96	707	178-64	14	23
Union City, Calif. (7)	P	65-50-40	25,350-30,636	None	3,248	2,673-82	2,296	272-105	...	575
	F	33-33-56	22,848-27,348	None	1,402	1,217-87	1,024	139-54	...	185
Upland, Calif. (7)	P	77-59-40	20,454-24,252	Y-24,552-20	3,299	2,513-76	2,045	378-90	56	730
	F	45-43-56	20,136-23,880	Y-24,180-20	1,968	1,687-86	1,359	274-54	37	244
Upper Arlington, Ohio	P	50-47-40	14,647-23,063	Y-23,663-21	1,678	1,525-91	1,196	206-123	54	99
	F	60-58-56	14,647-23,063	Y-23,663-21	2,208	2,062-93	1,559	353-150	21	125
	R	28-3-40	14,872-16,952	None	1,140	652-57	533	75-44	146	342
Upper Merion tp, Pa.	P	56-46-40	19,389-25,852	Y-27,477-25	2,096	1,687-80	1,358	143-186	180	229
Upper Moreland tp, Pa. (1)	P	42-33-40	20,593-24,352	Y-26,300-20	1,308	1,134-87	975	81-78	29	145
	F	...-...-..	...-...	..-...-..	87	...-..	...	...-...	...	87
	R	18-0-40	13,936-16,910	Y-18,263-20	559	337-60	278	33-26	91	131
Urbana, Ill. (7)	P	50-42-40	20,646-21,846	Y-24,031-10	1,773	1,444-81	1,154	259-31	12	317
	F	44-43-56	18,218-20,618	Y-22,680-10	1,660	1,440-87	1,034	375-31	13	207
Vacaville, Calif. (7)	P	66-44-42	22,482-26,661	Y-30,863-20	2,688	2,199-82	1,749	332-118	22	467
	F	38-37-56	23,115-27,410	Y-31,732-20	2,020	1,616-80	1,282	244-90	...	404
Valdosta, Ga.	P	78-63-40	11,566-14,289	Y-17,718-6	1,353	1,353-100	1,137	165-51	...	...
	F	76-74-56	11,038-13,631	Y-16,902-6	1,446	1,446-100	1,217	179-50	...	...
	R	50-20-40	8,686-10,528	Y-12,885-6	747	747-100	623	87-37	...	...
Visalia, Calif.	P	88-61-40	18,694-23,346	None	3,450	2,561-74	2,270	290-1	15	874
	F	36-34-56	16,442-20,534	None	1,374	1,088-79	955	132-1	8	278
	R	29-3-40	14,969-18,694	None	2,161	511-24	459	52-...	43	1,607
Vista, Calif. (7)	F	39-38-56	17,178-20,448	None	1,958	1,369-70	1,057	269-43	53	536
Walla Walla, Wash. (7)	P	34-17-40	18,792-24,000	Y-24,384-15	1,380	1,253-91	1,081	78-94	12	115
	F	34-33-56	...-...	Y-...-15	1,148	1,007-88	884	50-73	16	125
	R	10-8-40	15,648-19,980	Y-20,160-15	676	249-37	210	28-11	23	404
Wallingford t, Conn. (7)	P	73-60-40	15,549-18,906	Y-19,159-15	1,878	1,533-82	1,533	...-...	65	280
	F	61-61-42	16,198-20,883	Y-21,136-15	2,452	1,600-65	1,600	...-...	522	330
Warner Robins, Ga.	P	75-62-40	12,730-14,061	None	1,814	1,482-82	1,130	170-182	98	234
	F	70-69-60	12,126-13,395	None	1,300	1,230-95	942	147-141	1	69
	R	73-3-40	9,048-9,963	None	1,210	1,020-84	761	125-134	29	161
Watertown, N.Y.	P	65-62-40	14,957-19,007	Y-19,982-18	2,326	2,049-88	1,507	542-...	49	228
	F	102-101-40	14,957-19,007	Y-19,982-18	3,478	3,244-93	2,396	848-...	19	215
	R	22-22-40	10,279-13,036	Y-14,011-18	654	420-64	342	78-...	...	234
Wausau, Wis. (7)	P	60-53-39	17,735-20,268	Y-20,748-20	1,894	1,660-88	1,284	301-75	10	224
	F	58-58-56	17,665-20,189	Y-20,669-20	1,992	1,664-84	1,244	352-68	248	80
Wayne tp, N.J. (1,7)	P	112-100-40	19,426-24,750	Y-28,587-20	4,051	3,816-94	3,143	419-254	96	139
	F	...-...-..	...-...	..-...-..	160	...-..	...	...-...	160	...
Wellesley t, Mass.	P	...-...-..	19,174-22,561	Y-23,161-..	1,777	1,601-90	1,601	...-...	36	140
	F	...-...-..	18,809-22,128	Y-22,728-30	1,631	1,529-94	1,529	...-...	18	84
West Jordan, Utah (7)	P	44-36-40	16,500-21,876	..-...-..	1,041	976-94	684	183-109	65	...
	F	6-6-40	16,500-21,876	..-...-..	288	256-89	186	55-15	32	...
West Memphis, Ark.	P	48-43-40	12,390-16,356	None	1,205	996-83	837	122-37	35	174
	F	47-46-56	12,390-16,356	None	891	836-94	774	32-30	12	43
	R	37-22-40	8,642-10,670	None	675	497-74	425	46-26	44	134
Wethersfield t, Conn. (1,7)	P	51-40-40	18,162-22,891	Y-23,241-15	2,099	1,791-85	1,288	271-232	156	152
	F	1-1-38	17,420-23,530	Y-23,880-15	285	36-13	20	2-14	121	128
Wheaton, Ill. (7)	P	67-50-40	17,772-26,684	None	2,583	2,111-82	1,664	330-117	5	467

Table 3/18 continued POLICE, FIRE, AND REFUSE COLLECTION AND DISPOSAL DEPARTMENTS: PERSONNEL, SALARIES, AND EXPENDITURES FOR CITIES OVER 10,000: 1984

City	Depart-ment	Total personnel, no. uniformed, duty hours per week	Entrance, maximum salary ($)	Longevity pay, maximum ($), no. years to max.	Reported expenditures (in thousands): Total expenditures (A) ($)	Total personnel expenditures (B), % of (A) ($)	Salaries and wages (C) ($)	City contrib. to employee retirement, insurance (D) ($)	Capital outlay (E) ($)	All other (F) ($)
25,000-49,999 continued										
Wheaton, Ill. (cont'd)	F	18-18-56	19,225-24,776	None	978	744-76	591	113-40	11	223
White Plains, N.Y.	P	196-155-40	16,750-24,680	Y-25,420-..	9,381	8,892-95	6,046	2,447-399	...	489
	F	165-158-40	16,750-24,680	Y-25,420-..	6,980	6,613-95	4,498	1,872-243	...	367
	R	82-56-40	16,388-18,001	Y-18,301-..	3,348	2,056-61	1,531	364-161	126	1,166
Willingboro tp, N.J. (7)	P	64-41-40	19,293-25,855	Y-29,767-20	2,709	2,701-100	2,254	343-104	8	...
	F	...-...-..	...-...	..-...-..	129	...-..	...	...-...	20	109
	R	...-...-..	...-...	..-...-..	830	...-..	...	...-...	...	830
Wilmette v, Ill. (7)	P	56-41-40	22,358-27,484	Y-30,129-20	2,227	1,966-88	1,555	317-94	54	207
	F	44-44-55	21,354-26,250	Y-28,776-20	1,847	1,765-96	1,257	422-86	21	61
Wilmington, N.C. (7)	P	122-104-42	13,238-16,374	..-...-..	3,190	2,601-82	2,166	358-77	105	484
	F	118-110-56	12,016-14,890	..-...-..	3,085	2,523-82	2,060	394-69	111	451
	R	40-20-40	8,641-10,681	..-...-..	1,129	580-51	499	61-20	53	496
Wilson, N.C.	P	85-73-40	12,514-16,769	Y-...-20	1,758	1,672-95	1,440	173-59	86	...
	F	84-83-56	11,918-17,943	Y-...-20	1,810	1,703-94	1,469	176-58	107	...
	R	35-35-40	8,469-12,143	Y-...-20	898	458-51	387	47-24	100	340
Winona, Minn. (7)	P	39-37-40	18,744-22,152	Y-23,038-20	1,484	1,325-89	956	302-67	30	129
	F	38-38-56	19,944-22,920	Y-23,836-20	1,766	1,548-88	987	493-68	18	200
Woonsocket, R.I. (7)	P	108-98-38	18,226-18,988	Y-19,937-21	3,099	2,777-90	2,077	472-228	44	278
	F	135-135-42	18,316-19,041	Y-19,993-20	3,551	3,357-95	2,810	330-217	47	147
	R	3-0-40	12,337-13,163	Y-13,288-21	317	68-21	45	8-15	...	249
Yakima, Wash.	P	115-87-40	19,908-26,998	Y-28,618-20	4,362	3,703-85	2,794	612-297	47	612
	F	83-73-46	19,140-25,471	Y-26,999-20	3,439	3,024-88	2,239	556-229	124	291
	R	21-2-40	15,804-18,449	Y-19,556-20	1,074	377-35	299	44-34	1	696
Yorba Linda, Calif. (1,4,7)										
Yuma, Ariz. (7)	P	102-70-40	18,078-25,523	Y-...-..	3,123	2,669-85	2,180	388-101	112	342
	F	69-65-56	17,201-22,670	Y-...-..	2,083	1,843-88	1,620	145-78	48	192
	R	24-0-40	15,591-21,135	Y-...-..	1,190	484-41	398	54-32	6	700
Zanesville, Ohio	P	77-61-40	13,312-20,467	Y-21,491-18	2,234	1,715-77	1,358	242-115	124	395
	F	53-52-56	15,230-19,248	Y-20,403-25	1,404	1,382-98	991	284-107	22	...
	R	17-0-40	11,482-13,333	Y-13,999-17	344	344-100	274	38-32	...	...
10,000-24,999										
Aberdeen, Wash. (7)	P	47-39-40	22,920-27,828	None	...	...-..	...	...-...	...	...
	F	47-46-51	22,920-27,828	None	...	...-..	...	...-...	...	...
Acton t, Mass.	P	27-27-40	18,381-20,565	None	815	785-96	776	...-9	...	30
	F	38-34-42	18,231-20,205	Y-...-20	1,020	974-95	966	...-8	2	44
Ada, Okla.	P	37-33-40	13,380-15,456	Y-16,896-30	884	767-87	644	82-41	47	70
	F	32-32-56	13,152-15,264	Y-16,224-20	697	599-86	521	36-42	39	59
	R	23-15-40	10,692-12,384	Y-13,824-30	533	394-74	308	60-26	47	92
Adrian, Mich. (7)	P	37-31-40	19,212-22,809	Y-24,809-..	1,236	1,099-89	930	93-76	13	124
	F	22-22-..	20,368-22,052	Y-24,257-..	756	700-93	572	78-50	2	54
	R	3-3-..	15,308-18,075	None	193	60-31	51	6-3	...	133
Alamogordo, N.M. (7)	P	62-47-42	13,003-23,822	None	1,200	1,125-94	978	109-38	75	...
	F	4-0-56	12,221-15,378	None	246	121-49	107	11-3	125	...
Albany, Calif. (7)	P	32-31-40	23,508-27,552	None	1,295	1,193-92	976	104-113	25	77
	F	23-23-56	21,036-25,596	None	794	747-94	589	85-73	13	34
Albert Lea, Minn. (7)	P	37-29-40	21,507-24,190	None	1,307	1,090-83	872	180-38	...	217
	F	24-24-56	23,168-23,913	Y-25,348-30	967	831-86	602	214-15	...	136
	R	2-0-40	...-...	..-...-..	189	61-32	52	7-2	...	128
Alexander City, Ala.	P	30-25-42	11,440-14,378	None	754	613-81	490	90-33	36	105
	F	25-25-56	11,440-14,378	None	466	407-87	326	59-22	16	43
	R	9-9-40	8,902-9,963	None	313	222-71	176	34-12	9	82
Alpena, Mich. (7)	P	21-21-40	16,619-19,760	Y-20,946-20	718	661-92	542	76-43	9	48
	F	29-29-56	16,526-19,186	Y-20,337-20	916	831-91	686	88-57	24	61
Altamonte Springs, Fla.	P	78-59-40	15,691-22,172	Y-...-..	1,793	1,653-92	1,355	256-42	54	86
	F	55-49-56	15,691-22,172	Y-...-..	1,441	1,299-90	1,064	205-30	78	64
	R	11-5-40	11,948-16,881	Y-...-..	405	207-51	171	30-6	79	119
Altus, Okla.	P	42-33-40	12,576-16,452	None	869	815-94	693	99-23	5	49
	F	31-31-60	10,524-14,892	None	521	494-95	442	35-17	13	14
	R	17-3-40	9,864-15,180	None	305	295-97	250	36-9	...	10
Alvin, Tex.	P	34-29-40	18,533-22,537	Y-24,537-20	965	725-75	626	63-36	80	160
	F	1-1-40	18,533-22,537	Y-24,537-20	103	22-21	19	2-1	8	73
	R	15-15-40	11,502-13,998	Y-18,998-20	600	285-48	247	24-14	115	200
Andalusia, Ala. (7)	P	25-25-42	10,140-15,812	None	299	299-100	260	39-...	...	...
	F	17-17-56	9,900-14,800	None	250	250-100	219	31-...	...	...
	R	11-11-40	7,072-10,787	None	118	118-100	103	15-...	...	...
Andrews, Tex. (1)	P	18-18-40	18,216-21,828	Y-23,268-30	420	364-87	311	44-9	...	56
	F	...-...-..	...-...	..-...-..	42	...-..	...	...-...	...	42
	R	8-8-40	15,984-19,236	Y-20,676-30	253	175-69	149	21-5	...	78
Ankeny, Iowa (1,7)	P	25-19-48	15,424-20,984	None	752	610-81	481	83-46	17	125
	F	2-2-40	...-...	..-...-..	126	61-48	47	10-4	14	51
Apple Valley, Minn. (1,7)	P	31-21-40	16,368-25,176	Y-27,444-16	956	827-87	711	86-30	129	...
Arcata, Calif. (1,7)	P	22-17-40	16,680-20,280	Y-21,294-5	964	701-73	538	122-41	1	262
Ardmore, Okla.	P	49-37-40	12,896-13,374	Y-15,756-3	880	725-82	636	59-30	42	113
	F	45-45-56	11,589-12,084	Y-14,004-3	913	693-76	602	48-43	192	28
	R	32-25-40	10,941-11,648	Y-13,560-4	752	573-76	475	60-38	77	102
Arkadelphia, Ark.	P	22-22-48	10,500-10,500	None	491	389-79	310	52-27	29	73
	F	4-4-72	12,000-12,000	None	105	68-65	61	2-5	27	10
	R	9-9-40	7,000-7,000	None	205	140-68	111	18-11	...	65
Arnold, Mo. (3,7)	P	43-31-40	15,933-21,237	Y-22,086-10	1,206	1,057-88	863	123-71	41	108

Table 3/18 continued **POLICE, FIRE, AND REFUSE COLLECTION AND DISPOSAL DEPARTMENTS: PERSONNEL, SALARIES, AND EXPENDITURES FOR CITIES OVER 10,000: 1984**

City	Department	Total personnel, no. uniformed, duty hours per week	Entrance, maximum salary ($)	Longevity pay, maximum ($), no. years to max.	Reported expenditures (in thousands): Total expenditures (A) ($)	Total personnel expenditures (B), % of (A) ($)	Salaries and wages (C) ($)	City contrib. to employee retirement, insurance (D) ($)	Capital outlay (E) ($)	All other (F) ($)
10,000-24,999 continued										
Artesia, N.M.	P	30-29-40	16,044-19,308	None	894	708-79	556	114-38	48	138
	F	15-15-56	16,044-19,308	None	543	322-59	261	47-14	187	34
	R	6-0-40	13,953-16,752	None	258	151-59	120	23-8	35	72
Asheboro, N.C.	P	40-40-42	11,918-15,591	Y-17,150-10	732	693-95	581	90-22	39	...
	F	39-39-56	11,918-15,591	Y-17,150-10	712	708-99	594	92-22	4	...
	R	24-14-40	8,893-11,634	Y-12,797-10	317	317-100	263	41-13	...	...
Ashland, Ohio	P	37-30-40	13,919-17,133	None	751	750-100	616	104-30	1	...
	F	30-26-56	13,837-17,057	None	749	739-99	581	127-31	10	...
	R	16-16-48	9,360-16,224	None	277	277-100	232	30-15	...	...
Ashland, Ore. (7)	P	21-14-40	16,650-20,568	None	1,240	778-63	592	117-69	462	...
	F	21-21-56	16,062-19,572	None	653	641-98	500	99-42	12	...
Ashtabula, Ohio	P	37-30-40	16,291-18,135	Y-...-..	1,231	979-80	725	130-124	47	205
	F	35-34-54	16,291-17,116	Y-18,076-..	1,087	927-85	658	148-121	44	116
	R	17-16-40	15,298-15,298	Y-15,898-..	634	386-61	282	41-63	60	188
Ashwaubenon v, Wis. (5)	P	29-25-56	24,000-...	None	1,165	890-76	650	184-56	100	175
	R	21-21-40	20,000-...	Y-...-..	145	145-100	107	38-...	...	...
Aston tp, Pa. (1)	P	19-17-40	21,138-24,237	Y-27,872-20	836	721-86	603	40-78	6	109
	R	6-6-40	17,180-17,659	None	276	145-53	127	9-9	48	83
Atascadero, Calif. (7)	P	28-22-40	19,471-19,471	Y-21,467-3	864	723-84	624	65-34	30	111
	F	11-10-56	17,742-17,742	Y-19,516-3	418	325-78	282	29-14	11	82
Atchison, Kan.	P	22-17-40	12,000-18,190	None	596	514-86	423	67-24	27	55
	F	21-21-56	12,000-17,020	None	724	424-59	361	38-25	150	150
	R	6-4-40	10,000-15,000	None	182	100-55	84	10-6	...	82
Athens, Tenn.	P	36-22-40	11,614-15,239	Y-16,382-6	656	530-81	457	55-18	30	96
	F	20-20-56	11,614-15,239	Y-16,382-6	457	361-79	312	39-10	2	94
	R	9-3-40	8,218-10,786	Y-11,595-6	181	125-69	105	13-7	1	55
Atwater, Calif. (7)	P	26-20-40	17,982-21,312	Y-22,380-5	923	773-84	597	140-36	21	129
	F	7-7-56	15,162-17,976	Y-18,420-5	255	159-62	121	29-9	57	39
Auburn, Me.	P	43-41-40	12,895-14,940	None	1,207	1,017-84	809	149-59	59	131
	F	66-61-42	11,913-13,798	None	1,745	1,574-90	1,156	326-92	9	162
	R	9-6-40	9,768-11,310	None	179	134-75	105	18-11	...	45
Augusta, Me.	P	48-39-42	12,701-15,128	None	1,138	1,028-90	782	180-66	43	67
	F	31-31-54	13,474-16,048	None	849	754-89	575	133-46	38	57
	R	6-0-40	9,942-10,941	None	163	112-69	80	18-14	2	49
Avon t, Conn.	P	33-30-40	17,840-22,580	None	1,293	984-76	859	72-53	63	246
	F	...-...-..	...-...	..-...-..	152	...-..	...	...-...	...	152
	R	...-...-..	...-...	..-...-..	93	51-55	44	3-4	...	42
Avon Lake, Ohio (7)	P	24-23-40	17,836-23,572	Y-24,572-22	881	764-87	612	102-50	39	78
	F	20-19-56	17,836-23,572	Y-24,572-22	1,062	694-65	535	117-42	316	52
Bainbridge, Ga.	P	24-19-40	9,422-15,371	None	629	464-74	393	40-31	8	157
	F	15-15-56	8,775-13,680	None	310	257-83	218	22-17	4	49
	R	18-8-40	9,000-11,460	None	555	242-44	185	26-31	125	188
Balch Springs, Tex. (7)	P	25-18-40	...-...	..-...-..	528	454-86	394	31-29	2	72
	F	19-18-56	...-...	..-...-..	479	274-57	236	19-19	86	119
Ballwin, Mo. (7)	P	35-27-38	16,000-23,000	None	997	781-78	665	85-31	50	166
Barrington t, R.I.	P	25-18-37	15,560-19,095	Y-20,241-5	770	770-100	624	119-27	...	...
	F	35-35-42	13,993-19,223	Y-20,280-5	845	845-100	682	130-33	...	...
	R	6-6-40	14,323-16,329	Y-16,982-..	168	105-63	91	7-7	63	...
Barstow, Calif. (3)	P	40-28-40	16,380-19,656	None	1,398	1,085-78	802	186-97	69	244
Bartlett v, Ill. (1,7)	P	25-16-40	19,614-23,608	Y-...-..	889	646-73	548	70-28	53	190
Bartow, Fla.	P	29-24-40	17,000-18,450	Y-18,634-20	1,072	941-88	882	59-...	31	100
	F	13-13-56	16,000-18,000	Y-18,180-20	376	302-80	280	22-...	...	74
	R	24-0-40	11,000-14,000	Y-14,140-20	662	431-65	404	27-...	20	211
Batavia, Ill. (7)	P	24-19-40	17,729-26,903	None	959	678-71	641	3-34	...	281
	F	6-5-56	17,604-23,701	None	533	240-45	229	1-10	...	293
Batavia, N.Y. (7)	P	35-33-40	15,790-19,185	Y-19,685-20	980	980-100	707	233-40	...	...
	F	41-40-40	16,234-19,176	Y-19,576-20	1,219	1,219-100	884	281-54	...	...
Bath, Me.	P	24-16-40	14,100-18,400	Y-...-4	569	492-86	492	...-...	13	64
	F	18-18-42	13,541-14,851	Y-15,119-4	548	435-79	435	...-...	65	48
Beatrice, Neb. (7)	P	27-19-..	13,752-18,432	None	660	540-82	447	59-34	32	88
	F	17-17-..	13,752-19,356	None	503	479-95	343	111-25	2	22
Bedford, Ind.	P	31-25-40	16,016-16,952	None	800	651-81	568	35-48	37	112
	F	37-36-56	16,016-16,952	None	864	693-80	596	40-57	31	140
	R	7-0-40	7,488-14,269	None	157	115-73	90	15-10	4	38
Bedford, Ohio (7)	P	31-26-40	23,009-25,141	Y-26,901-20	1,247	1,115-89	853	153-109	2	130
	F	20-19-56	23,009-25,141	Y-26,901-20	777	710-91	520	110-80	11	56
Bedford Heights, Ohio	P	40-40-40	21,797-25,063	Y-26,563-20	782	782-100	782	...-...	...	...
	F	27-27-52	21,797-25,063	Y-26,563-20	699	699-100	699	...-...	...	...
	R	23-0-40	17,700-25,001	Y-26,499-20	512	512-100	512	...-...	...	...
Bellaire, Tex. (7)	P	43-38-40	16,510-24,622	Y-24,922-8	1,542	1,164-75	1,057	38-69	82	296
	F	23-22-56	16,510-24,622	Y-24,922-8	846	639-76	588	21-30	106	101
	R	12-0-40	13,910-20,748	Y-21,048-8	885	318-36	282	10-26	8	559
Belle Glade, Fla.	P	57-50-40	14,435-22,422	None	1,524	1,199-79	1,027	127-45	55	270
	F	15-14-56	13,016-20,209	None	365	312-85	271	31-10	3	50
	R	21-9-40	9,297-14,435	None	834	308-37	270	28-10	48	478
Bellefontaine, Ohio	P	18-18-40	15,400-18,400	Y-19,000-20	584	478-82	368	68-42	5	101
	F	15-15-56	15,400-18,400	Y-19,000-20	435	406-93	305	72-29	6	23
	R	11-11-40	13,125-15,413	Y-16,013-20	286	209-73	166	25-18	5	72

Table 3/18 continued **POLICE, FIRE, AND REFUSE COLLECTION AND DISPOSAL DEPARTMENTS: PERSONNEL, SALARIES, AND EXPENDITURES FOR CITIES OVER 10,000: 1984**

City	De-part-ment	Total personnel, no. uniformed, duty hours per week	Entrance, maximum salary ($)	Longevity pay, maximum ($), no. years to max.	Reported expenditures (in thousands): Total expendi-tures (A) ($)	Total personnel expendi-tures (B), % of (A) ($)	Salaries and wages (C) ($)	City contrib. to employee retirement, insurance (D) ($)	Capital outlay (E) ($)	All other (F) ($)
10,000-24,999 continued										
Bellevue, Neb. (1,7)	P	51-40-40	14,700-21,192	Y-22,092-21	1,414	1,273-90	1,062	119-92	49	92
	F	2-1-40	...-...	..-...-..	277	42-15	34	3-5	21	214
Belmont, Calif. (3,7)	P	38-30-40	21,852-26,556	None	1,851	1,539-83	1,246	226-67	19	293
Belton, Mo. (1)	P	27-21-40	17,328-21,576	None	750	593-79	493	56-44	47	110
	F	12-12-40	17,328-21,576	None	450	324-72	271	33-20	38	88
Belton, Tex. (7)	P	26-18-40	12,688-13,998	Y-...-..	543	390-72	337	37-16	49	104
	F	16-16-56	12,609-13,978	Y-...-..	383	263-69	230	23-10	27	93
	R	10-4-40	10,379-10,920	None	298	156-52	139	12-5	93	49
Belvidere, Ill. (7)	P	23-21-40	17,762-20,631	Y-22,011-25	610	523-86	492	3-28	11	76
	F	21-21-56	17,762-20,631	Y-22,011-25	570	521-91	489	5-27	20	29
Bend, Ore. (7)	P	42-32-40	18,588-22,044	None	1,423	1,250-88	927	239-84	35	138
	F	44-42-56	17,796-21,108	None	1,444	1,265-88	938	248-79	20	159
Benicia, Calif. (7)	P	35-24-..	21,834-25,896	None	1,383	1,303-94	986	244-73	4	76
	F	30-29-..	20,724-24,576	None	1,249	1,037-83	774	214-49	67	145
Bennington t, Vt. (1,7)	P	27-24-35	13,000-15,500	None	734	584-80	512	39-33	...	150
Bensenville v, Ill. (7)	P	38-26-40	17,100-26,450	Y-27,450-15	1,239	961-78	874	23-64	85	193
	F	24-23-56	17,100-24,100	Y-25,600-15	1,007	587-58	550	2-35	174	246
Benton, Ark.	P	29-21-40	12,660-16,420	Y-20,000-2	414	414-100	367	29-18	...	...
	F	34-32-55	11,673-...	Y-15,500-3	549	549-100	529	...-20	...	...
	R	7-4-40	13,500-...	Y-14,000-..	76	76-100	68	5-3	...	...
Berkeley, Mo. (7)	P	45-38-40	16,232-20,173	None	1,233	1,085-88	891	114-80	18	130
	F	30-30-54	16,232-20,173	None	725	685-94	562	72-51	1	39
Berkeley Heights tp, N.J. (1)										
Berkley, Mich. (7)	P	21-18-40	18,505-26,844	Y-28,992-20	1,034	898-87	709	137-52	19	117
	F	11-11-40	18,505-26,844	Y-28,992-25	598	472-79	372	68-32	5	121
Berlin, N.H.	P	27-25-40	16,494-17,347	Y-17,587-20	703	630-90	497	80-53	18	55
	F	26-24-42	15,804-16,459	Y-16,629-20	694	620-89	505	74-41	45	29
	R	7-4-40	15,184-15,704	None	145	144-99	120	8-16	...	1
Berwick b, Pa. (1,7)	P	12-12-40	16,182-17,232	Y-18,132-..	408	367-90	342	...-25	...	41
Bethany, Okla.	P	35-33-40	...-...	Y-...-25	863	765-89	637	92-36	47	51
	F	26-26-56	...-...	Y-...-25	667	605-91	538	37-30	15	47
	R	23-23-40	...-...	Y-...-25	560	388-69	323	47-18	70	102
Beverly Hills v, Mich. (5,7)	P	29-26-40	20,840-26,375	Y-...-..	1,415	1,191-84	912	197-82	49	175
Biddeford, Me.	P	39-39-40	12,667-15,580	Y-16,358-15	1,101	852-77	703	80-69	34	215
	F	30-30-56	11,182-14,153	Y-14,860-15	755	613-81	490	67-56	8	134
	R	9-6-40	12,148-12,148	Y-13,084-20	170	131-77	107	12-12	...	39
Big Rapids, Mich.	P	15-13-40	17,050-19,000	Y-19,760-20	361	357-99	312	21-24	...	4
	F	9-9-54	15,913-18,317	Y-18,867-20	233	227-97	196	13-18	...	6
Big Spring, Tex.	P	63-48-40	16,050-16,980	Y-17,250-25	1,632	1,325-81	1,130	154-41	109	198
	F	51-50-56	15,150-16,080	Y-16,350-25	1,238	1,106-89	952	121-33	17	115
	R	23-9-40	9,919-11,761	Y-...-25	524	403-77	342	47-14	8	113
Bloomfield t, Conn. (1)										
Bloomingdale v, Ill.	P	38-27-40	17,971-24,066	None	1,055	868-82	755	68-45	16	171
Bloomsburg t, Pa. (1,7)	P	14-11-40	13,315-16,901	Y-...-..	345	293-85	270	3-20	11	41
	F	...-...-..	...-...	..-...-..	53	...-..	...	...-...	4	49
Blytheville, Ark. (7)	P	47-43-40	11,808-12,712	Y-13,348-15	925	740-80	642	74-24	52	133
	F	28-28-56	12,050-12,716	Y-13,352-15	506	444-88	411	16-17	9	53
	R	35-20-40	7,960-8,266	Y-8,679-15	721	359-50	322	22-15	248	114
Bogalusa, La.	P	43-34-42	10,695-12,050	None	1,032	887-86	724	137-26	63	82
	F	40-40-60	10,695-12,288	None	1,122	1,013-90	649	337-27	98	11
	R	37-37-40	9,630-13,312	None	543	458-84	391	41-26	6	79
Boone, Iowa (7)	P	15-14-40	15,696-19,884	Y-...-..	560	505-90	403	60-42	...	55
	F	17-17-56	15,648-21,540	Y-...-..	536	462-86	362	55-45	59	15
Boone t, N.C. (1)	P	27-27-42	10,877-16,144	None	472	380-81	320	47-13	48	44
	R	7-4-40	10,428-13,518	None	157	104-66	87	13-4	28	25
Borger, Tex. (7)	P	31-22-40	16,248-18,348	Y-19,548-25	719	610-85	544	52-14	28	81
	F	27-27-56	15,480-17,484	Y-18,684-25	771	581-75	519	48-14	62	128
	R	9-0-40	13,503-16,644	Y-17,844-25	491	163-33	146	14-3	92	236
Bourbonnais v, Ill. (1,7)	P	18-12-40	16,700-22,000	None	531	471-89	410	29-32	18	42
	F	...-...-..	...-...	..-...-..	150	42-28	37	3-2	2	106
Bourne t, Mass.	P	36-30-40	13,975-18,977	Y-19,327-30	1,130	941-83	834	46-61	58	131
	F	32-29-42	15,176-19,929	Y-20,329-30	975	826-85	736	41-49	67	82
	R	7-7-38	13,887-17,332	Y-17,732-25	200	145-73	128	8-9	...	55
Bozeman, Mont.	P	32-25-40	13,488-16,668	Y-16,848-2	752	752-100	608	79-65	...	...
	F	20-20-48	15,138-18,048	Y-18,318-3	583	583-100	471	72-40	...	...
	R	8-0-40	18,044-18,408	Y-18,768-5	193	193-100	157	20-16	...	...
Brainerd, Minn. (7)	P	18-18-40	19,332-22,260	None	629	482-77	369	84-29	13	134
	F	7-7-40	19,839-21,955	None	233	186-80	128	47-11	3	44
Brattleboro t, Vt. (7)	P	35-25-40	13,475-15,977	None	772	636-82	571	63-2	38	98
	F	23-21-56	13,475-15,977	None	555	422-76	380	41-1	21	112
Brawley, Calif.	P	24-17-40	15,924-18,948	None	1,226	1,042-85	795	169-78	21	163
	F	18-18-58	14,604-17,376	None	838	589-70	447	97-45	218	31
	R	12-8-40	12,216-14,496	None	396	275-69	203	42-30	3	118
Brecksville, Ohio (1)	P	21-21-40	20,000-26,332	Y-26,692-3	1,126	915-81	719	126-70	74	137
	F	10-10-56	19,400-25,732	Y-26,092-3	673	263-39	215	29-19	14	396
	R	5-5-40	17,784-22,984	Y-23,344-5	1,459	848-58	674	94-80	136	475
Brenham, Tex.	P	26-19-40	14,810-18,533	Y-20,033-25	687	499-73	432	42-25	37	151
	F	9-9-56	14,124-17,680	Y-19,180-25	319	232-73	201	20-11	5	82

Table 3/18 continued **POLICE, FIRE, AND REFUSE COLLECTION AND DISPOSAL DEPARTMENTS: PERSONNEL, SALARIES, AND EXPENDITURES FOR CITIES OVER 10,000: 1984**

					Reported expenditures (in thousands)					
City	De-part-ment	Total personnel, no. uniformed, duty hours per week	Entrance, maximum salary ($)	Longevity pay, maximum ($), no. years to max.	Total expendi-tures (A) ($)	Total personnel expendi-tures (B), % of (A) ($)	Salaries and wages (C) ($)	City contrib. to employee retirement, insurance (D) ($)	Capital outlay (E) ($)	All other (F) ($)
10,000-24,999 continued										
Brenham, Tex. (cont'd)	R	16-8-40	10,056-13,296	Y-14,796-25	500	288-58	249	24-15	16	196
Brentwood b, Pa. (1)										
Bridgeton, Mo. (3)										
Bridgeton, N.J.	P	52-46-40	15,292-19,863	Y-...-..	1,563	1,563-100	1,352	139-72	...	...
	F	12-12-40	12,250-19,366	Y-...-..	401	401-100	351	32-18	...	...
Brighton, Colo. (1)	P	31-23-40	18,490-24,370	None	991	772-78	674	49-49	56	163
Bristol b, Pa. (7)	P	13-12-40	18,183-21,305	Y-22,105-20	520	431-83	388	1-42	15	74
	F	4-4-42	16,663-17,843	None	149	115-77	98	6-11	...	34
Bristol t, R.I. (1)	P	36-30-..	15,681-18,829	..-...-..	1,041	924-89	719	139-66	...	117
	F	...-...-..	...-...	..-...-..	130	11-8	11	...-...	20	99
	R	34-2-..	13,666-13,666	..-...-..	863	580-67	484	43-53	...	283
Bristol, Va.	P	44-37-40	9,942-15,671	None	1,050	888-85	746	113-29	21	141
	F	42-41-56	9,942-15,671	None	902	791-88	657	106-28	48	63
	R	19-11-40	7,300-11,648	None	421	270-64	218	36-16	79	72
Brookfield v, Ill. (7)	P	31-27-40	20,856-25,896	None	959	842-88	842	...-...	31	86
	F	13-13-54	20,856-25,896	None	426	386-91	386	...-...	11	29
Brookings, S.D. (1,7)	P	28-24-..	15,900-19,500	Y-20,000-20	987	872-88	705	106-61	25	90
	R	10-6-..	12,708-17,000	Y-17,500-20	290	229-79	180	34-15	5	56
Broomfield, Colo. (3,7)	P	45-33-40	19,860-27,012	None	1,650	1,423-86	1,223	123-77	27	200
Brown Deer v, Wis. (5,7)	P	30-22-40	21,005-25,307	None	1,024	959-94	749	174-36	4	61
	F	12-12-56	20,501-25,200	None	577	444-77	348	84-12	1	132
Brownfield, Tex.	P	20-14-48	15,444-15,444	None	576	473-82	378	65-30	7	96
	F	3-3-56	13,212-13,212	None	158	87-55	70	12-5	6	65
	R	11-0-40	9,624-9,624	None	420	192-46	154	25-13	106	122
Brownwood, Tex.	P	31-25-40	13,896-15,876	Y-17,076-25	670	536-80	485	39-12	43	91
	F	29-29-56	12,408-13,572	Y-14,772-25	526	469-89	415	43-11	13	44
	R	17-17-40	10,800-10,920	Y-11,520-25	364	199-55	178	15-6	9	156
Brunswick, Ga.	P	78-68-40	12,397-18,678	None	1,738	1,339-77	1,339	...-...	145	254
	F	38-37-54	11,856-17,846	None	691	574-83	574	...-...	...	117
	R	47-25-40	8,736-12,979	None	684	497-73	497	...-...	2	185
Brunswick t, Me.	P	36-28-40	13,333-16,614	None	905	772-85	576	148-48	40	93
	F	24-23-50	12,683-15,678	None	558	496-89	383	80-33	24	38
	R	8-5-40	13,083-15,184	None	329	142-43	120	18-4	28	159
Bucyrus, Ohio	P	22-18-40	15,412-15,912	Y-17,112-24	612	519-85	402	73-44	32	61
	F	17-17-56	14,352-15,558	Y-16,758-24	505	490-97	361	94-35	...	15
	R	8-8-40	14,164-15,364	Y-15,364-24	288	164-57	129	18-17	56	68
Buffalo Grove v, Ill. (7)	P	43-33-40	19,542-27,144	Y-27,644-20	1,529	1,292-84	1,071	130-91	87	150
	F	22-21-40	19,542-27,144	Y-27,644-20	956	627-66	531	52-44	220	109
Burkburnett, Tex.	P	17-12-40	...-...	..-...-..	359	329-92	281	38-10	29	1
	F	3-3-40	...-...	..-...-..	58	41-71	35	4-2	17	...
	R	11-5-40	...-...	..-...-..	156	156-100	131	18-7	...	...
Burlington t, Mass. (7)	P	59-55-40	18,573-22,473	Y-25,844-25	2,225	2,050-92	1,792	179-79	46	129
	F	53-53-42	17,688-21,403	Y-23,256-30	2,148	1,959-91	1,716	170-73	118	71
Burlington, N.J. (1)	P	41-36-40	19,157-23,742	Y-26,116-20	1,539	1,376-89	1,189	115-72	...	163
	F	...-...-..	...-...	..-...-..	54	...-..	...	...-...	...	54
	R	7-4-40	15,779-16,401	Y-18,041-20	198	173-87	143	16-14	...	25
Burrillville t, R.I.	P	21-16-80	16,588-16,588	Y-16,988-..	423	412-97	375	5-32	11	...
Butler, Pa. (7)	P	26-26-40	14,438-20,722	Y-21,947-..	886	750-85	651	30-69	...	136
	F	29-29-42	13,750-21,298	..-...-..	874	755-86	662	15-78	...	119
Cadillac, Mich. (7)	P	15-15-40	17,792-20,883	Y-21,433-26	594	535-90	382	111-42	10	49
	F	14-14-56	16,378-17,691	Y-18,116-20	443	421-95	293	82-46	3	19
Cambridge, Md. (1)	P	...-...-..	10,613-15,686	None	705	705-100	660	45-...	...	...
Cambridge, Ohio (7)	P	34-30-40	15,995-17,763	Y-17,787-15	865	688-80	543	112-33	69	108
	F	20-20-56	15,995-17,763	Y-17,787-15	691	552-80	402	112-38	90	49
Camden, Ark.	P	35-27-40	11,939-14,830	Y-...-..	620	565-91	504	23-38	55	...
	F	28-28-56	11,586-14,394	Y-...-..	599	517-86	461	18-38	27	55
	R	12-7-40	8,715-10,608	Y-...-..	157	149-95	127	9-13	8	...
Campbell, Ohio (7)	P	16-16-40	13,260-15,060	..-...-..	479	403-84	301	57-45	6	70
	F	10-10-42	13,260-15,060	..-...-..	290	266-92	193	44-29	...	24
Canandaigua, N.Y.	P	28-26-38	...-...	None	933	788-84	604	150-34	80	65
	F	14-14-40	14,927-19,035	None	425	358-84	319	21-18	18	49
	R	4-2-40	12,500-14,310	Y-14,935-20	174	89-51	69	15-5	28	57
Canon City, Colo.	P	32-24-40	17,934-20,376	Y-20,580-5	812	681-84	578	33-70	32	99
	F	19-19-56	17,934-20,376	Y-20,580-5	621	594-96	486	62-46	3	24
Canonsburg b, Pa. (1,7)	P	13-13-40	19,850-20,750	None	309	309-100	309	...-...	...	...
	F	...-...-..	...-...	..-...-..	30	...-..	...	...-...	30	...
Canyon, Tex.	P	14-12-40	14,946-19,608	Y-20,808-25	373	326-87	291	29-6	13	34
	F	3-3-40	12,882-16,908	Y-18,108-25	195	129-66	111	17-1	8	58
	R	5-0-40	10,062-13,200	Y-14,400-25	245	124-51	111	11-2	77	44
Carlisle b, Pa. (1,7)	P	29-28-40	14,830-18,158	Y-18,933-13	837	729-87	609	82-38	24	84
	F	...-...-..	...-...	..-...-..	324	44-14	7	37-...	24	256
Carpinteria, Calif. (3,7)	P	21-16-40	20,317-23,977	Y-26,377-15	781	585-75	529	15-41	21	175
Carrollton, Ga.	P	40-33-42	12,400-15,200	Y-16,200-10	968	805-83	650	94-61	2	161
	F	29-29-56	11,000-11,900	Y-12,500-10	492	448-91	359	43-46	...	44
	R	17-17-44	10,500-11,400	None	408	244-60	201	22-21	48	116
Carthage, Mo. (7)	P	26-24-40	13,816-16,000	None	664	561-84	453	71-37	23	80
	F	25-25-56	14,304-16,037	None	689	587-85	472	78-37	11	91
Cary t, N.C.	P	26-24-42	14,779-19,822	None	477	457-96	428	29-...	20	...

Table 3/18 continued **POLICE, FIRE, AND REFUSE COLLECTION AND DISPOSAL DEPARTMENTS: PERSONNEL, SALARIES, AND EXPENDITURES FOR CITIES OVER 10,000: 1984**

City	De-part-ment	Total personnel, no. uniformed, duty hours per week	Entrance, maximum salary ($)	Longevity pay, maximum ($), no. years to max.	Reported expenditures (in thousands): Total expendi-tures (A) ($)	Total personnel expendi-tures (B), % of (A) ($)	Salaries and wages (C) ($)	City contrib. to employee retirement, insurance (D) ($)	Capital outlay (E) ($)	All other (F) ($)
10,000-24,999 continued										
Cary t, N.C. (cont'd)	F	27-26-60	13,416-17,971	None	602	512-85	480	32-...	90	...
	R	26-26-40	10,504-14,081	None	467	333-71	312	21-...	134	...
Casa Grande, Ariz.	P	50-34-40	18,312-24,672	None	1,446	1,172-81	1,003	134-35	44	230
	F	15-14-56	18,312-24,672	None	583	467-80	424	32-11	16	100
	R	13-0-40	12,666-17,112	None	576	263-46	224	31-8	77	236
Casselberry, Fla.	P	48-34-40	13,546-17,992	None	1,140	950-83	774	148-28	67	123
	F	19-18-56	13,546-17,992	None	499	391-78	319	62-10	20	88
Castle Shannon b, Pa. (1,7)	P	11-11-40	11,400-19,718	Y-20,704-20	454	343-76	310	1-32	12	99
Cathedral City, Calif. (2,4,7)	F	3-3-40	17,150-21,204	None	60	60-100	56	...-4	...	...
Cayce, S.C.	P	31-29-40	11,792-16,096	None	489	430-88	430	...-...	59	...
	F	15-15-56	10,696-14,599	None	206	198-96	198	...-...	8	...
	R	12-7-40	7,203-9,848	None	247	131-53	131	...-...	116	...
Cedar City, Utah	P	15-14-40	15,587-19,481	None	59	22-37	...	12-10	9	28
	F	3-3-40	15,587-19,481	None	12	9-75	...	4-5	...	3
	R	1-0-40	15,587-19,481	None	137	10-7	...	4-6	...	127
Centerville, Ohio (3)	P	24-19-40	19,105-24,980	None	790	699-88	559	98-42	12	79
	R	7-4-40	12,255-16,016	None	360	239-66	210	16-13	2	119
Centralia, Ill.	P	35-28-40	17,008-18,564	Y-21,349-20	892	743-83	672	...-71	...	149
	F	22-21-56	17,455-18,626	Y-21,420-20	587	511-87	467	...-44	...	76
	R	4-2-40	17,893-18,842	Y-20,195-20	257	138-54	118	13-7	30	89
Chambersburg b, Pa. (7)	P	27-25-40	15,152-19,793	None	846	660-78	574	53-33	3	183
	F	20-19-56	14,845-19,844	None	630	441-70	372	46-23	3	186
	R	6-0-40	15,392-17,742	None	541	133-25	106	20-7	12	396
Chanute, Kan.	P	24-20-40	14,094-15,702	Y-15,806-3	556	551-99	436	27-88	5	...
	F	16-16-40	13,850-15,284	Y-15,388-3	336	336-100	285	19-32	...	...
	R	6-0-40	11,337-12,799	Y-12,903-3	171	171-100	106	7-58	...	...
Chillicothe, Ohio	P	43-41-40	15,496-18,450	Y-18,750-6	1,370	1,212-88	939	179-94	3	155
	F	46-46-56	15,142-18,374	Y-18,675-6	1,553	1,466-94	1,077	288-101	10	77
	R	12-7-40	15,059-16,037	Y-16,337-6	362	280-77	223	30-27	...	82
Christiansburg t, Va. (1)	P	...-...-40	11,799-14,990	Y-15,780-..	477	377-79	321	39-17	19	81
	F	...-...-...	...-...	..-...-..	55	2-4	...	...-2	9	44
	R	...-...-40	8,385-10,975	Y-11,524-..	181	120-66	106	8-6	4	57
Circleville, Ohio (7)	P	29-20-40	11,440-13,998	Y-14,598-30	675	581-86	471	81-29	20	74
	F	19-19-56	11,648-13,948	Y-14,548-30	612	459-75	362	80-17	132	21
Clairton, Pa. (7)	P	16-16-40	...-21,184	Y-23,293-5	2,602	560-22	542	15-3	...	2,042
	F	11-11-40	...-21,184	Y-23,293-5	2,380	338-14	273	15-50	...	2,042
Claremore, Okla.	P	21-21-40	12,828-12,828	None	605	512-85	402	110-...	15	78
	F	21-21-48	12,540-12,540	None	416	353-85	327	26-...	10	53
	R	18-7-40	11,484-11,484	None	517	239-46	191	48-...	132	146
Clarksburg, W.Va.	P	41-30-40	11,171-15,279	Y-16,359-20	1,157	984-85	780	115-89	2	171
	F	41-41-55	10,859-15,279	Y-16,359-20	924	841-91	668	106-67	5	78
	R	28-7-40	12,792-12,792	Y-13,872-20	795	506-64	393	68-45	33	256
Clawson, Mich. (1)										
Clayton, Mo. (7)	P	55-45-40	20,652-23,928	Y-...-..	2,047	1,805-88	1,466	176-163	62	180
	F	34-32-56	20,652-23,928	Y-...-..	1,009	959-95	794	88-77	2	48
Clearfield, Utah (1)	P	23-15-40	16,046-...	None	658	557-85	435	86-36	30	71
	F	1-1-40	...-...	None	122	65-53	45	5-15	21	36
	R	4-4-40	12,306-...	None	132	76-58	60	13-3	4	52
Cleburne, Tex.	P	41-34-34	15,978-18,312	Y-21,012-..	940	852-91	718	88-46	...	88
	F	43-41-41	15,978-18,312	Y-21,012-..	1,056	975-92	843	78-54	...	81
	R	23-23-23	10,374-12,036	Y-14,736-..	157	121-77	101	12-8	...	36
Cocoa, Fla.	P	45-33-40	13,000-21,445	Y-22,196-15	1,366	1,057-77	892	124-41	...	309
	F	35-34-56	12,143-19,884	Y-20,580-15	979	775-79	638	104-33	7	197
	R	21-11-40	8,278-13,437	Y-13,907-15	633	378-60	306	53-19	...	255
Cocoa Beach, Fla. (7)	P	40-32-40	12,813-16,806	Y-19,459-10	950	752-79	660	62-30	100	98
	F	24-24-56	12,376-16,249	Y-18,804-10	905	458-51	404	39-15	392	55
College Park, Md.	R	31-1-40	12,242-13,977	None	982	637-65	497	59-81	133	212
Collinsville, Ill. (7)	P	37-28-40	22,911-23,171	Y-25,043-18	1,256	1,063-85	830	177-56	47	146
	F	25-25-42	22,091-22,364	Y-24,155-16	978	832-85	618	173-41	63	83
Colonial Heights, Va. (1,7)	P	32-25-40	14,040-19,754	None	916	739-81	582	101-56	75	102
	F	3-3-40	14,040-19,754	None	94	70-74	54	10-6	3	21
	R	..-..-..	...-...	..-...-..	400	4-1	4	...-...	...	396
Columbia Heights, Minn. (7)	P	23-19-40	18,681-26,688	Y-29,090-16	985	877-89	643	204-30	19	89
	F	7-7-40	20,168-25,087	None	433	359-83	239	112-8	31	43
Columbus, Neb.	P	37-26-40	13,944-18,024	None	832	698-84	597	62-39	23	111
	F	12-12-56	13,248-17,472	None	337	244-72	198	33-13	24	69
Commerce, Calif. (2,4,7)										
Commerce City, Colo. (1,7)	P	52-40-42	18,564-22,272	None	1,760	1,401-80	1,187	95-119	2	357
Concord t, Mass. (7)	P	38-34-40	16,430-20,586	Y-21,086-20	1,015	891-88	891	...-...	40	84
	F	33-33-42	16,119-20,026	Y-20,626-20	892	813-91	813	...-...	25	54
	R	2-2-40	...-...	..-...-..	108	48-44	48	...-...	...	60
Concord, N.C.	P	50-45-40	13,875-17,708	Y-20,499-..	1,395	1,045-75	903	142-...	52	298
	F	40-40-40	12,585-16,062	Y-18,594-..	1,050	838-80	720	118-...	11	201
	R	36-24-58	8,944-11,415	Y-13,214-..	764	510-67	434	76-...	54	200
Conneaut, Ohio (7)	P	24-19-40	16,442-17,139	Y-17,799-25	628	508-81	379	67-62	9	111
	F	14-14-48	15,300-15,625	Y-16,110-25	425	379-89	283	55-41	2	44
Connellsville, Pa. (7)	P	18-18-40	14,500-16,500	Y-17,100-20	454	381-84	332	...-49	8	65
	F	10-10-56	14,300-16,141	Y-17,101-25	272	203-75	178	...-25	...	69
Conroe, Tex.	P	59-42-40	16,620-20,040	Y-21,240-25	1,616	1,292-80	1,121	103-68	15	309

Table 3/18 continued POLICE, FIRE, AND REFUSE COLLECTION AND DISPOSAL DEPARTMENTS: PERSONNEL, SALARIES, AND EXPENDITURES FOR CITIES OVER 10,000: 1984

City	Depart-ment	Total personnel, no. uniformed, duty hours per week	Entrance, maximum salary ($)	Longevity pay, maximum ($), no. years to max.	Reported expenditures (in thousands): Total expenditures (A) ($)	Total personnel expenditures (B), % of (A) ($)	Salaries and wages (C) ($)	City contrib. to employee retirement, insurance (D) ($)	Capital outlay (E) ($)	All other (F) ($)
10,000-24,999 continued										
Conroe, Tex. (cont'd)	F	32-29-56	16,290-19,740	Y-20,940-25	1,002	766-76	655	76-35	69	167
	R	23-14-40	10,830-13,860	Y-15,060-25	792	389-49	333	31-25	11	392
Conway, S.C.	P	33-25-40	11,652-15,237	None	719	570-79	466	77-27	39	110
	F	8-8-56	11,652-15,237	None	193	152-79	123	21-8	5	36
	R	16-0-40	7,956-15,237	None	375	197-53	164	20-13	72	106
Cookeville, Tenn.	P	50-39-40	12,845-...	Y-17,617-..	1,127	916-81	762	82-72	56	155
	F	36-36-56	11,618-...	Y-15,974-..	673	627-93	509	69-49	12	34
	R	11-7-40	9,796-...	Y-13,145-..	256	200-78	158	21-21	...	56
Cooper City, Fla. (7)	P	32-23-40	17,435-22,252	None	899	787-88	677	75-35	28	84
	F	5-5-40	15,529-20,810	None	154	94-61	82	7-5	5	55
Copperas Cove, Tex.	P	38-29-40	13,896-14,088	Y-15,432-..	774	520-67	520	...-...	32	222
	F	36-32-64	12,933-13,344	Y-14,688-..	666	483-73	483	...-...	22	161
	R	19-8-34	10,566-11,796	Y-13,140-..	468	217-46	217	...-...	10	241
Coronado, Calif. (7)	P	33-22-40	18,474-21,912	None	1,497	1,359-91	1,027	294-38	5	133
	F	31-30-56	17,664-20,940	None	1,305	1,191-91	915	248-28	4	110
Corsicana, Tex.	P	38-30-..	15,570-17,508	Y-17,556-1	903	763-84	646	97-20	...	140
	F	34-33-..	15,570-17,508	Y-17,556-1	723	662-92	555	91-16	8	53
	R	35-18-..	11,784-11,784	Y-11,832-1	725	462-64	388	58-16	92	171
Cortland, N.Y.	P	39-36-40	14,226-...	Y-20,185-19	1,336	1,230-92	877	293-60	...	106
	F	44-43-40	14,226-...	Y-20,186-19	1,322	1,226-93	866	292-68	...	96
	R	6-0-40	15,433-15,443	Y-...-..	157	139-89	101	28-10	...	18
Cottage Grove, Minn. (2,7)	P	27-17-40	22,614-27,909	Y-30,421-16	931	770-83	658	79-33	27	134
	F	9-8-40	22,730-26,977	Y-29,857-14	408	316-77	269	29-18	23	69
Cranberry tp, Pa. (1)	P	13-11-40	21,008-23,004	None	436	373-86	272	67-34	11	52
Crestwood, Mo. (7)	P	32-26-40	15,845-19,395	None	958	822-86	672	98-52	33	103
	F	29-29-56	14,496-17,724	None	833	773-93	644	88-41	10	50
Creve Coeur, Mo. (7)	P	39-32-38	20,532-24,972	Y-27,132-30	1,457	1,231-84	945	173-113	57	169
Crystal Lake, Ill. (1,7)	P	37-24-40	18,300-25,000	None	1,329	1,248-94	1,031	153-64	64	17
	F	7-6-40	18,300-25,000	None	515	401-78	350	31-20	38	76
Cudahy, Calif. (3,4,7)										
Cumru tp, Pa. (1)										
Dania, Fla. (7)	P	53-41-40	18,512-23,628	Y-25,990-6	1,578	1,416-90	1,124	218-74	38	124
	F	30-26-49	19,052-24,336	Y-26,769-6	1,161	1,062-91	844	173-45	42	57
	R	16-0-40	11,413-14,456	Y-15,901-6	587	275-47	204	52-19	4	308
Danvers t, Mass. (7)	P	44-40-39	18,200-21,653	Y-22,078-30	1,350	1,153-85	1,112	...-41	60	137
	F	50-50-42	18,215-21,665	Y-21,965-25	1,506	1,343-89	1,276	...-67	90	73
Danville, Ky.	P	26-21-40	10,284-12,511	None	626	483-77	383	88-12	40	103
	F	22-22-56	11,123-13,530	None	465	402-86	320	72-10	9	54
	R	7-7-40	8,127-9,888	Y-...-..	123	79-64	63	12-4	2	42
Darien, Ill. (2,7)	P	20-13-40	18,380-26,603	Y-27,400-10	980	654-67	584	4-66	41	285
Davie t, Fla. (7)	P	79-58-40	18,589-33,200	Y-34,700-3	2,705	2,164-80	1,808	215-141	216	325
	F	39-38-48	17,295-28,600	Y-30,600-3	1,393	1,073-77	888	134-51	5	315
De Land, Fla.	P	55-39-40	13,936-18,387	Y-...-25	1,419	1,093-77	981	95-17	...	326
	F	30-29-56	12,525-16,492	Y-...-25	829	603-73	537	52-14	...	226
	R	21-8-40	8,070-10,628	None	399	261-65	220	32-9	5	133
De Soto, Tex. (7)	P	30-23-40	17,592-20,436	Y-21,636-25	804	605-75	523	53-29	85	114
	F	32-31-48	17,592-20,436	Y-21,636-25	850	730-86	626	62-42	45	75
Decatur, Ga.	P	48-41-40	13,988-19,219	None	1,205	966-80	882	84-...	38	201
	F	44-44-56	13,988-19,219	None	979	891-91	817	74-...	24	64
	R	19-3-40	9,921-13,000	None	668	410-61	354	56-...	31	227
Deer Park, Tex. (1)	P	37-31-40	23,046-28,246	Y-34,460-5	1,715	1,441-84	1,165	165-111	67	207
	F	2-2-40	23,046-28,246	Y-34,460-5	328	126-38	103	15-8	25	177
	R	21-12-40	18,574-22,256	Y-27,152-5	1,066	576-54	471	64-41	5	485
Deerfield v, Ill. (3,7)	P	43-33-40	20,001-28,312	None	1,568	1,375-88	1,202	102-71	46	147
Defiance, Ohio (7)	P	30-22-40	13,000-18,500	Y-19,055-5	871	721-83	559	94-68	18	132
	F	18-18-48	13,000-17,250	Y-17,775-5	660	516-78	389	87-40	82	62
Delano, Calif.	P	42-37-40	16,775-20,378	Y-20,872-..	1,374	1,165-85	975	111-79	24	185
	F	13-13-56	14,957-18,157	Y-18,637-..	435	374-86	317	44-13	34	27
	R	8-8-40	12,299-14,957	Y-15,377-..	330	150-45	129	14-7	100	80
Delaware, Ohio	P	38-30-40	17,851-22,352	Y-23,252-20	1,088	1,028-94	827	134-67	...	60
	F	28-27-56	17,851-22,352	Y-23,252-20	927	878-95	669	157-52	3	46
	R	10-0-40	14,477-17,082	Y-17,982-20	532	200-38	181	...-19	121	211
Denville tp, N.J. (1)										
Derby, Conn. (1,7)	P	22-22-40	18,074-19,272	Y-19,622-1	494	494-100	396	40-58	...	...
Derry tp, Pa. (1,7)	P	29-24-40	15,000-20,000	None	864	735-85	641	49-45	2	127
	R	1-0-40	14,574-20,837	None	102	30-29	25	3-2	...	72
Dickinson, N.D.	P	42-42-40	15,506-18,996	Y-19,032-5	1,114	878-79	712	109-57	77	159
	F	4-4-40	17,179-20,952	Y-20,988-5	172	121-70	101	13-7	...	51
	R	3-0-40	15,506-18,996	Y-19,032-5	181	67-37	54	8-5	...	114
Dodge City, Kan.	P	35-27-40	13,279-...	Y-...-..	899	720-80	578	62-80	54	125
	F	22-22-56	12,280-...	Y-...-..	491	432-88	345	40-47	10	49
	R	9-1-40	12,277-...	Y-...-..	380	210-55	166	21-23	10	160
Douglas, Ariz.	P	39-31-40	14,046-18,834	None	930	787-85	646	62-79	25	118
	F	24-23-56	14,046-17,926	None	579	526-91	417	54-55	12	41
	R	10-4-40	10,820-13,398	None	215	180-84	135	18-27	...	35
Douglas, Ga.	P	33-28-60	11,523-17,035	None	704	627-89	519	98-10	28	49
	F	26-26-50	9,464-15,153	None	486	457-94	370	87-...	17	12
	R	26-3-40	7,696-11,981	None	329	165-50	133	32-...	87	77

Table 3/18 continued **POLICE, FIRE, AND REFUSE COLLECTION AND DISPOSAL DEPARTMENTS: PERSONNEL, SALARIES, AND EXPENDITURES FOR CITIES OVER 10,000: 1984**

					Reported expenditures (in thousands)					
City	Department	Total personnel, no. uniformed, duty hours per week	Entrance, maximum salary ($)	Longevity pay, maximum ($), no. years to max.	Total expenditures (A) ($)	Total personnel expenditures (B), % of (A) ($)	Salaries and wages (C) ($)	City contrib. to employee retirement, insurance (D) ($)	Capital outlay (E) ($)	All other (F) ($)
10,000-24,999 continued										
Dover, Del. (1)	P	72-56-40	13,624-17,347	None	1,769	1,735-98	1,268	371-96	...	34
	R	10-6-40	7,696-9,838	None	388	174-45	138	21-15	...	214
Dover, N.H. (7)	P	47-38-40	15,891-18,304	Y-18,720-6	1,301	1,136-87	992	143-1	12	153
	F	36-35-42	12,601-14,609	Y-15,129-5	1,008	835-83	735	99-1	41	132
Dover, Ohio (7)	P	22-19-40	16,453-17,950	Y-18,325-5	688	585-85	466	81-38	30	73
	F	13-13-56	16,569-17,967	Y-18,342-5	482	445-92	333	87-25	3	34
Dover tp, Pa. (7)	P	24-21-40	14,990-24,589	Y-26,960-19	837	587-70	550	1-36	20	230
	F	...-...-..	...-...	..-...-..	68	...-..	...	...-...	22	46
Dublin, Ga.	P	37-33-40	11,815-15,060	None	835	692-83	598	69-25	33	110
	F	29-28-60	11,004-14,061	None	611	562-92	489	54-19	2	47
	R	30-8-..	8,674-11,066	None	473	390-82	333	37-20	...	83
Dumas, Tex.	P	27-27-40	17,654-18,311	Y-...-..	714	590-83	499	85-6	13	111
	F	8-8-52	16,966-17,604	Y-...-..	220	164-75	135	27-2	...	56
	R	11-0-40	14,858-15,331	Y-...-..	303	211-70	178	31-2	12	80
Dumont b, N.J. (1,7)	P	33-30-40	19,970-25,118	Y-30,016-24	1,355	1,247-92	1,072	150-25	...	108
	F	...-...-..	...-...	..-...-..	125	...-..	...	...-...	66	59
Duncan, Okla.	P	45-39-40	12,000-13,380	None	1,326	1,214-92	984	158-72	77	35
	F	32-32-56	11,130-12,120	None	782	744-95	610	89-45	17	21
	R	29-29-40	8,775-9,600	None	706	545-77	452	52-41	136	25
Durango, Colo.	P	43-29-40	14,935-21,394	None	2,260	1,033-46	844	93-96	97	1,130
	F	17-16-56	14,935-21,394	None	1,609	427-27	346	49-32	755	427
	R	8-0-40	11,183-16,180	None	397	173-44	141	12-20	57	167
Lake Station, Ind. (1)	P	19-18-40	...-18,755	..-...-..	543	543-100	458	33-52	...	...
	R	10-0-40	10,379-15,642	None	205	205-100	168	25-12	...	...
East Grand Rapids, Mich.	P	20-16-40	19,734-24,986	Y-25,986-25	612	611-100	525	54-32	1	...
	F	16-16-54	17,082-22,412	Y-23,412-25	477	474-99	412	43-19	3	...
	R	5-0-40	15,756-19,136	Y-20,136-25	95	95-100	74	12-9	...	...
East Greenwich t, R.I. (3,7)	P	33-25-38	15,835-19,257	Y-19,657-4	917	786-86	635	108-43	41	90
East Liverpool, Ohio	P	25-21-40	10,634-15,630	Y-16,290-20	655	614-94	468	78-68	...	41
	F	23-23-56	10,634-15,630	Y-16,290-20	830	597-72	416	118-63	201	32
	R	13-6-40	13,853-15,163	Y-15,763-25	332	266-80	205	29-32	...	66
East Longmeadow t, Mass. (7)	P	26-24-40	16,795-17,759	Y-18,284-25	706	611-87	594	...-17	35	60
	F	8-8-40	17,148-18,495	Y-19,045-25	236	197-83	191	...-6	5	34
East Moline, Ill.	P	37-31-40	24,070-24,564	Y-25,249-15	1,595	1,376-86	1,046	285-45	61	158
	F	32-32-42	24,070-24,564	Y-25,249-15	1,231	1,129-92	831	258-40	59	43
	R	13-13-40	21,132-22,025	Y-22,734-15	689	379-55	286	51-42	121	189
East Norriton tp, Pa. (1)	P	20-19-40	20,090-25,300	Y-26,050-15	706	588-83	508	34-46	27	91
	F	...-...-..	...-...	..-...-..	66	2-3	2	...-...	1	63
East Pennsboro tp, Pa. (1)										
East Ridge t, Tenn. (2)	P	28-22-40	14,976-15,496	Y-15,546-5	579	556-96	472	44-40	23	...
	R	22-14-40	13,260-13,260	Y-13,310-5	355	355-100	299	26-30	...	...
East Rockaway v, N.Y. (4)										
East Windsor tp, N.J. (1)	P	51-39-40	18,528-26,670	Y-27,750-..	1,528	1,528-100	1,269	209-50	...	...
	R	6-2-40	16,209-19,069	Y-20,149-..	104	104-100	90	9-5	...	...
Easton t, Mass.	P	29-28-38	17,210-21,269	Y-21,519-25	935	793-85	753	...-40	29	113
	F	27-26-42	15,139-20,264	Y-20,514-25	747	652-87	611	...-41	23	72
	R	8-5-40	15,028-15,028	Y-15,278-20	172	129-75	117	...-12	...	43
Edinburg, Tex. (1)	P	45-30-40	12,750-14,331	Y-14,709-1	782	670-86	579	65-26	77	35
	F	...-...-..	...-...	..-...-..	107	27-25	...	26-1	39	41
	R	40-19-40	7,924-8,403	Y-8,419-1	793	390-49	326	37-27	83	320
Edwardsville, Ill. (7)	P	25-18-40	17,906-22,383	Y-23,870-15	649	557-86	504	14-39	10	82
	F	17-17-56	16,260-21,685	Y-23,172-15	363	321-88	295	...-26	3	39
Effingham, Ill. (7)	P	32-22-40	15,652-19,526	Y-...-..	840	676-80	547	91-38	31	133
	F	14-14-48	15,652-19,526	Y-...-..	538	409-76	299	91-19	33	96
El Centro, Calif. (7)	P	56-38-40	17,514-20,772	Y-20,952-5	1,709	1,658-97	1,240	322-96	51	...
	F	34-33-56	16,644-19,728	Y-19,908-5	1,056	1,026-97	771	210-45	30	...
El Cerrito, Calif. (7)	P	35-30-40	21,240-25,596	None	1,877	1,532-82	1,107	347-78	...	345
	F	24-23-56	20,626-26,124	None	1,185	1,084-91	855	195-34	...	101
El Dorado, Kan.	P	23-17-40	14,083-21,534	Y-22,038-5	557	452-81	372	44-36	24	81
	F	13-13-72	14,083-21,534	Y-22,038-5	514	417-81	343	41-33	22	75
	R	9-0-40	10,877-13,882	Y-15,809-5	308	74-24	47	16-11	1	233
El Segundo, Calif. (7)	P	78-59-40	22,500-30,504	Y-35,556-21	4,388	3,676-84	2,671	699-306	9	703
	F	59-55-56	19,122-28,320	Y-33,588-21	3,527	3,159-90	2,408	559-192	28	340
Elizabeth City, N.C.	P	36-34-40	9,706-16,286	None	833	687-82	555	106-26	28	118
	F	36-35-58	9,706-13,397	None	703	594-84	489	82-23	8	101
	R	23-23-40	7,280-7,462	None	581	344-59	284	45-15	82	155
Elizabethton, Tenn.	P	32-30-42	12,536-13,147	None	588	546-93	443	63-40	18	24
	F	25-25-56	12,536-13,147	None	524	412-79	333	50-29	103	9
	R	10-7-40	10,304-11,355	None	1,086	110-10	84	12-14	425	551
Elizabethtown, Ky.	P	27-22-40	10,545-15,284	None	681	538-79	475	49-14	51	92
	F	28-27-56	12,409-16,003	None	663	585-88	517	52-16	31	47
Ellensburg, Wash. (7)	P	15-13-40	18,156-22,824	None	648	512-79	413	45-54	26	110
	F	18-18-56	18,168-22,644	None	656	569-87	493	26-50	7	80
Elmwood Park v, Ill. (7)	P	32-27-..	17,900-23,612	Y-25,501-12	1,360	1,229-90	954	180-95	26	105
	F	24-24-..	17,900-23,612	Y-25,501-12	964	894-93	646	165-83	25	45
Emmaus b, Pa. (1,7)	P	15-14-40	18,668-22,743	Y-24,243-15	512	407-79	376	1-30	2	103
	F	3-0-40	...-...	..-...-..	163	71-44	71	...-...	10	82
Englewood, Ohio (7)	P	17-13-40	16,661-21,258	None	640	508-79	403	69-36	3	129

Table 3/18 continued POLICE, FIRE, AND REFUSE COLLECTION AND DISPOSAL DEPARTMENTS: PERSONNEL, SALARIES, AND EXPENDITURES FOR CITIES OVER 10,000: 1984

					Reported expenditures (in thousands)					
City	Depart-ment	Total personnel, no. uniformed, duty hours per week	Entrance, maximum salary ($)	Longevity pay, maximum ($), no. years to max.	Total expendi-tures (A) ($)	Total personnel expendi-tures (B), % of (A) ($)	Salaries and wages (C) ($)	City contrib. to employee retirement, insurance (D) ($)	Capital outlay (E) ($)	All other (F) ($)
10,000-24,999 continued										
Ennis, Tex.	P	30-19-40	16,432-17,222	Y-18,422-25	749	581-78	486	72-23	51	117
	F	27-26-56	17,006-17,821	Y-19,021-25	712	521-73	440	61-20	89	102
	R	15-1-40	12,584-13,166	Y-14,366-25	301	231-77	189	32-10	...	70
Ephrata b, Pa. (7)	P	15-14-40	15,175-20,039	Y-...-..	566	463-82	401	31-31	30	73
Erlanger, Ky. (1,7)	P	21-17-40	12,394-16,380	None	588	471-80	359	79-33	29	88
	F	1-1-40	...-...	..-...-..	106	23-22	18	3-2	21	62
Escanaba, Mich. (5)	P	21-16-40	16,453-18,283	Y-18,683-20	765	656-86	479	132-45	1	108
	F	21-19-40	16,453-18,283	Y-18,683-20	752	644-86	479	125-40	...	108
	R	6-0-40	14,934-16,598	Y-16,998-20	237	163-69	128	26-9	...	74
Euless, Tex. (7)	P	55-48-40	18,372-20,592	Y-20,652-2	1,435	1,110-77	1,010	57-43	166	159
	F	43-42-40	18,372-20,592	Y-20,652-2	1,380	967-70	880	50-37	350	63
Fairfax, Va.	P	51-27-40	17,688-27,440	None	2,676	2,381-89	1,736	615-30	39	256
	F	39-38-56	17,688-27,440	None	1,778	1,558-88	1,095	387-76	21	199
	R	18-12-40	10,857-16,846	None	525	357-68	255	80-22	...	168
Fairfield, Ala.	P	30-25-40	16,952-20,571	Y-22,319-20	887	745-84	618	100-27	...	142
	F	21-21-56	16,952-20,571	Y-22,319-20	617	535-87	442	72-21	7	75
	R	15-5-40	16,161-17,784	Y-19,295-20	578	299-52	249	36-14	22	257
Fairmont, Minn. (1,7)	P	15-14-40	20,496-21,936	Y-22,000-25	495	420-85	369	17-34	...	75
Fairmont, W.Va. (7)	P	52-34-40	13,700-17,600	Y-18,200-20	1,122	1,069-95	822	225-22	53	...
	F	48-46-72	13,700-17,600	Y-18,200-20	1,124	1,124-100	863	140-121	...	...
Fairview tp, Pa. (1,7)	P	10-9-40	13,320-21,251	Y-22,551-16	478	395-83	275	100-20	19	64
Fairview Heights, Ill. (1,7)	P	38-28-40	19,854-22,057	Y-24,864-20	1,223	1,113-91	947	82-84	48	62
Fairview Park, Ohio	P	31-29-40	17,790-22,375	Y-23,717-26	1,111	927-83	763	121-43	...	184
	F	31-31-51	17,790-22,375	Y-23,717-26	1,047	982-94	756	175-51	...	65
	R	8-4-40	17,306-18,450	Y-19,557-26	317	189-60	153	20-16	...	128
Faribault, Minn. (7)	P	21-21-40	18,803-24,252	Y-26,192-5	747	600-80	540	16-44	36	111
	F	16-16-56	18,112-23,354	Y-25,222-5	519	481-93	449	2-30	5	33
Farmers Branch, Tex.	P	62-55-40	21,840-24,900	Y-26,400-25	3,941	1,812-46	1,575	177-60	106	2,023
	F	59-58-56	22,920-24,960	Y-26,460-25	884	742-84	629	64-49	140	2
	R	28-26-40	12,240-15,900	Y-17,400-25	1,000	778-78	683	70-25	220	2
Farmington, Mich. (5,7)	P	30-23-40	16,535-24,978	Y-26,078-20	1,226	1,026-84	779	150-97	88	112
Fergus Falls, Minn. (1)	P	22-20-40	17,364-20,736	Y-21,980-18	644	621-96	497	59-65	23	...
	R	12-7-40	14,748-15,948	Y-16,745-20	375	326-87	191	23-112	49	...
Ferguson, Mo.	P	59-53-42	17,144-20,835	Y-21,906-20	1,884	1,551-82	1,283	155-113	2	331
	F	17-17-59	15,756-19,157	Y-20,124-20	650	453-70	370	47-36	...	197
	R	11-7-48	13,628-16,598	Y-17,422-20	532	294-55	239	30-25	...	238
Floral Park v, N.Y. (1)	P	34-34-40	18,886-31,773	Y-34,573-..	2,230	2,230-100	1,511	650-69	...	...
	R	14-9-40	18,246-20,398	None	346	346-100	255	61-30	...	...
Florence, Ky. (2,7)	P	31-25-40	17,118-17,118	..-...-..	1,027	823-80	644	121-58	64	140
Forest Grove, Ore. (7)	P	22-16-40	16,652-21,611	None	711	588-83	452	92-44	10	113
	F	11-10-56	16,031-20,820	None	455	321-71	246	53-22	35	99
Forest Hill, Tex. (5)	P	31-30-40	15,600-16,380	Y-...-..	794	614-77	527	74-13	40	140
Forest Park, Ohio (1,7)	P	23-23-40	19,780-24,299	Y-24,541-20	883	747-85	583	105-59	35	101
Forrest City, Ark.	P	26-25-40	14,114-15,317	None	674	465-69	412	28-25	58	151
	F	13-13-56	12,844-14,844	None	275	227-83	212	...-15	9	39
	R	14-7-40	8,378-8,378	None	226	119-53	103	7-9	48	59
Fort Madison, Iowa	P	31-25-40	14,007-17,450	Y-17,930-20	861	730-85	566	117-47	25	106
	F	23-23-56	14,007-17,488	Y-17,968-20	729	614-84	474	107-33	54	61
	R	7-4-40	12,646-14,040	Y-14,556-20	148	119-80	98	11-10	...	29
Fort Thomas, Ky.	P	22-21-40	17,725-18,432	..-...-..	641	536-84	467	34-35	27	78
	F	16-16-56	17,378-18,397	..-...-..	436	389-89	342	21-26	...	47
	R	9-5-40	16,381-16,381	..-.. -..	247	186-75	161	13-12	...	61
Fort Walton Beach, Fla.	P	42-33-40	13,312-17,826	Y-...-..	1,326	1,110-84	909	155-46	26	190
	F	33-32-56	13,047-17,482	Y-...-..	846	715-85	599	84-32	21	110
	R	29-17-40	9,006-12,064	Y-...-..	1,034	457-44	370	61-26	396	181
Foster City, Calif. (7)	P	34-29-40	22,311-27,120	None	1,552	1,233-79	1,063	96-74	37	282
	F	28-27-56	21,768-26,460	None	1,198	999-83	856	86-57	14	185
Fostoria, Ohio (7)	P	34-27-40	18,845-21,778	Y-23,693-20	1,284	1,037-81	830	141-66	41	206
	F	20-20-54	18,845-21,778	Y-23,693-20	866	741-86	567	132-42	3	122
Frankfort, Ind.	P	35-25-40	16,720-16,720	None	714	607-85	538	7-62	8	99
	F	50-38-40	16,720-16,720	None	772	699-91	606	4-89	1	72
	R	8-5-40	12,190-12,190	None	118	95-81	75	7-13	...	23
Franklin, Ind. (7)	P	25-20-40	15,838-15,838	Y-19,005-20	587	479-82	401	40-38	8	100
	F	31-30-40	15,838-15,838	Y-19,005-20	666	607-91	513	50-44	16	43
	R	8-0-40	11,408-13,312	None	123	106-86	89	6-11	...	17
Murrysville, Pa. (1,7)	P	18-14-40	17,255-23,000	Y-28,750-25	794	685-86	509	119-57	21	88
Franklin, Wis. (1,7)	P	32-25-38	19,848-24,948	Y-25,716-25	1,299	1,168-90	909	203-56	38	93
	F	9-9-45	17,653-22,167	Y-22,971-25	628	488-78	395	75-18	102	38
Franklin Park v, Ill. (7)	P	63-46-40	18,712-...	Y-...-..	1,737	1,586-91	1,379	...-207	35	116
	F	46-45-51	24,432-...	Y-...-..	1,519	1,420-93	1,299	...-121	61	38
Fraser, Mich. (5,7)	P	49-41-48	21,892-27,800	Y-30,468-..	...	...-..	...	...-..	...	...
Fredericksburg, Va.	P	48-41-40	13,707-17,410	Y-20,155-20	1,053	903-86	724	140-39	4	146
	F	22-22-48	13,707-17,410	Y-20,155-20	492	371-75	297	57-17	66	55
	R	12-6-40	8,923-11,357	Y-13,062-20	291	243-84	195	38-10	...	48
Freehold tp, N.J. (3)										
Fremont, Neb.	P	29-24-40	14,112-17,820	Y-18,216-6	870	736-85	629	73-34	1	133
	F	29-29-56	14,112-17,820	Y-18,216-6	681	612-90	551	27-34	6	63
Fremont, Ohio	P	35-32-40	14,056-17,572	Y-18,532-20	1,172	916-78	702	144-70	42	214
	F	25-25-54	14,649-17,395	Y-18,532-20	1,016	658-65	477	136-45	207	151

Table 3/18 continued **POLICE, FIRE, AND REFUSE COLLECTION AND DISPOSAL DEPARTMENTS: PERSONNEL, SALARIES, AND EXPENDITURES FOR CITIES OVER 10,000: 1984**

City	Department	Total personnel, no. uniformed, duty hours per week	Entrance, maximum salary ($)	Longevity pay, maximum ($), no. years to max.	Reported expenditures (in thousands): Total expenditures (A) ($)	Total personnel expenditures (B), % of (A) ($)	Salaries and wages (C) ($)	City contrib. to employee retirement, insurance (D) ($)	Capital outlay (E) ($)	All other (F) ($)
10,000-24,999 continued										
Front Royal t, Va.	P	30-23-40	13,458-18,138	None	604	519-86	433	51-35	11	74
	F	4-0-40	12,397-17,566	None	68	68-100	56	7-5	...	...
	R	13-0-40	10,462-13,270	None	233	189-81	155	18-16	...	44
Fulton, Mo.	P	31-21-40	12,283-15,353	None	648	495-76	399	63-33	6	147
	F	18-18-48	10,809-15,353	None	350	284-81	223	36-25	31	35
	R	12-12-40	7,589-10,509	None	325	138-42	103	20-15	40	147
Gahanna, Ohio (2,7)	P	26-26-40	13,104-22,058	Y-22,458-5	896	813-91	657	86-70	49	34
Gainesville, Ga.	P	67-58-40	12,896-19,614	None	1,520	1,174-77	1,056	77-41	48	298
	F	50-49-56	12,896-19,614	None	1,070	937-88	845	63-29	3	130
	R	43-40-40	10,088-15,350	None	875	607-69	541	38-28	101	167
Gainesville, Tex.	P	38-30-40	15,684-15,684	Y-15,744-1	1,022	769-75	651	92-26	66	187
	F	20-20-60	15,684-15,684	Y-15,744-1	527	427-81	352	62-13	...	100
	R	17-4-40	10,824-10,824	Y-10,884-1	417	286-69	244	30-12	46	85
Galion, Ohio	P	23-23-40	17,992-...	Y-...-..	831	674-81	498	127-49	...	157
	F	13-13-55	18,117-...	Y-...-..	619	532-86	371	127-34	...	87
Gallatin, Tenn.	P	40-32-40	13,562-14,144	Y-16,203-10	904	718-79	598	59-61	1	185
	F	33-30-56	12,637-14,414	None	712	599-84	486	53-60	1	112
	R	17-1-40	11,461-12,251	None	539	313-58	252	28-33	...	226
Galloway tp, N.J.	P	29-26-40	15,402-20,883	Y-...-..	979	800-82	647	107-46	...	179
Garden City, Kan. (1)	P	55-38-40	15,084-18,996	None	1,601	1,300-81	1,006	123-171	66	235
	F	...-...-..	...-...	..-...-..	175	88-50	84	4-...	67	20
	R	11-4-40	11,436-14,340	None	671	250-37	195	22-33	111	310
Garden City v, N.Y.	P	57-44-40	20,677-28,987	Y-30,377-15	2,755	2,488-90	1,810	581-97	90	177
	F	33-33-40	20,922-25,455	Y-26,155-15	1,737	1,384-80	991	328-65	74	279
	R	35-18-40	14,692-17,117	Y-17,717-15	1,905	939-49	716	164-59	398	568
Georgetown, Ky. (1,7)	P	23-15-40	9,500-14,000	None	444	365-82	304	41-20	...	79
	F	2-0-40	9,500-14,000	None	45	30-67	27	2-1	...	15
	R	17-11-40	7,488-9,568	None	437	211-48	173	23-15	...	226
Georgetown, S.C.	P	39-32-40	11,070-15,498	None	923	751-81	610	81-60	55	117
	F	24-23-56	10,395-14,552	None	501	429-86	348	47-34	22	50
	R	13-8-40	8,370-11,717	None	231	190-82	152	20-18	...	41
Germantown, Tenn. (7)	P	35-25-40	14,700-16,800	None	767	559-73	481	47-31	49	159
	F	27-27-56	13,764-18,708	None	648	509-79	444	42-23	21	118
Germantown v, Wis. (2,7)	P	23-19-40	21,518-25,775	Y-26,075-13	965	806-84	598	140-68	4	155
Gillette, Wyo.	P	48-37-40	20,319-27,820	None	1,762	1,409-80	1,202	139-68	89	264
	R	7-4-40	16,820-20,181	None	428	206-48	178	20-8	15	207
Gilroy, Calif. (7)	P	47-37-40	24,654-29,232	None	1,994	1,772-89	1,470	228-74	59	163
	F	21-20-56	22,020-26,112	None	930	866-93	720	112-34	30	34
Girard, Ohio (7)	P	20-20-40	19,918-19,918	Y-...-..	646	580-90	503	76-1	...	66
	F	17-17-54	19,918-19,918	Y-...-..	484	454-94	386	66-2	...	30
Gladstone, Mo. (5)	P	53-43-40	17,424-22,572	None	1,491	1,252-84	1,036	123-93	47	192
Glastonbury t, Conn. (1,7)	P	53-40-40	17,500-23,821	Y-24,206-21	1,970	1,711-87	1,312	255-144	91	168
	F	...-...-..	...-...	..-...-..	286	113-40	113	...-...	45	128
	R	5-0-40	12,688-15,392	Y-15,777-21	176	130-74	95	21-14	...	46
Glen Cove, N.Y. (1,7)	P	49-48-37	18,850-31,906	Y-33,905-19	2,908	2,564-88	1,807	634-123	25	319
	F	4-4-42	16,610-18,756	Y-21,135-30	315	129-41	95	26-8	10	176
	R	8-3-40	12,211-13,827	Y-15,410-30	817	330-40	235	67-28	...	487
Glen Ellyn v, Ill. (1,7)	P	45-32-40	19,219-25,834	None	1,704	1,270-75	1,061	203-6	42	392
Glen Rock b, N.J. (1)	P	26-21-40	19,200-28,625	Y-30,625-24	1,005	911-91	732	129-50	26	68
	F	...-...-..	...-...	..-...-..	14	...-...	...	...-...	14	...
	R	12-10-40	17,000-18,366	Y-20,569-24	502	368-73	322	21-25	...	134
Glendale Heights v, Ill. (1)										
Glenwood v, Ill. (7)	P	22-15-40	17,700-23,000	None	602	531-88	472	38-21	37	34
	F	3-3-40	17,700-23,000	None	244	136-56	123	10-3	2	106
Gloversville, N.Y. (7)	P	35-31-40	14,473-18,491	Y-18,891-20	900	875-97	752	74-49	25	...
	F	44-40-40	12,282-12,282	Y-12,782-20	1,284	1,279-100	841	371-67	5	...
Golden, Colo.	P	34-25-40	19,380-24,744	None	954	816-86	676	66-74	22	116
	F	1-0-40	16,932-21,624	None	71	39-55	30	3-6	28	4
Goose Creek, S.C.	P	22-14-40	10,649-21,746	None	474	426-90	371	37-18	48	...
	F	8-8-60	8,819-17,992	None	195	114-58	102	7-5	81	...
	R	13-13-40	8,819-17,992	None	256	158-62	142	9-7	98	...
Gorham t, Me. (1)	P	13-9-40	14,309-18,456	None	340	307-90	254	39-14	...	33
	F	...-...-..	...-...	..-...-..	72	30-42	30	...-...	...	42
Goshen, Ind. (7)	P	32-25-40	15,007-15,187	Y-17,737-17	1,032	875-85	643	179-53	43	114
	F	34-34-56	15,022-15,202	Y-17,752-20	1,024	953-93	667	236-50	4	67
Grand Haven, Mich. (7)	P	20-12-40	18,022-23,642	None	885	709-80	621	57-31	21	155
	F	16-16-54	16,443-20,252	None	436	377-86	327	29-21	...	59
Grandville, Mich. (1)	P	17-13-40	17,596-23,750	Y-24,350-15	628	496-79	396	62-38	34	98
	F	...-...-..	...-...	..-...-..	80	29-36	27	2-...	10	41
Grants, N.M. (7)	P	36-32-36	12,916-16,485	Y-17,685-..	681	478-70	414	53-11	41	162
	F	12-12-48	10,120-12,916	Y-14,160-..	237	162-68	140	18-4	1	74
Grants Pass, Ore. (7)	P	32-32-40	17,052-21,792	None	1,294	1,072-83	786	183-103	...	222
	F	17-16-56	15,324-19,620	None	859	667-78	485	116-66	4	188
Grapevine, Tex. (7)	P	46-34-40	16,992-20,520	Y-21,480-20	1,538	1,114-72	988	49-77	149	275
	F	43-42-56	16,992-20,520	Y-21,480-20	1,133	1,014-89	901	45-68	19	100
Great Bend, Kan. (7)	P	43-35-42	15,000-17,525	Y-17,965-40	1,108	844-76	734	52-58	68	196
	F	28-27-63	15,000-17,585	Y-18,025-40	806	652-81	563	50-39	15	139
Green River, Wyo. (1)	P	32-31-40	20,592-33,550	Y-...-..	1,354	1,092-81	867	160-65	60	202

Table 3/18 continued **POLICE, FIRE, AND REFUSE COLLECTION AND DISPOSAL DEPARTMENTS: PERSONNEL, SALARIES, AND EXPENDITURES FOR CITIES OVER 10,000: 1984**

City	Depart-ment	Total personnel, no. uniformed, duty hours per week	Entrance, maximum salary ($)	Longevity pay, maximum ($), no. years to max.	Reported expenditures (in thousands): Total expendi-tures (A) ($)	Total personnel expendi-tures (B), % of (A) ($)	Salaries and wages (C) ($)	City contrib. to employee retirement, insurance (D) ($)	Capital outlay (E) ($)	All other (F) ($)
10,000-24,999 continued										
Green River, Wyo. (cont'd)	F	...-...-..	...-...	..-...-..	160	52-33	42	8-2	8	100
	R	9-0-40	16,931-27,602	Y-...-..	432	300-69	236	42-22	54	78
Greenbelt, Md. (1)	P	27-21-40	16,931-22,422	None	1,098	805-73	655	115-35	54	239
	R	8-8-40	11,565-15,725	None	296	165-56	136	22-7	20	111
Greenfield t, Mass.	P	35-31-40	14,477-16,848	None	817	745-91	704	...-41	22	50
	F	27-26-42	14,426-16,794	None	702	649-92	617	...-32	5	48
	R	11-1-40	14,234-14,234	None	259	189-73	179	...-10	70	...
Greensburg, Pa. (1,7)	P	34-29-40	20,262-24,315	None	897	802-89	782	10-10	26	69
	F	...-...-..	...-...	..-...-..	110	...-..	...	...-...	39	71
Greenville, Ohio (7)	P	26-22-40	13,457-18,928	None	691	559-81	445	81-33	23	109
	F	21-20-56	12,247-18,500	None	651	578-89	436	106-36	18	55
	R	2-0-40	...-...	..-...-..	384	58-15	54	...-4	...	326
Greenville, Tex. (7)	P	46-38-40	15,973-19,570	Y-20,770-25	1,078	935-87	812	91-32	51	92
	F	60-59-56	15,217-18,641	Y-19,841-25	1,479	1,339-91	1,168	126-45	35	105
Greenwood, S.C.	P	43-29-42	10,565-14,867	None	1,219	990-81	811	137-42	28	201
	F	48-47-42	10,565-14,867	None	919	822-89	694	92-36	18	79
	R	16-4-40	7,509-10,565	None	696	377-54	316	43-18	110	209
Greer, S.C.	P	30-30-40	11,752-15,662	None	681	542-80	448	76-18	39	100
	F	14-14-40	11,149-14,872	None	247	216-87	178	31-7	...	31
	R	24-0-40	9,838-13,021	None	565	330-58	280	37-13	82	153
Gretna, La. (7)	P	56-56-40	12,000-12,000	Y-13,740-10	1,423	877-62	730	105-42	70	476
	F	...-...-..	...-...	..-...-..	211	...-..	...	...-...	...	211
	R	...-...-..	...-...	..-...-..	332	...-..	...	...-...	...	332
Griffin, Ga.	P	61-44-40	13,748-14,349	Y-14,949-25	1,703	1,179-69	999	99-81	68	456
	F	58-57-56	13,250-13,865	Y-14,465-25	1,177	985-84	864	48-73	1	191
	R	70-38-40	9,082-10,219	Y-10,819-25	1,675	935-56	784	64-87	289	451
Grosse Pointe Park, Mich.	P	30-30-40	16,625-25,506	Y-26,306-29	1,288	1,146-89	887	175-84	30	112
	F	19-19-54	14,670-24,500	Y-25,300-29	754	708-94	550	110-48	10	36
	R	11-5-40	15,870-16,910	Y-17,510-18	683	245-36	190	25-30	120	318
Grosse Pointe Woods, Mich. (5)	P	41-33-40	23,355-27,780	..-...-..	1,270	1,270-100	1,270	...-...	...	...
	R	4-2-40	15,787-17,035	..-...-..	78	78-100	78	...-...	...	...
Grove City, Ohio (7)	P	32-26-40	15,018-22,755	Y-23,280-16	1,107	205-19	...	120-85	26	876
Groves, Tex.	P	11-10-40	18,970-21,965	Y-23,165-25	522	401-77	330	52-19	20	101
	F	8-8-56	18,970-21,965	Y-23,165-25	355	257-72	209	35-13	64	34
	R	15-15-40	14,497-16,786	Y-17,986-25	633	355-56	285	46-24	69	209
Gulfport, Fla. (1)	P	26-25-40	15,195-20,016	None	822	661-80	562	50-49	7	154
	F	...-...-..	...-...	..-...-..	84	45-54	41	1-3	8	31
	R	12-8-40	10,523-13,862	None	650	208-32	170	18-20	222	220
Haddon tp, N.J. (1)	P	29-24-40	16,203-21,762	Y-23,503-20	661	661-100	661	...-...	...	...
	R	6-0-40	8,684-15,570	Y-16,816-20	94	94-100	94	...-...	...	...
Haddonfield b, N.J.	P	28-22-42	17,561-23,066	Y-24,795-..	854	756-89	614	118-24	...	98
	F	6-6-42	19,965-23,666	Y-25,440-..	195	170-87	154	10-6	...	25
	R	8-5-40	12,040-13,708	Y-14,736-..	378	135-36	121	7-7	177	66
Haines City, Fla.	P	33-26-40	13,286-14,827	Y-...-5	680	558-82	485	49-24	43	79
	F	14-14-56	11,660-14,688	Y-...-5	281	242-86	211	20-11	3	36
	R	19-0-40	8,908-12,241	Y-...-5	403	233-58	197	23-13	50	120
Hamburg v, N.Y. (1)										
Hampton t, N.H.	P	29-29-40	13,395-17,077	Y-17,727-20	991	805-81	671	83-51	...	186
	F	36-36-42	13,543-16,477	Y-16,977-20	1,018	940-92	776	103-61	...	78
	R	6-1-40	12,813-15,538	Y-16,188-20	598	119-20	103	9-7	...	479
Hampton tp, Pa. (7)	P	18-17-40	19,962-23,879	Y-24,254-15	720	516-72	453	2-61	12	192
Hamtramck, Mich.	P	49-42-40	17,308-18,168	Y-18,768-30	2,749	2,628-96	1,088	1,309-231	10	111
	F	39-39-50	17,308-18,168	Y-18,768-30	1,916	1,878-98	868	844-166	25	13
	R	14-8-40	17,092-17,976	Y-18,676-35	458	378-83	247	78-53	...	80
Hanahan, S.C.	P	22-19-40	10,663-13,350	None	353	311-88	254	41-16	37	5
	F	19-19-72	11,196-13,314	None	377	337-89	274	49-14	35	5
	R	9-9-40	8,320-10,460	None	121	116-96	97	12-7	4	1
Hanford, Calif.	P	44-35-40	19,074-22,443	None	1,674	1,258-75	1,029	202-27	74	342
	F	25-24-56	15,336-18,025	None	771	689-89	545	125-19	5	77
	R	14-12-40	13,200-15,496	None	815	352-43	283	60-9	77	386
Hannibal, Mo. (7)	P	48-33-40	14,181-15,060	Y-16,641-25	966	844-87	711	85-48	17	105
	F	39-38-56	14,181-15,060	Y-16,641-25	820	791-96	678	74-39	6	23
Hanover t, Mass.	P	23-21-40	15,514-18,579	None	623	552-89	528	...-24	29	42
	F	11-11-40	14,425-17,200	None	370	322-87	313	...-9	...	48
	R	3-0-40	...-...	None	205	40-20	39	...-1	...	165
Harrison, N.Y.	P	70-65-40	23,904-27,010	Y-27,485-20	3,398	3,022-89	2,071	677-274	69	307
	F	12-11-40	22,057-25,966	Y-26,411-20	1,402	1,236-88	330	131-775	21	145
	R	29-21-40	20,310-20,810	None	1,278	762-60	495	161-106	87	429
Harvard t, Mass. (1)	P	5-5-40	20,580-22,470	..-...-..	137	118-86	118	...-...	19	...
Hastings, Minn. (7)	P	16-15-40	...-26,448	Y-26,998-15	700	598-85	495	59-44	26	76
	F	8-8-56	...-23,748	None	390	317-81	268	29-20	22	51
Havre, Mont.	P	16-15-40	14,177-15,734	Y-...-.	315	256-81	206	29-21	4	55
	F	17-16-40	13,440-16,236	Y-...-.	316	283-90	219	39-25	4	29
	R	5-0-40	16,307-18,096	Y-...-.	337	133-39	112	7-14	56	148
Hawaiian Gardens, Calif. (2,4,7)										
Hays, Kan.	P	29-29-40	14,520-19,416	Y-20,775-25	878	672-77	548	59-65	69	137
	F	17-17-42	14,520-19,416	Y-20,775-25	493	436-88	360	38-38	15	42
	R	10-0-40	11,328-14,520	Y-15,536-25	283	186-66	157	17-12	2	95

Table 3/18 continued **POLICE, FIRE, AND REFUSE COLLECTION AND DISPOSAL DEPARTMENTS: PERSONNEL, SALARIES, AND EXPENDITURES FOR CITIES OVER 10,000: 1984**

					Reported expenditures (in thousands)					
City	Depart-ment	Total personnel, no. uniformed, duty hours per week	Entrance, maximum salary ($)	Longevity pay, maximum ($), no. years to max.	Total expendi-tures (A) ($)	Total personnel expendi-tures (B), % of (A) ($)	Salaries and wages (C) ($)	City contrib. to employee retirement, insurance (D) ($)	Capital outlay (E) ($)	All other (F) ($)
10,000-24,999 continued										
Hazel Crest v, Ill. (7)	P	25-24-40	18,127-24,981	Y-26,481-20	892	769-86	641	66-62	50	73
	F	8-8-56	17,680-24,981	Y-26,481-20	324	238-73	182	37-19	6	80
Hazel Park, Mich.	P	42-35-40	24,171-26,384	Y-28,355-5	1,705	1,555-91	1,423	10-122	35	115
	F	20-20-56	24,891-26,300	Y-28,268-5	761	712-94	654	...-58	1	48
Hazelwood, Mo. (7)	P	46-37-40	17,769-25,120	None	1,596	1,258-79	1,037	133-88	40	298
	F	33-30-56	15,702-25,508	None	1,202	985-82	812	103-70	40	177
Hazlet tp, N.J. (1,7)	P	36-36-40	18,646-23,824	Y-24,574-15	...	...-..	...	...-...	...	...
Helena, Mont. (7)	P	41-32-40	13,867-16,400	Y-17,126-12	1,038	823-79	642	144-37	2	213
	F	28-27-40	14,790-17,376	Y-17,916-15	731	656-90	555	80-21	...	75
	R	13-0-40	15,766-16,660	Y-17,200-15	981	291-30	245	29-17	421	269
Hemet, Calif.	P	46-36-40	21,204-25,776	None	1,736	1,105-64	1,105	...-...	108	523
	F	34-33-56	20,184-24,540	None	1,486	889-60	889	...-...	139	458
	R	9-0-40	15,000-18,228	None	740	217-29	217	...-...	113	410
Henderson, Ky.	P	49-43-40	12,522-15,288	None	1,049	927-88	800	53-74	67	55
	F	52-51-56	12,513-15,276	None	1,114	1,025-92	890	60-75	34	55
	R	21-1-40	9,069-11,045	None	333	269-81	209	25-35	39	25
Henderson, Nev. (7)	P	40-40-40	19,805-23,880	Y-26,268-20	1,482	1,272-86	1,042	176-54	62	148
	F	39-39-56	19,732-22,580	Y-24,838-20	1,324	1,220-92	997	174-49	7	97
Henderson, N.C.	P	45-40-40	11,908-15,236	None	616	616-100	546	70-...	...	...
	F	33-32-72	11,336-14,508	None	503	503-100	434	69-...	...	...
	R	28-17-40	8,476-10,816	None	298	298-100	257	41-...	...	...
Hereford, Tex. (1)	P	27-21-40	15,000-17,040	Y-17,400-10	714	537-75	465	55-17	45	132
	R	8-2-40	12,600-12,600	Y-12,960-10	317	160-50	135	19-6	47	110
Herrin, Ill.	P	13-10-40	16,400-19,600	None	415	287-69	224	40-23	9	119
	F	8-8-56	14,500-19,200	None	263	217-83	161	42-14	6	40
	R	5-3-40	20,800-21,632	None	160	15-9	...	6-9	32	113
Hermitage, Pa. (1,7)	P	30-24-40	19,160-21,894	Y-22,551-6	921	784-85	673	58-53	17	120
	F	2-1-40	...-...	Y-...-6	123	48-39	41	5-2	3	72
Hickory Hills, Ill. (3,7)	P	26-21-40	18,468-25,535	Y-28,089-13	1,010	822-81	721	46-55	52	136
Highland Park b, N.J.	P	27-21-35	12,185-23,759	Y-24,947-..	1,066	981-92	944	...-37	...	85
	F	5-5-42	12,185-23,759	Y-24,947-..	166	135-81	128	...-7	...	31
	R	18-17-40	12,667-14,164	Y-14,872-..	298	298-100	241	36-21	...	...
Hillsdale b, N.J. (1)	P	19-19-38	17,375-26,737	Y-27,987-20	854	854-100	716	98-40	...	...
	R	22-13-40	12,305-21,187	Y-22,437-20	220	220-100	186	12-22	...	...
Hinsdale v, Ill. (7)	P	32-25-40	21,339-25,960	None	1,056	945-89	791	148-6	57	54
	F	15-14-56	21,339-25,960	None	578	545-94	426	113-6	8	25
Hobart, Ind.	P	30-22-38	16,500-17,500	Y-18,140-13	816	728-89	581	64-83	58	30
	F	24-23-56	16,500-17,500	Y-18,140-13	554	528-95	421	45-62	15	11
	R	11-11-40	14,456-14,456	None	268	204-76	162	21-21	30	34
Holden t, Mass. (1)	P	19-17-42	15,688-18,411	None	464	365-79	343	13-9	28	71
	F	2-1-40	...-...	..-...-..	165	108-65	108	...-...	...	57
Holliston t, Mass. (1,7)	P	18-18-38	14,456-20,124	Y-20,509-5	564	564-100	523	26-15	...	...
	F	..-...-..	...-...	..-...-..	86	86-100	55	1-30	...	...
Homewood v, Ill. (1,7)	P	45-34-40	18,924-27,468	Y-28,224-15	1,582	1,511-96	1,261	180-70	7	64
	F	14-11-56	17,856-25,944	Y-26,694-15	575	477-83	402	57-18	14	84
Hopatcong b, N.J.	P	25-22-40	15,948-23,968	Y-25,406-5	735	702-96	570	95-37	...	33
	F	..-...-..	...-...	..-...-..	23	...-..	...	...-...	...	23
	R	13-8-40	13,416-15,000	Y-17,496-5	616	500-81	398	82-20	...	116
Hopewell tp, N.J. (1,7)	P	22-22-40	14,500-24,250	None	700	599-86	483	66-50	32	69
Hopewell tp, Pa. (1,7)	P	..-...-..	14,500-20,116	Y-...-..	348	295-85	251	16-28	...	53
	F	..-...-..	...-...	..-...-..	25	...-..	...	...-...	...	25
Hopkins, Minn. (1,7)	P	28-20-40	22,236-27,792	Y-30,293-16	1,049	872-83	740	88-44	26	151
	F	..-...-..	...-...	..-...-..	172	82-48	77	3-2	3	87
Hudson t, N.H.	P	35-27-40	14,248-17,513	None	630	630-100	517	113-...	...	...
	F	18-16-58	14,500-17,500	None	434	434-100	363	71-...	...	...
	R	2-2-40	13,500-13,500	None	...	...-..	...	...-...	...	...
Hueytown, Ala. (7)	P	15-11-40	16,993-20,633	None	466	372-80	317	39-16	8	86
	F	11-11-53	16,993-20,633	None	421	299-71	254	33-12	63	59
Huntington, Ind.	P	34-29-40	15,974-15,974	Y-18,849-18	780	735-94	576	157-2	...	45
	F	38-38-40	15,974-15,974	Y-18,849-18	849	819-96	675	142-2	3	27
	R	19-0-40	11,274-12,438	None	344	286-83	253	31-2	10	48
Huntsville, Tex. (1,7)	P	39-29-40	18,408-24,384	Y-24,408-6	1,213	916-76	815	66-35	80	217
	F	3-3-40	18,408-24,384	Y-24,408-6	256	86-34	77	6-3	33	137
	R	23-11-40	13,086-15,912	Y-15,930-5	854	471-55	418	33-20	72	311
Hyattsville, Md. (2)										
Imperial Beach, Calif.	P	20-20-40	18,564-22,008	None	742	22-3	...	16-6	...	720
	F	13-13-56	16,074-19,080	Y-19,440-8	425	314-74	256	35-23	...	111
	R	10-10-40	14,688-18,312	None	314	219-70	189	12-18	...	95
Independence, Kan.	P	22-22-40	...-...	None	575	459-80	396	45-18	41	75
	F	17-17-56	...-...	None	350	333-95	287	32-14	5	12
	R	12-8-40	...-...	None	249	179-72	152	17-10	...	70
Indiana b, Pa. (1,7)	P	..-...-..	20,331-21,590	Y-23,749-15	909	801-88	690	45-66	16	92
	F	..-...-..	...-...	..-...-..	78	...-..	...	...-...	...	78
Indianola, Iowa (1,7)	P	13-9-40	14,685-18,720	None	401	311-78	247	38-26	20	70
	F	..-...-..	...-...	..-...-..	145	...-..	...	...-...	110	35
Inver Grove Heights, Minn. (1,7)	P	25-18-40	20,070-27,324	Y-29,304-14	818	688-84	564	68-56	58	72
	F	..-...-..	...-...	..-...-..	81	10-12	...	10-...	...	71
Ipswich t, Mass. (7)	P	22-21-38	16,828-18,768	None	691	621-90	508	81-32	28	42

Table 3/18 continued POLICE, FIRE, AND REFUSE COLLECTION AND DISPOSAL DEPARTMENTS: PERSONNEL, SALARIES, AND EXPENDITURES FOR CITIES OVER 10,000: 1984

City	Department	Total personnel, no. uniformed, duty hours per week	Entrance, maximum salary ($)	Longevity pay, maximum ($), no. years to max.	Reported expenditures (in thousands): Total expenditures (A) ($)	Total personnel expenditures (B), % of (A) ($)	Salaries and wages (C) ($)	City contrib. to employee retirement, insurance (D) ($)	Capital outlay (E) ($)	All other (F) ($)
10,000-24,999 continued										
Ipswich t, Mass. (cont'd)	F	16-16-42	16,892-18,840	None	482	437-91	359	57-21	7	38
	R	1-1-40	13,177-14,165	None	17	16-94	13	2-1	...	1
Ironton, Ohio	P	19-19-40	15,757-16,657	None	539	439-81	344	60-35	7	93
	F	15-15-56	15,757-16,657	None	404	365-90	273	65-27	6	33
	R	10-0-40	15,000-15,000	None	358	214-60	171	22-21	48	96
Jacksonville, Ill. (7)	P	39-31-40	16,768-21,779	None	879	860-98	806	7-47	19	...
	F	25-25-40	16,768-21,412	None	624	599-96	576	1-22	25	...
Jacksonville, N.C.	P	89-73-40	12,909-16,224	None	1,635	1,390-85	1,222	135-33	60	185
	F	60-59-60	12,173-13,998	None	1,061	978-92	841	111-26	19	64
	R	35-25-40	8,893-9,256	None	689	383-56	329	44-10	112	194
Jacksonville Beach, Fla.	P	46-32-40	14,156-19,302	Y-...-..	1,291	1,004-78	824	138-42	60	227
	F	33-32-56	12,954-18,026	Y-...-..	908	760-84	617	120-23	26	122
	R	20-14-40	9,083-12,433	Y-...-..	485	253-52	206	30-17	6	226
Jamestown, N.D. (7)	P	31-27-40	14,580-19,512	Y-20,293-20	732	635-87	533	71-31	6	91
	F	7-7-56	14,580-19,512	Y-20,293-20	235	183-78	157	18-8	11	41
	R	12-6-40	11,178-14,964	Y-20,293-20	324	235-73	198	23-14	24	65
Jasper, Ala.	P	34-28-40	14,423-14,663	Y-14,783-5	1,123	817-73	647	118-52	...	306
	F	16-16-40	13,013-13,013	Y-13,133-5	397	280-71	226	37-17	...	117
	R	16-16-40	11,998-11,998	Y-12,118-5	344	249-72	203	29-17	...	95
Jefferson tp, N.J. (1,7)	P	35-29-40	15,900-25,500	Y-27,046-5	1,339	1,224-91	975	186-63	40	75
Jeffersonville, Ind.	P	49-43-40	17,081-17,281	Y-20,698-20	1,227	1,019-83	900	88-31	23	185
	F	47-46-56	17,081-17,281	Y-20,698-20	1,155	971-84	891	48-32	...	184
	R	39-31-40	15,200-15,429	None	850	649-76	567	64-18	...	201
Jennings, La.	P	28-21-40	12,500-14,130	Y-19,782-23	834	529-63	460	46-23	54	251
	F	9-5-56	12,492-14,385	Y-20,139-23	513	247-48	194	42-11	65	201
	R	14-14-40	9,901-12,085	Y-16,919-23	555	247-45	200	31-16	91	217
Junction City, Kan.	P	68-48-40	13,395-15,974	Y-15,998-18	1,453	1,142-79	924	197-21	75	236
	F	31-31-56	12,371-17,598	Y-17,622-18	698	607-87	464	130-13	1	90
	R	15-10-40	7,280-11,440	None	280	182-65	155	24-3	...	98
Juneau, Alaska	P	40-21-40	32,016-38,028	Y-43,632-18	2,184	1,562-72	1,273	225-64	14	608
	F	36-35-56	28,248-34,938	Y-38,832-18	2,172	1,509-69	1,211	213-85	36	627
Kearney, Neb. (1)	P	35-28-42	14,772-18,864	Y-20,808-10	938	744-79	659	48-37	38	156
	F	...-...-..	...-...	..-...-..	225	...-..	...	...-...	135	90
	R	16-8-40	10,488-13,392	Y-14,772-10	614	324-53	281	28-15	67	223
Keene, N.H.	P	41-38-40	13,401-17,197	Y-17,697-..	1,235	1,018-82	819	117-82	14	203
	F	37-37-42	13,907-17,845	None	1,001	900-90	734	94-72	1	100
Kelso, Wash.	P	21-21-40	20,350-22,874	Y-...-5	819	672-82	567	69-36	...	147
	F	15-15-..	22,170-25,249	Y-...-5	555	524-94	456	24-44	1	30
	R	5-5-40	...-...	Y-...-5	197	129-65	111	14-4	...	68
Kenmore v, N.Y.	P	29-29-40	16,573-20,571	Y-21,071-20	1,113	1,029-92	740	286-3	...	84
	F	4-4-40	16,697-21,079	Y-21,579-20	225	150-67	108	41-1	...	75
	R	20-13-40	12,904-16,286	Y-16,866-20	556	443-80	355	86-2	...	113
Kent, Wash. (7)	P	74-53-40	23,568-29,016	Y-29,041-10	3,333	2,564-77	2,095	252-217	123	646
	F	88-77-54	20,496-31,968	Y-33,252-10	2,981	2,515-84	2,142	132-241	33	433
Key West, Fla. (7)	P	71-62-40	15,372-20,242	None	1,642	1,584-96	1,372	155-57	58	...
	F	54-53-56	16,467-21,683	None	1,335	1,317-99	1,138	133-46	18	...
	R	19-7-40	...-...	None	...	...-..	...	...-...	...	...
Kilgore, Tex.	P	39-34-40	16,824-16,824	Y-20,108-..	1,118	779-70	711	37-31	54	285
	F	63-53-40	16,332-16,332	Y-16,524-..	1,295	1,061-82	969	52-40	99	135
	R	19-0-40	15,060-15,060	..-...-..	552	315-57	286	14-15	109	128
Killingly t, Conn. (1,4)										
Kingston, Pa.	P	23-22-..	...-17,700	Y-19,470-..	408	408-100	408	...-...	...	...
	F	...-...-..	...-17,200	Y-18,920-..	254	254-100	254	...-...	...	...
	R	...-...-..	...-13,900	..-...-..	83	83-100	83	...-...	...	...
Kirkland, Wash. (7)	P	...-...-..	23,592-30,720	None	1,564	1,296-83	1,063	134-99	10	258
	F	...-...-..	21,588-30,372	None	1,318	962-73	828	55-79	60	296
Kissimmee, Fla. (7)	P	80-53-40	14,623-22,901	Y-23,401-10	1,414	1,187-84	987	165-35	129	98
	F	45-44-56	13,891-21,724	Y-22,224-10	1,081	929-86	787	113-29	30	122
	R	10-1-40	10,962-17,140	Y-17,640-10	393	148-38	125	17-6	36	209
Klamath Falls, Ore. (7)	P	35-28-40	15,504-23,808	None	1,361	1,222-90	941	211-70	40	99
	F	32-28-56	15,480-18,708	None	1,264	1,167-92	915	199-53	35	62
La Grange, Ga.	P	82-73-40	11,619-14,000	None	1,709	1,341-78	1,152	150-39	50	318
	F	68-60-60	11,134-13,339	None	1,313	1,108-84	951	125-32	15	190
	R	40-26-40	8,444-10,164	None	1,217	490-40	419	54-17	510	217
La Grange v, Ill. (7)	P	28-28-40	22,632-25,980	None	1,180	1,046-89	946	...-100	47	87
	F	18-18-48	22,632-25,980	None	842	645-77	587	...-58	37	160
La Grange Park v, Ill. (1)	P	25-20-40	19,152-26,064	None	1,002	939-94	698	188-53	4	59
La Palma, Calif. (2,7)	P	23-18-36	21,768-26,460	None	969	840-87	719	121-...	48	81
La Porte, Ind. (7)	P	43-43-40	15,496-15,496	Y-17,356-18	892	754-85	631	37-86	55	83
	F	44-44-56	15,496-15,496	Y-17,356-18	948	876-92	767	20-89	7	65
La Porte, Tex.	P	52-36-40	20,190-26,508	Y-27,948-30	2,799	1,498-54	1,260	146-92	96	1,205
	F	10-10-72	20,478-32,760	Y-34,200-30	969	387-40	323	38-26	93	489
	R	17-14-40	16,880-27,560	Y-29,000-30	1,286	496-39	419	49-28	99	691
La Verne, Calif. (7)	P	37-31-40	21,684-26,364	None	1,838	1,655-90	1,145	284-226	32	151
	F	16-15-56	21,372-25,968	None	1,250	830-66	596	140-94	72	348
Lacey, Wash. (2,7)	P	26-23-40	22,320-28,212	None	1,138	820-72	650	108-62	8	310
Lackawanna, N.Y.	P	51-51-40	17,819-21,180	Y-21,580-20	2,237	2,170-97	2,170	...-...	1	66
	F	64-64-40	13,768-20,217	Y-20,617-20	1,760	1,646-94	1,646	...-...	3	111

Table 3/18 continued **POLICE, FIRE, AND REFUSE COLLECTION AND DISPOSAL DEPARTMENTS: PERSONNEL, SALARIES, AND EXPENDITURES FOR CITIES OVER 10,000: 1984**

					Reported expenditures (in thousands)					
City	Department	Total personnel, no. uniformed, duty hours per week	Entrance, maximum salary ($)	Longevity pay, maximum ($), no. years to max.	Total expenditures (A) ($)	Total personnel expenditures (B), % of (A) ($)	Salaries and wages (C) ($)	City contrib. to employee retirement, insurance (D) ($)	Capital outlay (E) ($)	All other (F) ($)
10,000-24,999 continued										
Lackawanna, N.Y. (cont'd)	R	13-13-40	13,582-13,582	Y-13,982-20	393	271-69	271	...-...	...	122
Laconia, N.H. (7)	P	37-29-40	13,395-17,368	Y-17,668-6	1,034	858-83	714	98-46	31	145
	F	29-27-56	11,725-14,596	Y-14,896-5	771	597-77	488	63-46	12	162
Lafayette, Calif. (3,4,7)										
Laguna Beach, Calif. (7)	P	54-37-40	21,960-26,700	None	2,751	2,289-83	1,985	238-66	27	435
	F	33-31-56	19,848-24,132	None	1,705	1,389-81	1,191	158-40	18	298
Lake Forest, Ill.	P	33-20-40	21,000-28,000	Y-28,050-5	1,821	1,617-89	1,205	303-109	47	157
	F	23-22-56	20,000-27,000	Y-27,050-5	1,108	1,002-90	692	252-58	48	58
	R	13-13-40	16,300-21,700	Y-21,750-5	575	400-70	322	46-32	35	140
Lake Havasu City, Ariz. (7)	P	38-33-40	14,747-22,880	Y-23,280-20	1,101	866-79	757	49-60	55	180
	F	54-44-55	14,747-22,880	Y-23,280-20	1,522	1,350-89	1,192	67-91	17	155
Lake Jackson, Tex. (1)	P	35-28-40	21,174-22,859	Y-...-..	1,008	789-78	674	89-26	59	160
	F	...-...-..	...-...	..-...-..	67	...-..	...	...-...	...	67
	R	20-8-40	15,371-16,660	None	650	386-59	326	43-17	87	177
Lake Oswego, Ore.	P	47-33-40	19,044-22,296	None	1,800	1,510-84	1,112	256-142	45	245
	F	39-38-56	17,406-22,260	None	1,740	1,515-87	1,129	253-133	39	186
Lamesa, Tex.	P	22-15-40	...-...	Y-...-..	545	483-89	396	65-22	...	62
	F	10-10-60	13,764-15,396	Y-...-..	266	216-81	177	29-10	...	50
	R	10-3-40	10,776-12,504	Y-...-..	264	177-67	141	25-11	...	87
Lancaster v, N.Y. (1)	P	16-12-37	16,125-23,714	Y-24,164-25	749	672-90	520	118-34	34	43
	R	33-6-40	16,424-16,744	Y-16,944-20	1,621	916-57	691	161-64	79	626
Lansdale b, Pa. (1)	P	24-18-40	18,981-26,157	Y-28,511-20	957	785-82	702	22-61	22	150
Lansdowne b, Pa.	P	16-13-40	23,257-25,582	Y-...-..	746	620-83	540	...-80	34	92
	F	...-...-..	...-...	..-...-..	5	...-..	...	...-...	5	...
	R	9-8-40	11,606-12,896	None	306	195-64	159	...-36	10	101
Las Vegas, N.M.	P	40-32-40	12,252-14,328	Y-14,472-4	1,110	676-61	563	80-33	98	336
	F	11-10-40	10,896-13,776	Y-13,920-4	308	161-52	129	22-10	42	105
	R	11-11-40	10,476-12,252	Y-12,396-4	421	179-43	150	23-6	75	167
Latrobe b, Pa. (1)	P	22-14-40	16,114-17,000	Y-21,400-20	419	419-100	285	78-56	...	...
	F	...-...-..	...-...	..-...-..	52	39-75	30	5-4	...	13
	R	8-8-40	15,000-15,000	Y-18,000-..	220	201-91	153	26-22	...	19
Laurel t, Md.	P	39-27-43	16,918-24,087	Y-24,087-3	1,035	827-80	827	...-...	5	203
	R	15-8-40	12,379-14,872	Y-15,496-3	278	159-57	159	...-...	3	116
Lawndale, Calif. (3,4)										
Lawrence tp, N.J. (1,7)	P	55-50-40	20,256-28,740	Y-30,540-28	2,023	1,871-92	1,587	217-67	45	107
	F	6-6-40	13,000-20,123	Y-21,923-28	71	10-14	...	3-7	44	17
League City, Tex. (7)	P	36-23-40	19,028-22,105	..-...-..	1,174	1,043-89	865	103-75	8	123
	F	1-0-40	23,762-...	..-...-..	34	29-85	24	3-2	...	5
Lebanon, Ore. (7)	P	21-20-40	17,262-22,037	None	780	684-88	511	123-50	20	76
	F	17-16-72	17,908-22,868	None	940	551-59	416	99-36	225	164
Lebanon, Tenn.	P	26-26-40	12,292-12,916	None	1,056	474-45	384	73-17	2	580
	F	27-27-56	13,220-13,511	None	977	450-46	363	70-17	31	496
	R	16-0-40	6,968-7,321	None	481	193-40	154	28-11	...	288
Ledyard t, Conn. (1)	P	10-9-40	12,288-17,588	None	250	191-76	169	11-11	1	58
	F	2-2-40	11,593-14,766	None	79	32-41	27	2-3	5	42
Lemon Grove, Calif. (7)	F	21-20-56	15,348-23,460	None	728	649-89	516	114-19	8	71
Lenexa, Kan. (7)	P	65-38-40	17,220-23,748	None	2,117	1,817-86	1,470	274-73	67	233
	F	34-33-56	16,404-22,620	None	1,108	986-89	785	162-39	51	71
Levelland, Tex.	P	26-19-40	16,800-18,792	Y-19,992-25	678	538-79	471	54-13	38	102
	F	7-7-56	16,800-18,792	Y-19,992-25	209	170-81	150	16-4	7	32
	R	9-0-40	12,900-14,016	Y-15,216-25	347	181-52	161	16-4	72	94
Lewisville, Tex. (7)	P	59-47-40	19,074-21,540	Y-22,740-25	2,629	1,252-48	1,127	83-42	978	399
	F	38-38-48	17,478-19,752	Y-20,952-25	1,306	920-70	829	64-27	98	288
Lexington, N.C.	P	60-53-48	11,814-15,080	None	1,374	1,090-79	930	144-16	92	192
	F	51-50-56	11,253-14,352	None	1,011	901-89	764	123-14	27	83
	R	49-30-40	8,403-10,712	None	902	570-63	493	65-12	55	277
Liberty, Mo. (7)	P	32-25-40	16,632-21,744	None	1,000	817-82	701	83-33	37	146
	F	24-24-56	16,632-21,744	None	773	651-84	560	63-28	16	106
Lighthouse Point, Fla. (7)	P	40-27-40	18,290-24,596	None	1,117	994-89	861	105-28	26	97
	F	17-17-54	15,780-21,172	None	462	426-92	362	51-13	...	36
	R	13-13-40	10,464-17,492	None	725	295-41	253	31-11	230	200
Lincolnwood v, Ill. (2)	P	30-26-40	14,750-28,500	..-...-..	...	...-..	...	...-...	...	...
Lisle v, Ill. (3)	P	35-25-40	19,139-25,641	None	1,257	958-76	787	110-61	69	230
Logansport, Ind. (7)	P	38-33-40	15,277-...	None	656	625-95	544	32-49	31	...
	F	45-45-72	15,277-...	None	802	801-100	709	27-65	1	...
	R	...-...-..	...-...	..-...-..	164	164-100	164	...-...	...	...
Loma Linda, Calif. (4,7)	F	11-10-67	19,259-22,334	None	472	218-46	183	26-9	3	251
Lomita, Calif. (3,4,7)										
Longwood, Fla. (7)	P	31-27-40	13,885-18,885	None	687	518-75	418	86-14	11	158
	F	15-15-56	13,885-18,885	None	326	278-85	225	46-7	26	22
Los Alamitos, Calif. (3,7)	P	25-20-40	22,680-27,876	None	1,300	1,133-87	833	213-87	53	114
Los Banos, Calif. (1,7)	P	21-14-40	17,244-20,832	None	983	737-75	545	120-72	37	209
	F	1-1-40	...-...	..-...-..	84	32-38	25	6-1	5	47
Loves Park, Ill. (1)	P	26-25-40	15,611-21,036	Y-21,877-10	645	614-95	556	...-58	31	...
Lower Makefield tp, Pa. (1)	P	23-23-40	18,935-24,038	Y-25,001-5	650	650-100	612	...-38	...	...
Lower Moreland tp, Pa. (1,7)	P	28-21-40	21,006-24,136	Y-26,550-20	943	755-80	669	...-86	92	96
	F	...-...-..	...-...	..-...-..	44	...-..	...	...-...	...	44
Lower Providence tp, Pa. (1)										

Table 3/18 continued **POLICE, FIRE, AND REFUSE COLLECTION AND DISPOSAL DEPARTMENTS: PERSONNEL, SALARIES, AND EXPENDITURES FOR CITIES OVER 10,000: 1984**

					Reported expenditures (in thousands)					
City	Depart-ment	Total personnel, no. uniformed, duty hours per week	Entrance, maximum salary ($)	Longevity pay, maximum ($), no. years to max.	Total expenditures (A) ($)	Total personnel expenditures (B), % of (A) ($)	Salaries and wages (C) ($)	City contrib. to employee retirement, insurance (D) ($)	Capital outlay (E) ($)	All other (F) ($)
10,000-24,999 continued										
Lower Southampton tp, Pa. (1)										
Lumberton, N.C. (7)	P	43-37-42	12,068-15,778	None	999	811-81	718	64-29	54	134
	F	48-47-56	11,639-15,977	None	934	773-83	671	77-25	80	81
	R	19-8-40	8,272-9,341	None	504	363-72	310	37-16	73	68
Lynnwood, Wash.	P	42-36-40	23,899-28,122	Y-28,842-10	1,807	1,487-82	1,219	148-120	36	284
	F	32-31-48	23,786-27,989	Y-28,709-10	1,380	1,079-78	926	52-101	34	267
Mc Alester, Okla.	P	37-31-40	11,280-13,704	Y-13,896-4	594	563-95	501	36-26	...	31
	F	38-37-56	11,280-13,704	Y-13,896-4	720	675-94	603	46-26	...	45
	R	17-8-40	8,592-10,452	Y-10,644-4	252	212-84	179	21-12	...	40
Mc Henry, Ill. (1,7)	P	34-25-40	17,500-21,800	Y-22,672-6	1,204	992-82	790	139-63	87	125
Mc Minnville, Ore.	P	25-23-40	17,232-21,840	Y-22,560-..	606	606-100	461	104-41	...	...
	F	10-10-40	17,316-21,948	Y-22,824-..	282	282-100	217	52-13	...	...
Mc Pherson, Kan. (7)	P	23-17-40	14,000-21,000	None	612	527-86	416	82-29	16	69
	F	14-14-56	14,000-21,000	None	422	357-85	282	56-19	15	50
Madera, Calif. (7)	P	45-34-40	16,980-22,923	None	1,344	1,333-99	1,002	229-102	11	...
	F	24-24-56	16,555-22,350	None	759	759-100	572	133-54	...	...
Madison t, Conn. (7)	P	26-26-40	15,634-18,820	Y-19,135-15	1,047	714-68	545	103-66	82	251
Madison, Ind. (1)	P	26-26-40	15,446-...	Y-...-..	417	417-100	417	...-...	...	...
	R	28-28-42	11,128-...	None	453	453-100	453	...-...	...	...
Mamaroneck v, N.Y. (1)	P	45-45-40	19,612-27,888	Y-28,178-5	2,164	2,005-93	1,428	490-87	37	122
	F	...-...-..	...-...	..-...-..	226	16-7	15	1-...	43	167
	R	14-0-40	16,492-18,993	Y-19,293-10	721	376-52	270	80-26	75	270
Manalapan tp, N.J. (1,7)	P	33-23-40	13,500-24,910	Y-25,159-10	1,185	1,046-88	849	133-64	...	139
Manassas, Va. (7)	P	43-37-40	15,184-19,365	Y-21,341-..	1,102	901-82	755	125-21	9	192
	F	3-3-40	14,456-18,450	Y-20,322-..	124	58-47	46	10-2	12	54
	R	...-...-..	...-...	..-...-..	330	...-..	...	...-...	...	330
Mansfield t, Conn. (1)	P	4-3-40	15,933-18,262	Y-18,787-6	163	101-62	82	11-8	11	51
	F	...-...-..	...-...	..-...-..	422	...-..	...	...-...	...	422
	R	2-0-40	...-...	..-...-..	54	43-80	35	4-4	...	11
Manville b, N.J.	P	21-21-40	17,950-22,475	Y-23,300-15	662	662-100	539	85-38	...	...
	R	6-5-40	12,648-17,555	None	135	135-100	109	15-11	...	...
Maple Grove, Minn.	P	19-17-40	19,292-26,486	None	692	597-86	500	60-37	31	64
	F	1-1-40	30,441-...	None	131	87-66	81	4-2	18	26
Maple Shade tp, N.J. (1,7)	P	34-29-40	17,654-22,750	Y-23,885-20	1,293	1,109-86	868	102-139	...	184
Maplewood, Mo. (7)	P	28-23-40	15,537-19,801	Y-21,801-25	765	640-84	584	23-33	10	115
	F	19-19-60	15,537-19,801	Y-21,801-25	499	446-89	422	3-21	29	24
Maplewood tp, N.J. (7)	P	50-50-40	19,520-23,826	Y-26,208-5	1,881	1,811-96	1,448	358-5	...	70
	F	43-43-42	19,230-22,267	Y-24,493-5	1,470	1,438-98	1,130	304-4	...	32
Marblehead t, Mass.	P	41-39-39	15,430-18,903	Y-19,403-25	1,656	1,527-92	1,230	221-76	22	107
	F	45-45-42	15,552-18,903	Y-19,628-30	1,547	1,408-91	1,127	203-78	80	59
	R	15-8-40	12,940-13,726	Y-14,376-30	629	289-46	224	40-25	...	340
Marina, Calif. (7)	P	17-17-40	15,600-19,500	None	4,313	1,058-25	825	196-37	14	3,241
	F	8-8-72	15,600-19,500	None	155	134-86	85	38-11	21	...
Marinette, Wis.	P	22-21-40	12,800-17,226	Y-...-3	784	651-83	487	121-43	9	124
	F	19-19-56	12,806-12,806	Y-...-3	636	503-79	396	71-36	89	44
	R	6-6-40	13,217-14,788	Y-...-3	356	195-55	146	36-13	...	161
Marion, Ill. (7)	P	19-18-40	15,480-16,640	Y-17,120-20	506	407-80	324	57-26	35	64
	F	13-13-56	17,328-18,096	Y-18,576-20	389	324-83	248	58-18	1	64
	R	5-3-40	15,080-15,080	Y-15,560-20	167	119-71	98	14-7	28	20
Marion, Iowa	P	29-23-40	14,550-18,519	Y-19,219-20	958	729-76	601	104-24	55	174
	F	15-15-56	14,782-17,979	Y-18,049-20	440	399-91	325	57-17	2	39
	R	5-0-40	13,895-17,145	Y-17,845-20	316	96-30	81	10-5	85	135
Markham, Ill.	P	35-35-40	17,107-20,127	None	998	213-21	77	44-92	...	785
	F	1-1-40	21,200-21,200	None	168	24-14	20	1-3	...	144
	R	6-3-40	17,940-17,940	None	400	101-25	81	5-15	...	299
Marple tp, Pa.	P	39-33-40	18,000-28,300	Y-33,600-20	1,435	1,271-89	1,102	12-157	29	135
	R	13-13-40	18,000-18,000	None	449	301-67	240	25-36	...	148
Marquette, Mich. (7)	P	33-28-40	17,190-22,176	Y-22,476-30	1,186	1,090-92	859	140-91	21	75
	F	22-22-54	15,456-20,616	Y-20,941-30	806	711-88	560	92-59	7	88
Marshall, Minn. (1,7)	P	19-15-40	18,636-24,898	None	643	510-79	434	50-26	22	111
Marshall, Mo.	P	30-22-40	13,495-15,101	None	602	486-81	408	50-28	19	97
	F	16-16-48	12,499-14,915	None	393	316-80	259	34-23	27	50
	R	12-5-40	9,984-15,080	None	542	273-50	232	29-12	164	105
Martinsville, Ind.	P	16-16-..	14,605-...	None	311	301-97	246	17-38	10	...
	F	10-10-..	14,605-...	None	219	195-89	155	17-23	24	...
	R	3-3-..	13,035-...	None	62	45-73	37	1-7	17	...
Martinsville, Va.	P	56-49-40	13,920-16,536	Y-19,164-21	1,377	1,148-83	950	158-40	44	185
	F	26-26-56	12,624-15,000	Y-17,388-21	636	545-86	452	75-18	41	50
	R	13-6-40	8,988-10,176	Y-11,796-21	289	181-63	150	23-8	35	73
Maryville, Tenn.	P	28-28-40	13,456-19,887	None	834	666-80	499	131-36	59	109
	F	28-28-60	11,612-17,174	None	760	677-89	498	140-39	15	68
	R	...-...-40	9,548-14,136	None	403	219-54	192	27-...	67	117
Massapequa Park v, N.Y. (7)										
Matteson v, Ill. (7)	P	33-28-40	19,722-24,830	None	1,148	916-80	792	58-66	37	195
	F	12-12-56	16,779-25,428	None	553	371-67	320	22-29	13	169
Maumee, Ohio (1,7)	P	35-30-40	19,165-23,870	..-...-..	1,429	1,137-80	905	158-74	...	292
	F	4-4-40	...-...	..-...-..	206	158-77	131	21-6	...	48
Mayfield, Ky. (7)	P	27-23-40	12,000-13,200	None	449	359-80	359	...-...	4	86

Table 3/18 continued **POLICE, FIRE, AND REFUSE COLLECTION AND DISPOSAL DEPARTMENTS: PERSONNEL, SALARIES, AND EXPENDITURES FOR CITIES OVER 10,000: 1984**

City	Depart-ment	Total personnel, no. uniformed, duty hours per week	Entrance, maximum salary ($)	Longevity pay, maximum ($), no. years to max.	Reported expenditures (in thousands): Total expendi-tures (A) ($)	Total personnel expendi-tures (B), % of (A) ($)	Salaries and wages (C) ($)	City contrib. to employee retirement, insurance (D) ($)	Capital outlay (E) ($)	All other (F) ($)
10,000-24,999 continued										
Mayfield, Ky. (cont'd)	F	39-39-56	11,160-11,400	None	619	531-86	531	...-...	7	81
Mayfield Heights, Ohio	P	38-32-40	19,009-25,750	Y-26,470-20	1,516	1,310-86	1,011	178-121	48	158
	F	25-25-56	19,009-25,750	Y-26,470-20	968	897-93	671	148-78	10	61
	R	9-9-40	13,665-17,950	Y-18,670-20	333	170-51	133	18-19	...	163
Meadville, Pa. (7)	P	25-24-40	15,205-19,169	Y-20,127-20	846	726-86	567	75-84	27	93
	F	19-19-56	17,473-18,968	None	606	511-84	371	78-62	19	76
Medford tp, N.J. (1)	P	31-28-40	17,575-26,275	Y-26,032-15	1,059	954-90	788	131-35	...	105
	R	8-8-40	10,010-20,002	None	273	164-60	139	17-8	...	109
Medina, Ohio (1)	P	29-27-40	15,101-19,261	Y-21,195-20	1,001	856-86	700	100-56	63	82
	R	12-0-40	12,418-15,850	Y-16,858-20	597	295-49	238	32-25	96	206
Melrose Park v, Ill. (7)	P	57-52-40	12,000-25,960	None	1,581	1,581-100	1,581	...-...	...	...
	F	61-61-..	12,000-24,860	None	1,529	1,529-100	1,529	...-...	...	...
Menasha, Wis.	P	49-33-40	19,968-23,268	None	1,578	1,466-93	1,103	250-113	43	69
	F	35-35-56	18,456-22,200	None	1,197	1,162-97	834	234-94	8	27
	R	5-0-40	18,824-18,824	None	261	159-61	134	11-14	60	42
Mequon, Wis. (1,7)	P	34-34-40	19,056-24,582	Y-24,657-4	1,422	1,250-88	961	229-60	58	114
Mercedes, Tex.	P	28-21-40	12,457-14,353	None	646	432-67	380	35-17	37	177
	R	15-8-40	8,404-8,412	None	315	149-47	128	12-9	62	104
Mercer Island, Wash. (5)										
Merriam, Kan. (7)	P	21-19-40	15,834-24,120	Y-...-..	719	595-83	491	62-42	...	124
	F	12-12-56	15,078-24,120	Y-...-..	331	308-93	243	36-29	...	23
Merrimack t, N.H.	P	33-29-40	14,850-17,035	Y-17,235-15	932	758-81	625	87-46	40	134
	F	20-19-56	12,000-17,037	None	535	428-80	351	42-35	18	89
	R	2-0-40	12,220-15,288	None	75	29-39	25	2-2	...	46
Metuchen b, N.J. (1)										
Miami Springs, Fla.	P	43-35-40	20,087-24,120	Y-25,120-15	1,489	1,343-90	1,018	259-66	47	99
	R	17-10-40	10,595-12,613	Y-13,613-15	489	305-62	247	36-22	4	180
Middlesex b, N.J. (1)	P	29-27-40	16,936-22,813	Y-24,634-20	1,408	1,357-96	780	124-453	...	51
	F	...-...-..	...-...	..-...-..	48	...-..	...	...-...	...	48
	R	8-5-40	11,690-17,379	Y-18,769-20	225	177-79	140	23-14	...	48
Middletown, N.Y.	P	49-44-40	16,044-22,882	None	1,386	1,174-85	1,174	...-...	42	170
	F	40-40-40	15,629-22,802	None	971	853-88	853	...-...	12	106
	R	9-9-40	12,769-16,790	None	239	157-66	157	...-...	...	82
Middletown tp, Pa. (1,4)										
Middletown b, Pa. (1,7)	P	13-13-40	13,807-20,189	None	406	336-83	287	19-30	15	55
Midlothian v, Ill. (7)	P	22-22-40	17,633-22,530	None	554	554-100	531	...-23	...	...
	F	11-11-48	16,789-20,926	None	272	272-100	258	...-14	...	...
Midvale, Utah (1,7)	P	22-21-40	13,475-18,105	None	734	610-83	386	206-18	7	117
	F	...-...-..	...-...	..-...-..	120	25-21	5	20-...	15	80
Mill Valley, Calif. (7)	P	27-21-40	23,172-27,480	None	1,210	908-75	746	117-45	32	270
	F	21-21-56	22,332-26,472	None	853	634-74	524	79-31	15	204
Millbrae, Calif. (7)	P	34-25-40	21,672-26,352	None	1,137	1,068-94	855	200-13	29	40
	F	23-22-40	20,532-24,948	None	774	758-98	606	141-11	3	13
Millburn tp, N.J.	P	63-58-40	19,500-24,982	Y-...-25	2,100	1,796-86	1,796	...-...	64	240
	F	48-47-42	19,500-24,982	Y-...-25	1,733	1,408-81	1,408	...-...	222	103
	R	11-11-40	16,165-19,956	Y-21,952-25	...	...-..	...	...-...	...	...
Millington, Tenn.	P	23-23-40	14,700-16,512	None	651	523-80	437	86-...	27	101
	F	14-14-56	13,080-14,388	None	308	245-80	205	40-...	9	54
	R	10-4-40	10,296-11,024	None	216	126-58	110	16-...	8	82
Millville, N.J.	P	60-48-40	10,338-21,453	Y-22,740-5	1,639	1,502-92	1,228	182-92	20	117
	F	4-4-40	10,338-21,453	Y-22,740-5	279	132-47	112	13-7	125	22
	R	11-8-40	7,308-17,477	Y-18,526-5	505	247-49	202	31-14	170	88
Milwaukie, Ore. (7)	P	30-23-40	20,052-23,664	None	1,097	983-90	753	175-55	5	109
	F	28-27-56	20,112-23,844	None	1,163	1,002-86	774	181-47	8	153
Mineola v, N.Y.	R	24-18-40	13,887-17,164	Y-17,664-15	588	528-90	389	69-70	60	...
Mineral Wells, Tex.	P	30-23-40	12,150-15,732	Y-15,780-1	891	560-63	469	49-42	22	309
	F	6-6-60	12,150-14,352	Y-14,400-1	166	110-66	91	10-9	26	30
	R	25-9-40	8,316-10,284	Y-10,332-1	431	337-78	280	22-35	37	57
Mission, Tex. (7)	P	48-36-40	13,546-14,742	Y-15,942-25	908	744-82	658	64-22	2	162
	F	11-10-40	12,220-14,924	Y-16,124-25	230	149-65	130	14-5	6	75
Missouri City, Tex. (7)	P	39-28-40	19,740-27,108	Y-29,508-25	1,466	1,152-79	976	100-76	83	231
	F	25-25-54	19,740-27,108	Y-29,508-25	1,088	822-76	703	71-48	127	139
Mitchell, S.D. (7)	P	28-24-40	13,690-14,143	Y-...-..	560	500-89	419	60-21	...	60
	F	13-13-56	13,477-14,716	Y-...-..	340	314-92	239	66-9	...	26
	R	11-0-40	11,823-11,823	Y-...-..	223	189-85	161	19-9	...	34
Moberly, Mo.	P	38-34-40	11,102-16,368	None	976	748-77	604	82-62	55	173
	F	23-23-56	10,017-14,758	None	487	450-92	351	63-36	11	26
	R	16-0-40	9,089-12,611	None	363	281-77	219	33-29	21	61
Monessen, Pa. (7)	P	16-16-40	17,014-20,051	Y-23,059-15	541	359-66	305	12-42	9	173
	F	4-4-48	17,014-20,051	Y-23,059-15	172	120-70	94	14-12	5	47
Monroe t, Conn.	P	36-30-40	15,959-21,212	Y-21,412-15	1,274	1,068-84	860	138-70	43	163
Monroe, Mich. (7)	P	53-49-40	17,638-24,877	Y-25,252-25	1,944	1,670-86	1,432	176-62	...	274
	F	47-47-55	17,647-24,840	Y-25,215-25	1,546	1,466-95	1,256	154-56	...	80
Monroe, N.C. (5)	P	76-71-40	12,646-20,446	None	2,499	1,649-66	1,350	257-42	341	509
	R	21-0-40	11,107-14,102	None	677	326-48	261	53-12	81	270
Montclair, Calif. (7)	P	59-42-40	22,434-26,605	None	2,639	2,045-77	1,578	280-187	67	527
	F	42-36-56	19,116-22,620	None	1,881	1,490-79	1,155	206-129	24	367
Montgomery, Ohio (3,7)	P	16-14-40	21,500-25,300	Y-25,975-5	641	531-83	414	74-43	25	85

Table 3/18 continued **POLICE, FIRE, AND REFUSE COLLECTION AND DISPOSAL DEPARTMENTS: PERSONNEL, SALARIES, AND EXPENDITURES FOR CITIES OVER 10,000: 1984**

City	De-part-ment	Total personnel, no. uniformed, duty hours per week	Entrance, maximum salary ($)	Longevity pay, maximum ($), no. years to max.	Reported expenditures (in thousands) Total expendi-tures (A) ($)	Total personnel expendi-tures (B), % of (A) ($)	Salaries and wages (C) ($)	City contrib. to employee retirement, insurance (D) ($)	Capital outlay (E) ($)	All other (F) ($)
10,000-24,999 continued										
Montville t, Conn. (1)	P	...-...-..	13,700-16,000	None	185	175-95	175	...-...	10	...
	F	...-...-..	12,300-12,300	None	115	65-57	65	...-...	50	...
Montville tp, N.J. (1)	P	32-28-40	...-...	Y-...-20	1,002	1,002-100	858	99-45	...	...
Moon tp, Pa. (1,7)	P	26-21-40	20,389-24,200	Y-25,000-23	901	745-83	648	13-84	...	156
Moraga t, Calif. (3,4,7)										
Morgan City, La.	P	59-47-40	15,271-17,678	Y-18,032-1	1,480	1,262-85	1,132	85-45	7	211
	F	34-33-40	13,851-14,544	Y-14,835-1	912	841-92	753	60-28	7	64
	R	16-12-47	11,817-15,126	Y-15,441-1	675	318-47	294	18-6	12	345
Morganton, N.C.	P	57-51-40	13,520-18,122	Y-18,847-15	1,398	1,111-79	945	126-40	91	196
	F	23-23-56	12,246-16,406	Y-17,062-15	461	424-92	356	50-18	5	32
	R	16-16-40	9,100-12,246	Y-12,736-15	399	227-57	187	28-12	76	96
Morristown, Tenn. (7)	P	48-42-40	14,165-18,138	Y-...-..	1,457	1,106-76	879	149-78	82	269
	F	48-48-56	...-...	Y-...-..	1,007	887-88	705	120-62	25	95
	R	18-7-40	...-...	Y-...-..	681	328-48	239	53-36	110	243
Morton v, Ill. (1,7)	P	15-12-40	16,536-24,900	Y-28,697-..	776	604-78	527	39-38	54	118
Morton Grove v, Ill. (7)	P	57-46-40	22,815-27,420	Y-27,730-15	1,670	1,476-88	1,476	...-...	55	139
	F	42-41-56	22,739-26,674	Y-26,984-15	1,340	1,167-87	1,167	...-...	21	152
Moscow, Idaho (1,7)	P	31-22-40	15,558-20,064	Y-...-..	995	758-76	602	103-53	24	213
	F	3-2-40	...-...	Y-...-..	200	110-55	78	28-4	30	60
Moses Lake, Wash. (7)	P	26-17-40	19,320-24,156	None	873	721-83	588	72-61	4	148
	F	13-13-52	18,000-22,500	None	499	435-87	364	39-32	23	41
Moultrie, Ga.	P	41-35-40	11,461-14,643	None	1,028	796-77	703	48-45	52	180
	F	41-40-60	10,920-13,936	None	735	679-92	587	42-50	8	48
	R	35-15-40	8,112-10,400	None	644	435-68	357	31-47	21	188
Moundsville, W.Va.	P	18-14-40	15,808-15,808	Y-17,536-20	545	472-87	379	55-38	24	49
	F	21-21-48	15,467-15,467	Y-17,262-20	451	424-94	377	6-41	2	25
	R	11-11-40	12,418-12,418	Y-13,618-20	276	176-64	144	12-20	41	59
Mount Holly tp, N.J. (1)	P	25-22-40	18,531-23,652	Y-25,835-4	815	731-90	646	62-23	...	84
	R	5-3-40	11,736-14,822	Y-15,563-4	76	65-86	61	4-...	...	11
Mount Laurel tp, N.J. (1)	P	37-30-40	18,276-24,050	Y-28,050-20	949	949-100	779	117-53	...	...
	R	11-8-40	13,307-16,277	Y-18,277-20	188	188-100	156	19-13	...	...
Mount Vernon, Ill.	P	37-34-40	18,505-19,173	Y-21,724-20	1,246	1,027-82	848	157-22	32	187
	F	28-28-56	18,505-19,173	Y-21,724-20	1,022	897-88	695	186-16	29	96
	R	9-5-40	18,505-18,834	None	785	240-31	204	28-8	302	243
Mount Vernon, Ohio	P	32-23-40	15,267-18,658	None	896	714-80	552	93-69	29	153
	F	30-29-56	15,288-18,695	None	815	740-91	562	113-65	7	68
Mountain Brook, Ala. (7)	P	52-44-40	17,362-20,715	Y-21,015-13	1,762	1,443-82	1,156	231-56	99	220
	F	56-55-52	17,362-20,715	Y-21,015-13	1,837	1,631-89	1,309	258-64	29	177
Mountlake Terrace, Wash. (7)	P	21-19-40	24,748-30,935	None	996	817-82	693	90-34	4	175
	F	10-9-42	24,096-27,415	None	542	352-65	301	33-18	9	181
Munster t, Ind. (1)	P	28-21-40	17,417-23,255	Y-23,795-..	859	732-85	732	...-...	22	105
	F	1-0-40	...-...	..-...-..	98	59-60	59	...-...	22	17
	R	18-18-40	14,500-18,600	None	210	206-98	206	...-...	3	1
Muskegon Heights, Mich. (7)	P	28-22-40	20,398-20,999	Y-23,099-25	960	818-85	660	110-48	29	113
	F	15-15-54	17,269-18,063	Y-19,869-25	429	408-95	332	50-26	7	14
Myrtle Beach, S.C. (7)	P	79-62-40	12,436-18,922	None	1,991	1,552-78	1,274	226-52	74	365
	F	46-46-48	11,266-17,143	None	940	745-79	603	113-29	132	63
	R	23-23-40	9,247-13,392	None	1,024	380-37	320	45-15	316	328
Naples, Fla.	P	75-57-41	16,253-21,453	None	1,843	1,602-87	1,461	98-43	32	209
	F	35-33-56	15,540-20,513	None	805	711-88	647	44-20	26	68
	R	34-28-40	12,862-15,814	None	1,140	617-54	550	37-30	155	368
Narragansett t, R.I. (7)	P	33-28-38	15,812-18,347	Y-19,972-25	1,090	922-85	705	173-44	11	157
	F	17-17-42	14,594-17,373	Y-19,323-30	585	489-84	414	55-20	18	78
Natchitoches, La.	P	46-45-40	9,027-11,448	None	767	560-73	523	37-...	79	128
	F	31-31-40	9,782-9,782	None	507	463-91	432	31-...	12	32
	R	56-28-40	7,280-...	None	929	561-60	524	37-...	131	237
Nederland, Tex.	P	22-18-40	20,760-24,000	Y-...-..	701	525-75	423	82-20	21	155
	F	11-9-56	20,760-24,000	Y-...-.	380	327-86	262	49-16	7	46
	R	7-0-40	17,388-18,512	Y-...-..	707	286-40	229	42-15	168	253
Neenah, Wis.	P	50-43-39	19,356-22,488	Y-22,788-20	1,962	1,782-91	1,286	353-143	65	115
	F	43-41-56	19,632-22,212	Y-22,512-20	1,609	1,554-97	1,117	324-113	5	50
	R	14-14-40	19,056-19,074	None	897	433-48	278	55-100	370	94
Nether Providence tp, Pa. (7)	P	11-11-40	23,076-24,254	Y-27,649-20	456	403-88	346	22-35	...	53
New Bern, N.C. (7)	P	55-45-42	12,090-16,201	Y-16,801-30	971	719-74	615	64-40	101	151
	F	30-29-56	11,514-15,430	Y-16,030-30	632	459-73	385	50-24	53	120
New Braunfels, Tex.	P	40-32-40	...-16,057	Y-16,657-25	1,164	891-77	787	88-16	90	183
	F	44-43-56	15,222-15,983	Y-16,583-25	1,072	944-88	842	89-13	22	106
	R	27-18-40	11,585-13,062	Y-13,662-20	667	426-64	382	37-7	70	171
New Canaan t, Conn.	P	47-43-40	20,230-23,786	Y-24,136-5	1,895	1,560-82	1,248	212-100	40	295
	F	8-8-42	17,234-21,999	Y-22,349-5	422	258-61	196	44-18	16	148
New Carrollton, Md.	R	12-8-40	9,588-15,201	None	...	...-..	...	...-...	...	...
New Castle, Ind.	P	45-42-48	13,152-13,711	Y-14,971-18	940	825-88	675	40-110	17	98
	F	33-33-56	13,152-13,711	Y-14,971-18	714	671-94	543	32-96	13	30
	R	35-20-40	11,650-11,650	Y-...-..	637	632-99	485	47-100	5	...
New Hope, Minn. (1)	P	23-20-..	18,018-26,688	Y-29,090-16	1,015	813-80	699	83-31	...	202
New Milford b, N.J. (1)										
New Port Richey, Fla. (7)	P	33-26-40	13,333-16,890	None	814	632-78	492	96-44	56	126
	F	18-17-56	12,376-17,792	None	499	391-78	306	61-24	63	45

Table 3/18 continued **POLICE, FIRE, AND REFUSE COLLECTION AND DISPOSAL DEPARTMENTS: PERSONNEL, SALARIES, AND EXPENDITURES FOR CITIES OVER 10,000: 1984**

					Reported expenditures (in thousands)					
City	Depart-ment	Total personnel, no. uniformed, duty hours per week	Entrance, maximum salary ($)	Longevity pay, maximum ($), no. years to max.	Total expenditures (A) ($)	Total personnel expenditures (B), % of (A) ($)	Salaries and wages (C) ($)	City contrib. to employee retirement, insurance (D) ($)	Capital outlay (E) ($)	All other (F) ($)
10,000-24,999 continued										
New Port Richey, Fla. (cont'd)	R	6-0-40	6,968-14,290	None	166	112-67	90	16-6	20	34
New Smyrna Beach, Fla.	P	54-41-42	13,051-18,595	Y-19,130-..	1,338	1,021-76	851	103-67	35	282
	F	48-46-48	11,207-13,703	Y-14,032-..	1,051	915-87	742	116-57	9	127
	R	31-15-40	9,167-13,416	Y-13,803-..	1,123	769-68	327	405-37	19	335
New Ulm, Minn. (1,7)	P	22-19-40	21,360-21,972	None	788	729-93	689	20-20	26	33
	F	...-...-..	...-...	..-...-..	254	136-54	76	60-...	118	...
Newark v, N.Y. (7)	P	19-17-40	15,056-15,864	Y-17,803-2	517	463-90	351	90-22	25	29
	F	5-5-40	14,335-14,335	Y-...-..	143	114-80	83	24-7	5	24
Newberg, Ore. (7)	P	24-17-40	18,912-24,132	Y-24,432-20	813	717-88	560	104-53	27	69
	F	7-5-40	18,444-23,544	Y-23,944-20	231	193-84	150	28-15	...	38
Newburyport, Mass. (7)	P	34-32-40	12,953-16,794	Y-17,044-5	830	760-92	760	...-...	10	60
	F	31-31-42	12,950-16,791	..-...-..	811	717-88	717	...-...	15	79
Newnan, Ga.	P	31-27-42	13,062-18,387	None	745	600-81	534	44-22	49	96
	F	23-23-56	13,155-18,469	None	472	440-93	397	25-18	12	20
	R	24-15-40	9,276-13,062	None	462	353-76	317	21-15	51	58
Newport, Ky. (7)	P	40-32-40	10,999-10,999	Y-11,999-20	1,020	839-82	570	176-93	13	168
	F	45-45-56	11,551-11,551	Y-12,551-20	970	954-98	679	189-86	16	...
Newton, Iowa	P	29-24-40	14,664-19,740	None	932	767-82	618	85-64	...	165
	F	25-25-56	13,968-19,968	None	1,003	766-76	605	122-39	...	237
	R	10-7-40	11,668-14,290	None	225	163-72	149	...-14	...	62
Newton, Kan.	P	22-18-40	14,326-17,836	Y-18,460-36	629	538-86	427	82-29	23	68
	F	22-22-54	14,326-17,836	Y-18,460-36	658	615-93	477	104-34	14	29
	R	13-8-40	11,206-13,988	Y-14,612-36	349	256-73	212	23-21	50	43
Newtown tp, Pa. (1)	P	13-13-40	...-24,582	..-...-..	607	488-80	369	77-42	...	119
Niles, Mich. (7)	P	26-18-40	...-21,247	Y-25,008-25	876	764-87	568	136-60	36	76
	F	17-17-54	...-20,652	Y-24,307-25	604	575-95	420	111-44	12	17
Norco, Calif. (4)										
Norfolk, Neb.	P	38-31-40	13,884-18,324	None	1,026	825-80	699	80-46	51	150
	F	25-24-56	13,236-17,508	None	789	631-80	476	123-32	76	82
Norridge v, Ill. (3,7)	P	27-21-45	15,000-26,450	None	1,186	1,022-86	875	80-67	25	139
North Attleborough t, Mass. (7)	P	38-32-40	15,745-17,925	Y-18,325-5	881	881-100	856	...-25	...	...
	F	39-37-..	15,096-18,018	Y-18,268-25	839	839-100	802	...-37	...	...
North Augusta, S.C. (5)	P	41-34-40	15,282-21,794	None	1,085	859-79	700	109-50	121	105
	R	19-12-40	9,848-10,294	None	384	255-66	209	27-19	42	87
North Branford t, Conn. (1)	P	15-14-38	15,229-19,716	None	606	514-85	353	91-70	23	69
	F	..-...-..	...-...	..-...-..	181	25-14	10	...-15	47	109
	R	2-0-40	...-...	..-...-..	55	23-42	18	2-3	...	32
North Brunswick tp, N.J. (1)										
North Canton, Ohio (1,7)	P	22-22-40	16,670-19,011	Y-19,511-20	749	621-83	501	82-38	15	113
	F	...-...-..	...-...	..-...-..	71	41-58	37	4-...	...	30
North College Hill, Ohio (1)										
North Haven t, Conn.	P	53-45-40	16,858-19,572	Y-19,923-15	1,696	1,480-87	1,066	286-128	51	165
	F	30-29-42	18,204-19,396	Y-19,720-15	1,146	916-80	679	157-80	104	126
	R	22-9-40	15,679-17,004	Y-17,220-16	786	506-64	412	45-49	22	258
North Lauderdale, Fla. (7)	P	50-38-40	18,105-22,825	None	1,420	1,170-82	1,005	107-58	46	204
	F	15-15-48	15,494-21,695	None	400	302-76	259	26-17	26	72
North Platte, Neb.	P	56-37-40	13,416-17,534	Y-17,714-15	1,384	1,231-89	1,033	116-82	40	113
	F	37-30-56	13,013-17,460	Y-17,640-15	956	807-84	719	30-58	13	136
	R	11-0-40	10,837-13,874	Y-14,054-15	380	204-54	176	15-13	37	139
North Royalton, Ohio	P	27-21-40	19,510-24,003	Y-25,443-20	1,083	890-82	664	147-79	...	193
	F	14-14-54	19,500-24,000	Y-25,440-20	535	461-86	326	96-39	...	74
	R	6-4-40	16,515-18,678	Y-20,118-20	268	163-61	128	22-13	...	105
North St. Paul, Minn.	P	11-9-40	18,213-28,020	Y-30,542-16	497	428-86	382	46-...	20	49
	F	1-1-..	...-...	..-...-..	104	51-49	46	3-2	15	38
North Versailles tp, Pa. (1)										
Northbridge t, Mass.	P	17-16-40	16,415-19,861	Y-20,261-30	534	487-91	427	50-10	8	39
	F	8-8-48	16,662-17,778	None	249	192-77	182	4-6	...	57
Northfield, Minn. (1,4,7)	P	20-15-40	...-...	Y-...-..	582	543-93	477	36-30	39	...
	F	1-0-..	...-...	..-...-..	33	25-76	25	...-...	8	...
Norton t, Mass.	P	20-20-40	14,000-18,980	Y-20,000-10	501	467-93	467	...-...	34	...
	F	16-16-42	14,000-18,980	Y-20,000-10	460	399-87	399	...-...	61	...
Norton Shores, Mich. (7)	P	23-22-40	19,824-23,508	Y-25,859-24	1,246	726-58	597	92-37	269	251
	F	8-8-48	17,513-20,876	Y-22,964-24	461	318-69	271	31-16	43	100
Norwalk, Ohio	P	19-15-40	18,109-20,644	Y-21,464-20	792	643-81	501	106-36	34	115
	F	14-14-56	18,109-20,644	Y-21,464-20	493	451-91	334	88-29	6	36
	R	6-6-40	12,893-16,858	Y-17,678-20	179	126-70	102	15-9	2	51
Novi, Mich. (1)										
Oak Harbor, Wash.	P	28-18-40	19,032-26,832	Y-27,100-9	675	652-97	559	62-31	9	14
	F	1-1-40	...-...	..-...-..	189	82-43	75	6-1	12	95
	R	6-6-40	16,308-20,796	Y-21,004-5	270	158-59	137	16-5	11	101
Oakland b, N.J. (1,7)	P	...-...-40	20,000-26,700	Y-29,103-5	1,279	1,247-97	1,020	182-45	...	32
	F	...-...-..	...-...	..-...-..	6	6-100	6	...-...	...	...
Oakland Park, Fla. (5)	P	100-84-40	18,497-24,787	Y-28,505-20	3,435	2,833-82	2,404	429-...	4	598
	F	40-40-52	17,616-23,607	Y-27,148-20	1,335	1,195-90	992	203-...	13	127
	R	25-17-40	13,474-18,056	Y-20,765-20	1,215	568-47	483	85-...	10	637
Ocean City, N.J. (7)	P	57-54-40	17,055-23,479	Y-25,827-25	2,030	2,030-100	1,659	283-88	...	...
	F	49-49-56	17,055-23,479	Y-26,296-30	2,461	1,741-71	1,416	252-73	720	...
Ogdensburg, N.Y.	P	31-27-40	16,576-20,331	None	873	789-90	601	142-46	2	82

Table 3/18 continued **POLICE, FIRE, AND REFUSE COLLECTION AND DISPOSAL DEPARTMENTS: PERSONNEL, SALARIES, AND EXPENDITURES FOR CITIES OVER 10,000: 1984**

					Reported expenditures (in thousands)					
City	Depart-ment	Total personnel, no. uniformed, duty hours per week	Entrance, maximum salary ($)	Longevity pay, maximum ($), no. years to max.	Total expendi-tures (A) ($)	Total personnel expendi-tures (B), % of (A) ($)	Salaries and wages (C) ($)	City contrib. to employee retirement, insurance (D) ($)	Capital outlay (E) ($)	All other (F) ($)
10,000-24,999 continued										
Ogdensburg, N.Y. (cont'd)	F	38-33-40	17,112-20,521	None	1,133	1,048-92	762	228-58	5	80
	R	2-2-40	17,472-17,534	None	71	56-79	44	9-3	2	13
Okmulgee, Okla.	P	34-27-40	12,172-13,372	Y-14,572-12	120	120-100	...	83-37	...	...
	F	29-29-56	11,208-13,260	Y-14,460-12	68	68-100	...	36-32	...	...
	R	7-0-40	11,328-11,932	Y-13,132-12	27	27-100	...	19-8	...	...
Oneida, N.Y. (7)	P	25-22-40	16,356-17,356	Y-18,356-20	755	683-90	498	128-57	25	47
	F	26-26-40	16,454-17,454	Y-18,454-20	749	715-95	538	122-55	10	24
Opelika, Ala.	P	66-55-40	11,835-15,475	Y-16,125-25	1,524	1,213-80	1,044	128-41	60	251
	F	56-55-56	11,274-14,747	Y-15,397-25	1,082	979-90	844	103-32	23	80
	R	37-17-40	11,274-14,747	None	940	371-39	322	32-17	46	523
Orange t, Conn. (1)										
Orange, Tex.	P	53-39-40	17,368-21,174	Y-22,374-25	1,477	1,233-83	1,040	122-71	43	201
	F	43-41-56	17,093-20,471	Y-21,671-25	1,238	1,086-88	894	123-69	45	107
	R	18-11-40	12,854-17,472	..-...-..	692	349-50	288	33-28	76	267
Orangeburg, S.C.	P	49-36-40	15,101-16,863	None	1,095	871-80	700	117-54	51	173
	F	38-38-60	12,767-15,943	None	764	698-91	552	97-49	10	56
	R	15-6-40	11,029-11,892	None	723	292-40	235	25-32	371	60
Oregon, Ohio	P	39-36-40	24,003-25,792	Y-26,308-..	1,518	1,368-90	1,044	191-133	1	149
	F	11-11-52	23,774-25,563	Y-26,074-..	922	639-69	509	84-46	180	103
Oregon City, Ore.	P	32-25-40	19,260-22,284	Y-23,616-30	...	...-..	...	...-...	...	...
	F	28-27-56	19,032-24,372	Y-25,836-30	...	...-..	...	...-...	...	...
Orland Park v, Ill. (3,7)	P	51-36-..	17,000-26,000	None	1,887	1,399-74	1,170	229-...	40	448
Ormond Beach, Fla. (5)	P	56-42-40	14,374-18,518	Y-19,166-10	1,448	1,074-74	935	93-46	74	300
	F	19-18-40	13,118-16,753	Y-17,339-10	477	369-77	332	22-15	22	86
	R	28-24-40	11,117-14,191	Y-14,688-10	1,188	491-41	407	61-23	176	521
Oskaloosa, Iowa	P	17-13-40	14,312-16,915	Y-17,815-20	504	425-84	345	66-14	2	77
	F	18-18-56	13,857-17,170	Y-18,070-20	432	387-90	337	35-15	19	26
Ossining v, N.Y.	P	44-42-40	18,500-25,000	Y-25,500-15	1,694	1,694-100	1,232	385-77	...	...
	R	10-0-40	15,500-18,000	Y-18,500-15	242	242-100	210	14-18	...	...
Oswego, N.Y. (7)	P	49-46-40	16,316-20,128	Y-22,274-23	1,615	1,508-93	1,131	308-69	40	67
	F	76-75-44	15,486-19,971	Y-22,045-20	3,883	2,168-56	1,620	445-103	1,577	138
Ottawa, Kan. (5)	P	42-34-40	15,054-19,213	None	1,088	910-84	772	92-46	52	126
Owatonna, Minn.	P	22-20-40	14,496-24,980	Y-25,854-5	664	591-89	506	60-25	35	38
	F	8-8-56	19,394-21,550	Y-22,150-5	293	250-85	218	22-10	14	29
Owosso, Mich. (5)	P	19-19-40	16,655-21,649	Y-22,197-20	706	611-87	475	92-44	7	88
	F	23-23-56	18,495-20,595	Y-21,127-20	740	663-90	503	105-55	3	74
Oxford, Ohio (1)	P	27-20-40	18,704-22,101	Y-22,761-30	952	819-86	662	101-56	57	76
	F	...-...-..	...-...	..-...-..	56	32-57	30	2-...	6	18
	R	9-6-40	13,355-15,213	Y-15,873-30	292	236-81	190	25-21	14	42
Palatka, Fla.	P	33-26-40	14,081-14,081	None	808	660-82	566	75-19	18	130
	F	28-28-56	12,919-12,919	None	714	555-78	485	52-18	84	75
	R	19-19-40	8,778-9,848	None	387	258-67	218	31-9	39	90
Palestine, Tex.	P	49-38-40	15,972-20,472	Y-21,672-25	946	779-82	623	115-41	1	166
	F	35-35-56	15,024-18,780	Y-19,980-25	741	659-89	519	102-38	...	82
	R	18-18-40	10,440-14,016	Y-15,216-25	414	236-57	184	35-17	17	161
Palm Bay, Fla. (7)	P	71-47-40	13,883-22,189	None	1,669	1,256-75	1,086	110-60	132	281
	F	44-41-56	12,468-17,133	None	921	676-73	578	62-36	139	106
Palm Beach Gardens, Fla. (7)	P	50-39-40	15,874-...	Y-19,165-12	1,325	1,249-94	1,055	107-87	76	...
	F	7-7-40	13,354-...	Y-18,281-12	224	162-72	130	17-15	62	...
Palm Desert, Calif. (3,4,7)										
Palmdale, Calif. (2,4,7)										
Palos Heights, Ill. (7)	P	22-22-40	12,100-...	None	925	820-89	706	47-67	...	105
Pampa, Tex.	P	42-31-40	15,546-17,556	Y-18,756-25	1,067	821-77	702	83-36	43	203
	F	40-40-56	14,100-15,924	Y-17,124-25	957	879-92	749	93-37	2	76
	R	16-2-40	11,118-12,540	None	847	279-33	235	29-15	213	355
Paradise t, Calif. (7)	P	32-23-40	18,548-22,589	None	1,152	958-83	766	106-86	...	194
	F	36-34-56	15,375-22,102	None	1,196	1,081-90	830	130-121	...	115
Paradise Valley t, Ariz.	P	25-18-40	20,766-26,504	None	913	732-80	617	91-24	121	60
Paragould, Ark.	P	30-26-40	11,265-11,752	Y-12,927-10	529	432-82	377	40-15	25	72
	F	18-18-60	12,194-12,459	Y-13,705-10	292	292-100	264	11-17	...	...
	R	16-10-40	9,654-9,718	Y-10,670-10	225	183-81	165	10-8	13	29
Paris, Tenn. (7)	P	27-21-40	13,635-15,054	None	580	488-84	398	64-26	28	64
	F	24-24-54	13,635-15,054	None	546	468-86	368	74-26	10	68
Parsons, Kan. (5)										
Patchogue v, N.Y.	F	4-0-40	13,811-13,811	None	215	96-45	75	15-6	3	116
	R	13-0-40	13,208-13,208	None	307	245-80	193	52-...	1	61
Pearl, Miss. (7)	P	31-28-40	12,108-30,012	None	662	547-83	446	72-29	19	96
	F	38-37-48	12,108-30,012	None	700	659-94	537	86-36	12	29
Pearland, Tex. (1)	P	32-26-40	20,124-20,571	Y-21,771-25	895	755-84	662	69-24	7	133
	R	13-13-40	15,267-18,741	Y-19,941-25	640	250-39	213	24-13	94	296
Pecos, Tex. (1)	P	22-17-40	17,111-17,476	Y-17,524-1	661	509-77	439	55-15	22	130
	F	...-...-..	...-...	..-...-..	90	22-24	22	...-...	8	60
	R	14-2-40	7,644-7,644	Y-7,692-1	368	180-49	156	19-5	76	112
Peoria, Ariz.	P	37-34-40	17,028-21,710	Y-...-20	1,088	844-78	699	108-37	82	162
	F	12-11-..	17,028-21,710	Y-...-20	351	245-70	216	16-13	49	57
	R	10-4-40	12,266-15,496	Y-...-20	846	266-31	221	30-15	332	248
Pequannock tp, N.J. (1)										
Peru, Ill. (1,7)	P	24-21-40	16,755-16,755	Y-20,105-20	778	655-84	527	92-36	26	97

Table 3/18 continued **POLICE, FIRE, AND REFUSE COLLECTION AND DISPOSAL DEPARTMENTS: PERSONNEL, SALARIES, AND EXPENDITURES FOR CITIES OVER 10,000: 1984**

City	De-part-ment	Total personnel, no. uniformed, duty hours per week	Entrance, maximum salary ($)	Longevity pay, maximum ($), no. years to max.	Reported expenditures (in thousands): Total expendi-tures (A) ($)	Total personnel expendi-tures (B), % of (A) ($)	Salaries and wages (C) ($)	City contrib. to employee retirement, insurance (D) ($)	Capital outlay (E) ($)	All other (F) ($)
10,000-24,999 continued										
Peru, Ill. (cont'd)	F	...-...-..	...-...	..-...-..	697	110-16	110	...-...	516	71
Peters tp, Pa. (7)	P	21-16-40	17,700-20,820	Y-23,890-15	769	589-77	436	92-61	87	93
	F	...-...-..	...-...	..-...-..	138	...-..	...	...-...	...	138
Phoenixville b, Pa. (1,7)	P	23-19-40	...-20,629	Y-22,280-20	857	726-85	646	6-74	18	113
	F	...-...-..	...-...	..-...-..	99	9-9	...	...-9	...	90
	R	...-...-..	...-...	..-...-..	186	...-..	...	...-...	...	186
Piedmont, Calif.	P	27-20-40	22,692-27,468	None	994	862-87	667	146-49	8	124
	F	22-22-56	22,788-26,184	None	884	840-95	669	134-37	11	33
Pierre, S.D. (1)	P	22-19-40	14,000-15,500	None	628	405-64	367	26-12	21	202
	F	2-0-40	...-...	..-...-..	127	31-24	27	3-1	19	77
	R	6-0-40	13,175-15,500	None	147	100-68	87	10-3	...	47
Piqua, Ohio	P	23-23-40	21,471-25,339	None	1,069	888-83	687	122-79	23	158
	F	26-26-56	13,080-16,511	None	951	878-92	652	153-73	4	69
	R	8-8-40	14,085-16,060	None	402	193-48	152	21-20	42	167
Pittsburg, Kan. (5)	P	31-27-40	13,272-17,352	None	823	656-80	497	105-54	51	116
	F	31-31-56	13,272-17,352	None	760	698-92	520	124-54	2	60
Plainfield t, Conn. (7)	P	15-15-40	13,208-15,787	None	527	347-66	295	34-18	14	166
Plainview, Tex.	P	38-29-40	13,905-...	Y-20,336-..	1,031	755-73	668	83-4	80	196
	F	29-29-56	13,162-...	Y-20,336-..	737	623-85	564	56-3	15	99
	R	14-14-40	11,637-...	Y-16,176-..	531	228-43	203	24-1	55	248
Plattsburgh, N.Y.	P	43-41-40	15,100-23,562	None	1,474	1,351-92	988	291-72	34	89
	F	49-47-40	12,606-23,706	None	1,745	1,531-88	1,124	330-77	143	71
	R	6-4-40	16,598-17,721	None	153	142-93	112	21-9	1	10
Pleasant Grove, Utah (7)	P	11-10-40	13,218-19,429	Y-...-..	359	250-70	190	39-21	29	80
Plymouth tp, Pa.	P	23-18-40	18,147-23,485	Y-24,860-20	907	801-88	672	71-58	...	106
	R	9-5-40	18,262-18,699	None	317	221-70	166	32-23	...	96
Pontiac, Ill.	P	23-17-40	14,442-19,945	Y-21,939-30	581	491-85	411	69-11	26	64
	F	7-7-56	14,442-19,945	Y-21,939-30	261	197-75	166	28-3	20	44
	R	3-2-40	11,126-15,396	Y-16,935-30	96	56-58	49	6-1	...	40
Port Chester v, N.Y.	P	59-56-40	16,763-26,369	Y-26,819-18	2,647	2,318-88	1,629	577-112	15	314
	F	14-14-40	17,802-24,314	Y-24,764-18	760	499-66	332	140-27	23	238
	R	20-13-40	14,001-16,631	Y-17,444-23	777	528-68	409	81-38	166	83
Port Hueneme, Calif. (2)										
Port Lavaca, Tex. (7)	P	21-16-44	16,026-17,318	Y-18,278-..	487	428-88	373	39-16	5	54
	F	13-13-48	16,494-17,657	Y-18,617-..	352	280-80	245	25-10	9	63
	R	...-...-..	...-...	..-...-..	443	...-..	...	...-...	...	443
Port Orange, Fla.	P	44-33-42	13,541-19,261	None	1,249	943-76	867	58-18	63	243
	F	38-36-56	12,896-18,366	None	945	686-73	630	42-14	69	190
	R	19-0-40	9,630-13,707	None	716	260-36	237	16-7	98	358
Port St. Lucie, Fla. (3,4)	P	30-21-42	15,179-15,179	None	1,067	803-75	661	97-45	35	229
Portsmouth t, R.I.	P	24-24-37	12,886-16,790	Y-17,126-10	765	647-85	473	139-35	34	84
	F	22-22-42	13,798-17,348	Y-18,215-20	681	626-92	462	130-34	...	55
Potsdam v, N.Y. (2,4)										
Pottstown b, Pa.	P	49-40-40	17,184-21,097	Y-22,785-20	1,454	1,320-91	1,118	94-108	16	118
	F	14-12-54	15,801-15,801	None	482	385-80	288	74-23	...	97
	R	7-4-40	11,149-14,144	Y-15,276-20	191	154-81	131	16-7	...	37
Prairie Village, Kan. (3,7)	P	49-36-40	15,900-21,500	Y-26,000-25	1,597	1,340-84	1,047	223-70	69	188
Prattville, Ala.	P	45-37-40	11,523-15,246	None	960	755-79	638	87-30	35	170
	F	32-31-56	11,003-14,560	None	702	607-86	513	73-21	8	87
	R	19-13-40	7,633-10,088	None	291	238-82	195	28-15	43	10
Princeton b, N.J. (1)										
Princeton tp, N.J. (1,7)	P	31-26-80	17,655-27,443	Y-28,693-24	1,033	948-92	823	125-...	15	70
Prospect Heights, Ill. (3,4)										
Pulaski t, Va.	P	28-21-40	11,917-15,970	Y-18,488-25	591	445-75	369	49-27	19	127
	F	11-11-56	10,809-13,796	Y-15,970-25	241	175-73	145	18-12	25	41
	R	11-7-40	7,316-9,338	Y-10,809-25	255	167-65	138	17-12	20	68
Pullman, Wash. (7)	P	30-22-40	17,364-21,288	None	1,015	806-79	668	77-61	...	209
	F	13-13-61	17,832-21,720	None	1,021	348-34	310	15-23	579	94
Radford, Va.	P	25-24-40	10,100-15,272	None	537	419-78	359	41-19	22	96
	F	12-12-56	13,063-14,468	None	271	202-75	172	21-9	6	63
	R	12-12-40	7,508-10,296	None	237	130-55	109	13-8	45	62
Ramsey, Minn. (1)	P	7-6-40	21,130-26,745	None	249	214-86	182	22-10	8	27
	F	...-...-..	...-...	..-...-..	34	...-..	...	...-...	...	34
Ramsey b, N.J. (1,7)	P	28-24-40	10,000-28,593	Y-31,452-20	1,078	1,067-99	898	120-49	11	...
	F	...-...-..	...-...	..-...-..	310	...-..	...	...-...	310	...
Randolph tp, N.J. (1)										
Rantoul v, Ill. (1,7)	P	23-18-40	18,240-22,608	None	623	510-82	480	12-18	40	73
Ravenna, Ohio (7)	P	17-17-40	14,580-18,553	Y-...-..	601	496-83	392	67-37	1	104
	F	18-18-56	14,580-18,553	Y-...-..	577	543-94	411	99-33	...	34
Rawlins, Wyo. (7)	P	23-12-40	16,584-23,592	None	968	802-83	704	23-75	10	156
	F	8-8-40	16,584-24,552	None	253	185-73	135	25-25	32	36
	R	4-0-40	15,953-17,929	None	200	84-42	71	6-7	34	82
Red Bank, Tenn.	P	25-20-40	13,800-13,900	None	429	409-95	357	31-21	20	...
	F	5-5-51	13,100-13,300	None	151	151-100	135	12-4	...	...
	R	7-5-40	10,600-10,600	None	151	106-70	91	7-8	45	...
Red Wing, Minn.	P	21-18-40	20,610-25,176	Y-26,171-14	1,029	853-83	565	257-31	23	153
	F	27-27-56	19,116-24,161	None	1,033	918-89	694	187-37	25	90
	R	9-6-40	17,941-19,261	None	290	194-67	156	24-14	...	96

Table 3/18 continued **POLICE, FIRE, AND REFUSE COLLECTION AND DISPOSAL DEPARTMENTS: PERSONNEL, SALARIES, AND EXPENDITURES FOR CITIES OVER 10,000: 1984**

					Reported expenditures (in thousands)					
City	Department	Total personnel, no. uniformed, duty hours per week	Entrance, maximum salary ($)	Longevity pay, maximum ($), no. years to max.	Total expenditures (A) ($)	Total personnel expenditures (B), % of (A) ($)	Salaries and wages (C) ($)	City contrib. to employee retirement, insurance (D) ($)	Capital outlay (E) ($)	All other (F) ($)
10,000-24,999 continued										
Reedley, Calif. (1)	P	22-18-40	17,640-20,904	None	781	587-75	501	38-48	14	180
	R	7-4-40	12,768-15,132	None	335	176-53	128	33-15	12	147
Reidsville, N.C.	P	41-39-42	13,416-18,878	Y-20,010-20	950	899-95	773	103-23	32	19
	F	23-23-56	13,416-18,878	Y-29,010-20	575	497-86	423	62-12	4	74
	R	28-28-40	9,081-12,778	Y-13,545-20	575	426-74	360	52-14	48	101
Reynoldsburg, Ohio (2,7)	P	30-21-40	17,763-22,672	Y-23,172-6	1,190	1,021-86	810	138-73	39	130
Richmond, Ky.	P	37-30-40	12,230-19,274	None	828	662-80	578	63-21	55	111
	F	51-51-54	12,342-19,108	None	943	889-94	780	84-25	3	51
	R	26-15-40	9,006-16,879	None	763	304-40	268	18-18	129	330
Richmond Heights, Mo. (7)	P	30-28-40	17,449-26,729	None	1,076	884-82	672	137-75	54	138
	F	19-19-56	17,449-26,729	None	641	560-87	424	81-55	29	52
Richmond Heights, Ohio	P	...-...-..	...-...	..-...-..	583	583-100	583	...-...	...	...
	F	...-...-..	21,166-23,289	Y-24,453-20	299	299-100	299	...-...	...	...
Ridgefield t, Conn. (7)	P	39-32-40	13,970-19,814	Y-20,114-20	1,131	937-83	763	98-76	73	121
	F	23-21-40	14,020-19,978	Y-20,278-20	701	584-83	469	72-43	59	58
Ridgefield b, N.J. (1,4)										
Ridgefield Park v, N.J. (1)										
River Edge b, N.J. (1,7)	P	21-18-40	18,306-24,910	Y-26,404-25	920	856-93	720	106-30	4	60
	F	...-...-..	...-...	..-...-..	45	...-..	...	...-...	...	45
	R	...-...-..	...-...	..-...-..	567	...-..	...	...-...	...	567
River Forest v, Ill. (7)	P	33-27-40	16,942-27,617	None	1,162	997-86	933	...-64	48	117
	F	21-21-56	16,908-27,101	None	737	668-91	627	...-41	31	38
Riverdale v, Ill.	P	24-20-40	16,848-22,560	None	672	566-84	534	5-27	14	92
	F	6-6-48	17,388-23,136	None	200	161-81	154	...-7	11	28
	R	6-0-40	16,890-20,280	None	288	160-56	132	21-7	65	63
Riverview, Mich. (7)	P	29-26-40	24,877-27,040	Y-27,540-5	1,185	1,118-94	884	156-78	29	38
	F	...-...-..	...-...	None	301	261-87	252	3-6	5	35
	R	10-10-40	24,544-27,352	None	1,217	475-39	398	33-44	326	416
Roanoke Rapids, N.C.	P	39-31-42	12,072-15,366	Y-16,288-15	829	673-81	558	82-33	42	114
	F	29-28-54	11,496-14,664	Y-15,544-15	564	518-92	427	67-24	2	44
	R	19-10-40	9,006-11,502	Y-12,192-15	472	265-56	215	34-16	93	114
Robbinsdale, Minn. (1,7)	P	25-17-40	17,351-26,686	Y-29,088-16	917	701-76	600	71-30	30	186
	F	...-...-..	...-...	..-...-..	238	121-51	56	65-...	73	44
	R	...-...-..	...-...	..-...-..	299	...-..	...	...-...	...	299
Robstown, Tex.	P	25-19-40	13,872-17,376	Y-18,576-25	703	576-82	502	58-16	17	110
	F	10-10-60	13,326-16,452	Y-17,652-25	245	194-79	168	19-7	...	51
	R	20-0-40	9,744-12,889	None	455	310-68	268	26-16	145	...
Rochester, N.H. (7)	P	35-30-40	14,176-17,300	Y-17,800-20	...	...-..	...	...-...	...	...
	F	22-21-40	12,247-15,422	Y-15,922-20	...	...-..	...	...-...	...	...
Rock Falls v, Ill. (5)	P	34-34-40	14,794-...	None	1,041	765-73	590	120-55	28	248
	R	5-3-40	14,071-...	None	206	113-55	92	11-10	8	85
Rock Springs, Wyo. (7)	P	64-38-40	22,344-23,784	None	2,359	1,773-75	1,460	167-146	128	458
	F	33-33-56	22,064-23,364	None	1,645	1,042-63	808	157-77	297	306
Rockledge, Fla.	P	26-20-40	12,700-15,362	None	669	514-77	439	53-22	28	127
	F	23-22-60	12,700-16,000	None	604	443-73	374	46-23	108	53
	R	11-8-40	8,320-13,353	None	437	193-44	159	20-14	127	117
Rocky Hill t, Conn. (1,7)	P	27-19-40	17,481-21,368	Y-22,043-15	1,147	942-82	805	85-52	32	173
	F	...-...-..	...-...	..-...-..	265	10-4	10	...-...	19	236
Rocky River, Ohio	P	35-31-40	17,288-22,753	Y-23,776-20	1,378	1,220-89	962	190-68	...	158
	F	29-29-56	17,288-22,753	Y-23,776-20	1,101	1,037-94	777	202-58	...	64
	R	18-11-40	12,979-16,515	Y-17,258-20	573	363-63	293	41-29	66	144
Rohnert Park, Calif. (5)										
Rolla, Mo.	P	31-24-40	13,368-15,864	Y-15,891-5	615	474-77	429	45-...	36	105
	F	16-16-56	9,090-10,816	Y-10,833-5	392	304-78	269	35-...	40	48
	R	17-0-40	9,914-10,890	Y-10,900-5	365	221-61	199	22-...	8	136
Romulus, Mich. (7)	P	38-36-40	17,500-21,000	None	811	811-100	811	...-...	...	...
	F	1-0-40	...-...	..-...-..	186	186-100	186	...-...	...	...
Roseburg, Ore. (7)	P	30-21-40	15,792-20,160	None	1,101	988-90	767	159-62	...	113
	F	31-31-56	15,792-20,160	None	981	901-92	693	154-54	...	80
Roselle Park b, N.J. (7)	P	31-31-40	14,106-22,203	Y-24,423-25	996	943-95	753	143-47	4	49
Roseville, Calif.	P	56-40-40	19,551-23,764	None	2,188	1,659-76	1,363	195-101	106	423
	F	36-35-56	18,611-22,621	None	1,491	1,249-84	1,037	146-66	23	219
	R	12-6-40	14,601-16,098	None	706	288-41	234	34-20	30	388
Round Lake Beach v, Ill. (7)	P	28-20-40	17,825-22,194	None	706	621-88	553	7-61	5	80
Roy, Utah (7)	P	23-17-40	16,647-22,703	None	688	592-86	472	106-14	11	85
	F	7-7-56	16,647-22,703	None	226	189-84	150	34-5	7	30
Russellville, Ark. (7)	P	28-19-40	11,189-13,357	None	600	469-78	405	47-17	...	131
	F	34-34-56	11,088-12,726	None	265	265-100	258	7-...	...	...
Ruston, La.	P	34-28-40	11,365-...	None	...	...-..	...	...-...	...	...
	F	40-40-60	11,017-15,832	Y-...-20	670	670-100	630	40-...	...	...
	R	28-12-40	8,216-10,712	None	314	314-100	314	...-...	...	...
Rutland, Vt.	P	45-35-40	15,460-15,460	Y-16,916-42	1,044	906-87	807	54-45	10	128
	F	37-37-56	15,460-15,460	Y-16,916-42	872	818-94	723	48-47	...	54
	R	2-0-40	12,667-12,667	Y-14,123-42	114	46-40	40	4-2	...	68
Rye, N.Y. (7)	P	35-30-40	19,274-26,649	Y-28,539-19	1,767	1,499-85	1,001	437-61	...	268
	F	16-16-40	17,338-23,234	Y-25,124-20	676	467-69	412	27-28	...	209
Saddle Brook tp, N.J. (1,7)	P	30-29-37	15,049-25,352	Y-27,890-30	1,292	1,175-91	840	185-150	50	67
	F	...-...-..	...-...	..-...-..	34	...-..	...	...-...	...	34

Table 3/18 continued **POLICE, FIRE, AND REFUSE COLLECTION AND DISPOSAL DEPARTMENTS: PERSONNEL, SALARIES, AND EXPENDITURES FOR CITIES OVER 10,000: 1984**

City	Depart-ment	Total personnel, no. uniformed, duty hours per week	Entrance, maximum salary ($)	Longevity pay, maximum ($), no. years to max.	Reported expenditures (in thousands): Total expendi-tures (A) ($)	Total personnel expendi-tures (B), % of (A) ($)	Salaries and wages (C) ($)	City contrib. to employee retirement, insurance (D) ($)	Capital outlay (E) ($)	All other (F) ($)
10,000-24,999 continued										
Saddle Brook tp, N.J. (cont'd)	R	...-...-..	...-...	..-...-..	313	...-..	...	...-...	...	313
St. George, Utah (1)										
St. Peters, Mo. (3,7)	P	39-32-40	15,725-20,946	None	1,226	961-78	733	116-112	53	212
Salem, Va.	P	59-47-40	12,875-18,990	None	1,230	1,184-96	977	162-45	46	...
	F	45-44-42	11,668-17,243	None	850	843-99	696	114-33	7	...
	R	72-34-40	9,568-14,185	None	792	792-100	648	110-34	...	...
Salisbury, N.C. (7)	P	67-52-40	12,370-16,365	None	1,400	1,091-78	947	115-29	74	235
	F	60-56-56	11,790-15,591	None	1,102	986-89	908	54-24	85	31
	R	31-0-40	8,570-11,275	None	661	365-55	314	39-12	17	279
Salisbury tp, Pa. (1)	P	10-9-40	16,407-21,064	Y-22,064-..	345	288-83	263	...-25	17	40
San Benito, Tex.	P	32-28-40	11,690-12,813	Y-13,604-1	616	459-75	403	39-17	55	102
	F	17-16-56	13,191-14,036	Y-14,889-1	360	274-76	242	23-9	41	45
	R	26-14-40	8,050-8,986	None	329	239-73	208	19-12	...	90
San Carlos, Calif. (3,7)	P	44-32-40	22,509-27,360	None	8,625	1,672-19	1,360	285-27	783	6,170
San Dimas, Calif. (3,4,7)										
San Fernando, Calif. (2,7)	P	46-35-40	22,188-27,468	Y-30,215-14	2,402	2,101-87	1,478	499-124	67	234
San Juan Capistrano, Calif. (2,4,7)										
San Marcos, Calif. (3,4,7)										
San Marcos, Tex. (5,7)	P	41-30-40	14,772-16,646	Y-24,046-15	937	769-82	671	78-20	26	142
	F	27-24-56	14,772-16,646	Y-24,046-15	637	561-88	486	61-14	21	55
	R	...-...-..	...-...	..-...-..	277	188-68	166	15-7	...	89
San Pablo, Calif. (2)	P	45-34-40	19,908-24,120	None	1,549	1,338-86	988	247-103	36	175
Sand Springs, Okla.	P	26-24-40	13,260-20,400	Y-20,480-20	648	561-87	457	69-35	...	87
	F	29-29-56	13,260-20,400	Y-20,480-20	598	573-96	491	39-43	8	17
	R	11-11-40	10,248-15,144	None	365	176-48	151	15-10	...	189
Sanford, Fla.	P	63-52-40	14,872-20,226	Y-...-30	1,737	1,396-80	1,170	183-43	110	231
	F	40-39-56	14,872-20,226	Y-...-30	1,279	998-78	833	138-27	82	199
	R	21-14-40	10,082-13,712	Y-...-30	579	342-59	274	45-23	...	237
Sanford, N.C. (7)	P	50-48-40	12,456-14,380	None	1,047	776-74	746	...-30	90	181
	F	35-34-40	12,456-14,380	None	645	514-80	491	...-23	72	59
Sanger, Calif.	P	28-23-40	17,478-20,724	None	699	698-100	533	119-46	1	...
	F	19-19-56	16,224-19,236	None	464	463-100	351	84-28	1	...
	R	11-9-40	13,656-16,188	None	256	242-95	185	37-20	14	...
Santa Fe Springs, Calif. (4,7)	F	69-66-56	23,238-28,140	Y-33,132-22	3,595	3,543-99	2,497	821-225	52	...
Santa Paula, Calif. (1)										
Saratoga Springs, N.Y. (7)	P	57-54-40	16,592-19,045	Y-20,045-20	1,802	1,736-96	1,272	349-115	66	...
	F	51-47-36	14,092-16,545	Y-17,545-20	1,478	1,455-98	1,057	287-111	23	...
Saugus t, Mass. (7)	P	53-51-40	17,544-20,390	Y-20,890-25	1,420	1,391-98	1,332	...-59	29	...
	F	49-44-42	17,380-20,200	Y-20,750-25	1,194	1,181-99	1,134	...-47	13	...
Sault Ste. Marie, Mich. (7)	P	28-27-40	16,268-18,024	None	882	802-91	583	184-35	22	58
	F	19-19-56	16,308-18,931	None	662	625-94	472	125-28	1	36
Scarborough t, Me. (1,7)	P	19-15-40	12,683-16,817	None	558	468-84	391	52-25	27	63
	F	1-1-40	...-...	..-...-..	176	75-43	72	1-2	29	72
Scarsdale v, N.Y.	P	48-43-40	15,000-26,284	Y-26,984-17	2,055	1,827-89	1,280	450-97	49	179
	F	44-44-40	12,000-24,393	Y-24,893-17	1,937	1,778-92	1,259	441-78	39	120
	R	32-25-40	11,000-21,202	Y-21,702-20	1,380	809-59	611	140-58	24	547
Scituate t, Mass. (7)	P	37-29-40	16,828-18,553	Y-18,853-20	884	748-85	725	...-23	36	100
	F	58-53-42	17,604-19,405	Y-19,655-20	1,373	1,306-95	1,269	...-37	4	63
Scott tp, Pa. (1)										
Scottsbluff, Neb.	P	34-28-40	13,665-16,973	Y-18,678-10	915	729-80	629	65-35	46	140
	F	17-17-56	13,075-15,957	Y-17,617-9	569	450-79	332	100-18	44	75
	R	11-3-40	10,358-12,604	Y-13,894-9	400	221-55	198	13-10	44	135
Searcy, Ark.	P	18-12-40	11,800-15,600	Y-...-..	374	330-88	330	...-...	44	...
	F	18-18-40	11,800-15,800	Y-...-..	285	280-98	280	...-...	5	...
	R	17-17-40	9,050-14,500	None	390	235-60	235	...-...	155	...
Secaucus t, N.J. (1,7)	P	65-60-40	18,599-27,617	Y-30,379-25	2,056	1,780-87	1,387	271-122	...	276
Seguin, Tex.	P	37-26-40	13,539-17,757	Y-18,957-..	875	665-76	573	78-14	73	137
	F	20-20-58	13,259-17,757	Y-18,957-..	436	367-84	315	44-8	3	66
	R	29-17-40	6,970-10,454	None	478	334-70	284	39-11	48	96
Selma, Calif. (7)	P	25-19-40	15,672-19,044	None	907	712-79	533	140-39	25	170
	F	11-11-56	13,860-16,860	None	500	338-68	253	68-17	81	81
Seven Hills, Ohio (1)	P	14-14-40	22,655-24,015	Y-24,915-15	513	460-90	361	37-62	...	53
	F	...-...-..	...-...	..-...-..	116	88-76	83	5-...	...	28
	R	16-16-40	15,787-...	Y-...-..	619	388-63	342	46-...	...	231
Shamokin, Pa. (1)	P	16-12-40	12,500-18,806	None	382	363-95	316	17-30	4	15
	F	...-...-..	...-...	..-...-..	77	11-14	11	...-...	6	60
Sharon t, Mass.	P	23-22-38	15,431-18,871	Y-19,071-20	783	623-80	623	...-...	31	129
	F	18-17-42	16,239-19,356	Y-19,606-20	476	417-88	417	...-...	3	56
Sharon, Pa. (7)	P	36-29-40	12,711-19,390	Y-20,002-19	984	922-94	778	65-79	25	37
	F	29-29-42	14,278-18,688	Y-19,240-19	810	725-90	562	91-72	5	80
Sharonville, Ohio (1,7)	P	24-20-40	18,144-23,764	Y-24,339-..	1,397	1,017-73	801	143-73	42	338
	F	3-3-40	18,144-23,764	Y-24,339-..	338	236-70	211	18-7	18	84
Sheffield Lake, Ohio (7)	P	10-7-40	15,271-19,384	None	373	301-81	225	42-34	24	48
	F	13-13-54	13,731-16,853	None	414	259-63	183	49-27	104	51
Shelby, N.C.	P	48-43-43	12,428-15,860	Y-16,260-15	1,251	996-80	813	158-25	87	168
	F	35-33-56	11,804-15,132	Y-15,532-15	850	687-81	563	107-17	26	137
	R	23-23-40	9,256-11,804	Y-12,204-15	343	295-86	239	45-11	...	48
Sheridan, Wyo.	P	49-29-40	17,118-22,942	Y-24,742-19	2,059	1,018-49	811	117-90	739	302

Table 3/18 continued **POLICE, FIRE, AND REFUSE COLLECTION AND DISPOSAL DEPARTMENTS: PERSONNEL, SALARIES, AND EXPENDITURES FOR CITIES OVER 10,000: 1984**

					Reported expenditures (in thousands)					
City	Department	Total personnel, no. uniformed, duty hours per week	Entrance, maximum salary ($)	Longevity pay, maximum ($), no. years to max.	Total expenditures (A) ($)	Total personnel expenditures (B), % of (A) ($)	Salaries and wages (C) ($)	City contrib. to employee retirement, insurance (D) ($)	Capital outlay (E) ($)	All other (F) ($)
10,000-24,999 continued										
Sheridan, Wyo. (cont'd)	F	19-18-56	16,432-22,069	Y-23,869-19	1,420	640-45	495	92-53	710	70
	R	11-0-40	14,789-19,843	Y-21,643-19	403	286-71	242	17-27	92	25
Sherwood, Ark. (1)	P	26-25-40	15,000-17,203	None	536	466-87	420	28-18	13	57
	R	6-4-40	11,544-...	Y-...-..	103	84-82	75	5-4	1	18
Shively, Ky.	P	23-20-40	16,851-18,746	Y-...-1	632	605-96	516	42-47	...	27
	F	23-22-56	18,170-20,134	Y-...-1	641	630-98	537	46-47	...	11
	R	19-0-40	14,248-14,518	Y-...-1	363	316-87	286	26-4	...	47
Shoreview, Minn. (2,4,7)										
Shorewood v, Wis.	P	30-24-38	21,564-24,528	None	1,098	1,054-96	817	181-56	44	...
	F	21-21-52	21,564-24,528	None	740	724-98	570	107-47	16	...
	R	3-3-40	20,425-20,925	None	83	83-100	64	11-8	...	...
Shrewsbury t, Mass. (7)	P	36-31-37	17,211-19,640	None	880	783-89	783	...-...	31	66
	F	33-32-42	17,217-19,640	Y-19,940-..	790	728-92	728	...-...	9	53
Sidney, Ohio	P	34-29-40	17,118-19,822	Y-20,813-25	1,212	1,000-83	797	147-56	9	203
	F	27-27-54	17,118-19,822	Y-20,813-25	889	804-90	614	146-44	13	72
	R	9-7-40	14,477-16,765	Y-17,603-25	396	227-57	187	26-14	2	167
Sierra Madre, Calif. (7)	P	18-18-40	20,400-24,348	None	891	629-71	450	135-44	12	250
	F	1-1-40	23,256-...	None	137	59-43	50	6-3	9	69
Sikeston, Mo. (5)										
Simsbury t, Conn. (1,7)	P	35-30-40	17,785-22,213	Y-22,713-20	1,240	1,002-81	771	163-68	...	238
Smyrna, Ga. (7)	P	67-53-40	12,343-17,876	None	1,239	1,027-83	860	89-78	...	212
	F	51-50-56	12,343-17,876	None	942	867-92	722	77-68	...	75
	R	23-12-40	8,735-12,652	None	709	336-47	276	30-30	...	373
Snyder, Tex.	P	22-17-40	16,872-19,704	Y-20,904-25	844	568-67	469	86-13	47	229
	F	10-10-60	16,476-18,396	Y-19,596-25	426	258-61	220	32-6	30	138
	R	9-1-40	15,126-15,132	Y-16,332-25	485	201-41	165	31-5	102	182
Solon, Ohio	P	38-29-40	21,788-26,052	Y-28,657-20	1,647	1,385-84	1,078	187-120	...	262
	F	27-27-54	21,788-26,052	Y-28,657-20	1,201	1,025-85	758	179-88	...	176
	R	46-0-40	19,198-23,129	Y-25,441-20	1,057	993-94	715	151-127	...	64
Somers Point, N.J. (7)										
Somerset, Ky.	P	28-28-40	10,442-15,059	None	707	481-68	381	85-15	24	202
	F	18-18-56	10,442-15,059	None	551	392-71	310	74-8	5	154
	R	6-6-40	8,174-11,814	None	172	87-51	72	12-3	23	62
Somerset t, Mass.	P	34-30-40	15,102-16,780	Y-...-..	748	671-90	671	...-...	30	47
	F	32-30-42	16,085-17,872	Y-...-..	744	657-88	657	...-...	62	25
	R	9-9-40	14,924-14,942	Y-...-..	209	131-63	131	...-...	59	19
Somersworth, N.H. (7)	P	23-17-40	12,844-16,224	Y-16,640-20	573	434-76	351	48-35	50	89
	F	12-11-40	11,607-14,442	Y-14,962-20	413	298-72	242	32-24	11	104
Somerville b, N.J. (1)										
South Brunswick tp, N.J. (1)										
South Charleston, W.Va.	P	25-23-40	14,434-19,061	None	902	783-87	564	140-79	34	85
	F	28-28-40	14,434-19,061	None	849	782-92	545	149-88	10	57
	R	25-14-40	10,475-12,950	None	826	700-85	517	84-99	34	92
South El Monte, Calif. (3,4)										
South Houston t, Tex. (1)										
South Kingstown t, R.I. (1)	P	54-42-40	12,750-17,598	Y-18,654-20	1,428	1,233-86	1,022	156-55	19	176
	R	4-0-40	12,898-14,448	Y-...-..	566	93-16	77	9-7	321	152
South Miami, Fla.	P	49-41-40	20,492-24,601	Y-26,077-15	1,260	1,189-94	1,043	73-73	52	19
	R	21-10-40	13,544-16,371	Y-17,353-15	667	392-59	338	23-31	...	275
South Milwaukee, Wis.	P	33-32-..	22,334-24,694	Y-24,994-25	1,312	1,312-100	972	232-108	...	...
	F	20-20-..	22,845-25,405	Y-25,705-25	857	857-100	621	169-67	...	...
	R	22-15-40	19,022-19,261	Y-19,561-25	520	520-100	478	22-20	...	...
South Orange Village tp, N.J. (7)	P	52-48-40	15,892-22,637	Y-24,900-25	2,277	2,046-90	1,545	407-94	...	231
	F	40-40-42	15,892-22,637	Y-24,900-25	1,432	1,374-96	1,006	301-67	...	58
South Pasadena, Calif. (7)	P	41-30-40	21,846-25,908	None	1,746	1,554-89	1,113	332-109	39	153
	F	23-23-56	21,084-25,020	None	1,177	977-83	717	199-61	17	183
South Plainfield b, N.J. (1)	P	50-50-40	19,664-25,173	Y-27,187-..	1,727	1,495-87	1,408	22-65	...	232
South St. Paul, Minn.	P	28-24-40	22,800-27,636	Y-29,018-20	1,470	1,324-90	826	445-53	24	122
	F	22-21-56	22,800-27,636	Y-29,018-20	996	928-93	633	254-41	2	66
South Salt Lake, Utah	P	27-21-40	14,616-16,752	None	1,044	727-70	522	186-19	60	257
	F	16-15-40	14,616-16,152	None	601	487-81	354	116-17	7	107
	R	5-0-40	12,636-14,652	None	160	119-74	90	29-...	...	41
South Whitehall tp, Pa. (1,4,7)	F	...-...-..	...-...	..-...-..	264	...-..	...	...-...	264	...
South Windsor t, Conn. (1,7)	P	34-28-40	14,868-19,766	Y-19,836-5	918	802-87	685	52-65	44	72
	F	1-1-35	...-...	..-...-..	39	28-72	24	2-2	9	2
Southaven, Miss. (7)	P	16-16-40	11,918-11,918	None	205	205-100	191	13-1	...	...
	F	12-12-40	11,918-11,918	None	154	154-100	143	10-1	...	...
Southbridge t, Mass. (7)	P	30-30-40	15,662-18,054	None	4,202	582-14	578	...-4	20	3,600
	F	28-28-42	14,815-16,663	None	532	522-98	518	...-4	10	...
Southbury t, Conn. (7)	P	10-10-40	14,646-14,646	None	206	182-88	158	11-13	5	19
	R	2-2-45	...-...	..-...-..	63	37-59	31	2-4	...	26
Speedway t, Ind. (7)	P	32-25-40	16,591-17,498	Y-18,498-20	842	637-76	562	49-26	7	198
	F	33-33-48	16,591-17,498	Y-18,498-20	763	682-89	581	72-29	6	75
Spencer, Iowa (7)	P	17-17-48	16,914-19,099	Y-20,177-15	480	458-95	378	...-80	22	...
	F	5-5-56	15,187-16,469	Y-17,549-15	155	145-94	88	...-57	10	...
Springdale, Ark. (7)	P	50-38-38	13,319-18,768	None	1,399	929-66	811	81-37	249	221
	F	43-43-56	13,308-18,216	None	880	809-92	742	29-38	1	70

Table 3/18 continued **POLICE, FIRE, AND REFUSE COLLECTION AND DISPOSAL DEPARTMENTS: PERSONNEL, SALARIES, AND EXPENDITURES FOR CITIES OVER 10,000: 1984**

City	Depart-ment	Total personnel, no. uniformed, duty hours per week	Entrance, maximum salary ($)	Longevity pay, maximum ($), no. years to max.	Reported expenditures (in thousands): Total expenditures (A) ($)	Total personnel expenditures (B), % of (A) ($)	Salaries and wages (C) ($)	City contrib. to employee retirement, insurance (D) ($)	Capital outlay (E) ($)	All other (F) ($)
10,000-24,999 continued										
Springettsbury tp, Pa. (7)	P	22-20-40	17,334-23,286	Y-26,779-20	781	651-83	558	37-56	34	96
	F	11-11-56	15,525-20,545	Y-23,325-20	342	300-88	257	17-26	...	42
Springfield tp, Pa. (1)										
Stanton, Calif. (7)	P	45-34-40	21,414-25,392	None	1,838	1,567-85	1,287	156-124	18	253
	F	26-26-56	19,914-23,616	None	1,234	950-77	788	99-63	58	226
Starkville, Miss.	P	30-26-40	12,600-13,891	None	648	438-68	360	62-16	41	169
	F	32-32-56	11,544-13,104	None	652	496-76	412	66-18	61	95
	R	23-11-40	7,280-8,216	None	503	291-58	251	38-2	58	154
Statesville, N.C.	P	66-59-40	11,650-14,868	Y-...-..	1,215	1,001-82	1,001	...-...	53	161
	F	58-57-56	11,095-14,161	Y-...-..	1,010	889-88	889	...-...	12	109
	R	49-33-40	7,885-10,063	Y-...-..	523	425-81	425	...-...	...	98
Stephenville, Tex. (7)	P	29-24-40	13,752-17,556	Y-19,644-..	806	604-75	525	57-22	66	136
	F	20-20-40	12,468-14,448	Y-18,804-..	508	419-82	367	39-13	23	66
	R	1-0-40	13,752-17,196	Y-20,520-..	72	33-46	28	4-1	...	39
Sterling, Colo.	P	28-22-40	15,715-18,792	None	752	632-84	519	52-61	53	67
	F	7-7-42	14,879-17,880	None	444	195-44	148	26-21	216	33
	R	7-4-40	10,665-15,046	None	208	113-54	86	11-16	3	92
Stillwater, Minn. (7)	P	15-15-40	18,012-26,760	Y-29,168-4	575	521-91	450	50-21	35	19
	F	6-6-56	21,348-25,524	Y-27,438-5	275	250-91	220	21-9	13	12
Stonington t, Conn. (1)	P	29-27-40	15,603-21,112	Y-21,262-5	1,208	884-73	732	98-54	205	119
Streamwood v, Ill. (7)	P	42-39-40	17,170-26,853	None	1,538	1,386-90	1,094	189-103	49	103
	F	14-13-52	17,170-26,853	None	732	593-81	451	99-43	9	130
Streator, Ill.	P	23-21-40	17,899-...	Y-19,174-23	688	688-100	479	161-48	...	...
	F	14-14-56	18,675-...	Y-19,950-23	490	490-100	289	167-34	...	...
	R	8-8-40	17,177-...	Y-18,377-15	181	181-100	139	23-19	...	...
Struthers, Ohio (7)	P	15-15-40	14,903-18,103	None	492	442-90	335	67-40	...	50
	F	8-8-55	14,903-18,103	None	291	259-89	193	45-21	...	32
Sumter, S.C.	P	79-53-40	11,313-15,225	None	1,728	1,337-77	1,074	177-86	110	281
	F	60-60-60	10,774-14,500	None	1,284	1,055-82	856	150-49	28	201
	R	57-36-40	7,019-8,902	None	1,546	569-37	447	58-64	214	763
Sunbury, Pa. (1,7)	P	21-14-40	14,000-21,695	None	373	373-100	373	...-...	...	...
Susquehanna tp, Pa. (7)	P	25-23-40	16,819-19,653	Y-20,153-20	919	715-78	535	118-62	75	129
Swansea t, Mass. (1,7)	P	30-28-37	...-...	..-...-..	656	656-100	638	...-18	...	...
	F	2-1-40	...-...	..-...-..	50	50-100	50	...-...	...	...
Sweetwater, Tex.	P	24-20-40	14,340-16,368	Y-17,568-25	653	486-74	406	56-24	32	135
	F	24-23-56	14,340-16,368	Y-17,568-25	671	518-77	451	39-28	17	136
	R	10-0-40	11,016-13,896	Y-15,096-25	468	170-36	144	16-10	20	278
Swissvale b, Pa.	P	18-18-40	17,468-19,222	Y-19,622-5	541	478-88	459	4-15	...	63
	F	6-6-60	17,199-18,414	Y-18,814-5	193	149-77	134	9-6	3	41
	R	7-7-40	17,493-17,826	None	227	161-71	133	22-6	...	66
Takoma Park, Md. (3)										
Tallmadge, Ohio (1)										
Tarpon Springs, Fla. (7)	P	37-28-40	14,498-22,464	None	854	770-90	677	64-29	2	82
	F	36-35-56	13,716-21,316	None	874	789-90	710	50-29	5	80
Taylor, Tex.	P	15-15-40	16,344-16,344	Y-...-..	355	285-80	248	29-8	17	53
	F	16-16-40	14,688-14,688	Y-...-..	278	248-89	215	25-8	5	25
	R	12-8-40	7,980-7,980	Y-...-..	298	179-60	155	18-6	51	68
Temple Terrace, Fla.	P	39-30-40	14,643-23,067	Y-24,067-20	1,056	828-78	705	91-32	47	181
	F	21-20-56	13,374-19,344	Y-20,344-20	445	371-83	314	37-20	12	62
	R	9-0-40	9,547-13,062	Y-14,062-20	452	146-32	117	22-7	...	306
Terrell, Tex.	P	26-26-40	14,622-19,128	Y-19,554-7	624	594-95	517	56-21	30	...
	F	8-8-56	14,280-18,216	Y-18,552-7	249	173-69	148	18-7	76	...
	R	16-13-40	9,906-12,936	None	342	225-66	198	14-13	117	...
Texarkana, Ark. (7)	P	45-30-40	13,720-15,940	Y-18,489-25	4,170	1,376-33	1,247	68-61	2	2,792
	F	36-35-56	12,953-14,392	Y-16,875-25	809	728-90	680	27-21	...	81
The Colony, Tex. (7)	P	15-15-40	17,886-21,204	Y-...-..	444	387-87	328	43-16	57	...
	F	8-8-56	17,886-21,204	Y-...-..	247	213-86	141	15-57	34	...
The Dalles, Ore. (7)	P	19-19-40	15,780-17,952	None	496	496-100	347	111-38	...	...
	F	14-14-56	16,584-18,480	None	511	461-90	353	80-28	50	...
The Village, Okla.	P	24-19-40	14,940-18,540	Y-17,629-18	656	590-90	494	48-48	8	58
	F	19-19-56	14,940-18,540	Y-17,629-18	495	455-92	398	19-38	6	34
	R	15-15-40	11,400-13,800	None	364	278-76	218	30-30	4	82
Thibodaux, La. (1,7)	P	64-43-40	11,707-17,710	None	991	791-80	713	48-30	10	190
	R	3-0-40	8,733-12,697	None	783	37-5	34	2-1	91	655
Thomasville, Ga.	P	44-35-44	11,748-24,526	Y-27,056-15	1,111	883-79	719	137-27	53	175
	F	40-40-56	13,919-25,771	Y-27,064-15	952	823-86	662	133-28	10	119
	R	42-22-40	7,550-13,998	Y-15,058-15	947	568-60	465	84-19	27	352
Thomasville, N.C.	P	43-37-42	11,270-14,937	None	826	691-84	574	72-45	36	99
	F	43-43-56	10,220-14,223	None	793	717-90	595	76-46	9	67
	R	29-18-40	8,089-11,825	None	580	331-57	277	36-18	111	138
Tiffin, Ohio (7)	P	43-34-40	14,140-16,421	Y-17,735-15	1,115	1,000-90	780	133-87	1	114
	F	30-29-52	14,103-16,240	Y-17,539-15	798	754-94	558	130-66	1	43
Tifton, Ga.	P	47-39-40	10,800-13,728	None	892	660-74	570	72-18	33	199
	F	22-22-68	10,800-14,456	None	372	321-86	277	34-10	11	40
	R	24-14-40	8,068-10,816	None	422	288-68	245	33-10	...	134
Tigard, Ore. (7)	P	29-22-40	18,720-22,392	Y-24,631-5	1,035	897-87	675	144-78	44	94
Tiverton t, R.I. (7)	P	26-18-38	13,845-16,536	Y-17,363-15	638	531-83	455	31-45	17	90
	F	18-18-42	14,665-17,865	Y-18,580-20	510	464-91	367	72-25	...	46

Table 3/18 continued **POLICE, FIRE, AND REFUSE COLLECTION AND DISPOSAL DEPARTMENTS: PERSONNEL, SALARIES, AND EXPENDITURES FOR CITIES OVER 10,000: 1984**

					Reported expenditures (in thousands)					
City	Depart-ment	Total personnel, no. uniformed, duty hours per week	Entrance, maximum salary ($)	Longevity pay, maximum ($), no. years to max.	Total expendi-tures (A) ($)	Total personnel expendi-tures (B), % of (A) ($)	Salaries and wages (C) ($)	City contrib. to employee retirement, insurance (D) ($)	Capital outlay (E) ($)	All other (F) ($)
10,000-24,999 continued										
Tooele, Utah (1,7)	P	21-19-40	14,578-20,349	None	734	547-75	423	93-31	67	120
	F	...-...-..	...-...	..-...-..	115	58-50	25	1-32	42	15
Towamencin tp, Pa.	P	13-13-40	21,849-24,688	Y-...-12	312	299-96	299	...-...	13	...
Tracy, Calif. (7)	P	42-30-40	18,270-21,696	None	1,505	1,270-84	968	223-79	69	166
	F	19-19-56	17,682-21,012	None	978	594-61	457	101-36	315	69
Traverse City, Mich.	P	25-25-40	19,356-21,800	Y-22,890-15	1,153	954-83	775	124-55	...	199
	F	23-23-56	18,688-20,905	Y-22,368-25	833	697-84	550	99-48	...	136
	R	4-0-40	15,798-17,555	Y-18,782-25	181	181-100	140	26-15	...	...
Tredyffrin tp, Pa.	P	51-43-40	22,305-25,974	Y-28,571-20	1,842	1,562-85	1,394	15-153	59	221
Trenton, Mich.	P	53-51-40	20,717-25,896	Y-26,496-21	2,253	2,057-91	1,676	381-...	...	196
	F	35-35-54	20,340-25,425	Y-26,025-21	1,532	1,401-91	1,148	253-...	...	131
	R	...-...-40	20,467-20,467	Y-21,067-21	436	192-44	192	...-...	...	244
Troy, Ohio	P	37-31-40	16,448-22,258	Y-...-5	1,209	1,027-85	799	137-91	19	163
	F	29-29-56	16,448-22,258	Y-...-5	1,110	964-87	721	165-78	38	108
	R	11-11-40	15,506-15,787	Y-...-5	508	258-51	208	25-25	...	250
Tullahoma, Tenn.	P	34-30-40	12,847-14,583	None	720	558-78	486	32-40	62	100
	F	23-23-40	14,206-14,206	None	498	409-82	355	26-28	7	82
	R	18-18-40	10,483-11,939	None	521	179-34	154	11-14	207	135
Two Rivers, Wis. (7)	P	30-21-38	17,045-20,007	Y-21,007-18	909	878-97	658	163-57	31	...
	F	20-19-56	17,607-19,698	Y-21,668-18	624	624-100	452	129-43	...	...
Ukiah, Calif. (7)	P	27-23-40	17,940-21,816	Y-22,470-14	1,274	1,034-81	769	207-58	23	217
	F	19-18-56	17,088-20,772	Y-21,395-14	898	719-80	512	166-41	50	129
	R	3-0-40	17,328-21,072	Y-21,704-14	186	63-34	47	8-8	...	123
Universal City, Tex. (1,7)	P	35-21-40	16,000-17,851	Y-18,811-..	615	485-79	437	36-12	1	129
University Park, Tex.	P	39-34-40	...-...	Y-...-..	1,450	1,120-77	956	135-29	110	220
	F	33-33-56	...-...	Y-...-..	1,291	958-74	807	127-24	103	230
	R	38-0-40	...-...	Y-...-..	913	571-63	483	66-22	92	250
Upper Allen tp, Pa. (1)										
Upper Dublin tp, Pa. (1)										
Upper Southampton tp, Pa. (1,7)	P	23-21-40	18,226-23,430	Y-23,730-5	867	729-84	621	44-64	27	111
Urbana, Ohio	P	22-18-40	16,138-17,742	Y-18,630-20	605	516-85	414	78-24	31	58
	F	19-18-56	15,392-18,642	Y-19,574-20	577	528-92	403	103-22	12	37
	R	7-0-40	13,333-15,912	None	256	127-50	105	15-7	16	113
Urbandale, Iowa (1)	P	33-27-40	16,805-20,168	Y-21,176-5	1,172	998-85	846	85-67	16	158
	R	6-3-40	15,374-16,086	Y-16,561-5	218	153-70	127	15-11	8	57
Valparaiso, Ind.	P	48-35-40	15,283-18,235	Y-18,715-12	993	976-98	890	70-16	17	...
	F	30-29-56	14,171-18,526	Y-19,006-12	673	620-92	575	35-10	53	...
	R	13-8-45	13,899-15,800	Y-16,280-12	221	221-100	192	24-5	...	...
Van Wert, Ohio (7)	P	25-20-40	15,500-15,500	Y-19,750-30	623	521-84	416	48-57	5	97
	F	19-19-56	18,500-18,500	Y-19,750-30	519	449-87	343	61-45	18	52
	R	...-...-..	...-...	..-...-..	4	2-50	2	...-...	...	2
Vandalia, Ohio (2)	P	31-21-40	16,680-23,127	None	980	840-86	670	114-56	33	107
	F	1-1-40	18,803-22,838	None	209	116-56	108	6-2	38	55
Venice, Fla.	P	52-36-40	14,000-21,396	..-...-..	1,665	1,335-80	1,124	172-39	48	282
	F	34-32-56	12,525-19,926	None	612	612-100	612	...-...	...	...
	R	...-...-..	9,443-13,437	None	1,046	233-22	175	32-26	167	646
Vermilion, Ohio (1,7)	P	22-18-40	15,091-15,091	None	800	712-89	584	75-53	4	84
Vero Beach, Fla. (3)	P	67-49-40	12,813-17,202	None	1,821	1,542-85	1,312	159-71	87	192
	R	38-25-40	9,464-14,165	None	1,297	622-48	490	91-41	45	630
Victorville, Calif. (4,7)	F	20-15-56	17,496-21,840	Y-24,024-5	646	518-80	410	85-23	14	114
Vidor, Tex. (1)	P	25-20-40	17,868-17,868	Y-...-1	562	549-98	499	48-2	13	...
	R	8-8-40	13,176-13,176	Y-...-1	175	175-100	160	14-1	...	...
Virginia, Minn.	P	27-26-40	22,791-23,196	None	827	773-93	665	18-90	2	52
	F	25-25-40	22,778-23,105	None	816	794-97	682	31-81	4	18
	R	5-1-40	18,957-18,957	Y-20,474-23	365	171-47	135	15-21	110	84
Wabash, Ind. (7)	P	26-26-45	16,211-...	Y-16,571-18	734	655-89	475	146-34	31	48
	F	31-31-56	16,211-...	Y-16,571-18	796	749-94	559	149-41	27	20
Waldwick b, N.J. (1,7)	P	18-18-40	15,800-26,025	Y-27,846-20	832	768-92	617	107-44	17	47
	F	...-...-..	...-...	..-...-..	195	6-3	6	...-...	139	50
Walker, Mich. (1,7)	P	...-...-..	20,133-25,166	Y-26,366-..	878	731-83	601	78-52	50	97
	F	...-...-..	...-...	..-...-..	176	122-69	117	3-2	16	38
Wall tp, N.J.	P	43-43-40	18,196-25,024	Y-27,526-20	1,689	1,408-83	1,208	185-15	...	281
	R	14-14-40	13,565-18,503	Y-20,353-20	350	295-84	267	23-5	...	55
Warren b, Pa. (7)	P	27-22-40	18,054-21,112	Y-21,814-20	795	650-82	590	4-56	14	131
	F	28-28-56	16,352-20,150	Y-22,285-20	869	751-86	647	44-60	13	105
Warren t, R.I. (1,7)	P	20-20-38	11,600-18,433	Y-19,723-5	541	541-100	409	105-27	...	...
	R	16-5-40	13,499-13,499	None	320	320-100	251	51-18	...	...
Warrensburg, Mo. (7)	P	21-19-40	12,510-15,120	None	388	355-91	302	34-19	33	...
	F	14-14-57	12,324-14,916	None	264	250-95	212	25-13	14	...
Warrington tp, Pa. (1,4,7)										
Washington, Ill. (1)	P	15-12-40	15,600-19,760	Y-21,341-12	682	549-80	429	87-33	22	111
Washington, Ind.	P	13-13-40	13,022-13,022	None	217	184-85	168	...-16	10	23
	F	15-15-60	12,905-12,905	None	336	205-61	187	...-18	99	32
	R	7-6-40	10,765-10,765	None	123	99-80	79	10-10	1	23
Washington (Morris) tp, N.J. (1,7)	P	19-18-40	18,460-25,250	Y-26,512-16	705	596-85	517	58-21	36	73
Washington, Ohio (7)	P	22-16-40	14,078-16,993	Y-17,193-25	560	478-85	372	64-42	4	78
	F	14-14-56	14,078-16,993	Y-17,193-25	480	380-79	283	66-31	7	93
Watertown t, Conn. (1,7)	P	33-27-40	19,910-19,910	Y-21,896-20	992	878-89	755	50-73	70	44

Table 3/18 continued **POLICE, FIRE, AND REFUSE COLLECTION AND DISPOSAL DEPARTMENTS: PERSONNEL, SALARIES, AND EXPENDITURES FOR CITIES OVER 10,000: 1984**

City	Department	Total personnel, no. uniformed, duty hours per week	Entrance, maximum salary ($)	Longevity pay, maximum ($), no. years to max.	Reported expenditures (in thousands): Total expenditures (A) ($)	Total personnel expenditures (B), % of (A) ($)	Salaries and wages (C) ($)	City contrib. to employee retirement, insurance (D) ($)	Capital outlay (E) ($)	All other (F) ($)
10,000-24,999 continued										
Watertown, S.D.	P	29-25-45	15,794-18,420	Y-19,164-2	757	685-90	567	82-36	30	42
	F	28-28-56	14,951-17,404	Y-18,148-2	594	577-97	518	24-35	7	10
	R	12-6-40	13,978-15,329	Y-16,013-2	397	254-64	215	24-15	80	63
Watertown, Wis. (7)	P	35-29-40	18,054-21,000	Y-21,527-16	1,035	958-93	723	172-63	30	47
	F	20-20-56	16,499-19,420	Y-19,947-16	631	579-92	427	116-36	26	26
	R	4-0-40	16,766-16,766	Y-17,293-16	119	95-80	75	13-7	...	24
Waterville, Me.	P	31-27-42	10,920-16,432	Y-...-6	903	798-88	651	113-34	16	89
	F	22-22-56	13,827-15,315	Y-...-6	648	584-90	480	79-25	10	54
	R	4-4-40	12,492-13,587	Y-...-6	116	105-91	94	6-5	...	11
Watsonville, Calif.	P	47-40-40	19,884-...	None	1,521	1,210-80	1,210	...-...	48	263
	F	27-26-56	18,948-...	None	1,023	822-80	822	...-...	53	148
	R	19-9-40	14,640-...	None	873	400-46	400	...-...	69	404
Waxahachie, Tex.	P	34-31-40	14,452-15,246	Y-...-..	822	643-78	564	61-18	36	143
	F	...-...-56	12,790-13,353	Y-...-..	508	451-89	396	41-14	2	55
	R	...-...-40	10,202-12,181	None	415	206-50	179	19-8	77	132
Waycross, Ga.	P	58-40-40	11,273-14,788	None	1,214	946-78	835	111-...	25	243
	F	45-44-56	10,753-14,102	None	663	584-88	516	68-...	28	51
	R	32-16-40	8,008-10,525	Y-...-..	503	361-72	320	41-...	57	85
Wayland t, Mass.	P	23-23-38	18,066-20,318	Y-20,668-30	766	670-87	624	29-17	32	64
	F	25-25-42	17,903-19,844	Y-20,194-30	748	706-94	654	29-23	...	42
Wayne, Mich. (7)	P	45-34-40	20,992-24,663	Y-25,363-26	1,991	1,696-85	1,322	256-118	83	212
	F	20-20-56	19,966-26,073	Y-26,773-26	927	822-89	638	124-60	17	88
Waynesboro, Va.	P	42-40-40	12,700-15,985	None	830	822-99	650	117-55	8	...
	F	16-16-56	11,174-13,025	None	318	314-99	247	46-21	4	...
	R	16-16-40	8,650-10,087	Y-11,172-6	239	239-100	183	38-18	...	...
Weatherford, Tex.	P	31-23-40	15,142-18,408	Y-19,608-26	846	635-75	542	70-23	52	159
	F	13-13-56	15,229-18,520	Y-19,720-26	313	241-77	207	25-9	16	56
	R	15-9-40	9,256-12,376	Y-13,576-26	432	230-53	195	24-11	...	202
Webster Groves, Mo. (7)	P	53-43-40	18,352-21,558	Y-22,208-25	1,513	1,296-86	1,109	138-49	58	159
	F	40-40-56	18,352-21,558	Y-22,208-25	1,150	1,079-94	947	90-42	15	56
Weslaco, Tex.	P	41-31-40	11,440-11,440	Y-11,488-..	797	651-82	570	59-22	1	145
	F	29-28-40	9,651-9,651	Y-9,699-..	467	285-61	244	30-11	2	180
	R	29-17-40	8,486-8,486	None	522	354-68	307	32-15	...	168
West Chester b, Pa. (1)	P	...-...-..	20,178-23,452	Y-25,797-25	1,241	1,148-93	1,026	9-113	11	82
	R	...-...-..	14,710-17,695	Y-...-..	234	160-68	132	12-16	...	74
West Chicago, Ill. (3)	P	32-25-40	17,318-29,982	Y-30,132-..	1,218	1,004-82	791	159-54	34	180
West Des Moines, Iowa (1)	P	33-28-40	17,490-21,862	Y-22,438-5	1,014	976-96	735	139-102	38	...
	F	...-...-..	...-...	..-...-..	166	106-64	93	10-3	60	...
	R	10-10-40	15,080-17,316	Y-17,892-5	288	233-81	179	24-30	55	...
West Fargo, N.D. (1)	P	17-14-40	17,016-20,964	None	401	376-94	337	31-8	25	...
	R	5-4-40	13,968-...	None	112	109-97	95	9-5	3	...
West Goshen tp, Pa. (2)										
West Linn, Ore. (7)	P	17-15-40	16,926-21,060	None	597	511-86	386	89-36	19	67
	F	5-5-56	16,668-20,796	None	262	166-63	119	37-10	39	57
West Manchester tp, Pa. (1,7)	P	17-16-40	15,330-21,520	Y-23,670-24	619	487-79	368	81-38	32	100
	F	...-...-..	...-...	..-...-..	45	...-..	...	...-...	45	...
West Milford tp, N.J. (7)	P	44-37-40	...-...	Y-...-20	366	198-54	...	138-60	40	128
West St. Paul, Minn. (7)	P	25-21-40	18,914-28,020	Y-30,542-16	894	776-87	668	79-29	25	93
	F	19-19-56	19,380-27,672	Y-29,232-15	778	710-91	539	147-24	10	58
West University Place, Tex.	P	28-21-40	17,080-22,468	Y-23,668-25	755	597-79	506	68-23	51	107
	F	20-20-52	15,629-21,085	Y-22,285-25	629	562-89	474	70-18	19	48
	R	12-12-40	11,178-13,985	None	557	303-54	277	17-9	94	160
Westborough t, Mass.	P	35-35-38	10,754-18,552	None	...	...-..	...	...-...	...	...
	F	13-13-42	15,593-20,900	None	...	...-..	...	...-...	...	...
Westbrook, Me. (7)	P	34-30-40	12,676-12,676	None	932	801-86	611	155-35	29	102
	F	27-26-42	13,414-16,769	Y-17,608-15	732	624-85	505	91-28	12	96
Westchester v, Ill. (7)	P	36-35-40	17,947-24,519	None	1,233	1,125-91	855	178-92	...	108
	F	23-23-56	18,518-24,295	None	898	853-95	614	180-59	4	41
Westerly t, R.I. (1,7)	P	32-28-40	12,017-23,924	None	1,278	995-78	782	155-58	45	238
	R	3-0-40	15,517-15,993	None	110	57-52	48	3-6	21	32
Western Springs v, Ill. (7)	P	19-13-40	20,123-26,160	None	868	765-88	597	136-32	43	60
	F	...-...-..	...-...	..-...-..	135	95-70	75	17-3	28	12
Westford t, Mass. (1)										
Westmont v, Ill. (1,7)	P	43-32-40	17,160-26,998	Y-29,120-..	1,604	1,294-81	1,137	85-72	119	191
	F	2-2-40	...-...	..-...-..	296	229-77	208	17-4	11	56
Wheeling v, Ill. (7)	P	48-36-40	20,628-27,803	Y-28,203-12	1,905	1,626-85	1,298	34-294	72	207
	F	40-38-56	18,704-25,219	Y-...-12	1,401	1,305-93	1,012	4-289	33	63
White Bear Lake, Minn. (1,7)	P	25-18-40	17,346-26,687	Y-29,088-16	1,151	1,019-89	877	104-38	24	108
	F	1-0-..	...-...	..-...-..	277	168-61	151	12-5	30	79
White Settlement, Tex. (7)	P	22-16-40	14,706-19,635	Y-...-..	552	422-76	358	45-19	35	95
	F	...-...-..	...-...	..-...-..	89	32-36	32	...-...	30	27
	R	11-6-40	8,159-10,774	None	357	107-30	89	11-7	103	147
Whitehall b, Pa. (1,7)	P	17-12-40	17,734-25,334	Y-26,854-20	722	650-90	571	6-73	21	51
Whitemarsh tp, Pa. (1)										
Whitewater, Wis. (1,7)	P	27-20-40	17,065-19,888	Y-20,888-8	728	664-91	532	73-59	...	64
	F	...-...-..	...-...	..-...-..	10	10-100	10	...-...	...	...
Whitpain tp, Pa. (1,7)	P	20-17-40	18,427-25,306	Y-26,506-20	646	553-86	487	14-52	18	75
Williston, N.D. (1)	P	33-33-40	20,192-...	Y-...-..	1,130	902-80	755	87-60	51	177

Table 3/18 continued **POLICE, FIRE, AND REFUSE COLLECTION AND DISPOSAL DEPARTMENTS: PERSONNEL, SALARIES, AND EXPENDITURES FOR CITIES OVER 10,000: 1984**

City	Department	Total personnel, no. uniformed, duty hours per week	Entrance, maximum salary ($)	Longevity pay, maximum ($), no. years to max.	Reported expenditures (in thousands): Total expenditures (A) ($)	Total personnel expenditures (B), % of (A) ($)	Salaries and wages (C) ($)	City contrib. to employee retirement, insurance (D) ($)	Capital outlay (E) ($)	All other (F) ($)
10,000-24,999 continued										
Williston, N.D. (cont'd)	R	14-9-40	15,000-...	Y-...-..	598	309-52	258	28-23	156	133
Willmar, Minn. (1,7)	P	28-22-40	19,458-23,472	Y-24,372-15	724	714-99	611	67-36	10	...
	F	2-0-40	14,046-17,388	None	153	121-79	115	4-2	32	...
	R	7-0-40	17,718-23,784	None	179	177-99	158	11-8	2	...
Willoughby, Ohio	P	45-35-40	21,112-26,520	None	1,914	1,618-85	1,256	262-100	...	296
	F	28-27-56	21,112-26,499	None	1,219	1,103-90	819	222-62	...	116
	R	14-6-40	14,768-16,016	None	424	305-72	241	39-25	...	119
Wilmington t, Mass. (7)	P	37-35-40	18,387-20,676	Y-22,016-25	1,165	1,014-87	924	42-48	54	97
	F	34-32-42	18,387-20,676	Y-22,016-25	949	883-93	803	40-40	10	56
Wilmington, Ohio	P	22-16-40	14,810-18,013	None	620	551-89	445	68-38	...	69
	F	14-14-56	14,810-18,013	None	455	391-86	299	66-26	...	64
	R	10-10-40	11,045-12,189	None	339	182-54	143	19-20	...	157
Wilton t, Conn. (7)	P	37-34-40	16,235-22,227	None	1,108	968-87	763	144-61	30	110
	F	20-18-42	16,176-19,523	None	652	507-78	433	47-27	29	116
Wilton Manors, Fla. (1)										
Winchester t, Conn. (1)	P	24-18-40	15,998-17,164	None	758	526-69	382	76-68	76	156
	F	2-0-40	...-...	..-...-..	168	51-30	41	4-6	...	117
Winchester, Va.	P	48-42-40	12,222-15,634	Y-17,223-9	1,204	997-83	851	99-47	36	171
	F	19-18-60	11,661-14,886	Y-16,405-9	465	350-75	292	42-16	2	113
	R	12-0-40	9,161-11,661	Y-12,853-9	275	172-63	138	20-14	...	103
Winfield, Kan.	P	23-23-40	14,706-18,304	None	749	661-88	459	151-51	22	66
	F	20-20-56	14,007-17,443	None	614	572-93	394	136-42	2	40
	R	9-9-40	11,513-15,059	None	527	185-35	150	17-18	134	208
Winnetka v, Ill.	P	34-27-40	20,820-28,272	None	1,628	1,404-86	998	313-93	72	152
	F	23-22-56	20,820-28,272	None	1,205	1,081-90	688	279-114	38	86
	R	20-16-40	18,300-20,760	None	599	455-76	340	60-55	...	144
Winter Haven, Fla.	P	40-17-40	14,481-15,205	None	1,558	1,055-68	927	88-40	60	443
	F	38-36-56	14,472-15,200	None	988	748-76	626	96-26	56	184
	R	9-2-40	8,881-11,914	None	932	282-30	247	22-13	...	650
Winter Park, Fla. (7)	P	61-48-40	15,891-22,173	Y-22,395-10	2,349	1,827-78	1,663	110-54	29	493
	F	46-45-56	12,463-17,326	Y-17,499-10	1,178	1,000-85	859	107-34	7	171
	R	17-0-40	11,544-16,037	Y-16,197-10	769	340-44	285	41-14	...	429
Winter Springs, Fla. (7)	P	28-21-40	13,044-17,530	None	578	472-82	422	28-22	37	69
	F	25-24-56	12,722-17,098	None	565	460-81	414	27-19	20	85
Wisconsin Rapids, Wis.	P	48-37-39	18,130-21,822	Y-22,302-20	1,640	1,445-88	1,088	276-81	45	150
	F	29-29-56	17,624-21,602	Y-22,082-20	995	928-93	719	158-51	7	60
	R	9-6-44	17,182-17,504	Y-18,044-30	668	219-33	178	29-12	...	449
Wolcott t, Conn. (7)	P	26-20-40	15,000-20,134	None	881	699-79	527	121-51	20	162
Wood River, Ill. (7)	P	24-18-40	18,075-19,541	Y-20,541-22	835	729-87	565	118-46	42	64
	F	8-8-56	18,075-19,541	Y-20,541-22	378	353-93	256	82-15	3	22
Woodburn, Ore. (7)	P	29-19-40	15,588-19,848	None	900	669-74	520	92-57	45	186
	F	13-12-56	15,072-17,928	None	470	327-70	247	52-28	32	111
Woodbury, Minn. (1,7)	P	12-10-40	22,248-26,940	Y-28,961-15	628	463-74	400	48-15	46	119
	F	...-...-..	...-...	..-...-..	98	24-24	24	...-...	5	69
Woodridge v, Ill. (3,7)	P	44-32-40	19,198-26,790	Y-27,150-6	1,694	1,355-80	1,161	110-84	84	255
Woodstock, Ill. (1,7)	P	32-22-40	18,292-25,269	..-...-..	...	...-..	...	...-...	...	...
	F	...-...-..	...-...	..-...-..	51	38-75	36	...-2	13	...
Woodward, Okla.	P	32-24-40	16,790-17,199	Y-19,599-20	906	729-80	631	93-5	64	113
	F	20-20-56	15,435-16,380	Y-18,780-20	500	416-83	382	31-3	40	44
	R	13-8-40	13,560-13,860	Y-16,260-20	396	211-53	184	24-3	65	120
Worthington, Minn. (1)	P	23-17-40	16,960-21,458	Y-22,403-..	561	510-91	426	52-32	51	...
	F	...-...-..	...-...	..-...-..	23	23-100	23	...-...	...	...
Worthington, Ohio (2,7)	P	35-21-40	16,916-23,715	None	1,206	1,064-88	849	147-68	46	96
Yuba City, Calif. (7)	P	48-33-40	20,037-23,603	None	1,692	1,391-82	1,057	172-162	23	278
	F	25-24-56	16,451-16,451	None	973	821-84	626	110-85	27	125

D Management Trends and Issues

1

Local Government Managers: Profile of the Professionals in a Maturing Profession*

Mary A. Schellinger
International City Management Association

On the surface, the job description of a local government manager hasn't changed much since the first person to fill such a job sat down at his desk in Staunton, Virginia, in 1908. Both then and now, a manager serves at the pleasure of the council and has overall responsibility for overseeing the day-to-day activities of the local government.

But that's where the difference between yesterday's managers and today's managers comes in—in the definition of day-to-day activities. The activities of today's local government managers bear little resemblance to those of managers at the time the local government management profession was in its infancy.

At the beginning of the twentieth century when the first city managers were defining their profession, their day-to-day activities focused on addressing the needs of growing metropolitan centers—building an infrastructure, expanding a school system, providing public transportation, and assuring public safety. Today, the complexities of a society directing itself into the twenty-first century have been interwoven into the day-to-day activities of local governments so that our cities and counties are sophisticated and intricately configured businesses and our managers are brokers, negotiators, communicators, and entrepreneurs.

Likewise, on the surface a composite of the local government management profession has remained unchanged as the profession evolved. In the early days, the profession was composed of white males who were well educated, happily married, and stood a fifty-fifty chance of subscribing to a conservative political philosophy. So, too, today . . . on the surface. But a closer look at the body of professionals who make up the local government management profession today shows some differences.

As the complexion of our local governments has become more diverse, more women and minorities have entered the profession. As the demands and pressures involved in managing complex government organizations have increased, members of the profession are getting a little more education and a little more experience before they take their first jobs as managers. The purpose of this article is to examine the characteristics of the people who make up the local government management profession and the changes that have occurred in that profile over time.

METHODOLOGY

In the spring and summer of 1984, ICMA conducted a mail survey of chief administrators in local governments having the council-manager form of government or providing for a position of overall general management.[1] Survey questionnaires were sent to a total of 3,315 municipalities, 238 counties, and 144 councils of governments. Additional surveys were sent in a follow up mailing to those who did not reply to the first request. Completed surveys were received from 2,131 municipalities (64%), 144 counties (61%), and 85 (59%) COGs. Table 1/1 displays the return rates by population group, geographic region and division, metro status, and form of government.

Many of the questions on the 1984 survey instrument were worded so that they would be comparable to results of earlier surveys of chief administrators and trends could be traced over time. Specifically, questions on personal characteristics and job tenure were designed to complement a 1971 study by Richard J. Stillman II and two major ICMA surveys, one in 1974 and the other in 1980.[2]

Throughout this article, the term *manager* is used to encompass city, village, town and township managers; county managers; chief administrative officers (CAOs); and executive directors (EDs). Specifically, *executive director* refers to the head of a council of governments. Although several differences distinguish the jobs of various managers, they are grouped together for the purposes of this article. As public administrators, they share common goals and common problems.

PROFILE

When the profession was scrutinized in 1980, the trends compared to earlier surveys that surfaced pointed to a younger, more mobile profession. Some of these trends have taken a different direction in the past four years.

Age. Many of the trends concerning the age of managers that appeared to be substantiated by the 1980s survey were reversed or modified by the 1984 study. Overall, the median age dropped from 43 in 1974 to 40 in 1980. However, in the four years since the 1980 survey, the median rose slightly to 41. The average age of a manager as of 1 June 1984 was 42.6 years (no table shown).

The trend toward greater numbers of older managers can be seen even more clearly when examining the change for various age groups. Between 1974 and 1980 there was significant growth in the number of managers 40 years of age and younger (Table 1/2). The proportion of managers in this group increased by nine percentage points while the proportion of older managers decreased accordingly. In 1984, the proportion of managers 30 and under fell off dramatically (five percentage points) while the proportion for all other age groups increased. The greatest increase was for the 31 to 40 age group, which increased by four percentage points.

It is not particularly surprising that 88% of the managers responding to the 1984 survey are between the ages of 30 and 60. That figure is, no doubt, not substantially different from the work force as a whole. However, some interesting variations appear when this grouping is examined on a regional basis. In the West, 95% of the responding managers are between 30 and 60 while in the Northeast only 81% of the managers fall between those ages (no table shown). In the West there are only 7 managers (1%) under 31 and 19 managers (4%) over 60; in the Northeast there are 50 managers (11%) under 31 and 35 managers (8%) over 60.

Sex. The number of women in the profession has grown significantly in recent years, especially in the last four years. In 1971, there were only 7 women managers. This figure represents less than 1% of the profession. In fact, it wasn't until the 1974 survey that the number of women managers was large enough to register on the trends table (Table 1/3). By the time of the 1984 survey, 5% of the responding managers were women.

The growth is more startling when the actual numbers are examined rather than the percentages. In the decade between 1971 and 1980, the number of women managers grew more than eightfold, going from 7 to 58. In the next four years, the number of female managers doubled, so that 116 of the managers who responded to the 1984 survey are female. Furthermore, women are taking jobs as managers in communities of all sizes today. In 1971, they generally worked in places under 2,500 population. In 1974, there were no women managers in places over 10,000 population (Table 1/3). By 1980, that statement was true only of places over 100,000. In 1984, women are spread throughout communities of all sizes. In fact, the largest places, those over 500,000 population, show the second largest percentage of female managers.

The incidence of women managers has spread across geographic regions as well as population groups. In 1974, women managers were found only in places in the Northeast. By 1980, there were women managers in all four regions. Between 1980 and 1984, the percentage of women managers doubled in the North Central region, the South, and the West while it increased by only 50% in the Northeast (Table 1/3).

The marked growth in the number of women managers may, in part, be explained by a similar growth in the number of female council members for the same period. The percentage of female council members nearly doubled between 1971 and 1974, going from 3.6% to 6.5%,

* Data for this article were collected from the survey *A Profile of the Local Government Manager/Chief Administrative Officer/Executive Director—1984* (CAO/84) conducted by the International City Management Association, Washington, D.C., 1984.

Table 1/1 SURVEY RESPONSE

Classification	All recognized local governments: No. surveyed (A)	No. responding	% of (A)	Recognized municipalities: No. surveyed (B)	No. responding	% of (B)	Recognized counties: No. surveyed (C)	No. responding	% of (C)	Recognized COGs: No. surveyed (D)	No. responding	% of (D)
Total	3,697	2,360	63.8	3,315	2,131	64.3	238	144	60.5	144	85	59.0
Population group												
Over 1,000,000	30	21	70.0	1	1	100.0	9	5	55.6	20	15	75.0
500,000–1,000,000	50	31	62.0	8	3	37.5	22	13	59.1	20	15	75.0
250,000– 499,999	77	54	70.1	19	14	73.7	22	14	63.6	36	26	72.2
100,000– 249,999	173	112	64.7	73	57	78.1	53	34	64.2	47	21	44.7
50,000– 99,999	247	169	68.4	183	131	71.6	49	31	63.3	15	7	46.7
25,000– 49,999	436	307	70.4	393	283	72.0	38	23	60.5	5	1	20.0
10,000– 24,999	911	611	67.1	875	591	67.5	36	20	55.6	...	...	...
5,000– 9,999	793	510	64.3	786	506	64.4	7	4	57.1	...	...	...
2,500– 4,999	605	358	59.2	605	358	59.2	...	...	...	...	...	...
Under 2,500	375	187	49.9	372	187	50.3	2	0	0.0	1	0	0.0
Geographic region												
Northeast	802	454	56.6	780	444	56.9	12	5	41.7	10	5	50.0
North Central	879	634	72.1	827	599	72.4	21	17	81.0	31	18	58.1
South	1,219	731	60.0	1,002	596	59.5	151	94	62.3	66	41	62.1
West	797	541	67.9	706	492	69.7	54	28	51.9	37	21	56.8
Geographic division												
New England	348	196	56.3	345	194	56.2	...	...	...	3	2	66.7
Mid-Atlantic	454	258	56.8	435	250	57.5	12	5	41.7	7	3	42.9
East North Central	495	365	73.7	465	343	73.8	12	10	83.3	18	12	66.7
West North Central	384	269	70.1	362	256	70.7	9	7	77.8	13	6	46.2
South Atlantic	722	470	65.1	542	358	66.1	150	94	62.7	30	18	60.0
East South Central	115	56	48.7	104	53	51.0	...	...	...	11	3	27.3
West South Central	382	205	53.7	356	185	52.0	1	0	0.0	25	20	80.0
Mountain	220	150	68.2	194	138	71.1	15	6	40.0	11	6	54.5
Pacific Coast	577	391	67.8	512	354	69.1	39	22	56.4	26	15	57.7
Metro status												
Central	327	245	74.9	296	220	74.3	...	...	...	...	...	...
Suburban	1,730	1,117	64.6	1,728	1,116	64.6	...	...	...	...	...	...
Independent	1,328	821	61.8	1,291	795	61.6	...	...	...	...	...	...
Metro	137	86	62.8	...	...	...	137	86	62.8	...	...	...
Nonmetro	101	58	57.4	...	...	...	101	58	57.4	...	...	...
Form of government												
Mayor-council	724	457	63.1	724	457	63.1	...	...	...	...	...	...
Council-manager	2,425	1,578	65.1	2,425	1,578	65.1	...	...	...	...	...	...
Commission	21	11	52.4	21	11	52.4	...	...	...	...	...	...
Town meeting	124	74	59.7	124	74	59.7	...	...	...	...	...	...
Rep. town meeting	21	11	52.4	21	11	52.4	...	...	...	...	...	...
With administrator	238	144	60.5	...	...	...	238	144	60.5	...	...	...

and nearly doubled again between 1974 and 1981 when the percentage of female council members stood at 12.8%.[3]

Race and Ethnic Background. Overall, the results of the 1984 survey show virtually no change in the racial composition of the profession compared to the 1980 survey results. In 1980 all of the responding managers were white except for 29; in 1984 there are 28 who are not white. The number of black managers has remained the same (15) although their distribution among geographic regions and population groups has changed somewhat (Table 1/4). There are two more Asian managers in 1984 than there were in 1980 and three fewer Indians.

The number of Hispanic managers nearly doubled between 1980 and 1984; there were 40 Hispanic managers responding to the survey in 1980 and 71 in 1984 (no table shown). (At the time of the 1971 survey, there were no Hispanic managers.) The percentages of Hispanic managers are distributed evenly among population groups. However, when examining the actual numbers, 56 of the 71 Hispanic managers (79%) serve communities with populations between 2,500 and 50,000 population. Similarly, Hispanic managers work in all geographic areas of the county but just over three-quarters of them (76%) work in the South or the West.

Table 1/2 LOCAL GOVERNMENT MANAGERS BY AGE GROUP

Age group	1974 No.	1974 %	1980 No.	1980 %	1984 No.	1984 %
Total	1,646	100	1,977	100	2,348	100
30 and under	189	12	256	13	178	8
31–40	490	30	756	38	995	42
41–50	503	31	493	25	605	26
51–60	367	22	378	19	461	20
Over 60	97	6	94	5	109	5

Note: Percentages may exceed 100% because of rounding.

Marital Status. The 1960s and 1970s saw many Americans weighing the pros and cons of alternative life styles. Now, the media is proclaiming the return of the public at large to "the traditional values" of marriage and family in the 1980s. Managers are not living by the media's prescription, however. During the past decade, the number of single managers has gradually increased. In 1974, just 3% of the reporting managers were single (Table 1/5). That figure increased to 4% in 1980 and to 5% in 1984.

Similarly, the number of divorced or separated managers increased during the past decade. In 1974, only 1% of the reporting managers were divorced or separated. This was followed by a sharp increase in the number of

Table 1/3 SEX OF LOCAL GOVERNMENT MANAGERS

Classification	Male 1974	Male 1980	Male 1984	Female 1974	Female 1980	Female 1984
Total, all managers	99%	97%	95%	1%	3%	5%
Population group						
Over 500,000	100	100	92	0	0	8
250,000–499,999	100	100	94	0	0	6
100,000–249,999	100	100	96	0	0	5
50,000– 99,999	100	99	97	0	1	3
25,000– 49,999	100	99	97	0	1	3
10,000– 24,999	100	99	97	0	1	3
5,000– 9,999	99	97	96	1	3	4
2,500– 4,999	100	96	94	0	4	6
Under 2,500	93	89	83	7	11	17
Geographic region						
Northeast	97	94	91	3	6	9
North Central	100	98	96	0	2	4
South	100	98	96	0	2	4
West	100	98	96	0	2	4

Table 1/4 RACE OF LOCAL GOVERNMENT MANAGERS

Classification	No. reporting (A)	White No.	White % of (A)	Black No.	Black % of (A)	Indian/Native American No.	Indian/Native American % of (A)	Asian No.	Asian % of (A)
Total, all managers	2,349	2,321	99	15	1	7	..[1]	6	..[1]
Population group									
Over 500,000	52	50	94	1	3	0	0	1	3
250,000–499,999	54	52	96	2	4	0	0	0	0
100,000–249,999	111	108	97	2	2	0	0	1	1
50,000– 99,999	169	168	99	0	0	0	0	1	1
25,000– 49,999	306	303	99	2	1	0	0	1	..[1]
10,000– 24,999	609	603	99	5	1	0	0	1	..[1]
5,000– 9,999	509	508	99	1	..[1]	0	0	0	0
2,500– 4,999	355	348	98	1	..[1]	6	2	0	0
Under 2,500	184	181	98	1	1	1	1	1	1
Geographic division									
New England	195	195	100	0	0	0	0	0	0
Mid-Atlantic	256	252	98	1	..[1]	1	..[1]	2	1
East North Central	363	359	99	4	1	0	0	0	0
West North Central	268	267	99	0	0	0	0	1	..[1]
South Atlantic	469	462	99	6	1	0	0	1	..[1]
East South Central	56	56	100	0	0	0	0	0	0
West South Central	204	200	98	1	1	3	2	0	0
Mountain	147	147	99	1	1	1	1	0	0
Pacific Coast	389	383	98	2	1	2	1	2	1

[1] Rounds to less than 0.5%.

Table 1/5 MARITAL STATUS OF LOCAL GOVERNMENT MANAGERS

Marital status	1974	1980	1984
Total, all managers	100	100	100
Single	3	4	5
Married	96	91	89
Divorced or separated	1	5	5

Note: Percentages may not equal 100% because of rounding.

divorced or separated managers between 1974 and 1980—from 1% to 5%. Although it was lost in rounding the numbers for Table 1/5 there was a very small increase (0.5%) in the number of divorced or separated managers between 1980 and 1984.

Corresponding to the increase in single, divorced, and separated managers is the decrease in married managers. The percentage of married managers has decreased from 96% in 1974 to 91% in 1980 to 89% in 1984 (Table 1/5).

Political Preference. Several subtle shifts in political preference have taken place among managers in the past decade. In both 1974 and 1980 the percentage of Republican managers was the same as the percentage of Democratic city managers (no table shown). The results of the 1984 survey—a survey taken in the heat of the 1984 presidential campaign which culminated in a Republican landslide election—show a slight preference for the Democratic party among managers over the Republican party when percentages are compared (Table 1/6).

Perhaps the most striking trend in political preference is the trend away from affiliation with either major political party. In 1974, 37% of the reporting managers said that they were independent or that they had no political preference. In 1980, 45% gave one of these answers, and, in 1984, the number was 47% (24% said they were independent and 23% said they had no preference).

Educational Attainment. While the local government management profession has always attracted (or demanded) highly educated individuals, the level of educational attainment among managers has risen sharply since the 1971 Stillman study (Table 1/7). At that time, 69% of the reporting managers had a bachelor's or master's degree.[4] A few managers had doctorates, but their numbers were so small that they did not equal one-half of one percentage point.

When the 1974 survey was taken, 76% of the managers reported having a bachelor's or master's degree. Again, there was a small number of managers with doctorates. By 1980, the percentage of managers with degrees had risen to 84%. Included in this figure are 1% of the managers who reported holding doctorates. At the time of the 1984 survey, 88% of the managers hold at least one degree. Of that figure, 30% hold bachelor's degrees, 57% hold master's degrees, and 1% hold doctorates.

There is a strong relationship between age and level of educational attainment that reflects the emphasis put on acquiring advanced degrees in the past two decades or so. Nearly all managers aged 30 or less have a degree (96%) (Figure 1/1). The ratio of managers in this age group with a master's degree is ten percentage points greater than the percentage for all managers. Likewise, the managers in the 31 to 40 age group have a much higher than average level of educational attainment—95% have a degree. In this age group the proportion of managers with master's degrees is even larger than in the 30 or less group and the percentage with a doctorate is the same as the percentage for all managers.

Whether it is the recent emphasis on advanced degrees or the radical changes in the way governments do business that has driven managers back to school to learn new skills, many managers have earned their advanced degrees at an age that is beyond the traditional age for a student going straight through school without a work break between degrees. Twenty percent of the managers whose highest degree is a master's earned that degree between the ages of 30 and 40, 6% earned a master's when they were between 40 and 50, and 1% earned a master's after they had reached the age of 50 (no table shown). Among managers with doctorates, 40% of them earned the degree between the ages of 30 and 40, 24% earned the degree between the ages of 40 and 50, and 4% earned the degree after 50.

JOB TENURE AND MOBILITY

The local government management profession is frequently characterized as being extremely mobile. The average number of years that the managers responding to the 1984 survey have served in their current positions is 5.4, but that is not an unusually brief period of employment

Table 1/6 POLITICAL PREFERENCE OF LOCAL GOVERNMENT MANAGERS

Classification	No. reporting (A)	Democrat No.	Democrat % of (A)	Republican No.	Republican % of (A)	Independent No.	Independent % of (A)	Other No.	Other % of (A)	No affiliation No.	No affiliation % of (A)
Total, all managers	2,324	643	28	609	26	545	24	2	..[1]	525	22
Population group											
Over 500,000	51	16	31	8	16	13	25	0	0	14	27
250,000–499,999	53	21	40	9	17	11	21	0	0	12	23
100,000–249,999	108	37	34	16	15	30	28	0	0	25	23
50,000– 99,999	168	43	26	43	26	44	26	0	0	38	23
25,000– 49,999	302	81	27	66	22	86	29	1	..[1]	68	23
10,000– 24,999	605	149	25	155	26	167	28	0	0	134	22
5,000– 9,999	506	126	25	171	34	94	19	0	0	115	23
2,500– 4,999	348	115	33	89	26	63	18	1	..[1]	80	23
Under 2,500	183	55	30	52	28	37	20	0	0	39	21
Geographic division											
New England	194	47	24	44	23	69	36	1	1	33	17
Mid-Atlantic	256	59	23	92	36	60	23	0	0	45	18
East North Central	358	36	10	84	24	102	29	0	0	136	38
West North Central	265	59	22	62	23	73	28	0	0	71	27
South Atlantic	464	191	41	75	16	83	18	0	0	115	25
East South Central	56	19	34	6	11	14	25	0	0	17	30
West South Central	199	67	34	28	14	60	30	0	0	44	22
Mountain	149	40	27	52	35	37	25	0	0	20	13
Pacific Coast	383	125	33	166	43	47	12	1	..[1]	44	12

[1] Rounds to less than 0.5%.

in today's job market. The perception of high mobility may be due more to the fact that when a manager moves from one job to another he or she generally moves from one community to another rather than to the length of time the manager spends in any given job. We may achieve a more accurate portrayal of the stability of managers and the stability of the profession by examining the length of a manager's current employment in tandem with the total number of years as a local government manager and the number of local governments served as manager.

Service in Current Position. As mentioned above, the average length of time managers have spent in their current positions is 5.4 years (Table 1/8). However, as a measure of distribution, averages tend to conceal the extremes. The figures used to calculate this average range from as little as 1 year (periods of less than a year were rounded to 1 year for the statistical tabulations) to 43 years (no table shown). Length of service is generally tied positively to population size, ranging from 10.2 years in places over 1,000,000 down to 4.3 years in places under 2,500. Geographic location appears to have little bearing on the length of tenure.

Just over one-quarter of the reporting managers (26%) have been in their current positions for 7 or more years (Table 1/9). Of that figure, 6% have been in their current positions 15 or more years; 8% have been there for 11 to 15 years; and 12% have served for 7 to 10 years. In general, a greater percentage of managers who have served 1 to 2 years are found in smaller communities while the percentages of managers who have served 15 or more years are higher in the larger places.

The length of service in a manager's current position is closely tied to age. The percentage of managers age 30 or less who have been in their current jobs for 1 or 2 years is just over

Table 1/7 HIGHEST LEVEL OF EDUCATIONAL ATTAINMENT OF LOCAL GOVERNMENT MANAGERS

Level of attainment	1971	1974	1980	1984
Doctorate degree	..[1]	..[1]	1%	1%
Master's degree	27%	38%	51	57
Bachelor's degree	42	38	32	30
Some college, no degree	26	18	12	10
High school diploma	3	5	3	2
Less than high school diploma	2	1	..[1]	..[1]

Note: Percentages, when totaled, may not equal 100% because of rounding.
[1] Rounds to less than 0.5%.

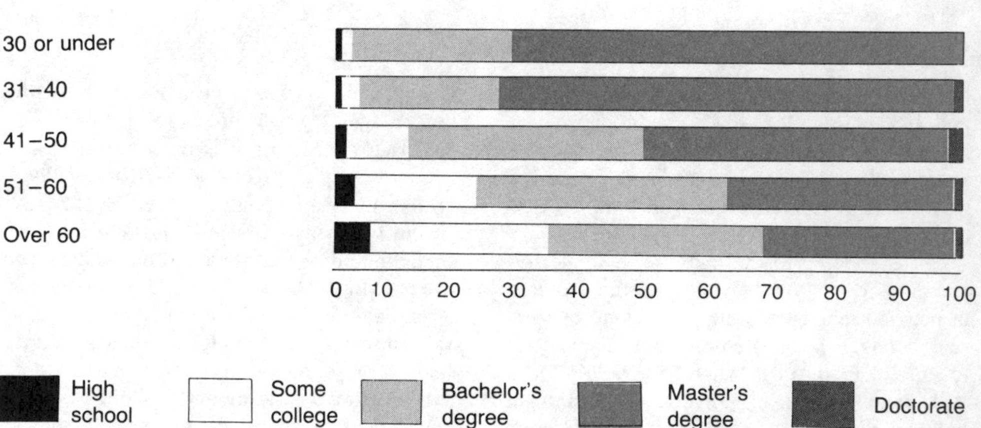

Figure 1/1 *Highest level of educational attainment by age group*

five and a half times greater than the percentage of managers 60 or over who have been in their positions for that amount of time (Figure 1/2). Conversely, the percentage of managers 60 and over who have served in their current positions for 7 to 10 years (the grouping showing the longest tenure for the youngest managers) is 16 times greater than the percentage of managers 30 or less who have served 7 to 10 years.

The 1980 data showed a trend toward shorter lengths of service for managers in all age groups except those in the 30 and under age group when compared with the 1974 data. The difference between average tenure in 1974 and in 1980 generally increased as age increased. As in the case of the age data discussed above, the 1984 data reversed the earlier trend (Table 1/10). The average number of years spent in their current position increased for managers in all age groups. The greatest increase was for managers in the 61 and over age group, whose tenure returned nearly to the level reported in 1974.

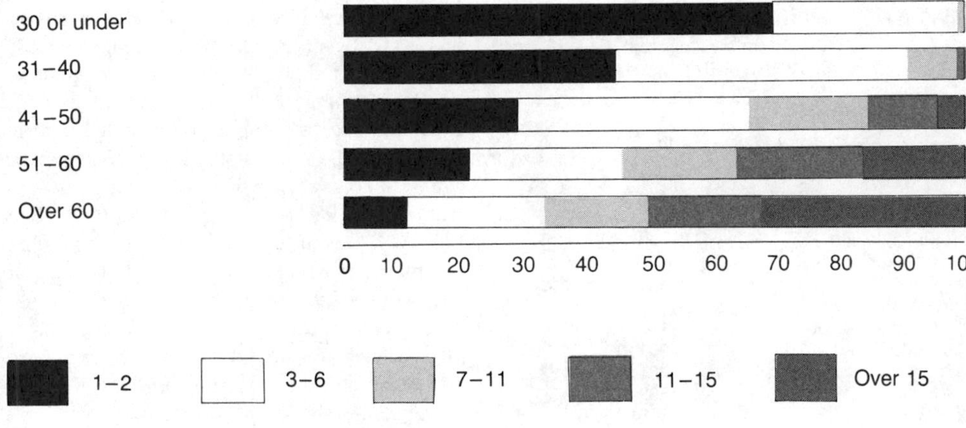

Figure 1/2 *Number of years in current position by age group*

Table 1/8 AVERAGE NUMBER OF YEARS IN CURRENT POSITION

Population group	No. reporting	Average no. of years
Total, all managers	2,331	5.4
Over 1,000,000	20	10.2
500,000–1,000,000	30	6.2
250,000– 499,999	52	6.4
100,000– 249,999	112	5.2
50,000– 99,999	167	5.7
25,000– 49,999	304	6.6
10,000– 24,999	605	5.6
5,000– 9,999	502	5.1
2,500– 4,999	354	4.5
Under 2,500	185	4.3

Table 1/10 AVERAGE NUMBER OF YEARS SPENT IN CURRENT POSITION, BY AGE GROUP

Age group	1974	1980	1984
30 and under	1.8	1.9	2.2
31–40	4.8	3.0	3.3
41–50	9.0	4.8	5.8
51–60	12.0	6.0	8.9
Over 60	13.0	8.7	12.2

Table 1/9 NUMBER OF YEARS IN CURRENT POSITION

Classification	No. reporting (A)	1–2		3–6		7–10		11–15		15 or more	
		No.	% of (A)	No.	% of (A)	No.	% of (A)	No.	% of (A)	No.	% of (A)
Total, all managers	2,331	826	35	892	38	279	12	194	8	140	6
Population group											
Over 500,000	50	9	18	17	34	7	14	12	24	5	10
250,000–499,999	52	14	27	18	35	9	17	7	14	4	8
100,000–249,999	112	38	34	48	43	8	7	12	11	6	5
50,000– 99,999	167	57	34	54	32	28	17	20	12	8	5
25,000– 49,999	304	91	30	110	36	44	15	29	10	30	10
10,000– 24,999	605	199	33	240	40	73	12	53	9	40	7
5,000– 9,999	502	177	35	209	42	56	11	37	7	23	5
2,500– 4,999	354	155	44	134	38	31	9	17	5	17	5
Under 2,500	185	86	47	62	34	23	12	7	4	7	4
Geographic division											
New England	193	67	35	76	39	19	10	15	8	16	8
Mid-Atlantic	252	75	30	92	37	35	14	30	12	20	8
East North Central	362	127	35	134	37	52	14	30	8	19	5
West North Central	266	93	35	121	46	31	12	11	4	10	4
South Atlantic	464	174	38	160	35	53	11	49	11	28	6
East South Central	55	24	44	20	36	5	9	4	7	2	4
West South Central	204	76	37	76	37	24	12	14	7	14	7
Mountain	147	64	44	58	40	15	10	6	4	4	3
Pacific Coast	388	126	33	155	40	45	12	35	9	27	7

Table 1/11 AVERAGE TOTAL NUMBER OF YEARS AS A LOCAL GOVERNMENT MANAGER

Population group	No. reporting	Average no. of years
Total, all managers	2,330	9.3
Over 1,000,000	20	13.2
500,000–1,000,000	28	10.4
250,000– 499,999	53	11.7
100,000– 249,999	112	10.5
50,000– 99,999	168	12.1
25,000– 49,999	303	11.7
10,000– 24,999	605	9.6
5,000– 9,999	503	8.3
2,500– 4,999	353	7.2
Under 2,500	185	6.4

Total Years as a Local Government Manager. The average number of years that the respondents to the 1984 survey have spent as local government managers is 9.3 (Table 1/11). That figure certainly appears low in light of the fact that ICMA awards plaques to an increasing number of managers who have served local government for 25, 30, and 35 years. In fact, in 1982 ICMA awarded a plaque for the first time to a manager who had served for 45 years. But this average includes all managers, those that have spent a short time at their first manager jobs as well as those that have been in the profession an award winning amount of time.

Figure 1/3 shows the distribution of career service by age. Viewed in this way, the amount of time spent in the profession by the managers who have more established careers can be clearly seen: 27% of the managers between 41 and 50, 53% of the managers between 51 and 60, and 65% of the managers 61 and over have served as managers for 15 years or more. Included in those figures are 18% of the managers in the 51 to 60 age group who have 25 or more years of service and 37% of the 61 and over group who have 25 or more years of service. Nine percent of the reporting managers (all in the 61 and over age group) have more than 34 years of service.

In Table 1/12 the distribution of career ser-

Table 1/12 TOTAL NUMBER OF YEARS AS A LOCAL GOVERNMENT MANAGER

Classification	No. reporting (A)	Less than 5		5–14		15–24		25–34		35 or more	
		No.	% of (A)	No.	% of (A)	No.	% of (A)	No.	% of (A)	No.	% of (A)
Total, all managers	2,330	732	31	1,114	48	357	15	115	5	12	1
Population group											
Over 500,000	48	7	15	21	44	16	33	4	8	0	0
250,000–499,999	53	12	23	24	45	11	21	6	11	0	0
100,000–249,999	112	29	26	55	49	22	20	6	5	0	0
50,000– 99,999	168	36	21	74	44	40	24	18	11	0	0
25,000– 49,999	303	76	25	128	42	67	22	29	10	3	1
10,000– 24,999	605	167	28	306	51	98	16	29	5	5	1
5,000– 9,999	503	162	32	268	53	56	11	16	3	1	..[1]
2,500– 4,999	353	152	43	162	46	32	9	5	1	2	1
Under 2,500	185	91	49	76	41	15	8	2	1	1	1
Geographic division											
New England	193	69	36	80	42	23	12	18	9	3	2
Mid-Atlantic	253	70	28	138	55	33	13	11	4	1	..[1]
East North Central	362	118	33	165	46	55	15	23	6	1	..[1]
West North Central	266	82	31	144	54	34	13	6	2	0	0
South Atlantic	465	143	31	223	48	73	16	22	5	4	1
East South Central	54	21	39	25	46	7	13	1	2	0	0
West South Central	203	65	32	93	46	34	17	10	5	1	1
Mountain	147	49	33	70	48	23	16	4	3	1	1
Pacific Coast	387	115	30	176	46	75	19	20	5	1	..[1]

[1]Rounds to less than 0.5%.

Table 1/13 TOTAL NUMBER OF GOVERNMENTS SERVED AS A LOCAL GOVERNMENT MANAGER

Classification	No. reporting (A)	One		2 or 3		4 to 6		7 or more	
		No.	% of (A)	No.	% of (A)	No.	% of (A)	No.	% of (A)
Total, all managers	2,321	1,139	49	967	42	190	8	25	1
Population group									
Over 500,000	50	15	50	12	40	2	7	1	3
250,000–499,999	51	26	51	16	31	8	16	1	2
100,000–249,999	111	51	46	46	41	14	13	0	0
50,000– 99,999	167	61	37	75	45	25	15	6	4
25,000– 49,999	301	130	43	133	44	34	11	4	1
10,000– 24,999	603	278	46	269	45	51	9	5	1
5,000– 9,999	502	252	50	213	42	33	7	4	1
2,500– 4,999	353	193	55	138	39	18	5	4	1
Under 2,500	183	120	66	59	32	4	2	0	0
Geographic division									
New England	193	96	50	76	39	19	10	2	1
Mid-Atlantic	252	140	56	97	39	13	5	2	1
East North Central	362	180	50	151	42	24	7	7	2
West North Central	265	128	48	120	45	16	6	1	..[1]
South Atlantic	464	219	47	203	44	39	8	3	1
East South Central	55	34	62	18	33	2	4	1	2
West South Central	201	90	45	82	41	26	13	3	2
Mountain	143	65	46	62	43	15	11	1	1
Pacific Coast	386	187	48	158	41	36	9	5	1

[1] Rounds to less than 0.5%.

Table 1/14 MANAGERS WHOSE IMMEDIATELY PREVIOUS POSITION WAS NOT AS A LOCAL GOVERNMENT MANAGER

Classification	No. reporting	No.	%
Total, all managers	2,302	1,359	59
Population group			
Over 500,000	46	34	74
250,000–499,999	50	32	64
100,000–249,999	111	68	61
50,000– 99,999	168	85	51
25,000– 49,999	303	159	53
10,000– 24,999	597	334	56
5,000– 9,999	500	291	58
2,500– 4,999	350	226	65
Under 2,500	177	130	73
Geographic division			
New England	189	100	53
Mid-Atlantic	248	162	65
East North Central	359	214	60
West North Central	265	152	57
South Atlantic	458	274	60
East South Central	52	35	67
West South Central	197	119	60
Mountain	146	76	52
Pacific Coast	388	227	59

vice is shown by population group and geographic division. The largest communities (those over 500,000 population) attract managers with 15 to 24 years of service at a rate twice that of the national rate; these communities also can boast having managers with 25 to 34 years of service at nearly twice the national rate.

Number of Governments Served. The average number of governments managers have served is 1.9. A whopping 91% have served three or fewer governments (Table 1/13). Again, age strongly affects these national figures. Two-thirds of the managers who have held four to six manager positions with different governments are 51 or older; 90% of the managers that have held more than six positions are 51 or older (Figure 1/4). Surprisingly, one manager under thirty has served four to six different governments and 67 managers in that age group have served two or three governments.

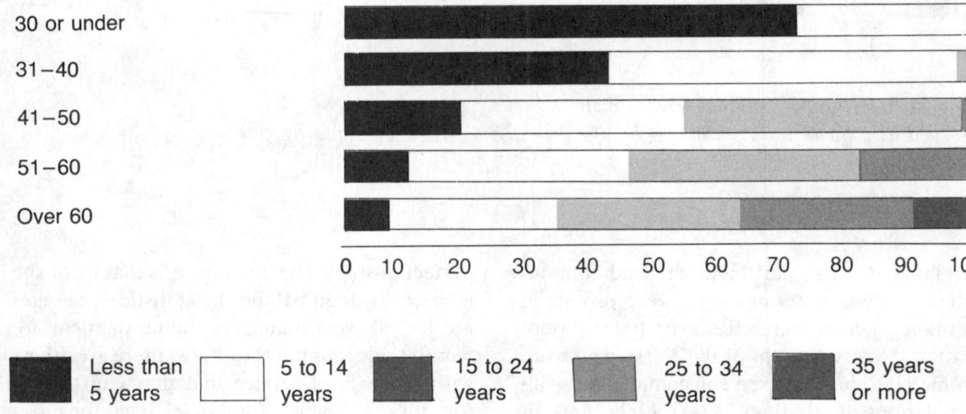

Figure 1/3 *Total number of years as a local government manager by age group*

CAREER PATH

Many of the figures presented in the section on job tenure and mobility seem to contradict what we *know* about the local government management profession. Our picture of the profession and the men and women who stand out in the profession focuses on the established manager, the manager who decided at an early age to enter public service, got a good education (if our manager is a post World War II baby boom baby, that education would certainly include an MPA), worked in one or two communities as an assistant, and has had two or three good manager jobs since then.

But the survey results paint quite a different picture. Over half (59%) of the survey respondents (representing 64% of the profession) were not working as local government managers immediately prior to taking their current positions (Table 1/14). Certainly, some of the respondents may have been managers at an earlier period and perhaps took an assistant manager's position in a larger community as a stepping stone to their current position. Others may have left the profession to pursue an advanced degree or work in the private sector and returned to it in their current position. This figure is, nevertheless, high. The largest communities (those 100,000 and over in population) and the smallest communities (those under 5,000 population) have the greatest proportion of managers who did not come immediately from another manager position.

The executive directors of councils of gov-

Table 1/15 MANAGERS WHO WERE PROMOTED TO THEIR CURRENT POSITION FROM WITHIN THE SAME GOVERNMENT

Classification	No. of managers whose previous position was not as a manager (A)	Managers promoted from within No. (B)	% of (A)	Deputy manager/CAO No.	% of (B)	Assistant manager/CAO No.	% of (B)	Assistant to the manager/CAO No.	% of (B)	Department head No.	% of (B)	Finance director No.	% of (B)	Engineer No.	% of (B)	Clerk No.	% of (B)	Elected official No.	% of (B)	Other No.	% of (B)
Total, all managers	1,325	549	41	35	6	183	33	37	7	120	22	47	9	16	3	41	7	15	3	47	9
Population group																					
Over 500,000	34	16	47	9	56	3	19	0	0	6	38	0	0	0	0	0	0	1	6	1	6
250,000–499,999	31	15	48	3	20	5	33	0	0	6	40	0	0	0	0	0	0	0	0	1	7
100,000–249,999	67	43	64	4	9	18	42	5	12	11	26	3	7	0	0	0	0	0	0	1	2
50,000– 99,999	83	55	66	4	7	21	38	2	4	12	22	6	11	1	2	1	2	1	2	5	9
25,000– 49,999	156	92	59	7	8	36	39	5	5	23	25	10	11	1	1	3	3	0	0	7	8
10,000– 24,999	324	133	41	2	2	54	41	13	10	25	19	14	11	4	3	8	6	4	3	9	7
5,000– 9,999	287	101	35	3	3	32	32	4	4	19	19	9	9	7	7	11	11	3	3	10	10
2,500– 4,999	219	52	24	3	6	11	21	5	10	9	17	3	6	3	6	9	17	4	8	5	10
Under 2,500	124	38	31	0	0	3	8	3	8	9	24	2	5	0	0	9	24	2	5	8	21
Geographic division																					
New England	94	35	37	1	3	10	29	3	9	3	9	0	0	1	3	3	9	5	14	5	14
Mid-Atlantic	159	66	42	4	6	21	32	4	6	8	12	5	8	3	5	7	11	4	6	9	14
East North Central	210	83	40	9	11	23	28	4	5	18	22	8	10	3	4	10	12	2	2	6	7
West North Central	147	52	35	2	4	7	13	8	15	11	21	5	10	3	6	8	15	0	0	7	13
South Atlantic	268	121	45	10	8	36	30	9	7	29	24	15	12	2	2	7	6	2	2	11	9
East South Central	34	11	32	0	0	2	18	1	9	5	45	0	0	1	9	1	9	1	9	0	0
West South Central	117	53	45	2	4	25	47	4	8	11	21	2	4	0	0	1	2	0	0	4	8
Mountain	75	35	47	3	9	15	43	1	3	7	20	4	11	2	6	2	6	1	3	0	0
Pacific Coast	221	93	42	4	4	44	47	3	3	28	30	8	9	1	1	2	2	0	0	5	5

ernments were more likely not to have served as managers immediately prior to taking their current positions than the other managers as a group, 82% of the COG directors did not come directly from another manager position (not shown in table).

This does not mean that councils and commissions are entrusting the welfare of our communities to rookies, however. When it comes time for councils to appoint a new manager to take charge of their community they appear to want someone who already has some knowledge about what works there and what doesn't. Forty-one percent of the managers who were not serving in a manager position immediately prior to taking their current position reported that they were promoted from some other position in the local government they are currently serving (Table 1/15).

All of the communities 10,000 and over promoted someone from within their government to the manager's position at a rate equal to or greater than the national rate. The greatest incidence of this practice is found in governments with populations of over 500,000 (47%), 100,000 to 249,999 (64%), and 50,000 to 99,999 (66%).

Most frequently, managers served as assistant managers immediately prior to taking their current positions; 34% of the managers who were promoted from within reported doing so. Surprisingly, only 7% of the respondents indicated that they served as deputy manager prior to taking their current position and this practice seems to be concentrated in larger cities (those over 250,000 population). It may be that the difference between an assistant manager and a deputy manager is more a matter of title than job description, particularly in smaller communities, and that, in fact, assistant managers perform many of the same functions in communities where there is no deputy manager.

If the respondents who served as assistants to the manager are combined with assistant managers and deputy managers, then nearly half (48%) of the respondents who were promoted from within were already working in the manager's office and had some advance knowledge of the workings of their community prior to taking their current position as manager.

The next most frequently reported source of manager talent within government is the department heads (22%). With the exception of cities over 500,000 and those 250,000 to 500,000 (38% and 40%, respectively) this practice is fairly evenly spread across population groups. Communities in the East South Central division reported this practice at a rate twice the national rate, while New England communities reported promoting department heads to managers at half the national rate.

Promotion to manager from other positions in the local government appears to be confined primarily to small and medium sized communities. No engineers or clerks were promoted to manager in communities over 100,000 population. Ninety percent of the clerks who were promoted to manager serve in communities with populations of less than 25,000. Only three finance directors and one elected official took manager positions in cities over 100,000.

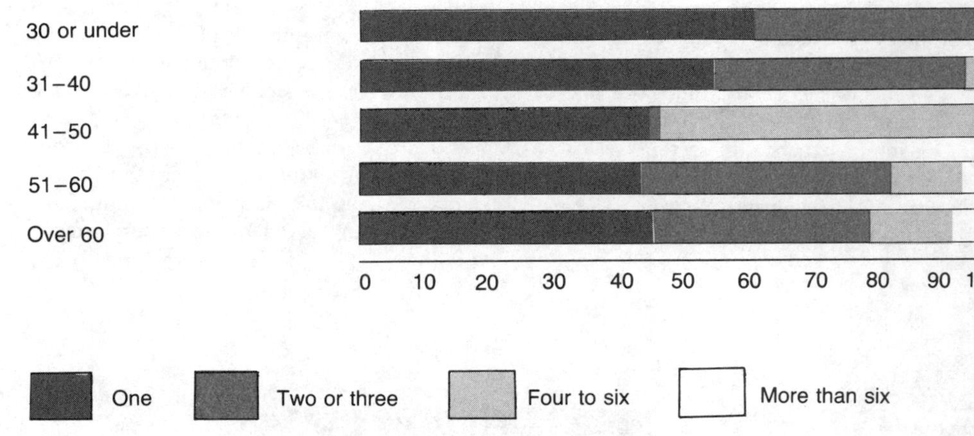

Figure 1/4 *Number of local governments served as a local public manager by age group*

CONCLUSION

The changes that have affected local governments in the recent past are not by the wildest stretch of the imagination a well-kept secret. In fact, we just have to look around us to see the changes caused by urban growth, technology, and the decentralization of government. The communities that have evolved as the result of all these changes cannot be lumped together without losing the special characteristics that make each community unique.

The same can be said when describing the recent information collected about local government managers. The average manager is a white male getting ready for his forty-third birthday. He got his bachelor's degree, worked for a while, and then went back to school to get an advanced degree. He is married and a member of the Democratic party. He's been in his current position just about four and a half years, but has been in the profession just over nine years. He took a break between his first and second manager jobs. He's a good manager and enjoys the challenges created by the changes in his community.

But what about the communities who need a manager who doesn't match this statistically perfect profile? The good news is that he or she is there. Hidden behind the statistical averages are today's real managers. Some of them are new at their jobs but they know there are others with 44 years of service that they can turn to for advice. Some of them change jobs frequently looking for new challenges and opportunities. Others have found challenges and opportunities in the same communities they've served for over 40 years.

---

[1] For an explanation of the criteria for ICMA recognition see: *Who's Who in Professional Local Government Management* (Washington, D.C.: International City Management Association, 1985).

[2] See: Richard J. Stillman II, *The Rise of the City Manager: A Public Professional in Local Government* (Albuquerque, N.M.: University of New Mexico Press, 1974); Laurie S. Frankel and Carol A. Pigeon, *Municipal Managers and Chief Administrative Officers*, Urban Data Service Reports, vol. 7 no. 2 (Washington, D.C.: International City Management Association, February 1975); Amy Cohen Paul, *Local Government Managers: On the Job and Off*, Urban Data Service Reports, vol. 13 no. 9 (Washington, D.C.: International City Management Association, September 1981); Richard J. Stillman II, "Local Public Management in Transition: A Report on the Current State of the Profession," in *The Municipal Year Book 1982* (Washington, D.C.: International City Management Association, 1982), pp. 161–73; and, Charles T. Henry, *Trends in City Management Careers 1970–1980: A Profession under Stress*, Urban Data Service Reports, vol. 14 no. 3 (Washington, D.C.: International City Management Association, March 1982).

[3] Mary A. Schellinger, *Council Profile*, Baseline Data Reports, vol. 15 no. 5 (Washington, D.C.: International City Management Association, May 1983), p. 8.

[4] Only the highest level of educational attainment is reported here.

D 2

The Irish City and County Management System*

Joseph F. Zimmerman
State University of New York at Albany

The local government system in the Republic of Ireland is distinguished by five major features: tight central government control; nomination of high-ranking local officials (after open competition) by a national commission; universal use of the council-manager plan; a sharp legal division between the respective powers of the council and the manager; and the sharing of a common manager by all local authorities within a county except in Cork, Limerick, and Waterford counties. Currently, there are 112 elected authorities—27 county councils, 4 county borough corporations (the cities of Cork, Dublin, Limerick, and Waterford), 7 borough corporations, 49 urban district councils, and 25 town commissioners.

The counties and county boroughs are the principal units of local government. Counties have councils with 21 to 46 members elected by proportional representation; vacancies are filled by co-option. The structure and responsibilities of county government are uniform. Each county has a manager and is responsible for physical planning and development, amenities, housing, roads, fire protection, assessment and collection of rates (property tax) and charges, sanitary services, and a number of less important functions.

De jure relations between the national government and local authorities are based upon a centralization paradigm embodied in the *Ultra Vires* Rule, that is, local authorities possess no inherent powers of self-government.

Tight central control of political subdivisions means local governments are enmeshed in national politics, since they must make representations to the central government to achieve their local goals. The three major political parties are active on both levels of government. As a consequence, national elected representatives tend to be involved deeply in local politics, and local elected representatives tend to have a similar involvement in national politics. One hundred and two (61.4%) of the 166 members of Dáil Eireann (House of Commons) serve on local councils; several serve on two separate local councils.[1]

THE MANAGER SYSTEM

Interest in the management system developed after 1923, when the Minister for Local Government and Public Health was granted power to dissolve local councils for failing to fulfill their responsibilities and appoint a commissioner(s) to perform the dissolved council's duties.[2] Several councils, including those in Cork and Dublin, were dissolved in 1924. The Minister appointed the Greater Dublin Commission of Inquiry, which in 1926 recommended the urbanized areas adjacent to Dublin be annexed to the city and a city manager appointed.[3] However, Cork, rather than Dublin, became the first local authority with a manager when the necessary enabling legislation was enacted in 1929 and a new council was elected to replace the commissioner appointed by the Minister.

The manager system, by special legislation, was extended to the city of Dublin and Dun Laoghaire Borough in 1930, the city of Limerick in 1934, and the city of Waterford in 1939. In Cork, Dublin, Limerick, and Waterford, the manager also serves as the town clerk. The system was extended to all counties by the County Management Act of 1940, which went into effect in 1942. The act stipulates that the county manager is the manager of all other local authorities—boroughs, urban districts, towns, and joint bodies—in the county, with the exceptions of the cities of Cork, Limerick, and Waterford, which have separate city managers. The 1940 County Management Act stipulates that the offices of Dublin city manager and Dublin county manager are to be held by the same person. That person also serves as the manager of Dun Laoghaire Borough and Balbriggan Town. (When Dun Laoghaire was brought under the Dublin authority, its manager was made an assistant Dublin city and county manager.)

Each manager is selected de facto by a national body, the Local Appointments Commission (which was created in 1926 and is financed by local authorities) since it nominates only one person for each vacancy.[4] Failure of the council concerned to appoint the nominee within three months results in automatic appointment.[5] A manager holds office for an indefinite term, but must retire at the age of 65. He may be suspended by a two-thirds vote of a city or county council while his fitness to hold office is investigated. Subsequently, with the sanction of the Minister for the Environment, the council may remove the manager from office by a two-thirds vote. Borough councils, urban district councils, and town commissioners lack the authority to suspend a manager. In the eyes of some early observers of the system, the manager was the "Minister's man" since his removal from office required the approval of the Minister and his salary was determined by the Minister.

The 1940 act makes a razor-sharp distinction between the powers assigned to the manager and the powers assigned to the council. The functions reserved to the council are specified, and include passage of by-laws, adoption of the budget, submission of applications to the Minister for the Environment to have boundaries altered, determinations of the rates (property taxes), borrowing of money, nomination of individuals to serve on committees and other public bodies, development of a priority list for the letting of council houses, disposal of municipal property, planning development, expanding the staff, and other functions. Section 31 of the County Management Act requires the manager to advise the council about these matters. The manager is entitled to attend and speak at council meetings, but lacks a vote. By law the manager possesses only administrative powers, but in fact he plays a major role in initiating policy, as will be pointed out in a subsequent section.

Executives functions, the responsibility of the manager, are defined as all local authority functions other than those reserved to the council. His authority in the area of personnel is restricted by the central government and may be restricted by his council. The manager appoints principal officers (those in higher administrative, professional, or technical positions), but he can appoint only people nominated by the Local Appointments Commission, and in practice the Commission nominates only one person for each position. Appointments are made on the basis of a national competition and examinations administered by the Commission. Usually officials advance within their own organization, but they must apply to the Commission for nomination to each new position (at the upper levels) before they can be appointed by the manager.

The law requires the manager to keep the council fully informed. The council can require the manager to provide information on any executive action other than staff matters that he plans to take. By law, the manager takes action by signing written orders: these orders must be made available at the next council meeting, and the manager must maintain a register of orders.

The county council is authorized to direct the manager at a specially called meeting to take a specific course of executive action in matters relating to staff and prosecution of individuals. The City and County Management (Amendment) Act of 1955 modifed the 1940 act by deleting the reference to prosecution and empowering a council to issue such a directive at any meeting. The 1955 act also authorizes councils to forbid the manager to carry out proposed works other than maintenance and repair work and activities required by law.

Apparently the manager continues to occupy the dominant position despite the 1955 legislation that strengthened council powers. In 1970, Professor Basil Chubb of Trinity College (Dublin) wrote, "The absence to a great extent of committees, the fact that the manager is necessarily in close touch with central departments, the existence of a County Managers' Association . . . all combine to make the manager the powerhouse of local government."[6]

*This article is based in part upon interviews conducted with Irish city and county managers and councillors in 1973 and 1983. Quotations from these interviews are not cited in the end notes.

THE MANAGERS

Almost all managers in the Republic of Ireland have spent most of their careers in local government service, rising to their current positions from a variety of entry level positions. Of those in office in 1983, only two had begun their careers not in local government but in the national Department of the Environment. Experience as an assistant manager in county Cork seems to be a major route to a position as a manager as the county has a de facto federal system, with an assistant manager in charge of each of the three administrative divisions of the county.

pointed out that "county managers have to spend too much of their time dealing with urban authorities, travelling to and attending council meetings and following up questions raised in the urbans. This attention to the detailed management of the smaller urbans limits the time spent on the longer term problems of the county as a whole."[7] By 1983, the time devoted to urban communities by managers was reduced substantially in seven counties as the result of the appointment of assistant managers in Clare, Galway (two positions), Limerick, Mayo, Meath, Tipperary North Riding, and Wexford. One manager who still had no assistant in 1983 reported that he was devoting an inordinate amount of time to the urbans because they were growing and experiencing problems.

Service on the Local Government Staff Negotiations Board, Computer Board, or various committees as well as the monthly meetings of the Managers' Association and meetings (held at the request of the managers) at the Department of the Environment bring many managers to Dublin an average of one to one and a half days a week.

In contrast to the American manager, the Irish manager never appoints citizen advisory committees for fear councillors will feel he is "going over their heads." (Traditionally, it is the function of councillors to help citizens who have questions or problems with the local authority.) What advice the manager receives from citizens usually comes through individual contacts, attendance at various functions, and citizen deputations. According to one manager in 1983, the number of deputations is increasing because of public frustration caused by scarce fiscal resources. Before meeting with a deputation of citizens, the typical manager invites the councillors who represent the citizens' area(s) to attend the meeting.

Councillors who were interviewed reported that they almost always deal with county officials other than the manager and will meet with the manager only if they have difficulties with the other officials. All councillors, except one, reported that relationships with these other officials were excellent. The managers themselves are generally well regarded. Recently, when a member of the Mayo County Council cast "slurs" on the manager's character, the councillor was rebuked by the other members of his party—Fine Gael—for "remarks which we feel have transgressed the reasonable bounds of normal debate."[8]

THE ROLE OF COUNCILLORS

City and county managers have a high regard for councillors and the role they play in the local government system. A manager interviewed in 1983 pointed out that the combined judgment of councillors is good and that councillors tie officials to reality. He added that the councillors act as ambassadors for the local authority and secure community acceptance for offical policies. In agreement, a second county manager stressed that councillors play a valuable role in explaining council policy to their constituents. Another manager explained that the manager system would be dangerous without a council. Another described the councillors as "good antennae," reflecting local opinion and reaction and expressing local needs. He added, "They must be listened to and interpreted properly. Sometimes for political or other reasons they may make indirect rather than explicit references. Other times they overstate their case."

All councillors interviewed agreed with these definitions. A borough councillor defined his role as that of a "mediator between the public and management," a "fact finder," a "go between," and a "buffer between the people and the management."

One county manager interviewed in 1983 identified an important function of councillors as that of ensuring that policies are carried out as defined by the council, rather than as interpreted by officials. A second county manager pointed out: "Having made policy decisions, councillors worry if anomalies appear at the working level or if it appears that individuals suffer due to the interpretations of a policy of which they have approved."

Councillors sometimes feel impatient with this somewhat limited role. A county manager interviewed explained that an individual deciding to be a candidate for the position of councillor has a sense of mission, a desire to do something to better local conditions. However, once in office, the councillor often finds the job is confined by regulations and rules of order. Although he or she started out to be a legislator concerned with making local laws, the councillor ends up devoting a great deal of time to seeking planning permission for constituents, getting relief for them, and so forth. All councillors interviewed reported that constituent functions are very time-consuming. One city councillor described himself as "a glorified social worker rather than a legislator," and an urban district councillor agreed, saying, "You are an unpaid social worker to a great extent." A county councillor reported, "You are the local messenger."

According to a county manager in 1983, clientelism is becoming more of a problem because people will not use all the facilities available to them and even ask their councillor to fill out their application forms. In the words of a second county manager, "Even if the citizen was not confused he may go to his local councillor (and sometimes more than one) on the basis that representations may not do his cause any harm and could possibly do some good."

As a consequence, perhaps, some councils deal with broad policy questions only at budget time. As one county councillor said, there is "pressure from constituents to devote time to nuts and bolts, but there is no pressure from constituents to devote time to major policy issues."

Nevertheless, the councillors' perception that they spend relatively little time on substantive legislative matters has a positive explanation as well. As one manager explained, the council may not discuss a major item on the agenda before approving it because they have confidence in the manager. Councillors generally agreed with this assessment of the reason they give little time to agenda items. From a county manager's perspective, "Councillors are prepared to make policy decisions provided data are put before them in a reasonable manner. Managers are expected to make clear which solutions they prefer and give reasons for their preference."

Managers interviewed in 1983 reported an improvement in the calibre of councillors in the period since 1975. Because of this trend, questions are more probing and are welcomed by the manager. One manager attributed the higher calibre of councillors to better education and the "European dimension"—councillors are aware of local government developments in European Economic Community nations, including reorganizations. Another manager interviewed in 1983 pointed out that by listening to the councillors, the manager encourages them to debate major issues.

To sharpen the definition of the role of the council, we asked managers to comment upon the extent to which their council systematically reviewed their total performance. The reader should bear in mind that Section 3 of the 1955 act authorizes the council to forbid the manager to carry out any proposed action with the exceptions of maintenance and repair work and activities required by law.

Interviews with managers in 1973 revealed that no council had employed Section 3, but in 1983 one manager reported that he had been stopped from an action by its use. A county manager reported in 1983 that while he had never had a Section 3 notice, his council occasionally suggested that something not be done. A second manager stated, "The council is not even aware of Section 3 and I could not conceive of it[s] being employed." This assessment seems generally accurate as no councillor interviewed was aware of the existence of the Section 3 provision.

John C. Bollens and John C. Ries wrote, with respect to American managers, that "activities which have an aura of science, system, and technology—that is to say, dimensions of civil affairs where laymen are least informed—are not only less apt to be challenged successfully by a critic, but are more likely to be left entirely to the discretion of the managers."[9] This seems to be true in Ireland. Councillors and managers unanimously agreed that there is no systematic review of the manager's total performance by the council.

A county manager emphasized that the council would check him if he did something and did not tell councillors about it. All managers interviewed stressed the critical importance of keeping the council informed. A number of managers attach copies of all pertinent reports and correspondence to the agenda for each council meeting.

Although the manager is required to maintain a register of his orders and present it at each council meeting, those interviewed in 1973 and 1983 reported that county councillors seldom read the orders. Urban councillors, on the other hand, tend to read the orders and raise questions on them at council meetings.

In describing the relationship between councillors and a manager and his staff, Chubb wrote that the role of the former tends to be rather that of "clients seeking favour than that of a board of directors and their top management."[10] Councillors and managers were split in their view of the accuracy of Chubb's statement. A county manager interviewed in 1983 disagreed entirely, saying, "I have never viewed a councillor as someone coming to look for a favor." But another manager reported that councillors believe they have a duty to obtain something for a constituent even if it is contrary to established council policy. He added he had been hard pressed by public representatives to take an action to which they knew he would not agree. According to a county councillor, "There are a lot of councillors who think they should do everything for anyone whether the constituent is entitled to something or not." A second county councillor was convinced that some councillors tell constituents they have obtained something for them even though the constituents are entitled to it. A county manager pointed out, "Councillors will sometimes try very hard for their constituents even if they know that it is highly unlikely that their request will be acceded to. This is because they wish to test out the practical working limits of the system or because they may wish to feel that they have done what they could for a deserving case." He added that council staff in order to ensure fairness "are careful not to do for one particular member what they are not prepared to do for another."

The Chairman. The chairman or mayor is usually selected by the majority party although several councils have agreed to alternate the chairmanship between the two major parties. Fianna Fail and Fine Gael members of one county council have been alternating the chairmanship in order to prevent the independent members, who otherwise would hold the balance of power, from dictating who is elected chairman.

Prior to the advent of the manager system, the chairman often was a very powerful political figure who dominated the council. As one would expect, the appearance of a professional manager has generally reduced the role of the chairman. Only one chairman was described in 1973 and in 1983 by a manager as dominating the council. Other chairmen were viewed as moderators. All councillors interviewed perceived the chairman of their council as strictly a presiding officer. Although the chairman's formal powers are negligible, the office has prestige, and most councillors aspire to being chairman.

The County Management Act of 1940 stipulates that the manager shall provide all information in his possession to the chairman of the council, but most chairmen do not confer regularly with the manager prior to council meetings to discuss the agenda. (Interestingly, one county manager reported that "my chairmen never trouble me for information.") Only one county manager stated that "there are things you will discuss with the chairman but not with an ordinary member of the council." Many councillors and managers indicated that the chairmen prefer not to be briefed prior to a council meeting. A chairman explained that if he was briefed by the manager, the other councillors would view him as the manager's man. In one county the chairman is briefed before an occasional council meeting, and in another county the chairman is briefed on controversial issues only. One county manager reported that he feels "a need to consult the chairman, but he is too ephemeral," because the chairmanship is rotated annually. The manager is convinced that "you need a good chairman to back you up and give you local background." Yet he agrees that regular manager-chairman conferences may lead the council to "regard the chairman as the manager's man."

Area Committees. Several county councils form "area," "district," or "roads" committees to deal with roads and other parochical matters that are not of interest to the entire council. Committees reduce the number of notices of motion on the council's agenda.

A manager interviewed in 1983 reported that the committees were very useful at estimates (budget) time because he can give councillors a private review of finances. Since the press does not attend committee meetings, matters can be discussed more frankly than at a council meeting.

In order to free their agendas, the Kilkenny and Wexford County councils decided area committees only would receive deputations of citizens. The committees also prove valuable in acting as a "safety valve" and affording opportunities for full debate of controversial issues. A national deputy-councillor reported he gets more publicity out of his area committee than he does by putting questions to the Dáil (House of Commons).

Area committees meet as often as once a month in Cork and as seldom as once a year or every two years in Mayo. In Mayo, a county councillor interviewed in 1983 reported that the committees meet infrequently because they have built up a large backlog of projects that cannot be financed.

Estimates Committees. The 1955 act authorizes councils to establish estimates (budget) committees. In 1973, three county councils—Monaghan, Waterford, and Westmeath—had such committees, but Waterford subsequently abandoned the committee because the derating (exemption from property tax) of domestic homes made it impossible to determine what funds would be available for the coming year.

Managers agreed that councils generally prefer not to have an estimates committee because the council wants to give the appearance of defending the ratepayers (taxpayers) against the spending plans of the manager. If the council prepares the estimates, it cannot blame the manager for increases in the rates. As a manager put it, the council does not want the blame for the rates rising even though they have been urging spending all year. A county secretary observed in 1973 that when the estimates are presented to the council by the committee, "some committee members act as if they were not on the committee."

THE MANAGER'S POLICY ROLE

Clarence E. Ridley wrote in 1958 that American council members "seldom initiate policy," but "are very active during the stages of consideration, review, hearings, and decision-making."[11] All Irish managers interviewed in 1973 and 1983 held a similar view, that is, that the managers are the major policy initiators and very few policy proposals are developed by the councils. Bollens and Ries wrote, with respect to American managers, "Citizens and public officials alike look to the manager to get things done."[12] A similar situation prevails in the Republic of Ireland. A former Dublin City Commissioner explained the dominant role of the manager in the following terms: "Due to the highly technical nature of some of the work, the wide scope of activities involved, the quality and quantity of the documentation issued, and the time restraints under which the elected representatives operate, the scales of the partnership are weighted towards the manager."[13] A county manager interviewed in 1983 pointed out that local government is very complex and there are huge files of departmental circulars. As a result, "the cards are stacked against the councillors."

In 1975, Dublin city councillor Pat Carroll wrote: "Given a choice between policy-making power and a handful of specific areas requiring an enormous commitment of time and interest to these at the expense of most other matters as against retaining the current situation of policy impotence but plenty of knowledge and help in the local implications of decisions, I believe that the vast majority will opt for the latter. Moreover, I suspect the people they represent would prefer it that way."[14] All councillors interviewed with one exception reported that their councils take no action on reserved functions without the manager's advice. A county councillor reported that the older and more experienced councillors will ask the manager for advice, but some of the younger councillors may resent this practice.

Managers interviewed in 1973 made a number of significant comments about the initiation of policy. One manager emphasized that "if anything new is needed, the manager and his staff recommend it." Another manager held that policy has to be formulated by the manager as the council lacks the capacity to develop plans. Regardless of whether it concerns an executive or a reserved function, all policy comes from the manager, according to a third county manager. He conceded that the manager may get the germ of good ideas from council discussions. A fourth manager described councillors as "policy makers in terms of alternatives put before them rather than initiators of policy." A city councillor reported that his council was "too involved in microdecisions and should get involved in macrodecisions."

In 1983, managers held similar views. One manager stated he could not recall a single new policy emanating from the council. A county secretary described his manager as the motivator of policies that gain acceptance, but added that the manager always stresses the primacy of the council.

A perceptive manager noted that "local government has become exceedingly complex," and councillors lack the time to become familiar with the details of national policies. Another manager mentioned that he always "tests the water" by talking to the chairman of the council or party whips before recommending a new policy. Still another manager explained that while he can initiate policies, achievement of many policy goals requires money, which is controlled by the elected representatives. A fourth manager said that a good manager can steer his council if he wants to, and most councils would not get off the ground in carrying out reserved functions without the assistance of the manager. The council will go along with the manager's policy recommendations, according to a fifth manager, provided they get the "kudos." And a county manager reported that the "him versus us" mentality is gone and all managers consult councils in advance even on executive matters.

While there is a sharp legal distinction between executive and reserved functions, there is unanimous agreement among councillors and managers interviewed that the distinction is blurred in practice and decision making is shared. The lack of a sharp distinction in practice is attributable in part to the fact that councillors generally are not fully aware of the precise legal distinction. Only a handful of councillors interviewed think members of their councils are aware of the functional distinctions. A city councillor and an urban district councillor reported members of their councils are hesitant to question long-term officials on the distinctions because the members are not fully certain of the legal provisions. Interviews in 1983 revealed that the terms "executive functions" and "reserved functions" are seldom mentioned in council chambers. One city councillor reported that "these words never come up at meetings."

One manager explained that it is a "deliberate policy not to make a sharp distinction." A county manager stated, "I act as if they are making the decision even if it is an executive function. I want [the councillors] to comment as there is a tendency for staff to think they know everything." A third manager reported that he brings matters to the council that do not require its approval in order to keep the members informed and involved, so that they will understand why he acted as he did. A fourth manager is careful to let it appear that all decisions are council decisions and gives the council credit for everything that is accomplished. A fifth manager related that "even on executive functions I give the council credit if a decision turns out well." A county manager believes he must give the council freedom to raise any issue "even if it is executive." He added, "I listen and then make my decisions." Expressing agreement with this practice, several councillors emphasized that they discuss executive functions in order to provide the manager with advice.

In effect, the managers agreed with the statement made by John J. Horgan of Cork in 1945: "The county and city managers must, therefore, if they are to succeed in their task, keep the public fully informed, listen patiently to complaints and secure the approval of their councils to changes in policy or administration. They must, in short, seek to lead rather than to drive, to persuade rather than to compel."[15] Bromage in 1961 wrote in a similar vein that "the teamwork between Irish councils and managers runs fairly parallel to that in many American cities. Managers must persuade and convince reluctant councilmen as to the appropriations and tax rates."[16]

There are some problems with shared responsibilities. According to a county manager in 1983, "A manager would need to be very careful in discussing executive functions. If he says he will be bound by their advice, he may be illegal and if he keeps bringing in executive functions to the members, he is undermining his own statutory position. There is, therefore, a tight rope to be walked. The desire to keep the members informed has to be balanced by his discharging his duties as laid down by statute."

It was suggested by another manager that some councillors would like to make more functions executive functions in order to escape responsibility.

Thirteen managers in 1973 qualified their statements about the blurring of functional responsibility by mentioning that they make a distinction with respect to staff. A county manager, however, pointed out that when a new councillor occasionally asks, "Why wasn't the council consulted on this appointment?" the manager does not even need to reply as an experienced councillor will explain that "staff is not a council function."

Managers make firm recommendations to the council on all policy matters, including controversial ones. Councils want to be guided and will ask for a recommendation if the manager has not provided one. A county manager observed in 1973 that councillors seldom declare a matter a reserved function, and frequently ask for the manager's advice. All but one councillor interviewed reported that their councils either solicited the manager's advice before exercising reserved functions or listened to advice volunteered by the manager. The exception—an urban district councillor—stated, "We do not ask the manager for advice as we try not to be a rubber stamp for the manager." A county councillor estimated that 50% of the reserved functions would not be carried out if the manager did not advise the council to exercise its powers.

In 1973, four managers reported that they made a firm recommendation on each issue to the council without mentioning alternatives because the council preferred a firm recommendation. Interviews in 1983 revealed that managers generally discuss alternatives when making a recommendation, but the alternatives, according to one manager, are discussed in negative terms. A second manager pointed out that on certain issues "you might want to get the benefit of council input and you lay out the issues and the options." He stressed that "you have to be flexible."

SECTION 4

Under provisions of the County Management Act of 1940, a council is authorized to direct the manager to take a certain course of executive action except in matters dealing with staff and prosecution and discontinuance of prosecution of individuals. This power was modified and extended to all councils by Section 4 of the City and County Management (Amendment) Act of 1955.

Public conflict between a majority of a council and the manager generally occurs only in instances involving a Section 4 motion. One of the older county managers interviewed in 1973 thought that the section relieved tension in situations in which the manager took the view that his word was absolute. This manager viewed Section 4 as a seldom used safety value. All councillors interviewed, with one exception, said the provision is a good one, but should not be used often. A county councillor offered the opinion that the section "should be used every now and then to reassert the balance of power with the manager." A county official mentioned that councillors in his county are loath to use Section 4, out of respect for the manager.

A county manager in 1983 described Section 4 as a good safeguard against bureaucracy, but added that the section should not be employed to reverse decisions to deny planning applications. According to a second county manager, use of the section is a reflection of the strength of the council and the inflexibility of the manager. A third county manager reported that some Section 4 motions were not genuine, and he could accommodate them.

The section never has been employed in Carlow, Cavan, Kildare, Longford, Meath, Roscommon, or the cities of Cork, Limerick, and Waterford. Elsewhere, the frequency of use since 1955 has varied from once in Clare (1983) to

150 a year in County Wicklow. The section has been invoked infrequently in the latter county since 1977. In Donegal, Galway, Kerry, Louth, and Mayo the county councils employ the section frequently to direct the manager to grant planning permission.

Concern over the use of Section 4 led Taoiseach (Prime Minister) Garret FitzGerald in 1983 to reaffirm a 1982 letter that he, as leader of the party, circulated to Fine Gael members of the Dublin Corporation directing them to support the recommendations of planning officials on land zoning matters.[17] An Taisce (National Trust for Ireland) in 1983 released a report condemning the use of the section for planning provisions:

> Many Section 4 motions . . . are passed without a vote. Furthermore, councillors are assenting to planning permissions on sites which they have not visited and for which detailed grounds for refusal are presented to them by authority officials.[18]

One of the major issues involving Section 4 in many counties is the use of land along the national primary routes, a new system of roads being financed by the national government. National and county policy is to discourage building along the new routes in order to ensure that traffic flows smoothly, but property owners frequently ask permission to build along the road, and councils feel themselves pressured to direct the manager to grant planning permission.

Councillors are not unaware that special planning permission can interfere with broad policy. In 1983, Mayo County Councillor Frank Durcan, while debating a Section 4 motion to allow a house along a newly constructed segment of a national primary route, stated, "What we have to decide is whether we are going to allow ribbon development along this route."[19] County Manager Michael O'Malley described the application as one of the worst submitted to the local authority.

Managers believe it is a serious mistake for a council to utilize Section 4 as it will be abused. A manager in 1973 described the section as "a sledgehammer approach" and held that "a man should not be manager if Section 4 has to be used." Ten years later, a different county manager stated that overuse of Section 4 debases it and that the manager should have the right of automatic appeal to An Bord Pleanála (the Irish planning appeals board).[20]

Managers interviewed in 1983 were unanimous in saying that Section 4 should not be employed to direct the manager to grant planning permission since a person whose application has been denied already has the right to appeal the denial to An Bord Pleanála. A county secretary stated that councillors have been hiding behind "executive functions" for years, and if the council employs Section 4, the public will recognize that executive functions are not "sacrosanct." One manager mentioned that the section was used once in his county, but the councillors regretted its use because of the flood of applications for special treatment that resulted when citizens saw that the council had the power to direct the manager to take certain actions. He did not anticipate that Section 4 would be employed in the future.

SYSTEMATIC CHANGES

In the past decade several significant developments have affected local government in Ireland. Rapid improvement in local infrastructure and services in the 1960s and 1970s raised public expectations, which cannot be satisfied now in a period of scarce fiscal resources. A related development was the national government's decision following the 1977 general elections to remove the tax on domestic homes (derating), thereby depriving local authorities of the power to raise a significant amount of funds on their own initiative. The 1983 decision of the Oireachtas (national legislature and president) authorizing local authorities to levy charges for service does not offset the lost revenue because service charges produce only a small fraction of the funds needed by local authorities.[21]

An unintended side affect of derating domestic homes has been a weakening of councils and a feeling among councillors that their limited role in the governance system has been debased further, since they must rely more heavily now upon the central exchequer for uncertain funds.

Work pressures on local authorities have become considerably heavier because of the sharp increase in national legislation relating to local governments—planning, housing, fire services, dangerous substances, litter control, casual trading, motor taxation licensing, and so forth. Departmental circulars inundate local officials who must also complete additional reports for the central government in order to get central funds.

The accelerating pace of development in urban areas has created problems for county managers and their staffs. Relief over the past decade has been provided in seven counties by the employment of assistant county managers.

Physical planning has become a most important activity of local authorities as reflected in the number of planning applications; the interest in such applications exhibited by the local press, councillors, and citizens; and the conflict generated in some local governments between the manager and the council over planning decisions.

Because of the greater complexity of local government and the scarcity of local fiscal resources, more citizens visit and telephone local authority offices. A related development has been the rise of residents' and tenant associations, including the Association of Combined Residents' Associations (ACRA) and the National Association of Tenant's Organizations (NATO), which lobby at the national and local levels.

SUMMARY AND CONCLUSIONS

The Irish local government system is centralized, the national government granting local authorities relatively little discretionary authority and closely regulating their actions. At the county level, national law vests major powers in the council. In practice, however, all major policy initatives flow from the manager instead of being developed collectively by the council independent of the manager in accordance with the original council-manager theory.

Elected representatives and officials interviewed agree that the Irish citizen has excellent access to elected representatives. Citizen access is offset, however, by the tight central government control of local authorities. In addition, the *Ultra Vires* Rule suppresses innovation at the local level and is frustrating for citizens, elected representatives, and staff.

The interviews reveal that councillors place great confidence in managers and rely heavily upon them for guidance in carrying out council functions. Councillors described relations between their councils and managers as very good to excellent. Only one council has employed Section 3 of the 1955 act to forbid the manager to carry out a proposed action, and, with the exception of a few counties, Section 4 has been employed sparingly to direct the manager to take a certain course of action.

Although the council legally appoints the manager and is responsible for supervising his performance of executive functions, no council systematically reviews the manager's total performance either on a continuing or a periodic basis. Two reasons account for the absence of a review: the special efforts made by managers to keep councils fully informed about executive actions reduce the councillors' need for a review, and councillors lack the expertise and the time to exercise close inspection of the chief administrator's activities.

The precise de jure allocation of power has become blurred in practice by the teamwork approach employed by most councils and managers. The manager's role as the chief policy innovator is due to his knowledge and expertise, and the limited time the average elected representatives can devote to official duties. The manager generally knows more about the law, about national policies outlined or determined by central government, about local administrative capacity, and about solutions to problems than do councillors.

Recognizing the manager's special knowledge and skills, councillors look to the manager to lead the local authority. While managers dominate the policy development process, they themselves point out that their councils make important contributions to policy formation and are careful to give the councils full credit for local authority accomplishments.

Councillors and managers see the council playing three roles. The most important one is representing citizens' views in the policy formulation process. The second role is being an ombudsman who ensures that citizens are treated fairly by officials and that grievances are rectified. Managers rate this role an important one. The third role is serving individuals. Managers are convinced councillors devote too much of their official time to this role and would welcome greater participation by councillors in the process of developing major policies for the local authority. The fact that Irish councillors know most people in their small constituencies personally is undoubtedly a major reason they devote a substantial amount of time to serving constituents.

Future changes in the local government system probably will be evolutionary and pragmatic in nature in contrast to the revolutionary changes introduced by adoption of the management system. Despite the widespread dissatisfaction with central control expressed by councillors and managers, traditional beliefs regarding the proper repository of legal authority apparently will prevent political subdivisions from receiving a broad grant of discretionary authority.

[1]The percentage of deputies with local government experience is considerably higher because of the tradition that local councillors resign their seats upon becoming a Minister or a Minister of State.

[2]*Local Government (Temporary Provisions) Act,* 1923.

[3]*Greater Dublin Commission of Inquiry: Report* (Dublin: The Stationery Office, 1926).

[4]*Local Authorities (Officers and Employees) Act,* 1926.

[5]*City and County Management (Amendment) Act,* 1955, § 5 (9) (b).

[6]Basil Chubb, *The Government and Politics of Ireland,* 1st ed. (London: Oxford University Press, 1970), pp. 286–87. In the 1982 edition, Chubb dropped the statement, but wrote "the manager tends to be the architect of community services." See the second edition, p. 305.

[7]McKinsey & Company, Incorporated, *Strengthening the Local Government Service: A Report Prepared for the Minister for Local Government* (Dublin: The Stationery Office, 1972), p. 20.

[8]"Fine Gael Rebukes Member over Remarks," *Western People,* April 11, 1984, p. 19.

[9]John C. Bollens and John C. Ries, *The City Manager Profession: Myths and Realities* (Chicago: Public Administration Service, 1969), p. 17.

[10]Chubb, *The Government and Politics of Ireland,* 2d ed., p. 306.

[11]Clarence E. Ridley, *The Role of the City Manager in Policy Formulation* (Chicago: The International City Managers' Association, 1958), p. 47.

[12]Bollens and Ries, *The City Manager Profession,* p. 20.

[13]Barry Early, "Dublin City Commissioners at Work," *Administration,* Winter 1973, p. 437. The Minister for Local Government in 1969 dissolved the Dublin Corporation for failure to strike a rate and appointed a single commissioner to perform the functions of the city council. The Coalition Government's Minister for Local Government in 1973 appointed the former city councillors as city commissioners, and a new city council was elected in 1974. The Minister for Local Government has been renamed the Minister for the Environment.

[14]Pat Carroll, "Who Controls City Hall?" *Hibernia,* January 10, 1975, p. 6.

[15]John J. Horgan, "Growth of Irish Manager Plan," *National Municipal Review,* June 1945, p. 282.

[16]Arthur W. Bromage, "The Council Manager Plan in Ireland," *Public Management,* February 1961, p. 30.

[17]Frank McDonald, "FitzGerald Interfered in Housing Plan, Claims Builder," *The Irish Times,* July 11, 1983, p. 9.

[18]*Planning: Use and Mis-Use of Section 4 Resolutions* (Dublin: An Taisce, 1983), p. 5.

[19]"Ribbons Development 'Butchers' Mayo Roads," *Western People,* June 29, 1982, p. 21.

[20]Joseph F. Zimmerman, "An Bord Pleanála (The Irish Planning Board)," *Administration,* vol. 28, no. 3, 1980, pp. 329–44.

[21]*Local Government (Finance Provisions) (No. 2) Act,* 1983.

D **3**

Intergovernmental Service Arrangements and the Transfer of Functions

Lori M. Henderson
Advisory Commission on Intergovernmental Relations

Service provision at the local level is continually evolving in the interests of reducing costs and improving performance. In recent years many local governments have had to cope with a harsh new climate of economic stress spawned by the 1981–1982 economic recession, the taxpayer revolt, and reduction in federal grants-in-aid. Despite indications that the national economy is on the rebound, the financial health of many localities remains infirm, as documented in a recent study by the Joint Economic Committee. It found a significant increase in the number and proportion of medium-sized cities operating with budget deficits, a problem previously limited mainly to larger cities,[1] and reports that in smaller communities fiscal problems also have become prevalent. As the mayor of one small town in Colorado commented, "Sharp reductions in resources, excessive inflation, and new programs and policies originating at the federal and state level have combined to make this decade one of the most difficult and challenging in the history of small towns."[2]

As fiscal pressures have intensified in recent years, localities have found themselves "on the receiving end of a sudden and dramatic shift in responsibility for providing many public services."[3] In an effort to do more with less, local officials have increasingly sought more economical alternatives to delivering services using only their own employees.

Intergovernmental approaches—intergovernmental service contracts, joint service agreements, and intergovernmental service transfers—are three such alternatives. *Intergovernmental service contracts* are agreements (formal and informal) between two units of government in which one pays the other for the delivery of a service to the inhabitants in the jurisdiction of the paying government. *Joint service agreements* are agreements between two or more governments for the joint planning, financing, and delivery of a service to the inhabitants of all jurisdictions participating in the agreement. *Intergovernmental service transfers* are the permanent transfer of total responsibility for the provision of a service from a governmental unit to another entity, either a government or a private organization.

Current practice and trends in their use since the early and mid-1970s are the focus of this article. Current data are derived from a survey conducted during the summer of 1983 by the Advisory Commission on Intergovernmental Relations (ACIR) and the International City Management Association (ICMA) with the financial assistance of the Department of Housing and Urban Development.

The survey instrument was similar in structure and content to those used in two earlier ACIR reports on intergovernmental arrangements in 1972 and 1975. It was sent to the chief administrative officer in all cities of 10,000 and over in population and to counties of 50,000 and over in population. In addition, it was sent to a one-in-eight sample of cities 2,500 to 9,999 in population and counties with population under 50,000. Finally, the cities with populations below 2,500 that are recognized as council-manager cities by the ICMA were also surveyed on a one-in-eight basis.

In all, 3,140 cities and 1,067 counties were asked to participate in the 1983 survey. Of that number, responses were received from 49.7%: 1,654 (52.7%) from cities and 435 (40.8%) from counties. Table 3/1 shows the distribution of responses by population, geographic region, metropolitan status, and form of government. These general breakdowns were used to analyze certain segments of the survey data.

As with any survey of this size and nature, several caveats should be kept in mind when interpreting the data.

First, mailing questionnaires can result in underreporting.[4] Most local governments do not keep a central file on all written and unwritten agreements, so it can be difficult for the official answering the questionnaire to report accurately all the intergovernmental activity that might be occurring in a given jurisdiction.

Second, the 1983 ACIR/ICMA survey instrument was designed to incorporate as many aspects of the earlier ACIR questionnaires on intergovernmental service arrangements as possible, but they were not identical. The differences between the questionnaires should be taken into consideration when evaluating trends.

Finally, many respondents had difficulty distinguishing among the various kinds of intergovernmental service arrangements. Although the definitions of these arrangements were included in the survey, respondents continued to misinterpret or confuse certain aspects of the various arrangements with one another and with other private and public service production and delivery mechanisms. Although several statistical techniques were used to minimize the potential impact of this problem, it may still have influenced some of the data included in this article.

These caveats, while worthy of mention, are not meant to detract from the overall utility of the data and findings.

The analysis of trends compares these 1983 data with the results of comparable surveys conducted by ACIR and ICMA in 1972 and 1975 and reported in two ACIR reports published in 1976: *The Challenge of Local Government Reorganization*[5] and *Pragmatic Federalism: The Reassignment of Functional Responsibility*.[6]

INTERGOVERMENTAL SERVICE CONTRACTS

In 1983, 52%, or 1,084 of the 2,069 responding cities and counties, reported entering into intergovernmental service contracts (Table 3/2). Almost twice as many jurisdictions have written contracts as have unwritten ones (not shown in table). This finding suggests that most local officials are cognizant of problems that may arise when contracting for services and are relying on a legally binding mechanism to ensure adequate service delivery.

A larger proportion of large governments enter into service contracts than small units. Combining the three largest population categories and the three smallest reveals that 60% of the responding cities and counties with populations of 250,000 and over enter into contracts, contrasted with 39% with populations under 10,000.

Cities and counties contract for delivery of services with about the same degree of frequency: 52% and 54%, respectively. However, some differences are evident between cities and counties. Although the percentage of both cities and counties with contracts generally declines as their populations decrease, the drop is considerably more pronounced among cities. Seventy-six percent of cities with populations of 250,000 and over report entering into contracts, but only 38% with populations under 10,000 did so. In contrast, the number of counties entering into contracts does not decline as steeply as population size decreases. Fifty-three percent of counties with populations of 250,000 and over report entering into contracts, compared to 44% of those under 10,000 population. Further differences are that cities of 250,000 and above report more written and unwritten contracts than counties of similar size, and cities under 10,000 population did more contracting than counties of that size.

Central cities (61%) have a slightly higher propensity to enter into contracts than suburban (56%) and independent cities (40%). Metropolitan and nonmetropolitan counties contract for services with about the same degree of frequency. Regional differences, however, are discernible. Contracting is most prevalent in the West (especially the Pacific Coast states) and least prevalent in the Northeast (especially the New England and Mid-Atlantic states).

As shown in Table 3/2, form of government also has some bearing on the tendency to enter into service contracts. Cities with council-manager governments and counties with appointed or elected executive forms of government do considerably more contracting than their counterparts having other governmental forms.

Most Frequently Purchased Services. The

Table 3/1 SURVEY RESPONSE

Classification	Cities surveyed	Total no. of cities responding (No.)	Total no. of cities responding (%)	Counties surveyed	Total no. of counties responding (No.)	Total no. of counties responding (%)	Total no. surveyed	Total no. responding (No.)	Total no. responding (%)
Total, all cities and counties	3,140	1,654	52.7	1,067	435	40.8	4,207	2,089	49.7
Population group									
Over 1,000,000	6	4	66.7	22	9	40.9	28	13	46.4
500,000–1,000,000	17	8	47.1	56	20	35.7	73	28	38.4
250,000– 499,999	34	18	52.9	94	47	50.0	128	65	50.8
100,000– 249,999	113	73	64.6	228	108	47.4	341	181	53.1
50,000– 99,999	278	143	51.4	375	138	36.8	653	281	43.0
25,000– 49,999	613	365	59.5	77	28	36.4	690	393	57.0
10,000– 24,999	1,535	759	49.4	116	43	37.1	1,651	802	48.6
5,000– 9,999	227	108	47.6	64	25	39.1	291	133	45.7
2,500– 4,999	268	142	53.0	18	8	44.4	286	150	52.4
Under 2,500	49	34	69.4	17	9	52.9	66	43	65.1
Geographic region[1]									
Northeast	904	393	43.5	141	55	39.0	1,045	448	42.9
North Central	905	478	52.8	313	136	43.4	1,218	614	50.4
South	830	463	55.8	452	175	38.7	1,282	638	49.8
West	501	320	63.9	161	69	42.9	662	389	58.8
Metro status[2]									
Central	432	248	57.4	...	...	...	432	248	57.4
Suburban	1,808	919	50.8	...	...	...	1,808	919	50.8
Independent	900	487	54.1	...	...	...	900	487	54.1
Metro	...	...	...	543	231	42.5	543	231	42.5
Nonmetro	...	...	...	524	204	38.9	524	204	38.9
Form of government[3]									
Mayor-council	1,436	647	45.0	...	...	...	1,436	647	45.0
Council-manager	1,409	894	63.6	...	...	...	1,409	896	63.6
Commission	111	45	40.5	...	...	...	111	45	40.5
Town meeting	137	52	38.0	...	...	...	137	52	38.0
Representative town meeting	47	14	29.8	...	...	...	47	14	29.8
Without administrator	...	...	...	660	244	37.0	660	244	37.0
With administrator	...	...	...	407	191	46.9	407	191	46.9

[1]*Geographic regions: Northeast*—Connecticut, Maine, Massachusetts, New Hampshire, New Jersey, New York, Pennsylvania, Rode Island, and Vermont; *North Central*—Illinois, Indiana, Iowa, Kansas, Michigan, Minnesota, Missouri, Nebraska, North Dakota, Ohio, South Dakota, and Wisconsin; *South*—Alabama, Arkansas, Delaware, District of Columbia, Florida, Georgia, Kentucky, Louisiana, Maryland, Mississippi, North Carolina, Oklahoma, South Carolina, Tennessee, Texas, Virginia and West Virginia; *West*—Alaska, Arizona, California, Colorado, Hawaii, Idaho, Montana, Nevada, New Mexico, Oregon, Utah, Washington, and Wyoming.

[2]*Metro status: Central*—the city(ies) actually appearing in the MSA title; *Suburban*—the city(ies) located within an MSA; *Independent*—the city(ies) not located within an MSA; *Metro*—a county located within an MSA; *Nonmetro*—a county located outside the boundaries of an MSA.

[3]*Forms of government: For cities: Mayor-council*—an elected council serves as the legislative body with a separately elected head of government; *Council-manager*—the mayor and council make policy and an appointed administrator is responsible for the administration of the city; *Commission*—a board of elected commissioners serves as the legislative body and each commissioner is responsible for the administration of one or more departments; *Town meeting*—qualified voters meet to make basic policy and choose a board of selectmen to carry out the policy; *Representative town meeting*—representatives selected by citizens vote at meetings, which may be attended by all town citizens. *For counties: Without administrator*—includes counties with the commission form of government; *With administrator*—includes counties with the council-elected executive form.

questionnaire inquired about contracting in seven broad service categories—public safety and corrections, public works and utilities, health and welfare, transportation, parks and recreation, education and culture, and general government and finance. Forty-two specific services were classified under these categories. Three of the seven categories accounted for 74% of the 4,328 contracts reported by all responding cities and counties. These were: public works and utilities (26%), public safety and corrections (24%), and health and welfare (24%). The order for responding cities was the same: public works and utilities (30%), public safety and corrections (23%), and health and welfare services (23%). For counties, the order was reversed: health and welfare (29%), public safety and corrections (26%), and public works and utilities (21%).

Breaking the data down by the 42 specific services reveals that jails and detention homes were the services most frequently contracted by both cities and counties. The ten services most frequently contracted are shown in Table 3/3 for cities, counties, and the two combined.

Service Providers. Table 3/4 shows the distribution of service contracts among various government entities. Cities entered into service contracts most frequently with counties (56%): for 35 of the 42 services listed in the questionnaire, counties were the cities' primary supplier. Cities contracted with other cities less frequently (25%): they were primary providers of 3 of the listed services. In contrast, counties indicate entering into contracts with other counties and with cities with about equal frequency.

As shown in Table 3/4, the dominance of the county as the city's main supplier under intergovernmental contracts stands out in four of the seven fields: public safety and corrections (63%), health and welfare (70%), education and culture (70%), and general government and finance (71%). In two others, public works and utilities and parks and recreation, counties also get more contracts. Only transportation contracts go more frequently to another entity: 42% go to special districts.

Service contracts between cities most often involve public works and utilities (35%). Other major providers for city services include school districts for parks and recreation (29%), and state government for both public safety and corrections (12%) and public works and utilities (13%).

Although counties' rather balanced use of other counties and cities is evident, they clearly lean toward contracting with other counties for services in health and welfare (50%), parks and recreation (50%), and general government and finance (67%), while contracting with cities for public works and utilities (63%) and education and cultural services (60%). Counties also rely significantly on school districts for parks and recreation (27%), on special districts for transportation (43%), and on the state for both health and welfare (30%) and public safety and corrections (19%).

Reasons for Entering into Service Contracts. Respondents were asked to identify which of seven reasons best explained their government's decision to contract with another government for the delivery of public services. The seven reasons listed were: lack of qualified personnel, lack of facilities, achieve economies of scale, eliminate service duplication, more logical to organize service beyond jurisdictional or areal limits, take politics out of service delivery, and citizen demand for service arrangement. Of the 4,328 contracts reported, 52% were entered into for "economies of scale." "More logical to organize services beyond jurisdictional or areal limits" was the next most frequently cited reason (38%).

"Economies of scale" was cited almost over-

Table 3/2 INTERGOVERMENTAL SERVICE CONTRACTS, BY CITIES AND COUNTIES

	Cities responding	Cities with contracts (No.)	Cities with contracts (%)	Counties responding	Counties with contracts (No.)	Counties with contracts (%)	Cities and counties responding	Cities and counties with contracts (No.)	Cities and counties with contracts (%)
Total	1,639	853	52	430	231	54	2,069	1,084	52
Population group									
Over 1,000,000	4	2	50	9	5	56	13	7	54
500,000–1,000,000	8	7	88	19	10	53	27	17	63
250,000– 499,999	18	14	78	47	25	53	65	39	60
100,000– 249,999	72	47	65	108	60	56	180	107	59
50,000– 99,999	141	88	62	138	80	58	279	168	60
25,000– 49,999	360	201	56	27	14	52	387	215	56
10,000– 24,999	753	386	51	43	20	47	796	406	51
5,000– 9,999	107	42	39	22	8	36	129	50	39
2,500– 4,999	142	53	37	8	2	25	150	55	37
Under 2,500	34	13	38	9	7	78	43	20	47
Geographic region									
Northeast	392	147	38	55	19	35	447	166	37
North Central	474	252	53	132	66	50	606	318	52
South	459	227	49	174	94	54	633	321	51
West	314	227	72	69	52	75	383	279	73
Metro status									
Central	246	149	61	...	...	...	246	149	61
Suburban	908	510	56	...	...	...	908	510	56
Independent	485	194	40	...	...	...	485	194	40
Metro	...	...	...	230	126	55	230	126	55
Nonmetro	...	...	...	200	105	53	200	105	53
Form of government									
Mayor-council	638	278	44	...	...	...	638	278	44
Council-manager	890	542	61	...	...	...	890	542	61
Commission	45	13	29	...	...	...	45	13	29
Town meeting	52	17	33	...	...	...	52	17	33
Representative town meeting	14	3	21	...	...	...	14	3	21
Without administrator	...	...	...	240	114	47	240	114	47
With administrator	...	...	...	190	117	62	190	117	62

Table 3/3 TEN MOST FREQUENTLY PURCHASED CONTRACT SERVICES, BY CITIES, COUNTIES, AND TOTAL

Rank	Cities: Service	No. of cities	Counties: Service	No. of counties	Total cities and counties: Service	No. of cities and counties
1	Jails/detention homes	257	Jails/detention homes	70	Jails/detention homes	327
2	Sewage disposal	243	Fire prevention/suppression	50	Sewage disposal	267
3	Tax assessing	187	Computer and data processing	46	Animal control	218
4	Animal control	175	Animal control	43	Tax assessing	210
5	Water supply	173	Solid waste disposal	43	Solid waste disposal	209
6	Solid waste disposal	166	Police/fire communications	38	Water supply	201
7	Police/fire communications	148	Libraries	36	Police/fire communications	186
8	Tax/utility bill processing	134	Mental health service	33	Fire prevention/suppression	159
9	Traffic signal installation/maintenance	131	Emergency medical/ambulance	33	Tax/utility bill processing	157
10	Sanitary inspection	130	Water supply	28	Sanitary inspection	150
			Police patrol	28		

whelmingly in all service categories by both cities and counties. Only transportation services were contracted for by cities primarily because it was "more logical to organize beyond jurisdictional boundaries," and for counties, the need to "eliminate service duplication" dominated as the primary reason for parks and recreation contracts.

JOINT SERVICE AGREEMENTS

Joint service agreements, like contracts, are a common alternative for delivering public services. Of the 2,039 responding cities and counties, 1,132 or 55% have entered into such agreements with other governmental entities.

As is true for intergovernmental service contracts, more populous cities and counties tend to enter into agreements more frequently than the less populous (Table 3/5). Seventy-two percent of the responding governments with populations of 250,000 and over have entered into joint service agreements compared to 41% of those with populations under 10,000.

Counties show a slightly higher tendency to

Table 3/4 SERVICES DELIVERED TO CITIES AND COUNTIES THROUGH INTERGOVERNMENTAL SERVICE CONTRACTS, BY SERVICE CATEGORY AND BY PROVIDER

		Number and percent of contracts for delivery of services by:									
		County		City		School district		Special district		State	
Service category	Total number of contracts	(No.)	(%)	(No.)	(%)	(No.)	(%)	(No.)	(%)	(No.)	(%)
Total, cities and counties	4,328	2,403	56	1,306	30	111	3	491	11	457	11
Services delivered to *cities*	3,419	1,929	56	870	25	78	2	402	12	295	9
Public safety and corrections	805	507	63	199	25	10	1	33	4	99	12
Public works and utilities	955	361	39	337	35	3	...[1]	157	16	126	13
Health and welfare	785	547	70	145	18	6	...[1]	79	10	36	5
Transportation	170	48	28	44	26	1	...[1]	71	42	9	5
Parks and recreation	93	33	35	25	27	27	29	7	8	7	8
Education and culture	119	84	70	31	26	3	2	16	13	3	2
General government and finance	492	349	71	89	18	28	6	39	8	15	3
Services delivered to *counties*	909	474	52	436	50	33	4	89	10	162	18
Public safety and corrections	234	122	52	125	52	3	1	8	3	44	19
Public works and utilities	189	94	50	120	63	0	0	11	6	24	13
Health and welfare	261	131	50	86	33	5	2	40	15	78	30
Transportation	30	10	33	11	37	0	0	13	43	1	3
Parks and recreation	22	11	50	9	41	6	27	1	5	2	9
Education and culture	40	17	42	24	60	3	7	6	15	4	10
General government and finance	133	89	67	61	46	16	12	10	8	9	7

Note: Percentages add to more than 100 because some contracts involve more than one provider.
[1] Less than 1%.

Table 3/5 JOINT SERVICE AGREEMENTS

		Cities with agreements			Counties with agreements			Total with agreements	
Classification	Total cities responding	(No.)	(%)	Total counties responding	(No.)	(%)	Total cities and counties responding	(No.)	(%)
Total	1,619	879	54	420	253	60	2,039	1,132	55
Population group									
Over 1,000,000	4	2	50	9	7	78	13	9	69
500,000–1,000,000	8	8	100	20	14	70	28	22	79
250,000– 499,999	16	15	94	47	29	62	63	44	70
100,000– 249,999	69	42	61	105	67	64	174	109	63
50,000– 99,999	140	87	62	130	77	59	270	164	61
25,000– 49,999	360	226	63	26	17	65	386	243	63
10,000– 24,999	742	385	52	42	23	55	784	408	52
5,000– 9,999	106	44	42	24	9	38	130	53	41
2,500– 4,999	141	58	41	8	4	50	149	62	42
Under 2,500	33	12	36	9	6	67	42	18	43
Geographic region									
Northeast	385	157	41	54	27	50	439	184	42
North Central	473	262	55	128	72	56	601	334	56
South	451	228	51	169	106	63	620	334	54
West	310	232	75	69	48	70	379	280	74
Metro status									
Central	241	160	66	...	...	...	241	160	66
Suburban	897	471	53	...	...	...	897	471	53
Independent	481	248	52	...	...	...	481	248	52
Metro	...	...	...	225	140	62	225	140	62
Nonmetro	...	...	...	195	113	58	195	113	58
Form of government									
Mayor-council	633	295	47	...	...	...	633	295	47
Council-manager	876	545	62	...	...	...	876	545	62
Commission	45	16	36	...	...	...	45	16	36
Town meeting	51	18	35	...	...	...	51	18	35
Representative town meeting	14	5	36	...	...	...	14	5	36
Without administrator	...	...	...	233	131	56	233	131	56
With administrator	...	...	...	187	122	65	187	122	65

Table 3/6 TEN SERVICES MOST FREQUENTLY PROVIDED UNDER JOINT AGREEMENTS, TO CITIES, COUNTIES, AND TOTAL

	Cities		Counties		Total cities and counties	
Rank	Service	No. of cities	Service	No. of counties	Service	No. of cities and counties
1	Police/fire communciations	149	Mental health	48	Libraries	195
2	Libraries	149	Libraries	46	Police/fire communications	193
3	Sewage disposal	138	Police/fire communciations	44	Fire prevention/suppression	165
4	Fire prevention/suppression	134	Jails/detention homes	42	Sewage disposal	160
5	Jails/detention homes	107	Solid waste disposal	41	Jails/detention homes	149
6	Solid waste disposal	106	Programs for elderly	40	Solid waste disposal	147
7	Emergency medical/ambulance	100	Emergency medical/ambulance	38	Emergency medical/ambulance	138
8	Animal control	95	Public health clinics	37	Animal control	122
9	Recreational facilities	89	Planning/zoning	35	Recreational facilities	113
10	Water supply	78	Fire prevention/suppression	31	Programs for the elderly	102

enter into joint service agreements than cities, 60% and 54%, respectively. However, cities with populations of 250,000 and above enter into agreements with a much higher degree of frequency (89%) than counties of comparable size (66%).

Joint agreements are more common among central cities than among suburban and independent cities, but only slightly more common among metropolitan counties than nonmetropolitan counties. Regional differences are evident: a larger percentage of localities in the western region make joint agreements than their counterparts in other regions.

Consistent with the findings on service contracts, a higher percentage of cities with council-manager governments make joint agreements than cities with other forms of government. Similarly, counties with an elected or appointed administrator enter into joint agreements more frequently than those without an administrator.

Joint Services Provided. As was found with contracts, agreements primarily involve three of the seven categories listed in the questionnaire. Sixty-nine percent of the 3,319 agreements reported were for services in the categories of health and welfare (26%), public safety and corrections (23%), and public works and utilities (20%). Cities entered into joint agreements most frequently for public safety and corrections (23%), health and welfare (23%), and public works and utilities (22%). Counties used joint agreements most often for health and welfare services (34%), public safety and corrections (21%), and public works and utilities (15%).

Although the three top service categories are the same for both joint agreements and contracts, breaking down the data by the 42 specific services reveals differences. Libraries and police and fire communications were the two services most frequently provided under joint agreements (Table 3/6), whereas jails and detention homes and sewage disposal were provided the most frequently on a contractual basis (Table 3/3).

Table 3/7 further compares the types of services for which cities and counties had the most contracts and joint agreements.

As the table shows, the eight functions most frequently provided on a contractual basis are relatively non-controversial. Joint agreements, on the other hand, are utilized more frequently for services that require more participation and local control, such as recreation facilities and programs for the elderly. This finding is in concert with earlier research conducted by ACIR which concluded that "joint agreements seem to be better adapted to providing services that require program development and policy decisions, e.g., recreation, planning, and urban renewal."[7]

Table 3/7 SERVICES MOST FREQUENTLY CITED, BY TYPE OF ARRANGEMENT, FOR CITIES AND COUNTIES COMBINED

Intergovernmental service contract		Joint service agreement	
Service	No. of cities and counties	Service	No. of cities and counties
Jails/detention homes	327	Libraries	195
Sewage disposal	267	Police/fire communications	193
Animal control	218	Fire prevention/suppression	165
Tax assessing	210	Sewage disposal	160
Solid waste disposal	209	Jails/detention homes	149
Water supply	201	Solid waste disposal	147
Police/fire communications	186	Emergency medical/ambulance	138
Fire prevention/suppression	159	Animal control	122
Tax/utility bill processing	157	Recreational facilities	113
Sanitary inspection	150	Programs for elderly	102
Libraries	147	Water supply	93
Emergency medical/ambulance	122	Tax assessing	91
Programs for the elderly	62	Sanitary inspection	83
Recreation facilities	59	Fire prevention/suppression	76

Participants in Joint Agreements. Responding cities report that 48% of all joint agreements were entered into with counties and 41% with other cities. Counties were the principal joint providers for 24 of the 42 services, and cities were the principal partners for 12.

As with intergovernmental service contracts, counties participated in joint agreements with cities and other counties with the same degree of frequency. Counties were the principal partner for 19 services and cities for 15.

Table 3/8 shows dominant participants in seven functional categories. For cities' joint agreements, counties dominated in the health and welfare (59%), education and culture (65%), and general government and finance (58%) categories. Cities dominated in public works and utilities (47%). Cities rely equally on other cities (39%) and on special districts (38%) for transportation services. Cities cooperate mainly with other cities (40%) and with school districts (43%) for parks and recreation.

For counties, other counties were dominant participants in parks and recreation (68%), transportation (58%), general government and finance (68%), and health and welfare agreements (57%); cities were the most frequent partner in public safety and corrections (77%), public works and utilities (66%), and education and culture (67%). When state governments were utilized it was most frequently for health and welfare (26%); special districts were used frequently for transportation services (33%).

Comparing Table 3/4 with Table 3/8, we see that cities participate with other cities more frequently in joint agreements than in service contracts (41% versus 25%).

Reasons for Entering into Joint Agreements. Taking advantage of "economies of scale" was again the most frequently cited reason for entering into joint agreements (53%), and "more logical to organize services beyond jurisdictional or areal limit" was the second most commonly cited reason (46%), particularly for transportation services. This reason was also cited frequently for agreements in the education and culture area, and by counties for agreements in the parks and recreation area.

INTERGOVERMENTAL SERVICE TRANSFERS

Transfer of responsibility for the provision of a service is yet another service delivery alternative commonly employed by local governments.

Table 3/8 SERVICES RECEIVED BY CITIES AND COUNTIES UNDER JOINT AGREEMENTS, BY SERVICE CATEGORY AND BY PARTICIPANT

Service category	Total number of agreements	Number and percent of agreements for delivery of services by joint participation with: County (No.)	County (%)	City (No.)	City (%)	School district (No.)	School district (%)	Special district (No.)	Special district (%)	State (No.)	State (%)
Total, cities and counties	3,319	1,703	52	1,492	45	142	4	511	15	374	11
Services received by *cities*	2,432	1,177	48	999	41	118	5	397	16	248	10
Public safety and corrections	565	273	48	275	49	8	1	61	11	69	12
Public works and utilities	543	202	37	258	47	6	1	102	19	82	15
Health and welfare	569	333	59	178	31	9	1	93	16	61	11
Transportation	153	49	32	59	39	0	0	58	38	6	4
Parks and recreation	144	44	30	57	40	62	43	12	8	3	2
Education and culture	165	107	65	54	33	6	4	24	15	13	8
General government/finance	293	169	58	118	40	27	9	47	16	14	5
Services received by *counties*	887	526	59	493	56	24	3	114	13	126	14
Public safety and corrections	184	107	58	142	77	3	2	6	3	17	9
Public works and utilities	135	76	56	89	66	1	1	14	10	15	11
Health and welfare	304	173	57	115	38	2	1	49	16	79	26
Transportation	55	32	58	27	49	1	2	18	33	4	7
Parks and recreation	47	32	68	29	62	4	8	4	8	1	2
Education and culture	52	31	60	35	67	2	4	6	11	5	10
General government and finance	110	75	68	56	51	11	10	17	15	5	4

Note: Percentages add to more than 100 because some agreements are with more than one other party.

Table 3/9 CITIES AND COUNTIES TRANSFERRING SERVICE RESPONSIBILITIES SINCE 1976

Classification	Cities responding	Cities with transfers away (No.)	Cities with transfers away (%)	Counties responding	Counties with transfers away (No.)	Counties with transfers away (%)	Total no. responding	Total number with transfers away (No.)	Total number with transfers away (%)
Total	1,413	565	40	373	145	39	1,786	710	40
Population group									
Over 1,000,000	3	3	100	9	4	44	12	7	58
500,000–1,000,000	7	6	86	17	7	41	24	13	54
250,000– 499,999	15	12	80	39	20	51	54	32	59
100,000– 249,999	66	36	55	98	53	54	164	89	54
50,000– 99,999	121	49	41	122	42	34	243	91	37
25,000– 49,999	324	152	47	26	5	19	350	157	45
10,000– 24,999	645	247	38	31	9	29	676	256	38
5,000– 9,999	90	28	31	16	3	19	106	31	29
2,500– 4,999	112	24	21	6	0	0	118	24	20
Under 2,500	30	8	27	9	2	22	39	10	26
Geographic region									
Northeast	325	109	34	47	19	40	372	128	34
North Central	408	155	38	109	35	32	517	190	37
South	394	176	45	154	59	38	548	235	43
West	286	125	44	63	32	51	349	157	45
Metro status									
Central	217	133	61	...	...	...	217	133	61
Suburban	783	289	37	...	...	...	783	289	37
Independent	413	143	35	...	...	...	413	143	35
Metro	...	...	...	208	98	47	208	98	47
Nonmetro	...	...	...	165	47	29	165	47	29
Form of government									
Mayor-council	523	177	34	...	...	...	523	177	34
Council-manager	801	357	45	...	...	...	801	357	45
Commission	35	14	40	...	...	...	35	14	40
Town meeting	43	13	30	...	...	...	43	13	30
Representative town meeting	11	4	36	...	...	...	11	4	36
Without administrator	...	...	...	198	71	36	198	71	36
With administrator	...	...	...	175	74	42	175	74	42

As noted earlier, transfers, unlike service contracts and joint agreements, involve the surrender to another entity of responsibility for providing a service. Of the 1,786 responding cities and counties, 710 or 40% report service transfers since 1976, to another governmental unit, to a private firm, or to a nonprofit agency (Table 3/9).

Again, transfer of responsibility for a service seems to be influenced by a jurisdiction's population size. Of all localities with populations 250,000 and above, 58% report financial transfers, in contrast to only 25% of the respondents with populations of 10,000 and under.

Cities and counties transferred services with nearly the same degree of frequency. However, a larger proportion of large cities transferred functions than counties of similar size. Of cities with populations of 250,000 and above 84% report transfers, compared to 48% of counties of comparable population size. Cities with populations of 10,000 and below also had a greater tendency to transfer functions than smaller counties.

As is the case with contracts and agreements, central cities (61%) transfer functions more frequently than suburban cities (37%) and inde-

Table 3/10 TEN SERVICES MOST FREQUENTLY TRANSFERRED FROM CITIES AND COUNTIES SINCE 1976

	From cities		From counties		From cities and counties	
Rank	Service	No. of cities	Service	No. of counties	Service	Total
1	Refuse collection	124	Emergency medical/ambulance	16	Refuse collection	139
2	Solid waste disposal	99	Alcohol and drug rehabilitation	16	Solid waste disposal	118
3	Animal control	62	Refuse collection	15	Animal control	72
4	Jails/detention homes	61	Jails/detention homes	10	Jails/detention homes	71
5	Tax assessing	55	Animal control	10	Tax assessing	58
6	Sewage disposal	49	Street and bridge construction/ maintenance	10	Sewage disposal	55
7	Police/fire communications	43	Recreational facilities	10	Emergency medical/ambulance	54
8	Computer and data processing	42	Mental health services	10	Police/fire communications	52
9	Tax/utility bill processing	41	Police/fire communications	9	Computer and data processing	50
10	Emergency medical/ambulance	38	Computer and data processing	8	Tax/utility bill processing	44
			Hospitals	8		

Table 3/11 SERVICES RECEIVED UNDER TRANSFER AGREEMENTS BY SERVICE CATEGORY AND BY RECIPIENT

		Number and percent of services transferred to:													
		County		City		Special district		Regional organization		State		Private firm		Nonprofit organization	
Service category	Total number of transfers	(No.)	(%)	(No.)	(%)	(No.)	(%)	(No.)	(%)	(No.)	(%)	(No.)	(%)	(No.)	(%)
Total, cities and counties	1,412	469	33	140	10	78	6	109	8	92	7	392	28	163	12
Services transferred by *cities*	1,168	436	37	75	6	67	6	84	7	68	6	330	28	107	9
Public safety and corrections	164	106	65	22	13	5	3	11	7	11	7	7	4	6	4
Public works and utilities	381	74	19	23	6	15	4	31	8	28	7	198	52	10	3
Health and welfare	257	127	49	16	6	10	4	12	5	13	5	26	20	57	22
Transportation	62	8	13	5	8	11	18	16	26	0	0	7	11	12	19
Parks and recreation	51	10	20	0	0	8	16	0	0	2	4	14	27	13	25
Education and culture	43	30	70	1	2	3	7	2	5	2	5	2	5	5	12
General government and finance	210	81	32	8	3	15	7	12	7	12	6	76	36	4	2
Services transferred by *counties*	244	33	14	65	27	11	5	25	10	24	10	62	25	56	23
Public safety and corrections	39	5	13	20	51	2	5	2	5	8	21	2	5	4	10
Public works and utilities	61	10	16	19	31	4	7	5	8	4	7	24	39	5	8
Health and welfare	92	15	17	13	14	4	4	8	9	11	12	17	21	34	37
Transportation	8	1	13	3	38	0	0	2	25	0	0	2	25	4	50
Parks and recreation	15	0	0	5	33	0	0	3	20	0	0	4	27	4	27
Education and culture	7	1	14	3	43	1	14	1	14	0	0	0	0	2	28
General government and finance	22	1	4	2	9	0	0	4	17	1	4	13	57	3	13

Note: Percentages add to more than 100 because some transfers involve more than one recipient.

pendent cities (35%). Metropolitan counties transfer functions more frequently (47%) than nonmetropolitan counties (29%).

The data reveal only slight differences geographically for cities. Forty-four percent of the respondents in the West report transfers, 45% in the South, 38% in the North Central region, and 34% in the Northeast.

Council-manager cities transfer functions more frequently than cities with other forms of government, and counties with administrators are similarly more active in transfers than counties with a chief administrator.

Most Frequently Transferred Services. Seventy-two percent of all service transfers primarily involve three of the seven categories. Among the 1,412 transfers reported, public works and utilities (31%), health and welfare (25%) and general government and finance (16%) transfers were the most frequently cited. Cities report the transfer of public works and utilities functions (33%), health and welfare functions (22%), and general government and finance functions (18%) with the highest degree of frequency. Responding counties most frequently transferred health and welfare functions (38%), public works and utilities functions (25%), and public safety and corrections functions (16%).

Care must be taken in interpreting these findings, particularly those transfers that involve general government and finance services. As stated earlier, the questionnaire defined intergovernmental service transfer as the permanent transfer of total responsibility for providing a service. It also differentiated between delivery and provision of service. The latter was defined as deciding that a service should be made available and then arranging for its funding and delivery. The emphasis on "permanent" and "providing" was intended mainly to help the respondents distinguish between merely contracting for services—in which the contracting unit maintains responsibility for provision of the service—and actually giving up that responsibility to another entity.

It is not clear that survey respondents always made this distinction, and to the extent they did not, some unknown number of reported "transfers" were probably contracts. For example, engineering and architectural services, street lighting, and building and ground maintenance are some of the most frequently cited services reportedly transferred to private firms. While it is apparent that a local government may choose an alternative method of delivery for these types of services, the responsibility for the provision of these services generally remains with the local government.

As shown in Table 3/10, refuse collection and solid waste disposal are the services most frequently transferred. As with the services most frequently delivered through joint agreements, most of these services are non-controversial.

Recipients of Service Transfers. Of city service transfers, 37% went to counties, 28% went to private firms, and much smaller percentages went to other service providers. Counties made 27% of their transfers to cities and 25% to private firms. As Table 3/11 shows, the counties were the primary recipient of three of the seven categories from cities: public safety and corrections (65%), health and welfare (49%), and education and culture service responsibilities (70%). Private firms received the bulk of public works and utilities (52%), parks and recreation (27%), and general government and finance (36%).

Counties primarily transferred responsibility for public safety and corrections (51%), parks and recreation (33%), and education and cul-

Table 3/12 CITIES' USE OF PRIVATE CONTRACTING AS PERCENTAGE OF THEIR USE OF ALL (PUBLIC PLUS PRIVATE CONTRACTING): 23 SELECTED SERVICES, 1972 AND 1982

	1972 survey, 2,375 cities responding	1982 survey, 1,439 cities responding
Services with similar names in both surveys		
Solid waste disposal	44%	46%
Street lighting	80	66
Utility billing	56	61
Ambulance services	57	60
Animal control	31	26
Housing	5	23
Hospitals	38	61
Recreational facilities	4	33
Parks	3	68
Museums	20	20
Legal services	84	90
Payroll	56	85
Tax assessing	14	15
Personnel services	8	73
Public relations	67	89
Services with slightly different names in both surveys		
Snow plowing	30%	85%
Crime prevention/patrol	2	42
Traffic control	4	20
Insect control	8	33
Public health	2	19
Drug/alcohol treatment	7	15
Mental health	18	14

Source: ACIR staff calculations using ACIR, *The Challenge of Local Governmental Reorganization* (Report A-44), Washington, D.C., U.S. Government Printing Office, 1974, Appendix Table III-A, and an unpublished printout on the cities part of Table B in Carl F. Valente and Lydia D. Manchester, *Rethinking Local Services: Examining Alternative Delivery Approaches*, Washington, D.C., International City Management Association, 1984.

ture (43%) to cities. Private firms were the recipient of public works and utilities (39%) and general government and finance (57%) transfers.

Reasons for Service Transfers. As in the case of contracts and agreements, achieving "economies of scale" was the primary reason given by the respondents for transferring services (50%). "More logical to organize beyond jurisdictional boundaries" (28%) and "elimination of duplication" (21%) were the next most frequently cited reasons.

Although both cities and counties indicated that they transferred services principally to take advantage of economies of scale, some differences between the two are evident. Cities (52%) tend to site economies of scale as the primary incentive more often than counties (43%), indicating that the only services for which this was not the major incentive were transportation and education and cultural services. In contrast, counties (75%) overwhelmingly transferred transportation services to take advantage of economies of scale. Education and culture services were transferred equally to achieve economies of scale and because counties lacked the appropriate facilities.

TRENDS IN CITIES' USE OF INTERGOVERMENTAL ARRANGEMENTS

As the preceding section indicates, intergovernmental arrangements are widely used by local governments. Other recent studies show that localities are using a growing variety of private service provision and delivery methods to deliver public services. Both the increasing availability of alternative services and the financial pressures to do more with less help to form the context in which recent changes in the use and extent of intergovernmental service arrangements have occurred.

Because the earlier ACIR/ICMA surveys did not yield comparable data on counties, this trend analysis looks only at cities.

Intergovernmental Service Contracts. Comparing the 1972 and 1983 survey data on intergovernmental service contracts reveals a marginal decline in the number of contracts reported by cities over the past decade. In 1972, 59% of the responding cities said they had such contracts; in 1983, the proportion had dropped to 52%. Considering the mounting interest in and publicity about contracting as a more cost-effective method of service delivery in recent years, this was a surprising finding. A number of factors may explain the apparent decline.

As noted above, one explanation is the increase in cities' contracting with private firms rather than with other governments. Table 3/12, based on data from the 1972 ACIR/ICMA survey on intergovernmental service agreements and a 1982 ICMA survey on private service delivery alternatives, illustrates the growth in the use of service contracting with private firms in 23 service areas.[8] From 1972 to 1982, all but four of the 23 services showed an increase in the use of contracts with private firms for service delivery when viewed as a percentage of all municipal service contracts. Substantial increases occured in housing, hospitals, recreational facilities, parks, payroll, personnel services, public relations, snow plowing, crime prevention/patrol, traffic control, insect control, and public health.

Another factor is cities' increased use of joint agreements (reported later in this section), in situations where contracts were used earlier. A third explanation is the expanded role of counties as deliverers of urban services.[9] To the extent that counties increasingly perform such services, there is no need for city action, either directly or via intergovernmental contracts.

Apart from the modest decline in the percentage of cities reporting intergovernmental service transers, the findings from the 1983 survey are similar to those documented in 1972. Then as now, the more populous units of government were more likely to enter into service contracts than smaller units. Central cities contracted for services more frequently than suburban and independent cities, and contracting was most prevalent among western cities. However, the 1972 survey reported the lowest incidence of contracting in southern cities, in contrast to the 1983 finding that northeastern cities contracted the least frequently for services. Cities with the council-manager form of government contracted more frequently than those with the mayor-council, commission, or town meeting form of government, but the margin of difference widened from 1972 to 1983.

Comparing the data from the two surveys on the types of services most frequently provided on a contractual basis reveals that: (1) the largest percentage of contracts was for jails and detention home services in both periods, (2) sewage disposal and animal control services were included in the list of the top ten services provided through contract in both periods, and (3) the primary functional emphasis in the top ten shifted from public safety in 1972 to public works and utilities in 1983.

In 1972 other general units of government were the primary providers in 68% of all service contracts; by 1983, 81% of all services were provided by other local governments. In 1972, 4% of the service contracts were entered into with local school districts, 19% with regional and other special districts, and 10% with state governments. In contrast, the 1983 survey revealed that 2% of the service contracts were provided by local school districts, 12% with special districts, and 9% with state governments.

Joint Service Agreements. As noted earlier, the number of cities participating in joint agreements increased significantly from 1972 to 1983; 35% reported entering into joint agreements in 1972 in contrast to 55% in 1983.

Aside from this major change, few other changes occurred in the use of joint agreements and those that did were similar to the trends in cities' use of contracts. Both surveys indicate that the tendency to enter into agreements is directly related to population size. In 1972, central cities participated in agreements more frequently than suburban and independent cities, and western cities participated in joint agreements more frequently than their counterparts. Southern cities utilized agreements least often in 1972, but in 1983 northeastern cities reported the lowest incidence of participation in joint agreements. Cities with council-manager forms of government were more likely to engage in agreements than cities with other forms of government.

Eight of the ten most frequently cited agreements were for functions in the same service areas in both years. Comparable data from the two surveys on participants in agreements were not available.

Intergovernmental Service Transfers. Consistent with the findings on intergovernmental contracts, the data indicate a slight decline in the number of intergovernmental service transfers since 1975, when ACIR conducted a nationwide survey on the subject. In 1975, 31% of the responding cities reported they had participated in a service transfer; in 1983, 25% indicated they had done so.[10]

Part of the explanation for this decline may lie in the financial stress experienced recently by many localities. The recessions since that time may have inhibited governmental units' ability or willingness to accept responsibility for a new service or continue with an old one. Also, as noted earlier, mounting interest in private alternatives and increased use of joint service agreements may have contributed to the drop in the number of transfers. For example, some cities expressed a preference for contracting with a private firm over transferring responsibility for the service to another governmental unit in their responses to an open-ended question in the 1983 survey. Respondents in the earlier survey indicated a preference for intergovernmental service agreements over service transfers.

Aside from the minor drop in the percentage of cities reporting service transfers, their use remained essentially the same from 1975 to 1983. Larger units of government in both surveys had a greater tendency to shift services away from their jurisdictions than smaller ones. Consistent with population size, central cities transferred services more frequently than suburban and independent cities in both years. Geographical differences were slight in 1975 and 1983. In 1975, only a slight variation was found in transfer practices, but in 1983 council-manager cities tended to transfer services most frequently.

The types of services transferred to other units of government in both years were quite similar. The most noticeable change was a shift from solid waste disposal to public health as the most frequently cited service. This finding offered no real surprise. In the past few years, literature in the field indicates that local governments are increasingly relying on contracts with private firms to provide solid waste collection and disposal services to their citizens.[11] Moreover, the role of counties as providers of public health services has been expanding.

In both years, counties were the primary recipient of cities' transfers. In 1975, 55% of the transfers were made to counties; in 1983, counties received 54% of the transfers. Special districts declined as recipients of service transfers, assuming responsibility for 19% of the transfers in 1975 and only 9% in 1983. On the other hand, councils of government or other regional bodies were on the receiving end of 14% of city transfers in 1983 compared with 4% in 1975.

"Economies of scale" remained the major incentive behind all such arrangements. This factor was cited in the 1972 survey on intergovernmental arrangements, the 1975 survey on functional transfers, and the 1983 survey for all such arrangements.

SUMMARY

Intergovernmental alternatives are common approaches employed by localities to reduce the cost and improve the performance of public services. Their popularity has generally endured since the early 1970s when their use and scope were examined in two nationwide surveys conducted by ACIR and ICMA.

During the ensuing decade, cities made only modest changes in these arrangements, but significantly increased their use of joint agreements for the provision of public services. They used fewer intergovernmental service contracts and transfers.

One explanation for these declines is an increase in the use of private alternatives. The private sector offers local officials economical methods for the delivery of public services, but the lack of conclusive evidence in the literature on the extent and use of these arrangements makes it impossible to assess empirically their impact on intergovernmental arrangements.

---

1 Jane Roberts, "States and Localities in 1983: Recession, Reform, Renewal," *Intergovernmental Perspective 10*, No. 1, U.S. Advisory Commission on Intergovernmental Relations, (Washington, D.C.: U.S. Government Printing Office, Winter 1984), citing the Joint Economic Committee, *Trends in the Fiscal Conditions of Cities: 1981–83*. (Washington, D.C.: November 1983).

2 Peter Kenney, "Declaration of Dependence," *Colorado Municipalities*, (November–December 1982).

3 Beth Walter Honadle, "Interlocal Cooperation," *National Civic Review*, (July–August 1982).

4 H. Paul Friesma, *Metropolitan Political Structures* (Iowa City: University of Iowa Press, 1971), Ch. 3, for a more thorough discussion of the problem of underreporting.

5 U.S. Advisory Commission on Intergovernmental Relations, *The Challenge of Local Government Reorganization*, Report A-44, (Washington, D.C.: U.S. Government Printing Office, 1976).

6 U.S. Advisory Commission on Intergovernmental Relations, *Pragmatic Federalism: The Reassignment of Functional Responsibility*, Report M-105, (Washington, D.C.: U.S. Government Printing Office, 1976).

7 U.S. Advisory Commission on Intergovernmental Relations, *A Handbook for Interlocal Agreements and Contracts*, Report M-29, (Washington, D.C.: U.S. Government Printing Office, 1967).

8 Data for Table 3/12 are based on staff calculations using ACIR, *The Challenge of Local Reorganization*, Report A-44, Appendix Table III-A, and an unpublished print-out on the cities' part of Table B in Carl F. Valente and Lydia D. Manchester, *Rethinking Local Service Delivery: Examining Alternative Delivery Approaches* (Washington, D.C.: International City Management Association, 1984). Several caveats should be taken into consideration when comparing the data in Table 3/12. In the 1972 survey, intergovernmental contracting was the central focus of the study; in 1983, private sector approaches were the major concern. The 1972 study surveyed 5,900 cities over 2,500 in population and received a 40% response rate. The 1982 study surveyed 3,130 cities over 10,000 population and a 1-in-8 sample for cities under 2,500 and received a 46% response rate. The 1972 survey included a list of 76 services; in 1982, 59 services were listed in the questionnaires. The 23 services in the comparison are based on comparable services listed in both. While comparability is a concern, the evidence generally indicates that private contracting among cities certainly did not diminish in the ten-year period and very likely increased.

9 U.S. Advisory Commission on Intergovernmental Relations, *State and Local Roles in the Federal System*, Report A-88, (Washington, D.C.: U.S. Government Printing Office, 1982).

10 These percentages are based on transfers away to other governmental entities *only*. The percentage (40%) reported in the preceding section is based on transfers away to governmental entities, private firms, and non-profit organizations.

11 E. S. Savas, *Privatizing the Public Sector*, (Chatham House, 1982); Savas cites: "New Orleans Hauler Makes Inroads with Competitive Pricing," *Solid Waste Management 20*, No. 5, (May 1977); "Oklahoma City Three-Way Split," *Solid Waste Management 21*, No. 3, (March 1978); Peter E. Heidenreich, "Public Versus Private Solid Waste Management: The Nashville Approach," *Solid Waste Management 21*, No. 5, (May 1978); Ronald Smothers, "City, as Test, to Seek Bids on Private Refuse Pickup," *New York Times*, 26 March 1980.

4

Human Services in Local Government: Patterns of Service at Metropolitan Levels*

Robert Agranoff
Indiana University–Bloomington

Alex N. Pattakos
University of Maine at Orono

What is the role of local governments in the implementation of social policy during an era when federal and state programs receive the greatest share of attention? This question is especially pertinent in the mid-1980s because growth of federal and state programs appears to be leveling off. Moreover, federal and state legislative decisions and administrative actions regularly concern local government obligations and responsibilities. Despite all the attention paid to human services as a function of government, however, there is very little comparative data available on the present roles of local governments in delivering these services. Little is known about what cities and counties are doing in the way of human services. This article draws upon a survey conducted by the International City Management Association (ICMA) in 1984 to profile the contemporary role of city and county governments in human services, including patterns of service operation.

Human services, to be sure, comprise key local government services. In this regard, despite federal and state sponsorship of major programs in income maintenance, health services and health financing, employment and training, education, low income housing, and social services, cities and counties are also *directly* or *indirectly* involved in many of these services. The people who need the services live at the local level and therefore even federal- and state-operated programs must meet clients in some locale. Consequently, although another unit of government or a private delivery agent provides services for some citizens within the local government jurisdiction, it is the local government that is often the first point of contact for many citizens in need. Even though the city or county may not operate programs to meet particular needs, local government officials often have to see that citizens gain access to service providers.

This situation is made more complex by the confusing myriad of jurisdictions involved in the delivery of contemporary human services in a community: units of local general purpose government (GPG), special purpose local governments, federal agency offices, state agency offices, substate districts, regional quasi-governments, voluntary or non-profit service agencies, for-profit agencies, and independent/group practitioners. What this means is that the GPG takes on somewhat different roles than its counterparts at the national and state levels. In addition to being a possible operator of services, a GPG may also become the primary actor in putting together the disparate pieces on the local scene. It also can be a partner, acting in concert with other governments and/or major private sector entities in planning and solving human service problems. These local roles have most recently been put to their greatest challenge by reductions in federal and state funding growth, as well as by attempts to devolve programs to the state and local sector.

Specific details regarding these patterns of human services operations at the local level were previously unknown. This article, however, reports study findings which provide for the sorting of key trends and patterns of human service provision within a distinctly local government context. While the primary unit of analysis is the city or county governmental unit, the study also looks at the types of relationships GPGs have with other "metropolitan" human service actors. Particular attention in the study is paid to the financing, management, and delivery of a range of services exclusive of medical and welfare programs: elderly, children and youth, handicapped, and a wide range of general population counseling, emergency, access, and advocacy services.

TRADITIONAL AND EMERGENT ROLES OF LOCAL GOVERNMENT IN HUMAN SERVICES

The local government role has changed from that of a predominant actor to a more uncertain and perhaps supportive position. Social welfare development began with the principle of local responsibility in the Elizabethan poor laws: public aid was the domain of small units of government.[1]

The Federal Role. Throughout the nineteenth century, attempts to involve the federal government were largely thwarted by arguments of basic state/local responsibility, manifested by the states' constitutional power to shape local government. During the early part of the twentieth century, the Progressive Era gave impetus to reform in public health and welfare, resulting in an initial shift of responsibility from small units to large city or county units. In addition, statewide standards were instituted as a way of guarding the public welfare. The depression conditions of the 1930s created a need for assistance among "nonpoor" people for the first time. Both the states and the federal government were targets of various interest groups. Many programs that had been tried locally or experimentally became the fabric of state human services programming efforts, but only in some states. Other states chose to ignore the widespread economic problems.

National efforts, therefore, began with attempts to address widespread economic distress under the New Deal. The Social Security Act and several other pieces of federal legislation encouraged a federal–state partnership which, in effect, nationalized many programs that had been conducted by individual states.[2] The past five decades have largely reinforced the pattern of increasing nationalization. Several studies have documented the increased role of the federal government in setting the human services policy agenda for other governments.[3]

The State Role. State government differences, plus the march of state and national categorical programs, have created a varied landscape of local general purpose government human services. In this regard, counties are quite significant in the sixteen "county-administered" welfare states. Not only do they have strong welfare responsibilities, including medical assistance and food stamps, but they also have considerable responsibilities for public health and personal social services functions as well. Recently, many of these states (e.g., California, Minnesota, and Wisconsin) have strengthened county roles even further by passing legislation enabling counties to consolidate programs and undertake broad-range planning and management actions. By contrast, where state governments have taken over most welfare and service programs, the county role is more uneven. A 1974 survey of county roles within the human services sector identified four out of five counties with some welfare responsibilities, 75% administering public health and medical assistance services, and, 60% administering mental health programs.[4]

The Local Government Role. Cities defy characterization even more. In a few states, cities actually perform traditional county functions, and, in a number of large cities, the municipality operates as a composite city–county and its role parallels that of the county. Larger cities tend to perform multiple human services functions, but, in most cases, cities have a *mixed* human services role. A survey of 120 cities conducted by the U.S. Conference of Mayors in 1977 revealed that in addition to housing and employment and training services, cities over 30,000 in population are most likely to have some involvement in thirteen general social service areas: aging, consumer protection, counseling, day care, drug and alcohol abuse, health, income maintenance, information and referral/outreach, income services, manpower, nutrition, recreation, and youth.[5]

Significant Developments. While the growth of federal and state programs masked the local government role as an actual or potential leader in human services, a series of developments

*Authors' note: The authors would like to thank the following people for their assistance in the preparation of this article: Barbara J. Gage, Lisa A. Miller, Wayne B. Persons, and Linda Vanags, University of Maine at Orono; and Anne Sutton and Sue Hopfensberger, Indiana University–Bloomington.

moved cities and counties back towards center stage. First, community action programs (CAPs) and Model Cities programs became the first local programs to deal with poverty, employability, and other problems of the disadvantaged. When local governments were thrust back into the human services arena, local officials had to forge new relationships with health and human services officials and agencies.

Second, federal block grants and other flexible funding programs afforded local governments the opportunity to approach human services more comprehensively. Programs such as Community Development Block Grants, the Older Americans Act, HUD 701 Planning, various employment and training titles, as well as the new block grants enacted in 1981, while presumably targeted at specific policy aims, gave local governments increased options to meet problems.

Third, general revenue sharing for local governments has added new opportunities to meet needs not directly met by other programs. Many local governments have used this nearly unrestricted funding source to support local agencies and programs outside of government, particularly those for which there are no alternative sources of funding.

Fourth, local governments have become more involved in human services in an indirect, or *nonservice* fashion. "Governance" powers can be used to assist a population in need, through such means as: regulation and deregulation, tax policy changes, administrative reform, collaboration with the nonpublic sector, promotion of self-help, advocacy, and so on.

Fifth, industrial decline and economic recessions coupled with federal and state funding reductions have made local governments the focal point of action on many issues and problems. When pressing human concerns such as child abuse, delinquency, refugee resettlement, homelessness, and mental illness, impact neighborhoods or communities, those who want action typically turn to city and county leadership for a remedy.

Sixth, collectively these developments have led to the resurgence of a local constituency for human services. In this regard, growing recognition that complex local problems cannot be solved in distant capitols, coupled with a national public policy which underscores the responsibility of the state and local sector for addressing human needs, have, in large measure, redirected advocates to city halls and county courthouses.

These same developments have prompted local governments to accelerate lateral relationships with other local governmental units and with nonpublic provider agencies. The devolution of programs and problems has led local governments to deal with local foundations, businesses and unions, public and private service agencies, and other governmental agencies operating locally. These developments have carried local governments beyond a residual service delivery role and have given them an opportunity to forge new partnerships with other local actors.

The New Challenges. With local governments again involved in human services, all levels of government have expanded roles. The human services establishment now cuts across numerous problem areas, levels of government, public and private sectors, and segments of the population. However, recent events—particularly political changes and economic difficulties—have raised serious questions about the shape and size of the human services effort.

A fundamental problem is the overall reduction of financial support for domestic social programs. The size and effects of these cuts have been documented elsewhere.[6] Meanwhile, demands for services for certain special populations (such as the elderly, children and youth, and the handicapped) and emergency services for the general population, continue to increase. Managers have had to maintain policy goals and ensure program survival while dealing with fiscal stress and fewer resources to meet basic objectives.

A second challenge is the transfer of responsibility from the federal to the state and local levels. A number of recent initiatives, such as block grants and more flexible categorical grants-in-aid, shifted financial responsibility and put even more of the leadership onus on local governments to anticipate and solve problems, as well as to plan and manage the "system" for local purposes.

Deregulation poses a third challenge. As a result of state and local concerns over the stringency of federal program and funding regulations, and a corresponding inability to design and use programs to meet local needs, the administrative burden associated with grants-in-aid is being reduced. The challenge to local governments is to take advantage of this developing flexibility and use the expanded residual authority, or "policy space," to plan and operate programs to serve the local community.

A fourth and final challenge appears to be the increased recognition by the public sector that it must operate *interdependently* with the private sector. Public growth in the past few decades has masked the significant achievements of private sector efforts—private funding, service agencies, voluntary efforts—in human services. Now that resources are more scarce, public managers must learn how to work with private sector agents to meet the challenges of the future.

Clearly, these issues indicate that the coming years will be both challenging and difficult for those who are responsible for authorizing, funding, and managing human service programs at the local level. The degree to which local managers are equipped to meet these challenges may, in fact, prove to be the real "acid test" of the federalism evolving under current national policy directives.

CONCERNS OF THE LOCAL GOVERNMENT MANAGER

Why should the local government manager be concerned about the development and operation of human services programs? Many local governments do not consider human services to be a core function like public works and public safety. Moreover, major human services functions in income maintenance, health, education, and housing are primarily the responsibility of other governmental jurisdictions. Nevertheless, the preservation and rehabilitation of human resources comprise basic functions of any government. In this regard, an effective local government needs to possess a number of bottom line assets: a viable economic base; a sound physical infrastructure, e.g., roads and transportation; a social and cultural environment that assures a good quality of life; and a vital work force and general population that can meet its needs in the community. The latter dimension is the managerial concern that is most related to human services, for without substantial investments in the development and renewal of people, the community lacks a part of its vitality. Just as a declining economic base will diminish occupational opportunity, an insufficient human development base (i.e., a social infrastructure comprising educational, cultural, and other human services elements), will serve to diminish the *human* stock of a community. For these reasons, human service programs should concern local managers. Indeed, because they help develop or renew the human capital of a community and, consequently, influence other aspects of the so-called "quality of life" within diverse community contexts, the "human services" of local government may be the most reliable measure of community well-being.

The populations of many cities and urban counties are becoming older and poorer. A disproportionate number of citizens with problems live in the central cities, particularly in the Northeast and Midwest. The manager of a community in decline is faced with a large disadvantaged population which must be included in the "renewal" effort. While many programs geared to the disadvantaged are run under federal and state auspices, human problems are individual and local. As a result, interest groups and advocates often bring their influence to bear on local legislators and executives, even though the problems are addressed by the services of another jurisdiction. This *local effect* of human problems has been seen most recently in plant closings and relocations caused by reduced employment in industry, in turn a result of the economic recession. The local communities have been the first line of defense in meeting emergencies and renewing resources. Moreover, because the human services picture is so fragmented, local GPG managers have had to interact with other governmental units and delivery agents to meet these needs, often playing key human services roles, in addition to other urban service responsibilities.

The complexity of human services and the fact that they are not considered a core service make them a difficult area for many managers to understand. Most managers are best acquainted with direct-line, operational functions: fire, police, roads, sanitation, recreation, and so on. In human services, the manager's role is often quite different and indirect, typically involving networking, advocacy, leveraging, and cooperative ventures. Complex human needs are often met most effectively by the creative ability of the manager to involve *other* actors in the community.

Finally, funding reductions and increased client demand have put the management of human services in bold relief. Several human services have moved from a period of growth to a period of management, in which the wise use of scarce resources is essential for survival. Details of both design and operations that make programs successful in achieving their aims are therefore valued very highly. This suggests further that local government managers have much to exchange with those who specialize in human services, and that local managers must put program effectiveness at the heart of their concerns. Expressed in such terms, the management of human services is not much different from other dimensions of contemporary public administration practice.

RESEARCH EFFORTS

Despite the increased importance and significance of city and county roles in human services, there is no comprehensive source of information on the types of human services offered by local governments, or on their planning and management roles either for their own governments or in conjunction with other jurisdictions and funding sources. In the late 1960s, ICMA's Management Information Service undertook the first attempt to describe local government roles, as new federal programs impacting cities were beginning.[7] In 1975, the National Association of Counties and ICMA jointly conducted a survey of county human services. This study concluded that the wide range of programs sponsored or operated by counties was, in fact, largely funded by federal and state sources, user fees, and private funding.[8]

As noted earlier, a 1977 survey conducted by the U.S. Conference of Mayors found cities operating multifaceted human services programs, involving both direct service delivery as well as community-based organizations' approaches. Since the time of these surveys, the area of human services has undergone great changes, and a number of publications have appeared on general human services policy[9] and management.[10] However, there have been no recent systematic attempts to gather comparative data on the role(s) of local governments in human services on a national scale. Given the number of changes which have occurred in the intergovernmental arena over the past few years, especially in regards to the administration of domestic social policy, the 1984 ICMA study could not be more timely.

Purpose. In the spring of 1984, ICMA surveyed cities and counties to determine which of a broad range of human services were being provided, either directly or indirectly, by local governments. While *human services* encompasses an extensive and almost endless list of service possibilities, the ICMA study focuses on those services in which previous surveys of this type suggest cities and counties were most likely to be involved, as well as on those services that are not primarily driven by *other* jurisdictions (e.g., welfare, education, medical, and housing services). Thus, the survey examined elderly, children and youth, handicapped, and a range of general population counseling, access, advocacy, and emergency services. It was designed to explore types and levels of service in these areas, including expenditures, means of service provision, and numbers of residents receiving services.

Another purpose of the survey was to determine the types and extensiveness of city and county planning and management of human services. Given the emergent opportunities for leadership identified earlier, it was thought important to examine the diversity of local government operations, financial bases, planning functions, and executive positions. In other words, "What does the human service function look like within the structural context of local government operations?"

An additional goal of the survey was to examine the degree to which local GPGs work with other governmental and nongovernmental entities to meet human needs at the community level. Since human services are spread across the local landscape, it is important to determine the extent and type of joint ventures that combine the efforts of local governments with other entities in the planning, management, and delivery of services. Also, various types of arrangements for the provision of services, such as grants, contracts, and in-kind contributions, were examined.

Finally, the survey attempted to gauge, in admittedly only broad terms, the effect of reduced funding and devolution of functional responsibilities within the human services sector, by comparing perceived changes in programs and numbers of clients served at the local government level over a three-year time period. This included the last fiscal year before major shifts in national human services policy occurred.

Methodology. To address these issues, a survey instrument was developed by the authors and ICMA, in consultation with representatives of federal agencies dealing with human services and other groups representing local government, such as the National Association of Counties and the U.S. Conference of Mayors. After pretesting and revision, the questionnaire was mailed in February 1984 to the chief administrative officers of 2,600 municipalities with populations 10,000 and over, and 775 counties with populations 50,000 and over; follow-up mailings were sent out in April 1984.

Of the total number of survey instruments mailed, 761 usable city and 112 county questionnaires were returned, for response rates of 29.3% and 14.5%, respectively. Table 4/1 arrays selected characteristics of those cities and counties responding as well as all those jurisdictions which received the survey instrument.

While the pool of city respondents is generally representative across population groups, geographic regions and divisions, and metropolitan status, the council–manager form of government is over-represented, making up 67.7% of the sample. The county sample is somewhat less representative overall, but still contains sufficient numbers of counties representing various population and regional categories. The county sample is over-represented by metropolitan counties and by those with an administrator. While the response rate for cities and particularly counties is smaller than similar ICMA surveys, it is by no means disappointing. Because human services is not a direct operational function of every local GPG, some managers receiving the questionnaire may have been uncertain as to its appropriateness. Moreover, in some localities there is no staff person specifically responsible for human services who can uncover the detailed information required by the survey. The survey also proved to be a very difficult and involved instrument to complete. For example, respondents were asked to select among six different options or modes for delivering services, and, in some cases, to provide specific figures on dollars spent for services, numbers of employees, as well as numbers of clients served for some 32 different service groupings. Complex survey instruments like these often have lower response rates. As a result, the lower response rate for this survey is understandable. Nevertheless, the data base of 112 urban counties and 761 cities is a substantial number, keeping in mind that comparable data bases do not exist.

PATTERNS OF LOCAL GOVERNMENT SERVICE DELIVERY

The first portion of the survey concerns the ways in which cities and counties provide various human services within their jurisdictions. Four classes of program recipients were identified as targets for investigation: elderly, children and youth, the handicapped, and the general population. Respondents were asked to report all programs in which the jurisdiction had some involvement.

A summary of the results is presented in Table 4/2, which reports the frequencies of city and county government involvement in the services assessed by "mode" of involvement. Basically, this table presents a picture of: 1) whether or not a local government is involved in a particular type of service; and, 2) if it is involved, what is the means of involvement. Table 4/2 arrays the four general types of services noted above by 32 different service possibilities (ranging from 3 distinct services for the handicapped to 12 for the general population). The modes of service delivery include six possible types: 1) direct service delivery, using city/county facilities and employees; 2) joint service operation with another government; 3) contracting with another government to deliver the services; 4) contracting with a nongovernmental group to deliver the services; 5) providing some financial support to a nongovernmental group that delivers the service; and, 6) providing some in-kind support (e.g., staff assistance, facilities, materials) to a nongovernmental group that delivers the service. A jurisdiction could report involvement through more than one mode of service delivery, as appropriate. Therefore, the last column in the table presents an *unduplicated* count of the number of jurisdictions reporting *at least one type* of involvement within each service category. This figure provides a more parsimonious measure of city and county government involvement in the various human services listed.

The results demonstrate numerous and interesting patterns of local government involvement in human services. The most striking finding is that if one measures "involvement" strictly by direct service operation, substantial levels of city and county participation in human services are overlooked. In this regard, the variety of service delivery options or modes reveals a substantial role beyond direct operation. Most significant of these indirect operational roles are those involving public–private interaction, either through financial or in-kind support or contracting. Together, these three show the extensive involvement of local governments (particularly counties) in human services. The most dramatic evidence of this pattern is revealed when one compares the direct service roles with the unduplicated count of governments involved in human service delivery. For example, only 10.5% of cities operate nutrition centers for the elderly, whereas nearly half (48.9%) have some level of involvement. Likewise, 13.4% of counties are directly involved in food distribution to the general population, whereas 39.3% report some type of involvement. The same pattern is seen through all the services examined.

It is not surprising that local jurisdictions are most likely to engage in extensions of their "traditional" public services. Cities, for example, have always had a considerable role in recreation and transportation programs, and these seem to have been extended to special populations, such as the elderly, children and youth, and the handicapped. Similarly, counties have traditionally been the local providers of child welfare and some emergency services. The higher levels of involvement reported here suggest an extension of these county functions into new services for these specific populations. In addition, emergent services for the general population related to employment and training, mental health, and substance abuse are all relatively significant. These services reflect increasing county-level responsibilities mandated through the enactment of new state service acts of the past two decades.

City Roles. An intensive look at city roles reconfirms that these jurisdictions are most active in extensions of their more traditional services of recreation and transportation to the special populations. Involvement in programs for the general population is most prevalent in the area of emergency services, including counseling (29.8% for substance abuse and 25.2% for personal and family counseling), food distribution (32.5%), advocacy and referral (23.8%), emergency financial aid (19.7%), and crisis shelters (19.4%). The survey data confirm that direct service operation is not cities' predominant mode of delivery. With the exception of the various types of recreation programs, about half of the elderly programs, and a few other programs, the typical city is more likely to become involved in most services by cooperating or collaborating with other governments or with private agencies. For 20 of the 32 services ex-

Table 4/1 SURVEY RESPONSE

	Cities surveyed		Cities responding			Counties surveyed		Counties responding		
Classification	No. (A)	% of sample	No.	% of sample	% of (A)	No. (A)	% of sample	No.	% of sample	% of (A)
Total, all cities/counties	2,600	100.0	761	100.0	29.3	775	100.0	112	100.0	14.5
Population group										
Over 1,000,000	6	0.2	1	0.1	16.7	22	2.8	4	3.6	18.2
500,000-1,000,000	17	0.6	4	0.5	23.5	56	7.2	9	8.0	16.1
250,000- 499,999	34	1.3	7	0.9	20.6	94	12.1	13	11.6	13.8
100,000- 249,999	113	4.3	47	6.2	41.6	228	29.4	50	44.6	21.9
50,000- 99,999	278	10.7	99	13.0	35.6	375	48.4	36	32.1	9.6
25,000- 49,999	614	23.6	191	25.1	31.1	...	...	...	...	...
10,000- 24,999	1,538	59.1	412	54.1	26.8	...	...	...	...	...
Geographic region										
Northeast	753	29.0	154	20.2	20.5	135	17.4	18	16.1	13.3
North Central	749	28.8	235	30.9	31.4	206	26.6	21	18.8	10.2
South	655	25.2	180	23.7	27.5	316	40.8	51	45.5	16.1
West	443	17.0	192	25.2	43.3	118	15.2	22	19.6	18.6
Geographic division										
New England	310	11.9	58	7.6	18.7	28	3.6	4	3.6	14.3
Mid-Atlantic	443	17.0	96	12.6	21.7	107	13.8	14	12.5	13.1
East North Central	540	20.8	150	19.7	27.8	154	19.9	14	12.5	9.1
West North Central	209	8.0	85	11.2	40.7	52	6.7	7	6.3	13.5
South Atlantic	273	10.5	96	12.6	35.2	170	21.9	29	25.9	17.1
East South Central	135	5.2	23	3.0	17.0	63	8.1	10	8.9	15.9
West South Central	247	9.5	61	8.0	24.7	83	10.7	12	10.7	14.5
Mountain	112	4.3	48	6.3	42.9	46	5.9	10	8.9	21.7
Pacific Coast	331	12.7	144	18.9	43.5	72	9.3	12	10.7	16.7
Metro status										
Central	432	16.6	146	19.2	33.8	...	...	...	...	...
Suburban	1,582	60.8	462	60.7	29.2	...	...	...	...	...
Independent	586	22.5	153	20.1	26.1	...	...	...	...	...
Metro	...	...	...	...	...	536	69.2	85	75.9	15.9
Nonmetro	...	...	...	...	...	239	30.8	27	24.1	11.3
Form of government										
Mayor–council	1,103	42.4	207	27.2	18.8	...	...	...	...	...
Council–manager	1,251	48.1	515	67.7	41.2	...	...	...	...	...
Commission	101	3.9	15	2.0	14.9	...	...	...	...	...
Town meeting	100	3.8	15	2.0	15.0	...	...	...	...	...
Rep. town meeting	45	1.7	9	1.2	20.0	...	...	...	...	...
Without administrator	...	...	...	...	...	408	52.6	39	34.8	9.6
With administrator	...	...	...	...	...	367	47.4	73	65.2	19.9

amined, less than 10% of the cities were involved in direct operation of the service, if involved at all. Again, most local governments relied on some form of public–private interaction, with financial and in-kind support by GPGs showing the greatest frequency of use.

These public–private interaction patterns carry through to the service categories in which cities appear to be most directly involved (particularly those dealing with the elderly) and, to a lesser but notable extent, to those services directed towards the general population. Thus, the variety of involvement reveals a level of involvement beyond that which first "meets the eye" when one examines the direct operations role alone.

Overall, the city role is a mixed one, including extensive involvement in areas other than traditional recreation services, extending to a number of different populations and interests, through a variety of patterns, including direct operation of services, as well as various cooperative schemes with other governments and with the private sector.

The survey data also show a considerable variation in the amount of money spent, numbers of full-time employees involved, and numbers of residents receiving human services from cities. (No table shown.) To highlight this variation, high and low ranges for these particular items will be illustrated. The widest ranges among *direct* service expenditures were found for food-related and emergency services. For example, expenditures for elderly nutrition centers ranged from $1,000 to $26 million, those for child nutrition from $7,000 to $1.3 million, and those for emergency food distribution from $1,000 to $1.4 million. Special transportation services for the elderly showed the widest expenditure range among *joint operations* between governments, from $1,000 to $60 million. Generally, smaller dollar ranges were reported for services contracted with private organizations and for contributions to private agencies. Illustrating the range of expenditures under service *contracts* were the following service areas: legal advice and services ($2,000 to $198,000); job training services for the handicapped ($5,000 to $427,000); and child day care centers ($3,000 to $4.2 million). With few exceptions, financial support to nongovernmental groups fell into smaller ranges. For example, financial support for elderly day care services ranged from $1,000 to $97,000, for children and youth foster homes from $2,000 to $50,000, and for emergency housing services from $9,000 to $99,000.

The number of full-time employees involved in the planning, management, or delivery of these human services programs also varied widely. (No table shown.) While 105 cities reported that they had only one staff person assigned to recreational services for the elderly, one city reported 124 employees assigned to such tasks. More typically, between 1 and 50 employees were reported for practically all other human services programs.

Variation in the number of clients served was also considerable. An examination of a mix of services revealed that some cities served 10 people while others served over 100,000. For example, the client range for "meals on wheels" was 10 to 191,625, for personal and family counseling services from 8 to 100,000, and clients for food distribution services ranged between 30 and 200,000. These ranges further demonstrate the considerable diversity among cities' human services roles.

County Roles. County government roles in human services demonstrate similar patterns, although the direct service role is notably greater in several service areas. These urban counties

Table 4/2 SERVICE DELIVERY MODES, BY TYPE OF SERVICE

	Service delivery modes used by cities[1]							Service delivery modes used by counties[2]						
Type of service	Direct service (%)	Joint service (%)	Contract with another government (%)	Contract with non-government (%)	Financial support (%)	In-kind support (%)	Unduplicated count (%)	Direct service (%)	Joint service (%)	Contract with another government (%)	Contract with non-government (%)	Financial support (%)	In-kind support (%)	Unduplicated count (%)
Elderly														
Nutrition centers	10.5	8.4	3.7	4.1	13.3	23.7	48.9	18.8	8.0	4.5	18.8	18.8	17.0	62.5
"Meals on wheels"	6.0	3.2	3.2	4.3	11.0	17.1	35.6	13.4	2.7	2.7	17.0	18.8	18.8	54.5
Homemaker services	4.1	1.6	2.0	3.7	5.9	5.5	17.9	32.1	10.7	1.8	17.0	15.2	8.0	63.4
Day care/respite care	3.0	0.9	0.5	3.4	4.5	5.7	14.1	9.8	4.5	0.9	8.0	9.8	5.4	27.7
Special transportation	21.4	7.5	3.4	11.3	10.4	12.1	51.8	32.1	8.0	5.4	19.6	17.9	10.7	70.5
Recreation programs	48.1	5.8	0.8	3.5	7.9	14.7	63.6	24.1	8.0	0.0	9.8	11.6	10.7	46.4
Job placement	5.8	1.2	1.2	1.7	2.5	6.4	14.8	17.0	3.6	2.7	9.8	3.6	9.8	35.7
Volunteer opportunities	17.9	4.1	1.7	3.5	5.3	14.1	35.1	22.3	6.3	0.9	5.4	11.6	12.5	48.2
Counseling	14.5	2.9	0.8	5.3	6.4	10.6	31.5	25.9	8.9	0.9	8.9	8.9	12.5	48.2
Children and youth														
Day care centers	6.7	1.7	0.7	5.1	8.3	6.8	23.0	12.5	7.1	0.0	8.9	13.4	4.5	47.3
Counseling	12.0	3.3	0.9	7.9	6.8	6.4	28.5	29.5	10.7	3.6	22.3	8.9	8.0	48.2
Job placement	7.9	1.4	1.3	2.5	2.1	5.0	16.4	9.8	4.5	3.6	14.3	2.7	5.4	24.1
Nutrition	3.2	0.8	0.8	0.7	1.6	2.1	7.0	11.6	0.9	2.7	6.3	2.7	6.3	19.6
Adoption services	1.3	0.0	0.1	0.1	0.1	0.5	2.0	30.4	3.6	0.0	1.8	0.9	4.5	35.7
Foster homes	1.4	0.5	0.0	1.2	0.9	1.3	4.2	33.0	6.3	3.6	3.6	4.5	6.3	44.6
Protective services/shelter	3.0	1.3	0.4	2.9	5.1	2.8	13.9	37.5	8.0	1.8	15.2	12.5	8.0	60.7
Youth recreation	56.9	4.5	0.9	6.0	7.6	12.7	67.0	19.6	4.5	3.6	14.3	5.4	8.9	35.7
Handicapped														
Special transportation	13.1	2.6	1.7	7.6	4.5	6.0	28.0	16.1	3.6	0.9	11.6	5.4	7.1	37.5
Job training	1.8	1.1	0.7	2.5	5.1	2.6	11.3	6.3	8.0	2.7	12.5	11.6	6.3	38.4
Recreation programs	26.5	2.5	0.4	2.8	4.6	6.8	35.1	8.0	1.8	0.0	8.9	5.4	2.7	22.3
General population														
Personal and family counseling	9.5	1.2	0.9	5.9	7.8	6.2	25.2	30.4	9.8	1.8	12.5	13.4	6.3	58.0
Career counseling	3.5	0.8	0.9	1.6	1.2	3.2	8.7	9.8	2.7	2.7	3.6	2.7	0.9	21.4
Job training	5.0	1.4	1.2	3.5	1.3	4.5	12.4	18.8	6.3	7.1	5.4	0.9	5.4	37.5
Job placement	5.3	1.4	1.1	2.6	1.8	4.2	12.4	20.5	4.5	4.5	6.3	0.9	7.1	35.7
Consumer protection	4.5	0.3	0.1	0.4	0.9	3.2	8.4	8.9	0.0	0.0	0.0	0.9	2.7	12.5
Alcohol/drug abuse counseling	7.8	1.6	1.4	6.0	11.3	8.4	29.8	21.4	11.6	1.8	22.3	7.9	9.8	59.8
Advocacy and referral	13.5	1.6	0.4	4.3	4.5	6.0	23.8	28.6	3.6	0.9	9.8	6.3	7.1	44.6
Legal advice and services	2.5	0.9	0.9	2.9	2.8	5.3	12.6	5.4	3.6	0.9	7.1	8.0	4.5	27.7
Emergency financial aid	12.1	1.7	0.5	1.4	3.3	5.3	19.7	30.4	6.3	2.7	6.3	8.0	5.4	50.0
Emergency housing	5.5	1.3	0.5	3.0	4.6	4.7	15.5	11.6	3.6	1.8	8.0	6.3	9.8	34.8
Crisis shelters	1.7	0.9	0.4	4.1	9.3	5.0	19.4	5.4	3.6	0.9	12.5	13.4	9.8	40.2
Food distribution	11.3	2.6	1.3	2.9	5.5	16.6	32.5	13.4	4.5	1.8	9.8	1.8	17.0	39.3

[1] Percentages are based on 761 cities responding.
[2] Percentages are based on 112 counties responding.

are often the primary operators of state-organized human services programs in their respective areas. As with cities, in many service areas a more mixed pattern of delivery modes did emerge and anywhere from one-fourth to one-third of the counties responding indicated that they were involved in some form of direct service operation.

The survey data also reveal that extensive public-private cooperation exists across all service categories. In this regard, counties have a widespread role in services for the elderly as well as those for children and youth, particularly in local implementation of state child welfare and youth delinquency statutes. At the same time, counties are less involved in services for the handicapped. Counties do provide, or otherwise are involved in, a variety of general population services. One cluster of this type, which includes counseling, alcohol/drug abuse, and advocacy services, again reflects the state service role mentioned previously. Another cluster, comprising the last four emergency services listed in Table 4/2, no doubt reflects the urban nature of these counties. The unduplicated count of county involvement generally reinforces these patterns, implying that from one-half to two-thirds of most counties are involved in some type of elderly services, that between one-third and one-half are engaged in some form of child welfare services, and that from one-third to one-half of the respondent counties take part in various counseling and emergency services.

In terms of modes of service delivery, county government appears slightly more likely than city government to engage in *joint operations* with another government, particularly for those services in which counties are most active. With few exceptions, however, county jurisdictions appear less likely to *contract* with other governments. Special transportation for the elderly and job training services surfaced as areas that did not seem to fit the overall pattern. On the other hand, purchase-of-service contracting with nongovernmental groups proved to be more prevalent among counties than among cities. Indeed, this form of public–private service venture ranked next to direct operation as an important means of county human services involvement. In this regard, private contracting was reported as the most prevalent means of service delivery in counseling for children and youth, job training for the handicapped, and alcohol and drug counseling. Moreover, it ran a close second in a number of other service areas. County provision of financial and in-kind support follows the same general pattern, with support for elderly programs being most prevalent, followed by general population, and children and youth services. Overall, these patterns again reveal an extensive urban orientation with respect to the county role in human services, both in traditional and newer services, particularly when the several service modes are examined in closer detail. The variety of options (other than directly providing a service) that are available to urban counties suggests that the more "traditional" role of local involvement in human services is returning at the county level. These roles include purchase-of-service contracting and support for private sector service delivery agencies.

Multiple county roles appear to be complemented by the range of dollars spent for services, number of employees working in programs, and number of clients served. In terms of their direct service operations, county expenditures ranged from lows generally under $10,000 to around $10 million annually. (No table shown.) For example, expenditures for nutrition programs for children and youth ranged from $9,000 to $6.8 million, protective services/shelter from $6,000 to $12.9 million, and foster homes from $10,000 to $5.9 million. One county reported spending over $19 million on shelters for abused spouses. The broadest ranges associated with county joint service operations were for emergency housing ($1,000 to $5 million) and financial assistance ($2,000 to $13 million), no doubt reflecting cooperation with housing authorities and township relief. The greatest ranges for contracting with other governments also occurred in these two areas, with emergency financial assistance expenditures ranging from $12,000 to $22.2 million.

Contracting with nongovernmental groups demonstrated the greatest levels of variation, ranging from low figures of $1,000 to $20,000 to estimates upwards of $65 million. For example, expenditures for general population personal and family counseling service ranged from $4,000 to $64.2 million according to the survey returns. More typical of this particular service mode were the ranges for elderly recreation programs ($5,000 to $276,000) and for general population advocacy and referral services ($10,000 to $212,000). This pattern proved to be consistent for county financial contributions to private sector agencies, although very few contributions exceeded $1 million.

The greatest number of county employees worked either in day care (actual numbers reported ranged from 1 to 206) or in traditional county child welfare services, such as foster homes (from 1 to 124) and protective services (from 1 to 341). Youth recreation and personal and family counseling services employed from 1 to 100 people.

The number of clients served ranged from 20 or less (fourteen counties so reported) to over 100,000 persons (as reported by seven counties). In this regard, the survey data indicate that in terms of numbers of people served, special transportation services for the elderly ranged from 20 to 200,000, and handicapped transportation services ranged from 15 to 250,000. Other ranges were more narrow: for career counseling (35 to 6,000), job training (32 to 2,866), and homemaker services for the elderly (17 to 11,500). Again, these ranges highlight the considerable variation of county government involvement in all aspects of human services programs. Indeed, the human services role of county government, like that of its city counterpart, varies widely by jurisdiction and service function, a characteristic easily misunderstood if not entirely overlooked.

LEVELS OF SERVICE INVOLVEMENT

The discussion up to this point has focused on city and county roles in providing specific types of human services. It has provided a profile of local government human services using single indicators of service involvement and mode of delivery. Intuitively, the next question to be asked should deal with a corollary concern—*to what extent* do cities and counties become involved in providing human services for populations-in-need?

In order to shed some light on this issue (even if only in a preliminary way), the authors computed a crude index of service "involvement" based on the number of service categories (or types) available within each target population cluster. For example, nine different services for the elderly were identified as part of the survey design. Respondents' levels of involvement in elderly services were gauged simply by totalling the services in each type in which the city or county reported involvement. This admittedly crude technique was employed across all six modes of service delivery for each of the four target populations, resulting in 24 different measures of service involvement for both city and county jurisdictions.

Table 4/3 shows the patterns that emerged from this data reduction technique arrayed by the number of service categories in which the respondents indicated that their jurisdictions were involved.

The pattern is not an unexpected one, given the report of the summary data presented earlier. The largest percentage of jurisdictions, of course, were not involved in the provision of any elderly service, irrespective of mode of delivery. Moreover, a substantial proportion were involved in only one or two services, smaller numbers reported involvement in three to six service categories, and extremely small numbers of cities or counties were involved in more than six services for the elderly. This pattern of variation generally held true for jurisdictions across all six service delivery modes. As Table 4/3 indicates, next to *direct service operation*, which shows the largest percentage of jurisdictions involved in one or two service categories, high levels of involvement are also evident in purchase-of-service contracting with nongovernmental groups (15.2% for counties, 11.2% for cities) as well as in the provision of financial (17% for counties, 12.7% for cities) and in-kind support (8.9% for counties, 15.5% for cities) to such groups. This pattern was particularly notable for up to three different categories of elderly services in which a jurisdiction reported being involved, although the data suggest that counties were able to sustain this pattern at somewhat higher levels for each of these service delivery modes.

Similar patterns were found when the same measures were applied to the other target groups, namely, services to children and youth, the handicapped, and the general population. (No table shown.) The survey data suggest that when a city or county becomes involved in a particular mode of service delivery, it generally does so

Table 4/3 CITY AND COUNTY USES OF SERVICE DELIVERY OPTIONS, BY NUMBER OF ELDERLY SERVICES PROVIDED

Number of services	Direct service (%)[1]	Joint service (%)[1]	Contract with another government (%)[1]	Contract with non-government (%)[1]	Financial support (%)[1]	In-kind support (%)[1]
	Service delivery option					
City						
None	42.8	80.6	91.1	80.4	71.4	59.8
One	25.2	12.4	4.7	11.2	12.7	15.5
Two	13.4	2.8	2.4	3.8	6.8	8.4
Three	7.1	1.8	0.9	0.8	3.7	5.9
Four	5.3	1.1	0.3	1.7	1.7	2.4
Five	2.8	0.9	0.4	1.1	1.6	2.5
Six	1.6	0.4	0.1	0.4	1.1	2.5
Seven	1.3	0.1	0.0	0.3	0.3	1.8
Eight	0.3	0.0	0.0	0.1	0.3	0.7
Nine	0.3	0.0	0.1	0.3	0.5	0.5
County						
None	43.8	78.6	86.6	62.5	55.4	67.0
One	14.3	8.0	9.8	15.2	17.0	8.9
Two	11.6	3.6	1.8	4.5	11.6	6.3
Three	6.3	3.6	0.9	5.4	6.3	9.8
Four	7.1	1.8	0.9	2.7	1.8	0.9
Five	7.1	0.9	0.0	1.8	2.7	1.8
Six	1.8	1.8	0.0	4.5	1.8	0.0
Seven	2.7	1.8	0.0	1.8	2.7	1.8
Eight	2.7	0.0	0.0	0.9	0.9	2.7
Nine	2.7	0.0	0.0	0.9	0.0	0.9

[1] Based on 761 cities and 112 counties responding.

Table 4/4 CITY AND COUNTY DIRECT SERVICES FOR THE ELDERLY, BY POPULATION

Classification	None No.	None (%)[1]	Low No.	Low (%)[1]	Medium No.	Medium (%)[1]	High No.	High (%)[1]
	Level of involvement							
Total, all cities	326	42.8	348	45.7	73	9.6	14	1.8
Population group								
Over 1,000,000	0	0.0	0	0.0	0	0.0	1	100.0
500,000–1,000,000	1	25.0	1	25.0	2	50.0	0	0.0
250,000– 499,999	2	28.6	3	42.9	2	28.6	0	0.0
100,000– 249,999	13	27.7	23	48.9	9	19.1	2	4.3
50,000– 99,999	21	21.2	61	61.6	14	14.1	3	3.0
25,000– 49,999	66	34.6	105	55.0	18	9.4	2	1.0
10,000– 24,999	223	54.1	155	37.6	28	6.8	6	1.5
Total, all counties	41	36.6	36	32.1	25	22.3	10	8.9
Population group								
Over 1,000,000	0	0.0	2	50.0	1	25.0	1	25.0
500,000–1,000,000	0	0.0	3	33.3	4	44.4	2	22.2
250,000– 499,999	1	7.7	3	23.1	7	53.8	2	15.4
100,000– 249,999	23	46.0	15	30.0	8	16.0	4	8.0
50,000– 99,999	17	47.2	13	36.1	5	13.9	1	2.8

[1] Based on 761 cities and 112 counties responding.

in a limited fashion. More often than not, local government jurisdictions will become involved in a relatively small number of service categories, usually not more than three.

CONTEXT OF LOCAL GOVERNMENT INVOLVEMENT IN HUMAN SERVICES

What factors account for the variation among jurisdictions, both in terms of levels of involvement in service provision and in terms of choice of options for delivering such services. Patterns of variation in the two dimensions of human services delivery under study (i.e., *what* and *how* services were being provided by local GPGs) were examined more closely within the context of selected characteristics of the respondent communities. For this purpose, the authors used the following items from the standard set of jurisdictional characteristics maintained by ICMA: population group; geographic region; metropolitan status; and form of government.

Since the total number of possible associations among the variables under investigation was too large to manipulate in "raw" form, and therefore too unwieldy to analyze and report, the authors grouped the services in four categories based on the four target population groups as described in the previous section. Cities and counties were assigned level of service involvement "scores" based on the number of services in which they were involved for each of the four categories and each of the six service delivery modes. Since there were different numbers of services within each target population category, arbitrary scores of *low*, *medium*, and *high* involvement were established, along with *no* involvement, for each service category. Based on the distribution of *direct service* involvement by both kinds of jurisdictions for each target population, similar to that shown in Table 4/3, the following coding scheme was adopted: *elderly* low = 1–3, medium = 4–6, high = 7–9; *children and youth*, low = 1, medium = 2–3, high = 4 or more; *handicapped*, low = 1, medium = 2, high = 3; and *general population*, low = 1–2, medium = 3–5, high = 6–9. Using services for the elderly as an example, a "low" level of involvement would indicate that one, two, or three of the nine services listed in Table 4/2 (e.g., nutrition centers, meals on wheels, etc.) were provided. Similarly, jurisdictions classified as being in the "medium" category of the general population services sector would be those that reported involvement in from three to five of the services listed for this group in Table 4/2 (e.g., personal and family counseling, career counseling, and so forth).

These levels of service involvement were crosstabulated with the four jurisdictional characteristics mentioned earlier for each of the six service delivery options. Even after the data reduction just described, the number of possible relationships between the variables used in this study was still substantial, and far exceeded what could be reasonably reported in this article. As a result, only selected crosstabulations are provided, to demonstrate what appear to be the most interesting and significant (in both the statistical and the practical sense) relationships between the items under investigation.

Population Differences. Table 4/4 displays data for both cities and counties on levels of involvement in direct services for the elderly, arrayed by population groups. For cities, although some cells contain small numbers or none at all, it is apparent that a significant relationship exists between population size and services to the elderly. Although the numbers are small at the very highest levels of involvement, what effort there is (low and medium) appears to be concentrated in larger cities.

A similar pattern emerges when the level of direct services for the elderly is compared across population groups for counties (Table 4/4). Once again, although some of the cells contain small numbers, the relationship is clear: counties with larger populations, particularly those over 250,000, seem to engage directly in a greater number of services for their elderly citizens. Furthermore, according to these survey data, the direct service delivery role vis-à-vis this specific target group is strikingly similar among both large city and county jurisdictions.

A similar pattern was discerned in purchase-of-service contracting with nongovernmental groups for the provision of elderly services. Table 4/5 displays data on county involvement by population size. While there are some empty cells, larger counties seem to do more contracting, with the exception of the very largest counties perhaps, where a more mixed pattern developed. In general, the survey data tend to confirm the population pattern revealed earlier, wherein levels of service involvement are positively associated with population size for both cities and counties.

Regional Effects. Regionally, the most noticeable findings were that local jurisdictions in the Northeast seemed to be more disposed to deliver services directly while those in the western part of the country tended to rely more heavily on purchase-of-service contracting with nongovernmental groups. Although a number of data crosstabulations supported the existence of these associations, many, including all county analyses, were not statistically significant. However, two relationships at the city level which—with contracting of services for children and youth, and with direct delivery of general population services—proved to be statistically meaningful. The data for these two areas are displayed in Tables 4/6 and 4/7, respectively. To the extent that regional differences can be detected, the data suggest that the spectrum of general population services delivered directly is widest among cities in the Northeast and most limited among those in the West. By the same token, the data in Table 4/6 reveal that, in relative terms, contracting for children and youth services occurs on a broader scale among cities in the West than in other parts of the country.

Metropolitan Status. Another way of examining, and perhaps even explaining, differences between jurisdictions is to look at their metropolitan standing. Metropolitan status for cities is defined in terms of whether (a) it is the "central" entity within a standard metropolitan area, (b) it is classified as a "suburban" city within the metropolitan area, or (c) it is an "independent" jurisdiction beyond the bounds of any given metropolitan area.

The most consistent relationship found was that, for almost all types of service involvement by cities, higher levels occurred among those classified as central cities within metropolitan areas. Moreover, intermediate levels of involvement were generally found among independent cities, and, the lowest levels were most often found among suburban jurisdictions according to this scheme. Tables 4/8 and 4/9 provide two illustrations of this phenomenon. In these two cases, one involving financial support to nongovernmental groups for children and youth services and the other dealing with contracting with such groups for general population services, central cities, and then independent cities, reported greater service involvement. This finding is not surprising given the greater concentrations of disadvantaged persons in cities as opposed to suburbs. These concentrations of people-in-need are no doubt reflected in the higher levels of involvement found in this survey.

Form of Government. Finally, the authors examined delivery patterns by cities and counties according to their form of government, another standard descriptor for jurisdictions within ICMA's data base. Here, cities were classified into five distinct groups for purposes of analysis: mayor–council, council–manager, commission, town meeting, and representative town meeting. Similarly, county governments were divided into two groups: with an appointed administrator and without an administrator.

Overall, the most consistent pattern pointed towards greater involvement in human services among jurisdictions with professional managers or administrators. This finding pertained to both cities and counties, and held true for all four target population groups and all six modes of

Table 4/5 COUNTY CONTRACTING WITH NONGOVERNMENTAL GROUPS FOR ELDERLY SERVICES, BY POPULATION

	Level of contracting for elderly services							
	None		Low		Medium		High	
Classification	No.	(%)[1]	No.	(%)[1]	No.	(%)[1]	No.	(%)[1]
Total, all counties	73	65.2	22	19.6	11	9.8	6	5.4
Population group								
Over 1,000,000	2	50.0	0	0.0	2	50.0	0	0.0
500,000–1,000,000	3	33.3	3	33.3	1	11.1	2	22.2
250,000– 499,999	8	61.5	4	30.8	0	0.0	1	7.7
100,000– 249,999	31	62.0	10	20.0	6	12.0	3	6.0
50,000– 99,999	29	80.6	5	13.9	2	5.6	0	0.0

[1] Based on 112 counties responding.

Table 4/6 CITY CONTRACTING WITH NONGOVERNMENTAL GROUPS FOR CHILDREN AND YOUTH SERVICES, BY REGION

	Level of contracting for services							
	None		Low		Medium		High	
Classification	No.	(%)[1]	No.	(%)[1]	No.	(%)[1]	No.	(%)[1]
Total, all cities	644	84.6	66	8.7	42	5.5	9	1.2
Geographic region								
Northeast	133	86.4	12	7.8	9	5.8	0	0.0
North Central	210	89.4	16	6.8	6	2.6	3	0.4
South	160	88.9	9	5.0	11	6.1	0	0.0
West	141	73.4	29	15.1	16	8.3	6	0.8

[1] Based on 761 cities responding.

Table 4/7 CITY DIRECT SERVICE DELIVERY FOR GENERAL POPULATION, BY REGION

	Level of involvement							
	None		Low		Medium		High	
Classification	No.	(%)[1]	No.	(%)[1]	No.	(%)[1]	No.	(%)[1]
Total, all cities	521	68.5	149	19.6	66	8.7	25	3.3
Geographic region								
Northeast	80	51.9	48	31.2	17	11.0	9	5.8
North Central	166	70.6	43	18.3	23	9.8	3	1.3
South	145	80.6	16	8.9	12	6.7	7	3.9
West	130	67.7	42	21.9	14	7.3	6	3.1

[1] Based on 761 cities responding.

Table 4/8 CITY FINANCIAL SUPPORT TO NONGOVERNMENTAL GROUPS FOR CHILDREN AND YOUTH SERVICES, BY METRO STATUS

	Level of involvement							
	None		Low		Medium		High	
Classification	No.	(%)[1]	No.	(%)[1]	No.	(%)[1]	No.	(%)[1]
Total, all cities	609	80.0	95	12.5	46	6.0	11	1.4
Metro status								
Central	105	71.9	21	14.4	15	10.3	5	3.4
Suburban	387	83.3	52	11.3	19	4.1	4	0.9
Independent	117	76.5	22	14.4	12	7.8	2	1.3

[1] Based on 761 cities responding.

service involvement. Although the number of cities and counties with managers comprises a very large proportion of the total sample, nevertheless, these particular jurisdictional types fell into the higher service involvement categories with greater frequency than would be expected given their sample proportions. Tables 4/10 and 4/11 provide two illustrations of this pattern at the city and county levels of operation, respectively. In both instances, higher levels of involvement were uncovered for jurisdictions with some form of administrator. In the case of the county illustration (Table 4/11), which shows contracting with nongovernmental groups for children and youth services, the relationship between level of involvement and form of government appeared most clearly. Although the explanation of these findings is not readily apparent, it is possible that managers, especially county managers, may be more disposed to work out an "administrative" solution to the many human problems which confront them on a daily basis. Similarly, there may be something unique about the populations-in-need in these two examples that accounts for the differences noted.

HUMAN SERVICES MANAGEMENT IN LOCAL GOVERNMENT

This last section addresses more explicitly the ways in which human services programs are administered within the city and county governments responding to this survey. Information was collected about organizational, fiscal, and operational characteristics to obtain a profile of human services management capacity at the local government level. The authors followed the line of analysis described in the previous section, looking for relationships between the items contained in this part of the survey and the jurisdictional characteristics available in ICMA's master data file.

Human Services Management Tools. Tables 4/12 and 4/13 display for cities and counties, respectively, the percentage response for each of five human services management areas.

Centralized Human Services Departments. The first item for discussion is an organizational characteristic, namely, whether or not the responding jurisdiction has a centralized human services department involved in two or more program areas. As the appropriate tables indicate, 24.2% of all cities and one-half of all counties reported the existence of this type of agency. Furthermore, for both levels of government, the only clear association (in a statistically significant sense) that emerged from the data pertained to size of population. The larger the jurisdiction, the more likely it is to have a centralized human services department. In terms of the other jurisdictional characteristics displayed in Tables 4/12 and 4/13, any differences are difficult to assess because of chance factors associated with the sample itself. The only exception worth noting involves what appears to be a moderate association between the existence of a human services department and city metro status, which is not at all surprising given the complexity of managing the public's business within large urban centers.

On the average, cities with centralized human services departments employed 32 full-time equivalent staff persons (not shown in table). Departmental budgets for FY 1983 varied widely as would be expected, and were skewed in a positive direction (average budget totalled $1.6 million; median totalled $385,000). For counties, the average number of full-time employees within centralized human services departments was 138, although again it was skewed high by a few very large departments. The same held true for departmental budget figures, with the average equalling $10.7 million!

Human services management tools are displayed in Figure 4/1. Without question, counties were more likely than cities to report the use of each of these items. The evolution of the county government role in human services may partially account for these differences. Likewise, the variation in response may reflect more the definitions attached to these areas, which may not be consistent across governmental levels and functions.

Figure 4/2 arrays the various functions that centralized human services departments may perform. The most striking difference between cities and counties in this regard concerns the use of purchase-of-service contracting, an area in which counties responded in far greater numbers (85.4% compared with 56%). Percentages for city governments exceeded those for counties in three functional areas—direct services delivery, joint services, and advocacy/information and referral—but only by small margins. Counties were more likely to identify services coordination, planning, and evaluation as areas of functional responsibility for their human services departments.

Human Services Coordinators. Establishing a separate department with comprehensive program responsibilities is, of course, not the only way that local governments organize their human services efforts. Another approach taken

Table 4/9 CITY CONTRACTING WITH NONGOVERNMENTAL GROUPS FOR GENERAL POPULATION SERVICES, BY METRO STATUS

	Level of involvement							
	None		Low		Medium		High	
Classification	No.	(%)[1]	No.	(%)[1]	No.	(%)[1]	No.	(%)[1]
Total, all cities	652	85.7	63	8.3	36	4.7	10	1.3
Metro status								
Central	97	66.4	21	14.4	19	13.0	9	6.2
Suburban	411	89.0	34	7.4	16	3.5	1	0.2
Independent	144	94.1	8	5.2	1	0.7	0	0.0

[1]Based on 761 cities responding.

Table 4/10 CITY DIRECT SERVICE DELIVERY FOR THE ELDERLY, BY FORM OF GOVERNMENT

	Level of involvement							
	None		Low		Medium		High	
Classification	No.	(%)[1]	No.	(%)[1]	No.	(%)[1]	No.	(%)[1]
Total, all cities	326	42.8	348	45.7	73	9.6	14	1.8
Form of government								
Mayor–council	104	50.2	82	39.6	15	7.2	6	2.7
Council–manager	211	41.0	246	47.8	50	9.7	8	1.6
Commission	4	26.7	10	66.7	1	6.7	0	0.0
Town meeting	4	26.7	6	40.0	5	33.3	0	0.0
Rep. town meeting	3	33.3	4	44.4	2	22.2	0	0.0

[1]Based on 761 cities responding.

Table 4/11 COUNTY CONTRACTING WITH NONGOVERNMENTAL GROUPS FOR CHILDREN AND YOUTH SERVICES, BY FORM OF GOVERNMENT

	Level of involvement							
	None		Low		Medium		High	
Classification	No.	(%)[1]	No.	(%)[1]	No.	(%)[1]	No.	(%)[1]
Total, all counties	68	60.7	16	14.3	21	18.8	7	6.3
Form of government								
Without administrator	30	76.9	3	7.7	4	10.3	2	5.1
With administrator	38	52.1	13	17.8	17	23.3	5	6.8

[1] Based on 112 counties responding.

by city and county governments is to designate a staff person(s) as "coordinator of human services" for the jurisdiction, oftentimes located within the office of the chief administrative officer. As Tables 4/12 and 4/13 show, the number of cities and counties reporting the position of coordinator within their organizational structure was very similar to those having centralized departments—28.8% of cities and 49.1% of counties reported having a coordinator. Typically, this position is full-time, and most commonly is located within a broad-based department that has some human services responsibilities, such as a department of community and economic development. The responses to this part of the survey, however, varied widely and are not easily summarized. Significantly, the same relationships that were found between centralized departments and jurisdictional characteristics appeared in the human services coordinator data. Population size was the most prominent factor for both cities and counties, and metro status showed a moderate relationship with the coordinator variable for cities.

Comprehensive Human Service Planning. Another important dimension of human ser-

Table 4/12 CITY HUMAN SERVICES MANAGEMENT, BY POPULATION, GEOGRAPHIC REGION, METRO STATUS, AND FORM OF GOVERNMENT

Classification	Number of cities in sample (A)	Centralized human services department No.	(%)[1]	Human services coordinator No.	(%)[1]	Comprehensive human services planning No.	(%)[1]	Joint ventures No.	(%)[1]	Human services innovations No.	(%)[1]
Total, all cities	761	182	24.2	214	28.8	130	18.2	443	63.0	97	13.7
Population group											
Over 1,000,000	1	1	100.0	1	100.0	1	100.0	1	100.0	1	100.0
500,000–1,000,000	4	4	100.0	3	75.0	4	100.0	3	75.0	3	75.0
250,000– 499,999	7	6	85.7	5	71.4	5	71.4	6	85.7	5	71.4
100,000– 249,999	47	19	41.3	23	50.0	17	37.8	39	84.8	20	43.5
50,000– 99,999	99	43	43.9	47	48.0	35	36.5	76	81.7	23	25.3
25,000– 49,999	191	55	29.6	64	34.4	38	21.0	125	70.6	27	14.8
10,000– 24,999	412	54	13.2	71	17.7	30	7.9	193	51.5	18	4.8
Geographic region											
Northeast	154	45	29.6	55	36.4	32	21.8	94	67.1	22	15.2
North Central	235	50	21.6	57	24.8	30	13.8	132	58.4	25	11.5
South	180	32	17.8	37	21.1	24	14.0	88	55.7	22	13.3
West	192	55	29.4	65	34.8	44	24.4	129	72.1	28	15.6
Metro status											
Central	146	47	33.1	52	36.4	38	27.3	103	72.5	39	28.7
Suburban	462	117	25.5	142	31.5	82	18.8	269	63.7	54	12.6
Independent	153	18	12.0	20	13.4	10	7.1	71	51.1	4	2.8
Form of government											
Mayor–council	207	38	18.6	46	23.0	25	13.1	109	56.2	20	10.3
Council–manager	515	136	26.7	158	31.2	98	20.1	316	66.5	74	15.5
Commission	15	1	7.1	2	14.3	1	6.7	7	53.8	1	8.3
Town meeting	15	3	20.0	5	33.3	3	21.4	5	38.5	0	0.0
Rep. town meeting	9	4	50.0	3	37.5	3	37.5	6	75.0	2	25.0

[1] Percentages are based on the number of valid respondents for each particular category.

Table 4/13 COUNTIES HUMAN SERVICES MANAGEMENT, BY POPULATION, GEOGRAPHIC REGION, METRO STATUS, AND FORM OF GOVERNMENT

Classification	Number of counties in sample (A)	Centralized human services department No.	(%)[1]	Human services coordinator No.	(%)[1]	Comprehensive human services planning No.	(%)[1]	Joint ventures No.	(%)[1]	Human services innovations No.	(%)[1]
Total, all counties	112	55	50.0	54	49.1	59	53.6	87	80.6	36	38.3
Population group											
Over 1,000,000	4	4	100.0	4	100.0	3	75.0	4	100.0	1	33.3
500,000–1,000,000	9	8	88.9	9	100.0	4	44.4	9	100.0	5	62.5
250,000– 499,999	13	9	69.2	11	84.6	10	83.3	10	90.9	8	72.7
100,000– 249,999	50	21	42.9	18	36.7	23	46.9	38	77.6	15	35.7
50,000– 99,999	36	13	37.1	12	34.3	19	52.8	26	74.3	7	23.3
Geographic region											
Northeast	18	8	44.4	10	58.8	11	61.1	15	83.3	7	43.8
North Central	21	10	50.0	8	38.1	13	61.9	18	90.0	4	26.7
South	51	25	50.0	25	50.0	23	46.9	37	75.5	13	31.0
West	22	12	54.5	11	50.0	12	54.5	17	81.0	12	57.1
Metro status											
Metro	85	45	54.2	43	51.8	45	54.2	68	82.9	29	41.4
Nonmetro	27	10	37.0	11	40.7	14	51.9	19	73.1	7	29.2
Form of government											
Without administrator	39	15	39.5	15	39.5	13	35.1	27	71.1	12	37.5
With administrator	73	40	55.6	39	54.2	46	63.0	60	85.7	24	38.7

[1] Percentages are based on the number of valid respondents for each particular category.

vices operations examined in this study concerned local governments' comprehensive planning. While this is admittedly a difficult concept to examine by survey, its importance to the ultimate effectiveness of human services efforts cannot be overstated. Local governments' capacity to respond holistically and creatively to calls for assistance in a host of areas requires comprehensive planning. Again, Tables 4/12 and 4/13 display the relevant data for both city and county governments. Putting definitional considerations aside, counties were clearly more likely to respond in the affirmative on this question than were cities (53.6% to 18.2%, respectively). This difference is highlighted graphically in Figure 4/1.

Several correlates of comprehensive human services planning emerged from the data and deserve mention. Among the cities responding, for example, a clear and fairly strong association with population size was once again evident. Interestingly, however, this relationship did not appear in the county data. Statistically, metro status proved to be an important factor for cities in terms of their inclinations to do comprehensive planning (Table 4/12). Whereas form of government did not seem to be associated to any appreciable degree with human services planning activities among the cities in our sample, it did reach a level of statistical and substantive significance for county governments. In effect, the pertinent data in Table 4/13 imply that the employment of a professional administrator does make a difference on such matters. At a minimum, there is a perception among a greater proportion of the county government respondents from jurisdictions *with* administrators that comprehensive planning efforts are under way.

Participation in Joint Ventures. The survey also asked officials at the city and county levels to indicate whether their jurisdiction participated with other entities in *joint ventures*, which combined the planning, management, or delivery of human services. In this regard, county respondents were again more likely to report that their governments engaged in such joint activities (80.6% compared with 63%). Tables 4/12 and 4/13, as well as Figure 4/1, highlight these differences. It is significant that relatively high proportions of both cities and counties reporting utilize this particular service approach.

In regard to the question "with whom" are the ventures undertaken, it is clear that the role of private, nonprofit agencies is of central importance (72.5% of the cities and 89.6% of the counties so reported) (Table 4/14). City governments, according to these data, were then most likely to participate in joint ventures with county governments (63%); volunteer organizations (54.2%); and some type of substate entity, e.g., job training, area agency on aging (44.9%), in that order. Counties, on the other hand, seemed inclined to choose substate districts (65.5%), volunteer organizations (60.9%), and special purpose districts (50.6%), before city governments as partners in joint ventures. It should also be noted that some respondents from both levels of government identified state government as a participant in their human services activities, although not frequently enough to justify a separate category of response. In light of the emerging importance of state/local relations within the intergovernmental arena, it is suspected that this situation will undergo substantial change in the years ahead. As Table 4/14 also shows, business and industry, which together comprise the other element of the "private sector initiative," ranked relatively low on the lists of participants for joint ventures with local governments. This finding is not at all surprising as it has been pointed out elsewhere that public–private partnerships of this type are extremely difficult to effect.[11]

Tables 4/12 and 4/13 also provide information regarding the possible correlates of joint ventures for cities and counties. At the county government level, no statistically significant relationships were discerned, which implies that any differences noted in the table can be reasonably attributed to chance. For cities, however, both population size and metro status once again show significant signs of influence, with large, central cities reporting that they pursue joint ventures more than any other group.

Human Services Innovations. The last item displayed in Tables 4/12 and 4/13 is the response to a question which attempted to ascertain the degree of implementation of various human services "innovations" among the cities and counties surveyed. This particular inquiry was not directed at any specific action on the part of local governments, and actually comprised a wide variety of possibilities, including such things as the installation of new management information systems, client referral procedures, use of volunteers, etc. The intent was to identify the frequency with which local jurisdictions said that they had developed new approaches for the purpose of improving service quality or cost-effectiveness in service delivery within the "past year." Because of the lack of specificity in this particular question, the figures shown should only be construed as rough estimates of "innovation." Significantly, very few of the cities responded in the affirmative to this question (13.7%), while county respondents again indicated a greater propensity to identify such activities (38.3% of those responding). For counties, the only jurisdictional characteristic that appeared to be related to this survey item was population size; larger counties, with the exception of those over one million population, reported implementing innovations more than those under 100,000 population. Among the cities responding, population size *and* metro status proved to be the characteristics of most importance: the larger the city, the more likely it was to report the implementation of a human services innovation. On the same plane, of course, the larger the city, the more likely it was to fall into the "central" status on the metropolitan variable.

Financial Considerations. Figure 4/3 displays the sources of revenue for human services, expressed as average percentages, for the city and county governments responding to this survey. Respondents from cities indicated that they were most reliant on "locally generated" revenues to support their human service efforts, whereas the respondents from counties identified "fees and charges" collected from clients as being the number one source of revenue. It is important to recognize that not all survey respondents answered this particular set of questions completely. Consequently, the data presented in Figure 4/3 are suggestive rather

Table 4/14 ENTITIES WITH WHICH JURISDICTIONS PARTICIPATE IN JOINT VENTURES

Entity	City[1] (%)	County[2] (%)
County government	63.0	43.7
City government	25.5	43.7
Township	8.8	18.4
School district	35.4	36.8
Special district	28.7	50.6
Substate district	44.9	65.5
Private, nonprofit agency	72.5	89.6
Business and industry	20.3	37.9
Volunteer organization	54.2	60.9

[1] Based on 443 cities responding.
[2] Based on 87 counties responding.

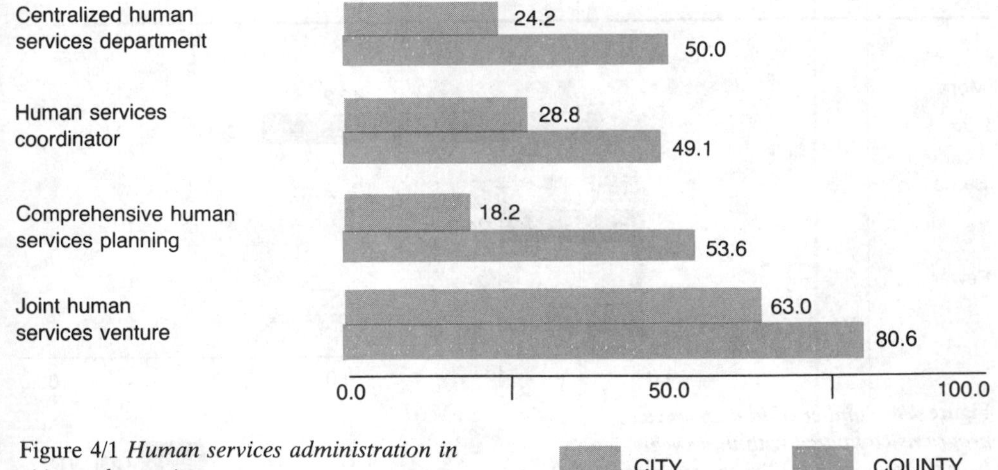

Figure 4/1 *Human services administration in cities and counties*

than definitive of patterns among local governments in the area of human services financing. Finally, it should be pointed out that the "other sources" category included the following: charges to other jurisdictions, donations, and financial support from nonprofit organizations and foundations.

Changes over Time. As indicated earlier in this article, one of the purposes of the survey was to assess, in admittedly very rough terms, the probable effects of changes in federal policies (specifically reduced funding and functional devolution) within the human services sector. The survey approached this issue by seeking to compare perceived changes in programs and numbers of clients served at the local government level over the preceding three-year period. The three-year timespan (roughly 1981 to 1984) was used since it corresponded to a period of major changes in national domestic policy direction.

The pertinent data for both city and county jurisdictions are displayed in Table 4/15, as well as in Figures 4/4 and 4/5. It is apparent from the data presented here that counties have experienced the greatest net effect, at least as viewed by those who responded to the survey, over this three-year period. The two figures speak most directly to this issue, highlighting the fact that the county respondents were less inclined than those representing cities to respond in the middle (i.e., same) category for either question. Moreover, the data from cities suggest that, over this three-year period, the number of human services programs within these jurisdictions was somewhat more likely to stay the same than to increase. On the other hand, the vast majority of city respondents perceived an increase in the numbers of people served by these programs. At the county level, over half of the jurisdictions responding reported increases in the number of programs *and* the number of people served. One possible interpretation of these findings is that federal and state funding reductions have forced local governments to at least maintain their services, and in a number of cases serve many more citizens in need. Again, the emergence of the county government role in human services, which was cited earlier, may account, at least in part, for these perceived changes.

No statistically significant jurisdictional characteristics were found to help account for the differences between the city and county perspectives presented. Of course, this conclusion may still be very significant in a practical, substantive sense. In effect, this finding implies that the changes (or lack thereof), perceived by city and county officials cannot be explained simply by considering differences in jurisdictional size, regional location, metropolitan status, or form of government. On the contrary, the survey data suggest that the perceptions of city and county officials are not that very different across these various jurisdictional types. By implication, then, it would be very difficult, indeed, to predict from these data the "most typical" city or county that has been affected in one way or another by the changing human services environment.

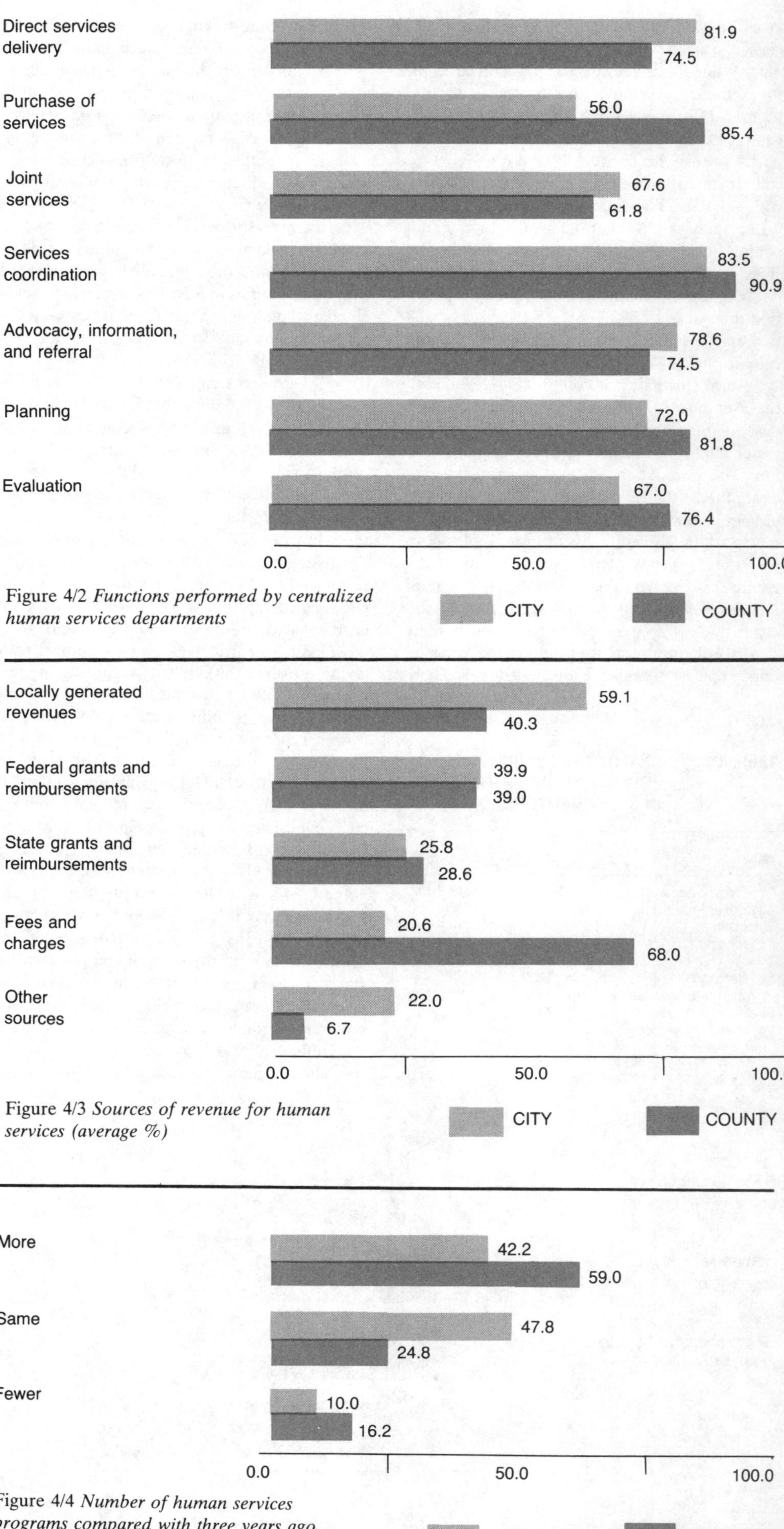

Figure 4/2 *Functions performed by centralized human services departments*

Figure 4/3 *Sources of revenue for human services (average %)*

Figure 4/4 *Number of human services programs compared with three years ago (survey was conducted in the spring of 1984)*

Table 4/15 CITY AND COUNTY HUMAN SERVICES COMPARED WITH THREE YEARS AGO[1]

	Cities						Counties					
	Number of programs			Number of people served			Number of programs			Number of people served		
Classification	More (%)	Same (%)	Fewer (%)	More (%)	Same (%)	Fewer (%)	More (%)	Same (%)	Fewer (%)	More (%)	Same (%)	Fewer (%)
Total, all cities/counties	42.2	47.8	10.0	62.4	30.8	6.8	59.0	24.8	16.2	76.7	9.7	13.6
Population group												
Over 1,000,000	0.0	100.0	0.0	0.0	100.0	0.0	50.0	25.0	25.0	50.0	0.0	50.0
500,000–1,000,000	75.0	25.0	0.0	100.0	0.0	0.0	55.6	22.2	22.2	77.8	11.1	11.1
250,000– 499,999	57.1	14.3	28.6	71.4	14.3	14.3	53.8	15.4	30.8	92.3	0.0	7.7
100,000– 249,999	38.6	38.6	22.7	60.5	18.6	20.9	59.6	25.5	14.9	73.9	8.7	17.4
50,000– 99,999	53.3	33.3	13.3	74.4	15.6	10.0	62.5	28.1	9.4	77.4	16.1	6.5
25,000– 49,999	45.6	42.2	12.2	69.1	24.7	6.2	...	...	...	...	...	...
10,000– 24,999	37.5	56.5	6.1	55.5	40.1	4.4	...	...	...	...	...	...
Geographic region												
Northeast	48.9	45.9	5.2	73.9	23.9	2.2	58.8	23.5	17.6	83.3	5.6	11.1
North Central	35.0	53.7	11.3	55.5	35.0	9.5	70.0	20.0	10.0	89.5	5.3	5.3
South	36.3	52.9	10.8	54.3	38.4	7.3	59.6	31.9	8.5	80.9	8.5	10.6
West	50.6	38.2	11.2	68.4	24.9	6.8	47.6	14.3	38.1	47.4	21.1	31.6
Metro status												
Central	39.6	47.0	13.4	61.4	28.8	9.8	...	...	...	...	...	...
Suburban	47.0	43.8	9.1	65.7	27.6	6.8	...	...	...	...	...	...
Independent	30.1	60.9	9.0	53.4	42.7	3.8	...	...	...	...	...	...
Metro	...	...	...	...	...	...	...	...	...	...	...	...
Nonmetro	...	...	...	...	...	...	...	...	...	...	...	...
Form of government												
Mayor–council	44.2	51.2	4.7	68.5	28.5	3.0	58.8	26.3	15.0	79.7	7.6	12.7
Council–manager	40.5	47.1	12.4	58.9	32.5	8.6	60.0	20.0	20.0	66.7	16.7	16.7
Commission	27.3	72.7	0.0	63.6	36.4	0.0	...	...	...	...	...	...
Town meeting	75.0	16.7	8.3	91.7	8.3	0.0	...	...	...	...	...	...
Rep. town meeting	66.7	33.3	0.0	88.9	11.1	0.0	...	...	...	...	...	...
With administrator	...	...	...	...	...	...	46.9	34.4	18.8	78.1	12.5	9.4
Without administrator	...	...	...	...	...	...	64.4	20.5	15.1	76.1	8.5	15.5

[1] Survey was conducted in the spring of 1984.

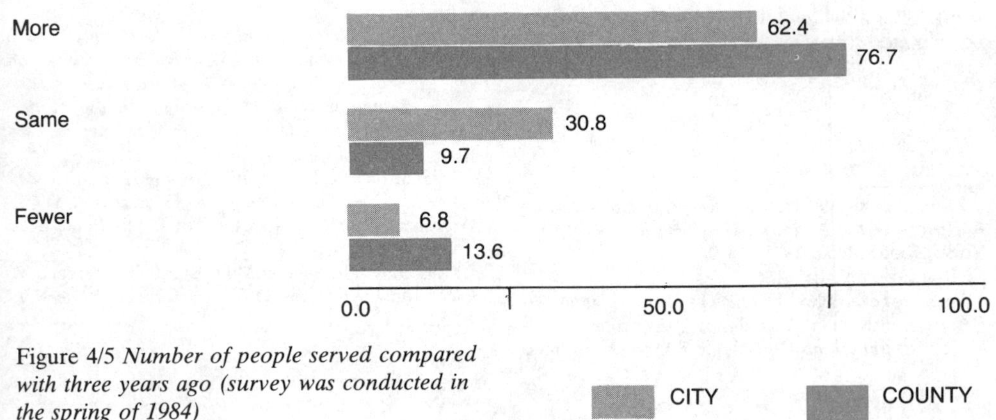

Figure 4/5 *Number of people served compared with three years ago (survey was conducted in the spring of 1984)*

CONCLUSIONS

The survey shows, quite clearly, that the roles of cities and counties in human services in the current era are multifaceted and hard to characterize with any precision. While local governments certainly have continued to maintain their traditional roles as providers of key public services, they have also moved into new areas of responsibility, sometimes directly and sometimes not, and sometimes deliberately and other times by default. As a consequence, the patterns revealed by the survey data reported in this article must be examined in broad perspective.

The survey showed that both cities and counties are involved in a wide variety of activities that fall under the human services umbrella. In addition to the more traditional types of recreation services, city governments seem most inclined to provide various kinds of transportation services to special populations-in-need within their jurisdictional boundaries. Likewise, they provide other forms of assistance to people in need, especially on an emergency basis.

At the county level, the human services function is much more spread out across programs and service types, according to these survey data. On balance, the counties responding to this survey were much more likely to provide different services *directly* than by any other mode of delivery. When they did use alternative service delivery approaches, they tended to collaborate with nongovernmental groups rather than rely on other public sector entities.

City governments followed this same pattern with the exception that they tended not to provide human services directly. This finding was not particularly surprising since cities have traditionally left the delivery of services to other jurisdictions, as well as to the private, nonprofit sector. Most cities, in fact, do not have statutory responsibilities for providing most of these human services.[12]

Service patterns for both cities and counties could best be described as multidimensional—most human services are not provided by any single mode of delivery. On the contrary, the survey shows that the mix of service delivery modes used by the responding jurisdictions is quite extensive across all of the service categories examined. Consequently, a cursory review of any one service delivery option, particularly the direct operation of services by local governments, leaves one with the impression that not much is going on in the way of human services. The survey demonstrated that this is especially the case among city governments. Yet, by looking at all alternative means of providing services, one finds that the environment of local government human services is much more dynamic. The fact that so many other jurisdictions and organizations deliver human services within the local community is itself a major challenge for local government managers to understand and "manage."

The management environment for local government human services, in its more traditional meaning, was also found to be quite diverse among the cities and counties surveyed. Overall, counties were more inclined than cities to use the different management tools under investigation. In this regard, the survey found that county governments: were more likely to centralize their human services efforts in a single department or unit; were more inclined to employ a "coordinator" of human services (whether or not they had a human services department); were more likely to engage in some form of comprehensive human services planning; and were somewhat more inclined to participate in joint ventures with nongovernmental groups for the provision of human services. Respondents from both types of jurisdictions did identify a variety of innovations designed presumably to improve service quality or enhance the cost-effectiveness of services. However, the number of responses from both groups was too low to report with confidence, although enough information was obtained to suggest that this area deserves further investigation.

The available data indicated that local governments are seeking out more "private sector" solutions to their human services problems, an approach which certainly reflects the current emphasis on privatization of public services, especially for meeting of human needs.[13] Moreover, there is some indication that many of the human services management "innovations" currently in vogue reflect advances in technology. We can expect the familiar buzzwords of information management to become an increasingly important part of the lexicon of local human services management.

The survey also suggests that local government human services have experienced some marked changes in recent years, in terms of the numbers of programs provided at the local level, as well as numbers of people receiving services. In this regard, county governments seem to have been affected most directly, with dramatic increases reported in both areas. The city respondents were more inclined to report increases in the number of people served and to indicate that the number of human services programs for which they had some responsibility stayed about the "same." By implication, the city human services effort may be operating under more pressure than are those at the county level, if for no other reason than that their finite resources are being stretched to meet escalating needs. The fact that the survey also indicated that cities were more likely than counties to rely on locally generated revenues to support human services makes this possibility even more striking from a policy management point of view. Indeed, in another survey conducted in October 1982 by the U.S. Conference of Mayors, 54% of the cities contacted reported using local general revenue to make up for federal budget cuts in various human services areas.[14]

All of these findings, in turn, underscore the need for local governments to explore with increased determination alternative financing and service delivery arrangements for meeting human needs. It is encouraging to see evidence in this survey that both cities and counties are working towards this end by collaborating with nongovernmental groups and other public sector entities. Local government human services in the remainder of the 1980s will certainly depend, in large measure, on the capability of both the public and private sectors to effect coordinated strategies for meeting human needs.

---

[1] June Axinn and Herman Levin, *Social Welfare: A History of the American Response to Need* (New York: Dodd, Mead, 1975), p. 9.

[2] Ibid., pp. 39, 124, 186.

[3] See, for example: Lawrence D. Brown, James W. Fossett, and Kenneth T. Palmer, *The Changing Politics of Federal Grants* (Washington, D.C.: Brookings Institution, 1984); Martha Derthick, *The Influence of Federal Grants* (Cambridge, Mass.: Harvard University Press, 1970); Harold Seidman, *Politics, Position and Power: The Dynamics of Federal Organization* (New York: Oxford, 1980); James L. Sundquist and David W. Davis, *Making Federalism Work* (Washington, D.C.: Brookings Institution, 1969).

[4] Al Templeton, "The County and the Community: Planning for and Delivering Human Services," *The County Year Book, 1975* (Washington, D.C.: International City Management Association, 1975), p. 108.

[5] See: U.S. Conference of Mayors, *Human Services in City Governments* (Washington, D.C.: 1977).

[6] See: Richard P. Nathan and Fred C. Doolittle, *The Consequences of Cuts* (Princeton, N.J.: Urban and Regional Research Center, Princeton University, 1983); John L. Palmer and Isabel V. Sawhill, eds., *The Reagan Experiment* (Cambridge, Mass.: Ballinger, 1984).

[7] See: Keith F. Mulrooney, *A Guide to Human Resources Development in Small Cities*, Management Information Service Report, Vol. 5, No. 10 (Washington, D.C.: International City Management Association, October 1973).

[8] See: Carolyn B. Lawrence and John M. DeGrove, "County Government Services," in *The County Year Book 1976* (Washington, D.C.: National Association of Counties and International City Management Association, 1976), pp. 91–129.

[9] For example, see: Robert Morris, *Social Policy and the American Welfare State* (New York: Longman, 1984); Sar A. Levitan and Clifford M. Johnson, *Beyond the Safety Net: Reviving the Promise of Opportunity in America* (New York: Ballinger, 1984).

[10] For example, see Robert Agranoff, ed., *Human Services on a Limited Budget* (Washington, D.C.: International City Management Association, 1983); Myron A. Weiner, *Human Services Management* (Homewood, Il.: Dorsey Press, 1982).

[11] Alex N. Pattakos, "In Search of Public/Private Partnerships: Good Intentions Aren't Enough," in Dennis L. Thompson, ed., *The Private Exercise of Public Functions* (Port Washington, N.Y.: Associated Faculty Press and Policy Studies Organization, 1985), pp. 173–188.

[12] U.S. Conference of Mayors/U.S. Conference of City Human Services Officials, *Human Services in FY82: Shrinking Resources in Troubled Times, A Survey of Human Services Officials in the Nation's Cities* (Washington, D.C.: U.S. Conference of Mayors, October 1982), p. 8.

[13] See: Jack A. Meyer, ed., *Meeting Human Needs: Towards a New Public Philosophy* (Washington, D.C.: American Enterprise Institute for Public Policy Research, 1982).

[14] U.S. Conference of Mayors/U.S. Conference of City Human Services Officials, *Human Services in FY82*, p. 12.

D 5

Motivating Local Government Employees with Incentives*

Amy Cohen Paul
International City Management Association

When productivity declines, management immediately begins to look for ways to correct the problem. Government, business, and industry in the United States have experienced major productivity problems in the past decade, all of which have been well documented and a cause for great national concern. This concern has helped make productivity improvement very big business and has prompted a myriad of productivity "experts" to tout "cures" to the problem (often sounding like sales persons for Doc Johnson's Magic Elixir).

While many fads and gimmicks have come and gone, one well-documented productivity improvement tool—the use of employee incentives—has remained popular over the years. Perhaps it is because incentives reward employees for their performance or ideas, while often providing the added benefit of increased participation. Or, it may be that incentives give employees the feeling that they have more control over their futures. In any event, the use of employee incentives by local governments has been increasing.

The logical question to ask, then, is "What are the best incentives to use?" The search for an answer stirs controversy because an incentive that motivates one person will not necessarily motivate another. As Philip C. Grant explains in "Motivation: Myths and Misnomers," economic issues no longer serve as primary motivators. "The average worker wants job security, interesting, challenging work, good relations with supervisors and peers, opportunities for advancement, and status and recognition in return for performance. All these are usually valued more than a paycheck."[1] Consequently, a great number of different approaches and incentive systems are being used in local governments today.

SURVEY METHODOLOGY

The data collected by ICMA in the summer of 1984 confirm the fact that incentives are quite popular in local governments. Mail questionnaires were sent to all municipalities 10,000 and over in population (2,603); those not responding to the initial mailing were sent a second request. A total of 1,265 (48.6%) cities responded (Table 5/1). Of those, 61.6% of the responses were from cities in the West while only 36.3% were from places in the South (not shown in table). In all cases respondents were instructed to exclude police, fire, and educational personnel when answering the questionnaire, since these local government employees are often covered by separate and very different personnel systems.

Because cities employing any type of incentive were more likely to answer the questionnaire, the respondents most definitely constitute a self-selected sample and may possibly overrepresent those local governments using employee incentives. This tendency is borne out by the fact that nine out of ten (91.6%) cities reported using at least one of the employee incentives queried in the survey (no table shown).

SELECTED INCENTIVES USED BY LOCAL GOVERNMENTS

This article presents only a snapshot of the employee incentive data collected by ICMA. Only those incentives and extraordinary benefits presented in the individual city table (Table 5/5) are discussed here. Several summary tables are included to provide some idea of the magnitude of the usage of incentives and to identify trends occuring since 1978. A detailed analysis of the survey results is covered in a separate forum, as a Baseline Data Report.[2]

Educational/Professional Development Incentives. Of all the incentives surveyed, educational incentives were by far the most widely used (Table 5/2). Almost three-quarters (74.2%) of the cities responding provided some form of educational incentive. For the purpose of this survey, educational and professional development incentives are defined as official monetary or nonmonetary rewards given to encourage employees to continue their professional or technical education. Although the most common form of this incentive is tuition reimbursement (98% of those cities reporting having any educational incentives provide some type of tuition reimbursement), other arrangements are also used. For example, 44.7% of the respondents allow time off with pay to attend courses.

Variation in Working Hours. One nonmonetary incentive that is popular in some local governments is to allow employees to have flexibility in determining their hours of work. Slightly over one-fourth (27.2%) of the respondents reported allowing flextime or a four-day work week. Of the two options, flextime (or gliding hours) was most popular, with 74.3% reporting this variation compared with only 40.9% using the four-day work week. Although the only two variations specifically queried were flextime and the four-day work week, other possibilities within

Table 5/1 SURVEY REPONSE

Classification	No. of cities surveyed[1] (A)	Cities responding No.	% of (A)
Total	2,603	1,265	48.6
Population group			
Over 1,000,000	6	1	16.7
500,000–1,000,000	17	6	35.3
250,000– 499,999	34	19	55.9
100,000– 249,999	113	61	54.0
50,000– 99,999	279	162	58.1
25,000– 49,999	615	334	54.3
10,000– 24,999	1,539	682	44.3
Geographic division[2]			
New England	310	109	35.2
Mid-Atlantic	443	164	37.0
East North Central	541	238	44.0
West North Central	209	134	64.1
South Atlantic	273	166	60.8
East South Central	135	61	45.2
West South Central	247	119	48.2
Mountain	112	68	60.7
Pacific Coast	333	206	61.9
Metro status[3]			
Central	508	270	53.1
Suburban	1.511	714	47.3
Independent	584	281	48.1
Form of government[4]			
Mayor-council	1 106	396	35.8
Council-manager	1 251	788	63.0
Commission	101	41	40.6
Town meeting	100	21	21.0
Rep. town meeting	45	19	42.2

[1] The term *cities* is used in this and the following tables to refer to cities, villages, towns, townships, and boroughs.
[2] Geographic divisions: *New England*—the states of Connecticut, Maine, Massachusetts, New Hampshire, Rhode Island, and Vermont; *Mid-Atlantic*—the states of New Jersey, New York, and Pennsylvania; *East North Central*—the states of Illinois, Indiana, Michigan, Ohio and Wisconsin; *West North Central*—the states of Iowa, Kansas, Minnesota, Missouri, Nebraska, North Dakota, and South Dakota; *South Atlantic*—the states of Delaware, Florida, Georgia, Maryland, North Carolina, South Carolina, Virginia, and West Virginia, plus the District of Columbia; *East South Central*—the states of Alabama, Kentucky, Mississippi, and Tennessee; *West South Central*—the states of Arkansas, Louisiana, Oklahoma, and Texas; *Mountain*—the states of Arizona, Colorado, Idaho, Montana, Nevada, New Mexico, Utah, and Wyoming; *Pacific Coast*—the states of Alaska, California, Hawaii, Oregon, and Washington.
[3] *Metro status: Central*—the city(ies) actually appearing in the standard metropolitan statistical area (SMSA) title; *Suburban*—the city(ies) located within an SMSA; *Independent*—the city(ies) not located within an SMSA.
[4] *Forms of government: Mayor-council*—an elected council serves as the legislative body with a separately elected head of government; *Council-manager*—the mayor and council make policy and an appointed administrator is responsible for the administration of the city; *Commission*—a board of elected commissioners serves as the legislative body and each commissioner is responsible for administration of one or more departments; *Town meeting*—qualified voters meet to make basic policy and choose a board of selectmen to carry out the policy; *Representative town meeting*—representatives selected by citizens vote at meetings, which may be attended by all town citizens.

*Data for this article were collected by the survey *Employee Incentives—1984* (INCT84) conducted by the International City Management Association in the spring and summer of 1984.

the purview of this category include staggered work hours and extended or compressed work weeks.

Task System. Another incentive that allows some variation in work hours is the task system. Of the cities reporting, 31% use this incentive for some of their employees. The task system allows an employee to leave work once an assigned task (e.g., sanitation collection route, parks maintenance) is completed and receive a full day's wage regardless of the time actually used to complete the task. When a good quality control system and periodic review of tasks are used in conjunction with the task system, this arrangement rewards efficiency with extra time off and often serves as a highly motivational incentive.

Attendance Incentives. Over half of the cities reporting (52.3%) use some type of monetary or nonmonetary inducements to improve attendance, reduce sick leave, or reduce lateness. By far, the method used most often (reported by 62.4% of those using attendance incentives) is to allow cash bonuses to be received for unused sick leave either at retirement or periodically. Other incentives include allowing unused sick leave to be converted to annual leave (28.3%), applying unused sick leave to early retirement (12.7%), granting "undesignated" leave days which can be used as either annual or sick leave (2.8%), and allowing sick leave to be "pooled" or donated for use by all employees (4.7%).

Job enrichment. Job enrichment, defined on the survey instrument as a "variety of formal processes for employees which help to make the job more interesting or more responsible," is probably the least quantifiable motivator included on the survey. However, it is an important incentive because, unlike some of the others, it satisfies the criteria for helping employees increase their self-esteem and self-actualize their needs. In spite of this, only 14.8% of the cities responding reported using any form of job enrichment as an employee incentive. Of those, job rotation and job redesign are widely used (94% and 93.4%, respectively, were so reported).

A more popular motivational incentive used by over one-third (37.5%) of the cities responding is management participation by employees (not shown in table). The survey defined this incentive as "formal efforts by the municipality to increase participation by nonmanagement employees in decision-making on day-to-day work or about government issues and policies." This incentive includes such techniques as labor-management committees (reported by 64.2% of the cities responding), quality circles (reported by 21.7%), and using a team approach of grouping employees to encourage cooperation and a broader view of the work process (reported by 42.5%) (not shown in table).

Awards Programs. A variety of incentive programs used by local governments involve rewarding employees for ideas that decrease costs, increase the quality of service, or otherwise improve the operations of the organization. Such programs often reward employees with monetary incentives, although nonmonetary incentives are also popular with the cities reporting. It appears from the data that monetary and nonmonetary awards are often used in conjunction with each other. For example, of the 216 cities reporting having a suggestion award program, 77.5% provide cash awards and 69.5% provide plaques, certificates, or other nonmonetary awards. Of the 318 cities using employee performance recognition programs (e.g., Employee-of-the-Month programs) less than half

Table 5/3 CITIES DISCONTINUING USE OF INCENTIVES, 1978 AND 1984

Incentive	1978[1] No.	1978[1] %	1984 No.	1984 %
Educational incentives	47	2.8	27	2.2
Variation in working hours	30	1.8	27	2.2
Task systems	59	3.6	60	4.8
Attendance incentives	15	0.9	13	1.1
Job enrichment	0	0.0	1	0.1
Suggestion awards	67	4.1	91	7.3
Safety awards	26	1.6	23	1.9

[1] Source: 1978 ICMA survey sent to all cities over 10,000 population. The response rate was 66.9% with 1,661 cities reporting.

Table 5/2 SELECTED INCENTIVES

Classification	Educational/ professional development		Variation in working hours		Task systems		Attendance incentives		Job enrichment		Suggestion awards		Safety incentives	
	No.[1]	%	No.[2]	%	No.[3]	%	No.[4]	%	No.[5]	%	No.[6]	%	No.[2]	%
Total	919	74.2	337	27.2	387	31.0	647	52.3	182	14.8	216	17.3	213	17.2
Population group														
Over 1,000,000	1	100.0	1	100.0	0	0.0	1	100.0	0	0.0	1	100.0	0	0.0
500,000–1,000,000	6	100.0	5	83.3	3	50.0	5	100.0	2	33.3	3	50.0	3	50.0
250,000– 499,999	16	84.2	12	63.2	14	73.7	14	73.7	3	16.7	8	42.1	7	36.8
100,000– 249,999	47	77.0	34	55.7	32	53.3	40	65.6	12	20.0	24	40.0	21	34.4
50,000– 99,999	119	76.3	44	28.0	62	38.5	97	61.0	23	14.6	52	32.9	41	25.6
25,000– 49,999	241	74.6	96	29.0	115	35.0	197	60.8	49	15.0	50	15.2	65	19.8
10,000– 24,999	489	72.7	145	21.8	161	24.0	293	43.9	93	14.0	78	11.6	76	11.4
Geographic division														
New England	70	68.0	21	20.2	20	18.9	59	56.2	8	7.5	15	14.2	18	17.0
Mid-Atlantic	96	60.4	29	17.8	43	26.2	87	53.4	20	12.5	20	12.3	13	8.1
East North Central	181	76.7	53	22.6	54	23.1	118	51.3	26	11.2	23	9.8	27	11.5
West North Central	104	79.4	35	26.9	25	18.8	58	43.6	24	18.2	16	12.1	14	10.4
South Atlantic	118	72.4	49	29.9	112	68.7	85	52.5	21	13.3	36	22.1	49	30.1
East South Central	39	63.9	13	21.3	22	36.1	27	45.0	4	6.7	6	9.8	8	13.3
West South Central	78	66.7	16	13.8	58	49.2	49	42.6	12	10.5	20	17.1	25	21.6
Mountain	62	91.2	40	59.7	29	44.6	44	65.7	21	30.9	25	37.3	18	27.3
Pacific Coast	171	85.1	81	40.5	24	11.8	120	59.7	46	22.9	55	27.1	41	20.5
Metro status														
Central	202	75.7	99	36.9	141	52.6	163	61.0	34	13.0	68	25.8	83	31.0
Suburban	513	73.7	174	24.9	154	21.9	368	52.9	115	16.5	113	16.1	92	13.2
Independent	204	73.9	64	23.4	92	33.1	116	42.3	33	11.9	35	12.6	38	13.9
Form of government														
Mayor-council	256	66.0	87	22.5	107	27.5	184	48.2	43	11.1	45	11.6	39	10.1
Council-manager	610	78.9	230	29.6	265	34.0	427	55.1	132	17.2	164	21.1	171	22.1
Commission	27	67.5	11	28.9	11	27.5	17	42.5	3	7.5	6	14.6	1	2.6
Town meeting	11	52.4	5	23.8	2	9.5	6	28.6	1	4.8	0	0.0	1	4.8
Rep. town meeting	15	88.2	4	23.5	2	11.1	13	72.2	3	16.7	1	5.6	1	5.6

[1] Based on 1,239 cities reporting.
[2] Based on 1,240 cities reporting.
[3] Based on 1,248 cities reporting.
[4] Based on 1,236 cities reporting.
[5] Based on 1,233 cities reporting.
[6] Based on 1,245 cities reporting.

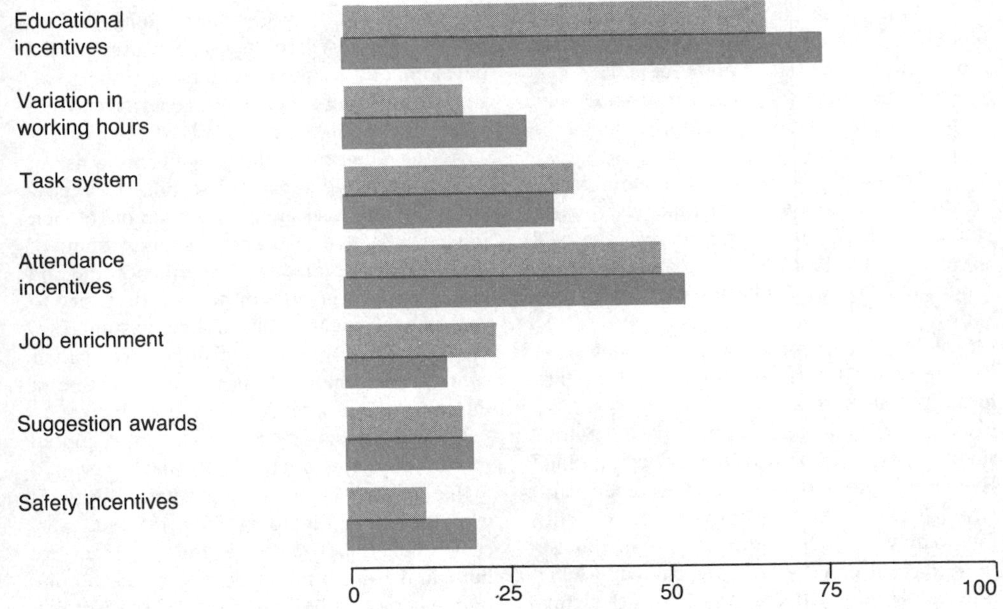

Source: 1978 ICMA survey sent to all cities over 10,000 population. The response rate was 66.9% with 1,661 cities reporting.

Figure 5/1 *Selected employee incentives, 1978 and 1984*

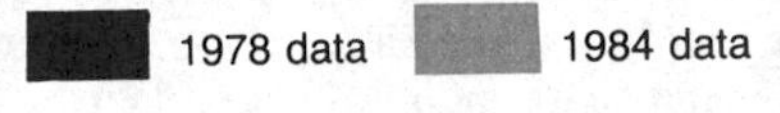

granted cash awards (46.4%) while almost three-quarters (73.3%) provide nonmonetary incentives. Safety awards were reported by 213 (17.2%) of the cities responding. Data on the exact nature of the awards were not collected.

TRENDS IN EMPLOYEE INCENTIVES

In 1978 ICMA sent a similar survey on employee incentives to 2,481 cities over 10,000 in population; two-thirds of the cities surveyed responded (66.9%) to that survey. The findings were published in several forms.[3] A synopsis of some of the comparable data is shown in Figure 5/1. As this figure shows, the use of employee incentives is definitely stronger now than six years ago.

For the seven incentives that are shown, all but two (task systems and job enrichment programs) became more widely used by local governments between 1978 and 1984. The front-runner, educational incentives (which were also the most widely used in 1978), showed an increase of 10.3 percentage points. Another incentive, variation in working hours, although not as commonly used as educational incentives, also experienced a considerable growth in popularity (an increase of nine percentage points) during the six-year period. Similarly, the use of attendance and safety incentives also grew in popularity during this period—an in-

Table 5/4 EXTRAORDINARY FRINGE BENEFITS

Classification	Dental insurance		Eye care		Substance abuse program		Personal counseling		Health counseling		Financial counseling		Free legal advice		Cafeteria-type selection of benefits		Daycare program	
	No.[1]	%	No.[2]	%	No.[3]	%	No.[4]	%	No.[5]	%	No.[6]	%	No.[7]	%	No.[8]	%	No.[7]	%
Total	739	64.2	304	27.6	272	25.6	349	32.6	318	31.0	225	22.5	34	3.2	58	5.6	4	0.4
Population group																		
Over 1,000,000	1	100.0	1	100.0	1	100.0	0	0.0	0	0.0	0	0.0	0	0.0	0	0.0	0	0.0
500,000–1,000,000	4	80.0	3	60.0	3	60.0	3	75.0	4	80.0	3	75.0	2	40.0	1	25.0	0	0.0
250,000– 499,999	13	72.2	6	35.3	11	61.1	10	55.6	10	58.8	8	50.0	0	0.0	1	7.1	0	0.0
100,000– 249,999	42	73.7	19	35.2	29	55.8	33	66.0	30	60.0	26	53.1	2	4.1	5	10.6	0	0.0
50,000– 99,999	115	76.7	43	30.7	60	45.8	77	55.8	70	53.4	48	38.7	7	5.0	10	7.5	1	0.7
25,000– 49,999	218	70.3	91	30.6	85	30.4	113	39.8	104	37.8	66	24.9	13	4.5	26	9.5	3	1.0
10,000– 24,999	346	56.7	141	24.0	83	14.4	113	19.7	100	18.2	74	13.7	10	1.7	15	2.6	0	0.0
Geographic division																		
New England	37	41.6	10	11.2	20	21.7	25	28.4	21	25.3	11	13.9	0	0.0	1	1.1	0	0.0
Mid-Atlantic	131	84.5	82	55.4	20	14.2	21	14.9	22	16.2	12	9.2	4	2.9	3	2.2	0	0.0
East North Central	131	60.1	55	26.8	49	25.4	52	26.9	50	26.6	35	19.0	1	0.5	4	2.0	0	0.0
West North Central	67	56.8	22	19.3	44	39.3	51	45.5	50	46.7	42	39.3	5	4.3	5	4.6	0	0.0
South Atlantic	53	35.8	17	11.3	40	26.7	53	35.8	49	33.6	36	24.8	6	4.0	6	4.1	0	0.0
East South Central	13	25.0	3	5.8	8	15.7	13	24.5	13	25.0	7	13.0	0	0.0	0	0.0	0	0.0
West South Central	61	56.5	5	5.2	17	18.1	30	30.0	24	24.5	18	19.1	3	3.1	1	1.1	1	1.0
Mountain	56	84.8	16	28.1	30	50.0	37	61.7	35	63.6	26	49.1	6	10.5	5	9.8	0	0.0
Pacific Coast	190	96.4	94	49.7	44	25.9	67	38.5	54	33.3	38	24.7	9	5.0	33	19.1	3	1.7
Metro status																		
Central	159	63.6	66	27.5	97	41.8	117	50.4	115	49.6	82	36.8	14	6.0	12	5.4	2	0.9
Suburban	478	72.9	205	32.6	127	21.2	185	30.5	154	27.2	106	19.2	15	2.4	44	7.4	2	0.3
Independent	102	41.6	33	14.2	48	20.8	47	20.4	49	21.4	37	16.4	5	2.1	2	0.9	0	0.0
Form of government																		
Mayor-council	227	63.4	99	28.9	78	23.7	82	25.0	80	25.5	56	18.4	7	2.1	8	2.4	0	0.0
Council-manager	482	66.9	189	27.4	178	26.8	249	37.1	222	34.5	161	25.6	25	3.7	49	7.6	4	0.6
Commission	22	56.4	14	36.8	9	25.0	10	28.6	9	25.0	5	14.3	2	5.6	1	2.8	0	0.0
Town meeting	5	26.3	1	5.3	3	15.8	3	16.7	2	11.1	1	5.6	0	0.0	0	0.0	0	0.0
Rep. town meeting	3	21.4	1	7.7	4	25.0	5	31.3	5	31.3	2	14.3	0	0.0	0	0.0	0	0.0

1 Based on 1,151 cities responding.
2 Based on 1,102 cities responding.
3 Based on 1,063 cities responding.
4 Based on 1,069 cities responding.
5 Based on 1,027 cities responding.
6 Based on 1,001 cities responding.
7 Based on 1,079 cities responding.
8 Based on 1,045 cities responding.

crease of 6 and 5.6 percentage points, respectively.

Other interesting trend data are found in Table 5/3, which examines cities that have discontinued using certain incentives. Although a slightly greater number of cities discontinued using incentives according to the 1984 survey, the actual numbers are still quite small. Suggestion incentives were discontinued by 91 cities reporting (7.3%) while 48 (4.8%) stopped using task systems. Other incentives were discontinued by fewer than 30 cities—clearly an indication that the majority of cities using incentives are satisfied and have found them to be valuable.

EXTRAORDINARY FRINGE BENEFITS

Are fringe benefits really employee incentives? For the most part, they probably are not, since they are usually available as a condition of employment. However, they certainly serve as an incentive when an employee is evaluating a job change. Since many local governments are in stiff competition with the private sector to attract top employees, fringe benefits cannot be ignored as important recruitment and retention factors.

Table 5/4 presents data on nine extraordinary fringe benefits queried in the survey. In general, when the range of benefits are examined geographically, it is clear that cities in the western part of the country are much more likely to provide extraordinary benefits than are those in other regions. This is particularly true and clearly exhibited by the data for some of the newest benefits. A good example is the use of cafeteria-type selection of benefits. While only 5.6% of the cities nationwide report allowing employees to choose benefits based on a a cafeteria-type plan, almost one-fifth (19.1%) of the cities in the Pacific Coast division and one-tenth (9.8%) of those in the Mountain division provide this much talked about benefit.

As Table 5/4 shows, dental insurance is by far the most widely used benefit included in the survey. Of the local governments reporting, almost two-thirds (64.2%) provide dental insurance. Use of this benefit has increased overwhelmingly in the six-year period since the 1978 survey. At that time, only 32.7% of the cities reporting provided dental insurance (no table shown.)

Following dental insurance, counseling services are the next most common benefits among local governments. Almost one-third (32.6%) provide personal counseling services while slightly fewer (31%) provide health counseling. Eye care is the next most popular benefit surveyed—27.6% of cities provide this benefit, followed by 25.6% who provide substance abuse programs for employees. Financial counseling is available to employees in 22.5% of the cities responding. Very few cities provide either free legal advice to employees (3.2%) or assist with day care programs (0.4%).

Data from the 1984 survey coupled with trend data from the 1978 survey clearly show that cities are responding to increased competition in the employment arena by providing more competitive benefits. Although the use of some benefits, such as counseling, is not widespread, the very fact that local governments have begun to offer more innovative benefits is very encouraging.

CONCLUSION

The continued growth in the use of incentives by local governments shows increased sensitivity to and recognition of the fact that not all employees are motivated by the same things and, especially, that they are not all motivated by money. Growth in the usage of professional development incentives underscores this point, since educational incentives generally do not result directly in monetary awards.

At the same time, the growth in the use of incentives would suggest that more local government employees are getting more out of their jobs. This would lead one to suppose some of those employees are happier on the job and find that their jobs give them more of a chance to continue their search for self-actualization. Employees certainly have a stronger say in their own destiny when they participate in some of the incentive programs surveyed.

Local governments that have not explored incentive systems might use the data presented in this article to begin a dialogue with colleagues who use them regarding their real and perceived benefits. The data in the individual city table make this a relatively easy task, and one that may pay off both in improved productivity and increased employee satisfaction.

---

[1] Philip C. Grant, "Motivation: Myths and Misnomers," in John Matzer, ed., *Creative Personnel Practices: New Ideals for Local Government,"* (Washington, D.C.: International City Management Association, 1984), p. 102.

[2] A forthcoming issue of the Baseline Data Reports will contain an indepth analysis of the survey results. Information about the report can be obtained from ICMA headquarters. The report will be published in late spring of 1985.

[3] See: John M. Greiner, "Incentives for Municipal Employees: An Update," *Urban Data Service Reports*, vol. 11 no. 8 (Washington, D.C.: International City Management Association, August 1978) and David S. Arnold, "Incentives for Municipal Employees: Data for Individual Cities, 10,000 and Over," *Urban Data Service Reports*, vol. 11 no. 9 (Washington, D.C.: International City Management Association, September 1979).

Table 5/5 SELECTED EMPLOYEE INCENTIVES IN CITIES 10,000 AND OVER

This table includes 1,265 municipalities (including cities as well as villages, boroughs, towns, and townships) 10,000 and over in population (based on U.S. Bureau of the Census April 1980 population counts). Data were collected from the survey *Employee Incentives—1984* conducted in the spring of 1984 by the International City Management Association. The survey specifically excluded police, fire, and education employees. Survey respondents are included in the following table only if the particular data items shown in the table are applicable to them and the survey response is usable. Leaders (..) indicate that the data are not reported. "Y" indicates yes; "N" indicates no.

Educational incentives: tuition reimbursement–amount–requirements to stay/time off/ salary increase/ available to all: indicates municipality's use of educational and professional development incentives: left, indicates municipality's use of tuition reimbursement; next, indicates type of tuition reimbursement (see key); next, indicates whether employee is required to remain with the municipality for a set period of time after receiving tuition reimbursement; next, indicates whether municipality allows time off with pay for employee to attend courses; next, indicates whether completion of a course with a passing grade usually results in a salary increase; right, indicates whether educational incentive program is available to all employees in the municipality.

Variation in working hours: 4-day work week/ flextime/ task system: left, indicates whether municipality allows a 4-day work week; next, indicates whether municipality allows flextime or gliding hours; right, indicates whether municipality allows employees to leave when they have completed the day's assigned tasks. "None" indicates that the municipality does not use any of these three incentives.

Attendance incentives: sick leave conversion/ cash bonuses/early retirement/personal leave/ pooling: left, indicates whether municipality converts unused sick leave to annual leave; next, municipality pays cash bonuses for unused sick leave periodically or at retirement; next, unused sick leave may be applied toward early retirement; next, total leave days can be used as either sick or annual leave; right, sick leave may be pooled or donated for use by all employees. "Not used" indicates that the municipality does not use any of these attendance incentives.

Job enrichment: job redesign/job rotation/labor–management committees/quality circles/ team approach: left, indicates whether municipality redesigns the day-to-day jobs of employees; next, municipality rotates employees through several different assignments (excluded is all rotation that is part of standard training programs for new employees); next, the municipality uses labor-management committees on noncontractual items such as productivity, working conditions, and safety; next, the municipality uses quality circles to identify, analyze, and solve problems in the work place; right, the municipality uses the team approach to encourage more cooperation and a broader view of the work process. "Not used" indicates that the municipality does not use any of these job enrichment incentives.

Awards: suggestion–cash–nonmonetary/performance–cash–nonmonetary/safety: left, indicates whether municipality gives suggestion awards; next, indicates whether cash awards are given; next, indicates whether nonmonetary suggestion awards are given; next, indicates whether municipality gives performance awards; next, indicates whether cash awards are given; next, indicates whether nonmonetary performance awards are given; right, indicates whether municipality gives safety awards. "Not used" indicates that the municipality does not use any of these awards.

Extraordinary benefits: indicates the type(s) of special incentives and fringe benefits the municipality provides (see key).

Key

Type of tuition reimbursement
- T–Total reimbursement
- P–Partial reimbursement
- D–Amount of reimbursement depends on course grade
- F–Fixed maximum amount for all employees

Extraordinary benefits
- A–Dental insurance
- B–Eye care
- C–Substance abuse programs
- D–Personal counseling
- F–Health counseling
- G–Financial counseling
- H–Free legal advice
- I–Cafeteria-type selection of benefits
- J–Day care program

Municipality	Educational incentives: tuition reimbursement-amount-requirements to stay-time off/ salary increase/ available to all	Variation in working hours: 4-day work week/ flextime/ task system	Attendance incentives: sick leave conversion/ cash bonuses / early retirement / personal leave / pooling	Job enrichment: job redesign/ job rotation/ labor-management committees / quality circles / team approach	Awards: suggestion-cash-nomonetary/ performance-cash-nomonetary / safety	Extraordinary benefits
ALABAMA						
Albertville	Y-D- Y-../../N	None	N/Y/N/N/N	Not Used	Not Used	...
Alexander City	N-...-..-Y/Y/N	None	N/N/N/N/N	Not Used	Y-N-Y/Y-N-Y/N	B,C
Anniston	Not Used	None	Not Used	Not Used	Not Used	...
Athens	Not Used	N/N/Y	N/Y/N/N/N	N/N/Y/N/N	Not Used	...
Auburn	Not Used	N/N/Y	Not Used	Not Used	N-N-N/Y-Y-Y/N	C
Bessemer	Not Used	N/N/Y	Not Used	Not Used	Not Used	B
Birmingham	Y-P- N-N/N/Y	Y/Y/Y	Not Used	N/N/Y/N/Y	Y-N-Y/N-N-N/Y	C,D,E,F
Enterprise	Not Used	None	Not Used	Not Used	Not Used	...
Eufaula	Y-T- N-N/N/Y	None	Not Used	Not Used	N-N-N/Y-N-Y/N	...
Fairfield	Not Used	N/N/Y	Not Used	Not Used	N-N-N/Y-N-N/N	A
Gadsden	Not Used	None	N/Y/N/N/N	Not Used	Not Used	A,C,D,E
Homewood	N-...-..-Y/N/Y	N/N/Y	Not Used	Not Used	Not Used	A
Hueytown	N-...-..-Y/N/N	None	Not Used	Not Used	Not Used	...
Huntsville	Y-P- Y-N/N/Y	N/N/Y	N/N/N/N/N	Not Used	N-N-N/N-N-N/Y	E
Mobile	Y-T,D-N-N/N/Y	None	Not Used	N/N/Y/N/N	Not Used	A
Mountain Brook	Y-T- N-N/N/N	N/Y/N	Not Used	Not Used	Not Used	...
Opelika	Y-T- N-Y/N/Y	N/N/Y	N/Y/N/N/N	N/Y/Y/N/Y	Y-N-Y/Y-N-Y/N	D,E,F
Tuscaloosa	Not Used	N/N/Y	Y/Y/N/N/N	Not Used	Not Used	D,E
ALASKA						
Juneau	N-...-..-Y/N/Y	Y/Y/N	Not Used	N/N/Y/N/N	N-N-N/N-N-N/Y	A,B
ARIZONA						
Casa Grande	Y-D- Y-Y/N/Y	N/Y/N	N/Y/N/N/N	Y/Y/N/N/Y	N-N-N/Y-N-Y/N	A,C,D,E,F,G
Chandler	N-...-Y-N/N/Y	Y/Y/N	Y/N/N/N/N	N/N/Y/N/N	Y-Y-Y/Y-Y-Y/Y	A,H
Douglas	Y-T- N-Y/N/Y	N/N/Y	N/Y/N/N/N	Not Used	Not Used	...
Flagstaff	Y-T- N-N/N/Y	Y/N/Y	Not Used	N/N/N/N/Y	N-N-N/Y-Y-Y/Y	A,D,E,H
Glendale	Y-F- N-N/N/Y	Y/N/N	Y/Y/N/N/N	N/N/Y/N/Y	N-N-N/N-N-N/Y	A,B,D,E
Lake Havasu City	Y-T- N-Y/N/Y	None	N/Y/N/N/N	Not Used	N-N-N/N-N-N/N	A
Mesa	Y-F- N-N/N/Y	Y/Y/Y	Y/Y/N/N/N	N/N/N/Y/N	Y-Y-Y/N-N-N/Y	A,B,C,D,E,F
Paradise Valley	Y-T- N-N/N/Y	None	Not Used	Not Used	Not Used	A
Phoenix	Y..- N-N/N/Y	Y/Y/Y	N/N/N/N/N	Not Used	Y-Y-Y/Y-Y-Y/N	A,D,E,F,G
Prescott	Y-T- N-N/N/Y	N/N/Y	Y/Y/N/N/N	Not Used	Y-Y-N/N-N-N/Y	A,D,E
Scottsdale	Y..- N-Y/N/Y	N/Y/N	N/N/N/N/N	N/N/N/N/N	N-N-N/Y-Y-Y/Y	A,B,D,E,F

Table 5/5 continued — SELECTED EMPLOYEE INCENTIVES IN CITIES 10,000 AND OVER

Municipality	Educational incentives: tuition reimbursement-amount-requirements to stay-time off/ salary increase/ available to all	Variation in working hours: 4-day work week/ flextime/ task system	Attendance incentives: sick leave conversion/ cash bonuses / early retirement / personal leave / pooling	Job enrichment: job redesign/ job rotation/ labor-management committees / quality circles / team approach	Awards: suggestion-cash-nomonetary/ performance-cash-nomonetary / safety	Extraordinary benefits
ARIZONA continued						
Sierra Vista	Not Used	N/N/Y	N/Y/N/N/Y	N/N/N/N/N	Y-Y-Y/Y-Y-Y/N	A,C,D
Tempe	Y-P- N-N/N/Y	N/N/Y	Y/Y/N/N/N	Not Used	N-N-N/N-N-N/Y	A,B
Tucson	Y-P- N-N/N/Y	N/Y/Y	Y/Y/N/N/N	N/Y/N/N/N	Y-Y-Y/N-N-N/N	A,B,C
Yuma	Y-P,F-N-N/N/Y	N/N/Y	Not Used	N/Y/N/N/Y	Y-Y-Y/N-N-N/Y	A,E
ARKANSAS						
El Dorado	Y-T-..-N/N/Y	N/N/Y	Not Used	Not Used	Not Used	...
Fort Smith	Y-T- N-N/N/Y	N/N/Y	N/N/N/N/N	N/N/Y/N/Y	Not Used	...
Hope	Not Used	N/N/Y	Not Used	Not Used	Not Used	A
Hot Springs	Not Used	N/N/Y	Not Used	Not Used	Not Used	A
Rogers	Not Used	None	N/N/Y/N/N	Not Used	N-N-N/Y-N-Y/N	A
Searcy	Not Used	N/N/Y	Not Used	Not Used	Not Used	A
Sherwood	Not Used	None	Y/N/N/N/N	...	N-N-N/Y-N-Y/Y	A
CALIFORNIA						
Alameda	Not Used	None	Not Used	Not Used	Not Used	A,D,E,F,H
Albany	N-...-N-Y/Y/N	Y/N/N	Not Used	Not Used	Not Used	A
Anaheim	Y-P- N-N/N/Y	N/Y/Y	N/N/N/N/N	Not Used	Y-N-Y/Y-Y-N/N	A,B,C,D,E,F
Arcadia	Y-F- Y-N/N/Y	None	Not Used	Not Used	N-N-N/Y-Y-Y/Y	A
Atwater	Y-P- N-N/N/Y	None	Not Used	Not Used	Not Used	A,B
Baldwin Park	Y-P,D-Y-N/N/Y	None	N/Y/N/N/N	Not Used	Not Used	A
Banning	Y-F- N-N/N/Y	None	Y/N/N/N/N	Not Used	Not Used	...
Barstow	Y-T- Y-N/N/Y	None	Not Used	Not Used	Y-Y-N/Y-N-N/N	A
Bell Gardens	N-...-..-Y/Y/N	None	Not Used	Not Used	Not Used	A,D,E,F
Bellflower	Not Used	None	N/Y/N/N/N	Not Used	Not Used	A
Belmont	Y-F- N-N/N/Y	None	N/Y/N/N/N	Y/N/N/N/N	Not Used	A,B
Berkeley	Not Used	N/Y/N	Not Used	N/N/Y/N/N	N-N-N/Y-N-Y/N	A,C
Beverly Hills	Not Used	None	Not Used	Not Used	N-N-N/N-N-N/Y	A,H
Brea	Y-F- N-N/N/Y	None	Not Used	Y/Y/N/N/Y	Not Used	A,D,E,F,G
Buena Park	Y-P- N-N/N/Y	None	N/Y/N/N/N	Not Used	Y-Y-Y/Y-N-Y/Y	A
Burbank	Y..- N-N/N/Y	N/N/Y	N/N/N/N/N	N/N/N/N/N	Y-Y-Y/N-N-N/N	D,E,F
Burlingame	Y..-..-N/N/..	N/Y/N	...	Not Used	N-N-N/N-N-N/N	A
Camarillo	Y-T,D-N-N/N/Y	None	N/Y/Y/N/N	Not Used	Not Used	A,D,E,F
Campbell	Y-F- N-N/N/Y	N/Y/N	N/N/N/N/N	Not Used	Not Used	A
Carlsbad	Y-T- Y-N/N/Y	Y/Y/N	Not Used	Not Used	Y-Y-Y/N-N-N/Y	A,B
Cathedral City	Y-T- N-N/N/Y	None	Not Used	Not Used	Not Used	A,B
Ceres	Y-T- N-Y/N/Y	N/N/N	N/Y/N/N/N	N/N/Y/N/N	Not Used	A,B,H
Cerritos	Y-F- Y-Y/N/Y	None	N/Y/N/N/N	N/Y/Y/N/N	Y-N-Y/Y-Y-Y/Y	A,D,E,F,G
Chico	Y..- N-N/N/N	None	N/N/Y/N/N	Not Used	Not Used	A
Chino	Y-P,F-N-../N/Y	None	N/N/N/N/N	N/N/Y/N/N	N-N-N/Y-N-Y/Y	A,B,D,E,F,G
Chula Vista	Y..- N-Y/N/Y	N/Y/N	N/Y/Y/N/N	Y/N/Y/N/N	Y-N-Y/N-N-N/N	A,B,C,D,E,F,H,I
Claremont	Y-T,F-Y-N/N/Y	N/N/Y	N/N/Y/N/N	N/N/Y/N/N	Not Used	A,H,I
Clovis	Y-T- N-N/Y/Y	None	Not Used	N/N/Y/N/Y	N-N-N/Y-N-Y/N	A,B
Colton	Y-T- N-Y/N/Y	None	N/N/N/N/N	Not Used	Not Used	...
Commerce	Y-F- Y-N/N/Y	None	N/Y/Y/N/N	N/N/N/N/Y	Not Used	A,B
Concord	Y-T- N-N/N/Y	Y/N/N	N/Y/N/N/N	Y/N/N/Y/N	N-N-N/Y-N-N/N	A,D,E
Corona	Y-F- N-Y/N/Y	None	N/Y/Y/Y/N	Not Used	Not Used	B,D
Coronado	Y-F- N-N/N/Y	N/Y/N	Y/N/N/Y/N	N/N/Y/Y/Y	Y-Y-Y/Y-N-Y/Y	...
Culver City	Not Used	N/N/Y	N/Y/N/N/N	Not Used	N-N-N/Y-N-N/N	A,C
Cypress	Y-F- Y-Y/N/Y	None	N/Y/N/N/N	Not Used	N-N-N/N-N-N/Y	A,B,C,D,E,F,G
Daly City	Not Used	None	Not Used	Not Used	Y-Y-N/N-N-N/Y	A,D,E,F
Davis	... ..-../../..	None	Not Used	Y/Y/Y/N/Y	N-N-N/N-N-N/Y	A,D
Delano	Y-T- N-Y/Y/N	N/N/N	Y/Y/N/N/N	Y/Y/Y/N/Y	Not Used	A
Downey	Y-T- N-N/N/Y	None	Not Used	Not Used	Not Used	A,C,D
Duarte	Y-P,F-N-N/N/Y	None	Y/N/N/N/N	N/Y/N/N/N	Not Used	A,B,E
El Centro	Not Used	None	N/N/Y/N/N	Not Used	Not Used	A,B
El Cerrito	Y-T- N-N/N/Y	None	Not Used	Not Used	Not Used	A
El Monte	N-...-..-../../..	None	Not Used	Not Used	Not Used	A,B,H
El Segundo	Y-T,D-Y-N/N/Y	None	N/Y/N/N/N	Y/Y/Y/N/Y	Y-Y-Y/Y-Y-N/N	A,D,H
Escondido	Y-F- N-Y/N/N	Y/Y/N	Y/N/N/N/N	Y/N/Y/N/N	Y-Y-Y/Y-Y-Y/Y	A,B,C,D,E,F,G,H
Fairfield	Y-T- N-Y/N/Y	None	N/Y/N/N/N	Not Used	Not Used	A,B,F
Folsom	Y-T- N-Y/Y/Y	None	N/Y/N/N/N	N/Y/N/N/N	Not Used	...
Fontana	Y-F- N-N/N/Y	None	N/N/N/Y/N	Y/Y/N/N/N	Y-Y-N/Y-Y-Y/N	A
Foster City	N-...-..-Y/N/Y	None	N/N/N/N/N	N/Y/N/N/N	Not Used	A,B
Fountain Valley	N-...-..-Y/N/..	N/N/N	N/Y/N/N/N	Not Used	Y-Y-N/N-N-N/N	A,B
Fremont	Not Used	Y/Y/N	N/Y/Y/Y/N	N/Y/N/Y/N	Not Used	A,D
Fresno	Y-T,F-Y-N/N/Y	N/N/Y	Y/N/N/N/Y	N/N/Y/Y/N	Y-Y-Y/N-N-N/Y	A,B,C,D
Fullerton	Y-F- Y-N/N/Y	N/Y/N	Y/Y/N/N/N	Y/N/N/Y/Y	Y-Y-Y/Y-Y-N/N	A,C,D,E,F,H
Gardena	Y-P- N-N/N/Y	N/Y/N	Not Used	Not Used	Not Used	A,B
Gilroy	Y..- N-Y/Y/N	N/Y/N	Not Used	Y/N/Y/N/N	Not Used	A,F
Glendale	Y-P,D-Y-N/N/Y	N/N/Y	Not Used	Not Used	Y-Y-N/N-N-N/N	A,B,C
Hanford	Y-F- Y-N/N/Y	None	Not Used	N/N/Y/N/N	N-N-N/Y-N-Y/N	A,H
Hayward	Y-T- N-N/N/Y	Y/N/N	N/Y/N/N/N	N/N/Y/Y/Y	N-N-N/N-N-N/Y	A,D,E,F,H
Hemet	Y-T- Y-N/N/Y	N/N/Y	Not Used	N/N/Y/N/N	Y-Y-Y/Y-Y-N/N	D
Hermosa Beach	Y-P- N-Y/N/Y	None	Not Used	Y/Y/N/N/N	N-N-N/N-N-N/N	A,B,C,D,E,H
Huntington Beach	Y..- N-N/N/Y	Y/N/N	N/Y/N/N/N	N/N/N/Y/N	Y-Y-N/N-N-N/N	A
Huntington Park	Y-T- N-Y/N/Y	Y/N/N	N/Y/N/N/N	N/Y/N/N/Y	Not Used	A,D
Indio	Not Used	None	Not Used	N/N/Y/N/N	N-N-N/N-N-N/Y	...
Inglewood	Y-F- N-N/N/Y	N/Y/N	Not Used	Not Used	Y-Y-Y/N-N-N/Y	A,B,C,D,E
La Mesa	Y-T- N-Y/N/Y	None	Y/N/N/N/N	N/N/N/N/Y	Y-Y-N/Y-N-N/N	A,B
La Mirada	Y-F- N-N/N/Y	Y/N/N	N/N/N/N/N	Not Used	N-N-N/Y-N-N/N	A,B,H
La Puente	Not Used	None	N/Y/Y/N/N	Not Used	Not Used	A,B

Table 5/5 continued SELECTED EMPLOYEE INCENTIVES IN CITIES 10,000 AND OVER

Municipality	Educational incentives: tuition reimbursement-amount-requirements to stay-time off/ salary increase/ available to all	Variation in working hours: 4-day work week/ flextime/ task system	Attendance incentives: sick leave conversion/ cash bonuses / early retirement / personal leave / pooling	Job enrichment: job redesign/ job rotation/ labor-management committees / quality circles / team approach	Awards: suggestion-cash-nomonetary/ performance-cash-nomonetary / safety	Extraordinary benefits
CALIFORNIA continued						
La Verne	N-...-..-N/N/N	None	N/Y/N/N/N	N/N/Y/N/N	Y-Y-Y/N-N-N/N	...
Lafayette	Not Used	None	Not Used	Y/N/N/N/Y	Not Used	...
Laguna Beach	Y-F- N-N/N/Y	None	N/Y/N/N/N	N/N/N/Y/Y	N-N-N/Y-Y-Y/N	C,D,E,F
Lakewood	... N-N/N/Y	None	N/Y/N/N/N	Not Used	N-N-N/Y-Y-N/N	A
Lancaster	Y-F- Y-N/N/Y	None	N/Y/N/N/N	N/N/Y/N/N	Not Used	A
Lawndale	Y-T- N-N/N/Y	None	Y/Y/N/N/N	Not Used	N-N-N/Y-Y-Y/N	A,D,E
Livermore	Y-P- N-N/N/Y	None	N/N/N/N/N	Not Used	N-N-N/Y-Y-N/N	A,B,H
Lodi	Y-P- N-Y/N/Y	N/Y/N	N/N/N/N/N	N/Y/N/N/N	Not Used	A,D,E
Loma Linda	Y-F- N-N/N/Y	N/Y/N	Y/N/N/N/N	Not Used	Y-N-N/Y-Y-Y/N	A,H
Lomita	Y-T- N-N/N/Y	None	Not Used	Not Used	N-N-N/Y-N-N/N	A
Lompoc	Y-P- Y-N/N/Y	N/N/N	N/Y/N/N/N	N/Y/N/N/N	Y-Y-N/N-N-N/Y	A
Los Alamitos	Y-T- N-N/N/N	None	N/Y/N/N/N	Not Used	Not Used	A,D,E,F
Los Altos	Y..-..-../../..	N/N/N	N/N/Y/N/N	N/N/Y/Y/Y	Not Used	A,D
Los Gatos	Y-F- N-N/N/N	N/Y/N	N/Y/N/N/N	N/N/N/N/Y	N-N-N/Y-Y-Y/N	A,B,D,E,F,H
Madera	Y-P- N-N/N/Y	N/Y/N	Not Used	N/N/Y/Y/N	N-N-N/N-N-N/Y	A,B
Manhattan Beach	Not Used	None	Y/N/Y/N/N	Not Used	Y-Y-Y/Y-Y-Y/Y	A,H
Manteca	Not Used	N/N/Y	Not Used	N/N/Y/N/N	N-N-N/Y-N-Y/N	A,B
Martinez	Y-T,F-N-N/N/Y	N/N/N	N/N/N/N/N	Not Used	Y-N-Y/Y-N-Y/N	A,B
Menlo Park	Y-F- N-N/N/Y	None	Y/Y/N/N/N	Not Used	Not Used	A
Merced	Not Used	None	Not Used	Not Used	Not Used	A,B,D
Milpitas	Y-P- N-Y/N/Y	Y/Y/N	N/Y/Y/N/N	Y/N/Y/N/Y	Y-Y-N/Y-Y-N/N	A,B
Modesto	Y-T- N-Y/N/Y	N/Y/N	Not Used	N/N/N/N/N	Y-Y-Y/N-N-N/N	A,B,C,D
Monrovia	Y-T,D-Y-N/N/Y	None	Not Used	Not Used	N-N-N/N-N-N/Y	A
Montclair	Y-F- N-Y/N/Y	None	N/Y/Y/N/N	Y/Y/Y/N/N	Y-Y-Y/N-N-N/N	A,B,D,E
Montebello	Y-T- N-N/N/Y	None	N/N/N/Y/N	N/N/Y/N/N	Y-Y-Y/Y-Y-Y/Y	A,B,C
Monterey	Y-P,F-N-Y/N/N	None	Not Used	Not Used	Not Used	A,B,H
Monterey Park	Y-T- N-N/N/Y	None	N/N/N/N/N	N/N/Y/N/Y	Y-N-Y/N-N-N/N	A
Moraga	Y-P- N-N/N/Y	N/Y/N	Not Used	Y/N/N/N/Y	Not Used	D,E
Newark	Y-F- N-N/N/Y	N/Y/N	N/Y/Y/N/N	Y/N/N/N/N	N-N-N/Y-Y-N/N	A,B,H
Newport Beach	... ..-../../..	N/N/Y	N/N/N/N/N	Not Used	Not Used	A
Norwalk	Y-F- N-N/N/Y	None	N/Y/N/N/N	N/N/Y/Y/Y	N-N-N/Y-N-Y/N	D,E,F
Novato	Y..- N-N/N/Y	N/Y/N	Not Used	N/N/N/N/N	N-N-N/Y-Y-N/N	A,B,H
Oakland	Y-T,D-Y-Y/N/Y	Y/Y/N	N/Y/N/N/N	Y/Y/Y/Y/Y	Not Used	A,B,C,D,E,F
Oceanside	Y-T,D-N-Y/N/Y	None	N/Y/N/N/N	Not Used	Y-Y-N/Y-Y-N/N	A,C,D,E,F
Ontario	... N-N/N/N	N/N/Y	N/N/Y/N/N	Not Used	Y-Y-Y/N-N-N/N	A,C,D,E,F,G,H
Orange	Y-F- N-../N/Y	None	Not Used	Not Used	Y-Y-Y/Y-N-Y/N	C,D,E
Oxnard	Y-P,F-N-N/N/Y	Y/N/Y	Y/N/N/N/N	N/Y/N/Y/N	Not Used	A,H
Palm Springs	Y-T- Y-N/N/Y	None	N/N/N/Y/N	N/N/N/Y/Y	Y-Y-Y/Y-Y-Y/N	A,B,C,D,E
Palmdale	Y-D- N-N/N/N	None	Not Used	Not Used	Not Used	A,B
Paramount	Y-T- N-N/N/N	None	N/Y/N/N/N	Not Used	Not Used	A,B
Petaluma	Not Used	N/Y/N	Not Used	Not Used	Not Used	I
Pico Rivera	Y-T- N-N/N/Y	N/Y/N	Not Used	N/Y/N/N/N	Not Used	A,B,D,G,H
Port Hueneme	Y-T- N-N/N/Y	None	Not Used	Y/N/Y/N/Y	Y-Y-Y/Y-N-Y/N	A,B,H
Porterville	Y-F- N-N/N/N	N/N/Y	N/N/N/N/N	Not Used	Y-Y-Y/N-N-N/N	A
Poway	Not Used	None	Not Used	N/N/N/N/N	Not Used	A,B,D
Rancho Cucamonga	Y-P- N-N/N/Y	None	Not Used	Not Used	Not Used	A,B
Rancho Palos Verdes	Y-P,F-N-N/N/Y	None	N/N/N/N/N	N/N/N/N/Y	Not Used	A,D
Redlands	N-...-N-N/N/Y	N/N/Y	N/N/N/N/N	Not Used	Not Used	A
Rialto	Y-D- N-Y/N/N	N/N/N	N/N/N/N/N	N/Y/N/N/N	N-N-N/N-N-N/Y	A,C,D,E,F
Richmond	Y-F- N-N/N/Y	None	Not Used	Not Used	Not Used	A
Ridgecrest	Y-P,F-N-Y/N/Y	None	Not Used	Not Used	Not Used	A
Riverside	Not Used	Y/N/Y	Not Used	Not Used	Y-Y-Y/Y-N-Y/N	A,C,D,E,F
Sacramento	Y-P- N-Y/N/Y	Y/Y/Y	N/Y/N/N/N	Not Used	Not Used	A,B,H
Salinas	Y-T- N-Y/N/Y	N/Y/N	N/Y/Y/N/N	N/N/Y/Y/N	N-N-N/Y-N-Y/N	A,B,G,H
San Carlos	Not Used	N/N/N	Not Used	Not Used	Not Used	A,D,E
San Clemente	Y-T,D-Y-Y/N/N	N/N/N	Not Used	N/N/Y/N/Y	Y-Y-Y/N-N-N/N	A,B
San Dimas	Y-F- N-N/N/N	Y/Y/N	N/Y/N/N/N	Y/Y/N/Y/Y	N-N-N/Y-N-Y/Y	A,C,G
San Fernando	Y-P- N-N/N/Y	None	Not Used	Not Used	Not Used	A
San Gabriel	Y-T- N-N/N/Y	None	N/Y/N/N/N	N/N/Y/N/N	Y-N-Y/Y-N-Y/N	A,D,E
San Juan Capistrano	Y-T- Y-N/N/Y	Y/N/N	Not Used	Not Used	N-N-N/Y-Y-Y/N	A
San Leandro	N-...-..-Y/N/..	None	Not Used	N/N/N/N/N	Y-Y-N/N-N-N/Y	A,D,E,F
San Luis Obispo	Not Used	Y/N/N	N/N/Y/N/N	N/N/Y/N/Y	N-N-N/N-N-N/Y	A,B,C
San Marcos	Not Used	N/Y/N	N/Y/N/N/N	N/N/N/N/N	Not Used	A
San Marino	Y-T- N-N/N/N	None	Not Used	Not Used	Not Used	A,B
San Pablo	Y-T,F-Y-N/N/Y	None	N/N/Y/N/N	N/N/Y/N/N	Not Used	A,D,E
San Rafael	Y-P- N-N/N/Y	N/Y/N	N/Y/N/N/N	N/N/Y/N/N	N-N-N/Y-Y-N/N	A,C,H
Sanger	Y-F- Y-N/N/N	Y/N/N	Y/N/N/N/N	N/N/Y/N/N	Not Used	A
Santa Cruz	Y-F- N-N/N/Y	Y/Y/Y	N/Y/N/N/N	N/N/Y/N/N	Not Used	A,B
Santa Fe Springs	Y-F- N-Y/N/N	None	N/Y/N/N/N	N/N/Y/N/Y	Y-Y-Y/Y-N-Y/N	A,C,D,E,F
Santa Monica	Y-F- N-N/N/Y	Y/N/Y	N/Y/N/N/N	N/N/Y/N/N	Not Used	A
Santa Paula	Y-P- N-N/N/Y	None	N/Y/N/N/N	Not Used	Not Used	A,B,H
Santa Rosa	Not Used	None	N/Y/N/N/N	N/Y/N/N/Y	N-N-N/Y-N-N/Y	A
Saratoga	Y-T,F-N-Y/N/Y	N/N/N	N/Y/N/N/N	Y/N/Y/N/Y	Not Used	A,C,D,E,F
Seal Beach	N-...-..-../../..	None	Not Used	Not Used	N-N-N/Y-N-Y/N	A,B
Seaside	Y-P,D-N-Y/N/N	None	Y/Y/N/N/N	N/N/Y/N/N	Y-Y-N/N-N-N/N	A
Simi Valley	Y-F-..-N/N/Y	None	N/Y/N/Y/N	Not Used	Y-N-Y/N-N-N/N	A,B
South Gate	Y-T,F-Y-N/N/Y	None	N/N/N/N/N	Not Used	Not Used	A,B,C,D,E
South Lake Tahoe	Y-T,D-N-Y/N/Y	Y/Y/N	Y/Y/N/N/N	Y/N/Y/Y/N	N-N-N/Y-Y-N/Y	A,B,C,D
Stockton	Y-T,D-N-N/N/Y	Y/Y/N	N/Y/N/N/N	N/N/Y/N/N	N-N-N/Y-Y-Y/Y	A,B,D,E,F
Suisun City	N-...-..-N/N/N	Y/Y/N	Not Used	Y/Y/N/N/Y	Not Used	A,B,C,D,F,H
Sunnyvale	Y..- N-Y/../Y	Y/Y/N	N/N/N/N/N	N/N/Y/N/Y	Y-Y-Y/N-N-N/N	A,D,E,F,H
Thousand Oaks	Y-T- N-Y/N/Y	Y/Y/N	Not Used	Not Used	Y-Y-N/Y-N-N/N	A,B

Table 5/5 continued SELECTED EMPLOYEE INCENTIVES IN CITIES 10,000 AND OVER

Municipality	Educational incentives: tuition reimbursement-amount-requirements to stay-time off/ salary increase/ available to all	Variation in working hours: 4-day work week/ flextime/ task system	Attendance incentives: sick leave conversion/ cash bonuses / early retirement / personal leave / pooling	Job enrichment: job redesign/ job rotation/ labor-management committees / quality circles / team approach	Awards: suggestion-cash-nomonetary/ performance-cash-nomonetary / safety	Extraordinary benefits
CALIFORNIA continued						
Tracy	Y-T- N-Y/N/Y	None	Y/N/N/N/N	N/N/Y/N/N	N-N-N/Y-N-Y/Y	A,B
Tulare	Y-F- N-N/N/Y	N/N/Y	N/Y/N/N/Y	Not Used	Not Used	A,C,E
Turlock	Not Used	None	N/Y/N/N/N	Not Used	N-N-N/Y-Y-N/N	A,B
Tustin	Y-P- Y-Y/N/N	N/Y/N	N/N/N/Y/N	Y/Y/Y/N/Y	N-N-N/Y-N-Y/N	A,C,D,E,F
Ukiah	Y-T- N-Y/N/Y	None	Not Used	Not Used	N-N-N/Y-Y-Y/N	A,B
Union City	Y-T- N-N/N/N	N/Y/N	Not Used	N/N/Y/N/Y	N-N-N/N-N-N/Y	A,C,D,E,F,H
Victorville	Y-P- N-Y/N/Y	None	Not Used	Not Used	N-N-N/N-N-N/Y	A
Vista	Y-T,F-N-N/N/Y	N/Y/N	Y/Y/N/N/N	N/N/Y/N/N	N-N-N/Y-N-Y/N	A,H
Walnut Creek	Y-F- N-N/N/Y	None	N/N/N/Y/N	Not Used	Y-Y-Y/N-N-N/N	A,C,D,E,F
Westminster	Y-P- Y-N/N/Y	None	Not Used	Not Used	Not Used	A,B
Whittier	Y-P- Y-N/N/Y	N/N/Y	N/N/Y/N/Y	Y/Y/Y/N/N	Y-Y-Y/N-N-N/Y	A,F
Yuba City	Not Used	...	...	...	...	A,B
COLORADO						
Arvada	Y-F- N-N/N/Y	Y/Y/N	Not Used	Y/Y/Y/Y/Y	Y-Y-N/N-N-N/Y	A,B,C,D,E,F
Aurora	Y-T,F-N-N/N/Y	Y/Y/N	Y/Y/N/N/N	Y/N/Y/N/Y	Y-Y-Y/Y-Y-N/Y	A,C,D,E,F
Brighton	Y-F- Y-N/N/Y	Y/Y/N	Not Used	N/N/Y/N/N	Y-Y-N/N-N-N/Y	F
Broomfield	Y-T- N-N/N/Y	N/Y/N	Not Used	N/N/N/N/N	N-N-N/Y-Y-Y/Y	A
Colorado Springs	Y-T- Y-N/N/Y	Y/Y/Y	Y/Y/N/N/N	Y/Y/Y/N/Y	N-N-N/Y-Y-N/N	A,C,D,E,F
Durango	Y-T,D-N-Y/N/Y	Y/Y/Y	N/Y/N/N/N	Not Used	Y-Y-Y/Y-Y-Y/N	E
Englewood	Y-T- Y-Y/N/Y	None	N/Y/N/N/N	N/N/Y/N/Y	Not Used	A,C,D,E,F
Grand Junction	Y-T- N-N/N/Y	Y/Y/Y	N/N/N/N/N	N/Y/N/N/N	Y-Y-N/Y-Y-Y/Y	A,C,D,E,F
Greeley	Y-T- Y-Y/N/Y	None	Not Used	N/N/N/Y/N	N-N-N/Y-N-Y/N	...
Lakewood	Not Used	Y/N/N	Y/N/N/N/Y	N/Y/Y/N/N	Y-Y-N/Y-Y-N/N	A,C,D,E,F
Littleton	Y-T,F-N-N/N/Y	...	...	Not Used	...	A,B,C,D,E,F
Longmont	Y-P- Y-Y/N/Y	N/N/Y	Not Used	Not Used	N-N-N/N-N-N/Y	A,C,D,E,F
Loveland	Y-T- Y-N/N/N	N/Y/Y	N/N/N/N/N	Y/N/Y/Y/Y	Y-Y-N/Y-Y-Y/Y	A,C,D,E,F
Northglenn	Not Used	Y/Y/Y	N/N/N/Y/N	Not Used	Not Used	A,D
Sterling	Y-P- N-N/N/Y	None	N/Y/N/N/N	Not Used	Not Used	A
Westminster	Y-T,F-Y-Y/N/Y	None	Not Used	N/N/Y/Y/N	Y-Y-N/N-N-N/N	A
CONNECTICUT						
Avon	Y-T- Y-Y/N/Y	None	N/Y/N/N/N	Y/N/Y/N/Y	Not Used	A
Bethel	Not Used	None	Not Used	Not Used	Not Used	C
Bristol	Not Used	None	Y/Y/N/N/N	Not Used	Not Used	A,C,D
Danbury	Y-P- N-N/Y/Y	None	Not Used	Not Used	N-N-N/Y-Y-N/N	A,D,E
Darien	Y-T- Y-Y/N/Y	None	Not Used	Not Used	N-N-N/N-N-N/Y	A
East Hartford	Y-T- Y-Y/N/N	N/N/Y	Y/N/Y/N/N	Not Used	Y-Y-N/N-N-N/N	A,B
Farmington	Y-T- N-Y/N/Y	None	Y/N/N/N/N	Not Used	Y-Y-N/N-N-N/Y	A,B,C,D,E
Glastonbury	Y-F- Y-../N/Y	...	...	N/N/Y/N/N	...	A,D
Greenwich	Y-P- N-Y/N/Y	None	N/N/Y/N/Y	N/N/Y/N/Y	Not Used	A,B,C,D,E,F
Groton	Y-D- Y-N/N/..	None	Not Used	Not Used	Not Used	A
Hamden	Not Used	None	...	Not Used	N-N-N/N-N-N/N	A,D
Killingly	Y-P- N-N/N/Y	None	N/Y/N/N/N	Not Used	N-N-N/N-N-N/Y	B
Ledyard	Not Used	None	Not Used	Not Used	Not Used	...
Manchester	Y-P-..-Y/N/N	None	N/N/N/N/N	N/N/Y/N/N	Y-Y-N/N-N-N/N	C
Mansfield	Y-T- N-N/N/Y	None	N/Y/N/N/N	Not Used	Y-Y-N/N-N-N/Y	C,D,E,F
Middletown	Not Used	None	N/Y/N/N/N	Not Used	N-N-N/N-N-N/Y	A,B
Milford	Not Used	N/N/Y	Not Used	Not Used	N-N-N/N-N-N/Y	A
Monroe	Not Used	None	Y/N/N/N/N	Not Used	Not Used	A
Montville	Y..- Y-Y/N/N	N/N/Y	Not Used	N/N/N/N/N	Not Used	D,E,F
New Fairfield	N-...-N-Y/N/N	None	Not Used	Not Used	Not Used	...
Newington	Y-F- N-N/N/Y	N/Y/N	...	N/N/N/N/N	Not Used	A
North Haven	Y-P,D-N-N/N/N	N/N/Y	Not Used	N/N/Y/N/Y	N-N-N/N-N-N/Y	A,C,D
Norwich	Not Used	None	Not Used	Not Used	Y-N-N/N-N-N/Y	...
Orange	Not Used	None	Not Used	Not Used	Not Used	A,D,E,F
Plainfield	Not Used	N/Y/N	N/Y/Y/N/N	N/N/Y/N/N	Not Used	...
Rocky Hill	Y..- N-Y/N/Y	None	Y/N/N/N/N	Not Used	N-N-N/Y-N-Y/Y	A
South Windsor	... ..-../../..	None	Y/N/N/N/N	Not Used	Not Used	A
Southbury	Y-T- N-../N/N	None	Not Used	Not Used	Not Used	A
Stonington	Not Used	N/Y/N	Not Used	Y/N/N/N/N	Not Used	A
Trumbull	Not Used	None	N/Y/N/N/N	Not Used	Not Used	A
Wallingford	... ..-../../..	None	...	Not Used	Not Used	A,C,D,E,F
West Hartford	Y-P- Y-Y/N/Y	N/N/Y	Y/N/N/N/N	N/N/Y/N/N	Not Used	...
Winchester	Y-T- N-Y/N/Y	N/Y/N	Y/N/Y/N/N	Y/N/N/N/Y	Not Used	A
Windsor	Y-P- Y-N/N/Y	None	Not Used	N/N/Y/N/N	Not Used	A,B,D,E,F
Wolcott	Not Used	N/N/Y	N/N/Y/Y/N	Not Used	Not Used	...
DELAWARE						
Dover	Y-F- Y-Y/N/Y	N/N/Y	N/N/Y/N/N	N/N/Y/N/Y	Not Used	...
Newark	Not Used	None	N/Y/N/N/N	N/N/Y/N/N	N-N-N/N-N-N/Y	A,C,D,E,F
Wilmington	Not Used	N/N/Y	Y/Y/N/N/N	Not Used	Y-Y-N/Y-N-N/N	C,D,E,F
FLORIDA						
Altamonte Springs	Y-T,D-Y-N/N/Y	Y/Y/Y	N/N/N/N/N	N/N/Y/N/N	N-N-N/Y-Y-Y/N	...
Belle Glade	Not Used	None	Not Used	Not Used	N-N-N/Y-Y-Y/N	...
Boca Raton	Y-P,D-Y-N/N/Y	N/N/Y	Not Used	N/N/Y/N/N	Y-Y-N/Y-N-Y/Y	C,D,E,F
Cape Coral	Y-T,D-N-N/Y/N	N/N/Y	N/N/Y/N/N	Not Used	Not Used	A,C
Clearwater	Y-F- Y-N/N/Y	N/Y/Y	N/N/Y/N/N	N/N/N/N/N	N-N-N/Y-Y-Y/N	A
Cocoa Beach	Y-T- N-N/N/Y	None	Not Used	Not Used	N-N-N/Y-N-Y/N	...
Cooper City	Y-P- Y-Y/N/Y	N/N/N	N/Y/N/N/N	Not Used	Not Used	A,B
Coral Gables	N-...-..-Y/N/Y	N/N/Y	Not Used	N/N/N/N/N	Not Used	D
Coral Springs	Y-P- Y-Y/N/Y	None	Y/Y/N/N/Y	Not Used	Not Used	A

Table 5/5 **SELECTED EMPLOYEE INCENTIVES IN CITIES 10,000 AND OVER**
continued

Municipality	Educational incentives: tuition reimbursement-amount-requirements to stay-time off/ salary increase/ available to all	Variation in working hours: 4-day work week/ flextime/ task system	Attendance incentives: sick leave conversion/ cash bonuses / early retirement / personal leave / pooling	Job enrichment: job redesign/ job rotation/ labor-management committees / quality circles / team approach	Awards: suggestion-cash-nomonetary/ performance-cash-nomonetary / safety	Extraordinary benefits
FLORIDA continued						
Dania	N-...-Y-Y/../Y	None	Y/Y/N/N/N	N/N/Y/N/N	N-N-N/N-N-N/Y	A
Davie	Y-T- N-N/Y/Y	None	Not Used	Not Used	Not Used	A,B
Daytona Beach	Y-F- Y-N/N/Y	None	N/Y/N/N/N	Not Used	Y-Y-Y/Y-Y-N/Y	B,C,E
Deerfield Beach	Y-T- N-Y/N/Y	N/N/Y	N/Y/N/N/N	Not Used	Not Used	...
Delray Beach	Not Used	None	N/Y/N/N/N	Not Used	N-N-N/N-N-N/Y	...
Dunedin	Y-T- Y-N/N/Y	N/Y/Y	N/Y/N/N/N	Not Used	N-N-N/N-N-N/Y	A,D,E,F
Fort Myers	Y-T,D-N-N/N/Y	N/N/Y	Not Used	Not Used	Not Used	A,D,E
Fort Pierce	Not Used	N/N/Y	N/Y/N/N/N	Not Used	Not Used	...
Gainesville	Y-P,F-Y-N/N/Y	N/Y/N	N/N/Y/N/N	Not Used	N-N-N/Y-N-Y/N	A
Gulfport	Not Used	N/N/Y	Y/N/N/N/N	N/Y/Y/N/N	Y-N-Y/N-N-N/Y	C,D,E,F
Haines City	Y-D- N-N/N/Y	N/N/Y	N/Y/N/N/N	Y/Y/N/N/Y	N-N-N/Y-N-Y/N	...
Hallandale	... ..-../../..	N/N/N	N/Y/N/N/N	Not Used	N-N-N/N-N-N/N	...
Hialeah	Y..- N-N/N/Y	N/N/Y	Y/N/N/N/N	N/N/N/N/N	N-N-N/Y-N-N/N	C
Hollywood	N-...-..-../../..	N/N/Y	Y/N/N/N/N	N/N/Y/N/N	Not Used	C,F
Homestead	Y-P- Y-N/N/Y	N/N/Y	Y/N/N/N/N	N/N/Y/N/N	Y-Y-N/N-N-N/N	...
Jacksonville	Y..- Y-N/N/Y	Y/Y/Y	...	N/N/Y/N/N	Y-Y-N/N-N-N/N	C
Key West	Not Used	None	N/N/N/N/N	Not Used	N-N-N/Y-Y-Y/N	...
Kissimmee	Y-T- Y-N/N/Y	N/Y/Y	Not Used	N/N/Y/N/Y	N-N-N/Y-Y-Y/N	D,F
Lakeland	Y-T,F-Y-N/N/Y	N/N/Y	N/Y/N/N/N	Not Used	Y-Y-Y/N-N-N/N	A,D,E
Largo	Y-D- N-N/N/Y	N/N/Y	Y/N/N/N/N	N/Y/N/Y/N	Y-N-Y/Y-Y-Y/N	C,D,E,F
Leesburg	Y..- Y-N/N/Y	N/N/Y	N/Y/N/N/N	Not Used	Not Used	...
Lighthouse Point	Not Used	...	...	...	...	...
Melbourne	Y-T- Y-N/Y/Y	None	N/Y/Y/N/N	N/N/N/Y/N	Y-Y-Y/Y-Y-N/Y	...
Miami	Y-P,F-Y-N/N/Y	N/N/Y	Y/Y/Y/N/N	Not Used	N-N-N/Y-Y-Y/N	A
Miami Beach	Y-F- Y-N/N/Y	N/N/Y	Y/N/N/N/Y	Not Used	N-N-N/Y-Y-Y/Y	A,C,D,E,F
Miami Springs	Not Used	N/N/Y	Not Used	Not Used	Not Used	D
Naples	Y-T,D-N-N/N/N	N/N/Y	Y/N/N/N/Y	Y/Y/Y/Y/N	Y-Y-N/N-N-N/Y	...
New Smyrna Beach	Y-T,D-Y-Y/N/Y	N/N/Y	N/Y/N/N/N	N/N/Y/N/Y	N-N-N/Y-N-Y/Y	A,C
North Miami	Y-F- N-Y/N/N	Y/Y/Y	Y/Y/Y/N/N	Y/Y/N/Y/N	Y-N-Y/Y-N-Y/N	A,C,E,H
North Miami Beach	Y-F- Y-Y/Y/Y	Y/N/Y	Y/Y/N/Y/N	Not Used	Y-Y-Y/Y-N-Y/Y	A,C
North Palm Beach	Y-P,F-Y-N/N/Y	N/N/Y	N/Y/N/N/Y	Y/N/Y/N/Y	N-N-N/Y-Y-Y/N	D
Oakland Park	Y-F- Y-N/N/Y	N/N/Y	N/Y/N/N/N	Not Used	Not Used	A
Ocala	Y-P- Y-Y/N/Y	N/N/Y	Y/Y/N/N/N	Not Used	Y-Y-Y/Y-Y-N/Y	A,D,E
Ormond Beach	Not Used	None	N/Y/N/N/N	N/N/Y/Y/N	Not Used	A,H
Palatka	Y-T- N-Y/../Y	N/N/Y	N/Y/N/N/N	Not Used	Not Used	...
Palm Bay	Y-D- Y-Y/N/Y	N/N/N	Y/N/N/N/N	N/N/Y/N/Y	Y-N-Y/Y-N-N/N	A,C,D,E,F,G
Palm Beach Gardens	Not Used	N/N/Y	N/Y/Y/N/N	Not Used	Not Used	G
Panama City	Y-P- N-N/N/Y	N/N/Y	N/Y/N/N/N	Not Used	Not Used	...
Pembroke Pines	Y-D- Y-N/N/Y	N/Y/N	N/N/N/N/N	Not Used	Y-Y-N/N-N-N/Y	...
Pensacola	Y-T- N-N/N/Y	N/N/Y	Y/Y/N/N/N	N/N/N/Y/N	N-N-N/Y-N-N/N	...
Plant City	N-...-..-Y/Y/N	N/N/Y	Y/Y/N/N/N	N/N/Y/N/N	N-N-N/N-N-N/Y	D,E
Plantation	Not Used	None	N/Y/N/N/N	Not Used	Not Used	A,B
Pompano Beach	Not Used	N/Y/N	Not Used	Not Used	Not Used	...
Port Orange	Y-F- N-N/N/Y	N/N/Y	N/Y/N/N/N	Not Used	N-N-N/Y-N-Y/N	B,C,D,E
Port St. Lucie	Not Used	None	Not Used	N/N/N/Y/N	Not Used	A,D,E,F,H
Riviera Beach	Y-D- N-../N/Y	N/N/Y	Not Used	Not Used	N-N-N/Y-Y-Y/N	A
Rockledge	Not Used	None	N/N/N/N/N	Not Used	Not Used	A
St. Petersburg	Not Used	N/Y/Y	Y/N/N/N/N	N/N/N/Y/N	Y-Y-Y/Y-N-Y/Y	D
Sunrise	Not Used	...	...	...	...	A
Tallahassee	Y-F- Y-N/N/Y	Y/N/Y	Not Used	N/N/N/N/N	N-N-N/N-N-N/Y	A,C,D,E,F
Tamarac	Y-T,D-Y-Y/N/Y	None	N/N/Y/N/Y	Not Used	Not Used	A
Tampa	Y-P,F-N-N/N/Y	N/N/Y	Y/N/N/N/N	Y/N/N/N/N	N-N-N/Y-N-Y/N	...
Tarpon Springs	Y-D-..-N/N/Y	None	Not Used	Not Used	Not Used	A
Temple Terrace	Not Used	N/N/Y	Y/N/N/N/N	N/N/Y/N/N	N-N-N/Y-N-Y/N	...
Titusville	Y-D- N-N/N/Y	N/N/Y	N/N/N/N/N	Not Used	N-N-N/Y-N-Y/Y	A,D,E,F
West Palm Beach	Y-T- Y-N/N/Y	N/N/Y	Not Used	Not Used	N-N-N/Y-N-Y/Y	...
Winter Haven	Y-T- Y-N/Y/Y	N/Y/Y	Not Used	Not Used	Not Used	...
Winter Springs	Not Used	None	Not Used	Not Used	Not Used	...
GEORGIA						
Athens	Not Used	N/Y/Y	Y/N/N/N/N	Y/Y/Y/N/N	N-N-N/Y-Y-N/Y	C,E
Atlanta	N-...-..-N/N/N	None	N/Y/N/N/N	Not Used	Not Used	A,C
College Park	Not Used	N/N/Y	Not Used	Not Used	Not Used	A
Cordele	Y-D- N-Y/Y/N	N/N/N	Not Used	Y/Y/N/N/Y	N-N-N/N-N-N/N	E
Decatur	Y-T- N-Y/N/Y	Y/N/Y	Not Used	Y/N/N/N/Y	Not Used	A,E
Douglas	Y-F- Y-N/N/Y	N/N/Y	Not Used	N/N/N/N/N	N-N-N/N-N-N/N	...
Dublin	Not Used	N/N/Y	Not Used	Not Used	N-N-N/Y-Y-Y/N	A
East Point	Not Used	None	Not Used	Not Used	N-N-N/N-N-N/Y	A
Fitzgerald	Y-T- N-Y/N/N	None	Not Used	Not Used	Not Used	...
Griffin	Y..- Y-N/N/Y	N/N/Y	N/Y/N/N/N	Not Used	N-N-N/N-N-N/N	D,E
Hinesville	... ..-../../..	N/N/N	N/N/N/N/N	Not Used	Not Used	...
La Grange	N-...-N-N/N/Y	N/N/Y	Not Used	Not Used	Not Used	...
Macon	Y-F- Y-N/N/Y	N/N/Y	N/Y/N/N/N	Not Used	Y-Y-Y/Y-Y-N/N	C,D,E,F
Marietta	Not Used	Y/N/Y	N/Y/N/N/N	Not Used	Y-Y-N/N-N-N/Y	A,B
Moultrie	Not Used	N/N/Y	N/Y/N/N/N	Not Used	Not Used	...
Newnan	Not Used	None	Not Used	Not Used	Not Used	...
Rome	Not Used	None	Not Used	Not Used	Not Used	...
Roswell	Y-D- Y-Y/N/Y	None	Not Used	Not Used	Not Used	E
Savannah	Y-T- Y-Y/N/N	Y/Y/Y	Y/N/N/N/N	Y/N/N/N/N	Y-N-Y/Y-N-Y/Y	C,D,E,F
Warner Robins	Not Used	N/N/Y	Not Used	Not Used	Not Used	A

Table 5/5 continued **SELECTED EMPLOYEE INCENTIVES IN CITIES 10,000 AND OVER**

Municipality	Educational incentives: tuition reimbursement-amount-requirements to stay-time off/ salary increase/ available to all	Variation in working hours: 4-day work week/ flextime/ task system	Attendance incentives: sick leave conversion/ cash bonuses / early retirement / personal leave / pooling	Job enrichment: job redesign/ job rotation/ labor-management committees / quality circles / team approach	Awards: suggestion-cash-nomonetary/ performance-cash-nomonetary / safety	Extraordinary benefits
HAWAII						
Hilo	Y..- Y-Y/N/Y	N/N/N	N/N/Y/N/N	Y/N/N/Y/N	Y-Y-N/Y-Y-Y/Y	A
Honolulu	Y-T,D-Y-N/N/Y	N/Y/Y	N/N/N/N/N	N/N/Y/Y/N	Y-Y-Y/Y-Y-Y/Y	A,B,D,E,F
IDAHO						
Coeur d'Alene	Y-P,F-N-N/N/Y	Y/N/N	Y/Y/N/N/N	Not Used	Y-Y-Y/N-N-N/N	A,C
Idaho Falls	Y-F- N-Y/N/Y	N/Y/Y	N/Y/N/N/N	N/Y/N/N/N	Not Used	A,B,C,D,E,F
Moscow	Y-T- N-Y/N/Y	None	Not Used	Not Used	Not Used	...
Pocatello	Y-T,F-N-N/N/N	Y/Y/Y	Not Used	N/N/N/Y/N	Not Used	...
Rexburg	Y-T- N-Y/Y/N	N/Y/N	Not Used	Not Used	Not Used	...
Twin Falls	Y-T- N-N/N/Y	Y/Y/N	Y/N/N/N/N	Y/N/N/N/N	Not Used	A,D,E
ILLINOIS						
Addison	Y-P- N-N/N/Y	N/Y/N	N/Y/N/N/N	N/N/N/N/Y	Not Used	A,B,D
Alton	Not Used	N/N/Y	N/N/N/N/N	N/N/Y/N/N	Not Used	...
Arlington Heights	Y-T,D-N-Y/N/Y	None	Not Used	N/Y/N/N/N	Not Used	B,C,D,E,F
Aurora	Y-T- Y-N/N/N	None	Not Used	Not Used	Not Used	...
Bartlett	Y-F- N-Y/N/Y	None	Not Used	Not Used	Not Used	...
Batavia	Y-P- N-N/N/Y	None	Not Used	Not Used	Not Used	A
Belleville	Not Used	None	N/Y/N/N/N	Not Used	Not Used	A,B
Belvidere	Y-D- N-Y/N/Y	None	Not Used	Not Used	Not Used	A
Bensenville	Y-D- N-N/N/Y	None	Not Used	Not Used	Not Used	...
Bloomington	Y-T,D-N-Y/N/Y	N/N/Y	Not Used	N/N/Y/N/N	Y-Y-Y/N-N-N/Y	C,D,E,F
Bolingbrook	Y-F- Y-N/N/Y	None	Not Used	Not Used	Not Used	...
Buffalo Grove	Y-T,D-N-Y/N/Y	Y/Y/N	Not Used	Not Used	N-N-N/Y-N-Y/N	A
Calumet City	Not Used	N/N/Y	Not Used	Not Used	Not Used	A,B
Carol Stream	Y-T- Y-N/N/Y	None	Not Used	Not Used	N-N-N/Y-Y-Y/N	...
Carpentersville	Y-T- N-N/N/Y	None	N/Y/N/N/N	Not Used	Not Used	D,E,F
Centralia	Y-T- Y-N/N/Y	N/N/Y	N/Y/N/N/N	N/N/Y/N/N	Not Used	...
Champaign	Not Used	None	Y/Y/N/N/N	Not Used	N-N-N/N-N-N/Y	...
Charleston	Y-T,D-N-N/Y/Y	N/Y/N	Not Used	Not Used	Y-N-Y/N-N-N/N	...
Chicago Heights	Y-T- N-N/N/Y	N/N/Y	Not Used	N/N/N/N/Y	Not Used	E,H
Country Club Hills	N-...-..-Y/N/..	None	N/Y/N/N/N	Not Used	Not Used	A
Crystal Lake	Y-T,D-N-N/N/Y	None	N/Y/N/N/N	N/N/N/Y/N	Not Used	...
Darien	Y-T-..-Y/Y/Y	None	N/N/N/N/N	Not Used	Not Used	...
Decatur	Y-F- N-Y/N/Y	None	N/Y/N/N/N	Not Used	Y-Y-N/Y-N-Y/Y	C,D,E,F
Deerfield	Y-F- Y-Y/Y/Y	N/Y/N	...	Y/N/N/N/Y	N-N-N/N-N-N/Y	A,C
Des Plaines	Not Used	N/Y/N	N/Y/N/N/N	N/N/Y/N/N	Not Used	E
Dixon	Not Used	None	Not Used	Not Used	Not Used	A,B
Downers Grove	Y-T- N-N/N/Y	None	N/N/N/N/N	Not Used	Y-Y-Y/Y-N-Y/N	A,B
East Peoria	Y-T- N-N/Y/Y	None	Y/Y/Y/N/N	Not Used	Not Used	...
Elgin	Y-T- N-N/N/Y	N/N/Y	N/Y/N/N/N	Not Used	N-N-N/Y-N-Y/N	C,D,E,F
Elk Grove Village	Not Used	None	Not Used	Y/Y/Y/N/N	Not Used	A
Elmwood Park	Y-T- N-Y/N/Y	None	Not Used	N/N/Y/N/N	N-N-N/Y-N-Y/Y	...
Evanston	Y-T- Y-Y/N/Y	N/N/Y	N/Y/N/N/N	N/N/Y/N/N	N-N-N/Y-N-Y/N	B,C,D,E,F
Fairview Heights	Y-D- Y-Y/N/N	None	Not Used	N/N/N/N/N	N-N-N/Y-N-Y/N	A,B
Glen Ellyn	Y-D- Y-N/N/Y	None	Not Used	N/N/Y/N/N	N-N-N/N-N-N/Y	...
Glendale Heights	Y-P,D-Y-Y/N/Y	None	Not Used	Not Used	Not Used	A,D,E,F
Glenview	Y-T- N-N/N/Y	None	Not Used	N/N/N/N/Y	Not Used	B,D,E,F
Glenwood	Not Used	N/Y/N	Not Used	Not Used	Not Used	...
Hanover Park	Y-D- Y-N/N/Y	None	N/Y/N/N/N	Not Used	N-N-N/Y-Y-Y/N	...
Highland Park	Y-D- N-N/N/Y	None	Not Used	Not Used	N-N-N/N-N-N/Y	A,C,D,E
Hoffman Estates	Y-T- N-N/N/Y	None	N/N/N/N/Y	N/Y/N/N/Y	N-N-N/Y-N-Y/N	A,C,D,E,F
Homewood	Y-D-..-../N/Y	None	Y/Y/N/N/N	N/N/Y/N/N	N-N-N/N-N-N/Y	...
Joliet	Y-T- N-N/N/Y	None	Not Used	N/N/N/Y/N	Not Used	A
Kewanee	... N-Y/N/Y	N/N/Y	...	Not Used	Not Used	...
La Grange	Y-T,D-Y-N/N/Y	None	Not Used	Not Used	N-N-N/N-N-N/Y	...
La Grange Park	Not Used	None	Not Used	N/N/Y/N/Y	Not Used	...
La Salle	Y-T- N-N/N/N	None	Not Used	Not Used	Not Used	A
Lake Forest	Y-T- N-Y/N/Y	N/N/Y	N/Y/N/N/N	N/N/N/Y/N	Y-Y-Y/Y-N-Y/N	A,C,D,E,F
Lisle	Y..- Y-N/N/Y	N/Y/N	N/N/N/N/N	N/N/Y/N/N	Not Used	A
Mc Henry	Y-T- N-N/N/Y	None	N/N/N/N/N	Not Used	Not Used	...
Machesney Park	Y-P- Y-N/Y/Y	N/Y/N	Not Used	N/Y/N/N/Y	Not Used	H
Matteson	Y-T,D-Y-N/N/Y	None	N/N/N/N/N	Not Used	Not Used	A
Midlothian	Not Used	None	Not Used	Not Used	Not Used	A
Moline	Y-T- Y-Y/N/Y	Y/N/Y	Y/Y/N/N/N	N/N/Y/N/N	N-N-N/Y-N-Y/Y	C,D,E,F
Monmouth	Y-T- N-Y/Y/Y	N/N/Y	Not Used	N/N/Y/N/N	Not Used	...
Morton	Y-T- N-N/N/Y	None	N/N/N/N/N	Not Used	N-N-N/Y-N-N/N	A
Mount Prospect	Y-P- N-N/Y/Y	N/Y/N	N/Y/N/N/N	Y/Y/Y/Y/Y	Y-N-Y/N-N-N/N	...
Mount Vernon	Y-T- N-N/Y/N	N/N/Y	Y/Y/N/N/N	Not Used	Not Used	...
Naperville	Y-T- Y-N/N/Y	None	Y/Y/N/N/N	N/Y/N/N/N	Y-Y-Y/Y-N-Y/Y	A
Niles	N-...-..-Y/N/..	None	Y/N/N/N/N	Not Used	N-N-N/Y-N-Y/N	A,D,E,F
Normal	Y-T- N-Y/N/Y	N/N/Y	Not Used	N/N/N/N/Y	Y-Y-Y/N-N-N/N	C,D,E,F
North Chicago	Y-P- N-Y/N/Y	None	Not Used	Not Used	Not Used	A
Northbrook	Y..- Y-N/Y/Y	None	N/Y/N/N/N	N/Y/N/N/Y	Not Used	B,D,E
Oak Lawn	Not Used	None	Not Used	Not Used	Not Used	A,C
Orland Park	Y-T- N-N/N/Y	None	Not Used	Not Used	Y-Y-N/N-N-N/N	A
Palatine	Y-P- Y-Y/N/Y	N/Y/N	N/Y/N/N/N	Y/Y/Y/Y/Y	N-N-N/N-N-N/Y	A
Palos Heights	Y-D- N-N/N/Y	None	Not Used	N/N/N/N/Y	Not Used	...
Peoria	Y-P- N-N/N/Y	None	Not Used	Not Used	Not Used	A
Peru	Not Used	None	Not Used	Not Used	Not Used	...
Prospect Heights	Not Used	N/Y/N	Not Used	Not Used	Not Used	...
Quincy	Y-D- N-N/N/N	N/N/Y	N/Y/N/N/N	Not Used	Not Used	C

Table 5/5 continued SELECTED EMPLOYEE INCENTIVES IN CITIES 10,000 AND OVER

Municipality	Educational incentives: tuition reimbursement-amount-requirements to stay-time off/ salary increase/ available to all	Variation in working hours: 4-day work week/ flextime/ task system	Attendance incentives: sick leave conversion/ cash bonuses / early retirement / personal leave / pooling	Job enrichment: job redesign/ job rotation/ labor-management committees / quality circles / team approach	Awards: suggestion-cash-nomonetary/ performance-cash-nomonetary / safety	Extraordinary benefits
ILLINOIS continued						
Rantoul	Y-T- N-N/N/Y	None	Not Used	Not Used	Not Used	D,E,F
River Forest	Y-T- N-N/N/N	None	Not Used	Not Used	Not Used	...
Rock Falls	Not Used	None	Not Used	Not Used	Not Used	...
Rock Island	Y-P,F-N-Y/N/Y	N/N/Y	N/N/N/N/N	Not Used	N-N-N/Y-N-Y/Y	C,D,E,F
Romeoville	Not Used	None	Not Used	Not Used	Not Used	...
St. Charles	Y-T- N-N/N/Y	None	N/Y/N/N/N	Not Used	Not Used	A
Schiller Park	Not Used	None	N/Y/N/N/N	N/N/Y/N/N	N-N-N/Y-N-Y/N	...
Skokie	Y-P- N-N/N/Y	N/N/Y	Y/N/N/N/N	N/N/Y/N/Y	N-N-N/Y-Y-Y/N	C,D,E
Sterling	Y-T- N-N/N/Y	N/N/Y	Not Used	Not Used	N-N-N/Y-Y-N/N	A
Streamwood	Y-P- N-Y/N/Y	N/N/N	Not Used	Not Used	Y-Y-Y/Y-N-Y/N	A,C
Tinley Park	N-...-..-N/Y/N	None	Not Used	Not Used	Not Used	...
Urbana	Y-T- N-Y/N/N	None	N/Y/N/N/N	N/N/Y/N/N	N-N-N/Y-N-Y/N	...
Washington	Y-T- N-N/N/Y	None	Not Used	Not Used	Not Used	A
Waukegan	Y-P- N-N/N/Y	None	N/Y/N/N/N	Not Used	Not Used	A
West Chicago	Y-P- N-N/N/Y	None	Not Used	Y/Y/N/N/N	Not Used	A
Westchester	Y-P,D-N-N/N/Y	None	N/Y/N/N/N	Not Used	Not Used	A
Western Springs	Y-T- N-Y/N/Y	N/N/N	N/Y/N/N/N	N/N/N/N/Y	Y-N-Y/Y-N-Y/N	...
Westmont	Y-T- N-Y/N/Y	None	N/Y/N/N/N	N/N/N/N/N	N-N-N/Y-Y-Y/Y	C
Wheaton	Y-T- N-N/N/Y	None	Y/N/Y/N/N	N/N/Y/N/N	N-N-N/Y-N-Y/Y	D
Wheeling	N-...-..-N/N/Y	None	Not Used	N/N/Y/N/N	Not Used	...
Wilmette	Y-P- N-Y/N/Y	Y/Y/N	Not Used	Not Used	Not Used	B
Wood River	Y-T- N-Y/N/N	None	N/Y/N/N/N	Not Used	N-N-N/Y-N-Y/N	A,B,D
Woodridge	Y-T- N-N/N/Y	None	Not Used	N/N/N/N/N	N-N-N/Y-N-Y/N	...
Woodstock	Not Used	None	N/Y/N/N/N	N/N/N/Y/Y	N-N-N/Y-N-Y/N	...
Zion	Not Used	N/N/Y	Y/N/N/N/N	Not Used	Not Used	...
INDIANA						
Bedford	Y-T- N-Y/N/Y	None	Not Used	Not Used	Not Used	...
Bloomington	Y-T- N-Y/Y/N	N/N/Y	Not Used	Not Used	N-N-N/Y-N-Y/N	A,D,E,G
Columbus	Not Used	N/N/Y	Not Used	Not Used	Not Used	...
Evansville	N-...-..-Y/N/..	N/N/N	Y/Y/N/N/N	N/N/N/N/N	Not Used	A,B
Franklin	Y..- N-Y/Y/N	None	Not Used	Not Used	Not Used	A,B
Greenfield	Y-P- N-N/Y/N	None	N/N/Y/N/N	Not Used	Not Used	...
Highland	Not Used	None	Not Used	Not Used	Not Used	A
Hobart	Y-T- N-Y/N/N	None	Not Used	Not Used	Not Used	...
Kokomo	Y-T- N-Y/N/N	N/N/Y	N/Y/N/N/Y	Not Used	Not Used	A
Lawrence	Not Used	None	Not Used	Not Used	Not Used	A,B
Marion	Not Used	N/N/Y	...	Not Used	N-N-N/Y-N-Y/N	...
Martinsville	... ..-Y/../..	...	...	...	...	...
Michigan City	Not Used	N/N/Y	N/Y/N/N/N	Not Used	Not Used	...
Munster	Y-F- N-N/N/Y	N/N/Y	Not Used	N/N/Y/N/N	Not Used	A
Speedway	Not Used	None	N/Y/Y/N/N	Not Used	Not Used	C
Washington	Y-T- N-Y/N/Y	None	Not Used	Not Used	Not Used	...
IOWA						
Ames	Y-T-..-Y/Y/..	N/Y/N	Not Used	N/N/N/N/N	Y-Y-N/N-N-N/N	D,E,F
Ankeny	Y-F- Y-N/N/..	None	N/N/N/N/N	Not Used	Not Used	A
Boone	Y-F- N-Y/Y/Y	None	N/Y/N/N/N	N/Y/N/N/Y	Not Used	...
Burlington	Y-T- N-Y/N/Y	N/Y/Y	N/Y/N/N/N	N/N/Y/N/N	N-N-N/Y-N-Y/N	A,C,D,E,F
Cedar Falls	Y-T,D-N-N/N/Y	Y/Y/Y	N/N/Y/N/N	Not Used	Not Used	...
Clinton	... ..-../../..	None	Not Used	Not Used	Not Used	A
Davenport	Y-P- N-N/N/..	None	Y/N/N/N/N	Not Used	Not Used	A,C,F
Fort Dodge	Y-D- N-Y/N/Y	None	N/Y/N/N/N	Not Used	Not Used	A,C
Fort Madison	Y-P- N-N/N/N	N/N/Y	Y/N/N/N/N	N/N/N/Y/N	Not Used	...
Indianola	Y-T- N-Y/N/Y	None	Not Used	N/N/Y/N/N	Y-Y-N/N-N-N/N	A
Iowa City	Not Used	N/N/Y	N/Y/N/N/Y	Not Used	Not Used	C,D,E
Marion	Not Used	N/N/Y	N/Y/N/N/N	N/N/N/N/N	Not Used	...
Marshalltown	Y-T- N-N/N/Y	None	Not Used	Not Used	Not Used	A
Newton	Y-T- Y-N/N/N	N/N/N	N/Y/N/N/N	N/N/N/N/Y	Not Used	A
Oskaloosa	Y-D- N-Y/N/Y	None	Not Used	Not Used	Not Used	...
Sioux City	Y-T- N-Y/N/Y	None	Not Used	N/N/Y/N/N	Not Used	...
Spencer	Y-T- N-Y/N/Y	None	N/N/N/N/N	N/Y/N/N/N	Not Used	...
Urbandale	N-...-N-N/N/N	N/Y/N	Not Used	Not Used	Not Used	...
Waterloo	Not Used	Y/Y/N	N/Y/N/N/N	N/N/Y/N/N	Not Used	A,C
KANSAS						
Chanute	Not Used	N/N/Y	Not Used	Not Used	N-N-N/Y-Y-N/N	...
Coffeyville	Not Used	None	Not Used	Not Used	Not Used	A
Dodge City	Y-T,D-Y-N/N/Y	None	Not Used	Not Used	Not Used	A
El Dorado	Y-P,D-Y-N/N/Y	N/N/Y	Not Used	Y/Y/N/N/N	Not Used	A,C,D,E,F
Emporia	Y-T- N-Y/N/Y	N/N/Y	N/Y/N/N/N	Y/N/N/N/N	N-N-N/N-N-N/Y	A,C,D,E,F
Garden City	Y-T- N-Y/Y/Y	None	N/Y/N/N/N	Y/N/N/N/Y	N-N-N/Y-N-Y/N	A,B,E,F
Hays	... ..-../../..	N/N/Y	Not Used	N/N/Y/N/N	Not Used	...
Hutchinson	Y-P- N-Y/N/Y	N/N/Y	Y/Y/N/N/N	Not Used	N-N-N/Y-N-Y/Y	A,C,E
Independence	Not Used	N/N/Y	Not Used	Not Used	N-N-N/Y-N-Y/N	...
Lawrence	Not Used	N/N/Y	Not Used	Not Used	Y-Y-N/Y-Y-Y/Y	C,D,E,F
Leavenworth	Y-T-..-../N/N	N/N/Y	...	Y/Y/N/N/N	Not Used	A,C,D,E
Leawood	Y-P,D-N-N/N/Y	None	Not Used	N/N/Y/N/N	Y-Y-Y/Y-N-Y/N	A
Lenexa	Y-T- Y-Y/N/Y	None	N/Y/N/N/N	Not Used	Not Used	A,D,E,F
Mc Pherson	N-...-N-Y/Y/Y	N/Y/N	Not Used	Not Used	Not Used	A
Manhattan	Y-D- N-Y/N/Y	None	N/N/N/N/N	Not Used	Not Used	A
Merriam	Y-D- N-N/N/Y	None	Not Used	Not Used	Not Used	...
Newton	Y-T- N-N/N/Y	Y/N/Y	N/Y/N/N/N	N/N/N/N/Y	Not Used	...

Table 5/5 continued SELECTED EMPLOYEE INCENTIVES IN CITIES 10,000 AND OVER

Municipality	Educational incentives: tuition reimbursement-amount-requirements to stay-time off/ salary increase/ available to all	Variation in working hours: 4-day work week/ flextime/ task system	Attendance incentives: sick leave conversion/ cash bonuses / early retirement / personal leave / pooling	Job enrichment: job redesign/ job rotation/ labor-management committees / quality circles / team approach	Awards: suggestion-cash-nomonetary/ performance-cash-nomonetary / safety	Extraordinary benefits
KANSAS continued						
Olathe	Y-P,D-N-Y/N/Y	N/N/Y	Not Used	Not Used	N-N-N/Y-Y-Y/N	A,B,C,D,E,F
Ottawa	Not Used	None	Not Used	Not Used	N-N-N/Y-N-N/N	A
Overland Park	Y-P- N-Y/N/Y	N/Y/N	Not Used	N/N/Y/N/N	N-N-N/N-N-N/Y	C,D,E,F
Pittsburg	Y-P,D-N-N/N/Y	None	Not Used	Not Used	Not Used	...
Prairie Village	Y-P- N-Y/Y/Y	N/N/N	Not Used	N/N/N/N/N	Not Used	...
Shawnee	Y-T,D-N-Y/N/Y	N/Y/N	Not Used	N/Y/N/N/Y	Not Used	...
Topeka	Y-F- Y-Y/N/Y	N/Y/Y	Not Used	N/N/Y/N/Y	Not Used	A,C,D,E,F,H
KENTUCKY						
Ashland	Not Used	None	N/Y/N/N/N	Not Used	N-N-N/N-N-N/Y	A
Bowling Green	Y-T- N-Y/N/Y	None	Not Used	N/N/Y/N/N	Not Used	...
Covington	Y-D-..-N/N/Y	N/Y/N	...	N/N/Y/Y/Y	Not Used	A,D,E
Danville	Not Used	N/Y/N	Not Used	N/N/N/N/Y	Not Used	...
Elizabethtown	Y-T- N-N/Y/..	None	Not Used	Not Used	Not Used	...
Erlanger	Not Used	None	Not Used	Not Used	Not Used	A
Fort Thomas	Y-F- N-N/N/Y	N/Y/N	N/Y/Y/N/Y	Not Used	Not Used	D
Hopkinsville	N-...-..-Y/N/..	None	Y/N/N/N/N	N/N/Y/N/N	N-N-N/N-N-N/Y	...
Lexington-Fayette	Not Used	N/N/Y	N/N/N/N/N	Not Used	Not Used	A,D,E,F
Louisville	Not Used	Y/Y/N	Not Used	N/N/N/Y/N	Not Used	C,D,E,F
Murray	Y-P,D-N-N/N/Y	N/N/Y	N/Y/Y/N/N	Not Used	Not Used	...
Newport	N-...-N-N/N/Y	None	Y/N/N/N/N	Not Used	Not Used	A
Nicholasville	Y-T- N-Y/N/..	None	N/Y/N/N/N	Not Used	Not Used	...
Richmond	Not Used	N/N/Y	Not Used	Not Used	Not Used	...
Shively	Not Used	Y/N/Y	N/Y/N/N/N	Not Used	Not Used	...
Somerset	Y-P,D-N-Y/Y/Y	N/N/Y	Not Used	Not Used	Not Used	...
Winchester	Y-F- Y-N/N/Y	N/Y/N	N/Y/N/N/N	N/Y/N/N/N	Not Used	...
LOUISIANA						
Abbeville	N-...-..-Y/N/N	N/N/Y	Not Used	Not Used	Not Used	A,C
Jennings	Y-T- N-Y/N/N	None	Not Used	N/Y/Y/Y/N	N-N-N/N-N-N/Y	A,C,D
Kenner	Not Used	N/Y/N	N/Y/N/N/N	N/N/N/N/Y	Y-N-Y/Y-N-Y/N	A,C,D,E,F
Monroe	Not Used	None	Not Used	Not Used	Not Used	A,D
Shreveport	Y-T- Y-N/N/Y	N/N/Y	Not Used	Not Used	Y-N-Y/Y-N-Y/N	A,C,D,E,F
MAINE						
Augusta	Y-T,D-N-Y/Y/Y	None	N/Y/N/N/N	Not Used	Not Used	...
Bangor	Y-D- N-Y/N/Y	None	Not Used	Not Used	Not Used	...
Biddeford	Y-T- N-Y/N/Y	N/N/N	Not Used	Not Used	Not Used	...
Brunswick	Y-P- N-Y/N/Y	N/N/Y	Not Used	Not Used	Not Used	...
Gorham	Y-T,D-N-Y/N/Y	None	Not Used	Not Used	Not Used	...
Lewiston	Y-P- N-Y/N/Y	N/N/Y	N/Y/N/N/N	N/N/Y/N/N	Y-Y-N/N-N-N/N	...
Orono	Not Used	Y/N/N	Not Used	N/N/Y/N/N	Not Used	F
Portland	Y..- N-Y/N/Y	Y/Y/Y	N/Y/N/N/N	N/N/Y/N/Y	Y-Y-Y/Y-N-Y/Y	C,D,E
Presque Isle	Not Used	None	Not Used	Not Used	Not Used	...
Saco	Not Used	N/N/Y	Y/N/N/N/N	Not Used	Not Used	B
Scarborough	N-...-N-Y/N/Y	Y/N/N	Not Used	Not Used	Not Used	...
Waterville	Y-D- N-Y/N/Y	N/Y/N	Y/Y/Y/N/N	N/N/N/N/Y	Y-N-Y/N-N-N/N	...
Windham	Y-T- N-Y/N/N	None	N/Y/N/N/N	Not Used	N-N-N/N-N-N/Y	...
MARYLAND						
Annapolis	Y-P- N-N/N/Y	N/N/Y	Not Used	Not Used	Y-N-N/N-N-N/N	B
Bowie	Y-P- N-N/N/Y	N/N/Y	Not Used	Not Used	Y-Y-N/Y-N-Y/N	B
College Park	Y-P- N-N/N/Y	N/N/Y	Not Used	N/N/N/N/Y	Y-Y-Y/Y-Y-Y/Y	B
Gaithersburg	Y-T- N-N/N/Y	N/Y/N	Not Used	Not Used	Not Used	A,C
Greenbelt	Y-F- Y-N/N/N	N/Y/Y	Not Used	N/N/N/Y/N	N-N-N/Y-Y-Y/N	D
Laurel	Y-T- N-Y/N/Y	N/N/Y	N/Y/N/N/N	N/N/N/N/Y	N-N-N/N-N-N/Y	A,B,D
Rockville	Y-P,D-N-Y/N/Y	N/N/Y	N/Y/N/N/N	N/N/Y/N/N	N-N-N/Y-N-Y/N	A,B,C,D,E,F,H
Takoma Park	Y-T- Y-N/N/Y	N/Y/Y	N/N/Y/N/N	Not Used	Not Used	...
MASSACHUSETTS						
Acton	Not Used	None	Not Used	Not Used	Not Used	...
Amesbury	Y-P- Y-N/N/N	None	Not Used	Not Used	Not Used	...
Amherst	Y-P- Y-Y/N/Y	None	N/Y/N/N/N	N/N/N/Y/N	Not Used	C,D,E,F
Arlington	Not Used	N/N/Y	Y/Y/N/N/N	Not Used	N-N-N/Y-N-Y/N	...
Brookline	N-...-Y-N/N/N	N/N/Y	Y/N/N/N/N	Not Used	Not Used	C,D,E
Cambridge	Y-F- N-Y/N/Y	Y/N/Y	Y/N/N/N/N	Not Used	Not Used	A
Concord	Y-F- N-N/N/Y	None	Not Used	N/N/Y/N/N	Not Used	B
Danvers	Y-T- N-N/N/Y	N/N/Y	N/Y/N/N/N	Y/N/Y/N/Y	Not Used	A,C
Easthampton	N-...-..-../../..	None	N/N/N/N/N	Not Used	Not Used	...
Falmouth	Y-F- N-N/N/N	N/Y/N	N/Y/N/N/N	N/Y/N/N/N	Not Used	...
Framingham	N-...-..-Y/N/N	None	Y/N/N/N/N	Not Used	Not Used	D,E
Gloucester	Y-T- N-N/N/Y	None	N/Y/N/N/N	Not Used	Not Used	...
Greenfield	Y-P- N-Y/N/N	N/N/N	Not Used	N/N/N/N/Y	Not Used	...
Hanover	Not Used	None	Not Used	Not Used	Not Used	...
Holden	Not Used	None	Not Used	Not Used	Not Used	C,D,E
Ipswich	Y-D- N-Y/N/N	N/Y/N	N/N/N/N/N	N/N/N/N/Y	Not Used	...
Lexington	Y-P- N-N/N/Y	None	Not Used	Not Used	Not Used	...
Marblehead	Not Used	None	N/Y/N/N/N	Not Used	Not Used	...
Medford	... N-N/N/N	None	Not Used	Not Used	Not Used	...
Melrose	Not Used	N/N/N	Not Used	Not Used	Not Used	...
Natick	... ..-Y/N/Y	N/N/Y	Y/N/N/N/N	Y/N/Y/N/Y	Not Used	...
Northampton	Not Used	None	Not Used	N/N/Y/N/N	Not Used	...
Northborough	Not Used	None	Not Used	Not Used	Not Used	...
Oxford	N-...-..-Y/N/..	None	Not Used	N/N/N/N/N	Not Used	...

Table 5/5 continued **SELECTED EMPLOYEE INCENTIVES IN CITIES 10,000 AND OVER**

Municipality	Educational incentives: tuition reimbursement-amount-requirements to stay-time off/ salary increase/ available to all	Variation in working hours: 4-day work week/ flextime/ task system	Attendance incentives: sick leave conversion/ cash bonuses / early retirement / personal leave / pooling	Job enrichment: job redesign/ job rotation/ labor-management committees / quality circles / team approach	Awards: suggestion-cash-nomonetary/ performance-cash-nomonetary / safety	Extraordinary benefits
MASSACHUSETTS continued						
Randolph	... ..-../N/..	None	N/Y/N/N/Y	Not Used	Not Used	C,D,E
Salem	Not Used	None	N/Y/N/N/N	N/N/Y/N/N	Not Used	...
Saugus	Not Used	None	N/N/Y/N/N	Not Used	Y-Y-N/N-N-N/N	...
Seekonk	Not Used	None	Not Used	Not Used	Not Used	...
Shrewsbury	Y-T- N-N/N/Y	None	Y/Y/N/N/N	Not Used	Not Used	...
Stoneham	Y-P- Y-Y/N/Y	None	Not Used	Not Used	Not Used	...
Watertown	Y-P- N-Y/N/Y	None	N/Y/N/N/N	N/N/Y/N/N	Not Used	C,H
Wayland	N-...-N-Y/N/Y	Y/Y/N	N/Y/N/N/N	N/N/Y/N/N	Not Used	...
Wellesley	Y-T- Y-N/N/N	N/Y/N	Y/N/N/N/N	Not Used	Not Used	D,E
Weymouth	Not Used	...	...	...	...	...
Wilmington	Not Used	None	Y/N/N/N/Y	Not Used	Not Used	...
Winchester	Y-T- N-N/Y/Y	None	Not Used	N/N/Y/N/N	Not Used	...
Worcester	Y-P- Y-N/N/N	N/N/Y	N/Y/N/N/N	N/N/Y/N/N	Not Used	C
Yarmouth	Y-T,D-Y-Y/N/Y	None	Not Used	Not Used	Not Used	...
MICHIGAN						
Adrian	Not Used	None	Y/Y/N/N/N	Not Used	Not Used	A,C,D,E,F
Albion	Y-P- N-N/N/Y	None	Not Used	N/N/Y/Y/Y	Not Used	A
Alpena	Not Used	None	Not Used	Not Used	Not Used	A
Ann Arbor	Y-T- Y-N/N/Y	N/N/Y	N/N/N/N/N	Y/Y/Y/N/N	N-N-N/Y-Y-N/N	A,B,D,E,F
Berkley	Y-T- N-Y/Y/Y	None	N/Y/N/N/N	Y/N/Y/N/N	Not Used	A,B
Beverly Hills	Y-T- N-N/N/Y	None	N/Y/N/N/N	N/N/Y/N/N	Not Used	A
Birmingham	Y-F- N-N/N/Y	None	N/Y/N/N/N	Not Used	Not Used	A,B
Cadillac	Y-T,D-N-Y/N/Y	None	Not Used	N/N/Y/N/Y	Not Used	A,B
Dearborn Heights	Not Used	None	N/Y/N/N/N	N/N/Y/N/N	Not Used	A
East Detroit	Y-T- Y-Y/N/Y	N/N/Y	N/Y/N/Y/Y	N/N/Y/N/Y	N-N-N/Y-N-Y/N	A,B,C,D,E
Escanaba	Y-T- Y-Y/N/Y	Y/N/Y	N/Y/N/N/N	Not Used	Not Used	...
Farmington	Y-T- N-N/N/Y	None	Y/N/N/N/N	Not Used	Not Used	A,B,C,D
Farmington Hills	Y-T- Y-N/N/Y	None	Not Used	Y/Y/N/N/N	Not Used	A,B
Flint	Y-P- N-N/N/Y	Y/Y/Y	Not Used	Not Used	N-N-N/N-N-N/Y	A,C
Garden City	N-...-N-Y/N/Y	N/N/Y	Not Used	Y/Y/Y/Y/Y	N-N-N/Y-N-Y/N	A,B
Grand Rapids	Not Used	None	Not Used	Not Used	Y-Y-N/Y-N-Y/N	A,C,D
Grosse Pointe Woods	Y-D- N-N/N/Y	None	N/Y/N/N/Y	Not Used	Not Used	A,B,D,E
Harper Woods	Y-D- N-N/N/Y	None	Not Used	N/N/Y/N/Y	Y-N-Y/N-N-N/N	A,B,D,E,F
Holland	Y-T,F-N-N/N/Y	None	Not Used	Not Used	Y-Y-N/N-N-N/N	...
Jackson	Y-T,D-N-N/N/Y	None	N/Y/N/N/N	Not Used	Not Used	A
Kalamazoo	Not Used	None	Not Used	Not Used	N-N-N/N-N-N/Y	A,C,D,E,F
Kentwood	Y-T- Y-N/N/Y	N/Y/N	N/N/N/N/N	Not Used	Not Used	A,D,E
Lansing	Y-F- N-N/N/N	None	Not Used	Not Used	N-N-N/N-N-N/N	A,B,C,D,E,F
Lincoln Park	Y-F- N-N/N/Y	None	Y/N/N/N/N	Not Used	Not Used	A,B
Livonia	Y-F- N-N/N/N	N/Y/N	Y/Y/N/N/N	Not Used	Not Used	A,B
Madison Heights	Y-F- Y-N/N/Y	N/N/Y	N/Y/N/N/N	Not Used	Not Used	A,B,C
Meridian	Y-T- Y-Y/N/Y	N/Y/N	N/Y/N/N/N	N/N/Y/N/N	Not Used	...
Midland	Y-T- N-N/N/Y	Y/Y/Y	Not Used	Y/Y/Y/N/N	Not Used	A,C,D,E,F
Monroe	Y-D- Y-N/N/Y	None	N/Y/N/N/N	Not Used	Not Used	A
Mount Clemens	Y-F- N-N/N/Y	Y/Y/Y	Y/N/N/N/N	N/N/Y/N/N	Not Used	A,C,D,E,F
Mount Pleasant	Y-T- N-Y/N/Y	Y/Y/N	N/Y/N/N/N	Not Used	Not Used	A
Muskegon	Y-T,D-N-N/N/Y	None	N/Y/N/N/Y	Not Used	Not Used	A,D,E,F
Niles	Y-D- N-N/N/Y	N/Y/N	N/Y/N/N/N	N/Y/Y/Y/Y	Not Used	A
Norton Shores	Y-T- N-N/N/Y	None	Not Used	N/Y/Y/N/N	Not Used	A
Novi	Y-P,F-N-N/N/Y	None	Y/Y/N/N/Y	N/N/Y/N/Y	Not Used	A,B
Owosso	Y-T- N-N/N/Y	N/Y/N	Not Used	N/N/Y/N/N	Not Used	A
Port Huron	Y-T- N-N/N/N	N/Y/N	Not Used	Not Used	N-N-N/N-N-N/Y	A,E
River Rouge	Y-F- N-N/N/Y	None	Not Used	Not Used	Not Used	...
Romulus	Not Used	None	Not Used	N/N/N/Y/N	N-N-N/Y-N-Y/N	A,B,D,E,F
Royal Oak	N-...-N-N/N/Y	None	N/N/N/N/N	N/N/N/N/N	Not Used	A,C,D
Saginaw	Y..- N-N/N/N	None	N/Y/N/N/N	Not Used	Not Used	A
Saginaw	Y-D- N-N/N/N	None	N/N/N/Y/N	Not Used	Not Used	A
Sault Ste. Marie	Y-P- N-N/N/Y	None	Not Used	Not Used	Not Used	A,C
Taylor	Y-P,D-Y-N/N/Y	None	...	N/N/Y/N/Y	N-N-N/Y-N-Y/N	A,B,C
Traverse City	Y-D- N-N/N/Y	Y/Y/N	N/N/N/N/N	N/Y/N/N/N	Not Used	C,D,E,F
Trenton	Not Used	N/N/N	Y/N/N/N/N	N/N/Y/N/N	Not Used	A,B
Warren	Not Used	N/Y/Y	Y/Y/N/N/N	N/N/N/N/Y	Not Used	A,B,H
Wyoming	Y-T- N-N/N/Y	None	Y/Y/N/N/N	Not Used	Y-Y-N/N-N-N/Y	A,D,E
Ypsilanti	Y-D- Y-Y/N/Y	N/Y/N	Y/N/N/N/N	Not Used	Not Used	A,B
MINNESOTA						
Albert Lea	Y-T- N-Y/N/N	None	N/N/N/N/N	Y/Y/Y/N/Y	Not Used	D,E,F,G
Anoka	Y-T- N-Y/N/Y	None	Not Used	Not Used	N-N-N/Y-N-Y/N	A,B,C,D,E,F
Apple Valley	Y-T- N-N/N/Y	N/N/N	N/Y/N/N/N	N/N/N/N/Y	Not Used	A,B,C,D,E,F,G
Austin	Not Used	None	Not Used	Not Used	Not Used	B,C,E
Bemidji	Y-T- N-Y/N/Y	None	N/Y/N/N/N	Not Used	Not Used	...
Blaine	Y-P,D-N-N/N/N	None	N/N/N/N/N	Not Used	Y-N-Y/Y-Y-N/Y	A,C,D,E,F,H
Brooklyn Center	Y-P- N-N/N/Y	None	Y/N/N/N/N	N/N/N/Y/N	Not Used	A,C,D,E,F
Brooklyn Park	Y-T- N-N/N/Y	N/Y/N	Not Used	Not Used	Y-Y-N/N-N-N/N	C,D,E,F
Columbia Heights	Y-T- N-N/N/Y	None	Y/Y/N/N/N	N/Y/Y/Y/Y	Y-N-Y/N-N-N/N	A,C,D,E,F
Coon Rapids	Y-F- Y-N/N/Y	Y/Y/N	Y/Y/N/N/N	Not Used	N-N-N/Y-Y-N/N	D,H
Cottage Grove	Y-T,D-N-N/N/Y	None	N/N/N/N/N	N/N/Y/N/Y	N-N-N/Y-Y-N/N	A,B,C,D,E,F
Crystal	Y-P,D-N-N/N/Y	None	Not Used	Not Used	N-N-N/N-N-N/Y	A,B,C,D,E
Eagan	Y-T- N-N/N/N	None	Not Used	Not Used	Not Used	D,E,F
Eden Prairie	Y-D- N-N/N/Y	N/Y/N	Y/Y/N/N/N	N/N/N/N/Y	Not Used	A,B,D,E,F
Edina	Y-D- Y-N/N/Y	None	Not Used	Y/Y/N/N/N	Not Used	C,D

Table 5/5 continued — SELECTED EMPLOYEE INCENTIVES IN CITIES 10,000 AND OVER

Municipality	Educational incentives: tuition reimbursement-amount-requirements to stay-time off/ salary increase/ available to all	Variation in working hours: 4-day work week/ flextime/ task system	Attendance incentives: sick leave conversion/ cash bonuses / early retirement / personal leave / pooling	Job enrichment: job redesign/ job rotation/ labor-management committees / quality circles / team approach	Awards: suggestion-cash-nomonetary/ performance-cash-nomonetary / safety	Extraordinary benefits
MINNESOTA continued						
Fairmont	Not Used	None	N/Y/N/N/Y	N/N/Y/Y/Y	Not Used	A
Faribault	Y-P- N-Y/N/Y	N/Y/N	N/Y/N/N/N	N/N/Y/N/Y	Not Used	...
Fergus Falls	Y-T- N-Y/N/Y	N/N/Y	Not Used	Not Used	N-N-N/N-N-N/Y	C,D,E,F
Golden Valley	Y-T- N-Y/N/Y	None	Y/Y/N/N/N	Not Used	Y-Y-N/N-N-N/N	B,D,E,F
Hastings	Y-T- N-N/N/N	None	Not Used	N/N/Y/N/N	Not Used	D,E,F
Mankato	Not Used	None	N/Y/N/N/N	Not Used	Not Used	...
Maplewood	N-...-..-N/N/N	None	Not Used	N/N/Y/N/N	Not Used	A,B,C,D,E,F
Minnetonka	... ..-../../..	None	N/Y/N/N/Y	N/N/Y/N/N	Not Used	B,H
Mounds View	Not Used	None	Not Used	N/N/N/N/Y	Not Used	B,C,D,E,F
New Hope	Y-P- N-N/N/Y	N/Y/N	Not Used	Y/Y/N/N/Y	Not Used	A,D,E,F
New Ulm	Y-T- N-N/N/Y	None	N/Y/N/N/N	Not Used	Not Used	...
North St. Paul	Y-T- N-N/N/Y	N/N/N	N/Y/N/N/N	N/Y/N/N/N	Not Used	A,D,E,F
Northfield	Y..- N-N/N/Y	N/N/N	Not Used	N/N/N/N/Y	Not Used	...
Oakdale	Not Used	None	Not Used	Not Used	N-N-N/Y-Y-N/Y	D,E,F
Plymouth	Y-T- N-Y/N/Y	Y/Y/N	N/Y/N/N/N	N/N/N/Y/Y	Y-N-Y/N-N-N/Y	A,B,D,E,F,G
Red Wing	Y-T- N-Y/N/Y	None	N/Y/N/N/N	N/N/Y/N/N	N-N-N/Y-N-Y/N	D,E,F
Richfield	Y-P- N-N/N/Y	Y/Y/N	N/N/N/Y/N	Not Used	N-N-N/Y-Y-Y/N	A,B,C
Robbinsdale	Y-T- N-Y/N/N	None	N/Y/N/N/N	N/N/N/Y/N	Not Used	A,C,D,E
Rochester	Y-D- Y-N/N/Y	N/Y/N	Not Used	N/N/Y/Y/N	Not Used	A,C,D,E,F
St. Cloud	N-...-..-Y/N/Y	N/N/Y	Not Used	Not Used	Not Used	A,B,C,D,E,F,G,H
St. Louis Park	Y-T- Y-N/N/Y	N/Y/N	N/Y/N/N/N	Not Used	Not Used	A,B,E
St. Paul	Y-F- Y-../N/Y	N/Y/N	Y/Y/N/N/N	N/N/Y/N/Y	N-N-N/Y-N-Y/N	A,B,C
Shoreview	Y-P- N-Y/N/Y	N/Y/N	Not Used	Y/Y/Y/N/N	Not Used	A,B
South St. Paul	Y-P- Y-N/N/Y	None	Y/N/N/N/N	N/N/N/N/N	Not Used	D,E,F
Stillwater	Not Used	N/N/N	N/Y/N/N/N	Not Used	Not Used	C,D,E,F
Virginia	Not Used	None	Not Used	Not Used	Not Used	A,B
West St. Paul	Y-T,F-Y-Y/N/Y	None	Not Used	N/N/N/N/Y	Not Used	...
Willmar	Y-T- N-Y/N/Y	None	N/Y/N/N/N	Not Used	Not Used	...
Woodbury	Y-T- N-N/N/N	None	N/N/N/N/N	Not Used	Not Used	A,C,D,E,F
MISSISSIPPI						
Biloxi	Y-T- N-Y/../Y	N/N/N	Not Used	Not Used	N-N-N/Y-N-Y/N	A
Clarksdale	Y-T- N-Y/Y/N	None	Not Used	Not Used	Not Used	...
Corinth	Y-T- N-Y/Y/N	N/N/Y	N/Y/N/N/N	Y/Y/N/N/N	Not Used	...
Grenada	Y-T- N-Y/N/Y	None	Not Used	Not Used	Not Used	...
Gulfport	Y-F- N-Y/Y/Y	None	Y/N/Y/N/N	Not Used	Not Used	...
Hattiesburg	Not Used	None	Not Used	Not Used	N-N-N/N-N-N/N	...
Meridian	Y-T- N-N/N/N	None	N/Y/N/N/N	N/N/N/N/N	N-N-N/Y-N-Y/N	...
Starkville	Y-D- N-Y/../Y	None	N/Y/N/N/N	Not Used	N-N-N/N-N-N/N	C,D,E
Tupelo	Y-T- N-Y/N/Y	None	Not Used	Not Used	Not Used	D,E,F
Vicksburg	Not Used	None	Not Used	Not Used	Not Used	...
MISSOURI						
Arnold	Y-D- Y-Y/N/Y	None	Not Used	Not Used	Not Used	A,D
Ballwin	Y-F- N-N/N/Y	None	Not Used	N/N/N/N/N	Y-N-N/Y-N-Y/N	A,E
Belton	Y-P- N-N/N/Y	None	N/N/N/N/Y	Not Used	Not Used	A
Berkeley	Y..- N-Y/N/Y	None	Not Used	N/N/Y/Y/Y	Not Used	C,D,F
Blue Springs	Y-T,D-Y-N/N/Y	Y/Y/N	N/N/N/N/N	Y/Y/N/Y/N	N-N-N/N-N-N/N	A,C,D,E,F
Bridgeton	Y-F- N-N/N/Y	None	Not Used	Not Used	Not Used	A
Cape Girardeau	Not Used	N/N/Y	Not Used	N/N/Y/Y/N	N-N-N/Y-N-Y/N	...
Carthage	Not Used	N/Y/N	Not Used	Not Used	Not Used	...
Clayton	Y..- Y-N/N/Y	None	Not Used	Not Used	Not Used	A,B,C
Creve Coeur	Y-T- Y-Y/Y/Y	None	Not Used	N/Y/N/N/N	N-N-N/Y-Y-Y/N	A,B
Excelsior Springs	Y-T- Y-N/N/Y	None	Not Used	Y/N/Y/N/N	Not Used	A
Gladstone	Y-D- N-Y/N/Y	None	Y/N/N/N/N	N/Y/Y/N/N	Y-Y-N/Y-N-Y/N	A
Grandview	Y-P- N-N/N/Y	None	N/N/N/N/N	N/Y/Y/N/N	Not Used	A
Hannibal	Y-D- Y-Y/N/Y	None	N/Y/N/N/N	Not Used	Not Used	A
Independence	Y-P- Y-Y/N/Y	None	Not Used	N/N/Y/N/N	Y-N-Y/N-N-N/N	...
Joplin	Y-P- N-N/N/Y	N/N/Y	Not Used	Not Used	Not Used	...
Kirksville	N-...-N-Y/N/Y	None	Y/N/Y/N/N	N/N/N/Y/N	N-N-N/Y-Y-Y/N	A
Kirkwood	Y-F- N-N/N/Y	N/N/Y	Not Used	Not Used	Not Used	A,B,C,D,E
Liberty	Y-T- Y-N/N/Y	N/Y/N	N/Y/N/N/N	Not Used	Not Used	A
Maplewood	Y-F- N-N/Y/Y	N/Y/N	Not Used	Not Used	Not Used	A,C,D
Moberly	Y-T- N-Y/N/Y	None	N/N/N/N/N	N/N/Y/N/N	N-N-N/Y-Y-Y/N	...
Overland	Not Used	None	Not Used	Not Used	Not Used	...
Richmond Heights	Y-D- N-N/Y/Y	None	Y/N/N/N/N	Not Used	Not Used	A
Rolla	Y-P,F-Y-N/N/Y	Y/N/Y	Not Used	Y/Y/Y/N/N	N-N-N/Y-Y-Y/N	A,D
St. Ann	Y..- N-N/N/Y	None	Not Used	Not Used	Not Used	...
St. Charles	Y-T,F-Y-N/N/N	None	N/Y/N/N/N	N/N/Y/N/N	N-N-N/N-N-N/Y	C,D,E,F
St. Louis	Y-P- N-N/N/Y	None	Y/N/N/N/N	Not Used	Y-Y-Y/N-N-N/N	A,C,D,E
Sedalia	Y-T- N-Y/N/N	None	Not Used	Not Used	N-N-N/N-N-N/Y	...
Springfield	Not Used	None	Not Used	Not Used	Not Used	...
University City	Y-F- N-N/N/Y	N/N/Y	Not Used	Not Used	N-N-N/Y-Y-N/N	C,D,E,F,G
Warrensburg	Not Used	None	Not Used	Not Used	Not Used	A
Webster Groves	Y-T- N-N/N/Y	N/N/N	Not Used	N/Y/Y/N/Y	Not Used	...
MONTANA						
Billings	Y-D- N-N/N/Y	Y/N/Y	Y/N/N/N/N	Not Used	N-N-N/Y-Y-N/N	A,C,D
Helena	Y-P- N-Y/N/Y	N/N/Y	N/N/N/N/N	Y/N/N/N/Y	N-N-N/Y-N-Y/N	A
Missoula	Y-F- N-Y/N/Y	Y/Y/N	Not Used	N/N/Y/N/N	Not Used	A
NEBRASKA						
Columbus	Not Used	None	Not Used	Not Used	Not Used	...

Table 5/5 continued SELECTED EMPLOYEE INCENTIVES IN CITIES 10,000 AND OVER

Municipality	Educational incentives: tuition reimbursement-amount-requirements to stay-time off/ salary increase/ available to all	Variation in working hours: 4-day work week/ flextime/ task system	Attendance incentives: sick leave conversion/ cash bonuses / early retirement / personal leave / pooling	Job enrichment: job redesign/ job rotation/ labor-management committees / quality circles / team approach	Awards: suggestion-cash-nomonetary/ performance-cash-nomonetary / safety	Extraordinary benefits
NEBRASKA continued						
Fremont	Y-P- N-N/N/Y	None	Not Used	N/N/Y/N/N	Not Used	...
Hastings	Not Used	None	Not Used	Not Used	Not Used	A
Norfolk	Y-T- N-N/N/Y	Y/N/N	Not Used	N/N/Y/N/N	Y-Y-Y/Y-Y-Y/Y	A,C
North Platte	Not Used	None	Not Used	Not Used	Not Used	...
Scottsbluff	N-...-N-Y/N/Y	N/N/Y	Y/N/N/N/N	N/N/N/N/Y	N-N-N/Y-N-Y/Y	...
NEVADA						
Carson City	Y-T,D-N-Y/N/Y	Y/N/N	N/Y/N/N/N	Not Used	Y-Y-N/N-N-N/N	A,B,C,D,E,F
Las Vegas	Y-P,D-Y-N/N/Y	Y/Y/N	N/Y/N/N/N	Y/Y/Y/N/N	N-N-N/Y-Y-Y/N	A,D,E,F
Sparks	Y-F- N-N/N/Y	None	Y/Y/N/N/N	Y/Y/Y/N/N	Y-Y-Y/Y-Y-Y/N	A,B,C,D,E
NEW HAMPSHIRE						
Berlin	N-...-..-Y/N/..	N/N/N	Not Used	N/N/N/N/Y	Not Used	...
Claremont	Y-P- N-N/N/Y	None	Y/Y/N/N/N	Not Used	Y-Y-N/N-N-N/N	...
Concord	Y-T- N-Y/N/Y	N/N/Y	N/N/N/N/N	Not Used	N-N-N/Y-Y-Y/N	...
Derry	Not Used	None	Not Used	Not Used	Not Used	...
Dover	Y-T- N-N/Y/Y	None	Not Used	Not Used	N-N-N/N-N-N/Y	A
Durham	Y-T- N-Y/N/Y	Y/N/N	Y/Y/N/N/N	Not Used	Not Used	...
Laconia	... ..-../../..	None	Y/N/N/N/N	Not Used	Y-Y-N/N-N-N/Y	...
Londonderry	N-...-..-Y/N/N	None	N/Y/N/N/N	Not Used	N-N-N/N-N-N/N	...
Manchester	Y-P,F-N-N/N/Y	Y/Y/N	Y/N/N/N/Y	N/N/Y/N/N	Not Used	C
Merrimack	Y-P- N-N/N/Y	None	Not Used	Not Used	Not Used	A
Nashua	Y-P- N-N/N/Y	N/N/Y	N/Y/N/N/N	Y/N/N/N/N	Y-Y-N/N-N-N/Y	C,D,E,F
Rochester	Not Used	None	Not Used	Not Used	Not Used	...
Somersworth	Y-T- N-Y/Y/N	Y/N/N	N/Y/N/N/N	N/N/N/Y/N	N-N-N/N-N-N/Y	...
NEW JERSEY						
Bayonne	Not Used	None	Not Used	Not Used	Not Used	A
Bergenfield	Not Used	N/N/Y	N/Y/N/N/N	N/Y/N/N/N	N-N-N/N-N-N/Y	A,C
Berkeley Heights	Not Used	None	Not Used	Not Used	Not Used	...
Bloomfield	Not Used	None	Not Used	Not Used	Not Used	A
Bridgeton	Y-D- Y-Y/N/Y	None	N/Y/N/N/N	Not Used	N-N-N/Y-N-Y/N	...
Cedar Grove	Not Used	None	N/Y/N/N/N	Not Used	Y-Y-N/N-N-N/N	A
Clifton	Y-T- N-N/Y/Y	None	N/Y/N/N/N	Not Used	N-N-N/Y-N-Y/N	A
Dumont	Y-T- N-Y/N/Y	N/N/Y	Not Used	Not Used	Not Used	...
East Brunswick	Y-P- N-N/N/Y	N/Y/N	N/Y/N/N/N	N/N/Y/N/N	Not Used	A
East Windsor	Y..- N-Y/N/Y	Y/Y/N	Not Used	Y/Y/Y/N/Y	N-N-N/Y-Y-N/N	A
Englewood	Not Used	None	N/Y/N/N/N	...	Y-Y-Y/Y-N-Y/N	...
Evesham	... ..-../../..	N/N/Y	N/N/N/N/N	N/N/N/N/Y	Not Used	A,B
Fair Lawn	Not Used	None	N/Y/N/N/N	Not Used	Y-Y-N/N-N-N/N	D
Fort Lee	Y..- N-Y/N/N	None	N/Y/N/N/N	Not Used	Not Used	A
Franklin	Y-T- N-Y/N/N	N/N/N	Not Used	Not Used	Not Used	A,B
Freehold	Y-T- N-Y/N/N	None	Not Used	Not Used	N-N-N/Y-Y-N/N	A
Galloway	Y-T- N-Y/N/N	None	Not Used	Not Used	Not Used	A,B
Glen Rock	Y-T- N-Y/N/Y	N/N/Y	N/Y/Y/N/N	Not Used	N-N-N/Y-Y-Y/N	...
Hackensack	Y-D- N-N/N/Y	N/N/Y	N/Y/N/N/N	Not Used	Not Used	A
Haddon	N-...-N-N/Y/Y	None	N/Y/N/N/N	Not Used	Not Used	...
Haddonfield	Not Used	N/Y/Y	Not Used	Not Used	Not Used	A
Hamilton	Y-P- N-N/N/Y	None	N/Y/N/N/N	Not Used	Y-N-Y/Y-Y-Y/N	A,B
Hawthorne	Not Used	None	Not Used	Not Used	Not Used	A
Highland Park	Not Used	None	N/Y/N/N/N	Not Used	Not Used	A
Hillside	Not Used	None	N/Y/N/N/N	Not Used	Not Used	A
Hoboken	Y-T- N-N/N/Y	None	N/Y/N/N/N	Not Used	Not Used	A,G
Hopewell	Y-P- Y-N/N/Y	None	Not Used	Not Used	Not Used	...
Irvington	Not Used	None	N/Y/N/N/N	Not Used	Not Used	A
Jackson	Y-T,D-Y-N/N/N	None	N/Y/Y/N/N	N/N/Y/N/Y	Not Used	A,B
Jersey City	N-...-..-Y/N/..	N/Y/N	N/Y/N/N/N	Y/N/N/N/N	Y-N-Y/N-N-N/N	A,B,G
Lindenwold	Not Used	None	N/N/Y/N/N	Not Used	Not Used	...
Livingston	Y-P- N-N/N/N	None	Not Used	Y/Y/Y/N/Y	Y-N-Y/Y-N-Y/N	A,D,E
Maple Shade	Not Used	None	Not Used	N/N/Y/N/Y	Not Used	A,B,C
Aberdeen	Y-T- N-Y/N/N	None	N/Y/N/N/N	N/N/Y/N/N	Not Used	A
Medford	N-...-N-Y/N/Y	None	Not Used	Not Used	Not Used	...
Metuchen	Y-P- N-Y/Y/N	N/Y/N	N/Y/N/N/N	Not Used	Not Used	A,C
Middlesex	Y-T- N-Y/N/Y	N/N/Y	N/Y/Y/N/N	Not Used	Y-Y-N/N-N-N/Y	A
Millburn	Not Used	N/N/Y	N/Y/N/N/N	Not Used	N-N-N/N-N-N/Y	A
Morristown	Not Used	None	Not Used	Not Used	Not Used	...
New Providence	Y-T- Y-Y/N/Y	None	Not Used	N/N/N/N/N	Not Used	A
Newark	Y-P,F-N-Y/N/Y	N/N/Y	N/Y/N/N/N	Not Used	Not Used	A,D,E,F
Oakland	N-...-..-Y/N/Y	None	N/Y/N/N/N	Not Used	Not Used	A,B
Ocean	N-...-..-../../..	N/N/Y	N/Y/Y/N/N	N/N/N/N/N	N-N-N/Y-N-Y/N	A,D
Pemberton	Y-T- N-Y/N/Y	None	Not Used	Not Used	Not Used	C,D
Pequannock	Y..- N-Y/N/Y	N/N/N	N/Y/N/N/N	Y/N/N/N/N	Not Used	...
Phillipsburg	Y-T- N-N/N/Y	None	N/Y/N/N/N	Not Used	Not Used	A
Pleasantville	Not Used	None	Not Used	Y/Y/N/N/Y	Not Used	A,B
River Edge	N-...-..-N/Y/N	None	Not Used	Not Used	Not Used	...
Rockaway	Y-T- N-Y/N/Y	N/Y/N	Not Used	N/N/Y/N/N	Not Used	A,B,C,E,G
Roxbury	Y-T- Y-N/N/N	N/Y/Y	N/Y/N/N/N	Not Used	Not Used	A
Rutherford	Y..- N-N/N/Y	N/N/Y	N/N/Y/N/N	Not Used	Not Used	A
Secaucus	Not Used	None	Not Used	Not Used	Not Used	A
Sparta	Y-P- N-Y/Y/Y	None	N/Y/N/N/N	Not Used	Not Used	A
Teaneck	Y-T- N-N/N/Y	None	Not Used	Not Used	Not Used	A
Trenton	N-...-..-Y/N/N	N/N/Y	Not Used	N/N/Y/N/N	N-N-N/Y-Y-Y/N	A,B,C,D,E,F
Union City	Y-T- N-N/Y/Y	N/N/N	Not Used	N/N/N/N/N	Not Used	A,B

Table 5/5 continued **SELECTED EMPLOYEE INCENTIVES IN CITIES 10,000 AND OVER**

Municipality	Educational incentives: tuition reimbursement-amount-requirements to stay-time off/ salary increase/ available to all	Variation in working hours: 4-day work week/ flextime/ task system	Attendance incentives: sick leave conversion/ cash bonuses / early retirement / personal leave / pooling	Job enrichment: job redesign/ job rotation/ labor-management committees / quality circles / team approach	Awards: suggestion-cash-nomonetary/ performance-cash-nomonetary / safety	Extraordinary benefits
NEW JERSEY continued						
Verona	Y-T- N-N/N/..	None	Not Used	Not Used	Not Used	A
Vineland	Y-T- N-N/N/N	None	N/Y/N/N/N	Not Used	Not Used	A
Wanaque	Y-F- N-N/N/Y	None	N/Y/N/N/N	Not Used	N-N-N/Y-N-Y/N	A,B
Wayne	Y-T- N-Y/N/Y	None	N/Y/N/N/N	Not Used	Not Used	A,C,D,E
West Deptford	Y-T- N-N/N/Y	N/N/Y	N/Y/N/N/N	N/N/Y/Y/Y	Y-Y-N/N-N-N/N	A,B,E,F
West Milford	Y-P- Y-N/N/Y	None	N/Y/N/N/N	Not Used	Not Used	A,B
West Orange	Not Used	None	N/Y/N/N/N	N/N/N/N/Y	Not Used	D,E,F
Westfield	Not Used	None	N/Y/N/N/N	Not Used	Not Used	...
Westwood	Y-T- N-Y/N/Y	N/N/Y	Not Used	Not Used	Not Used	A,D,E,F
Willingboro	N-...-..-Y/Y/Y	Y/N/N	Y/N/N/N/N	Not Used	Not Used	A,B,C
NEW MEXICO						
Albuquerque	Y..- N-Y/N/Y	Y/Y/Y	Not Used	N/N/Y/Y/Y	Y-Y-Y/Y-Y-Y/Y	A,C,D,E,F
Hobbs	N-...-..-N/N/Y	None	Y/N/N/N/N	Not Used	N-N-N/N-N-N/Y	A,C,D,E,F,G
Las Cruces	N-...-..-Y/N/Y	N/Y/Y	Y/Y/N/N/N	Not Used	N-N-N/Y-Y-Y/Y	C,D,E,G
Las Vegas	N-...-..-Y/N/N	N/Y/Y	Not Used	Y/N/N/N/N	Not Used	...
Roswell	Y-T- N-Y/N/Y	None	Y/N/N/N/N	N/N/Y/N/N	N-N-N/Y-N-Y/N	...
Santa Fe	Y-T- Y-Y/N/Y	None	Not Used	N/N/N/N/Y	N-N-N/Y-Y-N/N	A,B,C,D,E,F
NEW YORK						
Auburn	Y-T,F-N-N/N/Y	N/N/Y	Not Used	Not Used	Not Used	A
Batavia	Y-T- N-N/N/Y	None	N/Y/N/N/N	Not Used	Not Used	...
Brighton	Y-F-..-Y/N/N	None	Not Used	N/N/N/N/Y	Not Used	A,C
Canandaigua	Y-D- N-N/N/N	None	N/N/Y/N/N	N/N/Y/N/N	Not Used	...
Elmira	Not Used	N/N/Y	Not Used	Not Used	Not Used	A,B
Endicott	Not Used	None	Not Used	N/N/Y/N/N	Not Used	...
Fredonia	Not Used	None	Not Used	Not Used	Not Used	A
Freeport	Not Used	None	N/Y/N/N/N	N/Y/N/N/N	Not Used	A,C,D,E,F,H
Fulton	Not Used	None	Not Used	Not Used	Not Used	A,B
Garden City	Y-T,D-N-N/Y/Y	N/N/Y	Y/N/N/N/N	Y/Y/Y/N/N	Y-Y-N/Y-N-N/N	A,C,D,E
Glens Falls	Y-T- N-Y/N/N	None	Not Used	Not Used	Not Used	A,E
New Rochelle	Not Used	N/N/Y	Not Used	Y/N/N/N/N	Y-Y-Y/N-N-N/Y	A
Newark	N-...-..-Y/N/N	None	Not Used	N/N/N/N/N	Not Used	...
Newburgh	Y-D- N-Y/N/N	N/N/Y	Not Used	Y/Y/Y/Y/Y	Y-N-Y/Y-Y-Y/N	...
Oneida	Y-P,D-N-N/N/Y	None	N/Y/N/N/N	Not Used	Not Used	...
Patchogue	Not Used	N/N/Y	Not Used	N/N/N/Y/N	Not Used	A
Peekskill	Y-F- N-N/N/Y	N/N/Y	N/Y/N/N/N	Not Used	Not Used	C
Plattsburgh	Not Used	N/Y/N	N/N/N/N/N	N/N/Y/Y/N	Y-Y-N/N-N-N/N	C
Rockville Centre	Not Used	N/N/Y	N/N/N/N/N	N/N/Y/N/Y	N-N-N/N-N-N/Y	A
Rome	Y..- N-Y/N/N	N/Y/N	N/Y/N/N/N	N/N/Y/N/Y	Not Used	A,B,D,E,F
Rye	Not Used	None	N/Y/N/N/N	Not Used	Not Used	A,B
Scarsdale	Y-F- N-N/N/N	N/N/Y	N/Y/N/N/N	N/N/Y/N/N	Y-Y-N/N-N-N/N	A,B,C,D,E
Tonawanda	Not Used	N/N/Y	Not Used	Not Used	Not Used	...
Troy	Y-T,D-N-Y/N/Y	N/N/Y	Y/N/Y/N/N	Y/N/Y/N/N	Y-Y-N/N-N-N/N	A
Utica	Not Used	None	Not Used	N/N/N/N/N	N-N-N/N-N-N/Y	A,B
West Seneca	Not Used	None	Not Used	Not Used	Not Used	A
White Plains	Y-P- N-../N/Y	N/N/Y	N/N/N/N/N	Y/Y/Y/N/N	N-N-N/Y-N-Y/N	A,C
Yonkers	Not Used	N/N/Y	N/Y/N/N/N	Not Used	N-N-N/N-N-N/Y	A,B,C,D,E,F
NORTH CAROLINA						
Asheboro	Y-P- N-Y/../Y	N/N/Y	Not Used	N/N/Y/N/Y	Y-N-Y/N-N-N/Y	A,H
Asheville	N-...-..-Y/N/Y	Y/Y/Y	Not Used	Y/Y/Y/N/Y	Y-N-Y/Y-Y-Y/N	B,C,D,E,F
Burlington	N-...-..-Y/N/Y	N/Y/Y	Not Used	Not Used	N-N-N/N-N-N/Y	A
Cary	Y-P,F-Y-Y/N/N	N/N/Y	Not Used	Y/Y/N/N/N	Y-Y-Y/N-N-N/N	A,D,F
Chapel Hill	Y-T,F-Y-Y/N/Y	N/N/Y	N/N/Y/N/N	Not Used	N-N-N/N-N-N/N	...
Charlotte	Y-T,D-N-N/N/Y	N/Y/Y	Y/N/Y/N/N	Not Used	N-N-N/Y-Y-Y/Y	...
Concord	Not Used	None	Not Used	Not Used	Not Used	...
Durham	Y-T- N-Y/N/Y	N/N/Y	N/N/Y/N/N	N/N/N/Y/N	Y-Y-Y/N-N-N/Y	D,E
Eden	Y-T- N-Y/Y/Y	N/N/Y	Not Used	Not Used	Y-N-Y/Y-N-Y/Y	...
Gastonia	Y-T,D-N-Y/N/Y	N/N/Y	N/N/Y/N/N	N/N/Y/N/Y	Not Used	B,C,D,E,F
Goldsboro	Y-T- Y-Y/N/Y	N/N/Y	Not Used	Not Used	Not Used	...
Greensboro	Y-F- N-N/N/Y	Y/Y/Y	N/N/N/N/N	N/N/Y/N/Y	Y-Y-Y/Y-Y-Y/Y	D,E
Greenville	Y-P- N-Y/N/Y	None	N/N/N/N/N	N/N/N/N/Y	N-N-N/N-N-N/Y	D,E,F
Henderson	Not Used	None	Not Used	Not Used	Not Used	...
Hickory	Y-T,D-N-N/N/Y	N/N/Y	N/N/Y/N/N	N/N/Y/N/N	Not Used	D,E
Laurinburg	Not Used	None	Not Used	N/N/N/N/Y	Not Used	...
Lexington	Y..- N-N/Y/Y	N/N/Y	Not Used	N/N/N/N/N	N-N-N/N-N-N/Y	C,D,E,F
Monroe	Not Used	N/N/Y	N/N/Y/N/N	Y/Y/Y/N/Y	Y-Y-N/Y-N-Y/N	...
Morganton	Y..- N-Y/Y/Y	N/N/Y	Not Used	N/N/N/N/N	Y-Y-Y/Y-N-Y/Y	D
New Bern	Y-F- Y-Y/N/Y	N/Y/Y	...	Y/Y/Y/N/Y	Not Used	D,E,F,G
Raleigh	Y-F- Y-Y/N/Y	Y/Y/Y	N/N/Y/N/N	Not Used	N-N-N/Y-Y-Y/Y	...
Reidsville	Y-T- Y-Y/Y/Y	N/N/Y	Not Used	N/N/N/Y/Y	N-N-N/Y-Y-Y/Y	C,D,E,F
Roanoke Rapids	Y-T- Y-N/N/Y	N/N/Y	Not Used	Not Used	Not Used	C,F
Rocky Mount	Y-P- N-Y/N/Y	Y/N/Y	N/N/Y/N/N	N/N/N/Y/N	Not Used	...
Statesville	Y-P- Y-Y/../Y	Y/Y/Y	Not Used	N/N/N/Y/N	Not Used	...
Wilmington	Y-T,D-N-Y/N/Y	N/N/Y	N/Y/N/N/N	N/Y/N/N/N	Y-Y-N/Y-Y-N/N	B,C,D,E,F,G,H
Wilson	Y-P,F-N-Y/N/Y	N/N/Y	Not Used	N/N/Y/N/N	N-N-N/Y-Y-N/N	C,D,E,F
NORTH DAKOTA						
Dickinson	Y-T- N-Y/N/Y	None	Not Used	Not Used	N-N-N/Y-N-Y/N	...
Minot	Not Used	N/N/Y	Not Used	N/N/Y/N/N	Not Used	...
Williston	Not Used	N/N/N	Not Used	Not Used	Not Used	...

Table 5/5 continued **SELECTED EMPLOYEE INCENTIVES IN CITIES 10,000 AND OVER**

Municipality	Educational incentives: tuition reimbursement-amount-requirements to stay-time off/ salary increase/ available to all	Variation in working hours: 4-day work week/ flextime/ task system	Attendance incentives: sick leave conversion/ cash bonuses / early retirement / personal leave / pooling	Job enrichment: job redesign/ job rotation/ labor-management committees / quality circles / team approach	Awards: suggestion-cash-nomonetary/ performance-cash-nomonetary / safety	Extraordinary benefits
OHIO						
Akron	Not Used	Y/Y/Y	Not Used	N/N/N/N/Y	Not Used	A,B,C,E
Athens	Y-T- N-Y/Y/N	None	Not Used	Not Used	Y-N-Y/Y-N-Y/N	...
Bedford	Y-T,D-N-Y/N/Y	None	N/Y/N/N/N	Y/Y/N/N/N	Not Used	A,B
Bexley	Not Used	None	Y/Y/N/N/N	N/N/Y/N/N	Y-N-Y/N-N-N/N	A,C
Bowling Green	Y..- N-Y/N/Y	None	N/N/N/N/N	N/N/Y/N/N	Not Used	...
Brunswick	Not Used	N/Y/N	Y/Y/N/N/N	Y/Y/Y/N/Y	N-N-N/Y-N-Y/N	A,B,E
Chillicothe	Y-F- N-Y/Y/Y	N/Y/Y	N/Y/N/N/N	N/N/N/N/Y	Y-N-N/N-N-N/Y	A,C,D
Cincinnati	Not Used	N/Y/Y	N/N/N/N/N	N/N/N/Y/N	Not Used	A,B,C,D,E,F
Circleville	Y-T- N-Y/N/Y	None	Y/Y/N/N/N	Not Used	N-N-N/Y-N-Y/N	...
Cleveland Heights	Y-T- Y-N/N/Y	N/N/Y	Not Used	N/N/N/N/Y	Not Used	A,C,D,E,F
Cuyahoga Falls	Y..- N-Y/N/N	N/N/Y	N/Y/N/N/N	Not Used	Not Used	A
Dayton	Y-P- Y-N/N/Y	N/Y/Y	Y/N/N/N/N	N/N/Y/N/N	N-N-N/Y-Y-Y/N	C,F
Delaware	Y-D- Y-N/../Y	Y/N/N	Y/N/N/N/N	Not Used	Not Used	A
Delhi	Y-D- N-N/N/Y	None	Not Used	Y/N/N/N/N	Not Used	...
East Cleveland	Y-P- N-N/N/Y	N/Y/N	Y/Y/N/N/N	Not Used	Not Used	A
Euclid	Y-P- N-Y/Y/Y	N/N/Y	Not Used	Y/Y/Y/Y/Y	Not Used	...
Forest Park	Y-F- N-Y/N/Y	None	N/Y/Y/N/N	Not Used	Not Used	A
Franklin	Y-T,D-N-Y/N/Y	None	Not Used	Not Used	Not Used	...
Gahanna	Y-P,D-Y-N/N/Y	Y/N/N	Not Used	Not Used	Not Used	A,B
Greenville	Y-T- N-Y/Y/Y	None	Not Used	Not Used	Not Used	...
Kent	Y-P- N-Y/N/Y	N/Y/N	N/N/N/N/N	N/N/Y/N/N	Not Used	A,B
Kettering	Y-P,D-Y-N/N/N	None	N/Y/N/N/N	N/N/Y/Y/Y	N-N-N/N-N-N/Y	...
Lakewood	Y-D- Y-N/N/N	None	N/Y/N/N/N	N/N/Y/N/N	Y-Y-Y/Y-N-Y/N	A,C,D,E,F
Maple Heights	Not Used	N/N/Y	N/Y/N/N/N	Not Used	Not Used	A,B,C,D,E,F
Miamisburg	Y-P,D-N-N/N/Y	None	Y/Y/N/N/N	Not Used	Not Used	A,F
Middletown	Y-P- N-N/N/Y	N/Y/N	Y/Y/N/N/N	Not Used	Not Used	A
Mount Vernon	Y-T- N-N/N/Y	None	...	N/N/Y/N/N	Not Used	B
North Canton	Y-T- N-N/N/Y	N/Y/N	Not Used	Not Used	Not Used	A
North Olmsted	Not Used	None	Not Used	Not Used	Not Used	...
North Royalton	Not Used	N/N/Y	Y/N/N/N/N	Not Used	Not Used	A
Parma	Not Used	None	Y/N/N/N/N	Not Used	Not Used	...
Parma Heights	Not Used	None	N/Y/N/N/N	Not Used	Not Used	...
Portsmouth	N-...-..-Y/N/..	N/N/Y	N/N/N/N/N	Not Used	Not Used	...
Reading	Y-T- N-Y/N/Y	Y/Y/Y	N/Y/N/N/N	Not Used	Not Used	A,B
Reynoldsburg	Y-D- N-Y/Y/Y	N/N/N	Not Used	Not Used	Not Used	A,B,C,D,H
Seven Hills	Not Used	...	...	...	...	...
Shaker Heights	Not Used	Y/N/Y	N/Y/N/N/N	Not Used	Not Used	A
Sheffield Lake	N-...-N-Y/Y/Y	None	...	Y/Y/Y/N/N	Y-N-Y/Y-N-Y/Y	B
Sidney	Y-T- N-Y/N/Y	N/N/Y	Not Used	Not Used	Not Used	...
Solon	Y-D- N-Y/N/Y	None	Not Used	Not Used	Not Used	A,B
Springdale	Not Used	None	N/Y/N/N/N	Not Used	N-N-N/Y-Y-N/N	A
Springfield	N-...-Y-Y/Y/N	N/Y/Y	Not Used	N/N/Y/N/N	N-N-N/N-N-N/N	C,D,E,F
Sylvania	Y-T- N-N/N/Y	None	Y/N/N/N/N	N/N/Y/N/N	Not Used	A,B,C,D,E
Troy	N-...-N-N/../N	N/N/Y	Not Used	Not Used	Not Used	...
University Heights	N-...-..-Y/N/N	None	N/Y/N/N/N	Not Used	Not Used	A
Upper Arlington	Not Used	None	Not Used	Not Used	Not Used	A
Urbana	N-...-..-N/N/N	Y/Y/N	N/Y/N/N/N	Not Used	Not Used	...
Vandalia	Y-F- N-N/N/Y	None	Not Used	Not Used	Not Used	A,B
Warren	Y-T- N-Y/N/Y	N/N/Y	Y/N/N/N/N	Not Used	Not Used	A
Washington	N-...-..-Y/N/Y	None	Not Used	Not Used	Not Used	...
West Carrollton	Y-P,F-Y-Y/N/Y	None	Y/Y/N/N/N	N/N/Y/N/N	Not Used	...
Westerville	Y-T- Y-Y/N/Y	None	N/N/Y/N/N	Not Used	Not Used	A,B
Westlake	Not Used	N/N/Y	Not Used	Not Used	Not Used	A
Willoughby	Not Used	None	Not Used	Not Used	Not Used	A,B
Worthington	Y-P- N-Y/N/Y	N/N/N	Y/Y/N/N/N	Not Used	N-N-N/Y-N-Y/N	A
Xenia	Not Used	N/N/Y	Not Used	Not Used	Not Used	...
OKLAHOMA						
Ada	Y-T- N-Y/N/Y	N/N/Y	Y/N/N/N/N	N/N/Y/N/N	Not Used	D,E,F
Altus	Y-T- N-N/../Y	N/Y/Y	...	N/N/N/Y/N	N-N-N/N-N-N/N	C,D,E,F
Ardmore	Y-T- Y-Y/N/Y	Y/N/Y	Y/N/N/N/N	N/N/N/Y/Y	N-N-N/Y-N-Y/Y	E
Bartlesville	Y-P- N-N/N/Y	N/N/Y	Not Used	N/N/Y/N/N	Y-Y-N/Y-N-Y/N	A
Bethany	Y-D- Y-N/../Y	None	Not Used	Not Used	N-N-N/N-N-N/Y	...
Broken Arrow	Y-P- N-Y/N/Y	N/N/Y	...	Not Used	Not Used	A
Del City	Y-T- N-N/N/Y	N/N/Y	N/Y/N/N/N	Not Used	Not Used	A
Duncan	Not Used	None	Not Used	Not Used	Not Used	...
Edmond	Not Used	N/N/Y	Not Used	Not Used	Not Used	A,D
Lawton	Y-P- N-Y/N/N	N/Y/Y	N/Y/N/N/N	Not Used	N-N-N/Y-N-Y/N	...
Midwest City	Y-P,D-Y-N/N/Y	N/N/Y	N/Y/N/N/N	Not Used	Y-Y-Y/Y-Y-Y/N	A,B
Moore	Not Used	N/N/Y	...	Not Used	Not Used	A
Okmulgee	Y-D- N-Y/N/Y	None	N/Y/N/N/N	N/N/N/N/Y	Not Used	A
Sand Springs	N-...-..-N/../N	None	Not Used	Not Used	Y-N-Y/Y-N-Y/N	A
Stillwater	Y-T,D-N-Y/N/Y	Y/Y/Y	Not Used	Not Used	Not Used	C,D,E,F
The Village	Y-T,D-N-N/N/Y	N/N/Y	N/N/Y/N/N	N/Y/N/N/N	N-N-N/Y-N-Y/N	A,B
Tulsa	Y-P- N-Y/N/Y	N/Y/Y	Y/Y/N/N/Y	Not Used	Y-Y-Y/N-N-N/Y	A,C,D,E,F
OREGON						
Ashland	Y-T- N-Y/N/N	None	Y/Y/N/N/N	Not Used	N-N-N/Y-Y-N/N	A,B,E
Beaverton	Y-T- N-N/N/Y	N/Y/N	...	N/N/Y/Y/N	Not Used	A,B
Coos Bay	Y-T- N-N/N/Y	None	Not Used	Y/Y/Y/Y/N	Not Used	A,C
Corvallis	Y-D- Y-N/N/Y	N/Y/N	Not Used	Y/Y/Y/N/Y	Not Used	A,C,D,E,F
Eugene	Not Used	Y/Y/N	Y/N/N/N/N	N/Y/Y/Y/N	N-N-N/N-N-N/Y	A,B

Table 5/5 continued SELECTED EMPLOYEE INCENTIVES IN CITIES 10,000 AND OVER

Municipality	Educational incentives: tuition reimbursement-amount-requirements to stay-time off/ salary increase/ available to all	Variation in working hours: 4-day work week/ flextime/ task system	Attendance incentives: sick leave conversion/ cash bonuses / early retirement / personal leave / pooling	Job enrichment: job redesign/ job rotation/ labor-management committees / quality circles / team approach	Awards: suggestion-cash-nomonetary/ performance-cash-nomonetary / safety	Extraordinary benefits
OREGON continued						
Grants Pass	Y-P- N-Y/N/Y	Y/Y/N	N/Y/N/N/N	Not Used	Not Used	A,B,E
La Grande	Y-T- N-N/N/Y	None	Not Used	Y/Y/Y/N/Y	N-N-N/N-N-N/N	A,B
Lake Oswego	Y-F- Y-N/N/Y	Y/Y/N	Not Used	N/N/Y/N/N	N-N-N/Y-Y-N/N	A,B
Lebanon	Y-T- N-Y/N/Y	None	Not Used	Not Used	Not Used	A,B
Mc Minnville	Y-T- N-N/N/Y	None	N/N/Y/N/N	Not Used	Not Used	A,B
Milwaukie	Y-T- Y-Y/N/N	N/Y/N	Not Used	Not Used	Not Used	A
Oregon City	Y-T- N-N/N/Y	None	Not Used	Not Used	Not Used	A,B
Pendleton	Y-P- N-Y/N/Y	None	Y/N/N/N/N	Not Used	Not Used	A,B,E
Roseburg	Y-P- N-N/N/Y	N/Y/Y	N/N/Y/N/N	N/Y/Y/N/Y	N-N-N/Y-Y-Y/Y	A
Salem	Y-P,D-N-N/N/Y	Y/N/N	Not Used	Y/Y/Y/N/Y	N-N-N/N-N-N/Y	A,B
Springfield	Y-P,D-N-Y/Y/Y	N/Y/N	Not Used	N/Y/N/N/Y	N-N-N/N-N-N/Y	A
The Dalles	Y-P,D-N-../N/Y	None	Not Used	Not Used	Not Used	A,B
Tigard	Not Used	None	N/N/N/N/N	N/N/Y/Y/N	Not Used	A
Woodburn	Y-T- N-N/N/Y	None	Not Used	Not Used	Not Used	A
PENNSYLVANIA						
Abington	Y-P,F-N-N/N/Y	N/N/Y	Not Used	Not Used	Y-Y-N/N-N-N/N	A,B
Allentown	Y-T,D-N-N/N/N	N/Y/N	Not Used	N/N/Y/N/N	N-N-N/N-N-N/Y	A,B,D,E,F
Beaver Falls	N-...-..-N/Y/N	None	N/Y/N/N/N	N/N/Y/N/N	Not Used	A,B
Bethel Park	Y-T- N-N/N/Y	Y/Y/Y	N/Y/N/N/N	Not Used	Not Used	A,B
Bethlehem	Not Used	None	N/Y/N/N/N	Not Used	N-N-N/Y-N-Y/Y	A
Bloomsburg	N-...-..-Y/N/N	None	Not Used	Not Used	Not Used	...
Bristol	Not Used	None	N/Y/N/N/N	Not Used	Not Used	A,B
Butler	Not Used	None	Not Used	Not Used	Not Used	A,B
Carlisle	Not Used	None	N/Y/N/N/Y	Not Used	Not Used	A,B
Carnegie	Not Used	None	N/Y/N/N/N	Not Used	Not Used	A,B
Castle Shannon	N-...-..-Y/N/Y	None	Not Used	Not Used	Not Used	A,B
Chambersburg	Y-T- N-Y/N/Y	N/Y/Y	Not Used	Y/N/Y/N/N	N-N-N/N-N-N/Y	...
Dover	Y-F- N-Y/N/Y	None	Not Used	N/N/N/Y/Y	Not Used	...
East Norriton	Y-T- N-N/N/Y	None	N/N/N/N/N	Not Used	N-N-N/N-N-N/N	A,B
Easton	N-...-..-Y/N/..	N/N/Y	Not Used	N/N/Y/N/Y	Not Used	A,B
Emmaus	Y-D- N-Y/N/N	None	Not Used	Not Used	Not Used	...
Ephrata	Not Used	None	N/Y/N/N/N	Y/Y/N/N/Y	Not Used	A,B
Erie	Not Used	N/N/Y	Y/N/N/N/N	N/N/Y/N/N	Not Used	A,B,C,D,E
Falls	Not Used	None	Not Used	Not Used	Not Used	A,B
Murrysville	N-...-..-Y/N/Y	None	Not Used	Not Used	Not Used	A,B
Hampton	Y-T,D-N-Y/N/Y	None	N/Y/N/N/N	Not Used	N-N-N/Y-N-Y/N	A,B
Hanover	Y-T- N-N/Y/Y	Y/Y/N	Not Used	Y/Y/Y/N/Y	N-N-N/Y-N-Y/N	A,B,D,E,F
Harrisburg	Not Used	None	N/Y/N/N/N	N/N/Y/N/N	Not Used	A,B,D,E,F
Harrison	Not Used	None	Not Used	Not Used	Not Used	B
Haverford	... ..-../../..	N/N/Y	N/Y/N/N/N	N/N/Y/N/N	Y-Y-N/N-N-N/N	A,B,C,D
Hermitage	Y-T- Y-Y/N/Y	N/Y/N	N/Y/N/N/N	Not Used	Not Used	A,B,E
Hopewell	Y-P- N-Y/N/N	None	Not Used	Y/N/N/N/N	Not Used	A,B
Kingston	N-...-..-Y/N/Y	None	N/Y/Y/N/N	Not Used	Not Used	A,B
Lebanon	Not Used	None	Not Used	Not Used	Not Used	B
Lower Merion	Y-T- N-N/N/Y	N/N/Y	Not Used	Not Used	Not Used	A,B
Mc Candless	Not Used	N/N/N	Not Used	Not Used	Not Used	A
Manheim	Y-T- N-N/N/Y	None	Not Used	N/N/N/N/Y	Not Used	A,B
Marple	Not Used	None	Not Used	Not Used	Not Used	A,B
Meadville	Y-T,D-Y-Y/N/Y	None	Y/Y/Y/N/N	N/N/Y/Y/N	N-N-N/N-N-N/Y	A,D,E,F
Middletown	Y-T- N-N/N/N	None	Y/N/N/N/N	Not Used	N-N-N/Y-N-Y/N	A,B,H
Middletown	Y-T- N-N/N/Y	N/Y/N	Not Used	Not Used	Y-N-Y/N-N-N/N	A
Monessen	Not Used	N/Y/N	Not Used	N/N/N/N/Y	Not Used	A,B
Monroeville	Y-T- Y-N/N/Y	N/N/Y	N/Y/Y/N/N	N/N/Y/N/Y	Y-Y-Y/Y-N-Y/Y	A,B,C,D,E,H
Moon	Y-P,D-N-Y/N/N	None	Not Used	Not Used	Not Used	A,B
Mt. Lebanon	Not Used	None	N/Y/N/N/N	Not Used	Not Used	A,B
Oil City	Not Used	None	Not Used	Not Used	Not Used	A,B
Penn Hills	Y-P- N-N/N/Y	None	Y/Y/N/N/N	N/N/Y/N/N	Not Used	A,B
Peters	Y-T- N-Y/N/Y	None	N/Y/N/N/N	N/N/N/Y/N	Not Used	A
Philadelphia	Y-P- Y-Y/N/N	N/Y/N	Y/Y/N/N/N	N/N/Y/N/N	Y-Y-Y/Y-Y-Y/N	A,B,C
Phoenixville	Not Used	None	Not Used	N/N/N/N/N	Not Used	A,B
Plum	Not Used	N/Y/Y	N/Y/N/N/N	Not Used	Not Used	A,B
Pottstown	Y-F- N-N/N/Y	N/N/Y	Not Used	Not Used	Not Used	A,B
Salisbury	Not Used	None	Not Used	Not Used	Not Used	A,B
Scott	Not Used	None	N/N/Y/N/N	N/N/Y/N/N	Not Used	A,B
Shaler	... ..-../../..	None	N/Y/N/N/N	Not Used	Not Used	A,B
Shamokin	Not Used	N/Y/N	Not Used	Not Used	Not Used	B
Sharon	Y-T- N-Y/N/Y	None	N/N/N/Y/N	N/N/Y/N/N	Not Used	B
South Park	Not Used	N/N/Y	N/Y/N/N/N	Not Used	Not Used	A,B
State College	Y-T,F-N-Y/N/Y	N/N/Y	N/Y/N/N/N	Not Used	Not Used	A,B
Swissvale	Y-T- N-Y/N/Y	N/N/Y	Not Used	Not Used	Not Used	A,B,G
Towamencin	Not Used	None	Not Used	N/N/Y/N/N	Not Used	A,B
Upper Allen	Y-T- N-Y/N/Y	N/N/N	N/Y/N/N/N	Y/N/N/N/Y	Not Used	A,B
Upper Dublin	Y-P- N-N/N/Y	N/Y/N	Not Used	Not Used	Not Used	A,B
Upper Merion	Y-F- N-N/N/Y	None	Y/N/N/N/N	Not Used	N-N-N/Y-Y-N/Y	A,B
Upper Moreland	Not Used	None	Y/N/N/N/N	N/N/Y/N/N	Not Used	A,B
Upper St. Clair	Not Used	N/Y/N	Not Used	N/N/Y/N/Y	Y-N-Y/N-N-N/N	A,B
West Chester	... ..-../../..	None	Not Used	Not Used	Not Used	A,B
West Manchester	Y-T- N-N/N/Y	N/Y/N	...	Y/N/N/N/N	N-N-N/Y-N-Y/N	A,B
West Mifflin	Not Used	None	Not Used	Not Used	Not Used	A,B
Whitehall	Not Used	None	N/N/N/N/N	Not Used	Not Used	A,B
Whitehall	Not Used	N/N/Y	Not Used	Not Used	Not Used	A

Table 5/5 continued **SELECTED EMPLOYEE INCENTIVES IN CITIES 10,000 AND OVER**

Municipality	Educational incentives: tuition reimbursement-amount-requirements to stay-time off/ salary increase/ available to all	Variation in working hours: 4-day work week/ flextime/ task system	Attendance incentives: sick leave conversion/ cash bonuses / early retirement / personal leave / pooling	Job enrichment: job redesign/ job rotation/ labor-management committees / quality circles / team approach	Awards: suggestion-cash-nomonetary/ performance-cash-nomonetary / safety	Extraordinary benefits
PENNSYLVANIA continued						
Whitemarsh	Not Used	N/Y/N	N/Y/N/N/N	Not Used	Not Used	A,B
Whitpain	Y-P- N-Y/N/Y	None	Not Used	Y/Y/Y/N/N	Not Used	A
Yeadon	Y-T- N-N/N/N	N/N/Y	Not Used	Not Used	Not Used	A,B
York	Y-P,D-N-Y/N/N	None	Not Used	N/N/Y/Y/N	N-N-N/Y-N-N/N	A,B
RHODE ISLAND						
Barrington	Y-T- N-Y/N/Y	N/N/Y	N/Y/N/N/Y	N/N/Y/Y/Y	N-N-N/N-N-N/Y	A,D,E,F
Coventry	Y-T- N-N/N/Y	None	N/Y/Y/N/N	Not Used	Not Used	A
Cranston	Y-F- N-N/N/N	None	N/Y/N/N/N	Not Used	Not Used	A,B,C,D,E
East Greenwich	Y-P- N-N/N/Y	None	Not Used	Not Used	Not Used	A
East Providence	Y-F- N-N/N/N	None	Not Used	Not Used	Not Used	A,C,D,E
Newport	Y-T- N-N/N/Y	None	N/N/N/N/Y	N/N/Y/N/N	Y-Y-N/Y-Y-N/N	A,B,E
Portsmouth	Y-T- N-N/N/N	None	Not Used	Y/N/N/N/N	Not Used	A
Warwick	N-...-..-N/Y/Y	N/N/Y	N/Y/N/N/N	N/N/Y/N/N	N-N-N/N-N-N/Y	A,D,E
Westerly	Not Used	N/Y/N	N/N/Y/N/N	N/N/Y/N/Y	Y-N-Y/N-N-N/N	A,D,F
SOUTH CAROLINA						
Aiken	Y-P- Y-Y/Y/Y	N/Y/Y	Y/N/N/N/N	Y/Y/Y/N/Y	N-N-N/Y-N-Y/Y	C,D,E,F
Anderson	Not Used	N/N/Y	Not Used	Not Used	N-N-N/Y-N-Y/N	...
Cayce	Not Used	Y/N/Y	Y/N/N/N/N	Not Used	Y-Y-N/Y-N-Y/Y	A,B,C,D,E,F
Charleston	Y-D- N-N/N/Y	N/N/Y	Not Used	Y/Y/N/N/N	N-N-N/Y-N-Y/Y	A
Columbia	Y-T- N-N/N/Y	None	Not Used	Not Used	N-N-N/Y-N-Y/N	...
Conway	Y-T-..-N/N/Y	None	Not Used	Not Used	N-N-N/Y-N-Y/N	...
Florence	Y-D- Y-N/N/Y	None	N/N/N/N/N	N/N/Y/N/N	N-N-N/Y-Y-Y/N	D,E
Gaffney	Not Used	N/N/Y	Not Used	Not Used	Not Used	...
Greenville	N-...-..-Y/N/..	N/N/Y	Not Used	Not Used	N-N-N/Y-Y-Y/N	A,C,D,E
Greenwood	Not Used	N/N/Y	Not Used	Not Used	Not Used	...
Greer	Y-P- N-N/Y/Y	N/N/Y	Not Used	Y/N/N/N/N	Not Used	A
Myrtle Beach	Y-T-..-N/N/Y	N/N/Y	Not Used	Not Used	N-N-N/Y-Y-Y/N	A,C,D
North Augusta	Not Used	N/Y/Y	Not Used	Y/N/N/N/N	N-N-N/Y-Y-N/N	...
North Charleston	Not Used	N/Y/Y	N/Y/N/N/N	Not Used	Not Used	A
Rock Hill	Y-T- N-Y/N/Y	N/N/Y	Y/N/N/N/N	N/N/N/N/N	N-N-N/N-N-N/Y	C,D,E,F
Spartanburg	... Y-Y/N/Y	N/Y/Y	N/N/Y/Y/N	...	N-N-N/N-N-N/Y	A,C,D,E,F
Sumter	Not Used	None	Not Used	Not Used	Not Used	A
Union	Not Used	N/N/Y	Not Used	N/N/N/N/N	Y-Y-N/Y-N-Y/N	...
SOUTH DAKOTA						
Brookings	Y-T- N-N/N/Y	Y/N/N	Not Used	Not Used	Not Used	...
Pierre	Y-P- N-N/N/Y	N/N/N	Not Used	Not Used	Not Used	...
Rapid City	Not Used	None	Y/Y/N/N/N	N/N/Y/N/N	Y-Y-Y/N-N-N/N	C,D,E,F
Sioux Falls	Y-P- Y-N/N/Y	N/Y/N	N/Y/N/N/N	N/N/Y/N/N	Y-Y-Y/N-N-N/N	A,C
Watertown	Not Used	None	Not Used	N/N/Y/N/N	Not Used	...
Yankton	Y-P- N-N/Y/N	None	Not Used	Y/N/N/N/N	N-N-N/N-N-N/Y	D,E,F
TENNESSEE						
Bartlett	Y-D- N-N/N/Y	None	Not Used	Not Used	Not Used	A,B
Bristol	N-...-N-Y/N/..	N/N/Y	N/N/Y/N/N	Not Used	N-N-N/N-N-N/Y	...
Columbia	Y-T- N-Y/Y/Y	None	Not Used	N/N/N/N/N	Not Used	...
Elizabethton	Not Used	N/N/Y	Not Used	Not Used	Not Used	...
Gallatin	Y-T- Y-Y/N/Y	None	Not Used	Not Used	N-N-N/Y-N-Y/Y	C,D,F
Johnson City	N-...-..-Y/N/Y	Y/Y/Y	N/Y/Y/N/N	N/N/N/Y/N	N-N-N/Y-Y-Y/N	D,E
Kingsport	Y-F- N-N/N/Y	None	N/N/Y/N/N	Not Used	Y-Y-Y/Y-N-Y/N	...
Mc Minnville	Not Used	None	Not Used	Not Used	Not Used	...
Maryville	Y-P- N-N/N/Y	Y/N/N	Not Used	N/N/N/Y/Y	N-N-N/Y-N-Y/N	E
Memphis	Y-P- Y-N/N/Y	None	Y/N/N/N/N	Y/Y/Y/N/Y	Not Used	...
Morristown	Not Used	N/N/Y	N/Y/N/N/N	Not Used	N-N-N/Y-Y-N/Y	A
Murfreesboro	Not Used	None	Not Used	Not Used	Not Used	A
Nashville-Davidson	Y-T- Y-Y/N/Y	Y/N/Y	N/Y/N/N/N	N/N/Y/N/N	Y-Y-Y/Y-N-Y/Y	C,D,E,F
Paris	Y-T- N-N/N/N	N/N/Y	Not Used	Not Used	Not Used	...
Springfield	Not Used	None	Not Used	Not Used	Not Used	...
Tullahoma	Y..- N-Y/N/..	N/N/Y	N/Y/N/N/N	Not Used	Y-Y-Y/N-N-N/N	...
TEXAS						
Abilene	Not Used	N/N/Y	Not Used	N/N/N/N/N	Y-Y-Y/N-N-N/N	D,E,F
Alice	Not Used	None	Not Used	Not Used	Not Used	A
Amarillo	Y-T- Y-N/N/Y	None	Not Used	N/N/N/Y/N	Y-N-Y/Y-N-Y/Y	D,E
Arlington	Y-P,D-Y-N/N/Y	None	N/Y/N/N/N	Not Used	N-N-N/N-N-N/Y	A,D,E,F
Athens	Y-T- N-Y/N/Y	None	Y/N/N/N/N	N/N/N/N/Y	Y-Y-Y/N-N-N/N	...
Baytown	Not Used	N/N/Y	N/N/N/N/N	Not Used	N-N-N/Y-N-Y/Y	A,C,D
Beaumont	Y-T- N-N/N/Y	None	Not Used	N/N/N/N/N	Y-N-Y/Y-N-Y/Y	A
Bellaire	Not Used	None	Not Used	Not Used	Not Used	...
Big Spring	Not Used	None	Not Used	Not Used	N-N-N/N-N-N/Y	...
Borger	Y-T- N-Y/Y/Y	None	Not Used	Not Used	Not Used	...
Brenham	Y-T,D-N-Y/N/Y	N/N/Y	Not Used	Y/N/N/Y/N	Not Used	...
Brownfield	Y-T- N-Y/Y/N	N/N/Y	Not Used	Not Used	Not Used	...
Brownsville	Y-T- Y-Y/N/Y	N/N/Y	Not Used	Y/Y/N/N/N	N-N-N/N-N-N/Y	...
Brownwood	Not Used	None	N/Y/N/N/N	Not Used	N-N-N/Y-N-Y/N	...
Canyon	Not Used	None	Y/N/N/N/N	Not Used	Not Used	...
Cleburne	Not Used	N/N/Y	Not Used	N/N/N/N/N	Not Used	A
Conroe	Not Used	None	N/Y/N/N/N	Not Used	N-N-N/Y-N-Y/N	E
Corpus Christi	Y-T- N-Y/N/Y	N/N/Y	N/Y/N/N/N	N/N/Y/Y/N	Y-Y-Y/Y-Y-Y/Y	C,D,E,F
Corsicana	Not Used	None	N/N/N/N/N	Not Used	Not Used	...
Dallas	Y-P,F-Y-N/N/N	Y/Y/N	Y/Y/N/N/N	N/N/N/Y/N	N-N-N/Y-N-Y/Y	A,B,C,D,E,F,G,H
De Soto	Not Used	None	N/Y/N/N/N	Not Used	Y-N-N/N-N-N/N	A

Table 5/5 continued **SELECTED EMPLOYEE INCENTIVES IN CITIES 10,000 AND OVER**

Municipality	Educational incentives: tuition reimbursement-amount-requirements to stay-time off/ salary increase/ available to all	Variation in working hours: 4-day work week/ flextime/ task system	Attendance incentives: sick leave conversion/ cash bonuses / early retirement / personal leave / pooling	Job enrichment: job redesign/ job rotation/ labor-management committees / quality circles / team approach	Awards: suggestion-cash-nomonetary/ performance-cash-nomonetary / safety	Extraordinary benefits
TEXAS continued						
Del Rio	Y-P,D-N-N/N/Y	N/Y/N	N/Y/Y/N/N	Not Used	Y-N-Y/N-N-N/Y	A
Denton	Y-T-..-Y/N/..	N/N/Y	Not Used	Y/Y/Y/N/Y	Not Used	D
Duncanville	N-...-N-N/Y/N	None	Y/N/N/N/N	Not Used	N-N-N/Y-Y-Y/N	A
Eagle Pass	Not Used	None	Not Used	Not Used	Not Used	...
Edinburg	Not Used	None	Not Used	N/N/N/N/N	N-N-N/Y-N-Y/N	A
El Paso	Not Used	N/N/Y	Not Used	Not Used	Y-Y-Y/N-N-N/N	A,B
Euless	Y-T- Y-N/N/Y	None	Y/N/N/N/N	Not Used	Not Used	A
Farmers Branch	Y-T- N-N/N/Y	N/N/Y	Not Used	Y/N/N/N/N	Not Used	A
Forest Hill	Y-T- N-Y/N/Y	None	Not Used	N/N/N/N/Y	N-N-N/Y-N-Y/N	A
Fort Worth	Y-P- N-N/Y/Y	N/N/Y	Not Used	N/N/Y/N/Y	N-N-N/N-N-N/Y	A,D,E
Friendswood	Y-P- N-N/N/Y	None	Not Used	Not Used	Not Used	A,C,D
Galveston	N-...-..-Y/N/N	N/N/Y	Not Used	Not Used	Not Used	...
Grapevine	Y-D- N-Y/N/Y	None	N/Y/N/N/N	Not Used	N-N-N/Y-N-Y/N	A
Greenville	Y-P,D-N-Y/N/Y	Y/N/N	Y/N/N/N/N	Not Used	N-N-N/Y-N-Y/N	A,C,D,E,F
Groves	Y-T- N-N/Y/Y	N/N/Y	N/N/Y/N/N	Not Used	Not Used	C
Haltom City	Not Used	None	N/Y/N/N/N	Y/Y/N/N/N	Not Used	A,G
Harlingen	Not Used	None	Not Used	Not Used	Not Used	...
Hereford	Not Used	...	...	...	...	...
Huntsville	Not Used	N/N/Y	Not Used	Not Used	N-N-N/N-N-N/Y	A
Hurst	Y-D- Y-N/N/Y	None	Not Used	Not Used	Not Used	A
Jacksonville	Y-T- N-Y/N/Y	N/N/Y	Not Used	N/N/Y/N/Y	Not Used	...
Kerrville	Y-T- Y-Y/N/Y	None	Not Used	Not Used	Not Used	...
Killeen	N-...-N-Y/N/N	N/N/Y	Not Used	Not Used	N-N-N/Y-Y-N/N	D
Kingsville	... ..-N/N/..	N/N/Y	Not Used	Not Used	N-N-N/Y-Y-N/N	...
Lake Jackson	Y-T- N-N/N/Y	None	Not Used	Not Used	Not Used	...
Lamesa	Y-D- N-Y/N/Y	None	Y/N/N/N/N	N/N/N/N/Y	Not Used	D,E,F
Lancaster	Not Used	None	Y/N/N/N/N	Not Used	Not Used	...
League City	Y-T- N-Y/N/Y	None	Not Used	Y/N/N/N/N	Not Used	A
Longview	Not Used	N/N/Y	N/Y/N/N/N	N/N/N/N/N	Y-Y-Y/Y-N-Y/N	A,D,E,F
Lubbock	N-...-N-Y/N/N	None	Not Used	Not Used	Not Used	...
Lufkin	Y-D- Y-Y/N/Y	None	Not Used	Not Used	Not Used	...
Mc Allen	Y-T- N-N/N/Y	N/N/Y	N/Y/N/N/N	Not Used	Not Used	A
Mc Kinney	Y-T- Y-N/N/Y	None	Not Used	Not Used	Not Used	...
Mesquite	Not Used	N/N/Y	N/N/N/N/N	N/N/Y/N/N	N-N-N/Y-Y-N/Y	C,D,E
Missouri City	Y-T- N-Y/Y/Y	None	Not Used	Not Used	Y-N-Y/Y-N-Y/N	A
Nederland	Y-T,D-N-Y/N/N	Y/N/Y	Y/N/N/N/N	N/N/Y/N/N	N-N-N/Y-N-Y/Y	...
New Braunfels	Not Used	N/N/Y	Not Used	Not Used	Not Used	A
North Richland Hills	Y-T- N-N/N/Y	None	Not Used	Not Used	Not Used	A
Odessa	Y-T,D-N-N/N/Y	N/Y/Y	N/N/N/N/N	Not Used	Y-Y-N/N-N-N/Y	A
Orange	Y-F- Y-Y/N/Y	None	Not Used	Y/Y/N/N/N	N-N-N/Y-Y-Y/Y	A
Palestine	N-...-N-Y/Y/N	None	Not Used	Not Used	Not Used	...
Paris	Y-T- N-Y/Y/N	N/N/Y	Y/N/N/N/N	Y/N/N/N/N	Not Used	...
Pearland	Not Used	N/N/Y	Not Used	Not Used	Not Used	A,D,E,F
Pharr	Y..- Y-Y/N/Y	N/Y/Y	Not Used	Not Used	Not Used	...
Plainview	N-...-N-N/Y/Y	None	N/Y/N/N/N	Not Used	Not Used	...
Plano	Y-P- Y-N/N/Y	Y/N/Y	Y/N/N/N/N	N/N/N/N/Y	N-N-N/Y-Y-N/Y	C,D,E,F
Port Arthur	Y-T- Y-N/N/Y	None	N/Y/N/N/N	Not Used	Not Used	A
Richardson	Y-F- N-N/N/Y	N/N/Y	Not Used	Not Used	Not Used	A
San Angelo	Y-T- N-N/N/Y	None	Not Used	Not Used	Y-Y-Y/Y-Y-N/N	A,D,E,F
San Marcos	Not Used	None	Not Used	N/Y/N/Y/Y	Y-N-Y/N-N-N/N	A,D
Sherman	Y-T,D-N-Y/N/Y	Y/N/Y	Y/N/N/N/N	Not Used	Not Used	A
Snyder	Y-T- N-Y/N/Y	None	N/Y/N/N/N	Not Used	N-N-N/Y-N-Y/N	...
South Houston	N-...-N-Y/N/N	None	N/N/N/N/N	Not Used	N-N-N/N-N-N/N	...
Stephenville	N-...-..-Y/N/N	None	Not Used	Not Used	Not Used	...
Sulphur Springs	Y-T- Y-Y/N/Y	N/N/Y	Not Used	N/N/N/N/Y	N-N-N/Y-N-Y/N	...
Temple	Not Used	N/N/Y	N/N/N/N/N	Not Used	N-N-N/Y-Y-Y/N	...
Texarkana	Y-T- N-N/N/Y	None	Not Used	Not Used	Not Used	A,I
The Colony	N-...-..-Y/N/Y	None	Not Used	Y/N/N/N/N	Not Used	A,B
Tyler	Y-P,D-N-N/N/Y	N/N/Y	Not Used	Not Used	N-N-N/Y-N-Y/N	A,C,D,E,F,G
University Park	Y-T,D-N-N/N/Y	N/N/Y	N/N/N/N/N	Y/Y/Y/Y/N	Not Used	...
Uvalde	Y-T- N-Y/N/Y	None	N/N/N/N/N	N/N/N/N/Y	Not Used	...
Vernon	Y-T- N-Y/Y/Y	None	Not Used	Not Used	Not Used	...
Victoria	Y-T- Y-N/../Y	None	Not Used	Not Used	Not Used	A,D,E
Waco	Not Used	None	Not Used	Not Used	N-N-N/N-N-N/Y	...
Waxahachie	Not Used	N/N/Y	Y/N/N/N/N	Not Used	Not Used	...
Weatherford	Not Used	N/N/Y	N/Y/N/N/N	Not Used	N-N-N/N-N-N/Y	...
Weslaco	Not Used	N/N/Y	Not Used	Not Used	Not Used	...
West University Place	... ..-../../..	N/N/Y	Not Used	Not Used	N-N-N/N-N-N/Y	A
Wichita Falls	Y-P- Y-Y/N/Y	N/N/Y	Y/N/N/N/N	N/N/N/N/Y	Y-Y-Y/Y-N-Y/Y	A,C,D,E,F
UTAH						
Cedar City	Y-T-..-Y/N/Y	None	Not Used	Not Used	Not Used	A
Clearfield	Y-F- Y-Y/N/Y	Y/Y/Y	Not Used	N/N/N/N/Y	N-N-N/Y-Y-Y/N	A
Logan	Not Used	Y/N/Y	Not Used	Not Used	Y-Y-Y/N-N-N/N	...
Murray	Y-T,D-Y-N/N/Y	None	N/Y/N/N/N	N/Y/Y/N/N	N-N-N/Y-Y-Y/N	A,B,D,E,F,G
Ogden	Not Used	Y/Y/Y	Y/Y/N/N/N	Y/Y/Y/N/N	Not Used	A,B,C,D,E
Orem	Y-P- Y-N/N/Y	Y/Y/Y	N/Y/N/N/N	N/N/N/N/Y	N-N-N/Y-Y-Y/N	A
Provo	Y-T- Y-N/N/Y	Y/Y/Y	N/Y/N/N/N	Y/Y/Y/N/N	N-N-N/Y-N-Y/N	A,B
Salt Lake City	Y-D- N-N/N/Y	Y/Y/N	Y/N/Y/N/N	N/N/Y/N/Y	N-N-N/Y-Y-Y/N	A,C,D,E,F,G
Sandy City	Y-T,D-N-N/N/Y	Y/Y/N	Y/N/N/N/N	Y/Y/Y/N/Y	Y-Y-Y/Y-N-Y/N	A,D,E,F,H

Table 5/5 continued SELECTED EMPLOYEE INCENTIVES IN CITIES 10,000 AND OVER

Municipality	Educational incentives: tuition reimbursement-amount-requirements to stay-time off/ salary increase/ available to all	Variation in working hours: 4-day work week/ flextime/ task system	Attendance incentives: sick leave conversion/ cash bonuses / early retirement / personal leave / pooling	Jcb enrichment: job redesign/ job rotation/ labor-management committees / quality circles / team approach	Awards: suggestion-cash-nomonetary/ performance-cash-nomonetary / safety	Extraordinary benefits
UTAH continued						
South Salt Lake	Y-T,D-N-N/N/Y	None	Not Used	N/Y/N/N/N	N-N-N/N-N-N/N	C,D,H
West Jordan	Y-P- Y-../N/Y	None	N/Y/N/N/N	N/N/N/N/N	Not Used	A,B
West Valley City	Y-P,D-Y-N/Y/Y	None	N/Y/Y/N/N	Y/N/N/N/Y	Y-Y-Y/Y-Y-Y/N	A,E
VERMONT						
Brattleboro	Not Used	N/Y/N	Not Used	N/N/N/N/N	Y-Y-Y/N-N-N/Y	...
VIRGINIA						
Blacksburg	Y-T- N-N/N/Y	None	Y/N/N/N/N	N/N/N/N/Y	N-N-N/N-N-N/Y	D
Charlottesville	Y-F- Y-Y/N/Y	Y/N/Y	Not Used	N/N/Y/Y/Y	N-N-N/Y-Y-Y/Y	C,D,E,F
Christiansburg	Y-T,D-N-Y/N/Y	N/N/Y	N/N/N/Y/N	N/N/N/N/Y	Not Used	...
Colonial Heights	Not Used	None	Not Used	Not Used	Not Used	...
Fredericksburg	Y..- N-Y/Y/N	None	Not Used	Not Used	Not Used	...
Front Royal	Y-T- N-../Y/Y	None	Not Used	Not Used	N-N-N/Y-N-N/N	...
Hopewell	Y-T,D-N-N/N/Y	N/Y/N	Not Used	Not Used	Y-N-Y/N-N-N/Y	C,D
Lynchburg	Y-T,F-Y-N/N/Y	N/Y/Y	Not Used	N/N/N/N/N	Y-Y-Y/N-N-N/Y	A,C,D,E,F
Manassas	Not Used	None	Not Used	Not Used	Not Used	A
Martinsville	Y-T,D-Y-N/N/Y	Y/N/Y	Not Used	Not Used	N-N-N/Y-Y-N/N	D,E,F
Newport News	Y-T,D-N-N/N/Y	Y/N/Y	Not Used	Not Used	Not Used	D,E,F
Norfolk	Y-P,F-N-N/N/Y	Y/Y/Y	N/N/N/N/N	N/Y/Y/N/Y	Y-Y-N/Y-N-N/Y	...
Petersburg	Y-P,F-N-N/N/Y	None	Not Used	N/N/N/N/N	N-N-N/Y-N-Y/N	E,F,G
Richmond	Y..- N-Y/N/Y	Y/Y/Y	Not Used	N/N/N/N/Y	N-N-N/Y-N-N/Y	...
Vienna	Y-T,F-N-Y/N/Y	N/N/Y	Not Used	Not Used	N-N-N/N-N-N/Y	D,E,F
Waynesboro	N-...-..-Y/N/..	None	Not Used	Not Used	Not Used	...
Winchester	Y-F- Y-N/N/Y	None	N/N/N/N/N	N/N/Y/N/N	N-N-N/Y-N-Y/Y	...
WASHINGTON						
Aberdeen	Y-T,D-N-Y/N/Y	Y/N/N	Not Used	N/N/Y/N/N	Y-Y-Y/N-N-N/Y	A,B,C
Bellevue	Y-T- N-N/N/Y	Y/Y/N	Y/N/N/N/N	N/N/N/N/N	N-N-N/Y-Y-N/N	A
Bremerton	Y-P- N-N/N/Y	Y/Y/N	Not Used	Not Used	Not Used	A,D,E
Edmonds	Y-P,F-N-N/N/Y	None	N/N/N/N/N	Not Used	Not Used	A,B
Ellensburg	N-...-N-Y/N/Y	None	Not Used	Not Used	Not Used	A,B
Everett	... ..-../../..	N/N/N	Not Used	N/N/N/N/N	Y-Y-Y/Y-N-Y/N	A,B
Kennewick	Y-P- N-N/N/N	Y/Y/N	N/Y/N/N/N	Not Used	Not Used	A
Kirkland	Not Used	N/Y/N	N/Y/N/N/N	Not Used	Y-N-Y/N-N-N/N	A,B,C
Lacey	Not Used	None	Not Used	N/Y/N/N/N	Not Used	A,H
Longview	Y-T,D-N-Y/N/Y	N/N/Y	N/Y/N/N/N	N/N/N/Y/N	Not Used	A
Lynnwood	Y-T- N-N/N/Y	None	Not Used	Not Used	Not Used	A,B
Moses Lake	Y-D- N-Y/N/Y	None	Y/N/N/N/N	N/N/N/N/N	N-N-N/Y-N-Y/N	A,B
Mountlake Terrace	Y-T- N-Y/N/Y	Y/N/N	N/Y/N/N/N	Y/Y/Y/N/Y	Not Used	A,D
Oak Harbor	Y..- N-N/N/Y	None	Not Used	Not Used	Not Used	...
Port Angeles	Y-T- N-N/N/Y	N/Y/N	...	N/N/Y/N/Y	Y-N-Y/Y-N-Y/Y	A,C
Pullman	Not Used	None	Not Used	N/N/Y/N/Y	Y-Y-N/N-N-N/N	A,B,C,D,E,F
Puyallup	N-...-N-Y/N/Y	N/Y/N	Not Used	N/N/N/N/Y	Not Used	A,B
Renton	Y-F- N-N/N/Y	N/Y/N	N/Y/N/N/N	N/N/Y/N/Y	Not Used	A,B,C
Richland	Not Used	N/N/Y	Y/Y/N/N/N	Not Used	Not Used	A
Spokane	Y-T- N-Y/N/Y	Y/Y/Y	N/Y/N/N/N	Y/N/Y/N/N	Y-Y-Y/Y-N-Y/N	A,B,C,D
Vancouver	Not Used	None	Not Used	Not Used	N-N-N/Y-N-N/Y	A,C,D,E
Wenatchee	Y-T- N-Y/N/N	N/N/N	...	Not Used	N-N-N/N-N-N/N	A,B,C
Yakima	N-...-N-Y/N/Y	None	Y/Y/N/N/N	N/N/Y/N/N	N-N-N/Y-N-Y/N	A,B
WEST VIRGINIA						
Bluefield	Y-T- N-N/N/Y	None	Not Used	Not Used	N-N-N/N-N-N/N	G
Fairmont	Y-P- Y-Y/N/Y	None	Y/N/N/N/N	N/N/N/Y/N	N-N-N/Y-Y-N/N	C
Huntington	Not Used	N/N/Y	Not Used	Not Used	Not Used	B
Moundsville	Not Used	N/Y/Y	Not Used	Not Used	Not Used	B
Parkersburg	Not Used	Y/N/N	Y/Y/N/N/N	Not Used	Not Used	...
South Charleston	Y-D- N-N/N/Y	N/Y/Y	Not Used	N/N/Y/N/N	Not Used	A
WISCONSIN						
Allouez	Not Used	None	N/N/N/N/N	Y/Y/N/N/N	Not Used	A
Brown Deer	Not Used	None	Not Used	Not Used	Not Used	...
De Pere	N-...-..-Y/N/N	None	Not Used	Not Used	Not Used	A
Eau Claire	Y-T- Y-N/N/N	None	Not Used	Not Used	Y-Y-N/N-N-N/N	A,B,C,D,E,F
Germantown	Y-D- Y-Y/Y/Y	N/Y/N	Not Used	Y/N/N/N/Y	Y-N-N/N-N-N/Y	...
Green Bay	Not Used	None	Not Used	N/N/N/Y/N	N-N-N/Y-N-Y/Y	A,C,D,F
Greendale	Not Used	None	Not Used	Not Used	Not Used	B,E
La Crosse	Not Used	None	Not Used	Not Used	Not Used	C,D,E,F
Marshfield	Y-P- N-N/N/Y	N/Y/N	Not Used	Not Used	Not Used	...
Menasha	Y-T- N-N/N/Y	None	N/N/N/N/N	Not Used	Not Used	A
Menomonee Falls	Y-T- Y-Y/N/Y	N/N/Y	Not Used	Not Used	Not Used	A,B
Mequon	Y-P,D-N-N/N/Y	None	N/Y/N/N/N	Not Used	Not Used	A
Milwaukee	Y-T,F-Y-Y/N/Y	N/Y/N	Y/Y/N/N/N	Y/Y/N/Y/Y	N-N-N/Y-Y-N/Y	A,B,C,E
New Berlin	Y-D- N-N/N/Y	None	Not Used	Not Used	Not Used	...
Racine	N-...-..-Y/N/Y	None	N/Y/N/N/N	Not Used	N-N-N/N-N-N/Y	C,D,E
Shorewood	Y-P- N-Y/N/Y	None	N/N/N/N/N	N/N/N/Y/N	N-N-N/N-N-N/Y	...
Sun Prairie	Y-T- N-Y/N/N	N/Y/Y	Not Used	N/N/N/N/Y	Not Used	A
Two Rivers	Y-P- N-N/N/Y	N/Y/N	N/Y/N/N/N	Not Used	N-N-N/Y-Y-N/N	...
Watertown	Not Used	None	Not Used	Not Used	Not Used	...
West Allis	Y-F- N-N/N/Y	N/N/Y	Not Used	Not Used	Y-Y-Y/N-N-N/N	A,C,D,E
West Bend	Y-T- N-N/N/N	None	Not Used	Not Used	Not Used	...
Whitewater	Not Used	None	Not Used	Not Used	Not Used	...

Table 5/5 continued **SELECTED EMPLOYEE INCENTIVES IN CITIES 10,000 AND OVER**

Municipality	Educational incentives: tuition reimbursement-amount-requirements to stay-time off/ salary increase/ available to all	Variation in working hours: 4-day work week/ flextime/ task system	Attendance incentives: sick leave conversion/ cash bonuses / early retirement / personal leave / pooling	Job enrichment: job redesign/ job rotation/ labor-management committees / quality circles / team approach	Awards: suggestion-cash-nomonetary/ performance-cash-nomonetary / safety	Extraordinary benefits
WYOMING						
Casper	Y-T- N-Y/N/Y	Y/N/Y	N/Y/N/N/N	N/N/Y/Y/Y	Y-N-Y/Y-N-N/N	A,C,D,E,F,H
Gillette	Y-T- N-N/N/Y	None	Not Used	Not Used	Y-N-Y/Y-N-Y/N	A,C,D,E,F
Green River	Y-P- Y-N/N/Y	N/Y/N	Not Used	N/N/N/N/Y	Not Used	A,C,D
Laramie	Y-D- N-Y/N/Y	N/N/Y	Not Used	N/N/Y/N/N	Not Used	A,C
Rawlins	Not Used	None	N/N/N/N/Y	N/N/Y/N/Y	Y-N-Y/Y-N-Y/N	A,C,D,E,F
Rock Springs	Y-T- Y-Y/N/Y	None	N/Y/N/N/N	Not Used	N-N-N/Y-N-Y/N	A,B
Sheridan	Y-T- N-Y/N/Y	None	N/Y/N/N/N	Not Used	Not Used	A

E Directories

1 The Year Book Directories

2 Professional, Special Assistance, and Educational Organizations Serving Local and State Governments

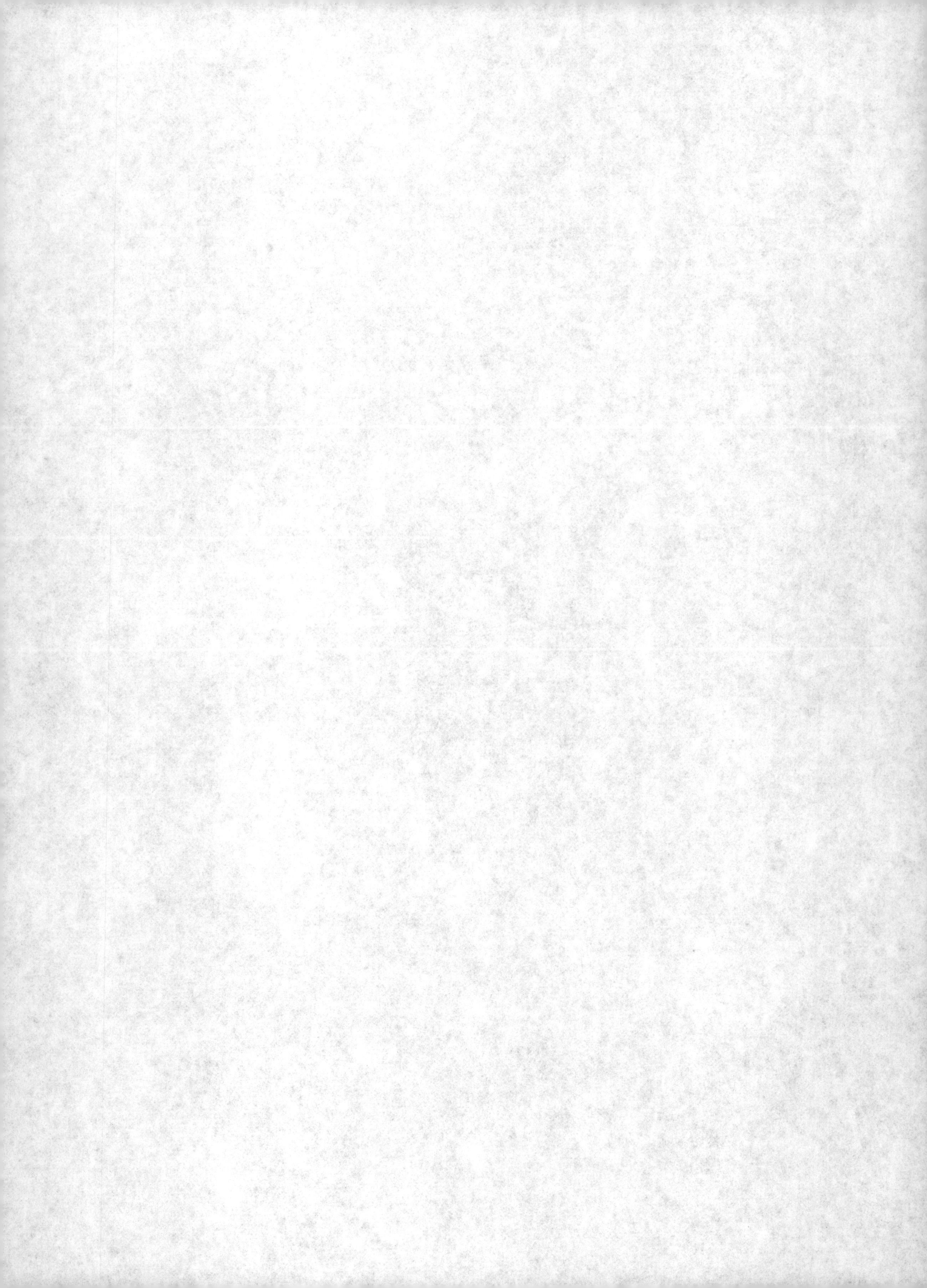

1

The Year Book Directories

The directories in this section of the Year Book contain the names of municipal and county officials in the United States as reported in the fall of 1984 along with the names of appointed chief administrative officers in Canada and other countries. In addition, this section includes directories for state municipal leagues; provincial associations and unions in Canada; state and territorial agencies for community affairs; provincial and territorial agencies for local affairs in Canada; state and provincial municipal management associations; state associations of counties; and directors of councils of governments recognized by ICMA.

The names of municipal and county managers and other chief appointed management executives for the United States and other countries are shown in Directories 1/8, 1/9, and 1/10. An asterisk (*) after the municipality name in these directories designates a municipality that has been recognized by the International City Management Association as having the council-manager form of local government, and a section mark (§) designates a municipality that has been recognized by ICMA as having a position of overall general management. Further information on these recognized places, including legal basis, title of position, form of government, and year of recognition, plus the number of administrators the community has had and information on the current administrator, is presented in the annual ICMA publication *Who's Who in Local Government*.

Information in Directories 1/1 through 1/8 was obtained from: the National League of Cities (1/1), the Federation of Canadian Municipalities (1/2 and 1/4), the Council of State Community Affairs Agencies (1/3), ICMA files (1/5, 1/7, and 1/8), and a telephone survey (1/6), and is current as of November 1984 unless otherwise indicated. Information for Directory 1/9 was obtained by a Year Book mailing to all county-type governments in July 1984. Information for Directory 1/10 was obtained by a similar mailing to all cities 2,500 and over in population and to recognized council-manager or general management places under 2,500 in July 1984.

The phone numbers in Directories 1/7, 1/8, 1/9, and 1/10, preceded by the area code, are for the city hall, municipal building, or county building, or for some municipal or county official such as the manager, clerk, or mayor, and were obtained by the Year Book mailings.

State Municipal Leagues. Directory 1/1 shows 49 state leagues of municipalities serving 49 states. (Hawaii does not not have a league.) Information includes league address, name of the executive director, phone number, and year organized. State municipal leagues provide a wide range of research, consulting, training, publications, and legislative representation services for their cities.

Provincial and Territorial Associations and Unions in Canada. Directory 1/2 shows 18 organizations serving the 11 provinces and the territories in Canada. The name of the president and a permanent officer are shown along with the address and phone number where available.

State Agencies for Community Affairs. Directory 1/3 presents the name and address of 50 agencies for community affairs in the United States. It includes the name of the executive director or head of the agency. These agencies of state governments offer a variety of research, financial information, and coordination services for cities and other local governments.

Provincial and Territorial Agencies for Local Affairs in Canada. Directory 1/4 shows 14 agencies for local affairs serving 11 provinces and the territories in Canada. The directory lists the name and address of the minister as well as the minister's phone number.

State Municipal Management Associations. Directory 1/5 shows the name, president, address, and phone number for 48 municipal management associations serving 48 of the United States, the District of Columbia, and 2 provinces in Canada. (The states of Wyoming, North Dakota, South Dakota, Idaho, and Montana are served by the Great Open Spaces City Management Association. In addition, Idaho is also served by its own association.)

State Associations of Counties. Directory 1/6 shows the name, address, phone number, name of executive director, and year organized for 48 county associations serving 47 states. (Two associations serve the state of Washington; three states do not have associations: Connecticut, Rhode Island, and Vermont.) Like their municipal league counterparts, these associations provide a wide range of research, training, consulting, publications, and legislative representation services.

Directors of Councils of Governments. Directory 1/7 gives the official name of the council of governments, the director and year appointed, and the telephone number for COGs recognized by ICMA.

International Administrators. Directory 1/8 gives the name of the appointed administrator and phone number, if available, for the chief appointed administrator in communities overseas. In Canada the communities listed are recognized by ICMA as having the council-manager plan or providing for a position of overall general management. In the other countries, the municipalities listed generally subscribe to the same standards of professional local government management.

County Officials in U.S. Counties. Directory 1/9 lists, alphabetically by state, all county-type governments. It shows the population (in thousands) according to the 1980 Census of Population; the county telephone number; name of the board chairman, county judge, or president; appointed administrator; clerk to the governing board; chief financial officer; county engineer; county health officer; and chief law enforcement official.

Municipal Officials in U.S. Cities. Directory 1/10 lists, alphabetically by state, all incorporated places in the United States 2,500 and over and those places under 2,500 recognized by ICMA. It shows the current form of government; ICMA recognition status; the population (in thousands) according to the 1980 Census of Population; municipal phone number; name of mayor; appointed administrator; city clerk; finance officer; fire chief; police chief; and public works director. Leaders (. .) in the population column mean that the population of the place is under 500.

Other Local Government Directories. The names of municipal officials not reported in the Year Book are available in many states through directories published by state municipal leagues, state municipal management associations, and state associations of counties. Names and addresses of these leagues and associations are shown in Directories 1/1, 1/5, and 1/6. In some states the secretary of state, the state agency for community affairs (Directory 1/3), or another state agency publishes a directory that includes municipal and county officials. In addition, several directories with national coverage are published for health officers, welfare workers, housing and urban renewal officials, and other professional groups.

Directory 1/1 STATE MUNICIPAL LEAGUES

State	Name of league and headquarters address	Name and title of executive director[1]	Phone number	Year first effort to cooperate[2]	Year first organized[3]
Alabama	Alabama League of Municipalities, P.O. Box 1270, Montgomery 36102	John F. Watkins, ED	205 262-2566	1914	1930
Alaska	Alaska Municipal League, 105 Municipal Way, Suite 301, Juneau 99801	Scott A. Burgess, ED	907 586-1325	1950	1950

Directory 1/1 continued **STATE MUNICIPAL LEAGUES**

State	Name of league and headquarters address	Name and title of executive director[1]	Phone number	Year first effort to cooperate[2]	Year first organized[3]
Arizona	League of Arizona Cities and Towns, 1820 West Washington Street, Phoenix 85007	John J. DeBolske, ED	602 258-5786	1925	1937
Arkansas	Arkansas Municipal League, P.O. Box 38, North Little Rock 72115	Don A. Zimmerman, ED	501 374-3484	1917	1934
California	League of California Cities, 1400 K Street, Sacramento 95814	Don Benninghoven, ED	916 444-5790	1898	1898
Colorado	Colorado Municipal League, 1500 Grant Street, Suite 200, Denver 80203	Kenneth G. Bueche, ED	303 831-6411	1900	1923
Connecticut	Connecticut Conference of Municipalities, 956 Chapel Street, New Haven 06510	Joel Cogen, ED	203 772-2168	...	1966
Delaware	Delaware League of Local Governments, P.O. Box 484, Dover 19903	Leon deValinger, Jr., ED	302 678-0991	1965	1965
Florida	Florida League of Cities, P.O. Box 1757, Tallahassee 32302	Raymond C. Sittig, ED	904 222-9684	1922	1922
Georgia	Georgia Municipal Association, 34 Peachtree Street, Suite 2300, Atlanta 30303	James V. Burgess, Jr., ED	404 688-0472	1916	1934
Idaho	Association of Idaho Cities, 3314 Grace Street, Boise 83703	Raymond Holly, ED	208 344-8594	1918	1941
Illinois	Illinois Municipal League, 1220 South 7th Street, Springfield 62708	Steven Sargent, ED	217 525-1220	1899	1914
Indiana	Indiana Association of Cities and Towns, 150 West Market Street, Room 600, Indianapolis 46204	Michael J. Quinn, ED	317 635-8616	1891	1899
Iowa	League of Iowa Municipalities, Suite 100, 900 Des Moines Street, Des Moines 50316	Robert W. Harpster, ED	515 265-9961	1898	1898
Kansas	League of Kansas Municipalities, 112 West 7th Street, Topeka 66603	E. A. Mosher, ED	913 354-9565	1910	1910
Kentucky	Kentucky Municipal League, P.O. Box 22736, Lexington 40522	Edwin L. Griffin, Jr., ED	606 257-3285	1929	1929
Louisiana	Louisiana Municipal Association, P.O. Box 4327, Baton Rouge 70821	Charles J. Pasqua, ED	504 344-5001	1935	1937
Maine	Maine Municipal Association, Local Government Center, Community Drive, Augusta 04330	Christopher G. Lockwood, ED	207 623-8429	1936	1936
Maryland	Maryland Municipal League, 76 Maryland Avenue, Annapolis 21401	Jon C. Burrell, ED	301 268-5514	1937	1948
Massachusetts	Massachusetts Municipal Association, 131 Tremont Street, Boston 02111	James W. Segel, ED	617 426-7272	1961	1961
Michigan	Michigan Municipal League, P.O. Box 1487, Ann Arbor 48106	George D. Goodman, D	313 662-3246	1899	1899
Minnesota	League of Minnesota Cities, 183 University Avenue East, Saint Paul 55101	Donald A. Slater, ED	612 227-5600	1903	1913
Mississippi	Mississippi Municipal Association, 455 North Lamar, Jackson 39202	Patrick A. Dunne, ED	601 353-5854	1918	1936
Missouri	Missouri Municipal League, 1913 William Street, Jefferson City 65101	Gary Markenson, ED	314 635-9134	1914	1927
Montana	Montana League of Cities and Towns, 130 Neill Avenue, Helena 59601	Alec Hansen, ED	406 442-8768	1910	1932
Nebraska	League of Nebraska Municipalities, 1335 L Street, Lincoln 68508	David Chambers, D	402 476-2829	1910	1910
Nevada	Nevada League of Cities, P.O. Box 2307, Carson City 89701	Gentty P. Etcheverry, ED	702 882-2121	...	1950
New Hampshire	New Hampshire Municipal Association, P.O. Box 617, Concord 03301	John B. Andrews, ED	603 224-7447	1955	1961
New Jersey	New Jersey State League of Municipalities, 407 West State Street, Trenton 08618	John E. Trafford, ED	609 695-3481	1915	1915
New Mexico	New Mexico Municipal League, P.O. Box 846, Santa Fe 87501	William F. Fulginiti, ED	505 982-5573	...	1958
New York	New York Conference of Mayors, 119 Washington Avenue, Albany 12210	Donald A. Walsh, AED	518 463-1185	1910	1910
North Carolina	North Carolina League of Municipalities, P.O. Box 3069, Raleigh 27602	S. Leigh Wilson, ED	919 834-1311	1908	1922
North Dakota	North Dakota League of Cities, P.O. Box 2235, Bismarck 58502	Robert E. Johnson, ED	701 223-3518	1912	1927
Ohio	Ohio Municipal League, 40 South Third Street, 5th Floor, Columbus 43215	John P. Coleman, ED	614 221-4349	1912	1952
Oklahoma	Oklahoma Municipal League, 201 N.E. 23rd Street, Oklahoma City 73105	Donald C. Rider, ED	405 528-7515	1913	1913

Directory 1/1 continued — STATE MUNICIPAL LEAGUES

State	Name of league and headquarters address	Name and title of executive director[1]	Phone number	Year first effort to cooperate[2]	Year first organized[3]
Oregon	League of Oregon Cities, P.O. Box 928, Salem 97308	Edward Ferguson, ED	503 588-6466	1913	1913
Pennsylvania	Pennsylvania League of Cities, 2608 North Third Street, Harrisburg 17110	John A. Garner, ED	717 236-9469	1900	1900
Rhode Island	Rhode Island League of Cities and Towns, 128 North Main Street, Providence 02903	Kenneth F. Payne, ED	401 272-3434	1959	1965
South Carolina	Municipal Association of South Carolina, P.O. Box 11558, Columbia 29211	J. McDonald Wray, ED	803 799-9574	1936	1939
South Dakota	South Dakota Municipal League, 214 East Capitol, Pierre 57501	Robert H. Miller, ED	605 224-8654	1925	1935
Tennessee	Tennessee Municipal League, Room 317, 226 Capitol Boulevard, Nashville 37219	Joseph A. Sweat, ED	615 255-6416	1913	1940
Texas	Texas Municipal League, 1020 Southwest Tower, Austin 78701	Ted C. Willis, ED	512 478-6601	1913	1913
Utah	Utah League of Cities and Towns, University Club Building, Suite 1240, 136 East South Temple, Salt Lake City 84111	Herschel G. Hester III, ED	801 328-1601	1907	1907
Vermont	Vermont League of Cities and Towns, 52 State Street, Montpelier 05602	Steven E. Jeffrey, ED	802 229-9111	1967	1967
Virginia	Virginia Municipal League, 311 Ironfronts, 1011 East Main Street, Richmond 23206	R. Michael Amyx, ED	804 649-8471	1905	1905
Washington	Association of Washington Cities, 1073 South Capitol Way, Olympia 98501	Kent E. Swisher, ED	206 753-4137	1910	1910
West Virginia	West Virginia Municipal League, 1615 Washington Street, East, Charleston 25311	Betty Dean, ED	304 343-9201	1917	1935
Wisconsin	League of Wisconsin Municipalities, 122 West Washington Avenue, Madison 53703	Stanley York, ED	608 255-9780	1898	1898
Wyoming	Wyoming Association of Municipalities, P.O. Box 2535, Cheyenne 82001	Robert R. Cantine, ED	307 632-1942	...	1952

[1] Titles abbreviated as follows: AED, Acting Executive Director; ED, Executive Director; D, Director.
[2] The date in this column refers in most instances to the beginning of a loosely knit organization of cities on a corporate basis for the purpose of presenting municipal problems before the legislature.
[3] This date is the year when an active organization, as now known, was established.

Directory 1/2 — PROVINCIAL AND TERRITORIAL ASSOCIATIONS AND UNIONS IN CANADA[1]

Province or Territory	Association/Union	President	Permanent Officer
Alberta	Alberta Association of Municipal Districts and Counties	Reeve W. Daley, Box 297, Granum, T0L 1A0	J. D. Edworthy, Secretary-Manager, 4504–101 Street, Edmonton, T6E 5G9 403 436-9375
	Alberta Urban Municipalities Association	Mayor G. Cuff, P. O. Box 130, Spruce Grove, T0E 2C2 403 962-2611	T. P. Buchanan, Executive Director, 10145-104 Street, Edmonton, T5J 1A4 403 433-4431
British Columbia	Union of British Columbia Municipalities	Mayor Audrey Moore, 460 Columbia Avenue, Castlegar, V1N 1G7 604 365-7227	C. S. J. McKelvey, Executive Director, 313-6th Street, New Westminster, V3L 3A7 604 526-4447
Manitoba	Manitoba Association of Urban Municipalities	Mayor E. J. Greenslade, P.O. Box 940, Portage-la-Prairie, R1N 3C1	Rochelle Zimberg, Executive Director 201-377 Henderson Highway, Winnipeg, R2K 2H2 204 667-6585
	Union of Manitoba Municipalities	Reeve D. Harms, P.O. Box 189 Manitou, R0G 1G0 204 242-2838	W. H. Rusk, Secretary-Treasurer, P. O. Box 536, Portage-la-Prairie, R1N 3B9
New Brunswick	Association of Villages of New Brunswick	Mayor R. Walls, P.O. Box 17, Blackville, E0C 1C0	Sandra Allen, Executive Director, 3-390 King Street, Fredericton, E3B 1E3 506 454-0240

Directory 1/2 continued **PROVINCIAL AND TERRITORIAL ASSOCIATIONS AND UNIONS IN CANADA**

Province or Territory	Association/Union	President	Permanent Officer
New Brunswick (cont'd.)	Cities of New Brunswick Association	Mayor E.C. Wilkins, P.O. Box 130, Fredericton, E3B 2Y1	D. W. Ellis, Executive Secretary, 3-390 King Street, Fredericton, E3B 1E3 506 454-0240
	Towns of New Brunswick Association	Mayor G. Carroll, P.O. Box 800, Grand Falls, E0J 1M0 506 455-9426	A. J. Savoie, Executive Secretary, 14 Guérette Street East, Edmundston, E3V 1N9
Newfoundland and Labrador	Newfoundland and Labrador Federation of Municipalities	Mayor A. Reid, P.O. Box 999, Carbonear, A0A 1T0 709 596-2701	D. Smith, Executive Director, P.O. Box 5756, St. John's, A1C 5X3 709 753-7820
Northwest Territories	Northwest Territories Association of Municipalities	Councillor D. Sian, P.O. Box 580, Yellowknife, X1A 2N4 403 873-2671	Anita Perry, Executive Director, P.O. Box 1529, Yellowknife, X0E 1H0 403 873-8359
Nova Scotia	Union of Nova Scotia Municipalities	Mayor D. Carter, 730 Prince Street, Truro, B2N 1G9 902 893-2438	S. Zwicker, Executive Director, Suite 132, 1657 Barrington Street, Halifax, B3F 2A1 902 423-8331
Ontario	Association of Municipalities of Ontario	Alderman M. Catterall, 111 Sussex Drive, Ottawa, K1N 5A1 613 563-1111	Macdonald Dunbar, Executive Director, 100 University Avenue, Toronto, M5J 1V6 416 593-1441
Prince Edward Island	Federation of Prince Edward Island Municipalities	Commissioner J. MacLean, 31 Gordon Drive, Sherwood, C1A 6B8 902 894-5041	J. Coady, Executive Director, P.O. Box 98, Charlottetown, C1A 7K2 902 894-5552
Québec	Union des Conseils de Comtés du Québec	J-M Moreau, 1081 route Marie-Victorin, Verchères 514 583-3077	A. Nadeau, Secrétaire-général, 2835 chemin Gomin, Ste-Foy 418 651-3343
	Union des Municipalités du Québec	Marie F. Dufour, C.P. 2000, Jonquière, G7S 4K8	Luc Lacharité, Directeur-général, 301-315 boul. Dorchester E., Montréal, H2X 3P3 514 288-1693
Saskatchewan	Saskatchewan Association of Rural Municipalities	Councillor C. A. Phelps, 2075 Hamilton Street, Regina, S4P 2E1 306 527-3577	L. Wilkinson, Executive Secretary, 2075 Hamilton Street, Regina, S4P 2E1 306 527-3577
	Saskatchewan Urban Municipalities Association	Alderman H. Taylor, 1053 Clifton Avenue, Moose Jaw, S6H 3L3 306 525-3727	R. A. Wankling, Executive Director, 200-1819 Cornwall Street, Regina, S4P 2K4 306 525-3727
Yukon	Association of Yukon Communities	Alderman M. Hampton, P.O. Box 112, Faro, Y0B 1K0 403 994-2510	A. Carrel, Executive Director, 2131 Second Avenue, Whitehorse, Y1A 1C3 403 667-6064

[1]Data for this directory were provided by the Federation of Canadian Municipalities in the fall of 1983.

Directory 1/3 STATE AGENCIES FOR COMMUNITY AFFAIRS

State or territory	Agency, address, and telephone number	Name and title of executive director
Alabama	Department of Economic and Community Affairs, 3465 Norman Bridge Road, Montgomery 36105	William Rushton Director
Alaska	Department of Community and Regional Affairs, Pouch B, Juneau 99811	Emil Notti Commissioner
Arizona	Governor's Office of Economic Planning and Development, 1700 West Washington, Room 505, Phoenix 85007	Beth Jarman Executive Director
Arkansas	Industrial Development Commission, 1 State Capitol Mall, Little Rock 72201	Robert K. Middleton, III Director of Planning
California	Department of Housing and Community Development, 921 Tenth Street, 7th Floor, Sacramento 95814	Susan DeSantis Director
Colorado	Department of Local Affairs, 1313 Sherman Street, Denver 80203	Morgan Smith Executive Director
Connecticut	Department of Housing, 1179 Main Street, Hartford 06101	Joseph E. Canale Commissioner
Delaware	Department of Community Affairs, 156 South State Street, P.O. Box 1401, Dover 19901	Frances M. West Secretary
Florida	Department of Community Affairs, 2571 Executive Center Circle East, Tallahassee 32301	John DeGrove Secretary
Georgia	Department of Community Affairs, 40 Marietta Street, N.W., 8th Floor, Atlanta 30303	Jim Higdon Commissioner
Hawaii	Department of Planning and Economic Development, P.O. Box 2359, Honolulu 96804	Hideto Kono Director
Idaho	Division of Economic and Community Affairs, State Capitol Building, Room 108, Boise 83720	David O. Porter Administrator
Illinois	Department of Commerce and Community Affairs, 620 East Adams Street, Springfield 62706	George Dinges Assistant Director
Indiana	Department of Commerce, 440 N. Meridian, Indianapolis 46204	Brian Bosworth Deputy Director
Iowa	Office for Planning and Programming, 523 East 12th Street, Des Moines 50319	Ed Stanek Director
Kansas	Department of Economic Development, 503 Kansas Avenue, 6th Floor, Topeka 66612	Charles Schwartz Secretary
Kentucky	Department of Local Government, Capital Plaza Tower, 2nd Floor, Frankfort 40601	Earl Campbell Assistant to the Secretary
Louisiana	Department of Urban and Community Affairs, 5790 Florida Boulevard, Baton Rouge 70806	Dorothy Taylor Secretary
Maine	State Planning Office, 184 State Street, State House Station 38, Augusta 04333	Richard E. Barringer Director
Maryland	Department of Economic and Community Development, 45 Calvert Street, Annapolis 21401	Ardath Cade Assistant Secretary for Community Development
Massachusetts	Executive Office of Communities and Development, 100 Cambridge Street, 14th Floor, Boston 02202	Amy Anthony Secretary
Michigan	Office of Business and Community Development, P.O. Box 30225 Lansing 48909	Carol Hoffman Director
Minnesota	Office of Community Development, Department of Energy, Planning, and Development, 940 American Center Building, 150 East Kellogg Boulevard, St. Paul 55101	Sam Newman Director
Mississippi	Department of Community Development, 1304 Sillers Building, Jackson 39201	Mark Nixon Director
Missouri	Division of Community and Economic Development, P.O. Box 118, Jefferson City 65102	Gary Taylor Acting Director
Montana	Department of Commerce, 1424 9th Avenue, Helena 59620	Gary Buchanan Director
Nebraska	Department of Economic Development, Division of Community Affairs, Box 94666, 301 Centennial Mall South, Lincoln 68509	George Garnett Director
Nevada	Office of Community Services, 1100 East William, Room 109, Carson City 89710	Linda A. Ryan Director
New Hampshire	State Planning Division, 2½ Beacon Street, Concord 03301	David Scott Director
New Jersey	Department of Community Affairs, 363 West State Street, Trenton 08625	John Renna Commissioner
New Mexico	Local Government Division, 206 Lamy Building, Santa Fe 87503	Clarence Lithgow Director
New York	Division of Housing and Community Renewal, Two World Trade Center, New York 10047	Yvonne Scruggs-Leftwich Commissioner
North Carolina	Department of Natural Resources and Community Development, P.O. Box 27687, Raleigh 27611	James A. Summers Secretary
North Dakota	Office of Intergovernmental Assistance, State and Local Planning Programs, State Capital, 9th Floor, Bismarck 58505	Ron Soderberg Director
Ohio	Department of Development, 30 East Broad Street, P.O. Box 1001, Columbus 43215	Al Dietzel Secretary
Oklahoma	Department of Economic and Community Affairs, 4545 North Lincoln, Lincoln Plaza #285, Oklahoma City 73105	Cindy Rambo Secretary
Oregon	Intergovernmental Relations Division, 155 Cottage, N.E., Salem 97310	Robert L. Montgomery Administrator
Pennsylvania	Department of Community Affairs, Forum Building, Harrisburg 17120	Shirley Dennis Secretary
Rhode Island	Department of Community Affairs, 150 Washington Street, Providence 02903	Frederick C. Williamson Director
South Carolina	Division of Community and Intergovernmental Affairs, 1205 Pendleton Street, Suite 308, Columbia 29201	Joe Murray Director
South Dakota	Department of Water and Natural Resources, Office of Water Policy, Pierre 57501	Bob Hartford
Tennessee	Department of Economic and Community Development, 1007 Andrew Jackson Building, Nashville 37219	Mike McGuire Assistant Commissioner
Texas	Department of Community Affairs, P.O. Box 13166, Capitol Station, Austin 78711	Rafael Quintanilla Executive Director

Directory 1/3 continued — STATE AGENCIES FOR COMMUNITY AFFAIRS

State or territory	Agency, address, and telephone number	Name and title of executive director
Utah	Department of Community and Economic Development, 6290 State Office Building, Salt Lake City 84114	Dale Carpenter, Director
Vermont	Department of Housing and Community Affairs, Pavilion Office Building, Montpelier 05602	Alexander Shak, Commissioner
Virginia	Department of Housing and Community Development, 205 North 4th Street, Richmond 23219	O. Gene Dishner, Director
Washington	Department of Community Development, 9th and Columbia Building, Olympia 98904	Pat Dunn, Director
West Virginia	Community Development Division, Governor's Office of Economic and Community Development, State Capitol Complex, Room 553B, Charleston 25305	Fred Cutlip, Director
Wisconsin	Department of Development, 123 West Washington Avenue, Madison 53702	Rolf Wegenke, Assistant to the Administrator
Wyoming	Department of Economic Planning and Development, Barrett Building, Cheyenne 82002	John Niland, Executive Director

Directory 1/4 — PROVINCIAL AND TERRITORIAL AGENCIES FOR LOCAL AFFAIRS IN CANADA[1]

Province or territory	Minister, address	Phone number
Alberta	Hon. Julian Koziak, Minister of Municipal Affairs, 423 Legislative Building, Edmonton, T5K 2B6	403 427-3744
British Columbia	Hon. W. S. Ritchie, Minister of Municipal Affairs, 747 Fort Street, Victoria, V8W 3E1	604 387-3602
Manitoba	Hon. Eugene Kostyra, Minister of Urban Affairs, 104 Legislative Building, Winnipeg, R3C 0V8	204 944-3729
	Hon. A. R. Adam, Minister of Municipal Affairs, 330 Legislative Building, Winnipeg, R3C 0V8	204 944-3788
New Brunswick	Hon. Y. R. Poitras, Minister of Municipal Affairs, P.O. Box 6000, Fredericton, E3B 5H1	506 453-2558
Newfoundland	Hon. Hazel R. Newhook, Minister of Municipal Affairs, Confederation Building, P.O. Box 4750, St. John's, A1C 5T7	709 737-3048
Northwest Territories	Hon. J. J. Wah-Shee, Minister of Local Government, Government of Northwest Territories, Yellowknife	403 873-7139
Nova Scotia	Hon. Thomas McInnes, Minister of Municipal Affairs and Housing, P.O. Box 216, Halifax, B3J 4M2	902 424-5550
Ontario	Hon. Claude Bennett, Minister of Municipal Affairs and Housing, 777 Bay Street, Toronto, M5G 2E5	416 585-6000
Prince Edward Island	Hon. Gordon Lank, Minister of Community and Cultural Affairs, P.O. Box 2000, Charlottetown, C1A 7N8	902 892-2659
Québec	Hon. Jacques Léonard, Ministre des Affaires Municipales, Hôtel du Gouvernement, Edifice A, Québec, G1A 1A5	418 643-2050
Saskatchewan	Hon. T. Embury, Minister of Urban Affairs, 302 Legislative Building, Regina, S4S OB3	306 565-6774
	Hon. Louis Demeter, Minister of Rural Development, 303 Legislative Building, Regina, S4S OB3	306 565-2260
Yukon	Hon. Dan Lang, Minister of Municipal and Community Affairs, P.O. Box 2703, Whitehorse, Y1A 2C6	403 667-5427

[1]Data for this directory were provided by the Federation of Canadian Municipalities in the fall of 1983.

Directory 1/5 — STATE AND PROVINCIAL MUNICIPAL MANAGEMENT ASSOCIATIONS

State	Association	President, address, phone number
Alabama	Alabama City Managers' Association	W. David Cobb, City Administrator, P.O. Box 636, Marion 36756, 205 688-6545
Alaska	Alaska City Managers' Association	Gene F. Moore, City Manager, P.O. Box 46, Kotzebue 99752, 907 442-3401

Directory 1/5 continued — STATE AND PROVINCIAL MUNICIPAL MANAGEMENT ASSOCIATIONS

State	Association	President, address, phone number
Arizona	Arizona City Managers' Association	Glenwood Wilson Community Services Manager Municipal Building Phoenix 85003 602 262-6941
Arkansas	Arkansas City Management Association	David M. McWethy Assistant City Manager P.O. Box F Fayetteville 72701 501 521-7700
California	City Managers' Department, League of California Cities	Robert W. Quinlan City Manager 10300 Torre Ave. Cupertino 95014 408 252-4505 213 577-4222
Colorado	Colorado Section of ICMA	John E. Arnold City Manager P.O. Box 580 Fort Collins 80522 303 484-4220
Connecticut	Connecticut Town and City Management Association	William N. Brady Town Manager 28 South Main Street West Hartford 06107 203 722-6620
Delaware	City Management Association of Delaware	Peter S. Marshall City Manager P.O. Box 390 Newark 19711 302 366-7020
District of Columbia	D.C. Urban Management Association	John E. Touchstone Director of Public Works District Building, Suite 511 1350 Pennsylvania Avenue Washington, D.C. 20004 202 727-1000
Florida	Florida City and County Management Association	Anthony L. Shoemaker City Manager P.O. Box 4748 Clearwater 33516 813-462-6500
Georgia	Georgia City-County Management Association	Wilbur Avera City Manager P.O. Box 672 Thomaston 30286 404-647-4242
Idaho	Idaho City Management Association	Charles W. Moss City Manager P.O Box 4169 Pocatello 83201 208 232-4311
Illinois	Illinois City Management Association	Jeffery Fuller Assistant to the City Manager 505 Park Place Park Ridge 60068 312 399-5200
Indiana	Indiana Chapter of ICMA	Larry J. Hessler Town Manager P.O. Box 273 Newburgh 47630 812 853-3578
Iowa	Iowa City Management Association	Carl E. Ramey City Manager 1100 8th Avenue Marion 52302 319 377-1581
Kansas	Kansas Association of City Managers	Carl M. Metzger City Manager 6th & Lincoln Concordia 66901 913 243-2670
Kentucky	Kentucky City Managers' Association	Gene H. Stinchcomb City Administrator/ Coordinator P.O. Box 8 Berea 40403 606 986-8528
Maine	Maine Town and City Management Association	David O. Cole Town Manager 75 Main Street Lincoln 04457 207 794-3372
Maryland	Maryland City Management Association	Patrick J. Prangley Town Administrator 5008 Queensburg Road Riverdale 20737 301 927-6381
Massachusetts	Massachusetts Municipal Management Association	Robert C. Lawton, Jr. Executive Secretary Town of Yarmouth 1146 Route 28 South Yarmouth 02664 617 398-2231
Michigan	Michigan City Management Association	William J. Baldridge City Manager 211 Williams Street Royal Oak 48068 313 546-1000
Minnesota	Minnesota City Management Association	Kenneth H. Huber City Administrator Municipal Building, Box 270 St. Peter 56089 507-931-4840
Mississippi	Mississippi City and County Administrators' Association	J. Larry Burris City Administrator P.O. Box 667 McComb 39648 601 684-3641
Missouri	Missouri City Management Association	John B. Morrison City Manager 4 E. Lockwood Avenue Webster Grove 63119 314 961-4100
Nebraska	City Management Association of Nebraska	Jan Beals City Manager 411 E. 2nd Street Ogallala 69153 308 284-6001
Nevada	Nevada City-County Management Association	Don W. Hataway City Manager 2621 Northgate Lane #2 Carson City 89701 702 887-2100
New Hampshire	New Hampshire City and Town Managers' Association	Peter Russell City Manger P.O. Box 373 Enfield 03748 603 632-5001
New Jersey	New Jersey Municipal Management Association	Reagan Burkholder Township Manager 16 Lanning Boulevard East Windsor 08520 609 443-4000
New Mexico	New Mexico City Management Association	James P. Jeffers City Manager 100 W. 1st Street Portales 88130 505 356-6662

Directory 1/5 continued — STATE AND PROVINCIAL MUNICIPAL MANAGEMENT ASSOCIATIONS

State	Association	President, address, phone number
New York	Municipal Management Association of New York State	Jerry C. Hiller Village Manager Village Hall 571 Main Street East Aurora 14052 716 652-6000
North Carolina	North Carolina City and County Management Association	John C. Munn County Manager Union County P.O. Box 218 Monroe 28110 704 289-8557
Ohio	Ohio City Management Association	Robert A. Trimble City Manager P.O. Box 321 Brunswick 44212 216 225-9144
Oklahoma	City Management Association of Oklahoma	Thomas Mikulecky City Manager 600 S. Dewey, Box 699 Bartlesville 74003 918 336-0000
Oregon	Oregon Section of ICMA	Kent L. Taylor City Manager P.O. Box 50 Lincoln City 97367 503 996-2151
Pennsylvania	Association of Pennsylvania Municipal Managers	Stephen Ross Township Manager West Whiteland Township P.O. Box 210 Exton 19341 215 363-9525
Rhode Island	Rhode Island City and Town Management Association	Glenn J. Miller Town Manager Town Hall, Broad Street Westerly 02891 401 596-0341
South Carolina	South Carolina City and County Management Association	Jack B. Ethredge, Jr. City Manager P.O. Box 1038 North Myrtle Beach 29482 803 272-4000
Tennessee	Tennessee City Management Association	James R. Johnson City Administrator City Hall 101 S. Walnut Collierville 38017 901 853-8501
Texas	Texas City Management Association	George Patterson City Administrator City of Highland Park 4700 Drexel Drive Dallas 75205 214 670-3011
Utah	Utah City Managers' Association	Arlene Loble City Manager Box 1480, City Hall Park City 84060 801 649-9321
Vermont	Vermont Town and City Management Association	Leo V. Clark Town Administrator P.O. Box 248 Stowe 05672 802 253-7350
Virginia	Virginia Section of ICMA	Edward L. Brower Town Manager P.O. Box 341 Warrenton 22186 703 347-1101
Washington	Washington City Management Association	Charles N. Earl Chief Administrative Officer Thurston County Thurston County Courthouse Olympia 98503 206 753-8325
West Virginia	West Virginia City Managers' Association	Edwin Daley City Manager 200 Jackson Street Fairmont 26554 304 366-6211
Wisconsin	Wisconsin City Management Association	Stephen Nenonen City Administrator City Hall 100 Jackson Street Ripon 54971 414 748-7771
Wyoming, North and South Dakota, Idaho, and Montana	Great Open Spaces City Management Association	Thomas Courtney City Manager City Hall P.O. Box 1907 Twin Falls 83301 208 733-0860
Alberta	Local Government Administrators of Alberta	Colin Dean Town of High River P.O. Bag 10 High River, T0L 1B0
Ontario	Ontario Municipal Administrators' Association	David J. Low Administrator Town of Ajax 65 Harwood Avenue South Ontario 61S 2H9 519 631-1680
Québec	Québec Association of Municipal Managers	Ghyslain Jobin Acting City Manager 7575 Boulevard Henri-Bourassa Charlesbourg G1H 3E7

Directory 1/6 STATE ASSOCIATIONS OF COUNTIES

State	State association and address	Name and title of executive director	Phone number	Year first organized
Alabama	Association of County Commissions of Alabama, 100 North Jackson Street, Montgomery 36104	O. H. Sharpless, Executive Director	205 263-7594	1929
Alaska	Alaska Municipal League, 105 Municipal Way, Suite 301, Juneau 99801	Scott A. Burgess, Executive Director	907 586-6526	1950
Arizona	Arizona Association of Counties, Room 100, 1820 West Washington, Phoenix 85007	Richard W. Casey, Executive Director	602 252-6563	1968
Arkansas	Association of Arkansas Counties, 314 South Victory Street, Little Rock 72201	Courtney Langston, Executive Director	501 372-7550	1968

Directory 1/6 continued **STATE ASSOCIATIONS OF COUNTIES**

State	State association and address	Name and title of executive director	Phone number	Year first organized
California	County Supervisors Association of California, Suite 101, 1100 K Street, Sacramento 95814	Larry Naake Executive Director	916 441-4011	1895
Colorado	Colorado Counties, Inc., Suite 301, 1177 Grant Street, Denver 80203	Harry P. Bowes Executive Director	303 861-4076	1915
Delaware	Delaware Association of Counties, 414 Federal Street, Dover, 19901	William Stevenson President	302 736-2040	....
Florida	State Association of County Commissioners of Florida, P.O. Box 549, Tallahassee 32302	John P. Thomas Executive Director	904 224-3148	1929
Georgia	Association of County Commissioners of Georgia, Rhodes-Haverty Bldg., Suite 1201, 134 Peachtree Street, Atlanta 30303	Hill R. Healan Executive Director	404 522-5022	1914
Hawaii	Hawaii Association of Counties, Inc. City and County of Honolulu, City Hall Honolulu 96813	Rudy Pacarro President	808 245-4771	1959
Idaho	Idaho Association of Counties, P.O. Box 1623, Boise 83701	Charles Holden Executive Director	208 345-9126	1960
Illinois	Illinois Association of County Board Members, 914 South 5th Street, Springfield 62703	Paul Bitschenauer Executive Secretary	217 528-5331	1973
Indiana	Association of Indiana Counties, Inc., 120 Monument Circle, Suite 217, Indianapolis 46204	Richard J. Cockrum Executive Director	317 632-7453	1958
Iowa	Iowa State Association of Counties, 1055 Sixth Avenue, Des Moines 50314	John T. Torbert Executive Director	515 244-7181	1971
Kansas	Kansas Association of Counties, Suite D, 112 West Seventh Street, Topeka 66603	Fred Allen Executive Secretary	913 233-2271	....
Kentucky	Kentucky Association of Counties, 205 Capital Avenue, Frankfort 40601	Fred Creasey Executive Director	502 223-7668	1973
Louisiana	Policy Jury Association of Louisiana, 707 North Seventh Street, Baton Rouge 70802	James T. Hays Executive Secretary	504 343-2835	1923
Maine	Maine County Commissioners Association, 124 State Street, Augusta 04330	....	207 623-4697	1939
Maryland	Maryland Association of Counties, Inc., 169 Conduit Street, Annapolis 21401	Tee O'Connor Executive Director	301 269-0043	1951
Massachusetts	County Commissioners' & Sheriffs' Association of Massachusetts, Main Street, Barnstable 02630	James J. Collins President	617 362-2511	....
Michigan	Michigan Association of Counties, 319 West Lenawee Street, Lansing 48933	James N. Callahan Executive Director	517 372-5374	1898
Minnesota	The Association of Minnesota Counties, 555 Park Street, Suite 300, St. Paul 55103	Morris Anderson Executive Director	612 224-3344	1909
Mississippi	Mississippi Association of Supervisors, P.O. Box 1314, Jackson 39215	Jesse Greer Executive Director	601 353-2741	1929
Missouri	Missouri Association of Counties, P.O. Box 234, Jefferson City 65102	Juanita Donehue Executive Director	314 634-2120	1972
Montana	Montana Association of Counties, 1802 11th Avenue, Helena 59601	Gordon Morris Executive Director	406 442-5209	1909
Nebraska	Nebraska Association of County Officials, 625 South 14th Street, Suite A, Lincoln 68508	Jack Mills Executive Director	402 474-3328	1937
Nevada	Nevada Association of Counties, 208 N. Fall Street, Carson City, 89701	James Shipman Executive Director	702 883-7863	1945
New Hampshire	New Hampshire Association of Counties, 163 North Main Street, Concord 03301	Peter J. Spaulding Executive Secretary	603 228-0331	1947
New Jersey	New Jersey Association of Counties, Suite 1428, 240 West State Street, Trenton 08608	Guy Millard Executive Director	609 394-3467	1921
New Mexico	New Mexico Association of Counties, 410 Don Gaster Avenue, Santa Fe 87501	Donna K. Smith Executive Director	505 983-2101	1926
New York	New York State Association of Counties, 150 State Street, Albany 12207	Edwin Crawford Executive Director	518 465-1473	1925
North Carolina	North Carolina Association of County Commissioners, P.O. Box 1488, Raleigh 27602	C. Ronald Aycock Executive Director	919 832-2893	1908
North Dakota	North Dakota Association of Counties, P.O. Box 417, Bismarck 58502	Mark A. Johnson Executive Director	701 258-4481	1906
Ohio	County Commissioners' Association of Ohio, Suite 510, 40 South 3rd Street, Columbus 42315	A. R. Maslar Executive Director	614 221-5627	1880
Oklahoma	Oklahoma County Commissioners Association, 3133 NW 63rd Street, Oklahoma City 73116	Ivan Simmons President	405 840-9582	....
Oregon	Association of Oregon Counties, P.O. Box 12729, Salem 97309	P. Jerry Orrick Executive Director	503 585-8351	1906
Pennsylvania	Pennsylvania State Association of County Commissioners, 17 North Front Street, Harrisburg 17101	Douglas E. Hill Executive Director	717 232-7554	1886
South Carolina	South Carolina Association of Counties, 1817 Hampton Street, Columbia 29201	Russell B. Shetterley Executive Director	803 252-7255	1967
South Dakota	South Dakota Association of County Commissioners, 214 East Capitol, Pierre 57501	Neal Strand Executive Director	605 224-4554	1914
Tennessee	Tennessee County Services Association, 226 Capitol Boulevard Building, Nashville 37219	Ralph J. Harris Executive Director	615 242-5591	1954
Texas	Texas Association of Counties, P.O. Box 2131, Austin 78768	Sam Clonts Executive Director	512 478-8753	1969
Utah	Utah Association of Counties, 10 West Broadway, Suite 311, Salt Lake City 84101	John F. Tanner Executive Director	801 364-3583	1923
Virginia	Virginia Association of Counties, Suite 1120, 1001 East Broad Street, Richmond 23219	Richard W. Hall-Sizemore Executive Director	804 973-7557	1935

Directory 1/6 continued — STATE ASSOCIATIONS OF COUNTIES

State	State association and address	Name and title of executive director	Phone number	Year first organized
Washington	Washington Association of County Officials, 105 East Eighth Avenue, Suite 307, Olympia 98501	Fred Saeger, Executive Director	206 943-1812	1959
	Washington State Association of Counties, 6730 Martin Way, N.E., Olympia 98506	Jim Metcalf, Executive Director	206 491-7100	1908
West Virginia	West Virginia Association of Counties, Suite 514, 922 Quarrier Street, Charleston 25301	Eugene Elkins, Executive Director	304 346-0592	1960
Wisconsin	Wisconsin Counties Association, 122 West Washington Avenue, Suite 200, Madison 53703	Mark Rogacki, Executive Director	608 266-6480	1935
Wyoming	Wyoming County Commissioners Association, P.O. Box 86, Cheyenne 82003	B. G. Mitchie, Executive Director	307 632-5409	1968

Directory 1/7 — DIRECTORS OF COUNCILS OF GOVERNMENTS RECOGNIZED BY ICMA[1]

County	Appointed administrator, year appointed	Phone number
ALABAMA-3		
Birmingham Regional Planning Commission	Paul G. Dentiste 80	205 251-8139
Central Alabama Regional Planning and Development Commission	Robert E. Grasser 73	205 271-2866
East Alabama Regional Planning and Development Commission	James W. Curtis 80	205 237-6741
ARIZONA-3		
District #4 COG	Frank G. Servin 75	602 782-1886
Maricopa Association of Governments	John J. DeBolske 67	602 254-6308
Northern Arizona COG	Christopher Bavasi 80	602 774-1895
ARKANSAS-3		
Metroplan	Jason Rouby 66	501 372-3300
Northwest Arkansas Regional Planning Commission	Larry R. Wood 82	501 751-7125
White River Planning and Development District	Van C. Thomas 77	501 793-5233
CALIFORNIA-14		
Association of Bay Area Governments	Revan A. F. Tranter 73	415 464-7900
Association of Monterey Bay Area Governments	Wilber E. Smith 76	408 624-2117
Central Sierra Planning Council	John L. Prentiss 76	209 532-8768
Coachella Valley Association of Governments	Lester Cleveland 84	714 346-1127
Council of Fresno County Governments	Jack W. Reagan 76	209 233-4148
Kern County COG	G. Mark Gibb 81	805 861-2191
Sacramento Area COG	James E. Williams 82	916 441-5930
San Bernardino Associated Governments	Wesley C. McDaniel 73	714 884-8276
San Diego Association of Governments	Richard J. Huff 69	714 236-5300
Santa Barbara County-Cities Area Planning Council	G. R. Lorden 81	805 963-7194
Southern California Association of Governments	Mark A. Pisano 76	213 385-1000
Stanislaus Area Association of Governments	Doyle D. Dodd 72	209 526-6200
Tulare County Association of Governments	Eugene E. Smith 78	209 733-6303
Ventura County Association of Governments	Norman Blacher 73	805 654-2888
COLORADO-2		
Colorado West Area COG	Jim Evans 82	303 625-1723
Denver Regional COG	Robert D. Farley 70	303 455-1000
CONNECTICUT-1		
Connecticut River Estuary Regional Planning Agency	Stanley V. Greimann 68	203 388-3497
DISTRICT OF COLUMBIA-1		
Metropolitan Washington COG	Walter A. Scheiber 66	202 223-6800
GEORGIA-4		
Atlanta Regional Commission	B. Harry West 73	404 656-7700
Coastal Area Planning and Development Commission	Vernon D. Martin 70	912 264-7363

Regional council	Appointed administrator, year appointed	Phone number
GEORGIA-4 continued		
Middle Georgia Area Planning and Development Commission	Charles H. Howell 69	912 744-6160
Southeast Georgia Area Planning and Development Commission	Ed Bodenhamer 75	912 285-6097
IDAHO-2		
Panhandle Area Council	Geraldine A. Perkins 82	208 667-1556
Southeast Idaho COG	Alan Lessler 83	208 233-4032
ILLINOIS-8		
Bi-State Metropolitan Planning Commission	Gary Vallem 81	309 793-6300
Greater Egypt Regional Planning and Development Commission	A. S. Kirkikis 78	618 549-3306
North Central Illinois COG	Frederic J. Kuzel 83	815 875-3396
Northeastern Illinois Planning Commission	Lawrence Christmas 80	312 454-0400
Northwest Municipal Conference	William G. Grams 79	312 253-6323
South Central Illinois Regional Planning and Development Commission	Fred W. Walker 73	618 548-4234
South Suburban Mayors' and Managers' Association	Beth Ruyle 78	312 687-4050
Tri-County Regional Planning Commission	Robert L. Pinkerton 75	309 694-4391
INDIANA-3		
Michiana Area COG	Charles W. Minkler 84	219 287-1829
Northwestern Indiana Regional Planning Commission	Norman E. Tufford 67	219 923-1060
Southwestern Indiana and Kentucky Regional COG	Mary Brown 78	812 426-5117
IOWA-4		
East Central Intergovernmental Association	William J. Baum 80	319 556-4166
Midas COG	Stephen F. Hoesel 80	515 576-7183
Siouxland Interstate Metropolitan Planning Council	Donald M. Meisner 66	712 279-6286
Southern Iowa Economic Development Association	Joseph D. Mondanaro 81	515 682-8741
KANSAS-2		
Chikaskia, Golden Belt, and Indian Hills Associations of Local Governments	Jerry W. Keene 84	316 672-5541
North Central Regional Planning Commission	Gary P. Graham 80	913 738-2218
KENTUCKY-6		
Barren River Area Development District	Jack Eversole 68	502 781-2381
Big Sandy Area Development District	Joseph L. McCauley 68	606 886-2374
Bluegrass Area Development District	Jas Sekhon 72	606 272-6656
Lincoln Trail Area Development District	James E. Greer 77	502 769-2393
Northern Kentucky Area Development District	Byron Mohr 83	606 283-1885
Purchase Area Development District	Henry Hodges 73	502 247-7171
LOUISIANA-1		
Shreve Area COG	Craig A. Bennight 83	318 226-6488

Directory 1/7 continued — DIRECTORS OF COUNCILS OF GOVERNMENTS RECOGNIZED BY ICMA[1]

Regional council	Appointed administrator, year appointed	Phone number
MAINE-1		
Greater Portland COG	John E. Walker 81	207 774-9891
MARYLAND-2		
Regional Planning Council	Walt J. Kowalczyk, Jr. 79	301 383-5830
Tri-county Council for Southern Maryland	Gary V. Hodge 80	301 884-2144
MASSACHUSETTS-1		
Merrimack Valley Planning Commission	Gaylord Burke 83	617 374-0519
MICHIGAN-1		
Southeast Michigan COG	John M. Amberger 82	313 961-4266
MISSISSIPPI-1		
Central Mississippi Planning and Development District	F. Clark Holmes 73	601 981-1511
MISSOURI-4		
East-West Gateway Coordinating Council	Les Sterman	314 421-4220
Mid-America Regional Council	Peter S. Levi 77	816 474-4240
Ozark Foothills Regional Planning Commission	Edward A. Friar 82	314 785-6402
South Central Ozark COG	Norman C. Hollis 81	417 256-8123
NEW MEXICO-2		
Southern Rio Grande COG	Albert T. Sanchez 79	505 523-7474
Southwest New Mexico COG	James W. Harrison 72	505 388-1974
NEW YORK-1		
Capital District Regional Planning Commission	Chungchin Chen 80	518 272-1414
NORTH CAROLINA-8		
Centralina COG	George J. Monaghan 74	704 372-2416
Land-of-Sky Regional Council	Robert E. Shepherd 73	704 254-8131
Lumber River COG	James B. Perry 81	919 738-8104
Neuse River COG	J. Roy Fogle 68	919 638-3185
Piedmont Triad COG	Lindsay W. Cox 69	919 294-4950
Region L. COG	Thomas W. Elkins 80	919 446-0411
Triangle J. COG	Bradley S. Barker 78	919 549-0551
Western Piedmont COG	Richard D. Taylor 71	704 322-9191
OHIO-4		
Miami Valley Regional Planning Commission	Nora E. Lake 82	513 223-6323
Ohio-Kentucky-Indiana Regional COG	Anthony H. Hessling 70	513 621-7060
Ohio Mid-Eastern Governments Association	Harry F. Smock 69	614 439-4471
Toledo Metropolitan Area COG	Calvin M. Lakin 70	419 241-9155
OKLAHOMA-3		
Association of Central Oklahoma Governments	Zach D. Taylor 79	405 848-8961
Central Oklahoma Economic Development District	Wayne J. Manley 81	405 273-6410
Northern Oklahoma Development Association	Charles Arnold 82	405 237-4810
OREGON-8		
Coos-Curry COG	Sandra Diedrich 74	503 756-2563
Lane Council of Governments	George W. Kloeppel 81	503 687-4283
Metropolitan Service District	Rick Gustafson 79	503 221-1646
Mid-Columbia Council of Governments	Richard A. Jentzsch 83	503 298-4101
Mid-Columbia Economic Development District	Keith Sutton 83	503 296-2266
Mid-Willamette Valley COG	Alan H. Hershey 77	503 588-6177
Oregon District 4 COG	William R. Wagner 82	503 757-6851
Umpqua Regional COG	Paul Howard 76	503 440-4231
PENNSYLVANIA-6		
Lower Dauphin COG	Marianne D. Faust	717 558-1093
North Central Pennsylvania Regional Planning and Development Commission	Ronald Kuleck 77	814 773-3162
Northwest Pennsylvania Regional Planning and Development Commission	Wm. R. Steiner 81	814 437-3024
South Hills Area COG	Ralph D. Bowen 75	412 653-7483
Twin Rivers COG	James Morrison 83	412 678-8651
West Shore COG	David Chuprinski 84	717 761-6211
SOUTH CAROLINA-4		
Central Midlands Regional Planning Council	Sidney F. Thomas 69	803 798-1243
Lower Savannah COG	Eric P. Thompson 81	803 649-7981
South Carolina Appalachian COG	Douglas E. Phillips 82	803 242-9733
Upper Savannah COG	Dan B. Mackey II 68	803 229-6627
SOUTH DAKOTA-3		
Fifth District Planning and Development Commission	Dennis W. Potter 74	605 224-1623
Northeast COG	Paul Hildebrandt 82	605 229-4740
Planning and Development District Three	Bryan L. Hisel 82	605 665-4408
TENNESSEE-1		
East Tennessee Development District	Allen W. Neel 78	615 584-8553
TEXAS-18		
Alamo Area COG	Al J. Notzon III 71	512 225-5201
Ark-Tex COG	James D. Goerke 75	214 774-3481
Capital Area Planning Council	Richard G. Bean 71	512 443-7653
Central Texas COG	Walton B. Reedy 76	817 939-1801
Coastal Bend COG	John P. Buckner 77	512 883-5743
Concho Valley COG	Robert R. Weaver 81	915 944-9666
Deep East Texas COG	E. Ray Hill 83	409 384-5704
East Texas COG	Glynn J. Knight 80	214 984-8641
Heart of Texas COG	Hugh W. Davis 76	817 756-6631
Houston-Galveston Area Council	Jack Steele 79	713 627-3200
Lower Rio Grande Valley Development Council	Robert A. Chandler 67	512 682-3481
Nortex Regional Planning Commission	Edwin B. Daniel 68	817 322-5281
North Central Texas COG	William J. Pitstick 66	817 461-3300
Panhandle Regional Planning Commission	Jerry S. McGuire 81	806 372-3381
South East Texas Regional Planning Commission	Don Kelly 70	713 727-2384
South Plains Association of Governments	Jerry D. Casstevens 79	806 762-8721
Texoma Regional Planning Commission	Larry Cruise 82	214 786-2955
West Central Texas COG	Brad Helbert 83	915 672-8544
UTAH-1		
Five County Association of Governments	John S. Williams 78	801 673-3548
VIRGINIA-7		
Central Shenandoah Planning District Commission	David W. Rundgren 75	703 885-5174
Central Virginia Planning District Commission	Wm. W. Hibbert III 72	804 845-3491
Crater Planning District Commission	Dennis K. Morris 82	804 861-1666
Northern Neck Planning District Commission	Stephen K. Whiteway 79	804 529-7400
Northern Virginia Planning District Commission	John W. Epling 72	703 642-0700
Southeastern Virginia Planning District Commission	Arthur L. Collins 79	804 461-3200
Southside Planning District Commission	Robt. P. Lawler, Jr. 81	804 447-7101
West Piedmont Planning District Commission	Mark Henne 81	703 638-3987
WASHINGTON-4		
Benton-Franklin Governmental Conference	Donald P. Morton 81	509 943-9185
Puget Sound COG	Mart Kask 71	206 464-7090
Regional Planning Council of Clark County	Richard T. Howsley 78	206 699-2361
Skagit COG	Stephen G. Ladd	206 757-4514
WEST VIRGINIA-3		
Bel-O-Mar Regional Council	William C. Phipps 78	304 242-1800
Mid-Ohio Valley Regional Council	R. Terry Tamburini 76	304 485-3801
Region One Planning and Development Council	Michael B. Jacobs 73	304 425-9508
WISCONSIN-2		
East Central Wisconsin Regional Planning Commission	Roy C. Willey, Jr. 72	414 729-1100
West Central Wisconsin Regional Planning Commission	Kevin W. Jones 81	715 836-2918
WYOMING-1		
Fremont County Association of Governments	Barry A. Cook 80	307 332-9208
CANADA-2		
Québec Urban Community (Québec)	....	418 681-9611
Regional District of Fraser-Fort George (British Columbia)	Ken Ball 81	604 563-9225

[1] This directory is limited to those councils of governments that have been recognized by ICMA as of 26 November 1984 as providing for a position of overall professional management.

Directory 1/8 LOCAL GOVERNMENT CHIEF APPOINTED ADMINISTRATORS IN CANADA AND OTHER COUNTRIES

Municipality	Appointed Administrator	Phone Number
AUSTRALIA		
New South Wales		
Blue Mountains	Ronald C. Fennell	....
Carrathool Shire	Shane T. Godbee	....
Eurobodalla Shire	Kerry M. Blanch	....
Hawkesbury Shire	Raymond L. Rawson	....
Hunters Hill	William E. G. Phipson	....
Penrith	Barry B. Long	....
Walcha Shire	Kenneth H. Croskell	....
Warringah Shire	Patrick T. Hynes	....
Windouran Shire	Michael P. Conallin	....
Woollahra	Michael R. Regnis	....
Queensland		
Beaudesert Shire	Keith W. Stuckey	....
Brisbane	Antony T. C. Philbrick	....
Caboolture Shire	Ian C. Warren	....
Cairns	Graeme L. Pearce	....
Ipswich	Harold B. Edmonds	....
Kensington & Norwood	Geoffrey T. Whitbread	....
MacKay	Stanley E. Fursman	....
Murgon	Warren John Hubner	....
South Australia		
Adelaide	Michael J. Llewellyn-Smith	....
Alice Springs	E. Roy Mitchell	....
Barossa	Keith H. Davis	....
Darwin	Garry P. Storch	....
Hindmarsh	John R. Langman	....
Salisbury	John R. Kleem	....
Tea Tree Gully	Ronald C. S. Hunter	....
Unley	Alfred G. Usher	....
Tasmania		
Glenorchy	Stewart A. Wardlaw	....
Lindisfarne	Ronald L. Marriott	....
Scottsdale	Thomas B. Ransom	....
Ulverstone	Alfred R. Mott	....
Victoria		
Benalla	John Francis Shaw	....
Berwick	Patrick J. Northeast	....
Brighton	Victor Faravoni	....
Broadmeadows	Bruce D. McGregor	....
Buln Buln Shire	Keith A. Pretty	....
Castlemaine	Geoffrey B. Kohlman	....
Coburg	Joseph R. Diffen	....
Corio Shire	Richard P. Metcalf	....
Cranbourne Shire	Terence Vickerman	....
Creswick Shire	Bernard C. Rees	....
Deakin Shire	Bruce Pearl	....
Dimboola Shire	Ronald G. Ferguson	....
Echuca	Kevin F. McCartney	....
Flinders	Larry M. Jones	....
Gisborne Shire	Terence H. Larkins	....
Hamilton	Russell J. Worland	....
Hastings Shire	William R. Featherston	....
Heidelberg	Alan Jones	....
Horsham	Robyn A. Marshall	....
Kew	Adrian Halliday	....
Knox	Timothy John Neville	....
Korumburra Shire	David A. Cartledge	....
Marong Shire	Graeme Elvey	....
Melbourne	Desmond N. Bethke	....
Melton Shire	Maxwell B. Watson	....
Mildura Shire	David J. McMillan	....
Moe	Robert J. Pugsley	....
Mordialloc	Douglas H. Corben	....
Morwell Shire	Ronald H. Waters	....
Myrtleford Shire	Suzanne M. Walker	....
Numurkah Shire	Lindsay G. Mitchell	....
Nunawading	Leslie Fell	....
Pakenham Shire	Barry J. Wallis	....
Preston	Donald O. McLean	....
Rodney Shire	John L. Purdey	....
Shepparton Shire	John W. Reed	....
South Gippsland Shire	Harold R. Lomax	....
South Melbourne	Neil L. Marshall	....
Swan Hill	Garry J. Mennie	....
Traralgon	John L. Mitchell	....
Werribee Shire	John T. Kerr	....
Whittlesea Shire	Lindsay G. Esmonde	....
Wonthaggi	A. A. Noel Deed	....
West Australia		
Albany	Ian R. Hill	....
Canning	Noel I. Dawkins	....
East Fremantle	Mervyn G. Cowan	....
Kwinana	Robert K. Smillie	....
West Australia continued		
Melville	Ralph H. Fardon	....
Mosman Park	D. A. Walker	....
Perth	Reginald F. Dawson	....
Stirling	Malcolm G. Sargant	....
Wickepin	Patrick J. Walker	....
CANADA		
Alberta		
Calgary	George H. Cornish	403 268-5861
Edson	David G. Jonews	403 723-4401
Fort McMurray	....	403 743-1000
Fort Saskatchewan	Glen Pitman	403 998-2266
Grande-Prairie	J. S. Burke	403 532-9722
Lethbridge	R. M. Bartlett	403 320-3000
St. Albert	Tom McKay	403 459-6601
British Columbia		
Burnaby	Melvin J. Shelley	604 294-7944
Kamloops	Grayden R. Hayward	604 374-3311
Kimberly	R. Barry Bennett	604 427-5311
Kitimat	J. A. Currier	604 632-2161
Nanaimo	Robert J. Boxwell	604 754-4251
North Vancouver	D. A. Welsh	604 985-7761
Prince George	Chester Jeffery	604 564-5151
Saanich	W. M. Tremayne	604 386-2241
Surrey	Michael J. Jones	604 591-4011
Terrace	G. W. Buchanan	604 635-6311
Trail	K. Wiesner	604 364-1262
Vancouver	Fritz Bowers	604 873-7011
Victoria	James H. Bramley	604 385-5711
West Vancouver	I. T. Lester	....
Manitoba		
Brandon	Earl E. Backman	204 728-2278
New Brunswick		
Bathurst	Robert A. Bouchard	506 546-6651
Fredericton	John C. Robison	506 455-9426
Moncton	Murray E. MacLean	506 853-3333
Saint John	Arthur G. McDermott	506 658-2800
Woodstock	T. L. Everett	506 328-3307
Newfoundland		
Corner Brook	Clarence Keeping	709 634-8291
Gander	Donald Walsh	709 651-2930
Nova Scotia		
Dartmouth	Clifford A. Moir	902 421-2111
Halifax	Paul Calda	902 477-6411
Ontario		
Ancaster	Robert G. Morrow	416 648-4401
Barrie	Benson Straughan	705 726-4242
Belleville	Wilbur C. Purcell	613 968-6481
Brockville	Douglas G. Ellis	613 342-8772
Burlington	Michael H. Boggs	416 335-7777
Cambridge	Blayne C. Rennick	519 623-1340
Chatham	Hugh J. Thomas	519 352-4500
Cornwall	C. F. Adams	613 932-6252
Regional Municipality of Durham (Whitby)	Donald R. Evans	416 686-2401
Essex County (Windsor)	John H. Curran	519 776-6441
Guelph	M. R. Sather	519 822-1260
Regional Municipality of Halton (Oakville)	Dennis Y. Perlin	416 827-2151
Hamilton	Lou Sage	416 526-2700
Hamilton-Wentworth	C. T. Armstrong	416 526-4111
Huron County-Goderich	Bill G. Hanly	519 524-8394
Kitchener	J. R. Darrah	519 885-7100
London	Maurice C. Engels	519 679-4550
Mississauga	C. M. Beckstead	416 279-7600
Niagara Falls	J. L. Collinson	416 356-7521
Oakville	Harry E. Henderson	416 845-6601
Ottawa	Sydney Baldwin	613 563-3396
Owen Sound	W. W. Thom	519 376-1440
Regional Municipality of Peel (Brampton)	Richard L. Frost	416 791-9400
Peterborough	David L. Hall	705 742-7441
Pickering	Noel C. Marshall	416 683-2760
Renfrew	R. G. Howse	613 432-4848
Richmond Hill	Charles D. Weldon	416 884-8101
St. Catharines	Hugh John Cook	416 688-5600
Sarnia	John C. Robertson	519 332-0330
Sault Ste. Marie	Allan A. Jackson	705 949-9111
Sudbury	William Rice	705 674-3141
Regional Municipality of Sudbury (Sudbury)	H. R. Akehurst	750 673-2171
Thunder Bay	Donald R. MacLeod	807 623-2711

Directory 1/8 continued — LOCAL GOVERNMENT CHIEF APPOINTED ADMINISTRATORS IN CANADA AND OTHER COUNTRIES

Municipality	Appointed Administrator	Phone Number
Ontario continued		
Timmins	J. E. Bergeron	705 264-1331
Trenton	Aubrey Sharp	613 392-2841
Vanier City	Michael Breton	613 746-8105
Wallaceburg	Scott C. Somerville	519 627-1603
Regional Municipality of Waterloo	Robert F. Richardson	519 885-9400
Windsor	Hilary G. Payne	519 255-6500
Woodstock	Kenneth Miller	519 539-1291
Prince Edward Island		
Summerside	Nelson Johnson	902 436-4222
Québec		
Alma	M. Gaetan Tremblay	418 662-6501
Anjou	Claude Donalson	514 352-4440
Baie-Comeau	Guy Massicotte	418 296-4931
Baie d'Urfé	A. W. Dancey	514 457-5324
Beaconsfield	Allen Mainville	514 697-4660
Beloeil	Jean J. Corbeil	514 467-2835
Boisbriand	Rosaire G. Brisson	514 435-1954
Boucherville	Ronald Beaupre	514 655-3131
Brossard	Richard Labrecque	514 676-0201
Cap-de-la-Madeleine	Roland Desaulniers	819 375-1661
Chambly	Jacques Vezina	514 658-8788
Chibougamau	Jean-Claude Audet	....
Chicoutimi	Benoit Simard	418 545-9550
Côte Nord-Beauport	Jean Paul Daigle	....
Côte-St-Luc	James G. Butler	514 489-9771
Cowansville	George H. Bernier	514 263-0141
Dolbeau	Jean Paul Benet	418 276-0160
Dollard-des-Ormeaux	....	....
Dorval	Jean-Louis Roy	514 636-4040
Forestville	Raymond Joncas	418 587-2285
Gagnon	....	418 532-6303
Grand' Mère	Jules Dube	819 538-9543
Greenfield Park	A. J. Burns	514 671-5955
Hampstead	W. Remington	514 487-1441
Hauterive	Jean-Guy Rousseau	....
Hull	Jean Aime Desjardins	819 777-2781
Jonquière	Jean Marc Gagnon	418 547-6631
Kirkland	Andre L. Houde	514 694-4100
La Tuque	Roger Berlinguet	819 523-5110
LaSalle	Robert Barbeau	514 367-1000
Laval	Marc Perron	514 688-6221
LeMoyne	Gilles Seguin	514 671-5948
Lebel-sur-Quevillon	Hector Landry	819 755-4826
Lévis	Andre Quellet	418 833-3261
Longueuil	Fernard Pore	514 670-2220
Lorraine	....	514 621-8550
Louisville	Ghislain Lessard	819 228-5115
Mirabel	Yves Lacroix	514 476-0360
Mont-St-Hilaire	Laurent Olivier	514 467-2854
Mount Royal	John R. Warren	514 737-1141
Murdochville	Michael Noy	418 784-2536
Outremont	J. R. Victor Mainville	514 274-9451
Pierrefonds	Gerard Le Page	514 684-4480
Pincourt	....	514 453-8981
Pointe-aux-Trembles	....	418 876-2233
Pointe Claire	Tom Buffitt	514 697-0770
Port Cartier	Medard Anctil	418 766-2343
Québec City	Jacques Perreault	418 694-6082
Québec Urban Community-Québec City	Maurice Bergeron	418 694-7041
Répentigny	Louis W. Le Page	514 585-2660
Rosemere	Guy Robitaille	514 621-3500
Rouyn	Guy Carle	819 767-1721
Roxboro	V. P. Gray	514 684-0555
Ste-Anne-des-Monts	Daniel Martineau	418 263-5511
St-Bruno-de-Montarville	....	514 653-2443
St-Laurent	Guy Jasmin	819 787-2380
Québec continued		
Ste-Thérèse	Claude Dagenais	514 434-1440
Schefferville	Jean-Yves Truchon	418 585-2471
Senneville	Leo Viau	514 457-6020
Sept-Iles	Roger A. Boudreau	418 962-2525
Shawinigan	Jacques Sansfacon	819 537-6626
Shawinigan-Sud	Charles J. Mills	819 536-5671
Sherbrooke	Roch Letourneau	819 565-3000
Thetford Mines	Andre Laramee	418 335-2981
Trois-Rivières	Jacques Charette	819 374-3521
Trois-Rivières Ouest	Marc Tessier	819 375-7731
Val-d'Or	Guy Faucher	819 824-9613
Valleyfield	Gaetan Rousse	....
Verdun	Jean-Paul Hebert	514 769-2701
Victoriaville	Levis Lupien	819 758-8291
Westmount	John M. McIver	514 935-8531
Saskatchewan		
Moose Jaw	W. L. Johnson	306 693-3621
Regina	William K. Mann	306 569-7262
Saskatoon	A. P. Gilewicz	306 644-9240
Uranium City	William S. Seaman	306 498-3441
ENGLAND		
Buckinghamshire County	Edward M. E. White	....
Dorset County	Kenneth A. Abel	....
East Sussex County	Robin M. Beechey	....
Kent County	William U. Jackson	....
Reading	Harry Tee	....
Salford	Roger C. Rees	....
South Wight	Colin M. Simpson	....
West Glamorgan County	Michael E. J. Rush	....
West Lancashire	John Cowdall	....
IRELAND		
Meath County	Francis J. O'Brien	....
ISRAEL		
Jerusalem	Shaul Sasson	....
NETHERLANDS		
Amsterdam	Henk Van Ruller	....
NEW ZEALAND		
Auckland	Bruce T. C. Anderson	....
Christchurch	John H. Gray	....
Hamilton	Stuart A. Lenz	....
Manukau	Ronald Wood	....
Matamata	William J. Curragh	....
Mount Eden	Noel Edward Ashby	....
One Tree Hill	Brian W. Archer	....
Taupo	Clifford J. Houston	....
Timaru	Douglas E. Pearson	....
Upper Hutt	Robert John Vine	....
NORWAY		
Oslo	Bernt H. Lund	....
Trysil	Martin Gran	....
SOUTH AFRICA		
Pieterburg	Jack A. Botes	....
SWEDEN		
Heby Kommun	Carl-Ake E. Elmersjo	....
Malungs Kommun	Olof E. Almkleven	....
SWITZERLAND		
Chur	Dieter Heller	....

Directory 1/9 COUNTY OFFICIALS IN ALL U.S. COUNTIES

The data for the directory of county officials were collected by the International City Management Association (ICMA) in the summer and fall of 1984 through a mail survey. The 3,108 counties surveyed include all county-type governments (including independent cities and city–county consolidations).

In addition to the names of officials (and the county phone number) data on race and sex were collected for the county board chairman, judge or president, the appointed administrator, clerk to the governing board, chief financial officer, county health officer, planning director, county engineer, director of welfare/human services, chief law enforcement official, purchasing director, and personnel director. The positions of planning director, welfare director, purchasing director, and personnel director are not shown in the individual county directory that follows. All data collected other than the names and phone number are treated with complete confidentiality, and only aggregate data are presented below.

Sex and Race of County Officials. Tables 1/9/a and 1/9/b present a breakdown of each sex by race for the county officials. Given the level of detail shown it is possible to reaggregate these data for other displays that would show race and sex characteristics for the total number of officials reporting.

The positions shown are most often held by males with the exception of clerk to the governing board; 58.9% of the persons holding that position are female. The position of chief financial officer is almost equally held by males and females (51% and 49%, respectively). Overall, females account for 24.2% of the total officials reporting.

Whites are predominant in each of the positions shown. Among the other racial groupings, blacks are most frequently found in the positions of board chairman, appointed administrator, planning director, welfare director, purchasing director, health officer, and personnel director.

The Directory. For convenience, the directory shows the names of counties in alphabetical order within each state. The 3,105 counties listed represent over 16,000 names listed in the directory. Other items indicated in the directory for each county-type government are the population and county phone number. Recognition by ICMA is also indicated as appropriate.

Table 1/9/a MALE COUNTY OFFICIALS BY RACE

				Race											
		Total males		White		Black		Asian		American Indian		Other		Race not reported	
Position	Total reporting (A)	No. (B)	% of (A)	No.	% of (B)	No.	% of (B)	No.	% of (B)	No.	% of (B)	No.	% of (B)	No.	% of (B)
Board chairmen	2,512	2,367	94.2	2,227	94.1	35	1.5	4	0.2	4	0.2	3	0.1	94	4.0
Appointed administrators	971	831	85.6	763	91.8	13	1.6	6	0.7	2	0.2	3	0.4	44	5.3
Clerks to the governing board	2,428	997	41.1	957	96.0	6	0.6	3	0.3	1	0.1	3	0.3	27	2.7
Planning directors[1]	1,154	1,050	91.0	979	93.2	14	1.3	7	0.7	1	0.1	7	0.7	42	4.0
Engineers	1,307	1,303	99.7	1,237	94.9	1	0.1	6	0.5	1	0.1	2	0.2	56	4.3
Welfare directors[1]	965	586	60.7	508	86.7	16	2.7	4	0.7	0	0.0	2	0.3	56	9.6
Chief law enforcement officials	2,497	2,486	99.6	2,363	95.1	19	0.8	2	0.1	5	0.2	6	0.2	91	3.7
Purchasing directors[1]	1,035	767	74.1	716	93.4	13	1.7	4	0.5	1	0.1	1	0.1	32	4.2
Chief finance officers	2,292	1,175	51.3	1,110	94.5	5	0.4	3	0.3	1	0.1	3	0.3	53	4.5
Health officers	1,766	1,309	74.1	1,210	92.4	16	1.2	9	0.7	1	0.1	11	0.8	62	4.7
Personnel directors[1]	898	643	71.6	584	90.8	18	2.8	4	0.6	1	0.2	3	0.5	33	5.1

Note: The sum of males and females does not correspond to the total reporting because the sex of some respondents was not indicated and could not be determined from the respondent's name.

[1] This position is not shown in the directory of county officials.

Table 1/9/b FEMALE COUNTY OFFICIALS BY RACE

				Race											
		Total females		White		Black		Asian		American Indian		Other		Race not reported	
Position	Total reporting (A)	No. (B)	% of (A)	No.	% of (B)	No.	% of (B)	No.	% of (B)	No.	% of (B)	No.	% of (B)	No.	% of (B)
Board chairmen	2,512	145	5.8	142	97.9	1	0.7	1	0.7	0	0.0	0	0.0	1	0.7
Appointed administrators	971	140	14.4	134	95.7	4	2.9	0	0.0	0	0.0	0	0.0	2	1.4
Clerks to the governing board	2,428	1,431	58.9	1,368	95.6	11	0.8	1	0.1	6	0.4	6	0.4	39	2.7
Planning directors[1]	1,154	104	9.0	94	90.4	3	2.9	0	0.0	0	0.0	0	0.0	7	6.7
Engineers	1,307	4	0.3	4	100.0	0	0.0	0	0.0	0	0.0	0	0.0	0	0.0
Welfare directors[1]	965	379	39.3	336	88.7	16	4.2	1	0.3	0	0.0	2	0.5	24	6.3
Chief law enforcement officials	2,497	11	0.4	11	100.0	0	0.0	0	0.0	0	0.0	0	0.0	0	0.0
Purchasing directors[1]	1,035	268	25.9	245	91.4	10	3.7	0	0.0	2	0.7	2	0.7	9	3.4
Chief finance officers	2,292	1,117	48.7	1,079	96.6	6	0.5	1	0.1	1	0.1	0	0.0	30	2.7
Health officers	1,766	457	25.9	439	96.1	2	0.4	1	0.2	2	0.4	0	0.0	13	2.8
Personnel directors[1]	898	255	28.4	224	87.8	16	6.3	0	0.0	1	0.4	2	0.8	12	4.7

Note: The sum of males and females does not correspond to the total reporting because the sex of some respondents was not indicated and could not be determined from the respondent's name.

[1] This position is not shown in the directory of county officials.

Directory 1/9 COUNTY OFFICIALS IN ALL U.S. COUNTIES

Population
.. Less than 500 population

County designation
C City-county consolidation
I Independtent city
B Borough
P Parish

Other codes
† Information from previous Year Books
* Recognized by ICMA as a county with the council-manager form of government
§ Recognized by ICMA as a county with a position of overall general management
.... Data not reported or not applicable

County, county seat, 1980 population (000 omitted),	County telephone number	Board chairman	Appointed administrator	Clerk to the governing board	Chief financial officer	County engineer	County health officer	Chief law enforcement official
ALABAMA (67)								
Autauga (Prattville) (32)	205 365-7914	(not reporting)						
Baldwin (Bay Minette) (78)	205 937-0200	(not reporting)						
Barbour (Clayton) (25)	205 775-8366	(not reporting)						
Bibb (Centreville) (16)	205 926-4745	(not reporting)						
Blount (Oneonta) (36)	205 274-2124	(not reporting)						
Bullock (Union Springs)† (11)	205 738-3883	John W Waters	Sylvia Dismukes	Sylvia Dismukes	Sylvia Dismukes	Wayne Brady	....	H O Williams
Butler (Greenville) (22)	205 382-3512	(not reporting)						
Calhoun (Anniston) (117)	205 236-0961	(not reporting)						
Chambers (Lafayette) (39)	205 864-8823	Doss D Leak	Dorothy T Powers	Dorothy T Powers	Dorothy T Powers	Charles P Markert	....	James C Morgan
Cherokee (Centre)† (19)	205 927-3668	Ralph A Meade	....	Trissi Lunsford	....	....	Terry Stephens	Jack E Smith
Chilton (Clanton)† (31)	205 755-1551	Thomas A Hayes	Margie E Headley	Margie E Headley	J Raymond Cox	Ray Edwards	....	James F Johnson
Choctaw (Butler)† (17)	205 459-2417	Charles V Ford	....	Pettus M Sparrow	Pettus M Sparrow	Timothy H Hornsby	Richard Jayne	Donald Lolley
Clarke (Grove Hill)† (28)	205 275-3251	Fred L Huggins	....	Ellen N Toland	....	Wilbur G Downey	....	Ray Sheffield
Clay (Ashland)† (14)	205 354-2198	C W Carpenter	John B McMahan	Jonell Bishop	John B McMahan	Larry C Phurrough	Robert Henderson	Billy G Morris
Cleburne (Heflin)† (13)	205 463-5656	Mac Smith	Cindy Gibbs	Cindy Gibbs	....	James L Deverell	Robert Henderson	Jack Norton
Coffee (Elba)† (39)	205 987-5430	Marion B Brunson	....	Brunease Winston	Brunease Winston	Frank Charlton	Kenneth Ball	Brice R Paul
Colbert (Tuscumbia) (55)	205 383-4981	Charles Thompson	....	Aurelia Lee	....	Larry Black	Roger Norris	John Aldridge
Conecuh (Evergreen)† (16)	205 578-2095	David L Burt Jr	Wayne Johnston	Wayne Johnston	Wayne Johnston	B B Murphy	C P St Amant	Edwin Booker
Coosa (Rockford) (11)	205 377-2420	Jasper Fielding	....	Betty T King	....	David Shaner	....	William A Evans
Covington (Andalusia)† (37)	205 222-3613	William P Smith	Keltys Powell	Keltys Powell	Keltys Powell	Wm J McClain	Ziba Anderson	Warren D Harrell
Crenshaw (Luverne) (14)	205 335-5357	I T Harbin	....	Mary C Capps	Mary C Capps	James M Tate	....	Frances A Smith
Cullman (Cullman) (62)	205 739-3530	Randall Shedd	....	Lucille Galin	Lucille Galin	Joseph T Miller	....	Wendell Roden
Dale (Ozark) (48)	205 774-6025	R E Don Turner	Shelia Turner	Kathy L Martin	....	Guy Payne	Charles Oliver	Bryant Mixon
Dallas (Selma) (54)	205 875-4401	John W Jones Jr	....	M A Butler	John N Jones Jr	Thomas Friday	Sam Waldrop MD	Walter D Nichols
De Kalb (Fort Payne) (54)	205 845-0541	(not reporting)						
Elmore (Wetumpka)† (43)	205 567-5241	Edward W Enslen	Cathy Traywick	Cathy Traywick	Betty P Murphy	James Cody	Ceri Williams	Sidney Thrash
Escambia (Brewton) (38)	205 867-3659	Devon Wiggins	Kenneth Taylor	Kenneth Taylor	....	Harry E Russell	C P St Amant Jr	Timothy A Hawsey
Etowah (Gadsden)† (103)	205 546-2821	Robert V Hitt	....	H J Martin Jr	....	Roger C Ellison	Jean Foster	Roy McDowell
Fayette (Fayette) (19)	205 932-4617	(not reporting)						
Franklin (Russellville) (28)	205 332-3814	(not reporting)						
Geneva (Geneva)† (24)	205 684-2276	Harold B Wise	....	Ellen H Laye	....	Lamar Peterman	Kenneth Ball	Douglas Whittle
Greene (Eutaw) (11)	205 372-3349	William M Branch	....	Evice P Alford	....	James C Jones Jr	....	James Flannigan
Hale (Greensboro) (16)	205 624-4334	Richard M Avery	....	Nell G McMillan	Nell G McMillan	E Riley Lucas	John Chism MD	Chester Colvin
Henry (Abbeville)† (15)	205 585-2753	....	Ron H Rabun	....	....	....	....	....
Houston (Dothan) (75)	205 793-1114	Charles Whiddon	Marjorie Hunt	Dianne Edgar	....	Oswald W Peters	Marilyn Crumpton	Lamar Hadden
Jackson (Scottsboro)† (51)	205 259-6617	Sam Gant II	Jocelyn Lamunyon	Sue Ward	Jocelyn Lamunyon	William T Hill	Betty Vaughn	William R Collins
Jefferson (Birmingham) (671)	205 325-5311	Chriss H Doss	Don Ammons	E H Gamble	C Dominick	Richard L Straub	Mary Tiller MD	Melvin Bailey
Lamar (Vernon)† (16)	205 695-7332	W H Allen	....	Rita Smith	Rita Smith	Robert V Hawkins	....	Richard Varnon
Lauderdale (Florence) (81)	205 766-5180	William B Duncan	Corrine Campbell	Corrine Campbell	....	Ronald P Griffith	....	Charles W Townsen
Lawrence (Moulton)† (30)	205 974-0663	Richard Proctor	Clyde Cameron	Joan Lang	....	Ronald Stroup	Betty Vaughan	Grady Rose
Lee (Opelika) (76)	205 745-6471	(not reporting)						
Limestone (Athens) (46)	205 232-1320	S J Johnston	....	Bonnie J Strain	S J Johnston	James O Birch	Betty Vaughan	Mike Blakely
Lowndes (Haynesville)† (13)	205 548-2331	Charles Smith	Jacqueline Thomas	Jacqueline Thomas	Jacqueline Thomas	Leonard W Nall	....	John Hulett
Macon (Tuskegee) (27)	205 727-5120	Ronald J Green	George S Bulls	George S Bulls	George S Bulls	William T Hill	Walter R Pack	Lucius D Amerson
Madison (Huntsville) (197)	205 532-3492	Mike Gillespie	George Plue	....	George Plue	David Pope	Dr Robey	Joe Patterson
Marengo (Linden) (25)	205 295-5364	A Glass	....	Patricia E Davis	Patricia E Davis	Hollis Glass	Charles Shields	William Smith Jr
Marion (Hamilton) (30)	205 921-3172	Brady Baccus	....	Gearldean Lindsey	....	E L Pearce	....	A C Tice
Marshall (Guntersville)† (66)	205 582-3642	Charles Wright	....	Pam Gilmore	....	Mac Watters	Hass Lule	John Colbert
Mobile (Mobile) (364)	205 690-8605	Dan Wiley	W C Helveston	W C Helveston	Ernest L Tones	Joe Ruffer	Alfred Stumppe	Tom Purvis
Monroe (Monroeville) (23)	205 743-2283	(not reporting)						
Montgomery (Montgomery) (197)	205 832-4950	Mack O McWhorter	David T Stockman	David T Stockman	David T Stockman	J H Trotter Jr	Mary G Dorrough	M S Butler
Morgan (Decatur) (90)	205 350-9600	W A Waddell Jr	Willa C Dockery	Syble W Kent	....	Bob Woodruff	Betty Vaughn MD	Buford Burgess
Perry (Marion) (15)	205 683-6106	(not reporting)						
Pickens (Carrollton) (21)	205 367-8179	(not reporting)						
Pike (Troy)† (28)	205 566-6374	S A Graham	....	Eloise Murphree	....	Herbert E Huner	....	Harold Anderson
Randolph (Wedowee) (20)	205 357-4551	(not reporting)						
Russell (Phenix City) (47)	205 298-0516	(not reporting)						
Shelby (Columbiana) (66)	205 669-4895	Thomas A Snowden	....	Myra B Davis	....	John Gary Ray	....	J F Glasgow
St. Clair (Ashville) (41)	205 594-3641	(not reporting)						
Sumter (Livingston)† (17)	205 652-2731	Claude Jackson	Lucinda Cockrell	Lucinda Cockrell	Lucinda Cockrell	Lamar Hardin	Bobby Stuart	Melvin Stephens
Talladega (Talladega) (74)	205 362-2112	(not reporting)						
Tallapoosa (Dadeville)† (39)	205 825-4268	Eldon Sharpe	....	Bruce Carleton	Bruce Carleton	Charles M Rooks	....	Joe Smith
Tuscaloosa (Tuscaloosa)† (137)	205 349-3870	W Hardy McCollum	Robert H Johnston	Robert J Johnston	Robert H Johnston	Samuel M Hill	Kenneth Aycock	Beasor Walker
Walker (Jasper) (69)	205 221-4994	Grady Perry	Frances O Knight	Frances O Knight	John Lynn	Rex A Wingo	Frank Lynn	Arthur Trotter Jr
Washington (Chatom) (17)	205 847-2208	John H Armstrong	....	Mary K Carpenter	Mary K Carpenter	Davis M Henson Jr	Wilson Turner	William J Wheat
Wilcox (Camden) (15)	205 682-9112	F R Albritton Jr	....	Ira Bradford	....	Mark Pool	S D Waldrop	Prince Arnold
Winston (Double Springs)† (22)	205 489-5026	James H Cagle	....	Lola Gilbreath	....	James H Lawrence	Tom Banks	Elton O Townsend
ALASKA (11)								
Anchorage C (173)	907 264-4111	Tony Knowles	Barbara Steckel	Ruby Smith	Bob Nelson	E Lee Browning	Rodman Wilson	Brian Porter
Bristol Bay (Naknek) b*† (1)	907 246-4224	....	F Mandeville	Betty J Thompson	F Mandeville		....	Larry H Owen
Fairbanks North Star (Fairbanks) b§ (49)	907 452-4761	Bb Allen	Gregory E Strong	Mona Drexler	Lynn Rice	Robert Shaw	....	....
Haines (Haines) b (2)	907 766-2711	Robert Henderson	....	Audrey Jackson	William Oliver	....	....	....

Directory 1/9 continued — COUNTY OFFICIALS IN ALL U.S. COUNTIES

County, county seat, 1980 population (000 omitted),	County telephone number	Board chairman	Appointed administrator	Clerk to the governing board	Chief financial officer	County engineer	County health officer	Chief law enforcement official
ALASKA (11) continued								
Juneau C (20)	907 586-3300	Fran Ulmer	N L Pat Teague	Peggie Garrison	Craig Duncan	George Porter	....	Joseph Ciraulo
Kenai Peninsula (Soldotna) b (25)	907 262-4441	Joseph Arness	Stanley Thompson	Joanne Brindley	Roy Barton	Bill Conyers	....	....
Ketchikan Gateway (Ketchikan) b* (11)	907 225-6151	Carroll Fader	David G Crow	Georgiana Booth	Al Learned	....	....	....
Kodiak Island (Kodiak) b§ (9)	907 486-5736	Phil C Anderson	Jerome M Selby	Shirley E Miller	Bryce S Weeks	David C Crowe	....	....
Matanuska Susitna (Palmer) b* (18)	907 745-4801	Edna DeVries	Gary Thurlow	Chris Seagraves	Vern Roberts	Rodger Lewerenz	....	....
North Slope (Barrow) b (4)	907 852-2611	Eugene Brower	....	Alice Ahgeak	Lloyd Ahvakana	....	Micheal Stackhous	John Winjum
Sitka C (8)	907 747-3516	John E Dapcevich	Richard Anderson	Delores Ingwerson	John D McCracken	Larry Harmon	Edward Spencer	Art Letourneau
ARIZONA (15)								
Apache (St. Johns) (52)	602 337-4364	Arthur N Lee	Clarence Bigelow	Clarence Bigelow	Karla F Rogers	Jesse Broadbent	Eleanor Fossett	C Arthur Lee
Cochise (Bisbee)† (87)	602 432-5703	V L Thompson	J Altenstadter	J Altenstadter	Marsha Bonham	Fred M Hewitt	Ron Maxwell	Jimmy V Judd
Coconino (Flagstaff) (75)	602 779-6691	Karan L English	Catherine R Eden	Ethel Ulibarri	Stan Kleinman	Bill Howells	William Thomas	Joe Richards
Gila (Globe) (37)	602 425-3231	Adolph B Trujillo	....	Rose M Phillips	John C Bartz	R Larry Morse	Martin Hetrick	Lyman Peace
Graham (Safford)† (23)	602 428-3250	Hugh Hamman	Hank Gietz	Barbara Felix	Evelyn Hughes	James Moser	Darvin Weddle	Roy Curtis
Greenlee (Clifton) (11)	602 865-2072	H J Miller	Tom Candelaria	Deborah K Gale	Jackie D Quinn	Fred Flohrschutz	Barbara Brutcher	Robert Gomez
La Paz (Parker) (12)	602 669-6115	(not reporting)						
Maricopa (Phoenix)§ (1508)	602 262-3011	Fred Koory	Robert Mauney	Cherie Ellig	Glenn Stapley	Bob Esterbrooks	Adolfo Echeveste	Jerry Hill
Mohave (Kingman) (56)	602 753-9141	W J Bill Roper	Bill Bixby	Bill Bixby	Grace Marlow	Harold Ganyo	Albert Rosenblatt	Bill Richardson
Navajo (Holbrook) (68)	602 524-6161	Percy Deal	Eddie Koury	Sharon R Keene	J R DeSpain	Jim Bruce	Ray Holmes	Marlin Gillespie
Pima (Tucson)* (531)	602 792-8126	Sam Lena	Craig A McDowell	Eugenia Wells	James Lee Kirk	C H Huckelberry	Patricia Nolan MD	Clarence Dupnik
Pinal (Florence) (91)	602 868-5801	Jimmie B Kerr	Jay Bateman	Charles A Guinn	Jim Turnbull	Charles B Minter	Bonnie Powers	Frank Reyes
Santa Cruz (Nogales)† (20)	602 287-4778	George R Proctor	....	Lillian Rainery	A DeLa Fuente	....	Tad Pfister	Jaime Teyechea
Yavapai (Prescott) (68)	602 445-7450	John Olsen	James M Holst	Ann Lawrie Aisa	Richard Jacobs	Joe Sarvis	John Lalla	Harold Moore
Yuma (Yuma) (91)	602 782-4534	R Pete Woodard	Andrew O Torres	Andrew O Torres	Frank L Crosby	Donald B Fortney	Larry A Leach	John R Phipps
ARKANSAS (75)								
Arkansas (Stuttgart) (24)	501 673-3181	(not reporting)						
Ashley (Hamburg) (27)	501 853-5144	Don Hartley	....	Sarah Atkins	....	....	Bub Wilson	Charles Wells
Baxter (Mountain Home)† (27)	501 425-2755	Joe Dillard	Guy Jones	Arnold Knight	Nancy Rorie	John Ed Isbell	Wm Snow	Joe H Edmonds
Benton (Bentonville)† (78)	507 273-2741	A E Norwood	....	Mary Slinkard	Ray Jefferson	....	....	Don Rystrom
Boone (Harrison)† (26)	501 741-5760	Clifford Tomlinso	....	David Witty	Lois Brown	....	....	Roy Norvell
Bradley (Warren) (14)	501 226-3853	Joe L Fowler	....	Ioma S McKinney	Joe L Fowler	....	....	Jack Gambill
Calhoun (Hampton) (6)	501 798-4818	William G Wylie	....	Harold L Watson	Jean Erickson	....	....	Ira V Dunn
Carroll (Berryville)† (16)	501 423-2022	Gaylord Farmer	....	Carol Worley	Wanda Mckinney	....	....	Leroy Shower
Chicot (Lake Village) (18)	501 265-2432	(not reporting)						
Clark (Arkadelphia) (23)	501 246-4491	(not reporting)						
Clay (Piggott)† (21)	501 598-2667	Rue C Mack	....	Lavon Sonny Smart	Buster Griggs	....	....	Cloyce Pierce
Cleburne (Heber Springs) (17)	501 362-8141	Harvey Adcock	....	Wetzel H Stark	Farris Moody	....	Marsha J McCurry	Ron Davis
Cleveland (Rison) (8)	501 325-6214	Tom Taylor	....	John T Reed	Mack McCallister	....	George Boyd	Joe P King
Columbia (Magnolia) (27)	501 234-4194	(not reporting)						
Conway (Morrilton) (20)	501 354-4506	T J Mahan	....	Jerry Scroggins	Noma Faye Sledge	....	Rose Robinson	Carl Stobaugh
Craighead (Jonesboro) (63)	501 932-2921	(not reporting)						
Crawford (Van Buren) (37)	501 474-1312	(not reporting)						
Crittenden (Marion) (49)	501 739-3383	(not reporting)						
Cross (Wynne)† (20)	501 238-3373	William Joe Wood	....	Joline Norris	Hansel Pitts	Shannon Nix	Patsy Edwards	Ronnie Huey
Dallas (Fordyce) (11)	501 352-2307	(not reporting)						
Desha (Arkansas City) (20)	501 877-2426	Bonnie Zook	....	....	Hazel Glass	....	Marty Chambers	Ben Williams
Drew (Monticello)† (18)	501 367-3574	Harold D West	....	....	Carolyn Brown	....	....	David T Hyatt Jr
Faulkner (Conway) (46)	501 327-6586	(not reporting)						
Franklin (Ozark)† (15)	501 667-3607	Joe W Powell	....	Jo Ann Barham	Jane Ferguson	....	....	Robt F Pritchard
Fulton (Salem)† (10)	501 895-3310	Vernon H Smith	....	Gene Maguffee	Boyd Hickinbotham	....	....	Earl Hurt
Garland (Hot Springs)† (70)	501 321-2819	Bud Williams	Larry Williams	Bill Ridgeway	Joe Poe	George Murphy	Bob Clark	Clay White
Grant (Sheridan)† (13)	501 942-2551	Roy E Bayley	....	Maurice Shoptaw	Billy Winkle	....	Terry Brumbelow	Robert Shepherd
Greene (Paragould) (31)	501 236-3133	(not reporting)						
Hempstead (Hope) (24)	501 777-2241	(not reporting)						
Hot Spring (Malvern)† (27)	501 332-2261	Bob Brandenburg	....	....	Hannah Weaver	....	Russel Cobb	Doyle Cook
Howard (Nashville) (13)	501 845-3622	(not reporting)						
Independence (Batesville) (30)	501 793-5126	Jim Pearson	Rita Potts	Margaret Boothby	Charles Barnett	....	....	Gerald Fulbright
Izard (Melbourne)† (11)	501 368-4328	Paul Weaver	....	Charles Cheatham	Linda Jeffery	....	Johnnie Sue Dunav	Jack Yancey
Jackson (Newport) (22)	501 523-3178	(not reporting)						
Jefferson (Pine Bluff)† (91)	501 541-5360	Earl Chadick	Lillian Rogers	A G Stone	W P Ellis	....	....	W C Brassell
Johnson (Clarksville) (17)	501 754-2175	Bobby Joe Wilkins	....	Elmo Cater	F D Goza	....	....	Elton D Brown
Lafayette (Lewisville) (10)	501 921-4633	(not reporting)						
Lawrence (Walnut Ridge) (18)	501 886-2167	Elmer Gibbs	....	Vurnece Jones	Bill Holder	....	Lillian Shumaker	Bob Tomlinson
Lee (Marianna) (16)	501 295-2339	Kenneth Hunter	....	Pat Wilson	Jack Gentry	Joe Moore	....	Robert May Jr
Lincoln (Star City) (13)	501 628-4147	J T Moncrief	....	Virginia B Adcox	Jerry Sanders	....	Thomas Lewellen	Billy B French
Little River (Ashdown) (14)	501 898-5021	Hoye Horn	Nolan T Hefner	Delores Pullen	Carlene Bishop	C T Patterson	Billie Mitchell	Marlin Surber
Logan (Paris) (20)	501 963-2618	Cissie Boyd	Joe Kearney	Susan Hixson	R Robberson	....	....	Bill Kimbriel
Lonoke (Lonoke) (35)	501 676-2368	(not reporting)						
Madison (Huntsville) (11)	501 738-6721	Chas Whorton Jr	....	Marolyn Green	....	....	....	Ralph Baker
Marion (Yellville) (11)	501 449-6231	Berry E Burleson	....	Edith Williams	Layne Milligan	....	Bob Ahrens	Roger Edmonson
Miller (Texarkana)† (38)	501 774-3256	Lee Overstreet	....	Ted Thomas	Howard Giles	....	Doyle Purifoy	Ken Sinyard
Mississippi (Blytheville) (60)	501 762-2411	(not reporting)						
Monroe (Clarendon) (14)	501 747-3632	(not reporting)						
Montgomery (Mount Ida) (8)	501 867-3521	D E Abernathy	....	....	....	....	....	James Roy Carmack
Nevada (Prescott)† (11)	501 887-3115	Bobby W Taylor	....	Nell Grifford	Dick Stewart	....	Blake Crow MD	Doc Delaughter
Newton (Jasper) (8)	501 446-5125	(not reporting)						
Ouachita (Camden) (31)	501 836-4116	Alfred Smith	....	Juanita Biggers	Bruce Harrell	....	Greg Adams	Jack Dews
Perry (Perryville)† (7)	501 889-5126	J R Paul	J R Paul	Christine Wright	Linda Cody	....	....	Ray L Byrd
Phillips (Helena) (35)	501 338-3486	A Y Gordon	Ray Culver Jr	Virginia Cooper	Irene N Adams	....	....	Marion S Hickey
Pike (Murfreesboro) (10)	501 285-2231	(not reporting)						
Poinsett (Harrisburg) (27)	501 578-5333	Stephen L Ryan	Stephen L Ryan	Ralph Walker	Charles Whitney	....	Billie Foster	Thomas Graves
Polk (Mena)† (17)	501 394-4945	Wingo Johnson	....	Pat Myers	June Wiles	....	Wanda Cogburn	A L Hadaway
Pope (Russellville) (39)	501 968-6064	(not reporting)						
Prairie (Des Arc) (10)	501 256-3741	Guyman DeVore	....	Billy M Garth	M C Barlow	....	G M Schumann MD	Dale Madden
Pulaski (Little Rock) (341)	501 372-8300	Don R Venhaus	Jim Finch	Shirley Smith	W L Tedford	John L Taylor	....	Tommy Robinson

Directory 1/9 continued **COUNTY OFFICIALS IN ALL U.S. COUNTIES**

County, county seat, 1980 population (000 omitted),	County telephone number	Board chairman	Appointed administrator	Clerk to the governing board	Chief financial officer	County engineer	County health officer	Chief law enforcement official
ARKANSAS (75) continued								
Randolph (Pocahontas) (17)	501 892-5822	(not reporting)						
Saline (Benton) (53)	501 778-2667	Wayne M Bishop	....	George Ramsey Jr	Tommy Adams	....	Sandra Krebs	James Steed
Scott (Waldron)† (10)	501 637-2155	James Jim Hunt	....	Evelyn Ammons	Glen Dale Sparks	....	Sherry Plummer RN	Jim Daggs
Searcy (Marshall) (9)	501 448-3554	Duford Taylor	....	D L Adams	Jerry L Wallis	....	Charles Daniel MD	John Kent Griggs
Sebastian (Fort Smith) (95)	501 783-6139	William R Harper	David O Hudson	....	Mary L Willsey	....	....	Bill Cauthron
Sevier (de Queen) (14)	501 642-2425	Bill Pogue	....	Sandra Dunn	Maxine W Vilanova	....	Shirley Hadley	David L Godwin
Sharp (Ash Flat) (15)	501 994-7338	Franklin D Arnold	....	Tommy Estes	Wanda Kunkel	Donna Gipson	Susan Barnes	T J Sonny Powell
St. Francis (Forrest City)† (31)	501 633-8640	Carl E Cisco	....	Dorothy C Bernard	Thomas Cope	George Trusty	Vance Crain	Coolidge Conlee
Stone (Mountain View)† (9)	501 269-3351	Coleman Gammill	....	Patsy Newcomb	Peggy Trammell	....	Jaunita Coleman	R C Alexander
Union (El Dorado) (50)	501 863-5244	(not reporting)						
Van Buren (Clinton)† (13)	501 745-2443	Bobby Woodard	Joy McKnight	Sammy Collums	Imogene Story	....	Jim Walls	Gus Anglin
Washington (Fayetteville) (100)	501 521-8400	Charles A Johnson	Roger L Haney	Karen Beeks	Joan Perry	....	Jim House	Bud Dennis
White (Searcy)† (51)	501 268-2950	David Morris	....	William O Moore	Harrell Greer	....	Tom Jenkins	Aden L Woodruff
Woodruff (Augusta) (11)	501 347-5206	John Davis	John Davis	Pat Rives	Shirley Stoner	....	Lorene Cooper	Leon Creasey
Yell (Danville) (17)	501 495-2630	James Lee Witt	....	Carolyn Morris	James C Pledger	....	Len Cotton	Denver Dennis
CALIFORNIA (58)								
Alameda (Oakland)§ (1105)	415 874-7861	John George	Mel Hing	William Mehrwein	Donald Parkin	H A Flertzheim	Carl Smith MD	Glenn E Dyer
Alpine (Markleeville) (1)	916 694-2281	William K Freeman	Earl H O'Neal	Karen Keebaugh	Dolores Clark	Thomas M Gau	Gregory J Hayes	Archie P Wood Jr
Amador (Jackson) (19)	209 223-3230	Ken H Deaver	....	Cathy Montgomery	Elmer Evans	Rod Schuler	James McClenahan	Robert Campbell
Butte (Oroville)§ (144)	916 534-4781	Al Saraceni	Martin J Nichols	Martin J Nichols	Richard Puelicher	William Cheff	Al Raitt	Hal Brooks
Calaveras (San Andreas)† (21)	209 754-4252	Suzanne Kuehl	John Crane	Nadine Jackson	Joann Long	....	Robert Marshall	Claud Ballard
Colusa (Colusa) (13)	916 458-2101	D G Womble	Jack F Lawrence	Martha Nannen	Myles Spann	Gary Plunkett	Louis Buonomo MD	Bobby D McWatter
Contra Costa (Martinez)§ (657)	415 372-2371	Thomas Torlakson	Phillip Batchelor	James Olsson	Alfred Lomeli	Michael Walford	William Walker MD	Richard Rainey
Del Norte (Crescent City) (18)	707 464-3101	Helga Burns	John W Anderson	Ellen P Brown	Sarah Decker	Max H Bridges	Paul W Anderson	G Thomas Hopper
El Dorado (Placerville) (86)	916 626-2238	Pat Lowe	Kent M Taylor	Ann Macy	Elvis Ferguson	G Arthur Cort	Curtiss Weidmer	Richard Pacileo
Fresno (Fresno)§ (515)	209 488-1710	Vernon Conrad	Bruce W Spaulding	Darlene J Bloom	Gary Peterson	Richard Welton	Donald Rowe	Harold McKinney
Glenn (Willows) (21)	916 934-3834	Joe Williams	....	Milton E Walker	Merlyn Head	Bob Townsend	Joseph R Duba	Roger Roberts
Humboldt (Eureka)§ (108)	707 445-7266	Harry Pritchard	Robert E Hendrix	Robert Hanley	Stephen Strawn	Guy Kulstad	Paul Anderson MD	Dave Renner
Imperial (El Centro)§ (92)	619 339-4375	Louis Curiel	David L Dolenar	Kathy Jones	Don Brown	S Harry Orfanos	Lee Cottrell	Oren Fox
Inyo (Independence) (18)	619 878-2411	Robert Bremmer	Michael B Hanford	Kelli Lanshaw	John Treacy	....	George Kibler MD	Donald Dorsey
Kern (Bakersfield) (403)	805 861-2371	Ben Austin	R S Holden	Mariam Rademacher	Bill J Jackson	L Dale Mills	Leon Hebertson MD	Larry Kleier
Kings (Hanford) (74)	209 582-3211	Joe Hammond	Milton D McCoy	Rosie Martinez	Marion Rose	Ray Nielsen	Sheldon R Minkin	Tom Clark
Lake (Lakeport) (36)	707 263-2367	Raymond Couch	....	Lois Hesterberg	Norma J Barker	Eugene Collins	....	Raymond Benevedes
Lassen (Susanville) (22)	916 257-8311	R Pete Vossler	....	Jacquelyn Fuller	Beatrice Price	John Mitchell	Sumner Cheeseman	Ronald Jarrell
Los Angeles (Los Angeles)§ (7478)	213 974-1234	Deane Dana	Harry L Hufford	Larry Monteilh	Mark H Bloodgood	Stephen J Koonce	....	Sherman Block
Madera (Madera) (63)	209 675-7703	Gail McIntyre	Donald Hanoly	Wanda Bradly	Glenn Jessing	Norman Hanson	C Dean Mcclure	Ovonual Berkley
Marin (San Rafael) (223)	415 499-7331	Al Aramburu	John F Barrows	Ms Van Gillespie	Joseph Coffrini	Tom Flinn	Theodore Hiatt	Charles Prandi
Mariposa (Mariposa)† (11)	209 966-2005	Eric J Erickson	....	Gerald McCarthy	Donald Z Phillips	William Lincoln	Avery E Sturm	Kenneth Matthys
Mendocino (Ukiah)§† (67)	707 468-4441	Dan Hamburg	Albert P Beltrami	Joyce A Beard	Irene Lange	C F Campbell	Craig McMillan	Tim Shea
Merced (Merced)§ (135)	209 726-7434	Al Goman	Clark G Channing	Kenneth Randol	Norman Fullerton	Verne Davis	....	William Amis
Modoc (Alturas) (9)	916 233-2215	M W Mick Jones	....	Maxine Madison	Maxine Gloster	Don E Polson	Ed Richert	Raymond Sweet
Mono (Bridgeport)§ (9)	619 932-7911	Robert J Stanford	N F Poppelreiter	Marjorie E Peigne	Claude E Olsen	Richard J Melim	Charles L Lear MD	Lloyd F Wilson
Monterey (Salinas) (290)	408 424-8611	Michal Moore	Ernest Morishita	Ernest Morishita	Jack Skillicorn	Bruce W McClain	Robert Melton MD	D B Cook
Napa (Napa) (99)	707 253-4421	William Chew	Albert J Haberger	Janice F Norton	Rose Burrell	Harry Hamilton	Robert Hill	Phillip Stewart
Nevada (Nevada City) (52)	916 265-1225	Ilse Barnhart	Gene Albaugh	Cathy R Thompson	E Christina Dabis	Terrance Lowell	Jerry Zarriello	William Heafey
Orange (Santa Ana)§ (1932)	714 834-2000	Harriett Wieder	Robert E Thomas	Linda Roberts	Robert Citron	Murray Storm	Rex Ehling MD	Brad Gates
Placer (Auburn) (117)	916 823-4011	Alex Ferreira	Tom Schopflin	Georgia Burge	F Earl Corin	John Maccoun	William E Fair MD	Donald Nunes
Plumas (Quincy) (17)	916 283-1060	Leonard Ross	....	Ila Diggs	Barbara Cokor	Lawrence J Brock	Albert Kiefer MD	Kenneth Shanks
Riverside (Riverside)§ (664)	714 787-2898	Patricia Larson	Gary N Cottrell	Gerald Maloney	R Wayne Watts	Leroy D Smoot	Ronald Hattis	Bernard Clark
Sacramento (Sacramento)*† (783)	916 366-2000	Ted Sheedy	Brian H Richter	Bev Williams	Gary Cassady	D W McKenzie	Ronald L Usher	Robbie Waters
San Benito (Hollister) (25)	408 637-3786	Harold J Cerrato	Patrick Bates	John R Hodges	John R Hodges	Keith Carlen	Peter Jones MD	Robert Scattini
San Bernardino (San Bernardino)§† (893)	714 383-2255	Robert L Hammock	Robert B Rigney	Andree Disharoon	Joe Bell	James Matthews	Louis E Mahoney	Frank Bland
San Diego (San Diego)§† (1862)	619 236-2121	Paul Fordem	Clifford W Graves	Porter Cremans	Rod Calvao	Rudolph J Massman	James A Forde	John F Duffy
San Francisco C (679)	415 558-2105	Dianne Feinstein	Roger Boas	John Taylor	John C Farrell	....	M Silverman MD	Cornelius Murphy
San Joaquin (Stockton) (347)	209 944-3211	George L Barber	David Rowlands Jr	Joretta Hayde	John A Prowse	Henry Hirata	Jack Williams	John Zunino
San Luis Obispo (San Luis Obispo)§ (155)	805 549-5011	J Diefenderfer	William Briam	Francis Cooney	Paul Floyd	George Protopapas	George Rowland MD	George Whiting
San Mateo (Redwood City)* (588)	415 363-4100	Wm J Schumacher	David L Nichols	Minerva Takis	Ross Conti	Robert L Sans	James M Bodie	Brendan McGuire
Santa Barbara (Santa Barbara)* (299)	805 966-0611	David M Yager	Larry Parrish	Howard C Menzel	Kristi M Johnson	James Stubchaer	Lawrence Hart MD	John Carpenter
Santa Clara (San Jose)* (1295)	408 299-2424	Zoe Lofgren	Sally R Reed	Donald M Rains	William Parsons	Mario Baratta	J K Bartholet	Robert Winter
Santa Cruz (Santa Cruz) (188)	408 425-2171	Robley Levy	George T Newell	Stephen M Quong	Arthur M Merrill	Donald A Porath	Elinor C Hall	Alfred F Noren
Shasta (Redding) (116)	916 246-5557	Don C Maddox	Ronald H Piorek	Ann Reed	Jacque Williams	Richard Curry	Steven Plank MD	Phillip Eoff
Sierra (Downieville) (3)	916 289-3295	(not reporting)						
Siskiyou (Yreka) (40)	916 842-3531	James Steinhaus	Richard E Sierck	Norma Price	Susan Reather	David Gravenkamp	Robert Bayuk	Bud Taylor
Solano (Fairfield)* (235)	707 429-6311	John Cunningham	Richard E Watson	Linda Terra	Bobby Stow	Eugene Knapp	Edward Lopez MD	Albert Cardoza
Sonoma (Santa Rosa)§ (300)	707 527-2431	Bob Adams	Leonard L Whorton	Athena Bemis	Don Merz	Donald Head	Robert Holtzer	Roger McDermott
Stanislaus (Modesto)§ (266)	209 571-6333	Rolland C Starn	Gardner L Hutchin	Beth M Martinez	Frank L DeCamp	Harold Callahan	Kem Kelly MD	Lynn Wood
Sutter (Yuba City) (52)	916 674-8650	Allen Eager	Larry T Combs	Lonna Smith	Daphne Schliesman	....	....	Roy Whiteaker
Tehama (Red Bluff) (39)	916 527-4655	Russell Frey	....	Floyd A Hicks	Doris Forward	Lawrence Coleman	Melvin Gumm	Ron E Koenig
Trinity (Weaverville) (12)	916 623-4000	Ralph R Modine	Dave Andres	Barbara M Rhodes	John D Larkin	John Tryon	Michael G Polka	Gil Brown
Tulare (Visalia)§ (246)	209 733-6531	Dolores E Mangine	John McClure II	John McClure II	C Ralph Howard	....	Ronald Probasco	Bob Wiley
Tuolumne (Sonora)§ (34)	209 533-5511	Clyde W May	Steven C Szalay	Lawrence G Lee	John Nicolini	Cyrus Hoblitt	M Ellen Vogel	Wallace C Berry
Ventura (Ventura)§ (530)	805 654-4000	S Lacey	R Wittenberg	R Dean	N Hawkes	A Goulet	S Miller MD	J Gillespie
Yolo (Woodland)* (113)	916 666-8150	(not reporting)						
Yuba (Marysville) (50)	916 741-6464	Charles D Center	Jay Hull	Patricia Stewart	James Kennedy	Donald Frost	Chas B Johnson MD	Robert Day
COLORADO (63)								
Adams (Brighton) (246)	303 659-2120	Leo Younger Jr	Robert Clifton	William Sokol	Helen Hill	Richard Marino	....	Bert Johnson
Alamosa (Alamosa) (12)	303 589-5887	Tim Gallagher	Gary T Suiter	Mary B Sparrow	Stella Mai Foster	....	Marlin E Luther	James P Drury
Arapahoe (Littleton) (294)	303 795-4400	Bettyann Dittemor	....	Marjorie Page	Dorothy Vogt	Ernest Hamilton	....	Patrick Sullivan
Archuleta (Pagosa Springs) (4)	303 264-2536	Chris L Chavez	Sylvia Carpenter	Martha Valdez	Tinnie E Lattin	....	....	Neal I Smith
Baca (Springfield)† (5)	303 523-4521	Roy Brinkley	Dana Christie	Sheila Ingle	....	....	Jacqueline Brown	W E Goff

Directory 1/9 continued — COUNTY OFFICIALS IN ALL U.S. COUNTIES

County, county seat, 1980 population (000 omitted),	County telephone number	Board chairman	Appointed administrator	Clerk to the governing board	Chief financial officer	County engineer	County health officer	Chief law enforcement official
COLORADO (63) continued								
Bent (Las Animas) (6)	303 456-0171	Glen Gill	....	Donetta Davidson	Mildred Sharp	Steve Whitehill	Steve Whitehill	Darrell Emrie
Boulder (Boulder) (190)	303 441-3131	Jack Murphy	....	....	....	....	....	Brad Leach
Chaffee (Salida) (13)	303 539-6031	....	Harold L Lewis	....	....	....	....	....
Cheyenne (Cheyenne Wells) (2)	303 767-5685	Floyd McEwen	....	Rita M Holthus	....	....	James L Blain MD	Walter E Hyle
Clear Creek (Georgetown) (7)	303 569-3251	James G Lucas	Julia Holmes	Julia Holmes	Helen R Holman	....	Carl Anderson MD	James R Bennett
Conejos (Conejos) (8)	303 376-5772	Dale N Sowards	Bertha N Montoya	Gracie Broyles	Dora Jiron	....	Lynn Mortensen	Gene DeHerrera
Costilla (San Luis)† (3)	303 672-3962	Epi Jaramillo	Allen Manzavares	Roy D Martinez	Alfredo Chavez	....	Louise Kahn	Ernest Sandoval
Crowley (Ordway) (3)	303 267-4643	Oran Burmood	Joe M Kinard	Marilou Geringer	Loie E Norris	....	....	Perfecto A Hijar
Custer (Westcliffe)† (2)	303 783-2441	Leonard Reis	....	Mary Kattnig	Doris J Porth	....	Kristine Striker	Robert Baker
Delta (Delta) (21)	303 874-7595	Ben O Sheldon	George H Gault	Josephine M Gore	Mildred Hamilton	....	Bonnie H Koehler	Richard A Miklich
Denver C (491)	303 575-5511	Federico Pena	....	Felicia Muftic	James A Murrdy	J A Bruce	....	T E Coogan
Dolores (Dove Creek) (2)	303 677-2383	Louis A Bucher	....	Maxine Sanders	Shirley Hasty	....	Joyce Waller	Charles Williams
Douglas (Castle Rock) (25)	303 688-6260	Sonya Blackstock	Donald A Klemme	Reta A Crain	Tony Sanfratello	Tom Schweitzer	....	Steve Zotos
Eagle (Eagle) (13)	303 328-7311	W Keith Troxel	Brad Jones	J Phillips	Mary Walker	Larry Metternick	Thomas Steinberg	A J Johnson
El Paso (Colorado Springs) (309)	303 471-0600	Terry Harris	Terry Storm	Ardis Schmitt	Sharon Shipley	Max Rothschild	John Muth	Bernard Barry
Elbert (Kiowa) (7)	303 621-2343	Glenn A Hart	Deena S Roe	John Peppel Jr	Suzie Graeff	....	Norma Rogers	George Yarnell
Fremont (Canon City) (29)	303 275-1511	(not reporting)						
Garfield (Glenwood Springs)† (23)	303 945-9158	E Jim Drinkhouse	S R Broome	Mildred Alsdorf	Ella Stephens	Leonard Bowlby	Mary Jo Jacobs	Verne Soucie
Gilpin (Central City) (2)	303 582-5214	Charles V Cullar	Lorraine P Crowe	Lorraine P Crowe	Virginia Starkey	Harold Donnelly	Janet Brower	Rosetta L Anderle
Grand (Hot Sulphur Springs)* (7)	303 725-3347	W A Bill Needham	R Howard Moody	Patricia L Appleb	Marge J Alt	Clark Branstetter	Marvin L Fischer	H L Henderson
Gunnison (Gunnison)* (11)	303 641-0248	David Leinsdorf	Michael J Rock	Lorna Dotts	C Fletcher	....	John Tarr MD	George Kenady
Hinsdale (Lake City) (..)	303 944-2225	James H Ryan	L F Jake Jacobs	Sara L Brown	Verna A Carl	....	....	Burton E Smith
Huerfano (Walsenburg)† (6)	303 738-2370	Joe B Rodriquez	Andrew P Nigrini	Barbara B Pullin	Thomas J Solomon	....	....	Harold Martinez
Jackson (Walden) (2)	303 723-4660	Robt E Manville	Wm Kent Crowder	Ruth M McGrew	Jill Potter	....	David W France	Gary L Cure
Jefferson (Golden) (372)	303 277-8508	Donald C Stanbro	Terry A Green	Eleanor V Martin	Donald E Couch	....	Charles Miller	Harold E Bray
Kiowa (Eads)† (2)	303 438-5810	Merle Crockett	Gary Woodward	....	Steve Baxter	....	....	Gary Rehm
Kit Carson (Burlington) (8)	303 346-8133	Egar Pratt	....	Iva Gross	Sandra Berry	....	R C Beethe MD	George R Hubbard
La Plata (Durango)† (27)	303 259-4000	Sara Duncan	Laurence Mills	Norma Hurford	Clyde Demel	Edward Bennett	Robert Balliger	Alvin Brown
Lake (Leadville)† (9)	303 486-0993	Carl Miller	A Peterson	June Ossman	Viola M Irwin	Ronald Dump	....	Chas Martschinske
Larimer (Fort Collins) (149)	303 221-7000	James D Lloyd	Arlen Stokes	John Ulvang	Charles Woodward	William Campton	Robert Sherwood	James W Black
Las Animas (Trinidad) (15)	303 846-3314	(not reporting)						
Lincoln (Hugo) (5)	303 743-2444	James D Clement	....	Marie Brockway	James R Covington	....	....	Leroy Yowell
Logan (Sterling) (20)	303 522-0888	Elda M Lousberg	Kent Gumina	Charlene Craddock	Barbara Kaiser	....	....	Donald Bollish
Mesa (Grand Junction)* (82)	303 244-1800	George R White	Gordon D Tiffany	Earl Sawyer	John P Morgan	Robert Carman	Kenneth Lampert	L R Williams
Mineral (Creede) (1)	303 658-2440	Nell Wyley	....	G Hargraves	....	....	....	Phillip Leggitt
Moffat (Craig) (13)	303 824-5517	Albert Camilletti	Cynthia Shanahan	Barbara L Terrill	Margaret Jones	....	Tom Told Do	S L Valdez Jr
Montezuma (Cortez) (17)	303 565-3728	(not reporting)						
Montrose (Montrose)† (24)	303 249-7755	Lyman Thomas	....	Patricia Vernon	Herbert Anderson	....	Robert Motley	Tom Gilmore
Morgan (Fort Morgan) (23)	303 867-8202	Robert Bauer	Mary E Wehrer	Fay A Vondy	Robert A Sagel	....	Herb Jaeger	Howard J Mann
Otero (La Junta) (23)	303 384-4221	Robert Bauserman	Barry Shioshita	Stella Sedillo	Dennis Smith	Rick Klein	Wanda Girard	John Eberly
Ouray (Ouray) (2)	303 325-4650	Howard B Williams	....	Addie A Sim	Ramona M Radcliff	....	....	Arthur Dougherty
Park (Fairplay) (5)	303 893-2282	John Crawford Sr	David Blackstock	Harriet Anderson	Etta Everett	....	Richard Worl	Norman Howey
Phillips (Holyoke)† (5)	303 854-2454	Leland H Miller	Leland H Miller	Mary Louise Evans	Lois Lipker	Louis Harmon	....	Clair Pillard
Pitkin (Aspen)† (10)	303 925-5232	George Madsen	Curt Stewart	Loretta Banner	Tom Oken	Pat Dobie	Tom Dunlop	Dick Kienast
Prowers (Lamar) (13)	303 336-9001	Joe Hasser	Carl F Winsor	Mildred Jones	Geneva Mosher	....	....	George Martin
Pueblo (Pueblo) (126)	303 543-3550	Jon H Giguere	Jack D Craddock	Lucille Wilson	L Reininger	Mark A Carmel	....	Dan Tihonovich
Rio Blanco (Meeker) (6)	303 878-5068	Kenneth O Kenney	Della L Wear	Veyon Wagner	Della L Wear	Jack Raley	Robert Dorsett MD	Ronald K Hilkey
Rio Grande (Del Norte) (11)	303 657-2580	Thad C Elliott	Suzanne Benton	Lela Ann Bennett	Billie Garretson	....	Mary J Sanderson	John Kammerzell
Routt (Steamboat Springs)† (13)	303 879-0108	Robert E McKune	Donald E Cluxton	Kim Sullivan	Dillon Rich	Jim Douglas	Mike Zopf	Tim Walsh
Saguache (Saguache) (4)	303 655-2231	Keith Edwards	John Bernhart	Mary Moore	John Bernhart	....	....	Larry Zimmer
San Juan (Silverton) (1)	303 387-5671	Ernest F Kuhlman	....	Mary L Andersen	C Martinez	....	Ruth B Ward	Susan R Kurtz
San Miguel (Telluride)† (3)	303 728-3372	Fred Ellerd	....	Shauna Palmer	Sherry Rose	Paul Sale	Barbara Mahoney	William Masters
Sedgwick (Julesburg) (3)	303 474-3346	Leo H Detamore	....	Maedine Nelson	Ruth L Schweitzer	....	....	Herbert Fliethman
Summit (Breckenridge)* (9)	303 453-2561	Don Peterson	Bruce Baumgartner	Colleen Richmond	Robert F Bell	Neil Kelly	William Smith	Delbert Ewoldt
Teller (Cripple Creek) (8)	303 633-5847	L June Fulhrodt	....	Shirley A Beach	Connie Copenhaver	....	Callie A Videtich	Gary Shoemaker
Washington (Akron) (5)	303 345-2701	Paul E Florian	....	Garland Wahl	Marijane Keim	....	....	William McDonald
Weld (Greeley) (123)	303 356-4000	Norman Carlson	Donald D Warden	M A Feuerstein	Francis Loustalet	Drew Scheltinga	Ralph R Wooley MD	Harold Andrews
Yuma (Wray) (10)	303 332-5796	Harvey W Pletcher	Melanie Mears	Margie Eyestone	Jane Clark	....	W S Kolling DV	Robert Murphy
DELAWARE (3)								
Kent (Dover) (98)	302 736-2000	(not reporting)						
New Castle (Wilmington)§ (399)	302 571-7500	Richard T Collins	John T McCool	Shirley A Agnor	William B Graden	....	....	John R McCarnan
Sussex (Georgetown)† (98)	302 856-7701	Ralph E Benson	Joseph T Conaway	Emogene P Ellis	Geo F Purpur Jr	....	....	Stephen E Rogers
D.C. (1)								
Washington I† (638)	202 727-1000	Marion Barry	Thomas Downs	....	Elizabeth Reveal	....	....	Maurice T Turner
FLORIDA (67)								
Alachua (Gainesville)§ (151)	904 374-5210	Thomas Coward	Jerry L Maxwell	A Curtis Powers	....	Edwin E Culpepper	....	L J Hindery
Baker (Macclenny) (15)	904 259-3121	Thomas A Fraser	....	Harry Richardson	Harry Richardson	Glenn Williamson	John Adams	Joe Newmans
Bay (Panama City) (98)	904 769-8306	Isaac W Byrd	Alton P Cape	Harold Bazzel	James R Maloy Sr	Steve Potter	A F Ullman	Lavelle Pitts
Bradford (Starke)† (20)	904 964-6280	George Pierce	....	Gilbert S Brown	....	James Ward	Joyce Riherd	Dolph E Reddish
Brevard (Titusville)§† (273)	305 269-8011	....	Peter J Hayes	Raymond Winstead	Douglas E Martin	Richard Driskell	Manuel J Garcia	....
Broward (Fort Lauderdale)§ (1014)	305 765-5121	Nicki E Grossman	Floyd Johnson	Floyd Johnson	Foster Muzea	....	Joan Heggen	George Brescher
Calhoun (Blountstown) (9)	904 674-4545	Drew Peacock Jr	....	Willie D Wise	Willie D Wise	Bob King	Dan Yoder	Buddy Smith
Charlotte (Port Charlotte)§ (59)	813 627-1101	Franz H Ross	W Wm Kiriloff	Buddy C Alexander	....	Paul G Vanbuskirk	....	Glenn E Sapp
Citrus (Inverness)§ (55)	904 726-8500	John T Barnes	Craig M Hunter	Walter D Connors	Gary Herndon	E L Dougherty	Landis Crockett	Charles Dean
Clay (Green Cove Springs) (67)	904 284-6300	Dale S Wilson	C Rosebrough	George L Carlisle	George L Carlisle	Jay Carver	Ed Stansel	Jennings Murrhee
Collier (Naples)§ (86)	813 774-8999	David C Brown	Donald Lusk	William J Reagan	James Giles	Tom Kuck	William Cox	Aubrey Rogers
Columbia (Lake City) (35)	904 755-4100	Jerry V Ward	Dale Williams	Mary B Childs	....	....	Dr Collins	Raymond Dyal
Dade (Miami)* (1626)	305 579-5900	Stephen P Clark	M R Stierheim	Richard P Brinker	Jose Pagan	William M Powell	Richard A Morgan	Bobby L Jones
De Soto (Arcadia) (19)	813 494-3773	(not reporting)						
Dixie (Cross City)† (8)	904 498-7021	C W Stephenson	....	Joe Hubert Allen	....	James D Ward	Charlotte G Liles	Glen Dyals
Escambia (Pensacola)§† (234)	904 436-5781	Gerald Woolard	Rodney L Kendig	Joe Flowers	Joe Flowers	Fred Hubacker	Robert K Wilson	Vince Seely
Flagler (Bunnell) (11)	904 437-2170	Thomas W Durrance	Hubert Pellicer	Shelton B Barber	Shelton B Barber	Donald Chinnery	Paul Fell	Robert McCarthy
Franklin (Apalachicola) (8)	904 653-8861	Willis Collins Jr	....	Lee R P Rivers	Lee R P Rivers	Walter Creekmore	Herbert Garfield	Jack Taylor Jr

Directory 1/9 continued — COUNTY OFFICIALS IN ALL U.S. COUNTIES

County, county seat, 1980 population (000 omitted),	County telephone number	Board chairman	Appointed administrator	Clerk to the governing board	Chief financial officer	County engineer	County health officer	Chief law enforcement official
FLORIDA (67) continued								
Gadsden (Quincy) (42)	904 875-4701	Earl W Lodge	....	Wayne Hanna	Wayne Hanna	E W Lee	Jerry Wynn	W A Woodham
Gilchrist (Trenton) (6)	904 463-2341	W B Mathis Jr	....	....	Jackie R Barron	....	....	....
Glades (Moore Haven) (6)	813 946-0113	Vance W Whidden	....	Jerry L Beck	Jerry L Beck	....	Mark Roston MD	Russell Henderson
Gulf (Port Saint Joe) (11)	904 229-6113	(not reporting)						
Hamilton (Jasper) (9)	904 792-1288	(not reporting)						
Hardee (Wauchula) (19)	813 773-6952	John R Gough	J Hetherington	Colemon W Best	....	....	George Heine	Doyle W Bryan
Hendry (La Belle) (19)	813 675-5217	C Harold White	Lionel Ebeatty	C R Fitzsimmons	....	George W Davis	....	Robert T Durkis
Hernando (Brooksville)§ (44)	904 796-4741	Henry D Ledbetter	David L Greene	Harold W Brown	Karen Nicolai	....	James M Stem MD	Melvin Kelly
Highlands (Sebring) (48)	813 385-2581	C J Buddy Wise	Cecil P Skipper	Earl Rich	....	Carl Cool	William Hill	Joe Sheppard
Hillsborough (Tampa)§ (647)	813 272-5000	Rodney C Colson	Norman W Hickey	James F Taylor Jr	William Goaziou	James Hatch	Donald S Kwalick	Walter Heinrich
Holmes (Bonifay)† (15)	904 547-2835	Gene Sims	....	Cody Taylor	....	....	....	Drew Galloway
Indian River (Vero Beach)*† (60)	305 567-8000	Don C Scurlock	Michael J Wright	Freda Wright	Jeffery Barton	James W Davis	J B Tucker MD	Tim Dobeck
Jackson (Marianna) (39)	904 482-2501	Alva Mercer	....	Daun Crews	....	....	....	J P McDaniels
Jacksonville-Duval C (541)	904 633-3131	Jake M Godbold	Donald R McClure	Ronald R Johnson	Ray Clardy	Stanley Nodland	Patricia Cowdery	Dale Carson
Jefferson (Monticello) (11)	904 997-3596	(not reporting)						
Lafayette (Mayo)† (4)	904 294-1600	Norman Jackson	....	Paul Trawick	....	....	John Lloyd	Bobby McCray
Lake (Tavares) (105)	904 343-9830	Glenn C Burhans	Michael C Willett	James C Watkins	....	Ben Benedum	June Atkinson	Noel E Griffin Jr
Lee (Fort Myers) (205)	813 335-2340	Roland Eastwood	Lavon Wisher	Sal Geraci	Gary Humphreys	Mike Carroll	Joseph Lawrence	Frank Wanicka
Leon (Tallahassee)§ (149)	904 488-4710	Doug Nichols	James W Parrish	Paul F Hartsfield	Paul F Hartsfield	Russell Tagliaren	....	Eddie Boone
Levy (Bronson) (20)	904 486-4311	(not reporting)						
Liberty (Bristol)† (4)	904 643-5404	James E Johnson	Duncan Hosford	Duncan Hosford	Duncan Hosford	William Bishop	Dan Yoder	Harrell W Revell
Madison (Madison) (15)	904 973-4176	Roy C Smith	....	Alfred F Welch	....	....	....	Joe C Peavy
Manatee (Bradenton)§ (148)	813 748-4501	Edward W Chance	Robt F Fernandez	R B Chips Shore	R B Chips Shore	Harry Ely	John Ambrusko	Thomas Burton
Marion (Ocala) (122)	904 622-0305	Murray E Fugate	F W Chambers	Frances Thigpin	....	B W Tenbroeck	N Grossman MD	Don Moreland
Martin (Stuart)§ (64)	305 283-6760	Alex L Haynes	Robert H Oldland	Louise V Isaacs	Louise V Isaacs	H Burt Smith	A McCallister MD	James Holt
Monroe (Key West)§ (63)	305 294-4641	Ken Sorensen	Kermit H Lewin	Danny Kolhage	Danny Kolhage	Vernon Page	Jose Bofill MD	William Freeman
Nassau (Fernandina Beach) (33)	904 261-6127	John F Claxton	....	Jerry Greeson	Jerry Greeson	Richard L King	N D Lund	R W Dougherty
Okaloosa (Crestview) (110)	904 682-2711	Larry Y Anchors	B B Sadler	Newman C Brackin	....	David Heinrich	Edmund Kielman MD	Larry Gilbert
Okeechobee (Okeechobee) (20)	813 763-6441	Sarah F Price	....	Clif Betts Jr	....	....	Neil Miller	John W Collier
Orange (Orlando)§ (472)	305 420-3122	Lou Treadway	James L Harris	Thomas H Locker	Thomas H Locker	George W Cole	John McGarry MD	Lawson L Lamar
Osceola (Kissimmee) (49)	305 817-1200	Michael D Bast	....	Mel Wills Jr	O E Tom Kessler	William Whitney	....	Ernest P Murphy
Palm Beach (West Palm Beach)* (573)	305 837-2059	Ken Spillias	John C Sansbury	John B Dunkle	Allen Clark	Herbert F Kahlert	Carl Brumback MD	Richard Wille
Pasco (New Port Richey)* (194)	813 847-2411	J L Hollingsworth	John J Gallagher	Jed Pittman	Jed Pittman	Jack D Easley	Robert May MD	John M Short
Pinellas (Clearwater)* (728)	813 462-3000	John Chesnut Jr	Fred E Marquis	Karleen DeBlaker	Robert Zinn	J Keith Wicks	Richard Levinson	Gerard A Coleman
Polk (Bartow) (322)	813 533-1161	Brenda Taylor	Frank B Smith Jr	E D Bud Dixon	James Roden	Gerald Towson	William Hill	Louie Mims
Putnam (Palatka) (51)	904 328-5181	J W Allenden	Gary Adams	Edward L Brooks	Robert Moore	Barry Harris	Charles Pierce	E W Pellicer
Santa Rosa (Milton)† (56)	904 623-3630	Jim Howell	....	Gerald F Barnes	Gus Schuster	Tom Justice	E W Sutton	Jim Powell
Sarasota (Sarasota)§ (202)	813 365-1000	Jerry L Hente	Ed Maroney	R H Hackney Jr	Rebecca Eger	Charles Goode	M J Magenheim MD	Jim Hardcastle
Seminole (Sanford)§ (180)	305 323-4330	Sandra S Glenn	T Duncan Rose III	Arthur H Beckwith	Arthur H Beckwith	William Bush Jr	Jorge Deju	John E Polk
St. Johns (St. Augustine) (51)	904 824-8131	Chester Benet	John L Harrington	Carl Markel	Henry S Hendrix	John L Harrington	James T McGibony	F O'Loughlin
St. Lucie (Fort Pierce)§ (87)	305 466-1100	Maurice Snyder	Weldon B Lewis	Roger Poitras	Daniel Kurek	Marcus Baggett	Neil Miller	Lanie Norvell
Sumter (Bushnell) (24)	904 793-2848	W Tom Blackmon	Bernard Dew	Bernard Shelnutt	....	....	June Atkinson	James L Adams
Suwannee (Live Oak) (22)	904 362-2827	Verneil Johnson	....	Jerry Scarborough	Jerry Scarborough	....	Melvin Kight	Robert Leonard
Taylor (Perry) (17)	904 584-3531	(not reporting)						
Union (Lake Butler) (10)	904 496-3711	Dale Smith	....	Margie F Cason	Margie F Cason	Lawrence Freeman	Glenn Howard	John H Whitehead
Volusia (De Land)* (259)	904 736-2700	P T Fleuchaus	Thomas C Kelly	Thomas C Kelly	Albert W Gault	Vohnnie L Pearson	William W Cox MD	Edwin H Duff
Wakulla (Crawfordville) (11)	904 926-3341	(not reporting)						
Walton (De Funiak Springs) (21)	904 892-3137	Sam Pridgen	....	Catherine King	....	W L Wilkinson	Howard Currie MD	Quinn McMillian
Washington (Chipley) (15)	904 638-7212	Albert E Davis	Roger D Hagan	T W Pitts	T W Pitts	....	Al Cleveland	Fred Peel
GEORGIA (159)								
Appling (Baxley)† (16)	912 367-7761	Kenneth Craven	Russell J Crosby	Russell J Crosby	Russell J Crosby	....	Ted Hallway	Lewis Parker
Atkinson (Pearson)† (6)	912 422-3391	Eston Metts	....	Tammy W Crosby	....	....	Margie N Giddens	Earl E Haskins
Bacon (Alma) (9)	912 632-5214	Cleon Carver	....	Mary Edna Wheeler	....	Payne Copeland	....	Russell Tanner
Baker (Newton) (4)	912 734-5294	(not reporting)						
Baldwin (Milledgeville) (35)	912 453-4007	(not reporting)						
Banks (Homer) (9)	404 677-2231	Harold Watkins	....	Avis Lewallen	....	....	....	Henry Crane
Barrow (Winder)† (21)	404 867-7581	Anne J Segars	....	Nelda B Brooksher	....	....	Ben Willingham	Joel H Robinson
Bartow (Cartersville)† (41)	404 382-4766	Frank Moore	Steve Bradley	Steve Bradley	....	Bob Peoples	....	Don Thurman
Ben Hill (Fitzgerald)† (16)	912 423-2455	Ed Drexler	James E Lee	Robin S Calhoun	....	....	James E Luckie	John N Hughes
Berrien (Nashville)† (14)	912 686-5421	Larry H Crumley	....	Gail Reynolds	Gail Reynolds	....	Jo Ann McGill	Robert M Swanson
Bibb (Macon) (151)	912 745-6871	Emory Greene	....	Hazel McCuen	Agnes Hatcher	Robert Fountain	....	Raymond Wilkes
Bleckley (Cochran)† (11)	912 934-4516	Jackie Holder	....	Sandra B Letson	....	....	....	Edward Coley Jr
Brantley (Nahunta) (9)	912 462-5256	Jimmy Woodard	....	Dale Halligan	....	....	Brenda Crews	Robert W Johns
Brooks (Quitman)† (15)	912 263-5561	J B Thagard	....	C E Taylor Jr	....	....	....	Hiram Bembry
Bryan (Pembroke)† (10)	912 653-4681	L Carlton Gill	....	Jetta E Foxworth	Jetta E Foxworth	....	Jewel Owens	Harry Williamson
Bulloch (Statesboro)† (36)	912 764-6245	Denver Lanier	....	Denver Lanier	....	....	....	Arnold R Akins
Burke (Waynesboro) (19)	404 554-2324	Ray Delaigle	C W Hopper Jr	C W Hopper Jr	C W Hopper Jr	....	Henry Tinley	Gregg Coursey
Butts (Jackson) (14)	404 775-7277	D W Bailey	....	Ruby Kate Moore	Billy Sutton	....	....	Billy Leverette
Calhoun (Morgan) (6)	912 849-4835	B Arlen Eubanks	....	Phyllis P Beard	....	....	Vivian Chancy	Charles E Cheney
Camden (Woodbine)* (13)	912 576-5621	(not reporting)						
Candler (Metter)† (8)	912 685-2835	George W Bird Jr	....	Debbie S Lanier	Debbie S Lanier	Billy Morgan	Diane Bryant	Homer Bell
Carroll (Carrollton)† (56)	404 832-3541	Horrie B Duncan	....	Susan N Allen	Bette Barnes	Douglas Crawford	Olan Ledford	Hugh Lee Lambert
Catoosa (Ringgold) (37)	404 935-4047	(not reporting)						
Charlton (Folkston) (7)	912 496-2549	William J Carter	....	Rosa Mae Brooks	....	....	J M Jackson MD	Ernest Conner
Chatham (Savannah) (202)	912 944-4984	Bill Stephenson	....	Jimmie L Szoke	Joseph E Mahany	Thomas A Smith	Wilbur Lundquist	Al St Lawrence
Chattahoochee (Cusseta)† (22)	404 989-3644	Julian Greer	....	H K Harp Jr	....	....	....	Glynn Cooper
Chattooga (Summerville) (22)	404 857-4021	Wayne Denson	....	Rebecca S Martin	....	....	....	Gary W McConnell
Cherokee (Canton)† (52)	404 479-1966	Willie M Johnson	T Carmichael	Charlotte Gray	Gene Hobgood	Grady Holcomb	Kathy Yarbrough	James Ballard
Clarke (Athens)§ (74)	404 354-2600	James R Holland	Roger H Alderman	William L Foster	John S Culpepper	George Chandler	John McKinley	Ronnie Chandler
Clay (Fort Gaines)† (4)	912 768-2631	Gerald Isler	....	Deanna Bertrand	Deanna Bertrand	....	Margaret Thornton	Roger Shivers
Clayton (Jonesboro)† (150)	404 471-1905	Charley Griswell	Milton Worsham	Milton Worsham	....	Steve Richardson	C W Sargent	James Parker
Clinch (Homerville) (7)	912 487-2667	George A Sirmans	....	Sherrie Peterson	....	....	Rosell Kearson	Cecil Barber
Cobb (Marietta) (298)	404 429-3000	Ernest W Barrett	James R Miller	Samuel M Young	Michael J Bolek	....	Elton Osborne MD	Bill Hutson
Coffee (Douglas) (27)	912 384-4799	Frank Jackson	....	Gail Hill	....	....	....	Paul Hutcheson
Colquitt (Moultrie)* (35)	912 985-6859	Wm D Kennedy	M Bruce Leigh	Yvonne Flowers	....	....	....	Eugene M Beard
Columbia (Appling)† (40)	404 863-7580	John A Dempsey Jr	....	James Emory Sayer	....	James W Ivey	Carol Davis	Tom Whitfield
Columbus-Muscogee C† (169)	404 324-7711	J W Feighner	Franklin Lambert	Lemuel Miller Jr	Irell Marshal	Larry Becknell	Leah R Camp	W J Wetherington

Directory 1/9 continued — COUNTY OFFICIALS IN ALL U.S. COUNTIES

County, county seat, 1980 population (000 omitted),	County telephone number	Board chairman	Appointed administrator	Clerk to the governing board	Chief financial officer	County engineer	County health officer	Chief law enforcement official
GEORGIA (159) continued								
Cook (Adel) (13)	912 896-7717	(not reporting)						
Coweta (Newnan)§† (39)	404 253-2728	....	Vernon Hunter	....	....	....	....	....
Crawford (Knoxville) (8)	912 836-3328	(not reporting)						
Crisp (Cordele) (19)	912 273-6251	W M Davis Jr	....	A J Smith Jr	....	W D Goff Jr	....	E W Forrest
Dade (Trenton)† (12)	404 657-4625	Larry Moore	....	Carrol Kirchmeyer	....	Irby Teet	....	Ronald C Steele
Dawson (Dawsonville) (5)	404 265-3164	Joe Lane Cox	....	Becky McCord	....	....	Don Flemmings	John Davis
De Kalb (Decatur) (483)	404 371-2881	Manuel J Maloof	Gretta M Dewald	David W Joyner	David W Joyner	....	Gunar Bohan	Dick Hand
Decatur (Bainbridge) (25)	912 246-3944	(not reporting)						
Dodge (Eastman) (17)	912 374-4361	Guy Tripp	....	Elaine Clements	Doyce Mullis	....	Earlene Williams	Jackson Jones
Dooly (Vienna) (11)	912 268-4228	Billy S Giles	....	Frances K Smith	Frances K Smith	....	Lawrence Nutt	Barney Thomas
Dougherty (Albany)* (101)	912 436-0514	Gil M Barrett	W Alan Reddish	W Alan Reddish	Robert I Bolton	Gerald Kirksey	Paul White	D Lamar Stewart
Douglas (Douglasville) (55)	404 949-2000	Jerry H Watson	Raymond Worthan	Helen Meade	....	Leland Pierce	Elton Osborne MD	Earl Lee
Early (Blakely) (13)	912 723-4304	Wilber A Evans	Billy Broadway	Billy Broadway	Billy Broadway	Lodge Holman	Bam Bridges	Oree Thompson
Echols (Statenville) (2)	912 559-6538	Donald Dukes	....	Mary Bell Carter	....	....	Rudene Moulton RN	Charles Carter
Effingham (Springfield) (18)	912 754-6071	(not reporting)						
Elbert (Elberton) (19)	404 283-5761	(not reporting)						
Emanuel (Swainsboro) (21)	912 237-8911	(not reporting)						
Evans (Claxton) (8)	912 739-1141	Carlon A Lewis Sr	....	Dorothea S West	Dorothea S West	....	Randy Sellars	Ben Sapp
Fannin (Blue Ridge) (15)	404 632-2039	(not reporting)						
Fayette (Fayetteville) (29)	404 461-6041	Jerry Barronton	....	Carol C Mundt	....	Don E Moore	Ferrol Sams Jr	Randall Johnson
Floyd (Rome) (80)	404 291-5110	Anne Rigas	R McCullouh	Sue Broome	Joy Turner	John Stewart	Virginia Hamilton	Jim Free
Forsyth (Cumming) (28)	404 887-5923	Donald Glover	A Lloyd Wagnon	Betty Shadburn	A Lloyd Wagnon	N Dale Bryant	Shannon Mize	Wesley Walraven
Franklin (Carnesville) (15)	404 384-2483	Terrell Roper	....	Gail P Walls	Terrell Roper	....	....	Joe Foster
Fulton (Atlanta)* (590)	404 572-2000	Michael L Lomax	Sam E Brownlee	Alice Smith	Virginia Stanton	Howard Frandsen	William Elsea MD	Clinton Chafin
Gilmer (Ellijay)† (11)	404 635-4361	Ben N Whitaker	....	Merle B Howell	....	....	....	Stanley Ferman
Glascock (Gibson) (2)	404 598-2671	Charles C Roberts	....	Elizabeth Hadden	Joe F Fordham	....	Mary Chalker	James L English
Glynn (Brunswick)* (55)	912 265-0585	....	Charles T Stewart	....	....	....	....	....
Gordon (Calhoun)§ (30)	404 629-3795	Harold Faith	Eddie Peterson	Clara G Ferguson	Harold Faith	Julian James	Jim Harris	Pat Baker
Grady (Cairo)† (20)	912 377-1512	John P Bell	Wm E Barrineaum	Bonnie H Maxwell	....	....	....	Gerald D Thomas
Greene (Greensboro) (11)	404 453-7716	Harvey Higdon	....	Gretchen Ott	....	....	Lee Parker	James Finch Jr
Gwinnett (Lawrenceville) (167)	404 962-1400	(not reporting)						
Habersham (Clarkesville) (25)	404 754-6270	Hebron Lovell	A Lloyd Wagnon	Ruby Fulbright	Ruby Fulbright	....	L G Hicks	Robert F Pitts
Hall (Gainesville)*† (76)	404 536-6681	Henry O Ward	Michael G Bryant	Sylvia G Cooper	Arlin W Pitts	James Shuler	....	Richard V Mecum
Hancock (Sparta)† (9)	404 444-5746	George Lott	Johnny Warren	Mamie D Smith	Sammy Warren	....	Hortonse Sigma	J T Walton
Haralson (Buchanan) (18)	404 646-5528	Robert E Richie	....	Louise Nix	George Kimball	....	George Hagood	Scott W Roberts
Harris (Hamilton) (15)	404 628-4958	Raymond E Grant	P Richard Ellis	Marian T Young	....	....	Ray King	John H Adams
Hart (Hartwell) (19)	404 376-2531	(not reporting)						
Heard (Franklin) (7)	404 675-3821	Steve Lipford	....	Barbara Rivers	Barbara Rivers	Samuel G Noles	Fred Harcrow	Doyle Scott
Henry (McDonough)* (36)	404 957-1538	Edward H Whiddon	Ron H Rabun	Beverly P McLeod	Jason Patrick	....	Ned Clarke	Steve Elkins
Houston (Warner Robins)† (78)	912 922-4471	Houston Porter Jr	J P Goodwin Jr	J P Goodwin Jr	Sandi Stalnaker	....	Jim Harden	Cullen Talton
Irwin (Ocilla) (9)	912 468-9441	J C Harper	....	Sue McClelland	....	....	....	Leonard Pope
Jackson (Jefferson)† (25)	404 367-9838	Henry D Robinson	Henry D Robinson	Mrs Dean Wilbanks	Mrs Dean Wilbanks	....	....	Neal Ward
Jasper (Monticello) (8)	404 468-6645	J Frank Atkins Jr	....	Betty C Miller	....	....	Sarah R Deleza RN	Jack Bailey
Jeff Davis (Hazlehurst) (11)	912 375-4263	Dan Mims	Lonnie V Roberts	Lonnie V Roberts	Lonnie V Roberts	Garner L Graham	....	Mark Hall
Jefferson (Louisville)† (18)	912 625-3332	T E Buchanan	....	Lucy S Williamson	Lucy S Williamson	....	Jewel Lamb	Zollie R Compton
Jenkins (Millen) (9)	912 982-2563	Charles F Bragg	....	D P Long Jr	....	....	Royce Taylor	L C William Jr
Johnson (Wrightsville) (9)	912 864-3484	(not reporting)						
Jones (Gray)† (17)	912 986-6405	Sterling Sumner	....	Starr Hudson	....	....	Victor Brown	Robert N Reece
Lamar (Barnesville) (12)	404 358-3624	Warren Bush	Robert Zellner	Robert Zellner	Robert Zellner	....	....	Frank Monaghan
Lanier (Lakeland)† (6)	912 482-2088	J L Gaskins Jr	....	Bonnie Ganas	....	....	....	James E Watson
Laurens (Dublin) (37)	912 272-4755	Mike Wolfe	Sara M Neal	Sara M Neal	Sara M Neal	....	....	Ronnie Rogers
Lee (Leesburg)† (12)	912 759-6875	A M Bruner	....	T P Tharp	T P Tharp	J R Littlefield	....	E J Bowyer
Liberty (Hinesville) (38)	912 876-2164	James M Floyd	Michael J Stewart	....	Michael J Stewart	....	Dr Whit Fraser	Robert V Sikes
Lincoln (Lincolnton)† (7)	404 359-4444	Walker T Norman	Bruce C Beggs	Linda B Penland	J Vincent Hogan	....	Frances Mims	B C Danner
Long (Ludowici) (5)	912 545-2123	(not reporting)						
Lowndes (Valdosta)* (68)	912 333-5116	Fred DeLoach Jr	Buford W McRae	Inez Pendleton	....	Earl Tyre	Lynne Feldman	Robert Carter
Lumpkin (Dahlonega) (11)	404 864-3736	(not reporting)						
Macon (Oglethorpe)† (14)	912 472-7021	Neal Bentley	....	Roselyn Starling	Roselyn Starling	....	....	Charles Cannon
Madison (Danielsville) (18)	404 795-3351	Vincent J Hix	....	Carolyn K Bagwell	....	Troy Adams	Tom Campbell	Jack D Fortson
Marion (Buena Vista) (5)	912 649-2603	(not reporting)						
McDuffie (Thomson) (19)	404 595-3982	Joyce R Blevins	....	Joyce R Blevins	Joyce R Blevins	....	John Tebeau	William B Swan
McIntosh (Darien) (8)	912 437-6671	R D Gardner	....	Maude Thagard	....	....	Warren Rasmussen	Lamar Echols
Meriwether (Greenville) (21)	404 672-4416	Grady Bradshaw Sr	Daniel J Moniz	Debbie S Flournoy	....	Fred W Smith	Henry J Barnes	Dan A Branch
Miller (Colquitt) (7)	912 758-2731	Frankie Phillips	....	Virginia Phillips	....	Horace Lovering	Maggie R Bell	C C Phillips
Mitchell (Camilla) (21)	912 336-5102	(not reporting)						
Monroe (Forsyth)† (15)	912 993-1029	Robt M Williams	....	Richard E Davis	Dell A Darden	Brack L Goolsby	Louis Hughes	John C Bittick
Montgomery (Mount Vernon) (7)	912 583-4401	(not reporting)						
Morgan (Madison) (12)	404 342-0725	William B Cochran	....	Doris J Harris	....	Bill Ponder	....	Henry Burge
Murray (Chatsworth)† (20)	404 695-2413	Kirby Patterson	....	Joyce Jones	....	J L Hufstetler	Mike Kelley	William Hansird
Newton (Covington)† (34)	404 786-2686	Roy L Varner	....	A T Stubbs	J S Brooks	....	....	Gerald Malcom
Oconee (Watkinsville) (12)	404 769-5120	Choyce A Johnson	....	Lourine Morrison	Reba Hammond	....	Jimmy Thumond	Charles Holcomb
Oglethorpe (Lexington)† (9)	404 743-5270	J W Griffith	....	Judy H Paul	....	....	Jane Ridgeway	Gene Smith
Paulding (Dallas) (26)	404 445-6668	(not reporting)						
Peach (Fort Valley) (19)	912 825-2535	H W Peavy Jr	Thomas J Franklin	Thomas J Franklin	Thos J Franklin	Jerry C Bryan	....	Johnnie V Becham
Pickens (Jasper)† (12)	404 692-2121	Fred K Stancil	Mamie L Forrester	Sharon D Troglin	....	Billy J Turner	Ruth Hinton	Billy P Wofford
Pierce (Blackshear) (12)	912 449-6648	Forrest W Sweat	....	Marlene T Dowling	....	....	....	Noah Strickland
Pike (Zebulon)† (9)	404 567-3406	Joanna G Angle	James J Germany	James J Germany	....	....	Rodney Hilley	William Riggins
Polk (Cedartown)† (32)	404 748-1305	Charles Kinney	J K McElwee	Jerry McDowell	....	....	....	Seals Swafford
Pulaski (Hawkinsville) (9)	912 783-1911	(not reporting)						
Putnam (Eatonton) (10)	404 485-4501	(not reporting)						
Quitman (Georgetown) (2)	912 334-4565	H L Balkcom Jr	....	Blanche W Jones	Kathryn B Rogers	....	Kathryn A Gary	I L Balkcom III
Rabun (Clayton) (10)	404 782-5271	Virgil P Ledford	....	Marilyn Rogers	....	....	....	Chester J York
Randolph (Cuthbert)† (10)	912 732-6440	R W Moore	....	Debbie L Devane	Debbie L Devane	....	....	T E Faircloth
Richmond (Augusta)§ (182)	404 828-6700	Jack Miles	Dayton Sherrouse	Dayton Sherrouse	Al Slavens	Ray Bailey	Maurice Patton	Charles Webster
Rockdale (Conyers)† (37)	404 922-7750	Charles Smith Jr	....	....	Sarah R Alexander	....	....	Victor B Davis
Schley (Ellaville) (3)	912 937-2101	(not reporting)						
Screven (Sylvania) (14)	912 564-7535	L C Oliver	J E Schotta Sr	Patsy B Moore	Patsy B Moore	....	William Pace	George F Bazemore
Seminole (Donalsonville) (9)	912 524-2878	Jack Brannon	....	Louise Alday	Eunyce M Lee	Earl Thursby	....	Jerry Godby

Directory 1/9 continued — COUNTY OFFICIALS IN ALL U.S. COUNTIES

County, county seat, 1980 population (000 omitted),	County telephone number	Board chairman	Appointed administrator	Clerk to the governing board	Chief financial officer	County engineer	County health officer	Chief law enforcement official
GEORGIA (159) continued								
Spalding (Griffin)§ (48)	404 228-9900	Ruth G Martin	Wayne Johnson	Maureen C Jackson	Michael E Smith	....	V Williams MD	James C Freeman
Stephens (Toccoa) (22)	404 886-9491	Evatt Thomason	....	Nancy Downs	....	....	Fred Williams	Don Shirley
Stewart (Lumpkin) (6)	912 838-6769	Perry T Usher	....	Rosemary Barbaree	....	....	....	Albert G Grimes
Sumter (Americus)† (29)	912 924-3090	W W Ferguson	....	Barbara McCarty	Barbara McCarty	....	....	Randy Howard
Talbot (Talbotton) (7)	404 665-3220	F Montgomery	....	Dorothy Self	....	....	Cindy Taylor	John Johnson
Taliaferro (Crawfordville) (2)	404 456-2494	Henry G Moore Jr	....	Josie Bird	....	....	....	Dorsey C Combs
Tattnall (Reidsville) (18)	912 557-6716	(not reporting)						
Taylor (Butler) (8)	912 862-3336	Murray Jarrell	....	Debra Bone	....	....	....	Nicholas E Giles
Telfair (McRae)† (11)	912 868-5688	Gene M Williams	....	Jo Anne Teate	....	....	....	Jack M Walker
Terrell (Dawson) (12)	912 995-2631	(not reporting)						
Thomas (Thomasville)* (38)	912 226-0516	Joe D Fallin	....	Ruth M Jones	....	Murray A Maxwell	....	R Carlton Powell
Tift (Tifton)† (33)	912 382-5255	Charles Kent	....	Imogene Register	....	Abel Walton	....	Edd Walker
Toombs (Lyons)† (23)	912 526-3311	Mell Taylor	....	Chris Humphrey	Chris Humphrey	....	Don Curry	Charles Durst
Towns (Hiawassee) (6)	404 896-3633	Truman Barrett	....	Betty Stroud	Tom Flanagan	....	....	Rudy Roach
Treutlen (Soperton)† (6)	912 529-3664	Jim L Gillis Jr	....	Sylvia Norris	Charles Carr	....	....	Joe C Mullis
Troup (La Grange)* (50)	404 882-1478	V Hawley Smith	Jack M Crook	Lurie R Cook	Jack N Crook	George Brand	Gus Morgan	Elton Jones
Turner (Ashburn) (10)	912 567-2041	Lester Adkison	Mary J Wynn	Mary J Wynn	Mary J Wynn	....	Karlene Martenn	Lamar Whiddon
Twiggs (Jeffersonville) (9)	912 945-3350	Millard Hendricks	Faye S Allen	Carmen M Stark	....	....	Christy L Sims	W E Hamrick
Union (Blairsville)† (9)	404 745-2654	Wayne E Colwell	....	Janie M Beavers	Bill J Dyer	....	....	Harlan Duncan
Upson (Thomaston) (26)	404 647-7012	J Irvin Hendricks	....	Gertrude L Taylor	....	....	....	Merrill Greathous
Walker (La Fayette)† (56)	404 638-1437	Roy E Parrish Jr	Bebe Heiskell	Faye W Shankles	Faye W Shankles	....	....	Ralph Jones
Walton (Monroe) (31)	404 267-7531	B R Anderson	Mearon Queen	Vickie M Gasaway	....	Richard D Brown	....	Franklin Thornton
Ware (Waycross) (37)	912 283-4904	(not reporting)						
Warren (Warrenton)† (7)	404 465-2171	Allen S May	....	Pauline Van Dyke	Geo C Garrett	....	Patsy Reese	R Dye
Washington (Sandersville) (19)	912 552-3186	(not reporting)						
Wayne (Jesup)* (21)	912 427-3789	John E Tyre	....	Nancy Jones	....	....	....	Jim Poindexter
Webster (Preston) (2)	912 828-5775	Lucius Black	....	Vivian Bankston	Peggy Kennedy	....	....	George Goare
Wheeler (Alamo) (5)	912 568-7137	(not reporting)						
White (Cleveland)† (10)	404 865-2235	M Lanier Chambers	....	Lois P Nix	....	....	Dorothy J Payne	Frank Baker
Whitfield (Dalton) (66)	404 278-2494	(not reporting)						
Wilcox (Abbeville)† (8)	912 467-2737	M D Brown	....	Gwen Gibbs	....	....	....	C E Bloodsworth
Wilkes (Washington) (11)	404 678-2511	Guy W Bufford Jr	....	David L Tyler	Guy W Bufford Jr	Guy W Bufford Jr	Mildred Hackney	Cecil A Moore
Wilkinson (Irwinton) (10)	912 946-2215	(not reporting)						
Worth (Sylvester) (18)	912 776-3456	W W Mims	....	Nell Ford	....	....	Fred L McLean MD	B L Pritchard
HAWAII (4)								
Hawaii (Hilo) (92)	808 961-8211	Megumi Kon	Barney Menor	Rudolph Legaspi	Stanley Nakamae	Edward Harada	Ben Hur MD	Guy Paul
Honolulu C (763)	808 523-4111	Patsy T Mink	Andrew I T Chang	Raymond K Pua	Peter D Leong	Michael J Chun	Anna Maria Brault	Douglas G Gibb
Kauai (Lihue)† (39)	808 245-3385	Tony T Kunimra	Joshua Hew	Jerome Hew	Cecelia Ramones	Larry Kitamura	....	Roy Hiram
Maui (Wailuku)† (71)	808 244-7711	Goro Hokama	Howard K Nakamura	James Ushijima	Henry Lav	Ralph Hayashi	....	Joseph Cravalho
IDAHO (44)								
Ada (Boise)† (173)	208 383-4400	Bill Gratton	....	John Bastida	Marjorie Jonasson	David Collins	Bob Des Aulniers	Chuck Palmer
Adams (Council) (3)	208 253-4561	C Keppinger	....	Michael Fisk	Nancy Armitage	Ronald Blakley	Clare Howland	Jim Hileman
Bannock (Pocatello) (65)	208 236-7012	Carolyn Meline	....	Larry W Ghan	Vivian Crozier	Jay Nelson	Jack Jelke	Shirley Gameson
Bear Lake (Paris) (7)	208 945-2212	George M Hulme	....	Joan P Eborn	Elaine Webb	Montain Kunz	George Spinner	Randall White
Benewah (St. Maries) (8)	208 245-3212	Jack A Buell	....	Beverly R Vallard	Juanita Lundt	....	....	Robert Kirts
Bingham (Blackfoot)† (36)	208 785-5005	W Christensen	....	Jean Esplin	Melva Clark	Robert Butler	....	Mike M Shiosaki
Blaine (Hailey) (10)	208 788-4290	Rupert House	....	Marie Ivie	Marilyn Lanier	James Koonce	Dave Dingman	Dennis Haynes
Boise (Idaho City) (3)	208 392-4431	J E Yensen	Arlene C Kolar	Arlene C Kolar	Arlene C Kolar	....	Martin O Jones	Lynn D Bowerman
Bonner (Sandpoint)† (24)	208 263-6841	Harold Anselmo	....	Clifford D Chapin	Alice M Nelson	Louis Vermeer	Sherry Dodson	Rocky Eveland
Bonneville (Idaho Falls) (66)	208 529-1100	Clyde Burtenshaw	....	L Ronald Longmore	Mable Bingham	Robert G Gray	Jeanine Doney	Richard Ackerman
Boundary (Bonners Ferry) (7)	208 267-2242	Bill Currie	....	Norma J Estep	Irma Merrifield	Charles Morgen	Maryjean Leach RN	Ronald Smith
Butte (Arco) (3)	208 527-3021	James O Andreason	....	Judith R Bailey	....	....	Lois Techick	Darrell G Richard
Camas (Fairfield) (1)	208 764-2242	(not reporting)						
Canyon (Caldwell)† (84)	208 454-7300	Carlos Bledsoe	....	Bill A Staker	Bill A Staker	....	Dick Adams	John D Prescott
Caribou (Soda Springs) (9)	208 547-4342	(not reporting)						
Cassia (Burley) (19)	208 678-7302	J Weldon Beck	Timothy A Hurst	Frank B Kearns	Shirley Povlsen	....	Debra Hieb	Ray G Mitchell
Clark (Dubois) (1)	208 374-5304	(not reporting)						
Clearwater (Orofino) (10)	208 476-3615	Donald Ponozzo	....	Allen Medalen	Mary J Wilmarth	William Bird	Robert Weddell	Nick Albers
Custer (Challis) (3)	208 879-2360	Frank Maraffio	....	Ethel M Peck	Judi Leuzinger	Charlie Burns	....	H Ken Bowers
Elmore (Mountain Home) (22)	208 587-7272	John W Shrum	....	Ramona E Yrazabal	....	....	Bob Fox	Robert W Mendiola
Franklin (Preston) (9)	208 852-1090	Robert M Hull	....	Michael D Kunz	....	....	....	Eudean H Gunnell
Fremont (St. Anthony) (11)	208 624-7332	(not reporting)						
Gem (Emmett)† (12)	208 365-4561	Tom Pasley	....	Thelma R Koldziej	Edith Sawyer	Ron Blakley	....	Wm C McConnel
Gooding (Gooding) (12)	208 934-4841	Will H Thomas	....	Margaret Clements	Doris O Robertson	Gerald Martens	Kathryn Goodwin	Robert Aja
Idaho (Grangeville) (15)	208 983-2751	Douglas Higgins	....	Joyce C Hart	Clarice Schmidt	Carl Edwards	....	Rodger Laughlin
Jefferson (Rigby)† (15)	208 745-7756	Clyde Terry	....	Robert J Barnes	Margaret Treasure	....	....	Garth Gunderson
Jerome (Jerome) (15)	208 324-8811	Carl Butler	....	Cheryl Watts	Elsie Childers	....	Eileen Weisman	Elza Hall
Kootenai (Coeur d'Alene) (60)	208 664-8291	Glenn R Jackson	....	Carol Deitz	Maxine McKinzie	John Carpita	Larry Belmont	Floyd E Stalder
Latah (Moscow)† (29)	208 882-8580	Jay A Nelson	....	Joan Bauer	Norma Slade	....	Rich Gabriel	Laune Odenberg
Lemhi (Salmon) (7)	208,756-2815	Louie Demick	....	Alberta Wiederric	Shirley R Hoy	....	....	William N Baker
Lewis (Nezperce) (4)	208 937-2261	(not reporting)						
Lincoln (Shoshone) (3)	208 886-7641	Douglas Hansen	....	Dana Sturgeon	Harriett Davidson	....	....	Darwin Mills
Madison (Rexburg)† (19)	208 356-3662	Dell Klingler	....	Nellis H Garner	Jayne R Green	....	....	Lionel V Koon
Minidoka (Rupert) (20)	208 436-9331	Lyle Barton	....	Duane Smith	Phyllis Norby	....	Sandra Stoller	Ray Jarvis
Nez Perce (Lewiston) (33)	208 799-3000	Robert Huddleston	....	James E Lloyd	Paulene Bennet	....	....	Ron Koeper
Oneida (Malad City)† (3)	208 766-4116	Conrad Alder	....	Joyce Freidenberg	Ila May Williams	....	....	Kenneth Wharthon
Owyhee (Murphy)† (8)	208 495-2421	Donald L Davis	....	Barbara Jayo	Joan Bachman	....	....	Tim Nettleton
Payette (Payette)† (16)	208 642-9371	Arnold Howard	Arnold Howard	Eula Cheese	Betty Adler	....	....	Robert Barowsky
Power (American Falls) (7)	208 226-2522	Seth Neibaur	....	Marjorie Glascock	Melba J Ferguson	Rick Rowe	....	Howard A Sprague
Shoshone (Wallace) (19)	208 752-3331	F W Cantamessa	....	Irene Nonini	Tammy House	Richard Gatten	Sharon Conners	Frank Crnkovich
Teton (Driggs) (3)	208 354-2905	(not reporting)						
Twin Falls (Twin Falls) (53)	208 734-3300	Ann S Cover	....	Richard A Pence	Juanita Stettler	....	....	James Munn
Valley (Cascade) (6)	208 382-4297	Adolf Heinrich	....	John W Crutcher	Carmen M Irwin	Les Ankenman	....	M Blair Shepherd
Washington (Weiser) (9)	208 549-2092	Jack Gardner	....	Mary Kautz	Irene E Goins	....	....	James R Johnston
ILLINOIS (102)								
Adams (Quincy) (72)	217 223-6300	(not reporting)						

Directory 1/9 continued — COUNTY OFFICIALS IN ALL U.S. COUNTIES

County, county seat, 1980 population (000 omitted),	County telephone number	Board chairman	Appointed administrator	Clerk to the governing board	Chief financial officer	County engineer	County health officer	Chief law enforcement official
ILLINOIS (102) continued								
Alexander (Cairo) (12)	618 734-3947	(not reporting)						
Bond (Greenville) (16)	618 664-1966	Edwin Davis	....	Eldon Roe	William E Johnson	....	James Tucker	Bill Willeford
Boone (Belvidere) (29)	815 544-3103	Leroy Schroeder	Bradford Townsend	D Weitemeyer	E Gunderson	James Gang	Carol Klint	Duane Wirth
Brown (Mount Sterling) (5)	217 773-3421	(not reporting)						
Bureau (Princeton)† (39)	815 875-2014	George E Gonigam	....	Tom Velon	....	David S Sullivan	....	Melvin L Hult
Calhoun (Hardin)† (6)	618 576-2351	Jerome Sibley	....	Orville H Johnes	Kenneth Taviner	Paul W Rust	Margaret Hillen	Richard C Meyer
Carroll (Mount Carroll)† (19)	815 244-9171	Donald G Swanson	....	Sandra K Brown	Doris G Kessler	Wm N Pottorff	....	Jimmy A Thulen
Cass (Virginia)† (15)	217 452-7217	Raymond Robinson	....	George J Petefish	Michael Barnett	Robert F Phelps	Carol Siltman	Carl Wubker
Champaign (Urbana) (168)	217 384-3772	J Wallace Rayburn	....	Dennis Bing	Roger Little	Glen Cougil	....	Joseph Brown
Christian (Taylorville) (36)	217 824-4969	(not reporting)						
Clark (Marshall)† (17)	217 826-8311	John L Hammond	....	Lester E Letteral	Carol A Cornwell	....	....	W Dan Crumrin
Clay (Louisville) (15)	618 665-3626	(not reporting)						
Clinton (Carlyle) (33)	618 594-2464	Robert Cohlmeyer	....	Alvin P Erlinger	Harold H Kueper	Ronald C Mitchell	Nancy C Huels	Gerald H Dall
Coles (Charleston) (53)	217 348-0501	Eugene Bauer	....	Jackie Bacon	Jackie Record	....	Fred Edgar	Charles Lister
Cook (Chicago) (5253)	312 443-5500	George W Dunne	William M Doyle	Stanley T Kusper	Edward J Rosewell	Richard Golterman	Karen L Scott MD	Richard J Elrod
Crawford (Robinson)† (21)	618 546-1212	Joe Bliss	....	Ruth Bradbury	Elaine Miller	David V Johnson	....	Richard Hunnicutt
Cumberland (Toledo) (11)	217 849-2631	Michael D Walk	....	John E Saathoff	Ralph R White	E J Huffington	Winona Saathoff	Luke F Holsapple
De Kalb (Sycamore) (75)	815 895-9161	Donald W Lundeen	Ray Bockman	Terry Desmond	Wesley Yeager	....	Richard Morgan	Wilbur B Scott
De Witt (Clinton) (18)	217 935-2119	Charles L Wilson	....	Joye Floyd	....	Philip Koeberlien	....	Donald E Massey
Douglas (Tuscola) (20)	217 253-2411	Virgil L Luth	....	Jack A Allen	Helen R Ziegler	....	Calvin Locker	Charles Conner
Du Page (Wheaton) (658)	312 682-7000	Jack T Knuepfer	Michael Linz	Jay C Bennett	John L Novak	Ron Dold	James Paulissen	Richard P Doria
Edgar (Paris) (22)	217 465-4151	James B Sullivan	....	Shirley Eldredge	Martha Reeley	Jack O Leathers	....	Jack Hood
Edwards (Albion) (8)	618 445-2115	(not reporting)						
Effingham (Effingham) (31)	217 342-4990	Ernest Garbe	....	Robert Behrman	Alma Croft	Jack Johnson	Ted Crump	Kenneth Moore
Fayette (Vandalia) (22)	618 283-0394	Glenn R Bunyard	....	Isabelle B Brandt	David C Marty	Charles Bowles	Cara Kelly	Leonard E Kelly
Ford (Paxton) (15)	217 379-2721	Donald O Nelson	....	Robert N Thompson	Barbara L Hoover	John E Mitchell	John A Pichering	Lloyd A Falck
Franklin (Benton) (43)	618 438-3221	(not reporting)						
Fulton (Lewistown) (44)	309 547-3041	Melba Ripper	....	Randal L Rumler	Bernard J Oaks	Robert Pedigo	Robert Klutts	Walter Fleisher
Gallatin (Shawneetown) (8)	618 269-3025	(not reporting)						
Greene (Carrollton) (17)	217 942-5443	Charles K Barnett	....	Eunice B Batty	Benjamin Goode	Gilbert Meyer	Kevin Hutchison	Francis Neubauer
Grundy (Morris) (31)	815 942-0335	(not reporting)						
Hamilton (McLeansboro) (9)	618 643-2721	Donald J Morris	....	Lovella Craddock	Keith Webb	....	Evelyn Barker	William Warren
Hancock (Carthage) (24)	217 357-3911	(not reporting)						
Hardin (Elizabethtown) (5)	618 287-2251	Harold Dutton	....	Sue McMaster	David M Humphrey	Frank Conci	....	Lowell D Lasater
Henderson (Oquawka) (9)	309 867-2911	John Weir	....	Eula M Rogers	Eileen Nolan	....	Joan Ray	Daryl Thompson
Henry (Cambridge) (58)	309 937-5192	Lauren Truninger	Richard Erickson	Dennis L Anderson	G Herbert Johnson	Nelson Taber	Louise Tharp	Gilbert Cady
Iroquois (Watseka) (33)	815 432-4911	Homer H Beall Jr	....	John M Kuntz	Shelby J Townsend	Bill Guill	John Pickering	Joe Mathy
Jackson (Murphysboro) (62)	618 684-2151	Eugene Chambers	....	Robert B Harrell	Shirley Booker	William Munson	F Siebenman Jr	William Kilquist
Jasper (Newton)† (11)	618 783-3124	Lowell E Kepley	....	Alma Lefever	Ilene Allison	Gary Maxwell	Mary Finley	Bob Finn
Jefferson (Mount Vernon) (36)	618 242-2590	J Eugene Wells	....	Frank A Wilson	Gaylord B Harlan	....	....	Robert Pitchford
Jersey (Jerseyville) (21)	618 498-5571	J Richard Allen	....	Linda J Crotchett	J Richard Allen	Jim Hill	Nola Kramer RN	Frank Yocom
Jo Daviess (Galena) (24)	815 777-0161	Thomas J Cullen	....	Ralph Schoenfeld	W C Burroughs	Gregory Stauder	Peggy Jackson	Marlo A Specht
Johnson (Vienna) (10)	618 658-3611	G W Phillips	....	Cletis Morris	Claude Harper	Jesse Johns	....	Elry Faulkner
Kane (Geneva) (278)	312 232-3400	Frank R Miller	....	David Pierce	Donald L Clute	....	....	George Kramer
Kankakee (Kankakee) (103)	815 937-2990	Roy M West	....	Albert Keller	John Novack	James Piekarczyk	....	William Sroggins
Kendall (Yorkville) (37)	312 553-7573	Frank Coffman	....	Jean P Brady	Elaine Mitchell	Joseph Gaesser	Ruth Ann Little	Charles McDonald
Knox (Galesburg) (62)	309 343-3121	Donald L Moffitt	....	Yvonne Tabb	Marian Fennig	Francis E Griffin	....	Donald Hulick
La Salle (Ottawa) (109)	815 434-8242	Joseph E Hettel	....	Tom Walsh	Roy Rathbun	....	....	Pete Wahl
Lake (Waukegan) (440)	312 689-6600	Glenn E Miller	Dwight A Magalis	Linda Ianuzi Hess	Jack Anderson	Marty Buehler	Steven Potsic MD	Robert Babcox
Lawrence (Lawrenceville)† (18)	618 943-2346	Harold Benson	....	Patricia O Groves	Larry Umfleet	R Trowbridge	Maxine Jackman	Eddie Ryan
Lee (Dixon) (36)	815 288-3309	Graham Huffman	....	Rosemary Emmert	Sharon Thompson	Ronald Brandau	Donna May	Raymond Nehring
Livingston (Pontiac) (41)	815 844-5166	Elton H Sancken	....	Arnold E Natzke	Sylvia L Bashore	Jon A Bourne	Gladys Kohrt	Robert W Jones
Logan (Lincoln) (32)	217 732-4148	Wayne A Conrady	....	Weldon B Frantz	....	Ronald Fox	Karen Rosenburg	Robert Patterson
Macon (Decatur) (131)	217 424-1470	Charles Bud Riley	....	William M Tangney	Jim O Edgcomb	Donald R Johnson	Robert Shrout	Stephen D Fisher
Macoupin (Carlinville) (49)	217 854-3214	George Caveny	....	John J Saracco	Michael A Zippay	Thomas D Gazda	June Weise	Richard Zarr
Madison (Edwardsville)† (248)	618 692-4341	Nelson Hagnauer	Mary Kane	Evelyn Bowles	Michael Henkhaus	David Dietzel	....	Emil Toffant
Marion (Salem)† (44)	618 548-3400	James E Sager	....	Ralph Johnnie	Sherman Doolen	Ralph Hilmes	Nellie Linder	Charles R Sanders
Marshall (Lacon) (14)	309 246-6325	James E Quinn	....	Marjorie Rossetti	....	Emil F Cramer	Beverly DeRubeis	James E Frawley
Mason (Havana) (19)	309 543-6661	(not reporting)						
Massac (Metropolis) (15)	618 524-5213	Eddie Cockrel	....	Dorothy S Gragg	Clinton English	....	....	Ronald Tucker
McDonough (Macomb) (37)	309 837-2308	Albert Lucas	....	Delmer Deems	Patricia Waggoner	....	Randall Haut	John Blevins
McHenry (Woodstock) (148)	815 338-2040	(not reporting)						
McLean (Bloomington)§ (119)	309 827-5311	Roscoe McPheren	B E Peterson	Jeanette Barret	James Boylan	H Bekermeier	Ben Boyd	Steven Brienen
Menard (Petersburg) (12)	217 632-2415	Merle Kirby	....	James C Combs	Jean Whitehurst	....	Charles Mertz	Ronald Phillips
Mercer (Aledo) (19)	309 582-7021	Fred W Allen	....	Lorena R Johnson	Verla D Thompson	Glenn D Worner	Linda Wilson	Marvin Thirtyacre
Monroe (Waterloo) (20)	618 939-8681	(not reporting)						
Montgomery (Hillsboro)† (32)	217 532-2552	Edmund F Spinner	....	Clinton F Kimbro	Ron Jenkins	Anthony Georgeff	Tom Larson	James Moore
Morgan (Jacksonville) (38)	217 245-4619	Donald H Blimling	Danny R Little	Barbara J Gross	Robert Hall	Calvin Hance	William Meyer	Henry G Jackson
Moultrie (Sullivan) (15)	217 728-4389	Don Harchous	....	Richard Purdeu	Johna Sims	Ben McRill	Joanna Cole	Russell Moore
Ogle (Oregon) (46)	815 732-3201	Robert Gingerich	....	Margaret Fridley	Chrissie E Martin	....	Michael Williams	Gerald D Brooks
Peoria (Peoria)§ (200)	309 672-6056	Gary F Stella	David J Krings	Mary Harkrader	Edward T O'Connor	Fred Rogers	Thomas Jackamore	George Shadid
Perry (Pinckneyville) (22)	618 357-5116	Gerald Hawkins	....	Judy Rennison	Frank Mangin	Roy Smith	....	Jerry Woolsey
Piatt (Monticello) (17)	217 762-9487	(not reporting)						
Pike (Pittsfield) (19)	217 285-6812	Lester L Vincent	....	Carrol K Hoover	Robert M Capps	....	Martha Lowry	Donald N Snyder
Pope (Golconda) (4)	618 683-8101	Johnny Climer	....	Twila G Thomas	Ann Ferrell	Frank Conci	....	Rodney J Brenner
Pulaski (Mound City) (9)	618 748-9360	Roy W Walls	....	Rosalie Basham	Edna Kerr	Joe O Plemon	....	Russell E Dakin
Putnam (Hennepin)† (6)	815 925-7129	John Petersen	....	Joseph R Panier	Chas H Kassabaum	J William Shafer	Donald Gallagher	Donald G Cioni
Randolph (Chester) (36)	618 826-2510	(not reporting)						
Richland (Olney)† (18)	618 392-3111	K G Ernst	....	Wayne D Seely	Virgle L Michels	....	Carolyn Hartrich	Joseph F Willis
Rock Island (Rock Island) (166)	309 786-4451	Paul E Mulcahey	....	John A Gianulis	Lester R Carlson	Gary Lange	Clayton C Pape	Gordon A Powell
Saline (Harrisburg)† (27)	618 252-6905	Bill Endsley Jr	....	David D Phelps	Clifton Jones	Rob Roy Brown	....	George Henley
Sangamon (Springfield)† (176)	217 753-6600	Richard G Austin	....	Gary Tumulty	Fred H Tomlin	John McCree	Frank Pickett	James Purdon
Schuyler (Rushville) (8)	217 322-4734	(not reporting)						
Scott (Winchester) (6)	217 742-3178	Richard Hoots	....	Loreita Ballard	Jackie Barber	Richard Brown	....	Roland L Wallis
Shelby (Shelbyville) (24)	217 774-4421	Marvin Jordan	....	Dwight Campbell	Barney R Melvin	Star Rheynard	Joel Clark	Robert A Collins
St. Clair (Belleville) (265)	618 277-6600	(not reporting)						
Stark (Toulon) (7)	309 286-5911	Melvin L Stahl	....	Patricia Plotner	Paula J Becket	Ronald D Wallace	Mary Ryan	Lonny G Dennison
Stephenson (Freeport) (50)	815 235-8289	Donald Petticoff	....	Dean W Amendt	Edith M Dadez	Douglas G Happ	F Dean Danner Jr	Glenn T Oefelein

Directory 1/9 continued — COUNTY OFFICIALS IN ALL U.S. COUNTIES

County, county seat, 1980 population (000 omitted),	County telephone number	Board chairman	Appointed administrator	Clerk to the governing board	Chief financial officer	County engineer	County health officer	Chief law enforcement official
ILLINOIS (102) continued								
Tazewell (Pekin)† (132)	309 347-6551	Dan Bell	Harold Kahn	Duane Gray	Russell Strauman	Terry Gardner	Gordon Poquette	James Donahue
Union (Jonesboro) (17)	618 833-5711	(not reporting)						
Vermilion (Danville) (95)	217 442-3700	Charles E Beckner	....	....	Robert Jones	Jesse Irvin	Steve Laker	Gene Hughes
Wabash (Mount Carmel)† (14)	618 262-4561	W Karl Herrick	....	Joan E Wolfe	Don L Birley	....	Michael Henry	Randy Grounds
Warren (Monmouth) (22)	309 734-8529	(not reporting)						
Washington (Nashville) (15)	618 327-8314	Lester D Campbell	....	Virgil May	William H Windler	William Jack	....	Albert Dinkelman
Wayne (Fairfield) (18)	618 842-5182	(not reporting)						
White (Carmi) (18)	618 382-7211	(not reporting)						
Whiteside (Morrison)† (66)	815 772-7201	Dean L Dahlgren	....	Dan Heusinkveld	Janet Buikema	James Schoenhard	Raymond Empereur	L L Kimmel
Will (Joliet)† (324)	815 727-8413	....	W Barry Baker	....	....	....	....	....
Williamson (Marion) (57)	618 997-1301	(not reporting)						
Winnebago (Rockford)§ (251)	815 987-2590	Pat L Scott	John Schoeberlein	Paul P Gill	Douglas R Aurand	....	Joseph Orthoefer	Donald Gasparini
Woodford (Eureka)† (33)	302 467-2822	Lawrence Guard	....	Cecil W Nohl	Pat Eckhoff	Robert Cherveny	....	Quentin J Durst
INDIANA (92)								
Adams (Decatur) (30)	219 724-2600	Loren D Caffee	....	Fred R Huppert	Galen A Sprunger	....	Terry R Smith	Thomas K Coolman
Allen (Fort Wayne) (294)	219 428-7555	Richard Regedanz	Sandra R Wolfe	Gloria Goeglein	Linda Bloom	Howard Biggs	Jane Irmscher MD	Daniel Figel
Bartholomew (Columbus)† (65)	812 372-6411	Marvin Finke	....	Betty Essex	Sheila Durham	Ronald May	Walter Dearmitt	Jimmie McKinney
Benton (Fowler) (10)	317 884-1687	James Gilbert	Linda Goodson	Irene Swartz	James McGrath	....	A L Coddens	James Patton
Blackford (Hartford City) (16)	317 348-1620	Donald Beal	...	Carolyn Gordon	Judith H Townsend	....	George D Parks	Richard Pickering
Boone (Lebanon) (36)	317 482-2940	Robert E Guernsey	...	Barbara Gray	Carol J Gorham	....	L S Bailey	Ern K Hudson
Brown (Nashville)† (12)	812 988-2788	Harold Seltz	...	....	Evon Weaver	Webber Hardin	Robert Seibel	Rex Kritzer
Carroll (Delphi) (20)	317 564-3172	Byron J Jervis	....	Lorna E Hicks	Deloris Mullin	Charles Ritzler	T Neal Petry	Don Roth
Cass (Logansport)† (41)	219 722-5050	Joe D Long	Joe D Long	Mary Muehlhausen	Margaret Bechdol	George Van Meter	Fred Hillis	Gene Powlen
Clark (Jeffersonville)† (89)	812 283-4451	Samuel K Gwin	Larry R Dean	John Gellhaus	James L Bottorff	Hyun T Lee	Robt McKechnie	Raymond J Parker
Clay (Brazil)† (25)	812 448-8044	Joseph A Knust	....	Helen Megenhardt	George C Lynch	....	S Rahim Farid MD	Wayne E Lucas
Clinton (Frankfort) (32)	317 654-8529	E Biesecker	....	Paul R Myers	....	....	Milton Erdel	Robert Payne
Crawford (English) (10)	812 338-2565	(not reporting)						
Daviess (Washington) (28)	812 254-1090	Judith Dwyer	....	Ron Frette	Wilbur Wise	Ralph Price	James Rohrer MD	Everett Beasley
De Kalb (Auburn) (34)	219 925-2362	James Herzer	....	Wilma Wilhelm	Kimbeline Folden	....	Mark Souder	Larry Metcalf
Dearborn (Lawrenceburg) (34)	812 537-2151	(not reporting)						
Decatur (Greensburg) (24)	812 663-8223	(not reporting)						
Delaware (Muncie) (129)	317 747-7730	Ron Quakenbush	....	Jack Donati	Lawrence Walsh	Stanley E Hiatt	Clyde Botkin	Gary Carmichael
Dubois (Jasper)† (34)	812 482-6545	....	....	H Hochgesang	Basil Kunkel	....	J P Salb MD	Ambrose Wilz
Elkhart (Goshen)† (137)	219 533-5250	Thomas Romberger	....	Charles R Miller	Wilbur Hostetler	Dale Myers	Stanley Reedy MD	Dick Bowman
Fayette (Connersville) (28)	317 825-1213	Joseph Heeb	....	Rita A Jinks	Jean K Bever	Jerry Gobin	Jack Lockhart	George Zimmerman
Floyd (New Albany) (61)	812 948-5400	V Freiberger	....	Lela L McBarron	Carolyn Eve	Garner D Willey	Everett Bickers	Jerome Schlinder
Fountain (Covington) (19)	317 793-2243	Charles Bowles	....	Debra Jahnke	Kathy Pugh	George Crowder	Herb Lawson	Dale Conrad
Franklin (Brookville) (20)	317 647-4631	Leroy Combs	....	Alberta Sauerland	Mary Lohrey	....	Perry F Seal MD	Donald Helms
Fulton (Rochester) (19)	219 223-2912	Everett Smith	....	Merrill O Kendall	Joan Bunn	....	Joseph Richardson	R A McLochlin
Gibson (Princeton) (33)	812 386-8401	(not reporting)						
Grant (Marion) (81)	317 668-8871	John Comer	....	Ray Hickam	Robert Gordon	....	John W Kennedy	Ronald Mowery
Greene (Bloomfield) (30)	812 384-8532	(not reporting)						
Hamilton (Noblesville)† (82)	317 776-9600	....	....	....	....	Jim Hufford	Jean Perrin MD	Robert Chandler
Hancock (Greenfield) (44)	317 462-1106	Noble N Snodgrass	....	Irene H Kramer	Byron Collier	J Wm Strange	Wm R Rhynearson	Nicholas Gulling
Harrison (Corydon) (27)	812 738-8241	J Frederick Royse	....	Joseph T Mattingl	Cletus Zollman	....	Richard Schroeder	Leonard McAfee
Hendricks (Danville) (70)	317 745-9231	(not reporting)						
Henry (New Castle) (53)	317 529-2800	John McGrady	....	Richard C Bailey	Brenda K Veach	....	Lynn Bowers MD	Paul A Piercy
Howard (Kokomo) (87)	317 456-2215	Dale Fawcett	....	Howard F Helms	Elva Ladow	William Schmidlin	Alan Adler	Earle Howard
Huntington (Huntington) (36)	219 356-0692	Meredith Helms	....	Bonnie S Ostrow	Brema Smith	Richard Thompson	Wallace Schoeff	C Ray Williams
Indianapolis-Marion C (701)	317 236-3200	Wm H Hudnut III	Don McPherson	Beverly Rippy	Fred Armstrong	Jack Irwin	Frank Johnson MD	Joseph McAtee
Jackson (Brownstown) (37)	812 358-4242	(not reporting)						
Jasper (Rensselaer) (26)	219 866-4681	Fred L Boissy Jr	....	Bessie Scheurich	Wilma E Hornbeck	V Christopher	Michael Louck MD	Terry L Gilliland
Jay (Portland)† (23)	219 726-7575	Herbert L Masters	....	Marilyn Coleman	Frances Weesner	Mikel Long	Eugene Gillum	George Meehan
Jefferson (Madison) (30)	812 265-4225	(not reporting)						
Jennings (Vernon) (23)	812 346-2131	Dale Pettit	....	Neal Custer	William Horstman	....	Louis Calli Sr	Richard H Wilson
Johnson (Franklin) (77)	317 736-9090	William A Ray	....	Sally L Higdon	Sally L Higdon	John Meyers	William Province	J Robert Haugh
Knox (Vincennes) (42)	812 882-3944	Gordon Stinebaugh	....	....	Delores Evans	....	Ralph Jacqmain	Fred Huffman
Kosciusko (Warsaw)† (60)	219 267-4444	Charles Lynch	....	....	Vickie Patterson	R Winebrenner	David Haines MD	Al Rovenstine
La Porte (La Porte) (109)	219 326-6808	Kenneth W Swanson	....	Sherry K Waters	Alyce Byrd	James Kiel	Donald Wingstrom	Jan Rose
Lagrange (Lagrange) (26)	219 463-3431	Earnest D Young	....	....	B Schemahorn	John Madden	Allen Martin	Dale Sturtz
Lake (Crown Point) (523)	219 738-2020	N A Spann	Betty A Mucha	Leslie O Pruitt	Irene Holinga	Steve Manich	Pearl Johnson	Rudy Bartolomei
Lawrence (Bedford)† (42)	812 275-3111	Stephen E Jones	....	Bernard M Edwards	Lois M Mitchell	....	Donald M Kerr	John McBride
Madison (Anderson) (139)	317 646-9325	(not reporting)						
Marshall (Plymouth) (39)	219 935-8555	Glenn Overmyer	....	Mary B Haas	Peggy Clevenger	....	J Robertson MD	Richard Tyson
Martin (Shoals) (11)	812 247-3731	John M O'Brien	....	Vincent Williams	Margaret A Smith	....	D R Beemblossom	Dave Qualkenbush
Miami (Peru) (40)	317 472-3901	James M Mock	....	Harold L Smith	Harold L Smith	Kenneth Einselen	Parker Snyder MD	Donald Howard
Monroe (Bloomington)† (98)	812 336-3757	Charlotte Zietlow	....	Vi Simpson	Vi Simpson	....	Steve Creech	Jim Young
Montgomery (Crawfordsville) (36)	317 362-1614	(not reporting)						
Morgan (Martinsville)† (52)	317 342-1102	James Jessup	....	Dan Bastin	Brenda Brittain	Delbert Hobson	Robert Beasley	Paul L Mason
Newton (Kentland) (15)	219 474-5842	Walter Miller	....	....	....	....	M F Guzman MD	Charles P Mullen
Noble (Albion) (35)	219 636-2658	Louis E Lash	....	Deedra L Kreager	Bonnie J Summe	....	Robert C Stone	Donald R Leitch
Ohio (Rising Sun) (5)	812 438-2610	(not reporting)						
Orange (Paoli) (19)	812 723-2649	(not reporting)						
Owen (Spencer) (16)	812 829-2260	Frank M Nardi	....	Margaret Tucker	Lois Bixler	....	Robert Rose	Harley E Melton
Parke (Rockville)† (16)	317 569-3872	Donald Rennick	Ronald J Meschen	Dolores Sparks	Ralph L Harrison	Edward Gould	R Bloomer MD	D M Eslinger
Perry (Cannelton) (19)	812 547-4411	Albert L Faulkner	....	Barbara Goffinet	Jean G Thomas	....	Stephen Syler MD	Warren J Taylor
Pike (Petersburg) (13)	812 354-6025	(not reporting)						
Porter (Valparaiso) (120)	219 464-8661	(not reporting)						
Posey (Mount Vernon) (26)	812 838-3266	G Straw	....	Manford E Mounts	Frances Crawford	Albert Holtz	Herman Hirsch	Carl J Dick
Pulaski (Winamac) (13)	219 946-3653	Marion Planck	....	Sheryl Passmore	Orval Burgess	....	William Thompson	Charlotte Ward
Putnam (Greencastle) (29)	317 653-4603	C James Malayer	....	Rose Marie Buis	Frances Harris	....	John Ellett Jr MD	Gerald A Hoffa
Randolph (Winchester) (30)	317 584-7070	Gerald Stephen	Carl O Gettinger	Carl O Gettinger	Lowell Fields	....	Judy Young	Richard Johnson
Ripley (Versailles)† (24)	812 689-6311	Kenneth Copeland	....	Rita A Hinners	William J Wagner	....	James Drummond	Kenneth Lovins
Rush (Rushville)† (20)	317 932-2077	Marvin Vannatta	....	Carole M Rigsbee	Joyce L Piper	....	Frank Green MD	Marvin L Hedrick
Scott (Scottsburg)† (20)	812 752-4745	Jim Peacock	....	Wanda Whitaker	Elsie Sharp	....	Marvin McClain	Marietta Hardy
Shelby (Shelbyville)† (40)	317 398-8306	Kenneth Nigh	....	Cheryl Glaub	Frank Zerr	....	Rick Roudebush	Rick Isgrigg
Spencer (Rockport) (19)	812 649-4376	Wayne A Roell	....	Mary E Haaff	Dennis Neuhoff	....	Michael O Monar	James E McDurmon

Directory 1/9 continued — COUNTY OFFICIALS IN ALL U.S. COUNTIES

County, county seat, 1980 population (000 omitted),	County telephone number	Board chairman	Appointed administrator	Clerk to the governing board	Chief financial officer	County engineer	County health officer	Chief law enforcement official
INDIANA (92) continued								
St. Joseph (South Bend) (242)	219 284-9534	Tom Catanzerite	Henry Ferrettie	Joseph Nagy	Joseph Doran	Robert Richardson	George Plain MD	Wm Richardson
Starke (Knox) (22)	219 772-3821	(not reporting)						
Steuben (Angola) (25)	219 665-3014	James Wyatt	....	Barbara Rose	Carolyn Bailey	Edward Kyle	Knight Kissinger	L McClelland
Sullivan (Sullivan) (21)	812 268-4491	Lee Hiatt	....	Judy K Harris	Alice Smiley	Sherril Page	Joseph E Dukes	David W Jones
Switzerland (Vevay) (7)	812 427-3302	James Lucas	....	Kathy L Carfield	....	....	Diego Valenzuela	J D Leap
Tippecanoe (Lafayette)† (122)	317 423-9215	Bruce V Osborn	William D Martin	Mora Dell Andrews	Betty Michael	A Dan Ruth	Robt Vermilya MD	Edgar Harger
Tipton (Tipton) (17)	317 675-2795	J Boyer	....	Amy E Holbrook	Amy E Holbrook	Bradley Rayl	Michael Harper	Frank Fritch
Union (Liberty) (7)	317 458-5464	Stanley G Fields	....	Virginia Bostick	Edith G Hahn	....	John T Hinton	Robert Walton
Vanderburgh (Evansville) (168)	812 426-5241	Richard J Borries	J Lindenschmidt	Margie Meeks	Lewis Volpe	Andy Easley	Samuel T Elder	Clarence Shepard
Vermillion (Newport) (18)	317 492-3570	Elmo H Riggen	....	Etta Waneta Ray	Anna M B Fravel	....	John W Somerville	Kim H Hawkins
Vigo (Terre Haute) (112)	812 238-8000	....	....	Ruel Burns Jr	Kenneth Thomas	Joseph Krueger	W W Drummy MD	Andy Atelski
Wabash (Wabash) (37)	219 563-5217	Philip G Magner	....	Philip Hegel	Samuel Schlemmer	Herbert Underwood	Frederick Poehler	Larry Rice
Warren (Williamsport) (9)	317 762-3510	(not reporting)						
Warrick (Boonville) (41)	812 897-3580	Keith Shelton	Roger Emmons	Thomas G Hess	Charles Ashby	Elmo Dockery	Bowen Hoover MD	Donald Gore
Washington (Salem) (22)	812 883-6717	Lester Walton	....	Lee H Peugh	Virginia Elrod	....	Edward R Apple MD	John Agan
Wayne (Richmond) (76)	317 966-7541	Jerry Dils	....	Richard W Thalls	Olen McMinn	Henry Gardner	Francis Warrick	Delbert Davis
Wells (Bluffton) (25)	219 824-3224	Ralph D Santon	....	Geoffrey E Frank	Loren Elzey	....	David Pietz	Nyal Frantz
White (Monticello) (24)	219 583-5761	Dean E Fleck	....	Kathryn A Barton	O D Ferguson	William L Altherr	Warren V Morris	Jerry W Johns
Whitley (Columbia City) (26)	219 248-8212	David A Rouch	....	Ruth Beers	Richard Harrold	George Atkinson	John S Wilson MD	Larry Helfrich
IOWA (99)								
Adair (Greenfield) (10)	515 743-6111	Richard Kuhl	....	Lorraine E Homan	Cora McClain	Donald J Lynam	Sharon Campbell	Donald W Carrick
Adams (Corning) (6)	515 322-3340	Verlyn Rice	....	Delores Hill	Delores Hill	Eldon Rike	....	Thomas M Nolan
Allamakee (Waukon) (15)	319 568-3522	John W Beisker	....	Kay Carter	Elsa Hager	William C Kerndt	Alden F Wiley MD	Neil E Becker
Appanoose (Centerville) (16)	515 856-6101	(not reporting)						
Audubon (Audubon) (9)	712 563-4275	(not reporting)						
Benton (Vinton) (24)	319 472-2365	Harry T Horak	....	Florence E Rippel	Warren Richart	Gerald Petermeier	Mark Greenlee	Kenneth Popenhage
Black Hawk (Waterloo) (138)	319 291-2500	Francis Messerly	....	Denise Dunn	Jerry Ellis	Larry Clark	William Mays	W Christensen
Boone (Boone)† (26)	515 432-1123	Dale Danilson	....	Albert G Sorenson	Richard F Sward	Carl F Schnoor	John F Murphy MD	Henry N Wallace
Bremer (Waverly) (25)	319 352-2523	Ralph W Juhl	....	Austa White	John Devries	W Jorgenrude	....	Wm Westendorf
Buchanan (Independence) (23)	319 334-2196	(not reporting)						
Buena Vista (Storm Lake) (21)	712 744-2545	Donald P Harjes	....	Lewis B Julius	Nina Roberts	Donald D Linnan	Darlene Peterson	John B Galbraith
Butler (Allison)† (18)	319 267-2670	William H Skinner	....	Donald G Johnson	Steven P Heerts	Robert L Haylock	Linda Truax	Russell D Vance
Calhoun (Rockwell City)† (14)	712 297-7741	Charles Moore	....	Joann Davis	Joyce McClintock	Jerry Weber	Ethel Mack RN	Jack Satern
Carroll (Carroll) (23)	712 792-4923	Walter Koster	....	Brian L Rupiper	Bernice Williams	Rich Michaelis	Lewis H Rich	John G Longnecker
Cass (Atlantic) (17)	712 243-4570	Marjorie Karns	....	Dale E Sunderman	Sharon B Winchell	William L Schultz	....	Larry Jones
Cedar (Tipton) (19)	319 886-3168	Mary Ann Dolan	....	Patricia Meixner	Gary Jedlicka	Billy G Conner	Rick Dvorak	Keith Whitlatch
Cerro Gordo (Mason City)† (48)	515 421-3099	John Fromm	....	Shirley E Cahalan	Michael Grandon	Warren G Davison	....	Steven Madson
Cherokee (Cherokee) (16)	712 225-4890	Donald Tietgen	....	Beverly Anderson	Patricia Carlson	William Bennett	Mavis Stoner	Darrel Bud Stroud
Chickasaw (New Hampton) (15)	515 394-2100	Sherry Wurzer	....	Gloria Putz	Sadie McFarland	William Baurer	Donna Schwickergt	Thomas Barnatz
Clarke (Osceola) (9)	515 342-2213	(not reporting)						
Clay (Spencer) (20)	712 262-1569	Duane F Fisk	....	Philip L Hurst	Bernard T Wheeler	Roger K Clark	Janice J Schmuck	Philip W Nelson
Clayton (Elkader) (21)	319 245-1106	Robert D Walke	....	Dennis Freitag	....	Glen Meisner	Steven R Helfer	Ronald H Rumph
Clinton (Clinton) (57)	319 243-6210	Howard K Carr	....	Walter W Killean	Homer B Hoskinson	Larry B Mattusch	Salvador R Borja	Dennis Kavanaugh
Crawford (Denison)† (19)	712 263-3045	John K Weiss	....	....	Donald J Groth	H Dale Wight	Donald J Soll MD	Donald D Stehr
Dallas (Adel) (30)	515 993-4751	Francis Weil	....	Roberta Burkhead	Murray Luther	Gene Hardy	Pat McPherson	Lee Struble
Davis (Bloomfield) (9)	515 664-2344	Jo Ella Cossel	....	Jeanine Wilfawn	....	Leroy Bergman	Ron Myrom MD	Ray Dykes
Decatur (Leon) (10)	515 446-4382	Graydon Griffin	....	Douglas Akers	Goldie Martin	Vaughn Clark	....	Steven E Layton
Delaware (Manchester) (19)	319 927-2515	Donald Atkinson	....	Sharon McCrabb	Helen McWilliams	Donald Smith	Gloria Rattenborg	Robert Campbell
Des Moines (Burlington) (46)	319 753-8203	Joseph Beckman	....	M Dockendorff	Katherine Masters	S J Klassen	Rollin Cowles	Russell Krieger
Dickinson (Spirit Lake) (16)	712 336-3356	Beverly Bergquist	....	Nancy Reiman	Marie Barrett	Kenneth Westergar	Vivian Lynn	Wendell Kilts
Dubuque (Dubuque) (94)	319 583-3511	Wilfred Bahl	Jan Hess	Terrence Hirsch	Tom Breitbach	Charles Baule	Paul Buss	Leo Kennedy
Emmet (Estherville) (13)	712 362-4261	Claire Nelson	....	Elmer A Weir	Russell L Smith	Gary Stribley	Madonna Johnson	Dan Gronbeck
Fayette (West Union) (25)	319 422-6061	Lois Miller	....	....	....	W Moellering	Anne Bodensteiner	Norman McCauley
Floyd (Charles City) (20)	515 228-7111	Dale Koehler	....	Janice Sherman	Allen Kellogg	Lyle Laartz	Forest Klages	L L Lane
Franklin (Hampton)† (13)	515 456-5621	Gilbert Behn	....	Delos Dohlman	Jane Lubkeman	Neil Jorgenson	Bernice Crabb	Duane Payne
Fremont (Sidney) (9)	712 374-2415	Richard Pullman	....	Jannet Whipple	Winifred Roades	Dale Miller	Lary Birby	Larry Gaylord
Greene (Jefferson) (12)	515 386-2316	R C Fredericksen	....	Rudolph Walter	Esther Fister	Ron Betterton	....	James Kurth
Grundy (Grundy Center) (14)	319 824-3122	Helen M Kopsa	....	Wilbur Rust	Deloris Bakker	Steven J Holcomb	Chas J Latendress	Rick Penning
Guthrie (Guthrie Center)† (12)	515 747-3512	Bob Burmeister	Darwin Hall	Darwin Hall	Beverly Kunkle	Stephen Akes	Stephen Patterson	Stuart Stringham
Hamilton (Webster City) (18)	515 832-3525	Marvin D Johnson	....	Lana D Hinderks	Dean C Erbes	Wesley D Smith	Marcill Johnson	....
Hancock (Garner)† (14)	515 923-3163	Gerald Burk	....	Dorothy DeVary	Rudy J Urich	J Wm Waddingham	L R Fuller	David Michel
Hardin (Eldora) (22)	515 858-3461	Millie Lloyd	....	Keith Van Patter	....	Rodney Vlotho	Sharon Brown RN	Jerry Sunken
Harrison (Logan) (16)	712 644-2665	John R Erixon	....	Elizabeth Harder	....	William Cook	Eileen Grundmeier	Merle E Sass
Henry (Mount Pleasant) (19)	319 385-2632	(not reporting)						
Howard (Cresco) (11)	319 547-2880	Robert Freel	....	Wilma Mohs	Helen Bateman	Richard Brown	Peter Kepros	Gary Cleviand
Humboldt (Dakota City) (12)	515 332-1571	Gary Kuehnast	....	Jerry C Diedrick	Patricia Albrecht	Paul Klevos	Lawrence Lerdal	Marvin Andersen
Ida (Ida Grove) (9)	712 364-2626	Raymond H Ernst	....	Helen J Wanberg	....	Marvin McGahuey	Janice A Rupert	Donald W Gebers
Iowa (Marengo)† (15)	319 642-3041	Leonard J Thys	....	Shirley N Dye	E Frontera	Donald A Torney	P Dellamuth	James F Slockett
Jackson (Maquoketa) (23)	319 652-3144	Barbara Wright	....	J W Brady Jr	Alfred Tebbe Jr	William D Upmeyer	Kimberly Deppe	Robert P Lyons
Jasper (Newton)† (36)	515 792-7016	Howard Peters Jr	....	Linda Gifford	Illa Guthrie	Charles Cabalca	Kathy Netzel	Allen Wheeler
Jefferson (Fairfield) (16)	515 472-3454	(not reporting)						
Johnson (Iowa City)† (82)	319 338-5442	Betty Ockenfels	....	....	Don Kral	O J Gote	Graham Dameron	Gary Huges
Jones (Anamosa) (20)	319 462-2282	S Strang	....	Linda Richardson	Grace Zimmermam	Earl Bissel	L Woeste RN	John Cook
Keokuk (Sigourney) (13)	515 622-2902	L Hollingsworth	....	Kathryn G Berg	Arlene Nilles	....	M Waechter RN	Ron Colin George
Kossuth (Algona) (22)	515 295-2718	Stanley Muckey	....	D Doddsthilges	Donald Jorgenson	Richard Schick	Mary Kahler	Charles Day
Lee (Fort Madison) (43)	319 372-6557	Charles Krogmeier	....	Anne M Pedersen	Carolyn E Norton	Dennis Osipowicz	M Archibald MD	Don E Arnold
Linn (Cedar Rapids)† (170)	319 398-4054	B Joseph Rinas	....	....	James M Hennessey	Jerry Nelson	Keith Erickson	Donald Sawyer
Louisa (Wapello) (12)	319 523-3371	Dean O Corey	....	Kay Skipton	Karen S Elkin	John F Pasch	Nancy P Pierce	Billy D Havenhill
Lucas (Chariton)† (10)	515 774-2018	John A Neighbour	....	Victoria Black	Martha Milnes	Nick Konrady	R E Anderson MD	Larry Lowe
Lyon (Rock Rapids) (13)	712 472-3713	Ralph F Kock	....	Kenneth Baldwin	Richard Heidloff	Jeffrey Williams	Kandace Koll	Luraine E Smith
Madison (Winterset)† (13)	515 462-3225	Paul W Binns	....	Kay Billeter	Jean Alles	....	Jerry Trevillyan	Paul Welch
Mahaska (Oskaloosa) (23)	515 673-3496	Daryl Denney	....	Jane L Coffey	Rex D Sherburne	Raymond Blessum	Tunis Den Hartog	Joe Beal
Marion (Knoxville) (30)	515 828-2207	(not reporting)						
Marshall (Marshalltown) (42)	515 754-6300	Richard C Blahnik	....	Sherrill A Snider	Carl Proescholdt	Royce Fichtner	Mary Lou Lapour	Derald Gonzales
Mills (Glenwood)† (13)	712 527-3146	Wayne Keith	....	Margaret Delavan	F M Robinson	Bill G Connors	E Kelleher	....
Mitchell (Osage)† (12)	515 732-5861	Betty McCarthy	....	Dorothy Kindschuh	Arlene Brown	Wilhelm Groskurth	Richard Gross	Richard E Jahnel
Monona (Onawa)† (12)	712 423-1585	Donald E Loomis	....	June Geadelmann	Donald W Comfort	Orville Ives	M Vandenhull	Dennis Smith

Directory 1/9 continued — COUNTY OFFICIALS IN ALL U.S. COUNTIES

County, county seat, 1980 population (000 omitted),	County telephone number	Board chairman	Appointed administrator	Clerk to the governing board	Chief financial officer	County engineer	County health officer	Chief law enforcement official
IOWA (99) continued								
Monroe (Albia) (9)	515 932-7706	Raymond Vance	....	David I Grimes	Ruth Morgan	Wendell W Folkert	Loretta Corso	Dennis M Carr
Montgomery (Red Oak) (13)	712 623-5127	David R England	....	Donna Mae Smith	Dale Lindner	Cleo W Smith	James Shehan	Richard E Harrell
Muscatine (Muscatine) (40)	319 263-5821	Paul Kemper	....	Marilyn J Hansen	....	Robert Simmering	Harlan Merrill	Richard D Oppelt
O'Brien (Primghar) (17)	712 757-3255	(not reporting)						
Osceola (Sibley)† (8)	712 754-2241	....	....	Jack A Davis	....	....	....	Robert Rolfes
Page (Clarinda) (19)	712 542-3219	Earl C Warner	....	Betty Stickelman	Donna Wheeler	Ralph Morrow	Joyce Hickey	Ron Franks
Palo Alto (Emmetsburg) (13)	712 852-2924	Charley Naig	....	George J Kliegl	Kathleen Thompson	William W Ellingt	Margaret Aldrich	J Albert Neary
Plymouth (Le Mars) (25)	712 546-6100	Herman Kluver	....	Claire Steele	Norman G Kehrberg	Thomas Rohe	Mary L Taylor	David P Stock
Pocahontas (Pocahontas) (11)	712 335-4127	Leonard J Sernett	....	Dorothea E Bowers	Berniece Hiatt	Robert Reinhart	....	Donald Schossow
Polk (Des Moines) (303)	515 286-3116	Tom Whitney	Ray Sears	Mike Mauro	Fred Horner	Richard Van Gundy	Julius Connor MD	Bob Rice
Pottawattamie (Council Bluffs) (87)	712 328-5644	Roy Geiger	....	Douglas D Primmer	Judy Ann Miller	Charles E Hales	....	Michael Kerns
Poweshiek (Montezuma) (19)	515 623-5443	Kenneth Richman	....	Jo Wray	Melvin M Mills	M O Hansen	Nancy Buitendorp	O Max Allen
Ringgold (Mount Ayr) (6)	515 464-3234	(not reporting)						
Sac (Sac City) (14)	712 662-7791	(not reporting)						
Scott (Davenport)§ (160)	319 326-8611	Bill Fennelly	F Glen Erickson	Karen Fitzsimmons	C Ray Wierson	Robert Dewys	Larry Barker	Forrest Ashcraft
Shelby (Harlan) (15)	712 755-3831	Burdette Poldberg	....	H Clay Pauley	Elizabeth Markham	Eldo Schornhorst	Ruth V Linton	Orrell D Gearhart
Sioux (Orange City) (31)	712 737-2216	Arie Schimmel	....	Dennis Lange	L Vander Esch	Douglas Julius	Sharon Bragg	Jim R Schwiesow
Story (Nevada) (72)	515 382-6581	W G Stucky	....	Alvina McHone	Doris M Samson	Del Jespersen	Don Nolting	John P Stark
Tama (Toledo)† (20)	515 484-3980	Mike Wentzien	....	Al Ohrt	Pauline Reinig	Robert Gumbert	Maryln Vale	Rex Cook
Taylor (Bedford) (8)	712 523-2280	Fred Helm	....	Carole Noer	Wanda Campbell	Thomas Nelson	Ann Maher	Marven Weed
Union (Creston) (14)	515 782-7218	Keith Sammons	Steven Wasteney	Jeannette Quick	Fran Bakerink	Tom Donahey	....	Donald Loy
Van Buren (Keosauqua) (9)	319 293-3129	Merle McDonald	Jon P Finney	Jon P Finney	Russell Boyd	Lewis Petersma	Laurie J Dorothy	Marvin J Story
Wapello (Ottumwa) (40)	515 684-4671	Dean Giltner	....	Paul Mottet	Paul Mottet	Milton C Johnson	....	Bud C Erwin
Warren (Indianola) (35)	515 961-2393	Ruth Hardin	Jerry Harmison	Beverly Dickerson	Betty K Conklin	Bob G Sandy	Barbara Booher	James W Lee
Washington (Washington)† (20)	319 653-3655	Elmer V Schneider	....	Curtis P Mineart	Charles H Pacha	Robert G Huber	....	Yale H Jarvis
Wayne (Corydon) (8)	515 872-2221	Ronald Green	....	Doris Ewing	Dean Besco	Rolley Glasgow	....	Jerry Street
Webster (Fort Dodge) (46)	515 573-7175	Leonard Hansch	....	V M Gudmonson	M L Hottman	Richard Sperry	Jacj Bradley	Charles Griggs
Winnebago (Forest City) (13)	515 582-4520	Don Grotewold	....	Robert D Paulson	Ruth Solomonson	A L Heeren	....	Donald O Vold
Winneshiek (Decorah) (22)	319 382-5085	Rufus J Moellers	....	Margaret Kruchek	Wayne H Walter	George Hanzlik	N Fenstermann	Melvin S Lee
Woodbury (Sioux City) (101)	712 279-6525	J C O'Sullivan	....	Donald Linduski	Hallie Sargisson	Lloyd Kallsen	Tom Corothers	Russell White Jr
Worth (Northwood)† (9)	515 324-2316	Jack Hanna	....	Morris Kalgaarden	James A Hanson	James E Hyde	Nancy Faber	Chas Stoffregen
Wright (Clarion) (16)	515 532-3262	Gene Sturgeon	....	Gladys Riley	Bernice Valley	Haydn E Jones	Jane Middleton RN	Vernon Elston
KANSAS (105)								
Allen (Iola) (16)	316 365-7491	R Keith Hobart	....	Jean M Barber	Betty L Jackson	George Jones	Eugene Myers	Ronald D Moore
Anderson (Garnett)† (9)	913 448-5924	Donald P Koontz	....	Judith Crismas	Opal Meyers	....	T O Osborn MD	Thomas J Hermreck
Atchison (Atchison)† (18)	913 367-1653	Tom Lykins	....	Pauline M Lee	Marian L Harrison	....	....	Hugh B Gillen
Barber (Medicine Lodge)† (7)	316 886-3212	I W Mease	....	Jeanne Peirson	Phyllis J Taylor	Joseph Reutter	Dean E Stucky	Dennis Stackley
Barton (Great Bend) (31)	316 792-7391	Robert R Hoyt	....	....	....	M Doolen Edman	Lillian Akings	Gene Marks
Bourbon (Fort Scott) (16)	316 223-1870	Roy Stewart	....	Barbara Wood	Opal Hess	....	Wilma Hibdon	Harold Stewart
Brown (Hiawatha) (12)	913 742-2581	Dallas L Corbet	....	Darlene Meyer	Thelma Lance	....	....	John J Wolney
Butler (El Dorado)† (45)	316 321-5056	J W Simmons	Stephen Seyb	Virginia Linden	Betty Orr	Ted Farmer	Beverly Summers	David Williams
Chase (Cottonwood Falls) (3)	316 273-6423	George J Beaver	....	Darwin K Reyer	Juanita Gibb	....	Kay Olson	Larry J Sigler
Chautauqua (Sedan) (5)	316 725-3370	Mitchell Foster	....	Margaret Stephens	Una Mae Harmon	....	William K Walker	William L Brooks
Cherokee (Columbus)† (22)	316 429-2042	Jack Boyes	....	Maurice Soper	Betty McBride	Perry Parker	Maurice Lamb	Charles Sharp
Cheyenne (St. Francis) (4)	913 332-2401	Wayne Goodell	....	Shirley B Bailey	....	Wayne Ritchey	Dr E R Cram	Ray Lee
Clark (Ashland) (3)	316 635-2813	Roy C Glaze Jr	....	Rogene Heugatter	Coleen Brown	Dean Adams	Barbara Strodtman	Loftis Meser
Clay (Clay Center) (10)	913 632-2552	Harold Holtz	....	Shirley Mackender	....	Frank Mayo	Cheryl Scott	Gary Caldwell
Cloud (Concordia) (12)	913 243-4319	Mark C Morgan	....	Betty L Dewitt	Alice M Walker	Doyle D Turner	Michael D Grant	Fred Modlin
Coffey (Burlington) (9)	316 364-2191	David J Beard	....	Jack E Scott	Dorothy Ellis	Norman Bowers	Susan Mueller	Earl Freeman
Comanche (Coldwater) (3)	316 582-2361	Vernon Huck	....	Bonnie Parcel	Ruth Morris	....	Lona Dowling	Jene Allen
Cowley (Winfield) (37)	316 221-4066	Marilyn J Johnson	....	Marjorie Williams	Ethel M White	....	Kenneth Stout	F Satterthwaite
Crawford (Girard) (38)	316 724-6115	A J Albertini	....	James McFarland	John E Westhoff	Noland Durnell	Wesley H Hall MD	John Chester
Decatur (Oberlin) (5)	913 475-2132	Jack Noone	....	C Walinder	Mildred Waldo	Melvin Kincaid	Eula Juenemann RN	Bob McLaughlin
Dickinson (Abilene) (20)	913 263-3774	(not reporting)						
Doniphan (Troy) (9)	913 985-3513	Richard Schultz	....	Wilma Williams	....	Charles Marker	Emerson Yoder M D	Jerry K Dubach
Douglas (Lawrence) (68)	913 841-7700	Beverly A Bradley	....	Rita Westerhaus	Ruth Vervynck	Frank Hempen	Kay Kent	Rex Johnson
Edwards (Kinsley) (4)	316 659-2583	Lloyd Britton	....	Bea Coats	W P Williamson	....	W L McKim	Leonard Carlson
Elk (Howard) (4)	316 374-2490	(not reporting)						
Ellis (Hays) (26)	913 625-6558	Harold G Kraus	....	Emery J Rome	Mike Billinger Jr	....	Dorothy Cody	Bruce A Hertel
Ellsworth (Ellsworth) (7)	913 472-4161	(not reporting)						
Finney (Garden City) (24)	316 276-3051	Clifford Hope Jr	....	Carol Brown	Donna Bradford	Max Morgan	Terry Hunsburger	Grover Craig
Ford (Dodge City)† (24)	316 227-3184	Edward Gibb	....	Lucille Keck	Dorothy Formm	Dale Smith	Dale R Boles	Richard Wolfe
Franklin (Ottawa) (22)	913 242-1471	(not reporting)						
Geary (Junction City)† (30)	913 238-3912	Keith F Devenney	....	Marjorie L Davis	Marie H Johnson	....	Leroy Wunder	Jim A Gross
Gove (Gove) (4)	913 938-2300	(not reporting)						
Graham (Hill City) (4)	913 674-5433	Darrol W Irby	....	Darlene Riggs	Shirley Pimlott	Gary L Cameron	Jackie Clark	Don E Scott
Grant (Ulysses) (7)	316 356-1335	Cecil L Pucket	....	Shirley McHenry	....	....	M A Brewer MD	Darrell Pflughoft
Gray (Cimarron)† (5)	316 855-3618	W W McFarland	....	Ann Koehn	Lovevilla C Lekey	Sam Moler	Donna Davis	Marvin A Kramer
Greeley (Tribune) (2)	316 376-4256	Floyd Kleymann	....	Emogene Wineinger	Joy Anne Sawyer	....	W F Werner	O B Rutherford
Greenwood (Eureka) (9)	316 583-7421	(not reporting)						
Hamilton (Syracuse)† (3)	316 384-5629	John Helfrich	....	Twyla Reed	Lucille Staats	....	C E Petterson MD	Thomas Lambeth
Harper (Anthony)† (8)	316 842-5555	....	....	....	Elva Harmon	....	P J Antrim	....
Harvey (Newton) (31)	316 283-6900	Dave Friesen	Gene R Kristenson	Margaret Wright	Sarah Fiedler	....	Jan Sauerwein	Galen Morford
Haskell (Sublette) (4)	316 675-2263	Gail Hale	....	Suwayne French	Nancy Weeks	Ted Berglund	A H Thiemann	Carl J Pettay
Hodgeman (Jetmore) (2)	316 357-6421	Charlie W Patchen	....	Everett Beltz	Jessie Mae Ling	Gary Burkhart	James O Shea	Harry Craghead Jr
Jackson (Holton)† (12)	913 364-2891	Otto E Dienstbeir	....	Edna Brock	Marjorie P Bruns	Melvin E Ralston	Jim Seeley	Don D Collins
Jefferson (Oskaloosa) (15)	913 863-2272	Richard Malm	....	Alyce P Riedesel	Virginia Reiling	L N Moffitt	Robert R Snook MD	Roy Dunnaway
Jewell (Mankato)† (5)	913 378-3700	John R Ross	....	Herschel Rhea	Lynn Scarrow	Warren Hardin	Richard Kimball	Donald Heskett
Johnson (Olathe)* (270)	913 782-5000	Bruce Craig	Frank Dixon	Donald J Curry	William O'Brien	James Pilley	B Sullivan RN	Fred Allenbrand
Kearny (Lakin) (3)	316 355-6422	(not reporting)						
Kingman (Kingman) (9)	316 532-3111	(not reporting)						
Kiowa (Greensburg) (4)	316 723-3366	Frank R Rinkel	....	Truman E Nash	Elsie Haraldson	....	Frank R Rinkel	Thomas Boman
Labette (Oswego) (26)	316 795-2138	Larry Dean Myers	....	Thelma Foster	Barbara Goodnight	Charles Smay	Stan Handshy	Murl T Bringle
Lane (Dighton) (2)	316 397-5356	Dean Hamilton	....	Leo S Brown	Elsie M Lawrence	Les M Sheahon	Pat Brown RN	Paul F Marsteller
Leavenworth (Leavenworth) (55)	913 682-7611	Dollie Scheller	....	Larry E Scheller	Shirley J Tate	Melvin L Hedrick	James B Lewis	Terry L Campbell
Lincoln (Lincoln)† (4)	913 524-4757	Robert O Neill	....	Loa Page	Doris Larsen	John Cashatt	Mary Luidens MD	Don Panzer

Directory 1/9 continued **COUNTY OFFICIALS IN ALL U.S. COUNTIES**

County, county seat, 1980 population (000 omitted),	County telephone number	Board chairman	Appointed administrator	Clerk to the governing board	Chief financial officer	County engineer	County health officer	Chief law enforcement official
KANSAS (105) continued								
Linn (Mound City) (8)	913 795-2668	John Rees	....	Marion R Johnson	Julia P Dunavan	Richard A Long	Fred E Dunlap	Donald E Troth
Logan (Oakley) (3)	913 672-4244	Robert K Scott	....	Judy L Litson	M Harvene Hoeb	Norman Boyd	Paula Marchbanks	Clarence Turley
Lyon (Emporia) (35)	316 342-5404	Gail W Gasche	Philip E Winter	Rosemary Spalding	Lula Hunt	Leu Lowrey	Eileen Greischar	Daniel Andrews
Marion (Marion) (14)	316 382-2185	Harold B Jost	....	Marquetta Eilerts	Kathryn Schimpf	Richard Teaford	Grace Utting	June Jost
Marshall (Marysville) (13)	913 562-5361	F A Long	....	Gayle Landoll	Dorothy Hula	Rollin Fincham	....	E Pennington
McPherson (McPherson) (27)	316 241-8149	Waldo Preheim	Wilva Hatfield	Margaret E Bryan	Lenora L Claypool	Melvin Ferguson	Carolyn Shuman	Harris Terry
Meade (Meade) (5)	316 873-2581	Fred Boyd	....	Velma Pemberton	....	Dean Adams	R H Hill MD	Michael Cox
Miami (Paola) (22)	913 294-3976	David O Smith	....	Clarice V Yackle	Berdene Welch	Larry Robinson	Wm Appenfeller	Charles Light
Mitchell (Beloit) (8)	913 738-3652	Lawrence Cordel	....	Joleen Walker	Carol Emmot	John Cashatt	Laura Otte	Gary T Reiter
Montgomery (Independence) (42)	316 331-2710	Raymond Caldwell	....	Arva D Chittum	Billie Lewark	Kurt Booe	Dr Barbera	Arthur Scherk
Morris (Council Grove)† (6)	316 767-5518	Earl Forsberg	....	Michelle Yadon	Donna Muller	....	James Bowers MD	Richard R Malek
Morton (Elkhart) (3)	316 697-2157	R L Arheart	....	Ruby Bultman	Lois Hall	Eldon Dunn	Josephine Carson	Merlin Stout
Nemaha (Seneca) (11)	913 336-2170	Jim D Brownlee	....	Alvin Bauman	Lawrence Eisenbar	....	James Lueger	W Duane Harvey
Neosho (Erie) (19)	316 244-3293	(not reporting)						
Ness (Ness City)† (4)	913 798-2401	M D Dewald	....	Verla Klitzke	David Jarvis	....	Joanne Stenzel	Gary O'Brien
Norton (Norton) (7)	913 877-2363	Ray H Ellis	....	Dorothy Shearer	Sally Breiner	....	Lila M Atwell RN	Harland Reusink
Osage (Lyndon) (15)	913 828-4812	Robert Markley	....	Virginia Kersten	Jo Ann Hamilton	....	Eva Anschutz	Robert E Masters
Osborne (Osborne) (6)	913 346-2431	Donald S Kiper	....	Gloria B Wood	Shirley Curry	Gerald Curry	Burton D Cox	Daryl Thornburg
Ottawa (Minneapolis) (6)	913 392-2279	Robert M Aylward	....	Yvonne J Hawkins	....	Dillard Wooley	....	Dean F Dunham
Pawnee (Larned)† (8)	316 285-3721	Don Foster	....	Ronald Young	Eleanor Zink	Gerald Prescott	O R Cram	C Atteberry
Phillips (Phillipsburg) (7)	913 543-5513	Leonard Archer	....	Margaret Malone	Judy Rowland	Eddy DeBoer	Eric Musser	LeRoy Stephen
Pottawatomie (Westmoreland) (15)	913 457-3314	Warren Nelson	....	Juanita Chilcott	Faye Pittenger	....	Rita McLean	Dean Taylor
Pratt (Pratt) (10)	316 672-5181	Ralph R Bales	Alma Walker	Alma Walker	Helen Parr	....	F P Wolff MD	Raymond McGuire
Rawlins (Atwood) (4)	913 626-3351	(not reporting)						
Reno (Hutchinson) (65)	316 665-2929	Richard Robl	....	G Heldenbrand	Annabel Miller	James Melvin	Judith Babbs	James Fountain
Republic (Belleville)† (8)	913 527-2508	Edward L Pachta	....	Carl E Larson	Emma Berggren	Warren L Hardin	C McCracken	Larry G Tebow
Rice (Lyons) (12)	316 257-2232	(not reporting)						
Riley (Manhattan) (64)	913 537-6300	Rosalys M Rieger	....	Wanda Coder	Mary Lowman	Dan Harden	Charles Murphy	Al Johnson
Rooks (Stockton) (7)	913 425-6391	Francis Malin	....	Clara Strutt	Peggy Sheffer	Wesley Wendt	W Votapka	Ronald Stithem
Rush (La Crosse) (5)	913 222-2731	John B Kober	....	Barbara Bortz	Ruth Anne Krug	....	Joan Harvey	Jack Mendenhall
Russell (Russell) (9)	913 483-4641	(not reporting)						
Saline (Salina) (49)	913 827-1961	Roy W Allen	....	Dan S Geis	Keith Lilly	Wesley N Moore	Wm Null	Al Naes
Scott (Scott City) (6)	316 872-2420	(not reporting)						
Sedgwick (Wichita)§ (367)	316 268-7011	Jack Spratt	F Tim Witsman	Dorothy White	Jerry Threlfall	Claud Shelor	Fred E Tosh MD	Johnnie Darr
Seward (Liberal) (17)	316 624-0211	Jim Rice	....	Dorothy Sanborn	Amy Jo Neese	....	Wm J Harrison MD	Charles Lucas
Shawnee (Topeka) (155)	913 295-4149	Richard A Maner	....	Patsy A McDonald	Marjorie Robards	John Tarasyn	Ray Baker MD	Ed Ritchie
Sheridan (Hoxie) (4)	913 675-3361	Joe C Haffner	....	Doreen Kennedy	Esther Bainter	Elmer Boxler	Barbara Corder	Roger Johnson
Sherman (Goodland) (8)	913 899-6125	John Golden	....	Janet R Rumpel	Shelby L Miller	James L Pickett	....	Jack W Armstrong
Smith (Smith Center) (6)	913 282-6533	(not reporting)						
Stafford (St. John)† (6)	316 549-3509	Walter S Jenkins	....	Pauline Duer	Eleanor M Young	....	Dr Brown	Bill D Christie
Stanton (Johnson) (2)	316 492-2140	Ivan L Nicholas	....	Sharon Dimitt	Phyllis Kistler	Gerald Nickell	Bill Troup	James R Garrison
Stevens (Hugoton) (5)	316 545-2541	Kenneth Lester	....	Sarah Reynolds	Belva Hickey	Leonard Baker	....	Russ Dewitt
Sumner (Wellington) (25)	316 326-3395	Elmer C Dill	....	Sibyl P Whippie	Loren L Hibbs	Rex Brunson	Larry R Anderson	Colin Wood
Thomas (Colby)† (8)	913 462-2561	Vera L Sloan	....	Rosalie Seemann	Luciel Taylor	Dean A Steward	Rex Kolste MD	Lloyd G Lunsway
Trego (Wakeeney) (4)	913 743-2114	Darlene Hille	....	Thomas W Rhoden	Margaret A Papes	Cloyce Randall	James Hamilton MD	Roger Sells
Wabaunsee (Alma) (7)	913 765-3414	Glen Heiser	....	Ruth Diepenbrock	C Westerhau	....	Anne Wigglesworth	Marion Cox
Wallace (Sharon Springs) (2)	913 852-4282	(not reporting)						
Washington (Washington)† (9)	913 325-2974	Dwain P Compton	....	Eileen Cox	LaDeane Crimmins	George P Sugars	....	Terry N Taylor
Wichita (Leoti) (3)	316 375-2731	Maurice Wikoff	....	Berneice Gilmore	Sharen A Altman	Norman Owings	Helen McClain RN	Melvin McKellips
Wilson (Fredonia) (12)	316 378-4337	Eugene Shockley	....	Marjoria Winn	Bernice Z Ritz	Allen Blaker	E A Rindt MD	Paul Ammann
Woodson (Yates Center) (5)	316 625-3162	(not reporting)						
Wyandotte (Kansas City) (172)	913 573-2876	Paul Antos	....	Wm Burns Jr	Robert Brown	Robert Wessel	Darrel Newkirk MD	John Quinn
KENTUCKY (120)								
Adair (Columbia)† (15)	502 384-4703	Jimmy D Firquin	Jimmy D Firquin	Robert M White	Roscoe Antle	....	David Upchurch	Gary Melton
Allen (Scottsville) (14)	502 237-3631	Edwin Ballard	....	Elvis Russell	Carol Thomas	A R Oliver	Vesper Jones	Jerry Wimpee
Anderson (Lawrenceburg) (13)	502 839-3041	(not reporting)						
Ballard (Wickliffe) (9)	502 335-3531	Michael Magee	....	Lynn Lane	Varlieu Perkins	Jim Hook	....	Jack Stevens
Barren (Glasgow) (34)	502 651-3783	Woody Gardner Jr	....	Wilmer L Hodges	Howard M Jones	Norris Johnson	....	Gale Wood
Bath (Owingsville) (10)	606 674-2613	Charles B Hart Sr	....	James D Evans	....	Sidney Butcher	....	James Razor
Bell (Pineville) (34)	606 337-3076	Darrell L Lewis	....	Joan A Cawood	Brenda Walters	....	Ron Oakes	Vernon Taylor Sr
Boone (Burlington) (46)	606 334-2240	Terry Roberts	....	Rose Mason	Charles Conrad	....	....	Thomas Schwatz
Bourbon (Paris) (19)	606 987-3010	Roy T Baber	....	Betty Jo Heick	Dollie J Young	....	....	Charles Hinkle
Boyd (Catlettsburg) (56)	606 739-4134	Paul F Purvis	....	Barbara Gunderson	Joyce Smoot	Boots Wright	Leslie Osborne	Troy Dixon
Boyle (Danville) (25)	606 236-2306	Mary Pendygraft	....	John B Nichols	Melvin Veatch	....	Harold Yankey	Tommy Sims
Bracken (Brooksville)† (8)	606 735-2300	Dwayne Jett	Dwayne Jett	Mary Bauer	David Appleman	Richard Hamilton	Mary Louise Kalb	Kenneth Garrison
Breathitt (Jackson) (17)	606 666-2818	(not reporting)						
Breckinridge (Hardinsburg) (17)	502 756-2246	James T Stinnett	....	Cathy S Moore	Mary C Dant	....	Lula B Carman	Bobby D Kennedy
Bullitt (Shepherdsville) (43)	502 543-2262	Clifford F Haley	Rose M Snodgrass	Nina Mooney	Elizabeth Deacon	....	Hubert Clay	Danny Thompson
Butler (Morgantown)† (11)	502 526-3433	David R Martin	David R Martin	Eva J Tuck	Kathryn W Brown	Raymond Givens	Alan Meredith	J V McKinney
Caldwell (Princeton)† (13)	502 365-6660	J D Jones	....	B Van Hooser	Debbie East	....	Raymond Giannini	Ewaylon Rogers
Calloway (Murray) (30)	502 753-2920	George H Weaks	....	....	Sue Outland	Joe Bruce Wilson	James Erwin	David Balentine
Campbell (Newport)† (83)	606 292-3838	Lloyd K Rogers	....	Vione D Clark	Erma Staton	Walter Deller	....	Thomas Bridges
Carlisle (Bardwell) (5)	502 628-3233	(not reporting)						
Carroll (Carrollton)† (9)	502 732-4426	Robert M Westrick	....	John P Tilley	Louise Supplee	William A Wilson	Gerald Eckler	George R Cayton
Carter (Grayson) (25)	606 474-5366	Joe D Kitchen	....	Ralph Cartee Jr	Joy C Nolan	....	Wm Matthes MD	Carl W Walker
Casey (Liberty) (15)	606 787-6154	Garland Hoskins	....	Ruth Smith	Micah S Beard	....	....	Carl E Meece
Christian (Hopkinsville) (67)	502 887-4105	(not reporting)						
Clark (Winchester) (28)	606 744-3189	James B Allen Jr	Lois McChrystal	B Shimfessle	Jean L Cole	L Willoughby	....	Gary Lawson
Clay (Manchester)† (23)	606 598-2071	Carl Sizemore	....	Florence Baker	Beula H Cornett	....	....	Harold Sizemore
Clinton (Albany)† (9)	606 387-5234	Donald Poore	Sheila Nuszbaum	Lloyd Stockton	Mary F Stockton	....	Kathy Bernard	Gordon Speck
Crittenden (Marion) (9)	502 965-3403	(not reporting)						
Cumberland (Burkesville) (7)	502 864-3726	(not reporting)						
Daviess (Owensboro) (86)	502 684-7285	(not reporting)						
Edmondson (Brownsville)† (10)	502 597-2819	Donald F Doyel	....	Richard Sanders	Charlene Vincent	Bennie Vincent	Barry Woods	Buddy Alford
Elliott (Sandy Hook)† (7)	606 738-5335	David Blair	Kelly B Howard	....	Elda Peters	....	....	....

Directory 1/9 continued — COUNTY OFFICIALS IN ALL U.S. COUNTIES

County, county seat, 1980 population (000 omitted),	County telephone number	Board chairman	Appointed administrator	Clerk to the governing board	Chief financial officer	County engineer	County health officer	Chief law enforcement official
KENTUCKY (120) continued								
Estill (Irvine) (14)	606 723-7524	Donnie Watson	....	Dora N Henry	Lydia McKinney	Thomas Hymer	....	Montie Parks
Fleming (Flemingsburg) (12)	606 845-8461	(not reporting)						
Floyd (Prestonsburg) (49)	606 886-9193	John M Stumbo	....	Carla R Boyd	David D Allen	Sam H Fitzpatrick	Earl Compton	Henry Hale
Franklin (Frankfort) (42)	502 875-8751	Robert T Harrod	Sue C Blakeman	Donald C Hulette	Kathleen Hughes	Ed Parris	....	Sam Harrod
Fulton (Hickman) (9)	502 236-2594	James M Everett	Karen Argo	Dee Langford	Bethel E Choate	Tommy Yarbro	Marian White	Marshal Jones
Gallatin (Warsaw) (5)	606 567-5691	Clarence Davis	....	Lavern Johns	....	....	....	Carole Wheeler
Garrard (Lancaster) (11)	606 792-3071	(not reporting)						
Grant (Williamstown) (13)	606 823-7561	Byron D Martin	....	John S McCoy	J W Rich	....	....	William G Points
Graves (Mayfield) (34)	502 247-1733	(not reporting)						
Grayson (Leitchfield)† (21)	502 259-3159	Charles L Lively	....	Margaret Woosley	Oran P Lawler	Gary Logsdon	Charles L Lively	Qulin Escue
Green (Greensburg) (11)	502 932-5386	(not reporting)						
Greenup (Greenup) (39)	606 473-3151	(not reporting)						
Hancock (Hawesville) (8)	502 927-8137	James H Fallin	....	Anita L Robertson	Glenn R Cox Jr	....	....	Phil Bozarth
Hardin (Elizabethtown) (89)	502 765-2350	R R Thomas	....	David Logsdon	Gilla Jenkins	Richard McDeavit	Richard Roush	Ralph Baskett
Harlan (Harlan)† (42)	606 573-2600	Hugh Hall	Connie Boggs	Tommy Lee	Raymond Cole	Leo Miller	....	William Redwine
Harrison (Cynthiana) (15)	606 234-4841	Charles Swinford	....	....	Scott McCauley	....	....	Warren Judy
Hart (Munfordville) (15)	502 524-2751	(not reporting)						
Henderson (Henderson)† (41)	502 826-3971	A C Pritchett	....	Virginia Clark	Mike Wathen	....	....	....
Henry (New Castle) (13)	502 845-2891	Ben A Elston	....	Rhonda Carpenter	Kathie J Bryant	Gayle Mann	Lloyd Penniston	Ray Powell
Hickman (Clinton) (6)	502 653-4369	Donnie Kell	Jenera Clark	Sophia Barclay	Barbara Tarver	R L Williams Jr	Betty Johnson	Virgil P Clark
Hopkins (Madisonville) (46)	502 821-7361	(not reporting)						
Jackson (McKee) (12)	606 287-8562	William O Smith	....	Charles A Kilburn	Patricia Gabbard	Jerry Lynch	....	Fred Hays
Jefferson (Louisville) (685)	502 581-6060	Mitch McConnell	David L Huber	Augusta Scott	Robert C Miller	James N Birch	Tom Wallace MD	G Edgar Helm Jr
Jessamine (Nicholasville)† (27)	606 885-4500	Sherman Dean Jr	....	Mildred Williams	Marie Frogge	B D Carroll	....	Leroy Hager
Johnson (Paintsville)† (24)	606 789-4616	Frank Johnson	Robert M Conley	Lonza Reed	Virginia Siler	....	Robert A Hall	Gene E Cyrus
Kenton (Covington) (137)	606 491-2800	James A Dressman	John Nienaber Jr	Carol Brockell	Ivan Frye	Don Graven	....	R C Richardson
Knott (Hindman)† (18)	606 785-5592	Sid Williams	Bobby Williams	Jim Rose	Ray Slone	Bruce Collins	Paul Prater	Thomas J Adams
Knox (Barbourville) (30)	606 546-3568	Homer Lee Jackson	....	Troy Hampton	Jack Ketcham	Leslie Mills	....	Wilbur Bingham
Larue (Hodgenville) (12)	502 358-4400	Joe Pearman	....	Helen O'Dell	Janet Propes	....	....	John O Lewis
Laurel (London) (39)	606 864-5158	(not reporting)						
Lawrence (Louisa) (14)	606 638-4108	Ray Williams	....	Amos See	....	Laban E Wallace	....	Arlie Workman
Lee (Beattyville) (8)	606 464-3678	D Brandenburg	Sharon Watterson	Erma Combs	Phyllis Fulks	....	....	Tracy Gross
Leslie (Hyden) (15)	606 672-3200	Kermitt Keen	....	Earl Fields	Mahala Duff	....	....	Henry Roberts
Letcher (Whitesburg) (31)	606 633-2432	(not reporting)						
Lewis (Vanceburg)† (15)	606 796-2722	Jackie Ray Cooper	Jack Lowder	Shirley A Hinton	Charles Jordan Jr	....	....	Jeffrey M Cooper
Lexington-Fayette C† (204)	606 255-5631	Scotty Baesler	....	....	Betty P Unseld	....	....	John P McFadden
Lincoln (Stanford) (19)	606 365-2601	(not reporting)						
Livingston (Smithland)† (9)	502 928-2106	Ralph Smith	....	James Jones	Rebecca Doom	....	Ray Grimmitt	Jack Day
Logan (Russellville) (24)	502 726-3116	James E Bailey	....	Kenny Chapman	Doris McMillen	Harry C Johnson	....	Robert Wilson
Lyon (Eddyville)† (6)	502 388-7311	Terry O McKinney	....	....	Martha D Wallace	....	....	William Craig
Madison (Richmond) (53)	606 623-2849	Harold K Botner	Joan S Perry	C S Wagers	Billy Cosby	Carl Webb	Sandra Touissant	Cecil Cochran
Magoffin (Salyersville)† (14)	606 349-2313	Paul H Salyer	Hargis Fletcher	Haden B Arnett	P Collinsworth	....	....	Pat Montgomery
Marion (Lebanon) (18)	502 692-3451	Randall Donahue	Lelia A Elden	Philip Jarboe	Donald George	Otis Shofner	Keith Brock	Edward Masterson
Marshall (Benton) (26)	502 527-3388	Mike Miller	....	James R English	Joe Williams	John Holland	Ron Lucas	Brian Roy
Martin (Inez) (14)	606 298-7723	John B Callaham	....	Samuel R Moore	Sharon R Harmon	....	....	Ray Fields
Mason (Maysville)† (18)	606 564-3341	Billy F Ross	....	Martha Tierney	Jeannine Dwelly	James H Pollitt	Dewey Applegate	Robert Case
McCracken (Paducah) (61)	502 444-4707	Raymond C Schultz	....	Shirley Renaud	Mary M Hoffman	Buddy J Smith	Harold Priddle	Howard Walker
McCreary (Whitley City) (16)	606 376-2413	Floyd R Frasure	....	Jo E Kidd	John A Crabtree	Onel Bryant	Earl Taylor	Lindell L Wilson
McLean (Calhoun) (10)	502 273-3082	(not reporting)						
Meade (Brandenburg) (23)	502 422-3967	Bert E Watts	....	Mike Jones	Charles Thompson	....	....	Joseph E Greer
Menifee (Frenchburg) (5)	606 768-3482	Henry Ratliff	....	....	Rita Helton	....	Joanne Egelston	Hershell Sexton
Mercer (Harrodsburg) (19)	606 734-5135	(not reporting)						
Metcalfe (Edmonton) (9)	502 432-4821	(not reporting)						
Monroe (Tompkinsville)† (12)	502 487-5505	Douglas Carter	....	Larry Pitcock	Katherine Burnett	....	....	Randall Curtis
Montgomery (Mount Sterling)† (20)	606 498-1992	Harry Hoffman II	....	Judy L Witt	Pat Harper	....	....	Bobby Joe Stamper
Morgan (West Liberty) (12)	606 743-3949	(not reporting)						
Muhlenberg (Greenville) (32)	502 338-2520	Robert Draper	....	Opal Dick	Charles R Lewis	....	....	Harold McElvain
Nelson (Bardstown) (28)	502 348-5941	(not reporting)						
Nicholas (Carlisle)† (7)	606 289-2404	Reese Smoot	....	Rose Scott	Lanny Hutchison	....	Lee Rose	Charles Ring
Ohio (Hartford)† (22)	502 298-7629	C B Embry Jr	....	Cecil Barnard	Sue Hitchell	Lantie Allen	....	Bobby Martin
Oldham (La Grange) (28)	502 222-9311	(not reporting)						
Owen (Owenton)† (9)	502 484-3405	Horace D West	....	Eugene Young	Nina Cobb	Byron Jacobs	Richard Hampton	Thomas Kemper Jr
Owsley (Booneville)† (6)	606 593-6202	Howard Moore	....	Wayne Marshall	Cale Turner	....	J B Bowman	Billy P McIntosh
Pendleton (Falmouth)† (11)	606 654-4321	David H Pribble	....	Carol W Ockerman	Patricia Downard	Hubert Dunn	Sharma Klee	Donald R Mays
Perry (Hazard) (34)	606 436-4614	Jesse P Engle	Bob Hammonds	....	Joyce Napier	....	....	Pearl Couch
Pike (Pikeville)† (81)	606 432-6243	Paul E Patton	Sanford Chaney	Laura Maynard	N Stephen Friend	....	Mary Pauline Fox	William Deskins
Powell (Stanton) (11)	606 663-2834	Bill Patrick	....	Anna M Baker	Louise Ashley	....	Linda Fagen	Elmo Congleton
Pulaski (Somerset) (46)	606 678-4853	John W Garner	....	Willard Hansford	Louise Simpson	Allen Rocky Hurt	M A Shepperd MD	John Adams
Robertson (Mount Olivet) (2)	606 724-5212	(not reporting)						
Rockcastle (Mount Vernon)† (14)	606 256-2856	Bob Jasper	Mark Jasper	....	....	....	....	....
Rowan (Morehead)† (19)	606 784-5151	Jim Nickell	....	Jean Bailey	....	....	....	Jack Carter
Russell (Jamestown) (14)	502 343-2112	Dwight C Hadley	K Higginbotham	Terry L Stephens	Osborn Roy	Logan Carnes	Paul Walkup	Wendell Wilson
Scott (Georgetown)† (22)	502 863-0349	Charlie Sutton	....	....	Raymond Morrison	....	....	Gary D Wainscott
Shelby (Shelbyville) (23)	502 633-1220	Bobby Stratton	Wayne Stratton	Sue Carole Perry	Mary S Bradshaw	James Rogers	Robert Moore	Fred A Ruble
Simpson (Franklin) (15)	502 586-7184	Kenneth Y Harper	....	Debbie Renick	Judy Hayes	Russell Delk	Barry Turner	G R DeWeese
Spencer (Taylorsville) (6)	502 477-8127	C L Glasscock Jr	....	Robin Greenwell	Margaret Veech	Collis Rogers	Robert Moore	Larry Lawson
Taylor (Campbellsville) (21)	502 465-6677	(not reporting)						
Todd (Elkton) (12)	502 265-2363	(not reporting)						
Trigg (Cadiz) (9)	502 522-8459	Zelner Cossey	....	V Alexander	Mary Graham	....	....	Kenneth Oakley
Trimble (Bedford)† (6)	502 255-7196	Clyde E Greenwood	Mary Ann Welty	Robert Moore	Bernice Liter	Bradford Andrew	Barry Wainscott	Wm Howard Long
Union (Morganfield)† (18)	502 389-1081	Bob White	Jane Hite	Sam T Hite	Sandra Butts	Thomas L Bishop	Bedford Walker	Billy S Peak
Warren (Bowling Green) (72)	502 843-4146	Basil W Griffin	Basil W Griffin	Charles Morehead	Cooper Smith	John Drennan	Charles Bunch	Wayne Constant
Washington (Springfield) (11)	606 336-3636	J Bourbon Elliott	....	A H Robertson	Olivia Montgomery	....	Joey Purdom	Bruce Burkhead
Wayne (Monticello) (17)	606 348-4241	Hallice Upchurch	Joy Smith	Robert A Parrigin	Charles Cowan	....	....	Joe Conn
Webster (Dixon) (15)	502 639-5042	C B Clark	....	....	Teresa Hibbs	....	....	Raymond Ray
Whitley (Williamsburg) (33)	606 549-0416	(not reporting)						
Wolfe (Campton)† (7)	606 668-3040	Danny Brewer	Danny Brewer	Kenneth Lindon	Riley Harris	....	A S Holmes	Roland Dunn
Woodford (Versailles) (18)	606 873-4139	Jenny K Given	....	Betty W Wilhoit	Merl Goldey	Arthur T Craig	....	Dennis Nunnelley

Directory 1/9 continued — COUNTY OFFICIALS IN ALL U.S. COUNTIES

County, county seat, 1980 population (000 omitted),	County telephone number	Board chairman	Appointed administrator	Clerk to the governing board	Chief financial officer	County engineer	County health officer	Chief law enforcement official
LOUISIANA (64)								
Acadia (Crowley) P (56)	318 783-0953	(not reporting)						
Allen (Oberlin) P (21)	318 639-4376	(not reporting)						
Ascension (Donaldsonville) P (50)	504 473-9866	(not reporting)						
Assumption (Napoleonville) P (22)	504 369-7435	Paul Cancienne	James M Clement	....	Stephen Fertitta	C J Savoie	Ellen Fingers	Anthony Faterman
Avoyelles (Marksville) P (41)	318 253-9203	(not reporting)						
Baton Rge-E Baton Rge C† (346)	504 389-3100	Pat Screen	....	....	O L Schofield	....	....	Pat Bonanno
Beauregard (de Ridder) P (30)	318 463-7019	Margaret Dees	....	Bobbie L Montague	Bobbie L Montague	Elton Pickering	Russell R Conley	Bolivar Bishop
Bienville (Arcadia) P (16)	318 263-2019	Tommie Uzzle	James W Martin	James W Martin	James W Martin	S E Huey Co	Ray Harmon	Arvis Whitman
Bossier (Benton) P (81)	318 965-2329	Boyd Montgomery	J W Ramsey	Cheryl G Martin	Cheryl G Martin	J W Ramsey	J W Thompson	Vol S Dooley
Caddo (Shreveport) P (252)	318 226-6780	(not reporting)						
Calcasieu (Lake Charles) P† (167)	318 439-3656	Anthony P Mayeux	Rodney M Vincent	Jennabeth Smythe	P Laroy Alston	Claude D Smart	W Edgar Percy MD	Wayne McElveen
Caldwell (Columbia) P (11)	318 649-2273	(not reporting)						
Cameron (Cameron) P (9)	318 775-5718	J B Braxton Blake	Garner Nunez	Hayes P Picou Jr	Garner Nunez	George Bailey	....	James R Savoie
Catahoula (Harrisonburg) P (12)	318 744-5435	Emmitt Taylor	Emmett Book	Emmett Book	Emmett Book	Alex Theriot	Dennis Dosher	Thomas Jackson
Claiborne (Homer) P (17)	318 927-9601	(not reporting)						
Concordia (Vidalia) P (23)	318 336-7151	Fred Falkenheiner	N S Hodges	N S Hodges	N S Hodges	James Hawkins	M McDonald	Hubert McGlothin
De Soto (Mansfield) P (26)	318 872-0738	L B Bagley	Betty A Woods	Betty A Woods	Betty A Woods	David A Renshaw	Roger Gingles	Floyd E Lambert
East Carroll (Lake Providence) P (12)	318 559-2399	(not reporting)						
East Feliciana (Clinton) P (19)	504 683-8577	Charles E Coleman	John Thomas	Judith G Kelly	Judith G Kelly	W C Monroe	Fred Alsup	Arch V Doughty
Evangeline (Ville Platte) P (33)	318 363-5651	Larry Buller	Wilbert J Ardoin	Wilbert J Ardoin	Wilbert J Ardoin	R J Landreneau	J S Guillory	Floyd Soileau
Franklin (Winnsboro) P (24)	318 435-9429	Gilmer Lee	Ann Ezell	Ann Ezell	Ann Ezell	Ken McManus	....	Eugene Parker
Grant (Colfax) P† (17)	318 627-9907	Dan Brown	William M Bell	J Elray Lemoine	William M Bell	....	Jerry Brevelle	L R Hataway
Iberia (New Iberia) P (64)	318 365-8246	Francis Romero	....	B Schoeffler	William Boudreaux	Wayne M Labiche	Dr J R Romero	Errol A Romero
Iberville (Plaquemine) P† (32)	504 687-6819	Ernest J Franchise	....	Carl F Grant	Andrew J Hargooa	Carl F Grant	Carl E Blunck MD	Freddie Pitre
Jackson (Jonesboro) P (17)	318 259-2795	(not reporting)						
Jefferson Davis (Jennings) P (32)	318 824-1160	(not reporting)						
Jefferson (Gretna) P (455)	504 367-6611	Joseph S Yenni	J E Martin Jr	Dolores Gonzales	Dennis A Dimarco	Ross W Ketchum	Molly Puneky MD	Harry Lee
La Salle (Jena) P (17)	318 992-2158	(not reporting)						
Lafayette (Lafayette) P (150)	318 233-0150	(not reporting)						
Lafourche (Thibodaux) P (82)	504 446-8427	Cyrus B Tardo	Charles P Maggio	....	Charles P Maggio	Robert H Simons	Larry Legendre	Duffy Breaux
Lincoln (Ruston) P† (40)	318 255-3663	Fredric Hoogland	....	Ruby Nell Cobb	C Reagan Sutton	Felix B Camors	....	Wayne Houck
Livingston (Livingston) P (59)	504 686-2266	James H Sibley	....	Robbie C Hill	Connie Allen	....	John Sziber	Odom Graves
Madison (Tallulah) P† (15)	318 574-3451	Joe W Thornton	Joe M Clark	Ann D Thomas	Jewel Claxton	....	....	R R Mitchell
Morehouse (Bastrop) P (35)	318 281-3343	(not reporting)						
Natchitoches (Natchitoches) P† (40)	318 352-2714	J L Ackel	Louis C Bernard	Louis C Bernard	Jo Ann Ward	....	....	Norman A Fletcher
New Orleans-Orleans C (557)	504 586-4311	Ernest N Morial	Erroll G Williams	Leatrice Seigel	Bobby Major	....	Brobson Lutz MD	Henry M Morris
Ouachita (Monroe) P (139)	318 323-5188	Billy Daniel	....	Nell C Mangham	Nell C Mangham	....	Ruth Vingiello	Laymon Godwin
Plaquemines (Pointe a la Hache) P (26)	504 682-0081	Germaine B Curley	....	Merl D Ansardi	Albert J Beshel	Arthur S Patron	Esther Wood RN	Ernest Wooton
Pointe Coupee (New Roads) P (24)	504 638-9596	(not reporting)						
Rapides (Alexandria) P† (135)	318 473-6660	L B Henry	Barry D Hines	Angie Murray	Barry D Hines	Cecil Raggio	John Yeager	Marshall T Cappel
Red River (Coushatta) P (10)	318 932-5719	Glen Jones	Francis Brown Jr	Emmitt V Womack	Francis Brown Jr	....	M D Cannon	Buddy Huckabay
Richland (Rayville) P† (22)	318 728-2061	Larry Branch	Virginia Caviness	Virginia Caviness	Virginia Caviness	Terry Denmon	Mrs Clem	J Foster Jones Jr
Sabine (Many) P (25)	318 256-5637	Brady Strahan Jr	....	Dolly M Knippers	Edna C Shirley	Wayne Westerman	Quinton Corley	Alfice Brumley Jr
St. Bernard (Chalmette) P (64)	504 277-6371	Charles Ponstein	David B Farber	Stephen W Price	Stephen W Price	Thomas P Reed	....	Jack A Stephens
St. Charles (Hahnville) P (37)	504 783-6246	Kevin M Friloux	Timmy Vial	Joan W Becnel	Roland Becnel Jr	....	Zeringue Leola RN	Johnny Marino
St. Helena (Greensburg) P (10)	504 222-4514	(not reporting)						
St. James (Convent) P (21)	504 562-7496	(not reporting)						
St. John the Baptist (Laplace) P (32)	504 652-9569	Arnold Labat	Maxie McGraw	Audrey Millet	Claudette Raphael	Ernest Bailey	Sidney Becnel	Lloyd B Johnson
St. Landry (Opelousas) P† (84)	318 948-3688	Ivan Buck Ryder	Ronnie Ortego	Kathy Moreau	Chas Richard Jr	Jim Reynolds	J J Stagg MD	Howard Zerangue
St. Martin (St. Martinville) P† (40)	318 394-3711	L Higginbotham	Nathan J Cormier	James Theriot	Nathan J Cormier	Hector Naquin	Alfred Potier	Charles Fuselier
St. Mary (Franklin) P (64)	318 828-4100	Harold G Clausen	Connie M Fournet	Connie M Fournet	Connie M Fournet	F K Clausen	Joan Adams	Huey Bourgeois
St. Tammany (Covington) P (111)	504 892-3955	Herman A Sharp	R Lee Gilmour	Dennis D Striz	R Lee Gilmour	William H Dobson	Hilda Reynuad MD	Pat J Canulette
Tangipahoa (Amite) P (81)	504 748-4146	(not reporting)						
Tensas (St. Joseph) P (9)	318 766-3542	Sam Dillard	Ronnie W Hopkins	Ronnie W Hopkins	Ronnie W Hopkins	C Keith Capdepon	Norma Ray	Fred Scott
Terrebonne C§ (94)	504 868-3000	Edward P Lyons	Henry Boese	Paul Labat	Hebert Fredericks	Robert Jones	Victor Todesco	Charlton Rozands
Union (Farmerville) P (21)	318 368-3055	(not reporting)						
Vermilion (Abbeville) P (48)	318 893-3641	(not reporting)						
Vernon (Leesville) P (53)	318 239-2444	(not reporting)						
Washington (Franklinton) P (44)	504 839-4582	(not reporting)						
Webster (Minden) P (44)	318 377-2144	(not reporting)						
West Baton Rouge (Port Allen) P (19)	504 383-4755	Leo Blaize	Ted Denstel	Thomas Leblanc	Ted Denstel	George Lefebvre	M Volentine	Belvin Bergeron
West Carroll (Oak Grove) P (13)	318 428-3281	Bill Anderson	....	Martha Stephens	....	Terry Denmon	....	Gary Bennett
West Feliciana (St. Francisville) P (12)	504 635-3794	(not reporting)						
Winn (Winnfield) P (17)	318 628-5824	Hiriam J Wright	Catherine Roberts	Catherine Roberts	Catherine Roberts	A W Weissman	Tom McConnell	Dal L Page
MAINE (16)								
Androscoggin (Auburn) (100)	207 786-3501	(not reporting)						
Aroostook (Caribou) (91)	207 493-3318	David V Bell	....	Linda Richardson	Harry F Rideout	....	....	Edgar Wheeler
Cumberland (Portland)† (216)	207 774-4258	Joseph Mazziotti	....	Elvira S Ridlon	Frank Mulkern	....	....	Martin Joyce Jr
Franklin (Farmington)† (27)	207 778-6614	Stanton F Yeaton	....	Marie A Andrews	Edwina M Green	....	....	Ronald A Durrell
Hancock (Ellsworth) (42)	207 667-9542	John E Jordan Jr	....	Eugenia L Labelle	....	....	....	William F Clark
Kennebec (Augusta) (110)	207 622-0971	Nancy G Rines	....	Carole Obery	Theodore H Russel	....	....	Leo Bazinet
Knox (Rockland) (33)	207 594-9379	Merrill W Payson	....	Lois Ann Lehn	Pauline Curtis	....	....	George Massie
Lincoln (Wiscasset)† (26)	207 882-6311	M Robert Barter	....	Rupert C Stevens	Chester F Fossett	....	....	William C Carter
Oxford (South Paris) (49)	207 743-6359	Norman K Ferguson	Carole G Mahoney	Carole G Mahoney	William Perkins	....	....	Alton Howe

Directory 1/9 continued — COUNTY OFFICIALS IN ALL U.S. COUNTIES

County, county seat, 1980 population (000 omitted),	County telephone number	Board chairman	Appointed administrator	Clerk to the governing board	Chief financial officer	County engineer	County health officer	Chief law enforcement official
MAINE (16) continued								
Penobscot (Bangor) (137)	207 942-8535	John W Bragg	....	Mary K Strathdee	Irene A Burke	Peter M Buchanan	....	T B Richardson
Piscataquis (Dover-Foxcroft) (18)	207 564-2161	Joseph L A Morin	....	Carolyn K Doore	Philip E Warren	....	....	Frank H Murch
Sagadahoc (Bath) (29)	207 443-9332	Harold B Leeman	....	Francine D Pecci	Ida C Stover	....	....	Arthur E Tainter
Somerset (Skowhegan) (45)	207 474-9861	Charles Carpenter	....	Cynthia Pomerleau	Ruth Poland	....	....	William T Wright
Waldo (Belfast) (28)	207 338-3282	(not reporting)						
Washington (Machias) (35)	207 255-3127	(not reporting)						
York (Alfred) (140)	207 324-1571	James K McMahon	David R Adjutant	Marcia L Boudreau	Deborah Plamondon	....	....	C Wesley Phinney
MARYLAND (24)								
Allegany (Cumberland) (81)	301 777-5911	Arthur T Bond	Howard H Bailey	Carol A Gaffney	....	W Stephen Young	Jane A Fiscus MD	Donald R Wade
Anne Arundel (Annapolis) (371)	301 224-0113	Virginia Clagett	Adrian G Teel	Judith C Holmes	Walter N Chitwood	....	J Howard Beard MD	William S Lindsey
Baltimore (Towson)* (656)	301 494-3100	D P Hutchinson	B Melvin Cole	Thomas Toporovich	Annette R Grim	Harry J Pistel	Donald J Roop	Cornelius Behan
Baltimore (Baltimore) I (787)	301 396-3100	Wm D Schaeffer	Joan B Bereska	....	Charles L Benton	....	....	Bishop Robinson
Calvert (Prince Frederick) (35)	301 535-1600	William T Bowen	Jack G Upton	Ann F O'Neill	Jessie Jo Bowen	Jack Thye	David L Rogers	Adrian Joy
Caroline (Denton)§ (23)	301 479-0660	Earl R Bell	Edwin G Richards	K Leigh Sands	Dorsey L Wooters	Alan Visintainer	John A Grant	Louis C Andrew
Carroll (Westminster) (96)	301 848-4500	John L Armacost	Robert A Bair	Virginia R Black	Eugene C Curfman	John T Sterling	Janet W Neslen	Grover Sensabaugh
Cecil (Elkton)† (60)	301 398-0200	Frank D Ragan	David T Pinder	David T Pinder	Norman Hasson	Clifford Houston	Virginia Bailey	John F Dewitt
Charles (La Plata) (73)	301 645-0500	Marland Deen	C W Chinault	Shirley M Gore	Thelma M Bowie	Roy E Hancock	Diane Matuszak MD	David D Fuller
Dorchester (Cambridge) (31)	301 228-1700	William I Wingate	Robert K Lloyd	....	Warren G Robinson	Charles Weber	Eugene Guthrie	Philip McKelvey
Frederick (Frederick) (114)	301 694-1100	Galen R Clagett	Kenneth R Coffey	Wanda V Weddle	Martha A Brittain	Maurice F Daly	Martha T Schipper	Snyder C Robert
Garrett (Oakland) (26)	301 334-3917	John G Braskey	Robert J Fousek	Robert J Fousek	Arzella T Parsons	Kenneth Metheny	William Pope	Franklin Finch
Harford (Bel Air) (146)	301 838-6000	John Hardwicke	Georgia Hodsdon	....	James M Jewell	Jerald Wheeler	Thomas M Thomas	Theodore S Moyer
Howard (Ellicott City) (119)	301 992-2011	J Hugh Nichols	William E Eakle	Raquel Sanudo	J D Campbell	Geo F Neimeyer	Joyce M Boyd MD	Paul H Rappaport
Kent (Chestertown) (17)	301 778-4600	Mary Roe Walkup	....	Janice F Fletcher	W Roger Williams	E Nick Kirsch	John A Grant	H Allen Blizzard
Montgomery (Rockville)§ (579)	301 279-1000	Charles Gilchrist	Lewis T Roberts	....	Max R Bohnstedt	....	Donald A Swetter	Bernard D Crooke
Prince George's (Upper Marlboro)§ (665)	301 952-3000	Floyd E Wilson Jr	John Wesley White	Jean M Schmuhl	William R Brown	James R Novak	Helen McAllister	Michael Flaherty
Queen Annes (Centreville) (26)	301 758-0322	Oscar A Schulz	Robert D Sallitt	Lynda H Palmatary	William H Tolson	Joseph T Brice	Robert C Duvall	Melville Sewell
Somerset (Princess Anne) (19)	301 651-0320	Dennett L Butler	Charles E Massey	Charles E Massey	Philip R Mahan	Robert W Maddox	Gladys Allen	Thomas Windsor
St. Marys (Leonardtown)† (60)	301 475-5621	George H Aud	Edward V Cox	Judith A Spalding	Joseph P O'Dell	John B Norris Jr	William Marek	Wayne L Pettit
Talbot (Easton) (26)	301 822-2401	Herbert L Andrew	Blenda Armistead	Mary C Foster	Blenda Armistead	....	Eugene H Guthrie	Robert W Gerlock
Washington (Hagerstown) (113)	301 791-3090	Ronald L Bowers	Barry A Teach	Kathryn F Short	Harry C Snook	Glenn L Dull	John S Neill MD	Glenn L Bowman
Wicomico (Salisbury) (65)	301 749-5127	Henry S Parker	Matthew E Creamer	Virginia P Carson	C Joseph Schiller	C Kirk Banks	James E Bowes	John W Baker
Worcester (Snow Hill) (31)	301 632-1194	Roland E Powell	John A Yankus	....	Margaret C Davis	E Victor Smullen	Donald Harting	G D McAllister
MASSACHUSETTS (14)								
Barnstable (Barnstable) (148)	617 362-2511	Charles W Eager	....	Barbara H Neil	Mary LeClair	....	Stetson Hall	John J Bowes
Berkshire (Pittsfield) (145)	413 448-8424	John J Pignatelli	....	Deborah Capeless	Joann H Wadsworth	Robert L Saulnier	....	Carmen Massimiano
Boston-Suffolk C† (563)	617 725-4000	Raymond Flynn	Edward T Sullivan	....	Lowell L Richards	....	....	Joseph M Jordan
Bristol (Taunton) (475)	617 824-9681	M Earle Gaudette	....	William P Grant	Frank Vieira	....	....	David R Nelson
Dukes (Edgartown) (9)	617 627-5535	John S Alley	....	Beverly Wright	Margaret O'Neill	....	....	C S Look Jr
Essex (Salem)† (634)	617 741-0201	John W McKean	John F Barry	James D Leary	Katherine O'Leary	Richard Gelotti	....	Charles H Reardon
Franklin (Greenfield) (64)	413 774-4015	Margaret Herlihy	Wayne C Melville	Helen L Pekenia	Jean M Smith	Andrew F Wait	....	Donald J McQuade
Hampden (Springfield) (443)	413 781-8100	Rita M Tremble	....	William Martin Jr	Daniel M Keyes	Frank Rueli	....	Michel J Ashe Jr
Hampshire (Northampton) (139)	413 584-0557	Robert J Garvey	....	Norma J Thibodo	William O'Connor	Almer Huntley	....	John F Boyle
Middlesex (East Cambridge) (1367)	617 494-4000	Bill Schmidt	Paul W Blazar	Edward J Sullivan	William J Gustus	Philip H Lynch	Eugene Arnold	Edwd F Henneberry
Nantucket C (5)	617 228-0790	B Grossman	Keith A Bergman	Patricia R Church	....	....	Richard Ray	Randolph P Norris
Norfolk (Dedham) (607)	617 326-1600	James J Collins	Henry W Ainslie	N Barbadoro	James M Collins	Alvah L Downs	....	Clifford Marshall
Plymouth (Plymouth) (405)	617 747-1350	Joseph McCarthy	Diana C Lothrop	Francis R Powers	John F McLellan	Joseph F Monahan	....	Peter Y Flynn
Worcester (Worcester) (646)	617 798-7700	Paul X Tivnan	....	Philip J Philbin	Michael Donoghue	John C O'Toole	....	Theodore M Herman
MICHIGAN (83)								
Alcona (Harrisville) (10)	517 724-6807	Gerald Jasinsii	....	Anne Moore	Gerald Jasinsii	....	....	Edward Schroeder
Alger (Munising) (9)	906 387-2076	Albert B Hill	....	Donald W Kinnunen	Nancy R Robare	M Hendrickson	John Clark	David Cromell
Allegan (Allegan)† (82)	616 673-8471	James S Rolfe	....	Russell Sill	F Edgerton	Fred Neils	David L Ohmart	Robert L Schra
Alpena (Alpena)† (32)	517 356-0930	Roger B Phillips	....	Clara H Noack	Mary A Werner	....	Brian Youngs MD	Thomas Male
Antrim (Bellaire) (16)	616 533-8607	Curtis Patrick	....	Laura Sexton	Beverly Edgington	....	Walter Franczk	Elwin Wilcox
Arenac (Standish) (15)	501 673-3181	E Schillinger	....	Douglas C Black	Pauline Hall	Stephen Gregorich	Richard Nowak	James Mosciski
Baraga (L'Anse) (8)	906 524-6183	Larry C Menard	....	....	....	....	....	Harold Heikkinen
Barry (Hastings) (46)	616 945-3953	Paul Kiel	....	Norval E Thaler	Elsie B Furrow	Ronald L Lear	....	David O Wood
Bay (Bay City) (120)	517 892-5535	William A Reder	....	Steven Toth	E Lewandowski	William A Lynch	Frederick Dryzga	Kevin F Green
Benzie (Beulah) (11)	616 882-4433	Uledene Merrill	....	Jean Bowers	Ronald Mead			Zane Gray
Berrien (St. Joseph) (171)	616 983-7111	David M Peterson	Roger W Petrie	Forrest Kesterke	William C Heyn	Robt T Billington	Jermone Erickson	Forrest N Jewell
Branch (Coldwater) (40)	517 279-8411	Jerry R Hubbard	Angela Mabin	Raymond Ehl	Harold Myers	Fredrick Lilue	Benjamin Johnson	Norman Heinemann
Calhoun (Marshall) (142)	616 781-1677	(not reporting)						
Cass (Cassopolis)† (49)	616 445-8621	Dennis H Stamp	....	Kenneth M Poe	Sharon K Hansell	....	Owen Gordon	James E Northrop
Charlevoix (Charlevoix) (20)	616 547-9272	(not reporting)						
Cheboygan (Cheboygan) (21)	616 627-4233	(not reporting)						
Chippewa (Sault Ste. Marie) (29)	906 635-6300	Daniel T Dorrity	Patricia L Caruso	John J Sherry	Vida P Tesch	....	James Terrian	Leroy Case
Clare (Harrison) (24)	517 539-7131	Wayne J Elton	....	Donna Carr	Ellen Ulch	....	Richard Nowak	Ghazey Aleck
Clinton (St. Johns) (56)	517 224-6761	Roger A Overway	William Lefevere	Jane Swanchara	Gerald Shepard	....	Joseph Latoff	Anthony A Hufnage
Crawford (Grayling) (9)	517 348-2841	Jeannette Kitchen	....	Elizabeth Wieland	Joseph V Wakeley	John Keir	Jack Cinco	John B Huss
Delta (Escanaba)† (39)	906 786-2237	Elnora S Vader	Edward J Maguire	Michael R Albert	Myrtle V Ottensma	....	Mary Cretens	John Robitaille
Dickinson (Iron Mountain) (25)	906 774-2573	Garland Mainville	William Marchetti	Susan Wicklund	Joanne Johnson	....		Elroy Mattson
Eaton (Charlotte) (88)	517 543-7500	Carroll H Moon	James Stewart	Linda M Twitchell	Robert Cole	Dean Delamater	Edwin Larkin MD	Arthur Kelsey
Emmet (Petoskey)† (23)	616 347-2801	Al Foster	James Houston	Irene Granger	John Banwell	Orval Cutshaw	Jerry Chase	Richard Zink
Genesee (Flint)† (450)	313 257-3034	Michael K Brown	Frank E Goodroe	John H Trecha	Richard McGraw	Robert L Chase	Bernard Berman MD	John P Obrien
Gladwin (Gladwin) (20)	517 426-7351	Clarence Brokoff	....	William Hall	Elizabeth Ridley		....	Lawrence Lawless
Gogebic (Bessemer)† (20)	906 667-0411	V Melvin Jacobson	Rick A Minkin	Melvin R Peterson	Katherine Karjala	David B Carpenedo	....	Donald B Pezzetti
Grand Traverse (Traverse City) (55)	616 941-2420	William Kurtz	K Ross Childs	Virginia Watson	Dean F Sheets	Wes Reincke	Gordon Rady MD	Jack Canfield
Gratiot (Ithaca) (40)	517 875-3343	(not reporting)						
Hillsdale (Hillsdale) (42)	517 437-3391	(not reporting)						
Houghton (Houghton) (38)	906 482-1150	G R Pini	G H Pyhtila	R J Hosking	G H Pyhtila	....	....	J N Ruotsala
Huron (Bad Axe) (36)	517 269-8242	Ronald J Knoblock	....	Dorothy Stoeckle	Roberta Moetteli	Robert Tufts	Dale Hippensteel	Richard V Stokan
Ingham (Lansing) (272)	517 676-5222	(not reporting)						
Ionia (Ionia)† (52)	616 527-0300	Elvon Rasmussen	....	P LaViolette	Lucille Heppe	....	Edwin Larkin	William Bensinger
Iosco (Tawas City) (28)	517 362-4212	Carlton Merschel	David R McManus	D Keith Papas	Edward J Nelkie	Allen Buchanan	....	George Westcott

Directory 1/9 continued — COUNTY OFFICIALS IN ALL U.S. COUNTIES

County, county seat, 1980 population (000 omitted),	County telephone number	Board chairman	Appointed administrator	Clerk to the governing board	Chief financial officer	County engineer	County health officer	Chief law enforcement official
MICHIGAN (83) continued								
Iron (Crystal Falls) (14)	906 875-3301	Fred M Saigh	Daniel R Hannigan	Susan I Yackel	Arthur G Hibbard	Raymond Ronquist	Barbara Serena	Harold N Gill
Isabella (Mount Pleasant) (54)	517 772-0911	James Schafer	Randolph Terronez	Betty Prout	J Bierschbach	Bruce Rohrer	Richard Nowak	James Mull
Jackson (Jackson) (151)	517 788-4333	Robert Cowing	Elwin M Johnson	Jean S Kahn	Janet C Rochefort	....	Dean Tribby MD	Henry C Zavislak
Kalamazoo (Kalamazoo) (212)	616 384-8411	Herman Drenth	David Kirby	Nancy Donovan	Win Scofield	....	Robert Tomchik MD	Thomas Edmunds
Kalkaska (Kalkaska) (11)	616 258-4176	Harry R Hall Sr	....	Patricia Rodgers	Harry R Hall Sr	....	Richard Courson	Alan L Hart
Kent (Grand Rapids) (445)	616 774-3679	(not reporting)						
Keweenaw (Eagle River) (2)	906 337-2229	Donna D Lassila	Marilyn Winquist	Ethel L Ketola	Joyce Haapala	James Heikkila	D Gilbert MD	Elroy Antilla
Lake (Baldwin) (8)	616 745-2721	Robert D Stark	....	Lucinda K Keefer	Ruth J Updegraff	Thomas Sage	David C Nolan MD	Robert G Blevins
Lapeer (Lapeer)† (70)	313 667-0200	Gail L Potter	....	Mary Ellen Thick	Mary Ellen Thick	David DeSandre	John Niederhauser	Ronald Kalanquin
Leelanau (Leland) (14)	616 256-9824	James A Meyer	....	D Wunderlich	James A Meyer	James Gilbo	Matthew Houghton	Fred Buehrer
Lenawee (Adrian) (90)	517 263-8831	Hugh Flippo	William Bacon	Patricia Johnston	....	....	....	Richard L Germond
Livingston (Howell)† (100)	517 546-3520	Richard I Slayton	Barbara M Cox	Joseph H Ellis	Louis Crandall	....	Robert Scranton	Dennis DeBurton
Luce (Newberry) (7)	906 293-5521	R Richards	....	Eva Danielson	Lois Fighter	....	James Terrian MD	K Erickson
Mackinac (St. Ignace) (10)	906 643-7300	Vernon T Hossack	....	L Marie Kaminsky	Charles Gustafson	....	F Howard Hague	Benjamin Thompson
Macomb (Mount Clemens) (695)	313 469-5100	Patrick J Johnson	David M Diegel	Edna Miller	Adam E Nowakowski	....	Daniel C Lafferty	William H Hackel
Manistee (Manistee) (23)	616 723-4575	Roy C Howes	S M Fredericks	Emily Iverson	Alan Ver Heek	....	William Moon MD	Ford Waterman
Marquette (Marquette)§ (74)	906 228-8500	Timothy J Lowe	Dennis Aloia	Henry A Skewis	James F Sodergren	John Beerling	Randy Johnson MD	Joseph I Maino
Mason (Ludington) (26)	616 843-8202	(not reporting)						
Mecosta (Big Rapids) (37)	616 796-5835	James Peek	Charles W Curtis	Elda H Wells	Virginia Tighe	....	David C Nolan	Gerald F Weis
Menominee (Menominee) (26)	906 863-9968	Thomas Zeratsky	....	Kenneth Krause	L Therriault	....	Mary Cretens	Herbert Marklein
Midland (Midland)§ (74)	517 832-6780	Scott MacDonald	Charles A Londo	Jeffrey Porter	William Case	A John Hatt	Winfred Oyen	James McNutt
Missaukee (Lake City) (10)	616 839-4967	Gerald DeRuiter	....	Don Molitor	Lorna Molitor	Henry Diemer	Gordon R Rady	Richard A Jenema
Monroe (Monroe) (135)	313 243-7011	Arden T Westover	John J Kryston	Warren J Labeau	Norman J Blanchet	....	David J Lieberman	Chas G Harrington
Montcalm (Stanton) (48)	517 831-5226	Lorena M Braendle	Nancy Hansing	Nyle Erskin	Rosmary Long	....	Joseph Latoff	Thomas Hebert
Montmorency (Atlanta) (7)	517 785-3358	Albert LaFleche	Paul B Goode	M Jeanne Clement	Gloria J Marlatt	....	....	Randall Wilson
Muskegon (Muskegon)§ (158)	616 724-6231	John Halmond	Ralph Precious	Sheryl L Albertie	William Andree	Robert Zettell	Anita Herald	Harry Pennington
Newaygo (White Cloud) (35)	616 689-7200	John Graves	Barbara A Geno	Maxwell L Jordan	Stanley Dekuiper	Norman Ochs	David Nolan	Leonard Somers
Oakland (Pontiac) (1012)	313 858-0480	Richard R Wilcox	....	Lynn D Allen	Louis A Mackenzie	Donald Malinowski	Robert L Locey MD	L Brookspatterson
Oceana (Hart) (22)	616 873-4835	John M Kirk	Paul E Inglis	Elizabeth A Field	George A Lambrix	....	....	John R Simmons
Ogemaw (West Branch) (16)	517 345-0714	John D Williams	....	Edwin D Ostrander	Beverly Bennett	Harold Smith	....	William Ehinger
Ontonagon (Ontonagon) (10)	906 884-4255	T J Domitrovich	James M Hainault	Bernice M Huotari	Diana J Killoran	Joseph Meagher	Marion Davison	Gerald Kitzman
Osceola (Reed City) (19)	616 832-3261	Robert Pontz	....	Carl L Wyman	Elizabeth Staffor	....	Richard Novak	David Needham
Oscoda (Mio) (7)	517 826-3241	(not reporting)						
Otsego (Gaylord) (15)	517 732-6484	J Richard Yuill	....	Ardis I Heacock	Erma Backenstose	....	Charles N Iknayan	Robert Dowker
Ottawa (Grand Haven) (157)	616 846-8326	Jack R Smant	....	Daniel C Krueger	Kurt W Humphrey	Ronald Bakker	William C Lamain	Robert Dykstra
Presque Isle (Rogers City) (14)	517 734-3288	Neil Whitsitt	....	Faye C Claus	William Furtaw	....	Brian Youngs	Myron E Peltz
Roscommon (Roscommon) (16)	517 275-5923	Eleanor Sliter	....	Robert W Smith	Dolores M Barber	....	....	Garth A Meyer
Saginaw (Saginaw) (228)	517 790-5200	Norman E Howell	J Marvin Baldwin	Gladys J Ormsby	Marvin D Hare	James F Clark	Senen L R Asuan	James L Kelly
Sanilac (Sandusky) (41)	313 648-2933	Robert L Warren	John Dean	Delene Schultheis	Ken Rhead	....	Dale Hippensteel	Ross Dundas
Schoolcraft (Manistique) (9)	906 341-5532	Lindsley Frenette	....	Ferdinand Lesica	William E Cowman	....	James Terrian	Lloyd E Gray
Shiawassee (Corunna) (71)	517 743-3421	Lloyd A Webster	....	Elna M Thatcher	Judith Kingsbury	....	Charles R Newell	A James LaJoye
St. Clair (Port Huron)§ (139)	313 985-9631	Alexander Wnuk	Samuel Grey	Marion Sargent	Donald E Dodge	Robert E D'Alcorn	Jon B Parsons	David J Doktor
St. Joseph (Centreville) (56)	616 467-6361	Arden Wright	....	Beverly J Burnham	Janet L Beals	....	Benjamin Johnson	Neubert D Balk
Tuscola (Caro) (57)	517 673-5999	Donna Rayl	....	Elsie Hicks	Elgene Keller	Robert Wellington	John Niederhauser	Paul Berry
Van Buren (Paw Paw) (67)	616 657-5581	Franklin Schurr	....	Shirley Jackson	Bee Lackey	....	James Davis MD	H Cal Rosema
Washtenaw (Ann Arbor)§ (265)	313 994-2400	Mary Egnor	David Hunscher	Robert Harrison	Steven Racine	Jack Durbin	John Atwater	Ron Schebil
Wayne (Detroit)† (2337)	313 224-0903	Samuel A Turner	....	Bernard E Hanus	Raymond Wojtowicz	....	Dennis J Dilworth	William Lucas
Wexford (Cadillac) (25)	616 779-9453	Robert Mackey	....	Donald Linn	Hubert L Toudin	....	....	Ronald J Jameson
MINNESOTA (87)								
Aitkin (Aitkin) (13)	218 927-2102	Melvin L Johnson	....	Helena C Dotzler	Veron Nelson	John Walkup	James Hover MD	William J Sobey
Anoka (Anoka) (196)	612 421-4760	Albert A Kordiak	Jay McLinden	....	Don Bailey	Paul Ruud	....	Buster Talbot
Becker (Detroit Lakes) (29)	218 847-7659	C A Boyer	....	Conrad Ohm	Conrad Ohm	Monte Berend	Virgil Watson	Terry Shannon
Beltrami (Bemidji) (31)	218 751-7300	Glidden Kenneth	....	Ruth Edevold	Tony Paxton	Raymond Sauve	Larry Schuette	Norland Orielle
Benton (Foley) (25)	612 968-6206	Emil Kelm Jr	Larry P Johnson	Larry P Johnson	Joan Neyssen	Dennis C Carlson	Vicki R Hoffman	L Trushenski
Big Stone (Ortonville) (8)	612 839-2105	Elwood Throndrud	....	Judith F Pattison	Donald Williams	James D Burgess	Robert Ross	Orin Haukos
Blue Earth (Mankato) (52)	507 625-3031	William A Maher	Pat McDonnel	Milton Owens	Pat McDonnel	Ralph Sleeper	Al Hanzel	Leroy Wiebold
Brown (New Ulm) (29)	507 359-7900	Conrad B Hilbert	Otis A Loose	Otis A Loose	Jerome R Bentz	James Sommer	Milton L Kaiser	Larry D Pederson
Carlton (Carlton)† (30)	218 384-4281	James Nynas	....	Allan W Naslund	Robert Sundeen	Boyd Paulu	R Christensen MD	Terry Twomey
Carver (Chaska) (37)	612 448-3435	Joe F Neaton	Gregory L Mangold	Gregory L Mangold	Donald F Dahlke	Donald Wisniewski	C L Provence MD	Jack Hendrickson
Cass (Walker) (21)	218 547-3300	M Hime	....	Robert F Hansen	Marge L Daniels	James Worcester	Dorothy J Opheim	Louis Chalich
Chippewa (Montevideo)† (15)	612 269-7447	Leonard Ward	....	Byron Zurn	Jon Clauson	Elroy Dragsten	....	Donald Skogrand
Chisago (Center City) (26)	612 257-1300	(not reporting)						
Clay (Moorhead) (49)	218 299-5002	Marvin Dauner	....	Jim Thoreen	Pauline Sarbaum	John Cousins	Jon Thomas	Jim Fischer
Clearwater (Bagley) (9)	218 694-6177	(not reporting)						
Cook (Grand Marais) (4)	218 387-2282	Chester Lindskog	....	Carol Gresczyk	Carol Gresczyk	David Zech	Stephen Lackore	John Lyght
Cottonwood (Windom) (15)	507 831-1905	Keith Madson	....	C W Langley	M M Wiens	Lynn Emerson	....	Glen Ward
Crow Wing (Brainerd)† (42)	218 829-1481	Mary Koep	....	Conrad A Bye	Conrad A Bye	Duane A Blanck	Edward Rosenbaum	Charles Warnberg
Dakota (Hastings) (194)	612 437-3191	J Voss	Frederick Joy Jr	Joan Kendall	Thomas V Novak	Robert Sandeen	....	Rodney Boyd
Dodge (Dodge Center)† (15)	507 635-2321	Harlan Buck	....	....	....	Vern Moll	Anne Hagler	Ernest Vanderhyde
Douglas (Alexandria) (28)	612 762-2381	Bill Collins	....	William Anderson	A C Olsen	E Lynn Olson	....	Terry Eilers
Faribault (Blue Earth) (20)	507 526-5145	Paul Beyer	Palmer N Eckhardt	Palmer N Eckhardt	Willert McRea	Hershel Koenig	....	Roger Fletcher
Fillmore (Preston)† (22)	507 765-4701	....		....	Philip Burkholder	Neil Britton	....	Donald Gudmundson
Freeborn (Albert Lea) (36)	507 373-0794	S L Johnson	Truman Thrond	Truman Thrond	William E Brown	David L Everds	....	Donald Nolander
Goodhue (Red Wing) (39)	612 388-8261	John E Davidson	....	William A Miller	....	M G Pinsonneault	....	Dale R Grote
Grant (Elbow Lake) (7)	218 685-4520	Robert Richards	....	Delores Flint	....	Otho C Buxton	....	Edward Williams
Hennepin (Minneapolis)§ (941)	612 348-3000	John E Derus	Dale A Ackmann	Kay Mitchell	Vernon Hoppe	A J Lee	....	Donald J Omodt
Houston (Caledonia) (20)	507 724-5211	Harold J Leary	....	Douglas K Moen	Stan Harris	....	Donna Herman	Dennis L Swedberg
Hubbard (Park Rapids) (14)	218 732-3196	Wayne Cochran	Roland K Vik	Roland K Vik	Irene S Toops	Douglas Goriesky	Robert J Rose MD	Larry Johnson
Isanti (Cambridge)§ (24)	612 689-3859	Frank Weisbrod	George Rindelaub	George Rindelaub	Wilfred Norman	Charles Gronberg	Lowell Becker MD	Kenneth Harder
Itasca (Grand Rapids) (43)	218 326-9777	Doug Carpenter	Robert R Olson	Robert R Olson	Dale M Virden	George Engstrom	Dennis Scherer	Russell Johannsen
Jackson (Jackson)† (14)	507 847-2763	Milford Gentz	....	Luther F Glaser	Clayton Eolson	Dwight M Herman	Dennis Hanselman	Gerald Benjamin
Kanabec (Mora)† (12)	612 679-1030	Percy Terpstra	....	Jerry T Tvedt	Elaine Harrison	Gregory Nikodym	Ronald K Menk MD	George L Anderson
Kandiyohi (Willmar) (37)	612 235-2727	Virgil M Olson	Wayne Thompson	Alvin H Hoogeveen	Zelda Minke	Gary Danielson	Richard Rasmussen	Larry Kleinhuizen
Kittson (Hallock) (7)	218 843-2655	Floyd L Sanner	....	Elden W Johnson	Robert Laude	David Olsonawski	Claudia Nyegaard	B Patrick Overend
Koochiching (International Falls) (18)	218 283-2581	Donald Sandbeck	....	Darlene Olsen	Robert Lovell	Douglas Grindall	Marc Gorden	William Elliott
Lac Qui Parle (Madison) (11)	612 598-7444	Alfred Gloege	....	Raymond L Olson	Marlyn Johnson	Marlyn Hanson	....	Graylen Carlson

Directory 1/9 continued

COUNTY OFFICIALS IN ALL U.S. COUNTIES

County, county seat, 1980 population (000 omitted),	County telephone number	Board chairman	Appointed administrator	Clerk to the governing board	Chief financial officer	County engineer	County health officer	Chief law enforcement official
MINNESOTA (87) continued								
Lake (Two Harbors) (13)	218 834-5581	Edwin W Hansen	Richard A Sigel	Richard A Sigel	Melroy Peterson	Alan D Goodman	Harold B Leppink	William DeRosier
Lake of the Woods (Baudette) (4)	218 634-1451	(not reporting)						
Le Sueur (Le Center) (23)	612 357-2251	Robert T Kaveney	....	Terry Overn	Robert F Tuma	Ronald Sandvik	Brian Smith	Pat W Smith
Lincoln (Ivanhoe) (8)	507 694-1529	Carl Hauschild	....	D D Sagmoe	Mark R Leibfried	Luthard Hagen	....	Albert Thompson
Lyon (Marshall) (25)	507 537-6728	William Merrit	....	Catherine Seifert	Catherine Seifert	Tom Behm	....	Don Stokke
Mahnomen (Mahnomen) (6)	218 935-2251	(not reporting)						
Marshall (Warren) (13)	218 745-4851	M Gonsorowski	....	Charles G Cheney	Charles G Cheney	....	W A Pinnsoneault	Dennis G Brekke
Martin (Fairmont) (25)	507 235-3261	(not reporting)						
McLeod (Glencoe) (30)	612 864-5551	(not reporting)						
Meeker (Litchfield) (21)	612 693-2887	Kermit Swanson	Donald Herzog	Donald Herzog	Allan Knutson	G Regenschied	Daniel Johnson	John Rogers
Mille Lacs (Milaca) (18)	612 983-2561	Fran Barg	....	Elmer Warolin	Elmer Warolin	Richard Larson	Julie A Johnston	Russell Iverson
Morrison (Little Falls)§ (29)	612 632-2941	Gilbert Kapsner	David Loch	David Loch	Rose Hubner	Ken Paulson	Mary Ann Blade	Paul Tschida
Mower (Austin)† (40)	507 433-2077	Robert Finbraaten	....	Graham R Uzlik	Eileen Tapager	Ray Guttormson	Gene C Muchow MD	Wayne Goodnature
Murray (Slayton) (12)	507 836-6163	Rimer Isder	....	Duane Q Bonohus	R Loosbrock	Donald M Barth	....	Ronald McKenzie
Nicollet (St. Peter) (27)	507 931-6800	Warren Rodning	....	Lawrence Overn	Richard Bresnahan	Mike Wagner	Larry Biederman	George T Witty
Nobles (Worthington) (22)	507 372-7711	Orville S Wee	Ken W Roberts	Ken W Roberts	Ken W Roberts	Steven Schnieder	....	Dale C Peters
Norman (Ada) (9)	218 784-7131	(not reporting)						
Olmsted (Rochester) (92)	507 285-8115	Joan T Sass	Richard G Devlin	Richard G Devlin	Robert Bendzick	John K Dolan	Arvid Houglum MD	Charles Von Wald
Otter Tail (Fergus Falls) (52)	218 739-2271	Sydney G Nelson	....	Sylvia G Bergerud	Steven Andrews	Dennis Berend	Larry Mathison	Glen M Melby
Pennington (Thief River Falls) (15)	218 681-4011	Glenn Tasa	Kenneth Olson	Kenneth Olson	A E Jorgenson	Wayne Olson	E O Thorsgaard	Charles Richards
Pine (Pine City) (20)	612 629-6781	C Camielewski	....	Frances Southwick	Ruth A Blahnik	David L Rholl	Ralph F Mach MD	John Kozisek
Pipestone (Pipestone) (12)	507 825-4494	Ray Haarsma	....	Gordon Baden	Ruth Wiese	Doug Haeder	....	Ronald Smidt
Polk (Crookston) (35)	218 281-5408	Don Bakken	John Schmalenberg	John Schmalenberg	Florence Rood	Bernard Lieder	R T Martin	Earl Mosher
Pope (Glenwood) (12)	612 634-5301	Ralph Ranum	Wm T Boyle	Wm T Boyle	David Troen	Otho Buxton	Elayne Schluter	Gerald Moe
Ramsey (St. Paul)§ (460)	612 298-4145	Warren W Schaber	R L Brubacher	Harry E Marshall	James Van Houdt	Kenneth E Weltzin	Raymond Cink	Charles Zacharias
Red Lake (Red Lake Falls) (5)	218 253-4281	(not reporting)						
Redwood (Redwood Falls) (19)	507 637-8325	Richard Jacobsen	....	Larry L Bunting	John R Mahoney	Peter Boomgarden	Sue Stout	Jerry Luttman
Renville (Olivia) (20)	612 523-2071	Palmer Brelie	Jim Tersteeg	Jim Tersteeg	Douglas Knutson	Dennis Stoeckman	Leo O Furr	Donald Davis
Rice (Faribault)§ (46)	507 334-2281	Warren Babcock	Nancy Hohbach	Lorraine Nelson	Dorothy Gallagher	Art Storhaug	Daniel Campbell	David Schweisthal
Rock (Luverne) (11)	507 283-8212	Slieter R Allan	....	Charles A Braa	Margaret Cook	Arnold W Johnson	D W Siebert	Ole Hommen
Roseau (Roseau) (13)	218 463-2541	(not reporting)						
Scott (Shakopee) (44)	612 445-7750	Anthony Worm	Joseph F Ries	Joseph F Ries	Thomas E Muelken	Bradley Larson	Anthony Spagnolo	Douglas L Tietz
Sherburne (Elk River) (30)	612 441-1441	Frank Madsen	....	E Dale Palmer	Lois Riecken	Russ Matchinsky	....	Richard Witschen
Sibley (Gaylord) (15)	612 237-2369	Leroy Pinske	Gene O Solmonson	Gene O Solmonson	Waldo Reckdahl	Gene Isakson	Lois Hacker	Roger M Graham
St. Louis (Duluth) (222)	218 726-2000	Gary E Cerkvenik	....	Raymond C Carlson	Russell Petersen	Ben Beauclair	Harold Leppink	Ernie Grams
Stearns (St. Cloud)§ (108)	612 251-1882	Clarence Kramer	Peter J Herlofsky	Henry J Kohorst	Thomas Winter	William Rice	....	Charles Grafft
Steele (Owatonna) (30)	507 451-8040	Les Oeltjenbruns	David Severson	John Hallenberger	Alphonso Langer	Richard Skalicky	Kenneth Buresh	Wm Hildebrandt
Stevens (Morris) (11)	612 589-4660	Paul W Larson	....	Dick Bluth	Dick Bluth	Lawrence Schaub	Michael Busian	Larry J Sayre
Swift (Benson) (13)	612 843-4069	John R Langan	....	Byron L Giese	Ronald A Vadnais	Tallack Johnson	Kathy Cavanaugh	Kenneth B Hanson
Todd (Long Prairie) (25)	612 732-6181	Robert George	....	Melvin Bense	Kathryn Gresser	Duane Lorsung	Guy Peterson	Kenneth Gothman
Traverse (Wheaton) (6)	612 563-4311	(not reporting)						
Wabasha (Wabasha)† (19)	612 565-3978	John Fitzgerald	Charles McDonald	Charles McDonald	Martin R Beyer	Robert Egan	Elaine Timmer	Robert Loechler
Wadena (Wadena) (14)	218 631-2425	Clarence Kreklau	....	Robert Fort	Robert C Lindberg	F Gene Mattern	Karen Nelson	H Michael Carr
Waseca (Waseca) (18)	507 835-7510	Robert L Peterson	Bruce M Boyce	Roy S Nelson	Roderick E Joyce	Robert McPartlin	S Normann MD	Edward Kubat
Washington (Stillwater)§ (114)	612 439-3220	Sally Evert	Charles Swanson	Charles Swanson	R H Stafford	....	Mary Luth	James Trudeau
Watonwan (St. James)† (12)	507 375-3341	Lyle Bergeman	....	Roald Revne	Lucy Burke	Gerald Engstrom	....	Vernie Engdahl
Wilkin (Breckenridge) (8)	218 643-4981	R Friederichs	....	Wm E McCullough	Francis W Ziegler	Thomas G Richels	....	Beryl D Osmondson
Winona (Winona) (46)	507 452-4174	Lee Luebbe	C Donald Gilomen	C Donald Gilomen	C Sherwood	Rick Arnebeck	Lynn Theurer	Vernon Spitzer
Wright (Buffalo) (59)	612 682-3900	Paul J McAlpine	Richard W Norman	Richard W Norman	....	Wayne Fingalson	Jannice Devens	E Darrell Wolff
Yellow Medicine (Granite Falls) (14)	612 564-3132	....	....	Mayme Kompelien	Sharon Schuler	Don Paulson	Carl Lundell	Richard Rollins
MISSISSIPPI (82)								
Adams (Natchez) (38)	601 446-6684	(not reporting)						
Alcorn (Corinth) (33)	601 286-6265	James Newcomb	....	Leon Fields	Leon Fields	....	Luther Adams	Bill O Gant
Amite (Liberty) (13)	601 657-8022	H K Barron	....	Reece Nunnery	Reece Nunnery	L H Clark	Dorothy Hess	Norman Travis
Attala (Kosciusko) (20)	601 289-2921	(not reporting)						
Benton (Ashland) (8)	601 224-6611	(not reporting)						
Bolivar (Cleveland) (46)	601 843-9413	J E Bobo	Wayne Cole	Jeanne R Walker	Jeanne R Walker	W M Thomas	....	H M Grimmett
Calhoun (Pittsboro)† (16)	601 983-2424	Robert E Clanton	....	Tommy Hallum	Tommy Hallum	Leland Cook	Thomas Waller MD	James Morgan
Carroll (Carrollton) (10)	601 237-9274	Don Conley	Ralph Self	Ralph Self	Ralph Self	Charles James	Alifo Rausa	C D Whitfield
Chickasaw (Houston) (18)	601 456-2513	(not reporting)						
Choctaw (Ackerman) (9)	601 285-6329	Kenneth A King	....	Donald Nunn	Donald Nunn	J C Patton	Virginia Ray	Boyce W Bruce
Claiborne (Port Gibson)† (12)	601 437-4992	William Matt Ross	....	Stella H Jenning	....	F Joe Speights	....	Frank Davis
Clarke (Quitman) (17)	601 776-2126	(not reporting)						
Clay (West Point) (21)	601 494-3124	(not reporting)						
Coahoma (Clarksdale) (37)	601 624-2286	(not reporting)						
Copiah (Hazlehurst)† (27)	601 894-3011	W E Hood	M E Keys	L E Hood	....	F J Speights	James Wooten	T L Jackson
Covington (Collins) (16)	601 765-4242	(not reporting)						
De Soto (Hernando) (54)	601 368-5011	(not reporting)						
Forrest (Hattiesburg) (66)	601 583-3551	Lynn Cartlidge	Herman Lee	Jimmy Havard	Jimmy Havard	Richard Simmons	Clay Hammack	Gene Walters
Franklin (Meadville) (8)	601 384-2330	Carl Ray Lehmann	Jimmy W Jones	Jimmy W Jones	Jimmy W Jones	Larry H Clark	Joyce Carlock	James H Newman
George (Lucedale) (15)	601 947-4801	Ralph Fairley	....	Jerry Ray Harvey	Jerry Ray Harvey	Wayne Brown	L B Barton	Eugene C Howell
Greene (Leakesville)† (10)	601 394-2377	Lauvon Pierce	....	Lavon Freeman	Lavon Freeman	Paul Conguista	....	Tommy Miller
Grenada (Grenada) (21)	601 226-1821	(not reporting)						
Hancock (Bay St. Louis) (25)	601 467-5404	Adolph Kellar	....	E Michael Necaise	E Michael Necaise	....	....	Ronald Peterson
Harrison (Gulfport) (158)	601 865-4001	Leroy Urie	....	G N Creel	G N Creel	A W Hagan	Martha Adams Hays	Larkin Smith
Hinds (Jackson) (251)	601 968-6500	(not reporting)						
Holmes (Lexington) (23)	601 834-2508	(not reporting)						
Humphreys (Belzoni) (14)	601 247-1740	(not reporting)						
Issaquena (Mayersville) (3)	601 873-2761	W E Holmb Jr	....	Mary Vandevender	....	Wallace Carter	....	Arthur Lawler
Itawamba (Fulton) (21)	601 862-3421	Billy Young	....	Betty Hood	Betty Hood	Claude Martin	....	Leland Taylor
Jackson (Pascagoula) (118)	601 769-3089	Peter Fierce	Jim Williams	Lynn Presley	Lynn Presley	James Fortenberry	....	Wallace Gill
Jasper (Bay Springs) (17)	601 764-3368	(not reporting)						
Jefferson Davis (Prentiss) (14)	601 792-4204	Ralph Daley	....	Jack D Berry	Jack D Berry	John L Anderson	Clay Hammock	Gary Jones
Jefferson (Fayette) (9)	601 786-3021	(not reporting)						

Directory 1/9 continued — COUNTY OFFICIALS IN ALL U.S. COUNTIES

County, county seat, 1980 population (000 omitted),	County telephone number	Board chairman	Appointed administrator	Clerk to the governing board	Chief financial officer	County engineer	County health officer	Chief law enforcement official
MISSISSIPPI (82) continued								
Jones (Laurel) (62)	601 428-0527	(not reporting)						
Kemper (de Kalb)† (10)	601 743-2460	Mike Luke	....	Betty Eldridge	Betty Eldridge	J W Kemp	Margaret Morrison	Joe Sciple
Lafayette (Oxford) (31)	601 234-2131	(not reporting)						
Lamar (Purvis) (24)	601 794-8504	Carley Parker	....	Carley Parker	Carley Parker	Bill Jordan	....	Estus Earlott
Lauderdale (Meridian) (77)	601 482-9701	(not reporting)						
Lawrence (Monticello) (13)	601 587-7162	(not reporting)						
Leake (Carthage) (19)	601 267-7371	Jack Jones	....	Neal Horn	Neal Horn	Joe A Waggoner	M Morrison MD	Joe M Thaggard
Lee (Tupelo)† (57)	601 842-2311	Alfred W Rice	Alfred W Rice	Jerry L Clayton	Jerry L Clayton	Ben Coggins	Will Denton	Robert Herring
Leflore (Greenwood) (42)	601 453-1041	(not reporting)						
Lincoln (Brookhaven) (30)	601 833-4911	(not reporting)						
Lowndes (Columbus) (57)	601 327-7880	Charles J Younger	....	....	Charles J Younger	Oliver Mitchell	....	Louis W Harper Sr
Madison (Canton) (42)	601 859-1177	Pat Luckett Jr	....	Billy J Cooper	....	Horace Lester	Alice Lee MD	William Noble
Marion (Columbia) (26)	601 736-2691	(not reporting)						
Marshall (Holly Springs)† (29)	601 252-4431	Joe Cooper	....	J M Flick Ash	J M Flick Ash	A L Goodman	....	Osborne Bell
Monroe (Aberdeen) (36)	601 369-8143	(not reporting)						
Montgomery (Winona) (13)	601 283-2333	(not reporting)						
Neshoba (Philadelphia) (24)	601 656-3581	Arlo Winstead	Mary B Beckham	Bobby G Posey	Bobby G Posey	Tom W Cox	....	Glen Waddell
Newton (Decatur) (20)	601 635-3370	H M Smith	....	Janice Nelson	Janice Nelson	Maury Gunter	....	M A Miles
Noxubee (Macon) (13)	601 726-4243	(not reporting)						
Oktibbeha (Starkville) (36)	601 323-5834	(not reporting)						
Panola (Batesville)† (28)	601 563-3171	M N Aldridge	....	C B Vance Jr	C B Vance Jr	R M Short	J O White	D M Bryan
Pearl River (Poplarville) (34)	601 795-2237	(not reporting)						
Perry (New Augusta) (10)	601 964-3218	Paul Johnston	....	Alfred Lott	Alfred Lott	Paul Conjustia	Clay Hammack	Jimmy Smith
Pike (Magnolia) (36)	601 783-3363	(not reporting)						
Pontotoc (Pontotoc) (21)	601 489-3451	Grady O Baker	Terry Donaldson	Terry Donaldson	Terry Donaldson	James E Akins	W E Riecken	John H Moore
Prentiss (Booneville) (24)	601 728-8151	J P Davis	....	Phillip Cole	Phillip Cole	Don Eubanks	Greg Geno	W V Horn
Quitman (Marks) (13)	601 326-2661	(not reporting)						
Rankin (Rankin) (69)	601 825-2217	(not reporting)						
Scott (Forest) (25)	601 469-1922	W J Measels Jr	....	Kenneth Gordon	....	Maurey E Gunter	Margaret Morrison	Glen L Warren
Sharkey (Rolling Fork) (8)	601 873-2755	Joe Carson	....	Don H Collins	Don H Collins	Wallace Carter	....	Joe Ford
Simpson (Mendenhall) (23)	601 847-1418	L C McAlpin	Hugh Jack Stubbs	Lennis Welch	Lennis Welch	Jerry Wallace	Bob Wolfe MD	Lloyd Jones
Smith (Raleigh) (15)	601 782-4463	(not reporting)						
Stone (Wiggins)† (10)	601 928-5266	O B Brown	....	Gerald W Bond	Gerald W Bond	Dan R O'Neal	Sue Batson	Eldon Ladner
Sunflower (Indianola) (35)	601 887-4703	James Corder	Jack E Harper Jr	Jack E Harper Jr	Jack E Harper Jr	G Wayne Gardner	Anne Sessums	C O Sessums
Tallahatchie (Charleston) (17)	601 647-5551	(not reporting)						
Tate (Senatobia) (20)	601 562-5661	(not reporting)						
Tippah (Ripley) (19)	601 837-7374	(not reporting)						
Tishomingo (Iuka) (18)	601 423-6021	(not reporting)						
Tunica (Tunica)† (10)	601 363-2451	Paul Battle Jr	Larry M Butler	Hugh J Hawkins	Hugh J Hawkins	Joe Lauderdale	James O White	Hugh M Monteith J
Union (New Albany) (22)	601 534-5284	(not reporting)						
Walthall (Tylertown) (14)	601 876-3553	(not reporting)						
Warren (Vicksburg)† (52)	601 636-4415	James R Andrews	....	Mark J Chaney	Mark J Chaney	Gerald Crout	John Campbell	Paul Barrett
Washington (Greenville) (72)	601 332-1595	(not reporting)						
Wayne (Waynesboro) (19)	601 735-2873	Artis L Clay	....	H H Hardee	H H Hardee	Lawrence R Clark	....	Marvin M Farrior
Webster (Walthall) (10)	601 258-4131	James Dean	....	J D Robertson	J D Robertson	Jack Willis	....	Bill Middleton
Wilkinson (Woodville)† (10)	601 888-4381	W B Netterville	....	Thomas C Tolliver	Thomas C Tolliver	Phillip Chaffin	....	H B McGraw
Winston (Louisville)† (19)	601 773-3319	Jack Warner	....	Bobby S Sullivan	Bobby S Sullivan	....	Jerry Hill	Cecil Jennings
Yalobusha (Water Valley)† (13)	601 473-2091	E Doke French	Bobby H Clark	Bobby H Clark	Bobby H Clark	Jack Willis	Ms Quay Jones	L A Jones
Yazoo (Yazoo City) (27)	601 746-2661	(not reporting)						
MISSOURI (115)								
Adair (Kirksville)† (25)	816 665-3350	Jack Shelton	....	Max W Patterson	Clara Wheeler	....	Claudine Frazier	Jim Kemp
Andrew (Savannah) (14)	816 324-3624	Donald L Phillipp	....	Francis E Turner	Doris L Franklin	....	....	Gary Howard
Atchison (Rockport) (9)	816 744-6214	(not reporting)						
Audrain (Mexico) (26)	314 581-8211	J W Toalson	....	John B Jesse	Mary E Davis	Bill Todd	William Johnson	James A Barber
Barry (Cassville) (24)	417 847-2561	Dilbeck Lloyd	Dilbeck Lloyd	....	....	George Ulmer	....	Jimmy Hopkins
Barton (Lamar) (11)	417 682-3529	G Douglas Haile	....	Bonda Rawlings	Marion Sprouls	....	....	L Ron Jeffries
Bates (Butler) (16)	816 679-3371	(not reporting)						
Benton (Warsaw) (12)	816 438-7326	(not reporting)						
Bollinger (Marble Hill) (10)	314 238-2126	Jerry Woodfin	....	Myra K Dickerson	Mary J Crader	....	....	Januar Peters
Boone (Columbia) (100)	314 874-7515	Norma Robb	....	Wendy Noren	Kay Murray	....	....	Charles Foster
Buchanan (St. Joseph) (88)	816 271-1412	(not reporting)						
Butler (Poplar Bluff) (38)	314 785-6201	(not reporting)						
Caldwell (Kingston)† (9)	816 586-2571	Maurice Houghton	....	Mayo J Anderson	Thomas W Holman	....	Linda McElwee	Maurice L Robison
Callaway (Fulton) (32)	314 642-5139	Charles E Ausfahl	....	Geo H Carrington	Irene Glascock	....	Effie Selby	Vollie Salmons
Camden (Camdenton) (20)	314 346-2250	(not reporting)						
Cape Girardeau (Jackson) (59)	314 243-1052	(not reporting)						
Carroll (Carrollton) (12)	816 542-0615	(not reporting)						
Carter (Van Buren) (5)	314 323-4527	(not reporting)						
Cass (Harrisonville) (51)	816 884-5100	(not reporting)						
Cedar (Stockton) (12)	417 276-3514	(not reporting)						
Chariton (Keytesville) (10)	816 288-3273	(not reporting)						
Christian (Ozark)† (22)	417 485-6360	Leslie Keltner	....	Junior Combs	Leland Nelton	....	Jean Edley	L E Lamb
Clark (Kahoka) (8)	816 727-3283	Harlan H Hunziker	....	James K Hayden	Harlan H Hunziker	....	Janet Nixon	Verlin W Waide
Clay (Liberty) (136)	816 781-7700	Edward J Bauman	Walter Van Asselt	Donald F Warren	Beverly Corum	Joe Davidson	Richard Janulewic	Jack Corum
Clinton (Plattsburg) (16)	816 539-2156	Eldon Hixson	....	John O'Day	Eleanor Crane	Melvin Johnson	Pat Kilpatrick RN	Bob Defreece
Cole (Jefferson City) (57)	314 634-9100	E I Hockaday	....	Stanley C Diemler	Maurice F Markway	Walt Johannpeter	....	Wyman S Easinger
Cooper (Boonville) (15)	816 882-2114	(not reporting)						
Crawford (Steelville)† (18)	314 775-2376	B L Halbert	....	A L Stubblefield	....	....		Johnny L Giles
Dade (Greenfield) (7)	417 637-2724	(not reporting)						
Dallas (Buffalo)† (12)	417 345-2632	Bryce Bradley	....	Janiece Duff	Nettie Baker	....	....	Russell Hill
Daviess (Gallatin) (9)	816 663-2641	Robert Owings	....	Edna R Wilson	Judy Carder	Artie Hightree	Valletta Danull	Tom Houghton
De Kalb (Maysville) (8)	816 449-5402	(not reporting)						
Dent (Salem) (15)	314 729-4144	(not reporting)						
Douglas (Ava) (12)	417 683-4714	(not reporting)						
Dunklin (Kennett) (36)	314 888-2796	(not reporting)						
Franklin (Union) (71)	314 583-2494	Hugh McCane	....	Emmett Reed	Tom Herbst	Steve Carey	....	Paul Bruns
Gasconade (Hermann) (13)	314 486-5427	Wilford Kallmeyer	....	Roger Prior	Ralph Grannemann	....	Linda Paubel	Elmer Gerloff

Directory 1/9 continued — **COUNTY OFFICIALS IN ALL U.S. COUNTIES**

County, county seat, 1980 population (000 omitted),	County telephone number	Board chairman	Appointed administrator	Clerk to the governing board	Chief financial officer	County engineer	County health officer	Chief law enforcement official
MISSOURI (115) continued								
Gentry (Albany) (8)	816 726-3525	Garel Rainey	....	Carolyn Stevens	....	....	....	Eugene Lupfer
Greene (Springfield)† (185)	417 868-4000	H C Compton	....	Roy Blunt	Carol Langsford	Clifford Clark	Harold Bengsch	John T Pierpont
Grundy (Trenton) (12)	816 359-6305	(not reporting)						
Harrison (Bethany) (10)	816 425-6424	Wm McIntosh	....	Robert McIntosh	....	....	....	Leon Riggs
Henry (Clinton)† (20)	816 885-5301	Waldo Feaster	Waldo Feaster	T R Hetherington	Leon Eidson	....	Anett Bailey	Peter Werner
Hickory (Hermitage) (6)	417 745-6450	(not reporting)						
Holt (Oregon) (7)	816 446-3303	(not reporting)						
Howard (Fayette) (10)	816 248-2284	Raymond Johnmeyer	....	William Shiflett	....	....	Erma Johnmeyer	Randall Yaeger
Howell (West Plains) (29)	417 256-2591	Don Holman	....	Dennis Vonallmer	Dennis Vonallmen	....	....	Hubert Holman
Iron (Ironton)† (11)	314 546-2912	Ronald Murphy	....	Ruth Ricketts	Floyd Myracle	....	....	Kenneth W Ruble
Jackson (Kansas City) (629)	816 881-3000	Bill Waris	Anthony Bartlett	Bernice J Conley	Gary Panethiere	Jim Kissick	....	Robert J Rennau
Jasper (Carthage) (87)	417 358-8800	Byron Fly	....	Roland Davis	Eva Mayfield	....	Bill Gory	Leland Boatwright
Jefferson (Hillsboro) (147)	314 789-3911	(not reporting)						
Johnson (Warrensburg)† (39)	816 747-2112	Hayes Finley	....	Wendell Davis	Shirley Coonrod	David Calhoon	....	Charles Norman
Knox (Edina) (6)	816 397-2184	Paul W Parsons	....	Kenneth Patterson	Kenneth James	....	....	Harold Foreman
Laclede (Lebanon) (24)	417 532-5471	(not reporting)						
Lafayette (Lexington) (30)	816 259-4315	(not reporting)						
Lawrence (Mount Vernon)† (29)	417 466-3666	Joe Mayberry	....	Bob Barteismeyer	Bill Hubbard	....	Harold E George	David Tatum
Lewis (Monticello) (11)	314 767-5205	Dennis McCutchan	....	Ronald D Hinton	Bill Schlager	....	Donna Pickins	Robert L Whitmer
Lincoln (Troy) (22)	314 528-4415	(not reporting)						
Linn (Linneus) (15)	816 895-5417	Harold R James	....	Bert L Summy	John F Ridgway	....	Margie McGahan	Clifford L Monroe
Livingston (Chillicothe) (16)	816 646-2293	Bill Hoyt	....	Madeline Hawkins	....	....	....	Leland Odell
Macon (Macon) (16)	816 385-4631	(not reporting)						
Madison (Fredericktown) (11)	314 783-2176	James D Rauls	....	....	....	....	....	Gary L Asher
Maries (Vienna) (8)	314 422-3924	Andrew Buschmann	....	Joe Clay Crum	Ronald Terrill	....	....	William M French
Marion (Palmyra)† (29)	314 769-2549	John E Yancey	....	W Ennis Sears	M Saffarrans	Henry Crane	Betty Nickel	Harold White
McDonald (Pineville) (15)	417 223-4717	(not reporting)						
Mercer (Princeton) (5)	816 748-4335	(not reporting)						
Miller (Tuscumbia)† (19)	314 369-2317	James M Myers	....	Clyde Lee Jenkins	F Blankenship	....	Rose M Boor	Gerald L Whittle
Mississippi (Charleston) (16)	314 683-2104	(not reporting)						
Moniteau (California) (12)	314 796-4661	J George Albin	....	Paul D Bloch	Edwina L Kay	....	Edna Potter	David Lamm
Monroe (Paris) (10)	816 327-5817	Cecil V Evans	....	Cloyce G Menefee	Estelle Wills	....	Diana Johannaber	Dean Mason
Montgomery (Montgomery City) (12)	314 564-3341	(not reporting)						
Morgan (Versailles) (14)	314 378-5300	J C Hatch	....	Mardella Raines	....	....	....	L M Earnest Jr
New Madrid (New Madrid) (23)	314 748-2524	(not reporting)						
Newton (Neosho)† (41)	417 451-4540	John Shonkwiler	....	Robert R Bridges	Avis Lankford	Lonnie McCumber	Gloria Davis	Joe Abramovitz
Nodaway (Maryville) (22)	816 582-2251	Edward R Dobbins	....	....	Thomas A Otte	....	....	Danny Estes
Oregon (Alton) (10)	417 778-7475	(not reporting)						
Osage (Linn) (12)	314 897-2139	(not reporting)						
Ozark (Gainesville) (8)	417 679-3516	Glenn Gardner	....	Dallas L Herd	Fred Jenkins	....	Marie Hicks	Herman Pierce
Pemiscot (Caruthersville) (25)	314 333-4203	(not reporting)						
Perry (Perryville) (17)	314 547-4242	(not reporting)						
Pettis (Sedalia)† (36)	816 827-3958	Gary C Hieronymus	....	Bette L Padgett	Mary H Grimes	Edward N Hall	Dianne Pilant	James Lawson
Phelps (Rolla) (34)	314 364-3503	W D McCall	....	William Huskey	Ray Noakes	Robert Elgin	Ron Barnes	Thomas Pasley
Pike (Bowling Green) (18)	314 324-2412	Robert Turpin	Jim Ford	....	Dolores F Tinsley	....	Martha Wahl RN	Dave Jenkins
Platte (Platte City) (46)	816 431-2232	(not reporting)						
Polk (Bolivar) (19)	417 326-4031	(not reporting)						
Pulaski (Waynesville) (42)	314 774-2241	George Berry	....	Alfred Lercher	Belva Hensley	....	....	Paul M Long
Putnam (Unionville)† (6)	816 947-2674	Bryce E Whitacre	....	Emery Welsh	Sharon Thompson	....	....	Danny Peto
Ralls (New London) (9)	314 748-2524	(not reporting)						
Randolph (Huntsville) (25)	816 277-4717	(not reporting)						
Ray (Richmond) (21)	816 776-3184	(not reporting)						
Reynolds (Centerville) (7)	314 648-2302	Arthur L Cook	....	James L Hill	....	....	....	Olver D Lawxhow
Ripley (Doniphan) (12)	314 996-3215	(not reporting)						
Saline (Marshall) (25)	816 886-3331	Lucile Hisle	....	Joseph A Carroll	M Arthur Twilling	....	B F Knipschild MD	Wally George
Schuyler (Lancaster) (5)	816 457-3842	(not reporting)						
Scotland (Memphis) (5)	816 465-7027	Ward Benson Jr	....	Roger M Riebel	Grace Brown	....	....	Billy J Snodgrass
Scott (Benton) (40)	314 545-3549	(not reporting)						
Shannon (Eminence) (8)	314 226-3414	(not reporting)						
Shelby (Shelbyville)† (8)	314 633-2181	Samuel Buckman	....	Gene Wiseman	Helen Duffy	....	....	Gerald Gander
St. Charles (St. Charles)† (143)	314 724-1209	Richard Green	....	Jimmy Primm	John Nichols	Joe Nichols	Paul Roberts	Edward Uebinger
St. Clair (Osceola)† (9)	417 646-2315	Leroy Russel	....	Donna D Houston	....	....	....	Shirley W Collins
St. Francois (Farmington) (43)	314 756-4551	(not reporting)						
St. Louis (Clayton) (975)	314 889-2041	Gene McNary	Ned Taddevcci	Daniel T O'Leary	John A Lucks	Jan H Paynton	Everard Rutledge	Gil Kleinknecht
St. Louis (St. Louis) I (453)	314 622-4000	Vincent Schoemehl	....	....	Paul Berra	William B Hope Jr	William B Hope Jr	John Berner
Ste. Genevieve (Ste. Genevieve) (15)	314 883-5589	Adrian J Ehler	....	Michael E Bauman	Peggy J Naeger	....	....	Clarence Basler
Stoddard (Bloomfield) (29)	314 568-3339	N Bud Temples Jr	....	John Capps	Harry Norman	....	....	Ralph Mouser
Stone (Galena)† (16)	417 357-6127	Kenneth Bowling	Larry D Baker	Larry D Baker	Larry D Baker	....	....	Richard R Barnes
Sullivan (Milan) (7)	816 265-3786	David T Wilson	....	Terry Alexander	Tommy Couch	....	....	Carl Mutt Ward
Taney (Forsyth) (20)	417 546-2241	John Strahan Jr	....	Ronald A Houseman	....	Quentin Moore	Lissie David	Charley Keithley
Texas (Houston)† (21)	417 967-2112	Sally Gladden	....	Donald R Troutman	Gene Rust	....	....	Ray Clayton
Vernon (Nevada) (20)	417 667-3157	(not reporting)						
Warren (Warrenton)† (15)	314 456-3331	Leonard Sutton	....	Janis Meyer	Alvin Brandt	Robert L Lewis	....	Melvin Twiehaus
Washington (Potosi) (18)	314 438-4346	Robert E Reed	....	Theresa E West	Judy Gilliam	....	Mamie L Wigger	Steven Richards
Wayne (Greenville) (11)	314 224-3513	(not reporting)						
Webster (Marshfield) (20)	417 468-2223	(not reporting)						
Worth (Grant City) (3)	816 564-2219	George Young	....	Robert E Pierce	Ann Fletchall	....	Carolyn Hunt RN	Jack Baker
Wright (Hartville) (16)	417 741-6661	(not reporting)						
MONTANA (56)								
Anaconda-Deer Lodge C§† (13)	406 563-8421	Stan Blaz	Daniel J Worsdell	....	Daniel J Wordsell	....	....	James Connors
Beaverhead (Dillon) (8)	406 683-2642	John L Eliel	....	Margaret Thompson	Margret Sturm	....	Andrew Juergens	Richard E Later
Big Horn (Hardin) (11)	406 665-3520	Dick Gregory	....	Debra L Johnson	Lorraine Hamilton	Dan Hamilton	John March	Bill Joy
Blaine (Chinook) (7)	406 357-3250	Ordell Klindworth	....	Lucille Oehmcke	Shirley Grubb	....	Samuel Kevan MD	Charles Hay
Broadwater (Townsend) (3)	406 266-3443	Ronald Sanderson	....	Judith R Doggett	Fleda I Brammer	....	Lois Breen MD	Rick Barthule
Butte-Silver Bow C (37)	406 723-8262	Donald R Peoples	....	William Driscoll	Gary Rowe	....	William Burke	Robert Butorovich
Carbon (Red Lodge)† (8)	406 446-1595	Frank Cole Jr	....	Tony F Zupan	John Michelcic	....	James J Kane	Gary R Dent

Directory 1/9 continued — COUNTY OFFICIALS IN ALL U.S. COUNTIES

County, county seat, 1980 population (000 omitted),	County telephone number	Board chairman	Appointed administrator	Clerk to the governing board	Chief financial officer	County engineer	County health officer	Chief law enforcement official
MONTANA (56) continued								
Carter (Ekalaka) (2)	406 775-8749	Joseph Padden	....	Jane M Brewster	Marjorie Justice	....	Richard Menger	Vernon G Preuss
Cascade (Great Falls) (81)	406 761-6700	(not reporting)						
Chouteau (Fort Benton) (6)	406 622-5151	Dale L Skaalure	....	Joann M Peres	Jean M Johnson	....	....	Paul F Williams
Custer (Miles City) (13)	406 232-1347	Bruce K Bergerson	....	D E Woolhiser	Byron Rogge	....	C C Kohn	F W Damm
Daniels (Scobey) (3)	406 487-5561	C William Tande	....	Carol Malone	Lorraine Jerome	....	Merle D Fitz	L Warner Harrison
Dawson (Glendive) (12)	406 365-3058	Alvin Mathison	....	Patricia Peterson	Betty Kegley	....	Camille Spitzer	Howard Hodous
Fallon (Baker) (4)	406 778-2846	Art Koenig	....	Mary Lee Dietz	Faye Koenig	....	John Obye	Leland Gundlach
Fergus (Lewistown) (13)	406 538-5321	Robert K Phillips	....	Debbie Pallet	Susan Spurgeon	....	Madonna Smith	Jack L Songer
Flathead (Kalispell) (52)	406 755-5300	Kenneth H Krueger	....	Martha Grewal	....	....	Althea Ginnebaugh	Chuck Rhodes
Gallatin (Bozeman) (43)	406 587-7316	Joy I Nash	Kenneth G Mosby	Vickie Jorgensen	Loy Carroll	....	Edward King MD	L John Onstad
Garfield (Jordan) (2)	406 557-2760	Kenneth A Coulter	....	Betty Stafford	Betty Jean Cooley	....	....	P T Cremer
Glacier (Cut Bank) (11)	406 873-2482	Donald Koepke	....	Donna E Lasorte	Bertha Dunnigan	Robert Flynn	Jospeh Meek	James Persling
Golden Valley (Ryegate) (1)	406 568-2231	Raymond Jeffers	....	Aileen Mattheis	Sharon Carpenter		....	Eugene Clark
Granite (Philipsburg) (3)	406 859-3771	(not reporting)						
Hill (Havre) (18)	406 265-5481	Arthur Rambo	....	Diane Mellem	Lowell Swenson	....	B Richardson MD	Howard Taylor
Jefferson (Boulder)† (7)	406 225-3332	Leslie J Sodorff	....	Joanne McFarlane	Eva O Rieker	....	....	Harold Demers
Judith Basin (Stanford) (3)	406 566-2301	(not reporting)						
Lake (Polson) (19)	406 883-6211	Harold Fitzner	....	Ethel M Harding	Marjorie D Knaus	....	Ralph K Campbell	D Glenn Frame
Lewis and Clark (Helena) (43)	406 443-1010	Linda Stoll-Ander	Ed Blackman	Sue Bartlett	....	Bob Hanson	Robert Johnson	Chuck O'Reilly
Liberty (Chester) (2)	406 759-5365	Marvin S Cheek	....	Alma Soper	Rose Campbell	....	Richard Buker Jr	Richard A Burrows
Lincoln (Libby) (18)	406 293-7781	R W Lindsey	....	Janet B F Siegel	Delores S Womack	....	Richard Irons	Donald Shaw
Madison (Virginia City) (5)	406 843-5311	(not reporting)						
McCone (Circle) (3)	406 485-3505	(not reporting)						
Meagher (White Sulphur Springs)† (2)	406 547-3612	A C Grande Jr	....	Dellamae O Lind	Joyce M Ringer	Eugene Dreidlein	....	Lloyd M Frisbie
Mineral (Superior) (4)	406 822-4541	Tom Marvin	....	Shirley Mancini	Billye A Bricker	....	James Hoyne MD	Wade Van Gilder
Missoula (Missoula) (76)	406 721-5700	Robert Palmer	Howard Schwartz	Fern Hart	Fern Hart	Bob Holm	Gary Boe	Ray Froehlich
Musselshell (Roundup) (4)	406 323-1104	O S Ellis	....	Frances L Dawson	Clinton J Moore	....	....	Brian Neidhardt
Park (Livingston) (13)	406 222-6120	James Todd	....	Janice Jennings	Louise Ammerman	Ed Gorton	Robert Childers	Robert Oakland
Petroleum (Winnett)*† (1)	406 429-5551	Brendan Murphy	Robert E Coffey	Rose Beanblossom	Robert E Coffey	....	Richard Isen	Robert Busenbark
Phillips (Malta)† (5)	406 654-2423	Duane W Compton	....	Ingelef Schwartz	Marion K Goulet	....	R M Wiprud	Michael R Camp
Pondera (Conrad) (7)	406 278-3226	Art Lindseth	....	Gladys Mortensen	Marlene Stoetzel	....	James Meyer	W L Hammermeister
Powder River (Broadus) (3)	406 436-2657	Alvin Raschkow	....	Karen D Amende	Glads Linville	Dave Worman	David Kidder	Don P Pertuit
Powell (Deer Lodge) (7)	406 846-3680	Thomas A Beck	....	Arthur L Jennings	Dalice M Cook	....	Don R Vidrine	David J Collings
Prairie (Terry) (2)	406 637-5431	Charles J Breen	....	Don G Hubber	Edna C Irion	....	Lorance Krogstad	Gary H Larsen
Ravalli (Hamilton) (22)	406 363-4790	Frank T Williams	Reba Falk	Darlene Hughes	Ruth Cleveland	L Higginbotham	Frederick Bell	Dale E Dye
Richland (Sidney)† (12)	406 482-1708	Bing C Poff	....	Helen Gierke	Gloria Paladichuk	Russell G Huotari	Richard Segnitz	Harold N Grinolds
Roosevelt (Wolf Point) (10)	406 653-1590	R Almont Harvey	....	Helen Eggebrecht	Virginia Plouffe	....	Mark B Listerud	Dean Mahlum
Rosebud (Forsyth) (10)	406 356-7318	(not reporting)						
Sanders (Thompson Falls)† (9)	406 827-3491	John Muster	....	Dixie Vaught	June M Thayer	....	....	James Doxtater
Sheridan (Plentywood) (5)	406 765-2310	C S Holje	....	Milton Hovland	....	....	Kirk Stoner MD	Ben Holt
Stillwater (Columbus) (6)	406 322-4546	Ezra G Rickman Jr	....	Lois R Van Every	....	Duane Christensen	....	Thos Blankenship
Sweet Grass (Big Timber) (3)	406 932-5152	Ole Oiestad	....	Hazel D Fallang	Linda Langhus	....	Rodney Fink	Svend Mauland
Teton (Choteau) (6)	406 466-2151	Erich E Keiper	....	Loretta J Young	M Connie Kuster	Monte Makin	Lora Wier	John L Howard
Toole (Shelby) (6)	406 434-2232	John G Nesbo	....	Elizabeth Munson	Judith J Nevins	....	Robert A Clary	Vern L Anderson
Treasure (Hysham)† (1)	406 342-5547	Alex Wetsch	....	S Van Hemelryck	Kathleen Thomas	....	Wm Anderson MD	Gary Fjelstad
Valley (Glasgow) (10)	406 228-4613	Earl Daley	....	Mary Lou Eide	Audrey I Parke	....	David J Hide	Daniel Taylor
Wheatland (Harlowton)† (2)	406 632-5621	Edgar Langston	....	Carol Clark	Rosemary Thompson	....	....	R Eggenbacken
Wibaux (Wibaux) (1)	406 795-2433	Dey Schlapia	....	Marlene J Blome	Sandra F Evans	....	Nancy H Raush MD	Arleigh H Meek
Yellowstone (Billings) (108)	406 256-2700	David Gorton	....	Merrill H Klundt	Jerry Thomas	....	George Sheckleton	Mike Schafer
NEBRASKA (93)								
Adams (Hastings) (31)	402 463-2491	Sharon L Bennett	....	Anita M Hawes	Julia M Moeller	Roger S Parks	....	Gregg A Magee
Antelope (Neligh) (9)	402 887-4410	Gordon C Baker	....	Eleanor Holm	Donna Payne	....	Kenneth Drobny	Kenneth Drobny
Arthur (Arthur)† (1)	308 764-2203	Harlan Anderberg	....	....	Lloydie Daly	....	....	....
Banner (Harrisburg) (1)	308 436-5265	(not reporting)						
Blaine (Brewster) (1)	308 547-2222	Walter L Rhoades	....	Edna D Spencer	Sue Clark	....	....	Lee Sinner
Boone (Albion) (7)	402 395-2055	(not reporting)						
Box Butte (Alliance) (14)	308 772-6565	John Ditsch	....	Kathryn M Hood	Gwen Warthen	....	....	M E Frerichs
Boyd (Butte)† (3)	402 775-2391	Wayne Kibby	....	....	Ione L Riesselman	....	....	....
Brown (Ainsworth) (4)	402 387-2705	(not reporting)						
Buffalo (Kearney) (35)	308 237-2289	(not reporting)						
Burt (Tekamah) (9)	402 374-1955	Robert C Betts Sr	....	A Dale French	C E Mock Jr	Joe P Neary	....	Leonard Canarsky
Butler (David City)† (9)	402 367-3091	Henry R Kobza	....	D E Struebing	Richard Liebrecht	Jerry Hain	Ronald Vaca	Leo F Meister
Cass (Plattsmouth) (20)	402 296-2164	Albert Ulrich	....	Alan D Wohlfarth	Richard Wassinger	....	....	Fred Tesch
Cedar (Hartington) (11)	402 254-3983	Joseph Keiter	....	Edward S Stevens	Roger J Schwartz	....	....	Gordon W Graham
Chase (Imperial) (5)	308 882-5266	(not reporting)						
Cherry (Valentine) (7)	402 376-2420	Zale Quible	....	Darlene Burge	Mary Rose Kuskie	Donald Pettigrew	Tim C Sutherland	Tim C Sutherland
Cheyenne (Sidney) (10)	308 254-2141	Dean Wilson	....	Robert Hossle	Clara Benisek	Richard Carman	....	Darrel Johnson
Clay (Clay Center) (8)	402 762-3463	Lawrence Griess	....	Janet Hajny	Virgie A McCune	Max L Bailey	Marge Etherton	Gary E Jones
Colfax (Schuyler)† (10)	402 352-3434	Joseph R Prusa	....	Lamar J Brdicko	Gladys M Swanson	James McMeekin	Evelyn Vanicek	Richard P Kruse
Cuming (West Point) (12)	402 372-2144	(not reporting)						
Custer (Broken Bow) (14)	308 872-5701	Grayston Cool	....	Marian J Woodward	Leadell Jones	Harry R Duryea	....	Neal Fink
Dakota (Dakota City)† (17)	402 987-3471	Neil R McCluhan	....	....	....	....	....	....
Dawes (Chadron) (10)	308 432-2863	Arnold E Johnson	....	Gealy W Mathis	Margy Stoner	W C Schaff	....	Lyle Fernau
Dawson (Lexington) (22)	308 324-2127	(not reporting)						
Deuel (Chappell) (2)	308 874-3308	Robert Robb	....	Claudia M Vogt	Kenneth Fornander	....	....	Floyd H Stahr
Dixon (Ponca)† (7)	402 755-2208	Jerry Knerl	....	Audrey Dohma	Nellie M Anderson	Sid Saunders	John Stander	Dean Chase
Dodge (Fremont) (36)	402 721-3494	Walt J Mruz	....	Fred Mytty	....	James Coen	....	Richard Wennstedt
Douglas (Omaha) (398)	402 444-7000	Michael Kelley	R Schoettger	Walter Spellman	....	Thomas Doyle	Daniel Worthing	Richard Roth
Dundy (Benkelman) (3)	308 423-2058	Mason Jones	....	Tony Lutz	Shirley I Baney	Charles Wright	....	John C Corder
Fillmore (Geneva) (8)	402 759-3018	Ernest Becwar	....	Willard H Foster	Marilyn Christian	....	Otis Mattox	William Burgess
Franklin (Franklin) (4)	308 425-3492	(not reporting)						
Frontier (Stockville) (4)	308 367-8641	Walter E Betz	....	Margaret Crawford	....	Charles E Wright	Lannie L Roblee	Lannie L Roblee
Furnas (Beaver City)† (6)	308 268-4145	Glenn Cowan	....	K McClelland	Grace C Faw	Charles E Wright	....	William O Bennett
Gage (Beatrice) (24)	402 223-1300	Steve Timm	....	Calvin H Gullion	Margaret Higgins	Lyle Tanderup	....	Ted E Henderson
Garden (Oshkosh) (3)	308 772-3924	Dale Kastens	....	Edward P Sullivan	Elaine Pebley	....	Ardis Shepherd	Jack L Hunt
Garfield (Burwell) (2)	308 346-4161	Gerald Quinn	....	Martin Robbins	Leila Flowers	J Harvey Johnson	....	Donald Mattern

Directory 1/9 continued

COUNTY OFFICIALS IN ALL U.S. COUNTIES

County, county seat, 1980 population (000 omitted),	County telephone number	Board chairman	Appointed administrator	Clerk to the governing board	Chief financial officer	County engineer	County health officer	Chief law enforcement official
NEBRASKA (93) continued								
Gosper (Elwood) (2)	308 785-2611	Donald J Foss	....	Alice Jean Dreher	Delores M Houlden	....	....	David W Schutz
Grant (Hyannis) (1)	308 458-2488	Leroy Evans	....	Delores M Blakey	Betty J Gentry	Bruce G Raddatz	....	John M Gentry
Greeley (Greeley Center) (3)	308 428-3625	B J Meyer	....	Sandra L Voboril	Miriam J Hickman	Bernard L Meyer	....	Doyal Keller
Hall (Grand Island) (48)	308 381-5080	Irene Abernethy	....	Marjorie Haubold	Keith F Schoel	....	Edward H Edwards	Charles Fairbanks
Hamilton (Aurora) (9)	402 694-3443	Paul M Kemling	....	Charlotte Baasch	Donald L Sorensen	Keith W Maw	....	Paul E Harding
Harlan (Alma)† (4)	308 928-2173	Edward H Backes	....	Verdeen Leopold	Diane Grotfeld	Wayne Dietz	....	Ronald Early
Hayes (Hayes Center) (1)	308 286-3413	Murel D McNutt	....	Darlene M Bixler	Stanley D Rucker	Marvin Athey	....	Greg T Otte
Hitchcock (Trenton) (4)	308 334-5646	C Poindexter	....	D Reynolds	Betty L Horinek	....	....	William W Cemer
Holt (O'Neill)† (14)	402 336-1762	Leonard Jungman	....	Gary Devall	John McCarville	....	....	Charles Fox
Hooker (Mullen) (1)	308 546-2244	(not reporting)						
Howard (St. Paul) (7)	308 754-4343	Linda Scarborough	Clifford Stefanow	Ranae Smith	Edna M Petersen	....	....	Ronald R Bryer
Jefferson (Fairbury) (10)	402 729-2323	William H Wrigley	....	Mary E Schmal	Alice Fall Nelson	....	....	Rex E Southwick
Johnson (Tecumseh) (5)	402 335-3246	Troy E Walters	....	Kathleen M Nievee	Margaret Parrish	Jack L Evans	Karen Zuhlke	Richard D Mahoney
Kearney (Minden) (7)	308 832-1172	Philip Anderbery	....	P Osterbuhr	Marcele D Schmidt	Gerald Carman	Donald M Prince	Marshall S Nelson
Keith (Ogallala) (9)	308 284-4726	Ron Siffring	....	Leota Wood	Norma J Morrell	....	....	Wayne L Young
Keya Paha (Springview)† (1)	402 497-3791	Larry Shepperd	....	W J Rowan	Tim A Stephen	....	....	Cary Sell
Kimball (Kimball) (5)	308 235-2241	Vernon J Bourlier	....	Elaine Sandridge	Arthur H Johnson	....	....	William J Thacker
Knox (Center) (11)	402 288-4282	Dale Stubben	....	Virginia Buerman	Sam Key	Donald Jiracek	....	Wes Eisenbeiss
Lancaster (Lincoln) (193)	402 471-7447	Mike Johanns	Wayne Hart	W Richard Baker	Richard Nuernberg	Don Thomas	M Jane Ford	Dale Adams
Lincoln (North Platte)† (36)	308 534-4350	Gerald K Brown	....	H Nadine Heath	Ilene G Rockwell	Lyle K Birkby	....	Gordon D Gilster
Logan (Stapleton) (1)	308 636-2311	Gene Tullis	....	Cora E Mahoney	Maureen Black	....	....	James E Wonch
Loup (Taylor) (1)	308 942-3135	Donald Cone	....	Debbie S Postany	Lois M Stone	Harvey Johnson	....	Philip M Hart
Madison (Madison) (31)	402 454-3311	(not reporting)						
McPherson (Tryon) (1)	308 587-2363	(not reporting)						
Merrick (Central City) (9)	308 946-2881	Leland Greving	....	Floyd M Gorgen	....	....	Ellen Campbell	D Schneiderheing
Morrill (Bridgeport) (6)	308 262-0860	R Reifschneider	....	Shirley C Avary	Irene Foster	William Keefover	....	Roger D Sterkel
Nance (Fullerton) (5)	308 536-2331	Theodore Prososki	....	Marvin McFee	Doris A Hardle	....	....	Sam R King
Nemaha (Auburn) (8)	402 274-4213	Wm Seibert	....	Joann Rohrs	Patricia Holtzman	John H Stevenson	Kay Oestmann	Gary Boan
Nuckolls (Nelson) (7)	402 225-4361	Joe Sullivan	....	Selma A Ferguson	....	Ardell Talkington	....	Donald Squires
Otoe (Nebraska City) (15)	402 873-3586	Patricia Ramald	....	Gerald Schmitz	Wilma King	....	....	....
Pawnee (Pawnee City) (4)	402 852-2962	Floyd Vrtiska	....	Kenneth A Bowman	....	Charles O Morin	....	Charles J Hall
Perkins (Grant)† (4)	308 352-4643	Warren Softley	....	Mary Buss	Anna Stephenson	....	C Colglazier	David Deaver
Phelps (Holdrege) (10)	308 995-4469	Willard Peterson	....	Lois E Young	Sharon Rupe	Dale Sall	....	Dwayne Newman
Pierce (Pierce) (8)	402 329-4225	(not reporting)						
Platte (Columbus) (29)	402 564-1311	Ronald Blaser	....	Milton J Langan	Marietta Newman	Ronald Rystrom	....	Neal Drum Jr
Polk (Osceola) (6)	402 747-5431	Dale Lindburg	....	Ruth N Stromberg	Dorothy Fjell	....	Katherine J Smoli	Timothy G Siemek
Red Willow (McCook) (13)	308 345-1552	(not reporting)						
Richardson (Falls City) (11)	402 245-2911	Gerald Bucher	....	Nevada Williams	....	....	....	Eugene D Ramer
Rock (Bassett) (2)	402 684-3933	(not reporting)						
Saline (Wilber)† (13)	402 821-2374	Joseph W Kovarik	....	Ray E Houska	Lila M Witt	Larry Lewis	Edward C Shimerda	Byron R Buzek
Sarpy (Papillion) (86)	402 339-3225	....	Laddie J Kozeny	Mary E Cowger	Kathleen Ingram	Norman Whitney	....	Patrick Thomas
Saunders (Wahoo) (19)	402 443-4335	Archie Hightshoe	....	Charles J Egr	James Fauver	William Lindholm	Thomas Svoboda	Ron Poskochil
Scotts Bluff (Gering) (38)	308 436-6600	William C Peters	....	Vera Dulaney	Darlene Robertson	Rick Meter	Jerry Taylor	David Schleve
Seward (Seward) (16)	402 643-2883	Carol S Beck	....	John D Gill	Geraldine Sleight	....	....	Roger W Anderson
Sheridan (Rushville) (8)	308 327-2633	(not reporting)						
Sherman (Loup City) (4)	308 745-1513	Wendell Glinsmann	....	....	Mildred Peterson	....	Virgil Kaminski	Virgil Kaminski
Sioux (Harrison) (2)	308 668-2443	Dean Lundy	....	Alvin Publow	Dale DeHaven	....	James G Robertson	James G Robertson
Stanton (Stanton) (7)	402 439-2222	Ray O Zoucha	....	Rita Roenfeldt	Sandra Zoubek	J Harvey Johnson	....	M Janulewicz
Thayer (Hebron) (8)	402 768-6126	Gary D Hergott	Gerald Voigt	Lefa M Sulz	Lefa M Sulz	William Wehling	....	Gary R Young
Thomas (Thedford)† (1)	308 645-2261	F Allen Naber	....	Marilyn Maseberg	....	Dennis Heermann	....	Donald D Keys
Thurston (Pender) (7)	402 385-2343	(not reporting)						
Valley (Ord) (6)	308 728-3700	Kenneth Collins	....	Claire D Hansen	Sharon Foth	Maxon Leth	....	Gerald Woodgate
Washington (Blair) (16)	402 426-2323	Jim Knag	....	C Petersen	Virginia Bauer	....	....	William Gutschow
Wayne (Wayne)† (10)	402 375-2288	Gerald Pospishil	....	Orgretta Morris	Leon F Meyer	....	....	Leroy Janssen
Webster (Red Cloud) (5)	402 746-2716	Lawrence J Goll	....	Leah L Deisley	Sandra Koler	C A Talkington	....	James L Disney
Wheeler (Bartlett) (1)	308 654-3235	(not reporting)						
York (York) (15)	402 362-7759	Harry A Dahlgren	....	Evelyn M Fouts	Marjorie King	John D Nordmeyer	....	Robert D Miller
NEVADA (17)								
Carson City-Ormsby C (32)	702 887-2100	H J Jacobsen	D W Hataway	Ted Thornton	William T Golden	Joseph Laird	....	Harold Dunn
Churchill (Fallon)† (14)	702 423-6028	Beale Cann	....	Manuel Barrenchea	Manuel Barrenchea	....	....	David M Banovich
Clark (Las Vegas)* (462)	702 383-3500	Thalia M Dondero	Joseph C Denny	Loretta Bowman	Keith Latham	Granville Bowman	Otto Ravenholt MD	John Moran
Douglas (Minden)§ (19)	702 782-9821	Herbert Witt	Robert S Hadfield	Yvonne Bernard	Robert S Hadfield	Warner Phillips	David Johnson	Jerry Maple
Elko (Elko)* (17)	702 738-5398	Ernie Hall	George R Boucher	Robert L Kane	Ceasar E Salicchi	E Larry White	Howard W Owen	James C Miller
Esmeralda (Goldfield) (1)	702 485-3406	W S Wright	Leila M Shrider	Celia M Ranson	Ora Roper	Kenneth Haskew	....	Glenn E Penson
Eureka (Eureka) (1)	702 237-5262	Charles A Vaccaro	....	Joan Shangle	Joan Shangle	....	....	Bruce Carlson
Humboldt (Winnemucca) (9)	702 623-6343	Vic V Botts	....	Susan E Harrer	Josephine Patters	....	....	James Bagwell
Lander (Austin) (4)	702 964-2447	(not reporting)						
Lincoln (Fioche) (4)	702 962-5390	(not reporting)						
Lyon (Yerington) (14)	702 463-3341	Joseph J Lommori	Betty Day	W J Parr	Rita Evasovic	Lester L Gobel	Eleanor Holman	Eugene Wilhelm
Mineral (Hawthorne) (6)	702 945-2446	Harry Poe	Patrick Landon	Martha G Barlow	Martha G Barlow	....	Richard Heffner	John Madraso Jr
Nye (Tonopah)† (9)	702 482-9291	Robert N Revert	P M Roy Neighbors	Karen Quilter	Rena Bailey	....	Eloise Reid	Harold E Davis
Pershing (Lovelock) (3)	702 273-2208	Robert N Maher	....	Louise Similey	Louise Similey	....	Stanley Mccart MD	James McIntosh
Storey (Virginia City) (1)	702 847-0577	(not reporting)						
Washoe (Reno)* (194)	702 785-4179	Belie Williams	John MacIntyre	Judi Bailey	Gary Simpson	Douglas Hopkins	Michael Ford	Vince Swinney
White Pine (Ely) (8)	702 289-2341	(not reporting)						
NEW HAMPSHIRE (10)								
Belknap (Laconia) (43)	603 524-3570	(not reporting)						
Carroll (Ossipee)† (28)	603 539-2428	Brenda M Presby	....	....	G Colby Weeks	....	Harry M Rose	Roy H Larson Jr
Cheshire (Keene)† (62)	603 352-0051	William F Lynch	Donna M Drouin	David G Adams	Whalen B Dunn	....	....	Kenneth N Lysitt
Coos (Berlin) (35)	603 752-2144	(not reporting)						
Grafton (Woodsville) (66)	603 787-6941	Dorothy Corcoran	Evelyn I Smith	Arthur E Snell	A F Stiegler III	....	....	Herbert W Ash
Hillsborough (Nashua) (277)	603 882-9471	(not reporting)						
Merrimack (Concord) (98)	603 228-0331	Peter Spaulding	Rodney Tenney	Wesley Haynes	Charles Carroll	....	....	Dana Smith
Rockingham (Exeter)† (190)	603 679-2256	Ernest P Barka	Roy Morrisette	Carrolle Hueter	Clarke Chandler	....	....	Charles F Vetter
Strafford (Dover) (85)	603 742-1458	Paul J Dumont	Glenn E Fratto	Laura Carey	Charles A Crocco	....	....	Richard Cavanaugh
Sullivan (Newport) (36)	603 863-2560	R Woodhull	....	Sydney J Clarke	Peter R Lovely	Leon H Geil	....	Edward J Bruno

Directory 1/9 continued — COUNTY OFFICIALS IN ALL U.S. COUNTIES

County, county seat, 1980 population (000 omitted),	County telephone number	Board chairman	Appointed administrator	Clerk to the governing board	Chief financial officer	County engineer	County health officer	Chief law enforcement official
NEW JERSEY (21)								
Atlantic (Atlantic City) (194)	609 345-6700	John F Gaffney	F Zavaglia	Thomas R Somers	Michael Dougherty	Eugene Petitt	Joseph Aiello	Mario Floriani
Bergen (Hackensack) (845)	201 646-2000	Gerald Calabrese	Richard L Nelson	Roberta Stern	Eugene F DiPaola	Edward R Ranuska	Michael A Guarino	Wm D McDowell
Burlington (Mount Holly) (363)	609 267-3300	Harold L Colburn	....	Charles T Juliana	Arthur Collins	James Quinn	Walter Trommelen	Francis P Brennan
Camden (Camden)§† (472)	609 757-8000	J V Borreggine	Siegfried Dahms	Francis J Ward	Nicholas A Rudi	Robert E Kelly	Jung H Cho	William J Simon
Cape May (Cape May Court House) (82)	609 465-7111	Anthony Catanoso	Kathryn Willis	Kathryn Willis	Philip Matalucci	Neil Clarke	Louis Lamanna	Beech Fox
Cumberland (Bridgeton) (133)	609 451-8000	Edward H Salmon	William Gehring	Sumner Lippincott	Louis C Totoro	....	Manuel Ostroff	George Castellini
Essex (Newark) (850)	201 961-7000	Jerome D Greco	David Williams	Daniel Gibson Jr	Thomas W Jordan	Frank M Cummins	James Jordan	James M Nixon
Gloucester (Woodbury) (200)	609 853-3200	John R Maier	Gary J Higham	John W Robertson	Jean Dubois	Jerry A Canter	Robert J Smith	George G Small
Hudson (Jersey City)† (557)	201 795-6000	Steve Cappiello	Aaron I Schulman	Daniel T Sansone	William Pearl	Michael Feury	William O'Brien	Peter DiNardo
Hunterdon (Flemington) (87)	201 782-4300	George D Muller	....	Dorthy K Bertany	Roland Hunter	David W Stem	Francis Piccola	Warren E Peterson
Mercer (Trenton) (308)	609 989-6631	Bill Mathesius	Walter A Deangelo	Joyce L McDade	Vito J Petrino	Donald T Harney	....	Gilbert J Lugossy
Middlesex (New Brunswick) (596)	201 745-3000	Stephen Capestro	John T McHugh	Marie MacWilliam	D Ferrazzoli	John J Reiser	Laszlo Szabo	Joseph Spicuzzo
Monmouth (Freehold) (503)	201 431-7391	Thomas J Lynch Jr	Robert J Collins	John E Westlake	Mark E Acker	C Van Benschoten	Lester Jargowsky	William Lanzaro
Morris (Morristown) (408)	201 285-6000	Carol J Rufener	Fred J Rossi	Virginia Shea	Robert T Natoli	George E Burke	....	John M Fox
Ocean (Toms River) (346)	201 244-2121	Damian G Murray	Benjamin H Mabie	Thomas Waskovich	James T Mullins	Richard E Lane	Charles Kauffman	Arthur F Brown
Passaic (Paterson) (448)	201 881-4405	William Pirone	Nicola R DiDonna	Edward Murphy	Nicola R DiDonna	Gaetano Farina	....	Edwin Englehardt
Salem (Salem) (65)	609 935-7510	Clinton H Ware	Lee M Munyon	Lee M Munyon	Rose Rice	Chris R Rehmann	Joseph LaCavera	Norris Williams
Somerset (Somerville) (203)	201 231-7000	John K Kitchen	Bjorn E Firing	Margaret Maccini	Fred G Thomas Jr	Thomas E Decker	....	L Nickolopoulos
Sussex (Newton)§ (116)	201 383-1023	James J Campbell	Donald E Welcome	Jean E Rose	A Thonnerieux	Eric Grove	Paul Wegmann	Fred W Cooper
Union (Elizabeth)* (504)	201 527-4000	Charlot Defilippo	Louis J Coletti	Eileen Chrenka	L Caroselli	Armand Fiorletti	....	John H Stamler
Warren (Belvidere) (84)	201 475-5361	Charles M Lee	Morris R Wilson	Morris R Wilson	Robert Leupo	David B Hicks	Emmett E Landiak	Edward Bullock
NEW MEXICO (33)								
Bernalillo (Albuquerque)§ (420)	505 766-4000	Lenton Malry	Alex Abeyta	Dolores Waller	James Lewis	....	Gene Clement	Bob Stover
Catron (Reserve) (3)	505 533-6423	David M Vackar	Mary Perdue	Robert A Atwood	Patty K Chaddick	....	....	Corwin Hulsey
Chaves (Roswell) (51)	505 623-4341	Clyde Allensworth	Curtis Woolf	Rhoda Goodloe	Lin M Hall Sr	....	....	Glen Dennis
Cibola (Grants)† (30)	505 287-9431	Bonifacio Chavez	Bruce Boynton	George Marquez	Jerry Killough	....	....	Bill Driggers
Colfax (Raton) (14)	505 445-9661	Waneta E Dabovich	Whitney O Hite	Stella M Lopez	Roselee Baca	....	....	Joe E Vigil
Curry (Clovis) (42)	505 763-5591	Travis Stovall	....	Florine Hawkins	....	....	....	Wesley Myers
De Baca (Fort Sumner) (2)	505 355-2601	Shell D Denison	....	Leila Kyle	Pat Propps	....	Mary Andreas RN	Earl Turnbow
Dona Ana (Las Cruces) (96)	505 523-5634	Fernando R Macias	Robert L Smith	Gladys Hansen	Natalia Dimatteo	Robert E Martinez	Frank Claus	Henry Diaz
Eddy (Carlsbad)§ (48)	505 887-9511	Ralph Callaway	Bob Stockwell	Virgie Cole	Louise Greene	John Lewis Jr	Shirley Kerns	Jack Childress
Grant (Silver City) (26)	505 538-3338	Manuel T Serna	Luis Cardoza	Isabel Quinones	Rusilia Benavidez	....	....	Mike Bethea
Guadalupe (Santa Rosa) (4)	505 472-3791	Richard Gutierrez	Johnny Marquez Jr	Naponeon Martinez	Viola Pacheco	....	Peggy Blair	Joe E Martinez
Harding (Mosquero) (1)	505 673-2301	Bennie Kirksey	....	Julie Martinez	....	Joseph Trujillo	Rita Weisdorfer	Robert Aragon
Hidalgo (Lordsburg)† (6)	505 542-9213	William B Collins	Tom E Anderson	Margaret P Coogan	June B Moore	....	....	William B Darnell
Lea (Lovington) (56)	505 396-8521	W H Brininstool	Leon Faris	Donna Benge	Dorothy Pruit	W P Greenhaw	....	Ralph Wrinkle
Lincoln (Carrizozo)§ (11)	505 648-2337	John A Hightower	Suzanne Cox	Jane McSwane	W Kay Allison	....	....	Tom Sullivan
Los Alamos (Los Alamos)* (18)	505 662-8000	Sidney Singer	Ronald C Jack	Lewis Muir	Robert W Bunkley	Richard J Fox	Robert O Penny	....
Luna (Deming) (16)	505 546-6501	Walter W Schultz	J Bullington	J Bullington	Fannie T Smyer	....	....	Jack D Coussons
McKinley (Gallup) (55)	505 722-3869	Richard Bowman	Donald L Jordan	Gloria Lente	George Galanis	....	Wade Parker	Benny Padilla
Mora (Mora)† (4)	505 387-5279	Mauricio E Duran	Ernesto Lovato	Rudy Montoya	Rosie Zamora	....	....	Palemon Chavez
Otero (Alamogordo) (45)	505 437-7427	William F Gage	Virginia Yearley	Katie Sanchez	Yemartha Nolan	....	....	Richard E Virden
Quay (Tucumcari) (11)	505 461-0510	Fred W Barnett	Glenn Briscoe	Pat Clark	Becky W Bryant	....	....	David J Garnett
Rio Arriba (Tierra Amarilla) (29)	505 588-7255	(not reporting)						
Roosevelt (Portales) (16)	505 356-8562	Robert Grider	....	Maudene Haragan	Pauline Clark	....	....	Stanley Bilberry
San Juan (Aztec)† (81)	505 334-9481	Jim T Dunlap	Sally Welles	Julien Ryner	Thomas Reynolds	C C Cash	Wade Parker	Earl Roberts
San Miguel (Las Vegas) (23)	505 425-9333	Gilbert G Ortiz	Edmundo Martinez	Rebecca Medina	Consuelo Trujillo	Pete Laumbach	Victor Lacerua	Luis Martinez
Sandoval (Bernalillo)† (35)	505 867-2341	Teofilo C Perea	Frank J Marquez	Sally G Padilla	Rosita Martinez	....	Maria Goldstein	Gennaro Ferrara
Santa Fe (Santa Fe)† (75)	505 988-8871	Samuel J Garcia	Michael Trujillo	C Leatherman	Rosina Martinez	....	....	Eddie Armijo
Sierra (Truth or Consequences) (8)	505 894-6215	John A Tipton	Noel B Mauldin	Lily Montoya	Diana Crowder	Hermilo Sedillo	....	Charlie Sedillo
Socorro (Socorro) (13)	505 835-0589	Vernon Cox	Eleanor W Oliver	Lorraine J Woodar	E G DeBrine	....	....	Hubert R Spurgin
Taos (Taos) (19)	505 758-8834	Eli Herrera	Richard LeDoux	Marie Gallegos	Roy Martinez	....	....	Felipe Cordova
Torrance (Estancia) (7)	505 384-2418	Wayne Connell	P Vespignani	Drese Sutherland	Mary Alice Graham	....	....	Richard Ness
Union (Clayton) (5)	505 374-9491	Jerome T Jones	....	Della Wetsel	....	....	....	Andres A Cordova
Valencia (Los Lunas) (31)	505 865-9681	Albert Olguin	Richard E Aragon	Moises Griego	Barbara Beattie	....	....	Lawrence Romero
NEW YORK (58)								
Albany (Albany) (286)	518 447-7040	Charles E Cahill	James J Coyne	Paul T Devane	Edward T Stack	Fred Doeing	Wm A Grattan MD	George L Infante
Allegany (Belmont) (52)	716 268-7612	(not reporting)						
Broome (Binghamton)† (214)	607 772-2109	Jeffrey Kraham	....	Kay Diekow	Brian Lind	Phillip Murphy	Kathleen Gaffney	Anthony Ruffo
Cattaraugus (Little Valley) (86)	716 938-9111	James J Snyder	....	William C Baker	Barbara Edwards	....	James M Garvey MD	John Kalamanka
Cayuga (Auburn) (80)	315 253-1011	Dale C Parmley	....	Robert B Weller	David A Farrell	William L Catto	William L Catto	Robert C Sponable
Chautauqua (Mayville) (147)	716 753-7111	Thomas Harte	....	Orlo Bartholomew	Marshall Nelson	George Riedesel	Robert Berke MD	John Bentley
Chemung (Elmira)† (98)	607 737-2912	John A Flory	....	Shirley M Erle	R Arden DeVore	....	Stanley Holland	Robert Bucher
Chenango (Norwich) (49)	607 335-4500	Robert Q Davy	....	Edwin Crumb	Albert Evans	....	Doreen Laing	Morris Eccleston
Clinton (Plattsburgh) (81)	518 561-8800	Robert Garrow	Francis Broderick	Francis Broderick	Roy McGee	....	John Andrus	Russell Trombly
Columbia (Hudson) (59)	518 828-1527	John H Hess	....	Mary Mazzacano	Anne Twaddle	Richard Brady	Lawrence Berg	Paul Proper
Cortland (Cortland) (49)	607 753-5052	James O'Mara	....	Mary Ellen Opera	Carl A Edlund	....	James Feuss	Duane Whiteman
Delaware (Delhi) (47)	607 746-2603	Donald C McKown	....	Arretta Early	Cyrus Schoonmaker	Richard Lanigan	....	Levon Telian
Dutchess (Poughkeepsie) (245)	914 431-2020	Douglas McHoul	....	Patricia Digrandi	M Philip Amodeo	Peter N Anagnos	John R Scott	F Scoralick
Erie (Buffalo) (1015)	716 846-8865	(not reporting)						
Essex (Elizabethtown) (36)	518 873-6301	Gifford Cross	....	Peter Mends	S Egglefield	Kenneth Wheeler	....	Robert Lavigne
Franklin (Malone) (45)	518 483-6767	J Patrick Timmons	John W Johnson	Gloria J Jandrew	William A Hughes	Arleigh Walker	Sue Desantis	Melvin D Nemier
Fulton (Johnstown) (55)	518 762-4128	Frank J Vacek	....	Peter S Wilson	Allen Bohne	....	....	Robert M Wandel
Genesee (Batavia)§ (59)	716 344-2550	Craig Yunker	Charles W Meyer	Georgia L Geissle	Richard E Siebert	....	Mary Stocum	W Douglas Call
Greene (Catskill) (41)	518 943-3080	Edmund Armstrong	William F Hagan	Richard Morse Sr	Gary Layman	....	C McRoberts	Charles Daucher
Hamilton (Lake Pleasant) (5)	518 548-6651	M J Hosley Jr	....	Natalie Williams	John E Heffernan	....	....	Douglas Parker
Herkimer (Herkimer)† (67)	315 867-1002	Robert E Vandusen	Victor B Norman	Russell C Roof	Martha B Zuris	A Frank Dolan	....	Edward W Casler
Jefferson (Watertown) (88)	315 785-3000	W Douglas Howland	....	James A Merritt	Kenneth F Rogers	....	....	Alfred P O'Neil
Lewis (Lowville) (25)	315 376-3560	Clifford Reinhard	....	Dorothy E Kotel	Urban Karcher	....	....	Floyd A Martin
Livingston (Geneseo) (57)	716 243-2500	James M Steele	....	Joyce Fitzgerald	Joseph F Griffo	Rodney Carpenter	Joan Helinski	Richard A Kane
Madison (Wampsville) (65)	315 366-2011	Don R Callahan	....	Cecelia S Paone	Harold Landers	....	....	Robert Ryan
Monroe (Rochester)* (702)	716 428-2380	John A Stanwix	....	Carol K Kaman	Lucien A Morin	Gerald McDonald	Joel L Nitzkin MD	Andrew P Meloni
Montgomery (Fonda) (53)	518 853-3431	Miles Frasier Jr	G C Dodd	G C Dodd	Norma Palmer	Donald Adamowski	....	Ronald Emery
Nassau (Mineola) (1322)	516 535-3131	Francis T Purcell	Henry W Dwyer	John DeGrace	John V Scaduto	Ludwig G Hasl Pe	J J Dowling MD	Samuel Rozzi

Directory 1/9 continued **COUNTY OFFICIALS IN ALL U.S. COUNTIES**

County, county seat, 1980 population (000 omitted),	County telephone number	Board chairman	Appointed administrator	Clerk to the governing board	Chief financial officer	County engineer	County health officer	Chief law enforcement official
NEW YORK (58) continued								
New York City C† (7071)	212 566-5700	Edward I Koch	....	....	Philip Michael	....	....	Robert J McGuire
Niagara (Lockport)† (227)	716 439-6126	Fremont C Ferchen	....	Ilene L Boyd	David S Broderick	J Robert O'Grady	Francis Clifford	Anthony Villella
Oneida (Utica) (253)	315 798-5790	William Bellinger	Richard Edwards	Robert Caswell	David Townsend	Anthony Doren	....	William Hasenauer
Onondaga (Syracuse) (463)	315 425-3421	Nicholas J Pirro	John H Mulroy	Nancy J Skahen	Raymond Banach	Bruce J Trexler	....	John C Dillon
Ontario (Canandaigua)† (89)	716 394-7070	William R Compton	Elwyn C Herendeen	Lillian C Boda	Francis J Finnick	William A Sage	....	Gary A Stewart
Orange (Goshen)† (260)	914 294-5151	Louis Heimbach	Joseph Braun	M Ronald Phillips	John Keller	Louis J Cascino	Russell Johnson	Roger Phillips
Orleans (Albion)† (38)	716 589-7053	Aruther Eddy	Stanley J Dudek	Lois M Brandt	Mary B Basinait	....	John Staeble	David M Green
Oswego (Oswego)§† (114)	315 349-3235	Robert P Jones	James W Wright	Ralph W Schmidt	William J Brouse	....	Rupert J Collins	Raymond Miller
Otsego (Cooperstown) (59)	607 547-4202	David W Brenner	....	Violet Schallert	James H Higgins	....	....	Martin A Ralph
Putnam (Carmel) (77)	914 225-3641	Kevin L Wright	David D Bruen	Rosemary L Braatz	John P Duffy	Julius I Cesare	John Simmons	R Weizenecker
Rensselaer (Troy) (152)	518 270-2700	William C Walsh	....	T William Bossidy	William St John	Larry Fairchild	Kenneth Vanpraag	Eugene Eaton
Rockland (New City) (260)	914 425-5000	Herbert Reisman	....	V K Seigerman	Joseph St Lawrenc	Joseph W Hornik	Israel Praiss MD	Thomas Goldrick
Saratoga (Ballston Spa)§ (154)	518 885-5381	Marshall Robinson	Howard H Bailey	Ardis Anderson	George Gasser	Joseph Ritchey	Stella Jivok	James D Bowen
Schenectady (Schenectady)* (150)	518 382-3280	Charles Drago Jr	Robert D McEvoy	Joseph Parillo Jr	Albert A Shapiro	Harry A Mason	....	Bernard T Waldron
Schoharie (Schoharie) (30)	518 295-7147	Stewart Mace	....	Elaine Cooper	Lawrence Tague	James Van Deusen	Carl Stefanik	Harvey Stoddard
Schuyler (Watkins Glen) (18)	607 535-6641	Philip Smith	....	Doris Craig	F Roger Eaton	....	....	Michael Maloney
Seneca (Waterloo) (34)	315 539-9285	(not reporting)						
St. Lawrence (Canton)§ (114)	315 379-2000	N Viskovich	John C Krol	Phyllis W McCall	Richard C Buckley	John C Cook	....	Keith K Knowlton
Steuben (Bath) (99)	607 776-7127	Lynn J Morse	....	Russell N Kemple	John W Young	....	....	Jack Lisi
Suffolk (Hauppauge) (1284)	516 360-4000	Peter F Cohalan	Louis Howard	William Rogers	Joseph R Caputo	A Barton Cass	David Harris MD	Dewitt C Treder
Sullivan (Monticello) (65)	914 794-3000	Brian Ingber	Paul Rouis	Morris Rosenbloom	Daniel Briggs	....	....	Joseph Wasser
Tioga (Owego) (50)	607 687-0100	Edward Hubbard	....	Constance L Trueb	Carl Saddlemire	Robert Korba	....	J Raymond Ayers
Tompkins (Ithaca) (87)	607 274-5551	Harris B Dates	John J Murphy	Phyllis Howell	John J Murphy	William Mobbs	Willard Schmidt	Robert Howard
Ulster (Kingston)† (158)	914 331-9300	Thomas W Roach	Calvin Cunningham	Randall V Roth	Lewis Kirschner	....	Peter Corsones MD	Walter Baschnagel
Warren (Lake George) (55)	518 761-6535	S J Goodspeed	Harold Robillard	Harold Robillard	John E Wertime	Fred Austin	....	Neil Tripp
Washington (Fort Edward) (55)	518 747-7791	Joseph T Rota	....	Malcolm B Douglas	Edmond A McMorri	Arthur Angrisani	....	Martin Wescott
Wayne (Lyons) (85)	315 946-9767	Marvin E Decker	....	Helen Maddock	Lois Van Hoover	....	....	Richard Pisciotti
Westchester (White Plains)§ (867)	914 285-2000	Andrew P O'Rourke	Edward M Gibbs	Anthony Giambruno	Joseph P Gulia	Frank Bohlander	Anita S Curran	Anthony Mosca
Wyoming (Warsaw) (40)	716 786-2840	Everett G Ahl	....	John B Edwards	Shirley Holbrook	Gary R Weidman	Suzanne Stopen	Allen Capwell
Yates (Penn Yan) (21)	315 536-4221	Gilbert C Smith	....	Martha Marchionda	Irene Jones	....	....	Jan Scofield
NORTH CAROLINA (100)								
Alamance (Graham)* (99)	919 228-1312	Paul C Davis	Robert C Smith	Rickey Moorefield	Colleen I Foust	Larry Alley	Timothy Green	John Stockard
Alexander (Taylorsville) (25)	704 632-9332	Elmer E Sipe	George Lee Rogers	Grace D Bebber	George Lee Rogers	....	Denese Houston	Tom Bebber
Alleghany (Sparta)† (10)	919 372-4179	Burton Osborne	Charles Dysart Jr	Charles Dysart Jr	Charles Dysart Jr	....	Eva Wooten RN	Joe Roberts
Anson (Wadesboro)* (26)	704 694-2796	F A Huntley	Taron S Jones	Julia H Brooks	Dorothy V Tyson	....	Henry Collins	Tommy W Allen
Ashe (Jefferson) (22)	919 246-8841	Stan Elliott	Larry G South	Pamalee O Neaves	Patricia T Fowler	....	V Addington	Eugene Goss
Avery (Newland) (14)	704 733-5186	Charles Von Canon	Robert C Wiseman	Nancy Cook	Patti Setzer	....	Cliff Aldridge	Clinton Phillips
Beaufort (Washington)* (40)	919 946-7721	O Ledrue Buck Jr	Don L Davenport	John I Morgan	Don L Davenport	Earl W Bonner	Gary Taylor	Nelson L Sheppard
Bertie (Windsor)§ (21)	919 794-4823	Charles H Edwards	John E Whitehurst	Peggy R Jones	John E Whitehurst	....	Elizabeth Joyner	James W Perry
Bladen (Elizabethtown)* (30)	919 862-4813	William V Clark	D L Evans	D L Evans	Ella Sue Bullock	Edwin Dowless	Steve Moffat	Earl Storms
Brunswick (Bolivia)§ (36)	919 253-4331	Pearly Vereen	William D Carter	Regina E White	Dennis A Harrison	Dan C Shields	Thomas Blum	John Carr Davis
Buncombe (Asheville)† (161)	704 255-5000	R Curtis Ratcliff	....	....	William Taylor	Joe Enderle	James Tenney	Tom Morrisey
Burke (Morganton)§ (73)	704 433-4000	James B Cates	James E Haynes	Debra M Smith	David G Smith	....	Charles Buckner	Jerry Richards
Cabarrus (Concord)§ (86)	704 786-3133	James W Lentz	Charles D McGinn	Frankie F Small	Blair D Bennett	....	W F Pilkington	Robert M Canaday
Caldwell (Lenoir)* (68)	704 758-8451	Alden E Starnes	William D Forbes	Betty Blankenship	Robert Query Jr	....	Marjorie O Strawn	Bliff Benfield
Camden (Camden) (6)	919 335-4077	Paul DeBerry	....	Randy Keaton	Clarann Mansfield	....	Howard Campbell	Robert F Berry
Carteret (Beaufort)* (41)	919 728-8400	Mary Sue Noe	James C Rickards	Virginia Edwards	Daphne Faircloth	....	Gordon M Davis	Ralph Thomas
Caswell (Yanceyville)§ (21)	919 694-4193	W W Pointer Jr	Neil Emory	Wanda P Smith	Helen W Guthrie	....	Tom Johnson	J I Smith Jr
Catawba (Newton)* (105)	704 464-7880	Gary A Whitener	J Thomas Lundy	Virginia W Sobotk	James L Westbrook	....	Barry A Blick	L David Huffman
Chatham (Pittsboro) (33)	919 542-2841	Earl D Thompson	Marvin K Hoffman	Hazel P Boone	V McConnell	....	Thomas Johnson	Jack Elkins
Cherokee (Murphy) (19)	704 837-2522	(not reporting)						
Chowan (Edenton)§† (13)	919 482-8431	Alton G Elmore	L C Copeland	Anne K Spruill	L C Copeland	....	H C Campbell	Troy E Toppin
Clay (Hayesville) (7)	704 389-6103	Harold E Lance	George Anderson	Ronald Patterson	Donna K Howell	....	Jackie Sellers	Howard D Barnard
Cleveland (Shelby)* (83)	704 484-4800	Jack Palmer Jr	Joseph R Hendrick	Catherine Cochran	Lane Alexander	....	Richard G Steeves	Buddy McKinney
Columbus (Whiteville)§ (51)	919 642-3860	Lynwood Norris	Richard B Self	Richard B Self	Emogene Suggs	....	Robert Holbrook	William G Rhodes
Craven (New Bern)§ (71)	919 637-3338	Sidney R French	Tyler Harris	Audrey Fields	Irma Tingle	....	Junius Davis	Calton W Bland
Cumberland (Fayetteville)§ (247)	919 483-8131	Charles M Speegle	C G Strassenburg	Marsha Fogle	John F Nalepa	Robert Stanger	Jesse Williams MD	Ottis F Jones
Currituck (Currituck)§ (11)	919 232-2075	Newton N Hampton	Wm S Richardson	Wm S Richardson	Wm S Richardson	....	John B Sledge Jr	W N Newbern Jr
Dare (Manteo) (13)	919 473-2950	(not reporting)						
Davidson (Lexington)* (113)	704 249-7011	E G Hargrave	Andrew D Flick Jr	Miriam Conner	Wm E Bryan Jr	....	Richard C Baxley	Paul R McCrary
Davie (Mocksville)§ (25)	704 634-5513	William L Foster	Charles Mashburn	Charles Mashburn	Reta Vogler	....	Connie Stafford	George E Smith
Duplin (Kenansville) (41)	919 296-1240	Allen D Nethercut	Ralph Cottle	Ralph Cottle	Russell Tucker	....	Joe Costin	Elwood Revelle
Durham (Durham)* (153)	919 688-3360	William V Bell	E S Swindell Jr	E S Swindell Jr	Paul N Warren	....	John Fletcher	Roland Leary
Edgecombe (Tarboro) (56)	919 823-8131	C B Martin	Allen Lee Harrell	Ellis Williford	Ellis Williford	....	Hugh G Young	Phil H Ellis
Forsyth (Winston-Salem)* (244)	919 727-2071	....	H L Pete Jenkins	Jane F Cole	Kenneth C Brennan	Edward Klevinski	Thomas R Dundon	Manly Lancaster
Franklin (Louisburg) (30)	919 496-5994	James S Hunt	James W Mills	Jean P Beckham	Allen W Shearin	....	Lorey H White	William T Dement
Gaston (Gastonia)* (163)	704 866-3100	Harley B Gaston	Philip L Hinely	Martha M Jordan	Ronald L Courtney	Richard Wyatt	John Shaw	A B Homesley
Gates (Gatesville) (9)	919 357-1240	Sherwood Eason	Edward McDuffie	Tazewell D Eure	Edward McDuffie	....	F James Boehm	Willie R Harrell
Graham (Robbinsville) (7)	704 479-3361	Tony T Ayers	Jacky M Ayers	Betty Waldroup	Patsy Irons	....	Jacky Ayers	Archie Peterson
Granville (Oxford) (34)	919 693-4761	James L Carey	Albert R Sharp	Bobbie R Wilson	Jean C Blackley	Bob Davis	Charles D Rollins	Arthur Ray Currin
Greene (Snow Hill) (16)	919 747-3446	Frank Walston Jr	Allen M Hardison	Allen M Hardison	Allen M Hardison	....	Bruce B Tingle	Early Whaley
Guilford (Greensboro)* (317)	919 373-2000	Forrest Campbell	John Witherspoon	Norma H Bodsford	Thomas H Cashwell	....	Joseph L Holliday	James L Proffitt
Halifax (Halifax)§ (55)	919 583-1131	Harry A Branch	M Thomas Barnes	Cathy M Lawrence	Linda Taylor	Leo Green	Virgil Cook	W C Bailey
Harnett (Lillington)† (60)	919 893-2091	Jesse Alphin	Jack Brock	Vanessa Young	Vanessa Young	....	Henry Thompson	Lewis Rosser
Haywood (Waynesville) (46)	704 456-9812	Edwin Russel	....	Charles Howell	Ralph J Rathbone	....	R S Robertson	C Jack Arrington
Henderson (Hendersonville) (59)	704 692-4213	William T Drake	William T Drake	Betty L Hyder	David E Nicholson	....	George Bond Jr	Albert Jackson
Hertford (Winton)* (23)	919 358-8151	Maynard W Callis	M Allen O'Neal	Patricia Weaver	Russell Overman	....	Jim Boehm	James Baker
Hoke (Raeford)§ (20)	919 875-8751	John G Balfour	James E Martin	James E Martin	Charles A Davis	....	Lloyd Horne	David Barrington
Hyde (Swanquarter) (6)	919 926-5711	J B Berry	Clifford Swindell	Douglas A Gibbs	Emily C Thomas	....	Willie J Shooter	Roland W Dale
Iredell (Statesville)* (83)	704 872-9501	Joe H Troutman	J Wayne Deal	Alice Fortner	F W Furches Jr	....	William Mashburn	Leroy Reavis
Jackson (Sylva) (26)	704 586-4226	Wayne Hooper	....	Darlene Fox	Darlene Fox	Woody Hampton	Randall Turpin	Fred Holcombe
Johnston (Smithfield) (71)	919 934-5969	Norman C Denning	Kramer Jackson	Eleanor N Creech	Kramer Jackson	....	Helen Ray	George Johnson
Jones (Trenton) (10)	919 448-7571	Osborne Coward	Larry Meadows	Larry Meadows	Larry Meadows	....	Doris Oliver	Wesley Mallard
Lee (Sanford) (37)	919 775-3515	Bertha L Matthews	Walter B Hartman	K R Hoyle	Beatrice C Fields	....	Thomas L Johnson	James S Holt
Lenoir (Kinston) (60)	919 527-6231	(not reporting)						

Directory 1/9 continued — COUNTY OFFICIALS IN ALL U.S. COUNTIES

County, county seat, 1980 population (000 omitted),	County telephone number	Board chairman	Appointed administrator	Clerk to the governing board	Chief financial officer	County engineer	County health officer	Chief law enforcement official
NORTH CAROLINA (100) continued								
Lincoln (Lincolnton) (42)	704 732-3361	Harry D Ritchie	Fred M Houser	Fred M Houser	Fred M Houser	....	Robert R Whittman	Harven A Crouse
Macon (Franklin)§ (20)	704 524-6421	C Siler Slagle	Sam K Greenwood	Sam K Greenwood	Evelyn J Southard	....	W David Simpson	George Moses
Madison (Marshall)† (17)	704 649-2300	James T Ledford	....	David P Caldwell	David P Caldwell	....	Edward A Morton	Elymas Y Ponder
Martin (Williamston) (26)	919 792-3345	John L House	Donnie H Pittman	Beverly S James	Danette B Minshew	....	Judy Wright	Willie R Rogers
McDowell (Marion)§ (35)	704 652-7121	John English	Jack H Harmon	Judy A Wright	Judy A Wright	....	Clifford Fields	Bob R Haynes
Mecklenburg (Charlotte)* (404)	704 374-2472	T L Odom	Gerald G Fox	Hazel H Hatley	H Weatherly Jr	E Kenneth Hoffman	Basil G Delta MD	Bruce Abercrombie
Mitchell (Bakersville)† (14)	704 688-2130	Hale Buchanan	David P Huskins	Judy Young	Johnny R Gouge	....	Connie Bowman	Coy D Hollifield
Montgomery (Troy) (22)	919 576-4221	C R Williams	Gary S McCaskill	Sally M Warner	Gary S McCaskill	....	Richard C Wori	Wayne Wooten
Moore (Carthage)§ (51)	919 947-5800	Arthur Purvis	Roy L Lowe	Lynn Hearne	Ella Boroughs	....	Alfred Siege	James Wise
Nash (Nashville)* (67)	919 459-4141	F B Cooper Jr	L R Holoman Jr	P Wayne Moore	L R Holoman	....	William W Hill Jr	Franklin D Brown
New Hanover (Wilmington)* (103)	919 341-7184	Karen E Gottovi	G Felix Cooper	Lucie F Smith	Andrew J Atkinson	Wyatt Blanchard	Robert S Parker	Joseph McQueen
Northampton (Jackson)*† (23)	919 534-2501	Jasper Eley	E Stewart Taylor	Rose R Sumner	E Stewart Taylor	Leo Green	....	Bob W Corey
Onslow (Jacksonville)* (113)	919 347-4717	Edward Hurst	Rick Leary	B Formyduval	....	....	Larry Pakowski	Billy G Woodward
Orange (Hillsborough)* (77)	919 732-8181	Don Willhoit	Kenneth Thompson	Beverly A Blythe	Wallace H Harding	....	Jerry Robinson	Lindy Pendergrass
Pamlico (Bayboro) (10)	919 745-3133	Robert A Paul	William R Rice	William R Rice	Dorothy Avent	....	James Baluss	Leland Brinson
Pasquotank (Elizabeth City) (28)	919 335-0865	W C Owens Jr	W David Harris	W David Harris	Mac M Miller	....	Howard Campbell	Davis M Sawyer
Pender (Burgaw) (22)	919 259-2307	(not reporting)						
Perquimans (Hertford)† (9)	919 426-5660	Joseph Nowell Jr	....	Jeanne C White	Durward F Reed Jr	....	Howard F Campbell	Julian Broughton
Person (Roxboro) (29)	919 599-0288	Malcolm Montgomer	Michael M Ruffin	Faye T Wilson	Patricia B Stutts	....	Thomas Johnson	Ernest T Dixon
Pitt (Greenville)§ (84)	919 752-2934	Kelly Barnhill	H R Gray	John Bulow	Margaret M Robert	....	Robert Ehinger	Ralph Tyson
Polk (Columbus)§ (13)	704 894-3301	Henry Huntsinger	Richard T Radford	Richard T Radford	Richard T Radford	....	....	Boyce Carswell
Randolph (Asheboro)† (92)	919 629-2131	William T Boyd	Bobby J Crumley	Annie C Shaw	Frank Willis	....	George Elliott	Robert Mason
Richmond (Rockingham)* (45)	919 997-2571	....	Jesse L Yeargan	....	....	....	....	....
Robeson (Lumberton)* (102)	919 738-9341	Carl L Britt	W Paul Graham	Linda A Hedgpeth	Emogene Chandler	....	Thad Wester MD	Hubert Stone
Rockingham (Wentworth)* (83)	919 349-2922	Troy C Hodges	Hugh P Griffin Jr	Odessa P Johnson	H Glenn Powell	....	William Thompson	C D Vernon
Rowan (Salisbury) (99)	704 636-0361	Hall Steele	Seth S Murdoch	Brenda Honeycutt	Timothy Russell	....	Herbert L Hawley	John F Stirewalt
Rutherford (Rutherfordton)† (54)	704 287-2211	Harvey Powell	Robert S Irvin	Robert S Irvin	Joe L Swing	....	Clifford Fields	Damon Huskey
Sampson (Clinton)§ (50)	919 592-6308	C Marion Butler	Wm Wyman Yelton	Wm Wyman Yelton	Jerry D Hobbs	....	Eugene Hines	W Cranford Fann
Scotland (Laurinburg)* (32)	919 277-0470	James A Gibson	John Q Byrd	John Q Byrd	John Q Byrd	....	Lucile Bridgeman	C Alfred White
Stanly (Albemarle)* (49)	704 983-2181	N A Tony Lowder	John M Link Jr	Rachel G Goins	....	....	Joseph B Bass	Ralph L McSwain
Stokes (Danbury)§ (33)	919 593-2811	Lee E Dunlap	Jerry W Rothrock	Jerry W Rothrock	Joyce Spencer	....	W H Johnson Jr	Tony Blalock
Surry (Dobson)* (59)	919 386-8676	W Fletcher Harris	W E Bondurant	....	Peggy H Johnson	....	Robert M Caldwell	W R Hall
Swain (Bryson City) (10)	704 488-9273	James Coggins	Barry Hipps	Barry Hipps	Oneal Muse	....	Russell Childers	William D Lewis
Transylvania (Brevard) (23)	704 884-3100	William M Ives	W David McNeill	Judith A Mathews	Debbie Buchanan	....	Jack McGinnis	Milford Hubbard
Tyrrell (Columbia)† (4)	919 796-1371	Durwood M Cooper	James Brickhouse	Kim V Suter	James Brickhouse	....	Judith Wright	Royce L Rhodes
Union (Monroe)* (70)	704 289-5511	Harry Myers	John C Munn	Barbara W Moore	Pearl F Helms	....	Howard Surface	W Frank McGuirt
Vance (Henderson) (37)	919 438-3207	Danny W Wright	....	Sandra Catherwood	Emily G Whitten	....	Charles D Rollins	F T McGhee
Wake (Raleigh)* (301)	919 755-6160	M Edmund Aycock	Richard Y Stevens	Alta B Chalmers	Garland H Jones	Jimmie B Holland	Robert M Hall MD	John H Baker Jr
Warren (Warrenton) (16)	919 257-3115	Eva M Clayton	Charles J Worth	Judy H Joyner	Susan W Whitley	....	Joseph Lennon	T R Williams
Washington (Plymouth)§ (15)	919 793-5823	Mayme W Davenport	Jack DiSarno	Lois C Askew	Gayle T Critcher	....	Judy Wright	James Whitehurst
Watauga (Boone)§ (32)	704 264-1300	J Paul Combs	James S Ratchford	Glenda D Stevens	W Donald Dotson	....	Carl Tuttle	James C Lyons
Wayne (Goldsboro)† (97)	919 735-4331	Deloit Cotton	Bruce S Grice Sr	Bruce S Grice Sr	Bruce S Grice Sr	....	O Aiken Mays	James L Sasser
Wilkes (Wilkesboro)§ (59)	919 651-7300	Max Bauguss	John T Barber	Eileen M Wilkins	Edward Bowers	....	Alton M Brown	Kyle Gentry
Wilson (Wilson)§ (63)	919 237-3913	Roy L Champion	Garry C Mercer	Garry C Mercer	Garry C Mercer	....	T Thurston Perry	Wayne V Gay
Yadkin (Yadkinville)§ (28)	919 679-8513	Grady J Hunter	Kennon D Briggs	Kennon D Briggs	Kennon D Briggs	....	Leonard Wood	Jack Henderson
Yancey (Burnsville) (15)	704 682-2122	(not reporting)						
NORTH DAKOTA (53)								
Adams (Hettinger)† (4)	701 567-2468	Leonard J Jacobs	....	Betty Svihovec	Marjorie Walby	....	Thos Jacobsen MD	Michael D Carroll
Barnes (Valley City)† (14)	701 845-0881	F J Vandrovec	....	Margaret A Conlon	Inga Hendrickson	Roger Lee	....	Rheinhold Weber
Benson (Minnewaukan) (8)	701 473-5340	Claire Paulson	....	Fay Huffman	Robert J Wallace	Gene Hager	....	Ned J Mitzel
Billings (Medora) (1)	701 623-4491	(not reporting)						
Bottineau (Bottineau) (9)	701 228-2225	Vern Berge	....	Mae Streich	Evelyn Kalk	Peter Wold	Viola Beyer	Lyle Lunde
Bowman (Bowman) (4)	701 523-5421	(not reporting)						
Burke (Bowbells) (4)	701 377-2861	Lavern Chrest	....	Herman Aufforth	Hazel Herman	....	....	Russell McIntyre
Burleigh (Bismarck)† (55)	701 222-6714	Deanna Hill	....	Bernice Asbridge	Helen D Schatz	Jon R Mill	D J Driscoll	Frederick Harvey
Cass (Fargo) (88)	701 241-5601	Jeannette Stanton	....	Ordelle Brua	Maxine Liversage	....	....	Donald J Rudnick
Cavalier (Langdon) (8)	701 256-2124	(not reporting)						
Dickey (Ellendale)† (7)	701 349-3249	Gene Young	....	....	Florence Klein	....	....	Walter Raugutt
Divide (Crosby) (3)	701 965-6351	R Christionson	....	Laila Findley	Jenora Carlson	....	M S Nandra MD	Irving Johnson
Dunn (Manning) (5)	701 573-4448	Albert Sickler	....	Rienhard Hauck	Connie Hawkinson	....	Linda Wallace	Douglas A Carlson
Eddy (New Rockford) (4)	701 947-2434	Robert Ludwig	....	....	Beverly Ehlers	....	A Leismeister	Edward Allmaras
Emmons (Linton) (6)	701 254-4807	....	....	Anna Mary Dockter	....	....	Henry Janssen MD	Art B Sauter
Foster (Carrington) (5)	701 652-2491	John Murphy	....	Roger R Schlotman	D S Peterson	....	Jean Kulla RN	James R Dunn
Golden Valley (Beach) (2)	701 872-4331	Don Abernethy	....	Earl L Fischer	Gene Skoglund	L W Veigel	M Wade MD	Donald Huso
Grand Forks (Grand Forks) (66)	701 775-2571	James Earl	Anita L Hansen	Anita L Hansen	Anita L Hansen	Richard Onstad	Ken Shultz	Gordon Taylor
Grant (Carson) (4)	701 622-3275	Norman V Schock	....	Ervin H Schatz	R Ruscheinsky	....	Vicki Siewert	Ron Eli
Griggs (Cooperstown) (4)	701 797-3117	Earny Ronningan	....	Walter F Kerbaugh	Willis Brekke	Ellsworth Brekke	Dale Iverson MD	Vernon Fuglestad
Hettinger (Mott) (4)	701 824-2515	Theo Strand	....	Roy J Steiner	Loran D Rixen	....	Jody Olson	Reinhold Schaible
Kidder (Steele) (4)	701 475-2632	Clois Hetletved	....	Eldora Berg	Joyce Solheim	....	....	Arnold Kraft
La Moure (La Moure) (6)	701 883-5179	(not reporting)						
Logan (Napoleon) (3)	701 754-2741	(not reporting)						
McHenry (Towner) (8)	701 537-5724	Duane Woodall	....	Francis R Hoynes	Francis R Hoynes	....	....	Clifford Larson
McIntosh (Ashley) (5)	701 288-3347	Leopold Rudolf	....	....	Ervin R Denning	....	Udom Tinsa MD	Milton O Wiest
McKenzie (Watford City)† (7)	701 842-3616	David L Jones	....	C G Wehrung	Phyliss McLees	Alan Estvold	....	Paul Larson
McLean (Washburn) (12)	701 462-8541	Donald Nordquist	Marlan Hvinden	Marlan Hvinden	Rodney Slagg	Ronald Wagner	....	Arlin Thompson
Mercer (Stanton) (9)	701 745-3292	Adolph Miller	....	Leora Retterath	Leora Rettrath	Rick West	Keith Johnson	Ronald Kessler
Morton (Mandan) (25)	701 663-4223	Michael V Schaaf	Paul E Trauger	Paul E Trauger	Mary M Dighton	Richard Kjonaas	Frank E Gilchrust	Leo Snider
Mountrail (Stanley)† (8)	701 628-2145	Kenneth O Lystad	....	Mary L Rolf	Bonnie M Eliason	....	....	Kenneth Halvorson
Nelson (Lakota) (5)	701 247-2463	Odell Flaagan	....	Wesley J Davidson	Evelyn Larson	....	Dr Iverson	Arthur Varty
Oliver (Center) (2)	701 794-8777	(not reporting)						
Pembina (Cavalier)† (10)	701 265-4231	J Oliver Johnson	....	Wm J Sturlaugson	Ruth Parnell	Fred A Karnik	Mary Sandison	Glenn E Wells
Pierce (Rugby) (6)	701 776-6161	(not reporting)						
Ramsey (Devils Lake) (13)	701 662-2189	Lloyd Stromme	....	Byrdia M Spidahl	Byrdia M Spidahl	....	Wm Turkula	Perry Horner
Ransom (Lisbon) (7)	701 683-5541	Francis Archbold	....	Patricia Carlblom	....	Russell Watts	A K Lewis MD	Calvin Dupree
Renville (Mohall) (4)	701 756-6301	Donald Hanson	....	Susan Ritter	....	Alan Melin	Debbie Brendel	Robert Thomas
Richland (Wahpeton) (19)	701 642-7700	Merlin Berg	....	Leona Hektner	Virginia Burshiem	....	G L Wiltse MD	Allen Prochnow

Directory 1/9 continued **COUNTY OFFICIALS IN ALL U.S. COUNTIES**

County, county seat, 1980 population (000 omitted),	County telephone number	Board chairman	Appointed administrator	Clerk to the governing board	Chief financial officer	County engineer	County health officer	Chief law enforcement official
NORTH DAKOTA (53) continued								
Rolette (Rolla) (12)	701 477-3816	(not reporting)						
Sargent (Forman) (6)	701 724-3361	(not reporting)						
Sheridan (McClusky) (3)	701 363-2205	Armin Erdmann	....	Robert R Neuharth	Shirley Jorgensen	....	....	Arlen E Shatz
Sioux (Fort Yates)† (4)	701 854-3481	Simon Dillman	....	Ernest Halverson	Michael Snider	....	....	Miles Utter
Slope (Amidon) (1)	701 879-6276	Merle Hayden	....	Robert Strommen	Teresa Buzalsky	....	....	Elmer C Morland
Stark (Dickinson)† (24)	701 225-2712	....	....	Paulette Reule	Kathryn Kary	....	....	Jim Rice
Steele (Finley) (3)	701 524-2110	John E Laughlin	....	Ruth Gullicks	Dorothy Thompson	....	....	Gilman H Johnson
Stutsman (Jamestown) (24)	701 252-9035	Vern Wahl	....	Lary J Olson	Wanda Kruger	....	Sharon Unruh	Dave Orr
Towner (Cando) (4)	701 968-3414	Duane Haugen	....	Verna M Martz	Eileen R Fiedler	....	G H Hilts MD	Howard Soderberg
Traill (Hillsboro) (10)	701 436-4458	Hartman Ulland	....	Joanne Haugen	Donna Oelrich	David Heyer	Kay Palan	Richard Fisher
Walsh (Grafton) (15)	701 352-2851	Leonard Agerholt	....	Lorraine Papenfus	Ann Thompson	Dennis Markusen	C C Rand	Joey L Pederson
Ward (Minot) (58)	701 852-5406	Orrin Luchsinger	....	Greg Nelson	Dave Senger	Gailen Narum	....	Arthur T Anderson
Wells (Fessenden) (7)	701 547-3521	Harvey Lenz	....	Vance L Kro	Vance L Kro	....	M J Towarnicky	Curtis D Pellett
Williams (Williston) (22)	701 572-6373	Lloyd A Johnson	....	M Gunderson	June Ford	Steve Robinson	....	Stan Lyson
OHIO (88)								
Adams (West Union) (24)	513 544-3286	(not reporting)						
Allen (Lima) (112)	419 228-3700	Robert R Cupp	Crit W Akers	Sally J Clemans	Herbert McElwain	Clayton T Bacon	David Rosenbrock	Charles W Harrod
Ashland (Ashland) (46)	419 289-0000	J Myron Leininger	....	Sue Norris	John Welch	Larry Chamberlain	Jack Lentz	Kenneth Etzwiler
Ashtabula (Jefferson) (104)	216 576-9090	Alfred W Mackey	Betty Johns	Betty Johns	Robert Harvey	John Smolen	Raymond Saporito	William Johnston
Athens (Athens) (56)	614 593-7988	Karen Harvey	....	Vada Poston	Thomas Steenrod	Archie W Stanley	Joe Kasler	Robert S Allen
Auglaize (Wapakoneta) (43)	419 738-3612	Robert V Vogel	....	Connie Lauth	Vernon E Doenges	Douglas Reinhart	David Rosebrock	James Knoch
Belmont (St. Clairsville)† (83)	614 695-2121	A J Sargus	....	Mary Kapolka	Joseph A Pappano	Fred F Bennett	D J Pickenpaugh	Richard Stobbs
Brown (Georgetown) (32)	513 378-3956	Earl B Berger	....	Deborah Goslin	Mary Jennings	James G Beasley	K C McGann	John W Wesseler
Butler (Hamilton) (259)	513 807-5800	Donald Schirmer	Donald B Brill	Diana Bradford	Mary C Law	William R Foster	Pat Burg	Robert Walton
Carroll (Carrollton) (26)	216 627-2250	Russell G Barrett	....	Richard C Walton	Richard G Walton	John H McClain	Jack L Maffett	Dean R Yeager
Champaign (Urbana)† (34)	513 653-5896	Grover Foulk	....	May Engle	J A Underwood	Jack Engle	V R Frederick MD	Roger Stillings
Clark (Springfield) (150)	513 328-2400	L F Kerrigan	W Darrell Howard	Martha I Fleck	Ralph H Stiers	Roger F Borchers	Dean Hodge	Raymond B Jordan
Clermont (Batavia) (128)	513 732-7110	Robert S Croswell	Patrick Dinan	Judith Kocica	David Smith	Walter C Carter	Harvey Hines	John Van Camp
Clinton (Wilmington)† (35)	513 382-2103	D M Fife	....	Nancy McKay	Drusilla Peelle	James Nimz	Howard Elerding	Patrick Haley
Columbiana (Lisbon) (114)	216 424-9511	David Halverstadt	....	Nancy Thompson	Ardel Strabala	Bert Dawson	Dr Paul Beaver	Richard Koffel
Coshocton (Coshocton) (36)	614 622-1753	William Hoop Jr	....	Esmond C Taylor	Michelle Darner	James Gute	Michael Wilson	David Corbett
Crawford (Bucyrus) (50)	419 562-5876	Burnell Shumaker	....	Blanche E Murr	Glen Cole	Randolph Strauch	Donald Campbell	Ronny Shawber
Cuyahoga (Cleveland) (1498)	216 443-7000	V C Campanella	William R Plato	Jeri Chaikin	Francis E Gaul	Thomas J Neff	Francis F Silver	Gerald T McFaul
Darke (Greenville) (55)	513 548-2035	(not reporting)						
Defiance (Defiance)† (40)	419 782-4761	Albert A Weber	....	Susan K Schelling	Karen A Tubbs	Dennis M Bell	Lucy M Weaver	Douglas B Ziegler
Delaware (Delaware) (54)	614 369-8761	Fay Parrott	Done Fisher	David R Thomas	Madge Conklin	Fred Stults	Fran Ververka	William B Lavery
Erie (Sandusky) (80)	419 627-7682	William P Scheid	Ray E Sherman	Vickie Johnson	Virginia Grathwol	Kenneth Polta	Don Ledwell	John Magnuson
Fairfield (Lancaster) (94)	614 654-6530	Henry Leckrone	....	Donna Noice	Sam LaFever	Robert Reef	Stephen Hodson	Jim Peck
Fayette (Washington Ct Hse) (27)	614 335-6371	(not reporting)						
Franklin (Columbus) (869)	614 462-3322	Hugh Demoss	D Keith Nichols	Barbara J Carter	Bobbie Hall	John Circle	John Stephens MD	Robert Berry
Fulton (Wauseon) (38)	419 335-5921	Al Kreuz	....	Mary Behnfeldt	Grace Amstutz	Thomas Stahl	Don Stotzer MD	L James Trigg
Gallia (Gallipolis) (30)	614 446-4612	Verlin Swain	....	Joan Davis	Myron McGhee	James Baird	Gerald Vallee	James Montgomery
Geauga (Chardon) (74)	216 285-2222	Tony Gall	George W Taylor	Alice Kritzer	Richard Makowski	Robert Phillips	Jane M Mahoney	James Todd
Greene (Xenia) (130)	513 376-5000	Thos Blessing III	Ralph C Harper	Nancy Boyer	James W Schmidt	Richard Eastman	Wm McCullough	Russell Bradley
Guernsey (Cambridge) (42)	614 432-2505	Samuel N Stover	....	Martha Porter	Charles Milligan	Thomas D Parnell	Tom Swan MD	James U Carpenter
Hamilton (Cincinnati)† (873)	513 632-8222	Robert A Taft II	Michael J Maloney	Angela Detzel	Wayne F Wilke	Donald C Schramm	Harold Jacobs	Lincoln Stokes
Hancock (Findlay) (65)	419 424-7044	(not reporting)						
Hardin (Kenton) (33)	419 673-0771	(not reporting)						
Harrison (Cadiz) (18)	614 942-3552	L Timmerman	....	Brenda K Graham	Michael Cope	Howard Stitt	James Lapp	Richard Rensi
Henry (Napoleon) (28)	419 592-4876	Stephen Kryder	....	Reva M Eisaman	Ruth Boyd	Charles McClure	Dr Stough	Irvin Flory
Highland (Hillsboro)† (33)	513 393-1911	Harriet F Stivers	....	Doris Edgington	Ann B Williams	Lowell McCarty	L T Odland MD	Hugh Rogers
Hocking (Logan) (24)	514 385-5195	Carl W Risch	....	Blanche Mowery	Francis E Myers	William Shaw	J Ward Doering	James P Jones
Holmes (Millersburg)† (29)	216 674-0286	....	....	Darrell O Conkle	Don W Miller	Robert L Kasner	Maurice E Mullet	P Phil Huff
Huron (Norwalk)† (55)	419 668-3092	Thomas W Carabin	Edward J Still	Christine Keller	Ardeth Chupp	Lawrence L Heit	Howard Sparks MD	John Borgia
Jackson (Jackson) (31)	614 286-3301	Joe Conger	....	Marianna Edwards	Andrew G Armbrist	Paul J Harris	Carl Greever MD	Charles Hunter
Jefferson (Steubenville) (92)	614 283-4111	(not reporting)						
Knox (Mount Vernon) (46)	614 397-2727	Richard K Mavis	....	D Joan Dailey	Joseph Mickley	Gary J Durbin	M McLarnan	Paul K Rowe
Lake (Painesville) (213)	216 357-2500	Daniel J Supanick	Charles A Crown	John S Crocker	Kathleen Cotter	Tom Gilles	Joel Lucia	Edwin Cunningham
Lawrence (Ironton) (64)	614 533-4368	(not reporting)						
Licking (Newark) (121)	614 349-8421	John L Eshelman	Glen K Porter	Glen K Porter	J Terry Evans	Jerry H Wray	Robert Mai	Gerry Billy
Logan (Bellefontaine) (39)	513 599-7283	Warren W Smith	....	Judith L Grove	Don Downing	Chester R Kurtz	W A Verbsky	Milt Watts
Lorain (Elyria) (275)	216 329-5000	Ron L Nabakowski	D A Dellisanti	Mona L Walsh	J Grant Keys	L McGlinchy	Ken Pearce	James A Mertz
Lucas (Toledo) (472)	419 245-4500	Francis Szollosi	Edward J Ciecka	Herbert O Hoehing	John McHugh	George Wilson	Richard Wenzel MD	Donald Hickey
Madison (London) (33)	614 852-2972	(not reporting)						
Mahoning (Youngstown) (289)	216 747-2000	Thomas J Carney	John Juhasz	John B Juhasz Jr	Michael Pope	Michael Fitas	Paul Cramer	James Traficant
Marion (Marion) (68)	614 387-5871	(not reporting)						
Medina (Medina)† (113)	216 723-3641	Sterling Sechrist	....	Thelma M Wegst	Betty J Rom	William Anderson	Leroy Dalheim MD	L John Ribar
Meigs (Pomeroy)† (24)	614 992-2895	David Koblentz	....	Mary Hobstetter	George M Collins	Philip Roberts	....	James Profitt
Mercer (Celina) (38)	419 586-3178	Edward Osterholt	Joan Bollenbacher	Joan Bollenbacher	Robert C King	Keith Earley	G McElroy MD	E Joseph Gilmore
Miami (Troy) (90)	513 335-8341	Robert Clawson	Judith F Foureman	Judith F Foureman	Ethel Felver	Douglas Christian	Charles Oxley MD	Luther Dunfee
Monroe (Woodsfield) (17)	614 472-1341	Bernard C Smith	....	Barbara Blattler	James N Neuhart	Gerald Sims	Jack M Matheny	F Sulsberger
Montgomery (Dayton)§ (572)	513 225-4690	Paula MacIlwaine	Claude Malone Jr	Juanita M Hunn	Joe Shump	Fred Frecker	Morton Nelson	Tom Wilson
Morgan (McConnelsville) (14)	614 962-4752	(not reporting)						
Morrow (Mount Gilead) (26)	419 947-4085	Wm J Turner	....	Elaine Keirns	Dwight McClarren	Justin Earley	Frances Veverka	Tom E Harden
Muskingum (Zanesville) (83)	614 452-4587	Don L Dilts	....	Rella K Sroufe	Norma J Bowman	Loren Camp	Ron Elble	Bernard Gibson
Noble (Caldwell) (11)	614 732-2969	James R Rayner	....	Donna J Boyd	W David Fleming	Robert C Paxton	Fredrick M Cox	Landon T Smith
Ottawa (Port Clinton) (40)	419 734-4431	James A Mazur	....	Barbara J Hermes	James Snider	John G Papcun	Jack Witker MD	John R Crosser
Paulding (Paulding) (21)	419 399-3786	(not reporting)						
Perry (New Lexington) (31)	614 342-2045	(not reporting)						
Pickaway (Circleville) (44)	614 474-5233	Donald E Strous	Gregory D Bigam	Gregory D Bigam	Gregory D Bigam	Robert Parker	William Myers MD	Dwight E Radcliff
Pike (Waverly)† (23)	614 947-4817	Samuel A Hughes	....	Paul T Barker	Homer L Scaggs	Richard L Craumer	Joseph Ramsey	James G Dixon
Portage (Ravenna)† (136)	216 296-6466	Thomas J Freeman	....	Eloise Ticknor	Maurice Kline	Leroy Satrom	Kenneth Rupp	Ross L Jamerson
Preble (Eaton) (38)	513 456-3746	Edwin S Brubaker	Sharon Shute	Sharon Maggard	Betty Mong	Kenneth Yost	James Lucas	Jan M Spitler
Putnam (Ottawa) (33)	419 523-3656	Vincent J Niese	....	Edna M Michel	Rosella C Verhoff	Terrance R Recker	Raymond H Meyer	Robert C Beutler
Richland (Mansfield) (131)	419 755-5500	Paul White	....	Naomi Carter	Daniel Smith	Marion Schaus	D Campbell MD	Richard Petty
Ross (Chillicothe)† (65)	614 773-5115	James M Caldwell	James L Kennard	Letitia S Dobbins	Bennett Junk	Paul M Miller	L T Odland	Thomas Hamman
Sandusky (Fremont) (63)	419 332-6411	Wesley R Fahrbach	....	T Druckenmiller	V Swartzlander	Donald Shaffer	Kenneth Kerik	Joseph Kindred
Scioto (Portsmouth) (85)	614 353-5111	Robert W Cross	....	Jeanne Schmidt	Ronald Greene	Jim Weaver	Roy Adams	John Knauff

Directory 1/9 continued — COUNTY OFFICIALS IN ALL U.S. COUNTIES

County, county seat, 1980 population (000 omitted),	County telephone number	Board chairman	Appointed administrator	Clerk to the governing board	Chief financial officer	County engineer	County health officer	Chief law enforcement official
OHIO (88) continued								
Seneca (Tiffin) (62)	419 447-4550	C Leverne Wertz	Dianne Vogelsong	Dianne Vogelsong	M Bernard	Preston R Spencer	....	Weldin Neff
Shelby (Sidney) (43)	513 498-7226	Bernard A Aselage	....	Susan Fair	Gerald F Billing	J Stephan Hubbell	Stephan Corthell	John Lenhart
Stark (Canton)† (379)	216 454-5651	Richard D Watkins	Robert A Fonte	William J Keen	Harold Roach	Joseph A Sturrett	William Franks	Robert C Berens
Summit (Akron) (524)	216 379-5110	John R Morgan	Jerry Sloan	Richard A Skraba	John Donofrio	Paul G Swanson	Martha Nelson MD	David W Troutman
Trumbull (Warren)† (242)	216 841-0400	Anthony Latell Jr	....	Roselyn J Ferris	Harold Williams	Edward Ryser	L A Loria MD	Richard Jakmas
Tuscarawas (New Philadelphia)† (85)	216 364-8811	William Winters	....	Edith Bair	Don Levergood	Charles Young	Robert Hastedt MD	Louis Clark
Union (Marysville)† (30)	513 642-4601	Glenn Irwin	....	L E Snider	Tomia Lowe	Donald Hart	Fran Veverka	John Overly
Van Wert (Van Wert) (30)	419 238-1022	(not reporting)						
Vinton (McArthur)† (12)	614 596-4571	John Simmons	....	Cora Pettet	Larry Clary	Ronald Sharrett	Donald Barton	Delno McClure
Warren (Lebanon) (99)	513 932-4040	G Terwilleger	....	Karen K Jones	Harry D Cornett	Craig R Pendleton	Ben Wahl	Robert Dalton
Washington (Marietta)† (64)	614 373-6623	Wayne A Schafer	....	Sandra I Matthews	Dorothy K Peppel	R V Schultheis	Mary Whitacre	Richard D Ellis
Wayne (Wooster) (97)	216 263-1111	(not reporting)						
Williams (Bryan) (36)	419 636-1551	(not reporting)						
Wood (Bowling Green)† (107)	419 352-6531	John G Ault	....	Margaret Savieo	Harold R Bateson	Anthony Allion	James Ryder	George Ginter
Wyandot (Upper Sandusky) (23)	419 294-1432	(not reporting)						
OKLAHOMA (77)								
Adair (Stillwell) (19)	918 696-7198	(not reporting)						
Alfalfa (Cherokee) (7)	405 596-2392	Paul Murrow	....	Kaye Jay	....	....	Dean Vaughn	Delmar Coppock
Atoka (Atoka) (13)	405 889-2643	Leo Evans	....	Troy Gammon	Richard Lillard	....	Jim Weaver	Robert Hearnell
Beaver (Beaver)† (7)	405 625-3191	Jim Lane	....	Audrey Parker	....	....	Ron Huffman	Deb McGuire
Beckham (Sayre) (19)	405 928-3330	(not reporting)						
Blaine (Watonga)† (13)	405 622-5890	Wendell Robison	....	Alveria McBee	....	....	....	James E Sinclair
Bryan (Durant) (31)	405 924-2202	(not reporting)						
Caddo (Anadarko) (31)	405 247-6609	(not reporting)						
Canadian (El Reno) (56)	405 262-1070	Penny Ferrell	....	Betty Eisenhour	Vernon Lawrence	....	....	Jerry Russell
Carter (Ardmore) (44)	405 223-8162	(not reporting)						
Cherokee (Tahlequah) (31)	918 456-3171	(not reporting)						
Choctaw (Hugo) (17)	405 326-5331	Leo Robertson	....	Mae Beason	L Massengale	Hal Lambert	Jack Hicks	Bill Hall
Cimarron (Boise City) (4)	405 544-2251	....	....	Cindi M Kincannon	Gayla James	....	....	Bob D White
Cleveland (Norman)† (133)	405 366-0200	Gordon L Jones	Carl E Remus	Billie Gatewood	Margaret Smith	....	Littleton Fowler	Bill Porter
Coal (Coalgate) (6)	405 927-3122	J N Flint	....	....	....	....	....	....
Comanche (Lawton)† (112)	405 353-3717	Gale Humble	....	Beverly Glasgow	R Bainbridge	....	Jim Booher	C M Hawkins Jr
Cotton (Walters) (7)	405 875-3026	M J Meaders	....	Linda Stack	Janie Sheppard	....	Don Morgan	Michael Fletcher
Craig (Vinita)† (15)	918 256-3564	Phil Beisly	....	Maxine Highsmith	Carol Paulding	....	Rex Netherton	Jess Walker
Creek (Sapulpa) (59)	918 224-0278	Dan Whitehouse	....	Rima Anhland	Nadine Thoos	....	Shirley Brooks	Bob Whitworth
Custer (Arapaho) (26)	405 323-4420	C M Reinhard	....	Calvin Klein	Inez Leavell	Robert Leonard	Lynn McElroy	Richard Mueller
Delaware (Jay) (24)	918 253-4520	Johnny Jackson	....	Sam Fields	Juanita Larmon	....	....	Bob Hughes
Dewey (Taloga) (6)	405 328-5361	(not reporting)						
Ellis (Arnett) (6)	405 885-2311	(not reporting)						
Garfield (Enid) (63)	405 237-0227	Ernest Reynolds	....	Robert G Graf	Joyce Postier	Merland G Wright	Kirk T Mosley	Ray Pickle
Garvin (Pauls Valley) (28)	405 238-2772	L C Stewart	....	Carole Richard	....	....	Dewey Smith	....
Grady (Chickasha) (39)	405 224-5211	James C Waldron	....	Betty Ballard	J G Mosley	....	Wes Bannister	Ron Taylor
Grant (Medford) (7)	405 395-2274	Howard W Guthrie	....	Elaine Blubaugh	Norma Kretchmar	....	Kirk T Mosley MD	Archie Yearick
Greer (Mangum)† (7)	405 782-3664	Curtis Wetsel	....	Dorothy Brooks	Helen Lively	....	Robert A Warner	Alfred Rogers
Harmon (Hollis) (5)	405 688-3658	(not reporting)						
Harper (Buffalo) (5)	405 735-2521	(not reporting)						
Haskell (Stigler) (11)	918 967-2107	Jethro Henry	....	Johnathan Turney	....	....	Ron Barnett	Jay Stout
Hughes (Holdenville)† (14)	405 379-2746	Lloyd Sanford	....	Nina Baxter	Bill Marsh	....	Paul Lanham	Orville Rose
Jackson (Altus) (30)	405 482-4070	(not reporting)						
Jefferson (Waurika) (8)	405 228-2029	Kenneth Smith	....	Sevelle Overstree	Bobbie Fitzgerald	....	Wes Bannister	Simon Kennedy
Johnston (Tishomingo) (10)	405 371-3184	Guy Combes	....	Norma Maytubby	Dortha Hailes	....	Ron Roberts	Sam Holt
Kay (Newkirk) (50)	405 362-2537	Vern E Willbanks	....	Norma Lee Cook	Luella Backhaus	....	Mike O Connor	Thomas Johnstone
Kingfisher (Kingfisher)† (14)	405 375-3887	Ron Lemon	....	Charlotte Simon	C Brownlee	....	Donald Hutcheson	Coye Lee Barker
Kiowa (Hobart) (13)	405 726-5286	(not reporting)						
Latimer (Wilburton) (10)	918 465-3543	Carl U McCullar	....	W E Tidwell	Bea Chronister	....	....	Burlen R Glenn
Le Flore (Poteau)† (41)	918 647-2527	Charles Cox	....	Darrel Gallegly	J Ben Goodin	Bob Booms	Wayne Lowery	Ray Kirkland
Lincoln (Chandler) (27)	405 258-1264	John J Ogez	....	Wilda Clark	Don Sporleder	....	Mike O'Connor	Ray McLain
Logan (Guthrie) (27)	405 282-0266	(not reporting)						
Love (Marietta) (7)	405 276-3059	Clifford Harris	....	Dora Jackson	Eloise Tipton	....	Ronald Roberts	Marvin Wade
Major (Fairview)† (9)	405 227-4732	W F Lakey	....	Willa Dean Tripp	Gloria J Fast	....	....	Bill Pool
Marshall (Madill) (11)	405 795-3220	Monroe Barwick	....	Dovie Johnson	....	....	....	Billy Jack Hewett
Mayes (Pryor) (32)	918 825-2426	Edgar True	....	Sammy A Howard	....	....	....	Paul Smith
McClain (Purcell) (20)	405 527-3360	(not reporting)						
McCurtain (Idabel)† (36)	405 286-2370	Gail Craytor	....	Dixie May	Kenneth Hughes	Herbert Dunlop	Doyle Carper	Alan Marston
McIntosh (Eufaula) (15)	918 689-2741	(not reporting)						
Murray (Sulphur)† (12)	405 622-3777	Glenn Kahlor	Gary Jones	Linda Warren	J A Dowling	....	Jerry Mobly	Ed Bristol
Muskogee (Muskogee) (67)	918 682-7781	(not reporting)						
Noble (Perry) (12)	405 336-2141	(not reporting)						
Nowata (Nowata) (11)	918 273-2480	Edward L Wallace	....	Marjorie Fuller	Helen Jo Yeiton	John Rains	....	Michael E Bird
Okfuskee (Okemah) (11)	918 623-0939	Wayne Root	Wayne Root	Jean Reno	Dane Unterkircher	....	Shirley Brooks	Roy Nichols
Oklahoma (Oklahoma City) (569)	405 236-2727	Fred Snyder	....	Jerry Dewoody	Joe Barnes	Nelson Ryan	G Dellaportas	J D Sharp
Okmulgee (Okmulgee) (39)	918 756-0788	(not reporting)						
Osage (Pawhuska) (39)	918 287-3136	(not reporting)						
Ottawa (Miami) (33)	918 542-9476	(not reporting)						
Pawnee (Pawnee) (15)	918 762-3741	H B Minney	....	Raymond Young	Fern Karraker	....	....	S L Butch Allen
Payne (Stillwater) (62)	405 624-9300	Karen Mullendore	....	Sherri Schieffer	Joretta Gillette	Jack Lawmaster	Mike O'Connor	Frank Phillips
Pittsburg (McAlester) (41)	918 423-4859	(not reporting)						
Pontotoc (Ada) (33)	405 332-1425	(not reporting)						
Pottawatomie (Shawnee)† (55)	405 273-4305	Bill Thompson	....	Georgia B Austin	Margaret Newell	Charles Johnson	Paul Lanman	Ruie Birks
Pushmataha (Antlers) (12)	405 298-3626	Finnis Whiteside	....	Shirley Pryor	Evalene Nabors	....	Billy Jack Hicks	Louis A Goheen
Roger Mills (Cheyenne) (5)	405 497-3365	George Bryan	....	Opal J Means	Glen Kendall	Robert Leonard	Frank K Buster	Bob Trammell
Rogers (Claremore) (46)	918 341-2518	(not reporting)						
Seminole (Wewoka) (27)	405 257-6236	(not reporting)						
Sequoyah (Sallisaw) (31)	918 775-4556	Gus E Fullbright	....	Nadine C Mitchell	Faye Sanders	....	Bert Corley MD	Sam Lockhart
Stephens (Duncan) (43)	405 255-8460	(not reporting)						
Texas (Guymon) (18)	405 338-3233	C R Depuy	....	Linda Bowman	Melvin Camp	....	W N Oxley	Robert Bauer

Directory 1/9 continued — **COUNTY OFFICIALS IN ALL U.S. COUNTIES**

County, county seat, 1980 population (000 omitted),	County telephone number	Board chairman	Appointed administrator	Clerk to the governing board	Chief financial officer	County engineer	County health officer	Chief law enforcement official
OKLAHOMA (77) continued								
Tillman (Frederick)† (12)	405 335-3421	James G Burks	....	John W Hartwig	Ava R Tidwell	....	....	Robert B Rowe
Tulsa (Tulsa) (471)	918 584-0471	Melvin C Rice	Clayton T Edwards	....	John Cantrell	Ray Jordan	....	Frank Thurman
Wagoner (Wagoner) (42)	918 485-2216	(not reporting)						
Washington (Bartlesville) (48)	918 336-0330	John Lanning	....	Fae A Moreland	Dean Bennett	....	Pat McLaury	Glen Codding
Washita (Cordell) (14)	405 832-2284	Alfred Miller	....	W B Sharp Jr	Dana Moore	....	....	Joe Ferrero
Woods (Alva) (11)	405 327-0998	(not reporting)						
Woodward (Woodward)† (21)	405 256-8097	J D Jackson	....	Stanley Fowler	Jane Hensley	....	Gary Reavis	A Creel Gaston
OREGON (36)								
Baker (Baker) (16)	503 523-6414	Larry L Smith	Tony Hamman	Julia Woods	Alice L Saunders	James Hanley	Gary Devos	Terry Speelman
Benton (Corvallis)† (68)	503 757-6800	Barbara Ross	Daniel Bartlett	Daniel Burk	Clark Ruggles	James Blair	Elizabeth Sazie	John T Dolan
Clackamas (Oregon City) (242)	503 655-8581	Robert Schumacher	Jerry G Justice	Juanita Orr	Thelma Hooper	Winston Kurth	John F Schilke	Bill Brooks
Clatsop (Astoria)† (32)	503 325-1000	Roger A Berg	....	Norma Hunsinger	Robert W Gazewood	Homer Tunks	K Hellberg	Almond Eastman
Columbia (St. Helens) (36)	503 397-3796	Robert L King	Roberta J Stubbs	Reta C Kerry	Corene Carlstrom	Ted Standen	....	Bruce Oester
Coos (Coquille) (64)	503 396-3121	(not reporting)						
Crook (Prineville) (13)	503 447-6553	Dick Hoppes	....	Grace Bannon	Leona Puckett	....	David Riggs	Tom Lowe
Curry (Gold Beach) (17)	503 247-7011	(not reporting)						
Deschutes (Bend) (62)	503 388-6570	Albert A Young	Michael A Maier	Susan E Stoneman	Helen Rastovich	David Hoerning	Steve Knap	Jim France
Douglas (Roseburg)† (94)	503 672-3311	Bill Vian	....	Judy Robison	Thomas J Eckerd	Kenneth Erickson	Sharon Thrall MD	Norman Neal
Gilliam (Condon) (2)	503 384-2311	(not reporting)						
Grant (Canyon City) (8)	503 575-0059	Lorene Allen	....	Carol Voigt	Kathy Smith	Bob Bagett	M T Merrill	Dave Hayne
Harney (Burns) (8)	503 573-6356	Dale White	....	Avel Diaz	Berneace Shelton	Charles F Palmer	John H Weare	R Keith Boggs
Hood River (Hood River)§ (16)	503 386-3970	Elmer W Murray	Kenneth W Kirby	Donna M Layman	Paul F Helton	James Lyon	W T Edmundson MD	Robert D Lynch
Jackson (Medford)§ (132)	503 776-7211	Jerry Barnes	Paul Steinbrenner	Kathy Beckett	Gary Cadle	....	Taira Fukushima	C W Smith
Jefferson (Madras) (12)	503 475-2449	Herschel Read	....	Elaine Henderson	Elva Townsend	....	....	Hamlin P Perkins
Josephine (Grants Pass) (59)	503 474-5100	Anthony Corriea	....	Gail J Gibson	Barbara Humberd	Robert Weber	Bill Dalton MD	M L Fanning
Klamath (Klamath Falls) (59)	503 882-2501	Roger Hamilton	Harry Jensen	Evelyn Biehn	F Jean Elzner	Earl Kessler	Perry Rickard	Tom Duryee
Lake (Lakeview) (8)	503 947-2421	George Carlon	....	Karen O'Conner	Rose Hollworth	....	Robert Bomengen	Bill Griffin
Lane (Eugene)§ (275)	503 687-4011	Peter A Defazio	Steven J Ickes	Debbie E Mohr	John E Faw	John Goodson	David L White	David N Burks
Lincoln (Newport)† (35)	503 265-6611	G E Stuart	....	Virginia L Kampf	Mary Kuenzli	Joe Steere	Hilda Moravick	Larry Spencer
Linn (Albany) (89)	503 967-3800	Carl J Stephani	William L Offutt	Del W Riley	Arlene Downing	Willis Grafe	Trin Dumlao	Kenneth Goin
Malheur (Vale) (27)	503 473-3123	E M Seuell	....	Robert L Morcom	Jean P Bond	William Weaver	David W Sarazin	Robert G Ingram
Marion (Salem) (205)	503 588-5212	Randall Franke	Kenneth Roudybush	Inice Haverkate	Ralph J Grim	Robert Hansen	Beverly Olsen MD	Chuck Foster
Morrow (Heppner) (8)	503 676-9233	Don McElligott	....	Lorayne Bowman	Margo Sherer	Otto Burden	Pat Wright	Roy Drago
Multnomah (Portland) (563)	503 248-3511	Dennis V Buchanan	....	Jane McGarvin	Andrew Thaler	Larry F Nicholas	Charles Schade MD	Fred Pearce
Polk (Dallas) (45)	503 623-8171	Henry A Dougherty	....	M Kaltenbach	Joe Cochrane	Clarence Swenson	E A Flaming MD	Bill Berlin
Sherman (Moro) (2)	503 565-3606	(not reporting)						
Tillamook (Tillamook) (21)	503 842-5511	Gerald A Woodward	....	Susan Becraft	Steven Simpson	Jon Oshel	Howard Kaliher	David Wilson
Umatilla (Pendleton) (59)	503 276-7111	A L Draper	....	Marcia Wells	Lillian Sorensen	C Van Elsberg	Dr Koch	James Carey
Union (La Grande) (24)	503 963-1001	Earle C Misener	Marlene Perkins	Shirley Bolin	Barbara Dean	Howard Perry	Wesley Allen MD	Robert Price
Wallowa (Enterprise) (7)	503 426-3226	Stanley J Farris	....	Marjorie L Martin	....	....	Lowell Euhus MD	Roger A Decker
Wasco (The Dalles) (22)	503 296-2207	William L Hulse	....	Kathryn McBride	Carole Wood	Dennis Kramer	Carla Chamberlain	Robert Brown
Washington (Hillsboro)* (245)	503 648-8611	Wes Myllenbeck	Donald D Stilwell	M Crutsinger	Cristi Cutler	....	Marietta Sorenson	Bill Probstfield
Wheeler (Fossil) (2)	503 763-2400	(not reporting)						
Yamhill (McMinnville) (55)	503 472-9371	David E Bishop	Kenneth Williams	Charles Stern	Marilyn Smith	Bill Gille	Mark Olson	Glenn Shipman
PENNSYLVANIA (67)								
Adams (Gettysburg) (68)	717 334-6781	Thomas L Collins	....	Darryl S Mummert	George W Stock	....	....	Bernard V Miller
Allegheny (Pittsburgh) (1450)	412 355-5300	Tom Foerster	Scott R O'Donnell	S M Sirabella	Jay Costa	J Fred Graham	N M Richards MD	Eugene L Coon
Armstrong (Kittanning) (78)	412 543-2500	Carl L Culp	....	Dorothy C Morris	Ray G Heilman	....	....	Joseph B Frick
Beaver (Beaver) (204)	412 728-5700	Joseph H Widmer	....	Robert W Cyphert	Kenneth Campbell	John Grant	....	Frank Policaro
Bedford (Bedford) (47)	814 623-1173	Joseph H Clapper	....	Patricia M Chapin	Rowland A Clark	P Joseph Lehman	....	Max Norris Sr
Berks (Reading) (313)	215 375-6121	Donald Bagenstose	....	Ronald R Seaman	Stella C Kompa	Ronald Weaver	....	John Kramer
Blair (Hollidaysburg)† (137)	814 695-5541	John W Gardner	Ralph T Mangus	Ralph T Mangus	Wm Collins Jr	....	....	Eugene Wegemer
Bradford (Towanda) (63)	717 265-5700	Marilyn A Bok	....	Gary L Wood	Michael Brutzman	....	....	Thomas Fairchild
Bucks (Doylestown) (479)	215 348-6000	Carl F Fonash	William H Rieser	William H Rieser	Richard C Gore	....	Edmund Lindemuth	Lawrence Michaels
Butler (Butler) (148)	412 285-4731	R M Patterson	Thomas D Lavorini	....	Joan T Chew	Marshall Kapp	....	....
Cambria (Ebensburg) (183)	814 472-5440	Joseph P Roberts	....	Thomas J Rafas	Esther M Donahue	....	....	Thomas P Burns
Cameron (Emporium) (7)	814 486-2315	Mary J Donovan	....	Verle M Jack	Richard D English	....	....	James J Fragale
Carbon (Jim Thorpe) (53)	717 325-2481	(not reporting)						
Centre (Bellefonte) (113)	814 355-6700	Jeffrey M Bower	....	Vicki L Bumbarger	Gino P Fornicola	Rodney M Hoy	....	Garry G Kunes
Chester (West Chester) (317)	215 431-6100	Robert J Thompson	James L Boling	Wayne R Rothermel	Armand Taraschi	Richard Wilking	John Maher MD	Fred Fulton
Clarion (Clarion) (43)	814 226-4000	(not reporting)						
Clearfield (Clearfield) (84)	814 765-2461	Harry Fred Bigler	....	Eleanor Ludwig	James W Laing Jr	....	....	Chester A Hawkins
Clinton (Lock Haven) (39)	717 748-7779	James E Bottorf	....	Diane L Lucas	Lee K Marshall Jr	....	....	William Maggs
Columbia (Bloomsburg) (62)	717 784-1991	Lucille Whitmire	Harry R Faux	Harry R Faux	Shirley F Drake	....	....	Victor B Vandling
Crawford (Meadville) (89)	814 336-1151	Ivan G Rose	....	H Richard Hays	Frederic A Wagner	....	....	Howard Stewart
Cumberland (Carlisle) (178)	717 249-1133	Marcia L Myers	Sandra Whittaker	Sandra Whittaker	Jerry L Nailor	....	....	William Beck
Dauphin (Harrisburg) (232)	717 255-2711	John E Minnich	....	Sidney A Reese	R F Dick	....	....	Wm H Livingston
Delaware (Media)* (555)	215 891-4000	Frank J Lynch	Matthew J Hayes	Carma M Mullen	Thomas J Monteith	Robert L Keates	Joan L Murray	John Taylor
Elk (Ridgway) (38)	814 776-1161	James C Yetzer	....	Pat Butler	John R Kestler	....	....	Raymond Krasinski
Erie (Erie)† (280)	814 452-3333	Judith M Lynch	Peter J Russo	Florindo Fabrizio	A Jake Gehrlein	....	John J Toth	Robert J Michel
Fayette (Uniontown)† (160)	412 437-4525	Fred L Lebder	....	Joseph Korona Jr	....	....	....	Thomas Hamilton
Forest (Tionesta) (5)	814 755-3537	William E Snyder	....	Avonelle Rudolph	Elizabeth Mealy	....	....	Harry E Tucker
Franklin (Chambersburg) (114)	717 264-4125	Fred J Rock Jr	....	Linford Pensingee	Mary Hockenberry	....	....	Raymond Z Hussack
Fulton (McConnellsburg) (13)	717 485-4212	(not reporting)						
Greene (Waynesburg) (40)	412 852-1171	Leonard R Santore	Herbert A Cox	Herbert A Cox	Joseph R Souders	....	....	Remo E Bertugli
Huntingdon (Huntingdon) (42)	814 643-3091	Larry O Sather	....	Louella C Coons	Richard E Kidd	Africa Engineers	....	Mark E Leamer Jr
Indiana (Indiana) (92)	412 465-2623	James E McQuown	....	Helen C Hill	Emma S Ober	Mark Gera	....	John R Gondal
Jefferson (Brookville)† (48)	814 849-8031	John R Caldwell	....	Gretchen H Grube	Dale Corbin	....	....	John Dinger
Juniata (Mifflintown) (19)	717 436-8991	(not reporting)						
Lackawanna (Scranton) (228)	717 961-6800	Joseph J Corcoran	Gerald Stanvitch	Ann Marie Regan	Robert Payton	Dominick Surace	....	John J Szymanski
Lancaster (Lancaster)† (362)	717 299-8000	Robert C Boyer	John H Hoober	John H Hoober	Robert E Fasnacht	Thomas F Shirk	....	Thomas Williams
Lawrence (New Castle) (107)	412 658-2541	Roger M DeCarbo	....	Charleen T Micco	Robert E Foht	....	....	George Sigler
Lebanon (Lebanon) (110)	717 274-2801	Lose M Swanger	Donald J Rhine	Donald J Rhine	Lois J Bomberger	....	....	Clifford A Roland
Lehigh (Allentown) (274)	215 820-3001	David K Bausch	Terry B Schutten	Lorraine R Berta	Thomas J Lazorik	Frank Moyer	....	Ronald L Neimeyer
Luzerne (Wilkes-Barre) (343)	717 825-1500	F J Trinisewski	....	Eugene R Klein	Michael Morreale	James J Brozena	....	Frank Jagodinski
Lycoming (Williamsport) (118)	717 327-2200	Gene Smith	John N Balog	John N Balog	Irene S Migrath	....	....	L Eugene Pauling
McKean (Smethport) (51)	814 887-5571	Raymond J Curtis	Audrey Irons	Audrey Irons	Connie Eaton	....	....	Richard J Miller

Directory 1/9 continued — COUNTY OFFICIALS IN ALL U.S. COUNTIES

County, county seat, 1980 population (000 omitted),	County telephone number	Board chairman	Appointed administrator	Clerk to the governing board	Chief financial officer	County engineer	County health officer	Chief law enforcement official
PENNSYLVANIA (67) continued								
Mercer (Mercer) (128)	412 662-3800	Harold E Bell	....	Robert S Gargasz	Nettie J Pantell	Mark Miller	....	Donald Marenchin
Mifflin (Lewistown) (47)	717 248-6733	H K Kochenderfer	....	Peggy G Yoder	....	....	....	Jay R Laub
Monroe (Stroudsburg) (69)	717 424-5100	James Cadue	Betsy Caprioli	....	Martin Stafanik	John Dennis	....	Forrest Sebring
Montgomery (Norristown) (644)	215 278-3000	Paul Baker Bartle	Robert W Graf	....	Floriana N Bloss	A W Martin	....	Frank W Jenkins
Montour (Danville) (17)	717 275-1331	Thomas E Herman	Susan M Kauwell	Susan M Kauwell	Robert P Love	....	....	Fred R Shepperson
Northampton (Easton)§ (225)	215 253-4111	Gerald E Seyfried	Joseph T Zajacek	Frank E Flisser	Charles Houck	....	....	Kenneth Stocker
Northumberland (Sunbury)† (100)	717 286-7721	James P Kelley	Laura Weir	Robert Rumberger	Ronald Schreffler	Charles Hopta	Ernest Korten	Russeell Wolfe
Perry (New Bloomfield) (36)	717 582-2131	R Elwood Mohler	....	L Dean McMillen	Margaret M Bolton	....	....	M C Raffensberger
Philadelphia C† (1688)	215 686-1776	Wilson Goode	Leo A Brooks	Joseph C Vignola	Richard G Gilmore	....	Stuart Shapiro MD	Gregore Sambor
Pike (Milford) (18)	717 296-7613	Willis J Gilpin	....	Centa T Quinn	Edward Delling	Fred Schoenagel	....	Arthur J Jebson
Potter (Coudersport) (18)	814 274-8290	Thomas O Bowman	F W Gunzburger	F W Gunzburger	Richard McCaigue	....	....	Dale W Russell
Schuylkill (Pottsville) (161)	717 622-5570	Paul Sheers	Robert B Hoppe	M Reddington	Gerald G Lengle	John C Briel	....	Daniel Grow
Snyder (Middleburg)† (34)	717 837-0691	Guy E Mitterling	Lee E Knepp	Lee E Knepp	Ann I Shadel	....	....	Richard Nornhold
Somerset (Somerset) (81)	814 443-1434	Paul L O'Conner	....	Kay F Slope	Lois Brougher	....	....	Guy Davis
Sullivan (Laporte) (6)	717 946-5201	(not reporting)						
Susquehanna (Montrose) (38)	717 278-3878	(not reporting)						
Tioga (Wellsboro) (41)	717 724-1906	Oliver R Bartlett	....	D H Blackwell	Edgar A Carlson	....	....	Richard L Hasting
Union (Lewisburg) (33)	717 524-4461	Sherman Doebler	Diana L Robinson	Diana L Robinson	Miriam H Dberdorf	Roger Hepner	....	Donald N Everitt
Venango (Franklin)† (64)	814 437-6871	Oscar W Bodamer	....	Naomi L Osborne	Margaret Spence	J Edward Adams	....	Harry Storm
Warren (Warren)† (47)	814 723-7550	D K Rice	....	Georgianna Shea	Bonnie Hoffman	....	....	Donnell Allen Jr
Washington (Washington) (217)	412 228-6700	Frank R Mascara	Louis L Lignelli	C Dallatore	John Yoney	....	....	James A Fazzoni
Wayne (Honesdale) (35)	717 253-5970	Earl J Simons	....	Reg Wayman	Alfred Perkins	James Knash	....	William Bluff
Westmoreland (Greensburg)† (392)	412 834-2191	Ted Simon	Jack W Simon	Elaine Oravets	Garrette Blubaugh	Henry G Fitz	....	John W Peck
Wyoming (Tunkhannock) (26)	717 836-3200	(not reporting)						
York (York) (313)	717 848-3301	W C McKinley	....	Lynwood Schleeter	....	....	....	Oliver Nace
SOUTH CAROLINA (46)								
Abbeville (Abbeville)† (23)	803 459-5312	W D Nixon	Joyce T Simpson	Carol A Chrisley	L Abner Hall	....	Stacia Hagen	Sam B Cann Jr
Aiken (Aiken)§ (106)	803 649-3481	Carrol H Warner	W Scott Barnes	Doris G Shulse	Frieda L Walker	Joe W Busby Jr	Charles M Garland	Wm Ralph Gunnells
Allendale (Allendale) (11)	803 584-2013	(not reporting)						
Anderson (Anderson)* (133)	803 261-4000	Robert L Wiles	Billy D O'Neal	Linda N Gilstrap	Betty Smith	Norman M Walters	Thomas Hyslop	E E Duck Cooley
Bamberg (Bamberg)§ (18)	803 245-5191	....	James H Zorn Jr	....	....	....	....	....
Barnwell (Barnwell) (20)	803 259-3464	T E Richardson	R E Hunter Jr	Peggy M Rhinehart	Pickens Williams	....	....	George Hogg
Beaufort (Beaufort)* (65)	803 525-7151	William McBride	Michael G O'Neill	Alice Glawson	Elrid Moody	Erik Freiesleben	Foster C McCaleb	M McCutcheon
Berkeley (Moncks Corner) (95)	803 761-8250	Johnnie T Flynn	....	Betty Lou Hanna	Carolyn M Umphlet	Dale Gregg	....	M C Cannon
Calhoun (St. Matthews)† (12)	803 874-2435	David Summers Jr	K T Rickenbaker	Lois H Inabinet	Jones E Carson	....	W B Fairey	Ronny Fickling
Charleston (Charleston)* (277)	803 577-7800	Charles T Wallace	Charles B Hetrick	Evelyn K Bonham	David P Edwards	James C Rogers	J C Chambers MD	Walter C Gay
Cherokee (Gaffney) (41)	803 489-5224	Fyunciz Wilhinz	Dolphus C Medley	Doris F Pearson	Catherine Gibson	....	....	Joe Wallace
Chester (Chester)† (30)	803 385-5133	R Carlisle Roddey	....	Marion M Thomas	Hall G Hunnery	....	Helen E Llewelyn	Robert H Orr Jr
Chesterfield (Chesterfield) (38)	803 623-2535	Charles Ingram	Chappell Hurst Jr	Chappell Hurst Jr	John W Sowell	William B Barfiel	Jackie Phillips	Ralph Freeman
Clarendon (Manning) (27)	803 435-8424	W Curtis Gibbons	John E Thames	Cindy Draton	Margaret Jackson	....	....	Horace F Swilley
Colleton (Walterboro)† (32)	803 549-1725	Thomas F Fennell	Bert Artlip	Bert Artlip	Bette R Fralick	....	....	C E Ackerman Jr
Darlington (Darlington) (63)	803 393-7602	(not reporting)						
Dillon (Dillon)† (31)	803 774-6030	Hubert Grice	Claude W Graham	Kathleen Lane	Mary Lou Parham	....	....	Jasper G Rogers
Dorchester (St. George)*† (58)	803 563-2331	George P Knight	J Marc Hehn	Betty P Judy	Patsy G Knigt	Thomas W Bailey	Richard Johnson	Carl Knight
Edgefield (Edgefield) (18)	803 637-5381	Charles E Lybrand	H O Carter	H O Carter	James W McCord	....	Don Padgett	R Billy Parker
Fairfield (Winnsboro) (21)	803 635-1411	Marion Stevenson	James H Lucas	Raye Duncan	G R Lauderdale	....	J B Floyd	L I Montgomery
Florence (Florence) (110)	803 665-3099	Herbet G Ham	M L Love Jr	Joann Welch	Barry L Elliott	M L Love Jr	....	William C Barnes
Georgetown (Georgetown) (42)	803 546-5011	Alfred B Schooler	....	Jacquelyn H Owens	....	....	....	Michael Carter
Greenville (Greenville)§ (288)	803 298-8551	....	Joel R Mashburn	....	George W Hendrix	Hank Ludwig	....	Johnny Mack Brown
Greenwood (Greenwood)§ (58)	803 229-6622	Carroll H Brooks	Robert M Haynie	Pamela S Spears	Ira Nell Smith	Ronald E Ehlinger	....	L Giles Daniel
Hampton (Hampton) (18)	803 943-4951	Charlie I Crews	Virginia D Lathan	Edna L Smith	Wilson P Tuten Jr	....	....	Isiah R Loadholt
Horry (Conway) (101)	803 248-6247	Laurie McLeod	....	Gladys A Allen	Roger G Hucks	....	M U Dantzler	M L Brown
Jasper (Ridgeland) (15)	803 726-8271	(not reporting)						
Kershaw (Camden) (39)	803 432-6194	(not reporting)						
Lancaster (Lancaster)* (53)	803 285-1565	L Eugene Hudson	Carroll P Huffman	Irene L Plyler	Ted O Wright	....	....	Carolyn Parks
Laurens (Laurens) (52)	803 984-3538	(not reporting)						
Lee (Bishopville) (19)	803 484-5341	(not reporting)						
Lexington (Lexington)§† (140)	803 359-8000	Jerrod F Howard	G F Broom Jr	Dorothy K Wingard	Marjorie H Sharpe	Huley G Shumpert	Richard O Ballew	James R Metts
Marion (Marion) (34)	803 423-3904	Marvin Stevenson	M Gault Beeson	Mary Lynn Hood	Joyce W Lett	....	....	Lonnie Richardson
Marlboro (Bennettsville) (32)	803 479-4462	Claude Driggers	....	Maxine D Townsend	Maria T Thomas	....	....	Jack N Weatherly
McCormick (McCormick) (8)	803 465-2231	Curtis E Baggett	....	Cathy McDaniel	Frances W Sibert	Raymond Edmunds	Waymon B Storey	James E Gable
Newberry (Newberry)† (31)	803 276-0681	Arthur C Sparks	Edward F Lominack	Jewell D Kibler	George W Summer	....	....	L L Henderson
Oconee (Walhalla) (49)	803 638-2532	Norman D Crain	....	Opal O Green	Henry A Cater	....	....	Earl Holcombe
Orangeburg (Orangeburg)*† (82)	803 533-1000	Vernon Ott Jr	Gary A Smoak	Eugenia Lightfoot	J Steve Summers	Gary N Adkins	....	Vance L Boone
Pickens (Pickens) (79)	803 878-7800	Marion C Owens	R Weldon Day	Doris Watson	Doris Watson	....	....	C David Stone
Richland (Columbia)* (268)	803 748-4600	James C Leventis	Richard L Black	Brenda Fuller	William H Linder	Ralph B Pearson	William Kemick	Frank Powell
Saluda (Saluda) (16)	803 445-2635	Alfred B Coleman	Ray E Frazier	Shirley P Boone	Gayle P Werts	....	....	George C Booth
Spartanburg (Spartanburg)§ (202)	803 596-2000	Lachlan L Hyatt	K Westmoreland	Carolyn P Parris	Oren L Brady III	Carey C Burnett	James Padgett Jr	Larry D Smith
Sumter (Sumter) (88)	803 773-1581	L P Booth	E M DuBose	Lorraine L Player	C E Stafford	T L Rogers	G A Cook	Hazel Reeves
Union (Union)† (31)	803 427-5655	John L Greer	....	Linda Jolly	James W Cheek	....	....	William A Jolly
Williamsburg (Kingstree) (38)	803 354-9321	Alex Chatman	....	Dorothy Thornhill	Pearl R Brown	....	....	Theo McFarlin
York (York)* (107)	803 684-9261	Harold Dickson	James E Klugh	Nancy B Moore	Clyde Nichols	Joel E Wood	....	Elbert Pope
SOUTH DAKOTA (66)								
Aurora (Plankinton) (4)	605 942-7752	Lex Weller	....	Darlene Haines	Arlene Staller	Ben Lagge	Margaret Swent	Evan Edinger
Beadle (Huron) (19)	605 352-2655	(not reporting)						
Bennett (Martin) (3)	605 685-6969	(not reporting)						
Bon Homme (Tyndall) (8)	605 589-3391	C Tjeerdsma	Jerra L Ferwerda	....	Mammie Rothscadl	Joseph Sykora	Michele Muller	....
Brookings (Brookings) (24)	605 692-7825	(not reporting)						
Brown (Aberdeen) (37)	605 225-1864	Merrill D Rix	....	Burlene Berg	Adeline Wiederich	....	....	Steve Oakes
Brule (Chamberlain) (5)	605 734-6521	Lawrence Swanson	....	James Gough	Blanche Stenson	William Nelson	Phyllis Soulek	Vernon Collins
Buffalo (Gannvalley) (2)	605 293-3217	F Armernalhy	....	Joseph Zastrow	Mary D Nelson	....	....	Melvin M Rank
Butte (Belle Fourche) (8)	605 892-2516	(not reporting)						
Campbell (Mound City) (2)	605 955-3366	Myron Johnson	....	Lenore Pfeifle	Karl Mitzel	....	....	Ervin Meidinger

Directory 1/9 continued **COUNTY OFFICIALS IN ALL U.S. COUNTIES**

County, county seat, 1980 population (000 omitted),	County telephone number	Board chairman	Appointed administrator	Clerk to the governing board	Chief financial officer	County engineer	County health officer	Chief law enforcement official
SOUTH DAKOTA (66) continued								
Charles Mix (Lake Andes) (10)	605 487-7511	(not reporting)						
Clark (Clark) (5)	605 532-5921	Russell Neal	....	Darlene Audus	Mary Helms	James Bjerke	Sally Waterfall	Virgil Wagner
Clay (Vermillion) (13)	605 624-2281	Daniel Bylander	....	Esther Girard	Helen Moore	Robert Johnson	H J Fletcher MD	Raymond Passick
Codington (Watertown) (21)	605 886-8497	Ralph Mack	....	Patricia Walder	Margaret McNulty	Hiene Junge	Connie Jones	Charles Schamens
Corson (McIntosh) (5)	605 273-4229	Cal Thorstenson	....	Bernita Moser	Joan Bauer	....	....	Lynn G Utter
Custer (Custer)† (6)	605 673-4815	John A Jack Lintz	....	Frances Hanson	Donna Palmer	....	Colleen Winters	DeWayne Glassgow
Davison (Mitchell) (18)	605 996-2450	Heinert Herbert	....	John Oster	Ervin Volk	....	Gail Johnson	Lyle Swenson
Day (Webster) (8)	605 345-3102	Ardis Abbott	....	A Gilbertson	Judith Barber	....	....	Sal Herrick
Deuel (Clear Lake)† (5)	605 874-2120	Ronald Boone	....	Audrey Ramynke	Audrey Ramynke	Kenneth S Korseth	H Dean Hughes MD	Patrick Culhane
Dewey (Timber Lake) (5)	605 865-3672	Paul Garr	....	Joan Sieker	John Alley	Ray Olson	....	Ted L Schweitzer
Douglas (Armour)† (4)	605 724-2423	John G Van Zee	....	Wilma Faller	Kenneth Peters	Emil Rothenberger	Ronald Price	Ronald L Morrow
Edmunds (Ipswich) (5)	605 426-6762	Robert C Stoecker	....	Irene Rissmann	Edith Baus	....	....	Dennis M Olson
Fall River (Hot Springs) (8)	605 745-5130	Franklin Manke	....	Sherrill A Dryden	Elma Strackbein	Orville Dryer	....	Leo Bray
Faulk (Faulkton) (3)	605 598-6224	Floyd Gjernes	Marlene Kern	Marlene Kern	Dorothy Shawgo	Ed Bowar	Maxine White RN	Kenneth Wherry
Grant (Milbank) (9)	605 432-6711	Rudolph A Nef	....	Elaine Hallberg	Maureen Dinter	Vernon Harms	E A Johnson MD	Garth E Thorpe
Gregory (Burke) (6)	605 775-2664	J C Engelmeyer	....	Julia Bartling	Ruth Jones	Raymond Roggow	E P Sweet	Lawrence Oliver
Haakon (Philip) (3)	605 859-2627	(not reporting)						
Hamlin (Hayti) (5)	605 783-3201	Roger Prouty	....	Dixie Opdahl	Theresia Svarvari	John Vanbemmel	Jill Kasten	Dan Mack
Hand (Miller) (5)	605 853-2182	Glenn Smith	....	Carol DeGeest	Ladonna Kindle	....	Nancy Mushitz	Charles Fechner
Hanson (Alexandria) (3)	605 239-4714	William Pierson	....	Rosemary Mayhew	Mary Erpenbach	M Blankenship	....	Robert Brown
Harding (Buffalo)† (2)	605 375-3313	Donald Wagner	....	Kay Baier	Dagny Burt	Eugene Bickerdyke	....	Roger Page
Hughes (Pierre)† (14)	605 224-7744	D J Hull	....	....	Bud Ray	Robert Meyer	....	Arlo Mortimer
Hutchinson (Olivet) (9)	605 387-2835	Leonard Wiens	....	Nora J Lee	Darlene J Schoon	Milton R Handel	....	Raymond Zeeb
Hyde (Highmore) (2)	605 852-2519	Roland R Jirsa	....	Eileen Bortness	G Louise Moss	Harold Kutz	Stephen Schroeder	L Mike McDonnell
Jackson (Kadoka) (3)	605 837-2121	(not reporting)						
Jerauld (Wessington Springs)† (3)	605 539-1202	Harold Olson	....	Verna M Satter	....	F McHenry	J Christensen	Lyle Weekly
Jones (Murdo) (1)	605 669-2242	G Liffengren	....	Wanda Iversen	Beverly Andrews	Jack Richards	....	Don Convey
Kingsbury (De Smet)† (7)	605 854-3832	Thomas J Duffy	....	Audrey L Magnuson	Marjorie J Jensen	Ron R Olson	....	Wm D Conn
Lake (Madison)† (11)	605 256-2068	G W Chalcraft	....	Mae Olson	Rhoda Benjamin	Milton Persoon	Lavonne Schlump	Thomas O Bakke
Lawrence (Deadwood) (18)	605 578-2040	(not reporting)						
Lincoln (Canton) (14)	605 987-2581	R Koopsma	....	Helen E Nelson	Beverly Myers	John L Frislie	Kay Reed	Kenneth D Albers
Lyman (Kennebec) (4)	605 869-2247	Beryl Tracy	....	Joan Brinckmeyer	Adelia B Olsen	Donald Hlavinka	....	Eugene Mertens
Marshall (Britton) (5)	605 448-2401	Leonard Eikamp	....	Marion Cusick	Nelva Kristoffers	James Osness	Phylis Johnson	Dale Elsen
McCook (Salem)† (6)	605 425-2791	Walter Stevens	....	Judith Heumiller	Lorraine Kessler	....	A Petres MD	Eugene Taylor
McPherson (Leola)† (4)	605 439-3314	Albert Fischer	....	Steven Serr	Lorraine Fauth	Elvin Feickert	George McIntosh	Keith Kunz
Meade (Sturgis) (21)	605 347-4513	(not reporting)						
Mellette (White River) (2)	605 259-3291	Eugene Strain	....	Judy K Brickman	M Knispel	....	....	George H Bouman
Miner (Howard) (4)	605 772-4671	Richard Jerlow	....	Cindy Callies	Mildred Hosmer	John Mentele	....	Timothy Reisch
Minnehaha (Sioux Falls) (109)	605 335-4220	Richard Flynn	Dale E Froehlich	Donna Thoms	Deloris Erickson	Kenneth Long	....	Lester Hawkey
Moody (Flandreau) (7)	605 997-3161	H Blankenfeld	Laurie Johnson	Laurie Johnson	Bruce Clark	James Prouty	B Schiefelbein	William Baer
Pennington (Rapid City) (70)	605 394-2171	Neil Van Sickle	....	Helen Daughenbaug	Winona Brady	....	Robert Wermers	Don Holloway
Perkins (Bison) (5)	605 244-5624	Alwyn Rose	....	Fern Brockel	Dolores Chapman	....	....	H J Kolb
Potter (Gettysburg) (4)	605 765-9472	(not reporting)						
Roberts (Sisseton) (11)	605 698-3395	(not reporting)						
Sanborn (Woonsocket) (3)	605 796-4515	(not reporting)						
Shannon (Hot Springs) (11)	605 745-3996	(not reporting)						
Spink (Redfield) (9)	605 472-1825	Duane Muxen	....	Rosemary Thomas	Lloyd W Buchholz	Randall A Gabriel	....	Gary L Newman
Stanley (Fort Pierre) (3)	605 223-2673	Gene Stoeser	....	Phyllis Kenzy	Catherine Pexa	....	....	Gary Miller
Sully (Onida) (2)	605 258-2541	Gene W Stampe	....	Eileen M Gerken	Edna M Brunmeier	....	Marvel Buhler	Maynard L Bloom
Todd (Winner) (7)	605 747-2664	(not reporting)						
Tripp (Winner) (7)	605 842-3727	Raymond Petersek	....	Shirley L Briggs	Lois Viedt	Martin Anderson	....	Darrell Meiners
Turner (Parker)† (9)	605 297-3153	H J Engbrecht	....	Darlene Peterson	Clara Jane Peters	....	....	Paul Morehouse
Union (Elk Point)† (11)	605 356-2041	M C Bak	....	Phyllis Limoges	Winna M Lanning	Bobby Lee Meister	....	Eugene Rasmussen
Walworth (Selby) (7)	605 649-7878	William Morrison	....	Mary L Bucklin	Phylliss Pudwill	Walter Lehrkamp	Roberta Atkinson	James Spiry
Yankton (Yankton) (19)	605 665-2143	Bennett Van Osdel	....	Carol Peterson	....	....	Jay W Hubner MD	....
Ziebach (Dupree) (2)	605 365-5157	Clinton Farlee	....	Lucille Fairbanks	Virginia Hertel	....	....	Michael Stocklin
TENNESSEE (95)								
Anderson (Clinton) (67)	615 457-5400	David O Bolling	David O Bolling	Kenneth Caldwell	Patsy Stair	Frank Sewell	Carlton Salyer	Thomas Van Riper
Bedford (Shelbyville) (28)	615 684-1921	(not reporting)						
Benton (Camden) (15)	901 584-6011	Joe E Wright	....	Gordon Pafford	G W Patterson	....	....	Robert T Shannon
Bledsoe (Pikeville)† (9)	615 447-6855	William C Deakins	William C Deakins	C D Mills Jr	Alton Anderson	....	Mike Stanifer	Carlton Nipper
Blount (Maryville)† (78)	615 982-1302	Robert J Davis	....	Milburn Waters	Charles J Powell	Tony Abbott	Mary Cragan	L B Sutton Jr
Bradley (Cleveland) (68)	615 472-1581	Eddie Cartwright	....	Claude H Climer	Anderson F Miller	Sam Hyberger	Bob Caylor	Robert Lawson
Campbell (Jacksboro) (35)	615 562-2526	Jack R Alexander	....	Brenda S Boshears	George R Asbury	....	Eddie Troxell	Harry E Cureton
Cannon (Woodbury)† (10)	615 563-2320	Nolan Northcutt	....	Robert P Smith	Joe Rogers	....	....	Robert Bogle
Carroll (Huntingdon) (28)	901 986-3762	Wesley Beal Jr	....	James McLemore	Walter Butler	....	....	Joe Parker
Carter (Elizabethton) (50)	615 542-2021	Truman Clark	....	Goldie B Pierce	Robert Ellis	....	....	William Crumley
Cheatham (Ashland City)† (22)	615 792-4316	Jimmy P Lockert	....	Eugene Knox	Donnie Jones	....	James Baldwin	Dorris Weakley
Chester (Henderson) (13)	901 989-7622	Neal Smith	....	Kimba Clayton	Barry Smith	....	Dr O McCallum	Eric Bell
Claiborne (Tazewell) (25)	615 626-5231	Bill D Hurst	....	Aillen Standifer	Elizabeth Wilmoth	....	Jack Brogan	Billy W Smith
Clay (Celina)† (8)	615 243-2161	Cecil F Langford	....	....	James R Bailey	....	John H Stone	Austin P Thompson
Cocke (Newport) (29)	615 623-8791	Jerry Clevenger	Charles Moore	Don Boley	Victor Webb	....	Barbara Donaldson	Roy J Keifer
Coffee (Manchester) (38)	615 728-3024	Don J Darden	....	Charles E Wells	Jesse E West	....	....	Bobby McCullough
Crockett (Alamo) (15)	901 696-2445	Jeff T Davis	....	Bobby Cates	Wayne Parlow	....	Charles N Hickman	Neal Klyce
Cumberland (Crossville)† (29)	615 484-6165	Jeannette Warner	....	Pete Stubbs	Burxie Copeland	....	....	Charles Shadden
De Kalb (Smithville) (14)	615 597-5177	(not reporting)						
Decatur (Decaturville) (11)	901 852-2231	Ann G Houston	....	R C Montgomery	Janis Wright	....	....	Ray Moore
Dickson (Charlotte) (30)	615 789-4171	William D Field	....	William E Brazzel	Jewel Bishop	Wm V Lightfoot	Charles Craft	C Don Martin
Dyer (Dyersburg) (35)	901 285-1692	Kenneth Westbrook	....	Jere Bradshaw	Judy Patton	....	J C Moore	Tommy B Cribbs
Fayette (Somerville) (25)	901 465-2461	(not reporting)						
Fentress (Jamestown) (15)	615 879-7713	Willie L Teague	....	Patricia Conatser	Tex Moles	....	Sharron Garrett	Tommy Williams
Franklin (Winchester)† (32)	615 967-2905	Andy L Henshaw	....	Flora Dixon	Barbara Nichols	....	....	Mike Kirk
Gibson (Trenton) (49)	901 855-4550	Ronnie A Riley	....	Josephine Jackson	Barbara Palmer	Jack Siler	C N Hickman	Robert Etheridge
Giles (Pulaski) (25)	615 363-1509	(not reporting)						
Grainger (Rutledge) (17)	615 828-3513	Norman Acuff	....	Barbara Jackson	Pauline Daniel	....	Phil Chambers	Earl Cameron
Greene (Greeneville)† (54)	615 638-8118	Philip B King	Philip B King	Freddie Shaw	Clay Woolsey	D C Bowman	Ken Matthews	Gail E Colyer

Directory 1/9 continued — COUNTY OFFICIALS IN ALL U.S. COUNTIES

County, county seat, 1980 population (000 omitted),	County telephone number	Board chairman	Appointed administrator	Clerk to the governing board	Chief financial officer	County engineer	County health officer	Chief law enforcement official
TENNESSEE (95) continued								
Grundy (Altamount) (14)	615 692-3455	(not reporting)						
Hamblen (Morristown)† (49)	615 586-1931	C L Jones	....	Wilburn Beck	Paul L Bruce	....	M Carver MD	Tom Sams
Hamilton (Chattanooga)† (288)	615 757-2496	Dalton Roberts	....	William F Knowles	Coy C Browder	Pat Fyie	Sharlinda Turner	H Q Evatt
Hancock (Sneedville) (7)	615 733-4341	Ray A Baker	....	Wayne Dean	Bruce Roberts	....	....	Ouglas Seal
Hardeman (Bolivar) (24)	901 658-3266	Claude M Foote Jr	....	Linda Y Simpson	Gaylon H Powell	....	....	Delphus Hicks Jr
Hardin (Savannah) (22)	901 925-9078	James R Patterson	....	Vernon J Plunk	Sam Armstrong Jr	....	....	David Seaton
Hawkins (Rogersville) (44)	615 272-7173	J B Howe	J B Howe	Darrell Rouse	Donna Alvis	Lynn K Newton	Jerry Stewart	Lee Justice
Haywood (Brownsville) (20)	901 772-1432	Dixon Hood	....	Ann Medford	Ms Dell Hopkins	Jerry Stoots	B D Hale	James Sullivan
Henderson (Lexington) (21)	901 968-7141	Bobby W Dyer	Bobby W Dyer	....	....	....	....	Jack Fowler
Henry (Paris) (29)	901 642-5212	James W Farmer	....	Dorris L Coley	....	....	....	R W Cole
Hickman (Centerville)† (15)	615 729-2492	Ralph A Fly	....	Edward Dotson	Billy Bryant	....	....	Mitchell Brady
Houston (Erin) (7)	615 289-3633	George E Clark	....	Robert Brown	Woodrow Adams	....	Julia Cook	James Mobley
Humphreys (Waverly) (16)	615 296-7795	L Barton Bone	....	A Taylor Hall	Sadie P Little	....	Dorsey Yates	Ronnie Toungette
Jackson (Gainesboro) (9)	615 268-9888	Doy T Wilson	....	Mildred Dennis	Billy Scott	....	Donald Tanell MD	Wayne Mahaney
Jefferson (Dandridge) (31)	615 397-3800	Paul D Goddard Jr	....	R E Farrar III	Florence Swann	....	....	Tom F Eslinger
Johnson (Mountain City) (14)	615 727-7853	(not reporting)						
Knox (Knoxville) (320)	615 521-2005	Dwight Kessel	....	Tommy Lowe	Herbert Acuff	Robert Brotherton	Mary Duffy MD	Joe Fowler
Lake (Tiptonville)† (7)	901 253-7382	James E Naifeh	James E Naifeh	Jo Ann Hicks	Dorothy J Tittle	....	Greg Williams	Joe L Jones
Lauderdale (Ripley) (25)	901 635-3500	Bill Pete Tucker	....	V McBride Jr	Paul Meadows	....	Jayaram Prasad	Milford Durham
Lawrence (Lawrenceburg)† (34)	615 762-3931	Jack N Benefield	....	Kenneth Weathers	....	....	....	Thomas Pyrdum
Lewis (Hohenwald)† (10)	615 796-3378	William T Rasbury	....	Paul L Spears	Charles Campbell	....	....	Robert Conner
Lincoln (Fayetteville)† (26)	615 433-3045	Thos W Redden Sr	....	Wilma F Moore	Knox Stewart	....	Walton Rich	Tom Bean
Loudon (Loudon) (29)	615 458-4663	H Ross Wilkerson	....	Riley Wampler	J D Click	Tom Davis	James R Proaps	Joe Sims
Macon (Lafayette) (16)	615 666-2363	Hillas Swindle	....	James R Howser	Maburn Dyer	....	Larry Tucker	Bill Music
Madison (Jackson) (75)	901 423-6020	J Alex Leech	....	Freddie Pruitt	Wilma Allen	Joe R Moling	A J Muellar	Warren Roberts
Marion (Jasper)† (24)	615 942-2552	Doug Fitz Gerald	....	Frank Minter	Bobby E Carter	....	Harold Deep	Loyd A Hood
Marshall (Lewisburg) (20)	615 359-1279	L L Isaacson	....	Tommy Higdon	Ruby Jean Ogilvie	....	....	Carlton Bless
Maury (Columbia) (51)	615 388-6233	Taylor Rayburn	....	Nancy Thompson	Polly Lovett	....	Nancy Penrod	William S Voss
McMinn (Athens) (42)	615 745-7634	Hugh L Lamb	....	Helen Haskins	Ed J Fiegle	....	....	Robert Richardson
McNairy (Selmer) (23)	901 645-3511	(not reporting)						
Meigs (Decatur)† (7)	615 334-5850	Raymond E Bivens	Raymond E Bivens	Chevi Shoemaker	Ricky Bivens	....	Anderson Hutsell	R L McKenzie
Monroe (Madisonville)† (29)	615 442-3981	Charles Wilkins	....	R Brian Tallent	T R Haun	....	Mary Cragan MD	R H Johnson
Montgomery (Clarksville) (83)	615 647-6787	Joel Plummer	....	Wilma K Drye	Elsie Johnson	Gus G Norfleet	Bland Skelton	Billy R Smith
Moore (Lynchburg) (5)	615 759-7076	John M Bennett	....	Bettie C Vaughan	....	....	....	John H Glassmeyer
Morgan (Wartburg) (17)	615 346-3881	(not reporting)						
Nashville-Davidson C (456)	615 259-6047	Richard Fulton	....	Ruth Judd	Charles Cardwell	....	Joseph M Bistowis	Joe Casey
Obion (Union City) (33)	901 885-9611	Robert Jarvis	....	Vollie Boehms	....	....	....	Nathan Cunningham
Overton (Livingston) (18)	615 823-5638	John C Houser	....	Hugh Ogletree	Kenneth Copeland	....	Clay Parsons	Herman Moody
Perry (Linden)† (6)	615 589-2216	D H Qualls	Janet Marshall	Jean E Smothers	Hollis R Hinson	....	Rex Patterson	Charles Qualls
Pickett (Byrdstown)† (4)	615 864-3798	Everett Asberry	....	Jack Storie	Howard Cross	....	Jimmy Clark	Edward Dowdy
Polk (Benton) (14)	615 338-2841	Charles E Stevens	....	Robert Hughes	Cooper Rogers	....	Ken Bishop	Frank R Payne
Putnam (Cookeville) (48)	615 526-6321	(not reporting)						
Rhea (Dayton) (24)	615 775-0187	Guy Price	....	Jimmy Wilkey	Dean Whitfield	....	Ed Kerley	Paul Smith
Roane (Kingston)† (48)	615 376-5578	Kenneth E Yager	Ronald B Woody	Dorothy Marshall	Jim D Shipley	....	Carolyn Beard	Arnold Clower
Robertson (Springfield) (37)	615 384-2476	Emerson Meggs	Angela Traughber	Connie Swann	Robert D Alley	....	....	Ted Emery
Rutherford (Murfreesboro)† (84)	615 893-6644	John B Mankin	....	....	....	....	....	....
Scott (Huntsville) (19)	615 663-2355	Dwight E Murphy	....	Vesta J Phillips	Clifford Thompson	....	Bill Bowling	Marion Carson
Sequatchie (Dunlap) (9)	615 949-3670	(not reporting)						
Sevier (Sevierville)† (41)	615 453-6136	Larry Waters	....	Paul Atchley	Larry Waters	....	Raymond Gann	Carmen L Townsend
Shelby (Memphis) (777)	901 528-3500	William N Morris	James Huntzicker	Richard Mashburn	Riley C Garner	George L Reed	....	Eugene Barksdale
Smith (Carthage) (15)	615 735-2092	(not reporting)						
Stewart (Dover) (9)	615 232-5371	Don Trawick	....	Jimmy Fitzhugh	Eugene McGregor	Jerry Cunningham	R Austin III	David Hicks
Sullivan (Blountville) (144)	615 323-7135	Lon V Boyd	James K White	Marjorie S Harr	Frances Harrell	....	Charles Chapman	Mike Gardner
Sumner (Gallatin) (86)	615 452-4282	(not reporting)						
Tipton (Covington) (33)	901 476-2604	Henry S Vaughan	....	Clara H McMillin	Don M Max	Van E Boals	Jayram Presad	Wayne Baskin
Trousdale (Hartsville) (6)	615 374-2461	G W Oldham	....	Harold Gregory	Betty Gregory	....	....	Charles Robinson
Unicoi (Erwin) (16)	615 743-9391	Howard T Garland	....	Fred E Congdon	....	....	....	Paul H White
Union (Maynardville) (12)	615 992-3061	Von Richardson	....	Roy Carter	James Phillips	....	Raymond Downing	Earl Loy
Van Buren (Spencer) (5)	615 946-2314	Herbert R Davis	....	Tony Bayless	Hobert Crain	....	....	Verbal Wheeler
Warren (McMinnville)† (33)	615 473-2505	H T Pelham	....	G Fred Martin	Joy Slatton	....	....	Billy Delaney
Washington (Jonesboro) (89)	615 753-6211	Robert J Good	....	Roy Phillips	Robert J Good	John Deakins	L Moffitt MD	Ronald England
Wayne (Waynesboro) (14)	615 722-5517	(not reporting)						
Weakley (Dresden) (33)	901 364-5413	H C Brundige	....	Faye Butts	John Prince	Jimmy Freeman	....	Michael Wilson
White (Sparta) (20)	615 836-3787	(not reporting)						
Williamson (Franklin) (58)	615 794-2559	Robert A Ring	....	Charlie Fox Jr	Lillie Buford	Howard D Wyatt	Doris G Spain	Fleming Williams
Wilson (Lebanon)† (56)	615 444-1383	Don Simpson	....	Benton Jennings	John Majors	....	Jerry Franklin	Terry Ashe
TEXAS (254)								
Anderson (Palestine) (38)	214 723-7428	Edward A Copeland	R S Berry	Jo Huddleston	R S Berry	....	....	Roy A Herrington
Andrews (Andrews) (13)	915 523-3062	Les M Brown	....	James Craddock	Reeder Price	James Tompkins	John Kantor	Wayne Farmer
Angelina (Lufkin) (64)	409 634-5413	Dan Jones	....	Pauline Grisham	E R Bush Jr	....	....	Sammy Leach
Aransas (Rockport)† (14)	512 729-2403	John D Wendell	John D Wendell	Val Jean Eaton	Marvine Wix	....	J Curtis Kovacs	Robert Hewes
Archer (Archer City) (7)	817 574-4811	B G Holder	....	Jane Adams	Betty Tarno	....	Paul Parkey MD	P L Pippin Jr
Armstrong (Claude) (2)	806 226-3221	Gladys A Posey	....	Betty Parker	B Stephenson	....	Gladysa Posey	Chas Strange
Atascosa (Jourdanton) (25)	512 769-3093	O B Gates	....	Elidia Segura	John N Self	....	Graves Young	Tommy Williams
Austin (Bellville)† (18)	409 865-5911	Leroy H Grebe	....	Dorothy Himly	Betty Krueger	....	J B Harle MD	T A Maddox
Bailey (Muleshoe) (8)	806 272-3077	Gordon H Green	....	Barbara McCamish	Dorothy Turner	....	Jerry D Gregory	Bobby Henderson
Bandera (Bandera)† (7)	512 796-3781	Tommy W Curbo	....	Vera King	Elizabeth James	....	....	Guy V Pickett
Bastrop (Bastrop) (25)	512 321-2579	Clyde E Clardy	....	Joyce Schaefer	Doris Oldfield	....	John W Barton	Tommy Moseley
Baylor (Seymour) (5)	817 888-3322	Joe Dickson	....	Wilburn Redwine	Pat Coker	....	C M Randal Jr MD	Don Mooney
Bee (Beeville)† (26)	512 358-1394	John B Hensley	....	Julia V Torres	Eudelia S Barrera	....	Harold H Harris	Robert L Horn
Bell (Belton)† (158)	817 939-3521	John Garth	....	....	Roy Sheppherd	Walter Neaves	G Womack MD	Lester Gunn
Bexar (San Antonio) (989)	512 220-2201	(not reporting)						
Blanco (Johnson City) (5)	512 868-4266	Charles Scott	....	Jeffy B Furber	....	....	....	Sherman Brodbeck
Borden (Gail) (1)	915 856-4391	Van York	....	Dorothy Browne	Melisa Ludecke	....	....	Norman Sneed
Bosque (Meridian) (13)	817 435-2382	Earl W Page	Nancy S McClure	Patsy Owen Mize	Hugh H Trotter	....	H Hildebrand	Denny Proffitt
Bowie (Boston)† (75)	214 628-2571	Edward Miller	....	Marylene Megason	Gerald L Freeman	....	....	Thomas Hodge
Brazoria (Angleton) (170)	713 849-5711	E E Brewer	Monroe Schrader	Dolly Bailey	Susan Neighbours	Gordon Hays	L D O'Gorman	Joe King
Brazos (Bryan) (94)	409 775-7400	R J Holmgreen	....	Frank Boriskie	B V Elkins	....	Roy Smith	Bobby Yeager
Brewster (Alpine) (8)	915 837-2412	Tom Connor	....	Helen Crone	Hortencia Ramos	....	W Lockhart Jr MD	Jack McDaniel

Directory 1/9 continued — COUNTY OFFICIALS IN ALL U.S. COUNTIES

County, county seat, 1980 population (000 omitted),	County telephone number	Board chairman	Appointed administrator	Clerk to the governing board	Chief financial officer	County engineer	County health officer	Chief law enforcement official
TEXAS (254) continued								
Briscoe (Silverton) (3)	806 823-2383	Fred W Mercer	....	Bess McWilliams	Mildred Reid	....	James Toan MD	Dick Roehr
Brooks (Falfurrias) (8)	512 325-3053	Joe B Garcia	....	Calixto Mora	Oscar Hinojosa	....	Richard Penly MD	Ramiro Castellano
Brown (Brownwood) (33)	915 643-2828	Ernest Cadenhead	....	Juanita Bailey	Connie Cline	....	Philip Gold	Melvin Stovall
Burleson (Caldwell) (12)	713 567-4326	(not reporting)						
Burnet (Burnet) (18)	512 756-4161	D C Kincheloe	....	Millie Williams	Katy Gilmore	....	Joe A Shepperd MD	Weldon Buck
Caldwell (Lockhart) (24)	512 398-2213	L W Scott	L W Scott	....	Amelia Rizzoto	....	M Silva MD	Elvin Hoskins
Calhoun (Port Lavaca) (20)	512 552-2967	R E Wyatt	....	Mary L McMahan	Sharron Marek	....	Larry W Dodd	A P Lacey
Callahan (Baird) (11)	915 854-1155	Mack Kniffen	....	Darlene Walker	Dora Hounshell	....	Raul Calvo	Bill Skinner
Cameron (Brownsville) (210)	512 544-0830	Moises V Vela	....	Maximo M Sheldon	W R MacNelly	Jack L Brown	David W Flory MD	Marshall Rousseau
Camp (Pittsburg) (9)	214 856-2731	(not reporting)						
Carson (Panhandle) (7)	806 537-3622	Jay R Roselius	....	Sue Persons	....	....	Dr Prendergast	Connie Reed
Cass (Linden) (29)	214 756-5181	Caver Johnson	....	Wilma O'Rand	Hazelle Carson	....	Jerry R Bailes MD	L M Rankin
Castro (Dimmitt)† (11)	806 647-4451	Ms M L Simpson Jr	....	Frances Joy Jones	Oleta Raper	....	B H Lee MD	Lonny Rhynes
Chambers (Anahuac) (19)	713 267-3671	Alma Turner	....	Norma Rowland	Jimmie Moorhead	R T Pinchback	Leonidas S Andres	C E Morris
Cherokee (Rusk) (38)	214 683-2350	(not reporting)						
Childress (Childress) (7)	817 937-2221	Clarence L Darter	....	Winona Furr	Tom K Newberry	....	Jack F Fox	Ronald B Sims
Clay (Henrietta) (10)	817 538-4651	Bill Nobles	....	John J McGee	Sue Brock	....	Leroy Schaffner	Jake Bogard
Cochran (Morton) (5)	806 266-5450	(not reporting)						
Coke (Robert Lee) (3)	915 453-2641	Aubrey Z Denman	....	Janet Baker	Stover Taylor	....	Zae Young Zeon MD	Marshall Millican
Coleman (Coleman) (10)	915 625-4218	Wm Skelton	....	Glenn Thomas	Barbara Freeman	....	Donald D Pope	H F Fenton
Collin (McKinney)† (144)	214 542-5017	William J Roberts	....	Franklin P Adams	Franklin P Adams	....	....	Joe Steenbergen
Collingsworth (Wellington)† (5)	806 447-5408	Zook Thomas	....	Helen Gollihugh	Yavonne Brewer	Earl Parker	Carter Holcomb	Kenneth Maxwell
Colorado (Columbus) (19)	713 732-2155	(not reporting)						
Comal (New Braunfels) (36)	512 625-4121	Fred R Clark	....	Mary Hill Brotze	Fred R Clark	Clark B McCoy	Robert D Martin	Walter Fellers
Comanche (Comanche) (13)	915 356-2466	Bobbye Allen	....	Betty Conway	Hazel Caruth	....	Roy D Mims	W G Garmon
Concho (Paint Rock) (3)	915 732-4322	(not reporting)						
Cooke (Gainesville)† (28)	817 665-3731	Jim A Robertson	....	Frank Scoggin	Irene Bryant	....	David Shauf	Dan Tiller
Coryell (Gatesville) (57)	817 865-5016	(not reporting)						
Cottle (Paducah) (3)	806 492-3613	Vana Tobias	....	Geneva Bragg	Atha Prater	....	M Gardiner MD	Frank Taylor
Crane (Crane) (5)	915 558-3581	(not reporting)						
Crockett (Ozona) (5)	915 392-2022	A O Fields	....	Debbi Puckett	Dick Kirby	Henry Elledge	R W Owensy	Billy Mills
Crosby (Crosbyton) (9)	806 675-2011	Robert Work	....	Floyd Mcginnes	Joyce Whitehead	....	....	Lavoice Riley
Culberson (Van Horn) (3)	915 283-2059	John Conoly	....	Rosalinda Abreo	Lola B McAfee	....	Gordon Cox MD	Richard Upchurch
Dallam (Dalhart) (7)	806 249-4751	(not reporting)						
Dallas (Dallas) (1557)	214 749-8361	Frank Crowley	Robt W Montgomery	Earl Bullock	Joe Jack Mills	J W Bryan	Gordon Green MD	Don Byrd
Dawson (Lamesa) (16)	806 872-7544	Glenn White	Don Stephens	Billie Bingham	Barbara Stone	....	Douglas B Black	Billy R Horton
De Witt (Cuero)† (19)	512 275-2116	Robert B Sheppard	Terry G Wyatt	K Ann Drehr	Walter R Wolf	....	Rick D Edwards MD	Bobby J McMahan
Deaf Smith (Hereford) (21)	806 364-1746	(not reporting)						
Delta (Cooper) (5)	214 395-2211	Fred Potts	....	Patsy Barton	Martha Jones	....	Gaza Janes	Mike Holbert
Denton (Denton) (143)	817 565-8500	Buddy Cole	....	....	Claudia Mulkey	....	Gerald O Flanagan	Kenneth George
Dickens (Dickens) (4)	806 623-5531	(not reporting)						
Dimmit (Carrizo Springs) (11)	512 876-2323	Rodrigo L Guerra	....	Mario Z Garcia	Arturo Juarez	....	Mary E Blackard	Ben Doc Murray
Donley (Clarendon)† (4)	806 874-3625	W R Christal	....	P C Messer	Frieda Gray	....	R L Gilkey MD	J W Thompson
Duval (San Diego) (13)	512 279-3322	Gilberto Uresti	....	Oscar Garcia Jr	Carmen B Oliveira	....	Luis Dehoyos	Raul Serna
Eastland (Eastland) (19)	817 629-1583	(not reporting)						
Ector (Odessa) (115)	915 332-8271	Jan Fisher	....	Lucille Wolz	Daniel G Ramirez	....	Ford Sweetman	Bob Brookshire
Edwards (Rocksprings) (2)	512 683-2235	(not reporting)						
El Paso (El Paso) (480)	915 546-2000	Pat F O'Rourke	....	Hector Enriquez	Steve E Seely	Robert Rivera	L Nickey MD	Michael P Davis
Ellis (Waxahachie) (60)	214 937-1290	(not reporting)						
Erath (Stephenville) (23)	817 965-4310	Randy Thomas	....	Pauline Chandler	Edith Carr	....	Kam W Ip	David Coffee
Falls (Marlin) (18)	817 883-2061	Burke Kirkpatrick	....	G L Burks	Marylyn Ejem	B J Jackson	C G Brown	Larry G Pamplin
Fannin (Bonham) (24)	214 583-9121	William C Terry	....	Margaret Gilbert	Florence Keahey	....	Lynn Fite	Sam Patton
Fayette (La Grange) (19)	409 968-3055	Dan R Beck	....	Irene Pratka	Dan Von Rosenberg	....	Bill D Nolen MD	Vastine Koopmann
Fisher (Roby) (6)	915 776-2151	Marshal Bennett	....	Bettie Rivers	Ilene Hale	....	C M Callan	Mickey Counts
Floyd (Floydada) (10)	806 983-2244	Choise Smith	....	Margaret Collier	Glenna M Orman	....	....	Fred A Cardinal
Foard (Crowell) (2)	817 684-1424	Charlie Bell	....	C McDaniel	Jan Bond	....	Walter H Stapp	Gene Sheppard
Fort Bend (Richmond)† (131)	713 342-3411	Jodie E Stavinoha	....	Pearl Ellett	E Williams	Stanley Kucherka	W Culpepper MD	Ervin Hurta
Franklin (Mount Vernon) (7)	214 537-2342	W B Meek	....	Wanda Johnson	Jennet O'Neal	....	....	Pete Holingsworth
Freestone (Fairfield) (15)	214 389-2635	H D Black Jr	....	Doris T Welch	Carolyn Cooper	....	Gibran Tallim MD	J R Sessions Jr
Frio (Pearsall) (14)	512 334-2214	(not reporting)						
Gaines (Seminole) (13)	915 758-3521	(not reporting)						
Galveston (Galveston)† (196)	409 762-8621	Ray Holbrook	....	Mary Christensen	R Kirkpatrick	G M Fitzgerald	W Kemmerer Jr MD	Joe Max Taylor
Garza (Post) (5)	806 495-2521	Giles W Dalby	....	....	Voda Beth Gradine	....	R Rodriquez MD	James Pippin
Gillespie (Fredericksburg) (14)	512 997-2854	Mark B Wieser	....	Doris Lange	Reuben Herbort	Charles Holmes	Charles E Burg	David Nehr
Glasscock (Garden City) (1)	915 354-2382	John E Robinson	....	Betty Pate	....	....	....	Royce Pruit
Goliad (Goliad) (5)	512 645-3337	John R Barnhill	....	Gail M Turley	Lanell Oehlke	....	Gustavo Diaz MD	Francis B Byrne
Gonzales (Gonzales) (17)	512 672-2327	Henry Vollentine	....	B J Fullilove	Kay Brzozowski	....	Robt A Williamson	Curtis Parsley
Gray (Pampa) (26)	806 665-2308	(not reporting)						
Grayson (Sherman)† (90)	214 868-9515	Horace Groff	....	Paul E Lee	Dora Agee	....	....	L E Jack Driscoll
Gregg (Longview) (99)	214 758-6181	Henry Atkinson	....	Janice Hancock	James Fuller	Elton Sanders	D M McLaughlin	Bobby Weaver
Grimes (Anderson)† (14)	713 873-2967	Ben F Swank Jr	....	Trinston Harris	Lena Mae Jarvis	Dennis Sanders	....	Bill Foster
Guadalupe (Seguin) (47)	512 379-0418	James Sagebiel	....	Cecil E Schulze	E Ray Zies	Steve Steinmetz	....	Leslie Kallies
Hale (Plainview) (38)	806 293-8481	(not reporting)						
Hall (Memphis) (6)	806 259-2511	James E Chappell	....	Phyllis Dunn	Sandra Bradcock	....	H R Stevenson	Albert Blanks
Hamilton (Hamilton)† (8)	817 386-3815	Betty Sue Jenkins	....	Virginia Lovell	Karen S Tyson	....	C B Wright MD	Cecil Proctor
Hansford (Spearman) (6)	806 659-2626	R L McClellan	....	Amelia Johnson	Verna Gail Keim	....	Dave Muthali	R L McFarlin
Hardeman (Quanah) (6)	817 663-2911	Lee Ross Greene	....	Loraine White	Lucille Jobe	....	....	Chester Ingram
Hardin (Kountze) (41)	409 246-3371	Milton McKinney	....	....	Henry Donelson	....	Allen Hooks MD	H R Holzapfel
Harris (Houston) (2410)	713 221-9500	Jon Lindsey	R L Raycraft	Nolan Bordelon	J F Flack	Richard P Doss	F Jensen MD	Jack Heard
Harrison (Marshall) (52)	214 938-4385	Richard Anderson	....	Glenn Link	Betty C Anderson	Art Knollman	Andrew Gwynn	Bill Oldham
Hartley (Channing) (4)	806 235-3582	Joe N Thomas	....	Grady Belew	....	....	....	Stewart C Johnson
Haskell (Haskell) (8)	817 864-2451	(not reporting)						
Hays (San Marcos) (41)	512 392-2601	(not reporting)						
Hemphill (Canadian)† (5)	806 323-6521	Bob Gober	....	G Vandiver	Lorene Burton	....	Rush Snyder Sr	C H Wright
Henderson (Athens) (43)	214 675-6120	Winston Reagan	....	Joe Dan Fowler	Carolyn Sorrell	....	Winston Reagan	Charlie Fields Jr
Hidalgo (Edinburg) (283)	512 383-2751	(not reporting)						
Hill (Hillsboro) (25)	817 582-2161	Larry Wright	....	Ruth Pelham	Jewel Burton	....	John M Johnson	Brent Button
Hockley (Levelland) (23)	806 894-6856	Robert L Bowman	....	Raymond O Dennis	Murry C Stewart	....	....	Leroy Schulle
Hood (Granbury)† (18)	817 573-1767	Milton Meyer	....	Doris Dyer	Buster Damron	....	Don D Davis	Edwin Tomlinson
Hopkins (Sulphur Springs) (25)	214 885-3926	H W Scott	....	Mary Attlesey	Donald J Rea	....	Don O'Neal	Charles Mitchel

Directory 1/9 continued **COUNTY OFFICIALS IN ALL U.S. COUNTIES**

County, county seat, 1980 population (000 omitted),	County telephone number	Board chairman	Appointed administrator	Clerk to the governing board	Chief financial officer	County engineer	County health officer	Chief law enforcement official
TEXAS (254) continued								
Houston (Crockett)† (22)	713 544-3263	Herbert L Morgan	....	John C Smith	Faye Hiroms	....	Chris R Haeckler	Morris Minter
Howard (Big Spring) (33).	915 263-7132	Milton L Kirby	....	Margaret J Ray	Bonnie J Franklin	Bill G Mims	....	Aubrey N Standard
Hudspeth (Sierra Blanca) (3) . . .	915 369-2301	(not reporting)						
Hunt (Greenville)† (55)	214 455-4504	Edwin L Terrell	....	Opal Johnson	Allie Cole Pearce	....	Jay Caudle	Bobby Young
Hutchinson (Stinnett) (26)	806 878-2801	Tom Wicker	....	Janice Knowles	June Christian	John Wise	....	Lon Blackmon
Irion (Mertzon) (1)	915 835-2421	V F Lindley	....	Jane Ethridge	Mildree James	....	....	Delmon West
Jack (Jacksboro) (7).	817 567-2241	Bobbie A Owen	....	Patsy Ramzy	Ruby Abernathie	....	H Counts	W B Mathis
Jackson (Edna) (13)	512 782-2352	Sam D Seale	....	Martha Knapp	Harrison Stafford	....	Patti Dodson MD	Harvey Reynolds
Jasper (Jasper)† (31)	713 384-2632	Harold E Kennedy	....	Evelyn Stott	Reba M Galloway	....	Chester Hooker	Aubrey E Cole
Jeff Davis (Fort Davis) (2).	915 426-3968	Ann Scudday	....	Peggy Robertson	Fern Fisher	....	....	W W McCutcheon
Jefferson (Beaumont) (251). . . .	409 835-3741	R P LeBlanc Jr	....	R L Barnes	Jerry Ware	Robert Stroder	Paul N Fortney MD	R E Culbertson
Jim Hogg (Hebbronville) (5) . . .	512 527-3015	Romeo J Vasquez	....	Lilia Pena	Linda Jo Soliz	....	F C Glendenning	Gilberto Ybanez
Jim Wells (Alice) (36)	512 664-3032	Roberto Guerra	....	Arnoldo Gonzalez	....	....	C H McDougall MD	Oscar Lopez
Johnson (Cleburne) (68)	817 645-2292	(not reporting)						
Jones (Anson) (17).	915 823-3741	Roy Thorn	....	Buryl Rye	L R Winkels Jr	....	Gopichand Kapu	Mike Middleton
Karnes (Karnes City) (14)	512 780-3732	Kenneth P Pearce	Clem R Cannon	Elizabeth A Swize	....	....	Causey C Quillian	Robert R Mutz
Kaufman (Kaufman) (39)	214 932-4331	Maxine Darst	....	Jimmy Graham	Mildred Becker	....	Wm Fortner MD	Roy Brockway
Kendall (Boerne) (11)	512 249-2131	Kenneth D Muller	....	Darlene Herrin	Joyce F George	....	H C Day	Lee H D'Spain Jr
Kenedy (Sarita) (1).	512 294-5220	J A Garcia Jr	....	Faye Chandler	J W Turcotte	....	....	James Chandler
Kent (Jayton)† (1)	806 237-3373	Mark A Geeslin	....	Cornelia Cheyne	Laverna Harrison	....	....	R G Goodall
Kerr (Kerrville)† (29).	512 896-1337	Gordon Morriss	....	Pat Dye	Dorothy Hilburn	....	T R Boyce	Clifton Greeson
Kimble (Junction) (4)	915 446-2724	Wilbur R Dunk	....	Louise P Oliver	Sue Stewart	....	Richard Respess	John A Lockett
King (Guthrie) (..)	806 596-4411	Lee Roy Dilliard	Evelyn Sursa	....	Alene Morris	....	....	Babe Oliver
Kinney (Brackettville)† (2).	512 563-2521	Albert A Postell	....	Delores Raney	....	....	....	Norman H Hooten
Kleberg (Kingsville) (33).	512 592-2411	W C McDaniel	....	Ura Dean Ware	W C McDaniel	Gil Cade	Dr L E Ramey	J S Scarbrough II
Knox (Benjamin) (5)	817 454-2191	H T Melton	....	Gloria L West	J T Cypert	....	W F Thompson	Morris E Nix
La Salle (Cotulla) (6).	512 879-2225	L Martinez Jr	....	Nora Mae Tyler	Jimmy Patterson	....	J M Barton	Jose T Garcia
Lamar (Paris)† (42)	214 784-4117	Brady Fisher	....	Margaret Coplin	Latricia Miller	....	Joe Hillhouse	Roger Peterson
Lamb (Littlefield) (19)	806 385-4222	Wayne Whiteaker	....	Bill Johnson	Lucy Morehand	....	J H Oyer	Ed McNeese
Lampasas (Lampasas) (12). . . .	512 556-3812	Dorothye G Harper	....	Connie Hartmann	Leona Hurst	....	....	Gordon Morris
Lavaca (Hallettsville) (19)	512 798-2301	Wilbert Roznovsky	....	Charles Strauss	Thomas M Grahmann	....	Thomas Halling	Hilmer W Woytek
Lee (Giddings)† (11).	713 542-3178	E W Kraus	....	Carol Dismukes	Bea Tschatschula	....	Charles Burns	Joe Goodson
Leon (Centerville) (10).	214 536-2352	(not reporting)						
Liberty (Liberty) (47).	409 336-8071	Dempsie Henley	Yvonne Ward	....	W O Mearns	J A Rice	Wm Castle MD	C L Eckols
Limestone (Groesbeck) (20) . . .	817 729-3810	Howard Smith	....	Deborah Goodrich	Sandra Rasco	Robert Archibald	J B Riggs MD	Dennis Walker
Lipscomb (Lipscomb) (4)	806 862-4131	James P Shearer	....	Coeta Sperry	Louise Mingus	....	Sam Christopher	Calvin Babitzke
Live Oak (George West) (10) . . .	512 449-1624	(not reporting)						
Llano (Llano) (10)	915 247-5054	W R Miller	....	Herman Raesener	Margaret Hardin	....	Howard Stitt	Gale Ligon
Loving (Mentone) (..)	915 377-2362	Donald C Creager	....	Edna R Dewees	Jeanetta F Busby	....	....	Elgin R Jones
Lubbock (Lubbock) (212)	806 741-8000	Rodrick L Shaw	....	Ann Davidson	Connie Nicholson	Bobby Beale	....	D L Keesee
Lynn (Tahoka) (9)	806 998-4750	J F Brandon	....	C W Roberts	....	....	....	Stanley Krause
Madison (Madisonville) (11) . . .	713 348-2670	James R Fite	....	Joyce Coleman	Inez Bates	....	J E Reed Jr MD	Ed Fannin
Marion (Jefferson) (10)	214 665-3971	Sonny Haggard	....	Clairece Ford	....	....	W S Terry MD	A G Whatley
Martin (Stanton) (5)	915 756-2231	Bob Deavenport	....	Doris Stephenson	H D Howard	....	Thomas Miller	Dan Saunders
Mason (Mason) (4).	915 347-5556	Fritz E Landers	....	Beatrice Langehen	Jane Hoerster	....	James Pettit	Don K Grote
Matagorda (Bay City) (38).	409 245-3620	Burt O'Connell	Burt O'Connell	Sarah Vaughn	Otis Bickham	....	Paul L Brewer	Samuel L Hurta
Maverick (Eagle Pass) (31)	512 773-3824	Rudy Bowles	....	Ermelinda Sumpter	Manuel Reyes	....	A E Batres	Tom Bowles
McCulloch (Brady) (9)	915 597-2977	Boyd Hunt	....	Rose M Luttrel	Norma Holloway	....	Charles Reynolds	Glenn Weatherman
McLennan (Waco) (171).	817 756-7171	(not reporting)						
McMullen (Tilden) (1)	512 274-3215	(not reporting)						
Medina (Hondo) (23).	512 426-2313	(not reporting)						
Menard (Menard) (2).	915 396-4682	(not reporting)						
Midland (Midland) (83)	915 682-9481	William B Ahders	....	Rosenelle Cherry	Dee Thompson	William R Harrel	Don Goodrum	Dallas Smith
Milam (Cameron) (23).	817 697-3581	D B Harden	....	Willie Mae Wieser	C J Maddox	....	S H Richardson	Leroy Broadus
Mills (Goldthwaite)† (4)	915 648-2222	T W Johnson	....	W A Bryant	Gloria Marler	....	Douglas Dennis MD	Ron Wetterman
Mitchell (Colorado City)† (9) . . .	915 728-2615	Bill F Carter	....	Joan Beach	Mildred Mann Boyd	....	W Kenneth Cowan	Wendell Bryant
Montague (Montague) (17)	817 894-2401	Thomas W Brown	....	Christine Cook	Brenda Milligan	....	....	William F Conway
Montgomery (Conroe) (128) . . .	713 756-0571	J C Edwards III	....	Roy Harris	Margaret Caskey	J D Blanton	Felix McGivney	Joe Corley
Moore (Dumas)† (17)	806 935-5588	Jack D Powell	....	Rhonnie Campbell	Phyllis Holmes	....	....	M R Weaver
Morris (Daingerfield) (15).	214 645-3691	Ronald M Cowan	....	Doris McNatt	Ann Clevenger	....	Buddy Smith MD	Joe Skipper
Motley (Matador)† (2)	806 347-2424	Billy J Whitaker	....	L Camphbell	Wilna Hobbs	....	....	Alton Marshal
Nacogdoches (Nacogdoches) (47)	713 564-0496	(not reporting)						
Navarro (Corsicana) (35)	214 872-8261	Gary B Bennett	....	James F Doolen	A G Dibble	....	J H Barnebee	Bobby Ross
Newton (Newton)† (13)	713 379-5341	Lee Roy Fillyaw	....	Melba Canty	....	....	....	Robert Woods
Nolan (Sweetwater)† (17).	915 235-2263	Donald A Menn	Willie F Arpe	Judy Brazelton	Naurvelle Rogers	....	S F Supowit MD	Don Underwood
Nueces (Corpus Christi) (268) . .	512 888-0580	(not reporting)						
Ochiltree (Perryton) (10)	806 435-2152	Howard E Stone	....	Mable McLarty	Ginger Hayes	....	Eugene Waide	Joe Hataway
Oldham (Vega)† (2)	806 267-2667	John P Gilter	....	....	....	....	....	....
Orange (Orange) (84)	713 883-7740	James D Stringer	....	Molly Theroit	Earlene Hillard	Richard Goad	Howard C Williams	Edward L Parker
Palo Pinto (Palo Pinto) (24) . . .	817 686-2227	(not reporting)						
Panola (Carthage) (21).	214 693-3245	Ruff Wall	....	Roy Cadenhead Jr	Sue Parker	Chris Mauritzen	....	Tommy Harris
Parker (Weatherford) (45).	817 599-6591	Gerald W Birdwell	....	Carrie Reed	Geneva Carter	....	....	Billy R Cain
Parmer (Farwell) (11)	806 481-3383	Porter Roberts	....	Bonnie Warren	Benna Felts	....	Paul Spring MD	M C Morgan Jr
Pecos (Fort Stockton) (15)	915 336-2792	Charles Warnock	Gilbert L Ray	Paul Yeager	G McCallister	Jack Silliman	Susan Morrey MD	Larry Gibbs
Polk (Livingston) (24)	713 327-8113	Wayne Baker	....	Aline Stephenson	Sally Kessler	Jim Benton	F Rodriguez MD	Ted Everitt
Potter (Amarillo)† (99).	806 379-2400	Ben Bynum	....	Sue Daniel	Lawrence Youngbld	Bob Harp	Ronald Lacy MD	J D Boydston
Presidio (Marfa) (5)	915 729-4452	C W Henderson Jr	....	Ramona Lara	Mario S Rivera	....	Paul T Armerding	R D Thompson
Rains (Emory) (5)	214 473-2461	(not reporting)						
Randall (Canyon)† (75)	306 655-3251	Charles M Purcell	....	Leroy Hutton	Judy Monk	....	Dudley Moore	W C Longest
Reagan (Big Lake)† (4)	915 884-2665	Frank Sandel	Jane Gay	Hazel Carr	Flora M McIntyre	....	John L Wright MD	Vick Atwood
Real (Leakey) (2)	512 232-5304	G W Twilligear Jr	....	Marjorie Kellner	Bonnie Crider	....	....	Buck B Miller
Red River (Clarksville) (16)	214 427-2680	Wm S Whiteman	Maurice H Isbell	Mary Hausler	Donna Townes	....	....	Bobby D Storey
Reeves (Pecos) (16)	915 445-5418	W O Bill Pigman	....	Cathrine Ashley	Nina Abila	....	....	Raul Florez
Refugio (Refugio) (9)	512 526-4434	Ginger D Fagan	Ginger D Fagan	Rebekah Scott	Ginger D Fagan	....	Lee Stevens MD	Jim Hodges
Roberts (Miami) (1)	806 868-3721	Newton M Cox	Debbie Stribling	Jackie M Jackson	Sarah Gill	....	S J Montgomery MD	Eddie Brines
Robertson (Franklin) (15)	713 828-3636	(not reporting)						
Rockwall (Rockwall)† (15)	214 722-5152	Harold Crawford	....	June Wimpee	J H Dudley	....	Randol P Sparks	John M Vance
Runnels (Ballinger) (12).	915 365-2720	(not reporting)						

Directory 1/9 continued — COUNTY OFFICIALS IN ALL U.S. COUNTIES

County, county seat, 1980 population (000 omitted),	County telephone number	Board chairman	Appointed administrator	Clerk to the governing board	Chief financial officer	County engineer	County health officer	Chief law enforcement official
TEXAS (254) continued								
Rusk (Henderson) (41)	214 657-2117	James B Porter	....	Helen Sillick	Virgil Cole	Loyd Johnson	Jeffrey Cahill MD	Michael J Strong
Sabine (Hemphill) (9)	409 787-3543	Royce C Smith	....	Minnie Gooch	Ollie Faye Sparks	....	G C Winslow MD	Blan Greer
San Augustine (San Augustine) (9)	409 275-2762	Jack B Nichols	....	....	Carol W Vaughn	....	....	Nathan L Tindall
San Jacinto (Coldspring) (11)	713 653-2324	(not reporting)						
San Patricio (Sinton) (58)	512 364-1120	J M Edmondson Jr	....	Dottie Maley	Ray Harris	....	A F Tasch MD	C Wayne Hitt
San Saba (San Saba) (6)	915 372-3635	Thomas Bowden	....	Nila Ruth Barker	Mada Lee Smith	....	Roy Lee MD	Brantley Barker
Schleicher (Eldorado) (3)	915 853-2833	(not reporting)						
Scurry (Snyder)† (18)	915 573-8576	Preston Wilson	....	Beverly Ainsworth	Billy W Thompson	....	Louie Vaughn	Keith Collier
Shackelford (Albany) (4)	915 762-2232	Ernest D Fincher	....	....	Alma Maxwell	....	L S Key	Ben J Riley
Shelby (Center) (23)	713 598-3611	(not reporting)						
Sherman (Stratford) (3)	806 396-2021	W S Frizzell	....	M L Albert	Linda Keener	....	Claude Harlow MD	Clois Vaughn
Smith (Tyler) (128)	214 595-4861	Robert H Hayes	....	Mary Morris	Nancy Braswell	Kennith Cline	Kerfoot Walker MD	Frank Brunt
Somervell (Glen Rose) (4)	817 897-2322	George R Crump	....	Dorothy McFall	Wynell Whitt	....	Roger Marks	Frank Laramore
Starr (Rio Grande City) (27)	512 487-2307	Blas Chapa	....	Arturo Clarke	Jose D Villarreal	....	Ramiro Narro MD	Eugenio Falcon
Stephens (Breckenridge) (10)	817 559-3700	(not reporting)						
Sterling (Sterling City) (1)	915 378-5191	Roland L Lowe	....	Sandra Peel	Beth Kilpatrick	....	W J Swaan MD	Tommy Wright
Stonewall (Aspermont) (2)	817 989-2272	George H Frazier	....	Betty L Smith	....	....	....	Leroy Morrow
Sutton (Sonora) (5)	915 387-3815	(not reporting)						
Swisher (Tulia) (10)	806 995-3294	Jay Johnson	....	Pat Wesley	Lanelle Dovel	....	....	John Gayler
Tarrant (Fort Worth) (861)	817 334-1195	(not reporting)						
Taylor (Abilene) (111)	915 677-1711	James R McMillon	....	Janice Lyons	Mozelle Thomas	....	Curzon Ferris Jr	John Middleton
Terrell (Sanderson) (2)	915 345-2391	(not reporting)						
Terry (Brownfield)† (15)	806 637-6421	Herbert Chesshir	....	Frank T Gray	Bobbie Montgomery	....	D B Black	Ralph Murry
Throckmorton (Throckmorton) (2)	817 849-3081	William T Lindsey	....	Cathey Mitchel	Margret Lilly	....	Sumal Gosh	Jerry Schrimsher
Titus (Mount Pleasant) (21)	214 572-8891	(not reporting)						
Tom Green (San Angelo) (85)	915 653-2385	Edd B Keyes	Gene Rowden	Marie Russell	Billie McDaniel	....	Wayne Farrell	Ernest D Haynes
Travis (Austin) (419)	512 473-9555	Mike Renfro	....	Doris Shropshire	Johnny Crow	David Preble	Albert Randall MD	Doyne Bailey
Trinity (Groveton) (9)	409 642-1443	Jimmie Thornton	....	Elaine Lockhart	Linda O'Neal	....	Lawrence Quan MD	Kenneth Moore
Tyler (Woodville) (16)	409 283-2141	Allen Sturrock	....	Grace Bostick	Ann Nichol	....	John Gilchrist MD	Leon Fowler
Upshur (Gilmer)† (29)	214 843-2823	Everett Dean	....	J B Hill Jr	C H Pitman	....	J L Fenlaw MD	Dale Jewkes
Upton (Rankin) (5)	915 693-2321	Peggy Garner	....	Buena Coffee	Doris Speed	....	....	S O Langford
Uvalde (Uvalde)† (22)	512 278-3216	J R White	....	Eileen Carlisle	Josephine Noble	Lee Hawkes	Jimmie V Stewart	Kenneth Kelley
Val Verde (Del Rio) (36)	512 774-3611	Sergio Gonzalez	Cecil Gutierrez	Mildred Hildreth	Cecil Adams	....	Conrado Galindo	James R Koog
Van Zandt (Canton)† (31)	214 567-4071	Sam Hillard	....	Steve Gandy	Shirley Morgan	....	....	Travis Shafer
Victoria (Victoria) (69)	512 575-4558	Norman D Jones	....	Val D Huvar	Pat Beck	....	Don L Wendt	Dalton Meyer
Walker (Huntsville) (42)	409 295-5787	Ralph A Davis Jr	....	James D Patton	B McGilberry	....	M G Selassie MD	Darrell White
Waller (Hempstead) (20)	713 826-3357	A M McCaig	....	Elva D Mathis	Patricia Sneed	John H Rafferty	E R Owens MD	Ronnie Sitton
Ward (Monahans) (14)	915 943-3209	Richard Sitz	....	Pat Finley	Audrey Harris	....	G R Albertson	D Hall
Washington (Brenham) (22)	409 836-9374	Gus F Mutscher	....	Gertrude Lehrmann	Rosa Lee Fuchs	....	W F Hasskarl Jr	Elwood Goldberg
Webb (Laredo) (99)	512 727-7272	C Y Benavides Jr	N R Hernandez	Henry Flores	Hector Farias Jr	Oscar Salinas	Jose Gonzalez	Mario Santos Jr
Wharton (Wharton) (40)	409 532-4612	Edward E Wuthrich	....	Delfin Marek	Gus Wessels Jr	....	Stanley Mcmasters	Rudy Machala
Wheeler (Wheeler) (7)	806 826-5544	(not reporting)						
Wichita (Wichita Falls) (121)	817 322-0721	Thomas H Bacus	....	Lydia Torres	Clifford Hagstrom	....	Rbt G Howell MD	William L Burrow
Wilbarger (Vernon) (16)	817 552-5486	Bob Arnold	....	Frances McGee	Janice King	....	Layne Collums MD	Gerald King
Willacy (Raymondville) (17)	512 689-2710	(not reporting)						
Williamson (Georgetown) (77)	512 863-3585	(not reporting)						
Wilson (Floresville) (17)	512 393-3126	W D Cox	....	Richard Bolf	Peggy Jaeggli	....	Calvin Daughtery	Marvin H Baumann
Winkler (Kermit) (10)	915 586-6658	Frances Clark	....	Ruth Godwin	John W Stout	....	W T Timmons MD	W H Sage
Wise (Decatur)† (27)	817 627-5743	Charles R Wilhite	....	Laverne Forman	Emma Ray	....	W E Huddleston	Carl Ramsey
Wood (Quitman) (25)	214 763-2711	Lee E Williams	S Kent Gibson	Martha Bridges	....	....	David Murley	Bill Edd Jones
Yoakum (Plains) (8)	806 456-2721	(not reporting)						
Young (Graham)† (19)	817 549-2030	N L Barrett	....	Hugh Grubbs	Vesta Cox	Kenneth Mobley	R G McDaniel	....
Zapata (Zapata) (7)	512 765-4342	Jake G Rathmell	....	Arnoldo Flores	Jose Luis Guevara	....	Jean Harris	Romeo R Ramirez
Zavala (Crystal City) (12)	512 374-2331	(not reporting)						
UTAH (29)								
Beaver (Beaver) (4)	801 438-2352	Chad W Johnson	....	Paul B Barton	Rondo T Farrer	....	David A Symond	G Lynn Cartwright
Box Elder (Brigham City)† (33)	801 734-2031	Don E Chase	....	Jay R Hirschi	Glen S Fife	Denton H Beecher	John Bailey	Robert E Limb
Cache (Logan) (57)	801 752-5935	Dean R Smith	Keith J Nelson	Seth S Allen	Lucile Ferguson	Preston Ward	John Bailey	D Douglas Bodrero
Carbon (Price) (22)	801 637-4700	(not reporting)						
Daggett (Manila) (1)	801 784-3154	(not reporting)						
Davis (Farmington) (147)	801 366-3000	Glen E Saunders	....	Michael G Allphin	Pauline McBride	H Glenn Austin	Enrico Leopardi	Brant L Johnson
Duchesne (Duchesne)† (13)	801 738-2437	Alton N Moon	....	Janet Cowan	Maxine Taylor	Georg Adams	Rand Web	George Marett
Emery (Castle Dale) (11)	801 381-2139	(not reporting)						
Garfield (Panguitch) (4)	801 676-8826	George Middleton	....	Dawna Barney	Merle Stowell	....	Jan Frandsen	Vic Middleton
Grand (Moab)† (8)	801 259-5645	William Hance	....	Barbara Domenick	....	John E Keogh	....	James D Nyland
Iron (Parowan)† (17)	801 477-3375	James C Robinson	....	Clair Hulet	Lamar G Jensen	Ralph B Platt	....	Ira Schoppmann
Juab (Nephi)† (6)	801 623-0271	Joseph A Bernini	....	Alice R Newton	Joyce C Pay	....	....	David H Carter
Kane (Kanab) (4)	801 644-2458	Calvin C Johnson	....	Kathy Chamberlain	V Weldon Glover	....	....	Benney R Riddle
Millard (Fillmore) (9)	801 743-6223	(not reporting)						
Morgan (Morgan) (5)	801 829-3311	Steven J Hopkin	....	Janis Widdison	Janice A Larson	Keith Hansen	Weber Morgan	Max T Robinson
Piute (Junction) (1)	801 577-2840	Afton G Blood	Bobbie G Barnson	Bobbie G Barnson	Betty C Wiley	....	....	Brent Gottfredson
Rich (Randolph) (2)	801 793-2415	(not reporting)						
Salt Lake (Salt Lake City) (619)	801 535-7307	D Michael Stewart	Diana D Felt	H Dixon Hindley	Arthur L Monson	Roy Baty	Harry L Gibbons	N D Hayward
San Juan (Monticello) (12)	801 587-2231	Calvin Black	....	Gail L Dalton	Marian Bayles	Douglas Pehrson	Carroll D Goon	S Rigby Wright
Sanpete (Manti) (15)	801 835-2131	Ned P Madsen	....	Wayne G Beck	Earl D Clark	....	....	Kennard Anderson
Sevier (Richfield) (15)	801 896-4870	(not reporting)						
Summit (Coalville) (10)	801 336-5951	Gerald E Young	Stanley Strebel	Reed D Pace	Robert Williams	....	Steve Jenkins	Fred Eley
Tooele (Tooele) (26)	801 882-5557	(not reporting)						
Uintah (Vernal) (21)	801 789-1622	Neal H Domgaard	Byron G Merrell	Dorothy C Luck	Amy G Pope	Nelson Marshall	Rand Webb	Arden W Stewart
Utah (Provo) (218)	801 373-5510	Keith J Richan	....	William F Huish	Elwood L Sundberg	Clyde R Naylor	Joseph K Miner MD	Mack Holley
Wasatch (Heber City) (9)	801 654-3211	(not reporting)						
Washington (St. George) (26)	801 673-4432	Jerry B Lewis	....	Marjorie Howell	R Lynn Gardner	Robert MacDonald	....	Kenneth Campbell
Wayne (Loa) (2)	801 836-2731	(not reporting)						
Weber (Ogden) (145)	801 399-8481	(not reporting)						
VERMONT (14)								
Addison (Middlebury) (29)	802 388-7741	(not reporting)						

Directory 1/9 continued **COUNTY OFFICIALS IN ALL U.S. COUNTIES**

County, county seat, 1980 population (000 omitted),	County telephone number	Board chairman	Appointed administrator	Clerk to the governing board	Chief financial officer	County engineer	County health officer	Chief law enforcement official
VERMONT (14) continued								
Bennington (Bennington)† (33)	802 442-8528	Victor K Harwood	Elizabeth A King	....	Herbert W Gall	....	....	John H Maloney
Caledonia (St. Johnsbury) (26)	802 748-3813	Paul J Sevigny	....	Barbara S Terrill	Edward F Senecal	....	....	Jeffrey N Bitcon
Chittenden (Burlington) (116)	802 863-3467	(not reporting)						
Essex (Guildhall) (6)	802 254-6857	(not reporting)						
Franklin (St. Albans) (35)	802 524-2739	(not reporting)						
Grand Isle (North Hero)† (5)	802 372-8350	George R Anderson	Frederick Hislop	Joanne Batchelder	Jean D Hutchins	....	....	John S Lawrence
Lamoille (Hyde Park) (17)	802 888-2207	Ronald N Terrill	Clifford Porter	Lorraine M Sweets	Jean Crary	....	....	Gardner G Manosh
Orange (Chelsea) (23)	802 685-4610	Olive P Angell	....	Ernest H Kennedy	Ernest H Kennedy	....	....	Gerald G Eldred
Orleans (Newport) (23)	802 334-2711	Robert H Nelson	....	Constance Daigle	Harold Bowen	....	....	James G Murphy
Rutland (Rutland) (58)	802 775-4394	(not reporting)						
Washington (Montpelier) (52)	802 223-2091	Willis C Bragg	Josephine Romano	....	Earl Hoffman	....	....	Ronald West
Windham (Brattleboro) (37)	802 254-4994	(not reporting)						
Windsor (Woodstock) (51)	802 457-2121	(not reporting)						
VIRGINIA (136)								
Accomack (Accomac)† (31)	804 787-4289	Donald L Hart Jr	C M Williams Jr	C M Williams Jr	Martha B Hundley	....	Thomas W Simpson	Robert L Tull Jr
Albemarle (Charlottesville)*† (51)	804 296-5822	Gerald E Fisher	Guy B Agnor Jr	Lettie E Neher	Ray B Jones	Maynard Elrod	Richard A Prindle	George W Bailey
Alexandria I (103)	703 838-4300	Chas E Beatley Jr	Douglas Harman	Helen M Holleman	....	Dayton L Cook	Anne J Albertson	Charles Strobel
Alleghany (Covington) (14)	703 862-4918	Clarence W Farmer	Randal E Arno	Randal E Arno	Dorothy P Brown	Noel P Beach	Dr Nancy Welch	Leon P Smith
Amelia (Amelia Court House)§ (8)	804 561-3039	Joe H Paulette	John A Anzivino	John A Anzivino	John F Deekens	....	Samuel Graham MD	Harold H Osborne
Amherst (Amherst) (29)	804 946-7206	Stanley C Harris	Stewart E Shaner	Stewart E Shaner	Donald T Wood	....	Joanna H Harris	Michael W Cox
Appomattox (Appomattox) (12)	804 352-5275	S R Lawson	....	Barbara Williams	Ida H Campbell	....	Joanna H Harris	James Richardson
Arlington (Arlington)*† (153)	703 558-0200	Ellen M Bozman	Larry J Brown	Jean C Julian	Bennie L Fletcher	....	Martin Wasserman	William K Stover
Augusta (Staunton) (54)	703 885-8931	B L Speck	R E Huff	R E Huff	Sue Lindamood	H H Ralston	C W Caplen MD	Glenn P Lloyd
Bath (Warm Springs) (6)	703 839-2361	(not reporting)						
Bedford I† (6)	703 586-0421	James D Harvey	D K Cook	....	....	....	....	T E King
Bedford (Bedford) (35)	703 586-0421	C Whitney Grove	Cecil C Knowles	Cecil C Knowles	Edna N Murray	....	Joanna Harris	Carl Wells
Bland (Rocky Gap) (6)	703 688-4562	(not reporting)						
Botetourt (Fincastle) (23)	703 473-8220	J M Peck Jr	William K Manion	William K Manion	A C Williamson	....	Nancy Welch MD	Norman Sprinkle
Bristol I (19)	703 466-2221	James F Rector	Hugh G Cooper	Emmett M Hoover	Hugh G Cooper	....	....	Thomas W Stone Jr
Brunswick (Lawrenceville)† (16)	804 848-3107	....	....	M Henry Turnbull	Clarence T Orgain	....	Stephen Childrey	Peter G Brockwell
Buchanan (Grundy) (38)	703 935-2745	William P Harris	Joseph W Bland	Joseph W Bland	J H Childress	....	Nellie Wright MD	Paul A Crouss
Buckingham (Buckingham)§ (12)	804 969-4242	Thomas B Hall Jr	Arthur L Lane Jr	Arthur L Lane Jr	Sandra H Blanks	....	William Atkinson	G A Shumaker Jr
Buena Vista I (7)	703 261-6121	Harold Kidd	Larry M Foster	....	....	....	....	Erskin K Campbell
Campbell (Rustburg)§ (45)	804 332-5161	Walter W Viohl	Donald N Johnston	Donald N Johnston	G Hunter Jones Jr	J L Noffsinger	Joanna Harris MD	Robert E Maxey Jr
Caroline (Bowling Green) (18)	804 633-5380	Robert C Doswell	Berkley Mitchell	Berkley Mitchell	William A Garrett	....	Charles B Mundy	Ottie J Moore
Carroll (Hillsville) (27)	703 728-3331	Billy C Barker	James L Surratt	James L Surratt	Guy R Padgett	James F Gates	Craig Smith MD	W Hassell Vass
Charles City (Charles City)§ (7)	804 829-2401	Henry O Hollimon	Lloyd O Jones	Lloyd O Jones	Jessie B Crewe	....	Curtis Thorpe	James H Bowman
Charlotte (Charlotte Crt House) (12)	804 542-5117	J Wayland Dunn	Russell B Clark	Russell B Clark	Madeline C Boliek	....	Samuel A Graham	Burrel A Brown
Charlottesville I (45)	804 971-3100	Francis L Buck	Cole Hendrix	Jeanne Cox	Robert Sheets	....	....	John D Bowen
Chesapeake C (114)	804 547-6166	J B Jennings Jr	....	E J Calloway	J A Sibley	J A O'Connor	Dr S Kendra	R A Lakoski
Chesterfield (Chesterfield)§ (141)	804 748-1000	H G Daniel	Richard L Hedrick	Joan S Dolezal	M Arline McGuire	....	W P Wagner	E L Wingo
Clarke (Berryville) (10)	703 955-3269	Eustace B Jackson	G Robert Lee	G Robert Lee	Edythe R Pifer	....	....	Albert Nicodemus
Clifton Forge I (5)	703 863-5091	George R Goode Sr	Roger D Baker	V Craig Hudson	Robert B Deaton	....	....	Dorsey G Huffman
Colonial Heights I (17)	804 526-7506	James B McNeer	Robert E Taylor	Dolores D Elmore	John H Mitchell	Robert V Cawthorn	....	R B Ellison
Covington (Covington) I (9)	703 962-4984	James L Jamison	Richard C Flora	Brenda H Falls	....	....	....	Donald Leet
Craig (New Castle)† (4)	703 864-5010	Zane M Jones	Jeffrey D Johnson	Jeffrey D Johnson	Sandra C Reynolds	....	Nancy M Welch MD	Billy McPherson
Culpeper (Culpeper)* (23)	703 825-3035	William C Chase	Franklin Bell Jr	Franklin Bell Jr	Clark Glass	....	John Einarison	Robert Peters
Cumberland (Cumberland)† (8)	804 492-4442	E W Sanderson	....	Imogene Tunstall	Irene D Speas	....	S A Graham MD	Henry Blanton III
Danville I (46)	804 799-5100	Samuel A Kushner	Charles F Church	Aubrey D Dodson	Aubrey D Dodson	Arthur Daniel Jr	Donald Stern MD	B C Elliott
Dickenson (Clintwood) (20)	703 926-4549	William A Patton	Jimmy Hawkins	Teddy Bailey	Paul E Moore	Jeff Yates	....	Edward C Fleming
Dinwiddie (Dinwiddie) (23)	804 469-3717	G S Bennett Jr	W C Knott	Annie L Williams	William E Jones	....	J R Tietjen MD	Bennie M Heath
Emporia I (5)	804 634-3332	William H Ligon	Tedd E Povar	Nell M Mitchell	Tedd E Povar	....	....	Elmer L Grizzard
Essex (Tappahannock)† (9)	804 443-4331	Alex F Dillard Jr	James F Moore	James F Moore	F H Ellis	....	Joanna S Owens	D W Insley
Fairfax I (19)	703 385-7855	George T Snyder	Edward A Wyatt	J Henderson	Edward J Cawley	John Veneziano	....	Loyd W Smith
Fairfax (Fairfax)* (597)	703 691-2000	John F Herrity	J H Lambert	Ethel A Register	Warren Hutchison	....	Richard K Miller	Carroll Buracker
Falls Church I (10)	703 241-5100	Carol W Delong	Anthony H Griffin	Mary C Gallagher	Halsey Green III	....	Richard K Miller	Stanley K Johnson
Fauquier (Warrenton)§ (36)	703 347-8600	John B Adams	Steve Crosby	Steve Crosby	J E Cox	....	Dr John Einarson	Ashby Olinger
Floyd (Floyd) (12)	703 745-2028	W L Whitlock	Henry E McDaniel	Henry E McDaniel	W G Cannaday	....	Jim Hall	Geo E Branscome
Fluvanna (Palmyra)§ (10)	804 589-3138	....	Gregory K Wolfrey	....	....	....	....	....
Franklin I (7)	804 562-4111	G Elliott Cobb Jr	Wayne G Reed	Wayne G Reed	Dorothy Saunders	David Jones	E D Harris	Grady Britt
Franklin (Rocky Mount)§ (36)	703 483-1315	Noell Parcell	Billy P Beckett	Billy P Beckett	Doris D Brown	....	Elizabeth Roycrof	W Q Overton
Frederick (Winchester)§ (34)	703 667-2365	Kenneth Y Stiles	John R Riley Jr	John R Riley Jr	Dorothy Keckley	Robert Harriman	Paul Pedersen	Roscoe Bruce
Fredericksburg I (15)	703 373-5011	Lawrence P Davies	Peter Kolakowski	C P Pugh	Peter Kolakowski	R Wayne Brooks	Charles Mundy	Harry Fleming Jr
Galax I (7)	703 236-3441	Glenn G Wilson	W Harold Snead	W Harold Snead	Doris J Bedwell	....	....	B R Melton
Giles (Pearisburg) (18)	703 921-2525	Howard C Morris	Barbara M Hobbs	Barbara M Hobbs	William D Bane	....	Gregory Corell	John E Hopkins
Gloucester (Gloucester)§ (20)	804 693-4042	George C Sterling	William H Whitley	William H Whitley	Mary F Altemus	Wesley D Jones	Joanna Owens	William G Gatling
Goochland (Goochland)§ (12)	804 556-4701	Andrew W Pryor	David A Clabo	David A Clabo	Malcolm W Amos	....	Curtis Thorpe MD	John W Amos
Grayson (Independence)† (17)	703 773-2471	Lewis P Kirk	Donald G Young	Donald G Young	Fields Young Jr	....	D Craig Smith	Herbert McKnight
Greene (Stanardsville) (8)	804 985-7803	Warner C Wood	Julius L Morris	Julius L Morris	E D Jarman	....	Richard Prindle	William L Morris
Greensville (Emporia)§ (11)	804 348-4205	Garland P Faison	David Whittington	David Whittington	Charles A Reid	....	Richard Mitchell	Earl Sasser
Halifax (Halifax)§ (30)	804 476-2141	Oscar Tate	Joseph N Morgan	Joseph N Morgan	W C Anderson	....	Steven Childrey	Woody Bane
Hampton C (123)	804 727-6000	James L Eason	Robert J O'Neill	Diana T Hughes	James A Peterson	Joseph L Womack	Carol C Hogg MD	Pat G Minetti
Hanover (Hanover)§ (50)	804 798-6081	E C C Woods Jr	John J Jackson	John J Jackson	G M Weems	Randy Guill	Curtis Thorpe	Harold Bradley
Harrisonburg I† (20)	703 434-6776	Walter Green III	Marvin B Milam	....	Beverly A Simmons	....	....	Richard Presgrave
Henrico (Richmond)* (181)	804 747-4000	John A Waldrop Jr	Wm F Lavecchia	Margaret B Baker	....	Philip T Rutledge	Forrest W Pitts	Leslie Sheppard
Henry (Collinsville) (58)	703 638-5311	Sammy Redd	C Lee Lintecum	Robert C Crouch	D W Turner	Whitmill C Brown	E Roycroft	James Rogers
Highland (Monterey) (3)	703 468-2447	M L Eagle	....	Sue K Dudley	William B Huffman	....	C W Caplen	C Milton Ralston
Hopewell I (23)	804 541-2200	Hilda M Traina	Clinton H Strong	Mary Frances Pito	Philip R Grant	Frederick Hughes	Dale Lasiter	Robert G Broyles
Isle of Wight (Isle of Wight)§ (22)	804 357-3191	Richard L Turner	W B Owen	W B Owen	Beryl H Perry Jr	....	....	B F Dixon
James City (Williamsburg)§ (23)	804 220-1122	Stewart U Taylor	James B Oliver Jr	James B Oliver Jr	John E McDonald	Wayland Bass	Robt McKeogh MD	Robert C Key
King and Queen (King & Queen Ct. Hse.) (6)	804 785-7955	Robt H Bourne Jr	Charles W Smith	Charles W Smith	Nita T Hollowell	....	Joanna Owens	Robert F Longest
King George (King George) (11)	703 775-9181	Woodrow W Saft	Kenneth M Scruggs	Kenneth M Scruggs	C Walter Gallahan	....	C G Chestnut	Clarence W Dobson
King William (King William)§ (9)	804 769-3011	J P Townsend	Dale R Burton	Dale R Burton	Wm N Campbell	....	Joanna Owens MD	W Wayne Healy
Lancaster (Lancaster) (10)	804 462-5220	John J Cardwell	Anita Sanders	Anita Sanders	Novella W Abbott	....	Edward Harris MD	Ronald D Crockett
Lee (Jonesville)† (26)	703 346-2691	Darvin J Barker	Edith Bowen	Edith Bowen	L E Jones	....	G Honeycutt MD	Robert V Chadwell

Directory 1/9 continued **COUNTY OFFICIALS IN ALL U.S. COUNTIES**

County, county seat, 1980 population (000 omitted),	County telephone number	Board chairman	Appointed administrator	Clerk to the governing board	Chief financial officer	County engineer	County health officer	Chief law enforcement official
VIRGINIA (136) continued								
Lexington I (7)	703 463-7133	Charles F Phillip	John V Doane	....	....	....	....	L O Sutton
Loudoun (Leesburg)§ (57)	703 777-0100	James F Brownell	Philip A Bolen	Philip A Bolen	George W Titus	Terrence Wharton	Earl Virts MD	John Isom
Louisa (Louisa) (18)	703 967-0401	Frank B Boxley Jr	Robert C Klepper	Robert C Klepper	Harry M Lumsden	....	Richard A Prindle	Henry A Kennon
Lunenburg (Lunenburg)† (12)	804 696-2230	C L Barens Jr	W R Moore	W R Moore	A C Vaughan	....	S A Graham MD	A G Daniel
Lynchburg I† (67)	804 847-1400	Elliott L Shearer	Edgar Culverhouse	Barbara J Gage	Michael W Hill	Raymond A Booth	Joanna Harris MD	C E Robertson
Madison (Madison)† (10)	703 948-6102	J T Williamson	....	Stephen L Utz	Ray E Gooding	....	John Einarson MD	Harry O Tinsley
Manassas I (15)	703 335-8200	Edgar E Rohr	C M Moyer Jr	R H Moore	Curtis L Mlsna	J E Harney	....	Samuel S Ellis
Manassas Park I (7)	703 361-0124	George R Maitland	Jerry W Davis	Lana A Conner	James E Norlund	....	....	Wilbur Hudson
Martinsville I (18)	703 638-3971	William C Cole Jr	Don R Edmonds	W H Yeaman	Richard D Fitts	Leon E Towarnicki	....	Terry L Roop
Mathews (Mathews) (8)	804 725-7171	C H Richardson Jr	Frank A Pleva	Frank A Pleva	Judy Oburroughs	....	Joanna Owens	Kenneth H Jordan
Mecklenburg (Boydton)§ (29)	804 738-6191	C O Johnson	B McCauley	Polly C Johnson	Robert Gregory	....	Stephen Childrey	Harold Harris
Middlesex (Saluda)† (8)	804 758-4330	A Carl Handley Jr	Stephen G Gadinis	Stephen G Gadinis	Anita S Wilson	....	Joanna Owens	Aubrey Packett
Montgomery (Christiansburg)§ (64)	703 382-1431	Mary R Fessler	Betty S Thomas	Betty S Thomas	Ellis D Meredith	Gary W Gibson	William Hattfield	Louis E Barber
Nelson (Lovingston) (12)	804 263-4873	(not reporting)						
New Kent (New Kent) (9)	804 966-9861	Richard S Ellyson	Royal E Wood	Royal E Wood	Louise C Williams	J L Gallaher	Randolph Burgess	F W Howard Jr
Newport News C (145)	804 247-8411	Joseph C Ritchie	Robert T Williams	Bernice I Berry	C S Sullivan	Mostafa A Sabbah	William H Cope	Darrel W Stephens
Norfolk I (267)	804 441-2000	Joseph A Leafe	Julian F Hirst	Louis S Hudgins	Jimmy D Clowers	Lawrence Gassman	H M Rimple	Charles D Grant
Northampton (Eastville) (15)	804 678-5148	J T Holland	R Keith Bull	R Keith Bull	E B Savage	....	....	W T Belote
Northumberland (Heathsville) (10)	804 580-7666	Edwin A Sisson	....	John E Burton	Ellen V Booker	....	Ed Appleby	S Bowles Jr
Norton I (5)	703 679-1160	George Hunnicutt	Charles R Brown	Jo K Nosler	Ernest W Ward	Ronald E Peaks	....	Samuel A Mongle
Nottoway (Nottoway) (15)	804 645-8696	Dick R Forrester	Ronald E Roark	Ronald E Roark	Annie T Ellett	....	Jamie S Hawley	Jesse E Powell
Orange (Orange) (18)	703 672-3313	Robert J Schwartz	A T Baskerville	A T Baskerville	W Eugene Bartley	....	John Einarson	William Faulconer
Page (Luray)§† (19)	703 743-4142	....	Ronald W Good	....	....	....	....	....
Patrick (Stuart) (18)	703 694-6094	Lowell A Layman	Barnie K Day	Barnie K Day	Mary M Arrington	....	E Roycroft	Jay E Gregory
Petersburg I (41)	804 733-6131	R Wilson Cheely	....	Barbara W Moore	Robertson Blount	....	John R Tietjen MD	Lawrence R Nowery
Pittsylvania (Chatham)§ (66)	804 432-2041	Claude Whitehead	William D Sleeper	William D Sleeper	Glenn A Brown	....	Donald R Stern MD	Taylor McGregor
Poquoson I (9)	804 868-7151	Joseph K Bunting	Robert M Murphy	Judy F Wiggins	Frances C Firth	Kristen Lawrence	....	John T White
Portsmouth I (105)	804 393-8000	James Holley III	George L Hanbury	Corinna Jeffreys	Roy W Cherry	Richard A Hartman	William Crawford	....
Powhatan (Powhatan)§ (13)	804 598-4271	Robert R Cosby	Edgar A Appling	Edgar A Appling	Ruth N Heath	....	W P Wagner MD	Garland K Stokes
Prince Edward (Farmville) (16)	804 392-8837	Hugh E Carwile Jr	Mildred B Hampton	Mildred B Hampton	Lucy W Shorter	....	Samuel A Graham	Gene A Southall
Prince George (Prince George)§ (26)	804 732-8818	Samuel L Bland	John G Kines Jr	Kenneth L Figg Jr	Elaine O Phillips	Roy A Trexler	John R Tietjen MD	John F Atwood
Prince William (Manassas)§ (145)	703 369-9235	Kathleen Seefeldt	Robert S Noe Jr	....	Connie Bawcum	Martin Crahan	Robert M Dean	G T Owens
Pulaski (Pulaski) (35)	703 980-8888	(not reporting)						
Radford I (13)	703 639-9626	Ted W Bess	Robt P Asbury Jr	Roy I Lloyd Jr	Jess W Cantline	....	....	James Whitt
Rappahannock (Washington) (6)	703 675-3621	(not reporting)						
Richmond (Warsaw) (7)	804 333-3415	W D Gray	....	Stephen Whiteway	Lois O Shockley	....	....	Lewis A Rock
Richmond I (219)	804 780-4000	Roy A West	Manuel Deese	Edgar Duffy	Neal Evans	....	....	Frank S Duling
Roanoke (Roanoke)§ (73)	703 772-2006	Harry C Nickens	Donald R Flanders	Donald R Flanders	Alfred C Anderson	John R Hubbard	Nancy M Welch MD	O S Foster
Roanoke I (100)	703 981-2000	Noel C Taylor	H Bernhard Ewert	Mary F Parker	Joel M Schlanger	Richard B Burrow	E J Clarke Jr MD	M David Hooper
Rockbridge (Lexington)† (18)	703 463-4361	Charles C Trimble	Donald G Austin	....	Charles A Potter	....	C W Caplen	S M Reynolds
Rockingham (Harrisonburg)§ (57)	703 434-4455	O Lynwood Byerly	William G O'Brien	William G O'Brien	Cecil L Wampler	Don E Krueger	C Caplan MD	Glenn Weatherholt
Russell (Lebanon) (32)	703 889-2372	Dr Roy R Smith	James A Gillespie	James A Gillespie	L Guy Plaster	....	....	J Trigg Fields
Salem I (24)	703 375-3016	James Taliaferro	W J Paxton Jr	....	Frank P Turk	....	....	Harry Haskins Jr
Scott (Gate City)§ (25)	703 386-6521	M C Price	Billie T Lynch	Billie T Lynch	Martha H Bledsoe	....	G C Honeycutt Jr	Darrel Mcmurray
Shenandoah (Woodstock) (28)	703 459-2195	Dennis M Morris	John D Cutlip	John D Cutlip	Elvin C Walker	....	Paul D Pedersen	Marshall Robinson
Smyth (Marion) (33)	703 783-3298	Fred B Frye	Marvin R Perry	Marvin R Perry	Ruth D Albert	....	Craig Smith	Jerry L Archer
South Boston I (7)	804 572-3621	William A Kent	J A Houghton	J Aubrey Houghton	Steve V Saunders	....	....	B H Covington
Southampton (Courtland) (19)	804 653-2465	A Meredith Felts	Joseph E Johnson	Joseph E Johnson	Fred D Worrell	....	John C Lipsey	Vernie W Francis
Spotsylvania (Spotsylvania) (34)	703 582-6361	Emmitt Marshall	Steven T Foster	Steven T Foster	Elizabeth Flippo	Lanny L Branner	Charles B Mundy	Thomas C Waddy Jr
Stafford (Stafford)§ (40)	703 659-8603	Alvin Y Bandy	C M Williams Jr	C M Williams Jr	Michael Saunders	James L Briggs	....	Richard L Ashby
Staunton I (22)	703 885-1251	Hugh B Sproul III	R Gene McCombs	Bette W Herr	Boyce Spinelli	....	....	Phillip Ash
Suffolk C (48)	804 934-3111	Andrew B Damiani	John L Rowe Jr	Henry C Murden	Leon Johnson	....	John Lipsey MD	Gilbert F Jackson
Surry (Surry) (6)	804 294-3137	M Sherlock Holmes	Beverly Brewer	Beverly Brewer	Anne T Seward	....	J R Tietjen	W C Andrews Jr
Sussex (Sussex) (11)	804 246-5511	J F Newsome	William J Hopkins	William J Hopkins	Onnie L Woodruff	....	....	E Stuart Kitchen
Tazewell (Tazewell) (51)	703 988-7541	Joseph E Peery Jr	C H Peery III	C H Peery III	Norman Cook	William N Lambert	Nellie Wright MD	William Osborne
Virginia Beach C (262)	804 497-4111	Harold Heischober	T H Muehlenbeck	Ruth Hodges Smith	Giles G Dodd	D R Trueblood	George Sjolund MD	Charles R Wall
Warren (Front Royal)§ (21)	703 636-9973	Robert F Looney	J Ronald George	J Ronald George	Doris D Miller	....	Paul D Pederson	Lynn Armentrout
Washington (Abingdon)§ (46)	703 628-2983	Clyde H King Jr	Richard Barton	....	Dan G Stevens	....	D Craig Smith	John A McCall
Waynesboro I (15)	703 949-8305	Warren F Kindt	Charles T Yancey	Margaret Gilmore	Frank Fletcher	Michael Murphy	....	Horace L Gleason
Westmoreland (Montross)§† (14)	804 493-8911	Everett W O'Neill	Thomas V Finan	Thomas V Finan	Margaret O Nash	....	George Moore	Charles W Jackson
Williamsburg I† (10)	703 229-4821	Robert C Walker	Frank Force	....	....	....	....	....
Winchester I (20)	703 667-1815	Chas M Zuckerman	Wendell L Seldon	Patricia B Ashby	B M Perrero	Ed J Jankiewicz	Paul Pedersen MD	F Allen Barley
Wise (Wise)* (44)	703 328-2321	Tom Pierce	Joel R Sikes	Joel R Sikes	Maude Hawkins	....	G C Hunnicutt	William Kelley
Wythe (Wytheville) (26)	703 228-5457	George F James	Billy R Branson	Billy R Branson	S Sutherland	Kenneth P Hurst	D Craig Smith	G Wayne Pike
York (Yorktown)§ (35)	804 898-0200	Rodgers A Smith	John M Richardson	John M Richardson	Arlene D Pollard	....	Robert P McKeogh	Preston Williams
WASHINGTON (39)								
Adams (Ritzville) (13)	509 659-0090	Richard A Coon	....	Monica Hanson	Louise Brewer	J R Kavanagh	James J Jardee MD	R D Snowden
Asotin (Asotin) (17)	509 243-4164	Neil C Ausman	....	Nancy Spears	Jerry McGuire	Roger N Diesen	Ronald Neu	Gary Gunkel
Benton (Prosser) (109)	509 786-4278	Ronald S Jones	....	Glennette Evans	Claude Oliver	Dennis Skeate	Herbert Cahn	Robert Rupp
Chelan (Wenatchee) (45)	509 663-1147	(not reporting)						
Clallam (Port Angeles)§ (52)	206 452-7831	Don Feeley	Michael R Wilson	Charlene Gau	Robert J Clark	Gene Unger	Stan Garlick	Steven T Kernes
Clark (Vancouver) (192)	206 699-2000	John S Mckibbin	....	Mary Ann Moroney	Doug Lasher	George Stillman	Tom Milne	Frank Kanekoa
Columbia (Dayton)† (4)	509 382-4542	Vernon Marll	....	Dorothy Hutchens	Robert Truesdale	Gary Gasaway	Donald Pittman	Rod Flint
Cowlitz (Kelso) (80)	206 577-3020	Van A Youngquist	....	Hettie Herron	Donna Rolfe	Ken Stone	Allen C Norman MD	Les Nelson
Douglas (Waterville) (22)	509 745-8527	Wm Schmidtman	....	Laurie Evenhus	Carol H Mires	Dwaine Townsend	....	Bill M Williams
Ferry (Republic) (6)	509 775-3161	Arthur L Cameron	....	Christy D Thomas	A Lee Gendron	Ralph W E Main	Edmund Gray	Richard Baldwin
Franklin (Pasco) (35)	509 545-3535	Ken Miller	....	Vera Green	Valoria Loveland	Bruce Gilkeson	Herbert C Kahn MD	Wallace Bradley
Garfield (Pomeroy) (2)	509 843-1391	Donne Stallcop	....	John F Carlson	....	Donald J Lyman Jr	R J Weiland	Bill Taylor
Grant (Ephrata) (49)	509 754-2011	Bill Frederickson	....	Frances Wadham	James Archer	Mike Murray	Wallace Ruthford	Felix Ramon
Grays Harbor (Montesano) (66)	206 249-3842	(not reporting)						
Island (Coupeville) (44)	206 679-7300	E Duane Kemp	....	Harry H Ferrier	Patricia Pfeifer	Roy L Allen	Terry Walker	Richard R Medina
Jefferson (Port Townsend) (16)	206 385-2016	B G Brown	....	Jerdine C Bragg	Frances H Hansen	Brian Shelton	J Fischnaller	Lelane B Smith
King (Seattle)§ (1270)	206 344-4100	Randy Revelle	Lauraine D Brekke	Dorothy Owen	Robert Cowan Jr	LaBelle Donald	Jesse Tapp	Vernon Thomas
Kitsap (Port Orchard) (147)	206 876-7053	William Mahan	....	Janet Banach	Billie Eder	Paul Dour	Willa Fisher	Pat Jones

Directory 1/9 continued — COUNTY OFFICIALS IN ALL U.S. COUNTIES

County, county seat, 1980 population (000 omitted),	County telephone number	Board chairman	Appointed administrator	Clerk to the governing board	Chief financial officer	County engineer	County health officer	Chief law enforcement official
WASHINGTON (39) continued								
Kittitas (Ellensburg) (25)	509 962-6811	Elizabeth McCune	....	Michelle Dufault	Bette Spence	Don Berdan	Robert Atwood	Tom Young
Klickitat (Goldendale)† (16)	509 773-4612	Fred Holly	....	Nancy J Evans	L Douvravsky	Edward A Hoyle	....	Richard Williams
Lewis (Chehalis) (55)	206 748-9121	Harold R Cooper	....	Gary E Zandell	Karl Kuehner	Vern Wagar	Robert Cole MD	William H Wiester
Lincoln (Davenport) (10)	509 725-2281	(not reporting)						
Mason (Shelton) (31)	206 426-3222	William O Hunter	....	Rebecca S Toebe	Lowell H Bamford	Marley Young	Joanne Hoover	Nathan Stairs
Okanogan (Okanogan) (31)	509 422-3521	Melvin E Kuhlmann	....	Armentia M Tenner	Walter Womack	Alan O King	Blackburn Joslin	S R Johnston
Pacific (South Bend) (17)	206 875-6541	Andrew L Monson	....	Vyrle L Hill	Robert Kain	John O Trent	R A Bussabarger	Herbert W Newton
Pend Oreille (Newport) (9)	509 447-4119	Harlan F Young	....	Lois J Reed	George Kimsey	Herb Pease	....	Anthony Bamonte
Pierce (Tacoma) (486)	206 593-4415	....	Terry Sebring	Marlene Ellsworth	Patrick Kenney	Fred Anderson	Ray Bud Nicola	Ray Fjetland
San Juan (Friday Harbor) (8)	206 378-2163	Thomas R Cowan	....	Diana G Sheffer	C Erickson	Ron P Loewen	Paul Chiles MD	Ray K Sheffer
Skagit (Mount Vernon) (64)	206 336-9300	Bud Norris	Robert W Taylor	Megan Cheney	Jerry McInturff	Gene Sampley	J K Neils MD	John Boynton
Skamania (Stevenson) (8)	509 427-5141	Ed Callahan	....	Gary M Olson	Wilma J Cornwall	Gail P Swaine	Wayne T Shandara	William R Closner
Snohomish (Everett) (337)	206 259-9411	Cliff Bailey	....	Ellie Snyder	Andy Urban	Jerry Weed	Claris Hyatt MD	Robert Dodge
Spokane (Spokane)§ (342)	509 456-2265	Keith Shepard	Marshall Farnell	Rosanne Montague	Dennis E Chilberg	Robert S Turner	Mary Luther MD	Larry V Erickson
Stevens (Colville)† (29)	509 684-3751	Jack E Cogswell	....	Maribeth Lilley	Frederick McCurd	Reid Wheeler	Ed Gray	Chan St Clair
Thurston (Olympia)§ (124)	206 753-8000	George Barner	Charles Earl	Patti Zech	Harris Hunter	Al Williams	Robert Murphy MD	Dan Montgomery
Wahkiakum (Cathlamet) (4)	206 795-3219	Joseph E Florek	....	Betty E Gregory	Sharon L Mast	Paul A Giaver	....	Eugene C Strong
Walla Walla (Walla Walla)† (47)	509 525-6161	Robert J Petersen	....	Lynn Smith	Vera Kanen	Steve Stanton	George Herbert MD	Kenneth J Klundt
Whatcom (Bellingham) (107)	206 676-6717	Craig W Cole	Shirley Vanzanten	Carol Ebergson	Landrum C Bowen	Edwin Henken	Philip Jones MD	Larry E Mount
Whitman (Colfax) (40)	509 397-4622	Dan Boone	....	James Repp	Mary Crawford	Marvin Carroll	Don Takush MD	Cleve D Hunter
Yakima (Yakima) (173)	509 575-4000	Jim Whiteside	....	Irene C Turner	Dale Gray	Daniel Hesse	Robert Atwood MD	Dick Nesary
WEST VIRGINIA (55)								
Barbour (Philippi) (17)	304 457-2232	(not reporting)						
Berkeley (Martinsburg) (47)	304 263-3511	Victor L Shockey	Norman Risavi	John W Small Jr	William Risner	....	Curtis G Powers	William N Kisner
Boone (Madison) (30)	304 369-3925	(not reporting)						
Braxton (Sutton) (14)	304 765-2881	Fred Delp	George J Welly	David L Jack	Connie Zummo	....	George T Hoylman	Connie Zummo
Brooke (Wellsburg) (31)	304 737-3661	Alfred Deangelis	....	Anthony J Filbert	Gary Young	....	John Bertram	Gary Young
Cabell (Huntington) (107)	304 525-7754	(not reporting)						
Calhoun (Grantsville) (8)	304 354-6725	(not reporting)						
Clay (Clay)† (11)	304 587-4259	Donald L Samples	....	Avis S Moore	Larry Conrad	....	....	Larry Conrad
Doddridge (West Union) (7)	304 873-2631	Raymond J Vanscoy	Vivian L Swisher	Dessie Daugherty	C K McCullough	....	Kenneth B Lauren	C K McCullough
Fayette (Fayetteville) (58)	304 574-1200	(not reporting)						
Gilmer (Glenville) (8)	304 462-7641	Earl J Gainer	....	Louella Stalnaker	Louella Stalnaker	....	Jack Heater	V Kirkpatrick
Grant (Petersburg) (10)	304 257-4422	A E Kessel	....	Harold Hiser	Edward Hiser	....	Lysle Veach	Edward Hiser
Greenbrier (Lewisburg) (38)	304 645-2373	(not reporting)						
Hampshire (Romney) (15)	304 822-5112	(not reporting)						
Hancock (New Cumberland) (40)	304 564-3311	George Gvoyich	Edwin J Thorne	Wilma Boring	William Webster	....	Thomas J Beynon	William Webster
Hardy (Moorefield) (10)	304 538-2929	Robert A Keller	....	Sue K Halterman	Gary B Stalnaker	....	M H Maxwell	Gary B Stalnaker
Harrison (Clarksburg) (78)	304 624-7431	(not reporting)						
Jackson (Ripley)† (26)	304 372-2011	Roger B Fisher	....	Annabelle Taylor	....	....	Perry Merritt	Homer Fisher
Jefferson (Charles Town)† (30)	304 725-9761	Garland Moore Jr	David L Ash	John E Ott	Donald R Giardina	Charles Sager	Earl D Allara	Donald R Giardina
Kanawha (Charleston) (231)	304 348-0750	F Douglas Stump	Susan M Harman	Margaret D Miller	Carl W Withrow	Bernard H Clark	Page H Seekford	Carl W Withrow
Lewis (Weston)† (19)	304 269-3371	Wm D Chapman	....	....	Ralph M Hall	....	....	....
Lincoln (Hamlin) (24)	304 824-3336	(not reporting)						
Logan (Logan) (51)	304 752-2000	(not reporting)						
Marion (Fairmont) (66)	304 366-2210	(not reporting)						
Marshall (Moundsville) (42)	304 845-1220	Richard B Ward	....	Norma Glover Sine	Robert L Lightner	Charles Eller	....	Robert L Lightner
Mason (Point Pleasant)† (27)	304 675-1110	Charles Fowler Jr	Kevin L Durst	Josephine T Hanes	Robert E Fruth	....	Richard Slack MD	Robert E Fruth
McDowell (Welch)† (50)	304 436-6218	Jennings B Boyd	....	Hilda J Taylor	Clark K Belcher	....	....	Clark K Belcher
Mercer (Princeton) (74)	304 425-8151	(not reporting)						
Mineral (Keyser) (27)	304 788-3924	Paul H Michael	Michael C Bland	Marshall E Nield	Jerry L Detrick	....	....	Jerry L Detrick
Mingo (Williamson) (37)	304 235-1638	(not reporting)						
Monongalia (Morgantown) (75)	304 291-7257	Eugene J Sellaro	Diane F DeMedici	Thelma Gibson	Joseph C Janco	....	Bette G Hinton MD	Joseph C Janco
Monroe (Union) (13)	304 772-3096	(not reporting)						
Morgan (Berkeley Springs) (11)	304 258-2774	J Brown Norton	Clyde M Graham	Clyde M Graham	James T Batt	....	Rick Hertges	James T Batt
Nicholas (Summersville) (28)	304 872-3630	Carroll T Lay	Patricia Neff	Tom Blankenship	Robert J Adams	....	William Lester MD	Robert J Adams
Ohio (Wheeling) (61)	304 234-3628	John I Tominack	Thomas C Samol	Thomas C Samol	Thomas Campbell	....	Thomas Thomas MD	Thomas Campbell
Pendleton (Franklin) (8)	304 358-2505	Morris M Homan	Thomas E Painter	Nancy K Gonshor	Leland E Propst	Thomas W Firor	Charles J Sites	Leland E Propst
Pleasants (St. Marys) (8)	304 684-3513	(not reporting)						
Pocahontas (Marlinton) (10)	304 799-4604	(not reporting)						
Preston (Kingwood)† (30)	304 329-1805	Ward Thomas	Richard L Weekly	Nancy Reckart	James Liller	....	Delroy Davis	James Liller
Putnam (Winfield) (38)	304 586-9036	(not reporting)						
Raleigh (Beckley) (87)	304 255-9146	Paul H Flanagan	Thomas P Vidovich	Elinor Hurt	Claude England	....	....	Claude England
Randolph (Elkins) (29)	304 636-0543	(not reporting)						
Ritchie (Harrisville) (11)	304 643-2164	(not reporting)						
Roane (Spencer) (16)	304 927-2860	(not reporting)						
Summers (Hinton)† (16)	304 466-4235	Billy Joe Edwards	....	Barbara N Carr	James H Blume Sr	....	Jack D Woodrum	James H Blume Sr
Taylor (Grafton) (17)	304 265-1401	(not reporting)						
Tucker (Parsons) (9)	304 478-2606	(not reporting)						
Tyler (Middlebourne) (11)	304 758-2311	(not reporting)						
Upshur (Buckhannon)† (23)	304 472-1068	....	Leslie Smith	....	....	....	....	....
Wayne (Wayne) (46)	304 272-5101	(not reporting)						
Webster (Webster Springs) (12)	304 847-2508	(not reporting)						
Wetzel (New Martinsville) (22)	304 455-1390	Norman E Morris	....	Pearl Frei	Ora E Stull	Henry Parsons	Rosario Suyao	Ora E Stull
Wirt (Elizabeth)† (5)	304 275-4222	Joseph M Handlan	....	....	Lloyd E Boston	....	....	Lloyd E Boston
Wood (Parkersburg) (94)	304 424-1976	William C Parrish	Mary R Rader	H K Smith	L W Bechtold	....	James Miller	L W Bechtold
Wyoming (Pineville) (36)	304 732-8000	William W Bailey	....	D Michael Goode	H L Hatfield	David Jackson	Samuel Muscari Jr	H L Hatfield
WISCONSIN (72)								
Adams (Friendship) (13)	608 339-4200	Casey Grabarski	....	Rita Pelton	Sharlene Klicko	....	Mary Mudge	Robert Farber
Ashland (Ashland) (17)	715 682-2533	Thomas Kieweg	....	Elaine A Stibbe	....	....	Ruth Johnson RN	Donald Wilmot
Barron (Barron) (39)	715 537-3212	Arnold Ellison	....	Judith A Genereau	Marla K Thompson	....	Kathleen Newman	Wallace Larson
Bayfield (Washburn)† (14)	715 373-5607	Edwin Rendos	....	James C Strom	Daniel R Anderson	Larry Young	Carol Deeth	R Fredericks
Brown (Green Bay)† (175)	414 497-3211	Larry Adams	Donald Holloway	Ronald DeLain	Harold Lemerond	....	Judy Pinkstaff RN	Leon Pieschek
Buffalo (Alma) (14)	608 685-4940	Duane Baertsch	Gale O Hoch	Gale O Hoch	Patricia J Wodele	Bergie Ritscher	....	Robert L Sing
Burnett (Webster) (12)	715 866-4155	Charles Tollander	....	Donald E Iverson	....	....	Dianne L Gravesen	Donald Chell
Calumet (Chilton) (31)	414 849-2361	Carl Wilberscheid	John J Keuler	Donna Hedrich	John J Keuler	....	Ella Guthrie	Dan Gillis
Chippewa (Chippewa Falls) (52)	715 723-4168	Wallace J Bowe	....	Jerome L Dachel	A M Zwiefelhofer	....	Peg Scherlin	James B Revoir

Directory 1/9 continued — COUNTY OFFICIALS IN ALL U.S. COUNTIES

County, county seat, 1980 population (000 omitted),	County telephone number	Board chairman	Appointed administrator	Clerk to the governing board	Chief financial officer	County engineer	County health officer	Chief law enforcement official
WISCONSIN (72) continued								
Clark (Owen) (33)	715 743-3301	Ray J Conzemius	....	Rosalind J Chubb	Ruby Meihack	....	Lois O Guest	David B Bertz
Columbia (Portage) (43)	608 742-2191	Dennis Dorn	....	Signe Johnson	Mary Grunke	....	....	Armin Ohnesorge
Crawford (Prairie du Chien) (17)	608 326-6431	Robert G Dillman	....	Paul Hazen	Martin E Sprosty	....	Rosemary Lochner	Wm C Fillbach
Dane (Madison) (324)	608 266-4599	Roderick Matthews	James N Hubing	Carol N Little	Gene Nelson	Thomas Martinelli	Richard Crim	Jerome Lacke
Dodge (Juneau) (75)	414 386-4411	H J Kreutzmann	G G Lichtenberg	Dorothy Ebert	Roger Gorst	....	Nancy Doepke	Ted Meekma
Door (Sturgeon Bay)† (25)	414 743-5511	Harvey J Malzahn	....	Robert Papke	Chester Ostram	Donald Richmond	John Beck MD	Leroy Klein
Douglas (Superior) (44)	715 394-0341	Douglas Finn	....	R Somerville	Mary Berg	Michael Strauman	Patrick Heiser	Frederick Johnson
Dunn (Menomonie)§† (34)	715 232-1677	....	John C Krizek	....	....	....	....	....
Eau Claire (Eau Claire) (79)	715 839-5106	C W Chatterson	Ronald T Wampler	Joanne Lester	Larry L Lokken	Thomas R Walther	John A Bacharach	Larry W Jacobson
Florence (Florence) (4)	715 528-3201	Edwin Kelley	....	Robert Anderson	Marilyn Harrison	Richard Leffler	Karen Wertanen	Jacob Neuens
Fond du Lac (Fond du Lac) (89)	414 929-3000	Wilbert Halbach	....	Joyce Buechel	Otto W Sutter	....	Diane Cappozzo	Thomas W Snyder
Forest (Crandon) (9)	715 478-2422	Erhard Huettl	....	Dora James	Marie Palmer	Ronald Brooks	Judy Hitchcock RN	Edgar Wilson
Grant (Lancaster) (52)	608 723-2711	Mary L Wirth	....	Dorothea Eck	Beverly Hartnett	Daniel Wagner	Linda Adrian	Herbert Hottenste
Green (Monroe) (30)	608 328-8288	(not reporting)						
Green Lake (Green Lake) (18)	414 294-6581	Herbert Dahlke	....	Edward Riggs	....	....	Betty Johnson	Herman Rasmussen
Iowa (Dodgeville) (20)	608 935-5445	Richard Scullion	....	Claire Olson	Clifford Olson	....	Joyce Berning	Nicholas Basting
Iron (Hurley) (7)	715 561-3375	(not reporting)						
Jackson (Black River Falls)† (17)	715 284-7441	Keith Ferries	....	Alice Larson	Delores Walton	Harlow Nelson	Karen Bryns	Craig Amidon
Jefferson (Jefferson)† (66)	414 674-2500	Hilmer H Groth	Willard D Hausen	Barbara A Geyer	Edward M Jensen	....	Eileen M Taylor	Keith L Mueller
Juneau (Mauston) (21)	608 847-5849	C F Saylor	....	Carl Wilke	Betty Siekert	....	....	Gervse Thompson
Kenosha (Kenosha) (123)	414 656-6455	Angelo Capriotti	....	John R Collins	Ruth Radatz	....	Esther Alexanian	D Piencikowski
Kewaunee (Kewaunee)† (20)	414 388-3580	Harold Reckelberg	....	Edward J Dorner	Roland L Baierl	....	R M Nesemann	Jerry H Coenen
La Crosse (La Crosse) (91)	608 785-9581	Charles H Pierce	....	Russell L Fiedler	Joann P Anderson	Harvey Shisler	Douglas Mormann	Sylvia Boma
Lafayette (Darlington)† (17)	608 776-4003	Richard McKnight	....	Stephen J Pickett	Lila M Benson	....	Mary E Oechlsin	Kenneth Pratt
Langlade (Antigo) (20)	715 627-6200	Marvin Tessmer	....	Norman J Cejka	Mary Novak	....	....	John H Hoffman
Lincoln (Merrill) (26)	715 536-7444	(not reporting)						
Manitowoc (Manitowoc) (83)	414 683-4000	Donald Vogt	....	James Kornely	Harold Blumer	Dale Wech	Helen Mueller	Thomas Kocourek
Marathon (Wausau)§ (111)	715 847-5000	Edward Fenhaus	Charles P Balczun	Raymond H Ott	....	....	George Million	Louis Gianoli
Marinette (Marinette) (39)	715 735-3371	Theodore J Sauve	....	Robert M Harbick	Roger L DeGroot	....	Mary T Mursau RN	Joseph M Larson
Marquette (Montello) (12)	414 297-2532	Thomas McDowell	....	Gary L Sorensen	Shirley Procknow	Larry Laing	Ruby Dow	Kelly Campion
Menominee (Keshena)† (3)	715 799-3311	Harley Lyons Sr	Hilary Waukau Sr	Carol A Latender	....	....	Ruth E Gatz	James Tourtillott
Milwaukee (Milwaukee) (965)	414 278-4223	F Thomas Ament	....	Thomas Zablocki	Emil Stanislawski	Gerald Schwerm	....	Richard E Artison
Monroe (Sparta) (35)	608 269-8718	Louis W Schlaver	....	David Hering	Patricia Harrie	George Baker	....	Timothy Donovan
Oconto (Oconto) (29)	414 834-5322	(not reporting)						
Oneida (Rhinelander) (31)	715 369-2727	(not reporting)						
Outagamie (Appleton) (129)	414 735-5255	George Schroeder	John R Schreiter	James Hensel	Peter L Berg	....	....	Thomas Drootsan
Ozaukee (Port Washington) (67)	414 284-9411	(not reporting)						
Pepin (Durand) (7)	715 672-8704	Donald A Sommers	Donna L Yenter	James R Bresina	Olga A Vogel	....	Richard J Bryant	Roger D Britton
Pierce (Ellsworth) (31)	715 273-5272	(not reporting)						
Polk (Balsam Lake) (32)	715 485-3161	George Vollert	....	Elroy Spangenberg	David Anderson	Wm Hansen	....	Kenneth Madsen
Portage (Stevens Point) (57)	715 346-1351	Robert Steinke	Jerry Glad	Roger Wrycza	Alfred Bartkowiak	....	....	Daniel Hintz
Price (Phillips) (16)	715 339-3325	Edgar Granberg	....	Clarence Cvengros	J Muriel Cress	....	Carol Dahlie	Michael Johnson
Racine (Racine)† (173)	414 636-3118	James F Rooney	....	Dennis Kornwolf	Douglas Stansil	Patrick Carroll	Grace Rose	Robert Rohner
Richland (Richland Center) (17)	608 647-2197	Merlyn Merry	....	Bernal W Coy	Marie F Davis	....	....	William Breneman
Rock (Janesville)§ (139)	608 755-2010	Donald E Upson	Craig G Knutson	Gregory Seefeldt	Nikolaus Korndorf	....	Larry M Eils	F Joseph Black
Rusk (Ladysmith) (16)	715 532-5579	Marvin Hanson	....	Richard B Sargent	Anne Gibbs	Ken Zimmer	Kathleen Mai	William Volkman
Sauk (Baraboo) (43)	608 356-5581	Melvin Rose	....	Opal Kohlmeyer	Melvin Brandt	Donald McConagy	Cathy Vanderboom	Alan B Shanks
Sawyer (Hayward) (13)	715 634-4866	(not reporting)						
Shawano (Shawano)† (36)	715 526-9150	Harry Bauman	....	....	....	....	....	....
Sheboygan (Sheboygan) (101)	414 459-3103	Harold Lindemann	....	P Jaschinski	Hans Fischer	Roger Lanning	....	Jhon Webb
St. Croix (Hudson) (44)	715 386-5581	Norman E Anderson	....	Jill Berke	M J Livermore	....	Agnes Welsch	Luverne Burke
Taylor (Medford) (19)	715 748-3131	Edwin Ahlers	....	Roger Emmerich	Alvin Sova	....	Mary Farning	Alfred Palmer
Trempealeau (Whitehall) (26)	715 538-2311	Earl Ryder	....	Harold Tomter	Vitus Kampa	....	....	Noble Kleven
Vernon (Viroqua) (26)	608 637-3569	(not reporting)						
Vilas (Eagle River) (17)	715 479-6469	(not reporting)						
Walworth (Elkhorn) (72)	414 723-4900	Robert Stevenson	....	....	....	....	....	....
Washburn (Shell Lake) (13)	715 468-7808	Eugene F Barret	....	John L Brown	Alta F Kallenbach	....	Ellen Erlandson	Marvin L Anderson
Washington (West Bend) (85)	414 338-4400	Reuben J Schmahl	....	George F Nehrbass	Fredric Seefeldt	....	Pauline Harder	Clarence Schwartz
Waukesha (Waukesha) (280)	414 548-7194	Betty Cooper	....	Audrey A Carlson	Dorothy Macdonald	Vincil Demshar	Herbert Ripley	Raymond Klink
Waupaca (Waupaca) (43)	715 258-2128	Loran H Frazier	....	Eleanor J Dretzke	John H Devaud	....	Duwayne Tanner RN	William E Mork
Waushara (Wautoma) (19)	414 787-4631	George Sorenson	....	Harold Prochnow	Mary L Oligney	....	E Ann Buck	Norman Weiss
Winnebago (Oshkosh) (132)	414 235-2500	Paul Stevenson	....	Dorothy L Propp	Delore LaMarche	....	Marsha Brightman	Terry Footit
Wood (Wisconsin Rapids) (73)	715 421-8460	David L Draves	....	Anthony Ruesch	David Goetz	....	Janet Mensching	Robert Bodette
WYOMING (23)								
Albany (Laramie)† (29)	307 742-2149	Max W Rardin	....	Linda C Darty	....	....	Galyn Stahl	Donald L Fritzen
Big Horn (Basin) (12)	307 568-2357	Kenneth Bullinger	....	Ellen Cowan Whipp	George H Hoffman	Herbert Jennerich	R McLean MD	Gary J Anders
Campbell (Gillette) (24)	307 682-7283	W B Fitch	....	Vivian E Addison	Shirley Study	Wm F Flaherty	George McMurtrey	D B Hladky
Carbon (Rawlins) (22)	307 328-2668	Robert Grieve	....	Mary G Bradford	Mary Aydelott	Frank Smith	Daniel S Klein MD	C W Ogburn
Converse (Douglas) (14)	307 358-2244	(not reporting)						
Crook (Sundance)† (5)	307 283-1975	Donald C Gose	....	Ruth E Davidson	Karen G Glover	....	Jerri Villano MD	Ronald H Pulse
Fremont (Lander)† (40)	307 322-2870	J M Kail	....	James A Farthing	Lew A Lee	....	John Gilbertson	Tim McKinney
Goshen (Torrington) (12)	307 532-4051	(not reporting)						
Hot Springs (Thermopolis) (6)	307 864-3515	Frank Rhodes	....	Bette R Anderson	Grace E Allard	....	Nels E Vicklunc	Deloyd Quarberg
Johnson (Buffalo) (7)	307 684-7555	Simon J Berlin	....	Carol J Barton	Dugal W Dickerson	....	Patrick D Nolan	Larry Kirkpatrick
Laramie (Cheyenne) (69)	307 638-4240	(not reporting)						
Lincoln (Kemmerer)† (12)	307 877-9056	Boyd L Eddins	....	Elisabeth Wade	Betty Des Rosiers	....	Janet Andrews	T Deb Wolfley
Natrona (Casper) (72)	307 235-9200	Frank L Schulte	R A Rowlands	John J Tobin	Edith Howard	....	Walter B Watson	John M Barrett
Niobrara (Lusk) (3)	307 334-2211	Lewis L Landkamer	....	Betty F Morgan	Dede Reed	....	William Craske	Gene H Bryson
Park (Cody) (22)	307 587-5548	(not reporting)						
Platte (Wheatland)† (12)	307 322-2315	Don Olson	....	D K Purcell	Betty Dunham	J K Kennedy	William Wilson MD	Einer Mickelsen
Sheridan (Sheridan) (25)	307 674-6722	W B Frith	....	Margaret Lewis	Sylvia Sadler	J T Hollingsworth	....	William H Johnson
Sublette (Pinedale) (5)	307 367-4372	Floyd E Bousman	....	Lois J Yake	Nylla Kunard	....	J Thomas Johnston	Wm P Slatter
Sweetwater (Green River) (42)	307 875-2611	Fred Radosevich	....	Albert B Vesco	Albert B Vesco	John T Nelson	Elmer McKay MD	James Stark
Teton (Jackson) (9)	307 733-4430	(not reporting)						
Uinta (Evanston) (13)	307 789-3815	(not reporting)						
Washakie (Worland) (9)	307 347-3131	Robert A Swander	....	Marion Barngrover	Maryellen Hampton	Donald Wolford	Edward C Horsley	Tim Upton
Weston (Newcastle) (7)	307 746-4744	(not reporting)						

Directory 1/10 MUNICIPAL OFFICIALS IN ALL U.S. CITIES OVER 2,500

The data for the directory of municipal officials were collected by the International City Management Association (ICMA) during the summer of 1984 through a mail survey. The 7,008 municipalities surveyed include all incorporated places with a population 2,500 and over and those places under 2,500 recognized by ICMA as having either the council-manager form of government or a position of overall general management.

In addition to the names of officials (and the municipal phone number) data on race and sex are collected for the mayor, appointed administrator, city clerk, finance director, personnel director, planning director, fire chief, police chief, public works director, and purchasing director. The positions of personnel director, planning director, and purchasing director are not shown in the individual city directory that follows. All data collected other than the names and phone number are treated with complete confidentiality, and only aggregate data are presented below.

Sex and Race of Municipal Officials. Tables 1/10/a and 1/10/b present a breakdown of each sex by race for the municipal officials. Given the level of detail shown it is possible to reaggregate these data for other displays that would show race and sex characteristics for the total number of officials reporting.

The positions shown are most often held by males with the exception of municipal clerk; 68.6% of the persons holding that position are female. Whites are predominant in each of the positions shown. Other than whites, blacks (male and female combined) are more dominant in the positions of mayor, city clerk, personnel director, planning director, police chief, fire chief, public works director, and purchasing director. In the other positions, the number of Mexican-Americans is equal to or greater than that of blacks.

Overall, females account for 17.5% of the total officials reporting. The number of females in 1984 is greater than the 1983 level for all positions except fire chief.

The Directory. For convenience, the directory shows the names of municipalities in alphabetical order within each state. The 7,008 municipalities listed represent over 48,000 names listed in the directory. Other items indicated in the directory for each municipality are the type of municipality (city, village, town, township, borough, or plantation), form of government, population, and municipal phone number. Recognition by ICMA is also indicated as appropriate.

Table 1/10/a MALE MUNICIPAL OFFICIALS BY RACE

		Total males		Race														Race not reported	
				White		Black		Mexican-American		American Indian		Oriental		Other					
Position	Total reporting (A)	No. (B)	% of (A)	No.	% of (B)	No.	% of (B)	No.	% of (B)	No.	% of (B)	No.	% of (B)	No.	% of (B)			No.	% of (B)
Mayors	6,707	6,146	91.6	5,657	92.0	96	1.6	71	1.2	12	0.2	10	0.2	5	0.1			295	4.8
Appointed administrators	4,424	4,009	90.6	3,697	92.2	37	0.9	51	1.3	5	0.1	5	0.1	9	0.2			205	5.1
Clerks	6,372	1,980	31.1	1,848	93.3	24	1.2	20	1.0	1	0.1	2	0.1	1	0.1			84	4.2
Finance directors	5,278	3,563	67.5	3,297	92.5	24	0.7	44	1.2	0	0.0	22	0.6	2	0.1			174	4.9
Personnel directors[1]	2,817	2,063	73.2	1,884	91.3	54	2.6	36	1.7	1	0.0	3	0.1	5	0.2			80	3.9
Planning directors[1]	3,296	2,960	89.8	2,689	90.8	39	1.3	44	1.5	3	0.1	22	0.7	3	0.1			160	5.4
Fire chiefs	6,154	6,131	99.6	5,704	93.0	42	0.7	43	0.7	13	0.2	4	0.1	2	0.0			323	5.3
Police chiefs	6,368	6,327	99.4	5,833	92.2	95	1.5	84	1.3	16	0.3	0	0.0	4	0.1			295	4.7
Public works directors	5,443	5,362	98.5	4,925	91.9	79	1.5	70	1.3	8	0.1	19	0.4	11	0.2			250	4.7
Purchasing directors[1]	2,359	1,798	76.2	1,632	90.8	32	1.8	38	2.1	1	0.1	7	0.4	3	0.2			85	4.7

Note: The sum of males and females does not correspond to the total reporting because the sex of some respondents was not indicated and could not be determined from the respondent's name.
Leaders (. . .) indicate less than 0.05%.
[1] This position is not shown in the directory of municipal officials.

Table 1/10/b FEMALE MUNICIPAL OFFICIALS BY RACE

		Total females		Race												Race not reported	
				White		Black		Mexican-American		American Indian		Oriental		Other			
Position	Total reporting (A)	No. (B)	% of (A)	No.	% of (B)	No.	% of (B)	No.	% of (B)	No.	% of (B)	No.	% of (B)	No.	% of (B)	No.	% of (B)
Mayors	6,707	536	8.0	491	91.6	6	1.1	4	0.7	0	0.0	0	0.0	0	0.0	35	6.5
Appointed administrators	4,424	374	8.5	344	92.0	5	1.3	4	1.1	1	0.3	0	0.0	0	0.0	20	5.3
Clerks	6,372	4,369	68.6	4,063	93.0	50	1.1	60	1.4	12	0.3	8	0.2	1	0.0	175	4.0
Finance directors	5,278	1,694	32.1	1,576	93.0	14	0.8	13	0.8	4	0.2	3	0.2	0	0.0	84	5.0
Personnel directors[1]	2,817	732	26.0	635	86.7	44	6.0	13	1.8	2	0.3	2	0.3	0	0.0	36	4.9
Planning directors[1]	3,296	322	9.8	287	89.1	11	3.4	3	0.9	2	0.6	3	0.9	0	0.0	16	5.0
Fire chiefs	6,154	0	0.0	0	89.1	0	3.4	0	0.9	0	0.6	0	0.9	0	0.0	0	5.0
Police chiefs	6,368	13	0.2	11	84.6	0	0.0	0	0.0	0	0.0	0	0.0	0	0.0	2	15.4
Public works directors	5,443	46	0.8	39	84.8	1	2.2	2	4.3	0	0.0	0	0.0	0	0.0	4	8.7
Purchasing directors[1]	2,359	538	22.8	488	90.7	16	3.0	11	2.0	5	0.9	2	0.4	0	0.0	16	3.0

Note: The sum of males and females does not correspond to the total reporting because the sex of some respondents was not indicated and could not be determined from the respondent's name.
Leaders (. . .) indicate less than 0.05%.
[1] This position is not shown in the directory of municipal officials.

Directory 1/10 MUNICIPAL OFFICIALS IN ALL U.S. CITIES OVER 2,500[1]

Form of government
CM Council-manager
CO Commission
MC Mayor-council
RT Representative town meeting
TM Town meeting

Municipal designation
b borough
pl plantation
t town
tp township
v village

Population
. . Less than 500 population

Other codes
† Information from previous Year Books
* Recognized by ICMA as municipality with council-manager form of government
§ Recognized by ICMA as municipality with position of overall general management
. . . . Data not reported or not applicable

City, 1980 population (000 omitted), form of government		Municipal phone number	Mayor	Appointed administrator	City clerk	Finance officer	Fire chief	Police chief	Public works director
ALABAMA (134)									
Abbeville (3)	MC	205 585-3221	C C Vickrey	....	J M Giganti Jr	J M Giganti Jr	Carroll Grimes	F E Deaton	Dickie Clark
Alabaster (7)	MC	205 663-3922	H A Rubin	....	Dorothy Henry	....	John C Cochran	C E Carter	....
Albertville (12)	MC	205 878-0431	Gordon Henderson	....	Frank B Volenvine	Frank B Volenvine	Johnny M Rollings	Tommie Cole	Herbert Chaffin
Alexander City (14)	MC	205 329-8426	Charles Bailey	....	George H Gordon	....	Marvin Still	Lynn Royall	Harold McClellan
Aliceville§ (3)	MC	205 373-6611	Roth Hook	B Tommy McKinstry	Annie M Russell	....	Everett Owens	David Markem	....
Andalusia† (10)	MC	205 222-3311	Benjamin T Williams	....	Roland Carter	Roland Carter	Phillip Hughes	John Ellis	....
Anniston* (30)	CM	205 236-3421	Gertrude R Williams	Robert C Cheatham	Mary Owen Brisky	Thomas N Wright	Horace Holland	C Wayne Chandler	Donald W Warden
Arab t (6)	CO	205 586-3544	Lamonte Davis	....	Barbara B White	....	Tommy Prestridge	Jack Banister	Bud Blakely
Athens (15)	MC	205 233-2220	Bobby Wood	....	Mignon Bowers	....	Wilson Craig	Richard H Faulk	Billy Swanner
Atmore (9)	MC	205 368-2246	Patricia McKenzie	....	Louise W Day	Louise W Day	Charles Rutherford	James Dixon	Lloyd Biggs
Attalla (8)	MC	205 538-9986	Garry W Shirley	....	Jane Phillips	Jane Phillips	Olin Eubanks	Earl Lee	Kermit Roberts
Auburn* (28)	CM	205 821-1900	Jan Dempsey	Douglas J Watson	Douglas J Watson	Levi A Knapp	Ellis Mitchell	Billy G Holder	Frank Scully
Bay Minette† (7)	MC	205 937-5502	John F Rhodes	Harry Still Sr	Tommy M Langham	Charles W Strong Jr	Tim Blakemore	John C Trough	Harry Still Sr
Bessemer† (32)	CO	205 424-4060	Ed Porter	....	H W Mitchell Jr	H W Mitchell Jr	Joe Roberson	Jenda Smith	Amos Hyche
Birmingham (284)	MC	205 254-2000	R Arrington Jr	Willie Davis	Jackson B Bailey	Richard Martin	Neal Gallant	Arthur Deutcsh	John Duncan
Boaz (7)	MC	205 593-5741	(not reporting)						
Brent (3)	MC	205 926-4643	(not reporting)						
Brewton (7)	MC	205 867-3281	Ray M Sherer	....	J P Maxwell Jr	....	J H Martin	H Glenn Holt	....
Bridgeport t† (3)	MC	205 495-3892	James Russell Lee	F M Lee	F M Lee		Jim Mashburn	Don Godfrey	James Russell Lee
Brighton (5)	MC	205 425-8934	Richard L Lewis	....	Ella P Hairston	Ella P Hairston	Warren Smith	Frank Ellington	....
Brundidge t† (3)	CO	205 735-2385	John H Senn	....	Britt Thomas	....	Douglas T Ingram	Joe F Connell	Rex O'Connell
Centreville (3)	MC	205 926-4995	(not reporting)						
Chickasaw† (7)	MC	205 452-2225	J C Davis Jr	....	Iris Evans	Iris Evans	C E Hollinghead	C E Hollinghead	Sam E Lee
Childersburg (5)	MC	205 378-5521	B J Meeks	....	J Derek Hill	J Derek Hill	Douglas Blair	Ira F Finn	....
Citronelle (3)	MC	205 866-7973	H C Bassett	....	Diane D Barnett		Golee Andrews	W Roy Mason	
Clanton† (6)	MC	205 755-1105	F Basil Clark	....	Faye Swanner	F Basil Clark	Johnny Smith	James Henderson	F Basil Clark
Columbiana (3)	MC	205 669-6242	J D Falkner	....	Mary D Largin	....	Johnny Farr	Howell Y Horn	James Palmer
Cordova t (3)	MC	205 483-9266	Boyd Jackson	....	Mary M Kelly	....	Joe Christian	Henry H Lynn	Jess Reed
Cullman (13)	MC	205 739-1212	Robert E McGukin	....	Elizabeth B Hughes	Elizabeth B Hughes	Junior Walker	Roy Wood Jr	Kenneth Speegle
Dadeville t (3)	MC	205 825-9242	(not reporting)						
Daleville† (4)	MC	205 598-2345	Gene L Hughes	....	Charles A Spencer	....	William L Ingram	William L Ingram	....
Daphne t† (3)	MC	205 626-2628	A Victor Guarisco	....	Barbara A Baggette	A Victor Guarisco	Boyd L Nelson	Joseph H Hall	Ray Simmons
Decatur (42)	MC	205 355-7410	Bill J Dukes	....	Gail Busbey	Dorothy O Lorenza	Paul Kilgore	Frank Shafer	C B Armstrong
Demopolis (8)	MC	205 289-0577	Hugh Allen	....	Dolly S Ward	....	Aubrey Randall	Johnie R Brock	....
Dothan§ (49)	MC	205 793-0100	Kenneth Everett	M D Cunningham	M D Cunningham	Frank Etheredge	Ben Ray Barnes	Kater W Williams	Gary Martin
East Brewton t (3)	MC	205 867-6092	Lovelace Parker	....	Karen H Singleton	....	Guyland E Langham	David Dixon	....
Elba (4)	MC	205 897-2333	Bob M English	....	Durward M English	....	....	John White	....
Enterprise† (18)	MC	205 347-2251	G C Donaldson	Carl Griffin	Carl Griffin	Carl Griffin	B J Watson	Robert Paschal	Henry Lunsford
Eufaula (12)	MC	205 687-6621	(not reporting)						
Evergreen† (4)	MC	205 578-1574	Lee F Smith	....	Miller T Sellers	....	Matthew Davis Jr	James Powell	....
Fairfield† (13)	MC	205 788-2492	Johnny T Nichols	....	Grady M Ellison	Grady M Ellison	Charley Carnes	Laird J Sharpe	Paul Domostoy
Fairhope (7)	MC	205 928-2136	James P Nix	....	Evelyn P Phillips	Richard Dunning	Donnie Walker	Leo Gilheart	Phil Rutherford
Fayette (5)	MC	205 932-5367	Guthrie J Smith	....	Patricia Durr	Patricia Durr	Robert Fulmer	Ralph Olive	....
Florence§ (37)	MC	205 764-7271	William E Batson	E Graham Edwards	James E Wilson	James E Wilson	W R Bevis	Leo Bailey	Ernest A Fite
Foley† (4)	MC	205 943-1545	Arthur A Holk	....	Fred G Mott	G Frank Smyth	Ralph Shumacher	Wilbur Willis	James E Wright
Fort Payne† (11)	MC	205 845-1524	Fred W Purdy	....	Marjorie Roden	....	Milton L Leath Jr	Frank D Parker	....
Fultondale† (6)	MC	205 841-6456	Curtis Parks Jr	....	Milton W Stuckey	....	Bruce C Coggin	William J Finn	George B Davidson
Gadsden† (48)	CO	205 543-9870	Steve Means	....	Martha A Elrod	Norman G Reaves	Gerald Mayo	M L Carter	E M Pledger
Gardendale (8)	MC	205 631-8787	G William Noble	....	Bettye Dickey	Bettye Dickey	Clint Doss	Hoyatt McCain	Wendell Phillips
Geneva† (5)	MC	205 684-9500	Hugh Herring Jr	....	Sheron Enfinger	....	Harry Chancy	Elray Derouen	O'Neal Jerkins
Glencoe t† (5)	MC	205 492-1424	John A Sewell	....	Rosa H St John	....	Jerry Lay	Charles Rutledge	David Hare
Graysville (3)	MC	205 674-5643	Wayne Tuggle	....	Judy Flippo	Wayne Tuggle	Russell D Riley	James R Martin	Paul D Busby
Greensboro† (3)	MC	205 624-8119	John C Jay Jr	....	Sharon Davis	John C Jay Jr	Alvin McCrory	Gary Bice	John C Jay Jr
Greenville (8)	MC	205 382-2647	(not reporting)						
Guntersville (7)	MC	205 582-2120	Robert L Hembree	....	Lena Kennamer	Robert L Hembree	Dewey F Wales	Jerry Gamble	....
Haleyville (5)	MC	205 486-3121	Larry Gilliland	....	Tommie L Robinson	....	Leon Bridges	Roger Cooper	....
Hamilton t (5)	MC	205 921-2121	E T Sims Jr	....	Barbara G Partain	Barbara G Partain	Billy H Loden	Willard Frye	E T Sims Jr
Hartford† (3)	MC	205 588-2245	John A Hughes Jr	H R Lee	Linda A Brannon	....	Gary L Adkison	Junior Smith	H R Lee
Hartselle§ (9)	MC	205 773-2535	Don Brown	....	Betty P Parker	Betty P Parker	P C Hill	J P Orr	Mel Waterman
Headland (3)	MC	205 693-3365	D Winston Griggs Jr	....	Elizabeth G White	....	Pete Brackin	Noel Manasco	....
Heflin t (3)	MC	205 463-2291	Ewell Parker	....	Jane Shockley	Ewell Parker	Rudell Perry	J C Lambert	....
Hokes Bluff t (3)	MC	205 492-2414	(not reporting)						
Homewood (21)	MC	205 877-8600	Robert G Waldrop	....	Marilyn W Grubbs	Marilyn W Grubbs	Albert Evans	Jerry T Haynes	Pierce J England
Hoover t† (15)	MC	205 979-1854	Frank S Skinner Jr	....	Anita Steiner	William Billingsley	Tom Bradley	David Cummings	....
Hueytown† (13)	MC	205 491-7010	Preston E Darden	....	Dan Tunmire	....	John M Bradley	Edw H Robinson Jr	....
Huntsville (143)	MC	205 532-7000	Joe W Davis	Ralph E Gipson	Ruby C Neeley	Ruby C Neeley	Hugh A Luna	Salvatore Vizzini	C D Black
Irondale† (7)	MC	205 956-9200	Charles H Eagar	....	Fay McCoy	Fay McCoy	John B McDanal	William C McSween	Thomas Bryant
Jackson (6)	MC	205 246-2461	James E Arrington	....	Wayne Brunson	....	Geo W Skipper Jr	William S Taylor	Charles A Walston
Jacksonville (10)	MC	205 435-7611	John B Nisbet Jr	....	Betty B Marbut	....	Ernest Henderson	Paul Locke	Curtis Cunningham
Jasper* (12)	CM	205 221-2100	John C Nicholson	Lucius G Freeman	Doris McAdams	Valerie Bulloch	Marion Cooner	Joe Filyaw	James E Haynes
Lafayette† (4)	MC	205 864-9812	J Edward Yeargan	....	....	....	Keith Wilkerson	Mike Looser	John Julian Cotter

Directory 1/10 continued — MUNICIPAL OFFICIALS IN ALL U.S. CITIES OVER 2,500[1]

City, 1980 population (000 omitted), form of government	Municipal phone number	Mayor	Appointed administrator	City clerk	Finance officer	Fire chief	Police chief	Public works director
ALABAMA (134) continued								
Lanett† (7) MC	205 644-2141	Mac H Langley	Charles Jennings	Linda Hamby	Shirley B Motley	Harry Hudson	James A Smith	Robert Boyd
Leeds (9) MC	205 699-2581	Jack Courson	....	Gladys D Prentice	....	Clark Kennedy	Clarence Bailey	Arnold Pike
Linden (3) MC	205 295-4121	Roy P Vice	William E Barley	Cheryl S Fultz	William E Barley	Brady W Creel	Brady W Creel	Alton R Anderson
Lipscomb (4) MC	205 428-6374	M T Wesson	....	Nelta Files	Donald Mooney	Larry Reaves	Johnny C Woods	....
Livingston*† (3) CM	205 652-2505	Thomas M Tartt	Thomas C Luke	Thomas C Luke	Thomas C Luke	John Snider	Larry Moody	Moreland Nixon
Luverne† (3) MC	205 335-3741	Clemant Carpenter	....	....	....	....	....	....
Madison (4) CO	205 772-0111	Burwell L Wilbanks	....	Betty T Benson	Burwell L Wilbanks	Charles Wallace	Charles Graves	Ray Sanderson
Marion§ (4) MC	205 683-6545	Douglas J Moore	W David Cobb	Carolyn G Thomas	Carolyn G Thomas	Vernon G Crocker	John W Anderson	....
Midfield (7) MC	205 923-7578	Arnold N Burgess	....	Alta Jean McQueen	....	....	James W Morris	Roy Keller
Millbrook† (3) MC	205 285-6428	L Reginald Minter	....	Rebecca Lott	Rebecca Lott	Brian Bodine	Donald W Buzbee	....
Mobile (200) CO	205 438-7411	Lambert C Mims	....	Richard L Smith	Patrick W Kelly	Lloyd J Freeman	Robert P Larison	Thomas K Peavy
Monroeville (6) MC	205 575-2081	B C Hornady	....	Mary S Myrick	Mary S Myrick	W D Pickens	Charles E Colbert	Lyle W Salter
Montevallo (4) MC	205 665-2555	Ralph W Sears	Donald H Hughes	....	....	S M Mahan Jr	Allen Needham	....
Montgomery† (178) MC	205 832-4417	Emory Folmar	John J Hogg Jr	John L Baker	Hugh S Austin	Jim Sutherland	Charles E Swindall	....
Moulton t (3) MC	205 974-5191	H A Alexander	....	Barbara Coffey	....	Lyndon Blaxton	J C Holliday	....
Mountain Brook* (17) CM	205 870-3532	T A Gaskin Jr	J Wayne Campbell	Ann R McCutcheon	J Sam Collins	Charles T Oakley	John F Haley	Cecil W Amason
Muscle Shoals t (9) CO	205 383-5675	(not reporting)						
Northport (14) MC	205 349-1133	(not reporting)						
Oneonta (5) MC	205 274-2150	Jack Fendley	....	Delene Gibbs	....	Charles Montgomery	Earl Fortenberry	....
Opelika (22) CO	205 745-3461	Guy Thompson	....	Zane E Burleson	Zane E Burleson	Albert Smith	Ronald L Dunson	Jack White
Opp (7) MC	205 493-4572	Malcom L Senn Sr	Carl M Cosby II	Carl M Cosby II	Roy R Jeffcoat	Jake J Benton	Jerry Brannon	Charles D McGowan
Oxford t (9) MC	205 831-7510	Therman Whitmore	....	Ernestine Boyles	Ernestine Boyles	Dewey Webb	Stanley Merrill	David Rooks
Ozark (13) MC	205 774-5393	Billy J Blackmon	....	Sam Parker	Sam Parker	Pat White	Allen Benefield	Billy Blackwell
Pelham t† (7) MC	205 663-3901	Burk Dunaway	....	Willie Mae Dennis	Ray Hamilton	William Bryars	Dave Watson	Paul Yeager
Pell City (7) MC	205 338-2244	Hugh H Williamson	S Con Coupland	Bettie Scott	....	Ben Windsor	Homer C Layton Jr	James A Tyus
Phenix City*† (27) CM	205 298-5649	Jane Gullatt	John M Franklin	O Neal Kindred	Jan Thomas	James Montgomery	Bobby F Ellis	Walter Sparks
Piedmont (6) MC	205 447-2511	(not reporting)						
Pleasant Grove (7) MC	205 744-7221	Hollis H Cain	....	Sarah A Mays	....	John Scholl	Robert L Love	Rufus Long
Prattville (19) MC	205 365-9997	C Gray Price	Jerry D Sims	Rubye E Kennedy	Rubye E Kennedy	Donald McGough	E R Crew	J N Buckner Jr
Prichard (40) MC	205 457-3381	John H Smith	Eva C Greene	Eva C Greene	Eva C Greene	Daniel Scoggin	Tyree Richberg	Malachi Jones
Rainbow City t (6) MC	205 442-2511	Sue L Glidewell	....	Dorothy T Lee	Sue L Glidewell	Jack Thornton	L Williason II	L A Dunn
Rainsville t† (4) MC	205 638-6331	Vaughn T Goggans	....	Sue Bowman	....	Freddie W Wilson	Jerry Fairris	....
Red Bay (3) MC	205 356-4473	(not reporting)						
Roanoke† (6) MC	205 863-4129	Henry V Bonner	....	Olin E Sheppard	....	Vernon Tobin	Floyd Fetner	....
Roosevelt (3) MC	205 426-1261	(not reporting)						
Russellville† (8) MC	205 332-6060	Leonard O Allen	....	Keith Gladney	....	Harlon Hutcheson	Burns Saint	Norris L Moore
Saraland (10) MC	205 675-5103	Charles W Harben	....	Mary L Potter	....	Ravon Allen	Franklin Pridgen	Ronald Brown
Satsuma† (4) MC	205 675-1440	Charles E Little	....	Earline F McKinley	....	Bonney B Barlow	Bonney B Barlow	....
Scottsboro (15) MC	205 574-3100	Lonnie E Crawford	....	Gail Duffey	....	Lonnie Webb	Keith Smith	Hollis Johnson
Selma (27) MC	205 875-3500	Joe T Smitherman	....	Hugh A Wall	Hugh A Wall	James W Foster	Melvin Summerlin	Carroll Shoultz
Sheffield† (12) CO	205 383-0250	Howard	....	James L Sparks	James L Sparks	Odell Murry	Warren Aycock	Charles Welch
Southside t† (5) MC	205 442-2255	W W Burns	....	Sue Price	....	Tom Russell	Johnnie T Huie	....
Stevenson (3) MC	205 437-2920	B R Thomas	....	Bettye T Jackson	....	Mack Morris	Jon W Steckel	....
Sumiton t (3) MC	205 648-3261	(not reporting)						
Sylacauga (13) MC	205 249-4353	Gene E Stewart	....	John Newberry	John Newberry	Prima Herd	Billy Hay	Eddie Bentley
Talladega (19) CO	205 362-8186	Larry H Barton	....	George C Montgomery	Ken Payne	Tom Jeff Partridge	Michael J Hamlin	James Perley
Tallassee (5) MC	205 283-6571	Thomas W Pollard	....	Betty J Elrod	Betty J Elrod	Fred Piper	Gordon Thornell	Charles Mulder
Tarrant City (8) MC	205 841-2758	Robert J Burns	Anne M Byrom	....	....	Herbert McAlpine	James D Phillips	W T Baggett
Thomasville (4) MC	205 636-5827	(not reporting)						
Troy† (13) CO	205 566-0177	G A Gibbs	....	Jimmy A Floyd	Jimmy A Floyd	A B Tillery	M D Benefield	Joe Lance Jackson
Trussville t (4) MC	205 655-7478	H David Nicodemus	....	Joellen Townsend	....	Jerrial Williams	Irving Nash	....
Tuscaloosa (75) CO	205 349-2010	Alvin P Dupont	....	George F Lamb	J V Dockery	James L Watts	Winston A Morris	Walter D Lawley Jr
Tuscumbia§ (9) CO	205 383-5463	Bendall W Hollis	....	Flora Hanback	Bendall W Hollis	Harold McKee	Charles Thompson	Charles Lewis
Tuskegee† (13) MC	205 727-2180	Johnny Ford	....	Linda J Carroll	Jesse Upshaw	Luther Curry	Joseph Walker	William Foster
Union Springs (4) MC	205 738-2720	Johnnie G McGowan	....	Doris B Roten	Joseph L Davis Jr	Thomas May	T W Tillery	Larry Singleton
Valley (9) MC	205 756-3131	John H Hood	....	Jennifer Abrams	....	....	Arthur E Carmack Jr	....
Vernon† (3) MC	205 695-7718	Allen McNees	....	....	....	....	....	....
Vestavia Hills (16) MC	205 979-6410	Sara W Wuska	....	Thelma Moon	Francis C Coggin	William F Towers	Douglas J Jefferson	James L Bonner
Warrior† (3) MC	205 647-0521	H Jean Gayle	....	LaBonne Gilliland	H Jean Gayle	Sam Ogletree	Roger Beam	....
Weaver t (3) MC	205 820-1120	(not reporting)						
Wetumpka (4) MC	205 567-5147	G Truman Welch	....	Velma N Gober	....	Jake Strickland	Jack Wood	Earl Allen
Winfield† (4) MC	205 487-4337	Hewitt Addison	....	Edrell S Reed	Edrell S Reed	Ellis R Westbrook	James T Holliman	Denver Miles
York t (3) MC	205 392-5231	Charles L Bellenger	....	Virginia P Miller	Virginia P Miller	Wayne Simmers	J B Mitchell	J Edwin Stallings
ALASKA (25)								
Anchorage§ (173) MC	907 264-4111	Tony Knowles	Barbara Steckel	Ruby Smith	Robert M Nelson	Ross Fosberg	Brian S Porter	Mike Bieger
Barrow*† (2) CM	907 852-5211	Nate Olemaun Jr	Marie P Adams	Emily Nusunginya	....	Tom Opie	....	....
Bethel* (4) CM	907 543-2297	John Guinn	Lyman Hoffman	Wayne Maiers	Pete Donnel	Mark Barker	Tom Varnell	Gary Volkman
Cordova* (2) CM	907 424-3237	Leonard V Pingatore	Richard J Leland	Donna M Sherby	Jack P Ference	Dewey G Whetsell	William T Bragron	William R Bernard
Dillingham* (2) CM	907 842-5211	Leon C Braswell	James D Dunn	Vivian M Braswell	Lila Tubbs	Robert W King	Glenn Herbst	William Tennyson
Fairbanks* (23) CM	907 452-1881	Bill Walley	W C Droz	Carma B Roberson	Robert R Wolting	Warren Tilman	Matthew K Kiernan	Lane Thompson
Fort Yukon* (1) CM	907 662-2479	Jonathan Solomon	James R Filip	Susan E Salmon	Nancy E Shewfelt	Grafton Bergman	Robert A Arnold	Grafton Bergman
Galena* (1) CM	907 656-1301	Vernon White	Patricia Myers	Patricia Myers	Bessie L Cleaver	Jessie R Crane Jr	Robert Harrington	James Walldow
Homer* (2) CM	907 235-8121	Erle Cooper	Philip C Shealy	Kathleen Herold	Cris Newby	Tom Craig	Michael Daugherty	John Morgan
Juneau* (20) CM	907 586-3300	Fran Ulmer	N L Pat Teague	Peggie Garrison	Mary Smith	Alan Judson	Joseph Ciraulo	Robert Johnson
Kenai* (4) CM	907 283-7535	Tom Wagoner	Wm J Brighton	Janet A Whelan	Charles A Brown	Walter Winston	Richard A Ross	Keith Kornelis
Ketchikan* (7) CM	907 225-3111	Edward W Zastrow	James Van Altvorst	Karen Miles	Allan B Learned	Michael G Fisher	Daniel Anslinger	John Pearson
Kodiak* (5) CM	907 486-3224	John R Pugh	Samuel C Gesko Jr	Marcella Dalke	Roy A Deebel	George Magnusen	Edgar E Martin	Herman T Beukers
Kotzebue* (2) CM	907 442-3401	Willie Goodwin Jr	Bruce Kovarik	Linda Brown	....	Donald Tucker	Donald Buehler	John Ward
Mountain Village§ (1) MC	907 591-2929	....	John G Peter	....	....	....	....	....
Nome* (2) CM	907 443-5242	Leo B Rasmussen	Lyle W Larson	Linda E Conley	Caroline C Reardon	Robert Lewis	Robert L Kauer	....
Palmer* (2) CM	907 745-3271	George W Carte	David L Soulak	David L Soulak	Peter Van Horsen	Daniel M Contini	John McKibbon	....
Petersburg* (3) CM	907 772-4511	Don Koenigs	R L Underkofler	Patricia L Curtiss	Jodell Jones	Norman Fredricksen	Robert Oszman	Elias Lucas
Seldovia* (..) CM	907 234-7643	Darlene Crawford	Carl L Hille	Elaine M Giles	Elaine M Giles	Duane Ihrie	A W Anderson	Rolland Grosdidier
Seward* (2) CM	907 224-3331	Donald W Cripps	Ronald A Garzini	Linda S Murphy	S Joseph Gale	John R Gage	Louis A Bencardino	Galen Albertson
Sitka§ (8) MC	907 747-3294	John E Dapcevich	Richard Anderson	Dolores M Ingwersen	John McCracken	Gerry Helland	Art Letourneau	Jerry Simpson
Skagway§† (1) MC	907 983-2297	R F Messegee	....	Ms L S Gordon	....	C E Mulvihill	J D Hester	D W Buttle
St. Mary's*† (..) CM	907 438-2515	....	Mark D Mayo	....	....	....	....	....
Valdez* (3) CM	907 835-4313	Susy Collins	Jim E Watson	Shirley Scott	Tom Gilson	Thomas W McAlister	Pat Shely	Lee Schlitz

Directory 1/10 continued — MUNICIPAL OFFICIALS IN ALL U.S. CITIES OVER 2,500[1]

City, 1980 population (000 omitted), form of government		Municipal phone number	Mayor	Appointed administrator	City clerk	Finance officer	Fire chief	Police chief	Public works director
ALASKA (25) continued									
Wrangell*† (2)	CM	907 874-2381	William B Privett	Joyce Rasler	Lanore K Gunderson	Jeff Jabusch	Gordon L Buness	William G Klein	Ken Davidson
ARIZONA (58)									
Apache Junction* (10)	CM	602 982-8002	Wendell J Clarke	Michael J McNulty	Kathleen Connelly	J Keith Lewis	....	Bill McDaniel	Richard Broman
Avondale* (8)	CM	602 932-2400	Dessie M Lorenz	Carlos V Palma	Linda Tyler	Raymond H Shuey	H L McCreary	John C Lopez	Larry Ramirez
Benson* (4)	CM	602 586-2245	Mary Dillon	Paul Nordin	Doris Humphrey	Doris Humphrey	Max Jones	George McMinimy	Gordon Douglas
Bisbee (7)	CM	602 432-5446	Frank N Peters	....	Nellie Hodges	Nellie Hodges	Norman Wymbs	Edward Lopez	Ramiro Ross
Buckeye t* (3)	CM	602 935-4532	Robert G Strander	Fred C Carpenter	Kaye Hughes	Kaye Hughes	Gene Ray	Jesse C Burton	Steve Villa
Casa Grande* (15)	CM	602 836-7413	Hugh N Guinn	Rodger L Bennett	Nelda Hooker	Frank N Brown	Jerry Donahue	George Coxey	....
Chandler* (30)	CM	602 899-9700	Jerrell W Brooks	....	Carolyn Dunn	Barry Webber	Bart Beckwith	Ron Danielson	Jim Goff
Chino Valley t (3)	MC	602 636-2646	LeRoy M Parker	Cathie G Rodman	Mildred C Hennessey	Mildred C Hennessey	James Edwardson	Joseph V Amore	....
Clifton t*† (4)	CM	602 865-4146	Thomas Aquilar	Manuel A Perea	Manuel A Perea	Manuel A Perea	Nazario Hernandez	Edward S Cramer	V P Roman
Coolidge* (7)	CM	602 723-5361	Gail M Murray	Eugene C Wieneke II	Vicki C Culp	Marlene Edwards	Will Wadkins	Robert C Bonney Jr	Ronald J Stewart
Cottonwood t* (5)	CM	602 634-5526	Donald Hahn	Steven L Thompson	Steven L Thompson	Charles F Sweet	James A Mullenix	Charles Keltner	....
Douglas (13)	CM	602 364-8405	Ben F Williams Jr	Bill R DaVee	Victor M Stevens	Victor M Stevens	William T Hudspeth	Alvaro H Fragoso	Ben LaForge
Eagar t (3)	CM	602 333-4128	George R Pena	Gordon C Henrie	....	Paul Watson	Howard Carlson	Terry J Ringey	....
El Mirage t*† (4)	MC	602 977-7177	....	Gil M Olguin	....	....	....	....	....
Eloy* (6)	CM	602 466-9201	Don Decker	James Wm Little	Barbara A Dunaway	Barbara A Dunaway	Dennis Decker	Edward L Cibbarelli	Leroy Williams
Flagstaff* (35)	CM	602 774-5281	Robert L Moody	Frank Abeyta	Linda Butler	John Surina	Dean Treadway	Tom James	Michael L Adams
Florence t (3)	MC	602 868-5889	James C England	Kenneth Buchanan	Laurie Borquez	....	Joe A Valdez	Tom J Rankin	Patrick S Granillo
Gila Bend t* (2)	CM	602 683-2255	Julius Fox	Richard McComb	Theresa Velasquez	Richard McComb	Gene Merritt	....	Gene Merritt
Gilbert t§ (6)	MC	602 892-0802	L J Reed	Kent L Cooper	Phyllis J Alberty	Rich Oesterle	Mike Casson	Fred J Dees	Charles H Strand
Glendale* (97)	CM	602 931-5400	George R Renner	John L Maltbie	Lavergne Behm	Jack Hale	Robert Sharps	Jack Rose	Tom Martinsen
Globe*† (7)	CM	602 425-7991	G H Williams	....	Georgia Humphrey	Georgia Humphrey	Hugh Martin	R M McGann	C S Collins
Goodyear t* (3)	CM	602 932-3910	Chauncey B Coor	Ernest Kleinschmidt	Stephen S Cleveland	John H Starks	Lee M Ullman	Seymour Nealis	Eric A Grendell
Guadalupe t* (5)	CM	602 839-2415	Patricio V Villa	Olmedo J Abeyta	Olmedo J Abeyta	Olmedo J Abeyta	Henry Bandin	John Guerra	Joe Ruiz
Hayden t* (1)	CM	602 356-7801	Carmelita C Hart	....	Carol J Flores	Glenda Huddleston	Ynez Lopez	Daryl N Reinertson	Robert S Lorona
Holbrook* (6)	CM	602 524-6225	Kitty Benson	Paul J Richards	Paul J Richards	Ray Alley	George Simpson	Lester James	George Despain
Kearny t* (3)	CM	602 363-5547	Ray Tennison	Leonard L Fuller	Carol Meadows	Leonard L Fuller	Basili O Hillan	Patricia Huntsman	Jan Szendzielorz
Kingman* (9)	CM	602 753-5561	Carol Anderson	Louis G Sorensen	Dorothy Helmer	Robert J DePoy	Charles Potter	Carroll O Brown	Charles L Boise
Lake Havasu City* (16)	CM	602 855-2116	James S Spezzano	Jon L Devner	Ann R Sayne	Vito J Tedeschi	Robert Weber	Victor Mike Wilkins	James J Schulte
Mesa* (152)	CM	602 834-2011	Sumner Al Brooks	Charles K Luster	Dorthe Dana	Calvin Herron	Donald Johnson	Leonard Kotsur	Dean Sloan
Miami t (3)	MC	602 473-2281	Elias Lazarin Jr	Thomas E McCoy	Thomas E McCoy	Thomas E McCoy	Sam Knight	Abraham J Castaneda	Elias Y Garcia
Nogales (16)	MC	602 287-6571	F D Fontes	Robert A Saldamando	Robert A Saldamando	Robert A Saldamando	Jose DeLa Ossa	Manuel Treto Jr	Gabriel Ramirez
Page* (5)	CM	602 645-8861	David A Pape	Jack S Reinhold	....	Jack S Reinhold	Robert L Nichols	Raymond McAlister	Roger French
Paradise Valley t* (11)	CM	602 948-7411	Joan R Lincoln	Oscar A Butt	Mary Ann Brines	....	....	Peter Wainwright	Don L Ferris Jr
Parker t§ (3)	MC	602 669-9265	Nell B Kulp	Shirley Bassford	Shirley Bassford	Martha Crewse	Shelby Harmon	Robert S Caples	Frank Savino Jr
Payson (5)	CM	602 474-5242	Eugene E Quigley	Jack W Monschein	Mary S Jones	Wm R Ingram Jr	Charles A Jacobs	David N Wilson	Eng Pek Tan
Peoria* (12)	CM	602 979-3720	Edmund Tang	James A Walker	Richard M Gomez	Ronald Brown	Michael Fusco	Donald Cuker	Richard Moran
Phoenix* (790)	CM	602 262-6941	Terry Goddard	Marvin A Andrews	Donna Culbertson	Alex Cordova	Alan V Brunacini	Ruben B Ortega	Ronald W Jensen
Prescott* (20)	CM	602 445-3500	William A Young	A D Tomlinson Jr	Marie Watson	James Culbreth	Robert McNabb	Max Merritt	Jerry Freund
Prescott Valley t* (2)	CM	602 772-9207	Carmelite Staker	Harold G Branch	Lyn Newton	Lyn Newton	....	Edward Seder	....
Safford* (7)	CM	602 428-2762	Carol MacDonald	William B Elliott	Pat Savage	Don Knight	Irvin Talley	Milton Rhea	Robert Porter
Scottsdale* (88)	CM	602 994-2521	Herbert Drinkwater	Roy R Pederson	Roy R Pederson	James A Jenkins	Ronald C Butler	Michael G Gannon	Tommy J Davis
Show Low* (4)	CM	602 537-5724	Joy J Harding	Ronald L Kiedrowski	William Puzz	William Puzz	K Sam Solomon	John Corder	Hollis Taylor
Sierra Vista* (26)	CM	602 458-3315	Jean Randle	Michael D Goyer	Bruce A Mordhorst	....	Donald R Newcomer	C Reed Vance	George P Michael
Snowflake t* (4)	CM	602 536-4412	Nonie Johnson	Steve H Thacker	Charleene Rogers	....	....	Sanford Flake	Eldon Stratton
Somerton (6)	MC	602 627-2551	Jess Vela	Nyla Wesner	Nyla Wesner	Nyla Wesner	Leland Young	Albert Garcia	Jessie Munoz
South Tucson* (7)	CM	602 792-2424	Dan Eckstrom	Enrique G Serna	William Ponder	William Ponder	George Felix	Charles Kalak	....
St. Johns (3)	MC	602 337-4517	Myrlan A Brown	....	Lee Waters	....	Lavere O'Connolly	Ronald Heap	William D Prentice
Superior t (5)	MC	602 689-5752	Manuel Ruiz Jr	....	Mellie P Bribiescas	....	....	Boyd R Beckstead	John Ward
Surprise t (4)	CM	602 977-8369	George Cumbie	Harold Yingling	Lovena Luttrell	Harold Yingling	Gilbert Balcom	F V Skip Luttrell	Arturo Quinones
Tempe* (107)	CM	602 967-2001	Harry E Mitchell	James L Alexander	Virginia S Thompson	Jerry E Geiger	William Hayes	A F Fairbanks Jr	Jim Jones
Thatcher t (3)	MC	602 428-2290	Ladd Mullenaux	....	Herbert Winsor	....	Jerry Robinson	James Mullenaux	Herbert Winsor
Tolleson* (4)	CM	602 936-7111	Charles P Hayes	Ralph Velez	Barbara C Williams	Bruce Johnson	Scott Butler	J Fred Davis	Rafael Moreno
Tucson* (331)	CM	602 791-4204	Lewis Murphy	Joel D Valdez	Don Dement	James Kay Jr	Richard Moreno	Peter Ronstadt	Hurvie E Davis
Wickenburg t* (4)	CM	602 684-5451	James M Mason	B J Ben Nardelli	Edna Grieves	....	Joe T Walters	Al Saulter	Coney Orosco
Willcox* (3)	CM	602 384-4271	Jonnie Belle Bethel	Richard L Cook	Bruce Kelly	Bruce Kelly	Bill Teeters	Bill Morales	Rene Diaz
Williams* (2)	CM	602 635-4413	James Hoffman	Leon H Berger	Leon H Berger	Andrew Tomlinson	Jimmie Walker	Edward J Durnez	....
Winslow§ (8)	MC	602 289-2422	Georgia Metzger	Frank Freeman	Lily Martinez	....	John Dalton	Frank Foley	Bill Barris
Yuma* (42)	CM	602 783-1271	Philip G Clark	Douglas W Lowe	....	Michael Fleetwood	William Steiert	David Brown	Larry Hunt
ARKANSAS (91)									
Alma† (3)	MC	501 632-4119	Manford N Burris	....	Ronald A Bennett	....	Tommy Wilson	Joe Don Gregory	James Thibault
Arkadelphia* (10)	CM	501 246-9864	Stell R Callaway	Ken Wasson	Shirley Ann Loy	....	Truman Still	Parvin Romines	Ron Bise
Ashdown (4)	MC	501 898-2622	J H Welch Jr	....	Curtis Daniel	Curtis Daniel	Dale Jones	James L Pynes	Gerald Smithpeters
Atkins† (3)	MC	501 641-7853	Dallas L Swain	....	Syble Marple	....	Clarence A Ehemann	James D Johnston	Alfred W Berry
Augusta (3)	MC	501 347-5656	Marjorie C Malin	....	Dorothy Willis	Sharon Rushing	Charles Hollis	Jimmy Moore	Ronnie Straccner
Bald Knob (3)	MC	501 724-6371	Raymond D Emde	....	Karon Miller	....	Robert N Hendrix	Dennis Pierce	....
Barling t (4)	MC	501 452-1550	Jerry Barling	Robert J Turner	Sheila Forget	....	Bill Turner	Paul Rivaldo	Charles Stites
Batesville (8)	MC	501 793-3420	Jim Shirrell	....	Larry Williams	....	J W Cummings	....	....
Beebe (4)	MC	501 882-3365	Roy Simmons	....	Maxine Harrell	Maxine Harrell	Bill Nick	James E Jackson	Roy Simmons
Benton (17)	MC	501 778-2546	George M Wagner	....	Martha J Lequieu	John P Walden	Dewell Anderson	Jim D Harris	....
Bentonville (9)	MC	501 273-9062	Richard Hoback	....	Blaine Jackson	David Hausam	Jerry Griffith	Dan M Moody	....
Berryville (3)	MC	501 423-2245	Hal Kennelley	....	Russell Atchley	Helen I Maples	Gene Chafin	David Muniz	Charles Lindt
Blytheville (24)	MC	501 763-3602	Tom A Little Jr	Elmer R Smith	Dorothy L Besharse	Jerald Haun	Danny Smothers	Charles B Dye	Homer Besharse
Booneville (4)	MC	501 675-3811	Cecil A Trowbridge	....	Rose Leftwich	Rose Leftwich	Omar Lee Godfrey	J H Parker Jr	Donald Hardin
Brinkley* (5)	CM	501 734-1382	Ralph H Wilson	Leroy D Alsup	Donna Pruitt	Geraldine Patrick	Robert Raney	George Bethell	Hayes Warren
Bryant (3)	MC	501 847-0292	Dean R Boswell Jr	....	Wanda Smith	Leta Boone	Raymond Pittman	James Hipps	J C Green
Cabot (5)	MC	501 843-3566	N E Smith	....	Katie Weeks	Katie Weeks	Carl Pickard	Jay W Verkler	....
Camden* (15)	CM	501 836-6436	Richard F Taylor	T Michael McDowell	Preston L Woods	Preston L Woods	Robert O Vaughan	Micheal J Paladino	Harlan B Benson
Carlisle (3)	MC	501 552-3120	James M Corkill	....	Kelly Stauber	Joe Cunningham	Marion Partain	Gary Gray	Ricky Sumner
Clarksville (5)	MC	501 754-6486	Marvin Vinson	Ann Schmatjen	Metta Holman	Metta Holman	Charles Callahan	Kyn Wilson	Foy Howard
Conway (20)	MC	501 329-3878	William L Wright	....	Martha Hartwick	Maxine Spruiell	Doyce Ballard	Vonnie Taylor	W K Stanford
Corning† (4)	MC	501 857-6716	E W Cochran	....	Carolyn Williams	Carolyn Williams	Fred Martin	Leonard Bell	Harry Hudson
Crossett (7)	MC	501 364-4131	Leslie Black	....	Nelson Toler	Sue Miller	James Launius	Derrell George	Thomas Goree
Dardanelle† (4)	MC	501 229-4500	Dana Merrit	....	Lucille Hodges	....	Bill George	John Blevins	William T Roach
De Queen*† (5)	CM	501 584-3445	Eddie Pulliam	Hut Greenwood	Ethel Fleenor	....	Paul Downs	Bill Jones	....
De Witt (4)	MC	501 946-2191	John Schallhorn	Ms Jerry Paxton	Willene Miller	....	Calvin Danner	Milton Peebles	Freemont Ferguson
Dermott (5)	MC	501 538-5251	Eugene R Farrell	....	Kathryn McDaniel	Eugene R Farrell	Morris Parker	Jerry Melton	Carrol Jackson

Directory 1/10 continued **MUNICIPAL OFFICIALS IN ALL U.S. CITIES OVER 2,500[1]**

City, 1980 population (000 omitted), form of government		Municipal phone number	Mayor	Appointed administrator	City clerk	Finance officer	Fire chief	Police chief	Public works director
ARKANSAS (91) continued									
Dumas (6)	MC	501 382-2121	Jessie M Free	....	Mary S Howard	....	Jimmy Blankenship	Jim Peterson	....
Earle (4)	MC	501 792-8909	James H King	....	Sylvia Layton	Sylvia Layton	Irby Campbell	Paul Green	Fred Russell
El Dorado† (27)	MC	501 863-8061	Larry Combs	....	Mary Hudson	....	James R Amason	John Morgan	W R Baker
England (3)	MC	501 842-2438	Roy Cox	....	Ruth Baker	....	Marvin Buffalo	Randy Krablin	....
Eudora (4)	MC	501 355-4545	Harlan Nunnelee	....	Lue Hart	Lois Worthington	Cois Martindale	Sam Bradley	Eugie Harrell
Fayetteville* (37)	CM	501 521-7700	Paul Noland	Donald L Grimes	Suzanne Kennedy	Scott Linebaugh	Paul D Logue	Bob Jones	Clayton Powell
Fordyce† (5)	MC	501 352-3988	Paul A Harrelson	Charles Hearne	Jan Doherty	Jan Doherty	Roy W Moseley	Joe Pennington	Bill Gober
Forrest City (14)	MC	501 633-1692	Danny Ferguson	....	C N Haven	C N Haven	Carl Pettus	Joe Goff	Jim Beazley
Fort Smith* (71)	CM	501 785-2801	William D Vines	William L Faught	Cindy Remler	Kara Bushkuhl	James W Moore	Keith E Daniels	H Richard Green
Gosnell (3)	MC	501 532-8544	Carl B Ledbetter	....	Janice Gray	....	Robert Penter	John Parish	....
Greenwood (3)	MC	501 996-2742	Troy Pete Brown	....	Bobbie Ray Jones	....	Bill Gann	Marvin Booker	....
Gurdon† (3)	MC	501 353-2515	Peter M Rudolph	....	Blanche Smith	S K Garrett	Carl Flowers	Charles Anderson	....
Hamburg (3)	MC	501 853-5300	Maxwell L Hill	....	Mary Ann White	Maxwell L Hill	Johnny Kilcrease	Richard Thomas	Earle Benson
Harrison (10)	MC	501 741-6666	William W Gregg	....	James Guy Roberts	....	Orville Main	Jerry W Edwards	Graham Roberts
Heber Springs (5)	MC	501 362-3635	Raymond Robus	....	Norma Jean Martin	....	James Morrow	Jim Thayer	....
Helena (10)	MC	501 338-9831	Thad Kelly	....	Mildred Sallis	Lillian W Hatfield	Alton Yancey	Leroy Davis	Bob Burge
Hope* (10)	CM	501 777-6701	Floyd Young	John D Swift	Leneta Hare	John D Swift	Joe Don Webb	Harvey Fullerton	Jewel May
Hot Springs (35)	MC	501 321-1113	Jim Randall	....	J Harold Smith	James Scott	John Wood	Marvin Owen	Jim Atchley
Hoxie (3)	MC	501 886-2742	J M Johnson	....	Betty Welch	....	James Pickney	Paul Hendrix	....
Jacksonville (28)	MC	501 982-3181	James G Reid	....	Lula M Leonard	Eugene Kelley	Wilbur Smart	Frank Neely	Bill Owens
Jonesboro (32)	MC	501 932-1052	Neil Stallings	....	Steve Kent	Herbert Davis	Fred Rorex	Edward Cunningham	Mike Cameron
Lake Village (3)	MC	501 265-2228	Jack R Rhodes	....	Joanne H Vencill	....	Larry Donaldson	James E Daniels	....
Little Rock* (158)	CM	501 371-4510	J W Benafield	Susan B Fleming	Jane Czech	E Jack Murphy	Rubin Webb	Walter Simpson	William Davies
Lonoke (4)	MC	501 676-7953	Jack O Smith	....	Carole Tefteller	Thomas Privett	Jack Wheat	John L Davis	Melvin O Murphy
Magnolia (12)	MC	501 234-1375	George Wheatley	....	Genevieve Baskin	George Wheatley	Herschel Hampton	Larry J Taylor	J C Allen
Malvern† (10)	MC	501 332-3638	Bill J Scrimshire	....	Phyllis Dial	Paul Bowdle	Thomas Taylor	Laney Phipps	Herman Higdon
Manila (3)	MC	501 561-3223	(not reporting)						
Marianna (6)	MC	501 295-6089	Martin Chaffin	....	Chas E Yancey III	J H Smithson	Joe Crawford	Mark Birchler	Jack Dilks Jr
Marion† (3)	MC	501 739-3071	E W Bigger Jr	....	....	....	Gary Rash	John W Griffin	....
Marked Tree (3)	MC	501 358-3216	Howard Dawson	....	George Crowell	George Crowell	Tom Williams	Elmer Bud Rollins	....
McGehee (6)	MC	501 222-3160	Rosalie S Gould	Frances Sims	Charles L Loyd	....	Bobby Hood	David Dupwe	....
Mena (5)	MC	501 394-4585	Paul T Autry	....	Monroe Drye	....	Odell Egger	Donald Allen	Lynn Harris
Monticello (8)	MC	501 367-2744	James T Jordan	....	Glenda F Nichols	Reva L Abbott	Jack Carson	Odis Allen	....
Morrilton† (7)	MC	501 354-3484	Gerald Laux	....	Maude White	....	Edward Lee Eddy	Robyn Massingill	....
Mountain Home† (7)	MC	501 425-5116	Ronald E Pierce	....	Connie House	Connie House	James A Ball	Paul A Doak	Robert E Hurst
Nashville† (5)	MC	501 845-1432	John H Ball II	....	June Floyd	....	Howard Shaw	Herbert N Turley Jr	....
Newport (8)	MC	501 523-6568	Wayne Beard Jr	Elwanda Templeton	J Paul Heard	Don Collins	Blanchard Cooley	John Max Jones	Burt Willard
North Little Rock† (64)	MC	501 374-2233	Reed W Thompson	....	Ms Jackie Neil	Bob Sisson	Charles W Redding	W D Younts	Charles Miller
Osceola (9)	MC	501 563-5102	R E Prewitt	....	Lynda Wells	Ed Lea	Fred Hendrix	Robert Womack	Charles Griffin
Ozark (4)	MC	501 667-2238	Gary E Briley	....	Donna Stacy	....	Robert Trotter	Artemus McElhaney	....
Paragould (15)	MC	501 236-6974	Charles R Partlow	....	Goldie Wise	....	Davey J Jackson	William W Lindley	Jacksie Jamison
Paris† (4)	MC	501 963-2450	Cecil Patterson	....	Billy L Rhineheart	Cecil Patterson	William J Wright	Richard C Arndt	....
Piggott (4)	MC	501 598-3791	George Cook	....	Monedith Wright	Monedith Wright	Marshall Wheeler	Kenneth Parker	....
Pine Bluff (57)	MC	501 534-5420	Dave Wallis	....	Edna Munn	Edward Bogy	Ray Jacks	James C Parker	....
Pocahontas (6)	MC	501 892-3924	Junior J Wooldridge	....	Elizabeth Penn	Elizabeth Penn	Jerry Matheny	J D Yancy	William P Crain
Prescott (4)	MC	501 887-2210	(not reporting)						
Rogers (17)	MC	501 636-4130	John W Sampier Jr	....	Mary E Kincy	Marshall L Bailey	Kenneth D Riley	Dennis Musteen	....
Russellville (15)	MC	501 968-2098	W H Hashbarger	....	Charles F Howell	Juanita Lee Edwards	Earl Price	Herbert Johnston	Charles Cochran
Searcy† (14)	MC	501 268-2483	Jack Wiseman	....	Truett Langley	Belinda LaForce	J W Morris	Dean Hunter	William Joyner
Sheridan (3)	MC	501 942-3921	Dalton V Walker	....	Joe Wise Jr	....	Norris Cash	David Hooks	....
Sherwood† (11)	MC	501 835-5319	Jack P Evans	....	Amy Sanders	G R Massey	Pete Lacey	Charles Seelinger	Jim Willis
Siloam Springs§ (8)	MC	501 524-5136	Bill Foreman	Jack Hoyt	Helen Allum	....	David Wesner	Tommy Himes	Hershel Daniels
Springdale (23)	MC	501 756-8200	Charles N McKinney	....	Mida Neff	Mida Neff	Mickey Jackson	Truman Brewer	....
Stamps (3)	MC	501 533-4771	Ronald Joe Cowling	....	Billie Nicholas	....	James H Goodwin	Jerry W Honeycutt	....
Stuttgart (11)	MC	501 673-3535	H E Raines	....	Ann Walker	Jane Jackson	Edward Lynch	Aubrey D Roswell	C E Snyder
Texarkana* (21)	CM	501 774-3161	Bobby F Ferguson	Kenneth W Parker	Sandra Powell	Pat Crumpton	Clinton McCormack	John Butler	Olin Crowell
Trumann †† (6)	MC	501 483-5355	Bobby L Ballard	Wilma Moss	Florence Wright	Martha Holmes	....	Jim Furnish	....
Van Buren (12)	MC	501 474-1541	Robert E Gene Bell	....	Ann Graham	....	Jerry McGraw	Gary Robertson	....
Waldron (3)	MC	501 637-3181	Carlton Roberds	....	O Ann Oliver	....	Curtis Billings	William E Luttrell	....
Walnut Ridge (4)	MC	501 886-6638	Tommy Holland	....	Benson Hart	....	Joe Coker	Larry Daniels	....
Warren (8)	MC	501 226-6743	John B Frazer	....	Bertia Mae Lassiter	Ms David B Fort	Eddie Wayne Lathan	David L Dunaway	....
West Helena (11)	MC	501 572-2528	Robert E Teeter	....	Julia S Adkins	....	Earl T Meiers	James T Cross	E L Cowsert
West Memphis (28)	MC	501 735-2720	Leo Chitman	....	Dan Craft	Wyman D Morgan	Tom Burkhart	Bill Ralph	....
Wynne† (8)	MC	501 238-9171	James C Luker	....	Olive M Bock	Doyl Brown	Wilbur English	N E Zachary	Henry Williams
CALIFORNIA (402)									
Adelanto* (2)	CM	714 246-8606	Edward A Dunagan	P Chamberlaine	Eunice L Puckett	Gerri Claude	John Luetke	John Morrissey	....
Agoura Hills* (11)	CM	818 889-9114	Carol Sahm	Michael W Huse	Michael W Huse	Michael W Huse	....	....	....
Alameda* (64)	CM	415 522-4100	Anne B Diament	J Bruce Rupp	Deen Speegle	William J Zenoni	Dick Quarante	Bob Shiells	Bill Norton
Albany* (15)	CM	415 528-5720	Edward McManus	William E Haden	Jacqueline Bucholz	Roy Paul Endserby	Horace I Koepke	James Simmons	Robert S Guletz
Alhambra*† (65)	CM	213 570-5111	Michael S Messina	Kevin J Murphy	Ms D M Outwater	Stephen W Helvey	Robert G Tolladay	Joseph T Molloy	Terry L James
Alturas (3)	MC	916 233-2512	Roger Dorris	....	Denise Utter	Kathie Utt	James W Porter	Ed Loveless	Elwyn K Doss
Anaheim* (222)	CM	714 999-5100	Don R Roth	William O Talley	Leonora N Sohl	George Ferrone	Robert Simpson	Jimmie Kennedy	James D Ruth
Anderson* (7)	CM	916 365-2521	John Stevens	William R Garr	Jacqueline Padilla	Bruce Johnson	Ross Phipps	Philip Raner	Robert Agee
Antioch* (44)	CM	415 778-4531	Verne L Roberts	Leland M Walton	Dorothy P Marks	Gene Poertner	Vince Aiello	Leonard Herendeen	Stanford Davis
Arcadia* (46)	CM	818 574-5400	David S Hannah	George J Watts	Ms C Van Maanen	Gerald Shuster	Gerald Gardner	Charles D Mitchell	Chester Howard
Arcata* (12)	CM	707 822-5951	Julie Fulkerson	Rory C Robinson	Rory C Robinson	David W Tyson	William McKenzie	Joseph L Maskovich	Frank R Klopp
Arroyo Grande* (11)	CM	805 489-1303	B'Ann Smith	Robert Mack	Nancy Davis	David E Bacon	Tony Marsalek	James C Clark	Paul Karp
Artesia* (14)	CM	213 865-6262	James A Van Horn	Harold Campbell	Margaret M Rittel	Laura Wise	....	....	Chuck Bernal
Arvin (7)	MC	805 854-3134	Billy F Owens	O L Wooner	Wilma J Bratton	....	....	Robert McIntosh	Robert Caferelli
Atascadero§ (16)	MC	805 466-8000	....	Murray L Warden	....	Ralph H Dowell Jr	Mike Hicks	Richard H McHale	Lawrence McPherson
Atherton t* (8)	CM	415 325-4457	John W Dinkelspiel	Ross G Hubbard	Ross G Hubbard	Ross G Hubbard	....	Richard L Moore	Ross G Hubbard
Atwater* (18)	CM	209 358-5606	Gregory R Olzack	Thomas I Smith	Frances M Barrett	....	Jim Laginha	Robert Calaway	....
Auburn* (8)	CM	916 885-5661	Gene Wise	Rodney K Haack	Florence Ladeck	Edna Casebeer	Henry Gietzen	Nicholas Willick	Scott Chadd
Avalon* (2)	CM	213 510-0220	Gilbert R Saldana	John R Longley	Shirley Davy	Richard E Ferguson	Jack T Goslin	Dale Goss	Peter Woolson
Avenal§ (4)	MC	209 386-5766	James Castleman	Homer L Bludau	Carolyn J Parks	Homer L Bludau	....	....	Howard Ricks
Azusa* (29)	CM	818 334-5125	Eugene F Moses	Lloyd J Wood	Adolph A Solis	Geoffrey J Craig	John B Littlefield	Lloyd Wood	William Cunningham
Bakersfield* (106)	CM	805 326-3711	Thomas A Payne	George A Caravalho	Marguerite Anderson	W D Higginbotham Jr	D S Needham	R O Price	J D Hawley
Baldwin Park* (51)	CM	213 960-4011	Jack B White	Ralph H Webb	Linda L Gair	Dennis R Halloway	....	David Snowden	Dick Smith

Directory 1/10 continued **MUNICIPAL OFFICIALS IN ALL U.S. CITIES OVER 2,500[1]**

City, 1980 population (000 omitted), form of government		Municipal phone number	Mayor	Appointed administrator	City clerk	Finance officer	Fire chief	Police chief	Public works director
CALIFORNIA (402) continued									
Banning* (14)	CM	714 849-4511	E Brigitte Page	Ray Windsor	Lucille M Elizondo	Willis S Olson	Carl Sparks	Louis Davison	Charles Stevens
Barstow* (18)	CM	714 256-3531	Bernard W Keller	E Wayne Lamoreaux	Jean K Blackwell	Evelyn Radel	David Matthews	H O Davis	Eric G Ziegler
Beaumont* (7)	CM	714 845-1171	James B Thompson	Norman J Davis	Irene Joyce Sweeney	Ronney Wong	Bill Farnham	Raymond Justus	Gary G Phelps
Bell* (25)	CM	213 588-6211	Clarence Knechtel	Byron L Woosley	Martha Guttierez	Steven Klotzsche	....	Franklin D Fording	Byron L Woosley
Bell Gardens*† (34)	CM	213 927-8301	Roy L Paul	Larry J Kosmont	Leanna Keltner	David A Bass	John Enright	William L Donohoe	Steve Steinbrecher
Bellflower* (53)	CM	213 804-1424	John Ansdell	Jack A Simpson	Deborah Harrington	Michael A Sakamoto	....	....	Wm O McConnell
Belmont* (25)	CM	415 573-2201	William H Hardwick	Edward P Everett	J W McLaughlin	Michael B Shelton	Gary Schmitz	Floyd D Sanderson	John Hopkins
Belvedere* (2)	CM	415 435-3838	George H Gnoss Jr	Edmund H San Diego	Edmund H San Diego	Edmund H San Diego	Frank Buscher	Gary J Lester	John Kottage
Benicia* (15)	CM	707 745-0510	Marilyn C O'Rourke	John F Silva	Frances D Greco	Ronald E Peterson	Hank A Howard	Pierre Bidou	Donald F Curtis
Berkeley* (103)	CM	415 644-6000	Eugene Gus Newport	Daniel Boggan Jr	Edythe Campbell	Bernon Erickson	Victor Porter	Ronald Nelson	Edward T Marshall
Beverly Hills* (32)	CM	213 550-4700	Annabelle Heiferman	Edward S Kreins	Jean Ushijima	Donald J Oblander	William Daley	Lee Tracy	Melton Odom
Big Bear Lake (5)	MC	714 866-5831	John Eminger	Robert L Van Nort	Ivy J Zobel	Jeffrey Brunsdon	Ed Kimbrough	Gary Huff	John Bruechle
Bishop§ (3)	MC	619 873-5863	Roger Rogers	Richard F Pucci	Richard F Pucci	Richard F Pucci	Phil Moxley	Frederick G Coburn	James Barnes
Blythe* (7)	CM	619 922-6161	Ernest E Weeks	Dick Milkovich	Jeanene Manly	Dick Milkovich	Ray Pease	Glen Mackey	Les Warning
Bradbury§ (1)	MC	213 358-3218	Ronald G Westmyer	Dolly Vollaire	Dolly Vollaire	Dolly Vollaire	....	....	Dolly Vollaire
Brawley* (15)	CM	619 344-1550	Robert Noriega	Joseph Mulloy	Janet P Smith	Joseph Mulloy	Les Torbett	Carleton Bradley	Charles Brown
Brea* (28)	CM	714 990-7600	Carrey J Nelson	Ed G Wohlenberg	Dorothy Storm	John M Stark	Jerry McDowell	Donald L Forkus	Pat McCarron
Brentwood* (4)	CM	415 634-3505	Roger P Moore	Harry E Gill	Harry E Gill	Harry E Gill	....	James A Frank	John S Jones
Brisbane* (3)	CM	415 467-1515	Jeannine Hodge	Richard B Kerwin	Richard B Kerwin	Roger A Kalil	C R Moritz	Elmer A Martini	C R Moritz
Buena Park* (64)	CM	714 521-9900	Don R Griffin	....	Marguerite Courson	Ted T Abo	Samuel J Winner	Robert T Reber	Don Kemp
Burbank* (85)	CM	818 953-9701	E Daniel Remy	Andrew C Lazzaretto	Evelyn Haley	Stephen W Helvey	Curt V Reynolds	Glen Bell	Steven M Magnuson
Burlingame* (26)	CM	415 342-8931	Irving S Amstrup	Dennis J Argyres	Judith A Malfatti	Helen Fricke	O Fred Fricke	Alfred J Palmer	Ralph E Kirkup
Calexico* (14)	CM	619 357-0981	Wm J Polkinhorn	Oscar G Rodriguez	A T Samaniego	Oscar G Rodriguez	Armando Zuniga	J Leonard Speer	Mariano Martinez Jr
California City* (3)	CM	714 373-8661	Lou Logue	Stanleigh Megargee	Thelma M Chance	Gary G Hill	David Crandell	William Dempsey	J Dean Stewart
Calipatria† (3)	MC	714 348-2293	Gene Sones	....	....	....	....	....	....
Calistoga† (4)	MC	707 942-5188	Robert B Wareham	Lester Cavagnaro	Mary M Duffy	Mary M Duffy	Don Meyer	James Anderson	Richard Avey
Camarillo* (38)	CM	805 482-8922	F Burrows Esty	Thomas W Oglesby	Marilyn J Thiel	Larry L Weaver	Stanley E Masson	John Gillespie	John M Bressan
Campbell* (27)	CM	408 866-2100	Ralph Doetsch Sr	Kevin C Duggan	Anne G Coyne	G H Whittaker	James F McMullen	Donald Burr	Joseph Elliott
Capitola* (9)	CM	408 475-7300	Michael R Routh	Stephen R Burrell	Pamela Greeninger	Ardath Fugate	Jerry Bowles	Robert L Allen	Craig French
Carlsbad* (35)	CM	714 438-5621	Mary H Casler	Frank D Aleshire	Aletha Rautenkranz	James Elliott	James K Thompson	Vincent Jimno	....
Carmel-by-the-Sea§ (5)	MC	408 624-2781	Charlotte Townsend	Douglas J Schmitz	Jeanne Brehmer	Gregory D'Ambrosio	Robert Updike	John McGilvray	William L Askew Jr
Carpinteria* (11)	CM	805 684-5405	John K Fukasawa	Allan R Coates Jr	Allan R Coates Jr	Allan R Coates Jr	....	John R Frontado	....
Carson* (81)	CM	213 830-7600	Kay Calas	Raymond L Meador	Helen Kawagoe	William Parrott	Ray Brunstrom	Bufford Smith	Harold Williams
Cathedral City*† (11)	CM	619 324-8388	V Harry Krings	Jack R Smith	Maxine E Clem	Curt DeCrinis	....	....	....
Ceres* (13)	CM	209 537-8911	Brian Carlin	James G Marshall	Ivy J Laffoon	D Cindy Higby	....	Gail W Peterson	Joachim Hollstein
Cerritos* (53)	CM	213 860-0311	Barry A Rabbitt	Gaylord F Knapp	Caroline DeLlamas	John Saunders	Paul Delaney	Stephen O Batchelor	William Morris Jr
Chico* (27)	CM	916 895-4800	Karl Ory	Fred Davis	Barbara A Evans	Robert E Shepherd	Charles Lowden	U F Bullerjaan	Allan J Savitz
Chino* (40)	CM	714 627-7577	Larry Walker	Roger A Storey	Lee Tyrrell	James S Diaz	Ora M Short	James Anthony	Ray Wellington
Chowchilla§† (5)	MC	209 665-4816	Reginald Upton	James W Peel	James W Peel	....	Frank Borba	James Curutchet	William Searcy
Chula Vista* (84)	CM	714 575-5111	Gregory R Cox	John D Goss	Jennie M Fulasz	Lyman Christopher	William J Winters	William J Winters	John Lippitt
Claremont* (31)	CM	714 624-4531	Enid H Douglass	Leonard G Wood	Barbara A Hallamore	Jim Dale	Morris Gregory	Charles R Lines	Tom Holland
Clayton (4)	CM	415 672-3622	Carolyn Bovat	Gary Knox	Ruth Scott	Everet Clift	....	Gary Knox	Michael Klein
Clearlake (8)	MC	707 994-8201	Doris C Logoteta	Ismael Rodriguez	Sharon Goode	Phyllis Burrows	Donald Parker	Raymond Skerry	David Byrnes
Cloverdale* (4)	CM	707 894-2521	Stephen Congdon	Michael A Wilson	Barbara Peugh	Carol Giovanatto	Milton C Holt	Rodney H Persons	Michael G Morris
Clovis* (33)	CM	209 298-8061	William H Armstrong	Allen L Goodman	Michael Prandini	Michael Prandini	James L Rankin	Gerald Galvin	Leon P Lancaster
Coachella* (9)	CM	714 398-6131	Manuel Arredondo	Raul T Romero	Sherwin W W Goynes	Anthony B Lopez	John M Rios	Arnold Jimenez	Dudley Hemphill
Coalinga* (7)	CM	209 935-1533	Donald D Dapelo	Glenn H Marcussen	Johnnie D Quinney	Gerald C Craig	Fred Frederickson	James Henry	Alan D Jacobsen
Colton* (27)	CM	714 370-5060	Albert A Huntoon	Phillip D Elliott	Helen Ramos	Ruby Andengaard	Ron Gemmell	Paul Connolly	John Hutton
Colusa (4)	MC	916 458-4941	John A Rogers	....	Joyce McCullough	Joyce McCullough	Daryl C Thompson	Raegene C Cation	Roy G Triplett
Commerce* (11)	CM	213 722-4805	Robert Bob Eula	Claude J Klug	Ruth Aldaco	John Mitsuuchi	John W Englund	Sherman Block	Manuel Jimenez
Compton* (81)	CM	213 537-8000	Walter R Tucker	Laverta Montgomery	Charles Davis	Tim Brown	Monroe Smith	James L Carrington	Angel Espiritu
Concord* (103)	CM	415 671-3000	Stephen L Weir	F A Stewart	Bernadette Carroll	Stanley Pinkoski	....	George Straka	Cosmo Tedeschi
Corcoran* (6)	CM	209 992-2151	Bruce George	George Lambert	Connie Harris	Joyce Denzinger	Ken Harp	Joel Patton	....
Corning* (5)	CM	916 824-5558	Gary R Strack	Ben B Anderson	A Darlene Dickison	Ben B Anderson	James Calbreath	John B Fulks	Terry N Snow
Corona* (38)	CM	714 736-2371	Richard A Deininger	James D Wheaton	Diedre Lingenfelter	John Grindrod	Harvey Simpson	Bob J Talbert	Joseph Palencia
Coronado* (19)	CM	714 435-2211	R H Dorman	Raymond R Silver	Thomas Patricola	James F Benson	Robert E Shanahan	Gerald W Boyd	Linwood Newton
Corte Madera †* (8)	CM	415 924-1700	Robert E Holmes	....	....	George T Warman Jr	Robert W Shearer	Phillip D Green	Clifford E Temps
Costa Mesa* (82)	CM	714 754-5327	Donn Hall	Fred Scrsabal	Eileen P Phinney	Robert A Oman	John Petruzziello	Roger Neth	Bruce Mattern
Cotati* (3)	CM	707 795-5478	Archie Stewart	Randy Johnsen	Rebecca Haynes	Kathy Kruger	Bob Rippin	Robert Stewart	Steve Nommsen
Covina* (34)	CM	213 331-0111	Charles G Colver	Richard A Miller	Frieda C Richardson	Stanley McCartney	Carl Johnson	John Lentz	Del Dewhirst
Crescent City* (3)	CM	707 464-7483	C Ray Smith	Roy D Bysegger	Debra E Witt	Rodney A Jahn	Donald Olson	Nicholson Pottorff	Dave Gustafson
Cudahy* (18)	CM	213 773-5143	Lynwood E Evans	Gerald M Caton	Gerald M Caton	Gerard Goedhart	George Harms	Frank Fording	Maynard Law
Culver City* (38)	CM	213 837-5211	Paul A Jacobs	Harry D Jones	Pauline C Dolce	Roger Mansfield	George Sweeny	Elwood E Ted Cooke	John Lathrop
Cupertino* (26)	CM	408 252-4505	John Plungy	Robert W Quinlan	Dorothy Cornelius	Blaine Snyder	Douglas Sporleder	Robert W Quinlan	Bert Viskovich
Cypress* (40)	CM	714 828-2200	Richard Partin	Darrell Essex	Darrell Essex	Lawrence Hurst	Larry J Holms	Ronald E Lowenberg	Robert Beardsley
Daly City* (79)	CM	415 991-8000	Michael D Nevin	David R Rowe	Betty Mazza	Susan B Merrill	Richard Bridges	David A Hansen	John C Martin
Danville§ (26)	MC	415 820-6337	....	Michael M Davis	....	....	....	....	....
Davis* (37)	CM	916 756-3745	Ann M Evans	Howard L Reese	Howard L Reese	William D Feldmeier	Donald J Sylvia	Vic Mentink	David B Pelz
Del Mar* (5)	CM	714 755-9313	James W Tetrault	Robert A Nelson	Diane Lennert	Gloria Curry	William H Tripp	....	Sam Nicosia
Delano* (16)	CM	805 725-0230	Leonard T Velasco	Dennis W McDuffie	Dorothy Dowell	Michael Corn	Don Gallagher	Mickey D Chernekoff	Larry B Inman
Desert Hot Springs* (6)	CM	714 329-6411	William L Gibson	Gerald F Johnson	Colleen J Nicol	Ronald D Peck	Robert Cox	Frank Robles	Robert J Oberstar
Dinuba* (10)	CM	209 591-1203	Raymond K Millard	Robt F D Adams	Noble Shaw	Noble Shaw	Art Gillespie	Edward M Hernandez	Stan Moore
Dixon* (8)	CM	916 678-2326	Joe F Anderson	David L Harris	Bea Fairfield	....	William Fairfield	Roy Ennes	....
Dos Palos* (3)	CM	209 392-2174	Mario Giannoni	Mark Bautista	Doran L Otterbein	Mark Bautista	Byron Johnson	Richard Farmer	Stephen Hamilton
Downey* (83)	CM	213 869-7331	Randall R Barb	Robert R Ovrom	Robert L Shand	Leroy Powell	George D Davis	William F Martin	William A Ralph
Duarte* (17)	CM	213 357-7931	Carlyle Falkenborg	J Kenneth Caresio	J Kenneth Caresio	Donald Pruyn	....	....	Dominic Milano
Dublin§ (13)	MC	415 829-4600	....	Richard C Ambrose	....	....	....	....	....
Dunsmuir* (2)	CM	916 235-4822	Emmet Hill	Jack L Hurlburt	Elizabeth Ritchie	Jack L Hurlburt	Robert L Kenoyer	John R Rowland	Jack L Hurlburt
East Palo Alto (18)	MC	415 853-3100	(not reporting)						
El Cajon* (74)	CM	714 440-1776	John W Reber	Robert T Acker	Marilynn Linn	Harvey H Henderson	Roger D House	Darwin R Sinclair	John F Pizzato
El Centro* (24)	CM	714 352-9440	Randal L Horton	Abdel Salem	Rita Noden	....	Tom Garner	Ralph Cordova	....
El Cerrito* (23)	CM	415 234-2323	Howard P Abelson	Ronald D Creagh	Lucille V Irish	Thomas C Sinclair	Reyes Barraza	Patrick T Reeve	....
El Monte* (79)	CM	818 575-2252	Donald McMillen	Greg Korduner	Kathy Kaplan	Marvin Louie	Charles Masten	Wayne Clayton	Robert J Pinniger
El Paso de Robles* (9)	CM	805 238-1515	Gary E Stemper	John R McCarthy	John R McCarthy	Phillip S Molina	Robert Adams	Vernon L Mathison	Jay Lyon
El Segundo* (14)	CM	213 322-4670	Charles K Armstrong	Arthur E Jones	Valerie Burrowes	Jose Sanchez	Laurence H Sheldon	J Clark Devilbiss	William A Glickman
Emeryville (4)	MC	415 654-6161	Dottie Heintz	Joseph Tanner	Odessa T Hall	James Lindsay	Ramon D Vittori	Joseph Maltby	Paul Soltow
Escalon* (3)	CM	209 838-3556	David C Ennis	Earl D Wilson Jr	Earl D Wilson Jr	Earl D Wilson Jr	....	Jack B Storne	Daniel L Braddock
Escondido* (62)	CM	714 741-4703	Ernie Cowan	Vernon G Hazen	Jeanne Bunch	Timothy R Huntley	Bob Watts	James Connole	Dennis Wilson
Eureka* (24)	CM	707 443-7331	Fred J Moore Jr	Robert Stockwell	Robert Stockwell	Joann Stanhope	Verne Cooney	O R Shipley	Grant Crammond
Exeter* (6)	CM	209 592-9244	Alvin B Miller	Roy Chace	Roy Chace	....	....	Frank Jeffers	Roy Chace

Directory 1/10 continued — MUNICIPAL OFFICIALS IN ALL U.S. CITIES OVER 2,500[1]

City, 1980 population (000 omitted), form of government		Municipal phone number	Mayor	Appointed administrator	City clerk	Finance officer	Fire chief	Police chief	Public works director
CALIFORNIA (402) continued									
Fairfax t* (7)	CM	415 453-1584	Frank J Egger	Richard V Brown	Mary Getty Hansen	Edward J Kelly	Robert Beedle	Charles A Grasso	Bill Street
Fairfield* (58)	CM	707 426-5500	Gary Falati	B Gale Wilson	Bess Day	Charles Long	....	Charles Huchel	Ronald Hurlbut
Farmersville* (6)	CM	209 747-0458	Charles Felix	Patrick M King	Lucille Scott	Patti Tedford	....	Gary Meek	Ruben DeLeon
Fillmore* (10)	CM	805 524-3701	Ernest J Morales	James E Robbins	Noreen H Withers	Veda Southwick	George R Campbell	William A Brewer	Jerome J Wedding
Firebaugh* (4)	CM	209 659-2043	Morris Kyle Jr	Pierce J Powers	Flora Mae Shuemake	Les Beshears	John G Borboa	Howard Manes	Robert Macias
Folsom* (11)	CM	916 355-7200	George E Hannaford	David M Mansfield	Arlene Soto	Neal Bearden	Robert Welch	Harold N Barker	William E Kime
Fontana* (37)	CM	714 823-3411	Nathan A Simon	Jean D Ratelle II	Patricia M Murray	Edwin E Luekemeyer	Ora Short	Ben L Abernathy	Robt J Schoenborn
Fort Bragg§ (5)	MC	707 964-5325	Bob Woelfel	Gary D Milliman	Deelynn Carpenter	John Deiderich	Robert Ramage	Jodean Mayberry	Larry Brooks
Fortuna§ (8)	MC	707 725-6125	Beth Rundell	Robert M Davis	Robert M Davis	David Bentley	Robert Sommerville	Wm P Terry	Thomas McWhorter
Foster City* (23)	CM	415 349-1200	Roger Chinn	Richard Wykoff	Marvell Herren	James Hardy	John Bettencourt	Robert Norman	David Miller
Fountain Valley* (55)	CM	714 963-8321	Mary Adler	Judy L Kelsey	Evelyn McClendon	Steve Chippas	Dick Jorgensen	Marvin Fortin	Wayne Osborne
Fremont* (132)	CM	415 791-4500	Leon J Mezzetti	Charles K McClain	Douglas Eads	Fred Stabell	Dean Holzgrafe	Robert Wasserman	Thomas M Blalock
Fresno* (218)	CM	209 488-1563	Daniel K Whitehurst	R M Christofferson	Jacqueline Ryle	Allen W Charkow	Bud Armstrong	Max Downs	James L Martin
Fullerton* (102)	CM	714 738-6300	A B Catlin	William C Winter	Anne M York	Barbara A Henderson	William Houser	Martin Hairabedian	Hugh L Berry
Galt§ (6)	MC	209 745-2961	Donald L Prachar Jr	Joseph M Tanner	Linda Stallings	Virginia E Twardy	....	....	Waldo Kolb
Garden Grove* (123)	CM	714 638-6673	Jonathan H Cannon	Delbert L Powers	Carolyn Morris	Anthony J Andrade	Douglas V Spickard	Francis Kessler	George L Tindall
Gardena* (45)	CM	213 327-0220	Donald L Dear	Martin H Reagan	May Y Doi	Keith Bennett	Andy Bero	Richard Propster	Ken Ayres
Gilroy* (22)	CM	408 842-3191	Roberta H Hughan	Jay Baksa	Ms S E Steinmetz	Cecil A Reinsch	Albert L Brittain	Gregory G Cowart	Richard L Cox
Glendale* (139)	CM	818 956-4000	Carroll W Parcher	James M Rez	Merle Hagemeyer	Brian A Butler	Allan R Stone	David J Thompson	George Miller
Glendora* (39)	CM	213 335-4071	John C Gordon	James M Evans	Culver E Heaton Jr	Samuel Shwetz	Morris Gregory	O B Posey	Arthur E Cook
Gonzales* (3)	CM	408 675-2321	Charles Villegas	Berkley H Brannon	Berkley H Brannon	Julia Mena	Rick Rubbo	Conrad Aponte	R David Garibay
Grand Terrace* (8)	CM	714 824-6621	Hugh J Grant	Seth Armstead	Myrna Erway	Thomas Schwab	Howard Wright	Jim Bradford	Joe Kicak
Grass Valley (7)	MC	916 273-2203	Dennis C Hill	David A Breninger	David A Breminger	Luther W Faler	John F Straka	Melvin W Mouser	Tim Hackworth
Greenfield§ (4)	MC	408 674-5591	Elias DeLeon Jr	George Scarborough	George Scarborough	Veeda Cumming	Victor Pura	Lamarr Sauer	John Alves
Gridley (4)	MC	916 846-3143	Doris Long	Henry E Ford	Henry E Ford	Evelene D Payne	Alvah McBride	John Donnahoe	....
Grover City* (9)	CM	805 489-4040	Juanita J Qualls	Arnold Dowdy	Alberta A Gallagher	Linda J Maher	Lowell Forister	David L Brown	Thomas Sullivan
Guadalupe* (4)	CM	805 343-1340	Frank T Almaguer	....	Nancy C Etteddgue	....	Henry J Lawrence	Raymond A Champagne	....
Gustine* (3)	CM	209 854-6471	Daniel Serpa	David K Witter	David K Witter	David K Witter	Richard Vierra	Robert Belmont	David K Witter
Half Moon Bay* (7)	CM	415 726-5566	Melvin A Mello Sr	W Fred Mortensen	Ralphena R Guest	Claudia P Snyder	Gildo Bustichi	John E Gonzales	Ronald G Young
Hanford* (21)	CM	209 582-2511	J Brent Madill	James L Armstrong	Dorothy A Mattos	Tom Dibble	George Watson	Lee Drummond	Donald M Dodge
Hawaiian Gardens* (11)	CM	213 420-2641	Jack M Myers	Douglas Dunlap	Carol J Dorfmeyer	....	....	....	Tom Tichenor
Hawthorne* (56)	CM	213 970-7902	Guy J Hocker Jr	R Kenneth Jue	Patrick Keller	Sam Takata	Ralph A Hardin	Kenneth Stonebraker	James Mitsch
Hayward* (94)	CM	415 581-2345	Alex Giuliani	Donald A Blubaugh	Paloma Weaver	John O'Sullivan	William Neville Jr	Charles Plummer	Edward E Phillips
Healdsburg§ (7)	MC	707 433-9425	Robert Rose	Michael McDonald	Jean McMellon	Kurt Hahn	Ken Hanley	Joe Palla	Richard Pusich
Hemet* (23)	CM	714 658-9411	Patricia L Herron	Lyle W Alberg	Edward J Rodeghier	Steve Temple	Lyle W Alberg	Roger Miller	David R Oltman
Hercules* (6)	CM	415 724-2489	John Cadigan	Steven M Salomon	Ellen M Zapata	William A Lindsay	Tom Birdwell	Russell S Quinn	William Chapman
Hermosa Beach* (18)	CM	213 376-6984	Gary Brutsch	Gregory T Meyer	Kathy Reviczky	Gregory T Meyer	Ronald Simmons	Frank Beeson	....
Hillsborough t* (10)	CM	415 343-2795	Patrick W Kelly	Robert M Davidson	Virginia Hvid	Virginia Hvid	Kenneth Newman	William A Key	Jack B Rush
Hollister* (11)	CM	408 637-8221	John Ivancovich	Paul Ogden	....	....	Tony Aguirre	Wayne Purvus	Jack LaPorte
Holtville (4)	MC	619 356-2912	Larry Martinez	....	Martha Miller	....	Giles A Nadey	Arlie P Henthorne	William E Bell
Hughson* (3)	CM	209 883-4054	William Trieweiler	Troy C Presley	Gayle Robertson	....	Robert Silva	L G Etherington Jr	Troy Presley
Huntington Park* (46)	CM	213 582-6161	William Cunningham	Donald L Jeffers	Marilyn A Boyette	Edward S Chow	....	Geano Contessotto	Ronald J Zapf
Huntington Beach* (171)	CM	714 536-5511	Jack Kelly	Chas W Thompson	Alicia M Wentworth	Robert J Franz	Raymond C Picard	Earle Robitaille	Paul Cook
Huron (3)	MC	209 945-2241	Tony E Silva	Frank V Filice	Barbara C Martinez	Norman Huebert	....	....	Steve Garza
Imperial (3)	MC	619 355-4371	Victor Mendoza	....	Betty Willett	Betty Willett	Lon Hettinger	Lon Hettinger	Stacy D Chase
Imperial Beach* (23)	CM	619 423-8300	Brian P Bilbray	Sherman T Stenberg	Sherman T Stenberg	Dante Dayacap	John A Holsenback	John F Duffy	Jerald D Johnson
Indian Wells* (1)	CM	714 346-2489	Frank Chilson	Prince E Pierson	Prince E Pierson	Thomas M Wood	William S Lord	Arthur Renney	Prince E Pierson
Indio* (22)	CM	714 347-2351	Roger Harlow	W Phillip Hawes	Saundra Juhola	Kenneth Adams	John Payne	Curtis R Cross	Roland Taatjes
Inglewood* (94)	CM	213 649-7301	Edward Vincent	Paul D Eckles	Iris A Crochet	Norman Y Cravens	Robert E Osby	Joseph Rouzan	William Mahar
Irvine* (62)	CM	714 660-3600	David G Sills	Wm Woollett Jr	Nancy C Lacey	Jeff Niven	Larry Holmes	Leo E Peart	G Brent Muchow
Irwindale* (1)	CM	818 962-3381	Michael Miranda	Charles R Martin	Margaret S Barbosa	Charles R Martin	....	Julian Miranda	....
Kerman§ (4)	MC	209 846-9384	Harry Pedersen	....	Edith M Forsstrom	Edward Watanabe	....	Kenneth W Stafford	Daniel F Ayala
King City* (5)	CM	408 385-3281	Irving J Copley	Damon B Edwards	Marjorie Sarina	Carlos Olvera	Floyd Owens	David Torres	Harlan Butler
Kingsburg* (5)	CM	209 897-5821	Gordon R Satterberg	Lawrence Butzlaff	Lawrence Butzlaff	Lawrence Butzlaff	Don Huddleston	James L Taylor	Lawrence Butzlaff
La Canada Flintridge*† (20)	CM	213 790-8880	O Warren Hillgren	George Caswell	Patricia Anderson	....	....	....	....
La Habra* (45)	CM	213 694-1011	John Holmberg	C Lee Risner	Katherine Adams	Sara Morris	Verl Griffin	Ron Meehan	James Harkins
La Habra Heights* (5)	CM	213 694-6302	Jean G Good	Robt G Gutierrez	Robt G Gutierrez	Robt G Gutierrez	Jerry Wilcut	Sherman Block	John E Maulding
La Mesa* (50)	CM	619 463-6611	George F Bailey	Ronald E Bradley	Anita Underwood	Dennis M Hackett	James O Orsborn	Donald G Fach	James O'Grady
La Mirada* (41)	CM	213 943-0131	C David Peters	Gary K Sloan	Anna J Martin	Gary K Sloan	John Englund	Sherm Block	Perry Turigliatto
La Palma* (16)	CM	714 523-7700	Edward J Bryne	Richard Rowe	Mary M O'Neil	....	....	Norman Hansen	Richard L Polen
La Puente* (31)	CM	818 330-4511	Max E Ragland	Frank Ruiz	Frank Ruiz	Donald O Withers	....	....	Frank Ruiz
La Quinta (4)	MC	619 564-2246	(not reporting)						
La Verne* (24)	CM	714 593-8726	Jon Blickenstaff	William Sheldon Jr	N Kathleen Hamm	Geraldine H Peck	Robert S Lapp	Wesley Stearns	Brian Bowcock
Lafayette* (21)	CM	415 284-1968	Gayle Vilkema	Maureen Cassingham	Maureen Cassingham	....	....	....	Joe Carrasco
Laguna Beach*† (18)	CM	714 497-3311	Robert F Gentry	Kenneth C Frank	Verna Rollinger	Richard R Reese	Ronald Adams	Neil J Purcell	Terry Brandt
Lake Elsinore* (6)	CM	714 674-3124	Arta E Valenzuela	J Michael Norton	Jo Ann Money	Jo Barrick	....	....	Loren Culp
Lakeport (4)	MC	707 263-5682	Arlin Pischke	....	Bernice M Hudson	Larry Jack	Don DeBolt	James Campbell	Jerry Ritchie
Lakewood* (75)	CM	213 866-9771	Jacqueline Rynerson	Howard L Chambers	Jack Huntsinger	Nancy Hicks	....	....	Leonard Biel
Lancaster* (48)	CM	805 945-7811	Barbara Little	James C Gilley	Christine E Root	William Redman	....	....	Richard Kopecky
Larkspur* (11)	CM	415 924-8084	Michael Wornum	Harlan Barry	Nancy Anthony	Rita Mott	William Lellis	Phil Green	Carolyn Campbell
Lawndale* (23)	CM	213 772-4191	Sarann Kruse	Paul J Philips	Joyce A South	Paul J Philips	Clyde A Bragdon	Sherman Block	Keene Wilson
Lemon Grove* (21)	CM	714 464-6934	James V Dorman	Jack D Shelver	Karen Thomson	Karen Thomson	Robert N Adams	....	....
Lemoore*† (9)	CM	209 924-5396	Donald W Casten	Wm R Drennen	Gloria Ornellas	Gloria Ornellas	Russell Kreps	William Young	Gary Misenhimer
Lincoln* (4)	CM	916 645-3314	Robert Flocchini	Richard J Ramirez	Linda Stackpoole	Richard J Ramirez	Al Gulliford	Robert Leighty	Jerry Judge
Lindsay* (7)	CM	209 562-2511	Douglas Bodine	John W Beene	Redoy Kiesz	Redoy Kiesz	John W Beene	John W Beene	John Dutton
Live Oak (3)	CM	916 695-2112	Douglas Dollar	....	Blanche Gillespie	Blanche Gillespie	Vernon Berry	....	Donald A Dosser
Livermore* (48)	CM	415 449-4000	Dale Turner	Leland J Horner	Carol Greany	Monica Potter	Michael J Sample	Melvin Nelson	Daniel J Lee
Livingston* (5)	CM	209 394-8041	Dwight Benafield	Paul E Lawrence	Elwood Campini	Paul E Lawrence	John Vance	Harold McKinney	Gary Petty
Lodi* (35)	CM	209 334-5634	John R Randy Snider	Henry A Glaves Jr	Alice M Reimche	Robert H Holm	Donald MacLeod	Floyd Williams	Jack L Ronsko
Loma Linda* (11)	CM	714 796-2531	Ardyce H Koobs	Robert R Mitchell	Robert R Mitchell	Robert R Mitchell	Peter R Hills	....	....
Lomita* (17)	CM	213 325-7110	Harold S Croyts	Walker J Ritter	Dawn R Tomita	....	....	....	....
Lompoc* (26)	CM	805 736-1261	Joe Andrew Salazar	Gene L Wahlers	Maureen Bosking	John Walk	J Michael Ellison	J D Smith	....
Long Beach* (361)	CM	213 590-6711	Ernie Kell	John E Dever	Shelba Powell	James A Algie	Robert E Leslie	Charles B Ussery	James T Pott
Los Alamitos* (12)	CM	213 431-3538	David A Lander	Michael A Graziano	Michael A Graziano	Richard A Patino	Larry Holmes	Kelson McDaniel	Vernon P Hee
Los Altos Hills t* (7)	CM	415 941-7222	Andrew Allison	Gordon Miller	Patricia Dowd	....	....	....	....
Los Altos*† (26)	CM	415 948-1491	Frank Verlot	Arne L Croce	....	John G Lovell	John T Sanders	Richard G Brannan	Ronald D Gruenwald
Los Angeles§ (2967)	MC	213 485-2121	Tom Bradley	Keith Comrie	Elias Martinez	James K Hahn	Donald O Manning	Daryl F Gates	Philip V King

Directory 1/10 continued — MUNICIPAL OFFICIALS IN ALL U.S. CITIES OVER 2,500[1]

City, 1980 population (000 omitted), form of government	Municipal phone number	Mayor	Appointed administrator	City clerk	Finance officer	Fire chief	Police chief	Public works director
CALIFORNIA (402) continued								
Los Banos* (10) CM	209 826-5119	Elmer K Austin	Loris T Broddrick	Tesse J Mazzina	James J Johnson	Roland Pimentel	Charles J Martin	....
Los Gatos* (27) CM	408 354-6832	Thomas Ferrito	David R Mora	Rose E Aldag	Rose E Aloag	....	J Frank Acosta	Robert Bryant
Lynwood* (49) CM	213 603-0220	E L Morris	Charles G Gomez	Andrea L Hooper	....	Ron Lathrope	....	....
Madera* (22) CM	209 674-8802	Edward J Boyle	Robert H Kelley	Edith J Fischer	Virgil L McDowell	Lawrence Sunia	Gordon E Skeels	David Chumley
Manhattan Beach* (32) CM	213 545-5621	Russell F Lesser	David J Thompson	John A Lacey	Merle Lundberg	Thomas P Wilson	Harry Kuhlmeyer	Mort August
Manteca* (25) CM	209 239-9511	Jack C Snyder	David M Jinkens	Joann Tilton	Leticia Allison	Larry Drager	Leonard Taylor	Michael Brinton
Marina* (21) CM	408 384-3715	George J Takahashi	Larry W Bagley	Larry W Bagley	Marty Silguero	Travis Jackson	Daniel G Givens	Vince DiMaggio
Martinez* (23) CM	415 372-4900	Michael M Menesini	Paul D Brotzman	Lawrence J Kowalski	Mike P Jones	....	Jack E Garner	Mohinder P Sharma
Marysville§† (10) MC	916 674-6633	Ronald A Haedicke	....	Elisabeth A Ahart	Leigh P Keicher	John Buchanan	John A Gust	J C Onderek
Maywood§ (22) MC	213 560-3197	William A Hamilton	Leonard R Locher	Leonard R Locher	Leonard R Locher	Clyde A Bragdon Jr	Theodore R Heidke	Leonard R Locher
McFarland (5) CM	805 792-3091	Donnie Campbell	....	Doris Wood	....	....	Vido Giuntoli	....
Mendota§ (5) MC	209 655-3291	Leo Capuchino	Paul K Owhadi	Paul K Owhadi	Dean Beyer	....	Jack Pina	Eliseo Garcia
Menlo Park* (26) CM	415 858-3360	Peg Gunn	Michael A Bedwell	Jaye Carr	Russell Scotten	Vincent Del Pozzo	Gerald McNamara	Lauren Mercer
Merced* (36) CM	209 385-6999	Samuel C Pipes	Wm H Cunningham	....	L Patrick Samsell	Kenneth Mitten	Patrick Lunney	Stevan Stroud
Mill Valley* (13) CM	415 388-4033	Joan Boessenecker	Douglas R Dawson	Elaine Carry	John Tweedie	William A Walsh	William A Walsh	Henry Van Dyke
Millbrae*† (20) CM	415 692-6890	Frank T Cannizzaro	James R Erickson	Alicia Magallanes	Joe Arch	William Moke	John Dineen	Lyle D Johnson
Milpitas* (38) CM	408 942-2310	James Rodgers	Michael Uberuaga	Gail Ranney	Lawrence Sabo	Michael N Harwood	James B Murray	Jerry Williams
Modesto* (106) CM	209 577-5200	Peggy Mensinger	Garth Lipsky	Norrine Coyle	Pete Brock	R Bruce Simons	Gerald McKinsey	Ed Walker
Monrovia* (31) CM	213 359-3231	Paul A Stuart	James E Starbird	Patricia Ostrye	Howard Longballa	George W Kahl	Bill Tubbs	Carl G Brooks
Montclair* (23) CM	714 626-8571	Harold M Hayes	G Michael Milhiser	Margaret A Crawford	G Michael Milhiser	Loren Pettis	Gregory C Caldwell	Carl Sawtell
Monte Sereno* (3) CM	408 354-7635	Dorothea F Bamford	Donald C Wimberly	Fay Furtado	....	....	....	Donald C Wimberly
Montebello* (53) CM	213 725-1200	Wm O Nighswonger	Joseph M Goeden	Andrew T Lambo	Grant Gundestrup	Robert J King	Leslie D Sourisseau	Robert Lata
Monterey* (28) CM	408 646-3761	Clyde W Roberson	John O Dunn Jr	Pat O'Hearn	Dewey Evans	John Montenero	Harold Benadom	L W McIntyre
Monterey Park* (54) CM	213 307-1255	David Almada	Lloyd DeLlamas	Pauline Lemire	David P Bentz	....	Jon D Elder	....
Moorpark (8) MC	805 529-7864	(not reporting)						
Moraga t* (15) CM	415 376-5200	William G Combs	Gary C Chase	Gary C Chase	Gary C Chase	....	Thomas H Simms	James E Grassi
Morgan Hill* (17) CM	408 779-7271	J Robert Foster	Charles R Cate	Barbara Little	Bill Mullen	Brad Spencer	Wm Dodeward	....
Morro Bay* (9) CM	805 772-1214	Eugene R Shelton	Gary Napper	Gary Napper	Louise Burt	Bernard C Zerr	Dave Howell	Nick Nichols
Mount Shasta (3) MC	916 926-2141	Richard Derwingson	....	Gino Marconi	Gino Marconi	Joe Spini	Lou Baldi	Robert Aberg
Mountain View* (59) CM	415 966-6304	Maryce Freelen	Bruce W Liedstrand	Alice Roylance	Ronald Beach	Wes Gunion	Robert Schatz	E Allen Shelley
Napa* (51) CM	707 252-7711	Robert G Pelusi	William Lee Bopf	Pamyla C Means	John Dannewitz	Vernon Hamilton	Kenneth Jennings	John W Lindblad
National City* (49) CM	714 477-1181	Kile Morgan	Tom G McCabe	Ione M Campbell	Alex Caloza	Randy Kimble	Terry Hart	Curtis Williams
Needles* (4) CM	619 326-2113	David B Daniel	Vernon Bailey	Cheryl K Sallis	Vernon Bailey	Herb Eberhardt	Bruce Weekley	Vernon Bailey
Nevada City* (2) CM	916 265-2496	Paul J Matson	Beryl P Robinson Jr	Maureen Ryan	....	Greg Wasley	Billy E Beard	Charles Adams
Newark* (32) CM	415 793-1400	David W Smith	Richard W Turnlund	Alberto T Huezo	Alberto T Huezo	F P Spalding	Carl W Pierce	P H B Tong
Newman* (3) CM	209 862-3725	Janet Carlsen	James D Holden	James D Holden	James D Holden	Kenneth Johnson	Thomas W Engstrom	Augustine A Alves
Newport Beach* (63) CM	714 640-2151	Evelyn Hart	Robert L Wynn	Wanda Andersen	George Pappas	James Reed	Charles Gross	Ben Nolan
Norco* (21) CM	714 735-3900	Naomi R Feagan	John W Donlevy	Muriel A Ruthrauff	Carolyn Bartleman	Richard Smetana	John Jones	James Ashcraft
Norwalk* (85) CM	213 929-2677	Cecil N Green	Raymond L Gibbs	Mary Paxon	Wiley Y Jung	....	....	Kenneth Montgomery
Novato* (44) CM	415 897-4311	Don Shank	Phillip J Brown	....	Marilyn Leuck	....	William Kirkpatrick	....
Oakdale* (8) CM	209 847-3031	Robert E Wikoff	Bruce W Bannerman	Rebecca A Peluso	Margery Cruz	Jack Criswell	David Sundy	Mike Pettinger
Oakland*† (339) CM	415 273-3301	Lionel J Wilson	Henry L Gardner	Arrece Jameson	Richard Digre	Samuel L Golden	George T Hart	Terry Roberts
Oceanside* (77) CM	619 439-7300	Larry M Bagley	Suzanne E Foucault	Barbara Bishop	Carl V Husby Jr	Jack Rosenquist	Larry Marshall	Glenn Prentice
Ojai* (7) CM	805 646-5581	Richard Conrad	Carl Hatfield Jr	Cyndi Reynolds	Cyndi Reynolds	S E Masson	Gary Markley	Kenneth C Gilbert
Ontario* (89) CM	714 986-1151	R E Ellingwood	Roger D Hughbanks	Deloris Arterburn	Samuel R Norris	David R Lee	Leroy M Kolbrek	Michael Teal
Orange* (92) CM	714 532-0321	James Beam	J William Little	Marilyn Jensen	Ted Schoettger	Martel Thompson	Norman A Traub	Frank Page
Orange Cove§ (4) MC	209 626-4488	Eugene Pinedo	Robert Trevino	Maria C Estrada	William Smith	George Winzer	George Garcia	Bayani Mauricio
Orland (4) MC	916 865-4741	Ernie Lohse	Al Calonico	Laura Blevins	Glendora Feil	Jack Bucke	William F Olney	Bernard Plants
Oroville* (9) CM	916 533-2575	Jana Wilson	Richard Copeland	Richard Copeland	Leo Burns	Dean Hill	Jan R Duke	Kirt Hunter
Oxnard* (108) CM	805 486-4311	Nao Takasugi	James E Frandsen	Mabi Covarrubias	Walt Yates	Ted Christensen	Robert P Owens	Ben Wong
Pacific Grove* (16) CM	408 375-3151	Florus C Williams	Gary W Bales	H Fred Smith	H Fred Smith	Donald Gasperson	John Matteson	Anthony Weeks
Pacifica* (37) CM	415 875-7300	Peter Loeb	David G Finigan	David G Finigan	Gul Ramchandani	....	Alfred Olson	Michael G Randolph
Palm Desert* (12) CM	619 346-0611	Walter H Snyder	Bruce A Altman	Sheila R Gilligan	Kirby J Warner	Eric Vogt	Michael Lewis	Barry McClellan
Palm Springs* (32) CM	714 323-8201	Frank M Bogert	Norman R King	Judith H Sumich	Paul R Howard	Byron Chaney	Tom Kendra	David Strecker
Palmdale* (12) CM	805 273-3162	Janis C Bales	Gregory McWilliams	Gregory McWilliams	Ray Wood	Clyde Bragdon	Sherman Block	Gregory McWilliams
Palo Alto* (55) CM	415 329-2392	Lawrence Klein	William Zaner	Ann J Tanner	Mark R Harris	Robert Wall	James C Zurcher	David Adams
Palos Verdes Estates* (14) CM	213 378-0383	Ronald M Florance	Thomas A Devereux	Ray Randolph	Ray Randolph	Richard Wendt	John Dollarhide	Ross Meadows
Paradise t§ (23) MC	916 872-8696	Curt Campion	George F Irving	Diana Kruger	David L Sanders	James P Gilpatrick	Leonard F Trombley	Jon Lander
Paramount* (36) CM	213 531-3503	Gerald Mulrooney	William A Holt	William A Holt	David Spilman	....	....	....
Parlier (3) MC	209 646-2767	Arcadio Viveros	Berton K Wills	Rosie D Flores	....	....	....	....
Pasadena* (119) CM	818 405-4222	William Bogaard	Donald F McIntyre	Pamela Swift	Harry Lauritzen	Kaya Pekerol	Robert McGowan	Arthur A Krieger
Patterson* (4) CM	209 892-2041	Pat D Maisetti	Henry G Hesling	Reta R Muller	Henry G Hesling	Richard Gaiser	Donald Braunton	Nicholas Pinhey
Perris* (7) CM	714 657-5115	Louis R Boettcher	Robert L Briscoe	Beti An Hynes	Ray L Leland	David L Flake	John L Kuykendall	Ronald Kwiatkowski
Petaluma* (34) CM	707 778-4345	Fred V Mattei	John L Scharer	Patricia E Bernard	Juelle Ann Boyer	Leslie H Lenz Jr	Robert B Murphy	Thomas S Hargis
Pico Rivera* (53) CM	213 942-2000	James M Patronite	Robert L Williams	Thelma M Kail	Randy L Rassi	George Harms	Robert Pash	John E Medina
Piedmont§ (10) MC	415 420-3040	Ted Normart	David A Berger	David A Berger	Carl R Kuney	L J Phillips	Craig T Steckler	Dan Masdeo
Pinole* (14) CM	415 724-9000	Louis Borges Jr	Donald E Bradley	Elizabeth Grimes	Joseph Meneghini	Alex A Clark	Theodore Barnes	G Keith Freeman
Pismo Beach* (5) CM	805 773-4657	Wm O Richardson	Les Crist	Terry A Briscoe	Margaret Vicars	Paul Henlin	Edward C Williams	Dave Watson
Pittsburg* (33) CM	415 439-4850	Joseph Detorres	S Anthony Donato	Mary Erbez	Ken Hammon	Vincent Aiello	Leonard Castiglione	Robert Soderbery
Placentia* (35) CM	714 993-8117	Richard E Buck	Roger L Kemp	Doris B Black	Frank B Dunnavant	Larry J Holms	Harold A Fischer	Robert Damato
Placerville* (7) CM	916 622-3515	Carl Borelli	Lee Yarborough	Lennie Mills	Lennie Mills	Albert G Herzig	Ted J Mertens	Michael W Foster
Pleasant Hill* (25) CM	415 934-6050	Paul L Cooper	James L Alkire	Wetona L Crawford	Virginia F O'Byrne	William Maxfield	James Nunes	W James See
Pleasanton* (35) CM	415 847-8000	Kenneth R Mercer	James R Walker	James R Walker	Emily Wagner	Joe Hill	William E Eastman	Robert L Warnick
Pomona* (93) CM	714 620-2051	G Stanton Selby	Ora E Lampman	Joyce Herr	Robert A Otto	John M Fowlkes	Donald Burnett	Ben Minamide
Port Hueneme* (18) CM	805 488-3625	Dorill B Wright	John R Velthoen	Karen B Jackson	James M Hanks	....	Robert A Anderson	John J Duffy
Porterville*† (20) CM	209 784-1400	Steven E Tree	Chas G Huffaker	Chas G Huffaker	William R McGuire	Jerry O Mainord	John C Smith	William R McGuire
Portola* (2) CM	916 832-4216	....	Earl W Morrison	Marsha L Frerking	Marsha L Frerking	Curtis Marshall	....	Verlin D Woods
Portola Valley† (4) CM	415 851-1700	Nancy Robertson	....	....	Henry P Huff III	Richard B Figoni	John McDonald Jr	Bruce E Kirk
Poway* (33) CM	619 748-6600	Bruce J Tarzy	James L Bowersox	Marjorie Wahlsten	Kathleen D Jimno	William Toon	....	Alan Archibald
Rancho Cucamonga* (55) CM	714 989-1851	Jon D Mikels	Lauren Wasserman	Beverly A Authelet	Harry Empey	Richard Feuerstein	John Futscher	Lloyd Hubbs
Rancho Mirage* (6) CM	619 324-4511	William D Wilson	Stephen A Birbeck	Barbara E Dohn	Herb Schmid	Dave Flake	Ben Clark	....
Rancho Palos Verdes* (35) CM	213 377-0360	Jacki Bacharach	Donald F Guluzzy	Jo Lofthus	Greg Beaubien	Ray Brunstrom	Elmer Omohundro Jr	Gordon Siebert
Red Bluff* (9) CM	916 527-2605	Velma A Trujillo	Dennis W Fischer	Jeanne L Saunders	Raymond Harrington	Charles T Gauthier	John E Faulkner	Harlan E Warwick
Redding* (42) CM	916 225-4090	Howard Kirkpatrick	Robert E Courtney	Ethel A Nichols	Linda R Downing	Kenneth Erichsrud	Robert H Whitmer	Carl H Arness Jr
Redlands* (44) CM	714 793-2641	Carole Beswick	John E Holmes	Lorrie Poyzer	Henry Lee Archbold	Ray Mills	Robert E Brickley	John Donnelly
Redondo Beach* (57) CM	213 372-1171	Barbara J Doerr	Timothy J Casey	John Oliver	....	James L Black	Roger M Moulton	James Bailey
Redwood City* (55) CM	415 369-6251	Britschgi C Brenton	James M Smith	J C Hildebrand	Peter Tasseff	Peter J O'Brien	Anthony L Guardino	Frank J Addiego

Directory 1/10 continued

MUNICIPAL OFFICIALS IN ALL U.S. CITIES OVER 2,500[1]

City, 1980 population (000 omitted), form of government	Municipal phone number	Mayor	Appointed administrator	City clerk	Finance officer	Fire chief	Police chief	Public works director
CALIFORNIA (402) continued								
Reedley§ (11) MC	209 638-6881	Lawrence R Wilder	Thomas M Butch	Raymond L Medcalf	Carlos Sanchez	Bill Jackson	Forrest Brown	Kent D Davis
Rialto* (36) CM	714 820-2525	Gerald R Eaves	Walter Pudinski	Joseph H Sampson	Arthur T College	Roger Purdie	Raymond Farmer	Renato Ranoa
Richmond* (75) CM	415 231-2030	Thomas J Corcoran	James M Fales Jr	Harlan J Heydon	....	Charles W Schwab	Earnest Clements	Lawrence Loder
Ridgecrest§ (16) MC	619 375-1321	Anna Marie Bergens	Lawrence M Cook	Joyce M Taft	C Roger Ward	....	Larry Brunson	Edgar E Edwards
Rio Dell (3) MC	707 764-3532	Craige McKnight	Wayne D Mayhall	Anita Potter	Wayne D Mayhall	Dave Ghilarducci	Rudolph Elendt	Frank Dodge
Rio Vista (3) CM	707 374-6451	Milton Wallace	Robert R Brown	Anita Reineke	Peter Woodruff	Stanford Simi	Richard D Cook	....
Ripon* (4) CM	209 599-2108	Edmund F Feichtmeir	Clarence Smit	Clarence Smit	Clarence Smit	Ed Bynum	Elden Nutt	....
Riverbank* (6) CM	209 869-3671	Charles E Neal	Gerald E Robirds	Gerald E Robirds	Brian E Cox	Robert P Tucker	Bernard J Remas Jr	Billy G Lee
Riverside* (171) CM	714 787-7557	Ab Brown	Douglas Weiford	Alice A Hare	Hal Brewer	Richard Bosted	L L Richardson	Bob Wales
Rocklin* (7) CM	916 624-3351	Will Linton	Carlos Urrutia	Sandra Bedwell	Rex E Miller	Randy Lavelock	James Simmons	Harold Peters
Rohnert Park* (23) CM	707 795-2411	A Hollingsworth	Peter M Callinan	Peter M Callinan	Joseph D Netter	Jerry R Bick	Robert E Dennett	Roland L Brust
Rolling Hills Estates* (9) CM	213 377-1577	Jerome Belsky	Harry R Peacock	Harry R Peacock	Phillip Keller	John Englund	Sherman Block	Harry R Peacock
Rolling Hills* (2) CM	213 377-1521	Ginny Leeuwenburgh	Ron Molendyk	Ron Molendyk	....	Clyde A Bragdon	Sherman Block	Martin Murphy
Rosemead* (43) CM	213 288-6671	Gary A Taylor	Frank G Tripepi	Ellen Poochigian	Frank G Tripepi	Clyde Bragdon	Sherman Block	Donald J Wagner
Roseville* (24) CM	916 783-9151	Harry Crabb Jr	Robt G Hutchison	Pauline Brockman	Robert L Hargrave	Carl J Green	James A Hall	Frederick Barnett
Ross † (3) MC	415 453-1453	R S Poore	....	Virginia Stott	....		Douglas Miller	Jorgen V Lunding
Sacramento* (276) CM	916 449-5011	Anne Rudin	Walter J Slipe	Lorraine Magana	Jack R Crist	William R Powell	John P Kearns	Melvin H Johnson
Salinas* (80) CM	408 758-7201	James B Barnes	William A Carlson	Dottie F Doughty	John Copeland	Thomas Campbell	R Fred Ferguson	Arnold C Joens
San Anselmo* (12) CM	415 453-0392	Pieter Toal	Michael P Garvey	Carolyn Foster	Michael P Garvey	Robert Beedle	Bernard Del Santo	George Davison
San Bernardino§ (118) MC	714 383-5122	W R Bob Holcomb	John Matzer Jr	Shauna Clark	Warren Knudson	Gerald Newcombe	Benjamin Gonzales	Roger G Hardgrave
San Bruno*† (35) CM	415 877-8897	Bob Marshall	Gerald D Minford	Terri Rasmussen	Robert Bodeman	Harper Petersen	Frank E Hedley	Robert Whitehair
San Buenaventura* (74) CM	805 654-7800	R Dennis Orrock	John Baker	Barbara J Kam	John R McMillan	Bob Horne	Raymond McLean	Shelley Jones
San Carlos* (25) CM	415 593-8011	William M Steele	Warren H Shafer	Margaret Hanley	Dianne L Gershuny	Gary W Schmitz	Owen McGuigan	Parviz Mokhtari
San Clemente* (27) CM	714 361-8200	Kenneth E Carr	....	Max L Berg	Dean A Porter	Ron Coleman	Gary E Brown	Donald R Duckworth
San Diego* (876) CM	714 236-6363	Roger Hedgecock	Ray Blair	Charles G Abdelnour	Libby Anderson	Roger C Phillips	William B Kolender	Terry Flynn
San Dimas* (24) CM	714 599-6713	Donald Haefer	Robert L Poff	Pamela J Jackson	Robert L Poff	....	....	Frank Basile
San Fernando* (18) CM	818 365-2541	Roy Richardson	Donald E Penman	Donald E Penman	Michael J Moon	....	Charles Sherwood	....
San Francisco§ (679) MC	415 558-6161	Dianne Feinstein	Roger Boas	John Taylor	John C Farrell	Emmet Condon	Cornelius P Murphy	Jeffrey Lee
San Gabriel* (30) CM	818 308-2800	Jeanne E Parrish	Robert D Clute	Charles H Faulkner	Mark M Uyeda	Charles F Brown	Don S Tutich	Frank F Forbes
San Jacinto*† (7) CM	714 654-7337	Joe Marthaller	Ross S Nammar	....		....	Larry Preston	Richar Bowser
San Jose* (637) CM	408 277-4000	Thomas McEnery	Gerald E Newfarmer	Helen Jackson	Ralph Hanley	Earl Thompson	Joseph D McNamara	D Kent Dewell
San Juan Capistrano* (19) CM	714 493-1171	Gary L Hausdorfer	Stephen B Julian	Mary Ann Hanover	Robert Boone	....	....	William D Murphy
San Leandro* (64) CM	415 577-3000	Valance Gill	Leroy E Riordan	Georgia L Dennehey	John J Jermanis	Harold L Hamilton	Donald F Becker	Philip H Long
San Luis Obispo* (34) CM	805 541-1000	Melanie C Billig	Paul A Lanspery	Pamela Voges	Roberta Goddard	Mike Dolder	Roger L Neuman	David F Romero
San Marcos* (17) CM	714 744-4020	Lionel G Burton	Rick Gittings	Sheila A Kennedy	G L Cano Jr	....	....	Richard Wygant
San Marino* (13) CM	818 300-0700	Benjamin F Hammon	Allen B Stephenson	Betty J Groomes	Betty J Groomes	James V Hawkins	James W Moore	....
San Mateo* (78) CM	415 377-3300	Florence Rhoads	Richard B DeLong	Doris Christen	John L Derussy	Arthur N Koron	Don Phipps	Robert G Bezzant
San Pablo* (20) CM	415 234-6443	Joseph M Gomes	Donald L Russell	Charlotte Maggard	Roy Endersby	....	David W Sylstra	Gary Leach
San Rafael* (45) CM	415 456-1112	Lawrence E Mulryan	Robert F Beyer	Jeanne M Leoncini	Ransom E Coleman	Robt Marcucci	Henry W Ingwersen	David Bernardi
San Ramon§ (21) MC	415 838-2424	Richard Harmon	James H Robinson	James H Robinson	....	....	John Gackowski	....
Sanger* (13) CM	209 875-2587	Thomas Olson	Kerry L Miller	Harriet Stephens	Michael Compton	D Dean Mobley	Charles Chrestman	Floyd Little
Santa Ana* (204) CM	714 834-4906	Robert Luxembourger	Robert C Bobb	Janice C Guy	Lawrence M Shaffer	William J Reimer	Raymond C Davis	David H Grosse
Santa Barbara* (75) CM	805 963-0611	Sheila Lodge	Richard D Thomas	Richard D Thomas	Theresa M Ruether	Alfred L Faoro	Gerald L Lowry	David H Johnson
Santa Clara* (88) CM	408 984-3000	William A Gissler	D R Von Raesfeld	J Boccignone	K Machnick	Donald P Visconti	Donald C Ferguson	Sam Cristofano
Santa Cruz* (41) CM	408 429-3540	John Laird	Richard C Wilson	Patricia M Kenyon	Robert J Shepherd	Tony Pini	Jack Bassett	Larry L Erwin
Santa Fe Springs* (15) CM	213 868-0511	Ronald S Kernes	Donald R Powell	Hazel L Thomas	Donald M Nuttall	Bernard Cannard	....	John R Price
Santa Maria* (40) CM	805 925-0951	George S Hobbs Jr	Robert F Grogan	Mary W O'Brien	Robert S Hossli	C Wright Crakes	Joseph Centeno	Reese N Riddiough
Santa Monica* (88) CM	213 393-9975	Kenneth Edwards	John H Alschuler	Ann Shore	C Michael Dennis	Thomas Tolman	James Keane	Stanley Scholl
Santa Paula* (21) CM	805 525-4478	Les Maland	James W Morrison	Stacey B MacDonald	Kent Parson	James Bensen	James Corrigan	Norman S Wilkinson
Santa Rosa* (83) CM	707 576-5361	Schuyler L Jeffries	Kenneth R Blackman	Kenneth R Blackman	John S Lindsay	Michael Turnick	Salvatore Rosano	Broydon J Riha
Santee*† (60) CM	714 562-6153	Jim Bartell	Ronald L Ballard	Loretta H Roper	Robert E Carter	Ronald S Berry	Ken Wigginton	John P Sullivan
Saratoga* (29) CM	408 867-3438	Virginia Fanelli	J Wayne Dernetz	J Wayne Dernetz	Steve Peterson	....	....	Dan Trinidad
Sausalito* (7) CM	415 332-0310	Alice T Rogers	Michael Fuson	Janet F Tracy	Carl Tregner	Stephen Bogel	William Fraass	N Wohlschlaeger
Scotts Valley* (7) CM	408 438-2324	Barbara Leichter	Robert J Rockett	Robert J Rockett	Joyce F Bray	C Bruce Scott	Gerald C Pittenger	Jack E Elzer
Seal Beach*† (26) CM	213 431-2527	Victor Grgas	Allen J Parker	Joanne M Yeo	Denis Thomas	....	Stacy T Picascia	Gary Johnson
Seaside* (37) CM	408 899-6200	Lancelot C McClair	Charles E McNeely	Dee Latimore	Roderick M Stewart	Charles King	Bennie W Cooper	Michael Obryon
Sebastapol* (6) CM	707 823-7863	Thomas F Miller	Melvin K Davis	Melvin K Davis	Charles L Foster	Russ Shura	Charles Baker	Larry R Koverman
Selma* (11) CM	209 896-1064	Larry Fitzpatrick	Nicholas Pavlovich	Gen Grutzmacher	....	David Haugen	James Brockett	....
Shafter§ (7) MC	805 746-6361	Donald C Zachary	August A Caires	Dolores Robinson	August A Caires	....	Frank Christensen	John Guinn
Sierra Madre*† (11) CM	213 355-7135	Clem L Bartolai	James E McRea	L Marie Warfel	Douglas Berkshire	Marc F Mueller	Irvin E Betts	Thomas P Kirk
Signal Hill* (6) CM	213 426-7333	Gerard Goedhart	David A Caretto	Kris Beard	Vicki Baker	Paul C Delaney	Michael R McCrary	James A Biery
Simi Valley* (78) CM	805 522-1333	Elton Gallegly	M L Lin Koester	M L Lin Koester	Loron Cox	Dick Wilson	Lindsay P Miller	Joseph Lopez
Soledad* (6) CM	408 678-3963	Graig R Stephens	Carlos Urrutia	Martha Magdaleno	Elizabeth Burns	Frank Johnson	Benjamin Jimenez	Clarence Nielsen
Sonoma* (6) CM	707 938-3681	Henry J Riboni	Brock T Arner	Eleanor Berto	Brock T Arner	Albert Mazza	Billy Rettle	Richard Rowland
Sonora§ (3) MC	209 532-4541	Ronald E Stearn	William R Smith	Betty M Castle	Patricia L Perry	Guy C Mills	Ralph D Hamilton	....
South El Monte* (17) CM	818 579-6540	John D Gonzales	Gregory D Korduner	Margaret M Garcia	Gregory D Korduner	....	....	....
South Gate* (67) CM	213 567-1331	Herbert W Cranton	Bruce C Spragg	Janet E Stubbs	George Wanner	....	Norman E Philipps	Victor Rollinger
South Lake Tahoe* (21) CM	916 541-2900	John Cefalu	Richard Milbrodt	Myrna Vindum	Jim Deaton	Bert Cherry	Dean Shelton	Ed Brauner
South Pasadena* (23) CM	213 799-9101	Ted R Shaw	Charles R Martin	Ruby W Kerr	Robert A Keil	Gene E Murry	Samuel L Buntyn	John J Bernardi
South San Francisco* (49) CM	415 877-8500	Mark N Addiego	C Walter Birkelo	Barbara A Battaya	Barry R Lipton	John L Drago	James Datzman	Robert S Yee
St. Helena (5) MC	707 963-2741	(not reporting)						
Stanton* (21) CM	714 891-2521	Martha V Weishaupt	Kevin O'Rourke	Kevin O'Rourke	James J Antoniono	Jerold L Hunter	Robert U Eason	Roy E Bruckner
Stockton* (150) CM	209 944-8212	Randy Ronk	Raymond Cezar	Frances Hong	Gary C Ingraham	Donald J Irvine	Julio Cecchetti	Harry Montgomery
Suisun City* (11) CM	707 429-2900	Bill Jenkins	Robert J Bounds	Anita L Skinner	Robert J Bounds	James W Pennington	Thomas D Alder	R E Roberts
Sunnyvale* (107) CM	408 738-5411	Lynn Briody	Thomas F Lewcock	Thomas F Lewcock	Amy Chan	Jess Barba	Jess Barba	Edward James
Susanville (7) MC	916 257-2174	Helen M Leve	Jeffrey G Foltz	Mary A Fahlen	....	Raymond A Berettini	Marcus D Murphy	Mario D Vial
Taft* (5) CM	805 763-3144	Bill Lackey	Stephen L Wright	Norma Robinson	Ms N Bazzell	Jim Gaither	Bill Schlieter	Bill Kytola
Tehachapi* (4) CM	805 822-3264	Franklin W Tharp	Steven A Kueny	Kathryn L Koski	Steven A Kueny	A A Anthony	Donald Trumble	George Marantos
Temple City* (29) CM	213 285-2171	Mary Lou Swain	Karl L Koski	Karl L Koski	Karl L Koski	....	....	....
Thousand Oaks* (78) CM	805 497-8611	A Lee Laxdal	Grant R Brimhall	Nancy A Dillon	Robert S Biery	....	....	J Louis Scherer
Tiburon †* (7) CM	415 435-0956	Larry Smith	Robert L Kleinert	Robert L Kleinert	Alan P Nadritch	....	John Bailey	Louis F Brunini
Torrance* (131) CM	213 328-5310	Jim Armstrong	LeRoy J Jackson	Donna M Babb	W W Dundore	Richard DeYoung	Donald E Nash	....
Tracy* (18) CM	209 836-2670	Don Simpson	Michael E Locke	Betty J Dani	Rodney Davenport	Dan Watrous	Larry Kissell	William Silva
Tulare* (22) CM	209 688-2001	C Duane Miller	W Lynn Dredge	William Fishbough	William Fishbough	Kenneth Bridges	Roger Hill	Richard Mangnall
Turlock* (26) CM	209 668-5500	Bradford A Bates	Steven H Kyte	Vera Sahlstrom	Larrie Sweet	Larry F Hughes	John R Johnson	Richard Martin
Tustin* (32) CM	714 544-8890	Ursula E Kennedy	William A Huston	Mary E Wynn	Ronald Nault		Charles Thayer	Robert Ledendecker
Ukiah* (12) CM	707 462-2971	Charles G Myers	D Kent Payne	D Kent Payne	G R Brosig	Lee Mitchell	David G Johnson	Robert Pedroncelli
Union City* (39) CM	415 471-3232	Tom Kitayama	Karen Smith	Karen Smith	Zenda James	Kenneth Garcia	Michael Manick	Paul Ove

Directory 1/10 continued **MUNICIPAL OFFICIALS IN ALL U.S. CITIES OVER 2,500[1]**

City, 1980 population (000 omitted), form of government	Municipal phone number	Mayor	Appointed administrator	City clerk	Finance officer	Fire chief	Police chief	Public works director
CALIFORNIA (402) continued								
Upland* (48) CM	714 982-1352	Richard G Anderson	S Lee Travers	Doreen K Carpenter	Phyllis Proctor	Donald R Justis	Coy D Estes	S Lee Travers
Vacaville* (43) CM	707 446-6700	William J Carroll	John P Thompson	Corinne L Grannen	Robert E Eaton	Robert Powell	Gary Tatum	Dale Pfeiffer
Vallejo* (80) CM	707 553-4275	Terry A Curtola Jr	Michael B Lynch	Mildred R Watson	Michael B Lynch	William Patchell	Roland C Dart	Glenn A Harris
Victorville* (14) CM	714 245-3411	Robert L Dolch	James L Cox	Paula Porter	Adair Most	Rodolfo N Cabriales	Michael L O'Rourke	Edmundo S Aguirre
Villa Park* (7) CM	714 998-1500	William J Odlum	Carolyn Veregge	Carolyn Veregge	....	....	....	....
Visalia* (50) CM	209 625-6313	Berkley R Johnson	Ted A Gaebler	Donna Hall	Tim Hansen	Jack Kennedy	Ray Forsyth	Bill Carr
Vista* (36) CM	619 726-1340	Nancy C Wade	Morris B Vance	Jean Brooks	Frank E Rowlen	Harry Kaylor	Robert DeSteunder	Joseph J Karrer
Walnut* (10) CM	714 595-7543	Bertha Ashley	Robert T Dickey	Beverly Sherwood	Robert T Dickey	John Englund	Sherman Block	Robert L Fleming
Walnut Creek* (54) CM	415 943-5800	Gail Murray	Thomas G Dunne	Barbara Rivara	Bernard Strojny	....	Karel Swanson	Darrell Mortensen
Wasco§ (10) MC	805 758-3003	Paul Neufeld	Pat E Davis	Pat E Davis	Pat E Davis	....	....	Julian Munoz
Waterford (3) MC	209 874-2328	Zane H Johnston	Robert B Fulton	Sally Fulton	....	Robert Rinehart	Robert B Fulton	Henry Rader
Watsonville* (24) CM	408 728-6011	Ann Soldo	John Radin	Lorraine Washington	Charles Comstock	....	Ray Belgard	L John Cooper
Weed* (3) CM	916 938-4842	Vince Tallerico	Steve Feldman	....	Dorian M Aiello	Lawrence Hogue	Charles Byrd	Rick Bothwell
West Covina* (80) CM	818 962-8631	Robert L Bacon	Herman R Fast	Helene Mooney	Leonard Eliot	Robert McClelland	Craig L Meacham	Harry W Thomas
Westlake Village* (6) CM	213 706-1613	....	James E Emmons	James E Emmons	Ray Wood	William Zeason	Michael Graham	R Dennis Delzeit
Westminster* (71) CM	714 898-3311	Kathy Buchoz	Chris Christiansen	Mary Lou Morey	Olinto Albert Ricci	Jim Weaver	Jackie Lee Shockley	John Cyprien
Whittier* (69) CM	213 698-2551	Myron D Claxton	Thomas G Mauk	Gertrude L Hill	Irwin B Bornstein	....	James F Bale	V Clyde Haight
Willits* (4) CM	707 459-4601	Harry E Brown	Clifford L Swanson	Frances Helton	Frances Helton	David J Thomen	Barry Kaler	Clifford L Swanson
Willows*† (5) CM	916 934-7041	James Jacobs	Russell Melquist	Russell Melquist	Russell Melquist	Bradley H Mallory	Robert A Shadley	Jon P Barker
Winters (3) CM	916 795-4910	J Robert Chapman	Gail A Wingard	Gale Bruhn	Larry G Smyres	Vernon C Bruhn	Steven C Godden	Mickey Gordon
Woodlake* (5) CM	209 564-8055	Bill Diamond	Jack R Justice	Ruth Gonzalez	James E Reed	....	Raymond Sands	Jack R Justice
Woodland* (30) CM	916 662-5416	Harry O Walker	Thomas A Peterson	Jean L Winnop	Kris B Kristensen	John Buchanan	William F Colston	Ron Tribbett
Woodside t* (5) CM	415 851-7764	Joan Stiff	Leslie L Doolitte	Joan Olson	John W Kruse	Art Kitto	Brendon Maguire	Richard I Whaley
Yorba Linda* (28) CM	714 777-5000	Henry Wedaa	Arthur C Simonian	Dianna M Higdon	Gordon Vessey	....	....	Roy Stephenson
Yountville t (3) MC	707 944-8851	W K Nelson	Robert E Myers	Frances E Field	Robert E Myers	....	....	Peter J Bardessono
Yreka* (6) CM	916 842-4386	Donald Pierce	James L Dillon	James L Dillon	....	Dean Jefferson	William E Duncan	Leroy P Manley
Yuba City* (19) CM	916 741-4601	Joseph Fraser	Dwane Milnes	Dwane Milnes	Jack Kurtz	William Spaller	Roy D Harmon	Keith W Fine
COLORADO (83)								
Alamosa* (7) CM	303 589-2593	Clifford J Hartman	....	Jean Buchanan	Josie Abeyta	Ron Green	Roy Orton	Joseph L Strahl
Arvada* (85) CM	303 431-3000	Robert G Frie	Don F Allard	Nelda Parker	Ruth Hogan	Lynn Sellers	Gerald L Williams	Ron Culbertson
Aspen* (4) CM	303 925-2020	William L Stirling	Harold Schilling	Kathryn S Koch	Sheree Sonfield	Steve Crockett	Richard Rianoshek	Jay Hammond
Aurora* (159) CM	303 695-7000	Dennis Champine	James R Griesemer	Al Howard	Al Howard	John Speed	Benny K Blake	Harry Labonde
Avon t* (1) CM	303 949-4280	Allan R Nottingham	Richard D Blodgett	William D James	William D James	Steven Miller	Robert Willcox	James Lamont
Boulder* (77) CM	303 441-3131	Ruth A Correll	James W Piper	Dave G Manzanares	Cappie I Fine	Charles Boyes	Jay Propst	David W Knapp
Breckenridge t* (1) CM	303 453-2251	Stephen C West	....	Rosemary Ahern	....	Virgil Davis	Ralph A Schultz	H J Stalf
Brighton* (13) CM	303 659-4050	Gary D Gilpin	Patrick McDermott	Arlene Haley	Wilkie Miller	....	....	Robert Sandquist
Broomfield* (21) CM	303 469-3301	Walter P Spader	George D DiCiero	Lucy Brown	Terry W Cole	David T McCarty	Patrick C Ahlstrom	Marvin Thurber
Brush§ (4) MC	303 842-5001	Lawrence Coughlin	Robt S McClary	Clara W Lassen	....	Donald P Ruhl	Kenneth Baker	David Baker
Buena Vista t§ (2) MC	303 395-8643	Jerome J Steinauer	Charles Hedgepeth	Julia E Hupper	Julia E Hupper	Randall B Loback	Charles O Campton	....
Burlington t† (3) MC	303 346-8652	Rol Hudler	Lester McLain	Phyllis Collins	....	Phil Woodrick	Carrol Johnston	....
Canon City* (13) CM	303 275-6814	George R Turner	John R McGinn	Ruth Tobey Hampson	Mary E Kienietz	Chris Canterbury	John W Wilson	Loren J Patton
Carbondale* (2) CM	303 963-2733	Bill Gray	Davis Farrar	Susanne Cerise	Nancy Barnett	Ron Leach	Fred Williams	Stan Wallis
Castle Rock t* (4) CM	303 688-3326	George J Kennedy	P Joseph Knopinski	Richard Wilson	Richard Wilson	Randall Stagner	Rodney Wright	Dan Bunting
Cherry Hills Village§ (5) MC	303 789-2541	Joan Duncan	Charles S Coward	Elizabeth N Noel	....	....	Charles B Wood	....
Colorado Springs* (215) CM	303 578-6699	Robert M Isaac	George H Fellows	Robert E Parker	J H B Wilson	Richard Smith	John L Tagert	Dewitt Miller
Commerce City* (16) CM	303 289-3600	Harold E Kite	Philip D Speight	Betty Martin	Don Wilson	....	Neal Wikstrom	Gregg Clements
Cortez* (7) CM	303 565-3402	William Mollenkopf	Susan M Sanfilippo	Glenn W Smith	Glenn W Smith	Harold Ford	Roy C Lane	....
Craig§ (8) MC	303 824-6560	Larry Polich	Donald B Cooper	Donald B Cooper	Donald B Cooper	David Dean	Glen P Sherman	....
Crested Butte t* (1) CM	303 349-5338	Thomas S Cox	William V Crank	Adele Bachman	Adele Bachman	....	Richard Largo	Fred Dyer
Del Norte t*† (2) CM	303 657-2708	Martin V Lull	Frank Ortega	Barbara Slade	....	Marlen Yates	Dennis Horney	Modesto Pacheco
Delta* (4) CM	303 874-7566	L T Mangum	Stephen D Schrock	Mary Lynn Williams	H Andrew Mason	Fay Mathews	Robert Elliott	Fred Kettle
Denver (491) MC	303 575-2601	Federico Pena	....	Felicia Muftic	James A Murray	Myrle K Wise	Thomas E Coogan	John Mrozek
Durango* (11) CM	303 247-5622	William F Casey	Robt F Ledger Jr	Pauline M Redman	Richard S Jung	D R Merry	Chris Wiggins	Otha J Rogers
Eagle t* (1) CM	303 328-6354	James H Seabry	William P Powell	Marilene Miller	Marilene M Miller	....	Daniel L Kneale	Duston D Walls
Edgewater (6) MC	303 238-7803	Rex E Swann	Julie A Boatman	Julie A Boatman	Julie A Boatman	Robert Rutt	Henry D Smith	Albert N Mackenson
Englewood* (30) CM	303 761-1140	Eugene L Otis	Andrew J McCown	Gary Higbee	Gary Higbee	James Broman	Robert R Holmes	Kells Waggoner
Estes Park t (3) MC	303 586-5331	H Bernerd Dannels	Dale G Hill	Vickie O'Connor	Monte L Vavra	Jack Rumley	Robert W Ault	Richard D Widmer
Evans* (5) CM	303 339-5344	Tom Bruner	Glenn Crowson	Steve Westerdahl	Jan Whittet	Gerald Hettinger	Jim Burns	Herbert Davidson
Federal Heights t (8) MC	303 428-3526	Lester M Bauer	Robert W Bridges	Margaret M French	Robert W Bridges	Jim Fyffe	Dwain D Farris	Robert W Bridges
Florence* (3) CM	303 784-4848	Charles McCall	John D West	Dana Angel	Dori Williams	James Myers	Duane Norton	Martin Duran
Fort Collins* (65) CM	303 221-6220	Gerry Horak	John E Arnold	Wanda Krajicek	James H Harmon	John D Mulligan	Bruce Glasscock	Roger E Krempel
Fort Lupton (4) MC	303 857-6667	Donald R Cummins	Rose M Bowles	Victor R Moculeski	....	Ronald Ceretto	Jack Hurst	Robert C Crumb
Fort Morgan† (9) MC	303 867-3001	Irven L Billiard	Glenn W Calvert	Wayne E Kellogg	Wayne E Kellogg	Gene Nelson	W Gale Davey	Michal Gay
Fountain*† (8) CM	303 382-5604	Harold D Thompson	Anthony Guiliano	Anna L Daugherty	Michael D Hall	Jack Lenn	R A Ritchey	Frank J Bustamento
Fruita§ (3) MC	303 858-3663	Robert P Pollock	Errol E Snider	Margaret Steelman	Kevin Swain	Kenneth Kendell	Jack Vanarsdol	Gary Hoffman
Glendale* (2) CM	303 759-1513	William J Convery	John L Baudek	John L Baudek	John L Baudek	Robert Quinlan	LaVonne W Brown	Herbert D Moore
Glenwood Springs* (5) CM	303 945-2575	Carl L Schiesser	Michael S Copp	Pamela K Smith	Bob Standerfer	L Zancanella	Robert Halbert	Kevin Kadlec
Golden* (12) CM	303 279-3331	Ruth A Maurer	Charles L Goudge	Sharon L Bennetts	Ronald Schonebaum	Stewart Reinhard	Donald J Jarvis	....
Grand Junction* (28) CM	303 244-1800	J P Mike Pacheco	Mark K Achen	Neva B Lockhart	John Tasker	Robert T Mantlo	Gary J Leonard	James Patterson
Greeley* (53) CM	303 353-6123	Mike Lehan	Peter A Morrell	Gayle L Voss	Leonard A Wiest	Gary Novinger	B J Edington	C William Hargett
Greenwood Village§ (6) MC	303 773-0252	Frederick C Fisher	James H Mullen	Lois Ann Iman	Mary B Skeen	....	Daryl G Gates	Clifton P Coleman
Gunnison*† (6) CM	303 641-2444	Jesse T Stone	Dale W Howard	Marian L Hicks	Marian L Hicks	Steve Williams	Floyd F Johnson	James C Buffington
Hayden t* (2) CM	303 276-3741	William Leisure	Daniel R Ellison	Jean Graham	Doug Monger	Terry McCarty	Cyril J Lenahan	Terry McCarty
Julesburg t*† (2) CM	303 474-3344	Clark D Bernhardt	Melvin G Mikelson	Muriel L Nelson	....	Jack Sheaffer	Melvin G Mikelson	....
La Junta* (8) CM	303 384-2578	Gary Freeman	C A Sarlo	Doris Houghton	Doris Houghton	Rodney Davidson	Charles Widup	Harold Scofield
Lafayette* (9) CM	303 665-2380	Bob L Burger	Mike Acimovic	Beverly A Smith	William Harrison	Dennis James	Larry Stallcup	Warren Williams
Lakewood* (113) CM	303 234-8605	Linda Shaw	William E Kirchhoff	Jean L Rogers	Lynn W Clannin	....	Charles Johnston	Richard Plastino
Lamar† (8) MC	303 336-4376	Joe Reichard	Darrell Bailey	Marvin Fowler	Fred Norman Jr	Harold Lorenson	Ben Franco	....
Las Animas† (3) MC	303 456-0422	Alferd Putnam	....	Lila M Maupin	Lila M Maupin	James E Pryor	Norman G Roberts	Dale Kortz
Leadville (4) MC	303 486-0349	Dennis F Reece	....	Eva Ann Fenske	Eva Ann Fenske	Donald Fabian	Fred Van Pelt Jr	Chris Kastrinos
Limon t* (2) CM	303 775-2346	Dennis E Coonts	Del Beattie	Teresa Odwyer	....	Vern Sallee	James C Trahern	Del Beattie
Littleton* (29) CM	303 795-3700	....	Gale D Christy	Janet H Breslin	Marvin Thrasher	Lee Daugherty	Craig Camp	Charles Blosten
Longmont* (43) CM	303 776-6050	William G Swenson	Alvin E Sweney	Alice Hamon	Steven Jessen	Robert Neiman	Fred Rainguet	Neal Renfroe
Louisville* (6) CM	303 666-6565	Norbert Meier	Terry Hundley	Cleo M Mudrock	Sharon Caranci	Dan Ross	Rodney Leesman	Karl Kasch
Loveland* (30) CM	303 667-6130	Ray Reeb	Jan H Winters	Victoria Sheneman	Robert Eichem	Jack Sullivan	Lawrence Seib	Paul Haines
Manitou Springs* (4) CM	303 685-5481	Russell S Lewis	Hugh J King Jr	Lois J Greenman	James G Pratt	Steven Hart	Harry F Greenman Jr	....
Meeker t* (2) CM	303 878-5344	Gus R Halandras	Duane L Rehborg	Duane L Rehborg	Duane L Rehborg	....	William L Elder III	Frank O Marsh
Monte Vista* (4) CM	303 852-5926	Ronald Schulz	Lewis A McGill	Neta Slingerland	Alfretta Danielewic	Don Loundsbury	Robert F King	Murlas R Sanders
Montrose* (9) CM	303 249-4534	Sue Merett	William R Robinson	Mary L Watt	Leona James	Leon Krebs	....	Jeffrey Willett

Directory 1/10 continued

MUNICIPAL OFFICIALS IN ALL U.S. CITIES OVER 2,500[1]

City, 1980 population (000 omitted), form of government		Municipal phone number	Mayor	Appointed administrator	City clerk	Finance officer	Fire chief	Police chief	Public works director
COLORADO (83) continued									
Northglenn* (30)	CM	303 451-8326	Charles C Winburn	David A Hawker	Joan M Baker	Michael Anderson	David McCarty	C A Gunderson	Jim Landeck
Pueblo* (102)	CM	303 545-0561	Mike Salardino	John M Bramble	Marian D Mead	Billy G Martin	Lewis A Quigley	Robert O Silva	Tom Cvar
Rangely t§ (2)	MC	303 675-8476	E W Long	Donald C Peach	Veda Muller	Daniel L Cooley	....	Joseph Lane	Donald W Fessler
Rifle* (3)	CM	303 625-2121	George E Mitchell	Ted C Anderson	Leona G Rains	Michael C Bestor	Robin Shreiner	Lawrence P Allec	Robert Whittington
Rocky Ford (5)	CM	303 254-7414	Jack Steir	Darryl L Schulz	Ellenor Brenneman	....	Robert Cadwallader	Chris Lucero	....
Salida (5)	MC	303 539-2311	Edward Touber	....	Anthony E Gentile	....	James M Gray	Leonard W Post	Ernest Criswell
Sheridan (5)	MC	303 795-3414	Roger B Rowland	Jimmy E Curnes	Dee Heath	Roger B Rowland	Roger K Steinberg	Joe Stephenson Jr	George D Knapp
Silverthorne t§ (1)	MC	303 468-2637	William J Schmidt	Gary L Sears	Jeannie Hayes	....	....	John Victoravich	Paul E Knight
Steamboat Springs* (5)	CM	303 879-2060	Phil Struble	Philip S Mahoney Jr	Vicki D Marcy	Charles S Gubisch	Delmar Coyner	Roger Jensen	Daniel Hartman
Sterling* (11)	CM	303 522-9700	Earl D Franklin Jr	Marvin G McElwain	Irvin G Christner	Irvin G Christner	Gerald Acre	Melvin Honebein	Ali Izadian
Telluride t* (1)	CM	303 728-3851	John Micetic	Joseph T Crain	Margaret R Howlett	Gary Beardsworth	....	Hank Smith	Raymond Hughes
Thornton*† (40)	CM	303 452-1001	Margaret Carpenter	Gerald E Hagman	Nancy A Vincent	Curtis Addison	George Buck	W Douglas Franks	Eric Pahlke
Trinidad* (10)	CM	303 846-9843	Roberta Cordova	William R Cordova	Lila Valdez	Larry Corradino	James C Perri	Richard L Scherwitz	John Digarbo
Vail t* (2)	CM	303 476-7000	Rodney E Slifer	....	Pamela A Brandmeyer	William Pyka	Richard Duran	Curt Ufkes	Stan Berryman
Walsenburg† (4)	MC	303 738-1048	Leo Maes	....	Paula Jo Sterk	Robert Holland	Mario Amidei	Octaviano Vigil	Gabe Gayton
Westminster* (50)	CM	303 429-1546	George Hovorka	Wm M Christopher	Michele Gallegos	Susann Stubbs	John A Dutch	Dan Montgomery	Ron Hellbusch
Wheat Ridge§ (30)	MC	303 237-6944	Frank Stites	Thomas H Palmer	Wanda Sang	James O Malone	....	Howard E Jaquay	Rodger O Young
Windsor t* (4)	CM	303 686-7476	W Wayne Miller	Richard Lessner	P Jeanne Brunner	Richard Lessner	Ed Fagler	John Micheals	Dennis Wagner
Winter Park t* (..)	CM	303 726-8081	Nick Teverbaugh	Patrick Guilfoyle	Karen Stewart	Patrick Guilfoyle	....	....	James Griffith
Woodland Park* (3)	CM	303 687-9243	John D Carr	Kirk D Relford	Cindy Morse	Rue Ann Vorhies	....	John W Hogue	Larry D Iverson
Wray t* (2)	CM	303 332-4431	Jack Sloniker	Robert W Snedeker	Charles Murphy	Milton Speicher	Gary Peterson	John W Courtney	....
Yuma§ (3)	MC	303 848-3878	Donald R Starnes	Paul Metcalf	Ronda Wright	....	Gary Snelling	Mike Murphy	Douglas Lasater
CONNECTICUT (153)									
Ansonia (19)	MC	203 735-6448	William J Menna	Sharon L Schwarz	Florence K Hoinski	Anthony Caserta	Edward McGoe	James Mcgrath	Arthur Anglace
Ashford t† (3)	TM	203 429-2750	David M Gardner	....	Barbara B Metsack	Anne M Supina	....	....	....
Avon t* (11)	CM	203 677-2634	Richard Hines	Philip K Schenck Jr	Caroline B Lamonica	Philip K Schenck Jr	Eric Ruppert	James A Martino	....
Barkhamsted t (3)	TM	203 379-8665	(not reporting)						
Beacon Falls t (4)	TM	203 729-4340	Leonard F D'Amico	....	Francis X Doiron	Mario G Fuoco	Harold Lennon	Leonard F D'Amico	Frank Del Vecchio
Berlin t (15)	TM	203 828-7000	Warren E Kingsbury	....	Joanne G Ward	Gary S Clinton	....	William Scalise	Morgan Seelye
Bethany t (4)	TM	203 393-2100	Gordon V Carrington	....	Joan C Simpson	....	George H Quinn Jr	Gordon V Carrington	....
Bethel t (16)	TM	203 743-9231	Clifford J Hurgin	....	Jane D Shannon	Barry Curina	Donald Clarke	John Basile	Edward M Reynolds
Bethlehem t (3)	TM	203 266-7510	Leonard J Assard	....	Lucy N Palangio	....	William Mastriano	Leonard J Assard	Gene E Heidenreich
Bloomfield t* (19)	CM	203 243-8971	David A Baram	R Gary Stenhouse	Elizabeth F Jolley	Alan Desmarais	Adolf Jacobsen	Philip R Lincoln	John Kazmarski
Bolton t (4)	CM	203 649-8743	Henry P Ryba	Karen R Levine	Catherine Leiner	Catherine Peterson	N James Preuss Jr	....	Donato Rattazzi Jr
Branford t (23)	RT	203 488-6305	Judy Gott	Joseph Mooney	Frank Kinney III	Robert M Geier	Peter Mullen	William Holohan	Jerry Bernardo
Bridgeport (143)	MC	203 576-7600	Leonard S Paoletta	....	Leonard Crone	Robert Lange	John Schmidlin	Patrick J Dolan	Ronald N DeFilippo
Bristol (57)	MC	203 584-7600	John J Leone Jr	....	Rita Brown	Theodore N Hamilton	Anthony D Basile	John F Oliver	John J Gavin
Brookfield t (13)	MC	203 775-2515	Kenneth V Keller	....	Ruth B Burr	Raymond G Waidelich	Howard Hantsch	John W Anderson	Malcolm R Grant
Brooklyn t (6)	TM	203 774-9452	Ernest Ouellet	....	Madeleine E Costa	Hans Koehl	Jeffrey Otto	Ernest Ouellet	Leonard Albee Sr
Burlington t (6)	TM	203 673-6789	Theodore C Scheidel	....	Kathleen K Zabel	A Gertrude Simmons	Erick B Tharau Jr	Theodore C Scheidel	....
Canterbury t (3)	TM	203 546-9377	Robert Manship	....	Marguerite Simpson	Henry Gerl	David Veit	....	....
Canton t (8)	TM	203 693-4093	Samuel S Humphrey	....	Shirley Krompegal	Francis X Bruton Jr	Dennis Lassen	Charles Keefe	Richard Negro
Cheshire t* (22)	CM	203 272-3501	Gilbert P Leslie Jr	Edw T O'Neill Jr	Mae R Tabor	Linda R Savitsky	Douglas Yocher	George R Merriam	Thomas F Crowe Jr
Chester t (3)	TM	203 526-9553	Robert J Blair	....	Elsie L Tarpill	Laura Straub	John M Divis	Robert J Blair	....
Clinton t (11)	TM	203 669-9333	Margery C Scully	....	Theodore Moser	Bion Shepard	Hugh Allen	Frank H Breiling	Milton Moritz
Colchester b (3)	MC	203 537-3250	Eugene P McGrath	....	Terri Weis	Robert Pulford	....	....	....
Colchester t (8)	TM	203 537-3461	Helen B Gay	....	Patrica A Lagrega	Robert Washburn	Jess McMinn	....	William Standish
Columbia t (3)	TM	203 228-3284	Leonard A Couchon	....	Eleanor Vickers	Joanne Gyure	Louis Scotti	Leonard A Couchon	....
Coventry t* (9)	CM	203 742-6324	Robert E Olmsted	David Berner	Ruth E Benoit	....	....	Frank Trzasko	Roger Bellard
Cromwell t (10)	TM	203 635-3380	Paul R Harrington	....	Bernard Neville	Edward Alsup	Donald Swanson	Eugene Rame	Michael Marino
Danbury† (60)	MC	203 797-4511	James E Dyer	Robert M Steinberg	Elizabeth Crudginto	Paul Shea	Chrles Monzillo	Nelson F Macedo	Daniel Garamella
Danielson b (5)	MC	203 774-4357	Frederick Hillmann	....	Louis Zipkin	Louis Zipkin	Richard Levola	Paul T Auger	....
Darien t§ (19)	RT	203 655-8927	William H Patrick	Norman A Lucas	Marilyn Van Sciver	John Fletcher	....	John W Jordan	A Walter Saburn
Deep River t (4)	TM	203 526-5783	Joseph P Miezejeski	....	Jean M Ressler	Arthur Thompson	Peter Woodcock	Joseph P Miezejeski	....
Derby (12)	MC	203 734-9203	John S DeBarbieri	....	Helen P Dripchak	Edward Brickett	Thomas Francione	Leo Herbette	Ronald Luneau
Durham t (5)	TM	203 349-3452	M Foster Mather	....	Marjorie C Hatch	William A Moore	George Planeta	M Foster Mather	....
East Granby t (4)	TM	203 653-2576	Frank R Rothammer	....	Miriam Viets	Charles W Chatey	Stewart Dewey	Frank R Rothammer	....
East Haddam t (6)	TM	203 873-8615	John Blaschik Jr	....	Mildred E Quinn	....	Edward Dombroski	....	Edward J Roczniak
East Hampton t§ (9)	MC	203 267-4468	George K White	Alan H Bergren	Pauline Markham	Alan H Bergren	Philip Visintainer	Dean True	Robert Drewry
East Hartford t (53)	MC	203 289-2781	George A Dagon	....	John J Barry Jr	Richard C Harvey	Thomas Dawson	Clarence A Drumm	Arthur J Mulligan
East Haven t (25)	MC	203 468-3204	Anthony Proto Jr	....	John Brereton	Louis Clini	Howard Weir	Joseph R Pascarella	Ralph Lambert
East Lyme t (14)	TM	203 739-6931	(not reporting)						
East Windsor t (9)	TM	203 623-8122	Robert M Watts	....	Claire S Badstubner	Kenneth E Pitney	....	....	....
Easton t (6)	TM	203 268-6291	Lois E Stueck	....	Carl Milnar	Hilmer Nelson	William Borofsky	Gerard Hance	Edward L Nagy
Ellington t (10)	TM	203 875-3190	Mary A Miller	....	Dorothy MacIntosh	Nicholas Dicorleto	Jerry B Connors	Mary A Miller	Peter H Michaud
Enfield t* (43)	CM	203 745-0371	Joseph O'Connor	Robert J Mulready	Michael Alexopoulos	V E Santacroce	David Luke	Walter J Skower	Roger J Mullins
Essex t (5)	TM	203 767-8201	Richard Riggio	....	Betty J Gaudenzi	John Greene	Paul Phoenix	Richard Riggio	Richard Riggio
Fairfield t (55)	RT	203 255-8200	Jacquelyn C Durrell	....	Evelyn Hiller	John Leahy	David W Russell Jr	William Mockalis	Frank Daniels
Farmington t* (16)	CM	203 673-8200	Andreas B Michale	Stephen A Flis	Edgar A King	Daniel P Costello	Lee Mahana	Leroy Bangham	Jon Streeter
Glastonbury t* (24)	CM	203 659-2711	Sonya Googins	Richard S Borden Jr	Edward J Friedeberg	G Ted Ellis	Thomas Manager	Francis Hoffman Jr	S Robert Pryzby
Granby t* (8)	CM	203 653-2538	David W Russell	William F Smith Jr	Cilesta V Adamick	William F Smith Jr	Raymond Salmonson	Terrance N Treschuk	William P Lyons
Greenwich t (60)	RT	203 622-7700	Roger J Pearson	William C Robinson	Rowland D Harris	William J Reynolds	John H Titsworth	Thomas G Keegan	John J Kennedy
Griswold t (9)	TM	203 376-2521	Donald E Burdick	....	Alice F Stradczuk	David S Drobiak	....	Donald E Burdick	Donald E Burdick
Groton (10)	MC	203 441-2103	Catherine Kolnaski	....	Anthony R Demarinis	Robert T Macri	William M Scarano	Joseph A Sandora	John Umryz
Groton t* (41)	CM	203 445-8551	Lawrence E Hurley	C Richard Foote	Ms S M Sawyer	Laverne A Henn	....	Thomas Falvey	Walter P Blanker
Guilford t (17)	TM	203 453-2763	Frank V Larkins Jr	....	Barbara E Rawson	John M Allan	Robert D Andrew	Samuel Downs Jr	James A Portley
Haddam t (6)	TM	203 345-8531	Mark P Lundgren	....	Ann P Huffstetler	Donald C Davis	....	Mark P Lundgren	Mark P Lundgren
Hamden t (51)	MC	203 288-5641	Peter F Villano	....	Roberta C O'Brien	Robert Zaorski	John Tramontano	John P Ambrogio	Anthony Mentone
Hartford* (136)	CM	203 722-6620	Thirman L Milner	Alfred A Gatta	Sebastian Santiglia	John T Walsh	John B Stewart Jr	Bernard R Sullivan	John Burke
Harwinton t (5)	TM	203 485-9612	Lloyd T Shanley Jr	....	Cherie D Shanley	....	....	....	Lloyd T Shanley Jr
Hebron t (5)	TM	203 228-9406	Raymond J Burt	....	Marian Celio	....	W V Borst	....	....
Jewett City b† (3)	MC	203 376-2443	Stanley Drobiak	....	Phyllis M Brown	Cynthia Kata	Donald Ouillette	Thurston Fields	Adam Keemon
Kent t (3)	TM	203 927-3989	Robert A Ward	....	Marian F Pacocha	Loretto Roney	John Howland	....	....
Killingly t* (15)	CM	203 774-8601	Joseph P Collison	Thomas E Dwyer	Ms M A McMerriman	Michelle Weiss	....	....	Dennis G Foran
Killingworth t† (4)	TM	203 663-1765	H E Bruce	....	Hazel C Haynes	Richard I Boyd	Alfred Dudek Jr	H E Bruce	H E Bruce
Lebanon t (5)	TM	203 642-6100	Edward O Clark	....	Joyce McGillicuddy	Ronald Bender	Harry Gendron	Richard R Bauwens	....
Ledyard t (14)	MC	203 464-8740	Mary K McGrattan	....	Patricia Karns	Barbara M Heineman	....	Mary K McGrattan	W Stanley Lamb
Lisbon t (3)	TM	203 376-3400	Jeremiah A Shea	....	Ms F Pawlikowski	Audrey Babbitt	John Crees	Jeremiah A Shea	....
Litchfield t (8)	TM	203 567-5133	Charles S Dobos	....	Evelyn N Goodwin	Norma Waldvogel	Joseph Weir	Charles S Dobos	Charles S Dobos

Directory 1/10 continued

MUNICIPAL OFFICIALS IN ALL U.S. CITIES OVER 2,500[1]

City, 1980 population (000 omitted), form of government		Municipal phone number	Mayor	Appointed administrator	City clerk	Finance officer	Fire chief	Police chief	Public works director
CONNECTICUT (153) continued									
Madison t (14)	TM	203 245-2465	Donald J LaChance	....	Milton Marcus	....	Thomas Lemley	Cyrus Gaeta	Stewart MacMillan
Manchester t* (50)	CM	203 647-3000	Barbara B Weinberg	Robert B Weiss	Edward J Tomkiel	Thomas S Moore	John C Rivosa	Robert D Lannan	George A Kandra
Mansfield t* (21)	CM	203 429-3336	Jane Ann Bobbitt	Martin H Berliner	Madelyn Eremita	....	George Thompson	Martin H Berliner	Lon R Hultgren
Marlborough t (5)	TM	203 295-9547	Anthony J Maiorano	....	Ethel M Fowler	....	Raymond K Weber	....	....
Meriden* (57)	CM	203 634-0003	Walter A Evilia	Terry V Sprenkel	Dolores G Pollard	Edward F Murphy	Ronald E Fontaine	George J Caffrey	J Bruce Marks
Middlebury t (6)	TM	203 758-2430	Edward B St John	....	Doris M Valentine	Karl M Mandl	John J Proulx Jr	A Frank Calabrese	....
Middlefield t (4)	TM	203 349-3446	James R Blois	....	Evelyn Konefal	James R Blois	Bruce Villwock	....	James R Blois
Middletown (39)	MC	203 344-3400	Sebastian Garafalo	Janet B Daniels	Anthony Sbona	James M Reynolds	John E Riordan	George R Aylward	Salvatore C Fazzino
Milford (49)	MC	203 783-3200	Alberta Jagoe	....	Margaret S Egan	Antonio D Giguere	William A Healey	William Bull	John Donnelly
Monroe t* (14)	CM	203 261-3651	Kenneth S Heitzke	Richard W Emerick	Thelma Inderdohnen	Jeffrey T Whone	Paul Devan	Robert Wesche	Michael J Gantick
Montville t (16)	MC	203 848-3030	Howard R Beetham Jr	....	Margret Skinner	Howard Beetham Jr	Ed Bradgon	Paul Mallon	Raymond Luty
Naugatuck t (26)	MC	203 729-4571	(not reporting)						
New Britain (74)	MC	203 224-2491	William J McNamara	Paul S Vayer	Richard T Murphy	Thomas M Doyle	Thomas Keough	Clifford J Willis	Richard Opulski
New Canaan t (18)	TM	203 966-3539	Charles P Morton	Edwin F Gutt	Mary L Ritter	Caroline Rothschild	Stephan Benko	Ralph M Scott	Louis J Moreno
New Fairfield t (11)	TM	203 746-2448	John Fairchild	....	Diana M Peck	....	Bruce Taylor	John Fairchild	....
New Hartford t (5)	TM	203 379-3389	Anita Baxter	....	Patricia Halloran	Barbara Lautenbach	Joseph Lavoie	Anita Baxter	Victor Vincent
New Haven (126)	MC	203 787-8200	Biagio Ben DiLieto	Paul Guidone	John A Keyes	Michael Milone	John P Reardon	William F Farrell	Thomas A Antollino
New London* (29)	CM	203 443-2861	Carl Stoner	C Francis Driscoll	Clark Van Der Lyke	Robert Smith	Frederick Philopena	Donald Sloan	Andrew H Sims Jr
New Milford t (19)	MC	203 354-5516	Clifford C Chapin	....	Anna E Chapin	August P Cicotti	David Lathrop	Theodore R Adams	Donald G Marsh
Newington t* (29)	CM	203 666-4661	Maryellen Andersen	Peter M Curry	Roberta Jenkins	Donald F McKay	Joseph Kalasky	Thomas G Ganley	....
Newtown t (19)	MC	203 426-8131	Jack Rosenthal	....	Elizabeth Smith	Benjamin B Spragg	....	Louis D Marchese	William Peck
North Branford t* (12)	CM	203 488-2537	Joanne Wentworth	Thomas J Wontorek	Yvonne Bartemy	Thomas J Wontorek	Ralph Thomas	....	Thomas J Wontorek
North Canaan t† (3)	TM	203 824-7246	Henry E Pozzetta	....	Josephine S Harris	Walter Arbo	Russell Crafts	....	....
North Haven t (22)	TM	203 239-5321	Walter J Gawrych	....	Amelia P Kennedy	Vincent E Palmeri	John E Obier Jr	Walter Berniere	Richard F Gillen
North Stonington t (4)	TM	203 535-2877	Nicholas H Mullane	....	Patricia P McGowan	Velda M Haskell	Donald W Howell	Nicholas H Mullane	....
Norwalk (78)	MC	203 838-7531	William A Collins	....	Marilyn Robinson	Jack Miller	John E Yost Jr	Carl LaBianca	Dominick DiGangi
Norwich* (38)	CM	203 887-6722	Kent S Baker	Charles C Whitty	Beverly C Muldoon	Angelo Sanquedolce	Harold H Lamphere	Richard J Abele	Walter J Wadja
Old Lyme t (6)	TM	203 434-1605	Wallace F Moore	....	Jessie F Smith	Edward Perkins	....	Wallace F Moore	Olcott W Harris Jr
Old Saybrook t (9)	TM	203 388-3401	Barbara J Maynard	....	Jeanne D Kelly	Burton Chapman	Wayne Wysocki	Edmund Mosca	Ronald Baldi
Orange t (13)	TM	203 795-0751	Ralph E Capecelatro	....	William J Heinrichs	Arthur B Williams	Frank Knight	James H Heinz	Robert Hiza
Oxford t (7)	TM	203 888-2543	William J Stakum	....	Beverly M Martinoli	Hubert B Piper	John G Tuz	William J Stakum	William J Stakum
Plainfield t (13)	TM	203 564-4071	Joseph Taverna	....	Patricia Carroll	Patricia Carroll	Kenneth Moffitt	Gary Sousa	Alex Zelinsky
Plainville t* (16)	CM	203 793-0221	Joseph Toner	....	Peter T Lennon Jr	....	Howard A Swanson	Francis Roche	Caryl P Bradt
Plymouth t (11)	MC	203 589-6330	Donna M Warkoski	....	Janet Scoville	David Barbieri	Charles Freimuth	....	Joseph N Caggiano
Pomfret t (3)	TM	203 974-0191	Raymond E Heath	....	Nora V Johnson	Nora V Johnson	Harley J Hill	Raymond E Heath	....
Portland t (8)	TM	203 342-2880	Robert E Cleary	....	Bernadette Dillon	John Jedrzejczyk	George V Johnson	Robert E Cleary	C Joseph Seiferman
Preston t (5)	TM	203 887-5581	Parke C Spicer	....	Janet E Perkins	Richard Camp	Paul MacDonald	Parke C Spicer	Parke C Spicer
Prospect t (7)	MC	203 758-4461	Robert J Chatfield	....	Ms P M Vaillancourt	Robert J Chatfield	Paul L Murray	Robert J Chatfield	....
Putnam t (9)	TM	203 928-6608	Everett G Shepard	....	Lillian M Newth	Patricia A Kowal	Donald A Gilman	Michael A Green	Maurice A Viens
Putnam† (7)	MC	203 928-5529	Stanley W Ozog	....	Josephine Kentile	R Roger Brodeur	Donald Gilman	Michael Green	Ernest Dumas
Redding t (7)	TM	203 938-2002	Mary Anne Guitar	Mary Anne Wiesner	Patricia A Creigh	Mary Anne Wiesner	....	....	....
Ridgefield t (20)	TM	203 438-7301	Elizabeth M Leonard	Raymond Astarita	Dora Cassavechia	Abraham Morelli	Richard T McGlynn	Thomas J Rotunda Jr	Frank Serfilippi
Rocky Hill t* (15)	CM	203 563-1451	Paul T Daukas	Dana Whitman Jr	Marion Palmer	Gene S Pianka	James Vinchetti	Philip H Schnabel	Dana Whitman Jr
Salisbury t (4)	TM	203 435-9512	Charlotte H Reid	....	....	....	....	Charlotte H Reid	....
Seymour t† (13)	TM	203 888-2511	Francis H Conroy Jr	....	Norma E Drummer	Alexander J Carpp	Donald Lesnick	Walter Trzcinski	Alvin MacBrien
Sharon t (3)	TM	203 364-5224	William A Wilbur	....	Anna M Johnson	....	John Murtagh	William A Wilbur	William A Wilbur
Shelton (31)	MC	203 736-2681	Eugene M Hope Jr	Clarence W Oppel	Beverly M Brown	Louis M Marusic	Ralph Hopkins	Peter J Siraco	Frank B Waldhaus
Simsbury t (21)	TM	203 651-3751	Margaret C Shanks	....	John W Case	Robert W Metcalf	....	Daniel J Coppinger	Frank V Rossi
Somers t (8)	TM	203 763-0841	Steven D Kominski	....	Irene Percoski	George Warner	Wolfgang Schiessel	Steven D Kominski	Steven D Kominski
South Windsor t* (17)	CM	203 644-2511	John J Mitchell	Richard J Sartor	....	George P Spring Jr	Philip Crombie	William Ryan	Robert Arsenault
Southbury t (14)	TM	203 264-0606	Harmon L Andrews	....	Joyce Hornbecker	Paul F Smith	Roy Baldwin	Harmon L Andrews	Eugene Metcalf
Southington t* (37)	CM	203 628-5553	Robert Cusano	John Weichsel	Juanine DePaolo	Daniel Armond	Arthur Toth	Philip D'Agostino	Anthony Tranquillo
Sprague t (3)	TM	203 822-6223	Matthew T Delaney	....	Mary M Stefon	Wilfred Blanchette	Thomas Girard	....	....
Stafford t† (9)	TM	203 684-2130	John E Julian	....	Pauline Laskow	Ronald Argenta	....	John E Julian	Dominic Campanelli
Stafford Springs b (3)	MC	203 684-3827	Norman Milliard	....	Kathleen M Walsh	Kathleen M Walsh	Dennis Littel	Anthony Ostrowski	Dock Sellers
Stamford (102)	MC	203 358-4150	Thom Serrani	....	Lois Pontbriant	Paul Pacter	Joseph Vitti	John Considine	John R Obrien
Stonington t (16)	TM	203 535-1566	James M Spellman	....	Ruth Waller	Ruth A Lancaster	....	Carl Johnson	Henry C Miner
Stratford t* (51)	CM	203 385-4000	Edward J Fennell	Ronald W Owens	Wm J Readey Jr	Ronald W Owens	Edwin Scheibel	C W Parniewski	F McDougall
Suffield t (9)	TM	203 668-7397	William G Harrison	Ronald W Birmingham	Dorothy McCarty	Lewis W Cannon	Thomas L Bellmore	Murray Phelps	....
Thomaston t (6)	TM	203 283-4421	Eugene McMahon	....	Edna Billings	Richard Chandon	Robert Brown	William F Flaherty	Richard Thompson
Thompson t (8)	TM	203 923-9561	Geri Langlois	....	Rachel Haggerty	Mercedes J Robbins	Paul Grenier	Geri Langlois	....
Tolland t* (10)	CM	203 872-4320	Stewart Joslin	John B Harkins	Elaine G Bugbee	John B Harkins	Ronald Littell	....	John B Harkins
Torrington (31)	MC	203 489-2228	Michael J Conway	....	Addo Bonetti	Dino M Borghesi	Francis Yanok	Anthony Neri	Robert Good
Trumbull t (33)	MC	203 261-3631	Paul Timpanelli Jr	....	Nancy Brown	Herbert Steinhardt	Joseph Adzima	Norman W Porteous	Paul Kallmeyer
Vernon t§ (28)	MC	203 872-8591	Marie A Herbst	Robert W Dotson	Henry F Butler	James M Luddecke	Donald J Maguda	Herman A Fritz	Ronald W Hine
Wallingford t (37)	MC	203 265-0911	William W Dickinson	....	Rosemary Rascati	Thomas A Myers	Jack K McElfish	Joseph J Bevan Jr	Steven Deak
Washington t (4)	TM	203 868-2786	John A Marsh	....	Doris K Welles	Ann Y Wyant	Duncan Woodruff	John A Marsh	....
Waterbury (103)	MC	203 574-6700	Edward D Bergin	Joseph R Carrah	Salvatore Jacaruso	Charles Donato	Ignazio Del Buono	Frederick Sullivan	William Spallone
Waterford t (18)	RT	203 442-4489	L Bettencourt	....	Calvin Brouwer	Arthur Davis	Douglas Peabody	James Perkins	Edward Steward
Watertown t* (19)	CM	203 274-5411	Barbara Hymel	James Troup	Mary B Canty	David Minnich	Avery W Lamphier	Frank Lecchi	Thomas Van
West Hartford t* (61)	CM	203 236-3231	Kevin B Sullivan	William N Brady	Nan L Glass	Edward A Lehan	Robert R Romanski	Francis G Reynolds	James F Kissane Jr
West Haven (53)	MC	203 934-3421	Lawrence Minichino	....	Julie Giordano	Kenneth E Ferris	William Johnson	Michael D'Errico	Frank Cusano
Westbrook t† (5)	TM	203 399-6236	Donald P Morrison	....	Johanna Schneider	Nicholas Lewitz	Loren Baker	Donald P Morrison	John P Riggio
Weston t (8)	TM	203 222-2656	Helen S Speck	Edward B Gomeau	Helen M Rosendahl	Edward B Gomeau	Frederick J Moore	Joseph McAleenan	Joseph Lametta
Westport t (25)	RT	203 226-8311	William Seiden	....	Joan M Hyde	Donald J Miklus	Donald A Byington	Ronald F Malone	Gerard A Smith
Wethersfield t* (26)	CM	203 529-8611	James R Boesch	Henry R Allen	W Dudley Birmingham	Lawrence J Guilmet	Clinton Hughes	T William Knapp	Henry R Allen
Willimantic*† (15)	CM	203 423-2559	John Lescoe	....	....	Elizabeth Hartt	Charles Monzillo	John Hussey	Joseph Dazy
Willington t (5)	TM	203 429-9965	Daniel Avery	....	Eleanor DuPilka	....	....	Daniel Avery	Elwood Jones
Wilton t (15)	TM	203 762-5578	Margaret S Gill	Eugene A Alexy	Mary Duffy	Eugene A Alexy	William Daskam	....	Thomas W Thurkettle
Winchester t* (11)	CM	203 379-2713	James Omeara	Jay A Gsell	Russell A Didsbury	Henry Centrella Jr	Frank Smith	John F Arcelaschi	Stephen M Eddy
Windham t† (21)	TM	203 423-1658	Louise M Guarnaccia	....	R James Sypher	....	....	....	....
Windsor t* (25)	CM	203 688-3675	John T Pier	Albert G Ilg	George J Tudan	Ruth M Levine	....	Maxie L Patterson	Ernest Phillips
Windsor Locks t (12)	TM	203 623-3458	Clifford Randall	....	Marie Dengemis	....	Raymond Ovellette	Bernard Kulas	Rudolph Fromm
Wolcott t (13)	MC	203 879-4666	E S Wilensky	....	Elaine King	Richard Semeraro	William McKinley	Roy Hoffman	Donald Sullivan
Woodbridge t (8)	TM	203 387-6639	Russell B Stoddard	....	Polly P Schulz	Martha H Mason	Emil Mattei	David Burke	Joseph C Kalson
Woodbury t (7)	TM	203 263-2141	Elizabeth A Adams	....	Jane Sandulli	John E Werner	Harris G Neal	Elizabeth A Adams	P Edward Lizauskas
Woodstock t (5)	TM	203 928-0208	Clarence C Child	....	F Veronica Hibbard	Barbara P Rich	....	Clarence H Child	....
DELAWARE (13)									
Bethany Beach t§ (..)	CO	302 539-8011	Jesse A Rawley Jr	Dean S Phillips	Bawn W Lawson	Murray D Snider	Daniel Orendorf	Herbert C Carey	James E Seabrease

Directory 1/10 continued — MUNICIPAL OFFICIALS IN ALL U.S. CITIES OVER 2,500[1]

City, 1980 population (000 omitted), form of government		Municipal phone number	Mayor	Appointed administrator	City clerk	Finance officer	Fire chief	Police chief	Public works director
DELAWARE (13) continued									
Delmar t* (1)	CM	302 846-2664	James L Smith	Karen E Horsman	Rebecca A Joseph	....	Joseph Morris	Harold E Saylor	Robert Handy
Dover* (24)	CM	302 736-7000	Crawford J Carroll	Robt J Bartolotta	William H Willis	Mike Karia	Wayne Hutchison	Joe A Klenoski	Richard E Scrafford
Elsmere t* (6)	CM	302 998-2215	John L Mitchell Sr	Joseph A Mangini Jr	....	Leslie Winkler	....	Patrick J Ramone	James Schneider
Laurel t (3)	CM	302 875-2277	William B Horner	Richard F Whaley	....	....	William Hearn	Donald J Edwards	....
Middletown t (3)	MC	302 378-2711	Charles E Price	....	Elizabeth S Burge	....	Kenneth L Branner	....	....
Milford* (5)	CM	302 422-6616	Joseph R Rogers	John F Frederick	Nancy J Daniels	Denise S Holleger	Wayne Hill	Richard Carmean	David J Coyle
New Castle (5)	MC	302 328-4804	John F Klingmeyer	....	Ann R Hushebeck	Thomas McGuire	Francis Suppe	Ray Wood	Charles Burris
Newark* (25)	CM	302 366-7000	Wm M Redd Jr	Peter S Marshall	Susan A Lamblack	A K Martin	Kenneth Farrell	William Brierley	Arthur W Fridl
Rehoboth Beach* (2)	CM	302 227-6181	John A Hughes	Gregory J Ferrese	Joyce Sutton	Catherine Batchelor	Howard Blizzard	Harry J Maichle Jr	James Hudson
Seaford (5)	CM	302 629-9173	Guy N Longo	Dolores F Jones	....	....	Michael Vincent	C Robert Miller	John D Holt
Smyrna t* (5)	CM	302 653-9231	George C Wright Jr	Edward R Stiff	Andrew P Johnson	....	....	Donald H McGinty	Wm E Hamburg
Wilmington§ (70)	MC	302 571-4011	Wm T McLaughlin	Bruce A Smith	Leo T Marshall	I G Cleaver	Jerome M Donohue	Dennis P Regan	Wm G Turner Jr
D.C. (1)									
Washington§ (638)	MC	202 727-1000	Marion Barry	Thomas Downs	Clifton Smith	Elizabeth Reveal	Theodore Coleman	Maurice T Turner	John Touchstone
FLORIDA (221)									
Alachua* (4)	CM	904 462-1231	James A Lewis	Mark Duchon	Mark Duchon	Sandy Burgess	Ron Prokop	Freddie Dampier	....
Altamonte Springs§ (22)	MC	305 830-3801	Raymond M Ambrose	Phillip D Penland	Penny Conahan	Mark Debord	T S Siegfried	William A Liquori	Donald F Newnham
Apalachicola (3)	MC	904 653-9319	Roger Newton	....	Dorothy Rolstad	Grady Lowe	Neuman Marshall	Warren Faircloth	Carl Gilbert
Apopka (6)	MC	305 889-2594	John H Land	....	Bonnie S Bray	Jack H Douglas Jr	Leon T Evett	Thomas A Collins Jr	Thomas E Richeson
Arcadia* (6)	CM	813 494-4114	Richard Fazzone	Edward J Strube	Margaret Way	Margaret Way	Anthony V Messina	Kenneth E Carlton	Harry Fowler
Atlantic Beach* (8)	CM	904 249-2395	William S Howell	A William Moss	Adelaide R Tucker	A William Moss	R Wayne Royal	David E Thompson	....
Atlantis* (1)	CM	305 965-1744	Joseph Veaner	E Earl Moore	Betty A Yon	Thomas Benham	....	Robert J Roberson	Bill Castaner
Auburndale* (7)	CM	813 967-1144	Charles W Johnson	Bruce Canova	Sandra Jackson	....	James A Hancock Jr	Allen J Hobbs	John A Johnson
Avon Park† (8)	MC	813 452-2221	David H Barefield	Larry W Sutton	....	....	H M Flowers	Paul Frost Jr	John Ziegler
Bal Harbour v* (3)	CM	305 866-4633	John S Sherman	Fred W Maley	Mary T Wetterer	Fred W Maley	....	Norman Staubesand	Robert Wheldon
Bartow* (15)	CM	813 533-0911	Orlando S Wright	James R O'Connor	Werner C Jones	John A Nickels	Tim Pitts	Charles A Fleming	J M Long
Bay Harbor Islands t* (5)	CM	305 866-6241	Stanley Goldsmith	Anthony Nales	Linda Karlsson	Cecil M Rash	....	Alex Spector	Kenneth Cassel
Bay Lake* (..)	CM	305 828-2034	Robert Streit	Stanley M Fletcher	Desiree L Horn	Reyna J Graham	....	....	....
Belle Glade* (17)	CM	305 996-0100	Thomas A Altman	W E Strang Jr	June H Boglioli	Frank C Anderson	Jesse Womack	D Bill Mathis	Frank Green
Belle Isle (3)	MC	305 851-7730	Frank A Borgon	Ann Byland	Ann Byland	Ann Byland	....	....	E Joseph McKinney
Belleair t* (4)	CM	813 584-7134	George E Mariani	Kurt D Peters	Lorain Blankenship	Kurt D Peters	Earl Lowe	Harry F Gwynne	....
Belleair Bluffs (3)	CO	813 584-2151	J Wilson Reed	....	Grace W Rulison	Barbara R Jonas	Karl D Diekman	James W Mangum	David R Sexsmith
Biscayne Park v† (3)	CO	305 893-7490	Edward J Burke	....	Jeanette Horton	Jeanette Horton	....	Daniel C Marx	Rollin E Johnson
Blountstown* (3)	CM	904 674-5488	Laddie Williams	Grant Gentry	Grant Gentry	Grant Gentry	Harvey Grantham	Winston Deason	....
Boca Raton* (50)	CM	305 393-7700	William A Konrad	James A Rutherford	Candace Bridgwater	Susan M Miller	John G Withrow	Peter A Petracco	John H Carroll
Bonifay (3)	MC	904 547-4238	Tom E Jenkins	R A Boswell	R A Boswell	R A Boswell	David O Perry	William Poole	Arelee Marell
Boynton Beach* (36)	CM	305 734-8111	Carl Zimmerman	Peter L Cheney	Betty Boroni	Grady Swann	James Rhoden	William Hamilton	Richard Walke
Bradenton† (30)	MC	813 748-0800	Bill Evers	W C Eyman	W C Eyman	W C Eyman	Gene Gallo	Charles B Wells	Earl Crawley
Brooksville* (6)	CM	904 796-4954	Franklin F Emerson	James G Cummings	Sandra L Woodall	Barry M Fredianelli	James Adkins	Timothy Vitt	Billy H Orr
Callaway† (7)	CO	904 769-4837	Ted Czupryk	....	Roy Kingsmill	Roy Kingsmill	James D Walls	Tommy Sims	Donald Minchew
Cape Canaveral* (6)	CM	305 783-1100	Wayne Rutherford	Frederick Nutt	Janet Leeser	Frederick Nutt	Patrick T Lee	....	Kenneth L Boring
Cape Coral* (32)	CM	813 574-3311	Joseph Mazurkiewicz	Robert D Proctor	Eula R Jorgensen	Charles D Tomlins	James L Hunt	James R White	Richard P Arson
Casselberry (15)	MC	305 831-3551	Charles H Glascock	....	Linda M Zike	Linda M Zike	Paul W Algeri	Frederick McGowan	Gage H Harvey
Chattahoochee† (5)	MC	904 663-4046	Robert D Hayes	....	Maidie Kingry	Maidie Kingry	F C Buddy Pfaender	David R Turnage	Clyde Hopkins
Chipley (3)	MC	904 638-1706	Colly V Williams	Lessie Boswell	Lessie Boswell	Lessie Boswell	Ira Carter	Robert Pleas	Fred A Buchanan
Clearwater* (85)	CM	813 462-6500	Kathleen F Kelly	Anthony Shoemaker	Lucille Williams	Daniel Deignan	Robert L Davidson	Sidney Klein	Max G Battle
Clermont* (5)	CM	904 394-4081	Charles B Beals	George D Forbes	....	D Wayne Saunders	Robert E Smythe	Prentice Tyndal	Robert E Smythe
Clewiston† (5)	CO	813 983-9191	Fred C Sikes	C F Blair	Leon Bembry	Cheryl Waters	W C Pelham Jr	Robert Dysart	I Raymond Pittman
Cocoa* (16)	CM	305 636-7121	Diane Tingley Gunn	Kenneth W Killgore	Linda C Knudson	Kenneth W Killgore	David Salisbury	Thomas F O'Connell	William Stephenson
Cocoa Beach* (11)	CM	305 783-4911	Robert E Lawton	James E Smith	Olive P Harness	William A Ryan	Robert B Walker	Robert E Wicker	William Straub
Coconut Creek* (6)	CM	305 972-4820	Louis J Schneider	Dennis D Mele	Angela A Bender	Harry Kilgore	John Whalen	John Whalen	....
Cooper City§ (10)	MC	305 434-4300	Suellen H Fardelman	Christopher Farrell	Susan Bernard	Frank Suozzo	Lenny Sanford	John J Pozar	John Flint
Coral Gables* (43)	CM	305 442-6400	William H Chapman	Donald E Lebrun	Virginia L Paul	James R Whitley	Philip F Sistik	Kenneth W Bush	Albert P Dusey
Coral Springs* (37)	CM	305 752-3410	O B Geiger	Dodd A Southern	Jonda K Joseph	Willard R Beck	John Dowling	Warren S Gilbert	G Robert Grube
Crestview (8)	MC	904 682-6131	Jerry W Milligan Sr	....	Edward M Neal	Edward M Neal	Dalton Brannon	James A Caton	Brady Ward
Crystal River (3)	CM	904 795-4216	Herbert D Williams	Wallace A Payne	Wallace A Payne	Eugene Williford	Morrow B Dumas II	James C Morgan	Donald A Sever
Dade City* (5)	CM	904 567-5148	William L Dennis	Ben Bolan	L C Smith	L C Smith	W B McKendree	Bernard R Enlow	Claude H Pike Jr
Dania* (12)	CM	305 921-8700	Byrd Chester	Richard Marant	Wanda Mullikin	Wanda Mullikin	Eugene Jewell	Rudolf Rigo	Vi Cooper
Davie t§ (21)	CM	305 584-1804	V J Jenkins	Irving Rosenbaum	Patricia McDaniel	Christopher Wallace	Michael Donati	Robert Weatherholt	Bruce Bernard
Daytona Beach Shores* (1)	CM	904 767-7121	Donald E Large	Robert D Holmquist	....	Gale B Sittig	Earl Free	Frank Dario	Joseph Fox
Daytona Beach* (54)	CM	904 252-6461	Lawrence J Kelly	Howard D Tipton	Rachel H Field	James C Maniak	Michael D McGibeny	C W Willits Jr	Russell E Hooper
De Funiak Springs (6)	MC	904 892-2156	John A McDonald	Michael G Standley	Wayne A Thompson	....	Warren McIntyre	Clinton Hooks	Aubrey McDonald
De Land* (15)	CM	904 736-1990	J E Summerhill	D Scott Rohlfs	Viola Ballentine	Janet W Brock	John C Wright	Richard Slaughter	Clarence Davenport
Deerfield Beach* (39)	CM	305 427-3331	Jean M Robb	J Eldon Mariott	Muriel Rickard	David P Bok	Tom Boylston	William Neal	John Vogel
Delray Beach* (34)	CM	305 278-2841	Doak S Campbell III	James L Pennington	Elizabeth Arnau	David M Huddleston	Michael T Jackson	Charles L Kilgore	Gerald Church
Dunedin* (30)	CM	813 733-4151	Mary Bonner	Parwez Alam	Robert Henderson	Philip McGuire	Robert Haworth	Robert Haworth	Parwez Alam
Edgewater (7)	MC	904 428-3245	David C Ledbetter	....	Connie A Kinsey	Connie A Kinsey	George Kennedy	Douglas W Betts	Earl Copeland
Eustis* (9)	CM	904 357-6991	S T E Pinkney	B F Jarrell	Jim R Myers	Jim R Myers	R A Shirk	R D Spears	Mike Stearman
Fernandina Beach* (7)	CM	904 261-6171	John G Haddock	F B Jones	Vicki P Wingate	Larry N Holton	James A Graves	Jerry Cameron	J B Higginbotham
Florida City (6)	MC	305 247-8221	Otis Wallace	....	....	Otis Wallace	....	John Folden	Clay Hoffheins
Fort Lauderdale* (153)	CM	305 761-2000	Robert A Dressler	Constance Hoffmann	Christine Anderson	Damon Adams	Fred Lane	Ronald Cochran	F T Kain
Fort Meade* (6)	CM	813 285-8191	Joseph E Davis	Robert F Bullard	Robert F Bullard	Robert F Bullard	Billy Gunter	Andrew Kovschak	Leonard Filyan
Fort Myers (37)	MC	813 334-1281	Ellis Solomon	....	Maynard W Matz	Maynard W Matz	Jack Kaune	Morgan House	Don McKenna
Fort Pierce* (34)	CM	305 464-5600	Wm R Dannahower	M Frank Blackwell	Inez Lowry	George J Bergalis	Russell Rogers	James A Powell	Vincent F Mannella
Fort Walton Beach* (21)	CM	904 243-3141	Kate Bagley	Chuck L Ingram	Helen Spencer	Chas H Evans	Billy Lee	Charles Keeler Jr	D Monty Jackson
Frostproof (3)	CM	813 635-2151	W C Funk	Dan H Ruhl Jr	Lillian J Amerson	....	Raymond Chatlos	Raymond L March	David F Hand
Fruitland Park* (2)	CM	904 787-6089	Thomas H Shepherd	Roman A Yoder Jr	Nancy S Eannarino	Sheryll Yoakum	Thomas Gamble	James L Yates Jr	James F Donovan
Gainesville* (81)	CM	904 374-2011	Jean Chalmers	Wm Higginbotham Jr	Mary Ann Frazer	Robert L Lockridge	Donald W Harkins Jr	Atkins W Warren	....
Graceville (3)	CO	904 263-3250	L H French Jr	George W Meadows	Kathleen B Turner	....	William Stob	Daniel B Ward	Charles J Shumaker
Green Cove Springs* (4)	CM	904 284-5621	Donald A Fullerton	Teddy C Ryan Jr	Marjorie Robertson	Ted Biggs	Reid Wager	William T Bland	R L Mckee
Greenacres City* (9)	CM	305 965-0388	James P Quigley	F W Douthwaite	Evelyn L Wheeles	Evelyn L Wheeles	Thomas C Rhodes	John T Treanor	Robert Flemming
Gulf Breeze* (5)	CM	904 932-3544	Joseph Reynes	Jackson C Tuttle II	Marita Rhodes	Jackson C Tuttle II	Edw L Bonifay Jr	Al Winfield	Floyd R Smith
Gulfport* (11)	CM	813 321-1158	Jay P Clymer	Ellis Shapiro	Lesley D Madison	Bruce T Haddock	L T McCarthy	Herman W Golliner	William F Brown
Haines City* (11)	CM	813 422-4986	Owen Flowers	Wm G Drummond	Eileen L Cummings	Sybil Burch	Wayne Walling	Kenneth Thompson	Lionel Carroll
Hallandale* (37)	CM	305 458-3251	Art Canon	Dean D Hunter Jr	June Watts Depp	Daryl Pokrana	Edward Proli	Richard C Fox	John C Depp
Havana t (3)	MC	904 539-6493	W K Cowart	Cecil G Trippe	Marjorie Underhill	....	....	P L Fusilier	....

Directory 1/10 continued — **MUNICIPAL OFFICIALS IN ALL U.S. CITIES OVER 2,500[1]**

City, 1980 population (000 omitted), form of government		Municipal phone number	Mayor	Appointed administrator	City clerk	Finance officer	Fire chief	Police chief	Public works director
FLORIDA (221) continued									
Hialeah (145)	MC	305 885-1531	Raul L Martinez	....	Daniel Deloach	Albert Turri	Thomas J Hyle	C B Seay	Jack Haygood
Hialeah Gardens (3)	MC	305 558-4114	Daniel M Riccio	....	Janet C Nusbaum	Janet C Nusbaum	....	Charles T Renegar	Willie Kelso
Highland Beach t* (2)	CM	305 278-4548	Louis Y Horton	Elaine W Roberts	Mary Ann Whaley	M Maree Birkbeck	....	William Cecere	....
Holly Hill (10)	CM	904 252-7631	Don Wiggins	Sue Blackwell	Sue Blackwell	L Virginia Wine	Dennis Bates	J Patrick Finn	Ronald F Emery
Hollywood* (117)	CM	305 921-3201	David R Keating	James E Chandler	Martha Lambos	Paul E Wimberly	James Ward	Samuel D Martin	Larry Roberts
Holmes Beach (4)	MC	813 778-2221	(not reporting)						
Homestead* (21)	CM	305 247-1801	Irving Peskoe	Alex Muxo Jr	Alphonso Milligan	Frank Del Toro	....	John Wall	Stanley Pacetti
Indialantic t* (3)	CM	305 723-2242	Andrea Deratany	H Blake Proctor	Carolyn Hazelgrove	Carolyn Hazelgrove	Robert Reed	Roger Skinner	John P Eddy
Indian Harbor Beach* (6)	CM	305 773-3181	Seymour Roth	Richard G Edgeton	Ruth H Grigsby	Lise Schroeder	Gil Grignon	Frederick J Fernez	Gil Grignon
Indian River Shores t* (1)	CM	305 231-1771	Fritz Gierhart	Joseph Dorsky	Virginia Blake	Joseph Dorsky	Ernest Polyerari	Ernest Polyerari	....
Indian Rocks Beach* (4)	CM	813 595-2517	Ralph H Finke	Dorothy A Cramer	Dorothy A Cramer	Dorothy A Cramer	....	Edward F Bulger	Virgil L Sawyer
Inverness† (4)	MC	904 726-2611	O J Humphries	Richard A Gilbert	Richard A Gilbert	Raymond Fitzgerald	....	Benjamin R Young	Daniel W Sawyer
Jacksonville Beach* (15)	CM	904 249-2381	Robert W O'Neill	John E White	Nancy Lee	Nancy Lee	Frank E Brunson Sr	Paul Brown	Melvin Heiman
Jacksonville (541)	MC	904 633-3700	Jake M Godbold	Donald R McClure	Ray Clardy	Ray Clardy	M D Gunn	Dale Carson	A J Kinard
Jupiter t* (10)	CM	305 746-5134	Mary Hinton	Griff H Roberts Jr	Jean H Beck	....	....	Glynn E Mayo	Jim Davis
Jupiter Island t* (..)	CM	305 546-5011	John H Mulliken Jr	R F Vande Weghe	Gloria D Schaus	....	Raymond F Lott	Jack G Curry	....
Kenneth City t (4)	MC	813 544-6655	Wm B Bartholomew	....	Joan D Musgrave	Carl F Schleck	Steve McCarthy	R E Webster	Charles B Knox
Key West* (24)	CM	305 294-3721	Richard A Heyman	Joel L Koford	Josephine Parker	Michael Simmons	Gilbert Gates	Larry Rodriquez	Puriegton Howanitz
Kissimmee* (15)	CM	305 847-2821	George A Gant	Arthur B Preston	....	Jean C Bennett	Kenneth Kemp	Frank J Ross	George W Mann
Lake Alfred* (3)	CM	813 956-3434	William K Hagy	Ivan L Carter Jr	Ellen M Newbern	Phyllis M Gregg	Donald W Ellis	Bruce J Efurd	James A Henson
Lake City* (9)	CM	904 752-2031	Gerald Witt	Ralph O Bowers	James R Minchin	James R Minchin	W V Wynn	Ray Simmons	John W Porter
Lake Clarke Shores t§ (3)	MC	305 964-1515	David E Fancher	Stuart Liberman	Stuart Liberman	....	....	Carl Valentine	....
Lake Mary (3)	MC	305 323-7910	Walter A Sorenson	Kathy S Rice	Carol A Edwards	Madeleine A Minns	James Orioles	Harry S Benson	James Orioles
Lake Park t* (7)	CM	305 848-3456	Max A Mickley	L Dennis Whitt	Debra M Laster	Kevin B Hollinger	George Long	Thomas J Cammarano	....
Lake Wales* (8)	CM	813 676-2533	R E Pilsbury	Ron R Russell	Josephine G Harper	Ron R Russell	John Busbee	John Busbee	Ron R Russell
Lake Worth* (27)	CM	305 586-1600	Betty Cortese	Kenneth S Nipper	Barbara A Forsythe	Carl J Gessler	Robert D Boike	C Lee Reese	Hubert Schmitz
Lakeland* (47)	CM	813 682-1141	Peggy C Brown	Robert V Youkey	Huretta Bassett	E C Trankle	J H Alford	Lawrence W Crow Jr	William P Warner
Lantana t (8)	MC	305 582-9095	Henry Johnson	Robert W Cameron	Robert W Cameron	Richard Kingrey	Howard Hartfelder	Charles Leonard	Richard J Parella
Largo* (59)	CM	813 584-8671	George C McGough	D Russell Barr	Kay H Klinsport	Jeffrey G Spies	Jerry Carter	Jerry Vaughn	Chris A Kubala
Lauderdale Lakes† (25)	MC	305 731-1212	Alfonso Gereffi	....	Audrey Tolle	....	Leonard J White	....	Roger Everly
Lauderdale-by-the-Sea t (3)	MC	305 776-0576	J R Forrest	....	Juanita Pendlebury	....	Dudley Greene	Joseph Fitzgerald	Dudley Greene
Lauderhill (37)	MC	305 739-0100	David Kaminsky	....	Muriel Trombley	Thomas R Camasso	Michael Cooper	George Slinkman	Louis Martin
Leesburg* (13)	CM	904 787-4313	Charles W Gregg	Rex A Taylor	James C Schuster	James C Schuster	Robert Taylor	James B Brown Jr	Richard G Shanklin
Lighthouse Point (11)	MC	305 943-6500	Frank J McDonough	Gerald J Renuart	Frances S Marsh	Gerald J Renuart	Charles E Malone	Paul Mannino	Wayne Stambaugh
Live Oak (7)	MC	904 362-2276	William W Howard	J Myron Holmes	Wm J McCullers	Troy E Roberts Jr	Howard Wright	Jack L Garrett	Williard Hewitt
Longboat Key t* (5)	CM	813 383-3721	Harry P Kirst	Dennis W Kelly	E Jane Pool	Walter Schmidt	Robert E Fakelman	Wayne McCammon	Albert T Cox Jr
Longwood (10)	CM	305 831-0555	J Russell Grant	David D Chacey	Donald L Terry	David D Chacey	Charles Chapman	Gregory Manning	Thomas Jackson Jr
Lynn Haven* (6)	CM	904 265-2121	Montel M Johnson	William V Kinsaul	Patricia H Mercer	....	John A Wright	Guy Tunnell	Bobby F Dutton
Macclenny t† (4)	MC	904 259-6251	A L Finley	J G Dopson	J G Dopson	J G Dopson	Stuart Nelson	....	Wendill Kirkland
Madeira Beach*† (5)	CM	813 391-9951	J Kenneth Jacobsen	Ralph W Rawson	Donna R Bender	Paul Williams	Charles W Beard	Bruno Kramer	Daryl Wilson
Madison* (3)	CM	904 973-4181	James O Catron	Thomas P Moffses Sr	Pearlie Mae Pearce	Pearlie Mae Pearce	Raymond Pinkard	Edward Odom	David Brown
Maitland* (9)	CM	305 644-8895	E X Blaschka	George E McMahon	Phyllis J Holvey	George E McMahon	Sid Ballou	John M Erwin	Matthew P Cross
Manalapan t* (..)	CM	305 585-9477	J Michael Curto	Shirley Kohl Vallan	Shirley Kohl Vallan	....	Ralph M Meadows	Ralph M Meadows	Richard L Paugh
Margate* (36)	CM	305 972-6454	Leonard Weisinger	Thomas H Hissom	Shirley J Baughman	Samuel Moschella	Robert Lindley	L A Christopher	James Hinds
Marianna* (7)	CM	904 482-4353	Bob Sanford	Julian E Laramore	Frances Ratzlaff	Frances Ratzlaff	Jack Barwick	Wiley G Pittman	Edward L Christmas
Mary Esther t (4)	MC	904 243-3566	(not reporting)						
Melbourne* (47)	CM	305 727-2900	Harry C Goode Jr	Samuel H Halter	Zella M Gaston	Amy Williams Stull	Jack R Dull	Bruce G Campbell	William Harper
Melbourne Beach t (3)	CO	305 724-5860	Louis W Conroy Jr	....	Virginia M Tuller	Michael J Block Jr	H Wayne Lynch	William C White	Martha M Remark
Miami* (347)	CM	305 579-6666	Maurice A Ferre	Howard V Gary	Ralph G Ongie	Carlos Garcia	K E McCullough	Kenneth I Harms	Don W Cather
Miami Beach* (96)	CM	305 673-7373	Malcolm C Fromberg	Rob W Parkins	Elaine M Baker	William MacDonald	Edward Walterman	Kenneth Glassman	Frank Aymonin
Miami Shores v* (9)	CM	305 758-8000	Kevin P O'Connor	L R Forney Jr	Antoinette Vigneron	Gail B Macdonald	....	John A Fletcher	Thomas J Benton
Miami Springs* (12)	CM	305 885-4581	John A Cavalier Jr	J Martin Gainer	Patricia A Cochran	Donald G Nelson	....	Michael A Koshock	Roland F Rivero
Milton* (7)	CM	904 623-3661	Clyde L Gracey	Russell L Harber	Dewitt Nobles	Dewitt Nobles	James D Cumbie	Charles E Manning	Russell L Harber
Miramar (33)	MC	305 989-6200	Frank R Branca	Charles G Strattan	Joseph J Tagg	Jack Neustadt	George Brown	Ed Werder	Edward O Frazier
Monticello (3)	MC	904 997-3312	R V Evans	Donald D Anderson	Betty W Bullock	Betty W Bullock	Johaan P Cooksey	George A Griffin	....
Mount Dora (6)	CM	904 383-2141	William O Boyd	Tony Segreto	Tony Segreto	Martha Danesky	Carroll Griggs	Earl Gooden	Joe Perry
Mulberry* (3)	CM	813 425-1125	Carl M Ellis	Robert O Wheeler	Patricia Richardson	Robert O Wheeler	Carl R Madebach	John W Hunter	H M Seigler
Naples* (18)	CM	813 262-7401	S R Billick	Franklin C Jones	Janet Davis Cason	Frank W Hanley	Norris Ijams	Paul C Reble Jr	William F Savidge
Neptune Beach (5)	MC	904 241-3191	Ish Brant	....	Donna L Williams	Linda Watson	Howard C Basil	Howard C Basil	Richard Hillard
New Port Richey* (11)	CM	813 849-2261	George W Henry	Charles W McCool	June S Bottner	Daniel R Klein	Roy Miller	James C Bottner	Nelson C Vogel
New Smyrna Beach* (14)	CM	904 427-4166	George E Musson	E Irene Beckham	Lynda L Schaidt	John E Hagood	Albert Bishop	Cody L Gear Jr	Melvin Phillips
Niceville* (9)	CM	904 678-4523	Randall Wise	Lannie L Corbin	George H Ireland	Brentwood Bryan	James C Davis	Edward W Holloway	Lannie L Corbin
North Bay Village* (5)	CM	305 756-7171	Paul Vogel	Nancy Ciummo	Susan Moody	Dale N Olson	....	Stanford C Blair	Everett L Johnson
North Lauderdale* (18)	CM	305 722-0900	John Hart	Eric M Soroka	C Milli Dyer	Stanley Hochman	Jess Boytell	Jess Boytell	Edward Goebel
North Miami* (43)	CM	305 893-6511	Marco B Loffredo Jr	Lawrence C Casey	Clair T Singerman	Thomas H Schnieders	....	Thomas H Flom	Alfred J Signore
North Miami Beach* (36)	CM	305 947-7581	Marjorie McDonald	William McGill	Solomon Odenz	Marilyn Spencer	....	Buford Whitaker	Herbert Lund
North Palm Beach v* (11)	CM	305 848-3476	V A Marks	Ray Howland	Dolores R Walker	Joan Bernola	Larry Joyce	John S Atwater	Charles R O'Meilia
North Port (6)	MC	813 426-1288	Margaret M Gentle	....	Lillian A Pedersen	Margaret M Gentle	William T Moore Jr	Victor Costello	Howard R Osborne
Oakland Park* (22)	CM	305 561-6250	Glenn J Dufek	Richard A Clark	Darleen Mitchell	Elbert E Wrains	Edward D Bailey	Edward P Turner	Harry L Wimberly
Ocala* (37)	CM	904 629-8401	Wayne L Rubinas	Scotty J Andrews	Mary Jane Milam	Robert F Sprinkle	William E Woods	A L McGehee	Gary R Stewart
Ocoee* (8)	CM	305 656-2322	Thomas Ison	Kenton Griffin	Clyde C Burgess	Ivan Poston	Ronnie Stroesnider	Leroy Turner	Cliff Burgess
Okeechobee (4)	MC	813 763-3372	Edward W Douglas	Richard C Fellows	Bonnie S Thomas	Bonnie S Thomas	Keith Tomey	Larry Mobley	Landon C Fortner Jr
Oldsmar* (3)	CM	813 855-4693	Sandy Francisco	Hugh D Williams	Cheryl D Mortenson	Sharon Harrell	Ross Wilman	....	Don McCullers
Opa-Locka* (14)	CM	305 688-4611	John Riley	Danny Alvarez	Sherrie Lovette	Danny Alvarez	....	Robert B Ingram	Don Samuels
Orange City (3)	MC	904 775-3333	Richard Attwood	James H Kerr III	Jean Emery	....	Ron Haire	Gerald Fleming	Walter Legacy
Orange Park t§ (9)	MC	904 264-9565	Hance R Bruce	....	Joyce Bryan	Dorothy Mollnow	Frank Parrish	....	Arthur W Berger
Orlando (128)	MC	305 849-2121	Bill Frederick	L A Hester	Grace A Chewning	G Michael Miller	F E Reynolds	Frederick J Walsh	Robert C Haven
Ormond Beach* (21)	CM	904 677-0311	Charles E Bailey	John H Leemkuil	Marian A Maxwell	John H Leemkuil	Harold E Burr	Harold E Burr	David Day
Oviedo (3)	MC	305 365-3287	Robert W Whittier	....	Nancy K Cox	....	Andrew McDaniel	Robert W Hancock	A M Jones
Pahokee t (6)	MC	305 924-5534	Duncan Padgett	....	Betty J McCoy	....	Cecil Phillps	C Salvatore III	Richard Mount
Palatka* (10)	CM	904 325-4591	Eugene L Walker	Allen R Bush	Allen R Bush	....	Jay Crawford	Jimmy Hill	....
Palm Bay* (19)	CM	305 727-7100	William F Madden	Robert G Matte	Alice Passmore	James H Demming	David Greene	Charles R Simmons	Eric S Meserve

Directory 1/10 continued — **MUNICIPAL OFFICIALS IN ALL U.S. CITIES OVER 2,500[1]**

City, 1980 population (000 omitted), form of government		Municipal phone number	Mayor	Appointed administrator	City clerk	Finance officer	Fire chief	Police chief	Public works director
FLORIDA (221) continued									
Palm Beach Gardens* (14)	CM	305 622-1200	Michael Martino	John L Orr	Linda M Ard	John L Orr	Edward Arrants	Edward Himmelsbach	Leonard Devine
Palm Beach t* (10)	CM	305 655-5341	Yvelyne DeM Marix	Douglas C Delano	Grace T Peters	Steven Driscoll	Vincent K Elmore	Joseph L Terlizzese	Samuel P Hadley
Palm Springs v* (8)	CM	305 965-4010	Richard Jette	Patrick D Miller	Patricia M Mallon	Patrick D Miller	Elmer W Hoagland	Elmer W Hoagland	....
Palmetto (9)	MC	813 722-4567	Robert E Hunt Sr	....	Steve Odem	....	William Bellamy	A E Hambacher	Lee Baten
Panama City* (33)	CM	904 763-6641	Girard L Clemons Jr	John E Baxter	Michael Bush	Michael Bush	Robert Richardson	Leroy French	Virgil Bass
Parker† (4)	MC	904 871-4104	Earl Gilbert	....	Bruce Anderson	....	Roy L Roberts	Joe B Walker	....
Pembroke Park t (5)	MC	305 966-4600	Dottie Johnston	Hewitt Wagner	Barbara R Powell	Benjamin M Linet	George Van Etveldt	Eugene O'Sullivan	Hewitt Wagner
Pembroke Pines* (36)	CM	305 431-4500	Charles W Flanagan	Woodward Hampton	Charles F Dodge	Rene Gonzalez	Phillip Rosenthal	John Tighe	Robert Perkins
Pensacola* (58)	CM	904 436-4111	Vince Whibbs	Stephen L Garman	Polly Johns	Walter D Parker	Raymon J Church	Louis L Goss	Tom Royster
Perry* (8)	CM	904 584-7161	J C Yarbrough	William J Noonan	William J Noonan	William T Powers	S D Sapp	Ronald D Smith	Barney E Johnson
Pinellas Park* (33)	CM	813 544-8831	Cecil W Bradbury	Ronald P Forbes	Grace Kolar	Paul Wunderlich	Kenneth Cramer	David Milchan	Klem Adamski
Plant City* (19)	CM	813 752-3125	J D Merrill	Nettie M Draughon	Richard M Olson	Richard M Olson	George Contner	Troy E Surrency	Salvador D Nabong
Plantation† (49)	MC	305 797-2220	Frank Veltri	....	Chester L Merrick	Robert E Brekelbaum	Robert Pudney	Morris Meek	J Robert Spero
Polk City t* (1)	CM	813 984-1375	Billy C Knight	Louise A Smith	Louise A Smith	....	Carmen Ray White	Tommy R Wood	....
Pompano Beach* (53)	CM	305 786-4050	Emma Lou Olson	James E Soderlund	Charlotte Burrie	Steve Weinstein	Ralph G Borger	Schuyler Ted Meyer	Jack Gumbart
Port Orange* (19)	CM	904 761-8000	James R Fisher	Kenneth W Parker	Ms Marion J Zeller	Michael R Saunders	Michael Ertz	David Solana	Steve White
Port St. Joe* (4)	CM	904 229-8261	Frank Pate Jr	Leslie A Farris	Leslie A Farris	Leslie A Farris	Bascom Hamm	Robert G Maige	Martin B Adkison
Port St. Lucie* (15)	CM	305 878-0097	W B McChesney	G Wayne Allgire	Sandra C Krause	Gerald Van Patten	Russell Rogers	O H Schlesselman	Ernest R Dike Jr
Punta Gorda* (7)	CM	813 639-2867	Charles D Burke	Bernard W Senkel	Mary Lou Hillenburg	William A Knoble	Donald J Romer	Donald R Bennett	Thomas C Roadman
Quincy* (9)	CM	904 627-7681	Eldon L Greene	William F Johnson	Sylvester Woodward	Kenneth A Cowen	Robert E Joyner	Edward M Spooner	Thad White
Riviera Beach* (27)	CM	305 845-4000	Bobbie E Brooks	William E Wilkins	Gwendolyn E Davis	Dennis Widlansky	Frank N Sulkowski	Frank M Walker III	Art Cobb Jr
Rockledge* (12)	CM	305 636-5711	J J Oates	John A Hipp	Dorathea Hamilton	John A Hipp	R D Nix Jr	Richard R Kallis	J J Gilliard
Royal Palm Beach v (3)	MC	305 793-3400	Sam Lamstein	Robert C Bryer	Beverly J Burcaw	Patricia Sage	Karl Combs	....	H Kenneth Osborne
Safety Harbor* (6)	CM	813 726-0780	John H Williams	John J Downes	Bonita J Haynes	Steve Moskun	Wm Jay Stout	....	Jamal S Nagamia
Sanford* (23)	CM	305 322-3161	Lee P Moore	Warren E Knowles	Henry N Tamm	Henry N Tamm	W C Gailey	Ben Butler	A Robert Kelly
Sanibel* (3)	CM	813 472-4135	Fred W Valtin	Gary Price	Gary Price	Mildred L Howze	....	John P Butler	Gary A Price
Sarasota* (49)	CM	813 365-2200	Lou Ann Palmer	Kenneth Thompson	Robert A McLelland	John T Haylett	Harold Stinchcomb	Earl D Parker	Gilbert J Leacock
Satellite Beach* (9)	CM	305 773-4407	Edward A Rainis	Richard H Shinn	Anne F Scanlon	Norma Tetrault	Jack Smith	Thomas T McCarthy	Gene Sorensen
Sebastian (3)	MC	305 589-5330	Jim Gallager	....	Deborah Krages	Carol Carswell	Ralph Arand	John L Emrick	Barton LaBar
Sebring (9)	MC	813 385-0549	Smith J Rudasill	....	Jack R Stroup	....	....	....	....
Seminole (5)	MC	813 391-0204	Holland G Mangum	Shirley Merrifield	June M Smith	Holland G Mangum	James R McConnell	Gerry Coleman	Mel Rackett
South Bay* (4)	MC	305 996-6751	Vernita Cox	Lomax Harrelle	Virginia K Walker	Virginia E Walker	Johnny Parchment	Roy Humston	Lomax Harrelle
South Daytona* (10)	CM	904 788-5000	Eugene E Rhodes Jr	Paul A Piller	....	Paul A Piller	John W Geissler	Gary A White	Sam Tucker
South Miami*† (11)	CM	305 667-5691	Jack Block	William E Godwin	Rosemary J Nayman	Richard K Solock	....	Murray L Selsky	James Simmons
South Pasadena (4)	MC	813 347-4171	Thomas A Ravelli	....	Ray Harbaugh	Dorothy M Bedford	Joseph G Novak	....	....
Springfield† (7)	MC	904 785-9516	Buddy McLemore	....	J C Scalf	Joyce Maynor	Herman L Self	John Sword	Philip Connor
St. Augustine* (12)	CM	904 829-5691	Ramelle Petroglou	Calvin E Glidewell	Paula B Owens	H Lee Burgess	T H Nelson	David Daniel	Jack Cubbedge
St. Cloud* (8)	CM	305 892-2161	Robert Lee Renick	James V Chisholm	James V Chisholm	John E Ford	Kermit Wheeler	E E Eunice	Donald A Kinsella
St. Petersburg* (237)	CM	813 893-7171	Corinne Freeman	Alan N Harvey	Brenda Jividen	Richard L Ashton	Jerry G Knight	Samuel F Lynn	Jordan M Rich
St. Petersburg Beach* (9)	CM	813 367-2735	Dan L Johnson	Max Royle	Ms D C Salsinger	D R Perkins	Charles Hartman	Thomas Lange	Charles Ames
Starke† (5)	MC	904 964-5027	Vernon Silcox	....	Neil L Tucker	Neil L Tucker	Robert Lewis	Jimmy Bowan	Merrill Dees
Stuart* (9)	CM	305 287-3444	Stewart Hershey	Robert McGrath	Betty Kenny	Marty Boatright	Louis J Papitto	Charles E White	Sandy Mitchell
Sunrise (40)	MC	305 741-2580	John Lomelo Jr	....	D DeBenedictis	Thomas J Mullen	John Komasa	Samuel A Ramputi	Louis J Perrotti
Surfside t* (4)	CM	305 861-4863	Ben Levine	Harold S Cohen	John Pine	Harold S Cohen	....	Terrill Williamson	Aaron Cohen
Sweetwater (8)	MC	305 221-0411	Armando A Penedo	....	Marie O Schmidt	Esther Colon	....	Charles Toledo	Armando A Penedo
Tallahassee* (82)	CM	904 599-8100	Kent Spriggs	Daniel A Kleman	Robert B Inzer	Philip Inglese	Edwin C Ragans	Melvin Tucker	Rhett A Miller Jr
Tamarac* (29)	CM	305 722-5900	Philip B Kravitz	Elly F Johnson	Marilyn Bertholf	Steven Wood	Bernard Simon	Joseph McIntosh	Gregory M Turek
Tampa† (272)	MC	813 223-8181	Bob Martinez	....	Frances Henriquez	Louis Russo	A S Coniglio Jr	Robert L Smith	Steve Tindale
Tarpon Springs* (13)	CM	813 938-3711	Bill Lane	Blaine P Lecouris	Kathy Alesafis	Robert Bublitz	Kenneth Ennis	Blaine Lecouris	Donald Ison
Tavares* (4)	CM	904 343-2121	Eugene Glenn	Robert E Phillips	Robert E Phillips	Robert E Phillips	E S Lane	Wm Brandt	Roger Pattullo
Temple Terrace* (11)	CM	813 988-5111	Edward B Simmon	Picot B Floyd	Patricia A Jones	Thomas J Bonfield	James W Bailey	Tom Matthews	Bob Fernandez
Tequesta v (4)	CM	305 746-7457	Carlton D Stoddard	Robert Harp	Cyrese Colbert	Bill Kascavelis	....	Franklin E Flannery	James W Worth
Titusville* (32)	CM	305 269-4400	T Scarborough Jr	Hector Figueredo	Janet R Camacho	Ray Deloach	Richard C Cherry	Charles L Ball	John Peterson
Treasure Island* (6)	CM	813 360-0811	Walter Stubbs	Peter G Lombardi	Peter G Lombardi	Charles D Francis	Charles J Fant	Cliff Frye	Ron Owen
Valparaiso (6)	MC	904 678-2912	John B Arnold Jr	....	Faye B Floyd	John B Arnold Jr	Charles Nieft	Lomax Donaldson	Claude H Vanderford
Venice* (12)	CM	813 485-3311	Richard W Louis	Dale E Rieth	Bernie N Simanskey	Wilburn H Kern	James J Culbert	Ray V Waymire Jr	Lawrence Heath
Vero Beach* (16)	CM	305 567-5151	David Gregg Jr	John V Little	Phyllis Neuberger	Thomas R Nason	Forrest Smith	Samuel P McCall	Donald Smoak
Wauchula (3)	MC	813 773-3131	E J Wilson	....	Mavis F Best	Mavis F Best	....	Ray Grimes	Thomas M Priest
West Melbourne* (5)	CM	305 727-7700	Frederick Winter	Mark K Ryan	Janice Daniels	Linda J Midtling	....	James Donnan	....
West Miami§ (6)	MC	305 266-1122	Pedro Reboredo	Fred M Bowen Jr	Yolanda Aguilar	Fred M Bowen Jr	....	Patrick Kiel	George Kulik
West Palm Beach* (63)	CM	305 659-8000	Dwight R Baber	Richard G Simmons	Agnes Hayhurst	Katherine Battern	Lamar W Bell	John Jamason	Benjamin T Nabors
Wildwood* (3)	CM	904 748-1223	R F Rector	John Phillips Jr	Joseph T Jacobs	....	T L Smart	Ed Lynum Jr	T L Smart
Wilton Manors§ (13)	MC	305 566-2467	Robert H Dubree Sr	J Scott Miller	Diane M Hominick	John J Ciullo	Richard Rothe	Bernard S Scott	Hesper Hudson
Winter Garden* (7)	CM	305 656-4111	Ralph Fulford	Ray Creech	Hugh O Grimes	Reed Watts	Roy E LaBossiere	Jimmie Yawn	William Faulk
Winter Haven* (21)	CM	813 294-3551	Paul B Cate	P E Kinsey	Vietta B Young	Calvin Bowen	Charles Brown	Ron Martin	Dale Smith
Winter Park* (22)	CM	305 644-9860	Hope Strong Jr	David T Harden	Sandra O Rozar	Robert Hague	Michael D Molthop	Raymond Beary	J O Compton
Winter Springs* (10)	CM	305 327-1800	John V Torcaso	Richard Rozansky	Mary T Norton	....	Charles Holzman	John Govoruhk	Charles Hassler
Zephyrhills*† (6)	CM	813 782-1525	Robert H Johnson	Louie H Holt	Joanne Good	Judson B Baggett	Carlton Galster	William R Eiland	Harold Bryant
GEORGIA (153)									
Acworth§ (4)	CM	404 974-3112	Joe T Chambers	K F Copeland	Bobbie J Davis	K F Copeland	....	R G Cantrell	Joe Griffis
Adel* (6)	CM	912 896-2821	Wm F Bozeman	John H Flythe	Jerry Permenter	Jerry Permenter	E O Frost	H G Philips	Ralph Hill
Albany* (74)	CM	912 883-1415	James H Gray Sr	Carl F Leavy	Joann Pope	T L McComb	C E Hysler Jr	Norman E Denney	W D Lanier
Alma* (4)	CM	912 632-5917	James E Deen	Jeff L Kinlaw	Mary Alice Stafford	Jeff L Kinlaw	Wayne Williams	L W Cartrett	Glover Scott
Alpharetta (3)	MC	404 475-9566	Jimmy Phillips	Albert E Johnson	Sue Rainwater	Albert E Johnson	Squire Ferguson	Larry Abernathy	Foster Cagle
Americus (16)	MC	912 924-4413	Russell Thomas Jr	....	Sybil Hamrick	Sybil Hamrick	Morris Smith	Richard M Bond	Jim Usry
Ashburn (5)	MC	912 567-3431	J I Youngblood	....	Marie Hudgins	Marie Hudgins	Billy Ray Royal	E L Bean	Donald Padgett
Athens (43)	MC	404 543-4191	Lauren M Coile	Al Crace	Johnny C Fowler	Johnny C Fowler	....	Everett E Price	Ben Williams
Atlanta§ (425)	MC	404 658-6100	Andrew Young	Shirley C Franklin	Larry Dingle	Pat Glisson	B J Thompson	Morris G Redding	Chester Funnye
Augusta (48)	MC	404 724-4391	(not reporting)						
Austell† (4)	MC	404 941-0228	John L Collar	R H Causey	D S Lockridge	D S Lockridge	Mike Smith	C W Hardin	R H Putman
Avondale Estates* (1)	CM	404 294-5400	Thomas E Brooks	Dewey C Brown Jr	Kathy R Swanson	Beatrice F Sutton	....	Dewey C Brown Jr	E Thomas Brown
Bainbridge* (11)	CM	912 246-2150	B K Reynolds	W Shelton Smith	W Shelton Smith	Florine King	James Duke	James Duke	Dave Holley
Barnesville (5)	MC	404 358-0181	(not reporting)						
Baxley* (4)	CM	912 367-4695	Wm Terry Turner	Samuel W Dunn	Jean W Spell	Jean W Spell	Mickey Bass	Charlie Beach	H L Crosby
Blackshear (3)	MC	912 449-5375	Harry G Adams	....	Gloria D Roberson	....	Arthur Kier	Dennis Martin	Arthur Kier
Blakely§ (6)	MC	912 723-3677	Billy Fleming	George A Loyed	Sterling P Jones	Sterling P Jones	Franklin Brown	Carl Gilbert	....
Bowdon§ (2)	MC	404 258-3725	T Raymon Morgan	Julian M Jones Sr	Betty B Cason	Julian M Jones Sr	....	James C Rooks	Leon H Word

Directory 1/10 continued

MUNICIPAL OFFICIALS IN ALL U.S. CITIES OVER 2,500[1]

City, 1980 population (000 omitted), form of government	Municipal phone number	Mayor	Appointed administrator	City clerk	Finance officer	Fire chief	Police chief	Public works director
GEORGIA (153) continued								
Bremen (4) MC	404 537-2331	Richard H Wheeler	Hoyt H Bilbo	Beverly H Cash	....	Clark Farr	Larry G Hembree	....
Brunswick* (18) CM	912 265-8210	A C Knight III	Homer L Wilson	Ms H S Jennings	S L Hall	Thomas R Nichols	J C Carter	Homer L Wilson
Buford* (7) CM	404 945-6761	Tommy Hughes	Earley Biffle	Judy Martin	....	A C Ehlert	Walter Gunter	Earley Biffle
Cairo* (9) CM	912 377-1722	Adrian P Clark	Dan A Wells	Martha Faye Lewis	....	Ronald Johnson	Marvin C Sasser	....
Calhoun (5) MC	404 629-0151	William C Burdette	James W Hobgood	Cathy Harrison	Cathy Harrison	Ferrell Grizzle	Hughdon Davis	Dean Harris
Camilla* (5) CM	912 336-5636	Arch McNeill Jr	Clarence H Bryant	Virginia McMinn	Clarence H Bryant	Lazelle McCook	Doug Adair	Paul Green
Canton (4) MC	404 479-2421	Odie P Galt Jr	William J Buckner	Judy G Wehunt	William A Teasley	Roy G Barber	Jimmy L Waters	Arnold Fowler
Carrollton* (14) CM	404 832-2443	Tracy Stallings	Dudley Crosson	Jewell Mashburn	Al Collins	L A Dukes	Jack Bell	Bob Tucker
Cartersville* (10) CM	404 382-1171	David Tillman	Walter K Mahone	Clarance Walker	Clarance Walker	Norris Westbrooks	Paul Whitley	Jerry E Milam
Cedartown* (9) CM	404 748-3220	Jerry W Walley	J J Brooks	Emily C Shaw	J J Brooks	Ellis Mauldin	W M Moss	J J Brooks
Centerville (3) MC	912 953-4734	Walker Fowler Jr	....	Virginia E Abbott	....	Robert A Smith Jr	Michael Sullivan	J D Boler
Chamblee (7) MC	404 458-0066	Johnson W Brown	....	Jo Anne Donaldson	....	....	T L Terrell	....
Clarkston t (5) MC	404 443-6489	(not reporting)						
Claxton (3) MC	912 739-1712	Perry Lee Deloach	....	Gayle K Durrence	Gayle K Durrence	Larry Rogers	Edward Oglesbee Jr	C W Young
Cochran (5) MC	912 934-6346	Charles D Killebrew	....	William J Lucas	....	....	Charles L McDonald	....
College Park* (25) CM	404 767-1537	T Owen Smith	Jerry L Gwaltney	Jean Cress	....	Winfred S Tucker	Garon L Glover	....
Columbus* (169) CM	404 571-4700	J W Feighner	Franklyn Lambert	Lemuel H Miller Jr	Catherine Howse	Robert Ledford	W J Wetherington	Richard McKee
Commerce (4) MC	404 335-3164	Tommy Stephenson	H Douglas Dorsey	Deborah Willoughby	Deborah Willoughby	Bubba McDonald	H G Perry	Daniel Strickland
Conyers* (7) CM	404 483-4411	Charles C Walker	Barbara D Bramblett	Debbie Everson	....	Jerry Norton	Roland Vaughn	Bobbie Hill
Cordele* (11) CM	912 273-3102	Perry Culpepper Sr	David E Scales	Jackie H Brown	Nancy W Brannon	Eugene Stephens	John Mapp	James W Watson
Cornelia*† (3) CM	404 778-4921	....	Sanford Blackburn	....	....	....	....	....
Covington* (11) CM	404 786-5324	W L Bill Dobbs	Frank B Turner	Betty L Schell	James H Mitcham	E Jack Parker	Bobby Moody	Sam Walton
Cuthbert† (4) MC	912 732-3161	Hiram Goodman	....	Trudie McDonald	C R Dixon	Albert Cole	Phillip V Jarrel	Steve Jackson
Dahlonega (3) MC	404 864-6133	Jack Roberts	Emory L Stephens	Jane Jarrard	Emory L Stephens	....	....	....
Dallas* (2) CM	404 445-4466	Coleman Camp	Kenneth Elsberry	Helon Wills	Kenneth Elsberry	Bill Patrick	Doug Gober	J T Cochran
Dalton (21) MC	404 278-9500	Jimmy L Young Sr	Albert Rollins	Faye L Martin	Albert Rollins	Clifford Maney	James Lowe	Richard Bramlett
Dawson* (6) CM	912 995-4444	J G Raines	D R Bell Jr	D R Bell Jr	D R Bell Jr	Jackie Lash	Jackie Lash	John Stokes
Decatur* (18) CM	404 377-9911	Robert E Carpenter	G Curtis Branscome	W Calvin Horton	V H Thornton	Sherrard E White	J Edwin Matthews	Charles M Gall
Donalsonville† (3) MC	912 524-2118	H M Shingler	Frank Bell	Dorothy E Johnson	Dorothy E Johnson	W T Williams	Frank Manley	W T Williams
Doraville (7) MC	404 451-8745	Gene Lively	J W Buechler	J W Buechler	Gene Lively	....	George Everett	....
Douglas* (11) CM	912 384-3302	Jim Minix	Olaf F Pearson	Hayvene McFall	John Lester	Freddie Davis	Clyde Purvis	Herschel Carver
Douglasville* (8) CM	404 942-5118	Charles L Camp	Jack H Banks	Mary Alice Wypasek	....	T D Pate	Joe L Whisenant	Keith L Williams
Dublin* (16) CM	912 272-1620	Albert Franks	Kenneth R Hammons	James E Shurley	James E Shurley	Robert Drew	Frank Owens	Jimmy Sawyer
Duluth† (3) MC	404 476-3434	Claude D Mason	....	Helen Banks	....	....	Darrell E Brown	Kenneth J Pittard
East Dublin t† (3) MC	912 272-6883	George H Gornto	....	Evelyn M Harrell	Evelyn M Harrell	William Crisp	Larry N Drew	A T Williams
East Point* (37) CM	404 765-1000	Walter A Ponder	Joseph Johnson Jr	Evelyne K Reeves	....	Edward J Elam	John L McClendon	J P Eidson
Eastman* (5) CM	912 374-7721	Marva M McGriff	John Reddock	Ann S Jones	Ann S Jones	Alfonso Stephens	Terry L Crowell	James T Burnham
Eatonton (5) MC	404 485-3311	James P Marshall	John R Davis	Audrey S Hightower	Audrey S Hightower	Orvin Vanlandingham	Billy Wooten	John R Davis
Elberton* (6) CM	404 283-5321	Joe H Fendley Sr	C A Brown	Iola S Stone	Iola S Stone	Niles T Poole	George W Ward	Barney Taylor
Fairburn§ (3) MC	404 964-2244	A J Green	Alex Howell Sr	Bobbie Langston	Alex Howell Sr	Welton Smith	C H Nave	John King
Fayetteville† (3) MC	404 461-6029	Jack D Dettmering	John Davidson	John Davidson	John Davidson	Harry D Huddleston	Charles K Gilbert	John Davidson
Fitzgerald§ (10) MC	912 423-9827	Gerald Thompson	Alvie L Dorminy	Louise T Wiggins	Alvie L Dorminy	I Willie Crawford	Drew Soloman	....
Forest Park* (19) CM	404 366-4720	Jerome Tomasello	John B Parker	John B Parker	Bob Bailey	L C Cole	Joseph Picard	O L Berry Jr
Forsyth (5) MC	912 994-5649	Richard W Truitt	....	Barbara Antonio	Barbara Antonio	H B Gunnell	Benjamin Ponder Jr	....
Fort Oglethorpe (5) CM	404 866-2544	John W Norris	Mitchell B Moore	Glenn E Parker	Mitchell B Moore	Harold Cook	John Allen	John F Fritts
Fort Valley (9) MC	912 825-8261	C W Peterson	M L Gilchrist	M L Gilchrist	Jack Hamilton	W H Jackson	John B Dankel	James Howard
Gainesville*† (15) CM	404 534-7321	James A Hartley	Ray Keith	Henry Pinyan	Henry Pinyan	Verner S Hamrick	George S Knapp	George Austin
Garden City§ (7) MC	912 964-1711	Ralph O Kessler	Robt P Schwartz	Robt P Schwartz	Robt P Schwartz	James D Crosby Jr	Jeffrey G Wood	George W Burke
Glennville (4) MC	912 654-2461	Charlie Rowland	Jean Bridges	Jean Bridges	Jean Bridges	Bobby Brannen	Harry Sands Jr	Dane DeLoach
Gordon t (3) MC	912 628-2222	Michael L Dennis	....	Fay B Garner	Fay B Garner	Terry Eady	Cuyler Payne	James E Dennard Jr
Greensboro (3) MC	404 453-7967	Dean Stewart	Charlton S Veazey	Charlton S Veazey	Charlton S Veazey	Omer Cook	Fred L Webb	Charlton S Veazey
Griffin* (21) CM	404 227-5288	Cecil L Davis	Frank C Schofield	Frank C Schofield	Frank C Schofield	Leonard J Pitts	Jimmy R Sutton	....
Grovetown (3) MC	404 863-4576	Leon R Davidson	....	Darleen H Plunkett	Darleen H Plunkett	Charles R Cramer	Peter P Zatorski	Bobby L Brinson
Hapeville (6) MC	404 768-8080	Barney L Sullivan	Robert A Forgay	....	Robert A Forgay	Jesse West	James E Clay	Joe D Hindman
Hartwell (5) MC	404 376-4756	Joan H Saliba	Ellis D Foster	Ellis D Foster	Ellis D Foster	Maurice Vickery	Cecil E Reno	....
Hawkinsville* (4) CM	912 892-3240	Lawrence L Bennett	Richard Hogg	Margaret C Walker	Margaret C Walker	Samuel G Clark	William L Poole	Lute Marshall
Hazlehurst (4) MC	912 375-2571	Lawrence G Contos	....	David L Griffin	M D Coleman	Larry L Anthony	Steven C Land	Bennie T Hughes
Hinesville (11) MC	912 876-3564	Carl R Dykes	Billy Edwards	Onetha Mingledorff	Onetha Mingledorff	Julien Mingledorff	Robert Ryon	Mark Copeland
Hogansville* (3) CM	404 637-8629	Douglas E Boatner	C Wesley Duffey	Diane Sherrer	Wesley Duffey	Wilson St Clair	Lewis Clay Bryant	....
Homerville (3) MC	912 487-2375	Chester Day	William C Vest	William C Vest	William C Vest	Tony Strickland	Donald Lee	Dell T Bennett
Jackson (4) MC	404 775-7535	C B Brown Jr	....	Judy Kelly	....	W L Vaughn	Dorsey Evans	Glenn L Smith
Jesup* (9) CM	912 427-2234	Joel R Greene	Ron McLemore	Sue R Sutton	Sue R Sutton	Kennic Yeomans	Mike Deal	Sumter Flowers
Jonesboro (4) MC	404 478-7407	(not reporting)						
Kennesaw (5) MC	404 424-8274	Darvin R Purdy	....	Susan Rackley	Jo Stephenson	....	Robert L Ruble	Richard Howard
La Fayette* (7) CM	404 638-1272	E R Gasque	Grady McCalmon	Glenna Thomas	Glenna Thomas	Jim Tom Maffett	Charles Richardson	James McAlister
La Grange* (24) CM	404 884-7386	J Gardner Newman	James R Hanson	John W Bell	John W Bell	Christopher Fowler	G R Shepherd	S L White
Lake City† (3) MC	404 366-8080	Harold L Bevis Jr	....	Alva O Inman	Alva O Inman	....	....	....
Lawrenceville† (9) MC	404 963-2414	Tom Cain	Don E Martin	Robert P Baroni	Robert P Baroni	....	Louie F Schneider	Don E Martin
Lilburn (4) MC	404 921-2210	Charles E Bannister	....	Jean Cole	....	....	Ronald H Houck	L N Hendrix
Lithonia (3) MC	404 482-8136	Allison Venable	....	Irene S Stewart	....	....	Jerome Woods	....
Louisville (3) MC	912 625-3166	Julian L Veatch	Wm A Summerford	Wm A Summerford	Wm A Summerford	John Livingston III	H J Tanner	John Livingston III
Lyons† (4) MC	912 526-6578	W T Aiken	....	Jackie Alexander	Norma S Moore	Jack Durst	Wayne Dees	Jim Cason
Macon§ (117) MC	912 744-7000	George M Israel III	William D Scalf	James Hunnicutt	Robert Loveland	James E Hinson	Jim Brooks	Robert E Bass
Madison† (3) MC	404 342-1251	R L Allgood	Charles Young	Harriett C Young	Harriett C Young	R A Norton	Harry N Thompson	....
Manchester* (5) CM	404 846-3141	James C Beavers	Gerald B Garr	Katherine M Jones	Gerald B Garr	Tony Floyd	Bruce Sanborn	Ralph Pearson
Marietta* (31) CM	404 429-4202	Robert E Flournoy	John M Crane	....	....	Howard Chastain	....	....
McDonough (3) MC	404 957-3915	Billy Copeland	James C Sanders Jr	Elvira B Phillips	....	Bill Fort	Thomas A Nale	Charles M Davis
McRae (3) MC	912 868-6051	(not reporting)						
Metter (4) MC	912 685-2527	John D Miles	....	Edna K Brinson	....	James W Brantley	Gordon M Lowe II	James W Brantley
Milledgeville (12) MC	912 453-9441	James E Baugh	....	Martha T Miller	....	Hayward Jackson	Hervey E Keator	Terrel O Simmons
Millen† (4) MC	912 982-4642	Robert W Fries	Carter Crawford	Nancy C Cobb	Nancy C Cobb	Stan Coleman	Neil M Casey	Jack Burke
Monroe (9) MC	404 267-7536	(not reporting)						
Montezuma (5) MC	912 472-8144	Pat Dozier	Robert Booth	....	Joyce Middlebrooks	James M Clark	James Haralson	Robert Booth
Morrow* (4) CM	404 961-4002	Ernest W Duffey	Robert A Hill	....	Liselotte E Coon	Henry E Phillips	David J Rayburn	....
Moultrie* (16) CM	912 985-1974	William M McIntosh	Robert Roberson	Richard Crowdis	Richard Crowdis	Frank Bannister	Robert N Livingston	Ralph Turner
Nashville (5) MC	912 686-5527	Dewey Hand	....	Elaine Giddens	Dewey Hand	Earl Powell	Wesley Griner	F A Nelson
Newnan* (11) CM	404 253-2682	Joe P Norman	Richard A Bolin	Martha C Ball	Richard A Bolin	Joel H Davis	Jerry Helton	....
Norcross† (3) MC	404 448-2122	Lillian Webb	....	Betty Mauldin	....	....	Jerry Griswell	Fred Chastain
Ocilla (3) MC	912 468-5141	Jim Wilkinson	....	Martha J Towson	....	Charlie Gainer Jr	Al Kelly	....
Palmetto (2) MC	404 463-3377	Tom Gibby	....	Valerie Sutton	....	Roger D Handley	John Clark Boddie	Anthony Bramlett

Directory 1/10 continued — MUNICIPAL OFFICIALS IN ALL U.S. CITIES OVER 2,500[1]

City, 1980 population (000 omitted), form of government		Municipal phone number	Mayor	Appointed administrator	City clerk	Finance officer	Fire chief	Police chief	Public works director
GEORGIA (153) continued									
Peachtree City† (6)	MC	404 487-7657	Frederick Brown Jr	....	Frances Meaders	....	Gerald Reed	Benjamin G Parks	Brant Keller
Pelham§ (4)	MC	912 294-7900	Wendell Adams	Henry G Boynton	Marie Stapleton	Henry G Boynton	Dabney Crosby	Larry Burkhead	Carol Whigham
Perry (9)	MC	912 987-1911	Barbara C Calhoun	....	F Marion Hay	F Marion Hay	Gary Hamlin	B E Dennard	Edward Warren
Pooler t (3)	MC	912 748-7261	Travis Nichols	Bonnie Cleland	....	....	Stan Riner	Milton Sills	Glen Greeson
Port Wentworth† (4)	MC	912 964-4379	James L Brown	Harold D Bennett	Harold D Bennett	Harold D Bennett	Gerald Boykin	Robert B Sellars	Tommy Thomas
Powder Springs (3)	CM	404 943-1666	John O Rogers	....	Leila Stephens	Leila Stephens	....	Gerald T Balas	Bobby C Elliott
Quitman*† (5)	CM	912 263-4166	Wayne Carroll	James H Kennedy	Annie Ruth Bower	....	Dewey Foster	Eddie Stroud	J P Griffin
Riverdale* (7)	CM	404 997-8989	Lamar Hutcheson	Charles F Laws	Elizabeth Iler	Elizabeth Iler	William C Nash	Wayne Phillips	Ronald Gossett
Rockmart* (4)	CM	404 684-5454	Steven B Smith	Ronald S Morgan	Helen A Hurt	....	Jeff Ellis	Buddy Cagle	Jimmy Hughes
Rome* (30)	CM	404 291-8222	Martin H Mitchell	John Bennett	Branson Gayler	Gary Burkhalter	Raymond Smith	Joe Cleveland	....
Rossville† (4)	MC	404 866-1325	Charlie B Sherrill	....	Bernice S Phillips	Bobbie Alexander	Lewis Palmer	Charles Dunn	Lee Britton
Roswell§† (23)	MC	404 993-9541	W L Mabry Jr	Elwyn Gaissert	Elvin Gaissert	Evelyn Callaway	Aubrey Reeves	Jerry King	Walter Rekuc
Sandersville (6)	MC	912 552-6006	Alfred F Haynes	....	John D Everett	John D Everett	Barney Riner	Royce Lord	Bobby Knight
Savannah* (142)	CM	912 233-9321	John P Rousakis	Arthur A Mendonsa	Sophie S Gottlieb	Richard M Evans	John M Schroder	David Gellatly	James E Hagin
Smyrna (20)	MC	404 434-6600	Arthur T Bacon	Willouise C Spivey	Willouise C Spivey	Willouise C Spivey	Hubert Cochran	R Everett Little Jr	J E David
Snellville (9)	MC	404 972-0200	W Emmett Clower	....	Betty B McMichael	Betty B McMichael	....	John D Hewatt	Steve E Carter
Social Circle (3)	MC	404 464-2380	Frank Sherrill	....	Anne S Peppers	....	Neal Knight	Franklin Thornton	Jimmy Bryant
Sopertont† (3)	MC	912 529-6173	Frank Radford Jr	....	Becky Hooks	....	Jakie E Young	Robert Moxley	....
St. Marys§ (4)	MC	912 882-5516	Ward Hernandez	Macon C Sammons Jr	Deborah Watts	Margie Funderburk	Jerry Lockhart	Robert Keele	Bennie Smith
Statesboro (15)	MC	912 764-5468	J Thurman Lanier	....	Julian B Hodges	Julian B Hodges	Joe Beasley	Merle Clark	Edward O Cone
Stone Mountain† (5)	MC	404 469-0101	Randolph Medlock	....	Luthy Kitts	Kathy Kitts	....	Charles Thompson	Henry Lee Shoemake
Summerville (5)	MC	404 857-3402	Sewell Cash	....	Ms Earl B Self	Ms Earl B Self	John B Echols Sr	Arlen S Thomas	Bob Maxey
Swainsboro (8)	MC	912 237-7025	(not reporting)						
Sylvania* (3)	CM	912 564-7411	W H Lariscy	E K Overstreet	F J Lee	....	H P Brown	W H Black Jr	T W Rhodes
Sylvester (6)	MC	912 776-3346	Oren H Harden J R	....	Juanita Willis	....	Tommy Marchman	Tommy Bozeman	....
Tallapoosa (3)	CM	404 574-2345	James L Walker	....	Philip B Eidson	....	Scotty McClain	Joe Williams	Edw A McLeroy Jr
Thomaston* (10)	CM	404 647-4242	Charles E Kersey	Wilbur K Avera	Wilbur K Avera	Wilbur K Avera	Frank Boyt	Tony McCard	Frank Spraggins
Thomasville* (18)	CM	912 228-7673	M Tom Faircloth	M H Allen	Carl L Rowland	Carl L Rowland	I D Golden	John Perry	....
Thomson (7)	MC	404 595-1781	Robert E Knox Jr	Steve Szablewski	....	Audrey G Eller	Raymond McHatton	Jack Garrison	Fay Smith
Tifton* (14)	CM	912 382-6231	W Cecil Evans	Webster B Morgan	Eloise Scarborough	Evelyn W Potts	Leroy Salter	Hugh E Smith	W A Harrison
Toccoa* (9)	CM	404 886-8451	Lee Bowen	James A Calvin	Josephine Gleason	Phil Jackson	Max Thomas	Tony Bryan	Avery Merry
Union City (5)	MC	404 964-2288	Fred T Etris	....	Sonya Carter	Sonya Carter	C M West	B L Fronebarger	J W Morris
Valdosta* (38)	CM	912 242-2600	Ernest Nijem	Michael Cason	Richard Hamlen	Richard Hamlen	Charles Ogburn	....	E R Brown
Vidalia* (10)	CM	912 537-7661	W N Rhodes	Robert T Kelley	Ola Mask	Robert T Kelley	Bobby Davidson	Bobby Davidson	Herman Burke
Vienna (3)	MC	912 268-4744	Hobby Stripling Sr	Stanley Gambrell	Stanley Gambrell	....	James Woodward III	Bobby Reed	Larry Allen
Villa Rica§ (3)	MC	404 459-3957	Bill Warren	J W Conner	J W Conner	Jean Spiva	....	Raymon Cole	Don McGill
Warner Robins† (40)	MC	912 923-2631	Foy Evans	....	Thomas E McMinn	....	Ernest Wood	Ernest Wood	Milton Grace Jr
Washington (5)	CM	404 678-2322	E B Pope	Warren Sisson	Virginia Ledbetter	Warren Sisson	Allan Poss	Frank Holley	....
Waycross* (19)	CM	912 287-2900	Janice Parks	Cloyd B Heys	Michael Stephenson	J Robert Day	Donald E Kovacs	W Lynn Taylor	Gary Bryson
Waynesboro (6)	MC	404 554-5112	George L DeLoach	T J Brantley	T J Brantley	....	Charles E Dickey	H L Ivey	R C Teague
West Point† (4)	MC	404 645-2226	John C Barrow	Joel T Wood	....	....	George L Reid	John R McCurry	Paul A Crook
Winder (7)	MC	404 867-3106	John O Mobley Jr	....	Ernie Graham III	Ernie Graham III	John Etheridge	James F Terrell	Myron Skinner
Woodbine§ (1)	MC	912 576-3211	Donald Mitchell	George L Hannaford	George L Hannaford	....	Sherman Kelly Sr	Edvin Cooler	Sherman Kelly Sr
Woodstock (3)	MC	404 926-8852	Evelyn W Chambers	....	Sheila A King	....	Joe Dodson	J L Vaughn	Clarence A Gaddis
Wrightsville† (3)	MC	912 864-3303	Willis R Wombles	....	Jewell R Parker	....	Roy Crawford	Marcus Miller	....
HAWAII (2)									
Hilo (37)	MC	808 961-8211	Megumi Kon	Barney B Menor	Rudy Legaspi	Stanley Nakamae	Shozo Nagao	Guy Paul	Edward K Harada
Honolulu (763)	MC	808 523-4111	Eileen R Anderson	Andrew I T Chang	Raymond K Pua	Peter D Leong	Melvin M Nonaka	Douglas G Gibb	Michael J Chun
IDAHO (42)									
American Falls (4)	MC	208 226-2569	Ken Morgan	....	Carol Gilson	....	Fred Aguirre	Walt Miller	....
Ammon (5)	MC	208 529-4211	Russell N Swensen	....	Deon Hemingway	....	Marvin McGary	....	Hayes L Whiteley
Blackfoot (10)	MC	208 785-0491	Delwin C Daniels	....	Donavan D Wren	Donavan Wren	Parley D Wynn	Ed Jones	....
Boise City (102)	MC	208 384-4422	Richard R Eardley	....	Anette Mooney	....	John Boros	James Montgomery	William J Ancell
Bonners Ferry§ (2)	MC	208 267-3105	Harold Sims	....	Billie Krause	....	T J Hopkins	Donald D Hamilton	Michael Woodward
Buhl (4)	MC	208 543-5650	James H Barker	....	Frances L McArthur	....	Mark Grimes	Lester B Cochran	Albert L Hodge
Burley (9)	MC	208 678-2224	Chuck Shadduck	....	Bud Brinegar	Bud Brinegar	Russell Vaughn	Leman Messley	Leon Bedke
Caldwell (18)	MC	208 459-3641	A H McCluskey	....	Betty Jo Keller	Donna Talley	Tom Burns	Richard W Dormois	Ron Redmond
Chubbuck (7)	MC	208 237-2400	John O Cotant Jr	....	Ron C Conlin	Ron C Conlin	Eldon Muir	Arnold J Stone	Steven M Smart
Coeur d'Alene§ (20)	MC	208 667-9533	James R Fromm	G Eugene McAdams	Lois Lawson	Kenneth Thompson	Frank M Sexton	Frank Premo	Thomas G Wells
Eagle (3)	MC	208 939-6813	(not reporting)						
Emmett (5)	MC	208 365-5055	Rod Morgan	....	Lois B Meserole	....	Orville Wright	Mike Priest	Jack Dodson
Garden City (5)	MC	208 342-5591	(not reporting)						
Gooding† (3)	MC	208 934-5669	Gene Heller	....	Isabelle Cahoon	Susan R Wilson	Pat Bishop	Bill Bunn	Lloyd McLeod
Grangeville† (4)	MC	208 983-2851	Ralph Bos	....	June Edwards	Leo G Myers	G W Eimers	Robert E Wilbanks	W A Canaan
Hayden (3)	MC	208 772-4411	Frank J Canale	....	Marian L Jobes	....	....	....	....
Heyburn (3)	MC	208 678-8158	Harold R Hurst	....	Ila D Despain	Ila D Despain	....	Robert M Vasquez	James A McGill
Idaho Falls (40)	MC	208 529-1100	Thomas V Campbell	....	Velma Chandler	John Evans	Doug Call	Robert Pollock	Donald F Lloyd
Jerome† (7)	MC	208 324-8189	Ralph B Peters	....	Marilyn Ann Bragg	....	Lynn A Bingham	Darryl Cameron	Lanny G Sloan
Kellogg (3)	MC	208 786-9131	(not reporting)						
Lewiston* (28)	CM	208 746-3671	Gene Mueller	Craig McMicken	Janice B Vassar	Ruth Beck	Merle Frank	Rodney Frederiksen	Michael Johnson
Meridian (7)	MC	208 888-4433	Grant Kingsford	....	Jack Niemann	Jack Niemann	Kenny Bower	Doug Nichols	Bruce D Stuart
Montpelier (3)	MC	208 847-0824	Farrell G Larsen	....	Renee H Bird	Doris Taylor	Richard A Merritt	Gary E Mills	Wendell Feinauer
Moscow§ (17)	MC	208 882-5553	Deanna Hager	William A Smith	Elaine Russell	James R Wallace	Ralph McAllister	David Cameron	....
Mountain Home (8)	MC	208 587-9041	Donald Etter	....	Betty Manning	Rita Harris	Tom Hiler	Bob George	Art Smith
Nampa† (25)	MC	208 466-9221	Winston K Goering	....	Camille Beaubien	Kendall Harward	Ronald Nihart	Marshall Brisbin	Larry Bledsoe
Orofino (4)	MC	208 476-4725	Helen K Hight	David R Colvin	....	....	Alan White	James D Pishl	Dennis P Abrams
Payette† (5)	MC	208 642-3377	Dick E Butcher	....	Barbara A Millard	Barbara A Millard	Steve Phillips	Floyd Moyer	....
Pocatello* (46)	CM	208 232-4311	L Ed Brown	Charles W Moss	Peter McDougall	....	H G Call	Norman Propst	John C Postlewait
Post Falls§ (6)	MC	208 773-3511	Kent Helmer	Lee H Dean	Marilyn J Fehling	Marilyn J Fehling	Calvin Frazey	Harlan E Fritzsche	Harold Johnson
Preston† (4)	MC	208 852-1817	Richard A Bowman	....	Arlene Nash	....	Tony Christensen	Ken McCollum	Gene R Larson
Rexburg (12)	MC	208 356-9331	John C Porter	....	Rose Bagley	Richard Horner	Rex Larsen	Blair Siepert	Ferrel Davidson
Rigby (3)	MC	208 745-8111	Claude C Tremelling	....	Lloyd C Gneiting	....	Eldon Poole	Larry G Anderson	Fred Hutchens
Rupert† (5)	MC	208 436-9608	W F Bill Whittom	....	Loretta Klingenberg	Teresa Stockton	Thayne Taylor	Paul Fries	Donald Courtright
Salmon (3)	MC	208 756-3214	Neal James	Polly Prchal	....	....	Frank Barsalou	Robert Nielson	Grant Davis
Sandpoint (4)	MC	208 263-3158	Marian L Ebbett	....	Helen M Newton	Joyce E Papke	Wade Brown	William Kice	Joel Petty
Shelley (3)	MC	208 257-3390	(not reporting)						
Soda Springs§ (4)	MC	208 547-2151	David H Clegg	Roy G Rainey	LaRae Rasmussen	....	Norman Bjorkman	Blynn B Wilcox	Gary Jensen
St. Anthony† (3)	MC	208 624-3494	Neils O Thueson	....	Lila H Gold	Lila H Gold	Gail Sutton	Rex F Powell	Arnold Rinehart

Directory 1/10 continued — MUNICIPAL OFFICIALS IN ALL U.S. CITIES OVER 2,500[1]

City, 1980 population (000 omitted), form of government	Municipal phone number	Mayor	Appointed administrator	City clerk	Finance officer	Fire chief	Police chief	Public works director
IDAHO (42) continued								
St. Maries† (3) MC	208 245-2577	Ernest Pendell	....	Ona L Hedgecock	....	Archie Sorenson	Douglas McPherson	Phillip Brown
Twin Falls* (26) CM	208 733-0860	Emery Petersen	Thomas J Courtney	Bryce King	Bryce King	Tim Qualls	Tim Qualls	Gary Young
Weiser (5) MC	208 549-1965	Clark Syme	R L Hogg	R L Hogg	R L Hogg	Edwin Dohrmann	Earl Flannery	....
ILLINOIS (398)								
Abingdon (4) MC	309 462-3182	Earnest L Curtis	....	Ray A Landon	....	Ross E Simkins	Ed Suter	Steve Murfin
Addison v§ (29) MC	312 543-4100	Angelo Chrysogelos	Anthony J LaRocca	Joan Forest	Bob Simpson	Mike Puntillo	Emil Novotny	Gerald Hoppenrath
Aledo (4) MC	309 582-7241	Virgil Giffin	....	J W Hemphill	....	....	Hugh D McAtee	Dale J Devore
Algonquin v (6) MC	312 658-4322	R G Bangert Jr	....	Thomas M Andrews	Wm P Caveny	John Helfert	Kenneth W Bartels	....
Alsip v† (17) MC	312 385-6902	Arnold A Andrews	....	Robert A Gruber	John Streeter	Wayne Rice	Warner T Huston	John Redmore
Alton (34) MC	618 463-3522	Paul A Lenz	....	Edward D Voumard Jr	John M Ryan	Donald Twichell	R C Sowders	Lucian A Harris
Anna† (5) MC	618 833-8528	Robert L Ferrell	....	Pearl A Baker	Thomas Campbell	Lawrence J Boyer	Lawrence J Boyer	Ben Edwards
Antioch v (4) MC	312 395-1000	Raymond P Toft	....	Marilyn Sterbenz	Marilyn Sterbenz	Charles Maplethorpe	Charles Miller	Charles Maplethorpe
Arcola (3) MC	217 268-4966	Jack Chaney	....	Raymond F Holterman	Larry L Bushu	Jim Monahan	John W Calhoun III	Jack Logan
Arlington Heights v* (66) CM	312 253-2340	James T Ryan	Kenneth M Bonder	John Gross	John Gross	John Hayden	Rodny Kath	Allen Sanders
Auburn (4) MC	217 438-6151	Loren Boesdorfer	Judith Stillwell	Michael Lewis	Clara Lou Bergman	William Herron	Roy Basiewicz	Frank Kazenske
Aurora (81) MC	312 892-8811	Jack Hill	....	E F Pietkiewicz	Roger Cantlin	John R Mangers	Robert E Brent	James Nanninga
Barrington v* (9) CM	312 381-2141	Robert A Woodsome	Bruce Trego	Doris W Dorzweiler	Leonard J Flood	Steven Figved	Jeffrey Marquette	Lawrence E Lux
Barrington Hills v (4) MC	312 428-1200	Barbara P Hansen	Lucille S Keating	Joan F Pope	Norman Tucker	....	Robert D Lamb	....
Bartlett v (13) MC	312 837-0800	Glen A Koehler	Valerie L Salmons	Linda Harper	Earl R Beckner	....	Frederick Ciccione	Orlo Benson
Bartonville v (6) MC	309 697-2323	William Pirtle	....	Kenneth Lane	....	Mike Helms	Lester Cooley	....
Batavia§ (13) MC	312 879-1424	Jeffery D Schielke	Ronald F Podschweit	Nancy H Roth	Ronald F Podschweit	Willim J Darin	Freeman S Reed	....
Beardstown (6) MC	217 323-3110	Robert E Summey	....	Janice M Schlueter	....	Richard B Harmon	Raymond G Taylor	Ronald Jones
Belleville (42) MC	618 233-6810	Richard A Brauer	....	Arthur Baum	H Kenneth Reynolds	Leland Knapp	Barry Biehl	John Holdener
Bellwood v (20) MC	312 547-3500	Sigel C Davis	....	Donald P Lemm	Harvey R Untiedt	Bernard Rubicz	Richard W Eastham	Carl Gottfried
Belvidere (15) MC	815 544-2612	Gaius L Barr	....	Romelle Cunningham	Robert L Bahling	Donald L Bland	Robert Bowley	Narayan D Kedare
Bensenville v§ (16) MC	312 766-8200	Larry C Bieneman	Wilma T Bartunek	Joseph R Henderson	Dorothy Allamian	Schoppe E Willard	Harold Nehmzow	Wilma T Bartunek
Benton† (8) CO	618 439-0421	Leland L Brown	....	Margaret Kelley	Charles R Webster	Paul A Rogers	Mark Drake	....
Berkeley v (5) MC	312 449-8840	Karl J Ermisch	....	Violet L Murphy	Alan V Hughes	Frank Sustr	Raymond Chapman	James Rich
Berwyn† (47) MC	312 788-2660	Thomas A Hett	....	Constance Michalek	Paul Los	William Glass	John Caithamer	Clement Lovisek
Bethalto v (9) MC	618 377-8723	William Stephenson	....	Wanda Taylor	Frank L Schoppet	John L Holmes	Lewis Dreith	Joseph Ricci
Bloomingdale v§ (13) MC	312 893-7000	Samuel J Tenuto	Robert F Reeves	Marie E Tayfel	Patricia A Just	Lawrence H Koehn	Gary J Schira	Daniel C Wennerholm
Bloomington* (44) CM	309 828-7361	Richard Buchanan	William L Vail	Sandra Cordero	Allan W Horsman	Michael Sinclair	Lewis Devault	George Swier
Blue Island (22) MC	312 597-8600	John D Rita	David S Carfello	George E Heitmann	Robert Helmin	Richard Holdefer	Richard Kooyenga	Vincent Egert
Bolingbrook v* (37) CM	312 759-0400	Edward L Rosenthal	Mark M Levin	Donna B Schmidt	Robert Kolodziej	Terrence Droogan	William Charnisky	Michael Drey
Bourbonnais v§ (13) MC	815 937-3570	Ernest J Mooney II	Thomas A Clark	Carol Harms	Barry Baron	Charles Tanner	Joseph E Beard	Richard Brooks
Bradley v† (11) MC	815 933-8533	Kenneth Hayes	Glenn Mulligann	Lily Zajc	Gregory Keller	Albert Wingo	Robert O Martin	Henry Wilkins
Braidwood (3) CO	815 458-2333	Jackie L Bunting	....	Carol A Deterding	John E Zilm	Chester Grygiel	....	Coy E Willis
Breese† (4) MC	618 526-7731	Wilfrid C Hilmes	....	Robert J Venhaus	....	Robert Dumstorff	Al Gebke	Martin Johnson
Bridge View v (14) MC	312 594-2525	(not reporting)						
Broadview v (9) MC	312 681-3600	Emil J Parkes	....	Robert C Matteoni	Robert C Matteoni	James G Cote Sr	Donald M George	Robert Macaluso
Brookfield v* (19) CM	312 485-7344	Pierce F McCabe	James R Mann	Linda L Sokol	George Turdik	Edward Gorniak	John C Hymel	Dennis Valentine
Buffalo Grove v* (22) CM	312 459-2500	Verna L Clayton	William Balling	Janet Sirabian	William Brimm	Wayne Winter	Leo McCann	Gregory Boysen
Burbank (28) MC	312 599-5500	John W Fitzgerald	Robert Herrmann	Rosemary Carpenter	Harry Klein	Martin Kreil	Robert Erickson	Jim Seiler
Burnham v (4) MC	312 862-9150	Eldreth A Rundlett	....	Nancy Dobrowski	Anthony C Avalos	Terrence E Spaniak	James D Crull	James Tancos
Burr Ridge v§ (4) MC	312 325-0420	Emil J Coglianese	James P Connors	Patrice Pecora	....	....	Don Deyoung	Howard Heil
Bushnell (4) MC	309 772-2521	David Ogle	....	Margaret Davis	Fred Oathout	Earl Niestrdt	Merville Hilliard	....
Cahokia v (19) MC	618 337-7182	Michael King	....	Jesse Brown	Kenneth Diers	Hershell Riddle	Richard K Odem	....
Cairo (6) CO	618 734-4127	Allen E Moss Sr	....	Martha A Smith	....	Raymond Hughes	Earl A Shepherd Jr	....
Calumet City† (40) MC	312 891-8100	Robert C Stefaniak	....	Mildred A Breclaw	Albert A Wisowaty	Charles O Reilly	James J Shutoski	Mickey Surdyk
Calumet Park v (9) MC	312 385-6862	Ronald P Romanowski	....	Roberta C Lundquist	Jim Riedel	Thomas Battistella	Thomas Zielinski	Robert Talski
Canton† (15) MC	309 647-0020	Donald E Edwards	David Dorgan	Nancy S Whites	Patricia Wright	Robert Derenzy	Robert W Molleck	Clifford L Sagaser
Carbondale* (27) CM	618 549-5302	Helen Westberg	William C Dixon	Janet Vaught	Paul Sorgen	Charles McCaughan	Edward J Hogan	Edward Reeder
Carlinville (5) MC	217 854-4076	Anna M Schoenherr	....	Joann Wiggins	....	William Pranger Sr	Lynn Angelo	....
Carlyle† (3) MC	618 594-2611	J Leo Davis	....	Jean Parson	B Leroy Seiffert	....	Earl Robert	....
Carmi (6) MC	618 382-8118	J B Brown	....	Frances Graves	....	Ray Yates	John Ziegler	....
Carol Stream v* (15) CM	312 665-7050	Janice Gerzevske	Gregory Bielawski	Clela A Montgomery	Michael J O'Keefe	Ted Tokarski	Wilbur Reichert	John A Turner
Carpentersville v* (23) CM	312 426-3439	Herbert A Radtke	Richard L Escalante	Lillian Burian	Lillian Burian	Richard Paul	John Skillman	Stephen Starek
Carrollton (3) MC	217 942-5517	Michael C Sullivan	....	Lois Gillingham	....	Donald Reynolds	Michael C Sullivan	Gene Wagener
Carterville† (3) MC	618 985-2252	Frank Samuel	....	Ron Wade	William Johnson	William Edwards	Norman Lewis	....
Cary v (7) MC	312 639-0003	Gus Alexakos	Thomas W Scanlan	Cecelia R Kotlaba	Roger Stoffer	Lester Macko	William H Moore	Gary Stauffer
Casey† (3) MC	217 932-2700	Bill Savage	....	Merle Fisher	....	Ben Fisher Jr	George Milbourn	....
Caseyville v† (4) MC	618 344-1233	George E Chance	....	Virgil E Kassing	Ada Knussmann	Gerard Scott	David Buckner	Gerard Scott
Centralia* (15) CM	618 532-5442	Jack Sligar	Warren B Browning	....	Earline Creed	Larry Smith	Kermit Justice	Richard Jones
Centreville† (10) MC	618 332-1021	Riley L Owens III	Amos E Green II	Vincent J Kiefer	Odie C Lacy	....	Theodore Shamalian	Willie Jackson
Champaign* (58) CM	217 351-4403	Robert W Dodd	John L Bloomberg	John T Lyons	John T Lyons	Douglas Forsman	Donald G Hanna	Richard J Larson
Channahon v (4) MC	815 467-5311	Wayne W Chesson	Almeda Moore	Eileen Clark	Michael Rittof	Kurt Boggs	Nicholas Priddy	Harold Randolph
Charleston§ (19) CO	217 345-7819	Clarence E Pfeiffer	Michael A Steele	Patsy J Loew	....	Les R Hickenbottom	Maurice Johnson	E O Reed
Chatham v† (6) MC	217 483-2451	John F Whitney	Gloria Richie	Donna Hedinger	William Smith	Gerry Hughes	Mark Gleason	Harold Bell
Chester (8) MC	618 826-2326	Stanley A Macieiski	....	Nancy J Eggemeyer	....	William L Brown	Jack L Houghlan	....
Chicago (3005) MC	312 744-4000	Harold Washington	William F Ware	Walter S Kozubowski	Walter K Knorr	Louis Galante	Fred Rice Jr	Jerome Butler
Chicago Heights (37) MC	312 756-5300	Charles Panici	Enrico J Doggett	John M Costabile	Dominic J Sesto	Arthur George	Douglas Barger	Ernest Molyneaux
Chicago Ridge v (13) MC	312 425-7700	Eugene L Siegel	....	Mary E Macarol	Mary E Macarol	Robt Miller	Jas O'Hara	Peter Chiappetti
Chillicothe (6) MC	309 274-2020	Richard L Fislar	....	Ms Ilion W Crabel	Richard L Fislar	Gail Myers	Steven R Maurer	Sid Crabel
Christopher (3) MC	618 724-2424	John Regis	....	Candice Cross	Max Heinzman	Ramon Bione	Homer Howell	....
Cicero t† (61) MC	312 656-3600	Henry J Klosak	....	John F Kimbark	Leroy Lawniczak	Mel Gregory Sr	Otto Svehla	Kenneth Rokowski
Clarendon Hills v§ (7) MC	312 323-3500	Alan I Hurd	F Edward Glatfelter	Mary Arnold	Edward F Hosek	....	Arthur Blackwell	Joseph Sulda
Clinton (8) CO	217 935-9438	Stanley J Stites	....	Ms R D Wickenhauser	Thomas Edmunds	Haskell Bohn	Michael Norrington	James Miller
Coal City v (3) MC	815 634-8608	Rick W Roseland	....	Carol L Haughtigan	Gerald Provance	Donald Ulivi	Dennis Neary	Jerry Campbell
Coal Valley v (4) MC	309 799-3604	Patrick A Huys	....	Louella C Smith	Henry DeVooght	Larry Fuhr	Lindy C Peterson	Keith E Glaus
Collinsville (20) CO	618 344-5252	Gene H Brombolich	....	Louis Jackstadt	William T Jenkins	Robert Jackson	Nick Mamino	....
Columbia (4) MC	618 281-7144	George W Eckert	....	Clifford H Schrader	Earl Stahlheber	Alan Holden	Walter Reibeling	....
Country Club Hills (15) MC	312 798-2616	David R Larson	Ottmar H Becker	Pearl L Shaffner	Henry A Pawlik	John Scanlan	Robert L Roberts	Albert Schnepf
Countryside† (7) MC	312 354-7270	Carl W LeGant	....	Walter H Klimcke	Donald M Orndorff	Richard Vachata	Kenneth G Wolf	Joseph McCormack
Crest Hill (9) MC	815 741-5100	Donald L Randich	....	Florine Kovalcik	Anthony Picciolo	....	Dennis Jaskoviak	James Murphy
Crestwood v (11) MC	312 371-4800	Chester Stranczek	Frank D Gassmere	Nancy C Venegas	....	A Kolasinski	Norman Griffin	....
Crete v (5) MC	312 672-5431	Ronald Christopher	....	Mariann Gemper	Charles Wisniewski	Earl Hothan	C Michael Seibert	Ronald Bremer
Creve Coeur v† (7) MC	309 699-6714	Merlin Kiesewetter	....	Suzanne Thatcher	Sue Starnes	Jack Harvey	Gerald Daughters	Dick Malson
Crystal Lake* (19) CM	815 459-2020	Carl Wehde	Joseph J Misurelli	Jerry D Heiman	Irvin Stroner	Harold Krecker	Sam Johns	Clyde Wakefield

Directory 1/10 continued — MUNICIPAL OFFICIALS IN ALL U.S. CITIES OVER 2,500[1]

City, 1980 population (000 omitted), form of government	Municipal phone number	Mayor	Appointed administrator	City clerk	Finance officer	Fire chief	Police chief	Public works director
ILLINOIS (398) continued								
Danville† (39). . . . . . . CO	217 431-2200	David S Palmer	....	Marjory Kair	Joe M Stroud	Richard Eaglen	Robert Dietzen	Ernie A Cox
Darien§ (15) . . . . MC	312 852-5000	Erwin A Sirovy	John D Marquart	Gert S Coit	Louis McGinley	....	David E Kohnke	Robert L Rodgers
De Kalb* (33). . . . . . . CM	815 756-4881	Greg Sparrow	Mark C Stevens	Peggy Hoyt	Calvin Henry	Albert Riippi	Joseph Maciejewski	Ronald Naylor
Decatur* (94). . . . . . . CM	217 424-2700	Gary Anderson	Leslie T Allen	Phyllis Sands	Ronald Lappi Jr	Donald Minton	Patrick Vaughan	William B Sands
Deerfield v* (17) . . . . . CM	312 945-5000	Bernard Forrest	Robert D Franz	Naomi Clampitt	George Valentine	Jack Gagne	Richard C Brandt	Edmund Klasinski
Des Plaines (54) . . . . . MC	312 391-5300	John E Seitz	Mary M Taylor	Donna McAllister	Duane L Blietz	Charles Gedroic	Leroy Alfano	Jerry Matula
Dixmoor v (4). . . . . . . MC	312 385-0319	Kenneth Fisher	....	Frieda Wakefield	Michael Cech	Kenneth Steinhagen	Leonard Brzinski	Frances Echols
Dixon (16). . . . . MC	815 288-1485	James E Dixon	....	Barbara J Graff	Rita Crundwell	Richard Clayton	Robert Short	Edward Slain
Dolton v (25) . . . . . . MC	312 849-4000	(not reporting)						
Downers Grove v* (39) CM	312 964-0300	Betty M Cheever	Stephen B Veitch	Barbara C Waldner	Susan M Behrens	John Wander	....	Gary Walk
Du Quoin (7) . . . . MC	618 542-3841	Robert M Armstrong	....	Cecil W Daily	Wayne Bigham	Richard Fronek	Kenneth DeMent	....
Dupo v (3) . . . . MC	618 286-3280	Virgil D Casey	....	Clint Proffer	Carl Chism	Dan Biggs	Walter J Ford	Chas Frederick
Dwight v§ (4). . . . . . . MC	815 584-3077	James P Moyemont	Richard A Carlucci	Jean H Louis	Robert F Klingler	G Wm Stevens	Richard D Irvin	J G Dransfeldt
East Alton v (7). . . . . . MC	618 259-7714	Frank Keasler	....	Jeanne Holt	M Wesley Tucker	William Shewmaker	George M Urban	Harry L Kuehnel
East Chicago Heights v (5). . . . . MC	312 758-3131	(not reporting)						
East Dundee v (3) . . . . MC	312 426-2822	David E Bartelt	....	Jill A Yucuis	....	....	David B Smith	Ron Bockenhauer
East Moline (21) . . . . . MC	309 755-3486	(not reporting)						
East Peoria (22) . . . . . CO	309 694-6251	James L Ranney	....	Robert L Arnold	Robert L Arnold	Terance Brewer	Walter Hellstrom	James D Thompson
East St. Louis (55). . . . MC	618 271-1080	Carl E Officer	Lamar D Gentry	Frank C Smith	Charles Powell	Bruce Hill	Charles Wren	Steve Collins
Edwardsville (12). . . . . MC	618 656-8010	Kenneth L Evers	....	Nina J Baird	Lawrence Hengehold	Stephen Deist	Bennett W Dickmann	Jack R Tolliver
Effingham (11) . . . . . . CO	217 347-5555	Charles W Stevens	....	Jack J Parks	....	Maurice Braun	Ronald F Rentfrow	....
El Paso§ (3). . . . . MC	309 527-4005	William Holt	Samuel E Tapson Jr	David W Fever	Sharon Duncan	Harold Benidict	Harold Shepherd	Wayne Miller
Eldorado (5). . . . . CO	618 273-6566	Carl D Johnson	....	Pat Mahoney	Helen Harper	Quentin Wilson	Glen Barrall	....
Elgin* (64) . . . . CM	312 695-6500	R L Verbic	....	Marie Yearman	James Bolerjack Jr	....	Robert L Baird	Melford Dahl
Elk Grove Village v* (29) . . . . CM	312 439-3900	Charles J Zettek	Charles A Willis	Patricia S Smith	George C Coney	Charles B Henrici	Fred J Engelbrecht	Thomas J Cech
Elmhurst* (44) . . . . . . CM	312 530-3000	Abner S Ganet	Thomas P Borchert	Elaine Libovicz	Robert B Cole	Richard R Swanson	Bernt A Monsen	William R Gray
Elmwood Park v* (24) CM	312 452-7300	Elmer W Conti	Richard B Nuzzo	Mary Fickenscher	Warren Kowalski	George Schlanger	Dewey Paoletti	John Litrenta
Eureka (4) . . . . MC	309 467-2113	Guiseppe Serangeli	Benny R Arbuckle	Robert Watson	....	Mike Lockhart	Gerald E Reinmann	....
Evanston* (74) . . . . . . CM	312 328-2100	James C Lytle	Joel M Asprooth	Sandra W Gross	Robert A Shonk	Sanders Hicks	William H Logan	Stephen T Pudloski
Evergreen Park v§ (22) MC	312 422-1551	Anthony Vacco	Richard DeBoer	Hamilton B Maher	James Haberkorn	John Hojek	Norbert F Smith	Edward Schuth
Fairbury (4) . . . . MC	815 692-2743	James E Steidinger	....	Patricia J Tetley	....	Keith Klitzing	William F Spray	Leroy E McPherson
Fairfield (6) . . . . MC	618 842-3871	Russell L Wilson	....	Annis Lea Doty	Billie R Anderson	Larry E McCoy	Murrel E Day	....
Fairview Heights (12) . . MC	618 397-9111	George A Lanxon	....	Harvey S Noubarian	James Jacob	Bernard Rowan	Roger A Richards	Robert Hotz
Farmington† (3) . . . . . MC	309 245-2011	R James Hurst	....	Roger Woodcock	Roger Woodcock	Donald Saunders	Fred L Smith	....
Flora (5) . . . . CO	618 662-8313	Chas E Overstreet	....	Laura E Hall	Douglas J Briscoe	Leo A Hettiger	Edwin L Guyott	....
Flossmoor v* (8). . . . . CM	312 798-2300	Bert H Reed Jr	Marilynne B Davis	Marjorie Conway	....	Greg Berk	John Barton	James Carney
Forest Park v (15) . . . . CO	312 366-2323	Fred E Marunde	....	William R McKenzie	Lorraine Popelka	Robert Hodges	Arthur Grams	....
Fox Lake v (7) . . . . . . MC	312 587-2151	Richard Hamm	....	Matthew Tierney	Marilyn J Skupien	Stuart Hoehne	Robert Trinski Sr	Dean Donner
Fox River Grove v§ (3) MC	312 639-3171	Daniel J Shea	....	Verda C Vrana	Deborah Buck	Donald Kohlhase	Robert H Polston	Richard Rohlfs
Frankfort v† (4). . . . . MC	815 469-2177	Glenn R Warning	Burton H Breidert	Johanna M Mark	....	Milton C Batson	Darrell L Sanders	Donald E Stephen
Franklin Park v (18) . . MC	312 671-4800	Jack B Williams	Arthur Whalen	John A Gregg Sr	Wilma Aletich	Kenneth Ryndek	James Bickley	John U Smyth
Freeburg v (3) . . . . . . MC	618 539-5545	Lester Fritz	....	Dora Becker	John Reuter	Robert Koerber	George Price	Quinten Laabs
Freeport (26) . . . . MC	815 235-8203	Mark B McLeroy	....	Lucille G Lattig	Frank Henry	Robert Pontius	Walter Holcomb	....
Fulton (4) . . . . MC	815 589-2616	Peter Maliszewski	....	Lavonne Huizenga	....	Del Huizenga	....	....
Galena (4). . . . . MC	815 777-1050	Frank Einsweiler	....	Gayle Burns	....	Donald Beadle	Kenneth Molitor	....
Galesburg* (35) . . . . . CM	309 343-4181	Jerry L Miller	Lawrence A Asaro	Anita Carlton	Don Viane	Dale May	James H Frakes	Lyman M Jensen
Galva (3). . . . . MC	309 932-2555	David E McClintic	....	Keith Carter	....	Keith Carter	George W Cannel	....
Geneseo (6). . . . . MC	309 944-6419	Eugene W Eiklor	Richard A Schnuer	....	....	....	Louis Bervid	Lawrence Lievens
Geneva§ (10) . . . . MC	312 232-7494	Edgar G Crane	Wayne L Heninger	Roberta L Harper	Ronald A Steele	Frank Johnson	Wm Kidwell	Thomas W Talsma
Genoa† (3) . . . . MC	815 784-2327	Clair Deming	....	Elizabeth Mahmoud	Edwin Drake	Elmer Hughes	Ray E Garrett	David Carroll
Georgetown (4). . . . . . MC	217 662-2525	Joseph S Dalida	....	Judy Sawyer	....	Claude Robertson	Jack Hart	Jesse Pritchett
Gibson City (3) . . . . . . MC	217 784-5872	Loel Jordan	....	Margaret J Anderson	....	....	Robert Brandkamp	Donald Ehlenfeld
Gillespie (4). . . . . MC	217 839-2919	Howard Carney	....	Shirley Zanter	....	Donald Westwood	Kenneth Robertson	....
Glen Carbon v (5) . . . . MC	618 288-5766	Ronald J Foster	....	Glenda J Kovarik	Evelyn Wiechman	Lynn Perry	Billy R Moore	Richard E Carter
Glen Ellyn v§ (24) . . . . MC	312 469-5000	Michael R Formento	Gary L Webster	Wilma Linde	Robert J Taylor	Stuart S Stone	James E Mullany	Frank E Reno
Glencoe v* (9) . . . . . . CM	312 835-4111	Florence H Boone	David J Cole	Donald C Duranso	Donald C Duranso	Robert B Bonneville	Robert B Bonneville	Carl F Peter
Glendale Heights v§† (23) . . . . MC	312 260-6000	Jeri Sullivan	Gerald Seals	Marge Peterson	Gerald Irwin	Ronald Dukes	Daniel McCollum	Subhash Raval
Glenview v* (31) . . . . . CM	312 724-1700	Thomas E Smith	Paul T McCarthy	Katherine Appert	Dennis Lauer	....	David J Kelly	....
Glenwood v (11) . . . . . MC	312 758-5150	Fred W Delaney	....	Carol Klein	John W Kerr	William Kennedy	Andrew Castner	Ted Wix
Granite City (37) . . . . . MC	618 452-6200	Paul Schuler	....	Robert Stevens	Robert W Stevens	Donald Parente	Ronald Veizer	Mac Warfield
Grayslake v (5) . . . . . . MC	312 223-8515	Edwin M Schroeder	....	Adell Laurin	....	Rodney Rockenbach	Edward Wunderle	John Schumacher
Green Rock (3) . . . . . . MC	309 792-0571	Terry Van Klavern	....	Martha Sawyer	....	....	C Robert Phillips	C Leroy Kelley
Greenville* (5) . . . . . . CM	618 664-1644	Charles Ireland	Harold Palmer	Harriet Taylor	Harriet Taylor	Gerald Foss	John King	Simon Brown
Gurnee v§ (7). . . . . . . MC	312 623-7650	Richard A Welton	Robert R Trigg	Norman C Balliet	Robert R Trigg	Sam Dada	Lawrence E Dluhos	Richard J Klein
Hamilton (4) . . . . MC	217 847-2936	Elmer L Metz	....	Diann Freeman	Kerry Asbridge	William Johnson	Robert McFarland	William Dobbins
Hanover Park v* (29) . . CM	312 837-3800	Louis F Barone	Dennis E Dawson	Sonya A Crawshaw	Robert H Whyte	William Gresher	Robert G Sauer	William A Rinne
Harrisburg (9) . . . . . . MC	618 253-7451	Ron Morse	....	Dorice Turner	John D Cummins	Looney Martin	Kennth Childers	Charles D Barrett
Harvard (5) . . . . MC	815 943-6468	Frank Godo	....	P Michael Bannwolf	William E Johnston	Aaron McConnell	Percy L Gibson	Harold Hooper
Harvey (36) . . . . CO	312 339-4200	David N Johnson	....	Walter J Johnson	E Berry-Beck	James E Eaves	Bruce P Terry	Frank A Piekarski
Harwood Heights v (8) MC	312 867-7200	Ray Willas	....	Walter F Silarski	Bruno Michelotti	Lucien Bond	Jack Pechous	Frank Bathauer
Havana (3) . . . . MC	309 543-3411	W Colleen Curless	....	Mary M Howerter	Cecil Gilson	Mike Noe	Ralph Howerter	....
Hazel Crest v* (14) . . . CM	312 335-9600	Martin J Kauchak	James D Prosser	Joan R Lippe	Bob M Marshall	Charles Prentiss	Harold V Moore	Chris W Wuellner
Henry (3) . . . . MC	309 364-3056	Arnold Parker	....	Irene Carlson	David Ward	Steve Hunt	Glen A Killen	Danny L Ziegler
Herrin† (10). . . . . MC	618 942-3175	Donald R Swinford	....	Ida Berra	Sharon A Ricketts	Laverne Kerley	Thomas Horn	James C Kirk
Hickory Hills (14) . . . . MC	312 598-4800	Raymond L Kay	....	Ms G R Magnuson	Voyle Mabbott	....	Peter F Hurst	Vydas Juskelis
Highland* (7). . . . . . . CM	618 654-9891	Homer Poss	Walter M Johnson	Lila Manville	Sharon Bellm	Norman Meyer	Carl Wolf	Michael DeSelm
Highland Park* (31) . . . CM	312 432-0800	Robert M Buhai	Larry L Rice	Carmen Rollery	Jim Kelly	Bart Moran	M Bonamarte Jr	George Bonnett
Highwood (5) . . . . MC	312 432-1924	Fidel Ghini	....	William J Biaggi	William J Lolli	David Biondi	Forest Grandi	Leo Bernardi
Hillsboro (4) . . . . MC	217 532-5566	James R Hart	....	C W Boone	Wm Baran	Richard Hewitt	John Downs	Richard L James
Hillside v (8) . . . . MC	312 449-6450	Joseph T Tamburino	Jeff L Thompson	Dorothy C Gehrke	....	James J Metzger	Charles R Janata	Carl McKinniss
Hinsdale v* (17) . . . . . CM	312 789-7000	William L Moore	Chas O Dobbins Jr	Ellen B Mooney	Richard H Skiba Jr	Kenneth L Felbinger	Kenneth L Felbinger	Bohdan J Proczko
Hoffman Estates v§ (38) MC	312 882-9100	Virginia M Hayter	John Fulton Dixon	Anne Von Sothen	Mike Ducharme	....	James R Taylor	Paul K Wattles
Hometown (5) . . . . . . MC	312 424-7500	Philip S Lucerto	....	Joan Dobrowits	Raymond J Czajka	Patrick Dunne	Nickolas Kolabusak	John Hennelly
Homewood v* (20) . . . CM	312 798-3000	R P Gooley	Larry A Lowery	Ms B A Van Antwerp	Richard A Mays	Joseph Klauk	William Nolan Jr	Don Habermehl
Hoopeston (6) . . . . . . MC	217 283-5833	Donald L Dukes	Kenneth R Collins	Donald Dean	....	James Hopkins	Orval Kaag	....
Indian Head Park v (3) MC	312 246-3080	Al Krisciunas	....	Mary G Radice	Gerald W Fox	....	Thomas J Rowan	James M Wilkinson
Inverness v (4) . . . . . . MC	312 358-7740	(not reporting)						

Directory 1/10 continued — MUNICIPAL OFFICIALS IN ALL U.S. CITIES OVER 2,500[1]

City, 1980 population (000 omitted), form of government	Municipal phone number	Mayor	Appointed administrator	City clerk	Finance officer	Fire chief	Police chief	Public works director
ILLINOIS (398) continued								
Itasca v† (8) MC	312 773-0835	Wesley G Usher	....	Elizabeth M Upstrom	Donald McLean	Alvin Lueth	Stanley Rossol	Alan Anderson
Jacksonville (20) MC	217 243-3391	Helen Foreman	....	Pauline W Newport	Joe Farran	Tom Spradlin	Wilbur Stafford	Jimmie Fernandes
Jerseyville v (8) MC	618 498-3312	Herman H Blackorby	....	Yvonne Hartmann	Carl Strube	Charles Updike	Thos Woelfel	....
Johnston City† (4) MC	618 983-6651	Bill Stevens	....	Eugenia Hatfield	....	Dennis Beaumont	Bennie Vick	....
Joliet* (78) CM	815 740-2495	John Bourg	Paul A Flynn	Nancy Vallera	Robert Fraser	George E Plese	Fred W Breen	John M Mezera
Justice v (11) MC	312 458-2520	David D Mack	....	Dolores R White	....	Ronald Szarzynski	Eugene Wroblewski	....
Kankakee (30) MC	815 933-0495	Thomas J Ryan Jr	....	Gene Glenzinski	Robert Kell	Leroy Sarowatz	Dean R Bauer	Richard A Tyson
Kenilworth v* (3) CM	312 251-1666	James M Roche	Kenneth A Terlip	John F Stewart	Roger R Nelson	Gilbert Schmidt	Vernon W Roddy	Ignazio Fiorentino
Kewanee (15) MC	309 852-2611	Alfred Hill	....	John R Anderson	Charles Warriner	Jerry Warner	David Anderson	Alfred Hill
Knoxville (3) MC	309 289-2814	Dale L Logsdon	....	Charles E Peck	....	....	R W Greene	....
La Grange Park v* (13) CM	312 354-0225	Robert F Huson	Timothy W Schuenke	Margaret M Foster	Joseph J Faber	Gilbert Welch	Richard J Savage	Max O'Bradovich
La Grange v* (16) CM	312 579-2300	John E Hausmann	Stephen Berley	Robert C Newman	Donald J Yucuis	Gerald W Granat	Roy J Lane	James Schnute
La Salle (10) MC	815 223-0077	Aloysius A Gunia	....	Frances Baratta	Frank Videgar	William Bacidore	Al Swierkosz	Quinto Pattelli
Lake Bluff v* (4) CM	312 234-0774	Phyllis H Albrecht	Kenneth E Long	Ethel O Tincher	Dale J Rudy	Robert B Graham	Fredrick C Day	Richard L Pelz
Lake Forest* (15) CM	312 234-2600	F C Farwell III	John F Fischbach	John J Fisher	Robert D Shaffer	Edward F Burns	Thomas L Trezise	....
Lake in the Hills v (6) CM	312 658-4213	Barbara Key	....	Pam Hopp	Trudy Bourassa	John Helfert	Irving Floress	Fred Kruse
Lake Zurich v§ (8) MC	312 438-5141	Henry J Paulus	Delmar Hosler	Wanda E Grever	Stan Helgenson	Robert Block	James Glogovsky	....
Lansing v† (29) MC	312 474-0176	Louis L LaMourie	....	Dorothy Hopkins	Thomas Schrode	Ralph Schauer Jr	Dean R Stanley	Lyndell Miller
Lawrenceville† (6) MC	618 943-2116	Gerald C Harper	....	Charles A Fiscus	Leslie Wright	Charles Potts	Donald S Foster	Chris Kelly
Lebanon (3) MC	618 537-4976	N James Lombardo	....	Edna M Frierdick	Donald Cornell	Jerry Bohnenstiel	Clifford Dawson	Gerald Cornell
Lemont v (6) MC	312 257-6421	Herbert A Zielke	George A Bracken	Pearl A Mentch	Jean Nona	Robert Kowalski	Donald Wiegand	Raymond Marciniak
Leroy (3) MC	309 962-3031	Jack W Moss	....	Juanita Dagley		Jack W Moss	James E Sandage	....
Lewistown† (3) MC	309 547-2113	Don R Braden	....	Melodee W Rudolph	L W Gillam	Kenneth Hyzer	Keith Hilton	....
Libertyville v*† (17) CM	312 362-2430	Paul M Neal	Allen H Schertz	Valerie A Dunn	Allen H Schertz	Jack Reitman Sr	Roger H Stricker	Victor Favia
Lincoln (16) MC	217 735-2815	Bill G Wilson	....	Robert Madigan	Robert Madigan	Wallace Sparks	Robert Hahn	Don Osborne
Lincolnshire v§ (4) MC	312 945-8500	Evelyn Cooper	David M Limardi	David M Limardi	Richard Hintz	Ted Tarr	Glenn H Larson	Steven R Weinstock
Lincolnwood v (12) MC	312 673-1540	John C Porcelli	Bernard H Arends	Robert L Harling	....	James Holiaw	D Martin	A F Tanovich
Lindenhurst v (6) MC	312 356-8252	Robert R Ratch	Paul L Ashley	Norma Cullis	Arthur Neubauer	....	Gary L Kupsak	Carl Norlin
Lisle v§ (14) MC	312 968-1200	George A Varney	Carl N Doerr	Marjorie M Connelly	Harold O'Keefe	Paul Boecker	Harold Fitzsimmons	....
Litchfield (7) MC	217 324-2022	Ralph R Redfern	....	Jesse P Yellowley	....	James Leitschuh	William A Dolahite	....
Lockport (9) MC	815 838-0549	Joseph Bolattino	Gordon M McCluskey	Edward J Rossetto	Phil Williams	James Miller	Robert P Miller	Gordon M McCluskey
Lombard v* (37) CM	312 620-5700	Mardyth E Pollard	....	Lorraine G Gerhardt	Eileen L Moeller	John E Corbly	William D Hogan	Richard V Doherty
Long Grove v§ (2) MC	312 634-9440	George G Dickson	Dwayne M Doughty	Lenore Simmons	....	....	....	....
Loves Park (13) MC	815 633-8121	Joseph F Sinkiawic	....	Lorraine Chaussee	Barbara Weyrauch	Phillip Foley	Darryl F Lindberg	Willis Niffenegger
Lynwood (4) MC	312 758-6101	Barclay W Fleming	....	Faye Berkheiser	Alan Montella	Rich Eriks	Greg Szymanski	Gene Hefner
Lyons v (10) MC	312 447-8886	William G Smith	....	William Polich	Joseph Lotarski	James Spolar	James Svoboda	Kenneth Couch
Machesney Park v (19) MC	815 877-5432	Charles E Beutell	....	Gladys Nelson	Benford Hamlin	....	....	Jeffrey Heid
Macomb (20) MC	309 833-2575	Robert Anstine	....	Lucille Gibson	Jim Schisler	Edward Holzwarth	Richard K Clark	Paul Johnston
Madison (6) MC	618 876-6268	Mike Sasyk	....	John N Bellcoff	Judy Donaldson	Mike Macek	Donald Bridick	....
Marengo (4) MC	815 568-7112	David J Klasing	....	Lucile Polnow	Fred M Spear	Ross Kitchen	William T Mullen	Donald Piskie
Marion (14) CO	618 997-6281	Robert L Butler	....	Maureen Johnston	Everett E Jeter	Charles Heyde	L B Hunter	Henry Burress
Marissa v (3) MC	618 295-2351	Arthur S Macke	....	Julietta M Bottiaux	Diane Peebles	Stanley Lewis	Alvin J Sievers	Danny Smith
Markham† (15) MC	312 331-4905	William A Sparger	....	Mary B Kraus	George Petersen	Walter McNeil	Robert D Wilson	William Relford
Marquette Heights (3) MC	309 382-3455	Gary Little	....	Vicki Crum	Lee A Ohlinger	Rick Crum	James Steele	....
Marseilles (5) CM	815 795-2133	J C Knudson	....	Lucille Sergenti	Joyce O Pomatto	Herbert Johnson	James Hollenbeck	....
Marshall (4) MC	217 826-2112	Francis Ted Trefz	Steve Calhoun	True Garwood	Larry Strohm	....	Murray Melton Sr	George Q Smith
Mascoutah* (5) CM	618 566-2965	Leroy Perrotet	D L Sitton	Lavern Bishcoff	Ann Winker	Kenneth Hamman	W E Beatty	....
Mason City (3) MC	217 482-3669	William H Zimmerman	....	M Joanne Burris	Dorrence Brucker	....	Thomas A Brewster	Joe T Burris
Matteson v (10) MC	312 748-1559	Mark W Stricker	Daniel E Dubruiel	Lois J Butler	....	Robert H Wilcox	Donald W Story	Frank Denman
Mattoon (20) CO	217 235-5654	Roger W Dettro	....	Janice M Strater	....	Roy G Sparks	Raymond E Senteney	....
Maywood v* (28) CM	312 344-1200	Joe Freelon	Harlan D Mayberry	William Travis	Richard Choinoski	Steven Persico	Andrew Rodez	Henderson Yarbrough
McHenry (11) MC	815 385-0947	Joseph B Stanek	....	Barbara E Gilpin	Jon J Meyer	Glenn Peterson	George R Pasenelli	Paul J Halvensleben
Melrose Park v† (21) MC	312 343-4000	C August Taddeo	....	John Otmaskin	Robert Guerine	Alfred Mueller	Ronald Belle	Ralph Tolomei
Mendota† (7) MC	815 539-7459	James A Strouss	....	Michael L Wasmer	Michael L Wasmer	James Johnson	Irvin McDougall	Joe Hochstatter
Metropolis (7) MC	618 524-4016	Richard Corzine	....	Bess LaVeau	....	Virgil Mescher	Robert Griffey	Virgil Elam
Midlothian v† (14) MC	312 389-0200	Harry Raday	....	Robert R Hansen	....	John Schaeffner	William Fischer	Edw Williquette
Milan v§ (6) MC	309 787-8500	James Hansen	Steven W Seiver	Nancy L Gosney	....	Daniel Mack	Wesley Greenwood	....
Millstadt v (3) MC	618 476-1514	Gary Shondy	....	Jane Kane		Robert Griebel	Gerald Gomric	
Mokena v† (5) MC	312 479-9311	Michael D Everett	Owen C Maue	Rita A Sorensen	Donald Baumhover	Delbert Yunker	Kenneth Gamache	Larry Haack
Moline§ (46) MC	309 796-0463	Robert W Anderson	Steven Carter	Jane E Lundeen	James R Nowicki	James L Woydziak	Thomas L Smaha	John P Hoffstatter
Momence (3) MC	815 472-2001	(not reporting)						
Monmouth (11) MC	309 734-2141	Pat L McManus	....	Elmo Ferrenburg	Elmo Ferrenburg	James Ray	George M Ferris	Stan Lemke
Montgomery v (3) MC	312 896-8080	Stu Johnson	....	Nan Cobb	Eileen Kell	Jack Steinhoff	Dennis Schmidt	William Curry
Monticello† (5) MC	217 762-2583	Phillip Blankenburg	....	Ronald G Ivall	Linda Ayers	Willard D Sumner	Ronald D Swan	Ronald G Ivall
Morris (9) MC	815 942-5438	James R Washburn	....	Marjorie Warren	Robert White	Robert Coleman	Alan Love	Wilfred Dix Jr
Morrison (5) MC	815 772-7657	W W Bull	Samuel E Tapson Jr	Nancy Poling	Jerry O Bogle	Jon Groharing	Robert Snodgrass	....
Morton v (14) MC	309 266-5361	R D Hertenstein	W W Moler	Harriett J Anderson	William Collingwood	Richard Cambell	Oval D Stephens	Robert Wraight
Morton Grove v§ (24) MC	312 965-4100	Richard Flickinger	Larry N Arft	Jerry Schuhrke	Thomas Downes	Bernard Brady	Larry Schey	James Dahm
Mount Carmel (9) MC	618 262-4822	George W Woodcock	Ronald E Anderson	Ronald E Anderson	Rudy Witsman	Jay Spencer	Dan DeWitt	Curtis C Williams
Mount Morris v† (3) MC	815 734-6425	Donald Mulcay	....	Lois A Hachmeister	Jon Murray	Carl Francis	John G Thompson	....
Mount Prospect v* (53) CM	312 392-6000	Carolyn H Krause	Terrance L Burghard	Carol A Fields	David C Jepson	Lawrence A Pairitz	Ronald W Pavlock	Herbert L Weeks
Mount Vernon* (17) CM	618 242-5000	William Thackrey	Paul A Berg	Paul Hayes	John F Lunini	Don Hahn	Ronald Massey	Dennis Shirley
Mount Zion v§ (5) MC	217 864-5424	James D Price	Scot Wrighton	Sherry French	Jana L Bridgman	....	Paul D Wood	W Jack Grider
Mundelein v§† (17) MC	312 566-7070	Colin L McRae	Kenneth Marabella	Colleen Kasting	Mary K Hatton	Edward Kalasa	Arthur T Glitz	....
Murphysboro (10) MC	618 684-4961	Sydney H Appleton	....	Phyllis M Gottlieb	Phyllis M Gottlieb	Chester Steele	Larry Tincher	James Shields
Naperville* (42) CM	312 420-6111	Margaret P Price	George D Smith	Suzanne Holt	John Lawlor	Donald Faulhaber	James A Teal Jr	Ned P Becker
Nashville (3) MC	618 327-3058	H Reinhardt	....	G Zimmerman	Carl Reuter	....	A Gilter	T McFeron
New Lenox v§ (6) MC	815 485-6452	Dennis Valy	Brian C Phillips	Marjorie Wajchert	Michael Treacy	Kenneth Hossack	Lawrence Anderson	Lewis Loebe Jr
Newton† (3) MC	618 783-8451	Jim Yates	....	Marcella Martin	Mary Evelyn Dhom	William Snyder	Michael Swick	....
Niles v* (30) CM	312 967-6100	Nicholas B Blase	Jack Hadge	Frank C Wagner Jr	Jeffrey Bell	Harry Kinowski	Clarence Emrikson	Keith Peck
Nokomis (3) MC	217 563-2514	Gene Adden	....	Mary Jean Scheller	Mary Lou Spengel	Martin Dawson	James Vazzi	Donald H Petty
Normal t* (36) CM	309 454-2444	Richard T Godfrey	David S Anderson	Marianne Edwards	Ronald Hill	George R Cermak	David C Lehr	Donald Hallowell
Norridge v† (16) MC	312 453-0800	Joseph Sieb	....	Irene Gdula	George R Dickinson	Lucien Bond	Medard Zabratanski	Herman A Capoccia
North Aurora v (5) MC	312 897-8228	(not reporting)						
North Chicago† (39) MC	312 578-7750	Bobby E Thompson	....	Rudolph B Grom	Daniel Pacenti	Robert Sandahl	Ernest Fisher	....
North Riverside v§ (7) MC	312 447-4211	James R Votava	Wayne E Pesek	Joseph J Spina Jr	Birger Nyborg	Thomas Wiencek	Thomas W Cernock	Robert G Mitchard
Northbrook v* (31) CM	312 272-5050	Lucinda W Kasperson	Robert A Weidaw	Sandra D Kent	Robert T Sutton	John G Julcher	Arthur K Schmidt	James M Reynolds
Northfield v* (6) CM	312 446-9200	George F Hartnett	John H Eckenroad	John H Eckenroad	Edward McKee	Glenn Bennett	Richard D Klatzco	Earl Nystrand
Northlake*† (12) CM	312 343-8700	Eugene C Doyle	Daniel A Joyce	Gloria Raitano	Fred A Mierendorf	Julius Sharpy	Lee Gehrke	Mario Grossi
O'Fallon§ (10) MC	618 624-4500	Gary C Mackey	Mike Bowen	Debra Kozsdiy	Robert Brown	Thomas R Bleau	Henry Wizeman	David Davis

Directory 1/10 continued — MUNICIPAL OFFICIALS IN ALL U.S. CITIES OVER 2,500[1]

City, 1980 population (000 omitted), form of government		Municipal phone number	Mayor	Appointed administrator	City clerk	Finance officer	Fire chief	Police chief	Public works director
ILLINOIS (398) continued									
Oak Brook v§ (7)	MC	312 654-2220	Wence F Cerne	John H Brechin	Marianne Lakosil	....	James E Clark	Albert G Ceren Jr	Floyd Wilson
Oak Forest§ (26)	MC	312 687-4050	James W Jesk Jr	....	Robt J Fitzpatrick	Mel Konrath	David Waite	Alvin Lexow	Michael Cozzo
Oak Lawn v* (61)	CM	312 636-4400	Ernest F Kolb	Richard E O'Neill	A Jayne Powers	Anne Spray Brooker	Elmore J Harker Jr	John Haberkorn	Donald Canning
Oak Park v* (55)	CM	312 383-6400	Sara G Bode	Ralph A DeSantis	Virginia R Cassin	Allen Dean Moore	John Sweeney	Keith R Bergstrom	Horst Melcher
Oglesby (4)	MC	815 883-8621	Gerald F Scott	....	Shaun West	Rose Zomboracz	Edward Koscielski	Rudolph Gandolfi	Joseph Popurella
Olney* (9)	CM	618 395-7302	Gail Lathrop	James A Stevens	Paul Abegglen	David P Van Vooren	Jerry Umfleet	Joseph Woith	James Sager
Olympia Fields v (4)	MC	312 748-8246	Anita W Healey	....	Margaret Belvedere	....	....	Fred M Unger	Fred Keuch
Oregon (4)	CO	815 732-6321	James Barnes	....	Julienne Crowley	Norman H Collins	Gary Griffin	Thomas Miller	....
Orland Park v* (23)	CM	312 349-5400	Melvin H Doogan	Ronald J Ruskey	Anne M Limanowski	Franklin Loebe	Arthur Granat	Duke Gorris	Richard J Dime
Oswego v (3)	MC	312 554-3259	(not reporting)						
Ottawa† (18)	MC	815 433-0161	James M Thomas	....	Wanda Eichelkraut	William Ferguson	Arthur Cunniham	Raymond Moore	George D Small
Palatine v* (32)	CM	312 358-7500	Robert J Guss Jr	Michael D Kadlecik	Rita L Mullins	....	Harvey C Carothers	Jerry Bratcher	John M Loete
Palos Heights (11)	MC	312 361-1800	Eugene G Simpson	....	Helen Mae Asmus	....	Bob Jacobs	Reed M Powers	J Martin
Palos Hills (17)	MC	312 598-3400	Gerald R Bennett	....	Crystal Petrulis	Kenneth Nolan	John Roe	Daniel Hurley	George T Lutz
Palos Park v (3)	CM	312 448-2700	Rosemary Kaptur	....	Patricia Jones	Edward Poe Jr	John Kettman	William Shanley	Daniel Snyder
Pana (6)	MC	217 562-3626	Henry R Suchard	....	Dolores E Klee	Florian L Scherzer	Bill Williamson	Mike Harris	Martin Cerven
Paris* (10)	MC	217 465-7601	Frank L Clinton	Ralph Jacob	Martha B Tuttle	Steven R Sabens	Carroll Hartley	Carter Metcalf	Ike Mitchell Iv
Park City (4)	MC	312 623-5030	Julian Guerrero Jr	....	Max Lingenfeiser	....	....	Michael L Luff	Jason P Sherrod
Park Forest v* (26)	CM	312 748-1112	Ronald Bean	John F Perry	Elva L Iid	Erica Buncis	John Morrissey	Fred Romano	Michael J Cap
Park Ridge* (39)	CM	312 399-5200	Martin J Butler	Gerald Hagman	Lesslie Ethridge	Ms C E Schmidt	....	....	T A Fredrickson
Pawnee v (3)	MC	217 625-7831	Arthur Brown	....	Renee Oliver	....	Larry Warrington	Bill Miller	....
Paxton (4)	MC	217 379-4022	James E Kingston	....	Bess Anderson	James P Graham	Gary Popel	Dennis Schneider	James Lynch
Pekin (34)	CO	309 346-6494	Willard E Birkmeier	....	James F Kautz	Ruth E Veerman	Donald L Benassi	Donald L Benassi	Thomas L Sassman
Peoria* (124)	CM	309 672-8500	Richard E Carver	James B Daken	Frances Schwenger	P G Bardezbanian	William Sollberger	Salvatore Pisano	Stephen Van Winkle
Peoria Heights v (7)	MC	309 682-0221	Raymond L Picl	Rick Williams	Audrey Smith	Joseph J Ricketts	William Bair	Michael McCoy	Steven Rettig
Peotone v (3)	MC	312 258-3279	Warren Baker	....	Elouise Clausing	Richard Anderson	Lanson Russell	Gary Bogart	Dennis Gribbins
Peru (11)	MC	815 223-0061	Donald L Baker	....	Patricia K Gately	Patricia K Gately	Donald Nowakowski	Roy White	Don Kowalczyk
Phoenix v† (3)	MC	312 331-2636	James C Harris Sr	Howard Edwards	Johnnie M Lane	Lacy L Thomas	James Cole	James P Morgan	Theodore Morgan
Pinckneyville (3)	CO	618 357-6916	Wm J Cunningham	....	Frances Thomas	Joseph M Holder	Jerry Smith	Thomas Denton Jr	Harlan M Yeager
Pittsfield (4)	MC	217 285-4484	W Dudley Williams	....	Donald F Hanback	....	Robert H Groom	Larry Snyder	Carrol I Mitchell
Plainfield v (4)	MC	815 436-7093	Richard J Selfridge	James E West	Vera J Krnac	Edward M Geschke	Richard Eldred	Melvin J Lantz	Harrison Countryman
Plano (5)	MC	312 552-8275	Verlin Akers	....	Paula Dimond	June Schumacher	Richard Konow	Dennis Harris	Gerald Canham
Pontiac§ (11)	MC	815 844-6752	Dale O Campbell	Robert M Karls	Marjorie M Ripsch	Mildred Bradley	Don Ford	John Swaufield	....
Pontoon Beach v (3)	MC	618 931-0738	Paul L Bennett	....	Mary Warren	Raymond L Gaudette	....	N Chet Ballew	....
Posen v† (5)	MC	312 385-0139	Joseph J Smaron	....	Jerry J Kuznieski	....	John Krizik	Mary Ann Gratkowski	....
Princeton (7)	MC	815 875-2631	William E Nelson	....	Eugene A Wolf	Richard Unholz	Terry Himes	Mel Hult	....
Prospect Heights§ (12)	MC	312 398-6070	John E Gilligan	Stephen Sturgell	Karen Pedersen	....	....	Errol Levy	Randall S Kuras
Quincy† (42)	MC	217 223-6370	C David Nuessen	....	Kenneth Kircher	John D Shull	James E Doellman	Charles Gruber	Leon K Kowalski
Rantoul v (20)	MC	217 893-1661	Katy B Podagrosi	....	Fred Bartell	Ken Modglin	Jack Jones	Tom Lindzy	Dave Willard
Red Bud† (3)	MC	618 282-2315	Curtis Kimzey	....	John W Faust	Loren Harms	Leroy Bievenue	Jacob Frisch	....
Richton Park v* (9)	CM	312 481-8950	Murell Reeves	A Douglas Fenske	Beverly Burke	Sarah Davis	James Waitekus	Jim R Klaman	Daniel Fielding
River Forest v (12)	CM	312 366-8500	Thomas Cusack Jr	James E Devine	Emerson K Houser	James E Devine	Warren Richardson	Nicholas M Coscino	Charles Barbier
River Grove v (10)	MC	312 453-8000	Elmer E Wolf	Frank J Loni	James R Domsenke	Joseph J Barzano Jr	Louis Schneiderwind	Donald Olsen	Robert O'Connor
Riverdale v (13)	MC	312 841-2200	Frank J Heenan	....	Marceline Phalen	Robert Brecheisen	William Taylor	Peter A Sanders	James Dempsey Jr
Riverside v* (9)	CM	312 447-2700	F Edward Meksto	Chester Kendzior Jr	Jane F Norman	Lillian Shramek	Anthony L Bedzarz	Donald Doneske	Neil Van Dyke
Riverton v† (3)	MC	217 629-9122	Joe Rusciolelli	....	....	....	....	....	....
Riverwoods v§ (3)	MC	312 945-3990	Daniel F Mangin III	Gladys A Grad	Gail Kalish	....	....	....	....
Robbins v (8)	CM	312 385-8940	Richard Ballentine	....	Irene H Brodie	Joann Kelly	Charles Lloyd	Carl Williams	James Jackson
Robinson† (7)	MC	618 544-7616	Richard D Morris	....	Patricia L Kerr	....	Samuel J Beard	Howard W Kirchhoff	....
Rochelle (9)	CO	815 562-6161	Dale R Vogeler	....	John T Havens	....	James McCaslin	Winston Brass	....
Rock Falls v† (11)	MC	815 625-6809	Glen R Kuhlemier	....	Margie C Sommers	....	Carl N Sommers	Carl N Sommers	William Wike
Rock Island* (47)	CM	309 793-3300	James R Davis	J Neil Nielsen	J Vander Meersch	Sheryl J Ligon	Donald Leslie	Ronald Hansen	Gregory Champagne
Rockford (140)	MC	815 987-5500	John F McNamara	John C Phillips	....	Ronald Malmberg	William Baylor	Delbert E Peterson	Ralph Speer
Rolling Meadows* (20)	CM	312 394-8500	William D Ahrens	James A Turi	Marylyn C Koch	....	Thomas C Quillin	Donald L Cundiff	Dennis S York
Romeoville v§† (16)	MC	815 886-2900	Howard Trippett	George M DeFrench	Gerald Ashfield	Linda Lindquist	A F Stadelmaier	Robert Starke	Robert A Braasch
Roselle v (17)	MC	312 980-2000	Sandra J Birdsall	Glenn F Spachman	Harriet Ward	A Donald Mazza	Steve Caravello	Dayle E Lites	Robert O Burns
Rosemont v (4)	MC	312 825-4404	Donald E Stephens	....	Irene Kolaski	Ray Gold	Gary Hopkins	Richard V Drehobl	Vito Corriero
Round Lake Beach v† (13)	MC	312 546-2351	Rodney Brenner	....	Carmen Reyes	Chris Russo	Ed Glower	Lawrence Pasquini	John Isbell
Round Lake Park v (4)	MC	312 546-1513	George Scherer	....	Edith C Heimos	Meredythe Scurto	....	John Robinson	Alfred Louden
Round Lake v† (3)	MC	312 325-0428	Rudolph Magna Sr	....	....	....	....	....	....
Rushville (3)	MC	217 322-3833	Robert McMillen	....	Ina Jane Patterson	Dean Houck	Karl Ford	Wayne Diseron	....
Salem* (8)	CM	618 548-2222	Leonard E Ferguson	Donald E Hahn	Marilyn K Steevens	....	....	William A Krueger	Clyde Scott
Sandwich (4)	MC	815 786-9321	Fred J Wehling	....	Carol J Erickson	Ronald Walker	Marvin Johnson	Glenn Huffman	Donald Clason
Sauk Village v (11)	MC	312 758-3330	Edward W Paesel	Theodore R Theodore	Agnes M Theodore	Edward S Zsido	Leroy Hawkins	Richard Rhodes	Edward Nieft
Savanna (5)	MC	815 273-2251	Donald H Nehrkorn	....	Ruth Kelly	Corine H Myers	Benny Hess	James P Moore	Paul E Hartman
Schaumburg v* (52)	CM	312 894-4500	Herbert J Aigner	Stephen J Atkins	Sandy Carsello	Keith Wendland	Robert Sutherland	Robert Hammond	Robert Miller
Schiller Park v (11)	MC	312 678-2550	Edward E Bluthardt	....	Walter Bykowski	John J Gregor Jr	Walter Siwek	Edward Bluthardt Jr	George J Sieracki
Shelbyville (5)	CO	217 774-5531	Marjorie Sylvester	Marjorie J Strohl	Marjorie J Strohl	Charles W Lloyd	....	Gary L Crowder	....
Shorewood v§ (5)	MC	815 725-2150	David A Barry	James P Shapard	Diana Schmitt	Gerald Clair	....	Donald R Lattin	Bernie Albright
Silvis† (7)	MC	309 792-9181	Stacy King	....	William L Tatman	....	Robert Leibovitz	Gary Williams	Wilbur Samuelson
Skokie v* (60)	CM	312 673-0500	Albert J Smith	Robert J Eppley	Marlene Williams	Daniel W Ryan	Thomas C Quillin	William D Miller	Don Manak
South Beloit (4)	MC	815 389-3023	Gary E Pierce	....	Kathleen A Murphy	Alan Palmer	Kenneth C Morse	Jack O Johnson	Maurice Kehoe
South Chicago Heights v† (4)	MC	312 755-1880	Donald A Prisco	Rennie R Smith III	Ms J Lawniczak	Eliseo Giannetta	Angelo J Petrarca	Rennie R Smith III	Felix Cristello
South Elgin v (6)	MC	312 742-5780	T J Rolando Jr	....	Dale D W Stevens	Joseph J Huber	Louis Oine	James A Bobik	John E Peters
South Holland v† (25)	MC	312 333-0572	Harold J Gouwens	....	Ruth DeVries	Willard Vander Zee	Harris Van Drunen	John Rinkema	Elmer DeYoung
South Jacksonville v (3)	MC	217 245-4803	Richard H Godfrey	....	Linda K Nichols	Ms Leslie Musch	Willard Hickox	Richard Evans	Garry Thomas
Sparta (5)	CO	618 443-2917	Thomas F Maybell	....	Ronald E Cavalier	....	Harry H Hermes	Jackie B Bivens	Eugene L Bigham
Spring Valley (6)	MC	815 664-4221	James Cinotto	....	Beverly West	Joseph Riva	Gene Scheri	James Smoode	William Becker
Springfield (100)	CO	217 789-2000	J Michael Houston	....	Candice D Trees	James E Norris	Thomas Hall	Stanley D Troyer	O C Langfelder
St. Charles (17)	MC	312 377-4400	Fred T L Norris	....	Jean Conners	Larry Maholland	Larry Swanson	William Burke	Darryll R Bauer
Staunton (5)	MC	618 635-2233	Fred Brauer	....	Delbert Stiegemeier	Larry Lux	Lowell Lovejoy	Larry Grabruck	Richard Kapp
Steger v (9)	MC	312 754-3395	Louis Sherman	....	William M Hodge	Milford Bisping	Elmer Joyce	Charles Tieri	John Gilkison
Sterling* (16)	CM	815 625-0485	William K Durham	Charles W Bell	Rosemary Coughlin	Joyce Frankfother	Arlyn Oetting	Cadet T Thorp	George Biszak
Stickney v† (6)	MC	312 749-4400	George B Rench	....	Arthur E Rawers	Mary Ellen Prerost	Joseph Steinhoff	James Dolezal	Charles Bachielli
Stone Park v† (4)	MC	312 345-5550	William J Francione	....	Harry Jack	Dorothy Caraher	John Davis	Harry E Testa	Sylvester L Palmer
Streamwood v* (23)	CM	312 837-0200	Stephen Gant	Edward Emond	Billie D Roth	Douglas Ellsworth	Thomas Holz	Paul Rauscher	John White
Streator (15)	MC	815 672-2517	Arthur P Dell	....	Edward G Vanko	Arthur P Dell	Richard Benner	Kenneth Sangston	....
Sullivan (5)	MC	217 728-7622	Thomas R Dean	....	Floyd Buckalew	....	....	Roger D Hansen	....

Directory 1/10 continued

MUNICIPAL OFFICIALS IN ALL U.S. CITIES OVER 2,500[1]

City, 1980 population (000 omitted), form of government	Municipal phone number	Mayor	Appointed administrator	City clerk	Finance officer	Fire chief	Police chief	Public works director
ILLINOIS (398) continued								
Summit v (10) . . . . . . MC	312 563-4800	Chester Strzelczyk	....	John J Kirk	Claude Aldridge	Joseph Bailey	James Vukovich	Albert Baker
Swansea v (5) . . . . . . MC	618 234-3292	Donald R Melhorn	....	Paul Krupp	Robert T Wiltshire	Dennis Thacker	Edward J Lintzenich	....
Sycamore (9). . . . . MC	815 895-4515	Harold L Johnson	....	Georgina L Yeager	Georgina L Yeager	Russell L Utter	Robert W Huber	Gene M Listy
Taylorville (11) . . . . . . MC	217 824-2101	Daniel G Reese	....	Frances Sutton	Fred J Torricelli	Keith Evrley	Roger E Jones	....
Thornton v† (3) . . . . . MC	312 877-6136	Charles P Nason	....	Marian Mikrut	Judy A Diekelman	William Marcum	Louis Wawrzyniak	Pete Den Hartog
Tinley Park v§ (26) . . . MC	312 532-7700	Edward J Zabrocki	Dennis A Kallsen	Frank W German Jr	Brad Bettenhausen	Robert Bettenhausen	Robert Long	Charles B Powers
Trenton† (3) . . . . MC	618 224-7323	Herbert Schlarmann	....	Doris M Jones	Mary B Wehrle	Paul Meyer	Ronald Dillow	....
Troy (4) . . . . MC	618 667-6741	Ron Criley	....	Mary Chasteen	David Roady	Jim Laughlin	Clarence Quinley	Bud Klaustermeir
Tuscola (4) . . . . MC	217 253-2112	Clarence Snyder	Wanda Long	Harold Scheu	Richard Parker	Dennis Dietrich	Ronald Earl	Eugene Williams
University Park v* (6) CM	312 534-6451	Earl Bell	Fred Bluestone	Wilma Jenkins	Ed Zsido	Michael Grubermann	Michael F Dooley	Frank Fouts
Urbana§ (36) . . . . MC	217 384-2366	Jeffrey T Markland	....	Ruth Brookens	Ronald Eldridge	John L Troeger	John L Troeger	James S Darling
Vandalia (5). . . . . MC	618 283-1196	Neil F Donnals	....	Rose Ann Mull	....	Jerry Beabout	Carrol Dugan	Carl Frailey
Venice (3) . . . . MC	618 877-2114	Tyrone Echols	....	Ralph D Brawley	James Gardner	William Meehan	Farris Smith	Thomas Scaturro
Vernon Hills v§ (10). . . MC	312 367-3700	Phillip L Ellis	Herbert W Kip	Joanne Korstanje	Donna Manahan	....	Larry L Laschen	Frank Cibulka
Villa Grove† (3). . . . . . CM	217 832-4721	John A Leon	....	Norma Miller	....	Gale Underwood	....	Carrol Grammer
Villa Park v* (23) . . . . CM	312 834-8500	Victor Lesch	Kevin O'Donnell	James St Louis	Richard J Thomas	Jerry Anderson	Roger Weiser	William C Boyd
Virden (4) . . . . MC	217 965-3711	Earl Bristow	....	Victoria Stewart	Ron Stevens	Albert B Fuiten	Gary Plessa	Allen Butcher
Warrenville† (8) . . . . . MC	312 393-9427	Richard M Volkmer	....	Lucy Bernard	Robert E Johnson	Cliff Johnson	Chester A Hall	Paul Mizevitz
Washington Park v (8) MC	618 874-0115	(not reporting)						
Washington§ (10) . . . . MC	309 444-3196	Ronald N Marshall	Fred J Snider	Deborah Robson	Robert H Gordon	Charles Slonneger	Harold E Marteness	Robert A Dudas
Waterloo (5) . . . . MC	618 939-8661	Jerry L Gum	Harold H Hirstein	Michael Raeber	Robert Jaenke	Don Toal	Charles Barnett	Arthur O Fischer
Watseka (6). . . . . MC	815 432-2711	Ernest A Grove	....	Helen M Harries	Esther B Johnson	Victor Cahoe	Kenneth German	Jerry Lacy
Wauconda v (6) . . . . . MC	312 526-8786	Kenneth McGill	....	Venita L McConnel	Mary J Slusser	Lyle Matthews	Paul M Hansen	Jeffery J Kuester
Waukegan (68). . . . . . . MC	312 689-7500	Bill Morris	Mezell L Williams	William F Durkin	John Dluhos	Hugh White	Ken Ryckman	Bob Johnson
West Chicago* (13) . . . CM	312 231-3322	A Eugene Rennels	George R Catalano	Richard J Truitt	George R Catalano	James Hamlin	John Bullaro	James D Foster
West Dundee v* (4) . . . CM	312 426-6161	Thomas Warner	William R Sommer	Margaret Jefferson	....	Larry McManaman	Allan Demien	Virgil Thorson
West Frankfort† (9) . . . CO	618 932-3262	Orville Nolen	....	Carolyn Martin	Jack Woolard	Tom Aaron	Charles Broy Jr	Bill Krah
Westchester v* (18). . . CM	312 345-0020	John J Sinde	Leonard W Weigel	Helen J Waters	James Fergle	Wayne R Horn	Donald R Musker	Robert G Mitchard
Western Springs v* (13) CM	312 246-1800	Louis F Schauer	Paul C Nicholson	Frank C Everitt	Richard F Ratkowski	Frank G Benak	George P Graves	Patrick R Higgins
Westhaven v† (3) . . . . MC	312 349-6666	James O Brien	Carolyn Wachowiak	Merril Singleterry	Walter Gacek	....	Timothy Presler	Charles Kidd
Westmont v* (17) . . . . CM	312 968-0560	Gregory S Szymski	Oliver R Bishop	Elmer Fries	Robert Sterkowitz	Frank Johanik	Richard Johnson	....
Westville v (4) . . . . . . MC	217 267-2131	Louis Zamberletti	....	Emmalu Brewer	Mary Langdon	Joseph Starks	John Mackiewicz	....
Wheaton* (43) . . . . . . CM	312 260-2000	Robert J Martin	Donald B Rose	Lillian Johnson	Kenneth McConnaugh	David Fleege	Carl Dobbs	Joseph R Knippen
Wheeling v* (23). . . . . CM	312 459-2600	Sheila H Schultz	Thomas M Markus	Elizabeth L Hartman	Gregory J Peters	Bernhardt Koeppen	Michael F Haeger	Robert D Gray Jr
White Hall (3). . . . . . . MC	217 374-2345	(not reporting)						
Willow Springs v (4). . . MC	312 839-2701	Frank L Militello	....	R Virginia Farrell	Dorothy Anderson	James A Musil	James Ross	....
Willowbrook v§ (5) . . . MC	312 323-8215	Edw Schmittschmitt	Bernard A Oglietti	Roberta Krause	Marion Van Stedum	....	Joseph A Pec	Mark C Pusinelli
Wilmette v* (28). . . . . CM	312 251-2700	Vernon T Squires	Stan E Kennedy	Stan E Kennedy	Robert N Amoruso	Robert Brady	Fred W Stoecker	Dick Hansen
Wilmington (4) . . . . . . MC	815 476-2176	Robert P Weidling	....	James C Johnston	Bonita L Hill	Randall Black	Franklin W Lyons	Frederick Richmond
Winfield v§ (4) . . . . . . MC	312 665-1778	Jim L Collins	Michael S Allison	Patricia A Stuart	James C Ford	John N Karwoski	Carl Sostak	Richard Ahrens
Winnetka v* (13). . . . . CM	312 446-2500	Gwendolyn H Trindl	Robert A Buechner	Robert A Buechner	Kenneth A Klein	John Schneider	Herbert A Timm	Max L Whitman
Winthrop Harbor v (5) MC	312 872-3846	Arthur E Fossland	....	Dawn L McLain	Margaret Blanchard	Kim Evans	William Pate	Robert F Williams
Wood Dale* (11). . . . . CM	312 766-4900	Jerry C Greer	Kurt Bressner	Geraldine Jacobs	Ralph Stephens	William Stanek	Frank Williams	....
Wood River* (12) . . . . CM	618 254-0123	Lon A Smith	Hiram Bill Watkins	Jean V Stanley	Michael Sweda	Don Greer	Don Greer	Ron Kincade
Woodridge v§ (22). . . . MC	312 852-7000	William F Murphy	Scott D Staples	Dorothy Stahl	....	....	James Keyes	Joseph Fennell
Woodstock* (12). . . . . CM	815 338-4300	Frances M Kuhn	Dennis L Anderson	Suzanne B Ehardt	Glendon M Kiger	Phil Parker	Herbert J Pitzman	John W Isbell
Worth v† (12) . . . . . . MC	312 448-1181	Daniel A Kumingo	....	Norma M Brewster	Edith Raimondi	Kenneth Murphy	Harry P Jenkins	Michael Cozzo
Yorkville (3). . . . . MC	312 553-6222	Robert E Davidson	....	Luanne J Erickson	Sandra L Loebbaka	Larry Bretthauer	Richard Randall	James T Johnson II
Zion (18) . . . . CO	312 872-4546	Howard P Everline	....	Wanda M Oleson	John Stark	Andrew Neargarder	Norman E Lee	James W Whitt
INDIANA (159)								
Albany t (3). . . . . MC	317 789-6112	(not reporting)						
Alexandria (6). . . . . . . MC	317 724-4633	Richard L Zarse	....	Almetta Johnson	Almetta Johnson	Fred R Haas	Ron Warner	....
Anderson (65) . . . . . . MC	317 644-8821	Thomas R McMahan	....	Marie Riggs	James H Steele Jr	Carl Greenlee	Frank Burrows	Doyle Wright
Angola (5). . . . . MC	219 665-2514	Gerald C Lett	....	Margaret Bledsoe	....	Raymond Meek	Kenneth B Ham	....
Attica (4) . . . . MC	317 762-2467	Avis L Hansley	....	Rachel Mathers	....	William McCall	Timothy Quinn	....
Auburn (8) . . . . MC	219 925-5430	B L Dickman	....	Patricia Clark	Patricia Clark	Bill L Walters	Duane Keesler	B L Dickman
Aurora (4). . . . . MC	812 926-1777	Paul O Alford	....	Micheal S Turner	Micheal S Turner	L Hafenbridle	Wm D McCartney	Paul O Alford
Austin t† (5) . . . . MC	812 794-2877	....	....	Mildred Hollan	....	....	John D Adams	....
Batesville (4) . . . . MC	812 934-2509	Victor E Kaiser	....	Allen M Beck	....	Donald Weigel	Daniel E Strecker	....
Bedford (14) . . . . MC	812 279-6555	John A Williams	Thomas J Fountaine	Mary Frances Duncan	Mary Frances Duncan	Don Tirey	Dean Duncan	John A Williams
Beech Grove (13) . . . . MC	317 784-3003	Elton H Geshwiler	....	Marcella L Miceli	Marcella L Miceli	Paul McDermott	Daniel Challis	M Allan Reece
Berne† (3). . . . . MC	219 589-2169	Gaylord Stuckey	....	Elmer Graber	....	Cletus Gifford	Merlin Bixler	....
Bicknell† (5) . . . . MC	812 735-4636	Jerry G Russell	....	Rita J Lee	....	Paul V Koenig	John J Vendes	....
Bloomington† (52). . . . MC	812 339-2261	Tomilea Allison	John Langley	Patricia Williams	Betty Merriman	Larry Fleener	Phil Riley	Pat Patterson
Bluffton (9) . . . . MC	219 824-1520	John Flaningam	....	Christie Petzel	....	Steven Fischer	Wayne Grove	....
Boonville (6) . . . . MC	812 897-1230	James T Pryor	....	Ruth Wire	Evelyn Hart	Vernon Knight Jr	Jerry Fuller	Bill O Utzman
Brazil (8). . . . . MC	812 443-2221	Norval Pickett Jr	....	John Johnson	....	Roy Kellar	Mose Marks	Norval Pickett Jr
Bremen t (4) . . . . MC	219 546-2471	....	....	Joanne Kimmell	....	Lowell Martin	James A Brown	....
Brookville t (3) . . . . . . MC	317 647-5681	Loren W Murphy	....	Sylvan Reiboldt	....	Daniel M Bruns	Thomas D Helms	....
Brownsburg t (6). . . . . MC	317 852-7905	(not reporting)						
Brownstown t (3) . . . . MC	812 358-5500	....	....	Patricia Forgey	....	Wilbert Wessel Jr	Russell Martin	....
Butler (3) . . . . MC	219 868-5200	Guy Mausteller	....	Sharon Spake	....	Larry Moore	Jerry Ladd	Franklin Brock
Carmel (18) . . . . MC	317 844-6433	(not reporting)						
Cedar Lake t (9) . . . . . MC	219 374-7000	Frank L King	....	Lillian E Falkiner	Lillian E Falkiner	....	James W Hunley	....
Chandler t (3). . . . . . . MC	812 925-6882	John M Hatcher	John F Hillenbrand	Nicholas J Galloway	....	Frank Shelton	George A Irvin	Robert Hess
Charlestown (6) . . . . . MC	812 256-3422	Clay Hall	....	Dorothea Jenkins	Dorothea Jenkins	Carl Hall	Ed McDonald	Clay Hall
Chesterfield t (3) . . . . . MC	317 378-3331	Tommie Grant	....	Patricia A Summers	....	Dale Sheedy	Moses G Beeman	....
Chesterton t* (9). . . . . CM	219 926-1641	....	Marilyn Dartz	Helen Wynder	A S Kipper	Walt Pliske	James Killosky	....
Cicero t† (3) . . . . MC	317 984-4900	David Clements	....	....	....	....	....	....
Clarksville t (15) . . . . . CO	812 288-7155	Albert Theriac	....	Gregory Isgrigg	....	James G Kaster	Gary Hall	....
Clinton (5). . . . . MC	317 832-9880	Domenic A Natale	....	H Marie Meadows	H Marie Meadows	Everett Barker	Larry W Stultz	Domenic A Natale
Columbia City (5) . . . . MC	219 244-5141	Joseph R Zickgraf	Anthony G Zickgraf	Rosie Coyle	....	Paul Shoda	John North	Anthony G Zickgraf
Columbus (30) . . . . . . MC	812 376-2500	Robert N Stewart	....	Jeanne Carteaux	Jeanne Carteaux	James M Miller	Jerry E Coon	Keith Reeves
Connersville (17). . . . . MC	317 825-1271	William F Collins	....	Henrietta Ripberger	Henrietta Ripberger	Stephen Freeman	Jerald L Weldin	Warren Sudhoff
Corydon t (3) . . . . MC	812 738-3958	Fred K Cammack	....	Mary H Merker	....	Donald Saulman	Richard O Yetter	....
Covington (3). . . . . . . MC	317 793-2331	Eugene Smail	....	Jo Ann Anderson	Jo Ann Anderson	Jeffrey Allison	Tony Knecht	Eugene Smail
Crawfordsville (13). . . . MC	317 362-3804	Glenn J Knecht	....	Jeanette Servies	Jeanette Servies	Fred Davis	Carlos Goode	....
Crown Point (16). . . . . MC	219 663-0257	James A Forsythe	....	Eileen V Shults	....	Roland E Wise	Charles Franko	James A Forsythe
Cumberland t (3). . . . . MC	317 894-3580	(not reporting)						

Directory 1/10 continued — MUNICIPAL OFFICIALS IN ALL U.S. CITIES OVER 2,500[1]

City, 1980 population (000 omitted), form of government		Municipal phone number	Mayor	Appointed administrator	City clerk	Finance officer	Fire chief	Police chief	Public works director
INDIANA (159) continued									
Danville t (4)	CO	317 745-4180	Norm Gulley	Marcel J Coulomb Jr	Pauletta Frye	....	Kent Hadley	Gary D Eakin	Terry Myers
De Motte t (3)	MC	219 987-3831	(not reporting)						
Decatur (9)	MC	219 724-7171	Harold B Miller	....	Patricia Mansfield	....	L Gene Moser	Dick Mansfield Jr	....
Dunkirk (3)	MC	317 768-6565	John D Mink	....	Beverly Holloway	....	Lawrence Dull	Gerald Kirby	....
Dyer t§† (10)	MC	219 865-6108	John P Quinn	....	Maryann Brown	Maryann Brown	Ewald Rietman	Charles Thompson	....
East Chicago (40)	MC	219 392-1600	Robert A Pastrick	....	George Cvitkovich	James W Knight	Solomon J Ard	Delbert Hartley	Andres Fernandez
Edinburg t† (5)	MC	812 526-2663	Larry Whitlock	Richard Galbreath	Eva May McMillan	Eva May McMillan	Paul Moore	Kenny Quinn	Richard Galbreath
Elkhart (41)	MC	219 294-5471	James P Perron	....	Nedra D Tripp	Maribeth Hicks	Douglas Bowlby	James Mable	Howard Hostetler
Ellettsville t† (3)	MC	812 876-2297	G L Chandler Jr	....	Rogette N Hector	....	Jim Davis	Donal Kuster	....
Elwood (11)	MC	317 552-5076	Phillip F Orbaugh	....	Bessie Strong	....	Jerry Wilson	Carl Ritter	Phillip F Orbaugh
Evansville (130)	MC	812 426-5000	Michael D Vandeveer	....	Betty Lou Jarboe	Leslie Blenner	John Behme	Ray Hamner	John Vezzoso
Fairmount t (3)	MC	317 948-4632	....	....	Milo B Brown	Clarence King	Ted Hiatt	Robert Curtis	....
Fort Branch t (3)	MC	812 753-7662	(not reporting)						
Fort Wayne (172)	MC	219 427-1111	Winfield C Moses Jr	David M Perlini	Sandra M Kennedy	Cozette Simon	Tom Heckman	David C Riemen	David Kiester
Fortville t (3)	MC	317 485-4044	(not reporting)						
Frankfort (15)	MC	317 654-5715	Don E Snyder	....	Deborah A Neal	....	Wayne Young	Roy Scott	Don E Snyder
Franklin† (12)	MC	317 736-3602	Charles R Littleton	....	Inalouis Matthews	....	Jack A Matthews	G Donald Linneman	....
Garrett (5)	MC	219 357-4033	Marcella M Zerns	....	Jennie L DePaolo	....	Harry G Jackson Jr	Jerry W Custer	William T Dembickie
Gary (152)	MC	219 881-1300	Richard G Hatcher	James Holland	Barbara Wesson	Charles Ruckman	Bobby Joiner	Frederick Kowsky	Jerome Fifer
Gas City (6)	MC	317 674-5728	Eugene Linn	....	Frank Hillman	....	Joe Miitsch	Larry Leach	....
Goshen† (20)	MC	219 533-8621	Max R Chiddister	....	Phyllis D Roose	Phyllis D Roose	Duane E Stoner	Devoe Stoner	Forrest Miller
Greencastle (8)	MC	317 653-9211	Gerald E Warren	....	Janice Inman	....	Robert Elmore	James Hendrich	Gerald E Warren
Greendale t (4)	MC	812 537-2125	James Irons	F R Rudolph	Deborah Rainey	F R Rudolph	Edward Noel	Jerry McAdams	F R Rudolph
Greenfield (11)	MC	317 462-8510	Keith J McClarnon	....	Patricia Elmore	....	....	Robert Butler	....
Greensburg† (9)	MC	812 663-3344	Sheldon Smith	....	David Hartwell	....	Jim Biltz	Les Gay	....
Greenwood (19)	MC	317 881-8527	Jeanette Surina	....	Martha Chitwood	....	Marion Kite	Charles Henderson	....
Griffith t (17)	MC	219 924-7500	....	....	Florence Kaegebein	Florence Kaegebein	George Thiel	William L Weddell	Glen Reyome
Hammond (94)	MC	219 853-6300	Thomas McDermott	Sandra Dempsey	Stanley Kulik	Edward Brown	Wayne Duncanson	James Bobowski	C Jerome Smith
Hanover t (4)	MC	812 866-2131	Jonathan Smith	....	Susan M Patterson	Susan M Patterson	....	Willie E Lucas Jr	Roy Poindexter
Hartford City (8)	MC	317 348-0412	Joseph Castelo Jr	....	Vera Pontius	Vera Pontius	O G Henderson	Doug Hall	Joseph Castelo Jr
Hebron t (3)	MC	219 996-4641	Ray Bales	....	Donna Taber	....	Allen Stembel	Ray Lockhardt	....
Highland t (26)	MC	219 838-1080	Carl J Miklusak	....	Paul L Doherty	Paul L Doherty	James Dale	James Turoci	R G Bradley
Hobart† (23)	MC	219 942-1940	Calvin E Green Jr	....	Margaret J Kuchta	Margaret J Kuchta	H Richard Harrigan	Lawrence Juzwicki	Calvin E Green Jr
Huntingburg (5)	MC	812 683-2211	Dale W Helmerich	....	Urban O Blessinger	Urban O Blessinger	Marvin L Boeglin	William L Wampler	....
Huntington (16)	MC	219 356-4714	Ronald D Schenkel	....	Joretta M Schoeff	John V Michael	Dennis Mick	Charles Crago	Ronald D Schenkel
Indianapolis (701)	MC	317 236-3200	Wm H Hudnut III	Don McPherson	Beverly Rippy	Fred L Armstrong	Don Strietlemeir	Joseph McAtee	Barbara Gole
Jasper (9)	MC	812 482-4255	Jerome Alles	....	Iris Gutgsell	....	Edward Eckert	Stephen Wagner	....
Jeffersonville (21)	MC	812 283-4451	Dale L Orem	....	C Richard Spencer	C Richard Spencer	Ronald Collins	Gerald Priest	Dale L Orem
Kendallville (7)	MC	219 347-0352	J W Riemke	....	Dorothy Pippenger	....	L McGahen	Craig Streich	Jerry L Luttman
Knox (4)	MC	219 772-4553	Robert W Lynch	....	Lilyan Armstrong	Lilyan Armstrong	Robert Sims	Donald Hansen	....
Kokomo (48)	MC	317 452-4058	Stephen J Daily	....	Carol Moberly Myers	Jone D Wilson	Joe Granson	Rodger L Fain	Kenneth J Ferries
La Porte (22)	MC	219 362-3175	Dennis F Smith	....	Florence G Chroback	Florence G Chroback	Thomas J Miller	Allen R Ott	Dennis F Smith
Lafayette (43)	MC	317 742-8404	James F Riehle	....	Eileen J Hession	Anne Glade	Robert E Taylor Jr	Ronald O Milks	Maurice E Callahan
Lake Station (14)	MC	219 962-3111	Arthur L Hartley	....	Rebecca Williams	....	Ronald Good	Thomas Pearson	Thomas Cogley
Lawrence† (26)	MC	317 545-6191	Morris Settles	....	William D Hall	William D Hall	Gerald Krug	Warren Wilkinson	Bill Gann
Lawrenceburg (4)	MC	812 537-1676	Carl Agner	Roland Horney	Elsie Massey	Elsie Massey	Paul Sartin	Donald Combs	Carl Agner
Lebanon (11)	MC	317 482-1218	Ann Garoffolo	....	Helen Harman	....	William Williams	Carl Jo Rady	....
Ligonier (3)	MC	219 894-4112	Grover Patrick	....	Lois Renner	....	Donald E Gillespie	Robert B Durham	Grover Patrick
Linton† (6)	MC	812 847-7754	Patrick F Turner	Walter B Watson	Evelyn L Runnels	Evelyn L Runnels	Delbert L Ferree	David L West	Patrick F Turner
Logansport (18)	MC	219 753-2551	John R Davis	....	Charles A Knepper	Charles A Knepper	Joseph B Casalini	Robert J Rozzi	Kenneth E Smith
Loogootee (3)	MC	812 295-4770	Ted M Killion	....	Doris Traylor	....	Gerald Huebner	Paul E Gee	Donald Grindstaff
Lowell t§ (6)	MC	219 696-7794	William Marshall	Timothy J Gagen	Marcia Carlson	....	Elmer Kender	George H Navarre	....
Madison (12)	MC	812 265-4033	Markt L Lytle	Julie A Jackson	Betty Brunton	Betty Brunton	James Edwards Jr	Jerry Sachleben	Randy Eggenspiller
Marion† (36)	MC	317 662-9931	Fred D Weagley	Evelyn Copeland	Mary Jane Hollway	Evelyn Copeland	Fred Shafer	Lee Mauldon	Jim Weagley
Martinsville (11)	MC	317 342-2861	Guy F Fogleman	....	Erma Scott	Erma Scott	Timothy Fraker	Terry Weddle	John Drapalik
Merrillville (28)	MC	219 769-3501	Albert S Wirtes	....	Merle Cook	Merle Cook	Roger Carter	Jerry L McCory	Richard Jewell
Michigan City (37)	MC	219 874-3288	Clifford D Arnold	Jerome L Eisele	Thomas F Fedder	Jerome L Eisele	Raymond Brooks	Barry L Nothstine	Jerome L Eisele
Middletown t (3)	MC	317 354-2911	(not reporting)						
Mishawaka (40)	MC	219 258-1622	Robert C Beutter	....	Janet A Opfel	Edwina C Kintner	Michael Portolese	Lawrence Stabrowski	Gary E West
Mitchell (5)	MC	812 849-2151	Jerry L Hancock	....	Shirley A Warren	Shirley A Warren	....	Phillip M Tincher	....
Monticello† (5)	MC	219 583-9889	Dixie Blair	....	Audrey Dixon	....	Dewitt Robinson	Robert E Fox	David Diener
Mooresville t (5)	MC	317 831-1608	Robert Farmer	....	Janet L Hood	....	James R Bruner	George A Ditton	....
Mount Vernon† (8)	MC	812 838-5576	Jackson L Higgins	....	Laura C Bullard	....	Leonard L Kuhn	Wilfred Clark Jr	....
Muncie† (77)	MC	317 747-4844	James P Carey	Roger Marsh	Billie Jo Burkett	William Barnes	Carl Lucas	Donald Scroggins	Stanley Hiatt
Munster t§ (21)	MC	219 836-8810	Gilbert L Moore	Thomas F DeGiulio	Phyllis Hayden	....	Robert C Nowaczyk	Thomas Rhind	James Mandon
Nappanee (5)	MC	219 773-2112	Robert W Callander	....	Kimberly A Ingle	....	Forrest G Reed	Bruce Thornton	....
New Albany† (37)	MC	812 948-5333	Robert L Real	....	Bonnie Rogers	William Chanley	Larry Denison	Roy Wolfe	Carl Pearcy
New Castle† (20)	MC	317 529-3502	Gerald Bud Ayers	....	Pamela S Jarvis	Pamela S Jarvis	Jack D Thurman	Dale L Salyers	Don Lundy
New Chicago t† (3)	MC	219 962-1157	Michael Minarich	....	....	....	....	....	....
New Haven† (7)	MC	219 749-1911	Terry A Werling	....	Helen L Purvis	....	R Schladenhauffen	Robert L Ladig	Terry A Werling
New Whiteland t† (5)	CM	317 535-9487	Elmer D Ford	....	Sandra Smoot	Sandra Smoot	Sam Williams	Joseph L Lasiter	....
Newburgh t† (3)	MC	812 853-3578	Elizabeth Sowa	Larry J Hessler	Sally K Diaz	Sally K Diaz	Gene Smith	Dennis Patton	....
Noblesville (12)	MC	317 773-4614	Patricia A Logan	....	Marilyn Conner	Marilyn Conner	Jeffrey L Reveal	David J Crose	....
North Manchester t† (6)	MC	219 982-6536	Jack J Williams	James C Taylor	Nancy J Reed	....	Herbert W Young	B R Hettmansperger	....
North Vernon (6)	MC	812 346-5907	Robert W Curry	Lulu Belle Webb	Lulu Belle Webb	Lulu Belle Webb	Robert J Ringer	Jim Lamb	Robert W Curry
Oakland City (3)	MC	812 749-3222	Everett E Robertson	....	Diana Cochren	....	Charles R Cochren	Robert Bigham	....
Paoli t (4)	MC	812 723-2739	(not reporting)						
Peru (14)	MC	317 472-2400	Robert L Haskett	....	Marylynn Black	Marylynn Black	Doyle Hunt	Jerrl Landis	John Biggs
Petersburg (3)	MC	812 354-8515	(not reporting)						
Plainfield t† (9)	MC	317 839-2561	Robin G Brandgard	....	Virginia H Weber	....	James Baxter	James R Pound	....
Plymouth† (8)	MC	219 936-2124	Charles O Glaub	....	Beverly J Curtis	....	Robert S Shaffer	Donald J Jefferies	....
Portage (27)	MC	219 762-5425	Robert E Goin	....	Anita L Bando	Anita L Bando	Thomas P Potts	Steven Chaddock	Robert E Goin
Porter t* (3)	CM	219 926-2771	Thomas Esgate	....	Lila L Hokanson	....	Raymond Wesley	Leonard Smith	James Phillips
Portland (7)	MC	219 726-9395	James E Luginbill	....	Betty Miller	....	Larry Petro	Raymond L Mock	Joe Arnold
Princeton (9)	MC	812 385-3498	L Frank Wade	....	Janet Jones	Janet Jones	Robert Embree	Howard Hardiman	....
Rensselaer (5)	MC	219 866-5212	Robert Dean Wilcox	....	Susan M Smith	....	....	Dennis J Anslover	....
Richmond (41)	MC	317 966-5561	Frank H Waltermann	Christopher G Klose	Mary Merchanthouse	Cathy Maness	Larry Bosell	Joseph Nimitz	Ralph Willis
Rochester† (5)	MC	219 223-2510	Donald E Cook	....	Janice K Roe	Janice K Roe	Robert Kramer	Dave Goss	Donald E Cook
Rockville t (3)	MC	317 569-6253	Donald C Swaim	....	Imogene Rahn	....	Jack Wilson	Dewey White	....
Rushville (6)	MC	317 932-2672	Joseph Delon	....	Sharon Bostic	Sharon Bostic	Noah Jacobs	Ron Cameron	Joseph Delon
Salem† (5)	MC	812 883-4265	Don R Humphrey	Jennifer Humphrey	Catherine L Moore	Bill Goen	Larry Cooper	Max Boling	Don R Humphrey

Directory 1/10 continued

MUNICIPAL OFFICIALS IN ALL U.S. CITIES OVER 2,500[1]

City, 1980 population (000 omitted), form of government		Municipal phone number	Mayor	Appointed administrator	City clerk	Finance officer	Fire chief	Police chief	Public works director
INDIANA (159) continued									
Schererville t* (13)	CM	219 322-4581	Paulette Stark	James B Stevens	Alice A Siebert	Alice A Siebert	Joseph Govert	Ronald Schweder	....
Scottsburg (5)	MC	812 752-4343	Edward W Cozart	....	Carol Robbins	....	Raymond Jones	John C Lizenby	....
Sellersburg t (3)	MC	812 246-3821	(not reporting)						
Seymour (15)	MC	812 522-4020	William W Bailey	....	M Carter	M Carter	John Terry	James Bullard	Jerry L Hartsell
Shelbyville (15)	MC	317 398-4131	Dan D Theobald	....	Betty L Worland	Betty L Worland	Robert Buckley	Robert Nolley	Michael R Babbitt
South Bend† (110)	MC	219 284-9011	Roger O Parent	Craig E Hartzer	Irene Gammon	Joseph E Kernan	Timothy Brassell	Dan D Thompson	John E Leszczynski
Speedway t (13)	MC	317 241-2566	Charles E Bowling	....	John R Sneyd	John R Sneyd	William Ermel	Bill Burgan	Gary L Cain
Spencer t (3)	MC	812 829-3213	Jack E Noel	....	....	....	Rick Shields	Gerry Sips	....
St. John t† (4)	MC	219 365-4800	Hal Foltz	....	Betty L Siedelmann	....	Samuel DeYoung	Robert Ponton	Clarence Monix
Sullivan (5)	MC	812 268-6077	Herman A Smith	....	Kathryn K Garrett	Kathryn K Garrett	John Hochstetler	Charles Butler	Lewis Brooks
Syracuse t (3)	MC	219 457-3216	Carl Myrick	....	Jennifer Hughes	Jennifer Hughes	Joe Anderson	Warren Swartz	Joe Dock
Tell City (9)	MC	812 547-3266	(not reporting)						
Terre Haute (61)	MC	812 232-9467	P Pete Chalos	....	Chuck Hanley	Tharon Geckeler	Bob Osborn	Gerald Loudermilk	John Wooden
Tipton (5)	MC	317 675-7561	Walter T Balser	....	John A McNeal	....	George Ogden	Gary L Stout	Noel Olse
Trail Creek t (3)	MC	219 872-2422	Daniel Tompkins	....	Rosalie Lasky	Rosalie Lasky	....	Michael Chastain	....
Union City (4)	MC	317 964-6534	Bill R Fulk	....	Wanda L Wood	Wanda L Wood	Richard A Wantz	Richard Addington	....
Upland t (3)	MC	317 998-2971	(not reporting)						
Valparaiso (22)	MC	219 462-1161	David A Butterfield	....	Sharon Emerson	....	Larry Linton	Richard Buchanan	David A Butterfield
Vincennes (21)	MC	812 882-7285	William D Rose	....	Marvin Westfall	Marvin Westfall	Ronald Thomas	Robert Goldman	William D Rose
Wabash† (13)	MC	219 563-4171	George Dingledy	....	Maxine Mullin	Maxine Mullin	Dallas Winchester	Jerry Mullett	Pat Ragan
Warsaw† (11)	MC	219 267-8894	P E Mike Hodges	....	Pamela Ward	....	Tom Burns	Sam Brown	....
Washington (11)	MC	812 254-0319	David W Abel	....	Doris Munning	....	Larry Turk	Garth P Riffey	....
West Lafayette† (21)	MC	317 463-3571	Sonya L Margerum	....	George R Fraser	George R Fraser	Richard Coddington	Mel Timmons	Paul J Couts
Westfield t (3)	MC	317 896-5577	James J Edwards	....	Mary Lou Thatcher	Mary Lou Thatcher	Robert E Mikesell	Kenneth D Peters	....
Whiting (6)	MC	219 659-7700	Joseph B Grenchik	P M Grenchik	Margaret Drewniak	....	Thomas Justak	Ambrose Kapitan	....
Winchester (6)	MC	317 584-6845	Jack Fowler	....	Marilyn Pash	Jack Fowler	Leon Leach	Don Hesser	Jack Fowler
Winona Lake t (3)	CM	219 267-7581	David Wolkins	....	Charlene Black	Charlene Black	Ed Purrington	John Trier	Gary Baker
Yorktown t§ (4)	MC	317 759-8521	Larry Applegate	Marc R Mansfield	Miriam Kay Sidey	....	John A Myers	James Ross	Maurice Masters
Zionsville t (4)	MC	317 873-2469	Henry Cole	....	Beverly Harves	Beverly Harves	....	....	....
IOWA (130)									
Adel (3)	MC	515 993-4771	Walter Flinn	....	Jerry Roberts	....	Robert Cadwell	Willard D Hanson	....
Albia (4)	MC	515 932-2129	Bernard Carr	....	Carl E Gragg	Carl E Gragg	Warren Woollums	David Speck	Thomas Murphy
Algona (6)	MC	515 295-5115	Harold Van Allen	....	Garlene Schmidt	Garlene Schmidt	Donald Peterson	Eric Swalwell	Lewis G Giesking
Altoona (6)	MC	515 967-5136	L J Sam Wise	....	Bettie Ballard	Bettie Ballard	Gordon Gill	Acel Bristoll	John Sommers
Ames* (46)	CM	515 232-6210	F Paul Goodland	Steven L Schainker	Nancy Gibbons	Betty Jo Harker	Ralph Parks	Dennis Ballantine	Arnold Chantland
Anamosa (5)	MC	319 462-3773	Al Schnieder	....	Suzanne Marek	Peggy Conrad	Ivan Eden	Richard Stivers	Harold Huston
Ankeny* (15)	CM	515 964-5500	Ollie J Weigel	Reid S Charles	Joann Goins	Joann Goins	Tom Strait	Dennis Ballard	Jay Schreiner
Atlantic (8)	MC	712 243-4810	Harry P Richardson	....	Debbie L Wheatley	....	Kendal C Warne	....	F W Retz
Audubon (3)	MC	712 563-3269	Jay Dee Mendenhall	....	Mary Herrig	....	Clifton Petersen	Arnold Krauel	Steve Stetzel
Belle Plaine (3)	MC	319 444-2200	Robert O Burrows	....	Helen M Uchytil	....	Maurice Van Hamme	Jerry Dejoode	Robert Wolfe
Belmond*† (3)	CM	515 444-3386	....	Wayne R Pals	....	....	....	....	....
Bettendorf† (27)	MC	319 355-1865	William C Glynn	James W Strieck	James W Strieck	James W Strieck	Hans Goettsch	Keith Chandler	Gerald F Springer
Bloomfield (3)	MC	515 664-2260	Michael Auguspurger	....	Marilyn McElderry	Marilyn McElderry	Rick Piper	Bill Foglesong	Marcus Irven
Boone (13)	MC	515 432-4211	Elmer H Ohlmann	....	Audrey Veldhuizen	Audrey Veldhuizen	Richard Littell	Donald Hart	Norman Vegors
Buffalo* (1)	CM	319 381-2226	Lewis M Adams	Carol A Bernauer	Carol A Bernauer	....	Kenneth Anderson	Gage D Adams	Ralph J Jewett
Burlington* (30)	CM	319 753-8101	Wayne W Hogberg	W G Lawley	Richard W Cain	Douglas J Worden	William Ell	Theodore A Behne	S J Klassen
Camanche (5)	MC	319 259-8446	Paul R Willis Jr	....	Jane Munksgaard	....	B J Tyler	Gerald R Edwards	B J Tyler
Carlisle t (3)	MC	515 989-3224	Leslie Lane	....	Kenneth G Miller	....	Terry Campbell	Terry B Hardy	....
Carroll* (10)	CM	712 792-1000	Aurthur A Neu	Richard J Hierstein	Leon P Oswald	Leon P Oswald	Harold Grundmeier	Gary Harm	Randall M Krauel
Carter Lake (3)	MC	712 347-6320	John D Lesley	....	Doreen D Mowery	....	Carl Wilson	John A Bruno	John Waltrip
Cedar Falls (36)	MC	319 277-4166	Douglas C Sharp	....	Kenneth Tewalt	Kenneth Tewalt	Dale Holmes	Paul Hoffey	James Glover
Cedar Rapids (110)	MC	319 398-5012	Donald J Canney	....	Lois Keller	Robert McMahan	Edsel McMickle	Ray Baker	....
Centerville (7)	MC	515 437-4339	Donald L Scott	....	Martin E Games	....	Marlin E Henderson	John T Riddick	Laverne Thomas
Chariton* (5)	CM	515 774-5991	Wm Paul Marner	Bernard W Aulwes	Ruth A Ryun	....	Ronald C Smith	Jay A Fisher	....
Charles City (9)	MC	515 228-2631	Gerald R Fisher	....	Helen B Webster	Helen B Webster	Keith J Oldham	Dean A Shoars	Daniel H Barrett
Cherokee§ (7)	MC	712 225-5749	James Clabaugh	G T Bremicker Jr	Debra L Taylor	Debra L Taylor	James Bleakly	Norman Hill	....
Clarinda*† (5)	CM	712 542-2136	Harold L Davis	Robert L Bailey	Robert L Bailey	Robert L Bailey	Michael Reed	Lowell L Adkins	....
Clarion* (3)	CM	515 532-2847	Dennis Colson	W Bruce Bierma	W Bruce Bierma	....	Maurice Riley	Robert Shaw	....
Clear Lake City† (7)	MC	515 357-5267	Carl Hankenson	....	Thomas Lincoln	Thomas Lincoln	Jim Dyre	James Frampton	Jim Leasure
Clinton (33)	MC	319 242-7545	Charles F Tillema	James C Richardson	Jody E Smith	....	Gary L Thoms	Russell A Bentley	Eugene F Niebuhr
Clive§ (6)	MC	515 223-6220	O Gene Maddox	Gary R Lago	Marjorie S Lee	....	John Schiefer	G Dean Dymond	Willard J Wray Jr
Coralville (8)	MC	319 351-1266	M Kattchee	....	Helen Gaut	....	Gary Kinsinger	Donald M Ewalt	Donald Slothower
Council Bluffs* (56)	CM	712 328-4601	William Ballenger	Michael G Miller	Olga Arellano	Shirley Runte	Delbert Burdick	Edward Dinovo	William Bittner
Cresco (4)	MC	319 547-3101	Vince Teetshorn	....	Evelyn C Baldner	....	Vincent Hornberger	Thomas G Heath Jr	Dirk Jablonski
Creston (8)	MC	515 782-2000	Terry L Donanue	Dennis Howard	Donna Benson	Dennis Howard	Lowell Willets	Robert Kessler	Arthur Becker
Davenport§ (103)	MC	319 326-7711	Charles K Peart	Bruce F Romer	Ruth Reynolds	Kent Kolney	Robert Schick	Charles Borgstadt	Rex D Matthews
De Witt (5)	MC	319 659-3811	Leo Maynard	....	Kay Ann Goddard	....	John Burken	Richard L Peasley	Everett H Schroeder
Decorah (8)	MC	319 382-3651	David T Nelson	....	Patricia A Luren	....	Bruce Meyer	Al Etteldorf	....
Denison (7)	MC	712 263-3143	James R Lodwick	....	O H Webb	....	Myron Eggers	Robert Schraeder	....
Des Moines* (191)	CM	515 283-4111	Peter Crivaro	Richard A Wilkey	Donna Boetel-Baker	Charles O'Connor	Lee Williams	Billie B Wallace	John Bellizzi
Dubuque* (62)	CM	319 589-4100	James E Brady	W Kenneth Gearhart	Mary A Davis	A G Heitzman	William Miller	Robert J O'Brien	Francis A Murray
Dyersville† (4)	MC	319 875-7724	John J Kirsch	....	Eileen L Huberty	....	Leland Nebel	Allen Clouse	Gustave C Wilhelm
Eagle Grove (4)	MC	515 448-4343	Jana Amdahl	Paul J Niebur	Paul J Niebur	Keith Riley	Harry Archie Lalor	Curtis L Green	Carl Halverson
Eldora (3)	MC	515 858-5182	Everett N Baldus	Jeffrey L Kooistra	....	....	John McBride	James K Collins	Merle Manning
Eldridge§ (3)	MC	319 285-4841	Frank E Pancratz	Donald L Sandor	Jean A Schilling	....	Barry Braack	George Gil Hansen	Roger K Kirby
Emmetsburg§† (5)	MC	712 852-4030	Carroll Currans	Patrick Kliegl	Ms R Argabright	....	Robert McNally	Dale Briggs	Leo Gilman
Estherville (8)	MC	712 362-3574	Elmer Jacob	Steven D Woodley	Tom Noteboom II	Tom Noteboom II	David Knox	Robert Knox	....
Evansdale (5)	MC	319 232-6683	Fred M Saul	....	....	....	Kenneth Loftus	Dan Vance	....
Fairfield (9)	MC	515 472-6193	Robert L Rasmussen	....	John Brown	John Brown	Jack Cavenee	Frank Johnson	Robert D Moore
Forest City (4)	MC	515 582-3574	Eugene Morris	David E Nolton	Paul D Boock	....	Cecil Olson	Douglas Book	....
Fort Dodge (29)	CO	515 576-4551	James A Janvrin	Richard J Nielsen	Dennis W Milefchik	....	Willard Whitcome	Don Hensley	Ronald Kirchner
Fort Madison* (14)	CM	319 372-7700	John E Einspanjer	David E Johnston	Joann Herold	....	John Schier	William L Link	Warren D Barnum
Garner (3)	MC	515 923-2588	Ivan D Dodd	....	Mildred M Bredlow	....	James W Meyer	David L Martin	Bradley A Miller
Glenwood† (5)	MC	712 527-4717	Gene A Schatz	Dale L Harper	Nancy L West	Nancy L West	Willard Stivers	Kenneth L Mead	Michael Bengtson
Grinnell* (9)	CM	515 236-2605	David E McConnell	Theodore K Clausen	Gary Goddard	....	Dave Barns	James Ahrens	....
Grundy Center† (3)	MC	319 824-6118	Michael D Ralston	....	Vance Koerner	....	Roger Mooty	Francis Gutosky	Edwin F Gibson
Guttenberg* (2)	CM	319 252-1161	Karen P Merrick	James R Webb	James R Webb	....	Owen Pufahl	Glenn Witham	Theodore Petsche
Hampton (5)	MC	515 456-4853	Howard W Werner	....	Kenneth Herwig	....	M E Taylor	Bud Nelson	Duane Stoltz
Harlan (5)	MC	712 755-5137	O B Roecker	....	Susan L Lambert	Ray Chipman	Larry Gustason	Ronald Rose	Terry L Cox

Directory 1/10 continued

MUNICIPAL OFFICIALS IN ALL U.S. CITIES OVER 2,500[1]

City, 1980 population (000 omitted), form of government		Municipal phone number	Mayor	Appointed administrator	City clerk	Finance officer	Fire chief	Police chief	Public works director
IOWA (130) continued									
Hawarden (3)	MC	712 552-2565	Ivoran Noe	....	Jeffrey Pederson	Jeffrey Pederson	Mose Hendricks	Melvin Hulleman	Russel Harris
Hiawatha (5)	MC	319 393-1515	Keith Kress	....	Joan L Biederman	....	Hugh Carney	David Saari	....
Humboldt (5)	MC	515 332-3435	Leroy Jorgensen	....	R D Hake	....	Sherman Silbaugh	Darrell Wiegand	....
Ida Grove§ (2)	MC	712 364-2428	Ivan A O'Tool	Diane F Campbell	Diane F Campbell	Diane F Campbell	Don Wunschel	Don Gebers	Diane F Campbell
Independence (6)	MC	319 334-2780	Frank R Brimmer	....	N Clark Madison	....	Charles Conklin	Daniel H Schremser	Vernon Bud Hall
Indianola* (11)	CM	515 961-5361	Irene Richardson	Charles A Button	R I Long	....	Dean Hutt	Earl D Pace	....
Iowa City* (51)	CM	319 356-5000	John McDonald	Neal G Berlin	Marian Karr	Rosemary Vitosh	Robert Keating	Harvey D Miller	Charles Schmadeke
Iowa Falls* (6)	CM	515 648-2527	Rocco Lavalle	Terri Lea Schroeder	Terri Lea Schroeder	Raymond McMullen	Marlyn Humphrey	Dennis Hawkins	....
Jefferson (5)	MC	515 386-3111	Charles F Davis	Richard J Crayne	Richard J Crayne	....	Bill Ecklund	John Grasso	Richard J Crayne
Johnston§ (3)	MC	515 278-2344	Mary Ann Roberts	Donald K Coates	Betty A Mulvihill	....	James Powell	David W Davis	Robert D Flaws
Keokuk (14)	MC	319 524-2050	J M MacLaw	....	J A Finerty	J A Finerty	Donald Jenkins	Ramon N Weldon	Scott Fehseke
Knoxville* (8)	CM	515 842-3146	James Bell	Joseph H Salitros	Margaret Sharp	....	Duane Robuck	Charles Wooldridge	Gary Cowman
Lamoni (3)	MC	515 784-6311	Rollin Bridge	....	Cora A Mullins	....	Mark Ballantyne	....	Robert Colyer
Le Claire*† (3)	CM	319 289-5441	Robert J Scannell	Edwin N Choate	Judy Olsen	Marie Spinsby	Harvey Phillips	Robert Utley	Herman Orman
Le Mars* (8)	CM	712 546-7018	Floyd Hall	James C Payne	Beverly Langel	....	Wayne Shipper	Joseph Melnichak	Charles Eufers
Manchester (5)	MC	319 927-3636	Milt L Kramer	Kim D Leinbach	Karen K Cole	....	Douglas Palmer	Bruce A Trapp	....
Maquoketa* (6)	CM	319 652-2484	Alvin F Barker	Patrick Callahan	Weotha Hinz	....	James Franks	Ronald Evans	John Olson
Marion* (19)	CM	319 377-1581	Wm J Grundy Jr	Carl E Ramey	Joy Sparenborg	....	James Ford	Christopher Ebert	John Bender
Marshalltown (27)	MC	515 754-5701	Stan Brown	....	Mary Skartvedt	Elaine Gundacker	James Hilsabeck	James Wilkinson	....
Mason City (30)	MC	515 423-2614	Kenneth E Kew	....	Carlene Davis	Charles B Hammen	Ron Van Horn	Eugene A Kleinow	Timothy Paranto
Missouri Valley (3)	MC	712 642-3502	Robert G Thompson	Bob Brooks	Vernon C Spilker	....	William Bugenhagen	Darrel D Cates	....
Monticello (4)	MC	319 465-4230	Keith Stamp	....	Mary Hunt	Mary Hunt	Clarence Goedken	Richard Castro	Keith Hagen
Mount Pleasant (7)	MC	319 385-4616	(not reporting)						
Mount Vernon (3)	MC	319 895-8742	James Hickey	....	Donald Siggins	Jay Fordyce	Thomas Kleineck	Marvin Kuehl	Donald Siggins
Muscatine* (23)	CM	319 264-1550	Donald R Platt	Soren Wolff	Soren Wolff	Deborah Rauh	Paul Zigenhorn	Jerry Tesmond	Ray Childs
Nevada† (6)	MC	515 382-5466	Burnell D Hagen	Darlene C Pallesen	Darlene C Pallesen	Darlene C Pallesen	Steven M Herr	Ray A Couser	....
New Hampton (4)	MC	515 394-2109	Harold F Gilbert	....	Robert P Gilbert	Robert P Gilbert	Peter Willadsen Jr	Duane Lampson	Donald J Markle
Newton* (15)	CM	515 792-4604	Robert L Smith	Rollie J Boeding	Rollie J Boeding	Sue Peters	Stacy Backus	Michael Quinn	Ken Clausen
Norwalk† (3)	MC	515 981-0228	David D Hoskins	....	Merle E Huff	....	....	M W Richardson	....
Oelwein* (8)	CM	319 283-5440	Beth MacFarlane	Steven H Kendall	Steven H Kendall	Steven H Kendall	Wallace A Rundle	James Fortsch	Lavern Varguson
Onawa (3)	MC	712 423-1181	George B King	Pearl G Doll	Pearl G Doll	Pearl G Doll	Jeff Sander	Cole B Shatswell	....
Orange City (5)	CM	712 737-4885	Robert Dunlop	Allen Roos	Don Schreur	....	Alfred Dykstra	Gordon Abels	....
Osage (4)	MC	515 732-3709	Elgin G Enabnit	....	Delia Erdmann	Delia Erdmann	Dave Smith	Edward Viskocil	William Bollinger
Osceola (4)	MC	515 342-2377	(not reporting)						
Oskaloosa§ (11)	MC	515 673-9431	Robert Lynn	James R Huff	Marilyn Sears	Marilyn Sears	Willard Ellis	Jim Brummel	Lyle Boender
Ottumwa (27)	CO	515 683-0600	Jerry L Parker	....	Ann Cullinan	Ed Moline	Frank Sylvester	Phil Gates	Darrell Adams
Pella (8)	MC	515 628-4173	(not reporting)						
Perry (7)	MC	515 465-2481	George P Soumas	....	Colleen Bice	Colleen Bice	....	Jim D Smith	William Simmer
Pleasant Hill (3)	MC	515 262-9368	Richard J Shaffer	....	Mark W Miller	Mark W Miller	Frank Grant Jr	Robert G Evans	Ronald A Brandt
Red Oak§ (7)	MC	712 623-4908	Ray Gustafson	Ronald A Crisp	Ronald A Crisp	....	Kenneth Wise	Elmer Ecthernach	....
Rock Rapids§ (3)	MC	712 472-2511	Duane L Moser	William G Tobin	....	....	Max Henry	James P Kille	....
Rock Valley§ (3)	MC	712 476-5707	Maurice Van Voorst	Wm J Van Maanen	Wm J Van Maanen	Wm J Van Maanen	Herman Dirksen	Dennis Feauto	Wm J Van Maanen
Sac City (3)	MC	712 662-7593	E Lynn Minnmann	Gary C Mahannah	....	....	James Joe Johnston	Michael Petricca	Robert Scheffler
Sanborn§ (1)	MC	712 729-3842	Don Kroese	Bret K Warnke	Bret K Warnke	Bret K Warnke	Randy Lyman	Gary Grapevine	Bret K Warnke
Sheldon*† (5)	CM	712 324-4651	Raymond Youngers	William Rush	Dorothy Mitchell	....	Merlynn Miller	Bill Van Rennes	Eldor Schuerman
Shenandoah* (6)	CM	712 246-4411	K R Norton	Merrill J Kruse	Merrill J Kruse	James Winegardner	....	Richard Hunt	....
Sibley* (3)	CM	712 754-2541	John Massa	Howard C Parrott	Dolores Fink	Howard C Parrott	Ted Krull	....	....
Sioux Center* (5)	CM	712 722-0761	William L Mouw	Darrel Rensink	Darrel Rensink	Eldon Westra	Stanley Altena	Paul Adkins	Harold Schiebout
Sioux City* (82)	CM	712 279-6102	John Van Dyke	J R Castner	George W Gross	John Meyers	John P Lovaas	Gerald P Donovan	William W Amundson
Spencer (12)	MC	712 262-6490	Edward K Johnson	....	Donna M Fisher	Donna M Fisher	Stewart Mackie	Don Wolford	Harold Sunday
Spirit Lake*† (4)	CM	712 336-1871	Robert Boettcher	Peter Hegeman	Peter Hegeman	Peter Hegeman	Robert H Bruett	Duane A Yager	Robert Kivela
Storm Lake* (9)	CM	712 732-5700	Wilbur Tucker	Clarence W Krepps	J A Fitzpatrick	....	Ronald C Wilson	Don Slazinik	....
Story City§ (3)	MC	515 733-2121	George Toft	Steven Carter	Pat Twedt	....	Michael Ose	Bruce Kann	Jim Skare
Tama† (3)	MC	515 484-3822	Ralph B Franklin	....	Inez Novotny	....	Larry Eisentrager	Shane Bingham	Richard Ervin
Tipton (3)	MC	319 886-6187	Wayne Deerberg	Robert E Snavely	Lora Ward	Roberta L Parker	Robert W Peck	Mike L Young	E Lee Johnson
Urbandale* (18)	CM	515 278-3900	E J Giovannetti	Robert L Layton	Margaret Parsons	Sandi Tompkins	Jack Gooding	David Hamlin	Cliff Gardiner
Villisca (1)	CM	712 826-2282	Janis Sue Enarson	....	Sharon Jo King	....	Michael Jackson	....	John Elliot
Vinton (5)	MC	319 472-4707	V E Blank	Dennis Dancker	Barbara J Smith	Barbara J Smith	Dave Hite	Carl Pippert	....
Washington (7)	MC	319 653-6584	Raymond L Minick	....	Cohen L Bond	....	Robert D Zager	Gene S Beinke	Stephen W Dodd
Waterloo (76)	MC	319 291-4311	Del Bowers	....	Larry Burger	Tom Campbell	Jerry Olson	Kenneth Huck	....
Waukon (4)	MC	319 568-2583	Thomas D Stone	....	Merlin F Kruger	Merlin F Kruger	Phillip Stone	Loren R Fiet	Francis D Kessel
Waverly* (8)	CM	319 352-4252	Evelyn Rathe	Michael R Schneider	Michael R Schneider	Julie Luther	John Ingersoll	Arthur Simpson	David M Six
Webster City* (9)	CM	515 832-5701	Donald E Bruer	Gerald K Kent	Gerald K Kent	Gerald K Kent	Terry A Johnston	Hans Dickinson	Greg Malmstrom
West Burlington (3)	MC	319 752-5451	Leland F Haring Jr	James H Spradling	Barbara J Benge	Lois E Martin	Robert E Elliott	Robert Linden	....
West Des Moines* (22)	CM	515 223-3250	George M Mills	John P Bryan	Jerry D Proudfit	Jerry D Proudfit	Randall L Bracken	Frederick V Carson	Lonnie D Hawbaker
West Liberty* (3)	CM	319 627-2418	Larry G Combs	Michael E Tholen	Michael E Tholen	Michael E Tholen	Ken Morrison	Marcus Montagna Sr	James Garner
West Point§ (1)	MC	319 837-6313	James C Crago	Dean Torreson	....	....	Delbert Moeller	Austin O'Brien	....
West Union (3)	MC	319 422-3320	Ann Hutchens	Sue Freidhof	Sue Freidhof	....	Charles Broghammer	Marvin Youngblood	....
Wilton§† (3)	MC	319 732-2115	Wilbert H Stoelk	R E Wardenburg	Shirley I Wacker	....	James Sheetz	Art F W Giese	Robert Coffey
Windsor Heights§ (6)	MC	515 279-3662	C D Millsap	Marjorie A Webb	....	....	A E Hunter	Wm Hitchcock	Robert E Burris
Winterset† (4)	MC	515 462-1422	Bernard Morrisey	....	Mark J Nitchals	....	Jerry Mease	Albert Lehman	....
KANSAS (109)									
Abilene* (7)	CM	913 263-2550	Clifford H Asling	Stan B Stewart	Mildred E Hanson	Mildred E Hanson	Dean Annis	Fred Garten	....
Andale (1)	MC	316 445-2351	Ron Seiler	....	Shirley Stuever	Kathleen O Scheer	....	Earl D Lathrom	James W Davidson
Andover (3)	MC	316 733-1303	Zack Wilkerson	Patricia M Stuenkel	Patricia M Stuenkel	Jane Beach	....	Myron Moen	James Dunn
Anthony (3)	CO	316 842-5434	Wilford Wyckoff	Jack C Scott	Robt E Henderson	....	Roger Andrews	Richard Happ	....
Arkansas City* (13)	CM	316 442-0280	Vern Case	Curtis H Snow	Rodney Franz	Rodney Franz	W E Rowe	William R Rice	....
Atchison* (11)	CM	913 367-5081	Norm Ellis	William H Sachs Jr	Mark Thelen	Mark Thelen	Michael E McDermed	Ronald E Pickman	Joe L McCoy
Augusta* (7)	CM	316 775-6301	Robert J Shryock	H Homer Bair	Elsie George	Elsie George	Steve Shafer	Steve Shafer	C R Dexter
Baxter Springs† (5)	MC	316 856-2114	Elmo Burrows	....	Barbara Spradling	Floyd Chase	Bill Lewman	Charles Scott	....
Belleville* (3)	CM	913 527-2288	Harold G Wilber	Richard D Ash	Catherin Derowitsch	Catherin Derowitsch	Mickey Ferguson	Martin Awalt	Donald Danielson
Beloit§ (4)	MC	913 738-3551	Don Pierce	Dan Moellenberndt	George Colby	....	Arnold Krone	Dave Sutter	....
Bonner Springs* (6)	CM	913 422-1020	Reece Kuhn	Robert W Evans	Sue Stinnett	Sue Stinnett	Warren Hanks	Frank Robertson II	John W Wasson
Burlington (3)	MC	316 364-5334	Floyd Lewis	....	Marion J Logan	....	Terry Reams	Ralph Romig	....
Chanute* (11)	CM	316 431-9300	John M Scully	Richard A Williams	Jim Youngberg	....	Jimmie Haines	Vernon Shultz	Howard Knox
Cheney§ (1)	MC	316 542-3622	Robert E Taylor	Douglas Fisher	Lois I Marteney	....	Lloyd Bledsoe	Robert Davidson	Randall Oliver
Cherryvale (3)	CO	316 336-2776	Warren Dewitt	....	Ruth Blome	W Alva Dodson	Darrel Trollope	Tim Downum	Charles L Caldwell
Clay Center (5)	MC	913 632-5454	(not reporting)						
Clearwater§ (2)	MC	316 584-2311	Don C Roth	Yvonne E Coon	Delores Williams	....	Wes Tackkett	John A Touhey	James E Murphy

Directory 1/10 continued — MUNICIPAL OFFICIALS IN ALL U.S. CITIES OVER 2,500[1]

City, 1980 population (000 omitted), form of government	Municipal phone number	Mayor	Appointed administrator	City clerk	Finance officer	Fire chief	Police chief	Public works director
KANSAS (109) continued								
Cofteyville* (15) CM	316 251-7000	Jack Anderson	William A Snell	Stacey Wood	Daniel Bryant	Gordon Fry	Otto Ivy	Arthur C Hyatt
Colby* (6) CM	913 462-3973	James L Kriss	Jack Heaton	Pearl Smith	Pearl Smith	Ivan Lee	Mark Spray	Cloyd Bray
Columbus† (3) MC	316 429-2159	W E Schaiff	....	Gail Houser	Robert Teel	Haskel Carter	Carl Cristiansen Jr	Gary Smith
Concordia* (7) CM	913 243-2670	William B Smith	Carl Metzger	Verna Scott	....	Phil Schlup	Dennis Rohr	Tom Fisher
Derby§ (10) MC	316 788-1519	Don Storck	Ward R Clements Jr	Geneva Moore	Ward R Clements Jr	Sam Austn	Delbert Fowler	Ed Kopyscinski
Dodge City* (18) CM	316 225-1391	Louis Sanchez	Robert Livingston	Ronald Thornburg	Ronald Thornburg	Geo G Daeschner	Oakley C Ralph	Harold Leedom
Edwardsville† (3) MC	913 441-3707	Lindy Trent	....	Helen M Beashore	....	Leland Jones	Dennis Robertson	....
El Dorado* (11) CM	316 321-9100	Edward L Blake	Richard B Chesney	Adam R Collins	Adam R Collins	Victor S Marshall	Victor S Marshall	Oral Taylor
Ellinwood§ (3) MC	316 564-3161	Ronald McCrary	Glen E Welden	Chris Brown	....	Art Huslig	Jerry Kaiser	Tom Wornkey
Emporia* (25) CM	316 342-5105	Clark Allemang	J Brent McFall	Stephen L Anderson	Steve Commons	Claude Lang Jr	Larry Blomenkamp	Lee Stolfus
Eudora (3) MC	913 542-2095	James Hoover	....	Arlene Lawson	....	Benny Dean	Bill Long	....
Eureka† (3) CO	316 583-6511	James L Saunders	....	Ruby Foster	Ray A McIlvain	Leo Butler	Ronald D Tompkins	....
Fairway (5) MC	913 262-0350	(not reporting)						
Fort Scott* (9) CM	316 223-0550	Claude W Norris	Donald D Munsell	Wilda Insley	Jon B Garrison	Don Hunziker	Dale Ogran	Charles Elliott
Fredonia† (3) CO	316 378-2231	William Falstad	....	Karen L Shinn	Lee W Spohn	Calvin Studebaker	Gerry Harding	....
Frontenac (3) MC	316 231-9210	O'Wen L O'Hara	....	Richard W Cicero	....	....	Carl Flora	....
Galena (4) MC	316 783-5265	James Bankson	....	Barbara Wilkins	Colleen Colgrove	Bill Hall	Bill Lyerla	Howard Jarvis
Garden City* (18) CM	316 276-8263	Bonnie Talley	Deane P Wiley	Timothy V Knoll	Timothy V Knoll	Allan Shelton	Jimmy Grenz	....
Garden Plain (1) MC	316 535-2563	Eugene H Heimerman	....	Betty L Rausch	....	Victor Simon	Armando Gutierrez	....
Garnett* (3) CM	913 448-5496	Claron G Cole	Richard G Doran	Joyce E Martin	Joyce E Martin	Gary Benjamin	Lawrence Kellerman	Paul Smitheran
Girard (3) CO	316 724-8918	Frankie D Dunnick	....	Jean M Bolin	Jack T Newberry	Joe Sands	Robert Orender	Tony Dechario
Goddard§ (1) MC	316 794-2441	Francis Langton	Douglas Fisher	Jackie Rundell	....	....	Merle J Nelson	Lyle Warfield
Goodland* (6) CM	913 899-2372	Wade Barnett	Keith D Jantz	Archie Wicke	Archie Wicke	Robert D Cowan	Steve Fenner	Eddie D Chatfield
Great Bend§ (17) MC	316 792-2121	Gail L Lupton	Howard D Partington	Howard Lindberg	....	Harold Walter	Dean Akings	....
Hays* (16) CM	913 625-2815	Melly Schmidt	Kenneth R Carter	Dorothy Soderblom	Dorothy Soderblom	Wayne Schwartz	Lawrence Younger	Leo Wellbrock
Haysville§ (8) MC	316 524-3243	Glenn O Crum	Charles F Vogt	V Faye Mallory	....	....	J Earl Kitchings	Bob Shipe
Herington* (3) CM	913 258-2271	Tom L Dutton	W A Wetmore	Debra Wendt	....	Terry Stroda	Jerry Payne	....
Hesston§ (3) MC	316 327-4412	Jos Swartzendruber	Maurice Bowersox	Jean Krehbiel	....	Weldon Bachman	Mickey DeHook	....
Hiawatha† (4) CM	913 742-7417	Jerry E Young	James M Haag Jr	Lois Heller	Gerald C Speidel	Harold Robertson	Curtis Shaver	....
Hillsboro (3) MC	316 947-3162	Harold J Wiebe	....	Janice K Meisinger	....	Wayne Lowry	Byron McCarty	Johnnie Liles
Hoisington* (4) CM	316 653-4125	Oliver M Sears	T M DeArman III	Mary Joan Ray	....	Vernon Skolaut	Glenn J Brack	Leroy P Rube
Holton*† (3) CM	913 364-2721	Keith Wagoner	C E Williams	Virginia Zibell	....	Warren Baum	Joan Winters	Rob Stephenson
Horton* (2) CM	913 486-2681	....	John Ruh	....	....	....	....	....
Hugoton (3) MC	316 544-8531	Robert Gill	....	Tom Hicks	Tom Hicks	....	R B Walter	Everett Rowden
Hutchinson* (40) CM	316 665-2614	Ralph Gingerich	George W Pyle	Vernon Stallman	Vernon Stallman	Dallas Jones	Jack Heidebrecht	Dennis Clennan
Independence* (11) CM	316 331-2500	Peggy Coder	Paul A Sasse	Fred Gress	Fred Gress	Clyde Huff	Lee Bynum	....
Iola† (7) CO	316 365-3211	John L Carder	....	V C Perkins	....	Tince Little	John Maier	Les Olm
Junction City* (19) CM	913 238-3103	James Smothers	John F Higgins	Frank Galliher	Frank Galliher	William D Ritter	Jerry Smith	Ernest Oppenlander
Kansas City* (161) MC	913 573-5000	John E Reardon	W James Medin	David T Isabell	David T Isabell	Lawrence Bowers	Allan P Meyers	Gary C Stubbs
Kingman (4) CO	316 532-3111	R L Pulliam	....	Mildred Boswell	....	Bydus Taber	Paul S Kalmar	Ben Payton
Kinsley* (2) CM	316 659-3611	Gary Meadows	Greg L Sparks	Elizabeth Brown	Ethyl Steele	Buford Brodbeck	James Kerr	Newton J Baker Jr
La Crosse* (2) CM	913 222-2511	Wendell Brozek	Dudley Schutte	Joan Dreher	Harry Grass	Armen Ideker	Steve Schroeder	Dudley Schutte
Lansing (5) MC	913 727-3233	Kenneth W Bernard	....	Regina L Marshall	Robert S Wagner	Jack Fitch	Michael W Smith	John Boley Jr
Larned* (5) CM	316 285-2149	W R Brenner	Ronald D Arnold	Vicki Gillett	Ronald D Arnold	Ralph Johnson	John E Slack	Ronald Arnold
Lawrence* (53) CM	913 841-7722	Ernest E Angino	Buford M Watson Jr	Vera Mercer	Ethan A Smith	James McSwain	R R Stanwix	George Williams
Leavenworth* (34) CM	913 682-9201	Lee Farnsworth	Harold A Anderson	M B Strange	G Harold Dawson	Richard Patzwald	Wm McKeel	David J Pennington
Leawood§ (13) MC	913 642-5555	Kent E Crippin	Richard J Garofano	Jinny Oberlander	Richard J Garofano	Jerry Strack	J Stephen Cox	Tom Bieszczat
Lenexa (19) MC	913 492-8800	Rich Becker	Donald R Capper	Sandra Howell	Sandra Howell	Kenneth Hobbs	John L Foster	Charles C Pond
Liberal* (15) CM	316 624-0101	Don Jones	Alan Morris	Craig Simons	Craig Simons	Milton L Rice	Rick Kistner	....
Lindsborg§ (3) MC	913 227-3355	Leland E Olson	Ann Gottberg	Ann Gottberg	....	G Willard Keding	Burl D Croomes Jr	Robert G Peterson
Lyons (4) MC	316 257-2320	Paul E Jones	Dewey D Breese	Norma A Miller	....	Jim Miller	Dennis L Luck	David Kendrick
Madison§† (1) MC	316 437-2556	Donald Birtciel	Leonard Biggs	Beth Rawlings	....	....	....	....
Maize§ (1) MC	316 722-7561	Dennie C Bretz	James M Heinicke	Karen Fitzmier	Susan Ethridge	....	Ed Green	William T Applegate
Manhattan* (33) CM	913 537-0056	David J Fiser	M Don Harmon	Gregg W Gibson	Bernie Hayen	William D Smith	....	Bruce K McCallum
Marysville (4) MC	913 562-5331	James L Lindeen	....	Jay M Funk	Jay M Funk	Charles A Lindeen	Randy Wiler	....
McCracken* (..) CM	913 394-2229	Byron Gilbert	Mildred Anderson	Mildred Anderson	....	Charles Jacobs	Joe Casey	....
McPherson (12) MC	316 241-6300	Delbert E Crabb	....	William Goering	William Goering	Lawrence Bruzda	Waldean Vincent	Gerry Bley
Merriam§ (11) MC	913 722-3330	Irene B French	Josephine McCauley	Barbara Young	Josephine McCauley	Richard Fredrick	James R Browning	Harold Hester
Mission (9) MC	913 722-3685	Sylvester Powell Jr	....	Suzanne G Gibbs	Suzanne G Gibbs	Murrel F Bruce	Robert A Sturm	Stephen L Weeks
Mission Hills§ (4) MC	913 362-9620	Hoyt H Thompson	Ray H Johnson	W M Schaefer	Ray H Johnson	R Wilcox	Louis LeManske	Ray H Johnson
Mulvane§ (4) MC	316 777-1111	James P Ford	Edward W Elam	Roberta Kimble	Wanda D Wells	Merle S McKee	William J Simmons	....
Neodesha (3) CO	316 325-2828	Murlin Blackstun	....	Jovonnah Boecker	....	Leland Reedy	Wes Sade	....
Newton* (16) CM	316 283-6900	Merrill Raber	Jay P Newton Jr	John Torline	John Torline	Clayton Sadowski	Dwain Kelsch	Gene Smallwood
Norton (3) MC	913 877-3355	H L Deines	Dennis McMullen	Carol Wertenberger	Carol Wertenberger	Alvin Mapes	Elmer Howell	Dennis McMullen
Olathe* (37) CM	913 782-2600	Herman Cline	Lee Brodbeck	Howard Pevehouse	Ron Mason	Dan Williams	Frank Barnes	Bill Ramsey
Osage City (3) MC	913 528-3714	Dwight Thompson	....	Nina D Gragg	....	John Earhart	Forrest W Gragg	....
Osawatomie* (4) CM	913 755-2146	Sherman W Cole	....	Edith Kester	....	Marion G Maxwell	John Cragg	Marion G Maxwell
Ottawa* (11) CM	913 242-2190	James R McCrea	David Watkins	Orlin W Smith	Orlin W Smith	Oren K Skiles	Oren K Skiles	Robert B Moore
Overland Park* (82) CM	913 381-5252	Ed Eilert	Donald E Pipes	Bernice Crummett	Bernice Crummett	....	Myron Scafe	Dennis Garrett
Paola* (5) CM	913 294-2497	William C Lawrence	Edward E Dawson	Jill A Holmes	Paul Grabill	Robert Harris	Bruce L Bowker	Lucky Meisel
Park City§ (4) MC	316 744-2026	Raymond Reiss	Bruce McCandless	Jerrie Molina	....	....	Ace Van Wey	Fred Sherwood
Parsons* (13) CM	316 421-5500	J William Orr	Dennis R Tinberg	Mildred C Vance	Mildred C Vance	Dean Sailsbury	Thomas D Barrett	....
Phillipsburg (3) MC	913 543-5234	Jim Kramer	....	Virginia J John	....	Joel Hiesterman	Willard Tyrrell	....
Pittsburg* (19) CM	316 231-4100	Ronnie Beach	Michael A Conduff	Karen K Garman	Robert K Biles	William J Scott	Ralph W Shanks	John D Van Gorden
Prairie Village§ (25) MC	913 381-6464	Sue Weltner	Barbara Vernon	Robert Kieber	Barbara Vernon	....	Louis Lemanske	Jerald Robnett
Pratt* (7) CM	316 672-5571	Quentin Hannawald	John S Beckman	Curt Wood	Curt Wood	Berkley Miller	Paul Garst Jr	....
Roeland Park (8) MC	913 722-2600	Michael E Shartzer	....	Gail J Sweany	....	....	Kenneth A Carpenter	....
Russell* (5) CM	913 483-6311	Roger W Williams	Glenn E Hill	Judy M Sargent	Judy M Sargent	Earl Hemphill	Bobby E Tyler	Frank Peirano
Sabetha§ (2) MC	913 284-2158	....	Royal R Kimmel	....	....	....	....	....
Salina* (42) CM	913 823-2277	Charles B Roth	Rufus L Nye	D L Harrison	D L Harrison	Dave Robertson	John W Woody	Dean Boyer
Scott City (4) MC	316 872-5322	Dainiel G Weides	....	Bertha Paul	....	J Kenneth Hoover	Peter Massey	Preston Stewart
Shawnee* (30) CM	913 631-2500	Thomas Soetaert	Gary K Montague	Barbara J Yardley	Lee Meyer	Jim Farthing	Charles J Stump	Dan L Noland
St. Marys* (2) CM	913 437-2311	Mary L Schumaker	Henry W Beseau	Jodeane Reese	....	James Keating	Gary Zinn	Donald Burrous
Sterling* (2) CM	316 278-3411	Nevin McMurphy	Randy A Wetmore	Ms E N Randles	....	Carl Vagts	Ronald R Groth	....
Stockton* (2) CM	913 425-6703	Kenneth Forssberg	Richard Nienstedt	Leta M Bouchey	Richard Nienstedt	Francis Cadoret	Gene Axelson	Leroy McLaughlin
Topeka (115) CO	913 295-3940	Douglas S Wright	....	Norma Robbins	Charles E Holt	Joe Douglas	Robert Weinkauf	Dave Gingrich
Ulysses§ (5) MC	316 356-4600	Bill Rogers	Gary Burr	Paula Shapland	....	Robert Spain	Darrell Pflughoft	Charles Cantrell
Valley Center§ (3) CM	316 755-1231	Marcelyn M Harris	Mac D Manning Jr	Carol A Reffner	....	Bob Tormey	Al Pitts	Michael R Freed
Wamego* (3) CM	913 456-9119	James B Meinhardt	Lyle H Dresher	Leroy Stewart	Sarah J Zoeller	Michael J Coon	Kenneth Seager	Claude Asbury
Wellington* (8) CM	316 326-3631	Kermit Quillen	Craig H Hubler	Joan Martin	....	Darle D Robinson	Rodney Oldridge	....

Directory 1/10 continued

MUNICIPAL OFFICIALS IN ALL U.S. CITIES OVER 2,500[1]

City, 1980 population (000 omitted), form of government	Municipal phone number	Mayor	Appointed administrator	City clerk	Finance officer	Fire chief	Police chief	Public works director
KANSAS (109) continued								
Wichita* (279) CM	316 268-4105	Robert G Knight	Eugene H Denton	Donald C Gisick	Russell L Brenner	Jim Sparr	Richard Lamunyon	David Stowe
Winfield* (11) CM	316 221-3060	Bill Dexter	David E Warren	Donald D Drennan	Dale Meyer	George Gurley	E D Winebrenner	....
KENTUCKY (112)								
Alexandria (5) MC	606 635-4125	Roger Steffen	James C Wolfe	Bill Smith	Susan Weinel	Val Lederer	Jack Bailey	Gene Studer
Ashland* (27) CM	606 325-8571	Everett B Reeves	Ronald W McBride	Robert W Johnson	P Gregory Walters	James C Hogsten	Tom E Kelley	J R Murphy
Barbourville (3) MC	606 546-3404	Charles Buchanan	....	Debbie Mills	Charles Buchanan	James Tye	Wilbert D Hughes	....
Bardstown (6) MC	502 348-5947	Guthrie Wilson	Larry Hamilton	Lonnie G Parrott	Lonnie G Parrott	Arch Pendergrass Jr	Robert L Sallee	Andrew Wolf
Beaver Dam (3) MC	502 274-7106	David C Taylor	Wendell Spencer	Carol J Vice	Deborah K Casey	Rodger Burgess	Alvin Tate	Wendell Spencer
Bellevue (8) MC	606 431-8888	Willard Hundemer	Donald Martin	Myrna Frischholz	Willard Hundemer	Jack Krogman	Elmer Corbin	Randall Grosch
Benton (4) MC	502 527-9338	(not reporting)						
Berea§ (8) MC	606 986-4976	C F Kerby	Gene Stinchcomb	Patricia D Abrams	Gene Stinchcomb	Jerry B Simpson	Billie R Moseley	Bill Hale
Bowling Green* (40) CM	502 782-2489	Charles Hardcastle	Chas W Coates	Orpha Davis	Kirby Ramsey	Hoyt Miller	Gary Raymer	James L Chaffee
Campbellsville (9) MC	502 465-7011	Robert L Miller	....	Donald Gaines	....	Jimmy E Cox	Kenneth Adams	....
Carrollton† (4) MC	502 732-4001	Charles W Webster	....	Perry M Harrell	Mable Shirley	Jack C Miles	Delbert Hudson	....
Catlettsburg† (3) MC	606 739-5223	Gary B Hunley	....	Kathy R Bennett	Pauline Hunt	Linzy Runyon	Ray F Castle	....
Central City§ (5) MC	502 754-5097	John A Lile	Kenneth Layman	Mildred E Tucker	....	Ferrell Christmas	Keith Nunley	....
Columbia (4) MC	502 384-2501	W J Flowers Jr	....	Jane B Akin	....	Mike Glasgow	Edwin Taylor	....
Corbin* (8) CM	606 528-1703	F D Jack Heath	Maurice A Ramsey	Betty Joe Perkins	....	Ova Hollingsworth	Philip L Martin	....
Covington* (49) CM	606 292-2236	Thomas Beehan	Donald B Eppley	Vivian Willman	Gregory H Engelman	Donald E Brown	Art Heeger	Robert Issenmann
Cumberland (4) MC	606 589-2106	Gene Mastin	....	Alice Hendrickson	Alice Hendrickson	Joe Carruba	Arthur Adams	Bob Bruner
Cynthiana (6) CO	606 234-4226	Melvin E Hampton	....	Janice F Tolle	William R Horn	Gregory T Lemons	Joe R Barkley	Joe Blackaby
Danville* (13) CM	606 236-2591	Roy W Arnold	Edward F Music	Dorothy Vangilder	....	Russell Phillips	Jim Ryan	Luther Galloway
Dawson Springs (3) MC	502 797-2781	Bethel N Morris	....	Denise W Ridley	....	Kenneth R Jackson	Barry E Boucher	Roger Rose
Dayton (7) MC	606 491-1600	G H Lynn	....	Geraldine Heeg	Geraldine Heeg	Charles Spreter	Gerald T Early	Earl Glasscock
Douglass Hills (4) MC	502 245-3600	Sharon Beals Leezer	....	Faye H Tanner	Thomas J Breslin	....	....	....
Edgewood (7) MC	606 331-5910	Louis A Noll	William Feeley	Bettie Kirst	Joseph Linton	Joseph Messmer	Charles Dickerson	Tim Bayer
Elizabethtown (15) MC	502 765-6121	Michael B Carroll	Charles A Ouellette	Elnora Fulkerson	Steve Park	Clifford Bowen	Edwin Tucker	William Owen
Elsmere (7) MC	606 341-7911	Albert Wermeling	....	Nancy Bowman	John Arrasmith Jr	Robert Landrum	William Hiler	Chester Brown
Erlanger (14) MC	606 727-2525	Fred H Thomas	Terry N Sapp	Patricia A Frakes	Mary E Golatzki	Jack Scheben	Orville J Johnson	Leon E Ryle
Flatwoods (8) MC	606 836-9661	T L Groves	....	Lucille Wright	Bob Caudill	J C Hughes	Edward J Kirk	Louis Maynard
Flemingsburg† (3) MC	606 845-5951	Kenneth Fern	Phillip Shay	James Berry	James Berry	John Byron	Thomas Helphenstine	Paul Schwartz
Florence§ (16) MC	606 371-5491	Roger W Rolfes	Bruce W Janken	Betsy R Conrad	Leon Munson	Donald Roberts	Charles R Callen	Robert Webster
Fort Mitchell§ (7) MC	606 331-1212	William H Goetz	John H Holman Jr	Dorothy Kuebbing	William Goetz	Victor Dietz	Larry Jones	Robert Lubrecht
Fort Thomas§ (16) MC	606 441-1055	Fred W Erschell Jr	David K Noran	Dorothy A Ivie	Elesteen Hagar	William E Dieckman	Norman H Hughes	Hershel Roell
Fort Wright (4) MC	606 331-1700	John J McCormack	Elmer A Muth	Elmer A Muth	Jean Warken	Robert Becker	Gene Weaver	Elmer Muth
Frankfort* (26) CM	502 875-8500	James C Burch	Paul H Royster	Ann C Hoover	James C Rogers	Joseph Jennings	Ted W Evans	Dennis E Minks
Franklin (8) MC	502 586-4497	Larry T Freas	....	Carol West	Kathy Gettings	Bobby Turner	Bruce Slate	Henry West
Fulton* (3) CM	502 472-1320	Kenneth Z Turner	John L Arntz	Barbara Rice	Bettie Robey	Richard Hartz	Milford Jobe	Bill McChesney
Georgetown† (11) MC	502 863-1707	Charles E Lenahan	....	Lucille Pollet	Maurice Alsop	Richard Covington	Eddie Chesser	Martin C Bramlett
Glasgow† (13) MC	502 651-5131	Luska J Twyman	Les Settle	Les Settle	Les Settle	Kenneth Pace	Jimmy Smith	James Atnip
Grayson (3) MC	606 474-6651	Frank Prater	....	Martha Lemaster	....	Billy B Jackson	Gary McClain	....
Greenville (5) MC	502 338-3966	Ben Topmiller Sr	Harold Sumner	Harold Sumner	Charles Dukes	Gary L Aders	Darrell R Curry	....
Harlan (3) MC	606 573-2912	L C Howard	....	Claudia Taylor	....	Bill Simms	Vernon Howard	Ken Hicks
Harrodsburg† (7) MC	606 734-2383	Charles E Carr	....	Marquita E Carey	Charles Yeast	Jack Trower	Timothy Bryant	B M Royalty
Hartford (3) MC	502 298-3612	Hayward Spinks	....	Mareta Andreas	....	Bobby Chinn	Daniel T McEnroe	Forrest D Jameson
Hazard*† (5) CM	606 436-3171	William D Gorman	Paul Feltner	Marbeth Nunn	Greeba Ven Davis	Wendell Ray Merrill	Edgar B Reynolds	Carlos Combs
Henderson* (25) CM	502 827-5671	William L Newman	Russell Sights	Theresa B Crafton	Robert N Hall	Charles Trodglen	Larry Ivie	Larry Fulkerson
Hickman*† (3) CM	502 236-2535	Joe H Rumfelt	Dan McKinnis	Lisa Prather	Dan McKinnis	Bill Ramsey	Henry White	Alvis DeHart
Highland Heights (4) MC	606 441-8575	(not reporting)						
Hillview (5) MC	502 587-3131	R L Carter	....	Myra Curry	....	....	Randall Hay	....
Hopkinsville (27) MC	502 887-4000	Sherrill L Jeffers	T Mark Withers	T Mark Withers	Win Wooton	Paul Barnes	Frank Boyer	Bob Valdez
Hurstbourne (4) MC	502 426-4808	(not reporting)						
Independence (8) MC	606 356-5302	Marion C Schadler	....	Pearl Carlisle	Frank Keller	Rick Messingshlager	Charles Donaldson	....
Irvine† (3) MC	606 723-2554	Leon Roberts	....	Eunice H Witt	Ora W Kirby	Fred Rogers	Marcus Cole	....
Jackson (3) MC	606 666-7069	Frank Noble	....	Marge Morrison	....	....	Doug Salyers	....
Jeffersontown (16) MC	502 267-8333	Daniel H Ruckriegel	....	Jeanne H Mattingly	Rita R Kelty	Robert Gaddie	Fred Roemele	Richard Dunn
Jenkins (3) MC	606 832-2141	(not reporting)						
La Grange (3) MC	502 222-1433	Robert B Theiss	....	Marjorie B Heilman	Marjorie B Heilman	Louis Powell	James E Robison	....
Lakeside Park (3) MC	606 341-6670	Henry M Mann	....	Sheila L Phelps	....	....	Larry L Hall	....
Lancaster† (3) MC	606 792-3023	Billy C Moss	....	Ginger L Ball	....	Kenneth Adams	Henry T Bell	....
Lawrenceburg (5) MC	502 839-5372	Kenneth P Hoskins	Robert D Bradshaw	Elizabeth C Hanks	Robert Thompson	Robert Cook	William J Kirby	....
Lebanon† (7) MC	502 692-6272	Maurice D Spalding	W Terry Ward	Joyce A Ford	....	....	Robert J Gutman	Kenneth W Graham
Leitchfield (5) MC	502 259-4034	(not reporting)						
Lexington-Fayette (204) MC	606 255-5631	Scotty Baesler	....	Kathryn W Johnson	Betty P Unseld	Earl McDaniel	John P McFadden	....
London (4) MC	606 864-4169	Edward E McFadden	....	Patricia A Depew	Patricia A Depew	Gilmore Phelps	William D Smith	....
Louisville (298) MC	502 587-3061	Harvey I Sloane	Burt J Deutsch	Claudine Washington	Robert Schwoeppe	Larry M Bonnafon	Richard Dotson	Michael French
Ludlow (5) MC	606 491-1233	Harold J Klosterman	David N Bloesing	W Lorraine Lyon	John Farrell	Norman Holbrook	Robert Highhouse	....
Madisonville (17) MC	502 821-3746	O L Lantaff	....	Gina W Munger	Lloyd Merrell	Howard Renfro	James E Bowles	Dennis Farris
Marion (3) MC	502 965-2266	Bobby R Fox	David G Cobb	Ann R Hill	Nina M Enoch	Ron Howton	William O Brown	Don Tinsley
Mayfield† (11) MC	502 247-1981	Virgil Gilliam	....	E D Bradford	Peggy Brady	Howard Dowdy	Charles Johnson	Raymond Hester
Maysville* (8) CM	606 564-9411	William M Boggs	Dennis D Redmond	Ann Brammer	Robert Smith	Stanley McGowan	Douglas Culp	Joseph Barrett
Middlesborough (12) MC	606 248-5670	Chester H Wolfe	....	Olive W Crockett	Jerry L Sharpe	R C Carter	James Pursifull	....
Monticello (6) MC	606 348-8473	Kenneth D Catron	....	B G Edwards	B G Edwards	Joseph B Gibson	Ralph Miniard	Donald Lester
Morehead (8) MC	606 784-8505	John W Holbrook Jr	Dan P Stewart	Diana Lindsey	P M Tackett	Eddie Holbrook	James Pelfrey	Alfred Ellis
Morganfield (4) MC	502 789-2525	(not reporting)						
Mount Sterling (6) MC	606 498-3785	Dorothy Lavoie	....	Doris W Baxter	....	James Halsey	Phillip M Fawns	Robert T Hiatt
Mount Washington† (4) MC	502 538-7346	Charles McMichael	....	Darrell Dickey	Darrell Dickey	Gayle Troutman	Leo Oliver	....
Murray (14) MC	502 753-1221	Holmes Ellis	....	Jo Crass	Jo Crass	James Hornbuckle	Paul Jerry Lee	Tommy Marshall
Newburg (6) MC	502 969-8859	(not reporting)						
Newport* (22) CM	606 292-3666	Steven Goetz	Dennis M Phelan	Frank Peluso	Richard Howe	Ralph Quitter	David Williams	Paul Baker
Nicholasville (10) CO	606 885-9473	Billy Lockridge	....	Bonnie Dean	Bonnie Dean	W T Brumfield	James M Cox Jr	....
Olive Hill† (3) MC	606 286-5532	J A Raybourn	Terry R Thompson	Terry R Thompson	....	James Cline	Lester Pelfrey	....
Owensboro* (54) CM	502 685-8200	Jack C Fisher	....	Carol Ann Blake	Ralph Rascoe	Walter Freeman	Ulysses Embry	Wm C Reynolds
Paducah* (29) CM	502 444-8503	Joe Viterisi	Carl G Holder Jr	Lenita S Smith	Thurman R Baker	Leon Dodge	J W Cunningham	....
Paintsville (4) MC	606 789-3664	James S Trimble	Ralph B Preston	Mary P Van Hoose	Patricia Colvin	Randell Hayslett	Ross W Spears	Paul Picklesimer
Paris§ (8) MC	606 987-2630	Douglas Castle	R L Brunner	Louis Elvove	Louis Elvove	Charles Peters	George Boling	Vernon Azevedo
Park Hills (4) MC	606 431-6252	Joseph B Niehaus	....	Evelyn Fogarty	Russell Clark	Robert Kaelin	F E Ostendorf Jr	Raymond Budde
Pikeville* (5) CM	606 432-3132	W C Hambley	Frank C Carlton	Ted Herring	Ted Herring	Charles T Smith	Eugene Edmonds	Cecil Ray
Pineville† (3) MC	606 337-2958	Robert L Madon	Charles Dean	Karen Hoskins	E J Farris	William A Robbins	David Hoskins	Cecil Miracle

Directory 1/10 continued

MUNICIPAL OFFICIALS IN ALL U.S. CITIES OVER 2,500[1]

City, 1980 population (000 omitted), form of government		Municipal phone number	Mayor	Appointed administrator	City clerk	Finance officer	Fire chief	Police chief	Public works director
KENTUCKY (112) continued									
Prestonsburg† (4)	MC	606 886-2335	Harold Cooley	David Evans	Sue Webb	Brenda Hayes	Thomas A Blackburn	Keith Lawson	Gervin Waddle
Princeton (7)	MC	502 365-9575	James E Ward Jr	....	Van Knight	Lana Fletcher	Regil B Hobby	Tennie Mitchell	Harley Lowery
Providence† (4)	MC	502 667-5463	James Gooch Jr	....	Charlotte Hendon	Charlotte Hendon	Donald Harris	Bobby Sauls	Wm E Winebarger
Radcliff (15)	MC	502 351-4477	(not reporting)						
Richmond* (22)	CM	606 623-7282	William Strong	Robert L Norris	Susan Higgins	H D Hurt Jr	William Lane	Walker J Howell	Dave Graham
Russell (4)	MC	606 836-9666	W Dulaney Wood	....	Peggy L Colvin	Peggy L Colvin	Harry J Thomas	Phillip Caskey	Mark Ballard
Russellville (8)	MC	502 726-6369	Kenneth Smith	....	Peggy S Jenkins	Edie Martin	J L Williamson	Mike Stratton	Ernie Cole
Scottsville (4)	MC	502 237-3238	George L Maxwell	....	Edith Parrish	Morris Grubbs	Herbert Fuqua	William Calvert	Greg Carver
Shelbyville (5)	MC	502 633-1835	Neil S Hackworth	....	Jess Puckett	Tom Hardesty	Bobby Whitaker	John Miller	Ernest Hawkins
Shepherdsville (4)	MC	502 543-2923	James T Sparrow	....	Neva L Ward	Neva L Ward	Everett R Waters	Benjamin Stillwell	....
Shively (17)	MC	502 448-5212	John W Burks	Rosemary Jacobs	Rosemary Jacobs	....	James Jenkins	Benjamin O Keutzer	Mary Carol Axman
Somerset§ (11)	MC	606 678-8185	Smith Van Hook	Jack J Early	David E Godsey	Jack J Early	Eugene Norfleet	Vertres B Jones	Jim Jones
Southgate (3)	MC	606 441-0075	James P Callahan	....	Rose M Welscher	Donald H Berkemeyer	Simon Jewell	Robert A Shields	Paul J Krebs
Springfield (3)	MC	606 336-7739	Dwight Wright	Mike Haydon	Mike Haydon	Mike Haydon	Jim Logsdon	Roy Fenwick	....
St. Matthews (13)	MC	502 895-9444	(not reporting)						
Stanford (3)	MC	606 365-7322	James C Harris	....	Wanda R Withrow	....	George Pennecuff	Don Young	....
Stanton† (3)	MC	606 663-2620	Hugh Tipton	....	Susie Fig	....	Wm Lawrence Rogers	William Thorpe	....
Taylor Mill (5)	MC	606 581-3234	Betty Clements	....	Mary Kordenbrock	Gary Wagner	Tim Cook	David B Wells	Roy Sandmann
Tompkinsville† (4)	MC	502 487-6776	Ralph T Hagan	....	Shera McClendon	Carol Moore	Charles Landrum	Johnny Graves	....
Versailles (6)	MC	606 873-5436	Paul Noel	....	Reata B Buffin	....	Paul Downey	Robert Y Brown	Mike Heathman
Villa Hills (4)	MC	606 331-4933	(not reporting)						
Vine Grove (4)	MC	502 877-2422	Wayne Vowels	....	Linda M Holeman	....	Deward A Lee	Patrick L Abshire	Roland E Carneal
Williamsburg (6)	MC	606 549-1616	Paul Estes	L P Partin	Anne L Pettit	....	Milton E Prewitt	H L Taylor	George Hayes
Williamstown (3)	MC	606 824-3352	Herbert Caldwell	Billy D Marksberry	William D Peddicord	....	William F Threlkeld	Freddie R Morgan	Billy D Marksberry
Wilmore (4)	MC	606 858-4411	Harold Rainwater	....	Colleen Brandenburg	....	James Anderson Sr	Roger Swallows	....
Winchester§ (15)	MC	606 744-7017	Carroll E Ecton	Ed Burtner	Marie Gainey	Wanda Hunt	Robert Monroe	Bill Claypoole	Jay Warden
LOUISIANA (98)									
Abbeville t (12)	MC	318 893-8550	Larry J Campisi	....	Suzanne Zaunbrecher	Ellis Bordelon	Nolan Frederick	Minos Hardy	Clifton Babineaux
Alexandria (52)	MC	318 473-1101	John K Snyder	Janet W Price	Jon Grafton	Velda L Lee	Charles Carruth	Glen E Beard	Anthony S D'Angelo
Amite City t (4)	MC	504 748-8761	Mildred B Easley	....	Verar Hayden	....	....	James C Ricks	Jerry J Trabona
Arcadia t (3)	MC	318 263-8455	Ray Dean Smith	....	Kay G Watson	Ray Dean Smith	Hubert Davis	B L Bob Murphy	Curtis Gipson
Baker† (13)	MC	504 778-0300	N E Pete Heine	....	....	Charlene Templeton	J E Carroll	Sidney Gautreaux	Parker Lee Nettles
Baldwin t† (3)	MC	318 923-7523	O O Longman	....	....	....	....	....	....
Ball t (3)	MC	318 640-9605	Clyde L Moore	....	Christine Covington	....	Evie Murrow	Daniel E Caldwell	....
Basile t (3)	MC	318 432-6693	Joe Toups	....	Rose Marie Johnson	....	Deo Guidry	Wilfred Lafleur	....
Bastrop (16)	MC	318 283-0250	John S Bond	....	Katie Martin	....	Ray Hobby	Stan Neathery	Calvin C Williams
Baton Rouge† (346)	MC	504 389-3100	Pat Screen	....	Don Nijoka	Otha Lynn Schofield	Marvin Castello	Pat Bonanno	William Addison
Berwick t (4)	MC	504 384-8858	Charles A Savoie	Gloria Nini	Gloria Nini	....	Vincent J Bella	Ovay Rogers	Stanley Boudreaux
Bogalusa† (17)	MC	504 732-2533	Louis Rawls	....	Ms Joel Foster	....	W F Raborn	Earl G Penton	Jerry Crain
Bossier City (50)	MC	318 424-8500	Don E Jones	....	Jewel Lewis	Charles Glover	J T Wallace	Bobby Gauthier	Ronnie Carlson
Breaux Bridge (6)	MC	318 332-2172	Vance J Theriot	Raymond J Guidry	Raymond J Guidry	Raymond J Guidry	John Allen Breaux	George Menard Sr	Norris Robert
Broussard t† (3)	MC	318 837-6681	Leroy J Miguez	....	....	....	....	Harold J Romero	....
Bunkie t (5)	MC	318 346-7494	Alfred Feeney	....	Deborah L Morace	....	Johnny Johns	Charles J Candella	Girard P Jusselin
Carencro t† (4)	MC	318 896-8481	Tommy J Angelle	....	Marie D Lemaire	James H Burleigh	Carroll E Guilbeau	Ms Arceneaux	....
Church Point t† (5)	MC	318 684-5693	John Harold Beaugh	....	Shirley D Kidder	....	Lloyd Latiolais	Floyd Lyons	....
Covington† (8)	MC	504 892-1811	Ernest J Cooper	Louis E Pauratore	Dianne Richardson	Louis E Pauratore	James Grogan	Al Strain	James Core
Crowley (16)	MC	318 783-1270	Robert L Istre	....	Kent Hoffpauir	Judy Istre	John Allen Leleux	John E Gibson	Oscar Primeaux
De Quincy t (4)	MC	318 786-8241	Gary W Cooper	....	Tommie Lou White	S E Snider	Roland Dudley	Dalbert R Fontenot	Ray M Cooley
De Ridder (11)	CM	318 462-2461	Creighton Pugh	Tommy Smith	Judy Kulaga	H W Bohon	Winfred Mitchell	Arvin Malone	Bernie Hatchett
Delhi t† (3)	MC	318 878-3792	Michael L Thompson	....	Gloria King	....	Willie Kennedy	Herman L Hoover	....
Denham Springs (8)	MC	504 665-8121	V H Hoover	....	Denver C Ballard	Magaret Stafford	C H Kennedy Jr	Scott Jones	B M McDonald
Donaldsonville† (8)	CM	504 473-4247	Ralph R Falsetta	Marvin Gros	Marvin Gros	Claude Bourg Jr	August Bradford	Murrel Hubble	Anthony Bonadona
Eunice (12)	MC	318 457-2601	Curtis Joubert	....	Shirley F Vige Sr	Shirley F Vige Sr	....	Calvin Morris	L J Aucoin
Farmerville t (4)	MC	318 368-9242	Tiny Talley	....	George C Miller	Tiny Talley	Michael Allen	George Cothran	Ferrel Thurston
Ferriday t (4)	MC	318 757-3411	Sammy Davis Jr	....	Judith P Boothe	Billy Rucker	Herman Smith	Lyle Schiele	Shelvey Duncan
Franklin† (10)	MC	318 828-3631	Sam Jones	....	Ray Robichaux	Lee Ann Mire	Lewis Rackley	David Naquin	Harold Thibodaux
Franklinton t (4)	MC	504 839-3569	Warren P Greer	....	Lorelle M Wood	....	Jerry Warren	Lynn Armand	....
Gonzales (7)	MC	504 644-2841	John A Berthelot	John A Berthelot	Terry S Tripp	Dalton Matchand	J C Walker	Barney Arceneaux	T V Featherston Jr
Grambling V† (4)	MC	318 247-6120	Richard J Gallot	....	Rosetta Days	....	Claud L Aker	....	....
Gramercy t (3)	MC	504 869-3975	(not reporting)						
Gretna (21)	MC	504 367-5591	William J White	....	Katherine R Weigel	Brenda L Schambach	Luke Labruzza Sr	B H Miller Jr	....
Hammond (15)	MC	504 345-3356	Debora Saik Pope	....	LaNita Earnest	....	Vito Collura	Roddy Devall	....
Harahan† (11)	MC	504 737-6383	Carlo R Ferrara	....	Barbara Butera	....	....	Michael A Ranatza	....
Haynesville t (3)	MC	318 624-0911	Carl Frasier	H U Slaid	H U Slaid	....	James Bailey	David C Mills	John D Amos
Homer t (4)	MC	318 927-3555	Joe Michael	....	....	Iris Sanders	Dennis Butcher	Clinton W Nelson	Jessie T Jones
Houma (94)	MC	504 868-5050	....	Henry A Boese	Paul Labat	Hebert F Frederick	Ernest Miller	Charles F Farmer	Baxter Wade
Jackson t (3)	MC	504 634-7777	Js M Norsworthy III	....	Gloria P Fontenot	....	Richard Dudley III	Ernest S Barnes	....
Jeanerette t (7)	MC	318 276-4587	Moise Guillotte Jr	....	Darryl Landry	Darryl Landry	Robert Grettner	Roman Wesley	John Landry
Jena t (4)	CM	318 992-2148	Orland Sandifer	....	Sharon Keel	....	John C Heath	George L King	....
Jennings† (12)	MC	318 824-0432	William T Cagnon	Jerry Mayeaux	S J Manuel	S J Manuel	Lisso Lawrence	Merrion S Taylor	Vicente Benaventie
Jonesboro t (5)	MC	318 259-2385	W Richard Zuber	....	Beatrice Rice	....	Maurice Newton	Mallory J Walker	W M Peel
Jonesville t† (3)	MC	318 339-8596	Janie S Morris	....	Judy Adams	Janie S Morris	Leland Adams	E M Pardue	Sim Nichols
Kaplan (5)	MC	318 643-8602	Dalfares J Trahan	Ouida M Broussard	Ouida M Broussard	....	Jerry Landry	Robert D Lege	....
Kenner† (66)	MC	504 468-7200	Aaron F Broussard	Jimmie Martinez	Gwen Boynton	Kenneth M Thompson	Dominick J Mumphrey	S J Lentini	Don Crimen
Kentwood t (3)	MC	504 229-3451	Nicholas A Saladino	....	Julia B Prescott	Julia B Prescott	Hubert Brown	Samuel Broyles	Hugh Douglas Cutrer
Kinder t (3)	MC	318 738-2620	Fred A Ashy	....	Dorothy T Langley	....	Charles W Reynolds	Edward Peloquin	....
Lafayette (82)	MC	318 261-8200	Dud Lastrapes	Glenn Weber	Glenn Duhon	Barry Berthelot	Jack Montoucet	James Romero	Jerry Trumps
Lake Arthur t (4)	MC	318 774-2211	E R Giles	....	Dorthy Charles	....	David Trahan	Jimmy Boudreaux	Donald Whitman
Lake Charles (75)	MC	318 491-1200	Paul A Savoie	James E Stainback	Elizabeth Eastman	Arthur Lee	Algie Breaux	Sam Ivey	Ron Rider
Lake Providence t (6)	MC	318 559-2288	General Trass Jr	....	Scottie Shirey	....	Jimmy McIntyre	Stewart Marshall	....
Leesville t (9)	CM	318 239-2444	Ralph D McRae Jr	Albert H Toombs	Delain P Prewitt	Delain P Prewitt	Allen R Williams	Gilmer Jeane Jr	Curtis Watkins
Lutcher t (5)	MC	504 869-5823	Elmore J Trosclair	....	Lloyd Dicharry	Lloyd Dicharry	Paul J Amato	Brian J Melancon	....
Mamou t (3)	MC	318 468-3272	Peter Savoy	....	Betty Newsom	Rayford Fontenot	Littell Fontenot	Bradley D Reed	Spencer Long
Mandeville t (6)	MC	504 626-3144	Ray Foil	....	Delia Hagan	Adelaide Boettner	Leonard Frosh	Tom Buell	....
Mansfield (6)	MC	318 872-0406	Druce A Chapman	....	Judy Wilkerson	....	Louie Melton	Lawrence Caston	Gene L Binning
Many t (4)	MC	318 256-3651	Mike Tarver	....	Loree Maxey	....	Reo Wright	Dean Lambert	Hildo Remedes
Marksville t† (5)	MC	318 253-9500	Richard R Michel	Hunter Dauzat	Hunter Dauzat	Hunter Dauzat	Ned J Bordelon	Michael F Neck	....
Minden† (15)	CO	318 377-2144	Noel E Byars	....	Wayne B Youngblood	Wayne B Youngblood	T C Bloxom Jr	Chester Adcock	Wayne Williamson
Monroe (58)	MC	318 329-2200	Robert E Powell	M J Cook	Gennie A Barnes	M J Cook	Bill Breland	Willie E Buffington	Loy Scarborough

Directory 1/10 continued

MUNICIPAL OFFICIALS IN ALL U.S. CITIES OVER 2,500[1]

City, 1980 population (000 omitted), form of government		Municipal phone number	Mayor	Appointed administrator	City clerk	Finance officer	Fire chief	Police chief	Public works director
LOUISIANA (98) continued									
Morgan City (16)	MC	504 385-1770	Cedric S Lafleur	Larry P Bergeron	....	Allen Templet	Gerald Price	Beverly Broussard	Donald Ray
Natchitoches (17)	MC	318 352-3661	Joe Sampite	....	Charles Powell	Charles Powell	Oscar R Vails	Burl D Lee	Clifford Walker
New Iberia (33)	MC	318 365-2471	J Allen Daigre	....	Willie M Ellis	Willie M Ellis	Bill Desormeaux	Steven L Davis	Austin Delahoussaye
New Orleans§ (557)	MC	504 586-4311	Ernest N Morial	Erroll Williams	Lea Siegel	Bobby Major Jr	W J McCrossen	Henry Morris	Harold J Gorman
New Roads t (4)	MC	504 638-7047	Trina O Scott	Joseph B Laurent	Mildred V Smith	Trina O Scott	Leslie Lindsly	Jules Hurst	Elie Part
Oakdale (7)	MC	318 335-3629	George B Mowad	....	Marie B West	....	Thomas Moore	V Chamberlain Jr	Donald Welch
Opelousas† (19)	MC	318 948-8294	Thomas R Edwards	Harold L Lastrapes	James R Bienvenu	Aline Miller	James Cahannin	Percy Lalonde	....
Patterson t† (5)	MC	504 395-5205	Fred Allen Mensman	David Lowery	Joann Smits	....	Steve Bierhorst	John L Robicheau	Edison Paul
Pineville (12)	MC	318 445-1431	Fred H Baden	....	Carol D Vermillion	Richard Brackney	James Wilson	Eldon Sayes	Truly Higgins
Plaquemine t (8)	MC	504 687-3116	Stanley R Hebert	....	Nell F Haynie	....	Charles Cranford	E J Leblanc	George Hernandez
Ponchatoula† (5)	MC	504 386-6484	Collins Bonicard	....	Ruby P Landry	....	Erlo McLaurin Jr	Ernest J Peltier	....
Port Allen (6)	MC	504 348-0441	(not reporting)						
Port Barre t (3)	MC	318 585-7646	Roy D Council	....	Janice L Burghooff	Gerald Bob Marks	Elvie Lanelos	Nolan Badeaux	....
Rayne† (9)	MC	318 334-3121	Ralph J Stutes	....	Robert D Hebert	Robert D Hebert	Ernest Boudreaux	Peter Haure	....
Rayville t (5)	MC	318 728-4142	Joe Kalil	....	Charles G Germany	....	Ralph Stephens	Wilburn Harris	J W McGlothin
Ruston (21)	MC	318 255-7000	Elton C Pody	....	James E Fletcher Jr	James E Fletcher Jr	James H Pipes	Bruce Thompson	Al Brewer
Shreveport§† (206)	MC	318 226-6001	John B Hussey	Stuart A Bach	Dianne Thomas	Jim Keyes	Dallas Greene	Cliff Heap	E J French
Slidell (27)	MC	504 643-3434	M W Webb Hart	Steve Buser	Gerri Ingrao	Virginia Roe	Edward Poplar	Max Rodriguez	Dan Yeates
Springhill† (7)	MC	318 539-5681	Johnny Herrington	....	Johnnie S McMahen	....	Billy Rasberry	Jerry L Stephens	Billy Castleberry
St. Martinville (8)	MC	318 394-6235	Earl H Willis	....	Leopold J Gary	Robert G Labbe	Leon J Bourque	Jerry C Curry	....
Sulphur† (20)	CO	318 527-7078	Dennis R Sumpter	John R Iles	Margret G Field	D J Guidry	C R Miller	Theron J Andrus	Dennis R Sumpter
Tallulah (10)	MC	318 574-0964	Leander A Anthony	....	Moses Jackson	Moses Jackson	Fred Washington	Andrew Bowman	C J Oney
Thibodaux (16)	MC	504 447-3767	Betran D F Hebert	Cleveland D Clement	Tommy Eschete	Kenneth Hoffmann	David Hebert	John R Bernard	Daisy Ledet
Vidalia t (6)	MC	318 336-5206	Sam Randazzo	....	Edith Spurlock	....	Jerry David	Delane Thornhill	....
Ville Platte t (9)	MC	318 363-2939	Hottell Fontendt	....	James E Demoruelle	....	Reinel Smith	James D Bordelon	....
Vinton t (4)	MC	318 589-7453	Raywood LeMaire	....	Melba Landry	Melba Landry	D J Schanz	Lionel Alamond	Raymond Guillery
Vivian t (4)	MC	318 375-3856	James W Williamson	....	Ruby P Cowgill	....	Fred W Brown	Donice Jones	Fred W Brown
Walker t (3)	MC	504 664-3123	Albert Pendarvis	....	Billie Herring	....	Richard Pettit	Rufus Hughes	Wilson Achord
Welsh t (4)	MC	318 734-2231	Charles L Bull Jr	....	Shirley C Meche	Harold J Daigle	Thomas J Schexnider	Robert L Hayes	Robert J Louviere
West Monroe (15)	MC	318 396-2600	Dave Norris	....	Donald L Taylor	Donald L Taylor	Robert R Roberts	Larry Laborde	Davis Cartlidge
Westlake t (5)	MC	318 433-0691	Dudley R Dixon	....	Peggy D McGee	....	Robert McClelland	Jim L Herford	Heard J Bertrand
Westwego (13)	MC	504 341-3424	Calvin A Galiano	....	Miriam Miller	Calvin A Galiano	Douglas Trauth	John Warden	....
Winnfield† (7)	MC	318 628-3939	J Maxwell Kelley	....	Pat Howell	....	Byron R Tullos	Cranford Jurden	Buford A Guilliams
Winnsboro t (6)	MC	318 435-9087	Herbert L Davis	....	William A Mulkey	....	Winfre D Welch	Aaron W Wright	....
Zachary (7)	MC	504 654-6871	John A Womack	....	Ms Merle W Johnston	....	Michael Ard	Dennis M Corban	Herman McKey
Zwolle t† (3)	MC	318 645-6141	Fred Roberson	....	....	....	....	....	....
MAINE (181)									
Amity t*† (..)	CM	....	....	Carletta Marshall	....	....	....	....	....
Ashland t* (2)	CM	207 435-2311	Melvin P Graham	Nancy E Farris	Nancy E Farris	Nancy E Farris	Donald O'Clair	J Vincent Malena	Nancy E Farris
Auburn* (23)	CM	207 786-2421	John J Cleveland	Charles A Morrison	Mary Lou Magno	George Kehoe	Clifton S Smith	Peter Mador	Robert F Belz
Augusta* (22)	CM	207 623-8540	Peter G Thompson	John G Edgerly	Madeline M Cyr	Ronald E Harvey	Leon Folger	Richard D Griffin	John H Charest
Baileyville t*† (2)	TM	207 427-3442	James L Wallace	E Jeffrey Barnes	Milton A Annis	Frank Besse	G Arthur Fleming	George Hammond	Frederick Berube
Bangor* (32)	CM	207 947-0341	Laurence Willey Jr	John W Flynn	Russell J McKenna	Theodore Jellison	Robert J Burke	Francis Woodhead	Henry Trahan
Bar Harbor t* (4)	CM	207 288-3329	Kenneth E Smith	Richard M Plante	Jean T Barker	Richard M Plante	Royal J Higgins	Craig B Hall Sr	Lawrence F Abbott
Bath* (10)	CM	207 443-4672	David A King	Peter A Garland	Beverly Henrikson	George W Sargent	Ronald Clark	Thomas J Landers	Kenneth Murray
Belfast* (6)	CM	207 338-3370	Monroe B Hall	David A Maynard	Wilma B Moses	....	James L Richards	Robert B Keating	Harold Young
Benedicta t*† (..)	CM	207 365-4160	....	Joseph P Rush	Lois McAvoy	....	....	....	....
Berwick t* (4)	CM	207 698-1101	Samuel Mathews	Norbert J Couture	Ann Stone	Norbert J Couture	Arthur J Plante	Asa C Morse	Norbert J Couture
Bethel t* (2)	TM	207 824-2669	Arlan R Jodrey	William H Judson	Merton T Brown Jr	....	Robert Davis	Robert Stearns	Robert L Davis
Biddeford† (20)	MC	207 283-0181	Martin J Rielly	Paul Gobeil	Luc Angers	Paul Gobeil	Raymond Parent	Roger Beaupre	T A Drouin Jr
Blaine t* (1)	TM	207 425-2611	Lawrence G Beals	Diana M Menendez	Diana M Menendez	....	....	....	....
Boothbay t* (2)	CM	207 633-2051	Thomas Nickerson	Russell B Peplaw	Joan M Rittall	Russell B Peplaw	Stanley W Lewis	....	Russell B Peplaw
Boothbay Harbor t* (2)	TM	207 633-3671	Don Wotton	Malcolm Hunter	M Robert Barter	....	Warren Page	Floyd McDunnah	Phil Andrews
Bowdoinham t* (2)	CM	207 666-5531	Gerard Curtis	Kathryn Ruth	Phyllis H Weeks	Kathryn Ruth	Allan C Frizzle Jr	Ryan Jennings	Kathryn Ruth
Brewer* (9)	CM	207 989-7500	Richard P Rublin	Reynold Perry	Arthur C Verow	Virgil S Pratt	John D Shaw Jr	David Koman	Arthur A Stockus
Bridgewater t* (1)	CM	207 429-9856	Boyd M Bradbury	Donna A Kingsbury	Paul Young	....	John Barker	....	....
Bridgton t* (4)	CM	207 647-5582	Robert McHatton	Philip M Tarr	Ruth Irish	....	Stevens Barker	Robert C Bell	Leo A Hamill Jr
Brownville t*† (2)	CM	207 965-2561	Neil B Arbo	David M Barrett	Jacqueline A Roy	David M Barrett	Henry Graves	David M Barrett	David M Barrett
Brunswick t* (17)	CM	207 725-7522	Robert Shepherd	John P Bibber	Gail Staley	Martin L Childs	Gary Howard	Dominic Vermette	Herbert W Watson
Bucksport t* (4)	CM	207 469-7368	Donald H Millett	Roger H Foster	Joyce Johnson	Roger H Foster	Paul McCann	Douglas Gray	Robert R Jardine
Buxton t (6)	TM	207 929-6171	....	....	Joan Plummer	....	....	....	....
Calais* (4)	CM	207 454-2521	Dayton J Dineen	William Bridgeo	Philip Manship	....	Jacob Brocato	James D Johnson	Maurice Barnard
Camden t* (5)	TM	207 236-3353	William Brawn	Elmer N Savage	Kimberly Cates	....	Robert Oxton	Albert M Smith	Elmer N Savage
Cape Elizabeth t* (8)	CM	207 799-0881	K Wayne Murray	John E Henchey	Natalie B Libby	Barbara E Jordan	William H Jordan	David W Pickering	Philip E Mullin Sr
Caribou* (10)	CM	207 493-3324	Roy Doak	Terrence St Peter	Ms C S Harrington	Paula Harris	Donald Woods	Verne B McKenney	Charles Huston
Carmel t* (2)	TM	207 848-3361	....	Glennis McSorley	Glennis McSorley	Glennis McSorley	Edward Crowley	Fred Emerson	....
Castle Hill t* (1)	CM	207 764-3754	Eugene Hoffses	Dennis P Gardner	Dennis P Gardner	Dennis P Gardner	....	....	Thomas Johnson
Chelsea t*† (3)	CM	207 582-4802	Everett Sidelinger	Maryfrances Bartlet	Virginia Keaton	....	Joseph Mills	....	....
Cherryfield t*† (1)	TM	207 546-2376	Charles Tehan	Liston Grant	Liston Grant	....	....	....	....
China t* (3)	TM	207 445-2014	Edward W French	Adele H Holmes	Joyce G Cowing	....	....	....	....
Clinton t* (3)	TM	207 426-8511	....	Harriet Lancaster	Dot Henry	....	Timothy Fuller	Gerald Sylvester	....
Corinna t* (2)	TM	207 278-4183	Roland V Buck	Philip B Swanson	Joanne K Metivier	....	Myron K Mullis	....	....
Corinth t* (2)	TM	207 285-3271	Russell V Broad	Donald A Strout	Donald A Strout	....	Gareth Blackwell	....	....
Crystal t* (..)	CM	207 463-2480	Vernon Anderson	Linda B York	Linda B York	Linda B York	Vernon L Anderson	....	Kenneth F Prescott
Cumberland t*† (5)	CM	207 829-5559	Alvin K Ahlers	Robert B Benson	Christine St Peter	Steven R Marriner	Kenneth Wagner	Leon H Planche	Philip M Wentworth
Danforth t*† (1)	CM	207 448-2321	Philip E Morse	Byron Gould	Byron Gould	Byron Gould	Luis Casanova	....	....
Dexter t* (4)	CM	207 924-7351	Roger S Brawn	David L Holt	Viola P Keyte	David L Holt	James H Silverman	David A Clukey	William A Keyte
Dover-Foxcroft t*† (4)	TM	207 564-3318	Hoyt M Fairbrother	Owen W Pratt	Philip E Warren	Philip E Warren	Harold Spearing	G Herbert Green	Robert Ladd
Dyer Brook t* (..)	TM	207 757-8302	Frazier Botting	Susan McLaughlin	Susan McLaughlin	....	....	....	....
Eagle Lake t* (1)	CM	207 444-5125	....	Reynold Raymond	Connie Morneault	Benjamin Ricciardi	....	....	....
Easton t§ (1)	TM	207 488-6652	Richard Kneeland	Duncan E Beaton Jr	Ruth A Fitzherbert	Ruth A Fitzherbert	Ira Dodge	....	Gary Flanagan
Eastport* (2)	CM	207 853-2300	Roger Conti	John E Madigan Jr	Carolyn Camick	Judith Hall	Merrill Conti	Richard Young	Rene O'Dell
Eliot t† (5)	TM	207 439-1813	Ralph K Chase	Daniel J Blanchette	Jane Vittum	Norma J Spinney	Walter Hoyt	Thomas Barr	Walter Spinney
Ellsworth* (5)	CM	207 667-2563	George W Spreng	Charles B Osgood	Fern A Kelley	Frank Myatt	Clayton E Torrey Jr	Albert E Carter	Charles B Osgood
Exeter t* (1)	CM	207 379-2191	Vernon R Crane	Jayne R Farrin	Jayne R Farrin	Jayne R Farrin	....	....	....
Fairfield t* (6)	CM	207 453-6404	Frank W Tozier	Roland J Dubay	Terry York	Karen A Bourque	Ralph Meader	Neil J Saucier	George H Taylor
Falmouth t* (7)	CM	207 781-5253	Jonathan S Piper	Doug Harris	Roberta Greenfield	Norma Holden	Freeman Cleaves	Clyde Leclair	Greg Apraham
Farmingdale t (3)	TM	207 582-2225	Harold F Hersom	Dawn S Richards	Dawn S Richards	....	David Richardson	....	....
Farmington t*† (7)	CM	207 778-6538	Ralph E Goodwin	Alan Gove	Fay B Adams	Beverly A Besaw	Robert McCleary	Sheridan Smith	Alan Gove

Directory 1/10 continued

MUNICIPAL OFFICIALS IN ALL U.S. CITIES OVER 2,500[1]

City, 1980 population (000 omitted), form of government		Municipal phone number	Mayor	Appointed administrator	City clerk	Finance officer	Fire chief	Police chief	Public works director
MAINE (181) continued									
Fort Fairfield t* (4)	CM	207 472-3801	Peter M LeVasseur	Alphonse R Dixon	Julie M Clark	Alphonse R Dixon	William Van Buskirk	Wendell Monson	Elson Cote
Fort Kent t* (5)	RT	207 834-3090	Marc Michaud	Claude Dumond	Lucille Audibert	Claude Dumond	Allan Dow	Kenneth Michaud	Claude Dumond
Freeport t* (6)	CM	207 865-4743	Hugh Phelps	Dale C Olmstead Jr	Phyllis Roy	Dale C Olmstead Jr	Darrel Fournier	William Stone	Alton Thompson
Frenchville t* (1)	CM	207 543-7301	Philip Pelletier	Philip Levesque	....	....	Bertrand Paradis	....	Bertrand Albert
Fryeburg t (3)	TM	207 935-2805	Hannah Hodsdon	Theresa G Shaw	Theresa G Shaw	Hannah Hodsdon	Corlis S Watson	Fred A Gould	Wilfred V Smith
Gardiner* (6)	CM	207 582-4200	William MacDonald	Kenneth J Kokernak	Kenneth J Kokernak	....	Frederick Hubbard	Gordon Glidden	James Pierce
Garland t* (1)	CM	207 924-6615	Arthur Jette	Edith P Stone	Susan Packard	....	Norman Packard	....	Edith P Stone
Gorham t* (10)	CM	207 839-3346	Carol P Day	Donald H Gerrish	D Brenda Caldwell	Jack R Gorsuch	Robert S Lefebure	Edmund Hagen	Lincoln F Hawkes
Gray t* (4)	CM	207 657-3339	Walter Riseman	Janis G McGrath	Janis G McGrath	Janis G McGrath	James Foster	James Purdy	Neal Lavallee
Greene t (3)	TM	207 946-5146	Kenneth B Fogg	....	Nellie S Fogg	....	Alden Peterson	....	Vern Ray
Greenville t* (2)	CM	207 695-2421	Richard Gould	David E Cota	David E Cota	David E Cota	Norman Grassette	Maximum Squires	John Ryder
Guilford t* (2)	TM	207 876-2202	Clifton Worthen	Robt O Littlefield	Peter Neal	Dorene Graf	Richard Williams	Robt O Littlefield	Robt O Littlefield
Hallowell* (3)	CM	207 623-4021	Barry S Timson	Cornell F Knight	Margaret Mosher	Carlene McQuarrie	Michael Grant	William W Ellis	Ed Rowe
Hampden t* (5)	CM	207 862-3034	Richard Jenkins	R Lewis Bone	Marie G Baker	Paula M Newcomb	Robert Bailey	Roland Huston	Sheldon Ryder
Harpswell t (4)	TM	207 833-2834	M B Whidden Jr	D G Black	Frances L Johnson	Anne F Anderson		....	Ronald A Webber
Hartland t* (2)	CM	207 938-4401	....	Peggy A Morgan	Erline Humphrey	....	Dana Cooper	....	....
Haynesville t*† (..)	TM	207 448-2239	....	Glenna Duguay	Eleanor McLaughlin	Glenna Duguay	Dale Clifford	....	....
Hermon t* (3)	CM	207 848-3386	Roger Harlbart	Ethan W Aronoff	Deborah Pfleiderer	Nancy M Nowell	Charles L Witham	....	....
Hodgdon t* (1)	CM	207 532-6498	Herman London	Kenneth R Knowles	Wilma M Welton	Kenneth R Knowles	....	....	....
Holden t§ (3)	TM	207 843-5151	George A McDonald	Thomas Hamilton	Thomas Hamilton	Thomas Hamilton	Donald F Hart	....	Ronnie Fowler
Hollis t† (3)	TM	207 929-8552	Philip Atkinson Jr	....	Sylvia N Smith	Marjorie A Plummer	....	....	Robert Hanson
Houlton t* (7)	CM	207 532-7111	Leigh E Cummings Jr	Philip McCarthy	Philip McCarthy	Nedra Hanson	Lawrence Haggerty	James W Brown	Ralph M Cleale
Island Falls t* (1)	TM	207 463-2246	Rodney L Willette	Pamela J York	Pamela J York	Pamela J York	Toby Lougee	....	....
Islesboro t* (1)	CM	207 734-6445	Cecil D Creelman	George L Martin	Beverly Caldwell	George L Martin	George A Durkee	....	....
Jackman t* (1)	TM	207 668-2111	Clifford Chandler	Elsie Crawford	Elsie Crawford	Elsie Crawford	William Shelley	Thomas Giroux	Henry J Morin
Jay t*† (5)	CM	207 897-6785	David Labbe	Michael J Houlihan	Cynthia A Badeau	Cynthia A Badeau	Larry Melcher	Erland Farrington	....
Kennebunk t* (7)	TM	207 985-2102	Dorothy E Stevens	Richard F Cahill	Edna L Wentworth	Richard F Cahill	Lloyd Nedeau	James A Lavalle	Richard F Cahill
Kennebunkport t (3)	TM	207 967-4243	Carl G Bartlett	....	Charles E Gould	....	Charles F Brown	John A Prescott	....
Kittery t* (9)	CM	207 439-1633	Gary H Reiner	Eric A Strahl	Dorothy F Kraft	....	George D Varney Jr	George E Huston	Richard Rossiter
Lebanon t (3)	TM	207 457-1171	Ronal N Patch	....	Lorraine Patch	Doris Woodman	Glen Gerrish	Gordon K Smith	Ernest Hartford
Lewiston* (40)	CM	207 784-2951	Alfred A Plourde	Lucien B Gosselin	Gerald P Berube	Richard T Metivier	Sherman Lahaie	Herve J Gendreau	Normand R Lamie
Limestone t* (9)	TM	207 325-3131	Poitras Oscar	Thomas R Stevens	Donna M Bernier	Thomas R Stevens	Paul Poitras	Jean Michaud	Dale R Brooker
Lincoln t* (5)	CM	207 794-3372	Eliz Butterfield	David O Cole	Maxine Worcester	Donna M Jandreau	David Smart	Robert Crockett	David Washburn
Linneus t* (1)	CM	207 532-6182	Fred Dunlop Jr	David Whittner	Frances M Hutchinso	David Whittner	Paul Scott	....	....
Lisbon t* (9)	CM	207 353-8634	William Donovan	John Bubier	Elsie M Sullivan	Rodney W Moody	Howard Ricker	David T Brooks	Wayne York
Litchfield t* (2)	TM	207 268-4721	George C Skelton	G David Byras Sr	G David Byras Sr	G David Byras Sr	Michael Eaton	Dale Cook	G David Byras Sr
Littleton t* (1)	TM	207 538-9862	Raymond A Wotton	Anna L Schools	Anna L Schools	....	....	....	Frederick McBride
Livermore Falls t* (4)	TM	207 897-3321	Roland Mercier	Nathaniel Tupper	Maxine L Bailey	....	Albert Jones Jr	Charles B Keene	....
Lubec t* (2)	CM	207 733-2202	Carlton R Leighton	Dana E Bradley	Marylyn C Curtis	Marylyn C Curtis	Errol F Tinker	John W Fuller	....
Ludlow t*† (..)	CM	207 532-5513	....	Russell F Taylor Jr	Marie Wright	....	Woodrow Hickling	....	....
Lyman t (3)	TM	207 499-2273	(not reporting)						
Machias t* (2)	CM	207 255-8683	Thomas G Wolverton	Oskar H Pedersen	Martha A Bagley	....	Philip A Roberts	Clifford A Braley	Richard D Wallace
Madawaska t* (5)	CM	207 728-6351	Beverly A Madore	Roland D Martin	Roland D Martin	Roland D Martin	Norman Cyr	Ronald Pelletier	George Daigle
Madison t* (4)	TM	207 696-3971	Norman A Dean	Richard R Michaud	Beverly J Hebert	Beverly J Hebert	Wilfred Dubois	Harley G Dunlap Jr	Philip Curtis
Mapleton t* (2)	TM	207 764-3754	Jeffrey Smith	Dennis P Gardner	Dennis P Gardner	Dennis P Gardner	Terry McPherson	Alex Cote	Thomas F Johnson
Mars Hill t* (2)	TM	207 425-3731	Thomas R York Jr	Thomas Saucier	Thomas Saucier	....	Norman McPherson	....	....
Masardis t* (..)	TM	207 435-2841	John Weeks	Julia MacDonald	Julia MacDonald	Julia MacDonald	Michael MacDonald		Clive A Bragdon
Mechanic Falls t* (3)	CM	207 345-2871	Lloyd A Boyd Sr	Adeline M Keene	Sheila A Gray	Adeline M Keene	Fenton Yates Jr	David J Miles	Adeline M Keene
Merrill t* (..)	CM	207 757-8286	Thomas Goff	Hazel E Beers	Hazel E Beers	Hazel E Beers	Robert N Furrow	Ralph Kennedy	....
Mexico t* (4)	TM	207 364-7971	Bertha A Barrett	Timothy E Kelcourse	Calvin P Lyons	Calvin P Lyons	William Whytock	Gregory Gallant	William Fisler
Milbridge t* (1)	CM	207 546-2422	John E Purington	Elliott L Foss	Esther Beal	Esther M Beal	Peter Sawyer	Colin Haskell	Elliott L Foss
Millinocket t*† (8)	CM	207 723-9701	Dean Beaupain	William J Ayoob	Philis Beaupain	William J Ayoob	Daniel Hart	Frank Friel	Robert E Lander
Milo t* (3)	CM	207 943-2202	Daniel Nutter	William F Brockman	Melinda Sherburne	Pauline Lewis	Albert Perkins	....	Harold Burton
Monmouth t* (3)	TM	207 933-2206	Bruce G Gray	Paul Bird	Paul Bird	Paul Bird	Laurence O Folsom	Daniel W McGinley	Herbert Whittier
Monroe t* (1)	TM	207 525-3515	Robert Dolloff	James Frost Sr	Vesta Rand	James Frost Sr	Reginald Mitchell	....	James Frost Sr
Monson t* (1)	TM	207 997-3641	Dwain Allen	Ruel P Cross	Jeanne Reed	....	Collin Bickford	....	Clarence Pratt
Monticello t*† (1)	TM	207 538-9500	Herschel Good	Norma Harper	Norma Harper	....	Morris Cole	....	Bernard Swimm
Mount Desert t* (2)	CM	207 276-5531	Durlin E Lunt Jr	Leonard H Kyle	Frederick Brown	Carlo Ninfi	Dana Haynes	Edward J Mandell	Robert W Hamblen
New Canada t*† (..)	CM	207 834-5617	Carrol Caron	Claude Dumond	Rita J Daigle	Claude Dumond	....	....	Claude Dumond
New Gloucester t* (3)	TM	207 926-4126	John Morrison	A Wayne Cobb	A Wayne Cobb	A Wayne Cobb	Willard Morrison	Herbert Thompson Jr	A Wayne Cobb
New Portland t* (1)	TM	207 628-4441	Breda Joy Stevens	Lena S Atwood	Lena S Atwood	Lena S Atwood	David Reed	....	....
Newport t (3)	TM	207 368-4410	Elmer W Wilcox	Edmond Bearor	Valarie Flanders	Evelyn M Ricker	Donald Brawn	Donald F Carnall	Harland Burke
Norridgewock t* (3)	TM	207 634-2252	Emery McIntyre	Irene Pion	Eloise B Libby	Irene Pion	David Jones	Leroy Jones	Irene Pion
North Berwick t (3)	TM	207 676-3353	(not reporting)						
Norway t*† (4)	TM	207 743-6651	Kenneth Kozak	Larry A Todd	Carol H Millett	Larry A Todd	Robert J Butters	James DeNormandie	Donald M Hunt
Oakfield t*† (1)	TM	207 757-8479	....	Candis Roy	Pansy L Burton	....	Gerald McGuire	....	Candis Roy
Oakland t* (5)	CM	207 465-7357	Robert Nutting	Robert J Quinn	Janice E Higgins	....	Charles Pullen	Joel R Abbot	....
Ogunquit t* (1)	CM	207 646-5139	John Miller	William Fraser	Madeline Brown	....	Bruce A Bernard	William P Hancock	Jonathan Webber
Old Orchard Beach t* (6)	CM	207 934-5714	Gerald F Verrier	Jerome G Plante	Maureen O'Leary	Lois A Benway	Thomas Smith	Paul A Tibbetts	Edward Coreau
Old Town* (8)	CM	207 827-5985	C Clark Young III	Stanton L McGowen	Shirley Stevens	Frank I Leathers	Kenneth Sirois	Dale Gauthier	Richard Lacadie
Orono t* (11)	CM	207 866-2241	David J Trefethen	Bruce A Locke	Wanda J Thomas	Wanda J Thomas	Gary J Robichaud	David J Dekanich	....
Orrington t* (3)	TM	207 825-3340	Rodney P Mann	John F White	Carole A Hardin	Amy L Waugh	Leslie E Grover	....	Amy L Waugh
Oxford t* (3)	CM	207 539-4431	Elton Record	Charles G Bourque	Anita Moulton	....	Ernest F Knightly	Ronald Kugell	....
Paris t*† (4)	TM	207 743-2501	Robert W Long	Paul C Brown	Elizabeth M Larson	....	John C Bryant	Lloyd C Herrick	Reginald Linindell
Patten t* (1)	TM	207 528-2215	Donald Adams	Rhonda J Harvey	Glenda Sommers	....	Waldo Harvey	Orrie L Hunt	....
Phillips t* (1)	TM	207 639-3561	Timothy E Abbott	Laura W Toothaker	Sylvia H Adams	Laura W Toothaker	Ronald H Buck	....	Stephen L Haines
Pittsfield t* (4)	CM	207 487-3136	Michael J Fendler	D Dwight Dogherty	Marie J Pennock	D Dwight Dogherty	Bernard C Williams	Spencer R Havey	....
Poland t* (4)	TM	207 998-4601	Lionel Ferland Jr	Richard L Chick	Judith A Akers	....	Ernest M Fitts	Eric Parker	....
Portage Lake t* (1)	TM	207 435-4361	Paul Nason	Velma P Casey	Gladys Cote	Velma P Casey	Herbert McPherson	....	Omar Paradis
Portland* (62)	CM	207 775-5451	David H Brenerman	Stephen T Honey	Jane Durgin	Richard Ranaghan Jr	Joseph E McDonough	Francis E Amoroso	George A Flaherty
Presque Isle* (11)	CM	207 764-4485	Dana Lougee	Gerald A Clark	Betty Merkel	Jere Sirois	Welden McPherson	R Peter Lavway	John V Carrier
Rangeley t* (1)	TM	207 864-3326	Howard E Gurney	Frank A Farnsworth	Audrey Hodge	Frank A Farnsworth	Brian Ellis	Ernest Allen	Jerome Gueuremont
Reed PL* (..)	TM	207 456-7546	Llewellyn Corbett	Joan Emery	Nyoka Irish	....	Blaine Irish Jr	....	....
Richmond t* (3)	CM	207 737-4305	Gordon Sherman	Ronnie Belanger	Gerald Brown	....	Dana Sullivan	Thomas P Fales Sr	Russ Williams
Rockland* (8)	CM	207 594-8431	Warren T Perry	Harold F Parks	Alton L Curtis	David F Hodges	Ernest F Daye	Richard D Hanley	David L St Peter
Rockport t* (3)	TM	207 236-3575	Howard Dearborn	R Paul Weston	Brenda S Richardson	R Paul Weston	Bruce C Woodward	Forest B Doucette	R Paul Weston
Rumford t* (8)	CM	207 364-4576	Jim Rinaldo	Robert L Noe	Mary Ann Prue	Robert L Noe	J Eugene Boivin	Dewey Robinson	Robey Welch
Sabattus t (3)	TM	207 375-4331	(not reporting)						
Saco* (13)	CM	207 282-4191	Eric Cote	Ronald E Stewart	Joan M LaMontagne	Cinthia Dyer	Larry Smith Sr	Richard L Nason	....

Directory 1/10 continued — MUNICIPAL OFFICIALS IN ALL U.S. CITIES OVER 2,500[1]

City, 1980 population (000 omitted), form of government	Municipal phone number	Mayor	Appointed administrator	City clerk	Finance officer	Fire chief	Police chief	Public works director
MAINE (181) continued								
Sanford t (18) RT	207 324-4121	David L Carpenter	David Y Miller	J Raymond Nadeau	Ms M C Gillings	David Rankin	Arthur J Kelly III	Anthony Hayes
Sangerville t*† (1) TM	207 876-2814	Judy Grant	Bradley Nuite	Ms G Rizzitello	Bradley Nuite	Dennis Pearl	....	Bradley Nuite
Scarborough t* (11) CM	207 883-4301	John W Griffin	Carl L Betterley	Marion L O'Roak	Ruth D Porter	Robert S Carson	Hollis G Dixon	William D Giguere
Searsport t* (2) TM	207 548-6372	Bruce G Mills	Donald C Grant	Susan Lessard	....	Dan Rich	Roger Ouellette	....
Sherman t* (1) TM	207 365-4260	Richard M McNally	Anna L Robinson	Anna Robinson	Anna L Robinson	Michael Elwell	....	....
Skowhegan t* (8) TM	207 474-3744	Warren S Shay	Patricia A Dickey	Dorothy E Cayford	Jean F Carrigan	Carl F McKenney	Larry Jones	Ray H Brown
Smyrna t* (..) CM	207 757-8286	Michael McCluskey	Hazel E Beers	Hazel E Beers	Hazel E Beers	Bryce Clark	Vinal Friel	....
South Berwick t*† (4) TM	207 384-2263	Richard R Goulet	John S Eldridge III	Beatrice Nutter	John S Eldridge III	George Gorman	Paul S Hunter	John S Eldridge III
South Portland* (23) CM	207 767-3201	Sidney H Schwartz	Robert B Ganley	Nadeen M Daniels	Rocco Marzilli Jr	Philip McGouldrick	Robert M Schwartz	Arvin D Erskine
Southwest Harbor t* (2) TM	207 244-5404	Robert E Stanwood	Michael K Knowles	Alice S Berry	Michael K Knowles	Wilbert Terry	John H Carroll	Michael K Knowles
St. Agatha t* (1) TM	207 543-7422	Francis Morin	Clarence Michaud	Clarence Michaud	Clarence Michaud	Joel Chamberland	....	Clarence Thibeault
St. Albans t* (1) TM	207 938-4568	Edward Walker	Larry Post	Angilee Seekins	....	Peter Duncombe	....	....
Stacyville t* (1) TM	207 365-4195	Gary H Moody	Mary Anne Guiggey	Mary Anne Guiggey	Mary Anne Guiggey	Dennis Gallagher	....	....
Standish t (6) TM	207 642-3466	Fred H Libby Jr	....	Elmer H Alley	....	William M Ward Jr	....	Jeffrey Richardson
Stockholm t*† (..) TM	207 896-5659	David Sterris	Helen A Holman	Albertine Dufour	Helen A Holman	Lewis Campbell	John Sjostedt	Simon Forsman
Stonington t*† (1) CM	207 367-2351	....	Earl Brill	Janice Turner	Earl Brill	....	Richard Sweetsir	....
Thomaston t* (3) TM	207 354-6272	Cecil Polky	Cathy A Smith	Cathy A Smith	Cathy A Smith	Malcolm Hyler	Burton Gale	David Taylor
Topsham t§ (6) TM	207 725-5821	Verdi L Tripp	Robert W Farrar	Margaret Munsey	Marjorie Randall	David A Dube	Paul J Lessard	Arthur Trusiani
Tremont t* (1) TM	207 244-7204	George Lawson	Gretchen K Strong	June E Thompson	Gretchen K Strong	Melvin Jewett	....	Gretchen K Strong
Turner t (4) TM	207 225-3414	Bernice Gilbert	Bernice Gilbert	Charlotte Ryan	....	Laurence Gagne	....	Bruce Leavitt
Van Buren t* (4) CM	207 868-2886	Verne Berube	Gerald E Blier	Kathleen Cyr	....	Chanel Bouchard	Herman Pelletier	Donald Dumond
Vassalboro t* (3) TM	207 872-2826	Philip Haines	Michael Roy	Vicki J Schad	Michael Roy	Gerald Dore	Richard Jerolmon	Michael Roy
Veazie t* (2) TM	207 945-9523	L William Demaso	Neils C Neilson	Neils C Neilson	Neils C Neilson	Jack Doyle	Joseph F Friedman	....
Waldoboro t* (4) TM	207 832-5369	Betty Lou Lee	Lee L Smith	Patricia L Chapman	Lee L Smith	Robert M Maxcy	Melvin M Spencer	Earl C Wallace
Wallagrass t* (1) CM	207 834-5515	....	Priscille Fournier	....	....	....	....	....
Warren t* (3) CM	207 273-2421	William W Cross	John Fraser	Avis M Luce	John Fraser	Edward Grinnell Jr	....	John Fraser
Washburn t* (2) TM	207 455-8485	Milford Libby	Sheldon Richardson	Glenis M Carter	Sheldon Richardson	Jasper K Umphrey	Gary Sanfacon	Richard Bragg
Waterboro t (3) TM	207 247-5166	Robert C Fay	....	Dianne Holden	John Monteith	Raymond Emmons Jr	....	Glenn Bean Sr
Waterville§ (18) MC	207 873-7131	Ann G Hill	John R Chmura	Ann B Peters	Carol Pickering	Frederick Brown	Ronald Laliberte	Luc J Carriere
Wells t* (7) TM	207 646-5113	Jamesl Wiggin	Fred T Breslin	Marion B Noble	....	....	Robert E Linscott	Fred T Breslin
Westbrook§ (15) MC	207 854-9105	Phillip D Spiller	Jonathan Carter	William L Clarke	Susan R Fitzpatrick	James F Rulman	Carmine Russo	Kenneth Eastman
Wilton t* (4) TM	207 645-4961	Harold Karkos	Paul T Soucie	Linda P Jellison	Paul T Soucie	Birdell Dunham	Parker James	Paul T Soucie
Windham t* (11) CM	207 892-2511	Brian Olson	Mark Green	Barbara E Strout	Melody Main	Timothy Dolby	Gregory C Hanscom	Steve Walker
Winslow t* (8) CM	207 872-2776	Kerry A Clark	Edward A Gagnon	Rosanne Boutin	....	Ansel Grindall	Ronald Whary	Lawrence Fortin
Winter Harbor t* (1) TM	207 963-2235	Vernon Joy	Allan L Smallidge	Allan L Smallidge	....	Dale F Torrey	F A Torrey	....
Winterport t* (3) TM	207 223-4433	Thomas Skratt	Richard A Erb	Cheryl Rancourt	Richard A Erb	Creighton L Parker	George Mele	Richard A Erb
Winthrop t* (6) CM	207 377-2286	Judith I Stebbins	Marshall Hills	Irma S Rice	Marshall Hills	Hartley Palleschi	Charles H Jackson	Marshall Hills
Wiscasset t (3) TM	207 882-6331	Lawrence R Gordon	....	Sheila R Leavitt	....	J Gordon Merry	Michael J Reidy	Roy E Barnes
Yarmouth t* (7) CM	207 846-9036	Clinton S Mason Jr	Osmond C Bonsey	Patricia A Merrill	Osmond C Bonsey	Carl Winslow	Richard Perry	Harold B Hutchinson
York t (8) MC	207 363-2660	Arthur A Berger	Donald P Cole III	Rega A Bridges	Margaret Law	Kenneth Towne	N Douglas Starbird	Leon R Moulton
MARYLAND (55)								
Aberdeen t* (12) CM	301 272-1600	Ronald Kupferman	Kenneth L Volkart	Sandra Ayres	Sandra Ayres	Bennet Smith	Lemuel Porter	Thomas C Wagman
Annapolis§ (32) MC	301 263-3322	Richard L Hillman	Anne E Pinckney	Patricia L Bembe	William S Tyler	Charles H Steele	John C Schmitt	William C Holland
Baltimore (787) MC	301 396-3100	Wm Donald Schaefer	Joan B Bereska	....	Charles L Benton	Peter O'Connor	Bishop Robinson	Francis W Kuchta
Bel Air t* (8) CM	301 838-5400	Geoffrey R Close	William N McFaul	Joanne L Russell	William N McFaul	Richard Woodward	James P Monaghan	D David Ranney Jr
Berwyn Heights t§ (3) MC	301 474-5000	William T Armistead	Bill Close	Suzan Lape	Bill Close	Sal Barille	Thomas Stoner	Howard F Moore
Bladensburg t§ (8) MC	301 927-7048	William R Seymour	T Eric Morsicato	Elsie S Morrison	Clare J Murtha	....	Robert M Zidek	John A Parker
Bowie* (34) CM	301 262-6200	Richard J Logue	G Charles Moore	Edith Maylack	Rosemary Moore	....	....	Chester Kreitzer
Brentwood t (3) MC	301 927-3344	George D Denny Jr	Lanny E Mummert	Mary E Reed	Mary E Tavel	Harold Hoffman	....	....
Brunswick t† (5) MC	301 834-7500	Jess D Orndorff	....	William L Roelke	William L Roelke	William Sauser	William F Miller Jr	Jack D Brawner
Cambridge (12) MC	301 228-4020	C Lloyd Robbins	....	Kenneth L Hughes	Kenneth L Hughes	James Raymond	Russell E Wroten	Charles W Parks
Capitol Heights t§ (3) MC	301 336-0626	Leo P Forami	Ralph A Lange	Margaret A McClary	....	....	....	Elmer Hockman
Centreville t* (2) CM	301 758-1180	F Dudley Benton	Scott A Hancock	Doris M Payne	....	G P Walls	Charles I Tarbutton	Paul I Roberts
Chestertown t (3) MC	301 778-0500	Elmer E Horsey	William S Ingersoll	....	Elmer E Horsey	Bruce Neal	Mauritz Stetson	Medford Capel
Cheverly t* (6) CM	301 773-8360	Robert W O'Connor	John L Fitzwater	Lenore B Lerch	....	....	Garrett T Kirwin Jr	Joseph C Hawkins
Chevy Chase t§ (3) MC	301 654-7144	....	Max E Bowen	....	....	....	....	....
Chevy Chase v§ (3) MC	301 654-7300	....	Roy A Burke	....	....	....	....	....
College Park* (24) CM	301 864-8877	Alvin J Kushner	Leon F Shore	Miriam P Wolff	Sterling B Cheatham	....	Donald L Byrd	James C Johnson
Crisfield (3) MC	301 968-1333	P J Purnell Jr	....	Julian C Tyler	....	Robt P Goldsborough	Wayne W Townsend	Robert L Bradford
Cumberland§ (26) MC	301 722-2000	George M Wyckoff Jr	Dennis E Piendak	Audrey C Wolford	William Z Burke	Russell L Livengood	Robet E Giles	John O Dewitt
Delmar t* (1) CM	301 896-2777	Frank E Gully	Karen E Horsman	Rebecca A Joseph	....	Joseph Morris	Harold E Saylor	Robert F Handy
District Heights t (7) MC	301 336-1402	William E Hay	....	Nora D Mencer	....	....	Ronald L Raycraft	Monroe G Chew Iv
Easton t (8) MC	301 822-2525	George P Murphy	....	Elizabeth M Willey	....	Thomas Harmon	R Edward Blessing	Roger C Judd
Elkton t† (6) CM	301 398-4170	James G Crouse	Robert R Reed	Naomi M Thomas	....	....	Calvin T Krammes	John W Peterson
Forest Heights t (3) MC	301 839-1030	Warren F Adams	....	Tillie T Luczak	Grover Dare	....	Harry Polis	Dionisio A Gabriel
Frederick (28) MC	301 662-5161	Ronald N Young	....	Carolyn R Greiner	Betty E Rice	Walter F Murray Jr	Richard J Ashton	Robert L Strine
Friendship Heights v§ (8) MC	301 656-2797	....	Alice M Bushnell	....	....	....	....	....
Frostburg (8) MC	301 689-6000	William R Davis	Dale E Iman	....	Dale E Iman	Gary Tummino	Lesie Bevan	Donald C Peck
Fruitland (3) MC	301 749-1276	Wendell G Mezick	Richard M Pollitt	Judith B Carey	James S Johnson	J Benny Malone	Donald E Bozman	....
Gaithersburg* (26) CM	301 948-3220	Bruce A Goldensohn	Sanford W Daily	Sanford W Daily	Roger L Anderson	....	George E Fusco	A M McLachlen
Glenarden t§ (5) MC	301 773-2100	Stanley D Brown	Eloise C Hall	Adelaide K Virgil	Shirley Allen	....	Frank T McGill	Lloyd Adams
Greenbelt* (16) CM	301 474-8000	Gil Weidenfeld	James K Giese	Gudrun H Mills	Casimir R Prybyl	....	William T Lane	George E Smith
Hagerstown (34) MC	301 790-3200	Donald R Frush	William M Breichner	Georgiann N Lucas	Alfred Martin	Richard Smith	Clinton Mowen	....
Havre de Grace (9) MC	301 939-1800	Charles Montgomery	....	Robert N Northwood	Robert N Northwood	Edward Rosenkrans	J Earl Walker Jr	David Himes
Hyattsville§† (13) MC	301 927-0194	Thomas L Bass	Robert T Johnson	Gertrude McCamley	James M Hannan	Donald B Moltrup	Robert T Perry	Daniel U Jones
Indian Head t* (1) CM	301 743-5511	Roy L Budd	....	Eleanor K Fuller	Eleanor K Fuller	Philip M Hamrick	Dave Fuller	Ross Metcalfe
La Plata t* (2) CM	301 934-8421	William F Eckman	Zakary A Krebeck	Betty J Taylor	Betty J Taylor	Kenneth Chaplin	Zakary A Krebeck	Zakary A Krebeck
Landover Hills t§ (1) MC	301 577-0101	James D Britt	David Felzenberg	....	Lorraine Zimmermann	....	Larry Sweeney	John Kerr
Laurel t (12) MC	301 725-5300	Robert J Dipietro	Roland B Sweitzer	Kaye M Sandul	Eleanor C Wolter	Richard Blakenship	Robert M Kaiser	Bruce M Dodgson
Mount Rainier (7) MC	301 927-0104	Stanley Prusch	Ralph C McGehee	....	....	Lawrence Trainum	Everett G Husk	Edward Posey
New Carrollton (13) MC	301 459-6100	Andrew C Hanko	John L Brunner	Eugenia V Czumak	Thomas A Patterson	....	....	Charles J Deitz
Ocean City t§ (5) MC	301 289-8221	Harry W Kelley	Anthony W Barrett	Sheldon E Dietert	Ron Bireley	Roger Steger	Frank Pappas	Dennis Dare
Pocomoke City* (4) CM	301 957-1333	J Dawson Clarke	Russell W Blake	Louise Northam	....	George Henderson Jr	Norwood Wimbrow	Dwight E Campbell
Poolesville t (3) CO	301 428-8927	Charles W Elgin Sr	....	Nancy I Fost	....	....	....	....
Princess Anne t* (1) CM	301 651-1818	Roland Collins	Wallace Dashiell	Goldie Brittingham	....	....	James C Bolden	....
Riverdale t§ (5) MC	301 927-6381	Guy Tiberio	Patrick J Prangley	....	Patrick J Prangley	James McGill	Leo W Link	Terence M Sheehan
Rockville* (44) CM	301 424-8000	John R Freeland	Larry N Blick	Helen Heneghan	Mary Parker	....	Jared Stout	Robert Goodin
Salisbury§ (16) MC	301 749-5723	W Paul Martin	Patrick J Fennell	Fara L Tawes	R T Baskerville	Francis Darling	Coulbourn Dykes	Ken Haensler

Directory 1/10 continued

MUNICIPAL OFFICIALS IN ALL U.S. CITIES OVER 2,500[1]

City, 1980 population (000 omitted), form of government	Municipal phone number	Mayor	Appointed administrator	City clerk	Finance officer	Fire chief	Police chief	Public works director
MARYLAND (55) continued								
Seat Pleasant (5) MC	301 336-2600	Frank J Blackwell	Eddie L Tobias	A Gloria Robinson	Dwain Lucas	....	....	William S Thomas
Snow Hill t§ (2) MC	301 632-2080	James R Freeny II	Douglas R Miller	Douglas R Miller	....	....	Orlando Blake	Robert Zueger
Takoma Park§† (16) MC	301 270-1700	Sammie A Abbott	James S Wilson Jr	M Sibyl Pusti	Richard A Schnuer	....	....	Richard Robbins
Taneytown (3) CM	301 756-2677	Henry Reindollar Jr	Neal W Powell	Linda Lingenfelder	....	....	Bruce W Moore	Elwood J Harner
Thurmont t (3) CO	301 271-7313	James F Black	....	Richard K May	Richard K May	James H Mackley	Herman D Shook	Marion W Rice
University Park t† (3) MC	301 927-2997	Ruth T Lutwack	....	Earl A Miller	Earl A Miller	....	John R Colister	....
Westernport t (3) MC	301 359-3932	James H Wills	....	Delores Y Rooney	Jerome Laffey	Daniel Taylor	James O Evans	Lacy L Tinsley
Westminster (9) MC	301 848-9000	Leroy L Conaway	....	John D Dudderar	Stephen V Dutterer	....	Sam R Leppo	Carroll R Dell
MASSACHUSETTS (267)								
Abington t (14) TM	617 878-0805	James E Franey	Arthur P Miller	Patricia A McKenna	Wilber G Hollis	Wallace A Howe	James J Healy	Richard G Burns
Acton t* (18) TM	617 263-8200	Donald R Gilberli	Bernard J Murphy Jr	Lydia R Lesure	Daniel Brosnan	Malcolm MacGregor	George W Robinson	Ralph Herrick
Acushnet t† (9) TM	617 995-1141	James S Madruga Jr	Alfred E Portway	Yvonne B Desroiers	Wilfred C Fortin	Arsene J Cusson	Michael R Poitras	Manuel A Sol Jr
Adams t§ (10) RT	413 743-1561	Joseph Dean Jr	Henry J Hill III	Paul Hutchenson	Charles F St John	William Chittenden	Bruce McLaren	Robert M Degen
Agawam t* (26) CM	413 786-0400	....	Edward A Caba	Richard M Theroux	David C Gallano	Russell D Jenks	Stanley Chmielewski	John P Stone
Amesbury t* (14) RT	617 388-0622	James N Thivierge	William J Grom	Josephine Jacques	Michael Basque	Arthur R Gaudet	Michael A Cronin	Harold Gillam
Amherst t* (33) RT	413 253-9708	Barbara K Griffith	Barry Del Castilho	Estelle M Matusko	James A Lindstrom	Victor J Zumbruski	Donald N Maia	Stanley P Ziomek
Andover t* (26) TM	617 470-3800	Donn B Byrne	Kenneth R Mahony	Elden R Salter	Anthony J Torrisi	William T Downs	James F Johnson	Robert E McQuade
Arlington t* (48) CM	617 643-6700	Robert Murray	Donald R Marquis	Ann Powers	Anello L Minervini	Warren R French	John F Carroll	Richard H Bowler
Ashburnham t (4) TM	617 827-5733	Leo P Collette Jr	Elaine McCarthy	Wesley P Landry	Raymond A Dennehy	A William Bickford	Ronald P Laplante	William Brennan Jr
Ashland t† (9) TM	617 881-1741	Rocco F Annesi	....	Anthony J Cunis	Paul R Romeo	Frank Karayianes	Robert J Gonfrade	Russell Pepper
Athol t (11) RT	617 249-2368	Michael R Davis	....	Mary M Erali	Charles E Baker	Brian Martin	Robert H Jillson	Noel J Ryan
Attleboro (34) MC	617 222-9610	Brenda L Reed	....	Virginia Holbrook	Richard V Boucher	Ronald M Churchill	Howard M Cruff	David Butterfield
Auburn t (15) RT	617 832-3761	Charles A Baker	Timothy J King	Doris M Hill	John J Nugent	Robert E Murray	Robert F Johnson	Joseph Luks
Avon t (5) TM	617 588-0414	John J DeMarco	....	Lorraine E Meninno	Lorraine E Meninno	John H Reid	Carl F Miller	James F Meninno
Ayer t (7) TM	617 772-2072	Thomas S Casey Jr	....	Beatrice L Briggs	Thomas F Callahan	G L Donahue Jr	Philip L Connors	William G Redfield
Barnstable t (31) RT	617 775-1120	John C Klimm	....	Francis A Lahteine	Daniel Kostreva	Richard Farrenkopf	Neil A Nightingale	Joseph Campo
Barre t (4) TM	617 355-2504	Earl N Sample	Lorraine S Leno	Alice C Orszulak	Arlene Betteridge	Richard Clark	Michael J Ryder	George F McDonald
Bedford t§ (13) TM	617 275-1111	Carol E Goldman	Richard J White	Muriel Wittenauer	Marcia Sternberg	William H Sullivan	Donald Eunson	Robert A Cassidy
Belchertown t† (8) TM	413 323-6901	Shirley A Dorey	William G Whitlock	George R Bach	Eleanor W Green	Donald F Bock	Robert A Knight	Harry Dodge
Bellingham t (14) TM	617 966-0990	Lawrence Cibley	....	B Z Remillard	Jeanne Mourey	Richard Ranieri	Joseph Grassi	Gerard Daigle
Belmont t (26) RT	617 484-2300	William P Monahan	Joan Garland	Ann Cresine-Wilson	Edwin R Sparrow Jr	James Murphy	Robert T Shea	James J Castanino
Berkley t (3) TM	617 824-6794	George A Moitoza	....	Francis Andrews	Kenneth E Combs	James R Barrow	David A Mason	....
Beverly (38) MC	617 927-0031	F John Monahan	....	Richard C Kelley	Harry A Gannon	Dean M Palmer	William D Cowles	Alan F Taubert
Billerica t§ (37) RT	617 667-7182	Thomas H Conway	Paul F Talbot	Myrtie Smith	Ralph McKenna	James Flavin	John Barretto	Jeffrey S Rider
Blackstone t* (7) CM	617 883-1500	Thomas E Devlin	Dan Doyle	Susan A Mellor	Earl E Robbins	John F Greene	Joseph Brouillette	Thomas F Devlin
Bolton t (3) TM	617 779-2297	(not reporting)						
Boston (563) MC	617 725-4000	Raymond L Flynn	Raymond Dooley	John P Campbell	George Russell Jr	Leo Stapleton	Joseph M Jordan	Joseph Casazza
Bourne t (14) TM	617 759-4486	Barry H Johnson	....	Mary C McDonough	Terrill Mark	Robert W Eldridge	Henry F Maiolini	Louis F Pellegrini
Boxborough t (3) TM	617 263-1116	Susan S Elenbaas	Thomas E Hauenstein	Virginia Richardson	....	Warren H Morse	Robert J Johnson	Warren H Morse
Boxford t (5) TM	617 887-8181	Enid E Thuermer	James A Aylward	Francis P Weatherby	Thomas M Blake	Damon J Dustin	Douglas A Warren	Thomas F Greene
Boylston t (3) TM	617 869-2234	Guy F Fuller	Suzanne C Olsen	Helen M Duffy	Lawrence Compton	Donald C Parker	David A Werme	Edward Kimball
Braintree t (36) RT	617 848-1870	Edward R Wynot	Robert R Sherman	Robert N Bruynell	Walter Kirkland	Carl R Vitagliano	John V Polio	Robert E Frazier
Brewster t (5) TM	617 896-3701	Robert A Sawtelle	Nancymarie Schwinn	Barbara A Vaughn	Ann E Hansen	Roy E Jones III	James R Ehrhart	Dennis D Hanson
Bridgewater t (17) TM	617 697-3700	David A Flynn	....	Ronald R Adams	George A Belcher	Clarence A Levy	William P Ferioli	....
Brockton (95) MC	617 580-1100	Carl Pitaro	....	John J Lyons	Dorothy R Donovan	James M Hallisey	Robert D Gillis	....
Brookline t§ (55) TM	617 232-9000	Edward Novakoff	Richard T Leary	William Sullivan	Shirley Sido	James P Fallon	George R Simard	William T Griffiths
Burlington t† (23) RT	617 272-6700	Albert J Kelley	Robert A Mercier	Catherine R McKim	Patrick J Mullin	Herbert W Crawford	Edw J McCafferty	Harold J Publicover
Cambridge* (95) CM	617 498-9000	Leonard J Russell	Robert W Healy	Paul Healy	James P Maloney Jr	Thomas V Scott	Anthony Paolillo	Everett Kennedy
Canton t (18) TM	617 828-0184	Richard R Staiti	Warren J Rutherford	Carlton B Taber	Donald E Cragen	James J Fitzpatrick	Joseph T Buckley	Henry L Munson
Carlisle t (3) TM	617 369-6155	David C Stewart	....	Eleanor S Cochran	....	Robert J Koning	David T Galvin	Roger A Davis
Carver t (7) TM	617 866-4551	(not reporting)						
Charlton t (7) TM	617 248-5900	Leonard Haebler	....	Mary S Sullivan	Paul Rogers	Maro Carrington	Phillip J Stevens	Maro Carrington
Chatham t (6) TM	617 945-2100	Wm G Litchfield	Elinore B Johnson	I Barbara Brown	Carol R Lund	Robert C Greenough	Barry D Eldredge	Gilbert R Borthwick
Chelmsford t (31) TM	617 256-2441	Bonita A Towle	Norman E Thidemann	Mary E St Hilaire	Ernest F Day	Frederick Reid	Raymond P McKeon	Harold P Gray
Chelsea† (25) MC	617 884-0407	Joel M Pressman	Paul G Casino	John Dalis	Valarie Connor	Herbert C Fothergil	Charles H Wilson	Jesse Neil
Cheshire t (3) TM	413 743-1690	Harvey J Daniels	....	Ruth Andrew	Donald Moore	Richard Francesconi	Richard Armstrong	Stanley F Krutiak
Chicopee (55) MC	413 594-4711	Richard S Lak	Matthew Zawidowski	John S Whalen Jr	Ernest LaFlamme Jr	Robert J Nunes	Edmund F Dowd	Edwin R Orwat
Clinton t (13) TM	617 365-4812	Alan D Jewett	....	Earl P Wilson	Lawrence F Burke	Thomas Moore	Martin F O'Toole	William G Gilmour
Cohasset t (7) TM	617 383-0187	Clifford Mitman Jr	Mark J Lanza	Frances L Marks	William Signorelli	Martin Dooley	Joseph Kealey	....
Concord t* (16) TM	617 369-2100	Terry W Rothermel	Steven E Sheiffer	Alice H Ingham	Anthony T Logalbo	Richard S Ryan	William J Costello	Harold W Storrs
Dalton t (7) TM	413 684-0032	William B Moody	Dorothy J Snyder	Alice B Andrews	....	Robert Kirchner	Anthony J Calabrese	Thomas J Callahan
Danvers t* (24) RT	617 777-0001	John D Crowley	Wayne P Marquis	Daniel J Toomey	Daniel J Toomey	Leland E Martin Jr	Christ J Bouras	Newton H Sweet
Dartmouth t§ (24) RT	617 997-0789	Walter P Faria	Lawrence Cameron	William B Mosher	William B Mosher	....	Stephen J Soares	Manuel Branco
Dedham t (25) RT	617 326-5770	Anthony V Taurasi	Robert B Hanson	Margaret M McGowan	Gerald J Leonard	John J Donovan	William C Kardas	Dominic DiVirgilio
Deerfield t (5) RT	413 665-4645	Elizabeth Kirkwood	....	Mary Ann Warner	Mary Ann Warner	....	David R Bell	John Kelleher
Dennis t§ (12) TM	617 394-8300	William Shanahan	Allan S Young	Elinor Slade	Elinor Slade	Robert S Hersey	Pasquale Santamauro	Robert E Crowell
Dighton t (5) TM	617 669-6431	Armand Gagne	....	Leanor Mendonca	Doris Hopkins	Joseph T White	Karl K Spratt Jr	Alfred A Perry
Douglas t (4) TM	617 476-3566	Patricia A Manning	....	Betty Ann McCallum	Paul Boutiette	Leon T Sochia III	John Koslak	Edward Therrien
Dover t (5) TM	617 785-0054	Walter Attrilge	Kevin E Paicos	Marcia E Mahoney	Kevin E Paicos	Francis A Luttazi	Carl E Sheridan	John Miele
Dracut t (21) TM	617 452-1908	Warren L Shaw Jr	Elizabeth White	Gary W McCarthy	Janice M Maclean	Gerard A Carle	Robert A Tyrrell	Paul G Dillon
Dudley t (9) TM	617 943-2792	Anthony B DiDonato	....	Freda Lambros	David Perry	John Cristina	Leon Holewa	Felix B Orlowski
Duxbury t (12) TM	617 934-6586	John P Leonard	Edmund A Dondero	Nancy M Oates	Rolando DeAguiar	Carl T O'Neil	Daniel Skelly	....
East Bridgewater t (10) TM	617 378-2291	Paul R Nisby	....	Elaine S Powers	Edward S Whitmarsh	Robert K Winsor	Edward E Arnold	Raymond E Tardie
East Longmeadow t (13) TM	413 525-3305	Stanley P Brown	....	Richard A Clark	Donald M Scott	Forrest R Goodrich	Paul D Erickson	Alfred A Melien Jr
Eastham t (3) TM	617 255-0333	Howard W Quinn	....	Lillian Lamperti	Carolyn Gifford	Jack Austin	Jerry J Emond	Steven Douglas
Easthampton t† (16) RT	413 527-0818	Angelo C Yacuzzo	....	Phillip J Campbell	Gloria M Schmitter	Leonard E Light	Robert Allen	Richard C Carey
Easton t* (17) TM	617 238-7951	Leo Harlow	Daniel J Morgado	Esther C Anderson	Esther C Anderson	David W Brown	Walter Healey	Howard S Shaevitz
Essex t (3) TM	617 768-6531	Harold C Addison	....	Sally Soucy	Trish Roach	Ivan Muise	James Platt	John E Doyle
Everett (37) MC	617 389-2100	Edward G Connolly	....	J Kevin Dunn	Dominic Mazzio	Robert E Melvin	John Houghton	Frederick Tavano
Fairhaven t (16) RT	617 992-5416	Robert W Foster	....	Joseph A Saladino	William R Markey	Donald Bernard	Peter F Barcellos	Victor Oliveira Jr
Fall River (93) MC	617 675-6011	Carlton M Viveiros	Daniel Rapoza	Joseph F Doran	Norman Bolger	Louis Shea	Raymond Conroy	James Miller
Falmouth t (24) RT	617 548-7611	Leonard L Costa	....	William H Callahan	....	James Rogers	Paul Rodriques	Wm B Owen
Fitchburg (40) MC	617 345-9550	Bernard F Chartrand	....	Marion Smith	Richard N Sarasin	James C Keane	Francis R Roddy	Joseph J Levanti Jr
Foxborough t (14) TM	617 543-5301	Richard P Thompson	Andrew A Gala Jr	Arlene M Crimmins	Anthony P Matthews	Thomas F Sheehan	John P Gaudet Jr	Louis A Truax
Framingham t§ (65) RT	617 620-4811	John F Delprete	Matthew P Clarke	Michael J Ward	Donald J Croatti	John J Hancock	Arthur F Martins	James E Hanscom
Franklin t§ (18) TM	617 528-0049	George Woods	O Paul Shew	Florence E Keras	Albert R Brunelli	Lawrence Howell	Lawrence Benedetto	Modris Pukulis
Freetown t (7) TM	617 644-2201	M Rezendes Jr	....	Virginia J Terry	Yolande Morency	Richard Buttermore	Norman Allison Jr	Joseph F Simmons Jr
Gardner† (18) MC	617 632-4350	Gerald E St Hilaire	....	Genia J Pacocha	Michael T Smith	Robert C Peterson	Richard L Gemborys	Ronald Albee
Georgetown t (6) TM	617 352-6424	William E Handren	Cathy L'Hommedieu	Kenneth B Owens	Ann Ambrey	Thomas Nagle	Richard Spencer	Ben Bailey

Directory 1/10 continued — MUNICIPAL OFFICIALS IN ALL U.S. CITIES OVER 2,500[1]

City, 1980 population (000 omitted), form of government	Municipal phone number	Mayor	Appointed administrator	City clerk	Finance officer	Fire chief	Police chief	Public works director
MASSACHUSETTS (267) continued								
Gloucester (28) MC	617 283-0043	Richard R Silva	Jeffrey Y Zager	Fred J Kyrouz	Richard R Silva	Barry S McKay	Earland Worthley	Edward S Parks
Grafton t† (11) TM	617 839-4722	Paul G Bazinet	....	Raymond D Jordan	....	Richard F Glispin	James P Kearnan	....
Granby t (5) TM	413 467-7177	Robert H Farr	....	Jean R Hudgik	Robert Ward	David J Seiffert	John R Kirchhof	Steve Szaban
Great Barrington t (7) TM	413 528-3140	Richard J Louison	....	James T Coffey Jr	James T Coffey Jr	Mortimer Cavanaugh	William R Walsh Jr	Francis Van Deusen
Greenfield t§ (18) RT	413 774-4840	Richard T Blackbird	....	Robert N DeRusha	Patricia M Allen	George E Herzig Jr	David F McCarthy	James P Mosseau
Groton t (6) TM	617 448-2069	Robert S Hargraves	Margaret Howe-Soper	Thomas L M Park	Ann F Walsh	James F Connolly	George D Rider Jr	John R Norstrom
Groveland t (5) TM	617 372-6861	Hobart B Esty	....	Richard C Abbott	Catherine Boisselle	Harold F Sturtevant	James J Shanahan	John Bisi
Hadley t (4) TM	413 584-1590	Donald J Pipczynski	....	Joanna P Devine	Paul J Mokrzecki	Bernard Martula	Adolph Pipczynski	Joseph I Pipczynski
Halifax t (6) TM	617 293-5761	Daniel J Clark	....	Ruth V Perkins	Ruth V Perkins	Kenneth P Calvin	James A Booth	Ralph Hayward Jr
Hamilton t (7) TM	617 468-4455	Leon K Purington	....	Helen R Broyles	Bradley Peterson	Robert McRae	Robert W Poole	Gordon L Thompson
Hampden t (5) TM	413 566-3713	John M Flynn	....	Rita Vail	Judith Mikkola	Richard H Hatch	George K Stone Jr	Homer L Fuller
Hanover t§ (11) MC	617 826-2691	A Donald Deluse	Gregory J Doyon	John W Murphy	Gregory J Doyon	Wendell D Blanchard	John B Lingley	Herbert W Simmons
Hanson t (9) TM	617 293-2131	Bruce R Young	Idella R Snow	E M Waterman	Barbara A Gomez	Peter S Huska	Barry S Ross	Richard A Harris
Harvard t (12) TM	617 456-3995	Peter T Koch	....	Sally A Woster	R Don Haney	John O Burdick	Charles A Perry	Phillip Bartlett
Harwich t (9) TM	617 432-0145	Norman Gledhill Jr	Juell E Buckwold	Ruth B Ericson	Philip T Sherman	John S Trocchi	John S Raneo	Albert H Raneo
Hatfield t (3) TM	413 247-9211	Edward W Lesko Jr	....	Louise Slysz	Louise Slysz	Myron Sikorski	David Hurley	Edwin Smith
Haverhill† (47) MC	617 373-3818	William H Ryan	....	Nancy F Driscoll	William J Klueber	Richard Borden	Daniel M Fasulo	Herbert Nickerson
Hingham t (20) TM	617 749-1683	Kate Mahony	....	John H Studley	Joseph E Chase	Fletcher K Patch	J Borowski	Brian J Sullivan
Holbrook t† (11) TM	617 767-4312	Frank W McGaughey	....	M Shirley Austin	Louis E Savoie	William D Marble	John F White	Thomas R Cummings
Holden t* (13) CM	617 829-6561	James S Demetry	Wm A Kennedy Jr	Kathleen Peterson	Marion E Hewson	Edward R Oberg	Charles Hicks	William V Oliver
Holliston t (13) TM	617 429-2944	Daniel A Miley	Paul D Lebeau	Nancy L Norris	Bernard Doherty	Donald Rawson	W Laurence Marsell	Kenneth Garrity
Holyoke (45) MC	413 532-2602	Ernest E Proulx	....	James J Shea	Daniel Owens	Leonard Angers	Harold Skelton	Craig Dolan
Hopedale t (4) TM	617 478-2140	Robert E Barrows	John A Hayes	Robert S Phillips	M Russell Dennett	Donald A Moore	Robert B Taylor Jr	George Moore
Hopkinton t (7) TM	617 435-3781	John P Hinckley	....	Mary B Nealon	Patricia Whalen	Arthur P Stewart	Francis X Bowker	Robert H Bartlett
Hudson t§ (16) TM	617 562-9963	William G Collette	Clayton R Carlisle	Ralph W Warner	Joseph C Shay Jr	William M Hollick	Robert Turner	Joseph H Rego
Hull t (10) TM	617 925-2000	Leonard Hersch	Chris McCabe	Janet Bennett	Virginia Capo	James N Russo	Donald F Brooker	....
Ipswich t* (11) TM	617 356-4848	David S Player Jr	George E Howe	Isobel N Coulombe	George E Howe	Edwin R Emerson	Armand Brouillette	Armand T Michaud
Kingston t (7) TM	617 585-2711	Thomas D Lawton	....	George W Cushman	Daniel J Murphy	Jon H Alberghini	Daniel A Welch	Carl G Atwood
Lakeville t (6) TM	617 947-3400	F James Healey	Beverly J Pullano	Marjorie Henderson	Kathleen A Bowles	Roger S Hamilton	Donald L Bowles	Roger S Hamilton
Lancaster t (6) TM	617 365-3326	Edward J Valley	....	Eunice L Janda	Eric K Ross	John E McLaughlin	William D Moran	William Brodmerkle
Lanesborough t (3) TM	413 442-1167	Donald C Sheldon	....	Bonnie A Andrews	L Ruth Brower	Peter J Pannesco	Stanley J Misiuk	Donald R Clairmont
Lawrence (63) CO	617 686-6177	John J Buckley	....	Charles F Nyhan	Joseph A Lannon	James Bradley	Joseph J Tylus	Richard D'Agostino
Lee t† (6) RT	413 243-2100	John E Devarennes	....	John J Nagle	Dayton Delorme	Ottavio Giarolo	Edward J Finnegan	J Peter Scolforo
Leicester t (9) TM	617 892-4011	Edgar A Poirier	Russell J Connor Jr	J H Williamson	Richard Salem	Lory C Russell	Robert D Whitney	James Coughlin
Lenox t† (7) TM	413 637-1511	George L Darey	Patricia A Whalen	Rita T Paysan	James F Kincaid	John C Stringer	David W Berkel	Allen R Sykes
Leominster (35) MC	617 537-6311	Richard J Girouard	....	Audrey J Johnson	Anthony J Cali	Frederick W Johnson	Alan J Gallagher	Steven J Whitman
Lexington t§ (29) RT	617 862-0500	Margery M Battin	Robt Hutchinson Jr	Mary R McDonough	Richard M Perry	John D Bergeron	Paul E Furdon	Walter J Tonaszuck
Lincoln t§ (7) TM	617 259-8850	John A Ritsher	William G Hinchey	Nancy J Zuelke	Betty Lang	Domenic J Arena	Domenic J Arena	Richard P Carroll
Littleton t (7) TM	617 486-3121	Joseph Knox	Charles L Sumner	Mary Crory	Thomas A Arrison	Gary McCarraher	Thomas W O'Dea	Michael A Crory
Longmeadow t (16) TM	413 567-1066	Adolph J Jakobek	Russell F Denver	Jacqueline Marcotte	Richard Micheals	James E O'Brien	John Donaldson	Joseph J Cote
Lowell* (92) CM	617 454-8821	Brian J Martin	Bernard J Tully	William F Busby	James T Kennedy	John J Mulligan	John J Sheehan	George P Legrand
Ludlow t (18) RT	413 589-9506	John B Randall Jr	James Saloio	Helen Lemek	George Rescia	Homer R Dubois	John R Jorge	Manuel Martins
Lunenburg t (8) TM	617 582-6853	August N Misner	Barry J Stell	Robert J Ebersole	Robert J Ebersole	Dennis M Carrier	Hector J Morin	George G Munyon Jr
Lynn (78) MC	617 598-4000	Antonio J Marino	....	Joseph F Martin	Vincent S Glowik	Joseph Scanlon	Thomas Fay Jr	Richard Moulison
Lynnfield t§† (11) TM	617 334-3128	Joseph F Moran	Jeffrey T Zager	Leonard A Marshall	Leonard A Marshall	Paul N Romano	Paul N Romano	A David Rodham
Malden (53) MC	617 324-6600	Thomas H Fallon	Thomas P Callaghan	Karen Chausse	Jean Carroll	Roy Nickerson	James Keohane	Jack Kelly
Manchester t (5) TM	617 526-1712	Louis J Barrier	....	Edward P Gavin	John A Eaton	Joseph P O'Malley	Felix Radack	Robert W Moroney
Mansfield t* (13) TM	617 339-8677	James A Wills	W C Maurer Jr	Judith Scott	Joan Cutillo	Edward A Sliney Jr	Jesse Earls	Joseph M Zeneski
Marblehead t (20) TM	617 631-4056	Thomas A McNulty	....	Betty J Brown	George B Snow	Edward G Creighton	John B Palmer	Thomas Hamond
Marion t (4) TM	617 748-2500	Joseph P Zora	Ray E Pickles	Pardon N Gibbs III	Pardon N Gibbs III	George D Jenney	Brian J Scott	Nathon B Nye
Marlborough (31) MC	617 485-0039	Kuson J Haddad	....	Lillian Haddad	Thelma Bertonassi	Robert McCarthy	Floyd Russell	Paul A Sharon
Marshfield t (21) TM	617 837-5141	James E Robinson	Richard Agnew	Constance Donahue	Henry B Adams	Frederick P Gibson	William P Sullivan	Leonard Landry
Mashpee t (4) MC	617 477-0222	Willard Hansen	Joseph F Murphy	Jane D Labute	Vernice Polka	....	Curtis W Frye	....
Mattapoisett t (6) TM	617 758-3758	John N Decosta	Carol J Adams	Lois Knight Ennis	Kathleen F Briggs	Donald C Wood	James Moran	Manuel R Nunes Jr
Maynard t (10) TM	617 897-2956	Mark L Waldron	Michael J Gianotis	Helen E Punch	Arthur Filz	Ronald Cassidy	Arner Tibbetts	Thomas Sheridan
Medfield t* (10) TM	617 359-8505	Kenneth M Childs Jr	Michael J Sullivan	Nancy J Preston	Francis J Cusack	Joseph E Ryan	William H Mann	Kenneth P Feeney
Medford* (58) CM	617 396-5500	Paul J Donato	John A Ghiloni	Joseph P McGonagle	Joseph D Callahan	Lawrence Sands	John Kirwan	Robert G O'Brien
Medway t (8) TM	617 533-2013	Edward A Borek	Patricia M Kennedy	Francis D Donovan	Frederick J Lee	Jerome A Hanlon	Wm David Lambirth	Patricia M Kennedy
Melrose (30) MC	617 665-2225	James E Milano	....	Jane B Munro	Jean S Macdonald	Francis B O'Brien	Robert T Lloyd	Richard Warrington
Mendon t† (3) TM	617 473-2312	Rolland J Morin Jr	....	Helen Gibson	Robert Kelly	Wesley Shattuck	Kelsie E Townsend	Francis Irons
Merrimac t (4) TM	617 346-8862	George P Stevens	....	Madeleine A Lay	Geraldine A Wallace	Richard J Powers	James A Flynn Jr	Francis Noone
Methuen* (37) CM	617 687-3867	Melvin C Weagle Jr	Richard Gladstone	James J Maloney	Richard Gladstone	Joseph J Nicolosi	Francis J Morse	Thomas F Doucette
Middleborough t* (16) TM	617 947-0928	Stephen Morris	Anders Martenson Jr	Sandra L Bernier	Ellen O Grant	Joseph F Oliver	William E Warner	Leighton F Peck
Middleton t§ (4) TM	617 774-3344	Robert D Twombly	Ira Singer	Marilynn Begrdsell	Patricia M Jordan	George W Nash	Edward Richardson	Kenneth J Bouffard
Milford t (23) RT	617 473-5115	Dino DeBartolomeis	Judith T Sparrow	Joseph Arcudi	Michael A Diorio	John S DePaolo	Vincent W Liberto	Ronald Speroni
Millbury t (12) TM	617 865-4710	John S Donnelly Jr	Earle W Chase Jr	Oran David Matson	David W Cofske	Thomas W Nault	George R Brady	Donald J Army
Millis t (7) TM	617 376-2634	Collins C O'Connor	Jacqueline Anderson	George G Ford	William Koney	Robert Volpicelli	David Egy	Robert N Leslie
Milton t§ (26) RT	617 698-0100	James G Mullen Jr	John A Cronin	James G Mullen Jr	Kevin G Sorgi	John T O'Neill	Gerard R Mattaliano	Lawrence W DeCelle
Monson t (7) TM	413 267-5555	Bernard E Pellisier	....	Muriel Sheridan	Muriel Sheridan	Elmer R Harris Jr	William F Picking	John R Morrell
Montague t (8) RT	413 863-4511	Gale Ann Allen	Frank Abbondanzio	Raymond J Zukowski	Leon A Momaney Jr	Francis Tognari	Richard H Cade	Joseph Janikas
Nahant t (4) TM	617 581-0088	Richard J Lombard	Doris P Patten	Harriet C Steeves	Barry Boyce	John P Quinn	Joseph Manley	Robert W Steeves
Nantucket t (5) TM	617 228-0790	Bernard D Grossman	Keith A Bergman	Madelyne G Perry	Joan Coffin	Bruce Watts	Randolph P Norris	Donald Oliver
Natick t§ (29) RT	617 653-9450	Susan G Salamoff	Frederick C Conley	Edward W Devereaux	John B Jennings	Robert E Morris	John Arena	Walter F Markett
Needham t§ (28) RT	617 444-5100	Marsha M Carlton	Harold W Noble	Theodora K Bertolet	Michael J Carroll	Charles M Bellomo	Louis Roman	Robert A MacEwen
New Bedford (98) MC	617 999-2931	Brian J Lawler	George G Mendon Ca	Janice A Davidian	Peter S Barney	Manuel Almeida	Arthur Oliveira	Robert J Couto
Newbury t (5) TM	617 465-9241	Angie Machiros	....	Ralph P Lowell	Dolores Krupowicz	Wallace O Pearson	George Riel	Ronald O Pearson
Newburyport (16) MC	617 465-8122	Richard E Sullivan	Sheila R Kennedy	George H Lawler Jr	Nolan Morris	Warren O Page	Joseph Garand	Joseph E Keefe
Newton (84) MC	617 552-7000	Theodore D Mann	Richard J Kelliher	Edward G English	David C Wilkinson	Edward B Reilly Jr	William F Quinn	James L Hickey
Norfolk t (6) TM	617 528-1400	Fred L Pfischner	Marilyn Morris	Elinor Pearson	Caroline Price	William Kelley	Samuel Johnston	F Arthur Woodworth
North Adams (18) MC	413 663-6685	(not reporting)						
North Andover t (20) TM	617 682-6521	John W Graham	John P Bohenko	Daniel Long	James H Dewhirst	William P Dolan	Edward Sullivan Jr	Joseph J Borgesi
North Attleborough t (21) TM	617 695-0981	Michael J Buckley	Joseph J Sullivan	Donald B Hussey	James P Cullen	Lester Caldwell	John D Coyle Jr	Raymond A Payson
North Brookfield t (4) TM	617 867-2907	Raymond H Small	Beverly A Lund	Doris Revane	Paul R Langevin	James Black	Harbig Thomasian	Raymond A Blake
North Reading t§ (11) TM	617 664-5731	William A Smith	Chester Spinney Jr	Betty J Vullo	Chester Spinney Jr	Nelson C Harris	Gordon F Berridge	Richard F Spindler
Northampton (29) MC	413 586-6950	David B Musante Jr	....	Adeline Murray	Michael Lyons	Jeremiah P Driscoll	Daniel Labato	Peter McNulty
Northborough t* (11) TM	617 393-6761	Simeon Fouracre	Rocco J Longo	Nancy J Reinschild	Paul R Gallagher	John Pierce	Kenneth G Hutchins	John R Schunder
Northbridge t (12) TM	617 234-2095	J Alfred Benoit	Spaulding R Aldrich	Muriel J Barry	Everett Burgess	Cornelius Madigan	Thomas Melia	Paul Sohigian
Norton t (13) TM	617 285-6301	Leonard P Silvia	Thomas G Younger	Diane Casagni	John F Hussey	George Burgess	Benton Keene Jr	Carl Jacobs
Norwell t* (9) TM	617 659-4946	J Richard Hartigan	Terence Finan	Lorraine Olsen	Camille Hudson	Warren P Merritt	David A Nichols	....

Directory 1/10 continued

MUNICIPAL OFFICIALS IN ALL U.S. CITIES OVER 2,500[1]

City, 1980 population (000 omitted), form of government		Municipal phone number	Mayor	Appointed administrator	City clerk	Finance officer	Fire chief	Police chief	Public works director
MASSACHUSETTS (267) continued									
Norwood t* (30)	CM	617 762-1240	Walter J Dempsey	John J Carroll	Robert M Thornton	Robert M Thornton	Thomas J Barry	George J Diblasi	Paul Wollenhaupt
Orange t (7)	TM	617 544-2254	(not reporting)						
Orleans t (5)	TM	617 255-0900	Mary C Smith	M Eleanor Bennison	Barbara F Ilkovich	Jean H Deschamps	Raphael A Merrill	Donald B Walsh	....
Oxford t* (12)	TM	617 987-0351	John G Saad	Dennis A Power	F Pansy Kennedy	....	Kenneth Prefontaine	Anthony E Sgariglia	Fred Adams
Palmer t (11)	TM	413 283-3711	Stephen Marhelewicz	....	Jacob Toshikian	Douglas C Calkins	Gus Theodore	Harold L Olson	Oliver A Beauregard
Paxton t (4)	TM	617 754-7638	Christian Baehrecke	Barbara A Scholl	June T Herron	James J Mellor	Brian C Murphy	Robert P Sheehan	Robert Hansson
Peabody (46)	MC	617 532-3000	Peter Torigian	....	Natalie Maga	John Ryan	Nick Gerakaris	Robert Costello	John Seites
Pembroke t† (13)	TM	617 293-7211	John Ahearn	Robert Hazlett	Richard Baltzer	Robert Kennedy	Earl Ford	George Shaw Jr	....
Pepperell t (8)	TM	617 433-6359	Wayne A Gray	Robert J Halpin	Ann W Sullivan	Suzanne Marchand	John S Marriner	David L Young	Kim C Spaulding
Pittsfield (52)	MC	413 499-1100	Charles L Smith	Lawrence A Grizey	Jacqueline Sachetti	Lawrence A Grizey	Joseph Coy	Stanley Stankiewicz	Gerald S Doyle
Plainville t (6)	TM	617 695-3142	Robert E Hartnett	Robert H Brothers	Kathleen Sandland	David Swanson	Edward D Devine	Walter Sandland	Ronald Fredrickson
Plymouth t§ (36)	RT	617 747-1620	Roger E Silva	William R Griffin	Andrew J Collas	Richard Drew	Eugene J Rasori	Richard H Nagle	Paul Hannigan
Provincetown t* (4)	CM	617 487-3900	Mary Jo Avellar	Rachel A White	Mary Deschene	Aubrey Wassyng	James F Meads	James F Meads	Peter J Markunas
Quincy (85)	MC	617 773-1380	Francis X McCauley	Peter M Kenney	John M Gillis	Robert Foy	Edward Barry	Francis X Finn	Paul Anderson
Randolph t (28)	RT	617 963-3212	Maureen A Dunn	Henry L Lowd	Joan F Ward	Henry L Lowd	Robert Teece	Osmond J Benjamino	Thomas W O'Dea
Raynham t (9)	TM	617 823-6600	Donald P Francis	Randall A Buckner	Helen Lounsbury	Robert P Smith	Raymond E Chappell	Peter King	Harry R Carey
Reading t (23)	RT	617 942-0500	Maureen O'Brien	John W Agnew Jr	Lawrence Drew	Raphael McDonald	Leonard J Redfern	Edward W Marchand	Anthoney Fletcher
Rehoboth t (8)	TM	617 252-3758	Michael J O'Hern	N Reichenberg	Suzanne Withers	Mildred J Hatten	Arthur T Hurrell Jr	George A Warish	Arthur J Smith
Revere (42)	MC	617 284-3600	George V Colella	....	John J Henry	....	James Connery	John DeLeire	Henry Trifone
Rochester t (3)	TM	617 763-2085	David L Hughes	....	Naida L Parker	John Bradford	Joseph H Clapp	Walter V Denham Jr	George M Leconte
Rockland t† (16)	TM	617 871-1874	Pauline A Pigeon	....	Mary Pickett	Ralph Rose	Ralph Tanzi	Angelo Umbrianna	George Domigan
Rockport t (6)	TM	617 546-6786	Chester Holgerson	....	F C Frithsen	....	Ernest A Niemi	Thomas O'Maley	Donald Atkinson
Rowley t (4)	TM	617 948-2081	Wendell R Hopkins	....	Jeanne P Grover	Betty George	John B Mighill	Kevin Barry	....
Rutland t (4)	TM	617 886-4551	George R Griffin	....	Irene Amsden	Joseph P Murphy	Thomas Ruchala	Ralph H Anderson Jr	James M Leger
Salem (38)	MC	612 744-0224	Anthony V Salvo	....	Josephine R Fusco	Richard Foley	Robert J Crowley	Charles J Connelly	Paul S Niman
Salisbury t (6)	TM	617 462-8232	Alfred V Sargent	....	Gertrude M Doyle	Josephine Kohan	Joseph P Callahan	Edwin J Oliveira	Joseph Thomas
Sandwich t (9)	TM	617 888-0157	H Eugene Carr	....	Barbara J Walling	Jean C Purrier	Ferdinand L Alvezi	Robt D Whearty Jr	James Crocker
Saugus t* (25)	RT	617 233-7000	David B Smith	Paul T Rabchenuk	Marcia R Wallace	Norman Hansen	George Parrott	Donald M Peters	Stanley Day
Scituate t* (17)	TM	617 545-6700	C Constantinides	Herbert W Gilsdorf	Pauline F Guivens	William Frugoli	Walter M Stewart	Walter Driscoll	Anthony Antoniello
Seekonk t§ (12)	TM	617 336-7400	John P Pozzi	Terry L Proctor	Emily Lagerquist	Rudolph Petorelli	David Bowden	Robert R Taylor	Joseph F Mello
Sharon t§ (14)	TM	617 784-6900	Colleen M Tuck	Benjamin E Puritz	Shirley S Davenport	....	James A Polito	Albert R Horan	....
Sheffield t† (3)	TM	413 229-2335	Dana A Bartholomew	....	Natalie Funk	....	Frank Smith	James M McGarry	Dana A Bartholomew
Sherborn t (4)	TM	617 653-3320	Lee R Supper	Carolyn F Landry	Lucy S Almasian	James T Campbell	Francis A Heffron	Daniel F Manning	Russell L Mailman
Shirley t (5)	TM	617 425-4331	Sylvia L Shipton	Arthur Scibelli	Donald K Delaite	Ruth Gendron	Alphee Levesque Jr	Enrico C Cappucci	Albert R Chevrette
Shrewsbury t* (23)	RT	617 844-4781	Robert Moroney	Richard D Carney	Donald R Gray	William A Garten	Andrew E LaFlamme	Robert K McGinley	Edward S Holland
Somerset t† (19)	TM	617 672-0651	Arthur Marchand Jr	....	Laura Courcier	Laura Courcier	Lionel Parent	Peter J Kerrigan	....
Somerville (77)	MC	617 625-6600	Eugene C Brune	....	William J Donovan	Gerald A McCue	Charles Donovan	Robert Carroll	John McMahon
South Hadley t (16)	RT	413 538-5017	Joseph W Long	Norman Cloutier	Mary L Couture	Douglas A Reney	David Daly	Henry A Decker	George E Daviau Jr
Southampton t (4)	TM	413 527-4920	James D Carey	....	Barbara A Schmidt	Lorraine R Thomas	Rheal Labrie	John F Skroski	John V Garstka
Southborough t (6)	TM	617 485-0710	Denson Satterfield	Jeffrey A Grossman	Paul J Berry	Willard S Putnam	Edward F Brock	William D Baker	John W Boland
Southbridge t* (17)	CM	617 765-0173	Daniel Morrill	Donald I Jacobs	Evelyn Baldyga	Richard H Genereux	Roger W Favreau	Bernard A Fiorelli	Hamer D Clarke
Southwick t (7)	TM	413 569-5504	Alan L Ferrigno	....	Robert E Girard	Eileen Whiting	Melbert Johnson	Charles Wolfe	Merton G Seibert
Spencer t (11)	TM	617 885-2578	(not reporting)						
Springfield (152)	MC	413 787-6000	Richard H Neal	....	William Metzger	Henry Piechota	Raymond Boudet	Paul J Fenton	John Lyons
Sterling t (5)	TM	617 422-8111	Dorothy M Barr	....	Lois Seifert	Catherine Bauman	John R Woodsmall	David J Pineo	Robert Cutler
Stoneham t* (21)	TM	617 438-7775	George D Lamantea	William Sequino Jr	Annamae Arsenault	Stephen J Szabo Jr	Raymond L Sorenson	Eugene M Passaro	William J Reid Jr
Stoughton t*† (27)	TM	617 344-6565	....	Philip Farrington	....	....	....	....	....
Stow t (5)	TM	617 897-4514	David M Lynch	....	Virginia I Hatch	Eila J Makey	Douglas V Trefry	Charles C Mayo	John A Makey
Sturbridge t (6)	TM	617 347-3108	Lloyd Pote	Wm Frangiamore	Susan T Blair	Lawrence Joseph	Leonard Senecal	Kevin Fitzgibbons	Karl Nauman
Sudbury t§ (14)	TM	617 443-8891	Anne W Donald	Richard E Thompson	Jean M MacKenzie	James Vanar	Michael C Dunne	....	Robert A Noyes
Sunderland t (3)	TM	413 665-4414	Paul S Hodgkins	Judy Tozloski	Ellen Korpita	Donald Mathison	Alec Kulessa	Kenneth J Heim	Charles Hepburn
Sutton t (6)	TM	617 865-5078	Carl A Licopoli	Robert T Reed	Ethel M O'Day	Jan Charity	Ellery Smith	Robert Conley	Raymond E Smith
Swampscott t (14)	RT	617 595-1645	Robert E Perry	....	Jack L Paster	Keith A Callahan	William R Hyde	Peter J Cassidy	Robert J Sotiros
Swansea t† (15)	TM	617 678-2981	Donald F Lesage	Michael W Finglas	Marion Audet	James Hodkinson	James R Eddy	Ralph T Lepore Jr	Michael E Ziobro
Taunton† (45)	MC	617 824-6942	Richard Johnson	Marc R Pacheco	Mary C Gordon	Robert L Quigley	George E Dexter	Roger J Renaud	Maynard D Spekin
Templeton t (6)	TM	617 939-8801	Robert Sabolefski	....	Dana G Putnam	David Bergeron	Richard Paine	John D Reardon	Steve Manty
Tewksbury t (25)	TM	617 851-4311	Paul H Sullivan	Ruth E Aubert	Elizabeth A Carey	Allan Port	William A Chandler	John F Sullivan	Philip L Pattison
Tisbury t (3)	TM	617 693-4204	James H Lobdell	William E Boerth	Marion A Mcclure	Frances M O'Neil	Richard Clark	John J McCarthy	....
Topsfield t (6)	TM	617 887-8571	William D Johnson	Deborah D Moulton	Elizabeth C Gill	Pauline M Evans	Ronald Giovannacci	Clifford L Keeling	William T Gamble
Townsend t (7)	TM	617 597-2837	Stephen M Dunbar	Kerry Codyer	Marilyn Maceachern	Howard Paulson	William Greenough	William May Jr	Raymond Bolden
Tyngsborough t (6)	TM	617 649-7441	Mary Rita Roberts	....	Dorothy Dunderdale	Roland Tourville	Joseph Knight Jr	Chas C Chronopolos	....
Upton t (4)	TM	617 529-6901	Richard Desjardins	....	Martha R Williams	Richard Karazia	Richard J Henderson	Rodney B Marchand	Henry J Poirier
Uxbridge t (8)	TM	617 278-2041	Edmond Lizotte	....	Ruth E Davis	Ronald Smith	William Albin	John J Emerick	John J Yerka
Wakefield t (25)	TM	617 245-8877	Eugene J Sullivan	John J McCarthy	Thelma E Rennard	John J McCarthy	Walter V Maloney Jr	William R Connors	Richard C Boutiette
Walpole t* (19)	RT	617 668-5400	Clement Boragine	James R Merriam	Louis E Hoegler	Kenneth S Crowell	Leonard Anderson	Armando C Betro	....
Waltham (58)	MC	617 893-4040	Arthur J Clark	Michael Lenza	Peter Koutoujian	George Gallitano	Joseph Steede	John F Rooney	Edward F Delaney
Ware t (9)	TM	413 967-5289	Richard L Jordan	Richard S Ellery	James M Roach	Madeleine Cebula	Richard W Pariseau	Stanley G Mettig Jr	Henry Desantis
Wareham t* (18)	TM	617 295-0800	Judith W Montminy	....	Jay K Montague	Manuel J Sylvia Jr	....	Robert C Hammond	Antone Fernandes
Warren t (4)	TM	413 436-5701	Edward Fleming	Thomas M Guerino	Beverly Russell	Jeffrey Dumas	William Witaszek	Sean R LeBoeuf	John F O'Neil Jr
Watertown t* (34)	CM	617 924-6890	J Malcolm Whitney	Peter F Boyer	James E Fahey Jr	Joseph O'Reilly Jr	Robert C O'Rielly	Walter T Munger	James P Clark
Wayland t§ (12)	TM	617 358-7701	L Thomas Linden	Edward N Perry	Grace I Bowen	Robert S Swain	Ronald F Profit	John Phylis	Anthony Marques
Webster t (14)	TM	617 943-0033	Henry P Slota	....	Regina Bugan	J S Chmielewicz	Gordon Wentworth	Roger Smith	Francis Walkowiak
Wellesley t (27)	RT	617 235-1617	Theodore F Parker	Thomas E Lee	Joan M Regan	R A Wakelin Jr	Stephen R Black	Leroy L Weaver	Maurice R Berdan
Wenham t (4)	TM	617 468-4468	Marjorie A Davis	....	Olga B Cousins	Nancy A Brown	Donald J Killam	Peter L Carnes	Peter J Burnham
West Boylston t (6)	TM	617 835-6091	Bruce L Shepard	Charles E Hudson	Doris Shepard	Francis M Bonci	Duncan Gillies	Geo Schwictenberg	Michael DeLiddo
West Bridgewater t (6)	TM	617 588-4820	Charles H Johnson	....	Anna E Brown	Elizabeth Zamaitis	Charles A Dyke	Ervin G Lothrop	Donald E Newman
West Brookfield t (3)	TM	617 867-6874	Peter C Magnante	....	Elizabeth Coulthard	Stanley Remiszewski	Peter J Wrobel	John S Zabek Jr	Daniel A Santos
West Newbury t (3)	TM	617 363-2341	Frank E Hobson Jr	....	Norman H Hobson	....	Richard Berkenbush	Richard Berkenbush	....
West Springfield t (27)	RT	413 781-7550	Richard C Newman	....	John F Crean Jr	Raymond N Spear	Emil J Polastri	Thomas F McNamara	Wallace W Wyman
Westborough t (14)	TM	617 366-7100	Richard N Foster	Dexter P Blois	Elizabeth D Amoroso	George C Lightbody	James W Parker Jr	Harry F Shepherd	Thomas Fryer
Westfield (36)	MC	413 568-9181	Michael E O'Connell	....	Patrick H Dowd	Ruth M Malanowski	Gerald J Fouche	Gerald O'Connor	Edward L Wielgus
Westford t (13)	TM	617 692-6511	David R Earl	Paul F Alphen	Elaine McKenna	Paula Brule	George Rogers	Joseph Connell	George Wyman
Westminster t (5)	TM	617 874-2184	Preston D Baker	Wayne R Walker	Denise Macaloney	Gilbert Parks	Ralph E Young	Robert R Cudak	William Wintturi
Weston t (11)	TM	617 893-7320	Harold B Wills Jr	J Ward Carter	Harry B Jones	Stephen S Rollins	John E Thorburn	Frank O Shaw	John J Ryan
Westport t (14)	TM	617 636-8822	George Leach	Julia S Enroth	Althea Manchester	Muriel Robbins	William Tripp	Rene D Dupre	Russell Hart
Westwood t (13)	TM	617 326-6450	Marcia A Hirshberg	Jos R Gallagher	Edith P McCracken	Peter J Dalton Jr	John J Sheehy	Francis Abbate	Ralph Phaneuf
Weymouth t (56)	RT	617 335-2000	Peg Goudy	....	Franklin Fryer	Allan J Masison	James Connor	Thomas J Higgins	Frank Lagrotteria
Whitman t (14)	TM	617 447-2561	Leo F Hurley	James M Jeffers	Grace E Ludwig	T M McWilliams	Richard Grenno	Francis Burley	N J Fredette
Wilbraham t (12)	TM	413 596-8111	Arthur F Dionne	James C Moynihan	Mary R Irla	Janet Gibson	Robert W Macaulay	Norton H Brainard	Herbert L Butler
Williamstown t* (9)	CM	413 458-3500	....	Steven L LeDoux	Betty F Kovacs	....	Gordan Noble	Joseph Zoito Jr	Richard S McFadden

Directory 1/10 continued — MUNICIPAL OFFICIALS IN ALL U.S. CITIES OVER 2,500[1]

City, 1980 population (000 omitted), form of government	Municipal phone number	Mayor	Appointed administrator	City clerk	Finance officer	Fire chief	Police chief	Public works director
MASSACHUSETTS (267) continued								
Wilmington t* (17) TM	617 658-3311	James C Stewart	R S Stapczynski	Priscilla R Lynch	Dorothy L Peters	Daniel Wandell	Bobby N Stewart	Robert P Palmer
Winchendon t (7) TM	617 297-0085	Raymond W Whitaker	Kathleen G Fallon	Lois A Abare	Charlotte Noponen	Richard B Williams	Selvino A Marinelli	Louis A Morneau
Winchester t*† (21) RT	617 729-1100	Edward F O'Connell	....	Carolyn Ward	A J Faggiano	Robert McElhinney	John P McHugh	Dominic J Serratore
Winthrop t (19) TM	617 846-1742	Robert A Deleo	Lester W Towlson	John A Clark	Fred Gillis	Charles J Flanagan	David C Rice	Donald Hodgkins
Woburn† (37) MC	617 933-0700	Thomas M Higgins	....	John J Ryan Jr	Robert J Foley	Robert E Doherty	Leo McElhiney	Robert Simonds
Worcester* (162) CM	617 799-1000	Joseph M Tinsley	Francis J McGrath	Robert J O'Keefe	George E O'Brien	James F Nally	Halstead Taylor	F Worth Landers
Wrentham t§† (8) TM	617 384-8918	Karen E Kohut	John D Midwood	Anthony M Marcelino	Richard A Mourey	Wendell McNamara	Paul Schwalbe	Everett W Skinner
Yarmouth t§ (18) TM	617 398-2231	Matthew J Steele	Robt C Lawton Jr	Kathleen D Johnson	Kathleen D Johnson	David P Akin	Robert F Chapman	Lloyd Dauphinais
MICHIGAN (250)								
Adrian* (21) CM	517 263-2161	Alden F Smith	James H Fridd	Marsha K Rowley	Larry L Opelt	Richard E Mohr	Terrence B Collins	D Jack Lemon
Albion* (11) CM	517 629-5535	James Young	George R Kolb	Larry L Hufnagel	Larry L Hufnagel	Jerry W Baker	Jerry W Baker	William Rieger
Algonac* (4) CM	313 794-9361	James R Steinmetz	Douglas C Larson	Mary L Jaros	Dianah Foster	Charles Johnson	....	Thomas Coppola
Allegan* (5) CM	616 673-5511	John N Wilson	Joanne C Wrench	Joanne C Wrench	Mary Lou Russell	Ronald Wedge	Edward Cone	Dale Commans
Allen Park (34) MC	313 928-1400	Frank J Lada	Richard A Huebler	Bernice R Weiss	Richard A Huebler	Raymond Bertoncelli	John McKeever	Leopold Kozuh
Alma* (10) CM	517 463-8336	Fred J Dorner	Blaine R Hinds	William M Stuckey	William M Stuckey	George E Blyton	Richard J Westgate	Alexander Radzibon
Almont v* (2) CM	313 798-8528	Dick Fitzwilson	James D Hock	Farel K Hinton	James D Hock	Norm Hamilton	....	Fred Treutle
Alpena* (12) CM	517 354-4158	William D Gilmet	Allan H Green	Rose E Brousseau	Rose E Brousseau	Julian Skiba	Lawrence Kunze	James Barnwell
Ann Arbor* (107) CM	313 994-2700	Louis D Belcher	Godfrey W Collins	Winifred Northcross	Donald D Ayers	Frederick Schmid	William J Corbett	John F Newman
Auburn§ (2) MC	517 662-6761	Lee O Kilbourn	Steven L Ledoux	Lucille Wiesenauer	Barbara Reiss	Richard Sugar	Thomas Gillman	Roye Burr
Auburn Hills§ (15) MC	313 373-5200	....	Leonard G Hendricks	....	....	....	....	....
Bad Axe* (3) CM	517 269-7681	Harold E Randall	Paul J McLean	Paul J McLean	Esther Motz	Peter Ney	John L Bodis	Peter Prill
Battle Creek* (36) CM	616 966-3000	Maude J Bristol	Gordon B Jaeger	Loraine Buckner	Merrill Stanley	Douglas Roach	William Kohnke	Rance L Leaders
Bay City* (42) CM	517 894-8200	Timothy G Sullivan	David D Barnes	Walter Wozniak Jr	Paul Kraft	Jerome Marchlewicz	Gerald Van Alst	Alexander Peterson
Belding* (6) CM	616 794-1900	Edward Jenkins	William H Fisher Jr	Mary Keena	Mary Keena	Fain Nickel	Roger Mason	Gerald Rawlings
Belleville (3) MC	313 697-9323	Howard Stinehour	Frank R Pascarella	Agnes Frisch	Agnes Frisch	Anthony Talaga Jr	Willard Dockter	Anthony Talaga Jr
Benton Harbor* (15) CM	616 927-8400	Wilce L Cooke	Ellis E Mitchell	Margaret Bowman	Ricardo Johnson	David Lincoln	Sam Watson Jr	Carl L Brown
Berkley* (19) CM	313 545-4500	Ronald G Norman	John H Kiracofe	Maryann Burton	Michael Tyler	Harry Anderson	Harry Anderson	Marvin Gensler
Bessemer* (3) CM	906 667-0333	Joseph Bonovetz	Bruce W Carlson	Bruce W Carlson	Isabelle E Haapoja	William C Nyman	....	William V Saily
Beverly Hills v* (12) CM	313 646-6404	William Hasserger	William M Israel	Daniel N Agacinski	Daniel N Agacinski	Thomas A Good	Thomas A Good	Charles F Comeau
Big Rapids* (14) CM	616 796-4823	Norman Mason	W Larry Collins	Roberta McCarthy	Lorraine Miedema	Ralph Wallace	Glen C Alber Jr	Glenn Potter
Birmingham* (22) CM	313 644-1800	Robert W Appleford	R S Kenning	Phyllis Armour	Donald E Johnson	Gary V Whitener	Edward P Ostin	Darrel Middlewood
Blissfield v (3) MC	517 486-4347	Byron A Cluckey Jr	....	Laura Neuman	Arthur Tormoehlen	Gary Crist	Arthur Gunter	Richard Frownfelter
Bloomfield Hills* (4) CM	313 644-1520	Marlynn Varbedian	Robert J Stadler	Robert J Stadler	Charles H Harmon Jr	Robert J Stadler	Robert J Stadler	Daniel Hamlin
Boyne City* (3) CM	616 582-6597	Keith Fitzpatrick	R Randolph Frykberg	Thomas Garlock	Edith Beck	Butch Erber	John Talboys	Basil Moore
Bridgman (2) MC	616 465-5144	(not reporting)						
Brighton* (4) CM	313 227-1911	Francis Criqui	....	Janice E Morrow	Mark R Christiansen	Melvin Sanch	Eugene Alli	John Beebe
Bronson* (2) CM	517 369-7334	Larry McConn	D Lee Ballard	Gerald A Hollister	Gerald A Hollister	Charles R Somerlott	Arvard Fountain	John Champion
Brown City§ (1) MC	313 346-2325	Norman Morrison	Thomas McCoy	Rae Ann Lee	Irene Weltin	William Pepper	Fred Maurer	William Dashluck
Buchanan* (5) CM	616 695-3844	Ray Berry	Clyde J Remmo	Herbert D Russell	Lorraine Moyer	Neal Burks	Clyde W Weaver	Joe Bachman
Burton (30) MC	313 743-1500	Jane L Nimcheski	Arnold James	Shirley Hillaker	Bradley C Becker	Elmer J Craft	Herman M Clark	James R Rabine
Cadillac* (10) CM	616 775-0181	Darrell Becker	Robert A Hamilton	Maurice S Evans	Dale M Walker	Herald Bassett	Lyle H Reddy	Michael R Wiesner
Capac v§ (1) MC	313 395-4355	William Stramaglio	....	Elberta Dodd	....	Carl Lang	Irene Schoenberg	Clarence Revitzer
Carleton v (3) MC	313 654-6255	(not reporting)						
Caro v (4) MC	517 673-2226	Kenneth Philp	W Donald Duggar	Charles Spaulding	....	David Mattlin	Kenneth Ball Sr	W Donald Duggar
Caspian* (1) CM	906 265-2514	John Archocosky	Rosalie King	Rosalie King	....	Archie Carlotto	Robert Remondini	....
Cedar Springs† (3) MC	616 696-1330	John T Teusink	....	Amber Bailey	Janet Riggle	Roger Scholz	Ronald Nielsen	James Haynes
Center Line* (9) CM	313 757-6800	Mary Ann Zielinski	P Van Den Branden	P Van Den Branden	James I Martin	Mark Grobbel	Mark Grobbel	Robert Jacob
Charlevoix* (3) CM	616 547-3270	Kenneth A Staley	....	James M Brinker	James M Brinker	John Martin	Jack R Mol	....
Charlotte* (8) CM	517 543-2750	L Daryl Baker	Robert H Lake	Irene Jewett	Howard Penrod	Cal Fullerton	Barton Howe	James Marry
Cheboygan* (5) CM	616 627-9931	Ellis N Olson	William E Chlopan	Patricia J St Jean	Patricia J St Jean	Al Bonsecours	Kurt R Jones	William E Chlopan
Chelsea V† (4) MC	313 475-1771	Charles S Ritter	F A Weber	Rose McGibbney	....	James Gaken	Robert Aeillo	F Petsch
Chesaning v* (3) CM	517 845-3800	Nathan Coon	....	Sandra Richardson	Elwin Harris	....	Howard Ormes	....
Clare* (3) CM	517 386-7541	Tom Johnson	F Bruce Wood	Phillip Belcher	F Bruce Wood	Jack Gibbis	Michael W Becker	Robert Bonham
Clawson*† (15) CM	313 435-4500	A D Brown	Edward Hermoyian	Clinton West	Clinton West	Richard LePla	Frank T Cribb	Les Tinson
Clio (3) MC	313 686-5850	Samuel W Geddes	George Atkin Jr	Alice E Grigar	George Atkin Jr	Jim K Chilson	Dale W Moore	George Atkin Jr
Coldwater* (9) CM	517 279-9501	Jerry L Ford	Gary P Kuckel	Marcelyn LaBelle	Marcelyn LaBelle	Wilford Loose	....	James Endicott
Constantine v§ (2) MC	616 435-2085	Patrick Benner	Steven R Aynes	Katie Hutson	....	Dale Jones	Robert E Brewer	Charles Hulse
Coopersville* (3) CM	616 837-9731	Raymond McCormick	Bryon L Mazade	....	Patricia Richards	Robert Grootenhuis	John Potts	....
Corunna§ (3) MC	517 743-3650	Ralph Atherton	Steve M Duchane	Linda Johnson	Ron Smith	Robert Volek	Herbert Jenkins	Roger Price
Croswell§ (2) MC	313 679-2299	Gary Macklem	Dale R Soumis	Diane A Black	....	Edward McLane	Jeffrey Dawson	Edward McLane
Crystal Falls* (2) CM	906 875-6647	Lawrence R Hegstrom	Walter E Hagglund	Barbara A Benda	Clarence S Hagglund	Leon Fabbri	Julius Simbob	Ballard V Dahl
Davison* (6) CM	313 653-2191	William J McGill	Jack N Abernathy	Jean C Kneeshaw	Nora E Wheeler	Keith Skellenger	Robert Johnson	Todd Scrima
De Witt (3) MC	517 669-2441	Lynn E Thayer	Robert L Peterson	Margie N Lotre	....	Arthur Newman	Wendell Myers	Carrol Ward
Dearborn (91) MC	313 943-2300	John B O'Reilly	Daniel S McCormick	Duane L Wydendorf	Robert Keith Archer	Gino H Polidori	John Connolly	Normand G Gomolak
Dearborn Heights (68) MC	313 277-7000	Donald H Bishop	W K McKersie	Robert G McLachlan	Frank Felice	Gordon Warren	Raymond E Collins	....
Delta tp† (24) MC	517 627-4031	....	Ivan Lootens	....	Ivan Lootens	....	....	....
Detroit (1203) MC	313 224-3400	Coleman A Young	Fred Martin	James H Bradley	Bella I Marshall	Melvin Jefferson	William L Hart	Alvin Johnson
Dowagiac* (6) CM	616 782-2195	Graham D Woodhouse	Karl S Tomion	James E Snow	David A Pilot	Wayne K Mattix	David Merwin	Larry Rohacs
Dundee v* (3) CM	313 529-3430	John R Williams	Eric A Anderson	Mary C Miller	....	Harold Dale Goetz	....	Harold Dale Goetz
Durand* (4) CM	517 288-3113	Paul Rearick	Dan J Post	Elizabeth A Miller	Robert Huska	Allan Pierce	Robert Eldridge	Dan J Post
East Detroit* (38) CM	313 445-5020	William A Mihelich	....	....	Silvio Marcozzi	Carl Gerds	Larry F Hitchcock	Ernest Scheeres
East Grand Rapids* (11) CM	616 949-2110	William Edison	Fred H Tholen	Timothy T Allard	Timothy T Allard	Peter J Gallagher	Peter J Gallagher	Clifford McMann
East Lansing* (48) CM	517 337-1731	John B Czarnecki	Thomas C Dority	Michael V Benedict	Gary Murphy	Jack Gregg	Robert Foster	Peter G Eberz
East Tawas (3) MC	517 362-6161	Robert C Bolen	....	Clyde L Soper	Norma Reinke	Wilfred Rapp	David J Foley	Jacob Montgomery
Eaton Rapids (5) CM	517 663-8118	Larry J Holley	Dennis O Craun	Dennis O Craun	Dennis O Craun	Richard F Freer	David A King	Howard Hillard
Ecorse (14) MC	313 386-2520	Kenneth Slifka	William H Polk	James Tassis	Thomas Enright	Louis Parker	Robert Short	Charles Weber
Escanaba* (14) CM	906 786-0240	Donald J Guindon	James J Hauser Jr	Joyce Osby	Michael Dewar	Wayne Heikkila	Wayne Heikkila	Wesley Chernick
Essexville* (4) CM	517 893-7192	C Donald Lowe	Richard G Runnels	Mary Monville	Marion D Skibinski	Terrence Hugo	Terrence Hugo	....
Farmington Hills* (58) CM	313 474-6115	Charles Williams	William M Costick	Floyd Cairns	Charles Rosch	Lawrence Karon	John Nichols	Thomas P Biasell
Farmington* (11) CM	313 474-5500	Ralph D Yoder	Robert F Deadman	Josephine Bushey	Winona Woods	G Robert Seifert	G Robert Seifert	Earl R Billing
Fenton* (8) CM	313 629-2261	Lucille M Brabon	Edw B Koryzno Jr	Eileen Roddy	Cynthia A Dethloff	Bruce E Dorland	Theodore E Glynn	Leslie P Bland
Ferndale* (26) CM	313 547-6000	James B Avery	Jess R Soltess	Valerie E Kitchen	Karen Harlick	Doyne Easterwood	Patrick T Sullivan	Kenneth G Bautel
Flat Rock† (7) MC	313 782-2455	Ted L Anders	....	Norman F Koszuta	Carolyn Beck	Chester L Hammond	Raymond Hoffman	Charles E Stedman
Flint (160) MC	313 766-7346	James A Sharpe Jr	Robert S Collier	Terry L Bankert	John Corbliss	Samuel Dixon	William Lyght	Kenneth Collard
Flushing* (9) CM	313 659-3139	William T Jakeway	Bernard Van Osdale	Shirley A Clark	Robert J Lawrence	David Bloss	Vernon L Royston	Archie Mark
Frankenmuth* (4) CM	517 652-9901	Richard Krafft Jr	Charles B Graham	Frederick W Geuder	John P Deterding	George Reinert	James R Petteys	Jack Schluckebier
Franklin v (3) MC	313 626-9666	John C Verdon	....	Rustle G Shand	....	Vernon Converse III	Edward A Glomb	....
Fraser* (15) CM	313 293-3102	Joseph F Boris Jr	....	Michael R Pohlod	Michael R Pohlod	James C Flynn	Lawrence Hofmann	Frank Rubino
Fremont* (4) CM	616 924-2101	Ken Longstreet	Henry Van Dop	Fred Dawe	Fred Dawe	Tom Bergklink	Galen Brookens	Jim Vedders

Directory 1/10 continued — **MUNICIPAL OFFICIALS IN ALL U.S. CITIES OVER 2,500[1]**

City, 1980 population (000 omitted), form of government		Municipal phone number	Mayor	Appointed administrator	City clerk	Finance officer	Fire chief	Police chief	Public works director
MICHIGAN (250) continued									
Garden City§ (36)	MC	315 525-8800	Vincent J Fordell	Cam Caldwell	Ronald D Showalter	Ronald D Showalter	Keith Nims	Charles Wilmoth	John Preston
Gaylord* (3)	CM	517 732-4060	Clark W Bates	Donald R Harmon	Jean L Tomaski	Elizabeth D Olund	David Duffield	Wayne Thomas	James E Cullen
Gibraltar (4)	MC	313 676-3900	Mary M Mellin	....	Jean E Thompson	Barbara A Papler	Jan Meyer	Jan Meyer	Arthur Redman
Gladstone* (5)	CM	906 428-2311	Leroy L Hamilton	Howard W Keeton	Howard W Keeton	Margaret A Gagnon	Paul L Dufresne	Paul L Dufresne	Philip N Gagnon
Grand Blanc† (7)	MC	313 694-1111	John M Carey	Randall D Byrne	Doris Lacina	Joanne Blom	Thomas H Ward	Jerry L Burr	Jack A Kipp
Grand Haven* (12)	CM	616 842-3210	Marge D Boon	Larry R Deetjen	William Swier	Phillip Moore	Joseph Bruneau	Richard Klempel	Jerry Lietzke
Grand Ledge (7)	MC	517 627-2149	Lewis D Gentry	Ronald Lee	Fay Shane	Joane Flitton	Robert G Briggs	David M Burtch	Harold Jolley
Grand Rapids* (182)	CM	616 456-3166	Gerald R Helmholdt	G Stevens Bernard	Sandra L Wright	Robert J White	Leon Williams	William G Hegarty	....
Grandville* (12)	CM	616 531-3030	James R Buck	Howard Nyenhuis	Marie A Gowell	Kathleen Lewis	Jack Scholten	Kenneth Madejczyk	Kenneth Jenison
Grayling* (2)	CM	517 348-2131	Gordon Thompson	Jerry W Morford	Jerry W Morford	Allen V Schreiner	David Reisinger	Peter Stephan	Donald Sorenson
Greenville* (8)	CM	616 754-5645	Robert Hewitt	Calvin L Teague	David R Moore	David R Moore	Garry Duram	Garry Duram	Gary Stacey
Grosse Pointe* (6)	CM	313 885-5800	Lorenzo D Browning	Thomas W Kressbach	Thomas W Kressbach	Dennis C Foran	Robert Marshall	Bruce D Kennedy	Douglas Collinson
Grosse Pointe Farms*† (11)	CM	313 885-6600	James H Dingeman	Andrew Bremer Jr	Richard Solak	Carrol Lock	Warren Schultz	Robert Ferber	Patrick Cosgrove
Grosse Pointe Park* (14)	CM	313 822-6200	Palmer T Heenan	John R Crawford	Nunzio J Ortisi	Nunzio J Ortisi	Phillip Costa	Henry O Coonce	James G Ellison
Grosse Pointe Shores v* (3)	CM	313 881-6565	G C Schroeder	Michael Kenyon	James T Wright	Michael Kenyon	....	J Vitale	T Maison
Grosse Pointe Woods* (19)	CM	313 343-2440	George S Freeman	Chester E Petersen	Chester E Petersen	F G Hornfisher	Jack Patterson	Jack Patterson	Leonard Ocelnik
Hamtramck (21)	MC	313 876-7703	Robert Kozaren	Frank Wasinski	Robert A Zwolak	Michael W Zebrowski	Samuel Dropchuk	Alex Shulgan	Carl G Karpinski
Hancock (5)	MC	906 482-1121	John Niemela	....	Karen Haischer	....	James Ahola	Jon Ahola	Wesley Keranen
Harbor Beach§ (2)	MC	517 479-3363	David Hunter	Michael Blau	David Dickinson	....	James Ritchie	Sidney Schock	Earl Learman
Harbor Springs* (2)	CM	616 526-2104	Lloyd Taylor	Ron M Howell	Dale Krajniak	Dale Krajniak	Douglas Jardine	C Dean Rye	Donald Gregory
Harper Woods* (16)	CM	313 343-2505	James R Haley	Elinor Cramer	Mickey D Todd	Terry T Hodgkinson	Howard LeFevre	Gary L Ford	Donald V Dayton
Hart* (2)	CM	616 873-2488	William Wells	Laverne A Serne	Laverne A Serne	Dorothy Cutter	Jerry Schaner	Daniel Leimback	Gary Hasty
Hastings (6)	MC	616 945-2468	William R Cook	....	Sharon Vickery	Sharon Vickery	Roger Caris	Mark Steinfort	M C Klovanich
Hazel Park* (21)	CM	313 546-7000	Stephen J Zervas	Dan W Potter	Marilyn S Manning	....	....	....	Calvin Strouse
Highland Park† (28)	MC	313 252-0030	Robert B Blackwell	....	Jean Green	James Lanum	Philip Ginotti	Carl Kerttu	Gene Ford
Hillsdale* (7)	CM	517 437-7312	Herbert H Hine	Gregg G Guetschow	Ruth K Ladd	Gregg G Guetschow	Larry Eichler	John J Kalusniak	Ron Neer
Holland* (26)	CM	616 396-2311	William Sikkel	Terry L Hofmeyer	Donald W Schipper	Larry Sandy	John DuMez	Charles Lindstrom	Tim Morawski
Holly v§ (5)	MC	313 634-9571	Ardath Regan	Thomas Bercher	Catherine Lane	Catherine Lane	Dick Swartout	William Sudbury	Ken Poff
Houghton§ (8)	MC	906 482-1770	Gerald S Bond	Raymond J Kestner	Kurt W Kuure	Raymond J Kestner	James Chappell	James Janda	Raymond J Kestner
Howell* (7)	CM	517 546-3500	James Young	John Szerlag	Don E Beach	Don E Beach	Robert Rose	Michel Oyler	Kenneth Thompson
Hudson* (3)	CM	517 448-3271	Joseph O'Reilly	Michael S Herman	Freda L Rodehaver	Chresteen Reuter	Richard Opsal	Albert T Clements	Sheldon Peltier
Hudsonville* (5)	CM	616 669-0200	Joan Edson	Henry Scholten	Joan Brouwer	Mark Rett	Roland DeWeerd	Richard W Honholt	Henry Scholten
Huntington Woods* (7)	CM	313 541-4300	Ronald F Gillham	Mark E Wollenweber	Mark E Wollenweber	Eugene Gardiner	James Y Stewart	....	....
Imlay City* (2)	CM	313 724-2135	Shirley Metcalf	Dennis Collison	Sandra Shene	Dennis Collison	Warner Hoeksema	Lawrence Dougherty	Douglas R Hill
Inkster* (35)	CM	313 565-4100	Betty G Miller	Gregory A Knowles	Delphine G Jones	James Klobuchar	Lyle Evon	James L Buckley	James Rance
Ionia† (6)	MC	616 527-4170	Fred Thwaites	Alan E Housler	Loraine Watson	Robert Baker	Gary Gonnella	Frank Lance	Donald Misner
Iron Mountain (8)	MC	906 774-8530	Ted Corombos	Jim Urbany	Louann Ebidon	Larry Swartout	Richard Rahoi	Vance T Sparpana	Jim Urbany
Iron River* (2)	CM	906 265-4719	Sylvester Nocerini	Francis A Wills	Alvilda Holm	....	Ellis Dobson	Floyd Van Wagner	Bruce Porier
Ironwood* (8)	CM	906 932-5050	James W Peterson	D Steve Worachek	Anita Zak	George E Anderson	Clifford Koivisto	Leroy Johnson	Gerald McGrath
Ishpeming* (8)	CM	906 486-6581	James F Tobin	....	Lambert L Chard	Richard D Colvin	Raymond Perrault	John A Healey	Robert E Dobson
Ithaca† (3)	MC	517 875-3160	Robert J Atkinson	Jack A Bouchey	Richard D Parling	Richard D Parling	Richard Lumsden III	William Osborn	Jack A Bouchey
Jackson* (40)	CM	517 788-4000	Albert W Stern	Wes McAllister Jr	Betty Granger	Betty Granger	Donald Braunreiter	James E Rice	Walter J Vaclavik
Kalamazoo* (80)	CM	616 385-8047	Francis P Hamilton	Sheryl L Sculley	Luann G Stampfler	Robert A Willard	John E Ross	John E Ross	William Nelson
Kalkaska v§† (2)	MC	616 258-9191	....	Wilbur Hatley	....	....	....	....	....
Keego Harbor* (3)	CM	313 682-1930	John J Nicol Jr	Wayne O'Neal	Katy Mann	....	Daniel L Miller	William E Holloway	Tony Hale
Kentwood (30)	MC	616 698-9610	Gerald L DeRuiter	Nancy M Shane	Beverly J Bacon	Donald Geelhoed	H W Thornton	Richard Dryer	John Heitman
Kingsford* (5)	CM	906 774-3526	Lawrence Berg	Robert H Langkawel	Robert H Langkawel	Mary H Moroni	Donald L Secrist	Donald L Secrist	Darryl K Wickman
L'Anse v (3)	MC	906 524-6116	Fred A Teddy	....	Roy A Kemppainen	Roy A Kemppainen	Gerald Johnson	Ray L Bailey	Frank Mervar
Lake Orion v* (3)	CM	313 693-8391	Fred C Cole	Christopher L Rose	Mary Simmons	Keith Sawdon	Jeffrey Key	James R Leach	John D Ranville
Lansing (130)	MC	517 487-1000	Terry J McKane	Ronald U DeMaagd	Rita M Bauman	James W Dowsett	Mark R Holliday	Richard A Gleason	Howard McCaffery
Lapeer* (6)	CM	313 664-2902	Barry E Shoults	Arnold B Whitney	Arnold B Whitney	Loretta Huntley	Louis Finsterwald	Terry L Fisk	Orville Gardner
Lathrup Village* (5)	CM	313 557-2600	Dorothy E Warren	Jerald D Stone	Doris Andrus	Jerald D Stone	....	Thomas Tellefsen	James Andrus
Laurium v (3)	MC	906 337-1600	Frank J Musich	Gary W Auge	Lucille M Kangas	Gary W Auge	Donald Julio	James J Lemler	David A Heinonen
Lincoln Park (45)	MC	313 386-1800	Frank M Sall	....	Irene B Bartal	Edward L Figure	Frank Ungar	Robert Heyer	W C Griffin
Litchfield* (1)	CM	517 542-2921	Woodrow Southfield	Ila J Smith	Marguerite Dooley	Marguerite Dooley	Richard Wade	John S Michelin	Dean Wooden
Livonia (105)	MC	313 421-2000	Edward H McNamara	....	Robert F Nash	Jack Dodge	Barney Knorp	William E Crayk	Russell Gronevelt
Lowell* (4)	CM	616 897-8457	James Maatman	Ray E Quada	Ray E Quada	Ray E Quada	Frank Baker	Barry D Emmons	A A Siciliano
Ludington* (9)	CM	616 845-6237	James R Braden	Gerald J Richards	Gerry Pehrson Klaft	John Villa	Gerald L Clark	Jack W Harper	Gerald L Clark
Madison Heights* (35)	CM	313 588-1200	George W Suarez	Dorothy M Lents	Geraldine A Case	Margaret P Birach	Donald L Hoskins	Frank Good	Peter Connors
Manistee* (8)	CM	616 723-2558	Vickers C Hansen	Robert C Lewis	Gerald Skiera	Kenneth J Oleniczak	John E Willett	John E Willett	....
Manistique* (4)	CM	906 341-2290	David Vaughn	Charles H Varnum	Patricia Erickson	Patricia Erickson	William Reno	James St Louis	Oliver Sholander
Marine City* (4)	CM	313 765-8830	Ervin LaBuhn	Loretta Vandric	Carol Ouellette	....	D P Stockwell	John Kelly	Jon E Stoppels
Marlette v* (2)	CM	517 635-7448	Dennis A Cargill	Charles Zampich	Robert C May	....	Robert Becker	James Lounsberry	Robert E Foster
Marquette* (23)	CM	906 228-8200	Robert C Stow Sr	David A Svanda	Norman L Gruber Jr	Robert Lawrence	George G Johnson	George G Johnson	Michael Etelamaki
Marshall* (7)	CM	616 781-5183	J Allen Bassage	Chester E Travis	Richard Watkins	....	L H Shellenberger	Roger A Graves	....
Marysville* (7)	CM	313 364-6613	David J Wright Jr	Jack M Schumacher	Robert C Maples	Robert C Maples	Larry D Garrow	Richard E Hinkley	Kenneth C Foerster
Mason* (6)	CM	517 676-9155	Gene Goodman	Patrick M Price	Patrick M Price	Norman L Austin	William Parsons	Clifford D Kline	Leslie Bruno Jr
Melvindale (12)	MC	313 389-2000	Thomas J Coogan	Thomas Norwood	Frances P Belanger	Joseph Gegus	Philip Christopher	William Donahue	Antonio Calderoni
Menominee (10)	MC	906 863-2656	Vernon L Anderle	....	Steven LeBoeuf	Steven LeBoeuf	Richard Schick	Michael Raygo	Robert Johnson
Meridian tp§ (29)	MC	517 349-1200	Carlene L Webster	Richard N Conti	Virginia L White	Thomas L Minter	Phillip C Johnson	John Amthor	Jon Mills
Midland* (37)	CM	517 835-7711	Joseph R Mann	Clifford R Miles	David W Wirth	Victor C Phillips	Robert J Fisher	Donald S Harcek	George W Shaffer
Milan* (4)	CM	313 439-1501	Ronald E Weber	Michael J Moran	Louise Burke	Louise Burke	Gary Brown	Chip Snider	Patrick McShane
Milford v* (5)	CM	313 684-1515	R Roy Danley	Bruce K Potthoff	Barbara Tressler	Herman Schneeman	James Caswell	Ronald Averill	T F Sutton
Monroe§ (24)	MC	313 243-0700	Kirk D McMullen	Timothy J Clifton	Robert L Dunbar	Thurman Liedel	Raymond R Soleau	Dalvin Arnold	Anthony Nowicki
Montrose* (2)	CM	313 639-6168	Edward F Ploucha	William E Space	Janice C Persons	Janice C Persons	Albert Huber	Ronald N Steinhorst	Paul Fejedelem
Mount Clemens* (19)	CM	313 469-6800	Ada Eisenfeld	Warren D Renando	Francis Pietrzak	William N Ringler	Charles Seehase	Max Patrick	Paul Hendricks
Mount Morris§ (3)	MC	313 686-2160	Allen J LaFurgey	William S Moore	Tamara J Miller	William S Moore	Orville L Stephens	Merle Sawyer	Max Wurn
Mount Pleasant* (24)	CM	517 773-7971	Gary G Knight	Thomas A Martin	Charles A Deibel	Charles A Deibel	Robert Denslow	Martin Trombley	Duane Ellis
Munising* (3)	CM	906 387-2095	Ruth M Snyder	Spencer R Nebel	Betty Ann Baker	Helen M Anderson	Theodore Belfry	Douglas Miron	Theodore Belfry
Muskegon* (41)	CM	616 724-6700	Elmer J Walcott	Robt F Hagemann III	Marva Vasquez	Betty Jean Walker	Robert Thue	Robert W Smith	Louis Van Dinther
Muskegon Heights* (15)	CM	616 733-1351	Robert A Warren	Emeterio A Cisneros	Lynne A Felt	James Stibitz	Duane Wilson	Willie R Howell	Henry Witherspoon
Negaunee* (5)	CM	906 475-7700	Edward Kinkella	Thomas R McNabb	Thomas R McNabb	Thomas R McNabb	Carl Rintala	William Treloar	Donald Robare
New Baltimore (5)	MC	313 725-2151	Frank Maskey	John B Hartner	Therese Orczykowski	Ina Rose Hubbard	William Schmid	Edward Reim	Harold Papaik
New Buffalo*† (3)	CM	616 469-1500	George Calnin	Thomas G Johnson	Joan Weishaupt	Susan Rogers	Ronald Bond	Edgar Caid	....
Newaygo* (1)	CM	616 652-1657	Douglas Day	....	....	Carol Sherwood	John Archbold Jr	Roger Chase	Brian Melvin
Niles§ (13)	MC	616 683-4700	Larry Clymer	Robert L Kufrin	Marjory Bachman	Marjory Bachman	Marion Fuller	Carl Lowell	Arthur Reed

Directory 1/10 continued **MUNICIPAL OFFICIALS IN ALL U.S. CITIES OVER 2,500[1]**

City, 1980 population (000 omitted), form of government		Municipal phone number	Mayor	Appointed administrator	City clerk	Finance officer	Fire chief	Police chief	Public works director
MICHIGAN (250) continued									
North Muskegon* (4)	CM	616 744-1621	C Max Fleischmann	Dennis W Stepke	Jean M Duplissis	Jeannette Gordon	James Kersman	Marvin H Wegner	Leonard Kaule
Northville* (6)	CM	313 349-1300	Paul R Vernon	Steven Walters	Joan McAllister	Steven Walters	James Allen	Rodney Cannon	Theodore Mapes
Norton Shores§ (22)	MC	616 798-4391	Merrill S Bailey	Herbert L Freye	Dorothy J Harjer	Russell Larsen	Harold P Wheeler	Charles Curtis	Rudolph J Chmelar
Norway* (3)	CM	906 563-8015	Daniel Stanchina	Raymond J France	Deborah L Hodge	Deborah L Hodge	William Johnson	Donald Calcatera	Joseph Flesatti
Novi* (23)	CM	313 349-4300	Robert Schmid	Ed F Kriewall Jr	Geraldine Stipp	Les Gibson	Arthur Lenaghan	Lee Begole	Robert A Shaw
Oak Park* (32)	CM	313 547-1331	Charlotte Rothstein	Aaron Marsh	Shirley M Pinson	James E Calder	....	....	Henry Lybeck
Ontonagon v§† (2)	MC	906 884-2975	....	Glenn Anderson	....	....	....	....	....
Otsego* (4)	CM	616 694-6146	Kenneth Bleeker	George J Strand	Jane L Tice	Joyce E Sanford	Darl Gilliland	Elton Goswick	Lester Goudy
Owosso* (16)	CM	517 723-8844	James P Capitan	Alex R Allie	Ruth M Coleman	Richard C Williams	Marvin Geeting	Harry Jankovic	Dale J Hexom
Oxford v* (3)	CM	313 628-2543	D Fortune	Brian G Arrowsmith	Nancy Miller	Nancy Miller	Dale Spiker	Frank C Huelsenbeck	Delbert Robinson
Paw Paw v† (3)	MC	616 657-3148	Charles F Smith	Harry L Bush	Charles R Cusumano	Charles R Cusumano	Ron Douglas	George Fadel	....
Petoskey* (6)	CM	616 347-4105	Joe Kilborn	George Korthauer	Leona Reissener	Leona Reissener	Simon Pennell	Ernest Kraus	Walter Goodwin
Pinconning* (1)	CM	517 879-2360	Charles Walworth	Norman E LaPorte	Caroline Card	Caroline Card	Harold Schumann	Peter LeFavour	Raymond Skowron
Plainwell§ (4)	MC	616 685-6821	James R Higgs	William R Stewart	William R Stewart	Karen Koehn	Bud Warnement	William J Drobny	Brian Whitney
Pleasant Ridge* (3)	CM	313 541-2900	Richard G Perkins	Louis G Barry	Barbara Joumas	Michael Lilly	Doyne Easterwood	Frank L Ockstadt	Louis G Barry
Plymouth*† (10)	CM	313 453-1234	Eldon W Martin	Henry E Graper Jr	Gordon G Limburg	Gordon G Limburg	Roy A Hall	....	Kenneth Vogras
Pontiac (77)	MC	313 857-7601	Wallace E Holland	....	Elizabeth Fletcher	K Joseph Young	Robert Lamson	James A Hildebrand	Donald L Kramer
Port Huron* (34)	CM	313 987-6000	James A Relken	G R Bouchard	Guy C Provost	Bruce A Seymore	Clifton A Friedland	Herman L Dusellier	Gerald Hummel
Portage* (38)	CM	616 327-4411	Engel Corstange	Donald P Ziemke	Lois B Johnson	....	James Reardon	George Von Behren	Jack Brodhagen
Portland*† (4)	CM	517 647-7531	Joseph V Tichvon	Rex Wambaugh	Kathleen Smith	Kathleen Smith	Larry Blundy	Richard White	Harold Ward
Reed City* (2)	CM	616 832-2245	Donald R Collison	William B McAfee	Marion A Fisher	Marion A Fisher	Gerald Kienitz	Phillip Rathbun	Kevin Rambadt
Richmond* (4)	CM	313 727-7571	Albert Bryant	Donald F Starr	William Commenator	William Commenator	Thomas McKiernan	John H Bridgewater	George L Klauka
River Rouge (13)	MC	313 842-4200	James Doig Jr	Anthony O Rinna	Park Richardson Jr	John Thomas Jr	Kevin Grignon	James Bates	Richard Crosson
Riverview* (15)	CM	313 283-2660	Peter Rotteveel	Harry J Kollman	Marilyn Girardin	Ms C Abercrombie	Donald Highfield	Donald J Highfield	Gerald N Perry
Rochester* (7)	CM	313 651-9061	Julia E Barrett	Kenneth A Johnson	Maxine Ross	Robert W Smalley	William Gray	Robert C Werth	Charles E Barker
Rockford* (3)	CM	616 866-2495	Jack Schwab	Daryl J Delabbio	....	....	Robert Van Der Mey	James Peterson	Robert Van Der Mey
Rockwood (3)	MC	313 379-9496	Melford Cunningham	Dale A Countegan	Nancy Dvorak Rich	James B Herzog	Frank Hinzmann	Gerald Norrix	Joseph Gonyea
Rogers City* (4)	CM	517 734-2191	James E Stewart	James E Leidlein	William R Froelich	William R Froelich	William R Froelich	Garnet P Robinson	Vernon E Langlois
Romeo v (4)	MC	313 752-3565	(not reporting)						
Romulus† (25)	MC	313 941-0666	William M Oakley	Patrick Hogan	Raymond C Antrell	Patsy Cantrell	Donald R Flood	Donald Flood	Dave Paul
Roosevelt Park* (4)	CM	616 755-3721	Donald D Kujawski	Robert L Kramer	Phyllis E Grams	Phyllis E Grams	....	Thomas M Kelenske	Michael R Chesher
Roseville* (54)	CM	313 445-5400	Jeanne A Riesterer	Thomas B Van Damme	Charles A LaGrant	John P Knapp	Morley Ireland	Thomas Asman	Larry McGrail
Royal Oak* (71)	CM	313 546-1000	Barbara A Hallman	Wm J Baldridge	Max LaValley	John L DaGiau	Wm H Crouch	John Taylor	James T Perry
Saginaw* (78)	CM	517 776-1480	Lawrence D Crawford	Tom Dalton	Enid G Davis	Mark Kennedy	Richard Hoffman	Alex Perez	James Ruhl
Saginaw tp§ (39)	MC	517 793-9540	George L Olson	Robert C Homan	Timothy J Braun	Virginia Gottschalk	Howard W Ihrke	Kenneth P Ott	Gerald C Francis
Saline (6)	MC	313 429-4907	Donald E Shelton	James L Levleit	Constance A Strait	Richard J Garay	Raymond Alber	James L Douglas	William Taylor
Sault Ste. Marie* (14)	CM	906 635-5261	James Alford	Neal A Godby	Audrey LeLievre	Elmer Adams	Gary Bennett	Robert Clary	Lyle E Jenks
Scottville* (1)	CM	616 757-4729	Clayton M Spencer	Blaine E Bacon	Blaine E Bacon	David L Hallberg	Donald V Engle	Evart T Cory	....
South Haven* (6)	CM	616 637-5211	Mary Buchert	Paul L Preston	Elizabeth Wagner	Sharon Onofrio	....	Thomas Allred	....
South Lyon* (5)	CM	313 437-1735	John M Renwick	Rodney L Cook	Norma Wallace	....	Charles Buhrs	Gerald L Smith	Bruce Jerome
Southfield* (76)	CM	313 354-1000	Donald F Fracassi	Del D Borgsdorf	Patrick G Flannery	Donald L Mason	Jerome McGrath	Edward Ritenour	Roger Smith
Southgate (32)	MC	313 246-1311	James A Kandrevas	Stephen J Bonczek	Robert M Alexander	Stephen J Bonczek	Thomas R Fisher	Robert J Perrin	Dennis E Gendron
Sparta v† (3)	MC	616 887-8251	Edward Soderstrom	....	Maizie Taylor	....	Paul Johnson	Len Sleutel	....
Spring Lake v* (3)	CM	616 842-1393	James D Christman	Eric R DeLong	Robert Lucking	Eric R DeLong	Mark Katt	Leon Langeland	John Hansen
Springfield* (6)	CM	616 965-2354	Adelbert E Bishop	Milford A Mellon	Carlene DeMaso	Carlene DeMaso	Robert Thomas	Gregory S Hansmeier	James Bracke
St. Charles v* (2)	CM	517 865-9791	Joyce Depre	....	Robert Grnak	Bertha Lavaley	....	Robert Meier	Willis R Boswell
St. Clair§ (5)	MC	313 329-7121	John A Sawher	Bruce D Banning	Janice B DiGiusto	Kathleen Haligowski	Perry Westrick	Joel Gorzen	....
St. Clair Shores* (76)	CM	313 445-5250	Ted B Wahby	Roy Stype	Robert S Helmer	A Kent Herbert	Henry C Graul	Elliott A Ewart	R Marlin Sumner
St. Ignace* (3)	CM	906 643-9671	Bruce Dodson	Rande J Wilson	Larry E Morris	Gary L Heckman	Leonard St Louis	Keith Pillsbury	....
St. Johns* (7)	CM	517 224-8944	John W Arehart	Randy L Humphrey	Richard L Coletta	Eugene W Simon	Clare Maier	Lyle French	Wendal Wagoner
St. Joseph* (10)	CM	616 983-6324	Franklin H Smith	William S Sinclair	Patrick D Phelan	Patrick D Phelan	Wm Moore	L Thomas Cooper	James Talbot
St. Louis* (4)	CM	517 681-2137	James E Ayers	Larry A Wernette	Leonard Johnson	Leonard Johnson	Larry Parsons	Howard Teed	Jim Pavlik
Stambaugh* (1)	CM	906 265-4213	Edward Van Ackeren	Albert K Silfven	Albert K Silfven	Joan B Brunswick	Thomas Korpi	Wayne Remondini	Albert K Silfven
Sterling Heights* (109)	CM	313 977-6123	Art Madar	Barry M Feldman	Mary T Zander	Robert Gulley	Eugene Schoenherr	Allan A Nalepa	Ray Filipchuk
Sturgis* (9)	CM	616 651-2321	Carlyle Kitson	John E Brand	Carol Rambadt	....	Robert Brown	Lyle Hopkins	....
Swartz Creek* (5)	CM	313 635-3600	Kay M Hart	Thomas L Hundley	Carol B Arvoy	....	Tom Spillane	Raymond L Adams	Michael R Shumaker
Sylvan Lake* (2)	CM	313 682-1440	Raymond C Dahlgren	....	Jeanette H Carey	Jeanette H Carey	Daniel Miller	Carl Fisher	....
Tawas City* (2)	CM	517 362-3731	David A Westcott	Jack H McNutt	Mary E Hilbert	Mary E Hilbert	Herbert Blust	George Westcott	Merlin Look
Taylor† (78)	MC	313 287-6550	Cameron G Priebe	....	John Sabo	Grant Alberts	Robert Diel	Joseph Forgays	George McGuckin
Tecumseh* (7)	CM	517 423-2107	Harold E Easton	Calvin Zorn	Vera Gardner	....	Wallace MacGeorge	Merlin Mowery	....
Three Rivers* (7)	CM	616 273-1075	Robert T McDonough	Gary L Word	Barbara Redford	Harold T Stock	S N Crose	Douglas Babcock	Thomas Tarkiewicz
Traverse City* (16)	CM	616 946-4800	Frederick D Nelson	Robt S Anderson	James Tompkins	Harry Zeeryp	Duane Mehl	Ralph Soffredine	Dale Majerczyk
Trenton (23)	MC	313 675-6500	George W Mans Jr	G Lloyd Silver	Marilyn F Reynolds	David Aronson	Russell D Stahl	William Lilienthal	Roy D Musselman
Troy* (67)	CM	313 524-3300	Richard Doyle	Frank Gerstenecker	Kenneth L Courtney	Kenneth L Courtney	James L Halsey	Lawrence Carey	Donald S Spurr
Utica (5)	MC	313 739-1600	Fred H Beck	....	Pat Delie	Shirley McMahon	Robert Beck	Reuben L Ricard	Joseph Francis
Vassar* (3)	CM	517 823-8517	James Hilligan	Dana J Reed	Carolyn Neuenfeldt	Edna A Eastham	Raymond O Hess Jr	John A Horwath	Raymond O Hess Jr
Wakefield* (3)	CM	906 229-5131	Charles Ludwick	Rudolph Mikulich	Marsha J Fetters	Patricia Mann	Lawrence Anderson	....	Nick Vidakovich
Walker* (15)	CM	616 453-6311	Adrian J Stehouwer	David Rubinstein	Linda Wiser	William Van Tuinen	William Burke	Walter Sprenger	John J Kinney
Walled Lake* (5)	CM	313 624-4847	Gaspare LaMarca	J Michael Dornan	Ruby Lewandowski	....	William Friar	Wilford G Hook	John E Nail
Warren (161)	MC	313 574-4500	James R Randlett	....	Carmella Sabaugh	Robert G Baker	Thomas Johnson	Max Durbin	Michael Servitto
Wayland* (2)	CM	616 792-2265	Donald Shafer	Carl W Fockler	Carl W Fockler	....	Hugh Deweerd	Harold Ernst	John Noordyke
Wayne* (21)	CM	313 722-2000	Patrick J Norton	Thomas G Daily	Norma M Collop	Edmund H Rothfelder	Kenneth Warfield	Ray Lecornu	James Law
West Branch* (2)	CM	517 345-0500	Richard W Werth	Gloria M Oswald	Gloria M Oswald	Debra Heisler	Joseph Rieger	Paul Longstreet	Thomas Brindley
Westland (85)	MC	313 721-6000	Charles W Pickering	Thomas Presnell	Diane Rohraff	John Sobleskie	Theodore Scott	Bill Rechlin	Henry Lundquist
Whitehall* (3)	CM	616 894-4048	Gordon E Huttenga	W David Boehm	....	Betty Jo Anderson	Gary Bohling	Orville M Smith	Howard Johnston
Williamston* (3)	CM	517 655-2774	Milton Steffes	Stephen Hughes	Mary F Haller	Wanda Piontkowski	Kurt Hunt	James LaClear	Ellis Wygant
Wixom (7)	MC	313 624-4557	Gary E Lentz	Keith A Salo	June Buck	Kevin Brady	George Spencer	Philip Leonard	Robert J Trombley
Wolverine Lake v (5)	CM	313 624-1710	Timmy Kozub	John D Berchtold	Donna Thorsberg	Frances Barber	....	John J O'Neill	John D Berchtold
Woodhaven† (11)	MC	313 675-3000	James D Lambert	David Flaten	Karen M Mazo	David Flaten	....	James A Caygill	Robert Thomas
Wyandotte (34)	MC	313 283-3800	James Wagner	....	William Griggs	Ralph Lesko	Bill Butch	Paul Mickel	Curt Burkett
Wyoming* (60)	CM	616 534-7671	Harold Isenga	James A Sheeran	Charles W Gress	John Schoolenberg	Harold Steenbergen	Lowell Henline	Gerald L Snyder
Ypsilanti* (24)	CM	313 483-1100	Peter J Murdock	Matt Hennessee	Robert A Slone Jr	Linda Brooks	John Coleman	W Robert Huff	....
Zeeland (5)	MC	616 772-4835	Donald Disselkoen	Leon Van Harn	Mary Richardson	Mary Richardson	Bill Gruppen	Lawrence Veldheer	Martin J Hieftje
Zilwaukee* (2)	CM	517 755-0931	James D Summerfield	Jack Tany	Rolland C Spencer	....	John Dammann	James R Stutesman	....
MINNESOTA (192)									
Afton (3)	MC	612 436-5090	George H Billmeyer	....	Linda Stancer	Evelyn Lane	Richard Johnson	....	....
Albert Lea* (19)	CM	507 373-2393	O H Hagen	Paul Sparks	Linda Oliver	D Rippentrop	E Grinolds	Clarence Ayers	R Johnson
Alexandria (8)	MC	612 763-6678	Paul F Nelson	....	Arlan E Johnson	....	Richard Nelson	George McKay	Earl LaMaack
Andover (9)	MC	612 755-5100	(not reporting)						

Directory 1/10 continued — **MUNICIPAL OFFICIALS IN ALL U.S. CITIES OVER 2,500[1]**

City, 1980 population (000 omitted), form of government	Municipal phone number	Mayor	Appointed administrator	City clerk	Finance officer	Fire chief	Police chief	Public works director
MINNESOTA (192) continued								
Anoka* (16) CM	612 421-6630	Lorraine Hostetler	Jerry Dulgar	Jerry Dulgar	Nancy Williams	Jacob Strouse	Andrew Revering	R B Johnson
Apple Valley (22) MC	612 432-0750	Willis E Branning	Richard G Asleson	Richard G Asleson	George Ballenger	Richard D Tuthill	Lloyd F Rivers	John B Gretz
Arden Hills v (8) MC	612 633-5676	Robert L Woodburn	....	Charlotte McNiesh	....	David Koch	....	Hans Johansen
Aurora v (3) MC	218 229-2614	John Niemi	....	Geraldine Boben	....	Robert Turk Jr	....	Walter Brune
Austin (23) MC	507 437-7671	Tom H Kough	Darrell Stacy	....	Richard Benzkofer	Dan Miller	Donald Hoffman	R F Murphy
Baxter (3) MC	218 829-7161	(not reporting)						
Bayport (3) MC	612 439-2530	Raoul Robledo	....	Dorothy R Smith	Raoul Robledo	Chas Schwartz	Stephen X Sullivan	Donald Gramenz
Belle Plaine§ (3) MC	612 873-5553	Frances Schuman	David Unmacht	David Unmacht	David Unmacht	Roger Mueller	Joe Lenz	Pat Fogarty
Bemidji* (11) CM	218 751-5610	Doug Peterson	Michael D McCurdy	Dorothy V Boe	Dale Page	Gerald Moen	Robert Tell	Michael Barclay
Benson* (4) CM	612 843-4775	Duaine Flanders	Edward Shukle	....	Ione Kellner	Calvin Lindblad	Wallace Weiss	Ken Ross
Blaine* (29) CM	612 784-6700	Francis Fogerty	Richard P Johnson	Joyce Twistol	....	Ronald Fagerstrom	Clayton Hogie	Kenneth Irvin
Bloomington* (82) CM	612 881-5811	James H Lindau	John G Pidgeon	Evelyn L Woulfe	Lyle R Olson	George Hayden	Jerry D Putman	Russell L Langseth
Blue Earth§ (4) MC	507 526-7336	John M Patton	John S Rudd	....	John S Rudd	Fritz Kriewall	Don Ficken	Jeffery Jansen
Brainerd (11) MC	218 829-2586	C Elmer Anderson	Richard M Johnson	Richard M Johnson	Richard M Johnson	Robert E Hannon	Ralph N Hitchens	Ronald Schweninger
Breckenridge (4) MC	218 643-1431	Marvin O Anderson	....	M D Casper	Mike Casper	James Severson	James C Worner	....
Brooklyn Center* (31) CM	612 561-5440	Dean A Nyquist	Gerald G Splinter	Gerald G Splinter	Paul Holmlund	Ronald Boman	James Lindsay	Sylvester Sy Knapp
Brooklyn Park* (43) CM	612 425-4502	James Krautkremer	R M Henneberger	Wesley Long	Charles Darth	Lyle Robinson	Donald E Davis	Neil M Johnson
Buffalo (5) CM	612 682-1181	Gerard Melgaard	Merton Auger	Merton Auger	Merton Auger	James O Nelson	Dan D Scott	Gary Mattson
Burnsville* (36) CM	612 890-4100	Connie Morrison	James K Spore	Evelyn M Kjos	Leslie J Anderson	Brian Holzer	Michael DuMoulin	Charles A Siggerud
Caledonia (3) MC	507 724-3450	Harold A Beth	....	Norman F Mechtel	Miles A Marnach	Dewayne Schroeder	Robert F Richards	....
Cambridge v (3) MC	612 689-3211	Lynn H Becklin	....	Scott G Larson	....	Tom Minar	Frank Akers	Tom Minar
Cannon Falls† (3) MC	507 263-3954	Robert Carnel	....	....	....	....	....	....
Champlin§ (9) MC	612 421-8064	Dale F Winch	Daniel Hartman	Doris Kemp	Connie Skarbakka	....	Ronald Harwood	Gerald Ruppelius
Chanhassen* (6) CM	612 937-1900	Thomas Hamilton	Don W Ashworth	Don W Ashworth	Kay Klingelhutz	Jack Kreger	Jerry Amrhein	William Monk
Chaska§† (8) MC	612 448-2851	Tracy D Swanson	William M Radio	Shirley Bruers	Bonita Carlson	James Worm	Greg Schol	Donald Fahey
Chisholm (6) MC	218 254-3353	Frank K Furlan	Ron Baron	Ron Baron	....	Dave Andrews	Robert Silvestri	George D Champa
Circle Pines§ (3) MC	612 784-5898	Marshall N Dahl	Craig R Rapp	Craig R Rapp	Craig R Rapp	Kelly Summerville	Ronald Nicholas	Jon M Thiel
Cloquet† (11) MC	218 879-3347	Mel Tan	....	Lawrence Gustafson	....	....	Bennett Roginski	James R Prusak
Cokato§ (2) MC	612 286-5813	Forrest Amundsen	Joel D Dhein	Peggy Carlson	....	Reed Carlson	....	....
Columbia Heights* (20) CM	612 788-9221	Bruce G Nawrocki	Robert S Bocwinski	William Elrite	William Elrite	Donald Johnson	Stuart Anderson	Fred Salsbury
Coon Rapids* (36) CM	612 755-2880	Robert B Lewis	Robert D Thistle	Betty Bell	Lyle Haney	William Thompson	Gerald D Nelson	William Ottensmann
Corcoran† (4) MC	612 420-2288	Harold Schutte	....	....	....	....	....	....
Cottage Grove† (19) CM	612 458-2800	Roger E Peterson	Carl F Meissner	Carl F Meissner	Randell J Winspear	Denis Erickson	Dennis Cusick	Frank Gaillard
Crookston† (9) MC	218 281-1232	Douglas A Oman	Raymond E Ecklund	Allen L Chesley	Allen L Chesley	George Jacobs	Dennis H Hogenson	Raymond E Ecklund
Crystal* (26) CM	612 537-8421	Thomas Aaker	John T Irving	Delores Ahmann	Miles D Johnson	Arthur Quady	James Mossey	William L Sherburne
Dawson§ (2) MC	612 769-4615	....	John J Frohrip	....	....	....	....	....
Dayton† (4) MC	612 427-4589	Hilmer J Hartman	....	Shirley Slater	Bruce Wasiloski	Robert Leger	Thomas Davison	....
Deephaven (4) MC	612 474-4755	Charles W Watson	Juliene Weidner	Juliene Weidner	....	....	James C Anderson	Wallace A Roholt
Delano§ (2) MC	612 479-1535	Chuck Theis	Baldev S Josan	Baldev S Josan	....	Winne Sinkel	....	....
Detroit Lakes (7) MC	218 847-5658	Loren Nelson	Richard Grabow	....	Louis Guzek	Arville Thompson	Alden Tyge	Herbert R Koenig
Dilworth (3) MC	218 287-2313	Arlo Brown	....	Gary Cowden	Ken Parke	Fred Doeden Jr	Stan Gordon	....
Duluth§ (93) MC	218 723-3297	John A Fedo	Richard A Ives	Jeff Cox	David Talbot	Gerald Behning	Eli Miletich	Roger A Kurrle
Eagan§ (21) MC	612 454-8100	Bea Blomquist	Thomas L Hedges	Gene Van Overbeke	Gene Van Overbeke	Robert Childers	Jay Berthe	Thomas Colbert
East Bethel† (7) MC	612 434-9569	Roger Grams	....	Sharon Hauschild	Sharon Anderson	Greg Henderson	....	Douglas Meyenburg
East Grand Forks (9) MC	218 773-2483	Louis A Murray	David E Mack	David E Mack	David E Mack	Daniel T Formato	Kermit W Sundin	Edwin J Osowski
Eden Prairie* (16) CM	612 937-2262	Wolfgang H Penzel	Carl J Jullie	John Frane	John Frane	Ray Mitchell	Jack Hacking	Gene Dietz
Edina* (46) CM	612 927-8861	C Wayne Courtney	Kenneth Rosland	Marcella Daehn	Jerry N Dalen	Bill Feck	Craig Swanson	Francis Hoffman
Elk River§ (7) MC	612 441-2052	Richard Hinkle	Robert C Middaugh	P Boedigheimer	P Boedigheimer	Russel D Anderson	Thomas Zerwas	Phil Hals
Ely (5) MC	218 365-3224	Gerard Bibeau	Arthur J Murphy	Arthur J Murphy	Arthur J Murphy	John Koshak	Joseph Baltich	Marvin Theno
Eveleth† (5) MC	218 744-4329	Patrick A Bastianel	....	Elmer A Milbridge	Elmer A Milbridge	Guido Rosati	James D Bozicevich	John Palo
Excelsior* (3) CM	612 474-5233	Richard Knapp	....	Jane Ann Peterson	Robert A Dietrick	William Rand	Richard Young	Carl Zieman
Fairfax§ (1) MC	507 426-7255	Kenneth Havemeier	....	Marcia Pelzel	....	Marlin Waibel	John Dover	....
Fairmont† (12) MC	507 238-9461	Robert N Malliet	Gary Klaphake	Lois J Cairns	Bryon A Karow	Randy Musser	Erwin Thiel	K M Mike Zarling
Falcon Heights (5) MC	612 644-5050	Ronald C Eggert	Dewan B Barnes	Dewan B Barnes	....	Jerry Renchin	Ronald E Eggert	....
Faribault§ (16) MC	507 334-2222	Robert W Heine	Robert H Yochum	....	Patrick Hentges	Dwight Hildebrandt	Gerald Reuvers	Glen D Hodgson
Farmington* (4) CM	612 463-7111	Patrick Akin	Larry Thompson	Larry Thompson	Wayne Henneke	David Pietsch	Stan Whittingham	William Hince
Fergus Falls§ (13) MC	218 739-2251	Kelly Ferber	James L Nitchals	....	Gary M Nelson	Kenneth Hovland	Harmarthur Hull	Donald G Eisenhuth
Forest Lake (5) MC	612 464-3550	John F Skoglund	Robert R Houle	Robert R Houle	Robert R Houle	Arthur E Jensen	David Schwartz	Arthur E Jensen
Franklin§ (1) MC	507 557-2259	Mary Ann Woelfel	....	Laurie Sherman	Laurie Sherman	Kermit Ness	Roger Degner	Kevin Thompson
Fridley* (30) CM	612 571-3450	William J Nee	Nasim M Qureshi	Sidney C Inman	Sidney C Inman	Robert Aldrich	James Hill	John F Flora
Gilbert (3) MC	218 741-9443	Herbert S Ocepek	Gary D Mackley	....	....	Thomas Indihar	Anthony Delzotto	Kenneth Kuitunen
Glencoe (4) MC	612 864-5586	Elf Austad	....	Gregory F Troska	....	Theophil Kostecka	Rudy Wittenberg	....
Golden Valley* (23) CM	612 545-3781	Mary E Anderson	William Joynes	Shirley Nelson	Donald Taylor	Bob Hennesy	Glen Olson	Lowell Odland
Goodview (3) MC	507 452-1630	(not reporting)						
Grand Rapids§ (8) MC	218 326-3246	John T Craig	Edward L Ericson	Edward L Ericson	Karlene Gale	Robert E Liebel	Harold Snyder	Richard Sackett
Granite Falls* (3) CM	612 564-3011	Gene Sannerud	Richard A Voller	Mrs Signe Maguire	Steven B Okins	Dan Schafer	Darryl Bulzomi	John Knutson
Ham Lake (8) MC	612 434-9555	Dennis J Landborg	....	Doris A Nivala	Doris A Nivala	Roger Mechels	....	....
Hastings§ (13) MC	612 437-4127	Luann Stoffel	Gary E Brown	....	....	Donald Latch	Daryl Plath	....
Hermantown (7) MC	218 729-6331	Helmer A Ruth	....	Nancy A Sirois	....	Reginald Royer	Terrance Ulshafer	Wallace Loberg
Hibbing (21) MC	218 262-3486	Richard A Nordvold	Harry Gherardi	Patrick L Garrity	Patrick L Garrity	O A Abate	William Grillo	Clyde Busby
Hopkins* (15) CM	612 935-8474	Robert Miller	William P Craig	J Scott Renne	John E Schedler	Raymond Petersen	Earl L Johnson	John J Strojan
Hoyt Lakes v† (3) MC	218 225-2344	Harry L Helmer	....	Richard J Bradford	....	Lynn Mugge	Donald Grivette	Emil Spielman
Hugo (4) MC	612 429-6676	Michael McAllister	....	Maryann Creager	....	Ronald Istvanovich	....	....
Hutchinson§ (9) MC	612 587-5151	Robert H Stearns	Gary D Plotz	Gary D Plotz	Ken Merrill	Orlin Henke	Dean O'Borsky	Marlow V Priebe
Independence (3) MC	612 479-2773	Marvin D Johnson	....	Earl H Taylor	....	....	W Henn	Earl H Taylor
International Falls (6) MC	218 283-9484	Robert W Anderson	....	Gary B Davison	Michael Stanich	Kenneth Hultman	Thomas Hardy	Gary Skallman
Inver Grove Heights* (17) CM	612 457-2111	William Saed	Robert W Schaefer	Robert W Schaefer	Douglas R Sell	Dale Beckman	Robert A Harris	James Kleinschmidt
Jackson (4) MC	507 847-4410	David Fell	David R Hartley	David R Hartley	David R Hartley	Richard Hample	Richard Seim	....
Jordan§ (3) MC	612 492-2535	Gail Andersen	Robert F Morgan	Robert F Morgan	Kathy C Lapic	William Busch	Alvin Erickson	Lawrence Jabs
Kasson† (3) MC	507 634-7071	Joseph Gronert	....	....	....	....	....	....
Kenyon§ (2) MC	507 789-6415	Mildred Lair	Coralee LaSell	....	....	Dave Morris	Ray Dawson	....
La Crescent† (4) MC	507 895-2595	Ottis Adamson	Stephan J Jilk	Stephan J Jilk	....	David Scroeder	Richard Johnson	....
Lake City† (5) MC	612 345-5383	Mary Lou Beckman	Richard Abraham	Bruce Schumacher	....	William Anderson	Gordon Vlasak	James Biggar
Lake Elmo§ (5) MC	612 777-5510	Maynard Eder	Patrick D Klaers	Patrick D Klaers	Marilyn Banister	Fran Pott	....	....
Lakeville§ (15) MC	612 469-4431	Duane Zaun	Patrick E McGarvey	Patrick E McGarvey	Dennis Feller	Barry Christiansen	Richard Radermacher	James Robinette
Le Sueur† (4) MC	612 665-6401	John K King	Allen Cords	Richard Almich	....	Dan Labelle	Harry Thorau	Dean Kunze
Lino Lakes† (5) MC	612 464-5562	Benjamin Benson	Randall Schumacher	Edna Sarner	Marilyn Anderson	Bruce MacDonald	Marvin Myhre	Donald Volk
Litchfield§ (6) MC	612 693-7201	Ronald L Johnson	Wayne R Carlson	Betty Anderson	Betty Anderson	Joe Tacheny	James Petersen	Robert Hendrickson
Little Canada v† (7) MC	612 484-2177	Raymound Hanson	....	Joseph Chlebeck	Joseph Chlebeck	Carl Spooner	....	Roger Glanzer

Directory 1/10 continued — MUNICIPAL OFFICIALS IN ALL U.S. CITIES OVER 2,500[1]

City, 1980 population (000 omitted), form of government		Municipal phone number	Mayor	Appointed administrator	City clerk	Finance officer	Fire chief	Police chief	Public works director
MINNESOTA (192) continued									
Little Falls (7)	MC	612 632-2341	Patricia B Spence	Thomas J Manninen	....	....	Charles Nieman	Clayton Olson	....
Long Prairie§† (3)	MC	612 732-2167	Donald F Moore	David Venekamp	....	Millie Steinberg	Larry Alsleben	Bob Ziegenhagen	Melvin Rahn
Luverne§ (5)	MC	507 283-2388	Harold Dueschle	Mary Guhin	....	Mark Lien	Jim Johannsen	Keith Aanenson	....
Madison* (2)	CM	612 598-3484	Robert Jette	William P Lavin	....	Alden Chester	Linia Nohrenberg	Reed Schmidt	Harold Hodge
Mahtomedi§ (4)	MC	612 426-3344	Henry DeWuske	Mark Lenz	Judy Elton	DeLossie Boldt	James Peloquin	....	Rollyn Young
Mankato* (29)	CM	507 625-3161	Herbert Mocol	William A Bassett	Carla Raberge	....	Ray Erlandson	Charles D Alexander	Paul Baker
Maple Grove§ (21)	MC	612 420-4000	James P Deane	Douglas S Reeder	Douglas S Reeder	Fred Christiansen	Roger Kuchera	Robert Burlingame	Gerald Butcher
Maplewood* (27)	CM	612 770-4500	John Greavu	Barry R Evans	Lucille E Aurelius	Daniel Faust	Alfred Schadt	Kenneth Collins	Kenneth Haider
Marshall§ (11)	MC	507 532-3231	Robert Schlagel	James R Heller	Thomas Meulebroeck	Thomas Meulebroeck	Edward Sheele	Marvin Bahn	Duane Aden
Medina v (3)	MC	612 473-4643	Thomas Anderson	....	Donna Roehl	Donna Roehl	....	Michael Sankey	James Dillman
Mendota Heights§ (7)	MC	612 452-1850	Robert G Lockwood	Kevin D Frazell	Kathleen Swanson	Larry Shaughnessy	Leroy Noack	Dennis Delmont	James Danielson
Milaca* (2)	CM	612 983-3141	Kenneth Trimble	Ralph K Hester	Ralph K Hester	Julie Bergstrom	Harry Totzke	Dennis Johnson	Harold Santema
Minneapolis§ (371)	MC	612 348-2032	Donald M Fraser	Lyall A Schwarzkopf	Lyall A Schwarzkopf	....	Thomas L Dickinson	Anthony Bouza	Perry D Smith
Minnetonka* (39)	CM	612 933-2511	Larry A Donlin	James F Miller	Dale L Eggenberger	Dale L Eggenberger	M Lindquist	Richard Setter	Donald L Asmus
Minnetrista§ (3)	MC	612 446-1660	Wally Clevenger	....	Charlotte Paterson	....	....	Timothy Thompson	Richard Bialon
Montevideo* (6)	CM	612 269-6575	L Steven Boehlke	R Ben Bifoss	Lavonne Sundlee	R Ben Bifoss	Marvin Garbe	Carl Sorensen	John Donahue
Monticello§ (3)	MC	612 295-2711	Arvie Grimsmo	Thomas A Eidem	....	Rick Wolfsteller	Williard Farnick	....	John Simola
Moorhead (30)	MC	218 299-5301	Morris L Lanning	....	Everett B Lecy	Gerald H Sorenson	Marlan Anderson	Leslie Sharrock	Everett B Lecy
Mora§ (3)	MC	612 679-1511	Robert L Ardner	Robert A Filson	Dorothea McCallum	Dorothea McCallum	Ron Naumann	David P Mawhorter	....
Morris* (5)	CM	612 589-3141	Merlin Beyer	Edward R Larson	Edward R Larson	....	Rick Eul	Henry Hull	William G Storck
Mound* (9)	CM	612 472-1155	Robert Polston	Jonathan R Elam	Francene C Clark	Sharon Legg	Robert Cheney	....	Eugene Hoff
Mounds View§ (13)	MC	612 784-3055	Duane McCarty	Donald F Pauley	....	Donald Brager	Ron Fagerstrom	Timothy Ramacher	Steve Thatcher
Mountain Iron§ (4)	MC	218 735-8267	Frank P Cerkvenik	Peter Von Drak	....	....	Mike Vidmar	....	Richard Anderson
New Brighton* (23)	CM	612 633-1533	Gregory Harcus	Henry D Sinda	Margaret Egan	Margaret Egan	Al Bauer	John Kelley	Les Proper
New Hope* (23)	CM	612 533-1521	Edward J Erickson	Daniel Donahue	Betty Pouliot	Larry Watts	William Reimer	Colin Kastanos	Roger Paulson
New Prague (3)	MC	612 758-4401	Raymond Schoenecker	Jerome Bohnsack	Jerome Bohnsack	Jerome Bohnsack	William Kajer	Dennis Rohloff	Melvin Stocker
New Ulm* (14)	CM	507 359-8233	Carl L Wyczawski	Richard D Salvati	Karl Huber Jr	Karl Huber Jr	L E Lowinske	Richard Gulden	Arnold A Putnam
Newport§ (3)	MC	612 459-5677	John Walker	John K Hawes	....	John K Hawes	Robert Engen	Fred Leimbek	Lee Flandrich Sr
North Mankato* (9)	CM	507 625-4141	David L Dehen	Robert Ringhofer	Laurie Rauenhorst	Wendell G Sande	Donald Benson	Dale Broughten	Robert Ringhofer
North Oaks† (3)	MC	612 484-5777	Warren Johnson	....	....	....	....	....	....
North St. Paul* (12)	CM	612 770-4450	William Sandberg	Robert E Gatti	Robert E Gatti	Glenn Anderson	Howard Anderson	Thomas J Langeslay	David Kotilinek
Northfield§ (13)	MC	507 645-8833	William Gill	Peter E Stolley	Evangline Hall	....	John Machacek	Mancel Mitchell	Larry Turner
Oak Park Heights (3)	MC	612 439-4439	Frank Sommerfeldt	Lavonne Wilson	....	Lavonne Wilson	....	Eugene Ostendorf	Roger Benson
Oakdale§ (12)	MC	612 739-5086	Leo Hudalla	Craig J Mattson	Craig J Mattson	Stephen Plaisance	....	Richard E Alstad	Roland Harrington
Olivia§ (3)	MC	612 523-2361	John R Stumpf	Richard N Carlson	Richard N Carlson	Richard N Carlson	John Stahl	Howard J Sander	Robert Ewer
Orono§ (7)	MC	612 473-7357	Mary C Butler	Walter R Benson	Alberta M Strom	Thomas M Kuehn	....	Melvin H Kilbo	John R Gerhardson
Ortonville† (3)	MC	612 839-3428	Harold G Van Winkle	....	Donald E Geier	....	Dale Hausauer	Quentin Larsen	....
Osseo (3)	MC	612 425-2624	Arnold Phenow	....	Richard E Setzler	....	Peter Phenow	Peter Weller	Andrew J Smith
Owatonna (19)	MC	507 451-4540	George E Kehoe	....	Thomas E Mealey	James A Moeckly	Frank B Anderson	Kenneth L Nissen	Maynard R Lueth
Park Rapids (3)	MC	218 732-3163	Gene Kinkel	....	Myron Harsha	Myron Harsha	Richard Harsha	James Scouton	....
Perham* (2)	CM	218 346-4455	Donald Swenson	Sandy L Dibrito	....	....	Jack Schmidt	Fay Botts	Frank Sczygiel
Pine Island§ (2)	MC	507 356-4591	Robert Fox	Paul Finocchio	Dawn M Boelke	....	John Archer	Dale Grote	....
Pipestone (5)	MC	507 825-3324	Steve Perkins	....	Dave Logan	....	Gordon Erickson	James Carstenson	Paul Miersma
Plymouth* (32)	CM	612 559-2800	David J Davenport	James G Willis	Laurie Houk	Lloyd J Ricker	Ralph Begin	Richard J Carlquist	Fred G Moore
Princeton* (3)	CM	612 389-2040	Faith N Zwemke	Gregory Withers	Gregory Withers	Steven Jackson	Douglas Patten	Thomas McCarthy	Eugene Zeroth
Prior Lake* (7)	CM	612 447-4230	Gary G Johnson	Michael McGuire	....	Ralph Teschner	Bob Mertens	Richard Powell	Larry J Anderson
Proctor (3)	MC	218 624-3641	Jimmie A Amundson	Daniel P Hoffman	....	....	James Parmeter	Scott H Schneider	Kenneth Erickson
Ramsey (10)	MC	612 427-1410	Thomas G Gamec	Lloyd G Schnelle	....	Jeanne A Haapala	....	Michael Auspos	Merle Mevissen
Red Wing§ (14)	MC	612 388-6734	Ed Powderly	Dean A Massett	Burton C Will	....	Richard Kosec	Forrest Wipperling	Tom Drake
Redwood Falls§ (5)	MC	507 637-5755	Richard S Anderson	Neil F Ruddy III	Neil F Ruddy III	Gordon Valle	Kenneth Kammerer	Mike Gerrety	Ronald Mannz
Richfield* (38)	CM	612 869-7521	John Hamilton	John G Cartwright	Sylvia K Bergh	Ronald S Rankin	....	Thomas A Morgan Jr	Donald Fondrick
Robbinsdale* (14)	CM	612 537-4534	Raymond A Mattson	Walter Fehst	Douglas Upton	Richard Gangelhoff	Thomas Sipe	Roland D Thurman	Reynold Eckstrom
Rochester§ (58)	MC	507 285-8086	Chuck Hazama	Stevan E Kvenvold	Carole Grimm	Paul Utesch	Orville Mertz	James M Macken Jr	Roger Plumb
Rosemount (5)	MC	612 423-4411	Leland S Knutson	....	Don F Darling	Francis J Goggin	Kenneth V Gist	James E Staats	Donald J Brown
Roseville* (36)	CM	612 484-3371	June Demos	James F Andre	James F Andre	Donald Sholund	James Dougherty	James Zelinsky	Charles Honchell
Rush City§ (1)	MC	612 358-4744	....	Joel R Hanson	....	....	....	....	....
Sartell§ (3)	MC	612 253-2171	Robert Bogard	....	Susan J Mueller	Susan J Mueller	Jan Bettenberg	Jerry O'Driscoll	Robert Raddatz
Sauk Centre (4)	MC	612 352-3467	Robert Wensman	....	Larry Bethel	....	David Meyer	George Trierweiler	....
Sauk Rapids§ (6)	MC	612 251-1022	Bernard Gratzek	Robert L Haarman	Robert L Haarman	Edward Schmidt	Dennis Schlichting	John Welsh	Richard Gronau
Savage§ (4)	MC	612 890-1045	Rodd Hopp	Mark H McNeill	Mark H McNeill	David Morrison	Tom Stang	Gordon Vlasak	Raymond Miller
Shakopee§ (10)	MC	612 445-3650	Eldon Reinke	John Anderson	Judith Cox	Gregg Voxland	Joe Ries	Thomas Brownell	Jim Karkanen
Shoreview§ (17)	MC	612 484-3353	Richard A Wedell	Gary L Dickson	Gary L Dickson	William W Stawarski	David Koch	....	Melvin Houle
Shorewood§ (5)	MC	612 474-3236	Bob Rascop	Daniel Vogt	Sandy Kennelly	Daniel Vogt	....	Richard Young	Don Zdrazil
Silver Bay (3)	MC	218 226-4408	Robert H Kind	....	Edward J Arola	Earl R Carman	Kenneth Tuorila	Robert M Sando	Toivo I Minkkinen
Sleepy Eye (4)	MC	507 794-3731	Harry Hornbrook	....	Edvin V Treml	....	Geo Ebenhoh	Otto W Klein	....
South Internatl Falls† (3)	MC	218 283-9461	Lloyd C Walls	....	....	....	....	....	....
South St. Paul§ (21)	MC	612 451-3226	Chas A Michelson	James P Cosgrove	C D McDermott	Marlin Amundson	Norman Nistler	Craig Kinney	Robert Simon
Spring Lake Park v† (6)	MC	612 784-6491	Don Masterson	Donald B Busch	Donald B Busch	Donald B Busch	Ron Fagerstrom	Otto J Lind	Chuck Rundle
Spring Valley v (3)	MC	507 346-7367	Wayne Fenske	Dan Elwood	Dan Elwood	Dan Elwood	Ivan Termat	....	Phillip Soltis
St. Anthony* (8)	CM	612 789-8881	Robert Sundland	David M Childs	Carol Johnson	Carol Johnson	Lee Entner	Donald Hickerson	Larry Hamer
St. Cloud§ (43)	MC	612 251-5541	R J Huston	Elmer J Malinen	Rob Grasslin	Marvin Brunsell	William Graham	Woody Bissett	John Dolentz
St. James§ (4)	MC	507 375-3241	Roger A Parsons	David M Osberg	Roy Trullinger	Roy Trullinger	Eldon Hovde	Don Mickelson	Craig Christiansen
St. Joseph v† (3)	MC	612 363-7541	Hugo B Weyrens	....	Robert G Johnson	....	Bill Wasner	William Lorentz	Herman Schneider
St. Louis Park* (43)	CM	612 920-3000	Lyle W Hanks	James Brimeyer	Beverly Flanagan	Harlan Syverson	John Kersey	....	Dick Koppy
St. Paul (270)	MC	612 298-4012	George Latimer	....	Albert B Olson	Peter Hames	Steve F Conroy	William McCutcheon	Donald E Nygaard
St. Paul Park† (5)	MC	612 459-9785	Steven J Abdella	Barry J Sittlow	Barry J Sittlow	Larry Shaughnessy	Russell Nelson	Virgil Gilbertson	Barry J Sittlow
St. Peter§ (9)	MC	507 931-4840	Douglas C Pyan	Kenneth H Huber	Cindy Underdahl	Ronald Otkin	Dennis Peterson	Bradley Kollman	Melvin Johnson
Staples (3)	MC	218 894-2550	(not reporting)						
Stewartville (4)	MC	507 533-4745	Harold W Johnson	Jonathan H Pearson	Jonathan H Pearson	DeAnna Burns	Phillip Denny	....	....
Stillwater§ (12)	MC	612 439-6121	Harry D Peterson	Nile L Kriesel	Bonnie J Kirtz	Betty J Caruso	David Chial	Wallace Abrahamson	John Shelton
Thief River Falls (9)	MC	218 681-2943	Bob Carlson	....	Gerald A Wigness	Roger I Delap	David Bjorkman	K Froscheiser	....
Tracy§ (2)	MC	507 629-3460	W Scott Keller	Audrey Koopman	Audrey Koopman	David Spencer	Morris Ohman	Curtis Wiese	Don Polzine
Two Harbors (4)	MC	218 834-4386	Wayne M Sletten	....	John D Olsvik	Roger P Simonson	Robert Sellman	Robert Sandness	Dale Hanson
Vadnais Heights (5)	MC	612 429-5343	Robert J Hohenauer	Gerald J Urban	Gerald J Urban	Gerald J Urban	Kenneth Lorenz	....	Leroy Urban
Virginia (11)	MC	218 741-3890	Jalmer T Johnson	....	Norma L Nekich	Greta Ocklind	Anteo Bocchi	Edward Snyder	Nicholas Dragisich
Waconia§ (3)	MC	612 448-5215	Gerald Bailey	Monte Eastvold	Esther Zellmann	....	Randall Sorensen	Jack Hendrickson	Randall Sorensen
Wadena (5)	MC	218 631-2383	Bruce H Nelson	....	Bruce L Brown	....	John Edinger	Joyce H Kopp	Ron Bucholz
Waite Park v (3)	MC	612 252-6822	(not reporting)						
Waseca* (8)	CM	507 835-3840	Avery Doc Hall	Timothy Madigan	Robert Jellum	....	Steven Werner	Bruce Stauffer	Orlin Ortloff

Directory 1/10 continued **MUNICIPAL OFFICIALS IN ALL U.S. CITIES OVER 2,500[1]**

City, 1980 population (000 omitted), form of government		Municipal phone number	Mayor	Appointed administrator	City clerk	Finance officer	Fire chief	Police chief	Public works director
MINNESOTA (192) continued									
Waterville§ (2)	MC	507 362-8300	Arthur Sorgatz	Larry Hansen	Luann Warner	Patricia Kelm	Elmer Stangler	Arle Bluhm	Robert Bittrich
Wayzata* (4)	CM	612 473-0234	Bill Humphrey	Allan Orsen	Allan Orsen	....	Bruce Day	David Brehm	Allan Orsen
Wells (3)	MC	507 553-5823	Bruce Steinhaus	....	Dolly Schultz	Dolly Schultz	Bruce Schulz	Orville Linde	Ray Wigern
West St. Paul* (19)	CM	612 455-9671	Kenneth Kube	Thomas A Hoban	Patricia J Morrison	John W Remkus	Richard B Krogh	Francis H Trost	Philip A Stefaniak
White Bear Lake*† (23)	CM	612 429-8526	Bradley Stanius	....	Raymond Siebenaler	David MacGillivray	Gordon Vadnais	Peter Korolchuk	Steve Gatlin
Willmar (16)	MC	612 235-4913	F J Ole Reynolds	....	Richard C Hoglund	Lawrence Haats	Douglas Lindblad	Lyle Goeddertz	Verne Carlson
Windom (5)	CM	507 831-2363	D Frederickson	....	D W Nelson	T N Weeks	Richard Jeffrey	Elton Wagner	....
Winona* (25)	CM	507 452-8550	Earl Laufenburger	D R Sollenberger	James G Pomeroy	Darrel R Johnson	Edward F Kohner	Jack Scherer	Robert J Bollant
Woodbury§ (10)	MC	612 739-5972	Daniel J Guider Jr	James V Lacina	William R Krueger	Thomas C Wright	Gene Johnson	Gregory T Orth	Howard C Radke
Worthington§ (10)	MC	507 376-3161	Harlin O Owens	Donald E Habicht	Garnet A Burns	M Tim Magee	Fred Weets	M D Rotschafer	Randy R Griffith
MISSISSIPPI (87)									
Aberdeen (7)	MC	601 369-8588	Frank W Harrington	R T Byars	Hershel D Williams	Glenn Howell	J P George	Russell Newman	Doyle Herndon
Amory (7)	MC	601 256-5721	Thomas Griffith	....	Rex Coker	Rex Coker	Earl Frye Jr	Carl Edward West	....
Baldwyn t (3)	MC	601 365-2383	Merle B Rowan	....	James P McWhorter	....	B E Ozbirn	Johnny W Conlee	Ted Crawford
Batesville t† (5)	MC	601 563-3131	B G Baker	....	Barbara L Broome	....	Larry Fisher	Donald C Christian	....
Bay St. Louis (8)	MC	601 467-9092	Larry J Bennett	....	Edward A Favre	Edward A Favre	Andrew B Lizana	Douglas Williams	Norbert Redmond
Belzoni† (3)	MC	601 247-1343	Tom N Turner Jr	....	R H Watson		Grady O Sanders	Romey Jones	Stephen Watsula
Biloxi (49)	MC	601 374-8600	Gerald H Blessey	Audrey A Lamey	Audrey A Lamey	Wade Fredricks	Guy B Roberts	Carl Short	Buddy Gillis
Booneville t† (6)	MC	601 728-6810	Charles Crabb	....	June Hutcheson	....	Frank Fleming	John O Lambert	....
Brandon (10)	MC	601 825-5021	Manning Cooper	....	Billy C Smith	Billy C Smith	William E Holmes	Jim Addy	
Brookhaven (11)	MC	601 833-2362	Harold Samuels	....	Irene H Byrne	....	Teunnison L Lea	L J McBride	James Griffin
Canton (11)	MC	601 859-4331	Sidney Runnels	....	Wanda A Baldwin	Wanda A Baldwin	Billy R Permenter	Bobby Winters	Frank Frazier
Carthage t† (3)	MC	601 267-9666	Jimmy D Wallace	....	Ann Hogue	....	Joey Robin Jones	Terry Jones	L F Chipley
Charleston (3)	MC	601 647-5841	Freeman Sanders	....	Diane Stanford	Diane Stanford	Phil P Shook	Ronnie W Nance	....
Clarksdale† (21)	MC	601 627-4761	Richard M Webster	....	H G Howell Jr	H G Howell Jr	John A Jones	L M Collins	Jim Wanamaker
Cleveland (15)	MC	601 846-1471	Martin T King Jr	Jerome Norwood	Virginia Wood	....	Charles Van Namen	Charles R Mosley	Kenneth McCool
Clinton t† (15)	MC	601 924-5462	Walter G Howell	....	Julia Harrison	Julia Harrison	Jeff Landrum	Jimmy Dukes	Edward Robertson
Columbia (8)	MC	601 736-8201	Robert R Bourne	....	D E Crawley	D E Crawley	Ted Thompson	Joe Sanders	....
Columbus (27)	MC	601 328-7021	James Trotter	....	A Y Lipsey	A Y Lipsey	R W Gale	Charlie M Watkins	....
Corinth (14)	MC	601 286-6644	John D Mercier	John D Mercier	James R Billingsley	James R Billingsley	James Young	Fred D Johnson	Sully D Ayers
Crystal Springs† (5)	MC	601 892-1212	John R Lang	....	Erma Deen Lewis	John R Lang	Buster Whittington	Tommy Jackson	Talmadge Jackson
Drew (3)	MC	601 745-8556	W O Williford	....	Frankye Manning	....	Raymond Stevens	J D Fleming	McArthur Benson
Durant (3)	MC	601 653-3221	Martin Frazure	....	George M Booker		Johnny A Toten	....	
Ellisville (5)	MC	601 477-3323	Howard W Laird	....	Lenora Roberts	Lenora Roberts	Frank E Williams	James E Polson	Ernest P Todd
Forest (5)	MC	601 469-2921	Erle Johnston	....	Patsy J McDill	Patsy J McDill	Paul Weems	....	John McElroy
Fulton t† (3)	MC	601 862-4929	Jack Creely	....	Betty Pearson	....	V H Pate Jr	Larry Poole	....
Greenville (41)	MC	601 335-2361	William C Burnley	....	Sam Adams		Paul Demoney	Robert Skinner	Vernon Alexander
Greenwood† (20)	MC	601 453-2246	Lanier Harper	....	Olene Lary	Lanier Harper	Jimmy Lord	James R Stevens	Darrell Winters
Grenada* (13)	CM	601 226-8820	Chuck Thomas	James J Turner	Edward W Ray Jr	....	Frank Morgan	Wayne Miley	J Kenneth Mixon
Gulfport (40)	CO	601 868-5700	Jack Barnett	....	Charles L Walker	Charles L Walker	James White	Hayward Hargrove	R C Randall
Hattiesburg (41)	CO	601 268-8500	Bobby L Chain	James B Borsig	W U Sigler	Kenneth Smith	Wayne Lee	Dempsey Lawler	G D Williamson
Hazlehurst† (4)	MC	601 894-3131	Percy S Milton	Betty Keywood	Betty Keywood	Percy S Milton	Ray White	Kenneth McLendon	J P Martin
Hernando† (3)	MC	601 368-9092	W Laney Funderburk	....	Hughleen W Tippitt	Hughleen W Tippitt	Jimmy L Word	Jim Bethune	Van Gates
Hollandale (4)	MC	601 827-2241	Charlie Abraham Jr	Van Richard Shirey	Jo Ann S Boykin	Charlie Abraham Jr	D A Furr	H H Atkinson	Lee Edwards
Holly Springs (7)	MC	601 252-4280	Sam D Coopwood	....	W W Newson	W W Newson	Joe S Fant	David Seale	Walter Paschal
Horn Lake (4)	MC	601 393-6178	Sammie M Dye	....	Linda S Coomer		Judd Killebrew	Mike Philley	Kerry Yopp
Houston† (4)	MC	601 456-2328	Harry G Robinson	....	Joyce Sullivan	Joyce Sullivan	....	Danny K Thomas	J D Walters
Indianola† (8)	MC	601 887-3101	Phillip Fratesi	....	Paul Pressgrove	W E Felts	Vincent Naticchioni	Kenneth Boutwell	C J Vanlandingham
Itta Bena t (3)	MC	601 254-7231	J K Bailey	....	Dianne Bennett	....	Troy Banks	Danny Banks	James Peeples
Iuka† (3)	MC	601 423-3781	John Biggs	....	Joyce Brumley	....	Floyd Whitaker	Jack Rye	....
Jackson (203)	CO	601 960-1000	Dale Danks Jr	....	Dorothy Coon	John Eley Warren	Edgar Bray	James L Black	William R Lewis
Kosciusko† (7)	CO	601 289-1226	Freddie George	....	Helen S Wasson	....	Wayne Rawson	Winnis W Cummins	Grover L Pope
Laurel (22)	CO	601 649-2601	Henry Bucklew	Mac Kitchens	Jolyn Sellers	Jolyn Sellers	Carlee Wedgeworth	David Lyons	T A Blackledge
Leland (7)	MC	601 686-4136	Fred J Weston	....	Mickey Fratesi	Mickey Fratesi	James Hastings	Bob McMaster	Dale Martin
Lexington† (3)	MC	601 834-1261	Billy Martin	....	Lee Meek	Lee Meek	W A Rathell	Ed Ellison	James Keith
Long Beach (8)	MC	601 863-1554	Glenn W Mitchell	....	Jeritza Pell	John J Charlton	Geo P Clegg	Ken Pell	John Becker
Louisville† (7)	MC	601 773-9201	Ralph L Hathorn	....	Charles S Lawrence	Ralph L Hathorn	Terrell Sinclair	Mack Parks	Tommy L Kirkpatrick
Magee t (3)	MC	601 849-3344	Pete Russell	....	James W Clyde	James W Clyde	Tommy Everett	Vernon B Turnage	John H Barnard
McComb§ (12)	MC	601 684-3641	Newton H James	James Larry Burris	Tommie G Jefcoat	Tommie G Jefcoat	....	Lee Barkdull	Paul Strittman
Mendenhall t (3)	MC	601 847-1212	Donnie Caughman	....	Judi May		Durr Mangum	Frank Thames	H C Duckworth
Meridian* (47)	CM	601 693-1820	I A Rosenbaum	Wallace Heggie	L E Skipper	L E Skipper	Homer Webb	Jerry Marlow	Jim Garrett
Moorhead t* (2)	CM	601 246-5461	Steve Oswalt	James W Griffin	Gloria Roberts	James W Griffin	Danny McCraney	James W Griffin	James W Griffin
Morton (3)	MC	601 732-6252	Ab Farris Jr	....	Marguerite H Lott	....	Dalton Denton	Clell Harrell	Oscar Tadlock
Moss Point (19)	MC	601 475-0300	(not reporting)						
Mound Bayou (3)	MC	601 741-2194	Earl S Lucas	....	Wanda C Stringer	Wanda C Stringer	James Carmicle	James Carmicle	Joseph Woods
Natchez (22)	MC	601 446-6641	Tony Byrne	....	Martha B Brown	....	Eugene Lewis	Kenneth Fairly	Herman Estes
New Albany† (7)	MC	601 534-6220	G W Henson	....	Ann Gregory		William G McGill	David Grisham	....
Newton (4)	MC	601 683-6181	W L Freeman Jr	....	Dale F Weaver	Dale F Weaver	Charles Vance	Joe Mowdy	Daryl W Ford
Ocean Springs† (15)	MC	601 875-4236	C McPhearson Jr	....	E M Tue	....	James A Murray	Fedrick O Sullivan	Mark Seymour
Okolona† (3)	MC	601 447-5461	Bill Whitt	....	Lynn Fair	....	Leslie H Bowen	James E Thornton	Therman Mitchel
Oxford (10)	MC	601 236-1310	John O Leslie	....	Virginia Chrestman	....	Terry McDonald	Billy White	Connie Lagrone
Pascagoula* (29)	CM	601 762-1020	Roy T O'Bryant Jr	Charles H Fulghum	Leona K McGinty	....	Robert E Pierce	William H Pope	John E Engel
Pass Christian (5)	MC	601 452-2626	Gordon E Bishop	....	Lorraine E Bowes	Lorraine E Bowes	George Mixon	John Dubuisson	James Welch
Pearl (21)	MC	601 932-2262	Vaughn Galloway	Ron Morgan	Shirley G Rogers	Vaughn Galloway	Robert Trigg	Tony Stuart	John McDill
Petal (8)	MC	601 545-1776	Sidney O Smith	....	Priscilla C Daniel	....	Ford Weatherford	Henry M Bounds	Robert W Powell
Philadelphia† (6)	MC	601 656-3612	Charles A McClain	....	Sara M Duett	....	W G Brunson	Fulton Jackson	....
Picayune*† (10)	CM	601 798-1506	Greg Mitchell	Kelly L McQueen	Kelly L McQueen	Kelly L McQueen	A F Vaughn	Lorance Lumpkin	W B Sheffield
Pontotoc (5)	MC	601 489-4321	Howard Stafford	....	Carolyn Lauderdale	....	Earl Carnes	Fulton Tutor	
Poplarville (3)	MC	601 795-8161	(not reporting)						
Quitman t (3)	MC	601 776-3728	Franklin L Slay	....	Lynda Sue Doggett		Steve Parker	Billy R Kemp	Harvey Underwood
Richland (4)	MC	601 932-3000	Lester J Spell Jr	....	Zenith S Lewis	Zenith S Lewis	Kary Whatley	Morris W Atkinson	....
Ridgeland (5)	MC	601 856-7113	Hite B Wolcott	....	Marcella Cannon	....	Kerry Minninger	Binford Watkins	Horace Ross
Ripley† (4)	MC	601 837-7154	Van Malone	....	Jean J Cappleman	....	Wayne Steverson	Jack Leisure	....
Rolling Fork (3)	MC	601 873-2814	John Pippin Jr	....	Nelda B Brown	....	Larry Ludwig	Charles McPhail	Billy G Johnson
Ruleville (3)	MC	601 756-2791	John G Burrell	....	Annell R Weed		William L Wilson	Ralph Breazeale	Walter H Williams
Senatobia (5)	MC	601 562-4474	W E Callicott	....	Lynn L Massey	....	Robert Latham	H B Grisham	
Shelby† (3)	MC	601 398-5156	Robert D Gray	....	James E Browning	....	James Nasser	Nathaniel Flowers	Eugene Royster
Southaven (16)	MC	601 393-5931	Carlton F Aldy	....	Marlene J Sprinkle	....	Vernon McCammon	Danny Vick	Barry Morgan
Starkville* (15)	CM	601 323-4813	Henry P Davis Jr	P C McLaurin Jr	Louise Thompson	P C McLaurin Jr	T J Bryant	Richard W Crouch	H W Webb Jr

Directory 1/10 continued — MUNICIPAL OFFICIALS IN ALL U.S. CITIES OVER 2,500[1]

City, 1980 population (000 omitted), form of government		Municipal phone number	Mayor	Appointed administrator	City clerk	Finance officer	Fire chief	Police chief	Public works director
MISSISSIPPI (87) continued									
Tupelo† (24)	MC	601 842-1725	James N Caldwell	....	David L Long	David L Long	Curtis Sanders	Ed Crider	....
Vicksburg (25)	CO	601 636-3411	Demery F Grubbs	....	Marie Pantoliano	Demery F Grubbs	James E Parker	A J Holliday	G H Van Norman
Water Valley (4)	MC	601 473-2431	Hamric Henry	....	Doris B Cox	....	Robert Ward	John D Watson	....
Waveland (4)	MC	601 467-4134	John Longo Jr	....	Arcelyn Dastugue	Arcelyn Dastugue	Don McIntyre	Donald A Dorn	John Longo Jr
Waynesboro t† (5)	MC	601 735-4874	Craig L Ezell	....	Allene Rigney	....	C L Westover Jr	Arthur Lee Nored	Martin L Stadalis
West Point (9)	MC	601 494-2573	Kenneth D Dill	Dewel G Brasher Jr	....	....	Caradine Young	Billy M Busby	E Clyde Woodson
Wiggins t (3)	MC	601 928-7221	R S Chatham	....	Ms Billie Hatten	....	Richard Tice	Joel A Simpson	....
Winona† (6)	MC	601 283-1232	Cecil Simpson	....	Jean Nail	Jean Nail	Travis McClure	W W Branch	Baine Hughes
Yazoo City (12)	MC	601 746-1401	Charles E Fulgham	....	P Harrell Granberry	....	Ken Woodard	Frank Coulter	David Street
MISSOURI (179)									
Arnold§ (19)	MC	314 296-2100	Alfred M Ems	Vilas S Gamble	Marion Becker	Frank Preswheat	Joe Wingbermuehle	James Curtis	Robert Cook
Aurora* (6)	CM	417 678-5121	Leonard Bisby	Randy Gustafson	Patricia Rinker	....	Barry Weber	Barry Weber	Joseph Tulgetske
Ava (3)	MC	417 683-4122	Lawrence Plaster	....	Marilyn S Alms	....	Bob Durham	Jerry Huffman	J L Liniger
Ballwin*† (13)	CM	314 227-8580	Richard G Andrews	Michael G Herring	....	Donette J Johnson	....	Donald J Loehr	Roger Shields
Bel-Ridge v (4)	MC	314 429-2878	Raymond Knapp	....	Dorothy M Bolbecher	Neva J Schaffner	....	Charles Hurt	James A Randolph
Bellefontaine Neighbors (12)	MC	314 867-0076	Joseph Berger	....	Mae McKay	Lawrence D Abeln	....	William J Cira	Frank W Kurz
Belton* (13)	CM	816 331-4331	Gary Mallory	Roger L Kroh	Alice M Strathman	Robert Steinshouer	Kirt Denkler	Jimmy B Luster	C Michael Rukgaber
Berkeley* (16)	CM	314 524-3313	Jack E Quigle	Nancy L Quigle	Eva Lee Monroe	Carl L Schwing	William Colson	Larry D Birkla	Vijay K Bhasin
Bethany† (3)	MC	816 425-3511	Leland G Magee	....	Ms Perky Premer	Marilyn Smith	John Gannon	....	....
Black Jack† (5)	MC	314 355-0400	Harold Evangelista	....	Gloria J Starzyk	John C Engelmeyer	....	Theodore G Starzyk	Nicholas C Pappas
Blue Springs* (26)	CM	816 228-0100	John R Michael	Frederick R Siems	Dianne Duff	Frederick R Siems	....	Howard Brown	Gordon Braun
Bolivar (6)	MC	417 326-5298	(not reporting)						
Bonne Terre* (4)	CM	314 358-2254	Faith C Bunch	Gayle Blackwell	Louise B Bouchard	....	Clarence Keen	Gene Archer	Clarence Keen
Boonville*† (7)	CM	816 882-2332	Dale Robinson	Irl W Tessendorf	Peggy J Geiger	....	Van A Warrick	Irvin Drew	George J Gering
Bowling Green (3)	MC	314 324-5451	James H Betz	....	Mayona Drennen	....	William J Hustedde	Jack L Floyd	Jack G Haley
Branson§† (3)	MC	417 334-3345	James A Martin	John F Gallagher	Pat Nash	Bonnie Robinson	Ernie Braswell	Larry P Burtman	Larry Van Gilder
Breckenridge Hills v (6)	MC	314 427-6868	Paul L Berry	Pamela Gnuse	Mary E Aman	Archie Ledbetter	....	Donald Black	Lee Roy Taylor
Brentwood§ (8)	MC	314 962-4800	Arthur J Oppenheim	David L Blackburn	David L Blackburn	David L Blackburn	Robert Niemeyer	Darold Sullins	L W Jim Brigham
Bridgeton (18)	MC	314 344-0600	E W Bill Abram	Don P Moschenross	Mary E Oellermann	Don P Moschenross	....	Eugene Broaders	Bryan Pearl
Brookfield* (6)	CM	816 258-3377	Rodger Timbers	Nancy R Olinger	Sarah L Turner	Nancy R Olinger	Walter Gordon Jr	David Hane	Donald Mudd
Buckner (3)	MC	816 249-3191	Charllynn Smith	....	Judy Buttress	....	Robert Pottberg	Claude Elliott	Henry Cable
Butler§† (4)	MC	816 679-4013	Bill D Thornton	James W Tucker	Cloteine Bartley	James W Tucker	James Henry	Wayne Conaway	Don Edmonds
Cabool§ (2)	MC	417 962-3136	Dale J Cartwright	Noah January	Billie L Stewart	....	Richard Hines	Lynn L Jones	....
California (3)	MC	314 796-2151	(not reporting)						
Cameron* (5)	CM	816 632-2177	Ernie McMullen	Robert Irvin	Lucille Osborn	Lucille Osborn	Glen Sherman	Harold L Riddle	David Mallen
Cape Girardeau* (34)	CM	314 334-1212	Howard C Tooke	Gary A Eide	Verna L Landis	John M Gilbert	Charles M Mills	D Ray Johnson	L W McDowell
Carl Junction (4)	MC	417 649-7237	Alva Donham	....	Nina Simpson	....	Bill Dunn	Don Williams	....
Carrollton (5)	MC	816 542-1414	Elisabeth A Daniels	....	Mary P Dean	....	Ronald Kellough	Robert D Corbett	Robert L Standley
Carthage§† (11)	MC	417 358-9025	Kent Neil	Dennis Kissinger	Barbara Welch	Barbara Welch	Don Simmons	Edward Ellefsen	David Clark
Caruthersville (8)	CM	314 333-2142	B F Rogers	....	Melinda Lee	....	Hardy Privett	Norman Howell	Champ Clark
Centralia (4)	MC	314 682-2139	David L Whitaker	Alfred J Figuly	Ruby McDonald	William H Miller	Lannie Patton	Jim Hollis	....
Chaffee (3)	MC	314 887-3558	Robert H Capshaw	....	Diane Eftink	Kenneth Cook	Bill Hagan	Ivan E McLain	Raymond Rowell
Charleston* (5)	CM	314 683-3325	Jackie Whiteside	Robert A Morris	Velna Brown	Gail B Davis	Thomas McKenzie	Robert Ritchey	David L Teeters
Chillicothe† (9)	MC	816 646-1877	Robert J Posch	....	Cora Stockwell	Theresa Figg	Joseph Rinehart	Maynard Hall	Keith Beardmore
Clayton* (14)	CM	314 727-8100	Richard T Stith Jr	Lee Roland Evett	Elizabeth A Dennis	Edward Doczy	Joseph J Morgan	Richard T Morris	E J Petersen Jr
Clinton§ (8)	MC	816 885-6121	Daniel B Miles	Allen D Gill	Ruth Barbee	....	Robert L Harrell	Gary L Wade	Edwin J Denman
Columbia* (62)	CM	314 874-7111	John Westlund	Richard N Gray	Patricia Scott	Harold E Boldt	William Westhoff	William E Dye	Raymond A Beck
Crestwood§ (13)	MC	314 966-4700	Patricia Killoren	D Kent Leichliter	Carol Schneiderhahn	David Watson	William J Kramer	Melvin P Loyd	Dale Houdeshell
Creve Coeur§ (13)	MC	314 432-6000	Harold L Dielmann	Clifford R James	LaVerne Collins	Clifford R James	....	Don Daniel	Elmer Belew
Crystal City† (4)	MC	314 937-4614	Terry M Yesberg	....	Debbie A Johns	....	Tony Picarella	O Glen Boyer	Robert Hastings
De Soto* (6)	CM	314 586-3326	Ron Watson	Lawrence C Palmer	Arlene Burt	Evelyn Lewis	Ivan Gibson	Lloyd Davis	....
Dellwood (6)	MC	314 521-4339	William R Dennis	....	Cecelia M Kilroy	....	....	Alfred H Alberda	....
Des Peres§ (8)	MC	314 966-4600	William F Morris	Tony G Riggs	Tony G Riggs	....	Ron Martin	Ron Martin	Kenneth C Kaller
Desloge (3)	MC	314 431-3700	Jack Rabaduex	Herbert Hoffman	Jean Peacock	D J Hughes	J D Hodge	Larry Dush	Kennard Skaggs
Dexter† (7)	MC	314 624-2547	Willis Conner	....	Mary M Poyner	....	Alphonse H Banken	Fredric S Fish	....
East Prairie* (4)	CM	314 649-3057	Martin K Hutcheson	Kathie Simpkins	Jerri Robison	Kathie Simpkins	Garry Ditto	Roger Gammons	William C Brown
Eldon§ (4)	MC	314 392-3129	Dwight Smittle	Richard D Franc	Laverne McLain	Richard D Franc	Charles Wilson	Robert E Hurtubise	Lloyd A Hoover
Eldorado Springs (4)	MC	417 876-6150	Raymond G Merryman	Ronald D Trivitt	M S Nunnelly	....	....	Don F Martin	Shirley Wagner
Ellisville (6)	MC	314 227-9660	Edward M O'Reilly	Victor J Reinke	Helen M Smith	Victor J Reinke	....	Joseph Starck	James W Merkle
Eureka (4)	MC	314 938-5233	Wm F Bud Weber	....	Irene Steward	....	....	Charles Branson	Wm F Bud Weber
Excelsior Springs* (10)	CM	816 637-0752	H B Carrell	Paul G Beecher	Sally Dixon	Linda Dreiling	Larry Glunt	John McGovern	Wallace McCrary
Farmington§ (8)	MC	314 756-1701	Ronald G Stevens	Ronald J Thomure	Phylis Hartrup	....	Phil Johnson	Walter Ellis	Ron Sheppard
Fayette§ (3)	MC	816 248-3154	Larry H Sapp Jr	John Bradshaw	Elaine Flippin	....	....	....	....
Ferguson* (25)	CM	314 521-7721	Charles H Grimm	James E Mello	Mary Jo Henckler	James E Mello	Don Parotte	Eston Randolph	Dan Fain
Festus§ (8)	MC	314 937-4694	Charles E Earls	Richard T Turley	Mark D Carroll	....	Donald D Declue	William N Pagano	....
Flat River* (4)	CM	314 431-3577	Marilyn Calvird	James B Blake	Katherine Holley	....	John L Daffron	Curtis Thurmond	Paul L Richardson
Florissant (55)	MC	314 921-5700	James J Eagan	....	Carol Fritschie	James May	....	Robert Lowery	Louis Jearls Jr
Fredericktown§ (4)	MC	314 783-3683	Leota Reagan	James Dismuke	Madge Strange	....	Darryl Asher	Jerry Umfleet	William King
Frontenac (4)	MC	314 994-3200	Morgan B Lawton	....	Mary B Colwell	Joan M Bayer	Robert R Bongner	David M Blazer	Donald J Rohlfing
Fulton (11)	MC	314 642-6826	George L Oestreich	....	Evelyn Hopkins	John Carter	Lloyd M Stiers	Richard Gillespie	....
Gladstone* (25)	CM	816 436-2200	Robert J Fairlie	Patrick J Reilly	Marilyn Ahnefeld	Antoinette Anderson	Kenneth Francis	Kenneth Francis	Steve Warger
Glendale§ (6)	MC	314 965-3600	Roger C Zimmermann	Douglas J Harms	Margaret Barham	Douglas J Harms	Ewart Ash	Cecil Livesay	Frederick I Horton
Grandview* (25)	CM	816 763-3900	Jan Martinette	Robert C Elliott	Ruth K Gray	J Michael Urie	Earl H England	John G Campbell	John G Rose
Hannibal† (19)	MC	314 221-0111	John Lyng	....	Marjorie H Deline	....	Delmar McClain	J Franklin Neff	Harvard F Ebers
Harrisonville* (6)	CM	816 884-3285	Howard R McHenry	David G Wilhite	Verda B Day	Verda B Day	Gene Self	William H Davis Jr	Don Gragg
Hayti (4)	MC	314 359-0632	Fred H Chaffin	....	Janet M Russell	Phil Bowen	Milford Chism	Barry E McKay	Leonard Plunkett
Hazelwood* (13)	CM	314 839-3700	Douglas W Palmer	Edwin G Carlstrom	Norma Caldwell	Edwin G Carlstrom	J Joseph McNamara	Robert Shockey	Jose M Hernandez
Hermann§ (3)	MC	314 486-5953	Daniel C Yoest	Perry D Lovett	Dolores Grannemann	....	Richard Michel	Robert O Sitton	....
Higginsville (5)	MC	816 584-2106	Buford Thurmon	....	Richard Reyna	....	Don Simpson	Ray Goring	Russell Ellis
Holts Summit† (3)	MC	314 896-4678	Richard M Griggs	....	....	....	....	....	....
Houston§† (2)	MC	417 967-3653	Melvin L Flowers	John P McDonald	Joyce P Campbell	....	Robert T Dunn	Keith Bobb	....
Independence* (112)	CM	816 836-8300	Barbara J Potts	Keith Wilson Jr	Bruce Lowrey	James Harlow	Norman Birch	Robert Rinehart	James F Merideth
Jackson§ (8)	MC	314 243-3568	Carlton G Meyer	Carl Talley	Dean Crites	....	Gary Niswonger	Robert Clifton	....
Jefferson City§ (34)	MC	314 634-6300	George Hartsfield	Gary J Hamburg	Phyllis Powell	Bob Cox	Robert F Rennick	Lawrence C Patton	Robert M Bates
Jennings† (17)	MC	314 388-1164	William D Tharp	....	Edna M Yowell	William Curtis	James Trentham	Harry G Slaten	....
Joplin* (39)	CM	417 624-0820	Kay Wells	Stribling Boynton	Joy Thompson	Jerry Potter	Harry Guinn	Larry Tennis	Harold McCoy
Kansas City* (448)	CM	816 274-2000	Richard L Berkley	....	E Richard Brenneman	John M Urie	Edward W Wilson Jr	Larry Joiner	Myron D Calkins
Kearney§† (1)	MC	816 635-4142	Dennis Watson	....	James Eldridge	....	Larry Pratt	Frank Vernon	Gary Lawson

Directory 1/10 continued **MUNICIPAL OFFICIALS IN ALL U.S. CITIES OVER 2,500[1]**

City, 1980 population (000 omitted), form of government	Municipal phone number	Mayor	Appointed administrator	City clerk	Finance officer	Fire chief	Police chief	Public works director
MISSOURI (179) continued								
Kennett (10) CM	314 888-9001	Warren Karsten Jr	....	Leverna S Moore	Norman P Bartmess	Bill McMahon	Jim Elliot	Larry Jones
Kinloch (4) MC	314 521-3335	Bernard L Turner Sr	Lorraine V Crawford	Sharon D Moore	Early Wilson	Lorenzo Robinson	Steven Haynes	William Whitley
Kirksville* (17) CM	816 627-1224	Russell Roberts	Wm A Galletly	Geraldine Riley	Kathleen Rogers	Ron Stewart	Wayne Martin	William Frogge
Kirkwood* (28) CM	314 822-5800	Herbert S Jones	Michael G Brown	Michael G Brown	Donald Vahey	Donald E Carter	Daniel B Linza	....
La Plata§ (1) MC	816 332-7166	Billie K Forbes	....	Ellen E Wood	....	Robert Couch	James L Dore	....
Ladue (9) MC	314 993-3439	Edith J Spink	....	E C Hankins	John E Angst	Elvi F Fava	Kenneth A Krueger	William F Heller
Lake Saint Louis§ (4) MC	314 625-1200	Stephen D Linehan	Ronald A Nelson	Mary Lou Von Blohn	Jean McDonough	Jeff Oldfield	John B Selby	Ronald A Nelson
Lamar (4) MC	417 682-5554	G W Gilkey	J A Roberts	Ms C Taffner	J A Roberts	Bill Rawlings	Emmett Hemphill	J A Roberts
Lebanon (10) MC	417 532-2157	(not reporting)						
Lee'S Summit§ (29) MC	816 251-2301	Gene H Rhodes	D John Edwards	Glenda F Shanks	Robert G Keefe	James Grigsby	D Gregg Henderson	James L Shanks
Lexington (5) MC	816 259-4633	Edward G Lee	....	Dorothy Stapleton	....	Bruce Wandell	Hershel L Hay	....
Liberty§ (16) MC	816 781-7100	K Russell Weathers	Lloyd V Harrell	Donna L Holloway	Meta Dillon	George Robinson	Clifton E Collins	Ronald L Norris
Louisiana (4) MC	314 754-4132	Junior Clark	....	Jane A Ray	W A Jordan Jr	Jerry Powell	William F Hughlett	Ray Geeson
Macon (6) MC	816 385-3173	Dale Whitley	....	Gerald D Maloney	Gerald D Maloney	Kenneth Cox	Herschel Williams	Paul Jensen
Malden† (6) MC	314 276-4502	Sparrel W Davis	....	Roscoe E Thornton	Roscoe E Thornton	Willard Rogers	Bob McDonald	Ray Lyons
Manchester§ (6) MC	314 227-1385	Glenn L Smith	Earle W Clifford	Earle W Clifford	....	....	John T Quinn	Charles Feldman
Maplewood* (11) CM	314 645-3600	Andrew L Hummert	Martin J Corcoran	Charlotte Green	Martin J Corcoran	Mervin Feick	Robert E Biggerstaf	Douglas A Hopkins
Marceline* (3) CM	816 376-3528	Duane Dorrell	Lee March	Teresa Fessler	....	Mervin Jones	Don Ross	Charles Tomlinson
Marshall (13) MC	816 886-2226	Shirley J Martin	Charles M Tryban	Dorothy Hughes	Ruth Gregory	John Rieves	James B Simmerman	Thomas Hill
Marshfield§ (4) MC	417 468-2310	Wayne Plunkett	Larry W Eaton	Glenña Lasater	....	Wayne Plunkett	Kenneth D Clardy	J E Jones
Maryville* (10) CM	816 562-2811	Lester Keith	Darrell P Dechant	Jo E Gill	Kevin W Huddleston	Larry Jackson	Larry Jackson	W D Driskel
Mexico* (12) CM	314 581-2100	Larry Webber	W Mark Pentz	Anne Shafer	....	Donald J Bolli	Donald J Bolli	Gilbert W Patrick
Moberly* (13) CM	816 263-4420	Jack Valentine	Paul J Walker	Carole Kehoe	Nick Burton	Luther K Davidson	Bill Pollard	Ron Wilson
Moline Acres (3) MC	314 868-2433	(not reporting)						
Monett (6) CO	417 235-3763	Floyd V Stewart	....	Doris Meyer	Jennings Conyers	James E Nolan	Wesley Thomas	Harlan Barekman
Monroe City (3) MC	314 735-4440	Stephen Ray Porter	....	Gary Osbourne	....	Carl Shively	Paul Clark	....
Montgomery City§ (2) MC	314 564-3160	....	Michael J Johnson	....	....	....	....	....
Mount Vernon (3) MC	417 466-2122	Neal S Underwood	....	Mary Walker	....	Melvin Owens	Fil Turk	....
Mountain Grove* (4) CM	417 926-4162	Joe Hylton	Terry Rickard	Judy Kjellberg	Shirley M Agee	Norman Jarrett	Bert Hopkins	Norman Jarrett
Neosho* (9) CM	417 451-1921	Merle D Jones Jr	William Beauvais	Wanda Campbell	Cheryl Mosby	Elmer Klein	George Kelly	James Cole
Nevada* (9) CM	417 667-7894	James A Novak	Douglas K Leslie	Virginia Shepherd	Ronald E Chandler	Donald Cox	Larry Moore	Ronald A Stratman
New Madrid* (3) MC	314 748-2458	W R Phillips Jr	Donald G Lloyd	Shelby Savat	....	Frank Hadder	James Helms	Donald G Lloyd
Nixa (3) MC	417 725-3785	Bill Chitwood	....	Coralee Patrick	....	Robert Lutgen	Joe Asher	....
Normandy (5) MC	314 385-3300	Patrick F Hambrough	....	Delores Westermeyer	James P Ferrario	....	Jerome Burke	John E Hutchinson
North Kansas City§ (5) MC	816 471-3030	Clark E Ferguson	Walter O Barry	Bonnie Harlin	Wendell Stevens	Clifton Fitzpatrick	Clarence Hoffman	Jerry Copeland
Northwoods† (6) MC	314 385-8000	James B Cunningham	Terry D Milam	Loretta Bewig	Joseph Schweitzer	....	Donald A McDonald	William Sago
O'Fallon§ (9) MC	314 272-6244	Jim Brown	Edward Brookshier	Ilene Galvin	Georgia Hoenig	David House	Daniel Granger	....
Oak Grove§ (4) MC	816 625-4012	Roy Meier	Larry D Smith	Peggy J Ewens	....	Robert Lowe	....	Anthony Lipari
Odessa (3) MC	816 633-4232	Charles A Fieth	....	Pamela Windsor	....	Orville Day	Robert W Kinder	Lee Barker
Olivette* (8) CM	314 993-0444	Charles G Berger	Jerome S Feldman	June Schrieber	Jerome S Feldman	Lavern Peters	Robert D Cole	Kenneth Rohan
Osage Beach§ (2) MC	314 348-3151	Joe Pottinger	Roy A Eckert	Linda Medlock	....	Jack Treasure	John W Page	....
Overland (20) MC	314 428-4321	Frank Munsch	....	Dorothy L Miller	Dorothy L Miller	Richard Paul	Eddy Williams	Robert B Brooks Jr
Ozark (3) MC	417 485-2407	Neal Grubaugh	....	Mary Lou Erhart	Roxanna Schwerdt	Bill McNabb	John S Whitney	Robert Snider
Pacific§ (4) MC	314 257-5187	Ron Sansone	William E Price	William E Price	Robert D Shaw	William Graf	Ronald F Reed	Edward O Gass
Pagedale (5) MC	314 726-1200	Mary Hall	....	Jerry Leon Simpson	Michael Asbury	....	Charles Johnson	....
Palmyra (3) MC	314 769-2223	L A Wellman	....	Dale S Barnett	....	Corbyn Jacobs	R W Chamberlain Jr	Bill Huffman
Perryville* (7) CM	314 547-2594	Robert J Miget	Alvin Stoverink	Richard Davis	Theo Wichern	Wayne Walker	L James Huber	Melvin Niswonger
Pevely (3) MC	314 479-4453	John O Baynes	....	Betty Stackley	....	....	Ron E Weeks	....
Pine Lawn (7) MC	314 261-5500	Roosevelt O'Kain	....	Steven McCall	Steven McCall	....	John L Pickens	Steve Marre
Pleasant Hill (3) MC	816 987-3135	Terry C Wilson	....	Sandra Beatty	Sandra Beatty	Bob Gray	Thomas D Bass	....
Poplar Bluff* (17) CM	314 785-7474	Bruce E Holloway	LaVern Bechtel	William W Pettet	....	John Jones	Cliff Hodge	Gene Brannum
Portageville (3) MC	314 379-5789	Arvil V Adams	....	George J Vogel	Arthur F Fisher	Bobby L Duggins	Joe Moore	Donald Swims
Potosi (3) MC	314 438-2767	P Russell Dessieux	....	Cecil D McCourtney	Roger Bilderback	....	Roy Logsden	P Russell Dessieux
Raymore§ (3) MC	816 331-0488	Donald W Mocker	Robert J Frank	....	....	....	Lee R Coleman	Jerry Davis
Raytown (32) MC	816 737-0550	Douglas Hall	....	Beverly Rolf	Beverly Rolf	Dale Collins	Kristofer Turnbow	Richard B Winner
Republic (4) MC	417 732-6065	Janet S Thompson	....	June Podoll	Jane Medlin	Bill Farr	Sam Hartsell	Garry Rudler
Richland§ (2) MC	314 765-4421	Charles P Parker	Bill Beydler	Clarice Payne	....	B P Thacker	Gerald Thaxton	Robert Starmer
Richmond (5) MC	816 776-3540	Ed LaBarr	....	Cynthia A Davidson	Ronnie M Haynes	Lonnie E Quick	John Moore	A Keith Sharp
Richmond Heights (12) CO	314 645-0404	Charles F Sargent	Mary M McAndrew	....	Richard H Riley	Lawrence E Santen	Ralph R Anderson	Harmony Lineback
Riverside (3) MC	816 741-3993	Michael D Holmes	....	Betty R Burch	....	....	Jerry V Wingo	....
Riverview (3) MC	314 868-0700	James W Watts	....	Theodore A Stocker	Thomas E Henderson	Leonard Aubuchon	Nelson Mamer	William T Carraway
Rock Hill (6) MC	314 968-1410	Jesse L Stroup	Larry W Hensley	....	....	Harold L Stroud	Donald McDonald	Lawrence Ott
Rolla§ (13) MC	314 364-1835	Floyd Ferrell	Leonard A Martin	Varonica Ragan	....	William Oliver	Stanley Spadoni	Donald Loomis
Salem (4) MC	314 729-5211	Ruth S Mullnack	....	Nadine L Victor	....	Kermit Allen	John Hudspeth	....
Savannah* (4) CM	816 324-3315	Reid Miller	....	Janice Hatcher	Janice Hatcher	Jim Edwards	Jerry Williams	Ken Lance
Scott City (3) MC	314 264-2157	H Alvie Modglin	....	Nona M Walls	....	C Leslie Crump	Gary Atchley	Harold Uelsmann
Sedalia§ (21) MC	816 827-3000	Larry G Foster	Mark E Durbin	Shirley Collins	Marvin K Mauck	C W Gordy	James E Carter	Gary Johnson
Shrewsbury (5) MC	314 647-5795	Karl G Odenwald	Wayne R Behney	Wayne R Behney	Barbara Smegner	Raymond Kranefuss	Fred J Huncke	....
Sikeston* (17) CM	314 471-2173	Bill Burch	Robert Knabel	Stephen L Matthews	Stephen L Matthews	....	Dan Hinton	H Jack Sargent
Slater* (2) CM	816 529-2271	Jim Gochenhour	Kevin G Kenzenkovic	Cheryl Fizer	....	Clifton H Reynolds	Ronald E Hager	Steve Ledman
Smithville§ (2) MC	816 532-0500	Willard C Pence	Wayne C Parker	Phyllis Edwards	Wayne C Parker	John Pinckard	Rick L Outersky	Gregg Protenic
Springfield* (133) CM	417 864-1000	George Scruggs	Don G Busch	Donald H Kelley	Fred Fantauzzi	William T Penland	Troy Majors	David G Snider
St. Ann (16) MC	314 427-8000	Clarence G Tiemeyer	....	Rhoda A Womack	Clarence G Tiemeyer	....	James F Ferrari	Timothy McNamee
St. Charles (37) MC	314 925-2000	Melvin G Wetter	John T Vinson	Linus H Lange	Margaret Christ	Edward Underwood	Frank Young	Paul Lorton
St. Clair (3) MC	314 629-0333	Patti M Huff	....	Darlene J Coons	....	Ferd Berkel	Carroll H Yoder	Harley Kamper
St. James (3) MC	314 265-7011	Nelson A Hart	....	Marilyn Linke	Ladonna Bailey	B H Green	Richard Woolsey	Kenneth Young
St. John*† (8) CM	314 427-8700	John Heidel	Eleanor Hines	Kathy Budde	....	Richard Paul	Ronald Pete Barteau	Ernie Brooks
St. Joseph* (77) MC	816 271-4600	David L Polsky	Hal C Kooistra	Walter T Welsh	Joseph Christoffel	John Rukavina	James R Hayes	Richard Ream
St. Louis (453) MC	314 622-4000	Vincent Schoemehl	John Temporiti	Veronica Braddy	Paul Berra	Thomas E Long	John Berner	Martin Walsh
St. Peters§ (16) MC	314 928-1800	Thomas W Brown	Robert R Irvin	Robert R Irvin	Stanley Richardson	....	Elwin L Chapman	Lionel Portell
Ste. Genevieve* (4) CM	314 883-5400	Ervin M Weiler	Phillip S Vawter	Richard A Rose	Phillip S Vawter	Jerry P Roth	Richard Lea	....
Sugar Creek (4) MC	816 252-4400	John C O'Renick	....	Veronica A Powell	John W Gavin	Emil Dykal	L Earle Conner	Ronald Martinovich
Sullivan† (5) MC	314 468-4612	Charles D Strauser	....	Florence Juergens	....	Robert Marsh	George R Counts	....
Sunset Hills (4) MC	314 849-3400	William A Wundrack	....	Patricia A Seabaugh	F H Brockman	....	Floyd C Dunlap	Denis G Knock
Town and Country (3) MC	314 432-6606	William A Schneider	....	....	S R Pylipow	....	Salvador Del Mar Jr	....
Trenton§ (7) MC	816 359-2013	William McHargue	Stan J Greil	Jolene Walker	....	William Vaughn	John Humphrey	Gary Whorton
Union§ (6) MC	314 583-3600	Charles R Parent	Bruce O Decker	Sharon Birkman	....	Gerald Borgmann	Donald Fowler	Robert E Thompson
University City* (43) CM	314 862-6767	Joseph W Mooney	Frank Ollendorff	Dolores A Miller	Michael T McPhail	William Markgraf	James P Damos	Allan Dieckgraefe
Valley Park (3) MC	314 225-5171	Fred L Palmer Jr	....	Glenn E Moon	Glenn E Moon	Wm J Brignole Jr	Louis C Brown	Roger Daegele
Vandalia (3) MC	314 594-2212	Archie Holt	....	Dolores Mottaz	J E Ed Cafer	Ramon Barnes	Lee H Barrett	Ray Callanan

Directory 1/10 continued — MUNICIPAL OFFICIALS IN ALL U.S. CITIES OVER 2,500[1]

City, 1980 population (000 omitted), form of government		Municipal phone number	Mayor	Appointed administrator	City clerk	Finance officer	Fire chief	Police chief	Public works director
MISSOURI (179) continued									
Warrensburg* (14)	CM	816 747-9131	Tim R Brooks	David A Greenamyre	Nancy Anderson	David A Greenamyre	Richard Stewart	Gene Burden	Larry Haugsness
Warrenton (3)	MC	314 456-3535	Fayette F Paul	....	Eileen C Boehm	....	John Drosselmeyer	Jane Logan	....
Washington§ (9)	MC	314 239-6710	Robert F Dierkes	David C Bell	Dolores Gerstenkorn	Janet Braun	Bill Halmich	Danny R Rowden	James A Briggs
Waynesville§ (3)	MC	314 774-6733	Keith Pritchard	Jim Lincoln	Rhonda Cristoffer	....	Danny Fry	Ferman Raines	....
Webb City (7)	MC	417 673-4651	Porter Don Crockett	....	Susan J Arft	Carolyn McGowan	Ronald F King	Robert Lawrence	Raymond Lawrence
Webster Groves* (23)	CM	314 961-4100	John W Cooper Jr	Joseph B Morrison	Mary Louise Miller	Joseph B Morrison	Fred H Entrikin Jr	Gene A Young	....
Wellston† (4)	MC	314 385-1015	Robert Powell	R Tinsley Parke	Valerie Smith	Frank McNeil	John King	Willie Ealy	Eldright White
Wentzville (3)	MC	314 327-5101	Donald Sheets	Milton L Roscoe	Lou Ann Crider	Lou Ann Crider	George Ehll	Sam Anselm	Clete Schulte
West Plains† (8)	CO	417 256-7176	Gerald E Elmore	....	Jeanie L Smith	Jeanie L Smith	Hubert Redburn	Edward L Reavis	Lowell B Patterson
Windsor (3)	MC	816 647-3512	Eugene Schell	....	Frances Nations	....	Steven Neill	Orville Wipperman	Elwood Chambers
Woodson Terrace (5)	MC	314 427-2600	James F Traube	....	Dorothy Rickard	Lois Rodebaugh	Lawrence Picker	Thomas A McKay	Howard Maassen
MONTANA (29)									
Anaconda-Deer Lodge† (13)	CM	406 563-8421	Stan Blaz	Daniel J Worsdell	Mary Chor	Daniel J Worsdell	Bob King	James Connors	Daniel J Worsdell
Billings* (67)	CM	406 657-8000	James W Van Arsdale	Alan A Thelen	Anna C Whorton	John Lawton	Robert Williams	Ellis E Kiser	Ken Haag
Bozeman* (22)	CM	406 586-3321	Kenneth L Weaver	James E Wysocki	Robin Sullivan	Amy Swan	Lee Lewis	George R Tate	Richard C Holmes
Butte-Silver Bow (37)	MC	406 723-8262	Donald R Peoples	....	William A Driscoll	Gary Rowe	Jim Leary	Robert Butorovich	James Johnston
Columbia Falls (3)	MC	406 892-4391	M Colleen Alison	....	Connie Konopatzke	Marlene C Ellman	Dennis McChesney	David G Konopatzke	John Perrin
Conrad† (3)	MC	406 278-3623	Donald F McClain	....	E J Jury	....	Marvin Klette	Gary Syvertson	Ralph Dunahoo
Cut Bank (4)	MC	406 873-5526	Joseph D Meagher	....	Eugene O Boyle	Eugene O Boyle	James D Newman	Joseph A Gauthier	Gary M Smith
Deer Lodge† (4)	MC	406 846-2238	John Wilson	....	Barbara McOmber	....	James L Gilbert	William Wood	....
Dillon (4)	MC	406 683-4245	James A Wilson	Richard Thorson	Bob Dwyer	George Joe Lane	Mike Swetish	Pat Clark	Richard Thorson
Forsyth (3)	MC	406 356-2521	Wm Lee Sitton	....	Daniel D Watson	Robert R Martinek	Karl Heberle	Robert Ash	Joseph G Foran
Glasgow† (4)	MC	406 228-2476	Larry Legare	....	Ramona M Tow	Ramona M Tow	Levon Johnson	Tom Grewe	Brent Magill
Glendive (6)	MC	406 365-3318	R E Dick Walsh	....	Shirley L Mohr	Kathleen C Sullivan	Paul J Latka	Larry D Marquart	Wilbur Wallace
Great Falls* (57)	CM	406 727-5881	Robert Worthington	G Allen Johnson	Kathryn E Wright	Nathan Tubergen	Michael Karlovich	Jack H Anderson	Robert Duty
Hamilton§ (3)	MC	406 363-2101	James J Whitlock	James D Menard	....	James D Menard	Lloyd Greenup	Gordon Klippenstien	....
Hardin (3)	MC	406 665-2113	Henry Hochhalter	....	Nancy Young	L Lachenmeier	Ron Johnson	....	....
Havre (11)	MC	406 265-6719	Raymond G Watson	....	Michael J Mariani	Michael J Mariani	James Cowan	Richard Stremcha	Fred Hartson
Helena* (24)	CM	406 442-9920	Russell J Ritter	Robert A Erickson	Barbara Montibeller	William Verwolf	Norm Gray	William Ware	Richard A Nisbet
Kalispell (11)	MC	406 755-5457	Leroy E McDowell	....	Marjorie Giermann	William Swanson	Gene Doty	Martin Stefanic	Kenneth Hammer
Laurel (5)	MC	406 628-8791	Albert Ehrlick	....	Donald L Hackmann	Peg J Kamerzel	Darrell L McGillen	Alan Crowe	Larry S Peterson
Lewistown (7)	MC	406 538-2302	C Wilbur Lindstrand	....	Sue E Glenn	Grace Ruggles	Thoralf Moline Jr	Russel Dunnington	Thomas Evans
Libby (3)	MC	406 293-5446	Fred A Brown	....	Virginia McGill	Virginia McGill	James E Davidson	....	William A Kemp
Livingston† (7)	MC	406 222-6120	S Charles Nicholson	Edward R Stern	Jennie Adams	Jennie Adams	Dave Fredricks	Mike Warren	John Orndorff
Miles City (10)	MC	406 232-3462	George T Kurkowski	Harvey Watts	Harvey L Watts	Lela F Togrimson	Russell Martin	Charles Beauchot	Dean Sloan
Missoula (33)	MC	406 721-4700	John H Toole	David Wilcox	Michael Young	Michael Young	Bernard Walsh	Eusebius Pfau	Joe Aldegerie
Polson† (3)	MC	406 883-2131	John A Dowdall	....	Kathy L Cox	....	Warren P Morse	Francis R Kis	Norman F Korf
Shelby (3)	MC	406 434-5222	Ronald Randall	....	Earl W Bennett	Earl W Bennett	James Horner	Vernon Anderson	Richard Voorhies
Sidney (6)	MC	406 482-2809	Charles Cummings	....	Ethel Sobolik	Louise Christensen	Terry Verhasselt	Frank DiFonzo	Harold Mercer
Whitefish* (4)	CM	406 862-2640	James Putnam	Jack B Arnold	Kay Beller	Helen M Doyle	David Sipe	....	H Sid Fredericksen
Wolf Point† (3)	MC	406 653-1852	Keith L Bryan	....	Marlene R Mahlum	....	Warren Evans	Robert Neumiller	Robert G Flynn
NEBRASKA (54)									
Alliance* (10)	CM	308 762-5400	Michael M Garwood	Wolfgang Bauer	Diane Gaughenbaugh	Leah King	Roger McGrath	Keith Rippy	Colin Halterman
Auburn (3)	MC	402 274-3420	John F George	....	Sherry Heskett	Harvey H Bergmann	Harlan Grable	Dennis Hogue	Lambert K Blecha
Aurora (4)	MC	402 694-6992	Ray A Griffin	....	Kent Heermann	....	Wm G Maahs	Wm G Gage	....
Beatrice§ (13)	MC	402 223-3569	Allen O Grell	Thomas Forslund	Thomas Forslund	Thomas Forslund	Leland D Gerwick	Don Luckeroth	Jim Bauer
Bellevue§ (22)	MC	402 291-8000	Joseph H Baldwin	Jeffrey L Renner	Beverly Hrdy	....	Donald E Knott	Warren Robinson	John Reding
Blair§† (6)	MC	402 426-4191	M Stanley Jensen	Douglas E Bullock	Verna R Bull	Douglas E Bullock	Donald Kuhr	Walter Groves	Raymond Fisher
Broken Bow§ (4)	MC	308 872-5831	Robert W Seeger	James E Peister	James E Peister	James E Peister	Frank Klapal	Loyal Muhlbach	Laverne H Martens
Central City (3)	MC	308 946-3806	D E Rutherford	....	David H Rish	....	August Fuehrer Jr	Ronnel L Spiegel	....
Chadron* (6)	CM	308 432-5986	Doug Bailey	Carl Dierks	Donna Rust	Carl Dierks	Gealy Mathis	Ted Vastine	Richard Halverson
Columbus§ (17)	MC	402 564-8584	Larry Marik	C Lloyd Castner	Lucille G Munson	C Lloyd Castner	R Hirschbrunner	Wesley J Baxa	Merlin E Lindahl
Cozad† (4)	MC	308 784-3907	Dean E Geihsler	Jim Morton	Percy Carl York	Percy Carl York	Gordon Lindstedt	Billy Stevenson	Lloyd Keller
Crete (5)	MC	402 826-4311	Ken Znamenacek	....	Gary L Yank	Gary L Yank	Clarence Vanourny	Howard Camp	George G Beyer
Dakota City§ (1)	MC	402 987-3331	Charles E Strong	Donald K McKinney	Donald K McKinney	Donald K McKinney	Jon Norris	Raymond Nance	....
David City§ (3)	MC	402 367-3135	Larry G Novak	Sid Magdanz	L Jean Hansen	....	Bill Ortmeier	Stephen M Sunday	Gene Grubaugh
Fairbury (5)	MC	402 729-2476	Shirley J Howell	....	Lila Hannappel	Lila Hannappel	Dennis Garton	Robert Gerhardt	Edward Brandt
Falls City† (5)	MC	402 245-2707	Paul M Weinert	Martin R Gist	Martin R Gist	Martin R Gist	August Strecker	Gary Spencer	Daryl Stockburger
Fremont§ (24)	MC	402 721-2860	Arthur L Peters	Jack J Sutton	Dorthy F Garrison	Jack J Sutton	Merlin A Olson	Francis L Hurt	Derril G Marshall
Geneva§† (2)	MC	402 759-3109	Reuben Lichti	Robert Higel	Irene Merrill	Willard Foster	Robert Hofferber	Murray Holmes	Robert Clark
Gering§ (8)	MC	308 436-5096	John McLellan Jr	Robert L Stull	Pamela K Johns	....	Robert Larsen	Kelly E Gaskill	Robert L Stull
Gordon* (2)	CM	308 282-0837	Jane Morgan	Geoffrey R Smith	Toni Siders	....	Dale Downing	Jack Hanham	Mike Winter
Gothenburg§† (3)	MC	308 537-3677	M A Rishel	....	Connie L Stull	....	Gary L Hicken	George R Shackleton	....
Grand Island§ (33)	MC	308 381-5450	Bill Wright	Dwight D Johnson	Richard L Retallick	Richard L Retallick	Ron Schwieger	Howard Bacon	Wayne L Bennett
Hastings (23)	MC	402 463-2411	William R Welton	....	Maurine Butterfield	....	Eugene Dean	James R Ruberson	Lee Blocker
Holdrege§ (6)	MC	308 995-8681	Helen D Anderson	....	Virginia L Steinke	Virginia L Steinke	James Wagner	Kenneth Jackson	Larry Duval
Kearney* (21)	CM	308 237-5133	Justus Dobesh	Clifford Stockmyer	Arlette Neal	Maxon E Brehm	Richard Rains	Robert Jatczak	George H Fairfield
Kimball (3)	MC	308 235-3639	Edith M Haines	Robert E Arraj	Florence LeMay	Robert E Arraj	Donald Story	Gerald R Holmes	Robert E Arraj
La Vista§ (10)	MC	402 331-4343	Harold C Leathers	Rodney E Austin	Dorothy McGinnis	Rodney E Austin	Les McCubbin	Dave Davenport	Ed McGinnis
Lexington* (7)	CM	308 324-2341	Clyde McCormick	Bill Podraza	Leon E Malzahn	....	Bob Martin	James E Joneson	....
Lincoln (172)	MC	402 471-7171	Roland A Luedtke	John C Evans	Paul Malzer Jr	Jack Vavra	Michael L Merwick	B Dean Leitner	Richard Erixson
Madison§ (2)	MC	402 454-3412	John Bomar	S Wells Williams	George Meonnert	Vern Peterson	Ray Keifer	Jeff Pradher	....
McCook* (8)	CM	308 345-2022	Gary V Rothmeyer	Curtis B Freeland	Kathy Casper	Debbie Jurgensen	Patrick Simpson	Richard D Brunswick	Jack G Lytle
Minden (3)	MC	308 832-1820	George Miller	Thomas Kenney	Richard G Young	....	Dick McBride	W P Peterson	....
Nebraska City (7)	CO	402 873-5515	Jack McIntire	....	Gladys Wenzel	Timothy W Nelsen	Thomas Hemphill	Kent R Roumpf	William Brockley
Norfolk§ (19)	MC	402 371-4566	Louis C Whitmore	Michael J Nolan	Betty Bohac	Randy Gates	Larry Reeves	James Brenneman	Dennis J Smith
North Platte§ (24)	MC	308 534-2610	Betty T Petersen	R L Grady	R L Grady	R L Grady	Charles Johnson	M Gutschenritter	....
O'Neill (4)	MC	402 336-3640	William S Mattern	....	James L Schwartz	....	Robert E Miles	Robert L Stahlecker	Ernie Lieb
Ogallala* (6)	CM	308 284-6001	C W Baltzell	Jan Beal	Paul Fisher	....	Virgil Beavers	Steve C Lamken	....
Omaha (312)	MC	402 444-5000	Michael Boyle	Lawrence Primeau	Mary G Cornett	William Miskell	Horton Dahlquist	Robert Wadman	James Suttle
Ord (3)	MC	308 728-5771	Alfred Burson	....	Wilma D Kroeger	....	Duane Carson	John Young	Gene Baugh
Papillion (6)	MC	402 339-3374	Robert A Wallace	Richard H Jensen Jr	W F Sullivan	Yvonne Bock	Richard Schmitz	S C Engberg	Albert L Vogel
Plainview (1)	MC	402 582-4928	Kenneth D Leiding	....	Jayne Gentzler	....	Kenneth L Hart	Jerry L Thackston	....
Plattsmouth (6)	MC	402 296-2522	Clayton J Rhylander	....	Rosalyn Covert	....	David Meisinger	Ronald Duckworth	Arthur A Hellwig
Ralston† (5)	MC	402 331-6677	Joseph Wager	....	C L Adams	C L Adams	James Barrett	Dale C Richardson	....
Scottsbluff* (14)	CM	308 632-4136	Donald E Overman	Frank U Koehler	W L Ferguson	W L Ferguson	Kenneth L Carter	James R Livingston	Paul M Sensibaugh
Seward§ (6)	MC	402 643-2928	Fred J Welsh	Don Eikmeier	Deb Schaefer	....	Richard Mailand	Ken Zike	....

Directory 1/10 continued — MUNICIPAL OFFICIALS IN ALL U.S. CITIES OVER 2,500[1]

City, 1980 population (000 omitted), form of government		Municipal phone number	Mayor	Appointed administrator	City clerk	Finance officer	Fire chief	Police chief	Public works director
NEBRASKA (54) continued									
Sidney* (6)	CM	308 254-5300	Richard Osterday	David C Weitzel	Geri Anthony	David C Weitzel	Jerry Lawson	George R Ward	Floyd Sanks
South Sioux City§ (9)	MC	402 494-5800	Vernie A Larson	Lance E Hedquist	Richard Berggren	Richard Berggren	Gerald Stolze	Robert G Claxton	Dave Lane
Superior (3)	MC	402 879-4711	Gary Kile	....	Dewayne L Aberg	....	Leo E Zadina	Robert F Allgood	Richard J Elliott
Valentine (3)	CM	402 376-2323	Allen Brott	Norma Jean New	....	Norma Jean Porath	Allen Brott	James Lutter	....
Valley (2)	MC	402 359-2251	John L Sullivan	....	Barbara Pforr	Barbara Pforr	Theodore Argintean	Charles Rehmeier	Timothy Klusaw
Wahoo (4)	MC	402 443-3222	Daryl Reitmajer	....	Phyllis J Nozicka	Phyllis J Nozicka	Donald Jelinek	John Kolterman	Donavon Larson
Wayne§ (5)	MC	402 375-1733	Wayne Marsh	Philip A Kloster	Norman Melton	Norman Melton	Dale Preston	Vern Fairchild	Vern Schulz
West Point§ (4)	MC	402 372-2466	Michael Wortman	James A Anderson	May Dee Stoltzman	....	Fred Schlueter	Pat Ell	....
York§ (8)	MC	402 362-4407	Donald A Grosshans	Jack R Kidder	C Jean Thiele	Jack R Kidder	Donald R Kohtz	F B Valentine	O R Davidson
NEVADA (11)									
Boulder City* (10)	CM	702 293-4302	Robert S Ferraro	....	Delia H Estes	Robert E Boyer	Robert L Sears	Robert T Lowrie	....
Carson City§ (32)	MC	702 887-2100	H J Jacobsen	D W Hataway	Ted P Thornton	William T Golden	Bernard Sease	Harold Dunn	Joseph Laird
Elko* (9)	CM	702 738-4213	D George Corner	Terry J Reynolds	Giuliana Murphy	....	Orvis P Cash	Gordon Fobes	Daryl Kofoed
Ely (5)	MC	702 289-2430	Barlow N White	Robert Spellberg	Robert Spellberg	Robert Spellberg	Raymond E Spear	....	Mike Kalleres
Fallon (4)	MC	702 423-5104	Merton E Domonoske	Ben T Bartlett	Jerry McKnight	Jerry J McKnight	James Allison	Danny J Wood	Daniel O'Brien
Henderson* (24)	CM	702 565-8921	Leroy Zike	Gary Bloomquist	Dorothy Vondenbrink	Robert M Kasner	Dale Starr	Jim Goff	Geoff Billingsley
Las Vegas* (165)	CM	702 386-6011	William H Briare	Ashley Hall	Carol Ann Hawley	Marvin E Leavitt	Clell West	....	D E Gene Donovan
North Las Vegas* (43)	CM	702 649-5811	James K Seastrand	Michael H Dyal	Esther Borden	Vytas Vaitkus	Frank D Larson	William Tharp	Gary Holler
Reno* (101)	CM	702 785-2020	Peter J Sferrazza	Chris E Cherches	Gilbert Mandagaran	Frank Kastory	Richard Minor	Robert Bradshaw	Robert Jackson
Sparks* (41)	CM	702 356-2279	James L Spoo	Patricia Thompson	Chloris Goodwin	Ralph Best	Don R Young	Thomas A Hill	Dave Roundtree
Winnemucca* (4)	CM	702 623-5081	Warren J Scott	....	Marguerite E Mowry	....	Walter Johnstone	....	D Stephen West
NEW HAMPSHIRE (83)									
Allenstown t (4)	TM	603 485-4276	Gabriel Daneault	....	Edward R Cyr	Catherine Valley	Roger Letender	Conner Norman	Joseph Benninghove
Amherst t† (8)	TM	603 673-6041	Edward C Masten	....	Bernice G Boothroyd	Marion M Sortevik	Marshall Strickland	John T Osborn Jr	Richard G Crocker
Atkinson t† (4)	TM	603 362-5266	William R Rollins	....	Linda Jette	Anthony Nobrega	David Weymouth	Philip V Consentino	Raymond H Morelli
Auburn t (3)	TM	603 483-2281	Daniel J Carpenter	....	Nancy Gagnon	....	Martin Sullivan	Lloyd P Wood	....
Barrington t† (4)	TM	603 664-9007	Patricia R Newhall	....	Muriel T Leocha	....	Sumner Hayes	Trafton Sprowl	Ronald D Landry
Bedford t (9)	RT	603 472-5242	Aubrey Robinson Jr	Donald Price	Edith P Schmidtchen	George Wiggin Jr	Ralph Wiggin	Richard Audette	Armand Dugas
Belmont t§ (4)	TM	603 267-6986	Julia Perkins	David R Caron	Calvin D Brown	John Moynihan	Albert Akerstrom	Douglas Boyd	Romeo Clairmont
Berlin* (13)	CM	603 752-7532	Joseph J Ottolini	Mitchell Berkowitz	Lise Malia	Aline Boucher	Robert Therriault	Joseph Martin	Maurice Wheeler
Boscawen t (3)	RT	603 796-2426	David R Plourde	....	Barbara M Holmes	Patricia Knight	Roland Bartlett	Brian Estee	Richard Hollins
Bow t (4)	TM	603 228-1187	Sara H Swenson	Donna M Brochu	Cynthia Batchelder	Joan P Lyford	Roger S Ordway	Peter A Cheney	....
Candia t (3)	TM	603 483-8101	Robert A Baker Sr	....	Christine Dupere	....	Leonard Wilson	Normand H St Onge	Ronald Severino
Charlestown t (4)	RT	603 826-4400	Cedric C Fisk	....	Charlene S Comstock	Mary R Gray	Robert W Burns	Robert A Colburne	Henry F Lake
Chesterfield t (3)	TM	603 363-8071	James C Milani	....	Betsey Chickering	....	William Vogeley	Robert Mills Jr	Alvin Davis
Claremont* (15)	CM	603 542-6262	James McCusker Jr	Peter Caputo	Rose Ellen Haugsrud	Jeannine Perry	Thomas Ford	Adam Bauer	....
Concord*† (30)	CM	603 224-0591	C David Coeyman	James C Smith	Elizabeth Campbell	James R Howard	Edward A Constant	David G Walchak	Ronald H Ford
Conway t* (7)	CM	603 447-3811	Charles Pinkham	Curtis H Lunt	John D Stevens	John D Edgerton	....	William Scaletti	....
Derry t (19)	TM	603 432-7724	Edward Anderson	William D Cox	Cecile Hoisington	Paul Martel	James Cote	Edward B Garone	Rodney A Bartlett
Dover* (22)	CM	603 742-3551	Robert L Whiting	Robert D Steele	Carol E Salava	Hoyt A Haney	David F Bibber	Charles Reynolds	Pierre R Bouchard
Durham t (11)	RT	603 868-5571	Norman Stiles	Deane Sweet	Linda Ekdahl	....	Raymond Dewhurst	Paul Gowen	George Crombie
Enfield t (3)	TM	603 632-4201	Carl F Patten	Peter G Russell	Ilene P Reed	....	Donald A Crate	Peter H Giese	Gerald Lashua
Epping t (3)	TM	603 679-5441	Roger E Gauthier	Hunter Rieseberg	Beatrice G Marcotte	Willis Baker	Richard Marcotte	Gregory Dodge	William G Parker
Epsom t (3)	TM	603 736-9002	George R Wiggin	....	Hazel P Steele	....	John Sawyer	Peter F Burgess	Robert Hutchins
Exeter t* (11)	CM	603 778-0591	Evelyn H Zarnowski	Donald E Chick	Thaddeus Klemarczyk	Donald R Brabant	William J Toland	Thomas F Powers III	Robert D Strout
Farmington t (5)	RT	603 755-2208	Joel D Plante	William N Cooper	L Kathy Vickers	Diane Berry	Richard Moulton	Carl Worster	Carl Baldwin
Franklin* (8)	CM	603 934-3900	Clayton Gassett	Frank P Edmunds	Elaine S Rayno	Kathleen T Bateson	Norman Beauchemin	John E Sims Jr	David Gloddy
Gilford t† (5)	RT	603 524-7438	Sandra T Mcgonagle	Phillippe A Arel	Debra E Eastman	....	Michael D Mooney	James L Martel	Richard E Lacasse
Goffstown t (11)	TM	603 497-3616	John C Sarette	David L Crowell	Elaine Emerton	Donna Brown	Richard E Fletcher	Stephen R Monier	Lorenzo J Perry
Gorham t* (3)	TM	603 466-3322	David W Murphy	Daniel C Ayer	Grace Savage	....	Wallace Martin	George T Gazey	....
Hampstead t† (4)	TM	603 329-5011	Kenneth H Clark	....	Alfred H Brickett	....	Walter Hastings	William J Letoile	....
Hampton t* (10)	CM	603 926-6766	Ashton J Norton	Philip G Richards	Jane P Kelley	Philip G Richards	Anthony H Kuncho	Robert Mark	George F Hardardt
Hanover t* (9)	TM	603 643-4123	Sharon L Nordgren	Clifford Vermilya	Frances G Wales	....	Stuart Corpieri	James H Collins	Richard Hauger
Haverhill t (3)	RT	603 747-3318	A Frank Stiegler Jr	Patricia G Klark	Helen M Smith	John S Cobb	....	Stephen C Savage	A James Boucher
Henniker t (3)	RT	603 428-3221	Tony E Fowler	....	Janet M Murdough	William McIver	F Benjamin Ayer	Thomas W Hassler	John L Brown
Hillsborough t (3)	RT	603 464-3877	Adelbert Skinner	Peter Chamberlin	Donald Knapton	Richard Baldwin	Richard Ritter	Richard Robbins Jr	....
Hinsdale t (4)	RT	603 336-5401	Delano Duffa	Jeffrey Francis	Eleanor Smith	....	Ralph Simonds	Lester Heath	Wayne Piquette
Hollis t (5)	RT	603 465-2209	Frederick Q Gemmill	Louise R King	Nancy B Jambard	Ralph J Hardy	Kenneth W Towne	Richard H Darling	Roy Wilkins
Hooksett t (7)	TM	603 485-8471	Sidney Baines Jr	....	Patricia Sack	Oscar Morin Jr	Alfred Law	James Oliver	Ed Haskell
Hopkinton t (4)	RT	603 746-3170	(not reporting)						
Hudson t† (14)	CM	603 889-1882	Leon F Malovin Jr	....	Karen Wisnosky	Theresa Dubowik	Frank A Nutting	....	Robert A Perreault
Jaffrey t (4)	TM	603 532-8322	Robert Chamberlain	....	Barry E Sasner	Elaine E Hautanen	Donald K Sawtelle	Eugene F O Brien	Kenneth E Saunders
Keene* (21)	CM	603 352-5211	L Edward Reyor	J Patrick MacQueen	Patricia A Little	Raymond P Tracy	Robert N Guyette	Harold A Becotte	John Ranagan
Kingston t (4)	RT	603 642-3342	John J Reinfuss	....	Bettie C Ouellette	....	Donald W Briggs Sr	Neil R Parker Sr	Michael D Smith
Laconia* (16)	CM	603 524-1520	Armand A Bolduc	Kenneth D Boehner	Ann G Dearborn	Carol A Lapointe	Louis T Wool	Bruce G Cheney	Frank R Denormandie
Lancaster t* (3)	CM	603 788-3391	Michael W Beattie	Donald E Crane	Jean E Oleson	Michael W Nadeau	Stephen Kipp	Allvin L Leonard	James Savage
Lebanon* (11)	CM	603 448-4220	Frank E Mastro	Alan H Edmond	Dorothy J Doyle	John P Aubin	Joseph Lariviere	Neal Wooley	Daniel A Nash
Litchfield t (4)	TM	603 424-4045	Stephen N Robinson	Cecile G Durocher	Diane L Jerry	....	Richard Jerry	John Simmons	....
Littleton t* (6)	RT	603 444-3996	Wayne P Golden	....	Thelma C Santy	Lucy M Peloquin	Richard Mackay	Louis Babin	William J Bedor
Londonderry t§ (14)	RT	603 434-8814	Gordon R Arnold	David B Wright	Alice M Taylor	Betsy McKinney	David A Hicks	Frederick A Ball	Robert Ross
Manchester (91)	MC	603 624-6455	Robert Shaw	John H Hoben	Joan E Walsh	Joseph J Acorace	John Lydon	Thomas J King	Theodore S MacLeod
Meredith t* (5)	TM	603 279-4538	Christine I Hayes	Edward L Schuette	Pauline L Fournier	Joyce M Bavis	Fred Copp	John P Curran	Carl L Smith
Merrimack t* (15)	TM	603 424-2331	Nancy R Gagnon	James A McSweeney	Robert R Morrill	Robert T Levan	Charles Q Hall	Joseph R Devine	Edward J Blaine Jr
Milford t (9)	RT	603 673-3403	(not reporting)						
Nashua (68)	MC	603 880-3300	Maurice L Arel	David B Campbell	Lionel Guilbert	Irving J Gallant	Richard J Navaroli	William Quigley	L Peter Benet
New London t (3)	TM	603 526-4821	Alf E Jacobson	....	Mary D Haddad	Benjamin Bucklin	Douglas Mathewson	Walter A Reney	William Green
Newmarket t (4)	RT	603 659-3617	Michael Cornelius	....	Eileen A Szeliga	....	Wilfred L Beaulieu	Paul T Gahan	Ronald M Bloom
Newport t* (6)	TM	603 863-1877	Arnold Greenleaf	Paul J Skowron	Sophie G Paul	....	E James Wright	Art Bastian	....
Newton t (3)	TM	603 382-4405	Kenneth L Bowers	....	Marjorie D Moisan	Marion L Kelly	Roland D Estabrook	David T Barrett	Dewey A Bowley
North Hampton t (3)	RT	603 964-8087	Robert A Southworth	....	Delores J Chase	Gail Johnson	Newman Goodwin Jr	Bruce I Golden	Vernon R Seavey
Northfield t† (3)	TM	603 286-4482	Roy L Jordan	....	Wanda P Jordan	Priscilla Beaulieu	Harold Harbour	Neal A Stone	Albert Cross
Northumberland t* (3)	CM	603 636-1450	Harold E Marshall	Ronald J Gilbert	Theresa Brooks	Pamela Styles	James Sanborn	Harry Lee Rice	Forest L Maguire
Pelham t (8)	RT	603 635-7811	Herbert Richardson	L Irja Sheppard	Cheryl B Rossi	Charlene F Takesian	Edmund Lapoint	William G Collis	....
Pembroke t (5)	RT	603 485-4747	Harold Paulsen	....	John Goff	....	Jacob Chase	Perry Eaton	Drew Richard Sr
Peterborough t (5)	TM	603 924-3201	Stanley Peters	John N Isham	Stella L Sumner	Kenneth Christian	Lawrence C Bishop	Joseph V McCarthy	John N Isham
Pittsfield t (3)	TM	603 435-6773	Leo W Fraser Jr	Mark T Fraser	Elizabeth Hast	Sandra M Marston	Frederick T Hast	David B Greenwood	Gordon W Foss
Plaistow t† (6)	RT	603 382-8469	Charles R Graham	Natalie K Kingsbury	Helen A Hart	Rosemarie L Bayek	John Fitzgerald	Alexander Brown Jr	Robert O'Hanley
Plymouth t (5)	RT	603 536-1731	Niels F Nielsen Jr	Thomas F Rankin	Carol A Elliott	Marilyn L Foley	Louis Sleeper	Donald A Young	Robert Kline
Portsmouth* (26)	CM	603 431-2000	Eileen Foley	Calvin Canney	Evelyn Hanscom	Kenneth C Dahl	Paul C Long	Stanton G Remick	Daniel Ayer

Directory 1/10 continued — MUNICIPAL OFFICIALS IN ALL U.S. CITIES OVER 2,500[1]

City, 1980 population (000 omitted), form of government		Municipal phone number	Mayor	Appointed administrator	City clerk	Finance officer	Fire chief	Police chief	Public works director
NEW HAMPSHIRE (83) continued									
Raymond t (5)	RT	603 895-4735	James Turner	Dana R Kingston	Gloria E Carney	Catherine Grant	Gordon Gould	Richard E Dolan	Lyman Hammond Jr
Rindge t† (3)	TM	603 899-5181	Redvers G White	....	Sharon H Wilkinson	Roland C Goddard Sr	Craig A Hoyt	David J Collum	Peter J Anderson
Rochester† (22)	MC	603 332-2130	Richard P Green	....	Gail Varney	Rita B George	Robert Duchesneau	Ken Hussey	Raymond Hancock
Rye t† (5)	TM	603 964-5523	J P Nadeau	Maynard L Young	Jane Ireland	....	George Moynahan Jr	Walter E Dockham Jr	Roger Philbrick
Salem t* (24)	CM	603 893-5731	Howard C Glynn	Michael J Valuk	Eleanor B Barron	Thomas W Sibalski	Donald P Bliss	John P Ganley	....
Seabrook t (6)	RT	603 474-3311	James C Falconer	Eric N Small	Virginia L Fowler	Carol L Perkins	Ernest B Sanborn	Roy F Crossland	Vernon Dow
Somersworth (10)	MC	603 692-4262	Charles D Burkam	....	Nancy Liebson	Thomas Marcoux	Paul Vallee	Ronald Perron	Norman Leclerc
Stratham t (3)	TM	603 772-4741	(not reporting)						
Swanzey t† (5)	RT	603 352-7411	David M Perry	....	Edith B Tobias	....	Henry Johnson	Richard A Wood Jr	Carl H Walden
Tilton t (3)	RT	603 286-4521	Maurice N Bowler	....	Gayle Twombly	Kenneth A Randall	Harold Harbour	George S Prescott	David E Wadleigh Sr
Walpole t (3)	TM	603 756-3672	Robert Graves	....	Virginia Baldwin	....	Geo Hurlbut	Thomas Baldwin	Robert Smith
Weare t (3)	TM	603 529-7575	(not reporting)						
Wilton t (3)	TM	603 654-9451	(not reporting)						
Winchester t (3)	RT	603 239-4951	Eugene Clark	Catherine I Burgess	Marjorie A Austin	Arnold B Conway	John L Sullivan	James E Harrison	Richard E Stetson
Windham t (6)	RT	603 432-7732	Douglas A Yennaco	....	Joan C Tuck	....	Stanley J Mackey	Norman J Crawford	....
Wolfeboro t* (4)	TM	603 569-3900	Peter Brewitt	Guy L Krapp	Patricia Waterman	....	Charles E Foss Jr	Stanley E Stevens	Curtis A Pike
NEW JERSEY (349)									
Aberdeen tp* (17)	CM	201 583-4200	Burton Morachnick	Mark Coren	Constance Petrillo	....	Louis Auriemma	Ralph E Wallace	Michael L Trotta
Absecon (7)	MC	609 641-0663	Orvis R Leopardi	William E Hurd	William E Hurd	Theadore E Nell	Oscar M Dutch	William C Steiner	....
Allendale b (6)	MC	201 825-3700	William A Simpson	Norma E Colburn	Norma E Colburn	Joshua Phillipson	John Holloway Jr	Frank A Parenti Jr	Franklin J Grieder
Alpha b (3)	MC	201 454-0088	Stephen Horvath Jr		Klara E Tarsi	Gloria M Babirak	George Cupon	George Duckworth	John Riggio
Andover tp* (5)	CM	201 383-6611	George M Matreyek	....	Mae Bauerlein	Judith L Tripodi	Paul Williams	George Smith	Walter Current Sr
Asbury Park* (17)	CM	201 775-2100	Ray Kramer	Samuel J Addeo	Stephen M Kay	Samuel W Siciliano	Quido Naplitani	Gary Wheary	Anthony J Del Pizzo
Atlantic City (40)	CO	609 347-5300	James L Usry	Carl Briscoe	Adelaide Deane	Arthur Bunting	John Jasper	Joseph Pasquale	Harvey Burns
Atlantic Highlands b (5)	MC	201 291-1444	Helen M Marchetti	Lane J Biviano	Ruth Carusoe	Joan A Smith	Marvin O Barrett	Samuel A Guzzi	James W Sage
Audubon b (10)	CO	609 547-0711	Francis J Ward	....	Lee C Daniels	Stanley S Mojta	Robert Hoover	William P Ulrich	Vincent L Lobascio
Barrington b (7)	MC	609 547-0706	Robert H Sullock	....	Thomas M Redanauer	Henry H Cohen	Charles J Houck	Howard T Page	William J Patton
Bayonne (65)	MC	201 858-6000	Dennis P Collins	Marvin A Eger	Robert F Sloan	Marvin Eger	John T Brennan	James F Sisk	Edward M Sweeney
Beachwood b (8)	MC	201 349-0245	William T Hornidge	....	E Mastropasqua	Bonnie Verga	John Weigand	John C Moody	H Wayne Swearingen
Belleville tp (35)	CO	201 759-9100	Michael V Marotti	....	Marylou Hood	Isadore Padula Jr	George Sbarra	George Lister	Joseph A Grande
Bellmawr b (14)	MC	609 933-1313	(not reporting)						
Belmar b (7)	CO	201 681-1176	Francis A Pyanoe	....	Charles F Ormsbee	....	....	....	....
Bergenfield b (26)	MC	201 384-3000	Charles J Odowd	Louis C Goetting	Louis C Goetting	Charles J Wood Jr	Robert Kirsch	Willard Burkart	Stephen T Corbett
Berkeley Heights tp§ (13)	MC	201 464-2700	James V Ralston	Thomas J Beisler	Gertrude Gonnelli	Thomas J Geraghty	Michael Amodeo	Ralph Del Duca	Thomas J Beisler
Berlin b† (6)	MC	609 767-7777	Millard Wilkinson		Paul W Breinig	Frances Cartwright	Wm Westcott Jr	William G Behnke	John C Williams
Bernards tp§ (13)	MC	201 766-2510	William B Wahl	Harold S Wood	James T Hart	James T Hart	....	Robert J Moore	George Moore
Bernardsville b§ (7)	MC	201 766-3000	Michael J Nervine	P J Passaro Jr	Ms H L Humiston	Ms H L Humiston	Louis Ferrante	Stanley Shapiro	....
Beverly (3)	MC	609 387-0205	Frank R Costello	....	Joseph J Rudnicki	Bruce Heller	Arthur Adams	Gene Difillipo	William Gaines
Bloomfield tp§ (48)	MC	201 743-4400	John W Kinder	H Joseph North	John J Galvin	Joseph R Auriemma	Robert G Melillo	Anthony J Castagno	Sam Deneka
Bloomingdale b (8)	MC	201 838-0778	Vincent A Sabio	Michael D Leary	Mildred C Bird	Theresa V Benack	George Bergested	Edward Fletcher	Robert Hudson
Bogota b (8)	MC	201 342-1736	Alexander F Kelemen	Geraldine L Morgan	Geraldine L Morgan	Janet M Rode	Edwin Wiemer	Henry J Smith	Otto F Knapp
Boonton t (9)	MC	201 335-2400	Anthony Bucco	Ricky L Prill	Ricky L Prill	William Demott	Frank Crocetti	Depalma Pascal	Albert Cronk
Bordentown (4)	CO	609 298-0604	Joseph R Malone III	....	Patricia D Borden	James F Kelly	Martin Gaynor	Francis H Lee	Joseph R Malone III
Bound Brook b (10)	MC	201 356-0833	Emil V Bonaduce	....	Anthony J Orlando	William Woldin	William Springer	Anthony M Cimino	Mark Cassebaum
Bradley Beach b (5)	CO	201 774-0588	Leonard W Riley	....	George H Moffett	Janet MacInnes	Andrew Hankins	Eugene T Myles	George A Denardo
Bridgeton (19)	MC	609 455-3230	Donald H Rainear	Elaine V Mitchell	Robert P McCormick	Terry C Delp	Charles Erianne	Richard H Gauntt	A A Fralinger Jr
Bridgewater tp§ (29)	MC	201 725-6300	James T Dowden	William J O'Neill	Bette B Nuse	John P Noguerol	....	Dix R M Fetzer	Richard F Walter
Brielle b (4)	MC	201 528-6600	Frank R Wesolowski	....	Thomas F Nolan	Wallace C Hartung	Jas F Langenberger	Arthur G Brandau	William A Burkhardt
Brigantine (8)	CO	609 266-7600	J Edward Kline	Charles E Fetter	Agnes C Simpson	Joseph R Greco	Ernest Westcott	John J O'Connor	Robert J Shipley
Buena b (4)	MC	609 697-1030	(not reporting)						
Burlington (10)	MC	609 386-0316	Herman T Costello	Douglas B Ayrer	David Vechesky	Douglas B Ayrer	John Ferry	Leroy Breece	Michael Carnivale
Butler b (8)	MC	201 838-7200	Claude C Post	Peter J Witschen	Doris Siek	....	James Soules	Gerald Napoleone	Joseph Mazurek
Byram tp (8)	MC	201 347-2500	John Reinbott	....	Frances H Webber	George Micklesavage	....	Eskil Danielson	....
Caldwell tp§ (8)	MC	201 226-6100	Peter L Buechner	Joseph O D'Arco	....	Louise Cetrangolo	Alfred Ward	Harry Johnson	Alfred Ward
Camden (85)	MC	609 757-7000	Melvin R Primas Jr	Richard H Cummings	John T Odorisio	Richard L Cinaglia	John Mogck Jr	R Douglas Holmes	Walter Richardson
Cape May* (5)	CM	609 884-8411	Arthur Blomkvest	Fred Coldren	Virginia E Petersen	Bruce MacLeod	J Howard Kelly	Harry A Stotz Jr	Jerome E Inderwies
Carlstadt b (6)	MC	201 939-2850	Dominick Presto	....	Frances Gomez	John Kilcullen	Burton Bello	Ernest Windfuhr	George Brown
Carteret b (21)	MC	201 541-4555	Peter J Sica	....	Anne N Szelag	Patrick Deblasio	Gerard Lausmohr	Robert D'Zurilla	George Coanshock
Cedar Grove tp* (13)	CM	201 239-1410	William McPhail	Joseph DiGiacomo	Marge Underhill	William Homa	Leigh Peterson	Donald Schneider	William Kowalski
Chatham b (9)	MC	201 635-0674	M Jacquelyn Marvin	Kenneth L Hetrick	Janet B Boyle	Barbara A Shepard	Harold A Sheats	David M Woodin	Herbert J Cannon
Cherry Hill tp§ (69)	MC	609 665-6500	Maria B Greenwald	Ronald S Miller	Eva Worrick	Jaqueline Lampert	....	Robert Tonczyczyn	Ronald Hepkin
Cinnaminson tp† (16)	MC	609 829-6000	Bradford S Smith	John T Hughes	Catherine E Obert	John T Hughes	Edward Miller	Thomas F Adams	James S Meckel
Clark tp† (17)	MC	201 388-3600	B G Yarusavage	Thomas E Connell	Ed R Padusniak	Betty Jo Ziemer	Vincent Pereira	Anthony T Smar	L Stanley Stires
Clayton b (6)	MC	609 881-2882	Charles A Ferrell	R J Devillasanta	Lydia Collins	R J Devillasanta	Donald Snipes	Richard Burke	Robert Sandelier
Clementon b (6)	MC	609 783-0284	Richard L Wooster	....	Grace V Pavlovec	Katherine V Stiles	Robert H Moran Jr	Edward A Lutz	....
Cliffside Park b (21)	MC	201 945-3456	Gerald Calabrese	....	Frank Olivieri	Vincent McKenna	Eugene Dickman	Louis Alfano	Walter P Okolita
Clifton* (74)	CM	201 473-2600	Gloria Kolodziej	Joseph J Lynn Sr	Betty J Lutz	Francis W Dorigatti	Joseph S Colca	Edward J Kredatus	Joseph J Lynn Sr
Closter b (8)	MC	201 784-0760	Joseph Bianco	Chas H Windeknecht	Charlotte E Masker	Norma J Gottemoller	Alfred Goodwin	James DiLuzio	Chas H Windeknecht
Collingswood b† (16)	CO	609 854-0720	Michael G Brennan	....	F Adelaide Spear	Marion S Flenard	Raymond Dobbs	William G Condon	Frank F Law
Cranford tp (25)	MC	201 276-8900	Gene Marino	Edward J Murphy	Linda S Wenz	Donald H Perlee	Leonard R Dolan II	Robert A Guertin	Manu K Patel
Cresskill b (8)	MC	201 569-5400	Michael R Dressler	....	Dorothy M Giguere	George W Stanton	Charles Stuart	Lester M DeVries	William E Cook
Delran tp§ (15)	MC	609 461-7734	Richard J Knight	Robert M Boyles III	Bernadette Porreca	Louis Kaniecki	James Turcich	David Banff	Richard Gilbert
Demarest b (5)	MC	201 768-0167	Richard D Schooler	Viola Laamanen	Viola Laamanen	Lore Lehmann	Theodore Polbos	Donald C Burgdorfer	Leo Lafferty
Denville tp§ (14)	MC	201 625-8300	John C O'Keeffe	Thomas J Grady	Donna I Costello	Patrick W Bailey	Henry Hammond	Howard Shaw	Thomas J Grady
Deptford tp* (23)	CM	609 845-5300	Joseph J Kivlen	Daniel J Mason	Kathleen W Maier	Lois G Demore	Albert Leidy	Joseph Michaels	Earl Moore
Dover t§ (15)	MC	201 366-2200	Aldo Cicchetti	....	Mildred Boyarski	Grace Tonini	Joseph Regelski	John A Albinson	Wilbur Downing
Dumont b (18)	MC	201 385-7000	David Dervitz	Mary C Price	Mary C Price	Joyce Crespo	James Molinaro	William Groesbeck	Michael Letizia
Dunellen b (7)	MC	201 968-3033	Lawrence Anzovino	....	Henry J Hodulik	Kathrine Gangemi	Jeffry Marren	William J Leary	Elston Snyder
East Brunswick tp (38)	MC	201 390-6820	William F Fox	David Weill	Elizabeth H Kiss	L Mason Neely	Vincent Grande	Thomas P Tyrrell	Thomas Shuster
East Hanover tp§ (9)	MC	201 887-5454	James R Marano	John W Hurst	Edith Jacquin	James R Marano	George Busold	William Scioscia	N Marcantonio
East Orange (77)	MC	201 266-5100	Thomas H Cooke Jr	William L Stevens	Earl Williams	A J Russoniello	Elliott Peterkin	George J Daher	Nelson Iglesias
East Rutherford b (8)	MC	201 933-3444	James L Plosia	....	Rose Staropoli	Patrick DeVasto	Kurt Dechert	Gilbert Logatto	....
East Windsor tp* (21)	CM	609 443-4000	Leonard J Millner	Reagan Burkholder	Elizabeth Nolan	Ralph Palmieri	....	Joseph G Michnisky	Ralph DiPaolo
Eastampton tp* (4)	CM	609 267-5723	....	John F Mason	....	....	....	....	....
Eatontown b (13)	MC	201 542-3303	J Joseph Frankel	Harold Grossman	Margaret L Smith	....	Allan Trask	Joseph Pelella	Edward J Stominski
Edgewater b (5)	MC	201 943-1700	Thomas J Tansey	Dominic Cacchiotti	Charles M Susskind	Michael Monaghan	James Murray	Edward Ring	Thomas Ring
Edison tp§ (70)	MC	201 287-0900	Anthony Yelencsics	John A Delesandro	Lucille Tucker	John H Fox Jr	H R Vliet	William Fisher	Julius Deri
Egg Harbor City (5)	MC	609 965-0081	Jack C Woerner	....	Ellan S Johns	Jill A Hayes	Barry Kienzle	John Baldi Jr	Harold Winkler

Directory 1/10 continued **MUNICIPAL OFFICIALS IN ALL U.S. CITIES OVER 2,500**[1]

City, 1980 population (000 omitted), form of government		Municipal phone number	Mayor	Appointed administrator	City clerk	Finance officer	Fire chief	Police chief	Public works director
NEW JERSEY (349) continued									
Elizabeth (106)	MC	201 820-4171	Thomas G Dunn	John F Papetti Sr	John J Dwyer	Linda Coleman	Charles R Swody	John J Brennan	Nicholas Schipani
Elmwood Park b§ (18)	MC	201 796-1457	Richard A Mola	....	Dolores Camlet	Joseph McQueeney	Patsy Pugliese	Michael Yachnik	Joseph Mulligan
Emerson b† (8)	MC	201 262-6086	Leo J Link	....	Arlene Raymond	Spencer A Tafuri	Michael D Falotico	Walter R Hackbarth	Joseph A Solimando
Englewood Cliffs b (6)	MC	201 569-5252	Joseph C Parisi	....	Joseph Favaro	Richard Nordlinger	John Obertlik	John F Murphy	Carmine Esposito
Englewood§ (24)	MC	201 567-1800	Steven R Rothman	William A Sommers	Jack Drakeford	Robert Benecke	Douglas Baker	Donald Rowan	Kenneth G Albert
Essex Fells tp§ (2)	MC	201 226-3400	Frank A Mingle	Robert DiTommaso	Robert DiTommaso	Marie B Addis	Harold E Sargent	George J Haydu	H L Ratzburg
Evesham tp* (22)	CM	609 983-2900	Raymond J Brosel	Burton T Conway	Florence Ricci	Thomas J Tontarski	....	Joseph Leedom	George Dechurch
Ewing tp† (35)	MC	609 883-2900	David C Evans	Fred R Walters	John A Garzio	John O Davies	....	Calvin R Steepy	Robert Dorio
Fair Haven b (6)	MC	201 747-0241	Nancy E Kern	William C Rue	William C Rue	William C Rue	Michael Connor	Lois A Devito	John C Riley
Fair Lawn b* (32)	CM	201 796-1700	Bernard Hersh	Joseph W Garger	Donald Debruin	Barry Eccleston	Edward Feldman	Robert Van Houten	William Davidson
Fairfield tp§ (8)	MC	201 227-0580	Theodore Nalesnik	Charles G Burns	Janet D Lemley	Molly Cusano	Kenneth Myron	George D Milne	Rocco Palmieri
Fairview b (11)	MC	201 943-3300	Mario Schettino	....	John G Tomaras	Anthony M Orecchio	Gaetano Galiardo	Samuel Linardi	Mario Saracino
Fanwood b (8)	MC	201 322-8236	Patricia M Kuran	Llewyellen Fisher	Llewyellen Fisher	Llewyellen Fisher	R E Hamill Jr	Anthony J Parenti	Raymond Manfra
Flemington b (4)	MC	201 782-8840	Herman E Kapp	....	Robert B Hauck	George Sirusas	Robert Evans	Peter J Tirpok	George Wilson
Florham Park b§ (9)	MC	201 377-5800	Dale A Anderson	Bert Esworthy	Joyce M Rawson	Linda S Reino	Andrew C Picone	Richard H Ruzicka	Kenneth S Gregory
Fort Lee b (32)	MC	201 592-3540	N Corbiscello	Stephen Cuccio	Carol Kohout	Dorothy Pagano	James Carney	Arthur Siebert	Arthur Ballant
Franklin tp* (31)	CM	201 873-2500	Robert Zaborowski	John C Lovell Jr	Madelyn Maak	George Ramsey	....	James Brown	Benjamin Walenczyk
Franklin b (4)	MC	201 827-9280	William J Hodas	....	Rose S Fletcher	Mildred Harden	John Doyle	Raymond Sweller	Frank Aumick
Franklin Lakes b (9)	MC	201 891-0048	William Vichiconti	....	Mary P Holly	....	James Webb	John E Bockhorn	Robert Brady
Freehold tp* (19)	CM	201 462-7900	David P Segal	Frederick E Jahn	Romeo Cascaes	Robert Jones	M Rossi	John Willis	Wm B Dickerson
Freehold b (10)	MC	201 462-1410	John G McGackin	Robert J Cabana	Vivian Taylor	Vivian Taylor	George H Hull	William R Burlew	....
Galloway tp* (12)	CM	609 965-4047	John W Mooney	Charles M Melchior	Audrey P Woods	Clare Mlynarczyk	Charles J Guenther	Roy Heintz	Erlin Perkins
Garfield*† (27)	CM	201 340-2000	Thomas J Duch	Robert Badini	Lorraine H Werner	John Nunno	Robert Krawiec	Carmine J Perrapato	Dominick Puzino
Garwood b (5)	MC	201 789-0710	Dominic V Carrea	....	Doris Polidore	Eileen Masterson	Edward Silver	Thomas J Colwell	....
Gibbsboro b (3)	MC	609 783-6655	John E White	....	Ellen M Egan	Rita DeProspo	James Johnston	Edward Heisler	....
Glassboro b (15)	MC	609 881-9230	William L Dalton	....	Carl Halpin	Mary E Weber	Louis E Corradetti	Robert Toughill	Clayton Platt
Glen Ridge tp† (8)	MC	201 748-8400	Donald E Lane	....	Stephen C Berry	Stephen C Berry	Marc Wegleski	Kenneth Swain	Maurits L Modin
Glen Rock b (11)	MC	201 447-2555	Eugene D Becken	Robert Freudenrich	Mary H Locke	Robert Freudenrich	Arthur Zanotti	Neil Finn	Harold Meeks
Gloucester City (13)	MC	609 456-0205	(not reporting)						
Gloucester tp† (45)	MC	609 228-4000	Ann A Mullen	John McPeak	Rose Marie Stortini	....	....	Seth Stichler	....
Guttenberg t† (7)	MC	201 868-3300	Raymond A Schnyder	....	Marion Glendinning	....	....	....	....
Hackensack*† (36)	CM	201 342-3000	Fred Cerbo	Joseph J Squillace	Doris L Dukes	James S Lacava	Anthony A Aiellos	Anthony J Iurato	Joseph J Casale
Hackettstown t† (9)	MC	201 852-3130	James G Smith	....	Wilbur C Willis	....	Kenneth Huyler	Richard L Armstrong	....
Haddon tp (16)	CO	609 854-1176	William Rohrer	....	Florence Black	Richard C Hardenber	Preston Morgan	Robert Saunders	William G Rohrer
Haddon Heights b (8)	MC	609 547-7164	A A Longo	....	W R Fannon	S D Troy	William Chain	R Battersby	Joan Elfreth
Haddonfield b§ (12)	CO	609 429-4700	John J Tarditi	Richard B Schwab	Janet G Betley	Edwin L Spragg	John Howarth	Roger Samartino	Theodore R Dorn
Haledon b (7)	MC	201 595-7766	Sam F Sibilio	....	Martha Haber	Regina Hartley	Edward Wilson	....	Fred Peloso
Hamilton tp† (83)	MC	609 890-3500	John K Rafferty	Arthur J Julian	Thomas J Warwick	Paul Kramer	....	George J Zimmer	Robert V Lewanowicz
Hammonton t† (12)	MC	609 561-0756	Russell P Clark	....	Diane Decicco	Theodore J Trauner	John B Berenato	Carmen Demarco	Joseph A Caruso
Harrington Park b (5)	MC	201 768-1700	Robert J Harrison	....	Don Horsey	Norman Brockmeier	Kenneth Hagemann	Robert A Demler	William Covert
Harrison t (12)	MC	201 483-7300	Frank E Rodgers	....	Ms J M Catrambone	Martin Polcari	John M Rodgers	Louis P Saporito	Robert S Baranowski
Hasbrouck Heights b (12)	MC	201 288-0195	(not reporting)						
Haworth b† (4)	MC	201 384-4785	John H Johl	Virginia Michel	Virginia Michel	Christine Teichmann	Jack Shea	Gaston F Michel	John Flaherty
Hawthorne b (18)	CO	201 427-1168	Louis Bay II	....	Eleanor F Tyther	Anthony Ross	James Aldi Jr	V J Mangiafico	Arthur A Brokaw
Hazlet tp§ (23)	MC	201 264-1700	Paul A Stallone	Robt G Weigand	David G Bryce	Ronald J Dobilas	John Beslanovitz	Holmes J Gormerley	Gilbert W Bennett
High Bridge b (3)	MC	201 638-6455	Carl J Lewis	....	Claire R Knapp	Deborah K Giordano	Gary Trimmer	Joseph M Lacey Sr	Gary Trimmer
Highland Park b (13)	MC	201 572-3400	Harold Berman	....	William F Ducca	Wanda E Hudson	Scott Lantz	Angelo Arrisi	Gerald T Kunkel
Highlands b (5)	MC	201 872-1515	(not reporting)						
Hightstown b† (5)	MC	609 448-2188	Richard Aughenbaugh	....	Sheila Clark	Edith V Erving	Carl Dye	Lawrence Archer	Laurence Blake
Hillsdale b (10)	MC	201 666-4800	Alfred J Murphy Jr	....	Elizabeth F Rotar	Margaret Nostrand	Keith I Durie	Philip J Varisco	Keith I Durie
Hillside tp† (21)	MC	201 926-3000	Louis A Santagata	....	C Mildred Karlik	Kevin P Davis	Thomas R Mateer	George A Shelbourne	Salvatore Lomonaco
Hoboken (42)	MC	201 420-2000	Steve Cappiello	Edwin J Chius	James J Farina	Matthew Cannarozzi	James R Houn	George W Crimmins	William Van Wie
Hohokus b (4)	MC	201 652-4400	Richard M Sayers	John B Shuart	John B Shuart	John B Shuart	Henry Lavit	Robert Re	Thomas J Dawson
Holmdel tp§ (8)	MC	201 946-4330	Joseph V Popolo	John Coughlin	John P Wadington	John P Wadington	Ralph Molzon	R Bruce Phillips	Edward Broberg
Hopatcong b (16)	MC	201 398-5200	Richard H Hodson	Robert Badini	Joan Dora	Jane Vonderheide	Paul Fischer	David DiMarco	Calvin D Bender
Hopewell tp§ (11)	MC	609 737-0638	William A Kampfer	James M Davy	Anna Hillman	James M Davy	....	Robert Ferrarin	Henry Burd
Irvington tp (61)	MC	201 399-8111	Anthony T Blasi	Henry Underhill	Jeffery Barnes	Vincent J Foti Jr	Joseph Gallagher	Herman G Fenchel	Adam Samiec
Jackson tp§ (26)	CO	201 928-1200	William L Schreiber	Francis J Savage	David T Miller Sr	Lawrence Williams	....	Walter McCurdy	John Smatusik Jr
Jamesburg b (4)	MC	201 521-2222	Joseph Tonkery	....	Edna E Gierman	Thomas Walker	Anthony Lamantia	Salvatore J Namio	Stanley Hawk
Jefferson tp§ (16)	MC	201 697-1500	Horace Chamberlain	Robert Bowden	June Cetro	Robert Bowden	Robert Emmetts	Robert Mosedale	Robert Cutter
Jersey City§ (224)	MC	201 547-5000	Gerald McCann	Frederick J Tomkins	Thomas F X Smith	Frederick Tomkins	Richard Harrison	....	Jack James
Keansburg b* (11)	CM	201 787-0215	Walter Farley	Edward C Weigand	Luke Shields	Vincent Indelicato	William P Riley	William Kryscnski	F Richard Smith
Kearny t (36)	MC	201 991-2700	Henry J Hill	....	James Cantlon	Dennis M Sherry	Joseph Philips	Bill G Comer	John Kurszwicz
Kenilworth b (8)	MC	201 276-9090	Livio Mancino	....	Margaret Adler	Dorothy A Himpele	Anthony Peters	Charles David	Frank Morro
Keyport b (7)	MC	201 739-3900	Richard W Bergen	John J Kennedy	Judith L Poling	John J Kennedy	John Jones	Michael E Kelley	Author S Rooke
Kinnelon b† (8)	MC	201 838-5401	Glenn L Sisco	....	Lucille Immen	Lucille Immen	Ralph P Grube	Allen R Maher	Robert G Sautter
Lakehurst b† (3)	MC	201 657-4141	Michael A Fuccile	....	Alyce M Fensterer	Alyce M Fenster	Richard Herrick	David Exel	John C Carr Foreman
Lakewood tp* (38)	CM	201 364-2500	H George Buckwald	Thomas L LaPointe	Gizella M Doyle	Carl A Inniss	John Deligny	Stephen Belitrand	Gilbert J Carlson
Lambertville (4)	CO	609 397-0110	Mary E Sheridan	....	Dorothy A Bolmer	Phillip L Pittore	Eugene Venettone	Jack Vennetone	Edward Nalence
Lawnside b (3)	MC	609 547-6133	Walter A Gaines	Jessie G Harris	Annette M Williams	Jessie G Harris	Samuel M Funches Jr	Richard Wise	Arnold Williams
Lawrence tp* (20)	CM	609 896-9400	Gretel Gatterdam	Robert J Albertson	Dorothea Simonelli	Allan D Pietrefesa	....	William Seabridge	Thomas Evans
Leonia b§ (8)	MC	201 944-4250	Robert R Bacicco	George D Haeuber	Anne G Williams	A Theodoracopoulos	Edmond J Hazlitt	Paul Dittmar	George D Haeuber
Lincoln Park b§ (9)	MC	201 694-6100	Stephen J Marabeti	Sanford Kaplan	Kay A Wittman	James A Anderson	Garry Morere	Michael Nowacki	Gregory Becker
Linden (38)	MC	201 486-3800	George Hudak	....	Val Imbriaco	Louise J Hasbrouck	Edwin Schulhafer	Domenic D Lello	John Mesler Jr
Lindenwold b (18)	MC	609 783-2121	John A Pregartner	....	Barbara L Dolchan	William J Sauerwine	....	Raymond Wilson	Patricia L Marshall
Linwood (6)	MC	609 927-4108	Donald B Vass	....	Mary E Boileau	Robert Matthews	Charles B Doughty	John J Wittenwiler	James Hutchins
Little Falls tp† (11)	MC	201 256-0170	Carmen J Gaita Jr	....	Ms M Montgomery	Nathan Honig	Donald Blackman	Bernard Terranova	Dennis Lindsay
Little Ferry b (9)	MC	201 641-9234	Charles C DiPaola	Spencer A Tafuri	Joan Heubel	Spencer A Tafuri	Michael Nunziato	Harold Schwartz	John A Bladek
Little Silver b† (6)	TM	201 842-2400	John A Marrah	Stephen Greenwood	Stephen Greenwood	Robert Frederickson	George Miller	James J Fagan	James Canneto
Livingston tp* (28)	CM	201 992-5000	Dominick A Crincoli	Robert H Harp	Renee Green	Robert H Harp	Charles W Schilling	Albert J Fachet	Arthur J Carson
Lodi b (24)	MC	201 365-4001	Chris M Paci	Frank J Loiacono	Steven Sireci Sr	Andrew L Pesenti	Salvatore Paci Jr	Andrew Voto	Kenneth G B Job
Long Branch (30)	MC	201 222-7000	Philip D Huhn	Anthony J Muscillo	Jennie C Defazio	Ronald J Mehlhorn	Frank Desantis	Robert Sartor	John Ferraro
Lyndhurst tp (20)	CO	201 438-5120	James M Guida	....	Herbert W Perry	John Gagliardi	....	William Jarvis	Evelyn Pezzolla
Madison b§ (15)	MC	201 377-8000	Eliz G Baumgartner	James R Allison	Fannie Stinson	Abraham Antun	James McCormack	Donald R Capen	Francis V Angri
Magnolia b (5)	MC	609 783-1520	M Mae McKenna	....	Joanmarie F Hunt	Joyce L Nutter	Emil G Altman	Henry Jefferson	John D Hunt
Mahwah tp§ (12)	MC	201 529-5757	Frank P Kraus	Robert P Hammer	Robert P Hammer	Stanley Newmark	Robert Baron	Robert Kratchman	Patrick H Malone
Manalapan tp§ (19)	MC	201 446-3200	George P Spodak	Debrah DeFeo	Catherine Haug	John O Malley	....	Thomas Wallace	Robert Paulsen
Manasquan b (5)	MC	201 223-0544	John L Winterstella	....	Mildred W Collard	Joanne S Madden	George Clayton	Paul R Lavance	Gerald G Evans
Manville b† (11)	MC	201 725-9478	Marion B Dudash	....	....	Dorothy Peltack	David Mroz	Michael Wass	Henry Cheesman

Directory 1/10 continued — **MUNICIPAL OFFICIALS IN ALL U.S. CITIES OVER 2,500[1]**

City, 1980 population (000 omitted), form of government		Municipal phone number	Mayor	Appointed administrator	City clerk	Finance officer	Fire chief	Police chief	Public works director
NEW JERSEY (349) continued									
Maple Shade tp* (21)	CM	609 779-9610	Joseph A Niceta	George D Haeuber	Rosemary Wallace	....	John Brasko	James T Ryan	....
Maplewood tp (23)	MC	201 762-8120	Robert H Grasmere	W David Carew	Robert F Gist	Joseph W Bonin	Sam Santucci	Francis J Torre	James F Burkhardt
Margate City (9)	CO	609 822-0424	William H Ross III	....	Robert A Gilchrist	Willim H Ross III	Edward Woods	James Creaghe	Russell C Roney Jr
Matawan b (9)	MC	201 566-3898	Victor R Armellino	Michael Piperno	Madeline H Bucco	....	Joseph Vaccarella	Robert V McGowan	....
Maywood b (10)	MC	201 845-6655	James J Panos	....	Patricia Allison	Joseph Iannaconi Jr	Bruce Schneider	Harry Kickuth	Ernest W Hanabergh
Medford tp* (17)	CM	609 654-2608	Steven J Corcoran	Richard W Deaney	Mildred Gager	....	Robert Merefield	John Foulk	Richard W Deaney
Medford Lakes b* (5)	CM	609 654-8898	John P Gaitens	John A Weaver Jr	John A Weaver Jr	John A Weaver Jr	John Lenhart	Roger N Smith	Carl Goodfellow
Mendham b (5)	MC	201 543-7152	Michael A Ackerman	Robert O Snedaker	....	Susan Giordano	Joseph Eible	James Cillo	David Crotsley
Merchantville b (4)	MC	609 662-2474	John F Morrissey	....	Daniel P Gotthold	Daniel P Gotthold	James F Brickley Jr	Gary R Cline	John L Hughes Jr
Metuchen b§ (14)	MC	201 632-8540	John Wiley Jr	David R Kochel	Eleanor M Brennan	Eleanor M Brennan	Geoffrey Pace	Joseph P Perrino	....
Middlesex b (13)	MC	201 356-7400	Ronald Dobies	....	Margaret Hanania	John H Ross	George Taylor	Sylvester Conrad	Vincent Lella
Middletown tp§ (63)	MC	201 671-3100	Robert B Waller	Herbert E Bradshaw	Frank Gleason	Herbert E Bradshaw	John Fricker	Joseph McCarthy	John McGowan
Midland Park b (7)	MC	201 445-5720	J William Van Dyke	Joseph Maddaloni Jr	Joseph Maddaloni Jr	Joseph Maddaloni Jr	Edward Hollema Jr	August Faber	Eugene Bellusci
Millburn tp§ (20)	MC	201 564-7000	Robert P Denise	John W Pritchard	John W Pritchard	John W Pritchard	Lawrence Zazzera	W P Tighe Jr	Anthony J Isaac
Milltown b (7)	MC	201 828-2100	Jack Whitman	....	Mary I Crabiel	James Lindsey	Alfred Bailey	William E Miller	Jack Scire
Millville (25)	CO	609 825-7000	Chester Goodwin III	....	Lewis N Thompson	Chester Goodwin III	Gary Wallen	Paul L Quinn	Dale Finch
Monmouth Beach b (3)	CO	201 229-2204	Louis P Sodano	....	Bonnie G Moore	Joan C Meyer	....	Richard L Keller	Louis Ferrugiaro
Montclair tp* (40)	CM	201 744-1400	James H Ramsey	Bertrand N Kendall	Constance B Arnott	Edward T Curtis	John W Gardner	Edward Giblin	Carl Guerrina
Montgomery tp* (7)	CM	201 359-8211	Catherine B Frank	Peter N Rayner	Lynn Rogers	Muriel K Page	Eugene Keller	Michael Szoke	Gary Garwacke
Montvale b (7)	MC	201 391-5700	David Metlitz	Allan C Bonhoff	Margaret W Palella	....	David Adams	John W Hanna	Paul Ramasco
Montville tp§ (14)	MC	201 334-1320	Frederick Eckhardt	Charles J Tahaney	Gladys Jarombek	Charles J Tahaney	....	James Gormley	Robert Cook
Moonachie b† (3)	MC	201 641-1813	Thomas Tucci	....	Kenneth Izzo	Kenneth Izzo	William Hunt	Stephen Garrand	John Miuccio
Moorestown tp*† (16)	CM	609 235-0912	Francis L Bodine	Alfred S Harding	John J Logue	David E Longacre Jr	....	Harry R Klatt	John T Carney
Morris Plains b (5)	MC	201 538-2224	Alan R Florin	....	Ruth C Romano	John J Doherty	Edward H Van Ness	H James Richardson	Robert H Sturtevant
Morristown t (17)	MC	201 538-4300	Emilio J Gervasio	Joseph S Rompala	William Chambers	Dorothy F Johnson	James Egbert	William E Pierson	Ron Assante
Mount Arlington b (4)	MC	201 398-6832	Roger A Maler	....	Mary Secola	....	Larry Elliott	William Morgan	Richard Barry
Mount Ephraim b (5)	CO	609 931-1546	William A Bradford	....	Catherine Pepe	William A Bradford	James Sylvester	Edward Dobleman	Harry J Hartman
Mount Holly tp* (11)	CM	609 267-0170	James B Smith	Barry Larson	Joan L Boas	Evelyn Bintliff	Theodore Gaskill	Eugene Stafford	Joseph Gregory Jr
Mount Laurel tp* (18)	CM	609 234-0001	Ronald A Graziano	Faneen M Cieslinski	Rita M Bovino	John G Bakos	Greg W Collier	Saunder Weinstein	Everett G Johnson
Mount Olive tp§ (19)	MC	201 691-0900	Charles H Johnson	Francis J Bastone	Anne Marie Haritos	Thomas McCann	Art Deden	....	Canger S Cassera
Mountain Lakes b*† (4)	CM	201 334-3131	Christopher Falcon	William F O'Brien	Alison M Wood	....	Skott Burkland	Joseph Spinozzi	Carl Danser
Mountainside b (7)	MC	201 232-2400	Bruce A Geiger	James Roberts	Katheen Toland	Janet Krommenhoek	Alan Hambacher	William A Alder	Robert Koser
National Park b† (4)	MC	609 845-3891	Francis A Witt	....	Robert Dougherty Jr	Joan Maska	James Trautner	William Stout Jr	Edward Hess
Neptune tp† (28)	CO	201 988-5200	Joseph M Pepe	Joseph E Bennett	Joseph E Bennett	William B Crelin	William Krayer	Anthony Paduano	Anthony J Molinaro
Neptune City b (5)	MC	201 776-7224	Holmes A Adams	....	Mildred M Adams	....	Owen Dunfee III	James Johnson	Norman Cottrell Sr
Netcong b (4)	MC	201 347-0252	Nicholas Pompilio	....	Thomasina Grogan	Joseph Togno	Richard Kelley	Louis Barbato	....
New Brunswick (41)	CO	201 745-5000	John A Lynch	Stanley Marcinczyk	William J Cahill	Alice Anne Hauck	Frank Hary	James V Gassaro	Thomas Weingartner
New Hanover tp (14)	CO	609 758-7149	Patrick G Malloy	James J Nash Jr	John Keller Jr	James J Nash Jr	Wayne Wharton	James J Nash Jr	....
New Milford b† (17)	MC	201 262-6100	Dan Longo	Frank J J Kehoe	Frank J J Kehoe	Gloria G Wolf	Ken Dreitlein	Patrick Jodice	John Roskovics
New Providence b (12)	MC	201 665-1400	Harold Weideli Jr	Edward M Bien	Ms L Schaffernoth	Richard O Burr	Emil Koref	James J Venezia	William Fitter
Newark§ (329)	MC	201 733-3600	Kenneth A Gibson	Elton E Hill	Frank D'Ascensio	Fleming Jones	John P Caufield	Hubert Williams	Vincent E Toma
Newton t* (8)	CM	201 383-3521	Nicholas A Masi	Theodore M Nelson	Douglas L Cummins	Camille Furgiuele	Richard J Blauvelt	Larry E Romyns	James D Jones
North Arlington b (17)	MC	201 991-6060	Leonard R Kaiser	Robert M Landolfi	Constance M Meehan	Anthony Blasi	Rolf Maris	Gerald Aponte	Joseph Mancuso
North Bergen tp (47)	CO	201 863-8500	Anthony DiVincent	Michael Pollotta	Joseph Picone	Charles Haas	George Franke	George Lehman	Nicholas Fortunato
North Brunswick tp (22)	TM	201 247-0922	Paul Matacera	....	Edna L Swanson	William Wright	Pete Micali	Carmen Canastra	Jake Thompson
North Caldwell tp (6)	MC	201 228-4444	Richard J Nelson	John S Kosko	Frances I Lucchind	John S Kosko	John D Ascensio	James C Rush	Stephen Petro
North Haledon b (8)	MC	201 427-7793	Peter Slootmaker	....	Lucille B Debiak	Cornelius LaFleur	Kenneth Hofer	Edward V Dombroski	....
North Plainfield b (19)	MC	201 756-4600	(not reporting)						
North Wildwood (5)	MC	609 522-2030	Anthony T Catanoso	Thomas W Flud	Jos J Stockridge	Rosario R Versaggi	Gordon L Mathis	William J Wizst	David E Blaker
Northfield (8)	MC	609 641-2832	William M Felton Jr	....	Carol A Raph	Jack Kelly	Ernest L Macomber	Robert E Shaw	Erland Chau
Northvale b (5)	MC	201 767-3330	John E Rooney	....	Ruth M Pribish	....	Edward Kammer	George E Vollmer	Peter Perretti
Norwood b (4)	MC	201 767-7200	Gus D'Ercole	Richard Vogler	Richard Vogler	Richard Vogler	Joseph Benardella	Frank D'Ercole	Rocco Cerbasi
Nutley tp (29)	CO	201 667-2800	Harry W Chenoweth	....	Jo Ann Hulin	Jerry J Amiano	Edward Fellrath	Salvatore Dimichino	Peter C Scarpelli
Oakland b* (13)	CM	201 337-8111	Wm Winterhalter	Sidney H Stone	Jeannine Hickey	Steven Schwager	Edwin Kimmel	Donald Hasenbalg	N David Fagerlund
Oaklyn b (4)	MC	609 858-2457	Bart R Mueller	....	Marie Hawkins	Charles Schaefer	Lee Ryan	John V Laggy	Vincent Scriboni
Ocean tp* (24)	CM	201 531-5000	Richard English III	Gregory Fehrenbach	Virginia K Bergeron	Herbert L Kushner	....	Neil Tantum	William J Taylor
Ocean City (14)	MC	609 399-6111	Jack Bittner	Joseph A Kane	Loretta C Marshall	....	Todd E Bower	Dominick Longo	....
Oceanport b† (6)	MC	201 222-8221	Clement V Sommers	Gene Valanzano	Patricia L Varca	Ida M Lancaster	Stephen Bray	Thomas L Byram	....
Ogdensburg b (3)	MC	201 827-3444	John F Kibildis	....	Jean Dickson	Joseph Fitzgibbons	....	James W Duke	....
Old Bridge tp* (52)	CM	201 721-5600	Russell J Azzarello	John M Morse	Mary M Brown	Robert Shrekgast	Frank Moscarello	William A Volkert	Rocco Donatelli
Old Tappan b (4)	MC	201 664-1849	Edward J Gallagher	Frank B Recktenwald	Frank B Recktenwald	Christine Cauvet	George Pomponio	John Kramer	Harry Lake
Oradell b (9)	MC	201 262-0558	Carl Marggraff	Stanley J Kufel	Stanley J Kufel	....	....	....	....
Orange tp (31)	MC	201 266-4200	Paul Monacelli	Leonard A Matarese	Felix DeFeo	Russell Jarger	Richard Franchino	Robert Sorge	Joseph Petrucelli
Palisades Park b (14)	MC	201 944-2753	Herman E Zuckerman	....	Marie D Russo	Patricia Albanese	Edward Lange	Martin T Faye	Anthony Casbar
Palmyra b (7)	MC	609 829-6100	John E Casey	Rudy Creyaufmiller	Grace A Carr	Anothy Giampaolo	Richard K Dreby	Robert A Fow	Donald L Johnson
Paramus b (26)	MC	201 265-2100	Joseph Cipolla	Clifford G Steele	Constance Sitek	Ann Brandsness	Robert Olson	Joseph Delaney	Jerry Rhodes
Park Ridge b§ (9)	MC	201 573-1800	David N Grubb	Charles E Gasior	Annaliese Krouse	Ann F Kilmartin	Robert R Ludwig	Ernest R Swanson	Theodore T Huff Jr
Parsippany-Troy Hills tp (50)	MC	201 263-4350	Frank B Priore	Gregory James Hill	Judith I Silver	Robert Griffith	Pat Lanza	Elwood Fox	Daniel Biondo
Passaic* (52)	CM	201 365-5500	Joseph Lipari	Imre Karaszegi Jr	Joseph Hirkala	Edward Routel	Kenneth Peterson	Kenneth Hill	Joseph Zangara
Paterson (138)	MC	201 881-3380	Frank X Graves Jr	Frank Del Monaco	Sylvia McEachern	Elmo Valle	Harold Kane	James T Hannan	Daniel Malatesta
Paulsboro b (7)	MC	609 423-1500	(not reporting)						
Pemberton tp§ (30)	MC	609 894-8201	Donald S Emmons	Carrol F Pickens	Charlotte C Newhart	George McGowan Jr	....	William Hann	Harold Lynch
Penns Grove b (6)	MC	609 299-0098	Kenneth James	....	Gilda T Gill	David W Livesay	Ralph Willis	Milton L Smith	....
Pennsauken tp (34)	CM	609 665-1000	Bill Orth	Kenneth W Carruth	Theresa R Brown	David Leonard	Timothy Sullivan	Nicholas Petitte	John Rothermel
Pequannock tp* (14)	CM	201 835-5700	Evelyn Justesen	Harold G Gerken	Elizabeth D Eley	Harold G Gerken	Edwin Verhage	Belwyn Harper	William Hutchison
Perth Amboy§ (39)	MC	201 826-0290	George J Otlowski	Gail P Feist	Harold E Augustine	C Marion Lipira	Joseph Deliman	Edward Mullen	Joseph Greiza
Phillipsburg t* (17)	CM	201 454-5500	Philip J Mugavero	Peter J Miller	Michele D Broubalow	Joseph Hriczak	Albert Pianelli	Charles E Erdie	Peter J Miller
Pine Hill b (9)	MC	609 783-0374	Joseph Nunes	....	Joan A Schneebele	Thomas Ciocco	William Duke	James LaGrande	Edward Hock Sr
Piscataway tp§ (42)	MC	201 981-0800	Robert G Smith	Paul A Abati	Ann Nolan	Michael Conti	....	Henry Knabe	Henry Zanetti
Pitman b (10)	CM	609 589-3522	Michael J Hannum	Gregory G Kahofer	Gregory G Kahofer	Earl Kelly	Coxie Brown	Joseph Foster	Ted Lewis
Plainfield§ (46)	MC	201 753-3000	Richard L Taylor	Jerome Harris	Emilia R Stahura	Peter P Sepelya Jr	....	John Propsner	Louis Jones
Plainsboro tp§ (6)	MC	609 799-0909	B W Wright	P I Hechenbleikner	P F Hullfish	P Rodefeld	Ted Wagner	C J Maurer Jr	P I Hechenbleikner
Pleasantville† (13)	MC	609 646-4130	George W Dix	Timothy P Gordon	George English	Gerard F Haugrich	Roger W Arlan	Ralph Peterson	Leroy S Stephens
Point Pleasant Beach b (5)	MC	201 892-1118	Daniel J Hennessy	....	Barbara Scharmann	Barbara Scharmann	Jos Wolfersberger	Charles Bertolatus	Lester W Dwyer
Point Pleasant b§ (18)	MC	201 892-3434	Marshall R Boggio	Paul Laracy	Margaret B Van Pelt	Judy Block	Bill Knect	Robert A Cooper	Albert Clifton
Pompton Lakes b (11)	MC	201 835-0143	Charles Romaine Jr	Donald W Krom	Marian Nicolosi	Donald W Krom	Thomas Duffy	Joseph Sisco	Joseph Black
Princeton tp* (14)	CM	609 924-5749	Winthrop S Pike	James J Pascale	Natalie Cruickshank	John S Clawson Jr	Clinton W Groover	A M Pinelli	Robert V Kiser
Princeton b (12)	MC	609 924-3119	Barbara B Sigmund	Mark S Gordon	Penelope S Carter	Decimus W Marsh	Clinton W Groover	Michael F Carnevale	....

Directory 1/10 continued — MUNICIPAL OFFICIALS IN ALL U.S. CITIES OVER 2,500[1]

City, 1980 population (000 omitted), form of government	Municipal phone number	Mayor	Appointed administrator	City clerk	Finance officer	Fire chief	Police chief	Public works director
NEW JERSEY (349) continued								
Prospect Park b (5) . . . MC	201 790-7903	Ronald M Trommelen	Judith Critchley	Judith Critchley	Marion DeYries	Robert Weir	Glenn Saltenberger	John Schaffer
Rahway§ (27). . . . . . . MC	201 381-8000	Daniel L Martin	Joseph M Hartnett	Francis R Senkowsky	Roger Pribush	James T Heller	Theodore Polhamus	Frank Koczur
Ramsey b (13) . . . . . . MC	201 825-3400	Emil L Porfido	Nicholas C Saros	Jeanette Szwec	Eleanor Ameye	Jack Schertel	Fred Smith	John Fecanin
Randolph tp* (18) . . . . CM	201 361-8200	Edward A Tamm	J Peter Braun	Doris M Ryan	Michael J Soccio	William Short	James McLagan	Michael Spillane
Raritan tp§ (8) . . . . . . MC	201 782-2919	Donald Gootee	Eugene Dunworth Jr	Hiram Ely Jr	Donald Bowlby	Roy Compton	Alfred Phillips	Robert Kling
Raritan b† (6). . . . . . . MC	201 231-1300	Steve Delrocco	....	Phillips Heathcote	Maryrose Moeller	Robert Comandini	John Soriano	....
Red Bank b (12) . . . . . MC	201 530-2740	Michael J Arnone	Lawrence M Riccio	Ruth M Eschelbach	Bruce Loversidge	Jack England	George Clayton Jr	Raymond England
Ridgefield Park v (13) CO	201 641-4950	Fred Criscuolo	....	Elizabeth Hannigan	John B Davis	Joseph Alberque	Walter J Grossmann	Fred Criscuolo
Ridgefield b (10). . . . . MC	201 943-5215	Stewart V Veale	Sophie Hegadorn	Sophie Hegadorn	Joseph Calabria	Joseph Gillespie	Arthur Hennessey	Robert Doidge
Ridgewood v* (25) . . . CM	201 444-5500	Bruce K Byers	Ronald Zweig	....	James Ten Hoeve	George Hamling	Frank Milliken	William J Cooke Jr
Ringwood b§ (13) . . . . MC	201 962-7037	P Cannici	Thomas F Kane	Kathleen D Cenicola	Charles DeDeyn	....	Roy Van Tassel	Harold McDowell
River Edge b (11) . . . . MC	201 262-1778	Edward P Raffo	Angela L Grillo	Angela L Grillo	Alan Negreann	Gerry Ryan	Kenneth J Quinn	Gerald Crum
River Vale tp§ (9) . . . . MC	201 664-2346	Burton T Cohen	Roy S Blumenthal	Corinne Ferrante	Ann Olivarius	John J Tobin	Thomas Simpson	Leonard Scott
Riverdale b (3) . . . . . . MC	201 835-4060	Michael Dedio	....	Christine Gregory	Frances Ball	James Reseling	Harry W Ressland	Barry Huber
Riverside tp (8). . . . . . TM	609 461-0284	Robert E Renshaw	Wm H Ruehmling	Michael F Chiaccio	Wm H Ruehmling	Michael Kranz	Thomas J Titto	Charles J Miller
Riverton b (3). . . . . . . MC	609 829-0120	David Styer Jr	....	Anna May Whitelock	....	A Charles Perkins	Thomas Gilbert	David I Wright
Rochelle Park tp (6) . . . MC	201 843-2266	Edward Bertsch	....	Irene McDermott	Philip J Galfo	Carmelo Dibartolo	Robert Diamond	Charles Lynch
Rockaway b (7). . . . . . . MC	201 627-2000	Robert H Johnson	Walter P Krich Jr	Ann M James	Walter P Krich Jr	Peter Baysa	Michael Bahnatka	Gilbert Graner
Rockaway tp§ (20). . . . . MC	201 627-7200	John Wojtaszek	Phyllis R Hantman	E Moran Jenins	Francis E McCudden	Art Crane	Steven J Dachisen	Ronald J McKinnon
Roseland b (5) . . . . . . MC	201 226-8080	Richard N Leonard	Gloria C Floyd	Gloria C Floyd	Gloria C Floyd	Jack Fallat	Walter R Critchett	William Howard
Roselle b (21) . . . . . . MC	201 245-5600	Elmer M Ertl	Vincent Belluscio	Johanna M Breden	V A Belluscio Jr	Robert Bloom	Vincent F Trolan	Thomas Nicholson
Roselle Park b (13) . . . MC	201 245-2300	Robert L Zeglarski	....	Jean Keenan	Jeanne Decker	Julius Swirz	Ben A Malaspina	Donald R Guarriello
Roxbury tp* (19). . . . . CM	201 584-7400	William Egbert	Robert F Casey	Carl White	Cecile Cole	Michael Brunson	George Fenske	....
Rumson b (8). . . . . . . MC	201 842-3300	Charles F Paterno	J Gary Sammon	J Gary Sammon	....	Bruce Kidd	John E Gaynor	William R Murphy Jr
Runnemede b (9) . . . . . MC	609 939-5161	David L Venella	....	Mary F Lafferty	David J Watson	Charles Romond	Vito Cimino	....
Rutherford b§ (19). . . . MC	201 939-0020	Barbara H Chadwick	....	Helen S Soroka	Edward Cortright	Charles Agel	William F Kraus	Peter Petronio
Saddle Brook tp (14) . . MC	201 843-7100	Raymond Santalucia	Harold C Marine	Dolores Johnson	Freda G Brett	Charles Cerone	Lars Olsen	Howard Boswell
Saddle River b (3) . . . . MC	201 327-2609	Walter R Ash Jr	....	Joanne Kwasniewski	Timothy M Tamblyn	William D'Elia	William J Smith	....
Salem (7) . . . . MC	609 935-0372	Kenneth R Lewis	....	John F McCarthy	David A Cawman	George Ahl	Louis Sullivan	Kenneth L Homan
Sayreville b (30) . . . . . MC	201 257-3200	John B McCormack	....	Margaret V Hahn	Wayne A Kronowski	Dennis Grobelny	Douglas A Sprague	Thomas Prusakowski
Scotch Plains tp* (21) CM	201 322-6700	Irene T Schmidt	Thomas E Atkins	Helen M Reidy	Dolores B Burns	Harry Messemer	Robert Luce	Ray D'Amato
Sea Girt b (3). . . . . . . MC	201 449-9433	Thomas Black	....	Helen B Brash	Helen B Brash	Albert Ratz	William Joule	Lawrence Duff
Sea Isle City† (3). . . . . CO	609 263-4461	Dominic C Raffa	....	Verna M Lynch	Gloria A Giampetro	John S Mazurie	Carl F Gansert	John H Fox
Secaucus t† (14). . . . . MC	201 863-2896	....	Philip J Kieffer	....	....	....	....	....
Shrewsbury b (3) . . . . MC	201 741-4200	Dorothy B Manson	....	Marlene Hotaling	Jane A Longo	Larry Johnson	Raymond Mass	Louis Longo
Somerdale b (6) . . . . . MC	609 783-6320	(not reporting)						
Somers Point (10) . . . . MC	609 927-9088	Frederick N Fontana	....	Mary C Lennie	Rosalie M Tebbs	Joseph Mackin	Lyn Bader	Howard Dill
Somerville b (12). . . . . MC	201 725-2300	Emanuel R Luftglass	Ralph D Sternadori	Ralph D Sternadori	Walter P Michaels	George Kavanaugh	Charles Niles	Edw R Westling III
South Amboy (8). . . . . . MC	201 727-4600	J Thomas Cross	Nicholas R Smolney	Natalie Brennan	William O'Leary	Francis Mulvey	Edward O'Leary	Richard M Muchanic
South Bound Brook b† (4). . . . . MC	201 356-0258	Stanley A Stavetski	....	Nicholas Rasnak	....	Jerome Bowers	Richard F Mignella	....
South Brunswick tp§ (17) . . . . MC	201 329-4000	Howard F Bellizio	Jerry A Bittner	Kathleen Thorpe	Joseph Rauch	....	Frank Simmons	Arthur Bifulco
South Orange Village tp (17) . . . . CO	201 762-6000	Bertrand Spiotta	Kenneth M Kroll	Kenneth M Kroll	John Mosca Jr	Pasquale Giordano	Fredrick Gayder	Arnold Knudsen
South Plainfield b (21) MC	201 754-9000	Michael English	....	William T DeSabato	Charles Haus	John R Cotone	Thomas Boyle	Julius Celentano
South River b† (14) . . . MC	201 257-1999	James W Genecki	W A Reichenbach	W A Reichenbach	Kathryn M Paprota	Stephen Kuzmack	George Cerekwas	....
South Toms River b† (4). . . . . MC	201 349-0403	Edward Mooney	....	Elizabeth Silvestri	Lucinda Dugan	....	Edward G Hughes	....
Sparta tp* (13). . . . . . CM	201 729-6174	Richard LaRuffa	David J Ferguson	Norma B Sisco	David J Ferguson	Howard Steepy	R Gordon Smith	James Mills
Spotswood b (8) . . . . . MC	201 251-3378	Wayne R Hamilton	Robert L Sabo	Ms R Pasterczyk	Ms J Gretch	Richard Drude	William Steindecker	Harvey L Lohr
Spring Lake Heights b (5). . . . . MC	201 449-3500	Frank E Adams	Frank B Horner	Dorothy C Gutierrez	Frank B Horner	John P Olesen	William D Fury	Frank Walton
Spring Lake b (4) . . . . MC	201 449-8920	Harry A Erbe	Theadore F Freeman	Theadore F Freeman	Mary Jane Sylvester	Edward V Willever	John M Sylvester	Robert A Pazienza
Springfield tp (14) . . . . MC	201 376-5800	Philip Feintuch	....	Helen Maquire	Barbara Thompson	Ted Johnson	George E Parsell	Walter Kozub
Stanhope b§ (4) . . . . . MC	201 347-0159	Michael Bender	Gary Kratz	Janice Martin	Gary Kratz	Thomas Donahue	Nicholas Grego	James Floyd
Stratford b (8) . . . . . . MC	609 783-0600	Frank W Stauss	....	Dorothy Carlson	Mary Jo Tate	Edward Herbert	Francis X Washart	Nancy Forsyth
Summit (21) . . . . MC	201 273-6400	Robert J Hartlaub	....	David L Hughes	Kenneth DeRoberts	J Douglas Bird	Frank Formichella	Carl J Bressan
Teaneck tp* (39). . . . . CM	201 837-1600	Bernard E Brooks	Werner H Schmid	Roslyn Endick	Gary Saage	Carl Anderson	Bryan E Burke	Milton S Robbins
Tenafly b (14). . . . . . . MC	201 568-6100	R K Van Nostrand	Richard O Griffith	Vivian M Purdy	Gerard V Leary	William Connolly	Nicodemus Amicucci	John Moscone
Tinton Falls b (8). . . . . MC	201 542-3400	Irving Cohen	Jerome S Reed	Jerome S Reed	Ann C Ervin	....	Wayne A White	Alexander G Nemeth
Totowa b (11) . . . . . . MC	201 956-1000	Samuel Cherba	....	S Del Vecchio	Robert Place	Allen Del Vecchio	Carmen Gaita	Paul Curcio
Trenton§ (92). . . . . . . MC	609 989-3000	Arthur J Holland	William J Guhl	Eugene Kalinowski	George Hannah	Daniel George	John Prihoda	Jos T Tuccillo Jr
Union tp (50). . . . . . . MC	201 688-2800	Michael T Bono	Thomas J Strapp	Nancy Derr	Joseph J Kmet	Edward Bachefski	John A Truhe	George J Salzmann
Union Beach b† (6) . . . MC	201 264-2277	Vincent L Farley	....	Mary Sabik	Eileen Schlemm	Joseph Koisa	Richard Trembley	Richard Pitcher
Union City† (56) . . . . . CO	201 348-5700	Arthur Wichert	....	Peter Leone	Evelyn Guerra	James W Moran	Herman Bolte	Michael Licameli
Upper Saddle River b (8). . . . . MC	201 327-2196	Merle C Worster	Rita M Hagen	Rita M Hagen	Merle C Worster	William Zabransky	Theodore Preusch	Jack Imperiale
Ventnor City (12). . . . . MC	609 823-7900	Scott E Becker	Joseph Verruni	Sandra M Biagi	Robert McLaughlin	William F Scull	Ronald W Fay	Charles Cianci
Verona tp§ (14) . . . . . MC	201 239-3220	James W Treffinger	Vincent A DiMauro	Vincent A DiMauro	Dorothy Trimmer	Joseph Gardner	William Wilkes	James Helb
Vineland§ (54) . . . . . . MC	609 691-3000	Joseph E Romano	Ronald P Sotak	Dolores Lopergolo	Joseph Leonardo	Biaggio Ciulla	Joseph Cassisi	C Thomas Kreck
Waldwick b (11) . . . . . MC	201 652-5070	Frank T McKenna	....	W Longson	Ms A M Portsmore	Joseph Agugliaro	Daniel Lupo	R Schmidt
Wall tp§ (19) . . . . MC	201 681-6300	Harry W Rash	Joseph N Ehret	Rita Fitterer	Betsy O'Toole	....	Leo Kubaitis	James White
Wallington b† (11). . . . MC	201 779-4879	Walter M Slomienski	....	Lorraine Klamerus	Joseph E Salko	Stephen Tomko	Edward Flejzor	William McNiff
Wanaque b (10) . . . . . MC	201 839-3000	Jud Colicchio	....	Dorothy Kuenzler	Ms C Spadaccini	Robert DeStaffen	David H Sisco	....
Washington (Morris) tp§ (11) . . . . MC	201 876-3315	Edward J Shields	Dianne S Gallets	Dianne S Gallets	Kevin Lifer	Mike Sabo	George Kluetz	Ralph DeFranzo
Washington (Warren) tp (4). . . . . MC	201 689-7200	Kenneth C Miller	....	Elizabeth H Opdyke	Arthur D Merrill	James Rush	John F Corrigan	....
Washington (Bergen) tp§ (10). . . . . MC	201 664-4404	Rudolph J Wenzel Jr	....	Julianna Zykoff	Jacqueline Do	Joseph Rinaldi	Justin Georgetti	Richard Koesel
Washington b* (6). . . . CM	201 689-3600	Joseph LaPrino	Alan M Fisher	Linda L Connelly	Alan M Fisher	Guy Burd	Anthony Terminelli	Alan M Fisher
Watchung b† (5) . . . . . MC	201 756-0080	Kenneth D Schmidt	....	Gladys Bartholomew	Gladys Bartholomew	Max P Weber	Richard R Ryan	Joseph Pagano
Wayne tp (46) . . . . . . MC	201 694-1800	Walter J Jasinski	John W Leidy	John R O'Brien	John Aitken	William Wiltshire	Robert Pringle	Anthony Buzzoni
Weehawken tp (13) . . . CO	201 867-1707	Stanley D Iacono	Richard F Turner	Theresa Ulrich	Rudolph Maurizi	Richard DeCosmis	Richard DeCosmis	Andrew Hogan
West Caldwell tp† (11) MC	201 226-2300	Robert L Reiher	Donald E West	Donald E West	Donald E West	Frank C Colavito	George E DeVaney	Kenneth F Matthews
West Deptford tp* (18) CM	609 845-4004	....	Raymond H Kromer	....	....	....	....	....
West Long Branch b (7) MC	201 229-1756	Frank Sorrentino	....	Mary F Gallagher	....	Frank Fasano	Ira E White	John F Schmitt
West Milford tp*† (23) CM	201 728-7000	Charles Slawinski	John T Terry	Kevin J Byrnes	Judith A Tiernan	B J McCaffrey	James Breslin	Andrew J Lycosky
West New York t† (39) CO	201 861-7000	Anthony M Defino	....	Raymond Gabriel	James F Langan	Robert Aiello	Herbert Haas	Mario Hernandez

Directory 1/10 continued — MUNICIPAL OFFICIALS IN ALL U.S. CITIES OVER 2,500[1]

City, 1980 population (000 omitted), form of government	Municipal phone number	Mayor	Appointed administrator	City clerk	Finance officer	Fire chief	Police chief	Public works director
NEW JERSEY (349) continued								
West Orange tp (41) MC	201 325-4200	Samuel A Spina	Marvin Corwick	Marie E Stopfer	Richard A Giuditta	Frank Capron	Edward M Palardy	John T McCann
West Paterson b (11) MC	201 345-8100	Alfred H Baumann	Alfred A Reda	Alfred A Reda	Andrew Carioti	Arnold Lijoi	George Furbacher	....
West Windsor tp§ (9) MC	609 799-2400	Stanley R Perrine	Edward C Madere	....	John J Hansen	....	Frank Cox	....
Westfield t (30) MC	201 232-8000	Ronald J Frigerio	John F Malloy	Joy Vreeland	James R Dickson	Walter J Ridge	James Moran	Edward A Gottko
Westville b† (5) MC	609 456-0030	Francis J Duer	Richard M Burr	Richard M Burr	Richard M Burr	John Flem	William J Bittner	William C Packer
Westwood b (11) MC	201 664-7100	Robert A Gardner	Joseph F Smith	Joseph F Smith	Eugene F Young	James D Hodges	John Cafaro	Robert Woods
Wharton b (5) MC	201 361-8444	T P Beirne	A P Guadagnino	A P Guadagnino	Jean Mench	Robert Omalley	Joseph Hornyok	F J Boyer
Wildwood (5) CO	609 522-2444	Earl B Ostrander	Marc Pfeiffer	Peter P Yecco	Stephen H Ritchie	Ernest Troiano	Ralph Sheets	Richard Harmon
Wildwood Crest b (4) CO	609 522-7788	John J Pantalone	....	Ethel A Filer	Charles Guhr	Gus Olson	Robert J Frederick	Frank J McCall
Willingboro tp* (40) CM	609 877-2200	Priscilla Anderson	John D Tegley	Lenore Stern	Sadie L Johnson	Norman Cheeseman	Robert A Rossell	Harry W McFarland
Wood-Lynne b (3) MC	609 962-8300	William M Terrell	....	Curtis Meyers	Alice E Meyers	Eric Schmidt	Wilmer D Wood	James Heffron
Wood-Ridge b (8) MC	201 939-0202	Herbert Gorab	Janet L Lynds	Janet L Lynds	Donald H Perlee	Thomas Bischoff	Paul G Haebler	Ellsworth Klotzbier
Woodbine b† (3) MC	609 861-2153	Ernest A Materio	....	Bea Eisenberg	Bea Eisenberg	Martin Bogushefsky	R Alexenberg	Seymour Benson
Woodbridge tp (90) MC	201 634-4500	Phil Cerria	....	Joseph V Valenti	John P Milano	....	Anthony O'Brien	Ralph P Barone
Woodbury (10) MC	609 845-1300	Richard L Skinner	Frederick K Bayer	Frederick K Bayer	Charles J Owens	Gregory Schaffer	F Dean Kimmel	Herbert H Hood
Woodbury Heights b (3) MC	609 848-2832	James J Master Jr	....	Frances Drill	Joan Maska	Donald W Steward	Thomas Reilly	Donald Ley Jr
Woodcliff Lake b (6) MC	201 391-4977	Bernard R Kettler	John T Doyle	Connie M Capodicasa	John T Doyle	Peter Van Riper	Dennis Winters	Edward Barboni
Woodstown b (3) MC	609 769-2200	Jan R Edwards	....	James M Edwards	James R Hackett	Jeffrey Mortimer	Walter J Simpkins	....
Wrightstown b (3) MC	609 723-4450	G Allen Miller	....	Linda Miller	Elizabeth Kirby	Larry Nixon	James Nash Jr	....
Wyckoff tp (16) MC	201 891-7000	J Gordon Stanley	Robert J Shannon Jr	Theresa M Moffa	Robert J Shannon Jr	John Myer	Donald D Stapleton	Donald G Hein
NEW MEXICO (42)								
Alamogordo* (24) CM	505 437-4530	Henry P Pacelli	Dan Malone	Angie J Rahn	Eduardo A Pacheco	Homer Houghtalin	Homer Houghtalin	Jon M Foulds
Albuquerque§ (332) MC	505 766-7550	Harry Kinney	Frank A Kleinhenz	Angie Ludi	Arthur A Blumenfeld	Leonard Ortega	Elroy C Hansen	Carl Rodolph
Artesia (10) MC	505 746-3593	Ernest C Thompson	Thomas L Howell	Edwin S Zendel	Edwin S Zendel	R H Castleberry	Bob Bishop	....
Aztec*† (6) CM	505 334-9456	Ken Good	Rolfe H Wagner	Dee Cornett	Charles Jordan	William Smith Jr	William Smith	....
Bayard v† (3) MC	505 537-3327	David C Conway	....	Jovita G Gonzales	....	Paul Martinez	A C Chon Manzano	Eddie Sedillos
Belen t* (6) CM	505 864-8221	Boleslo Lovato	Bonnie Lopez	Bonnie Lopez	Mildred Garley	Frank Ortega	Danny J Gabaldon	Joe Pena
Bernalillo t† (3) MC	505 867-2304	Michael W Foster	....	Ruth Lopez	....	Michael Carroll	Carlos Pino	Richard Arellanes
Bloomfield (5) MC	505 632-8096	Erva Lynch	Shirley Willis	Patsy Milligan	....	George Duncan	William Trotter	Jim Moore
Bosque Farms v† (3) MC	505 869-2358	Sharon M Eastman	Sharon M Eastman	Ahnawake Saunier	Ahnawake Saunier	Walter Shoemaker	Carl R Chamberlain	....
Carlsbad*† (25) CM	505 887-1191	Walter Gerrells	Claude F Tabor	Claude F Tabor	Wanda Baxter	Ronald Hopkins	Charles A Galloway	Harold May
Clayton t* (3) CM	505 374-8331	Jimmie Butt	Eli Garcia	Ann Porter	Ann Porter	Dwayne Massey	Roy C Carter	Eli Garcia
Clovis* (31) CM	505 762-2921	Frank A Murray Jr	Donald E Clifton	Roy H Hagler	Roy H Hagler	Bill Dunn	Caleb Chandler	Carl F Caspers
Corrales v (3) MC	505 897-0502	Thomas N Gentry	....	Carol Paradiso	Karen C Kegler	Gayle Gentry	Benjie Torres	....
Deming§ (10) MC	505 546-8848	Lloyd Pratz	John Strand	John Strand	John Strand	Fred Rossiter	C C Gray	James Harris
Espanola* (7) CM	505 753-2377	Consuelo S Thompson	Vidal N Martinez	Connie M Marquez	....	Terry Norris	....	Rupert Sanchez
Eunice (3) MC	505 394-2576	Ross L Robinson	....	Harriet P Reed	....	Clayton Wooten	Harlon Howell	....
Farmington* (31) CM	505 327-7701	Dee J Montano	William Manchester	Joyce G Harris	Pete McArthur	Al Conners	Calvin Shields	Robert Metzler
Gallup t* (18) CM	505 863-6871	Frank Colaianni	Ms Dani Frye	Dorothy Radosevich	Helen Kirk	Alfred Abeita	Frank Gonzales	G W Petranovich
Grants* (11) CM	505 287-7927	Dave Zerwas	Frank King	Eileen M Martinez	Martin Allex	R C Evans	William Snodgrass	John Thompson
Hobbs* (29) CM	505 397-3636	Roy Showalter	Kenneth E Martin Jr	Joyce Edmiston	Ken Gleason	Bob Gallagher	Robert Bob Cheney	Russell Doss
Jal (3) MC	505 395-2222	Gary Blocker	....	Aubrey Hobson	Aubrey Hobson	Robert Holzhueser	Claude H Simpson	L W Ragain
Las Cruces* (45) CM	505 526-0280	David M Steinborn	Dana A Miller	Karen P Stevens	Bruno Zaldo	A F Gomez	A F Gomez	Duane Greenfield
Las Vegas* (14) CM	505 454-1401	Steve R Franken	Daniel R Dible	Carmen Gonzales	Kathy Tapia	Tony Ludi	Tom Gillespie	Pete Ortiz
Lordsburg*† (3) CM	505 542-3421	Stephen D Hill	....	Lupe P Rivera	....	Charles R Walter	....	....
Los Lunas v (4) MC	505 865-9689	Louis F Huning	Eloy E Romero	Eloy E Romero	Shirley Walker	Atilano Chavez	William L Place	....
Los Ranchos de Albuquerque v (3) MC	505 344-6582	Warren J Gray	....	Annette Stafford	....	Jose Jaramillo	Ken Kingsbury	....
Lovington* (10) CM	505 396-2884	Keith Spradlin	Bob G Carter	Peggy Mann	Peggy Mann	Jack Davis	Archie Cummingham	Merle A Kindel
Milan v (4) MC	505 285-6694	Toby Michael	....	Agnes S Lopez	Ray Garcia	George Knotts	Alfonso Martinez	Arthur Gomez
Portales* (10) CM	505 356-6662	D K Shafer	Jim Jeffers	Evelyn Wright	Evelyn Wright	Floyd Cooper	Ron Walker	....
Raton* (8) CM	505 445-9551	Donald M Romero	John W Elwell	Eva Mae Sproule	....	Donald Lark	John L Garcia	J Felipe Silva
Rio Rancho† (10) MC	505 892-6704	David E Bruening	....	Joanne McGlothlin	Joanne McGlothlin	John Kearney	Dencil Haycox	....
Roswell* (40) CM	505 622-5811	Peter R York	James B Whitford	Sarah L Carter	Sarah L Carter	Don W French	Steve S Wisniewski	John J Miscavage
Ruidoso (4) MC	505 258-4014	George P White	James L Hine	Leon Eggleston	James L Hine	Virgil Reynolds	Dick Swenor	Frank Potter
Santa Fe* (49) CM	505 982-4471	Louis R Montano	Jerry Manzagol	Helen Trujillo	David Sena	Tom Broome	Andrew Leyba	Edward Ortiz
Santa Rosa§ (2) MC	505 472-3404	Albert Campos	....	Rita F Sanchez	....	Gilbert Romero	Joe H Chavez	William Capps
Silver City t* (10) CM	505 538-3731	Lucy Stermer	Sal Morales Jr	Maria Elena Lozano	Maria Elena Lozano	Daniel C Vasquez	Thomas J Ryan	David R Lozano
Socorro† (8) MC	505 835-0241	Tony J Jaramillo	....	Valentin Anaya	Genevie Baca	Felipe Baca	Santiago Naranjo	James B Cole
Sunland Park (4) MC	505 589-7565	(not reporting)						
Taos t§ (3) MC	505 758-4282	Philip Lovato	Carlos M Miranda	Josephine Gonzales	Josephine Gonzales	Ed Nettleton	Jose Lucero	Walter Vigil
Truth or Consequences* (5) CM	505 894-6674	Andy Garcia	Quentin Drunzer	Evelyn B Renfro	....	Mike Tooley	John Sawyer	Alfred Armijo
Tucumcari* (7) CM	505 461-3451	Jene Klaverweiden	Peter F Rivera	Bernadette Becker	Peter F Rivera	Butch Hoskins	Santiago Santillan	....
Tularosa v (3) MC	505 585-2771	Ramona A Vallejos	....	Margaret G Gonzales	....	Ralph Vigil	Ernest Sanchez	....
NEW YORK (271)								
Akron v (3) MC	716 542-9636	Donald J Whiting	....	Raymond J Carlo Jr	Raymond J Carlo Jr	Brian W Murray	....	Robert P Gaddis
Albany (102) MC	518 462-8600	Thomas M Whalen III	....	T Garry Burns	Charles M Hemingway	Forrest Bruce	Thomas H Burke	Harry Maikels
Albion v (5) MC	716 589-9176	J Donald Brace Jr	....	Kathleen R Ludwick	....	Richard Tibbits	Walter Schutt	Jose Palacios
Alfred v (5) MC	607 587-9188	Robert Sloan	....	John C Bridge	John C Bridge	Douglas Barber	L E Jamison Jr	....
Amityville v† (9) MC	516 264-6000	Victor S Niemi	....	Gordon H Moore	Ronald D Burns	Raymond Fleming	James C Oliver	Charles Lazaro
Amsterdam (22) MC	518 841-4307	Mario Villa	....	Carolyn Caldwell	John Bintz	Anthony Baldine	Kenneth Trzaskos	Kenneth Korona
Ardsley v* (4) CM	914 693-1550	Marie J Stimpfl	Vincent Atalese	Mary Kamens	Lynne Schiraldi	James Macri	Stephen Blaha	Lydia L Dallis
Attica v (3) MC	716 591-0898	Dale L Slocum	....	Kathleen Sennott	Kathleen Sennott	William Lepsch	Daniel Norcross	William Mooney
Auburn* (33) CM	315 252-9531	Edward L Lauckern	Bruce L Clifford	Philip J Conboy	Leo G McGee	William D Maywalt	John T Costello	Michael D O'Neill
Avon v (3) MC	716 226-8118	Donald E Mastin	....	....	Norma K Stapley	Kevin Quinlan	Ronald E McAfee	Jerry L Rowe
Babylon v (12) MC	516 669-1212	Gilbert C Hanse	....	Audrey McIntyre	Marilyn T Dowd	Bill Froehlich	....	John McKeown
Baldwinsville v (6) MC	315 635-3521	Thomas J Doris	....	Janet St John	Donald F Colon	Thomas Perkins	Timothy D Paul	Claude Sykes
Ballston Spa v† (5) MC	518 885-5711	Bert C Grandin	....	Bernhard Puckhaber	Daniel Murray	James Thomas	Raymond McCarthy	George Wescott
Batavia* (17) CM	716 343-8180	Bruce R Tehan	Ira M Gates	Rebecca J Tiede	Ira M Gates	Ralph Hyde	David G Mullen	Dennis Larson
Bath v (6) MC	607 776-3811	Warren H Hopkins	....	Lois Warren	....	Spencer Longwell	Larry Barnes	W Neal Wrinkle
Bayville v (7) MC	516 628-1439	Victoria Siegel	....	Vera S Ellison	Victoria Siegel	Dwight McKinney	Joseph Rodgers	Mike Symanski
Beacon† (13) CO	914 831-0302	George F Tomlinson	....	Joseph Gallio	Joseph MacAvery	Peter Hackbart	William Ashburn	John E Joseph
Bellport v (3) MC	516 286-0327	Frank C Trotta	....	Robert L Hawkins	Gail M Brisson	....	....	....
Binghamton (56) MC	607 772-7000	Juanita M Crabb	Michael T Fiur	Margery F Conlon	Donald Freed	Edwin A Faughnan	John Sejan	Timothy Grippen
Blasdell v (3) MC	716 822-1921	Michael W McGuire	Francis Larosa	Francis Larosa	Francis Larosa	Michael Miller	Robert Palmer	Adalbert Rojek
Briarcliff Manor v* (7) CM	914 941-4800	Edward T Dorsey	Lynn M McCrum	Imogene N Fink	Elsa Colt	Joseph E Piazzi	Arthur W Johnson Jr	Anthony J Decesaris
Brighton t (36) MC	716 473-8800	Richard D Wiles	....	Edwin R Jeffries	Warren Deroo	....	Eugene Shaw	Robert D Evans

Directory 1/10 continued MUNICIPAL OFFICIALS IN ALL U.S. CITIES OVER 2,500[1]

City, 1980 population (000 omitted), form of government		Municipal phone number	Mayor	Appointed administrator	City clerk	Finance officer	Fire chief	Police chief	Public works director
NEW YORK (271) continued									
Brightwaters v (3)	MC	516 665-1280	Gregory M Gibson	....	Anna May Garbedian	Charles A Hughes	....	....	Michael Harrington
Brockport v (10)	MC	716 637-5300	(not reporting)						
Bronxville v* (6)	CM	914 337-6500	William J Murphy	James E Gordon	....	John Gallaway	....	Carl Steinmuller	Joseph Palumbo
Brookville v (3)	MC	516 626-1792	Michael P Galgano	Robert Kops	Norman Burkhardt	Norman Burkhardt	August Schneider	Chas Capobianco	Harold Dougherty
Buffalo (358)	MC	716 855-4200	James D Griffin	Joseph J Scinta	Charles L Michaux	Robert E Whelan	Frederick Langdon	John B Myers	John C Friedline
Camden v† (3)	MC	315 245-0560	Henry C Spellicy	....	....	Charlene M Phinney	Ronald Corcoran	Richard Paul	David O Barker
Canandaigua* (10)	CM	716 394-6230	Patricia Boland	Carl F Luft	Stuart E Moore	Stuart E Moore	James E Farrell	Patrick W McCarthy	Louis Loy
Canastota v (5)	MC	315 697-7559	Donald F Cerio Sr	....	Joyce K Gustin	....	....	John V James	Joseph C Capparelli
Canisteo v (3)	MC	607 698-4553	L Burnett Jones	....	Marion Campbell	Marion Campbell	Lewis Martin	Phillip H Earley	Clement Pierce
Canton v (7)	MC	315 386-2871	Richard Lobdell	....	Marlene Thompson	Charles Carvel	Oglierd Weiss	Robert Ames	Larry Bovay
Carthage v† (4)	CO	315 493-1060	C Robert Rich	....	M Linda Weir	....	Charles Hoffman	Vincent J Frank	Kenneth Lanning
Catskill v (5)	MC	518 943-3830	John R Sencabaugh	....	Carolyn S Pardy	Carolyn S Pardy	Richard Overbaugh	Gerald E Cosenza	Thomas V Porto
Cayuga Heights v (3)	MC	607 257-1238	F G Marcham	....	Anne M Krohto	Gordon B Wheeler	Francis Miller	Harlin R McEwen	John B Rogers
Cazenovia v† (3)	MC	315 655-3041	Edward R Clarke	....	Elizabeth Marshall	....	John Durfee	Ralph Lamaitis	Francis Van Deusen
Cedarhurst v (6)	MC	516 295-5770	Nicholas A Farina	....	Daryl Ann Smallwood	....	....	....	Thomas Cittadino
Chittenango v (4)	MC	315 687-3936	Robert D Evans	....	Theresa Vincelette	Mary L Cerruti	Robert Freunscht	Richard Carbery	Norman McGowan
Cobleskill v (5)	MC	518 234-3891	Leon E Wilson	....	Marion Byrnes	....	Richard Cooper	Alfred Toohig	Clarence Kilmer III
Cohoes (18)	MC	518 237-7811	Ronald Canestrari	....	Marion Archambeault	Steven Niedbalec	Raymond K Lamora	Michael Robich	Donald Senecal
Colonie v† (9)	MC	518 869-7562	Hebert B Kuhn	....	Marjorie L Smith	Marjorie L Smith	James Frank	....	Ralph Warren
Corinth v (3)	MC	518 654-2012	Donald E Williams	....	Warren Saunders Jr	Ellen L Mosher	David Woodcock	Richard Crannell	Calvin Butler
Corning (13)	MC	607 962-7922	Daniel L Killigrew	....	Rose M Stranges	Kathryn Ann Howland	Charles F Houper	Arthur R Webster	James Moore
Cornwall-on-Hudson v† (3)	MC	914 534-4200	Edward C Moulton Jr	....	Jean Scofield	Edward C Moulton Jr	Charles Tonneson	Richard Douglass	....
Cortland (20)	MC	607 756-6521	Francis Quinlan	....	Irving Rothenburg	Dominic Mazza	Brian H Wilbur	Philip A Cinquanti	Robert Spada
Coxsackie v (3)	MC	518 731-2718	Robert D Brennan	....	Nancy M Bender	Nancy M Bender	Richard Anable	Gerald Girard	Robert Baker
Croton-on-Hudson v* (7)	CM	914 271-4781	Roland H Bogardus	Richard F Herbek	Richard F Herbek	Richard J Campbell	Martin Fiorito	Reginald Lambruschi	Howard Davis
Dannemora v (4)	MC	518 492-7000	Ellison R Carter	....	Nancy A Mazdzer	Nancy A Mazdzer	Harlan Jarvis	Ellison R Carter	Wilmer Barber
Dansville v† (5)	MC	716 335-5330	C Arthur Seymour	....	Nancy J Wise	Nancy J Wise	Dennis Mahus	Marc Vernam	Robert Sawdey
Delhi v (3)	MC	607 746-2258	Marc E Guy	....	Faith E Olson	....	Glen Brady	Francis Harmer	Jerry Brown
Depew v (20)	MC	716 683-1400	Arthur J Domino	....	Dorothy F Wojtylak	Leonard Grzybowski	Francis W Roscoe	John Maccarone	Vincent Lipuma
Dobbs Ferry v§ (10)	MC	914 693-2203	Gisela S Knight	Margaret M Slavin	Matthew P Carey	Matthew P Carey	Daniel Minozzi	James F Neal	Margaret M Slavin
Dolgeville v (3)	MC	315 429-9775	Lawrence J Sugar	....	Elaine S Salek	Donna L Loucks	Gary Wormer	James F Grose	Robert Sheppard
Dunkirk† (15)	MC	716 366-0777	Edwin L Gregoreski	....	Diane Trezenski	Norman Woloszyn	James Mead	Edward J Mulville	Carl Heck
East Aurora v (7)	MC	716 652-6000	John V Pagliaccio	Jerry C Hiller	Roy Decker	....	Mark Hartley	James I Wilson	Roy W Lang
East Hills v (7)	MC	516 621-4251	William R Fleischer	Earl R Ueckerman	....	....	....	....	Angelo DeCurtis
East Rochester v (8)	MC	716 586-3553	Peter D Quinzi	....	Frances R Cimicata	....	Thomas Ross	S Clyde Bussey	Edward Van Thof
East Rockaway v (11)	MC	516 599-1211	Theodore S Reinhard	....	Phyllis J Rand	Phyllis J Rand	Guy Donza	....	Eugene Torborg
East Syracuse v (3)	MC	315 437-3541	(not reporting)						
East Williston v (3)	MC	516 746-0782	Ronald G McKay	....	Joane A Lauman	Richard S Camp	John Schroeder	....	Donald W Smith
Ellenville v* (4)	CM	914 647-7080	Edward Jacobs	Anthony Guiliano	Elaine F Rivenburg	Linda Polkowski	Bruce Distel	George A Sheeley	....
Elmira* (35)	CM	607 734-2044	Stephen J Fesh Jr	John C Gridley	Kathryn Peterson	Lawrence Kay	Edward T Hintz	Richard Wandell	William D Roe
Elmira Heights v (4)	MC	607 733-6589	Chester F Lunner	....	Esther B Ladd	....	David L Padgett	Henry C Oneill	Jean Cazorla
Elmsford v (3)	MC	914 592-6555	(not reporting)						
Endicott v (14)	MC	607 757-2411	Marion L Corino	....	Mary Jane Sedlack	Mary Jane Sedlack	Joseph F Scordino	Walter Ford Jr	Eugene A Kudgus
Fairport v (6)	MC	716 223-0313	Vincent G Kennelley	Donald Aures	Nancy E Loughney	Nancy E Loughney	Edmund P Welch Jr	Joseph Picciotti	Harold DeWitt
Falconer v (3)	MC	716 665-4400	Louis A Schrader	....	Zira P James	Zira P James	Glen Dickerson	....	Norman R Mosher
Fallsburg t* (10)	CM	914 434-8810	Brian Ingber	Patricia Davis	Rita Balbirer	Karen Wilson	....	Samuel Siegel	John Bowers
Farmingdale v (8)	MC	516 249-0093	Willis B Carman Jr	John Luck	John Luck	John Luck	Kenneth Tortoso	....	Rocco Posillico
Fayetteville v (5)	MC	315 637-9864	James H Lannon	....	Martin E Lynch	....	Robert Grevelding	Michael L Darmento	Robert Grevelding
Floral Park v (17)	MC	516 354-6200	Thomas J Hayden	....	John G Lernihan	....	Kenneth Fairben	Benjamn Kilichowski	John J Monz
Flower Hill v† (5)	MC	516 627-2253	Louis B Resnick	....	Margaret D Reynolds	Margaret D Reynolds	....	....	....
Fort Edward v (4)	MC	518 747-4023	Leonard J King	....	Daniel J Smatko	Daniel J Smatko	Olin Oliver	Mitchell Suprenant	Robert Dickinson
Fort Plain v† (3)	MC	518 993-4271	Richard Jacksland	....	....	Ruby Rockefeller	Louis Conrad	Harold Wilday	Anthony Ciani
Frankfort v† (3)	MC	315 894-8811	Joseph F Grates	....	Molly M Moracco	Joseph F Grates	James Sgroi	Alvin Taylor	John Migliore
Fredonia v (11)	CM	716 673-1325	Louis C Mancuso	....	James M Sedota	....	Ray Beach	Loren Pabody	Philip Dejoe
Freeport v (38)	MC	516 378-4000	William H White	....	Thomas Devincenzo	Thomas Molloy	Lester Fieldsa	Anthony Elar	David Lovejoy
Fulton (13)	MC	315 592-5390	Verner M Drohan	....	John F Walsh Sr	John Ciciarelli	Dean Stuber	Walter Hanlon	Raymond Graham
Garden City v§ (23)	MC	516 742-5800	William O Dwyer	Robt L Schoelle Jr	Robt L Schoelle Jr	Robt L Schoelle Jr	Andrew McCaffrey	Ernest J Cipullo	B J Gorman
Gates t (30)	TM	716 247-6100	Jack C Hart	....	Richard A Warner	John Asam	Richard Ambeau	Thomas Roche	John O Lathrop
Geneseo v (7)	MC	716 243-1177	Robert J Eaton	....	William E Genesky	William E Genesky	Dale Ludwig	....	James Kershner
Geneva* (15)	CM	315 789-2603	Frank J Cecere Jr	Steven R Sarkozy	Phyllis M Anastasi	David Stowell	Carlton Naegle	Herman J Garrow	Herbert R Anderson
Glen Cove (25)	MC	516 676-2000	Vincent A Suozzi	....	Rita Auciello	Frank Macedonia	Michael Maher	Maurice O'Brien	Robert Mangan
Glens Falls† (16)	MC	518 761-3800	Edward Bartholomew	....	Magdalena S Cafaro	Robert Newton	Edward Butler	James E Duggan	Nicholas Sciartelli
Gloversville† (18)	MC	518 773-7527	Eugene D Reppenhage	....	Mario S Balzano	William E Russo	Kenneth E Green	Michael J Gancarz	Brian O Rowback
Goshen v (5)	MC	914 294-6750	Stephen O Hopkins	....	Ronald J Bally Sr	Frederick W Nowak	James Felczak	John Egbertson	Conrad A Kroll Jr
Gouverneur v† (4)	MC	315 287-1720	Curran E Wade	Scott A Hudson	Sarah P Hatline	Sarah P Hatline	Charles Halpin	James Griffith	Ronald D Cochrane
Gowanda v (3)	MC	716 532-3353	David C Schaack	Jeffrey R Smith	Jeffrey R Smith	....	Nicholas C Crassi	Richard A Stitzel	....
Granville v (3)	MC	518 642-2640	Wayne D Williams	....	Richard T Roberts	....	James Buxton	Keith Sweet	John T O'Brien
Great Neck v† (9)	MC	516 482-0019	Howard C Miskin	....	Joseph G Rose	Joseph G Rose	....	....	Lawrence Dunn
Great Neck Estates v (3)	MC	516 482-8283	Stanley Cohen	....	Betty Gordon	....	....	Thomas J Monahan	William R Howe
Great Neck Plaza v† (6)	MC	516 482-4500	Allan J Gussack	....	Annette Bergman	Annette Bergman	....	....	Harry Perlman
Green Island v (3)	MC	518 273-2201	John J McNulty	John J Brown	Anne M Iannone	John R Lamb	Robert J Clancy	Thomas F McGivern	Henry C Carl
Greenwood Lake v (3)	MC	914 477-8110	John J Santy	....	Doris F Hawkins	James M Dougherty	Charles Spalthoff	Edward Baldesweiler	Mario Yannitty
Hamburg v (11)	MC	716 649-0200	Karl A Henry	....	Coleta A Glass	Coleta A Glass	Patrick McPartland	Francis L Conroy	Gerald Knoll
Hamilton v (4)	MC	315 824-1111	Edward K Vantine Jr	....	James P Morgan	James P Morgan	John Basher	James Tilbe	John Rathbone
Harrison (23)	MC	914 835-2000	Pat V Angarano	....	Joseph Fiore	Charles DeMicco	Daniel E Berry	William Harris	James Monteiro
Hastings-on-Hudson v* (9)	CM	914 478-3400	Frances MacEachron	Neil P Hess	Mary Callas	Neil P Hess	Robert Schnibbe	Joseph Marsic	Edmund Maleska
Haverstraw v (9)	MC	914 429-5413	Frank J Haera	....	Deborah P Smith	Alice Facciola	Vincent T Ryan Sr	Michael Holland	Ralph Naples
Hempstead v (40)	MC	516 489-3400	George Milhim	David L Stewart	David L Stewart	Donald M Hollman	Lester Arsell	Thomas H Scott	Joseph A Franco
Herkimer v† (8)	MC	315 866-3303	Charles P Patterson	Philip R Streeter	Victoria Baggetta	Victoria Baggetta	James English	Robert B Hart	Philip R Streeter
Highland Falls v† (4)	MC	914 446-3400	Benedict J Eazzetta	....	John E Bourke	John E Bourke	John J Gunza	Linwood Rhodes Jr	John J Gunza
Hilton v (4)	MC	716 392-4144	Larry Gursslin	James Ingham	Janet Surridge	....	Steven Speer	....	George Sheffield
Homer v (4)	MC	607 749-3322	Harry A Calale	....	Ms A W Jebbett	Ms A W Jebbett	Donald Butler	....	Carleton G Thiel
Hoosick v† (4)	MC	518 686-7072	Donald S Bogardus	....	Nancy Taber	Nancy Taber	Donald McCabe	William Chapones	John Cuddihy
Hornell† (10)	MC	607 324-1044	Richard L Dunning	....	Neil C Crandall	Thelma A Pelych	James Mehlenbacher	Mark Whitman	John McAnany
Horseheads v* (7)	CM	607 739-5691	Robert G Chapman	Daniel Ammerman	John Wayne Bowers	....	Richard Sullivan	Robert Hendershott	Ernest Jansen
Hudson (8)	MC	518 828-1030	Michael Yusko Jr	....	Michael F Troy	Vincent J Kenney	James A Coons	John C Halloran	Ludwig Polidor
Hudson Falls v† (7)	MC	518 747-5426	Morris A Nassivera	....	Marie E Philo	Marie E Philo	Richard Sarazen	Rudy Stautner	George Chadwick

Directory 1/10 continued — MUNICIPAL OFFICIALS IN ALL U.S. CITIES OVER 2,500[1]

City, 1980 population (000 omitted), form of government		Municipal phone number	Mayor	Appointed administrator	City clerk	Finance officer	Fire chief	Police chief	Public works director
NEW YORK (271) continued									
Ilion v† (9)	MC	315 895-7449	David L Wickersham	Charles P Haggerty	Paul L Miller	Paul L Miller	Charles Schierholtz	Lloyd Wadsworth	James Rowland
Irondequoit t (58)	MC	716 467-8840	Eugene C Mazzola Jr	....	E Ann Long	Lawrence R Merritt	John Holtz	William H Frey	Brad Upson
Irvington v† (6)	MC	914 591-7070	Reginald F Marra	....	John J Irwin	John J Irwin	Nicholas Gasparre	James W Mondelli	Thomas E Depaoli
Island Park v (5)	MC	516 431-0600	Michael A Parente	....	Harold J Scully	Veronica Donohue	Laborio S Dangelo	....	Michael Masone
Ithaca (29)	MC	607 272-1713	John C Gutenberger	....	Joseph A Rundle	Joseph Spano	Charles Tuckerman	James Herson	Peter Novelli
Jamestown (36)	MC	716 661-2200	Steven B Carlson	....	Shirley A Bratt	Douglas M Anderson	William L Baglia Jr	Richard Ream	Jack O Thompson
Johnson City v (17)	MC	607 729-2296	(not reporting)						
Johnstown (9)	MC	518 762-3911	Donald F Murphy	....	Constance L Kesner	Frank S Kovarik	Edward W Heberer	James L Cook	Chas R Ackerbauer
Kenmore v (18)	MC	716 873-5700	Arthur A Nist	....	Phyllis G Higgins	Phyllis G Higgins	Gary J Armstrong	Elmer A Arnet	Charles J Sottile
Kings Point v (5)	MC	516 482-7872	Michael C Kalnick	....	Anita O Nidel	Anita O Nidel	....	Peter Kelly	Charles Angelo
Kingston (24)	MC	914 331-0080	Peter Mancuso	....	Louis F DeCicco	Walter Gardecki	William J Schreiber	Julius M Glassman	Jay Hogan
Lackawanna (23)	MC	716 827-6444	Thomas E Radich	Charles Barone	Gerald S Depasquale	Robert C Marciniak	John Baran	Joseph Deren	Anthony Collareno
Lake Grove v (10)	MC	516 585-2000	Lillian B Griffin	....	Mary C Brady	George A Davis	....	....	Douglas Colino
Lake Success v* (2)	CM	516 482-4411	Reuben L Kershaw	John Giordano	Christine A Reed	John Giordano	....	John Haeselin	George Hislop
Lakewood v† (4)	MC	716 763-8557	Anthony C Caprino	....	J Parker Swanson	Patricia B Moran	Jackson W Knowlton	James L Young	Wayne Tyler
Lancaster v (13)	MC	716 683-3100	Burt T Lyon	....	Rosemary Babcock	Burt T Lyon	Gerald A Smith	William E Hastrich	Richard C Bulman
Lansing v† (3)	MC	607 257-0424	Ann Furry	....	....	....	....	....	....
Larchmont v (6)	MC	914 834-6230	Miriam Curnin	....	Barbara Wood	Carmine DeLuca	Malcolm Whittemore	A V Lowman	F F Kellogg Jr
Lawrence v† (6)	MC	516 239-4600	Stanley D Kahn	Peter W Overs	Peter W Overs	Peter W Overs	....	....	Michael Perone Jr
Le Roy v§ (5)	MC	716 768-2527	Raymond Yacuzzo	Leonard Iannello	Leonard Iannello	Leonard Iannello	W Sidney Horgan	Samuel Steffenilla	Kermit Arrington
Lewiston v† (3)	MC	716 754-8271	Marilyn Toohey	....	June Morrison	June Morrison	William Kilmer	Lawrence Stuart	Ernest Murdoch
Liberty v* (4)	CM	914 292-6820	Ida Frankel	Jeffrey A Carmen	Bernice Nicholson	....	Donald Kortwright	Edward A Gisley	Donald Watson
Lindenhurst v (27)	MC	516 957-5700	Thomas H Kost	....	Robert K Sweeney	Louis Nemeth	Alex Marold	....	Frank Asselta
Little Falls (6)	MC	315 823-2400	(not reporting)						
Liverpool v (3)	MC	315 457-3441	James L Moore	....	Elaine B Miles	....	James F Galli	Raymond H Piper	Harold F Preston Sr
Lloyd Harbor v† (3)	MC	516 423-9044	William A McAneny	....	Irene K Alexander	Irene K Alexander	....	Ralph A Hummel	Arnold B Hedlund
Lockport (25)	MC	716 439-6667	Thomas C Rotondo Jr	....	Kenneth F Anderson	James W Ashcraft Jr	Thomas J Darroch	J Paul Leyden	William J Gerner
Long Beach* (34)	CM	516 431-1000	....	Edwin L Eaton	Frieda Levi	Sal Lombardi	Herbert Goldstein	Sol Barnett	Joseph P Hurley
Lowville v (3)	MC	315 376-6711	(not reporting)						
Lynbrook v (20)	MC	516 599-8300	William P Geier	....	A J Schuermann	Joseph P Larocco	John Crowley	Frank F Kehr	Frank Hillgardner
Lyons v (4)	MC	315 946-4531	John J Dashney	....	Corrine A Kleisle	Corrine A Kleisle	Arthur Schutt Sr	John S Lese	Charles Bowers Jr
Malone v (8)	MC	518 483-4570	James Auger	....	Elizabeth Bessette	Richard R Robare	....	Richard Brown	William Handly
Malverne v (9)	MC	516 599-1200	S R Morrow	....	William H Gaddis	William H Gaddis	Richard Lang	Raymond Garrigan	Al Severinsen
Mamaroneck v* (18)	CM	914 381-5500	Suzi Oppenheimer	Joseph P Fraioli	Leonard M Verrastro	Leonard M Verrastro	Dan Smyth	Joseph Del Bianco	Walter Webber
Manlius v† (5)	MC	315 682-9171	Angelo Albanese	....	Mary Jane Mercier	Mary Jane Mercier	Paul Whorrall	Thomas C Whorrall	Elvin C Hodge
Manorhaven v (5)	MC	516 883-7000	James F Mattei	....	Oliver J Longden	....	....	....	Joseph Nittolo
Massapequa Park v (20)	MC	516 798-0244	Robert S Thompson	William H Applegate	....	....	....	....	William E Colfer
Massena v (13)	MC	315 769-6924	Arsen Markarian	....	Sandra A Smith	Joseph F Trombino	Alex Krywanczyk	Dale D Wright	R D Cross
Mechanicville (6)	CO	518 664-4521	(not reporting)						
Medina v† (6)	MC	716 798-0710	Marcia B Tuohey	Emerson B Carlton	E Margaret Slack	....	Dell C Stork	Homer H Phillips	Edward Houseknecht
Menands v (4)	MC	518 434-2922	Thomas A Gibbs	....	William J Jones	William J Jones	Richard Rogozinski	Francis Kemprowski	Clyde Henderson
Middletown (21)	MC	914 343-4189	Richard A Hutchings	....	Douglas B Eaton	Sandra Kaminski	Merritt Winner	Harold Weigele	Alfred A Fusco Jr
Mineola v (21)	MC	516 746-0750	Edward S Smith	....	Richard M Devoe	Richard M Devoe	Albert Angelos	....	William d'Avanzo
Minoa v (4)	MC	315 656-3100	Donald C Crossett	....	Loretta I Sturick	....	David Van Marter	Leo N Capria Jr	Gordon Teska
Mohawk v (3)	MC	315 866-4312	(not reporting)						
Monroe v (6)	MC	914 782-8341	William E Trimble	....	Virginia T Carey	Marcella Hopwood	David Board	Andrew Margillo	Michael Mancino
Monticello v* (6)	CM	914 794-6130	Louis Harmin	Louis Bernstein	Lucille Weiler	Phil Giustra	William Culligan	Roger Bisland	Chester Williams
Morrisville v (3)	MC	315 684-3214	(not reporting)						
Mount Kisco v* (8)	CM	914 241-0500	Ferdinand Vetare	John N Crary	John N Crary	Carmen Defrancesco	Anthony Prigitano	William Nelligan	Howard L Zane
Mount Morris v (3)	MC	716 658-4160	L Richard Provino	Lois J Sciotti	Lois J Sciotti	Lois J Sciotti	Donald Taber	Charles D Pasquale	Joseph Muscarella
Mount Vernon (67)	MC	914 668-2200	Thomas E Sharpe	....	Ronald Iaboni	Peter Pucillo	Joseph Hammond	Anthony J Sarvaideo	Frederick Cardillo
Munsey Park v (3)	MC	516 365-7790	Louise V Reebel	....	Jacquelyn W Wright	Jacquelyn W Wright	....	....	....
Muttontown v (3)	MC	516 364-2240	George Henning	....	Barbara W Errett	....	....	....	....
New Hempstead v (4)	MC	914 354-8100	(not reporting)						
New Hyde Park v (10)	MC	516 354-0022	William G Gill	....	Jeanette Mosca	Julius Caccopola	....	....	Edward Bruhl
New Paltz v (5)	MC	914 255-0130	Robert I Remsnyder	....	Steve Ruelke	Steve Ruelke	David Butler	Charles Bogdanowicz	John W Logan
New Rochelle* (71)	CM	914 632-2021	Leonard C Paduano	C Samuel Kissinger	Angela LaRocca	Richard Devine	Donald A Baxter	Michael J Armiento	William Costa
New York City (7071)	MC	212 566-5700	Edward I Koch	....	David Dinkins	Philip Michael	Joseph E Spinnato	Benjamin Ward	Robert M Litke
New York Mills v (4)	MC	315 736-9212	John Pietryka	....	Hazel Topor	Edmund Waitr	Ronald Roman	Donald Wolanin	Walter Czajkowski
Newark v (10)	MC	315 331-4750	James E Praino	....	William J Maddock	....	James E Sadler	Edward Hethcoat	Steven Vanderbrook
Newburgh* (23)	CM	914 565-3333	Joan M Shapiro	Matthew B Galligan	Marlene A Koisch	Hargovind S Patel	James A Barry	Christopher Gershel	Thomas Shafer
Niagara Falls* (71)	CM	716 278-8000	Michael O'Laughlin	Nicholas Marchelos	Elsie Paradise	Leonard Bartos	Kenneth Bowser	Anthony C Fera	George Morreale
North Syracuse v§ (8)	MC	315 458-0900	Russell R Rhea	Douglas H Shupe	....	....	Michael Grillo	Robert Newman	Douglas G Goettel
North Tarrytown v (8)	MC	914 631-0113	Philip E Zegarelli	....	Filomena Fallacaro	Irene Amato	Larry Kosilla	Richard Spota	John Biros
North Tonawanda (36)	MC	716 693-0451	Elizabeth C Hoffman	....	George D Maziarz	Leslie Stolzenfels	Joseph J Belczak	Frank Malone	Gary J Franklin
Northport v (8)	MC	516 261-7502	Peter J Nolan	....	Dorothy Dugan	Dorothy Dugan	Bruce Berglund	Robert A Howard	....
Norwich (8)	MC	607 334-6001	Casey Jones	....	Gary Clark	Gary R Clark	Richard Phillips	Gary Follett	Thomas J Natoli
Nyack v† (6)	MC	914 358-0548	Alexander Caglione	....	Joseph Guerrieri	Michael Condello	Howard G Williams	Thomas G Coffey	Andrew G Kolb Jr
Ocean Beach v§† (..)	MC	516 835-5940	Thomas J Schwarz	W Thomas Potter	Nancy Balarezo	....	William J Wirostek	Joseph Loeffler	....
Ogdensburg* (12)	CM	315 393-6100	Richard G Lockwood	Daniel Fitzpatrick	Mary K Fredericks	S Erno Moore	A Walter Read	Robert J Cutt	Richard Marshall
Old Westbury v (3)	MC	516 626-0800	(not reporting)						
Olean (18)	MC	716 372-2200	William O Smith	....	John W Orcutt	Theodore Luty	C James Young	Michael S Luty	Robert D Carr
Oneida (11)	MC	315 363-4800	Jeannette E Kidd	....	Grace Perretta	Joan Cukierski	Robert Burgdoff	John C McClellan	W Robert Mayer
Oneonta (15)	MC	607 432-6450	James F Lettis	....	Michael W Lisa	Paul C Kogut	Francis R Russo	John J Donadio	Richard C Olton
Orchard Park v (4)	MC	716 662-9327	George F Knaisch	....	Carol A Stressinger	....	....	....	Nicholas Zilak
Ossining v* (20)	CM	914 941-1005	Joseph G Caputo	Geo R Kupchynsky	Lester M Kimball	Stephen T Tavano	Donald L Apostolico	Ronald A Goldfarb	Michael R Sterlacci
Oswego (20)	MC	315 342-5600	William S Cahill Jr	William J McCarthy	Robert Riggio	Paul Miller	Donald Beauchene	Floyd Kunzwiler	James A Matteson
Owego v (4)	MC	607 687-3555	Gertrud E Baker	....	Dora Marie Ritter	Dora Marie Ritter	Donald Warner	Robert Williams	Roy E Hulbert
Palmyra v† (4)	MC	315 597-4849	Mary Lou Wilson	....	Ethel B Johnson	Phyllis G Dickinson	David McGuire	Donald Henry	....
Patchogue v (11)	MC	516 475-4300	Norman Lechtrecker	....	Rose Marie Berger	Gerard R Nocita	Thomas Ferrante	....	....
Peekskill* (18)	CM	914 737-3400	George E Pataki	Joseph J Seymour	Joseph J Seymour	Patrick J Hayes	Dominic Dipierro Jr	Walter D Kirkland	John Faile
Pelham v§ (7)	MC	914 738-2015	Paul A Daronco	....	Claire Ferrante	....	Louis Ruggiero	Anthony Quatroni	....
Pelham Manor v§ (6)	MC	914 738-2030	John M Deakins	Richard R Blessing	Richard R Blessing	James B Huff	P Mancuso	P Zambernardi	Richard R Blessing
Penn Yan v (5)	MC	315 536-3015	R Bruce LeClaire	....	Shirley Condella	John Banach	Bart Winslow	Raymond K Stewart	Richard G Yonge
Perry v (4)	MC	716 237-2216	Terrence Murphy	....	Deborah J Shepard	Deborah J Shepard	Bruce Billings	Gary G Jurkowski	Roger T Bauer
Plattsburgh (21)	MC	518 563-7701	Carlton E Rennell	....	Aline G Cote	John J Lang	James E Duffany	Leo H Connick	Joseph L Pelkey
Pleasantville v* (7)	CM	914 769-1900	John Farrington	John S St Leger	Beatrice Wienkoop	Kathryn Gale	....	Calvin H Manning	Gilbert C Wienkoopm
Port Chester v* (24)	CM	914 939-2200	Peter Iasillo	Michael D Ritchie	Richard Falanka	Arnold Bernfeld	Harry Hayes	John Grosse	....
Port Jefferson v (7)	MC	516 473-4724	Harold Sheprow	....	Gordon Thomsen	Helen Ward	Richard Byrnes	Francis Burke	Michael Verruto
Port Jervis (9)	MC	914 856-2312	E Arthur Gray	....	James J Hinkley	James J Hinkley	Michael Innella	Frank A Masanotti	Richard L Onofry

Directory 1/10 continued **MUNICIPAL OFFICIALS IN ALL U.S. CITIES OVER 2,500[1]**

City, 1980 population (000 omitted), form of government		Municipal phone number	Mayor	Appointed administrator	City clerk	Finance officer	Fire chief	Police chief	Public works director
NEW YORK (271) continued									
Port Washington North v (3)	MC	516 883-5900	T J Pellegrino	....	Ms D Levine	Milton Rabinowitz	....	....	....
Potsdam v (11)	MC	315 265-7480	Paul J Claffey	Victor Bortnick	Margaret Robinson	Mary M Welch	Steven E Miles	Clinton R Matott	Roger Fadden
Poughkeepsie* (30)	CM	914 431-8500	Thomas Aposporos	William J Theysohn	Patricia Havens	Herbert C Bennett	James Davison	Stewart G Bowles	John DeZuane
Ravena v (3)	MC	518 756-8233	(not reporting)						
Rensselaer (9)	MC	518 462-9511	Joseph E Harrigan	....	John W Yonkers	John J Dwyer	James M West	James Stark	Joseph I Forcinella
Rhinebeck v (3)	MC	914 876-7015	Peter F Sipperley	....	Valerie Kilmer	Valerie Kilmer	Robert Ellsworth	Peter F Sipperley	John Marks
Rochester* (242)	CM	716 428-7000	Thomas P Ryan Jr	Peter A Korn	William McDonough	Vincent J Carfagna	Leonard Heuther	Delmar Leach	James E Malone
Rockville Centre v (25)	MC	516 766-0300	Donald F Browne	William H Cook	William H Cook	William H Cook	John A Nanavrakis	Alfred L Shull	Warren R Brenner
Rome† (44)	MC	315 336-6000	Carl J Eilenberg	....	Quintin E Barry	William A Glasso	William L Castor	Joseph A Grande	Frank Clark
Rye* (15)	CM	914 967-5400	Fred J Hunziker Jr	Francis J Culross	Michael J Rich	Harold J Aspesi	Walter Roode	Anthony J Schembri	Philip J Mercier
Rye Brook (8)	MC	914 939-0077	(not reporting)						
Sag Harbor v (3)	MC	516 725-0222	Ferdinand Runco	Joan Schoen	Joan Schoen	Joan Schoen	Brian Gilbride	John Harrington	Patrick Kern
Salamanca (7)	MC	716 945-4620	John F Gould	....	Kenneth W McClune	Linda J Rychcik	Howard Barton	Albert Agnelli	Anthony Pascarella
Sands Point v (3)	MC	516 883-3044	Edward N Madison	....	Evan Stephens	John A Burns	....	Michael Connolly	....
Saranac Lake v* (6)	CM	518 891-4150	Timothy L Jock	E J Lawless	Marilyn Clement	Marilyn Clement	Donald Duso	Gilles Miron	Steven Natoli
Saratoga Springs (24)	MC	518 587-3550	Ellsworth Jones	....	Edward Valentine	John T Butler	John Lanzara	Peter Pemberton	Thomas G McTygue
Saugerties v (4)	MC	914 246-2321	Robert M Moser	....	Muriel T McIntosh	Barbara Griffis	Joseph Doyle	William B Kimble	Edward Haines
Scarsdale v* (18)	CM	914 723-3300	Seymour Sims	Lowell J Tooley	Lowell J Tooley	David Coldrick	Raymond J White	Donald Ferarro	Peter J Woodcock
Schenectady (68)	MC	518 382-5000	Karen B Johnson	Anthony G Insogna	Katherine Ackerman	Bruno L Pezzano	Ralph Ruggiero	Richard G Nelson	Paul Cassillo
Scotia v† (7)	MC	518 374-1071	John F Ryan Jr	....	Catherine H Hurley	....	Donald W Wayand	William J Benosky	William J Adams
Sea Cliff v (5)	MC	516 671-0080	Norman Parsons	....	Nancy H Rose	Leo Hesselman	Jim Martin	Edwin R Neice	Edwin Rubick
Seneca Falls v (7)	MC	315 568-8107	Robert G Freeland	....	....	Scott A Smith	Alex Carissimi	A J Casamassima	Richard Lapp
Sherrill* (3)	CM	315 363-2440	James E Dunn	Wallace G Glasgow	Sidney Burgess	Kathryn B Conniff	Thomas White	Francis S Broski	Larry Herzog
Sidney v (5)	MC	607 563-3571	Elwood F Davis	....	Christine R Davis	....	Joseph A Maddalone	E Charles Bessett	Harlan Stringer
Silver Creek v† (3)	MC	716 934-3240	George S Borrello	....	Cynthia Hoisington	....	Harold Anger Jr	John M Yannie	John B Wright
Skaneateles v (3)	MC	315 685-3440	Carl H Fisher	....	Sally L Darrow	Sally L Darrow	Paul D Murphy	William M Angyal	John O Abbott
Sloan v† (5)	MC	716 897-1560	Bernard Wojtkowiak	....	Roslyn T Surdej	Roslyn T Surdej	Lawrence Dubaj	....	Anthony Sisti
Sloatsburg v (3)	MC	914 753-2727	Samuel J Abate	....	T F Bollatto Jr	T F Bollatto Jr	Michael Yorke	James A Ballard Jr	Thomas B Smith
Solvay v (7)	MC	315 468-1679	W L Campagnoni	....	P Mortas Piperno	Michael L Pestillo	Donald Mosher	Rocco Femano	Luke Cardone
South Glens Falls v (4)	MC	518 793-1455	Harry Van Scoy	....	Joyce M Leombruno	Joyce M Leombruno	James Boucher	....	John J Donohue
South Nyack v (4)	MC	914 358-0287	Raymond G Esposito	....	Mary G Martini	Bradford Hartwick	Dana Weishaar	Robert Booth	Richard Ambrey
Southampton v† (4)	MC	516 283-0247	Roy L Wines Jr	....	George A Andrews	Alison M Burrell	Herbert Raynor	Donald J Finlay	Richard L Fowler
Spencerport v† (3)	MC	716 352-4771	John G Hubbard	....	Gary R Boughter	....	Dale Wohlers	....	James C Bleier
Spring Valley v (21)	MC	914 352-1100	(not reporting)						
Springville v (4)	MC	716 592-4936	J James Neff	....	Gail M Riggs	Gail M Riggs	Donald Blakely	....	....
Suffern v† (11)	MC	914 357-2600	Joseph Savarese	....	Virginia Menschner	Lawrence Alberts	Harold Dawson	Richard Hasbrouck	Donald Grosso
Syracuse (170)	MC	315 473-2850	Lee Alexander	Kenneth Mokrzycki	Robert Visser	Eugene Marjinsky	Thomas Hanlon	Thomas Sardino	Vito Sciscioli
Tarrytown v§ (11)	MC	914 631-1106	Peter Barbella	Gennaro J Faiella	Louise E Camilliere	Gerald Barbelet	Robert Stiloski	Robert Lipsky	Martin Annicchiarico
Thomaston v (3)	MC	516 482-3110	Charles Betz	....	Gladys M Landau	....	....	....	William R Howe
Ticonderoga v (3)	MC	518 585-7404	Virginia R Smith	....	M McCormick	June Borho	Michael Parent	....	William E Rooker
Tonawanda (19)	MC	716 695-1800	David L Miller	....	James A Coogan	Alan P Minney	Jay R Ralph	Edward J Ringler	Ralph E Akins
Troy* (57)	CM	518 270-4401	William L Carley	John P Buckley	Joan A Piscitella	Joseph Mazzariello	William E Phoenix	William P Miller	Thomas M Murley
Tuckahoe v (6)	MC	914 961-3100	Philip D Tobin	....	Susan Ciamarra	Donald M Bonforte	Arthur Reid	Henry Norman	Anthony S Cacciola
Tupper Lake v (4)	MC	518 359-3341	Roger W Pickering	....	Kenneth Hollenbeck	Dean Lefebvre	Roger Demars	Rene Lavallee	Ronald Martin
Union t (61)	MC	607 754-2102	Richard H Miller	....	James L Hackett	Steven Lee Osser	....	....	....
Utica (76)	MC	315 798-3200	Louis D LaPolla	Alfred A Barbato	Ms P F Talerico	Thomas Nelson	Robert Manfredo	Benny Rotundo	Seth Cornish
Valley Stream v (36)	MC	516 825-4100	Ralph P Greco	....	Craig Weeden	James A Olsen	Neil Wallach	....	Michael Pender
Voorheesville v (3)	MC	518 765-2692	Richard Lennon	....	Judith A Gray	....	....	....	....
Walden v* (6)	CM	914 778-2177	Marcy L Sperry	David R Heacock	Nancy Mitchell	May L Bucklen	William Dunn	Harold Brilliant	T Williamson
Walton v (3)	MC	607 865-4358	Burtis W Budine	....	Doris P Rowell	Doris P Rowell	Robert Lang	Melvin Woodin	Percy Budine
Wappingers Falls v (5)	MC	914 297-8773	J Donald Synnet	....	Leo D Lowney	Anthony V Campilii	Francis Farrell	....	Fred Sidote
Warsaw v (4)	MC	716 786-2120	Robert B Brown	....	Ms C Eccleston	Ms C Eccleston	Jack Fisher	Douglas Brooks	Gerrard Miller
Warwick v (4)	MC	914 986-2031	Nicholas Papaceno	....	Carole Paffenroth	Linda Carr	....	Russell Granger	Carl Quackenbush
Waterloo v (5)	MC	315 539-9131	Lee Patchenn	....	Roscoe Bartran	Roscoe Bartran	William Herman	Doyle L Marquart	Robert McGhan
Watertown* (28)	CM	315 788-0722	T Urling Walker	Karl Amylon	May A Coleman	Douglas Danforth	Ronald Damon	John R Cascanette	William T Morris Jr
Watervliet* (11)	CM	518 270-3800	J Leo O'Brien	Michael E Gilchrist	Paul S Murphy	John P Heid	Edward J McCarthy	Francis A Landrigan	....
Waverly v (5)	MC	607 565-8106	Thomas J Mullen	....	Dorris A Gressel	Sondra Casterline	Gary Coleman	James Jackson	....
Webster v (5)	MC	716 265-3770	Robert R Johnville	William R Shearer	Dorothy Hinxman	Robert R Johnville	Gary Partridge	....	David M Galeazzo
Wellsville v (6)	MC	716 593-1121	Robert G Gardner	....	Janice A Givens	Janice A Givens	Richard Fleischman	Stephen L Margeson	D A Macfarquhar
Wesley Hills v (4)	MC	914 354-0400	(not reporting)						
West Haverstraw v (9)	MC	914 947-2800	Edward Zugibe	....	O Fred Miller	Fred Vanwort Jr	Michael Anderson	....	James Mackey
West Seneca t (51)	MC	716 674-5600	Joan F Lillis	....	M Ruth Harris	Joan F Lillis	George Davis	Bruce Manning	Edward Penders
Westbury v (14)	MC	516 334-1700	Ernest J Strada	....	John A Sharkey	John A Sharkey	....	....	John Ingram
Westfield v† (3)	MC	716 326-4961	Anthony J Monta Sr	Daniel Vendel	Daniel Vendel	Peter B Best	Ronald Trippy	Samuel P Arcadipane	....
White Plains (47)	MC	914 682-4200	Alfred Del Vecchio	....	William F Maguire	Dorothy Erard	William J McMahon	Patrick Gleason	Samuel Bartholomew
Whitehall v (3)	MC	518 499-0770	Lawrence J Varney	....	Joan C Douglas	....	Harold Martell	Bruce Angus	M Hakim Parwana
Whitesboro v (4)	MC	315 736-1613	Ambrose Carey Sr	....	Beverly Sperry	Mary E Reilly	David Jacobowitz	William M McMyler	Alan J Lazenby
Williamsville v (6)	MC	716 632-4120	Gordon J Kuzon	....	Theresa L Cummins	....	Richard Andrews	Herbert E Zimmerman	Philip J Boudreau
Williston Park v† (8)	MC	516 746-2193	Carl F Del Vecchio	....	....	Clement P Murphy	Robert C Schnall	....	John Bialobrzeski
Woodridge v*† (1)	CM	914 434-7855	Richard Elliott	....	Diane Sennett	Diane Sennett	Steve Proyect	Eugene Ackerley	Irvin S Newmark
Yonkers* (195)	CM	914 964-3000	Angelo R Martinelli	Rodney H Irwin	A Moczydlowski	Harold Peterson	William McLaughlin	Joseph Fernandes	Frank J Sisto
Yorkville v (3)	MC	315 736-9391	(not reporting)						
NORTH CAROLINA (158)									
Ahoskie t*† (5)	CM	919 332-5146	....	Robert C Elliott	....	....	....	....	....
Albemarle* (15)	CM	704 982-0131	Carlton B Holt	Jack F Neel	Raymond I Allen	William B Morris	Clyde R Calloway	Don C Frey	D L Smith Jr
Apex t* (3)	CM	919 362-8661	Larry M Jordan	Steven E Stewart	Sonja Lumley	Sonja Lumley	....	Leo W Shores	Ronald D Wicker
Archdale (5)	MC	919 431-9141	Henry H Darr	Dalton C Fulcher	Maxine Renn	....	Larry Brower	Darrel Arney	Vestal M Hill
Asheboro* (15)	CM	919 625-6131	William J Trogdon	T J McIntosh Jr	David B Leonard	David B Leonard	John A McGlohon	J D Bulla	Dumont Bunker
Asheville* (53)	CM	704 255-5000	Larry McDevitt	....	Wm F Wolcott Jr	Larry A Fisher	Powell N Ball	Fred W Hensley	T Clark Brown
Ayden t*† (..)	CM	919 746-4152	Ross S Persinger	Donald E Russell	Ralph Ford	Donald E Russell	Calvin Hardee	Thomas Burney	Raymond Eakes
Beaufort t (4)	MC	919 728-2141	Joyce Fulford	A C Blankenship	A C Blankenship	A C Blankenship	Bryan Loftin	Marvin P Knox	Curtis Perry
Belhaven t* (2)	CM	919 943-3105	C O Boyette	....	Deborah M Hollowell	Deborah M Hollowell	Shelton Williams	Bruce L Smith	....
Belmont*† (5)	CM	704 825-5586	Billy W Joye Jr	Carl W Howie	Mary G Queen	Carl W Howie	John A Limerick	Bill Joye Sr	John Lamar Henkle
Benson t* (3)	CM	919 894-3553	Charles Matthews	Steven L Harrell	Carolyn A Nordan	Steven L Harrell	Clifton Raynor	Charles L Nordan	L Walton Johnson
Bessemer City* (5)	CM	704 629-5542	Richard B Lackey Jr	Ralph S Messera	Janice C Costner	Ralph S Messera	Johnny C Goines	Robert D Colvin	Johnny C Goines
Biltmore Forest t§ (1)	MC	704 274-0824	Canie B Smith	Robt R Musselwhite	Robt R Musselwhite	Robt R Musselwhite	Rickman Fred	Rickman Fred	Swain Ballard
Black Mountain t*† (4)	CM	704 669-9102	Chester T Sobol Jr	Al Richardson Jr	Suzanne Turner	Al Richardson Jr	Gary D Bartlett	Crait Slagle	Al White
Boone t* (10)	CM	704 264-4364	Hadley Wilson	Len D Hagaman Jr	Lend Hagaman Jr	Bonnie F Greene	Jack Roark	Clyde Tester	....

Directory 1/10 continued — MUNICIPAL OFFICIALS IN ALL U.S. CITIES OVER 2,500[1]

City, 1980 population (000 omitted), form of government	Municipal phone number	Mayor	Appointed administrator	City clerk	Finance officer	Fire chief	Police chief	Public works director
NORTH CAROLINA (158) continued								
Brevard* (5) CM	704 884-4123	Opal C Hahn	Dee A Freeman	Glenda W Sansosti	Michael D Whitney	Gordon Byrd	L B Vaughan	Carroll Byers
Burlington* (37) CM	919 227-3603	K L Ketchum	J D Mackintosh Jr	W R Baker	W R Baker	John D Love	R F Shelton	Ronald R Sewell
Canton t* (5) CM	704 648-2363	C W Hardin	Wm G Stamey	Jimmy Flynn	Wm G Stamey	Leo Cayton	Charles Calloway	Roger M Lyda
Carolina Beach t* (2) CM	919 458-8291	J Neil Pharr	Richard A McLean	Lona B Thompson	Lona B Thompson	Robert Weeks	H G Grohman	Gilmer A Thompson
Carrboro t* (8) CM	919 942-8541	James V Porto Jr	Robert W Morgan	Sarah C Williamson	Don W Casper	Robert Swiger	Arvid Herje	Chris Peterson
Cary t* (22) CM	919 469-4000	Harold D Ritter	Braxton R Matthews	Marilyn D Ryan	Gary L McConkey	Ned Perry	John Boles	Jack Scoville
Chadbourn t* (2) CM	919 654-4146	S G Koonce	Steven D Wyatt	Lois Hope	....	Edwin Nance	Leo Herring	Spurgeon Duncan
Chapel Hill t* (32) CM	919 968-2700	Joseph L Nassif	David R Taylor	....	James M Baker	Everette Lloyd	Herman L Stone	Harold M Harris
Charlotte* (314) CM	704 374-2040	Harvey B Gantt	O Wendell White	Pat Sharkey	Douglas E Carter	R L Blackwelder	M M Vines	Pressly Beaver
Cherryville* (5) CM	704 435-4184	J Ralph Beam Jr	Janice L Hovis	Jean A Beam	....	Joe C Van Dyke	Michael Dellinger	Ted L Mace
Claremont* (1) CM	704 459-7009	Joseph M Chandler	Robert G Bernot	Patricia C Miller	Patricia C Miller	Michael Y Baker	Gerald R Tolbert	Jimmy L Campbell
Clayton t* (4) CM	919 553-5866	James A Bailey	Steven S Weatherman	Fran C Davis	Marc P Jones	Larry W Castleberry	Paul W Keene	Charles L Everette
Clinton t* (8) CM	919 592-3063	A E Kennedy Jr	Tommy M Combs	Elizabeth W Fortner	Peggy B Wiggins	Harold Maxton Price	Joseph J Puett	Wayne Hollowell
Concord* (17) CM	704 786-6161	Bernie A Edwards	Jesse L Greeson	Vickie C Weant	Kenneth Goble	Fred W Lippard	Jack K Moore	Donald T Howell
Conover* (4) CM	704 464-1191	Harvey O Hawn	J E Robinette	Frances L Kincaid	Dorothy M Warlick	J Reid Poovey Jr	Franklin L Travis	Jim Robinson
Cornelius t§† (2) MC	704 892-6031	....	Donald N Brookshire	....	....	....	....	....
Dallas t (3) MC	704 922-3176	W W Fogle	....	N E Vlaservich	N E Vlaservich	David Calahan	Harold Guffey	Scott A Braddy
Davidson t (3) MC	704 892-7591	Nancy H MacCormac	....	W E Brannon	W E Brannon	R W Gurley	J F Warlick	D B Fisher
Drexel t* (1) CM	704 437-7421	Kenneth Harris	Morris Baker	Barbara Ritchie	....	Benny Orders	Terry B Yount	Bill Dowdle
Dunn* (9) CM	919 892-2633	Ralph L Barefoot	Robt C W Nicholl	Louise A Hudson	....	Joseph T Campbell	Hargus Davidson	Ronald D Autry
Durham* (101) CM	919 683-4100	Charles B Markham	Orville W Powell	Margaret M Bowers	Robert A Slade	Talmadge H Lassiter	Talmadge H Lassiter	....
Eden* (16) CM	919 623-8468	Lawrence W Cox Jr	Charles E Hafter	Mary W Lambert	Joseph E Porter	Larry Rhodes	Garnet N Smart	John H Stevens
Edenton t§ (5) MC	919 482-2155	Roy L Harrell	S W Noble Jr	S W Noble Jr	Linda D Edmundson	Lynn C Perry	J D Parrish	William A Crummey
Elizabeth City* (14) CM	919 338-3981	John F Weeks III	Ronald L Matthews	S P Aydlett	S P Aydlett	Floyd Douglas Allen	W C Owens	Ray W Rogerson
Elizabethtown t§ (4) MC	919 862-2066	William C Keith	James W Freeman	Margie Thompson	....	Jack Cross	Charles Taylor	Tom Roberts
Elkin t (3) CM	919 835-2255	Thomas M Gwyn	....	Joe C Layell	Joe C Layell	A L Brown	John A Corder	Porter Childress
Elon College t (3) MC	919 584-0282	Parker Timothy	Roxie E Hetzel	Roxie E Hetzel	Roxie E Hetzel	Eddie King	Dan W Ingle	Donald K Wagoner
Enfield t (3) MC	919 445-3146	Leo Bellamy	Thomas A Lynn	Julius G Woody Jr	Simon J Meyer	Maurice Barnhill	James C Williams	Milton W Myers
Erwin t* (3) CM	919 897-8953	Cecil Moore	Kenneth Windley	Ramona Warren	Kenneth Windley	Louis Joseph	William Fuller	Frank Ralph Jr
Fairmont t* (3) CM	919 628-9766	W B Webster Sr	Leamon B Brice	Shirley Price	Helen Elliott	John R Jackson	....	Arthur A Shull
Farmville t§ (5) MC	919 753-5116	John T Walston	Frank L Bradham	Margie N Tripp	Margie N Tripp	H P Norman	Wilbur G Barber	Willie R Oakley
Fayetteville* (60) CM	919 483-1762	John W Hurley	John P Smith	M W Downs	William F Epps	Wilbur D Johnson	Ronald E Hansen	R A Muench
Forest City t§ (8) MC	704 245-0148	T Pryor Smith	Charles E Butler	Mary Lee C Curtis	Mary Lee C Curtis	Robert G Harrill	Tom McDevitt	Herbert Toms Jr
Franklin t (3) MC	704 524-2516	David E Henson	Jim Williamson	Frances C Collins	Frances C Collins	Furman Shook	Ernest C Wright	Al Ledford
Fuquay-Varina t* (3) CM	919 552-3178	Alfred M Johnson	William U Lee	Rachel B Turner	William U Lee	T C O'Connell	Angus W Hair	Larry W Bennett Jr
Gamewell (3) MC	704 758-2581	(not reporting)						
Garner t* (10) CM	919 772-4688	John W Watkins Jr	Gustav M Ulrich	Mary Lou Rand	Ted Prather	Phil Mitchell	P L McIver	William Pinch
Gastonia* (47) CM	704 864-3211	Thebaud Jeffers	Gary D Hicks	Brenda P Byrd	James A Philyaw	R L Murray	C C Elmore Jr	Samuel L Wilkins
Gibsonville t* (3) CM	919 449-4144	Ginger S Jarrett	John H Bain	John H Bain	Kay D Howe	James Reid Thomas	Robert I Tickle	Thomas G Evans Jr
Goldsboro* (32) CM	919 735-6121	Hal K Plonk	Kenneth L Collings	Sadie Whitfield	Richard M Slozak	Willard R Herring	C M Gilstrap	C R Southerland
Graham* (8) CM	919 228-8362	Troy W Woodard	Ray Fogleman	Nita G McMullan	Rebecca S Shoffner	Don Bulla	William F Miles	Thomas E Berry
Granite Falls t* (3) CM	704 396-3131	A W Huffman Jr	Linda K Story	Judy L Mackie	Linda K Story	Michael Coffey	Jerry J Bumgarner	Dewey Cook
Greensboro* (156) CM	919 373-2000	John W Forbis	Wm H Carstarphen	Nancy McPeak	C M Conway	R L Powell	C D Wade	James M Dawkins
Greenville* (36) CM	919 752-4137	Janice B Buck	Gail B Meeks	Lois D Worthington	Ronald R Kimble	Jeness Allen	Floyd H Holmes	Mayo E Allen
Hamlet* (5) CM	919 582-2651	Thomas E Smart	Ronald M Niland	Rhonda H Mills	Roger K Lowery	David Fuller	Robert F Beck Sr	Charles B Utter III
Havelock† (18) CM	919 447-8152	Eugene P Smith	H Ralph Kennedy	Vira M Watson	Patricia A Jones	James R Nobles	Michael J Campbell	James W Shank
Henderson* (14) CM	919 492-6111	R G Young Jr	Eric M Williams	....	Jerry L Moss	T O Wilkerson	K K Roberson	Ronald W Phillips
Hendersonville* (7) CM	704 692-7296	Don Michalove	....	Martha Bresnahan	Martha Bresnahan	F C Hendrix	Larry M Hesser	William V Powers
Hickory* (21) CM	704 322-2605	William R McDonald	B Gary McGee	Patricia W Williams	Joyce D Sipe	Larson H Moore	Floyd W Lucas	Cecil Clark
High Point* (64) CM	919 887-2511	Robert O Wells	H Lewis Price	Patricia P Simmons	William A Gear	Hannis L Thompson	Joseph Faircloth	Carl Wills
Hillsborough t† (3) MC	919 732-2104	Lucius Cheshire Jr	....	Agatha Johnson	Agatha Johnson	John Forrest	Arnold Hamlett	Clarence Rosemond
Hope Mills t* (5) CM	919 424-4513	A N Brafford	J R Pick	Erika U Santiago	Erika U Santiago	John B McLean Jr	Robert A Coller	Ben Holloman
Hudson t* (3) CM	704 728-8272	Joseph W Icard	Charles L Fox	Evelyn Raby	Barbara Harris	Mack Whiteside	Kenneth Bumgarner	Carl V Henderson
Jacksonville* (17) CM	919 455-2600	A D Zander Guy Jr	Patrick A Thomas	C W Hemmingway	James Featherstone	Franklin L Barger	Roger E Halbert	Michael B Ellzey
Kenansville t (1) CM	919 296-0369	Don Suttles	....	Mary Anne Jenkins	Mary Anne Jenkins	Ronnie Bostic	Glenn T Braswell	Stephen W Drew
Kernersville t* (7) CM	919 996-3121	Roger Swisher	D Kelly Almond	Betty B Teague	Betty B Teague	J L Barrow	G C Neal Stockton	Robert K Campbell
Kill Devil Hills t* (2) CM	919 441-7236	Lowell M Perry	Lloyd R Ballance	Bonnie J Bradley	Claire M Waterfield	William E Gard	C E Bray III	J Michael Luhouse
King (4) MC	919 983-8265	(not reporting)						
Kings Mountain (9) MC	704 739-2563	John H Moss	....	Joe H McDaniel	John H Moss	Gene Tignor	J D Barrett	....
Kinston* (25) CM	919 527-2111	Dudley D Foster	Robert G Brigman	Nell D Patrick	Nell D Patrick	Carl F Davis	Ross D Hagler	Grover Cole
La Grange t (3) MC	919 566-3186	Woodard H Gurley	....	Geraldine L Alphin	Geraldine L Alphin	Milton F Jones	Robert Pelletier	E B Walters
Laurinburg* (11) CM	919 276-8324	W Charles Barrett	P G Vandenberg	Betty R Childress	P G Vandenberg	James Lytch	N W Quick	Harold W Smith
Lenoir* (14) CM	704 758-0011	Robert A Gibbons	James H Hipp	James H Hipp	Betsy Wilson	Sam Williams	Terry A Crisp	Lex E Honeycutt
Lexington* (16) CM	704 243-2423	Dwight B Hinkle	Belvin B Beck Jr	Belvin B Beck Jr	Jack Yarbrough	Tommy Williams	Calvin Layton	Ken Foster
Lincolnton t* (5) CM	704 732-2281	Carroll Heavner	David E Lowe	Kay B Polhill	George E Heavner	Don Wise	T J Burgin	Max D Abernethy
Long Beach t* (2) CM	919 278-5011	Ben C Thomas Jr	Steven H Foster	Sylvia Butterworth	Sylvia Butterworth	Billy F Travis	James Sloop	Charles P Derrick
Longview t (4) MC	704 322-3921	Fred J Dale	Elsie L Wycoff	Elsie L Wycoff	Elsie L Wycoff	Ernest E Riley	Carl F Hawn	Joe W McConnell
Louisburg t* (3) CM	919 496-4145	V A Peoples	C L Gobble	Elmar N Holmes	Elmar N Holmes	Karl Pernell	Ned I Lloyd	Charles W Wynne
Lowell* (3) CM	704 824-3518	Harold Rankin	Reva Braswell	Lucille Jones	Reva Braswell	Wallace A Saunders	Harold Sprinkles	Edward Buchanan
Lumberton* (18) CM	919 739-6031	Coble D Wilson Jr	A Ray Griffin Jr	Janie L Oxendine	Dorothy McG Biggs	Sam Byrd	H C Britt	Dixon Ivey
Madison t* (3) CM	919 427-0221	J P Carter	Steven L Routh	Brenda D Moore	Philip M Pulliam	Early Ray Tucker	Jerry H Welch	Johnnie R Martin
Maiden t* (3) CM	704 428-8178	Robert L Smyre	David R Walker	R Irene Campbell	R Irene Campbell	Robert L Poovey	Donald Ray Walker	Billy R Price
Marion* (4) CM	704 652-3551	James H Segars	James Earl Daniels	James Earl Daniels	James Earl Daniels	Arthur C Edwards	Henry H Trent	Alvin Callahan
Maxton t (3) MC	919 844-5231	Robert W Fisher	Paul G Davis	Theresa Driggers	Paul G Davis	James R Driggers	Bobby Thompson	Bob Waldron
Mayodan t* (3) CM	919 427-0241	James A Collins	Jerry R Carlton	Debra E Cardwell	....	Thomas Williams	Ed Shelton	Bill Redmond
Mebane t (3) CM	919 563-5901	E Brooks Gardner	Richard L French	Elaine J Hicks	Elaine J Hicks	Timothy Bradley	Grady L Caviness	Delmar C Lankford
Mint Hill t§ (10) MC	704 545-9726	Troy D Pollard	Joan P Shaw	Ms Bobbie H Meacham	Troy D Pollard	....	....	....
Mocksville t† (3) MC	704 634-2259	D J Mando	Terry L Bralley	Catherine Collins	....	L Pete Dwiggins	Alton Carter	Andrew Lagle
Monroe* (13) CM	704 289-8557	Fred C Long	J E Hinkel	Claudette H Smith	J E Hinkel	William W House	Malcolm S Niven	P Wilson Crook
Mooresville t*† (9) CM	704 663-3800	Joe V Knox	Troy R Scoggins Jr	Troy R Scoggins Jr	Kenneth Kistler	Howard E Pender	Frank L Upright	Lynn M Barnette
Morehead City t* (4) CM	919 726-6848	Edward S Dixon	C David Harris	Marjorie S Holland	C David Harris	James B Griffin	William J Condie	X F Mason
Morganton* (14) CM	704 437-8863	Andrew M Kistler II	Douglas O Bean	Douglas O Bean	Billy R Truett	....	Billy J Hamrick	F A Traynham
Mount Airy* (7) CM	919 786-6523	W M Beamer	S L Spencer	Nancy B Nichols	Nancy B Nichols	B J Woodruff	Joe L Simmons	S L Spencer
Mount Holly* (5) CM	704 827-3931	Charles B Black Jr	Greg E Young	Greg E Young	....	Ray Massey	Jimmy D Hufstetler	Eddie Nichols
Mount Olive t (5) MC	919 658-9536	D F Odom Jr	Sidney C Mallory	Arlene G Talton	Arlene G Talton	Joseph W Caveness	John W Hodges	Lloyd Warren
Murfreesboro t (3) MC	919 398-4665	W W Hill	Edward F Burchins	Molly Eubank	Edward F Burchins	Gene Byrd	Robert E Harris Jr	Jack Beatty
Nags Head t* (1) CM	919 441-5508	Donald W Bryan	J Webb Fuller	Constance V Hardee	Doris O'Neal Gard	Paul Royston	....	Harry Lange
Nashville t* (3) CM	919 459-4511	Rex A Paramore	Raymond Boutwell	Billie G Kennedy	Billie G Kennedy	L R Bass Jr	Donald R Skinner	Harold D Pittman
New Bern* (15) CM	919 633-5161	Paul M Cox	Anthony I Hooper	Annette F West	Kai D Helson	Reid Whitford	John W Worsham	Charles H Kimbrell
Newton* (8) CM	704 464-1282	Wayne Dellinger	R D Whisenant	Rita K Williams	John A Sofley Jr	William Russell	James C Masters	Jack Matthews

Directory 1/10 continued **MUNICIPAL OFFICIALS IN ALL U.S. CITIES OVER 2,500[1]**

City, 1980 population (000 omitted), form of government		Municipal phone number	Mayor	Appointed administrator	City clerk	Finance officer	Fire chief	Police chief	Public works director
NORTH CAROLINA (158) continued									
North Wilkesboro t* (3)	CM	919 667-7129	Neil G Cashion Jr	Charles B Lott	Barbara V Stone	Charles B Lott	Conley Call	David T Felts	J J Bentley
Oxford t* (8)	CM	919 693-2195	Allie G Ellington	H T Ragland Jr	Ann S Parrott	Kelway L Howard II	John B Norris	James H Griffin	Jimmy Crews Jr
Pembroke t* (3)	CM	919 521-9758	Milton Hunt	McDuffie Cummings	Ruby Smith	....	Ray Hunt	Kirby Ammons	James Locklear
Pinehurst v* (2)	CM	919 295-1901	Edgar J Roberts	George A Wood	Melodie F Frye	George A Wood	Wayne Brower	Charles A Wilson	James Ritter
Pineville t*† (2)	CM	704 889-2291	G C Fowler	Jos E Baker Jr	Mary A Creech	Jos E Baker Jr	Don Boatwright	M T Rogers	William Hopkins
Pittsboro t* (1).	CM	919 542-4621	Jack P Justice	Robert J Touhey	Lois H Moore	....	Burnice Griffin	Larry O Hipp	James N Stevenson
Plymouth t* (5)	CM	919 793-3622	William R Flowers	Matt Matteson	Anita N Sawyer	Anita N Sawyer	William L Whitley	Floyd M Woodley	Robbie G Jones
Raeford* (4)	CM	919 875-8161	John K McNeill Jr	Thomas A Phillips	Thomas A Phillips	Helen H Huffman	Crawford Thomas	V Leonard Wiggins	Willis C Sellars
Raleigh* (150)	CM	919 890-3070	Avery C Upchurch	D E Benton Jr	Gail Smith	Z B Hill	Thomas T Kuster	F K Heineman	Lynn Baird
Red Springs t* (4). . . .	CM	919 843-5849	George T Paris	Thomas Wayne Horne	Doris Berrier	Doris Berrier	William D McPhaul	Luther W Haggins	Cleveland Parker
Reidsville* (12).	CM	919 349-7013	Earl M Grogan	Wm E Gentner	Ann S Bradsher	Bernice P Phillips	J H Monsees	James K Festerman	Fred W Goodman
Roanoke Rapids* (15)	CM	919 535-2031	J Lloyd Andrews	Victor H Denton	George W Morgan	George W Morgan	A E Dixon	D N Beale	Wilmer Whitfield
Rockingham* (8).	CM	919 895-9088	G R Kindley Jr	A Lee Galloway	Wm C Reynolds	Wm C Reynolds	Larry C Carter	Eddie R Martin	....
Rocky Mount* (41) . . .	CM	919 972-1111	Frederick Turnage	William Batchelor	Jean M Bailey	Ernest J Ward	John E Hawkins	Joseph Brown	Francis E Beaudry
Roxboro*† (8)	CM	919 599-3116	Revis L Carver	Clarence Burch	Margie L Adcock	Beatrice W Patton	Roy W Hall	Franklin R Edwards	John H Blanks
Rutherfordton t (3). . . .	CM	704 287-3520	Ray A Morris	John W Condrey	John W Condrey	Janet W Nix	William O Wells	Kenneth Hunsucker	Welford L Rogers
Salisbury* (23).	CM	704 637-2200	Wiley Lash	Harvey R Mathias	Frances C Beaver	Donald F Miller	Tedd Melvin	David L Fortson	John Vest
Sanford* (15).	CM	919 774-6501	Rex McLeod	O B Stokes	O B Stokes	Tom Spivey	Sam Bost	R V Yarborough	Larry B Thomas
Scotland Neck t (3) . . .	MC	919 826-3152	Ferd L Harrison	William R Flowers	Patsy A Faithful	....	Wayne Smith	William W Joyner	S R Williams
Selma t* (5)	CM	919 965-9841	Grover T Dees	Joe Edwards Jr	Ann Vause	Allen R Hayes	Joe Price	Charles Hicks	Terry Keen
Seven Devils t* (..) . . .	CM	704 963-5342	Kenneth B McLean	Christopher D May	Christopher D May	James Albert Greene	....	Joe Ray Buchanan	Gary C Fox
Shelby* (15)	CM	704 487-4066	George W Clay Jr	D M Wilkison	Mary E Cole	John S Hudson	Glenn Barrett	James D Fish	Hugh L Humphries
Siler City t* (4).	CM	919 742-4731	Earl B Fitts	Benjamin T Shivar	Wanda G Ingold	Wanda G Ingold	Jim Dixon	Lewis S Phillips	Herbert A Smith
Smithfield t* (7)	CM	919 934-2116	Kenneth B Baker	Anthony C Robertson	Robert E Plowman Jr	Robert E Plowman Jr	Chas P Strickland	Joseph N Pearce	Thurman Pilkington
Southern Pines t* (9)	CM	919 692-7021	Jane M Clark	William B Coleman	Blanche R Woodruff	William B Coleman	Peter Rapatas	Earl S Seawell	Richard Lazenby
Southport* (3)	CM	919 457-5460	Norman R Holden	Nelson E Smith	C B Caroon	Harold F Aldridge	Harold F Aldridge	William F Coring Jr	Gary Ammons
Spencer* (3)	CM	704 633-2231	C E Spear Jr	Hilda B Palmer	Peggy C Whitley	Hilda B Palmer	Howard Everhart	Larry H Jones Sr	Donald Walser
Spindale t (4).	MC	704 286-3466	Jack W Metcalf	Bill Penson	Faye Chester	Faye Chester	John A Horne	J Harvey Moore	Michael Brooks
Spring Lake t*† (6) . . .	CM	919 436-0241	Evelyn Q Parker	Richard P Higgins	Carolyn J Powers	Carolyn J Powers	Patrick A Stevens	Victor D Latham	Joseph W Walthall
Statesville* (19)	CM	704 873-2121	David L Pressly Jr	Peter T Connet	Ralph M Sisk	Patrick J O'Connor	Glenn D O'Ferrell	James D Myers	A E Pettit
Stoneville t* (1)	CM	919 573-9695	....	Michael Roche	....	....	....	....	....
Tabor City t† (3)	MC	919 653-3458	Marion S Baxter	....	....	....	....	....	....
Tarboro t* (9)	CM	919 823-8121	John D Pigg	Robert R Collins	W Logue Corbett	....	George G Cherry Jr	Harry W Alderman	John Chapman
Thomasville* (14)	CM	919 475-1321	Nancy R Myers	Kyle Williams	Ben L Maree	Tony C Jarrett	Oscar Parrish	Donald W Truell	....
Troy t* (3)	CM	919 572-3661	Roy J Maness	Bruce A Radford	Cathy Maness	Bruce A Radford	John Wallace	Everett L Norton Jr	Howard Nooe
Tryon t* (2).	CM	704 859-6654	Kenneth L Tucker	Glenn M Rhodes	Maisie Edwards	Glenn M Rhodes	Clarence Scoggins	Jerry Ross	Clarence B Henson
Valdese t* (3).	CM	704 874-2279	Jimmy C Draughn	Jeffrey V Morse	Harold Passmore	Billy Chapman	Sherrill Brittain	Oscar Pascal	Howard Barlow
Wadesboro t*† (4). . . .	CM	704 694-5171	William F Short Jr	William B Chewning	Nancy G Huntley	William B Chewning	Mack Davis	Robert F Kendall	Harold D Carpenter
Wake Forest t* (4). . . .	CM	919 556-2024	Thomas J Byrne	Jerry A Walters	Carol G Kinton	Phyllis Chalk	Donnie Hight	Harvey Newsom	....
Wallace t (3)	MC	919 285-4136	Melvin G Cording	Robert C Hyatt	....	....	Thomas Townsend	Roscoe B Rich	John Murray
Warrenton t* (1)	CM	919 257-3315	B G White	V R Vaughan	Carolyn M Robertson	V R Vaughan	Leon Cheek	Freddie Robinson	W B Neal
Warsaw t (3)	MC	919 293-7814	Samuel E Godwin Sr	Alfred Herring	Alfred Herring	....	Cecil Guy	R P Wood Jr	Larry Simmons
Washington* (8)	CM	919 946-1033	J Stancil Lilley	Ralph A Clark	Plummer A Daniel	Plummer A Daniel	Hugh M Sterling Jr	Johnny R Rose	....
Waynesville t* (7)	CM	704 456-3515	S Ronnie James	William M Sutton	Jacklyn G Messer	Bill Green	Leonard B Messer	Coleman Moody	....
Wendell t* (2)	CM	919 365-4444	Candace S Tongue	Ira C Fuller	Ira C Fuller	Ms B A Raper	Herbert Ramsey Jr	John W Horton	Donnie M Ayscue
Whiteville* (6)	CM	919 642-8046	Horace B Whitley	Howard A Jones	Susan E Duncan	Jean Babson	Charles D Trotter	Douglas J Keller	Charles E Heye
Williamston t (6).	MC	919 792-5142	R H Cowen	J B Godwin	J B Godwin	J B Godwin	T E Price	James Thompson	W M Long Jr
Wilmington* (44)	CM	919 762-4323	William Schwartz	William B Farris	Claire Hughes	J D Harrell	Lloyd H Wolfe	Darryl L Bruestle	R F Coleman Jr
Wilson* (34)	CM	919 291-8111	Ralph El Ramey	T Bruce Boyette	C W Pittman III	C W Pittman III	Ben Williams	Thomas C Younce	Wm P Bartlett
Winston-Salem* (132)	CM	919 727-2123	Wayne A Corpening	Bryce A Stuart	Marie Matthews	Loris R Colclough	Lester E Ervin Jr	L A Powell	P W Swann
Woodfin t† (3)	CM	704 253-4887	Coy F Rice	....	Anna H Gardner	Anna H Gardner	....	Eugene F Rice	....
Wrightsville Beach t (3)	MC	919 256-2245	Eugene N Floyd	Hugh H Perry Jr	Hugh H Perry Jr	Hugh H Perry Jr	Everett K Ward	George M Antley	John T Nesbitt
Zebulon t* (2)	CM	919 269-7455	Frank B Wall	Donald E Horton	Donald E Horton	Donald E Horton	Sidney C Perry	Windel H Perry	L Wilson Stallings
NORTH DAKOTA (18)									
Beulah (3).	MC	701 873-4637	Darold Benz	Robert F Wendel	Bev Sullivan	Robert F Wendel	Lester Schiltz	Dave Paetz	....
Bismarck (44).	CO	701 222-6471	Bus Leary	Dan Dahlgren	Grant Bergquist	....	Jack Hegadus	Kenneth Medeiros	Raymond Jundt
Bottineau† (3)	MC	701 228-3232	Mona Marchus	....	William Woolcott	Rueben Ellingson	Thomas Acheson	....	John Wilcox
Carrington (3).	MC	701 652-2102	Norman H Hanson	Karen Hafner	Verna Freeman	Karen Hafner	Arnold Schroeder	Leon Helton	Dale Townsend
Devils Lake† (7)	CO	701 662-4098	Dennis L Riggin	Michael J Connor	Margie A Austin	Michael J Connor	William Oehlke	Christian Mathieson	Glenn Olson
Dickinson† (16)	CO	701 225-6765	A E Baumgartner	James K Gerou	James K Gerou	James K Gerou	Joe Boespflug	Gerald Barnhart	Bruce Pier
Fargo (61).	CO	701 241-1300	Jon G Lindgren	....	F R Fahrlander	F R Fahrlander	Lansford Josal	Edwin R Anderson	Wilbur K Michelson
Grafton† (5).	MC	701 352-1561	Warner K Taylor	Robert L Lerud	E F Machart	....	Clayton Lamont	Leroy McCann	Lester Eaton
Grand Forks (44).	MC	701 775-8103	H C Wessman	Pat Owens	Don Tingum	....	Richard Aulich	James Clague	F B Orthmeyer
Harvey (3).	MC	701 324-2000	Gary Bergstrom	Jennifer Hogue	Jennifer Hogue	Gary Bergstrom	Loren Pellett	Larry Hoffer	Gary Keller
Jamestown (16)	MC	701 252-5900	James T Lusk	....	Rex C Brisben	Rex C Brisben	Melvin J Kachel	Thomas W Jensen	Waice D Kritsky
Mandan (16)	CO	701 663-9546	Sharon Schafer	Lynn A Lander	Phyllis Graner	Lynn A Lander	Pete Gartner	Mark Moline	Pete Snider
Minot* (33).	CM	701 857-4750	Chester Reiten	Robert A Schempp	David Waind	Robert Frantsvog	Duwayne Ward	Carrol Erickson	Lyle Weeks
Rugby (3)	MC	701 776-6181	Al Wentz	L A Johnson	....	Curtis Teigen	David Schneibel	Charles Hilyard	....
Valley City (8).	CO	701 845-1700	Dale Olson	....	Raymond G Larson	....	Geo Schlittenhardt	Jack F Ladbury	Leif Ravnaas
Wahpeton† (9)	MC	701 642-8448	Warren E Schuett	Arden C Anderson	Arden C Anderson	Arden C Anderson	Kermit Wateland	Delano A Lotzer	Jerry C Lein
West Fargo† (10)	CO	701 282-3843	Clayton A Lodoen	....	....	Michael D McLeod	Roger Olson	Kenneth Hansen	Richard Fuller
Williston (13)	CO	701 572-8161	J A Haugen	Rodger A Neumann	Rodger A Neumann	Rodger A Neumann	Orlin Kirby	Raymond Atol	Gene Emery
OHIO (348)									
Ada v (6)	MC	419 634-8876	Robert Allen Jr	James Meyer	Merle E Wirt	Merle E Wirt	....	Thomas Gibson Jr	....
Akron (237).	MC	216 375-2121	Thomas Sawyer	....	Edward Davis	Bartley Hildreth	James H Harris	Philip G Barnes	Ray Kapper
Alliance (24)	MC	216 821-3110	Francis Carr	John Benincasa	Joanne Burr	Paul L Cironi	Eugene Drummond	George Ziga	John Benincasa
Amberley v* (3)	CM	513 531-8675	John L Muething	Bernard E Boraten	Betty J Sizemore	....	Garry H Benner	Garry H Benner	....
Amherst (11)	MC	216 988-4380	John C Jaworski	....	Olga Sivinski	Marilyn Jacobcik	Walter Gambish	William Hall	....
Archbold v (3)	CM	419 445-4726	William Lovejoy	Nolan Tuckerman	Gladys Winzeler	Gladys Winzeler	Richard Erbskorn	Richard Purdy	....
Ashland (20)	MC	419 289-8622	Don M Richey	....	William E Strine	William E Strine	Ronald E Baker	Donald Townsend	....
Ashtabula (23)	MC	216 997-5791	Robert J Bollman Jr	....	Robert J Sabo	Robert J Bollman Jr	Charles L Moiser	Howard S Stewart	Michael Rossitti
Athens (20)	MC	614 593-7322	Edward R Beckett	James Deardorff	Harriet Trevas	Mary J Alex-Krusac	Richard Cooley	Theodore Jones	Harry Kacenski
Aurora† (8)	MC	216 562-6131	Matthew Mattmuller	....	Lunette J Baldwin	Dennis E Golem	F J Barnoff	Theodore George	Charles N Brown
Avon (7).	MC	216 934-6192	Thomas L Wearsch	....	Pearl B Olearcik	William D Hyde	Donald Casper	Roy T Dreger	John Smitek
Avon Lake† (13)	MC	216 933-6141	Robert E Allen	....	Kathy Lynch	Ernest Palmer	Richard Butler	Thomas Quinn	John Kniepper
Baltimore v (3)	MC	614 862-4491	Dennis R Keller	....	Robert C Kalish	Robert C Kalish	Fred Reedy	Robert Newbold	Fredrick A Landis
Barberton (30)	MC	216 753-6611	William J Judge	....	....	Raymond Flickinger	Harry Hummel	Gene R Mosley	Jack M Wood
Barnesville v (5)	MC	614 425-3444	Allen Phillips	....	Marie McCrate	Marie McCrate	Harold Arnold	Chris Ditto	Okey Curtis

Directory 1/10 continued

MUNICIPAL OFFICIALS IN ALL U.S. CITIES OVER 2,500[1]

City, 1980 population (000 omitted), form of government	Municipal phone number	Mayor	Appointed administrator	City clerk	Finance officer	Fire chief	Police chief	Public works director
OHIO (348) continued								
Bay Village (18) MC	216 871-2200	James H Cowles	....	Audrey Greaser	Bruce E Warnock	Gregory D Jackson	Peter J Gray	Gordon Forsmark
Beachwood (10) MC	216 464-1070	Harvey E Friedman	....	Eugene J Pesti	Eugene J Pesti	William S Kaselak	Robert H Abrams	Gerry Cipra
Beavercreek§ (32) MC	513 426-5170	Paul T Dunnigan	Robert J Froehlich	Carol A Becker	Paul Scarborough	....	Billy E Perry	David J Baker
Bedford* (15) CM	216 232-1600	Donald Grossenbaugh	Arthur V Dickard	Edna Jaklitch	Kenneth E Kleppel	Jeffrey L Duber	James Cooper	Sherman S Webb
Bedford Heights (13) MC	216 439-1600	Jimmy Dimora	....	Ann Pocaro	William L Fenton	Eugene Gehri	Dominic Meuti	Phillip Zito
Bellaire (8) MC	614 676-6539	Pete Kovalyk	....	Donna J Landers	Anthony G DeMarco	Michael Wallace	Ralph W Weeks	Richard L Croweii
Bellbrook* (5) CM	513 848-4666	G David Buccalo	David E Hamilton	Pamela D Loper	Betty Kent	Joe Knopp	Richard Frederick	Charles Henderson
Bellefontaine (12) MC	513 592-4376	Richard J Vicario	....	Ardythe Predmore	Michael Yoder	James R Furby	John W Harvey	William C Atkinson
Bellevue (8) MC	419 483-7720	Donald C Tedhams	Michael J Sigg	Linda Connors	Ethel Foti	Larry Gregory	Russell Hetrick	....
Belpre (7) MC	614 423-7592	Ivan C Smith	Garrett C Brown	Sharon Kemper	Benjamin R Grant	Wesley Walker	Larry Baxter	Lester A Pittenger
Berea (20) MC	216 826-5800	John G Whipple	....	....	John R Hauff	Robert P Strong	John A Cook Jr	Paul McCumbers
Bexley (13) MC	614 235-8694	David H Madison	....	John W Hornberger	John W Hornberger	....	Thomas W Tobin	Stanley H Sheehan
Blanchester v† (3) MC	513 783-2431	Stephen Valentine	....	Janelle Swearingen	....	Donald Walker	Richard R Payton	Edward Bailey
Blue Ash* (10) CM	513 745-8500	Stephanie Stoller	Marvin D Thompson	Mary E Malone	James S Pfeffer	Glenford Ross	Elisha N Sturgill	Preston M Combs
Bluffton v (3) MC	419 358-2961	James Porter King	....	Thomas Foltz	....	Darrel Huber	James Hicks	Larry Core
Bowling Green (26) MC	419 352-3541	Bruce H Bellard	Wesley K Hoffman	Jorja Gladden	Charles E Kerr	Elmer Gonyer	Galen L Ash	David Barber
Brecksville (10) MC	216 526-4351	(not reporting)						
Bridgeport v (3) MC	614 635-2424	Charles W Furbee	....	Carole Lyle	Arthur Timberlake	Russell C Hores	Carl Smith	....
Broadview Heights† (11) MC	216 526-4357	William M Bittle	....	Linda Cloonan	Michael Cassidy	Leonard Masek	Edward O'Toole	Dean Sisler
Brook Park (26) MC	216 433-1300	Thomas J Coyne Jr	Jone B Weist	Audrey Zeiger	Shelby J Lawhun	Ernest Conrad	Thomas Dease	Thomas J Coyne
Brooklyn (12) MC	216 351-2133	John M Coyne	....	Frank P Scarano	Frank P Scarano	Joseph V Pucci	James F Maloney	Peter R Laudi
Brookville v (4) CM	513 833-2135	George E Brown	John R Wright	E Eugene Roeser	E Eugene Roeser	Thomas Dafler	Larry Rose	John R Wright
Brunswick* (28) CM	216 225-9144	Stan Umpleby	Robert A Trimble	Sheryll Lulas	Joan M Thesling	Martin Rooy	Clayton Crook	Gregory Crane
Bryan (8) MC	419 636-4232	William C Runkle	....	Robert C Hoffman	Robert C Hoffman	Gerald Robinson	James Phillips	....
Buckeye Lake v (3) MC	614 928-7100	Charles E Slater	....	Toni Yarman	....	Dana Moran	Pat Mullins	....
Bucyrus† (13) MC	419 562-6767	Paul R Outhwaite	Francis X Anderson	Della K Hildebrand	....	Gordon Grove	Charles McDonald	Bernard Piper
Byesville v (3) MC	614 685-5901	Arthur Valentine	....	Marjorie J Roller	....	Randy Wray	John Reid	....
Cadiz v† (4) MC	614 942-8844	Raymond Jones	....	Donna J Barnhart	Donna J Barnhart	John Francis	....	Arthur Barcus
Cambridge (14) MC	614 439-1050	C Charles Schaub II	....	Linda Waller	Donna Frisbee	James Cropper	Frank Stroud	Robert E Hormberg
Campbell (12) MC	216 755-1451	James J Vargo	Gus Kust	Judith C Mihin	Steve Odea	William Vrabel	Frank Phillips	Gus Kust
Canal Fulton v (3) MC	216 854-2225	S R McLaughlin	S E Singleton	H W Price	H W Price	R T Kroeger	R J Hanus	....
Canal Winchester v† (3) MC	614 837-7493	K L Miller	....	Arthur C Ferber	....	Larry L Flowers	Robert C Miller	....
Canfield* (6) CM	216 533-1101	Francis McLaughlin	James A McFellin	Pat Matevich	James A McFellin	Robert J Tieche	Terrence Shidel	Ronald W Wiant
Canton (95) MC	216 489-3000	Sam D Purses	....	Albert Artimez	Richard Mallonn	Thomas Kilcullen	Thomas W Wyatt	Thomas Ascani
Carey v (4) MC	419 396-7681	Jon W Updegraff	Ernest M Zmyslinski	Gladys Richardson	Gladys Richardson	Clement Hoepf	Jack E Orians	Roy Coppler
Carlisle v (4) MC	513 746-0555	Kelly C Borad	....	Robert Flischel	Robert Flischel	B J Carpenter	Gary Long	....
Carrollton v (3) MC	216 627-2411	Denver I Dever	....	Betty Davis	....	Robert Herron	W R McAfee	....
Cedarville v (3) MC	513 766-2911	(not reporting)						
Celina (9) MC	419 586-6464	Blair Williams	Thomas A Schwartz	Cynthia Woten	Patrick Smith	Jerry Bauchar	Leroy Felver	Tom Anderson
Centerville* (19) CM	513 433-7151	Shirley F Heintz	Darryl K Kenning	Marilyn McLaughlin	William Bettcher	Randall L Staley	J William Lickert	Richard Bishop
Chagrin Falls v† (4) MC	216 247-5050	....	Robert C McKay	....	....	....	....	....
Chardon v* (4) CM	216 285-3585	Robert H Eldridge	Daniel A Anslinger	Shirley Bellamy	Shirley Bellamy	Phil King	William Niehus	Daniel A Anslinger
Cheviot (10) MC	513 661-2700	J Michael Laumann	Robert S Buchanan	Darryl Ambach	Joseph Wilson	Clarence Borntrager	Donald Mackie	Robert S Buchanan
Chillicothe (23) MC	614 774-1185	Leonard L Freeman	....	Donald Schofield	William B Morrissey	David Carnes	Timothy Crawford	Jack R Lallier
Cincinnati* (385) CM	513 352-3000	Arn Bortz	Sylvester Murray	Webster W Posey	Frank Dawson	Norman L Wells	Myron J Leistler	George Rowe
Circleville (12) MC	614 477-2551	John W Jenkins	....	June Gazdik	Madeline L Sanders	Ronald Sowers	Robert L Temple	Atwood P Jones
Cleveland Heights* (56) CM	216 371-6600	Alan J Rapoport	Richard V Robinson	Robert Rink	Robert Rink	Robert Marth	Martin G Lentz	Dominic A Tomaro
Cleveland (574) MC	216 664-2000	George V Voinovich	....	Mercedes Cotner	Daniel Neckel	James McNamee	William Hanton	Ernest Cedroni
Clyde* (5) CM	419 547-0575	Patrick Wadsworth	Nelson E Summit	James Watt	Betty L Scheer	David E Moyer	John Scheer Jr	Bradley A Biggs
Coal Grove v† (3) MC	606 532-7447	Bernard T McKnight	Mike Myers	Juanita Markel	Juanita Markel	James Sherman	John Goldcamp	....
Coldwater v (4) MC	419 678-4881	Maurice G Cron	Raymond Kremer	Betty M Dilworth	....	Paul Streacker	Dean F Schaller	....
Columbiana v* (5) CM	216 482-2173	Richard G Simpson	Albert E Wardingley	....	Albert E Wardingley	Charles Flohr	Mark A Shaffer	Donald J Shaffer
Columbus (565) MC	614 222-8100	Dana G Rinehart	R Scott Spriggs	Francine C Ryan	Patrick H Power	Donald Werner	Dwight Joseph	Gisela Rosenbaum
Conneaut (14) MC	216 593-4357	(not reporting)						
Cortland v (5) MC	216 637-3916	(not reporting)						
Coshocton† (13) MC	614 622-1373	Daniel L Moody	Chas A Turner Sr	Janet S Mosier	Martha Salrin	Charles Turner Jr	....	Forrest Hudson
Covington v (3) MC	513 473-2102	Donald E Garman	....	Kay E Mckinney	Luther Landis Jr	Richard F Minnich	Norman L Swartz	Richard McMaken
Crestline (5) MC	419 683-3800	Henry Peresie	....	....	....	....	....	....
Crooksville v (3) MC	614 982-2656	James W Cannon	....	Mildred Wayne	Durwood Neff	Norton Claypool	Robin Zinn	Robert Bentley
Cuyahoga Falls (44) MC	216 923-9921	Robert J Quirk	....	Thomas A Mitchel	Frank J Sherman	Wayne Bowen	Charles Elum	Albert P Ganocy
Dayton* (204) CM	513 443-3600	Paul R Leonard	....	Don L Crawford	Robert Cramer	Glen Alexander	Tyree Broomfield	James L Francis
Deer Park (7) MC	513 791-1081	Francis R Healy	David A O'Leary	Harry Gilligan III	Geo A Diersing Jr	Michael J Hagy	Donald J Lally	....
Defiance§ (17) MC	419 784-2101	W Thomas Wiseman	Michael L Abels	Joyce A Rohrs	Rita A Kissner	Robert Marihugh	Gary Shafer	....
Delaware* (19) CM	614 363-1965	Michael R Shade	Jewel D Scott	Elizabeth F Speese	....	James V Pliickebaum	Ronald L Poulton	Robert J Harmon
Delhi tp§ (29) MC	513 922-3111	Dusty Rhodes	Joseph R Morency	James W Holtel	James W Holtel	Donald Ohmer	Howard R Makin	Robert W Bass
Delphos (7) MC	419 695-4010	Harold A Wieging	....	....	John Dickman	Donald Schimmoeller	Dennis M Kimmet	Charles Verhoff
Delta v§ (3) MC	419 822-3190	Bernard Spangler	....	....	Helen M Harris	George R Dick	Robert Taylor	....
Dennison v (3) MC	614 922-2067	(not reporting)						
Dover (12) MC	216 343-7725	Guy M Smith	....	Neva Jerome	Zoe Ann Kelley	Fred Nixon	Jack Griffin	Richard C Shaw
Dublin v (4) CM	614 889-2175	James E Lewis	Sherman Sheldon	Fran Urban	Nan Prushing	....	Robert Mayer	Bruce Warner
East Cleveland* (37) CM	216 681-5020	Wallace Davis	Elijah A Wheeler	Vivian Logan	John Urban	Lavalle Dorsey	William Kelly	Ross Brankatelli
East Liverpool† (17) MC	216 385-3381	John H Payne	....	Jerry L Summers	Patrica Hadley	James Pelley	Milton Fowler	James R Walker
East Palestine (5) MC	216 426-4345	Donald E Smith	....	Bruce Van Fossen	....	Merle Stewart	Gary A Clark	William McCormick
Eastlake (22) MC	216 951-1416	Morris Becker	....	Marge Hlebak	David D Miller	Charles Musser	William DePledge	Ronald Stackhouse
Eaton* (7) CM	513 456-5561	Eric W Daily	J Steven Morris	Betty J Sowder	Betty J Sowder	Dean Steinke	James Dearth	Eugene F Copp
Elmwood Place v (3) MC	513 242-0563	Emmitt Spears	....	Ray Baker	Raymond G Spears	William Siegel	Stanley Wilkymacky	....
Elyria (58) MC	216 322-1829	Michael B Keys	....	Jack Lesnick	Beverly J Renner	Ronald Novak	Rodger Griffith	Charles R Hoagland
Englewood*† (11) CM	513 836-5106	Edward S Kemper	Eric A Smith	Karen Winkler	Joan M Huls	David Evans	Erik Dam	Victor W Roberts
Enon v† (3) MC	513 864-5577	Charles Koons	....	....	....	....	William Sorg	....
Euclid (60) MC	216 289-2700	Anthony J Giunta	John Piscitello	Lucille Kucharski	Richard T Balazs	George R Langa	Frank W Payne	Louis C Dommer
Fairborn* (30) CM	513 879-1730	Georgia P Hale	William W Burns	Jack Pope	Jack Pope	Robert M Haun	Robert Cox	....
Fairfield tp§† (39) MC	513 863-5414	....	Donald B Brill	....	....	....	....	....
Fairfield* (31) CM	513 867-5300	Robert J Wolpert	Robert J Gerhardt	Dena Napier	James A Hanson	Donald Bennett	Gary Rednour	Robert M Dettmer
Fairlawn (6) MC	216 666-8875	Louis A Mangels	....	Lawrence W Pelland	Lawrence W Pelland	John M Gemind	Michael J LaMonica	....
Fairport v (3) MC	216 352-3620	(not reporting)						
Fairview Park (19) MC	216 333-2200	Joseph M Gaul	John E Schirmer	Rosalie Karaba	Thomas K Malone	William M Curran	Chester Kluth	John E Schirmer
Findlay† (36) MC	419 424-7137	W Bentley Burr	David J Wobser	Eunice A Davenport	Al Hofer	George Kennedy	David B Clark	....
Forest Park* (19) CM	513 595-5200	Brandon H Wiers	Claire R Kuhlman	Kathy Lives	Lois Reynolds	Robert Stegeman	James B Nieman	David J Stenger
Fort Shawnee v (5) MC	419 991-2015	Karen A Garrett	....	R Elizabeth Smith	Diane L Barnes	....	Gene S Sharp	....
Fostoria (16) MC	419 435-8282	Kenneth A Beier	J Charles Macias	Jacquelyn E Peiffer	Clarence L Jacob	William D Woods	James T Keckler	J Charles Macias

Directory 1/10 continued — MUNICIPAL OFFICIALS IN ALL U.S. CITIES OVER 2,500[1]

City, 1980 population (000 omitted), form of government		Municipal phone number	Mayor	Appointed administrator	City clerk	Finance officer	Fire chief	Police chief	Public works director
OHIO (348) continued									
Franklin* (11)	CM	513 746-9921	William Thomas	Phillip A Herrick	Jane McGee	Sandra Morgan	Forrest Johnson	George Hamilton III	Thomas Davis
Fremont (18)	MC	419 334-9556	Richard D Maier	Warren T Curtis	John Newcomer	Fred W Recktenwald	Alvin Whittaker	Richard L Joseph	Warren T Curtis
Gahanna (18)	MC	614 471-2563	James F McGregor	....	M Peg Cunningham	Donald E Britton	....	Roger Schirtzinger	Gene Baugh
Galion† (12)	MC	419 468-1857	Paulette K Ritchey	....	Garland Gledhill	E Roberta Wade	M G Enders Jr	John Swain	Kenneth E Durtsche
Gallipolis* (6)	CM	614 446-1789	....	Christian P Morris	Alma D Martin	Alma D Martin	Ray Bush	Garland Nibert	....
Garfield Heights (33)	MC	216 475-1100	Thomas J Longo	....	Margaret Sikon	Richard W Obert	Paul E Unger	J L Hopkins	Alex J Piekarczyk
Geneva* (7)	CM	216 466-4675	Charles K Castle	Marc J Thompson	Nancy Bowdler	Marc J Thompson	Gary Farley	James Pearson	Marc J Thompson
Georgetown v (3)	MC	513 378-6395	Joseph C Rose	Milford Fisher	Bonnie Jones	....	Joseph Brookbank	Harry L Graves	....
Germantown§ (5)	MC	513 855-6567	Dale E Shafer Jr	Sam Steadman Jr	Kathy E Blevins	Doris M Amburgey	Richard Zechar	James J Desch	Steven A Fugate
Girard† (13)	MC	216 545-3879	Joseph J Melfi	....	Helen Bornemiss	Regina Demas	Sam Revella	Anthony M Ross	Nicholas J Melfi
Golf Manor (4)	MC	513 531-7491	Dennis J Puthoff	David L Foglesong	Jack Nathan	....	Michael B Gunn	Jackie R McDaniel	....
Grandview Heights (7)	MC	614 488-3159	Lawrence E Pierce	James M Blackburn	Frank L Godorhazy	....	Charles W Hovermale	Charles L Cotton	Sam A Troiano
Granville v* (4)	CM	614 587-0707	Thomas F Gallant	Douglas E Plunkett	Catherine M Miller	Shirley A Robertson	James Dumbauld	Franklin L Sorrell	Ralph Blackstone
Green tp§ (51)	MC	513 385-3283	Stephen G Brinker	Raymond Schlinkert	Cheryl J Winkler	....	Robert Weitzel	James Suder	Joseph Florian
Greenfield (5)	MC	513 981-3500	William B Wisecup	Berlin Whitley	Roberta Cowgill	Maxine Palmer	T Steven Campbell	Gregory L Barr	....
Greenhills v (5)	MC	513 825-2100	Robert G Carlson	David B Moore	H Clifft Rotherum	H Clifft Rotherum	Herbert Burns	Donald L Slaughter	....
Greenville (13)	MC	513 548-1482	Richard B Birt	....	Marvella Fletcher	Marvella Fletcher	Willie Beaver	Dwight Williamson	Walter Hocevar
Grove City (17)	MC	614 875-6368	Robert E Evans	Charles W Boso Jr	June Cook	Robert E Behlen	Donald Reese	Ronald R Gabriel	James McDonald
Groveport v (3)	MC	614 836-5301	J Harold Carley	G Roland Williams	Opal Rohr	Opal M Rohr	....	Roger Adams	G Roland Williams
Hamilton* (63)	CM	513 868-5800	George V McNally	William G Tallman	Anna Manna Hubbard	Jack Becker	Donald Lickert	Charles T Knox	Michael Samoviski
Harrison v (6)	MC	513 367-4313	Harry A Rolfes	....	Geraldine R Dole	Geraldine R Dole	Alan Kinnett	Frank R Mondary	....
Heath† (7)	MC	614 522-1420	John C Geller	Al Lallathin	Ms C Lederer	Ms C Lederer	Richard Padar	Thomas Ewing	Stan Holmquist
Hicksville v (4)	MC	419 542-5011	(not reporting)						
Highland Heights (6)	MC	216 461-2440	Thomas A Hughes	....	Jean A Buchak	D Wm Weber	Edward S Bencin	Keith H Woodie	Joseph Morscher
Hilliard (8)	MC	614 876-7361	R A Reynolds	....	Robert Stewart	L A Skeels	....	Edgel Maynard	Robert Tucker
Hillsboro (6)	MC	513 393-3447	Betty Bishop	Kelly Shelton	Rebecca A Tharp	Elizabeth Musser	Thomas J Stephens	Michael Lengefeld	....
Hubbard (9)	MC	216 534-3090	William S Colletta	....	Dorothy Booth	John Glod	Robert Strachen	Louis P Carsone	Thomas J Bolchalk
Huber Heights (35)	MC	513 233-1423	(not reporting)						
Hudson v* (5)	CM	216 650-1799	Harold L Bayless	S S Schweikert	Mary A George	Barbara J Harder	Paul Martin	Ronald Michalec	James Cox
Huron* (7)	CM	419 433-5000	Vera M McComb	Richard H Witker	Phyllis Wassner	Harold Holzhauser	John A Zimmerman	Louis P Wargo	Richard H Witker
Independence (8)	MC	216 524-4131	Winfred Wisnieski	....	Ms E Hackett	Louis Onders	Carl M Frimel	Louis Narduzzi	George Walkowiak
Indian Hill v* (6)	CM	513 561-6500	William W Ventress	James D Jester	Paul C Riordan	Paul C Riordan	Robert Coy	William C Wiebold	John N McBride
Ironton† (14)	MC	614 532-3833	William R Sheridan	....	Janet Miller	James Tordiff	James Brown	William Ackison	James E Meyers
Jackson (7)	MC	614 286-3224	Burleigh F Oiler	....	Barbara Leach	Edward R Jarvis	Richard Eubanks	Wayne Kight	Ronald B Speakman
Jefferson (Madison) v (4)	MC	614 879-7674	Charlie M Miller	....	Eleanor Baker	....	....	Frank E Cox	....
Jefferson (Ashtabula) v (3)	MC	216 576-3941	Kenneth Fertig	B D Westfall	Gertrude Armstrong	Gertrude Armstrong	John Wayman	Kenneth Johnson	....
Johnstown v (3)	MC	614 967-3177	Charles W White	....	Charles E Williams	....	John Johnson	Alvey L Gussler	....
Kent* (26)	CM	216 678-8100	Nancy Hansford	James C Bacon Jr	Carol Lockhart	Daniel S Foecking	Raymond Dietz	William Lillich	Priscilla Blanchard
Kenton (9)	MC	419 675-5292	Ray O Thompson	John J Krock	Dorothy M Gibson	Robert R Brown	Charles Wilson	L K Fisher	John J Krock
Kettering* (61)	CM	513 296-2400	Gerald E Busch	Robert F Walker	Virginia J Schulke	P Michael Robinette	James C Frey	Randall E Barney	....
Kirtland (6)	MC	216 256-3332	Mario V Marcopoli	Harold E Brichford	Pamela Lewis	Richard L Martinet	Ralph Dyke	Dennis T Yarborough	Phillip W Shrout
Lakemore v (3)	MC	216 733-6125	Charles A Carr	Gerald Sanner	Sandra L Stafford	Sandra L Stafford	James Brown	Daniel O Conner	William Bookman
Lakewood (62)	MC	216 521-7580	Anthony C Sinagra	....	Madeline A Cain	Leonard A Mikula	Byron Cook	Edmund Mecklenburg	Robert Kleinweber
Lancaster (35)	MC	614 653-1201	Edward C Rutherford	....	James C Russell	A Gene Ash	Wilbur Welch	Flaveon E Augg	Sam Barney
Lebanon* (10)	CM	513 932-3060	Mark R Bogen	Timothy C Hansley	....	George S Perrine	Michael T Hannigan	Ronald G Ferrell	....
Leipsic v§ (2)	MC	419 943-2009	James Russell	Wm Grunkemeyer	Christine Schroeder	Polly Mangold	Robert Dietsch	Jeff Schreiber	Ken Teders
Lexington v (4)	MC	419 884-1329	Eugene R Parkison	Charles Pscholka	Dianna Braden	Mary Ellen Algire	Richard Carter	James Hoffer	....
Lima (47)	MC	419 228-5462	Harry J Moyer	....	Margaret Griffith	G Hobart Reinier	John C Brookman	Frank L Catlett	David J Grisez
Lincoln Heights* (5)	CM	513 733-5900	Arthur Dawson	....	Dorothy Fletcher	Rosa M Blair	Ernest McCowen	Ervin Martin	Fletcher Strayhorn
Lisbon v (3)	MC	216 424-5503	Joseph E Chapman Jr	....	Thelma Culbertson	Thelma Culbertson	Harold J Adams	Charles Carlisle	....
Lockland† (4)	MC	513 761-1124	Jim Brown	....	Stan Heideman	Douglas Sand	Thomas E Grau	Eugene Robinson	....
Lodi v (3)	MC	216 948-2040	Edward Richardson	....	Carline M Ferguson	Donald Gilbert	Larry Cradock	Michael A Jones	Carl Zdelar
Logan† (7)	MC	614 385-8310	Evans S Hand Jr	C T Grey	Albert Elick	Betty Kuhn	Robert Courter	Charles Barron	....
London (7)	MC	614 852-1111	Edward A Bower	Bill Ames	....	Mary Louise Alcott	Richard Minner	James R Bates	Joseph Londergan
Lorain (75)	MC	216 244-3204	Joseph J Zahorec	....	Arlene K Kokinda	Kenneth J Koscho	Alfred W Damm	John Malinovsky	Richard J Koba
Lordstown v† (3)	MC	216 824-2283	Burnell Muth	....	....	....	....	....	....
Loudonville v (3)	MC	419 994-3214	M D Shilling	....	....	Ruth E Ferris	Burley Saunier	Wm E Porter	Thomas Sellers
Louisville* (8)	CM	216 875-3321	Donald D Marshall	Roger H Howard	Barbara Calvert	William G Hamilton	Lynn E Kerstetter	Richard A Deitrick	Richard J Menegay
Loveland* (9)	CM	513 683-0150	Roland Boike	Wayne Barfels	Barbara A Casey	Bill Taphorn	Jim Hunter	George T Brockman	Jim Benedict
Lyndhurst (18)	MC	216 442-5777	Leonard M Creary	....	Dan M Patrick II	Dan M Patrick II	Joseph A Sweeney	Roger M Smyth	Steve Settevendemie
Macedonia (7)	MC	216 468-1300	Stuart W Feils	....	Mary P Hegidus	Margret Gillenkirk	Carl E Stewart	Bryce Acheson	James R Lawton
Madeira* (9)	CM	513 561-7228	Mary Anne Christie	William S Toth	Patrica A Smith	Steven A Soper	....	Phillip R Hudson	Floyd H Poppenhouse
Mansfield (54)	MC	419 526-2600	Edward T Meehan	William O Friend	....	L Norman Walker	Dyce Kopcial	Mathew Benick	Francis Fischer
Maple Heights (30)	MC	216 662-6000	William T Voll	Michael S Dernyar	George S Matejka	George S Matejka	Vincent J Jacobs	Dennis J Love	Frank Novak
Mariemont v† (3)	MC	513 271-3246	Clarence M Erickson	....	Robert V Naugle	....	Thomas A Driggers	Donald Shanks	....
Marietta (16)	MC	614 373-1387	Nancy P Hollister	Lance Hinson	Pauline Jorgensen	Thomas F O'Brien	William D Eagleson	Roger E Phillis	Lance Hinson
Marion (37)	MC	614 387-2020	Ronald L Malone	Ronald L Malone	Joan Steward	Robert Cramer	Phillip Reid	Robert Exley	Robert E Malone
Martins Ferry (9)	MC	614 633-2876	John Regis	....	....	Andrew Sutak	Jeff Sommer	Lloyd Shrodes	Joseph E Minder
Marysville (7)	MC	513 642-6015	Thomas O Nuckles	Wilfred E Conrad	Lois J Reese	Marjorie M Wilcox	Ralph A Burns	Vernon E Bright	....
Mason* (9)	CM	513 398-8010	Louis Eves	Thomas W Moeller	Betty Baysore	Betty Baysore	Donald Walker	James Edwards	Max T Chesney
Massillon (31)	MC	216 833-4625	Delbert A Demmer	....	Barbara Workman	Barbara Workman	Tom Matthews	Richard Bryan	Ted C Willoughby
Maumee (16)	MC	419 893-8751	James B Dussel	Richard A Krieger	Charles H Beard	Charles H Beard	Frederic R Burdo	Thomas E Bodi	F Joseph Cory
Mayfield v (4)	MC	216 461-2210	Fred N Carmen	Gus Amendola	Donna J Heath	Steven M Toth	Allan L Hejcl	Donald H Stevens	....
Mayfield Heights (22)	MC	216 442-2626	Ross C DeJohn	....	Robert G Tribby	Robert G Tribby	Wayne R Jacobson	Dominic M Caprara	Andrew D Fornaro
McDonald v (4)	MC	216 530-5471	Robert W Zajack	....	Joseph R McHale	Robert Alexander	Daniel Nagy	John Golubic	John Tote
Medina (15)	MC	216 725-8861	William C Lamb	Jeffrey B Kehnle	Catherine L Horn	Wayne Hamilton	Thurston Berry	H C Davis Jr	Thos C Cunningham
Mentor* (42)	CM	216 255-1100	Donald E Krueger	Edward J Podojil	Carolyn C Haddock	Morris Beverage	John D Preuer	Joseph S Koziol	Alvin E Beasley
Mentor-on-the-Lake (8)	MC	216 257-7216	Franklin T Stroud	Kip L Molenaar	Judith Davis	Kip L Molenaar	Donald Cunningham	William Chamar	....
Miamisburg* (15)	CM	513 866-3303	Robert H Mears	Mark A Gibson	Ms Anthony Clark	Kermit E Simmons	Robert Menker	Robert F Goenner	....
Middleburg Heights (16)	MC	216 234-8811	Gary W Starr	....	Barbara Becker	Mildred C Babich	James M McCarthy	Robert Blatnica	Charles R Henke
Middleport v (3)	MC	614 992-3145	Fred L Hoffman	....	Jon P Buck	Carl Horky	Jeff Darst	J J Cremeans	....
Middletown* (44)	CM	513 425-7766	James W Saunders	Dale F Helsel	Bettie J Arthur	Robert F Ritter	Roger South	Russell L Dwyer	Richard D Goecke
Milford* (5)	CM	513 831-4192	Douglas W Thomson	James D Buckner	Sharon D Marsh	Stephen Wagner	John Cooper	David A Smith	Elmer R Weigel
Millersburg v (3)	MC	216 674-1886	David Shrock	William D Marks	Harold Wheaton	Ronald Stutzman	Raymond Eyler	Darryl Weiss	....
Minerva v* (5)	CM	216 868-7705	Dick W Mount Sr	Gregory B Horn	Rhea L Cochran	Joanne Chuckalovcha	Ray Willett	Ronald W Jornd	Milton J Eichman
Mingo Junction v (5)	MC	614 535-1511	John L Lewis	....	....	Richard Crugnale	John L McGuire	Geo Dodsworth	Lawrence Fristick
Minster v (3)	MC	419 628-2595	Elmer A Weaver	....	Vernon Naber	Vernon Naber	Donald Lampert	William Poeppelman	Joseph Bruns
Mogadore v† (4)	MC	216 628-4896	George H Wear	....	Ruth S Frieden	Ruth S Frieden	Edward O Jenkins	Marvin G Wilmoth	....

Directory 1/10 continued — MUNICIPAL OFFICIALS IN ALL U.S. CITIES OVER 2,500[1]

City, 1980 population (000 omitted), form of government		Municipal phone number	Mayor	Appointed administrator	City clerk	Finance officer	Fire chief	Police chief	Public works director
OHIO (348) continued									
Monroe v§ (4)	MC	513 539-7374	A Seth Johnston	Derek L Conklin	Linda Brower	Frank C Pahr	Mark Neu II	Michael Lawhorn	....
Montgomery† (10)	MC	513 891-2424	Florence W Kennedy	Dean E Sterling	....	Ralph C Lottes	....	Charles F Sellars	Thomas Keissler
Montpelier v (4)	MC	419 485-4015	Roger Thorp	John Bitler	Betty M Allman	Betty M Allman	Lewis Hendricks	William Mapes	John Bitler
Moraine* (5)	CM	513 299-7312	Harold L Johnson	James R Harville	Pamela M Conley	Ora F Allen	Harold Sigler	Glenn Carmichael	....
Moreland Hills v† (3)	MC	216 248-1188	Alvin T Croucher	....	Kathy Konicky	David W Rowlinson	....	James E Codney Sr	Robert J Potts
Mount Gilead v (3)	MC	419 946-3926	Charles Giauque	....	Betty Williams	Betty Williams	Richard K Young	Robert D Ruhl	....
Mount Healthy (8)	MC	513 931-8840	David C Stockdale	Lois R Melvin	Vera S Adkins	William Bobinger	Arthur Girty	George Hunt	Lois R Melvin
Mount Vernon (14)	MC	614 397-3917	Betty K Winand	J Kenneth Grove Jr	Martha J Lemasters	Margaret Ann Ruhl	Ernie Farmer	Thomas Bartlett	J Vernon Hall
Munroe Falls v (5)	MC	216 688-7491	Gerald L Hupp	....	Douglas F Scott	Douglas F Scott	Charles Rush	Steve A Stahl	Edgar E Carpenter
Napoleon* (9)	CM	419 592-4010	Robert G Heft	Richard A Hayward	R W Schweinhagen	R W Schweinhagen	James Hershberger	Richard Rudolph	....
Nelsonville† (5)	MC	614 753-1314	Wilbur D Mender	Paul Wolfe	Jane Heintzelman	Catherine I Giffin	Danny Knight	Gregory Smith	Paul Wolfe
New Boston (3)	MC	614 456-5347	(not reporting)						
New Carlisle* (6)	CM	513 845-9493	H Ruth Schaffer	Carole S Hoffman	Clair Miller	Madge Shellhaas	Harold L Lucas	Ronald Gregory	George Hahnemann
New Lebanon v (5)	MC	513 687-1341	James E Teer Jr	Michael J Dickey	E Karen Grimmett	E Karen Grimmett	Charles S Crotty	Michael J Dickey	Charles S Crotty
New Lexington v† (5)	MC	614 342-1633	Delmar Danison	John Tincher	Virginia Treadway	Virginia Treadway	Brenton Taylor	Randy Barker	....
New Miami v (3)	MC	513 892-1141	Earcel Cheek	....	Virginia A Hensley	Virginia A Hensley	Robert Carberry	Ben Kidd	....
New Philadelphia† (17)	MC	216 364-4491	Leo Benjamin	....	James Huff	John Comanita	Eugene Parson Jr	James Locker	G Michael Coutts
New Richmond v (3)	MC	513 553-4684	(not reporting)						
Newark (41)	MC	614 349-2214	William S Moore	....	Diana Hufford	G Leonard Feightner	Clarence E Huston	Robert T Post	Bryce R Peterson
Newburgh Heights v† (3)	MC	216 641-4650	Ronald D Sulik	....	Maxine Grissman	Maxine Grissman	John Martin	James Lukas	....
Newcomerstown v (4)	MC	614 498-6313	Charles R Yingling		Donald L Porcher	....	Edward Groff	John E Lawver	....
Newton Falls* (5)	CM	216 872-0806	Lester Irwin	Hiram W Watkins III	Patricia Swimmer	Dolores Stoner	Kenneth Whetzel	Ellis Thompson	Robert Eakins
Niles (23)	MC	216 652-3415	John P Shaffer	....	....	Ann Ford	Charles Semple	John Ross	Lewis M Slanina
North Baltimore v (3)	MC	419 257-2394	Robert A Patteson	Donald Aitman	Nancy Richmond	Nancy Richmond	Frank W Paden	Donald Hendren	....
North Canton (14)	MC	216 499-8223	William Hines	A Michael Sumser	Marion J Wilson	V Magaret Loretto	Glen A Forney	Charles D Henley	....
North College Hill† (11)	MC	513 521-7413	Charles L Woeste	....	Diane Heller	George Snyder	Wilbert Koch	Peter A Zappulla	C Jack Pelzel
North Kingsville v (3)	MC	216 224-0091	Woodrow McConnell	....	Elizabeth Terrill	....	Carl Oxley	Nicholas H Walker	
North Olmsted (36)	MC	216 777-8000	R W Swietyniowski	....	Florence E Campbell	Edward J Boyle	John Van Kuren	Marion R Taylor	J P Corrigan
North Ridgeville† (22)	MC	216 327-6811	Richard J Noll	....	John Zywczyk	Chris Costin	Eugene Diederich	Thomas A Sigsworth	Robert Kleinoeder
North Royalton (18)	MC	216 237-5686	John G Halak	....	June Lusk	Leonore Chidsey	Lloyd Leimbach	James Zindrowski	Richard Esdinsky
Northfield v (4)	MC	216 467-7139	Charles A Greenlee	....	Patricia M Burger	Patricia M Burger	Curtis Pavlick	S Gilbert Backus	....
Northwood§ (5)	MC	419 693-9328	John R Hageman	Alden E Hatch	Marsha J Kurek	Marsha J Kurek	Merlin H Rolfes	Sidney R Lark	Russell B Slocum
Norton† (12)	MC	216 825-7815	Walter C Peterman	John R Sanders	Fred C Sommer	Fred C Sommer	Michael Antoniotti	Forest Diefendorff	....
Norwalk (14)	MC	419 668-4159	R Thomas Cochran	....	Patricia Matheny	Vernis O George	David D Caprara	Donald Ratliff	James Cochran
Norwood (26)	MC	513 396-8200	Joseph E Sanker	Darrell Maxwell	Joseph W Sanker	Paul R Piening Jr	Leon Hughes	Carl Motz	Joe Geers
Oak Harbor v (3)	MC	419 898-5561	Willard Bloom	Henry Brooks	Sandra Baumgartner	....	Tom Almendinger	William Paulsen	....
Oakwood v (4)	MC	419 594-3352	(not reporting)						
Oakwood* (9)	CM	513 298-0600	E E Storms Jr	J David Foell	Cathy Dewire	Callie Rehrig	Michael J Kelly	Michael J Kelly	R C Reece
Oberlin* (9)	CM	216 775-1531	Harriet A Arnold	Dale S Sugerman	Julie A Simonson	Douglas E Ward	Doyle Jones	Robert K Jones	J Chris Nielson
Obetz v (3)	MC	614 491-1080	Mark Froehlich	Don Tussing	Helen Hayes	Helen Hayes	....	David Jones	....
Olmsted Falls† (6)	MC	216 235-5550	William P Mahoney	....	Geraldine Geist	Geraldine Geist	John Calogar	....	
Ontario v (4)	MC	419 529-3818	Chas K Hellinger		Ann L Wolfe	....	Wayne E Danals	Robert E Krauss	John P McPherson
Oregon† (19)	MC	419 698-7045	Stephen J Toth	R Brooks Whitmore	Mary A Taylor	Mary A Taylor	Gene Groll	William Hoefflin	Donald A Surface
Orrville (8)	MC	216 683-8715	Howard E Wade	Peter Guster	Patricia Ayers	Charles E Horst	Chester LeFever	William Stocker	Robert A Nichols
Ottawa v (4)	MC	419 523-5020	Louis H Macke		Mack Schaffer	Mack Schaffer	Roger Trenkamp	Eugene Fischbach	Dewey M William
Ottawa Hills v (4)	MC	419 536-1111	S Stewart Cochrane	Robert M Jeffrey	....	Robert Reinbolt	Fred L Yeager	Joseph H A Eich	Robert M Jeffrey
Oxford* (18)	CM	513 523-2171	Stephen D Snyder	Dennis R Stuckey	Evelyn Webb	Evelyn Webb	Len Endress	Joseph L Statum	Richard W Fink
Painesville* (16)	CM	216 352-9301	....	Lester N Nero	Shirley A Farren	Robert J Wooten	Jack A Martin	....	Raymond L Dray
Parma (93)	MC	216 886-2323	John Petruska	....	Bernard J Survoy	Joseph S Lime	Thomas Romeo	Francis Szabo	Howard Trumble
Parma Heights (23)	MC	216 884-9600	Paul W Cassidy	....	Carla Binder	Alice J Felice	Ronald B Hutchings	Edward Mudra	Daniel A Tobik
Paulding v§ (3)	MC	419 399-4011	Albert Rife	Harry Wiebe	Rosalee Armstrong	Rosalee Armstrong	Robert Unger	Paul Keeler	
Pepper Pike† (6)	MC	216 831-8500	John T Avery		....	Rosemary David	William E Gorris	Stephen A Toth	Frank Csiszko
Perrysburg (10)	MC	419 874-7913	Samuel F Hunter	....	Wayne D Tuckerman	....	Merlin J Artz	C M Descamps	James M Bagdonas
Pickerington v§ (4)	MC	614 837-3974	Thomas H Burkhardt	R Steven Bailey	Evelyn Strawn	Linda Fersch	....	Donald Pruden	Harold Rarey
Piqua* (20)	CM	513 778-2051	Charles E Stevens	Frank Patrizio Jr	Lucy D Laug	Robert N Slagle	Robert Bowman	Donald White	....
Poland v (3)	MC	216 757-2112	(not reporting)						
Pomeroy v (3)	MC	614 992-2246	Richard Seyler	....	William Snouffer	William Snouffer	Charles Legar	George Z Stitt	....
Port Clinton (7)	MC	419 734-5522	John F Fritz	Max E McLaury	Laurie Eberle	Nancy O'Neal	John Drummer	Henry Jacoby	
Portsmouth* (26)	CM	614 354-8807	Richard Grimm	Richard T Roberts	Ruth J Coriell	James F Stewart	William Medley	James A Workman	Paul R Ison
Ravenna (12)	MC	216 296-3864	Donald J Kainrad	....	Frank Polichene	Ralph O Lewis	Larry Shafer	Douglas Peters	William E Hale
Reading (13)	MC	513 733-3725	Anthony J Gertz	Dennis E Albrinck	Denise L Jones	Donald A Dawdy	Robert Hollmeyer	Robert Huelsman	Dennis E Albrinck
Reynoldsburg (21)	MC	614 866-6391	John K Francis		Sonja A Herd	Mary M Funk	....	Jess E Moore	Ronald R Morrison
Richfield v (3)	MC	216 659-9201	E June Feiber	Larry P Wilson	....	Libby Peters	Russell English	Thomas Fisher	....
Richmond Heights (10)	MC	261 486-2474	Robert J Boyle	....	Marcia S Morgan	Sylvania Stanek	Robert A Stefancik	Joseph Collins	Jack DeFranco
Rittman* (6)	CM	216 925-2045	Ashton O Hall	Julian M Suso	Judith A Emery	Donna F Fite	Gary Larch	Larry A Boggs	....
Rocky River (21)	MC	216 331-0600	Earl Martin	....	Susan Weschler	Susan Wollenzier	Donald Chessar	James Pancoast	Don Umerley
Rossford (6)	MC	419 666-0210	Louis Bauer Jr	Milan L Vavrik	Edward Tucholski	David A Weaks	John Lonchyna	Mathew J Vedra	....
Sabina v† (3)	MC	513 584-2123	Edward Hodge	....	Barbara A Scranton		Guy Riddle	Richard May	....
Salem (13)	MC	216 332-4241	Robert E Sell	....	Kathleen Utterback	Frances Dickey	Lee Cranmer	John L Sommers III	John P Dwyer
Sandusky* (31)	CM	419 627-5861	George L Mylander	Frank A Link	Sarah A White	Carol M Steensen	Owen R Reed	Gerald A Lechner	Paul C Fogle
Sebring* (5)	CM	216 938-9340	J Michael Pinkerton	Charles Tieche	Judy Snyder	Charles Tieche	James Cannell	Paul E Freer	
Seven Hills (14)	MC	216 524-4421	John F Kelley		Rose Marie Gavula	Jack E Evans	Charles Hosta	John Fechko	Irvin Gallagher
Shadyside (4)	MC	614 676-5972	Ronald P Kaluger	....	Wm E Johnson	Wm E Johnson	Dan Boyd	Kenneth Perigloisi	David E Manner
Shaker Heights (32)	MC	216 752-5000	Stephen J Alfred	William J Schuchart	William J Schuchart	William J Schuchart	Ronald Specht	George J Lamboy	Walter Ugrinic
Sharonville (10)	MC	513 563-1144	John S Dowlin	Rex E Baysore	....	James Greensfelder	Dale Duermit	William Nuss	
Sheffield Lake (10)	MC	216 949-7141	Daniel Fragassi		Paul Stockert	William Andersen	Eugene Rouse	Thomas Walther	Mearl Walton
Shelby (10)	MC	419 347-5131	Garland John Gates	....	John R DeVito	John R DeVito	Ned Reed	John Van Wagner	....
Sidney* (18)	CM	513 498-2335	James P Humphrey	Steven E Husemann	Tanyce M Lang	Michael Puckett	Lyle Baker	Jack L Wilson	Roger M Hoersten
Silver Lake v (3)	MC	216 923-5233	Clyde L Conn	....	William V Curry	William V Curry	....	Raymond Bellinger	Milton R Bertka
Silverton (6)	MC	513 793-7980	Richard F Hunter	....	John W Davis	Shirley J Larkin	Paul J Steman	William F Eggers	Paul J Steman
Solon (14)	MC	216 248-1155	Charles J Smercina	....	Thelma Linton	Thelma Linton	Julius Oriti	Robert W Bruckner	Anthony Picone
South Charleston v*† (2)	CM	513 462-8888	Thos L Rutschilling	Clayton Mercer	Wanda L Rice	....	Roger Giffin	Gary L Owens	Clayton Mercer
South Euclid (26)	MC	216 381-0400	Arnold D'Amico	....	Celeste DiCillo	Celeste DiCillo	Fred R Rothaermel	William Van Veghel	Kevin P Lynch
South Lebanon v (3)	MC	513 494-2211	Vernon E Hogan	Sheila R Campbell	Diana Mitchem	....	Albert Clark	Lester Kilburn	....
South Point v (4)	MC	614 377-4838	William A Gaskin	Earl Blake	Ralph Early	....	J F Eldridge	Carl Vance	....
South Russell v (3)	MC	216 338-7843	Thomas F Harvey	Wallace H King	Jane G Stern	Carl Groth	....	Robert Hamilton	
Springboro v§ (5)	MC	513 748-1041	James H Eyler	William R Covell	Gayle Bennett	Sue Morris	Richard Chenault	Carl Hirschback	George Brackney
Springdale§ (10)	MC	513 671-0885	Vernon P French	Cecil W Osborn	Doyle H Webster	Doyle H Webster	Robert J Posega	James I Freland	Robert N Sears

Directory 1/10 continued — MUNICIPAL OFFICIALS IN ALL U.S. CITIES OVER 2,500[1]

City, 1980 population (000 omitted), form of government		Municipal phone number	Mayor	Appointed administrator	City clerk	Finance officer	Fire chief	Police chief	Public works director
OHIO (348) continued									
Springfield* (73)	CM	513 324-7700	Leland L Schuler	W Gregg Lamar	Priscilla Smithers	Keith Overly	William Casey	....	Alvin Wansing
St. Bernard (5)	MC	513 242-7770	Chas Von Der Meulen	....	Terry Grant	Edward J Geiser	Leon Boyd	Robert Heller	Jack Hausfeld
St. Clairsville† (5)	CM	614 695-1324	Edgar White	Harry Myers Jr	Virginia Stidd	Lois Pugh	Bruce Henderson	Martin Kendzora	Dennis Bigler
St. Marys (8)	MC	419 394-3303	William T Sell	Thomas L Brodbeck	Frances L Wehnes	Pamela J Edgar	Ron Hunter	George Henderson	Kenneth Hegemann
Steubenville (26)	MC	614 283-6133	Michael J Walkosky	James Lord	Lillian Lloyd	J A Quattrone Jr	John Prayso	Geo Mavromatis	Joseph Scalise
Stow (25)	MC	216 688-8206	C Paul Hutchison	....	Bonnie Emahiser	John A Earle	Robert Dauchy	Paul F Long	Gerald R Dolson
Streetsboro (9)	MC	216 626-4942	David Pavlick	....	Nancy Davis	David L Williams	Homer Templeton	James D Brown	Joseph A Collica
Strongsville (29)	MC	216 238-5720	Walter F Ehrnfelt	....	Martha Finn	Thomas Zammikiel	William M McKinley	Frank Papp	Walter F Ehrnfelt
Struthers (14)	MC	216 755-2181	Howard W Heldman	....	Amelia DeLost	Mary Ellen Jones	Harold L Milligan	Valent Granchie	George J Stanko
Swanton v (3)	CM	419 826-9515	Richard C Peters	Carla R Christy	Ardys Slaninka	Carla R Christy	Lewis W Taylor	Frederick J Ray	Lewis W Taylor
Sylvania (16)	MC	419 882-7102	James E Seney	....	Clayton F Fischer	Clayton F Fischer	David Drake	Gerald A Sobb	Ronald S Carmichael
Tallmadge (15)	MC	216 633-0850	Robert S Merriman	....	Frances Cochran	John Wray	Dennis Crossen	Gale G Gault	Robert E Victory
Tiffin (20)	MC	419 447-3440	Thomas L Yager	Robert M Blair	....	Letha Mount	Thomas Huss	David Martien	William Shumaker
Tipp City* (6)	CM	513 667-8424	Carl Suerdieck	....	Nancy Arnett	Richard Drennen	Clarence Drewing	Ronald Spring	....
Toledo* (355)	CM	419 245-1000	Donna Owens	David A Boston	Larry J Brewer	James E Kasch	William H Winkle	John W Mason	Eugene R Kasper
Toronto† (7)	MC	614 537-2750	Andrew J Blaner	....	Inzy R Markle	Ralph R Tarulli	Larry Lukacena	Paul McCarthy	Harry Crouch
Trenton* (6)	CM	513 988-6304	John Madoffori	Melvin P Ruder	Marcia M Szala	Gregory S Watson	Larry Beiser	Joe E Richard	Freelen Whitt
Trotwood* (8)	CM	513 837-7771	Richard J Haas	Robert A Kuntz	Jeri Jewett	Robert A Kuntz	....	Jon Schweigert	Curtis Eagle
Troy§ (19)	MC	513 335-1725	Douglas A Campbell	Arthur D Haddad	Sue G Knight	Chris A Peeples	Robert M Counts	Charles W Frank	....
Twinsburg (8)	MC	216 425-7161	Anthony A Perici	....	Catherine Hamilton	Jo Anne Terry	Roy Watson	Robert Knaack	....
Uhrichsville† (6)	MC	614 922-1243	Burton E Peck	....	Joanne L Dunlap	Joanne L Dunlap	Dale Grandison	Frank Barker	Robert W Stevenson
Union* (5)	MC	513 836-8624	David R Stamper	John P Applegate	Mary H Hewell	Mary H Hewell	....	....	....
Union tp§ (28)	MC	513 752-1741	Catherine Wuerdeman	Mary Lou Evans	Rozanne Evans	....	....	Willis Russell	....
University Heights (15)	MC	216 932-7800	Beryl E Rothschild	....	Jeune McCormick	Margaret O Patrick	Ralph T Ballard	Phillip J Carr Jr	Marshall J Wien
Upper Arlington* (36)	CM	614 457-5080	Richard H Moore	Richard A King	Margaret C Halk	Denham Pride	John C Haney	Kenneth W Borror	....
Upper Sandusky (6)	MC	419 294-3862	Donald Hall	....	Maureen Houser	Sharon Lee	Rex Vent	Mel Sanford	....
Urbana§ (11)	MC	513 653-3812	Lewis B Moore	N Lawrence Wolke	Patricia King	....	E A Branstiter	Bill Lingrell	Arthur D Baer
Van Wert (11)	MC	419 238-0308	Stan Agler	Warren Foy	Susan K Bagley	Clyde W Bellinger	Paul H Baer	Ronald C Treon	....
Vandalia* (13)	CM	513 898-5891	Michael Robinette	Michael Ratcliff	Michael Ratcliff	William Hoffman	Robert Treiber	James Higgins	Theodore Rusen
Vermilion (11)	MC	216 967-0123	Hobart A Johnson	....	Eileen Bulan	Robert H Martin	Eugene Kropf	Roland Fleming	George Phillips
Versailles v§ (2)	MC	513 526-3294	C W McClurg	David J Seibel	Mary Ann Reed	....	Paul Pierron	George Frantz	Ramon Nickol
Wadsworth (15)	MC	216 335-1521	Charles R Danals	....	Linda Gehring	Lynda C Carrino	Chester Fish	Michael L King	William J Lyren
Walbridge v (3)	MC	419 666-1830	Forrest Scarberry	....	Mary Jane Finch	....	Donald Smothers	W Tom Wilson	....
Wapakoneta (8)	MC	419 738-6111	William V Lietz	Wayne A York	....	Janet Winkler	Edward J Schaub	Billy D Wolfe	....
Warren (57)	MC	216 841-2601	Daniel J Sferra	....	Barbara Busko	Anthony Iannucci	Roger Hernon	Richard Galgozy	Stephen J Papalas
Warrensville Heights (17)	MC	216 662-5858	Raymond J Grabow	....	Pauline Lowe	William Zadeskey	Kenneth Rosenlieb	Craig Merchant	....
Washington tp§ (40)	MC	513 433-0152	Douglas R Fink	Michael E Morton	Rita C Shear	....	Randall L Staley	Bill Daniel	Bill Johnson
Washington* (13)	CM	614 335-5720	Willard W Wilson	Douglas R Elliott	John I Stackhouse	John I Stackhouse	John Rockhold	William Robinson	....
Waterville v* (4)	CM	419 878-8107	Charles Peyton	....	Barbara Crandall	Velma L Gosden	Carl Conrad	Lowell S Gingrich	Ken Blair
Wauseon† (6)	MC	419 335-9022	Richard G Volk	....	Cora B Fraker	Cora B Fraker	Robert Barnes	Larry Sluder	Elmer Krieger
Waverly v (5)	MC	614 947-5162	Howard L Galloway	....	Jane McFarland	R E Childers	Lanny Claytor	Carson Newman	Marion Kiotz
Wellington v† (4)	MC	216 647-4626	Rudolph C J Neumann	....	Lyle Clarr	Lyle Clarr	Tony C Marley	Walter McCreery	Robert Dupee
Wellston (6)	MC	614 384-2720	H N Winters	....	Mary Ann Jarvis	Kathleen Mulhern	R A Hollingshead	Freddie D Kendrick	Ronnie M Potts
Wellsville (5)	MC	216 532-2524	Nunzio Lombardozzi	John Call	Cris McNicol	James R Haddock	David Lloyd	Martin Thorn	....
West Carrollton* (13)	CM	513 859-5181	A A Hintermeister	Glen T Williams	Don E Holycross	Kenneth F Glover	William Ennis	Kenneth M Spencer	Merle Neyman
West Milton v* (4)	CM	513 698-4191	Don Thompson	Robert Hemmerich	Joyce Knife	Dolores Frantz	Joseph Frantz	David Mote	....
West Union v (3)	MC	513 544-5326	C Robert Blake	....	Joy L Miller	....	William Kirker	Daniel Davis	Milford Kirker
Westerville* (23)	CM	614 890-8542	James A Tressler	Maynard W Dils	Sharon L Hahn	G David Lindimore	Richard C Morrison	Harry Schutte	Michael J Wasylik
Westlake† (19)	MC	216 871-3300	Theodore R Busch	....	Louise Hall	W G Fritzsche	Robert Patton	John Fleischer	Joseph Skodis
Whitehall (21)	MC	614 237-8611	John A Bishop	....	Nancy J Raab	Ginny Phillips	James Nessley	....	William H Roby
Wickliffe (17)	MC	216 944-4000	William R Reid	....	Angela Trimboli	Joseph A Unetic	Edward Bochenek	Andrew Zambory	Darryl Crossman
Willard* (6)	CM	419 933-2581	Kenneth Sommers	Paul W Capelle	Joann Jones	Eugene McEndree	George Yacob	David Sattig	....
Willoughby Hills (9)	MC	216 946-1234	Melvin G Schaefer	....	Marilyn Monzula	Steven Toth	William Heckler	Fred Heyer	....
Willoughby (19)	MC	216 951-2800	Eric R Knudson	....	Loretta Radebaugh	Chalmers H Glover	Kenneth F Stafford	William E Crosier	George W Tegner
Willowick (18)	MC	216 585-3700	Ralph J Gilfether	....	Edward H Zupancic	Edward H Zupancic	George Rupena	Ronald F Dopirak	David G Webster
Wilmington (10)	MC	513 382-3833	Clifford N Eveland	....	Linda Eichelberger	C Kent Vandervort	Joseph E Spicer	Michael Hatten	Robert W Holmes
Windham v (4)	MC	216 326-2622	Maurice E Hankins	....	Rachel Barrett	....	Donald Miller	Glenwood Barker	....
Wintersville v (5)	MC	614 264-5533	Frank P Layman	....	John M Lenhart	John M Lenhart	Rob Herrington	Victor Calabrese	John Weaver
Woodlawn v (3)	MC	513 771-6130	Lawyer Lawson	Wm J Spraul	Roy Bornemann	....	Kenneth Frankl	John E Williams Jr	....
Woodsfield v (3)	MC	614 472-0418	C E Knowlton II	....	Esther McIntire	Dorothy Ricer	J Ward Strickling	Manifred Keylor	....
Wooster (19)	MC	216 263-5200	J Clyde Breneman	Thomas D Spitler	Virginia Angert	James B Pyers	Edward Schuch	James Pearce	Donald Detrow
Worthington* (15)	CM	614 436-3100	Lawrence W Braun	David B Elder	Janice M McNeel	Barry A Brooks	....	P R Abbott	Judth A Zimomra
Wyoming* (8)	CM	513 821-7600	Frederic L Goeddel	Randolph Forrester	Bonnie S Jones	Mary Ann Engel	James Benken	Robert W Hess	John Wirtz
Xenia* (25)	CM	513 372-7611	Walter L Marshall	Robert Stewart	Ronald F Cousino	Ronald F Cousino	Charles L Beason	Dan H Aultman	Steven W Weaver
Yellow Springs v* (4)	CM	513 767-7202	Joseph Dowdell	D Kent Bristol	Veronica Meyers	....	....	James A McKee	....
Youngstown (115)	MC	216 746-1892	Patrick J Ungaro	Robert A Noday	William Holt	Dominic Conti	Gerald Kernan	Randall Wellington	Richard A Marsico
Zanesville (29)	MC	614 455-0600	Donald L Mason	George Thomas	Betty S Colopy	Joseph W Quinn	William Wagner	Earl D Moore	Frederick J Grant
OKLAHOMA (129)									
Ada* (16)	CM	405 436-6300	Bill Thompson	Leonard D Briley	Jerry Farnham	Jerry Farnham	William Gray	Richard Gray	Wilfrid Stride
Altus (23)	MC	405 477-1950	Leo Houck	Jerald D Stone	Bernice Padgham	Bernice Padgham	Carl Stout	Hoyt Benedict	Bobbie E Hubert
Alva§† (6)	MC	405 327-1340	Jones Clyde	Dean Calhoon	Lester McKee	....	Jack P Haltom	Arlo Darr	Albert L Rose
Anadarko* (6)	CM	405 247-2481	E E Otey	Robt M Williamson	Bob Wilkerson	Vonda Neal	Johnnie Beeler	Ron Poolaw	Billy R Newell
Antlers †† (3)	MC	405 298-3756	Finis Amend	Clyde E Bell	Lena Lawless	Clyde Allen	Lanny Nash	Craig Wilson	Bill Hampton
Ardmore* (24)	CM	405 223-2933	L S Morrison	G Craig Weinaug	Penny Hobbs	Penny Hobbs	James B Mercer	Bill Culley	Ronald Holt
Atoka*† (3)	CM	405 889-3341	Vincent Howard	Harold Thomas	Clydene West	....	Charles Meade	George Brewster	Elgin Justus
Bartlesville* (35)	CM	918 336-0000	Arch Robbins	Thomas J Mikulecky	George Jones	George Jones	George Oates	Charles Spencer	....
Bethany* (22)	CM	405 789-2146	James L Falkner	Richard G Gertson	J B Hill	J B Hill	Tom Barnett	Bill R Bowen	Charles B Smoot
Bixby (7)	CM	918 366-8280	John E Spring	Fred Keas	Johnie Baker	Wayne K Meyer	Gary Brooner	Dale Davis	Fred Keas
Blackwell* (8)	CM	405 363-3282	John Stauffacher	Bruce K Stone	Lottie Schone	....	Phil Carroll	Mel Roberts	Leroy Harris
Bristow (5)	MC	918 367-2237	Marvin L Veit	....	Sharie R Long	Bill Jenkins	Harold Aston	Mike Newell	Jack Richardson
Broken Arrow* (36)	CM	918 251-5311	Nick Hood Jr	Jim Whitlock	Larry Spurlock	Jim Whitlock	Melvin Mashburn	James Stover	Gary Blackford
Broken Bow* (4)	CM	405 584-2282	Wanda Roark	George A Puckett	Carolyn Buckner	....	Robert Peavy	Marvin Hill	Dale Batson
Chandler*† (3)	CM	405 258-0890	Eula Mae Cross	Robert James	Ethel Payton	....	David Hoover	Jerry Bryant	....
Checotah (3)	MC	918 473-2311	Floyd Beaird	....	Walter B Frost	....	Donald Ray	Ronald Beaver	Floyd Beaird
Cherokee* (2)	CM	405 596-3326	Bill West	Don Groves	Geraldine McMahan	....	Don Arganbright	Charlie Tucker	....
Chickasha* (16)	CM	405 222-2100	Bruce Storms	Lloyd Rinderer	Donna Jones	....	John Clift	Edward L Smith	Larry Fuchs
Choctaw (8)	CM	405 390-8198	Ron Briggs	Gene Fisher	Joy Well Cook	John T Whetsel	David Newby	John T Whetsel	Bill Story
Claremore† (12)	MC	918 341-2365	Elizabeth K Gordon	....	Margaret Robertson	Margaret Robertson	Walter Ross Boyd	Charles Williams	....

Directory 1/10 continued **MUNICIPAL OFFICIALS IN ALL U.S. CITIES OVER 2,500[1]**

City, 1980 population (000 omitted), form of government	Municipal phone number	Mayor	Appointed administrator	City clerk	Finance officer	Fire chief	Police chief	Public works director
OKLAHOMA (129) continued								
Cleveland* (3) CM	918 358-3121	Elgin Thomas	Jimmie D Martin	Jacqueline Brower	Larry Gilbert	Donald Cochran	Ted Blackburn	Luther Sisk
Clinton* (9) CM	405 323-0217	Patrick T Cornell	James Luckett	Glendene Goucher	Rex Madden	John Kinder	Jay Green	....
Coalgate* (2) CM	405 927-2241	Richard A Nordvold	J Roy Toney	Edna Tate	J Roy Toney	James Harris	William Grillo	Roy Dan Burns
Collinsville† (4) MC	918 371-2811	Gerald G Carlburg	....	Brenda G Lamberson	....	Lee R Harrold	Edward Scott	Frank D Morland
Comanche* (2) CM	405 439-8832	Anna Schaak	Bill Parese	Carla Hulin	Carla Hulin	C P Watson	Ron Hunter	....
Commerce (3) MC	918 675-4373	J C Jeffery	....	Tina L Wilson	Tina L Wilson	John Sooter	John Sooter	George F Roberts
Coweta (5) CM	918 486-2189	Harry Tracy	Lee Wert	Betty Booth	....	David Pool	Dale Keeler	Elmer Dodson
Crescent*† (2) CM	405 969-2538	Evelyn M Mefferd	Boyd W Fisher	Sadie J Pierson	Velma Hildreth	Phillip Yenzer	Roy Wileman	....
Cushing* (8) CM	918 225-0277	Don Kindley Jr	R G Annis Jr	Maxine Kautz	Maxine Kautz	Lloyd Slater	Don Gourley	John McPherson
Davis* (3) CM	405 369-2323	John Powell	Jerry Fullerton	Reba Roper	Jerry Fullerton	....	Joe Ayers	....
Del City* (28) CM	405 677-5741	James Nolen	Dennis W Beach	Kathy Burkhart	Melba J Bleigh	Tom Tollison	Tom Rogers	Dave Hopkins
Dewey* (4) CM	918 534-2272	Gary Taylor	Paul B Allee	Betty Catron	....	Jim Eppler	Leonard Ames Sr	Leroy Stevens
Drumright* (3) CM	918 352-2631	Paul R Branch	James F Palone	Sandra Brock	Sandra Brock	Jerry Slane	Burney Felton	Henry Randall
Duncan* (23) CM	405 252-0250	Bobby Pollock	Bill J Dashner	Clyde Shaw	Clyde Shaw	....	Dale Anderson	James Carver
Durant*† (12) CM	405 924-7200	Ed Mittelstet	....	Frances Malzahn	Frances Malzahn	E C Morriss	Coleman Townsend	....
Edmond* (35) CM	405 348-8830	Carl F Reherman	Dallas D Graham	Patsy Sandefur	Patsy Sandefur	Ron Lloyd	Al Newport	Ron Shaw
El Reno* (15) CM	405 262-4070	Ed Metz	....	Wilfred Tate	Wilfred Tate	Ray Ludlow	Roy Bourquin	Gene Watts
Elk City* (10) CM	405 225-3230	Harold R Wehrenberg	Wm Bois Marable	Ella Mae Walker	Frank H Whitney	Jim Cross	Randy Smith	A T Jones
Enid* (50) CM	405 234-0400	John McMillen	Lyle D Smith	Ilene Butler	Gary L Cole	Everette Brewer	George Stover	Jerry Smith
Eufaula (3) MC	918 689-2534	Joe Johnson	....	Hattie Shropshire	....	Bud Kelso	Bill Day	....
Fairview* (3) CM	405 227-4416	K Ewald	Dixie J Blackledge	Irene Howerton	....	Mike Howerton	Jack Kelly	Calvert Garman Jr
Frederick (6) MC	405 335-7571	Charles Greenfield	Wm Charles Martin	Evelyn Young	Orvel Gibson	Joe Bradley	David Larocque	....
Glenpool (3) CM	918 224-5409	Larry Blackburn	Roger Miner	Daniel D Gibson	Daniel D Gibson	Randy Hunter	Larry Bible	Leo Rodebush
Grandfield* (1) CM	405 479-5215	Mary F Gebhart	Glynn Weaver	Donna Nill	....	Kenneth Smith	Roy L Wales	....
Grove* (3) CM	918 786-6107	Huber Logue	Max Sanks	Becky Holt	Terri Harris	Jim Barrett	Raymond Johnson	Duane Brown
Guthrie* (10) CM	405 282-0493	Bill Merrell	Daniel G Ward	Betty Wrede	C Franklin Sanders	William A Ward	Thomas Tindall	Larry J Shelton
Guymon*† (8) CM	405 338-3396	J D Braley	Terry H Powell	Joyce Scott	Julian Schaub	Fontaine L Cooley	Duane Boren	Damon Hamilton
Harrah t* (3) CM	405 454-2951	Mark Seikel	Vertus Dan Brandt	Irene Burrus	Dan Brandt	Dewayne Coleman	Hubert Gilbert	John Inglehart
Healdton* (4) CM	405 229-1283	Delbert Lambert	Bill Rowton	Vivian Adams	....	Mike Hunt	Bobby Spradling	Wesley Fondren
Heavener* (3) CM	918 653-2217	Curtis Norvell	Joe R Johnson	Hope Hembree	Richard Steed	Freddie Cox	Gerald Branam	Johnny Woodral
Henryetta* (6) CM	918 652-3489	H E Greenley	Irl E Wall Jr	Lo Reese Brown	....	Georage Gulley	Everett G Allen	Basil Vaughn
Hobart (5) MC	405 726-3100	A C Aker	....	Charlene Pulley	....	Dale Lafever	Vernard Holbrook	Glenn Garrison
Holdenville (5) MC	405 379-3397	Beverly Rodgers	....	Brenda Gooden	Eldine Nichols	Bob Brittain	Ben Aguirre	Beverly Rodgers
Hollis* (3) CM	405 688-2167	Dewey Heath	Doug Burns	Mary Mullins	James Mahan	Clyde H Whitman	Kenneth Woods	....
Hominy§ (3) CM	918 885-2164	E G Guy Reed	Paul D O'Keefe	Betty Yarbrough	Charles Slamans	Phillip Wilson	Charles Crawford	....
Hugo† (7) MC	405 326-2722	Gene Thomson	....	Waldo J Beadle	Doris Tucker	Billy Hardaway	Ocie Clifton	Larry Hobgood
Idabel (8) MC	405 286-7600	Rex Helms	....	Rosalind Holman	Martin J Bell	Joe Brown	William B Denison	Dean Justus
Jenks* (6) CM	918 299-9102	Wayne Parker Jr	Victor R Ewing	Bernice Foster	Dianna Pritchard	Bill Heinen	Lloyd Ruddell	Leon Earp
Kingfisher (4) MC	405 375-3705	George Brownlee	Vernie Snow	Dorothy Burns	....	Jim Bengs	Ronnie Ronspeiz	Oral Stake
Konawa* (2) CM	405 925-3775	William Tucker Jr	Ralph Veltema	Wanda Lowry	....	Mike Boren	Troy Dame	....
Lawton* (80) CM	405 357-6100	Wayne Gilley	Robt E Metzinger	Jean McGavic	Robert McCaffree	Richard Tannery	Robert Gillian	Bill Baker
Lindsay* (3) CM	405 756-2019	James Harrison	Bill Cowan	Linda Newby	....	Allen R Wilson	Duke Morrison	Bill Cowan
Lone Grove t (3) MC	405 657-3111	Lincoln Stanley	....	Virginia Vigil	....	Leo Potts	Dearl Cathey	....
Madill* (3) CM	405 795-3378	Ralph Thompson	Henry Walt Allen	Marilyn McAdoo	Marilyn McAdoo	Carl Reed	Buford Huff	Tom Reynolds
Mangum* (4) CM	405 782-2256	Charles Yoder	Gerald Hukill	Teresa Barrett	....	Claude Goade	Jerry Nelson	....
Marlow* (5) CM	405 658-5401	Delton Lamb	Wallace R Stovall	Maxine Price	....	Frank Tow	Ralph Abney	....
McAlester* (17) CM	918 423-9300	W B Rayburn	Randy S Green	Bobbi Lanz	Marilyn Belote	Freddie Sanders	Dale Nave	Commodora Howard
McLoud t (4) MC	405 964-5264	Joe Ross	R McClanathan	Christina Polach	Charlotte Banks	Robert Lempges	Wayne Heath	Eugene Stevens
Medford* (1) CM	405 395-2823	W R Mortimer	Warren Beggs	Frances E Mark	Barbra Bush	Lloyd Williamson	Jack Delay	Charles Jones
Miami (14) CO	918 542-3041	Wm E Goodman	H Alton Rivers	Dee G Watters	Pauline Wilson	Robert L Turner	Bill G Melton	Dillard L Rose
Midwest City* (50) CM	405 732-2281	Dave Herbert	Charles Johnson	Tommy Melton	Tommy Melton	Tom Canfield	James M Cox	....
Moore* (35) CM	405 799-4411	Louis Kindrick	Robert W Swanagon	Maxine Evers	Priscilla Hargis	John Knight	Richard Mills	....
Muldrow t (3) MC	918 427-3296	Tommy Treat	....	Deane Rogers	....	David Taylor	....	....
Muskogee* (40) CM	918 682-6602	Virgil James	Walter G Beckham	Diana Lee Sweeden	Carl C Cole	Marshall Beard	Henry Sharp	Don Younger
Mustang* (7) CM	405 376-4521	Richard L Weathers	....	Lee Clark	Linda R Hazell	Arlon Hadlock	Ken McNair	Michael D Pence
New Cordell† (3) MC	405 832-3826	Floyd W Craig	....	Jean Smith	....	Tommy Merrill	J D Dobbs	....
Newcastle* (3) CM	405 387-4427	Sherrell Griffith	James R Branum	Loycie Kerr	....	Billy Mack Keith	Rae Neal	....
Newkirk* (2) CM	405 362-2117	Lanio Roberts	David E Haynes	David E Haynes	Larry Ralph	Joe Colclasure	Leslie Johnston	Donald Stephens
Nichols Hills* (4) CM	405 843-6637	John M Mee	Douglas Henley	Douglas Henley	Huston Huffman Jr	Charles Wallace	James P Stoddard	Russell Fields
Nicoma Park t (3) MC	405 769-5673	Leland L Fox	....	Mary Belle Sparks	....	James D Shonts	Jim Roberson	....
Noble t† (3) MC	405 872-3355	Joe Work	....	Margaret Leslie	T Harding	J Farris	....	James L Clark
Norman* (68) CM	405 321-1600	Steve R Thrower	James D Crosby	Mary P Hatley	Gerald L Carlson	Jim Davis	Don Holyfield	David A Rennie
Nowata* (4) CM	918 273-3532	Don Turner	Jack L Hughes	Pat M Reeder	....	Jack Hughes	Mike Richardson	Chester Christian
Okemah* (3) CM	918 623-1050	Bobby Massey	Bruce L Mahaffey	Evalyn Herring	Evalyn Herring	Leland Scrimshire	David Hardin	Charles R Stotts
Oklahoma City* (403) CM	405 231-2011	Andy Coats	C Scott Johnson	Tom Hurley	Don Bown	Jimmie R Catlege	Lloyd Gramling	Merrel Medley
Okmulgee* (16) CM	918 756-4060	James L Milroy	David M Harris	James Brian	James Brian	Ernest Ledbetter	Chester Hodge	....
Owasso* (6) CM	918 272-2251	Boyd Spencer	Dan Galloway	Ann Hendrickson	Lee Dawson	Bob Allen	Robert Morgan	Lloyd Hubbs
Pauls Valley* (6) CM	405 238-3308	Billy O Wilson	Bob Martin	Ann Tate	Pearce Blake	Dwain Pearson	Jim Jarman	Earl Cobb
Pawhuska* (5) CM	918 287-3576	Billy L Todd	Harvey K Massey	Opal Hamlin	Kathrine Ross	Bob Sholl	John Boone	James L Sweeden
Perry (6) MC	405 336-4241	Max Adams	....	Bonnita M Johnson	....	Tom Moore	Paul Pritchett	Charles J Bezdicek
Pocola t (3) MC	918 436-2477	Donald Lairamore	Jack Yates	Gearldene Reeder	Gearldene Reeder	Donald Williamson	Jim J Howard	....
Ponca City* (26) CM	405 762-2494	E Lee Brown	Marion E Thorpe	Donald Wolff	Ralph Bowman	Jim Bates	Norman Coffelt	Gary Martin
Poteau (7) MC	918 647-4191	Melvin L Taylor	....	Launa E Pate	Phil McGehee	Tom C Cabe	W R Seale	Charley Brese
Prague* (2) CM	405 567-2279	Howard Dawkins	Hugh Power	Laura J Epperson	Juanita Kelton	Rayburn Moses	James C Hall	Robert B Love
Pryor (8) MC	918 825-0888	Carl C Curry	Gerald H Clack	Erma E Rogers	Jewelene Pierson	David Harrison	Wiley Backwater	....
Purcell* (5) CM	405 527-6561	J C Miller	Royce Hunter	Elizabeth Norvell	Elizabeth Norvell	Joseph G Wallace	Frank Lindsay	....
Sallisaw* (6) CM	918 775-6241	George Glenn	James R Hudgens	H R Park	....	R L Smith	Wayne Craghead	B Q Callahan
Sand Springs* (13) CM	918 245-8751	Jerry Hanner	Inez Kirk	Mary Sue Overbey	Mary Sue Overbey	Sam Harvey	Odean Helm	Vernon Smith
Sapulpa* (16) CM	918 224-6660	Louis Whittaker	Nellie Skaggs	Shirley Burzio	Vicky Roberson	Tony Woodall	Jack McKenzie	Larry Coggins
Sayre† (3) MC	405 928-2260	Jerald E Hansen	Paul Buntz	Bonita J Matlock	....	John Hill	Lonnie Risenhoover	....
Seminole* (9) CM	405 382-4330	Fred Gipson	....	Jo Mills	Jo Mills	Maurice Martin	Bill Jordan	Dennis Roesler
Shawnee* (27) CM	405 273-1250	Jerry E Ozeretny	Ron Bourbeau	Clara Hurst	Bertha Ann Young	Tommy Whitecotton	Mel Webb	Raymond Block
Skiatook t† (4) MC	918 396-2797	Bob G Kehler	Monte Gondles Jr	Freddie Billups	Monte Gondles Jr	Wm Bennett	Walter Spurgeon	....
Spencer*† (4) CM	405 771-3226	....	Kenneth R Beal	....	....	....	....	Kenneth R Beal
Stigler* (3) CM	918 967-2164	Lonnie Davis	Robert L Floyd	Louise Smith	Shirley Cross	Charles Owen	Jack Spradling	....
Stillwater* (38) CM	405 372-0025	Christine Salmon	Carl D Weinaug	Dan Winders	Dan Winders	Jim Smith	Mike Strope	Harold Gibson
Stroud* (3) CM	918 968-2571	Aubrey E Christy	E Wesley Devero	Ann Thompson	Lorene Evans	Lavon Ward	Glover Crittenden	E Wesley Devero
Sulphur (6) MC	405 622-5096	Ray Goodwin	Eugene L Copenhaver	Wanda Frantz	Donna Payne	Joe Mayfield	Ronald Thomas	Ralph Watson
Tahlequah (10) MC	918 456-0651	Anthony Stockton	Robert V Schwabe	Eunice B Ross	Robert Hensley	Sam Pinson	Boyd Hamby	J M Hicks

Directory 1/10 continued — **MUNICIPAL OFFICIALS IN ALL U.S. CITIES OVER 2,500[1]**

City, 1980 population (000 omitted), form of government		Municipal phone number	Mayor	Appointed administrator	City clerk	Finance officer	Fire chief	Police chief	Public works director
OKLAHOMA (129) continued									
Tecumseh* (5)	CM	405 598-2189	Mary Jo Copeland	Randy Swinson	Ann Atwater	Ann Atwater	Bill Trammel	Richard Holland	....
The Village* (11)	CM	405 751-8861	Robert Blakeley	John Zakariassen	John Zakariassen	Cathy Keller	Roy Brock	Phyllip Olive	Larry Walton
Tishomingo (3)	MC	405 371-2191	Norma Chaney	....	Geneva Carr	Geneva Carr	Danny Parker	Billy Joe Hutchins	....
Tonkawa* (4)	CM	405 628-2508	Ronnie Blubaugh	J E Ditmore	Jean Muegge	....	John Ramey	Frank A Hall	Joe Byers
Tulsa (361)	CO	918 592-7777	Terry Young	....	Francis F Campbell	Edward C Koepsel	E S Hawkins	Harry G Stege	Harold Miller
Tuttle† (3)	MC	405 381-2335	Lee Franklin	Bob McKittrick	Mary Jo Haywood	John King	David Williams	Bob McKittrick	Bob McCathern
Vinita† (7)	MC	918 256-6468	Bobby G Wiles	....	Wilma C Woolman	Lester Davis	Jack Melton	Eugene Williams	Harley Cotrill
Wagoner (6)	MC	918 485-4586	Leo M Scott	Dwight Mays	Jane Teel	Fred R Jackson	Ray Ferguson	Leroy Champlain	Dwight Mays
Walters* (3)	CM	405 875-3337	W K Boyer Jr	Buddy Veltema	Judy Reece	....	Ray Ewing	Don Fowler	Jess Sheppard
Warr Acres† (10)	MC	405 789-2892	John Rost	Frank V Wood Jr	Jean Drake	Jean Drake	Roger Leonard	William Selby	Raymond Bryant
Watonga (4)	MC	405 623-4669	R B Chapman		Pat DeSpain	Donald Clewell	Fred Espy	Lonnie Rickey	....
Waurika*† (2)	CM	405 228-2713	Ceburn Lovett	Stan Patty	Kathy Harris	Donalda Showalter	Dutch Elkins	Lyndel Harris	Virgil Fielding
Weatherford (10)	MC	405 772-7454	Everett Gartrell	George Wilkinson	Tony Davenport	Tony Davenport	Jack Brown	Paul Gaines	....
Wetumka*† (2)	CM	405 452-3153	Cloyce Heath	Joel Heathcott	Joey Beth Graves	Pat Stuckey	Kenny Maxwell	Clark Chastain	Lyndon Cline
Wewoka* (5)	CM	405 257-2413	Leodus Banks	Kenneth Lee Resor	Jaxcine Lee Orr	Jaxcine Lee Orr	Dwight Argo	Jack Harris	Kenneth Lee Resor
Wilburton (3)	MC	918 465-2262	Gerald D Hood	....	Mary L Wartick	....	Eugene Taylor	Robert Joe Hokit	Teresa Hollingback
Woodward* (14)	CM	405 256-2280	Ken Smith	Delbert Self	Gary L Lyon	Juanita Camp	Charles Gieswein	Bruce Storm	Bennie Davis
Wynnewood (3)	MC	405 665-2307	Jim Motes	....	Hazel Wilbanks	....	Bill Hughes	John Ozment	Don Harmon
Yale* (2)	CM	918 387-2121	F A Olinghouse Jr	Robert Wherry	Dorothy Hixson	....	Charles Strader Jr	Walter Tappan	Kenneth Thurman
Yukon* (17)	CM	405 354-1895	Robert Nelson	David H Pence	Mary Lee Huckaba	Mary Lee Huckaba	Bob Noll	Sam Ervin	....
OREGON (89)									
Albany* (27)	CM	503 967-4311	Donald W Brudvig	William B Barrons	D Gary Holliday	D Gary Holliday	Daniel P Bolis	Darrell L Pepper	John Joyce
Ashland§ (15)	MC	503 482-3211	L Gordon Medaris	Brian L Almquist	Nan E Franklin	Robert D Nelson	Lee Roy King	S Victor Lively	Allen A Alsing
Astoria* (10)	CM	503 325-5821	Edith Henningsgaard	James M Flint	Ronald D Caton	Ronald D Caton	Eugene P Robertson	Robert W Johnson	John Crockett
Baker* (9)	CM	503 523-6541	George W Gwilliam	Arthur F Reiff	Roland C Campbell	Roland C Campbell	Don Everson	Douglas Humphress	James Adamson
Bandon§ (2)	MC	503 347-2437	Raymond H Kelley	Ben M McMakin	Blythe Tiffany	Ben M McMakin	Lanny Boston	Donald S MacDonald	Don M Pierce
Beaverton (31)	MC	503 644-2191	Larry Cole	....	Nancy Wilcox	David Chen	Hueston Reynolds	Don Newell	Noel Klein
Bend* (17)	CM	503 388-5505	Craig C Coyner III	Arthur R Johnson	James W Kerfoot	James W Kerfoot	Thomas P Hansen	David Malkin	Thomas L Gellner
Boardman§ (1)	MC	503 481-9252	G W Peck	Larry D Dalrymple	Shirley Zielinski	....	Robert McKinley	Robert McKinley	Larry Phillips
Brookings* (3)	CM	503 469-2163	Robert L Kerr	Lynn R Stuart	Naomi Bradfield	Naomi Bradfield	Tom Kerr	Sam Dotson	C K Smith
Brownsville* (1)	CM	503 466-5666	....	Allen L Henderson	Dianne M Gann	....	....	....	....
Burns (4)	MC	503 573-5255	Joe F Hayse	....	Mary Ann Robinson	John Cater	Pat Ward	Aaron Richardson	Dave Clayton
Canby§ (8)	MC	503 266-4021	Michael L Gabrion	Bud Atwood	Marilyn K Perkett	Virginia L Graham	Smith French III	Jerry Giger	Bud Atwood
Cascade Locks§ (1)	MC	503 374-8484	Eugene Miller	Kenneth D Hobson	Donald W Kitchens	Donald W Kitchens	Donald Hensgen	....	Richard McCulley
Central Point§ (6)	MC	503 664-3321	Don Jones	E David Kucera	....	George C Jacobs	Don Paul	....	Vern Capps
Coos Bay* (14)	CM	503 269-1181	Charles Holbert	William H Curtis	Dana Lafferty	Gail George	Andy Anderson	Rollie T Pean	Joe Schwarm
Coquille* (4)	CM	503 396-2116	Hugh Pinkston	Patricia Strain	Shirley Patterson	Patricia Strain	Jerry McCue	E N Daniels	John Higgins
Cornelius* (4)	CM	503 648-1197	Jim Larkins	Mark F Arbuthnot	Mildred Otto	Mildred Otto	Chris Asanovic	Ralph Blair	Merritt Newdall
Corvallis* (41)	CM	503 757-6901	Alan Berg	Gary F Pokorny	Hazel Stratton	James E Todd	Walter Pflughaupt	....	Rolland Baxter
Cottage Grove* (7)	CM	503 942-5501	William A Whiteman	Bruce G Williams	Lois G Howes	Lois G Howes	Bruce Lamb	Richard L Hoffer	Robert Sisson
Dallas* (9)	CM	503 623-2338	Gwen Vandenbosch	Roger G Jordan	Roger G Jordan	Del Funk	John C Barnard	Donald L Pursel	David Shea
Eagle Point§ (3)	MC	503 826-4212	Donna G Butchino	Richard C Box	Nita Gosnell	Nita Gosnell	Dennis Jordan	Leon C Sherman	Leroy Bedingfield
Estacada* (1)	CM	503 630-3223	John Rowley	Duane E Robinson	Lucille Beckman	Yvonne Vavla	....	....	Larry Stevens
Eugene* (106)	CM	503 687-5010	Gus Keller	Michael D Gleason	Karen Goldman	Warren Wong	Everett G Hall	James L Packard	Christine Anderson
Florence§ (4)	MC	503 997-3436	Greg Anderson	Clayton Schmitt	Alice M Hunt	Clayton Schmitt	Vern Passinger	M J Shaw	Gregory Hamman
Forest Grove* (11)	CM	503 357-7151	W G Peterson	Michael E Solomon	....	Ivan M Burnett	Robert M Davis	Gary K Tyler	John D Burdett
Gladstone§ (10)	MC	503 656-5223	H Wade Byers Jr	Ronald J Partch	Verna Howell	Ronald J Partch	Robert K Nelson	Max W Patterson	Alvin C Kolb
Grants Pass* (15)	CM	503 474-6360	Bruce M McGregor	J Michael Casey	....	Dorothy Tryk	Jerry Ryan	Ernie Woolf	H Jack Shipley
Gresham* (33)	CM	503 661-3000	Margaret Weil	James R Keller	Maureen Swaney	Martin F Wynne	Joe Parrott	Kent R Reesor	William E Cameron
Hermiston*† (9)	CM	503 567-5521	Raymond R Schroth	L T Harper	Robert D Irby	L T Harper	John C Shull	Robert J Shannon	....
Hillsboro* (28)	CM	503 681-6100	J W Derr	Eldon S Mills	Margaret M Bauer	Margaret M Bauer	Dayton Arruda	Herman Woll	Stanley Dillon
Hood River§ (4)	MC	503 386-1488	James T Walker	Peter R Harris	Dorothy M Swyers	Dorothy M Swyers	Wayne Dehart	Richard Kelly	....
Independence§ (4)	MC	503 838-1212	Marion Rossi	Lloyd Halverson	Dorothy Pugh	Lloyd Halverson	Dan Greer	George E Weaver	John Snitker
Junction City (3)	MC	503 998-2153	Larry Crowley	....	Roberta Likens	Melodese Korstad	Jim Pate	John W Peterson III	Robert L Fountain
Keizer* (20)	CM	503 390-3700	Robert Simon	Roy L Payne	Susan Biasi Darby	....	Duane Sanford	Robert Thomas	
Klamath Falls* (17)	CM	503 883-5310	George C Flitcraft	Harold J Derrah	Karren Fowler	Karren Fowler	Bruce Caldwell	Dan Tofell	Ray Bidegary
La Grande* (11)	CM	503 963-7161	Suzan Turley	Lynnwood Hamilton	Eldon Slippy	Eldon Slippy	Bill White	John Courtney	Ron Gross
Lake Oswego* (23)	CM	503 636-3601	C Herald Campbell	Peter C Harvey	Rosemary A Mader	Fred Matthias	Jack Snook	Thomas E Webster	John M Godsey Jr
Lakeview† (3)	MC	503 947-2029	L Lane Thornton	Delores Edmonson	Opal Murphy	Delores Edmonson	Del Lepley	Troy Riblett	David T Schaer
Lebanon* (10)	CM	503 258-3185	Robert G Smith	James D Thompson	....	Joseph A Windell	Bruce Perkins	Delmer D Johnson	Stanley Stevenson
Lincoln City§ (5)	MC	503 996-2151	Alice S Sim	Kent L Taylor	D W Bill Works	D W Bill Works	....	Michael E Holden	....
McMinnville§ (14)	MC	503 472-9371	Donald D Porter	Joe W Dancer	Marjorie E Kerber	....	Jerry Smith	Kenneth E Gudeman	William M Blum
Medford* (40)	CM	503 770-4432	Lou Hannum	John R Thomson	Emily H Kirkham	Jonathan J Jalali	Waitman S Boddy	Glen D Johnston	Lewis N Powell
Milton-Freewater* (5)	CM	503 938-5532	Dale Courtney	James A Swayne	....	Debra Grant	Dorsey Sherman	William Biggs	Jack D King
Milwaukie* (18)	CM	503 659-5171	Ronald D Kinsella	Hugh H Brown	Laurie L Perkin	Margaret A Post	Richard Bailey	Ronald Goodpaster	Steven Hall
Molalla (3)	MC	503 829-6855	Kerry Kilbride	C D Haynes	C D Haynes	C D Haynes	....	Roger Roth	John Whiteside
Monmouth§† (6)	MC	503 838-0722	William Horner	Stan J Kenyon	Joan E Howard	Joan E Howard	Donald C Milligan	Rick Brungardt	Russ Faust
Mt. Angel§ (3)	MC	503 845-9291	Margaret Hoffer	Pete Wall	Sharon Todd	Pete Wall	Victor Hoffer	Kimball Vickery	Phillip Meissner
Myrtle Creek (3)	CM	503 863-3171	Marilyn West	Donald P Dodge	Ms Lou Pringle	Donald P Dodge	Bill Leming	Mike Cramer	....
Myrtle Point§ (3)	CM	503 572-2626	Jean Coffman	David C Aper	Rosemary Padgett	....	J M Myers	William Gillock	....
Newberg§ (10)	MC	503 538-9421	Elvern Hall	Michael D Warren	Arvilla Page	Brenda Stroud	Elmer Christensen	David Bishop	Robert S Sanders
Newport* (8)	CM	503 265-5331	John D Brenneman	Donald A Davis	Patricia P Bearden	....	Dennis McManus	James Rivers	Larry Crisler
North Bend* (10)	CM	503 756-6311	William E Smith	Alfred Roth	James C Johnson	James C Johnson	A Kenneth Daugherty	George P Booras	Ronald F Stillmaker
Nyssa* (3)	CM	503 372-2264	Glade Chadwick	Max Brittingham	Sandi Jasper	Max Brittingham	Delbert Malloy	Terry Thompson	Ralph T Lowe
Oakridge§ (4)	MC	503 782-2258	Arion Redmond	Robert D DeLong	Laura J Stalcup	....	Marshall Mikesell	Robert H Peterson	Jerald A Shanbeck
Ontario* (9)	CM	503 889-7684	Robert Widmer	E Dick Franks	....	Roger C Dexter	Larry E Roberts	James H Jones	Doug Tietze
Oregon City* (15)	CM	503 657-0891	Ronald D Thom	....	Jean K McNulty	William J Ruddy	Harold Nunn	Richard Martin	William C Parrish
Pendleton* (15)	CM	503 276-1811	Joe McLaughlin	C David Crumpton	Jill Turner	Jill Turner	Richard D Hopper	E E Gallaher	Gerald L Odman
Philomath (3)	MC	503 929-3001	Janet Tunison	R Lyman Houk	Margaret J Nyman	Margaret J Nyman	David Harlacher	Richard Raleigh	....
Pilot Rock* (2)	CM	503 443-2811	John R Standley	....	Toni Hamby	....	....	Richard Chavez	....
Portland (366)	CO	503 248-4078	J E Bud Clark	....	Jewel Lansing	Mark Gardiner	Kenneth Owens	Ronald R Still	Geoff Larkin
Prineville* (5)	CM	503 447-5627	David C Asher	C Henry Hartley	....	....	John Ferguson	James H Soules	Tom Basey
Redmond§ (6)	MC	503 548-2148	Bob Riggs	Robt L McWilliams	Toni Buettner	Joanne Holcomb	Hoy Fultz	Clarence Durgan	Gerald Knippel
Reedsport* (5)	CM	503 271-3603	Ronald O Hanson	Robert D Richardson	Sandra K Hanson	Sandra K Hanson	Zack Turner	Stephen Evans	Jeff McIlvenna
Roseburg* (17)	CM	503 672-7701	John W Dunn	George C Stubbert	George C Stubbert	Robert D Barbee	Charles F Wuergler	Charles Wuergler	Al R Hooten
Salem* (89)	CM	503 588-6255	Sue Harris	Russell E Abolt	Patricia Wolfe	Richard Armstrong	James Bone	Brian Riley	Ronald Merry
Sandy§ (3)	MC	503 668-5533	Ruth Loundree	Thomas S Reber	....	June M Peterson	Bob Rathke	Fred W Punzel	Roy Gochnour
Scappoose (3)	MC	503 543-7146	Elizabeth E Huser	Evelyn J Hudson	....	....	Richard Hoffmann	Carl A Wonderly	Martin Renwick
Seaside* (5)	CM	503 738-5511	Joyce C Williams	Lawrence L Lehman	Marie Chestnut	Estelle O'Conner	James Puckett	John M West	Robert D Chisholm

Directory 1/10 continued — MUNICIPAL OFFICIALS IN ALL U.S. CITIES OVER 2,500[1]

City, 1980 population (000 omitted), form of government		Municipal phone number	Mayor	Appointed administrator	City clerk	Finance officer	Fire chief	Police chief	Public works director
OREGON (89) continued									
Sheridan§ (2)	MC	503 843-2347	Art Hebert	W Bruce Peet	Yvonne J Garcia	Art Hebert	Eugene Smail	Richard A Hoeppner	Stanley Turnidge
Sherwood* (3)	CM	503 625-5522	....	James H Rapp	....	....	....	....	....
Silverton* (5)	CM	503 873-5321	John M Middlemiss	Douglas K Robinson	Douglas K Robinson	Carol Petersen	Carl Brown	Cliff Bethschieder	Richard Barstad
Springfield* (42)	CM	503 726-3700	John D Lively	Steven C Burkett	Anne L Pflug	Anne L Pflug	Donald L Herschel	Robert E Deu Pree	Michael A Kelly
St. Helens (7)	MC	503 397-6272	Geneva M Shadley	Rosaline L Mallory	Rosaline L Mallory	Marilyn L McCarty	Donald Armintrout	Reginald Bowles	Nate Waldron
Stayton (4)	MC	503 769-3425	Henry A Porter	Ellis Vandehey	....	Elaine Fisk	Ron Tegen	A A Allen	George Hall
Sutherlin* (5)	CM	503 459-2856	Gil Leinonen	Lloyd E Norris	Della M Mattingly	Roy M Stulken	Bernard Warnken	Cecil G Holley	Dan Daniels
Sweet Home* (7)	CM	503 367-5128	Ruth Ganta	Max C Thompson	....	Barbara Shaw	Gerry Wooley	Ed Savage	David Monson
Talent† (3)	MC	503 535-1566	Duane Johnson	....	....	Jo James	Owen E Kruger	Charles H Roberts	George C Gleim
The Dalles* (11)	CM	503 296-5481	John Lundell	Del Cesar	John B Thomas	John B Thomas	Albert Jones	Paul J Nagy	Rod McKee
Tigard* (14)	CM	503 639-4171	John E Cook	Robert W Jean	Loreen Wilson	Jerri Widner	....	Robert Adams	Frank Currie
Tillamook* (4)	CM	503 842-2472	Don Normile	Jerry Green	Joanne Boggs	Joanne Boggs	James Jaqua	David Rogers	Michael Mahoney
Toledo* (3)	CM	503 336-2247	Donald Knapp	Dan Ousley	Jeanette Gray	....	Dick White	Jerry L Pryor	Doyle Thorne
Troutdale§ (6)	MC	503 665-5175	Sam K Cox	Pamelia L Christian	Nancy B Nixon	Nancy B Nixon	....	George Haddock	F Gregory Wilder
Tualatin§ (7)	MC	503 692-2000	Roy R Rogers	Stephen A Rhodes	....	Marilyn M Matthias	....	....	Michael McKillip
Umatilla§ (3)	MC	503 922-3226	Donald Armstrong	Hartley Seeger	Eve Foote	....	James Roxbury	Eldon Olson	Hartley Seeger
Warrenton* (2)	CM	503 861-2233	Robert C Pollard	Gilbert G Gramson	Jayne W Ballman	Kathy L Hanna	Duane A Mullins	William L Humphrey	James B Rankin
West Linn* (13)	CM	503 656-4261	Larry McIntyre	John A Buol	Diana J Nicolay	Wayne L Paterson	Russ Castlemann	Art Enderlin	Al Steininger
Wilsonville§ (3)	MC	503 682-1011	A G Meyer	Daniel O Potter	Deanna J Thom	Ray Shorten	....	....	Larry Blanchard
Winston§ (3)	MC	503 679-6739	Marjorie Brady	David R Waffle	Margo S Champion	....	....	George D Jacobs	Jim McClendon
Woodburn* (11)	CM	503 982-5222	William J Costine	Max L Pope	Barney O Burris	Barney O Burris	Martin Krupicka	Lyle Henderson	G S Frank Tiwari
PENNSYLVANIA (540)									
Abington tp§ (59)	CO	215 884-5000	William D C Dennis	Albert L Herrmann	Albert L Herrmann	Robert L Graves	Adolph J Rebelo	....	William Kalkbrenner
Abington tp§ (1)	MC	717 586-0111	John M Hennemuth	Ronald G Bray	....	....	....	Daniel J Mooney	Harry F Derr Jr
Akron b† (3)	MC	717 859-1600	Guy B Zell	Wilmer E Hall	W Richard Goshert	....	J Herbert Beard	Clarence P Fasnacht	J Howard Wolf
Aldan b (5)	MC	215 626-3553	Howard R Walker Jr	....	Janet E Morris	Curtis C Wise	....	Myron Blankley	David McLaughlin
Aliquippa b§† (17)	MC	412 375-5188	Daniel Britza	Samuel L Coxson	....	Mary Alviani	James Piroli	Albert A Merruli	Joseph V Nardo
Allentown (104)	MC	215 437-7546	Joseph S Daddona	N James Fluck	Elizabeth Borneman	N James Fluck	Ernest E Toth	David M Howells Sr	Harry Bisco
Altoona (57)	MC	814 944-7131	David L Jannetta	....	Constance J Hilling	Leonard L Bettwy	Reynold Santone Jr	Peter N Starr	Paul Daley
Ambler b§ (7)	CM	215 646-1000	William G Young Jr	Edward J Heimel	George W Benigno	Edward J Heimel	Joseph Schneider	Frank A Wack	....
Ambridge b§ (10)	MC	412 266-4070	Walter Panek	Andrew Pugar	....	....	Orlando Gagliardi	George A Kyrargyros	Satino Maruca
Amity tp*† (6)	CM	215 689-9415	....	John C Korst	....	....	....	....	....
Archbald b (6)	MC	717 876-1800	Joseph J Daley	....	Ann Jones	....	Robert Harvey	John McHale	Robert Munley
Arnold (7)	MC	412 337-4441	William DeMao	....	Domenic A Saulle	Elias E Moses	Casomir Gentile	William C Clark	....
Ashland b† (4)	MC	717 875-2411	F Staudenmeier	Ronald E Maurer	....	....	Thomas P Towers	Thomas W Joyce	....
Ashley b† (4)	MC	717 822-7518	Helen Kolbicka	....	....	Bernard Szot	Philip Collotty	Joseph Bishop	....
Aspinwall b§ (3)	MC	412 781-0213	Arthur G Esser	William F Eckert	....	....	Arthur G Esser	William L Eckert	....
Aston tp§ (15)	MC	215 494-1636	Peter J M Rohall	John Marcarelli	....	....	....	James C McCarthy	Richard Lehr
Athens b† (4)	MC	717 888-2120	Lawrence E Canavan	....	Beverly J Walker	....	David Whipple	Charles T Strange	John Pollock
Avalon b* (6)	CM	412 761-5820	Joseph F Elm	Ethel C Carlin	....	Edwin B Geier	William Carney	John J Downey	William R Bender
Avoca b (4)	MC	717 457-4011	(not reporting)						
Baden b (5)	MC	412 869-2411	Louis F Marsilio Jr	Susan A Yount	....	....	Mark K Wolz	Frank N Tavern Jr	....
Baldwin b (25)	CM	412 882-9600	Samuel L McPherson	Shirley A Kuchta	Shirley A Kuchta	Mary M Romanus	....	Aldo Gaburri	Joseph Pogany
Bally b§ (1)	MC	215 845-2351	William C Stompf	Eugene D Smith	Mary Cressman	Robert Moll	Leo Mutter	Philip Ferrizzi	Eugene D Smith
Bangor b† (5)	MC	215 588-2216	Duane E Miller	....	Mildred Scheffler	....	Kenneth Beegle	Donald Gillingham	Anthony Priori Sr
Barnesboro b (3)	MC	814 948-8230	William Bland	Fred C Nastasi	Irma Shea	Samuel Rocco	Robert Hineman	John Sharkey	Paul Lubert
Beaver b§ (5)	MC	412 774-6134	Robert P Linn	Robert N Robinson	Jean T Barber	....	Fred E Weigle	Anthony Hovanec	....
Beaver Falls (13)	MC	412 847-2800	Leo J Hegner	Perry C Wayne Jr	Perry C Wayne Jr	Erma J Camp	Rocco Capoza	Lloyd Haswell	Esther M Berry
Beavertown b§ (1)	MC	717 658-2505	William Kepner	Lewis B Ritter	Dixie Baker	....	George Benfer	George Aumiller	Lewis B Ritter
Bedford b† (3)	MC	814 623-8192	Richard L Letrent	John L Montgomery	Helen Cuppett	....	Jay F Speicher	Joseph B Clark	....
Bellefonte b§ (6)	MC	814 355-1501	Gino Fornicola	Walter B Peterson	Walter B Peterson	Kit Kennedy	Richard Brown	Donald Smith	Willard E Schultz
Bellevue b§† (10)	MC	412 766-6164	....	Robert E Lee	....	....	....	....	....
Bensalem tp* (52)	CM	215 639-2500	Stephen J Kelly	Natalie A Strange	Natalie A Strange	Natalie A Strange	John C Matter Jr	Theodore Zajac	Nicholas Pasqualone
Bentleyville b (3)	MC	412 239-2112	Gail Ames	....	Lena Greenfield	Joseph Brown	Walter Wisniewski	Wm Stankovich	....
Benzinger tp§ (9)	MC	814 781-1274	Thomas Fleming Jr	James E Newell	....	....	Michael Bauer	Gary G Eckert	Steven Samick
Berwick b (12)	CM	717 752-2723	Lou Biacchi	Clarence O'Dell	Clarence O'Dell	Frances Dietrichson	Norman Fowler	Charles Robsock	Leo Talanca
Bethel Park* (35)	CM	412 831-6800	Reno Virgili	Matthew J Kridler	Matthew J·Kridler	Timothy Babik	Daniel Moore	Joseph M Kletch	George McTall
Bethlehem§ (70)	MC	215 865-7014	Paul M Marcincin	Edward J Downing	James B Earley	Ms T M Bartholomew	Celestino O Freitas	John C DiDonato	Wendell S Sherman
Bethlehem tp (12)	MC	215 865-5563	(not reporting)						
Big Beaver b† (3)	MC	412 827-2416	Anthony T Prato	....	....	....	John Pinkerton	Albert Cunning	....
Birdsboro b* (3)	CM	215 582-1173	Russell H Mountz	Thomas B Adams	Thomas B Adams	Thomas B Adams	Michael Hernandez	Warren Delp	Thomas B Adams
Blairsville b§ (4)	MC	412 459-9100	Dean C Zug	Larry W Garner	....	....	Robert C Thompson	Joseph R Cameron	....
Blakely b† (7)	MC	717 489-5660	Robert Klinko	Harold McCusker Jr	....	....	Thomas Taylor	Thomas Dubas	....
Bloomsburg t (12)	MC	717 784-7703	Daniel J Bauman	Gerald E Depo	Gerald E Depo	Geraldine Kern	Ralph Magill	Larry Smith	Bruce Keller
Blossburg b§† (2)	MC	717 638-2452	....	John D Davies	....	....	....	....	....
Boyertown b§ (4)	MC	215 367-2688	Robert L Fleming	Robert Layman	....	....	....	Darius M Puff	....
Brackenridge b† (4)	MC	412 224-0800	Charles F Hanna	Cynthia Swigart	....	....	Dennis Vrotney	Ralph DeSanto	....
Braddock b (6)	MC	412 271-1018	(not reporting)						
Braddock Hills b† (3)	MC	412 241-5080	Richard Foster	Marilyn Pazehoski	....	....	Herman Funk	Daniel Blystone	Peter Zenter
Bradforbt (11)	CM	814 362-3884	Ronald L Orris	....	....	Robert F Steckmeyer	Theodore Shay	Vincent Borrelli	....
Brentwood b (12)	MC	412 884-1500	James H Joyce	....	Lorraine Trainor	....	Gary Weinheimer	Robert Hartshorn	Paul Klauck
Bridgeport b† (5)	MC	215 272-1811	Daniel H Deorzio	....	Joseph G Homa	Samuel R Santoro	Frank Makowiak	Joseph D Collilouri	....
Bridgeville b* (6)	CM	412 221-6012	Pasquale V Deblasio	Ernest McNeely	Ellen Roessler	....	Jeffrey Sharp	Leonard Villani	Robert Fleming
Brighton tp§† (8)	MC	412 495-6313	....	Howard E Noll	....	....	....	....	....
Bristol b§ (11)	MC	215 788-3828	Margaret Stakenas	Fidel Esposito	Fidel Esposito	Fidel Esposito	Michael Plebani	John Tortu	Pat Yezzie
Bristol tp* (59)	CM	215 785-0500	Robert Lewis Jr	Stanley P Gawel	....	Andrew A Koch	William Jones	John Tegzes	William Surrick
Brookhaven b† (8)	MC	215 874-2557	Ralph A Garzia	John Moccia	Joan Arnold	Benjamin Linowski	Robert Ricks	John Eller	Richard Denza
Brookville b (5)	MC	814 849-5325	Mary Helen Haugh	Charles C Maxwell	....	Charles C Maxwell	Robert Magill	Earl G Smith	John Crooks
Brownsville b (4)	MC	412 785-3363	Barry Cook	....	Elizabeth Laver	....	Clark Sealy	Samuel J Nicola	....
Buckingham tp§ (9)	MC	215 794-8834	David A Downs	Joseph W Golden	Bernadette Glenn	Beverly Weitzel	Wayne Ewer	Stephen Daniels	Donald Naylor
Butler (17)	MC	412 285-4124	Ronald E Forcht	....	Alice S Johnston	William M Hulton Jr	George Smith	Henry E Clauser	Chester F Sikora
California b† (6)	MC	412 938-7202	Joseph Dochinez	....	Bernadine Mudry	Virginia Pipik	Thomas Hartley	Nelson J Horner	Dale Huffman
Callimont b§† (..)	MC	....	....	Wm A Merrill III	....	....	....	....	....
Caln tp§ (10)	MC	215 384-0600	Charles F O'Donnell	Tom Zalewski	Joan Gross	Paul Woodruff	Fred Eckenbach	Edw W Masterstefone	Samuel V Moore
Cambridge Springs b* (2)	CM	814 398-2311	Carlton R Andrews	David W Stone	Esther B Houpt	....	Eugene Shearer	....	Ken Dine
Camp Hill b* (8)	CM	717 737-3456	Ruth C Wrye	Andrew C Janssen	Andrew C Janssen	Andrew C Janssen	David Apgar	Andrew C Janssen	Andrew C Janssen
Canonsburg b* (10)	CM	412 745-1800	Jack Passante	Paul W Amic	Paul W Amic	Steve Lombardi	Harold Coleman	R T Bell	Raymond Sifinski

Directory 1/10 continued

MUNICIPAL OFFICIALS IN ALL U.S. CITIES OVER 2,500[1]

City, 1980 population (000 omitted), form of government		Municipal phone number	Mayor	Appointed administrator	City clerk	Finance officer	Fire chief	Police chief	Public works director
PENNSYLVANIA (540) continued									
Carbondale§ (11)	MC	717 282-4110	Charlotte V Moro	Robert Davis	Mary Milligan	John J Kearney	William Burrell	Francis Dottle	Frank J Mancuso
Carlisle b* (18)	CM	717 249-4422	John E Lebo	Allen L Loomis Jr	Alice Stine	Timothy J Paul	David Boyles	Frank Giordano	Bert Davis
Carnegie b† (10)	MC	412 276-1414	L J Harkovich	R J Cicconi	Carol Goldbach	Albert Falcioni	Lawrence Collins	Harry W Smith	Lud Hanczar
Carroll Valley b§ (1)	MC	717 642-8269	Daniel E McGarry	Aylwyn D Williams	Virginia A Ciliotta	Aylwyn D Williams	....	Steven E Feeser	....
Castle Shannon b (10)	MC	412 561-9200	George W Evans	Veronica T Recker	Veronica T Recker	....	James O'Brien	James L Campbell	Merle M Michelucci
Catasauqua b* (8)	CM	215 264-0571	Richard Deibert	Eugene L Goldfeder	....	....	Richard K Fehnel	Wayne W Muffley	Elias F Grim
Centerville b (4)	MC	412 757-6307	Dewey Milich	Linda McCloskey	....	....	Robert Bitner	Frank D Clish	....
Chalfont b† (3)	MC	215 822-0991	Andrew H Stoler	....	....	....	Curtis Martin	Harry M Gacad	
Chambersburg b* (16)	CM	717 264-5151	Samuel A Ferraro	Julio D Lecuona	Julio D Lecuona	Cleveland Forrester	William E Sheppard	Michael T Defrank	John Taylor
Charleroi b† (6)	MC	412 483-6011	Fred P McLuckie	Ronald G Halkias	Elaine T Martinko	Fred Briggs	David Moody	Larry Celaschi	....
Cheltenham tp§ (36)	MC	215 887-1000	Robert J Hannum	Nicholas Melair Jr	Nicholas Melair Jr	Darrell D Bottorff	Michael L Moonblatt	Stephen W Ott	William J Bryant
Chester (46)	MC	215 447-7700	Joseph F Battle	....	Samuel Poliafico	Timothy J Gorbey	James MacDonald	John Owens	....
Chippewa tp* (7)	CM	412 843-8177	Delmer V Forsberg	Bruce E Hamer	....	....	Okey T Cline	C Douglas Loughner	Raymond Gilliland
Churchill b§ (4)	MC	412 241-7113	Frank Comunale III	Robert F Lutz	....		Donald M Cunningham	Charles R Stahl	
Clairton† (12)	MC	412 233-8113	Rose M Busch	Pauline M Branik	Pauline M Branik	Daniel Pastore	Kenneth Ujevich	....	John Hronakes
Clarion b*† (7)	CM	814 226-7707	Melvin G Riffer	David A Blaner	Carol LaPinto	David A Blaner	Robert Gourley	R Eric Shaffer	Arthur Wencil
Clarks Summit b§ (5)	MC	717 586-9316	Wm J Westington	Robert A Thorne	Frances L Jones	Robert A Thorne	Louis J Vitale Jr	James Rosencrance	Robert A Thorne
Clearfield b (8)	MC	814 765-7817	Clifford J Mann	Allan L Martin	Kathy Spears	....	Jeffrey Williams	William M Mohney Jr	....
Clifton Heights b (7)	MC	215 623-1000	Evelyn A Hess	....	Marie Melbourne	Ralph Delucia	Edward Volante	Ronald A Berry	John Goff
Coaldale b (3)	MC	717 645-9377	Theodore Bortnick	....	Lyle Augustine Jr	Lyle Augustine Jr	Andrew Sotak	Donald Butts	....
Coatesville§ (11)	MC	215 384-0300	....	Dennis Paul Elko	....	Lewis J Gay	John Jacoby	John Griffy	
College tp* (6)	CM	814 234-7200	....	C Thomas Lechner	....	C Thomas Lechner	....	....	C Thomas Lechner
Collegeville b (3)	MC	215 489-9208	David A Cornish	....	Phyllis Parsons	Kenneth L Schaefer	Dennis Parker	John R Clawson	....
Collingdale b (10)	MC	215 586-0500	(not reporting)						
Columbia b* (10)	CM	717 684-2468	Elliot William	Gary L Myers	Ms M L Meyers	Gerald Nikolaus	Tim Deeg	Bern F Edelman	Jack Leahy
Colwyn b (3)	MC	215 461-2000	Anthony F Franco	Jack Frazier	Mary Martin	Doris Cinclair	Al Rasley	William Garrity	....
Concord tp* (6)	CM	215 459-8911	Robert C Hench	John N Cornell	....	....	Steve Cooper	....	....
Connellsville† (10)	MC	412 628-2020	Ronald J Haggerty	....	Marsha A Bower	Joan D Miller	Francis J Childs	Walter F Weimer	Louis S Chroyer
Conshohocken b (8)	MC	215 828-1092	Francis J Ruggiero	....	Elizabeth V Brandt	Elizabeth V Brandt	George Metz	Adam J Pagliaro	G McTamney
Conway b (3)	MC	412 869-5550	Jack Andolina	Sandra Brandenburg	....	....	Wilbert D Falk Jr	Vince Bozza	Frank Panzanella
Coopersburg b (3)	MC	215 282-3307	Thelma M Kiess	Roberta M Shelly	....	....	Robert C Gaugler	Robert W Snyder Sr	....
Coplay b (3)	MC	215 262-2288	Josephine Shemanski	....	Warren Miller	Martin Anthony	Bruce G Korsak	William Balliet	....
Coraopolis b† (7)	MC	412 264-3002	Joseph V Divito Sr	....	Oliver Cassasanta	....	Nathan Spaniol	Howard White	Robert Barone
Cornwall b† (3)	MC	717 274-3436	William Smith	....	....	....	....	....	....
Corry (7)	MC	814 663-7041	David E Mitchell	Robert E Grice	Marie McCray	Ivan G Bennink	James Maloney	James F Hurlbut	David A Johnson
Coudersport b§ (3)	MC	814 274-9776	William Schroecer	Janet Horvath	....	....	John Hetrick	James Minor	Joseph P Milchuck
Crafton b (8)	MC	412 921-2014	Richard F Welch	....	Patricia Kozlowski	Harry Rieder	H Roy Hermes	John T Daniels	....
Cranberry tp§ (11)	MC	412 776-4806	....	Allan J Te Desco	....	....	David Berneburg	John Scarfo	....
Cumru tp§ (11)	CO	215 777-1343	Richard F Venne	William S Shea	Carol J Steffy	Curtis S Mohn	....	John Halstead	Bruce E Reppert
Curwensville b (3)	MC	814 236-1840	David A McNaul	....	Emma Guarino	....	Robert Decker	John Confer	John Rumsky
Dallas b† (3)	MC	717 675-1389	James B Davies III	Ralph Garris	....	....	Donald Shaffer	Edward Lyons	....
Dallastown b (4)	MC	717 244-6626	Charles E Gross	Walter M Ehrhart	....	....	James Raffensberger	William Donivan	....
Danville b† (5)	MC	717 275-3091	William C Leighow	Frederick O Yohn	....	Frederick O Yohn	Richard L Blosky	Lewis R Lee	Bruce G Earlston Sr
Darby b§† (12)	MC	215 586-1100	....	N J DiGregorio	....	....	....	....	....
Darby tp§† (12)	CO	215 586-1514	Lawrence Patterson	Harry Modesti	Bennetta A Scott	John McGowan	....	William Johnson	James Sandone
Derry b (3)	MC	412 694-2030	Richard K Thomas	Mary J Geary	....	....	Frederick Squib	Ronald T Bolen	Edward E Shomo
Derry tp* (18)	CM	717 533-2057	Leonard I Hill	John H Weigel III	....	John H Weigel III	John D Payne	Donald J Hack	Donald B Kaylor
Dickson City b (7)	MC	717 489-5758	Vincent Wiercinski	....	....	....	Bill Bilinski Jr	William Stadnitski	George Slocum
Dillsburg b§ (2)	MC	717 432-9969	Donald S Karns	J Chadwick Wagner	Beverly A Davis	....	....	Glenn E Smith	....
Donora b (8)	MC	412 379-6600	George Saxon	Robert Paraschak	Robert Paraschak	....	John Sabo	Jose Alvarez	Michael J Rodjom
Dormont b§ (11)	MC	412 561-8900	W H Moreland Jr	Stanley L Gorski	Stanley L Gorski	Stanley L Gorski	William H Sampson	Charles J Lee Jr	....
Dover tp* (13)	CM	717 292-3634	Donald J Deitz	Leon B Lankford	....	Betty A Shoemaker	Gary Shearer	Ronald Smeal	Jack L Caplinger
Downingtown b* (8)	CM	215 269-0344	George Quinn Sr	Donald J Greenleaf	....	Anthony Gambale	James McGowan III	Vernon Osborne	Patrick Noles
Doylestown b* (9)	CM	215 345-4140	Vincent C Gorman	Robert M Pellegrino	Robert M Pelligrino	Timothy J Zaro	Donald Tilley	Paul P Brady	Lewis Arthur Logan
Doylestown tp§ (12)	MC	215 348-9915	Diane M Hering	John W Snyder	Joan Krysiak	....	....	Robert T Cobb	....
Dravosburg b (3)	MC	412 466-5200	William A Linn Sr	....	Donna Thorpe	....	Lawrence Page	John P Rufft	Tony Guglielmo
Du Bois§ (9)	MC	814 371-2000	Leo Karoleski	....	Walter F Lepionka	Walter F Lepionka	William Kotzbauer	James R Beers	John Miknis
Duncannon b* (2)	CM	717 834-4311	Russel E Hammaker	Thomas M Evans	Shirley H Leedy	....	....	Joseph C Sebacius	....
Dunmore b (17)	MC	717 343-7611	Joseph J Domnick	Frank J Muraca	Arthur J Moran	Frank Padula	Carmen Magnotta	Frank Occulto	James Miller
Dupont b† (3)	MC	717 655-6216	Frederick P Lokuta	Edward Vogue Jr	Methislaus Szumski	....	Edward Twardowski	Edwin Kuzinski	Fran Drost
Duquesne (10)	MC	412 469-3770	Leo E Zabelsky	David P Poljak	Phyllis Senato	Charles Scalise	Bernard A Marino	William Yunn	Raymond R Terza
Duryea b (5)	MC	717 457-6784	Eugene Chromey	....	Lois Morreale	Emily Romanczuk	Gene Evaskitis	Leonard Ash	John Abent
East Caln tp§ (2)	MC	215 269-1989	William E Augustine	Edwin R Hill	....	Edwin R Hill	....	....	Edwin R Hill
East Lansdowne b (3)	MC	215 623-7131	William M Smyrl Jr	....	Joan T Binder	....	David J Lauro	Samuel S Ziviello	....
East McKeesport b (3)	MC	412 824-0324	Edwin S Bradley	....	Suzanne Charley	Mary Jean Strawins	Terance Rannigan	Harry C Keller	Samuel Pack
East Norriton tp§ (13)	MC	215 275-2800	Joseph C Ronca Jr	Helmuth J Baerwald	Helmuth J Baerwald	Helmuth J Baerwald	Ronald Stralkowski	James J Cotter	Norman A Milnes
East Pennsboro tp§ (14)	CO	717 732-0711	....	Robert L Gill	....	Robert L Gill	James N Bumgardner	James J Corbett	Gary S Walters
East Petersburg b (4)	MC	717 569-9282	David E Brian	Kathleen Fry	....	....	Mervin G Hess	David E Moore	....
East Stroudsburg b* (8)	CM	717 421-8300	David L Miller	Larry Comunale	....	....	Kenneth L Miller	Charles L McDonald	Kenneth R Brown
East Whiteland tp*† (8)	CM	215 648-0600	....	J D Reimenschneider	....	J D Reimenschneider	Donald Fonda	Robert Redzig	Edward W Galante
Easton (26)	MC	215 253-7141	Salvatore Panto Jr	....	Joseph Mauro	Robert Rush	Frank A Bruneio	William Cunningham	John A Cappellano
Easttown tp§† (9)	MC	215 644-9000	A John May	Gene R Williams	Gene R Williams	Gene R Williams	John C Stillwell	John C Stillwell	Russell K McCulley
Ebensburg b (4)	MC	814 472-8930	(not reporting)						
Economy b† (10)	MC	412 869-4779	Kenneth E Campbell	Marie Hagg	Sandra Hendricks	Vince Testa	Blaine Hendrickson	Thomas C Harrington	....
Eddystone b† (3)	MC	215 876-3106	Curtis Wood	....	John W Snyder	Florence Dubois	Robert Gliem	Wm J Maitland	....
Edgewood b§ (4)	MC	412 242-4824	William K Vincett	Christopher Lochner	Christopher Lochner	Christopher Lochner	Robert L Bozurich	Peter D Messina	Richard Christenson
Edgeworth b* (2)	CM	412 741-9400	John C Oliver Jr	Douglas C Arndt	....	Douglas C Arndt	Harvey Lauderbaugh	Harlan Goerman	Douglas C Arndt
Edinboro b§ (6)	MC	814 734-1812	Gregory D Lessig	Randy R Sanders	Randy R Sanders	....	Jon Graff	Ralph E Barone	Randy R Sanders
Edwardsville b§† (6)	MC	717 288-6484	B P Kaczynowski	....	Leo J Martin Jr	George Tomasak	Hugh Jones	Louis Bryski	Donald Kulick
Elizabethtown b* (8)	CM	717 367-1700	Daniel Mader	Nick Viscome	Nick Viscome	Peter J Whipple	Harvey Kleinfelter	Anthony Meridionale	Wayne Devan
Ellwood City b* (10)	CM	412 758-5576	Frank Zona	Frank J Strange	Mary Ann Fleo	Frank J Strange	Jack Brest	Thomas Magnifico	George Hulick
Emmaus b (11)	MC	215 965-9292	William L Lobb	Bruce E Fosselman	Bruce E Fosselman	Bruce E Fosselman	Robert R Reiss	Earl Brensinger	Bruce E Fosselman
Emporium b*† (3)	CM	814 483-5678	James Gennocro	Augustus A Zito	Shirley A McDonald	Geo D Coppersmith	Richard Aikens	James R Urey	Augustus A Zito
Emsworth b† (3)	MC	412 761-1729	William Moul	....	Jean Simmons	Ronald Kracht	Richard J Weinzierl	Hermann Pappert Jr	Sam Boyd
Ephrata b§ (11)	MC	717 733-1277	Clair L Wolf	L Victor Dickinson	L Victor Dickinson	Joel E Callihan	John Eitnier	Timothy Burkholder	....
Erie (119)	MC	814 456-8561	Louis J Tullio	....	James Klemm	Patricia J Liebel	James R Breon	Richard Skonieczka	Robt J Waytenick
Etna b† (5)	MC	412 781-0569	John Tuttle	William M Skertich	....	William M Skertich	Charles Pugar	Ron Harris	John Yagusic
Exeter b (5)	MC	717 654-3001	Andrew C Mauriello	....	....	....	Paul Smith	Bernard Pepperling	....
Exeter tp (14)	MC	215 779-5660	William H Becker	Richard D Fisher	Doris T Concordia	....	Terry L Francis	A U Brintzenhoff	John M Vitillo
Fairview tp* (12)	CM	717 774-3190	Arthur L Shaffer	E R McCollum	....	....	Kenneth B Snyder	William R Collins	....

Directory 1/10 continued

MUNICIPAL OFFICIALS IN ALL U.S. CITIES OVER 2,500[1]

City, 1980 population (000 omitted), form of government	Municipal phone number	Mayor	Appointed administrator	City clerk	Finance officer	Fire chief	Police chief	Public works director
PENNSYLVANIA (540) continued								
Falls tp* (36)	CM 215 295-4176	Willard C Wamsley	Ray A Nearhood	....	Helen Bondurant	George Hoffman	James Kettler	Brooks Jackson
Farrell* (9)	CM 412 981-6500	Eugene Pacsi	Charles A Nath	Lavon Saternow	Charles A Nath	....	William L Caputo	Donald Pisegna
Ferguson tp§ (8)	MC 814 238-4651	Mary Dunkel	Donald A Bachman	....	....	....	David S Nale	....
Fleetwood b (3)	MC 215 944-8220	E Richard Boyer	....		Lester A Hoch	Martin Yourkavitch	Leonard O Greth	Gary Ebeling
Folcroft b† (8)	MC 215 534-5823	William J Monteith	....	Jean Bozzelli	Hinckley Greenlaw	Robert Thompson	Theodore Pastore	....
Ford City b (4)	MC 412 763-3081	Joseph Kovalovsky	....	Anna Warnick	....	Robert Duncan	Jan Lysakowski	Henry Fijal
Forest Hills b* (8)	CM 412 351-7330	Alfred McCloy	Mary Jane K Hirt	Mary Jane K Hirt	Carol Wilson	Raymond Heller	James Lapaglia	Richard J Branzel
Forty Fort b (6)	MC 717 287-8586	Sheldon Glahn	Carl Scarantino	Carl Scarantino	Boyd Hoats	Louis G Wagner Jr	Henry Winters	Harold Taylor
Foster tp (5)	CO 814 362-4656	Frank Milks	....	Jo Ann Hoover	....	....	Donald Boyer	....
Fountain Hill b§† (5)	MC 215 867-0301	George A Laughlin	Ralph M Hutchison	....	....	James J Bobal	Karl H Wied	Robert F Hercik
Fox Chapel b* (5)	CM 412 781-1637	Philip W Osborne	Richard R Moore	....	....	Alfred Humes	Robert C Marshall	Albert M Biernesser
Frackville b (5)	MC 717 874-3860	Raymond J Tomko	....	Emanuel Lightstone	....	Robert Thomas	Edward Shearn	Nicholas Borzak
Franconia tp* (7)	CM 215 723-1137	....	J Delton Plank	....	J Delton Plank	....	Paul R Hunsberger	Franklin D Kerver
Franklin* (8)	CM 814 437-1485	Guy Mammolite	Wm P Buchanan	E William Gabrys	E William Gabrys	Bill Snyder	Robert D Cardy	Joseph Griswold
Franklin Park b (6)	MC 412 364-4115	George R Wist	....	....	....	Ronald A Merriman	Norbert L Micklos	Albert H Lively
Freeland b (4)	MC 717 636-0111	Joseph J Brogan	....	John Herkalo	Daniel Ravina	John E Teliho	Michael Mistiszyn	David Karpovich
Geistown b (3)	MC 814 266-8313	George Borischak	....	A Elaine Fuller	Donald P Scott	Patrick Seigh	Louis Valle	....
Gettysburg b* (7)	CM 717 334-1160	Robert N Heflin	Charles W Sterner	Hazel M Dillman	Charles W Sterner	Timmon Linn	Russel H Potter Jr	Charles W Sterner
Girard b* (3)	CM 814 774-3012	Paul Grettler	Richard H Gebhardt	Richard H Gebhardt	Richard H Gebhardt	Louis Hannah	Gerald Moryc	Richard H Gebhardt
Glassport b† (6)	MC 412 672-7400	Samuel Demarco	....	Rosemary Bradley	Albert Halucha	Joseph Salzman	Lawrence Oley	Joseph Capozzoli
Glenolden b (8)	MC 215 583-3221	John MacVeigh III	....	Sarah A Dougherty	Francis X Foster	Leonard Ley	Joseph Grant	....
Green Tree b* (6)	CM 412 921-1110	Edward S Crawford	Harry R Dunhoff	....	....	Wm Schwartzmiller	Carl E Wolcutt	Robert Johnson
Greencastle b† (4)	MC 717 597-2047	Charles J Witmer	Edwin C Bittner	....	....	Gary R Hawbaker	Harold J Benchoff	....
Greensburg† (18)	MC 412 834-3800	Scott L Brown	....	R Edward Jackson	George S Rugh	John E Hutchinson	Domenick Felice	John R Finfrock
Greenville b* (8)	CM 412 588-4193	Joseph P Walton	Marie H Julian	....	....	Hugh F Shields	Joseph J Pinkle	Paul D Boyer
Grove City b* (8)	CM 412 458-7060	Karl A Bubeck	Terence W Farren	Nancy S Albright	Bette J Shipton	Donald E Beightol	Earl E Dulaney	Donald E Beightol
Hamburg b§ (4)	MC 215 562-7821	James F Holtzer	Lynda G Albright	Lynda G Albright	....	Ray L Hartman	Gene Schappell	....
Hampden tp§† (17)	MC 717 761-0119	John V Thomas	Chas M Kemberling	Chas M Kemberling	John V Thomas	Daniel J Hurley	Kenneth E Fetrow	....
Hampton tp* (14)	CM 412 486-0400	....	Steven H Perry	Anna M Frketic	Marion King	....	Chester J Kline	Edward J Berzonski
Hanover b* (15)	CM 717 637-3877	John C Harman	Joseph B O'Brien	Ronald Birgensmith	Joseph B O'Brien	James A Roth	E G Margelot Jr	Allen T Staub
Hanover tp* (2)	CM 215 264-1069	Randall C Atkinson	Bryan D Coleman	Sandra A Kutos	Bryan D Coleman	Philip Beil	....	Jay D Mosser
Harmony tp (4)	CO 412 266-1910	August Antonini	Candace Shuster	Lyla Swan	....	Dave Finch	Jack Lively	
Harris tp* (3)	CM 814 466-6228	Christopher Lee	James P Murphy	James P Murphy	James P Murphy	Glenn Dry	....	Harold L Wingard
Harrisburg§ (53)	MC 717 255-3011	Stephen R Reed	David C Latshaw	Rosemary B Berry	Bruce A Barnes	Donald H Konkle	Richard J Vajda	James Close
Harrison tp (13)	CO 412 226-1393	George E Conroy	....	Faith A Payne	William R Poston	Jack Wetzel	Fred L Phillippi	Harry B Gourley
Hatboro b§ (8)	MC 215 443-9100	Joseph Celano	David L Woglom	David L Woglom	John F McKean	W Robert Stauch	Joseph J Camp Sr	James W Greener
Hatfield tp§ (13)	CO 215 855-0900	John R Greene	Sydney C Brittin	....	Harry M Rutherford	Abe Rittenhouse	M Robert Turner	Willis K Alderfer
Hatfield b (3)	CM 215 855-0781	Luther Moyer	Leonard Perrone	....	Leonard Perrone	Ralph Rehig	Robert Turner	Robert Hickson
Haverford tp§ (52)	CO 215 446-1000	Joseph F Kelly	Thomas J Bannar	....	Paul A Leonard	Harry N Sauder	James A Myers	Alfonso Digirolamo
Hazleton (27)	MC 717 459-4960	James Paisley	....	Joseph M Demarinis	....	Girard A Caso	Louis Farnell	....
Hellertown b* (6)	CM 215 838-7041	Donald C Zimpfer	Leo Fetzer	Leo Fetzer	Leo Fetzer	Gerald Malone	Alfred R Shaw Jr	Lorrain Cawley
Hempfield tp (43)	CO 412 834-7232	(not reporting)						
Hermitage* (16)	CM 412 981-0800	Len W Krichko	Terry S Fedorchak	Terry S Fedorchak	Terry S Fedorchak	Robert S Goeltz	John A Marriott	....
Highspire b* (3)	CM 717 939-3303	James Baker	James R Brokenshire	....	....	Larry Byers	Ralph J Sherin	....
Hollidaysburg b* (6)	CM 814 695-7543	C G Harclerode	Roy E Davis	Roy E Davis	Roy E Davis	Robert E Kerns	Edward Plowman	Roy E Davis
Homer City b* (2)	CM 412 479-9190	Boyd G Simmons	Anthony T Lenze	Anthony T Lenze	Anthony T Lenze	Fred Smith	Mark A Succheralli	Anthony T Lenze
Homestead b (5)	MC 412 461-1340	Stephen Simko	Louis J Pastor	....	Maureen Sharbaugh	....	Christopher T Kelly	Edward Adkins
Honesdale b (5)	MC 717 253-0731	Richard L Kreitner	....	Jean Joseph	....	Lawrence Martone	Frank M Rosler	Maurice Brown
Hopewell tp§ (15)	CO 412 378-1460	Vincent D'Eramo	Carol Pancurak	....	....	William Clawson	Fred David	Sharp Davidson
Horsham tp* (16)	CM 215 643-3131	....	Michael J McGee	....	....	William J Williams	John L Donovan	Stanley J Mroz
Hughesville b*† (2)	CM 717 584-2041	Pauline Montgomery	Maxine E Secules	Maxine E Secules	....	Gene Cahn	John J Rechel	....
Hummelstown b§ (4)	MC 717 566-2555	Marion F Alexander	Michael J O'Keefe	Michael J O'Keefe	Michael J O'Keefe	Richard Leader	Roy C Bridges	Richard J Engle
Huntingdon b* (7)	CM 814 643-3966	Charles L Jamison	Willis L Shore	Willis L Shore	Willis L Shore	Robert Jessel	Daniel L Varner	Willis L Shore
Indiana b§ (16)	MC 412 465-6691	George E Thompson	E W Harkless	E W Harkless	Patrick J Ward	Richard Sherry	Charles R McAdoo	E W Harkless
Indiana tp* (6)	CM 412 767-5333	George Erceg	James Phillips	Helen Fannie	....	....	Lawrence Curti	Richard Shock
Ingram b† (4)	MC 412 921-3625	James G Hellmann	....	Gladys S Ryser	....	Robert N Depp	Robert B Clark	....
Irwin b§ (5)	MC 412 863-0630	J Kenneth Tray	Joseph R Plues	....	....	Benjamin Perkins	Benjamin Perkins	Arthur C Youngstead
Jeannette† (13)	MC 412 523-8411	M J Salvatore	....	Richard S Laskey	A B Elias	Kenneth Brinton	Leo Caranese	Charles Copeland
Jefferson b (9)	MC 412 384-4750	Michael Stanton	Saundra J Walsh	....	....	....	Edward S Stanton	....
Jenkintown b* (5)	CM 215 885-0700	J Theo Jensen Jr	Wm J Richardson Jr	Wm J Richardson Jr	Wm J Richardson Jr	Gary Bachman	James J Lavin	Charles Ladley
Jersey Shore b* (5)	CM 717 398-0104	George W Teufel	Donald W Packer	Deborah M Colocino	Donald W Packer	Terry Mantle	Gary L Reighard	Donald W Packer
Jessup b† (5)	MC 717 489-0411	John Mancak	....	Lavinia Walsh	Kenneth Marchegiani	Danial Faramelli	Patrick Kane	Rudy Vangarelli
Jim Thorpe b (5)	MC 717 325-3025	Michael Hichok	....	Charlotte Malchon	Edith Crossin	Joseph Steber	Thomas L Mase	....
Johnsonburg b* (4)	CM 814 965-5682	Pat Cherry	Richard S Beaver	Richard S Beaver	Richard S Beaver	William Keneski	George T King	James DiJulio
Johnstown (35)	MC 814 539-8761	Herbert Pfuhl Jr	....	Virginia Slivosky	Kenneth Bopp	Charles Krumenack	John Kucenski	Louis Torak
Kane b* (5)	CM 814 837-9240	Edgar D James	Lori Andrusis	Lori Andrusis	Lori Andrusis	Joseph Stauffer	R A Fisher	Rowland E Proashas
Kenhorst b (3)	MC 215 777-7327	Frank Quattrock	Frank Garbini	Mary Baxewanis	....	Ronald Yeity	Arthur Raybuck	....
Kennett Square b§ (5)	MC 215 444-4590	J Stephen Little	Douglas P Marguriet	....	....	....	....	....
Kingston§ (16)	MC 717 288-4576	Charles Bankes	Kenneth P Johnson	Carol Urban	Kenneth P Johnson	Dave Long	John Reese	Bernard R Biga
Kingston tp* (7)	CM 717 696-3809	Daniel Wisnieski	Mark A Kunkle	Carole Loberg	....	Gerald Kapral	Paul Sabol	Robert Chamberlain
Kittanning b (5)	MC 412 543-2091	George E Harvey	....	Betty Thompson	Betty Thompson	Edward Atwood	Robert J Hulings	Reedy J Adams
Kulpmont b (4)	MC 717 373-1521	Walter Stavinski	....	Peter P Avellino Jr	Paul A Niglio Jr	Al Politza	Peter Wasilewski	....
Kutztown b† (4)	MC 215 683-6131	James W Schwoyer	....	Carl H Bortz	Donald L Boyer	C Leibensberger	Edmund F Pilarski	....
Lancaster tp (11)	MC 717 291-1213	(not reporting)						
Lancaster (55)	MC 717 291-4711	Arthur E Morris	Howard F Goldberg	Faye A Williams	Bernard J Ziegler	J Donald Mummaw	John Ulrich	Alan Gesford
Lansdale b* (17)	CM 215 368-1691	Michael DiNunzio	F Lee Mangan	....	Edward Lindinger	Jay Daveler	James W Hansley	Jacob I Ziegler
Lansdowne b§ (12)	MC 215 623-7300	William D Johnston	R J Robinson	....	....	Paul Wentzel	Charles Lausch	....
Lansford b† (4)	MC 717 645-5844	Joseph C Genits	....	Richard E Forgay	....	George S Krajnak Sr	Joseph Delpero	....
Larksville b (4)	MC 717 288-6619	Robert Kopka	....	....	....	James Brennan	Joseph Sindrick	....
Latrobe b§ (11)	MC 412 539-8548	Angelo Caruso	Robert Barto	Kathy J Baum	Robert Barto	J Regis Kessler	Francis D Plyler	David Williams
Laureldale b (4)	MC 215 929-8700	George D Sobresky	....	Violet E Schaeffer	....	Ted Feltenberger	Barry F Schaeffer	....
Lebanon (26)	CO 717 273-6711	Martin Schneider	Debra J Gates	Debra J Gates	Linnea Miller	Gary Hammer	M J DeLeo	....
Leechburg b† (3)	MC 412 842-8511	Samuel P Catalino	....	....	....	Andrew Palczer	Larry Kulick	....
Lehighton b* (6)	CM 215 377-4002	Clinton J Williams	M L Smedley	Betty Frable	....	Edward Conarty Jr	Lionel Cote	M L Smedley
Lemoyne b§† (4)	MC 717 737-6843	Robert W Farver	Joseph W Golden	Joseph W Golden	Joseph W Golden	Gary S Anderson	Howard E Dougherty	Gary S Anderson
Lewisburg b† (5)	MC 717 523-3614	Lewis Hendricks Jr	Donald E Vaughan	Janice L Stamfel	Donald E Vaughan	William L Sartwell	Donald L Heiter	Donald E Vaughan
Lewistown b§ (10)	MC 717 248-1361	William Chamberlin	Eleanor A Stimely	Eleanor A Stimely	Eleanor A Stimely	Kenneth J Powell	James A Wagner	Burle Fisher
Liberty b† (3)	MC 717 324-3461	Robert A Black	Beverly H Mase	....		Roy Reed	....	....
Lititz b† (8)	MC 717 626-2044	Raymond S Reedy	Kenneth P Wiest	Ellen R Chandler	....	Jere Buchter	George C Hicks	David R Anderson

Directory 1/10 continued

MUNICIPAL OFFICIALS IN ALL U.S. CITIES OVER 2,500[1]

City, 1980 population (000 omitted), form of government		Municipal phone number	Mayor	Appointed administrator	City clerk	Finance officer	Fire chief	Police chief	Public works director
PENNSYLVANIA (540) continued									
Littlestown b (3)	MC	717 359-5101	Frank E Basehoar Sr	....	Samuel B Michael	Richard E Selby	Donald R Morgret	Roger C Gouker	Samuel B Michael
Lock Haven* (10)	CM	717 748-9513	Diann H Stuempfle	Frank L Taggart	Frank L Taggart	Paul D Welch	Lawrence E Neff	James E Belcher	Richard C Ardner
Logan tp§† (12)	MC	814 944-5340	Cloyd Forsht	Frank L Noye	Frank L Noye	Frank L Noye	....	John Reeder	....
Lower Allen tp§ (14)	MC	717 737-8681	R F Hawley	Ronald J Mull	Ronald J Mull	Ronald J Mull	Glen Hawbecker	Mitchell Smith	David R Lenker
Lower Burrell (13)	MC	412 335-9875	Dennis L Kowalski	....	Frank B Duda	Jack R Anderson	David Swick	John T McKillop	Mr Van Ernest
Lower Gwynedd tp§ (7)	MC	215 646-5302	Janet Kirch	Edward Hancock	Linda Koch	Ruth Dunn	Joseph Schneider	Gary Oconnor	....
Lower Makefield tp* (17)	CM	215 493-3646	Grace Godshalk	James J Dillon	....	....	....	Charles E Ronaldo	....
Lower Merion tp§ (60)	MC	215 649-4000	Charles F Ward	Patrick J Joyce	Eileen R Trainer	Lois S Nichols	Harry R Knorr Jr	Salvatore Frustaci	Bert L Williams
Lower Moreland tp§ (12)	MC	215 947-3100	....	Alison D Winter	....	Robert Slauch	Thomas Spangler	Robert R Hamilton	H Will Lawrence
Lower Paxton tp§ (35)	MC	717 657-5600	Richard N Koch	Jack F Hurley	Helen K Kirk	....	....	Stanley V Holsinger	....
Lower Pottsgrove tp§ (7)	MC	215 323-1380	Gerald Richards	Raymond Umstead	Eleanor Rosen	Sally Moyer	Lewis Babel	Richard Lengel	....
Lower Providence tp* (19)	CM	215 539-8020	Richard T Brown	John F Mikowychok	....	....	Harry Miller	Thomas P Rogers	....
Lower Saucon tp* (7)	CM	215 865-1161	Mark Chehi	Mary Curtin	....	....	Joseph J Luybli	Guy Lesser	Andrew Hayes
Lower Southampton tp§ (18)	CO	215 357-7300	Charles Raudenbush	Leon LaRosa	....	Vicky Walters	Steven Eckman	Edward F Wunsch	Warne W Clayton
Lower Swatara tp§ (7)	MC	717 939-9377	Franklin P Linn Sr	Frank R Siffrinn	....	Edward A Gingrich	....	Richard Malwitz Jr	Earl W Condran Sr
Luzerne b† (4)	MC	717 287-4312	Nevin L Gorki	Michael Hardik	Marion Cecconi	....	Jeff Rifenberry	William Tregan	....
Mahanoy City b (6)	MC	717 773-2150	Vincent E Zelonis	....	P R Kaczmarczyk	Thomas Homa	Paul MacLeary	Jack P McElhenny	....
Malvern b* (3)	CM	215 644-2602	Jarold J Sedlacek	Richard DiPrimio	....	Richard DiPrimio	John O Stebbins	Bruce T Evarts	Ira Dutter
Manchester tp* (8)	CM	717 764-4646	Tim L Horner	David A Raver	....	Vivian J Smith	Paul L Schaefer	W Ronald Smeal	David A Raver
Manheim b* (5)	CM	717 665-2463	James R Brosey	Dan W Lane	....	....	David J Carpenter	John Winters	....
Manheim tp§ (26)	CO	717 569-6406	....	James M Martin	James M Martin	James M Martin	....	David E Moore	Carl L Neff
Mansfield b§ (3)	MC	717 662-2315	Benjamin Hutcheson	Robert O Dewey	....	Ethel E Hanford	Joseph S Thompson	James A Pratt	....
Marcus Hook b§ (3)	MC	215 485-1341	James F Jackson	Bruce A Dorbian	Dolores Kowac	Joseph Gattone	Robert Sides	George McClure	Raymond Garzia
Marietta b (3)	MC	717 426-4143	Oliver Overlander	Cynthia L Hughes	....	....	Barry Eppley	William B Roberts	....
Marple tp§ (24)	MC	215 356-4040	Patricia A Keates	Joseph W Flicker	....	Hugo N Yannelli	Thomas Murray	Daniel S Hennessey	Edward T Cross
Marysville b* (2)	CM	717 957-3110	Charlotte N Rowe	Larry N Wilfong	....	....	Charles K Good	Leonard Lotrick	....
Masontown b (5)	MC	412 583-7731	George R Standish	....	Patrick Del Grosso	Paul Cassidy	Russell King	Robert Salipek	Peter Mitchell
McAdoo b† (3)	MC	717 929-2504	Joseph Billet	Edward J Bielen	Mary A Labert	Barbara A Kalena	Robert Leshko	Joseph Litchko	....
McCandless t* (26)	CM	412 364-0616	....	Tobias M Cordek	....	Tobias M Cordek	....	Patrick B McCabe	Mark Sabina
McDonald b (3)	MC	412 926-8711	Lyman Bellaire	Ralph G Schwartz	Gloria J Noble	Ralph G Schwartz	William W Dickinson	Bruce E Barnhart	....
McKees Rocks b (9)	MC	412 331-2498	Thomas H Connolly	William C Beck	....	....	Edward M Maritz	Ronald Panyko	Richard Naughton
McKeesport (31)	MC	412 675-5050	Louis Washowich	Karen Supansic	Johanna Bell	Christine Smeltzer	Robert Matwick	James J Lundie	Daryl Segina
McSherrystown b† (3)	MC	717 637-1838	Thomas J Weaver	Richard Smith	Patricia M Groft	Martin J Weaver	Wm Livelsberger	D Michael Vial	William H Smith Jr
Meadville* (16)	CM	814 724-6000	James J DiMaria	David L Wendtland	Ronald Rushton	Danial Smith	George Cullum	Robert Fischer	Kenneth A Beers
Mechanicsburg b* (9)	CM	717 766-5431	Samuel L Nedrow	D E Sultzaberger	D E Sultzaberger	....	James Neff	Rodney L Whitcomb	....
Media b† (6)	MC	215 566-5210	Frank W Daly	....	James J Loughran	Francis J Marabella	James Jefferies	Gerald F Olmsted	James J Loughran
Mercer b (3)	MC	412 662-3980	William T Wardle	....	Diana L Jackal	Majorie Palmer	James Minner	Frank J Detelich	James M Hovis
Mercersburg b§† (2)	MC	717 328-3321	....	Paul Clugston	....	....	....	....	....
Meyersdale b (3)	CM	814 634-5110	(not reporting)						
Middletown tp* (12)	CM	215 565-2700	Alfred A Gollatz	W Bruce Clark	W Bruce Clark	Celeste M Dunion	John T McKeown	....	Arthur W Rothe
Middletown tp* (34)	CM	215 943-0300	Richard J Scott	John J Burke	John J Burke	Nancie Cossman	Lyle Winters	Michael J Chitwood	Joseph Giacomuzzi
Middletown b*† (10)	CM	717 944-4686	Robert G Reid	Paul H Bradtmiller	Suzan K Sides	James C Harper	William C Weaver	Ronald F Wells	....
Midland b (4)	MC	412 643-4170	(not reporting)						
Mifflinburg b* (3)	CM	717 966-1013	John E Schnure	George M Steese	Doris A Guffey	Steven E Dodge	Duane L Zimmerman	Hall E Solomon	George M Steese
Millcreek tp (44)	MC	814 833-1111	Paul J Martin	....	Dorothy M Young	Gerald M Wolf	....	Merrill T Dever	Paul J Martin
Millersburg b (3)	MC	717 692-4711	Baylor Custer	Kenneth L Rose Jr	Edra E Carvell	Robert Koppenhaver	Robert Lehman Sr	Kenneth L Rose Jr	....
Millersville b§ (8)	MC	717 872-4645	William E Moyer	Stephen L Sechriest	Stephen L Sechriest	Stephen L Sechriest	James D Eshleman	....	Frank Neff
Millvale b (5)	MC	412 821-1356	(not reporting)						
Milton b* (7)	CM	717 742-8759	Henry Longenberger	Harold L Mertz	Carrie M Thomas	....	William Bastian	Michael T Warns	....
Minersville b† (6)	MC	717 544-2149	John Smythe	....	G M Volkay	James Cleary	George Ulmer	Joseph A Willinsky	....
Monaca b* (8)	CM	412 775-3321	John A Antoline	Thomas A Stoner	Doreen M Vincenti	....	William Raisley	Lawrence Conti	William Keefer
Monessen§ (12)	MC	412 684-9712	James A Sepesky	Paul J Shives	Paul J Shives	Ernest S Wisyanski	Robert H Leone	Steve Hazy	Andrew Freeman
Monongahela (6)	MC	412 258-5501	John Moreschi	....	Carole Foglia	Joseph Jordan	George Devore	Owen Burns Jr	James Harrison
Monroeville* (31)	CM	412 823-5100	Michael P Lynch	Marshall W Bond	Marshall W Bond	Janet Hufford	....	George Gregowich Jr	Jack Speelman
Montgomery tp§ (6)	MC	215 855-1771	Robert R Kuhn	Daniel P Olpere	Daniel P Olpere	Janet E Cherrington	James Swartley	Richard J Brady	Paul Henning
Montgomery b* (2)	CM	717 547-1671	Richard D Thomas Jr	Richard Zika	....	....	John Grove	Richard M Knaur	....
Montoursville b (5)	MC	717 368-2486	John Dorin	Eugene E Boyles	Eugene E Boyles	....	Lynn Welty	Brian Aldinger	H L Dieffenbacher
Moon tp§ (21)	CO	412 262-1700	Jack Wise	Gregory G Smith	....	Robert W Currie	Charles Belgie Jr	H Thomas Krance	John Kennedy
Moosic b (6)	MC	717 457-5480	Frank J Assaf	Clare Conaboy	....	....	....	William Salmon	John Thiel
Morrisville b* (10)	CM	215 295-8181	Lee D Rockafellow	Harry F Falkenstein	....	....	R Gary Davis	Harry G Merke	Howard Wilmot
Mount Carmel b* (8)	CM	717 339-4486	Joseph V Honecker	Joseph K Bass	Marian E Muldowney	Marian M Muldowney	Joseph Gula	Edward J Strike	Victor Kornaski
Mount Joy b* (6)	CM	717 653-2300	Robert D Stoner	Paul E Stehman Jr	Paul E Stehman Jr	Mark D Gainer	George Hedrick	J Bruce Kline	Amos D Hershey
Mount Oliver b (5)	MC	412 431-8107	John W Smith	Freda A Froelich	Alice A Dedig	Carl M Patrick	James Cassidy	John V Hindmarch	William Holzer
Mount Penn b (3)	MC	215 779-5151	John Becker	Regina Skrincosky	Pamela Eisele	Ralph Orlando	Richard Hawk	Barry Cardell	Robert Moyer
Mount Pleasant b (5)	MC	412 547-6745	William Potoka	....	....	Lois S Reese	Thomas Sweitzer	John Galbraith	....
Mount Union b§ (3)	MC	814 542-4051	Luke C Riley	Ronald G Fortney	....	....	Mike Goodman	Lawrence Knable Jr	....
Mt. Lebanon* (34)	CM	412 343-3400	James M Delsole	James P Cain	....	Marcia L Taylor	Stephen C Walther	David A Varrelman	James W Harrod
Muncy b (3)	MC	717 546-3952	(not reporting)						
Munhall b† (15)	MC	412 461-2526	William W Knight	....	....	....	....	....	....
Murrysville§ (16)	MC	412 327-2100	Barbara B Redding	John M Lynch	John M Lynch	John M Lynch	....	Edward D Roberts	Thomas M Stout
Myerstown b§ (3)	MC	717 866-5038	Malcolm R Seager	Edward H Treat	John S Brown III	Lee C Smith	Frederick Shaak	Daryl G Layser	....
Nanticoke† (13)	MC	717 735-2200	Edward J Butkiewicz	....	Paul J Barron	Eugene Ruminski	Donald Casey	Wasil Kobela	Henry Krasucki
Nanty-Glo b (4)	MC	814 749-0331	Arthur C Price Sr	....	Jennie M Mulato	Mary A Mychajlonka	Thomas Waltz	Ronald P Brown	James Stephens
Narberth b§ (4)	MC	215 664-2840	Dennis J Sharkey	William J Martin	Betty J Willard	Isabel W Pittenger	John R Thomas	....	Harry Girvin
Nazareth b (5)	MC	215 759-2540	Charles J Peischl	Jean Stewart	Paul Kokolus	Paul Kokolus	Richard Garren	Joseph Roccosanto	....
Nesquehoning b (3)	MC	717 669-9588	Frank Jacobs	....	Joseph G Greco Jr	....	Bernard Gogal	Joseph Tout	....
Nether Providence tp§ (13)	CO	215 566-4516	Eugene G Monaco	Gary J Cummings	Sarah Lukens	Gary J Cummings	Robert Foltz	Francis Corbett	Virgil Mills
New Brighton b*† (7)	CM	412 846-1870	Paul Spickerman	Larry R Morley	....	....	David Hickey	Philip Rini	Jerry Feit
New Britain t (3)	MC	215 348-4586	George W Taylor	....	Janis B Brandt	....	....	Austin Brown	....
New Castle§ (34)	MC	412 652-7781	Dale Yoho	Dennis P Lemieux	Jack H Fritz	Dennis P Lemieux	James Antonio	Vince Russo	Joseph Cook
New Cumberland b* (8)	CM	717 774-0404	Terry A Stoner	S Sultzaberger	....	....	George R Ebersole	Earle R Sweikert Jr	Elmer Wertz
New Eagle b† (3)	MC	412 258-4477	Thomas McGinty	Linda J Hall	Mary Ann Lopresti	....	Adrian Martello	Charles Ziska	John Zelinski
New Hanover tp§ (5)	MC	215 323-1008	Harold V Lohmiller	Anita B John	Eileen Pogany	....	....	Lloyd K Kline	C Ray Batchelder
New Holland b* (4)	CM	717 354-4567	Gene A Lowry	Kenneth Minier	....	....	Larry G Usner	Harry M Erb Jr	Barry G Eitnier

MUNICIPAL DIRECTORIES

Directory 1/10 continued **MUNICIPAL OFFICIALS IN ALL U.S. CITIES OVER 2,500[1]**

City, 1980 population (000 omitted), form of government		Municipal phone number	Mayor	Appointed administrator	City clerk	Finance officer	Fire chief	Police chief	Public works director
PENNSYLVANIA (540) continued									
New Hope b§ (1)	MC	215 862-3347	....	Bettylou Balderston	....	....	....	....	....
New Kensington (18)	MC	412 337-4525	John J Monaco	....	Anna Marie Domenick	David M Hanna	Edward Saliba	Edward L McAfoose	Bernard T Kubiak
New Stanton b† (3)	MC	412 925-9700	John G Reagan	....	Cynthia L Walthour	....	David Hauger	....	Harry C Kauffman
New Wilmington b (3)	MC	412 946-8167	Guy McCrumb	....	Peggy Sherrod	Thomas J O'Shane	James Schiek	Richard Hanna	Edward Garrett
Newtown b† (3)	MC	215 968-2109	Harry W Weber Jr	Martin P Sutton	Lois B Saurman	....	George Forsyth Sr	Martin C Duffy	
Newtown tp§ (12)	MC	215 356-0200	Joseph L Crawford	Paul D West	....	....	....	Stanley R Short	Paul M McDonald
Norristown b§ (35)	MC	215 272-8080	John Marberger	John Plonski	Gail Polvino	Mary Ralston	George Dewees	William J Bambi	Fred J Von Hacht
North Braddock b§ (9)	MC	412 271-1306	Norman Irvin	Edward Calabria	Edward Calabria	Edward Calabria	James Novak	Fred Burdell Jr	Roman Petrusky
North Catasauqua b† (3)	MC	215 264-1504	Roy K Hodes	....	Julia V Superka	Joseph J Holena	Greg Loch	....	Frank Hacker
North East b (5)	MC	814 725-8611	Thomas Scrimenti	Kenneth Maas	....	....	Roy T Huber	Roy T Huber	Herbert Mallick
North Huntingdon tp (32)	CM	412 863-3806	(not reporting)						
North Middleton tp§ (9)	MC	717 243-8550	Charles E King	....	Joyce L Brehm	....	Robert L Hays	William S Weaver	....
North Versailles tp (13)	MC	412 823-6602	Robert Vuyanich	....	Alice Shearer	Edward R McGuire	Darryl Roher	Vincent Dicenzo	Jesse Reed
North Wales b (3)	MC	215 699-4424	Frank M Hartman	Gregory E Prowant	....	....	Joseph Pelletier	Kenneth C Veit	Richard E Schatz
Northampton tp§ (27)	MC	215 357-6800	Albert Wiley Jr	D Bruce Townsend	....	....	Thomas Briggs	William Feeney	Pat Giradi
Northampton b* (8)	CM	215 262-2576	Paul E Kutzler	Carl F DiCello	....	Patricia Walter	Joseph Kochenash	Joseph J Handler Jr	Gregory Gorsky
Northumberland b (4)	MC	717 473-3414	L Robert Waltz	William A Sabo	Jane G Sanders	Ernest Gessner	William Winters	Ron L Ray	Clair Lenig
Norwood b (7)	MC	215 586-5800	(not reporting)						
O'Hara tp* (9)	CM	412 782-1400	William H Crooks Jr	Carol T Young	....	Carol T Young	Frank DeBlasio	Raymond A Schafer	Charles Clinton
Oakmont b§ (7)	MC	412 828-3232	Donald H Eaton	Adeline Brown	Adeline Brown	Adeline Brown	Sam Brocato	Donald V Smith	Adeline Brown
Ohio tp§ (2)	MC	412 364-6321	John McDonald	Joseph J Start	....	Joseph J Start	Thomas Larkin	Brian S Kording	Gerald Reichart
Ohioville b† (4)	MC	412 643-8061	Eli Sainovich	....	....	....	....	Bernard Zlatovich	....
Oil City* (14)	CM	814 677-1241	Leonard M Abate	Terence W Farren	Terence W Farren	Terence W Farren	James Stack	Richard Bucholz	James H Hicks
Old Forge b† (9)	MC	717 457-7441	Frank G Digennari	....	....	....	Edward Rishko	Stanley Lisowski	Anthony Tagliaterra
Olyphant b (5)	MC	717 489-2135	Michael Chekansky	....	Edith Kenny	Phil Condella	Al Caines Jr	Walter Demain	Thomas Keegan
Orwigsburg b§ (3)	MC	717 366-2285	Everit Binns	George R Zimmer	Anna L Shiffert	....	Adam H Faust	Stanley P Brozana	....
Oxford b§ (4)	MC	215 932-2500	Paul E Andriole	Neil R Phillips	Virginia M Holt	Grace Peterson	Larry Sherrow	James E Peters	Daniel Hoffman
Palmerton b§ (5)	CM	215 826-2505	Guy F Zern	John W Kasten	Teresa M Vargo	John W Kasten	David M Lucia	John O Rupell	....
Palmyra b§ (7)	MC	717 838-6361	Clifford K Mark	Paul J Garber	Paul J Garber	....	....	Gary D Garman	....
Parkesburg b (3)	MC	215 857-2616	William E Wilson Jr	....	Joann Reynolds	Alan M Wolfe	Richard Klingler	Lester J Thomas	Rawlins Engle
Patton tp§ (7)	MC	814 234-0271	Victor Dupuis	Thomas S Kurtz	Christine Spearly	....	....	Gary B Davenport	....
Pen Argyl b (3)	MC	215 863-4119	Frank S Brumbaugh	....	Dolores B Savitz	....	Peter Thomas Jr	Dwayne R Honey	Alvin E Englert
Penbrook b§ (3)	MC	717 232-3733	Timothy J Dailey	Wendy J Rotz	Linda S Bartholomeo	Ronda A White	J Edward Crum Jr	Edward A Katz	....
Penn tp* (9)	CM	717 632-7366	Nevin Musselman Jr	Philip F Hertz	Dorothy Ernst	Steve W Thomas	Richard Rorrer	Ronald R Beeler	P F Hertz
Penn Hills§ (58)	MC	412 795-3500	Roy C Ritenour	Harry R McIndoe	Harry R McIndoe	Edw P Schrecengost	John D Mason	Kenneth J Sechoka	Daniel P Farabaugh
Penndel b (3)	MC	215 757-5153	John M Smith	....	....	....	William Davis	Stephen M Burke	....
Perkasie b§ (5)	MC	215 257-5065	Winfred O Kulp	Gary A Nace	Gary A Nace	Gary A Nace	Robert S Graham	Claude E Nase	Martin O Grossmyer
Peters tp§ (13)	MC	412 941-4180	....	Michael A Silvestri	Madeline M Farkas	....	Dan Coyle	Robert M Clark	Peter Overcashier
Philadelphia† (1688)	MC	215 686-1776	Wilson Goode	Leo A Brooks	Joseph C Vignola	Richard G Gilmore	William Richmond	Gregore Sambor	Dudley R Sykes
Philipsburg b (3)	MC	814 342-3440	Nick T Drivas	Donald P Enck	Peggy J Eyerly	J Stephen Garner	Jerry Woods	Robert E Trump	Donald Enck
Phoenixville b* (14)	CM	215 933-8801	Robert M Gray	William P Herman	Patricia M Garrison	Frank R Edinger	Ollie Sims	Henry Rodrique	....
Pine tp§ (4)	MC	412 625-1591	Gerald W Weaver	William D Marsh	....	....	....	....	....
Pitcairn b (4)	MC	412 372-3116	(not reporting)						
Pittsburgh (424)	MC	412 255-2100	Richard S Caliguiri	David Matter	Michael Perry	Thomas Flaherty	Charles Lewis	Robert Coll	Louis Gaetano
Pittston (10)	MC	717 654-0513	Thomas A Walsh	....	Paul McGarry	P J Melvin	Francis McDonnell	Joseph Delaney	Thomas J Reilley
Pleasant tp§† (3)	MC	814 723-5240	....	Marshall L Gern	....	....	....	....	....
Pleasant Hills b (10)	MC	412 655-3300	Eldon D Snyder	R H Knefelkamp	Nancy J Rodgers	Warren F Bourgeois	H James Hosfield	Stanley A Smith	George Lamars
Plum b (25)	CM	412 795-6800	A E Oblock	Alberta L Horner	....	Alberta L Horner	....	Robert A Alexander	John E Walters
Plymouth tp§ (17)	MC	215 277-4100	Robert D Wurzbach	James T Mitchell	....	Peter T Dipasquale	....	John A Volpe	Charles F Oyler
Plymouth b (8)	MC	717 779-9552	Edward F Burns	Elaine Marvinski	....	Barbara Burk	Ralph Delong	John Z Thomas	Chester D Rydzefski
Port Allegany b* (3)	CM	814 642-2526	Richard Kallenborn	L O Griffith	Susan E Robbins	....	Dennis Williams	Donald G Carley	....
Port Carbon b† (3)	MC	717 622-5411	Francis Lubinsky	....	....	Donald Kerns	Burtis Bennsinger	William Bradley	....
Port Vue b (5)	MC	412 664-9323	Edward A Pollack	....	Joann M Gubanic	....	Todd Shultz	Howard T Judy	....
Portage b (4)	MC	814 736-4330	Howard W Smith	....	Joseph E Shandor	Frank Portash	John Walkovich	Carl D Chappell	Darryl Hanna
Pottstown b*† (23)	CM	215 326-3100	Edward W Jameson	Eugene G Moody	Helene M Foley	Eugene G Moody	Harold Moyer	James E Rodgers	Earl J Case
Pottsville (18)	CO	717 622-1234	Anthony J Pacenta	....	Carol Chickersky	Thomas J Pellish	Todd March	John Mushock	....
Prospect Park b† (7)	MC	215 532-1007	John E Costello	Mary Pepe	Anna May Depew	Raymond Malseed	Tony Maffie	William H Young	Frank Natoli
Punxsutawney b* (7)	CM	814 938-4800	J C Nelles	Stephen L Johnson	Stephen L Johnson	Stephen Johnson	Thomas Chelgrin	Ronald P Krolick	Edward Shaw
Quakertown b*† (9)	CM	215 536-5001	....	Nicholas Luca	Nicholas Luca	....	Jeff Stump	Chief McFadden	John Cain
Radnor tp§ (28)	MC	215 688-5600	Andrew A Orr	Chas B Guernsey	....	Edward Hayes	Donald A Wood	Maurice L Hennessy	Ernest L Marmer
Rankin b (3)	MC	412 271-1027	Matthew Furjanic	Mary Koval	....	....	David Mozeik	Nekodie Mudd	Charles B Simone
Reading (79)	CO	215 320-6000	Karen A Miller	....	Ruth M Thompson	Thomas W Gajewski	Charles Schaeffer	Rodney E Steffy	Edw W Leonardziak
Red Lion b*† (6)	CM	717 244-3475	C Martin Neff	Raymond E Arnold Jr	....	Jeffrey E Fix	Rodney R Brenneman	John H Ruby	....
Reynoldsville b (3)	MC	814 653-2110	Gloria V Rankus	....	Jacqueline K Beck	....	Ralph T August	Robert E Milliren	Jackson Shepler
Richland tp§† (8)	MC	412 443-5921	....	Dean Bastianini	....	....	....	....	....
Ridgway b* (6)	CM	814 776-1125	Robert V Howard	Martin R Schuller	....	....	William Gausman	Burton Shaver	Albert Paladino
Ridley tp§ (34)	CO	215 534-4800	Joseph P Cronin Jr	Anne E Howanski	....	Daniel E Mingis	Paul Ong	Charles C Randell	Joseph H Rafferty
Ridley Park b† (8)	MC	215 532-2100	Joseph Kilkenny	Larry J Wygant	....	Harry McGrady	Paul Bustin	Charles E Miller	Richard Miles
Roaring Spring b (3)	MC	814 224-4814	Vance D Myers	Charles F Yingling	....	....	Kenneth Pote	Kenneth M Bathurst	Max W Burke
Robinson tp (9)	CM	....	(not reporting)						
Rochester b§ (5)	CM	412 774-6928	Gerald J LaValle	Timothy E Vail	Joyce A Cutshall	Timothy E Vail	Ronald Hogue	Felix Deluca	Howard Begley
Ross tp§ (35)	MC	412 931-0558	Arthur F White	A Leathery	....	....	Joseph Franks	Earl K Grabenstein	Raymond G Hale
Royersford b* (4)	CM	215 948-3737	John M Salamone	Robert L Weikel	Robert L Weikel	....	Richard M Saylor Sr	Harry E Van Horn	Otto J Fox
Salisbury tp* (12)	CM	215 797-4000	Janet B Keim	Clifford G Steff	Wm J Ganster	Wm J Ganster	....	Charles Durner Jr	Stanley Fries
Sayre b*† (7)	CM	717 888-7739	Nicholas Chacona	Eugene T Osmun	Audrey A Garfield	....	Thomas Yonkin	Richard Verstreate	....
Schuylkill Haven b* (6)	CM	717 385-2841	Paul R Donmoyer	Ronald L Waller	John F Marshall	John F Marshall	Kenneth R Reed	Thomas G Smith	....
Scott tp§ (20)	CO	412 276-5300	Domenic Colarosa	P A Wodnicki	P A Wodnicki	Arthur J Komoroski	....	Marino Zarolli	Harold McGowan
Scottdale b (6)	MC	412 887-8220	Eugene J Beran	Barry D Whoric	Barry D Whoric	....	Patsy A Slate	Ralph M Rich Jr	....
Scranton (88)	MC	717 348-4100	James B McNulty	Richard Rossi	Frank Naughton	Henry McNulty	Robert Ruddy	Robert Williams	Joseph Loughney
Selinsgrove b* (5)	CM	717 374-2311	Kenneth Mease	George Kinney	....	....	George Haas	James Hartley	Gary Klingler
Sellersville b§ (3)	MC	215 257-5075	J Hufnagle Sr	Richard D Coll	Richard D Coll	Richard D Coll	Thomas Hufnagle	Robert E Burke	Alan S Frick
Sewickley Heights b§ (1)	MC	412 741-5111	C J Ramsburg Jr	G Robert Surls	William P Rohe	....	Alan E Farrier	Alan Farrier	Herbert C Ford
Sewickley b* (5)	CM	412 741-4015	David P Guilot	Martin C McDaniel	Elizabeth M Pflugh	Martin C McDaniel	Hugh A McMaster Jr	Walter J Brannon	Herbert Dittrich
Shaler tp§† (34)	MC	412 486-9700	....	Wm L Crawford	....	Lois M Daviess	....	Edw Sobehart	W C Shomaker
Shamokin (10)	MC	717 644-0876	William L Rickert	....	William R Strausser	Warren C Schriver	Robert E Milbrand	Ronald A Wagner	Claude E Kehler Jr
Sharon (19)	MC	412 347-7503	Robert T Price	....	Judith A Morrison	Robert M Crofford	Paul E McSherry	Robert J Truitt	Robert T Price
Sharon Hill b (6)	MC	215 586-8200	Ronald C Raymond	Mildred Enderle	Mildred Enderle	Mildred Enderle	Robert Lauer	William E Hanna	....

Directory 1/10 continued

MUNICIPAL OFFICIALS IN ALL U.S. CITIES OVER 2,500[1]

City, 1980 population (000 omitted), form of government	Municipal phone number	Mayor	Appointed administrator	City clerk	Finance officer	Fire chief	Police chief	Public works director
PENNSYLVANIA (540) continued								
Sharpsburg b (4) MC	412 781-0546	Marion A Gerardi	Marianne L Burkarth	Mary Jane Szwedko	Mary Jane Szwedko	Anthony J Scalise	Donald F Ferraro	Carl J Ferraro
Sharpsville b* (5) CM	412 962-7896	Eugene M Blair	Robert H Glass	Jill M Miller	....	Paul E Mehalko	Rocco Del Fratte	Dale E Bucher
Shenandoah b† (8) MC	717 462-1918	John Reese	L Breznik	L A Sewastynowicz	J J Stascavage	A Bubnis	....	....
Shillington b§ (6) MC	215 777-1338	George W Kochard	Michael D Mountz	Jam M Squibb	....	E M Squibb Jr	Quentin T Hamory	Frank A Riegel
Shippensburg b* (5) CM	717 532-2147	Jerry A Weigle	Frederick A Reddig	Frederick A Reddig	....	Edward Goodhart	Michael J Lynch	....
Shrewsbury b (3) MC	717 235-4371	Dennis S Bradfield	....	....	....	Dennis A Wertz	David D Weston	John B Myers
Silver Spring tp§† (7) MC	717 766-0178	....	Robt O McCarthy	....	....	....	....	....
Sinking Spring b (3) MC	215 678-4903	Richard H Miller	Dorothy E Behm	Bonnie B Yoder	Robert Clark	Richard Good	John Habecker	....
Slatington b† (4) MC	215 767-2131	Paul H Handwerk	Bertha M Griffith	....	....	Gary Phillips	Arthur Kistler	Robert Labold
Slippery Rock b (3) MC	412 794-6391	Frank Monteleone	....	....	Ruth West	Tom Davis	L J Thompson	Paul Dickey
Somerset b* (6) CM	814 443-2661	Elmer D Kline	Michael G Mahaney	Mathilda Brown	....	J R Lehman	Geo Jock	Park Stoy
Souderton b* (7) CM	215 723-4371	C H Allebach Jr	P Michael Coll	Elaine G Frederick	....	Paul Stoudt	Charles A Quinn	....
South Fayette tp (10) CM	412 221-8700	(not reporting)						
South Greensburg b (3) MC	412 837-8858	James T Fetsko	....	Donna P Ickes	Donna P Ickes	Charles W Giron	Jerome M Todaro Jr	....
South Hanover tp§ (4) MC	717 566-8253	Donald W Vachon	Dennis H Barr	....	....	....	....	....
South Lebanon tp§ (7) CO	717 274-0481	Paul E Krause	Walter A Herr	Phyllis I McGann	James G Loser Sr	Dennis Trainor	George Gettler	....
South Park tp§ (14) MC	412 831-7000	David S Woods	Harry J Mertz	Harry J Mertz	Harry J Mertz	....	Edward Strimlan	William Spagnol
South Strabane tp§ (7) MC	412 225-9055	Edward Mazur	Mae C Reynolds	....	....	....	Donald M Zofchak Jr	William H Orndoff
South Whitehall tp* (16) CM	215 398-0401	Charles E Mackenzie	Chester W Gilkey	....	Ronnie Rice	....	Donald MacConnell	Ralph H Kocher Sr
South Williamsport b (7) MC	717 322-0158	R David Frey	Joanne C Ackerman	....	Charles Luppert	David L Huyck	Charles E Smith	C Robert Lutcher
Southmont b† (3) MC	814 255-3104	Robert Morgan	....	Lois J Smith	Thomas Dailey	Michael Butler	Anthony Wilt	Jan Bosley
Southwest Greensburg b (3) MC	412 834-0360	James L Hayden Jr	....	....	....	John Ackerman	James Santmyer	....
Spring tp† (17) MC	215 678-5393	....	J George French	....	....	....	....	....
Spring City b (3) MC	215 948-3660	Jean Jeffries	Calvin M Adams	Sara L Robinson	Adele T Groman	Keith Bliss	Donald Widdecombe	....
Spring Garden tp† (11) MC	717 848-2858	Clarence H Gotwalt	Carl L Hykes	Carl L Hykes	Donald H Sterner	George Williams III	S W Lehman Jr	Geo F Himmelright
Springdale b† (4) MC	412 274-6800	John S Palovcak	Bob P Playfair	Burnette Coulter	Charles J Hawk	Henry Mink	Ron Rivers	Joseph Paukoucek
Springettsbury tp* (20) CM	717 757-3521	Albert H Spinner	David J Deutsch	David J Deutsch	S S Olewiler Jr	Glenn Kline	Harold D Kessler	George Gemmill
Springfield tp† (25) CO	215 544-1300	Robert M DiOrio	....	Harry A Bornman	Joseph Harrity	Joseph S Burns	George W Hill	Thomas R Behmke
Springfield tp* (20) CM	215 836-7600	....	J R Fulginiti	J R Fulginiti	J R Fulginiti	....	Earl M Hopkins	Robert S Wilmot
St. Clair b† (4) MC	717 429-2240	Joseph H Long	Donald C Hosler	Roland Price Jr	Carol Sutzko	Robert F Greenback	Thomas I Maley	....
St. Marys b* (6) CM	814 781-1718	Ulmar Fritz	Leo A Weichman	Leo A Weichman	....	Michael Bauer	Donald Wilhelm	Richard Nussbaum
State College b§ (36) MC	814 234-7100	Arnold Addison	Carl B Fairbanks	Carl B Fairbanks	Ronald A Davis	C Marvin Robinson	E G Williams Jr	Donald R Dorneman
Steelton b (6) MC	717 939-9842	J Richard Stouffer	Frank P Fisher	Frank P Fisher	Kathrine Kocevar	Robert Butts	Kenneth J Tindal	Thomas L Reider
Stowe tp (9) CO	412 771-4877	Joseph Patrowsky	....	Julienne Pawlowski	Wallace Akanowicz	Martin A Jacobs	Stephen Homer	James A Mollica
Stroudsburg b* (5) CM	717 421-5444	Chester L Gross	Bradley A Blubaugh	Bradley A Blubaugh	James A Somers	Richard Seip	Gary J Roberts	Frank Labar
Sugar Creek b* (6) CM	814 432-4717	John D McClelland	James W Sigworth	Inez C Redmond	....	....	Charles R Tarr	....
Summit Hill b† (3) MC	717 645-2305	Kenneth Frassinelli	....	Kathryn Chickilly	....	Carl Gray	John Crampsie	....
Sunbury (12) MC	717 286-7820	William E Gass	....	Linda Smith	Edward M Neff	Don Pyers	Charles T McAndrew	Charles Schlegel
Susquehanna tp§ (18) MC	717 545-4751	Jack S Pincus	Miles A Caughey	Miles A Caughey	Miles A Caughey	John C Brindle	William C Trapnell	Walter A Waddell
Swarthmore b§† (6) MC	215 543-4599	Charles D Hummer Jr	Richard E Hunt	Margaret K Crompton	....	Philip Layton	William Weidner	....
Swissvale b (11) MC	412 271-7101	Charles Martoni	Thomas J Esposito	....	Thomas J Esposito	Albert Lukac	Ronald Lees	....
Swoyersville b (6) MC	717 288-6581	Anthony Stefanoski	....	Joseph Koval	Joseph Koval	Vince Velikis	William Dorman	John Saxon
Tamaqua b* (9) CM	717 668-3444	William W Yost	Donald Matalavage	Joan D Snyder	Charles H Reaman	Robert Delay	Robert Neifert	....
Tarentum b† (6) MC	412 224-1818	James Wolfe	....	Joseph Davidek	....	....	Frank Prazenica	....
Taylor b (7) MC	717 562-1400	David Noakes	Daniel P Zeleniak	June W Kacaba	Archabald Stone	Willian Nash	James M Thomas	....
Telford b§ (4) MC	215 723-5000	H Arden Kinsey	Charles R Feindler	Charles R Feindler	....	Malcolm R Jacobs	Douglas E Bickel	Donald F Beck
Throop b† (4) MC	717 489-8311	John J Stecco	Frank Eshmont	Frank Eshmont	Vincent Cesari	Edward Barbolish	Andrew A Tomchack	Francis Hughes
Titusville* (7) CM	814 827-9651	Eugene C Mitcham	Dennis E Peden	Dennis E Peden	James R Graff	Richard L Barker	David E Burk	Walter F Gibbs
Towamencin tp* (11) CM	215 368-7602	Joseph L Stack	Cecile Daniel	....	Cecile Daniel	Clair Clemens	Joseph Kirschner	....
Towanda b* (4) CM	717 265-2696	Dewitt Hild	Frederick A Lohman	Mary Ann Mace	....	T Arthur Johnson	Dale Cole	Paul Clugston
Trafford b (4) MC	412 372-6559	Robert Skatell	....	Mary Ann Bitzer	Jerry C Marchitello	Dennis Wiser	James J Mastroianni	Louis S Petrini
Tredyffrin tp§ (23) MC	215 644-1400	....	Norman Mawby	....	....	Thos J Robinson III	Thomas H Baynard	Frank D Kelley
Troy b* (1) CM	717 297-2966	Donald O Rockwell	John Parsell	....	....	Robert Reynolds	Harry Corey	Sevelon Smith
Turtle Creek b (7) MC	412 824-2500	James DeMuzzio	Mary C Grubbs	Dolores R Porter	Joseph Pantalone	John Morenzi	William Hopbell	Nick Bianchi
Tyrone b (6) MC	814 684-1140	Stephen L Beals Sr	James DiBasillio	James DiBasillio	James DiBasillio	James R Beckwith	Thomas Cooper	James DiBasillio
Union tp§† (3) MC	717 935-2890	....	Donald F Smith	....	....	....	....	....
Union City b (4) MC	814 438-2331	Ralph E Kreps	Richard A Russell	....	Cyrus D Gilson	David Shreve	Norman Hanby	Leo Pfister
Uniontown (15) MC	412 438-9210	Paul H Bortz	....	Grace Giachetti	Harry Mulligan	Carl W Sneddon	Andrew Zawelensky	Charles B Smiley
Upland b (3) MC	215 874-7317	Richard McClintock	John Piccinino	....	....	Joseph Poliafico	Robert C Love	....
Upper Allen tp§ (11) MC	717 766-0756	Ray E Trimmer	George R Easton	George R Easton	George R Easton	Don Waardenburg	Clyde R King	George Anderson
Upper Darby tp§ (84) MC	215 352-4100	James J Ward	F Raymond Shay	Margaret M Murdoch	Joseph F Dolan III	Victor N Darmiento	Martin J Kerns	Joseph W Vasturia
Upper Dublin tp* (22) CM	215 643-1600	Patrick J Zollo	Gregory N Klemick	....	Martha L Perego	Stuart Pennypacker	Raymond O Polett	William Grove
Upper Gwynedd tp§ (9) MC	215 699-7777	Jean Debarth	Michael A Iacocca	....	....	....	William E Herr	....
Upper Merion tp* (26) CM	215 265-2600	Ralph P Volpe	Ronald G Wagenmann	....	William R Kelser	....	Clement G Reedel	....
Upper Moreland tp§ (26) MC	215 659-3100	Wm C Seiberlich Jr	Brian L Mook	Brian L Mook	Patria A Burns	Rickie Hostvedt	Edward O Stauch Jr	Joseph R Ceniviva
Upper Providence tp* (10) CM	215 933-9179	Virgil P Templeton	George W Waterman	Evelyn Tomko	....	....	Edmund Fenyus	Frank W McGregor
Upper Providence tp§† (9) MC	215 565-4944	Robert Williams	....	....	....	John Ramsey	William Hampton	....
Upper Saucon tp§ (10) MC	215 282-1171	Donald C Clum	Bernard A Rodgers	....	....	Glenn Scholl	William J Edmond Sr	Joseph F Black
Upper Southampton tp§ (16) MC	215 357-1582	Thomas L Farrington	David P Cooper	Ida R Weidman	David Shafter	Alan D Ridge	Walter C Stevens	Harry Wonderland
Upper St. Clair tp* (19) CM	412 831-9000	....	Douglas A Watkins	Douglas A Watkins	Diane Kosarek	John Best	John P Kelly	K Chambon
Uwchlan tp§ (8) CO	215 363-9450	....	Douglass D Hanley	....	....	Richard Ruth	....	....
Vandergrift b† (7) MC	412 567-7818	Richard J Hunger	....	Stephen Delledonne	....	James Kerr	Guido DePaul	Alfred Ciuca
Verona b (3) MC	412 828-6034	William A Futules	....	....	....	James Broderick	Ken Eicheldinger	Stanley Dudczak
Warminster tp§ (36) MC	215 443-2900	Carl J Messina	Jack E Lantrip	....	....	Charles F Moyer	Elmer Clawges	Joshua Beatty
Warren b* (12) CM	814 723-6300	Gary E Olson	Michael P Crotty	Michael P Crotty	Michael P Crotty	Frank Viola	James W Neall	Keith Ludwig
Warrington tp§ (11) MC	215 822-1318	Vincent Charpentier	Teresa S Thomas	....	Teresa S Thomas	John Paul	John D Bonargo	....
Warwick tp§ (8) MC	717 626-8900	....	Karen L Koncle	....	Karen L Koncle	....	Harry T Aichele	James H Maser
Washington† (18) MC	412 228-5400	Leah S Driehorst	....	Sharon E Wright	Susanne E Gomez	Paul H Brookman	Anthony Popeck	John A Manning
Watsontown b§ (2) MC	717 538-1000	Oliver H Wetten	Barbara M Hyde	Doris M Garthwaite	David L Smith	Russell McClintock	James B Croft Jr	Robert Deacon Barr
Waynesboro b* (10) CM	717 762-2101	Thomas M Painter	Lloyd R Hamberger	....	M Arlene Morrison	Terry L Reiber	Charles E McCleary	Paul L Doub
Waynesburg b* (4) CM	412 627-8111	Roy L Huffman	....	Dreama Swanson	....	Pete Walker	Timothy M Hawfield	Robert A Johnson
Weatherly b§ (3) MC	717 427-8640	Rosebud Leppler	Beverly E Knepper	Eloise Hinterleiter	Beverly Knepper	Richard D Knepper	Larry Fedorick	....
Wellsboro b* (4) CM	717 724-3186	Guy Morral	John E Dugan	John E Dugan	....	John E Dugan	Michael J Gough	Martin J Beck
Wesleyville b (4) MC	814 899-9124	Betty Palmer	Mary B Ripley	Jennie Berti	Richard Klopfer	Robert Sprouse	James E Moore	Emory Hinkler
West Caln tp§† (5) MC	215 384-5643	....	Gary L Dunlap	Margaret Sweney	....	....	....	....

Directory 1/10 continued — MUNICIPAL OFFICIALS IN ALL U.S. CITIES OVER 2,500[1]

City, 1980 population (000 omitted), form of government	Municipal phone number	Mayor	Appointed administrator	City clerk	Finance officer	Fire chief	Police chief	Public works director
PENNSYLVANIA (540) continued								
West Chester b* (17) CM	215 692-7574	Craig J Milliken	Robert J Shaw	Robert J Shaw	Robert J Shaw	Robert Brice	John O Green	Leroy Bryant
West Goshen tp* (16) CM	215 696-5266	Thomas G Gavin	Patricia Mizzau	Patricia Mizzau	Patricia Mizzau	....	Michael F Dunn	....
West Hazleton b (5) MC	717 455-3694	Bernard Rockovich	....	Alice E Robinson	....	Robert J Ward	Neil S Blasko	....
West Homestead b (3) MC	412 461-1844	John J Dindak	....	Elsie Fekety	....	William Reagan	Chester Wrobel	William Reagan
West Manchester tp* (13) CM	717 792-3505	Michael J March	W Lee Woodmansee	....	Betty L Keller	....	Harold L Easter	....
West Mifflin b (26) MC	412 461-5619	Peter W Richards	Theresa Corso	....	....	....	Michael Babjak	Donald Finney
West Newton b† (3) MC	412 872-6860	Thomas O Filbern	....	Mary Ruppert	Daniel Donohoe	William Hoffman	John E Gregory	Stanley Indof
West Norriton tp (14) CO	215 631-0450	Theodore Heske	....	Mary Mahlfeld	Margaret A Bailey	Robert McGettigan	Paul J Scharff Jr	Joseph G Koegel
West Pittston b (6) MC	717 655-5566	Merle Bainbridge	Chester Newhart	....	....	James Hudelson	Thomas Dale	Joseph Raieski
West Pottsgrove tp§† (4) MC	215 323-7717	Richard D Bacchi	Robert E Wood	....	....	Joseph Shemansky	Frank J Holden	....
West Reading b§ (5) MC	215 374-8273	Edward I Wayne	Thomas H Bagenstose	....	....	Rodney Baer	Jack Crawford	....
West View b§† (8) MC	412 931-2800	Richard E Powell	Harry H Gruener	Audrey Steuernagel	....	Ronald George	Nicholas Buchlmayer	Harry H Gruener
West Whiteland tp§ (10) MC	215 363-9525	....	Stephen J Ross	....	Stephen J Ross	George Turner	Robert Bitter	Joseph Roscioli
West Wyoming b† (3) MC	717 693-1311	John Mizin	Alfred Evans	Tony Berkant	James Maira	Guilford Atherholt	Bert A Mangino	....
West York b† (5) MC	717 846-8889	Charles A Slenker	Kathy L Shultz	....	William V Valentine	Morris K Baker Jr	S Marshall Roser Jr	....
Westmont b† (6) MC	814 255-3865	Eugene Riek	....	Gail Heeter	John P Roddy	Austin M Greenland	....	Robert A Batey
White Oak b (9) MC	412 672-9727	Jack T Croushore	....	Nancy J Greenland	....	....	John Salopek	Jack E Lynch
Whitehall tp (22) MC	215 437-5524	M P Harakal Jr	John Marcarelli	....	Marion Gownaris	William F Balliet	Frederic A Conjour	Edward J Hochmiller
Whitehall b (15) MC	412 884-0505	Edwin F Brennan	Edmond J Reddy	....	Vanessa W Gleason	Jerry Fagan	J William Schmitt	Martin A Bruce
Whitemarsh tp§ (15) MC	215 825-3535	John P McCarthy	Lawrence J Gregan	....	John Donnelly	....	Richard Zolko	Harold Gans
Whitpain tp* (12) CM	215 277-2400	....	Phyllis C Lieberman	Phyllis C Lieberman	Rita M Eagan	James T Mitchell	Joseph C Stemple	John W Coyne
Wilkes-Barre§ (52) MC	717 826-8200	Thomas McLaughlin	Harold J Miller	William G Brace	John J Rollman	William J Milz	John R Swim	Robert F McGinley
Wilkins tp* (8) CM	412 824-6650	Joseph J Dombrosky	Wilmer K Baldwin	Wilmer K Baldwin	F R Kuszajewski	....	Victor A Dinzeo	....
Wilkinsburg b* (24) CM	412 244-2900	Richard C Depperman	Andrew Dent Jr	....	Edward Funkhauser	Daryle J Emeigh	Robert K Thomas	John J Curry
Williamsport (33) MC	717 326-2831	Stephen J Lucasi	....	Elda C Pagana	James Cooney	William Hayes	Matthew Rook	John Grado
Willistown tp§ (8) MC	215 647-5300	D Garth Wise	William L Tarr	....	Marcella S Boose	....	Robert M Valyo	John D DiMascio
Wilson b† (8) MC	215 258-6142	Edward A Miller	....	Janet K Siegfried	....	Willis L Weioner	Richard A Nace	Richard Siegfried
Wind Gap b (3) MC	215 863-9300	George L Andrew	....	Ralph H Wagner	Emilia Ronalds Kolb	Richard Davis	Robert Ambrose	....
Windber b (6) CM	814 467-9014	Oscar S Ripple	George Marcinko	....	Thomas Petrilla	Danny Digiulio	Edward Stopko	....
Windsor tp* (9) CM	717 244-3512	Paul M Smith	Henry B Sprenkle	....	....	....	Earle K Shenk	....
Wormleysburg b (3) MC	717 238-3861	(not reporting)						
Wyoming b (4) MC	717 693-0291	George Metcalfe	Bernard J Gilligan	Bernard J Gilligan	Joseph Chorba	Kirk Carey	John F Gilligan	Gene Allegrucci
Wyomissing b§† (7) MC	215 376-7481	Frederick Klein	Frank M Kauffman	A Drayovitch Jr	....	....	David Y Bausher	....
Yardley b (3) MC	215 493-6832	Edward E Robinson	Robert G Dellapelle	Jeanne W Ruttle	Robert G Dellapelle	C M Winslade	Thomas L Carroll	....
Yeadon b§ (12) MC	215 284-1606	James F Mollan Jr	Daniel C Fox	Dolores Danese	....	George Morris	Charles Trofe	Frank Camp
York (45) MC	717 843-8841	William J Althaus	Kathleen Pforr	Miriam L Neff	Joe Robinson	George Kroll	William Hose	John Hykes
York tp§ (17) MC	717 741-3861	Robert R Jacobs	Richard E Burrows	....	....	Kim Geesey	Raymond R LeRendu	Richard E Burrows
Youngsville b§ (2) MC	814 563-4604	Robert P Williams	William W Saunders	Margaret A Nelson	William W Saunders	Douglas Peterson	....	William W Saunders
Youngwood b (4) MC	412 925-3660	Albert N Hopfer	Roseann Freeman	....	Roseann Freeman	Michael Pacelli Jr	Scott R Adamson	....
Zelienople b (4) MC	412 452-6610	William E Slack	Charles K Jones Jr	Jack Hockenberger	Mary Santoro	Robert E Blum	Lewis A Pizer	....
RHODE ISLAND (38)								
Barrington t* (16) CM	401 245-3103	Allan C Klepper	Robt J Schiedler	Lorraine A Derois	Jerome F Williams	C S Dumican Jr	Alfred T Oliver Jr	William A Scheibl
Bristol t (20) TM	401 253-7000	Thomas J DaPonte	Thomas H Byrnes Jr	Orlando J Bisbano	John M Day	David G Sylvaria	Joseph P Green	Joseph Cavallaro
Burrillville t (13) MC	401 568-4300	....	....	Norman Mainville	Carlton F Brown	....	Joseph A Menard	Francis J Minutelli
Central Falls (17) MC	401 724-4500	Carlos A Silva Jr	....	Thomas Lazieh	Daniel J Vassett	Robert Coutu	James F Galligan	John Rodrigues
Charlestown t (5) RT	401 364-7718	Gary W Anderson Sr	Wm J McCauley	Cora F Burrows	Clement Stapleton	John Rousseau	G J DiChristofaro	Alan Arsenault
Coventry t* (27) CM	401 821-6400	Harold L Trafford	Ronald W Owens	Monique Capwell	Albin Richtarik	....	Carl Brown	Dennis Smith
Cranston (72) MC	401 461-1000	Edward D DiPrete	Michael M Doyle	Joseph L Gerardi	Mary V Gliottone	Ronald S Jones	Thomas M Harrington	Joseph V Pezza
Cumberland t† (27) MC	401 728-2400	Francis Stetkiewicz	....	Frances M Audette	George Cross	Raymond J Vallee	John J Partington	Thomas R Walker
East Greenwich t* (10) CM	401 884-4410	Alfred J Verrecchia	John C Simmons	Norma A Mahoney	Richard Bartlett	William G Brennan	John A Murray	John K Cook
East Providence* (51) CM	401 434-3311	Edward J Doyle	Earl P Sandquist	James H Beeley Jr	Charles H O'Connell	Ernest E Currier	George Rocha	Vartges Engustian
Exeter t (4) RT	401 294-3891	(not reporting)						
Foster t (3) RT	401 397-7771	A Edward Pearson	....	Margery F Borders	Richard C Hearn	....	John B Murray Jr	Robert C Schultz
Glocester t (8) RT	401 568-6206	....	....	Ethel A Jarvis	....	....	Richard B Tooher	Cliton E Gustafson
Hopkinton t (6) MC	401 377-2220	Thurman M Silks	....	Ms J T Langworthy	Arthur M Cottrell	....	John M Beatrice	Ralph L Ahern Jr
Jamestown t§ (4) RT	401 423-0200	Jerry McIntyre	Robt W Sutton Jr	Lois Coons	Robt W Sutton Jr	Joseph W Tiexiera	James G Pemantell	Steven J Goslee
Johnston t (25) MC	401 351-6618	Ralph R Arusso	....	Lucy F Countie	Attilio Verrengia	Angelo Cappelli	William P Tocco Jr	Ralph R Arusso
Lincoln t (17) MC	401 333-1100	Burton Stallwood	....	David Wilkie	Claudette Paine	Oliver H J Perry	William Strain	Allen Cullion
Little Compton t (3) MC	401 635-4658	(not reporting)						
Middletown t* (17) CM	401 847-0009	Edward B Corcoran	John F Fitzgerald	Frank N Campagna	Charles C Roberts	Joseph Burns	Robert Gibson	Raymond Jacome
Narragansett t* (12) CM	401 789-1044	Maurice Loontjens	Patrick C Scheidel	Ms A Klingensmith	Laura K Kenyon	Otis C Wyatt	James J Martin	George R Allaire
Newport* (29) CM	401 846-9600	Patrick G Kirby	John E Connors Jr	Jane McManus	Gary R Esposito	Paul W Gagne	John C Beebe	William V Gurney Jr
North Kingstown t* (22) CM	401 294-3331	Lloyd J Sherman	John A Mulligan	Lillian L Hackett	Thomas F Moon	Fenwick G Gardiner	John J Leyden	....
North Providence t (29) MC	401 232-0900	Salvatore Mancini	Donald Oliver	Pauline M Andre	Madeline Ferrante	Ralph Charello	Ernest Ricci	Frank Quinterno
North Smithfield t (10) MC	401 767-2200	Arthur Denomme	....	Gregory McPherson	Mary L Fagan	Edward J Cournoyer	Richard J Brady	Philip Fielding
Pawtucket (71) MC	401 728-0500	Henry S Kinch	John Burgess	Paul Breault	Al Papineau	Ronald Doire	Joseph C Roy	Wayne M Stetson
Portsmouth t (14) MC	401 683-2101	Hubert E Little	John O Thayer	Ernest Platt	Paul S McBride	Peter R Wilkey	Madison A Bailey	Marcel B Napert
Providence† (157) MC	401 421-7740	Vincent A Cianci Jr	Charles Mansolillo	Rose M Mendonca	Jerome Baron	Michael F Moise	Anthony J Mancusco	Joseph C Disanto
Richmond t† (4) RT	401 539-2497	F Bradford Pride	....	Carolyn S Richard	Florence N Corr	....	Neil C Place Sr	....
Scituate t (8) MC	401 647-2822	Robert A Crowley	....	Roger D Medbury	Robert L Harris	....	William J Lawton	Lloyd L Colvin
Smithfield t (17) MC	401 231-2460	Anthony B Simeone	Edith C Poirier	Flora A Simeone	Lilianne Rainville	Walter C Passano	Robert J Voas	James C Boyle
South Kingstown t* (20) CM	401 789-9331	Gilbert V Indeglia	Stephen A Alfred	Elizabeth M Wilson	Alan R Lord	Peter J Holland	Vincent Vespia	Alfred J Curnow
Tiverton t (14) TM	401 624-4277	Granger Jerome	....	William J French	Raymond Dias	Charles McDermott	Asa W Davol Jr	William R Grota
Warren t† (11) TM	401 245-7340	Paul J Harvey	....	Charles H Alfred	Shirley A McCanna	John E Conley Jr	Emilio Squillante	William J Tavares
Warwick (87) MC	401 738-2000	Joseph W Walsh	Henry A Johnson	Thomas Wilson	James Hagerty	Robert F Hutchinson	John F Coutcher	David Small
West Greenwich t† (3) TM	401 397-5016	Robert H Maguire	....	Cora M Lamoureux	Vinnie Richmond	....	Robert J Andrews	....
West Warwick t† (27) TM	401 828-0020	Joyce G Bulger	....	A Quarto	David C Brindamour	Maurice Boisclair	Danny Petrarca	Bernard F Magiera
Westerly t* (19) CM	401 596-0341	Samuel J Urso Jr	Glenn J Miller	Mary Levcowich	Genevieve Kurdziel	Robert Mackey	Nunzio Cimalore	Anthony Chiaradio
Woonsocket (46) MC	401 762-6400	Gaston A Ayotte Jr	....	John R Reynolds	G Edgar Parenteau	Gerald P Landry	Francis J Lynch	Makram H Megalli
SOUTH CAROLINA (93)								
Abbeville* (6) CM	803 459-5017	Jimmy Davis	David H Krumwiede	Thomas W Chandler	Joann Nabors	J T Nabors	Joseph M Creswell	Miike Moorhead
Aiken* (15) CM	803 648-5461	H O Weeks	Roland H Windham	I M Hendrix	I M Hendrix	J C Busbee	J C Busbee	Wyatt M Johnson
Allendale t (4) MC	803 584-4619	William Holmes	....	Bruce McGougan	Dwight Williams	John Marshal Lawson	M P Laurenzano	Addison McMillan
Anderson* (27) CM	803 226-7403	Darwin H Wright	Richard L Woodruff	John R Moore	John R Moore	Odis Gilreath	James Burriss	....
Andrews t (3) MC	803 264-8666	(not reporting)						
Bamberg t (4) MC	803 245-5128	J Virgil Hicks	....	M M Clinkscales	M M Clinkscales	B E Drawdy	G W Folk Sr	B E Ellis

Directory 1/10 continued

MUNICIPAL OFFICIALS IN ALL U.S. CITIES OVER 2,500[1]

City, 1980 population (000 omitted), form of government	Municipal phone number	Mayor	Appointed administrator	City clerk	Finance officer	Fire chief	Police chief	Public works director
SOUTH CAROLINA (93) continued								
Barnwell (6) MC	803 259-3266	Rodman Lemon	A P Black	Peggy S Main	Peggy S Main	Lloyd Vickery Jr	Eugene Darnell	Albert L Carroll
Batesburg t (4) MC	803 532-9231	William A Slover	....	Nelva L Ferriter	....	Elza S Spradley	Wallace Oswald	Lanyce Hatcher
Beaufort* (9) CM	803 524-4171	Henry C Chambers	Jack E Miller	Doris A Incas	Bernard L Bressette	Wendell Wilburn	Jesse L Altman Jr	Clayton H Cooler
Belton t (5) MC	803 338-7773	Leo Fisher	Joseph D McGee	Elizabeth C Darby	Sue Compton	Terry Sheridan	N Dean Bannister	Vernon Rhodes
Bennettsville§ (9) MC	803 479-9001	John J Weaver III	John M Holpe	John M Holpe	William C Jennings	Gerald R Raley	Eugene Copeland	Gene Harris
Bishopville t (3) MC	803 484-9418	Thomas A Drayton	Allan P Blum	Thelma Baker	....	Ronnie Williams	Odell Corbett	Ben T Galloway Jr
Blackville t (3) MC	803 284-2444	Eugene B Fickling	Don Lewis	Amelia S Martin	....	Charles Epps	E S McDonald	Steab Grayson
Camden* (7) CM	803 432-2421	H B Marshall Jr	Gary M Cannon	W A Smyrl	W A Smyrl	A Guy Mayer	John T Arledge	W H Davis
Cayce* (12) CM	803 796-9020	Stanley L Goodwin	E H Heustess Jr	Johnny Sharpe	Johnny Sharpe	James T Smith	Lavern Jumper	G Carroll Moore
Charleston (70) MC	803 577-6970	Joseph P Riley Jr	James G Budds	Mary R Wrixon	James W Etheredge	W E Guthke	Reuben M Greenberg	George H Aull
Cheraw t§ (6) MC	803 537-7283	Howard E Duvall Jr	J Wm Taylor	Helen D Funderburk	W E Watkins	Jimmy Thomas	L E Covington Jr	James T Morris
Chester* (7) CM	803 385-2123	W A Cranford	W Penn Colvin	Gwendolyn H Osment	W Penn Colvin	J R Franklin	Lawrence Strait	Paul L Land
Clemson§† (8) MC	803 654-2636	Hubert J Webb	Charles F Helsel Jr	Dianne J Bitzer	Herman A Linn	Charles W Owen	Wayne Wardlaw	Don G Curtis
Clinton t* (9) CM	803 833-1350	David E Tribble Jr	J Russell Allen	Mary F Pinson	Mary F Pinson	Troy N Bentley	Chesley L Richards	Charles J Harris
Clover t (3) MC	803 222-9494	William H White	....	Hazel Topor	Betty R Ferguson	Mack E McCarter	Lloyd C Hopper	Mack E McCarter
Columbia* (99) CM	803 733-8200	Kirkman Finlay Jr	Graydon V Olive Jr	Gladys L Brown	G C Robinett	Harvey W Evans	Robert A Wilbur	Miles Hadley
Conway* (10) CM	803 248-7351	Ike G Long Jr	John Patterson	Linda K Holland	Dolores Beverly	S E Hendrick	Larry Barnhill	Russell King
Darlington§ (8) MC	803 393-5838	J Ronald Ward	Cecil E Ward	Josephine G Ward	....	James C Stone Jr	Row Williams Jr	....
Denmark t (4) MC	803 793-3734	S A Neeley	....	....	Gerald E Wright	Otis P Sandifer Jr	Franklin D Gibson	J P Robinson
Dillon t* (7) CM	803 774-2431	W B Carmichael	Stephen J Sobers	Frances Leatherman	Frances Leatherman	W H King	Jack Carter	Troy P Price
Easley (14) MC	803 859-3890	William A Carr	....	Margaret M Gibson	Margaret M Gibson	Jimmie H Cobb	Kenneth Holcombe	Ray Hamby
Edgefield t† (3) MC	803 637-3935	Robert H McKie Jr	....	Charlotte L Coleman	....	Robert T Reel	M L Ryans	....
Florence* (30) CM	803 665-3113	Joe W Pearce Jr	Thos W Edwards Jr	W C Snow	W C Snow	Jerome E Register	Ralph R Porter	Harold G Huff
Folly Beach* (1) CM	803 588-2434	Richard L Beck	William E Griffin	Marlene B Estridge	....	George E Tittle Jr	George E Tittle Jr	Edward E Wilder
Forest Acres* (6) CM	803 782-9446	Royce G Waites	Jimmie C Wright	Jimmie C Wright	....	....	J C Rowe	....
Fort Mill t (4) MC	803 547-2034	Charles E Powers	J Mitchell Sizemore	Lucienne W Hinceman	Martha C Reid	W B Benfield	Robert E Kimbrell	W Waddell Gibson
Fountain Inn t (4) MC	803 862-4421	Paul E Gault Sr	....	Barbara S Brown	Paul E Gault Sr	Bobby C McKelvey	Lewis V Masters	Jack C Casey
Gaffney§ (13) MC	803 489-8174	John Q Little	Ben L Clary	Ben L Clary	Ben L Clary	Charles Petty	Mack R Jolley	Dick Crater
Georgetown§ (10) MC	803 546-2556	Douglas L Hinds	David W Treme	Joseph C Steen Jr	R Cobb Bell	Odell Avant	James F Elders	Rupert Green
Goose Creek§ (18) MC	803 797-6220	Michal J Heitzler	Dennis C Harmon	Paula A Nunimaker	....	L B Holland	Richard P Ruonala	John P Askins
Great Falls t (3) MC	803 482-2055	Tony P Paulos	....	Jackie L Payne	Raymond Case	George R Roof	Ralph Smith	Frank L Wood
Greenville* (58) CM	803 242-1250	William D Workman	John J Dullea	Barbara B Poole	Jack Howley	J T Roper	Harold C Jennings	Joe M Beam
Greenwood* (22) CM	803 229-0211	Thomas D Wingard	R T Higginbotham	Edna S McDaniel	Edna S McDaniel	S H Camp	J H Young	L D Adams
Greer§ (11) MC	803 877-9061	Don Smith	James J Forth Jr	Wilma Gosnell	Mary Greer	Mack Bailey	Jim Beason	Kenneth Smith
Hampton t (3) MC	803 943-2951	Harold S McMillan	....	Ms Ernie D Glynn	Harold S McMillan	Wade Freeman	Jerry M Thomas III	Richard H Pope
Hanahan§ (13) MC	803 554-4221	Marion T Dudley	Quinton T Martin	Anne S Farley	....	Billy L Hendricks	Melvin C Bellew	Jerry W Stegall
Hartsville* (8) CM	803 383-4551	Glenn J Lawhon Jr	Jesse E Stewart	Myrtle O Luther	....	Tommy W Livingston	Richard F Ritch Jr	Wilmont Berry
Hemingway t§ (1) MC	803 558-2824	W B Harmon	Cecil Kimrey	Cecil Kimrey	Cecil Kimrey	Herbert Tanner	Glen Ard	Kenneth Laster
Hilton Head Island t* (11) CM	803 785-2329	B M Racusin	Carey F Smith	Barbara G Anderson	....	....	....	Russell Byrd
Honea Path t (4) CM	803 369-2466	W E Gilmer	William Hall	Evelyn McKinney	....	R L Thornton	J L Parham	Ray Cox
Irmo t (4) MC	803 781-7050	Harry T Heizer Jr	....	Priscilla McMahon	Priscilla McMahon	....	Raymond Nash Jr	....
Isle of Palms (3) MC	803 886-6428	Clay Cable	....	Nellie S McDuffie	Nellie S McDuffie	Cal Cochrane	Fred E Thompson	Andrew J Parrish
Johnston t (3) MC	803 275-2488	E Forrest Edwards	....	Donna E Lybrand	....	Billy Parker	Charles E Waldrop	....
Kershaw t§ (2) MC	803 475-6065	Pauline Bailey	....	Phyllis Dorman	....	W T Clyburn	Danny C Williams	Ronnie A Martin
Kingstree t§ (4) MC	803 354-7484	John Yancey McGill	Robert G Cox	Lena D Wall	Robert G Cox	Bill Horton	C B Shorter Jr	Mike Tisdale
Lake City* (6) CM	803 394-5421	Carlton J Gaskins	Heyward Robinson	Cherline Howard	Ann Locke	Lide Moody	M E Brumbles	Carol Lawrence
Lancaster§ (10) MC	803 286-8414	Joseph Shaw	Paul S Paskoff	Jerry Witherspoon	Jerry Witherspoon	Donald Adams	Frank Harris	Douglas Latham
Laurens (11) MC	803 984-3933	L Bob Dominick	Paul M Willett	Patricia Beeks	Paul M Willett	Leon N Davis	James M Barrett	Sam W Wallace
Liberty t† (3) MC	803 843-6011	George E Jackson	....	William R Oliver	George E Jackson	M Steven Smith	N Willie Bagwell	James A Harris
Manning* (5) CM	803 435-8477	Pansy Ridgeway	W Ray Brown	Dorothy T Rawlinson	W Ray Brown	Carter H Jones	L Keith Josey Jr	David Hardin Jr
Marion t (8) MC	803 423-5962	T C Atkinson Jr	William R Jones	Mary C Batson	Wanda G Lee	James H Grice	Raymond E Britt	Billy Strange
Mauldin§ (8) MC	803 288-4910	A Wayne Crick	David M Bates	Eileen T Garrett	....	James G Moore Jr	William T Bishop	Lloyd Richards
McColl t (3) MC	803 523-5341	James S Coleman	....	Elizabeth B Foley	....	Lucky Farris	Larry V Ransom	Aubrey L Price
Moncks Corner t (4) MC	803 761-8036	Imogene T Russell	Samuel M Brown Jr	Grace S Wall	Samuel M Brown Jr	Pope Cook	Osborne L Morris	Samuel M Brown Jr
Mount Pleasant t (14) MC	803 884-8517	John J Dodds Jr	A Criscitiello	Colleen C Wolpert	Colleen C Wolpert	Cyrus T Pye	....	William H Mitchell
Mullins t (6) MC	803 464-9583	James F Ramsey	William S Bryan	Brenda H Ivey	James W Daniel	Clarence Causey	Dewey Proctor	William S Bryan
Myrtle Beach* (19) CM	803 626-7645	Erick B Ficken	Richard M Marvin	Mandy W Tomz	William C Doar	Fernie E Faulk	J Stanley Bird	E Ronald Andrews
Newberry*† (10) CM	803 276-4193	C A Shealy Jr	W Alfred Harvey	Tina P Wicker	Jess Torres	Lewis B Lee	Andrew Shealy	J A Jackson
North Augusta* (14) CM	803 279-0330	D Kim Ledford	Charles B Martin	Leona J Lewis	John P Potter Jr	W E Newman	W E Newman	Roger P Leduc
North Charleston (66) MC	803 554-5700	John E Bourne Jr	....	Cynthia E Stewart	Harley Henderson	William F New	James Alton Cannon	Ross F Walker
North Myrtle Beach* (4) CM	803 272-4000	Henry C Hester	Jack Ethredge	Sandra Todd	John Smithson	Charles Flick	Johnny Causey	Robert Alford
Orangeburg* (15) CM	803 534-2525	E O Pendarvis	L Hugh Smith	Henry S Domeracki	Henry S Domeracki	Marion F Inabinet	Eugene A Brant	B Reese Earley
Pageland t (3) MC	803 672-7292	James L Kirk	R Powell Black	Virginia H Outen	....	....	William Mills	....
Pendleton t† (3) MC	803 646-3622	J C Sloan	....	Joyce G Elrod	Joyce G Elrod	H B Barnette	James O Cleveland	Claude Williams
Pickens t (3) MC	803 878-6421	Calhoun N Hinton	....	Mary A Childs	....	T H Nealy	Wendal Jenkins	Jack G Black
Port Royal t§ (3) MC	803 524-5125	Henry Robinson	Bruce A Drawdy	Hazel Fier	Hazel Fier	Dan Lemieux	G D Smith	Harvey W Cawthorn
Ridgeland t§ (1) MC	803 726-3351	Wyman D Nettles	Thomas B Austin	Glondell M Walters	....	Tommie Jenkins	H L Ables	Joseph M Altman
Rock Hill* (35) CM	803 328-6171	J Emmett Jerome	Joe B Lanford	Gerald E Schapiro	Gerald E Schapiro	Crawford A Howell	Clyde C Long	Patrick A Brackett
Saluda t (3) MC	803 445-3522	James S Corley Sr	....	Annie M Smith	....	B W Smith	Michael Stancell	Keith Berry
Seneca t (7) MC	803 882-8457	H P Covington Jr	H J Balding	Barbara J B Whitney	....	Lawton O Bruce	Sam Shaw	H J Balding
Simpsonville t† (9) MC	803 963-3461	Ralph S Hendricks	....	Ms Clafton M Hinkle	Ms Lou Stiles	J D Stenhouse	D B McCartney	....
Spartanburg* (44) CM	803 596-2000	E Lewis Miller	Wayne Bowers	Oles C Womick	Katherine M Moore	Albert W Tillotson	W C Bain Jr	....
Springdale t (3) MC	803 794-0408	F Richard Bryant	....	Felton C Benton	Felton C Benton	....	Barron A Moreland	....
Summerville t† (6) MC	803 871-6000	Berlin G Myers	John F Wilbanks	John F Wilbanks	....	Rich G Waring III	James M Farmer	Roy C Winey
Sumter* (25) CM	803 773-3371	W A McElveen Jr	Horace B Curtis	Lourena N English	Talmadge Tobias Jr	Larry F Causey	Joe Brunson	Thomas W Evans
Surfside Beach t§ (3) MC	803 238-2590	H Blue Huckabee	Frank O Roberts III	Sheila Wiggins	Neil Ferguson	Jesse D Thomas	Henry K Meeks	J D Felix
Travelers Rest (3) CO	803 834-8740	C Murray Garrett	Charles H Hendrix	Gail Braziel	....	Glenn M Pace	Samuel B Clark	....
Union (11) MC	803 427-2691	J T Gregory	....	Bobbie Jean Lawson	Kenneth Barnette	Wilburn Lawson	Russell Roark	Fred Young
Walhalla t (4) MC	803 638-5833	Paul M Brown	....	Glenn C Martin	Glenn C Martin	Fred Finkenstadt	J Furman Nicholson	Frank D Clary
Walterboro* (6) CM	803 549-2545	Elton Culpepper	L Chriswell Bickley	Sherry Steedley	Julia M Sauls	W Harry Cone Jr	Thomas L McJunkin	T H Hydrick Jr
West Columbia (10) MC	803 791-1880	Paul E Waites	C M Carraway	Jennifer Cunningham	Jennifer Cunningham	H Barry Anderson	Vernon L Boatwright	Alton Hallman
Westminster t (3) MC	803 647-5071	David Johnson	....	Mike Lipscomb	....	Lamar Hardee	Mike McGuffiw	....
Williamston t† (4) MC	803 847-7473	Marion W Middleton	....	Frances Adams	....	Tommy Walker Jr	James E Erwin	Raymond A Roache
Williston t† (3) MC	803 266-7015	A W Flynn	....	Patty Shipes	....	Norman Widener	Charles Bechtold	Robert Augustine
Winnsboro t* (3) CM	803 635-3333	Quay W McMaster	L C Greene	Blanche C Robertson	L C Greene	John K Gillis	Larry Gainey	Walter E Taylor Jr
Woodruff t (5) MC	803 476-8154	Guy S Blakely Sr	....	Beverley Maddox	....	Robert Granger	Tommy Jennings	C B Parsons
York* (6) CM	803 684-2341	Eugene L Barnwell	Jimmy M Varner	Margie M Meek	Margie M Meek	Thomas C Kiser	Clyde David Morton	Charles Helms

Directory 1/10 continued — MUNICIPAL OFFICIALS IN ALL U.S. CITIES OVER 2,500[1]

City, 1980 population (000 omitted), form of government		Municipal phone number	Mayor	Appointed administrator	City clerk	Finance officer	Fire chief	Police chief	Public works director
SOUTH DAKOTA (24)									
Aberdeen (26)	CO	605 622-7000	Delphine E Janusz	....	Candace Lindskov	Bruce Nelson	Paul Lingor	Dave Sauer	Francis Brink
Belle Fourche (5)	MC	605 892-2494	Leslie C Snoozy	....	....	William S Noziska	Dale Gillette	Gary Fuller	Kenneth Pedersen
Box Elder (3)	MC	605 923-1401	Sam Boykin Jr	....	Dinah Lefler	Vernon H Wallace	Dennis Sutherland	Elmer Smith	Harold O'Neill
Brandon (3)	MC	605 582-6515	Edwin F Gruhot	Bruce Miller	....	Eloise Stensaas	....	Philip Youngdale	....
Brookings (15)	CO	605 692-6281	Roger Prunty	....	....	Boyce E Smith	Curtis Jensen	Gordon Miller	Lloyd L Darnall
Canton (3)	CO	605 987-2881	John J Fox	....	Lorraine Bulley	Lorraine Bulley	Robert Sanderson	Robert Van Zee	Donald Ulrikson
Hot Springs (5)	MC	605 745-3135	Carl Oberlitner	....	Debbie Romey	Cheryl Gunwall	Fred Engelbert	Gary Larson	....
Huron (13)	CO	605 352-6791	Paul K Flanagan	....	....	Roger Voigt	H B Harryman	Richard DeVries	Glenn Housiaux
Lead (4)	CO	605 584-1401	Kenneth S Bauman	Harley A Lux	....	Dorothy Keil	Walter Keil	Charles David Elver	....
Madison† (6)	CO	605 256-4586	Tom L Kommes	....	....	David R Schornack	Alden Erstad	Lester Seitz	....
Milbank (4)	MC	605 432-5775	Ralph Stinson	Dean Webb	....	....	James Berkner	Jerry Jutting	....
Mitchell (14)	MC	605 996-6452	Paul Tobin	....	Kathleen Rudloff	Clarice Nutter	John Neihart	Lawrence E Addy	Larry Little
Mobridge (4)	MC	605 845-3509	Darrell Bender	....	Darlene Zahn	Darlene Zahn	Don Opie	Brooks Johnson	....
Pierre (12)	CO	605 224-5921	Grace Petersen	....	....	Kenneth L Hericks	John Culberson	Harold Eberhard	Dave Padgett
Rapid City (46)	MC	605 394-4110	Arthur P LaCroix	....	....	Kent Brugger	Ken Johnson	Tom Hennies	Leonard Swanson
Redfield† (3)	MC	605 472-0660	Duane Sanger	....	....	A A Conrade	Tony Gabriel	Ronald Tennill	Royce Bush
Sioux Falls (81)	CO	605 339-7200	Joe Cooper	....	Florayne Tiemyer	Manfred Szameit	Orlan Norgaard	David F Green	R N Jorgenson
Sisseton* (3)	CM	605 698-3391	Edward L Buck	Rachel Stapleton	Gayle M Kriz	Rachel Stapleton	Richard Oien	Herbert Mussetter	Wayne Erickson
Spearfish (5)	MC	605 642-7775	Wilbur S Trethway	....	....	Elizabeth A Swift	Mike Kyte	Richard Mowell	Paul Dahl
Sturgis (5)	MC	605 347-4422	Robert L Voorhees	....	Beverly A Patterson	Sandra K Hale	Lloyd Erickson	Carl W Schaefer	Clacy Walsh
Vermillion* (10)	CM	605 624-2668	Merle Offerdahl	James W Antonen	....	Joe Conroy	Doug Brunick	Gary Wright	Joseph W Gillen
Watertown (16)	MC	605 886-4057	Herb B Jenson	....	....	Lauretta Hoff	Al Satter	LaVerne McPeek	J R Harty
Winner (3)	MC	605 842-2606	Steve Clark	....	....	Rosalee Ernest	Ray Anderson	Paul Schueth	....
Yankton* (12)	CM	605 665-4501	John Varvel	William R Ross	Jerald Knodel	Jerald Knodel	Patrick C Smith	Marvin Gifford	Gene Hoag
TENNESSEE (137)									
Adams t* (1)	CM	615 696-2593	John W Strange	Rachel Nolen	Rachel Nolen	....	Omer G Brooksher	....	Tim Henson
Alamo t (3)	MC	901 696-2506	C H Conley	Frances B Carlton	Joyce J Byrd	....	Jerry Pittman	Thomas Hutchison	John S Overton
Alcoa* (7)	CM	615 982-4190	Donald R Mull	Mickey J Bentley	Richard M Patterson	Richard M Patterson	Clifford G Freeman	William R Thomas	Don O Bledsoe
Athens* (12)	CM	615 745-3140	Burkett L Witt	Marvin S Bolinger	Kaye J Burton	Eunice Buttram	W Knox	Sidney Mathews	Mike Stone
Bartlett t (17)	MC	901 386-1414	Bobby K Flaherty	....	Martha W Chambliss	Stephen C Smith	George J Rieder	Roy Cheatham	....
Beersheba Springs t* (1)	CM	615 692-3508	John Richardson	....	Lonnie Whitman	....	Charles Hobbs	....	Michael Walker
Belle Meade* (3)	CM	615 297-6041	Elizabeth C Proctor	Robert H Thomas	....	....	....	Dan Binkley	....
Berry Hill* (1)	CM	615 292-5531	James K Cox	Jerome P Hartman	Ouida J Martin	....	....	Ronald H Drew	James E Haskins
Bolivar t (7)	MC	901 658-2020	Harold L Fitts	Fred F Kessler	....	....	Joe Shearin	Don Clifton	....
Brentwood* (9)	CM	615 373-3011	Brian J Sweeney	Robert B Adgent	Audrey J McCrary	Gregory V Howell	Louis J Baltz Jr	Howard Buttrey	Louis J Baltz III
Bristol* (24)	CM	615 968-9141	Ewell L Easley	B Thomas Moore	Nancy June Sparger	Nancy June Sparger	Phil W Vinson	Robert E Adams	....
Brownsville t† (9)	MC	901 772-1212	Jos G Taylor	....	Wm Jerry Taylor	....	L A Pattat	Jerry Wyatt	Jimmy Halbrook
Camden t (3)	MC	901 584-4656	Elvin W Johnson	....	Jesse L Byrn	....	Tom Bordanaro	Melvin Johnson	....
Carthage (3)	MC	615 735-1881	Benton M Lowe Jr	....	Joyce Rollins	....	Hollis Petty	Scotty Lewis	....
Centerville t† (3)	MC	615 729-4246	William N Steber	....	Myra Sullivan	....	James K Thompson	Donnie E Shelton	Wayne Prince
Charleston t* (1)	CM	615 336-3788	R D Lyle	Caroline Newport	Connie Haynie	....	David Thompson	Charles Parker	....
Chattanooga (170)	CO	615 757-5152	Gene Roberts	Evelyn M Shankles	H D Miller	H D Miller	J H Knowles	Eugene McCutcheon	Paul F Clark
Church Hill t (4)	MC	615 357-6161	Randall Housewright	Carroll Jenkins	Teresea J Wells	Carroll Jenkins	Dan Dewald	Wylie Cooper Jr	Freeman Chappell
Clarksville (55)	MC	615 645-2306	Ted A Crozier	....	Kaye Beasley	Clint Daniel	Finis Gray	Ira Nunley	C B Smith
Cleveland† (26)	CO	615 472-4551	Harry L Dethero	....	Janice S Casteel	Martin B Evans Jr	David May Jr	Arnold Botts	Richard T Lyles
Clifton City t* (1)	CM	615 676-3370	L Dewayne Staggs	Virgil W Morris	Ocie M Powell	Barbara A Culp	Glenn Prater	Billy W Burns	....
Clinton t§ (5)	MC	615 457-0424	Howard M Poly	Charles G Seivers	Patsy A Meredith	C G Seivers	Jack E Owens	Clifton Melton	....
Collegedale*† (5)	CM	615 396-3135	Wayne E Vandevere	Lee Holland	Gladys Mather	Donna Taylor	Duane Pitts	Thomas G Keaton	William Magoon
Collierville t§ (8)	MC	901 853-8501	H W Cox Jr	Jay R Johnson	Mary Lee Burley	Mary Lee Burley	Ben F Wilson	Dennis E Joyner	James Mathis
Collinwood*† (1)	CM	615 724-9227	James Dicus	Jasper Chambers	Willodean Hill	Willodean Hill	Russell Chambers	Coy Milton Watson	Jasper Chambers
Columbia* (26)	CM	615 388-5432	James L Bailey	Barrett H Jones	Betty R Modrall	Betty R Modrall	Wayne Hickman	Edward L Holton	....
Cookeville* (20)	CM	615 526-9591	Vaughn Howard	Luther Mathis	Jimmy Dale Shipley	....	Emil Jensen	Paul Jackson	William Ogletree
Covington (6)	MC	901 476-9613	John L Turner	....	Jere H Hadley	Jere H Hadley	Elmer H K Fiedler	Ronald J Gagnon	Tom Fullerton
Crossville* (6)	CM	615 484-5113	Ross Payne	Thomas E Potts	Donna Loveday	....	Gifford Adcox	Mel Sage	....
Dayton* (6)	CM	615 775-1817	Wendell Brown	....	....	Victor F Welch	Jack Arnold	Jack Carothers	....
Dickson t (7)	MC	615 446-5101	Tom H Waychoff	Doris R Sensing	Peggy Mason	Sue Lyle	Clayton Brazzell	Stephen Gray	Larry Gardner
Ducktown† (1)	CM	615 496-3341	U H Taylor Jr	....	Jan Russell	....	....	Kenneth Cheathan	....
Dunlap (4)	MC	615 949-2115	Danny Wallace	....	Clara Turner	Larry Hixson	Raymond Walker	Ricky Smith	Robertson Hobbs
Dyersburg (16)	MC	901 285-2642	Bill Revell	....	Van Williams	W C Moore	Billy Taylor	Bobby Williamson	Marion J Long
East Ridge t (21)	CO	615 867-7711	Brad Smith	David Mays	Charles Gass	Brad Smith	Ralph Pendergrass	Jerry McCullough	Don Huskey
Elizabethton* (12)	CM	615 543-3551	G Richard Sharpin	Thomas M Hord	Jasper Williams	Jasper Williams	Billy Jack Carter	Harry T Nave	Lynn Patillo
Erwin t (5)	MC	615 743-6231	Herman J May	Joe E Frazier	Doris Hensley	Joe E Frazier	R J Whitson	Bill Bogart	Paul Griffith
Etowah t (4)	MC	615 263-2102	James Mike Cantrell	Adele H Lattimore	Jean B James	Leon Green	Johnny Witt	George E Jorgenson	M L Stone
Fairview* (4)	CM	615 799-2484	Lawrence Nave	Gordon Lampley	Kathleen Daugherty	Gordon Lampley	John Stark	Robert M Odom	....
Farragut t (6)	MC	615 966-7057	Robert H Leonard	Jack S Hamlett	Mary Lou Koepp	....	....	....	William C Maney
Fayetteville t (8)	MC	615 433-6154	Tom Strong	....	Terry L Bedwell	....	Robert Strope	Thomas H Barnes	Lynn Wampler
Forest Hills* (5)	CM	615 383-8447	Richard Norvell	Julia E Baker	Julia E Baker	....	....	....	....
Franklin t (12)	MC	615 794-4572	A J Bethurum	R M Liggett	....	....	J W Culberson	David E Lewis	....
Gallatin (17)	MC	615 452-5400	John P Hancock	....	Robert W Lankford	David M Cooper	Joe M Womack	Wayne T Womack	John T Bracey
Gatlinburg* (3)	CM	615 436-7803	Zeno Wall	Jack Arthur	....	David A Beeler	Clell Ogle	James Kelly	....
Germantown§ (20)	MC	901 755-3000	Boyd Arthur Jr	James N Holgersson	Frances Sparkman	Hal W Canary Jr	John O'Bryan	Robert A Cochran	Jay Hollingsworth
Goodlettsville* (8)	CM	615 859-4078	J David Wilson	Timothy Jay Myers	Nancy Allen	Virginia Wright	John B Hunnicutt	John B Hunnicutt	William J Martin
Greenbrier t (3)	MC	615 643-4531	(not reporting)						
Greeneville t (14)	MC	615 639-7105	G Thomas Love	Thomas S Leonard	Thomas S Leonard	Thomas S Leonard	James Parman	Kenneth Rollins	J T Shell
Harriman (8)	MC	615 882-9414	Harold L Wester	....	Jane Palko	Nancy Oran	K Homer Scarbrough	Donald E Day	W T Wampler
Hartsville (3)	MC	615 374-3074	(not reporting)						
Henderson (4)	MC	901 989-4628	Charles R Fitts	....	Lyman D Cook	Lyman D Cook	John D Bryant	Perry M Hearn	....
Hendersonville* (27)	CM	615 822-1000	Earl Durham	Stephen W Raper	Larry Morris	Larry Morris	William E Posey	David Key	Charles Hasty
Hohenwald (4)	MC	615 796-2231	Guy Nicholson	Dolene Rogers	Peggy Dye	Guy Nicholson	Waymer Staggs	Charles Sealey	Guy Nicholson
Humboldt† (10)	MC	901 784-2511	Tom McCaslin	....	....	....	Wayne L Day	Raymond Kolwyck	Stan Little
Huntingdon t (4)	MC	901 986-8211	Jesse B Pinckley	....	J Kenneth Houston	J Kenneth Houston	J A Pendergrass	A J Taylor	James M Boyd
Iron City (..)	CM	615 845-4520	Loys G Sledge	....	Pat L Rhodes	....	Rayford Kimbrell	Frank D Murdock	Algie N Forsythe
Jackson (49)	CO	901 424-3440	Bob Conger	....	James Wolfe	Bob Conger	Thomas Alderson	Edward Alderson	Johnny Parham
Jasper t (3)	MC	615 942-3180	(not reporting)						
Jefferson City* (6)	CM	615 475-9071	Clyde Pike	Beverly R Cameron	Ms Jimmie Shelnutt	....	Robert Kinder	Rockie Fuller	Tex R Cooper
Jellico (3)	MC	615 424-6351	(not reporting)						
Johnson City* (40)	CM	615 929-9171	Raymond E Huff	John G Campbell	James Crumley	James Crumley	Clarence H Eades	Fred Phillips	Charles Harmon

Directory 1/10 continued — MUNICIPAL OFFICIALS IN ALL U.S. CITIES OVER 2,500[1]

City, 1980 population (000 omitted), form of government		Municipal phone number	Mayor	Appointed administrator	City clerk	Finance officer	Fire chief	Police chief	Public works director
TENNESSEE (137) continued									
Jonesboro t (3)	MC	615 753-6128	Tommy Dillow	….	Norman Francis	Norman Francis	Norman Francis	Bobby S Howell	Steve McCracken
Kingsport* (32)	CM	615 245-5131	C Norman Spencer	William R Cook	Thomas L McPherson	Thomas L McPherson	C L Caldwell	Jay Ralph Deal	S Roger Clark
Kingston t* (4)	CM	615 376-6584	Ruby Luckey	Chester Fultz	Mary B Barger	Carolyn Brewer	Mitchell Brummitt	Gary Humphreys	Charles Clark
Knoxville (183)	MC	615 521-2040	Kyle Testerman	….	Cindy Mitchell	Richard Dulaney	A Bruce Cureton	Robert Marshall	Herb Kidd
La Follette§ (8)	MC	615 562-4961	R C Alley	….	Debbie Pierce	Wanda Dower	Clyde Wilson	Boyd Carson	Max Robinson
La Vergne (5)	MC	615 793-6295	Vester Waldron	Richard Anderson Jr	Virginia C Frizzell	….	….	Terrell W Greene	….
Lafayette (4)	MC	615 666-2194	Will T Colter	Ruby Flowers	Opal Johnson	….	Loryn Atwell	Buford Wix	David Shrum
Lakewood* (2)	CM	615 847-3711	Charles K Donoho	Webster Lawrence	Jacqueline Morris	W C Gibbs Jr	….	….	….
Lawrenceburg (10)	MC	615 762-4459	Ivan Johnston	Charles T Brown	Charles T Brown	Billy Ray Helton	Roy Holloway	Earl Hollis	Sam Garrard
Lebanon (12)	MC	615 444-6300	Willis H Maddox	….	….	James F Boyd	Reid Major	Lawuel Jones	Jesse F Coe
Lenoir City§ (5)	MC	615 986-2715	Charles T Eblen	Edwin T Smith	Harold E Proaps	Idus D Conner	David Denton	W E Brown	Tom McCarroll
Lewisburg* (9)	CM	615 359-1544	John E Derryberry	James Lee Moss Jr	….	A C Sweeney Jr	John Redd	Ray Green	Ray Farley
Lexington† (6)	MC	901 968-6657	Jeffrey Davies	David Hopper	….	….	Wyatt Threadgill	Clifton Grissom	Jerrel D Jones
Livingston t (3)	MC	615 823-1269	H Winningham	….	Ms G DeRosett	H Winningham	A B Coleman	Howard Garrett	C Fletcher
Lobelville (1)	CM	615 593-2640	Steven D Hester	….	Barbara Hinson	Barbara DePriest	Frank Barber Jr	Robert White	….
Loudon§ (4)	MC	615 458-2033	Eugene Lambert	James M Smith Jr	Eldred D Smith	Eldred D Smith	Charles Jones Jr	John R Lennex	Ray Lovin
Madisonville t† (3)	MC	615 442-9416	Bobby Tallent	….	Anna Lou Newman	Frances H Wilson	Sam Tallent	Don Steel	….
Manchester (7)	MC	615 728-4652	Roy L Worthington	….	Nina H Moffitt	Nina H Moffitt	David Freeze	H Guinn Walker	Robert A Bailey
Martin (9)	MC	901 587-3126	Virginia B Weldon	Robert N Glasgow	Elizabeth Hammer	Robert N Glasgow	N B Williams	Jackie R Moore	….
Maryville* (17)	CM	615 984-7900	Stanley B Shields	Gary H Hensley	Ray Richesin	Allan T Bright	Bruce Hill	Don E Boring	….
Maynardville* (1)	CM	615 992-3821	Ronald Irick	Kyle Richardson	Hazel Gillenwater	Hazel Gillenwater	Coy Graves	Kyle Richardson	….
McKenzie (5)	MC	901 352-2264	Joe Morris	….	Bob Perkins	….	Bailey Wrinkle	Raymond W McDade	….
McMinnville (11)	MC	615 473-6691	Franklin P Blue	John H Biddle	Nancy Rogers	John H Biddle	William H Baker	Bobby G Southard	Duke Brown
Memphis (646)	MC	901 528-3131	Richard C Hackett	Donald A White	Robert Tamboli	Virginia Rutledge	James R Smith	John D Holt	Maynard C Stiles
Milan t (8)	MC	901 686-3301	Herb Davis	….	Oliver Radford	Richard Burrow	Robert Floersch	James Bratton	Billy Armstrong
Millington (20)	MC	901 872-2211	Thomas F Hall	….	M Fisher	James Knipple	Gordon Armour	Anthony Dingman	Jack Huffman
Monterey t† (3)	MC	615 839-2323	W H Wiggins Jr	….	Debbie Stephens	John Lusk	Richard Milligan	William Swallows	Cecil Garrett
Morristown* (20)	CM	615 581-0100	John R Johnson	R Keith Jackson	James B Gratz	….	Al Pitts	Joel K Seal	Carl Gilbert
Mount Carmel t† (4)	MC	615 357-7311	C Sidney Snodgrass	….	Sonda Creasy	Sonda Creasy	Dan Dewald	Ronald Collier	Carl Cradic
Mount Juliet* (3)	MC	615 758-9324	Grady Lynn	Danny C Farmer	Charmaine Major	Charmaine Major	Doug McQuary	Charles R McCrary	….
Mount Pleasant*† (3)	CM	615 379-7717	G Ray Wilson	Robert A Murray	Carolyn M Douglas	….	Marshall H Massey	Harlon McKissick	Larry Holden
Murfreesboro* (33)	CM	615 893-5210	Joe B Jackson	E C Fite Jr	John Barber	John Barber	Bobby J Swann	E N Brown	Jack Jones
Nashville-Davidson (456)	MC	615 259-6047	Richard Fulton	….	Ruth Judd	Charles Cardwell	Fred Davis	Joe Casey	Peter Heidenreich
Newbern (3)	MC	901 627-3221	Haskins Ridens	….	Robert O Dunfee	….	Bill Berry	William M Hinson	Don Campbell
Newport t (8)	MC	615 623-7323	Jeannie Y Wilson	….	Jack Shepherd	Jack Shepherd	Roger Butler	Buddy Don Ramsey	Lindsey Boyd
Norris* (1)	CM	615 494-7645	Armond L Arnurius	Kenneth F Vittum	….	….	Dudley Williams	Dudley Williams	William M Pointer
Oak Hill* (5)	CM	615 297-6153	Paul C Simpson	George W Morris	….	….	….	….	….
Oak Ridge* (28)	CM	615 483-5671	Roy F Pruett	M Lyle Lacy III	Jacquelyn J Bernard	W David Morris	William D Harris	….	Lowell Strunk
Oliver Springs t (4)	MC	615 435-7722	Keith C Jamerson	Richard W Hughes	Chester Spradlin	Lorena Abston	Carlis Phillips	Grant Lowe	Dean J Devaney
Oneida t (3)	MC	615 569-4295	(not reporting)						
Paris* (11)	CM	901 642-1212	William Culley	T Randy Williams	Mark L Johnson	Mark L Johnson	George Atkins	Richard Dunlap	Richard Collins
Pigeon Forge* (2)	CM	615 453-9061	Jimmy R Reagan	Earlene M Teaster	Mable O Ellis	Ms C M Quilliams	Denny Clabo	Jack Baldwin	Garland Harmon
Portland t (4)	MC	615 325-6776	Lloyd E Deasy	….	Ms Paul Keen	R D Dickens	Ernest Jones	Joe Coffeit	Lloyd Wayne Walker
Pulaski (7)	MC	615 363-2516	Stacey A Garner	R A Abernathy	….	R A Abernathy	Frank Collins	Stanley Newton	Brown Harwell
Ramer* (..)	CM	901 645-3728	….	George Armstrong	….	….	O D Pratt	Billy Jackson	….
Red Bank* (13)	CM	615 877-1103	Ralph C Barger	Larry Eaton	….	Glenn A Thompson	Lee Hustead	Ronald E Schroyer	Randy Taylor
Ripley (6)	MC	901 635-4000	Rozelle Criner	….	Verble M Mueller	….	Hubert Criner	Robert P White	Charlie Moore
Rockwood† (6)	CO	615 354-0163	Charles Robinson	….	….	Howard Butler	Fred Eachus Jr	….	W Allen Cisson
Rogersville t (4)	MC	615 272-7497	Jim Sells	William H Lyons	….	William H Lyons	Bill Henderson	William Livesay	Claude Peeks
Samburg t* (..)	CM	901 538-2556	J T Spicer	Tim Bunch	Clara Gant	….	Tim Bunch	Ken Shipley	….
Savannah* (7)	CM	901 925-3300	Joe W Barker	A D Caldwell	Doris Hudson	Mark B Alexander	Jim Berry	Donald B Cannon	….
Selmer t† (4)	MC	901 645-3242	Billy Joe Glover	….	….	Arnold Hurst	….	Donald W Fulghum	Bob Graham
Sevierville* (5)	CM	615 453-5504	Gary R Wade	Russell G Treadway	….	Pat Valentine	James Atchley	Anthony Thomas	Bob Robbins
Shelbyville* (14)	CM	615 684-2691	H V Griffin	Burtis W Landers	Kenneth McBee	Alton E Hale	Garland J King	Jesse B Blanton	W J Sullivan
Signal Mountain t (6)	CO	615 886-2177	Anne Nolan	….	Chuck Conner	Marion Summerville	Ray Francis	Boyd Veal	Mitchell Lawson
Smithville t (4)	MC	615 597-4745	Waniford A Cantrell	Cecil R Burger	Joyce Haas	….	W J Keith	Thomas Hopkins	Cecil R Burger
Smyrna t (9)	MC	615 459-2553	Sam Ridley	Michael Woods	Michael Woods	….	James Farmer	Charles Vance	Ben Andrews
Soddy-Daisy* (8)	CM	615 332-5323	Bryson Johnson	Paul R Page	Sara Burris	….	Hardie Stulce	Robert D Eckard	Jack Parker
South Fulton*† (3)	CM	901 479-2151	James V Henry	Charles E Reams	Elizabeth Liliker	Elizabeth Liliker	Lewis Bizzle	Elmer Mansfield	Bo Marlar
South Pittsburg (4)	MC	615 837-7511	John F Thompson	M M Burnett	Frances Walker	M M Burnett	James Humble	Richard B Morgan	David Payne
Sparta (5)	MC	615 836-3269	Robert F Baker	Hugh M Carmichael	….	Hugh M Carmichael	Charles L Hyder	Ernest W Cotten Jr	Herbert Hutchings
Spring City t* (2)	CM	615 365-6441	Park Hale	Joseph Garbarino	Martha White	Cathy McClendon	Cliff Newby	John James	….
Springfield (11)	CO	615 384-3561	William P Carneal	….	Steven J Gregg	….	David Greer	James Johnson	Billy B Gray
St. Joseph* (1)	CM	615 845-4141	Charles Sandy	Robert B Russ	Jean Hill	….	Walter Shelton	Dennis Daniels	….
Sweetwater (5)	MC	615 337-6979	Billy R Ridenour	….	Charlotte Starnes	….	James Lynn Phillips	Kenneth D Wilson	Wayne Roach
Tennessee Ridge t* (1)	CM	615 721-3385	John T Deason	J Milton Thomason	Karen T Harris	Woodrow Adams	Jerry W Clark	….	….
Trenton (5)	MC	901 855-2013	Tommie Goodwin	….	James B Burress	….	Travis Phillips	O B Campbell	Paul W Bennett
Tullahoma§ (16)	MC	615 455-2648	George Orr	Ron Darden	Patricia H Williams	Patricia H Williams	C B Watkins	Jack Welch	Ron Greene
Tusculum*† (1)	CM	615 638-6211	J E Walker	Wayne Taylor	B A Fitzgerald	B A Fitzgerald	Wallace Combs	Dennis J Johnston	Wayne Taylor
Union City* (10)	CM	901 885-1341	C H Adams	Don Thornton	Mildred Roberts	….	Dale Burress	Raymond Hutchens	Talmadge Simmons
Watauga* (..)	CM	615 928-3490	Holly Davison	Jerry Crowe	Hattie Skeans	….	Benny Calbough	Kenneth Potter	….
Waverly t (4)	MC	615 296-2101	Harold Ray Bell	Van Kemp	Louise S Mathias	….	J M Traylor	W B Frazier	John Whitfield Jr
Waynesboro* (2)	CM	615 722-5458	Floyd S Merriman	Howard Riley	….	Flora E Lacher	Harold Edwards	Billy H Brewer	….
Whitwell*† (2)	CM	615 658-5210	….	Richard Bryson	….	….	….	….	….
Winchester t (6)	MC	615 967-4771	Howard Hall	Faye Morrow	Jimmy W Crownover	Jimmy W Crownover	Bobby Scharber	Ray Commers	Bill Holliday
TEXAS (423)									
Abernathy* (3)	CM	806 298-2546	J Pete Thompson	G Rodney Ellis	Otelia Clement	….	Tommy Overstreet	Ray Naron	Tommy Overstreet
Abilene* (98)	CM	915 676-6206	David Stubbeman	Jim C Blagg	Patricia Patton	David M Wright	Richard Knopf	Warren Dodson	Robert Whitehead
Addison§ (6)	MC	214 450-7000	Jerry Redding	Ronald N Whitehead	Cindy Miller	Ralph Seeley	Robert A Minor	Richard Sullivan	….
Alamo (6)	MC	512 787-0006	Rodolfo Villarreal	Brijido Ysquierdo	Rosalinda Garcia	Brijido Ysquierdo	Neal Pearson	Ruben DeLeon	Procoro Barrientes
Alamo Heights (6)	MC	512 822-3331	William D Balthrope	….	G Courtney Goodin	G Courtney Goodin	W E Renken	Roger L Terry	K N Ports
Alice* (21)	CM	512 668-7210	Octavio Figueroa Jr	Roel G Valadez	Sandi McCumber	Tracy Herschap	Lee Gibson	Pedro Hinojosa Sr	….
Allen* (8)	CM	214 727-9171	Donald P Rodenbaugh	Jonathan McCarty	Marty A Hendrix	Brenton Lewis	Ronald Gentry	Richard Carroll	Ernie Hoback
Alpine t (5)	MC	915 837-3301	Delbert A Dyke	Tom Longman	Shirley Scholl	Tomi McDaniel	Ernest O Reesing Jr	Ruben D Melgoza	Ted Scown
Alton (3)	CM	512 581-2733	San Juanita Zamora	Romeo DeLa Garza	Lesvia Peralez	Vidal Roman	Oscar Guajardo	Ricardo Veliz Sr	….
Alvarado (3)	MC	817 783-3351	(not reporting)						
Alvin* (17)	CM	713 585-6165	Ted C Hermann	Donald R Birkner	Wynette Stoner	Susanne Barnett	Donald R Eernissee	Michel Jez	….
Amarillo* (149)	CM	806 378-3000	R P Rick Klein	John Q Ward	Marvell Marshall	Don C Cates	Curtis V Richards	Jerry Neal	Pat Christal

Directory 1/10 continued

MUNICIPAL OFFICIALS IN ALL U.S. CITIES OVER 2,500[1]

City, 1980 population (000 omitted), form of government		Municipal phone number	Mayor	Appointed administrator	City clerk	Finance officer	Fire chief	Police chief	Public works director
TEXAS (423) continued									
Andrews* (11)	CM	915 523-4820	Windle Harper	Len L Wilson	Kitty F Bristow	Kitty F Bristow	H L Jack Clements	Douglas W Gaines	Joel Locke
Angleton* (14)	CM	713 849-4364	Emmett C Adair	Clifford Hicks	Ruth Hertel	Clifford Hicks	A L Kelley	Harry Park	Melvin Leonard
Anson (3)	MC	915 823-2411	Gene Rodgers	....	Dottie Spraberry	Dottie Spraberry	Bill Cromeens	Johnny Graham	Carrol Greenwood
Anthony (3)	MC	915 886-3944	Adrian E Baca	....	Margarito Soliz	Saul Moreno	Bernard Deragowski	Bernard Deragowski	Jesus Almaraz
Aransas Pass*† (7)	CM	512 758-5301	Tommy Knight	Albert A Holguin	Natalia Smith	Albert A Holguin	Pete Martinez	Melvin Shedd	Allen Berna
Arlington* (160)	CM	817 275-3271	Harold E Patterson	....	Bobbye Ray	Keith E Reed	Bill Strickland	Roy Ables	K F Schnellenbach
Athens*† (10)	CM	214 675-5131	Tommy G Smith	....	Janice Whatley	Faye Crawfodd	A L Jones	David W Harris	....
Atlanta* (6)	CM	214 796-7153	Elston R Law	Sidney R Davis	Sylvia Cornbest	....	John Bailey	Jerry Walraven	Edward Groves
Austin* (345)	CM	512 477-6511	Ron Mullen	Jorge Carrasco	James E Aldridge	Ron Wood	Billy Glen Roberts	Frank Dyson	Richard Ridings
Azle (6)	CM	817 444-2541	C Y Rone	Harry Dulin	Kim Shelton	....	T O Brown	Dave Wilhelm	Albert L Dugger
Balch Springs (14)	MC	214 286-4444	Brent Erickson	Mozelle Strain	....	....	W E McCarter	Thomas McGee	William Vaughn
Balcones Heights (3)	MC	512 735-9148	Kirk K Colyer	Roy L Miller	Roy L Miller	William F Hill	Charles W Matthies	Herbie D Myers	....
Ballinger*† (4)	CM	915 365-3511	Wayne Irby	Dennis M Jones	....	....	Odell Denton	Paul Boggess	....
Bastrop§ (4)	MC	512 321-3941	David Lock	Marvin Patterson	Artie McLaurin	....	Cruz Galvan	Adell N Powell	....
Bay City (18)	MC	713 245-2137	Glen White	....	Carolyn Broughton	Glen White	Morris Richardson	Barney Mason	Jim Kashiwada
Baytown* (57)	CM	713 422-8281	Allen Cannon	Fritz Lanham	Eileen Hall	Ken Mitchell	Vance McBride	A W Henscey	Norman Dykes
Beaumont* (118)	CM	409 838-0600	William E Neild	Karl F Nollenberger	Myrtle Corgey	Robert Nachlinger	C A Shelton	John Swan	Joe Ternus
Bedford* (21)	CM	817 283-4646	L Don Dodson	Jim W Walker	Beth Davis	Charles Gardner	E M Bilger Jr	Glen Lightford	Gregory Dickens
Beeville* (15)	CM	512 358-4641	Jesse D Russe Jr	Joe B Montez	Tomas P Saenz	Ford Patton	Donnie Morris	W G McConnell	Phillip L Pacheco
Bellaire* (15)	CM	713 662-8222	Sam McKinney	William K Cole	Roena Loftin	Douglas Seckel	Rufus Summers	Jerry Loftin	Fred Childs
Bellmead*† (8)	CM	817 799-2436	....	B K West	....	....	....	....	....
Bellville (3)	MC	409 865-3136	Abner E Jackson	John Mumme	John Mumme	John Mumme	Warren Klump	Billy J Parker	John Mumme
Belton*† (11)	CM	817 939-5851	Clyde S Jones	Jeffrey B Holberg	Nola Kinney	R K Utley Jr	Larry Youngblood	Roy Kneese	Louis Griffin
Benbrook* (14)	CM	817 249-3000	Jerry Dunn	Kennith R Neystel	Pat Rutherford	David Ragsdale	Bill Trammell	Bob Richardson	Cary Conklin
Big Lake † (3)	MC	915 884-2511	H F Ritchie	Tony Wille	Tony Wille	....	Doc Robertson	....	Bobby Gay
Big Spring* (25)	CM	915 263-8311	Clyde Angel	Donald B Davis	Tom Ferguson	Tom Ferguson	Jim Ryals	Rick Turner	Tom Decell
Bishop † (4)	MC	512 584-2351	Eudocio Garcia	Emilia Rios	Shirley Sliger	Emilia Rios	Barry Fuhrken	G Frankenberger	John Blount
Boerne§ (3)	MC	512 249-9511	A E Howell Jr	Ronald C Bowman	Gloria G Stunz	....	Jeffrey Fincke	Walter E Myers	John B Moring Jr
Bonham* (7)	CM	214 583-2157	Roy Floyd	Thomas R Taylor	Sue Selph	....	James Ray Clark	Mike Bankston	Clyde Towbry
Borger* (16)	CM	806 273-2881	Frank Selfridge	A C Spears	Wanda Klause	James G Layton	John W Waldrep	Michael C Smith	Howard Griggs
Bowie (6)	CM	817 872-1114	John W Middleton	H H Cunningham Jr	Joan Durham	H H Cunningham Jr	Darrell Bell	James L Wade	Kenneth Polk
Brady§ (6)	MC	915 597-2152	John Bucy	Stephen W Nordholt	Dorene Patterson	Dorene Patterson	Garon Salter	Bill Stirman	Mike Hagan
Brazoria§ (3)	MC	409 798-9131	Paul Harang	Kenneth Timmermann	Betty M Wilson	....	Marvin R Setzer	Jack Kinslow	....
Breckenridge* (7)	CM	817 559-8287	Roger Wootton	Dwain Tolle	Gary G Ernest	Dwain Tolle	Roger McMullen	Ronnie Pendleton	
Brenham§ (11)	MC	713 836-7911	Dorothy Flisowski	Jim McAlister	Melvin Pohlmeyer	Leonard Addicks	Don Hoffman	Alfred Becker	Steve Kerbow
Bridge City* (8)	CM	409 735-5513	John W Banken	C R Nash	Ange Hebert	....	Paul Fournier	Andrew Verrett	Lloyd J Suire
Bridgeport (4)	MC	817 683-5906	Walter Hales	....	Patsy Sides	....	David McComis	....	....
Brownfield* (10)	CM	806 637-4547	T A Hicks	R C Fletcher	Zelma Miller	R C Fletcher	Marvin Dawson	J T Churchwell	Joe Cardenas
Brownsville* (85)	CM	512 542-4391	Emilio A Hernandez	Kenneth J Lieck	Yolanda Ramos	Pete Gonzalez	Ramon Garcia	Andy Vega	....
Brownwood*† (19)	CM	915 646-6056	W T Harlow	Virgil C Gray	Valree Evans	Gary Butts	R P Ferguson	V P Fowler	Richard Boston
Bryan* (44)	CM	409 779-5622	Ron Blatchley	Ernest R Clark	Dorothy Mallett	Scott McGough	Herman Rice	Charles W Phelps	Jack Cornish
Bunker Hill Village† (4)	MC	713 467-9762	Donald H Fidler	Harry E Uhlig	Virginia Johnson	Donald H Fidler	Abe Lamb	J M Schultea	Harry E Uhlig
Burkburnett* (11)	CM	817 569-2263	Pat Yarmoski	Gary Bean	Ms Lahoma Wood	Ms Lahoma Wood	John Brown	Dale L Bryan	John A Brookman
Burleson* (12)	CM	817 295-1113	Jerry Boone	Ronald V Crabtree	Jean Phillips	Frank Trando	Bob Green	Don Maxon	Bill Davison
Burnet †* (3)	CM	512 756-4501	Howard R Benton	Kenneth A Taylor	Pat Williams	Pat Williams	William Deleon	Eugene Schillings	J Lawson Gibbs
Caldwell* (3)	CM	409 567-3271	William L Broaddus	J D Teague	Edgar R Plemper	J D Teague	Kenneth B Clark	Al C Schmidt	J D Teague
Cameron (6)	MC	817 697-6646	Milton J Schiller	Lanny C French	Janet Sheguit	Lanny C French	Felix Matula	Leonard Doscocil	Walter Wallace
Canadian †* (3)	CM	806 323-6473	Therese Abraham	Van James	Yolanda Mooney	Linda Truitt	Gene Mathews	Bill Guinn	Lester Hodges
Canton (3)	MC	214 567-6556	Billy J Peace	Gerald Turner	....	Gerald Turner	Cecil Tawater	Delmer G Williams	Gerald Turner
Canyon* (11)	CM	806 655-7136	Phillip D Langen	Glen R Metcalf	Alex K Vaughn	C Howard Morris	Aubrey McDowell	Jesse McMullen	Robert R Rogers
Carrizo Springs* (7)	CM	512 876-5125	Ralph E Salinas	Gilbert Perales	Mario A Martinez	Gilbert Perales	Joe L Rodriguez	Ben Murray	Jose Mireles
Carrollton* (41)	CM	214 323-5000	Kenny Marchant	Mike Eastland	Janice Garrison	Dewey Jones	Harold Bessire	Vernon Campbell	Charles Bresett
Carthage*† (6)	CM	214 693-3868	Carson C Joines	Charles Thomas	Elizabeth Bonner	....	Brodie Akins	Carson N Parks	....
Castle Hills§ (5)	MC	512 342-2341	H P Lundblade	D R Seyfarth	Dawn Rogers	D R Seyfarth	William Duggins	Douglas L Crow Sr	....
Cedar Hill§ (7)	MC	214 291-4211	Archie A Hall	Gregory T Vick	Frankie M Lee	Wilma Crenshaw	Charles R Sims	William S Campbell	Bob Moore
Cedar Park (3)	MC	512 258-4121	George B Bowling	Stephen K Shutt	Nancy M Faulkner	....	....	Randolph N Doyer	....
Center§ (6)	MC	713 598-4693	George W Ihlo	Ronald E Cox	Lou Adams	Wilma Adams	Tommie C Fenley	Jimmy Matthews	Bertie Koonce
Childress* (6)	CM	817 937-3684	....	David Galligan	David Galligan	David Galligan	Lloyd Luck	Robert Seagroves	....
Cisco* (5)	CM	817 442-2111	Eris Ritchie	Michael D Moore	Ginger Johnson	Pablo Rodriguez	C W Guthrie	Billy Rains	Frank V Young
Clarksville* (5)	CM	214 427-3834	L D Williamson	James L Pryor	Olivia G Minter	James L Pryor	Bill Rains	J W Sims	Jack Holt
Cleburne* (19)	CM	817 641-3321	George W Marti	Lloyd E Moss	Jean Hamilton	Joel Victory	Lloyd McVicker	Claude Zachary	Andy Anderson
Cleveland§† (6)	MC	713 592-2667	Ronnie McWaters	S M Chittenden	Louise Liska	....	Charles Coe	Harley Lovings	
Clifton (3)	MC	817 675-8337	Charles R Rummel	James O Womack	Sue Pierce	M E Barron	Jamie Zanders	Robert M Brennand	Barney Eary
Clute (10)	MC	713 265-2541	Jerry Adkins	Wm M Pennington	Barbara R Hester	Wm M Pennington	R E Dunn	Eleazar Cortez	W I Edwards
Clyde † (3)	MC	915 893-4234	Alan Johnson	....	Ruby Cutbirth	....	Don Haley	William Miller	....
Cockrell Hill (3)	MC	214 339-4141	(not reporting)						
Coleman* (6)	CM	915 625-5114	Hugh Stempel	Roy McCorkle	Danny V Jameson	Roy McCorkle	Wade Turner	S H Johnson	James Hammonds
College Station* (37)	CM	409 764-3500	Gary M Halter	North Bardell	Dian B Jones	Alonzo E Van Dever	Douglas Landua	Marvin Byrd	Alfred Miller
Colleyville*† (7)	CM	817 281-4044	Robert E Neely	C R Ballenger	LaVada W Johnson	Pat Cox	Darrel Red Bailey	Joseph P Tozzi	William D LeGrand
Colorado City* (5)	CM	915 728-3464	Elmer Martin	Brenda Tarter	Rita Espinoza	Brenda Tarter	L O Schafer	Kenneth Farrow	Buford Rich Jr
Columbus§ (4)	MC	713 732-2366	Richard Heffley	George Purefoy		....		Tom Wine	....
Comanche† (4)	MC	915 356-2616	Johnny Livingston	Wade Pyburn	Wade Pyburn	Wade Pyburn	Dale Nowlin	Charles Anders	Wade Pyburn
Commerce* (8)	CM	214 886-2105	Thomas F Young	W W Cox	Jane P House	W W Cox	Jimmy Buchanan	James Peek	....
Conroe (18)	MC	409 539-4431	Carl Barton	Olen R Petty	Elizabeth C French	Hattie D Weisinger	John Cook	Don Massey	William Garrett
Converse* (5)	CM	512 658-1965	Harold G Bauman	Kent A Myers	Gracie Beane	Kent A Myers	Red Schumann	Mark Ospain	Robert McNair
Coppell§ (4)	MC	214 462-0022	Andrew Brown Jr	Ron Ragland	Dorothy Timmons	....	Jackie R Mayfield	Tommy W Griffin	....
Copperas Cove* (19)	CM	817 547-4221	Kenneth J Ambler	Mark B Roath	Rose M Mansfield	....	Raymond Ashcraft	Robert H McDonald	Lester D Peck
Corpus Christi* (232)	CM	512 884-3011	Luther Jones	Edward A Martin	Bill G Read	Charles Daley	Ralph Rogers	William C Banner	
Corsicana* (22)	CM	214 872-4811	Sue Youngblood	Craig Lonon	Nelda J Neal	Nelda J Neal	Duane Womack	John R Landers	Larry J Demoss
Cotulla† (4)	MC	512 879-2367	Danny C Garcia Jr	....	Glenda K Janek	....	Larry Griffin	....	Mauro Perez Jr
Crane† (4)	MC	915 558-3563	Jack Atkinson	Bill F Sanders	Geraldine Curfew	....	Glen Grissom	Jack R Crawford	....
Crockett* (7)	CM	713 544-5156	Howard Edmiston	Philip G Cook	Cary Ann Alford	Philip G Cook	Elmer Beard	Thomas Lee	Harold Thomas
Crowley (6)	CM	817 297-2201	Walton G Eller	....	Alyce E Deering	Alyce E Deering	Steve Buncik	Henri Eckhardt	James McDonald
Crystal City* (8)	CM	512 374-3478	Ray Espinosa	Jose Luis Balderas	Jose Luis Lopez	Roberto Maldonado	Delwin Hale	Luis Contreras Jr	....
Cuero* (7)	CM	512 275-6114	Ben E Prause	James H Pratt	Corlis Riedesel	Evelyn Barfield	Eldred G Schultz	B W Adams Jr	James R Margraves
Daingerfield (3)	CM	214 645-3906	Jerry Grainger	....	Margie Hargrove	....	Wayne Campbell	Scott Sartain	A W Lawton
Dalhart* (7)	CM	806 249-5511	Lorraine Wardell	David N Maddox	Elizabeth Knight	J C Potter	Marvin Gaddy	Ken Carley	David N Maddox
Dallas* (904)	CM	214 670-3302	A Starke Taylor	Charles S Anderson	Robert S Sloan	Winston C Evans	Dodd Miller	Billy D Prince	Clifford V Keheley
Dayton † (5)	MC	713 258-2642	W M Moreau	Louis N Neumeyer	Trudy Williams	Louis N Neumeyer	Bill Boyett	Ken Defoor	....
De Soto* (16)	CM	214 223-4120	Ernest Roberts	Clifford A Johnson	Jean Garner	Clifford A Johnson	Murrell Porter	Kenneth Hood	Herb Warren

Directory 1/10 continued
MUNICIPAL OFFICIALS IN ALL U.S. CITIES OVER 2,500[1]

City, 1980 population (000 omitted), form of government		Municipal phone number	Mayor	Appointed administrator	City clerk	Finance officer	Fire chief	Police chief	Public works director
TEXAS (423) continued									
Decatur (4)	MC	817 627-2741	Bobby Wilson	Sam Renshaw	Sam Renshaw	Sam Renshaw	Mike Atkins	Rex A Hoskins	James Luttrell
Deer Park* (23)	CM	713 479-2394	Jimmy A Burke	Floyd O Socia	Dorothy S Martin	Glenn Windsor	Horace Stack	Kenneth Gage	D R Jones
Del Rio* (30)	CM	512 774-2781	Roger S Cerny	James A Miceli	Bessie M Locker	Florencio Sauceda	Howard Baughman	James Riggs	James Henrikson
Denison* (24)	CM	214 465-2720	Ronnie Cole	James P Stiff	Barbara D Forrest	John E Wilkins	G L Cravens	E E Eubank	....
Denton* (48)	CM	817 566-8200	Richard O Stewart	Chris Hartung	Charlotte Allen	John McGrane	Jack Gentry	Hugh Lynch	Rick Svehla
Denver City t (5)	MC	806 592-5426	Kenneth Brown	Paul Grohman	....	....	Lewis Welch	Aj Fowler	....
Devine† (4)	MC	512 663-2804	Harvey O Squire	Jake McCarty	Larry J Capps	Jake McCarty	....	John DeLa Cruz	....
Diboll§ (5)	MC	409 829-4757	C H Sheperd Jr	Vernon Cupit	Geneva Ard	Geneva Ard	Gary Jones	Danny Ray	Moy D Scarborough
Dickinson v (8)	MC	713 337-2489	Joseph F Molloy	Luther G Morgan	Phyllis B Bricker	....	Pete Ozenberger	Wayne T Broussard	....
Dilley t (3)	MC	512 965-1624	Inez Asher	H G Bert Lumbreras	H G Bert Lumbreras	H G Bert Lumbreras	Gerald Burris	Eliodoro Gonzales	Ignacio Cortez
Dimmitt t (5)	MC	806 647-2155	Wayne Collins	Paul Catoe	Paul Catoe	Jo Hamilton	Steve Jameson	Don G Franklin	James Killough
Donna* (10)	CM	512 464-3315	Jose M Yanez	Luciano Ozuna Jr	Arcelia L Felix	Maria S Rocha	Isabel Infante	Fernando Castaneda	Manuel Rodriguez
Dublin† (3)	MC	817 445-3331	Jack Pratt	John David Johnson	Lillian Watson	....	James Fritts	David Johnson	Jack James
Dumas§† (12)	MC	806 935-4101	Mike Salim	Larry A Smith	Larry A Smith	Ernestine Martin	Wilmer Crain	F Hudson	Larry A Smith
Duncanville* (28)	CM	214 296-1401	Cliff Boyd	Dan Dodson	Laurie Lane	Jerry Striplin	Robert S O'Burke	Michael Courville	Robert B Lee
Eagle Lake* (4)	CM	409 234-2640	Elmer Struss	Robert Klockman	Lucille J Perry	....	L J Sonny Spanihel	Coulter Charles	Harry Supak
Eagle Pass* (21)	CM	512 773-1111	Enrique Montalvo	Roberto Barrientos	Gloria C Bewley	Manuel Contreras Jr	Guadalupe Cardona	Salvador Rios	Roberto Barrientos
Eastland* (4)	CM	817 629-8321	Charles P Marshall	J B Arther	....	....	....	....	....
Edcouch t† (3)	MC	512 262-2149	Jose C Hinojoso	Vivian Bentsen	....	Ramiro Rosa	Leonard Leggett	Primitivo Rodriquez	Homero DeLeon
Edgecliff v (3)	MC	817 293-4313	Tony Sims	....	Nancy Eller	Nancy Eller	Charles Talbot	Charles Talbot	Charles Talbot
Edinburg* (24)	CM	512 383-5661	Richard R Alamia	A Brent Branham	Maria M Corona	Tony Layton	Johnny Economedes	A C Gonzalez	Sam Horne
Edna* (6)	CM	512 782-3122	Richard E Browning	Larry W Kessler	Beverly Curlee	....	Robert Drexler	Norman Glaze	Paul Garza
El Campo* (10)	CM	713 543-5361	R Cecil Davis	Robert R Lundy	Brenda G Adams	Robert R Lundy	Larry Staff	Jimmie C Elliott	Fred Ehrhardt
El Lago (3)	MC	713 334-1951	Elizabeth F Lenoir	Jean Raffetto	June Larsen	John Petersen	Randy Zimmer	John Perez	....
El Paso (425)	MC	915 541-4000	Jonathan W Rogers	K E Beasley	W L Rieger Jr	J R Higdon	Joe Wilson	William E Rodriquez	David Harned
Electra* (4)	CM	817 495-2146	Ray B Dickey	Roger L Dunlap	Jean Mengwasser	....	Larry Huffstuttler	Richard Beck	Edward Helton
Elgin (5)	MC	512 285-3373	Marvin Carter	Alva McDonald	P Abel	Alva McDonald	W Alexander	Dan Gibson	Ralph Shafer
Elsa (5)	MC	512 262-2127	Antonio Barco	Ramiro Rosa	Ninfa Ozuna	....	Gregorio Madrigal	Lee Perez	....
Ennis* (12)	CM	214 875-9081	W D Murff	Steve Howerton	Wynell Rose	Wynell Rose	Rocky Harber	Dale Holt	Roy Callahan
Euless* (24)	CM	817 283-5381	Harold D Samuels	W M Sustaire	Kay Rainey	James R Hickerson	John K Scott	Johnnie M Wilson	James Knight
Everman (5)	MC	817 293-0525	Troy Daffron	Denton W Miller	Ms J Schlangenstein	....	Jerry Gibson	Randy G Sanders	J L Carroll
Fairfield (4)	MC	214 389-2633	W F Daniel	G M Dennis	Amanda Carroll	Amanda Carroll	H C Pagitt Jr	Jim Kellum	Charles Myers
Falfurrias (6)	CO	512 325-2420	E Villarreal Jr	....	Aurora C Rodriguez	....	David Zarate	Ruben M Longoria	Otis Goldman
Farmers Branch* (25)	CM	214 247-3131	John D Dodd	Paul M West	J W Wade	J W Wade	Jack Dyer	Roger Robbins	Earl Deland
Floresville (4)	CM	512 393-3105	Roy G Sanchez	L Jack Chaney	Barbara Brown	Roy G Sanchez	Harvey Elliott	Antonio Griego	Vicente Greigo
Flower Mound t* (4)	CM	214 539-8511	Andy Bukaty	Steven Lewis	Margaret Maxwell	....	C A Martin	Dennis Hazelwood	Tony Anderson
Floydada t* (4)	CM	806 983-2834	Parnell Powell	Wm A Feuerbacher	Jimmie Lou Stewart	Jimmie Lou Stewart	Bobby Welborn	Riley D Brewer	Jimmy M Green
Forest Hill* (12)	CM	817 293-3695	J Maurice Oakes	Rebecca Stark	Peggy Spain	Michael Phemister	R R Jordan	R R Jordan	W K Knight
Fort Stockton* (9)	CM	915 336-8525	Bruce McKenzie	Jesse Garcia	Aurora Gutierrez	Kenneth Johnson	Jimmy Jackson	Dale Cope	Dan McCarty
Fort Worth* (385)	CM	817 870-6000	Bob Bolen	Robert L Herchert	Ruth Alexander	Morris Matson	Howard L McMillen	H F Hopkins	Gary Santerre
Fredericksburg t (6)	MC	512 997-7521	Boyd Harper	....	Gary Neffendorf	Gary Neffendorf	David Burrier	Allen Mauldin	Allen Oestreich
Freeport* (13)	CM	713 233-3526	Tobey L Davenport	Earl W Heath	Janice L Spencer	Earl Heath	W R Johnson	Charles Bankston	Meryl Walters
Freer (3)	MC	512 394-6612	Malloy Hamilton	....	Hilda Rosales	....	....	J Hector Doria Jr	....
Friendswood* (11)	CM	713 482-3323	Ralph L Lowe	James C Morgan	Deloris McKenzie	David E Quick	Ken Honnoll	J M Wright	Melvin Meinecke
Friona* (4)	CM	806 247-2761	Clarence Monroe	Bee Lee Goodwin	....	Paula Wilson	Ralph Shirley	Bill Thieman	Clyde Fields
Frisco (3)	MC	214 377-2161	John Clanton	Mack Borchardt	Barbara Chandler	....	Mack Borchardt	Jerry Burton	....
Fritch§ (2)	MC	806 857-3143	Dane Welch	Jody P Butler	Jody P Butler	....	Don Wright	J Hudson	Calvin Hearron
Gainesville* (14)	CM	817 665-4323	Harry M Roark	Wm A Gaither	Rita Price	Lewis McLain	Charles D Brown	James R Boone	Ross Tamplin
Galena Park (10)	MC	713 672-2556	Alvin D Baggett	....	Barbara Nugent	Barbara Nugent	Randal Nordin	W E Cook	Michael Montgomery
Galveston* (62)	CM	409 766-2150	Janice R Coggeshall	Stephen N Huffman	Patsy Poole	Robt D Richardson	Paul Stanforth	E Barr	James D Havens
Garland* (139)	CM	214 494-7100	Charles R Matthews	Fred G Greene	Aleta Watson	Dean Ransom	B G Burkhart	Jesse Youngblood	Bill Dollar
Gatesville (6)	CM	817 865-5812	Creston Brazzil	Bob R Stevens	James McGlothlin	Evelyn Millsap	Billy Vaden	Floyd Williams	James Fowler
George West (3)	MC	512 449-1556	Albert T Brown	Brad Arvin	Robin McKinney	....	Frank Sales	Ed Olehy	Bob Baker
Georgetown* (9)	CM	512 863-5533	Carl Doering	Leo Wood	Pat Caballero	Barbara Raney	Les Bunte	Travis Thomas	W L Walden
Giddings* (4)	CM	713 542-2311	Robert L Placke	Larry Pippen	Lucille Walther	Larry Pippen	Mike Maass	E Chas Rost	Serapio Garza
Gilmer* (5)	CM	214 843-2553	Orear Watson	Thomas E Brymer	Linda Williams	Thomas E Brymer	Bobby Whiteside	Bill Wells	John Corley
Gladewater* (7)	CM	214 845-2196	James N Walker	H R Macomber	Sue Wilson	....	Jaye J Frost	James Keene	Roy Perryman
Gonzales*† (7)	CM	512 672-2815	....	Calvin E Spacek	....	Calvin E Spacek	....	....	Calvin E Spacek
Graham* (9)	CM	817 549-3322	Edwin S Graham III	Larry M Fields	Rogers Nanny	Rogers Nanny	Hall Cutshall	William A Paul Jr	....
Granbury (3)	MC	817 573-1114	Enar B Olson	Robert K Coffelt	Terry Smith	Michael W Easley	Kelton Conner	Donald F Steele	Felix Schmidt
Grand Prairie* (71)	CM	214 263-5221	Jerry Debo	Ted C Willis	Sue Shawver	Glenn Harriss	James Robertson	David Kunkle	Wendel Hulse
Grand Saline (3)	MC	214 962-3122	M P Pugh Sr	....	Chad E Grant	....	Ted Anderson	Robert Bradford	J C Gipson
Grapevine* (12)	CM	817 488-8521	W D Bill Tate	James L Hancock	Karen Spann	Jim Cook	J C Greener	H A Deggans	Jim Baddaker
Greenville* (22)	CM	214 455-2880	Leo Hackney	Kenneth O White	Pat Adams	William White	Claude Jenkins	Leon Powers	....
Gregory (3)	MC	512 643-6562	Celestino Zambrano	....	Olivia Saldivar	....	Ysidro Pena	Ruben Duran	....
Groesbeck (3)	MC	817 729-3293	Jim Longbotham	....	Martha Stanton	....	Eugene Dick	Charles H Walker	Eugene Dick
Groves* (17)	CM	713 962-4471	Sylvester Moore	Randy Kimler	Gene K Graham	Randy Kimler	Fred McAlpine	Mark Domingue	Harold Locke
Hallettsville (3)	MC	512 798-3681	Troy H Deavers	Maxine Mikulenka	Maxine Mikulenka	....	Roy Kalisek	Elmo E Grant	T H Kostelnik
Haltom City* (29)	CM	817 834-7341	Jack O Lewis	Roy L Moffatt	Linda Tidwell	Robert L Hurley	David Rainey	Jerry Robbins	Bill Sharp
Hamilton (3)	MC	817 386-8116	J L Hamilton	Cad W Berry	Ida Wulf	....	Tommy McKay	....	Syl Dyer
Hamlin (3)	MC	915 576-2711	Robert Fowler	Jenny White	....	....	Jerry Farnsworth	Ronnie Hill	Ellis West
Harker Heights* (7)	CM	817 699-2301	Danny Hurd	Fred A Coley	Fred A Coley	....	Bobby Barao	Robert Naramore	Richard Bone
Harlingen* (44)	CM	512 423-4230	Samuel C Lozano	Gavino D Sotelo	Jean Nesmith	Fernando Ramos	Elias Zamora	Guy Anderson	Raoul Campos
Haskell (4)	MC	817 864-2333	Abe Turner	Robert Baker	Robert Baker	Robert Baker	Tom Watson	Tom Paul Barnett	Dave Smith
Hearne* (5)	CM	409 279-3461	Guy Chandler	Steven K Carpenter	Dorothy J Kloss	Floyd Hafley	Horace Mathews	James Sparks	Roger Malone
Hedwig Village (3)	MC	713 465-6009	T W Bartlett	Lana Rizzuto	Lana M Rizzuto	Lana M Rizzuto	....	Marion G Reese	Edward V Dorr
Hempstead (4)	MC	409 826-2486	Leroy Singleton	....	Willie Mae Burch	Willie Mae Burch	L J Lecamu Jr	....	James Vines
Henderson (11)	CM	214 657-6551	Lester Brown	Jack Dickerson	Patsy Farley	Patsy Farley	Billy Parker	J T Ackerman	....
Henrietta t (3)	CM	817 538-4316	Charles Hilliard	George Hicks	Betty Thorn	George Hicks	Larry Crowley	Jake Bogart	George Hicks
Hereford* (16)	CM	806 364-2123	Wesley S Fisher	C Dudley Bayne	Bonna R Duke	C Dudley Bayne	David Spain	Caydon Brush	C Dudley Bayne
Hewitt§ (5)	MC	817 666-6171	Louis Mexia	Douglas Henderson	Betty A Orton	Carlo Jones	Jerry Howard	Jack L Caswell	Edward O Mirick
Highland Park t* (9)	CM	214 521-4161	John L Lancaster	L A Patterson	James Fisher	Bill Pollock	Henry Gardner	Henry Gardner	James Fisher
Highland Village (3)	MC	214 221-2558	Art Newman	Joseph M Gambill Jr	Ruth Baker	Maurine Smith	Charles Barfknecht	Fred Chance	Scott Cisney
Hillsboro* (7)	CM	817 582-3271	Ronald R Rhoads	Joe E Ward	Patricia Pollock	....	Norman Honeycutt	Ed Wheat	....
Hitchcock (7)	MC	409 986-5591	Dorothy A Childress	....	Joyce Balke	Dorothy A Childress	Billy Scott	Benjimen B Clawson	Ken Van Nostrand
Hollywood Park (3)	MC	512 494-2023	Ruby Weinholt	....	Rosamond Adair	Ms Charlie Hoover	Marvin Matter	Ronald Edwards	Marvin Matter
Hondo (6)	MC	512 426-3378	Andrew Patterson	Mike Rhea	Vangie Pimentel	Vickie L Smith	John L Sturm	Jerry Smith	Mike Rhea
Houston (1594)	MC	713 222-3011	Kathy Whitmire	....	Anna Russell	William R Brown	Raymond Harrison	Lee P Brown	Jon Vanden Bosch
Humble§† (7)	MC	713 446-3061	H E McKay	Denzel Percifull	Georgia Fields	Denzel Percifull	Lawrence C Clark	Lenny Hendrick	James P Baker

Directory 1/10 continued **MUNICIPAL OFFICIALS IN ALL U.S. CITIES OVER 2,500[1]**

City, 1980 population (000 omitted), form of government	Municipal phone number	Mayor	Appointed administrator	City clerk	Finance officer	Fire chief	Police chief	Public works director
TEXAS (423) continued								
Hunters Creek Village								
(4) MC	713 465-2150	Cebe Sue Barnett	Nancy J Parks	Kenna McAndrews	Francis G Winters	Bob Bredehoeft	Joe M Schultea Sr	Ross H Bird
Huntsville* (24) CM	409 295-6471	William V Nash	Gene Pipes	Ruth DeShaw	Patricia Allen	Joe French	David Farrar	Johnny Poteete
Hurst* (31) CM	817 281-6160	William D Souder	Jim Starr	Pat Evans	Dale Schultz	Joe Erwin	Joe Watson	Jim McMeans
Hutchins (3) MC	214 225-6121	(not reporting)						
Ingleside* (5) CM	512 776-2517	J G Herrington	Del Lewis	Leona Tiner	Gayle Goble	James Wright	Skip Rohrer	George Kneuper
Iowa Park§ (6) MC	817 592-2131	Timothy W Hunter	James S Barrington	Ithama Jolley	....	Danny Skinner	Tom Fenley	....
Irving* (110) CM	214 253-2600	Bobby Joe Raper	Jack D Huffman	Lester G Ford	Ralph Ellis Jr	Gene Spillman	Benny Newman	Lewis Patrick
Jacinto City† (9) CM	713 674-8424	Mike Blasingame	Joann Griggs	May Smith	Joann Griggs	Lon Squyres	Wayne Speaks	John L Cooper
Jacksboro* (4) CM	817 567-6321	Arthur S Shanafelt	Jerry R Lewis	Jerry R Lewis	Harva K Payne	Bill Craft	Arthur Reaves	John W Ash
Jacksonville* (12) CM	214 586-3510	Harry G Tilley	Gordon Pierce	Shine Chancellor	Shine Chancellor	Clem Cecil Jr	John F Brewer	Christopher Pledger
Jasper* (7) CM	409 384-4651	W L Neal	Wayne DuBose	Charles E Duckworth	Charles E Duckworth	Dallas Matthews III	Harlan Alexander	James Sheffield
Jefferson (3) CO	214 665-3922	Ruel D Young Sr	Sara K Hernandez	Anita Wyatt	....	Harold Clark	Frank D Williams	....
Jersey Village (4) MC	713 466-6159	Leonard J Terrien	Carol H Fox	Wanda J Parker	Carol H Fox	Frank Maher	R L Parsley	Robert E Moore
Jones Creek v (3) MC	409 233-1826	Lawrence A Willis	....	Anita Y McCoy	....	William Tidwell	Howard P Rape	....
Jourdanton (3) MC	512 769-3589	Austin Teutsch	Louis C Tarazon	Ann P Foster	Ann P Foster	Eddie Trimble	David W Ricks	Manuel Q Martinez
Junction§ (3) MC	915 446-2622	W Keaton Blackburn	Dale Norton	Frederica Wyatt	Dale Norton	Edward Stewart	Hubert L Hubbard	....
Karnes City †† (3) CO	512 780-3422	Benhardt Ahrens	....	Charles R Tiemann	....	Adolph Boelter	Nolan A Jonas	C Bartkoviak
Katy (6) MC	713 391-9181	Johnny Nelson	Betty H Murray	Virginia Maddox	Diana Ulbig	Billy F Patton	Pat O Adams	William P Cardiff
Kaufman§ (5) MC	214 932-2216	Harry H Holcomb	Norman Smith	Billie Ruth Keith	....	Eddie Brown	Robert Harris	Norman Smith
Keene (3) MC	817 641-3336	Roger L Ackermann	....	Beverly Barton	Margie Wilkes	Ed Cheever	Regan Scherencel	Jim Dyche
Keller§ (4) MC	817 431-1517	Bruce Lee	Johnny Sartain	Sheila Stephens	Johnny Sartain	Mike Stephens	Tom Cowan	....
Kenedy (4) CO	512 583-2230	R C Franklin	....	Marjorie Barber	Marjorie Barber	Robert Alexander	Juan F Salinas	Joe Ed Ponish
Kennedale (3) MC	817 478-5512	Danny Taylor	Ted Rowe	....	Ted Rowe	Jim Smith	Terry Ahrendt	Gene Henick
Kermit* (8) CM	915 586-3460	O L Marshall	Randall E Holly	Randall E Holly	Randall E Holly	Leroy Leard	Melvin Bartley	Wayne Reynolds
Kerrville* (15) CM	512 257-8000	A J Brough	James L Odle	Sheila L Brand	D D Crawford	Raymond Holloway	L Scott Evans	Calvin Neely
Kilgore* (11) CM	214 984-5081	Mickey D Smith	Ronald E Cox	Betty Robertson	Charles Johnson	Paul E Duckworth	Johnny E Bradley	....
Killeen* (46) CM	817 634-2191	Allen C Cloud	Robert M Hopkins	Nancy L Dibert	Daniel J Bray	Keith Langford	F L Giacomozzi	Michael H Barnes
Kingsville* (29) CM	512 592-5235	Billie Gunter	George K Noe	Randolph C Moravec	Randolph C Moravec	Tony Torres	Gerard V Gutierrez	Carlos Lerma
Kirby (6) CM	512 661-3198	Gary West	George Fetterman	Margaret Halbardier	George Fetterman	Jerry Kneupper	Allen Johnson	Donald Hand
Kountze (3) MC	409 246-3463	Robert T Fife	....	Vickie Carter	....	Dale Williford	Wilson Roberts	....
La Feria (3) CM	512 797-2261	Scott Sloane	Thomas V Kolterman	Lois Hargrove	Sunny K Phipp	Gene S Briones	John D Bryson	Daniel Perez
La Grange (4) MC	409 968-5805	Charlie Jungmichel	J D Legler	Violet Zbranek	....	Rudolph Voss	Lawrence Ulbrich	....
La Marque*† (15) CM	713 938-7201	Ron Crowder	Ivan Langford	Carol McLemore	....	Bob Doolittle	Richard Duroux	....
La Porte* (17) CM	713 471-5020	Virginia Cline	B Jack Owen	Cherie Black	Debra Cole	Joe Sease	Herb Freeman	Jerry Hodge
Lacy-Lakeview (3) MC	817 799-1366	Glover Laird	Jean Stangroom	Jean Stangroom	Jean Stangroom	Wayne Hutchison	Bruce Donley	William M Lanier
Lake Dallas (3) MC	817 497-2226	Johnny J Vinson	M Jean Chambers	Margaret Coulter	M Jean Chambers	Jerry McCutcheon	Alex F Williams Jr	Elmer Crawford
Lake Jackson* (19) CM	713 297-2481	V Vickers	A A MacLean	Chas Smith	A A MacLean	Paul Isreal	P C Miller	Dean Morgan
Lake Worth Village (4) MC	817 237-1211	Richard W Trimble	L O Irby	Linda A Haskell	L O Irby	Curtis M McKay Jr	Bert Campbell	Clifton Petrea
Lamesa* (12) CM	806 872-2121	Donald R Bethel	James P Feazelle	Robert Gorsline	J H McAllister	Audie Hughes	Gerry Brown	....
Lampasas (6) CM	512 556-3641	Henry V Campbell Jr	....	Carole Heller	....	John Rathman	J O Tanner	Evon Self
Lancaster* (15) CM	214 227-2111	Don Welch	Carl Tomerlin	Frances H Goodman	Pauline Hodges	Donald McMullan	John K Whitehead	John Pitstick
Laredo* (91) CM	512 726-1900	Aldo Tatangelo	R Marvin Townsend	Hortencia Gonzalez	....	Mike Perez	Victor L Garcia	Joe Guerra
League City† (17) MC	713 332-3431	Joe L Lamb	Paul Nutting	Leta Willoughby	Cathy Floyd	Craig Johnson	Ron Wrobleski	Larry Webb
Leon Valley§ (9) MC	512 684-1391	Irene Baldridge	Donald R Manning	Margaret Goodwin	L J Cott	Curtis Dunn	Bill Stannard	Jim Malone
Levelland* (14) CM	806 894-0113	Tony Malouf	Greg Ingham	Chris Wade	Judy Stehens	Thurman Davis	Ted Holder	Kenneth Rumbaugh
Lewisville* (24) CM	214 436-2591	Wayne Ferguson	R Darwin McGill	Bettye Harris	Bettye Harris	Randy Corbin	Steve McFadden	Tom Dingler
Liberty* (8) CM	713 336-3684	C Scott Parker	Roy N Bennett	Dale Alford	Dale Alford	Ben E Pickett	Fred Clements	....
Littlefield* (7) CM	806 385-5161	Clifton C Cutshall	George Shackelford	Amalia Martinez	Bonnie Massengale	Larry Buster	Mike Smith	Leon Durham
Live Oak* (8) CM	512 653-9140	Ralph Cullip	Charles W Pinto	Marian Elbel	Harry Martin	Heinz G Mueller	Mark Jackley	Heinz G Mueller
Livingston* (5) CM	409 327-4311	Joe Pedigo	Tom Nevinger	Joyce Rash	Joyce Rash	C L Cochran Jr	Larry M Macomber	Richard Walker
Llano (3) MC	915 247-4158	John Landon	George C Rogers	Imogene T Donop	....	Beverley Harden	Randy R Crider	....
Lockhart* (8) CM	512 398-3461	Maxine R Goodman	Cecil E Massey	Cecil E Massey	....	Jack Hay	Mark Hinnenkamp	Ralph Gerald
Longview* (63) CM	214 757-6666	Mitch Henderson	C Ray Jackson	Jo Ann H Metcalf	Jo Ann H Metcalf	Tommie McMaster	James McLaughlin	L K Smith Jr
Lubbock* (174) CM	806 762-6411	Alan Henry	Larry J Cunningham	....	Robert Massengale	Tom Foster	Thomas Nichols	Sam Wahl
Lufkin* (29) CM	713 634-8881	Pitser H Garrison	Harvey Westerholm	Ann Griffin	Rita Jinkins	Billy Stephens	Leonard Latham	Ron Wesch
Luling* (5) CM	512 875-2115	W S Hooper	Jack Caffall	Pat Williamson	Harold Watts	Paul Stahl	Bobby Johnson	Sam Jernigan
Madisonville (4) MC	713 348-2748	Joe H Drew	Joe Manning	Joe Manning	Joe Manning	Donnie Teague	David Burr	Jerry L Gafford
Mansfield* (8) CM	817 473-9371	Wayne Wilshire	Clayton Chandler	Kathryn T Howard	....	Bobby Looney	Michael Leyman	Chris Burkett
Manvel (4) MC	713 489-0630	Ron Kitchens	....	Marie George	Diane Pierson	Delbert Burleson	E C Hooker	....
Marble Falls †† (3) CM	512 693-3611	Robert A Pittman	Dick Zimmerman	Ms Bobbie Stueler	Dick Zimmerman	Johnny Thompson	Frank Steggall	Tommy Allison
Marlin§ (7) MC	817 883-5542	H B Stallworth Jr	Harold Underwood	Rosemary Lawler	Harold Underwood	Ben Markowski	R Riemenschneider	Billy L Roberts
Marshall* (25) CM	214 935-5241	Lane Strahan	Tony Williams	Betty Crenshaw	Betty Crenshaw	Gene Walker	Chuck Williams	Cecil Forester
Mathis (6) MC	512 547-3343	James T Knight	....	Maria O Sarate	Diana Self	Larry Wallek	Pete J Anzaldua	Fred F Farias
McAllen* (67) CM	512 686-2351	Othal E Brand	J A Escamilla	Natividad Sanchez	Guillermo Seguin	Everett H Derr	Lee Spradlin	Mel Placilla
McGregor (5) MC	817 840-2806	Felix A Morris	Kyle H McCain	Christine Otter	Kyle H McCain	John Blake	William M Copeland	Davis Faubion
McKinney* (16) CM	214 542-2675	Jim C Ledbetter	Donald E Paschal Jr	Jennifer G Cravens	Kyle Sonnenberg	E L Tinker Taylor	Ken A Walker	Harold Clary
Meadows (4) MC	806 539-2377	(not reporting)						
Memphis (3) MC	806 259-3001	Kenneth Dale	....	Nelwyn Ward	....	Jerry Smith	William Tuey	Michael S Branigan
Menard§ (2) MC	915 396-4616	William A Wilkinson	James F Cannon	Dorothy M Bundick	....	....	....	....
Mercedes*† (12) CM	512 565-3114	Gilberto Dominguez	Linda K Gulley	Jane Luera	Ernesto Briones	Rudy Garza	Robert Nunley	Albert Zavala
Mesquite* (67) CM	214 288-7711	Brunhilde Nystrom	C K Duggins	Lynn Prugel	James Prugel	Don Nelson	Glen Grayson	Dale Williams
Mexia* (7) CM	817 562-5385	Sidney Johnston	Joe C Benton	Cloyce Tyner	Cloyce Tyner	Aaron Thompson	Rodger Cotton	Gerald R Yarbrough
Midland* (71) CM	915 683-4281	G Thane Akins	James W Brown	Bill C Clanton	Troy Gifford	James Roberts	Wayne Gideon	Fred G Baker
Midlothian (3) MC	214 775-3481	(not reporting)						
Mineola (4) MC	214 569-5301	E M Bradshaw	Joe W Deupree	Joe W Deupree	Joe W Deupree	Ray Humphreys	Joe D Bevill	E M Bradshaw
Mineral Wells* (14) CM	817 328-1211	H Arthur Zappe	Sam Phelps	Neta Mason	John H Reagan	B H Gilstrap	Donald Fairrel	H C Powell
Mission* (23) CM	512 581-2101	Fernando Ortegon	Benito A Lopez	Criselda Briones	J Rolando Gonzalez	Rene Alaniz	Robert J Garza	....
Missouri City§ (25) MC	713 499-1681	John B Knox	David A Harner	Alice Church	Dorothy N Seckel	L C Guillot	L C Guillot	Thomas M Anderson
Monahans* (8) CM	915 943-4343	Richard J Hoyer	Jack Forga	Margie Wilson	Helen Shoemake	Lawrence Dain	David Mills	Jack Forga
Morton t (3) MC	806 266-8850	Howell Ray Luper	Albert L Field	Albert L Field	Albert L Field	J D Wiseley	....	John C Vasquez
Mount Pleasant* (11) CM	214 572-3412	Jerry Boatner	Paul W Henderson	Charles Nugent	Charles Nugent	Taft Nelson	B C Sustaire	Weldon Davis
Muleshoe* (5) CM	806 272-4528	Charles Bratcher	Dave W Marr Jr	Mary Hicks	....	Jack Dunham	Leslie D Irvin	L M Bell
Nacogdoches* (27) CM	713 564-4693	A L Mangham	Jarvis T Ammons	Cleon Compton	Cleon Compton	Charles Duffin	Don Barlow	John Phillips
Nassau Bay* (5) CM	713 333-2108	Gerald Allen	Howard L Ward	Nancy Sweningson	....	Douglas Harris	Jim Graves	Phil Briscoe
Navasota* (6) CM	409 825-6408	Morris Weaver	Edward D Thatcher	Geraldine Binford	Edward D Thatcher	Paul Scrivener	James W Campbell	Walter Hardin
Nederland* (17) CM	409 727-2711	Homer E Nagel	Howard McDaniel	Chris Serres	J B McKinney	Mike Lovelady	Billy Neal	John I Bamber
New Boston t (5) MC	214 628-5596	John H McCoy	....	Carol Ensey	Carol Ensey	Billy House	Otis Scott Jr	Robert L Walker
New Braunfels* (22) CM	512 625-3425	Barbara Tieken	Joe M Michie	Veronica Sarkozi	James A Jeffers	Jack L Wilson	Burney C Boeck	Fred R Ryden

Directory 1/10 continued — MUNICIPAL OFFICIALS IN ALL U.S. CITIES OVER 2,500[1]

City, 1980 population (000 omitted), form of government		Municipal phone number	Mayor	Appointed administrator	City clerk	Finance officer	Fire chief	Police chief	Public works director
TEXAS (423) continued									
Nocona (3)	MC	817 825-3281	Lynn Roberts	Tommy Sparks	Minnie Walker	Tommy Sparks	Kenneth Grant	Fred Castle	Tommy Sparks
North Richland Hills* (31)	CM	817 281-0041	Dan Echols	Rodger N Line	Jeanette Moore	Lou Spiegel	Stan R Gertz	Jerry McGlasson	Gene Riddle
Oak Ridge North (3)	MC	713 292-4648	Frederick M Wagner	....	Kathy Moore	....	Ed Robinson	G M Cox	Ed Robinson
Odessa* (90)	CM	915 337-7381	John B Minor	John D Harrison	Tena Walker	Frank Muser	W J Childress	Alan R Stewart	Bobby Tucker
Olmos Park* (2)	CM	512 824-3281	Woodward W Altgelt	E Gene Sprague	Terry L Storm	E Gene Sprague	Vincent J Lancaster	Michael K Ullevig	E Gene Sprague
Olney§ (4)	MC	817 564-2102	David H Penn	Jack Northrup	Jean Clifton	....	Eddie Pulliam	Van Perryman	Billy Perry
Orange* (24)	CM	409 886-3611	James R Dunaway	Charles L Curry	Mavis McClure	Karen S Johnson	M J Girlinghouse	C Jack McClelland	James Foyle
Palacios (5)	MC	512 972-2414	Leonard Lamar	....	Veronica Greene	Suzanne Henson	S L Davidson Jr	J R Wilson	Robert E Brewer
Palestine* (16)	CM	214 729-2181	Jack K Selden Jr	Kenneth N Berry	Jan Kaase	William Vick	Vernon Hamby	Hunter Williams	James Dean
Pampa* (21)	CM	806 665-8481	Calvin Whatley	Mack Wofford	Erma L Hipsher	Frank T Smith	Paul Jones	John J Ryzman	Allyn Moore
Panhandle* (2)	CM	806 537-3517	Leslie L McNeill	Larry D Gilley	Ann Mills	....	Mike Atchley	Ronald Spears	Len Jennings
Pantego t*† (2)	CM	817 274-1381	....	Robt T McDaniel	....	....	....	....	....
Paris* (25)	CM	214 785-7511	Joe Graham	David H Doty	H C Greene	H C Greene	Steve Burgin	Charles Whitley	Dan Brotton
Pasadena† (113)	MC	713 477-1511	Johnny Isbell	....	Jennings L Pitre	Jaime Valderrama	Jay Goyer	David Mullican	Joe Costanza
Pearland§ (13)	MC	713 485-2411	Thomas J Reid	Ronald J Wicker	Dorothy L Cook	Dorothy S Thompson	Larry Steed	Glen Stanford	William Thomasset
Pearsall* (7)	CM	512 334-3676	Ruben Leal	Andres Garza Jr	....	Andres Garza Jr	Billy Hal Woodward	Crispin Trevino	Alex Hernandez
Pecos* (13)	CM	915 445-2421	Frank Sanchez	William E Hopper	Marilea Parsons	Carroll W Thomson	J T Prewit	James W Wilson	....
Perryton* (8)	CM	806 435-4014	Mike R Richardson	J B Whigham Jr	Dan Graves	Dan Graves	C B Luther	Joe Hannon	David Landis
Pharr (21)	CO	512 787-2704	Fidencio R Barrera	Reyes Vela	Dora H Garza	Ernesto Ayala Jr	Burgess E Cook	Anacleto Martinez	Rene Castellanos
Pinehurst (3)	MC	713 886-2221	Grady L Johnson	Joseph L Runnels	Frances M McGee	Frances M McGee	Freddie Yust	Donald Hartsfield	....
Piney Point Village† (3)	MC	713 782-0271	A Lee Smith	....	Ann T Tatum	....	Robert Bredehoeft	Joe Schultea	Ross Bird
Pittsburg* (4)	CM	214 856-5475	D H Abernathy	Winfred T Newsome	Sue Sharp	Sue Sharp	David Abernathy	Weldon Reynolds	....
Plainview* (22)	CM	806 293-4171	E V Ridlehuber	John K Hatchel	Buddy Dodson	Norman Huggins	Joe Ferguson	Hugh Anderson	Bill Hogge
Plano* (72)	CM	214 424-6531	Jack Harvard	David A Griffin	Ms Jackie Blakely	James Forte	William Peterson	Jame McCarley	David Neeley
Pleasanton* (6)	CM	512 569-3867	Danny Qualls	R F Wehman	Kathy McMullen	....	R A Troell	Lester Fuller	R F Wehman
Port Aransas* (2)	CM	512 749-4111	Dale Bietendorf	Joyce Pulich	Esther Arzola	Diane Leucht	Norman White	David Hudiburgh	Carl Castell
Port Arthur* (61)	CM	713 983-3321	Malcolm L Clark	George E Dibrell	Carolyn Dixon	J Lowery	Clifford Barbay	J R Newsom	Robert Bowers
Port Isabel* (4)	CO	512 943-2682	Baldemar U Alaniz	James Elium III	Ernestina Barrera	James R Elium III	Robert Harris	Lorenzo Rosalez Jr	Pete Vela
Port Lavaca*† (11)	CM	512 552-9795	Kenneth D Lester	M H Gildon	Lorene S Sulton	....	Ray Stringham	W T Steen	Thomas B Hargrove
Port Neches*† (14)	CM	713 727-2181	G C Graham Sr	Charles E Norwood	Renella Babin	Charles E Norwood	James Harrington	Charles Bennefield	Elwyn L Graham
Portland* (12)	CM	512 643-6501	Bobby Whittington	William H Lewis	Judi Carson	William H Lewis	Calvin Jones	Harold White	Cesario Vela
Post (4)	MC	806 495-2811	G C McCrary	W G Pool	Wanda Wilkerson	....	Delbert Rudd	....	Mike Sanchez
Poteet (3)	MC	512 742-3574	Salvdor Almanza Jr	....	Carmen L Garcia	....	Ted Garcia	James R Spence	Carlos S Casas
Prairie View (4)	MC	409 857-3711	Ronald Leverett	Tanya Thomas	....	....	....	Daniel Bennett	Cecil Richards
Premont (3)	MC	512 348-3912	F Tino Perez	Idolina Perez	Idolina Perez	Idolina Perez	Ricardo Lopez	Erasmo Rodriguez	Idolina Perez
Princeton t (3)	MC	214 736-3700	James Funsch	Lee S Vickers	Donna Price	....	Mike Woody	....	Roy Jenkins
Quanah (4)	MC	817 663-5336	Randy Akers	H R Hamilton	H R Hamilton	H R Hamilton	Jimmy Edmonds	Skip Cargile	B Lorance
Ranger (3)	CO	817 647-3522	Raymond Hart	Barbara Wheat	Joyanne Hoover	Buddy Vinson	Darrell Fox	James C Rose Jr	Ron Butler II
Raymondville (9)	MC	512 689-2443	Joe Alexandre	C M Crowell	C M Crowell	C M Crowell	Dale Messinger	Sabas Garza Jr	Amado E Salinas Jr
Refugio (4)	MC	512 526-5361	Judy Williamson	....	Lillian Linney	....	Don Pullin	Wallace Maley	Joe Bell
Richardson* (72)	CM	214 235-8331	Martha E Ritter	Bob Hughey	Virginia Gruben	Daniel W Parker	Richard Russell	Kenneth R Yarbrough	Marshall L Haney
Richland Hills t (8)	MC	817 284-4901	David L Ragan	Dennis H Woodard	Pauline Kempe	Pauline Kempe	Don Steward	Barbara Childress	Roger Hokanson
Richmond t (10)	MC	713 342-5456	H G Moore	Keith A Crawford	Mona Matak	....	Frank Fishar	Dalton R Hargis	....
Richwood (3)	MC	409 265-2082	Tommy Jones	....	Linda Patterson	Linda Patterson	Rick Cary	Glenn Patton	Mike Harper
River Oaks (7)	MC	817 626-5421	Thomas M Holland	W C Ray	W C Ray	W C Ray	George Norton	Walter Schertz	Bobby Mayo
Robinson† (6)	MC	817 662-1415	Clint Capers	Robert Groth	Robert Groth	Robert Groth	James Threakeld	Cook Mike	Orville Johnson
Robstown† (12)	MC	512 387-4589	Julio Garcia Jr	Roy Gutierrez	Roy Gutierrez	Roy Gutierrez	Henry W Harms	James Torrez	John J Foster
Rockdale (6)	MC	512 446-2511	Bill T Avrett	Elizabeth Fenter	Brenda Surovik	Brenda Surovik	Earl Whitmore	Marshall Martin	James Fischer
Rockport (4)	MC	512 729-2213	C H Mills Jr	Herman C Johnson	Helen G Braffett	Herman C Johnson	John H Ray	J M Hinojosa	James C Gurley
Rockwall§ (6)	MC	214 722-1111	Leon Tuttle	Jesse E Gilbert Jr	Julie Couch	Claude Sturgeon	Benny Gracey	Bruce Beaty	Ed Heath
Roma (3)	MC	512 849-1411	Jose Carlos Saenz	Antioco Canales	Elizabeth Garza	America Bates	....	Leonel R Alvarez	....
Rosebud* (2)	CM	817 583-7926	Clarence Wolf	Wanda Fischer	Meolody McElyea	Wanda Fischer	E O Mier	Edward McElyea	Coy Smith
Rosenberg (18)	MC	713 342-2531	Ben Babovec	....	Alice Skalski	Ben Babovec	Gerald Matheaus	Dwayne Sparks	Ben Babovec
Round Rock*† (12)	CM	512 255-3612	Larry L Tonn	Robert L Bennett Jr	Joanne Land	Sam Huey	Lynn Bizzell	Gene Collier	Jack A Harzke
Rowlett* (8)	CM	214 475-3841	Bill Payne	John R Milford	Glenna Bean	Bob Harrison	Dennis Thomas	Tom Dunphy	Edward Richie
Rusk t* (5)	CM	214 683-2213	James B Long	Bill Lindley	Dolores Bongard	Bill Lindley	Jamie Weaver	Randy Hatch	Orville L Johnson
Saginaw (6)	CM	817 232-4640	J D Johnson	Jon Ed Robbins	Jon Ed Robbins	Jon Ed Robbins	James Judge	Gene Springer	Edwin Larson
San Angelo* (73)	CM	915 655-9121	Tom R Parrett	Stephen Brown	Peggy J Gilmore	Roland Howard	Gene Kilgore	Travis P Johnson	Cloice Whitley
San Antonio* (785)	CM	512 299-7011	Henry G Cisneros	Louis J Fox	Norma Rodriguez	Carl White	I O Martinez	Charles Rodriguez	Frank Kiolbassa
San Augustine t (3)	MC	713 275-2121	Walter Richey	Alton B Shaw	Amelia Jeanes	Frances Maxwell	Oran Davis	....	....
San Benito* (18)	CM	512 399-5344	Cesar Gonzalez	Domingo Ramirez	Lupita Passement	Roy DeNoyette	Guillermo Garcia Jr	Encarnacion Claudio	Hector Jalomo
San Diego (5)	MC	512 279-3341	Rupert Canales	....	Juanita T Saenz	....	Eladio Gonzalez	Oscar C Hughes	....
San Juan§ (8)	MC	512 787-9923	Hector Palacios	Ricardo Gomez	Enedelia Campos	Erasmo Ramos	Lowell Neubauer	Efrain Soto	Ted Trevino
San Marcos* (23)	CM	512 353-4444	Emmie Craddock	A C Gonzalez Jr	Janis K Womack	Wayne Moore	Oscar Carpenter	Myron L Calchutt	George W Boeker
Sanger§ (3)	MC	817 458-7930	Nel Armstrong	Lloyd Henderson	Mary Jo Stover	....	Merwyn Tucker	Sidney George	Billy Barclay
Sansom Park Village (4)	MC	817 626-3791	George Worley	....	Deana Keplinger	....	Mike Wasser	Kenneth P McMullen	Jim Mathis
Santa Fe (6)	MC	713 925-6412	John A Roberts	William R Lambert	Mafie McMath	....	....	Bryan M Lamb	....
Schertz* (7)	CM	512 658-7477	Earl W Sawyer	Jimmy G Gilmore	June G Krause	Jimmy G Gilmore	Ed Melton	James W Keith	....
Seabrook* (5)	CM	713 474-3201	L W Dickerson	Steven M Walters	Evelyn Purswell	....	Randy Zimmer	Robert W Kerber	Gary W Jones
Seagoville* (7)	CM	214 287-2050	B M Foster	Al Maddox	Ruth Sorrells	....	George Melaun	....	Don Hamon Sr
Seagraves (3)	MC	806 546-2593	Glenn Lewis	....	Catherin Mitchell	....	Manuel Davila	Billy Jones	Tom McCollister
Sealy (4)	MC	409 885-3511	Jim Walters	Charles Hinze Jr	Frank Krampitz Jr	Charles Hinze Jr	Robert Park	Roy Phillips	....
Seguin (18)	MC	512 379-3212	Betty Jean Jones	....	Linnette Habermann	Nora Chavez	Roger G Mycue	Leroy Schneider	Bill E Polasek Jr
Selma§ (1)	MC	512 651-6661	Steve Gose	Margie Lubianski	Margie Lubianski	Margie Lubianski	Billy Mueller	Benjamin F Wolfe	Pat Britt
Seminole* (6)	CM	915 758-3622	Jameil Aryain	Lanny S Lambert	Vickie Jones	Vickie Jones	Wayland McCullough	L M Blackmon	Randy Zelner
Seymour§ (4)	MC	817 888-3148	Charles T Sessions	Kevin P Evans	Mary Alice Smith	Kevin P Evans	Gene Robinson	Floyd Burke	....
Shamrock§ (3)	MC	806 256-3281	Douglas O V Rives	....	Linda L Amos	....	M O Lowe Sr	Art L Taylor	Johnny W Rhodes
Sherman* (30)	CM	214 892-4545	David Sprowl	Talmadge N Buie	Helen Friend	Michael Van Wickler	Phillip Allison	J D Pickens	David E Gattis
Silsbee*† (8)	CM	713 246-3372	....	Richard Hickerson	....	....	....	....	....
Sinton t* (6)	CM	512 364-2381	Rosalie Brown	Walter W Hill Jr	Archie Lea Rigby	Walter W Hill Jr	Owen Dragod	Sam Schwartz	Ronald N Garrison
Slaton* (7)	CM	806 828-6505	Donald R Sikes	Robert J Estes III	Kay Ella Bruedigam	Robert J Estes III	Bob Kern	Barbara Fowler	....
Smithville (3)	MC	512 237-3282	Bill Davison	....	Gwen Caldwell	....	Robert Reader	Jim Hutson	....
Snyder* (13)	CM	915 573-4957	Rod Waller	John W Gayle	Jeanne Johnson	John W Gayle	....	William A Stone	....
Sonora (4)	CM	915 387-2558	Billy C Gosney	James E Dover	Becky Covington	Becky Covington	Louis Olenick	Raymond Brent Gesch	Gene West
South Houston t (13)	MC	713 944-2330	Lynn W Brasher	....	Toy Ann Harp	Toy Ann Harp	James Sybert	Ray Jones	John Booher
South Padre Island t* (1)	CM	512 943-6456	Minnie Solomonson	Johnny P Smith	June E Tallant	....	Dwight Davis	Arthur Garcia	....
Southlake† (3)	MC	817 481-5581	Sam Sparger	....	....	....	....	....	....
Spearman* (3)	CM	806 659-2524	C Ralph Blodgett	Jim R Murray	Charlotte A Sheets	....	Steven Slater	D J Alberts	Ted Scroggs

Directory 1/10 continued — MUNICIPAL OFFICIALS IN ALL U.S. CITIES OVER 2,500[1]

City, 1980 population (000 omitted), form of government		Municipal phone number	Mayor	Appointed administrator	City clerk	Finance officer	Fire chief	Police chief	Public works director
TEXAS (423) continued									
Spring Valley† (3)	MC	713 465-8308	Diane D Tate	G R Parker	Charlene M Taylor	Samuel H Kemp	Robert C Bredehoft	John C Cook	....
Stafford t (5)	MC	713 499-4537	Leonard Scarcella	Lawrence Vaccaro Jr	Mary Burger	Joe Stibora	Andrew J Grahmann	Bonny R Krahn	Lawrence Vaccaro Jr
Stamford* (5)	CM	915 773-2591	Robert A Prichard	Mark S Watson	Olive A Casady	Mark S Watson	Bill Lawson	D Medford	Mark S Clark
Stephenville* (12)	CM	817 965-7887	David Clayton	Kurt J Ackermann	Joyce Pemberton	Charlene Young	Jimmy Mooney	Douglas Conner	Danny R Johnson
Sugar Land (9)	CM	713 494-3176	Walter S McMeans	Marina M Sukup	Glenda Gundermann	Jo Lanier	Johnnie J Pokluda	L B Ross	....
Sulphur Springs* (13)	CM	214 885-7541	David Baucom	David R Tooley	Sandy Beach	Wendell Sapaugh	C D Bolding	Donnie Lewis	Bill Farler
Sundown* (2)	CM	806 229-3131	Randy Winfrey	Thomas L Adams	Anna Emory	Dorothy F Dominguez	Doug Barry	Bobby Leo Barley	Frank Hernandez
Sunray t§ (2)	MC	806 948-4111	John Humphreys	Darce Foshee	Darce Foshee	....	Eddie Brown	....	....
Sweeny t† (4)	MC	713 548-3321	A M Anderson	....	Exa Keller	....	Charles Woodrow	Jerry Murphy	Kenneth Lott
Sweetwater* (12)	CM	915 236-6313	Tom E Wideman Jr	Bob Hart	Kenneth Roussel	Kenneth Roussel	Odell W Gillian	Jim Kelley	D M Teel
Taft§ (4)	MC	512 528-3512	H O Grebe	Zachary Z Zoul	Darlene Williams	Zachary Z Zoul	Jim Vogt	Ray Zapata	Elmo Acousta
Tahoka (3)	CM	806 998-4211	Meldon Leslie	Carl Reynolds	Hazel Connolly	....	J T Miller	W H Jack Miller	....
Taylor* (11)	CM	512 356-3675	George Ruzicka	Dan Mize	Sherry Morrison	David N Weber	Haywood Stanford Jr	Stafford Bengtson	....
Taylor Lake Village (4)	MC	713 474-2843	Marta R Greytok	....	Alice C Riley	....	....	John E Terrill	....
Teague (3)	MC	817 739-2504	Clydell R Webb	Emory D Partin	Emory D Partin	Emory D Partin	Leslie Welch	Robert Slaughter	Fred McKinley
Temple* (42)	CM	817 778-5561	John F Sammons Jr	Barney L Knight	Jorge Cruz-Aedo	Jorge Cruz-Aedo	Wallace A Bearor	Thomas H Vannoy	Leonard Henry
Terrell* (13)	CM	214 563-2681	John R Briggs Jr	Michael H Talbot	Bobby Bishop	J O Springer	Michael J Roscoe	Jim Donaldson	....
Terrell Hills (5)	CM	512 824-7401	George C Mead	Meredith E Murphy	Meredith E Murphy	Meredith E Murphy	Arnold Rose	Barney R Flowers	Meredith E Murphy
Texarkana* (31)	CM	214 794-3434	Durwood Swanger	H Russell Crider	Christie Hardin	Clint Harper	B J Fox	Wm H McGee	Bill Kimzey
Texas City (41)	CO	409 948-3111	E F Lowry	....	Bobby Earle	E F Lowry	Roy McKinney	Joe M Standley	George Stapelton
The Colony* (12)	CM	214 370-1756	Larry D Sample	Janice Carroll	Janet Gadd	Janice Carroll	Ronnie Gothard	N C Ristagno	....
Tomball t (4)	MC	713 351-5484	Lee Tipton	Don R Badeaux	Kathy L Morgan	Jerold Judkowitz	Daniel Matt	Derwood Kennedy	Don R Badeaux
Tulia* (5)	CM	806 995-3547	T A Hayhurst	Marshall Shelton	Barbara Cabe	Marshall Shelton	Louis Bice	Tom Rolen	Kenneth McCaslin
Tyler* (71)	CM	214 597-6651	Charles R Halstead	Gary E Gwyn	Ann Lanier	H V Bryan	Jerry Weaver	Larry Robinson	Tom Mallory
Universal City* (11)	CM	512 659-0333	Bruce A Barnard	Michael A Tanner	....	Karl D McCormick	Ross V Wallace	Albert J Lilly	Steve C Steinmetz
University Park* (22)	CM	214 363-1644	Edward J Drake	Leland Nelson	Leland Nelson	Robert E Hicks Jr	David Beidelman	David Beidelman	Jim Murphy
Uvalde* (14)	CM	512 278-3315	John H Harrell	James Thurmond	James Thurmond	Delia Hernandez	Charles Ham	Vance Chisum	C G Graham
Van Horn† (3)	CM	915 283-2050	Okey D Lucas	Rebecca L Brewster	Rebecca L Brewster	Rebecca L Brewster	Lyndon McDonald	....	Manuel Urias
Vernon* (13)	CM	817 552-2581	George E Maxon Jr	Fred H Hays	Paul Hawkins	Robert Eskridge	Charles Stewart	Wayne Hendrix	....
Victoria* (51)	CM	512 573-2401	Ted B Reed	James J Miller	Virginia K Beller	Charles E Windwehen	Henry C Juenke	K A Rosenquest	Richard A Voigt
Vidor† (12)	MC	409 769-5473	Dru Stephenson	Jenny Norris	....	....	Bill Gier	J L Reynolds	Robert Ewart
Waco* (101)	CM	817 756-6161	Malcolm Duncan	David F Smith Jr	Nana Cornwell	Robert H Salter	Robert Mercer	Larry Scott	C Wayne Dickens
Wake Village (4)	MC	214 838-0515	Patrick A Cherry	....	Montrose Ardeneaux	Patrick A Cherry	Larry Graves	Derrell T Hampton	....
Watauga (10)	MC	817 281-8047	Virgil Anthony Sr	W E Keating	Nancy J Meadows	W E Keating	Larry Glover	W E Keating	Richard Bee
Waxahachie* (15)	CM	214 937-7330	John Snider	Robert W Sokoll	Nancy J Ross	Mary Winn	Wendel Presler	Pierce Padgett Jr	Jack Matthews
Weatherford* (12)	CM	817 594-5441	Tom Vick	Kenneth Reneau	Gloria C Wood	Bill Davis	George Teague	Elwood Hoherz	Edgar Banks
Weimar* (2)	CM	409 725-8554	Tommy Brasher	F E Parks	Gene Rosenauer	F E Parks	Wilbur Grohmann Jr	Joey Stan Targac	Frankie Vana
Wellington (3)	MC	806 447-2363	Ralph Owens	Glen Taylor	Nell McKinney	Glen Taylor	Danny Gray	....	Eddie Davis
Weslaco* (19)	CM	512 968-3181	Hector Farias	....	Hilda R Adame	Minerva Martinez	Tony Abrigo	Gerald Jacobs	Juan P Flores
West Columbia* (4)	CM	409 345-3123	M A Brooks	....	Vicki S Knight	Vicki S Knight	R B Loggins III	Earl Winebrenner	....
West Orange (5)	MC	713 883-3468	Glenn F Seale	Walter Schexnyder	Tammy Willis	Walter Schexnyder	Bert Aven	Toney Taylor	Walter Schexnyder
West University Place* (12)	CM	713 668-4441	Marla Forristall	Richard Rockenbaugh	Ms Lee Lockard	Donna Sims	Terry Stevenson	Walter Snitken	....
Westworth Village (4)	MC	817 738-3673	Harry Ward	....	Debbie Wilkins	....	Frank Brock	Noel Lewis	....
Wharton* (9)	CM	409 532-2491	Donald R Carlson	Don E Taylor	D T Fordham	Elizabeth Bayliss	Ray Williamson	Jack O Kemp	V O Hollingsworth
White Oak t (4)	MC	214 759-3936	Marshall Cline	....	Sue Spruell	....	James Nall	Payton Hass	Dewayne Ham
White Settlement* (14)	CM	817 246-4971	James M Herring	Mike Groomer	Frances Colwell	....	Mike Burris	Glenn Tischler	Bob Salinas
Whitesboro t (3)	MC	214 564-3311	Charles Winchester	Faye Lynn Anderson	Sammie Nell Hedges	....	Ricky Baugh	Donald L Morgan	Joseph M Fenton
Wichita Falls* (94)	CM	817 322-5611	Gary D Cook	James P Berzina	Wilma J Thomas	Fred L Werner	Jim Jameson	Curtis R Harrelson	....
Wills Point (3)	MC	214 873-2578	Robert W Gilbreth	Wilson Read	Nancy A Browber	....	C C Girdley	B J McDonald	....
Windcrest (5)	MC	512 655-0022	Robert O Whitmore	....	Lillian D Burrowes	Robert O Whitmore	Stephen Takas	C H Grumbles	....
Winnsboro (3)	MC	214 342-5312	John G Cain	L E Guess Jr	Linda Miller	....	Harvey Welch	Gary Lile	Charles Stephens
Winters* (3)	CM	915 754-4424	W Lee Colburn	V Scott Epperson	LaMoyne Moore	V Scott Epperson	Johnny Merrill	L C Foster	....
Woodville t (3)	MC	713 283-2182	(not reporting)						
Woodway* (7)	CM	817 772-4480	Paul Hubbard	John T Lynch Jr	Margie Barker	Carl S Dossey	Joe Grubessich	Lloyd A Behm	Dean Conner
Wylie* (3)	CM	214 442-2236	John W Akin	Gus H Pappas	Carolyn Jones	....	Larry Allen	Royce D Abbott	....
Yoakum* (6)	CM	512 293-5481	M W Harbus Jr	Terry K Roberts	Dorothy R Moore	Charlotte R Morrow	Phillip R Baker	Thomas P Linn	....
UTAH (66)									
Alpine (3)	MC	801 756-6347	(not reporting)						
American Fork (12)	MC	801 756-3571	Malcolm H Beck	Robert W Warnick	Robert W Warnick	Carl Wanlass	Paul Peters	Randy Johnson	G Preston Taylor
Blanding (3)	MC	801 678-2791	(not reporting)						
Bountiful* (33)	CM	801 298-6140	Dean S Stahle	Thomas R Hardy	Arden F Jenson	Ira Todd	Jerry Lemon	Larry D Higgins	Jack Balling
Brigham City (16)	MC	801 734-2001	Peter C Knudson	Roger K Handy	Michael T Cosgrove	....	Lee D Packer	Jay M Herbert	Roland F Nuetzman
Cedar City§ (11)	MC	801 586-6514	Robert H Linford	Joe Melling	Jacqueline Bulloch	Marilyn Prince	David Bentley	Dennis Anderson	John Corry
Centerville (8)	MC	801 295-3477	Neil L Blackburn	Mark R Palesh	Suzanne B Wright	Mark R Palesh	....	Clifford Russell	Randy K Randall
Clearfield* (18)	CM	801 773-3301	Neldon E Hamblin	Don W Baird	Bonnie Hodge	Bonnie Hodge	Roger M Bodily	Daren Green	Sherman Schofield
Clinton§ (6)	MC	801 825-5398	Dennis C Smith	Nolan K Young	Jennette Wood	Nolan K Young	Lloyd H Brown	Leroy E Webb	Mel H Wood
Draper (6)	MC	801 571-4121	Glen B Cannon	Andrew Hatton-Ward	....	Barbara L Sadler	Calvin R Allen	F R Long	Tom L Spencer
Ephraim (3)	MC	801 283-4631	(not reporting)						
Farmington† (5)	CM	801 451-2383	Merrill R Petty	Max Forbush	Lynette Bingham	Donna Scharp	Don C Ball	Val J Morton	A Ron Nelson
Fruit Heights (3)	MC	801 546-0861	Dean O Brand	Ray W Phillips	Belva M Provost	....	....	....	....
Grantsville (4)	MC	801 884-3411	Fred L Hale	....	Patricia Hunter	....	Butch Barton	Richard Maycock	....
Heber (4)	MC	801 654-0757	Jan T Furner	....	Eleanor J Duke	....	Steven G Ivie	Bobby L Nelson	Bob J Muir
Helper (3)	MC	801 472-5391	Robert E Olsen	....	Lucy Richeda	....	James Pugliese	Karl Stavar	....
Hyrum (4)	MC	801 245-6033	Bruce E Darley	....	D Brent Jensen	D Brent Jensen	Kent Larsen	....	Derle Nielsen
Kaysville (10)	MC	801 546-1235	Gerald A Purdy	John W Thacker	Linda Ross	John W Thacker	Don Howard	Lyle Larkins	Max B Major
Layton† (26)	MC	801 544-3441	Lewis G Shields	Randall J Heaps	Randall J Heaps	Randall J Heaps	John H Adams	Lamar T Chard	Terry R Coburn
Lehi† (7)	MC	801 768-3545	Garry R Sampson	Gary H Lewis	....	Joyce S Wilson	Grant B Smith	William L Gibbs	Karl E Webb
Lindon (3)	MC	801 785-5043	Kenneth D McMillan	Wendyl L Jarvis	Wendyl L Jarvis	Wendyl L Jarvis	....	....	William G Green
Logan (27)	MC	801 752-3060	Newel G Daines Jr	....	Venal Jones	Donald L Fulton	Albern L Allen	Ferris Groll	Ray Hugie
Mapleton (3)	MC	801 489-5744	Wendell B Johnson	Marjorie M Stokes	Grace Bennett	Harold V Gividen	Gene Nielsen	Michael J Taylor	Kent Wheeler
Midvale (10)	MC	801 561-1418	Trent G Jeppson	David G Jorgensen	David G Jorgensen	....	Merrill Ross	Gerald W Maughan	Duane D Goodyear
Moab (5)	CM	801 259-5121	Thomas A Stocks	Thomas A Stocks	....	Lynda Moore	Troy Black	Daniel K Ison	Ross Leech
Monticello* (2)	CM	801 587-2271	Keith Redd	Richard C Terry	Shirley Redd	Richard C Terry	John Himmelberger	Everett Johnson	Clyde Christensen
Murray (26)	CO	801 262-2421	Larell D Muir	....	Ludell P Pierson	Clifford J Brown	Wendell Coombs	Calvin Gillen	Charles D Clay
Nephi (3)	MC	801 623-0822	Robert Steele	J Randy McKnight	Faye Greenhalgh	J Randy McKnight	Vard White	B Wayne Hoaldridge	Gary Howarth
North Ogden† (9)	MC	801 782-7211	Don F Colvin	Dennis R Shupe	Cleo M Christensen	Cecil E Robinson	Terry Call	Polo Afuvai	Dale E Chatelain
North Salt Lake (6)	MC	801 298-3877	Robert D Palmquist	Collin H Wood	Collin H Wood	Debra Kimber	Earl Littlewood	Val Wilson	Ray C Rasmussen

Directory 1/10 continued — MUNICIPAL OFFICIALS IN ALL U.S. CITIES OVER 2,500[1]

City, 1980 population (000 omitted), form of government		Municipal phone number	Mayor	Appointed administrator	City clerk	Finance officer	Fire chief	Police chief	Public works director
UTAH (66) continued									
Ogden* (64)	CM	801 399-8301	Robert A Madsen	B Cowles Mallory	Donna Adam	J Norman Burden	Joe Hilton	Joseph H Ritchie	Edgar Reed
Orem* (52)	CM	801 224-7000	Delance W Squire	Daryl Berlin	Phillip C Goodrich	Phillip C Goodrich	R Ted Peacock	R Ted Peacock	John W Jones
Panquitch§† (1)	MC	801 676-2311	....	K Bruce Fullmer	....	....	....	....	....
Park City§ (3)	MC	801 649-9321	John Green Jr	Arlene B Loble	....	Donn Kaynor	....	Frank Bell	Jerry W Gibbs
Payson§ (8)	MC	801 465-9226	Gary D Tassainer	Rodney W Watkins	....	Ronal J Crump	Blair Andreason	James E Box	....
Pleasant Grove (11)	MC	801 785-5045	David R Holdaway	Mark Johnson	Robert Williams	Mark Johnson	Frank Mills	Michael Ferre	Frank Mills
Pleasant View (4)	MC	801 782-8529	Peary B Barker	....	G W Downs	....	....	Rex Cragun	Paul Ellsworth
Price§ (9)	MC	801 637-5010	Art L Martines	Jeffrey W Killian	P Hampton McArthur	P Hampton McArthur	David A Barrett	Luther Owings	Vern Jones
Providence (3)	MC	801 752-9441	Clyde F Braegger	....	Kathleen H Gale	....	....	....	Darrell L Bodrero
Provo (74)	MC	801 375-1822	James E Ferguson	Chester L Waggener	Jean Eklund	George Karlsven	Boyd Carter	Swen C Nielsen	Nicholas Jones
Richfield*† (5)	CM	801 896-6439	Sue Marie Young	Woody Farnsworth	Marial Peterson	Woody Farnsworth	Stan Poulson	G Duane Ross	Jerry Watts
Riverdale (4)	MC	801 394-5541	L Leon Poulsen	James M Young	James M Young	James M Young	....	Glen Clarey	....
Riverton (7)	MC	801 254-0704	Dale F Gardiner	Michael Siler	Sandra Lloyd	....	Robert L Webster	John Patience	Richard Mumford
Roosevelt§ (4)	MC	801 722-5001	Lawrence Yack	Glen K Vernon	Carolyn Krissman	Jerry Murray	Edwin Richmond	Cecil Gurr	Bernell Buchanan
Roy§† (20)	MC	801 825-2205	Jack F Pierce	Richard Kirkwood	Richard Kirkwood	Richard Kirkwood	Richard Waters	Julian R Green	Max A Reeves
Salem§ (2)	MC	801 423-2770	Harold E Davis	....	Paul J Hair	Paul J Hair	Erman Stone	Dean W Wolf	Michael P Swenson
Salt Lake City (163)	CO	801 535-7611	Ted L Wilson	Albert E Haines	Kathryn Marshall	Lance Bateman	Peter O Pederson	E L Willoughby	Palmer DePaulis
Sandy City§ (51)	MC	801 566-1561	Lawrence P Smith	David F Dixon	Shirley Bloxham	Arthur Hunter	William Clough	Anton C Gustin	Randy G Taylor
Smithfield (5)	MC	801 563-6226	Robert J Chambers	....	Betty J Hatch	....	Lyman Hansen	....	James P Gass
South Jordan (7)	MC	801 254-3742	T Kay Edmunds	Richard N Warne	Stephen L Ames	Richard N Warne	Ted W Sandstrom	Duane H Sutherland	Alden Winters
South Ogden (11)	MC	801 392-9321	Ralph Cottrell Jr	F Stanley Nielson	Kathy Vandrimmelen	Ida Mae Bankhead	James Minster	Jim Wold	Glen Moore
South Salt Lake (11)	MC	801 535-7113	James W Davis	....	Beth M Jensen	James W Davis	Robert W Adams	Val W Bess	James W Davis
Spanish Fork§ (10)	MC	801 798-3568	Enoch A Ludlow	David A Oyler	Clyde A Swenson	Clyde A Swenson	Allen Jarvis	James McGowan	David A Oyler
Springville† (12)	MC	801 489-5121	John T Marshall	....	Verl S Dallin	....	Merlin Fox	Leland Bowers	Carl Curtis
St. George§ (11)	MC	801 673-3593	Karl Brooks	Gary Esplin	Maxine Smith	Joe Vincent	Wayne Houston	Joseph K Hutchings	Larry Bulloch
Sunset† (6)	MC	801 825-1628	Norm Sant	....	George Dickson	Larry Ashdown	Arley J Wallace	Archie Searle	Jerry Ellsworth
Syracuse (4)	MC	801 825-1477	Boyd T Thurgood	Phil C Barber	Joann Roberts	Boyd T Thurgood	Roy Miya	John W Gardiner	Blaine McDermott
Tooele§ (14)	MC	801 882-0110	George Diehl	....	Blanche Pratt	Paul V Kroff	Thomas T Tate	Jesse Peterson	Joe Busico
Tremonton (3)	MC	801 257-3324	G Melvin Foxley	....	W Paul Buys III	W Paul Buys III	Norvel Estep	Ronald Ogborn	Garry Carter
Vernal* (7)	CM	801 789-2255	Samuel Snyder	Kenneth L Bassett	Kenneth L Bassett	Harley R Hales	Dale Slaugh	Robert Downard	Kay Overson
Washington Terrace (8)	MC	801 393-8681	Lola R Morgan	....	Sheralle L Ito	Sheralle L Ito	David W Parkinson	Gary W Tracy	Richard E Nelson
Washington (3)	MC	801 628-1666	Robert A Slack	James A Reams	....	James A Reams	Richard Wilcox	Brent Chandler	Roy Reidhead
West Bountiful† (4)	MC	801 292-4486	Grant H Secrist	....	....	....	....	....	....
West Jordan* (27)	CM	801 561-1463	Dennis Randall	Ronald L Olson	Betty Kim Smith	Betty Kim Smith	Kal Farr	Kal Farr	Darrell Jones
West Valley City§ (73)	MC	801 974-5501	Gerald K Maloney	John D Newman Jr	Kathleen B Kaumans	Russell Sanderson	Darrell McIlrath	David Campbell	Glenn Weaver
Woods Cross† (4)	MC	801 292-4421	Lawrence W Urry	....	Alan P Low	....	....	Niles Stahle	....
VERMONT (72)									
Barre t* (7)	CM	802 479-9391	Mayo Sanborn	Paul D McGinley	Ruth A Finn	Ruth A Finn	J Rene Larouche	Raymond Jacobs	Curtis L Spring
Barre* (10)	CM	802 476-5246	Robert A Bergeron	Richard H Cate	Vico F Masi	Vico F Masi	Thomas F Venner	David I Palmer Jr	Reginald T Abare
Barton t (3)	TM	802 525-6222	Wallace Russell Jr	....	Doris L Kennison	Doris L Kennison	Howard Damon	....	Bickford Libby
Bellows Falls v*† (3)	CM	802 463-3964	James Tolaro	Lawrence McAuliffe	Patricia Lucia	....	John Wood Jr	Francis Aumand III	Maurice Kelly
Bennington t§ (16)	TM	802 447-1171	Timothy R Corcoran	James H Colvin	Mary Hodeck	William Hartington	Francis A Buck	Peter D Barton	Merton Cross
Bethel t* (2)	TM	802 234-9340	Richard Edmonds	Theodore M Nelson	Jean Burnham	Theodore M Nelson	Robert M Dean	Theodore M Nelson	Theodore M Nelson
Brandon t* (4)	CM	802 247-3635	Brian River	Patricia J Scott	Wilda Harris	Wilda Harris	Murray Knapp	....	Patricia J Scott
Brattleboro t* (12)	CM	802 257-5262	Hugh Bronson	Corwin S Elwell	Wardner C Angell	David M Sichel	T Howard Mattison	Marcel H Leclaire	Orman A Holden
Bristol t*† (3)	CM	802 453-2486	....	R W Smith	....	....	....	....	....
Bristol v*† (2)	CM	802 453-2410	....	R W Smith	....	....	....	....	....
Burlington† (38)	MC	802 862-5719	Bernard Sanders	....	James E Rader	Jonathan Leopold	Patrick T Brown	Richard E Beaulieu	James R Ogden
Castleton t* (4)	TM	802 468-5319	Eleanor Anderson	Betty Wheeler	Sara Grey	Robert McClure	Patrick Traverse	George Traverse	....
Cavendish v*† (1)	CM	802 226-7291	....	Rolf Van Schaik	Ronald Butler Jr	Ronald Butler Sr	Arthur Briggs	....	Joe Blanchard
Cavendish t*† (1)	CM	802 226-7291	Gary W Lazetera	Rolf Van Schaik	Ronald Butler Jr	Ronald Butler Sr	Arthur Briggs	....	Joe Blanchard
Charlotte t (3)	TM	802 425-3071	(not reporting)						
Chester t*† (3)	TM	802 875-2173	....	Prentice F Hammond	Sandra K Walker	Sandra K Walker	Arnold Stoddard	Gilbert E Carey	....
Colchester t* (13)	CM	802 655-0811	Robert Campbell	Francis J Taginski	Maxine McGinn	Coral Coleman	....	Charles Kirker	John Douglas
Derby t (4)	TM	802 766-4906	George Fuller	....	Pauline S Glover	Pauline S Glover	Craig Ellam	....	Curtis Brainard
Dorset t* (2)	CM	802 362-1178	William Mahlmann	Vernon C Squiers	Denise Hebert	....	....	....	....
Essex t* (14)	TM	802 879-0413	Peter Lyon	Kevin D Ryan	Jane M Yandow	....	George Bartley	John Terry	Dennis Lutz
Essex Junction v* (7)	CM	802 878-6944	William Adams	William K Dugan	Susan Hill	Gerald Malloy	Joseph Jacob	....	Craig L Cushing
Fair Haven t* (3)	CM	802 265-3610	John Tobin	Albert M Paulger	Caroline Levesque	Albert M Paulger	Donald Ward	Andrew Brown	....
Georgia t (3)	TM	802 524-2739	(not reporting)						
Hardwick t* (3)	TM	802 472-6120	Wyman Lanphear	Larry R Wood	Gerald S Hall	Larry R Wood	Erwin Gilcris	Donald R Stubbs	Larry R Wood
Hartford t* (8)	CM	802 295-9353	Stephen V P Mairs	Ralph W Lehman	Deborah A Adams	Robert A Simonds	Walter O Morancy	Alfonzo Guarino	....
Hartland t* (2)	TM	802 436-2119	Larry J Frazer	Hiram E Allen	Mary W Davis	Mary W Davis	William Riley	Leonard Eastman	....
Hinesburg t† (3)	TM	802 482-2281	Larry B Stevens	....	Gay A Muller	Gay A Muller	Bernard A Giroux	....	Stan J Bissonette
Jericho t† (4)	TM	802 899-4936	Donald B Fay	....	Phyllis Farrell	....	Randall Clark	....	....
Johnson t (3)	TM	802 635-2611	(not reporting)						
Ludlow t* (2)	CM	802 228-2841	Thomas Lazerta	Dean R Brown Jr	Jane Creaser	Dean R Brown Jr	Richard Harrison	Dan C Harvie	John T Davis
Ludlow v* (1)	TM	802 228-2841	Herbert B Vanguilde	Dean R Brown Jr	Dorothy S Bragg	Dean R Brown Jr	Richard Harrison	Dan C Halvie	John T Davis
Lyndon t† (5)	TM	802 626-5785	Douglas Townsend	....	Robert E Lawrence	....	Wendall P Cassady	J Leo Desjardins	....
Manchester t* (3)	CM	802 362-1313	Orland Campbell Jr	Harry J Henderson	Barbara Cross	David Feilding	Laurence Grant	W Manfred Wessner	....
Middlebury t* (8)	TM	802 388-4041	George W Foster	Richard A McGuire	Richard A Goodro	Richard A McGuire	Ralph Hayes Sr	Al Watson	George Gline
Milton t* (7)	TM	802 893-6655	Marty Branch	V Michael Duffy	John P Cushing	John P Cushing	Mike Adams	....	V Michael Duffy
Montpelier* (8)	CM	802 223-3031	Frank D Romano	John A MacLean	Jean R Hart	Jean R Hart	Ernest C Flanders	Douglas S Hoyt	Stephen A Gray
Morristown t (4)	TM	802 888-5147	Brian Greenia	Paul W Hughes	Sydney Mander	Carol Bradley	Wayne Camley	Lawrence C Laclair	....
Newport* (5)	CM	802 334-5136	Betty Jane Durkee	Peter Robinson	Charles Blake	....	Leo Parenteau	Curtis Hardy	Raymond Norris Jr
North Troy v*† (1)	CM	802 988-2663	....	Howard Cota	....	....	....	....	....
Northfield t*† (5)	CM	802 485-6121	David A MacDougall	Edgar C Gadbois	Martha Mahan	Martha Mahan	James Demasi	Burton C Sanders	....
Northfield v*† (2)	CM	802 485-6121	Bertha Pierce	Edgar C Gadbois	Richard L Cleveland	Richard L Cleveland	....	....	....
Poultney t* (3)	CM	802 287-9751	Morris Panoushek	Paul H Hermann	Josephine Williams	Josephine Williams	James Jordan	....	....
Poultney v* (2)	CM	802 287-4003	William D Lenz II	Charles Shenkel	Patricia J Roberts	....	James Jordan Jr	....	....
Pownal t (3)	TM	802 823-7757	Henry M Strohmaier	....	Rachel Mason	....	....	....	....
Randolph t* (5)	CM	802 728-5433	Lawrence Townsend	Ken Mencier	Doris M Bowman	Doris M Bowman	....	....	....
Richmond t (3)	TM	802 434-2221	(not reporting)						
Rockingham t* (6)	CM	802 463-3964	John Cook	Lawrence McAuliffe	Rita M Bruce	Lawrence McAuliffe	Denis Jeffrey	....	Harold Dodge
Rutland† (18)	MC	802 773-2000	John J Daley	....	Rosemary F Finley	Ronald J Graves	Richard M Barron	Charles Spoon	Thomas G Macaulay
Rutland t (3)	TM	802 773-2528	(not reporting)						
Shaftsbury t (3)	TM	802 442-4038	(not reporting)						
Shelburne t*† (5)	TM	802 985-2342	William A R Deming	Bert Moffatt	Colleen T Haag	Colleen T Haag	F Galipeau Jr	Wendell Worth	....
Sherburne t* (1)	TM	802 422-3241	Enrico Monti	David W Lewis	Josephine Blanchard	Patricia Keim	....	....	....

Directory 1/10 continued — MUNICIPAL OFFICIALS IN ALL U.S. CITIES OVER 2,500[1]

City, 1980 population (000 omitted), form of government		Municipal phone number	Mayor	Appointed administrator	City clerk	Finance officer	Fire chief	Police chief	Public works director
VERMONT (72) continued									
South Burlington* (11)	CM	802 658-7953	Paul A Farrar	Wm J Szymanski	Margaret A Picard	....	James W Goddette	Richard G Carter	Albert C Audette
Springfield t* (10)	TM	802 885-2104	Kenneth J Robinson	Paul W Ruse Jr	Bonnie B Greer	Paul W Ruse Jr	Ernest Lamphere	Francis Chadbourne	Jeffery E Slade
St. Albans* (7)	CM	802 524-2511	Floyd E Handy	James B Pignona	Patricia M Bronson	Jacques Bergeron	Reginald Austin	James W Warden	William H Scott Jr
St. Albans t (4)	CM	802 524-2415	Fred Bonnett	....	Eleanor G Goodrich	Eleanor G Goodrich	Roy Parah	....	John Blouin
St. Johnsbury t* (8)	CM	802 748-3926	Maurice Chaloux	David T Clark	N D Sleeper	N D Sleeper	Jerald Fournier	W Bruce Pratt	David T Clark
Stowe t (3)	TM	802 253-7350	Herbert J O'Brien	Leo V Clark	Marie N Betterley	Marie N Betterley	Wendall M Mansfield	Kenneth W Libby	David H Lavanway
Swanton v (3)	CM	802 868-3397	Leon Babbie	Orman E Croft	Carol N Edwards	....	Marcus Bostwick Sr	William Leahy	Harvey Amilhat
Swanton t (5)	TM	802 868-4421	Girard Lamphere	....	Francisco G Cavazos	....	....	....	....
Troy t*† (1)	TM	802 988-2663	....	Howard Cota	....	....	....	....	....
Waterbury t*† (4)	TM	802 244-7033	Edward Steele	Robert W Winchell	Edward Finn	Claude Baucher	Sydney Thurston	....	Robert W Winchell
Weathersfield t (3)	TM	802 674-2626	John R Fuller	Ernest Torpey	Helen W May	Carolyn Johnson	Rodney Spaulding	Douglas Howe	Ernest Torpey
West Rutland t* (2)	TM	802 438-2263	Daniel Deuel	William H Finger	Vic Sevigny	William H Finger	Joe Skaza Jr	Bob Geryk	William H Finger
Westminster t§† (2)	TM	802 722-4255	John F H Cook	William E O'Connor	Betty J Holton	....	Robert Lober	....	....
Williamstown t* (2)	TM	802 433-6671	Donald Brown	J Leo Donahue	Helen Murray	Helen Murray	Stuart Riddel	....	....
Williston t (4)	TM	802 878-5121	John C Heins	....	Arlene H Degree	Arlene H Degree	Howard Lunderville	Howard Lunderville	Emerson J Miles
Wilmington t* (2)	CM	802 464-8591	Jean Canedy	Sonia DeLury	Mari-Lou Rich	Janice Karwoski	Brian Johnson	....	Albert O'Neil
Windsor t* (4)	CM	802 674-6786	Wesley Hrydziusko	Harold R Sanders	Gertrude S McGuire	Nancy M Husband	Bruce W Stearns	Thomas T Taylor	Duane C Bandy
Winooski* (6)	CM	802 655-0571	Donald R Brunelle	Brendan S Keleher	Pauline K Schmoll	Pauline K Schmoll	Joseph Bourgeois	Armand R Vallee	Jerry O'Neal
Woodstock t* (3)	CM	802 457-3456	John L Audsley	Albert Gray Jr	Fred A Doubleday	Scott Dudley	James Paul	Paul West	Albert Gray Jr
Woodstock v* (1)	CM	802 457-3456	W Smith Thompson	Albert Gray Jr	Donald Wheeler	Scott Dudley	....	Paul K Chase Jr	Albert Gray Jr
VIRGINIA (91)									
Abingdon t* (4)	CM	703 628-3167	French H Moore Jr	Graham M Newman	Graham M Newman	Graham M Newman	H M McCormick Jr	William S Phillips	Claude M Vernon Jr
Alexandria* (103)	CM	703 838-4000	Chas E Beatley Jr	Douglas Harman	Helen Holleman	....	James Hicks	Charles Strobel	Dayton L Cook
Altavista t* (4)	CM	804 369-5001	D M Holland	S I Goldsmith	Ms B C Smither	Ms B C Smither	Jeffery A Cocke	Thomas L Neal	Clarence Dawson Sr
Appalachia t* (2)	CM	703 565-1174	James Clark	E E Brooks	Ms M D Reece	E E Brooks	R W Blair	....	Bobby G Reynolds
Arlington County*† (153)	CM	703 558-2401	Ellen M Bozman	Larry J Brown	Jean C Julian	Anton S Gardner	Thomas M Hawkins	William K Stover	H S Hulme Jr
Ashland t* (5)	CM	804 798-9219	Richard S Gillis	David W Reynal	Betty K Kennon	Harold W Mitchell	Wesley Carneal	John M Wolford	Gene W Hatcher
Bedford* (6)	CM	703 586-8974	James D Harvey	Jack A Gross	Teresa W Hatcher	C D Klotz Jr	J H Howard	T E King	....
Berryville t* (2)	CM	703 955-1099	J C Huffman	Stephen F Owen	Desiree A Allder	Stephen F Owen	Wayne R Whetzel	D Elden Nesselrodt	James E O'Brien
Big Stone Gap t* (5)	CM	703 523-0115	Jerry R Jessee	George R Polly	Joyce M Collins	George R Polly	W R Mumpower	Michael J Bentoski	George R Polly
Blacksburg t* (31)	CM	703 961-1100	Roger Hedgepeth	C Robert Stripling	Donna W Boone	Mervyn Timberlake	Keith Bolte	Donald L Carey	Randy W Bartlett
Blackstone t* (4)	CM	804 292-7251	James S Harris	Richard Lee	Ercelle P Dewey	Richard Lee	Wallace Hardaway	Wayne S Shields	Fred Sanger
Bluefield t* (6)	CM	703 322-4626	Cecile S Richardson	Alfred C Mead Jr	Alfred C Mead Jr	Harry Burton	E L Honaker	Jack W Asbury	James F Mayo
Bridgewater t† (3)	MC	703 828-3390	Roland Z Arey	Bob Holton	Sandra Caricofe	Nancy Price	John Bill Humes	Mark Payne	Bob Holton
Bristol* (19)	CM	703 466-2221	James F Rector	Hugh G Cooper	Emmett M Hoover	Hugh G Cooper	Charles Denton	Thomas W Stone Jr	W A Stephenson
Buena Vista* (7)	CM	703 261-6121	Harold F Kidd	Larry M Foster	Mary B Shaner	Curtis F Higgins	David Grow	Erskin K Campbell	Roy Coleman
Cape Charles t* (2)	CM	804 331-3259	Herman M Brown	Charles C Saddler	Elise H Dodd	....	Rodney Lewis	Charles J Powell	Norman Bell
Charlottesville* (45)	CM	804 971-3100	Francis L Buck	Cole Hendrix	Jeanne Cox	Robert Sheets	Julian Taliaferro	John Dekoven Bowen	John V Berberich
Chase City t* (3)	CM	804 372-5136	Charles L Duckworth	Fred A Darden	Cynthia G Gordon	Rickey G Reese	C Wayne Carter	Fred A Parsons	Jack Pruett Jr
Chatham t* (1)	CM	804 432-9515	Andrew W Todd	....	Margie H Dawson	Margie H Dawson	Landon Worsham	William D Thomas	Sherman Calloway
Chesapeake* (114)	CM	804 547-6166	S M Oman	....	Betty Calloway	J A Sibley	R G Bagley	R A Lakoski	John A O'Connor
Christiansburg t* (10)	CM	703 382-6128	Joe B Hornbarger	John E Lemley	Frank P Bersch	Jackie Sue Epperly	James W Epperly	Alvin L Hale	Robert M Gearheart
Clarksville t* (1)	CM	804 374-8178	Robert E Buchanan	Carl G Dean	Patricia S Yeates	Patricia S Yeates	Raymond Hite	Wayne Hogan	A Marshall Owen
Clifton Forge* (5)	CM	703 863-5091	George R Goode Sr	Roger D Baker	V Craig Hudson	Robert B Deaton	Sidney A Tyler	Dorsey G Huffman Jr	Donald E Allen
Coeburn t (3)	CM	703 395-3323	Harold L Ringley	Terry L Gibson	Sherry B McConnell	Sherry B McConnell	Randy Holbrook	Harold Markham	Terry L Gibson
Colonial Heights* (17)	CM	804 526-7506	James B McNeer	Robert E Taylor	Dolores Elmore	John H Mitchell	Robert E Williams	R B Ellison	Robert V Cawthorne
Covington* (9)	CM	703 962-4984	James L Jamison	Richard C Flora	Brenda Falls	Ray Heironimus	Gerald Burks	Donald Leet	
Crewe t* (2)	CM	804 645-9453	H L Taylor Jr	V C Bozman	Louise Shown	V C Bozman	Carlton Moore	Tony Shelton	V C Bozman
Culpeper t* (7)	CM	703 825-4700	Richard M Rosenberg	Jack E Dorman Jr	Guilford W Griffin	Gloria C Mills	Irvin Breeden	Charles B Jones	W T Beales
Danville* (46)	CM	804 799-5100	Samuel A Kushner Jr	....	Aubrey D Dodson	Aubrey D Dodson	W C Bray	....	W Victor Cousins
Dumfries t (3)	MC	703 221-3400	Olney A Brawner		Retta Ladd	Joann F Amidon	....	Harvey C Anderson	
Emporia* (5)	CM	804 634-3332	William H Ligon	Tedd E Povar	Nell Mitchell	Tedd E Povar	Warren C Rawlings	Elmer L Grizzard	Linwood Pope
Fairfax* (19)	CM	703 385-7855	George T Snyder Jr	Edward A Wyatt	Jacqueline Mauro	Edward J Cawley Jr	Harold E Dailey	Loyd W Smith	James Shull
Falls Church* (10)	CM	703 241-5100	Carol W Delong	Anthony H Griffin	Mary C Gallagher	Halsey T Green III	Bruce V Turner	Stanley K Johnson	Richard J Durgin
Farmville t* (6)	CM	804 392-5686	J David Crute	Gerald J Spates	Robert M Hazelwood	....	Phillip Gay	Otto S Overton	Eugene M Philbeck
Franklin* (7)	CM	804 562-4111	G Elliott Cobb Jr	Wayne G Reed	Wayne G Reed	Wayne G Reed	James M Wagenbach	J Grady Britt	David L Jones Jr
Fredericksburg* (15)	CM	703 373-5011	Lawrence A Davies	Peter R Kolakowski	Christie Pugh	Peter R Kolakowski	Carlyle Fines	Harry F Fleming Jr	R Wayne Brooks
Front Royal t* (11)	CM	703 635-3111	John K Marlow	Walter M Duncan	Vernon T Macturk	....	Robin B Cary	Milton L Robertson	Eugene Tewalt
Galax* (7)	CM	703 236-3441	Glenn G Wilson	W Harold Snead	W Harold Snead	Doris J Bedwell	Joe Crockett	B R Melton	Junior R Vass
Glasgow t* (1)	CM	703 258-2246	S H Blackburn	William S Knick	William S Knick	William S Knick	James McFadden	Richard Hostetter	William S Knick
Grundy t* (2)	CM	703 935-2551	W Miller Richardson	Gladys J Keen	Katie Yates	....	Ralph Hagy	Buford L Ratliff	Don Hawks
Hampton*† (123)	CM	804 727-6000	James L Eason	Thomas I Miller	Kathann Hollomon	Darlus Cook	Kenneth R Lavoie	Pat G Minetti	Frank Miller Jr
Harrisonburg* (20)	CM	703 434-6776	Walter F Green III	Marvin B Milam	N Arlene Loker	Beverly A Simmons	Larry W Shifflett	Richard W Presgrave	John Driver
Herndon t* (11)	CM	703 435-6800	Richard C Thoesen	Edwin D Martin	Mary E Ingram	Craig D Anderson	....	George W Winkel	David P Larsen
Hopewell* (23)	CM	804 541-2200	Hilda M Traina	Clinton H Strong	Mary F Pito	Philip R Grant	Edward L Bell	Robert G Broyles	Henry A Wilde
Lebanon t* (3)	CM	703 889-3191	George P Thomas	....	J Harold Jessee	....	Giles T Fields	....	....
Leesburg t* (8)	CM	703 777-2420	Robert E Sevila	John Niccolls	Dorothy B Rosen	Donald O Taylor		James M Kidwell	Juan F Chaves
Lexington* (7)	CM	703 463-7133	Charles F Phillips	John V Doane	Sandra Stuart	....	Keith Irvine	L O Sutton	David A Woody
Luray t* (4)	CM	703 743-5511	Ralph H Dean	Donald A Smith	Ethel Vaughan	Donald A Smith	Dan Seal	Jerry M Schiro	Rufus Breeden
Lynchburg* (67)	CM	804 847-1400	Jimmie B Bryan	Edgar A Culverhouse	Barbara J Gage	Michael W Hill	William A Anderson	C E Robertson	Raymond A Booth
Manassas* (15)	CM	703 335-8200	Edgar E Rohr	C M Moyer Jr	Ralph H Moore	Curtis L Mlsna	Wade C House	Samuel S Ellis	Clyde D Wimmer
Manassas Park* (7)	CM	703 361-0124	G Robert Maitland	Jerry W Davis	Lana A Conner	James E Norlund	Carl Winstead	Wilbur Hudson	Chet Lanum
Marion t* (7)	CM	703 783-4113	W W Scott Jr	Carl A Taylor	Ms C A Stump	Ms Dixie O Sheets	Stuart Buchanan	John H Grubb Jr	Bobby Cline
Martinsville* (18)	CM	703 638-3971	William C Cole Jr	Don R Edmonds	W Holladay Yeaman	Richard D Fitts	John Lloyd Gregory	Terry L Roop	George W Brown
Middleburg t§ (1)	MC	703 687-5152	Loyal D McMillin	Gerard F Rogers	Betty D Patterson	Jane C James	Edward C Swain	Charles E Craun	....
Narrows t* (3)	CM	703 726-3020	Edward G Skidmore	William C Rolfe	Ms C T Lloyd	Lois M Arrington	J Dunford	Daniel G Hare	Jerry Atwell
Newport News* (145)	CM	804 247-8411	Joseph C Ritchie	Robert T Williams	Bernice I Berry	Carter S Sullivan	T S Walls	Darrell W Stephens	Max T Palmer
Norfolk* (267)	CM	804 441-2000	Joseph A Leafe	Julian F Hirst	Louis S Hudgins	Jimmy D Clowers	Thomas E Gardner	Charles D Grant	Lawrence Gassman
Norton* (5)	CM	703 679-1160	George Hunnicutt	Charles R Brown	Jo Nosler	Ernest W Ward	Earle Brown	Samuel A Mongle	James C Hall
Orange t*† (3)	CM	703 672-1020	....	E L Lax	....	....	....	....	....
Pearisburg t* (2)	CM	703 921-1222	C J Taylor	John R Strutner	Judy R Harrell	Judy R Harrell	....	Ronald L Lemons	Glen W Allen
Petersburg* (41)	CM	804 733-6131	R Wilson Cheely	Richard M Brown	Barbara W Moore	Robertson Blount	M Russell Rakestraw	Lawrence R Nowery	M Guthrie Smith
Poquoson* (9)	CM	804 868-7151	Joseph K Bunting	Robert M Murphy	Judy F Wiggins	Frances C Firth	Jackie W Holloway	John T White	J L Montgomery
Portsmouth* (105)	CM	804 393-8641	James W Holley III	George L Hanbury	Corinna B Jeffreys	Roy W Cherry	Odell Benton	....	Ellis B Hilton
Pulaski t* (10)	CM	703 980-1000	Raymond F Ratcliff	Daniel E McKeever	Ruth A Harrell	Gary L Cutlip	William A Hall	Edgar J Williams	E L Early
Purcellville t§ (2)	MC	703 338-7421	Ronald M Masters	Gordon D Jones	Juanita S Rose	....	....	James Y Leake Sr	John W Creamer
Radford* (13)	CM	703 639-9626	Thomas Starnes	Robert P Asbury Jr	Roy I Lloyd	Jess W Cantline	Calvin C Whitt	James Whitt	James H Hurt

Directory 1/10 continued — MUNICIPAL OFFICIALS IN ALL U.S. CITIES OVER 2,500[1]

City, 1980 population (000 omitted), form of government		Municipal phone number	Mayor	Appointed administrator	City clerk	Finance officer	Fire chief	Police chief	Public works director
VIRGINIA (91) continued									
Richlands t* (6)	CM	703 964-2566	Paul E Cook	C P Mahaffey	Elva Lee Van Dyke	C P Mahaffey	Andrew Puckett	Jack F Young	George W Brown Jr
Richmond* (219)	CM	804 780-4000	Roy A West	Manuel Deese	Edgar A Duffy	Neal Evans	Ronald Lewis	Frank S Duling	Robert E Sarver
Roanoke* (100)	CM	703 981-2333	Noel C Taylor	H Bernhard Ewert	Mary L Parker	Joel M Schlanger	Jerry Kerley	M David Hooper	Thomas F Brady
Rocky Mount t (4)	MC	703 483-5243	Allen O Woody Jr	....	Nancy H Lynch	Nancy H Lynch	Danny Altice	Billy G Pickeral	H Hester Dudley
Salem* (24)	CM	703 375-3000	James E Taliaferro	W J Paxton Jr	R M Smith	Frank P Turk	Ronald T Hartman	Harry T Haskins Jr	....
Smithfield t* (4)	CM	804 357-3247	Armistead Jones	Elsey Harris Jr	Helen G Barrett	Helen G Barrett	J R Stallings	Claiborne A Havens	Wm Russell Batten
South Boston* (7)	CM	804 572-3621	William A Kent	J A Houghton	J A Houghton	S V Saunders	L W Osborne	B H Covington	G C Carrington Jr
South Hill t*† (4)	CM	804 447-3191	S H Raines	G Morris Wells Jr	....	Barbara H Hudson	Jimmy Crowder	G R Tolbert	Clarence Ezell
Staunton* (22)	CM	703 885-1251	Dolores Lescure	R Gene McCombs	Bette W Herr	Boyce Spinelli	William A Shaver	Phillip Ash	Frank S Wiggins
Strasburg t* (2)	CM	703 465-9197	Arthur Artz	Vincent Poling	Mary Taylor Price	Vincent Poling	William W Walton	James E Hall	John H Rhodes
Suffolk* (48)	CM	804 934-3111	Andrew B Damiani	John L Rowe Jr	Henry C Murden	Leon Johnson	J S Carter	Gilbert F Jackson	Thomas G Hines
Tappahannock t*† (2)	CM	804 443-3336	George C Clanton	George G Belfield	Beverley J Corrieri	George G Belfield	Edwin Smith	....	Ernest J King
Tazewell t*† (4)	CM	703 988-2501	Lockard E Conley	Dean Henderson	Lucy P Cruey	....	A D Buchanan	Brown Harman Jr	Alfred Webb
Victoria t* (2)	CM	804 696-2343	Harry A Wellons	Robert W Williams	Hazel J Abbitt	Shirley J Chappell	E T Harrell	....	S M Powell
Vienna t* (15)	CM	703 938-8000	Chas A Robinson Jr	Brack H Bentley	Marian S Wallace	W Gordon Brady	George W Ellis	....	John W Stockton
Vinton t* (8)	CM	703 982-0230	Charles R Hill	George W Nester	Ayles Brogan	....	Barry Fuqua	Clarence F Irby Jr	James A McClung
Virginia Beach* (262)	CM	804 427-4111	Harold Heischober	Thomas Muehlenbeck	Ruth H Smith	Giles G Dodd	Harry Diezel	Charles R Wall	C Oral Lambert Jr
Warrenton t* (4)	CM	703 347-1101	J W Lineweaver	E L Brower	Judy C Funkhouser	Frances Timberlake	Dale L Koglin	H Gary Heath	....
Waynesboro* (15)	CM	703 949-8305	Warren F Kindt	Charles T Yancey	Margaret B Gilmore	Frank Fletcher	Harvey L Kelley	Horace L Gleason	H Jax Bowman
West Point t (3)	MC	804 843-3330	William T Robinson	Ralph R Racioppi	Mary S Dunn	Mary S Dunn	Charles E Carlton	....	....
Williamsburg* (10)	CM	804 229-4821	Robert C Walker	Frank Force	Lois S Bodie	Raymond A Adams	J Robert Bailey Jr	Larry G Vardell	Frederick C Allison
Winchester* (20)	CM	703 667-1815	Charles M Zuckerman	Wendell L Seldon	Michael M Foreman	B M Perrero	Lynn A Miller	F Allen Barley	Edward J Jankiewicz
Wise t* (4)	CM	703 328-6013	Glenn Craft	Simeon E Ewing	....	Mayo Steffey	D Kelly	R D Dixon	Alvin Collins
Woodstock t* (3)	CM	703 459-3621	Oliver L Burkett Jr	J H Blount Jr	Carolyn C Mauck	Jean L Copp	Gary Yew	Jerry P Miller	Robert L Neff
Wytheville t* (7)	CM	703 228-3111	Carl E Stark	Wayne Sutherland	Sharon P Waller	Mary M Bourne	Dewey M Hagy	Robert A Doyle	W H Jones
WASHINGTON (101)									
Aberdeen (19)	MC	206 533-4100	George Irwin	....	Fred J Thurman	Fred J Thurman	Neil Laughead	William Ellis	Rudy Balgaroo
Anacortes† (9)	MC	206 293-5131	James Rice	....	George Khtaian	George Khtaian	Cecil Little	Myron Lippe	David Ford Jr
Arlington (3)	MC	509 435-5785	(not reporting)						
Auburn (26)	MC	206 931-3000	Bob Roegner	....	Coralee McConnehey	Dan Clements	Robert K Johnson	N Jim Gibson	Keith P Nevins
Battle Ground (3)	MC	206 687-7131	Everett Eaton	....	Judie Wegener	....	Jerry Nies	Ron Johnson	Larry McAndrews
Bellevue* (74)	CM	206 455-6800	Cary E Bozeman	Andrea Beatty	Marie O'Connell	Richard L Saunders	Dan Sterling	Donald Vanblaricom	C Hugh Warren
Bellingham (46)	MC	206 676-6900	Tim Douglas	....	Jennifer Olson	Donald K Hoffman	Gary Hedberg	Terence Mangan	John M Garner
Blaine* (2)	CM	206 332-8311	....	Dale A Ennor	Laura Amundson	....	....	James Hinchey	John Hergesheimer
Bonney Lake (5)	MC	206 862-8602	Carle Whisler	....	Diane Jenks	Diane Jenks	Alden Dobson	Donald Frazier	Terry Ward
Bothell* (8)	CM	206 486-3256	Clair C Inghram	Jerald L Osterman	Betty Keeney	Nancy Crossley	Richard Duncan	Jim McMahon	Frank Hansche
Bremerton (36)	CO	206 478-5252	Morrie Dawkins	....	Kathleen McCluskey	Leo Olney	....	....	....
Brier (3)	MC	206 775-5440	Wayne E Kaske	....	Norma L Schultz	....	....	....	Ralph H Klei Sr
Buckley (3)	MC	206 829-1921	Eugene E Robertson	Bernard Parker	Bernard Parker	Bernard Parker	Jon W Streepy	Arthur W McGehee	P Mikel Brendel
Burlington (4)	MC	206 755-0531	Raymond C Henery	Stanley P Kersey	Evelyn Fischer	Stanley P Kersey	Theodore N Banta	Edward Goodman	Stanley P Kersey
Camas (6)	MC	206 834-2462	Nan Henriksen	....	Dale E Scarbrough	Dale E Scarbrough	Maynard Erickson	Wm Hillgaertner	Mel H Avery
Centralia (11)	CO	206 736-5323	John Gelder	....	Rich Hanna	William Richard	Charles Newbury	R J Winter	Peter Corwin
Chehalis* (6)	CM	206 748-6664	Joyce E Venemon	Lloyd E Willis	Jo Ann Hakola	Jo Ann Hakola	Anthony L Keeling	Donald C Schwartz	Barry Heid
Chelan§ (3)	MC	509 682-4037	Earl Skip Gors	Armand E Werle	Robert J Daykin	Robert J Daykin	....	Marrian Peebles	J Wm Greenway
Cheney§ (8)	MC	509 235-6211	Tom Trulove	James Reinbold	Grant Murie	Grant Murie	John Montague	Jerome Garoner	Richard Johnson
Clarkston (7)	MC	509 758-5541	(not reporting)						
Clyde Hill t† (3)	MC	206 454-2351	Dwayne Richards	....	Ruth Saari	John McNamara	....	Kenneth Weinstein	....
Colfax (3)	MC	509 397-3861	L H Riedner	....	Marguerite Cain	Joe Goodrich	James Krouse	Rolland Watts	Robert Moorhead
College Place (6)	MC	509 529-1200	George W Fernald	....	Frances Henderson	....	Emanuel Rudolf	Dennis Lepiane	Chas B Chamberlain
Colville (5)	MC	509 684-5094	Helen J White	....	May G Fedric	....	Jack Citkovich	Robert Cole	Larry Schrader
Dayton (3)	MC	509 382-2361	Carl Rowe Jr	....	Carolyn Gilbreath	Carolyn Gilbreath	Robert Budig	Chester Powers	Jerry Dunlap
Des Moines* (7)	CM	206 878-4595	Pat DeBlasio	Stan E McNutt	Denis Olsen	Betty Hayes	Bob Arnold	Martin Pratt	Ron Longhi
Edmonds† (28)	MC	206 775-2525	Harve H Harrison	....	Irene Varney Moran	Art Housler	Jack D Weinz	Marlo M Foster	Bobby Mills
Ellensburg* (12)	CM	509 962-9863	Larry Nickel	Douglas G Williams	Gene R Triplett	Gene R Triplett	William E West	Lawrence Loveless	Thomas J Chini
Elma t (3)	MC	206 482-2212	William L Eaton	....	Nina M Georg	....	Merle Gowan	Delbert McNeal	Harry R Henneck
Enumclaw§ (5)	MC	206 825-3591	Robert F Denison	Lynn Karl Nordby	Lois A Parker	Alvena L Sumner	Joseph M Kolisch	Bruce Guenther	Lynn Karl Nordby
Ephrata (5)	MC	509 754-4601	O Richard Matheny	....	Rex L Mather	....	Ralph Groom	Sam Shiflett	Wayne Hampton
Everett† (54)	MC	206 259-8701	William E Moore	James W Langus	Elaine Moschilli	William Cushman	Douglas McNall	Allen Shelstad	Al Theal
Ferndale* (4)	CM	206 384-4302	Jack Williams	Ronald S Peterson	Roland Signett	....	Lorne Jensen	Roger Hintgen	John Eley
Fircrest t (5)	MC	206 564-8900	Lawrence Cavanaugh	James R Valentine	Juliann Beggs	Juliann Beggs	Jan L Chamberland	Ronald F Ames	....
Forks t (3)	MC	206 374-5412	Warren W Paul	....	R Daniel Leinan	....	Phil Arbeiter	Ken Bryson	....
Gig Harbor t§ (2)	MC	206 851-8137	Ruth M Bogue	Jeffrey R Snider	....	Evelyn Pior	....	James Pettersen	Tom Heineke
Goldendale (3)	MC	509 773-4288	Cyrus G Forry	....	Betty McKee	Betty McKee	Wes Loftin	Norman G Evans	Art Anderson
Grandview§ (6)	MC	509 882-1237	Dale H Burgeson	David C Veley	Nancy E Davidson	John Myers	William C Moore	David R Charvet	Karen A Brooks
Hoquiam (10)	MC	206 532-9330	J E McGuire	....	Joann Stover	Joann Stover	Lance Talley	Gordon Bunker	Dennis Priebe
Issaquah§ (6)	MC	206 392-6477	A J Culver	Leon Kos	Linda S Ruehle	Aagot Hess	Anthony J Singleton	Duaine A Garrison	Douglas J Crumley
Kelso* (11)	CM	206 423-0900	Richard I Woods	Jay Haggard	Shirley Heitzmann	Shirley Heitzmann	Lyn T Stoutt	Lyn T Stoutt	Sid Klein
Kennewick* (34)	CM	509 586-4181	James A Bates	Joseph W Painter	Marjorie A Price	Robert F Noland	Donald E Graves	Robert C Farnkoff	Ervin Bader
Kent§ (23)	MC	206 872-3300	Isabel Hogan	Richard Cushing	Marie Jensen	Laurence McCarthy	Norman Angelo	Jay Skewes	Donald Wickstrom
Kirkland* (19)	CM	206 828-1100	Doris Cooper	Allen Locke	Thomas Anderson	Thomas Anderson	Robert Ely	Arthur Clifford Jr	Larry Larse
Lacey* (14)	CM	206 491-3210	Mark O Brown	Vernon E Stoner	Timothy McGuire	Blaine Martin	....	John Mansfield	....
Longview* (31)	CM	206 577-3300	Weber Dennis	J Walter Barham	Thomas D Riffe	Thomas D Riffe	Robert E Heideman	Edward Bourdage	Nelson A Graham
Lynden (4)	MC	206 354-4270	Egbert Maas	....	Victoria Zukowski	John Heutink	Bryant Smit	Ronald Goad	Dwight Davis
Lynnwood§ (22)	MC	206 775-1971	Meryl J Hrdlicka	Michael G Caldwell	....	Robert W Noack	Alan M Dillon	John L Paddock	William E Nims
Marysville§ (5)	MC	206 659-8477	Norman Anderson	John L Garner	Phillip E Dexter	Phillip E Dexter	Douglas Ronning	John G Faulkner	William Butler
Medical Lake§ (4)	MC	509 299-7712	Don Johns	Tom Bumgarner	Georgette Wendt	Georgette Wendt	Bertram Revill	Donald State	Earl Davis
Medina* (3)	CM	206 454-9222	Gordon Griffes	Edward Pefferman	Della M Wyatt	Della M Wyatt	....	Albert L Anglin	Richard Renaud
Mercer Island* (22)	CM	206 232-6400	Fred Jarrett	Lawrence D Rose	Debra Symmonds	David A Osterholt	Jan P Deveny	Jan P Deveny	Richard Williams
Mill Creek* (2)	CM	206 745-1891	....	Charles Dibble	....	....	....	....	....
Milton t† (3)	MC	206 922-8733	Dick T Osaka	....	Gayla L Puckett	....	Ronald D Garton	Harold Burton	Ivan Stevica
Monroe t (3)	MC	206 794-7400	Gordon Tjerne	....	Betty King	....	Pat Vollandt	John Hovde	Joe Bredstrand
Montesano (3)	MC	206 249-3021	Michael F Daniels	....	Marie Fry	....	Wallace Vincent	F Ronald Bradbury	Robert Manley
Moses Lake* (11)	CM	509 766-9214	Norman Johnson	Joseph K Gavinski	Walter Fry	Walter Fry	Russell Beeman	Glen Sharp	Rita Perstac
Mount Vernon† (13)	MC	206 336-6585	Ruth E Gidlund	....	Michael Woodmansee	....	Thomas A H Pate	Ronald Tarry	....
Mountlake Terrace* (17)	CM	206 776-1161	Lois Anderson	Robert G White	Ron Swanson	Ron Swanson	Donald Garberg	Loren Watson	Carl Rautenberg
Normandy Park* (4)	CM	206 824-2602	John T Dawson	Donna K Hanson	Jacquelyn Wieland	Connie J Baccetti	....	Donald G Pierce	Keith A Harris
Oak Harbor (12)	MC	206 679-5551	Al Koetje	Robt H Walker	Terry G Hicks	Terry G Hicks	Jay Gunsauls	Frankie L Orr	Ed Boonstra
Ocean Shores* (2)	CM	206 289-2486	David Tips	Robt L Olander	Hester Ihrig	Hester Ihrig	Richard Jansen	Gale Stokes	Doug Hoflin

Directory 1/10 continued — MUNICIPAL OFFICIALS IN ALL U.S. CITIES OVER 2,500[1]

City, 1980 population (000 omitted), form of government	Municipal phone number	Mayor	Appointed administrator	City clerk	Finance officer	Fire chief	Police chief	Public works director
WASHINGTON (101) continued								
Olympia* (27) MC	206 753-8325	David A Skramstad	Robert W Murray	....	....	James Rambo	John H Wurner	Chuck Neumayer
Omak (4) MC	509 826-1170	Ray Treiber	....	Nancy McKain	Nancy McKain	Cal R Bowling	Byron Perkins	....
Othello (4) MC	509 488-5686	Stanley K Case	....	Gloria L Kennelly	Hazel M Gallinger	C Duane Van Beek	George Morton	....
Pasco* (18) CM	509 545-3404	Joe W Jackson	Leland F Kraft	Evelyn Wells	Jerry Conner	Larry Dickinson	Donald J Francis	Jim Ajax
Port Angeles* (17) CM	206 457-0411	Dorothy Duncan	David T Flodstrom	Merri E Lannoye	Robert E Orton	Larry Glenn	Michael A Cleland	Jack N Pittis
Port Orchard (5) MC	206 876-4407	Lesie J Weatherill	....	Robert G Lloyd	Kristine L Miller	Joseph L Snow	Joseph L Mathews Jr	Lawrence J Curles
Port Townsend (6) MC	206 385-3333	Brent S Shirley	....	David A Grove	David A Grove	Robert Jones	Robert Hinton	Ted Stricklin
Poulsbo (3) MC	206 779-3901	June Atack	....	Karol Jones	Paulette Alvarado	Larry Dibble	Richard Lang	Richard Mitchusson
Prosser (4) MC	509 786-2332	Robert J White	Walter M Titus	Helen P Carrell	Lelah A Fiker	Roger L Elliott	Melvin E Walker	....
Pullman§ (24) MC	509 334-4555	Pete A Butkus	John Sherman	John D Tonkovich	John D Tonkovich	Pat Wilkens	Ted Weatherly	James Hudak
Puyallup* (18) CM	206 841-4321	Ron S Crowe	Richard J Thompson	Paul Androes	Karen R A Clements	Ronald Haworth	Lawrence E Nash	Larry Werner
Quincy t (4) MC	509 787-3523	Kenneth K McGrew	....	Jean Lindberg	Jean Lindberg	Don Simmons	Kenneth G Carlile	Michael R Konen
Raymond† (3) CO	206 942-3451	Rance Freeman	....	Ronald L Hatfield	Ronald L Hatfield	Robert P Jones	William P Lee	Kreg Martin
Redmond (23) MC	206 882-6400	Doreen Marchione	....	Doris A Schaible	Paul F Kusakabe	....	Steven R Harris	Fred F Herzberg
Renton (31) MC	206 235-2500	Barbara Y Shinpoch	Michael W Parness	Maxine Motor	Michael Mulcahy	A Lee Wheeler	Alan Wallis	Richard Houghton
Richland* (34) CM	509 943-9161	John M Poynor	Neal J Shulman	Leslie Smith	Ron D Musson	Robert Panuccio	Bernard Colligan	William Gilbert
Seattle (494) MC	206 625-4000	Charles Royer	....	Tim Hill	Gary Zarker	Robert L Swartout	Patrick Fitzsimons	Barbara K Taber
Sedro-Woolley (6) MC	206 855-1661	Donald T Walley	....	Eric K Stendal	Eric K Stendal	Pete D Kelly	Ronald D John	Thomas E Oakes
Selah§ (4) MC	509 697-7215	Harold E Tayer	Michael I Quinn	Roy Lewis	....	John Soden	George Boyd	Dwain Jones
Sequim† (3) MC	206 683-4139	James Dinan	....	....	....	....	....	....
Shelton (8) CO	206 426-4491	Joyce E Jaros	Michael A McCarty	Tanya M Nolte	Dave Kneeland	George Hunter	Frank Rains	Chris T Thomson
Snohomish* (5) CM	206 568-3115	Ralph Davis	Kelly Robinson	Frank R Grigas	Frank R Grigas	Robert Merritt	Patrick Murphy	Tim Heydon
Spokane* (171) CM	509 456-3232	James E Chase	Terry L Novak	Marilyn Montgomery	Peter G Fortin	Paul Olsen	Robert Panther	Irving Reed
Stanwood (3) MC	206 629-2181	Kenneth E Day	....	Donald L Glancy	....	Walter G Hood	Robert B Kane	....
Steilacoom t† (5) MC	206 581-1900	Robert Anderson Jr	Dennis Clarke	Susan Wilson	....	Joel Anderson	Richard Amundsen	Jim Richards
Sumner (5) MC	206 863-5263	Lewis Noel	....	Loretta Shumake	Ms S Kristoffeson	Tom Myers	Ronald G Hyland	Glen Sherwood
Sunnyside* (9) CM	509 837-3997	Don Hughes	Leo S Fancey	Irene H Alseth	Hugo Schatz	Gary L Cole	Al M Tebaldi	Calvin Bowersox
Tacoma* (159) CM	206 591-5130	Doug Sutherland	Erling O Mork	Genelle Birk	David H Dow	Tony F Mitchell	Dean Phillips	Ronald M Button
Toppenish* (7) CM	509 865-5000	Norman M Johnson	James M Southworth	Troy R Emmons	....	Jerry V Donaldson	Karl B Hutchinson	Gary A Armstrong
Tukwila§ (4) MC	206 433-1800	Gary L Van Dusen	Don A Morrison	Maxine Anderson	Alan Doerschel	Hubert Crawley	Patrick Lowery	Byron G Sneva
Tumwater (7) MC	206 753-8550	Philip H Schmidt	Leonard L Smith	Mary J Benson	Mary J Benson	Richard Ridgeway	H M Vandiver	James G Brown
Union Gap (3) MC	509 248-0432	John P Hodkinson	Paul Burlingame	Regina Williams	Regina Williams	Donald W Linder	Richard Simmons	Kenneth W Harris
Vancouver* (43) CM	206 696-8121	Bryce Seidl	Paul M Grattet	H Kent Shorthill	H Kent Shorthill	Otto Jensen	Leland S Davis	John Ostrowski
Walla Walla* (26) CM	509 527-4522	William P Fleenor	Edwin R Ivey	Harry Kinzer	Harry Kinzer	Tom R Anderson	Charles Fulton	Duane Scroggins
Wapato (3) MC	509 877-2334	Richard C Calahan	....	Irene McAuliffe	....	James Dekker	Robert Wilson	....
Washougal† (4) MC	206 835-8501	Mike Johnson	....	R J Rust	R J Rust	Darrell Alder	Rich Williams	Don MacFadden
Wenatchee (17) CO	509 663-0551	Jim Lynch	....	David J Thrush	David J Thrush	Michael Brown	Kenneth Badgley	Norman Delabarre
West Richland (3) MC	509 967-3431	S Daniel Rosier	....	Grace Higgins	Grace Higgins	Lyman Nelson	John H Ritchie	Ralph Menasco
Yakima* (50) CM	509 575-6000	Clarence Barnett	Richard A Zais Jr	Karen S Roberts	John R Hanson	Edward Carroll	Pleas Green	David A Rhodes
WEST VIRGINIA (59)								
Barboursville v† (3) MC	304 736-8994	William E Rucker	....	Betty A Adkins	....	Stephen Parsons	Robert Smith	....
Beckley (20) MC	304 256-1750	Charles F Shoemaker	Robert L Cannon	Kenneth W Richmond	Kenneth W Richmond	Alvin L Wood	Carl J Legursky	Robert Robinson
Bethlehem v (3) MC	304 242-4180	John S Daniel	....	Avonel Bero	....	Robert Weisner	John S Daniel	....
Bluefield* (16) CM	304 327-2401	Paul Cole Jr	Fred P Burton	Dora M Hendrick	Fred P Burton	Richard Poe	James E Dent	Wm H Looney Jr
Bridgeport t (7) MC	304 842-6201	Charles M Loar	....	....	Keith L Boggs	Kelly Blackwell	Jack Clayton	Mason W Steele
Buckhannon (7) MC	304 472-1651	William R Short	....	Ms E J Poundstone	Ms E J Poundstone	C R Bud Bennett	Richard Osburn	Harley A Brown
Charles Town† (3) MC	304 725-2311	D C Master	J Robert Cain	Rufus Park	J Robert Cain	K Willingham	Charles Stebbins	Hebert McDaniel
Charleston (64) MC	304 348-8033	James E Roark	Charles R Gardner	Alma King	Harry F Price	John W Britton	Jack R Buckalew	Richard Cooke
Chester† (3) MC	304 387-2820	William E Scarry	....	Perry E Ross	Perry E Ross	Rodney Coen	Robert Pugh	....
Clarksburg* (22) CM	304 623-2936	William R Reynolds	Patsy S Trecost	Mildred A Zink	Frank Ferrari	Charles Lantz	Thomas C Durrett	Jon Kerns
Dunbar (9) MC	304 766-0222	Frank B Leone	....	Betty Janney	Betty Janney	Gary L Bowles	W W Wallace	Robert Young
Elkins (9) MC	304 636-1414	(not reporting)						
Fairmont* (24) CM	304 366-6211	Gregory T Hinton	Edwin C Daley	Helen F Tennant	Louis A Chico	David Wimer	Wayne Stutler	Thomas Arnold
Fayetteville t* (2) CM	304 574-0101	David L Hypys	Henry H Niday	Stephen Cruinkshank	Henry H Niday	Stephen Cruinkshank	Tunney Hunsaker	Henry H Niday
Follansbee* (4) CM	304 527-1330	Adam Dalessio	Raymond L Stoaks	Rudy Cipriani	Raymond L Stoaks	Larry Rea	Steve Perna	Grover Pugh
Grafton* (7) CM	304 265-1412	Paul E Elder	Frank F Robinette	Janie Ives	James A Spear	Bill Workman	Richard Utt	Clyde Henderson
Hinton (5) MC	304 466-3255	James A Leslie Jr	Jack L Scott	Jack L Scott	....	Leon R Pivont Jr	Ty Wayne Deeds	Ralph L Trout Jr
Huntington* (64) CM	304 696-5580	Joseph L Williams	....	Mary L Neely	R Clifton Duncan	H H Johnson	Norman E Noble	Ancher Madison
Hurricane v (4) MC	304 757-6751	Raymond Peak	....	Alwilda M Johnson	Linda Gibson	Jarrell Bledsoe	Richard Gillispie	Ernest P Stricklin
Kenova (4) MC	304 453-1571	(not reporting)						
Keyser† (7) MC	304 788-1511	H Edward Miller	Jeffrey Rhodes	....	Charles N Wimer	David Harman	Harry A Stewart	....
Kingwood t† (3) MC	304 329-1225	Patrick R Crogan	....	Amy L Snyder	Amy L Snyder	....	Roger L Menear	Claude Waugerman
Lewisburg (3) MC	304 645-2080	P L Gainer	....	Patricia Pennington	Hetta McMillion	Joe B Hayes	Richard E Weikle	Herb Montgomery
Logan t (3) MC	304 752-4044	Gary H Hylton	....	Violet Miller	....	Fred Thompson	Robert Mathis	Benny Eplin
Madison (3) MC	304 369-2762	James V Burgess Jr	....	Ferris L Jones	....	Stephen A Ball	Charles D Keglor	....
Mannington t (3) MC	304 986-2700	Drexil E Powell	....	Michele R Fluharty	....	Harold Moran	Gary M Roberts	Richard Stevens
Martinsburg* (13) CM	304 263-0805	Edward W Dockeneyjr	J Hutchins-Zachman	Karen M Foltz	....	Glenwood Hayes	Ronald Banta	Ralph Long
Montgomery t (3) MC	304 442-5181	(not reporting)						
Morgantown* (28) CM	304 291-7401	Harold Lipscomb	Doug Fawcett	Patricia Campbell	James R White	Edward J Nabors	John Cease	Howard Ralls
Moundsville* (12) CM	304 845-6300	Ronald Wood	James A Williams	Loretta J Francis	Naomi Simms	Oliver Jenkins	J G Watson	Cecil Blake
Mullens t (3) MC	304 294-7132	Paul J Clowers	....	Mervin C Cook	....	Paul J Clowers	Charles W Ross	....
New Martinsville (7) MC	304 455-2311	Howard T Jeffers	....	Faye R Smith	Faye R Smith	Robert Delancey	Carl E Kocher	....
Nitro t (8) MC	304 755-0701	Arden Ashley	....	John Santrock	Michael Greenleaf	Ernest Hedrick	Clifford Cochran	Gene Williams
Oak Hill* (7) CM	304 469-9541	Frederick Neudek	Kurt E Ankrom	Virginia Fox	Virginia Fox	Delbert Cordle	Jackie Roberts	Kurt E Ankrom
Paden City t (4) MC	304 337-2295	John H Ice	....	Bernidene Culp	....	James Richmond	John Lyons	Clifford Duke
Parkersburg (40) MC	304 424-8400	Ms Pat S Pappas	....	Connie Harper	Steve Leuliette	Stephen E Gainer	James G Midkiff	Michael Taylor
Philippi† (3) MC	304 457-3701	D B Baughman	Joseph P Mattaliano	Joseph P Mattaliano	Joseph P Mattaliano	Tommy Poling	Rodney W Snider	Mike Scott
Point Pleasant (6) MC	304 675-2360	Jimmy Joe Wedge	....	Laura Gaskins	Laura Gaskins	Jimmie L Woods	James F Gaskins	Dannie Rodgers
Princeton* (7) CM	304 425-9546	James L Cannon	James L Juhl	Virginia Wohlford	James L Juhl	John M Hyatt	George W Johnson	James E Brennan
Ranson§ (2) MC	304 725-1010	Robert G Lance	Dawn D Blackstock	Mildred Chambers	....	....	Edward Hutto	Dennis W Dillow
Ravenswood (4) CM	304 273-2621	Robert L Dittmar	....	Joan Turner	M Bowman Beverly	Earl Wolfe	Edward E Speece	....
Richwood (4) MC	304 846-2596	Hyer Sutton	John David Hicks	Dixie Cornell	Verina Haga	Ed Buck	William B Ward	Henry Scarber
Ripley (3) MC	304 372-3482	Ronald L Whiting	....	Elsa Morris	Charles Cottrill	John Landfried	Rowland Carper	Kenna Tolley
Shinnston* (3) CM	304 592-5631	Frank Bowman	John S Manna	Rosalee H Dolan	John S Manna	David Harmer	Donald W Book	Robin Drain
South Charleston§ (16) MC	304 744-5301	Richard A Robb	....	Winnie Atkinson	Richard A Atkinson	Larry Cox	Ronald L Willamson	Lee Dent
Spencer† (3) MC	304 927-1640	Terry A Williams	....	Eleneva Southall	Terry A Williams	Aaron Cottle	Jim Hardman	....
St. Albans (12) MC	304 727-2971	Averil L Ramsey	....	Peter J Maruish Jr	Peter J Maruish Jr	James L Beane	Robert C Barnette	Charles L Huffman
St. Marys* (2) CM	304 684-2401	Arthur G Olds	Geo E Hendricks	Kay Guess	Kay Guess	Goff Carpenter	Dallas Flowers	Roy Hearn
Summersville t (3) MC	304 872-1211	Thomas J Trent	....	G Dale Bailes	....	Joe Boso	D Garry Evans	Bobby R Hughes

Directory 1/10 continued **MUNICIPAL OFFICIALS IN ALL U.S. CITIES OVER 2,500**[1]

City, 1980 population (000 omitted), form of government		Municipal phone number	Mayor	Appointed administrator	City clerk	Finance officer	Fire chief	Police chief	Public works director
WEST VIRGINIA (59) continued									
Vienna† (12)	MC	304 295-6081	Walter E Pifer	....	Louise I Fleming	Louise I Fleming	George Scholl	Gary Deem	Robert Eschbacher
Weirton* (25)	CM	304 748-5050	Donald T Mentzer	William DuFour Jr	Susan E Foster	Thomas Koumaros	Dean Allen	William Hair	Dave Hair
Welch* (4)	CM	304 436-3114	John W Wilson	....	Charles W Blevins	Charles W Blevins	Jerry Rotenberry	Mike Nasser	Robert Lee
Wellsburg* (4)	CM	304 737-2104	Anthony Cipriani	Curtis Shook	Billie J Robinson	Agnes Harvey	Richard E Kins	Terrance P Dick	Douglas Hervey
Weston (6)	MC	304 269-6141	Wendell E Hayes	....	Jean Bennett	....	John H Shea	George E Blake	....
Westover (5)	MC	304 296-6860	Thomas K Chaplin	....	Elizabeth J Miranov	Francis L Teter Sr	David Clawges	Larry G Speicher	....
Wheeling* (43)	CM	304 234-0211	William H Muegge	F Wayne Barte	Betty Lou Palmer	Wilson Murray	Cliff Sligar	Edward Weith Jr	Lloyd P Adams
White Sulphur Springs (3)	MC	304 536-1454	John H Bowling	....	Margaret L Lewis	....	James Fife	Luther C Stacy	....
Williamson (5)	MC	304 235-1510	Sam G Kapourales	....	June Blevins	....	Grover C Phillips	Wilburn C Smith	Jennings Gannon
Williamstown† (3)	MC	304 375-7761	R E Leach	....	W W Cutlip	....	Austin Dallison	Donald E White Jr	....
WISCONSIN (170)									
Algoma (4)	MC	414 487-2163	(not reporting)						
Allouez t (15)	MC	414 432-5291	James R Charneski	Clarence Matuszek	Susan L Catlin	Clarence Matuszek	Richard Panure	....	Thomas Obenberger
Altoona† (4)	MC	715 834-2808	Delvin Eberlein	....	Alice M Schroeder	....	Robert Wagner	David J O'Donahoe	Edwin Duszynski
Amery§ (2)	MC	715 268-7486	Luther Toftness	Ralph Mickelson	Ralph Mickelson	....	Ric Van Blarcom	Michael Holmes	Warren Marquand
Antigo (9)	MC	715 623-3033	(not reporting)						
Appleton (59)	MC	414 735-6443	Dorothy Johnson	....	Jadell K Ferge	Reynold L Running	Fred J Selig	David L Gorski	Robert G Miller
Ashland (9)	MC	715 682-9333	James S Monroe	....	Jane S Smith	James A Bay	Gerald Giese	Gordon Gilbertson	James Hegbloom
Ashwaubenon v† (14)	MC	414 435-3751	Tony J Frigo	Tony J Frigo	Charlotte E Nelson	....	....	John Konopacki	....
Baraboo† (8)	MC	608 356-8361	Donald R Pierce	....	Dean T Bothell	....	Ronald G Federman	Michael J Lien	Harold A Platt
Barron (3)	MC	715 537-5631	Rodney A Peterson	....	Tony L Slagstad	....	John Kallenback	Oie E Severude	....
Bayside v* (5)	CM	414 352-7896	Marshall A Loewi	Joseph A Tanski	Joseph A Tanski	Joseph A Tanski	Benjamin J Fiedler	Benjamin J Fiedler	Ernest Cartwright
Beaver Dam (14)	MC	414 885-5541	John F Omen	....	Gary H Dummer	Roy Erickson	Peter S Westra	Douglas Randall	Bruce L Gall
Beloit* (35)	CM	608 364-6600	Everett C Haskell	H Herbert Holt	Henry C Schreve	Henry C Schreve	Paul J Athens	John M Mizerka	Frank J Zuicarelli
Berlin (5)	MC	414 361-0800	Harold R Klassa	....	Louise Sedarski	....	Donald Trampf	Germain Beck	....
Black River Falls† (3)	MC	715 284-5514	Louis Perry	....	William Arndt	William Arndt	Jeffrey Amo	Dan Gomer	James Schoolcraft
Bloomer (3)	MC	715 568-3032	LeRoy E Reetz	....	Charles H Cole	Charles H Cole	Rolland Prince	Jon Parkhurst	....
Boscobel (3)	MC	608 375-5001	Leo E Johnson	....	John E Ducharme	....	Jerry R Haney	Gerald Staskal	David Mikonowicz
Brillion (3)	MC	414 756-2250	Clarence F Wolf	....	Donald Brixius	....	Gerald Martinson	James Horvath	William Schuman
Brodhead (3)	MC	608 897-4018	Bruce W Timm	....	Nancy J Schoeller	....	Philip McManus	....	Harold D Schulz
Brookfield (34)	MC	414 782-9650	William A Mitchell	....	Gary L Rasmussen	Arlin R Wesner	James Mehring	Jerome Wolff	William A Muth Jr
Brown Deer v* (13)	CM	414 355-5220	Earl McGovern	Gerald J Seeber	Gerald J Seeber	Gary E Karshna	Donald Rosenbauer	Donald Rosenbauer	Richard Halfman
Burlington§ (8)	MC	414 763-3717	Martin J Itzin	Thomas R Lebak	Ralph F Epping	Ralph F Epping	Charles Hewitt	Walter E Gabriel	....
Butler v§ (2)	MC	414 781-9056	Harold Pulvermacher	Charles Erickson	Charles Erickson	Charles Erickson	Robert Zoulek	Raymond Thompson	Raymond Grzys
Cedarburg† (9)	MC	414 377-4500	Quentin F Schenk	....	Dorothy M Marks	Dorothy M Marks	Wayne A Fischer	George R Rees	Russell A Dimick
Chilton† (3)	MC	414 849-2451	A W Larson	....	Arthur T Pohland	....	Arno J Bruckner	Daniel Albedyll	Tim Foster
Chippewa Falls (12)	MC	715 723-3800	Leo R Hamilton	....	Lucyann Lecleir	Walter A Boos	Edward W Mishefske	Joseph S Coughlin	Rodney G Pike
Clintonville (5)	MC	715 823-6584	Karen M Siewert	....	Nancy Harris	Nancy Harris	Donald Johnson	Gerald R Blum	Steve Bernot
Columbus§ (4)	MC	414 623-3250	Peter Kaland	Donald A Yecke	Albert H Abrams	Donald A Yecke	James Boness	Lee Erdmann	Donald A Yecke
Combined Locks v (3)	MC	414 788-2059	George Bosch	....	Mark Van Thiel	Leroy Devalk	Charles Jansen	Chester Athey	William DeGoey
Cudahy (20)	MC	414 769-2200	Lawrence P Kelly	....	Frank Janicek	Frank Janicek	Norbert Olson	Anthony M Wise	Ronald Rutkowski
De Forest v† (3)	MC	608 846-4751	Royce Zum Brunnen	....	....	....	....	....	....
De Pere§ (15)	MC	414 336-5761	John Nusbaum	Jerome J Smits	Clayton Arndt	Jerome J Smits	Donald Vissers	Armand Wecker	Andrew S Radetski
Delafield (4)	MC	414 646-3395	Robert Savrnoch	....	Lois Jensen	....	Harold Roberts	James Vanderwerker	Sylvester Krueger
Delavan§ (6)	MC	414 728-5585	Charles W Brunswick	John M Stack	Betty L Statz	Pearl Canales	Neill Flood	Lawrence H Malsch	Lyle A Smith
Dodgeville† (3)	MC	608 935-5228	Frank Hess	....	Cheryl Voigts	Mildred Blabaum	Ronald Severson	Richard Hiemerl	....
Eau Claire* (52)	CM	715 839-4902	Shirley Crinion	Eric A Anderson	James Fering	Donald Norrell	John Brown	James McFarlane	Michael T Cousino
Edgerton (4)	MC	608 884-3341	David P Gorski	....	Norman L Burdick	Norman L Burdick	Charles Edwardson	Russell B Laine	Robert Strandlie
Elkhorn§ (5)	MC	414 723-2219	Gerhardt Immega	Martin J Rafferty	Phyllis Patek	Phyllis Patek	Pete Kelley	John Giese	Martin J Rafferty
Elm Grove v* (7)	CM	414 782-6700	Margaret A Farrow	Edmund M Henschel	Wayne D Bisek	Henry L Yulga	William Schneider	William I Vanark	Kenneth Blaedow
Evansville (3)	MC	608 882-4424	John E Jones Jr	....	R A Zilliox	Ron Pierce	Charles Nordeng	Richard J Luers	K Grenawalt
Fitchburg t (12)	MC	608 271-4551	(not reporting)						
Fond du Lac* (36)	CM	414 929-3320	Gerald H Ewert	Daniel R Thompson	Thomas M Lehman	G A Rebensburg	Harold C Munson	Melvin E Heller	J William Roemer
Fort Atkinson* (10)	CM	414 563-5584	John Behrend	Robert C Martin	John Wilmet	John Wilmet	Phil Doerching	William R Ciske	Steven Jankowski
Fox Point v* (8)	CM	414 352-8113	F R Dengel	Henry A Scholz	Noreen R Cook	....	Gerd J Hodermann	Gerd J Hodermann	William Gardner
Franklin (17)	MC	414 425-7500	Theodore J Fadrow	....	Gregory P Gregory	Willard L Crain Jr	....	Norman J Pollman	John M Bennett
Germantown v (11)	CM	414 251-1211	Marshall D Paust	Jerome A O'Connor	Susan Smith Johns	Fredric G Lex	Gene Arnold	Frank J Riemer Jr	Lloyd L Turner
Glendale§ (14)	MC	414 228-1700	Nobert Hynek	Richard Maslowski	June Joswick	Grace Fleisner	Robert Yourich	James Cotter	David Weis
Grafton v§ (8)	MC	414 377-3610	Ralph Laubenstein	Emory R Sacho	Emory R Sacho	....	Carl Wegner	Howard Thiede	Wilmer Helm
Green Bay (88)	MC	414 497-3600	Samuel J Hallion	Dave S Nennig	Paul J Janquart	Rudy G Reinhard	Gerald Selissen	Donald Cuene	Clyde S Crabb
Greendale v* (17)	CM	414 421-1300	Bernard Schroedl	Donald Fieldstad Jr	Harold H Lutz	Harold H Lutz	Earl King	Myron Ratkowski	Nick Paulos
Greenfield (31)	MC	414 543-5500	David Kaczynski	....	Henry Rajachel	....	Ray Szalacinski	Chester Kass	Raymond Dwyer
Hales Corners v§ (7)	MC	414 425-3355	Frederick L Licau	James C Hurm	James C Hurm	....	K Kearns	Duwayne Dzibinski	Ronald J Romeis
Hartford (7)	MC	414 673-4000	Richard W Witt	....	John C Spielmann	Shirley Ritger	Robert Baus	David C Henry	Lucian Darin
Hartland v (6)	MC	414 367-2714	Wilfred J Zeirke	....	Karen M Compton	David Wolken	Allen A Wilde	Mort Hetznecker	Robert Heise
Horicon (4)	MC	414 485-4701	David A Westimayer	....	David J Pasewald	David J Pasewald	Reinhardt Kiesow	Erwin G Bullette	Lloyd A Wagener
Hortonville v§ (2)	MC	414 779-6011	Donald E Briggs Sr	George Protogere	Corrine Radichel	Corrine Radichel	Raymond Weiland	Douglas Jones	Robert Henrickson
Howard v (8)	MC	414 497-4477	Roger Sachs	....	Bettie J Farr	....	Don Marks	....	Robert Redeling
Hudson (5)	MC	715 386-5821	Mary L Hallen	....	Gerald P Berning	Gerald P Berning	Herbert Frye	David C Burke	Henry M Paulson
Janesville* (51)	CM	608 754-2811	Thomas Stehura	Philip L Deaton	Frank L Spoden	Herbert H Stinski	Arthur P Stearns	Ray Voelker	Thomas Rogers
Jefferson§ (6)	MC	414 674-3443	Richard J Fischer	Denise Pieroni	....	Denise Pieroni	Donald Wegner	Chas Johnson	Reuben F Schulz
Kaukauna† (11)	MC	414 766-4682	Ronald L Van DeHey	....	Joan M Cleveland	....	Theodore Smits	William Appleton	Kenneth Schoenike
Kenosha (78)	MC	414 656-8000	John D Bilotti	John A Serpe	Gail F Procarione	Eugene R Schulz	Gerald J Poltrock	Joseph H Trotta	Donald K Holland
Kewaskum v§ (2)	MC	414 626-4060	....	Daniel S Schmidt	....	....	....	....	....
Kewaunee (3)	MC	414 388-2670	Ray C Burmeister	....	James Stadler	James Stadler	Orvel R Schultz	David Decramer	....
Kiel (3)	MC	414 894-2909	John Stroschine	....	Thomas Karls	Jerome Mertens	Robert Hennings	Ricky Sloan	Randall Neils
Kimberly v (6)	MC	414 788-3839	Charles Rundquist	....	Rick Hermus	....	Eugene Vandenberg	D L Jansen	R Van Den Boogaard
La Crosse (48)	MC	608 782-5655	Patrick Zielke	....	Aubrey Kroner	Eugene Pfaff	Irvin R C Kahler	William R Reynolds	Bob D Schroeder
Ladysmith† (4)	MC	715 532-5411	Lynn E Fredrick	....	Ed Arntson	Gordon Pedersen	Ron Barfknecht	Arlin Hanson	Bill Cristianson
Lake Geneva§† (6)	MC	414 248-3673	Richard C Folman	Roger D Schneider	Colleen Alexander	....	Thomas Derrick	Richard Newberry	Robert McLernon
Lake Mills* (4)	CM	414 648-2344	Harold N Lee Jr	Thomas G Popp Jr	Jean Abplanalp	Jean Abplanalp	Charles Sanft	Lee Bush	Jerry Wolff
Lancaster (4)	MC	608 723-4246	Albert D Weber	....	Vanda F Vorwald	Gregg Berry	Carl Muench	Rodger Janssen	Duane Wepking
Little Chute v (8)	MC	414 788-1521	Donald DeGroot	....	Lloyd Vanden Heuvel	....	Tom Lamers	Robert Nechodom	Martin T Jansen
Madison (171)	MC	608 266-4611	F J Jensenbrenner	....	Eldon L Hoel	Andre Blum	Edward Durkin	David C Couper	Jerome Franklin
Manitowoc (33)	MC	414 683-4440	Anthony V Dufek	....	June E Fetzer	Robert Ziegelbauer	Reinie E Herzog	Leroy Strauss	Michael E Hawley
Marinette (12)	MC	715 735-7427	Harold Pierce	....	Fred Westphal	Bonnie Branstrom	William Brown	Donald Schuchart	Norman A Dahl
Marshfield (18)	MC	715 384-2919	Marilyn Hardacre	....	G E Michaelsen	Michael Brehm	Clayton Simonson	Harold Burgess	Fred Haerter
Mauston† (3)	MC	608 847-6676	Terry K Welch	....	Russell W Bergh	....	Richard Hale	Otis J Foster	Adrian Madsen

Directory 1/10 continued — MUNICIPAL OFFICIALS IN ALL U.S. CITIES OVER 2,500[1]

City, 1980 population (000 omitted), form of government		Municipal phone number	Mayor	Appointed administrator	City clerk	Finance officer	Fire chief	Police chief	Public works director
WISCONSIN (170) continued									
Mayville§ (4)	MC	414 387-3800	Craig Donovan	Mark E Grams	Mark E Grams	Kenneth E Jaeger	Earl Sternat	Eugene Zangl	Vern Hilker
McFarland v (4)	MC	608 838-3153	Frank C Dresen	....	Ann L Davis	Ann L Davis	Gayhart Swenson	Kenneth Iwen	Otto J Driewer
Medford (4)	MC	715 748-4321	Arthur Salzwedel	....	William Mattson	....	Glenn Pat Doyle	Jack Kay	William Tylka
Menasha† (15)	MC	414 729-5100	Thom A Ciske	....	Raymond C Zielinski	Thomas R Stoffel	Thomas Miller	Roman Rappert	Ronald Mueller
Menomonee Falls v§ (28)	MC	414 251-7800	Robert J Steliga	Frederick Gottlieb	Patricia A Struve	Frederick Gottlieb	John Fulcher	David O Steingraber	Max A Vogt
Menomonie* (13)	CM	715 232-2180	Glen Schuknecht	G A Langmack Jr	Anita K Klamm	Vada M Husby	Charles Vind	Edward E Moffett	....
Mequon§ (16)	MC	414 242-3100	Lynn W Eley	Donald A Roensch	Charles V Treadwell	Charles V Treadwell	Curtis Witzlib	Carl N Schoeni	Donald A Roensch
Merrill† (10)	MC	715 536-5594	Richard F Holt	....	Judith A Stockowitz	....	Harvey Emanuel	Charles Johnson	....
Middleton† (12)	MC	608 836-7481	Dan A Ramsey	Joel G DeVore	Sylvia J Dennis	Timothy R Studer	Al Stucki	Wm S Franken	John A Lichtenheld
Milton (4)	MC	608 868-7679	Richard W Dabson	William Wachtendonk	Doris E Viney	....	Gene Kumlien	Donald H Chesmore	Charles Bingham
Milwaukee (636)	MC	414 278-3200	Henry W Maier	Jeff Musche	Ben Johnson	James A McCann	William Stamm	Harold A Breier	David A Kuemmel
Mondovi (3)	MC	715 926-3866	Gaylord Schultz	....	Jeffrey J Smith	....	Herman Berger	Michael A Birtzer	....
Monona§ (9)	MC	608 222-2525	Robert J Olson	Charles R Wilson	Shirley A Nicholson	Charles R Wilson	Eugene Hanson	Paul Welch	Richard W Freese
Monroe (10)	MC	608 325-4101	Patrick F Thorpe	....	James R Myers	....	Thomas L Casey	Richard L Busch	Jeffrey J Stewart
Mosinee (3)	MC	715 693-2275	Jack Maguire	....	Dennis Ann Nichols	Dennis Ann Nichols	Norbert Feit	Glen Thanig	James Daublender
Mount Horeb v† (3)	CM	608 437-3084	Peter J Waltz	Allen J Wood	Mickey Deneen	....	Charles Himsel	George Mayerhofer	Donald Olson
Mukwonago v (4)	MC	414 363-4081	Dennis A Behling	....	Bernard W Kahl	Bernard W Kall	George Schmidt	James Frank	Jerome Dettmann
Muskego (15)	MC	414 679-2660	Wayne G Salentine	....	Charlotte L Stewart	....	....	Richard Scholz	Willard Bertram
Neenah† (23)	MC	414 729-4600	Marigen Carpenter	....	J J Kraus	Theodore H Bauer	Robert Hoffman	Vernise Wollerman	Charles Maney
Neillsville (3)	MC	715 743-2105	Robert F Lulloff	....	Rex R Roehl	....	Charles Urban	Thomas Woods	Francis Laatch
Nekoosa (3)	MC	715 886-3811	John Voss	....	Kenneth Lang	....	Donald Walrath	Kenneth Ruder	Floyd Hohenstein
New Berlin (31)	MC	414 786-8610	John J Malone	....	Donald W DeBruin	Larry L Lange	Charles Conway	Michael Hanrahan	Ralph Becker
New Holstein (3)	MC	414 898-5766	Dennis Rybicke	....	Leland J Tikalsky	Paul W Depies	Donald Spletter	Theodore H Pagel	Carl Busse
New London (6)	MC	414 982-3323	Wayne Toltzman	....	James R Villiesse	James R Villiesse	Wayne Wilfuer	Jack V Algiers	W Robert Martin
New Richmond (4)	MC	715 246-4268	Kenneth Cernohous	....	Eloise M Anton	Eloise M Anton	Wade T Johnson	Dave Levi	....
North Fond du Lac v† (4)	MC	414 922-3240	Betty Ziewacz	....	Barbara Klingbile	....	Earl Pieper	James Sebestyen	Robert T Hinn
Oak Creek† (17)	MC	414 768-6500	Donald W Hermann	....	LaVerne Gutknecht	P Harry Eberle	Paul Manderle	Edmund Siarkiewicz	....
Oconomowoc§ (10)	MC	414 567-2133	Florence Whalen	Richard P Mercier	Ardyce Senfleben	George Langohr	Charles Witte	Leonard Schacht	Bernard Schultz
Oconto (5)	MC	414 834-2844	Glenn Garvey	....	Marcella Cook	Joseph McTavish	Michael Hoppe	Clark Longsine	....
Omro (3)	MC	414 685-5693	Aaron Fink	....	Janet Schettl	....	David Treleven	John Vonderloh	Gary Henke
Onalaska† (9)	MC	608 783-5666	Shirleigh Van Riper	....	Donald E Huggett	Leo Landsinger	Stanley Borchert	John Dlouhy	Mark Smick
Oregon v (4)	MC	608 835-3909	Roger Wetzel	....	Jeanette H Forman	....	Richard Andersen	Daniel Dahlke	Sylvandean D Farris
Oshkosh* (50)	CM	414 236-5000	Kathleen M Propp	William D Frueh	Donna Luebke	Edward Nokes	Calvin Phillipps	Donald Utecht	Gerald Konrad
Park Falls (3)	MC	715 762-2436	George Warshall	....	Neil D Hagmann	....	George Schneider	George Daniels	George Striegel
Peshtigo (3)	MC	715 582-3041	Henry Drees	....	Melvin G Sharpe	Melvin G Sharpe	Harvey R Behnke	Thomas Strouf	Peter A Kachel
Pewaukee v (5)	MC	414 691-3900	Lawrence E Farrell	Frank M Paulus	Elizabeth Williams	Lawrence E Farrell	James Babe	Edward M Baumann	Louis Thibault
Platteville* (10)	CM	608 348-9741	Lenny Glass	Merle L Strouse	Dean G Williams	Duane H Borgen	John Reiter	James L Enfelt	Mike Lewis
Plover v (5)	MC	715 346-2373	Daniel Schlutter	George T Bauman	Emmajane H Lee	Debra Sniadajewski	Joseph Radomski	Roger W Zebro	George T Bauman
Plymouth (6)	MC	414 893-1271	William B Kiley	....	Walter A Bein	Walter A Bein	Ronald Nicolaus	R H Bournoville	George F Schwartz
Port Washington§ (9)	MC	414 284-5585	George O Lampert	Stephen M Stapleton	Mary Downing	Stephen M Stapleton	Marc Eernisse	Edward Rudolph	Robert Dreblow
Portage (8)	MC	608 742-2176	Vincent P Smith	....	Alma M Braun	....	Claude B Hinickle	Thomas M Maloney	Michael T Horkan
Prairie du Chien (6)	MC	608 326-6406	(not reporting)						
Prescott (3)	MC	715 262-5544	Dean C Hauscaildt	....	Gordon M Johnson	....	Donald A Johnson	Myron H Dehning	Donald J Gutting
Racine (86)	MC	414 636-9011	Stephen F Olsen	....	Anthony J Schlaffer	Jerome J Maller	Ronald W Chiapete	James J Carvino	Fred H Larson
Reedsburg (5)	MC	608 524-6404	John W Bernien	....	Caroline R Held	....	Donald H Lichte	Reed A Woodward	Chester R Vogel
Rhinelander (8)	MC	715 362-7440	Joseph E Bloom	....	Deborah J Breivogel	Lorraine I Klug	Wallace Ritchie	Tony Paris	Eugene Oettinger
Rice Lake (8)	MC	715 234-7088	Alan D Arnold	....	Rhoda A Schnacky	....	Robert Reiten	Emmett Engstro	....
Richland Center (5)	MC	608 647-3466	LaVerne Hardy	....	Raymond Lawton	Eldon J Storer	Ralph Klinzing	Carter Harrison	Richard J Steiner
Ripon§ (7)	MC	414 748-7771	Warren C Bredahl	Stephen T Nenonen	Stephen T Nenonen	Stephen T Nenonen	Robert Lukoski	Dennis K Waller	Christopher Zoppa
River Falls§ (9)	MC	715 425-2447	Jerry E Wilkens	Eric Sorensen	Loyd E Ostness	Harris Kittelson	Butch Kahut	Perry Larson	David J Sonnenberg
River Hills v* (2)	CM	414 352-8213	Robert W Kasten	John M Fredrickson	Gladys B Cayze	....	Harold F Block	Harold F Block	....
Rothschild v (3)	MC	715 359-3660	Daniel Gorski	....	Sheila Pudelko	Sheila Pudelko	Calvin Bennett	Joseph E Toth	Merlin Owen
Sauk City v (3)	MC	608 643-3932	Maurice Schaefer	Paul Bartlett	....	....	S A Wipperfurth	Robert Rentmeester	Paul Patterson
Saukville v§ (3)	MC	414 284-9423	Paul E Miller	Kevin M Brunner	Kevin M Brunner	Kevin M Brunner	Paul Albinger Jr	William D Meloy	Bert Dietrich
Seymour (3)	MC	414 833-2209	Lowell Veitch	....	Judith I Zeuske	....	Robert Mory	John P Salchow	Earl R Gosse
Shawano (7)	MC	715 526-6138	Lee M Schrader	....	Rosella N Gartzke	Rosella N Gartzke	Melvin Knope	Donald Thaves	Maurice Rott
Sheboygan (48)	MC	414 459-3300	Richard W Suscha	....	Lawrence Felten	Richard C Gebhart	Bud Wagner	Victor O Keitel	Robert C F Kuhlmann
Sheboygan Falls (5)	MC	414 459-3191	Robert E Born	....	Corby D Felsher	Corby D Felsher	Raymond Schmitt	Jacob J Hermann Jr	Kenneth A Clark
Shorewood v* (14)	CM	414 332-4200	John J Mann	Shirl C Abbey	Robert M Stoffel	Robert M Stoffel	Alvin J Berndt	Alvin J Berndt	Chester Ignasiak
South Milwaukee (21)	MC	414 762-2222	C W Grobschmidt	Norbert S Theine	Jacqueline Johnson	Fred Brutvan	Russell Wendt	William Redding	William Lecher
Sparta (7)	MC	608 269-4340	M L Hulsether	....	Eleanor A Brooks	Theresa M Kowalski	Theodore Storandt	David P Kemp	James V Richgruber
St. Francis§† (10)	MC	414 481-2300	Milton Vretenar	Ralph Voltner Jr	Harriet Schwalbe	....	Robert Schwingle	Gerald G Barrett	Jack Schultz
Stevens Point (23)	MC	715 346-1570	Michael D Haberman	....	Phyllis Wisniewski	William Siebert	Peter Ugorek	Joseph Fandre	Jon Van Alstine
Stoughton (8)	MC	608 873-6677	Douglas Pfundheller	....	Helen J Johnson	John D Neal	Oscar J Forton	Stephen F Grady	Robert P Kardasz
Sturgeon Bay (9)	MC	414 743-3361	William O Wright	Edgar R Allingham	Paul C Bellin	Lawrence Bongle	Glen Anderson	Michael Nordin	Gary Blish
Sturtevant v† (4)	MC	414 886-4300	Abe Kirkorian	....	Barbara E Pauls	....	Fred Wright	Ronald R Kittel	....
Sun Prairie (13)	MC	608 837-2511	Donald N Foulke	....	Michael J Puksich	Michael J Puksich	Gene Hensen	Raymond C Boehlert	....
Superior (30)	MC	715 394-0200	Bruce C Hagen	....	Janet M Hennekens	Timothy M Nelson	John R Raaflaub	Robert L Bennett	C Robert Inglimo
Sussex v§ (3)	MC	414 246-8044	John H Tews	David Anderson	Lois Wandsneider	Lois Wandsneider	George Kaestner	....	Robert F Hutter
Thiensville v§ (3)	CO	414 242-3720	Robert Warber	Edward A Geick	John Gibbons	Edward A Geick	William Rausch	Kenneth Tushaus	Robert Gehrke
Tomah (7)	MC	608 372-5948	James F Ebert	....	Phillis Zimmerman	....	Howard Giesler	Duane E Owen	Keith C Keene
Tomahawk (4)	MC	715 453-4040	Harold F Burton	....	W F Hupfer	....	L Hanke	J Duplayee	....
Twin Lakes v (3)	MC	414 877-2858	James H Mayer	....	Jean Erickson	Jack Green	Donald Amborn	Peter DeMarco	Merlin Jahns
Two Rivers* (13)	CM	414 793-1191	....	James R Grassman	Gerald A Kasten	Gerald A Kasten	Ray J Kanugh	James F Thome	J J Kulhanek
Union Grove v (4)	MC	414 878-1818	Thomas Sorenson	....	Loretta Geason	Glen Cayemberg	Harmon Swantz	....	L Wm Behling
Verona§ (3)	MC	608 845-6495	R Thomas Moore	Beverly J Beyer	Beverly J Beyer	....	Donald D Stephens	Lynn Marquardt	Donald J Crownhart
Viroqua (4)	MC	608 637-7154	(not reporting)						
Washington t* (6)	CM	715 834-3257	Kenneth Stelzig	Ronald Funk	Helen Leipnitz	....	....	....	....
Watertown (18)	MC	414 261-4500	Kenneth P Thiel	....	Michael Hoppenrath	Michael Hoppenrath	Donald Asmus	Richard L Reynolds	Edward C Bennett
Waukesha (50)	MC	414 549-8000	Paul Keenan	....	Ruth Goetz	William Dick	Fred Baumgart	Thomas H Stigler	Rodney Vanden Noven
Waunakee v (4)	MC	608 849-5626	Math J Laufenberg	....	Robert H Ohlsen	....	John Joseph Kopp Jr	Frank A Balistreri	John Joseph Kopp Jr
Waupaca (4)	MC	715 258-2044	Daniel Schommer	....	Beverly Sather	Beverly Sather	Lee Thompson	Fred Rasmussen	Gene Sorensen
Waupun (8)	MC	414 324-5535	Robert Pease	....	Kyle J Clark	....	Norman D Lenz	Robert H Kindschuh	Ronald Beer
Wausau (32)	MC	715 845-5279	John L Kannenberg	....	Ernest J Cherney	Donald H Schultz	Kenneth Szeklinski	Sylvester Gajewski	....
Wauwatosa§ (51)	MC	414 258-3000	James A Brundahl	....	J R Neuman	....	Donald Bloedorn	Roy Wellnitz	J William Little
West Allis (64)	MC	414 476-4340	Jack F Barlich	....	Eldon Rinka	Paul M Ziehler	William Beres	Floyd Andrich	Leroy Krafcheck
West Bend§ (21)	MC	414 338-5103	Donald L Gonring	Dennis W Melvin	....	Claudine Kircher	Brian Mayer	James Skidmore	James J Schlosser

Directory 1/10 continued — MUNICIPAL OFFICIALS IN ALL U.S. CITIES OVER 2,500[1]

City, 1980 population (000 omitted), form of government	Municipal phone number	Mayor	Appointed administrator	City clerk	Finance officer	Fire chief	Police chief	Public works director
WISCONSIN (170) continued								
West Milwaukee v§ (4) MC	414 645-1530	Jenny Schuler	Frederick J Patrie	Frederick J Patrie	Frederick J Patrie	George F Heuer	Gerald S Gorlewski	Frederick J Patrie
West Salem v (3) . . . . MC	608 786-1858	Martin Hass	Kenneth Knutson	....	....	Harley Gilbertson	Thomas Suhr	....
Whitefish Bay v* (15) CM	414 962-6690	F Patrick Matthews	Michael C Harrigan	Lois M Tetzner	Lois M Tetzner	Alan N Myszewski	Alan N Myszewski	Carl Butz
Whitewater* (12). . . . . CM	414 473-3982	....	Paul B Webber	Wava Jean Nelson	Quinn C Smet	Larry Zimmerman	Bruce R Lyon	Leanne Miller
Wisconsin Rapids (18) MC	715 421-8200	James Paul Kubisiak	....	Robert O Boyarski	Donald C Zager	Donald Hafermann	Allen T Spencer	Roy G Elmhorst
Wisconsin Dells† (3) . . MC	608 254-2012	Richard Schauf	Robert Hillman	Robert Hillman	Robert Hillman	Robert McClyman	Elmer Fisher	Kenneth Weber
WYOMING (24)								
Buffalo t (4). . . . . MC	307 684-5566	Emil O Hecht	....	Nadine Gross	....	Robert L Hancock	Terrill G Barnhart	Bob Borgialli
Casper* (51) . . . . CM	307 235-8400	Joseph H Corrigan	Kenneth Erickson	Calvin L Chadsey	Calvin L Chadsey	Ronald R Baum	Edward F Kinion	James D Couch
Cheyenne (47) . . . . . . MC	307 637-6200	Don Erickson	Mick Snapp	Diana Deaguero	Ross Johnson	Charles Garey	Byron Rookstool	Gary Grunkemeyer
Cody (7). . . . . MC	307 527-7511	Dorse Miller Jr	....	James S Smiley	James S Smiley	Kirk Waggoner	Fred Wyatt	....
Douglas t§ (6) . . . . . . MC	307 358-3462	Dick George	Duane F Wroe	Betty Krivanec	Lauri Gillam	William Roberts	L W Majerus	Stephen F Bennett
Evanston t (6) . . . . . . MC	307 789-9690	Eugene B Martin	John F Hendrickson	Don U Welling	Lee Galeotos	Jon M Lunsford	Dennis Harvey	Wayne Shepherd
Evansville t (3) . . . . . . MC	307 234-6530	Norman D Anthony	Patricia Spaulding	Joyce D Hill	Vicki L Allen	Patrick A Terry	Donald McHattie	Maurice F Boyd
Gillette* (12) . . . . CM	307 686-5200	H A Carter	Alan E Tandy	Mildred Huravitch	David Layden	Sam Weinger	Bob Hartman	Glen M Taylor
Glenrock t§ (3) . . . . . . MC	307 436-9294	Robert Harper	Joseph G Wolf	Barbara Ann Bolton	Carol A Hampton	Vince Wickett	M C Chris Matson	David M Eason
Green River§ (13) . . . . MC	307 875-5000	Bonnie Pendleton	Randall H Reid	Norman Stark	Norman Stark	Glenn Hill	Reed Hayes	Richard Lemke
Jackson t* (5) . . . . . . CM	307 733-3932	Robert L Shervin	Melvin Webb	Jackie Lynes	Melvin Webb	George Shearer	Richard Hays	Mike Yokel
Kemmerer (3). . . . . . . MC	307 877-9007	Kaye Jones	John David Johnson	Evelyn Peterson	Agnes Scott	Robert Brunski	Wayne Wright	Jim White
Lander (9). . . . . MC	307 332-2870	Del Mc Omie	Alan O'Hashi	Paul J Freese	....	Wendell R Hudson	Bob Campbell	Darrell E Allen
Laramie* (24). . . . . . . CM	307 721-5200	Peggy A Deaver	Geo P McConnaughey	Jean Karch	William H Morrison	Don E Young	Gerald E Overman	Wesley James Nelson
Newcastle† (4) . . . . . . MC	307 746-3535	Louis W Carlson	....	Patricia Trosello	Aaron G Tunnell	Gene Diedtrich	Howard Snider	Cledus M Highland
Powell (5) . . . . MC	307 754-5106	Richard W Heasler	Raymond J Lutterman	Ross J Buchan	Ross J Buchan	Joe Darrah	Robert Coorough	Richard Myrick
Rawlins* (12). . . . . . . CM	307 324-2411	Glen A Woodbury	John C Darrington	Donald A Urban	Harriett M Carlson	Carol Allen	Norman A Wilson	....
Riverton* (10) . . . . . . CM	307 856-2227	James Soumas	William A Peterson	Dorothy C Shoup	Dorothy C Shoup	Dale Hinton	Dennis F Horyza	George Oetken
Rock Springs (19) . . . . MC	307 362-2330	C Keith West	Brian Rick	Jeanne Brinkerhoff	Jeanne Brinkerhoff	Harvey Cozad	Lawrence Levitt	Glenn Sugano
Sheridan† (15) . . . . . . MC	307 674-6483	M Dean Marshall	....	Arthur W Elkins	....	Aaron Holst	Roger F Krout	Tony Pelesky Jr
Thermopolis t§ (4). . . . MC	307 864-3838	Clark E Mortimore	R A Schaumleffeljr	Sharon Basse	....	Vincent Hanson	Harlan Sundermeyer	Russell Sorensen
Torrington t (5). . . . . . MC	307 532-5666	Blaine Ronne	....	Glen R Arends	Glen R Arends	Mike Vick	William P Reeves	John Tucker
Wheatland t (6). . . . . . MC	307 322-2962	Charles Parsons	James R Dunham	James R Dunham	James R Dunham	Leo Urbanek	Arnold Evans	James R Dunham
Worland (6) . . . . MC	307 347-4255	Timothy E McHenry	....	Dennis P Smith	Dennis P Smith	Robert Taylor	Allen B Tolley	John P Miller

E 2

Professional, Special Assistance, and Educational Organizations Serving Local and State Governments

This article briefly describes 76 organizations that provide services of particular importance to cities, counties, and other local and state governments. Most of the organizations are membership groups—school administrators, health officers, city planners, city managers, public works directors, city attorneys, and other administrators who are appointed rather than elected. Several are general service and representational organizations for states, cities, counties, and administrators and citizens. Several provide distinctive research, technological, consulting, and educational programs on a cost-of-service basis and have been established to meet specific needs of state and local governments. The others support educational activities in urban affairs or government administration and/or conduct research and other educational activities and thereby indirectly serve to strengthen professionalism in government administration.

Shown below are: (1) a listing of the 76 organizations with name, address, name of executive director or other administrator, major publications, purpose of the organization, and date established; and (2) Table 2/1 with information on these 76 organizations with respect to membership, number of chapters, services, conferences, staff, and expenditures.

The advisory aids available through the secretariats of these national organizations provide an excellent method of obtaining expert advice and actual information on specific problems. The information secured in this way enables local and state officials to improve administrative practices, organization, and methods and thus to improve the quality of services rendered to the people. Many of these organizations also are active in raising their standards of membership through in-service training, special conferences and seminars, and other kinds of professional development.

Research on current problems is a continuing activity of many of these groups, and all issue a variety of publications ranging from a minimum of a newsletter and occasional bulletins to diversified books, monographs, research papers, conference proceedings, and regular and special reports.

These organizations provide many of the services that in other countries would be the responsibility of the national government. They arrange annual conferences, publish newsletters and magazines, answer inquiries, provide in-service training and other kinds of professional development, provide placement services for members, and develop service and cost standards for various activities.

Most of the organizations in Table 2/1 have individual memberships, and several also have agency or institutional memberships. Some of these organizations have service memberships which may be based on the population of the jurisdiction, the annual revenue of the jurisdiction or agency, or other criteria that roughly measure the costs of providing service.

In addition to these kinds of membership fees, some of the organizations provide specialized consulting, training, and information services both by annual subscription and by charges for specific projects.

LISTING OF ORGANIZATIONS

Academy for State and Local Government, 444 North Capitol Street, N.W., Room 349, Washington, D.C. 20001. (202) 638-1445. Director: Enid Beaumont. Major publications: Publications list available on request. Purpose: To serve as the research, training, and management foundation for joint projects and programs of Council of State Governments, International City Management Association, National Association of Counties, National Conference of State Legislatures, National Governors' Association, National League of Cities, and U.S. Conference of Mayors. An arm of the Academy, the State and Local Legal Center, is devoted to the interests of state and local governments in the Supreme Court. Established 1971.

Airport Operators Council International, 1700 K Street, N.W., Washington, D.C. 20006. (202) 296-3270. Executive Director: J. Donald Reilly. Major publication: *Airport Highlights*. Purpose: To promote sound policies dealing with financing, construction, management, operations, and development of airports; to provide reference and resource facilities and information for airport operators; and to act as a voice to the public on the problems and solutions as well as the potential of airport operations. Established 1948.

American Association of Airport Executives, 2301 M Street, N.W., Washington, D.C. 20037. (202) 331-8994. Executive Vice President: Charles M. Barclay. Major publications: *Airport Report*; the Executive Manuals. Purpose: To assist the airport manager in performing responsibilities to the airport and community through an airport management reference library; a consulting service; publications containing technical, administrative, legal, and operational information. Established 1928.

American Association of Port Authorities, 1612 K Street, N.W., Washington, D.C. 20006. (202) 331-1263. President: J. Ron Brinson. Major publication: *World Ports*. Purpose: To exchange information relative to port construction, maintenance, operation, organization, administration, and management; to standardize and establish uniformity in operation, construction, and management of port facilities; and to promote port authorities and the development and encouragement of waterborne transportation. Established 1912.

American Association of School Administrators, 1801 North Moore Street, Arlington, Virginia 22209. (703) 528-0700. Executive Director: Paul B. Salmon. Major publications: *The School Administrator*; Critical Issues Series. Purpose: To develop highly qualified educational leaders and support excellence in educational administration; to initiate and support laws, policies, research and practice that will improve education; to promote programs and activities that focus on leadership for learning and excellence in education; and to cultivate a climate in which quality education can thrive. Established 1865.

American College of Hospital Administrators, 840 North Lake Shore Drive, Chicago 60611. (312) 943-0544. President: Stuart A. Wesbury, Jr., Ph.D. Major publications: *Hospital and Health Services Administration; ACHA News; Directory* (biennial); and miscellaneous task force, committee, and seminar reports. Purpose: To elevate the standards of competency for hospital and health services administrators through programs which include continuing education, professional certification, research, publications, and the recognition of managerial distinction and contributions to the health service delivery field. Established 1933.

American Institute of Architects, 1735 New York Avenue, N.W., Washington, D.C. 20006. (202) 626-7300. Executive Vice President: David Olan Meeker, Jr., FAIA. Major publications: *AIA Journal; AIA Memo*. Purpose: To promote professionalism in the field; to promote aesthetic, scientific, and practical efficiency of the profession; to advance the science and art of planning and building by advancing the standards of architectural education, training, and practice; and to coordinate the building industry and the profession of architecture to ensure the advancement of the standard of living through an improved environment. Established 1857.

American Library Association, 50 East Huron Street, Chicago 60611. (312) 944-6780. Executive Director: Robert Wedgworth. Major publications: *American Libraries*; *Booklist*; *Choice*. Purpose: To assist libraries and librarians in promoting and improving library service and librarianship. Established 1876.

American Planning Association. Including the American Institute of Certified Planners (AICP). 1776 Massachusetts Avenue, N.W., Washington, D.C. 20036. (202) 872-0611. With an office also at: 1313 East 60th Street, Chicago 60637. (312) 955-9100. Executive Director: Israel Stollman. Major publications: *Journal of the APA*; *Planning*; *Planning Advisory Service Reports*; *Land-Use Law & Zoning Digest*. Purpose: To advance the art and science of urban and regional planning; to promote effective techniques for development in cities, regions, and states; to provide research for planners and information on new developments; and to bring together the professional planner, citizen, elected official, developer, and practitioner. AICP provides an examination for certification, promotes professional continuing education, and administers accreditation of university planning curricula. Established 1978.

American Public Gas Association, P.O. Box 1426, Vienna, Virginia 22180. (703) 281-2910. Executive Director: Arie M. Virrips. Major publications: *Newsletter*; *Publicly Owned Natural Gas System* (annual); *Energy Saving Handbook for Homeowners*. Purpose: To provide professional assistance to public gas systems. Established 1961.

American Public Health Association, 1015 15th Street, N.W., Washington, D.C. 20005. (202) 789-5600. Executive Director: William H. McBeath. Major publication: *American Journal of Public Health*. Purpose: To protect the health of the public through the maintenance of standards for scientific procedures, legislative education, and practical application of innovative health care programs. Established 1872.

American Public Power Association, 2301 M Street, N.W., Washington, D.C. 20037. (202) 775-8300. Executive Director: Alex Radin. Major publications: *Public Power*; *Weekly Newsletter*. Purpose: To promote the efficiency of publicly owned electric systems; to achieve greater cooperation among public systems; to protect the interest of publicly owned utilities; and to provide services in the fields of management and operation, energy conservation, consumer services, public relations, engineering, design, construction, research and accounting practice, and legal policy. Established 1942.

American Public Transit Association, 1225 Connecticut Avenue, N.W., Washington, D.C. 20036. (202) 828-2800. Executive Vice President: Jack R. Gilstrap. Major publications: *Passenger Transport*; *Transit Factbook*; *Annual Labor Review*. Purpose: To represent the operators of and suppliers to public transit; to provide a medium for exchange of experiences, discussion, and comparative study of industry affairs; to research and investigate methods to improve public transit; to provide assistance in dealing with special issues; and to collect, compile, and make available data and information relative to public transit. Established 1882.

American Public Welfare Association, 1125 15th Street, N.W., Washington, D.C. 20005. (202) 293-7550. Executive Director: Edward T. Weaver. Major publications: *Public Welfare*; *Public Welfare Directory*; *This Week in Washington*; *W-Memo*; *Congressional Record Index*. Purpose: To promote the professional development of persons working in the field of public welfare; and to work for more effective federal policy in human services including income assistance, social services, health care, and employment services. Established 1930.

American Public Works Association, 1313 East 60th Street, Chicago 60637. (312) 667-2200. Executive Director: Robert D. Bugher. Major publications: *APWA Reporter*; bi-annual *Directory*; research reports; technical publications and manuals. Purpose: To advance the theory and practice of all aspects of public works facilities and services; to disseminate information on improved practices; to encourage high professional standards; and to promote cooperation in the field of public works. Established 1894.

American Society for Public Administration, 1120 G Street, N.W., Washington, D.C. 20005. (202) 393-7878. Executive Director: Keith F. Mulrooney. Major publications: *Public Administration Review*; *Public Administration Times*. Purpose: To improve the management of public service at all levels of government; to advance the science, processes, and art of public administration; and to disseminate information and facilitate the exchange of knowledge among persons interested in the practice or teaching of public administration. Established 1939.

American Water Works Association, 6666 West Quincy Avenue, Denver 80235. (303) 794-7711. Executive Director: David Preston. Major publications: *Journal AWWA*; *Mainstream*; *Op Flow*. Purpose: To promote public health, safety, and welfare through the improvement of the quality and quantity of water for the public. Established 1881.

Associated Public-Safety Communications Officers, Inc., P.O. Box 669, New Smyrna Beach, Florida 32070. (904) 427-3461. Executive Director: Robert E. Tall. Major publications: *APCO Bulletin*; *The Journal of Public Safety Communications*; *Public Safety Operating Procedures Manual; Frequency Coordination Manual; Police Telecommunication Systems Text; Theory of Waiting Times; Lifeline Dispatcher Training Course*. Purpose: To promote the development and progress of public safety telecommunications through research, planning, and training; to promote cooperation among public safety agencies; and to act as a liaison with federal regulatory bodies. Established 1935.

Building Officials and Code Administrators International, 4051 West Flossmoor Road, Country Club Hills, Illinois 60477. (312) 799-2300. Executive Director: Clarence R. Bechtel. Major publications: National Basic Code Series; *The Building Official and Code Administrator; BOCA Bulletin;* Research Reports; Professional Development Series. Publications catalog available on request. Purpose: To promulgate a complete package of performance model codes; to assist the user through training and educational services; and to provide technical services such as plan reviews, product evaluations, inspections, and administrative and management reviews. Established 1915.

Cable Television Information Center, 1500 North Beauregard Street, Suite 205, Alexandria, Virginia 22311. (703) 845-1700. President: Harold E. Horn. Major publications: *CTIC Cable Reports*, monthly newsletter. Purpose: To help local officials make informed decisions about cable television; to provide a centralized cable resource and information center to local governments across the country; to provide background information, valuable contacts and suggestions to local governments; and to represent local government interests in the formation of cable policy at the federal level. Established 1972.

Canadian Association of Municipal Administrators, 1318–112 Kent Street, Ottawa, Ontario K1P 5P2, Canada. (613) 237-5221. Executive Secretary: Jack Willis. Purpose: To improve the capability of Canadian municipal administrators and assist municipalities in providing effective and efficient local government services. Established 1972. An affiliate, the Canadian Municipal Personnel Association, serves as a major resource group in the area of urban personnel and labor relations. Established 1977.

Council for International Urban Liaison, 1120 G Street, N.W., Washington, D.C. 20005. (202) 626-4624. President: John Garvey, Jr. Purpose: To service the state, county, and city governmental and professional associations that formed the Council by strengthening their capabilities in international exchanges; to provide the members of these associations and other public and private organizations information on useful ideas; and to encourage the adaptation and practical usage of ideas where they fill a local need. Located in the offices of the International City Management Association. CIUL provides additional services to ICMA by contract.

Council on Municipal Performance, 30 Irving Place, New York, New York 10003. (212) 420-5950. President: John Tepper Marlin. Major publications: annual reports, Government Accounting and Auditing Series; *Contracting Municipal Services;* papers; Securities Regulation Series; *The Book of American City Rankings* (Facts on File, 1983); newsletter. Purpose: To publish comparative data on local governments; to promote more effective delivery of municipal services; and to provide business approaches to government operations. Established 1973.

Council of State Community Affairs Agencies, 444 North Capitol Street, Room 349, Washington, D.C. 20001. (202) 393-6435. Executive Director: John Sidor. Major publications: *State CDBG Update; State Enterprise Zones; States, Affordable Housing, and Land Use; Using Revolving Loan Funds in CDBG;* and others. Purpose: To help state agencies keep abreast of state and federal initiatives in local assistance; and to improve state programs through interstate coordination. Established 1974.

Council of State Governments, Iron Works Pike, P.O. Box 11910, Lexington, Kentucky 40578. (606) 252-2291. Executive Director: Carl W. Stenberg. Major publications: *Book of the States; State Government; State Government News*. Purpose: To strengthen state government in the federal system; to assist states in improving their legislative, administrative, and judicial practices; to promote state-local and interstate cooperation; and to facilitate state-federal relations. Established 1933.

Federation of Canadian Municipalities, 1318–112 Kent Street, Ottawa, Ontario K1P 5P2, Canada. (613) 237-5221. Executive Director: James W. Knight. Major publications: *Management and Planning Capabilities in Small Communities; Municipal Government in a New Canadian Federal System, vols. 1 and 2; FCM Forums* (newsletter); a series of six bilingual lexicons on administrative and technical municipal terminology; *Six, Five & Counting: Innovations in Municipal Economy*; and a brief to the Macdonald Commission on the economy. Purpose: To represent the national interest of local governments in Canada; and to act as a spokesman for Canadian local governments and as a clearinghouse for the collection, exchange, and dissemination of statistical data and information on Canadian municipal practices and procedures. Established 1937.

Government Finance Officers Association (formerly Municipal Finance Officers Association), 180 North Michigan Avenue, Suite 800, Chicago 60601. (312) 977-9700. With an office at 1750 K Street, N.W., Suite 200, Washington, D.C. 20006. (202) 466-2014. Executive Director: Jeffrey L. Esser. Major publications: *MFOA Newsletter; Governmental Finance Magazine; Resources in Review; Public Investor; GAAFR Review; Creative Capital Financing; Costing Government Services; Micro-computers in Government;* and *A Guide to Municipal Leasing*. Purpose: To establish professional policies and practices of government finance by: researching and establishing technical practices and policies of government finance management for state and local government; expanding the opportunities for professional recognition and career development of all persons who serve in the financial and related areas of government; identifying and researching major issues of intergovernmental fiscal policy and informing those interested in such issues; and extending cooperation and assistance to other associations and professional organizations concerned with government finance. Established 1906.

Governmental Refuse Collection and Disposal Association, P.O. Box 7219, Silver Spring, Maryland 20910. (301) 585-2898. Executive Director: H. Lanier Hickman, Jr. Purpose: To disseminate information through education programs and research projects in such areas as legislative activities, institutional constraints, engineering principles, operational functions, and standards of the solid waste management industry in order to achieve an environmentally sound, economically competitive, and effective system for solid waste management. Established 1962.

Governmental Research Association, 24 Province Street, Boston, Massachusetts 02109. (617) 357-8500. President: Earl M. Ryan. Major publications: *GRA Directory; GRA Reporter*; bibliography. Purpose: To promote and coordinate the activities of governmental research agencies; to encourage the development of effective organization and methods for the administration and operation of government; to encourage the development of common standards for the appraisal of results; to facilitate the exchange of ideas and experiences; and to serve as a clearinghouse. Established 1914.

ICMA Retirement Corporation, 1120 G Street, N.W., Washington, D.C. 20005. (202) 737-6616. President: Peter L. DeGroote. Purpose: To administer retirement plans as an aid to units of government in their overall personnel management programs. Included are supplemental and deferred programs as well as portable retirement plans for mobile personnel. Established 1972.

Institute of Internal Auditors, Inc., P.O. Box 1119, 249 Maitland Avenue, Altamonte Springs, Florida 32701. (305) 830-7600. President: Stanley C. Gross, CIA. Major publication: *The Internal Auditor*. Purpose: To provide comprehensive professional development activities and the standards for the practice of internal auditing; to research, disseminate, and promote knowledge and information about internal auditing and internal control. Of special interest to government auditors are the Institute's activities in governmental and public affairs. Established 1941.

Institute of Public Administration, 55 West 44th Street, New York 10036. (212) 730-5480. With offices at 1717 Massachusetts Avenue, N.W., Washington, D.C. 20036, (202) 667-6551, and Banco de Ponce Building, Suite 1102, Hato Rey, San Juan, Puerto Rico 00918, (809) 753-6399. President: Annmarie H. Walsh. Major publications: IPA Report (quarterly); list of other publications available on request. Purpose: To provide research, training, education, and advisory services in areas of public policy, government structure, public authorities, personnel management and training, public-private sector improvements, economic development, charter revision, planning and management, and intergovernmental program responsibilities and relationships. Established 1906.

Institute of Transportation Engineers (formerly Institute of Traffic Engineers), 525 School Street, S.W., Washington, D.C. 20024. (202) 554-8050. Executive Director: Thomas W. Brahms. Major publications: *ITE Journal*; Transportation Training Series; *Transportation and Traffic Engineering Handbook; Manual of Traffic Signal Design; Manual of Traffic Engineering Studies; Introduction to Transportation Engineering; Trip Generation Rates*. Purpose: To promote professional development in the field through support and encouragement of education, research, development of public awareness, and exchange of information. Established 1930.

International Association of Assessing Officers, 1313 East 60th Street, Chicago 60637. (312) 947-2069. Executive Director: Richard R. Almy. Major publications: *Assessment Digest; Property Tax Journal; Assessment and Valuation Legal Reporter; Property Assessment Valuation; Improving Real Property Assessment: A Reference Manual;* Bibliographic Series; Research and Information Series; Assessment Standards. Purpose: To improve standards and develop better techniques in assessment administration. Established 1934.

International Association of Auditorium Managers, 500 North Michigan Avenue, Suite 1400, Chicago 60611. (312) 661-1700. Executive Director: Richard E. Kinville. Major publications: *Auditorium News; Membership Directory; Facility Operations Manual; Industry Profile Survey*. Purpose: To promote professional development in the public assembly field and provide assistance to members. Membership consists of the managers of arenas, convention centers, auditoriums, and stadiums. Established 1924.

International Association of Chiefs of Police, 13 Firstfield Road, Gaithersburg, Maryland 20878. (301) 948-0922. Executive Director: Norman Darwick. Major publications: *Police Chief; Journal of Police Science and Administration; Law Enforcement Legal Review; Training Key; Police Reference Notebook*. Purpose: To advance the art of police science through development and dissemination of improved administrative, technical, and operational practices and to promote their use in police work; to foster police cooperation and exchange of information and experience among police administrators; to recruit and train qualified persons; and to encourage adherence of all police officers to high professional standards of performance and conduct. Established 1893.

International Association of Fire Chiefs, 1329 18th Street, N.W., Washington, D.C. 20036. (202) 833-3420. General Manager: Donald D. Flinn. Major publications: *The International Fire Chief; Washington Scene; The Management Report*. Purpose: To provide an information resource for those charged with the task of administering fire prevention, protection, and suppression efforts in the United States, Canada, and abroad. Established 1873. An affiliate is the International Association of Fire Chiefs Foundation. President: Arthur J. Glatfelter. Purpose: To promote the public good through fire service. The foundation will create and carry out programs that result in increased fire department efficiency and heightened public awareness of the need for ongoing programs of fire prevention, fire detection, and fire protection. Established 1974.

International City Management Association, 1120 G Street, N.W., Washington, D.C. 20005. (202) 626-4600. Executive Director: William H. Hansell, Jr. Major publications: *Public Management; ICMA Newsletter;* Municipal Management Series; *Municipal Year Book;* Baseline Data Reports; Management Information Service Reports; Practical Management Series; *Compensation 84*. Purpose: To strengthen the quality of urban government through professional management; to strengthen the competence of appointed urban managers and ensure qualified talent to meet urban government needs; to provide information and analysis of data, management ideas, and methods for urban government management; and to participate in the development and translation of new concepts for urban government management. Established in 1914.

International Conference of Building Officials, 5360 South Workman Mill Road, Whittier, California 90601. (213) 699-0541. Executive Director: James E. Bihr, P.E. Major publications: Uniform building code and related codes, mechanical, plumbing, housing, signs, dangerous buildings, and fire prevention; textbooks on building department administration, building inspection, plan review, mechanical inspection, concrete inspection; instructor guides and student workbooks on fire protection, building department administration, all phases of building inspection; *Building Standards* magazine and newsletter. Purpose: To develop and maintain uniform codes for the benefit of member city, county, and state agencies; to provide a research service on new building products and systems; to develop educational programs and seminars and certification programs for inspectors; to provide management studies of building department operations; and to provide engineering consultative services on code matters including plan review and interpretation and application of code requirements. Established 1922.

International Institute of Municipal Clerks, 160 North Altadena Drive, Pasadena, California 91107. (818) 795-6153. Executive Director: John J. Hunnewell. Major publications: *IIMC News Digest;* Case Study Packets; *IIMC Ordinance File; Consent Agenda; Indexing and Filing Council Minutes; Computerization of Licenses; Computer/Word Processing Use in the Municipal Clerk's Office.* Purpose: To improve administration of state, provincial, county, and local government through the position of clerk, secretary, or recorder—by maintaining central facilities for study and research devoted to improvement of methods and procedures relating to the municipal clerk's duties; by sponsoring professional career development institutes in 34 universities; by maintaining an Academy for Advanced Education with seminars at 26 universities; by offering a home study course in supervision; and by administering a professional certification program. Established 1947.

International Personnel Management Association—United States, 1850 K Street, N.W., Suite 870, Washington, D.C. 20006. (202) 833-5860. Executive Director: Donald K. Tichenor. Major publications: *Public Personnel Management; Agency Issues; IPMA News; Pay Rates in the Public Service;* Public Employee Relations Library (PERL) Series. Purpose: To promote public personnel management with emphasis on the merit system; to provide for the exchange of information relating to public personnel management; and to provide services and assistance to public personnel agencies. Established 1973.

Labor-Management Relations Service, 1620 Eye Street, N.W., 4th Floor, Washington, D.C. 20006. (202) 293-6790. Director: Roger Dahl. Major publications: *LMRS Newsletter;* Labor Relations Monographs; LMRS Special Reports. Purpose: Sponsored by the United States Conference of Mayors to respond to inquiries from local officials; to conduct special research studies; and to provide training services including scheduled state workshops, regional conferences, workshops at state and national conferences, and on-the-job training fellowships. LMRS also makes available to local government jurisdictions an array of management development and productivity improvement programs. Established 1970.

League of Women Voters of the United States, 1730 M Street, N.W., Washington, D.C. 20036. (202) 429-1965. Executive Director: Carol Parr. Major publications: *The National Voter; Report from the Hill; Action Alerts.* Purpose: The League is a nonpartisan organization encouraging citizens to participate actively in government and politics at the national, state, and local levels and to study, monitor, and lobby on public policy issues including water resources, clean air, nuclear energy, national security, voting rights, election laws, and women's employment. Established 1920. The League of Women Voters Education Fund, a separate but complementary organization, provides research, educational publications, and services to league members and the public and conducts citizen education and election-related projects. Executive Director: Carol Parr. Major publications: *Nuclear Power Primer; Blueprint for Clean Air; Tell It to Washington; Choosing the President; Hazardous Waste Primer; Pick a Candidate; U.S. National Security: Fact and Assumptions.* Established 1957.

Maritime Municipal Training and Development Board, 6209 University Avenue, Halifax, Nova Scotia B3H 3J5 Canada. (902) 424-3712. Executive Director: A. Donald Smeltzer. Major publications: *Municipal Personnel Policy and Procedure Resource Manual; Cash Management Handbook for Local Government; Training and Development for Local Government; The Boardroom Files; Roles, Responsibilities and Operating Procedures for New Brunswick Local Government; Productivity in Municipal Government: Concepts, Measurement and Improvement.* Purpose: To improve administrative operations in Maritime local government through the facilitation of information services, research and resource development, and the identification and resolution of administrative problems. Established 1974.

National Animal Control Association, P.O. Box 187, Colorado Springs, Colorado 80901. (303) 473-1741. Secretary: Phil Arkow. Major publications: *The NACA News*, newsletter. Purpose: To provide training for animal control personnel; to provide consultation and guidance for city governments on animal control ordinances, animal shelter design, budget and program planning, and staff training; and to provide public education. Established in 1978.

National Association of Counties, 440 First Street, N.W., Washington, D.C. 20001. (202) 393-6226. Executive Director: Matthew Coffey. Major publication: *County News.* Purpose: To serve as the voice of county government at the national level; to promote county government's heritage and its future; to serve as a liaison between county government and other levels of government; to achieve public understanding of the role of counties in the federal system; to provide information and analysis of data. Established 1935. Through the National Association of Counties Research Foundation (NACoRF), NACo maintains expertise in major problems and programs of county governments. Through the National Association of Counties Research, Inc. (NACoR, Inc.), NACo undertakes research pursuant to governmental grants and other grants. NACoR, Inc., was established in 1977.

National Association of Housing and Redevelopment Officials, 2600 Virginia Avenue, N.W., Washington, D.C. 20037. (202) 333-2020. Executive Director: Robert W. Maffin. Major publications: *Journal of Housing; NAHRO Monitor;* Rehabilitation and Neighborhood Conservation Series; *Housing for the Handicapped and Disabled: A Guide for Local Action; Directory of Local Agencies; Handbook for Commissioners.* Purpose: To serve as the professional organization for policymakers, administrators, program professionals, and technicians who deal with the planning, development, and management of housing for low and moderate income families and with the community development field. Established 1933.

National Association of Regional Councils, 1700 K Street, N.W., Washington, D.C. 20006. (202) 457-0710. Executive Director: Richard C. Hartman. Major publications: *Washington Report; Directory of Regional Councils.* Purpose: To promote the development and understanding of regional councils; to provide up-to-date information and technical assistance to councils; to assist in the expansion of regional council program opportunities; to develop and communicate national policy proposals on issues of regional impact; and to act as a liaison with federal and state agencies in order to promote the use of regional councils and present their needs. Established 1967.

National Association of Schools of Public Affairs and Administration, Suite 520, 1120 G Street, N.W., Washington, D.C. 20005. (202) 628-8965. Executive Director: Alfred M. Zuck. Major publications: *Guidelines/Standards for Undergraduates/Graduates in Public Affairs/Administration;* Peer Review Process Series; *Programs in Public Affairs and Administration 1984.* Purpose: To serve as a national center for information about programs and developments in the area of public affairs and administration; to foster goals and standards of educational excellence; and to represent members' concerns and interests in the formulation and support of national, state, and local policies for education and research. Established 1970.

National Association for State Information Systems, Iron Works Pike, Lexington, Kentucky 40578. (606) 252-2291. Executive Director: Carl Vorlander. Major publications: *NASIS Newsletter; NASIS Annual Report*. Purpose: To strengthen state government through the application of information systems technology; to act as a liaison with federal agencies; and to promote the development and transferal of information systems between states. Established 1969.

National Association of Towns and Townships, 1522 K Street, N.W., Suite 730, Washington, D.C. 20005. (202) 737-5200. Executive Director: Barton D. Russell. Major publication: *National Community Reporter*. Purpose: To offer technical assistance, educational services, and public policy support to local government officials from towns, townships, and other small communities across the country; to conduct research and to develop public policy recommendations scaled to the unique needs and nature of rural governments and small towns; to keep local officials abreast of decisions and actions of national import. Established 1963.

National Conference of State Legislatures, 1125 17th Street, Denver 80202. (303) 292-6600. Executive Director: Earl S. Mackey. Major publication: *State Legislatures*. Purpose: To improve the quality and effectiveness of state legislatures; to assure states a strong, cohesive voice in the federal decisionmaking process; and to foster interstate communication and cooperation. Established 1975. The Conference's Office of State-Federal Relations, 444 North Capitol Street, Washington, D.C. 20001, (202) 737-7004, produces *Capital to Capital*.

National Council for Urban Economic Development, 1730 K Street, N.W., Washington, D.C. 20006. (202) 223-4735. Executive Director: James E. Peterson. Major publications: *Urban Economic Developments; Economic Development Commentary; Legislative Report*. Purpose: To research and disseminate information on urban economic development and to strengthen the role and capacity of urban economic development organizations. Established 1967.

National Environmental Health Association, 1200 Lincoln Street, Suite 704, Denver 80203. (303) 861-9090. Executive Director: Nelson E. Fabian. Major publication: *Journal of Environmental Health*. Purpose: To maintain and improve the standards of performance in environmental health by promoting and encouraging research, education, and the dissemination of information; to publish information relating to environmental health; and to promote professionalism in the field. Established 1937.

National Fire Protection Association, Batterymarch Park, Quincy, Massachusetts 02269. (617) 328-9290. President: Robert W. Grant. Major publications: *National Fire Codes; Fire Protection Handbook; Fire Journal; Fire Service Today; Fire Technology;* textbooks, manuals, training packages, detailed analyses of important fires, fire officers guides, and others. Purpose: To safeguard people and their environment from destructive fire using scientific and engineering techniques and education; to develop and publish consensus standards intended to minimize the possibility and effects of fire; and to educate the public in ways to avoid loss of life and property from fire by making good fire safety habits a way of life. Established 1896.

National Governors' Association, Hall of the States, 444 North Capitol Street, Washington, D.C. 20001. (202) 624-5300. Director: Raymond C. Scheppach. Major publications: *Governors' Bulletin; Fiscal Survey of the States;* reports on a wide range of state issues. Purpose: To act as a liaison with the federal government; and to serve as a clearinghouse for information and ideas on how state and national issues can be resolved. Established 1908.

National Housing Conference, 1126 16th Street, N.W., Suite 211, Washington, D.C. 20036. (202) 223-4844. Executive Director: Jon W. Linfield. Major publications: *NHC Legislative Resolutions; NHC Reports from Washington*. Purpose: To promote better communities and housing for Americans through legislative action. Established 1931.

National Institute of Governmental Purchasing, 115 Hillwood Avenue, Suite 201, Falls Church, Virginia 22046. (703) 533-7300. Executive Vice President: Lewis E. Spangler. Major publications: *NIGP Letter Service Bulletin; NIGP Technical Bulletin; Dictionary of Purchasing Terms; Value Analysis Program Guide; Basic Public Purchasing and Materials Management; Intermediate Public Purchasing and Materials Management; Advanced Public Purchasing and Materials Management; Competitive Sealed Proposals; Competitive Negotiation Seminar Course; Universal Certification Requirements for Public Purchasing Personnel*. Purpose: To raise the standards of the public purchasing profession through the interchange of information and ideas. Established 1944.

National Institute of Municipal Law Officers, 1000 Connecticut Avenue, N.W., Suite 800, Washington, D.C. 20036. (202) 460-5424. General Counsel: Charles S. Rhyne. Major publications: *Municipal Attorney; Municipal Ordinance Review; Municipal Law Court Decisions; Municipal Law Docket; Municipal Newsletter*. Purpose: To provide law information, research, library services, and publications on law information to member municipal law officers. Established 1935.

National League of Cities, 1301 Pennsylvania Avenue, N.W., Washington, D.C. 20004. (202) 626-3000. Executive Director: Alan Beals. Major publications: *Nation's Cities Weekly; Urban Affairs Abstracts; National Municipal Policy; Priorities for American Cities; Directory of Local Officials*. Purpose: To strengthen the role and capacity of state leagues and municipal governments through research programs, information exchange, legislative representation, and federal liaison activities. Established 1924.

National Municipal League/Citizens Forum on Self-Government, 55 West 44th Street, New York 10036. (212) 730-7930. Executive Director: William N. Cassella, Jr. Major publication: *National Civic Review*. Purpose: To serve as a clearinghouse for information on methods of improving state and local government; to encourage citizen participation in state and local government; and to provide guides, model charters, and laws on specific subjects. Operates computer-assisted Civic Information and Techniques Exchange (CIVITEX) and sponsors the All-America Cities Awards program. Established 1894.

National Public Employer Labor Relations Association, 1620 Eye Street, N.W., 4th Floor, Washington, D.C. 20006. (202) 296-2230. President: Peter Vallone. Executive Director: Roger E. Dahl. Major publications: *NPELRA Newsletter;* contract clause reference manual; strike contingency planning manual; and arbitration manual. Purpose: To further the professional interests of federal, state, county, school/special district, and municipal government managers in the area of labor relations through training programs and the dissemination and exchange of information and policy pertaining to all areas of public sector labor relations; and to promote cooperation among members and professional standards in the field. Established 1971.

National Recreation and Park Association, 3101 Park Center Drive, Alexandria, Virginia 22302. (703) 525-0606. Executive Director: John H. Davis. Major publications: *Parks & Recreation; Journal of Leisure Research; Therapeutic Recreation Journal; Recreation & Park Law Reporter; Park Practice Program; Dateline: NRPA* (newsletter). Purpose: To improve and expand park and recreation systems and leisure services for the public through assisting park and recreation officials in the development and administration of physical, human, and financial resources. Established 1898.

National School Boards Association, 1680 Duke Street, Alexandria, Virginia 22314. (703) 838-6722. Executive Director: Thomas A. Shannon. Major publications: *The American School Board Journal; The Executive Educator; The School Administrator's Policy Portfolio; Research Reports; School Board News*. Purpose: To advance the quality of education by preserving and strengthening the concept of local lay control of, and accountability for, public education. Established 1940.

National Society for Internships and Experiential Education, 122 St. Mary's Street, Raleigh, North Carolina 27605. (919) 834-7536. Executive Director: Jane C. Kendall. Major publications: *Experiential Education* (newsletter); *Directory of Washington Internships;*

Directory of Public Service Internships: Opportunities for the Graduate, Post-Graduate, and Mid-Career Professional; Directory of Undergraduate Internships; Directory of Internships for Women; Panel Resource Papers on issues of quality program design and administration. Purpose: To promote quality programs in experiential education and encourage its acceptance as an integral part of American education. Established 1971.

Public Administration Service, 1497 Chain Bridge Road, McLean, Virginia 22101. (703) 734-8970. President and Executive Director: Theodore Sitkoff. Purpose: To provide management and specialized consulting services and conduct research for public jurisdictions and public managers—domestic and international—in order to improve the quality and delivery of public services. Consulting and research services provided include the development and installation of modern management systems, methods, techniques, and practices in many different functional fields such as: local, state, and federal organization and reorganization; personnel administration; criminal justice; public works; intergovernmental relations; telecommunications; office automation; and public sector productivity and responsiveness. Established 1933.

Public Risk and Insurance Management Association, 1120 G Street, N.W., Washington, D.C. 20005. (202) 737-7556. Executive Director: Natalie Wasserman. Major publications: *Primaletter; Basic Risk Management Manual; Public Officials at Risk,* outreach service. Purpose: To increase the proficiency of risk and insurance management in local government by providing an information network between government officials and employees involved in risk management, by assisting in the establishment of effective risk management programs, and by conducting research projects and training programs to aid in the development of more effective techniques. Established 1978.

Public Technology, Inc., 1301 Pennsylvania Avenue, N.W., Washington, D.C. 20004. (202) 626-2400. Major publications: *The PTI Catalog: Programs, Services, and Publications of Public Technology, Inc.; Public Technology* (newsletter); *Solutions for Technology-Sharing Networks; SMD Briefs; Transit Actions; Transit Technology Briefs;* guides, manuals, and reports. Purpose: To help member local and state governments improve services and cut costs through practical use of applied science and technology; to identify common needs susceptible to technological solution and to adapt or develop solutions in concert with public and private organizations; to assist with on-site evaluation, adaptation, and implemention; and to foster the exchange of technology among government agencies. Established 1971.

Southern Building Code Congress International, Inc., 900 Montclair Road, Birmingham, Alabama 35213. (205) 591-1853. Executive Director: William J. Tangye, P.E. Major publications: *The Standard Codes.* A *Directory of Services* listing other publications and services is available on request. Purpose: To provide a forum for governments, design professionals, and industry to join together to democratically promulgate and maintain a set of model regulatory construction codes. Established 1940.

Special Libraries Association, 235 Park Avenue South, New York 10003. (212) 477-9250. Executive Director: David R. Bender. Major publications: *Special Libraries*; *SpeciaList*; publications list available on request. Purpose: To provide an association of individuals and organizations having a professional, scientific or technical interest in library and information science, especially as these are applied in the recording, retrieval, and dissemination of knowledge and information in areas such as the physical, biological, technical and social sciences and the humanities; and to promote and improve the communication, dissemination and use of such information and knowledge for the benefit of libraries or other educational organizations. Established 1909.

Town Affiliation Association of the United States (Sister Cities International), 1625 Eye Street, N.W., Suite 424–26, Washington, D.C. 20006. (202) 293-5504. Executive Vice President: Thomas W. Gittins. Major publications: *Your City and the World; A Sister City Handbook; Sister City News; Washington Report.* Purpose: To provide a national forum for the interchange of ideas and resources to help local communities further their international programs. Established 1967.

United States Conference of Mayors, 1620 Eye Street, N.W., Washington, D.C. 20006. (202) 293-7330. Executive Director: John J. Gunther. Major publications: *The Mayor; City Problems; Mayors of America's Principal Cities.* Purpose: To promote cooperation between cities and the federal government; to promote responsible and responsive local government and effective municipal administration; and to promote exchanges of information and experiences among elected city officials. Established 1932.

Urban Affairs Association, University of Delaware, Newark, Delaware 19716. (302) 451-2394. Chairperson: Bernard H. Ross. Major publications: *UAA Communication*; *Journal of Urban Affairs; Directory of University Urban Programs*; selected papers of annual meetings; other special studies and reports. Purpose: To encourage the dissemination of information and research findings about urbanism and urbanization; to support the development of university education, research, and service programs in urban affairs; to promote more effective policies and procedures relating to university urban centers and institutes; to provide a forum for the exchange of information concerning problems faced by urban affairs institutes and centers; to facilitate the dissemination of information about urban affairs programs; and to foster the development of urban affairs as a professional academic field. Established 1969.

The Urban Institute, 2100 M Street, N.W., Washington, D.C. 20037. (202) 833-7200. President: William Gorham. Major publication: *Policy and Research Report*; publication catalog and annual report available on request. Purpose: To respond to needs for objective analyses and basic information regarding social and economic problems confronting the nation and government policies and programs designed to alleviate such problems. Established 1968.

Water Pollution Control Federation, 2626 Pennsylvania Avenue, N.W., Washington, D.C. 20037. (202) 337-2500. Executive Director: Robert A. Canham. Major publications: *Journal Water Pollution Control Federation; Operations Forum;* series of Manuals of Practice. Purpose: To develop and disseminate technical information concerning the nature, collection, treatment, and disposal of domestic and industrial waste-water. The Federation has held as an integral component of its mandate the pledge to act as a source of education to the general public as well as to individuals engaged in the field of water pollution control. Established 1928.

Table 2/1 PROFESSIONAL ORGANIZATIONS SERVING LOCAL AND STATE GOVERNMENTS

Data for 76 professional organizations are presented in this table, based on a survey conducted in August 1984.

Membership services

1 — Advisory or information services
2 — Annual conference report
3 — Directory
4 — On-site technical assistance
5 — Journal
6 — Newsletter
7 — Personnel placement service
8 — Special service reports
9 — Training
10 — Yearbook
11 — Legislative representation
12 — Professional accreditation
13 — Research projects

Services available to other than membership

1 — Advisory or information services
2 — Annual conference report
3 — Directory
4 — On-site technical assistance
5 — Journal
6 — Newsletter
7 — Personnel placement service
8 — Special service reports
9 — Training
10 — Yearbook
11 — Legislative representation
12 — Professional accreditation
13 — Research projects

Organization	No. of individual members	No. of agency members	No. of state or regional chapters	Membership services	Nonmembership services	Conferences: national-state or regional	No. of full-time staff	Operating expenditures ($000)
Academy for State and Local Government	...	...	...	...	1,13	...	8	320
Airport Operators Council International	210	...	...	1,2,3,6,8,11,13	2,3,6,8	Yes-Yes	19	800
American Association of Airport Executives	1,700	...	6	1,2,3,6,7,8,10,11,12	2,6,7	Yes-Yes	7	400
American Association of Port Authorities	350	...	...	1,2,3,4,6,8,9,11,13	1,4	Yes-No	9	450
American Association of School Administrators	18,000	150	50	1,2,3,4,5,6,7,8,9,10,11,12,13	1,7	Yes-Yes	65	5,600
American College of Hospital Administrators	18,500	...	...	1,2,3,5,6,7,8,9,10,12,13	2,3,5,6,10	Yes-Yes	56	...
American Institute of Architects	37,000	...	278	1,2,3,5,6,8,9,11,13	1,2,3,5,6,9	Yes-Yes	135	12,000
American Library Association	37,148	...	57	1,3,5,7,9,10,11,12,13	1,3,5,7,9,10,11,12,13	Yes-Yes	185	8,000
American Planning Association	21,000	...	47	3,5,7,9,11,12	1,3,4,5,7,8,9,13	Yes-Yes	54	4,200
American Public Gas Association	170	100	...	1,2,3,4,6,7,8,9,11,13	1,2,3,8	Yes-Yes	3	110
American Public Health Association	30,258	194	49	5,6,11,12,13	5,6,12	Yes-Yes	89	6,271
American Public Power Association	1,200	...	...	1,6,11	...	Yes-No	55	4,200
American Public Transit Association	...	780	...	1,2,3,4,5,6,7,8,9,11,12,13	2,4,5,6,9,11,12	Yes-Yes	54	5,400
American Public Welfare Association	6,300	700	...	1,3,4,5,6,8,9,13	3,4,5,6,8,9,13	No-Yes	34	1,400
American Public Works Association	22,151	1,692	62	1,3,5,6,8,9,12,13	3,8,9,13	Yes-Yes	43	3,818
American Society for Public Administration	16,443	35	117	1,5,6,9,11	1,6,9,11	Yes-Yes	18	1,427
American Water Works Association	30,500	3,800	40	1,2,5,6,7,8,9,11,13	1,2,7,8,9	Yes-Yes	73	6,151
Associated Public-Safety Communications Officers, Inc.	5,100	...	41	1,5,6,8,9,11,13	1,5,6,8,9,13	Yes-Yes	7	300
Building Officials and Code Administrators International	7,000	...	35	1,2,3,4,6,9,12,13	1,12	Yes-Yes	35	2,000
Cable Television Information Center	...	170	...	1,4,6,8,9,11,13	1	No-Yes	12	...
Canadian Association of Municipal Administrators	300	...	...	6	...	Yes-No	...[1]	30
Council for International Urban Liaison	...	...	...	6	1,4,6,8	No-No	4	200
Council on Municipal Performance	900	50	...	1,4,6,8,9,13	1,4,6,8,9,13	Yes-Yes	8	200
Council of State Community Affairs Agencies	...	49	...	1,3,4,6,8,9,11,13	6	Yes-No	7	480
Council of State Governments	50	...	...	1,2,3,4,5,6,8,9,11,13	1,2,3,5,6,8	Yes-Yes	85	3,000
Federation of Canadian Municipalities	...	269	...	1,2,3,6,8,13	3,6	Yes-Yes	11	...
Government Finance Officers Association[2]	9,500	...	...	1,3,4,5,6,7,8,9,11,13	1,3,4,5,6,7,9,11,13	Yes-Yes	55	4,000
Governmental Refuse Collection and Disposal Association	2,000	...	24	1,2,4,6,7,9,11	1,2,7	Yes-Yes	3	500
Governmental Research Association	300	...	...	1,3,6,8,13	3,6,8,13	Yes-No	...	20
ICMA Retirement Corporation	35,000	1,800	...	...	...	No-No	51	4,000
Institute of Internal Auditors, Inc.	27,000	...	170	1,2,3,5,6,9,12,13	2,5,9,12,13	Yes-Yes	70	6,000
Institute of Public Administration	...	...	...	...	1,4,6	No-No	60	520
Institute of Transportation Engineers	6,700	...	42	1,2,3,5,7,8,9,13	1,2,3,5,7,8,9,13	Yes-Yes	9	928
International Association of Assessing Officers	8,200	170	15	1,3,4,5,6,8,9,12,13	1,3,4,5,8,9,13	Yes-No	16	1,850
International Association of Auditorium Managers	900	...	7	1,2,3,6,7,11,12,13	1,3,4,5,7,13	Yes-Yes	2	400
International Association of Chiefs of Police	14,000	...	...	1,2,3,4,5,6,7,8,9,10,11,12,13	1,2,3,4,5,6,9,10,12,13	Yes-Yes	65	4,500
International Association of Fire Chiefs	8,500	102	8	1,2,4,5,6,8,9,11,13	1,2,4,5,6,8,13	Yes-Yes	15	1,300
International City Management Association	6,894	...	47	1,2,3,6,8,9,10,13	1,2,3,8,9,10,13	Yes-No	80	5,490
International Conference of Building Officials	5,043	1,704	56	...	...	Yes-Yes	60	5,000
International Institute of Municipal Clerks	7,100	...	...	1,3,6,7,8,9,11,12,13	3,6,7,9,13	Yes-No	6	340
International Personnel Management Association	4,730	1,070	...	1,3,5,6,7,8,9,11,13	1,3,5,6,7,8,9,11,13	Yes-Yes	14	1,465
Labor-Management Relations Service	1,000	...	...	1,4,6,9,13	6,9	Yes-Yes	2	100

Table 2/1 continued **PROFESSIONAL ORGANIZATIONS SERVING LOCAL AND STATE GOVERNMENTS**

Organization	No. of individual members	No. of agency members	No. of state or regional chapters	Membership services	Nonmembership services	Conferences: national-state or regional	No. of full-time staff	Operating expenditures ($000)
League of Women Voters Education Fund	...	...	...	...	1,8,13	Yes-Yes	30	1,655
League of Women Voters of the U.S.	110,000	...	1,300	1,2,4,6,8,9,11,13	1,6,8	Yes-Yes	47	2,127
Maritime Municipal Training and Development Board	...	...	...	1,4,5,7,8,9,13	1,5,7,13	No-No	4	252
National Animal Control Association	2,000	3,800	38	1,4,6,7,8,9,12,13	1,4,6,7,8,9,12,13	Yes-Yes	...	60
National Association of Counties	...	1,900	...	1,2,4,6,11,13	...	Yes-Yes	46	6,000
National Association of Housing and Redevelopment Officials	5,500	2,200	43	1,3,4,5,6,8,9,11,12,13	3,5,8,9,12,13	Yes-Yes	24	1,500
National Association of Regional Councils	...	300	...	1,3,6,11,13	1,3,6	Yes-Yes	12	856
National Association of Schools of Public Affairs and Administration	...	23	...	1,2,3,4,6,12	1,3,6	Yes-Yes	8	...
National Association for State Information Systems	...	50	4	1,3,6,8,10,13	1,6,8,10	Yes-Yes	2	100
National Association of Towns and Townships	80	...	13	1,4,6,8,11,13	6,8,13	Yes-Yes	8	270
National Conference of State Legislatures	...	55	...	1,4,5,6,9,11,13	...	Yes-Yes	100	6,000
National Council for Urban Economic Development	1,000	100	...	1,3,4,5,6,8,13	4,5,8	Yes-Yes	16	900
National Environmental Health Association	3,510	28	...	1,2,5,6,7,12,13	1	Yes-Yes	5	...
National Fire Protection Association	31,500	150	...	1,4,5,6,7,8,9,10,11,13	1,4,8,9,13	Yes-Yes	235	15,000
National Governors' Association	50	...	...	1,2,3,4,6,8,9,11,13	...	Yes-No	75	5,000
National Housing Conference	450	...	4	1,6,11,13	1	Yes-Yes	5	...
National Institute of Governmental Purchasing	70	1,270	34	1,2,3,4,5,6	1,2,3,4,6,7,8,9,12,13	Yes-No	8	450
National Institute of Municipal Law Officers	1,700	...	...	1,2,5,6,13	...	Yes-Yes	12	...
National League of Cities	...	1,175	49	1,3,6,8,9,11,13	1,6,8,9,13	Yes-Yes	57	5,200
National Municipal League/Citizens Forum on Self-Government	4,500	...	...	1,2,4,5,8,13	1,2,4,8,13	Yes-Yes	15	675
National Public Employer Labor Relations Association	1,300	...	13	1,2,3,4,6,7,8,9,11,13	1,8,9	Yes-Yes	4	...
National Recreation and Park Association	...	...	...	1,2,5,6,7,9,11,12	1,5,7,9	Yes-Yes	40	3,300
National School Boards Association	95,000	...	52	1,2,3,4,5,6,7,8,9,10,11,13	1,2,5,10	Yes-Yes	85	9,500
National Society for Internships and Experiential Education	600	100	...	1,3,4,6,8,13	1,3,6,8,13	Yes-Yes	2	...
Public Administration Service	...	...	...	...	1,4,9,13	No-No	50	3,000
Public Risk and Insurance Management Association	...	850	15	1,3,6,9,13	1,6,9	Yes-Yes	3	250
Public Technology, Inc.	...	175	1	1,2,3,4,6,8,9,13	2,3,4,6,8,9	Yes-Yes	65	4,000
Southern Building Code Congress International	2,400	1,500	32	1,2,3,4,5,6,7,8,9,10,11,12,13	2,3,4,5,9,10,12,13	...	...	...
Special Libraries Association	11,500	...	54	1,3,4,5,6,7,11,13	1,3,4,5,6	Yes-No	27	1,500
Town Affiliation Association of the U.S.	...	720	...	1,2,3,4,6,8,9	1	Yes-Yes	10	750
U.S. Conference of Mayors	...	750	...	1,2,3,6,8,9,11,13	1,2,3,6,8,13	Yes-No	65	3,000
Urban Affairs Association[3]	120	70	...	1,2,3,4,5,6,7,8,9,13	1,2,3,6,7	Yes-No	1	30
The Urban Institute	...	...	...	...	1,4,5,6,13	No-No	170	9,864
Water Pollution Control Federation	28,000	350	65	...	...	Yes-No	52	4,500

Leaders (. . .) indicate not applicable or data not reported.
[1] Staff support for the Canadian Association of Municipal Administrators is provided by the Federation of Canadian Municipalities.
[2] Formerly the Municipal Finance Officers Association.
[3] Formerly the Council of University Institutes of Urban Affairs.

F References

1 Sources of Information

1

Sources of Information

Edited by Mary L. Knobbe
Library Consultant, MLK/LC

The following pages offer an update to the selected bibliography for major areas of local government administration that appeared in the previous editions of *The Municipal Year Book*. These listings are compiled for reference primarily for urban administrators, staff members of government or research bureaus and other research and service organizations, and staff members of state and federal government agencies with a direct involvement in urban affairs.

This year's edition, like that of 1984, presents functional area references that have been compiled by librarians and other persons familiar with the particular functional areas. The names of the compilers and their organizations immediately follow the functional area headings given in the text.

Few sources listed in the 1985 *Municipal Year Book* were included in preceding editions. Nearly all sources listed have been published since January 1982. For a complete picture of publications issued during the past several years in this field, it is necessary to use this edition in conjunction with the Sources of Information in the nine preceding editions of *The Municipal Year Book*.

The present updated bibliography includes a section on Basic References and another on Basic Statistical Resources, followed by 15 functional area subject headings. Under each subject heading are two sections: the first includes books, reports, monographs, bibliographies, and reference works and is intended to keep the urban administrator informed of the latest thinking in various fields. The second section lists periodicals and includes magazines, journals, and newsletters. Frequency of publication is indicated as follows: (W) weekly, (BW) biweekly, (M) monthly, (BM) bimonthly, (Q) quarterly, (SM) semimonthly, (SA) semiannually, (BA) biannually.

Some (but not all) federal government publications are available through the U.S. Government Printing Office (GPO). Citations including the notation "GPO" should be ordered from the Superintendent of Documents, U.S. Government Printing Office, Washington, D.C. 20402.

Many items included were prepared under contract to the federal government by private agencies. These publications are often available from the National Technical Information Service (NTIS), 5285 Port Royal Road, Springfield, Virginia 22151. Publications which may be purchased from the National Technical Information Service have the notation "NTIS" following the publisher and date. NTIS publication numbers are provided when known.

Many references listed here are written and/or published by well-known public interest groups or professional associations. In these cases the name of the organization is not written in full. An abbreviation of the organization's name is used. For example, "APA" refers to the American Planning Association, "IPMA" refers to the International Personnel Management Association, etc. All abbreviations are included in the publishers' list at the end of this bibliography. Where they appear, they precede the full name and address of the organization and are followed by the word "for." The publishers' list also provides the full name and address of other publishers whose publications have been listed in this bibliography.

The items listed below are *not* available from the International City Management Association (ICMA) unless so noted in the entry or unless ICMA is the publisher.

Many ICMA publications are included in this bibliography. The notation "UDS" refers to Urban Data Service Reports; "MIS" refers to the reports of the Management Information Service; "BDR" refers to Baseline Data Reports. The reports of these services are available by subscription and by individual copy; information may be obtained by writing to ICMA.

Subject headings (2 basic reference headings followed by 15 functional area headings) used in this bibliography are:

Basic References
Basic Statistical Resources
Emergency Management
Environment and Energy
Fire Protection
Housing
Human Resources and Services
Information Technologies
Intergovernmental Relations
Law Enforcement and Criminal Justice
Local Government Organization and Management
Personnel and Labor Relations
Planning and Development
Public Finance
Public Works and Utilities
Recreation and Leisure
Transportation and Roads

The editor thanks those who have prepared the subject sections.

Basic References

Mary L. Knobbe
Library Consultant, MLK/LC

BOOKS, REPORTS, MONOGRAPHS, BIBLIOGRAPHIES, AND REFERENCE SOURCES

BLACK ELECTED OFFICIALS: A NATIONAL ROSTER, 1984. Prepared by the Joint Center for Political Studies. UNIPUB. 1984. 319 pp. Gives essential information on nearly 6,000 black elected officials in the U.S. today.

THE BOOK OF THE STATES 1984–85. Council of State Governments. 1984. 544 pp. Annual.

CANADIAN ALMANAC & DIRECTORY, 1984. 137th ed. By International Publications Service. Taylor & Francis, Inc. 1983. 1,122 pp. Annual directory lists officials of government departments, boards and commissions, and more.

THE CITY. By James A. Clapp. Rutgers University. 1984. 288 pp. A dictionary of quotable thought on cities and urban life.

DIRECTORY AND COMPILATION OF TECHNICAL AND ADMINISTRATIVE REQUIREMENTS IN ENERGY CODES FOR NEW BUILDING CONSTRUCTION USED IN THE UNITED STATES. National Conference of States on Building Codes and Standards, 1983. 198 pp.

ENERGY HANDBOOK. 2d ed. By Robert L. Loftness. Van Nostrand Reinhold. 1984. 763 pp. Emphasis is on newer energy technologies.

GOVERNMENT AGENCIES. Edited by Donald R. Whitnah. The Greenwood Encyclopedia of American Institutions Series, no. 7. 1983. 683 pp. Alphabetical with cross-references of over 100 government agencies and bureaus.

A HANDBOOK FOR EVALUATING THE CITY ADMINISTRATOR. League of Oregon Cities. 1983. 53 pp.

HANDBOOK OF THE AGED IN THE UNITED STATES. Edited by Erdman P. Palmore. Greenwood. 1984. Appendices list major academic research centers, statistics, references, and a bibliography.

HANDBOOK OF WAGE AND SALARY ADMINISTRATION. 2d ed. Edited by Milton L. Rock. McGraw-Hill. 1984. How to put a compensation program in action, manage and communicate it, record and research it, and keep it up to date.

NATIONAL DIRECTORY OF CORPORATE PUBLIC AFFAIRS 1984. Columbia Books. 1984. 429 pp. Over 1,500 corporations and 8,000 public affairs personnel.

NATIONAL TRADE AND PROFES-

SIONAL ASSOCIATIONS OF THE UNITED STATES. 19th ed. Columbia Books. 1984. 404 pp. About 6,000 active U.S. national organizations, including address, telephone number, name and title of chief executive, and much more.

1984 WASHINGTON REPRESENTATIVES. 8th ed. Columbia Books. 1984. 604 pp. Lists private individuals and firms which serve American and foreign companies and governments, trade and professional associations, labor unions, consumer, and other special interest groups seeking access to and influence with the federal government.

THE SOLAR ENERGY DIRECTORY. Edited by Sandra Oddo. Grey House. 1983. 312 pp. Lists people and organizations—professional and trade, advisory groups, government agencies, and manufacturers.

STATE ADMINISTRATIVE OFFICIALS CLASSIFIED BY FUNCTION 1983–1984. Compiled by Council of State Governments. 1984. 257 pp. This is supplement 3 to *The Book of the States*.

STATE AND LOCAL CAPITAL SPENDING AND BORROWING. Government Finance Research Center. 1984. 15 pp. Levels of need and costs of financing.

STATISTICAL ABSTRACT OF THE UNITED STATES, 1984. 104th ed. By U.S. Bureau of the Census. GPO. 1983. 1,015 pp. The national data book and guide to sources of statistics of the U.S.

STATISTICS SOURCES: A SUBJECT GUIDE TO DATA ON INDUSTRIAL, BUSINESS, SOCIAL, EDUCATIONAL, FINANCIAL, AND OTHER TOPICS FOR THE UNITED STATES AND INTERNATIONALLY. 8th ed. 2 vols. Ed. by Paul Wasserman and Jacqueline O'Brien. Gale Research. 1983. Expanded edition features more than 20,000 subject headings.

THE UNITED STATES GOVERNMENT MANUAL 1983/84. GPO. 1983. 908 pp.

WANT'S FEDERAL-STATE COURT DIRECTORY. By Want Publications. 1984. 127 pp. Gives complete addresses and telephone numbers for all 50 states and territories.

WIND ENERGY DIRECTORIES. By Frederick Frankena. Vance Bibliographies. 1984. 20 pp.

PERIODICALS

CURRENT MUNICIPAL PROBLEMS. (Q) Callaghan & Co.

GRANTSMANSHIP CENTER NEWS. (6/year) Grantsmanship Center.

IPA REPORT. (Q) Institute of Public Administration.

MEETINGS AND CONVENTIONS. (M) Ziff-Davis Publishing Company.

PUBLIC ADMINISTRATION QUARTERLY. (Q) Southern Public Administration Education Foundation.

URBAN INNOVATION ABROAD. (M) Council for International Urban Liaison.

Basic Statistical Resources

Grace Waibel
Library and Information Services Branch
Bureau of the Census

BOOKS, REPORTS, MONOGRAPHS, BIBLIOGRAPHIES, AND REFERENCE SOURCES

ICMA often receives requests from urban administrators concerning the availability of data sources. In response to these requests, the following list has been compiled of selected publications of the U.S. Departments of Commerce and Labor. The publications are divided into Employment, Finance, Population, and Housing, followed by the 1982 Census of Governments with descriptions of each volume and number. Other Basic Data Sources are included at the end of this list. All publications that appear in this section of the Year Book are available from the GPO.

EMPLOYMENT

U.S. Department of Labor
Bureau of Labor Statistics

ANALYSIS OF WORK STOPPAGES. Annual statistical analysis.

CURRENT WAGE DEVELOPMENTS. Monthly report summarizing wage and benefit changes in major collective bargaining situations. Compiled primarily from newspapers and other secondary sources.

NATIONAL SURVEY OF PROFESSIONAL, ADMINISTRATIVE, TECHNICAL, AND CLERICAL PAY. Annual bulletin summarizing the Bureau's annual survey of selected professional, administrative, technical, and clerical pay in industry.

STATE AND LOCAL GOVERNMENT EMPLOYMENT AND PAYROLLS. Monthly publication.

WORK STOPPAGES. Preliminary statistical estimates of work stoppages for the entire year.

U.S. Bureau of Commerce
Bureau of the Census

CITY EMPLOYMENT. Annual national totals on employment and payrolls of municipal governments, by function, with figures individually for the cities having 50,000 inhabitants or more.

FINANCES OF EMPLOYEE-RETIREMENT SYSTEMS OF STATE AND LOCAL GOVERNMENTS. Annual publication describing employee retirement systems, covering such items as receipts, benefits, and withdrawal payments, and cash and security holdings at the end of the fiscal year. Data are categorized by state, city, and other locally administered programs for selected individual systems.

LOCAL GOVERNMENT EMPLOYMENT IN SELECTED METROPOLITAN AREAS AND LARGE COUNTIES. Annual data for 74 SMSAs, their county areas, and other county areas of 200,000 population or more.

PUBLIC EMPLOYMENT. Annual national totals on employment of all governments (including the federal government), by function and by type of government. Also shows state-by-state statistics on federal civilian employees and, by function, statistics on employment and payrolls of state and local governments.

FINANCE

U.S. Department of Labor
Bureau of Labor Statistics

THE CONSUMER PRICE INDEX. Monthly report on consumer price movements, including statistical tables and technical notes.

U.S. Department of Commerce
Bureau of the Census

CITY GOVERNMENT FINANCES. Annual national and size group totals of municipal government finances, with comparative totals for previous years. Supplies financial statistics for individual cities and selected urban towns of over 50,000 and supplies additional detail for the 46 largest cities.

GOVERNMENTAL FINANCES. Annual national totals covering all governments—federal, state, and local—with comparative summary data for previous years, and financial statistics for state and local governments by states.

LOCAL GOVERNMENT FINANCES IN SELECTED METROPOLITAN AREAS AND LARGE COUNTIES. Annual data on revenue, expenditure, and debt of local governments for each of 74 populous SMSAs.

QUARTERLY SUMMARY OF FEDERAL, STATE, AND LOCAL TAX REVENUE. Four quarterly reports provide nationwide figures on tax revenue by level of government and types of tax; data on property tax collections in major county areas; and collections of selected state taxes.

STATE GOVERNMENT FINANCES. Annual detailed statistics nationally and by state, with comparative totals for previous years. This report covers revenue by source, expenditure by function and by character and object, indebtedness and debt transactions, and cash and security holdings.

STATE GOVERNMENT TAX COLLECTIONS. Annual national and state figures on tax collections of state governments, by type of tax. Includes detailed breakdowns of major tax categories.

POPULATION

U.S. Department of Commerce
Bureau of the Census

1980 Census of Population

VOL. 1. CHARACTERISTICS OF THE POPULATION. This volume presents final population counts and statistics on population characteristics. There are reports for 57 areas: the United States, each of the 50 states, the District of Columbia, Puerto Rico, and the outlying areas. The volume consists of four chapters designated as A, B, C, and D (described below).

Chapter A. Number of Inhabitants. Final official population count is presented for states, counties, SCSAs, SMSAs, urbanized areas, county subdivisions, incorporated places, and census designated places.

Chapter B. General Population Characteristics. Statistics on age, sex, race, Spanish origin, marital status, and household relationship are presented for states, counties, SCSAs, SMSAs, urbanized areas, county subdivisions, places of 1,000 or more inhabitants, American Indian reservations, and Alaskan native villages.

Chapter C. General Social and Economic Characteristics. These reports focus on the population subjects reported in Chapter B that were collected on a sample basis. In addition, statistics are given on nativity, state or country of birth, citizenship and year of immigration for foreign-born population, family composition, marital history, journey to work, and other characteristics. Each subject is shown for some or all of the following areas: states, counties, SCSAs, SMSAs, urbanized areas, places of 2,500 or more inhabitants, Indian reservations, and Alaskan native villages.

Chapter D. Detailed Population Characteristics. These reports cover most of the population subjects collected on a sample basis, presenting the data in considerable detail, cross-classified by age, race, and other characteristics. Each subject is shown for the state and the large SMSAs. Some subjects are also shown for central cities of large SMSAs.

VOL. 2. SUBJECT REPORTS. Each report in this volume concentrates on a particular subject. Detailed sample information and cross-relationships are generally provided on a national and/or regional level; in a few reports, data for states, large cities, SMSAs, or Indian reservations are also shown.

SUPPLEMENTARY REPORTS. These reports present special compilations of 1980 Census statistics and specific population subjects. The reports include population and households by states and counties, and race of the population by states.

Results of the 1980 decennial census began publication in 1980. The Bureau of the Census announces publication of reports (those listed here and others) in its *Monthly Product Announcement* and in its annual catalogue.

In addition to the findings of the Census of Population conducted every ten years, the Bureau of the Census publishes continuing and up-to-date statistics on population counts, characteristics, and other special studies on the American people. Several of these are individually described below, although all are issued under the general title *Current Population Reports*.

LOCAL POPULATION ESTIMATES. (P–26 Series.) Population estimates for counties for selected states in which the figures are prepared by a state agency as part of the Federal-State Cooperative Program for Local Population Estimates.

POPULATION CHARACTERISTICS. (P–20 Series.) Current national and, in some cases, regional data on geographic residence and mobility, fertility, education, school enrollment, marital status, numbers and characteristics of households and families.

POPULATION ESTIMATES AND PROJECTIONS. (P–25 Series.) Monthly estimates of the total population of the United States; annual midyear estimates of the population of states. Estimates of the population of selected metropolitan areas and their component counties. Projections of the future population of the United States and individual states.

SPECIAL STUDIES. (P–23 Series.) Studies on methods, concepts, and specialized data. Includes occasional reports on the Black population, metropolitan–nonmetropolitan population, youth, women, the older population, and other categories.

SPECIAL CENSUSES. (P–28 Series.) Results of population censuses generally taken at the request and expense of city or other local governments are summarized in this series of reports.

HOUSING

U.S. Department of Commerce
Bureau of the Census

1980 Census of Housing

VOL. 1. CHARACTERISTICS OF HOUSING UNITS. This volume presents final housing unit counts and statistics on housing characteristics. It consists of reports for 57 areas: the United States, each of the 50 states, the District of Columbia, Puerto Rico, and the outlying areas. The volume consists of two chapters for each area, designated as A and B.

Chapter A. General Housing Characteristics. Statistics are presented on 100 percent housing subjects: units at address, tenure, condominium status, number of rooms, persons per room, plumbing facilities, value, contract rent, and other characteristics. Statistics are presented for the following areas or their equivalents: states, counties, SCSAs, SMSAs, urbanized areas, county subdivisions, places of 1,000 or more inhabitants, American Indian reservations, and Alaskan native villages.

Chapter B. Detailed Housing Characteristics. These reports include some subjects covered in Chapter A. Additional subjects, collected on a sample basis, are: units in the structure, year occupant moved into unit, year structure was built, heating equipment, and other characteristics. Statistics are shown for some or all of the following areas or their equivalents: states, counties, SCSAs, SMSAs, urbanized areas, places of 2,500 or more inhabitants, American Indian reservations, and Alaskan native villages.

VOL. 2. METROPOLITAN HOUSING CHARACTERISTICS. These reports cover most of the 1980 Census housing subjects with considerable detail and cross-classification. There is one report for each SMSA, presenting data for the SMSA and its component large cities, as well as a report for each state.

VOL. 3. SUBJECT REPORTS. Each report in this volume concentrates on a particular subject. Detailed information and cross-classification are generally provided on a national and/or regional level.

VOL. 4. COMPONENTS OF INVENTORY CHANGE. A series of reports for the United States is based on a sample survey conducted in the fall of 1980. Subject content is similar to that of 1970 Housing Census, Vol. IV.

VOL. 5. RESIDENTIAL FINANCE. This volume presents data regarding the financing of privately owned nonfarm residential properties for the United States and regions.

SUPPLEMENTARY REPORT: SELECTED HOUSING CHARACTERISTICS BY STATES AND COUNTIES: 1980. This report presents statistics from the 1980 Census of Housing on general characteristics of housing units for the 50 states and the District of Columbia, counties, and independent cities.

1980 Census of Population and Housing

Population and Housing (final counts).

Block Statistics. PHC80–1–. One report for each SMSA shows data for individual blocks on selected 100 percent housing and population subjects. The series also includes a report for each state presenting block statistics for cities of 10,000 or more population outside SMSAs and for communities outside SMSAs which have contracted with the Census Bureau to provide block statistics from the 1980 Census.

Census of Population and Housing, 1980: P.L. 94–171 Population Counts. Provides substate data for total population, counts of five major race groups—white, black, American Indian (including Eskimo and Aleut), Asian and Pacific Islander—and other races, and a separate count of persons of Spanish/Hispanic origin.

Census Tracts. PHC80-2-. One report for each SMSA and one for the tracted balance of each state show data for most of the population and housing subjects included in the 1980 Census. Some tables are based on the 100 percent tabulations, others on the sample tabulations. Statistics are presented for SMSAs, central cities, and places of 10,000 or more inhabitants by census tracts.

Summary Characteristics for Governmental Units and Standard Metropolitan Statistical Areas. PHC80-3-. Statistics are presented on total population and on complete-count and sample population characteristics such as age, race, education, disability, etc., and on total housing units and housing characteristics such as value, age of structure, etc., for each SMSA and the 39,000 general purpose local governments in the United States.

Summary Tape Files. Results of the 1980 Census are also provided on computer tapes for the United States and Puerto Rico in the form of Summary Tape Files (STFs). The tapes provide statistics with greater subject and geographic detail than is available in printed or microfiche reports.

More complete descriptions of the reports issued can be found in the *1980 Census of Population and Housing User's Guide.*

ANNUAL HOUSING SURVEY

Current Housing Reports Series H-150-Year

The Annual Housing Survey, which is sponsored by the U.S. Department of Housing and Urban Development and the U.S. Bureau of the Census, was started in 1973. In addition to the six basic annual reports listed below, one or more supplementary reports (Series H-151) may be published for the United States.

A series of reports (H-170) will also be published for 60 selected standard metropolitan statistical areas. The data for the SMSAs are based on an independent sample of the 60 SMSAs divided into three groups of approximately 20 each, with one group interviewed every three years on a rotating basis.

Pt. A. General Housing Characteristics for the United States and Regions.

Pt. B. Indicators of Housing and Neighborhood Quality for the United States and Regions.

Pt. C. Financial Characteristics of the Housing Inventory for the United States and Regions.

Pt. D. Housing Characteristics of Recent Movers for the United States and Regions.

Pt. E. Urban and Rural Housing Characteristics for the United States and Regions.

Pt. F. Financial Characteristics by Indicators of Housing and Neighborhood Quality for the United States and Regions.

1982 CENSUS OF GOVERNMENTS

U.S. Department of Commerce Bureau of the Census

Conducted every five years, the Census of Governments provides data on the number and characteristics of state and local governments in the United States, the value of taxable property, public employees and payrolls, and governmental revenue, expenditure, debt, and financial assets.

Final reports on the 1982 Census of Governments are issued, beginning in 1983, following a format similar to that of the 1977 Census of Governments described below. All release dates are tentative.

As they are published, reports are announced in *Monthly Product Announcement,* published by the Bureau of the Census.

VOL. 1. GOVERNMENTAL ORGANIZATION.

No. 1. Governmental Organization. Governmental units and public school systems as of the beginning of 1982. Detailed data are shown for the United States, individual states, and SMSAs on such subjects as county, municipal, and township governments, by size of population; school districts and other public school systems by size of enrollment, by kind of area served, by grades provided, and by number of schools operated; and special districts, by function performed. Also shown is the number of local governments, by type, in each county in the United States. This report includes a summary description of governmental structure in each state.

No. 2. Popularly Elected Officials. Data on elected officials by state, inside and outside SMSAs, by type of government, and by type of office. Also included is a tabular presentation of elective offices authorized by state constitution and general laws, with information for each office on length of term, geographic area for election, and basis of compensation.

VOL. 2. TAXABLE PROPERTY VALUES AND ASSESSMENT—SALES PRICE RATIOS. Provides statistics, based on sample, on real properties involved in measurable sales during a six-month period of 1981. Statistics on effective tax rates, assessment-sales price ratios, and dispersion coefficients for certain realty are presented.

VOL. 3. PUBLIC EMPLOYMENT.

No. 1. Employment of Major Local Governments. October 1982 employment and payrolls of individual county governments, major city governments, school districts, and special districts.

No. 2. Compendium of Public Employment. October 1982 civilian employment and payrolls, by type of government and governmental function, including the federal government. This report presents, for states, detailed data on state and local government employment and payrolls, by function, and average October 1982 earnings of full-time employees. Summary statistics are presented for local government employment and payrolls in SMSAs and for coverage of full-time employees by contributory retirement systems; health, hospital, or disability insurance plans; and life insurance plans.

No. 3. Labor-Management Relations in State and Local Governments. State and local government organized employees, labor relations policies and agreements, and work stoppages. This report presents national and state data on employees who belonged to an employee organization in October 1982, the type of labor relations policies practiced by state and local governments, and written management-labor agreements, by type of government. Extensive data are also presented on state and local government work stoppages by state, by type of government, and for selected governmental functions.

VOL. 4. GOVERNMENTAL FINANCES.

No. 1. Finances of School Districts. Revenue, expenditure, debt, and financial assets of school districts.

No. 2. Finances of Special Districts. Detailed data on the finances of special districts for the United States and individual states; summary statistics are presented for selected special districts.

No. 3. Finances of County Governments. Revenue, expenditure, debt, and financial assets of county governments. Data are shown for the United States and for each state. Selected financial items are also shown for groups of counties classified by size of population and for individual county governments.

No. 4. Finances of Municipalities and Township Governments. Revenue, expenditure, debt, and financial assets of municipalities and townships. Detailed statistics are shown for states and for the United States.

No. 5. Compendium of Government Finances. A comprehensive summary of the Census findings on governmental finances. U.S. totals are provided for the federal government, states, and local governments by type of government. Data are also shown by states for state and local governments, including a breakdown by type of government and local government totals for counties. Also shown are per capita figures and percentage distributions and state rankings.

VOL. 5. LOCAL GOVERNMENT IN METROPOLITAN AREAS. This volume presents the Census findings for SMSAs in three major subject fields: numbers of local governments by type and size, local government employment, and local government finances. Data are shown in terms of nationwide aggregates for population-size groups of SMSAs and for the SMSA portion of each state, as well as for individual SMSAs and their component counties. Data are also shown for selected items of direct state expenditure in these areas.

VOL. 6. TOPICAL STUDIES.

No. 1. Employee Retirement Systems of State and Local Governments. Membership, receipts, benefit payments and beneficiaries, and financial assets of more than 3,000 state and local government employment retirement systems. National data are by system characteristics. State summaries include number, membership size, and financial and beneficiary characteristics. Statistics are shown individually for retirement systems having 200 members or more.

No. 2. Personnel and Selected Employee Benefit Expenditures by State and Major Local Governments. Data on state and local government expenditures for salaries and wages and selected fringe benefits for each state and major counties, cities, school districts, and special districts. No national or state aggregates are included.

No. 3. State Payments to Local Governments. Summary description for each state of programs involving grants and reimbursements to local governments, arranged by function (education, highways, public welfare, health and hospitals, and other), indicating the basis of allocation and amounts distributed under each program during fiscal year 1976–77.

No. 4. Historical Statistics on Governmental Finances and Employment. Nationwide figures on governmental revenue, expenditure, and indebtedness, by federal, state, and local levels of government for selected years from 1902 to 1981–82 and annually from 1956.

No. 5. Graphic Summary of the 1982 Census of Governments. Charts and maps first issued in the various reports of the Census are brought together in a single report with a brief explanatory text. A reference guide to the reports where the underlying statistics appear is also furnished.

No. 6. Regional Organizations. Contains information on structure, employment, and financial transactions of certain types of local regional organizations.

VOL. 7. GUIDE TO THE 1982 CENSUS OF GOVERNMENTS. Presents detailed samples of tables published in the 1982 Census of Governments report series. It is a descriptive source for users and potential users of data produced during the Census of Governments.

For a fuller description of 1982 Census of Governments reports, see Vol. 7 (listed immediately above).

OTHER BASIC DATA SOURCES

U.S. Department of Commerce
Bureau of the Census

COUNTY AND CITY DATA BOOK, 1982. Statistical data for counties, states, regions, divisions, and cities.

DIRECTORY OF FEDERAL STATISTICS FOR LOCAL AREAS: A GUIDE TO SOURCES. 1976.

DIRECTORY OF FEDERAL STATISTICS FOR LOCAL AREAS: A GUIDE TO SOURCES—URBAN UPDATE 1977–1978. 1979.

GUIDE TO RECURRENT AND SPECIAL GOVERNMENTAL STATISTICS. Summarizes the tabular presentations produced as part of the Census Bureau's program of state and local government statistics. Covers governmental finances; state, city, county governmental finances; public employment; city employment, etc.

POCKET DATA BOOK USA. Biennial. Graphic and tabular presentation of summary statistics on a wide variety of subjects.

STATE AND LOCAL GOVERNMENT SPECIAL STUDIES. Irregular series of publications based on data collected through the Census Bureau's program of state and local government statistics.

STATE AND METROPOLITAN AREA DATA BOOK, 1982. Presents a variety of statistical information for states and metropolitan areas. For each state, 2,008 statistical items are presented. Comparable totals are shown for Census divisions and regions and for the United States as a whole. For metropolitan areas, 440 items are shown.

STATISTICAL ABSTRACT OF THE UNITED STATES. Annual. National data book and guide to sources. Standard summary of statistics on social, political, and economic organization of the United States.

PERIODICALS, INDEXES, ABSTRACTS, AND OTHER SERVICES

The items listed here are of general interest to local government administrators. All cover a variety of subjects and are not specific to a particular functional area of local government.

AMERICAN CITY & COUNTY. (M) Buttenheim Publishing.

CITY HALL DIGEST: THE MUNICIPAL GOVERNMENT NEWSLETTER. (M) City Hall Communications. Covers topics of interest to municipal administrators.

CIVIC AFFAIRS. (Q) Bureau of Municipal Research. Bulletins issued on a variety of problems facing municipal governments in Canada.

COUNCIL OF PLANNING LIBRARIANS BIBLIOGRAPHIES. The council issues bibliographies on various aspects of city and regional planning and on all aspects of urban affairs on a continuing basis. More than 600 are currently available. Complete backlist with prices available from the council.

HOUSING AND PLANNING REFERENCES. (BM) U.S. Department of Housing and Urban Development. GPO. Covers all aspects of local government, not just housing and planning.

HUD USER. Distribution center for HUD Office of Policy Development and Research reports. Service includes customized literature searches. Publishes bibliographies.

INDEX TO CURRENT URBAN DOCUMENTS. (Q) Greenwood Press. Designed to provide a record of the official publications of the largest cities and counties.

MANAGEMENT INFORMATION SERVICE. (M) ICMA. Monthly reports on subjects of practical interest to local government managers plus other publications and an inquiry service. Available only to local governmental units (cities and counties).

MUNICIPAL WORLD. (M) Municipal World, Canadian.

NATION'S CITIES WEEKLY. (W) NLC.

PUBLIC ADMINISTRATION TIMES. (BW) ASPA.

PUBLIC AFFAIRS INFORMATION SERVICE BULLETIN. (W) PAIS. Quarterly and annual cumulations. An index covering public administration and economic and social conditions. Includes latest books, pamphlets, governmental and public agency publications, and periodical articles.

PUBLIC MANAGEMENT. (M) ICMA.

READER'S GUIDE TO PERIODICAL LITERATURE. (W) Wilson.

RECENT PUBLICATIONS ON GOVERNMENTAL PROBLEMS. (BW) Charles E. Merriam Center for Public Administration Library.

SAGE PUBLIC ADMINISTRATION ABSTRACTS. (Q) Sage Publications. Covers the literature on all aspects of public administration including public management.

SAGE URBAN STUDIES ABSTRACTS. (Q) Sage Publications. Covers all aspects of urban studies with cumulative annual index. Entries drawn from books, articles, pamphlets, and other sources.

SEARCH. (M) Urban Institute. Reports research findings and opinions of the Urban Institute, a nonprofit research institute founded to study the problems of the nation's communities.

SOCIAL SCIENCES INDEX. (Q) Wilson.

STATE MUNICIPAL LEAGUE MAGAZINES.

URBAN AFFAIRS ABSTRACTS. (W) NLC Library. A comprehensive weekly urban information service abstracting over 800 periodicals, newsletters, and journals; semi-annual and annual cumulations.

URBAN AFFAIRS QUARTERLY. (Q) Sage Publications.

URBAN AFFAIRS REPORTER. Commerce Clearinghouse. Loose-leaf service covering all aspects of urban affairs. Expensive.

URBAN DATA SERVICE. (M) ICMA. Includes monthly data reports on a wide range of municipal activities.

URBAN AND REGIONAL REFERENCES. Canadian Council on Urban and Regional Research. First volume issued in 1969 covering 1945–69; yearly supplements thereafter.

URBAN RESEARCH NEWS. (BW) Sage Publications. Offers concise information from all over the world on the latest developments in the diverse aspects of urban affairs. Sources of information are cited in each article.

Emergency Management

Mary L. Knobbe
Library Consultant, MLK/LC

BOOKS, REPORTS, MONOGRAPHS, BIBLIOGRAPHIES, AND REFERENCE SOURCES

BEYOND DUMPING: NEW STRATEGIES FOR CONTROLLING TOXIC CONTAMINATION. Edited by Piasecki. Quorum. 1984. 239 pp. Gives legal, technical, and public policy information on new ways to arrest toxic contamination.

DIASTER MANAGEMENT: WARNING RESPONSE AND COMMUNITY RELOCATION. By Ronald W. Perry and Alvin H. Mushkatel. Greenwood. 1984. 368 pp. Addresses two common problems: how to ensure citizen compliance with evacuation warnings and how to permanently relocate families threatened by hazards.

EMERGENCY MANAGEMENT IN THE STATES. By Edward D. Feigenbaum and Mark L. Ford. Council of State Governments. 1984. 56 pp. Summaries of legal provisions for each state.

EMERGING TECHNOLOGIES FOR THE CONTROL OF HAZARDOUS WASTES. By B. H. Edwards and others. Noyes. 1983. 146 pp. Major technologies covered are molten salt combustion, fluidized bed incineration, and ultraviolet/ozone destruction.

EVACUATION PLANNING IN EMERGENCY MANAGEMENT. By Ronald W. Perry et al. Lexington. 1981. 199 pp. A systematic and comprehensive study of evacuation designed to reduce the impact of an impending disaster.

HAZARDOUS MATERIALS INCIDENTS: IMPROVING COMMUNITY RESPONSE. By John A. Granito. MIS 16 (1). ICMA. January 1984. 12 pp. Provides a framework for community action in response to hazardous materials incidents.

HAZARDOUS WASTE: AN INTRODUCTION. Central States Education Center. 1984. 83 pp. Advocates the destruction or neutralization of wastes as alternatives to dumping and filling. Disposal techniques are discussed.

HOME MORTGAGE LENDERS, REAL PROPERTY APPRAISERS AND EARTHQUAKE HAZARDS. By Risa I. Palm et al. University of Colorado. 1983. 152 pp.

HURRICANE EMERGENCY PLANNING. By John R. Stone. North Carolina State University. 1983. 33 pp. Estimates evacuation times for nonmetropolitan coastal communities.

INNOVATIONS IN EARTHQUAKE AND NATURAL HAZARDS RESEARCH. By Gwendolyn B. Moore. Cosmos Corporation. 1983. 51 pp.

LANDSLIDES AND LAND USE CAPABILITY ANALYSIS: A SELECTED BIBLIOGRAPHY. By Jerry E. Green. Vance Bibliographies. 1984. 16 pp.

LAND TREATMENT OF HAZARDOUS WASTES. Edited by James F. Parr et al. Noyes. 1983. 422 pp. Land treatment offers the potential for safe, acceptable, effective management of certain hazardous wastes.

MANAGEMENT OF HAZARDOUS WASTE: POLICY GUIDELINES AND CODE OF PRACTICE. Edited by Michael J. Suess and Jan W. Huismans. World Health Organization. 1983. 100 pp.

PERIODICALS

DANGEROUS PROPERTIES OF INDUSTRIAL MATERIALS REPORT. (BM) Van Nostrand Reinhold.

EMERGENCY PREPAREDNESS NEWS. (BW) Business Publishers.

HAZARDOUS MATERIALS NEWSLETTER. (BM) John R. Cashman.

HAZARDOUS WASTE NEWS. (W) Business Publishers.

NATURAL HAZARDS OBSERVER. (BM) Natural Hazards Research and Applications Information Center.

Environment and Energy

Barbara Rodes
Conservation Foundation

BOOKS, REPORTS, MONOGRAPHS, BIBLIOGRAPHIES, AND REFERENCE SOURCES

ACID DEPOSITION: ATMOSPHERIC PROCESSES IN EASTERN NORTH AMERICA, A REVIEW OF CURRENT SCIENTIFIC UNDERSTANDING. National Research Council, Environmental Studies Board. National Academy Press. 1983. Illuminates the critical issues concerning acid rain and evaluates currently available scientific evidence.

APPLIED SOCIAL SCIENCE FOR ENVIRONMENTAL PLANNING. By William Millsap. Westview Press. 1984. 278 pp. Nineteen papers show how social sciences can assist other disciplines in understanding changes in natural and social environments.

CHANGES IN THE LAND: INDIANS, COLONISTS, AND THE ECOLOGY OF NEW ENGLAND. By William Cronon. Hill and Wang. 1983. An ecological and cultural analysis of the history of colonial New England; a deeply researched interdisciplinary look at the changes that followed the Europeans' arrival.

COASTAL ECOSYSTEM MANAGEMENT: A TECHNICAL MANUAL FOR CONSERVATION OF COASTAL ZONE RESOURCES. 2d ed. By John R. Clark. Robert E. Krieger. 1983. 928 pp. County and Municipal regulatory programs.

CONTROLLING INDUSTRIAL POLLUTION: THE ECONOMICS AND POLITICS OF CLEAN AIR. By Robert W. Crandall. Studies in the Regulation of Economic Activity Series. Brookings Institution. 1983. A synthesis of major controversies surrounding the Clean Air Act.

DISTRICT HEATING AND COOLING: A 28-CITY ASSESSMENT. By Michael J. Beshenberg. NTIS. 1983. 67 pp.

ECOTOXICOLOGY: THE STUDY OF POLLUTANTS IN ECOSYSTEMS. By F. Moriarty. Academic Press. 1983. The usefulness of acute toxicity tests, the predictive value of model ecosystems, and the problems of monitoring wildlife populations for the effects of pollutants.

ENERGY AND RESOURCE RECOVERY FROM WASTE. By Stephen C. Schwarz and Calvin R. Brunner. Noyes. 1983. 272 pp. A complete guide to techniques available for recovering energy and resources from waste.

ENERGY CONSERVATION TECHNIQUES FOR ENGINEERS. By Harry B. Zackrison, Jr. Van Nostrand Reinhold. 1984. 332 pp. A comprehensive technical manual.

ENERGY HANDBOOK. 2d ed. By Robert L. Loftness. Van Nostrand Reinhold. 1984. A comprehensive reference book.

ENVIRONMENTAL CONSULTATION. By C. Wesley Morse. Praeger. 1984. 193 pp. Offers consultation as an alternative to our current regulatory system.

ENVIRONMENTAL POLICY IN THE 1980s: REAGAN'S NEW AGENDA. Edited by Norman J. Vig and Michael E. Kraft. CQ Press. 1984. Argues that many of Reagan's policy changes will not be successful because they lack both political legitimacy and a rational foundation in technical and economic analysis.

ENVIRONMENTAL QUALITY 1983: 14th ANNUAL REPORT OF THE COUNCIL ON ENVIRONMENTAL QUALITY. GPO. 1984. 341 pp. In accordance with Section 201 of the National Environmental Policy Act, this report assesses status and trends of major environmental resources and identifies persisting issues. A basic reference.

EQUITY AND ENERGY: RISING ENERGY PRICES AND THE LIVING STANDARDS OF LOWER INCOME AMERICANS. By Mark N. Cooper et al. Westview Press. 1983. 302 pp. Explores economic trends worsening the plight of lower income citizens.

NATURAL RESOURCES AND THE ENVIRONMENT: THE REAGAN APPROACH. Edited by Paul R. Portney. Changing Domestic Priorities Series. The Urban Institute Press. 1984. Papers first presented at a conference held in June 1983, sponsored by the Urban Institute and Resources for the Future.

PUBLIC LANDS AND THE U.S. ECONOMY: BALANCING CONSERVATION AND DEVELOPMENT. Edited by George

M. Johnston and Peter M. Emerson. Westview Press. 1984. A wide-ranging discussion of how lands and resources administered by the Forest Service and the Bureau of Land Management can better serve present and future needs.

THE RESOURCEFUL EARTH: A RESPONSE TO GLOBAL 2000. Edited by Julian L. Simon and Herman Kahn. Basil Blackwell. 1984. A compendium that attempts to show that the free market can take care of mankind.

SETTLING THINGS: SIX CASE STUDIES IN ENVIRONMENTAL MEDIATION. By Allan R. Talbot. Published in cooperation with the Ford Foundation by the Conservation Foundation. 1983. Evaluation of the mediation efforts in six site-specific controversies. Concludes that mediation can resolve a broad array of environmental conflicts more quickly and enduringly than litigation.

THE SOLAR-HYDROGEN ENERGY ECONOMY: BEYOND THE AGE OF FIRE. Van Nostrand Reinhold. 1984. 197 pp. A future based on solar energy is discussed.

STATE OF THE ENVIRONMENT: AN ASSESSMENT AT MID-DECADE. By Dr. Edwin H. Clark II and the Conservation Foundation staff. The Conservation Foundation. 1984. An update of a 1982 edition, this book analyzes status and trend data and examines risk assessment, cross-media pollution, water resources, and the distribution of environmental management responsibilities among several levels of government.

STATE OF THE WORLD. By Lester R. Brown et al. Worldwatch Institute. 1984. A "report card," to be published annually, on changes in the global resource base. Analysis focuses on how these changes affect the economy.

TECHNOLOGIES AND MANAGEMENT STRATEGIES FOR HAZARDOUS WASTE CONTROL. Office of Technology Assessment, Hazardous Waste Control Assessment Project. GPO. 1983. Identifies four policy options that could form the basis for a comprehensive approach to protecting human health and the environment from hazardous waste.

TRANSITIONS TO ALTERNATIVE ENERGY SYSTEMS: ENTREPRENEURS, NEW TECHNOLOGIES, AND SOCIAL CHANGE. By Thomas Baumgartner and Tom R. Burns. Westview Press. 1984. 282 pp. Sections include: The shaping of alternative energy systems; consumer-oriented technologies; producer-oriented technologies; and analysis, theory, and normative consideration.

UNCERTAIN POWER: THE STRUGGLE FOR A NATIONAL ENERGY POLICY. Edited by Dorothy S. Zinberg. Pergamon Press. 1983. 260 pp. Energy and the Public, Energy and the Evaluation of Risk, Energy and Government, and Toward a Solution are the four major sections.

WETLANDS: THEIR USE AND REGULATION. Office of Technology Assessment. GPO. 1984. A policy perspective designed to manage the competing uses of wetlands.

PERIODICALS

AMICUS JOURNAL. (Q) Natural Resources Defense Council.

CONSERVATIONIST. (BM) New York State Department of Environmental Conservation.

ENERGY CONSERVATION DIGEST. (BM) Energy Conservation Digest.

ENVIRONMENTAL ACTION. (M) Environmental Action.

ENVIRONMENTAL FORUM. (M) Environmental Law Institute.

ENVIRONMENTAL LITERATURE. (BA) Yale University.

THE ENVIRONMENTAL PROFESSIONAL. (Q) Pergamon Press.

ENVIRONMENTAL SCIENCE AND TECHNOLOGY. (M) American Chemical Society.

EPA JOURNAL. (M) U.S. Environmental Protection Agency, Office of Public Affairs.

HAZARDOUS WASTE REPORT. (BM) Aspen Systems.

INSIDE EPA. (W) U.S. Environmental Protection Agency.

MONTHLY ENERGY REVIEW. (M) GPO.

NATIONAL WILDLIFE. (BM) National Wildlife Federation.

Fire Protection

Gerard J. Hoetmer
International City Management Association

BOOKS, REPORTS, MONOGRAPHS, BIBLIOGRAPHIES, AND REFERENCE SOURCES

AUTOMATIC SPRINKLER SYSTEMS HANDBOOK. NFPA. 1983. The only comprehensive sprinkler code handbook available. Contains the complete texts of the three most important sprinkler codes, NFPA 13, 13a and 13d. Includes clarifications and interpretations and detailed commentary by experts.

EXECUTIVE SUMMARY OPERATION SAN FRANCISCO. IAFC. 1984. 32 pp. The executive summary of the technical report of the Operation San Francisco Smoke Sprinkler Tests. Using full-scale fire tests, Operation San Francisco assessed the performance of fire sprinklers, early detection and alarm systems, and smoke removal systems in an apartment, jail cell, and hotel.

FIRE AND EMERGENCY RESOURCE DIRECTORY. NFPA. 1984. 956 pp. A convenient, up-to-date directory of people, organizations, and other resources for emergency planning and response. The directory covers such areas as EMS, hazardous materials incidents, mass casualty situations, arson, inspection and code enforcement, and public education.

FIRE CHIEFS DISASTER PLANNING MANUAL. IAFC. 1984. A revision of an earlier manual prepared by the IAFC. Includes new material on the functional planning concepts of integrated emergency management, as well as planning and management guidelines, suggestions for organizing emergency management, checklists for specific hazards, and a resource directory.

FIRE INSPECTION MANAGEMENT GUIDELINES. NFPA. 1982. Set of eleven "how to" guidelines for the fire inspection program manager. Handy reference for managers who must review an existing code enforcement program or establish a new one.

FIRE PROTECTION HANDBOOK. 15th ed. NFPA. 1981. 1,400 pp. A single source reference book on contemporary fire protection practices.

500 COMPETENCIES FOR FIREFIGHTER CERTIFICATION. IFSTA. 1983. Outlines exactly what a firefighter must be able to demonstrate to be certified. This book can be used as a learning tool, a training outline, an instructor's guide, or as a permanent record of training.

FUNDING SOURCES FOR FIRE DEPARTMENTS NFPA. 1983. Provides information on a wide variety of funding sources for emergency services, from federal assistance programs to private foundation grants.

THE GREATER METROPOLITAN WASHINGTON AREA POLICE AND FIRE/RESCUE SERVICES MUTUAL AID OPERATIONAL PLAN. Metropolitan Washington Council of Governments. 1983. 43 pp.

MANAGING PEOPLE: FIRE SERVICE PERSONNEL STRATEGIES. By Pam Powell. NFPA. 1984. Discusses widely accepted and time-tested methods for improving morale and increasing productivity in the fire department. Offers advice on a wide range of personnel management topics, and gives examples to illustrate the text.

NATIONAL FIRE CODES. 8 volumes. NFPA Annual. A compilation of the latest edition of NFPA's 246 fire safety standards and codes.

1984 FIRE ALMANAC. NFPA. 1984. One-stop reference for information about the fire protection field. It includes the year in review, fire department profiles, fire related national organizations, who's who in the fire field, fire statistics, career information, funding sources, etc.

OPERATION SAN FRANCISCO: SMOKE/SPRINKLER TESTS. IAFC. 1984. 120 pp. The results of Operation San Francisco, a major test of fire sprinklers and early warning and detection systems. Compares traditional and state-of-the-art fire protection systems.

POLICE, FIRE, AND REFUSE COLLECTION. BDR. 16(7). ICMA. July 1984. Examines number of employees, length of work week, minimum and maximum salaries, longevity pay, retirement insurance, capital outlays, and other expenditures. Comparisons are made with previous years' survey results.

PERIODICALS

FIRE CHIEF. (M) Ginn.
FIRE HOUSE. (M) American Firefighter Association.
FIRE JOURNAL. (BM) NFPA.
FIRE COMMAND. (M) NFPA.
INTERNATIONAL FIRE CHIEF. (M) IAFC.
JEMS: A Journal of Emergency Medical Services. (M) Backdraft Publications.
THE MANAGEMENT REPORT. (A) IAFC.

Housing

Mary L. Knobbe
Library Consultant, MLK/LC

BOOKS, REPORTS, MONOGRAPHS, BIBLIOGRAPHIES, AND REFERENCE SOURCES

AMERICA'S HOUSING CRISIS: WHAT IS TO BE DONE? Edited by Chester Hartman and William E. Bivens. Routledge & Kegan Paul. 1983. 184 pp. Syndication strategies for community-based development organizations.

BUILDING SOLAR: HOW THE PROFESSIONAL BUILDER IS MAKING SOLAR CONSTRUCTION WORK. By Karen Muller Wells. Van Nostrand Reinhold. 1984. 209 pp. What builders' hands-on experiences in constructing active and passive solar homes have taught them.

CHARACTERISTICS OF HOUSING UNITS. BDR 16(5). ICMA. 1984. 17 pp. Statistical data on housing in cities with populations of 25,000 or more, assembled from the U.S. Census Bureau's 1980 Decennial Census of Population and Housing.

DECENT HOUSING FOR THE POOR. By Janice Bryon. Housing Resource Center. 1983. 83 pp. Is it possible in the private sector?

ENERGY COSTS, URBAN DEVELOPMENT, AND HOUSING. By Anthony Downs and Katharine L. Bradbury. Brookings Institution. 1984. 296 pp. Statistics show that energy costs rose 232 percent between 1974 and 1980, while median household income rose only 68.6 percent.

THE GREAT HOUSING EXPERIMENT. Edited by Joseph Friedman and Daniel H. Weinberg. Sage. 1983. 288 pp. (*Urban Affairs Annual Review*, 24). Essays evaluating the Experimental Housing Allowance Program, 1973–1982.

HANDBOOK OF BUILDING MAINTENANCE MANAGEMENT. By Mel A. Shear. Reston. 1983. 612 pp. Describes how to develop a building profile, determine what jobs need to be done to maintain it properly, and then develop job descriptions.

HOUSING ABANDONMENT: A LOOK AT POSSIBLE CAUSES. By Susumu Kudo and William A. Peterman. University of Illinois, Nathalie P. Voorhees Center for Neighborhood and Community Improvement. 1984. 19 pp.

HOUSING AND LOCAL GOVERNMENT. By Mary K. Nenno and Paul C. Brophy. NAHRO. 1982. 256 pp. The latest source of information on housing management and adjusting local policies to accommodate national policies and trends.

HOUSING ASSISTANCE FOR OLDER AMERICANS: THE REAGAN PRESCRIPTION. By James Zais, Raymond J. Struyk, and Thomas Thibodeau. Urban Institute. 1982. 125 pp. A look at how older Americans will fare under the housing voucher approach.

HOUSING INTERIORS FOR THE DISABLED AND ELDERLY. By Bettyann Boeticher Raschlo. NAHRO. 1982. 360 pp. Practical applications in architecture, technique, and product design.

INCREASING HOUSING OPPORTUNITIES FOR THE ELDERLY. By Carole R. Shifman. PAS. 1983. 16 pp. (PAS Rept. No. 381.) Considers arguments for and against age-specific zoning for the elderly. (PAS subscribers only.)

MANUFACTURED HOMES: MAKING SENSE OF A HOUSING OPPORTUNITY. By Thomas E. Nutt-Powell. Auburn House. 1982. 193 pp. An illuminating status report, which sees the 1980s as a pivotal time.

METROPOLITAN HOUSING NEEDS FOR THE 1980s. By John C. Weicher, Lorene Yap, and Mary S. Jones. Urban Institute. 1982. 138 pp. An introduction projecting future housing needs.

NEIGHBORHOOD MOBILIZATION: REDEVELOPMENT AND RESPONSE. By Jeffrey R. Henig. Rutgers University Press. 1982. 283 pp. Focus is on neighborhood mobilization in response to urban development plans.

PROJECT MANAGEMENT: TECHNIQUES IN PLANNING AND CONTROLLING CONSTRUCTION PROJECTS. By Hira N. Ahuja. John Wiley. 1984. 470 pp. "The introduction of more quantitative analysis cannot itself solve management problems; it is necessary to synthesize quantitative facts with the human element to achieve professional project management."

REAL ESTATE: A BIBLIOGRAPHY OF THE MONOGRAPHIC LITERATURE. Edited by Peter D. Kaikalis and Jean K. Freeman. Greenwood. 1983. 317 pp. Over 2,600 monographic titles arranged by subject category.

RESCUING THE AMERICAN DREAM: PUBLIC POLICIES AND THE CRISIS IN HOUSING. By Rolf Goetze. Holmes & Meier. 1983. 150 pp. Discusses difficulties of finding affordable housing to rent or buy, as well as tax laws and credit policies that favor the affluent.

RETIREMENT COMMUNITIES: AN AMERICAN ORIGINAL. By Michael E. Hunt. Haworth. 1984. 278 pp. Focuses on a wide variety of retirement communities in the United States. Over a million older adults live in these planned settings.

THE SUBSIDIZED HOUSING HANDBOOK. National Housing Law Project, Multifamily Demonstration Program. 1982. A guide for Legal Service attorneys and their clients, which covers providing, managing, and preserving housing for lower-income families.

UNDERGROUND BUILDING DESIGN: COMMERCIAL AND INSTITUTIONAL STRUCTURES. By John Carmody and Raymond Sterling. Van Nostrand Reinhold. 1983. 254 pp. Information presented in three forms—general information, case studies, and technical information.

PERIODICALS

COMMUNITY DEVELOPMENT DIGEST. (BM) CD Publications.
COOPERATIVE HOUSING BULLETIN. (6/year) National Association of Housing Cooperatives.
HABITAT. (Q) Canada Mortgage and Housing Corporation.
HOUSING AUTHORITY JOURNAL. (BM) Housing Authority.
HOUSING FINANCE REVIEW. (Q) Federal Home Loan Mortgage Corporation.
HOUSING LAW BULLETIN. (BM) National Housing Law Project.
HOUSING THE ELDERLY REPORT. (M) CD Publications.
LANDLORD-TENANT RELATIONS REPORT. (M) CD Publications.
THE NEIGHBORHOOD WORKS. (M) Center for Neighborhood Technology.
PLACE. (M) Partners for Livable Places.
URBAN & HOUSING RESEARCH REPORT. (M) CD Publications.

Human Resources and Services

Diane R. DiPirro
American Public Welfare Association

BOOKS, REPORTS, MONOGRAPHS, BIBLIOGRAPHIES, AND REFERENCE SOURCES

ADVOCATING TODAY: A HUMAN SERVICE PRACTITIONER'S HANDBOOK. By Robert Sunley. Family Service Association of America. 1983. Describes the principles and practices of advocating at local, state, and federal levels of government.

APPLIED POVERTY RESEARCH. Edited by Richard Greenstein and Stephen M. Sachs. Rowman and Allanheld. 1983. An evaluation of the literature on poverty and poverty programs by sociologists, economists, and political scientists.

CONSUMERISM IN MEDICINE: CHALLENGING PHYSICIAN AUTHORITY. By Marie Haug and Bebe Lavin. Sage. 1983. Explores the causes and manifestations of medical consumerism and its implications for health care policy and utilization.

DECISION MAKING AT CHILD WELFARE INTAKE: A HANDBOOK FOR PRACTITIONERS. By Theodore J. Stein and Tina L. Rzepnicki. Child Welfare League of America. 1983. Comprehensive and systematic manual for any practitioner who works with cases involving possible child abuse.

DEVELOPMENTAL DISABILITIES: NO LONGER A PRIVATE TRAGEDY. Edited by Lynn Ekler and Maryanne P. Keenan. National Association of Social Workers and American Association on Mental Deficiency. 1983. Describes the social issues related to developmental disabilities at four levels of intervention: the individual, the family, the group, and the community.

DISABILITY, WORK AND SOCIAL POLICY: MODELS FOR SOCIAL WELFARE. By Aliki Coudroglou and Dennis L. Poole. Springer. 1984. Addresses the social and moral problems of caring for disabled persons.

ETHICAL DECISIONS FOR SOCIAL WORK PRACTICE. By Frank Loewenberg and Ralph Dolgoff. F.E. Peacock. 1982. Contains case studies and exercises to help practitioners analyze the ethics of situations faced daily in social work.

FAMILIES: WHAT MAKES THEM WORK: By David H. Olson, Hamilton I. McCubbin, et al. Sage. 1983. Describes the past and present direction of social policies for the aged at state and local levels.

FISCAL AUSTERITY AND AGING: SHIFTING GOVERNMENT RESPONSIBILITY FOR THE ELDERLY. By Carroll L. Estes, Robert J. Newcomer, et al. Sage. 1983. Examines 1,000 intact families at all stages of the life cycle.

GUARANTEED INCOME: THE RIGHT TO ECONOMIC SECURITY. By Allan Sheahen. Gain. 1983. Explanation of and rationale for providing a guaranteed income to all Americans.

HUMAN SERVICES ON A LIMITED BUDGET. Edited by Robert Agranoff. Practical Management Series. ICMA. 1983. 240 pp. Addresses the shift in emphasis from growth to efficient management in the area of human services.

LAST RESORTS: EMERGENCY ASSISTANCE AND SPECIAL NEEDS PROGRAMS IN PUBLIC WELFARE. By Joel F. Handler and Michael Sosin. Academic Press. 1983. Presents original work on how the welfare system meets emergencies and special needs.

LEGAL RIGHTS OF CHILDREN. Edited by Robert M. Horowitz and Howard A. Davidson. McGraw-Hill, Shepard's Division. 1984. A comprehensive legal reference book that covers a range of issues concerning children, such as abuse and neglect, adoption, health and welfare programs, and school and institutional rights.

MANAGING THE HUMAN SERVICES IN HARD TIMES. By David A. Bresnick. 1983. 221 pp. Human Services Press. A hands-on approach to management training provides comprehensive framework for human services managers operating in a variety of organizations.

MANAGING WITHOUT MANAGERS: ALTERNATIVE WORK ARRANGEMENTS IN PUBLIC ORGANIZATIONS. By Shan Martin. Sage. 1983. 176 pp. Describes a strategy for redistributing the managing functions and increasing the frequency of "doing" activities.

MASS MEDIA AND HUMAN SERVICES: GETTING THE MESSAGE ACROSS. By Edward A. Brawley. Sage. 1983. Describes how human services professionals can educate the public about what they do.

OUR ENDANGERED CHILDREN: GROWING UP IN A CHANGING WORLD. By Vance Packard. Little, Brown and Company. 1983. Argues that our institutions are "seriously malfunctioning" in preparing children for adulthood and tells what can be done.

POLITICAL ECONOMY OF AGING: THE STATE, PRIVATE POWER AND SOCIAL WELFARE. By Laura Katz Olson. Columbia University Press. 1982. Examines the role of traditional American institutions in fostering the social problem of old age.

PRIMARY HEALTH CARE: MORE THAN MEDICINE. Edited by Rosalind S. Miller. Prentice-Hall. 1983. Health planners, physicians, nurses, and social workers propose new solutions for a health care system that has become inefficient and too costly.

REAGONOMICS: A MIDTERM REPORT. Edited by William Craig Stubblebine and Thomas D. Willett. Institute for Contemporary Studies Press. 1983. Evaluation of the successes and failures of the first two years of the Reagan administration.

RESEARCH AND EVALUATION IN THE HUMAN SERVICES. By John R. Schuerman. Free Press. 1983. Basic, comprehensive introduction to research in social work and other human services professions.

SOCIAL POLICY IN AMERICAN SOCIETY. By Robert S. Magill. Human Services Press. 1984. Presents American social policy from descriptive, historical, and analytical perspectives.

SOCIAL SUPPORT NETWORKS: INFORMAL HELPING IN THE HUMAN SERVICES. By James K. Whittaker and James Garbarino. Aldine. 1983. Defines social support networks and tells how they fit into an overall framework of human services.

STATE AND THE POOR IN THE 1980's. Edited by Manuel Carballo and Mary Jo Bane. Auburn House. 1984. 350 pp. A comprehensive examination of the poor and the policies that affect them.

TASK-CENTERED MANAGEMENT IN HUMAN SERVICES. By Bageshwari Parihar. Charles C. Thomas. 1984. Provides a problem-oriented, short-term approach to decision making and problem resolution that emphasizes involvement, agreement, and communication.

WHEN BONDING FAILS: CLINICAL ASSESSMENT OF HIGH-RISK FAMILIES. By Frank G. Bolton, Jr. Sage. 1983. Practical guide suggests methods for easy identification of the high-risk family and ways of screening out families not likely to benefit from intervention.

WOMEN'S WELFARE, WOMEN'S RIGHTS. Edited by Jane Lewis. Croom Helm. 1983. Discusses changes in social policies necessary to alter the whole—not just one area—of women's lives.

PERIODICALS

ADMINISTRATION IN SOCIAL WORK. (Q) Haworth Press.

AGING. (BM) GPO.

CHILD PROTECTION REPORT. (BW) Child Protection Report.

CHILD WELFARE. (BM) Child Welfare League of America.

JOURNAL OF HUMAN SERVICES ABSTRACTS. (Q) Project SHARE.

NUTRITION WEEK. (W) Community Nutrition Institute.

PUBLIC WELFARE. (Q) American Public Welfare Association.

SOCIAL CASEWORK: THE JOURNAL OF CONTEMPORARY SOCIAL WORK. (M) Family Service Association of America.

SOCIAL SERVICE REVIEW. (Q) University of Chicago Press.

SOCIAL WORK RESEARCH AND ABSTRACTS. (Q) National Association of Social Workers.

Information Technologies

Mary L. Knobbe
Library Consultant, MLK/LC

BOOKS, REPORTS, MONOGRAPHS, BIBLIOGRAPHIES, AND REFERENCE SOURCES

ELECTRONIC MAIL. By Stephen Connell and Ian A. Galbraith. Knowledge Industry. 1982. 141 pp. A revolution in business communications.

THE EXECUTIVE'S GUIDE TO TV AND RADIO APPEARANCE. By Michael Bland. Knowledge Industry. 1980. 138 pp. How to prepare for being on TV or radio.

THE FUTURE OF VIDEOTEXT. By Elfrem Sigel. Knowledge Industry. 1983. 197 pp. The future of this industry.

A GUIDE TO SELECTING AND USING MICROCOMPUTERS IN GOVERNMENT. Arthur Anderson & Co. GFOA. A layman's guide to the new world of microcomputers in government.

INFORMATION SYSTEMS FOR MODERN MANAGEMENT. 3d ed. By Robert G. Murdick, Joel E. Ross, and James R. Claggett. Prentice-Hall. 1984. 466 pp. An up-to-date and integrated treatment of organization and management, emphasizing the use of management information systems.

MICROCOMPUTERS IN LOCAL GOVERNMENT. By James R. Griesemer. Practical Management Series. ICMA. 1983. 148 pp. A nontechnical reader for managers, elected officials, and department heads.

OFFICE AUTOMATION. Edited by Nancy M. Edwards. Knowledge Industry. A glossary of more than 7,000 terms from the major technologies.

OPTIONS FOR ELECTRONIC MAIL. By Libby Trudell with Janet Bruman and Dennis Oliver. Knowledge Industry. 1984. 160 pp. Explains and compares the major types of electronic mail services.

TAKING CONTROL OF YOUR OFFICE RECORDS. Edited by Katherine Aschner. Knowledge Industry. 1983. 264 pp. A book to help you organize your office paper work and manage your information efficiently.

TELECOMMUNICATIONS FOR LOCAL GOVERNMENT. Edited by Fred S. Knight, Harold E. Horn, and Nancy J. Jesuale. Practical Management Series. ICMA. 1982. 217 pp. A description of cable and other systems and how they are used, as well as guidelines for telecommunication planning.

THE TELECONFERENCING HANDBOOK. By Ellen A. Lazer, Martin C. J. Elton, and James W. Johnson, with others. Knowledge Industry. 1983. A new way to communicate that promises efficient management of money and time.

THE WORD PROCESSING HANDBOOK. By Katherine Aschner. Knowledge Industry. 1982. 193 pp. A step-by-step guide to automating your office.

PERIODICALS

COMPUTER GRAPHICS WORLD. (M) Pennwell Publishing.

COMPUTERS AND SECURITY. (3/year) North-Holland Publishing.

COMPUTERWORLD. (W) C.W. Communications.

DATAMATION. (M) Technical Publishing.

EMMS (Electronic Mail and Message Systems.) (SM) International Resources Development.

GOVERNMENT DATA SYSTEMS. (BM) United Business Publications.

INFORMATION AND WORD PROCESSING REPORT. (SM) (Formerly WORD PROCESSING REPORT.) Geyer-McAllister.

MICROSOFTWARE NEWS. (BM) ICMA and Product Information Network, McGraw-Hill.

OFFICE ADMINISTRATION AND AUTOMATION. (M) Geyer-McAllister.

RECORDS MANAGEMENT QUARTERLY. (Q) (Formerly R.M.A. RECORDS MANAGEMENT.) Association of Records Managers and Administrators.

Intergovernmental Relations

Carolyn A. Moore
Municipal Reference Library

BOOKS, REPORTS, MONOGRAPHS, BIBLIOGRAPHIES, AND REFERENCE SOURCES

ALABAMA AND NEW FEDERALISM. By William H. Wallace. Alabama Office of State Planning and Federal Programs. 1982. Description of how one state plans to deal with its changing responsibilities under block grants and new federalism programs.

AMERICAN FEDERALISM: A NEW PARTNERSHIP FOR THE REPUBLIC. Edited by Robert B. Hawkins Jr. Institute for Contemporary Studies. 1982. 281 pp. Proceedings of a September 1981 conference presenting an in-depth look at federalism.

AN ANALYSIS OF STATE, COUNTY, AND CITY GOVERNMENT POLICY STATEMENTS ON FEDERALISM. Academy for State and Local Government. 1982. 38 pp. Outlines the agreements, disagreements, and other characteristics found in each of the federalism policy proposals of the nine major national governmental associations.

THE BUDGET AND THE REGION. Northeast-Midwest Institute. 1984. Each chapter covers a budget topic of major importance to areas of the country hard-hit by the recent recession.

COOPERATION IN THE PROVISION OF SERVICES: A STUDY OF MASSACHUSETTS AND RHODE ISLAND TOWNS. By Catherine L. Flynn and others. Cooperative Extension Service, University of Massachusetts. 1982. 42 pp. Interlocal relationships occur among most of the surveyed communities, the majority of which are informal and mainly involve informational exchange.

DIRECTORY '84. National Association of Regional Councils. 1984. 55 pp. Provides a nationwide, current list of councils, their addresses, and main officers.

FEDERAL-STATE RELATIONS IN TRANSITION: IMPLICATIONS FOR ENVIRONMENTAL POLICY. Congressional Research Service for U.S. Senate Committee on Environment and Public Works. GPO. 1982. 99 pp. Traces evolution of national environmental programs from state and local problems. Emphasizes need for adequate analysis before policies are reversed or changed.

GOVERNING URBAN AMERICA: A POLICY FOCUS. By Bryan D. Jones. Little. 1983. 432 pp. Examines current urban policy while looking to the future and the problems imposed by resource limitations and complex political and governmental structures.

IMPLEMENTATION OF THE STATE MANDATES ACT IN ILLINOIS. Illinois Commission on Intergovernmental Cooperation. Research Memorandum No. 70. 1982. 9 pp. First year analysis of Illinois' legislation addressing state mandates and their impact on local government budgets.

INTERRELATIONSHIP OF FUNDING FOR THE ARTS AT THE STATE AND LOCAL LEVELS. 18th Report by U.S. House Committee on Government Operations. HR98-547. GPO. 1983. 60 pp. Findings and proposals based on an investigation of private and corporate support, impacts on economy and employment, and the influences of each level of government on the other.

INTERGOVERNMENTAL RESPONSIBILITIES FOR FINANCING PUBLIC TRANSIT SERVICES. By Robert Cervero. University Research and Training Programs, UMTA. GPO. 1983. DOT-1-83-30. 181 pp. Emphasis on sharing of public transit costs, since benefits fall on all governmental levels, while some of the increases in costs are due to regulations imposed from above.

THE ISSUE OF 1982: A BRIEFING BOOK. Conference on Alternative State and Local Policies. 1982. 233 pp. Directed to the "new" leaders who will make decisions under the "new federalism."

JAILS: INTERGOVERNMENTAL DIMENSIONS OF A LOCAL PROBLEM. ACIR. 1984. 247 pp. Examines jail issues, correctional alternatives, interlocal relations and jail management, and federal policies influencing jail management, and recommends specific actions.

LOCAL ENFORCEMENT OF STATE BUILDING AND FIRE CODES. By A. M. Westling. Bureau of Governmental Research and Service, University of Oregon. League of Oregon Cities. 1982. 29 pp. An example of coordination by state, county, and local levels in enforcement of interlocking codes.

POLITICS OF STATE AND LOCAL GOVERNMENT. 3d ed. By Duane Lockard. Macmillan. 1983. 280 pp. Extensively revised edition reflecting changes in government since the 1960s.

REDUCTIONS IN U.S. DOMESTIC SPENDING: HOW THEY AFFECT STATE AND LOCAL GOVERNMENTS. Edited by John William Ellwood. Transaction Books. 1982. 377 pp. An examination of budget reductions by program beginning in 1981.

REGIONAL PERSPECTIVES ON NEW FEDERALISM. By Peter H. Doyle. Northeast-Midwest Institute. 1982. 38 pp. Evaluates states' ability to accept responsibility for programs previously supported by federal outlays, particularly in serving lower income areas.

STATE AND LOCAL FISCAL RELATIONS IN EARLY 1980's. By Steven D. Gold. Urban Institute. 1983. 76 pp. Analyzes changes in fiscal policies under the current federal administration that have led to significant adjustments in state and local budgets.

STATE-LOCAL RELATIONS AND URBAN TECHNOLOGY: A STUDY IN INTERGOVERNMENTAL DECISION MAKING. Syracuse Research Corporation.

1982. NTIS (PB83-146332) Uses specific cooperative and innovative programs as examples of service systems operating in the political context that have been affected by federal policies.

TO COOPERATE OR NOT TO COOPERATE: A REPORT ON INTERGOVERNMENTAL COOPERATION IN ALLEGHENY COUNTY. Allegheny Conference on Community Development. 1982. 70 pp. Appendix. Proposes three recommendations to foster cooperation among area municipalities, regardless of size, since their basic municipal service needs are the same.

PERIODICALS

CITIZEN PARTICIPATION. (BM) Lincoln Filene Center for Citizenship and Public Affairs, Tufts University.

THE GAO REVIEW. (Q) GPO.

EAST-WEST DIRECTIONS. (Irregular) East-West Gateway Coordinating Council.

GOVERNMENTAL RISK MANAGEMENT REPORTS. (M) Risk Planning Group.

POLICY AND RESEARCH REPORT. (Q) Urban Institute.

POPULAR GOVERNMENT. (Q) Institute of Government, University of North Carolina.

PUBLIC AFFAIRS. (Irregular) Governmental Research Bureau, University of South Dakota.

STATE AND LOCAL GOVERNMENT REVIEW. (3/year) Carl Vinson Institute of Government, University of Florida.

WAYS AND MEANS. (Q) Conference on Alternative State and Local Policies.

Law Enforcement and Criminal Justice

National Criminal Justice Reference Service, National Institute of Justice

BOOKS, REPORTS, MONOGRAPHS, BIBLIOGRAPHIES, AND REFERENCE SOURCES

BATTERED WOMEN AND THEIR FAMILIES: INTERVENTION STRATEGIES AND TREATMENT PROGRAMS. Edited by Albert R. Roberts. (Social Work Series, vol. 1.) Springer. 1984. 209 pp. Intended for social workers, psychologists, and other practitioners, this book provides in-depth material on the most recent advances in family violence intervention.

THE COMMON SECRET: SEXUAL ABUSE OF CHILDREN AND ADOLESCENTS. By Ruth S. Kempe and C. Henry Kempe. W. H. Freeman. 1984. 284 pp. Examines the 200 percent increase in child sexual abuse, from pedophilia to rape to child pornography, and discusses the role of the family in this dilemma.

COMPENSATING VICTIMS OF CRIME: AN ANALYSIS OF AMERICAN PROGRAMS. By Daniel McGillis and Patricia Smith. Issues and Practices in Criminal Justice Series. National Institute of Justice. 1983. 218 pp. Describes policies and procedures of victim compensation programs across the country.

CONTROLLING PRIVATE SECURITY SYSTEM FALSE ALARMS. By F. Michael McLaurin. MIS 16(7). ICMA. July 1984. 12 pp. Reviews methods currently employed by local governments to reduce false alarms from private security systems.

ELDERLY CRIMINALS. By Evelyn S. Newman, Donald J. Newman, and Mindy L. Gewirtz. Oelgeschlager, Gunn & Hain. 1984. 252 pp. Focuses on the causes of the growing problem of elderly crime and on how our criminal justice system deals with the elderly criminal.

GUIDELINES FOR PRISON INDUSTRIES. By Robert C. Grieser, Neal Miller, and Gail S. Funke. National Institute of Corrections. 1984. 133 pp. Reports on the current status of prison industries across the nation, provides guidelines to help a state create or modify its authorizing legislation and operational procedures, and assesses the implications of court actions and standards pertaining to prison industries' accountability.

INNOVATIONS IN THE PROSECUTION OF CHILD SEXUAL ABUSE CASES. Edited by Josephine Bulkley. American Bar Association/National Legal Resource Center for Child Advocacy and Protection. 1981. 176 pp. The findings of a survey to obtain information on a wide range of prosecutorial issues in child abuse cases is presented in this volume. Also discussed are comprehensive and innovative programs for the treatment of incest offenders, victims, and their families.

THE INSANITY DEFENSE AND ITS ALTERNATIVES: A GUIDE FOR POLICYMAKERS. By Ingo Keilitz and Junius P. Fulton. National Center for State Courts. 1984. 88 pp. This monograph focuses on those areas of the insanity defense that form the core of the current debate: definitions of insanity, burdens of proof, verdicts, the disposition of insanity acquittees, and the abolition of the insanity defense.

INTRODUCTION TO CRIMINAL EVIDENCE. 2d ed. By Jon R. Waltz. Nelson-Hall. 1983. 470 pp. Intended for both a professional and a general audience, this text describes all the important rules of evidence in detail, with attention to their applicability in criminal proceedings.

JAIL OVERCROWDING: IDENTIFYING CAUSES AND PLANNING FOR SOLUTIONS—A HANDBOOK FOR ADMINISTRATORS. By Walter Busher. Office of Justice Assistance, Research, and Statistics. 1983. 117 pp. Describes dealing with jail overcrowding through comprehensive planning based on sound data and provides a step-by-step guide.

OPPORTUNITIES IN LAW ENFORCEMENT AND CRIMINAL JUSTICE. By James D. Stinchcomb. VGM Career Horizons. 1984. 152 pp. Discusses career opportunities at the city, county, and state levels as well as in the military and federal services.

POLICE FIELD OPERATIONS. By Thomas F. Adams. Prentice-Hall. 1985. 385 pp. Outlines police office and field procedures and the law enforcement officer's role in the community. Topics covered include routine assignments, interview and interrogation techniques, field notetaking, basic report writing, handling crimes in progress, crowd control, arrest, search, custody, and more.

THE PURSUIT OF CRIMINAL JUSTICE: ESSAYS FROM THE CHICAGO CENTER. Edited by Gordon Hawkins and Franklin E. Zimring. Studies in Crime and Justice Series. University of Chicago Press. 1984. 358 pp. Eighteen essays, written by scholars of the Chicago Center for Studies in Criminal Justice, deal with such diverse topics as the death penalty, organized crime, deterrence, sentencing, and corrections. A bibliography lists the Center's publications for 1965–1982.

REPORT TO THE NATION ON CRIME AND JUSTICE. Compiled by the Bureau of Justice Statistics. GPO. 1983. 108 pp. This nontechnical report digests the latest available data to give the reader a clear, accurate overview of crime, victims, offenders, and the criminal justice system and its costs.

THE SEARCH FOR EVIDENCE. By Art Buckwalter. Butterworth. 1984. 288 pp. Twenty chapters discuss fundamentals of evidence, verbal evidence, written evidence, physical evidence, and photographing and recording evidence.

SECURITY DESIGN FOR MAXIMUM PROTECTION. By Richard J. Gigliotti and Ronald C. Jason. Butterworth. 1984. 352 pp. Sixteen chapters discuss the various components that, when combined in the right proportions, result in maximum security. Topics considered include levels of physical security, the psychology of maximum security, the value of planning, and the security plan. Physical barriers and alarm systems are discussed.

TIME TO BUILD?: THE REALITIES OF PRISON CONSTRUCTION. By Bruce Cory and Stephen Gettinger. Edna McConnell Clark Foundation. 1984. 64 pp. In focusing on issues associated with prison and jail overcrowding, this booklet considers the costs and benefits of constructing new facilities, planning for construction, and managing the criminal justice system to reduce jail and prison populations.

TOWARD BETTER AND SAFER SCHOOLS: A SCHOOL LEADER'S GUIDE TO DELINQUENCY PREVENTION. National School Boards Association. 1984. 236 pp. Strategies for school delinquency prevention outlined in this handbook emphasize sound disciplinary policies and practices that improve the school climate by involving disruptive students in constructive activities rather than alienating them.

UNDERSTANDING POLICE AGENCY PERFORMANCE. Edited by Gordon P. Whitaker. National Institute of Justice. GPO. 1984. 182 pp. This report examines both the processes by which police resources are transformed into service activities and the effects those activities have on the community. Models for assessing performance are discussed in the context of police patrol operations.

USING CABLE TELEVISION FOR PUBLIC SAFETY IN SMALL COMMUNITIES. By Michael Dolhancryk and Thomas E. Kathman. MIS 16(2). ICMA. February 1984. 10 pp.

VIOLENT INDIVIDUALS AND FAMILIES: A HANDBOOK FOR PRACTITIONERS. Edited by Susan Saunders, Ann M. Anderson, Cynthia Allen Hart, and Gerald M. Rubenstein. Charles C. Thomas. 1984. 265 pp. The developmental and family origins of violence, methods for assessing the potential for violence in individuals, and strategies for intervention with victims of violence are discussed in this comprehensive text.

YOUTH GANGS. By Edward F. Dolan, Jr., and Shan Finney. Julian Messner. 1984. 141 pp. After outlining the history of juvenile gangs, this book addresses the numbers and criminal activities of gangs today, gang characteristics, ethnic gangs, the gang's daily life, and ways of countering the gang problem.

PERIODICALS

CORRECTIONS TODAY. (BM) American Correctional Association.

CRIME AND DELINQUENCY. (Q) Published by Sage in cooperation with the National Council on Crime and Delinquency.

JOURNAL OF CRIMINAL JUSTICE. (BM) Pergamon Press.

JOURNAL OF POLICE SCIENCE AND ADMINISTRATION. (Q) International Association of Chiefs of Police.

JOURNAL OF RESEARCH IN CRIME AND DELINQUENCY. (SA) Published by Sage in cooperation with the National Council on Crime and Delinquency.

JUDICATURE. (M) American Judicature Society.

JUVENILE AND FAMILY COURT JOURNAL. (Q) National Council of Juvenile and Family Court Judges.

POLICE CHIEF. (M) International Association of Chiefs of Police.

POLICE STRESS. (Q) International Law Enforcement Stress Association.

SECURITY MANAGEMENT. (M) American Society for Industrial Security.

Local Government Organization and Management

Linda J. Benigno
Municipal Reference Library

BOOKS, REPORTS, MONOGRAPHS, BIBLIOGRAPHIES, AND REFERENCE SOURCES

DOING MORE WITH LESS: CUTBACK MANAGEMENT IN NEW YORK CITY. By Demetrios Caraley et al. Graduate Program in Public Policy and Administration, Columbia University. 1982. 154 pp. Contains round-table discussions and interviews with New York City officials on how to spend less and produce more.

COSTING GOVERNMENT SERVICES: A GUIDE FOR DECISION MAKING. By Joseph T. Kelley. GFOA. 1984. 154 pp. Cost analysis is an important tool for managerial decision making. Examples, techniques, and various applications are outlined.

THE ENTREPRENEUR IN LOCAL GOVERNMENT. Edited by Barbara H. Moore. Practical Management Series. ICMA. 1983. 214 pp. Local government managers sometimes become entrepreneurs in response to fiscal pressures; they redefine the role of local government and make innovations.

A GUIDE TO SELECTING AND USING MICROCOMPUTERS IN GOVERNMENT. GFOA. 1984. 184 pp. Popular uses of microcomputers as well as selection and implementation procedures are discussed.

HOW TO MANAGE IN THE PUBLIC SECTOR. By Gordon Chase and Betsy Reveal. Addison-Wesley. 1983. 182 pp. Explains approaches that work.

INFORMATION MANAGEMENT IN PUBLIC ADMINISTRATION: AN INTRODUCTION TO GOVERNMENT IN THE INFORMATION AGE. Edited by Forest W. Horton and Donald A. Marchand. Information Resources Press. 1982. 588 pp. Data are a valuable resource that need to be carefully managed and controlled by public administrators.

ISSUES MANAGEMENT: ORIGINS OF THE FUTURE. By W. Howard Chase. Issue Action Publications. 1984. 170 pp. Municipal leaders must learn to create their own agendas and manage without giving in to outside forces in order to deal effectively with future issues.

LOCAL GOVERNMENT ASSISTANTS—1983. BDR 16(4). ICMA. 1984. 54 pp. Statistical profile of local government assistant managers, covering personal data as well as salaries, duties, mobility, and career goals.

THE MANAGEMENT IDEA BOOK: A PLANNING DIRECTOR LOOKS BACK AND HELPS YOU LOOK FORWARD. By Paul C. Zucker. West Coast Publishers. 1983. 112 pp. Practical, down-to-earth approaches for governmental officials with little or no formal training in management.

MANAGING CRISIS CITIES: THE NEW BLACK LEADERSHIP AND THE POLITICS OF RESOURCE ALLOCATION. By Bette Woody. Greenwood. 1982. 228 pp. Fiscal and other types of problems in older cities are examined in light of the "new black politics."

MANAGING PUBLIC RESOURCES. By Barry M. Mundt and others. Peat Marwick International. 1982. 143 pp. Managing public resources "is a complicated and sometimes unconventional art"; each management process involves a set of interacting steps.

MODERN PUBLIC ADMINISTRATION. 6th ed. By Felix A. Nigro and Lloyd G. Nigro. Harper & Row. 1984. 401 pp. Covers various aspects of administration, including basic problems of management, and has a new section on administration and politics.

ORGANIZATIONAL GOAL SETTING IN LOCAL GOVERNMENT. MIS 16(5). ICMA. May 1984. 17 pp. Four case studies.

PLANNING FOR CAPITAL IMPROVEMENTS. MIS 16(8). ICMA. August 1984. 19 pp. Presents a framework for planning the maintenance and replacement of existing capital equipment and facilities, and the acquisition or construction of new facilities.

THE PUBLIC MANAGER'S GUIDE. By Donald P. Crane and William A. Jones, Jr. BNA. 1982. 287 pp. This college level text describes the various roles that public managers take on, and emphasizes the primary concepts of public management.

RESULTS-ORIENTED BUDGETING FOR LOCAL PUBLIC MANAGERS IN THE 1980s. By Richard J. Stillman II. Bureau of Governmental Research and Service, University of South Carolina. 1982. 89 pp. Results budgeting emphasizes managerial effectiveness as opposed to financial techniques. This guide explains how to adapt results budgeting to a standard local government budget.

RETHINKING LOCAL SERVICES: EXAMINING ALTERNATIVE DELIVERY APPROACHES. By Carl Valente and Lydia Manchester. MIS Special Report No. 12. ICMA. March 1984. 289 pp. Discusses seven alternative systems for delivering services: purchase of service contracting, franchise agreements, subsidy arrangements, vouchers, volunteer personnel, self-help, and regulatory and tax incentives. Includes case studies.

SMALL CITIES AND COUNTIES: A GUIDE TO MANAGING SERVICES. Edited by James M. Banovetz. ICMA. 1984. 356 pp. Practitioner's book on management in the small community, covering laws, local offices, planning, economic development, municipal services, and intergovernmental relations.

A STATISTICS PRIMER FOR MANAGERS: HOW TO READ A STATISTICAL REPORT OR A COMPUTER PRINT OUT AND GET THE RIGHT ANSWERS. By John J. Clark and Margaret T. Clark. The

Free Press. 1983. 258 pp. Informed management decisions depend upon careful analysis of data.

PERIODICALS

CITY HALL DIGEST. (M) City Hall Communications.

CURRENT MUNICIPAL PROBLEMS. (Q) Callaghan Publishing.

GOVERNMENT EXECUTIVE. (M) Executive Publishers.

THE GUIDE TO MANAGEMENT IMPROVEMENT PROJECTS IN LOCAL GOVERNMENT. (Q) ICMA.

MANAGEMENT REVIEW. (M) AMA.

MUNICIPAL MANAGEMENT. (Q) Municipal Management Publishing Company.

PUBLIC ADMINISTRATION TIMES. (BW) ASPA.

PUBLIC MANAGEMENT. (M) ICMA.

Personnel and Labor Relations

Marilyn J. Modlin
The Bureau of National Affairs, Inc.

BOOKS, REPORTS, MONOGRAPHS, BIBLIOGRAPHIES, AND REFERENCE SOURCES

ALCOHOL AND DRUGS: ISSUES IN THE WORKPLACE. By Tia Schneider Denenberg and R. V. Denenberg. BNA. 1983. The industrial relations issues raised by the impact of alcohol and drugs in the workplace; intended for industrial relations practitioners.

COMPARATIVE INDUSTRIAL RELATIONS: A TRANS-ATLANTIC DIALOGUE. Edited by John V. Schappi. BNA and Oxford University. 1984. The proceedings of the first Oxford University/BNA symposium, August 3–17, 1983, at Oxford University.

CREATIVE PERSONNEL PRACTICES: NEW IDEAS FOR LOCAL GOVERNMENTS. Edited by John Matzer, Jr. Practical Management Series. ICMA. 1984. 256 pp. Topics include performance appraisal, employee motivation, bargaining, flexible benefits, and comparable worth.

DESIGNING EMPLOYEE ASSISTANCE PROGRAMS. By Dale A. Masi. AMACOM. 1984. A practical handbook for persons interested in setting up employee assistance programs. Contains descriptions of three successful programs operating today.

THE ECONOMICS OF NON-WAGE LABOUR COSTS. By Robert A. Hart. Allen & Unwin. 1984. The effects of non-wage labor costs on the cyclical behavior of employment, output and wages, and on the average working hours required by a company given recognition of these costs.

EFFECTIVE SUPERVISORY PRACTICES: BETTER RESULTS THROUGH TEAMWORK. 2d ed. ICMA. 1984. 215 pp. Basic training text in principles of supervision and guidelines for applying them on the job.

EMPLOYMENT AND TRAINING R & D LESSONS LEARNED AND FUTURE DIRECTIONS. Edited by R. Thayne Robson. W. E. Upjohn Institute for Employment Research. 1984. Conference proceedings of the National Council on Employment Policy, January 26–27, 1984. Papers by Eli Gineberg, Daniel H. Saks, Howard Rosen, and Gary Burtless and Robert H. Haveman.

THE EVALUATION INTERVIEW. 3d ed. By Richard A. Fear. McGraw-Hill. 1984. A complete guide to interviewing: how to evaluate a job candidate, what questions not to ask, how to establish rapport, what "employment at will" means today. Contains sample interview questions, rating forms, after-interview write-ups, and more.

HOW TO MEASURE HUMAN RESOURCE MANAGEMENT. By Jac Fitz-enz. McGraw-Hill. 1984. How to quantify four human resource functions: planning and staffing, compensation and benefits, employee relations, and training and development.

HUMAN RESOURCE DIRECTOR'S HANDBOOK. By Mary F. Cook. Prentice-Hall. 1984. A description and analysis of 12 human resource functions and how they can contribute to the organization's business plan and profitability.

HUMAN RESOURCES MANAGEMENT IN THE 1980's. Edited by Stephen J. Carroll and Randall S. Schuler. BNA. 1983. Supplement to the ASPA handbook of personnel and industrial relations.

INNOVATIONS IN MANAGING HUMAN RESOURCES. By Harriet Gorlin and Lawrence Schein. The Conference Board. 1984. An analysis of innovative approaches to raising productivity, improving product quality, increasing work participation, etc.

LABOR LAW AND INDUSTRIAL RELATIONS IN THE UNITED STATES OF AMERICA. 2d ed. By Alvin L. Goldman. BNA. 1984. Revision of 1979 edition.

THE LAW OF THE WORKPLACE: RIGHTS OF EMPLOYERS AND EMPLOYEES. By James Hunt. BNA. 1984. A summary of current workplace laws, their effect on both employers and employees, and the agencies and programs which administer these laws.

MAJOR ISSUES IN THE FEDERAL LAW OF EMPLOYMENT DISCRIMINATION. By George Rutherglen. The Federal Judicial Center. 1983. An analysis of the provisions of Title VII of the Civil Rights Act of 1964, together with a brief discussion of other federal remedies for employment discrimination.

NEGOTIATING A LABOR CONTRACT: A MANAGEMENT HANDBOOK. By Charles S. Loughran. BNA. 1984. Written for those persons responsible for the employer's side of labor contract negotiations, this work covers the complete bargaining process.

OUTPLACEMENT AND INPLACEMENT COUNSELING. By Lawrence M. Brammer and Frank E. Humberger. Prentice-Hall. 1984. How to implement both types of counseling within an existing human resources department.

PERFORMANCE APPRAISAL. 2d ed. By Richard L. Henderson. Reston. 1984. An analysis of the technical issues relating to performance appraisal: how to accurately describe a job, identify rating and measuring procedures, set up information systems and audit programs, etc.

THE PLANT CLOSURE POLICY DILEMMA: LABOR LAW AND BARGAINING. By Wayne R. Wendling. The W. E. Upjohn Institute for Employment Research. 1984. The role of collective bargaining in plant closure situations, and how collective bargaining can work to solve the problems of plant closure.

PRODUCTIVITY IMPROVEMENT OPPORTUNITIES IN POLICE OPERATIONS. MIS 16(4). ICMA. April 1984. 23 pp. Suggests operational improvements to increase productivity.

PUBLIC WORKS PRODUCTIVITY IMPROVEMENT. MIS 16(6). ICMA. June 1984. 20 pp. Examples from five cities of various sizes.

QUALITY OF WORKING LIFE IN INTERNATIONAL PERSPECTIVE. By Yves Delamotte and Shin-ichi Takezawa. International Labour Office. 1984. Examines the quality-of-working-life movement and its relationship to modern labor policies worldwide.

THE RIGHTS OF EMPLOYEES. By Wayne N. Outten, and Noah A. Kinigstein. Bantam Books. 1984. Published in conjunction with the American Civil Liberties Union, this book uses a question-and-answer format to elucidate the laws which regulate the employment relationship.

SALARIES OF MUNICIPAL OFFICIALS 1984. BDR 16(3). ICMA. 1984. 27 pp.

STAFFING THE PUBLIC SERVICE. By Albert P. Maslow. Published by the author. 1983. The staffing function of human resources management in the public sector.

A SURVEY OF UNION REPRESENTATION PROVISIONS IN FEDERAL LABOR AGREEMENTS. Prepared and issued by the Office of Employee, Labor and Agency Relations, U.S. Office of Personnel Management. NTIS. 1984. A review of contracts in the Labor Agreements Information Retrieval System (OPM) as of February 1, 1984.

UNION ORGANIZING AND STAYING ORGANIZED. By Ken Gagala. Reston. 1983. A book for both sides of the labor/management world, it describes how effective unions operate, and what happens when they cease to be viable (i.e., the decertification process).

WORKERS, JOBS, AND STATISTICS:

QUESTIONS AND ANSWERS ON LABOR FORCE STATISTICS. U.S. Bureau of Labor Statistics (Report 698). 1983. The collection, measurement, and use of statistics concerning the labor force and employment and unemployment.

PERIODICALS

AMERICAN DEMOGRAPHICS. (M) American Demographics.
THE BEST OF BUSINESS. (SA) 13-30 Corporation.
BULLETIN OF LABOUR STATISTICS. (Q) International Labour Office.
COMPENSATION REVIEW. (Q) AMA.
EMPLOYEE BENEFIT PLAN REVIEW. (M) Charles D. Spencer & Associates.
EMPLOYEE RELATIONS LAW JOURNAL. (Q) Executive Enterprises Publications.
HUMAN RESOURCE PLANNING. (Q) Human Resource Planning Society.
INDUSTRIAL AND LABOR RELATIONS REVIEW. (Q) New York State School of Industrial and Labor Relations.
INDUSTRIAL RELATIONS. (3 issues per year) Institute of Industrial Relations.
PERSONNEL LITERATURE. (M) GPO.
PERSONNEL MANAGEMENT ABSTRACTS. (Q) Personnel Management Abstracts.
PUBLIC PERSONNEL MANAGEMENT. (Q) IPMA.
SAM ADVANCED MANAGEMENT JOURNAL. (Q) Society for Advancement of Management.

Planning and Development

Camille A. Motta
The Urban Institute

BOOKS, REPORTS, MONOGRAPHS, BIBLIOGRAPHIES, AND REFERENCE SOURCES

BEYOND THE WASTE LAND: A DEMOCRATIC ALTERNATIVE TO ECONOMIC DECLINE. By Samuel Bowles. Anchor Press/Doubleday. 1983. 465 pp. Proposes an alternative to trickle-down economics as cure to our ailing economy. A 24-point economic program is presented that addresses the basic sources of waste in our corporate, capitalistic economy.
CAN AMERICA COMPETE? By Robert Z. Lawrence. Brookings Institution. 1984. 156 pp. Another opinion in the debate over U.S. structural policy. Lawrence analyzes sources of structural change in U.S. manufacturing and finds that America is not deindustralizing.
CITIES AND THE WEALTH OF NATIONS: PRINCIPLES OF ECONOMIC LIFE. By Jane Jacobs. Random House. 1984. 251 pp. Argues that we should look at the cities rather than the national economy in order to understand economic life. Many examples from history and contemporary society are used to add interest.
CONTESTED CITY. By John H. Mollenkopf. Princeton University Press. 1983. 328 pp. Delineates the causes and consequences of federal urban development programs established by New Deal democrats.
DIRECTORY OF INCENTIVES FOR BUSINESS INVESTMENT AND DEVELOPMENT IN THE UNITED STATES: A STATE-BY-STATE GUIDE. National Association of State Development Agencies, National Council for Urban Economic Development and the Urban Institute. Urban Institute Press. 1983. 652 pp. A major new sourcebook on business incentive programs of all categories in all states. Contains a 56-page overview presenting elements common to most state programs, the state-by-state guide, and an index of incentives.
ENERGY COSTS, URBAN DEVELOPMENT, AND HOUSING. Edited by Anthony Downs and Katharine Bradbury. Brookings Institution. 1984. 296 pp. Six papers from a 1981 Brookings conference show how higher energy prices affect future housing and urban development policies. Also considered is the effect of rising energy costs on the location of industry.
GROWTH INDUSTRIES IN THE 1980's: CONFERENCE PROCEEDINGS. Sponsored by Federal Reserve Bank of Atlanta. Quorum. 1983. 196 pp. Why do some firms prosper and grow even in bad times? Key growth characteristics are examined: location, size of firm, corporate structure, management, etc.
IMMODEST AGENDA: REBUILDING AMERICA BEFORE THE TWENTY-FIRST CENTURY. By Amitai Etzioni. McGraw-Hill. 1983. 418 pp. Grapples with the issues of rehabilitating America's individuals as government is cut: rebuilding the community and reindustrializing America.
INDUSTRIAL RENAISSANCE: PRODUCING A COMPETITIVE FUTURE FOR AMERICA. By William J. Abernathy, Kim B. Clark, and Alan M. Kantrow. Basic Books. 1983. 194 pp. Using the example of the automobile industry the authors focus on the new industrial competition and technological innovations to chronicle the "natural" evolution of mature industrial sectors.
LAND USE ISSUES OF THE 1980's. Edited by James H. Carr and Edward E. Duensing. Center for Urban Policy Research. 1983. 325 pp. Presents an analysis of current land use controls, reviews the shortcomings of the current system, and suggests modifications to improve urban spatial development patterns.
MANAGEMENT OF LOCAL PLANNING. By David C. Slater. ICMA. 1984. 288 pp. Focuses on the blending of two professional disciplines: planning and management in local government.
MANAGING URBAN CHANGE. 2 volumes. Organization for Economic Cooperation and Development. 1983. Vol. 1: POLICIES AND FINANCE; Vol. 2: THE ROLE OF GOVERNMENT. Results of a three-year, five-country analysis of policy options available to address the serious urban problems faced by many of the advanced industrial OECD countries. Discusses infrastructure, urban revitalization, urban public finance, the structure of urban policymaking, and so on.
NEIGHBORHOOD POLICY AND PLANNING. Edited by Phillip Clay and Robert Hollister. Lexington. 1983. 228 pp. Attempts to tie together current research and provide a framework for action on the various interventions in neighborhoods: resettlement, gentrification, neighborhood development organizations, and so on, in order to promote revitalization and improve the quality of life.
NEXT AMERICAN FRONTIER. By Robert B. Reich. Times Books. 1983. 324 pp. A historical view of the new economic realities that are leading to America's economic decline. The adaptations that must occur are referred to as America's next frontier. Proposes that social justice is essential to economic growth.
PUBLIC-PRIVATE PARTNERSHIP: NEW OPPORTUNITIES FOR MEETING SOCIAL NEEDS. Edited by Harvey Brooks, Lance Liebman, and Corinne Schelling. Published by Ballinger for American Academy of Arts and Sciences. 1984. 374 pp. Contributors approach the topic from various viewpoints: historical, practical (case studies), theoretical, and futuristic.
REBUILDING AMERICA'S CITIES: ROADS TO RECOVERY. Edited by Paul R. Porter and David C. Sweet. Center for Urban Policy Research. 1984. 255 pp. City "success stories" as reported at the Cities Congress on Roads to Recovery (CSU College of Urban Affairs) provide the material for this upbeat piece.
REVIEW OF PRIVATE APPROACHES FOR DELIVERY OF PUBLIC SERVICES. By Harry Hatry. Urban Institute Press. 1983. 105 pp. Focuses on various alternatives to delivery of basic services by local government employees, including contracting out, user fees, franchises, vouchers, volunteers, and grants and subsidies.
REVITALIZING THE OLDER SUBURB. By David Listokin and W. Patrick Beaton. Center for Urban Policy Research. 1983. 243 pp. A study of the fiscal stresses on mature suburbs, focusing on Englewood, New Jersey. A good review of the literature is presented.
SHAPING THE LOCAL ECONOMY: CURRENT PERSPECTIVES ON ECONOMIC DEVELOPMENT. Edited by Cheryl Farr. Practical Management Series. ICMA. 1984. 182 pp. Covers organizing economic development programs, forming public-private partnerships, using tax incentives, encouraging infill, and attracting high-tech development.
STRATEGIC PLANNING AND FORE-

CASTING: POLITICAL RISK AND ECONOMIC OPPORTUNITY. By William Ascher and William H. Overholt. Wiley. 1983. 311 pp. Systematic delineation of how forecasting exists to facilitate planning. Attempts to put political forecasting firmly into its policy advising context.

STREAMLINING LOCAL REGULATIONS: A HANDBOOK FOR REDUCING HOUSING AND DEVELOPMENT COSTS. By Stuart S. Hershey and Carolyn Garmise. MIS Special Report No. 11. ICMA. May 1983. 59 pp. Practical guidebook for reforming zoning, building codes, and other local regulations and permit procedures to reduce costs of housing and encourage community and economic development.

TAX INCENTIVES AND ECONOMIC GROWTH. By Barry P. Bosworth. Brookings Institution. 1984. 208 pp. Examines the efficacy of tax incentives as a means of increasing economic growth. Discusses the supply-side debate and the role of capital formation in productivity.

PERIODICALS

AMERICAN CITY & COUNTY. (M) Communication Channels.

AMERICAN REAL ESTATE AND URBAN ECONOMICS ASSOCIATION JOURNAL. (Q) American Real Estate and Urban Economics Association.

DEVELOPMENTS. (Q) National Development Council.

ECONOMIC DEVELOPMENT AND CULTURAL CHANGE. (Q) University of Chicago Press, Journals Division.

ECONOMIC DEVELOPMENT AND LAW CENTER REPORT. (BM) National Economic Development and Law Center.

ECONOMIC DEVELOPMENT COMMENTARY. (Q) National Council for Urban Economic Development.

ENTREPRENEURIAL ECONOMY. (M) Corporation for Enterprise Development.

ENVIRONMENT AND PLANNING C: GOVERNMENT AND POLICY. (Q) Pion Limited.

FINANCE AND DEVELOPMENT. (Q) International Monetary Fund.

INDUSTRY WEEK. (W) Penton/IPC.

LAND USE DIGEST. (M) Urban Land Institute.

LOCAL ECONOMIC GROWTH AND NEIGHBORHOOD REINVESTMENT REPORT. (BM) CD Publications.

NATION'S BUSINESS. (M) Chamber of Commerce of the U.S.

NORTHEAST JOURNAL OF BUSINESS AND ECONOMICS. (SA) University of Rhode Island, College of Business Administration.

PLANNING. (M) APA.

REGIONAL DEVELOPMENT DIALOGUE. (SA) United Nations Centre for Regional Development.

URBAN RESOURCES. (3/year) University of Cincinnati, Division of Metropolitan Services.

Public Finance

Laurence A. Himelfarb
Electronic Industries Association

BOOKS, REPORTS, MONOGRAPHS, BIBLIOGRAPHIES, AND REFERENCE SOURCES

ANALYSIS OF THE GRACE COMMISSION'S MAJOR PROPOSALS FOR COST CONTROL. Congressional Budget Office. GPO. 1984. 397 pp. Report focuses on those recommendations that the Grace Commission says would produce major budgetary savings.

BENCHMARKS OF URBAN CAPITAL CONDITION. By George E. Peterson and others. Urban Institute. 1983. 76 pp. Describes indicators of capital conditions to provide guidance in assessing capital plant needs and improving capital budgeting decisions; based on sample data from 62 cities.

CITY FISCAL CONDITIONS AND OUTLOOK FOR FISCAL 1984: RESOURCEFULNESS VS. RESOURCES. By Francis Viscount. National League of Cities. 1983. 29 pp. Reports on a survey of 300 city officials in leadership roles in the NLC.

CREATING AND FINANCING PUBLIC ENTERPRISES. By Arthur Gitajn. Government Financial Research Center, GFOA. 1984. 143 pp. Provides basic information on the creation and financing of public enterprises. Covers user charges, revenue debt, accounting for public enterprises, special districts and other pay approaches, and creating a public enterprise. Includes a useful bibliography.

CRISIS IN URBAN PUBLIC FINANCE: A CASE STUDY OF THIRTY-EIGHT CITIES. By Pearl M. Kamer. Praeger. 1983. 310 pp. Presents case studies of 38 of the largest U.S. cities, looking at fiscal strain and options for cutbacks.

FISCAL ADMINISTRATION: ANALYSIS AND APPLICATIONS FOR THE PUBLIC SECTOR. By John L. Mikesell. Dorsey. 1982. 433 pp. A thorough text on the practicalities of public agency operations and the development of an analytic framework. Includes sections on budgeting, revenue sources and structure, and the administration of public debt and idle fund management.

GEOGRAPHIC LIVING-COST DIFFERENCES. By Richard Cebula. Lexington. 1983. 190 pp. Variables and determinants of geographic living costs in the U.S.: an analytical approach.

GOVERNMENTAL ACCOUNTING. By Cornelius Tierney and Philip Calder. Elsevier Science Publishing. 1983. 223 pp. A useful reference work for finance officers, accountants, auditors, attorneys, and CPAs auditing financial statements for governments.

INFRASTRUCTURE INVENTORY AND CONDITION ASSESSMENT: TOOLS FOR IMPROVING CAPITAL PLANNING AND BUDGETING. By Stephen R. Godwin and George E. Peterson. Urban Institute. 1983. 59 pp. Identifies basic information needed to monitor capital facility conditions; explains how it can be used for better planning and capital management.

MUNICIPAL BONDS: PLANNING, SALE AND ADMINISTRATION. By Lennox C. Moak. MFOA. 1982. 405 pp. A textbook treatment of the entire field of the municipal bond market.

MUNICIPAL EXPENDITURES, REVENUES, AND SERVICES: ECONOMIC MODELS AND THEIR USE BY PLANNERS. Edited by W. Patrick Beaton. Center for Urban Policy Research. 1983. 255 pp. Tools for the planner to use in the face of federal cutbacks, high interest rates, and economic uncertainty.

THE MUNICIPAL MONEY CHASE: THE POLITICS OF LOCAL GOVERNMENT FINANCE. Edited by Alberta M. Sbragia. Westview. 1983. 251 pp. Deals with local government financing, municipal bonding and finance, and the relationship between congressional politics, federal grants, and local needs.

PENSION FUNDS INVESTMENTS IN REAL ESTATE. By Natalie McKelvey. Greenwood. 1983. 299 pp. A guide for pension fund managers wishing to invest in real estate.

PRACTICAL FINANCIAL MANAGEMENT: NEW TECHNIQUES FOR LOCAL GOVERNMENT. Edited by John Matzer, Jr. Practical Management Series. ICMA. 1984. 207 pp. Introduction to current techniques for improving efficiency and effectiveness of local government financial management.

THE PROPERTY TAX AND LOCAL FINANCE. Edited by C. Lowell Harris. Academy of Political Science. 1983. 242 pp. Discusses the politics of property taxation, problems of administration, property tax reform, and the future of the property tax.

PROPOSITION 2½: ITS IMPACT ON MASSACHUSETTS. Edited by Lawrence E. Susskind. Oelgeschlager, Gunn & Hain. 1983. 530 pp. Discusses history of Proposition 2½ and gives case studies and an analysis.

PUBLIC CHOICES—PRIVATE RESOURCES: FINANCING CAPITAL INFRASTRUCTURE FOR CALIFORNIA'S GROWTH THROUGH PUBLIC-PRIVATE BARGAINING. By Anne M. Kirlin and John J. Kirlin. California Tax Foundation. 1982. 101 pp. With increasing frequency, jurisdictions and developers "bargain" over capital investments needed to accommodate growth.

RETIREMENT AND INCOME. By Louis Harris. Garland. 1983. 120 pp. Survey of the attitudes of employees, retirees, and business leaders toward pensions and the retirement income system.

STATE AND LOCAL GOVERNMENT PURCHASING. Council of State Governments. 1983. 295 pp. Textbook including data on specific practices at the state and local level.

STATE TAXATION POLICY. Edited by Michael Barker. Policy Studies Series. Duke University Press. 1983. 284 pp. Explores the relationship between state taxation and economic development.

TAX INCENTIVES AND ECONOMIC GROWTH. By Barry P. Bosworth. Brookings Institution. 1984. 220 pp. Summarizes the effects of taxes on savings, investments, and work effort. Also examines the problems of coordinating measures to change tax incentives with fiscal and monetary policies.

TECHNOLOGY, INNOVATION AND REGIONAL ECONOMIC DEVELOPMENT. U.S. Congress, Office of Technology Assessment. GPO. 1984. 167 pp. Assesses the potential for local economic growth offered by high-technology industries. Describes programs used by state and local groups to encourage development of these industries.

THE TWENTY-YEAR CENTURY: ESSAYS ON ECONOMICS AND PUBLIC FINANCE. By Felix G. Rohatyn. Random House. 1984. 175 pp. Financier Rohatyn, the man who "saved NYC," calls for balanced responses to upheavals in the economic system rather than reliance on the whims of the market. He suggests the need for an industrial policy to make the U.S. more competitive.

PERIODICALS

THE APPRAISAL JOURNAL. (Q) American Institute of Real Estate Appraisers.

BUILDINGS: THE CONSTRUCTION AND BUILDINGS MANAGEMENT JOURNAL. (M) Stamats Publishing.

BUSINESS HORIZONS. (BM) School of Business. Indiana University.

CREDIT UNION NEWS. (BW) John Leaman.

FINANCIAL EXECUTIVE. (M) Financial Executives Institute. Publishes articles on pension fund management.

INDUSTRIAL DEVELOPMENT. (BM) Conway Publications.

JOURNAL OF PURCHASING AND MATERIALS MANAGEMENT. (Q) National Association of Purchasing Agents.

JOURNAL OF URBAN ECONOMICS. (BM) Academic Press.

PUBLIC BUDGETING AND FINANCE. (Q) Public Financial Publications.

PURCHASING. (SM) Cahners Publishing.

TAXES: THE TAX MAGAZINE. (M) Commerce Clearing House.

Public Works and Utilities

Mary K. Simon
American Public Works Association
Mary Beth Sasso
Arthur Andersen & Company

BOOKS, REPORTS, MONOGRAPHS, BIBLIOGRAPHIES, AND REFERENCE SOURCES

BETTER COMMUNICATION: THE KEY TO PUBLIC WORKS PROGRESS AND PUBLIC WORKS COMMUNICATION MANUAL. 2 volumes. Task Force on Communication, APWA. 1984. Contains guidelines for local officials who wish to improve their communication to a variety of audiences.

CENTRALIZED ADMINISTRATION OF PUBLIC BUILDINGS. Institute for Buildings and Grounds, APWA. 1984. Reference guide for the public building manager. Contains sections on custodial staffing, energy management, space considerations, and other topics.

COSTING GOVERNMENT SERVICES: A GUIDE FOR DECISION MAKING. By Joseph T. Kelley. 1984. Government Finance Research Center, GFOA. Offers advice to practitioners on how to use cost analysis to develop a workable budget for local jurisdictions. Instructions on how to define and cost basic services.

EXISTING SEWER EVALUATION AND REHABILITATION. ASCE and WPCF. 1983. (ASCE Manuals and Reports on Engineering Practice No. 62 and WPCF Manual of Practice No. FD-6.) Provides guidelines for the evaluation and rehabilitation of sanitary sewers. Major emphasis is on infiltration and inflow reduction, with lesser emphasis on maintaining the structural integrity of the sanitary sewer.

GROUNDS MAINTENANCE MANAGEMENT GUIDELINES. Edited by Jeffrey A. Bourne. Professional Grounds Management Society. n.d. This reference manual contains examples of maintenance standards, operating manuals, and contract specifications. Serves as a companion piece to *Guide to Grounds Maintenance Estimating*.

A GUIDE TO PUBLIC WORKS STANDARDS—AN INTRODUCTION TO LOCAL GOVERNMENT PUBLIC WORKS STANDARDS AND SPECIFICATIONS. Municipal Technical Advisory Service, University of Tennessee. 1984. A supplement to accompany *Local Government Public Works Standards and Specifications.* Useful handbook for elected officials, planning commissions, and administrators who must understand the need for public works standards and specifications.

HAZARDOUS WASTE AND THE PUBLIC WORKS OFFICIAL. By George Noble, P.E. APWA. 1984. Prepares local authorities for emergencies. Points out that public works plays the key role in an emergency.

INFRASTRUCTURE. BDR 16(1). ICMA. 1984. 10 pp. Based on a survey conducted by the National League of Cities and the U.S. Conference of Mayors, report covers the state of the nation's local infrastructure in December 1982.

AN INTERVIEW WITH WILLIAM D. HURST. Edited by Howard Rosen. Comments by Robert F. Legget and Dr. A. E. Berry. Public Works Historical Society. 1984. (Public Works Oral History Interview No. 5.) Recollections and reflections of one of Canada's leading engineers, researchers, and international diplomats.

1984 MUNICIPAL INDEX. Communication Channels. Annual. A useful buyer's guide to vendors of materials, equipment, and services for municipal use. The emphasis is on public works items. Also provides a small directory of municipal officials.

OUR HIGHWAYS: WHY DO THEY WEAR OUT? WHO PAYS FOR THEIR UPKEEP? Subcommittee on Highway Transport, AASHTO. 1984. Presents basic information to help the average citizen understand highway maintenance.

PASSING THE BUCKS: THE CONTRACTING OUT OF PUBLIC SERVICES. AFSCME. 1984. Discusses the impact of contracting out public services—the use of private companies to perform the work of state and local governments.

PAVEMENT PATCHING GUIDELINES. By Kamran Majidzadeh and Michael S. Luther. NTIS. 1983. Presents guidelines for constructing patches during cold weather (emergency and routine), and warm weather (routine). Patching of flexible, rigid, and composite pavements is addressed.

PAYING FOR TRANSPORTATION AT THE LOCAL LEVEL: 17 STRATEGIES. Institute for Transportation, APWA. 1984. A reference guide for the individual responsible for raising the revenue necessary to maintain the local transportation system.

PUBLIC AUTOMOTIVE FLEET ADMINISTRATION. Vol. 1. By Robert G. Edwards. CFN Publishing. 1983. Explores the options available to the fleet administrator in vehicle procurement and utilization. (Fleet operations, economics, and disposition are covered in Volume 2, to be published at a later date.)

SAFETY: TAILGATE TALKS. APWA. 1983. Practical outlines of talks on the various aspects of safety—street maintenance, lifting and carrying, solid waste collection, and other topics. Convenient format with flip-out card for trainer to carry easily.

PERIODICALS

AMERICAN CITY & COUNTY. (M) Communication Channels.

APWA REPORTER. (M) APWA.

CIVIC: THE PUBLIC WORKS MAGAZINE. (Canada). (M) Maclean-Hunter Press.

CIVIL ENGINEERING. (M) ASCE.

ENGINEERING NEWS-RECORD. (W) McGraw-Hill.
JOURNAL: AMERICAN WATER WORKS ASSOCIATION. (M) AWWA.
JOURNAL: WATER POLLUTION CONTROL FEDERATION. (M) WPCF.
PUBLIC WORKS. (M) Public Works Journal Corporation.
WASTE AGE. (M) National Solid Wastes Management Association.
WORLD WASTES. (M) Communication Channels.

Recreation and Leisure

Mary L. Knobbe
Library Consultant, MLK/LC

BOOKS, REPORTS, MONOGRAPHS, BIBLIOGRAPHIES, AND REFERENCE SOURCES

AMERICA'S CITY HALLS. By William L. Lebovich. Preservation Press. 1983. 224 pp. City halls show the evolution of city government as well as the development of American architecture.
AMERICA'S NATIONAL PARKS AND THEIR KEEPERS. By Ronald A. Foresta. Resources for the Future. 1984. 382 pp. Origin of National Park Service, and the new urgency of historic preservation and political pressure to make park land accessible to everyone.
BOTANICAL GARDENS, ARBORETUMS AND GREENHOUSES: A BIBLIOGRAPHY. By Coppa & Avery, Consultants. Vance Bibliographies. 1983. 11 pp.
BUILDING FOR THE ARTS. By Catherine R. Brown, William B. Fleissig, and William R. Morrish. Western States Arts Foundation. 1984. 260 pp. A guide to the planning and design of cultural facilities.
MANAGEMENT STRATEGIES IN FINANCING PARKS AND RECREATION. By Theodore R. Deppe. Wiley. 1983. 166 pp. A valuable fiscal management resource for middle-level managers.
MARINAS: A WORKING GUIDE TO THEIR DEVELOPMENT AND DESIGN. 3d ed. Nicholas Publications. 1984. 367 pp. Comprehensive coverage of subject.
MARINAS: RECOMMENDATIONS FOR DESIGN, CONSTRUCTION AND MANAGEMENT. 3d ed. Vol. 1 National Marine Manufacturers Association. 1983. 169 pp. An update of the 1961 edition considers all the new developments in the field.
OUTDOOR RECREATION. Rev. ed. By Douglas M. Knudson. Macmillan. 1984. 568 pp. Written for college students looking forward to professional work in parks.
OUTDOOR RECREATION AND RESOURCE MANAGEMENT. By John Pigram. St. Martin's Press. 1983. 262 pp. Concerns the implications of the "leisure revolution" and in particular the "potential of recreation to contribute to pleasurable, satisfying use of leisure time."
PARK MANAGEMENT. By Grant W. Sharpe. 1983. 340 pp. A typical day for the park manager suggests topics of concern. References are cited at the end of each chapter.
PRINCIPLES OF LEISURE COUNSELING. By Larry C. Loesch and Paul T. Wheeler. Educational Media Corporation. 1982. Presents counseling as a tool for overcoming problems associated with leisure time.
STAFF MANAGEMENT IN LIBRARY AND INFORMATION WORK. By Noragh Jones and Peter Jordan. Lexington. 1982. 215 pp. A handbook useful for library and information managers.

PERIODICALS

HISTORIC PRESERVATION. (BM) National Trust for Historic Preservation.
INFORMATION RETRIEVAL & LIBRARY AUTOMATION. (M) Lomond Publications.
LANDSCAPE JOURNAL. (SA) University of Wisconsin Press.
LIBRARY OF CONGRESS INFORMATION BULLETIN. (BM) Library of Congress Information Office.
PARK MAINTENANCE. (M) Madison Publishing Division.
PARKS & SPORTS GROUNDS. (M) Clarke and Hunter Ltd.
RECLAMATION & REVEGETATION RESEARCH. (Q) Elsevier Science Publishing.
RECREATIONAL SAFETY NEWSLETTER. (BM) National Safety Council.
RECREATION RESEARCH REVIEW. (Q) Ontario Research Council on Leisure.

Transportation and Roads

Janice W. Bain
Transportation Research Board

BOOKS, REPORTS, MONOGRAPHS, BIBLIOGRAPHIES, AND REFERENCE SOURCES

BICYCLES AND PUBLIC TRANSPORTATION: NEW LINKS TO SUBURBAN TRANSIT MARKETS. By Michael A. Replogle. The Bicycle Federation. 1984.
CLEANING TRANSIT BUSES: EQUIPMENT AND PROCEDURES. TRB. 1982. (National Cooperative Transit Research and Development Program Synthesis of Transit Practice #1.) 39 pp. Presents detailed information on procedures, equipment, and materials used in cleaning transit buses.
CONSTRUCTION CONTRACT CLAIMS: CAUSES AND METHODS OF SETTLEMENT. TRB. 1983. (National Cooperative Highway Research Program Synthesis of Highway Practice #105.) 58 pp. Identifies the most common types of highway construction contract claims, their causes, and settlement procedures.
COST-EFFECTIVENESS OF TRANSPORTATION SERVICES FOR HANDICAPPED PERSONS—RESEARCH REPORT. TRB. 1983. (National Cooperative Highway Research Program Report #261.) 130 pp. Documents a study of the cost-effectiveness of alternative transportation services for handicapped persons. A companion User's Guide (National Cooperative Highway Research Program Report #262) provides planners and decision makers with guidelines for evaluating alternative transportation services for handicapped persons and identifying the most cost-effective solutions for their communities.
DEVELOPMENTS IN AIRCRAFT AND AIRPORT COMPATIBILITY. TRB. 1984. (Circular #274.) 50 pp. A series of papers exploring airport/aircraft compatibility issues.
DIAL-A-RIDE: ASSESSING THE VARIABLES. By Martha A. Shulman. MIS 16(3). ICMA. March 1984. 12 pp. Reviews potential costs, opportunities, and limitations of dial-a-ride services.
THE DIMENSIONS OF PARKING. 2d ed. Parking Consultants Council, Urban Land Institute. 1983. 153 pp. Covers 18 topics related to parking. A guide to the best practices.
ECONOMIC BENEFITS AND FINANCING OF GENERAL AVIATION AIRPORTS. TRB. 1983. (Circular #259.) 65 pp. Fourteen papers covering the economics of general aviation airports and hub airports with a preponderance of general aviation activity.
ENFORCEMENT OF PRIORITY TREATMENT FOR BUSES ON URBAN STREETS. TRB. 1982. (National Cooperative Transit Research and Development Program Synthesis #2.) 30 pp. Presents information on the role of enforcement in bus priority operations and recommends enforcement measures.
IMPROVING DECISION-MAKING FOR MAJOR URBAN TRANSIT INVESTMENTS. TRB. 1983. (National Cooperative Transit Research and Development Program Report #4.) 47 pp. Assesses the federal, state, and local decision-making process for major urban mass transportation investments by evaluating recent alternatives, analysis, and related study experiences. Case studies are presented, as are recommendations for improvements in decision-making and research.
INTERCEPTING DOWNTOWN-BOUND TRAFFIC. Public Technology, Inc. GPO. 1982. 66 pp. Discusses traffic intercept strategies—techniques aimed at reducing the volume of traffic headed into downtown areas. Overall aim is to reduce central business district congestion and improve transit service efficiency.

MICROCOMPUTERS IN TRANSPORTATION. TRB. 1983. (Transportation Research Record #932.) 23 pp. Includes papers on applications of microcomputers in transportation planning, transit, traffic engineering, railroad engineering, and civil engineering.

MODEL PARKING CODE PROVISIONS TO ENCOURAGE RIDE-SHARING AND TRANSIT USE. JHK & Associates. NTIS. 1984. Proposes a model local parking code whose provisions are designed to reduce parking requirements by increasing use of public transit and ride-sharing.

PROCEEDINGS OF THE CONFERENCE ON ENERGY CONTINGENCY PLANNING IN URBAN AREAS. TRB. 1983. (Special Report #203.) 103 pp. Assesses the state of energy contingency planning since the 1979 energy crisis; examines the roles of the public and private sectors in contingency planning; examines the impact of deregulation on energy contingency planning; and suggests strategies for coping with future energy emergencies affecting the transportation sector.

RISK ASSESSMENT PROCESSES FOR HAZARDOUS MATERIALS. TRB. 1983. (National Cooperative Highway Research Program Synthesis of Highway Practice #103.) 27 pp. Presents detailed information on estimation of risk as part of a mitigation strategy to reduce vulnerability in transportation of hazardous materials, including hazardous wastes, through communities.

SHARED PARKING. Barton-Aschman Associates, Inc. Urban Land Institute. 1983. 86 pp. Studies multiple uses of parking lots and garages in 163 development projects both downtown and in the suburbs. Gives methods of estimating peak demands in shared parking areas.

SIMPLIFIED PROCEDURES FOR EVALUATING LOW-COST TSM PROJECTS—USER'S MANUAL. TRB. 1983. (National Cooperative Highway Research Program Report #263.) 209 pp. Identifies planning and programming approaches to implementation and management of effective TSM projects.

SOURCES OF INFORMATION IN TRANSPORTATION. 2d ed. Ad Hoc Committee of Transportation Librarians. NTIS. 1981. 308 pp. (3d ed. forthcoming from Vance Bibliographies in 1985.) The only reference work of its kind. Contains sections on highway, air, rail, water, urban, and pipeline modes of transportation. Each section suggests general reference works, journals, indexing/abstracting journals and data bases, conferences, statistical sources, dictionaries and glossaries, and so forth.

SPECIFICATION GUIDE FOR SMALL TRANSIT VEHICLES. Division of Public Transportation, Indiana Department of Transportation. 1984. A guide to preparation of specifications for small transit vehicles (vans, modified vans, small heavy-duty buses, body-on-chassis vehicles).

STARTING SHARED-RIDE TAXI SERVICES: AN OPERATOR'S GUIDEBOOK. TRB. 1983. 24 pp. Based on a workshop as well as experiences of taxi operators who have started shared-ride taxi services; discusses services, fares, and interaction with local government.

SYNTHESIS OF PRACTICE PLANNING FOR SMALL AND MEDIUM-SIZED COMMUNITIES. TRB. 1984. (Circular #283.) 29 pp. Case studies of small urban areas focusing on four topic areas: growth effects; data collection and management information systems; public transportation services; and programming, financing, and communicating with decision makers.

TRANSIT OWNERSHIP/OPERATIONS OPTIONS FOR SMALL URBAN AND RURAL AREAS. TRB. 1982. (National Cooperative Highway Research Program Synthesis of Highway Practice #97.) 28 pp. Identifies the major transit ownership/operation options for rural and small urban areas, reviews major advantages and disadvantages of options, and develops a framework to assist in the decision-making process.

TRANSPORTATION AND TRAFFIC ENGINEERING HANDBOOK. 2d ed. Edited by Wolfgang S. Homberger. Prentice-Hall. 1982. 883 pp. Classic work in traffic engineering since 1941. Earlier editions titled *Traffic Engineering Handbook*.

TRANSPORTATION INNOVATIONS: RIDESHARING TECHNIQUES AND PUBLIC-PRIVATE COOPERATION. TRB. 1983. (Transportation Research Record #914.) 71 pp. Eleven papers covering administrative and operational aspects of ridesharing, including the public sector role.

THE TROLLEY BUS: WHERE IT IS AND WHERE IT'S GOING. TRB. 1983. (Special Report #200.) 64 pp. Presents the history, operations, and implications (for energy conservation, the environment, and infrastructure) of the trolley bus.

URBAN BUSES: PLANNING AND OPERATIONS. TRB. 1983. (Transportation Research Record #915.) 48 pp. A series of papers exploring travel, economic, operational, and maintenance issues in urban transit bus operations.

PERIODICALS

CIVIL ENGINEERING. (M) ASCE.

ENGINEERING NEWS-RECORD. (W) McGraw-Hill.

ITE JOURNAL. (M) Institute of Transportation Engineers.

MASS TRANSIT. (M) Mass Transit.

PEDESTRIAN RESEARCH. (Q) American Pedestrian Research.

PUBLIC TRANSIT REPORT. (BW) Business Publishers.

PUBLIC WORKS. (M) Public Works Journal Corporation.

ROADS. (M) Scranton Gillette Communications. (Formerly *Rural and Urban Roads*.)

TRANSPORTATION ENGINEERING JOURNAL. (BM) ASCE.

List of Publishers

AASHTO for American Association of State Highway and Transportation Officials, 444 North Capitol Street, N.W., Washington, DC 20001.

ACA for American Correctional Association, 4321 Hartwick Road, Suite L-208, College Park, MD 20740.

Academic Press, Inc., 111 Fifth Avenue, New York, NY 10003.

Academy of Political Science, 2852 Broadway, New York, NY 10025.

AFSCME for American Federation of State, County and Municipal Employees, 1625 L Street, N.W., Washington, DC 20036.

Aldine Publishing, 200 Saw Mill River Road, Hawthorne, NY 10532.

Allen & Unwin, Inc., 9 Winchester Terrace, Winchester, MA 01890. P.O. to Box 978, 424 Raritan Center, Edison, NJ 08817.

Alternative Sources of Energy, Inc., 107 South Central Avenue, Milaca, MN 56353.

AMACOM, a division of American Management Association, 135 West 50th Street, New York, NY 10020.

American Association of State Highway and Transportation Officials, see AASHTO.

American Bar Association, 1800 M Street, N.W., S-200, Washington, DC 20036.

American Chemical Society, 1155 16th Street, N.W., Washington, DC 20036.

American Correctional Association, see ACA.

American Demographics Inc., P.O. Box 68, Ithaca, NY 14851.

American Federation of State, County and Municipal Employees, see AFSCME.

American Firefighter Association, 515 Madison Avenue, New York, NY 10022.

American Institute of Real Estate Appraisers, National Association of Real Estate Boards, 430 North Michigan Street, Chicago, IL 60611.

American Judicature Society, 200 West Monroe Street, Suite 1606, Chicago, IL 60606.

American Management Association, see AMA.

American Pedestrian Research, Box 624, Forest Hills Station, Forest Hills, NY 11375.

American Planning Association, see APA.

American Public Works Association, see APWA.

American Real Estate and Urban Economics Association, Georgia State University, Atlanta, GA 30303.

American Society for Industrial Security, 2000 K Street, N.W., Suite 651, Washington, DC 20006.

American Society for Public Administration, see ASPA.

American Society of Civil Engineers, see ASCE.

American Water Works Association, see AWWA.

APA for American Planning Association, 1313 East 60th Street, Chicago, IL 60637.

APWA for American Public Works Association, 1125 15th Street, N.W., Suite 300, Washington, DC 20005.

ASCE for American Society of Civil Engineers, 345 East 47th Street, New York, NY 10017.

ASPA for American Society for Public Administration, 1120 G Street, N.W., Washington, DC 20005.

Aspen Systems Corporation, 166 Research Boulevard., Rockville, MD 20850.

Association of Records Managers and Administrators, Box 8540, Prairie Village, KS 66208.

Auburn House Publishing Co., 131 Clarendon Street, Boston, MA 02216.

AWWA for American Water Works Association, 6666 West Quincy Avenue, Denver, CO 80235.

Backdraft Publication, Box 152, Morristown, NJ 07960.

Ballinger Publishing Co., Harvard Square, 17 Dunster Street, Cambridge, MA 02138.

Bantam Books, Inc., 666 Fifth Avenue, New York, NY 10019.

Basic Books, Inc., 10 East 53rd Street, New York, NY 10022.

Basil Blackwell, 432 Park Avenue, South, Suite 1505, New York, NY 10016.

Baywood Publishing Company, Inc., 120 Marine Street, Box D, Farmingdale, NY 11735.

The Bicycle Federation, 1055 Thomas Jefferson Street, N.W., Suite 316, Washington, DC 20007.

BNA for Bureau of National Affairs, Inc., 1231 25th Street, N.W., Washington, DC 20037.

Brookings Institution, 1775 Massachusetts Avenue, N.W., Washington, DC 20036.

Bureau of Municipal Research, 2 Toronto Street, Suite 306, Toronto, Ontario M5C 2B6, Canada.

Bureau of National Affairs, see BNA.

Business Publishers, Inc., 951 Pershing Drive, Silver Spring, MD 20910.

Buttenheim Publishing Corporation, Berkshire Common, Pittsfield, MA 01201.

Butterworth Publisher, 80 Montvale Avenue, Stoneham, MA 02180.

Cahners Publishing, 270 St. Paul Street, Denver, CO 80206.

California Tax Foundation, 921 11th Street, Suite 903, Sacramento, CA 95814.

Callaghan & Company, 165 North Archer Avenue, Mundelein, IL 60060.

Callahan Publishing, Box 3751, Washington, DC 20007.

Canada Mortgage and Housing Corporation, Montreal Road, Ottawa, Ontario K1A OP7, Canada.

Canadian Council on Urban and Regional Research, Suite 1100, 251 Laurier Avenue, N.W., Ottawa K1P 5I6, Canada.

Canadian Institute of Public Health Inspectors, P.O. Box 130, Etobicoke, Ontario M9C 4V2, Canada.

John R. Cashman, Ed. & Pub., Box 204, Barre, VT 05641.

CD Publications, 8555 16th Street, Silver Spring, MD 20910.

Center for Neighborhood Technology, Community Renewal Society, 111 North Wabash, Chicago, IL 60602.

CGN Publishing, 5443 Cribari Green, San Jose, CA 95135.

Chamber of Commerce of the U.S., 1615 H Street, N.W., Washington, DC 20062.

Child Protection Report, 1301 20th Street, N.W., Washington, DC 20036.

Child Welfare League of America, Inc., 67 Irving Place, New York, NY 10003.

City Hall Communications, Box 309, Seabrook, MD 20801.

Edna McConnell Clark Foundation, 250 Park Avenue, New York, NY 10017.

Clarke & Hunter Ltd., 61 London Road, Staines Middlestex TW18 4BN, England.

Columbia Books, 777 14th Street, N.W., Washington, DC 20005.

Columbia University Press, 136 South Broadway, Irvington-on-Hudson, NY 10533.

Commerce Clearing House, Inc., 4025 West Peterson Avenue, Chicago, IL 60646.

Communication Channels, Inc., 6285 Barfield Road, Atlanta, GA 30328.

Community Nutrition Institute, 1146 19th Street, N.W., Washington, DC 20036.

The Conference Board, Inc., 845 Third Avenue, New York, NY 10022.

Congressional Quarterly, Inc., 1414 22nd Street, N.W., Washington, DC 20036.

Conservation Foundation, 1717 Massachusetts Avenue, N.W., Washington, DC 20037.

Conway Publications, Peachtree Air Terminal, 1954 Airport Road, Atlanta, GA 20241.

Corporation for Enterprise Development, 1211 Connecticut Avenue, N.W., Suite 710A, Washington, DC 20036.

Cosmos Corporation, 1730 K St., N.W., Suite 1301, Washington, DC 20006.

Council for International Urban Liaison, 1120 G Street, N.W., Suite 300, Washington, DC 20005.

Council of Foundations, 1828 L Street, N.W., Washington, DC 20036.

Council of Planning Librarians, see CPL.

Council of State Governments, Iron Work Pike, Box 11910, Lexington, KY 40578.

CPL for Council of Planning Librarians, 1313 East 60th Street, Chicago, IL 60637.

CQ Press, see Congressional Quarterly.

Croom Helm Ltd., 2010 Street Johns Road, London SW11, England.

C.W. Communications, Inc., 375 Cochituate Road, Box 888, Framingham, MA 01701.

Marcel Dekker, Inc., 270 Madison Avenue, New York, NY 10016.

Doubleday & Company, Inc., 501 Franklin Avenue, Garden City, NY 11530.

Duke University Press, Box 6697, College Station, Durham, NC 27708.

Elsevier Science Publishing Company, Inc., 52 Vanderbilt Avenue, New York, NY 10017.

Energy Conservation Digest, Inc., 239 National Press Building, Washington, DC 20045.

Environmental Action, Inc., Room 731, 1346 Massachusetts Avenue, N.W., Washington, DC 20036.

Environmental Law Institute, 1346 Connecticut Avenue, N.W., Washington, DC 20036.

Executive Enterprises Publishing Company, 33 West 60th Street, New York, NY 10023.

Family Service Association of America, 44 East 23rd Street, New York, NY 10010.

Federal Home Loan Mortgage Corporation, Box 37248, Washington, DC 20013.

Federal Judicial Center, 1520 H Street, N.W., Washington, DC 20005.

Financial Executives Institute, 633 Third Avenue, New York, NY 10017.

W. H. Freeman and Company, 41 Madison Avenue, New York, NY 10010.

Free Press (Division of Macmillan Publishing Company), 866 3rd Avenue, New York, NY 10022.

Gain Publications, Inc., P.O. Box 2204, Van Nuys, CA 91404.

Garland STPM Press, 136 Madison Avenue, New York, NY 10016.

Geyer-McAllister Publishing Co., 51 Madison Avenue, New York, NY 10010.

Ginn & Company, 191 Spring Street, Lexington, MA 02173.

Government Finance Officers Association, formerly MFOA (Municipal Finance Officers Association).

Government Finance Research Center, 1750 K Street, N.W., Suite 200, Washington, DC 20006.

Government Research Corporation, 1750 M Street, N.W., Washington, DC 20036.

GPO for U.S. Government Printing Office, Superintendent of Documents, Washington, DC 20402.

Grantsmanship Center, 1031 South Grand Avenue, Los Angeles, CA 90015.

Greenwood Press, 88 Post Road West, Westport, CT 06881.

Grey House, 229 East 79th Street, Suite 3F, New York, NY 10021.

Haworth Press, Inc., 149 Fifth Avenue, New York, NY 10010.

Hill and Wang, 19 Union Square West, New York, NY 10003.

Holmes & Meier, IUB Building, 30 Irving Place, New York, NY 10003.

Housing Authority, 250 Broadway, New York, NY 10007.
Housing Resource Center, 4520 North Beacon, Chicago, IL 60640.
Human Resource Planning Society, Box 2553, Grand Central Station, New York, NY 10017.
Human Sciences Press, 72 Fifth Avenue, New York, NY 10011.

IAFC for International Association of Fire Chiefs, 1329 18th Street, N.W., Washington, DC 20036.
ICMA for International City Management Association, 1120 G Street, N.W., Washington, DC 20005.
IFSTA for International Fire Service Training Association, Fire Service Training, Oklahoma State University, Stillwater, OK 74074.
Indiana Department of Transportation, Division of Public Transportation, 143 West Market Street, Indianapolis, IN 46204.
Information Resources Press, Suite 700, 1700 North Moore Street, Arlington, VA 22209.
Inside E.P.A. Weekly Report, Box 7167, Ben Franklin Station, Washington, DC 20044.
Institute for Contemporary Studies Press, 260 California Street, Suite 811, San Francisco, CA 94111.
Institute of Industrial Relations, University of California, Berkeley, Berkeley, CA 94720.
Institute of Public Administration, 55 West 44th Street, New York, NY 10036.
Institute of Transportation Engineers, 525 School Street. S.W., Washington, DC 20024.
International Association of Chiefs of Police, Inc., Box 6010, 13 Firstfield Road, Gaithersburg, MD 20878.
International Association of Fire Chiefs, see IAFC.
International City Management Association, see ICMA.
International Fire Service Training Association, see IFSTA.
International Labour Office, 1750 New York Avenue, N.W., Suite 311, Washington, DC 20006.
International Labour Office, CH-1211, Geneva 22, Switzerland.
International Law Enforcement Stress Association, Box 156, Mattapan, MA 02126.
International Monetary Fund, 700 19th Street, N.W., Washington, DC 20431.
International Personnel Management Association, see IPMA.
International Resources Development, Inc., 30 High Street, Norwalk, CT 06851.
International Publication Service, see ips.
IPMA for International Personnel Management Association, 1850 K Street, N.W., Washington, DC 20006.
ips, a Division of Taylor & Francis, Inc., 242 Cherry Street, Philadelphia, PA 19106.

Knowledge Industry Publications, Inc., 701 Westchester Avenue, White Plains, NY 10604.

Law of Local Government Project, 1000 Connecticut Avenue, N.W., Suite 800, Washington, DC 20036.
League of Oregon Cities, 1201 Court Street, N.W., Box 928, Salem, OR 97308.
John Leaman, 150 Nassau Street, Suite 2030, New York, NY 10028.
Lexington Books (Division of D.C. Heath and Company), 125 Spring Street, Lexington, MA 01731.
Library of Congress, Information Office, Washington, DC 20540.
Little, Brown and Company, 34 Beacon Street, Boston, MA 01114.
Lomond Publications, Inc., P.O. Box 88, Mt. Airy, MD 21771.

McGraw-Hill Book Company, 1221 Avenue of the Americas, New York, NY 10036.
Maclean-Hunter Press, 481 University Avenue, Toronto, Ontario, Canada.
Madison Publishing Division, Box 1936, Appleton, WI 54913.
Albert P. Maslow, Staffing, Basswood Plaza-11c, Cranbury, NJ 08512.
Mass Transit, Inc., 337 National Press Building, Washington, DC 20045.
Charles E. Merriam Center for Public Administration Library, 1313 East 60th Street, Chicago, IL 60637.
Julian Messner, Simon & Schuster Building, 1230 Avenue of the Americas, New York, NY 10020.
Metropolitan Washington Council of Governments, see MWCOG.
MFOA for Municipal Finance Officers Association, 180 North Michigan Avenue, Chicago, IL 60601, now Government Finance Officers Association.
Michigan Society of Planning Officials, P.O. Box 1817, Lansing, MI 48901.
Morgan-Grampian Publishing Company, Berkshire Common, Pittsfield, MA 01201.
Municipal Finance Officers Association, see MFOA.
Municipal Management Publishing Company, 39 Pearl Street, Brandon, VT 05703.
Municipal Technical Advisory Service, University of Tennessee, 891 20th Street, Knoxville, TN 37996.
MWCOG for Metropolitan Washington Council of Governments, 1875 Eye Street, N.W. Washington, DC 20006.

NAHRO for National Association of Housing and Redevelopment Officials, 2600 Virginia Avenue, N.W., Washington, DC 20037.
National Academy Press, 2101 Constitution Avenue, N.W., Washington, DC 20418.
National Association of Housing and Redevelopment Officials, see NAHRO.
National Association of Housing Cooperatives, 2501 M Street, N.W., Washington, DC, 20037.
National Association of Purchasing Agents, 49 Sheridan Avenue, Albany, NY 12210.
National Association of Social Workers, 7981 Eastern Avenue, Silver Spring, MD 20910.
National Center for State Courts, 300 Newport Avenue, Williamsburg, VA 23185.
National Conference of States on Building Codes and Standards, 481 Carlisle Drive, Herndon, VA 22070.
National Council for Urban Economic Development, 1730 K Street, N.W., Washington, DC 20006.
National Council of Juvenile and Family Court Judges, Box 8979, University of Nevada, Reno, NV 89507.
National Development Council, 1025 Connecticut Avenue, N.W., Washington, DC 20036.
National Economic Development and Law Center, 1950 Addison Street, Berkeley, CA 94704.
National Fire Protection Association, see NFPA.
National Housing Law Project, 2150 Shattuck Avenue, Suite 300, Berkeley, CA 94704.
National League of Cities, see NLC.
National Marine Manufacturers Association, 401 North Michigan Avenue, Chicago, IL 60611.
National Safety Council, 444 North Michigan Avenue, Chicago, IL 60611.
National School Boards Association, 1680 Duke Street, Alexandria, VA 22314.
National Solid Wastes Management Association, Suite 930, 1120 Connecticut Avenue, N.W., Washington, DC 20036.
National Technical Information Service, see NTIS.
National Trust for Historic Preservation, 1785 Massachusetts Avenue, N.W., Washington, DC 20036.
National Wildlife Federation, Inc., 8925 Leesburg Pike, Vienna, VA 22180.
Natural Hazards Research and Applications Information Center, University of Colorado, IBS #6, Boulder, CO 80309.
Natural Resources Defense Council, Inc., 122 East 42nd Street, New York, NY 10168.
Nelson-Hall, 111 Canal Street, Chicago, IL 60606.
New York State Department of Environmental Conservation, 50 Wolf Road, Albany, NY 12205.
New York State School of Industrial and Labor Relations, Cornell University, Ithaca, NY 14853.
NFPA for National Fire Protection Association, 470 Atlantic Avenue, Boston, MA 02110.
Nicholas Publications, 155 West 72nd Street, New York, NY 10023.
NLC for National League of Cities, 1301 Pennsylvania Avenue, N.W., Washington, DC 20004.
North Carolina State University, Department of Civil Engineering, Raleigh, NC 27650.
North-Holland Publishing Co., Box 211, 1000 AE Amsterdam, Netherlands.
Noyes Data Corporation, Mill Road at Grand Avenue, Park Ridge, NJ 07656.
NTIS for National Technical Information Service, 5285 Port Royal Road, Springfield, VA 22161.

Oelgeschlager, Gunn & Hain, 1278 Massachusetts Avenue, Cambridge, MA 02138.
Ontario Research Council on Leisure, 77 Bloor Street, West, 8th Floor, Toronto, Ontario M7A 2R9, Canada.
Organization for Economic Cooperation and Development, 1750 Pennsylvania Avenue, N.W., Suite 1207, Washington, DC 20006.

PAIS for Public Affairs Information Service, 11 West 40th Street, New York, NY 10018.

Partners for Livable Places, ATTM: Livability Clearinghouse, 1429 21st Street, N.W., Washington, DC 20036.

PAS for Planning Advisory Service, 1313 East 60th Street, Chicago, IL 60637.

F. E. Peacock Publishers, Inc., 401 West Irving Park Road, Itasca, IL 60143.

Pennwell Publishing Co., Advanced Technology Group, 1714 Stockton Street, San Francisco, CA 94133.

Penton/IPC, Penton Plaza, 1111 Chester, Cleveland, OH 44114.

Pergamon Press, Maxwell House, Fairview Park, Elmsford, NY 10523.

Personnel Management Abstracts, 704 Island Lake Road, Chelsea, MI 48118.

Pion Limited, 207 Brondesbury Park, London NW2 5JN, England.

Planning Advisory Service, see PAS.

Praeger Publishers, Inc., 383 Madison Avenue, New York, NY 10017.

Prentice-Hall, Inc., Englewood Cliffs, NJ 07632.

Princeton University Press, 41 William Street, Princeton, NJ 08540.

Professional Grounds Management Society, 7 Church Lane, Pikesville, MD 21208.

Project Share, P.O. Box 2309, Rockville, MD 20852.

Public Affairs Information Service, see PAIS.

Public Financial Publications, Inc., P.O. Box 23474, Washington, DC 20024.

Public Technology, Inc., 1301 Pennsylvania Avenue, N.W., Washington, DC 20004.

Public Works Historical Society, 1313 East 60th Street, Chicago, IL 60637.

Public Works Journal Corporation, 200 South Broadway Street, Ridgewood, NJ 07451.

Quorum Books, Box 5007, 88 Post Road West, Westport, CT 06881.

Random House, Inc., 400 Hahn Road, Westminster, MD 21157.

Research Center in Business & Economics, College of Business Administration, University of Rhode Island, 210 Ballentine Hall, Kingston, RI 02881.

Resources for the Future, 1755 Massachusetts Avenue, N.W., Washington, DC 20036.

Reston Publications, 11480 Sunset Hills Road, Reston, VA 22090.

Routledge & Kegan Paul, Nine Park Street, Boston, MA 02108.

Rowman and Allanheld, 81 Adams Drive, Totowa, NJ 07512.

Rutgers University, Center for Urban Policy Research, P.O. Box 489, Piscataway, NJ 08854.

Rutgers University Press, 30 College Avenue, New Brunswick, NJ 08903.

Sage Publications, Inc., 275 South Beverly Drive, Beverly Hills, CA 90212.

School of Business, Indiana University, Bloomington, IN 47405.

Scranton Gillette Communications, 380 Northwest Highway, Des Plaines, IL 60016.

Society for Advancement of Management, 2331 Victory Parkway, Cincinnati, OH 45206.

Solar Age, P.O. Box 985, Farmingdale, NY 11737.

Southern Public Administration Education Foundation, Box 4434, Montgomery, AL 35101.

Charles D. Spencer & Associates, Inc., 222 West Adams Street, Chicago, IL 60606.

Springer Publishing Co., 200 Park Avenue South, New York, NY 10003.

Stamats Publishing Company, 427 Sixth Avenue, S.E., Cedar Rapids, IA 54206.

Technical Publishing Co., 875 Third Avenue, New York, NY 10022.

13-30 Corporation, 505 Market Street, Knoxville, TN 37902.

Charles C. Thomas, Publishers, 301-27 East Lawrence Ave., Springfield, IL 62717.

Times Books, 3 Park Avenue, New York, NY 10016.

Transportation Research Board, see TRB.

TRB for Transportation Research Board, 2101 Constitution Avenue, N.W., Washington, DC 20418.

UNIPUB, 205 East 42nd Street, New York, NY 10017.

United Business Publications, 475 Park Avenue, South, New York, NY 10016.

United Nations Centre for Regional Development, Marunounchi 2-4-7, Nakaku, Nagaya, 460 Japan.

U.S. Bureau of Labor Statistics, 441 G Street, N.W., Washington, DC 20212.

U.S. Department of Justice, National Institute of Corrections, Washington, DC 20534.

U.S. Department of Justice, National Institute of Justice, Washington, DC 20531.

U.S. Department of Justice, Office of Justice Assistance Research and Statistics, Washington, DC 20531.

U.S. Government Printing Office, see GPO.

University of Chicago Press, 5801 Ellis Avenue, Chicago, IL 60637.

University of Chicago Press, Journal Division, Box 37005, Chicago, IL 60637.

University of Cincinnati, Division of Metropolitan Services, Mail Location #175, Cincinnati, OH 45221.

University of Colorado, Institute of Behavioral Science, Boulder, CO 80309.

University of Illinois at Chicago, Nathalie P. Voorhees Center for Neighborhood and Community, Box 4348, Chicago, IL 60680.

University of Wisconsin Press, 114 North Murray Street, Madison, WI 53715.

University Press of America, Inc., 4720 Bostonway, Lanham, MD 20801.

The W. E. Upjohn Institute for Employment Research, 300 South Westnedge Avenue, Kalamazoo, MI 49007.

Urban Institute Press, Customer Service, P.O. Box 19958, Hampden Station, Baltimore, MD 21211.

Urban Land Institute, 1090 Vermont Avenue, N.W., Washington, DC 20036.

Vance Bibliographies, P.O. Box 229, Monticello, IL 61856.

Van Nostrand Reinhold Company, 135 West 50th Street, New York, NY 10020.

VGM Career Horizons, National Textbook Company, 4255 West Touhy Avenue, Lincolnwood, IL 60646.

Want Publications, 1511 K Street, N.W., Washington, DC 20005.

Water Pollution Control Federation, see WPCF.

Western States Arts Foundation, 141 East Palace Avenue, Santa Fe, NM 87501.

Westview Press, 5500 Central Avenue, Boulder, CO 80301.

John Wiley & Sons, Inc., 605 Third Avenue, New York, NY 10158.

H.W. Wilson Company, 950 University Avenue, Bronx, NY 10452.

World Health Organization, WHO Publication Centre, 49 Sheridan Avenue, Albany, NY 12210.

World Watch Institute, 1776 Massachusetts Avenue, N.W., Washington, DC 20036.

WPCF for Water Pollution Control Federation, 2626 Pennsylvania Avenue, N.W., Washington, DC 20037.

Yale School of Forestry and Environmental Studies, 205 Prospect Street, New Haven, CT 06511.

Ziff-Davis Publishing Company, One Park Avenue, New York, NY 10016.